Profiles
of
Ohio

2006

Profiles of Ohio

A UNIVERSAL REFERENCE BOOK

Grey House Publishing

PUBLISHER: Leslie Mackenzie
EDITOR: David Garoogian
EDITORIAL DIRECTOR: Laura Mars-Proietti
RESEARCH ASSISTANTS: Karynn Ketiinq

MARKETING DIRECTOR: Jessica Moody

Grey House Publishing, Inc.
185 Millerton Road
Millerton, NY 12546
518.789.8700
FAX 518.789.0545
www.greyhouse.com
e-mail: books @greyhouse.com

While every effort has been made to ensure the reliability of the information presented in this publication, Grey House Publishing neither guarantees the accuracy of the data contained herein nor assumes any responsibility for errors, omissions or discrepancies. Grey House accepts no payment for listing; inclusion in the publication of any organization, agency, institution, publication, service or individual does not imply endorsement of the editors or publisher.

Errors brought to the attention of the publisher and verified to the satisfaction of the publisher will be corrected in future editions.

Except by express prior written permission of the Copyright Proprietor no part of this work may be copied by any means of publication or communication now known or developed hereafter including, but not limited to, use in any directory or compilation or other print publication, in any information storage and retrieval system, in any other electronic device, or in any visual or audio-visual device or product.

This publication is an original and creative work, copyrighted by Grey House Publishing, Inc. and is fully protected by all applicable copyright laws, as well as by laws covering misappropriation, trade secrets and unfair competition.

Grey House has added value to the underlying factual material through one or more of the following efforts: unique and original selection; expression; arrangement; coordination; and classification.

Grey House Publishing, Inc. will defend its rights in this publication.

Copyright©2006 Grey House Publishing, Inc
All rights reserved

First edition published 2006
Printed in the USA

ISBN 10: 1-59237-175-2
ISBN 13: 978-1-59237-175-4

Table of Contents

Introduction

User's Guide

Profiles
- Alphabetical by County/Place...1
- Alphabetical Place Index..345
- Comparative Statistics..353

Education
- State Public School Profile..386
- School District Rankings...387
- National Assessment of Educational Progress (NAEP)................409
- Ohio Achievement Tests (OAT).......................................417
- Proficiency Tests (PT)...419
- Ohio Graduation Tests (OGT)..420

Ancestry
- Ancestry Rankings..423

Hispanic Population
- Hispanic Rankings..467

Asian Population
- Asian Rankings...491

Climate
- State Summary...511
- Weather Stations Map..513
- Weather Stations by County..514
- Weather Stations by City..516
- Weather Stations by Elevation.....................................517
- National Weather Service Stations.................................518
- Cooperative Weather Stations......................................526
- Weather Station Rankings..547
- Storm Events..554

Maps
- Congressional Districts...557
- Counties and Metro Areas..558
- Population..559
- Household Size..564
- Median Age..565
- Income and Poverty..566
- Median Home Value...568
- Homeownership Rate..569
- Educational Attainment..570
- 2004 Presidential Election..572

Introduction

This is the first edition of *Profiles of Ohio – Facts, Figures & Statistics for all 1,197 Populated Places in Ohio.* As for the other titles in our *State Profiles* series, we built this work using content from Grey House Publishing's award-winning *Profiles of America* – a 4-volume compilation of data on more than 42,000 places in the United States. We have updated and included the Ohio chapter from *Profiles of America,* and added entire fresh chapters of demographic information and ranking sections, so that *Profiles of Ohio* is the most comprehensive portrait of the state of Ohio ever published.

This first edition provides data on all populated communities and counties in the state of Ohio, from bustling urban centers to the hard-to-find outposts. It includes seven major sections that cover everything from **Education** to **Ethnic Backgrounds** to **Climate.** All sections include **Comparative Statistics** or **Rankings**, and full-color **Maps** at the back of the book provide valuable information in a quickly processed, visual format. Here's an overview of each section:

1. Profiles
This section, organized by county, gives detailed profiles of 1,197 places plus 88 counties, and is based on the 2000 Census. This core Census data has been so extensively updated, however, that nearly 80% of this section has 2005 numbers. In addition, we have added current government statistics and original research, so that these profiles pull together statistical and descriptive information on every Census-recognized place in the state. Major fields of information include:

Geography	*Housing*	*Education*	*Religion*
Ancestry	*Transportation*	*Population*	*Climate*
Economy	*Industry*	*Health*	

In addition to place profiles, this section includes an **Alphabetical Place Index** and **Comparative Statistics** that compare Ohio's 100 largest communities by dozens of data points.

2. Education
This section begins with an *Educational State Profile,* summarizing number of schools, students, diplomas granted and educational dollars spent. Following the state profile are **School District Rankings** on 16 topics ranging from *Teacher/Student Ratios* to *High School Drop-Out Rates.* Following these rankings are *2005 National Assessment of Educational Progress (NAEP), March 2006 Ohio Achievement Test (OAT), March 2005 Proficiency Test (PT), and March 2005 Ohio Graduation Test (OGT)* results.

3. Ancestry
This section provides a detailed look at the ancestral and racial makeup of Ohio. 217 ethnic categories are ranked three ways: 1) by number, based on all places regardless of population; 2) by percent, based on all places regardless of population; 3) by percent, based on places with populations of 10,000 or more. You will discover, for example, that Columbus in Franklin County has the greatest number of Greeks in the state at 2,702, and that Russians make up 15.5% of the population of Beachwood in Cuyahoga County.

4. Hispanic Population
This section defines Ohio's Hispanic population by 23 Hispanic backgrounds from *Argentinian* to *Venezuelan.* It ranks each of 15 categories, from Median Age to Median Home Value, by each Hispanic background. For example, you'll see that Painesville in Lake County has the highest percentage of

Mexicans who speak Spanish at home, and that Cleveland in Cuyahoga County has the greatest number of *Puerto Ricans* who own their own home.

5. Asian Population

Similar in format to the section on Hispanic Population, this section defines Ohio's Asian population by 21 Asian backgrounds from *Bangladeshi* to *Vietnamese*. It ranks each of 14 categories, from *Median Age* to *Median Home Value*, by each Asian background. You will learn that Columbus in Franklin County is the place with the greatest number of *Chinese* in the state, and that Cincinnati in Hamilton County has the highest percent of *Filipinos* who are college graduates.

6. Weather

This important topic is explored in detail in this section, which includes a *State Summary*, a *map* of the state's weather stations, and profiles of both *National* and *Cooperative Weather Stations*. In addition, you'll find *Weather Station Rankings*, where you'll see that, over the 30-year recorded period, Danville 2 W reported the lowest annual extreme minimum temperature at –35 degrees.

This section also includes current *Storm* data, with the most destructive storms ranked by both fatalities and property damage, from 1981-2006. Here you will learn that an F5 tornado in May 1985 caused $250 million in damage in Portage County and that extreme heat was responsible for 13 fatalities in northern Ohio in August 1995.

7. Maps

For a more visual point of view, there are 16 full-color maps of Ohio at the back of the book. They provide information on topics such as Core-Based Statistical Areas and Counties, Population Demographics, Household Size, Median Age, Income, Median Home Values, Educational Attainment, Congressional Districts, and another look at who voted for George Bush in 2004.

Note: The extensive **User's Guide** that follows this Introduction is segmented into six sections and examines, in some detail, each data field in the individual profiles and comparative sections for all chapters. It provides sources for all data points and statistical definitions as necessary.

User's Guide: Profiles

PLACES COVERED

All 88 counties.

942 incorporated municipalities. Municipalities are incorporated as either cities or villages.

112 census designated places (CDP). The U.S. Bureau of the Census defines a CDP as "a statistical entity, defined for each decennial census according to Census Bureau guidelines, comprising a densely settled concentration of population that is not within an incorporated place, but is locally identified by a name. CDPs are delineated cooperatively by state and local officials and the Census Bureau, following Census Bureau guidelines. Beginning with Census 2000 there are no size limits."

143 unincorporated communities. The communities included have both their own zip code and statistics for their ZIP Code Tabulation Area (ZCTA) available from the Census Bureau. They are referred to as "postal areas." A ZCTA is a statistical entity developed by the Census Bureau to approximate the delivery area for a US Postal Service 5-digit or 3-digit ZIP Code in the US and Puerto Rico. A ZCTA is an aggregation of census blocks that have the same predominant ZIP Code associated with the mailing addresses in the Census Bureau's Master Address File. Thus, the Postal Service's delivery areas have been adjusted to encompass whole census blocks so that the Census Bureau can tabulate census data for the ZCTAs. ZCTAs do not include all ZIP Codes used for mail delivery and therefore do not precisely depict the area within which mail deliveries associated with that ZIP Code occur. Additionally, some areas that are known by a unique name, although they are part of a larger incorporated place, are also included as "postal areas."

Important Notes

- *Profiles of Ohio* uses the term "community" to refer to all places except counties. The term "county" is used to refer to counties and county-equivalents. All places are defined as of the 2000 Census.
- In each community profile, only school districts that have schools that are physically located within the community are shown. In addition, statistics for each school district cover the entire district, regardless of the physical location of the schools within the district.
- Special care should be taken when interpreting certain statistics for communities containing large colleges or universities. College students were counted as residents of the area in which they were living while attending college (as they have been since the 1950 census). One effect this may have is skewing the figures for population, income, housing, and educational attainment.
- Some information (e.g. unemployment rates) is available for both counties and individual communities. Other information is available for just counties (e.g. election results), or just individual communities (e.g. local newspapers).
- Some statistical information is available only for larger communities. In addition, the larger places are more apt to have services such as newspapers, airports, school districts, etc.
- For the most complete information on any community, you should also check the entry for the county in which the community is located. In addition, more information and services will be listed under the larger places in the county.
- For a more in-depth discussion of geographic areas, please refer to the Census Bureau's Geographic Areas Reference Manual at http://www.census.gov/geo/www/garm.html.

DATA SOURCES

CENSUS 2000

The parts of the data which are from the 2000 Decennial Census are from the following sources: *U.S. Bureau of the Census, Census of Population and Housing, 2000: Summary Files 1 and 3.* Summary File 3 (SF 3) consists of 813 detailed tables of Census 2000 social, economic and housing characteristics compiled from a sample of approximately 19 million housing units (about 1 in 6 households) that received the Census 2000 long-form questionnaire. Summary File 1 (SF 1) contains 286 tables focusing on age, sex, households, families, and housing units. This file presents 100-percent population and housing figures for the total population, for 63 race categories, and for many other race and Hispanic or Latino categories.

Comparing SF 3 Estimates with Corresponding Values in SF 1

As in earlier censuses, the responses from the sample of households reporting on long forms must be weighted to reflect the entire population. Specifically, each responding household represents, on average, six or seven other households who reported using short forms.

One consequence of the weighting procedures is that each estimate based on the long form responses has an associated confidence interval. These confidence intervals are wider (as a percentage of the estimate) for geographic areas with smaller populations and for characteristics that occur less frequently in the area being examined (such as the proportion of people in poverty in a middle-income neighborhood).

In order to release as much useful information as possible, statisticians must balance a number of factors. In particular, for Census 2000, the Bureau of the Census created weighting areas—geographic areas from which about two hundred or more long forms were completed—which are large enough to produce good quality estimates. If smaller weighting areas had been used, the confidence intervals around the estimates would have been significantly wider, rendering many estimates less useful due to their lower reliability.

The disadvantage of using weighting areas this large is that, for smaller geographic areas within them, the estimates of characteristics that are also reported on the short form will not match the counts reported in SF 1. Examples of these characteristics are the total number of people, the number of people reporting specific racial categories, and the number of housing units. The official values for items reported on the short form come from SF 1 and SF 2.

The differences between the long form estimates in SF 3 and values in SF 1 are particularly noticeable for the smallest places, tracts, and block groups. The long form estimates of total population and total housing units in SF 3 will, however, match the SF 1 counts for larger geographic areas such as counties and states, and will be essentially the same for medium and large cities.

SF 1 gives exact numbers even for very small groups and areas, whereas SF 3 gives estimates for small groups and areas such as tracts and small places that are less exact. The goal of SF 3 is to identify large differences among areas or large changes over time. Estimates for small areas and small population groups often do exhibit large changes from one census to the next, so having the capability to measure them is worthwhile.

2005 Estimates and 2010 Projections

Some 2000 Census data has been updated with data provided by Claritas. Founded in 1971, Claritas is the industry leader in applied demography and the preeminent provider of small-area demographic estimates.

INFORMATION FOR COMMUNITIES

PHYSICAL CHARACTERISTICS

Place Type: Lists the type of place (city, town, village, borough, special city, CDP, township, plantation, gore, district, grant, location, reservation, or postal area). *Source: U.S. Bureau of the Census, Census of Population and Housing, 2000: Summary File 1 and U.S. Postal Service, City State File.*

Land and Water Area: Land and water area in square miles. *Source: U.S. Bureau of the Census, Census of Population and Housing, 2000: Summary File 1.*

Latitude and Longitude: Latitude and longitude in degrees. *Source: U.S. Bureau of the Census, Census of Population and Housing, 2000: Summary File 1.*

Elevation: Elevation in feet. *Source: U.S. Geological Survey, Geographic Names Information System (GNIS).*

HISTORY

History: Historical information. *Source: Columbia University Press, The Columbia Gazetteer of North America; Original research.*

POPULATION

Population: 1990 and 2000 figures are a 100% count of population. 2005 estimates and 2010 projections were provided by Claritas. *Source: Claritas; U.S. Bureau of the Census, Census of Population and Housing, 2000: Summary File 1.*

Population by Race: 2005 estimates includes the U.S. Bureau of the Census categories of White alone; Black alone; Asian alone; and Hispanic of any race. Alone refers to the fact that these figures are not in combination with any other race.

The concept of race, as used by the Census Bureau, reflects self-identification by people according to the race or races with which they most closely identify. These categories are socio-political constructs and should not be interpreted as being scientific or anthropological in nature. Furthermore, the race categories include both racial and national-origin groups.

- **White.** A person having origins in any of the original peoples of Europe, the Middle East, or North Africa. It includes people who indicate their race as "White" or report entries such as Irish, German, Italian, Lebanese, Near Easterner, Arab, or Polish.
- **Black or African American.** A person having origins in any of the Black racial groups of Africa. It includes people who indicate their race as "Black, African American, or Negro," or provide written entries such as African American, Afro-American, Kenyan, Nigerian, or Haitian.
- **Asian.** A person having origins in any of the original peoples of the Far East, Southeast Asia, or the Indian subcontinent including, for example, Cambodia, China, India, Japan, Korea, Malaysia, Pakistan, the Philippine Islands, Thailand, and Vietnam. It includes "Asian Indian," "Chinese," "Filipino," "Korean," "Japanese," "Vietnamese," and "Other Asian."
- **Hispanic.** The data on the Hispanic or Latino population, which was asked of all people, were derived from answers to long-form questionnaire Item 5, and short-form questionnaire Item 7. The terms "Spanish," "Hispanic origin," and "Latino" are used interchangeably. Some respondents identify with all three terms, while others may identify with only one of these three specific terms. Hispanics or Latinos who identify with the terms "Spanish," "Hispanic," or "Latino" are those who classify themselves in one of the specific Hispanic or Latino categories listed on the questionnaire — "Mexican," "Puerto Rican," or "Cuban" — as well as those who indicate that they are "other Spanish, Hispanic, or Latino." People who do not identify with one of the specific origins listed on the questionnaire but indicate that they are "other Spanish, Hispanic, or Latino" are those whose origins are from Spain, the Spanish-speaking countries of Central or South America, the Dominican Republic, or people identifying themselves generally as Spanish, Spanish-American, Hispanic, Hispano, Latino, and so on. All write-in responses to the "other Spanish/Hispanic/Latino" category were coded. Origin can be viewed as the heritage, nationality group, lineage, or country of birth of the person or the person's parents or ancestors before their arrival in the United States. People who identify their origin as Spanish, Hispanic, or Latino may be of any race.

Population Density: 2005 population divided by the land area in square miles. *Source: Claritas; U.S. Bureau of the Census, Census of Population and Housing, 2000: Summary File 1.*

Average Household Size: Average household size was calculated by dividing the total population by the total number of households. Figures are 2005 estimates. *Source: Claritas.*

Median Age: Figures are 2005 estimates. *Source: Claritas.*

Male/Female Ratio: Number of males per 100 females. Figures are 2005 estimates. *Source: Claritas.*

Marital Status: Percentage of population never married, now married, widowed, or divorced. *Source: U.S. Bureau of the Census, Census of Population and Housing, 2000: Summary File 3.*

The marital status classification refers to the status at the time of enumeration. Data on marital status are tabulated only for the population 15 years old and over. Each person was asked whether they were "Now married," "Widowed," "Divorced," or "Never married." Couples who live together (for example, people in common-law marriages) were able to report the marital status they considered to be the most appropriate.

- **Never married.** Never married includes all people who have never been married, including people whose only marriage(s) was annulled.
- **Now married.** All people whose current marriage has not ended by widowhood or divorce. This category includes people defined as "separated."
- **Widowed.** This category includes widows and widowers who have not remarried.
- **Divorced.** This category includes people who are legally divorced and who have not remarried.

Foreign Born: Percentage of population who were not U.S. citizens at birth. Foreign-born people are those who indicated they were either a U.S. citizen by naturalization or they were not a citizen of the United States. *Source: U.S. Bureau of the Census, Census of Population and Housing, 2000: Summary File 3.*

Ancestry: Largest ancestry groups reported (up to five). Includes multiple ancestries. *Source: U.S. Bureau of the Census, Census of Population and Housing, 2000: Summary File 3.*

The data represent self-classification by people according to the ancestry group or groups with which they most closely identify. Ancestry refers to a person's ethnic origin or descent, "roots," heritage, or the place of birth of the person, the person's parents, or their ancestors before their arrival in the United States. Some ethnic identities, such as Egyptian or Polish, can be traced to geographic areas outside the United States, while other ethnicities such as Pennsylvania German or Cajun evolved in the United States.

The ancestry question was intended to provide data for groups that were not included in the Hispanic origin and race questions. Therefore, although data on all groups are collected, the ancestry data shown in these tabulations are for non-Hispanic and non-race groups. Hispanic and race groups are included in the "Other groups" category for the ancestry tables in these tabulations.

The ancestry question allowed respondents to report one or more ancestry groups, although only the first two were coded. If a response was in terms of a dual ancestry, for example, "Irish English," the person was assigned two codes, in this case one for Irish and another for English. However, in certain cases, multiple responses such as "French Canadian," "Greek Cypriote," and "Scotch Irish" were assigned a single code reflecting their status as unique groups. If a person reported one of these unique groups in addition to another group, for example, "Scotch Irish English," resulting in three terms, that person received one code for the unique group (Scotch-Irish) and another one for the remaining group (English). If a person reported "English Irish French," only English and Irish were coded. Certain combinations of ancestries where the ancestry group is a part of another, such as "German-Bavarian," were coded as a single ancestry using the more specific group (Bavarian). Also, responses such as "Polish-American" or "Italian-American" were coded and tabulated as a single entry (Polish or Italian).

The Census Bureau accepted "American" as a unique ethnicity if it was given alone, with an ambiguous response, or with state names. If the respondent listed any other ethnic identity such as "Italian-American," generally the "American" portion of the response was not coded. However, distinct groups such as "American Indian," "Mexican American," and "African American" were coded and identified separately because they represented groups who considered themselves different from those who reported as "Indian," "Mexican," or "African," respectively.

The data is based on the total number of ancestries reported and coded. Thus, the sum of the counts in this type of presentation is not the total population but the total of all responses.

ECONOMY

Unemployment Rate: 2005 annual average. Includes all civilians age 16 or over who were unemployed and looking for work. *Source: U.S. Department of Labor, Bureau of Labor Statistics, Local Area Unemployment Statistics (http://www.bls.gov/lau/home.htm).*

Total Civilian Labor Force: 2005 annual average. Includes all civilians age 16 or over who were either employed, or unemployed and looking for work. *Source: U.S. Department of Labor, Bureau of Labor Statistics, Local Area Unemployment Statistics (http://www.bls.gov/lau/home.htm).*

Single-Family Building Permits Issued: Building permits issued for new single-family housing units in 2005. *Source: U.S. Census Bureau, Manufacturing and Construction Division (http://www.census.gov/const/www/permitsindex.html).*

Multi-Family Building Permits Issued: Building permits issued for new multi-family housing units in 2005. *Source: U.S. Census Bureau, Manufacturing and Construction Division (http://www.census.gov/const/www/permitsindex.html).*

Statistics on housing units authorized by building permits include housing units issued in local permit-issuing jurisdictions by a building or zoning permit. Not all areas of the country require a building or zoning permit. The statistics only represent those areas that do require a permit. Current surveys indicate that construction is undertaken for all but a very small percentage of housing units authorized by building permits. A major portion typically get under way during the month of permit issuance and most of the remainder begin within the three following months. Because of this lag, the housing unit authorization statistics do not represent the number of units actually put into construction for the period shown, and should therefore not be directly interpreted as "housing starts."

Statistics are based upon reports submitted by local building permit officials in response to a mail survey. They are obtained using Form C-404 const/www/c404.pdf, "Report of New Privately-Owned Residential Building or Zoning Permits Issued." When a report is not received, missing data are either (1) obtained from the Survey of Use of Permits (SUP) which is used to collect information on housing starts, or (2) imputed based on the assumption that the ratio of current month authorizations to those of a year ago should be the same for reporting and non-reporting places.

Employment by Occupation: Percentage of the employed civilian population 16 years and over in management, professional, service, sales, farming, construction, and production occupations. *Source: U.S. Bureau of the Census, Census of Population and Housing, 2000: Summary File 3.*

- **Management** includes management, business, and financial operations occupations:
  Management occupations, except farmers and farm managers
  Farmers and farm managers
  Business and financial operations occupations:
    Business operations specialists
    Financial specialists

- **Professional** includes professional and related occupations:
  Computer and mathematical occupations
  Architecture and engineering occupations:
    Architects, surveyors, cartographers, and engineers
    Drafters, engineering, and mapping technicians
  Life, physical, and social science occupations
  Community and social services occupations
  Legal occupations
  Education, training, and library occupations
  Arts, design, entertainment, sports, and media occupations
  Healthcare practitioners and technical occupations:
    Health diagnosing and treating practitioners and technical occupations
    Health technologists and technicians

- **Service** occupations include:
  Healthcare support occupations
  Protective service occupations:
    Fire fighting, prevention, and law enforcement workers, including supervisors

Other protective service workers, including supervisors
Food preparation and serving related occupations
Building and grounds cleaning and maintenance occupations
Personal care and service occupations

- **Sales** and office occupations include:
    Sales and related occupations
    Office and administrative support occupations

- **Farming,** fishing, and forestry occupations

- **Construction,** extraction, and maintenance occupations include:
    Construction and extraction occupations:
        Supervisors, construction, and extraction workers
        Construction trades workers
        Extraction workers
    Installation, maintenance, and repair occupations

- **Production,** transportation, and material moving occupations include:
    Production occupations
    Transportation and material moving occupations:
        Supervisors, transportation, and material moving workers
        Aircraft and traffic control occupations
        Motor vehicle operators
        Rail, water, and other transportation occupations
        Material moving workers

INCOME

Per Capita Income: Per capita income is the mean income computed for every man, woman, and child in a particular group. It is derived by dividing the total income of a particular group by the total population in that group. Per capita income is rounded to the nearest whole dollar. Figures shown are 2005 estimates. *Source: Claritas.*

Median Household Income: Includes the income of the householder and all other individuals 15 years old and over in the household, whether they are related to the householder or not. The median divides the income distribution into two equal parts: one-half of the cases falling below the median income and one-half above the median. For households, the median income is based on the distribution of the total number of households including those with no income. Median income for households is computed on the basis of a standard distribution and is rounded to the nearest whole dollar. Figures shown are 2005 estimates. *Source: Claritas.*

Average Household Income: Average household income is obtained by dividing total household income by the total number of households. Figures shown are 2005 estimates. *Source: Claritas.*

Percent of Households with Income of $100,000 or more: Figures shown are 2005 estimates. *Source: Claritas.*

Poverty Rate: Percentage of population with income in 1999 below the poverty level. Based on individuals for whom poverty status is determined. Poverty status was determined for all people except institutionalized people, people in military group quarters, people in college dormitories, and unrelated individuals under 15 years old. *Source: U.S. Bureau of the Census, Census of Population and Housing, 2000: Summary File 3.*

The poverty status of families and unrelated individuals in 1999 was determined using 48 thresholds (income cutoffs) arranged in a two-dimensional matrix. The matrix consists of family size (from 1 person to 9 or more people) cross-classified by presence and number of family members under 18 years old (from no children present to 8 or more children present). Unrelated individuals and 2-person families were further differentiated by the age of the reference person (RP) (under 65 years old and 65 years old and over).

To determine a person's poverty status, one compares the person's total family income with the poverty threshold appropriate for that person's family size and composition. If the total income of that person's family is less than the threshold appropriate for that family, then the person is considered poor, together with every member of his or her family. If a person is not living with anyone related by birth, marriage, or adoption, then the person's own income is compared with his or her poverty threshold.

TAXES

Total City Taxes Per Capita: Total city taxes collected divided by the population of the city. *Source: U.S. Bureau of the Census, State and Local Government Finances, 2002 (http://www.census.gov/govs/www/estimate.html).*

Taxes include:
- Property Taxes
- Sales and Gross Receipts Taxes
- Federal Customs Duties
- General Sales and Gross Receipts Taxes
- Selective Sales Taxes (alcoholic beverages; amusements; insurance premiums; motor fuels; pari-mutuels; public utilities; tobacco products; other)
- License Taxes (alcoholic beverages; amusements; corporations in general; hunting and fishing; motor vehicles motor vehicle operators; public utilities; occupation and business, NEC; other)
- Income Taxes (individual income; corporation net income; other)
- Death and Gift
- Documentary & Stock Transfer
- Severance
- Taxes, NEC

Total City Property Taxes Per Capita: Total city property taxes collected divided by the population of the city. *Source: U.S. Bureau of the Census, State and Local Government Finances, 2002 (http://www.census.gov/govs/www/estimate.html).*

Property Taxes include general property taxes, relating to property as a whole, taxed at a single rate or at classified rates according to the class of property. Property refers to real property (e.g. land and structures) as well as personal property; personal property can be either tangible (e.g. automobiles and boats) or intangible (e.g. bank accounts and stocks and bonds). Special property taxes, levied on selected types of property (e.g. oil and gas properties, house trailers, motor vehicles, and intangibles) and subject to rates not directly related to general property tax rates. Taxes based on income produced by property as a measure of its value on the assessment date.

EDUCATION

Educational Attainment: Figures shown are 2005 estimates and show the percent of population age 25 and over with a:

- **High school diploma (including GED) or higher:** includes people whose highest degree was a high school diploma or its equivalent, people who attended college but did not receive a degree, and people who received a college, university, or professional degree. People who reported completing the 12th grade but not receiving a diploma are not high school graduates.
- **Bachelor's degree or higher**
- **Master's degree or higher:** Master's degrees include the traditional MA and MS degrees and field-specific degrees, such as MSW, MEd, MBA, MLS, and Meng. *Source: Claritas.*

School Districts: Lists the name of each school district, the grade range (PK=pre-kindergarten; KG=kindergarten), the student enrollment, and the district headquarters' phone number. In each community profile, only school districts that have schools that are physically located within the community are shown. In addition, statistics for each school district cover the entire district, regardless of the physical location of the schools within the district. *Source: U.S. Department of Education, National Center for Educational Statistics, Directory of Public Elementary and Secondary Education Agencies, 2003-04.*

Four-year Colleges: Lists the name of each four-year college, the type of institution (private or public; for-profit or non-profit; religious affiliation; historically black college), the student enrollment, the phone number, and the annual tuition (including fees) for full-time, first-time undergraduate students (in-state and out-of-state). *Source: U.S. Department of Education, National Center for Educational Statistics, Directory of Postsecondary Institutions, 2004-05.*

Two-year Colleges: Lists the name of each two-year college, the type of institution (private or public; for-profit or non-profit; religious affiliation; historically black college), the student enrollment, the phone number, and the annual tuition (including fees) for full-time, first-time undergraduate students (in-state and out-of-state). *Source: U.S. Department of Education, National Center for Educational Statistics, Directory of Postsecondary Institutions, 2004-05.*

HOUSING

Homeownership Rate: Percentage of housing units that are owner-occupied. Figures shown are 2005 estimates. *Source: Claritas.*

Median Home Value: Median value of all owner-occupied housing units as reported by the owner. Figures shown are 2005 estimates. *Source: Claritas.*

Median Rent: Median monthly contract rent on specified renter-occupied and specified vacant-for-rent units. Specified renter-occupied and specified vacant-for-rent units exclude 1-family houses on 10 acres or more. Contract rent is the monthly rent agreed to or contracted for, regardless of any furnishings, utilities, fees, meals, or services that may be included. For vacant units, it is the monthly rent asked for the rental unit at the time of enumeration. *Source: U.S. Bureau of the Census, Census of Population and Housing, 2000: Summary File 3.*

Median Age of Housing: Median age of housing was calculated by subtracting median year structure built from 2000 (e.g. if the median year structure built is 1967, the median age of housing in that area is 33 years—2000 minus 1967). Year structure built refers to when the building was first constructed, not when it was remodeled, added to, or converted. For housing units under construction that met the housing unit definition—that is, all exterior windows, doors, and final usable floors were in place—the category "1999 or 2000" was used for tabulations. For mobile homes, houseboats, RVs, etc, the manufacturer's model year was assumed to be the year built. The data relate to the number of units built during the specified periods that were still in existence at the time of enumeration. *Source: U.S. Bureau of the Census, Census of Population and Housing, 2000: Summary File 3.*

HOSPITALS

Lists the hospital name and the number of licensed beds. *Source: Grey House Publishing, Directory of Hospital Personnel, 2005.*

SAFETY

Violent Crime Rate: Number of violent crimes reported per 10,000 population. Violent crimes include murder, forcible rape, robbery, and aggravated assault. *Source: Federal Bureau of Investigation, Uniform Crime Reports 2004 (http://www.fbi.gov/ucr/ucr.htm).*

Property Crime Rate: Number of property crimes reported per 10,000 population. Property crimes include burglary, larceny-theft, and motor vehicle theft. *Source: Federal Bureau of Investigation, Uniform Crime Reports 2004 (http://www.fbi.gov/ucr/ucr.htm).*

NEWSPAPERS

Lists the names of daily and weekly newspapers. Also includes the newspaper type and circulation, if available. *Source: BurrellesLuce MediaContacts 2005 (http://www.burrellesluce.com/MediaConnect).*

TRANSPORTATION

Commute to Work: Percentage of workers 16 years old and over that use the following means of transportation to commute to work: car; public transportation; walk; work from home. *Source: U.S. Bureau of the Census, Census of Population and Housing, 2000: Summary File 3.*

The means of transportation data for some areas may show workers using modes of public transportation that are not available in those areas (e.g. subway or elevated riders in a metropolitan area where there actually is no subway or elevated service). This result is largely due to people who worked during the reference week at a location that was different from their usual place of work (such as people away from home on business in an area where subway service was available) and people who used more than one means of transportation each day but whose principal means was unavailable where they lived (e.g. residents of non-metropolitan areas who drove to the fringe of a metropolitan area and took the commuter railroad most of the distance to work).

Travel Time to Work: Travel time to work for workers 16 years old and over. Reported for the following intervals: less than 15 minutes; 15 to 30 minutes; 30 to 45 minutes; 45 to 60 minutes; 60 minutes or more. *Source: U.S. Bureau of the Census, Census of Population and Housing, 2000: Summary File 3.*

Travel time to work refers to the total number of minutes that it usually took the person to get from home to work each day during the reference week. The elapsed time includes time spent waiting for public transportation, picking up passengers in carpools, and time spent in other activities related to getting to work.

Amtrak: Indicates if Amtrak service is available. Please note that the cities being served continually change. *Source: National Railroad Passenger Corporation, Amtrak National Timetable, 2005 (www.amtrak.com).*

AIRPORTS

Lists the local airport(s) along with type of service and hub size. *Source: U.S. Department of Transportation, Bureau of Transportation Statistics (http://www.bts.gov).*

ADDITIONAL INFORMATION CONTACTS

The following phone numbers are provided as sources of additional information: Chambers of Commerce; Economic Development Agencies; Boards of Realtors; Convention & Visitors Bureaus. Efforts have been made to provide the most recent area codes. However, area code changes may have occurred in listed numbers. *Source: Original research.*

INFORMATION FOR COUNTIES

PHYSICAL CHARACTERISTICS

Physical Location: Describes the physical location of the county. *Source: Columbia University Press, The Columbia Gazetteer of North America and original research.*

Land and Water Area: Land and water area in square miles. *Source: U.S. Bureau of the Census, Census of Population and Housing, 2000: Summary File 1.*

Time Zone: Lists the time zone. *Source: Original research.*

Year Organized: Year the county government was organized. *Source: National Association of Counties (www.naco.org).*

County Seat: Lists the county seat. If a county has more than one seat, then both are listed. *Source: National Association of Counties (www.naco.org).*

Metropolitan Area: Indicates the metropolitan area the county is located in. Also lists all the component counties of that metropolitan area. The Office of Management and Budget (OMB) defines metropolitan and micropolitan statistical areas. The current definitions are as of November 2004. *Source: U.S. Bureau of the Census (http://www.census.gov/population/www/estimates/metrodef.html).*

Climate: Includes all weather stations located within the county. Indicates the station name and elevation as well as the monthly average high and low temperatures, average precipitation, and average snowfall. The period of record is generally 1970-1999, however, certain weather stations contain averages going back as far as 1900. *Source: Grey House Publishing, Weather America: A Thirty-Year Summary of Statistical Weather Data and Rankings, 2001.*

POPULATION

Population: 1990 and 2000 figures are a 100% count of population. 2005 estimates and 2010 projections were provided by Claritas. *Source: Claritas; U.S. Bureau of the Census, Census of Population and Housing, 2000: Summary File 1.*

Population by Race: 2005 estimates includes the U.S. Bureau of the Census categories of White alone; Black alone; Asian alone; and Hispanic of any race. Alone refers to the fact that these figures are not in combination with any other race.

The concept of race, as used by the Census Bureau, reflects self-identification by people according to the race or races with which they most closely identify. These categories are socio-political constructs and should not be interpreted as being scientific or anthropological in nature. Furthermore, the race categories include both racial and national-origin groups.

- **White.** A person having origins in any of the original peoples of Europe, the Middle East, or North Africa. It includes people who indicate their race as "White" or report entries such as Irish, German, Italian, Lebanese, Near Easterner, Arab, or Polish.
- **Black or African American.** A person having origins in any of the Black racial groups of Africa. It includes people who indicate their race as "Black, African American, or Negro," or provide written entries such as African American, Afro-American, Kenyan, Nigerian, or Haitian.
- **Asian.** A person having origins in any of the original peoples of the Far East, Southeast Asia, or the Indian subcontinent including, for example, Cambodia, China, India, Japan, Korea, Malaysia, Pakistan, the Philippine Islands, Thailand, and Vietnam. It includes "Asian Indian," "Chinese," "Filipino," "Korean," "Japanese," "Vietnamese," and "Other Asian."
- **Hispanic.** The data on the Hispanic or Latino population, which was asked of all people, were derived from answers to long-form questionnaire Item 5, and short-form questionnaire Item 7. The terms "Spanish," "Hispanic origin," and "Latino" are used interchangeably. Some respondents identify with all three terms, while others may identify with only one of these three specific terms. Hispanics or Latinos who identify with the terms "Spanish," "Hispanic," or "Latino" are those who classify themselves in one of the specific Hispanic or Latino categories listed on the questionnaire — "Mexican," "Puerto Rican," or "Cuban" — as well as those who indicate that they are "other Spanish, Hispanic, or Latino." People who do not identify with one of the specific origins listed on the questionnaire but indicate that they are "other

Spanish, Hispanic, or Latino" are those whose origins are from Spain, the Spanish-speaking countries of Central or South America, the Dominican Republic, or people identifying themselves generally as Spanish, Spanish-American, Hispanic, Hispano, Latino, and so on. All write-in responses to the "other Spanish/Hispanic/Latino" category were coded. Origin can be viewed as the heritage, nationality group, lineage, or country of birth of the person or the person's parents or ancestors before their arrival in the United States. People who identify their origin as Spanish, Hispanic, or Latino may be of any race.

Population Density: 2005 population divided by the land area in square miles. *Source: Claritas; U.S. Bureau of the Census, Census of Population and Housing, 2000: Summary File 1.*

Average Household Size: Average household size was calculated by dividing the total population by the total number of households. Figures are 2005 estimates. *Source: Claritas.*

Median Age: Figures are 2005 estimates. *Source: Claritas.*

Male/Female Ratio: Number of males per 100 females. Figures are 2005 estimates. *Source: Claritas.*

RELIGION

Religion: Lists the largest religious groups (up to five) based on the number of adherents divided by the population of the county. Adherents are defined as "all members, including full members, their children and the estimated number of other regular participants who are not considered as communicant, confirmed or full members." The data is based on a study of 149 religious bodies sponsored by the Association of Statisticians of American Religious Bodies. The 149 bodies reported 268,254 congregations and 141,371,963 adherents. *Source: Glenmary Research Center, Religious Congregations & Membership in the United States 2000.*

ECONOMY

Unemployment Rate: 2005 annual average. Includes all civilians age 16 or over who were unemployed and looking for work. *Source: U.S. Department of Labor, Bureau of Labor Statistics, Local Area Unemployment Statistics (http://www.bls.gov/lau/home.htm).*

Total Civilian Labor Force: 2005 annual average. Includes all civilians age 16 or over who were either employed, or unemployed and looking for work. *Source: U.S. Department of Labor, Bureau of Labor Statistics, Local Area Unemployment Statistics (http://www.bls.gov/lau/home.htm).*

Leading Industries: Lists the three largest industries (excluding government) based on the number of employees. *Source: U.S. Bureau of the Census, County Business Patterns 2004 (http://www.census.gov/epcd/cbp/view/cbpview.html).*

Farms: The total number of farms and the total acreage they occupy. *Source: U.S. Department of Agriculture, National Agricultural Statistics Service, 2002 Census of Agriculture (http://www.nass.usda.gov/census).*

Companies that Employ 500 or more persons: The numbers of companies that employ 500 or more persons. Includes private employers only. *Source: U.S. Bureau of the Census, County Business Patterns 2004 (http://www.census.gov/epcd/cbp/view/cbpview.html).*

Companies that Employ 100 - 499 persons: The numbers of companies that employ 100 - 499 persons. Includes private employers only. *Source: U.S. Bureau of the Census, County Business Patterns 2004 (http://www.census.gov/epcd/cbp/view/cbpview.html).*

Companies that Employ 1 - 99 persons: The numbers of companies that employ 1 - 99 persons. Includes private employers only. *Source: U.S. Bureau of the Census, County Business Patterns 2004 (http://www.census.gov/epcd/cbp/view/cbpview.html)*

Black-Owned Businesses: Number of businesses that are majority-owned by a Black or African-American person(s). Majority ownership is defined as having 51 percent or more of the stock or equity in the business. Black or African American is defined as a person having origins in any of the black racial groups of Africa, including those who consider themselves to be "Haitian." *Source: U.S. Bureau of the Census, 2002 Economic Census, Survey of Business Owners: Black-Owned Firms, 2002 (http://www.census.gov/csd/sbo/index.html).*

Hispanic-Owned Businesses: Number of businesses that are majority-owned by a person(s) of Hispanic or Latino origin. Majority ownership is defined as having 51 percent or more of the stock or equity in the business. Hispanic or

User's Guide: Profiles

Latino origin is defined as a person of Cuban, Mexican, Puerto Rican, South or Central American, or other Spanish culture or origin, regardless of race. *Source: U.S. Bureau of the Census, 2002 Economic Census, Survey of Business Owners: Hispanic-Owned Firms, 2002 (http://www.census.gov/csd/sbo/index.html).*

Women-Owned Businesses: Number of businesses that are majority-owned by a woman. Majority ownership is defined as having 51 percent or more of the stock or equity in the business. *Source: U.S. Bureau of the Census, 2002 Economic Census, Survey of Business Owners: Women-Owned Firms, 2002 (http://www.census.gov/csd/sbo/index.html).*

The Survey of Business Owners (SBO), formerly known as the Surveys of Minority- and Women-Owned Business Enterprises (SMOBE/SWOBE), provides statistics that describe the composition of U.S. businesses by gender, Hispanic or Latino origin, and race. Additional statistics include owner's age, education level, veteran status, and primary function in the business; family- and home-based businesses; types of customers and workers; and sources of financing for expansion, capital improvements, or start-up. Economic policymakers in federal, state and local governments use the SBO data to understand conditions of business success and failure by comparing census-to-census changes in business performances and by comparing minority-/nonminority- and women-/men-owned businesses.

Retail Sales per Capita: Total dollar amount of estimated retail sales divided by the estimated population of the county in 2006. *Source: Editor & Publisher Market Guide 2006*

Single-Family Building Permits Issued: Building permits issued for new, single-family housing units in 2005. *Source: U.S. Census Bureau, Manufacturing and Construction Division (http://www.census.gov/const/www/permitsindex.html).*

Multi-Family Building Permits Issued: Building permits issued for new, multi-family housing units in 2005. *Source: U.S. Census Bureau, Manufacturing and Construction Division (http://www.census.gov/const/www/permitsindex.html).*

Statistics on housing units authorized by building permits include housing units issued in local permit-issuing jurisdictions by a building or zoning permit. Not all areas of the country require a building or zoning permit. The statistics only represent those areas that do require a permit. Current surveys indicate that construction is undertaken for all but a very small percentage of housing units authorized by building permits. A major portion typically get under way during the month of permit issuance and most of the remainder begin within the three following months. Because of this lag, the housing unit authorization statistics do not represent the number of units actually put into construction for the period shown, and should therefore not be directly interpreted as "housing starts."

Statistics are based upon reports submitted by local building permit officials in response to a mail survey. They are obtained using Form C-404 const/www/c404.pdf, "Report of New Privately-Owned Residential Building or Zoning Permits Issued." When a report is not received, missing data are either (1) obtained from the Survey of Use of Permits (SUP) which is used to collect information on housing starts, or (2) imputed based on the assumption that the ratio of current month authorizations to those of a year ago should be the same for reporting and non-reporting places.

INCOME

Per Capita Income: Per capita income is the mean income computed for every man, woman, and child in a particular group. It is derived by dividing the total income of a particular group by the total population in that group. Per capita income is rounded to the nearest whole dollar. Figures shown are 2005 estimates. *Source: Claritas.*

Median Household Income: Includes the income of the householder and all other individuals 15 years old and over in the household, whether they are related to the householder or not. The median divides the income distribution into two equal parts: one-half of the cases falling below the median income and one-half above the median. For households, the median income is based on the distribution of the total number of households including those with no income. Median income for households is computed on the basis of a standard distribution and is rounded to the nearest whole dollar. Figures shown are 2005 estimates. *Source: Claritas.*

Average Household Income: Average household income is obtained by dividing total household income by the total number of households. Figures shown are 2005 estimates. *Source: Claritas.*

Percent of Households with Income of $100,000 or more: Figures shown are 2005 estimates. *Source: Claritas.*

Poverty Rate: Estimated percentage of population with income in 2003 below the poverty level. *Source: U.S. Bureau of the Census, Small Area Income & Poverty Estimates.*

Bankruptcy Rate: The personal bankruptcy filing rate is the number of bankruptcies per thousand residents in 2005. Personal bankruptcy filings include both Chapter 7 (liquidations) and Chapter 13 (reorganizations) based on the county of residence of the filer. *Source: Federal Deposit Insurance Corporation, Regional Economic Conditions (http://www2.fdic.gov/recon/index.html).*

TAXES

Total County Taxes Per Capita: Total county taxes collected divided by the population of the county. *Source: U.S. Bureau of the Census, State and Local Government Finances, 2002 (http://www.census.gov/govs/www/estimate.html).*

Taxes include:
- Property Taxes
- Sales and Gross Receipts Taxes
- Federal Customs Duties
- General Sales and Gross Receipts Taxes
- Selective Sales Taxes (alcoholic beverages; amusements; insurance premiums; motor fuels; pari-mutuels; public utilities; tobacco products; other)
- License Taxes (alcoholic beverages; amusements; corporations in general; hunting and fishing; motor vehicles motor vehicle operators; public utilities; occupation and business, NEC; other)
- Income Taxes (individual income; corporation net income; other)
- Death and Gift
- Documentary & Stock Transfer
- Severance
- Taxes, NEC

Total County Property Taxes Per Capita: Total county property taxes collected divided by the population of the county. *Source: U.S. Bureau of the Census, State and Local Government Finances, 2002 (http://www.census.gov/govs/www/estimate.html).*

Property Taxes include general property taxes, relating to property as a whole, taxed at a single rate or at classified rates according to the class of property. Property refers to real property (e.g. land and structures) as well as personal property; personal property can be either tangible (e.g. automobiles and boats) or intangible (e.g. bank accounts and stocks and bonds). Special property taxes, levied on selected types of property (e.g. oil and gas properties, house trailers, motor vehicles, and intangibles) and subject to rates not directly related to general property tax rates. Taxes based on income produced by property as a measure of its value on the assessment date.

EDUCATION

Educational Attainment: Figures shown are 2005 estimates and show the percent of population age 25 and over with a:

- **High school diploma (including GED) or higher:** includes people whose highest degree was a high school diploma or its equivalent, people who attended college but did not receive a degree, and people who received a college, university, or professional degree. People who reported completing the 12th grade but not receiving a diploma are not high school graduates.
- **Bachelor's degree or higher**
- **Master's degree or higher:** Master's degrees include the traditional MA and MS degrees and field-specific degrees, such as MSW, MEd, MBA, MLS, and Meng. *Source: Claritas.*

HOUSING

Homeownership Rate: Percentage of housing units that are owner-occupied. Figures shown are 2005 estimates. *Source: Claritas.*

Median Home Value: Median value of all owner-occupied housing units as reported by the owner. Figures shown are 2005 estimates. *Source: Claritas.*

Median Rent: Median monthly contract rent on specified renter-occupied and specified vacant-for-rent units. Specified renter-occupied and specified vacant-for-rent units exclude 1-family houses on 10 acres or more. Contract rent is the monthly rent agreed to or contracted for, regardless of any furnishings, utilities, fees, meals, or services that may be included. For vacant units, it is the monthly rent asked for the rental unit at the time of enumeration. *Source: U.S. Bureau of the Census, Census of Population and Housing, 2000: Summary File 3.*

Median Age of Housing: Median age of housing was calculated by subtracting median year structure built from 2000 (e.g. if the median year structure built is 1967, the median age of housing in that area is 33 years — 2000 minus 1967). Year structure built refers to when the building was first constructed, not when it was remodeled, added to, or converted. For housing units under construction that met the housing unit definition—that is, all exterior windows, doors, and final usable floors were in place—the category "1999 or 2000" was used for tabulations. For mobile homes, houseboats, RVs, etc, the manufacturer's model year was assumed to be the year built. The data relate to the number of units built during the specified periods that were still in existence at the time of enumeration. *Source: U.S. Bureau of the Census, Census of Population and Housing, 2000: Summary File 3.*

HEALTH AND VITAL STATISTICS

Birth Rate: Estimated number of births per 10,000 population in 2004. *Source: U.S. Census Bureau, Population Estimates, July 1, 2003 - July 1, 2004 (http://www.census.gov/popest/births.html).*

Death Rate: Estimated number of deaths per 10,000 population in 2004. *Source: U.S. Census Bureau, Population Estimates, July 1, 2003 - July 1, 2004 (http://www.census.gov/popest/births.html).*

Age-adjusted Cancer Mortality Rate: Number of age-adjusted deaths from cancer per 100,000 population in 2002. Cancer is defined as International Classification of Disease (ICD) codes C00 - D48.9 Neoplasms. *Source: Centers for Disease Control, CDC Wonder (http://wonder.cdc.gov).*

Age-adjusted death rates are weighted averages of the age-specific death rates, where the weights represent a fixed population by age. They are used because the rates of almost all causes of death vary by age. Age adjustment is a technique for "removing" the effects of age from crude rates, so as to allow meaningful comparisons across populations with different underlying age structures. For example, comparing the crude rate of heart disease in New York to that of California is misleading, because the relatively older population in New York will lead to a higher crude death rate, even if the age-specific rates of heart disease in New York and California are the same. For such a comparison, age-adjusted rates would be preferable. Age-adjusted rates should be viewed as relative indexes rather than as direct or actual profiles of mortality risk.

Death rates based on counts of twenty or less (<=20) are flagged as "Unreliable". Death rates based on fewer than three years of data for counties with populations of less than 100,000 in the 1990 Census counts, are also flagged as "Unreliable" if the number of deaths is five or less (<=5).

Air Quality Index: The percentage of days in 2005 the AQI fell into the Good (0-50), Moderate (51-100), Unhealthy for Sensitive Groups (101-150), and Unhealthy (151+) ranges. *Source: Air Quality Index Report, 2005, U.S. Environmental Protection Agency, Office of Air and Radiation (http://www.epa.gov/oar).*

The AQI is an index for reporting daily air quality. It tells you how clean or polluted your air is, and what associated health concerns you should be aware of. The AQI focuses on health effects that can happen within a few hours or days after breathing polluted air. EPA uses the AQI for five major air pollutants regulated by the Clean Air Act: ground-level ozone, particulate matter, carbon monoxide, sulfur dioxide, and nitrogen dioxide. For each of these pollutants, EPA has established national air quality standards to protect against harmful health effects.

The AQI runs from 0 to 500. The higher the AQI value, the greater the level of air pollution and the greater the health danger. For example, an AQI value of 50 represents good air quality and little potential to affect public health, while an AQI value over 300 represents hazardous air quality. An AQI value of 100 generally corresponds to the national air quality standard for the pollutant, which is the level EPA has set to protect public health. So, AQI values below 100 are generally thought of as satisfactory. When AQI values are above 100, air quality is considered to be unhealthy—at first for certain sensitive groups of people, then for everyone as AQI values get higher. Each category corresponds to a different level of health concern. For example, when the AQI for a pollutant is between 51 and 100, the health concern is "Moderate." Here are the six levels of health concern and what they mean:

- "Good" The AQI value for your community is between 0 and 50. Air quality is considered satisfactory and air pollution poses little or no risk.
- "Moderate" The AQI for your community is between 51 and 100. Air quality is acceptable; however, for some pollutants there may be a moderate health concern for a very small number of individuals. For example, people who are unusually sensitive to ozone may experience respiratory symptoms.
- "Unhealthy for Sensitive Groups" Certain groups of people are particularly sensitive to the harmful effects of certain air pollutants. This means they are likely to be affected at lower levels than the general public. For example, children and adults who are active outdoors and people with respiratory disease are at greater risk from exposure to ozone, while people with heart disease are at greater risk from carbon monoxide. Some people may be sensitive to more than one pollutant. When AQI values are between 101 and 150, members of sensitive groups may experience health effects. The general public is not likely to be affected when the AQI is in this range.
- "Unhealthy" AQI values are between 151 and 200. Everyone may begin to experience health effects. Members of sensitive groups may experience more serious health effects.
- "Very Unhealthy" AQI values between 201 and 300 trigger a health alert, meaning everyone may experience more serious health effects.
- "Hazardous" AQI values over 300 trigger health warnings of emergency conditions. The entire population is more likely to be affected.

Number of Physicians: The number of active, non-federal physicians per 10,000 population in 2004. *Source: Area Resource File (ARF). February 2005. U.S. Department of Health and Human Services, Health Resources and Services Administration, Bureau of Health Professions, Rockville, MD.*

Number of Hospital Beds: The number of hospital beds per 10,000 population in 2003. *Source: Area Resource File (ARF). February 2005. U.S. Department of Health and Human Services, Health Resources and Services Administration, Bureau of Health Professions, Rockville, MD.*

Number of Hospital Admissions: The number of hospital admissions per 10,000 population in 2003. *Source: Area Resource File (ARF). February 2005. U.S. Department of Health and Human Services, Health Resources and Services Administration, Bureau of Health Professions, Rockville, MD.*

ELECTIONS

Elections: 2004 Presidential election results. *Source: Dave Leip's Atlas of U.S. Presidential Elections (http://www.uselectionatlas.org).*

NATIONAL AND STATE PARKS

Lists National and State parks located in the area. *Source: U.S. Geological Survey, Geographic Names Information System.*

ADDITIONAL INFORMATION CONTACTS

The following phone numbers are provided as sources of additional information: Chambers of Commerce; Economic Development Agencies; Boards of Realtors; Convention & Visitors Bureaus. Efforts have been made to provide the most recent area codes. However, area code changes may have occurred in listed numbers. *Source: Original research.*

User's Guide: Education

School District Rankings

Number of Schools: Total number of schools in the district. *Source: U.S. Department of Education, National Center for Education Statistics, Common Core of Data, Public Elementary/Secondary School Universe Survey: School Year 2003-2004.*

Number of Teachers: Teachers are defined as individuals who provide instruction to pre-kindergarten, kindergarten, grades 1 through 12, or ungraded classes, or individuals who teach in an environment other than a classroom setting, and who maintain daily student attendance records. Numbers reported are full-time equivalents (FTE). *Source: U.S. Department of Education, National Center for Education Statistics, Common Core of Data, Local Education Agency (School District) Universe Survey: School Year 2003-2004.*

Number of Students: A student is an individual for whom instruction is provided in an elementary or secondary education program that is not an adult education program and is under the jurisdiction of a school, school system, or other education institution. *Sources: U.S. Department of Education, National Center for Education Statistics, Common Core of Data, Local Education Agency (School District) Universe Survey: School Year 2003-2004 and Public Elementary/Secondary School Universe Survey: School Year 2003-2004*

Individual Education Program (IEP) Students: A written instructional plan for students with disabilities designated as special education students under IDEA-Part B. The written instructional plan includes a statement of present levels of educational performance of a child; statement of annual goals, including short-term instructional objectives; statement of specific educational services to be provided and the extent to which the child will be able to participate in regular educational programs; the projected date for initiation and anticipated duration of services; the appropriate objectives, criteria and evaluation procedures; and the schedules for determining, on at least an annual basis, whether instructional objectives are being achieved. *Source: U.S. Department of Education, National Center for Education Statistics, Common Core of Data, Local Education Agency (School District) Universe Survey: School Year 2003-2004*

English Language Learner (ELL) Students: Formerly referred to as Limited English Proficient (LEP). Students being served in appropriate programs of language assistance (e.g., English as a Second Language, High Intensity Language Training, bilingual education). Does not include pupils enrolled in a class to learn a language other than English. Also Limited-English-Proficient students are individuals who were not born in the United States or whose native language is a language other than English; or individuals who come from environments where a language other than English is dominant; or individuals who are American Indians and Alaskan Natives and who come from environments where a language other than English has had a significant impact on their level of English language proficiency; and who, by reason thereof, have sufficient difficulty speaking, reading, writing, or understanding the English language, to deny such individuals the opportunity to learn successfully in classrooms where the language of instruction is English or to participate fully in our society. *Source: U.S. Department of Education, National Center for Education Statistics, Common Core of Data, Local Education Agency (School District) Universe Survey: School Year 2003-2004*

Migrant Students: A migrant student as defined under federal regulation 34 CFR 200.40: 1) (a) Is younger than 22 (and has not graduated from high school or does not hold a high school equivalency certificate), but (b), if the child is too young to attend school-sponsored educational programs, is old enough to benefit from an organized instructional program; and 2) A migrant agricultural worker or a migrant fisher or has a parent, spouse, or guardian who is a migrant agricultural worker or a migrant fisher; and 3) Performs, or has a parent, spouse, or guardian who performs qualifying agricultural or fishing employment as a principal means of livelihood; and 4) Has moved within the preceding 36 months to obtain or to accompany or join a parent, spouse, or guardian to obtain, temporary or seasonal employment in agricultural or fishing work; and 5) Has moved from one school district to another; or in a state that is comprised of a single school district, has moved from one administrative area to another within such district; or resides in a school district of more than 15,000 square miles, and migrates a distance of 20 miles or more to a temporary residence to engage in a fishing activity. Provision 5 currently applies only to Alaska. *Source: U.S. Department of Education, National Center for Education Statistics, Common Core of Data, Public Elementary/Secondary School Universe Survey: School Year 2003-2004*

Students Eligible for Free Lunch Program: The free lunch program is defined as a program under the National School Lunch Act that provides cash subsidies for free lunches to students based on family size and income criteria. *Source: U.S. Department of Education, National Center for Education Statistics, Common Core of Data, Public Elementary/Secondary School Universe Survey: School Year 2003-2004*

Students Eligible for Reduced-Price Lunch Program: A student who is eligible to participate in the Reduced-Price Lunch Program under the National School Lunch Act. *Source: U.S. Department of Education, National Center for Education Statistics, Common Core of Data, Public Elementary/Secondary School Universe Survey: School Year 2003-2004*

Student/Teacher Ratio: The number of students divided by the number of teachers (FTE). See Number of Students and Number of Teachers above for for information.

Student/Librarian Ratio: The number of students divided by the number of library and media support staff. Library and media support staff are defined as staff members who render other professional library and media services; also includes library aides and those involved in library/media support. Their duties include selecting, preparing, caring for, and making available to instructional staff, equipment, films, filmstrips, transparencies, tapes, TV programs, and similar materials maintained separately or as part of an instructional materials center. Also included are activities in the audio-visual center, TV studio, related-work-study areas, and services provided by audio-visual personnel. Numbers are based on full-time equivalents. *Source: U.S. Department of Education, National Center for Education Statistics, Common Core of Data, Local Education Agency (School District) Universe Survey: School Year 2003-2004.*

Student/Counselor Ratio: The number of students divided by the number of guidance counselors. Guidance counselors are professional staff assigned specific duties and school time for any of the following activities in an elementary or secondary setting: counseling with students and parents; consulting with other staff members on learning problems; evaluating student abilities; assisting students in making educational and career choices; assisting students in personal and social development; providing referral assistance; and/or working with other staff members in planning and conducting guidance programs for students. The state applies its own standards in apportioning the aggregate of guidance counselors/directors into the elementary and secondary level components. Numbers reported are full-time equivalents. *Source: U.S. Department of Education, National Center for Education Statistics, Common Core of Data, Local Education Agency (School District) Universe Survey: School Year 2003-2004.*

Current Spending per Student: Expenditure for Instruction, Support Services, and Other Elementary/Secondary Programs. Includes salaries, employee benefits, purchased services, and supplies, as well as payments made by states on behalf of school districts. Also includes transfers made by school districts into their own retirement system. Excludes expenditure for Non-Elementary/Secondary Programs, debt service, capital outlay, and transfers to other governments or school districts. This item is formally called "Current Expenditures for Public Elementary/Secondary Education."

Instruction: Includes payments from all funds for salaries, employee benefits, supplies, materials, and contractual services for elementary/secondary instruction. It excludes capital outlay, debt service, and interfund transfers for elementary/secondary instruction. Instruction covers regular, special, and vocational programs offered in both the regular school year and summer school. It excludes instructional support activities as well as adult education and community services. Instruction salaries includes salaries for teachers and teacher aides and assistants.

Support Services: Relates to support services functions (series 2000) defined in Financial Accounting for Local and State School Systems (National Center for Education Statistics 2000). Includes payments from all funds for salaries, employee benefits, supplies, materials, and contractual services. It excludes capital outlay, debt service, and interfund transfers. It includes expenditure for the following functions:

- Business/Central/Other Support Services
- General Administration
- Instructional Staff Support
- Operation and Maintenance
- Pupil Support Services
- Pupil Transportation Services
- School Administration
- Nonspecified Support Services

Values shown are dollars per pupil per year. They were calculated by dividing the total dollar amounts by the fall membership. Fall membership is comprised of the total student enrollment on October 1 (or the closest school day to October 1) for all grade levels (including prekindergarten and kindergarten) and ungraded pupils. Membership includes students both present and absent on the measurement day. *Source: U.S. Department of Education, National Center for Education Statistics, Common Core of Data, School District Finance Survey (F-33), Fiscal Year 2001.*

Number of Diploma Recipients: A student who has received a diploma during the previous school year or subsequent summer school. This category includes regular diploma recipients and other diploma recipients. A High School Diploma is a formal document certifying the successful completion of a secondary school program prescribed by the state education agency or other appropriate body. *Source: U.S. Department of Education, National Center for Education Statistics, Common Core of Data, Local Education Agency (School District) Universe Survey: School Year 2003-2004.*

High School Drop-out Rate: A dropout is a student who was enrolled in school at some time during the previous school year; was not enrolled at the beginning of the current school year; has not graduated from high school or completed a state or district approved educational program; and does not meet any of the following exclusionary conditions: has transferred to another public school district, private school, or state- or district-approved educational program; is temporarily absent due to suspension or school-approved illness; or has died. The values shown cover grades 9 through 12. *Source: U.S. Department of Education, National Center for Education Statistics, Common Core of Data, Local Education Agency Universe Dropout File: School Year 2000-2001*

Note: n/a indicates data not available.

Ohio Educational Profile

Please refer to the District Rankings section in the front of this User's Guide for an explanation of data for all items except for the following:

Average Salary: The average teacher salary in 2003-2004. *Source: American Federation of Teachers, Survey & Analysis of Teacher Salary Trends 2004*

College Entrance Exam Scores:

    Scholastic Aptitude Test (SAT). *Note: The College Board strongly discourages the comparison or ranking of states on the basis of SAT scores alone. Source: The College Board, Mean SAT Reasoning Test™ Verbal and Math Scores by State, with Changes for Selected Years, 2005*

    American College Testing Program (ACT). *ACT, 2005 ACT National and State Scores*

National Assessment of Educational Progress (NAEP)

The National Assessment of Educational Progress (NAEP), also known as "the Nation's Report Card," is the only nationally representative and continuing assessment of what America's students know and can do in various subject areas. As a result of the "No Child Left Behind" legislation, all states are required to participate in NAEP. For more information please visit the U.S. Department of Education, National Center for Education Statistics at http://nces.ed.gov/nationsreportcard.

Ohio Achievement Tests (OAT) and Proficiency Tests (PT)

In 2004-2005, Ohio administered achievement tests in grades 3, 4, 5, 7 and 8 to assess whether students met its new academic content standards in core subjects. Ohio also used proficiency tests to measure whether students in grades 4 and 6 met grade-level standards in several subjects (note that these tests are being phased out and will be fully replaced by the achievement tests in 2005-2006).

The Ninth-Grade Proficiency Test, which is currently a high school graduation requirement, was administered in grades 11 and 12 during 2004-2005 (previously it was also administered in grade 9). Beginning with the class of 2007, this test will be fully replaced with the Ohio Graduation Tests (OGT), which are given to grade 10 students.

The achievement tests include portions on reading and math for grades 3 and 8, reading and writing for grade 4, reading for grade 5, and math for grade 7. The grade 4 proficiency test covers math, science and citizen/social studies. The grade 6 and 9 proficiency tests and the OGT all cover reading, writing, math, science and citizen/social studies.

The proficiency, achievement and OGT results report the level of proficiency a student demonstrates in each of the subject areas tested. Students are rated at one of the following five levels: advanced, accelerated, proficient, basic and limited.

Ohio Graduation Tests (OGT)

The new Ohio Graduation Tests are a key part of Ohio's education reform to establish an aligned system of standards, assessments (tests) and accountability for Ohio schools. The testing requirements were established by the Ohio General Assembly in 2001 based on recommendations by the Governor's Commission for Student Success, a broad-based group appointed by Governor Taft to improve Ohio's schools. Five tests in reading, writing, mathematics, science and social studies will make up the OGT.

The purposes of the OGT are to:

- Ensure that students who receive a high school diploma demonstrate at least high school levels of achievement;
- Measure the level of reading, writing, mathematics, science and social studies skills expected of students at the end of the 10th grade;
- Meet federal requirement for high school testing.

The new graduation tests will eventually replace the Ohio Ninth-Grade Proficiency Tests. The new tests are a more rigorous measure of students' high school achievement. They measure content learned through the end of the 10th-grade and are aligned to the new academic content standards. The OGT was originally set to be implemented with the graduating class of 2005. State leaders decided a delay was needed to ensure that students have the opportunity to learn the material included in the new academic content standards. As of December, 2002, the Board has adopted new content standards for English language arts, mathematics, science and social studies. For more information please visit the Ohio Department of Education at http://www.ode.state.oh.us/

User's Guide: Ancestry

Places Covered

The ranking tables are based on 1,054 places in Ohio. Places covered fall into one of the following categories: 243 cities; 699 villages; and 112 Census Designated Places (CDP). The U.S. Bureau of the Census defines a CDP as "a statistical entity, defined for each decennial census according to Census Bureau guidelines, comprising a densely settled concentration of population that is not within an incorporated place, but is locally identified by a name. CDPs are delineated cooperatively by state and local officials and the Census Bureau, following Census Bureau guidelines. Beginning with Census 2000 there are no size limits."

Source of Data

The ancestries shown in this chapter were compiled from three different sections of the 2000 Census: Race; Hispanic Origin; and Ancestry. While the ancestries are sorted alphabetically for ease-of-use, it's important to note the origin of each piece of data. Data for Race and Hispanic Origin was taken from Summary File 1 (SF1) while Ancestry data was taken from Summary File 3 (SF3). The distinction is important because SF1 contains the 100-percent data, which is the information compiled from the questions asked of all people and about every housing unit. SF3 was compiled from a sample of approximately 19 million housing units (about 1 in 6 households) that received the Census 2000 long-form questionnaire.

Ancestries Based on Race

The data on race were derived from answers to the question on race that was asked of all people. The concept of race, as used by the Census Bureau, reflects self-identification by people according to the race or races with which they most closely identify. These categories are sociopolitical constructs and should not be interpreted as being scientific or anthropological in nature. Furthermore, the race categories include both racial and national-origin groups.

If an individual did not provide a race response, the race or races of the householder or other household members were assigned using specific rules of precedence of household relationship. For example, if race was missing for a natural-born child in the household, then either the race or races of the householder, another natural-born child, or the spouse of the householder were assigned. If race was not reported for anyone in the household, the race or races of a householder in a previously processed household were assigned.

African-American/Black:	Creek	Yaqui	Other Asian, not specified
Not Hispanic	Crow	Yuman	Hawaii Native/Pacific Islander:
Hispanic	Delaware	All other tribes	Melanesian:
Alaska Native tribes, specified:	Houma	American Indian tribes,	Fijian
Alaska Athabascan	Iroquois	not specified	Other Melanesian
Aleut	Kiowa	Asian:	Micronesian:
Eskimo	Latin American Indians	Bangladeshi	Guamanian/Chamorro
Tlingit-Haida	Lumbee	Cambodian	Other Micronesian
All other tribes	Menominee	Chinese, except Taiwanese	Polynesian:
Alaska Native tribes, not specified	Navajo	Filipino	Native Hawaiian
American Indian or Alaska Native	Osage	Hmong	Samoan
tribes, not specified	Ottawa	Indian	Tongan
American Indian tribes, specified:	Paiute	Indonesian	Other Polynesian
Apache	Pima	Japanese	Other Pacific Islander,
Blackfeet	Potawatomi	Korean	specified
Cherokee	Pueblo	Laotian	Other Pacific Islander,
Cheyenne	Puget Sound Salish	Malaysian	not specified
Chickasaw	Seminole	Pakistani	White:
Chippewa	Shoshone	Sri Lankan	Not Hispanic
Choctaw	Sioux	Taiwanese	Hispanic
Colville	Tohono O'Odham	Thai	
Comanche	Ute	Vietnamese	
Cree	Yakama	Other Asian, specified	

African American or Black: A person having origins in any of the Black racial groups of Africa. It includes people who indicate their race as "Black, African Am., or Negro," or provide written entries such as African American, Afro American, Kenyan, Nigerian, or Haitian.

American Indian or Alaska Native: A person having origins in any of the original peoples of North and South America (including Central America) and who maintain tribal affiliation or community attachment. It includes people who classified themselves as described below.

American Indian - Includes people who indicated their race as "American Indian," entered the name of an Indian tribe, or reported such entries as Canadian Indian, French American Indian, or Spanish-American Indian.

Respondents who identified themselves as American Indian were asked to report their enrolled or principal tribe. Therefore, tribal data in tabulations reflect the written entries reported on the questionnaires. Some of the entries (for example, Iroquois, Sioux, Colorado River, and Flathead) represent nations or reservations. The information on tribe is based on self identification and therefore does not reflect any designation of federally or state-recognized tribe. Information on American Indian tribes is presented in summary files. The information for Census 2000 is derived from the American Indian Tribal Classification List for the 1990 census that was updated based on a December 1997 Federal Register Notice, entitled "Indian Entities Recognized and Eligible to Receive Service From the United States Bureau of Indian Affairs," Department of the Interior, Bureau of Indian Affairs, issued by the Office of Management and Budget.

Alaska Native - Includes written responses of Eskimos, Aleuts, and Alaska Indians, as well as entries such as Arctic Slope, Inupiat, Yupik, Alutiiq, Egegik, and Pribilovian. The Alaska tribes are the Alaskan Athabascan, Tlingit, and Haida. The information for Census 2000 is based on the American Indian Tribal Classification List for the 1990 census, which was expanded to list the individual Alaska Native Villages when provided as a written response for race.

Asian: A person having origins in any of the original peoples of the Far East, Southeast Asia, or the Indian subcontinent including, for example, Cambodia, China, India, Japan, Korea, Malaysia, Pakistan, the Philippine Islands, Thailand, and Vietnam. It includes "Asian Indian," "Chinese," "Filipino," "Korean," "Japanese," "Vietnamese," and "Other Asian."

Asian Indian - Includes people who indicated their race as "Asian Indian" or identified themselves as Bengalese, Bharat, Dravidian, East Indian, or Goanese.

Chinese - Includes people who indicate their race as "Chinese" or who identify themselves as Cantonese, or Chinese American.

Filipino - Includes people who indicate their race as "Filipino" or who report entries such as Philipino, Philipine, or Filipino American.

Japanese - Includes people who indicate their race as "Japanese" or who report entries such as Nipponese or Japanese American.

Korean - Includes people who indicate their race as "Korean" or who provide a response of Korean American.

Vietnamese - Includes people who indicate their race as "Vietnamese" or who provide a response of Vietnamese American.

Cambodian - Includes people who provide a response such as Cambodian or Cambodia.

Hmong - Includes people who provide a response such as Hmong, Laohmong, or Mong.

Laotian - Includes people who provide a response such as Laotian, Laos, or Lao.

Thai - Includes people who provide a response such as Thai, Thailand, or Siamese.

Other Asian - Includes people who provide a response of Bangladeshi; Bhutanese; Burmese; Indochinese; Indonesian; Iwo Jiman; Madagascar; Malaysian; Maldivian; Nepalese; Okinawan; Pakistani; Singaporean; Sri Lankan; or Other Asian, specified and Other Asian, not specified.

Native Hawaiian or Other Pacific Islander: A person having origins in any of the original peoples of Hawaii, Guam, Samoa, or other Pacific Islands. It includes people who indicate their race as "Native Hawaiian," "Guamanian or Chamorro," "Samoan," and "Other Pacific Islander."

> *Native Hawaiian* - Includes people who indicate their race as "Native Hawaiian" or who identify themselves as "Part Hawaiian" or "Hawaiian."
>
> *Guamanian or Chamorro* - Includes people who indicate their race as such, including written entries of Chamorro or Guam.
>
> *Samoan* - Includes people who indicate their race as "Samoan" or who identify themselves as American Samoan or Western Samoan.
>
> *Other Pacific Islander* - Includes people who provide a write-in response of a Pacific Islander group, such as Carolinian, Chuukese (Trukese), Fijian, Kosraean, Melanesian, Micronesian, Northern Mariana Islander, Palauan, Papua New Guinean, Pohnpeian, Polynesian, Solomon Islander, Tahitian, Tokelauan, Tongan, Yapese, or Pacific Islander, not specified.

White: A person having origins in any of the original peoples of Europe, the Middle East, or North Africa. It includes people who indicate their race as "White" or report entries such as Irish, German, Italian, Lebanese, Near Easterner, Arab, or Polish.

Ancestries Based on Hispanic Origin

Hispanic or Latino:	Salvadoran	Argentinean	Uruguayan
Central American:	Other Central American	Bolivian	Venezuelan
Costa Rican	Cuban	Chilean	Other South American
Guatemalan	Dominican Republic	Colombian	Other Hispanic/Latino
Honduran	Mexican	Ecuadorian	
Nicaraguan	Puerto Rican	Paraguayan	
Panamanian	South American:	Peruvian	

The data on the Hispanic or Latino population were derived from answers to a question that was asked of all people. The terms "Spanish," "Hispanic origin," and "Latino" are used interchangeably. Some respondents identify with all three terms while others may identify with only one of these three specific terms. Hispanics or Latinos who identify with the terms "Spanish," "Hispanic," or "Latino" are those who classify themselves in one of the specific Spanish, Hispanic, or Latino categories listed on the questionnaire ("Mexican," "Puerto Rican," or "Cuban") as well as those who indicate that they are "other Spanish/Hispanic/Latino." People who do not identify with one of the specific origins listed on the questionnaire but indicate that they are "other Spanish, Hispanic, or Latino" are those whose origins are from Spain, the Spanish-speaking countries of Central or South America, the Dominican Republic, or people identifying themselves generally as Spanish, Spanish-American, Hispanic, Hispano, Latino, and so on. All write-in responses to the "other Spanish/Hispanic/Latino" category were coded.

Origin can be viewed as the heritage, nationality group, lineage, or country of birth of the person or the person's parents or ancestors before their arrival in the United States. People who identify their origin as Spanish, Hispanic, or Latino may be of any race.

In all cases where the origin of households, families, or occupied housing units is classified as Spanish, Hispanic, or Latino, the origin of the householder is used. If an individual could not provide a Hispanic origin response, their origin was assigned using specific rules of precedence of household relationship. For example, if origin was missing for a natural-born daughter in the household, then either the origin of the householder, another natural-born child, or spouse of the householder was assigned. If Hispanic origin was not reported for anyone in the household, the Hispanic origin of a householder in a previously processed household with the same race was assigned.

Other Ancestries

Acadian/Cajun	Moroccan	French, except Basque	Scottish
Afghan	Palestinian	French Canadian	Serbian
African, Subsaharan:	Syrian	German	Slavic
African	Other Arab	German Russian	Slovak
Cape Verdean	Armenian	Greek	Slovene
Ethiopian	Assyrian/Chaldean/Syriac	Guyanese	Soviet Union
Ghanian	Australian	Hungarian	Swedish
Kenyan	Austrian	Icelander	Swiss
Liberian	Basque	Iranian	Turkish
Nigerian	Belgian	Irish	Ukrainian
Senegalese	Brazilian	Israeli	United States or American
Sierra Leonean	British	Italian	Welsh
Somalian	Bulgarian	Latvian	West Indian, excluding Hispanic:
South African	Canadian	Lithuanian	Bahamian
Sudanese	Carpatho Rusyn	Luxemburger	Barbadian
Ugandan	Celtic	Macedonian	Belizean
Zairian	Croatian	Maltese	Bermudan
Zimbabwean	Cypriot	New Zealander	British West Indian
Other Subsaharan African	Czech	Northern European	Dutch West Indian
Albanian	Czechoslovakian	Norwegian	Haitian
Alsatian	Danish	Pennsylvania German	Jamaican
Arab:	Dutch	Polish	Trinidadian and
Arab/Arabic	Eastern European	Portuguese	Tobagonian
Egyptian	English	Romanian	U.S. Virgin Islander
Iraqi	Estonian	Russian	West Indian
Jordanian	European	Scandinavian	Other West Indian
Lebanese	Finnish	Scotch-Irish	Yugoslavian

The data on ancestry were derived from answers to long-form questionnaire Item 10, which was asked of a sample of the population. The data represent self-classification by people according to the ancestry group or groups with which they most closely identify. Ancestry refers to a person's ethnic origin or descent, "roots," heritage, or the place of birth of the person, the person's parents, or their ancestors before their arrival in the United States. Some ethnic identities, such as Egyptian or Polish, can be traced to geographic areas outside the United States, while other ethnicities, such as Pennsylvania German or Cajun, evolved in the United States.

The intent of the ancestry question was not to measure the degree of attachment the respondent had to a particular ethnicity. For example, a response of "Irish" might reflect total involvement in an Irish community or only a memory of ancestors several generations removed from the individual. Also, the question was intended to provide data for groups that were not included in the Hispanic origin and race questions. Official Hispanic origin data come from long-form questionnaire Item 5, and official race data come from long-form questionnaire Item 6. Therefore, although data on all groups are collected, the ancestry data shown in these tabulations are for non-Hispanic and non-race groups.

The ancestry question allowed respondents to report one or more ancestry groups, although only the first two were coded. If a response was in terms of a dual ancestry, for example, "Irish English," the person was assigned two codes, in this case one for Irish and another for English. However, in certain cases, multiple responses such as "French Canadian," "Greek Cypriote," and "Scotch Irish" were assigned a single code reflecting their status as unique groups. If a person reported one of these unique groups in addition to another group, for example, "Scotch Irish English," resulting in three terms, that person received one code for the unique group (Scotch-Irish) and another one for the remaining group (English). If a person reported "English Irish French," only English and Irish were coded. Certain combinations of ancestries where the ancestry group is a part of another, such as "German-Bavarian," were coded as a single ancestry using the more specific group (Bavarian). Also, responses such as "Polish-American" or "Italian-American" were coded and tabulated as a single entry (Polish or Italian).

The Census Bureau accepted "American" as a unique ethnicity if it was given alone, with an ambiguous response, or with state names. If the respondent listed any other ethnic identity such as "Italian-American," generally the "American" portion of the response was not coded. However, distinct groups such as "American Indian," "Mexican American," and "African American" were coded and identified separately because they represented groups who considered themselves different from those who reported as "Indian," "Mexican," or "African," respectively.

Census 2000 tabulations on ancestry are presented using two types of data presentations — one using total people as the base, and the other using total responses as the base. This chapter uses total responses as the base and includes the total number of ancestries reported and coded. If a person reported a multiple ancestry such as "French Danish," that response was counted twice in the tabulations — once in the French category and again in the Danish category. Thus, the sum of the counts in this type of presentation is not the total population but the total of all responses.

An automated coding system was used for coding ancestry in Census 2000. This greatly reduced the potential for error associated with a clerical review. Specialists with knowledge of the subject matter reviewed, edited, coded, and resolved inconsistent or incomplete responses. The code list used in Census 2000, containing over 1,000 categories, reflects the results of the Census Bureau's experience with the 1990 ancestry question, research, and consultation with many ethnic experts. Many decisions were made to determine the classification of responses. These decisions affected the grouping of the tabulated data. For example, the Italian category includes the responses of Sicilian and Tuscan, as well as a number of other responses.

Although some people consider religious affiliation a component of ethnic identity, the ancestry question was not designed to collect any information concerning religion. Thus, if a religion was given as an answer to the ancestry question, it was listed in the "Other groups" category which is not shown in this chapter.

Ancestry should not be confused with a person's place of birth, although a person's place of birth and ancestry may be the same.

Ranking Section

In the ranking section of this chapter, each ancestry has three tables. The first table shows the top 10 places sorted by number (based on all places, regardless of population), the second table shows the top 10 places sorted by percent (based on all places, regardless of population), the third table shows the top 10 places sorted by percent (based on places with populations of 10,000 or more).

Within each table, column one displays the place name, the state, and the county (if a place spans more than one county, the county that holds the majority of the population is shown). Column two displays the number of people reporting each ancestry, and column three is the percent of the total population reporting each ancestry. For tables representing ancestries based on race or Hispanic origin, the 100-percent population figure from SF1 is used to calculate the value in the "%" column. For all other ancestries the sample population figure from SF3 is used to calculate the value in the "%" column.

Alphabetical Ancestry Cross-Reference Guide

Acadian/Cajun
Afghan
African *See African, sub-Saharan: African*
African American/Black
African American/Black: Hispanic
African American/Black: Not Hispanic
African, sub-Saharan
African, sub-Saharan: African
African, sub-Saharan: Cape Verdean
African, sub-Saharan: Ethiopian
African, sub-Saharan: Ghanian
African, sub-Saharan: Kenyan
African, sub-Saharan: Liberian
African, sub-Saharan: Nigerian
African, sub-Saharan: Other
African, sub-Saharan: Senegalese
African, sub-Saharan: Sierra Leonean
African, sub-Saharan: Somalian
African, sub-Saharan: South African
African, sub-Saharan: Sudanese
African, sub-Saharan: Ugandan
African, sub-Saharan: Zairian
African, sub-Saharan: Zimbabwean
Alaska Athabascan *See Alaska Native: Alaska Athabascan*
Alaska Native tribes, not specified
Alaska Native tribes, specified
Alaska Native: Alaska Athabascan
Alaska Native: Aleut
Alaska Native: All other tribes
Alaska Native: Eskimo
Alaska Native: Tlingit-Haida
Albanian
Aleut *See Alaska Native: Aleut*
Alsatian
American *See United States or American*
American Indian or Alaska Native tribes, not specified
American Indian tribes, not specified
American Indian tribes, specified
American Indian: All other tribes
American Indian: Apache
American Indian: Blackfeet
American Indian: Cherokee
American Indian: Cheyenne
American Indian: Chickasaw
American Indian: Chippewa
American Indian: Choctaw
American Indian: Colville
American Indian: Comanche
American Indian: Cree
American Indian: Creek
American Indian: Crow
American Indian: Delaware
American Indian: Houma
American Indian: Iroquois
American Indian: Kiowa
American Indian: Latin American Indians
American Indian: Lumbee
American Indian: Menominee
American Indian: Navajo
American Indian: Osage
American Indian: Ottawa
American Indian: Paiute
American Indian: Pima
American Indian: Potawatomi
American Indian: Pueblo
American Indian: Puget Sound Salish
American Indian: Seminole
American Indian: Shoshone

American Indian: Sioux
American Indian: Tohono O'Odham
American Indian: Ute
American Indian: Yakama
American Indian: Yaqui
American Indian: Yuman
Apache *See American Indian: Apache*
Arab
Arab/Arabic *See Arab: Arab/Arabic*
Arab: Arab/Arabic
Arab: Egyptian
Arab: Iraqi
Arab: Jordanian
Arab: Lebanese
Arab: Moroccan
Arab: Other
Arab: Palestinian
Arab: Syrian
Argentinean *See Hispanic: Argentinean*
Armenian
Asian
Asian: Bangladeshi
Asian: Cambodian
Asian: Chinese, except Taiwanese
Asian: Filipino
Asian: Hmong
Asian: Indian
Asian: Indonesian
Asian: Japanese
Asian: Korean
Asian: Laotian
Asian: Malaysian
Asian: Other Asian, not specified
Asian: Other Asian, specified
Asian: Pakistani
Asian: Sri Lankan
Asian: Taiwanese
Asian: Thai
Asian: Vietnamese
Assyrian/Chaldean/Syriac
Australian
Austrian
Bahamian *See West Indian: Bahamian, excluding Hispanic*
Bangladeshi *See Asian: Bangladeshi*
Barbadian *See West Indian: Barbadian, excluding Hispanic*
Basque
Belgian
Belizean *See West Indian: Belizean, excluding Hispanic*
Bermudan *See West Indian: Bermudan, excluding Hispanic*
Blackfeet *See American Indian: Blackfeet*
Bolivian *See Hispanic: Bolivian*
Brazilian
British
British West Indian *See West Indian: British West Indian, excluding Hispanic*
Bulgarian
Cambodian *See Asian: Cambodian*
Canadian
Cape Verdean *See African, sub-Saharan: Cape Verdean*
Carpatho Rusyn
Celtic
Central American: *See Hispanic: Central American*
Cherokee *See American Indian: Cherokee*

Cheyenne *See American Indian: Cheyenne*
Chickasaw *See American Indian: Chickasaw*
Chilean *See Hispanic: Chilean*
Chinese, except Taiwanese *See Asian: Chinese, except Taiwanese*
Chippewa *See American Indian: Chippewa*
Choctaw *See American Indian: Choctaw*
Colombian *See Hispanic: Colombian*
Colville *See American Indian: Colville*
Comanche *See American Indian: Comanche*
Costa Rican *See Hispanic: Costa Rican*
Cree *See American Indian: Cree*
Creek *See American Indian: Creek*
Croatian
Crow *See American Indian: Crow*
Cuban *See Hispanic: Cuban*
Cypriot
Czech
Czechoslovakian
Danish
Delaware *See American Indian: Delaware*
Dominican Republic *See Hispanic: Dominican Republic*
Dutch
Dutch West Indian *See West Indian: Dutch West Indian, excluding Hispanic*
Eastern European
Ecuadorian *See Hispanic: Ecuadorian*
Egyptian *See Arab: Egyptian*
English
Eskimo *See Alaska Native: Eskimo*
Estonian
Ethiopian *See African, sub-Saharan: Ethiopian*
European
Fijian *See Hawaii Native/Pacific Islander: Fijian*
Filipino *See Asian: Filipino*
Finnish
French Canadian
French, except Basque
German
German Russian
Ghanian *See African, sub-Saharan: Ghanian*
Greek
Guamanian or Chamorro *See Hawaii Native/Pacific Islander: Guamanian or Chamorro*
Guatemalan *See Hispanic: Guatemalan*
Guyanese
Haitian *See West Indian: Haitian, excluding Hispanic*
Hawaii Native/Pacific Islander
Hawaii Native/Pacific Islander: Fijian
Hawaii Native/Pacific Islander: Guamanian or Chamorro
Hawaii Native/Pacific Islander: Melanesian
Hawaii Native/Pacific Islander: Micronesian
Hawaii Native/Pacific Islander: Native Hawaiian
Hawaii Native/Pacific Islander: Other Melanesian
Hawaii Native/Pacific Islander: Other Micronesian

Hawaii Native/Pacific Islander: Other Pacific Islander, not specified
Hawaii Native/Pacific Islander: Other Pacific Islander, specified
Hawaii Native/Pacific Islander: Other Polynesian
Hawaii Native/Pacific Islander: Polynesian
Hawaii Native/Pacific Islander: Samoan
Hawaii Native/Pacific Islander: Tongan
Hispanic or Latino
Hispanic: Argentinean
Hispanic: Bolivian
Hispanic: Central American
Hispanic: Chilean
Hispanic: Colombian
Hispanic: Costa Rican
Hispanic: Cuban
Hispanic: Dominican Republic
Hispanic: Ecuadorian
Hispanic: Guatemalan
Hispanic: Honduran
Hispanic: Mexican
Hispanic: Nicaraguan
Hispanic: Other
Hispanic: Other Central American
Hispanic: Other South American
Hispanic: Panamanian
Hispanic: Paraguayan
Hispanic: Peruvian
Hispanic: Puerto Rican
Hispanic: Salvadoran
Hispanic: South American
Hispanic: Uruguayan
Hispanic: Venezuelan
Hmong *See Asian: Hmong*
Honduran *See Hispanic: Honduran*
Houma *See American Indian: Houma*
Hungarian
Icelander
Indian, American *See American Indian*
Indian, Asian *See Asian: Indian*
Indonesian *See Asian: Indonesian*
Iranian
Iraqi *See Arab: Iraqi*
Irish
Iroquois *See American Indian: Iroquois*
Israeli
Italian
Jamaican *See West Indian: Jamaican, excluding Hispanic*
Japanese *See Asian: Japanese*
Jordanian *See Arab: Jordanian*
Kenyan *See African, sub-Saharan: Kenyan*
Kiowa *See American Indian: Kiowa*
Korean *See Asian: Korean*
Laotian *See Asian: Laotian*
Latin American Indians *See American Indian: Latin American Indians*
Latino *See Hispanic or Latino*
Latvian
Lebanese *See Arab: Lebanese*
Liberian *See African, sub-Saharan: Liberian*
Lithuanian
Lumbee *See American Indian: Lumbee*
Luxemburger
Macedonian
Malaysian *See Asian: Malaysian*
Maltese
Melanesian: *See Hawaii Native/Pacific Islander: Melanesian*

Menominee *See American Indian: Menominee*
Mexican *See Hispanic: Mexican*
Micronesian: *See Hawaii Native/Pacific Islander: Micronesian*
Moroccan *See Arab: Moroccan*
Native Hawaiian *See Hawaii Native/Pacific Islander: Native Hawaiian*
Navajo *See American Indian: Navajo*
New Zealander
Nicaraguan *See Hispanic: Nicaraguan*
Nigerian *See African, sub-Saharan: Nigerian*
Northern European
Norwegian
Osage *See American Indian: Osage*
Ottawa *See American Indian: Ottawa*
Paiute *See American Indian: Paiute*
Pakistani *See Asian: Pakistani*
Palestinian *See Arab: Palestinian*
Panamanian *See Hispanic: Panamanian*
Paraguayan *See Hispanic: Paraguayan*
Pennsylvania German
Peruvian *See Hispanic: Peruvian*
Pima *See American Indian: Pima*
Polish
Polynesian: *See Hawaii Native/Pacific Islander: Polynesian*
Portuguese
Potawatomi *See American Indian: Potawatomi*
Pueblo *See American Indian: Pueblo*
Puerto Rican *See Hispanic: Puerto Rican*
Puget Sound Salish *See American Indian: Puget Sound Salish*
Romanian
Russian
Salvadoran *See Hispanic: Salvadoran*
Samoan *See Hawaii Native/Pacific Islander: Samoan*
Scandinavian
Scotch-Irish
Scottish
Seminole *See American Indian: Seminole*
Senegalese *See African, sub-Saharan: Senegalese*
Serbian
Shoshone *See American Indian: Shoshone*
Sierra Leonean *See African, sub-Saharan: Sierra Leonean*
Sioux *See American Indian: Sioux*
Slavic
Slovak
Slovene
Somalian *See African, sub-Saharan: Somalian*
South African *See African, sub-Saharan: South African*
South American: *See Hispanic: South American*
Soviet Union
Sri Lankan *See Asian: Sri Lankan*
sub-Saharan African *See African, sub-Saharan*
Sudanese *See African, sub-Saharan: Sudanese*
Swedish
Swiss
Syrian *See Arab: Syrian*
Taiwanese *See Asian: Taiwanese*
Thai *See Asian: Thai*

Tlingit-Haida *See Alaska Native: Tlingit-Haida*
Tohono O'Odham *See American Indian: Tohono O'Odham*
Tongan *See Hawaii Native/Pacific Islander: Tongan*
Trinidadian and Tobagonian *See West Indian: Trinidadian and Tobagonian, excluding Hispanic*
Turkish
U.S. Virgin Islander *See West Indian: U.S. Virgin Islander, excluding Hispanic*
Ugandan *See African, sub-Saharan: Ugandan*
Ukrainian
United States or American
Uruguayan *See Hispanic: Uruguayan*
Ute *See American Indian: Ute*
Venezuelan *See Hispanic: Venezuelan*
Vietnamese *See Asian: Vietnamese*
Welsh
West Indian, excluding Hispanic
West Indian: Bahamian, excluding Hispanic
West Indian: Barbadian, excluding Hispanic
West Indian: Belizean, excluding Hispanic
West Indian: Bermudan, excluding Hispanic
West Indian: British West Indian, excluding Hispanic
West Indian: Dutch West Indian, excluding Hispanic
West Indian: Haitian, excluding Hispanic
West Indian: Jamaican, excluding Hispanic
West Indian: Other, excluding Hispanic
West Indian: Trinidadian and Tobagonian, excluding Hispanic
West Indian: U.S. Virgin Islander, excluding Hispanic
West Indian: West Indian, excluding Hispanic
White
White: Hispanic
White: Not Hispanic
Yakama *See American Indian: Yakama*
Yaqui *See American Indian: Yaqui*
Yugoslavian
Yuman *See American Indian: Yuman*
Zairian *See African, sub-Saharan: Zairian*
Zimbabwean *See African, sub-Saharan: Zimbabwean*

User's Guide: Hispanic Population

Places Covered

Ranking tables cover all counties and all places in Ohio with populations of 10,000 or more.

Source of Data

CENSUS 2000

Data for this chapter was derived from following source: *U.S. Bureau of the Census, Census of Population and Housing, 2000: Summary File 4*. Summary File 4 (SF 4) contains sample data, which is the information compiled from the questions asked of a sample (generally 1-in-6) of all people and housing units. Summary File 4 is repeated or iterated for the total population and 335 additional population groups. This chapter focuses on the following 24 population groups:

Hispanic or Latino (of any race)
    Central American
        Costa Rican
        Guatemalan
        Honduran
        Nicaraguan
        Panamanian
        Salvadoran
    Cuban
    Dominican (Dominican Republic)
    Mexican
    Puerto Rican
    South American
        Argentinian
        Bolivian
        Chilean
        Colombian
        Ecuadorian
        Paraguayan
        Peruvian
        Uruguayan
        Venezuelan
    Spaniard
    Other Hispanic or Latino

Please note that the above list only includes Spanish-speaking population groups. Groups such as Brazilian are not classified as Hispanic by the Bureau of the Census because they primarily speak Portugese.

In order for any of the tables for a specific group to be shown in Summary File 4, the data must meet a minimum population threshold. For Summary File 4, all tables are repeated for each race group, American Indian and Alaska Native tribe, and Hispanic or Latino group if the 100-percent count of people of that specific group in a particular geographic area is 100 or more. There also must be 50 or more unweighted people of that specific group in a particular geographic area. For example, if there are 100 or more 100-percent people tabulated as Chilean in County A, and there are 50 or more unweighted people, then all matrices for Chilean are shown in SF 4 for County A.

To maintain confidentiality, the Census Bureau applies statistical procedures that introduce some uncertainty into data for small geographic areas with small population groups. Therefore, tables may contain both sampling and nonsampling error.

In an iterated file such as SF 4, the universes *households, families,* and *occupied housing units* are classified by the race or ethnic group of the householder. In any population table where there is no note, the universe classification is always based on the race or ethnicity of the person. In all housing tables, the universe classification is based on the race or ethnicity of the householder.

Comparing SF 4 Estimates with Corresponding Values in SF 1 and SF 2

As in earlier censuses, the responses from the sample of households reporting on long forms must be weighted to reflect the entire population. Specifically, each responding household represents, on average, six or seven other households who reported using short forms. One consequence of the weighting procedures is that each estimate based on the long form responses has an associated confidence interval. These confidence intervals are wider (as a percentage of the estimate) for geographic areas with smaller populations and for characteristics that occur less frequently in the area being examined (such as the proportion of people in poverty in a middle-income neighborhood). In order to release as much useful information as possible, statisticians must balance a number of factors. In particular, for Census 2000, the Bureau of the Census created weighting areas—geographic areas from which about two hundred or more long forms were completed—which are large enough to produce good quality estimates. If smaller weighting areas had been used, the confidence intervals around the estimates would have been significantly wider, rendering many estimates less useful due to their lower reliability. The disadvantage of using weighting areas this large is that, for smaller geographic areas within them, the estimates of characteristics that are also reported on the short form will not match the counts reported in SF 1 or SF 2. Examples of these characteristics are the total number of people, the number of people reporting specific racial categories, and the number of housing units. The official values for items reported on the short form come from SF 1 and SF 2. The differences between the long form estimates in SF 4 and values in SF 1 or SF 2 are particularly noticeable for the smallest places, tracts, and block groups. The long form estimates of total population and total housing units in SF 4 will, however, match the SF 1 and SF 2 counts for larger geographic areas such as counties and states, and will be essentially the same for medium and large cities. This phenomenon also occurred for the 1990 Census, although in that case, the weighting areas included relatively small places. As a result, the long form estimates matched the short form counts for those places, but the confidence intervals around the estimates of characteristics collected only on the long form were often significantly wider (as a percentage of the estimate). SF 1 gives exact numbers even for very small groups and areas; whereas, SF 4 gives estimates for small groups and areas such as tracts and small places that are less exact. The goal of SF 4 is to identify large differences among areas or large changes over time. Estimates for small areas and small population groups often do exhibit large changes from one census to the next, so having the capability to measure them is worthwhile.

Topics

POPULATION

Total Population: Sample count of total population.

Hispanic Population: The data on the Hispanic or Latino population, which was asked of all people, were derived from answers to long-form questionnaire Item 5, and short-form questionnaire Item 7. The terms "Spanish," "Hispanic origin," and "Latino" are used interchangeably. Some respondents identify with all three terms, while others may identify with only one of these three specific terms. Hispanics or Latinos who identify with the terms "Spanish," "Hispanic," or "Latino" are those who classify themselves in one of the specific Hispanic or Latino categories listed on the questionnaire — "Mexican," "Puerto Rican," or "Cuban" — as well as those who indicate that they are "other Spanish, Hispanic, or Latino." People who do not identify with one of the specific origins listed on the questionnaire but indicate that they are "other Spanish, Hispanic, or Latino" are those whose origins are from Spain, the Spanish-speaking countries of Central or South America, the Dominican Republic, or people identifying themselves generally as Spanish, Spanish-American, Hispanic, Hispano, Latino, and so on. All write-in responses to the "other Spanish/Hispanic/Latino" category were coded. Origin can be viewed as the heritage, nationality group, lineage, or country of birth of the person or the person's parents or ancestors before their arrival in the United States. People who identify their origin as Spanish, Hispanic, or Latino may be of any race.

Population groups whose primary language is not Spanish are not classified as Hispanic by the Bureau of the Census and are not included in this chapter (eg. Brazilian).

AGE

Median Age: Divides the age distribution into two equal parts: one-half of the cases falling below the median age and one-half above the median. Median age is computed on the basis of a single year of age standard distribution.

The data on age, which was asked of all people, were derived from answers to the long-form questionnaire Item 4 and short-form questionnaire Item 6. The age classification is based on the age of the person in complete years as of April 1, 2000. The age of the person usually was derived from their date of birth information. Their reported age was used only when date of birth information was unavailable.

HOUSEHOLD SIZE

Average Household Size: A measure obtained by dividing the number of people in households by the total number of households (or householders). In cases where household members are tabulated by race or Hispanic origin, household members are classified by the race or Hispanic origin of the householder rather than the race or Hispanic origin of each individual. Average household size is rounded to the nearest hundredth.

LANGUAGE SPOKEN AT HOME

English Only: Number and percentage of population 5 years and over who report speaking English-only at home.

Spanish: Number and percentage of population 5 years and over who report speaking Spanish at home.

Language spoken at home data were derived from answers to long-form questionnaire Items 11a and 11b, which were asked of a sample of the population. Data were edited to include in tabulations only the population 5 years old and over. Questions 11a and 11b referred to languages spoken at home in an effort to measure the current use of languages other than English. People who knew languages other than English but did not use them at home or who only used them elsewhere were excluded. Most people who reported speaking a language other than English at home also speak English. The questions did not permit determination of the primary or dominant language of people who spoke both English and another language.

FOREIGN-BORN

Foreign Born: Number and percentage of population who were not U.S. citizens at birth. Foreign-born people are those who indicated they were either a U.S. citizen by naturalization or they were not a citizen of the United States.

Foreign-Born Naturalized Citizens: Number and percentage of population who were not U.S. citizens at birth but became U.S. citizens by naturalization.

The data on place of birth were derived from answers to long-form questionnaire Item 12 which was asked of a sample of the population. Respondents were asked to report the U.S. state, Puerto Rico, U.S. Island Area, or foreign country where they were born. People not reporting a place of birth were assigned the state or country of birth of another family member or their residence 5 years earlier, or were imputed the response of another person with similar characteristics. People born outside the United States were asked to report their place of birth according to current international boundaries. Since numerous changes in boundaries of foreign countries have occurred in the last century, some people may have reported their place of birth in terms of boundaries that existed at the time of their birth or emigration, or in accordance with their own national preference.

EDUCATIONAL ATTAINMENT

High School Graduates: Number and percentage of the population age 25 and over who have a high school diploma or higher. This category includes people whose highest degree was a high school diploma or its equivalent, people who attended college but did not receive a degree, and people who received a college, university, or professional degree. People who reported completing the 12th grade but not receiving a diploma are not high school graduates.

4-Years College Graduates: Number and percentage of the population age 25 and over who have a 4-year college, university, or professional degree.

Data on educational attainment were derived from answers to long-form questionnaire Item 9, which was asked of a sample of the population. Data on attainment are tabulated for the population 25 years old and over.

The order in which degrees were listed on the questionnaire suggested that doctorate degrees were "higher" than professional school degrees, which were "higher" than master's degrees. The question included instructions for people currently enrolled in school to report the level of the previous grade attended or the highest degree received. Respondents who did not report educational attainment or enrollment level were assigned the attainment of a person of the same age, race, Hispanic or Latino origin, occupation and sex, where possible, who resided in the same or a nearby area. Respondents who filled more than one box were edited to the highest level or degree reported.

The question included a response category that allowed respondents to report completing the 12th grade without receiving a high school diploma. It allowed people who received either a high school diploma or the equivalent (Test of General Educational Development—G.E.D.) and did not attend college, to be reported as "high school graduate(s)." The category "Associate degree" included people whose highest degree is an associate degree, which generally requires 2 years of college level work and is either in an occupational program that prepares them for a specific occupation, or an academic program primarily in the arts and sciences. The course work may or may not be transferable to a bachelor's degree. Master's degrees include the traditional MA and MS degrees and field-specific degrees, such as MSW, MEd, MBA, MLS, and MEng. Some examples of professional degrees include medicine, dentistry, chiropractic, optometry, osteopathic medicine, pharmacy, podiatry, veterinary medicine, law, and theology. Vocational and technical training such as barber school training; business, trade, technical, and vocational schools; or other training for a specific trade, are specifically excluded.

INCOME AND POVERTY

Median Household Income (in dollars): Includes the income of the householder and all other individuals 15 years old and over in the household, whether they are related to the householder or not. The median divides the income distribution into two equal parts: one-half of the cases falling below the median income and one-half above the median. For households, the median income is based on the distribution of the total number of households including those with no income. Median income for households is computed on the basis of a standard distribution and is rounded to the nearest whole dollar.

Per Capita Income (in dollars): Per capita income is the mean income computed for every man, woman, and child in a particular group. It is derived by dividing the total income of a particular group by the total population in that group. Per capita income is rounded to the nearest whole dollar.

The data on income in 1999 were derived from answers to long-form questionnaire Items 31 and 32, which were asked of a sample of the population 15 years old and over. "Total income" is the sum of the amounts reported separately for wage or salary income; net self-employment income; interest, dividends, or net rental or royalty income or income from estates and trusts; social security or railroad retirement income; Supplemental Security Income (SSI); public assistance or welfare payments; retirement, survivor, or disability pensions; and all other income.

Receipts from the following sources are not included as income: capital gains, money received from the sale of property (unless the recipient was engaged in the business of selling such property); the value of income "in kind" from food stamps, public housing subsidies, medical care, employer contributions for individuals, etc.; withdrawal of bank deposits; money borrowed; tax refunds; exchange of money between relatives living in the same household; and gifts and lump-sum inheritances, insurance payments, and other types of lump-sum receipts.

The eight types of income reported in the census are defined as follows:

Wage or salary income. Wage or salary income includes total money earnings received for work performed as an employee during the calendar year 1999. It includes wages, salary, armed forces pay, commissions, tips, piece-rate payments, and cash bonuses earned before deductions were made for taxes, bonds, pensions, union dues, etc.

Self-employment income. Self-employment income includes both farm and nonfarm self-employment income. Nonfarm self-employment income includes net money income (gross receipts minus expenses) from one's own business, professional enterprise, or partnership. Gross receipts include the value of all goods sold and services rendered. Expenses include costs of goods purchased, rent, heat, light, power, depreciation charges, wages and salaries paid, business taxes (not personal income taxes), etc. Farm self-employment income includes net money income (gross receipts minus operating expenses) from the operation of a farm by a person on his or her own account, as an owner, renter, or sharecropper. Gross receipts include the value of all products sold, government farm programs, money received from the rental of farm equipment to others, and incidental receipts from the sale of wood, sand, gravel, etc. Operating expenses include cost of feed, fertilizer, seed, and other farming supplies, cash wages paid to farmhands, depreciation charges, cash rent, interest on farm mortgages, farm building repairs, farm taxes (not state and federal personal income taxes), etc. The value of fuel, food, or other farm products used for family living is not included as part of net income.

Interest, dividends, or net rental income. Interest, dividends, or net rental income includes interest on savings or bonds, dividends from stockholdings or membership in associations, net income from rental of property to others and receipts from boarders or lodgers, net royalties, and periodic payments from an estate or trust fund.

Social Security income. Social security income includes social security pensions and survivors benefits, permanent disability insurance payments made by the Social Security Administration prior to deductions for medical insurance, and railroad retirement insurance checks from the U.S. government. Medicare reimbursements are not included.

Supplemental Security Income (SSI). Supplemental Security Income (SSI) is a nationwide U.S. assistance program administered by the Social Security Administration that guarantees a minimum level of income for needy aged, blind, or disabled individuals. The census questionnaire for Puerto Rico asked about the receipt of SSI; however, SSI is not a federally administered program in Puerto Rico. Therefore, it is probably not being interpreted by most respondents as the same as SSI in the United States. The only way a resident of Puerto Rico could have appropriately reported SSI would have been if they lived in the United States at any time during calendar year 1999 and received SSI.

Public assistance income. Public assistance income includes general assistance and Temporary Assistance to Needy Families (TANF). Separate payments received for hospital or other medical care (vendor payments) are excluded. This does not include Supplemental Security Income (SSI).

Retirement income. Retirement income includes: (1) retirement pensions and survivor benefits from a former employer; labor union; or federal, state, or local government; and the U.S. military; (2) income from workers' compensation; disability income from companies or unions; federal, state, or local government; and the U.S. military; (3) periodic receipts from annuities and insurance; and (4) regular income from IRA and KEOGH plans. This does not include social security income.

All other income. All other income includes unemployment compensation, Veterans' Administration (VA) payments, alimony and child support, contributions received periodically from people not living in the household, military family allotments, and other kinds of periodic income other than earnings.

Poverty Status: Number and percentage of population with income in 1999 below the poverty level. Based on individuals for whom poverty status is determined. Poverty status was determined for all people except institutionalized people, people in military group quarters, people in college dormitories, and unrelated individuals under 15 years old.

The poverty status of families and unrelated individuals in 1999 was determined using 48 thresholds (income cutoffs) arranged in a two dimensional matrix. The matrix consists of family size (from 1 person to 9 or more people) cross-classified by presence and number of family members under 18 years old (from no children present to 8 or more children present). Unrelated individuals and 2-person families were further differentiated by the age of the reference person (RP) (under 65 years old and 65 years old and over).

To determine a person's poverty status, one compares the person's total family income with the poverty threshold appropriate for that person's family size and composition. If the total income of that person's family is less than the threshold appropriate for that family, then the person is considered poor, together with every member of his or her family. If a person is not living with anyone related by birth, marriage, or adoption, then the person's own income is compared with his or her poverty threshold.

HOUSING

Homeownership: Number and percentage of housing units that are owner-occupied.

The data on tenure, which was asked at all occupied housing units, were obtained from answers to long-form questionnaire Item 33, and short-form questionnaire Item 2. All occupied housing units are classified as either owner occupied or renter occupied.

A housing unit is owner occupied if the owner or co-owner lives in the unit even if it is mortgaged or not fully paid for. The owner or co-owner must live in the unit and usually is Person 1 on the questionnaire. The unit is "Owned by you or someone in this household with a mortgage or loan" if it is being purchased with a mortgage or some other debt arrangement, such as a deed of trust, trust deed, contract to purchase, land contract, or purchase agreement. The unit is also considered owned with a mortgage if it is built on leased land and there is a mortgage on the unit. Mobile homes occupied by owners with installment loans balances are also included in this category.

Median Gross Rent (in dollars): Median monthly gross rent on specified renter-occupied and specified vacant-for-rent units. Specified renter-occupied and specified vacant-for-rent units exclude 1-family houses on 10 acres or more.

The data on gross rent were obtained from answers to long-form questionnaire Items 45a-d, which were asked on a sample basis. Gross rent is the contract rent plus the estimated average monthly cost of utilities (electricity, gas, water and sewer) and fuels (oil, coal, kerosene, wood, etc.) if these are paid by the renter (or paid for the renter by someone else). Gross rent is intended to eliminate differentials that result from varying practices with respect to the inclusion of utilities and fuels as part of the rental payment. The estimated costs of utilities and fuels are reported on an annual basis but are converted to monthly figures for the tabulations. Renter units occupied without payment of cash rent are shown separately as "No cash rent" in the tabulations.

Housing units that are renter occupied without payment of cash rent are shown separately as "No cash rent" in census data products. The unit may be owned by friends or relatives who live elsewhere and who allow occupancy without charge. Rent-free houses or apartments may be provided to compensate caretakers, ministers, tenant farmers, sharecroppers, or others.

Contract rent is the monthly rent agreed to or contracted for, regardless of any furnishings, utilities, fees, meals, or services that may be included. For vacant units, it is the monthly rent asked for the rental unit at the time of enumeration.

If the contract rent includes rent for a business unit or for living quarters occupied by another household, only that part of the rent estimated to be for the respondent's unit was included. Excluded was any rent paid for additional units or for business premises.

If a renter pays rent to the owner of a condominium or cooperative, and the condominium fee or cooperative carrying charge also is paid by the renter to the owner, the condominium fee or carrying charge was included as rent.

If a renter receives payments from lodgers or roomers who are listed as members of the household, the rent without deduction for any payments received from the lodgers or roomers was to be reported. The respondent was to report the rent agreed to or contracted for even if paid by someone else such as friends or relatives living elsewhere, a church or welfare agency, or the government through subsidies or vouchers.

The median divides the rent distribution into two equal parts: one-half of the cases falling below the median contract rent and one-half above the median. Median contract rents are computed on the basis of a standard distribution and are rounded to the nearest whole dollar. Units reported as "No cash rent" are excluded.

Median Home Value (in dollars): Reported by the owner of specified owner-occupied or specified vacant-for-sale housing units. Specified owner-occupied and specified vacant-for-sale housing units include only 1-family houses on less than 10 acres without a business or medical office on the property. The data for "specified units" exclude mobile homes, houses with a business or medical office, houses on 10 or more acres, and housing units in multi-unit buildings.

The data on value (also referred to as "price asked" for vacant units) were obtained from answers to long-form questionnaire Item 51, which was asked on a sample basis at owner-occupied housing units and units that were being bought, or vacant for sale at the time of enumeration. Value is the respondent's estimate of how much the property (house and lot, mobile home and lot, or condominium unit) would sell for if it were for sale. If the house or mobile home was owned or being bought, but the land on which it sits was not, the respondent was asked to estimate the combined value of the house or mobile home and the land. For vacant units, value was the price asked for the property. Value was tabulated separately for all owner-occupied and vacant-for-sale housing units, owner-occupied and vacant-for-sale mobile homes, and specified owner-occupied and specified vacant-for-sale housing units.

The median divides the value distribution into two equal parts: one-half of the cases falling below the median value of the property (house and lot, mobile home and lot, or condominium unit) and one-half above the median. Median values are computed on the basis of a standard distribution and are rounded to the nearest hundred dollars.

User's Guide: Asian Population

Places Covered

Ranking tables cover all counties and places in Ohio with Asian and/or Native Hawaiian and other Pacific Islander residents.

Source of Data

CENSUS 2000

Data for this chapter was derived from following source: *U.S. Bureau of the Census, Census of Population and Housing, 2000: Summary File 4.* Summary File 4 (SF 4) contains sample data, which is the information compiled from the questions asked of a sample (generally 1-in-6) of all people and housing units. Summary File 4 is repeated or iterated for the total population and 335 additional population groups. This chapter focuses on the following 23 population groups:

Asian
- Asian Indian
- Bangladeshi
- Cambodian
- Chinese (except Taiwanese)
- Filipino
- Hmong
- Indonesian
- Japanese
- Korean
- Laotian
- Malaysian
- Pakistani
- Sri Lankan
- Taiwanese
- Thai
- Vietnamese

Native Hawaiian and Other Pacific Islander
- Fijian
- Guamanian or Chamorro
- Hawaiian, Native
- Samoan
- Tongan

Please note that this chapter only includes people who responded to the question on race by indicating only one race. These people are classified by the Census Bureau as the race *alone* population. For example, respondents reporting a single detailed Asian group, such as Korean or Filipino, would be included in the Asian *alone* population. Respondents reporting more than one detailed Asian group, such as Chinese and Japanese or Asian Indian and Chinese and Vietnamese would also be included in the Asian *alone* population. This is because all of the detailed groups in these example combinations are part of the larger Asian race category. The same criteria apply to the Native Hawaiian and Other Pacific Islander groups.

In order for any of the tables for a specific group to be shown in Summary File 4, the data must meet a minimum population threshold. For Summary File 4, all tables are repeated for each race group, American Indian and Alaska Native tribe, and Hispanic or Latino group if the 100-percent count of people of that specific group in a particular geographic area is 100 or more. There also must be 50 or more unweighted people of that specific group in a particular geographic area. For example, if there are 100 or more 100-percent people tabulated as Korean in County A, and there are 50 or more unweighted people, then all matrices for Korean are shown in SF 4 for County A.

To maintain confidentiality, the Census Bureau applies statistical procedures that introduce some uncertainty into data for small geographic areas with small population groups. Therefore, tables may contain both sampling and nonsampling error.

In an iterated file such as SF 4, the universes *households, families,* and *occupied housing units* are classified by the race or ethnic group of the householder. In any population table where there is no note, the universe classification is always based on the race or ethnicity of the person. In all housing tables, the universe classification is based on the race or ethnicity of the householder.

Comparing SF 4 Estimates with Corresponding Values in SF 1 and SF 2

As in earlier censuses, the responses from the sample of households reporting on long forms must be weighted to reflect the entire population. Specifically, each responding household represents, on average, six or seven other households who reported using short forms. One consequence of the weighting procedures is that each estimate based on the long form responses has an associated confidence interval. These confidence intervals are wider (as a percentage of the estimate) for geographic areas with smaller populations and for characteristics that occur less frequently in the area being examined (such as the proportion of people in poverty in a middle-income neighborhood). In order to release as much useful information as possible, statisticians must balance a number of factors. In particular, for Census 2000, the Bureau of the Census created weighting areas—geographic areas from which about two hundred or more long forms were completed—which are large enough to produce good quality estimates. If smaller weighting areas had been used, the confidence intervals around the estimates would have been significantly wider, rendering many estimates less useful due to their lower reliability. The disadvantage of using weighting areas this large is that, for smaller geographic areas within them, the estimates of characteristics that are also reported on the short form will not match the counts reported in SF 1 or SF 2. Examples of these characteristics are the total number of people, the number of people reporting specific racial categories, and the number of housing units. The official values for items reported on the short form come from SF 1 and SF 2. The differences between the long form estimates in SF 4 and values in SF 1 or SF 2 are particularly noticeable for the smallest places, tracts, and block groups. The long form estimates of total population and total housing units in SF 4 will, however, match the SF 1 and SF 2 counts for larger geographic areas such as counties and states, and will be essentially the same for medium and large cities. This phenomenon also occurred for the 1990 Census, although in that case, the weighting areas included relatively small places. As a result, the long form estimates matched the short form counts for those places, but the confidence intervals around the estimates of characteristics collected only on the long form were often significantly wider (as a percentage of the estimate). SF 1 gives exact numbers even for very small groups and areas; whereas, SF 4 gives estimates for small groups and areas such as tracts and small places that are less exact. The goal of SF 4 is to identify large differences among areas or large changes over time. Estimates for small areas and small population groups often do exhibit large changes from one census to the next, so having the capability to measure them is worthwhile.

Topics

POPULATION

Total Population: Sample count of total population of all races.

Asian Population: A person having origins in any of the original peoples of the Far East, Southeast Asia, or the Indian subcontinent including, for example, Cambodia, China, India, Japan, Korea, Malaysia, Pakistan, the Philippine Islands, Thailand, and Vietnam. It includes Asian Indian, Bangladeshi, Cambodian, Chinese (except Taiwanese), Filipino, Hmong, Indonesian, Japanese, Korean, Laotian, Malaysian, Pakistani, Sri Lankan, Taiwanese, Thai, and Vietnamese.

Native Hawaiian or Other Pacific Islander (NHPI) Population: A person having origins in any of the original peoples of Hawaii, Guam, Samoa, or other Pacific Islands. It includes people who indicate their race as Fijian, Guamanian or Chamorro, Native Hawaiian, Samoan, and Tongan.

The data on race, which was asked of all people, were derived from answers to long-form questionnaire Item 6 and short-form questionnaire Item 8. The concept of race, as used by the Census Bureau, reflects self-identification by people according to the race or races with which they most closely identify. These categories are socio-political constructs and should not be interpreted as being scientific or anthropological in nature. Furthermore, the race categories include both racial and national-origin groups.

If an individual did not provide a race response, the race or races of the householder or other household members were assigned using specific rules of precedence of household relationship. For example, if race was missing for a natural-born child in the household, then either the race or races of the householder, another natural-born child, or the spouse of the householder were assigned. If race was not reported for anyone in the household, the race or races of a householder in a previously processed household were assigned.

AGE

Median Age: Divides the age distribution into two equal parts: one-half of the cases falling below the median age and one-half above the median. Median age is computed on the basis of a single year of age standard distribution.

The data on age, which was asked of all people, were derived from answers to the long-form questionnaire Item 4 and short-form questionnaire Item 6. The age classification is based on the age of the person in complete years as of April 1, 2000. The age of the person usually was derived from their date of birth information. Their reported age was used only when date of birth information was unavailable.

HOUSEHOLD SIZE

Average Household Size: A measure obtained by dividing the number of people in households by the total number of households (or householders). In cases where household members are tabulated by race or Hispanic origin, household members are classified by the race or Hispanic origin of the householder rather than the race or Hispanic origin of each individual. Average household size is rounded to the nearest hundredth.

LANGUAGE SPOKEN AT HOME

English Only: Number and percentage of population 5 years and over who report speaking English-only at home.

Language spoken at home data were derived from answers to long-form questionnaire Items 11a and 11b, which were asked of a sample of the population. Data were edited to include in tabulations only the population 5 years old and over. Questions 11a and 11b referred to languages spoken at home in an effort to measure the current use of languages other than English. People who knew languages other than English but did not use them at home or who only used them elsewhere were excluded. Most people who reported speaking a language other than English at home also speak English. The questions did not permit determination of the primary or dominant language of people who spoke both English and another language.

FOREIGN-BORN

Foreign Born: Number and percentage of population who were not U.S. citizens at birth. Foreign-born people are those who indicated they were either a U.S. citizen by naturalization or they were not a citizen of the United States.

Foreign-Born Naturalized Citizens: Number and percentage of population who were not U.S. citizens at birth but became U.S. citizens by naturalization.

The data on place of birth were derived from answers to long-form questionnaire Item 12 which was asked of a sample of the population. Respondents were asked to report the U.S. state, Puerto Rico, U.S. Island Area, or foreign country where they were born. People not reporting a place of birth were assigned the state or country of birth of another family member or their residence 5 years earlier, or were imputed the response of another person with similar characteristics. People born outside the United States were asked to report their place of birth according to current international boundaries. Since numerous changes in boundaries of foreign countries have occurred in the last century, some people may have reported their place of birth in terms of boundaries that existed at the time of their birth or emigration, or in accordance with their own national preference.

EDUCATIONAL ATTAINMENT

High School Graduates: Number and percentage of the population age 25 and over who have a high school diploma or higher. This category includes people whose highest degree was a high school diploma or its equivalent, people who attended college but did not receive a degree, and people who received a college, university, or professional degree. People who reported completing the 12th grade but not receiving a diploma are not high school graduates.

Four-Year College Graduates: Number and percentage of the population age 25 and over who have a 4-year college, university, or professional degree.

Data on educational attainment were derived from answers to long-form questionnaire Item 9, which was asked of a sample of the population. Data on attainment are tabulated for the population 25 years old and over.

The order in which degrees were listed on the questionnaire suggested that doctorate degrees were "higher" than professional school degrees, which were "higher" than master's degrees. The question included instructions for people currently enrolled in school to report the level of the previous grade attended or the highest degree received. Respondents who did not report educational attainment or enrollment level were assigned the attainment of a person of the same age, race, Hispanic or Latino origin, occupation and sex, where possible, who resided in the same or a nearby area. Respondents who filled more than one box were edited to the highest level or degree reported.

The question included a response category that allowed respondents to report completing the 12th grade without receiving a high school diploma. It allowed people who received either a high school diploma or the equivalent (Test of General Educational Development—G.E.D.) and did not attend college, to be reported as "high school graduate(s)." The category "Associate degree" included people whose highest degree is an associate degree, which generally requires 2 years of college level work and is either in an occupational program that prepares them for a specific occupation, or an academic program primarily in the arts and sciences. The course work may or may not be transferable to a bachelor's degree. Master's degrees include the traditional MA and MS degrees and field-specific degrees, such as MSW, MEd, MBA, MLS, and MEng. Some examples of professional degrees include medicine, dentistry, chiropractic, optometry, osteopathic medicine, pharmacy, podiatry, veterinary medicine, law, and theology. Vocational and technical training such as barber school training; business, trade, technical, and vocational schools; or other training for a specific trade, are specifically excluded.

INCOME AND POVERTY

Median Household Income (in dollars): Includes the income of the householder and all other individuals 15 years old and over in the household, whether they are related to the householder or not. The median divides the income distribution into two equal parts: one-half of the cases falling below the median income and one-half above the median. For households, the median income is based on the distribution of the total number of households including those with no income. Median income for households is computed on the basis of a standard distribution and is rounded to the nearest whole dollar.

Per Capita Income (in dollars): Per capita income is the mean income computed for every man, woman, and child in a particular group. It is derived by dividing the total income of a particular group by the total population in that group. Per capita income is rounded to the nearest whole dollar.

The data on income in 1999 were derived from answers to long-form questionnaire Items 31 and 32, which were asked of a sample of the population 15 years old and over. "Total income" is the sum of the amounts reported separately for wage or salary income; net self-employment income; interest, dividends, or net rental or royalty income or income from estates and trusts; social security or railroad retirement income; Supplemental Security Income (SSI); public assistance or welfare payments; retirement, survivor, or disability pensions; and all other income.

Receipts from the following sources are not included as income: capital gains, money received from the sale of property (unless the recipient was engaged in the business of selling such property); the value of income "in kind" from food stamps, public housing subsidies, medical care, employer contributions for individuals, etc.; withdrawal of bank deposits; money borrowed; tax refunds; exchange of money between relatives living in the same household; and gifts and lump-sum inheritances, insurance payments, and other types of lump-sum receipts.

The eight types of income reported in the census are defined as follows:

Wage or salary income. Wage or salary income includes total money earnings received for work performed as an employee during the calendar year 1999. It includes wages, salary, armed forces pay, commissions, tips, piece-rate payments, and cash bonuses earned before deductions were made for taxes, bonds, pensions, union dues, etc.

Self-employment income. Self-employment income includes both farm and nonfarm self-employment income. Nonfarm self-employment income includes net money income (gross receipts minus expenses) from one's own business, professional enterprise, or partnership. Gross receipts include the value of all goods sold and services rendered. Expenses include costs of goods purchased, rent, heat, light, power, depreciation charges, wages and salaries paid, business taxes (not personal income taxes), etc. Farm self-employment income includes net money income (gross receipts minus operating expenses) from the operation of a farm by a person on his or her own account, as an owner, renter, or sharecropper. Gross receipts include the value of all products sold, government farm programs, money received from the rental of farm equipment to others, and incidental receipts from the sale of wood, sand, gravel, etc. Operating expenses include cost of feed, fertilizer, seed, and other farming supplies, cash wages paid to farmhands, depreciation charges, cash rent, interest on farm mortgages, farm building repairs, farm taxes (not state and federal personal income taxes), etc. The value of fuel, food, or other farm products used for family living is not included as part of net income.

Interest, dividends, or net rental income. Interest, dividends, or net rental income includes interest on savings or bonds, dividends from stockholdings or membership in associations, net income from rental of property to others and receipts from boarders or lodgers, net royalties, and periodic payments from an estate or trust fund.

Social Security income. Social security income includes social security pensions and survivors benefits, permanent disability insurance payments made by the Social Security Administration prior to deductions for medical insurance, and railroad retirement insurance checks from the U.S. government. Medicare reimbursements are not included.

Supplemental Security Income (SSI). Supplemental Security Income (SSI) is a nationwide U.S. assistance program administered by the Social Security Administration that guarantees a minimum level of income for needy aged, blind, or disabled individuals. The census questionnaire for Puerto Rico asked about the receipt of SSI; however, SSI is not a federally administered program in Puerto Rico. Therefore, it is probably not being interpreted by most respondents as the same as SSI in the United States. The only way a resident of Puerto Rico could have appropriately reported SSI would have been if they lived in the United States at any time during calendar year 1999 and received SSI.

Public assistance income. Public assistance income includes general assistance and Temporary Assistance to Needy Families (TANF). Separate payments received for hospital or other medical care (vendor payments) are excluded. This does not include Supplemental Security Income (SSI).

Retirement income. Retirement income includes: (1) retirement pensions and survivor benefits from a former employer; labor union; or federal, state, or local government; and the U.S. military; (2) income from workers' compensation; disability income from companies or unions; federal, state, or local government; and the U.S. military; (3) periodic receipts from annuities and insurance; and (4) regular income from IRA and KEOGH plans. This does not include social security income.

All other income. All other income includes unemployment compensation, Veterans' Administration (VA) payments, alimony and child support, contributions received periodically from people not living in the household, military family allotments, and other kinds of periodic income other than earnings.

Poverty Status: Number and percentage of population with income in 1999 below the poverty level. Based on individuals for whom poverty status is determined. Poverty status was determined for all people except institutionalized people, people in military group quarters, people in college dormitories, and unrelated individuals under 15 years old.

The poverty status of families and unrelated individuals in 1999 was determined using 48 thresholds (income cutoffs) arranged in a two dimensional matrix. The matrix consists of family size (from 1 person to 9 or more people) cross-classified by presence and number of family members under 18 years old (from no children present to 8 or more children present). Unrelated individuals and 2-person families were further differentiated by the age of the reference person (RP) (under 65 years old and 65 years old and over).

To determine a person's poverty status, one compares the person's total family income with the poverty threshold appropriate for that person's family size and composition. If the total income of that person's family is less than the threshold appropriate for that family, then the person is considered poor, together with every member of his or her family. If a person is not living with anyone related by birth, marriage, or adoption, then the person's own income is compared with his or her poverty threshold.

HOUSING

Homeownership: Number and percentage of housing units that are owner-occupied.

The data on tenure, which was asked at all occupied housing units, were obtained from answers to long-form questionnaire Item 33, and short-form questionnaire Item 2. All occupied housing units are classified as either owner occupied or renter occupied.

A housing unit is owner occupied if the owner or co-owner lives in the unit even if it is mortgaged or not fully paid for. The owner or co-owner must live in the unit and usually is Person 1 on the questionnaire. The unit is "Owned by you or someone in this household with a mortgage or loan" if it is being purchased with a mortgage or some other debt arrangement, such as a deed of trust, trust deed, contract to purchase, land contract, or purchase agreement. The unit is also considered owned with a mortgage if it is built on leased land and there is a mortgage on the unit. Mobile homes occupied by owners with installment loans balances are also included in this category.

Median Gross Rent (in dollars): Median monthly gross rent on specified renter-occupied and specified vacant-for-rent units. Specified renter-occupied and specified vacant-for-rent units exclude 1-family houses on 10 acres or more.

The data on gross rent were obtained from answers to long-form questionnaire Items 45a-d, which were asked on a sample basis. Gross rent is the contract rent plus the estimated average monthly cost of utilities (electricity, gas, water and sewer) and fuels (oil, coal, kerosene, wood, etc.) if these are paid by the renter (or paid for the renter by someone else). Gross rent is intended to eliminate differentials that result from varying practices with respect to the inclusion of utilities and fuels as part of the rental payment. The estimated costs of utilities and fuels are reported on an annual basis but are converted to monthly figures for the tabulations. Renter units occupied without payment of cash rent are shown separately as "No cash rent" in the tabulations.

Housing units that are renter occupied without payment of cash rent are shown separately as "No cash rent" in census data products. The unit may be owned by friends or relatives who live elsewhere and who allow occupancy without charge. Rent-free houses or apartments may be provided to compensate caretakers, ministers, tenant farmers, sharecroppers, or others.

Contract rent is the monthly rent agreed to or contracted for, regardless of any furnishings, utilities, fees, meals, or services that may be included. For vacant units, it is the monthly rent asked for the rental unit at the time of enumeration.

If the contract rent includes rent for a business unit or for living quarters occupied by another household, only that part of the rent estimated to be for the respondent's unit was included. Excluded was any rent paid for additional units or for business premises.

If a renter pays rent to the owner of a condominium or cooperative, and the condominium fee or cooperative carrying charge also is paid by the renter to the owner, the condominium fee or carrying charge was included as rent.

If a renter receives payments from lodgers or roomers who are listed as members of the household, the rent without deduction for any payments received from the lodgers or roomers was to be reported. The respondent was to report the rent agreed to or contracted for even if paid by someone else such as friends or relatives living elsewhere, a church or welfare agency, or the government through subsidies or vouchers.

The median divides the rent distribution into two equal parts: one-half of the cases falling below the median contract rent and one-half above the median. Median contract rents are computed on the basis of a standard distribution and are rounded to the nearest whole dollar. Units reported as "No cash rent" are excluded.

Median Home Value (in dollars): Reported by the owner of specified owner-occupied or specified vacant-for-sale housing units. Specified owner-occupied and specified vacant-for-sale housing units include only 1-family houses on less than 10 acres without a business or medical office on the property. The data for "specified units" exclude mobile homes, houses with a business or medical office, houses on 10 or more acres, and housing units in multi-unit buildings.

The data on value (also referred to as "price asked" for vacant units) were obtained from answers to long-form questionnaire Item 51, which was asked on a sample basis at owner-occupied housing units and units that were being bought, or vacant for sale at the time of enumeration. Value is the respondent's estimate of how much the property (house and lot, mobile home and lot, or condominium unit) would sell for if it were for sale. If the house or mobile home was owned or being bought, but the land on which it sits was not, the respondent was asked to estimate the combined value of the house or mobile home and the land. For vacant units, value was the price asked for the property. Value was tabulated separately for all owner-occupied and vacant-for-sale housing units, owner-occupied and vacant-for-sale mobile homes, and specified owner-occupied and specified vacant-for-sale housing units.

The median divides the value distribution into two equal parts: one-half of the cases falling below the median value of the property (house and lot, mobile home and lot, or condominium unit) and one-half above the median. Median values are computed on the basis of a standard distribution and are rounded to the nearest hundred dollars.

User's Guide: Weather

Inclusion Criteria — How the Data and Stations Were Selected

There were two central goals in the preparation of the weather chapter. The first was to select those data elements which would have the broadest possible use by the greatest range of potential users. For most of the National Weather Service stations there is a substantial quantity and variety of climatological data that is collected, however for the majority of stations the data is more limited. After evaluating the available data set, the editors chose nine temperature measures, five precipitation measures, and heating and cooling degree days — sixteen key data elements that are widely requested and are believed to be of the greatest general interest.

The second goal was to provide data for as many weather stations as possible. Although there are over 10,000 stations in the United States, not every station collects data for both precipitation and temperature, and even among those that do, the data is not always complete for the last thirty years. As the editors used a different methodology than that of NCDC to compute data, a formal data sufficiency criteria was devised and applied to the source tapes in order to select stations for inclusion.

Sources of the Data

The data in the weather chapter is compiled from several sources. The majority comes from the original National Climactic Data Center computer tapes (TD-3220 Summary of Month Co-Operative). This data was used to create the entire table for each Cooperative station and part of each National Weather Service station. The remainder of the data for each NWS station comes from the International Station Meteorological Climate Summary, Version 4.0, September 1996, which is also available from the NCDC.

NCDC has two main classes or types of weather stations; first order stations which are staffed by professional meteorologists and cooperative stations which are staffed by volunteers. In the weather chapter all first order stations operated by the National Weather Service are included, as well as every cooperative station that met our selection criteria.

Potential Cautions

First, as with any statistical reference work of this type, users need to be aware of the source of the data. The information here comes from NOAA, and it is the most comprehensive and reliable core data available. Although it is the best, it is not perfect. Most weather stations are staffed by volunteers, times of observation sometimes vary, stations occasionally are moved (especially over a thirty year period), equipment is changed or upgraded, and all of these factors affect the uniformity of the data. the weather chapter does not attempt to correct for these factors, and is not intended for either climatologists or atmospheric scientists. Users with concerns about data collection and reporting protocols are both referred to NCDC technical documentation, and also, they are perhaps better served by using the original computer tapes themselves as well.

Second, users need to be aware of the methodology used, which is described later in this User's Guide. Although this methodology has produced fully satisfactory results, it is not directly compatible with other methodologies, hence variances in the results published here and those which appear in other publications will doubtlessly arise.

Third, is the trap of that informal logical fallacy known as "hasty generalization," and its corollaries. This may involve presuming the future will be like the past (specifically, next year will be an average year), or it may involve misunderstanding the limitations of an arithmetic average, but more interestingly, it may involve those mistakes made most innocently by generalizing informally on too broad a basis. As weather is highly localized, the data should be taken in that context. A weather station collects data about climatic conditions at that spot, and that spot may or may not be an effective paradigm for an entire town or area. For example, the weather station in Burlington, Vermont is located at the airport about 3 miles east of the center of town. Most of Burlington is a lot closer to Lake Champlain, and that should mean to a careful user that there could be a significant difference between the temperature readings gathered at the weather station and readings that might be gathered at City Hall downtown. How much would this difference be? How could it be estimated? There are no answers here for these sorts of questions, but it is important for users of this book to raise them for themselves. (It is interesting to note that similar situations abound across the country. For example, compare different readings for the multiple stations in San Francisco, CA or for those around New York City.)

Our source of data has been consistent, so has our methodology. The data has been computed and reported consistently as well. As a result, the the weather chapter should prove valuable to the careful and informed reader.

Weather Station Tables

The weather station tables are grouped by type (National Weather Service and Cooperative) and then arranged alphabetically. The station name is almost always a place name, and is shown here just as it appears in NCDC data. The station name is followed by the county in which the station is located, the elevation of the station (at the time beginning of the thirty year period) and the latitude and longitude.

The National Weather Service Station tables contain 30 data elements which were compiled from two different sources, the International Station Meteorological Climate Summary (ISMCS) and NCDC TD-3220 data tapes. The following 14 elements are from the ISMCS: maximum precipitation, minimum precipitation, maximum 24-hour precipitation, maximum snowfall, maximum 24-hour snowfall, thunderstorm days, foggy days, predominant sky cover, relative humidity (morning and afternoon), dewpoint, wind speed and direction, and maximum wind gust. The remaining 16 elements come from the TD-3220 data tapes. The period of record (POR) for data from the TD-3220 data tapes is 1970-1999. The POR for ISMCS data varies from station to station.

Weather Elements (National Weather Service and Cooperative Stations)

The following elements were compiled by the editor from the NCDC TD-3220 data tapes using a period of record of 1970-1999.

The average temperatures (maximum, minimum, and mean) are the average (see Methodology below) of those temperatures for all available values for a given month. For example, for a given station the average maximum temperature for July is the arithmetic average of all available maximum July temperatures for that station. (Maximum means the highest recorded temperature, minimum means the lowest recorded temperature, and mean means an arithmetic average temperature.)

The extreme maximum temperature is the highest temperature recorded in each month over the period 1970-1999. The extreme minimum temperature is the lowest temperature recorded in each month over the same time period.

The days for maximum temperature and minimum temperature are the average number of days those criteria were met for all available instances. The symbol >= means greater than or equal to, the symbol <= means less than or equal to. For example, for a given station, the number of days the maximum temperature was greater than or equal to 90°F in July, is just an arithmetic average of the number of days in all the available Julys for that station.

Heating and cooling degree days are based on the median temperature for a given day and its variance from 65°F. For example, for a given station if the day's high temperature was 50°F and the day's low temperature was 30°F, the median (midpoint) temperature was 40°F. 40°F is 25 degrees below 65°F, hence on this day there would be 25 heating degree days. The also applies for cooling degree days. For example, for a given station if the day's high temperature was 80°F and the day's low temperature was 70°F, the median (midpoint) temperature was 75°F. 75°F is 10 degrees above 65°F, hence on this day there would be 10 cooling degree days. All heating and/or cooling degree days in a month are summed for the month giving respective totals for each element for that month. These sums for a given month for a given station over the past thirty years are again summed and then arithmetically averaged. It should be noted that the heating and cooling degree days do not cancel each other out. It is possible to have both for a given station in the same month.

Precipitation data is computed the same as heating and cooling degree days. Mean precipitation and mean snowfall are arithmetic averages of cumulative totals for the month. All available values for the thirty year period for a given month for a given station are summed and then divided by the number of values. The same is true for days of greater than or equal to 0.1" and 1.0" of precipitation, and days of greater than or equal to 1.0" of snow depth on the ground. The word trace appears for precipitation and snowfall amounts that are too small to measure.

Finally, remember that all values presented in the tables and the rankings are averages of available data (see Methodology below) for that specific data element for the last thirty years (1970-1999).

Weather Elements (National Weather Service Stations Only)

The following elements were taken directly from the International Station Meteorological Climate Summary. The periods of records vary per station.

Maximum precipitation, minimum precipitation, maximum 24-hour precipitation, maximum snowfall, maximum 24-hour snowfall, thunderstorm days, foggy days, relative humidity (morning and afternoon), dewpoint, prevailing wind speed and direction, and maximum wind gust are all self-explanatory.

The word trace appears for precipitation and snowfall amounts that are too small to measure.

Predominant sky cover contains four possible entries: CLR (clear); SCT (scattered); BRK (broken); and OVR (overcast).

How Cooperative Stations Were Selected

The basic criteria is that a station must have data for temperature, precipitation, heating and cooling degree days of sufficient quantity in order to create a meaningful average. More specifically, the definition of sufficiency here has two parts. First, there must be 22 values for a given data element (with the exception of cooling degree days which required only 14 values in order to be considered sufficient- more about this later), and second, eight of the sixteen elements included in the table must pass this sufficiency test. For example, in regard to average maximum temperature (the first element on every data table), a given station needs to have a value for every month of at least 22 of the last thirty years in order to meet the criteria, and, in addition, every station included must have at least eight of the sixteen elements at least this minimal level of completeness in order to fulfill the criteria. By using this procedure, 3,933 stations met these requirements and are included here.

Methodology

The following discussion applies only to data compiled from the NCDC TD-3220 data tapes.

The weather chapter is based on an arithmetic average of all available data for a specific data element at a given station. For example, the average maximum daily high temperature during July for Cleveland, Ohio was abstracted from NCDC source tapes for the thirty Julys, starting in July, 1970 and ending in July, 1999. These thirty figures were then summed and divided by thirty to produce an arithmetic average. As might be expected, there were not thirty values for every data element on every table. For a variety of reasons, NCDC data is sometimes incomplete. Thus the following standards were established.

For those data elements where there were 26-30 values, the data was taken to be essentially complete and an average was computed. For data elements where there were 22-25 values, the data was taken as being partly complete but still valid enough to use to compute an average. Such averages are shown in **bold italic** type to indicate that there was less than 26 values. For the few data elements where there were not even 22 values, no average was computed and 'na' appears in the space. If any of the twelve months for a given data element reported a value of 'na', no annual average was computed and the annual average was reported as 'na' as well.

This procedure was followed for 15 of the 16 data elements. The one exception is cooling degree days. The collection of this data began in 1980 so the following standards were adopted: for those data elements where there were 17-20 values, the data was taken to be essentially complete and an average was computed. For data elements where there were 14-16 values, the data was taken as being partly complete but still valid enough to use to compute an average. Such averages are shown in **bold italic** type to indicate that there was 14-16 values. For the few data elements where there were not even 14 values, no average was computed and 'na' appears in the space. If any of the twelve months for a given data element reported a value of 'na', no annual average was computed and the annual average was reported as 'na' as well.

Thus the basic computational methodology of the weather chapter is to provide an arithmetic average. Because of this, such a pure arithmetic average is somewhat different from the special type of average (called a "normal") which NCDC procedures produces and appears in federal publications.

Perhaps the best outline of the contrasting normalization methodology is found in the following paragraph (which appears as part of an NCDC technical document titled, CLIM81 1961-1990 NORMALS TD-9641 prepared by Lewis France of NCDC in May, 1992):

Normals have been defined as the arithmetic mean of a climatological element computed over a long time period. International agreements eventually led to the decision that the appropriate time period would be three consecutive decades (Guttman, 1989). The data record should be consistent (have no changes in location, instruments, observation practices, etc.; these are identified here as "exposure changes") and have no missing values so a normal will reflect the actual average climatic conditions. If any significant exposure changes have occurred, the data record is said to be "inhomogeneous," and the normal may not reflect a true climatic average. Such data need to be adjusted to remove the nonclimatic inhomogeneities. The resulting (adjusted) record is then said to be "homogeneous." If no exposure changes have occurred at a station, the normal is calculated simply by averaging the appropriate 30 values from the 1961-1990 record.

In the main, there are two "inhomogeneities" that NCDC is correcting for with normalization: adjusting for variances in time of day of observation (at the so-called First Order stations data is based on midnight to midnight observation times and this practice is not necessarily followed at cooperative stations which are staffed by volunteers), and second, estimating data that is either missing or incongruent.

A long discussion of the normalization process is not required here but a short note concerning comparative results of the two methodologies is appropriate.

When the editors first started compiling the weather chapter a concern arose because the normalization process would not be replicated: would our methodology produce strikingly different results than NCDC's? To allay concerns, results of the two processes were compared for the time period normalized results are available (1961-1990). In short, what was found was that the answer to this question is no. Never-the-less, users should be aware that because of both the time period covered (1970-1999) and the methodology used, data in the weather chapter is not compatible with data from other sources.

Adams County

Located in southern Ohio; bounded on the south by the Ohio River and the Kentucky border. Covers a land area of 583.91 square miles, a water area of 1.88 square miles, and is located in the Eastern Time Zone. The county government was organized in 1797. County seat is West Union.

Population: 25,371 (1990); 27,330 (2000); 28,392 (2005); 29,498 (2010 projected); Race: 97.6% White, 0.2% Black, 0.2% Asian, 0.8% Hispanic of any race (2005); Density: 48.6 persons per square mile (2005); Average household size: 2.56 (2005); Median age: 36.7 (2005); Males per 100 females: 96.7 (2005).

Religion: Five largest groups: 5.2% Christian Churches and Churches of Christ, 4.9% The United Methodist Church, 2.1% Presbyterian Church (U.S.A.), 2.0% Christian Union, 1.5% Church of the Nazarene (2000).

Economy: Unemployment rate: 8.3% (2005); Total civilian labor force: 13,149 (2005); Leading industries: 23.6% retail trade; 21.2% health care and social assistance; 16.4% manufacturing (2004); Farms: 1,320 totaling 198,277 acres (2002); Companies that employ 500 or more persons: 0 (2004); Companies that employ 100 to 499 persons: 7 (2004); Companies that employ less than 100 persons: 427 (2004); Black-owned businesses: n/a (2002); Hispanic-owned businesses: n/a (2002); Women-owned businesses: 628 (2002); Retail sales per capita: $8,579 (2006). Single-family building permits issued: 0 (2005); Multi-family building permits issued: 0 (2005).

Income: Per capita income: $16,779 (2005); Median household income: $33,313 (2005); Average household income: $42,520 (2005); Percent of households with income of $100,000 or more: 6.4% (2005); Poverty rate: 14.9% (2003); Bankruptcy rate: 8.54% (2005).

Education: Percent of population age 25 and over with: High school diploma (including GED) or higher: 68.7% (2005); Bachelor's degree or higher: 7.3% (2005); Master's degree or higher: 2.8% (2005).

Housing: Homeownership rate: 74.3% (2005); Median home value: $79,246 (2005); Median rent: $273 per month (2000); Median age of housing: 26 years (2000).

Health: Birth rate: 137.2 per 10,000 population (2004); Death rate: 101.5 per 10,000 population (2004); Age-adjusted cancer mortality rate: 272.1 deaths per 100,000 population (2002); Air Quality Index: 99.7% good, 0.3% moderate, 0.0% unhealthy for sensitive individuals, 0.0% unhealthy (percent of days in 2005); Number of physicians: 5.3 per 10,000 population (2004); Hospital beds: 13.2 per 10,000 population (2003); Hospital admissions: 598.9 per 10,000 population (2003).

Elections: 2004 Presidential election results: 63.8% Bush, 35.7% Kerry, 0.0% Nader, 0.3% Badnarik

National and State Parks: Adams Lake State Reserve; Ohio State Park; Serpent Mound State Memorial; Shawnee State Wilderness; Tranquility State Wildlife Area

Additional Information Contacts
Adams County Government. . . . . (937) 544-3286
  http://www.adamscountyohio.com/
Adams County Chamber of Commerce . . . . (937) 544-5454
  http://www.adamscountytravel.org

Adams County Communities

BLUE CREEK (unincorporated postal area, zip code 45616). Covers a land area of 69.973 square miles and a water area of 0.027 square miles. Located at 38.78° N. Lat.; 83.31° W. Long. Elevation is 680 feet.
Population: 1,382 (2000); Race: 96.8% White, 0.0% Black, 0.0% Asian, 0.0% Hispanic of any race (2000); Density: 19.8 persons per square mile (2000); Age: 25.8% under 18, 11.3% over 64 (2000); Marriage status: 19.4% never married, 68.7% now married, 5.3% widowed, 6.7% divorced (2000); Foreign born: 0.5% (2000); Ancestry (includes multiple ancestries): 31.8% United States or American, 9.8% German, 7.8% Other groups, 6.2% Irish, 4.1% English (2000).
Economy: Employment by occupation: 7.4% management, 5.9% professional, 21.0% services, 17.2% sales, 1.1% farming, 14.2% construction, 33.3% production (2000).
Income: Per capita income: $13,915 (2000); Median household income: $21,313 (2000); Poverty rate: 31.6% (2000).
Education: Percent of population age 25 and over with: High school diploma (including GED) or higher: 55.3% (2000); Bachelor's degree or higher: 4.6% (2000).
Housing: Homeownership rate: 75.4% (2000); Median home value: $60,600 (2000); Median rent: $281 per month (2000); Median age of housing: 24 years (2000).
Transportation: Commute to work: 88.5% car, 0.0% public transportation, 1.5% walk, 5.8% work from home (2000); Travel time to work: 15.2% less than 15 minutes, 23.1% 15 to 30 minutes, 34.6% 30 to 45 minutes, 13.3% 45 to 60 minutes, 13.8% 60 minutes or more (2000)

CHERRY FORK (village). Covers a land area of 0.122 square miles and a water area of 0 square miles. Located at 38.88° N. Lat.; 83.61° W. Long. Elevation is 890 feet.
Population: 178 (1990); 127 (2000); 137 (2005); 145 (2010 projected); Race: 100.0% White, 0.0% Black, 0.0% Asian, 0.0% Hispanic of any race (2005); Density: 1,122.1 persons per square mile (2005); Average household size: 2.63 (2005); Median age: 29.8 (2005); Males per 100 females: 107.6 (2005); Marriage status: 19.8% never married, 59.4% now married, 1.0% widowed, 19.8% divorced (2000); Foreign born: 0.0% (2000); Ancestry (includes multiple ancestries): 37.8% United States or American, 16.2% German, 12.8% Other groups, 4.1% English, 2.7% Irish (2000).
Economy: Employment by occupation: 0.0% management, 13.8% professional, 24.1% services, 25.9% sales, 0.0% farming, 13.8% construction, 22.4% production (2000).
Income: Per capita income: $14,234 (2005); Median household income: $30,455 (2005); Average household income: $37,500 (2005); Percent of households with income of $100,000 or more: 3.8% (2005); Poverty rate: 26.7% (2000).
Education: Percent of population age 25 and over with: High school diploma (including GED) or higher: 81.7% (2005); Bachelor's degree or higher: 9.8% (2005); Master's degree or higher: 4.9% (2005).
Housing: Homeownership rate: 65.4% (2005); Median home value: $73,333 (2005); Median rent: $296 per month (2000); Median age of housing: 54 years (2000).
Transportation: Commute to work: 96.4% car, 0.0% public transportation, 0.0% walk, 0.0% work from home (2000); Travel time to work: 25.0% less than 15 minutes, 17.9% 15 to 30 minutes, 12.5% 30 to 45 minutes, 16.1% 45 to 60 minutes, 28.6% 60 minutes or more (2000)

MANCHESTER (village). Covers a land area of 1.078 square miles and a water area of 0.015 square miles. Located at 38.69° N. Lat.; 83.60° W. Long. Elevation is 520 feet.
History: Manchester was founded in 1791 by General Nathaniel Massie. The town was an important steamboat landing in the mid-1800's, and in the later 1800's offered excursions on the river and showboats at the wharf.
Population: 2,333 (1990); 2,043 (2000); 1,996 (2005); 1,963 (2010 projected); Race: 97.3% White, 0.2% Black, 0.5% Asian, 0.4% Hispanic of any race (2005); Density: 1,850.9 persons per square mile (2005); Average household size: 2.26 (2005); Median age: 37.1 (2005); Males per 100 females: 90.8 (2005); Marriage status: 21.0% never married, 53.5% now married, 11.2% widowed, 14.4% divorced (2000); Foreign born: 0.1% (2000); Ancestry (includes multiple ancestries): 31.2% United States or American, 9.6% Other groups, 8.6% German, 8.4% Irish, 5.8% English (2000).
Economy: Single-family building permits issued: 0 (2005); Multi-family building permits issued: 0 (2005); Employment by occupation: 11.1% management, 10.0% professional, 18.1% services, 17.8% sales, 0.3% farming, 15.6% construction, 27.2% production (2000).
Income: Per capita income: $15,615 (2005); Median household income: $25,522 (2005); Average household income: $35,337 (2005); Percent of households with income of $100,000 or more: 4.3% (2005); Poverty rate: 23.3% (2000).
Education: Percent of population age 25 and over with: High school diploma (including GED) or higher: 62.7% (2005); Bachelor's degree or higher: 6.1% (2005); Master's degree or higher: 3.5% (2005).
School District(s)
Adams County/Ohio Valley Local SD (PK-12)
  2003-04 Enrollment: 5,098 . . . . (937) 544-5586
Manchester Local SD
  2003-04 Enrollment: n/a . . . . (740) 354-7761
Housing: Homeownership rate: 62.6% (2005); Median home value: $56,571 (2005); Median rent: $263 per month (2000); Median age of housing: 39 years (2000).
Safety: Violent crime rate: 19.5 per 10,000 population; Property crime rate: 150.9 per 10,000 population (2004).
Newspapers: The Manchester Signal (General - Circulation 5,500)
Transportation: Commute to work: 93.0% car, 0.0% public transportation, 3.7% walk, 2.0% work from home (2000); Travel time to work: 34.1% less

than 15 minutes, 32.5% 15 to 30 minutes, 11.9% 30 to 45 minutes, 3.9% 45 to 60 minutes, 17.6% 60 minutes or more (2000)

PEEBLES (village). Covers a land area of 1.213 square miles and a water area of 0 square miles. Located at 38.94° N. Lat.; 83.40° W. Long. Elevation is 829 feet.
Population: 1,793 (1990); 1,739 (2000); 1,682 (2005); 1,682 (2010 projected); Race: 97.6% White, 0.4% Black, 0.6% Asian, 0.4% Hispanic of any race (2005); Density: 1,386.5 persons per square mile (2005); Average household size: 2.42 (2005); Median age: 35.7 (2005); Males per 100 females: 90.7 (2005); Marriage status: 23.2% never married, 51.1% now married, 10.8% widowed, 14.9% divorced (2000); Foreign born: 0.0% (2000); Ancestry (includes multiple ancestries): 20.4% United States or American, 9.6% German, 9.4% Other groups, 5.6% Irish, 4.6% English (2000).
Economy: In agricultural area. Employment by occupation: 5.4% management, 12.5% professional, 18.0% services, 20.8% sales, 1.3% farming, 12.4% construction, 29.6% production (2000).
Income: Per capita income: $14,172 (2005); Median household income: $23,205 (2005); Average household income: $33,851 (2005); Percent of households with income of $100,000 or more: 3.7% (2005); Poverty rate: 28.2% (2000).
Education: Percent of population age 25 and over with: High school diploma (including GED) or higher: 63.0% (2005); Bachelor's degree or higher: 5.4% (2005); Master's degree or higher: 2.6% (2005).
School District(s)
Adams County/Ohio Valley Local SD (PK-12)
    2003-04 Enrollment: 5,098 . . . . (937) 544-5586
Housing: Homeownership rate: 57.3% (2005); Median home value: $63,523 (2005); Median rent: $276 per month (2000); Median age of housing: 38 years (2000).
Transportation: Commute to work: 92.3% car, 0.2% public transportation, 4.6% walk, 1.4% work from home (2000); Travel time to work: 32.6% less than 15 minutes, 28.3% 15 to 30 minutes, 11.9% 30 to 45 minutes, 7.1% 45 to 60 minutes, 20.2% 60 minutes or more (2000)

ROME (village). Aka Stout. Covers a land area of 0.266 square miles and a water area of 0.027 square miles. Located at 38.66° N. Lat.; 83.38° W. Long.
History: Also called Stout.
Population: 99 (1990); 117 (2000); 108 (2005); 105 (2010 projected); Race: 95.4% White, 0.0% Black, 0.0% Asian, 0.0% Hispanic of any race (2005); Density: 405.9 persons per square mile (2005); Average household size: 2.51 (2005); Median age: 35.9 (2005); Males per 100 females: 86.2 (2005); Marriage status: 20.2% never married, 59.6% now married, 6.4% widowed, 13.8% divorced (2000); Foreign born: 0.0% (2000); Ancestry (includes multiple ancestries): 35.3% Other groups, 25.2% United States or American, 7.6% German, 6.7% Irish, 2.5% English (2000).
Economy: Employment by occupation: 8.6% management, 14.3% professional, 20.0% services, 25.7% sales, 0.0% farming, 11.4% construction, 20.0% production (2000).
Income: Per capita income: $15,116 (2005); Median household income: $37,885 (2005); Average household income: $37,965 (2005); Percent of households with income of $100,000 or more: 2.3% (2005); Poverty rate: 24.4% (2000).
Education: Percent of population age 25 and over with: High school diploma (including GED) or higher: 70.0% (2005); Bachelor's degree or higher: 2.9% (2005); Master's degree or higher: 0.0% (2005).
Housing: Homeownership rate: 67.4% (2005); Median home value: $45,000 (2005); Median rent: $329 per month (2000); Median age of housing: 47 years (2000).
Transportation: Commute to work: 91.2% car, 0.0% public transportation, 8.8% walk, 0.0% work from home (2000); Travel time to work: 17.6% less than 15 minutes, 41.2% 15 to 30 minutes, 23.5% 30 to 45 minutes, 5.9% 45 to 60 minutes, 11.8% 60 minutes or more (2000)

SEAMAN (village). Covers a land area of 1.021 square miles and a water area of 0 square miles. Located at 38.93° N. Lat.; 83.57° W. Long. Elevation is 900 feet.
Population: 1,009 (1990); 1,039 (2000); 916 (2005); 895 (2010 projected); Race: 98.8% White, 0.0% Black, 0.0% Asian, 0.8% Hispanic of any race (2005); Density: 897.2 persons per square mile (2005); Average household size: 2.51 (2005); Median age: 33.3 (2005); Males per 100 females: 84.7 (2005); Marriage status: 24.3% never married, 52.2% now married, 12.0% widowed, 11.5% divorced (2000); Foreign born: 0.4% (2000); Ancestry (includes multiple ancestries): 17.6% United States or American, 14.8% Irish, 12.2% German, 9.9% English, 6.3% Other groups (2000).
Economy: In agricultural area. Single-family building permits issued: 0 (2005); Multi-family building permits issued: 0 (2005); Employment by occupation: 9.7% management, 15.8% professional, 14.5% services, 19.9% sales, 0.3% farming, 14.5% construction, 25.3% production (2000).
Income: Per capita income: $15,096 (2005); Median household income: $28,776 (2005); Average household income: $37,884 (2005); Percent of households with income of $100,000 or more: 4.1% (2005); Poverty rate: 21.7% (2000).
Education: Percent of population age 25 and over with: High school diploma (including GED) or higher: 76.4% (2005); Bachelor's degree or higher: 9.3% (2005); Master's degree or higher: 3.2% (2005).
School District(s)
Adams County/Ohio Valley Local SD (PK-12)
    2003-04 Enrollment: 5,098 . . . . (937) 544-5586
Housing: Homeownership rate: 62.7% (2005); Median home value: $81,500 (2005); Median rent: $316 per month (2000); Median age of housing: 36 years (2000).
Transportation: Commute to work: 93.3% car, 0.0% public transportation, 3.6% walk, 3.1% work from home (2000); Travel time to work: 26.6% less than 15 minutes, 25.0% 15 to 30 minutes, 16.5% 30 to 45 minutes, 12.8% 45 to 60 minutes, 19.1% 60 minutes or more (2000)

WEST UNION (village). Covers a land area of 2.568 square miles and a water area of 0 square miles. Located at 38.79° N. Lat.; 83.54° W. Long. Elevation is 967 feet.
History: Laid out 1804.
Population: 3,234 (1990); 2,903 (2000); 3,025 (2005); 3,151 (2010 projected); Race: 98.1% White, 0.3% Black, 0.1% Asian, 0.5% Hispanic of any race (2005); Density: 1,177.9 persons per square mile (2005); Average household size: 2.29 (2005); Median age: 39.6 (2005); Males per 100 females: 79.4 (2005); Marriage status: 20.8% never married, 49.2% now married, 15.6% widowed, 14.4% divorced (2000); Foreign born: 0.3% (2000); Ancestry (includes multiple ancestries): 20.7% United States or American, 20.6% German, 12.6% Irish, 6.2% Other groups, 5.4% English (2000).
Economy: In tobacco and grain area. Employment by occupation: 2.5% management, 9.6% professional, 19.8% services, 24.7% sales, 1.4% farming, 10.3% construction, 31.6% production (2000).
Income: Per capita income: $14,909 (2005); Median household income: $23,333 (2005); Average household income: $32,316 (2005); Percent of households with income of $100,000 or more: 4.6% (2005); Poverty rate: 21.8% (2000).
Education: Percent of population age 25 and over with: High school diploma (including GED) or higher: 66.8% (2005); Bachelor's degree or higher: 3.8% (2005); Master's degree or higher: 0.7% (2005).
School District(s)
Adams County/Ohio Valley Local SD (PK-12)
    2003-04 Enrollment: 5,098 . . . . (937) 544-5586
Housing: Homeownership rate: 55.3% (2005); Median home value: $69,032 (2005); Median rent: $256 per month (2000); Median age of housing: 32 years (2000).
Hospitals: Adams County Hospital (60 beds)
Newspapers: People's Defender (General - Circulation 9,100)
Transportation: Commute to work: 90.4% car, 0.8% public transportation, 6.3% walk, 2.4% work from home (2000); Travel time to work: 50.3% less than 15 minutes, 20.4% 15 to 30 minutes, 8.7% 30 to 45 minutes, 8.8% 45 to 60 minutes, 11.7% 60 minutes or more (2000)
Additional Information Contacts
Adams County Chamber of Commerce . . . . (937) 544-5454
    http://www.adamscountytravel.org

WINCHESTER (village). Covers a land area of 2.685 square miles and a water area of 0.017 square miles. Located at 38.94° N. Lat.; 83.65° W. Long. Elevation is 970 feet.
History: In agricultural area.
Population: 995 (1990); 1,025 (2000); 1,041 (2005); 1,035 (2010 projected); Race: 98.9% White, 0.0% Black, 0.6% Asian, 0.7% Hispanic of any race (2005); Density: 387.8 persons per square mile (2005); Average household size: 2.46 (2005); Median age: 34.0 (2005); Males per 100 females: 91.4 (2005); Marriage status: 18.6% never married, 60.7% now married, 7.9% widowed, 12.8% divorced (2000); Foreign born: 1.0% (2000); Ancestry (includes multiple ancestries): 17.7% United States or

American, 16.4% German, 9.6% Irish, 9.4% Other groups, 7.0% English (2000).
Economy: Employment by occupation: 9.7% management, 10.8% professional, 12.9% services, 21.0% sales, 0.0% farming, 14.7% construction, 30.9% production (2000).
Income: Per capita income: $18,249 (2005); Median household income: $35,882 (2005); Average household income: $44,805 (2005); Percent of households with income of $100,000 or more: 6.4% (2005); Poverty rate: 14.2% (2000).
Education: Percent of population age 25 and over with: High school diploma (including GED) or higher: 77.4% (2005); Bachelor's degree or higher: 6.7% (2005); Master's degree or higher: 2.9% (2005).
Housing: Homeownership rate: 61.6% (2005); Median home value: $85,469 (2005); Median rent: $289 per month (2000); Median age of housing: 42 years (2000).
Transportation: Commute to work: 95.4% car, 0.0% public transportation, 4.2% walk, 0.5% work from home (2000); Travel time to work: 21.6% less than 15 minutes, 26.0% 15 to 30 minutes, 14.2% 30 to 45 minutes, 16.0% 45 to 60 minutes, 22.1% 60 minutes or more (2000)

Allen County

Located in western Ohio; crossed by the Ottawa and Auglaize Rivers. Covers a land area of 404.43 square miles, a water area of 2.46 square miles, and is located in the Eastern Time Zone. The county government was organized in 1820. County seat is Lima.

Allen County is part of the Lima, OH Metropolitan Statistical Area. The entire metro area includes: Allen County, OH

Weather Station: Lima WWTP   Elevation: 849 feet

	Jan	Feb	Mar	Apr	May	Jun	Jul	Aug	Sep	Oct	Nov	Dec
High	33	38	48	61	72	81	85	82	77	64	50	39
Low	18	21	30	40	51	60	64	62	55	44	34	25
Precip	2.2	1.9	2.7	3.5	3.9	4.0	4.4	3.3	3.1	2.4	3.1	2.7
Snow	na	na	na	0.1	0.0	0.0	0.0	0.0	0.0	tr	tr	na

High and Low temperatures in degrees Fahrenheit; Precipitation and Snow in inches

Population: 109,755 (1990); 108,473 (2000); 108,317 (2005); 108,117 (2010 projected); Race: 84.5% White, 12.1% Black, 0.9% Asian, 1.5% Hispanic of any race (2005); Density: 267.8 persons per square mile (2005); Average household size: 2.63 (2005); Median age: 36.6 (2005); Males per 100 females: 100.2 (2005).
Religion: Five largest groups: 22.7% Catholic Church, 7.7% The United Methodist Church, 3.2% Evangelical Lutheran Church in America, 2.2% United Church of Christ, 2.0% Church of the Nazarene (2000).
Economy: Unemployment rate: 6.2% (2005); Total civilian labor force: 52,653 (2005); Leading industries: 20.0% health care and social assistance; 17.9% manufacturing; 15.7% retail trade (2004); Farms: 968 totaling 188,150 acres (2002); Companies that employ 500 or more persons: 8 (2004); Companies that employ 100 to 499 persons: 73 (2004); Companies that employ less than 100 persons: 2,684 (2004); Black-owned businesses: 255 (2002); Hispanic-owned businesses: n/a (2002); Women-owned businesses: 2,361 (2002); Retail sales per capita: $18,637 (2006); Single-family building permits issued: 267 (2005); Multi-family building permits issued: 53 (2005).
Income: Per capita income: $19,968 (2005); Median household income: $40,927 (2005); Average household income: $51,415 (2005); Percent of households with income of $100,000 or more: 9.5% (2005); Poverty rate: 11.3% (2003); Bankruptcy rate: 10.46% (2005).
Taxes: Total county taxes per capita: $270 (2004); County property taxes per capita: $106 (2004).
Education: Percent of population age 25 and over with: High school diploma (including GED) or higher: 82.7% (2005); Bachelor's degree or higher: 13.7% (2005); Master's degree or higher: 5.1% (2005).
Housing: Homeownership rate: 72.7% (2005); Median home value: $95,428 (2005); Median rent: $362 per month (2000); Median age of housing: 41 years (2000).
Health: Birth rate: 142.0 per 10,000 population (2004); Death rate: 104.5 per 10,000 population (2004); Age-adjusted cancer mortality rate: 240.4 deaths per 100,000 population (2002); Air Quality Index: 89.1% good, 10.3% moderate, 0.6% unhealthy for sensitive individuals, 0.0% unhealthy (percent of days in 2005); Number of physicians: 26.1 per 10,000 population (2004); Hospital beds: 65.9 per 10,000 population (2003); Hospital admissions: 2,230.4 per 10,000 population (2003).

Elections: 2004 Presidential election results: 66.1% Bush, 33.4% Kerry, 0.0% Nader, 0.3% Badnarik
Additional Information Contacts
Allen County Government . . . . (419) 228-3700
  http://www.co.allen.oh.us/
Bluffton Area Chamber of Commerce . . . . (419) 358-5675
  http://www.bluffton-ohio.com/bacc
City of Lima . . . . (419) 228-5462
  http://www.cityhall.lima.oh.us
Delphos Area Chamber of Commerce . . . . (419) 695-1771
  http://www.delphos-ohio.com
Lima Allen County Chamber of Commerce . . . . (419) 222-6045
  http://www.limachamber.com
Spencerville Chamber of Commerce . . . . (419) 647-2020
  http://www.noacc.org

Allen County Communities

BEAVERDAM (village). Aka Beaver Dam. Covers a land area of 0.629 square miles and a water area of 0 square miles. Located at 40.83° N. Lat.; 83.97° W. Long. Elevation is 860 feet.
Population: 487 (1990); 356 (2000); 376 (2005); 395 (2010 projected); Race: 99.2% White, 0.0% Black, 0.0% Asian, 0.5% Hispanic of any race (2005); Density: 598.1 persons per square mile (2005); Average household size: 2.54 (2005); Median age: 38.1 (2005); Males per 100 females: 94.8 (2005); Marriage status: 22.4% never married, 57.7% now married, 5.2% widowed, 14.7% divorced (2000); Foreign born: 0.9% (2000); Ancestry (includes multiple ancestries): 42.9% German, 7.7% Irish, 6.9% Swiss, 5.1% French (except Basque), 5.1% United States or American (2000).
Economy: In stock-raising area. Single-family building permits issued: 0 (2005); Multi-family building permits issued: 0 (2005); Employment by occupation: 8.9% management, 5.7% professional, 21.0% services, 12.7% sales, 0.0% farming, 10.2% construction, 41.4% production (2000).
Income: Per capita income: $19,076 (2005); Median household income: $46,250 (2005); Average household income: $48,463 (2005); Percent of households with income of $100,000 or more: 6.1% (2005); Poverty rate: 8.9% (2000).
Education: Percent of population age 25 and over with: High school diploma (including GED) or higher: 75.7% (2005); Bachelor's degree or higher: 2.8% (2005); Master's degree or higher: 0.0% (2005).
Housing: Homeownership rate: 85.1% (2005); Median home value: $61,481 (2005); Median rent: $275 per month (2000); Median age of housing: 60+ years (2000).
Transportation: Commute to work: 95.1% car, 0.0% public transportation, 2.1% walk, 0.0% work from home (2000); Travel time to work: 33.3% less than 15 minutes, 45.1% 15 to 30 minutes, 14.6% 30 to 45 minutes, 5.6% 45 to 60 minutes, 1.4% 60 minutes or more (2000)

BLUFFTON (village). Covers a land area of 3.329 square miles and a water area of 0.030 square miles. Located at 40.89° N. Lat.; 83.89° W. Long. Elevation is 824 feet.
History: Bluffton was founded in 1833 and named for a Mennonite community in Indiana. Many of the early residents were Mennonites of Swiss descent. Limestone outcroppings in the vicinity created a crushed stone and lime industry here.
Population: 3,480 (1990); 3,896 (2000); 3,962 (2005); 4,042 (2010 projected); Race: 97.8% White, 0.7% Black, 0.6% Asian, 1.2% Hispanic of any race (2005); Density: 1,190.0 persons per square mile (2005); Average household size: 2.89 (2005); Median age: 33.1 (2005); Males per 100 females: 76.2 (2005); Marriage status: 33.8% never married, 48.3% now married, 11.9% widowed, 6.0% divorced (2000); Foreign born: 2.3% (2000); Ancestry (includes multiple ancestries): 37.7% German, 12.1% English, 10.4% Swiss, 8.9% Irish, 8.8% Other groups (2000).
Economy: Single-family building permits issued: 8 (2005); Multi-family building permits issued: 2 (2005); Employment by occupation: 11.7% management, 26.1% professional, 21.8% services, 19.5% sales, 0.0% farming, 5.8% construction, 15.1% production (2000).
Income: Per capita income: $22,116 (2005); Median household income: $49,268 (2005); Average household income: $59,684 (2005); Percent of households with income of $100,000 or more: 14.7% (2005); Poverty rate: 5.7% (2000).
Education: Percent of population age 25 and over with: High school diploma (including GED) or higher: 88.3% (2005); Bachelor's degree or higher: 30.7% (2005); Master's degree or higher: 11.7% (2005).

School District(s)
Bluffton Ex Vill SD (PK-12)
  2003-04 Enrollment: 1,185 . . . . (419) 358-5901

Four-year College(s)
Bluffton University (Private, Not-for-profit, Mennonite Church)
  Fall 2004 Enrollment: 1,191. . . . . (419) 358-3000
  2005-06 Tuition: In-state $19,028; Out-of-state $19,028

Housing: Homeownership rate: 70.3% (2005); Median home value: $124,621 (2005); Median rent: $327 per month (2000); Median age of housing: 42 years (2000).
Newspapers: The Bluffton News (General - Circulation 2,900)
Transportation: Commute to work: 71.5% car, 0.0% public transportation, 23.7% walk, 2.4% work from home (2000); Travel time to work: 60.7% less than 15 minutes, 26.3% 15 to 30 minutes, 10.4% 30 to 45 minutes, 0.8% 45 to 60 minutes, 1.8% 60 minutes or more (2000)
Additional Information Contacts
Bluffton Area Chamber of Commerce . . . . (419) 358-5675
  http://www.bluffton-ohio.com/bacc

CAIRO
(village). Covers a land area of 0.242 square miles and a water area of 0 square miles. Located at 40.83° N. Lat.; 84.08° W. Long. Elevation is 815 feet.
Population: 473 (1990); 499 (2000); 503 (2005); 505 (2010 projected); Race: 98.4% White, 0.4% Black, 0.4% Asian, 1.0% Hispanic of any race (2005); Density: 2,080.5 persons per square mile (2005); Average household size: 2.73 (2005); Median age: 34.0 (2005); Males per 100 females: 92.0 (2005); Marriage status: 20.9% never married, 58.8% now married, 7.9% widowed, 12.5% divorced (2000); Foreign born: 0.0% (2000); Ancestry (includes multiple ancestries): 41.5% German, 15.4% English, 11.9% Irish, 8.5% Other groups, 7.1% Welsh (2000).
Economy: Single-family building permits issued: 4 (2005); Multi-family building permits issued: 0 (2005); Employment by occupation: 5.6% management, 13.1% professional, 15.4% services, 22.9% sales, 0.0% farming, 15.4% construction, 27.6% production (2000).
Income: Per capita income: $15,641 (2005); Median household income: $38,333 (2005); Average household income: $42,758 (2005); Percent of households with income of $100,000 or more: 2.7% (2005); Poverty rate: 6.9% (2000).
Education: Percent of population age 25 and over with: High school diploma (including GED) or higher: 90.1% (2005); Bachelor's degree or higher: 7.9% (2005); Master's degree or higher: 4.0% (2005).
Housing: Homeownership rate: 88.0% (2005); Median home value: $86,000 (2005); Median rent: $469 per month (2000); Median age of housing: 59 years (2000).
Transportation: Commute to work: 99.0% car, 0.0% public transportation, 1.0% walk, 0.0% work from home (2000); Travel time to work: 18.6% less than 15 minutes, 57.6% 15 to 30 minutes, 9.5% 30 to 45 minutes, 6.7% 45 to 60 minutes, 7.6% 60 minutes or more (2000)

DELPHOS
(city). Covers a land area of 2.903 square miles and a water area of 0 square miles. Located at 40.84° N. Lat.; 84.33° W. Long. Elevation is 780 feet.
History: Delphos was platted in 1845 by Ferdinand Bredeick. Its location on the Miami & Erie Canal and the Pennsylvania Railroad brought it early growth. Large-scale honey production was one of the leading industries.
Population: 7,436 (1990); 6,944 (2000); 6,905 (2005); 6,853 (2010 projected); Race: 98.3% White, 0.4% Black, 0.3% Asian, 0.7% Hispanic of any race (2005); Density: 2,378.4 persons per square mile (2005); Average household size: 2.50 (2005); Median age: 36.3 (2005); Males per 100 females: 95.9 (2005); Marriage status: 22.8% never married, 60.2% now married, 8.7% widowed, 8.3% divorced (2000); Foreign born: 0.8% (2000); Ancestry (includes multiple ancestries): 53.4% German, 7.3% United States or American, 7.0% Irish, 5.6% Other groups, 4.8% English (2000).
Economy: Single-family building permits issued: 18 (2005); Multi-family building permits issued: 0 (2005); Employment by occupation: 7.8% management, 14.0% professional, 14.7% services, 22.4% sales, 0.2% farming, 8.8% construction, 32.1% production (2000).
Income: Per capita income: $18,307 (2005); Median household income: $38,550 (2005); Average household income: $45,380 (2005); Percent of households with income of $100,000 or more: 5.2% (2005); Poverty rate: 6.8% (2000).
Education: Percent of population age 25 and over with: High school diploma (including GED) or higher: 84.0% (2005); Bachelor's degree or higher: 8.5% (2005); Master's degree or higher: 2.6% (2005).

School District(s)
Delphos City SD (PK-12)
  2003-04 Enrollment: 1,140 . . . . (419) 692-2509

Housing: Homeownership rate: 77.0% (2005); Median home value: $80,048 (2005); Median rent: $347 per month (2000); Median age of housing: 49 years (2000).
Newspapers: Delphos Daily Herald (Circulation 3,675)
Transportation: Commute to work: 95.6% car, 0.2% public transportation, 2.3% walk, 1.7% work from home (2000); Travel time to work: 42.7% less than 15 minutes, 35.6% 15 to 30 minutes, 16.8% 30 to 45 minutes, 1.8% 45 to 60 minutes, 3.1% 60 minutes or more (2000)
Additional Information Contacts
Delphos Area Chamber of Commerce . . . . (419) 695-1771
  http://www.delphos-ohio.com

ELIDA
(village). Covers a land area of 1.035 square miles and a water area of 0 square miles. Located at 40.78° N. Lat.; 84.19° W. Long. Elevation is 800 feet.
Population: 1,569 (1990); 1,917 (2000); 1,964 (2005); 2,047 (2010 projected); Race: 94.3% White, 2.5% Black, 1.1% Asian, 1.4% Hispanic of any race (2005); Density: 1,897.5 persons per square mile (2005); Average household size: 2.72 (2005); Median age: 37.4 (2005); Males per 100 females: 95.2 (2005); Marriage status: 21.0% never married, 64.8% now married, 5.7% widowed, 8.5% divorced (2000); Foreign born: 0.7% (2000); Ancestry (includes multiple ancestries): 41.6% German, 13.7% Irish, 7.7% United States or American, 7.6% Other groups, 7.4% English (2000).
Economy: Single-family building permits issued: 7 (2005); Multi-family building permits issued: 0 (2005); Employment by occupation: 14.3% management, 20.7% professional, 15.8% services, 25.5% sales, 0.0% farming, 7.8% construction, 15.9% production (2000).
Income: Per capita income: $24,495 (2005); Median household income: $55,183 (2005); Average household income: $66,539 (2005); Percent of households with income of $100,000 or more: 18.7% (2005); Poverty rate: 3.1% (2000).
Education: Percent of population age 25 and over with: High school diploma (including GED) or higher: 92.4% (2005); Bachelor's degree or higher: 22.6% (2005); Master's degree or higher: 8.3% (2005).

School District(s)
Elida Digital Academy (08-12)
  2003-04 Enrollment: 34 . . . . (419) 331-4155
Elida Local SD (PK-12)
  2003-04 Enrollment: 2,591 . . . . (419) 331-4155

Housing: Homeownership rate: 89.5% (2005); Median home value: $126,339 (2005); Median rent: $368 per month (2000); Median age of housing: 32 years (2000).
Transportation: Commute to work: 93.9% car, 0.3% public transportation, 1.7% walk, 4.1% work from home (2000); Travel time to work: 37.7% less than 15 minutes, 49.3% 15 to 30 minutes, 7.8% 30 to 45 minutes, 2.5% 45 to 60 minutes, 2.6% 60 minutes or more (2000)

FORT SHAWNEE
(village). Covers a land area of 7.205 square miles and a water area of 0 square miles. Located at 40.68° N. Lat.; 84.13° W. Long. Elevation is 866 feet.
Population: 4,128 (1990); 3,855 (2000); 3,869 (2005); 3,878 (2010 projected); Race: 93.3% White, 3.3% Black, 1.2% Asian, 1.3% Hispanic of any race (2005); Density: 537.0 persons per square mile (2005); Average household size: 2.48 (2005); Median age: 39.6 (2005); Males per 100 females: 96.6 (2005); Marriage status: 20.0% never married, 64.5% now married, 5.0% widowed, 10.5% divorced (2000); Foreign born: 0.3% (2000); Ancestry (includes multiple ancestries): 39.2% German, 14.2% Irish, 9.8% United States or American, 9.7% English, 9.0% Other groups (2000).
Economy: Single-family building permits issued: 3 (2005); Multi-family building permits issued: 0 (2005); Employment by occupation: 5.6% management, 18.0% professional, 15.5% services, 26.3% sales, 0.0% farming, 11.1% construction, 23.4% production (2000).
Income: Per capita income: $23,166 (2005); Median household income: $51,250 (2005); Average household income: $57,437 (2005); Percent of households with income of $100,000 or more: 10.2% (2005); Poverty rate: 2.7% (2000).
Education: Percent of population age 25 and over with: High school diploma (including GED) or higher: 90.1% (2005); Bachelor's degree or higher: 11.3% (2005); Master's degree or higher: 4.5% (2005).

Housing: Homeownership rate: 89.9% (2005); Median home value: $102,405 (2005); Median rent: $424 per month (2000); Median age of housing: 35 years (2000).
Safety: Violent crime rate: 12.9 per 10,000 population; Property crime rate: 90.0 per 10,000 population (2004).
Transportation: Commute to work: 96.7% car, 0.9% public transportation, 0.7% walk, 1.5% work from home (2000); Travel time to work: 37.3% less than 15 minutes, 50.8% 15 to 30 minutes, 5.9% 30 to 45 minutes, 2.4% 45 to 60 minutes, 3.6% 60 minutes or more (2000)

GOMER (unincorporated postal area, zip code 45809). Covers a land area of 0.582 square miles and a water area of 0 square miles. Located at 40.84° N. Lat.; 84.18° W. Long. Elevation is 780 feet.
Population: 208 (2000); Race: 100.0% White, 0.0% Black, 0.0% Asian, 0.0% Hispanic of any race (2000); Density: 357.4 persons per square mile (2000); Age: 18.6% under 18, 12.6% over 64 (2000); Marriage status: 17.9% never married, 60.1% now married, 4.0% widowed, 17.9% divorced (2000); Foreign born: 0.0% (2000); Ancestry (includes multiple ancestries): 26.6% German, 16.1% United States or American, 14.1% Irish, 7.5% Welsh, 3.5% Dutch (2000).
Economy: Employment by occupation: 11.5% management, 23.0% professional, 0.0% services, 28.7% sales, 0.0% farming, 0.0% construction, 36.9% production (2000).
Income: Per capita income: $28,434 (2000); Median household income: $54,583 (2000); Poverty rate: 0.0% (2000).
Education: Percent of population age 25 and over with: High school diploma (including GED) or higher: 100.0% (2000); Bachelor's degree or higher: 12.2% (2000).
Housing: Homeownership rate: 79.2% (2000); Median home value: $83,300 (2000); Median rent: $464 per month (2000); Median age of housing: 60+ years (2000).
Transportation: Commute to work: 95.1% car, 0.0% public transportation, 0.0% walk, 0.0% work from home (2000); Travel time to work: 31.1% less than 15 minutes, 54.1% 15 to 30 minutes, 4.9% 30 to 45 minutes, 4.9% 45 to 60 minutes, 4.9% 60 minutes or more (2000)

HARROD (village). Aka Harrods. Covers a land area of 0.224 square miles and a water area of 0 square miles. Located at 40.70° N. Lat.; 83.92° W. Long. Elevation is 991 feet.
Population: 541 (1990); 491 (2000); 459 (2005); 448 (2010 projected); Race: 98.7% White, 0.0% Black, 0.0% Asian, 0.7% Hispanic of any race (2005); Density: 2,050.2 persons per square mile (2005); Average household size: 2.78 (2005); Median age: 32.7 (2005); Males per 100 females: 101.3 (2005); Marriage status: 22.5% never married, 65.7% now married, 6.5% widowed, 5.2% divorced (2000); Foreign born: 0.4% (2000); Ancestry (includes multiple ancestries): 24.7% German, 18.1% United States or American, 10.0% Irish, 6.2% English, 3.0% Welsh (2000).
Economy: In agricultural area; wood products. Single-family building permits issued: 0 (2005); Multi-family building permits issued: 0 (2005); Employment by occupation: 5.0% management, 7.1% professional, 19.7% services, 22.6% sales, 0.8% farming, 17.6% construction, 27.2% production (2000).
Income: Per capita income: $17,200 (2005); Median household income: $43,269 (2005); Average household income: $47,848 (2005); Percent of households with income of $100,000 or more: 5.5% (2005); Poverty rate: 7.0% (2000).
Education: Percent of population age 25 and over with: High school diploma (including GED) or higher: 80.9% (2005); Bachelor's degree or higher: 4.0% (2005); Master's degree or higher: 3.3% (2005).

School District(s)
Allen East Local SD (PK-12)
    2003-04 Enrollment: 1,123 . . . . (419) 648-3333

Housing: Homeownership rate: 81.2% (2005); Median home value: $81,818 (2005); Median rent: $342 per month (2000); Median age of housing: 58 years (2000).
Transportation: Commute to work: 95.0% car, 1.7% public transportation, 2.1% walk, 1.3% work from home (2000); Travel time to work: 18.6% less than 15 minutes, 47.0% 15 to 30 minutes, 23.3% 30 to 45 minutes, 5.1% 45 to 60 minutes, 5.9% 60 minutes or more (2000)

LAFAYETTE (village). Aka La Fayette. Covers a land area of 0.205 square miles and a water area of 0 square miles. Located at 40.75° N. Lat.; 83.94° W. Long. Elevation is 927 feet.
Population: 449 (1990); 304 (2000); 304 (2005); 301 (2010 projected); Race: 99.0% White, 1.0% Black, 0.0% Asian, 0.0% Hispanic of any race (2005); Density: 1,483.3 persons per square mile (2005); Average household size: 2.53 (2005); Median age: 36.5 (2005); Males per 100 females: 88.8 (2005); Marriage status: 25.5% never married, 62.1% now married, 3.8% widowed, 8.5% divorced (2000); Foreign born: 0.0% (2000); Ancestry (includes multiple ancestries): 37.3% German, 20.2% United States or American, 13.9% Irish, 11.1% English, 7.0% French (except Basque) (2000).
Economy: Limestone quarrying. Employment by occupation: 2.9% management, 21.9% professional, 10.9% services, 32.1% sales, 0.0% farming, 11.7% construction, 20.4% production (2000).
Income: Per capita income: $21,990 (2005); Median household income: $45,000 (2005); Average household income: $55,708 (2005); Percent of households with income of $100,000 or more: 13.3% (2005); Poverty rate: 3.5% (2000).
Education: Percent of population age 25 and over with: High school diploma (including GED) or higher: 91.6% (2005); Bachelor's degree or higher: 8.9% (2005); Master's degree or higher: 2.5% (2005).
Housing: Homeownership rate: 88.3% (2005); Median home value: $86,923 (2005); Median rent: $338 per month (2000); Median age of housing: 60+ years (2000).
Transportation: Commute to work: 97.8% car, 1.4% public transportation, 0.7% walk, 0.0% work from home (2000); Travel time to work: 18.1% less than 15 minutes, 53.6% 15 to 30 minutes, 8.7% 30 to 45 minutes, 0.0% 45 to 60 minutes, 19.6% 60 minutes or more (2000)

LIMA (city). Covers a land area of 12.785 square miles and a water area of 0.097 square miles. Located at 40.74° N. Lat.; 84.11° W. Long. Elevation is 875 feet.
History: Lima was laid out on the Ottawa River in 1831 as the seat of Allen County. The name, the suggestion of minister and congressman Patrick Good, was drawn from a hat. Lima was incorporated in 1842. Oil was found here in 1885, bringing prosperity for a time until local industry turned to manufacturing railroad locomotives. It was in Lima that the Dillinger gang murdered Sheriff Jesse Sarber, starting a nation-wide hunt that ended in Dillinger's death and the end of his gang.
Population: 45,620 (1990); 40,081 (2000); 38,585 (2005); 37,150 (2010 projected); Race: 68.6% White, 26.4% Black, 0.8% Asian, 2.1% Hispanic of any race (2005); Density: 3,018.0 persons per square mile (2005); Average household size: 2.57 (2005); Median age: 33.3 (2005); Males per 100 females: 101.8 (2005); Marriage status: 33.6% never married, 43.0% now married, 8.5% widowed, 14.9% divorced (2000); Foreign born: 1.1% (2000); Ancestry (includes multiple ancestries): 27.6% Other groups, 20.9% German, 11.0% Irish, 9.6% United States or American, 5.2% English (2000).
Economy: Unemployment rate: 7.1% (2005); Total civilian labor force: 17,558 (2005); Single-family building permits issued: 6 (2005); Multi-family building permits issued: 3 (2005); Employment by occupation: 6.4% management, 12.0% professional, 20.8% services, 22.0% sales, 0.5% farming, 8.5% construction, 29.9% production (2000).
Income: Per capita income: $14,977 (2005); Median household income: $29,353 (2005); Average household income: $37,337 (2005); Percent of households with income of $100,000 or more: 4.2% (2005); Poverty rate: 22.7% (2000).
Taxes: Total city taxes per capita: $406 (2004); City property taxes per capita: $27 (2004).
Education: Percent of population age 25 and over with: High school diploma (including GED) or higher: 75.8% (2005); Bachelor's degree or higher: 9.8% (2005); Master's degree or higher: 3.1% (2005).

School District(s)
Allen East Local SD (PK-12)
    2003-04 Enrollment: 1,123 . . . . (419) 648-3333
Allen Educational Service Center (09-12)
    2003-04 Enrollment: n/a . . . . (419) 222-1836
Apollo Joint Vocational SD (09-12)
    2003-04 Enrollment: n/a . . . . (419) 998-2908
Bath Local SD (PK-12)
    2003-04 Enrollment: 2,085 . . . . (419) 221-0807
Lima City SD (PK-12)
    2003-04 Enrollment: 4,994 . . . . (419) 996-3400
Lima Digital Academy
    2003-04 Enrollment: n/a . . . . (419) 998-2400
Perry Local SD (PK-12)
    2003-04 Enrollment: 844 . . . . (419) 221-2770
Quest Academy Community (KG-05)
    2003-04 Enrollment: 96 . . . . (419) 227-7730

Shawnee Local SD (PK-12)
  2003-04 Enrollment: 2,657 .... (419) 998-8031
The Heir Force Academy
  2003-04 Enrollment: n/a

Four-year College(s)
Ohio State University-Lima Campus (Public)
  Fall 2004 Enrollment: 1,281....................... (419) 221-1641
  2005-06 Tuition: In-state $5,310; Out-of-state $16,533
University of Northwestern Ohio (Private, Not-for-profit)
  Fall 2004 Enrollment: 2,971....................... (419) 227-3141
  2005-06 Tuition: In-state $12,708; Out-of-state $12,708

Two-year College(s)
Apollo Career Center (Public)
  Fall 2004 Enrollment: 210 .... (419) 998-3000
James A Rhodes State College (Public)
  Fall 2004 Enrollment: 2,865....................... (419) 221-1112
  2005-06 Tuition: In-state $3,951; Out-of-state $7,902
Ohio State Beauty Academy (Private, For-profit)
  Fall 2004 Enrollment: 151 .... (419) 229-7896

Housing: Homeownership rate: 57.4% (2005); Median home value: $64,297 (2005); Median rent: $344 per month (2000); Median age of housing: 51 years (2000).
Hospitals: Lima Memorial Hospital (308 beds); St. Rita's Medical Center (424 beds)
Safety: Violent crime rate: 114.4 per 10,000 population; Property crime rate: 697.0 per 10,000 population (2004).
Newspapers: The Lima News (Circulation 35,979)
Transportation: Commute to work: 94.0% car, 1.7% public transportation, 1.7% walk, 1.6% work from home (2000); Travel time to work: 50.7% less than 15 minutes, 34.3% 15 to 30 minutes, 8.1% 30 to 45 minutes, 3.3% 45 to 60 minutes, 3.5% 60 minutes or more (2000)
Additional Information Contacts
City of Lima .... (419) 228-5462
  http://www.cityhall.lima.oh.us
Lima Allen County Chamber of Commerce .... (419) 222-6045
  http://www.limachamber.com

SPENCERVILLE
(village). Covers a land area of 0.910 square miles and a water area of 0 square miles. Located at 40.70° N. Lat.; 84.35° W. Long. Elevation is 833 feet.
History: Laid out 1844-1845, incorporated 1866.
Population: 2,293 (1990); 2,235 (2000); 2,183 (2005); 2,161 (2010 projected); Race: 97.2% White, 0.7% Black, 0.2% Asian, 0.2% Hispanic of any race (2005); Density: 2,397.8 persons per square mile (2005); Average household size: 2.59 (2005); Median age: 35.5 (2005); Males per 100 females: 90.5 (2005); Marriage status: 18.9% never married, 56.6% now married, 9.7% widowed, 14.9% divorced (2000); Foreign born: 0.6% (2000); Ancestry (includes multiple ancestries): 37.0% German, 10.9% United States or American, 8.0% Irish, 5.9% Other groups, 5.8% English (2000).
Economy: Trade center in agricultural area: dairy products; livestock; grain, soybeans. Manufacturing: furniture, metal products, cement, tile. Oil wells. Single-family building permits issued: 6 (2005); Multi-family building permits issued: 0 (2005); Employment by occupation: 3.9% management, 13.5% professional, 12.5% services, 21.6% sales, 0.1% farming, 8.8% construction, 39.6% production (2000).
Income: Per capita income: $17,964 (2005); Median household income: $35,762 (2005); Average household income: $45,513 (2005); Percent of households with income of $100,000 or more: 5.8% (2005); Poverty rate: 13.0% (2000).
Education: Percent of population age 25 and over with: High school diploma (including GED) or higher: 82.2% (2005); Bachelor's degree or higher: 8.5% (2005); Master's degree or higher: 2.0% (2005).

School District(s)
Spencerville Local SD (PK-12)
  2003-04 Enrollment: 1,013 .... (419) 647-4111

Housing: Homeownership rate: 77.5% (2005); Median home value: $78,782 (2005); Median rent: $309 per month (2000); Median age of housing: 49 years (2000).
Safety: Violent crime rate: 4.5 per 10,000 population; Property crime rate: 187.9 per 10,000 population (2004).
Newspapers: The Journal-News (General - Circulation 2,080)
Transportation: Commute to work: 90.7% car, 0.6% public transportation, 6.3% walk, 1.2% work from home (2000); Travel time to work: 35.4% less than 15 minutes, 35.2% 15 to 30 minutes, 20.3% 30 to 45 minutes, 3.9% 45 to 60 minutes, 5.2% 60 minutes or more (2000)
Additional Information Contacts
Spencerville Chamber of Commerce .... (419) 647-2020
  http://www.noacc.org

Ashland County

Located in north central Ohio; drained by forks of the Mohican River. Covers a land area of 424.37 square miles, a water area of 2.47 square miles, and is located in the Eastern Time Zone. The county government was organized in 1846. County seat is Ashland.

Ashland County is part of the Ashland, OH Micropolitan Statistical Area. The entire metro area includes: Ashland County, OH

Weather Station: Ashland 2 SW · Elevation: 1,263 feet

	Jan	Feb	Mar	Apr	May	Jun	Jul	Aug	Sep	Oct	Nov	Dec
High	32	36	47	59	70	79	83	81	74	62	49	38
Low	15	18	26	36	47	56	60	58	51	40	31	22
Precip	2.4	2.1	2.8	3.6	4.1	4.0	4.2	4.1	3.4	2.6	3.2	2.7
Snow	10.0	7.9	5.4	1.5	tr	0.0	0.0	0.0	0.0	tr	2.1	7.1

High and Low temperatures in degrees Fahrenheit; Precipitation and Snow in inches

Population: 47,507 (1990); 52,523 (2000); 54,434 (2005); 56,423 (2010 projected); Race: 97.5% White, 0.9% Black, 0.6% Asian, 0.6% Hispanic of any race (2005); Density: 128.3 persons per square mile (2005); Average household size: 2.66 (2005); Median age: 36.8 (2005); Males per 100 females: 97.0 (2005).
Religion: Five largest groups: 8.8% The United Methodist Church, 8.7% Evangelical Lutheran Church in America, 3.6% Catholic Church, 3.2% Greek Orthodox Archdiocese of America, 1.9% Independent, Non-Charismatic Churches (2000).
Economy: Unemployment rate: 6.2% (2005); Total civilian labor force: 27,084 (2005); Leading industries: 28.1% manufacturing; 11.6% health care and social assistance; 11.4% retail trade (2004); Farms: 1,089 totaling 161,100 acres (2002); Companies that employ 500 or more persons: 5 (2004); Companies that employ 100 to 499 persons: 20 (2004); Companies that employ less than 100 persons: 1,067 (2004); Black-owned businesses: n/a (2002); Hispanic-owned businesses: n/a (2002); Women-owned businesses: 671 (2002); Retail sales per capita: $8,861 (2006). Single-family building permits issued: 162 (2005); Multi-family building permits issued: 196 (2005).
Income: Per capita income: $19,532 (2005); Median household income: $42,761 (2005); Average household income: $51,254 (2005); Percent of households with income of $100,000 or more: 9.1% (2005); Poverty rate: 8.9% (2003); Bankruptcy rate: 8.55% (2005).
Education: Percent of population age 25 and over with: High school diploma (including GED) or higher: 83.2% (2005); Bachelor's degree or higher: 15.8% (2005); Master's degree or higher: 5.3% (2005).
Housing: Homeownership rate: 76.3% (2005); Median home value: $124,183 (2005); Median rent: $370 per month (2000); Median age of housing: 41 years (2000).
Health: Birth rate: 127.5 per 10,000 population (2004); Death rate: 93.3 per 10,000 population (2004); Age-adjusted cancer mortality rate: 229.6 deaths per 100,000 population (2002); Number of physicians: 10.6 per 10,000 population (2004); Hospital beds: 13.0 per 10,000 population (2003); Hospital admissions: 654.0 per 10,000 population (2003).
Elections: 2004 Presidential election results: 64.9% Bush, 34.3% Kerry, 0.0% Nader, 0.3% Badnarik
National and State Parks: Mohican State Forest
Additional Information Contacts
Ashland County Government....................... (419) 289-0000
  http://www.ashlandcounty.org/
Ashland Chamber of Commerce .... (419) 281-4584
  http://www.ashlandoh.com
City of Ashland .... (419) 289-8622
  http://www.ashland-ohio.com
Loudonville Chamber of Commerce .... (419) 994-4789
  http://www.loudonville-mohican.com

Ashland County Communities

ASHLAND (city). Covers a land area of 10.358 square miles and a water area of 0.038 square miles. Located at 40.86° N. Lat.; 82.31° W. Long. Elevation is 1,080 feet.

History: Ashland was platted in 1815 by William Montgomery, who called it Uniontown. In 1822 the town was renamed Ashland, for Henry Clay's estate at Lexington, Kentucky. A memorial to Johnny Appleseed, who often came through Ashland, was erected in 1915 through the donations of Ashland County children.
Population: 20,355 (1990); 21,249 (2000); 21,362 (2005); 21,638 (2010 projected); Race: 96.5% White, 1.1% Black, 1.2% Asian, 0.7% Hispanic of any race (2005); Density: 2,062.5 persons per square mile (2005); Average household size: 2.52 (2005); Median age: 35.1 (2005); Males per 100 females: 88.1 (2005); Marriage status: 26.6% never married, 54.8% now married, 8.1% widowed, 10.5% divorced (2000); Foreign born: 1.5% (2000); Ancestry (includes multiple ancestries): 31.5% German, 11.7% Irish, 11.3% United States or American, 10.8% English, 7.0% Other groups (2000).
Economy: Single-family building permits issued: 41 (2005); Multi-family building permits issued: 128 (2005); Employment by occupation: 9.6% management, 17.9% professional, 15.5% services, 24.8% sales, 0.4% farming, 6.8% construction, 24.9% production (2000).
Income: Per capita income: $18,518 (2005); Median household income: $36,311 (2005); Average household income: $45,292 (2005); Percent of households with income of $100,000 or more: 7.0% (2005); Poverty rate: 10.5% (2000).
Education: Percent of population age 25 and over with: High school diploma (including GED) or higher: 83.6% (2005); Bachelor's degree or higher: 19.7% (2005); Master's degree or higher: 6.8% (2005).

School District(s)
Ashland City SD (PK-12)
  2003-04 Enrollment: 3,817 . . . . (419) 289-1117
Ashland County-West Holmes Joint Vocational SD (11-12)
  2003-04 Enrollment: n/a . . . . (419) 289-3313
Crestview Local SD (PK-12)
  2003-04 Enrollment: 1,279 . . . . (419) 895-1700
Mapleton Local SD (PK-12)
  2003-04 Enrollment: 1,046 . . . . (419) 945-2123

Four-year College(s)
Ashland University (Private, Not-for-profit, Brethren Church)
  Fall 2004 Enrollment: 6,922 . . . . (419) 289-4142
  2005-06 Tuition: In-state $19,853; Out-of-state $19,853

Two-year College(s)
Ashland County-West Holmes Career Center (Public)
  Fall 2004 Enrollment: 49 . . . . (419) 289-3313

Housing: Homeownership rate: 64.6% (2005); Median home value: $107,516 (2005); Median rent: $370 per month (2000); Median age of housing: 45 years (2000).
Hospitals: Samaritan Regional Health System (110 beds)
Safety: Violent crime rate: 9.8 per 10,000 population; Property crime rate: 272.6 per 10,000 population (2004).
Newspapers: Ashland Times-Gazette (Circulation 12,434)
Transportation: Commute to work: 90.3% car, 0.6% public transportation, 5.7% walk, 2.4% work from home (2000); Travel time to work: 64.9% less than 15 minutes, 17.9% 15 to 30 minutes, 10.1% 30 to 45 minutes, 2.7% 45 to 60 minutes, 4.4% 60 minutes or more (2000)

Additional Information Contacts
Ashland Chamber of Commerce . . . . (419) 281-4584
  http://www.ashlandoh.com
City of Ashland . . . . (419) 289-8622
  http://www.ashland-ohio.com

BAILEY LAKES (village). Covers a land area of 0.406 square miles and a water area of 0.059 square miles. Located at 40.94° N. Lat.; 82.35° W. Long.
Population: 367 (1990); 397 (2000); 460 (2005); 520 (2010 projected); Race: 99.1% White, 0.0% Black, 0.0% Asian, 0.0% Hispanic of any race (2005); Density: 1,133.4 persons per square mile (2005); Average household size: 2.56 (2005); Median age: 36.1 (2005); Males per 100 females: 115.0 (2005); Marriage status: 24.7% never married, 63.7% now married, 3.4% widowed, 8.2% divorced (2000); Foreign born: 0.2% (2000); Ancestry (includes multiple ancestries): 34.1% German, 20.7% Irish, 10.6% Other groups, 9.7% English, 3.9% Scotch-Irish (2000).
Economy: Employment by occupation: 5.8% management, 27.2% professional, 7.6% services, 18.8% sales, 0.0% farming, 6.3% construction, 34.4% production (2000).
Income: Per capita income: $18,391 (2005); Median household income: $42,500 (2005); Average household income: $47,000 (2005); Percent of households with income of $100,000 or more: 3.9% (2005); Poverty rate: 11.8% (2000).
Education: Percent of population age 25 and over with: High school diploma (including GED) or higher: 84.0% (2005); Bachelor's degree or higher: 15.3% (2005); Master's degree or higher: 5.4% (2005).
Housing: Homeownership rate: 67.8% (2005); Median home value: $125,000 (2005); Median rent: $370 per month (2000); Median age of housing: 38 years (2000).
Transportation: Commute to work: 99.1% car, 0.0% public transportation, 0.0% walk, 0.9% work from home (2000); Travel time to work: 27.6% less than 15 minutes, 47.5% 15 to 30 minutes, 16.1% 30 to 45 minutes, 4.1% 45 to 60 minutes, 4.6% 60 minutes or more (2000)

HAYESVILLE (village). Covers a land area of 0.742 square miles and a water area of 0 square miles. Located at 40.77° N. Lat.; 82.26° W. Long. Elevation is 1,244 feet.
History: Hayesville was laid out in 1830 by Linus Hayes, a tavern owner, and Reverend John Cox. It was in Hayesville that William McKinley pleaded his first law case.
Population: 457 (1990); 348 (2000); 319 (2005); 316 (2010 projected); Race: 97.8% White, 1.6% Black, 0.0% Asian, 0.0% Hispanic of any race (2005); Density: 429.8 persons per square mile (2005); Average household size: 2.51 (2005); Median age: 46.1 (2005); Males per 100 females: 98.1 (2005); Marriage status: 22.2% never married, 64.9% now married, 2.5% widowed, 10.5% divorced (2000); Foreign born: 0.0% (2000); Ancestry (includes multiple ancestries): 20.2% German, 12.7% English, 11.7% United States or American, 8.5% Irish, 5.9% Italian (2000).
Economy: Single-family building permits issued: 2 (2005); Multi-family building permits issued: 0 (2005); Employment by occupation: 6.4% management, 12.1% professional, 17.2% services, 22.9% sales, 0.0% farming, 14.0% construction, 27.4% production (2000).
Income: Per capita income: $24,119 (2005); Median household income: $47,750 (2005); Average household income: $57,224 (2005); Percent of households with income of $100,000 or more: 8.7% (2005); Poverty rate: 8.0% (2000).
Education: Percent of population age 25 and over with: High school diploma (including GED) or higher: 80.7% (2005); Bachelor's degree or higher: 11.3% (2005); Master's degree or higher: 3.8% (2005).

School District(s)
Hillsdale Local SD (PK-12)
  2003-04 Enrollment: 1,172 . . . . (419) 368-8231

Housing: Homeownership rate: 84.3% (2005); Median home value: $97,857 (2005); Median rent: $468 per month (2000); Median age of housing: 60 years (2000).
Transportation: Commute to work: 93.0% car, 2.5% public transportation, 1.9% walk, 1.3% work from home (2000); Travel time to work: 30.3% less than 15 minutes, 52.9% 15 to 30 minutes, 6.5% 30 to 45 minutes, 6.5% 45 to 60 minutes, 3.9% 60 minutes or more (2000)

JEROMESVILLE (village). Covers a land area of 0.365 square miles and a water area of 0 square miles. Located at 40.80° N. Lat.; 82.19° W. Long. Elevation is 1,012 feet.
History: Jeromesville was named for a French trader, Jean Baptiste Jerome, who lived here. The town grew as a rural trading center.
Population: 582 (1990); 478 (2000); 430 (2005); 417 (2010 projected); Race: 97.0% White, 0.7% Black, 0.0% Asian, 2.3% Hispanic of any race (2005); Density: 1,178.1 persons per square mile (2005); Average household size: 2.34 (2005); Median age: 37.1 (2005); Males per 100 females: 91.1 (2005); Marriage status: 24.6% never married, 53.7% now married, 7.3% widowed, 14.4% divorced (2000); Foreign born: 1.2% (2000); Ancestry (includes multiple ancestries): 31.8% German, 11.0% United States or American, 8.4% Irish, 8.2% English, 7.3% Other groups (2000).
Economy: Employment by occupation: 4.4% management, 19.2% professional, 16.4% services, 21.6% sales, 0.8% farming, 9.6% construction, 28.0% production (2000).
Income: Per capita income: $20,756 (2005); Median household income: $42,969 (2005); Average household income: $48,505 (2005); Percent of households with income of $100,000 or more: 5.4% (2005); Poverty rate: 6.1% (2000).
Education: Percent of population age 25 and over with: High school diploma (including GED) or higher: 94.4% (2005); Bachelor's degree or higher: 14.0% (2005); Master's degree or higher: 4.2% (2005).

School District(s)
Hillsdale Local SD (PK-12)
　2003-04 Enrollment: 1,172 . . . . (419) 368-8231
Housing: Homeownership rate: 72.3% (2005); Median home value: $102,119 (2005); Median rent: $373 per month (2000); Median age of housing: 60+ years (2000).
Transportation: Commute to work: 94.4% car, 0.4% public transportation, 2.4% walk, 2.8% work from home (2000); Travel time to work: 23.7% less than 15 minutes, 56.4% 15 to 30 minutes, 14.5% 30 to 45 minutes, 2.1% 45 to 60 minutes, 3.3% 60 minutes or more (2000)

LOUDONVILLE (village). Covers a land area of 2.486 square miles and a water area of 0.010 square miles. Located at 40.63° N. Lat.; 82.23° W. Long. Elevation is 974 feet.
History: Loudonville was laid out in 1814 and named for a Revolutionary War soldier, James Louden Priest, who helped to survey the town. An early industry was the building of buses and ambulances.
Population: 3,142 (1990); 2,906 (2000); 2,967 (2005); 3,046 (2010 projected); Race: 99.0% White, 0.0% Black, 0.2% Asian, 0.4% Hispanic of any race (2005); Density: 1,193.3 persons per square mile (2005); Average household size: 2.42 (2005); Median age: 39.7 (2005); Males per 100 females: 94.7 (2005); Marriage status: 16.9% never married, 58.7% now married, 11.1% widowed, 13.3% divorced (2000); Foreign born: 0.6% (2000); Ancestry (includes multiple ancestries): 36.5% German, 11.3% United States or American, 10.7% English, 9.2% Irish, 3.9% Dutch (2000).
Economy: Single-family building permits issued: 6 (2005); Multi-family building permits issued: 0 (2005); Employment by occupation: 5.9% management, 10.2% professional, 16.4% services, 27.4% sales, 0.4% farming, 5.7% construction, 34.1% production (2000).
Income: Per capita income: $18,627 (2005); Median household income: $39,912 (2005); Average household income: $43,493 (2005); Percent of households with income of $100,000 or more: 4.5% (2005); Poverty rate: 13.2% (2000).
Education: Percent of population age 25 and over with: High school diploma (including GED) or higher: 84.0% (2005); Bachelor's degree or higher: 12.8% (2005); Master's degree or higher: 4.4% (2005).
School District(s)
Loudonville-Perrysville Ex Vill SD (PK-12)
　2003-04 Enrollment: 1,317 . . . . (419) 994-3912
Housing: Homeownership rate: 68.3% (2005); Median home value: $95,911 (2005); Median rent: $358 per month (2000); Median age of housing: 60+ years (2000).
Newspapers: The Loudonville Times (General - Circulation 2,300)
Transportation: Commute to work: 89.6% car, 0.3% public transportation, 4.9% walk, 3.1% work from home (2000); Travel time to work: 55.7% less than 15 minutes, 17.4% 15 to 30 minutes, 19.6% 30 to 45 minutes, 1.8% 45 to 60 minutes, 5.5% 60 minutes or more (2000)
Additional Information Contacts
Loudonville Chamber of Commerce . . . . (419) 994-4789
　http://www.loudonville-mohican.com

MIFFLIN (village). Covers a land area of 0.260 square miles and a water area of 0 square miles. Located at 40.77° N. Lat.; 82.36° W. Long. Elevation is 1,070 feet.
Population: 162 (1990); 144 (2000); 145 (2005); 144 (2010 projected); Race: 99.3% White, 0.0% Black, 0.7% Asian, 0.0% Hispanic of any race (2005); Density: 557.1 persons per square mile (2005); Average household size: 2.23 (2005); Median age: 39.3 (2005); Males per 100 females: 93.3 (2005); Marriage status: 47.0% never married, 27.8% now married, 5.2% widowed, 20.0% divorced (2000); Foreign born: 0.0% (2000); Ancestry (includes multiple ancestries): 23.5% German, 12.9% Irish, 9.1% Other groups, 5.3% United States or American, 4.5% Dutch (2000).
Economy: Single-family building permits issued: 0 (2005); Multi-family building permits issued: 0 (2005); Employment by occupation: 11.5% management, 3.8% professional, 19.2% services, 23.1% sales, 0.0% farming, 3.8% construction, 38.5% production (2000).
Income: Per capita income: $17,207 (2005); Median household income: $34,667 (2005); Average household income: $38,385 (2005); Percent of households with income of $100,000 or more: 0.0% (2005); Poverty rate: 12.9% (2000).
Education: Percent of population age 25 and over with: High school diploma (including GED) or higher: 78.3% (2005); Bachelor's degree or higher: 0.0% (2005); Master's degree or higher: 0.0% (2005).

Housing: Homeownership rate: 70.8% (2005); Median home value: $76,364 (2005); Median rent: $331 per month (2000); Median age of housing: 50 years (2000).
Transportation: Commute to work: 80.4% car, 7.8% public transportation, 7.8% walk, 3.9% work from home (2000); Travel time to work: 32.7% less than 15 minutes, 44.9% 15 to 30 minutes, 8.2% 30 to 45 minutes, 0.0% 45 to 60 minutes, 14.3% 60 minutes or more (2000)

NOVA (unincorporated postal area, zip code 44859). Covers a land area of 31.226 square miles and a water area of 0.054 square miles. Located at 41.02° N. Lat.; 82.33° W. Long. Elevation is 1,030 feet.
Population: 1,759 (2000); Race: 99.3% White, 0.0% Black, 0.0% Asian, 0.7% Hispanic of any race (2000); Density: 56.3 persons per square mile (2000); Age: 26.2% under 18, 10.8% over 64 (2000); Marriage status: 20.1% never married, 68.1% now married, 3.7% widowed, 8.1% divorced (2000); Foreign born: 1.2% (2000); Ancestry (includes multiple ancestries): 25.2% German, 18.9% United States or American, 12.8% Irish, 7.5% English, 5.9% Italian (2000).
Economy: Employment by occupation: 5.6% management, 6.7% professional, 12.0% services, 17.1% sales, 1.3% farming, 14.9% construction, 42.3% production (2000).
Income: Per capita income: $18,340 (2000); Median household income: $47,667 (2000); Poverty rate: 5.0% (2000).
Education: Percent of population age 25 and over with: High school diploma (including GED) or higher: 80.3% (2000); Bachelor's degree or higher: 6.4% (2000).
School District(s)
Mapleton Local SD (PK-12)
　2003-04 Enrollment: 1,046 . . . . (419) 945-2123
Housing: Homeownership rate: 93.5% (2000); Median home value: $105,000 (2000); Median rent: $398 per month (2000); Median age of housing: 27 years (2000).
Transportation: Commute to work: 92.0% car, 0.6% public transportation, 3.2% walk, 3.4% work from home (2000); Travel time to work: 18.7% less than 15 minutes, 35.6% 15 to 30 minutes, 15.7% 30 to 45 minutes, 15.8% 45 to 60 minutes, 14.2% 60 minutes or more (2000)

PERRYSVILLE (village). Covers a land area of 0.776 square miles and a water area of 0 square miles. Located at 40.65° N. Lat.; 82.31° W. Long. Elevation is 1,050 feet.
Population: 874 (1990); 816 (2000); 845 (2005); 865 (2010 projected); Race: 98.6% White, 0.6% Black, 0.0% Asian, 0.4% Hispanic of any race (2005); Density: 1,089.5 persons per square mile (2005); Average household size: 2.44 (2005); Median age: 33.7 (2005); Males per 100 females: 93.4 (2005); Marriage status: 24.0% never married, 52.1% now married, 7.8% widowed, 16.2% divorced (2000); Foreign born: 0.0% (2000); Ancestry (includes multiple ancestries): 29.4% German, 19.4% United States or American, 8.4% Irish, 6.8% English, 6.2% Other groups (2000).
Economy: Machining industry. Single-family building permits issued: 1 (2005); Multi-family building permits issued: 0 (2005); Employment by occupation: 4.0% management, 6.1% professional, 19.8% services, 19.5% sales, 1.3% farming, 10.2% construction, 39.0% production (2000).
Income: Per capita income: $13,749 (2005); Median household income: $30,786 (2005); Average household income: $33,480 (2005); Percent of households with income of $100,000 or more: 0.6% (2005); Poverty rate: 18.3% (2000).
Education: Percent of population age 25 and over with: High school diploma (including GED) or higher: 79.9% (2005); Bachelor's degree or higher: 9.2% (2005); Master's degree or higher: 2.9% (2005).
School District(s)
Department of Youth Services (06-12)
　2003-04 Enrollment: 1,333 . . . . (614) 728-2489
Loudonville-Perrysville Ex Vill SD (PK-12)
　2003-04 Enrollment: 1,317 . . . . (419) 994-3912
Housing: Homeownership rate: 66.3% (2005); Median home value: $72,353 (2005); Median rent: $305 per month (2000); Median age of housing: 60+ years (2000).
Transportation: Commute to work: 89.6% car, 0.0% public transportation, 7.4% walk, 1.6% work from home (2000); Travel time to work: 47.5% less than 15 minutes, 23.3% 15 to 30 minutes, 21.7% 30 to 45 minutes, 2.2% 45 to 60 minutes, 5.3% 60 minutes or more (2000)

POLK (village). Covers a land area of 1.008 square miles and a water area of 0.028 square miles. Located at 40.94° N. Lat.; 82.21° W. Long. Elevation is 1,270 feet.
Population: 355 (1990); 357 (2000); 419 (2005); 471 (2010 projected); Race: 98.6% White, 0.0% Black, 0.0% Asian, 0.0% Hispanic of any race (2005); Density: 415.6 persons per square mile (2005); Average household size: 2.83 (2005); Median age: 36.9 (2005); Males per 100 females: 87.9 (2005); Marriage status: 29.2% never married, 58.7% now married, 7.9% widowed, 4.3% divorced (2000); Foreign born: 0.0% (2000); Ancestry (includes multiple ancestries): 30.0% German, 18.3% United States or American, 14.6% Irish, 9.5% English, 5.8% Other groups (2000).
Economy: In agricultural area; fireworks. Single-family building permits issued: 0 (2005); Multi-family building permits issued: 0 (2005); Employment by occupation: 7.3% management, 6.4% professional, 20.5% services, 21.5% sales, 0.0% farming, 10.0% construction, 34.2% production (2000).
Income: Per capita income: $17,064 (2005); Median household income: $44,512 (2005); Average household income: $48,311 (2005); Percent of households with income of $100,000 or more: 3.4% (2005); Poverty rate: 5.0% (2000).
Education: Percent of population age 25 and over with: High school diploma (including GED) or higher: 78.1% (2005); Bachelor's degree or higher: 6.6% (2005); Master's degree or higher: 1.1% (2005).

School District(s)
Mapleton Local SD (PK-12)
    2003-04 Enrollment: 1,046 . . . . (419) 945-2123

Housing: Homeownership rate: 86.5% (2005); Median home value: $91,667 (2005); Median rent: $400 per month (2000); Median age of housing: 59 years (2000).
Transportation: Commute to work: 92.5% car, 0.0% public transportation, 0.9% walk, 6.5% work from home (2000); Travel time to work: 24.5% less than 15 minutes, 55.5% 15 to 30 minutes, 11.5% 30 to 45 minutes, 5.5% 45 to 60 minutes, 3.0% 60 minutes or more (2000)

SAVANNAH (village). Covers a land area of 0.443 square miles and a water area of 0 square miles. Located at 40.96° N. Lat.; 82.36° W. Long. Elevation is 1,101 feet.
Population: 363 (1990); 372 (2000); 432 (2005); 489 (2010 projected); Race: 99.3% White, 0.5% Black, 0.0% Asian, 0.0% Hispanic of any race (2005); Density: 974.4 persons per square mile (2005); Average household size: 2.73 (2005); Median age: 33.7 (2005); Males per 100 females: 103.8 (2005); Marriage status: 27.9% never married, 54.7% now married, 6.2% widowed, 11.2% divorced (2000); Foreign born: 0.0% (2000); Ancestry (includes multiple ancestries): 27.2% United States or American, 19.7% German, 8.3% Irish, 7.5% Other groups, 4.4% Polish (2000).
Economy: In agricultural area. Single-family building permits issued: 0 (2005); Multi-family building permits issued: 0 (2005); Employment by occupation: 3.3% management, 13.3% professional, 13.3% services, 19.4% sales, 1.1% farming, 12.8% construction, 36.7% production (2000).
Income: Per capita income: $16,603 (2005); Median household income: $40,114 (2005); Average household income: $45,396 (2005); Percent of households with income of $100,000 or more: 4.4% (2005); Poverty rate: 9.6% (2000).
Education: Percent of population age 25 and over with: High school diploma (including GED) or higher: 75.5% (2005); Bachelor's degree or higher: 14.9% (2005); Master's degree or higher: 3.3% (2005).
Housing: Homeownership rate: 81.0% (2005); Median home value: $95,758 (2005); Median rent: $343 per month (2000); Median age of housing: 60+ years (2000).
Transportation: Commute to work: 98.3% car, 0.0% public transportation, 1.1% walk, 0.6% work from home (2000); Travel time to work: 29.4% less than 15 minutes, 42.4% 15 to 30 minutes, 12.4% 30 to 45 minutes, 5.6% 45 to 60 minutes, 10.2% 60 minutes or more (2000)

SULLIVAN (unincorporated postal area, zip code 44880). Covers a land area of 31.376 square miles and a water area of 0.074 square miles. Located at 41.03° N. Lat.; 82.21° W. Long. Elevation is 1,126 feet.
Population: 2,359 (2000); Race: 97.2% White, 1.1% Black, 0.5% Asian, 0.0% Hispanic of any race (2000); Density: 75.2 persons per square mile (2000); Age: 32.6% under 18, 10.7% over 64 (2000); Marriage status: 22.0% never married, 63.1% now married, 7.1% widowed, 7.8% divorced (2000); Foreign born: 1.4% (2000); Ancestry (includes multiple ancestries): 24.6% German, 18.1% Irish, 9.6% English, 8.9% United States or American, 7.8% Other groups (2000).
Economy: Employment by occupation: 9.8% management, 9.9% professional, 12.7% services, 17.8% sales, 1.9% farming, 12.4% construction, 35.5% production (2000).
Income: Per capita income: $15,646 (2000); Median household income: $43,929 (2000); Poverty rate: 13.0% (2000).
Education: Percent of population age 25 and over with: High school diploma (including GED) or higher: 78.0% (2000); Bachelor's degree or higher: 6.9% (2000).

School District(s)
Black River Local SD (PK-12)
    2003-04 Enrollment: 1,669 . . . . (419) 736-3300

Housing: Homeownership rate: 86.7% (2000); Median home value: $111,800 (2000); Median rent: $480 per month (2000); Median age of housing: 23 years (2000).
Transportation: Commute to work: 87.8% car, 0.0% public transportation, 5.1% walk, 7.1% work from home (2000); Travel time to work: 23.5% less than 15 minutes, 24.2% 15 to 30 minutes, 16.0% 30 to 45 minutes, 28.7% 45 to 60 minutes, 7.6% 60 minutes or more (2000)

Ashtabula County

Located in northeastern Ohio; bounded on the north by Lake Erie; crossed by the Grand and Ashtabula Rivers. Covers a land area of 702.44 square miles, a water area of 666.03 square miles, and is located in the Eastern Time Zone. The county government was organized in 1807. County seat is Jefferson.

Ashtabula County is part of the Ashtabula, OH Micropolitan Statistical Area. The entire metro area includes: Ashtabula County, OH

Weather Station: Dorset   Elevation: 977 feet

	Jan	Feb	Mar	Apr	May	Jun	Jul	Aug	Sep	Oct	Nov	Dec
High	31	35	44	57	68	77	81	80	73	61	48	37
Low	15	16	25	34	44	53	57	56	50	39	32	22
Precip	2.6	2.3	3.2	3.6	3.7	4.5	4.2	4.1	4.3	3.8	3.9	3.3
Snow	17.5	12.9	12.1	2.9	tr	0.0	0.0	0.0	0.0	0.6	8.7	18.4

High and Low temperatures in degrees Fahrenheit; Precipitation and Snow in inches

Population: 99,821 (1990); 102,728 (2000); 103,323 (2005); 103,908 (2010 projected); Race: 93.9% White, 3.1% Black, 0.3% Asian, 2.6% Hispanic of any race (2005); Density: 147.1 persons per square mile (2005); Average household size: 2.58 (2005); Median age: 38.4 (2005); Males per 100 females: 95.9 (2005).
Religion: Five largest groups: 18.0% Catholic Church, 5.2% The United Methodist Church, 2.1% Evangelical Lutheran Church in America, 1.8% United Church of Christ, 1.8% Church of the Nazarene (2000).
Economy: Unemployment rate: 7.2% (2005); Total civilian labor force: 50,869 (2005); Leading industries: 32.1% manufacturing; 18.3% health care and social assistance; 16.2% retail trade (2004); Farms: 1,283 totaling 170,424 acres (2002); Companies that employ 500 or more persons: 2 (2004); Companies that employ 100 to 499 persons: 44 (2004); Companies that employ less than 100 persons: 2,192 (2004); Black-owned businesses: n/a (2002); Hispanic-owned businesses: n/a (2002); Women-owned businesses: 1,954 (2002); Retail sales per capita: $10,922 (2006). Single-family building permits issued: 214 (2005); Multi-family building permits issued: 0 (2005).
Income: Per capita income: $19,244 (2005); Median household income: $39,944 (2005); Average household income: $49,008 (2005); Percent of households with income of $100,000 or more: 8.0% (2005); Poverty rate: 12.0% (2003); Bankruptcy rate: 12.50% (2005).
Taxes: Total county taxes per capita: $255 (2004); County property taxes per capita: $178 (2004).
Education: Percent of population age 25 and over with: High school diploma (including GED) or higher: 79.8% (2005); Bachelor's degree or higher: 11.0% (2005); Master's degree or higher: 3.6% (2005).
Housing: Homeownership rate: 74.4% (2005); Median home value: $106,335 (2005); Median rent: $374 per month (2000); Median age of housing: 45 years (2000).
Health: Birth rate: 117.1 per 10,000 population (2004); Death rate: 109.3 per 10,000 population (2004); Age-adjusted cancer mortality rate: 241.6 deaths per 100,000 population (2002); Air Quality Index: 87.8% good, 10.2% moderate, 1.9% unhealthy for sensitive individuals, 0.0% unhealthy (percent of days in 2005); Number of physicians: 7.9 per 10,000 population (2004); Hospital beds: 31.2 per 10,000 population (2003); Hospital admissions: 903.8 per 10,000 population (2003).

Elections: 2004 Presidential election results: 46.3% Bush, 53.0% Kerry, 0.0% Nader, 0.3% Badnarik
National and State Parks: Geneva-On-The-Lake State Park; Orwell State Wildlife Area; Pymatuning State Park
Additional Information Contacts
Ashtabula County Government . . . . (440) 576-3750
  http://www.co.ashtabula.oh.us/
Andover Chamber of Commerce . . . . (440) 293-5895
  http://www.ashtabula.net/andover
Ashtabula Chamber of Commerce . . . . (440) 998-6998
  http://www.ashtabulachamber.net
Ashtabula County Convention & Visitors Bureau . . . . (440) 275-3202
  http://www.visitashtabulacounty.com
City of Ashtabula . . . . (440) 992-7103
  http://ci.ashtabula.oh.us
City of Conneaut . . . . (440) 593-7401
  http://www.conneaut.net
Conneaut Chamber of Commerce . . . . (440) 593-2402
  http://www.conneautchamber.org
Geneva Chamber of Commerce . . . . (440) 466-8694
  http://www.genevachamber.org
Geneva on the Lake Chamber of Commerce . . . . (800) 862-9948
  http://www.visitgenevaonthelake.com
Geneva on the Lake Visitors Bureau . . . . (440) 466-8600
  http://www.visitgenevaonthelake.com
Village of Orwell . . . . (440) 437-6549
  http://www.orwellvillage.org

Ashtabula County Communities

ANDOVER (village). Covers a land area of 1.366 square miles and a water area of 0 square miles. Located at 41.60° N. Lat.; 80.57° W. Long. Elevation is 1,085 feet.
Population: 1,216 (1990); 1,269 (2000); 1,294 (2005); 1,316 (2010 projected); Race: 95.5% White, 3.2% Black, 0.0% Asian, 1.8% Hispanic of any race (2005); Density: 947.5 persons per square mile (2005); Average household size: 2.93 (2005); Median age: 44.0 (2005); Males per 100 females: 89.5 (2005); Marriage status: 22.5% never married, 47.9% now married, 12.8% widowed, 16.8% divorced (2000); Foreign born: 0.5% (2000); Ancestry (includes multiple ancestries): 20.4% German, 17.2% United States or American, 13.4% English, 12.6% Irish, 9.8% Other groups (2000).
Economy: In agricultural area. Employment by occupation: 6.8% management, 10.1% professional, 13.8% services, 23.3% sales, 1.4% farming, 7.2% construction, 37.2% production (2000).
Income: Per capita income: $16,717 (2005); Median household income: $33,309 (2005); Average household income: $44,456 (2005); Percent of households with income of $100,000 or more: 7.3% (2005); Poverty rate: 10.7% (2000).
Education: Percent of population age 25 and over with: High school diploma (including GED) or higher: 74.0% (2005); Bachelor's degree or higher: 9.2% (2005); Master's degree or higher: 3.7% (2005).
School District(s)
Pymatuning Valley Local SD (PK-12)
  2003-04 Enrollment: 1,418 . . . . (440) 293-6488
Housing: Homeownership rate: 59.6% (2005); Median home value: $83,485 (2005); Median rent: $355 per month (2000); Median age of housing: 60+ years (2000).
Newspapers: Pymatuning Area News (General - Circulation 2,100)
Transportation: Commute to work: 87.3% car, 0.4% public transportation, 6.6% walk, 3.4% work from home (2000); Travel time to work: 58.6% less than 15 minutes, 11.4% 15 to 30 minutes, 8.8% 30 to 45 minutes, 10.1% 45 to 60 minutes, 11.2% 60 minutes or more (2000)
Additional Information Contacts
Andover Chamber of Commerce . . . . (440) 293-5895
  http://www.ashtabula.net/andover

ASHTABULA (city). Covers a land area of 7.551 square miles and a water area of 0.172 square miles. Located at 41.87° N. Lat.; 80.79° W. Long. Elevation is 680 feet.
History: The surveying party of Moses Cleaveland stopped here in 1796, and two members of the group remained as settlers. The town that was incorporated in 1831 was named Ashtabula for the river that emptied into Lake Erie at the site. Ashtabula developed as a shipping center for coal and iron ore, and as a fishing and farm trading center. Strong abolitionist sentiment made it a key station on the Underground Railroad.
Population: 21,626 (1990); 20,962 (2000); 20,138 (2005); 19,353 (2010 projected); Race: 83.2% White, 10.5% Black, 0.4% Asian, 6.6% Hispanic of any race (2005); Density: 2,666.8 persons per square mile (2005); Average household size: 2.47 (2005); Median age: 35.4 (2005); Males per 100 females: 89.7 (2005); Marriage status: 27.4% never married, 49.1% now married, 9.8% widowed, 13.8% divorced (2000); Foreign born: 2.7% (2000); Ancestry (includes multiple ancestries): 18.7% Other groups, 16.9% German, 15.0% Italian, 11.5% Irish, 9.2% English (2000).
Economy: Single-family building permits issued: 3 (2005); Multi-family building permits issued: 0 (2005); Employment by occupation: 6.6% management, 13.1% professional, 19.4% services, 23.7% sales, 0.3% farming, 8.4% construction, 28.5% production (2000).
Income: Per capita income: $15,252 (2005); Median household income: $29,914 (2005); Average household income: $37,328 (2005); Percent of households with income of $100,000 or more: 3.7% (2005); Poverty rate: 21.4% (2000).
Education: Percent of population age 25 and over with: High school diploma (including GED) or higher: 77.5% (2005); Bachelor's degree or higher: 10.4% (2005); Master's degree or higher: 3.1% (2005).
School District(s)
Ashtabula Area City SD (KG-12)
  2003-04 Enrollment: 4,661 . . . . (440) 993-2500
Buckeye Local SD (PK-12)
  2003-04 Enrollment: 2,287 . . . . (440) 998-4411
Two-year College(s)
Kent State University-Ashtabula Campus (Public)
  Fall 2004 Enrollment: 1,474 . . . . (440) 964-3322
  2005-06 Tuition: In-state $4,586; Out-of-state $12,018
Housing: Homeownership rate: 58.3% (2005); Median home value: $81,612 (2005); Median rent: $369 per month (2000); Median age of housing: 52 years (2000).
Hospitals: Ashtabula County Medical Center (241 beds)
Newspapers: The Star-Beacon (Circulation 19,935)
Transportation: Commute to work: 92.6% car, 2.1% public transportation, 2.9% walk, 1.6% work from home (2000); Travel time to work: 50.1% less than 15 minutes, 27.5% 15 to 30 minutes, 9.8% 30 to 45 minutes, 6.7% 45 to 60 minutes, 5.9% 60 minutes or more (2000)
Additional Information Contacts
Ashtabula Chamber of Commerce . . . . (440) 998-6998
  http://www.ashtabulachamber.net
City of Ashtabula . . . . (440) 992-7103
  http://ci.ashtabula.oh.us

AUSTINBURG (unincorporated postal area, zip code 44010). Covers a land area of 18.451 square miles and a water area of 0.144 square miles. Located at 41.75° N. Lat.; 80.86° W. Long. Elevation is 817 feet.
Population: 1,764 (2000); Race: 98.3% White, 0.0% Black, 0.0% Asian, 1.0% Hispanic of any race (2000); Density: 95.6 persons per square mile (2000); Age: 22.3% under 18, 16.8% over 64 (2000); Marriage status: 20.6% never married, 61.5% now married, 8.5% widowed, 9.4% divorced (2000); Foreign born: 1.3% (2000); Ancestry (includes multiple ancestries): 25.8% English, 21.1% German, 16.0% Irish, 7.5% Welsh, 7.2% Italian (2000).
Economy: Employment by occupation: 11.4% management, 15.6% professional, 14.9% services, 18.9% sales, 1.0% farming, 15.1% construction, 23.1% production (2000).
Income: Per capita income: $24,447 (2000); Median household income: $46,490 (2000); Poverty rate: 3.3% (2000).
Education: Percent of population age 25 and over with: High school diploma (including GED) or higher: 89.6% (2000); Bachelor's degree or higher: 20.0% (2000).
School District(s)
Geneva Area City Schools (PK-12)
  2003-04 Enrollment: 3,011 . . . . (440) 466-4831
Housing: Homeownership rate: 87.8% (2000); Median home value: $109,900 (2000); Median rent: $237 per month (2000); Median age of housing: 39 years (2000).
Transportation: Commute to work: 94.0% car, 0.5% public transportation, 0.6% walk, 4.9% work from home (2000); Travel time to work: 25.4% less than 15 minutes, 49.8% 15 to 30 minutes, 14.9% 30 to 45 minutes, 7.3% 45 to 60 minutes, 2.6% 60 minutes or more (2000)
Additional Information Contacts

Ashtabula County Convention & Visitors Bureau......... (440) 275-3202
http://www.visitashtabulacounty.com

CONNEAUT (city). Aka Lakeville. Covers a land area of 26.373 square miles and a water area of 0.057 square miles. Located at 41.94° N. Lat.; 80.56° W. Long. Elevation is 662 feet.
History: Conneaut was settled in 1799 by Thomas Montgomery and Aaron Wright. The village grew around the natural harbor, which attracted shipping of coal and ores.
Population: 13,241 (1990); 12,485 (2000); 12,630 (2005); 12,764 (2010 projected); Race: 96.2% White, 1.1% Black, 0.5% Asian, 1.2% Hispanic of any race (2005); Density: 478.9 persons per square mile (2005); Average household size: 2.44 (2005); Median age: 38.8 (2005); Males per 100 females: 95.1 (2005); Marriage status: 21.6% never married, 56.8% now married, 9.7% widowed, 11.8% divorced (2000); Foreign born: 1.0% (2000); Ancestry (includes multiple ancestries): 23.7% German, 16.4% Irish, 14.6% Italian, 14.2% English, 5.9% Finnish (2000).
Economy: Employment by occupation: 7.1% management, 12.6% professional, 19.0% services, 18.9% sales, 0.1% farming, 10.6% construction, 31.6% production (2000).
Income: Per capita income: $16,495 (2005); Median household income: $34,345 (2005); Average household income: $39,867 (2005); Percent of households with income of $100,000 or more: 3.4% (2005); Poverty rate: 13.0% (2000).
Education: Percent of population age 25 and over with: High school diploma (including GED) or higher: 81.2% (2005); Bachelor's degree or higher: 10.0% (2005); Master's degree or higher: 3.7% (2005).

School District(s)
Conneaut Area City SD (PK-12)
    2003-04 Enrollment: 2,527 .... (440) 593-7200
Housing: Homeownership rate: 70.0% (2005); Median home value: $86,722 (2005); Median rent: $363 per month (2000); Median age of housing: 57 years (2000).
Hospitals: Brown Memorial Hospital (86 beds)
Safety: Violent crime rate: 16.5 per 10,000 population; Property crime rate: 441.2 per 10,000 population (2004).
Transportation: Commute to work: 94.5% car, 0.6% public transportation, 2.1% walk, 1.6% work from home (2000); Travel time to work: 49.8% less than 15 minutes, 27.6% 15 to 30 minutes, 12.8% 30 to 45 minutes, 3.2% 45 to 60 minutes, 6.6% 60 minutes or more (2000)
Additional Information Contacts
City of Conneaut .... (440) 593-7401
    http://www.conneaut.net
Conneaut Chamber of Commerce..................... (440) 593-2402
    http://www.conneautchamber.org

DORSET (unincorporated postal area, zip code 44032). Covers a land area of 38.633 square miles and a water area of 0.035 square miles. Located at 41.67° N. Lat.; 80.66° W. Long. Elevation is 985 feet.
Population: 1,494 (2000); Race: 98.9% White, 0.6% Black, 0.0% Asian, 0.0% Hispanic of any race (2000); Density: 38.7 persons per square mile (2000); Age: 28.8% under 18, 10.1% over 64 (2000); Marriage status: 21.1% never married, 62.8% now married, 6.4% widowed, 9.7% divorced (2000); Foreign born: 1.1% (2000); Ancestry (includes multiple ancestries): 23.1% German, 17.6% Other groups, 16.7% Irish, 16.0% United States or American, 8.7% English (2000).
Economy: Employment by occupation: 7.5% management, 9.7% professional, 22.1% services, 14.6% sales, 3.8% farming, 15.6% construction, 26.7% production (2000).
Income: Per capita income: $13,828 (2000); Median household income: $37,281 (2000); Poverty rate: 12.0% (2000).
Education: Percent of population age 25 and over with: High school diploma (including GED) or higher: 72.5% (2000); Bachelor's degree or higher: 6.0% (2000).
Housing: Homeownership rate: 83.0% (2000); Median home value: $79,300 (2000); Median rent: $468 per month (2000); Median age of housing: 55 years (2000).
Transportation: Commute to work: 89.8% car, 1.4% public transportation, 4.0% walk, 2.1% work from home (2000); Travel time to work: 14.5% less than 15 minutes, 35.6% 15 to 30 minutes, 16.5% 30 to 45 minutes, 10.8% 45 to 60 minutes, 22.7% 60 minutes or more (2000)

EDGEWOOD (CDP). Covers a land area of 6.748 square miles and a water area of 0.006 square miles. Located at 41.87° N. Lat.; 80.75° W. Long. Elevation is 700 feet.
Population: 5,189 (1990); 4,762 (2000); 4,659 (2005); 4,566 (2010 projected); Race: 96.8% White, 1.3% Black, 0.7% Asian, 1.3% Hispanic of any race (2005); Density: 690.4 persons per square mile (2005); Average household size: 2.28 (2005); Median age: 42.3 (2005); Males per 100 females: 93.2 (2005); Marriage status: 17.7% never married, 61.8% now married, 7.5% widowed, 13.1% divorced (2000); Foreign born: 2.0% (2000); Ancestry (includes multiple ancestries): 23.4% German, 15.6% English, 15.3% Irish, 12.0% Italian, 7.7% Other groups (2000).
Economy: Employment by occupation: 6.5% management, 17.8% professional, 18.0% services, 24.8% sales, 0.3% farming, 9.8% construction, 22.9% production (2000).
Income: Per capita income: $22,481 (2005); Median household income: $43,241 (2005); Average household income: $51,120 (2005); Percent of households with income of $100,000 or more: 6.7% (2005); Poverty rate: 6.8% (2000).
Education: Percent of population age 25 and over with: High school diploma (including GED) or higher: 82.6% (2005); Bachelor's degree or higher: 10.2% (2005); Master's degree or higher: 4.8% (2005).
Housing: Homeownership rate: 79.8% (2005); Median home value: $89,243 (2005); Median rent: $389 per month (2000); Median age of housing: 44 years (2000).
Transportation: Commute to work: 97.4% car, 0.3% public transportation, 0.9% walk, 0.6% work from home (2000); Travel time to work: 57.1% less than 15 minutes, 25.2% 15 to 30 minutes, 6.6% 30 to 45 minutes, 6.4% 45 to 60 minutes, 4.6% 60 minutes or more (2000)

GENEVA (city). Covers a land area of 3.996 square miles and a water area of 0 square miles. Located at 41.80° N. Lat.; 80.94° W. Long. Elevation is 673 feet.
History: Geneva was founded in 1805. In Geneva's cemetery is a monument to Platt R. Spencer (1800-1864) who founded business schools in many cities and created the Spencerian penmanship system.
Population: 6,740 (1990); 6,595 (2000); 6,546 (2005); 6,476 (2010 projected); Race: 94.8% White, 1.3% Black, 0.2% Asian, 6.7% Hispanic of any race (2005); Density: 1,638.1 persons per square mile (2005); Average household size: 2.58 (2005); Median age: 40.2 (2005); Males per 100 females: 94.1 (2005); Marriage status: 26.5% never married, 53.4% now married, 8.6% widowed, 11.6% divorced (2000); Foreign born: 0.7% (2000); Ancestry (includes multiple ancestries): 25.4% German, 16.0% Irish, 11.8% English, 9.4% Other groups, 9.0% United States or American (2000).
Economy: Employment by occupation: 8.8% management, 17.0% professional, 15.4% services, 21.6% sales, 3.3% farming, 7.1% construction, 26.8% production (2000).
Income: Per capita income: $19,070 (2005); Median household income: $39,470 (2005); Average household income: $47,159 (2005); Percent of households with income of $100,000 or more: 6.8% (2005); Poverty rate: 9.4% (2000).
Education: Percent of population age 25 and over with: High school diploma (including GED) or higher: 77.5% (2005); Bachelor's degree or higher: 11.1% (2005); Master's degree or higher: 4.2% (2005).

School District(s)
Geneva Area City Schools (PK-12)
    2003-04 Enrollment: 3,011 .... (440) 466-4831
Housing: Homeownership rate: 63.7% (2005); Median home value: $109,549 (2005); Median rent: $360 per month (2000); Median age of housing: 46 years (2000).
Hospitals: UHHS Memorial Hospital of Geneva (46 beds)
Transportation: Commute to work: 91.2% car, 3.4% public transportation, 2.5% walk, 1.1% work from home (2000); Travel time to work: 38.1% less than 15 minutes, 27.7% 15 to 30 minutes, 24.5% 30 to 45 minutes, 5.9% 45 to 60 minutes, 3.8% 60 minutes or more (2000)
Additional Information Contacts
Geneva Chamber of Commerce .... (440) 466-8694
    http://www.genevachamber.org

GENEVA-ON-THE-LAKE (village). Covers a land area of 2.030 square miles and a water area of 0.015 square miles. Located at 41.85° N. Lat.; 80.94° W. Long. Elevation is 605 feet.
Population: 1,626 (1990); 1,545 (2000); 1,528 (2005); 1,517 (2010 projected); Race: 95.5% White, 0.7% Black, 0.4% Asian, 3.0% Hispanic of any race (2005); Density: 752.5 persons per square mile (2005); Average household size: 2.27 (2005); Median age: 35.7 (2005); Males per 100 females: 101.3 (2005); Marriage status: 24.9% never married, 48.8% now married, 7.2% widowed, 19.1% divorced (2000); Foreign born: 0.6%

(2000); Ancestry (includes multiple ancestries): 26.2% German, 20.4% Irish, 11.5% English, 10.9% Other groups, 8.6% Italian (2000).
Economy: Employment by occupation: 10.5% management, 9.1% professional, 18.1% services, 20.3% sales, 0.4% farming, 9.1% construction, 32.6% production (2000).
Income: Per capita income: $17,986 (2005); Median household income: $32,864 (2005); Average household income: $40,836 (2005); Percent of households with income of $100,000 or more: 5.3% (2005); Poverty rate: 19.1% (2000).
Education: Percent of population age 25 and over with: High school diploma (including GED) or higher: 73.2% (2005); Bachelor's degree or higher: 11.1% (2005); Master's degree or higher: 5.1% (2005).
Housing: Homeownership rate: 54.1% (2005); Median home value: $77,368 (2005); Median rent: $413 per month (2000); Median age of housing: 41 years (2000).
Transportation: Commute to work: 91.3% car, 0.9% public transportation, 3.5% walk, 3.4% work from home (2000); Travel time to work: 26.5% less than 15 minutes, 31.9% 15 to 30 minutes, 16.3% 30 to 45 minutes, 11.7% 45 to 60 minutes, 13.6% 60 minutes or more (2000)
Additional Information Contacts
Geneva on the Lake Chamber of Commerce . . . . (800) 862-9948
   http://www.visitgenevaonthelake.com
Geneva on the Lake Visitors Bureau . . . . (440) 466-8600
   http://www.visitgenevaonthelake.com

JEFFERSON (village). Covers a land area of 2.280 square miles and a water area of 0 square miles. Located at 41.73° N. Lat.; 80.77° W. Long. Elevation is 967 feet.
History: Jefferson was named by Gideon Granger, Postmaster General in Jefferson's cabinet. The Republican Party's first national platform was written here at the law office of Joshua R. Giddings.
Population: 3,389 (1990); 3,572 (2000); 3,598 (2005); 3,645 (2010 projected); Race: 97.4% White, 1.4% Black, 0.2% Asian, 0.7% Hispanic of any race (2005); Density: 1,577.9 persons per square mile (2005); Average household size: 2.58 (2005); Median age: 37.7 (2005); Males per 100 females: 87.0 (2005); Marriage status: 23.0% never married, 52.6% now married, 11.4% widowed, 12.9% divorced (2000); Foreign born: 1.1% (2000); Ancestry (includes multiple ancestries): 20.4% German, 17.4% Irish, 16.2% English, 11.0% Italian, 8.4% United States or American (2000).
Economy: Employment by occupation: 10.0% management, 18.5% professional, 22.1% services, 24.1% sales, 0.0% farming, 5.9% construction, 19.3% production (2000).
Income: Per capita income: $20,106 (2005); Median household income: $42,073 (2005); Average household income: $47,891 (2005); Percent of households with income of $100,000 or more: 7.5% (2005); Poverty rate: 5.8% (2000).
Education: Percent of population age 25 and over with: High school diploma (including GED) or higher: 86.8% (2005); Bachelor's degree or higher: 19.6% (2005); Master's degree or higher: 5.4% (2005).
School District(s)
Ashtabula County Joint Vocational SD (08-12)
   2003-04 Enrollment: n/a . . . . (440) 576-6015
Jefferson Area Local School District (PK-12)
   2003-04 Enrollment: 2,257 . . . . (440) 576-9180
Two-year College(s)
Ashtabula County Joint Vocational School (Public)
   Fall 2004 Enrollment: 163 . . . . (440) 576-6015
Housing: Homeownership rate: 61.7% (2005); Median home value: $120,549 (2005); Median rent: $392 per month (2000); Median age of housing: 36 years (2000).
Safety: Violent crime rate: 2.8 per 10,000 population; Property crime rate: 265.5 per 10,000 population (2004).
Newspapers: Sentinel (General - Circulation 7,000); The Courier (General - Circulation 3,000); The Gazette (General - Circulation 3,058); The Shores News (General - Circulation 1,200); The Valley News (General - Circulation 1,300); Vistas (Senior Lifestyles) (Senior Citizen - Circulation 5,000)
Transportation: Commute to work: 93.4% car, 0.0% public transportation, 5.1% walk, 1.0% work from home (2000); Travel time to work: 43.4% less than 15 minutes, 32.1% 15 to 30 minutes, 9.4% 30 to 45 minutes, 9.4% 45 to 60 minutes, 5.7% 60 minutes or more (2000)

KINGSVILLE (unincorporated postal area, zip code 44048). Covers a land area of 30.436 square miles and a water area of 0.043 square miles. Located at 41.86° N. Lat.; 80.65° W. Long. Elevation is 789 feet.
Population: 2,553 (2000); Race: 97.1% White, 0.3% Black, 0.0% Asian, 0.0% Hispanic of any race (2000); Density: 83.9 persons per square mile (2000); Age: 26.2% under 18, 17.4% over 64 (2000); Marriage status: 20.3% never married, 57.8% now married, 11.8% widowed, 10.0% divorced (2000); Foreign born: 1.0% (2000); Ancestry (includes multiple ancestries): 15.9% German, 12.9% United States or American, 12.6% English, 10.2% Irish, 6.1% Finnish (2000).
Economy: Wood products. Employment by occupation: 5.5% management, 13.7% professional, 19.7% services, 21.7% sales, 0.0% farming, 13.7% construction, 25.6% production (2000).
Income: Per capita income: $16,884 (2000); Median household income: $38,750 (2000); Poverty rate: 6.5% (2000).
Education: Percent of population age 25 and over with: High school diploma (including GED) or higher: 75.6% (2000); Bachelor's degree or higher: 9.5% (2000).
School District(s)
Buckeye Local SD (PK-12)
   2003-04 Enrollment: 2,287 . . . . (440) 998-4411
Housing: Homeownership rate: 82.8% (2000); Median home value: $95,600 (2000); Median rent: $324 per month (2000); Median age of housing: 34 years (2000).
Transportation: Commute to work: 95.7% car, 0.0% public transportation, 1.6% walk, 0.7% work from home (2000); Travel time to work: 32.7% less than 15 minutes, 41.3% 15 to 30 minutes, 10.6% 30 to 45 minutes, 5.9% 45 to 60 minutes, 9.5% 60 minutes or more (2000)

NORTH KINGSVILLE (village). Covers a land area of 8.903 square miles and a water area of 0.019 square miles. Located at 41.91° N. Lat.; 80.67° W. Long. Elevation is 715 feet.
Population: 2,672 (1990); 2,658 (2000); 2,659 (2005); 2,665 (2010 projected); Race: 97.4% White, 0.4% Black, 0.6% Asian, 1.5% Hispanic of any race (2005); Density: 298.7 persons per square mile (2005); Average household size: 2.53 (2005); Median age: 41.9 (2005); Males per 100 females: 97.3 (2005); Marriage status: 18.9% never married, 66.0% now married, 8.7% widowed, 6.4% divorced (2000); Foreign born: 1.5% (2000); Ancestry (includes multiple ancestries): 20.6% German, 18.5% English, 13.4% Italian, 12.8% Irish, 9.8% United States or American (2000).
Economy: Employment by occupation: 8.9% management, 18.1% professional, 13.0% services, 26.7% sales, 0.0% farming, 9.5% construction, 23.7% production (2000).
Income: Per capita income: $25,873 (2005); Median household income: $50,742 (2005); Average household income: $65,332 (2005); Percent of households with income of $100,000 or more: 15.5% (2005); Poverty rate: 7.0% (2000).
Education: Percent of population age 25 and over with: High school diploma (including GED) or higher: 83.6% (2005); Bachelor's degree or higher: 14.0% (2005); Master's degree or higher: 5.6% (2005).
School District(s)
Buckeye Local SD (PK-12)
   2003-04 Enrollment: 2,287 . . . . (440) 998-4411
Housing: Homeownership rate: 86.8% (2005); Median home value: $127,469 (2005); Median rent: $332 per month (2000); Median age of housing: 33 years (2000).
Transportation: Commute to work: 93.8% car, 0.8% public transportation, 1.6% walk, 3.6% work from home (2000); Travel time to work: 41.1% less than 15 minutes, 40.9% 15 to 30 minutes, 7.4% 30 to 45 minutes, 4.1% 45 to 60 minutes, 6.5% 60 minutes or more (2000)

ORWELL (village). Covers a land area of 1.664 square miles and a water area of 0 square miles. Located at 41.53° N. Lat.; 80.85° W. Long. Elevation is 902 feet.
Population: 1,387 (1990); 1,519 (2000); 1,560 (2005); 1,603 (2010 projected); Race: 96.1% White, 0.9% Black, 0.6% Asian, 1.3% Hispanic of any race (2005); Density: 937.6 persons per square mile (2005); Average household size: 2.44 (2005); Median age: 34.9 (2005); Males per 100 females: 90.9 (2005); Marriage status: 23.7% never married, 55.6% now married, 8.4% widowed, 12.3% divorced (2000); Foreign born: 0.9% (2000); Ancestry (includes multiple ancestries): 26.0% German, 16.5% Irish, 13.3% Other groups, 12.3% English, 8.9% Polish (2000).
Economy: In dairy, grain, and poultry area. Employment by occupation: 8.1% management, 9.1% professional, 13.8% services, 19.9% sales, 0.6% farming, 9.8% construction, 38.8% production (2000).
Income: Per capita income: $18,999 (2005); Median household income: $37,860 (2005); Average household income: $44,632 (2005); Percent of

households with income of $100,000 or more: 5.9% (2005); Poverty rate: 10.9% (2000).
Education: Percent of population age 25 and over with: High school diploma (including GED) or higher: 77.7% (2005); Bachelor's degree or higher: 8.5% (2005); Master's degree or higher: 3.0% (2005).

School District(s)
Grand Valley Local SD (PK-12)
   2003-04 Enrollment: 1,456 . . . . (440) 437-6570
Housing: Homeownership rate: 61.7% (2005); Median home value: $96,957 (2005); Median rent: $395 per month (2000); Median age of housing: 29 years (2000).
Transportation: Commute to work: 95.2% car, 0.0% public transportation, 4.1% walk, 0.7% work from home (2000); Travel time to work: 36.6% less than 15 minutes, 21.9% 15 to 30 minutes, 25.1% 30 to 45 minutes, 8.9% 45 to 60 minutes, 7.5% 60 minutes or more (2000)
Additional Information Contacts
Village of Orwell . . . . (440) 437-6549
   http://www.orwellvillage.org

PIERPONT (unincorporated postal area, zip code 44082).
Covers a land area of 33.432 square miles and a water area of 0.020 square miles. Located at 41.76° N. Lat.; 80.57° W. Long. Elevation is 995 feet.
Population: 1,469 (2000); Race: 100.0% White, 0.0% Black, 0.0% Asian, 2.2% Hispanic of any race (2000); Density: 43.9 persons per square mile (2000); Age: 33.1% under 18, 11.0% over 64 (2000); Marriage status: 18.5% never married, 64.9% now married, 6.9% widowed, 9.6% divorced (2000); Foreign born: 2.5% (2000); Ancestry (includes multiple ancestries): 23.3% German, 11.0% English, 6.5% Hungarian, 6.4% Irish, 6.2% Other groups (2000).
Economy: Employment by occupation: 5.7% management, 5.9% professional, 20.0% services, 12.3% sales, 1.4% farming, 15.8% construction, 38.9% production (2000).
Income: Per capita income: $13,594 (2000); Median household income: $36,071 (2000); Poverty rate: 24.1% (2000).
Education: Percent of population age 25 and over with: High school diploma (including GED) or higher: 76.1% (2000); Bachelor's degree or higher: 1.6% (2000).

School District(s)
Buckeye Local SD (PK-12)
   2003-04 Enrollment: 2,287 . . . . (440) 998-4411
Housing: Homeownership rate: 89.5% (2000); Median home value: $84,200 (2000); Median rent: $338 per month (2000); Median age of housing: 27 years (2000).
Transportation: Commute to work: 94.4% car, 1.1% public transportation, 0.0% walk, 4.5% work from home (2000); Travel time to work: 15.8% less than 15 minutes, 42.1% 15 to 30 minutes, 30.5% 30 to 45 minutes, 4.2% 45 to 60 minutes, 7.4% 60 minutes or more (2000)

ROAMING SHORES (village).
Covers a land area of 2.079 square miles and a water area of 0.719 square miles. Located at 41.63° N. Lat.; 80.82° W. Long. Elevation is 870 feet.
Population: 790 (1990); 1,239 (2000); 1,242 (2005); 1,241 (2010 projected); Race: 97.4% White, 1.9% Black, 0.0% Asian, 0.6% Hispanic of any race (2005); Density: 597.5 persons per square mile (2005); Average household size: 2.50 (2005); Median age: 41.5 (2005); Males per 100 females: 109.8 (2005); Marriage status: 16.4% never married, 71.8% now married, 4.4% widowed, 7.5% divorced (2000); Foreign born: 1.0% (2000); Ancestry (includes multiple ancestries): 28.4% German, 20.4% Irish, 15.3% English, 10.8% Italian, 8.6% United States or American (2000).
Economy: Employment by occupation: 14.8% management, 21.8% professional, 7.6% services, 25.4% sales, 0.0% farming, 9.0% construction, 21.5% production (2000).
Income: Per capita income: $33,402 (2005); Median household income: $68,945 (2005); Average household income: $83,639 (2005); Percent of households with income of $100,000 or more: 25.8% (2005); Poverty rate: 1.0% (2000).
Education: Percent of population age 25 and over with: High school diploma (including GED) or higher: 90.2% (2005); Bachelor's degree or higher: 20.5% (2005); Master's degree or higher: 4.6% (2005).
Housing: Homeownership rate: 94.0% (2005); Median home value: $179,358 (2005); Median rent: $569 per month (2000); Median age of housing: 18 years (2000).
Transportation: Commute to work: 96.7% car, 0.0% public transportation, 0.3% walk, 3.0% work from home (2000); Travel time to work: 9.4% less than 15 minutes, 27.6% 15 to 30 minutes, 28.2% 30 to 45 minutes, 17.6% 45 to 60 minutes, 17.2% 60 minutes or more (2000)

ROCK CREEK (village).
Covers a land area of 0.904 square miles and a water area of 0 square miles. Located at 41.66° N. Lat.; 80.85° W. Long. Elevation is 812 feet.
Population: 553 (1990); 584 (2000); 614 (2005); 641 (2010 projected); Race: 97.7% White, 1.1% Black, 0.0% Asian, 0.3% Hispanic of any race (2005); Density: 679.4 persons per square mile (2005); Average household size: 2.94 (2005); Median age: 32.7 (2005); Males per 100 females: 93.7 (2005); Marriage status: 32.2% never married, 52.4% now married, 7.3% widowed, 8.2% divorced (2000); Foreign born: 0.0% (2000); Ancestry (includes multiple ancestries): 40.9% German, 21.6% Irish, 10.7% Other groups, 9.5% English, 8.7% Italian (2000).
Economy: Employment by occupation: 4.4% management, 8.1% professional, 19.7% services, 20.7% sales, 0.0% farming, 16.6% construction, 30.5% production (2000).
Income: Per capita income: $16,258 (2005); Median household income: $41,500 (2005); Average household income: $47,763 (2005); Percent of households with income of $100,000 or more: 6.2% (2005); Poverty rate: 9.6% (2000).
Education: Percent of population age 25 and over with: High school diploma (including GED) or higher: 83.8% (2005); Bachelor's degree or higher: 7.4% (2005); Master's degree or higher: 1.9% (2005).

School District(s)
Jefferson Area Local School District (PK-12)
   2003-04 Enrollment: 2,257 . . . . (440) 576-9180
Housing: Homeownership rate: 78.5% (2005); Median home value: $100,008 (2005); Median rent: $428 per month (2000); Median age of housing: 60+ years (2000).
Hospitals: Glenbeigh Hospital of Rock Creek (80 beds)
Transportation: Commute to work: 88.9% car, 0.7% public transportation, 5.4% walk, 2.9% work from home (2000); Travel time to work: 25.8% less than 15 minutes, 30.3% 15 to 30 minutes, 24.7% 30 to 45 minutes, 5.5% 45 to 60 minutes, 13.7% 60 minutes or more (2000)

ROME (unincorporated postal area, zip code 44085).
Covers a land area of 46.385 square miles and a water area of 0.141 square miles. Located at 41.61° N. Lat.; 80.83° W. Long. Elevation is 853 feet.
Population: 2,943 (2000); Race: 97.4% White, 0.2% Black, 0.0% Asian, 1.6% Hispanic of any race (2000); Density: 63.4 persons per square mile (2000); Age: 30.8% under 18, 9.0% over 64 (2000); Marriage status: 19.3% never married, 62.9% now married, 6.0% widowed, 11.8% divorced (2000); Foreign born: 3.2% (2000); Ancestry (includes multiple ancestries): 21.9% German, 18.8% Irish, 11.8% English, 11.7% United States or American, 9.6% Polish (2000).
Economy: Employment by occupation: 9.4% management, 11.9% professional, 12.2% services, 18.3% sales, 1.8% farming, 17.1% construction, 29.4% production (2000).
Income: Per capita income: $18,049 (2000); Median household income: $44,514 (2000); Poverty rate: 9.8% (2000).
Education: Percent of population age 25 and over with: High school diploma (including GED) or higher: 84.4% (2000); Bachelor's degree or higher: 8.5% (2000).

School District(s)
Grand Valley Local SD (PK-12)
   2003-04 Enrollment: 1,456 . . . . (440) 437-6570
Housing: Homeownership rate: 84.8% (2000); Median home value: $98,000 (2000); Median rent: $452 per month (2000); Median age of housing: 31 years (2000).
Transportation: Commute to work: 93.9% car, 0.7% public transportation, 0.7% walk, 4.7% work from home (2000); Travel time to work: 14.3% less than 15 minutes, 30.6% 15 to 30 minutes, 26.4% 30 to 45 minutes, 13.0% 45 to 60 minutes, 15.8% 60 minutes or more (2000)

WILLIAMSFIELD (unincorporated postal area, zip code 44093).
Covers a land area of 33.132 square miles and a water area of 0.079 square miles. Located at 41.52° N. Lat.; 80.58° W. Long. Elevation is 1,135 feet.
Population: 1,525 (2000); Race: 90.7% White, 4.0% Black, 0.5% Asian, 0.0% Hispanic of any race (2000); Density: 46.0 persons per square mile (2000); Age: 29.9% under 18, 12.8% over 64 (2000); Marriage status: 23.9% never married, 63.2% now married, 5.2% widowed, 7.7% divorced (2000); Foreign born: 2.8% (2000); Ancestry (includes multiple ancestries):

21.2% German, 14.7% Irish, 11.4% Other groups, 11.1% English, 8.8% Polish (2000).
Economy: Employment by occupation: 6.7% management, 6.8% professional, 24.2% services, 24.5% sales, 2.2% farming, 9.1% construction, 26.5% production (2000).
Income: Per capita income: $13,780 (2000); Median household income: $30,417 (2000); Poverty rate: 14.2% (2000).
Education: Percent of population age 25 and over with: High school diploma (including GED) or higher: 77.6% (2000); Bachelor's degree or higher: 4.2% (2000).
Housing: Homeownership rate: 87.9% (2000); Median home value: $74,900 (2000); Median rent: $408 per month (2000); Median age of housing: 42 years (2000).
Transportation: Commute to work: 94.4% car, 0.0% public transportation, 4.4% walk, 0.0% work from home (2000); Travel time to work: 37.0% less than 15 minutes, 24.6% 15 to 30 minutes, 24.5% 30 to 45 minutes, 7.7% 45 to 60 minutes, 6.2% 60 minutes or more (2000)

WINDSOR (unincorporated postal area, zip code 44099). Covers a land area of 19.249 square miles and a water area of 0.038 square miles. Located at 41.54° N. Lat.; 80.96° W. Long. Elevation is 834 feet.
Population: 1,647 (2000); Race: 97.4% White, 1.2% Black, 0.0% Asian, 0.8% Hispanic of any race (2000); Density: 85.6 persons per square mile (2000); Age: 29.9% under 18, 12.7% over 64 (2000); Marriage status: 24.3% never married, 63.7% now married, 6.3% widowed, 5.7% divorced (2000); Foreign born: 0.8% (2000); Ancestry (includes multiple ancestries): 17.8% German, 17.0% United States or American, 14.0% Other groups, 12.5% Irish, 8.3% Hungarian (2000).
Economy: Employment by occupation: 5.0% management, 4.4% professional, 11.0% services, 18.0% sales, 1.3% farming, 32.2% construction, 28.1% production (2000).
Income: Per capita income: $19,014 (2000); Median household income: $40,586 (2000); Poverty rate: 11.3% (2000).
Education: Percent of population age 25 and over with: High school diploma (including GED) or higher: 65.7% (2000); Bachelor's degree or higher: 10.1% (2000).

School District(s)
Grand Valley Local SD (PK-12)
    2003-04 Enrollment: 1,456 . . . . (440) 437-6570

Housing: Homeownership rate: 86.8% (2000); Median home value: $91,500 (2000); Median rent: $382 per month (2000); Median age of housing: 42 years (2000).
Transportation: Commute to work: 91.6% car, 0.8% public transportation, 0.0% walk, 4.6% work from home (2000); Travel time to work: 10.7% less than 15 minutes, 37.4% 15 to 30 minutes, 17.7% 30 to 45 minutes, 8.4% 45 to 60 minutes, 25.8% 60 minutes or more (2000)

Athens County

Located in southeastern Ohio; bounded on the southeast by the Ohio River and the West Virginia border. Covers a land area of 506.76 square miles, a water area of 1.78 square miles, and is located in the Eastern Time Zone. The county government was organized in 1805. County seat is Athens.

Athens County is part of the Athens, OH Micropolitan Statistical Area. The entire metro area includes: Athens County, OH

Population: 59,549 (1990); 62,223 (2000); 65,328 (2005); 68,569 (2010 projected); Race: 93.5% White, 2.2% Black, 2.2% Asian, 1.0% Hispanic of any race (2005); Density: 128.9 persons per square mile (2005); Average household size: 2.71 (2005); Median age: 28.7 (2005); Males per 100 females: 96.2 (2005).
Religion: Five largest groups: 4.5% The United Methodist Church, 3.1% Catholic Church, 3.1% Christian Churches and Churches of Christ, 2.6% The Wesleyan Church, 1.2% Presbyterian Church (U.S.A.) (2000).
Economy: Unemployment rate: 6.0% (2005); Total civilian labor force: 30,060 (2005); Leading industries: 24.5% retail trade; 20.1% health care and social assistance; 19.5% accommodation & food services (2004); Farms: 673 totaling 104,816 acres (2002); Companies that employ 500 or more persons: 0 (2004); Companies that employ 100 to 499 persons: 13 (2004); Companies that employ less than 100 persons: 1,153 (2004); Black-owned businesses: n/a (2002); Hispanic-owned businesses: n/a (2002); Women-owned businesses: 1,157 (2002); Retail sales per capita: $7,869 (2006). Single-family building permits issued: 17 (2005); Multi-family building permits issued: 9 (2005).
Income: Per capita income: $16,766 (2005); Median household income: $30,884 (2005); Average household income: $43,852 (2005); Percent of households with income of $100,000 or more: 8.6% (2005); Poverty rate: 18.3% (2003); Bankruptcy rate: 3.77% (2005).
Taxes: Total county taxes per capita: $232 (2004); County property taxes per capita: $137 (2004).
Education: Percent of population age 25 and over with: High school diploma (including GED) or higher: 83.2% (2005); Bachelor's degree or higher: 27.0% (2005); Master's degree or higher: 13.6% (2005).
Housing: Homeownership rate: 60.5% (2005); Median home value: $91,697 (2005); Median rent: $380 per month (2000); Median age of housing: 30 years (2000).
Health: Birth rate: 100.8 per 10,000 population (2004); Death rate: 76.0 per 10,000 population (2004); Age-adjusted cancer mortality rate: 297.2 deaths per 100,000 population (2002); Air Quality Index: 60.7% good, 37.7% moderate, 0.0% unhealthy for sensitive individuals, 1.6% unhealthy (percent of days in 2005); Number of physicians: 23.2 per 10,000 population (2004); Hospital beds: 23.3 per 10,000 population (2003); Hospital admissions: 558.6 per 10,000 population (2003).
Elections: 2004 Presidential election results: 36.1% Bush, 63.2% Kerry, 0.0% Nader, 0.3% Badnarik.
National and State Parks: Gifford State Forest; Stroud Run State Park; Trimble State Wildlife Area; Waterloo State Forest
Additional Information Contacts
Athens County Government . . . . (740) 592-3219
    http://www.athenscountygovernment.com/
Athens Chamber of Commerce . . . . (740) 594-2251
    http://www.athenschamber.com
City of Athens. . . . . (740) 592-3338
    http://www.ci.athens.oh.us

Athens County Communities

ALBANY (village). Covers a land area of 1.244 square miles and a water area of 0.005 square miles. Located at 39.22° N. Lat.; 82.20° W. Long. Elevation is 755 feet.
History: Albany was laid out in 1831 and named for Albany, New York.
Population: 822 (1990); 808 (2000); 797 (2005); 798 (2010 projected); Race: 98.0% White, 0.6% Black, 0.1% Asian, 1.6% Hispanic of any race (2005); Density: 640.8 persons per square mile (2005); Average household size: 2.26 (2005); Median age: 39.4 (2005); Males per 100 females: 96.3 (2005); Marriage status: 22.6% never married, 54.9% now married, 8.9% widowed, 13.7% divorced (2000); Foreign born: 1.6% (2000); Ancestry (includes multiple ancestries): 15.1% United States or American, 14.7% German, 13.4% Irish, 10.2% English, 6.8% Other groups (2000).
Economy: Single-family building permits issued: 2 (2005); Multi-family building permits issued: 0 (2005); Employment by occupation: 5.3% management, 23.0% professional, 20.0% services, 26.5% sales, 0.0% farming, 16.0% construction, 9.3% production (2000).
Income: Per capita income: $20,267 (2005); Median household income: $38,047 (2005); Average household income: $45,447 (2005); Percent of households with income of $100,000 or more: 7.1% (2005); Poverty rate: 13.2% (2000).
Taxes: Total city taxes per capita: $85 (2004); City property taxes per capita: $75 (2004).
Education: Percent of population age 25 and over with: High school diploma (including GED) or higher: 85.8% (2005); Bachelor's degree or higher: 19.3% (2005); Master's degree or higher: 6.6% (2005).

School District(s)
Alexander Local SD (PK-12)
    2003-04 Enrollment: 1,679 . . . . (740) 698-8831

Housing: Homeownership rate: 73.6% (2005); Median home value: $101,577 (2005); Median rent: $355 per month (2000); Median age of housing: 34 years (2000).
Transportation: Commute to work: 94.3% car, 0.5% public transportation, 1.2% walk, 4.0% work from home (2000); Travel time to work: 19.2% less than 15 minutes, 64.0% 15 to 30 minutes, 7.8% 30 to 45 minutes, 1.3% 45 to 60 minutes, 7.8% 60 minutes or more (2000)

AMESVILLE (village). Covers a land area of 0.222 square miles and a water area of 0 square miles. Located at 39.40° N. Lat.; 81.95° W. Long. Elevation is 660 feet.
Population: 250 (1990); 184 (2000); 185 (2005); 187 (2010 projected); Race: 95.7% White, 0.5% Black, 0.0% Asian, 2.2% Hispanic of any race (2005); Density: 834.3 persons per square mile (2005); Average household

size: 2.61 (2005); Median age: 35.2 (2005); Males per 100 females: 96.8 (2005); Marriage status: 20.4% never married, 62.0% now married, 8.8% widowed, 8.8% divorced (2000); Foreign born: 0.0% (2000); Ancestry (includes multiple ancestries): 15.3% German, 14.2% Irish, 12.6% United States or American, 9.5% Dutch, 6.3% Scotch-Irish (2000).
Economy: In livestock area. Employment by occupation: 12.0% management, 20.7% professional, 18.5% services, 34.8% sales, 0.0% farming, 3.3% construction, 10.9% production (2000).
Income: Per capita income: $20,541 (2005); Median household income: $42,500 (2005); Average household income: $53,521 (2005); Percent of households with income of $100,000 or more: 8.5% (2005); Poverty rate: 8.0% (2000).
Education: Percent of population age 25 and over with: High school diploma (including GED) or higher: 87.4% (2005); Bachelor's degree or higher: 22.7% (2005); Master's degree or higher: 5.9% (2005).

School District(s)
Federal Hocking Local SD (PK-12)
    2003-04 Enrollment: 1,422 . . . . (740) 662-6691

Housing: Homeownership rate: 78.9% (2005); Median home value: $79,028 (2005); Median rent: $275 per month (2000); Median age of housing: 60+ years (2000).
Transportation: Commute to work: 90.2% car, 0.0% public transportation, 3.3% walk, 6.5% work from home (2000); Travel time to work: 12.8% less than 15 minutes, 54.7% 15 to 30 minutes, 16.3% 30 to 45 minutes, 8.1% 45 to 60 minutes, 8.1% 60 minutes or more (2000)

ATHENS (city). Covers a land area of 8.335 square miles and a water area of 0 square miles. Located at 39.32° N. Lat.; 82.09° W. Long. Elevation is 723 feet.
History: Athens was selected by the territorial legislature as the site of a university, which was chartered in 1804 and became Ohio University. Athens was incorporated as a city in 1912.
Population: 21,362 (1990); 21,342 (2000); 22,292 (2005); 23,320 (2010 projected); Race: 89.3% White, 3.4% Black, 4.9% Asian, 1.2% Hispanic of any race (2005); Density: 2,674.4 persons per square mile (2005); Average household size: 3.32 (2005); Median age: 22.6 (2005); Males per 100 females: 88.6 (2005); Marriage status: 70.0% never married, 24.6% now married, 2.3% widowed, 3.1% divorced (2000); Foreign born: 6.3% (2000); Ancestry (includes multiple ancestries): 28.3% German, 17.1% Irish, 12.6% Other groups, 10.6% English, 8.3% Italian (2000).
Economy: Single-family building permits issued: 15 (2005); Multi-family building permits issued: 5 (2005); Employment by occupation: 8.2% management, 37.4% professional, 22.5% services, 24.8% sales, 0.1% farming, 2.3% construction, 4.7% production (2000).
Income: Per capita income: $12,107 (2005); Median household income: $18,625 (2005); Average household income: $35,625 (2005); Percent of households with income of $100,000 or more: 8.0% (2005); Poverty rate: 51.9% (2000).
Taxes: Total city taxes per capita: $460 (2004); City property taxes per capita: $28 (2004).
Education: Percent of population age 25 and over with: High school diploma (including GED) or higher: 92.9% (2005); Bachelor's degree or higher: 61.4% (2005); Master's degree or higher: 35.1% (2005).

School District(s)
Athens City SD (PK-12)
    2003-04 Enrollment: 2,975 . . . . (740) 797-4544

Four-year College(s)
Ohio University-Main Campus (Public)
    Fall 2004 Enrollment: 20,143. (740) 593-1000
    2005-06 Tuition: In-state $8,235; Out-of-state $17,199

Housing: Homeownership rate: 29.6% (2005); Median home value: $138,848 (2005); Median rent: $423 per month (2000); Median age of housing: 37 years (2000).
Hospitals: O' Bleness Memorial Hospital (114 beds)
Safety: Violent crime rate: 17.1 per 10,000 population; Property crime rate: 238.5 per 10,000 population (2004).
Newspapers: Athens News (Alternative, General - Circulation 17,500); The Athens Messenger (Circulation 10,678)
Transportation: Commute to work: 51.1% car, 1.0% public transportation, 40.6% walk, 4.2% work from home (2000); Travel time to work: 74.2% less than 15 minutes, 20.0% 15 to 30 minutes, 3.3% 30 to 45 minutes, 0.6% 45 to 60 minutes, 1.8% 60 minutes or more (2000)
Additional Information Contacts
Athens Chamber of Commerce . . . . (740) 594-2251
    http://www.athenschamber.com

City of Athens. . . . . (740) 592-3338
    http://www.ci.athens.oh.us

BUCHTEL (village). Covers a land area of 0.481 square miles and a water area of 0 square miles. Located at 39.46° N. Lat.; 82.18° W. Long. Elevation is 690 feet.
Population: 650 (1990); 574 (2000); 576 (2005); 570 (2010 projected); Race: 96.5% White, 0.2% Black, 0.2% Asian, 1.7% Hispanic of any race (2005); Density: 1,198.3 persons per square mile (2005); Average household size: 2.42 (2005); Median age: 36.1 (2005); Males per 100 females: 94.6 (2005); Marriage status: 21.0% never married, 55.1% now married, 8.6% widowed, 15.3% divorced (2000); Foreign born: 0.0% (2000); Ancestry (includes multiple ancestries): 23.2% United States or American, 13.4% Irish, 12.7% German, 9.3% Other groups, 6.8% English (2000).
Economy: Employment by occupation: 11.8% management, 13.2% professional, 18.9% services, 22.8% sales, 0.9% farming, 9.2% construction, 23.2% production (2000).
Income: Per capita income: $13,898 (2005); Median household income: $28,415 (2005); Average household income: $33,634 (2005); Percent of households with income of $100,000 or more: 2.9% (2005); Poverty rate: 20.5% (2000).
Education: Percent of population age 25 and over with: High school diploma (including GED) or higher: 77.3% (2005); Bachelor's degree or higher: 6.6% (2005); Master's degree or higher: 1.8% (2005).
Housing: Homeownership rate: 80.7% (2005); Median home value: $66,667 (2005); Median rent: $317 per month (2000); Median age of housing: 26 years (2000).
Transportation: Commute to work: 97.3% car, 0.0% public transportation, 1.8% walk, 0.0% work from home (2000); Travel time to work: 37.8% less than 15 minutes, 28.9% 15 to 30 minutes, 8.9% 30 to 45 minutes, 4.9% 45 to 60 minutes, 19.6% 60 minutes or more (2000)

CHAUNCEY (village). Covers a land area of 0.670 square miles and a water area of 0 square miles. Located at 39.40° N. Lat.; 82.12° W. Long. Elevation is 659 feet.
History: Chauncey was first a salt town, and later a coal town.
Population: 1,173 (1990); 1,067 (2000); 1,054 (2005); 1,067 (2010 projected); Race: 91.7% White, 1.9% Black, 4.2% Asian, 0.9% Hispanic of any race (2005); Density: 1,572.7 persons per square mile (2005); Average household size: 2.45 (2005); Median age: 34.5 (2005); Males per 100 females: 92.7 (2005); Marriage status: 24.6% never married, 50.5% now married, 9.9% widowed, 15.0% divorced (2000); Foreign born: 5.2% (2000); Ancestry (includes multiple ancestries): 15.3% United States or American, 11.4% English, 10.9% Other groups, 9.6% German, 7.9% Irish (2000).
Economy: Employment by occupation: 6.6% management, 11.7% professional, 28.1% services, 28.1% sales, 0.0% farming, 8.3% construction, 17.1% production (2000).
Income: Per capita income: $13,316 (2005); Median household income: $26,538 (2005); Average household income: $32,640 (2005); Percent of households with income of $100,000 or more: 0.7% (2005); Poverty rate: 25.6% (2000).
Education: Percent of population age 25 and over with: High school diploma (including GED) or higher: 74.3% (2005); Bachelor's degree or higher: 11.8% (2005); Master's degree or higher: 3.4% (2005).

School District(s)
Athens City SD (PK-12)
    2003-04 Enrollment: 2,975 . . . . (740) 797-4544

Housing: Homeownership rate: 66.0% (2005); Median home value: $55,641 (2005); Median rent: $338 per month (2000); Median age of housing: 43 years (2000).
Transportation: Commute to work: 97.8% car, 1.2% public transportation, 0.5% walk, 0.5% work from home (2000); Travel time to work: 34.2% less than 15 minutes, 51.1% 15 to 30 minutes, 4.2% 30 to 45 minutes, 4.7% 45 to 60 minutes, 5.7% 60 minutes or more (2000)

COOLVILLE (village). Covers a land area of 0.842 square miles and a water area of 0.026 square miles. Located at 39.22° N. Lat.; 81.79° W. Long. Elevation is 700 feet.
Population: 663 (1990); 528 (2000); 570 (2005); 615 (2010 projected); Race: 98.8% White, 0.0% Black, 0.0% Asian, 0.0% Hispanic of any race (2005); Density: 677.0 persons per square mile (2005); Average household size: 2.43 (2005); Median age: 37.2 (2005); Males per 100 females: 102.1 (2005); Marriage status: 22.7% never married, 53.0% now married, 10.4%

widowed, 13.9% divorced (2000); Foreign born: 0.6% (2000); Ancestry (includes multiple ancestries): 19.8% German, 18.9% English, 17.0% Irish, 14.3% United States or American, 8.1% Other groups (2000).
Economy: Employment by occupation: 7.4% management, 9.4% professional, 24.1% services, 23.2% sales, 0.0% farming, 13.8% construction, 22.2% production (2000).
Income: Per capita income: $22,167 (2005); Median household income: $41,150 (2005); Average household income: $53,766 (2005); Percent of households with income of $100,000 or more: 8.5% (2005); Poverty rate: 15.6% (2000).
Education: Percent of population age 25 and over with: High school diploma (including GED) or higher: 70.8% (2005); Bachelor's degree or higher: 7.4% (2005); Master's degree or higher: 1.0% (2005).

School District(s)
Federal Hocking Local SD (PK-12)
    2003-04 Enrollment: 1,422 . . . . (740) 662-6691
Housing: Homeownership rate: 80.9% (2005); Median home value: $69,804 (2005); Median rent: $348 per month (2000); Median age of housing: 45 years (2000).
Transportation: Commute to work: 94.5% car, 0.5% public transportation, 2.5% walk, 0.0% work from home (2000); Travel time to work: 24.4% less than 15 minutes, 24.4% 15 to 30 minutes, 30.8% 30 to 45 minutes, 8.0% 45 to 60 minutes, 12.4% 60 minutes or more (2000)

GLOUSTER (village).
Covers a land area of 1.341 square miles and a water area of 0 square miles. Located at 39.50° N. Lat.; 82.08° W. Long. Elevation is 700 feet.
Population: 2,037 (1990); 1,972 (2000); 2,165 (2005); 2,326 (2010 projected); Race: 96.1% White, 0.9% Black, 0.0% Asian, 1.2% Hispanic of any race (2005); Density: 1,614.9 persons per square mile (2005); Average household size: 2.46 (2005); Median age: 32.1 (2005); Males per 100 females: 91.3 (2005); Marriage status: 27.4% never married, 49.9% now married, 10.8% widowed, 11.9% divorced (2000); Foreign born: 0.3% (2000); Ancestry (includes multiple ancestries): 14.3% Irish, 12.5% German, 12.3% United States or American, 10.3% English, 7.7% Other groups (2000).
Economy: Employment by occupation: 7.5% management, 14.3% professional, 23.6% services, 19.8% sales, 0.5% farming, 13.8% construction, 20.4% production (2000).
Income: Per capita income: $14,143 (2005); Median household income: $27,904 (2005); Average household income: $34,835 (2005); Percent of households with income of $100,000 or more: 3.6% (2005); Poverty rate: 28.2% (2000).
Education: Percent of population age 25 and over with: High school diploma (including GED) or higher: 71.2% (2005); Bachelor's degree or higher: 5.4% (2005); Master's degree or higher: 1.9% (2005).

School District(s)
Trimble Local SD (PK-12)
    2003-04 Enrollment: 1,071 . . . . (740) 593-8001
Housing: Homeownership rate: 67.8% (2005); Median home value: $54,911 (2005); Median rent: $298 per month (2000); Median age of housing: 60+ years (2000).
Transportation: Commute to work: 96.2% car, 0.5% public transportation, 1.1% walk, 2.2% work from home (2000); Travel time to work: 18.8% less than 15 minutes, 31.6% 15 to 30 minutes, 25.0% 30 to 45 minutes, 6.7% 45 to 60 minutes, 17.9% 60 minutes or more (2000)

GUYSVILLE (unincorporated postal area, zip code 45735).
Covers a land area of 51.112 square miles and a water area of 0.006 square miles. Located at 39.26° N. Lat.; 81.93° W. Long. Elevation is 652 feet.
History: Guysville developed as a coal-mining center.
Population: 1,692 (2000); Race: 97.1% White, 0.9% Black, 0.5% Asian, 2.0% Hispanic of any race (2000); Density: 33.1 persons per square mile (2000); Age: 25.1% under 18, 13.0% over 64 (2000); Marriage status: 20.1% never married, 64.0% now married, 5.6% widowed, 10.3% divorced (2000); Foreign born: 1.2% (2000); Ancestry (includes multiple ancestries): 20.4% United States or American, 18.3% English, 15.1% German, 13.9% Irish, 4.2% Other groups (2000).
Economy: Employment by occupation: 10.6% management, 13.1% professional, 17.4% services, 24.8% sales, 0.0% farming, 14.7% construction, 19.4% production (2000).
Income: Per capita income: $13,460 (2000); Median household income: $28,580 (2000); Poverty rate: 23.1% (2000).
Education: Percent of population age 25 and over with: High school diploma (including GED) or higher: 75.6% (2000); Bachelor's degree or higher: 9.3% (2000).
Housing: Homeownership rate: 85.5% (2000); Median home value: $68,300 (2000); Median rent: $268 per month (2000); Median age of housing: 22 years (2000).
Transportation: Commute to work: 89.8% car, 1.1% public transportation, 0.0% walk, 6.7% work from home (2000); Travel time to work: 6.0% less than 15 minutes, 34.9% 15 to 30 minutes, 29.8% 30 to 45 minutes, 14.4% 45 to 60 minutes, 15.0% 60 minutes or more (2000)

JACKSONVILLE (village).
Covers a land area of 0.257 square miles and a water area of 0 square miles. Located at 39.47° N. Lat.; 82.08° W. Long. Elevation is 700 feet.
Population: 544 (1990); 544 (2000); 505 (2005); 499 (2010 projected); Race: 97.4% White, 0.0% Black, 0.0% Asian, 0.4% Hispanic of any race (2005); Density: 1,966.3 persons per square mile (2005); Average household size: 2.40 (2005); Median age: 36.9 (2005); Males per 100 females: 84.3 (2005); Marriage status: 21.5% never married, 57.0% now married, 11.7% widowed, 9.8% divorced (2000); Foreign born: 0.2% (2000); Ancestry (includes multiple ancestries): 14.1% United States or American, 13.2% Irish, 10.5% Other groups, 8.8% German, 5.9% English (2000).
Economy: In coal mining area. Employment by occupation: 6.8% management, 9.7% professional, 25.6% services, 22.2% sales, 1.0% farming, 13.5% construction, 21.3% production (2000).
Income: Per capita income: $15,163 (2005); Median household income: $26,563 (2005); Average household income: $36,464 (2005); Percent of households with income of $100,000 or more: 4.8% (2005); Poverty rate: 24.5% (2000).
Education: Percent of population age 25 and over with: High school diploma (including GED) or higher: 77.2% (2005); Bachelor's degree or higher: 0.6% (2005); Master's degree or higher: 0.0% (2005).
Housing: Homeownership rate: 75.2% (2005); Median home value: $49,444 (2005); Median rent: $335 per month (2000); Median age of housing: 60+ years (2000).
Transportation: Commute to work: 95.5% car, 0.0% public transportation, 2.0% walk, 2.5% work from home (2000); Travel time to work: 18.3% less than 15 minutes, 39.6% 15 to 30 minutes, 25.9% 30 to 45 minutes, 6.6% 45 to 60 minutes, 9.6% 60 minutes or more (2000)

MILLFIELD (unincorporated postal area, zip code 45761).
Covers a land area of 33.193 square miles and a water area of 0.010 square miles. Located at 39.43° N. Lat.; 82.10° W. Long. Elevation is 678 feet.
History: Millfield, a coal town, was the scene of a mine disaster in 1930 when Mine No. 6 of the Sunday Creek Coal Company was engulfed in flames.
Population: 1,773 (2000); Race: 98.9% White, 0.0% Black, 0.3% Asian, 0.5% Hispanic of any race (2000); Density: 53.4 persons per square mile (2000); Age: 29.0% under 18, 8.0% over 64 (2000); Marriage status: 32.0% never married, 51.1% now married, 7.5% widowed, 9.4% divorced (2000); Foreign born: 0.5% (2000); Ancestry (includes multiple ancestries): 18.6% German, 12.4% United States or American, 11.5% Irish, 8.4% English, 5.3% Other groups (2000).
Economy: Employment by occupation: 9.3% management, 10.1% professional, 32.0% services, 16.1% sales, 2.1% farming, 13.3% construction, 17.2% production (2000).
Income: Per capita income: $12,565 (2000); Median household income: $27,083 (2000); Poverty rate: 19.4% (2000).
Education: Percent of population age 25 and over with: High school diploma (including GED) or higher: 78.5% (2000); Bachelor's degree or higher: 11.5% (2000).
Housing: Homeownership rate: 80.6% (2000); Median home value: $72,500 (2000); Median rent: $325 per month (2000); Median age of housing: 25 years (2000).
Transportation: Commute to work: 96.1% car, 0.0% public transportation, 1.0% walk, 3.0% work from home (2000); Travel time to work: 25.9% less than 15 minutes, 42.4% 15 to 30 minutes, 8.8% 30 to 45 minutes, 8.4% 45 to 60 minutes, 14.5% 60 minutes or more (2000)

NELSONVILLE (city).
Covers a land area of 4.972 square miles and a water area of 0 square miles. Located at 39.45° N. Lat.; 82.22° W. Long. Elevation is 680 feet.

History: First called Englishtown, the name was changed in 1824 to Nelsonville, in honor of Daniel Nelson, an enterprising citizen. Nelsonville developed as a coal town.
Population: 4,914 (1990); 5,230 (2000); 5,327 (2005); 5,459 (2010 projected); Race: 95.3% White, 2.2% Black, 0.4% Asian, 1.3% Hispanic of any race (2005); Density: 1,071.4 persons per square mile (2005); Average household size: 2.51 (2005); Median age: 29.8 (2005); Males per 100 females: 111.1 (2005); Marriage status: 38.6% never married, 42.8% now married, 7.4% widowed, 11.1% divorced (2000); Foreign born: 2.2% (2000); Ancestry (includes multiple ancestries): 15.7% German, 14.5% United States or American, 11.2% Irish, 11.0% Other groups, 10.7% English (2000).
Economy: Employment by occupation: 8.8% management, 10.1% professional, 28.5% services, 29.3% sales, 1.2% farming, 11.6% construction, 10.5% production (2000).
Income: Per capita income: $12,428 (2005); Median household income: $22,651 (2005); Average household income: $29,777 (2005); Percent of households with income of $100,000 or more: 3.3% (2005); Poverty rate: 33.9% (2000).
Education: Percent of population age 25 and over with: High school diploma (including GED) or higher: 73.2% (2005); Bachelor's degree or higher: 7.2% (2005); Master's degree or higher: 3.0% (2005).

School District(s)
Nelsonville-York City SD (PK-12)
   2003-04 Enrollment: 1,330 . . . . (740) 753-4441
Tri-County Joint Vocational SD (06-12)
   2003-04 Enrollment: n/a . . . . (740) 753-3511

Two-year College(s)
Hocking College (Public)
   Fall 2004 Enrollment: 4,458 . . . . (740) 753-3591
   2005-06 Tuition: In-state $3,348; Out-of-state $6,696
Tri-County Adult Career Center (Public)
   Fall 2004 Enrollment: 43 . . . . (740) 753-5464

Housing: Homeownership rate: 49.3% (2005); Median home value: $69,816 (2005); Median rent: $301 per month (2000); Median age of housing: 40 years (2000).
Hospitals: Doctors Hospital of Nelsonville (50 beds)
Safety: Violent crime rate: 56.4 per 10,000 population; Property crime rate: 502.4 per 10,000 population (2004).
Transportation: Commute to work: 88.3% car, 0.3% public transportation, 7.9% walk, 2.5% work from home (2000); Travel time to work: 39.8% less than 15 minutes, 34.0% 15 to 30 minutes, 11.6% 30 to 45 minutes, 4.4% 45 to 60 minutes, 10.2% 60 minutes or more (2000)

NEW MARSHFIELD (unincorporated postal area, zip code 45766). Covers a land area of 30.325 square miles and a water area of 0.017 square miles. Located at 39.32° N. Lat.; 82.25° W. Long. Elevation is 840 feet.
Population: 1,386 (2000); Race: 97.7% White, 0.0% Black, 1.4% Asian, 0.0% Hispanic of any race (2000); Density: 45.7 persons per square mile (2000); Age: 25.9% under 18, 9.7% over 64 (2000); Marriage status: 22.0% never married, 58.4% now married, 5.3% widowed, 14.3% divorced (2000); Foreign born: 1.0% (2000); Ancestry (includes multiple ancestries): 23.4% German, 19.7% Irish, 13.4% English, 9.2% United States or American, 7.4% Other groups (2000).
Economy: Employment by occupation: 1.4% management, 22.3% professional, 20.0% services, 24.3% sales, 0.0% farming, 16.5% construction, 15.5% production (2000).
Income: Per capita income: $15,285 (2000); Median household income: $40,491 (2000); Poverty rate: 14.1% (2000).
Education: Percent of population age 25 and over with: High school diploma (including GED) or higher: 80.6% (2000); Bachelor's degree or higher: 15.2% (2000).

School District(s)
Alexander Local SD (PK-12)
   2003-04 Enrollment: 1,679 . . . . (740) 698-8831

Housing: Homeownership rate: 78.8% (2000); Median home value: $55,000 (2000); Median rent: $276 per month (2000); Median age of housing: 25 years (2000).
Transportation: Commute to work: 93.8% car, 0.0% public transportation, 2.6% walk, 3.6% work from home (2000); Travel time to work: 14.8% less than 15 minutes, 64.6% 15 to 30 minutes, 8.5% 30 to 45 minutes, 5.5% 45 to 60 minutes, 6.6% 60 minutes or more (2000)

SHADE (unincorporated postal area, zip code 45776). Covers a land area of 19.470 square miles and a water area of 0 square miles. Located at 39.19° N. Lat.; 82.01° W. Long. Elevation is 820 feet.
Population: 798 (2000); Race: 96.6% White, 0.6% Black, 0.0% Asian, 0.0% Hispanic of any race (2000); Density: 41.0 persons per square mile (2000); Age: 26.4% under 18, 13.5% over 64 (2000); Marriage status: 14.0% never married, 59.1% now married, 9.7% widowed, 17.2% divorced (2000); Foreign born: 0.0% (2000); Ancestry (includes multiple ancestries): 20.8% Irish, 17.8% German, 13.5% Other groups, 13.4% English, 12.1% United States or American (2000).
Economy: Employment by occupation: 12.6% management, 16.7% professional, 23.6% services, 18.9% sales, 0.0% farming, 10.1% construction, 18.2% production (2000).
Income: Per capita income: $14,626 (2000); Median household income: $29,688 (2000); Poverty rate: 14.3% (2000).
Education: Percent of population age 25 and over with: High school diploma (including GED) or higher: 74.4% (2000); Bachelor's degree or higher: 12.2% (2000).

School District(s)
Alexander Local SD (PK-12)
   2003-04 Enrollment: 1,679 . . . . (740) 698-8831

Housing: Homeownership rate: 88.8% (2000); Median home value: $76,700 (2000); Median rent: $325 per month (2000); Median age of housing: 28 years (2000).
Transportation: Commute to work: 92.8% car, 2.8% public transportation, 0.0% walk, 4.4% work from home (2000); Travel time to work: 4.6% less than 15 minutes, 53.9% 15 to 30 minutes, 26.0% 30 to 45 minutes, 4.9% 45 to 60 minutes, 10.5% 60 minutes or more (2000)

STEWART (unincorporated postal area, zip code 45778). Covers a land area of 28.571 square miles and a water area of 0 square miles. Located at 39.34° N. Lat.; 81.88° W. Long. Elevation is 667 feet.
Population: 960 (2000); Race: 82.8% White, 7.5% Black, 1.4% Asian, 3.1% Hispanic of any race (2000); Density: 33.6 persons per square mile (2000); Age: 35.1% under 18, 4.7% over 64 (2000); Marriage status: 22.9% never married, 64.8% now married, 3.1% widowed, 9.2% divorced (2000); Foreign born: 1.4% (2000); Ancestry (includes multiple ancestries): 20.7% Other groups, 14.1% German, 11.8% Irish, 8.3% United States or American, 4.7% Scottish (2000).
Economy: Employment by occupation: 8.5% management, 10.7% professional, 17.7% services, 26.4% sales, 1.7% farming, 11.4% construction, 23.6% production (2000).
Income: Per capita income: $15,314 (2000); Median household income: $34,063 (2000); Poverty rate: 20.1% (2000).
Education: Percent of population age 25 and over with: High school diploma (including GED) or higher: 74.6% (2000); Bachelor's degree or higher: 8.5% (2000).

School District(s)
Federal Hocking Local SD (PK-12)
   2003-04 Enrollment: 1,422 . . . . (740) 662-6691

Housing: Homeownership rate: 85.5% (2000); Median home value: $63,000 (2000); Median rent: $420 per month (2000); Median age of housing: 26 years (2000).
Transportation: Commute to work: 92.0% car, 0.0% public transportation, 2.9% walk, 1.6% work from home (2000); Travel time to work: 17.9% less than 15 minutes, 42.1% 15 to 30 minutes, 22.0% 30 to 45 minutes, 8.4% 45 to 60 minutes, 9.5% 60 minutes or more (2000)

THE PLAINS (CDP). Covers a land area of 2.297 square miles and a water area of 0 square miles. Located at 39.37° N. Lat.; 82.13° W. Long. Elevation is 725 feet.
Population: 2,523 (1990); 2,931 (2000); 3,250 (2005); 3,547 (2010 projected); Race: 93.2% White, 2.9% Black, 1.5% Asian, 0.8% Hispanic of any race (2005); Density: 1,414.7 persons per square mile (2005); Average household size: 2.37 (2005); Median age: 35.5 (2005); Males per 100 females: 83.1 (2005); Marriage status: 25.7% never married, 56.9% now married, 6.4% widowed, 11.1% divorced (2000); Foreign born: 1.3% (2000); Ancestry (includes multiple ancestries): 14.5% German, 14.4% Irish, 11.3% United States or American, 10.7% English, 7.6% Other groups (2000).
Economy: Employment by occupation: 14.6% management, 23.4% professional, 17.2% services, 28.8% sales, 0.0% farming, 10.0% construction, 6.0% production (2000).

Income: Per capita income: $19,137 (2005); Median household income: $33,164 (2005); Average household income: $43,959 (2005); Percent of households with income of $100,000 or more: 6.4% (2005); Poverty rate: 17.7% (2000).
Education: Percent of population age 25 and over with: High school diploma (including GED) or higher: 86.6% (2005); Bachelor's degree or higher: 25.7% (2005); Master's degree or higher: 9.4% (2005).

School District(s)
Athens City SD (PK-12)
    2003-04 Enrollment: 2,975 . . . . (740) 797-4544

Housing: Homeownership rate: 55.1% (2005); Median home value: $98,833 (2005); Median rent: $402 per month (2000); Median age of housing: 21 years (2000).
Transportation: Commute to work: 94.4% car, 0.0% public transportation, 1.9% walk, 3.7% work from home (2000); Travel time to work: 70.5% less than 15 minutes, 22.0% 15 to 30 minutes, 1.5% 30 to 45 minutes, 2.1% 45 to 60 minutes, 3.9% 60 minutes or more (2000)

TRIMBLE (village). Covers a land area of 0.653 square miles and a water area of 0 square miles. Located at 39.48° N. Lat.; 82.07° W. Long. Elevation is 690 feet.
Population: 441 (1990); 466 (2000); 472 (2005); 483 (2010 projected); Race: 98.5% White, 0.0% Black, 0.2% Asian, 0.0% Hispanic of any race (2005); Density: 722.3 persons per square mile (2005); Average household size: 2.62 (2005); Median age: 32.1 (2005); Males per 100 females: 100.0 (2005); Marriage status: 24.0% never married, 54.9% now married, 7.2% widowed, 13.9% divorced (2000); Foreign born: 0.0% (2000); Ancestry (includes multiple ancestries): 19.4% United States or American, 11.2% English, 9.7% German, 9.1% Other groups, 5.7% Irish (2000).
Economy: Employment by occupation: 5.2% management, 12.6% professional, 17.8% services, 21.8% sales, 0.0% farming, 19.5% construction, 23.0% production (2000).
Income: Per capita income: $15,344 (2005); Median household income: $36,829 (2005); Average household income: $40,236 (2005); Percent of households with income of $100,000 or more: 3.9% (2005); Poverty rate: 26.1% (2000).
Education: Percent of population age 25 and over with: High school diploma (including GED) or higher: 74.6% (2005); Bachelor's degree or higher: 2.4% (2005); Master's degree or higher: 0.0% (2005).
Housing: Homeownership rate: 75.0% (2005); Median home value: $48,043 (2005); Median rent: $292 per month (2000); Median age of housing: 56 years (2000).
Transportation: Commute to work: 85.5% car, 0.0% public transportation, 6.9% walk, 5.7% work from home (2000); Travel time to work: 28.0% less than 15 minutes, 31.3% 15 to 30 minutes, 16.0% 30 to 45 minutes, 5.3% 45 to 60 minutes, 19.3% 60 minutes or more (2000)

Auglaize County

Located in western Ohio; drained by the Auglaize and St. Marys Rivers; includes part of Grand Lake. Covers a land area of 401.25 square miles, a water area of 0.47 square miles, and is located in the Eastern Time Zone. The county government was organized in 1848. County seat is Wapakoneta.

Auglaize County is part of the Wapakoneta, OH Micropolitan Statistical Area. The entire metro area includes: Auglaize County, OH

Population: 44,585 (1990); 46,611 (2000); 46,802 (2005); 46,984 (2010 projected); Race: 98.0% White, 0.2% Black, 0.5% Asian, 0.8% Hispanic of any race (2005); Density: 116.6 persons per square mile (2005); Average household size: 2.64 (2005); Median age: 37.7 (2005); Males per 100 females: 96.8 (2005).
Religion: Five largest groups: 26.3% Catholic Church, 10.0% United Church of Christ, 9.0% The United Methodist Church, 6.2% Evangelical Lutheran Church in America, 2.2% The Christian and Missionary Alliance (2000).
Economy: Unemployment rate: 4.5% (2005); Total civilian labor force: 26,219 (2005); Leading industries: 41.1% manufacturing; 11.7% retail trade; 11.4% health care and social assistance (2004); Farms: 1,020 totaling 217,916 acres (2002); Companies that employ 500 or more persons: 4 (2004); Companies that employ 100 to 499 persons: 18 (2004); Companies that employ less than 100 persons: 1,004 (2004); Black-owned businesses: n/a (2002); Hispanic-owned businesses: n/a (2002); Women-owned businesses: 753 (2002); Retail sales per capita: $11,460 (2006). Single-family building permits issued: 174 (2005); Multi-family building permits issued: 16 (2005).
Income: Per capita income: $22,267 (2005); Median household income: $47,910 (2005); Average household income: $58,220 (2005); Percent of households with income of $100,000 or more: 11.8% (2005); Poverty rate: 6.7% (2003); Bankruptcy rate: 7.98% (2005).
Education: Percent of population age 25 and over with: High school diploma (including GED) or higher: 85.8% (2005); Bachelor's degree or higher: 13.5% (2005); Master's degree or higher: 4.7% (2005).
Housing: Homeownership rate: 78.2% (2005); Median home value: $112,883 (2005); Median rent: $360 per month (2000); Median age of housing: 41 years (2000).
Health: Birth rate: 130.5 per 10,000 population (2004); Death rate: 92.6 per 10,000 population (2004); Age-adjusted cancer mortality rate: 199.2 deaths per 100,000 population (2002); Number of physicians: 12.6 per 10,000 population (2004); Hospital beds: 19.3 per 10,000 population (2003); Hospital admissions: 852.1 per 10,000 population (2003).
Elections: 2004 Presidential election results: 73.9% Bush, 25.6% Kerry, 0.0% Nader, 0.3% Badnarik.
National and State Parks: Fort Amanda State Park
Additional Information Contacts

Auglaize County Government . . . . (419) 739-6710
   http://www.auglaizecounty.org/
New Bremen Chamber of Commerce . . . . (419) 629-0313
   http://www.swauglaizechamber.com
Saint Mary's Chamber of Commerce. . . . . (419) 394-4611
   http://www.bright.net/~stmarys
Village of Minster . . . . (419) 628-3497
   http://www.minsteroh.com
Village of New Bremen . . . . (419) 629-2447
   http://www.newbremen.com
Village of New Knoxville. . . . . (419) 753-2160
   http://www.newknoxville.com
Wapakoneta Chamber of Commerce . . . . (419) 738-2911
   http://www.wapakoneta.com

Auglaize County Communities

BUCKLAND (village). Covers a land area of 0.256 square miles and a water area of 0 square miles. Located at 40.62° N. Lat.; 84.26° W. Long. Elevation is 855 feet.
Population: 239 (1990); 255 (2000); 237 (2005); 233 (2010 projected); Race: 97.9% White, 0.0% Black, 0.0% Asian, 0.0% Hispanic of any race (2005); Density: 925.2 persons per square mile (2005); Average household size: 2.39 (2005); Median age: 33.2 (2005); Males per 100 females: 95.9 (2005); Marriage status: 18.6% never married, 65.0% now married, 6.6% widowed, 9.8% divorced (2000); Foreign born: 0.8% (2000); Ancestry (includes multiple ancestries): 46.9% German, 18.5% United States or American, 8.2% Irish, 7.0% English, 5.8% Other groups (2000).
Economy: Employment by occupation: 8.7% management, 9.4% professional, 18.1% services, 24.4% sales, 2.4% farming, 7.9% construction, 29.1% production (2000).
Income: Per capita income: $18,281 (2005); Median household income: $36,500 (2005); Average household income: $43,763 (2005); Percent of households with income of $100,000 or more: 5.1% (2005); Poverty rate: 4.9% (2000).
Education: Percent of population age 25 and over with: High school diploma (including GED) or higher: 89.5% (2005); Bachelor's degree or higher: 2.0% (2005); Master's degree or higher: 0.7% (2005).

School District(s)
Wapakoneta City City SD (PK-12)
    2003-04 Enrollment: 3,160 . . . . (419) 739-2900

Housing: Homeownership rate: 84.8% (2005); Median home value: $68,889 (2005); Median rent: $250 per month (2000); Median age of housing: 60+ years (2000).
Transportation: Commute to work: 90.5% car, 0.0% public transportation, 7.1% walk, 2.4% work from home (2000); Travel time to work: 26.8% less than 15 minutes, 51.2% 15 to 30 minutes, 17.9% 30 to 45 minutes, 3.3% 45 to 60 minutes, 0.8% 60 minutes or more (2000)

CRIDERSVILLE (village). Covers a land area of 0.912 square miles and a water area of 0 square miles. Located at 40.65° N. Lat.; 84.14° W. Long. Elevation is 890 feet.
Population: 1,930 (1990); 1,817 (2000); 1,784 (2005); 1,738 (2010 projected); Race: 96.3% White, 0.2% Black, 0.0% Asian, 2.9% Hispanic of

any race (2005); Density: 1,956.6 persons per square mile (2005); Average household size: 2.44 (2005); Median age: 36.7 (2005); Males per 100 females: 85.6 (2005); Marriage status: 20.2% never married, 57.8% now married, 9.7% widowed, 12.3% divorced (2000); Foreign born: 0.8% (2000); Ancestry (includes multiple ancestries): 33.7% German, 14.9% United States or American, 14.2% Irish, 10.6% Other groups, 6.4% English (2000).
Economy: Single-family building permits issued: 0 (2005); Multi-family building permits issued: 0 (2005); Employment by occupation: 6.4% management, 13.2% professional, 15.6% services, 24.8% sales, 0.0% farming, 8.7% construction, 31.2% production (2000).
Income: Per capita income: $16,815 (2005); Median household income: $34,929 (2005); Average household income: $40,468 (2005); Percent of households with income of $100,000 or more: 3.7% (2005); Poverty rate: 12.3% (2000).
Education: Percent of population age 25 and over with: High school diploma (including GED) or higher: 79.3% (2005); Bachelor's degree or higher: 6.2% (2005); Master's degree or higher: 1.7% (2005).

School District(s)
Wapakoneta City City SD (PK-12)
    2003-04 Enrollment: 3,160 . . . . (419) 739-2900
Housing: Homeownership rate: 74.5% (2005); Median home value: $85,798 (2005); Median rent: $324 per month (2000); Median age of housing: 35 years (2000).
Transportation: Commute to work: 95.1% car, 0.0% public transportation, 3.0% walk, 1.6% work from home (2000); Travel time to work: 33.0% less than 15 minutes, 47.2% 15 to 30 minutes, 15.5% 30 to 45 minutes, 2.6% 45 to 60 minutes, 1.6% 60 minutes or more (2000)

MINSTER (village). Covers a land area of 1.878 square miles and a water area of 0 square miles. Located at 40.39° N. Lat.; 84.37° W. Long. Elevation is 967 feet.
History: Incorporated 1833.
Population: 2,733 (1990); 2,794 (2000); 2,774 (2005); 2,776 (2010 projected); Race: 99.7% White, 0.0% Black, 0.1% Asian, 0.2% Hispanic of any race (2005); Density: 1,477.4 persons per square mile (2005); Average household size: 2.74 (2005); Median age: 37.8 (2005); Males per 100 females: 94.5 (2005); Marriage status: 22.3% never married, 68.5% now married, 6.4% widowed, 2.8% divorced (2000); Foreign born: 0.7% (2000); Ancestry (includes multiple ancestries): 75.4% German, 7.2% Irish, 6.6% French (except Basque), 6.4% United States or American, 1.8% Other groups (2000).
Economy: Single-family building permits issued: 6 (2005); Multi-family building permits issued: 0 (2005); Employment by occupation: 12.2% management, 24.8% professional, 11.3% services, 20.9% sales, 0.2% farming, 5.2% construction, 25.4% production (2000).
Income: Per capita income: $25,887 (2005); Median household income: $63,133 (2005); Average household income: $70,565 (2005); Percent of households with income of $100,000 or more: 20.2% (2005); Poverty rate: 3.6% (2000).
Education: Percent of population age 25 and over with: High school diploma (including GED) or higher: 88.0% (2005); Bachelor's degree or higher: 22.3% (2005); Master's degree or higher: 8.5% (2005).

School District(s)
Minster Community School
    2003-04 Enrollment: n/a . . . . (419) 628-3397
Minster Local SD (PK-12)
    2003-04 Enrollment: 926 . . . . (419) 628-3397
Housing: Homeownership rate: 83.8% (2005); Median home value: $140,987 (2005); Median rent: $356 per month (2000); Median age of housing: 39 years (2000).
Newspapers: The Community Post (General - Circulation 2,500)
Transportation: Commute to work: 92.3% car, 0.0% public transportation, 3.1% walk, 1.9% work from home (2000); Travel time to work: 59.6% less than 15 minutes, 25.2% 15 to 30 minutes, 11.9% 30 to 45 minutes, 1.2% 45 to 60 minutes, 2.2% 60 minutes or more (2000)
Additional Information Contacts
Village of Minster . . . . (419) 628-3497
    http://www.minsteroh.com

NEW BREMEN (village). Covers a land area of 2.062 square miles and a water area of 0 square miles. Located at 40.43° N. Lat.; 84.38° W. Long. Elevation is 941 feet.
History: Incorporated 1833.
Population: 2,797 (1990); 2,909 (2000); 2,882 (2005); 2,883 (2010 projected); Race: 98.0% White, 0.0% Black, 0.7% Asian, 0.4% Hispanic of any race (2005); Density: 1,397.4 persons per square mile (2005); Average household size: 2.67 (2005); Median age: 35.5 (2005); Males per 100 females: 97.3 (2005); Marriage status: 21.7% never married, 65.5% now married, 6.2% widowed, 6.5% divorced (2000); Foreign born: 0.9% (2000); Ancestry (includes multiple ancestries): 66.0% German, 9.2% Irish, 8.8% United States or American, 4.8% English, 4.6% Other groups (2000).
Economy: Agriculture: dairy products. Manufacturing: rubber goods, machinery. Single-family building permits issued: 17 (2005); Multi-family building permits issued: 0 (2005); Employment by occupation: 9.2% management, 18.9% professional, 12.9% services, 20.9% sales, 0.0% farming, 7.3% construction, 30.9% production (2000).
Income: Per capita income: $22,706 (2005); Median household income: $53,977 (2005); Average household income: $60,537 (2005); Percent of households with income of $100,000 or more: 11.7% (2005); Poverty rate: 1.4% (2000).
Education: Percent of population age 25 and over with: High school diploma (including GED) or higher: 93.2% (2005); Bachelor's degree or higher: 17.9% (2005); Master's degree or higher: 5.8% (2005).

School District(s)
New Bremen Local SD (PK-12)
    2003-04 Enrollment: 992 . . . . (419) 629-8606
Housing: Homeownership rate: 78.8% (2005); Median home value: $128,818 (2005); Median rent: $399 per month (2000); Median age of housing: 43 years (2000).
Transportation: Commute to work: 89.0% car, 0.0% public transportation, 3.8% walk, 2.5% work from home (2000); Travel time to work: 65.4% less than 15 minutes, 23.9% 15 to 30 minutes, 6.1% 30 to 45 minutes, 2.5% 45 to 60 minutes, 2.2% 60 minutes or more (2000)
Additional Information Contacts
New Bremen Chamber of Commerce . . . . (419) 629-0313
    http://www.swauglaizechamber.com
Village of New Bremen . . . . (419) 629-2447
    http://www.newbremen.com

NEW KNOXVILLE (village). Covers a land area of 0.785 square miles and a water area of 0 square miles. Located at 40.49° N. Lat.; 84.31° W. Long. Elevation is 903 feet.
Population: 854 (1990); 891 (2000); 895 (2005); 896 (2010 projected); Race: 98.2% White, 0.2% Black, 0.6% Asian, 0.1% Hispanic of any race (2005); Density: 1,140.5 persons per square mile (2005); Average household size: 2.51 (2005); Median age: 36.0 (2005); Males per 100 females: 92.5 (2005); Marriage status: 26.6% never married, 60.4% now married, 5.8% widowed, 7.2% divorced (2000); Foreign born: 0.4% (2000); Ancestry (includes multiple ancestries): 64.0% German, 11.4% Irish, 7.0% English, 5.4% Other groups, 4.2% United States or American (2000).
Economy: Lumber, clay products. Single-family building permits issued: 2 (2005); Multi-family building permits issued: 0 (2005); Employment by occupation: 6.6% management, 17.5% professional, 11.0% services, 26.1% sales, 1.6% farming, 10.4% construction, 26.7% production (2000).
Income: Per capita income: $22,045 (2005); Median household income: $47,885 (2005); Average household income: $55,421 (2005); Percent of households with income of $100,000 or more: 11.2% (2005); Poverty rate: 4.7% (2000).
Education: Percent of population age 25 and over with: High school diploma (including GED) or higher: 93.7% (2005); Bachelor's degree or higher: 13.3% (2005); Master's degree or higher: 5.8% (2005).

School District(s)
New Knoxville Local SD (PK-12)
    2003-04 Enrollment: 459 . . . . (419) 753-2431
Housing: Homeownership rate: 75.0% (2005); Median home value: $94,079 (2005); Median rent: $363 per month (2000); Median age of housing: 50 years (2000).
Transportation: Commute to work: 87.8% car, 0.0% public transportation, 7.4% walk, 3.7% work from home (2000); Travel time to work: 54.6% less than 15 minutes, 34.5% 15 to 30 minutes, 5.8% 30 to 45 minutes, 2.1% 45 to 60 minutes, 3.0% 60 minutes or more (2000)
Additional Information Contacts
Village of New Knoxville . . . . (419) 753-2160
    http://www.newknoxville.com

SAINT MARYS (city). Covers a land area of 4.330 square miles and a water area of 0.032 square miles. Located at 40.54° N. Lat.; 84.39° W. Long. Elevation is 871 feet.

History: St. Marys began as a trading post, and was organized as a town after 1818. It was called Girty's Town when it served as headquarters and supply depot for Generals Harmar, Wayne, and Harrison. Later, its location on the Miami & Erie Canal made it a shipping center for farm produce, which arrived in St. Marys by boat and was transferred to wagons for the overland haul to the Ohio River.
Population: 8,601 (1990); 8,342 (2000); 8,239 (2005); 8,173 (2010 projected); Race: 97.2% White, 0.3% Black, 1.3% Asian, 0.5% Hispanic of any race (2005); Density: 1,902.9 persons per square mile (2005); Average household size: 2.56 (2005); Median age: 36.1 (2005); Males per 100 females: 94.5 (2005); Marriage status: 20.6% never married, 58.6% now married, 10.2% widowed, 10.6% divorced (2000); Foreign born: 2.6% (2000); Ancestry (includes multiple ancestries): 45.8% German, 13.7% Irish, 8.4% Other groups, 8.2% United States or American, 5.5% English (2000).
Economy: Single-family building permits issued: 19 (2005); Multi-family building permits issued: 12 (2005); Employment by occupation: 8.3% management, 17.6% professional, 16.6% services, 16.8% sales, 0.4% farming, 6.6% construction, 33.7% production (2000).
Income: Per capita income: $18,856 (2005); Median household income: $41,645 (2005); Average household income: $47,842 (2005); Percent of households with income of $100,000 or more: 6.3% (2005); Poverty rate: 7.3% (2000).
Taxes: Total city taxes per capita: $589 (2004); City property taxes per capita: $137 (2004).
Education: Percent of population age 25 and over with: High school diploma (including GED) or higher: 82.0% (2005); Bachelor's degree or higher: 11.8% (2005); Master's degree or higher: 4.1% (2005).

School District(s)
Saint Marys City SD (PK-12)
   2003-04 Enrollment: 2,591 . . . . (419) 394-4312

Housing: Homeownership rate: 70.7% (2005); Median home value: $91,036 (2005); Median rent: $364 per month (2000); Median age of housing: 47 years (2000).
Hospitals: Joint Township District Memorial Hospital (130 beds)
Newspapers: The Evening Leader (Circulation 5,412)
Transportation: Commute to work: 94.3% car, 1.0% public transportation, 1.9% walk, 1.0% work from home (2000); Travel time to work: 53.8% less than 15 minutes, 26.2% 15 to 30 minutes, 13.2% 30 to 45 minutes, 3.7% 45 to 60 minutes, 3.1% 60 minutes or more (2000)

Additional Information Contacts
Saint Mary's Chamber of Commerce. . . . . (419) 394-4611
http://www.bright.net/~stmarys

UNIOPOLIS (village). Covers a land area of 0.156 square miles and a water area of 0 square miles. Located at 40.60° N. Lat.; 84.08° W. Long. Elevation is 935 feet.
Population: 261 (1990); 256 (2000); 265 (2005); 269 (2010 projected); Race: 99.6% White, 0.0% Black, 0.0% Asian, 1.9% Hispanic of any race (2005); Density: 1,698.0 persons per square mile (2005); Average household size: 2.85 (2005); Median age: 35.3 (2005); Males per 100 females: 110.3 (2005); Marriage status: 11.2% never married, 69.8% now married, 5.6% widowed, 13.4% divorced (2000); Foreign born: 0.8% (2000); Ancestry (includes multiple ancestries): 47.9% German, 13.6% Irish, 13.6% Dutch, 7.6% Other groups, 5.5% French (except Basque) (2000).
Economy: In agricultural area. Employment by occupation: 1.6% management, 11.2% professional, 20.8% services, 18.4% sales, 0.0% farming, 13.6% construction, 34.4% production (2000).
Income: Per capita income: $18,774 (2005); Median household income: $48,929 (2005); Average household income: $53,495 (2005); Percent of households with income of $100,000 or more: 4.3% (2005); Poverty rate: 0.0% (2000).
Education: Percent of population age 25 and over with: High school diploma (including GED) or higher: 70.2% (2005); Bachelor's degree or higher: 5.3% (2005); Master's degree or higher: 4.7% (2005).
Housing: Homeownership rate: 88.2% (2005); Median home value: $73,125 (2005); Median rent: $375 per month (2000); Median age of housing: 60+ years (2000).
Transportation: Commute to work: 96.6% car, 0.0% public transportation, 0.8% walk, 2.5% work from home (2000); Travel time to work: 28.7% less than 15 minutes, 56.5% 15 to 30 minutes, 11.3% 30 to 45 minutes, 3.5% 45 to 60 minutes, 0.0% 60 minutes or more (2000)

WAPAKONETA (city). Covers a land area of 5.657 square miles and a water area of 0.055 square miles. Located at 40.56° N. Lat.; 84.19° W. Long. Elevation is 901 feet.
History: Wapakoneta was platted in 1833 and settled by people of German heritage. Woodworking industries provided the economic base in the late 1800's. The town's name was first Wapaghkonetta, a combination of two Indian names, Wapaugh and Konetta.
Population: 9,559 (1990); 9,474 (2000); 9,401 (2005); 9,335 (2010 projected); Race: 97.9% White, 0.2% Black, 0.4% Asian, 1.0% Hispanic of any race (2005); Density: 1,661.8 persons per square mile (2005); Average household size: 2.45 (2005); Median age: 36.6 (2005); Males per 100 females: 90.5 (2005); Marriage status: 21.6% never married, 54.7% now married, 11.2% widowed, 12.5% divorced (2000); Foreign born: 0.9% (2000); Ancestry (includes multiple ancestries): 43.1% German, 10.6% United States or American, 10.2% Irish, 9.9% English, 6.9% Other groups (2000).
Economy: Single-family building permits issued: 45 (2005); Multi-family building permits issued: 0 (2005); Employment by occupation: 9.5% management, 12.2% professional, 18.5% services, 23.1% sales, 0.3% farming, 10.7% construction, 25.8% production (2000).
Income: Per capita income: $21,595 (2005); Median household income: $42,098 (2005); Average household income: $52,462 (2005); Percent of households with income of $100,000 or more: 8.3% (2005); Poverty rate: 8.9% (2000).
Taxes: Total city taxes per capita: $344 (2004); City property taxes per capita: $47 (2004).
Education: Percent of population age 25 and over with: High school diploma (including GED) or higher: 83.1% (2005); Bachelor's degree or higher: 12.8% (2005); Master's degree or higher: 4.2% (2005).

School District(s)
Auglaize County Educational Academy
   2003-04 Enrollment: n/a
Auglaize County Special Needs School
   2003-04 Enrollment: n/a
Auglaize Educational Service Center (07-12)
   2003-04 Enrollment: n/a . . . . (419) 738-3422
Saint Marys City SD (PK-12)
   2003-04 Enrollment: 2,591 . . . . (419) 394-4312
Wapakoneta City City SD (PK-12)
   2003-04 Enrollment: 3,160 . . . . (419) 739-2900

Housing: Homeownership rate: 69.9% (2005); Median home value: $91,400 (2005); Median rent: $349 per month (2000); Median age of housing: 41 years (2000).
Safety: Violent crime rate: 11.5 per 10,000 population; Property crime rate: 139.5 per 10,000 population (2004).
Newspapers: Shelby County Review (General - Circulation 4,500); Wapakoneta Daily News (Circulation 5,300)
Transportation: Commute to work: 94.9% car, 0.1% public transportation, 2.2% walk, 1.8% work from home (2000); Travel time to work: 49.6% less than 15 minutes, 30.9% 15 to 30 minutes, 15.2% 30 to 45 minutes, 2.5% 45 to 60 minutes, 1.8% 60 minutes or more (2000)

Additional Information Contacts
Wapakoneta Chamber of Commerce . . . . (419) 738-2911
http://www.wapakoneta.com

WAYNESFIELD (village). Covers a land area of 0.706 square miles and a water area of 0 square miles. Located at 40.60° N. Lat.; 83.97° W. Long. Elevation is 1,054 feet.
Population: 851 (1990); 803 (2000); 742 (2005); 732 (2010 projected); Race: 97.3% White, 0.1% Black, 0.0% Asian, 1.6% Hispanic of any race (2005); Density: 1,051.0 persons per square mile (2005); Average household size: 2.56 (2005); Median age: 32.8 (2005); Males per 100 females: 93.7 (2005); Marriage status: 17.9% never married, 62.3% now married, 8.2% widowed, 11.6% divorced (2000); Foreign born: 0.5% (2000); Ancestry (includes multiple ancestries): 32.1% German, 14.4% United States or American, 13.3% Irish, 10.2% English, 5.6% Other groups (2000).
Economy: In agricultural area. Employment by occupation: 11.5% management, 6.8% professional, 19.7% services, 27.1% sales, 0.0% farming, 9.1% construction, 25.9% production (2000).
Income: Per capita income: $16,021 (2005); Median household income: $33,475 (2005); Average household income: $40,991 (2005); Percent of households with income of $100,000 or more: 5.9% (2005); Poverty rate: 10.6% (2000).

Education: Percent of population age 25 and over with: High school diploma (including GED) or higher: 84.5% (2005); Bachelor's degree or higher: 4.9% (2005); Master's degree or higher: 1.6% (2005).

School District(s)

Waynesfield-Goshen Local SD (PK-12)
    2003-04 Enrollment: 636 .... (419) 568-2391

Housing: Homeownership rate: 81.0% (2005); Median home value: $76,316 (2005); Median rent: $333 per month (2000); Median age of housing: 47 years (2000).

Transportation: Commute to work: 92.0% car, 0.0% public transportation, 3.8% walk, 4.1% work from home (2000); Travel time to work: 23.1% less than 15 minutes, 36.0% 15 to 30 minutes, 28.6% 30 to 45 minutes, 6.8% 45 to 60 minutes, 5.5% 60 minutes or more (2000)

Belmont County

Located in eastern Ohio; bounded on the east by the Ohio River and the West Virginia border. Covers a land area of 537.35 square miles, a water area of 4.04 square miles, and is located in the Eastern Time Zone. The county government was organized in 1801. County seat is St. Clairsville.

Belmont County is part of the Wheeling, WV-OH Metropolitan Statistical Area. The entire metro area includes: Belmont County, OH; Marshall County, WV; Ohio County, WV

Weather Station: Barnesville   Elevation: 1,240 feet

	Jan	Feb	Mar	Apr	May	Jun	Jul	Aug	Sep	Oct	Nov	Dec
High	35	38	49	60	70	78	82	81	75	63	51	40
Low	17	19	28	37	47	56	61	59	52	40	32	24
Precip	3.0	2.7	3.5	3.9	4.4	4.9	4.7	3.9	3.5	3.0	3.7	3.2
Snow	11.6	7.6	5.1	1.2	tr	0.0	0.0	tr	0.0	tr	1.7	5.7

High and Low temperatures in degrees Fahrenheit; Precipitation and Snow in inches

Population: 71,074 (1990); 70,226 (2000); 69,510 (2005); 68,758 (2010 projected); Race: 94.8% White, 3.9% Black, 0.3% Asian, 0.4% Hispanic of any race (2005); Density: 129.4 persons per square mile (2005); Average household size: 2.45 (2005); Median age: 41.8 (2005); Males per 100 females: 96.9 (2005).

Religion: Five largest groups: 13.1% Catholic Church, 10.1% The United Methodist Church, 4.9% Presbyterian Church (U.S.A.), 3.0% Christian Churches and Churches of Christ, 2.0% Churches of Christ (2000).

Economy: Unemployment rate: 6.4% (2005); Total civilian labor force: 32,391 (2005); Leading industries: 25.6% retail trade; 20.4% health care and social assistance; 13.7% accommodation & food services (2004); Farms: 753 totaling 141,908 acres (2002); Companies that employ 500 or more persons: 1 (2004); Companies that employ 100 to 499 persons: 35 (2004); Companies that employ less than 100 persons: 1,599 (2004); Black-owned businesses: n/a (2002); Hispanic-owned businesses: n/a (2002); Women-owned businesses: 937 (2002); Retail sales per capita: $16,395 (2006). Single-family building permits issued: 19 (2005); Multi-family building permits issued: 22 (2005).

Income: Per capita income: $18,584 (2005); Median household income: $33,801 (2005); Average household income: $44,351 (2005); Percent of households with income of $100,000 or more: 6.4% (2005); Poverty rate: 14.3% (2003); Bankruptcy rate: 10.10% (2005).

Taxes: Total county taxes per capita: $332 (2004); County property taxes per capita: $159 (2004).

Education: Percent of population age 25 and over with: High school diploma (including GED) or higher: 80.8% (2005); Bachelor's degree or higher: 11.1% (2005); Master's degree or higher: 4.1% (2005).

Housing: Homeownership rate: 75.2% (2005); Median home value: $74,952 (2005); Median rent: $280 per month (2000); Median age of housing: 46 years (2000).

Health: Birth rate: 97.9 per 10,000 population (2004); Death rate: 121.4 per 10,000 population (2004); Age-adjusted cancer mortality rate: 220.1 deaths per 100,000 population (2002); Air Quality Index: 99.2% good, 0.8% moderate, 0.0% unhealthy for sensitive individuals, 0.0% unhealthy (percent of days in 2005); Number of physicians: 13.7 per 10,000 population (2004); Hospital beds: 52.1 per 10,000 population (2003); Hospital admissions: 1,422.2 per 10,000 population (2003).

Elections: 2004 Presidential election results: 46.8% Bush, 52.7% Kerry, 0.0% Nader, 0.3% Badnarik

National and State Parks: Belmont Lake State Reserve

Additional Information Contacts

Belmont County Government .... (740) 699-2155
    http://www.belmontcountyohio.org/
Barnesville Area Chamber of Commerce .... (740) 425-4300
    http://www.barnesvilleohio.com
Bellaire Chamber of Commerce .... (740) 676-9723
    http://www.bellairechamber.com
Brideport Chamber of Commerce .... (740) 635-3377
    http://www.belmontcountyohio.org/connections/community.htm
City of Saint Clairsville .... (740) 695-1410
    http://www.stclairsville.com
Martins Ferry Chamber of Cmmrc .... (740) 633-2565
    http://www.martinsferrychamber.com
Saint Clairsville Chamber of Commerce .... (740) 695-9623
    http://www.stclairsville.com

Belmont County Communities

ALLEDONIA (unincorporated postal area, zip code 43902). Covers a land area of 7.818 square miles and a water area of 0 square miles. Located at 39.89° N. Lat.; 80.97° W. Long. Elevation is 830 feet.

Population: 212 (2000); Race: 100.0% White, 0.0% Black, 0.0% Asian, 0.0% Hispanic of any race (2000); Density: 27.1 persons per square mile (2000); Age: 25.3% under 18, 11.8% over 64 (2000); Marriage status: 17.2% never married, 65.5% now married, 3.4% widowed, 13.8% divorced (2000); Foreign born: 0.0% (2000); Ancestry (includes multiple ancestries): 29.8% English, 10.7% Czech, 9.0% United States or American, 5.1% Polish, 5.1% German (2000).

Economy: Employment by occupation: 5.1% management, 15.4% professional, 0.0% services, 10.3% sales, 0.0% farming, 28.2% construction, 41.0% production (2000).

Income: Per capita income: $16,104 (2000); Median household income: $52,692 (2000); Poverty rate: 20.5% (2000).

Education: Percent of population age 25 and over with: High school diploma (including GED) or higher: 100.0% (2000); Bachelor's degree or higher: 12.7% (2000).

Housing: Homeownership rate: 100.0% (2000); Median home value: $74,200 (2000); Median rent: $n/a per month (2000); Median age of housing: 48 years (2000).

Transportation: Commute to work: 94.9% car, 0.0% public transportation, 0.0% walk, 5.1% work from home (2000); Travel time to work: 0.0% less than 15 minutes, 33.8% 15 to 30 minutes, 25.7% 30 to 45 minutes, 17.6% 45 to 60 minutes, 23.0% 60 minutes or more (2000)

BARNESVILLE (village). Covers a land area of 1.923 square miles and a water area of 0.005 square miles. Located at 39.98° N. Lat.; 81.17° W. Long. Elevation is 1,280 feet.

Population: 4,350 (1990); 4,225 (2000); 4,118 (2005); 4,086 (2010 projected); Race: 98.7% White, 0.5% Black, 0.2% Asian, 0.2% Hispanic of any race (2005); Density: 2,141.0 persons per square mile (2005); Average household size: 2.35 (2005); Median age: 39.7 (2005); Males per 100 females: 83.4 (2005); Marriage status: 25.3% never married, 49.0% now married, 16.3% widowed, 9.4% divorced (2000); Foreign born: 0.9% (2000); Ancestry (includes multiple ancestries): 18.4% German, 16.7% Irish, 15.7% English, 10.6% United States or American, 4.3% Other groups (2000).

Economy: Manufacturing: glass, machinery. Single-family building permits issued: 7 (2005); Multi-family building permits issued: 0 (2005); Employment by occupation: 6.0% management, 14.3% professional, 22.4% services, 22.9% sales, 0.9% farming, 12.5% construction, 21.1% production (2000).

Income: Per capita income: $15,100 (2005); Median household income: $25,979 (2005); Average household income: $34,518 (2005); Percent of households with income of $100,000 or more: 2.5% (2005); Poverty rate: 22.1% (2000).

Education: Percent of population age 25 and over with: High school diploma (including GED) or higher: 77.5% (2005); Bachelor's degree or higher: 6.5% (2005); Master's degree or higher: 3.3% (2005).

School District(s)

Barnesville Ex Vill SD (PK-12)
    2003-04 Enrollment: 1,297 .... (740) 425-3615

Housing: Homeownership rate: 69.6% (2005); Median home value: $61,158 (2005); Median rent: $218 per month (2000); Median age of housing: 58 years (2000).

Hospitals: Barnesville Hospital Association (85 beds)

Newspapers: Barnesville Enterprise (General - Circulation 4,825)

Transportation: Commute to work: 89.1% car, 0.5% public transportation, 4.7% walk, 4.6% work from home (2000); Travel time to work: 43.3% less

than 15 minutes, 21.4% 15 to 30 minutes, 23.5% 30 to 45 minutes, 4.9% 45 to 60 minutes, 6.9% 60 minutes or more (2000)
Additional Information Contacts
Barnesville Area Chamber of Commerce . . . . (740) 425-4300
http://www.barnesvilleohio.com

BELLAIRE (city). Covers a land area of 1.759 square miles and a water area of 0.010 square miles. Located at 40.01° N. Lat.; 80.74° W. Long. Elevation is 667 feet.
History: Bellaire was named for the home of a Maryland settler who purchased part of the townsite in 1802. After 1900, coal mining and the manufacture of glass and enamel ware became the leading industries.
Population: 5,736 (1990); 4,892 (2000); 4,731 (2005); 4,565 (2010 projected); Race: 93.1% White, 4.9% Black, 0.3% Asian, 0.3% Hispanic of any race (2005); Density: 2,690.0 persons per square mile (2005); Average household size: 2.31 (2005); Median age: 40.1 (2005); Males per 100 females: 84.9 (2005); Marriage status: 27.2% never married, 45.9% now married, 14.4% widowed, 12.5% divorced (2000); Foreign born: 0.8% (2000); Ancestry (includes multiple ancestries): 20.1% Irish, 20.1% German, 12.9% Italian, 11.5% United States or American, 9.9% Other groups (2000).
Economy: Single-family building permits issued: 1 (2005); Multi-family building permits issued: 0 (2005); Employment by occupation: 7.8% management, 12.4% professional, 28.1% services, 25.4% sales, 0.0% farming, 7.9% construction, 18.4% production (2000).
Income: Per capita income: $14,284 (2005); Median household income: $21,568 (2005); Average household income: $32,523 (2005); Percent of households with income of $100,000 or more: 4.0% (2005); Poverty rate: 27.1% (2000).
Education: Percent of population age 25 and over with: High school diploma (including GED) or higher: 74.1% (2005); Bachelor's degree or higher: 6.0% (2005); Master's degree or higher: 2.2% (2005).
School District(s)
Bellaire Local SD (PK-12)
    2003-04 Enrollment: 1,549 . . . . (740) 676-1826
Housing: Homeownership rate: 56.1% (2005); Median home value: $49,581 (2005); Median rent: $259 per month (2000); Median age of housing: 58 years (2000).
Hospitals: Belmont Community Hospital (99 beds)
Safety: Violent crime rate: 14.7 per 10,000 population; Property crime rate: 475.3 per 10,000 population (2004).
Transportation: Commute to work: 91.9% car, 1.2% public transportation, 5.7% walk, 0.6% work from home (2000); Travel time to work: 41.7% less than 15 minutes, 43.3% 15 to 30 minutes, 8.6% 30 to 45 minutes, 2.3% 45 to 60 minutes, 4.2% 60 minutes or more (2000)
Additional Information Contacts
Bellaire Chamber of Commerce. . . . . (740) 676-9723
http://www.bellairechamber.com

BELMONT (village). Covers a land area of 0.282 square miles and a water area of 0 square miles. Located at 40.02° N. Lat.; 81.04° W. Long. Elevation is 1,200 feet.
Population: 471 (1990); 532 (2000); 527 (2005); 518 (2010 projected); Race: 96.2% White, 1.1% Black, 0.0% Asian, 1.1% Hispanic of any race (2005); Density: 1,868.9 persons per square mile (2005); Average household size: 2.50 (2005); Median age: 39.6 (2005); Males per 100 females: 98.1 (2005); Marriage status: 26.8% never married, 54.1% now married, 7.9% widowed, 11.2% divorced (2000); Foreign born: 0.0% (2000); Ancestry (includes multiple ancestries): 24.4% German, 15.7% United States or American, 13.2% Irish, 8.1% English, 5.0% Italian (2000).
Economy: In coal-mining area. Single-family building permits issued: 0 (2005); Multi-family building permits issued: 0 (2005); Employment by occupation: 5.8% management, 9.9% professional, 24.7% services, 25.5% sales, 1.2% farming, 11.5% construction, 21.4% production (2000).
Income: Per capita income: $15,119 (2005); Median household income: $32,875 (2005); Average household income: $37,761 (2005); Percent of households with income of $100,000 or more: 2.8% (2005); Poverty rate: 12.0% (2000).
Education: Percent of population age 25 and over with: High school diploma (including GED) or higher: 91.1% (2005); Bachelor's degree or higher: 5.0% (2005); Master's degree or higher: 0.8% (2005).
School District(s)
Union Local SD (PK-12)
    2003-04 Enrollment: 1,553 . . . . (740) 695-5776

Housing: Homeownership rate: 79.1% (2005); Median home value: $52,909 (2005); Median rent: $239 per month (2000); Median age of housing: 60+ years (2000).
Transportation: Commute to work: 95.5% car, 0.0% public transportation, 1.7% walk, 1.7% work from home (2000); Travel time to work: 23.1% less than 15 minutes, 41.6% 15 to 30 minutes, 23.1% 30 to 45 minutes, 3.8% 45 to 60 minutes, 8.4% 60 minutes or more (2000)

BETHESDA (village). Covers a land area of 0.642 square miles and a water area of 0.012 square miles. Located at 40.01° N. Lat.; 81.07° W. Long. Elevation is 1,200 feet.
Population: 1,161 (1990); 1,413 (2000); 1,388 (2005); 1,368 (2010 projected); Race: 99.1% White, 0.1% Black, 0.0% Asian, 0.4% Hispanic of any race (2005); Density: 2,160.8 persons per square mile (2005); Average household size: 2.34 (2005); Median age: 35.9 (2005); Males per 100 females: 90.7 (2005); Marriage status: 22.0% never married, 55.7% now married, 9.0% widowed, 13.3% divorced (2000); Foreign born: 0.6% (2000); Ancestry (includes multiple ancestries): 24.3% German, 16.6% Irish, 12.6% English, 11.5% United States or American, 4.6% Polish (2000).
Economy: Lumber mills. Single-family building permits issued: 1 (2005); Multi-family building permits issued: 0 (2005); Employment by occupation: 6.0% management, 12.6% professional, 23.8% services, 28.9% sales, 0.0% farming, 12.0% construction, 16.6% production (2000).
Income: Per capita income: $15,119 (2005); Median household income: $27,337 (2005); Average household income: $35,388 (2005); Percent of households with income of $100,000 or more: 2.2% (2005); Poverty rate: 18.5% (2000).
Education: Percent of population age 25 and over with: High school diploma (including GED) or higher: 81.9% (2005); Bachelor's degree or higher: 5.9% (2005); Master's degree or higher: 1.8% (2005).
Housing: Homeownership rate: 67.5% (2005); Median home value: $74,769 (2005); Median rent: $249 per month (2000); Median age of housing: 47 years (2000).
Safety: Violent crime rate: 7.1 per 10,000 population; Property crime rate: 135.5 per 10,000 population (2004).
Transportation: Commute to work: 94.5% car, 0.6% public transportation, 1.7% walk, 1.4% work from home (2000); Travel time to work: 21.0% less than 15 minutes, 48.7% 15 to 30 minutes, 21.0% 30 to 45 minutes, 5.6% 45 to 60 minutes, 3.7% 60 minutes or more (2000)

BRIDGEPORT (village). Covers a land area of 1.393 square miles and a water area of 0 square miles. Located at 40.07° N. Lat.; 80.74° W. Long. Elevation is 680 feet.
History: Bridgeport was platted by Ebenezer Zane in 1806, when it was called Canton. The present name was given in 1836. An early boatbuilding industry was replaced by glass-making in the late 1800's.
Population: 2,318 (1990); 2,186 (2000); 2,037 (2005); 1,930 (2010 projected); Race: 92.3% White, 6.3% Black, 0.1% Asian, 0.5% Hispanic of any race (2005); Density: 1,462.0 persons per square mile (2005); Average household size: 2.21 (2005); Median age: 41.4 (2005); Males per 100 females: 88.6 (2005); Marriage status: 22.5% never married, 50.1% now married, 9.3% widowed, 18.2% divorced (2000); Foreign born: 0.2% (2000); Ancestry (includes multiple ancestries): 27.9% German, 24.9% Irish, 12.8% English, 11.7% Other groups, 7.5% Italian (2000).
Economy: Single-family building permits issued: 1 (2005); Multi-family building permits issued: 0 (2005); Employment by occupation: 5.4% management, 10.9% professional, 26.0% services, 31.5% sales, 0.0% farming, 11.6% construction, 14.7% production (2000).
Income: Per capita income: $16,994 (2005); Median household income: $28,796 (2005); Average household income: $37,348 (2005); Percent of households with income of $100,000 or more: 3.8% (2005); Poverty rate: 16.2% (2000).
Taxes: Total city taxes per capita: $111 (2004); City property taxes per capita: $85 (2004).
Education: Percent of population age 25 and over with: High school diploma (including GED) or higher: 84.2% (2005); Bachelor's degree or higher: 10.4% (2005); Master's degree or higher: 3.7% (2005).
School District(s)
Bridgeport Ex Vill SD (PK-12)
    2003-04 Enrollment: 764 . . . . (740) 635-1713
Housing: Homeownership rate: 64.2% (2005); Median home value: $46,966 (2005); Median rent: $260 per month (2000); Median age of housing: 59 years (2000).

Safety: Violent crime rate: 9.4 per 10,000 population; Property crime rate: 187.9 per 10,000 population (2004).
Transportation: Commute to work: 94.3% car, 2.9% public transportation, 1.3% walk, 1.0% work from home (2000); Travel time to work: 48.8% less than 15 minutes, 36.9% 15 to 30 minutes, 10.2% 30 to 45 minutes, 0.8% 45 to 60 minutes, 3.3% 60 minutes or more (2000)
Additional Information Contacts
Brideport Chamber of Commerce . . . . (740) 635-3377
http://www.belmontcountyohio.org/connections/community.htm

BROOKSIDE (village).
Covers a land area of 0.173 square miles and a water area of 0 square miles. Located at 40.07° N. Lat.; 80.76° W. Long. Elevation is 700 feet.
History: Brookside was settled along Wheeling Creek, where grist mills, sawmills, and woolen mills were established. Later it became a coal mining town.
Population: 665 (1990); 644 (2000); 617 (2005); 595 (2010 projected); Race: 98.2% White, 1.1% Black, 0.0% Asian, 0.0% Hispanic of any race (2005); Density: 3,558.9 persons per square mile (2005); Average household size: 2.23 (2005); Median age: 44.7 (2005); Males per 100 females: 82.0 (2005); Marriage status: 19.7% never married, 59.8% now married, 10.2% widowed, 10.4% divorced (2000); Foreign born: 1.6% (2000); Ancestry (includes multiple ancestries): 31.4% German, 22.2% Irish, 15.2% Polish, 13.8% English, 9.3% Italian (2000).
Economy: Single-family building permits issued: 0 (2005); Multi-family building permits issued: 0 (2005); Employment by occupation: 10.5% management, 15.7% professional, 18.1% services, 33.4% sales, 0.0% farming, 9.9% construction, 12.3% production (2000).
Income: Per capita income: $20,385 (2005); Median household income: $37,500 (2005); Average household income: $45,406 (2005); Percent of households with income of $100,000 or more: 3.2% (2005); Poverty rate: 7.8% (2000).
Education: Percent of population age 25 and over with: High school diploma (including GED) or higher: 91.2% (2005); Bachelor's degree or higher: 13.1% (2005); Master's degree or higher: 2.8% (2005).
Housing: Homeownership rate: 79.4% (2005); Median home value: $76,757 (2005); Median rent: $352 per month (2000); Median age of housing: 56 years (2000).
Transportation: Commute to work: 93.1% car, 1.6% public transportation, 1.6% walk, 3.6% work from home (2000); Travel time to work: 40.3% less than 15 minutes, 46.8% 15 to 30 minutes, 7.5% 30 to 45 minutes, 1.7% 45 to 60 minutes, 3.7% 60 minutes or more (2000)

FLUSHING (village).
Covers a land area of 0.604 square miles and a water area of 0 square miles. Located at 40.14° N. Lat.; 81.06° W. Long. Elevation is 1,132 feet.
Population: 1,042 (1990); 900 (2000); 848 (2005); 810 (2010 projected); Race: 99.1% White, 0.6% Black, 0.0% Asian, 0.0% Hispanic of any race (2005); Density: 1,404.9 persons per square mile (2005); Average household size: 2.32 (2005); Median age: 40.2 (2005); Males per 100 females: 98.6 (2005); Marriage status: 25.1% never married, 50.5% now married, 8.2% widowed, 16.1% divorced (2000); Foreign born: 0.6% (2000); Ancestry (includes multiple ancestries): 21.4% Irish, 18.9% German, 11.6% Italian, 10.3% English, 9.4% United States or American (2000).
Economy: In coal-mining area. Employment by occupation: 4.5% management, 11.0% professional, 19.5% services, 29.4% sales, 0.0% farming, 13.2% construction, 22.4% production (2000).
Income: Per capita income: $17,491 (2005); Median household income: $32,153 (2005); Average household income: $40,637 (2005); Percent of households with income of $100,000 or more: 5.8% (2005); Poverty rate: 17.4% (2000).
Education: Percent of population age 25 and over with: High school diploma (including GED) or higher: 80.5% (2005); Bachelor's degree or higher: 7.6% (2005); Master's degree or higher: 2.1% (2005).
Housing: Homeownership rate: 76.7% (2005); Median home value: $63,077 (2005); Median rent: $269 per month (2000); Median age of housing: 58 years (2000).
Transportation: Commute to work: 95.1% car, 0.0% public transportation, 2.6% walk, 1.8% work from home (2000); Travel time to work: 20.5% less than 15 minutes, 52.5% 15 to 30 minutes, 14.4% 30 to 45 minutes, 8.1% 45 to 60 minutes, 4.5% 60 minutes or more (2000)

HOLLOWAY (village).
Covers a land area of 0.870 square miles and a water area of 0 square miles. Located at 40.16° N. Lat.; 81.13° W. Long. Elevation is 909 feet.
Population: 349 (1990); 345 (2000); 403 (2005); 440 (2010 projected); Race: 99.0% White, 0.0% Black, 0.0% Asian, 0.0% Hispanic of any race (2005); Density: 463.2 persons per square mile (2005); Average household size: 2.44 (2005); Median age: 39.0 (2005); Males per 100 females: 103.5 (2005); Marriage status: 22.6% never married, 54.7% now married, 10.8% widowed, 11.8% divorced (2000); Foreign born: 2.9% (2000); Ancestry (includes multiple ancestries): 18.3% Irish, 14.6% German, 12.3% Italian, 10.0% Other groups, 9.5% English (2000).
Economy: In coal mining area. Single-family building permits issued: 0 (2005); Multi-family building permits issued: 0 (2005); Employment by occupation: 7.4% management, 3.3% professional, 22.1% services, 19.7% sales, 0.0% farming, 18.0% construction, 29.5% production (2000).
Income: Per capita income: $13,579 (2005); Median household income: $27,763 (2005); Average household income: $33,167 (2005); Percent of households with income of $100,000 or more: 1.8% (2005); Poverty rate: 20.3% (2000).
Education: Percent of population age 25 and over with: High school diploma (including GED) or higher: 76.8% (2005); Bachelor's degree or higher: 3.6% (2005); Master's degree or higher: 0.4% (2005).
Housing: Homeownership rate: 87.9% (2005); Median home value: $34,490 (2005); Median rent: $255 per month (2000); Median age of housing: 60+ years (2000).
Transportation: Commute to work: 95.9% car, 0.0% public transportation, 0.8% walk, 1.6% work from home (2000); Travel time to work: 15.0% less than 15 minutes, 24.2% 15 to 30 minutes, 20.0% 30 to 45 minutes, 15.8% 45 to 60 minutes, 25.0% 60 minutes or more (2000)

JACOBSBURG (unincorporated postal area, zip code 43933).
Covers a land area of 54.419 square miles and a water area of 0.110 square miles. Located at 39.93° N. Lat.; 80.89° W. Long. Elevation is 1,300 feet.
Population: 1,744 (2000); Race: 98.2% White, 0.8% Black, 0.0% Asian, 0.3% Hispanic of any race (2000); Density: 32.0 persons per square mile (2000); Age: 24.0% under 18, 17.4% over 64 (2000); Marriage status: 19.1% never married, 68.9% now married, 7.4% widowed, 4.6% divorced (2000); Foreign born: 1.0% (2000); Ancestry (includes multiple ancestries): 24.3% German, 12.8% Irish, 12.3% English, 9.1% United States or American, 7.3% Other groups (2000).
Economy: Employment by occupation: 5.0% management, 9.9% professional, 14.9% services, 25.2% sales, 1.9% farming, 17.6% construction, 25.6% production (2000).
Income: Per capita income: $14,331 (2000); Median household income: $31,205 (2000); Poverty rate: 12.8% (2000).
Education: Percent of population age 25 and over with: High school diploma (including GED) or higher: 82.4% (2000); Bachelor's degree or higher: 6.7% (2000).
Housing: Homeownership rate: 86.4% (2000); Median home value: $60,200 (2000); Median rent: $215 per month (2000); Median age of housing: 41 years (2000).
Transportation: Commute to work: 89.3% car, 2.0% public transportation, 1.4% walk, 7.3% work from home (2000); Travel time to work: 10.8% less than 15 minutes, 43.8% 15 to 30 minutes, 24.4% 30 to 45 minutes, 14.6% 45 to 60 minutes, 6.4% 60 minutes or more (2000)

MARTINS FERRY (city).
Covers a land area of 2.160 square miles and a water area of 0 square miles. Located at 40.09° N. Lat.; 80.72° W. Long. Elevation is 700 feet.
History: The settlement that formed here in the 1780's was known as Norristown. In 1795 Absalom Martin laid out a town that he called Jefferson, but he later voided his town plat when he failed to get the county seat. Settlers continued to come, and in 1835 Absalom's son, Ebenezer Martin, replatted the town and named it Martinsville. Because Martin owned the ferry, the town became known as Martins Ferry. Writer William Dean Howells was born here in 1837.
Population: 8,085 (1990); 7,226 (2000); 6,931 (2005); 6,622 (2010 projected); Race: 93.7% White, 4.7% Black, 0.0% Asian, 0.6% Hispanic of any race (2005); Density: 3,208.6 persons per square mile (2005); Average household size: 2.23 (2005); Median age: 42.3 (2005); Males per 100 females: 84.4 (2005); Marriage status: 23.0% never married, 51.0% now married, 13.0% widowed, 13.0% divorced (2000); Foreign born: 0.6%

(2000); Ancestry (includes multiple ancestries): 26.7% German, 17.9% Irish, 12.7% Polish, 8.1% English, 8.0% Italian (2000).
Economy: Single-family building permits issued: 1 (2005); Multi-family building permits issued: 0 (2005); Employment by occupation: 9.1% management, 12.2% professional, 20.3% services, 31.0% sales, 0.2% farming, 8.2% construction, 19.1% production (2000).
Income: Per capita income: $17,943 (2005); Median household income: $26,804 (2005); Average household income: $39,773 (2005); Percent of households with income of $100,000 or more: 5.1% (2005); Poverty rate: 18.3% (2000).
Taxes: Total city taxes per capita: $203 (2004); City property taxes per capita: $60 (2004).
Education: Percent of population age 25 and over with: High school diploma (including GED) or higher: 80.2% (2005); Bachelor's degree or higher: 10.6% (2005); Master's degree or higher: 3.0% (2005).

School District(s)

Martins Ferry City SD (PK-12)
    2003-04 Enrollment: 1,522 . . . . (740) 633-1732
Housing: Homeownership rate: 62.1% (2005); Median home value: $62,102 (2005); Median rent: $271 per month (2000); Median age of housing: 58 years (2000).
Hospitals: East Ohio Regional Hospital (250 beds)
Newspapers: The Times-Leader (Circulation 18,318)
Transportation: Commute to work: 90.2% car, 1.1% public transportation, 5.2% walk, 2.4% work from home (2000); Travel time to work: 41.3% less than 15 minutes, 41.6% 15 to 30 minutes, 9.7% 30 to 45 minutes, 3.2% 45 to 60 minutes, 4.2% 60 minutes or more (2000)
Additional Information Contacts
Martins Ferry Chamber of Cmmrc . . . . (740) 633-2565
    http://www.martinsferrychamber.com

MORRISTOWN (village). Covers a land area of 0.505 square miles and a water area of 0 square miles. Located at 40.06° N. Lat.; 81.07° W. Long. Elevation is 1,300 feet.
History: Morristown was laid out in 1802 and served as a toll station on the National Road.
Population: 296 (1990); 299 (2000); 288 (2005); 280 (2010 projected); Race: 99.0% White, 0.7% Black, 0.0% Asian, 1.4% Hispanic of any race (2005); Density: 570.0 persons per square mile (2005); Average household size: 2.40 (2005); Median age: 39.8 (2005); Males per 100 females: 93.3 (2005); Marriage status: 27.4% never married, 58.5% now married, 8.9% widowed, 5.2% divorced (2000); Foreign born: 1.0% (2000); Ancestry (includes multiple ancestries): 16.1% Irish, 16.1% German, 11.5% English, 9.2% Polish, 8.5% Other groups (2000).
Economy: Employment by occupation: 10.9% management, 17.0% professional, 16.3% services, 30.6% sales, 0.0% farming, 10.9% construction, 14.3% production (2000).
Income: Per capita income: $19,366 (2005); Median household income: $44,000 (2005); Average household income: $46,479 (2005); Percent of households with income of $100,000 or more: 1.7% (2005); Poverty rate: 7.2% (2000).
Education: Percent of population age 25 and over with: High school diploma (including GED) or higher: 86.1% (2005); Bachelor's degree or higher: 14.4% (2005); Master's degree or higher: 1.5% (2005).
Housing: Homeownership rate: 80.0% (2005); Median home value: $82,222 (2005); Median rent: $375 per month (2000); Median age of housing: 60+ years (2000).
Transportation: Commute to work: 93.2% car, 0.0% public transportation, 0.0% walk, 4.1% work from home (2000); Travel time to work: 44.7% less than 15 minutes, 20.6% 15 to 30 minutes, 14.9% 30 to 45 minutes, 9.2% 45 to 60 minutes, 10.6% 60 minutes or more (2000)

NEFFS (CDP). Covers a land area of 4.010 square miles and a water area of 0 square miles. Located at 40.02° N. Lat.; 80.81° W. Long. Elevation is 735 feet.
Population: 1,320 (1990); 1,138 (2000); 1,056 (2005); 1,006 (2010 projected); Race: 99.1% White, 0.4% Black, 0.0% Asian, 0.1% Hispanic of any race (2005); Density: 263.3 persons per square mile (2005); Average household size: 2.49 (2005); Median age: 41.8 (2005); Males per 100 females: 98.1 (2005); Marriage status: 18.4% never married, 65.5% now married, 9.4% widowed, 6.8% divorced (2000); Foreign born: 0.0% (2000); Ancestry (includes multiple ancestries): 31.1% Irish, 26.7% German, 19.2% Polish, 9.9% English, 7.3% United States or American (2000).
Economy: In coal-mining area. Employment by occupation: 14.8% management, 7.0% professional, 21.4% services, 27.5% sales, 0.0% farming, 7.4% construction, 21.8% production (2000).
Income: Per capita income: $15,883 (2005); Median household income: $30,507 (2005); Average household income: $39,558 (2005); Percent of households with income of $100,000 or more: 5.2% (2005); Poverty rate: 13.8% (2000).
Education: Percent of population age 25 and over with: High school diploma (including GED) or higher: 69.8% (2005); Bachelor's degree or higher: 2.6% (2005); Master's degree or higher: 0.0% (2005).
Housing: Homeownership rate: 84.7% (2005); Median home value: $59,620 (2005); Median rent: $237 per month (2000); Median age of housing: 60+ years (2000).
Transportation: Commute to work: 97.1% car, 0.0% public transportation, 2.9% walk, 0.0% work from home (2000); Travel time to work: 10.7% less than 15 minutes, 77.0% 15 to 30 minutes, 5.7% 30 to 45 minutes, 2.5% 45 to 60 minutes, 4.1% 60 minutes or more (2000)

POWHATAN POINT (village). Aka Powhatan. Covers a land area of 1.557 square miles and a water area of 0.150 square miles. Located at 39.86° N. Lat.; 80.80° W. Long. Elevation is 641 feet.
History: Powhatan Point was established in the 1820's along the Ohio River. A coal boom during the 1920's brought growth to the town.
Population: 1,807 (1990); 1,744 (2000); 1,657 (2005); 1,617 (2010 projected); Race: 98.8% White, 0.3% Black, 0.0% Asian, 0.1% Hispanic of any race (2005); Density: 1,063.9 persons per square mile (2005); Average household size: 2.25 (2005); Median age: 41.0 (2005); Males per 100 females: 90.7 (2005); Marriage status: 18.1% never married, 62.5% now married, 10.3% widowed, 9.0% divorced (2000); Foreign born: 0.8% (2000); Ancestry (includes multiple ancestries): 18.5% German, 15.6% Irish, 11.5% United States or American, 10.9% English, 7.4% Polish (2000).
Economy: Single-family building permits issued: 3 (2005); Multi-family building permits issued: 0 (2005); Employment by occupation: 5.9% management, 15.7% professional, 19.4% services, 24.2% sales, 0.0% farming, 15.2% construction, 19.6% production (2000).
Income: Per capita income: $18,054 (2005); Median household income: $30,769 (2005); Average household income: $40,645 (2005); Percent of households with income of $100,000 or more: 6.8% (2005); Poverty rate: 19.8% (2000).
Education: Percent of population age 25 and over with: High school diploma (including GED) or higher: 75.6% (2005); Bachelor's degree or higher: 7.6% (2005); Master's degree or higher: 2.8% (2005).

School District(s)

Switzerland of Ohio Local SD (PK-12)
    2003-04 Enrollment: 2,764 . . . . (740) 472-5801
Housing: Homeownership rate: 71.6% (2005); Median home value: $60,753 (2005); Median rent: $258 per month (2000); Median age of housing: 48 years (2000).
Transportation: Commute to work: 96.5% car, 0.0% public transportation, 1.4% walk, 0.5% work from home (2000); Travel time to work: 23.2% less than 15 minutes, 37.1% 15 to 30 minutes, 24.8% 30 to 45 minutes, 7.3% 45 to 60 minutes, 7.6% 60 minutes or more (2000)

SAINT CLAIRSVILLE (city). Covers a land area of 2.148 square miles and a water area of 0 square miles. Located at 40.07° N. Lat.; 80.90° W. Long. Elevation is 1,284 feet.
History: St. Clairsville was named for Arthur St. Clair, first governor of the Northwest Territory. It became the seat of Belmont County in 1804.
Population: 5,456 (1990); 5,057 (2000); 5,083 (2005); 5,112 (2010 projected); Race: 95.0% White, 2.3% Black, 1.7% Asian, 0.5% Hispanic of any race (2005); Density: 2,366.3 persons per square mile (2005); Average household size: 2.19 (2005); Median age: 47.7 (2005); Males per 100 females: 83.5 (2005); Marriage status: 16.2% never married, 63.1% now married, 11.9% widowed, 8.8% divorced (2000); Foreign born: 2.9% (2000); Ancestry (includes multiple ancestries): 28.1% German, 14.0% Irish, 13.8% English, 12.9% Italian, 11.3% Polish (2000).
Economy: Single-family building permits issued: 3 (2005); Multi-family building permits issued: 4 (2005); Employment by occupation: 16.3% management, 27.2% professional, 14.0% services, 27.9% sales, 0.0% farming, 6.4% construction, 8.1% production (2000).
Income: Per capita income: $26,915 (2005); Median household income: $41,515 (2005); Average household income: $58,452 (2005); Percent of households with income of $100,000 or more: 11.6% (2005); Poverty rate: 6.7% (2000).

Education: Percent of population age 25 and over with: High school diploma (including GED) or higher: 88.4% (2005); Bachelor's degree or higher: 28.8% (2005); Master's degree or higher: 12.6% (2005).

School District(s)
Belmont-Harrison Joint Vocational SD (09-12)
    2003-04 Enrollment: n/a .... (740) 695-9130
Saint Clairsville-Richland City SD (PK-12)
    2003-04 Enrollment: 1,579 .... (740) 695-1624

Four-year College(s)
Ohio University-Eastern Campus (Public)
    Fall 2004 Enrollment: 862 .... (740) 695-1720
    2005-06 Tuition: In-state $4,323; Out-of-state $8,646

Two-year College(s)
Belmont Technical College (Public)
    Fall 2004 Enrollment: 1,740 .... (740) 695-9500
    2005-06 Tuition: In-state $4,058; Out-of-state $6,938

Housing: Homeownership rate: 71.1% (2005); Median home value: $124,100 (2005); Median rent: $392 per month (2000); Median age of housing: 36 years (2000).
Transportation: Commute to work: 94.8% car, 0.0% public transportation, 1.7% walk, 3.2% work from home (2000); Travel time to work: 42.6% less than 15 minutes, 37.2% 15 to 30 minutes, 8.8% 30 to 45 minutes, 4.4% 45 to 60 minutes, 7.0% 60 minutes or more (2000)

Additional Information Contacts
City of Saint Clairsville .... (740) 695-1410
    http://www.stclairsville.com
Saint Clairsville Chamber of Commerce .... (740) 695-9623
    http://www.stclairsville.com

SHADYSIDE (village). Covers a land area of 0.956 square miles and a water area of 0.020 square miles. Located at 39.97° N. Lat.; 80.75° W. Long. Elevation is 690 feet.
History: Shadyside was platted in 1901. It developed as a residential town, with casket making as a primary industry.
Population: 3,867 (1990); 3,675 (2000); 3,580 (2005); 3,479 (2010 projected); Race: 99.3% White, 0.1% Black, 0.1% Asian, 0.2% Hispanic of any race (2005); Density: 3,745.2 persons per square mile (2005); Average household size: 2.11 (2005); Median age: 46.1 (2005); Males per 100 females: 87.4 (2005); Marriage status: 15.1% never married, 62.0% now married, 14.5% widowed, 8.4% divorced (2000); Foreign born: 1.8% (2000); Ancestry (includes multiple ancestries): 25.4% German, 19.9% Irish, 11.5% United States or American, 9.5% English, 9.3% Italian (2000).
Economy: Single-family building permits issued: 2 (2005); Multi-family building permits issued: 0 (2005); Employment by occupation: 8.5% management, 19.3% professional, 18.6% services, 25.2% sales, 0.0% farming, 10.8% construction, 17.3% production (2000).
Income: Per capita income: $19,191 (2005); Median household income: $32,689 (2005); Average household income: $40,461 (2005); Percent of households with income of $100,000 or more: 5.4% (2005); Poverty rate: 9.2% (2000).
Education: Percent of population age 25 and over with: High school diploma (including GED) or higher: 84.7% (2005); Bachelor's degree or higher: 13.5% (2005); Master's degree or higher: 4.8% (2005).

School District(s)
Shadyside Local SD (PK-12)
    2003-04 Enrollment: 874 .... (740) 676-3121

Housing: Homeownership rate: 71.5% (2005); Median home value: $74,303 (2005); Median rent: $355 per month (2000); Median age of housing: 53 years (2000).
Safety: Violent crime rate: 0.0 per 10,000 population; Property crime rate: 188.1 per 10,000 population (2004).
Transportation: Commute to work: 93.8% car, 1.9% public transportation, 1.9% walk, 2.4% work from home (2000); Travel time to work: 41.2% less than 15 minutes, 37.7% 15 to 30 minutes, 10.8% 30 to 45 minutes, 3.2% 45 to 60 minutes, 7.1% 60 minutes or more (2000)

Brown County

Located in southwestern Ohio; bounded on the south by the Ohio River and the Kentucky border. Covers a land area of 491.76 square miles, a water area of 3.46 square miles, and is located in the Eastern Time Zone. The county government was organized in 1817. County seat is Georgetown.

Brown County is part of the Cincinnati-Middletown, OH-KY-IN Metropolitan Statistical Area. The entire metro area includes: Dearborn County, IN; Franklin County, IN; Ohio County, IN; Boone County, KY; Bracken County, KY; Campbell County, KY; Gallatin County, KY; Grant County, KY; Kenton County, KY; Pendleton County, KY; Brown County, OH; Butler County, OH; Clermont County, OH; Hamilton County, OH; Warren County, OH

Weather Station: Ripley Exp. Farm   Elevation: 879 feet

	Jan	Feb	Mar	Apr	May	Jun	Jul	Aug	Sep	Oct	Nov	Dec
High	38	43	53	64	73	81	85	84	78	66	54	43
Low	20	23	31	41	51	60	64	62	54	42	34	25
Precip	2.8	2.8	4.1	4.2	5.0	4.5	4.6	4.1	3.3	3.1	3.4	3.6
Snow	7.5	5.6	4.1	0.5	tr	0.0	0.0	0.0	0.0	tr	0.9	2.9

High and Low temperatures in degrees Fahrenheit; Precipitation and Snow in inches

Population: 34,966 (1990); 42,285 (2000); 44,467 (2005); 46,745 (2010 projected); Race: 97.9% White, 1.0% Black, 0.2% Asian, 0.3% Hispanic of any race (2005); Density: 90.4 persons per square mile (2005); Average household size: 2.69 (2005); Median age: 36.7 (2005); Males per 100 females: 97.2 (2005).
Religion: Five largest groups: 6.6% Christian Churches and Churches of Christ, 6.5% Catholic Church, 6.1% Southern Baptist Convention, 3.2% The United Methodist Church, 1.5% Church of the Nazarene (2000).
Economy: Unemployment rate: 6.8% (2005); Total civilian labor force: 22,045 (2005); Leading industries: 22.4% health care and social assistance; 20.7% retail trade; 12.3% accommodation & food services (2004); Farms: 1,400 totaling 220,729 acres (2002); Companies that employ 500 or more persons: 0 (2004); Companies that employ 100 to 499 persons: 6 (2004); Companies that employ less than 100 persons: 572 (2004); Black-owned businesses: n/a (2002); Hispanic-owned businesses: n/a (2002); Women-owned businesses: n/a (2002); Retail sales per capita: $6,705 (2006); Single-family building permits issued: 162 (2005); Multi-family building permits issued: 40 (2005).
Income: Per capita income: $19,614 (2005); Median household income: $43,203 (2005); Average household income: $52,216 (2005); Percent of households with income of $100,000 or more: 8.8% (2005); Poverty rate: 10.5% (2003); Bankruptcy rate: 10.90% (2005).
Taxes: Total county taxes per capita: $128 (2004); County property taxes per capita: $58 (2004).
Education: Percent of population age 25 and over with: High school diploma (including GED) or higher: 74.5% (2005); Bachelor's degree or higher: 8.8% (2005); Master's degree or higher: 3.3% (2005).
Housing: Homeownership rate: 79.6% (2005); Median home value: $106,701 (2005); Median rent: $331 per month (2000); Median age of housing: 24 years (2000).
Health: Birth rate: 131.6 per 10,000 population (2004); Death rate: 101.9 per 10,000 population (2004); Age-adjusted cancer mortality rate: 269.9 deaths per 100,000 population (2002); Number of physicians: 7.9 per 10,000 population (2004); Hospital beds: 13.4 per 10,000 population (2003); Hospital admissions: 418.9 per 10,000 population (2003).
Elections: 2004 Presidential election results: 63.6% Bush, 35.9% Kerry, 0.0% Nader, 0.3% Badnarik

Additional Information Contacts
Brown County Government .... (937) 378-3956
    http://www.county.brown.oh.us/
Georgetown Chamber of Commerce .... (937) 378-4784
    http://www.villagegeorgetown.com

Brown County Communities

ABERDEEN (village). Covers a land area of 1.414 square miles and a water area of 0.284 square miles. Located at 38.66° N. Lat.; 83.76° W. Long. Elevation is 510 feet.
History: Aberdeen was the Ohio River terminus of Zane's Trace, and a ferry point for people and goods going across the river to Kentucky.
Population: 1,586 (1990); 1,603 (2000); 1,653 (2005); 1,711 (2010 projected); Race: 96.5% White, 2.0% Black, 0.2% Asian, 0.8% Hispanic of any race (2005); Density: 1,169.1 persons per square mile (2005); Average household size: 2.30 (2005); Median age: 37.2 (2005); Males per 100 females: 88.1 (2005); Marriage status: 20.4% never married, 49.9% now married, 10.2% widowed, 19.6% divorced (2000); Foreign born: 1.1% (2000); Ancestry (includes multiple ancestries): 34.0% United States or American, 13.6% German, 10.1% Irish, 7.0% English, 6.0% Other groups (2000).

Economy: Employment by occupation: 7.4% management, 12.3% professional, 16.1% services, 23.6% sales, 0.3% farming, 13.2% construction, 27.1% production (2000).
Income: Per capita income: $17,565 (2005); Median household income: $32,240 (2005); Average household income: $40,254 (2005); Percent of households with income of $100,000 or more: 5.1% (2005); Poverty rate: 21.9% (2000).
Education: Percent of population age 25 and over with: High school diploma (including GED) or higher: 75.6% (2005); Bachelor's degree or higher: 7.4% (2005); Master's degree or higher: 3.6% (2005).

School District(s)
Ripley-Union-Lewis-Huntington Local SD (PK-12)
   2003-04 Enrollment: 1,440 . . . . (937) 392-4396

Housing: Homeownership rate: 60.6% (2005); Median home value: $81,818 (2005); Median rent: $305 per month (2000); Median age of housing: 22 years (2000).
Transportation: Commute to work: 93.6% car, 0.0% public transportation, 2.2% walk, 2.8% work from home (2000); Travel time to work: 44.1% less than 15 minutes, 32.4% 15 to 30 minutes, 6.7% 30 to 45 minutes, 3.1% 45 to 60 minutes, 13.6% 60 minutes or more (2000)

FAYETTEVILLE (village).
Covers a land area of 0.501 square miles and a water area of 0 square miles. Located at 39.18° N. Lat.; 83.93° W. Long. Elevation is 944 feet.
History: Fayetteville was settled in 1811 and became a village in 1868. St. Aloysius Academy, a Catholic school for boys, was founded here in 1850.
Population: 433 (1990); 372 (2000); 371 (2005); 386 (2010 projected); Race: 98.9% White, 0.5% Black, 0.0% Asian, 0.0% Hispanic of any race (2005); Density: 740.4 persons per square mile (2005); Average household size: 2.54 (2005); Median age: 33.5 (2005); Males per 100 females: 91.2 (2005); Marriage status: 19.9% never married, 60.1% now married, 9.4% widowed, 10.5% divorced (2000); Foreign born: 0.0% (2000); Ancestry (includes multiple ancestries): 31.6% German, 25.9% Irish, 13.2% French (except Basque), 12.2% United States or American, 7.8% English (2000).
Economy: Single-family building permits issued: 0 (2005); Multi-family building permits issued: 3 (2005); Employment by occupation: 9.4% management, 12.3% professional, 7.6% services, 26.3% sales, 0.0% farming, 17.5% construction, 26.9% production (2000).
Income: Per capita income: $21,523 (2005); Median household income: $40,526 (2005); Average household income: $54,692 (2005); Percent of households with income of $100,000 or more: 11.0% (2005); Poverty rate: 8.5% (2000).
Education: Percent of population age 25 and over with: High school diploma (including GED) or higher: 79.4% (2005); Bachelor's degree or higher: 7.7% (2005); Master's degree or higher: 3.4% (2005).

School District(s)
Fayetteville-Perry Local SD (PK-12)
   2003-04 Enrollment: 1,045 . . . . (513) 875-2423

Housing: Homeownership rate: 74.0% (2005); Median home value: $94,000 (2005); Median rent: $375 per month (2000); Median age of housing: 50 years (2000).
Transportation: Commute to work: 91.7% car, 1.2% public transportation, 4.1% walk, 3.0% work from home (2000); Travel time to work: 25.0% less than 15 minutes, 14.6% 15 to 30 minutes, 23.8% 30 to 45 minutes, 16.5% 45 to 60 minutes, 20.1% 60 minutes or more (2000)

GEORGETOWN (village).
Covers a land area of 3.702 square miles and a water area of 0 square miles. Located at 38.86° N. Lat.; 83.90° W. Long. Elevation is 930 feet.
History: Georgetown was surveyed in 1819 and named for Georgetown, Kentucky. In the second half of the 1800's, the town was a distribution point for tobacco grown in the area.
Population: 3,925 (1990); 3,691 (2000); 3,772 (2005); 3,890 (2010 projected); Race: 96.4% White, 1.9% Black, 0.6% Asian, 0.3% Hispanic of any race (2005); Density: 1,018.9 persons per square mile (2005); Average household size: 2.32 (2005); Median age: 36.3 (2005); Males per 100 females: 85.2 (2005); Marriage status: 23.7% never married, 50.3% now married, 10.9% widowed, 15.2% divorced (2000); Foreign born: 0.0% (2000); Ancestry (includes multiple ancestries): 30.5% German, 15.0% Irish, 14.9% United States or American, 11.9% Other groups, 11.7% English (2000).
Economy: Employment by occupation: 7.7% management, 13.3% professional, 18.6% services, 23.8% sales, 1.1% farming, 12.5% construction, 23.0% production (2000).
Income: Per capita income: $20,006 (2005); Median household income: $32,996 (2005); Average household income: $44,982 (2005); Percent of households with income of $100,000 or more: 8.2% (2005); Poverty rate: 14.5% (2000).
Education: Percent of population age 25 and over with: High school diploma (including GED) or higher: 77.3% (2005); Bachelor's degree or higher: 12.1% (2005); Master's degree or higher: 4.3% (2005).

School District(s)
Georgetown Ex Vill SD (PK-12)
   2003-04 Enrollment: 1,115 . . . . (937) 378-3730
Southern Hills Joint Vocational SD (07-12)
   2003-04 Enrollment: n/a . . . . (937) 378-6131

Housing: Homeownership rate: 62.9% (2005); Median home value: $92,653 (2005); Median rent: $323 per month (2000); Median age of housing: 38 years (2000).
Hospitals: Brown County General Hospital (127 beds)
Newspapers: Georgetown News Democrat (General - Circulation 16,900)
Transportation: Commute to work: 96.4% car, 0.0% public transportation, 1.6% walk, 2.0% work from home (2000); Travel time to work: 42.0% less than 15 minutes, 14.8% 15 to 30 minutes, 16.0% 30 to 45 minutes, 8.6% 45 to 60 minutes, 18.7% 60 minutes or more (2000)

Additional Information Contacts
Georgetown Chamber of Commerce . . . . (937) 378-4784
   http://www.villagegeorgetown.com

HAMERSVILLE (village).
Covers a land area of 0.374 square miles and a water area of 0 square miles. Located at 38.91° N. Lat.; 83.98° W. Long. Elevation is 968 feet.
Population: 586 (1990); 515 (2000); 523 (2005); 534 (2010 projected); Race: 99.4% White, 0.2% Black, 0.0% Asian, 0.0% Hispanic of any race (2005); Density: 1,398.0 persons per square mile (2005); Average household size: 2.84 (2005); Median age: 34.2 (2005); Males per 100 females: 89.5 (2005); Marriage status: 23.0% never married, 62.3% now married, 7.3% widowed, 7.3% divorced (2000); Foreign born: 0.4% (2000); Ancestry (includes multiple ancestries): 20.0% German, 18.5% Irish, 14.7% English, 12.3% United States or American, 9.7% Other groups (2000).
Economy: In agricultural area. Employment by occupation: 8.4% management, 4.2% professional, 13.1% services, 19.4% sales, 0.8% farming, 14.3% construction, 39.7% production (2000).
Income: Per capita income: $16,439 (2005); Median household income: $41,702 (2005); Average household income: $46,726 (2005); Percent of households with income of $100,000 or more: 7.1% (2005); Poverty rate: 6.4% (2000).
Education: Percent of population age 25 and over with: High school diploma (including GED) or higher: 65.4% (2005); Bachelor's degree or higher: 5.7% (2005); Master's degree or higher: 2.1% (2005).

School District(s)
Western Brown Local School District (PK-12)
   2003-04 Enrollment: 3,418 . . . . (937) 444-2044

Housing: Homeownership rate: 72.8% (2005); Median home value: $86,087 (2005); Median rent: $408 per month (2000); Median age of housing: 45 years (2000).
Transportation: Commute to work: 91.8% car, 0.9% public transportation, 3.4% walk, 3.0% work from home (2000); Travel time to work: 16.9% less than 15 minutes, 24.0% 15 to 30 minutes, 26.2% 30 to 45 minutes, 15.1% 45 to 60 minutes, 17.8% 60 minutes or more (2000)

HIGGINSPORT (village).
Covers a land area of 0.223 square miles and a water area of <.001 square miles. Located at 38.79° N. Lat.; 83.96° W. Long. Elevation is 510 feet.
Population: 298 (1990); 291 (2000); 312 (2005); 332 (2010 projected); Race: 99.7% White, 0.0% Black, 0.0% Asian, 0.3% Hispanic of any race (2005); Density: 1,399.2 persons per square mile (2005); Average household size: 2.54 (2005); Median age: 40.1 (2005); Males per 100 females: 89.1 (2005); Marriage status: 19.4% never married, 64.0% now married, 5.8% widowed, 10.7% divorced (2000); Foreign born: 0.0% (2000); Ancestry (includes multiple ancestries): 30.5% German, 11.8% Irish, 9.5% Italian, 8.3% United States or American, 5.2% French (except Basque) (2000).
Economy: Employment by occupation: 5.6% management, 4.0% professional, 12.8% services, 27.2% sales, 0.0% farming, 12.8% construction, 37.6% production (2000).
Income: Per capita income: $16,034 (2005); Median household income: $37,177 (2005); Average household income: $40,671 (2005); Percent of

households with income of $100,000 or more: 4.9% (2005); Poverty rate: 11.5% (2000).
Education: Percent of population age 25 and over with: High school diploma (including GED) or higher: 70.8% (2005); Bachelor's degree or higher: 4.2% (2005); Master's degree or higher: 1.9% (2005).
Housing: Homeownership rate: 74.8% (2005); Median home value: $72,500 (2005); Median rent: $360 per month (2000); Median age of housing: 60+ years (2000).
Transportation: Commute to work: 85.6% car, 0.0% public transportation, 7.2% walk, 0.0% work from home (2000); Travel time to work: 11.2% less than 15 minutes, 30.4% 15 to 30 minutes, 15.2% 30 to 45 minutes, 20.0% 45 to 60 minutes, 23.2% 60 minutes or more (2000)

MOUNT ORAB (village). Aka Mount Oreb. Covers a land area of 3.796 square miles and a water area of 0 square miles. Located at 39.03° N. Lat.; 83.92° W. Long. Elevation is 922 feet.
History: The name of Mount Orab was derived from the biblical Horeb.
Population: 2,055 (1990); 2,307 (2000); 2,614 (2005); 2,906 (2010 projected); Race: 99.1% White, 0.2% Black, 0.1% Asian, 0.1% Hispanic of any race (2005); Density: 688.6 persons per square mile (2005); Average household size: 2.62 (2005); Median age: 31.9 (2005); Males per 100 females: 87.2 (2005); Marriage status: 21.1% never married, 58.0% now married, 6.7% widowed, 14.2% divorced (2000); Foreign born: 0.5% (2000); Ancestry (includes multiple ancestries): 19.7% German, 17.7% United States or American, 13.6% Irish, 8.1% Other groups, 6.9% English (2000).
Economy: Employment by occupation: 7.9% management, 11.0% professional, 16.6% services, 24.3% sales, 0.3% farming, 12.2% construction, 27.7% production (2000).
Income: Per capita income: $19,128 (2005); Median household income: $40,324 (2005); Average household income: $49,429 (2005); Percent of households with income of $100,000 or more: 8.9% (2005); Poverty rate: 14.6% (2000).
Taxes: Total city taxes per capita: $380 (2004); City property taxes per capita: $150 (2004).
Education: Percent of population age 25 and over with: High school diploma (including GED) or higher: 75.7% (2005); Bachelor's degree or higher: 9.2% (2005); Master's degree or higher: 4.1% (2005).
School District(s)
Western Brown Local School District (PK-12)
    2003-04 Enrollment: 3,418 . . . . (937) 444-2044
Housing: Homeownership rate: 62.0% (2005); Median home value: $104,891 (2005); Median rent: $301 per month (2000); Median age of housing: 26 years (2000).
Newspapers: The Brown County Press (General - Circulation 15,750)
Transportation: Commute to work: 93.3% car, 0.6% public transportation, 1.5% walk, 2.9% work from home (2000); Travel time to work: 23.4% less than 15 minutes, 26.6% 15 to 30 minutes, 22.9% 30 to 45 minutes, 13.7% 45 to 60 minutes, 13.4% 60 minutes or more (2000)

RIPLEY (village). Covers a land area of 1.013 square miles and a water area of 0.065 square miles. Located at 38.73° N. Lat.; 83.84° W. Long. Elevation is 520 feet.
History: Ripley was laid out in 1812 by Colonel James Poage of Virginia. It was an early center for steamboat building, and for piano manufacturing. The 1937 flooding of the Ohio River ruined Ripley's wharf area. The Rankin House in Ripley was a station on the Underground Railroad.
Population: 1,867 (1990); 1,745 (2000); 1,790 (2005); 1,842 (2010 projected); Race: 90.4% White, 7.8% Black, 0.3% Asian, 0.5% Hispanic of any race (2005); Density: 1,766.6 persons per square mile (2005); Average household size: 2.34 (2005); Median age: 38.2 (2005); Males per 100 females: 85.5 (2005); Marriage status: 22.1% never married, 53.3% now married, 10.7% widowed, 13.9% divorced (2000); Foreign born: 0.2% (2000); Ancestry (includes multiple ancestries): 25.5% German, 16.7% United States or American, 11.8% Other groups, 11.4% English, 10.3% Irish (2000).
Economy: Employment by occupation: 7.4% management, 8.6% professional, 19.2% services, 27.4% sales, 0.6% farming, 8.3% construction, 28.4% production (2000).
Income: Per capita income: $17,013 (2005); Median household income: $33,140 (2005); Average household income: $39,755 (2005); Percent of households with income of $100,000 or more: 5.2% (2005); Poverty rate: 15.5% (2000).

Education: Percent of population age 25 and over with: High school diploma (including GED) or higher: 69.8% (2005); Bachelor's degree or higher: 6.8% (2005); Master's degree or higher: 3.1% (2005).
School District(s)
Ripley-Union-Lewis-Huntington Local SD (PK-12)
    2003-04 Enrollment: 1,440 . . . . (937) 392-4396
Housing: Homeownership rate: 63.7% (2005); Median home value: $82,821 (2005); Median rent: $253 per month (2000); Median age of housing: 49 years (2000).
Newspapers: Ripley Bee (General - Circulation 2,100)
Transportation: Commute to work: 85.7% car, 1.0% public transportation, 8.0% walk, 4.6% work from home (2000); Travel time to work: 36.9% less than 15 minutes, 29.6% 15 to 30 minutes, 5.9% 30 to 45 minutes, 11.7% 45 to 60 minutes, 16.0% 60 minutes or more (2000)

RUSSELLVILLE (village). Covers a land area of 0.778 square miles and a water area of 0 square miles. Located at 38.86° N. Lat.; 83.78° W. Long. Elevation is 975 feet.
Population: 459 (1990); 453 (2000); 471 (2005); 489 (2010 projected); Race: 98.1% White, 1.5% Black, 0.0% Asian, 0.8% Hispanic of any race (2005); Density: 605.4 persons per square mile (2005); Average household size: 2.33 (2005); Median age: 37.5 (2005); Males per 100 females: 89.9 (2005); Marriage status: 18.4% never married, 58.5% now married, 13.0% widowed, 10.0% divorced (2000); Foreign born: 0.0% (2000); Ancestry (includes multiple ancestries): 23.2% German, 14.3% United States or American, 14.1% English, 9.6% Irish, 5.3% Other groups (2000).
Economy: In agricultural area. Employment by occupation: 10.7% management, 16.5% professional, 12.1% services, 26.7% sales, 0.0% farming, 12.1% construction, 21.8% production (2000).
Income: Per capita income: $15,758 (2005); Median household income: $31,667 (2005); Average household income: $36,114 (2005); Percent of households with income of $100,000 or more: 1.5% (2005); Poverty rate: 7.0% (2000).
Education: Percent of population age 25 and over with: High school diploma (including GED) or higher: 72.2% (2005); Bachelor's degree or higher: 8.9% (2005); Master's degree or higher: 5.4% (2005).
School District(s)
Eastern Local SD (PK-12)
    2003-04 Enrollment: 1,543 . . . . (937) 378-3981
Housing: Homeownership rate: 79.7% (2005); Median home value: $80,227 (2005); Median rent: $317 per month (2000); Median age of housing: 53 years (2000).
Transportation: Commute to work: 89.6% car, 1.0% public transportation, 5.0% walk, 4.5% work from home (2000); Travel time to work: 28.6% less than 15 minutes, 20.3% 15 to 30 minutes, 12.0% 30 to 45 minutes, 12.5% 45 to 60 minutes, 26.6% 60 minutes or more (2000)

SAINT MARTIN (village). Covers a land area of 1.162 square miles and a water area of 0 square miles. Located at 39.21° N. Lat.; 83.89° W. Long. Elevation is 979 feet.
Population: 141 (1990); 91 (2000); 82 (2005); 81 (2010 projected); Race: 100.0% White, 0.0% Black, 0.0% Asian, 1.2% Hispanic of any race (2005); Density: 70.5 persons per square mile (2005); Average household size: 2.83 (2005); Median age: 44.2 (2005); Males per 100 females: 127.8 (2005); Marriage status: 28.8% never married, 65.2% now married, 6.1% widowed, 0.0% divorced (2000); Foreign born: 2.3% (2000); Ancestry (includes multiple ancestries): 31.8% German, 22.7% United States or American, 10.2% English, 9.1% Irish, 5.7% Dutch (2000).
Economy: Employment by occupation: 11.1% management, 6.7% professional, 4.4% services, 55.6% sales, 0.0% farming, 2.2% construction, 20.0% production (2000).
Income: Per capita income: $27,866 (2005); Median household income: $73,438 (2005); Average household income: $78,793 (2005); Percent of households with income of $100,000 or more: 31.0% (2005); Poverty rate: 0.0% (2000).
Education: Percent of population age 25 and over with: High school diploma (including GED) or higher: 86.2% (2005); Bachelor's degree or higher: 20.7% (2005); Master's degree or higher: 12.1% (2005).
Two-year College(s)
Chatfield College (Private, Not-for-profit, Roman Catholic)
    Fall 2004 Enrollment: 248 . . . . (513) 875-3344
    2005-06 Tuition: In-state $7,340; Out-of-state $7,340
Housing: Homeownership rate: 100.0% (2005); Median home value: $172,500 (2005); Median rent: $375 per month (2000); Median age of housing: 30 years (2000).

Transportation: Commute to work: 80.0% car, 2.2% public transportation, 0.0% walk, 17.8% work from home (2000); Travel time to work: 13.5% less than 15 minutes, 35.1% 15 to 30 minutes, 18.9% 30 to 45 minutes, 16.2% 45 to 60 minutes, 16.2% 60 minutes or more (2000)

SARDINIA (village). Covers a land area of 0.641 square miles and a water area of 0 square miles. Located at 39.00° N. Lat.; 83.80° W. Long. Elevation is 962 feet.
Population: 906 (1990); 862 (2000); 888 (2005); 916 (2010 projected); Race: 98.5% White, 0.2% Black, 0.0% Asian, 0.8% Hispanic of any race (2005); Density: 1,384.4 persons per square mile (2005); Average household size: 2.59 (2005); Median age: 33.1 (2005); Males per 100 females: 89.3 (2005); Marriage status: 19.0% never married, 61.0% now married, 6.7% widowed, 13.3% divorced (2000); Foreign born: 0.4% (2000); Ancestry (includes multiple ancestries): 24.3% German, 15.6% United States or American, 12.5% English, 11.8% Irish, 7.0% Other groups (2000).
Economy: Employment by occupation: 3.6% management, 10.9% professional, 19.6% services, 21.5% sales, 0.0% farming, 18.4% construction, 26.0% production (2000).
Income: Per capita income: $14,646 (2005); Median household income: $32,281 (2005); Average household income: $36,647 (2005); Percent of households with income of $100,000 or more: 2.3% (2005); Poverty rate: 20.1% (2000).
Education: Percent of population age 25 and over with: High school diploma (including GED) or higher: 69.7% (2005); Bachelor's degree or higher: 5.9% (2005); Master's degree or higher: 4.1% (2005).
School District(s)
Eastern Local SD (PK-12)
    2003-04 Enrollment: 1,543 . . . . (937) 378-3981
Housing: Homeownership rate: 58.9% (2005); Median home value: $71,176 (2005); Median rent: $319 per month (2000); Median age of housing: 49 years (2000).
Transportation: Commute to work: 96.2% car, 0.0% public transportation, 2.5% walk, 1.3% work from home (2000); Travel time to work: 21.3% less than 15 minutes, 27.0% 15 to 30 minutes, 25.4% 30 to 45 minutes, 12.4% 45 to 60 minutes, 14.0% 60 minutes or more (2000)

Butler County

Located in southwestern Ohio; bounded on the west by Indiana; crossed by the Great Miami River. Covers a land area of 467.27 square miles, a water area of 2.93 square miles, and is located in the Eastern Time Zone. The county government was organized in 1803. County seat is Hamilton.

Butler County is part of the Cincinnati-Middletown, OH-KY-IN Metropolitan Statistical Area. The entire metro area includes: Dearborn County, IN; Franklin County, IN; Ohio County, IN; Boone County, KY; Bracken County, KY; Campbell County, KY; Gallatin County, KY; Grant County, KY; Kenton County, KY; Pendleton County, KY; Brown County, OH; Butler County, OH; Clermont County, OH; Hamilton County, OH; Warren County, OH

Population: 291,479 (1990); 332,807 (2000); 347,942 (2005); 363,728 (2010 projected); Race: 89.7% White, 5.9% Black, 2.0% Asian, 1.7% Hispanic of any race (2005); Density: 744.6 persons per square mile (2005); Average household size: 2.68 (2005); Median age: 35.0 (2005); Males per 100 females: 95.8 (2005).
Religion: Five largest groups: 13.0% Catholic Church, 6.3% Southern Baptist Convention, 2.8% The United Methodist Church, 2.5% Church of God (Cleveland, Tennessee), 1.5% Presbyterian Church (U.S.A.) (2000).
Economy: Unemployment rate: 5.3% (2005); Total civilian labor force: 185,325 (2005); Leading industries: 16.1% manufacturing; 12.6% health care and social assistance; 12.2% retail trade (2004); Farms: 1,060 totaling 138,044 acres (2002); Companies that employ 500 or more persons: 14 (2004); Companies that employ 100 to 499 persons: 199 (2004); Companies that employ less than 100 persons: 6,679 (2004); Black-owned businesses: 434 (2002); Hispanic-owned businesses: 180 (2002); Women-owned businesses: 5,515 (2002); Retail sales per capita: $10,033 (2006); Single-family building permits issued: 2,573 (2005); Multi-family building permits issued: 204 (2005).
Income: Per capita income: $25,042 (2005); Median household income: $53,874 (2005); Average household income: $66,475 (2005); Percent of households with income of $100,000 or more: 18.1% (2005); Poverty rate: 8.9% (2003); Bankruptcy rate: 10.67% (2005).
Taxes: Total county taxes per capita: $155 (2004); County property taxes per capita: $97 (2004).

Education: Percent of population age 25 and over with: High school diploma (including GED) or higher: 83.5% (2005); Bachelor's degree or higher: 23.6% (2005); Master's degree or higher: 8.1% (2005).
Housing: Homeownership rate: 72.0% (2005); Median home value: $143,052 (2005); Median rent: $463 per month (2000); Median age of housing: 28 years (2000).
Health: Birth rate: 129.9 per 10,000 population (2004); Death rate: 78.5 per 10,000 population (2004); Age-adjusted cancer mortality rate: 216.2 deaths per 100,000 population (2002); Air Quality Index: 53.7% good, 41.4% moderate, 4.7% unhealthy for sensitive individuals, 0.3% unhealthy (percent of days in 2005); Number of physicians: 13.1 per 10,000 population (2004); Hospital beds: 20.1 per 10,000 population (2003); Hospital admissions: 996.2 per 10,000 population (2003).
Elections: 2004 Presidential election results: 65.9% Bush, 33.7% Kerry, 0.0% Nader, 0.2% Badnarik

Additional Information Contacts
Butler County Government	(513) 887-3247
http://www.butlercountyohio.org/	
City of Fairfield	(513) 867-5300
http://www.fairfield-city.org	
City of Hamilton	(513) 785-7000
http://www.hamilton-city.org	
City of Middletown	(513) 425-7730
http://www.ci.middletown.oh.us	
City of Monroe	(513) 539-7374
http://www.monroeohio.org	
City of Oxford	(513) 524-5200
http://www.cityofoxford.org/index.asp	
City of Trenton	(513) 988-6304
http://www.ci.trenton.oh.us/default.asp	
Fairfield Chamber of Commerce	(513) 881-5500
http://www.fairfieldchamber.com	
Hamilton Chamber of Commerce	(513) 844-1500
http://www.hamilton-ohio.com	
Mid Miami Valley Chamber of Commerce	(513) 422-4551
http://www.mmvchamber.org	
Middletown Convention & Visitors Bureau	(513) 422-3030
http://www.visitmiddletown.org	
Oxford Chamber of Commerce	(513) 523-5200
http://www.oxfordchamber.org	
Oxford Visitors Bureau	(513) 523-8687
http://www.enjoyoxford.org	
The Chamber of Commerce	(513) 422-4551
http://www.mmvchamber.org	
West Chester Chamber of Commerce	(513) 777-3600
http://www.sebcchamber.com	

Butler County Communities

BECKETT RIDGE (CDP). Covers a land area of 4.864 square miles and a water area of 0 square miles. Located at 39.34° N. Lat.; 84.43° W. Long.
Population: 4,503 (1990); 8,663 (2000); 9,109 (2005); 9,602 (2010 projected); Race: 84.0% White, 6.3% Black, 7.9% Asian, 1.9% Hispanic of any race (2005); Density: 1,872.6 persons per square mile (2005); Average household size: 2.73 (2005); Median age: 36.0 (2005); Males per 100 females: 98.8 (2005); Marriage status: 19.2% never married, 69.0% now married, 2.3% widowed, 9.5% divorced (2000); Foreign born: 8.6% (2000); Ancestry (includes multiple ancestries): 33.6% German, 18.0% Irish, 14.1% Other groups, 13.0% English, 5.4% Italian (2000).
Economy: Employment by occupation: 26.7% management, 29.9% professional, 5.4% services, 29.9% sales, 0.0% farming, 2.4% construction, 5.6% production (2000).
Income: Per capita income: $36,242 (2005); Median household income: $81,609 (2005); Average household income: $99,049 (2005); Percent of households with income of $100,000 or more: 36.9% (2005); Poverty rate: 1.5% (2000).
Education: Percent of population age 25 and over with: High school diploma (including GED) or higher: 96.2% (2005); Bachelor's degree or higher: 54.2% (2005); Master's degree or higher: 21.0% (2005).
Housing: Homeownership rate: 84.0% (2005); Median home value: $194,835 (2005); Median rent: $884 per month (2000); Median age of housing: 9 years (2000).
Transportation: Commute to work: 96.0% car, 0.8% public transportation, 0.2% walk, 2.9% work from home (2000); Travel time to work: 20.0% less

than 15 minutes, 47.4% 15 to 30 minutes, 23.6% 30 to 45 minutes, 7.2% 45 to 60 minutes, 1.8% 60 minutes or more (2000)

FAIRFIELD (city). Covers a land area of 20.990 square miles and a water area of 0.087 square miles. Located at 39.33° N. Lat.; 84.54° W. Long. Elevation is 590 feet.

History: The pioneers gave this area the name of Fairfield for the natural beauty of the surrounding fields. The City of Fairfield was originally a part of Fairfield Township, one of 13 townships in Butler County, Ohio. Fairfield was first incorporated as a village on July 10, 1954, and then by way of special census became a city on October 20, 1955. In 1979, the citizens of Fairfield voted to accept a charter that established a council-manager form of government.

Population: 40,084 (1990); 42,097 (2000); 42,564 (2005); 43,263 (2010 projected); Race: 87.3% White, 7.6% Black, 2.9% Asian, 1.8% Hispanic of any race (2005); Density: 2,027.8 persons per square mile (2005); Average household size: 2.45 (2005); Median age: 36.2 (2005); Males per 100 females: 95.2 (2005); Marriage status: 25.3% never married, 59.1% now married, 5.0% widowed, 10.6% divorced (2000); Foreign born: 3.6% (2000); Ancestry (includes multiple ancestries): 31.7% German, 14.4% Irish, 12.9% Other groups, 11.2% English, 9.0% United States or American (2000).

Economy: Unemployment rate: 4.8% (2005); Total civilian labor force: 25,057 (2005); Single-family building permits issued: 93 (2005); Multi-family building permits issued: 0 (2005); Employment by occupation: 15.9% management, 23.5% professional, 10.4% services, 30.6% sales, 0.1% farming, 7.1% construction, 12.4% production (2000).

Income: Per capita income: $27,178 (2005); Median household income: $56,022 (2005); Average household income: $66,299 (2005); Percent of households with income of $100,000 or more: 16.2% (2005); Poverty rate: 4.2% (2000).

Taxes: Total city taxes per capita: $556 (2004); City property taxes per capita: $107 (2004).

Education: Percent of population age 25 and over with: High school diploma (including GED) or higher: 89.1% (2005); Bachelor's degree or higher: 27.6% (2005); Master's degree or higher: 8.3% (2005).

School District(s)
Fairfield City SD (PK-12)
    2003-04 Enrollment: 9,547 . . . . (513) 829-6300

Two-year College(s)
Moler-Pickens Beauty Academy (Private, For-profit)
    Fall 2004 Enrollment: 119 . . . . (513) 874-5116
    2005-06 Tuition: In-state $7,260; Out-of-state $7,260

Housing: Homeownership rate: 65.8% (2005); Median home value: $141,031 (2005); Median rent: $593 per month (2000); Median age of housing: 23 years (2000).

Hospitals: Mercy Hospital - Fairfield (167 beds)

Safety: Violent crime rate: 28.4 per 10,000 population; Property crime rate: 358.9 per 10,000 population (2004).

Newspapers: Fairfield Echo (General - Circulation 20,000)

Transportation: Commute to work: 95.7% car, 1.1% public transportation, 0.5% walk, 2.3% work from home (2000); Travel time to work: 27.1% less than 15 minutes, 43.9% 15 to 30 minutes, 20.5% 30 to 45 minutes, 6.1% 45 to 60 minutes, 2.4% 60 minutes or more (2000)

Additional Information Contacts
City of Fairfield . . . . (513) 867-5300
    http://www.fairfield-city.org
Fairfield Chamber of Commerce . . . . (513) 881-5500
    http://www.fairfieldchamber.com

HAMILTON (city). Covers a land area of 21.612 square miles and a water area of 0.465 square miles. Located at 39.39° N. Lat.; 84.56° W. Long. Elevation is 600 feet.

History: Settlement at Hamilton began in 1791 when General St. Clair built Fort Hamilton as a military and trading post. The town was platted in 1794 by Colonel Israel Ludlow, and named Fairfield, but the site was abandoned in 1796. When the plat was recorded in 1802, the town was named Hamilton for the fort, and became the seat of Butler County. In 1854 Rossville, settled in 1804 on the other side of the Great Miami River, became part of Hamilton. It was the Hamilton Hydraulic water-power plant completed in 1852 that changed Hamilton into an industrial center. A resident here at that time was William Dean Howells, who describes the city in "A Boy's Town."

Population: 61,618 (1990); 60,690 (2000); 60,873 (2005); 61,383 (2010 projected); Race: 87.9% White, 7.8% Black, 0.6% Asian, 3.2% Hispanic of any race (2005); Density: 2,816.7 persons per square mile (2005); Average household size: 2.48 (2005); Median age: 35.4 (2005); Males per 100 females: 93.7 (2005); Marriage status: 24.7% never married, 52.5% now married, 8.6% widowed, 14.2% divorced (2000); Foreign born: 2.2% (2000); Ancestry (includes multiple ancestries): 21.6% German, 15.0% United States or American, 14.7% Other groups, 11.8% Irish, 8.6% English (2000).

Economy: Unemployment rate: 6.0% (2005); Total civilian labor force: 29,771 (2005); Single-family building permits issued: 171 (2005); Multi-family building permits issued: 119 (2005); Employment by occupation: 8.8% management, 13.7% professional, 16.7% services, 28.0% sales, 0.1% farming, 10.8% construction, 21.8% production (2000).

Income: Per capita income: $19,467 (2005); Median household income: $38,957 (2005); Average household income: $47,559 (2005); Percent of households with income of $100,000 or more: 7.1% (2005); Poverty rate: 13.4% (2000).

Taxes: Total city taxes per capita: $468 (2004); City property taxes per capita: $109 (2004).

Education: Percent of population age 25 and over with: High school diploma (including GED) or higher: 73.6% (2005); Bachelor's degree or higher: 12.4% (2005); Master's degree or higher: 3.7% (2005).

School District(s)
Butler Technology & Career Development Schools (07-12)
    2003-04 Enrollment: n/a . . . . (513) 868-1911
Edgewood City School District (PK-12)
    2003-04 Enrollment: 3,595 . . . . (513) 863-4692
Fairfield City SD (PK-12)
    2003-04 Enrollment: 9,547 . . . . (513) 829-6300
Hamilton City SD (PK-12)
    2003-04 Enrollment: 9,607 . . . . (513) 887-5000
New Miami Local SD (PK-12)
    2003-04 Enrollment: 868 . . . . (513) 863-0833
Richard Allen Academy III (KG-05)
    2003-04 Enrollment: 93 . . . . (513) 868-2900
Ross Local SD (PK-12)
    2003-04 Enrollment: 2,580 . . . . (513) 863-1253

Four-year College(s)
Miami University-Hamilton (Public)
    Fall 2004 Enrollment: 2,590 . . . . (513) 785-3000
    2005-06 Tuition: In-state $4,104; Out-of-state $15,636

Two-year College(s)
Butler Tech-D Russel Lee Career Center (Public)
    Fall 2004 Enrollment: 542 . . . . (513) 868-6300

Housing: Homeownership rate: 61.0% (2005); Median home value: $101,323 (2005); Median rent: $402 per month (2000); Median age of housing: 47 years (2000).

Hospitals: Fort Hamilton Hospital (307 beds)

Safety: Violent crime rate: 88.7 per 10,000 population; Property crime rate: 856.8 per 10,000 population (2004).

Newspapers: Journal-News (Circulation 22,650)

Transportation: Commute to work: 94.2% car, 1.0% public transportation, 2.5% walk, 1.5% work from home (2000); Travel time to work: 32.2% less than 15 minutes, 36.9% 15 to 30 minutes, 20.0% 30 to 45 minutes, 6.5% 45 to 60 minutes, 4.4% 60 minutes or more (2000)

Additional Information Contacts
City of Hamilton . . . . (513) 785-7000
    http://www.hamilton-city.org
Hamilton Chamber of Commerce . . . . (513) 844-1500
    http://www.hamilton-ohio.com

JACKSONBURG (village). Covers a land area of 0.019 square miles and a water area of 0 square miles. Located at 39.53° N. Lat.; 84.50° W. Long. Elevation is 960 feet.

History: Sometimes spelled Jacksonburgh.

Population: 50 (1990); 67 (2000); 81 (2005); 94 (2010 projected); Race: 95.1% White, 0.0% Black, 0.0% Asian, 0.0% Hispanic of any race (2005); Density: 4,154.7 persons per square mile (2005); Average household size: 2.89 (2005); Median age: 37.5 (2005); Males per 100 females: 113.2 (2005); Marriage status: 35.3% never married, 54.9% now married, 3.9% widowed, 5.9% divorced (2000); Foreign born: 0.0% (2000); Ancestry (includes multiple ancestries): 31.4% German, 20.0% United States or American, 17.1% Irish, 11.4% English, 7.1% Polish (2000).

Economy: Single-family building permits issued: 0 (2005); Multi-family building permits issued: 0 (2005); Employment by occupation: 7.1%

management, 17.9% professional, 7.1% services, 39.3% sales, 0.0% farming, 10.7% construction, 17.9% production (2000).
Income: Per capita income: $16,821 (2005); Median household income: $45,000 (2005); Average household income: $48,661 (2005); Percent of households with income of $100,000 or more: 0.0% (2005); Poverty rate: 0.0% (2000).
Education: Percent of population age 25 and over with: High school diploma (including GED) or higher: 83.0% (2005); Bachelor's degree or higher: 11.3% (2005); Master's degree or higher: 0.0% (2005).
Housing: Homeownership rate: 85.7% (2005); Median home value: $100,750 (2005); Median rent: $563 per month (2000); Median age of housing: 60+ years (2000).
Transportation: Commute to work: 89.3% car, 0.0% public transportation, 0.0% walk, 10.7% work from home (2000); Travel time to work: 16.0% less than 15 minutes, 48.0% 15 to 30 minutes, 16.0% 30 to 45 minutes, 8.0% 45 to 60 minutes, 12.0% 60 minutes or more (2000)

MIDDLETOWN
(city). Covers a land area of 25.657 square miles and a water area of 0.144 square miles. Located at 39.50° N. Lat.; 84.37° W. Long. Elevation is 665 feet.
History: Middletown was platted in 1802 by Stephen Vail and James Sutton, who named it for its position midway between Cincinnati and Dayton. It was in Middletown in 1825 that Governor DeWitt Clinton of New York took the first shovelful of dirt to signify the beginning of the Miami & Erie Canal.
Population: 52,003 (1990); 51,605 (2000); 51,958 (2005); 52,598 (2010 projected); Race: 85.5% White, 11.5% Black, 0.5% Asian, 1.1% Hispanic of any race (2005); Density: 2,025.1 persons per square mile (2005); Average household size: 2.37 (2005); Median age: 36.6 (2005); Males per 100 females: 92.3 (2005); Marriage status: 23.7% never married, 53.5% now married, 8.3% widowed, 14.6% divorced (2000); Foreign born: 1.0% (2000); Ancestry (includes multiple ancestries): 17.2% Other groups, 16.9% German, 15.4% United States or American, 11.5% Irish, 10.0% English (2000).
Economy: Unemployment rate: 6.1% (2005); Total civilian labor force: 26,152 (2005); Single-family building permits issued: 34 (2005); Multi-family building permits issued: 22 (2005); Employment by occupation: 8.3% management, 16.0% professional, 16.3% services, 25.5% sales, 0.1% farming, 9.6% construction, 24.2% production (2000).
Income: Per capita income: $21,409 (2005); Median household income: $39,851 (2005); Average household income: $50,344 (2005); Percent of households with income of $100,000 or more: 9.2% (2005); Poverty rate: 12.6% (2000).
Taxes: Total city taxes per capita: $489 (2004); City property taxes per capita: $133 (2004).
Education: Percent of population age 25 and over with: High school diploma (including GED) or higher: 77.2% (2005); Bachelor's degree or higher: 13.2% (2005); Master's degree or higher: 5.0% (2005).

School District(s)
Lakota Local SD (PK-12)
   2003-04 Enrollment: 16,358 . . . . (513) 874-5505
Life Skills Center-Middletown (09-12)
   2003-04 Enrollment: 322 . . . . (513) 423-1800
Madison Local SD (PK-12)
   2003-04 Enrollment: 1,590 . . . . (513) 420-4750
Middletown City SD (PK-12)
   2003-04 Enrollment: 7,296 . . . . (513) 423-0781
Middletown Fitness & Prep Acad (KG-06)
   2003-04 Enrollment: 158 . . . . (513) 424-6110
Summit Academy-Middletown (02-08)
   2003-04 Enrollment: 77 . . . . (513) 420-9767

Four-year College(s)
Miami University-Middletown (Public)
   Fall 2004 Enrollment: 2,032 . . . . (513) 727-3200
   2005-06 Tuition: In-state $4,104; Out-of-state $15,636

Two-year College(s)
Carousel Beauty College (Private, For-profit)
   Fall 2004 Enrollment: 73 . . . . (937) 223-3572
Tri State Semi Driver Training Inc (Private, For-profit)
   Fall 2004 Enrollment: 1 . . . . (513) 424-1237

Housing: Homeownership rate: 60.0% (2005); Median home value: $109,145 (2005); Median rent: $414 per month (2000); Median age of housing: 41 years (2000).
Hospitals: Middletown Regional Hospital (310 beds)
Safety: Violent crime rate: 29.6 per 10,000 population; Property crime rate: 660.0 per 10,000 population (2004).
Newspapers: Middletown Journal (Circulation 20,916)
Transportation: Commute to work: 94.7% car, 1.1% public transportation, 1.8% walk, 1.7% work from home (2000); Travel time to work: 42.5% less than 15 minutes, 32.4% 15 to 30 minutes, 17.0% 30 to 45 minutes, 4.7% 45 to 60 minutes, 3.3% 60 minutes or more (2000)

Additional Information Contacts
City of Middletown . . . . (513) 425-7730
   http://www.ci.middletown.oh.us
Mid Miami Valley Chamber of Commerce . . . . (513) 422-4551
   http://www.mmvchamber.org
Middletown Convention & Visitors Bureau . . . . (513) 422-3030
   http://www.visitmiddletown.org
The Chamber of Commerce . . . . (513) 422-4551
   http://www.mmvchamber.org

MILLVILLE
(village). Covers a land area of 0.591 square miles and a water area of 0 square miles. Located at 39.38° N. Lat.; 84.65° W. Long. Elevation is 630 feet.
Population: 837 (1990); 817 (2000); 889 (2005); 957 (2010 projected); Race: 97.9% White, 0.9% Black, 0.2% Asian, 0.0% Hispanic of any race (2005); Density: 1,504.7 persons per square mile (2005); Average household size: 2.59 (2005); Median age: 39.4 (2005); Males per 100 females: 87.6 (2005); Marriage status: 22.9% never married, 60.0% now married, 4.2% widowed, 12.9% divorced (2000); Foreign born: 1.2% (2000); Ancestry (includes multiple ancestries): 19.3% German, 17.2% United States or American, 10.0% English, 6.6% Irish, 4.9% Dutch (2000).
Economy: Employment by occupation: 8.7% management, 10.8% professional, 12.5% services, 25.5% sales, 0.0% farming, 20.0% construction, 22.6% production (2000).
Income: Per capita income: $22,731 (2005); Median household income: $48,942 (2005); Average household income: $58,914 (2005); Percent of households with income of $100,000 or more: 11.1% (2005); Poverty rate: 7.0% (2000).
Education: Percent of population age 25 and over with: High school diploma (including GED) or higher: 79.9% (2005); Bachelor's degree or higher: 9.3% (2005); Master's degree or higher: 2.1% (2005).
Housing: Homeownership rate: 82.8% (2005); Median home value: $120,149 (2005); Median rent: $408 per month (2000); Median age of housing: 31 years (2000).
Transportation: Commute to work: 97.6% car, 0.5% public transportation, 1.2% walk, 0.7% work from home (2000); Travel time to work: 17.8% less than 15 minutes, 39.4% 15 to 30 minutes, 33.3% 30 to 45 minutes, 6.4% 45 to 60 minutes, 3.2% 60 minutes or more (2000)

MONROE
(city). Covers a land area of 15.509 square miles and a water area of 0.023 square miles. Located at 39.44° N. Lat.; 84.36° W. Long. Elevation is 823 feet.
Population: 6,078 (1990); 7,133 (2000); 9,375 (2005); 11,409 (2010 projected); Race: 96.5% White, 1.7% Black, 0.5% Asian, 0.8% Hispanic of any race (2005); Density: 604.5 persons per square mile (2005); Average household size: 2.59 (2005); Median age: 40.1 (2005); Males per 100 females: 92.8 (2005); Marriage status: 16.5% never married, 67.7% now married, 6.9% widowed, 8.9% divorced (2000); Foreign born: 0.9% (2000); Ancestry (includes multiple ancestries): 26.0% German, 13.9% Irish, 13.8% English, 13.1% United States or American, 7.4% Other groups (2000).
Economy: Single-family building permits issued: 248 (2005); Multi-family building permits issued: 46 (2005); Employment by occupation: 12.4% management, 21.7% professional, 7.5% services, 29.0% sales, 0.0% farming, 12.7% construction, 16.7% production (2000).
Income: Per capita income: $28,427 (2005); Median household income: $64,063 (2005); Average household income: $72,021 (2005); Percent of households with income of $100,000 or more: 17.9% (2005); Poverty rate: 1.9% (2000).
Taxes: Total city taxes per capita: $593 (2004); City property taxes per capita: $131 (2004).
Education: Percent of population age 25 and over with: High school diploma (including GED) or higher: 90.6% (2005); Bachelor's degree or higher: 24.3% (2005); Master's degree or higher: 7.1% (2005).

School District(s)
Monroe Local Sd (PK-12)
   2003-04 Enrollment: 1,521 . . . . (513) 539-2536

Housing: Homeownership rate: 79.3% (2005); Median home value: $146,680 (2005); Median rent: $470 per month (2000); Median age of housing: 27 years (2000).
Safety: Violent crime rate: 87.6 per 10,000 population; Property crime rate: 593.0 per 10,000 population (2004).
Transportation: Commute to work: 96.5% car, 0.3% public transportation, 0.8% walk, 1.8% work from home (2000); Travel time to work: 25.2% less than 15 minutes, 47.0% 15 to 30 minutes, 17.0% 30 to 45 minutes, 5.3% 45 to 60 minutes, 5.5% 60 minutes or more (2000)
Additional Information Contacts
City of Monroe .... (513) 539-7374
http://www.monroeohio.org
The Chamber of Commerce .... (513) 422-4551
http://www.mmvchamber.org

NEW MIAMI (village).
Covers a land area of 0.887 square miles and a water area of 0.042 square miles. Located at 39.43° N. Lat.; 84.54° W. Long. Elevation is 590 feet.
Population: 2,598 (1990); 2,469 (2000); 2,634 (2005); 2,802 (2010 projected); Race: 93.3% White, 4.6% Black, 0.1% Asian, 1.0% Hispanic of any race (2005); Density: 2,968.1 persons per square mile (2005); Average household size: 2.77 (2005); Median age: 34.2 (2005); Males per 100 females: 99.1 (2005); Marriage status: 22.2% never married, 59.9% now married, 7.2% widowed, 10.7% divorced (2000); Foreign born: 1.2% (2000); Ancestry (includes multiple ancestries): 21.4% United States or American, 13.2% Other groups, 9.0% German, 5.7% Irish, 4.9% English (2000).
Economy: Employment by occupation: 5.4% management, 6.9% professional, 19.0% services, 24.8% sales, 0.0% farming, 16.3% construction, 27.6% production (2000).
Income: Per capita income: $17,693 (2005); Median household income: $40,862 (2005); Average household income: $48,952 (2005); Percent of households with income of $100,000 or more: 8.4% (2005); Poverty rate: 11.0% (2000).
Education: Percent of population age 25 and over with: High school diploma (including GED) or higher: 61.5% (2005); Bachelor's degree or higher: 2.4% (2005); Master's degree or higher: 1.0% (2005).
Housing: Homeownership rate: 70.9% (2005); Median home value: $77,076 (2005); Median rent: $407 per month (2000); Median age of housing: 42 years (2000).
Transportation: Commute to work: 98.5% car, 0.3% public transportation, 0.4% walk, 0.0% work from home (2000); Travel time to work: 27.3% less than 15 minutes, 39.1% 15 to 30 minutes, 19.7% 30 to 45 minutes, 7.2% 45 to 60 minutes, 6.7% 60 minutes or more (2000)

OKEANA (unincorporated postal area, zip code 45053).
Covers a land area of 26.293 square miles and a water area of 0 square miles. Located at 39.35° N. Lat.; 84.78° W. Long. Elevation is 645 feet.
Population: 3,047 (2000); Race: 98.2% White, 0.0% Black, 0.0% Asian, 0.0% Hispanic of any race (2000); Density: 115.9 persons per square mile (2000); Age: 30.6% under 18, 5.6% over 64 (2000); Marriage status: 21.3% never married, 70.0% now married, 2.3% widowed, 6.5% divorced (2000); Foreign born: 0.9% (2000); Ancestry (includes multiple ancestries): 43.7% German, 15.1% United States or American, 11.9% Irish, 8.5% English, 6.7% Italian (2000).
Economy: Employment by occupation: 14.9% management, 12.9% professional, 8.3% services, 22.5% sales, 1.8% farming, 19.2% construction, 20.5% production (2000).
Income: Per capita income: $23,329 (2000); Median household income: $60,530 (2000); Poverty rate: 4.4% (2000).
Education: Percent of population age 25 and over with: High school diploma (including GED) or higher: 87.9% (2000); Bachelor's degree or higher: 16.3% (2000).
Housing: Homeownership rate: 94.0% (2000); Median home value: $175,600 (2000); Median rent: $465 per month (2000); Median age of housing: 21 years (2000).
Transportation: Commute to work: 94.9% car, 1.3% public transportation, 0.9% walk, 1.3% work from home (2000); Travel time to work: 15.1% less than 15 minutes, 24.6% 15 to 30 minutes, 37.4% 30 to 45 minutes, 14.8% 45 to 60 minutes, 8.1% 60 minutes or more (2000)

OLDE WEST CHESTER (CDP).
Covers a land area of 0.348 square miles and a water area of 0 square miles. Located at 39.33° N. Lat.; 84.40° W. Long.

Population: 152 (1990); 232 (2000); 224 (2005); 196 (2010 projected); Race: 88.8% White, 5.8% Black, 1.3% Asian, 2.2% Hispanic of any race (2005); Density: 643.8 persons per square mile (2005); Average household size: 2.70 (2005); Median age: 38.8 (2005); Males per 100 females: 100.0 (2005); Marriage status: 37.3% never married, 50.2% now married, 10.1% widowed, 2.3% divorced (2000); Foreign born: 7.9% (2000); Ancestry (includes multiple ancestries): 36.5% German, 12.0% French (except Basque), 10.2% Swiss, 9.4% English, 8.6% United States or American (2000).
Economy: Employment by occupation: 9.4% management, 37.4% professional, 10.1% services, 21.6% sales, 0.0% farming, 13.7% construction, 7.9% production (2000).
Income: Per capita income: $36,127 (2005); Median household income: $78,676 (2005); Average household income: $97,500 (2005); Percent of households with income of $100,000 or more: 32.5% (2005); Poverty rate: 7.9% (2000).
Education: Percent of population age 25 and over with: High school diploma (including GED) or higher: 83.6% (2005); Bachelor's degree or higher: 41.4% (2005); Master's degree or higher: 9.2% (2005).
Housing: Homeownership rate: 79.5% (2005); Median home value: $160,870 (2005); Median rent: $950 per month (2000); Median age of housing: 35 years (2000).
Transportation: Commute to work: 94.2% car, 0.0% public transportation, 0.0% walk, 5.8% work from home (2000); Travel time to work: 29.0% less than 15 minutes, 31.3% 15 to 30 minutes, 27.5% 30 to 45 minutes, 6.1% 45 to 60 minutes, 6.1% 60 minutes or more (2000)

OXFORD (city).
Covers a land area of 5.876 square miles and a water area of 0.003 square miles. Located at 39.50° N. Lat.; 84.74° W. Long. Elevation is 972 feet.
History: Named for Oxford, the university town in Oxfordshire, England. Oxford was planned, even before the land had been surveyed and cleared, as the site of Miami University, authorized by the Ohio Legislature in 1809. The University actually opened in 1824, and the town grew around it. It was joined in 1848 by the Oxford College for Women, which flourished for 80 years before it was absorbed by Miami University. One of the instructors at the University was William Holmes McGuffey, whose name became synonymous with the "Eclectic Readers" that he compiled to help children learn to read.
Population: 21,307 (1990); 21,943 (2000); 22,509 (2005); 23,193 (2010 projected); Race: 90.0% White, 4.7% Black, 2.8% Asian, 1.7% Hispanic of any race (2005); Density: 3,830.7 persons per square mile (2005); Average household size: 3.69 (2005); Median age: 22.0 (2005); Males per 100 females: 89.7 (2005); Marriage status: 70.4% never married, 24.1% now married, 2.4% widowed, 3.2% divorced (2000); Foreign born: 3.7% (2000); Ancestry (includes multiple ancestries): 31.6% German, 15.9% Irish, 11.1% Other groups, 10.8% English, 8.2% Italian (2000).
Economy: Single-family building permits issued: 38 (2005); Multi-family building permits issued: 17 (2005); Employment by occupation: 8.3% management, 31.3% professional, 25.6% services, 24.1% sales, 0.1% farming, 3.7% construction, 7.0% production (2000).
Income: Per capita income: $13,934 (2005); Median household income: $27,850 (2005); Average household income: $46,638 (2005); Percent of households with income of $100,000 or more: 12.8% (2005); Poverty rate: 43.7% (2000).
Education: Percent of population age 25 and over with: High school diploma (including GED) or higher: 90.0% (2005); Bachelor's degree or higher: 54.2% (2005); Master's degree or higher: 29.5% (2005).
School District(s)
Talawanda City SD (PK-12)
  2003-04 Enrollment: 3,104 .... (513) 523-4716
Four-year College(s)
Miami University-Oxford (Public)
  Fall 2004 Enrollment: 17,161 .... (513) 529-1809
  2005-06 Tuition: In-state $21,487; Out-of-state $21,507
Housing: Homeownership rate: 34.0% (2005); Median home value: $153,865 (2005); Median rent: $443 per month (2000); Median age of housing: 27 years (2000).
Hospitals: McCullough-Hyde Memorial Hospital (60 beds)
Safety: Violent crime rate: 37.6 per 10,000 population; Property crime rate: 329.6 per 10,000 population (2004).
Newspapers: The Oxford Press (General - Circulation 4,500)
Transportation: Commute to work: 63.5% car, 2.0% public transportation, 27.7% walk, 3.9% work from home (2000); Travel time to work: 63.9% less

than 15 minutes, 17.9% 15 to 30 minutes, 8.4% 30 to 45 minutes, 6.1% 45 to 60 minutes, 3.7% 60 minutes or more (2000)

Additional Information Contacts

City of Oxford . . . . (513) 524-5200
http://www.cityofoxford.org/index.asp
Oxford Chamber of Commerce . . . . (513) 523-5200
http://www.oxfordchamber.org
Oxford Visitors Bureau . . . . (513) 523-8687
http://www.enjoyoxford.org

ROSS (CDP). Aka Venice. Covers a land area of 1.695 square miles and a water area of 0.021 square miles. Located at 39.31° N. Lat.; 84.64° W. Long. Elevation is 558 feet.

Population: 2,140 (1990); 1,971 (2000); 2,083 (2005); 2,189 (2010 projected); Race: 97.5% White, 0.2% Black, 0.3% Asian, 0.9% Hispanic of any race (2005); Density: 1,228.8 persons per square mile (2005); Average household size: 2.66 (2005); Median age: 36.4 (2005); Males per 100 females: 92.9 (2005); Marriage status: 17.0% never married, 68.1% now married, 8.0% widowed, 7.0% divorced (2000); Foreign born: 0.9% (2000); Ancestry (includes multiple ancestries): 18.9% German, 18.7% Irish, 18.2% United States or American, 12.2% English, 8.9% Other groups (2000).
Economy: Employment by occupation: 4.7% management, 15.2% professional, 9.1% services, 25.4% sales, 0.0% farming, 19.8% construction, 25.7% production (2000).
Income: Per capita income: $21,049 (2005); Median household income: $47,021 (2005); Average household income: $55,996 (2005); Percent of households with income of $100,000 or more: 11.1% (2005); Poverty rate: 3.6% (2000).
Education: Percent of population age 25 and over with: High school diploma (including GED) or higher: 76.5% (2005); Bachelor's degree or higher: 8.4% (2005); Master's degree or higher: 2.3% (2005).
Housing: Homeownership rate: 72.8% (2005); Median home value: $119,643 (2005); Median rent: $422 per month (2000); Median age of housing: 35 years (2000).
Transportation: Commute to work: 94.4% car, 0.0% public transportation, 2.3% walk, 3.4% work from home (2000); Travel time to work: 18.9% less than 15 minutes, 28.7% 15 to 30 minutes, 32.3% 30 to 45 minutes, 12.7% 45 to 60 minutes, 7.5% 60 minutes or more (2000)

SEVEN MILE (village). Covers a land area of 0.758 square miles and a water area of 0 square miles. Located at 39.48° N. Lat.; 84.55° W. Long. Elevation is 655 feet.

Population: 868 (1990); 678 (2000); 653 (2005); 649 (2010 projected); Race: 97.7% White, 0.5% Black, 1.1% Asian, 0.9% Hispanic of any race (2005); Density: 861.6 persons per square mile (2005); Average household size: 2.61 (2005); Median age: 38.8 (2005); Males per 100 females: 92.1 (2005); Marriage status: 22.9% never married, 62.0% now married, 6.6% widowed, 8.5% divorced (2000); Foreign born: 1.3% (2000); Ancestry (includes multiple ancestries): 27.8% German, 14.2% United States or American, 14.1% English, 9.2% Irish, 8.2% Other groups (2000).
Economy: Employment by occupation: 4.3% management, 15.2% professional, 17.2% services, 24.7% sales, 0.0% farming, 13.8% construction, 24.7% production (2000).
Income: Per capita income: $22,583 (2005); Median household income: $50,746 (2005); Average household income: $58,670 (2005); Percent of households with income of $100,000 or more: 10.8% (2005); Poverty rate: 4.1% (2000).
Education: Percent of population age 25 and over with: High school diploma (including GED) or higher: 81.0% (2005); Bachelor's degree or higher: 9.4% (2005); Master's degree or higher: 3.7% (2005).

School District(s)

Edgewood City School District (PK-12)
2003-04 Enrollment: 3,595 . . . . (513) 863-4692
Housing: Homeownership rate: 78.8% (2005); Median home value: $121,221 (2005); Median rent: $444 per month (2000); Median age of housing: 56 years (2000).
Transportation: Commute to work: 97.1% car, 0.0% public transportation, 0.6% walk, 2.3% work from home (2000); Travel time to work: 21.4% less than 15 minutes, 43.6% 15 to 30 minutes, 21.4% 30 to 45 minutes, 8.6% 45 to 60 minutes, 5.0% 60 minutes or more (2000)

SOMERVILLE (village). Covers a land area of 0.290 square miles and a water area of 0 square miles. Located at 39.56° N. Lat.; 84.63° W. Long. Elevation is 765 feet.

Population: 279 (1990); 294 (2000); 335 (2005); 373 (2010 projected); Race: 99.4% White, 0.0% Black, 0.6% Asian, 0.0% Hispanic of any race (2005); Density: 1,155.9 persons per square mile (2005); Average household size: 2.72 (2005); Median age: 36.4 (2005); Males per 100 females: 105.5 (2005); Marriage status: 25.5% never married, 54.3% now married, 7.0% widowed, 13.2% divorced (2000); Foreign born: 0.0% (2000); Ancestry (includes multiple ancestries): 29.5% United States or American, 14.6% German, 7.1% Other groups, 3.1% Scottish, 3.1% Italian (2000).
Economy: Employment by occupation: 4.7% management, 2.3% professional, 16.4% services, 27.3% sales, 0.0% farming, 21.9% construction, 27.3% production (2000).
Income: Per capita income: $15,351 (2005); Median household income: $35,250 (2005); Average household income: $41,809 (2005); Percent of households with income of $100,000 or more: 3.3% (2005); Poverty rate: 10.3% (2000).
Education: Percent of population age 25 and over with: High school diploma (including GED) or higher: 59.2% (2005); Bachelor's degree or higher: 0.0% (2005); Master's degree or higher: 0.0% (2005).
Housing: Homeownership rate: 73.2% (2005); Median home value: $85,600 (2005); Median rent: $458 per month (2000); Median age of housing: 60+ years (2000).
Transportation: Commute to work: 82.6% car, 2.5% public transportation, 7.4% walk, 4.1% work from home (2000); Travel time to work: 11.2% less than 15 minutes, 35.3% 15 to 30 minutes, 12.9% 30 to 45 minutes, 25.0% 45 to 60 minutes, 15.5% 60 minutes or more (2000)

SOUTH MIDDLETOWN (CDP). Covers a land area of 0.107 square miles and a water area of 0 square miles. Located at 39.48° N. Lat.; 84.41° W. Long.

Population: 288 (1990); 264 (2000); 265 (2005); 262 (2010 projected); Race: 97.4% White, 0.8% Black, 0.0% Asian, 0.8% Hispanic of any race (2005); Density: 2,481.6 persons per square mile (2005); Average household size: 2.65 (2005); Median age: 31.7 (2005); Males per 100 females: 85.3 (2005); Marriage status: 7.3% never married, 60.6% now married, 5.1% widowed, 27.0% divorced (2000); Foreign born: 0.0% (2000); Ancestry (includes multiple ancestries): 52.3% United States or American, 10.3% German, 5.7% Other groups, 5.2% Swedish, 2.9% Scotch-Irish (2000).
Economy: Employment by occupation: 19.5% management, 13.4% professional, 26.8% services, 15.9% sales, 0.0% farming, 3.7% construction, 20.7% production (2000).
Income: Per capita income: $18,462 (2005); Median household income: $53,571 (2005); Average household income: $48,925 (2005); Percent of households with income of $100,000 or more: 7.0% (2005); Poverty rate: 5.7% (2000).
Education: Percent of population age 25 and over with: High school diploma (including GED) or higher: 68.4% (2005); Bachelor's degree or higher: 13.3% (2005); Master's degree or higher: 7.6% (2005).
Housing: Homeownership rate: 63.0% (2005); Median home value: $86,250 (2005); Median rent: $475 per month (2000); Median age of housing: 52 years (2000).
Transportation: Commute to work: 89.0% car, 0.0% public transportation, 11.0% walk, 0.0% work from home (2000); Travel time to work: 46.3% less than 15 minutes, 53.7% 15 to 30 minutes, 0.0% 30 to 45 minutes, 0.0% 45 to 60 minutes, 0.0% 60 minutes or more (2000)

TRENTON (city). Covers a land area of 3.786 square miles and a water area of 0 square miles. Located at 39.48° N. Lat.; 84.45° W. Long. Elevation is 653 feet.

History: In 1799, Michael Pearce, a native of Essex County, New Jersey, founded the community that was to become Trenton, Ohio. The land deed, signed by President Thomas Jefferson and Secretary of State James Madison, established a parcel of 1,500 acres stretching from the Miami River on the east, to the present State Street on the north, and on towards the present Wayne Madison Road as the western boundary. Pearce platted 33 lots in 1816 and selected the name of Bloomfield for the new community. In 1820 an application for a post office was filed. To avoid confusion with another Ohio town, Pearce renamed the village as a remembrance of his birthplace, New Jersey's state capital Trenton. Growth was slow in the village, and it was not until 1971 that the population had grown to the required 5,000 to be classified as a city.
Population: 6,630 (1990); 8,746 (2000); 10,445 (2005); 12,022 (2010 projected); Race: 97.8% White, 0.6% Black, 0.4% Asian, 1.1% Hispanic of any race (2005); Density: 2,759.2 persons per square mile (2005); Average

household size: 2.71 (2005); Median age: 32.5 (2005); Males per 100 females: 97.4 (2005); Marriage status: 18.6% never married, 66.1% now married, 5.1% widowed, 10.3% divorced (2000); Foreign born: 1.6% (2000); Ancestry (includes multiple ancestries): 21.3% German, 15.3% United States or American, 12.8% Irish, 9.2% Other groups, 7.7% English (2000).
Economy: Single-family building permits issued: 98 (2005); Multi-family building permits issued: 0 (2005); Employment by occupation: 10.5% management, 13.8% professional, 12.0% services, 25.7% sales, 0.1% farming, 11.7% construction, 26.1% production (2000).
Income: Per capita income: $23,444 (2005); Median household income: $57,135 (2005); Average household income: $63,285 (2005); Percent of households with income of $100,000 or more: 13.4% (2005); Poverty rate: 3.7% (2000).
Education: Percent of population age 25 and over with: High school diploma (including GED) or higher: 85.0% (2005); Bachelor's degree or higher: 10.0% (2005); Master's degree or higher: 2.8% (2005).

School District(s)
Edgewood City School District (PK-12)
    2003-04 Enrollment: 3,595 . . . . (513) 863-4692

Housing: Homeownership rate: 74.4% (2005); Median home value: $133,022 (2005); Median rent: $457 per month (2000); Median age of housing: 25 years (2000).
Safety: Violent crime rate: 1.0 per 10,000 population; Property crime rate: 154.4 per 10,000 population (2004).
Transportation: Commute to work: 97.5% car, 0.6% public transportation, 0.5% walk, 1.0% work from home (2000); Travel time to work: 23.6% less than 15 minutes, 45.3% 15 to 30 minutes, 19.2% 30 to 45 minutes, 7.8% 45 to 60 minutes, 4.1% 60 minutes or more (2000)

Additional Information Contacts
City of Trenton . . . . (513) 988-6304
    http://www.ci.trenton.oh.us/default.asp
The Chamber of Commerce . . . . (513) 422-4551
    http://www.mmvchamber.org

WETHERINGTON
(CDP). Covers a land area of 0.698 square miles and a water area of 0 square miles. Located at 39.36° N. Lat.; 84.37° W. Long.
Population: 737 (1990); 1,010 (2000); 1,174 (2005); 1,316 (2010 projected); Race: 94.1% White, 3.1% Black, 1.4% Asian, 2.0% Hispanic of any race (2005); Density: 1,683.0 persons per square mile (2005); Average household size: 2.74 (2005); Median age: 41.8 (2005); Males per 100 females: 98.3 (2005); Marriage status: 10.4% never married, 88.2% now married, 0.0% widowed, 1.5% divorced (2000); Foreign born: 2.7% (2000); Ancestry (includes multiple ancestries): 37.2% German, 11.1% English, 10.1% Irish, 9.3% Polish, 6.1% French (except Basque) (2000).
Economy: Employment by occupation: 32.1% management, 18.2% professional, 3.2% services, 37.8% sales, 0.0% farming, 0.0% construction, 8.7% production (2000).
Income: Per capita income: $87,445 (2005); Median household income: $188,393 (2005); Average household income: $239,860 (2005); Percent of households with income of $100,000 or more: 80.8% (2005); Poverty rate: 2.4% (2000).
Education: Percent of population age 25 and over with: High school diploma (including GED) or higher: 98.6% (2005); Bachelor's degree or higher: 55.8% (2005); Master's degree or higher: 24.2% (2005).
Housing: Homeownership rate: 98.4% (2005); Median home value: $388,125 (2005); Median rent: $625 per month (2000); Median age of housing: 4 years (2000).
Transportation: Commute to work: 85.5% car, 3.8% public transportation, 0.0% walk, 8.7% work from home (2000); Travel time to work: 6.0% less than 15 minutes, 48.9% 15 to 30 minutes, 32.1% 30 to 45 minutes, 8.2% 45 to 60 minutes, 4.9% 60 minutes or more (2000)

Carroll County

Located in eastern Ohio; drained by Small Sandy, Conotton, and Yellow Creeks. Covers a land area of 394.67 square miles, a water area of 4.33 square miles, and is located in the Eastern Time Zone. The county government was organized in 1832. County seat is Carrollton.

Carroll County is part of the Canton-Massillon, OH Metropolitan Statistical Area. The entire metro area includes: Carroll County, OH; Stark County, OH

Population: 26,521 (1990); 28,836 (2000); 30,017 (2005); 31,248 (2010 projected); Race: 98.4% White, 0.5% Black, 0.2% Asian, 0.6% Hispanic of any race (2005); Density: 76.1 persons per square mile (2005); Average household size: 2.55 (2005); Median age: 39.6 (2005); Males per 100 females: 97.0 (2005).
Religion: Five largest groups: 10.0% The United Methodist Church, 6.6% Catholic Church, 4.9% Evangelical Lutheran Church in America, 2.1% Presbyterian Church (U.S.A.), 2.0% Christian Churches and Churches of Christ (2000).
Economy: Unemployment rate: 6.6% (2005); Total civilian labor force: 14,296 (2005); Leading industries: 29.9% manufacturing; 15.4% retail trade; 13.6% health care and social assistance (2004); Farms: 749 totaling 123,506 acres (2002); Companies that employ 500 or more persons: 0 (2004); Companies that employ 100 to 499 persons: 7 (2004); Companies that employ less than 100 persons: 466 (2004); Black-owned businesses: n/a (2002); Hispanic-owned businesses: n/a (2002); Women-owned businesses: 732 (2002); Retail sales per capita: $7,606 (2006). Single-family building permits issued: 5 (2005); Multi-family building permits issued: 0 (2005).
Income: Per capita income: $18,690 (2005); Median household income: $39,266 (2005); Average household income: $47,315 (2005); Percent of households with income of $100,000 or more: 6.4% (2005); Poverty rate: 10.7% (2003); Bankruptcy rate: 9.63% (2005).
Education: Percent of population age 25 and over with: High school diploma (including GED) or higher: 79.9% (2005); Bachelor's degree or higher: 9.2% (2005); Master's degree or higher: 3.0% (2005).
Housing: Homeownership rate: 80.3% (2005); Median home value: $111,164 (2005); Median rent: $322 per month (2000); Median age of housing: 31 years (2000).
Health: Birth rate: 126.3 per 10,000 population (2004); Death rate: 94.4 per 10,000 population (2004); Age-adjusted cancer mortality rate: 177.6 deaths per 100,000 population (2002); Number of physicians: 5.1 per 10,000 population (2004); Hospital beds: 0.0 per 10,000 population (2003); Hospital admissions: 0.0 per 10,000 population (2003).
Elections: 2004 Presidential election results: 54.5% Bush, 44.6% Kerry, 0.0% Nader, 0.4% Badnarik
National and State Parks: Leesville State Wildlife Area

Additional Information Contacts
Carroll County Government . . . . (330) 627-4869
    http://www.carrollcountyohio.net/
Carroll County Chamber of Commerce . . . . (330) 627-4811
    http://pages.eohio.net/carrollchamber

Carroll County Communities

CARROLLTON
(village). Covers a land area of 2.379 square miles and a water area of 0 square miles. Located at 40.57° N. Lat.; 81.08° W. Long. Elevation is 1,130 feet.
History: Laid out 1815.
Population: 3,194 (1990); 3,190 (2000); 3,306 (2005); 3,432 (2010 projected); Race: 98.8% White, 0.2% Black, 0.1% Asian, 0.6% Hispanic of any race (2005); Density: 1,389.7 persons per square mile (2005); Average household size: 2.20 (2005); Median age: 43.0 (2005); Males per 100 females: 81.4 (2005); Marriage status: 19.8% never married, 55.9% now married, 12.4% widowed, 11.9% divorced (2000); Foreign born: 0.4% (2000); Ancestry (includes multiple ancestries): 25.5% German, 17.8% Irish, 10.9% United States or American, 10.3% English, 5.3% Other groups (2000).
Economy: In agricultural area: grain, wool. Rubber goods, chinaware, brick. Single-family building permits issued: 4 (2005); Multi-family building permits issued: 0 (2005); Employment by occupation: 9.1% management, 17.0% professional, 15.7% services, 23.7% sales, 0.0% farming, 7.7% construction, 26.8% production (2000).
Income: Per capita income: $16,221 (2005); Median household income: $28,533 (2005); Average household income: $34,948 (2005); Percent of households with income of $100,000 or more: 2.5% (2005); Poverty rate: 17.0% (2000).
Education: Percent of population age 25 and over with: High school diploma (including GED) or higher: 76.2% (2005); Bachelor's degree or higher: 11.4% (2005); Master's degree or higher: 2.8% (2005).

School District(s)
Carrollton Ex Vill SD (PK-12)
    2003-04 Enrollment: 2,932 . . . . (330) 627-2181
Warrior Digital Academy
    2003-04 Enrollment: n/a

Housing: Homeownership rate: 61.9% (2005); Median home value: $112,683 (2005); Median rent: $287 per month (2000); Median age of housing: 49 years (2000).
Newspapers: The Free Press Standard (General - Circulation 7,550)
Transportation: Commute to work: 86.9% car, 4.1% public transportation, 4.8% walk, 2.9% work from home (2000); Travel time to work: 47.4% less than 15 minutes, 18.6% 15 to 30 minutes, 11.7% 30 to 45 minutes, 14.5% 45 to 60 minutes, 7.8% 60 minutes or more (2000)
Additional Information Contacts
Carroll County Chamber of Commerce . . . . (330) 627-4811
http://pages.eohio.net/carrollchamber

DELLROY
(village). Covers a land area of 0.171 square miles and a water area of 0.040 square miles. Located at 40.55° N. Lat.; 81.19° W. Long. Elevation is 960 feet.
Population: 314 (1990); 294 (2000); 342 (2005); 389 (2010 projected); Race: 99.1% White, 0.0% Black, 0.0% Asian, 0.0% Hispanic of any race (2005); Density: 1,994.7 persons per square mile (2005); Average household size: 2.39 (2005); Median age: 38.7 (2005); Males per 100 females: 92.1 (2005); Marriage status: 12.3% never married, 66.4% now married, 11.4% widowed, 10.0% divorced (2000); Foreign born: 0.0% (2000); Ancestry (includes multiple ancestries): 25.1% German, 16.9% Irish, 11.2% English, 7.9% French (except Basque), 7.9% Dutch (2000).
Economy: Employment by occupation: 17.6% management, 15.5% professional, 14.2% services, 17.6% sales, 0.0% farming, 8.8% construction, 26.4% production (2000).
Income: Per capita income: $16,418 (2005); Median household income: $30,968 (2005); Average household income: $39,266 (2005); Percent of households with income of $100,000 or more: 6.3% (2005); Poverty rate: 9.1% (2000).
Education: Percent of population age 25 and over with: High school diploma (including GED) or higher: 80.5% (2005); Bachelor's degree or higher: 12.1% (2005); Master's degree or higher: 3.9% (2005).
School District(s)
Carrollton Ex Vill SD (PK-12)
  2003-04 Enrollment: 2,932 . . . . (330) 627-2181
Housing: Homeownership rate: 76.9% (2005); Median home value: $70,435 (2005); Median rent: $321 per month (2000); Median age of housing: 60+ years (2000).
Transportation: Commute to work: 87.6% car, 0.0% public transportation, 10.9% walk, 1.5% work from home (2000); Travel time to work: 23.0% less than 15 minutes, 34.8% 15 to 30 minutes, 23.7% 30 to 45 minutes, 3.7% 45 to 60 minutes, 14.8% 60 minutes or more (2000)

LEESVILLE
(village). Covers a land area of 0.257 square miles and a water area of 0 square miles. Located at 40.45° N. Lat.; 81.21° W. Long. Elevation is 985 feet.
Population: 156 (1990); 184 (2000); 190 (2005); 196 (2010 projected); Race: 99.5% White, 0.5% Black, 0.0% Asian, 1.1% Hispanic of any race (2005); Density: 739.2 persons per square mile (2005); Average household size: 2.53 (2005); Median age: 35.5 (2005); Males per 100 females: 90.0 (2005); Marriage status: 21.2% never married, 62.8% now married, 10.9% widowed, 5.1% divorced (2000); Foreign born: 0.0% (2000); Ancestry (includes multiple ancestries): 29.0% German, 10.1% Other groups, 8.2% English, 6.8% United States or American, 5.8% Welsh (2000).
Economy: Flood-control dam nearby impounds Leesville Reservoir in a small tributary of Tuscarawas River. Employment by occupation: 10.5% management, 2.3% professional, 24.4% services, 10.5% sales, 0.0% farming, 7.0% construction, 45.3% production (2000).
Income: Per capita income: $19,053 (2005); Median household income: $43,804 (2005); Average household income: $48,267 (2005); Percent of households with income of $100,000 or more: 6.7% (2005); Poverty rate: 0.5% (2000).
Education: Percent of population age 25 and over with: High school diploma (including GED) or higher: 75.8% (2005); Bachelor's degree or higher: 5.6% (2005); Master's degree or higher: 5.6% (2005).
Housing: Homeownership rate: 93.3% (2005); Median home value: $57,692 (2005); Median rent: $n/a per month (2000); Median age of housing: 60+ years (2000).
Transportation: Commute to work: 97.6% car, 2.4% public transportation, 0.0% walk, 0.0% work from home (2000); Travel time to work: 21.4% less than 15 minutes, 32.1% 15 to 30 minutes, 34.5% 30 to 45 minutes, 8.3% 45 to 60 minutes, 3.6% 60 minutes or more (2000)

MALVERN
(village). Covers a land area of 0.682 square miles and a water area of 0 square miles. Located at 40.69° N. Lat.; 81.18° W. Long. Elevation is 997 feet.
Population: 1,215 (1990); 1,218 (2000); 1,183 (2005); 1,197 (2010 projected); Race: 92.1% White, 5.8% Black, 0.4% Asian, 1.1% Hispanic of any race (2005); Density: 1,733.5 persons per square mile (2005); Average household size: 2.24 (2005); Median age: 39.2 (2005); Males per 100 females: 90.2 (2005); Marriage status: 23.2% never married, 53.4% now married, 9.6% widowed, 13.7% divorced (2000); Foreign born: 1.0% (2000); Ancestry (includes multiple ancestries): 27.5% German, 13.5% Other groups, 12.1% Irish, 11.7% Italian, 7.7% English (2000).
Economy: In dairying area; makes clay products. Single-family building permits issued: 1 (2005); Multi-family building permits issued: 0 (2005); Employment by occupation: 5.3% management, 12.5% professional, 22.6% services, 18.1% sales, 0.3% farming, 10.0% construction, 31.1% production (2000).
Income: Per capita income: $17,418 (2005); Median household income: $32,169 (2005); Average household income: $39,099 (2005); Percent of households with income of $100,000 or more: 3.6% (2005); Poverty rate: 12.8% (2000).
Education: Percent of population age 25 and over with: High school diploma (including GED) or higher: 74.6% (2005); Bachelor's degree or higher: 9.4% (2005); Master's degree or higher: 2.6% (2005).
School District(s)
Brown Local Digital Academy
  2003-04 Enrollment: n/a
Brown Local SD (KG-12)
  2003-04 Enrollment: 897 . . . . (330) 863-1170
Housing: Homeownership rate: 58.4% (2005); Median home value: $90,617 (2005); Median rent: $305 per month (2000); Median age of housing: 53 years (2000).
Transportation: Commute to work: 87.8% car, 0.0% public transportation, 9.4% walk, 1.4% work from home (2000); Travel time to work: 41.7% less than 15 minutes, 30.2% 15 to 30 minutes, 17.9% 30 to 45 minutes, 7.2% 45 to 60 minutes, 2.9% 60 minutes or more (2000)

MECHANICSTOWN
(unincorporated postal area, zip code 44651). Covers a land area of 22.988 square miles and a water area of 0.009 square miles. Located at 40.62° N. Lat.; 80.96° W. Long. Elevation is 1,240 feet.
Population: 833 (2000); Race: 99.3% White, 0.0% Black, 0.0% Asian, 0.0% Hispanic of any race (2000); Density: 36.2 persons per square mile (2000); Age: 31.0% under 18, 13.9% over 64 (2000); Marriage status: 15.4% never married, 69.9% now married, 9.8% widowed, 4.8% divorced (2000); Foreign born: 0.0% (2000); Ancestry (includes multiple ancestries): 25.4% German, 20.0% Irish, 9.7% English, 8.3% United States or American, 6.4% Italian (2000).
Economy: Employment by occupation: 8.4% management, 6.4% professional, 14.8% services, 27.2% sales, 1.7% farming, 5.5% construction, 35.9% production (2000).
Income: Per capita income: $12,568 (2000); Median household income: $24,219 (2000); Poverty rate: 16.2% (2000).
Education: Percent of population age 25 and over with: High school diploma (including GED) or higher: 76.8% (2000); Bachelor's degree or higher: 3.6% (2000).
School District(s)
Carrollton Ex Vill SD (PK-12)
  2003-04 Enrollment: 2,932 . . . . (330) 627-2181
Housing: Homeownership rate: 70.9% (2000); Median home value: $85,800 (2000); Median rent: $453 per month (2000); Median age of housing: 38 years (2000).
Transportation: Commute to work: 94.2% car, 0.0% public transportation, 2.4% walk, 3.3% work from home (2000); Travel time to work: 27.4% less than 15 minutes, 34.9% 15 to 30 minutes, 14.8% 30 to 45 minutes, 9.7% 45 to 60 minutes, 13.2% 60 minutes or more (2000)

SHERRODSVILLE
(village). Covers a land area of 0.316 square miles and a water area of 0 square miles. Located at 40.49° N. Lat.; 81.24° W. Long. Elevation is 960 feet.
Population: 283 (1990); 316 (2000); 304 (2005); 303 (2010 projected); Race: 97.7% White, 0.3% Black, 0.3% Asian, 0.3% Hispanic of any race (2005); Density: 961.8 persons per square mile (2005); Average household size: 2.53 (2005); Median age: 38.8 (2005); Males per 100 females: 88.8 (2005); Marriage status: 15.2% never married, 61.2% now married, 7.6%

widowed, 16.1% divorced (2000); Foreign born: 0.0% (2000); Ancestry (includes multiple ancestries): 27.6% German, 18.8% Irish, 11.5% United States or American, 8.6% English, 7.9% Other groups (2000).
Economy: Employment by occupation: 7.7% management, 7.7% professional, 19.4% services, 31.0% sales, 0.0% farming, 11.6% construction, 22.6% production (2000).
Income: Per capita income: $13,997 (2005); Median household income: $31,000 (2005); Average household income: $35,458 (2005); Percent of households with income of $100,000 or more: 1.7% (2005); Poverty rate: 19.1% (2000).
Education: Percent of population age 25 and over with: High school diploma (including GED) or higher: 87.6% (2005); Bachelor's degree or higher: 5.0% (2005); Master's degree or higher: 1.5% (2005).

School District(s)
Conotton Valley Union Local SD (PK-12)
   2003-04 Enrollment: 547 . . . . (740) 269-2000

Housing: Homeownership rate: 78.3% (2005); Median home value: $60,952 (2005); Median rent: $293 per month (2000); Median age of housing: 50 years (2000).
Transportation: Commute to work: 90.1% car, 3.3% public transportation, 6.6% walk, 0.0% work from home (2000); Travel time to work: 25.8% less than 15 minutes, 38.4% 15 to 30 minutes, 15.2% 30 to 45 minutes, 14.6% 45 to 60 minutes, 6.0% 60 minutes or more (2000)

Champaign County

Located in west central Ohio; crossed by the Mad River, and Darby, Small Buck, and Little Darby Creeks. Covers a land area of 428.56 square miles, a water area of 1.15 square miles, and is located in the Eastern Time Zone. The county government was organized in 1805. County seat is Urbana.

Champaign County is part of the Urbana, OH Micropolitan Statistical Area. The entire metro area includes: Champaign County, OH

Weather Station: Urbana WWTP   Elevation: 997 feet

	Jan	Feb	Mar	Apr	May	Jun	Jul	Aug	Sep	Oct	Nov	Dec
High	33	37	48	60	71	80	84	83	76	64	50	39
Low	17	19	28	38	49	58	61	59	51	41	32	23
Precip	2.3	2.1	2.9	3.5	4.4	4.5	5.0	3.6	2.9	2.8	3.1	2.9
Snow	na	na	na	0.5	0.0	0.0	0.0	0.0	0.0	0.1	0.3	na

High and Low temperatures in degrees Fahrenheit; Precipitation and Snow in inches

Population: 36,019 (1990); 38,890 (2000); 39,910 (2005); 40,967 (2010 projected); Race: 95.6% White, 2.3% Black, 0.4% Asian, 0.9% Hispanic of any race (2005); Density: 93.1 persons per square mile (2005); Average household size: 2.56 (2005); Median age: 38.1 (2005); Males per 100 females: 96.6 (2005).
Religion: Five largest groups: 7.3% The United Methodist Church, 3.8% American Baptist Churches in the USA, 3.1% Catholic Church, 2.1% Evangelical Lutheran Church in America, 1.6% Church of the Nazarene (2000).
Economy: Unemployment rate: 5.7% (2005); Total civilian labor force: 20,881 (2005); Leading industries: 36.0% manufacturing; 19.4% health care and social assistance; 11.5% retail trade (2004); Farms: 937 totaling 207,554 acres (2002); Companies that employ 500 or more persons: 3 (2004); Companies that employ 100 to 499 persons: 12 (2004); Companies that employ less than 100 persons: 692 (2004); Black-owned businesses: n/a (2002); Hispanic-owned businesses: n/a (2002); Women-owned businesses: 683 (2002); Retail sales per capita: $8,486 (2006). Single-family building permits issued: 114 (2005); Multi-family building permits issued: 0 (2005).
Income: Per capita income: $21,754 (2005); Median household income: $47,478 (2005); Average household income: $55,224 (2005); Percent of households with income of $100,000 or more: 10.4% (2005); Poverty rate: 8.2% (2003); Bankruptcy rate: 11.31% (2005).
Education: Percent of population age 25 and over with: High school diploma (including GED) or higher: 82.4% (2005); Bachelor's degree or higher: 10.6% (2005); Master's degree or higher: 3.5% (2005).
Housing: Homeownership rate: 76.1% (2005); Median home value: $120,285 (2005); Median rent: $367 per month (2000); Median age of housing: 36 years (2000).
Health: Birth rate: 135.9 per 10,000 population (2004); Death rate: 96.3 per 10,000 population (2004); Age-adjusted cancer mortality rate: 232.5 deaths per 100,000 population (2002); Number of physicians: 4.0 per 10,000 population (2004); Hospital beds: 6.3 per 10,000 population (2003); Hospital admissions: 234.9 per 10,000 population (2003).

Elections: 2004 Presidential election results: 62.4% Bush, 37.1% Kerry, 0.0% Nader, 0.3% Badnarik
National and State Parks: Cedar Bog State Nature Preserve; Kiser Lake State Park
Additional Information Contacts
Champaign County Government . . . . (937) 484-1611
   http://www.co.champaign.oh.us/
City of Urbana . . . . (937) 652-4300
   http://urbanaohio.com
Urbana Chamber of Commerce . . . . (937) 653-5764
   http://www.champaignohio.com

Champaign County Communities

CABLE (unincorporated postal area, zip code 43009). Covers a land area of 33.823 square miles and a water area of 0.044 square miles. Located at 40.17° N. Lat.; 83.64° W. Long. Elevation is 1,170 feet.
Population: 1,775 (2000); Race: 99.3% White, 0.0% Black, 0.0% Asian, 0.7% Hispanic of any race (2000); Density: 52.5 persons per square mile (2000); Age: 28.5% under 18, 7.6% over 64 (2000); Marriage status: 14.9% never married, 74.2% now married, 3.5% widowed, 7.3% divorced (2000); Foreign born: 0.6% (2000); Ancestry (includes multiple ancestries): 22.2% German, 21.3% English, 16.4% Irish, 15.8% United States or American, 4.6% Other groups (2000).
Economy: Employment by occupation: 12.1% management, 11.0% professional, 8.4% services, 24.9% sales, 0.0% farming, 7.8% construction, 35.7% production (2000).
Income: Per capita income: $20,446 (2000); Median household income: $53,105 (2000); Poverty rate: 4.6% (2000).
Education: Percent of population age 25 and over with: High school diploma (including GED) or higher: 85.7% (2000); Bachelor's degree or higher: 10.2% (2000).
Housing: Homeownership rate: 90.8% (2000); Median home value: $108,300 (2000); Median rent: $350 per month (2000); Median age of housing: 32 years (2000).
Transportation: Commute to work: 94.7% car, 0.3% public transportation, 0.9% walk, 4.2% work from home (2000); Travel time to work: 15.8% less than 15 minutes, 48.3% 15 to 30 minutes, 20.7% 30 to 45 minutes, 7.1% 45 to 60 minutes, 8.1% 60 minutes or more (2000)

CHRISTIANSBURG (village). Covers a land area of 0.216 square miles and a water area of 0 square miles. Located at 40.05° N. Lat.; 84.02° W. Long. Elevation is 1,116 feet.
Population: 594 (1990); 553 (2000); 603 (2005); 644 (2010 projected); Race: 98.5% White, 0.5% Black, 0.3% Asian, 0.5% Hispanic of any race (2005); Density: 2,795.1 persons per square mile (2005); Average household size: 2.52 (2005); Median age: 37.4 (2005); Males per 100 females: 90.2 (2005); Marriage status: 22.3% never married, 59.2% now married, 7.9% widowed, 10.6% divorced (2000); Foreign born: 1.2% (2000); Ancestry (includes multiple ancestries): 22.6% German, 16.5% United States or American, 11.8% Other groups, 10.8% Irish, 5.9% English (2000).
Economy: In agricultural area. Single-family building permits issued: 0 (2005); Multi-family building permits issued: 0 (2005); Employment by occupation: 5.3% management, 7.8% professional, 10.2% services, 24.6% sales, 0.0% farming, 9.4% construction, 42.6% production (2000).
Income: Per capita income: $17,226 (2005); Median household income: $36,557 (2005); Average household income: $43,462 (2005); Percent of households with income of $100,000 or more: 3.3% (2005); Poverty rate: 6.7% (2000).
Education: Percent of population age 25 and over with: High school diploma (including GED) or higher: 72.2% (2005); Bachelor's degree or higher: 5.1% (2005); Master's degree or higher: 1.2% (2005).
Housing: Homeownership rate: 80.3% (2005); Median home value: $87,667 (2005); Median rent: $305 per month (2000); Median age of housing: 60+ years (2000).
Transportation: Commute to work: 95.0% car, 0.0% public transportation, 2.5% walk, 1.7% work from home (2000); Travel time to work: 10.9% less than 15 minutes, 50.8% 15 to 30 minutes, 29.4% 30 to 45 minutes, 5.5% 45 to 60 minutes, 3.4% 60 minutes or more (2000)

MECHANICSBURG (village). Covers a land area of 1.026 square miles and a water area of 0.007 square miles. Located at 40.07° N. Lat.; 83.55° W. Long. Elevation is 1,100 feet.

Population: 1,803 (1990); 1,744 (2000); 1,751 (2005); 1,769 (2010 projected); Race: 97.6% White, 0.7% Black, 0.0% Asian, 0.7% Hispanic of any race (2005); Density: 1,706.3 persons per square mile (2005); Average household size: 2.43 (2005); Median age: 35.3 (2005); Males per 100 females: 95.6 (2005); Marriage status: 26.5% never married, 52.2% now married, 8.5% widowed, 12.8% divorced (2000); Foreign born: 0.8% (2000); Ancestry (includes multiple ancestries): 17.4% German, 14.0% United States or American, 10.7% Irish, 10.6% English, 6.8% Other groups (2000).
Economy: In agricultural area; drugs, tools, farm equipment. Employment by occupation: 7.6% management, 8.7% professional, 16.4% services, 21.1% sales, 0.0% farming, 8.2% construction, 37.9% production (2000).
Income: Per capita income: $19,363 (2005); Median household income: $37,632 (2005); Average household income: $46,960 (2005); Percent of households with income of $100,000 or more: 8.4% (2005); Poverty rate: 14.9% (2000).
Education: Percent of population age 25 and over with: High school diploma (including GED) or higher: 74.0% (2005); Bachelor's degree or higher: 7.2% (2005); Master's degree or higher: 2.4% (2005).

School District(s)

Mechanicsburg Ex Vill SD (PK-12)
   2003-04 Enrollment: 850 . . . . (937) 834-2453

Housing: Homeownership rate: 66.8% (2005); Median home value: $93,770 (2005); Median rent: $316 per month (2000); Median age of housing: 60+ years (2000).
Transportation: Commute to work: 94.3% car, 0.2% public transportation, 2.4% walk, 2.1% work from home (2000); Travel time to work: 18.1% less than 15 minutes, 37.2% 15 to 30 minutes, 28.3% 30 to 45 minutes, 11.4% 45 to 60 minutes, 5.1% 60 minutes or more (2000)

MUTUAL (village).
Covers a land area of 0.136 square miles and a water area of 0 square miles. Located at 40.07° N. Lat.; 83.63° W. Long. Elevation is 1,190 feet.
Population: 126 (1990); 132 (2000); 140 (2005); 146 (2010 projected); Race: 100.0% White, 0.0% Black, 0.0% Asian, 2.9% Hispanic of any race (2005); Density: 1,028.4 persons per square mile (2005); Average household size: 2.55 (2005); Median age: 39.3 (2005); Males per 100 females: 77.2 (2005); Marriage status: 16.5% never married, 67.1% now married, 11.4% widowed, 5.1% divorced (2000); Foreign born: 0.0% (2000); Ancestry (includes multiple ancestries): 34.9% German, 17.0% United States or American, 13.2% English, 6.6% Other groups, 5.7% Dutch (2000).
Economy: Employment by occupation: 3.4% management, 16.9% professional, 8.5% services, 11.9% sales, 0.0% farming, 5.1% construction, 54.2% production (2000).
Income: Per capita income: $20,571 (2005); Median household income: $48,929 (2005); Average household income: $52,364 (2005); Percent of households with income of $100,000 or more: 5.5% (2005); Poverty rate: 1.0% (2000).
Education: Percent of population age 25 and over with: High school diploma (including GED) or higher: 90.4% (2005); Bachelor's degree or higher: 10.6% (2005); Master's degree or higher: 1.1% (2005).
Housing: Homeownership rate: 85.5% (2005); Median home value: $99,167 (2005); Median rent: $525 per month (2000); Median age of housing: 60+ years (2000).
Transportation: Commute to work: 98.2% car, 0.0% public transportation, 0.0% walk, 1.8% work from home (2000); Travel time to work: 26.8% less than 15 minutes, 33.9% 15 to 30 minutes, 33.9% 30 to 45 minutes, 1.8% 45 to 60 minutes, 3.6% 60 minutes or more (2000)

NORTH LEWISBURG (village).
Covers a land area of 0.894 square miles and a water area of 0 square miles. Located at 40.22° N. Lat.; 83.55° W. Long. Elevation is 1,087 feet.
Population: 1,275 (1990); 1,588 (2000); 1,767 (2005); 1,928 (2010 projected); Race: 96.9% White, 1.0% Black, 0.0% Asian, 0.8% Hispanic of any race (2005); Density: 1,976.9 persons per square mile (2005); Average household size: 2.62 (2005); Median age: 30.9 (2005); Males per 100 females: 102.6 (2005); Marriage status: 20.8% never married, 58.8% now married, 5.5% widowed, 14.9% divorced (2000); Foreign born: 0.8% (2000); Ancestry (includes multiple ancestries): 21.5% German, 14.1% United States or American, 11.1% Irish, 9.8% Other groups, 8.8% English (2000).
Economy: In agricultural area. Employment by occupation: 8.7% management, 9.9% professional, 10.5% services, 20.1% sales, 0.6% farming, 11.5% construction, 38.6% production (2000).

Income: Per capita income: $21,041 (2005); Median household income: $50,565 (2005); Average household income: $55,081 (2005); Percent of households with income of $100,000 or more: 8.9% (2005); Poverty rate: 7.3% (2000).
Education: Percent of population age 25 and over with: High school diploma (including GED) or higher: 87.4% (2005); Bachelor's degree or higher: 6.6% (2005); Master's degree or higher: 1.3% (2005).

School District(s)

Triad Local SD (PK-12)
   2003-04 Enrollment: 1,109 . . . . (937) 826-4961

Housing: Homeownership rate: 72.1% (2005); Median home value: $104,596 (2005); Median rent: $378 per month (2000); Median age of housing: 22 years (2000).
Transportation: Commute to work: 95.8% car, 0.0% public transportation, 1.8% walk, 2.0% work from home (2000); Travel time to work: 25.3% less than 15 minutes, 46.8% 15 to 30 minutes, 12.6% 30 to 45 minutes, 8.3% 45 to 60 minutes, 6.9% 60 minutes or more (2000)

SAINT PARIS (village).
Covers a land area of 0.868 square miles and a water area of 0 square miles. Located at 40.12° N. Lat.; 83.96° W. Long. Elevation is 1,200 feet.
History: St. Paris was settled in 1813 by David Huffman, when it was called simply Paris.
Population: 1,851 (1990); 1,998 (2000); 1,995 (2005); 2,021 (2010 projected); Race: 98.3% White, 0.2% Black, 0.0% Asian, 0.8% Hispanic of any race (2005); Density: 2,299.1 persons per square mile (2005); Average household size: 2.52 (2005); Median age: 33.8 (2005); Males per 100 females: 88.7 (2005); Marriage status: 22.1% never married, 60.8% now married, 6.6% widowed, 10.5% divorced (2000); Foreign born: 0.4% (2000); Ancestry (includes multiple ancestries): 24.2% German, 12.4% United States or American, 11.2% Irish, 11.1% English, 8.7% Other groups (2000).
Economy: Employment by occupation: 6.6% management, 13.1% professional, 12.3% services, 22.8% sales, 0.4% farming, 10.5% construction, 34.3% production (2000).
Income: Per capita income: $19,301 (2005); Median household income: $43,676 (2005); Average household income: $48,679 (2005); Percent of households with income of $100,000 or more: 4.9% (2005); Poverty rate: 8.8% (2000).
Education: Percent of population age 25 and over with: High school diploma (including GED) or higher: 80.8% (2005); Bachelor's degree or higher: 9.7% (2005); Master's degree or higher: 2.7% (2005).

School District(s)

Graham Digital Academy
   2003-04 Enrollment: n/a . . . . (937) 663-4123
Graham Local SD (PK-12)
   2003-04 Enrollment: 2,189 . . . . (937) 663-4123

Housing: Homeownership rate: 71.8% (2005); Median home value: $98,776 (2005); Median rent: $375 per month (2000); Median age of housing: 50 years (2000).
Transportation: Commute to work: 93.3% car, 0.7% public transportation, 4.6% walk, 1.2% work from home (2000); Travel time to work: 34.0% less than 15 minutes, 26.0% 15 to 30 minutes, 24.9% 30 to 45 minutes, 10.7% 45 to 60 minutes, 4.3% 60 minutes or more (2000)

URBANA (city).
Covers a land area of 6.822 square miles and a water area of 0 square miles. Located at 40.11° N. Lat.; 83.75° W. Long. Elevation is 1,050 feet.
History: Urbana was laid out in 1805, and selected in 1812 by General Hull as the site of a training camp. After the war, many of the soldiers who had trained here remained as residents.
Population: 11,436 (1990); 11,613 (2000); 11,590 (2005); 11,609 (2010 projected); Race: 91.0% White, 5.9% Black, 0.4% Asian, 1.5% Hispanic of any race (2005); Density: 1,698.9 persons per square mile (2005); Average household size: 2.35 (2005); Median age: 37.9 (2005); Males per 100 females: 88.9 (2005); Marriage status: 22.7% never married, 54.8% now married, 9.1% widowed, 13.4% divorced (2000); Foreign born: 0.6% (2000); Ancestry (includes multiple ancestries): 19.3% German, 16.3% United States or American, 12.7% Irish, 11.7% Other groups, 8.2% English (2000).
Economy: Employment by occupation: 8.6% management, 14.7% professional, 16.5% services, 19.2% sales, 0.7% farming, 10.0% construction, 30.3% production (2000).
Income: Per capita income: $18,769 (2005); Median household income: $35,713 (2005); Average household income: $43,067 (2005); Percent of

households with income of $100,000 or more: 5.5% (2005); Poverty rate: 10.9% (2000).
Taxes: Total city taxes per capita: $457 (2004); City property taxes per capita: $54 (2004).
Education: Percent of population age 25 and over with: High school diploma (including GED) or higher: 78.9% (2005); Bachelor's degree or higher: 11.3% (2005); Master's degree or higher: 4.0% (2005).

School District(s)
Urbana City School District (PK-12)
    2003-04 Enrollment: 2,353 . . . . (937) 653-1402
Urbana Community School
    2003-04 Enrollment: n/a . . . . (937) 653-1402

Four-year College(s)
Urbana University (Private, Not-for-profit)
    Fall 2004 Enrollment: 1,557. . . . . (937) 484-1301
    2005-06 Tuition: In-state $15,050; Out-of-state $15,050

Housing: Homeownership rate: 60.7% (2005); Median home value: $97,983 (2005); Median rent: $361 per month (2000); Median age of housing: 48 years (2000).
Hospitals: Mercy Memorial Hospital (73 beds)
Safety: Violent crime rate: 10.3 per 10,000 population; Property crime rate: 340.8 per 10,000 population (2004).
Newspapers: Sunday Extra (General - Circulation 14,200); Urbana Daily Citizen (Circulation 6,362)
Transportation: Commute to work: 93.9% car, 0.0% public transportation, 3.5% walk, 1.2% work from home (2000); Travel time to work: 51.3% less than 15 minutes, 24.9% 15 to 30 minutes, 14.5% 30 to 45 minutes, 4.7% 45 to 60 minutes, 4.7% 60 minutes or more (2000)

Additional Information Contacts
City of Urbana . . . . (937) 652-4300
    http://urbanaohio.com
Urbana Chamber of Commerce . . . . (937) 653-5764
    http://www.champaignohio.com

WOODSTOCK (village). Covers a land area of 0.272 square miles and a water area of 0 square miles. Located at 40.17° N. Lat.; 83.52° W. Long. Elevation is 1,042 feet.
Population: 296 (1990); 317 (2000); 304 (2005); 301 (2010 projected); Race: 97.7% White, 0.0% Black, 0.0% Asian, 0.0% Hispanic of any race (2005); Density: 1,119.2 persons per square mile (2005); Average household size: 3.10 (2005); Median age: 29.3 (2005); Males per 100 females: 87.7 (2005); Marriage status: 14.7% never married, 70.6% now married, 4.4% widowed, 10.3% divorced (2000); Foreign born: 0.0% (2000); Ancestry (includes multiple ancestries): 18.4% United States or American, 11.6% German, 11.3% Other groups, 5.2% English, 4.2% Irish (2000).
Economy: In agricultural area. Single-family building permits issued: 0 (2005); Multi-family building permits issued: 0 (2005); Employment by occupation: 5.5% management, 8.2% professional, 11.8% services, 16.4% sales, 2.7% farming, 20.9% construction, 34.5% production (2000).
Income: Per capita income: $19,301 (2005); Median household income: $49,000 (2005); Average household income: $59,872 (2005); Percent of households with income of $100,000 or more: 8.2% (2005); Poverty rate: 10.9% (2000).
Education: Percent of population age 25 and over with: High school diploma (including GED) or higher: 71.2% (2005); Bachelor's degree or higher: 8.2% (2005); Master's degree or higher: 2.4% (2005).
Housing: Homeownership rate: 81.6% (2005); Median home value: $93,913 (2005); Median rent: $297 per month (2000); Median age of housing: 60+ years (2000).
Transportation: Commute to work: 93.3% car, 0.0% public transportation, 6.7% walk, 0.0% work from home (2000); Travel time to work: 11.4% less than 15 minutes, 47.6% 15 to 30 minutes, 29.5% 30 to 45 minutes, 10.5% 45 to 60 minutes, 1.0% 60 minutes or more (2000)

Clark County

Located in west central Ohio; crossed by the Mad and Little Miami Rivers. Covers a land area of 399.86 square miles, a water area of 3.70 square miles, and is located in the Eastern Time Zone. The county government was organized in 1817. County seat is Springfield.

Clark County is part of the Springfield, OH Metropolitan Statistical Area. The entire metro area includes: Clark County, OH

Weather Station: Springfield New Water Works   Elevation: 928 feet

	Jan	Feb	Mar	Apr	May	Jun	Jul	Aug	Sep	Oct	Nov	Dec
High	34	38	49	60	71	80	84	82	76	64	51	40
Low	17	19	28	38	48	58	62	59	52	40	32	23
Precip	2.3	1.8	2.5	3.4	4.3	4.5	4.2	3.6	2.9	2.6	3.0	2.7
Snow	na	na	na	tr	0.0	0.0	0.0	0.0	0.0	tr	0.1	na

High and Low temperatures in degrees Fahrenheit; Precipitation and Snow in inches

Population: 147,540 (1990); 144,742 (2000); 142,815 (2005); 140,811 (2010 projected); Race: 87.9% White, 8.7% Black, 0.7% Asian, 1.4% Hispanic of any race (2005); Density: 357.2 persons per square mile (2005); Average household size: 2.52 (2005); Median age: 38.4 (2005); Males per 100 females: 93.0 (2005).
Religion: Five largest groups: 8.4% Catholic Church, 5.0% The United Methodist Church, 4.1% Evangelical Lutheran Church in America, 2.1% Southern Baptist Convention, 1.9% Christian Churches and Churches of Christ (2000).
Economy: Unemployment rate: 6.4% (2005); Total civilian labor force: 70,441 (2005); Leading industries: 17.1% manufacturing; 16.8% health care and social assistance; 15.9% retail trade (2004); Farms: 756 totaling 165,366 acres (2002); Companies that employ 500 or more persons: 8 (2004); Companies that employ 100 to 499 persons: 59 (2004); Companies that employ less than 100 persons: 2,562 (2004); Black-owned businesses: 229 (2002); Hispanic-owned businesses: n/a (2002); Women-owned businesses: 2,407 (2002); Retail sales per capita: $11,909 (2006); Single-family building permits issued: 247 (2005); Multi-family building permits issued: 40 (2005).
Income: Per capita income: $21,935 (2005); Median household income: $44,259 (2005); Average household income: $54,567 (2005); Percent of households with income of $100,000 or more: 11.2% (2005); Poverty rate: 11.3% (2003); Bankruptcy rate: 12.65% (2005).
Taxes: Total county taxes per capita: $200 (2004); County property taxes per capita: $109 (2004).
Education: Percent of population age 25 and over with: High school diploma (including GED) or higher: 81.5% (2005); Bachelor's degree or higher: 15.1% (2005); Master's degree or higher: 5.5% (2005).
Housing: Homeownership rate: 72.2% (2005); Median home value: $104,810 (2005); Median rent: $376 per month (2000); Median age of housing: 41 years (2000).
Health: Birth rate: 128.3 per 10,000 population (2004); Death rate: 115.9 per 10,000 population (2004); Age-adjusted cancer mortality rate: 205.3 deaths per 100,000 population (2002); Air Quality Index: 68.8% good, 28.8% moderate, 2.5% unhealthy for sensitive individuals, 0.0% unhealthy (percent of days in 2005); Number of physicians: 15.6 per 10,000 population (2004); Hospital beds: 27.5 per 10,000 population (2003); Hospital admissions: 1,353.3 per 10,000 population (2003).
Elections: 2004 Presidential election results: 50.8% Bush, 48.7% Kerry, 0.0% Nader, 0.3% Badnarik
National and State Parks: Buck Creek State Park; Buck Creek State Park

Additional Information Contacts
Clark County Government . . . . (937) 328-2405
    http://www.clarkcountyohio.gov/
City of Springfield . . . . (937) 324-7700
    http://www.ci.springfield.oh.us
New Carlisle Chamber of Commerce . . . . (937) 845-3911
    http://www.carlisleoh.org
Springfield/Clark County Chamber . . . . (937) 325-7621
    http://www.springfieldnet.com

Clark County Communities

CATAWBA (village). Covers a land area of 0.255 square miles and a water area of 0 square miles. Located at 40.00° N. Lat.; 83.62° W. Long. Elevation is 1,237 feet.
Population: 268 (1990); 312 (2000); 334 (2005); 354 (2010 projected); Race: 95.2% White, 0.6% Black, 0.0% Asian, 0.0% Hispanic of any race (2005); Density: 1,307.3 persons per square mile (2005); Average household size: 2.88 (2005); Median age: 32.2 (2005); Males per 100 females: 104.9 (2005); Marriage status: 20.4% never married, 59.9% now married, 0.0% widowed, 19.7% divorced (2000); Foreign born: 0.0% (2000); Ancestry (includes multiple ancestries): 25.4% German, 24.9% Irish, 15.0% Dutch, 8.8% Other groups, 7.8% Welsh (2000).
Economy: In agricultural area. Single-family building permits issued: 0 (2005); Multi-family building permits issued: 0 (2005); Employment by

occupation: 13.0% management, 4.3% professional, 19.6% services, 18.5% sales, 0.0% farming, 12.0% construction, 32.6% production (2000).
Income: Per capita income: $19,603 (2005); Median household income: $51,974 (2005); Average household income: $56,444 (2005); Percent of households with income of $100,000 or more: 5.2% (2005); Poverty rate: 0.0% (2000).
Education: Percent of population age 25 and over with: High school diploma (including GED) or higher: 84.2% (2005); Bachelor's degree or higher: 14.3% (2005); Master's degree or higher: 11.3% (2005).
Housing: Homeownership rate: 86.2% (2005); Median home value: $85,385 (2005); Median rent: $275 per month (2000); Median age of housing: 60+ years (2000).
Transportation: Commute to work: 100.0% car, 0.0% public transportation, 0.0% walk, 0.0% work from home (2000); Travel time to work: 5.4% less than 15 minutes, 46.7% 15 to 30 minutes, 32.6% 30 to 45 minutes, 5.4% 45 to 60 minutes, 9.8% 60 minutes or more (2000)

CRYSTAL LAKES (CDP).
Covers a land area of 0.456 square miles and a water area of 0.033 square miles. Located at 39.88° N. Lat.; 84.02° W. Long. Elevation is 855 feet.
Population: 1,613 (1990); 1,411 (2000); 1,336 (2005); 1,306 (2010 projected); Race: 96.0% White, 0.4% Black, 0.1% Asian, 2.8% Hispanic of any race (2005); Density: 2,926.8 persons per square mile (2005); Average household size: 2.46 (2005); Median age: 37.6 (2005); Males per 100 females: 101.5 (2005); Marriage status: 29.7% never married, 53.7% now married, 1.4% widowed, 15.2% divorced (2000); Foreign born: 1.8% (2000); Ancestry (includes multiple ancestries): 27.2% German, 23.7% United States or American, 19.2% English, 9.0% Irish, 5.9% Other groups (2000).
Economy: Employment by occupation: 3.5% management, 7.8% professional, 16.4% services, 25.9% sales, 0.0% farming, 11.7% construction, 34.7% production (2000).
Income: Per capita income: $18,235 (2005); Median household income: $43,563 (2005); Average household income: $44,866 (2005); Percent of households with income of $100,000 or more: 3.7% (2005); Poverty rate: 14.6% (2000).
Education: Percent of population age 25 and over with: High school diploma (including GED) or higher: 73.9% (2005); Bachelor's degree or higher: 1.1% (2005); Master's degree or higher: 0.3% (2005).
Housing: Homeownership rate: 83.2% (2005); Median home value: $78,705 (2005); Median rent: $360 per month (2000); Median age of housing: 44 years (2000).
Transportation: Commute to work: 100.0% car, 0.0% public transportation, 0.0% walk, 0.0% work from home (2000); Travel time to work: 20.4% less than 15 minutes, 56.4% 15 to 30 minutes, 15.9% 30 to 45 minutes, 1.2% 45 to 60 minutes, 6.1% 60 minutes or more (2000)

DONNELSVILLE (village).
Covers a land area of 0.388 square miles and a water area of 0 square miles. Located at 39.91° N. Lat.; 83.94° W. Long. Elevation is 950 feet.
Population: 349 (1990); 293 (2000); 295 (2005); 297 (2010 projected); Race: 95.3% White, 0.3% Black, 0.0% Asian, 3.7% Hispanic of any race (2005); Density: 761.2 persons per square mile (2005); Average household size: 2.95 (2005); Median age: 32.8 (2005); Males per 100 females: 110.7 (2005); Marriage status: 20.1% never married, 66.7% now married, 5.2% widowed, 8.0% divorced (2000); Foreign born: 0.8% (2000); Ancestry (includes multiple ancestries): 15.2% German, 13.2% United States or American, 8.6% Irish, 8.6% English, 6.6% Polish (2000).
Economy: Employment by occupation: 15.9% management, 18.9% professional, 11.4% services, 20.5% sales, 0.0% farming, 16.7% construction, 16.7% production (2000).
Income: Per capita income: $24,212 (2005); Median household income: $70,833 (2005); Average household income: $71,425 (2005); Percent of households with income of $100,000 or more: 21.0% (2005); Poverty rate: 9.5% (2000).
Education: Percent of population age 25 and over with: High school diploma (including GED) or higher: 87.7% (2005); Bachelor's degree or higher: 19.3% (2005); Master's degree or higher: 4.1% (2005).
School District(s)
Tecumseh Local SD (PK-12)
   2003-04 Enrollment: 3,578 . . . . (937) 845-3576
Housing: Homeownership rate: 81.0% (2005); Median home value: $126,351 (2005); Median rent: $383 per month (2000); Median age of housing: 45 years (2000).

Transportation: Commute to work: 95.5% car, 0.0% public transportation, 0.0% walk, 4.5% work from home (2000); Travel time to work: 15.1% less than 15 minutes, 54.0% 15 to 30 minutes, 26.2% 30 to 45 minutes, 0.0% 45 to 60 minutes, 4.8% 60 minutes or more (2000)

ENON (village).
Covers a land area of 1.326 square miles and a water area of 0 square miles. Located at 39.87° N. Lat.; 83.93° W. Long. Elevation is 900 feet.
Population: 2,653 (1990); 2,638 (2000); 2,543 (2005); 2,442 (2010 projected); Race: 96.6% White, 0.6% Black, 0.6% Asian, 1.1% Hispanic of any race (2005); Density: 1,918.0 persons per square mile (2005); Average household size: 2.31 (2005); Median age: 46.0 (2005); Males per 100 females: 97.7 (2005); Marriage status: 17.8% never married, 65.7% now married, 7.3% widowed, 9.2% divorced (2000); Foreign born: 2.7% (2000); Ancestry (includes multiple ancestries): 24.9% German, 14.9% Irish, 14.5% English, 12.0% United States or American, 5.9% Other groups (2000).
Economy: Single-family building permits issued: 10 (2005); Multi-family building permits issued: 0 (2005); Employment by occupation: 14.3% management, 20.9% professional, 10.4% services, 33.0% sales, 0.0% farming, 8.9% construction, 12.5% production (2000).
Income: Per capita income: $30,421 (2005); Median household income: $62,339 (2005); Average household income: $70,200 (2005); Percent of households with income of $100,000 or more: 19.2% (2005); Poverty rate: 2.8% (2000).
Education: Percent of population age 25 and over with: High school diploma (including GED) or higher: 91.3% (2005); Bachelor's degree or higher: 28.1% (2005); Master's degree or higher: 13.2% (2005).
School District(s)
Greenon Local SD (PK-12)
   2003-04 Enrollment: 1,980 . . . . (937) 328-5351
Springfield Preparatory and Fitness Academy
   2003-04 Enrollment: n/a
Housing: Homeownership rate: 79.8% (2005); Median home value: $142,236 (2005); Median rent: $396 per month (2000); Median age of housing: 30 years (2000).
Transportation: Commute to work: 95.3% car, 0.3% public transportation, 2.1% walk, 1.0% work from home (2000); Travel time to work: 25.1% less than 15 minutes, 48.2% 15 to 30 minutes, 20.3% 30 to 45 minutes, 2.8% 45 to 60 minutes, 3.6% 60 minutes or more (2000)

GREEN MEADOWS (CDP).
Covers a land area of 0.609 square miles and a water area of 0 square miles. Located at 39.86° N. Lat.; 83.94° W. Long.
Population: 2,526 (1990); 2,318 (2000); 2,232 (2005); 2,146 (2010 projected); Race: 97.2% White, 0.9% Black, 0.6% Asian, 0.9% Hispanic of any race (2005); Density: 3,666.6 persons per square mile (2005); Average household size: 2.48 (2005); Median age: 36.6 (2005); Males per 100 females: 95.8 (2005); Marriage status: 19.0% never married, 63.8% now married, 6.2% widowed, 11.0% divorced (2000); Foreign born: 0.9% (2000); Ancestry (includes multiple ancestries): 30.7% German, 16.1% English, 11.4% Irish, 10.3% United States or American, 9.9% Other groups (2000).
Economy: Employment by occupation: 11.3% management, 21.2% professional, 14.1% services, 24.8% sales, 0.0% farming, 12.5% construction, 16.1% production (2000).
Income: Per capita income: $19,948 (2005); Median household income: $44,083 (2005); Average household income: $49,472 (2005); Percent of households with income of $100,000 or more: 6.7% (2005); Poverty rate: 4.5% (2000).
Education: Percent of population age 25 and over with: High school diploma (including GED) or higher: 87.1% (2005); Bachelor's degree or higher: 16.0% (2005); Master's degree or higher: 6.2% (2005).
Housing: Homeownership rate: 75.2% (2005); Median home value: $117,857 (2005); Median rent: $494 per month (2000); Median age of housing: 35 years (2000).
Transportation: Commute to work: 98.3% car, 0.0% public transportation, 0.3% walk, 0.6% work from home (2000); Travel time to work: 24.9% less than 15 minutes, 48.6% 15 to 30 minutes, 19.9% 30 to 45 minutes, 3.0% 45 to 60 minutes, 3.6% 60 minutes or more (2000)

HOLIDAY VALLEY (CDP).
Covers a land area of 2.074 square miles and a water area of 0 square miles. Located at 39.85° N. Lat.; 83.97° W. Long. Elevation is 860 feet.
Population: 1,243 (1990); 1,712 (2000); 1,717 (2005); 1,729 (2010 projected); Race: 95.7% White, 1.5% Black, 0.6% Asian, 1.3% Hispanic of

any race (2005); Density: 827.9 persons per square mile (2005); Average household size: 2.97 (2005); Median age: 45.3 (2005); Males per 100 females: 88.5 (2005); Marriage status: 15.9% never married, 63.8% now married, 8.8% widowed, 11.5% divorced (2000); Foreign born: 2.5% (2000); Ancestry (includes multiple ancestries): 28.7% German, 13.2% English, 12.3% Scotch-Irish, 11.6% Irish, 9.7% Other groups (2000).
Economy: Employment by occupation: 17.8% management, 20.9% professional, 11.5% services, 25.8% sales, 0.0% farming, 13.0% construction, 11.0% production (2000).
Income: Per capita income: $25,175 (2005); Median household income: $62,898 (2005); Average household income: $69,892 (2005); Percent of households with income of $100,000 or more: 21.3% (2005); Poverty rate: 12.2% (2000).
Education: Percent of population age 25 and over with: High school diploma (including GED) or higher: 89.3% (2005); Bachelor's degree or higher: 22.9% (2005); Master's degree or higher: 8.9% (2005).
Housing: Homeownership rate: 95.5% (2005); Median home value: $130,102 (2005); Median rent: $664 per month (2000); Median age of housing: 29 years (2000).
Transportation: Commute to work: 94.0% car, 3.0% public transportation, 0.0% walk, 3.1% work from home (2000); Travel time to work: 20.7% less than 15 minutes, 47.1% 15 to 30 minutes, 10.5% 30 to 45 minutes, 7.3% 45 to 60 minutes, 14.5% 60 minutes or more (2000).

LAWRENCEVILLE (village). Covers a land area of 0.135 square miles and a water area of 0 square miles. Located at 39.98° N. Lat.; 83.87° W. Long. Elevation is 1,110 feet.
Population: 304 (1990); 302 (2000); 334 (2005); 364 (2010 projected); Race: 94.3% White, 1.5% Black, 0.0% Asian, 0.0% Hispanic of any race (2005); Density: 2,480.9 persons per square mile (2005); Average household size: 2.74 (2005); Median age: 35.6 (2005); Males per 100 females: 111.4 (2005); Marriage status: 20.6% never married, 59.7% now married, 3.3% widowed, 16.5% divorced (2000); Foreign born: 0.0% (2000); Ancestry (includes multiple ancestries): 28.6% German, 18.7% United States or American, 11.6% Irish, 11.2% English, 10.2% Other groups (2000).
Economy: Employment by occupation: 6.3% management, 20.3% professional, 12.7% services, 31.6% sales, 1.9% farming, 12.0% construction, 15.2% production (2000).
Income: Per capita income: $21,931 (2005); Median household income: $56,897 (2005); Average household income: $60,041 (2005); Percent of households with income of $100,000 or more: 13.1% (2005); Poverty rate: 3.1% (2000).
Education: Percent of population age 25 and over with: High school diploma (including GED) or higher: 85.8% (2005); Bachelor's degree or higher: 13.7% (2005); Master's degree or higher: 2.8% (2005).
Housing: Homeownership rate: 67.2% (2005); Median home value: $113,514 (2005); Median rent: $498 per month (2000); Median age of housing: 47 years (2000).
Transportation: Commute to work: 95.5% car, 0.0% public transportation, 1.3% walk, 3.2% work from home (2000); Travel time to work: 30.9% less than 15 minutes, 48.3% 15 to 30 minutes, 14.1% 30 to 45 minutes, 1.3% 45 to 60 minutes, 5.4% 60 minutes or more (2000).

MEDWAY (unincorporated postal area, zip code 45341). Covers a land area of 7.094 square miles and a water area of 0.214 square miles. Located at 39.88° N. Lat.; 84.02° W. Long. Elevation is 849 feet.
Population: 4,110 (2000); Race: 94.7% White, 0.8% Black, 0.7% Asian, 0.6% Hispanic of any race (2000); Density: 579.3 persons per square mile (2000); Age: 21.8% under 18, 18.4% over 64 (2000); Marriage status: 24.1% never married, 55.4% now married, 7.1% widowed, 13.3% divorced (2000); Foreign born: 1.3% (2000); Ancestry (includes multiple ancestries): 24.8% German, 21.4% United States or American, 14.5% English, 11.2% Irish, 6.8% Other groups (2000).
Economy: Employment by occupation: 8.4% management, 13.0% professional, 12.6% services, 26.2% sales, 0.4% farming, 11.6% construction, 27.8% production (2000).
Income: Per capita income: $19,156 (2000); Median household income: $38,191 (2000); Poverty rate: 7.5% (2000).
Education: Percent of population age 25 and over with: High school diploma (including GED) or higher: 77.1% (2000); Bachelor's degree or higher: 8.4% (2000).
School District(s)
Tecumseh Local SD (PK-12)
  2003-04 Enrollment: 3,578 . . . . (937) 845-3576

Housing: Homeownership rate: 84.4% (2000); Median home value: $81,600 (2000); Median rent: $368 per month (2000); Median age of housing: 37 years (2000).
Transportation: Commute to work: 95.0% car, 0.8% public transportation, 0.5% walk, 1.3% work from home (2000); Travel time to work: 26.0% less than 15 minutes, 52.2% 15 to 30 minutes, 16.5% 30 to 45 minutes, 2.1% 45 to 60 minutes, 3.1% 60 minutes or more (2000).

NEW CARLISLE (city). Covers a land area of 1.932 square miles and a water area of 0.007 square miles. Located at 39.94° N. Lat.; 84.03° W. Long. Elevation is 906 feet.
History: Founded 1810.
Population: 6,066 (1990); 5,735 (2000); 5,626 (2005); 5,505 (2010 projected); Race: 95.5% White, 0.4% Black, 0.3% Asian, 3.5% Hispanic of any race (2005); Density: 2,911.8 persons per square mile (2005); Average household size: 2.58 (2005); Median age: 36.2 (2005); Males per 100 females: 90.5 (2005); Marriage status: 20.6% never married, 59.6% now married, 6.8% widowed, 13.1% divorced (2000); Foreign born: 1.2% (2000); Ancestry (includes multiple ancestries): 22.7% German, 16.4% United States or American, 11.3% Other groups, 11.0% Irish, 10.1% English (2000).
Economy: In agricultural area; food products. Employment by occupation: 7.8% management, 14.2% professional, 19.0% services, 25.7% sales, 0.9% farming, 11.2% construction, 21.3% production (2000).
Income: Per capita income: $18,498 (2005); Median household income: $42,515 (2005); Average household income: $46,697 (2005); Percent of households with income of $100,000 or more: 5.2% (2005); Poverty rate: 11.5% (2000).
Education: Percent of population age 25 and over with: High school diploma (including GED) or higher: 82.2% (2005); Bachelor's degree or higher: 12.7% (2005); Master's degree or higher: 3.3% (2005).
School District(s)
Tecumseh Local SD (PK-12)
  2003-04 Enrollment: 3,578 . . . . (937) 845-3576
Housing: Homeownership rate: 73.2% (2005); Median home value: $99,201 (2005); Median rent: $379 per month (2000); Median age of housing: 38 years (2000).
Newspapers: Enon Messenger (General - Circulation 3,100); New Carlisle Sun (General - Circulation 4,200)
Transportation: Commute to work: 96.9% car, 0.2% public transportation, 1.0% walk, 1.1% work from home (2000); Travel time to work: 27.6% less than 15 minutes, 37.6% 15 to 30 minutes, 27.4% 30 to 45 minutes, 3.7% 45 to 60 minutes, 3.6% 60 minutes or more (2000)
Additional Information Contacts
New Carlisle Chamber of Commerce . . . . (937) 845-3911
  http://www.carlisleoh.org

NORTH HAMPTON (village). Covers a land area of 0.257 square miles and a water area of 0 square miles. Located at 39.99° N. Lat.; 83.94° W. Long. Elevation is 1,083 feet.
Population: 417 (1990); 370 (2000); 402 (2005); 435 (2010 projected); Race: 95.8% White, 0.0% Black, 1.5% Asian, 0.0% Hispanic of any race (2005); Density: 1,565.3 persons per square mile (2005); Average household size: 2.68 (2005); Median age: 35.5 (2005); Males per 100 females: 103.0 (2005); Marriage status: 22.5% never married, 67.6% now married, 8.1% widowed, 1.8% divorced (2000); Foreign born: 0.0% (2000); Ancestry (includes multiple ancestries): 23.5% German, 22.5% United States or American, 15.0% English, 13.9% Irish, 4.8% Welsh (2000).
Economy: Employment by occupation: 12.0% management, 22.0% professional, 4.0% services, 10.0% sales, 0.0% farming, 26.0% construction, 26.0% production (2000).
Income: Per capita income: $21,076 (2005); Median household income: $45,714 (2005); Average household income: $56,483 (2005); Percent of households with income of $100,000 or more: 12.0% (2005); Poverty rate: 0.0% (2000).
Education: Percent of population age 25 and over with: High school diploma (including GED) or higher: 90.4% (2005); Bachelor's degree or higher: 22.3% (2005); Master's degree or higher: 13.9% (2005).
Housing: Homeownership rate: 78.7% (2005); Median home value: $119,737 (2005); Median rent: $315 per month (2000); Median age of housing: 46 years (2000).
Transportation: Commute to work: 94.0% car, 0.0% public transportation, 6.0% walk, 0.0% work from home (2000); Travel time to work: 18.0% less than 15 minutes, 50.0% 15 to 30 minutes, 22.0% 30 to 45 minutes, 6.0% 45 to 60 minutes, 4.0% 60 minutes or more (2000)

NORTHRIDGE (CDP). Covers a land area of 3.053 square miles and a water area of 0 square miles. Located at 39.99° N. Lat.; 83.77° W. Long. Elevation is 1,090 feet.
Population: 5,939 (1990); 6,853 (2000); 6,675 (2005); 6,634 (2010 projected); Race: 97.4% White, 1.3% Black, 0.5% Asian, 0.5% Hispanic of any race (2005); Density: 2,186.4 persons per square mile (2005); Average household size: 2.38 (2005); Median age: 43.5 (2005); Males per 100 females: 93.1 (2005); Marriage status: 16.2% never married, 68.0% now married, 8.4% widowed, 7.4% divorced (2000); Foreign born: 0.4% (2000); Ancestry (includes multiple ancestries): 29.9% German, 14.6% United States or American, 13.6% Irish, 9.5% English, 5.6% Other groups (2000).
Economy: Employment by occupation: 9.6% management, 19.5% professional, 14.0% services, 25.7% sales, 0.2% farming, 8.1% construction, 22.8% production (2000).
Income: Per capita income: $24,413 (2005); Median household income: $54,254 (2005); Average household income: $58,013 (2005); Percent of households with income of $100,000 or more: 10.0% (2005); Poverty rate: 2.4% (2000).
Education: Percent of population age 25 and over with: High school diploma (including GED) or higher: 89.8% (2005); Bachelor's degree or higher: 17.6% (2005); Master's degree or higher: 5.1% (2005).
Housing: Homeownership rate: 84.9% (2005); Median home value: $122,875 (2005); Median rent: $436 per month (2000); Median age of housing: 28 years (2000).
Transportation: Commute to work: 96.5% car, 0.7% public transportation, 0.2% walk, 2.6% work from home (2000); Travel time to work: 27.5% less than 15 minutes, 50.1% 15 to 30 minutes, 11.8% 30 to 45 minutes, 7.2% 45 to 60 minutes, 3.4% 60 minutes or more (2000)

PARK LAYNE (CDP). Covers a land area of 1.488 square miles and a water area of 0 square miles. Located at 39.88° N. Lat.; 84.04° W. Long.
Population: 4,795 (1990); 4,519 (2000); 4,409 (2005); 4,280 (2010 projected); Race: 96.1% White, 0.5% Black, 0.2% Asian, 1.7% Hispanic of any race (2005); Density: 2,962.6 persons per square mile (2005); Average household size: 2.79 (2005); Median age: 33.0 (2005); Males per 100 females: 95.4 (2005); Marriage status: 21.2% never married, 60.8% now married, 5.1% widowed, 13.0% divorced (2000); Foreign born: 1.2% (2000); Ancestry (includes multiple ancestries): 27.0% United States or American, 17.5% German, 12.3% Irish, 8.1% Other groups, 6.4% English (2000).
Economy: Employment by occupation: 5.3% management, 11.1% professional, 14.9% services, 24.4% sales, 1.8% farming, 14.3% construction, 28.3% production (2000).
Income: Per capita income: $16,327 (2005); Median household income: $40,618 (2005); Average household income: $45,560 (2005); Percent of households with income of $100,000 or more: 4.8% (2005); Poverty rate: 6.6% (2000).
Education: Percent of population age 25 and over with: High school diploma (including GED) or higher: 75.6% (2005); Bachelor's degree or higher: 3.6% (2005); Master's degree or higher: 0.6% (2005).
Housing: Homeownership rate: 79.4% (2005); Median home value: $89,742 (2005); Median rent: $433 per month (2000); Median age of housing: 35 years (2000).
Transportation: Commute to work: 96.8% car, 0.0% public transportation, 1.4% walk, 1.7% work from home (2000); Travel time to work: 22.1% less than 15 minutes, 51.9% 15 to 30 minutes, 16.6% 30 to 45 minutes, 4.4% 45 to 60 minutes, 4.9% 60 minutes or more (2000)

SOUTH CHARLESTON (village). Covers a land area of 1.297 square miles and a water area of 0 square miles. Located at 39.82° N. Lat.; 83.63° W. Long. Elevation is 1,124 feet.
History: South Charleston developed as a rural distributing center.
Population: 1,681 (1990); 1,850 (2000); 1,910 (2005); 1,967 (2010 projected); Race: 96.3% White, 1.5% Black, 0.8% Asian, 0.2% Hispanic of any race (2005); Density: 1,472.3 persons per square mile (2005); Average household size: 2.52 (2005); Median age: 33.5 (2005); Males per 100 females: 88.0 (2005); Marriage status: 22.3% never married, 56.5% now married, 9.4% widowed, 11.9% divorced (2000); Foreign born: 0.3% (2000); Ancestry (includes multiple ancestries): 22.0% German, 14.4% Irish, 12.5% United States or American, 10.5% English, 8.7% Other groups (2000).
Economy: Employment by occupation: 9.8% management, 14.1% professional, 17.2% services, 23.2% sales, 0.4% farming, 10.4% construction, 25.0% production (2000).
Income: Per capita income: $19,300 (2005); Median household income: $42,793 (2005); Average household income: $48,696 (2005); Percent of households with income of $100,000 or more: 5.8% (2005); Poverty rate: 8.4% (2000).
Education: Percent of population age 25 and over with: High school diploma (including GED) or higher: 81.8% (2005); Bachelor's degree or higher: 9.9% (2005); Master's degree or higher: 4.2% (2005).
School District(s)
Southeastern Local SD (PK-12)
    2003-04 Enrollment: 876 . . . . (937) 462-8388
Housing: Homeownership rate: 65.0% (2005); Median home value: $98,611 (2005); Median rent: $369 per month (2000); Median age of housing: 46 years (2000).
Transportation: Commute to work: 93.8% car, 0.4% public transportation, 2.1% walk, 3.3% work from home (2000); Travel time to work: 20.3% less than 15 minutes, 41.5% 15 to 30 minutes, 21.1% 30 to 45 minutes, 10.8% 45 to 60 minutes, 6.3% 60 minutes or more (2000)

SOUTH VIENNA (village). Aka Vienna. Covers a land area of 0.405 square miles and a water area of 0 square miles. Located at 39.92° N. Lat.; 83.61° W. Long. Elevation is 1,200 feet.
Population: 550 (1990); 469 (2000); 481 (2005); 490 (2010 projected); Race: 97.5% White, 0.4% Black, 0.0% Asian, 2.3% Hispanic of any race (2005); Density: 1,187.4 persons per square mile (2005); Average household size: 2.75 (2005); Median age: 32.7 (2005); Males per 100 females: 91.6 (2005); Marriage status: 20.1% never married, 57.0% now married, 5.0% widowed, 17.9% divorced (2000); Foreign born: 0.8% (2000); Ancestry (includes multiple ancestries): 27.9% German, 15.2% English, 13.9% United States or American, 7.1% Irish, 6.3% Scottish (2000).
Economy: Employment by occupation: 7.5% management, 9.2% professional, 14.0% services, 28.9% sales, 0.4% farming, 8.3% construction, 31.6% production (2000).
Income: Per capita income: $19,257 (2005); Median household income: $44,671 (2005); Average household income: $52,929 (2005); Percent of households with income of $100,000 or more: 8.6% (2005); Poverty rate: 8.2% (2000).
Education: Percent of population age 25 and over with: High school diploma (including GED) or higher: 82.3% (2005); Bachelor's degree or higher: 8.1% (2005); Master's degree or higher: 3.2% (2005).
School District(s)
Northeastern Local SD (PK-12)
    2003-04 Enrollment: 3,628 . . . . (937) 325-7615
Housing: Homeownership rate: 71.4% (2005); Median home value: $116,797 (2005); Median rent: $460 per month (2000); Median age of housing: 60+ years (2000).
Transportation: Commute to work: 86.4% car, 0.9% public transportation, 7.3% walk, 5.5% work from home (2000); Travel time to work: 23.1% less than 15 minutes, 49.5% 15 to 30 minutes, 17.8% 30 to 45 minutes, 5.8% 45 to 60 minutes, 3.8% 60 minutes or more (2000)

SPRINGFIELD (city). Covers a land area of 22.473 square miles and a water area of 0.045 square miles. Located at 39.92° N. Lat.; 83.80° W. Long. Elevation is 1,000 feet.
History: Springfield's first settler was James Demint, who came in 1799. Surveyor John Daugherty platted a town in 1801. The settlement was called Springfield for the spring water coming down the cliffs that bordered the valley of Buck Creek. Simon Kenton from Kentucky set up a gristmill and sawmill on the site that was later the International Harvester plant. The National Road, completed in 1838, put Springfield on the route of the Ohio Stage Company and provided a means for the area's produce to get to a market. In the 1850's the Champion Binder Company was producing farm machinery here, its facility later purchased by the McCormick interests, which were subsequently acquired by International Harvester Company.
Population: 71,064 (1990); 65,358 (2000); 62,899 (2005); 60,477 (2010 projected); Race: 77.6% White, 17.9% Black, 0.9% Asian, 1.4% Hispanic of any race (2005); Density: 2,798.8 persons per square mile (2005); Average household size: 2.46 (2005); Median age: 35.2 (2005); Males per 100 females: 90.1 (2005); Marriage status: 29.0% never married, 47.6% now married, 9.7% widowed, 13.6% divorced (2000); Foreign born: 1.2% (2000); Ancestry (includes multiple ancestries): 21.9% Other groups, 17.9% German, 13.8% United States or American, 10.4% Irish, 6.5% English (2000).
Economy: Unemployment rate: 7.1% (2005); Total civilian labor force: 29,055 (2005); Single-family building permits issued: 20 (2005);

Multi-family building permits issued: 6 (2005); Employment by occupation: 8.5% management, 16.0% professional, 17.9% services, 25.2% sales, 0.3% farming, 8.1% construction, 24.1% production (2000).
Income: Per capita income: $18,549 (2005); Median household income: $34,713 (2005); Average household income: $44,850 (2005); Percent of households with income of $100,000 or more: 7.1% (2005); Poverty rate: 16.9% (2000).
Taxes: Total city taxes per capita: $482 (2004); City property taxes per capita: $40 (2004).
Education: Percent of population age 25 and over with: High school diploma (including GED) or higher: 77.0% (2005); Bachelor's degree or higher: 13.1% (2005); Master's degree or higher: 4.9% (2005).

School District(s)

Clark-Shawnee Local SD (PK-12)
   2003-04 Enrollment: 2,547 . . . . (937) 328-5378
Greenon Local SD (PK-12)
   2003-04 Enrollment: 1,980 . . . . (937) 328-5351
Greenon Virtual School
   2003-04 Enrollment: n/a
Life Skills Center-Springfield (09-12)
   2003-04 Enrollment: 254 . . . . (937) 322-2940
Northeastern Local SD (PK-12)
   2003-04 Enrollment: 3,628 . . . . (937) 325-7615
Northwestern Local SD (PK-12)
   2003-04 Enrollment: 1,951 . . . . (937) 964-1318
Springfield Academy of Excellence (KG-05)
   2003-04 Enrollment: 190 . . . . (937) 325-0933
Springfield City SD (PK-12)
   2003-04 Enrollment: 9,358 . . . . (937) 328-2000
Springfield-Clark County Joint Vocational SD (07-12)
   2003-04 Enrollment: n/a . . . . (937) 325-7368

Four-year College(s)

Wittenberg University (Private, Not-for-profit, Lutheran Church in America)
   Fall 2004 Enrollment: 2,182. . . . . (937) 327-6231
   2005-06 Tuition: In-state $27,542; Out-of-state $27,542

Two-year College(s)

Carousel Beauty College (Private, For-profit)
   Fall 2004 Enrollment: 50 . . . . (937) 223-3572
Clark State Community College (Public)
   Fall 2004 Enrollment: 3,510. . . . . (937) 328-6070
   2005-06 Tuition: In-state $3,492; Out-of-state $6,492
Community Hospital School of Nursing (Private, Not-for-profit)
   Fall 2004 Enrollment: 206 . . . . (937) 328-8900
   2005-06 Tuition: In-state $6,068; Out-of-state $6,068
Springfield Clark County Joint Vocational School (Public)
   Fall 2004 Enrollment: 206 . . . . (937) 325-7368

Housing: Homeownership rate: 57.8% (2005); Median home value: $81,498 (2005); Median rent: $364 per month (2000); Median age of housing: 50 years (2000).
Hospitals: Community Hospital (324 beds); Mercy Medical Center (329 beds)
Safety: Violent crime rate: 75.8 per 10,000 population; Property crime rate: 954.4 per 10,000 population (2004).
Newspapers: Springfield News-Sun (Circulation 30,746)
Transportation: Commute to work: 91.7% car, 1.5% public transportation, 4.2% walk, 1.6% work from home (2000); Travel time to work: 45.8% less than 15 minutes, 33.3% 15 to 30 minutes, 11.3% 30 to 45 minutes, 5.4% 45 to 60 minutes, 4.2% 60 minutes or more (2000)

Additional Information Contacts
City of Springfield. . . . . (937) 324-7700
   http://www.ci.springfield.oh.us
Springfield/Clark County Chamber . . . . (937) 325-7621
   http://www.springfieldnet.com

TREMONT CITY (village). Covers a land area of 0.267 square miles and a water area of 0 square miles. Located at 40.01° N. Lat.; 83.83° W. Long. Elevation is 950 feet.
Population: 477 (1990); 349 (2000); 345 (2005); 338 (2010 projected); Race: 96.5% White, 1.7% Black, 0.0% Asian, 0.3% Hispanic of any race (2005); Density: 1,291.5 persons per square mile (2005); Average household size: 2.54 (2005); Median age: 32.8 (2005); Males per 100 females: 94.9 (2005); Marriage status: 24.5% never married, 60.6% now married, 4.8% widowed, 10.0% divorced (2000); Foreign born: 0.6% (2000); Ancestry (includes multiple ancestries): 32.2% German, 15.1% Other groups, 13.6% English, 12.3% Irish, 7.2% United States or American (2000).
Economy: Single-family building permits issued: 0 (2005); Multi-family building permits issued: 0 (2005); Employment by occupation: 2.2% management, 10.6% professional, 14.0% services, 22.9% sales, 0.0% farming, 12.3% construction, 38.0% production (2000).
Income: Per capita income: $23,203 (2005); Median household income: $56,731 (2005); Average household income: $58,860 (2005); Percent of households with income of $100,000 or more: 6.6% (2005); Poverty rate: 5.8% (2000).
Education: Percent of population age 25 and over with: High school diploma (including GED) or higher: 90.3% (2005); Bachelor's degree or higher: 9.3% (2005); Master's degree or higher: 1.4% (2005).
Housing: Homeownership rate: 65.4% (2005); Median home value: $95,000 (2005); Median rent: $460 per month (2000); Median age of housing: 60 years (2000).
Transportation: Commute to work: 98.2% car, 1.2% public transportation, 0.0% walk, 0.6% work from home (2000); Travel time to work: 22.5% less than 15 minutes, 55.0% 15 to 30 minutes, 14.2% 30 to 45 minutes, 5.9% 45 to 60 minutes, 2.4% 60 minutes or more (2000)

Clermont County

Located in southwestern Ohio; bounded on the southwest by the Ohio River and the Kentucky border, and on the northwest by the Little Miami River. Covers a land area of 451.99 square miles, a water area of 5.68 square miles, and is located in the Eastern Time Zone. The county government was organized in 1800. County seat is Batavia.

Clermont County is part of the Cincinnati-Middletown, OH-KY-IN Metropolitan Statistical Area. The entire metro area includes: Dearborn County, IN; Franklin County, IN; Ohio County, IN; Boone County, KY; Bracken County, KY; Campbell County, KY; Gallatin County, KY; Grant County, KY; Kenton County, KY; Pendleton County, KY; Brown County, OH; Butler County, OH; Clermont County, OH; Hamilton County, OH; Warren County, OH

Weather Station: Chilo Meldahl Lock & Dam   Elevation: 498 feet

	Jan	Feb	Mar	Apr	May	Jun	Jul	Aug	Sep	Oct	Nov	Dec
High	38	43	53	65	74	82	86	85	79	68	55	44
Low	20	23	31	40	50	59	64	63	56	44	35	26
Precip	3.0	3.0	4.2	3.8	4.5	4.3	3.8	3.9	3.1	2.9	3.3	3.3
Snow	na	na	1.0	0.0	0.0	0.0	0.0	0.0	0.0	0.0	tr	1.5

High and Low temperatures in degrees Fahrenheit; Precipitation and Snow in inches

Weather Station: Milford   Elevation: 518 feet

	Jan	Feb	Mar	Apr	May	Jun	Jul	Aug	Sep	Oct	Nov	Dec
High	37	41	52	64	75	82	87	85	79	67	54	42
Low	19	21	30	39	49	58	63	61	53	40	32	24
Precip	3.1	2.6	3.8	4.2	5.0	4.5	4.0	4.2	3.2	3.1	3.7	3.4
Snow	5.8	4.9	2.1	0.4	tr	0.0	0.0	tr	0.0	0.1	0.4	2.2

High and Low temperatures in degrees Fahrenheit; Precipitation and Snow in inches

Population: 150,129 (1990); 177,977 (2000); 189,380 (2005); 201,303 (2010 projected); Race: 96.6% White, 0.9% Black, 1.0% Asian, 0.9% Hispanic of any race (2005); Density: 419.0 persons per square mile (2005); Average household size: 2.65 (2005); Median age: 35.9 (2005); Males per 100 females: 96.8 (2005).
Religion: Five largest groups: 14.6% Catholic Church, 4.2% The United Methodist Church, 3.5% Southern Baptist Convention, 3.2% Christian Churches and Churches of Christ, 0.8% Church of the Nazarene (2000).
Economy: Unemployment rate: 5.4% (2005); Total civilian labor force: 103,918 (2005); Leading industries: 20.2% retail trade; 13.4% manufacturing; 11.4% accommodation & food services (2004); Farms: 973 totaling 116,026 acres (2002); Companies that employ 500 or more persons: 6 (2004); Companies that employ 100 to 499 persons: 76 (2004); Companies that employ less than 100 persons: 3,524 (2004); Black-owned businesses: 105 (2002); Hispanic-owned businesses: n/a (2002); Women-owned businesses: 3,932 (2002); Retail sales per capita: $14,253 (2006). Single-family building permits issued: 1,196 (2005); Multi-family building permits issued: 332 (2005).
Income: Per capita income: $26,221 (2005); Median household income: $56,041 (2005); Average household income: $69,158 (2005); Percent of households with income of $100,000 or more: 19.0% (2005); Poverty rate: 6.9% (2003); Bankruptcy rate: 10.90% (2005).

42 PROFILES OF OHIO / Clermont County

Taxes: Total county taxes per capita: $261 (2004); County property taxes per capita: $111 (2004).
Education: Percent of population age 25 and over with: High school diploma (including GED) or higher: 82.0% (2005); Bachelor's degree or higher: 20.7% (2005); Master's degree or higher: 6.8% (2005).
Housing: Homeownership rate: 75.2% (2005); Median home value: $139,485 (2005); Median rent: $473 per month (2000); Median age of housing: 23 years (2000).
Health: Birth rate: 145.6 per 10,000 population (2004); Death rate: 73.6 per 10,000 population (2004); Age-adjusted cancer mortality rate: 206.9 deaths per 100,000 population (2002); Air Quality Index: 64.1% good, 34.0% moderate, 1.9% unhealthy for sensitive individuals, 0.0% unhealthy (percent of days in 2005); Number of physicians: 15.0 per 10,000 population (2004); Hospital beds: 8.8 per 10,000 population (2003); Hospital admissions: 341.8 per 10,000 population (2003).
Elections: 2004 Presidential election results: 70.7% Bush, 29.1% Kerry, 0.0% Nader, 0.2% Badnarik
National and State Parks: East Fork State Park; Stonelick Lake State Park
Additional Information Contacts
Clermont County Government . . . . (513) 732-7300
  http://www.co.clermont.oh.us/
Clermont County Convention and Visitors Bureau . . . . . . (513) 796-4282
  http://www.visitclermontohio.com
Milford-Miami Twp. Chamber of Commerce . . . . (513) 831-2411
  http://www.milfordmiamitownship.com
Village of Bethel . . . . (937) 845-8472
  http://www.betheltownship.org

Clermont County Communities

AMELIA (village). Covers a land area of 1.371 square miles and a water area of 0 square miles. Located at 39.02° N. Lat.; 84.22° W. Long. Elevation is 880 feet.
Population: 2,226 (1990); 2,752 (2000); 3,174 (2005); 3,584 (2010 projected); Race: 96.4% White, 0.7% Black, 0.4% Asian, 1.1% Hispanic of any race (2005); Density: 2,315.0 persons per square mile (2005); Average household size: 2.54 (2005); Median age: 31.0 (2005); Males per 100 females: 91.0 (2005); Marriage status: 23.3% never married, 59.9% now married, 5.6% widowed, 11.3% divorced (2000); Foreign born: 1.9% (2000); Ancestry (includes multiple ancestries): 30.4% German, 16.7% Irish, 16.1% United States or American, 9.0% Other groups, 8.3% English (2000).
Economy: Manufactures furniture. Employment by occupation: 14.9% management, 14.1% professional, 16.4% services, 25.9% sales, 0.3% farming, 13.1% construction, 15.3% production (2000).
Income: Per capita income: $20,332 (2005); Median household income: $49,108 (2005); Average household income: $51,711 (2005); Percent of households with income of $100,000 or more: 7.0% (2005); Poverty rate: 7.6% (2000).
Education: Percent of population age 25 and over with: High school diploma (including GED) or higher: 82.9% (2005); Bachelor's degree or higher: 13.5% (2005); Master's degree or higher: 2.7% (2005).
School District(s)
West Clermont Local SD (PK-12)
  2003-04 Enrollment: 9,189 . . . . (513) 943-5000
Housing: Homeownership rate: 53.6% (2005); Median home value: $125,605 (2005); Median rent: $448 per month (2000); Median age of housing: 20 years (2000).
Transportation: Commute to work: 94.1% car, 2.4% public transportation, 1.7% walk, 1.8% work from home (2000); Travel time to work: 16.4% less than 15 minutes, 29.4% 15 to 30 minutes, 28.7% 30 to 45 minutes, 18.5% 45 to 60 minutes, 7.0% 60 minutes or more (2000)

BATAVIA (village). Covers a land area of 1.463 square miles and a water area of 0.025 square miles. Located at 39.07° N. Lat.; 84.17° W. Long. Elevation is 594 feet.
History: Settled c.1797, laid out 1814, incorporated 1842.
Population: 1,700 (1990); 1,617 (2000); 1,674 (2005); 1,751 (2010 projected); Race: 95.0% White, 2.6% Black, 0.4% Asian, 0.3% Hispanic of any race (2005); Density: 1,144.3 persons per square mile (2005); Average household size: 2.49 (2005); Median age: 37.4 (2005); Males per 100 females: 97.4 (2005); Marriage status: 22.0% never married, 61.1% now married, 5.2% widowed, 11.7% divorced (2000); Foreign born: 0.6% (2000); Ancestry (includes multiple ancestries): 30.1% German, 17.2% United States or American, 14.4% Irish, 11.1% English, 9.7% Other groups (2000).
Economy: Tools, machinery, grain products. Manufacturing: auto transmissions. Employment by occupation: 12.0% management, 17.5% professional, 13.9% services, 33.1% sales, 0.0% farming, 8.3% construction, 15.2% production (2000).
Income: Per capita income: $22,679 (2005); Median household income: $45,512 (2005); Average household income: $56,580 (2005); Percent of households with income of $100,000 or more: 15.1% (2005); Poverty rate: 6.6% (2000).
Education: Percent of population age 25 and over with: High school diploma (including GED) or higher: 90.6% (2005); Bachelor's degree or higher: 17.8% (2005); Master's degree or higher: 8.0% (2005).
School District(s)
Batavia Local SD (PK-12)
  2003-04 Enrollment: 1,924 . . . . (513) 732-2343
Clermont Northeastern Local SD (PK-12)
  2003-04 Enrollment: 1,972 . . . . (513) 625-5478
West Clermont Local SD (PK-12)
  2003-04 Enrollment: 9,189 . . . . (513) 943-5000
Two-year College(s)
University of Cincinnati-Clermont College (Public)
  Fall 2004 Enrollment: 2,765. . . . . (513) 732-5200
  2005-06 Tuition: In-state $4,299; Out-of-state $10,785
Housing: Homeownership rate: 64.8% (2005); Median home value: $127,023 (2005); Median rent: $463 per month (2000); Median age of housing: 46 years (2000).
Hospitals: Clermont Mercy Hospital (157 beds)
Newspapers: The Clermont Sun (General - Circulation 3,300)
Transportation: Commute to work: 91.3% car, 1.4% public transportation, 5.9% walk, 1.5% work from home (2000); Travel time to work: 32.4% less than 15 minutes, 23.4% 15 to 30 minutes, 27.3% 30 to 45 minutes, 11.5% 45 to 60 minutes, 5.4% 60 minutes or more (2000)
Additional Information Contacts
Clermont County Convention and Visitors Bureau . . . . . . (513) 796-4282
  http://www.visitclermontohio.com

BETHEL (village). Covers a land area of 1.339 square miles and a water area of 0 square miles. Located at 38.96° N. Lat.; 84.08° W. Long. Elevation is 892 feet.
History: Settled 1797.
Population: 2,500 (1990); 2,637 (2000); 2,530 (2005); 2,487 (2010 projected); Race: 97.9% White, 0.1% Black, 0.3% Asian, 0.9% Hispanic of any race (2005); Density: 1,889.3 persons per square mile (2005); Average household size: 2.59 (2005); Median age: 31.5 (2005); Males per 100 females: 88.8 (2005); Marriage status: 24.0% never married, 53.5% now married, 9.4% widowed, 13.1% divorced (2000); Foreign born: 0.4% (2000); Ancestry (includes multiple ancestries): 19.9% German, 16.5% United States or American, 15.5% Irish, 13.5% English, 12.5% Other groups (2000).
Economy: In agricultural area; nurseries. Employment by occupation: 9.2% management, 10.5% professional, 19.9% services, 27.0% sales, 0.0% farming, 16.9% construction, 16.3% production (2000).
Income: Per capita income: $16,010 (2005); Median household income: $33,633 (2005); Average household income: $40,418 (2005); Percent of households with income of $100,000 or more: 5.5% (2005); Poverty rate: 20.1% (2000).
Education: Percent of population age 25 and over with: High school diploma (including GED) or higher: 71.8% (2005); Bachelor's degree or higher: 11.6% (2005); Master's degree or higher: 3.6% (2005).
School District(s)
Bethel-Tate Local SD (PK-12)
  2003-04 Enrollment: 1,970 . . . . (513) 734-2238
U S Grant Joint Vocational SD (11-12)
  2003-04 Enrollment: n/a . . . . (513) 734-6222
Two-year College(s)
US Grant Joint Vocational School (Public)
  Fall 2004 Enrollment: 34 . . . . (513) 734-6222
  2005-06 Tuition: In-state $4,050; Out-of-state $4,050
Housing: Homeownership rate: 49.7% (2005); Median home value: $102,684 (2005); Median rent: $415 per month (2000); Median age of housing: 48 years (2000).
Transportation: Commute to work: 90.2% car, 2.3% public transportation, 5.0% walk, 0.8% work from home (2000); Travel time to work: 25.4% less

than 15 minutes, 24.2% 15 to 30 minutes, 19.3% 30 to 45 minutes, 19.6% 45 to 60 minutes, 11.5% 60 minutes or more (2000)
Additional Information Contacts
Village of Bethel................................. (937) 845-8472
http://www.betheltownship.org

CHILO (village).
Covers a land area of 0.199 square miles and a water area of 0.039 square miles. Located at 38.79° N. Lat.; 84.13° W. Long. Elevation is 500 feet.
History: Chilo was a boat-building center and river port before the 1937 floods destroyed most of the town.
Population: 130 (1990); 97 (2000); 111 (2005); 124 (2010 projected); Race: 97.3% White, 0.0% Black, 0.0% Asian, 0.0% Hispanic of any race (2005); Density: 557.6 persons per square mile (2005); Average household size: 2.36 (2005); Median age: 47.0 (2005); Males per 100 females: 122.0 (2005); Marriage status: 18.3% never married, 62.0% now married, 12.7% widowed, 7.0% divorced (2000); Foreign born: 2.2% (2000); Ancestry (includes multiple ancestries): 40.7% German, 17.6% Other groups, 16.5% Irish, 12.1% English, 11.0% United States or American (2000).
Economy: Employment by occupation: 10.7% management, 14.3% professional, 14.3% services, 32.1% sales, 0.0% farming, 17.9% construction, 10.7% production (2000).
Income: Per capita income: $20,766 (2005); Median household income: $46,591 (2005); Average household income: $49,043 (2005); Percent of households with income of $100,000 or more: 4.3% (2005); Poverty rate: 12.4% (2000).
Education: Percent of population age 25 and over with: High school diploma (including GED) or higher: 70.5% (2005); Bachelor's degree or higher: 16.7% (2005); Master's degree or higher: 12.8% (2005).
Housing: Homeownership rate: 74.5% (2005); Median home value: $68,750 (2005); Median rent: $550 per month (2000); Median age of housing: 59 years (2000).
Transportation: Commute to work: 92.9% car, 0.0% public transportation, 3.6% walk, 3.6% work from home (2000); Travel time to work: 37.0% less than 15 minutes, 0.0% 15 to 30 minutes, 7.4% 30 to 45 minutes, 22.2% 45 to 60 minutes, 33.3% 60 minutes or more (2000)

DAY HEIGHTS (CDP).
Covers a land area of 1.203 square miles and a water area of 0 square miles. Located at 39.17° N. Lat.; 84.23° W. Long.
Population: 2,812 (1990); 2,823 (2000); 2,847 (2005); 2,890 (2010 projected); Race: 97.0% White, 1.1% Black, 0.4% Asian, 0.6% Hispanic of any race (2005); Density: 2,367.0 persons per square mile (2005); Average household size: 2.76 (2005); Median age: 40.2 (2005); Males per 100 females: 100.1 (2005); Marriage status: 20.1% never married, 66.7% now married, 6.7% widowed, 6.5% divorced (2000); Foreign born: 0.5% (2000); Ancestry (includes multiple ancestries): 36.7% German, 23.9% Irish, 13.1% United States or American, 12.0% English, 6.2% Other groups (2000).
Economy: Employment by occupation: 16.7% management, 17.2% professional, 14.4% services, 29.4% sales, 0.0% farming, 6.3% construction, 15.9% production (2000).
Income: Per capita income: $29,644 (2005); Median household income: $69,692 (2005); Average household income: $81,781 (2005); Percent of households with income of $100,000 or more: 25.9% (2005); Poverty rate: 2.3% (2000).
Education: Percent of population age 25 and over with: High school diploma (including GED) or higher: 85.1% (2005); Bachelor's degree or higher: 22.4% (2005); Master's degree or higher: 6.7% (2005).
Housing: Homeownership rate: 94.6% (2005); Median home value: $139,248 (2005); Median rent: $622 per month (2000); Median age of housing: 35 years (2000).
Transportation: Commute to work: 94.6% car, 2.6% public transportation, 0.0% walk, 2.3% work from home (2000); Travel time to work: 18.7% less than 15 minutes, 35.8% 15 to 30 minutes, 31.1% 30 to 45 minutes, 11.1% 45 to 60 minutes, 3.3% 60 minutes or more (2000)

FELICITY (village).
Covers a land area of 0.267 square miles and a water area of 0 square miles. Located at 38.83° N. Lat.; 84.09° W. Long. Elevation is 922 feet.
Population: 775 (1990); 922 (2000); 844 (2005); 846 (2010 projected); Race: 97.7% White, 0.8% Black, 0.2% Asian, 1.1% Hispanic of any race (2005); Density: 3,158.9 persons per square mile (2005); Average household size: 2.62 (2005); Median age: 31.9 (2005); Males per 100 females: 92.3 (2005); Marriage status: 25.4% never married, 51.9% now married, 9.2% widowed, 13.5% divorced (2000); Foreign born: 1.1% (2000); Ancestry (includes multiple ancestries): 22.2% German, 22.1% United States or American, 14.9% English, 14.7% Irish, 8.3% Other groups (2000).
Economy: Employment by occupation: 6.4% management, 15.7% professional, 20.4% services, 21.8% sales, 1.1% farming, 15.7% construction, 18.9% production (2000).
Income: Per capita income: $12,210 (2005); Median household income: $24,057 (2005); Average household income: $32,003 (2005); Percent of households with income of $100,000 or more: 3.1% (2005); Poverty rate: 34.9% (2000).
Education: Percent of population age 25 and over with: High school diploma (including GED) or higher: 56.8% (2005); Bachelor's degree or higher: 7.1% (2005); Master's degree or higher: 2.8% (2005).
School District(s)
Felicity-Franklin Local SD (PK-12)
2003-04 Enrollment: 1,182 .... (513) 876-2113
Housing: Homeownership rate: 44.7% (2005); Median home value: $69,714 (2005); Median rent: $365 per month (2000); Median age of housing: 50 years (2000).
Transportation: Commute to work: 82.1% car, 0.0% public transportation, 14.6% walk, 3.4% work from home (2000); Travel time to work: 29.3% less than 15 minutes, 9.3% 15 to 30 minutes, 15.4% 30 to 45 minutes, 31.7% 45 to 60 minutes, 14.3% 60 minutes or more (2000)

GOSHEN (unincorporated postal area, zip code 45122).
Covers a land area of 45.909 square miles and a water area of 0.221 square miles. Located at 39.22° N. Lat.; 84.11° W. Long. Elevation is 820 feet.
Population: 11,406 (2000); Race: 98.3% White, 0.4% Black, 0.2% Asian, 0.7% Hispanic of any race (2000); Density: 248.4 persons per square mile (2000); Age: 27.6% under 18, 8.6% over 64 (2000); Marriage status: 19.3% never married, 65.2% now married, 5.3% widowed, 10.2% divorced (2000); Foreign born: 0.2% (2000); Ancestry (includes multiple ancestries): 24.6% German, 20.8% United States or American, 12.4% Irish, 8.2% English, 7.3% Other groups (2000).
Economy: Employment by occupation: 6.6% management, 9.2% professional, 15.4% services, 26.2% sales, 0.1% farming, 17.2% construction, 25.3% production (2000).
Income: Per capita income: $18,963 (2000); Median household income: $45,513 (2000); Poverty rate: 7.3% (2000).
Education: Percent of population age 25 and over with: High school diploma (including GED) or higher: 73.7% (2000); Bachelor's degree or higher: 6.6% (2000).
School District(s)
Goshen Local SD (PK-12)
2003-04 Enrollment: 2,525 .... (513) 722-2222
Housing: Homeownership rate: 85.4% (2000); Median home value: $98,700 (2000); Median rent: $502 per month (2000); Median age of housing: 25 years (2000).
Transportation: Commute to work: 95.8% car, 0.5% public transportation, 1.5% walk, 1.3% work from home (2000); Travel time to work: 12.0% less than 15 minutes, 30.3% 15 to 30 minutes, 37.3% 30 to 45 minutes, 15.0% 45 to 60 minutes, 5.4% 60 minutes or more (2000)

MILFORD (city).
Covers a land area of 3.758 square miles and a water area of 0.067 square miles. Located at 39.17° N. Lat.; 84.28° W. Long. Elevation is 639 feet.
History: Milford was settled in an area of glacial moraines, on the Little Miami River. A prehistoric civilization left mounds in this region.
Population: 5,773 (1990); 6,284 (2000); 6,372 (2005); 6,513 (2010 projected); Race: 94.7% White, 3.6% Black, 0.6% Asian, 0.9% Hispanic of any race (2005); Density: 1,695.5 persons per square mile (2005); Average household size: 2.08 (2005); Median age: 40.4 (2005); Males per 100 females: 83.5 (2005); Marriage status: 20.5% never married, 52.5% now married, 13.5% widowed, 13.5% divorced (2000); Foreign born: 1.5% (2000); Ancestry (includes multiple ancestries): 31.5% German, 15.7% Irish, 14.9% English, 11.2% United States or American, 8.9% Other groups (2000).
Economy: Single-family building permits issued: 2 (2005); Multi-family building permits issued: 0 (2005); Employment by occupation: 12.4% management, 19.3% professional, 19.4% services, 26.5% sales, 0.0% farming, 9.2% construction, 13.2% production (2000).
Income: Per capita income: $25,213 (2005); Median household income: $35,861 (2005); Average household income: $52,015 (2005); Percent of households with income of $100,000 or more: 11.8% (2005); Poverty rate: 7.8% (2000).

Education: Percent of population age 25 and over with: High school diploma (including GED) or higher: 77.8% (2005); Bachelor's degree or higher: 23.5% (2005); Master's degree or higher: 8.6% (2005).

School District(s)

Great Oaks Inst of Technology Joint Vocational SD (07-12)
   2003-04 Enrollment: n/a . . . . (513) 771-8840
Milford Ex Vill SD (PK-12)
   2003-04 Enrollment: 6,225 . . . . (513) 831-1314

Housing: Homeownership rate: 49.9% (2005); Median home value: $133,141 (2005); Median rent: $438 per month (2000); Median age of housing: 34 years (2000).
Safety: Violent crime rate: 12.5 per 10,000 population; Property crime rate: 263.4 per 10,000 population (2004).
Transportation: Commute to work: 90.8% car, 1.2% public transportation, 2.1% walk, 4.7% work from home (2000); Travel time to work: 26.7% less than 15 minutes, 41.8% 15 to 30 minutes, 23.4% 30 to 45 minutes, 5.2% 45 to 60 minutes, 2.9% 60 minutes or more (2000)

Additional Information Contacts
Milford-Miami Twp. Chamber of Commerce . . . . (513) 831-2411
   http://www.milfordmiamitownship.com

MOSCOW (village).
Covers a land area of 0.402 square miles and a water area of 0.009 square miles. Located at 38.85° N. Lat.; 84.22° W. Long. Elevation is 500 feet.
History: Moscow was one of the first stations on the Underground Railroad. During the Reconstruction Period, Moscow was a busy shipping point, and a producer of large quantities of brandy.
Population: 269 (1990); 244 (2000); 253 (2005); 259 (2010 projected); Race: 96.4% White, 0.4% Black, 0.4% Asian, 0.0% Hispanic of any race (2005); Density: 628.7 persons per square mile (2005); Average household size: 2.61 (2005); Median age: 37.9 (2005); Males per 100 females: 97.7 (2005); Marriage status: 21.8% never married, 54.8% now married, 7.4% widowed, 16.0% divorced (2000); Foreign born: 0.8% (2000); Ancestry (includes multiple ancestries): 32.2% German, 16.9% English, 11.9% United States or American, 11.5% Irish, 4.6% Other groups (2000).
Economy: Employment by occupation: 4.6% management, 4.6% professional, 16.7% services, 19.4% sales, 1.9% farming, 24.1% construction, 28.7% production (2000).
Income: Per capita income: $15,049 (2005); Median household income: $36,023 (2005); Average household income: $39,253 (2005); Percent of households with income of $100,000 or more: 4.1% (2005); Poverty rate: 19.9% (2000).
Education: Percent of population age 25 and over with: High school diploma (including GED) or higher: 68.7% (2005); Bachelor's degree or higher: 1.8% (2005); Master's degree or higher: 1.8% (2005).
Housing: Homeownership rate: 77.3% (2005); Median home value: $94,583 (2005); Median rent: $388 per month (2000); Median age of housing: 60+ years (2000).
Transportation: Commute to work: 98.1% car, 0.0% public transportation, 0.0% walk, 1.9% work from home (2000); Travel time to work: 12.3% less than 15 minutes, 19.8% 15 to 30 minutes, 37.7% 30 to 45 minutes, 19.8% 45 to 60 minutes, 10.4% 60 minutes or more (2000)

MOUNT CARMEL (CDP).
Covers a land area of 1.683 square miles and a water area of 0 square miles. Located at 39.09° N. Lat.; 84.29° W. Long. Elevation is 880 feet.
Population: 4,462 (1990); 4,308 (2000); 3,774 (2005); 3,321 (2010 projected); Race: 96.6% White, 0.8% Black, 0.4% Asian, 1.2% Hispanic of any race (2005); Density: 2,242.1 persons per square mile (2005); Average household size: 2.47 (2005); Median age: 35.2 (2005); Males per 100 females: 98.5 (2005); Marriage status: 26.3% never married, 55.4% now married, 5.4% widowed, 12.9% divorced (2000); Foreign born: 1.9% (2000); Ancestry (includes multiple ancestries): 38.0% German, 15.3% Irish, 13.2% United States or American, 9.8% English, 7.5% Other groups (2000).
Economy: Employment by occupation: 12.6% management, 10.6% professional, 16.5% services, 29.7% sales, 0.0% farming, 10.9% construction, 19.6% production (2000).
Income: Per capita income: $19,959 (2005); Median household income: $40,643 (2005); Average household income: $49,379 (2005); Percent of households with income of $100,000 or more: 10.0% (2005); Poverty rate: 9.3% (2000).
Education: Percent of population age 25 and over with: High school diploma (including GED) or higher: 78.7% (2005); Bachelor's degree or higher: 10.9% (2005); Master's degree or higher: 1.4% (2005).
Housing: Homeownership rate: 63.6% (2005); Median home value: $119,027 (2005); Median rent: $441 per month (2000); Median age of housing: 33 years (2000).
Transportation: Commute to work: 93.6% car, 2.0% public transportation, 1.4% walk, 2.8% work from home (2000); Travel time to work: 32.0% less than 15 minutes, 31.6% 15 to 30 minutes, 27.5% 30 to 45 minutes, 6.6% 45 to 60 minutes, 2.3% 60 minutes or more (2000)

MOUNT REPOSE (CDP).
Covers a land area of 1.950 square miles and a water area of 0 square miles. Located at 39.18° N. Lat.; 84.22° W. Long. Elevation is 860 feet.
Population: 4,062 (1990); 4,102 (2000); 4,360 (2005); 4,583 (2010 projected); Race: 96.4% White, 1.0% Black, 1.2% Asian, 0.9% Hispanic of any race (2005); Density: 2,235.9 persons per square mile (2005); Average household size: 2.71 (2005); Median age: 36.3 (2005); Males per 100 females: 96.2 (2005); Marriage status: 20.9% never married, 65.8% now married, 5.9% widowed, 7.4% divorced (2000); Foreign born: 2.1% (2000); Ancestry (includes multiple ancestries): 30.2% German, 16.9% Irish, 13.4% Other groups, 11.5% English, 8.6% United States or American (2000).
Economy: Employment by occupation: 14.0% management, 18.9% professional, 12.0% services, 29.7% sales, 0.0% farming, 12.7% construction, 12.7% production (2000).
Income: Per capita income: $24,353 (2005); Median household income: $61,773 (2005); Average household income: $65,991 (2005); Percent of households with income of $100,000 or more: 15.6% (2005); Poverty rate: 5.1% (2000).
Education: Percent of population age 25 and over with: High school diploma (including GED) or higher: 87.9% (2005); Bachelor's degree or higher: 21.8% (2005); Master's degree or higher: 5.9% (2005).
Housing: Homeownership rate: 84.9% (2005); Median home value: $138,757 (2005); Median rent: $419 per month (2000); Median age of housing: 25 years (2000).
Transportation: Commute to work: 93.8% car, 1.5% public transportation, 1.0% walk, 3.3% work from home (2000); Travel time to work: 18.9% less than 15 minutes, 41.5% 15 to 30 minutes, 26.5% 30 to 45 minutes, 9.5% 45 to 60 minutes, 3.6% 60 minutes or more (2000)

MULBERRY (CDP).
Covers a land area of 1.514 square miles and a water area of 0 square miles. Located at 39.19° N. Lat.; 84.25° W. Long. Elevation is 840 feet.
Population: 2,856 (1990); 3,139 (2000); 3,468 (2005); 3,756 (2010 projected); Race: 96.8% White, 1.1% Black, 1.1% Asian, 0.7% Hispanic of any race (2005); Density: 2,289.9 persons per square mile (2005); Average household size: 2.52 (2005); Median age: 44.3 (2005); Males per 100 females: 80.3 (2005); Marriage status: 17.7% never married, 56.0% now married, 13.1% widowed, 13.2% divorced (2000); Foreign born: 2.9% (2000); Ancestry (includes multiple ancestries): 33.6% German, 14.8% Irish, 13.3% English, 8.6% United States or American, 5.5% Other groups (2000).
Economy: Employment by occupation: 17.4% management, 23.9% professional, 10.7% services, 30.3% sales, 0.0% farming, 9.6% construction, 8.0% production (2000).
Income: Per capita income: $30,292 (2005); Median household income: $58,664 (2005); Average household income: $74,762 (2005); Percent of households with income of $100,000 or more: 21.5% (2005); Poverty rate: 4.2% (2000).
Education: Percent of population age 25 and over with: High school diploma (including GED) or higher: 89.1% (2005); Bachelor's degree or higher: 33.6% (2005); Master's degree or higher: 9.4% (2005).
Housing: Homeownership rate: 80.6% (2005); Median home value: $139,153 (2005); Median rent: $537 per month (2000); Median age of housing: 16 years (2000).
Transportation: Commute to work: 95.6% car, 0.7% public transportation, 0.0% walk, 3.0% work from home (2000); Travel time to work: 25.6% less than 15 minutes, 40.2% 15 to 30 minutes, 25.9% 30 to 45 minutes, 7.1% 45 to 60 minutes, 1.1% 60 minutes or more (2000)

NEVILLE (village).
Covers a land area of 0.417 square miles and a water area of 0.043 square miles. Located at 38.81° N. Lat.; 84.21° W. Long. Elevation is 500 feet.
History: Neville was founded in 1808 and named for a Virginia officer in the Revolutionary War who was given land here for his military service. More than half of the houses in Neville were destroyed by the 1937 flooding of the Ohio River.

Population: 226 (1990); 127 (2000); 134 (2005); 139 (2010 projected); **Race:** 98.5% White, 1.5% Black, 0.0% Asian, 0.0% Hispanic of any race (2005); **Density:** 321.3 persons per square mile (2005); Average household size: 2.68 (2005); Median age: 35.0 (2005); Males per 100 females: 100.0 (2005); Marriage status: 22.9% never married, 56.3% now married, 7.3% widowed, 13.5% divorced (2000); Foreign born: 3.0% (2000); Ancestry (includes multiple ancestries): 26.1% German, 24.6% Irish, 24.6% English, 11.9% United States or American, 4.5% Other groups (2000).
Economy: Employment by occupation: 11.1% management, 3.7% professional, 24.1% services, 35.2% sales, 3.7% farming, 11.1% construction, 11.1% production (2000).
Income: Per capita income: $17,257 (2005); Median household income: $40,625 (2005); Average household income: $46,250 (2005); Percent of households with income of $100,000 or more: 6.0% (2005); Poverty rate: 19.4% (2000).
Education: Percent of population age 25 and over with: High school diploma (including GED) or higher: 60.5% (2005); Bachelor's degree or higher: 4.9% (2005); Master's degree or higher: 0.0% (2005).
Housing: Homeownership rate: 82.0% (2005); Median home value: $81,111 (2005); Median rent: $400 per month (2000); Median age of housing: 48 years (2000).
Transportation: Commute to work: 98.1% car, 0.0% public transportation, 1.9% walk, 0.0% work from home (2000); Travel time to work: 16.7% less than 15 minutes, 20.4% 15 to 30 minutes, 20.4% 30 to 45 minutes, 27.8% 45 to 60 minutes, 14.8% 60 minutes or more (2000)

NEW RICHMOND (village). Covers a land area of 3.442 square miles and a water area of 0.096 square miles. Located at 38.95° N. Lat.; 84.28° W. Long. Elevation is 495 feet.
History: New Richmond was created when two villages were joined. One of them, Susanna, had been laid out in 1816 by Thomas Ashburn as a model town. The 1937 flooding of the Ohio River devastated New Richmond.
Population: 2,408 (1990); 2,219 (2000); 2,362 (2005); 2,517 (2010 projected); Race: 96.7% White, 1.7% Black, 0.1% Asian, 0.9% Hispanic of any race (2005); Density: 686.1 persons per square mile (2005); Average household size: 2.75 (2005); Median age: 33.6 (2005); Males per 100 females: 100.5 (2005); Marriage status: 25.7% never married, 54.8% now married, 6.1% widowed, 13.4% divorced (2000); Foreign born: 0.7% (2000); Ancestry (includes multiple ancestries): 27.3% German, 21.9% Irish, 12.9% United States or American, 10.9% Other groups, 6.0% English (2000).
Economy: Employment by occupation: 10.1% management, 11.6% professional, 19.1% services, 26.5% sales, 0.0% farming, 14.9% construction, 17.6% production (2000).
Income: Per capita income: $20,519 (2005); Median household income: $45,182 (2005); Average household income: $55,822 (2005); Percent of households with income of $100,000 or more: 13.1% (2005); Poverty rate: 17.7% (2000).
Education: Percent of population age 25 and over with: High school diploma (including GED) or higher: 73.2% (2005); Bachelor's degree or higher: 15.5% (2005); Master's degree or higher: 4.7% (2005).
School District(s)
New Richmond Ex Vill SD (PK-12)
    2003-04 Enrollment: 2,411 . . . . (513) 553-2616
Housing: Homeownership rate: 59.3% (2005); Median home value: $120,455 (2005); Median rent: $415 per month (2000); Median age of housing: 53 years (2000).
Transportation: Commute to work: 88.2% car, 1.4% public transportation, 4.8% walk, 1.5% work from home (2000); Travel time to work: 27.1% less than 15 minutes, 30.4% 15 to 30 minutes, 27.4% 30 to 45 minutes, 8.7% 45 to 60 minutes, 6.5% 60 minutes or more (2000)

NEWTONSVILLE (village). Covers a land area of 0.243 square miles and a water area of 0 square miles. Located at 39.18° N. Lat.; 84.08° W. Long. Elevation is 905 feet.
Population: 427 (1990); 492 (2000); 500 (2005); 511 (2010 projected); Race: 99.6% White, 0.0% Black, 0.2% Asian, 0.4% Hispanic of any race (2005); Density: 2,054.7 persons per square mile (2005); Average household size: 2.75 (2005); Median age: 36.2 (2005); Males per 100 females: 97.6 (2005); Marriage status: 27.2% never married, 55.6% now married, 3.4% widowed, 13.8% divorced (2000); Foreign born: 0.0% (2000); Ancestry (includes multiple ancestries): 32.0% United States or American, 17.3% German, 5.3% Other groups, 5.0% Irish, 4.3% English (2000).

Economy: Employment by occupation: 7.6% management, 5.4% professional, 19.6% services, 28.3% sales, 0.0% farming, 13.6% construction, 25.5% production (2000).
Income: Per capita income: $20,835 (2005); Median household income: $47,209 (2005); Average household income: $57,239 (2005); Percent of households with income of $100,000 or more: 11.5% (2005); Poverty rate: 15.5% (2000).
Education: Percent of population age 25 and over with: High school diploma (including GED) or higher: 63.8% (2005); Bachelor's degree or higher: 3.4% (2005); Master's degree or higher: 0.9% (2005).
Housing: Homeownership rate: 78.0% (2005); Median home value: $104,918 (2005); Median rent: $375 per month (2000); Median age of housing: 42 years (2000).
Transportation: Commute to work: 92.7% car, 3.9% public transportation, 2.2% walk, 1.1% work from home (2000); Travel time to work: 16.4% less than 15 minutes, 24.3% 15 to 30 minutes, 27.1% 30 to 45 minutes, 18.1% 45 to 60 minutes, 14.1% 60 minutes or more (2000)

OWENSVILLE (village). Covers a land area of 0.396 square miles and a water area of 0 square miles. Located at 39.12° N. Lat.; 84.13° W. Long. Elevation is 862 feet.
Population: 872 (1990); 816 (2000); 749 (2005); 744 (2010 projected); Race: 97.1% White, 0.8% Black, 0.1% Asian, 1.5% Hispanic of any race (2005); Density: 1,892.4 persons per square mile (2005); Average household size: 2.20 (2005); Median age: 35.6 (2005); Males per 100 females: 88.2 (2005); Marriage status: 27.5% never married, 39.5% now married, 15.1% widowed, 17.9% divorced (2000); Foreign born: 0.6% (2000); Ancestry (includes multiple ancestries): 25.3% German, 19.4% United States or American, 12.9% Irish, 5.1% English, 3.8% Other groups (2000).
Economy: Limestone quarry. Employment by occupation: 7.7% management, 14.1% professional, 23.3% services, 26.2% sales, 0.0% farming, 11.5% construction, 17.3% production (2000).
Income: Per capita income: $18,009 (2005); Median household income: $27,386 (2005); Average household income: $39,304 (2005); Percent of households with income of $100,000 or more: 7.0% (2005); Poverty rate: 18.6% (2000).
Education: Percent of population age 25 and over with: High school diploma (including GED) or higher: 69.7% (2005); Bachelor's degree or higher: 7.4% (2005); Master's degree or higher: 3.4% (2005).
School District(s)
Clermont Northeastern Local SD (PK-12)
    2003-04 Enrollment: 1,972 . . . . (513) 625-5478
Housing: Homeownership rate: 42.8% (2005); Median home value: $116,667 (2005); Median rent: $264 per month (2000); Median age of housing: 27 years (2000).
Transportation: Commute to work: 90.3% car, 0.0% public transportation, 2.9% walk, 5.5% work from home (2000); Travel time to work: 15.4% less than 15 minutes, 41.1% 15 to 30 minutes, 28.4% 30 to 45 minutes, 11.0% 45 to 60 minutes, 4.1% 60 minutes or more (2000)

SUMMERSIDE (CDP). Covers a land area of 2.277 square miles and a water area of 0.003 square miles. Located at 39.11° N. Lat.; 84.29° W. Long. Elevation is 870 feet.
Population: 4,573 (1990); 5,523 (2000); 5,763 (2005); 6,075 (2010 projected); Race: 95.3% White, 1.2% Black, 1.7% Asian, 1.2% Hispanic of any race (2005); Density: 2,530.6 persons per square mile (2005); Average household size: 2.45 (2005); Median age: 34.3 (2005); Males per 100 females: 92.2 (2005); Marriage status: 24.0% never married, 60.2% now married, 5.3% widowed, 10.5% divorced (2000); Foreign born: 1.2% (2000); Ancestry (includes multiple ancestries): 32.3% German, 21.0% Irish, 11.5% United States or American, 11.3% English, 9.0% Other groups (2000).
Economy: Employment by occupation: 15.4% management, 17.8% professional, 11.3% services, 31.6% sales, 0.3% farming, 7.6% construction, 15.9% production (2000).
Income: Per capita income: $23,870 (2005); Median household income: $49,077 (2005); Average household income: $58,437 (2005); Percent of households with income of $100,000 or more: 13.2% (2005); Poverty rate: 6.2% (2000).
Education: Percent of population age 25 and over with: High school diploma (including GED) or higher: 83.2% (2005); Bachelor's degree or higher: 22.1% (2005); Master's degree or higher: 4.5% (2005).

Housing: Homeownership rate: 66.2% (2005); Median home value: $125,794 (2005); Median rent: $499 per month (2000); Median age of housing: 25 years (2000).
Transportation: Commute to work: 93.8% car, 2.9% public transportation, 1.0% walk, 2.1% work from home (2000); Travel time to work: 22.6% less than 15 minutes, 36.2% 15 to 30 minutes, 32.5% 30 to 45 minutes, 6.1% 45 to 60 minutes, 2.6% 60 minutes or more (2000)

WILLIAMSBURG (village).
Covers a land area of 1.908 square miles and a water area of 0.023 square miles. Located at 39.05° N. Lat.; 84.05° W. Long. Elevation is 850 feet.
History: Incorporated 1800.
Population: 2,552 (1990); 2,358 (2000); 2,425 (2005); 2,523 (2010 projected); Race: 98.5% White, 0.2% Black, 0.2% Asian, 0.2% Hispanic of any race (2005); Density: 1,270.7 persons per square mile (2005); Average household size: 2.48 (2005); Median age: 34.5 (2005); Males per 100 females: 89.7 (2005); Marriage status: 23.8% never married, 53.1% now married, 7.7% widowed, 15.4% divorced (2000); Foreign born: 0.7% (2000); Ancestry (includes multiple ancestries): 25.9% German, 17.1% United States or American, 14.1% English, 12.2% Irish, 12.0% Other groups (2000).
Economy: Agriculture: corn, wheat, tobacco. Manufacturing of chairs. Employment by occupation: 9.8% management, 10.3% professional, 14.1% services, 30.1% sales, 0.9% farming, 12.5% construction, 22.3% production (2000).
Income: Per capita income: $21,040 (2005); Median household income: $42,807 (2005); Average household income: $51,590 (2005); Percent of households with income of $100,000 or more: 7.7% (2005); Poverty rate: 11.3% (2000).
Education: Percent of population age 25 and over with: High school diploma (including GED) or higher: 73.3% (2005); Bachelor's degree or higher: 10.4% (2005); Master's degree or higher: 2.8% (2005).

School District(s)
Clermont County Educational Service Center
    2003-04 Enrollment: n/a . . . . (513) 735-8300
Williamsburg Local SD (PK-12)
    2003-04 Enrollment: 1,028 . . . . (513) 724-3077

Housing: Homeownership rate: 59.8% (2005); Median home value: $103,125 (2005); Median rent: $448 per month (2000); Median age of housing: 42 years (2000).
Transportation: Commute to work: 95.2% car, 0.5% public transportation, 2.3% walk, 0.6% work from home (2000); Travel time to work: 23.4% less than 15 minutes, 26.9% 15 to 30 minutes, 21.9% 30 to 45 minutes, 19.6% 45 to 60 minutes, 8.1% 60 minutes or more (2000)

WITHAMSVILLE (CDP).
Covers a land area of 1.750 square miles and a water area of 0 square miles. Located at 39.05° N. Lat.; 84.27° W. Long. Elevation is 900 feet.
Population: 2,720 (1990); 3,145 (2000); 3,011 (2005); 3,059 (2010 projected); Race: 96.6% White, 0.9% Black, 1.4% Asian, 1.0% Hispanic of any race (2005); Density: 1,720.3 persons per square mile (2005); Average household size: 2.35 (2005); Median age: 36.5 (2005); Males per 100 females: 99.0 (2005); Marriage status: 27.3% never married, 57.9% now married, 5.7% widowed, 9.1% divorced (2000); Foreign born: 0.3% (2000); Ancestry (includes multiple ancestries): 28.9% German, 21.3% Irish, 11.5% English, 9.6% United States or American, 9.4% Other groups (2000).
Economy: Employment by occupation: 8.9% management, 14.0% professional, 14.2% services, 29.7% sales, 0.0% farming, 14.4% construction, 18.8% production (2000).
Income: Per capita income: $25,653 (2005); Median household income: $55,319 (2005); Average household income: $60,250 (2005); Percent of households with income of $100,000 or more: 14.7% (2005); Poverty rate: 7.8% (2000).
Education: Percent of population age 25 and over with: High school diploma (including GED) or higher: 81.6% (2005); Bachelor's degree or higher: 15.4% (2005); Master's degree or higher: 4.2% (2005).
Housing: Homeownership rate: 62.7% (2005); Median home value: $133,057 (2005); Median rent: $429 per month (2000); Median age of housing: 32 years (2000).
Transportation: Commute to work: 95.4% car, 0.9% public transportation, 0.0% walk, 3.3% work from home (2000); Travel time to work: 21.0% less than 15 minutes, 28.8% 15 to 30 minutes, 38.5% 30 to 45 minutes, 8.6% 45 to 60 minutes, 3.1% 60 minutes or more (2000)

Clinton County

Located in southwestern Ohio; drained by forks of the Little Miami River and Caesar Creek. Covers a land area of 410.88 square miles, a water area of 1.41 square miles, and is located in the Eastern Time Zone. The county government was organized in 1810. County seat is Wilmington.

Clinton County is part of the Wilmington, OH Micropolitan Statistical Area. The entire metro area includes: Clinton County, OH

Weather Station: Wilmington 3 N   Elevation: 1,026 feet

	Jan	Feb	Mar	Apr	May	Jun	Jul	Aug	Sep	Oct	Nov	Dec
High	35	39	50	62	72	80	84	83	77	65	52	41
Low	18	21	30	39	49	58	62	60	53	41	33	24
Precip	2.6	2.4	3.4	4.1	4.8	4.3	4.4	3.3	2.8	2.9	3.4	2.9
Snow	8.2	6.3	3.9	0.7	tr	0.0	0.0	0.0	0.0	0.2	1.4	3.0

High and Low temperatures in degrees Fahrenheit; Precipitation and Snow in inches

Population: 35,415 (1990); 40,543 (2000); 42,351 (2005); 44,236 (2010 projected); Race: 95.8% White, 2.1% Black, 0.6% Asian, 0.8% Hispanic of any race (2005); Density: 103.1 persons per square mile (2005); Average household size: 2.60 (2005); Median age: 36.0 (2005); Males per 100 females: 96.7 (2005).
Religion: Five largest groups: 7.0% The United Methodist Church, 6.1% Catholic Church, 5.5% Christian Churches and Churches of Christ, 3.2% Southern Baptist Convention, 2.1% Friends (Quakers) (2000).
Economy: Unemployment rate: 5.5% (2005); Total civilian labor force: 22,333 (2005); Leading industries: 19.4% manufacturing; 9.3% retail trade; 8.8% health care and social assistance (2004); Farms: 811 totaling 238,805 acres (2002); Companies that employ 500 or more persons: 6 (2004); Companies that employ 100 to 499 persons: 21 (2004); Companies that employ less than 100 persons: 780 (2004); Black-owned businesses: n/a (2002); Hispanic-owned businesses: n/a (2002); Women-owned businesses: 583 (2002); Retail sales per capita: $16,481 (2006). Single-family building permits issued: 264 (2005); Multi-family building permits issued: 0 (2005).
Income: Per capita income: $20,552 (2005); Median household income: $44,597 (2005); Average household income: $53,079 (2005); Percent of households with income of $100,000 or more: 9.4% (2005); Poverty rate: 9.0% (2003); Bankruptcy rate: 12.07% (2005).
Taxes: Total county taxes per capita: $231 (2004); County property taxes per capita: $120 (2004).
Education: Percent of population age 25 and over with: High school diploma (including GED) or higher: 83.0% (2005); Bachelor's degree or higher: 14.2% (2005); Master's degree or higher: 4.9% (2005).
Housing: Homeownership rate: 69.1% (2005); Median home value: $120,972 (2005); Median rent: $393 per month (2000); Median age of housing: 34 years (2000).
Health: Birth rate: 133.2 per 10,000 population (2004); Death rate: 86.0 per 10,000 population (2004); Age-adjusted cancer mortality rate: 212.8 deaths per 100,000 population (2002); Air Quality Index: 72.6% good, 26.0% moderate, 1.4% unhealthy for sensitive individuals, 0.0% unhealthy (percent of days in 2005); Number of physicians: 18.5 per 10,000 population (2004); Hospital beds: 19.4 per 10,000 population (2003); Hospital admissions: 1,115.6 per 10,000 population (2003).
Elections: 2004 Presidential election results: 70.3% Bush, 29.4% Kerry, 0.0% Nader, 0.2% Badnarik
National and State Parks: Cowan State Park
Additional Information Contacts
Clinton County Government. . . . . (937) 382-2103
   http://co.clinton.oh.us/
Blanchester Chamber of Commerce . . . . (937) 783-3601
   http://www.clintoncountyohio.com
City of Wilmington . . . . (937) 382-5458
   http://ci.wilmington.oh.us
Clinton County Convention & Visitors Bureau . . . . (937) 382-1965
   http://www.clintoncountyohio.com
Wilmington Chamber of Commerce. . . . . (937) 382-2737
   http://www.wccchamber.com

Clinton County Communities

BLANCHESTER (village). Covers a land area of 2.962 square miles and a water area of 0.052 square miles. Located at 39.29° N. Lat.; 83.98° W. Long. Elevation is 971 feet.

Population: 4,293 (1990); 4,220 (2000); 4,320 (2005); 4,436 (2010 projected); Race: 98.5% White, 0.1% Black, 0.6% Asian, 0.7% Hispanic of any race (2005); Density: 1,458.6 persons per square mile (2005); Average household size: 2.52 (2005); Median age: 36.3 (2005); Males per 100 females: 87.5 (2005); Marriage status: 20.4% never married, 56.2% now married, 12.3% widowed, 11.2% divorced (2000); Foreign born: 0.1% (2000); Ancestry (includes multiple ancestries): 21.6% United States or American, 18.1% German, 11.3% English, 7.6% Irish, 6.3% Other groups (2000).
Economy: In livestock-raising and farming area. Manufacturing of pumps, clothing, canned foods. Employment by occupation: 8.7% management, 10.7% professional, 16.9% services, 23.1% sales, 0.0% farming, 12.2% construction, 28.4% production (2000).
Income: Per capita income: $18,264 (2005); Median household income: $38,883 (2005); Average household income: $45,513 (2005); Percent of households with income of $100,000 or more: 5.3% (2005); Poverty rate: 11.0% (2000).
Education: Percent of population age 25 and over with: High school diploma (including GED) or higher: 71.3% (2005); Bachelor's degree or higher: 10.9% (2005); Master's degree or higher: 3.7% (2005).

School District(s)
Blanchester Local SD (PK-12)
    2003-04 Enrollment: 1,771 .... (937) 783-3523
Little Miami Local School District (KG-12)
    2003-04 Enrollment: 3,201 .... (513) 899-2264

Housing: Homeownership rate: 65.4% (2005); Median home value: $98,079 (2005); Median rent: $362 per month (2000); Median age of housing: 38 years (2000).
Newspapers: The Star-Republican (General - Circulation 21,500)
Transportation: Commute to work: 91.6% car, 0.0% public transportation, 4.5% walk, 3.9% work from home (2000); Travel time to work: 29.6% less than 15 minutes, 17.3% 15 to 30 minutes, 29.1% 30 to 45 minutes, 13.9% 45 to 60 minutes, 10.1% 60 minutes or more (2000)

Additional Information Contacts
Blanchester Chamber of Commerce .... (937) 783-3601
    http://www.clintoncountyohio.com

CLARKSVILLE (village).
Covers a land area of 0.485 square miles and a water area of 0 square miles. Located at 39.40° N. Lat.; 83.98° W. Long. Elevation is 850 feet.
Population: 485 (1990); 497 (2000); 483 (2005); 482 (2010 projected); Race: 95.9% White, 0.4% Black, 0.2% Asian, 1.4% Hispanic of any race (2005); Density: 994.9 persons per square mile (2005); Average household size: 2.56 (2005); Median age: 32.9 (2005); Males per 100 females: 90.2 (2005); Marriage status: 30.1% never married, 48.7% now married, 5.6% widowed, 15.7% divorced (2000); Foreign born: 0.0% (2000); Ancestry (includes multiple ancestries): 18.9% United States or American, 16.5% Irish, 15.0% German, 13.0% Other groups, 9.1% English (2000).
Economy: Employment by occupation: 6.1% management, 7.8% professional, 21.2% services, 17.3% sales, 0.0% farming, 14.3% construction, 33.3% production (2000).
Income: Per capita income: $17,158 (2005); Median household income: $40,147 (2005); Average household income: $43,849 (2005); Percent of households with income of $100,000 or more: 2.6% (2005); Poverty rate: 9.0% (2000).
Education: Percent of population age 25 and over with: High school diploma (including GED) or higher: 81.3% (2005); Bachelor's degree or higher: 3.6% (2005); Master's degree or higher: 1.3% (2005).

School District(s)
Clinton-Massie Local SD (PK-12)
    2003-04 Enrollment: 1,774 .... (937) 289-2471

Housing: Homeownership rate: 72.0% (2005); Median home value: $83,158 (2005); Median rent: $346 per month (2000); Median age of housing: 60+ years (2000).
Transportation: Commute to work: 90.3% car, 0.0% public transportation, 0.9% walk, 8.8% work from home (2000); Travel time to work: 10.2% less than 15 minutes, 64.6% 15 to 30 minutes, 9.2% 30 to 45 minutes, 7.8% 45 to 60 minutes, 8.3% 60 minutes or more (2000)

MARTINSVILLE (village).
Covers a land area of 0.442 square miles and a water area of 0 square miles. Located at 39.32° N. Lat.; 83.81° W. Long. Elevation is 1,087 feet.
Population: 476 (1990); 440 (2000); 474 (2005); 508 (2010 projected); Race: 96.4% White, 1.1% Black, 0.4% Asian, 0.4% Hispanic of any race (2005); Density: 1,073.3 persons per square mile (2005); Average household size: 2.71 (2005); Median age: 35.9 (2005); Males per 100 females: 100.0 (2005); Marriage status: 20.6% never married, 54.1% now married, 12.4% widowed, 12.9% divorced (2000); Foreign born: 0.5% (2000); Ancestry (includes multiple ancestries): 31.4% United States or American, 11.0% Irish, 9.6% Other groups, 9.4% English, 8.2% German (2000).
Economy: Employment by occupation: 6.9% management, 10.3% professional, 17.2% services, 27.9% sales, 1.0% farming, 10.3% construction, 26.5% production (2000).
Income: Per capita income: $16,382 (2005); Median household income: $41,085 (2005); Average household income: $44,371 (2005); Percent of households with income of $100,000 or more: 2.3% (2005); Poverty rate: 8.5% (2000).
Education: Percent of population age 25 and over with: High school diploma (including GED) or higher: 69.9% (2005); Bachelor's degree or higher: 6.3% (2005); Master's degree or higher: 1.7% (2005).
Housing: Homeownership rate: 78.9% (2005); Median home value: $89,500 (2005); Median rent: $454 per month (2000); Median age of housing: 50 years (2000).
Transportation: Commute to work: 91.7% car, 0.0% public transportation, 2.9% walk, 3.4% work from home (2000); Travel time to work: 11.2% less than 15 minutes, 61.4% 15 to 30 minutes, 8.1% 30 to 45 minutes, 5.1% 45 to 60 minutes, 14.2% 60 minutes or more (2000)

MIDLAND (village).
Aka Midland City. Covers a land area of 0.352 square miles and a water area of 0 square miles. Located at 39.30° N. Lat.; 83.90° W. Long. Elevation is 994 feet.
History: Midland developed as a junction town for two branches of the Baltimore & Ohio Railroad.
Population: 341 (1990); 265 (2000); 263 (2005); 262 (2010 projected); Race: 95.4% White, 0.0% Black, 0.0% Asian, 3.0% Hispanic of any race (2005); Density: 747.3 persons per square mile (2005); Average household size: 2.66 (2005); Median age: 32.7 (2005); Males per 100 females: 108.7 (2005); Marriage status: 21.8% never married, 69.5% now married, 3.3% widowed, 5.4% divorced (2000); Foreign born: 0.0% (2000); Ancestry (includes multiple ancestries): 30.8% United States or American, 13.4% German, 10.7% Other groups, 7.4% English, 6.0% Irish (2000).
Economy: Employment by occupation: 1.6% management, 0.0% professional, 12.0% services, 24.8% sales, 0.0% farming, 12.0% construction, 49.6% production (2000).
Income: Per capita income: $16,549 (2005); Median household income: $42,500 (2005); Average household income: $43,965 (2005); Percent of households with income of $100,000 or more: 2.0% (2005); Poverty rate: 16.7% (2000).
Education: Percent of population age 25 and over with: High school diploma (including GED) or higher: 65.5% (2005); Bachelor's degree or higher: 2.3% (2005); Master's degree or higher: 1.2% (2005).

School District(s)
Blanchester Local SD (PK-12)
    2003-04 Enrollment: 1,771 .... (937) 783-3523

Housing: Homeownership rate: 74.7% (2005); Median home value: $70,000 (2005); Median rent: $410 per month (2000); Median age of housing: 47 years (2000).
Transportation: Commute to work: 96.6% car, 0.0% public transportation, 0.0% walk, 0.0% work from home (2000); Travel time to work: 11.9% less than 15 minutes, 32.2% 15 to 30 minutes, 23.7% 30 to 45 minutes, 14.4% 45 to 60 minutes, 17.8% 60 minutes or more (2000)

NEW VIENNA (village).
Covers a land area of 0.799 square miles and a water area of 0 square miles. Located at 39.32° N. Lat.; 83.69° W. Long. Elevation is 1,119 feet.
Population: 961 (1990); 1,294 (2000); 1,355 (2005); 1,417 (2010 projected); Race: 97.5% White, 0.1% Black, 0.0% Asian, 0.8% Hispanic of any race (2005); Density: 1,695.3 persons per square mile (2005); Average household size: 2.58 (2005); Median age: 31.9 (2005); Males per 100 females: 84.1 (2005); Marriage status: 19.7% never married, 56.0% now married, 6.4% widowed, 17.9% divorced (2000); Foreign born: 0.5% (2000); Ancestry (includes multiple ancestries): 25.0% United States or American, 19.2% German, 10.6% Irish, 10.3% Other groups, 7.3% English (2000).
Economy: Single-family building permits issued: 6 (2005); Multi-family building permits issued: 0 (2005); Employment by occupation: 5.8% management, 5.8% professional, 9.5% services, 28.6% sales, 0.7% farming, 12.8% construction, 36.8% production (2000).

Income: Per capita income: $15,799 (2005); Median household income: $35,005 (2005); Average household income: $40,699 (2005); Percent of households with income of $100,000 or more: 4.0% (2005); Poverty rate: 10.8% (2000).
Education: Percent of population age 25 and over with: High school diploma (including GED) or higher: 81.5% (2005); Bachelor's degree or higher: 4.5% (2005); Master's degree or higher: 1.6% (2005).

School District(s)
East Clinton Local SD (PK-12)
   2003-04 Enrollment: 1,571 . . . . (937) 584-2461

Housing: Homeownership rate: 66.0% (2005); Median home value: $81,071 (2005); Median rent: $343 per month (2000); Median age of housing: 29 years (2000).
Transportation: Commute to work: 95.2% car, 0.3% public transportation, 1.2% walk, 1.9% work from home (2000); Travel time to work: 20.1% less than 15 minutes, 55.8% 15 to 30 minutes, 8.1% 30 to 45 minutes, 6.2% 45 to 60 minutes, 9.7% 60 minutes or more (2000)

PORT WILLIAM
(village). Covers a land area of 0.116 square miles and a water area of 0 square miles. Located at 39.55° N. Lat.; 83.78° W. Long. Elevation is 1,028 feet.
Population: 250 (1990); 258 (2000); 261 (2005); 266 (2010 projected); Race: 93.9% White, 0.0% Black, 0.0% Asian, 1.1% Hispanic of any race (2005); Density: 2,248.4 persons per square mile (2005); Average household size: 2.64 (2005); Median age: 30.8 (2005); Males per 100 females: 103.9 (2005); Marriage status: 19.4% never married, 60.0% now married, 8.3% widowed, 12.2% divorced (2000); Foreign born: 1.6% (2000); Ancestry (includes multiple ancestries): 27.6% United States or American, 25.5% Other groups, 17.3% German, 8.2% English, 5.8% Irish (2000).
Economy: Employment by occupation: 6.8% management, 6.8% professional, 14.4% services, 28.8% sales, 0.0% farming, 19.5% construction, 23.7% production (2000).
Income: Per capita income: $15,431 (2005); Median household income: $36,563 (2005); Average household income: $40,682 (2005); Percent of households with income of $100,000 or more: 3.0% (2005); Poverty rate: 16.0% (2000).
Education: Percent of population age 25 and over with: High school diploma (including GED) or higher: 74.5% (2005); Bachelor's degree or higher: 7.0% (2005); Master's degree or higher: 0.0% (2005).
Housing: Homeownership rate: 61.6% (2005); Median home value: $89,310 (2005); Median rent: $365 per month (2000); Median age of housing: 60+ years (2000).
Transportation: Commute to work: 95.7% car, 0.0% public transportation, 4.3% walk, 0.0% work from home (2000); Travel time to work: 20.7% less than 15 minutes, 50.9% 15 to 30 minutes, 11.2% 30 to 45 minutes, 6.0% 45 to 60 minutes, 11.2% 60 minutes or more (2000)

SABINA
(village). Covers a land area of 1.293 square miles and a water area of 0 square miles. Located at 39.48° N. Lat.; 83.63° W. Long. Elevation is 1,045 feet.
Population: 2,698 (1990); 2,780 (2000); 2,862 (2005); 2,956 (2010 projected); Race: 97.2% White, 0.6% Black, 0.7% Asian, 1.5% Hispanic of any race (2005); Density: 2,213.0 persons per square mile (2005); Average household size: 2.56 (2005); Median age: 34.2 (2005); Males per 100 females: 93.6 (2005); Marriage status: 23.2% never married, 55.2% now married, 7.4% widowed, 14.2% divorced (2000); Foreign born: 0.3% (2000); Ancestry (includes multiple ancestries): 23.7% United States or American, 18.3% German, 10.9% Irish, 8.5% Other groups, 8.0% English (2000).
Economy: Single-family building permits issued: 4 (2005); Multi-family building permits issued: 0 (2005); Employment by occupation: 5.9% management, 7.4% professional, 12.5% services, 25.4% sales, 1.3% farming, 10.3% construction, 37.2% production (2000).
Income: Per capita income: $18,650 (2005); Median household income: $38,735 (2005); Average household income: $47,440 (2005); Percent of households with income of $100,000 or more: 7.2% (2005); Poverty rate: 12.9% (2000).
Education: Percent of population age 25 and over with: High school diploma (including GED) or higher: 78.6% (2005); Bachelor's degree or higher: 7.2% (2005); Master's degree or higher: 1.7% (2005).

School District(s)
East Clinton Local SD (PK-12)
   2003-04 Enrollment: 1,571 . . . . (937) 584-2461

Housing: Homeownership rate: 67.1% (2005); Median home value: $84,703 (2005); Median rent: $354 per month (2000); Median age of housing: 40 years (2000).
Transportation: Commute to work: 93.2% car, 0.0% public transportation, 3.1% walk, 2.6% work from home (2000); Travel time to work: 30.6% less than 15 minutes, 49.5% 15 to 30 minutes, 8.8% 30 to 45 minutes, 2.9% 45 to 60 minutes, 8.2% 60 minutes or more (2000)

WILMINGTON
(city). Covers a land area of 7.451 square miles and a water area of 0 square miles. Located at 39.44° N. Lat.; 83.82° W. Long. Elevation is 1,025 feet.
History: Seat of Wilmington College. Settled 1810, incorporated 1828.
Population: 11,421 (1990); 11,921 (2000); 12,312 (2005); 12,721 (2010 projected); Race: 90.5% White, 6.6% Black, 1.0% Asian, 1.1% Hispanic of any race (2005); Density: 1,652.4 persons per square mile (2005); Average household size: 2.42 (2005); Median age: 33.0 (2005); Males per 100 females: 91.2 (2005); Marriage status: 29.5% never married, 49.0% now married, 8.6% widowed, 12.8% divorced (2000); Foreign born: 2.3% (2000); Ancestry (includes multiple ancestries): 20.6% German, 14.8% United States or American, 13.4% Other groups, 13.3% Irish, 10.2% English (2000).
Economy: In a farm area: chiefly corn and hogs. Tools, machinery, fabricated metal products and transportation equipment are made. Single-family building permits issued: 74 (2005); Multi-family building permits issued: 0 (2005); Employment by occupation: 10.8% management, 15.3% professional, 16.9% services, 23.4% sales, 0.3% farming, 7.9% construction, 25.3% production (2000).
Income: Per capita income: $18,385 (2005); Median household income: $36,266 (2005); Average household income: $43,672 (2005); Percent of households with income of $100,000 or more: 5.2% (2005); Poverty rate: 11.7% (2000).
Taxes: Total city taxes per capita: $509 (2004); City property taxes per capita: $169 (2004).
Education: Percent of population age 25 and over with: High school diploma (including GED) or higher: 85.0% (2005); Bachelor's degree or higher: 16.6% (2005); Master's degree or higher: 6.8% (2005).

School District(s)
Great Oaks Inst of Technology Joint Vocational SD (07-12)
   2003-04 Enrollment: n/a . . . . (513) 771-8840
Wilmington City SD (PK-12)
   2003-04 Enrollment: 3,195 . . . . (937) 382-1641

Four-year College(s)
Wilmington College (Private, Not-for-profit, Friends)
   Fall 2004 Enrollment: 1,755 . . . . (800) 341-9318
   2005-06 Tuition: In-state $19,206; Out-of-state $19,206

Housing: Homeownership rate: 50.8% (2005); Median home value: $110,151 (2005); Median rent: $405 per month (2000); Median age of housing: 38 years (2000).
Hospitals: Clinton Memorial Hospital (150 beds)
Safety: Violent crime rate: 55.7 per 10,000 population; Property crime rate: 561.7 per 10,000 population (2004).
Newspapers: Wilmington News Journal (Circulation 7,400)
Transportation: Commute to work: 88.8% car, 1.0% public transportation, 7.2% walk, 2.8% work from home (2000); Travel time to work: 59.1% less than 15 minutes, 19.0% 15 to 30 minutes, 8.2% 30 to 45 minutes, 8.4% 45 to 60 minutes, 5.2% 60 minutes or more (2000)

Additional Information Contacts
City of Wilmington . . . . (937) 382-5458
   http://ci.wilmington.oh.us
Clinton County Convention & Visitors Bureau . . . . (937) 382-1965
   http://www.clintoncountyohio.com
Wilmington Chamber of Commerce . . . . (937) 382-2737
   http://www.wccchamber.com

Columbiana County

Located in eastern Ohio; bounded on the east by Pennsylvania, and on the southeast by the Ohio River; drained by the Little Beaver River. Covers a land area of 532.46 square miles, a water area of 2.73 square miles, and is located in the Eastern Time Zone. The county government was organized in 1803. County seat is Lisbon.

Columbiana County is part of the East Liverpool-Salem, OH Micropolitan Statistical Area. The entire metro area includes: Columbiana County, OH

Weather Station: Millport 2 NW Elevation: 1,148 feet

	Jan	Feb	Mar	Apr	May	Jun	Jul	Aug	Sep	Oct	Nov	Dec
High	35	39	50	61	71	80	83	82	75	63	51	40
Low	17	19	27	36	45	54	58	56	50	39	31	23
Precip	2.5	2.3	3.1	3.2	4.1	3.8	4.2	3.1	3.3	2.5	3.3	3.1
Snow	7.8	6.7	6.1	1.3	tr	0.0	0.0	0.0	0.0	tr	2.2	6.1

High and Low temperatures in degrees Fahrenheit; Precipitation and Snow in inches

Population: 108,276 (1990); 112,075 (2000); 111,424 (2005); 110,718 (2010 projected); Race: 96.3% White, 2.2% Black, 0.4% Asian, 1.3% Hispanic of any race (2005); Density: 209.3 persons per square mile (2005); Average household size: 2.58 (2005); Median age: 39.4 (2005); Males per 100 females: 99.2 (2005).
Religion: Five largest groups: 11.8% Catholic Church, 6.4% The United Methodist Church, 4.5% Presbyterian Church (U.S.A.), 3.5% Christian Churches and Churches of Christ, 3.0% Evangelical Lutheran Church in America (2000).
Economy: Unemployment rate: 7.1% (2005); Total civilian labor force: 53,667 (2005); Leading industries: 23.9% manufacturing; 18.6% health care and social assistance; 17.4% retail trade (2004); Farms: 1,184 totaling 136,080 acres (2002); Companies that employ 500 or more persons: 5 (2004); Companies that employ 100 to 499 persons: 26 (2004); Companies that employ less than 100 persons: 2,333 (2004); Black-owned businesses: n/a (2002); Hispanic-owned businesses: n/a (2002); Women-owned businesses: 1,877 (2002); Retail sales per capita: $11,247 (2006); Single-family building permits issued: 138 (2005); Multi-family building permits issued: 55 (2005).
Income: Per capita income: $18,721 (2005); Median household income: $38,444 (2005); Average household income: $47,177 (2005); Percent of households with income of $100,000 or more: 7.2% (2005); Poverty rate: 11.5% (2003); Bankruptcy rate: 13.63% (2005).
Taxes: Total county taxes per capita: $185 (2004); County property taxes per capita: $99 (2004).
Education: Percent of population age 25 and over with: High school diploma (including GED) or higher: 80.5% (2005); Bachelor's degree or higher: 10.8% (2005); Master's degree or higher: 3.4% (2005).
Housing: Homeownership rate: 76.4% (2005); Median home value: $95,595 (2005); Median rent: $327 per month (2000); Median age of housing: 43 years (2000).
Health: Birth rate: 112.4 per 10,000 population (2004); Death rate: 108.7 per 10,000 population (2004); Age-adjusted cancer mortality rate: 210.4 deaths per 100,000 population (2002); Air Quality Index: 97.5% good, 2.5% moderate, 0.0% unhealthy for sensitive individuals, 0.0% unhealthy (percent of days in 2005); Number of physicians: 11.4 per 10,000 population (2004); Hospital beds: 28.4 per 10,000 population (2003); Hospital admissions: 1,180.5 per 10,000 population (2003).
Elections: 2004 Presidential election results: 52.1% Bush, 47.4% Kerry, 0.0% Nader, 0.3% Badnarik
National and State Parks: Beaver Creek State Forest; Guilford Lake State Park

Additional Information Contacts

Columbiana County Government	(330) 424-9511
http://www.columbianacounty.org/	
Calcutta Area Chamber of Commerce	(330) 386-6060
http://www.calcuttaohiochamber.com	
City of East Liverpool	(330) 385-3381
http://www.eastliverpool.com	
City of East Palestine	(330) 426-4367
http://www.eastpalestineohio.org	
Columbiana Chamber of Commerce	(330) 482-3822
http://www.columbianachamber.com	
East Liverpool Chamber of Commerce	(330) 385-0845
http://www.elchamber.com	
East Palestine Chamber of Commerce	(330) 426-2128
http://www.eastpalestineohio.org	
Lisbon Chamber of Commerce	(330) 424-5503
http://www.columbianachamber.com	
Salem Chamber of Commerce	(330) 337-3473
http://www.salemohio.com/chamber	
Salem Convention & Visitors Bureau	(330) 337-2536
Wellsville Chamber of Commerce	(330) 532-2120
http://www.columbianacounty.org	

Columbiana County Communities

CALCUTTA (CDP). Covers a land area of 11.748 square miles and a water area of 0.015 square miles. Located at 40.68° N. Lat.; 80.57° W. Long. Elevation is 1,160 feet.
Population: 3,211 (1990); 3,491 (2000); 3,502 (2005); 3,534 (2010 projected); Race: 98.4% White, 0.1% Black, 0.9% Asian, 0.6% Hispanic of any race (2005); Density: 298.1 persons per square mile (2005); Average household size: 2.42 (2005); Median age: 46.4 (2005); Males per 100 females: 87.5 (2005); Marriage status: 20.2% never married, 59.8% now married, 10.1% widowed, 9.9% divorced (2000); Foreign born: 0.3% (2000); Ancestry (includes multiple ancestries): 22.3% German, 16.9% English, 16.4% Irish, 12.3% United States or American, 8.5% Italian (2000).
Economy: Employment by occupation: 11.4% management, 16.7% professional, 14.7% services, 25.9% sales, 1.1% farming, 11.8% construction, 18.3% production (2000).
Income: Per capita income: $20,553 (2005); Median household income: $38,534 (2005); Average household income: $49,151 (2005); Percent of households with income of $100,000 or more: 8.4% (2005); Poverty rate: 8.3% (2000).
Education: Percent of population age 25 and over with: High school diploma (including GED) or higher: 80.9% (2005); Bachelor's degree or higher: 13.2% (2005); Master's degree or higher: 5.8% (2005).
School District(s)
Buckeye On-Line School for Success
  2003-04 Enrollment: n/a
Housing: Homeownership rate: 78.8% (2005); Median home value: $114,130 (2005); Median rent: $268 per month (2000); Median age of housing: 29 years (2000).
Transportation: Commute to work: 94.8% car, 0.0% public transportation, 2.0% walk, 1.4% work from home (2000); Travel time to work: 41.6% less than 15 minutes, 31.1% 15 to 30 minutes, 18.2% 30 to 45 minutes, 4.9% 45 to 60 minutes, 4.2% 60 minutes or more (2000)

COLUMBIANA (village). Covers a land area of 6.057 square miles and a water area of 0.128 square miles. Located at 40.88° N. Lat.; 80.68° W. Long. Elevation is 1,118 feet.
History: Columbiana was laid out in 1805, when it was called Dixonville for its founder, Joshua Dixon. Harvey S. Firestone (1868-1938), who had the idea of making rubber tires for buggies, was born in Columbiana.
Population: 5,443 (1990); 5,635 (2000); 5,726 (2005); 5,821 (2010 projected); Race: 98.7% White, 0.1% Black, 0.3% Asian, 0.3% Hispanic of any race (2005); Density: 945.4 persons per square mile (2005); Average household size: 2.19 (2005); Median age: 47.0 (2005); Males per 100 females: 89.5 (2005); Marriage status: 16.9% never married, 61.6% now married, 11.1% widowed, 10.3% divorced (2000); Foreign born: 0.8% (2000); Ancestry (includes multiple ancestries): 30.8% German, 15.2% English, 14.4% Irish, 6.9% United States or American, 6.2% Italian (2000).
Economy: Single-family building permits issued: 81 (2005); Multi-family building permits issued: 8 (2005); Employment by occupation: 7.6% management, 18.9% professional, 16.5% services, 29.0% sales, 0.5% farming, 9.9% construction, 17.6% production (2000).
Income: Per capita income: $21,511 (2005); Median household income: $36,532 (2005); Average household income: $45,552 (2005); Percent of households with income of $100,000 or more: 7.8% (2005); Poverty rate: 6.5% (2000).
Education: Percent of population age 25 and over with: High school diploma (including GED) or higher: 85.7% (2005); Bachelor's degree or higher: 15.1% (2005); Master's degree or higher: 5.4% (2005).
School District(s)
Columbiana Ex Vill SD (PK-12)
  2003-04 Enrollment: 1,016 . . . . (330) 482-5352
Crestview Local SD (PK-12)
  2003-04 Enrollment: 1,137 . . . . (330) 482-5526
Housing: Homeownership rate: 67.4% (2005); Median home value: $117,546 (2005); Median rent: $377 per month (2000); Median age of housing: 37 years (2000).
Transportation: Commute to work: 95.2% car, 0.3% public transportation, 3.1% walk, 1.1% work from home (2000); Travel time to work: 35.7% less than 15 minutes, 42.3% 15 to 30 minutes, 17.2% 30 to 45 minutes, 3.0% 45 to 60 minutes, 1.8% 60 minutes or more (2000)
Additional Information Contacts
Columbiana Chamber of Commerce . . . . (330) 482-3822
  http://www.columbianachamber.com

EAST LIVERPOOL (city). Covers a land area of 4.348 square miles and a water area of 0.181 square miles. Located at 40.62° N. Lat.; 80.56° W. Long. Elevation is 689 feet.
History: East Liverpool was called St. Clair in 1798 by its founder, Thomas Fawcett of Ireland. Early residents called it Fawcett's Town, but in 1860 the name became Liverpool, because many of the residents had come from the English pottery city. James Bennett, a young potter from England, arrived here in 1838, and East Liverpool began the pottery production that shaped its character for many years.
Population: 13,654 (1990); 13,089 (2000); 12,342 (2005); 11,643 (2010 projected); Race: 93.8% White, 3.9% Black, 0.1% Asian, 0.6% Hispanic of any race (2005); Density: 2,838.5 persons per square mile (2005); Average household size: 2.48 (2005); Median age: 36.1 (2005); Males per 100 females: 87.4 (2005); Marriage status: 21.9% never married, 56.1% now married, 8.4% widowed, 13.7% divorced (2000); Foreign born: 0.5% (2000); Ancestry (includes multiple ancestries): 16.8% German, 14.9% Irish, 13.4% United States or American, 12.5% English, 12.3% Other groups (2000).
Economy: Single-family building permits issued: 0 (2005); Multi-family building permits issued: 2 (2005); Employment by occupation: 4.4% management, 11.3% professional, 25.0% services, 22.9% sales, 0.2% farming, 9.2% construction, 27.0% production (2000).
Income: Per capita income: $13,981 (2005); Median household income: $25,250 (2005); Average household income: $34,107 (2005); Percent of households with income of $100,000 or more: 4.0% (2005); Poverty rate: 25.2% (2000).
Education: Percent of population age 25 and over with: High school diploma (including GED) or higher: 73.6% (2005); Bachelor's degree or higher: 7.3% (2005); Master's degree or higher: 2.6% (2005).

School District(s)
Beaver Local SD (PK-12)
   2003-04 Enrollment: 2,455 . . . . (330) 385-6831
East Liverpool City SD (PK-12)
   2003-04 Enrollment: 3,082 . . . . (330) 385-7132

Two-year College(s)
Kent State University-East Liverpool Campus (Public)
   Fall 2004 Enrollment: 768 . . . . (330) 382-7400
   2005-06 Tuition: In-state $4,586; Out-of-state $12,018
Ohio Valley College of Technology (Private, For-profit)
   Fall 2004 Enrollment: 157 . . . . (330) 385-1070
   2005-06 Tuition: In-state $7,100; Out-of-state $7,100

Housing: Homeownership rate: 59.8% (2005); Median home value: $53,201 (2005); Median rent: $284 per month (2000); Median age of housing: 60 years (2000).
Hospitals: East Liverpool City Hospital (199 beds)
Newspapers: The Review (Circulation 10,937)
Transportation: Commute to work: 92.2% car, 1.5% public transportation, 4.5% walk, 1.5% work from home (2000); Travel time to work: 48.4% less than 15 minutes, 22.8% 15 to 30 minutes, 14.5% 30 to 45 minutes, 9.8% 45 to 60 minutes, 4.5% 60 minutes or more (2000)

Additional Information Contacts
Calcutta Area Chamber of Commerce. . . . . (330) 386-6060
   http://www.calcuttaohiochamber.com
City of East Liverpool. . . . . (330) 385-3381
   http://www.eastliverpool.com
East Liverpool Chamber of Commerce . . . . (330) 385-0845
   http://www.elchamber.com

EAST PALESTINE (city). Covers a land area of 2.775 square miles and a water area of 0 square miles. Located at 40.83° N. Lat.; 80.54° W. Long. Elevation is 1,020 feet.
History: East Palestine was established in 1828 by Thomas McCalla and William Grate. It developed as a pottery town, first using deposits of local clay, but later employing finer materials.
Population: 5,168 (1990); 4,917 (2000); 4,736 (2005); 4,585 (2010 projected); Race: 98.5% White, 0.3% Black, 0.3% Asian, 0.5% Hispanic of any race (2005); Density: 1,706.9 persons per square mile (2005); Average household size: 2.45 (2005); Median age: 39.4 (2005); Males per 100 females: 94.5 (2005); Marriage status: 22.8% never married, 57.8% now married, 10.5% widowed, 8.9% divorced (2000); Foreign born: 0.8% (2000); Ancestry (includes multiple ancestries): 26.5% German, 20.0% English, 19.9% Irish, 10.8% Italian, 9.0% United States or American (2000).
Economy: Single-family building permits issued: 8 (2005); Multi-family building permits issued: 0 (2005); Employment by occupation: 6.9% management, 13.3% professional, 14.8% services, 29.2% sales, 0.0% farming, 11.3% construction, 24.6% production (2000).
Income: Per capita income: $18,058 (2005); Median household income: $39,059 (2005); Average household income: $44,143 (2005); Percent of households with income of $100,000 or more: 4.3% (2005); Poverty rate: 10.0% (2000).
Education: Percent of population age 25 and over with: High school diploma (including GED) or higher: 84.2% (2005); Bachelor's degree or higher: 11.9% (2005); Master's degree or higher: 4.1% (2005).

School District(s)
East Palestine City SD (PK-12)
   2003-04 Enrollment: 1,442 . . . . (330) 426-4191

Housing: Homeownership rate: 75.4% (2005); Median home value: $93,371 (2005); Median rent: $363 per month (2000); Median age of housing: 60+ years (2000).
Safety: Violent crime rate: 16.5 per 10,000 population; Property crime rate: 322.0 per 10,000 population (2004).
Transportation: Commute to work: 91.6% car, 0.4% public transportation, 4.9% walk, 2.7% work from home (2000); Travel time to work: 38.9% less than 15 minutes, 28.0% 15 to 30 minutes, 22.7% 30 to 45 minutes, 7.2% 45 to 60 minutes, 3.2% 60 minutes or more (2000)

Additional Information Contacts
City of East Palestine. . . . . (330) 426-4367
   http://www.eastpalestineohio.org
East Palestine Chamber of Commerce . . . . (330) 426-2128
   http://www.eastpalestineohio.org

EAST ROCHESTER (unincorporated postal area, zip code 44625). Covers a land area of 21.408 square miles and a water area of 0.138 square miles. Located at 40.75° N. Lat.; 81.00° W. Long. Elevation is 1,094 feet.
Population: 1,603 (2000); Race: 100.0% White, 0.0% Black, 0.0% Asian, 0.0% Hispanic of any race (2000); Density: 74.9 persons per square mile (2000); Age: 31.3% under 18, 11.2% over 64 (2000); Marriage status: 21.4% never married, 66.7% now married, 3.8% widowed, 8.1% divorced (2000); Foreign born: 0.0% (2000); Ancestry (includes multiple ancestries): 37.8% German, 19.2% Irish, 15.6% English, 6.9% United States or American, 6.8% Italian (2000).
Economy: Employment by occupation: 13.3% management, 7.8% professional, 19.0% services, 17.5% sales, 1.8% farming, 9.3% construction, 31.4% production (2000).
Income: Per capita income: $13,537 (2000); Median household income: $38,068 (2000); Poverty rate: 10.5% (2000).
Education: Percent of population age 25 and over with: High school diploma (including GED) or higher: 81.3% (2000); Bachelor's degree or higher: 4.8% (2000).

School District(s)
Minerva Local SD (PK-12)
   2003-04 Enrollment: 2,202 . . . . (330) 868-4332

Housing: Homeownership rate: 78.7% (2000); Median home value: $85,400 (2000); Median rent: $362 per month (2000); Median age of housing: 39 years (2000).
Transportation: Commute to work: 87.5% car, 0.0% public transportation, 6.2% walk, 5.1% work from home (2000); Travel time to work: 32.7% less than 15 minutes, 39.8% 15 to 30 minutes, 17.9% 30 to 45 minutes, 6.2% 45 to 60 minutes, 3.4% 60 minutes or more (2000)

GLENMOOR (CDP). Covers a land area of 2.797 square miles and a water area of 0 square miles. Located at 40.66° N. Lat.; 80.61° W. Long. Elevation is 1,127 feet.
Population: 2,307 (1990); 2,192 (2000); 2,139 (2005); 2,113 (2010 projected); Race: 97.8% White, 1.0% Black, 0.2% Asian, 0.8% Hispanic of any race (2005); Density: 764.7 persons per square mile (2005); Average household size: 2.46 (2005); Median age: 42.1 (2005); Males per 100 females: 94.1 (2005); Marriage status: 18.8% never married, 59.1% now married, 12.2% widowed, 9.9% divorced (2000); Foreign born: 0.0% (2000); Ancestry (includes multiple ancestries): 13.2% Other groups, 13.1% English, 12.3% United States or American, 9.8% Irish, 8.5% German (2000).
Economy: Employment by occupation: 5.8% management, 12.8% professional, 16.4% services, 24.6% sales, 0.0% farming, 12.6% construction, 27.8% production (2000).

Income: Per capita income: $17,230 (2005); Median household income: $34,198 (2005); Average household income: $42,362 (2005); Percent of households with income of $100,000 or more: 5.5% (2005); Poverty rate: 6.9% (2000).
Education: Percent of population age 25 and over with: High school diploma (including GED) or higher: 77.3% (2005); Bachelor's degree or higher: 7.6% (2005); Master's degree or higher: 1.8% (2005).
Housing: Homeownership rate: 83.7% (2005); Median home value: $81,316 (2005); Median rent: $311 per month (2000); Median age of housing: 41 years (2000).
Transportation: Commute to work: 88.8% car, 0.0% public transportation, 7.5% walk, 1.7% work from home (2000); Travel time to work: 36.8% less than 15 minutes, 41.3% 15 to 30 minutes, 11.9% 30 to 45 minutes, 3.1% 45 to 60 minutes, 6.9% 60 minutes or more (2000)

HANOVERTON (village). Covers a land area of 0.707 square miles and a water area of 0 square miles. Located at 40.75° N. Lat.; 80.93° W. Long. Elevation is 1,137 feet.
Population: 434 (1990); 387 (2000); 389 (2005); 388 (2010 projected); Race: 98.5% White, 0.0% Black, 0.0% Asian, 0.3% Hispanic of any race (2005); Density: 550.2 persons per square mile (2005); Average household size: 2.43 (2005); Median age: 37.5 (2005); Males per 100 females: 87.9 (2005); Marriage status: 20.7% never married, 68.1% now married, 7.4% widowed, 3.7% divorced (2000); Foreign born: 3.9% (2000); Ancestry (includes multiple ancestries): 31.1% German, 14.3% English, 14.3% Irish, 8.5% United States or American, 5.1% Polish (2000).
Economy: Single-family building permits issued: 2 (2005); Multi-family building permits issued: 0 (2005); Employment by occupation: 2.8% management, 16.9% professional, 7.9% services, 19.2% sales, 0.0% farming, 15.8% construction, 37.3% production (2000).
Income: Per capita income: $18,156 (2005); Median household income: $41,429 (2005); Average household income: $44,141 (2005); Percent of households with income of $100,000 or more: 2.5% (2005); Poverty rate: 3.2% (2000).
Education: Percent of population age 25 and over with: High school diploma (including GED) or higher: 83.6% (2005); Bachelor's degree or higher: 10.3% (2005); Master's degree or higher: 0.8% (2005).
School District(s)
United Local SD (PK-12)
    2003-04 Enrollment: 1,537 . . . . (330) 223-1521
Housing: Homeownership rate: 85.0% (2005); Median home value: $88,000 (2005); Median rent: $272 per month (2000); Median age of housing: 60+ years (2000).
Transportation: Commute to work: 95.3% car, 0.0% public transportation, 2.3% walk, 1.2% work from home (2000); Travel time to work: 34.3% less than 15 minutes, 38.5% 15 to 30 minutes, 20.1% 30 to 45 minutes, 4.7% 45 to 60 minutes, 2.4% 60 minutes or more (2000)

HOMEWORTH (unincorporated postal area, zip code 44634). Covers a land area of 16.212 square miles and a water area of 0.028 square miles. Located at 40.83° N. Lat.; 81.05° W. Long. Elevation is 1,155 feet.
Population: 2,083 (2000); Race: 98.1% White, 0.0% Black, 0.8% Asian, 0.0% Hispanic of any race (2000); Density: 128.5 persons per square mile (2000); Age: 27.7% under 18, 10.6% over 64 (2000); Marriage status: 23.7% never married, 65.0% now married, 5.4% widowed, 5.8% divorced (2000); Foreign born: 1.4% (2000); Ancestry (includes multiple ancestries): 25.8% German, 10.4% Irish, 7.3% Italian, 7.0% United States or American, 6.9% Other groups (2000).
Economy: Employment by occupation: 16.9% management, 14.0% professional, 9.0% services, 16.6% sales, 6.1% farming, 13.0% construction, 24.6% production (2000).
Income: Per capita income: $18,980 (2000); Median household income: $48,393 (2000); Poverty rate: 2.6% (2000).
Education: Percent of population age 25 and over with: High school diploma (including GED) or higher: 90.2% (2000); Bachelor's degree or higher: 14.5% (2000).
Housing: Homeownership rate: 86.1% (2000); Median home value: $100,500 (2000); Median rent: $417 per month (2000); Median age of housing: 42 years (2000).
Transportation: Commute to work: 94.4% car, 0.5% public transportation, 1.2% walk, 3.4% work from home (2000); Travel time to work: 23.1% less than 15 minutes, 46.0% 15 to 30 minutes, 18.5% 30 to 45 minutes, 8.3% 45 to 60 minutes, 4.1% 60 minutes or more (2000)

KENSINGTON (unincorporated postal area, zip code 44427). Covers a land area of 31.741 square miles and a water area of 0.045 square miles. Located at 40.72° N. Lat.; 80.94° W. Long. Elevation is 1,119 feet.
Population: 1,728 (2000); Race: 99.6% White, 0.0% Black, 0.0% Asian, 0.0% Hispanic of any race (2000); Density: 54.4 persons per square mile (2000); Age: 29.1% under 18, 11.0% over 64 (2000); Marriage status: 17.7% never married, 70.3% now married, 3.9% widowed, 8.1% divorced (2000); Foreign born: 0.9% (2000); Ancestry (includes multiple ancestries): 24.6% German, 11.9% Irish, 11.3% United States or American, 7.8% English, 6.0% Dutch (2000).
Economy: Employment by occupation: 9.2% management, 12.0% professional, 16.7% services, 14.8% sales, 1.5% farming, 10.5% construction, 35.2% production (2000).
Income: Per capita income: $21,147 (2000); Median household income: $39,265 (2000); Poverty rate: 21.3% (2000).
Education: Percent of population age 25 and over with: High school diploma (including GED) or higher: 74.1% (2000); Bachelor's degree or higher: 7.0% (2000).
Housing: Homeownership rate: 87.8% (2000); Median home value: $75,500 (2000); Median rent: $325 per month (2000); Median age of housing: 39 years (2000).
Transportation: Commute to work: 88.2% car, 1.4% public transportation, 2.8% walk, 6.5% work from home (2000); Travel time to work: 22.3% less than 15 minutes, 27.7% 15 to 30 minutes, 24.2% 30 to 45 minutes, 16.7% 45 to 60 minutes, 9.1% 60 minutes or more (2000)

LA CROFT (CDP). Covers a land area of 1.139 square miles and a water area of 0 square miles. Located at 40.64° N. Lat.; 80.59° W. Long. Elevation is 1,180 feet.
Population: 1,427 (1990); 1,307 (2000); 1,298 (2005); 1,282 (2010 projected); Race: 98.8% White, 0.4% Black, 0.2% Asian, 0.4% Hispanic of any race (2005); Density: 1,139.8 persons per square mile (2005); Average household size: 2.52 (2005); Median age: 40.4 (2005); Males per 100 females: 95.8 (2005); Marriage status: 19.8% never married, 57.1% now married, 11.4% widowed, 11.7% divorced (2000); Foreign born: 0.0% (2000); Ancestry (includes multiple ancestries): 26.2% English, 16.8% German, 11.2% Irish, 8.8% Other groups, 7.0% United States or American (2000).
Economy: Employment by occupation: 8.1% management, 8.7% professional, 17.0% services, 21.8% sales, 0.0% farming, 6.7% construction, 37.6% production (2000).
Income: Per capita income: $15,152 (2005); Median household income: $32,794 (2005); Average household income: $38,115 (2005); Percent of households with income of $100,000 or more: 2.9% (2005); Poverty rate: 11.5% (2000).
Education: Percent of population age 25 and over with: High school diploma (including GED) or higher: 73.5% (2005); Bachelor's degree or higher: 3.6% (2005); Master's degree or higher: 0.9% (2005).
Housing: Homeownership rate: 86.2% (2005); Median home value: $65,876 (2005); Median rent: $348 per month (2000); Median age of housing: 46 years (2000).
Transportation: Commute to work: 95.4% car, 1.0% public transportation, 1.2% walk, 1.4% work from home (2000); Travel time to work: 44.0% less than 15 minutes, 38.7% 15 to 30 minutes, 7.3% 30 to 45 minutes, 4.1% 45 to 60 minutes, 5.9% 60 minutes or more (2000)

LEETONIA (village). Covers a land area of 2.112 square miles and a water area of 0.006 square miles. Located at 40.87° N. Lat.; 80.75° W. Long. Elevation is 1,021 feet.
History: Laid out 1866.
Population: 2,070 (1990); 2,043 (2000); 1,933 (2005); 1,861 (2010 projected); Race: 98.9% White, 0.2% Black, 0.1% Asian, 0.9% Hispanic of any race (2005); Density: 915.4 persons per square mile (2005); Average household size: 2.66 (2005); Median age: 35.6 (2005); Males per 100 females: 99.7 (2005); Marriage status: 25.5% never married, 56.3% now married, 6.5% widowed, 11.7% divorced (2000); Foreign born: 1.7% (2000); Ancestry (includes multiple ancestries): 29.3% German, 16.3% Irish, 15.5% Italian, 13.8% English, 7.0% United States or American (2000).
Economy: Single-family building permits issued: 3 (2005); Multi-family building permits issued: 0 (2005); Employment by occupation: 12.5% management, 10.7% professional, 19.2% services, 20.2% sales, 0.0% farming, 10.6% construction, 26.8% production (2000).

Income: Per capita income: $16,721 (2005); Median household income: $40,542 (2005); Average household income: $44,521 (2005); Percent of households with income of $100,000 or more: 3.2% (2005); Poverty rate: 7.0% (2000).
Education: Percent of population age 25 and over with: High school diploma (including GED) or higher: 83.3% (2005); Bachelor's degree or higher: 9.9% (2005); Master's degree or higher: 2.0% (2005).

School District(s)
Leetonia Exempted Village School District (PK-12)
    2003-04 Enrollment: 867 . . . . (330) 427-6594

Housing: Homeownership rate: 82.6% (2005); Median home value: $82,222 (2005); Median rent: $398 per month (2000); Median age of housing: 60+ years (2000).
Transportation: Commute to work: 93.0% car, 1.8% public transportation, 0.8% walk, 4.3% work from home (2000); Travel time to work: 36.2% less than 15 minutes, 36.2% 15 to 30 minutes, 16.4% 30 to 45 minutes, 5.7% 45 to 60 minutes, 5.6% 60 minutes or more (2000)

LISBON (village). Covers a land area of 1.106 square miles and a water area of 0 square miles. Located at 40.77° N. Lat.; 80.76° W. Long. Elevation is 968 feet.
History: Lisbon was founded in 1802, and grew as a coal and pottery town. This was the birthplace of politicians Marcus A. Hanna (1837-1904) and Clement L. Vallandigham (1820-1871).
Population: 3,037 (1990); 2,788 (2000); 2,606 (2005); 2,498 (2010 projected); Race: 97.9% White, 0.7% Black, 0.2% Asian, 0.6% Hispanic of any race (2005); Density: 2,356.5 persons per square mile (2005); Average household size: 2.42 (2005); Median age: 38.8 (2005); Males per 100 females: 90.2 (2005); Marriage status: 24.9% never married, 53.9% now married, 9.8% widowed, 11.5% divorced (2000); Foreign born: 1.4% (2000); Ancestry (includes multiple ancestries): 26.1% German, 18.7% Irish, 15.0% English, 9.7% Italian, 5.9% Other groups (2000).
Economy: Single-family building permits issued: 0 (2005); Multi-family building permits issued: 0 (2005); Employment by occupation: 5.2% management, 16.1% professional, 16.9% services, 28.4% sales, 0.7% farming, 12.4% construction, 20.3% production (2000).
Income: Per capita income: $15,992 (2005); Median household income: $30,748 (2005); Average household income: $37,639 (2005); Percent of households with income of $100,000 or more: 4.1% (2005); Poverty rate: 14.1% (2000).
Education: Percent of population age 25 and over with: High school diploma (including GED) or higher: 78.4% (2005); Bachelor's degree or higher: 12.7% (2005); Master's degree or higher: 4.4% (2005).

School District(s)
Beaver Local SD (PK-12)
    2003-04 Enrollment: 2,455 . . . . (330) 385-6831
Columbiana County Joint Vocational SD (08-12)
    2003-04 Enrollment: n/a . . . . (330) 424-9561
Lisbon Ex Vill SD (PK-12)
    2003-04 Enrollment: 1,154 . . . . (330) 424-7714

Two-year College(s)
Columbiana County Vocational School (Public)
    Fall 2004 Enrollment: 160 . . . . (330) 424-9561
    2005-06 Tuition: In-state $4,050; Out-of-state $4,050

Housing: Homeownership rate: 64.3% (2005); Median home value: $90,930 (2005); Median rent: $341 per month (2000); Median age of housing: 60+ years (2000).
Newspapers: Morning Journal (Circulation 14,059)
Transportation: Commute to work: 89.9% car, 3.1% public transportation, 4.2% walk, 2.9% work from home (2000); Travel time to work: 39.7% less than 15 minutes, 40.5% 15 to 30 minutes, 10.4% 30 to 45 minutes, 5.7% 45 to 60 minutes, 3.7% 60 minutes or more (2000)
Additional Information Contacts
Lisbon Chamber of Commerce . . . . (330) 424-5503
    http://www.columbianachamber.com

NEGLEY (unincorporated postal area, zip code 44441). Covers a land area of 15.834 square miles and a water area of 0.198 square miles. Located at 40.77° N. Lat.; 80.55° W. Long. Elevation is 850 feet.
Population: 1,573 (2000); Race: 99.5% White, 0.0% Black, 0.0% Asian, 0.4% Hispanic of any race (2000); Density: 99.3 persons per square mile (2000); Age: 24.1% under 18, 8.0% over 64 (2000); Marriage status: 18.9% never married, 62.0% now married, 5.9% widowed, 13.1% divorced (2000); Foreign born: 0.0% (2000); Ancestry (includes multiple ancestries): 21.6% German, 19.1% English, 18.4% United States or American, 13.6% Irish, 5.6% Italian (2000).
Economy: Employment by occupation: 3.6% management, 7.6% professional, 13.9% services, 25.6% sales, 0.0% farming, 9.2% construction, 40.1% production (2000).
Income: Per capita income: $18,439 (2000); Median household income: $40,288 (2000); Poverty rate: 12.2% (2000).
Education: Percent of population age 25 and over with: High school diploma (including GED) or higher: 77.5% (2000); Bachelor's degree or higher: 7.9% (2000).
Housing: Homeownership rate: 85.2% (2000); Median home value: $103,900 (2000); Median rent: $318 per month (2000); Median age of housing: 27 years (2000).
Transportation: Commute to work: 97.9% car, 0.9% public transportation, 0.0% walk, 1.2% work from home (2000); Travel time to work: 18.0% less than 15 minutes, 34.3% 15 to 30 minutes, 24.1% 30 to 45 minutes, 18.9% 45 to 60 minutes, 4.8% 60 minutes or more (2000)

NEW WATERFORD (village). Covers a land area of 0.889 square miles and a water area of 0 square miles. Located at 40.84° N. Lat.; 80.61° W. Long. Elevation is 1,053 feet.
Population: 1,278 (1990); 1,391 (2000); 1,361 (2005); 1,343 (2010 projected); Race: 98.7% White, 0.0% Black, 0.0% Asian, 0.1% Hispanic of any race (2005); Density: 1,530.3 persons per square mile (2005); Average household size: 2.40 (2005); Median age: 38.6 (2005); Males per 100 females: 94.2 (2005); Marriage status: 22.5% never married, 57.6% now married, 7.1% widowed, 12.7% divorced (2000); Foreign born: 0.1% (2000); Ancestry (includes multiple ancestries): 33.4% German, 14.1% Irish, 11.5% English, 7.5% Italian, 6.9% United States or American (2000).
Economy: In agricultural and coal area; furniture, pottery. Employment by occupation: 10.0% management, 9.4% professional, 17.3% services, 27.1% sales, 0.6% farming, 8.3% construction, 27.3% production (2000).
Income: Per capita income: $20,191 (2005); Median household income: $40,667 (2005); Average household income: $48,380 (2005); Percent of households with income of $100,000 or more: 6.9% (2005); Poverty rate: 9.5% (2000).
Education: Percent of population age 25 and over with: High school diploma (including GED) or higher: 82.9% (2005); Bachelor's degree or higher: 8.5% (2005); Master's degree or higher: 2.3% (2005).
Housing: Homeownership rate: 75.0% (2005); Median home value: $97,778 (2005); Median rent: $288 per month (2000); Median age of housing: 27 years (2000).
Transportation: Commute to work: 97.1% car, 0.6% public transportation, 0.8% walk, 1.2% work from home (2000); Travel time to work: 29.5% less than 15 minutes, 38.1% 15 to 30 minutes, 20.6% 30 to 45 minutes, 6.6% 45 to 60 minutes, 5.3% 60 minutes or more (2000)

ROGERS (village). Covers a land area of 0.235 square miles and a water area of 0 square miles. Located at 40.79° N. Lat.; 80.62° W. Long. Elevation is 1,023 feet.
Population: 247 (1990); 266 (2000); 282 (2005); 295 (2010 projected); Race: 98.9% White, 0.0% Black, 0.0% Asian, 0.7% Hispanic of any race (2005); Density: 1,200.5 persons per square mile (2005); Average household size: 2.79 (2005); Median age: 35.8 (2005); Males per 100 females: 108.9 (2005); Marriage status: 27.5% never married, 60.1% now married, 5.2% widowed, 7.3% divorced (2000); Foreign born: 1.6% (2000); Ancestry (includes multiple ancestries): 21.1% German, 19.9% Irish, 12.9% English, 8.2% Italian, 5.9% Welsh (2000).
Economy: In agricultural and coal area. Employment by occupation: 1.9% management, 2.8% professional, 27.1% services, 17.8% sales, 1.9% farming, 11.2% construction, 37.4% production (2000).
Income: Per capita income: $15,842 (2005); Median household income: $35,375 (2005); Average household income: $44,233 (2005); Percent of households with income of $100,000 or more: 5.9% (2005); Poverty rate: 14.7% (2000).
Education: Percent of population age 25 and over with: High school diploma (including GED) or higher: 76.4% (2005); Bachelor's degree or higher: 2.3% (2005); Master's degree or higher: 0.0% (2005).

School District(s)
Beaver Local SD (PK-12)
    2003-04 Enrollment: 2,455 . . . . (330) 385-6831

Housing: Homeownership rate: 80.2% (2005); Median home value: $62,500 (2005); Median rent: $275 per month (2000); Median age of housing: 60+ years (2000).

Transportation: Commute to work: 97.2% car, 0.0% public transportation, 0.0% walk, 1.9% work from home (2000); Travel time to work: 14.3% less than 15 minutes, 62.9% 15 to 30 minutes, 15.2% 30 to 45 minutes, 5.7% 45 to 60 minutes, 1.9% 60 minutes or more (2000)

SALEM (city).
Covers a land area of 5.474 square miles and a water area of 0 square miles. Located at 40.90° N. Lat.; 80.85° W. Long. Elevation is 1,226 feet.
History: The Quakers came to Salem in 1801 from Salem, New Jersey, and were joined by others from Pennsylvania and Virginia. The town was a station on the Underground Railroad.
Population: 12,796 (1990); 12,197 (2000); 11,726 (2005); 11,379 (2010 projected); Race: 98.3% White, 0.4% Black, 0.5% Asian, 0.5% Hispanic of any race (2005); Density: 2,142.2 persons per square mile (2005); Average household size: 2.34 (2005); Median age: 40.3 (2005); Males per 100 females: 85.7 (2005); Marriage status: 22.9% never married, 56.4% now married, 9.9% widowed, 10.8% divorced (2000); Foreign born: 1.2% (2000); Ancestry (includes multiple ancestries): 28.3% German, 16.7% Irish, 12.5% English, 10.6% Italian, 6.6% United States or American (2000).
Economy: Single-family building permits issued: 27 (2005); Multi-family building permits issued: 0 (2005); Employment by occupation: 7.8% management, 15.3% professional, 15.8% services, 24.3% sales, 0.6% farming, 8.9% construction, 27.4% production (2000).
Income: Per capita income: $18,717 (2005); Median household income: $33,228 (2005); Average household income: $43,012 (2005); Percent of households with income of $100,000 or more: 5.7% (2005); Poverty rate: 11.7% (2000).
Taxes: Total city taxes per capita: $386 (2004); City property taxes per capita: $71 (2004).
Education: Percent of population age 25 and over with: High school diploma (including GED) or higher: 82.0% (2005); Bachelor's degree or higher: 14.9% (2005); Master's degree or higher: 4.1% (2005).

School District(s)
Salem City SD (PK-12)
    2003-04 Enrollment: 2,445 . . . . (330) 332-0316
South Range Local SD (PK-12)
    2003-04 Enrollment: 1,318 . . . . (330) 549-5226
West Branch Local SD (PK-12)
    2003-04 Enrollment: 2,443 . . . . (330) 938-9324

Four-year College(s)
Allegheny Wesleyan College (Private, Not-for-profit, Other Protestant)
    Fall 2004 Enrollment: 57 . . . . (330) 337-6403
    2005-06 Tuition: In-state $4,280; Out-of-state $4,280
Kent State University-Salem Campus (Public)
    Fall 2004 Enrollment: 1,371 . . . . (330) 332-0361
    2005-06 Tuition: In-state $4,586; Out-of-state $12,018

Two-year College(s)
Hannah E Mullins School of Practical Nursing (Public)
    Fall 2004 Enrollment: 53 . . . . (330) 332-8940

Housing: Homeownership rate: 65.8% (2005); Median home value: $92,922 (2005); Median rent: $361 per month (2000); Median age of housing: 48 years (2000).
Hospitals: Salem Community Hospital (140 beds)
Safety: Violent crime rate: 0.8 per 10,000 population; Property crime rate: 65.1 per 10,000 population (2004).
Newspapers: The Salem News (Circulation 7,531)
Transportation: Commute to work: 92.5% car, 0.4% public transportation, 4.3% walk, 2.5% work from home (2000); Travel time to work: 55.1% less than 15 minutes, 21.1% 15 to 30 minutes, 13.6% 30 to 45 minutes, 6.3% 45 to 60 minutes, 3.9% 60 minutes or more (2000)
Additional Information Contacts
Salem Chamber of Commerce . . . . (330) 337-3473
    http://www.salemohio.com/chamber
Salem Convention & Visitors Bureau . . . . (330) 337-2536

SALINEVILLE (village).
Covers a land area of 2.223 square miles and a water area of 0 square miles. Located at 40.62° N. Lat.; 80.83° W. Long. Elevation is 1,084 feet.
History: Salineville was named for the salt springs nearby. A salt well was sunk here in 1809, and by 1835 twenty salt wells were operating along Little Yellow Creek. The arrival of the railroad in 1852 led to the opening of drift coal mines, bringing prosperity to Salineville after the Civil War.
Population: 1,474 (1990); 1,397 (2000); 1,305 (2005); 1,269 (2010 projected); Race: 99.3% White, 0.0% Black, 0.0% Asian, 0.7% Hispanic of any race (2005); Density: 587.2 persons per square mile (2005); Average household size: 2.57 (2005); Median age: 34.3 (2005); Males per 100 females: 98.9 (2005); Marriage status: 23.9% never married, 59.2% now married, 8.6% widowed, 8.3% divorced (2000); Foreign born: 0.1% (2000); Ancestry (includes multiple ancestries): 20.4% German, 14.0% Irish, 12.9% English, 12.4% United States or American, 5.8% Other groups (2000).
Economy: Employment by occupation: 4.1% management, 8.7% professional, 14.0% services, 19.9% sales, 0.4% farming, 6.3% construction, 46.8% production (2000).
Income: Per capita income: $14,863 (2005); Median household income: $30,682 (2005); Average household income: $37,790 (2005); Percent of households with income of $100,000 or more: 5.3% (2005); Poverty rate: 15.7% (2000).
Education: Percent of population age 25 and over with: High school diploma (including GED) or higher: 74.8% (2005); Bachelor's degree or higher: 4.4% (2005); Master's degree or higher: 1.7% (2005).

School District(s)
Southern Local SD (PK-12)
    2003-04 Enrollment: 903 . . . . (330) 679-2343

Housing: Homeownership rate: 72.4% (2005); Median home value: $43,516 (2005); Median rent: $281 per month (2000); Median age of housing: 60+ years (2000).
Transportation: Commute to work: 95.5% car, 0.4% public transportation, 0.4% walk, 3.2% work from home (2000); Travel time to work: 21.6% less than 15 minutes, 21.2% 15 to 30 minutes, 31.3% 30 to 45 minutes, 14.4% 45 to 60 minutes, 11.5% 60 minutes or more (2000)

SUMMITVILLE (village).
Covers a land area of 0.930 square miles and a water area of 0.024 square miles. Located at 40.67° N. Lat.; 80.88° W. Long. Elevation is 1,098 feet.
Population: 125 (1990); 108 (2000); 119 (2005); 125 (2010 projected); Race: 96.6% White, 0.0% Black, 0.0% Asian, 1.7% Hispanic of any race (2005); Density: 127.9 persons per square mile (2005); Average household size: 2.38 (2005); Median age: 41.1 (2005); Males per 100 females: 80.3 (2005); Marriage status: 7.2% never married, 68.1% now married, 14.5% widowed, 10.1% divorced (2000); Foreign born: 0.0% (2000); Ancestry (includes multiple ancestries): 14.6% Irish, 13.5% German, 11.2% United States or American, 7.9% Scottish, 7.9% English (2000).
Economy: Employment by occupation: 0.0% management, 0.0% professional, 19.1% services, 10.6% sales, 0.0% farming, 8.5% construction, 61.7% production (2000).
Income: Per capita income: $18,761 (2005); Median household income: $32,500 (2005); Average household income: $44,650 (2005); Percent of households with income of $100,000 or more: 10.0% (2005); Poverty rate: 15.7% (2000).
Education: Percent of population age 25 and over with: High school diploma (including GED) or higher: 79.7% (2005); Bachelor's degree or higher: 6.3% (2005); Master's degree or higher: 6.3% (2005).
Housing: Homeownership rate: 82.0% (2005); Median home value: $91,667 (2005); Median rent: $325 per month (2000); Median age of housing: 47 years (2000).
Transportation: Commute to work: 85.1% car, 8.5% public transportation, 6.4% walk, 0.0% work from home (2000); Travel time to work: 23.4% less than 15 minutes, 38.3% 15 to 30 minutes, 8.5% 30 to 45 minutes, 14.9% 45 to 60 minutes, 14.9% 60 minutes or more (2000)

WASHINGTONVILLE (village).
Covers a land area of 0.669 square miles and a water area of 0 square miles. Located at 40.89° N. Lat.; 80.76° W. Long. Elevation is 1,069 feet.
Population: 894 (1990); 789 (2000); 815 (2005); 859 (2010 projected); Race: 98.3% White, 0.1% Black, 0.0% Asian, 0.7% Hispanic of any race (2005); Density: 1,218.5 persons per square mile (2005); Average household size: 2.46 (2005); Median age: 36.4 (2005); Males per 100 females: 94.5 (2005); Marriage status: 24.8% never married, 56.3% now married, 4.8% widowed, 14.1% divorced (2000); Foreign born: 0.3% (2000); Ancestry (includes multiple ancestries): 25.4% German, 16.3% English, 13.0% Italian, 11.5% Irish, 11.3% United States or American (2000).
Economy: Employment by occupation: 3.4% management, 12.3% professional, 14.9% services, 22.0% sales, 0.6% farming, 14.9% construction, 32.0% production (2000).
Income: Per capita income: $15,417 (2005); Median household income: $32,540 (2005); Average household income: $37,961 (2005); Percent of households with income of $100,000 or more: 3.6% (2005); Poverty rate: 19.9% (2000).

Education: Percent of population age 25 and over with: High school diploma (including GED) or higher: 82.1% (2005); Bachelor's degree or higher: 10.1% (2005); Master's degree or higher: 3.1% (2005).
Housing: Homeownership rate: 64.0% (2005); Median home value: $79,216 (2005); Median rent: $287 per month (2000); Median age of housing: 54 years (2000).
Transportation: Commute to work: 92.2% car, 0.0% public transportation, 3.3% walk, 3.9% work from home (2000); Travel time to work: 29.5% less than 15 minutes, 44.4% 15 to 30 minutes, 19.3% 30 to 45 minutes, 4.7% 45 to 60 minutes, 2.2% 60 minutes or more (2000)

WELLSVILLE (village). Covers a land area of 1.760 square miles and a water area of 0.114 square miles. Located at 40.60° N. Lat.; 80.65° W. Long. Elevation is 690 feet.
History: Wellsville was founded in 1797 by William Wells, and grew as a stagecoach stop, a shipping center during the steamboat era, and the location of brickyards, potteries, and tile plants.
Population: 4,508 (1990); 4,133 (2000); 4,046 (2005); 3,959 (2010 projected); Race: 92.2% White, 5.6% Black, 0.1% Asian, 0.4% Hispanic of any race (2005); Density: 2,298.9 persons per square mile (2005); Average household size: 2.42 (2005); Median age: 37.0 (2005); Males per 100 females: 88.1 (2005); Marriage status: 25.9% never married, 50.3% now married, 9.8% widowed, 14.0% divorced (2000); Foreign born: 1.2% (2000); Ancestry (includes multiple ancestries): 15.6% German, 15.2% Italian, 13.5% Other groups, 12.8% United States or American, 10.6% Irish (2000).
Economy: Single-family building permits issued: 0 (2005); Multi-family building permits issued: 0 (2005); Employment by occupation: 7.0% management, 13.6% professional, 17.1% services, 23.1% sales, 0.0% farming, 7.4% construction, 31.6% production (2000).
Income: Per capita income: $16,032 (2005); Median household income: $29,939 (2005); Average household income: $38,683 (2005); Percent of households with income of $100,000 or more: 4.4% (2005); Poverty rate: 17.1% (2000).
Education: Percent of population age 25 and over with: High school diploma (including GED) or higher: 79.9% (2005); Bachelor's degree or higher: 6.3% (2005); Master's degree or higher: 0.8% (2005).

School District(s)
Wellsville Local SD (PK-12)
    2003-04 Enrollment: 976 . . . . (330) 532-2643

Housing: Homeownership rate: 63.4% (2005); Median home value: $47,591 (2005); Median rent: $283 per month (2000); Median age of housing: 60+ years (2000).
Safety: Violent crime rate: 65.9 per 10,000 population; Property crime rate: 236.8 per 10,000 population (2004).
Transportation: Commute to work: 89.2% car, 0.5% public transportation, 5.3% walk, 4.9% work from home (2000); Travel time to work: 31.9% less than 15 minutes, 44.8% 15 to 30 minutes, 11.2% 30 to 45 minutes, 7.2% 45 to 60 minutes, 4.9% 60 minutes or more (2000)
Additional Information Contacts
Wellsville Chamber of Commerce . . . . (330) 532-2120
    http://www.columbianacounty.org

Coshocton County

Located in central Ohio; drained by the Muskingum, Tuscarawas, and Walhonding Rivers. Covers a land area of 564.07 square miles, a water area of 3.51 square miles, and is located in the Eastern Time Zone. The county government was organized in 1811. County seat is Coshocton.

Coshocton County is part of the Coshocton, OH Micropolitan Statistical Area. The entire metro area includes: Coshocton County, OH

Weather Station: Coshocton Agr. Res. Station   Elevation: 1,138 feet

	Jan	Feb	Mar	Apr	May	Jun	Jul	Aug	Sep	Oct	Nov	Dec
High	33	37	47	59	70	78	82	81	74	62	50	39
Low	18	20	29	40	51	59	63	62	55	43	34	24
Precip	2.3	2.0	2.9	3.3	3.8	4.0	4.0	3.5	3.0	2.4	3.1	2.7
Snow	na	na	na	tr	0.0	0.0	0.0	0.0	0.0	tr	0.2	na

High and Low temperatures in degrees Fahrenheit; Precipitation and Snow in inches

Weather Station: Coshocton WPC Plant   Elevation: 757 feet

	Jan	Feb	Mar	Apr	May	Jun	Jul	Aug	Sep	Oct	Nov	Dec
High	36	40	51	63	73	80	84	83	76	65	52	41
Low	18	21	29	38	48	57	61	60	52	40	32	24
Precip	2.5	2.4	3.2	3.8	4.1	4.0	4.5	4.2	3.2	2.7	3.5	3.0
Snow	8.8	5.6	3.0	0.8	tr	0.0	0.0	0.0	0.0	tr	0.9	3.6

High and Low temperatures in degrees Fahrenheit; Precipitation and Snow in inches

Population: 35,427 (1990); 36,655 (2000); 37,357 (2005); 38,081 (2010 projected); Race: 97.3% White, 1.1% Black, 0.4% Asian, 0.8% Hispanic of any race (2005); Density: 66.2 persons per square mile (2005); Average household size: 2.53 (2005); Median age: 38.3 (2005); Males per 100 females: 95.7 (2005).
Religion: Five largest groups: 14.6% The United Methodist Church, 4.4% Catholic Church, 2.9% American Baptist Churches in the USA, 2.5% Church of the Nazarene, 2.5% Presbyterian Church (U.S.A.) (2000).
Economy: Unemployment rate: 8.3% (2005); Total civilian labor force: 18,063 (2005); Leading industries: 28.9% manufacturing; 14.8% health care and social assistance; 12.1% retail trade (2004); Farms: 1,043 totaling 179,643 acres (2002); Companies that employ 500 or more persons: 3 (2004); Companies that employ 100 to 499 persons: 17 (2004); Companies that employ less than 100 persons: 705 (2004); Black-owned businesses: 121 (2002); Hispanic-owned businesses: n/a (2002); Women-owned businesses: 747 (2002); Retail sales per capita: $8,375 (2006). Single-family building permits issued: 5 (2005); Multi-family building permits issued: 0 (2005).
Income: Per capita income: $18,658 (2005); Median household income: $38,562 (2005); Average household income: $46,856 (2005); Percent of households with income of $100,000 or more: 7.1% (2005); Poverty rate: 10.3% (2003); Bankruptcy rate: 11.07% (2005).
Taxes: Total county taxes per capita: $193 (2004); County property taxes per capita: $107 (2004).
Education: Percent of population age 25 and over with: High school diploma (including GED) or higher: 78.6% (2005); Bachelor's degree or higher: 9.8% (2005); Master's degree or higher: 3.5% (2005).
Housing: Homeownership rate: 76.4% (2005); Median home value: $93,504 (2005); Median rent: $303 per month (2000); Median age of housing: 39 years (2000).
Health: Birth rate: 121.9 per 10,000 population (2004); Death rate: 127.6 per 10,000 population (2004); Age-adjusted cancer mortality rate: 178.6 deaths per 100,000 population (2002); Number of physicians: 6.7 per 10,000 population (2004); Hospital beds: 36.2 per 10,000 population (2003); Hospital admissions: 1,194.5 per 10,000 population (2003).
Elections: 2004 Presidential election results: 56.9% Bush, 42.6% Kerry, 0.0% Nader, 0.1% Badnarik
Additional Information Contacts
Coshocton County Government . . . . (740) 622-1753
    http://www.co.coshocton.oh.us/
City of Coshocton . . . . (740) 622-1373
    http://www.coshoctoncityhall.com
Coshocton County Chamber of Commerce . . . . (740) 622-5411
    http://www.coshoctonchamber.com

Coshocton County Communities

CONESVILLE (village). Covers a land area of 0.152 square miles and a water area of 0 square miles. Located at 40.18° N. Lat.; 81.89° W. Long. Elevation is 780 feet.
Population: 420 (1990); 364 (2000); 344 (2005); 340 (2010 projected); Race: 99.7% White, 0.0% Black, 0.0% Asian, 1.2% Hispanic of any race (2005); Density: 2,256.2 persons per square mile (2005); Average household size: 2.49 (2005); Median age: 36.9 (2005); Males per 100 females: 96.6 (2005); Marriage status: 18.5% never married, 60.4% now married, 12.2% widowed, 8.9% divorced (2000); Foreign born: 0.0% (2000); Ancestry (includes multiple ancestries): 16.7% German, 12.8% United States or American, 10.8% Other groups, 9.4% English, 5.3% Irish (2000).
Economy: Employment by occupation: 6.1% management, 9.5% professional, 15.0% services, 22.4% sales, 0.0% farming, 8.8% construction, 38.1% production (2000).
Income: Per capita income: $18,314 (2005); Median household income: $36,429 (2005); Average household income: $45,652 (2005); Percent of households with income of $100,000 or more: 6.5% (2005); Poverty rate: 10.0% (2000).

Education: Percent of population age 25 and over with: High school diploma (including GED) or higher: 82.0% (2005); Bachelor's degree or higher: 1.8% (2005); Master's degree or higher: 0.0% (2005).

School District(s)

River View Local SD (PK-12)
    2003-04 Enrollment: 2,586 .... (740) 824-3521

Housing: Homeownership rate: 85.5% (2005); Median home value: $64,615 (2005); Median rent: $363 per month (2000); Median age of housing: 60+ years (2000).
Transportation: Commute to work: 92.5% car, 1.4% public transportation, 6.1% walk, 0.0% work from home (2000); Travel time to work: 31.3% less than 15 minutes, 57.1% 15 to 30 minutes, 6.1% 30 to 45 minutes, 1.4% 45 to 60 minutes, 4.1% 60 minutes or more (2000).

COSHOCTON (city). Covers a land area of 7.479 square miles and a water area of 0.111 square miles. Located at 40.26° N. Lat.; 81.85° W. Long. Elevation is 800 feet.
History: Coshocton was established on a plateau southeast of the juncture of the Walhonding and Tuscarawas Rivers, and developed as an industrial city. The town's name is of Indian origin. An advertising novelty plant built in 1887 by J.F. Meek was a leading industry. Coshocton suffered repeated floodings from the rivers until Wills Creek Dam and Mohawk Dam were built on the Walhonding in the 1930's.
Population: 12,193 (1990); 11,682 (2000); 11,634 (2005); 11,671 (2010 projected); Race: 95.8% White, 1.8% Black, 0.9% Asian, 0.8% Hispanic of any race (2005); Density: 1,555.7 persons per square mile (2005); Average household size: 2.30 (2005); Median age: 41.1 (2005); Males per 100 females: 87.7 (2005); Marriage status: 19.4% never married, 58.8% now married, 11.1% widowed, 10.7% divorced (2000); Foreign born: 2.3% (2000); Ancestry (includes multiple ancestries): 23.1% German, 14.4% United States or American, 12.3% Irish, 11.3% English, 7.7% Other groups (2000).
Economy: Single-family building permits issued: 3 (2005); Multi-family building permits issued: 0 (2005); Employment by occupation: 8.4% management, 15.4% professional, 13.6% services, 22.9% sales, 0.0% farming, 6.7% construction, 33.0% production (2000).
Income: Per capita income: $19,502 (2005); Median household income: $33,445 (2005); Average household income: $44,166 (2005); Percent of households with income of $100,000 or more: 6.2% (2005); Poverty rate: 8.3% (2000).
Taxes: Total city taxes per capita: $384 (2004); City property taxes per capita: $51 (2004).
Education: Percent of population age 25 and over with: High school diploma (including GED) or higher: 80.4% (2005); Bachelor's degree or higher: 13.1% (2005); Master's degree or higher: 4.4% (2005).

School District(s)

Coshocton City SD (PK-12)
    2003-04 Enrollment: 1,978 .... (740) 622-1901
Coshocton County Joint Vocational SD (10-12)
    2003-04 Enrollment: n/a .... (740) 622-0211
River View Local SD (PK-12)
    2003-04 Enrollment: 2,586 .... (740) 824-3521

Two-year College(s)

Coshocton County Joint Vocational Career Center (Public)
    Fall 2004 Enrollment: 32 .... (740) 622-0211

Housing: Homeownership rate: 64.9% (2005); Median home value: $92,048 (2005); Median rent: $306 per month (2000); Median age of housing: 52 years (2000).
Hospitals: Coshocton County Memorial Hospital (61 beds)
Newspapers: The Coshocton Tribune (Circulation 7,085)
Transportation: Commute to work: 91.9% car, 1.0% public transportation, 3.7% walk, 2.6% work from home (2000); Travel time to work: 62.9% less than 15 minutes, 21.1% 15 to 30 minutes, 8.2% 30 to 45 minutes, 3.9% 45 to 60 minutes, 3.9% 60 minutes or more (2000)
Additional Information Contacts
City of Coshocton .... (740) 622-1373
    http://www.coshoctoncityhall.com
Coshocton County Chamber of Commerce .... (740) 622-5411
    http://www.coshoctonchamber.com

FRESNO (unincorporated postal area, zip code 43824). Covers a land area of 77.896 square miles and a water area of 0.020 square miles. Located at 40.35° N. Lat.; 81.75° W. Long. Elevation is 900 feet.
Population: 3,396 (2000); Race: 98.0% White, 0.0% Black, 0.1% Asian, 0.0% Hispanic of any race (2000); Density: 43.6 persons per square mile (2000); Age: 31.0% under 18, 9.1% over 64 (2000); Marriage status: 24.9% never married, 65.3% now married, 3.9% widowed, 5.9% divorced (2000); Foreign born: 0.0% (2000); Ancestry (includes multiple ancestries): 24.7% German, 11.8% United States or American, 8.5% English, 7.1% Irish, 3.4% Other groups (2000).
Economy: Employment by occupation: 11.6% management, 11.8% professional, 8.4% services, 17.2% sales, 3.1% farming, 12.4% construction, 35.5% production (2000).
Income: Per capita income: $14,240 (2000); Median household income: $36,820 (2000); Poverty rate: 12.8% (2000).
Education: Percent of population age 25 and over with: High school diploma (including GED) or higher: 67.5% (2000); Bachelor's degree or higher: 5.9% (2000).

School District(s)

Ridgewood Local SD (PK-12)
    2003-04 Enrollment: 1,501 .... (740) 545-5312

Housing: Homeownership rate: 89.9% (2000); Median home value: $79,400 (2000); Median rent: $430 per month (2000); Median age of housing: 24 years (2000).
Transportation: Commute to work: 84.4% car, 2.0% public transportation, 5.0% walk, 7.1% work from home (2000); Travel time to work: 20.9% less than 15 minutes, 41.7% 15 to 30 minutes, 22.5% 30 to 45 minutes, 5.4% 45 to 60 minutes, 9.4% 60 minutes or more (2000)

NELLIE (village). Covers a land area of 0.710 square miles and a water area of 0 square miles. Located at 40.33° N. Lat.; 82.06° W. Long. Elevation is 817 feet.
Population: 130 (1990); 134 (2000); 142 (2005); 150 (2010 projected); Race: 96.5% White, 0.7% Black, 0.0% Asian, 0.0% Hispanic of any race (2005); Density: 199.9 persons per square mile (2005); Average household size: 2.49 (2005); Median age: 34.0 (2005); Males per 100 females: 89.3 (2005); Marriage status: 16.3% never married, 75.0% now married, 3.8% widowed, 4.8% divorced (2000); Foreign born: 0.0% (2000); Ancestry (includes multiple ancestries): 24.4% English, 17.0% German, 12.6% Irish, 11.9% United States or American, 4.4% Swiss (2000).
Economy: Mohawk Dam is nearby. Single-family building permits issued: 0 (2005); Multi-family building permits issued: 0 (2005); Employment by occupation: 14.7% management, 11.8% professional, 16.2% services, 16.2% sales, 5.9% farming, 8.8% construction, 26.5% production (2000).
Income: Per capita income: $18,908 (2005); Median household income: $42,500 (2005); Average household income: $47,105 (2005); Percent of households with income of $100,000 or more: 1.8% (2005); Poverty rate: 3.0% (2000).
Education: Percent of population age 25 and over with: High school diploma (including GED) or higher: 91.0% (2005); Bachelor's degree or higher: 20.2% (2005); Master's degree or higher: 3.4% (2005).
Housing: Homeownership rate: 89.5% (2005); Median home value: $82,500 (2005); Median rent: $n/a per month (2000); Median age of housing: 36 years (2000).
Transportation: Commute to work: 87.5% car, 0.0% public transportation, 3.1% walk, 9.4% work from home (2000); Travel time to work: 10.3% less than 15 minutes, 43.1% 15 to 30 minutes, 31.0% 30 to 45 minutes, 8.6% 45 to 60 minutes, 6.9% 60 minutes or more (2000)

PLAINFIELD (village). Covers a land area of 0.419 square miles and a water area of 0 square miles. Located at 40.20° N. Lat.; 81.71° W. Long. Elevation is 900 feet.
Population: 178 (1990); 158 (2000); 163 (2005); 168 (2010 projected); Race: 99.4% White, 0.0% Black, 0.6% Asian, 0.0% Hispanic of any race (2005); Density: 389.3 persons per square mile (2005); Average household size: 2.36 (2005); Median age: 41.5 (2005); Males per 100 females: 94.0 (2005); Marriage status: 21.9% never married, 67.2% now married, 7.0% widowed, 3.9% divorced (2000); Foreign born: 0.0% (2000); Ancestry (includes multiple ancestries): 41.0% German, 9.6% English, 8.3% French (except Basque), 6.4% Hungarian, 5.8% Other groups (2000).
Economy: Single-family building permits issued: 1 (2005); Multi-family building permits issued: 0 (2005); Employment by occupation: 2.6% management, 11.7% professional, 19.5% services, 19.5% sales, 0.0% farming, 24.7% construction, 22.1% production (2000).
Income: Per capita income: $18,742 (2005); Median household income: $41,300 (2005); Average household income: $44,275 (2005); Percent of households with income of $100,000 or more: 5.8% (2005); Poverty rate: 2.6% (2000).

Education: Percent of population age 25 and over with: High school diploma (including GED) or higher: 81.8% (2005); Bachelor's degree or higher: 14.9% (2005); Master's degree or higher: 8.3% (2005).

School District(s)
Ridgewood Local SD (PK-12)
    2003-04 Enrollment: 1,501 . . . . (740) 545-5312

Housing: Homeownership rate: 79.7% (2005); Median home value: $75,455 (2005); Median rent: $338 per month (2000); Median age of housing: 60+ years (2000).

Transportation: Commute to work: 96.1% car, 0.0% public transportation, 3.9% walk, 0.0% work from home (2000); Travel time to work: 9.1% less than 15 minutes, 64.9% 15 to 30 minutes, 9.1% 30 to 45 minutes, 6.5% 45 to 60 minutes, 10.4% 60 minutes or more (2000)

WALHONDING (unincorporated postal area, zip code 43843).
Covers a land area of 45.353 square miles and a water area of 0 square miles. Located at 40.34° N. Lat.; 82.17° W. Long. Elevation is 897 feet.

Population: 890 (2000); Race: 99.0% White, 0.0% Black, 0.0% Asian, 0.0% Hispanic of any race (2000); Density: 19.6 persons per square mile (2000); Age: 27.6% under 18, 14.5% over 64 (2000); Marriage status: 12.6% never married, 73.0% now married, 8.6% widowed, 5.9% divorced (2000); Foreign born: 0.4% (2000); Ancestry (includes multiple ancestries): 20.3% German, 11.9% United States or American, 5.2% Italian, 4.9% Irish, 4.5% Other groups (2000).

Economy: Employment by occupation: 6.3% management, 17.0% professional, 7.9% services, 11.5% sales, 0.0% farming, 20.0% construction, 37.3% production (2000).

Income: Per capita income: $12,908 (2000); Median household income: $33,657 (2000); Poverty rate: 18.0% (2000).

Education: Percent of population age 25 and over with: High school diploma (including GED) or higher: 74.5% (2000); Bachelor's degree or higher: 6.6% (2000).

Housing: Homeownership rate: 83.6% (2000); Median home value: $48,900 (2000); Median rent: $n/a per month (2000); Median age of housing: 24 years (2000).

Transportation: Commute to work: 86.9% car, 0.0% public transportation, 5.8% walk, 3.6% work from home (2000); Travel time to work: 20.8% less than 15 minutes, 23.7% 15 to 30 minutes, 19.1% 30 to 45 minutes, 18.2% 45 to 60 minutes, 18.2% 60 minutes or more (2000)

WARSAW (village).
Covers a land area of 0.436 square miles and a water area of 0.016 square miles. Located at 40.33° N. Lat.; 82.00° W. Long. Elevation is 805 feet.

Population: 758 (1990); 781 (2000); 728 (2005); 719 (2010 projected); Race: 97.1% White, 1.1% Black, 0.0% Asian, 1.2% Hispanic of any race (2005); Density: 1,668.8 persons per square mile (2005); Average household size: 2.47 (2005); Median age: 35.2 (2005); Males per 100 females: 90.1 (2005); Marriage status: 20.9% never married, 55.8% now married, 8.7% widowed, 14.6% divorced (2000); Foreign born: 0.4% (2000); Ancestry (includes multiple ancestries): 30.9% German, 16.0% United States or American, 14.3% Irish, 13.3% English, 8.5% Other groups (2000).

Economy: Molding sand, leather goods, food products. Single-family building permits issued: 0 (2005); Multi-family building permits issued: 0 (2005); Employment by occupation: 7.1% management, 9.4% professional, 17.1% services, 20.2% sales, 1.1% farming, 9.4% construction, 35.6% production (2000).

Income: Per capita income: $17,047 (2005); Median household income: $36,205 (2005); Average household income: $42,068 (2005); Percent of households with income of $100,000 or more: 6.1% (2005); Poverty rate: 6.7% (2000).

Education: Percent of population age 25 and over with: High school diploma (including GED) or higher: 84.7% (2005); Bachelor's degree or higher: 11.8% (2005); Master's degree or higher: 6.2% (2005).

School District(s)
River View Local SD (PK-12)
    2003-04 Enrollment: 2,586 . . . . (740) 824-3521

Housing: Homeownership rate: 74.9% (2005); Median home value: $76,512 (2005); Median rent: $303 per month (2000); Median age of housing: 40 years (2000).

Transportation: Commute to work: 94.5% car, 0.0% public transportation, 2.9% walk, 2.6% work from home (2000); Travel time to work: 18.8% less than 15 minutes, 54.9% 15 to 30 minutes, 14.6% 30 to 45 minutes, 5.4% 45 to 60 minutes, 6.3% 60 minutes or more (2000)

WEST LAFAYETTE (village).
Covers a land area of 0.660 square miles and a water area of 0 square miles. Located at 40.27° N. Lat.; 81.75° W. Long. Elevation is 807 feet.

History: West Lafayette began when John Coles, an Englishman, opened a store here in 1850. The town prospered with the arrival of the Pennsylvania Railroad. Early industries were an enameling plant, a metal-products company, and a novelty factory.

Population: 2,226 (1990); 2,313 (2000); 2,337 (2005); 2,380 (2010 projected); Race: 98.5% White, 0.3% Black, 0.0% Asian, 0.5% Hispanic of any race (2005); Density: 3,539.7 persons per square mile (2005); Average household size: 2.50 (2005); Median age: 36.1 (2005); Males per 100 females: 90.5 (2005); Marriage status: 20.8% never married, 55.8% now married, 9.1% widowed, 14.3% divorced (2000); Foreign born: 0.5% (2000); Ancestry (includes multiple ancestries): 28.1% German, 11.9% United States or American, 11.2% English, 9.9% Irish, 6.8% Other groups (2000).

Economy: Single-family building permits issued: 1 (2005); Multi-family building permits issued: 0 (2005); Employment by occupation: 6.0% management, 14.0% professional, 12.7% services, 25.3% sales, 0.0% farming, 9.2% construction, 32.7% production (2000).

Income: Per capita income: $16,959 (2005); Median household income: $34,104 (2005); Average household income: $42,189 (2005); Percent of households with income of $100,000 or more: 5.8% (2005); Poverty rate: 8.1% (2000).

Education: Percent of population age 25 and over with: High school diploma (including GED) or higher: 77.5% (2005); Bachelor's degree or higher: 10.9% (2005); Master's degree or higher: 4.2% (2005).

School District(s)
Ridgewood Local SD (PK-12)
    2003-04 Enrollment: 1,501 . . . . (740) 545-5312

Housing: Homeownership rate: 74.7% (2005); Median home value: $72,197 (2005); Median rent: $325 per month (2000); Median age of housing: 35 years (2000).

Transportation: Commute to work: 95.5% car, 0.4% public transportation, 2.0% walk, 1.3% work from home (2000); Travel time to work: 31.0% less than 15 minutes, 49.2% 15 to 30 minutes, 9.1% 30 to 45 minutes, 5.3% 45 to 60 minutes, 5.3% 60 minutes or more (2000)

Crawford County

Located in north central Ohio; drained by the Sandusky and Olentangy Rivers. Covers a land area of 402.11 square miles, a water area of 0.72 square miles, and is located in the Eastern Time Zone. The county government was organized in 1820. County seat is Bucyrus.

Crawford County is part of the Bucyrus, OH Micropolitan Statistical Area. The entire metro area includes: Crawford County, OH

Weather Station: Bucyrus   Elevation: 954 feet

	Jan	Feb	Mar	Apr	May	Jun	Jul	Aug	Sep	Oct	Nov	Dec
High	31	35	46	59	70	79	83	81	75	62	49	37
Low	16	18	27	37	47	57	61	59	51	40	32	22
Precip	2.2	1.9	2.7	3.5	4.0	4.4	4.5	3.8	3.2	2.4	3.1	2.8
Snow	7.9	5.9	3.6	0.8	tr	0.0	0.0	0.0	0.0	tr	1.0	4.0

High and Low temperatures in degrees Fahrenheit; Precipitation and Snow in inches

Population: 47,870 (1990); 46,966 (2000); 45,727 (2005); 44,471 (2010 projected); Race: 98.0% White, 0.5% Black, 0.4% Asian, 0.9% Hispanic of any race (2005); Density: 113.7 persons per square mile (2005); Average household size: 2.44 (2005); Median age: 39.4 (2005); Males per 100 females: 93.2 (2005).

Religion: Five largest groups: 16.1% Catholic Church, 12.1% Evangelical Lutheran Church in America, 8.3% The United Methodist Church, 3.9% United Church of Christ, 2.9% Church of the Nazarene (2000).

Economy: Unemployment rate: 6.7% (2005); Total civilian labor force: 22,842 (2005); Leading industries: 38.0% manufacturing; 14.2% health care and social assistance; 11.0% retail trade (2004); Farms: 693 totaling 234,204 acres (2002); Companies that employ 500 or more persons: 2 (2004); Companies that employ 100 to 499 persons: 23 (2004); Companies that employ less than 100 persons: 931 (2004); Black-owned businesses: n/a (2002); Hispanic-owned businesses: n/a (2002); Women-owned businesses: 931 (2002); Retail sales per capita: $8,160 (2006). Single-family building permits issued: 56 (2005); Multi-family building permits issued: 4 (2005).

Income: Per capita income: $19,882 (2005); Median household income: $40,027 (2005); Average household income: $47,879 (2005); Percent of households with income of $100,000 or more: 7.2% (2005); Poverty rate: 10.5% (2003); Bankruptcy rate: 10.90% (2005).
Education: Percent of population age 25 and over with: High school diploma (including GED) or higher: 80.2% (2005); Bachelor's degree or higher: 9.9% (2005); Master's degree or higher: 3.2% (2005).
Housing: Homeownership rate: 72.8% (2005); Median home value: $95,827 (2005); Median rent: $317 per month (2000); Median age of housing: 46 years (2000).
Health: Birth rate: 127.5 per 10,000 population (2004); Death rate: 103.3 per 10,000 population (2004); Age-adjusted cancer mortality rate: 184.9 deaths per 100,000 population (2002); Number of physicians: 9.4 per 10,000 population (2004); Hospital beds: 32.8 per 10,000 population (2003); Hospital admissions: 545.1 per 10,000 population (2003).
Elections: 2004 Presidential election results: 63.7% Bush, 35.7% Kerry, 0.0% Nader, 0.3% Badnarik
Additional Information Contacts
Crawford County Government . . . . (419) 562-5876
    http://www.crawford-co.org/
Bucyrus Chamber of Commerce . . . . (419) 562-4811
    http://www.bucyrusohio.com
City of Galion . . . . (419) 468-1857
    http://www.ci.galion.oh.us
Crestline Chamber of Commerce . . . . (419) 683-3818
    http://www.crestlineoh.com/Chamber%20of%20Commerce.html
Galion Chamber of Commerce . . . . (419) 468-7737
    http://www.galionchamber.org
Village of Crestline . . . . (419) 683-3800
    http://www.crestlineoh.com

Crawford County Communities

BUCYRUS (city). Covers a land area of 7.298 square miles and a water area of 0.015 square miles. Located at 40.80° N. Lat.; 82.97° W. Long. Elevation is 995 feet.
History: The site of Bucyrus was purchased by Samuel Norton and Colonel James Kilbourne in 1819, and settled by a group from Pennsylvania. Kilbourne surveyed the village in 1822 and named it for Cyrus, an ancient Persian leader. He prefixed it with "bu" to suggest "beautiful."
Population: 13,632 (1990); 13,224 (2000); 12,792 (2005); 12,352 (2010 projected); Race: 97.2% White, 0.8% Black, 0.7% Asian, 1.2% Hispanic of any race (2005); Density: 1,752.8 persons per square mile (2005); Average household size: 2.34 (2005); Median age: 38.9 (2005); Males per 100 females: 90.0 (2005); Marriage status: 22.6% never married, 52.9% now married, 10.8% widowed, 13.7% divorced (2000); Foreign born: 0.6% (2000); Ancestry (includes multiple ancestries): 30.6% German, 15.2% United States or American, 9.6% Irish, 9.4% English, 8.2% Other groups (2000).
Economy: Single-family building permits issued: 16 (2005); Multi-family building permits issued: 0 (2005); Employment by occupation: 7.9% management, 11.3% professional, 14.2% services, 23.9% sales, 0.3% farming, 8.6% construction, 33.8% production (2000).
Income: Per capita income: $19,311 (2005); Median household income: $35,295 (2005); Average household income: $43,877 (2005); Percent of households with income of $100,000 or more: 6.2% (2005); Poverty rate: 12.0% (2000).
Taxes: Total city taxes per capita: $371 (2004); City property taxes per capita: $62 (2004).
Education: Percent of population age 25 and over with: High school diploma (including GED) or higher: 75.9% (2005); Bachelor's degree or higher: 9.6% (2005); Master's degree or higher: 2.9% (2005).
School District(s)
Bucyrus City SD (PK-12)
    2003-04 Enrollment: 1,891 . . . . (419) 562-4045
Colonel Crawford Local SD (PK-12)
    2003-04 Enrollment: 1,004 . . . . (419) 562-4666
Wynford Local Schools (PK-12)
    2003-04 Enrollment: 1,146 . . . . (419) 562-7828
Housing: Homeownership rate: 64.2% (2005); Median home value: $90,067 (2005); Median rent: $316 per month (2000); Median age of housing: 45 years (2000).
Hospitals: Bucyrus Community Hospital (25 beds)
Newspapers: Telegraph-Forum (Circulation 7,216)

Transportation: Commute to work: 92.0% car, 0.1% public transportation, 3.4% walk, 2.1% work from home (2000); Travel time to work: 55.4% less than 15 minutes, 25.5% 15 to 30 minutes, 14.0% 30 to 45 minutes, 1.8% 45 to 60 minutes, 3.4% 60 minutes or more (2000)
Additional Information Contacts
Bucyrus Chamber of Commerce . . . . (419) 562-4811
    http://www.bucyrusohio.com

CHATFIELD (village). Covers a land area of 0.297 square miles and a water area of 0 square miles. Located at 40.95° N. Lat.; 82.94° W. Long. Elevation is 980 feet.
Population: 206 (1990); 218 (2000); 204 (2005); 194 (2010 projected); Race: 100.0% White, 0.0% Black, 0.0% Asian, 3.9% Hispanic of any race (2005); Density: 686.9 persons per square mile (2005); Average household size: 2.46 (2005); Median age: 37.5 (2005); Males per 100 females: 104.0 (2005); Marriage status: 25.2% never married, 62.6% now married, 9.2% widowed, 3.1% divorced (2000); Foreign born: 2.7% (2000); Ancestry (includes multiple ancestries): 42.4% German, 6.7% United States or American, 6.3% English, 4.5% Irish, 4.5% Other groups (2000).
Economy: Single-family building permits issued: 0 (2005); Multi-family building permits issued: 0 (2005); Employment by occupation: 13.9% management, 12.0% professional, 10.2% services, 14.8% sales, 4.6% farming, 13.9% construction, 30.6% production (2000).
Income: Per capita income: $17,365 (2005); Median household income: $40,417 (2005); Average household income: $42,681 (2005); Percent of households with income of $100,000 or more: 1.2% (2005); Poverty rate: 5.4% (2000).
Education: Percent of population age 25 and over with: High school diploma (including GED) or higher: 86.7% (2005); Bachelor's degree or higher: 10.4% (2005); Master's degree or higher: 3.7% (2005).
School District(s)
Buckeye Central Local SD (KG-12)
    2003-04 Enrollment: 708 . . . . (419) 492-2864
Housing: Homeownership rate: 92.8% (2005); Median home value: $75,217 (2005); Median rent: $325 per month (2000); Median age of housing: 60+ years (2000).
Transportation: Commute to work: 90.6% car, 0.9% public transportation, 4.7% walk, 1.9% work from home (2000); Travel time to work: 28.8% less than 15 minutes, 46.2% 15 to 30 minutes, 15.4% 30 to 45 minutes, 1.9% 45 to 60 minutes, 7.7% 60 minutes or more (2000)

CRESTLINE (village). Covers a land area of 2.888 square miles and a water area of 0 square miles. Located at 40.78° N. Lat.; 82.74° W. Long. Elevation is 1,160 feet.
History: Crestline (Crest Line) was established when the Pennsylvania Railroad became the second line in the area. It joined Livingston, founded two years earlier when the first railroad came through. When the two villages grew to the point where their borders touched, they joined as Crestline.
Population: 4,947 (1990); 5,088 (2000); 4,904 (2005); 4,718 (2010 projected); Race: 97.2% White, 1.3% Black, 0.4% Asian, 0.7% Hispanic of any race (2005); Density: 1,698.1 persons per square mile (2005); Average household size: 2.43 (2005); Median age: 36.7 (2005); Males per 100 females: 92.1 (2005); Marriage status: 26.0% never married, 53.8% now married, 8.5% widowed, 11.8% divorced (2000); Foreign born: 0.8% (2000); Ancestry (includes multiple ancestries): 30.8% German, 16.3% United States or American, 11.8% Irish, 10.5% Other groups, 8.9% English (2000).
Economy: Single-family building permits issued: 5 (2005); Multi-family building permits issued: 0 (2005); Employment by occupation: 7.2% management, 13.0% professional, 16.7% services, 22.0% sales, 0.4% farming, 8.5% construction, 32.1% production (2000).
Income: Per capita income: $18,728 (2005); Median household income: $36,694 (2005); Average household income: $45,004 (2005); Percent of households with income of $100,000 or more: 6.9% (2005); Poverty rate: 12.4% (2000).
Education: Percent of population age 25 and over with: High school diploma (including GED) or higher: 80.1% (2005); Bachelor's degree or higher: 8.6% (2005); Master's degree or higher: 2.8% (2005).
School District(s)
Crestline Ex Vill SD (PK-12)
    2003-04 Enrollment: 945 . . . . (419) 683-3647
Housing: Homeownership rate: 71.1% (2005); Median home value: $83,614 (2005); Median rent: $298 per month (2000); Median age of housing: 45 years (2000).

Hospitals: MedCentral Health System/Crestline Hospital (40 beds)
Newspapers: The Crestline Advocate (General - Circulation 2,000)
Transportation: Commute to work: 95.6% car, 0.2% public transportation, 3.0% walk, 0.9% work from home (2000); Travel time to work: 39.6% less than 15 minutes, 39.2% 15 to 30 minutes, 12.2% 30 to 45 minutes, 3.3% 45 to 60 minutes, 5.7% 60 minutes or more (2000)
Additional Information Contacts
Crestline Chamber of Commerce . . . . (419) 683-3818
  http://www.crestlineoh.com/Chamber%20of%20Commerce.html
Village of Crestline . . . . (419) 683-3800
  http://www.crestlineoh.com

GALION (city). Covers a land area of 4.960 square miles and a water area of 0.011 square miles. Located at 40.73° N. Lat.; 82.78° W. Long. Elevation is 1,166 feet.
History: Galion was setttled by German Lutherans from Pennsylvania in 1831. In the 1890's C.H. North organized a company for the manufacture of telephone equipment, inventing improvements that made Galion a pioneering center for this industry.
Population: 11,867 (1990); 11,341 (2000); 10,972 (2005); 10,627 (2010 projected); Race: 98.1% White, 0.2% Black, 0.4% Asian, 1.0% Hispanic of any race (2005); Density: 2,212.1 persons per square mile (2005); Average household size: 2.33 (2005); Median age: 37.9 (2005); Males per 100 females: 85.6 (2005); Marriage status: 21.7% never married, 53.9% now married, 9.7% widowed, 14.7% divorced (2000); Foreign born: 0.6% (2000); Ancestry (includes multiple ancestries): 28.1% German, 16.4% United States or American, 10.9% Other groups, 10.8% Irish, 9.3% English (2000).
Economy: Single-family building permits issued: 6 (2005); Multi-family building permits issued: 0 (2005); Employment by occupation: 7.6% management, 13.1% professional, 15.4% services, 22.0% sales, 0.0% farming, 9.2% construction, 32.7% production (2000).
Income: Per capita income: $17,999 (2005); Median household income: $34,412 (2005); Average household income: $41,537 (2005); Percent of households with income of $100,000 or more: 4.7% (2005); Poverty rate: 14.7% (2000).
Education: Percent of population age 25 and over with: High school diploma (including GED) or higher: 77.6% (2005); Bachelor's degree or higher: 8.8% (2005); Master's degree or higher: 2.9% (2005).
School District(s)
Galion City SD (PK-12)
  2003-04 Enrollment: 2,238 . . . . (419) 468-3432
Northmor Local SD (PK-12)
  2003-04 Enrollment: 1,243 . . . . (419) 946-8861
Housing: Homeownership rate: 63.3% (2005); Median home value: $84,520 (2005); Median rent: $328 per month (2000); Median age of housing: 49 years (2000).
Hospitals: Galion Community Hospital (178 beds)
Safety: Violent crime rate: 21.7 per 10,000 population; Property crime rate: 450.8 per 10,000 population (2004).
Newspapers: The Galion Inquirer (Circulation 4,000)
Transportation: Commute to work: 93.6% car, 0.4% public transportation, 3.6% walk, 1.7% work from home (2000); Travel time to work: 46.7% less than 15 minutes, 32.8% 15 to 30 minutes, 13.2% 30 to 45 minutes, 3.1% 45 to 60 minutes, 4.2% 60 minutes or more (2000)
Additional Information Contacts
City of Galion . . . . (419) 468-1857
  http://www.ci.galion.oh.us
Galion Chamber of Commerce . . . . (419) 468-7737
  http://www.galionchamber.org

NEW WASHINGTON (village). Covers a land area of 1.269 square miles and a water area of 0 square miles. Located at 40.96° N. Lat.; 82.85° W. Long. Elevation is 990 feet.
Population: 1,057 (1990); 987 (2000); 856 (2005); 808 (2010 projected); Race: 99.3% White, 0.0% Black, 0.6% Asian, 0.0% Hispanic of any race (2005); Density: 674.5 persons per square mile (2005); Average household size: 2.47 (2005); Median age: 38.3 (2005); Males per 100 females: 95.0 (2005); Marriage status: 24.3% never married, 61.6% now married, 6.7% widowed, 7.4% divorced (2000); Foreign born: 0.4% (2000); Ancestry (includes multiple ancestries): 50.0% German, 9.6% United States or American, 6.6% Other groups, 4.5% English, 4.2% Irish (2000).
Economy: Fabricated metal products, food products. Single-family building permits issued: 2 (2005); Multi-family building permits issued: 0 (2005); Employment by occupation: 9.2% management, 13.7% professional, 10.0% services, 21.4% sales, 1.4% farming, 10.4% construction, 33.9% production (2000).
Income: Per capita income: $20,049 (2005); Median household income: $44,094 (2005); Average household income: $49,352 (2005); Percent of households with income of $100,000 or more: 4.3% (2005); Poverty rate: 6.3% (2000).
Education: Percent of population age 25 and over with: High school diploma (including GED) or higher: 87.6% (2005); Bachelor's degree or higher: 14.3% (2005); Master's degree or higher: 5.8% (2005).
School District(s)
Buckeye Central Local SD (KG-12)
  2003-04 Enrollment: 708 . . . . (419) 492-2864
Housing: Homeownership rate: 83.9% (2005); Median home value: $86,379 (2005); Median rent: $254 per month (2000); Median age of housing: 60+ years (2000).
Newspapers: New Washington Herald (General - Circulation 1,500)
Transportation: Commute to work: 89.2% car, 0.0% public transportation, 6.5% walk, 2.0% work from home (2000); Travel time to work: 42.5% less than 15 minutes, 34.8% 15 to 30 minutes, 12.7% 30 to 45 minutes, 7.1% 45 to 60 minutes, 2.9% 60 minutes or more (2000)

NORTH ROBINSON (village). Aka Robinson. Covers a land area of 0.098 square miles and a water area of 0 square miles. Located at 40.79° N. Lat.; 82.85° W. Long. Elevation is 1,075 feet.
Population: 216 (1990); 211 (2000); 235 (2005); 255 (2010 projected); Race: 99.1% White, 0.0% Black, 0.0% Asian, 0.0% Hispanic of any race (2005); Density: 2,398.3 persons per square mile (2005); Average household size: 2.55 (2005); Median age: 43.2 (2005); Males per 100 females: 92.6 (2005); Marriage status: 15.9% never married, 71.6% now married, 5.1% widowed, 7.4% divorced (2000); Foreign born: 0.0% (2000); Ancestry (includes multiple ancestries): 33.9% United States or American, 23.7% German, 5.4% Irish, 4.0% Other groups, 3.1% English (2000).
Economy: Single-family building permits issued: 0 (2005); Multi-family building permits issued: 0 (2005); Employment by occupation: 6.1% management, 0.0% professional, 17.2% services, 26.3% sales, 0.0% farming, 8.1% construction, 42.4% production (2000).
Income: Per capita income: $14,681 (2005); Median household income: $32,500 (2005); Average household income: $37,500 (2005); Percent of households with income of $100,000 or more: 0.0% (2005); Poverty rate: 8.9% (2000).
Education: Percent of population age 25 and over with: High school diploma (including GED) or higher: 75.9% (2005); Bachelor's degree or higher: 1.8% (2005); Master's degree or higher: 0.0% (2005).
School District(s)
Colonel Crawford Local SD (PK-12)
  2003-04 Enrollment: 1,004 . . . . (419) 562-4666
Housing: Homeownership rate: 85.9% (2005); Median home value: $71,935 (2005); Median rent: $357 per month (2000); Median age of housing: 58 years (2000).
Transportation: Commute to work: 97.9% car, 0.0% public transportation, 2.1% walk, 0.0% work from home (2000); Travel time to work: 31.3% less than 15 minutes, 40.6% 15 to 30 minutes, 5.2% 30 to 45 minutes, 7.3% 45 to 60 minutes, 15.6% 60 minutes or more (2000)

TIRO (village). Covers a land area of 0.412 square miles and a water area of 0 square miles. Located at 40.90° N. Lat.; 82.77° W. Long. Elevation is 1,050 feet.
Population: 246 (1990); 281 (2000); 304 (2005); 311 (2010 projected); Race: 98.0% White, 0.0% Black, 1.6% Asian, 2.3% Hispanic of any race (2005); Density: 738.2 persons per square mile (2005); Average household size: 2.67 (2005); Median age: 33.7 (2005); Males per 100 females: 104.0 (2005); Marriage status: 16.4% never married, 68.3% now married, 2.6% widowed, 12.7% divorced (2000); Foreign born: 0.0% (2000); Ancestry (includes multiple ancestries): 20.6% German, 11.4% Other groups, 9.6% United States or American, 8.9% Irish, 7.8% English (2000).
Economy: In agricultural and timber area. Employment by occupation: 5.1% management, 2.6% professional, 11.1% services, 12.0% sales, 0.0% farming, 15.4% construction, 53.8% production (2000).
Income: Per capita income: $15,337 (2005); Median household income: $35,556 (2005); Average household income: $40,899 (2005); Percent of households with income of $100,000 or more: 0.9% (2005); Poverty rate: 13.2% (2000).
Education: Percent of population age 25 and over with: High school diploma (including GED) or higher: 69.7% (2005); Bachelor's degree or higher: 0.0% (2005); Master's degree or higher: 0.0% (2005).

School District(s)
Buckeye Central Local SD (KG-12)
  2003-04 Enrollment: 708 . . . . (419) 492-2864
Housing: Homeownership rate: 75.4% (2005); Median home value: $69,032 (2005); Median rent: $318 per month (2000); Median age of housing: 60+ years (2000).
Transportation: Commute to work: 98.2% car, 0.0% public transportation, 0.0% walk, 1.8% work from home (2000); Travel time to work: 10.7% less than 15 minutes, 62.5% 15 to 30 minutes, 24.1% 30 to 45 minutes, 0.0% 45 to 60 minutes, 2.7% 60 minutes or more (2000)

Cuyahoga County

Located in northern Ohio; bounded on the north by Lake Erie; drained by the Cuyahoga and Rocky Rivers. Covers a land area of 458.49 square miles, a water area of 787.07 square miles, and is located in the Eastern Time Zone. The county government was organized in 1808. County seat is Cleveland.

Cuyahoga County is part of the Cleveland-Elyria-Mentor, OH Metropolitan Statistical Area. The entire metro area includes: Cuyahoga County, OH; Geauga County, OH; Lake County, OH; Lorain County, OH; Medina County, OH

Weather Station: Cleveland Hopkins Int'l Airport   Elevation: 767 feet

	Jan	Feb	Mar	Apr	May	Jun	Jul	Aug	Sep	Oct	Nov	Dec
High	33	36	46	58	69	78	82	80	74	62	50	39
Low	19	21	29	38	48	58	63	61	54	44	35	25
Precip	2.4	2.3	3.0	3.3	3.4	3.9	3.6	3.6	3.8	2.8	3.4	3.1
Snow	16.4	13.4	10.8	2.5	tr	tr	tr	0.0	tr	0.4	4.9	12.6

High and Low temperatures in degrees Fahrenheit; Precipitation and Snow in inches

Population: 1,412,140 (1990); 1,393,978 (2000); 1,350,482 (2005); 1,306,708 (2010 projected); Race: 65.7% White, 28.3% Black, 2.3% Asian, 3.6% Hispanic of any race (2005); Density: 2,945.5 persons per square mile (2005); Average household size: 2.42 (2005); Median age: 38.7 (2005); Males per 100 females: 90.0 (2005).
Religion: Five largest groups: 34.9% Catholic Church, 5.7% Jewish Estimate, 2.2% The United Methodist Church, 1.7% American Baptist Churches in the USA, 1.7% Lutheran Church—Missouri Synod (2000).
Economy: Unemployment rate: 6.1% (2005); Total civilian labor force: 669,568 (2005); Leading industries: 17.0% health care and social assistance; 12.6% manufacturing; 10.3% retail trade (2004); Farms: 159 totaling 4,086 acres (2002); Companies that employ 500 or more persons: 104 (2004); Companies that employ 100 to 499 persons: 1,055 (2004); Companies that employ less than 100 persons: 36,033 (2004); Black-owned businesses: 9,809 (2002); Hispanic-owned businesses: 1,109 (2002); Women-owned businesses: 28,243 (2002); Retail sales per capita: $13,946 (2006). Single-family building permits issued: 1,748 (2005); Multi-family building permits issued: 245 (2005).
Income: Per capita income: $25,085 (2005); Median household income: $43,657 (2005); Average household income: $60,050 (2005); Percent of households with income of $100,000 or more: 14.4% (2005); Poverty rate: 13.5% (2003); Bankruptcy rate: 15.13% (2005).
Taxes: Total county taxes per capita: $356 (2004); County property taxes per capita: $202 (2004).
Education: Percent of population age 25 and over with: High school diploma (including GED) or higher: 81.7% (2005); Bachelor's degree or higher: 25.3% (2005); Master's degree or higher: 9.6% (2005).
Housing: Homeownership rate: 63.5% (2005); Median home value: $133,213 (2005); Median rent: $463 per month (2000); Median age of housing: 46 years (2000).
Health: Birth rate: 130.6 per 10,000 population (2004); Death rate: 112.8 per 10,000 population (2004); Age-adjusted cancer mortality rate: 214.6 deaths per 100,000 population (2002); Air Quality Index: 61.9% good, 34.2% moderate, 3.3% unhealthy for sensitive individuals, 0.5% unhealthy (percent of days in 2005); Number of physicians: 58.6 per 10,000 population (2004); Hospital beds: 48.4 per 10,000 population (2003); Hospital admissions: 2,020.7 per 10,000 population (2003).
Elections: 2004 Presidential election results: 32.9% Bush, 66.6% Kerry, 0.0% Nader, 0.3% Badnarik.
National and State Parks: Chagrin State Scenic River; Cleveland Lakefront State Park; Edgewater State Park
Additional Information Contacts

Cuyahoga County Government . . . . (216) 443-7000
  http://www.cuyahogacounty.us
Beachwood Chamber of Commerce . . . . (216) 831-0003
  http://www.beachwood.org
Bedford Heights Chamber of Commerce . . . . (440) 232-3369
  http://www.bedfordheightschamber.com
Berea Chamber of Commerce . . . . (440) 243-8415
  http://www.bereaohio.com
Brecksville Chamber of Commerce . . . . (440) 526-7350
  http://www.brecksvillechamber.com
Broadview Heights Chamber of Commerce . . . . (440) 838-4510
  http://www.broadviewhts.org
Chagrin Falls Chamber of Commerce . . . . (440) 247-6607
  http://www.cvcc.org
City of Bay Village . . . . (440) 899-3415
  http://www.cityofbayvillage.com
City of Beachwood . . . . (216) 464-1070
  http://www.beachwoodohio.com
City of Bedford . . . . (440) 735-6514
  http://www.bedfordoh.gov
City of Berea . . . . (440) 826-5800
  http://www.bereaohio.com
City of Broadview Heights . . . . (440) 526-4357
  http://www.broadview-heights.org
City of Brook Park . . . . (216) 433-1300
  http://www.cityofbrookpark.com
City of Cleveland . . . . (216) 664-3990
  http://www.city.cleveland.oh.us
City of Cleveland Heights . . . . (216) 291-4444
  http://www.clevelandheights.com
City of Euclid . . . . (216) 289-2751
  http://www.ci.euclid.oh.us
City of Fairview Park . . . . (440) 333-2200
  http://www.fairviewpark.org
City of Garfield Heights . . . . (216) 475-1100
  http://www.garfieldhts.org
City of Independence . . . . (216) 524-4131
  http://www.independenceohio.org
City of Lakewood . . . . (216) 521-7580
  http://www.ci.lakewood.oh.us
City of Maple Heights . . . . (216) 662-6000
  http://www.mapleheightsohio.com
City of Mayfield Heights . . . . (440) 449-7545
  http://www.mayfieldheights.org
City of North Olmsted . . . . (440) 777-8000
  http://www.north-olmsted.com
City of North Royalton . . . . (440) 237-4300
  http://www.northroyalton.org
City of Olmsted Falls . . . . (440) 235-5550
  http://www.olmstedfalls.org
City of Parma . . . . (440) 885-8000
  http://www.cityofparma-oh.gov
City of Pepper Pike . . . . (216) 831-8500
  http://www.pepperpike.org
City of Rocky River . . . . (440) 331-0600
  http://www.rrcity.com
City of Seven Hills . . . . (216) 524-4421
  http://www.sevenhillsohio.org
City of Shaker Heights . . . . (216) 491-1400
  http://www.shakeronline.com
City of Solon . . . . (440) 248-1155
  http://www.solonohio.org
City of South Euclid . . . . (216) 381-0400
  http://www.cityofsoutheuclid.com
City of Strongsville . . . . (440) 580-3100
  http://www.strongsville.org/content
City of University Heights . . . . (216) 932-7800
  http://www.universityheights.com
City of Westlake . . . . (440) 871-3300
  http://www.cityofwestlake.org
Convention & Visitors Bureau of Greater Cleveland . . . . . (216) 621-4110
  http://www.travelcleveland.com
Euclid Chamber of Commerce . . . . (216) 731-9322
  http://www.euclidchamberofcommerce.com
Garfield Heights Chamber of Commerce . . . . (216) 475-7775
  http://chamberplace.ghiis.com/1003/index.cfm
Greater Cleveland Partnership . . . . (216) 621-3300
  http://www.clevelandgrowth.com

Heights Regional Chamber of Commerce . . . . (216) 397-7322
http://www.hrcc.org
Korean America Association of Greater Cleveland . . . . (216) 689-2999
http://www.kaagc.org
Lakewood Chamber of Commerce . . . . (216) 226-2900
http://www.lakewoodchamber.org
Middleburg Heights Chamber . . . . (440) 243-5599
http://middleburgheightschamber.com
Olmsted Chamber of Commerce . . . . (440) 235-0032
http://www.olmstedchamber.org
Parma Area Chamber of Commerce . . . . (440) 886-1700
http://www.parmaareachamber.org
Rocky River Chamber of Commerce . . . . (440) 331-1140
http://www.rockyriverchamber.com
Solon Chamber of Commerce . . . . (440) 248-5080
http://www.solonchamber.com
Strongsville Chamber of Commerce . . . . (440) 238-3366
http://strongsvillecofc.com
Tri-City Chamber of Commerce . . . . (216) 454-0199
http://www.tricitychamber.com
Village of Bentleyville . . . . (440) 247-5055
http://www.villageofbentleyville.com
Village of Chagrin Falls . . . . (440) 247-5050
http://www.chagrin-falls.org
Village of Mayfield . . . . (440) 461-2210
http://www.mayfieldvillage.com
Village of Moreland Hills . . . . (440) 248-1188
http://www.morelandhills.com
Village of Orange . . . . (440) 498-4400
http://www.orangevillage.com
Village of Valley View . . . . (216) 524-6511
http://www.valleyview.net
West Shore Chamber of Commerce . . . . (440) 835-8787
http://www.westshorechamber.org
Westshore Chamber of Commerce . . . . (440) 835-8787
http://www.westshorechamber.org

Cuyahoga County Communities

BAY VILLAGE (city). Aka Bay. Covers a land area of 4.631 square miles and a water area of 2.454 square miles. Located at 41.48° N. Lat.; 81.92° W. Long. Elevation is 645 feet.
History: Named for its location on a bay of Lake Erie. Incorporated 1903.
Population: 17,000 (1990); 16,087 (2000); 15,580 (2005); 15,050 (2010 projected); Race: 97.8% White, 0.3% Black, 0.7% Asian, 1.0% Hispanic of any race (2005); Density: 3,364.0 persons per square mile (2005); Average household size: 2.53 (2005); Median age: 42.4 (2005); Males per 100 females: 92.0 (2005); Marriage status: 19.0% never married, 66.4% now married, 7.0% widowed, 7.6% divorced (2000); Foreign born: 4.4% (2000); Ancestry (includes multiple ancestries): 31.2% German, 26.8% Irish, 15.5% English, 9.6% Italian, 7.0% Polish (2000).
Economy: A residential community with some light industry. Single-family building permits issued: 14 (2005); Multi-family building permits issued: 0 (2005); Employment by occupation: 24.0% management, 28.2% professional, 7.7% services, 28.5% sales, 0.1% farming, 4.5% construction, 7.1% production (2000).
Income: Per capita income: $40,403 (2005); Median household income: $80,892 (2005); Average household income: $101,983 (2005); Percent of households with income of $100,000 or more: 36.6% (2005); Poverty rate: 3.1% (2000).
Education: Percent of population age 25 and over with: High school diploma (including GED) or higher: 96.5% (2005); Bachelor's degree or higher: 54.2% (2005); Master's degree or higher: 18.1% (2005).
School District(s)
Bay Village City SD (PK-12)
   2003-04 Enrollment: 2,455 . . . . (440) 617-7300
Housing: Homeownership rate: 92.3% (2005); Median home value: $198,077 (2005); Median rent: $381 per month (2000); Median age of housing: 44 years (2000).
Transportation: Commute to work: 89.2% car, 3.1% public transportation, 0.7% walk, 6.1% work from home (2000); Travel time to work: 26.8% less than 15 minutes, 36.5% 15 to 30 minutes, 26.1% 30 to 45 minutes, 7.4% 45 to 60 minutes, 3.1% 60 minutes or more (2000)
Additional Information Contacts
City of Bay Village . . . . (440) 899-3415
http://www.cityofbayvillage.com

BEACHWOOD (city). Covers a land area of 5.281 square miles and a water area of 0.012 square miles. Located at 41.48° N. Lat.; 81.50° W. Long. Elevation is 1,190 feet.
History: Beachwood Village was part of Warrensville Township until 1915, when it seceded following a decision by township officials to close a school in that area. On May 29, 1915, a petition signed by 57 freeholders of the northeastern part of the township was filed with the trustees. They asked that their section, containing a population of 151, be permitted to incorporate as a village. On June 15, 1915, an election was held at the schoolhouse at the corner of Richmond Road and North Woodland Road (officially renamed Fairmount Boulevard in September, 1925). Out of 47 votes, only one was against the proposal. On June 26, 1915, the trustees of Warrensville Township ordered the incorporation of Beachwood Village. In 1960, Beachwood attained city status, with the census showing a population of 6,089. Beachwood received its name from the beech trees that once covered the majority of the city. Rumor has it that an early Village Hall clerk misspelled the name on some official documents, giving us today's current spelling.
Population: 10,677 (1990); 12,186 (2000); 11,805 (2005); 11,456 (2010 projected); Race: 84.9% White, 9.3% Black, 4.3% Asian, 0.8% Hispanic of any race (2005); Density: 2,235.4 persons per square mile (2005); Average household size: 2.38 (2005); Median age: 53.4 (2005); Males per 100 females: 79.1 (2005); Marriage status: 13.7% never married, 63.7% now married, 16.4% widowed, 6.1% divorced (2000); Foreign born: 15.5% (2000); Ancestry (includes multiple ancestries): 19.1% Other groups, 15.5% Russian, 9.9% United States or American, 8.2% Polish, 6.8% Hungarian (2000).
Economy: Suburb of Cleveland. Single-family building permits issued: 5 (2005); Multi-family building permits issued: 0 (2005); Employment by occupation: 19.9% management, 39.7% professional, 5.3% services, 30.0% sales, 0.1% farming, 2.3% construction, 2.7% production (2000).
Income: Per capita income: $42,362 (2005); Median household income: $67,182 (2005); Average household income: $99,124 (2005); Percent of households with income of $100,000 or more: 32.0% (2005); Poverty rate: 4.3% (2000).
Education: Percent of population age 25 and over with: High school diploma (including GED) or higher: 91.6% (2005); Bachelor's degree or higher: 50.3% (2005); Master's degree or higher: 26.1% (2005).
School District(s)
Beachwood City SD (PK-12)
   2003-04 Enrollment: 1,596 . . . . (216) 464-2600
Four-year College(s)
Siegal College (Private, Not-for-profit, Jewish)
   Fall 2004 Enrollment: 146 . . . . (216) 464-4050
   2005-06 Tuition: In-state $12,000; Out-of-state $12,000
Housing: Homeownership rate: 63.8% (2005); Median home value: $286,275 (2005); Median rent: $1,076 per month (2000); Median age of housing: 29 years (2000).
Newspapers: Bedford Sun Banner (General - Circulation 5,052); Chagrin Herald Sun (General - Circulation 17,695); Euclid Sun Journal (General - Circulation 14,909); Solon Herald Sun (General - Circulation 17,675); Sun Scoop Journal (General - Circulation 14,909); The Sun Messenger (General - Circulation 14,018); The Sun Press (General - Circulation 20,040); West Geauga Sun (General - Circulation 17,695)
Transportation: Commute to work: 89.7% car, 1.4% public transportation, 0.7% walk, 7.6% work from home (2000); Travel time to work: 32.2% less than 15 minutes, 37.2% 15 to 30 minutes, 25.7% 30 to 45 minutes, 2.4% 45 to 60 minutes, 2.6% 60 minutes or more (2000)
Additional Information Contacts
Beachwood Chamber of Commerce . . . . (216) 831-0003
http://www.beachwood.org
City of Beachwood . . . . (216) 464-1070
http://www.beachwoodohio.com

BEDFORD (city). Covers a land area of 5.357 square miles and a water area of 0 square miles. Located at 41.39° N. Lat.; 81.53° W. Long. Elevation is 960 feet.
History: Named for Bedford in Bedfordshire, England. The first settlement at Bedford was made in 1786 by a group of Moravian missionaries, and was called Pilgerruh, meaning pilgrim's rest. In 1810 the town site was surveyed by the Connecticut Land Company, and in 1813 permanent

settlers arrived. Benjamin Fitch, who began the manufacture of chairs in Bedford, was one of the first settlers.
Population: 14,922 (1990); 14,214 (2000); 13,598 (2005); 12,965 (2010 projected); Race: 73.1% White, 22.7% Black, 1.4% Asian, 1.1% Hispanic of any race (2005); Density: 2,538.3 persons per square mile (2005); Average household size: 2.09 (2005); Median age: 40.7 (2005); Males per 100 females: 89.9 (2005); Marriage status: 27.8% never married, 51.3% now married, 9.6% widowed, 11.4% divorced (2000); Foreign born: 3.3% (2000); Ancestry (includes multiple ancestries): 19.8% Other groups, 19.1% German, 13.3% Irish, 11.7% Polish, 10.8% Italian (2000).
Economy: Single-family building permits issued: 3 (2005); Multi-family building permits issued: 2 (2005); Employment by occupation: 9.4% management, 17.6% professional, 14.2% services, 30.2% sales, 0.0% farming, 9.9% construction, 18.7% production (2000).
Income: Per capita income: $22,044 (2005); Median household income: $39,666 (2005); Average household income: $45,949 (2005); Percent of households with income of $100,000 or more: 5.8% (2005); Poverty rate: 7.6% (2000).
Taxes: Total city taxes per capita: $977 (2004); City property taxes per capita: $244 (2004).
Education: Percent of population age 25 and over with: High school diploma (including GED) or higher: 83.3% (2005); Bachelor's degree or higher: 18.1% (2005); Master's degree or higher: 5.5% (2005).

School District(s)
Bedford City SD (PK-12)
    2003-04 Enrollment: 3,890 . . . . (440) 439-1500

Housing: Homeownership rate: 59.8% (2005); Median home value: $111,580 (2005); Median rent: $539 per month (2000); Median age of housing: 43 years (2000).
Hospitals: UHHS Bedford Medical Center (110 beds)
Newspapers: Bedford Times-Register (General - Circulation 3,400); Maple Heights Press (General - Circulation 1,900); The News Leader (General - Circulation 10,000)
Transportation: Commute to work: 94.7% car, 1.7% public transportation, 2.0% walk, 1.4% work from home (2000); Travel time to work: 30.4% less than 15 minutes, 43.7% 15 to 30 minutes, 19.7% 30 to 45 minutes, 3.7% 45 to 60 minutes, 2.6% 60 minutes or more (2000)
Additional Information Contacts
City of Bedford . . . . (440) 735-6514
    http://www.bedfordoh.gov

BEDFORD HEIGHTS (city). Covers a land area of 4.537 square miles and a water area of 0 square miles. Located at 41.40° N. Lat.; 81.50° W. Long. Elevation is 1,040 feet.
History: Named for Bedford in Bedfordshire, England. Incorporated 1951.
Population: 12,131 (1990); 11,375 (2000); 11,102 (2005); 10,818 (2010 projected); Race: 22.2% White, 72.5% Black, 2.2% Asian, 1.8% Hispanic of any race (2005); Density: 2,447.2 persons per square mile (2005); Average household size: 2.20 (2005); Median age: 40.4 (2005); Males per 100 females: 87.0 (2005); Marriage status: 30.9% never married, 46.8% now married, 6.9% widowed, 15.4% divorced (2000); Foreign born: 2.1% (2000); Ancestry (includes multiple ancestries): 62.5% Other groups, 5.8% Italian, 4.6% German, 4.1% Irish, 2.8% Polish (2000).
Economy: Single-family building permits issued: 7 (2005); Multi-family building permits issued: 0 (2005); Employment by occupation: 12.0% management, 18.1% professional, 15.1% services, 26.9% sales, 0.1% farming, 7.5% construction, 20.3% production (2000).
Income: Per capita income: $24,067 (2005); Median household income: $41,606 (2005); Average household income: $52,446 (2005); Percent of households with income of $100,000 or more: 10.3% (2005); Poverty rate: 7.6% (2000).
Education: Percent of population age 25 and over with: High school diploma (including GED) or higher: 82.6% (2005); Bachelor's degree or higher: 16.2% (2005); Master's degree or higher: 5.3% (2005).
Housing: Homeownership rate: 53.1% (2005); Median home value: $125,558 (2005); Median rent: $551 per month (2000); Median age of housing: 35 years (2000).
Safety: Violent crime rate: 18.7 per 10,000 population; Property crime rate: 239.9 per 10,000 population (2004).
Transportation: Commute to work: 89.7% car, 6.0% public transportation, 2.3% walk, 1.5% work from home (2000); Travel time to work: 24.4% less than 15 minutes, 38.6% 15 to 30 minutes, 26.5% 30 to 45 minutes, 4.6% 45 to 60 minutes, 6.0% 60 minutes or more (2000)
Additional Information Contacts

Bedford Heights Chamber of Commerce. . . . . (440) 232-3369
    http://www.bedfordheightschamber.com

BENTLEYVILLE (village). Covers a land area of 2.607 square miles and a water area of 0.011 square miles. Located at 41.41° N. Lat.; 81.41° W. Long. Elevation is 938 feet.
Population: 674 (1990); 947 (2000); 942 (2005); 938 (2010 projected); Race: 96.8% White, 0.6% Black, 2.2% Asian, 1.1% Hispanic of any race (2005); Density: 361.4 persons per square mile (2005); Average household size: 3.22 (2005); Median age: 40.3 (2005); Males per 100 females: 102.1 (2005); Marriage status: 19.1% never married, 76.4% now married, 1.8% widowed, 2.7% divorced (2000); Foreign born: 7.4% (2000); Ancestry (includes multiple ancestries): 24.8% German, 14.8% English, 14.4% Italian, 11.4% Irish, 6.9% Polish (2000).
Economy: Suburb of Cleveland. Single-family building permits issued: 0 (2005); Multi-family building permits issued: 0 (2005); Employment by occupation: 36.2% management, 34.4% professional, 5.5% services, 21.6% sales, 0.0% farming, 0.5% construction, 1.8% production (2000).
Income: Per capita income: $80,918 (2005); Median household income: $201,639 (2005); Average household income: $260,154 (2005); Percent of households with income of $100,000 or more: 72.7% (2005); Poverty rate: 1.0% (2000).
Education: Percent of population age 25 and over with: High school diploma (including GED) or higher: 99.3% (2005); Bachelor's degree or higher: 77.6% (2005); Master's degree or higher: 37.4% (2005).
Housing: Homeownership rate: 98.0% (2005); Median home value: $581,897 (2005); Median rent: $1,208 per month (2000); Median age of housing: 13 years (2000).
Transportation: Commute to work: 92.4% car, 0.3% public transportation, 1.0% walk, 5.8% work from home (2000); Travel time to work: 24.5% less than 15 minutes, 30.4% 15 to 30 minutes, 34.5% 30 to 45 minutes, 8.1% 45 to 60 minutes, 2.5% 60 minutes or more (2000)
Additional Information Contacts
Village of Bentleyville. . . . . (440) 247-5055
    http://www.villageofbentleyville.com

BEREA (city). Covers a land area of 5.458 square miles and a water area of 0.108 square miles. Located at 41.37° N. Lat.; 81.86° W. Long. Elevation is 800 feet.
History: Named for the city in ancient Syria, mentioned in the Bible. Berea was founded by John Baldwin in 1827, on land owned by Gideon Granger, Postmaster General under President Jefferson. Baldwin discovered the vein of abrasive sandstone that provided the early industry for the community.
Population: 19,045 (1990); 18,970 (2000); 18,333 (2005); 17,728 (2010 projected); Race: 91.0% White, 5.1% Black, 1.1% Asian, 1.6% Hispanic of any race (2005); Density: 3,359.2 persons per square mile (2005); Average household size: 2.62 (2005); Median age: 37.1 (2005); Males per 100 females: 90.8 (2005); Marriage status: 33.1% never married, 48.7% now married, 7.3% widowed, 10.9% divorced (2000); Foreign born: 3.2% (2000); Ancestry (includes multiple ancestries): 27.8% German, 17.8% Irish, 13.5% English, 10.7% Polish, 9.8% Italian (2000).
Economy: Single-family building permits issued: 100 (2005); Multi-family building permits issued: 0 (2005); Employment by occupation: 12.1% management, 21.4% professional, 13.3% services, 33.5% sales, 0.3% farming, 6.7% construction, 12.8% production (2000).
Income: Per capita income: $24,047 (2005); Median household income: $50,164 (2005); Average household income: $61,592 (2005); Percent of households with income of $100,000 or more: 15.4% (2005); Poverty rate: 5.5% (2000).
Taxes: Total city taxes per capita: $700 (2004); City property taxes per capita: $225 (2004).
Education: Percent of population age 25 and over with: High school diploma (including GED) or higher: 89.1% (2005); Bachelor's degree or higher: 28.9% (2005); Master's degree or higher: 9.7% (2005).

School District(s)
Berea City SD (PK-12)
    2003-04 Enrollment: 8,027 . . . . (440) 243-6000

Four-year College(s)
Baldwin-Wallace College (Private, Not-for-profit, United Methodist)
    Fall 2004 Enrollment: 4,600 . . . . (440) 826-2900
    2005-06 Tuition: In-state $20,518; Out-of-state $20,518

Housing: Homeownership rate: 70.9% (2005); Median home value: $139,582 (2005); Median rent: $508 per month (2000); Median age of housing: 42 years (2000).

Safety: Violent crime rate: 18.3 per 10,000 population; Property crime rate: 197.4 per 10,000 population (2004).
Newspapers: Parma Sun Post (General - Circulation 23,828); The News Sun (General - Circulation 16,255); The Sun Star (General - Circulation 12,022)
Transportation: Commute to work: 86.6% car, 2.8% public transportation, 7.1% walk, 2.7% work from home (2000); Travel time to work: 33.0% less than 15 minutes, 36.4% 15 to 30 minutes, 21.3% 30 to 45 minutes, 6.0% 45 to 60 minutes, 3.3% 60 minutes or more (2000)
Additional Information Contacts
Berea Chamber of Commerce . . . . (440) 243-8415
  http://www.bereaohio.com
City of Berea . . . . (440) 826-5800
  http://www.bereaohio.com

BRATENAHL (village).
Covers a land area of 1.025 square miles and a water area of 0.600 square miles. Located at 41.55° N. Lat.; 81.60° W. Long. Elevation is 620 feet.
Population: 1,399 (1990); 1,337 (2000); 1,330 (2005); 1,325 (2010 projected); Race: 82.9% White, 13.6% Black, 0.8% Asian, 1.4% Hispanic of any race (2005); Density: 1,297.3 persons per square mile (2005); Average household size: 1.84 (2005); Median age: 52.8 (2005); Males per 100 females: 94.2 (2005); Marriage status: 21.2% never married, 56.3% now married, 8.6% widowed, 13.9% divorced (2000); Foreign born: 6.7% (2000); Ancestry (includes multiple ancestries): 21.1% German, 16.9% Irish, 15.6% English, 15.0% Other groups, 6.9% Italian (2000).
Economy: Suburb surrounded on three sides by Cleveland. Single-family building permits issued: 4 (2005); Multi-family building permits issued: 0 (2005); Employment by occupation: 32.1% management, 33.4% professional, 6.4% services, 22.4% sales, 0.0% farming, 2.0% construction, 3.8% production (2000).
Income: Per capita income: $75,155 (2005); Median household income: $87,784 (2005); Average household income: $135,883 (2005); Percent of households with income of $100,000 or more: 44.0% (2005); Poverty rate: 4.3% (2000).
Education: Percent of population age 25 and over with: High school diploma (including GED) or higher: 95.9% (2005); Bachelor's degree or higher: 63.6% (2005); Master's degree or higher: 35.7% (2005).
Housing: Homeownership rate: 84.6% (2005); Median home value: $241,797 (2005); Median rent: $550 per month (2000); Median age of housing: 39 years (2000).
Transportation: Commute to work: 88.2% car, 2.4% public transportation, 0.9% walk, 7.2% work from home (2000); Travel time to work: 28.8% less than 15 minutes, 53.2% 15 to 30 minutes, 13.4% 30 to 45 minutes, 1.9% 45 to 60 minutes, 2.7% 60 minutes or more (2000)

BRECKSVILLE (city).
Covers a land area of 19.611 square miles and a water area of 0.005 square miles. Located at 41.31° N. Lat.; 81.62° W. Long. Elevation is 960 feet.
History: Brecksville was settled about 1811 and named for John and Robert Breck, early residents.
Population: 11,818 (1990); 13,382 (2000); 13,489 (2005); 13,610 (2010 projected); Race: 94.7% White, 1.8% Black, 2.8% Asian, 1.0% Hispanic of any race (2005); Density: 687.8 persons per square mile (2005); Average household size: 2.61 (2005); Median age: 46.2 (2005); Males per 100 females: 99.2 (2005); Marriage status: 19.1% never married, 68.3% now married, 6.6% widowed, 6.0% divorced (2000); Foreign born: 6.6% (2000); Ancestry (includes multiple ancestries): 22.1% German, 18.3% Polish, 13.4% Irish, 12.6% Italian, 8.9% English (2000).
Economy: Single-family building permits issued: 40 (2005); Multi-family building permits issued: 0 (2005); Employment by occupation: 26.9% management, 28.3% professional, 8.1% services, 26.2% sales, 0.0% farming, 4.3% construction, 6.2% production (2000).
Income: Per capita income: $43,975 (2005); Median household income: $83,555 (2005); Average household income: $113,200 (2005); Percent of households with income of $100,000 or more: 39.7% (2005); Poverty rate: 2.5% (2000).
Taxes: Total city taxes per capita: $1,191 (2004); City property taxes per capita: $240 (2004).
Education: Percent of population age 25 and over with: High school diploma (including GED) or higher: 92.9% (2005); Bachelor's degree or higher: 47.3% (2005); Master's degree or higher: 22.2% (2005).
School District(s)
Brecksville-Broadview Heights City SD (KG-12)
  2003-04 Enrollment: 4,666 . . . . (440) 740-4010
Cuyahoga Valley Career Center (10-12)
  2003-04 Enrollment: n/a . . . . (440) 526-5200
Two-year College(s)
School of Nursing at Cuyahoga Valley Career Center (Public)
  Fall 2004 Enrollment: 102 . . . . (440) 746-8200
Housing: Homeownership rate: 88.1% (2005); Median home value: $251,450 (2005); Median rent: $999 per month (2000); Median age of housing: 28 years (2000).
Safety: Violent crime rate: 3.7 per 10,000 population; Property crime rate: 54.1 per 10,000 population (2004).
Transportation: Commute to work: 91.2% car, 1.4% public transportation, 1.0% walk, 5.8% work from home (2000); Travel time to work: 20.5% less than 15 minutes, 39.9% 15 to 30 minutes, 30.0% 30 to 45 minutes, 6.8% 45 to 60 minutes, 2.8% 60 minutes or more (2000)
Additional Information Contacts
Brecksville Chamber of Commerce . . . . (440) 526-7350
  http://www.brecksvillechamber.com

BROADVIEW HEIGHTS (city).
Covers a land area of 13.059 square miles and a water area of 0 square miles. Located at 41.32° N. Lat.; 81.67° W. Long. Elevation is 1,150 feet.
History: Named for the beautiful local views. Incorporated 1926.
Population: 12,219 (1990); 15,967 (2000); 17,199 (2005); 18,285 (2010 projected); Race: 94.2% White, 0.7% Black, 3.8% Asian, 0.9% Hispanic of any race (2005); Density: 1,317.1 persons per square mile (2005); Average household size: 2.47 (2005); Median age: 40.3 (2005); Males per 100 females: 92.5 (2005); Marriage status: 23.0% never married, 60.0% now married, 7.2% widowed, 9.8% divorced (2000); Foreign born: 8.9% (2000); Ancestry (includes multiple ancestries): 23.6% German, 16.8% Italian, 16.1% Polish, 13.4% Irish, 7.4% Slovak (2000).
Economy: Single-family building permits issued: 177 (2005); Multi-family building permits issued: 0 (2005); Employment by occupation: 19.6% management, 25.6% professional, 9.6% services, 28.3% sales, 0.1% farming, 5.7% construction, 11.1% production (2000).
Income: Per capita income: $35,520 (2005); Median household income: $65,081 (2005); Average household income: $87,483 (2005); Percent of households with income of $100,000 or more: 27.6% (2005); Poverty rate: 3.2% (2000).
Education: Percent of population age 25 and over with: High school diploma (including GED) or higher: 90.4% (2005); Bachelor's degree or higher: 36.9% (2005); Master's degree or higher: 13.1% (2005).
School District(s)
Brecksville-Broadview Heights City SD (KG-12)
  2003-04 Enrollment: 4,666 . . . . (440) 740-4010
North Royalton City SD (PK-12)
  2003-04 Enrollment: 4,496 . . . . (440) 237-8800
Two-year College(s)
Vatterott College-Cleveland (Private, For-profit)
  Fall 2004 Enrollment: 129 . . . . (440) 526-1660
  2005-06 Tuition: In-state $8,357; Out-of-state $8,357
Housing: Homeownership rate: 76.7% (2005); Median home value: $200,639 (2005); Median rent: $637 per month (2000); Median age of housing: 25 years (2000).
Safety: Violent crime rate: 11.3 per 10,000 population; Property crime rate: 65.1 per 10,000 population (2004).
Transportation: Commute to work: 92.9% car, 1.9% public transportation, 0.6% walk, 3.5% work from home (2000); Travel time to work: 16.6% less than 15 minutes, 43.9% 15 to 30 minutes, 29.4% 30 to 45 minutes, 7.2% 45 to 60 minutes, 2.9% 60 minutes or more (2000)
Additional Information Contacts
Broadview Heights Chamber of Commerce . . . . (440) 838-4510
  http://www.broadviewhts.org
City of Broadview Heights . . . . (440) 526-4357
  http://www.broadview-heights.org

BROOK PARK (city).
Covers a land area of 7.537 square miles and a water area of 0 square miles. Located at 41.40° N. Lat.; 81.81° W. Long. Elevation is 790 feet.
History: Named for its location near a branch of the Rocky River. Incorporated 1914.
Population: 22,961 (1990); 21,218 (2000); 20,434 (2005); 19,658 (2010 projected); Race: 93.6% White, 2.2% Black, 1.6% Asian, 2.0% Hispanic of any race (2005); Density: 2,711.0 persons per square mile (2005); Average household size: 2.54 (2005); Median age: 41.9 (2005); Males per 100 females: 95.1 (2005); Marriage status: 23.8% never married, 58.2% now

married, 8.4% widowed, 9.5% divorced (2000); Foreign born: 4.3% (2000); Ancestry (includes multiple ancestries): 26.5% German, 18.5% Irish, 14.1% Polish, 13.2% Italian, 7.2% English (2000).
Economy: Major office complex here; Cleveland municipal airport. Major transportation equipment and casting plants. Unemployment rate: 5.9% (2005); Total civilian labor force: 10,778 (2005); Single-family building permits issued: 8 (2005); Multi-family building permits issued: 0 (2005); Employment by occupation: 9.7% management, 12.3% professional, 16.0% services, 30.1% sales, 0.1% farming, 11.3% construction, 20.6% production (2000).
Income: Per capita income: $23,328 (2005); Median household income: $50,791 (2005); Average household income: $58,842 (2005); Percent of households with income of $100,000 or more: 11.4% (2005); Poverty rate: 4.6% (2000).
Taxes: Total city taxes per capita: $1,196 (2004); City property taxes per capita: $114 (2004).
Education: Percent of population age 25 and over with: High school diploma (including GED) or higher: 80.7% (2005); Bachelor's degree or higher: 9.8% (2005); Master's degree or higher: 2.5% (2005).

School District(s)
Berea City SD (PK-12)
    2003-04 Enrollment: 8,027 . . . . (440) 243-6000
Housing: Homeownership rate: 83.5% (2005); Median home value: $129,948 (2005); Median rent: $565 per month (2000); Median age of housing: 38 years (2000).
Safety: Violent crime rate: 9.2 per 10,000 population; Property crime rate: 37.2 per 10,000 population (2004).
Transportation: Commute to work: 94.1% car, 2.5% public transportation, 0.9% walk, 1.3% work from home (2000); Travel time to work: 30.8% less than 15 minutes, 43.0% 15 to 30 minutes, 18.6% 30 to 45 minutes, 4.5% 45 to 60 minutes, 3.1% 60 minutes or more (2000)
Additional Information Contacts
City of Brook Park . . . . (216) 433-1300
    http://www.cityofbrookpark.com

BROOKLYN (city).
Covers a land area of 4.284 square miles and a water area of 0.018 square miles. Located at 41.43° N. Lat.; 81.74° W. Long. Elevation is 765 feet.
History: The west side municipality of Brooklyn, distinguished from the Brooklyn portion of the city of Cleveland (Old Brooklyn) and located six miles southwest of downtown, lies contiguous to Cleveland on its east, north, and west borders, and to the city of Parma on its southern boundary. Brooklyn Township, organized June 1, 1818, occupied a significant part of Cleveland's early west side territory, and was bounded on the north by Lake Erie, on the east by the Cuyahoga River, on the west by Rockport, and on the south by the Parma and Independence townships. The incorporation of separate municipalities, along with subsequent annexations by the city of Cleveland, throughout the nineteenth and early twentieth centuries (Ohio City, Old Brooklyn, Linndale, and Brooklyn Heights) left only a small area in the southwest corner of the original Brooklyn township. That portion of the former township became Brooklyn Village on 16 March 1927, and was chartered as the city of Brooklyn in 1950. Primarily a residential suburb, in 1966 Brooklyn became the first community in the nation to mandate use of seatbelts in automobiles. It was also the first community to ban the use of non-hands free cell phones while driving. John M. Coyne served as Brooklyn mayor for 52 years, from 1948-1999, the longest consecutive term of service by any mayor in the nation.
Population: 11,706 (1990); 11,586 (2000); 11,131 (2005); 10,682 (2010 projected); Race: 91.0% White, 2.0% Black, 3.1% Asian, 4.3% Hispanic of any race (2005); Density: 2,598.2 persons per square mile (2005); Average household size: 2.14 (2005); Median age: 43.3 (2005); Males per 100 females: 92.4 (2005); Marriage status: 25.4% never married, 50.7% now married, 11.2% widowed, 12.7% divorced (2000); Foreign born: 9.0% (2000); Ancestry (includes multiple ancestries): 23.6% German, 14.1% Polish, 13.6% Irish, 12.4% Italian, 9.4% Slovak (2000).
Economy: Incorporated 1927. Single-family building permits issued: 0 (2005); Multi-family building permits issued: 0 (2005); Employment by occupation: 10.0% management, 14.9% professional, 14.4% services, 31.3% sales, 0.0% farming, 8.2% construction, 21.2% production (2000).
Income: Per capita income: $23,615 (2005); Median household income: $41,054 (2005); Average household income: $50,547 (2005); Percent of households with income of $100,000 or more: 8.5% (2005); Poverty rate: 6.6% (2000).

Education: Percent of population age 25 and over with: High school diploma (including GED) or higher: 80.1% (2005); Bachelor's degree or higher: 13.2% (2005); Master's degree or higher: 4.1% (2005).

School District(s)
Brooklyn City SD (PK-12)
    2003-04 Enrollment: 1,359 . . . . (216) 485-8100

Two-year College(s)
Total Technical Institute (Private, For-profit)
    Fall 2004 Enrollment: 105 . . . . (216) 485-0900
    2005-06 Tuition: In-state $9,300; Out-of-state $9,300
Housing: Homeownership rate: 62.3% (2005); Median home value: $129,127 (2005); Median rent: $446 per month (2000); Median age of housing: 42 years (2000).
Safety: Violent crime rate: 17.7 per 10,000 population; Property crime rate: 352.2 per 10,000 population (2004).
Transportation: Commute to work: 93.4% car, 2.5% public transportation, 2.3% walk, 1.2% work from home (2000); Travel time to work: 29.8% less than 15 minutes, 50.6% 15 to 30 minutes, 13.6% 30 to 45 minutes, 3.7% 45 to 60 minutes, 2.4% 60 minutes or more (2000)

BROOKLYN HEIGHTS (village).
Covers a land area of 1.773 square miles and a water area of 0 square miles. Located at 41.41° N. Lat.; 81.67° W. Long. Elevation is 710 feet.
Population: 1,450 (1990); 1,558 (2000); 1,549 (2005); 1,543 (2010 projected); Race: 96.6% White, 1.0% Black, 1.0% Asian, 1.5% Hispanic of any race (2005); Density: 873.6 persons per square mile (2005); Average household size: 2.61 (2005); Median age: 43.3 (2005); Males per 100 females: 92.4 (2005); Marriage status: 21.2% never married, 58.9% now married, 8.1% widowed, 11.8% divorced (2000); Foreign born: 2.7% (2000); Ancestry (includes multiple ancestries): 25.6% German, 23.3% Polish, 18.2% Italian, 10.7% Irish, 7.6% Slovak (2000).
Economy: Suburb of Cleveland. Single-family building permits issued: 1 (2005); Multi-family building permits issued: 0 (2005); Employment by occupation: 19.3% management, 22.0% professional, 12.7% services, 24.7% sales, 1.7% farming, 3.5% construction, 15.9% production (2000).
Income: Per capita income: $27,605 (2005); Median household income: $53,529 (2005); Average household income: $69,196 (2005); Percent of households with income of $100,000 or more: 26.1% (2005); Poverty rate: 2.2% (2000).
Education: Percent of population age 25 and over with: High school diploma (including GED) or higher: 86.4% (2005); Bachelor's degree or higher: 27.0% (2005); Master's degree or higher: 7.6% (2005).
Housing: Homeownership rate: 89.7% (2005); Median home value: $172,452 (2005); Median rent: $525 per month (2000); Median age of housing: 42 years (2000).
Safety: Violent crime rate: 0.0 per 10,000 population; Property crime rate: 174.0 per 10,000 population (2004).
Transportation: Commute to work: 97.4% car, 1.0% public transportation, 0.9% walk, 0.0% work from home (2000); Travel time to work: 42.9% less than 15 minutes, 39.1% 15 to 30 minutes, 14.7% 30 to 45 minutes, 0.0% 45 to 60 minutes, 3.4% 60 minutes or more (2000)

BROOKPARK (unincorporated postal area, zip code 44142).
Covers a land area of 7.685 square miles and a water area of 0 square miles. Located at 41.40° N. Lat.; 81.82° W. Long.
Population: 21,132 (2000); Race: 94.2% White, 2.0% Black, 1.4% Asian, 1.6% Hispanic of any race (2000); Density: 2,749.6 persons per square mile (2000); Age: 22.8% under 18, 17.2% over 64 (2000); Marriage status: 23.8% never married, 58.3% now married, 8.4% widowed, 9.4% divorced (2000); Foreign born: 4.4% (2000); Ancestry (includes multiple ancestries): 26.5% German, 18.6% Irish, 14.1% Polish, 13.3% Italian, 7.3% English (2000).
Economy: Employment by occupation: 9.7% management, 12.2% professional, 15.9% services, 30.2% sales, 0.1% farming, 11.3% construction, 20.6% production (2000).
Income: Per capita income: $20,436 (2000); Median household income: $46,280 (2000); Poverty rate: 4.7% (2000).
Education: Percent of population age 25 and over with: High school diploma (including GED) or higher: 80.6% (2000); Bachelor's degree or higher: 9.6% (2000).
Housing: Homeownership rate: 83.6% (2000); Median home value: $112,400 (2000); Median rent: $567 per month (2000); Median age of housing: 38 years (2000).
Transportation: Commute to work: 94.2% car, 2.5% public transportation, 0.9% walk, 1.3% work from home (2000); Travel time to work: 30.9% less

than 15 minutes, 42.8% 15 to 30 minutes, 18.7% 30 to 45 minutes, 4.4% 45 to 60 minutes, 3.2% 60 minutes or more (2000)

CHAGRIN FALLS (village).
Covers a land area of 2.071 square miles and a water area of 0.037 square miles. Located at 41.43° N. Lat.; 81.38° W. Long. Elevation is 927 feet.

History: Noah Graves from Massachusetts built a grist mill here in 1833, and the town of Chagrin Falls developed as a residential community. The town was named for the Chagrin River, said to have been named by surveyor Moses Cleaveland to express his embarrassment at mistaking it for the Cuyahoga River.

Population: 4,146 (1990); 4,024 (2000); 3,861 (2005); 3,692 (2010 projected); Race: 98.5% White, 0.0% Black, 0.5% Asian, 1.1% Hispanic of any race (2005); Density: 1,864.5 persons per square mile (2005); Average household size: 2.17 (2005); Median age: 44.7 (2005); Males per 100 females: 85.5 (2005); Marriage status: 22.0% never married, 55.3% now married, 11.0% widowed, 11.8% divorced (2000); Foreign born: 3.8% (2000); Ancestry (includes multiple ancestries): 28.7% German, 22.1% English, 17.6% Irish, 8.5% Italian, 4.5% United States or American (2000).

Economy: Single-family building permits issued: 2 (2005); Multi-family building permits issued: 0 (2005); Employment by occupation: 27.8% management, 29.2% professional, 9.6% services, 27.0% sales, 0.1% farming, 2.4% construction, 3.9% production (2000).

Income: Per capita income: $48,710 (2005); Median household income: $72,721 (2005); Average household income: $105,030 (2005); Percent of households with income of $100,000 or more: 35.6% (2005); Poverty rate: 3.6% (2000).

Education: Percent of population age 25 and over with: High school diploma (including GED) or higher: 95.3% (2005); Bachelor's degree or higher: 61.2% (2005); Master's degree or higher: 23.2% (2005).

School District(s)
Chagrin Falls Ex Vill SD (PK-12)
   2003-04 Enrollment: 1,970 . . . . (440) 247-5500
Kenston Local SD (KG-12)
   2003-04 Enrollment: 3,134 . . . . (440) 543-9677

Housing: Homeownership rate: 73.3% (2005); Median home value: $271,566 (2005); Median rent: $799 per month (2000); Median age of housing: 40 years (2000).

Hospitals: BHC Windsor Hospital (71 beds)

Newspapers: Chagrin Valley Times/Solon Times (General - Circulation 20,000)

Transportation: Commute to work: 89.5% car, 1.8% public transportation, 3.2% walk, 5.1% work from home (2000); Travel time to work: 28.4% less than 15 minutes, 30.1% 15 to 30 minutes, 27.8% 30 to 45 minutes, 9.5% 45 to 60 minutes, 4.2% 60 minutes or more (2000)

Additional Information Contacts
Chagrin Falls Chamber of Commerce . . . . (440) 247-6607
   http://www.cvcc.org
Village of Chagrin Falls . . . . (440) 247-5050
   http://www.chagrin-falls.org

CLEVELAND (city).
Covers a land area of 77.580 square miles and a water area of 4.844 square miles. Located at 41.48° N. Lat.; 81.67° W. Long. Elevation is 690 feet.

History: Moses Cleaveland platted the city of Cleveland on the shores of Lake Erie in 1796 for the Connecticut Land Company, but stayed only a few months in the town that would bear his name. It was Lorenzo Carter who pulled the community together, and launched the first boat from Cleveland harbor in 1804, a prophesy of the many freighters and passenger steamers that would one day enter this harbor. The spelling of the town's name changed from Cleaveland to Cleveland about 1832, when a newspaper editor had to drop one letter from his masthead to make it fit the space, and decided to drop the "a" from Cleaveland. Cleveland expanded when the Ohio & Erie Canal was completed, becoming a commercial center. In 1836 it was incorporated as a city, and over the next half-century developed into an industrial giant. The Cuyahoga Steam Furnace Company began making locomotives, the Cleveland Iron Company and the Standard Oil Company were organized, along with many other industries.

Population: 505,333 (1990); 478,403 (2000); 455,038 (2005); 432,022 (2010 projected); Race: 39.2% White, 52.3% Black, 1.7% Asian, 7.9% Hispanic of any race (2005); Density: 5,865.4 persons per square mile (2005); Average household size: 2.50 (2005); Median age: 34.2 (2005); Males per 100 females: 90.8 (2005); Marriage status: 38.9% never married, 38.2% now married, 9.0% widowed, 13.9% divorced (2000); Foreign born: 4.5% (2000); Ancestry (includes multiple ancestries): 50.9% Other groups, 9.2% German, 8.1% Irish, 4.8% Polish, 4.6% Italian (2000).

Economy: Unemployment rate: 7.9% (2005); Total civilian labor force: 191,940 (2005); Single-family building permits issued: 345 (2005); Multi-family building permits issued: 98 (2005); Employment by occupation: 8.2% management, 14.3% professional, 20.9% services, 26.7% sales, 0.1% farming, 7.5% construction, 22.3% production (2000).

Income: Per capita income: $15,729 (2005); Median household income: $28,802 (2005); Average household income: $38,551 (2005); Percent of households with income of $100,000 or more: 5.3% (2005); Poverty rate: 26.3% (2000).

Taxes: Total city taxes per capita: $822 (2004); City property taxes per capita: $135 (2004).

Education: Percent of population age 25 and over with: High school diploma (including GED) or higher: 69.1% (2005); Bachelor's degree or higher: 11.7% (2005); Master's degree or higher: 3.9% (2005).

School District(s)
Academy of Cleveland (KG-06)
   2003-04 Enrollment: 108 . . . . (216) 271-0237
Berea City SD (PK-12)
   2003-04 Enrollment: 8,027 . . . . (440) 243-6000
Citizens Academy (KG-05)
   2003-04 Enrollment: 290 . . . . (216) 791-4195
Cleve Academy of Math, Sci & Tech (KG-05)
   2003-04 Enrollment: 114 . . . . (216) 391-3752
Cleveland Municipal City SD (PK-12)
   2003-04 Enrollment: 69,655 . . . . (216) 574-8000
Cuyahoga Heights Local SD (PK-12)
   2003-04 Enrollment: 869 . . . . (216) 429-5700
Garfield Heights Community School
   2003-04 Enrollment: n/a
General Johnnie Wilson Military Academy (09-09)
   2003-04 Enrollment: 78
Greater Achievement Community (KG-07)
   2003-04 Enrollment: 59 . . . . (216) 781-6031
Greater Cleveland Academy for Gifted Students
   2003-04 Enrollment: n/a
Greater Heights Academy
   2003-04 Enrollment: n/a
Hope Academy Broadway Campus (KG-09)
   2003-04 Enrollment: 544 . . . . (216) 271-7747
Hope Academy Cathedral Campus (KG-09)
   2003-04 Enrollment: 589 . . . . (216) 721-6909
Hope Academy Chapelside Campus (KG-09)
   2003-04 Enrollment: 496 . . . . (216) 283-6589
Hope Academy Cuyahoga Campus (KG-08)
   2003-04 Enrollment: 306 . . . . (216) 251-5450
Hope Academy East Campus (KG-08)
   2003-04 Enrollment: 290 . . . . (216) 383-1214
Hope Academy Lincoln Park (KG-06)
   2003-04 Enrollment: 176 . . . . (216) 263-7008
Hope Northcoast Academy (KG-08)
   2003-04 Enrollment: 309
Horizon Science Academy Cleveland (06-12)
   2003-04 Enrollment: 370 . . . . (216) 432-3660
Horizon Science Academy Toledo
   2003-04 Enrollment: n/a
Imani Leadership Institute (KG-10)
   2003-04 Enrollment: 126 . . . . (216) 771-7501
Intergenerational School, The (KG-04)
   2003-04 Enrollment: 93 . . . . (216) 721-0120
International Preparatory (KG-12)
   2003-04 Enrollment: 838 . . . . (216) 791-2602
Life Skills Center of Cleveland (09-12)
   2003-04 Enrollment: 619 . . . . (216) 431-7571
Life Skills Center of Lake Erie (09-12)
   2003-04 Enrollment: 576 . . . . (216) 631-1090
Lorain Academy for Gifted Students
   2003-04 Enrollment: n/a
Madison Community School
   2003-04 Enrollment: n/a
Mansfield Academy for Gifted Students
   2003-04 Enrollment: n/a
Marcus Garvey Academy (06-08)
   2003-04 Enrollment: 59 . . . . (216) 451-7995

Mayfield City SD (PK-12)
   2003-04 Enrollment: 4,331 . . . . (440) 995-6800
Old Brooklyn Montessori School (KG-08)
   2003-04 Enrollment: 259 . . . . (216) 661-7888
Polaris Joint Vocational SD (09-12)
   2003-04 Enrollment: n/a . . . . (440) 891-7600
Puritas Community School (KG-03)
   2003-04 Enrollment: 62
Rising Star Elementary School
   2003-04 Enrollment: n/a
South Euclid-Lyndhurst City SD (PK-12)
   2003-04 Enrollment: 4,583 . . . . (216) 691-2000
Summit Academy High School Parma
   2003-04 Enrollment: n/a
Village Community School
   2003-04 Enrollment: n/a
Westpark Community-Cleveland (KG-05)
   2003-04 Enrollment: 170 . . . . (216) 688-0271
Westside School for the Arts
   2003-04 Enrollment: n/a

Four-year College(s)
Bryant and Stratton College-Cleveland (Private, For-profit)
   Fall 2004 Enrollment: 254 . . . . (216) 771-1700
   2005-06 Tuition: In-state $11,820; Out-of-state $11,820
Case Western Reserve University (Private, Not-for-profit)
   Fall 2004 Enrollment: 9,095 . . . . (216) 368-2000
   2005-06 Tuition: In-state $28,678; Out-of-state $28,678
Cleveland Institute of Art (Private, Not-for-profit)
   Fall 2004 Enrollment: 607 . . . . (216) 421-7000
   2005-06 Tuition: In-state $27,017; Out-of-state $27,017
Cleveland Institute of Music (Private, Not-for-profit)
   Fall 2004 Enrollment: 422 . . . . (216) 791-5000
   2005-06 Tuition: In-state $27,860; Out-of-state $27,860
Cleveland State University (Public)
   Fall 2004 Enrollment: 15,664 . . . . (216) 687-2000
   2005-06 Tuition: In-state $7,394; Out-of-state $13,850
David N Myers University (Private, Not-for-profit)
   Fall 2004 Enrollment: 1,004 . . . . (216) 391-6937
   2005-06 Tuition: In-state $12,300; Out-of-state $12,300
John Carroll University (Private, Not-for-profit, Roman Catholic)
   Fall 2004 Enrollment: 4,101 . . . . (216) 397-1886
   2005-06 Tuition: In-state $23,630; Out-of-state $23,630
Notre Dame College (Private, Not-for-profit, Roman Catholic)
   Fall 2004 Enrollment: 1,299 . . . . (216) 381-1680
   2005-06 Tuition: In-state $19,220; Out-of-state $19,220
Ohio College of Podiatric Medicine (Private, Not-for-profit)
   Fall 2004 Enrollment: 244 . . . . (216) 231-3300
The Cleveland Clinic Foundation-Dietetic Internship (Private, Not-for-profit)
   Fall 2004 Enrollment: 6 . . . . (216) 444-6487

Two-year College(s)
Academy of Court Reporting-Cleveland (Private, For-profit)
   Fall 2004 Enrollment: 483 . . . . (216) 861-3222
   2005-06 Tuition: In-state $8,000; Out-of-state $8,000
Beatrice Academy of Beauty (Private, For-profit)
   Fall 2004 Enrollment: 21 . . . . (216) 421-2313
Central School of Practical Nursing (Private, For-profit)
   Fall 2004 Enrollment: 87 . . . . (216) 391-8434
Cleveland Institute of Dental-Medical Assistants (Private, For-profit)
   Fall 2004 Enrollment: 182 . . . . (216) 241-2930
Cleveland Municipal School District Adult and Cont (Public)
   Fall 2004 Enrollment: 125 . . . . (216) 634-2157
Cuyahoga Community College District (Public)
   Fall 2004 Enrollment: 24,664 . . . . (800) 954-8742
   2005-06 Tuition: In-state $3,042; Out-of-state $6,228
Huron School of Nursing (Private, Not-for-profit)
   Fall 2004 Enrollment: 193 . . . . (216) 761-7996
   2005-06 Tuition: In-state $7,236; Out-of-state $7,236
Lincoln Welding School (Private, Not-for-profit)
   Fall 2004 Enrollment: n/a . . . . (216) 481-8100
Ohio Technical College (Private, For-profit)
   Fall 2004 Enrollment: 613 . . . . (216) 881-1700
Remington College-Cleveland Campus (Private, For-profit)
   Fall 2004 Enrollment: 657 . . . . (216) 475-7520
Vocational Guidance Services (Private, Not-for-profit)
   Fall 2004 Enrollment: 32 . . . . (216) 431-7800

Housing: Homeownership rate: 48.5% (2005); Median home value: $84,970 (2005); Median rent: $379 per month (2000); Median age of housing: 60 years (2000).
Hospitals: Cleveland Clinic (1113 beds); Cleveland Clinic Children's Hospital for Rehabilitation (52 beds); Columbia St. Vincent Charity Hospital (492 beds); Deaconess Hospital LLC; Fairview Hospital (511 beds); Grace Hospital (87 beds); Hillcrest Hospital/Cleveland Clinic Health System (311 beds); Lakewood Hospital (410 beds); Louis Stokes Cleveland Veterans Affairs (688 beds); Lutheran Hospital (209 beds); Marymount Hospital (279 beds); Meridia Euclid Hospital (377 beds); Meridia Huron Hospital (346 beds); MetroHealth Medical Center (728 beds); Northcoast Behavioral Health Care Systems - Cleveland Campus (399 beds); Parma Community General Hospital (348 beds); Saint Luke's Medical Center (474 beds); University Hospitals of Cleveland (1009 beds)
Safety: Violent crime rate: 129.4 per 10,000 population; Property crime rate: 584.3 per 10,000 population (2004).
Newspapers: Cincinnati Call and Post (General - Circulation 12,000); Cleveland Call and Post (Black - Circulation 32,000); Cleveland Free Times (Alternative - Circulation 90,000); Cleveland Jewish News (General, Jewish, Religious - Circulation 15,500); Columbus Call and Post (Black, General - Circulation 13,753); Daily Legal News (Circulation 1,000); Dirva (Ethnic, General - Circulation 2,500); State Edition Call and Post (General - Circulation 10,000); The Plain Dealer (Circulation 354,309)
Transportation: Commute to work: 81.3% car, 12.0% public transportation, 4.0% walk, 1.6% work from home (2000); Travel time to work: 22.0% less than 15 minutes, 45.0% 15 to 30 minutes, 20.7% 30 to 45 minutes, 5.6% 45 to 60 minutes, 6.7% 60 minutes or more (2000); Amtrak: Service available.

Additional Information Contacts
City of Cleveland . . . . (216) 664-3990
   http://www.city.cleveland.oh.us
Convention & Visitors Bureau of Greater Cleveland . . . . . . (216) 621-4110
   http://www.travelcleveland.com
Greater Cleveland Partnership . . . . (216) 621-3300
   http://www.clevelandgrowth.com
Heights Regional Chamber of Commerce . . . . (216) 397-7322
   http://www.hrcc.org
Middleburg Heights Chamber . . . . (440) 243-5599
   http://middleburgheightschamber.com
Solon Chamber of Commerce . . . . (440) 248-5080
   http://www.solonchamber.com
Westshore Chamber of Commerce . . . . (440) 835-8787
   http://www.westshorechamber.org

CLEVELAND HEIGHTS (city).
Covers a land area of 8.110 square miles and a water area of 0.015 square miles. Located at 41.51° N. Lat.; 81.56° W. Long. Elevation is 950 feet.
History: Named for Moses Cleaveland (1754-1806), surveyor of the Western Reserve. Cleveland Heights was established in 1905, and became a city in 1921. It grew as a collection of neighborhoods serving as residential suburbs for Cleveland.
Population: 54,052 (1990); 49,958 (2000); 47,431 (2005); 44,980 (2010 projected); Race: 49.8% White, 43.6% Black, 3.0% Asian, 1.7% Hispanic of any race (2005); Density: 5,848.6 persons per square mile (2005); Average household size: 2.35 (2005); Median age: 37.0 (2005); Males per 100 females: 87.7 (2005); Marriage status: 36.7% never married, 47.5% now married, 6.1% widowed, 9.7% divorced (2000); Foreign born: 8.3% (2000); Ancestry (includes multiple ancestries): 44.5% Other groups, 12.1% German, 10.3% Irish, 7.5% English, 5.8% Italian (2000).
Economy: Unemployment rate: 4.6% (2005); Total civilian labor force: 27,735 (2005); Single-family building permits issued: 6 (2005); Multi-family building permits issued: 0 (2005); Employment by occupation: 15.3% management, 38.2% professional, 12.0% services, 22.6% sales, 0.0% farming, 3.3% construction, 8.6% production (2000).
Income: Per capita income: $29,789 (2005); Median household income: $51,138 (2005); Average household income: $69,604 (2005); Percent of households with income of $100,000 or more: 18.7% (2005); Poverty rate: 10.6% (2000).
Taxes: Total city taxes per capita: $640 (2004); City property taxes per capita: $218 (2004).
Education: Percent of population age 25 and over with: High school diploma (including GED) or higher: 91.6% (2005); Bachelor's degree or higher: 50.0% (2005); Master's degree or higher: 25.3% (2005).

School District(s)

Casa De Sol Community
  2003-04 Enrollment: n/a
Cleveland Hts-Univ Hts City SD (KG-12)
  2003-04 Enrollment: 6,887 . . . . (216) 371-7171

Housing: Homeownership rate: 62.8% (2005); Median home value: $134,303 (2005); Median rent: $580 per month (2000); Median age of housing: 60+ years (2000).

Safety: Violent crime rate: 2.6 per 10,000 population; Property crime rate: 136.2 per 10,000 population (2004).

Transportation: Commute to work: 85.7% car, 5.8% public transportation, 3.6% walk, 3.8% work from home (2000); Travel time to work: 22.3% less than 15 minutes, 44.3% 15 to 30 minutes, 23.8% 30 to 45 minutes, 4.9% 45 to 60 minutes, 4.7% 60 minutes or more (2000)

Additional Information Contacts
City of Cleveland Heights. . . . . (216) 291-4444
  http://www.clevelandheights.com

CUYAHOGA HEIGHTS (village). Covers a land area of 3.208 square miles and a water area of 0 square miles. Located at 41.43° N. Lat.; 81.65° W. Long. Elevation is 718 feet.

Population: 682 (1990); 599 (2000); 568 (2005); 537 (2010 projected); Race: 98.1% White, 0.0% Black, 1.2% Asian, 0.0% Hispanic of any race (2005); Density: 177.0 persons per square mile (2005); Average household size: 2.25 (2005); Median age: 44.1 (2005); Males per 100 females: 91.2 (2005); Marriage status: 25.1% never married, 48.4% now married, 12.2% widowed, 14.3% divorced (2000); Foreign born: 6.3% (2000); Ancestry (includes multiple ancestries): 39.9% Polish, 21.0% Italian, 15.9% German, 12.2% Irish, 6.0% Slovak (2000).

Economy: Industrial village. Single-family building permits issued: 0 (2005); Multi-family building permits issued: 0 (2005); Employment by occupation: 13.6% management, 10.7% professional, 24.3% services, 30.1% sales, 0.0% farming, 7.4% construction, 14.0% production (2000).

Income: Per capita income: $22,126 (2005); Median household income: $42,692 (2005); Average household income: $49,871 (2005); Percent of households with income of $100,000 or more: 7.5% (2005); Poverty rate: 5.7% (2000).

Education: Percent of population age 25 and over with: High school diploma (including GED) or higher: 81.8% (2005); Bachelor's degree or higher: 9.6% (2005); Master's degree or higher: 2.2% (2005).

Housing: Homeownership rate: 74.6% (2005); Median home value: $130,380 (2005); Median rent: $427 per month (2000); Median age of housing: 57 years (2000).

Transportation: Commute to work: 90.0% car, 0.0% public transportation, 7.4% walk, 2.2% work from home (2000); Travel time to work: 56.1% less than 15 minutes, 33.0% 15 to 30 minutes, 8.7% 30 to 45 minutes, 1.5% 45 to 60 minutes, 0.8% 60 minutes or more (2000)

EAST CLEVELAND (city). Covers a land area of 3.106 square miles and a water area of 0 square miles. Located at 41.53° N. Lat.; 81.58° W. Long. Elevation is 820 feet.

History: Named for its location east of Cleveland. The original East Cleveland was annexed by Cleveland in 1872, and the name disappeared from the map until 1892, when the neighboring Collamer became East Cleveland Hamlet. In 1911 the village became a city.

Population: 33,096 (1990); 27,217 (2000); 25,814 (2005); 24,428 (2010 projected); Race: 4.6% White, 93.0% Black, 0.2% Asian, 0.8% Hispanic of any race (2005); Density: 8,310.2 persons per square mile (2005); Average household size: 2.40 (2005); Median age: 35.0 (2005); Males per 100 females: 80.4 (2005); Marriage status: 42.3% never married, 32.0% now married, 10.5% widowed, 15.3% divorced (2000); Foreign born: 2.9% (2000); Ancestry (includes multiple ancestries): 80.1% Other groups, 1.1% African, 1.1% United States or American, 0.7% German, 0.6% Italian (2000).

Economy: Unemployment rate: 8.3% (2005); Total civilian labor force: 9,959 (2005); Single-family building permits issued: 2 (2005); Multi-family building permits issued: 0 (2005); Employment by occupation: 6.6% management, 13.8% professional, 27.4% services, 27.2% sales, 0.0% farming, 6.0% construction, 19.0% production (2000).

Income: Per capita income: $13,488 (2005); Median household income: $22,123 (2005); Average household income: $31,864 (2005); Percent of households with income of $100,000 or more: 3.5% (2005); Poverty rate: 32.0% (2000).

Taxes: Total city taxes per capita: $386 (2004); City property taxes per capita: $72 (2004).

Education: Percent of population age 25 and over with: High school diploma (including GED) or higher: 69.1% (2005); Bachelor's degree or higher: 8.9% (2005); Master's degree or higher: 3.7% (2005).

School District(s)

East Cleveland City SD (PK-12)
  2003-04 Enrollment: 5,092 . . . . (216) 268-6570

Housing: Homeownership rate: 34.9% (2005); Median home value: $79,053 (2005); Median rent: $397 per month (2000); Median age of housing: 56 years (2000).

Safety: Violent crime rate: 23.9 per 10,000 population; Property crime rate: 2.7 per 10,000 population (2004).

Transportation: Commute to work: 75.5% car, 17.9% public transportation, 3.9% walk, 1.9% work from home (2000); Travel time to work: 17.8% less than 15 minutes, 37.6% 15 to 30 minutes, 26.8% 30 to 45 minutes, 8.1% 45 to 60 minutes, 9.7% 60 minutes or more (2000)

EUCLID (city). Covers a land area of 10.708 square miles and a water area of 0.858 square miles. Located at 41.59° N. Lat.; 81.51° W. Long. Elevation is 618 feet.

History: Euclid was settled in 1798 and named for the Greek mathematician by surveyors in the party of Moses Cleaveland. Euclid developed as a residential community near Cleveland.

Population: 54,875 (1990); 52,717 (2000); 50,579 (2005); 48,413 (2010 projected); Race: 60.3% White, 36.1% Black, 1.1% Asian, 1.2% Hispanic of any race (2005); Density: 4,723.5 persons per square mile (2005); Average household size: 2.15 (2005); Median age: 40.5 (2005); Males per 100 females: 84.8 (2005); Marriage status: 30.3% never married, 45.8% now married, 10.4% widowed, 13.5% divorced (2000); Foreign born: 5.3% (2000); Ancestry (includes multiple ancestries): 29.9% Other groups, 15.2% German, 12.6% Irish, 9.6% Italian, 8.8% Slovene (2000).

Economy: Unemployment rate: 6.2% (2005); Total civilian labor force: 26,000 (2005); Single-family building permits issued: 9 (2005); Multi-family building permits issued: 0 (2005); Employment by occupation: 11.9% management, 18.7% professional, 15.2% services, 30.8% sales, 0.0% farming, 6.8% construction, 16.5% production (2000).

Income: Per capita income: $21,440 (2005); Median household income: $37,719 (2005); Average household income: $45,894 (2005); Percent of households with income of $100,000 or more: 6.6% (2005); Poverty rate: 9.7% (2000).

Taxes: Total city taxes per capita: $544 (2004); City property taxes per capita: $185 (2004).

Education: Percent of population age 25 and over with: High school diploma (including GED) or higher: 82.1% (2005); Bachelor's degree or higher: 19.7% (2005); Master's degree or higher: 5.8% (2005).

School District(s)

Euclid City SD (PK-12)
  2003-04 Enrollment: 6,420 . . . . (216) 261-2900

Two-year College(s)

Cleveland Clinic Health System-School of Diagnostic Imaging (Private, Not-for-profit)
  Fall 2004 Enrollment: 37 . . . . (216) 692-8708
Euclid Beauty College (Private, For-profit)
  Fall 2004 Enrollment: 108 . . . . (216) 261-2600

Housing: Homeownership rate: 59.2% (2005); Median home value: $109,599 (2005); Median rent: $483 per month (2000); Median age of housing: 45 years (2000).

Hospitals: Euclid Hospital (371 beds)

Safety: Violent crime rate: 38.0 per 10,000 population; Property crime rate: 344.4 per 10,000 population (2004).

Transportation: Commute to work: 90.6% car, 5.7% public transportation, 1.7% walk, 1.5% work from home (2000); Travel time to work: 25.1% less than 15 minutes, 43.3% 15 to 30 minutes, 22.7% 30 to 45 minutes, 4.2% 45 to 60 minutes, 4.8% 60 minutes or more (2000)

Additional Information Contacts
City of Euclid . . . . (216) 289-2751
  http://www.ci.euclid.oh.us
Euclid Chamber of Commerce. . . . . (216) 731-9322
  http://www.euclidchamberofcommerce.com

FAIRVIEW PARK (city). Aka Fairview. Covers a land area of 4.696 square miles and a water area of 0 square miles. Located at 41.44° N. Lat.; 81.85° W. Long. Elevation is 750 feet.

History: Named to promote the town as a good place to live. Incorporated 1950.

Population: 18,028 (1990); 17,572 (2000); 16,855 (2005); 16,149 (2010 projected); Race: 95.1% White, 0.8% Black, 1.9% Asian, 1.6% Hispanic of any race (2005); Density: 3,589.5 persons per square mile (2005); Average household size: 2.21 (2005); Median age: 42.3 (2005); Males per 100 females: 89.3 (2005); Marriage status: 25.7% never married, 55.7% now married, 8.8% widowed, 9.8% divorced (2000); Foreign born: 5.8% (2000); Ancestry (includes multiple ancestries): 29.7% German, 26.7% Irish, 10.7% English, 8.9% Polish, 8.8% Italian (2000).
Economy: A residential suburb of Cleveland. Single-family building permits issued: 2 (2005); Multi-family building permits issued: 0 (2005); Employment by occupation: 16.1% management, 25.2% professional, 10.6% services, 31.7% sales, 0.1% farming, 6.7% construction, 9.6% production (2000).
Income: Per capita income: $29,609 (2005); Median household income: $55,183 (2005); Average household income: $65,208 (2005); Percent of households with income of $100,000 or more: 16.7% (2005); Poverty rate: 4.1% (2000).
Taxes: Total city taxes per capita: $527 (2004); City property taxes per capita: $223 (2004).
Education: Percent of population age 25 and over with: High school diploma (including GED) or higher: 91.6% (2005); Bachelor's degree or higher: 36.7% (2005); Master's degree or higher: 11.9% (2005).

School District(s)
Fairview Park City SD (PK-12)
    2003-04 Enrollment: 1,831 . . . . (440) 331-5500

Two-year College(s)
Fairview Beauty Academy (Private, For-profit)
    Fall 2004 Enrollment: 60 . . . . (216) 734-5555

Housing: Homeownership rate: 73.8% (2005); Median home value: $158,765 (2005); Median rent: $527 per month (2000); Median age of housing: 44 years (2000).
Transportation: Commute to work: 90.5% car, 4.5% public transportation, 1.6% walk, 3.0% work from home (2000); Travel time to work: 28.7% less than 15 minutes, 40.2% 15 to 30 minutes, 21.5% 30 to 45 minutes, 6.4% 45 to 60 minutes, 3.3% 60 minutes or more (2000)
Additional Information Contacts
City of Fairview Park . . . . (440) 333-2200
  http://www.fairviewpark.org

GARFIELD HEIGHTS (city).
Covers a land area of 7.226 square miles and a water area of 0.081 square miles. Located at 41.42° N. Lat.; 81.60° W. Long. Elevation is 900 feet.
History: Founded 1904, incorporated 1932.
Population: 31,739 (1990); 30,734 (2000); 29,471 (2005); 28,215 (2010 projected); Race: 79.7% White, 17.3% Black, 1.2% Asian, 1.3% Hispanic of any race (2005); Density: 4,078.2 persons per square mile (2005); Average household size: 2.44 (2005); Median age: 39.5 (2005); Males per 100 females: 88.3 (2005); Marriage status: 26.6% never married, 52.8% now married, 10.4% widowed, 10.2% divorced (2000); Foreign born: 4.4% (2000); Ancestry (includes multiple ancestries): 26.1% Polish, 17.4% Other groups, 14.9% German, 14.0% Italian, 10.2% Irish (2000).
Economy: Oil refineries and steel industry. Unemployment rate: 6.5% (2005); Total civilian labor force: 15,007 (2005); Single-family building permits issued: 18 (2005); Multi-family building permits issued: 0 (2005); Employment by occupation: 9.7% management, 14.2% professional, 15.1% services, 34.6% sales, 0.0% farming, 8.0% construction, 18.3% production (2000).
Income: Per capita income: $21,232 (2005); Median household income: $43,949 (2005); Average household income: $51,376 (2005); Percent of households with income of $100,000 or more: 7.6% (2005); Poverty rate: 8.5% (2000).
Taxes: Total city taxes per capita: $559 (2004); City property taxes per capita: $251 (2004).
Education: Percent of population age 25 and over with: High school diploma (including GED) or higher: 80.1% (2005); Bachelor's degree or higher: 11.9% (2005); Master's degree or higher: 3.3% (2005).

School District(s)
Cleveland Municipal City SD (PK-12)
    2003-04 Enrollment: 69,655 . . . . (216) 574-8000
Garfield Heights City SD (PK-12)
    2003-04 Enrollment: 3,859 . . . . (216) 475-8100

Housing: Homeownership rate: 79.7% (2005); Median home value: $107,963 (2005); Median rent: $483 per month (2000); Median age of housing: 47 years (2000).
Hospitals: Marymount Hospital (312 beds)
Safety: Violent crime rate: 31.4 per 10,000 population; Property crime rate: 279.9 per 10,000 population (2004).
Transportation: Commute to work: 92.5% car, 3.2% public transportation, 2.0% walk, 1.6% work from home (2000); Travel time to work: 25.5% less than 15 minutes, 47.0% 15 to 30 minutes, 20.5% 30 to 45 minutes, 3.2% 45 to 60 minutes, 3.9% 60 minutes or more (2000)
Additional Information Contacts
City of Garfield Heights . . . . (216) 475-1100
  http://www.garfieldhts.org
Garfield Heights Chamber of Commerce . . . . (216) 475-7775
  http://chamberplace.ghiis.com/1003/index.cfm

GATES MILLS (village).
Covers a land area of 9.093 square miles and a water area of 0.005 square miles. Located at 41.53° N. Lat.; 81.41° W. Long. Elevation is 750 feet.
Population: 2,508 (1990); 2,493 (2000); 2,404 (2005); 2,311 (2010 projected); Race: 92.6% White, 1.2% Black, 4.5% Asian, 1.6% Hispanic of any race (2005); Density: 264.4 persons per square mile (2005); Average household size: 2.68 (2005); Median age: 48.4 (2005); Males per 100 females: 96.9 (2005); Marriage status: 17.3% never married, 71.8% now married, 4.8% widowed, 6.0% divorced (2000); Foreign born: 12.3% (2000); Ancestry (includes multiple ancestries): 14.9% Irish, 14.3% German, 12.8% Italian, 12.5% English, 9.8% Other groups (2000).
Economy: Single-family building permits issued: 2 (2005); Multi-family building permits issued: 0 (2005); Employment by occupation: 32.5% management, 35.2% professional, 5.4% services, 23.1% sales, 0.0% farming, 1.3% construction, 2.4% production (2000).
Income: Per capita income: $75,419 (2005); Median household income: $142,164 (2005); Average household income: $199,972 (2005); Percent of households with income of $100,000 or more: 62.6% (2005); Poverty rate: 1.1% (2000).
Education: Percent of population age 25 and over with: High school diploma (including GED) or higher: 96.0% (2005); Bachelor's degree or higher: 66.6% (2005); Master's degree or higher: 37.0% (2005).

School District(s)
Mayfield City SD (PK-12)
    2003-04 Enrollment: 4,331 . . . . (440) 995-6800

Housing: Homeownership rate: 92.7% (2005); Median home value: $491,667 (2005); Median rent: $703 per month (2000); Median age of housing: 36 years (2000).
Safety: Violent crime rate: 0.0 per 10,000 population; Property crime rate: 12.3 per 10,000 population (2004).
Transportation: Commute to work: 83.5% car, 4.5% public transportation, 1.1% walk, 9.8% work from home (2000); Travel time to work: 17.4% less than 15 minutes, 33.8% 15 to 30 minutes, 33.2% 30 to 45 minutes, 8.5% 45 to 60 minutes, 7.1% 60 minutes or more (2000)

GLENWILLOW (village).
Aka Falls Junction. Covers a land area of 2.715 square miles and a water area of 0.005 square miles. Located at 41.36° N. Lat.; 81.47° W. Long. Elevation is 950 feet.
Population: 455 (1990); 449 (2000); 520 (2005); 582 (2010 projected); Race: 92.9% White, 5.4% Black, 0.0% Asian, 0.8% Hispanic of any race (2005); Density: 191.5 persons per square mile (2005); Average household size: 2.16 (2005); Median age: 42.7 (2005); Males per 100 females: 113.1 (2005); Marriage status: 25.4% never married, 51.6% now married, 6.1% widowed, 17.0% divorced (2000); Foreign born: 1.1% (2000); Ancestry (includes multiple ancestries): 21.8% German, 13.0% Italian, 11.2% Irish, 10.8% Polish, 9.2% English (2000).
Economy: Single-family building permits issued: 20 (2005); Multi-family building permits issued: 0 (2005); Employment by occupation: 12.0% management, 10.3% professional, 20.2% services, 28.8% sales, 0.0% farming, 13.3% construction, 15.5% production (2000).
Income: Per capita income: $23,897 (2005); Median household income: $44,214 (2005); Average household income: $50,954 (2005); Percent of households with income of $100,000 or more: 7.9% (2005); Poverty rate: 5.0% (2000).
Education: Percent of population age 25 and over with: High school diploma (including GED) or higher: 90.2% (2005); Bachelor's degree or higher: 16.9% (2005); Master's degree or higher: 2.1% (2005).
Housing: Homeownership rate: 75.5% (2005); Median home value: $126,471 (2005); Median rent: $194 per month (2000); Median age of housing: 40 years (2000).
Transportation: Commute to work: 97.4% car, 0.9% public transportation, 0.0% walk, 1.8% work from home (2000); Travel time to work: 33.2% less

than 15 minutes, 41.3% 15 to 30 minutes, 19.7% 30 to 45 minutes, 2.2% 45 to 60 minutes, 3.6% 60 minutes or more (2000)

HIGHLAND HEIGHTS (city). Covers a land area of 5.131 square miles and a water area of <.001 square miles. Located at 41.55° N. Lat.; 81.47° W. Long. Elevation is 934 feet.
Population: 6,249 (1990); 8,082 (2000); 8,676 (2005); 9,203 (2010 projected); Race: 90.9% White, 1.8% Black, 6.3% Asian, 0.4% Hispanic of any race (2005); Density: 1,690.8 persons per square mile (2005); Average household size: 2.91 (2005); Median age: 43.5 (2005); Males per 100 females: 95.5 (2005); Marriage status: 20.8% never married, 66.4% now married, 8.5% widowed, 4.3% divorced (2000); Foreign born: 11.1% (2000); Ancestry (includes multiple ancestries): 31.3% Italian, 16.0% German, 10.4% Irish, 9.0% Other groups, 8.6% Polish (2000).
Economy: Single-family building permits issued: 41 (2005); Multi-family building permits issued: 20 (2005); Employment by occupation: 20.8% management, 30.6% professional, 10.1% services, 29.7% sales, 0.2% farming, 4.6% construction, 4.0% production (2000).
Income: Per capita income: $37,862 (2005); Median household income: $84,669 (2005); Average household income: $109,860 (2005); Percent of households with income of $100,000 or more: 41.5% (2005); Poverty rate: 4.0% (2000).
Education: Percent of population age 25 and over with: High school diploma (including GED) or higher: 89.9% (2005); Bachelor's degree or higher: 42.5% (2005); Master's degree or higher: 20.0% (2005).
Two-year College(s)
ATS Institute of Technology
    Fall 2004 Enrollment: 349 . . . . (440) 449-1700
    2005-06 Tuition: In-state $9,570; Out-of-state $9,570
Housing: Homeownership rate: 97.3% (2005); Median home value: $268,809 (2005); Median rent: $828 per month (2000); Median age of housing: 30 years (2000).
Safety: Violent crime rate: 2.3 per 10,000 population; Property crime rate: 107.9 per 10,000 population (2004).
Transportation: Commute to work: 92.3% car, 1.0% public transportation, 0.9% walk, 5.1% work from home (2000); Travel time to work: 32.9% less than 15 minutes, 45.1% 15 to 30 minutes, 18.9% 30 to 45 minutes, 1.8% 45 to 60 minutes, 1.3% 60 minutes or more (2000)

HIGHLAND HILLS (village). Covers a land area of 1.978 square miles and a water area of 0.003 square miles. Located at 41.44° N. Lat.; 81.52° W. Long. Elevation is 1,106 feet.
Population: 1,677 (1990); 1,618 (2000); 1,625 (2005); 1,594 (2010 projected); Race: 29.4% White, 66.1% Black, 0.8% Asian, 1.8% Hispanic of any race (2005); Density: 821.7 persons per square mile (2005); Average household size: 6.53 (2005); Median age: 39.8 (2005); Males per 100 females: 203.2 (2005); Marriage status: 56.4% never married, 25.7% now married, 8.9% widowed, 9.0% divorced (2000); Foreign born: 0.7% (2000); Ancestry (includes multiple ancestries): 45.0% Other groups, 7.4% German, 5.2% English, 5.1% Hungarian, 2.2% Dutch (2000).
Economy: Single-family building permits issued: 0 (2005); Multi-family building permits issued: 0 (2005); Employment by occupation: 11.5% management, 14.2% professional, 19.9% services, 26.1% sales, 0.0% farming, 7.5% construction, 20.8% production (2000).
Income: Per capita income: $14,318 (2005); Median household income: $38,167 (2005); Average household income: $49,227 (2005); Percent of households with income of $100,000 or more: 8.4% (2005); Poverty rate: 22.9% (2000).
Education: Percent of population age 25 and over with: High school diploma (including GED) or higher: 61.4% (2005); Bachelor's degree or higher: 18.7% (2005); Master's degree or higher: 5.7% (2005).
School District(s)
Department of Youth Services (06-12)
    2003-04 Enrollment: 1,333 . . . . (614) 728-2489
Housing: Homeownership rate: 53.4% (2005); Median home value: $106,746 (2005); Median rent: $469 per month (2000); Median age of housing: 44 years (2000).
Safety: Violent crime rate: 18.7 per 10,000 population; Property crime rate: 6.2 per 10,000 population (2004).
Transportation: Commute to work: 90.5% car, 7.7% public transportation, 1.8% walk, 0.0% work from home (2000); Travel time to work: 16.3% less than 15 minutes, 43.0% 15 to 30 minutes, 29.4% 30 to 45 minutes, 5.9% 45 to 60 minutes, 5.4% 60 minutes or more (2000)
Additional Information Contacts

Tri-City Chamber of Commerce . . . . (216) 454-0199
http://www.tricitychamber.com

HUNTING VALLEY (village). Covers a land area of 7.980 square miles and a water area of 0.002 square miles. Located at 41.47° N. Lat.; 81.40° W. Long. Elevation is 772 feet.
Population: 799 (1990); 735 (2000); 710 (2005); 684 (2010 projected); Race: 99.0% White, 0.1% Black, 0.7% Asian, 0.4% Hispanic of any race (2005); Density: 89.0 persons per square mile (2005); Average household size: 2.56 (2005); Median age: 52.3 (2005); Males per 100 females: 102.9 (2005); Marriage status: 16.2% never married, 74.3% now married, 6.2% widowed, 3.3% divorced (2000); Foreign born: 5.0% (2000); Ancestry (includes multiple ancestries): 23.3% English, 22.3% German, 15.5% Irish, 7.5% Italian, 6.5% Russian (2000).
Economy: Single-family building permits issued: 2 (2005); Multi-family building permits issued: 0 (2005); Employment by occupation: 36.5% management, 30.0% professional, 8.8% services, 17.9% sales, 1.3% farming, 3.3% construction, 2.3% production (2000).
Income: Per capita income: $114,338 (2005); Median household income: $260,135 (2005); Average household income: $293,069 (2005); Percent of households with income of $100,000 or more: 71.1% (2005); Poverty rate: 2.3% (2000).
Education: Percent of population age 25 and over with: High school diploma (including GED) or higher: 98.4% (2005); Bachelor's degree or higher: 73.4% (2005); Master's degree or higher: 34.9% (2005).
Housing: Homeownership rate: 85.9% (2005); Median home value: $1 million+ (2005); Median rent: $725 per month (2000); Median age of housing: 42 years (2000).
Safety: Violent crime rate: 0.0 per 10,000 population; Property crime rate: 27.9 per 10,000 population (2004).
Transportation: Commute to work: 85.7% car, 0.0% public transportation, 4.7% walk, 8.3% work from home (2000); Travel time to work: 29.7% less than 15 minutes, 28.3% 15 to 30 minutes, 32.6% 30 to 45 minutes, 6.5% 45 to 60 minutes, 2.9% 60 minutes or more (2000)

INDEPENDENCE (city). Covers a land area of 9.586 square miles and a water area of 0 square miles. Located at 41.38° N. Lat.; 81.64° W. Long. Elevation is 856 feet.
Population: 6,500 (1990); 7,109 (2000); 7,079 (2005); 7,019 (2010 projected); Race: 97.1% White, 0.7% Black, 1.7% Asian, 0.8% Hispanic of any race (2005); Density: 738.5 persons per square mile (2005); Average household size: 2.63 (2005); Median age: 45.5 (2005); Males per 100 females: 90.3 (2005); Marriage status: 22.3% never married, 63.9% now married, 9.0% widowed, 4.8% divorced (2000); Foreign born: 5.3% (2000); Ancestry (includes multiple ancestries): 32.3% Polish, 20.2% German, 16.7% Italian, 10.7% Irish, 7.3% English (2000).
Economy: Chemical manufacturing headquarters. Single-family building permits issued: 21 (2005); Multi-family building permits issued: 0 (2005); Employment by occupation: 20.0% management, 25.4% professional, 7.9% services, 29.4% sales, 0.3% farming, 8.1% construction, 8.9% production (2000).
Income: Per capita income: $30,540 (2005); Median household income: $65,980 (2005); Average household income: $79,896 (2005); Percent of households with income of $100,000 or more: 30.3% (2005); Poverty rate: 3.6% (2000).
Taxes: Total city taxes per capita: $2,982 (2004); City property taxes per capita: $349 (2004).
Education: Percent of population age 25 and over with: High school diploma (including GED) or higher: 88.9% (2005); Bachelor's degree or higher: 28.9% (2005); Master's degree or higher: 10.7% (2005).
School District(s)
Independence Local SD (PK-12)
    2003-04 Enrollment: 1,141 . . . . (216) 642-5850
Four-year College(s)
University of Phoenix-Cleveland Campus (Private, For-profit)
    Fall 2004 Enrollment: 824 . . . . (216) 447-8807
    2005-06 Tuition: In-state $11,550; Out-of-state $11,550
Housing: Homeownership rate: 94.4% (2005); Median home value: $237,274 (2005); Median rent: $497 per month (2000); Median age of housing: 42 years (2000).
Transportation: Commute to work: 94.8% car, 2.0% public transportation, 0.0% walk, 3.2% work from home (2000); Travel time to work: 25.8% less than 15 minutes, 48.6% 15 to 30 minutes, 20.9% 30 to 45 minutes, 2.0% 45 to 60 minutes, 2.6% 60 minutes or more (2000)
Additional Information Contacts

City of Independence............................(216) 524-4131
http://www.independenceohio.org

LAKEWOOD (city). Covers a land area of 5.549 square miles and a water area of 1.150 square miles. Located at 41.48° N. Lat.; 81.80° W. Long. Elevation is 710 feet.
History: Named for its location on the wooded shores of Lake Erie. Lakewood was known as East Rockport until 1889, when its name was changed to Lakewood, referring to its location on the wooded shore of Lake Erie. Lakewood was incorporated as a city in 1911.
Population: 59,718 (1990); 56,646 (2000); 53,350 (2005); 50,144 (2010 projected); Race: 91.7% White, 2.4% Black, 1.7% Asian, 2.3% Hispanic of any race (2005); Density: 9,614.5 persons per square mile (2005); Average household size: 2.09 (2005); Median age: 36.5 (2005); Males per 100 females: 93.0 (2005); Marriage status: 38.3% never married, 43.1% now married, 6.5% widowed, 12.1% divorced (2000); Foreign born: 8.7% (2000); Ancestry (includes multiple ancestries): 25.2% German, 23.6% Irish, 9.8% English, 8.9% Italian, 7.8% Polish (2000).
Economy: Unemployment rate: 5.0% (2005); Total civilian labor force: 32,809 (2005); Single-family building permits issued: 1 (2005); Multi-family building permits issued: 0 (2005); Employment by occupation: 15.9% management, 25.1% professional, 13.8% services, 28.0% sales, 0.0% farming, 6.7% construction, 10.4% production (2000).
Income: Per capita income: $26,934 (2005); Median household income: $43,940 (2005); Average household income: $55,969 (2005); Percent of households with income of $100,000 or more: 12.0% (2005); Poverty rate: 8.9% (2000).
Taxes: Total city taxes per capita: $537 (2004); City property taxes per capita: $224 (2004).
Education: Percent of population age 25 and over with: High school diploma (including GED) or higher: 88.7% (2005); Bachelor's degree or higher: 35.8% (2005); Master's degree or higher: 12.1% (2005).

School District(s)
Lakewood City SD (PK-12)
   2003-04 Enrollment: 7,083......................(216) 529-4092

Two-year College(s)
Virginia Marti College of Art and Design (Private, For-profit)
   Fall 2004 Enrollment: 252.......................(216) 221-8584
   2005-06 Tuition: In-state $15,960; Out-of-state $15,960

Housing: Homeownership rate: 45.1% (2005); Median home value: $138,852 (2005); Median rent: $492 per month (2000); Median age of housing: 60+ years (2000).
Hospitals: Lakewood Hospital (400 beds)
Safety: Violent crime rate: 22.9 per 10,000 population; Property crime rate: 215.5 per 10,000 population (2004).
Transportation: Commute to work: 85.1% car, 7.8% public transportation, 3.6% walk, 2.6% work from home (2000); Travel time to work: 26.4% less than 15 minutes, 45.9% 15 to 30 minutes, 20.4% 30 to 45 minutes, 4.3% 45 to 60 minutes, 2.9% 60 minutes or more (2000)

Additional Information Contacts
City of Lakewood.................................(216) 521-7580
http://www.ci.lakewood.oh.us
Lakewood Chamber of Commerce...................(216) 226-2900
http://www.lakewoodchamber.org

LINNDALE (village). Covers a land area of 0.088 square miles and a water area of 0 square miles. Located at 41.44° N. Lat.; 81.76° W. Long. Elevation is 760 feet.
Population: 159 (1990); 117 (2000); 115 (2005); 113 (2010 projected); Race: 67.0% White, 17.4% Black, 0.0% Asian, 9.6% Hispanic of any race (2005); Density: 1,310.0 persons per square mile (2005); Average household size: 2.02 (2005); Median age: 36.3 (2005); Males per 100 females: 105.4 (2005); Marriage status: 36.8% never married, 25.3% now married, 12.6% widowed, 25.3% divorced (2000); Foreign born: 0.0% (2000); Ancestry (includes multiple ancestries): 32.2% Other groups, 19.0% Irish, 11.6% German, 7.4% Slovak, 5.8% English (2000).
Economy: Single-family building permits issued: 0 (2005); Multi-family building permits issued: 0 (2005); Employment by occupation: 14.0% management, 10.5% professional, 12.3% services, 15.8% sales, 5.3% farming, 19.3% construction, 22.8% production (2000).
Income: Per capita income: $16,978 (2005); Median household income: $22,500 (2005); Average household income: $34,254 (2005); Percent of households with income of $100,000 or more: 5.3% (2005); Poverty rate: 15.7% (2000).

Education: Percent of population age 25 and over with: High school diploma (including GED) or higher: 76.8% (2005); Bachelor's degree or higher: 0.0% (2005); Master's degree or higher: 0.0% (2005).
Housing: Homeownership rate: 43.9% (2005); Median home value: $74,000 (2005); Median rent: $350 per month (2000); Median age of housing: 60+ years (2000).
Transportation: Commute to work: 80.7% car, 8.8% public transportation, 10.5% walk, 0.0% work from home (2000); Travel time to work: 19.3% less than 15 minutes, 35.1% 15 to 30 minutes, 22.8% 30 to 45 minutes, 8.8% 45 to 60 minutes, 14.0% 60 minutes or more (2000)

LYNDHURST (city). Covers a land area of 4.390 square miles and a water area of 0 square miles. Located at 41.52° N. Lat.; 81.49° W. Long. Elevation is 1,015 feet.
History: Incorporated 1917.
Population: 15,982 (1990); 15,279 (2000); 14,692 (2005); 14,122 (2010 projected); Race: 96.1% White, 1.6% Black, 1.3% Asian, 0.8% Hispanic of any race (2005); Density: 3,346.4 persons per square mile (2005); Average household size: 2.26 (2005); Median age: 45.9 (2005); Males per 100 females: 86.4 (2005); Marriage status: 19.9% never married, 62.1% now married, 11.2% widowed, 6.8% divorced (2000); Foreign born: 7.1% (2000); Ancestry (includes multiple ancestries): 23.9% Italian, 18.4% German, 15.9% Irish, 9.4% English, 8.0% Polish (2000).
Economy: Single-family building permits issued: 10 (2005); Multi-family building permits issued: 0 (2005); Employment by occupation: 20.6% management, 24.1% professional, 10.6% services, 32.5% sales, 0.0% farming, 4.8% construction, 7.5% production (2000).
Income: Per capita income: $30,908 (2005); Median household income: $57,448 (2005); Average household income: $69,281 (2005); Percent of households with income of $100,000 or more: 19.6% (2005); Poverty rate: 2.5% (2000).
Education: Percent of population age 25 and over with: High school diploma (including GED) or higher: 92.9% (2005); Bachelor's degree or higher: 37.8% (2005); Master's degree or higher: 13.6% (2005).

School District(s)
South Euclid-Lyndhurst City SD (PK-12)
   2003-04 Enrollment: 4,583......................(216) 691-2000

Two-year College(s)
Cleveland Institute of Dental-Medical Assistants (Private, For-profit)
   Fall 2004 Enrollment: 92........................(216) 241-2930
Inner State Beauty School (Private, For-profit)
   Fall 2004 Enrollment: 43........................(440) 461-1000

Housing: Homeownership rate: 88.7% (2005); Median home value: $158,711 (2005); Median rent: $748 per month (2000); Median age of housing: 44 years (2000).
Safety: Violent crime rate: 0.7 per 10,000 population; Property crime rate: 27.5 per 10,000 population (2004).
Transportation: Commute to work: 93.5% car, 1.5% public transportation, 0.5% walk, 4.2% work from home (2000); Travel time to work: 30.5% less than 15 minutes, 43.6% 15 to 30 minutes, 18.9% 30 to 45 minutes, 4.9% 45 to 60 minutes, 2.0% 60 minutes or more (2000)

MAPLE HEIGHTS (city). Covers a land area of 5.191 square miles and a water area of 0 square miles. Located at 41.41° N. Lat.; 81.56° W. Long. Elevation is 936 feet.
History: Named for its abundance of maple trees. Incorporated 1932.
Population: 27,089 (1990); 26,156 (2000); 25,175 (2005); 24,157 (2010 projected); Race: 43.7% White, 51.5% Black, 2.2% Asian, 1.3% Hispanic of any race (2005); Density: 4,850.1 persons per square mile (2005); Average household size: 2.48 (2005); Median age: 38.8 (2005); Males per 100 females: 88.2 (2005); Marriage status: 27.4% never married, 52.1% now married, 10.0% widowed, 10.6% divorced (2000); Foreign born: 2.9% (2000); Ancestry (includes multiple ancestries): 42.4% Other groups, 10.0% Italian, 9.9% Polish, 8.6% German, 6.4% Irish (2000).
Economy: Chiefly a residential suburb of Cleveland, major shopping centers and miscellaneous manufacturing. Unemployment rate: 6.4% (2005); Total civilian labor force: 12,872 (2005); Single-family building permits issued: 14 (2005); Multi-family building permits issued: 0 (2005); Employment by occupation: 9.7% management, 15.5% professional, 14.8% services, 30.6% sales, 0.2% farming, 7.2% construction, 21.9% production (2000).
Income: Per capita income: $20,351 (2005); Median household income: $43,831 (2005); Average household income: $50,170 (2005); Percent of households with income of $100,000 or more: 7.0% (2005); Poverty rate: 5.9% (2000).

Taxes: Total city taxes per capita: $472 (2004); City property taxes per capita: $186 (2004).
Education: Percent of population age 25 and over with: High school diploma (including GED) or higher: 82.2% (2005); Bachelor's degree or higher: 12.9% (2005); Master's degree or higher: 3.0% (2005).

School District(s)

A World of Learning
   2003-04 Enrollment: n/a
Maple Heights City SD (PK-12)
   2003-04 Enrollment: 3,686 . . . . (216) 587-6100
Housing: Homeownership rate: 83.7% (2005); Median home value: $98,297 (2005); Median rent: $462 per month (2000); Median age of housing: 45 years (2000).
Transportation: Commute to work: 92.8% car, 4.1% public transportation, 1.5% walk, 1.0% work from home (2000); Travel time to work: 24.9% less than 15 minutes, 43.6% 15 to 30 minutes, 21.7% 30 to 45 minutes, 5.9% 45 to 60 minutes, 3.9% 60 minutes or more (2000)

Additional Information Contacts

City of Maple Heights . . . . (216) 662-6000
   http://www.mapleheightsohio.com

MAYFIELD (village).
Covers a land area of 3.925 square miles and a water area of 0.004 square miles. Located at 41.54° N. Lat.; 81.44° W. Long. Elevation is 927 feet.
Population: 3,462 (1990); 3,435 (2000); 3,309 (2005); 3,178 (2010 projected); Race: 93.1% White, 1.8% Black, 4.4% Asian, 0.8% Hispanic of any race (2005); Density: 843.1 persons per square mile (2005); Average household size: 2.44 (2005); Median age: 47.2 (2005); Males per 100 females: 92.3 (2005); Marriage status: 21.3% never married, 63.7% now married, 8.7% widowed, 6.4% divorced (2000); Foreign born: 11.7% (2000); Ancestry (includes multiple ancestries): 25.1% Italian, 23.0% German, 17.3% Irish, 9.2% English, 7.6% Polish (2000).
Economy: Insurance is major employer. Single-family building permits issued: 5 (2005); Multi-family building permits issued: 0 (2005); Employment by occupation: 22.2% management, 25.7% professional, 11.8% services, 28.4% sales, 0.0% farming, 6.7% construction, 5.2% production (2000).
Income: Per capita income: $40,296 (2005); Median household income: $72,274 (2005); Average household income: $98,479 (2005); Percent of households with income of $100,000 or more: 34.3% (2005); Poverty rate: 2.6% (2000).
Education: Percent of population age 25 and over with: High school diploma (including GED) or higher: 93.9% (2005); Bachelor's degree or higher: 45.3% (2005); Master's degree or higher: 18.0% (2005).

School District(s)

Mayfield City SD (PK-12)
   2003-04 Enrollment: 4,331 . . . . (440) 995-6800
Housing: Homeownership rate: 82.6% (2005); Median home value: $242,456 (2005); Median rent: $978 per month (2000); Median age of housing: 37 years (2000).
Safety: Violent crime rate: 3.0 per 10,000 population; Property crime rate: 253.1 per 10,000 population (2004).
Transportation: Commute to work: 91.3% car, 1.5% public transportation, 1.2% walk, 5.3% work from home (2000); Travel time to work: 30.8% less than 15 minutes, 35.6% 15 to 30 minutes, 24.2% 30 to 45 minutes, 3.2% 45 to 60 minutes, 6.2% 60 minutes or more (2000)

Additional Information Contacts

Village of Mayfield . . . . (440) 461-2210
   http://www.mayfieldvillage.com

MAYFIELD HEIGHTS (city).
Covers a land area of 4.218 square miles and a water area of 0 square miles. Located at 41.51° N. Lat.; 81.45° W. Long. Elevation is 1,080 feet.
History: Named either for Mayfield in Derby, England, or for the month of May. Incorporated 1925.
Population: 19,847 (1990); 19,386 (2000); 18,721 (2005); 18,045 (2010 projected); Race: 90.1% White, 3.4% Black, 5.2% Asian, 1.1% Hispanic of any race (2005); Density: 4,438.4 persons per square mile (2005); Average household size: 1.95 (2005); Median age: 45.3 (2005); Males per 100 females: 82.8 (2005); Marriage status: 24.4% never married, 50.7% now married, 14.0% widowed, 10.9% divorced (2000); Foreign born: 18.1% (2000); Ancestry (includes multiple ancestries): 26.1% Italian, 15.4% German, 12.6% Other groups, 9.0% Irish, 6.8% Russian (2000).
Economy: Single-family building permits issued: 44 (2005); Multi-family building permits issued: 0 (2005); Employment by occupation: 14.5% management, 23.5% professional, 14.0% services, 31.5% sales, 0.1% farming, 7.1% construction, 9.3% production (2000).
Income: Per capita income: $27,825 (2005); Median household income: $42,308 (2005); Average household income: $53,964 (2005); Percent of households with income of $100,000 or more: 10.0% (2005); Poverty rate: 6.3% (2000).
Education: Percent of population age 25 and over with: High school diploma (including GED) or higher: 85.7% (2005); Bachelor's degree or higher: 27.7% (2005); Master's degree or higher: 10.7% (2005).
Housing: Homeownership rate: 50.5% (2005); Median home value: $147,058 (2005); Median rent: $624 per month (2000); Median age of housing: 36 years (2000).
Hospitals: Hillcrest Hospital (327 beds)
Transportation: Commute to work: 91.5% car, 2.1% public transportation, 2.5% walk, 3.1% work from home (2000); Travel time to work: 32.4% less than 15 minutes, 40.3% 15 to 30 minutes, 20.3% 30 to 45 minutes, 4.3% 45 to 60 minutes, 2.7% 60 minutes or more (2000)

Additional Information Contacts

City of Mayfield Heights . . . . (440) 449-7545
   http://www.mayfieldheights.org

MIDDLEBURG HEIGHTS (city).
Covers a land area of 8.075 square miles and a water area of 0.016 square miles. Located at 41.36° N. Lat.; 81.80° W. Long. Elevation is 880 feet.
History: Rumor has it that the founder of Middleburg Heights conceived the city's name when he accidentally chopped off his finger at the "middle knuckle" while mincing onions. He mistakenly shipped the finger, with the onions, to University Heights. The home city of the fingerless founder was thereafter known as Middleburg Heights.
Population: 14,667 (1990); 15,542 (2000); 15,742 (2005); 15,906 (2010 projected); Race: 93.8% White, 1.5% Black, 2.6% Asian, 1.3% Hispanic of any race (2005); Density: 1,949.6 persons per square mile (2005); Average household size: 2.29 (2005); Median age: 45.5 (2005); Males per 100 females: 89.9 (2005); Marriage status: 24.3% never married, 55.9% now married, 9.9% widowed, 9.8% divorced (2000); Foreign born: 9.0% (2000); Ancestry (includes multiple ancestries): 26.6% German, 16.1% Irish, 14.3% Italian, 11.9% Polish, 7.9% Slovak (2000).
Economy: Single-family building permits issued: 40 (2005); Multi-family building permits issued: 0 (2005); Employment by occupation: 14.8% management, 20.2% professional, 14.8% services, 32.4% sales, 0.0% farming, 7.5% construction, 10.3% production (2000).
Income: Per capita income: $27,647 (2005); Median household income: $53,111 (2005); Average household income: $62,365 (2005); Percent of households with income of $100,000 or more: 15.2% (2005); Poverty rate: 3.0% (2000).
Education: Percent of population age 25 and over with: High school diploma (including GED) or higher: 85.4% (2005); Bachelor's degree or higher: 23.9% (2005); Master's degree or higher: 7.1% (2005).

Two-year College(s)

Polaris Career Center (Public)
   Fall 2004 Enrollment: 100 . . . . (440) 891-7600
   2005-06 Tuition: In-state $4,025; Out-of-state $4,025
Sanford-Brown Institute (Public)
   Fall 2004 Enrollment: 447 . . . . (440) 239-9640
Southwest General Health Care School of Medical Technology (Private, Not-for-profit)
   Fall 2004 Enrollment: 5 . . . . (440) 816-8859
Housing: Homeownership rate: 73.5% (2005); Median home value: $171,526 (2005); Median rent: $577 per month (2000); Median age of housing: 32 years (2000).
Hospitals: Southwest General Health Center (336 beds)
Transportation: Commute to work: 93.6% car, 1.5% public transportation, 1.4% walk, 2.9% work from home (2000); Travel time to work: 30.6% less than 15 minutes, 40.9% 15 to 30 minutes, 19.4% 30 to 45 minutes, 6.3% 45 to 60 minutes, 2.8% 60 minutes or more (2000)

MORELAND HILLS (village).
Covers a land area of 7.249 square miles and a water area of 0.004 square miles. Located at 41.44° N. Lat.; 81.42° W. Long. Elevation is 1,037 feet.
Population: 3,354 (1990); 3,298 (2000); 3,244 (2005); 3,187 (2010 projected); Race: 91.8% White, 3.6% Black, 3.8% Asian, 0.6% Hispanic of any race (2005); Density: 447.5 persons per square mile (2005); Average household size: 2.51 (2005); Median age: 49.0 (2005); Males per 100 females: 93.6 (2005); Marriage status: 18.1% never married, 71.1% now married, 6.2% widowed, 4.6% divorced (2000); Foreign born: 10.2%

(2000); Ancestry (includes multiple ancestries): 17.0% German, 14.0% English, 10.0% Russian, 9.4% Other groups, 8.1% Irish (2000).
Economy: Single-family building permits issued: 8 (2005); Multi-family building permits issued: 0 (2005); Employment by occupation: 30.3% management, 29.4% professional, 6.5% services, 28.0% sales, 0.0% farming, 2.9% construction, 2.9% production (2000).
Income: Per capita income: $75,730 (2005); Median household income: $123,703 (2005); Average household income: $190,198 (2005); Percent of households with income of $100,000 or more: 57.8% (2005); Poverty rate: 3.3% (2000).
Education: Percent of population age 25 and over with: High school diploma (including GED) or higher: 97.4% (2005); Bachelor's degree or higher: 66.2% (2005); Master's degree or higher: 31.1% (2005).
Housing: Homeownership rate: 95.0% (2005); Median home value: $409,202 (2005); Median rent: $1,000 per month (2000); Median age of housing: 37 years (2000).
Transportation: Commute to work: 86.9% car, 0.8% public transportation, 2.3% walk, 9.7% work from home (2000); Travel time to work: 25.7% less than 15 minutes, 38.1% 15 to 30 minutes, 30.0% 30 to 45 minutes, 2.8% 45 to 60 minutes, 3.4% 60 minutes or more (2000)
Additional Information Contacts
Village of Moreland Hills . . . . (440) 248-1188
  http://www.morelandhills.com

NEWBURGH HEIGHTS (village). Covers a land area of 0.582 square miles and a water area of 0 square miles. Located at 41.45° N. Lat.; 81.66° W. Long. Elevation is 690 feet.
Population: 2,495 (1990); 2,389 (2000); 2,243 (2005); 2,095 (2010 projected); Race: 92.9% White, 4.1% Black, 0.1% Asian, 2.8% Hispanic of any race (2005); Density: 3,853.5 persons per square mile (2005); Average household size: 2.23 (2005); Median age: 38.9 (2005); Males per 100 females: 93.4 (2005); Marriage status: 30.7% never married, 42.3% now married, 10.5% widowed, 16.5% divorced (2000); Foreign born: 2.5% (2000); Ancestry (includes multiple ancestries): 29.6% Polish, 21.6% German, 16.7% Irish, 12.2% Other groups, 11.1% Italian (2000).
Economy: Ceramic plants. Single-family building permits issued: 0 (2005); Multi-family building permits issued: 0 (2005); Employment by occupation: 10.4% management, 10.0% professional, 16.6% services, 29.5% sales, 0.0% farming, 10.8% construction, 22.7% production (2000).
Income: Per capita income: $20,792 (2005); Median household income: $40,320 (2005); Average household income: $46,359 (2005); Percent of households with income of $100,000 or more: 5.6% (2005); Poverty rate: 12.0% (2000).
Education: Percent of population age 25 and over with: High school diploma (including GED) or higher: 77.0% (2005); Bachelor's degree or higher: 10.6% (2005); Master's degree or higher: 3.4% (2005).
School District(s)
Washington Park Community (KG-06)
  2003-04 Enrollment: 181 . . . . (216) 271-6055
Housing: Homeownership rate: 63.1% (2005); Median home value: $83,974 (2005); Median rent: $414 per month (2000); Median age of housing: 60+ years (2000).
Transportation: Commute to work: 94.2% car, 3.0% public transportation, 2.2% walk, 0.3% work from home (2000); Travel time to work: 31.2% less than 15 minutes, 51.7% 15 to 30 minutes, 11.1% 30 to 45 minutes, 2.1% 45 to 60 minutes, 3.9% 60 minutes or more (2000)

NORTH OLMSTED (city). Covers a land area of 11.631 square miles and a water area of 0 square miles. Located at 41.41° N. Lat.; 81.91° W. Long. Elevation is 756 feet.
History: Named for Charles H. Olmsted. First U.S. municipal bus line began operations in North Olmstead in 1931. Incorporated as a city 1951.
Population: 34,240 (1990); 34,113 (2000); 33,153 (2005); 32,193 (2010 projected); Race: 92.8% White, 1.1% Black, 3.5% Asian, 1.7% Hispanic of any race (2005); Density: 2,850.4 persons per square mile (2005); Average household size: 2.47 (2005); Median age: 41.3 (2005); Males per 100 females: 93.3 (2005); Marriage status: 23.9% never married, 59.6% now married, 7.3% widowed, 9.2% divorced (2000); Foreign born: 7.8% (2000); Ancestry (includes multiple ancestries): 29.9% German, 22.8% Irish, 10.7% Italian, 9.9% Polish, 9.6% English (2000).
Economy: Mainly residential; chief industry, printed materials. Unemployment rate: 4.8% (2005); Total civilian labor force: 18,683 (2005); Single-family building permits issued: 36 (2005); Multi-family building permits issued: 0 (2005); Employment by occupation: 16.1% management, 21.6% professional, 12.4% services, 30.6% sales, 0.2% farming, 7.3% construction, 11.8% production (2000).
Income: Per capita income: $27,719 (2005); Median household income: $59,354 (2005); Average household income: $68,164 (2005); Percent of households with income of $100,000 or more: 19.0% (2005); Poverty rate: 4.1% (2000).
Taxes: Total city taxes per capita: $674 (2004); City property taxes per capita: $296 (2004).
Education: Percent of population age 25 and over with: High school diploma (including GED) or higher: 90.4% (2005); Bachelor's degree or higher: 27.2% (2005); Master's degree or higher: 9.2% (2005).
School District(s)
North Olmsted City Schools (PK-12)
  2003-04 Enrollment: 4,573 . . . . (440) 779-3549
Two-year College(s)
Remington College-Cleveland West Campus (Private, For-profit)
  Fall 2004 Enrollment: 368 . . . . (440) 777-2560
Housing: Homeownership rate: 79.8% (2005); Median home value: $164,723 (2005); Median rent: $577 per month (2000); Median age of housing: 34 years (2000).
Safety: Violent crime rate: 9.5 per 10,000 population; Property crime rate: 149.6 per 10,000 population (2004).
Newspapers: Lakewood Sun Post (General - Circulation 9,981); The Sun (General - Circulation 3,409); The Sun Herald (General - Circulation 15,830); West Side Sun News (General - Circulation 16,699)
Transportation: Commute to work: 92.4% car, 2.7% public transportation, 1.5% walk, 2.9% work from home (2000); Travel time to work: 25.5% less than 15 minutes, 41.2% 15 to 30 minutes, 23.3% 30 to 45 minutes, 6.6% 45 to 60 minutes, 3.5% 60 minutes or more (2000)
Additional Information Contacts
City of North Olmsted. . . . . (440) 777-8000
  http://www.north-olmsted.com

NORTH RANDALL (village). Covers a land area of 0.782 square miles and a water area of 0 square miles. Located at 41.43° N. Lat.; 81.53° W. Long. Elevation is 1,043 feet.
Population: 977 (1990); 906 (2000); 880 (2005); 852 (2010 projected); Race: 17.4% White, 74.8% Black, 1.0% Asian, 8.9% Hispanic of any race (2005); Density: 1,125.5 persons per square mile (2005); Average household size: 1.99 (2005); Median age: 41.7 (2005); Males per 100 females: 96.0 (2005); Marriage status: 36.6% never married, 35.9% now married, 7.5% widowed, 20.0% divorced (2000); Foreign born: 8.1% (2000); Ancestry (includes multiple ancestries): 72.6% Other groups, 4.3% Polish, 3.3% Italian, 3.0% African, 1.5% German (2000).
Economy: Site of Randall Park Mall, one of the largest shopping center in U.S. Extensive retailing; thoroughbred racing at Randall Park. Single-family building permits issued: 0 (2005); Multi-family building permits issued: 0 (2005); Employment by occupation: 9.3% management, 18.1% professional, 20.4% services, 29.0% sales, 5.4% farming, 2.0% construction, 15.9% production (2000).
Income: Per capita income: $22,342 (2005); Median household income: $32,500 (2005); Average household income: $42,155 (2005); Percent of households with income of $100,000 or more: 7.0% (2005); Poverty rate: 11.4% (2000).
Education: Percent of population age 25 and over with: High school diploma (including GED) or higher: 67.9% (2005); Bachelor's degree or higher: 10.7% (2005); Master's degree or higher: 3.6% (2005).
Housing: Homeownership rate: 28.1% (2005); Median home value: $120,667 (2005); Median rent: $527 per month (2000); Median age of housing: 39 years (2000).
Transportation: Commute to work: 76.0% car, 6.3% public transportation, 10.5% walk, 1.2% work from home (2000); Travel time to work: 34.2% less than 15 minutes, 33.6% 15 to 30 minutes, 23.9% 30 to 45 minutes, 5.7% 45 to 60 minutes, 2.6% 60 minutes or more (2000)
Additional Information Contacts
Tri-City Chamber of Commerce. . . . . (216) 454-0199
  http://www.tricitychamber.com

NORTH ROYALTON (city). Covers a land area of 21.286 square miles and a water area of 0 square miles. Located at 41.32° N. Lat.; 81.74° W. Long. Elevation is 1,197 feet.
History: Dairy-processing and sawmilling center in the 19th century, North Royalton has since developed a variety of light industries. Settled 1811, incorporated as a village 1927, as a city 1960.

Population: 23,197 (1990); 28,648 (2000); 30,102 (2005); 31,448 (2010 projected); Race: 95.5% White, 0.8% Black, 2.3% Asian, 1.0% Hispanic of any race (2005); Density: 1,414.2 persons per square mile (2005); Average household size: 2.52 (2005); Median age: 39.9 (2005); Males per 100 females: 94.8 (2005); Marriage status: 24.8% never married, 59.8% now married, 6.9% widowed, 8.5% divorced (2000); Foreign born: 6.8% (2000); Ancestry (includes multiple ancestries): 25.4% German, 18.4% Polish, 14.0% Irish, 12.3% Italian, 8.3% English (2000).
Economy: Light industry. Unemployment rate: 4.6% (2005); Total civilian labor force: 17,397 (2005); Single-family building permits issued: 174 (2005); Multi-family building permits issued: 35 (2005); Employment by occupation: 17.2% management, 19.9% professional, 11.6% services, 30.1% sales, 0.2% farming, 8.4% construction, 12.7% production (2000).
Income: Per capita income: $30,991 (2005); Median household income: $64,674 (2005); Average household income: $77,734 (2005); Percent of households with income of $100,000 or more: 25.1% (2005); Poverty rate: 2.3% (2000).
Taxes: Total city taxes per capita: $411 (2004); City property taxes per capita: $134 (2004).
Education: Percent of population age 25 and over with: High school diploma (including GED) or higher: 88.0% (2005); Bachelor's degree or higher: 29.4% (2005); Master's degree or higher: 8.4% (2005).
School District(s)
North Royalton City SD (PK-12)
    2003-04 Enrollment: 4,496 . . . . (440) 237-8800
Housing: Homeownership rate: 74.7% (2005); Median home value: $198,126 (2005); Median rent: $587 per month (2000); Median age of housing: 21 years (2000).
Safety: Violent crime rate: 8.8 per 10,000 population; Property crime rate: 43.5 per 10,000 population (2004).
Transportation: Commute to work: 92.8% car, 1.7% public transportation, 1.0% walk, 3.9% work from home (2000); Travel time to work: 18.3% less than 15 minutes, 37.6% 15 to 30 minutes, 28.6% 30 to 45 minutes, 10.4% 45 to 60 minutes, 5.1% 60 minutes or more (2000)
Additional Information Contacts
City of North Royalton . . . . (440) 237-4300
    http://www.northroyalton.org

OAKWOOD (village). Covers a land area of 3.459 square miles and a water area of <.001 square miles. Located at 41.36° N. Lat.; 81.50° W. Long. Elevation is 1,079 feet.
Population: 3,385 (1990); 3,667 (2000); 3,641 (2005); 3,622 (2010 projected); Race: 37.4% White, 59.1% Black, 0.4% Asian, 1.6% Hispanic of any race (2005); Density: 1,052.6 persons per square mile (2005); Average household size: 2.55 (2005); Median age: 45.0 (2005); Males per 100 females: 88.3 (2005); Marriage status: 28.1% never married, 44.8% now married, 12.2% widowed, 14.9% divorced (2000); Foreign born: 1.2% (2000); Ancestry (includes multiple ancestries): 53.4% Other groups, 13.6% German, 5.7% English, 5.5% Polish, 4.9% Irish (2000).
Economy: Single-family building permits issued: 35 (2005); Multi-family building permits issued: 0 (2005); Employment by occupation: 12.7% management, 16.2% professional, 11.9% services, 26.1% sales, 0.0% farming, 10.3% construction, 22.9% production (2000).
Income: Per capita income: $24,210 (2005); Median household income: $46,965 (2005); Average household income: $59,806 (2005); Percent of households with income of $100,000 or more: 15.7% (2005); Poverty rate: 6.3% (2000).
Education: Percent of population age 25 and over with: High school diploma (including GED) or higher: 76.4% (2005); Bachelor's degree or higher: 17.3% (2005); Master's degree or higher: 6.0% (2005).
Housing: Homeownership rate: 72.3% (2005); Median home value: $138,613 (2005); Median rent: $420 per month (2000); Median age of housing: 36 years (2000).
Safety: Violent crime rate: 13.5 per 10,000 population; Property crime rate: 173.8 per 10,000 population (2004).
Transportation: Commute to work: 94.0% car, 1.8% public transportation, 2.2% walk, 1.2% work from home (2000); Travel time to work: 20.3% less than 15 minutes, 43.7% 15 to 30 minutes, 26.3% 30 to 45 minutes, 5.0% 45 to 60 minutes, 4.8% 60 minutes or more (2000)

OLMSTED FALLS (city). Covers a land area of 4.131 square miles and a water area of 0 square miles. Located at 41.36° N. Lat.; 81.90° W. Long. Elevation is 774 feet.
Population: 6,784 (1990); 7,962 (2000); 8,628 (2005); 9,236 (2010 projected); Race: 96.1% White, 1.6% Black, 0.9% Asian, 1.4% Hispanic of any race (2005); Density: 2,088.4 persons per square mile (2005); Average household size: 2.50 (2005); Median age: 38.7 (2005); Males per 100 females: 92.6 (2005); Marriage status: 22.6% never married, 63.2% now married, 5.0% widowed, 9.2% divorced (2000); Foreign born: 2.4% (2000); Ancestry (includes multiple ancestries): 32.4% German, 21.2% Irish, 12.9% Italian, 11.9% English, 10.1% Polish (2000).
Economy: Manufacturing of tools. Single-family building permits issued: 23 (2005); Multi-family building permits issued: 0 (2005); Employment by occupation: 17.4% management, 24.1% professional, 10.6% services, 29.7% sales, 0.5% farming, 8.2% construction, 9.4% production (2000).
Income: Per capita income: $30,342 (2005); Median household income: $65,386 (2005); Average household income: $75,658 (2005); Percent of households with income of $100,000 or more: 22.3% (2005); Poverty rate: 2.1% (2000).
Education: Percent of population age 25 and over with: High school diploma (including GED) or higher: 94.0% (2005); Bachelor's degree or higher: 36.6% (2005); Master's degree or higher: 11.8% (2005).
School District(s)
Olmsted Falls City SD (PK-12)
    2003-04 Enrollment: 3,342 . . . . (440) 427-6000
Housing: Homeownership rate: 83.7% (2005); Median home value: $164,762 (2005); Median rent: $552 per month (2000); Median age of housing: 26 years (2000).
Safety: Violent crime rate: 9.5 per 10,000 population; Property crime rate: 151.3 per 10,000 population (2004).
Transportation: Commute to work: 93.0% car, 3.5% public transportation, 0.3% walk, 2.5% work from home (2000); Travel time to work: 20.4% less than 15 minutes, 37.7% 15 to 30 minutes, 26.8% 30 to 45 minutes, 8.9% 45 to 60 minutes, 6.1% 60 minutes or more (2000)
Additional Information Contacts
City of Olmsted Falls . . . . (440) 235-5550
    http://www.olmstedfalls.org
Olmsted Chamber of Commerce . . . . (440) 235-0032
    http://www.olmstedchamber.org

ORANGE (village). Covers a land area of 3.801 square miles and a water area of 0 square miles. Located at 41.44° N. Lat.; 81.47° W. Long. Elevation is 1,158 feet.
Population: 2,810 (1990); 3,236 (2000); 3,398 (2005); 3,547 (2010 projected); Race: 79.3% White, 13.7% Black, 5.1% Asian, 0.6% Hispanic of any race (2005); Density: 894.0 persons per square mile (2005); Average household size: 2.73 (2005); Median age: 45.1 (2005); Males per 100 females: 97.4 (2005); Marriage status: 18.8% never married, 68.9% now married, 6.8% widowed, 5.6% divorced (2000); Foreign born: 8.9% (2000); Ancestry (includes multiple ancestries): 19.8% Other groups, 10.6% United States or American, 10.3% German, 9.9% Russian, 6.4% Hungarian (2000).
Economy: Single-family building permits issued: 10 (2005); Multi-family building permits issued: 0 (2005); Employment by occupation: 21.5% management, 37.0% professional, 9.9% services, 23.5% sales, 0.0% farming, 4.8% construction, 3.2% production (2000).
Income: Per capita income: $50,602 (2005); Median household income: $97,055 (2005); Average household income: $138,029 (2005); Percent of households with income of $100,000 or more: 48.2% (2005); Poverty rate: 3.6% (2000).
Education: Percent of population age 25 and over with: High school diploma (including GED) or higher: 95.6% (2005); Bachelor's degree or higher: 58.4% (2005); Master's degree or higher: 27.2% (2005).
Housing: Homeownership rate: 95.6% (2005); Median home value: $307,328 (2005); Median rent: $931 per month (2000); Median age of housing: 32 years (2000).
Transportation: Commute to work: 91.6% car, 2.2% public transportation, 0.6% walk, 5.5% work from home (2000); Travel time to work: 28.4% less than 15 minutes, 33.4% 15 to 30 minutes, 29.4% 30 to 45 minutes, 6.3% 45 to 60 minutes, 2.5% 60 minutes or more (2000)
Additional Information Contacts
Village of Orange . . . . (440) 498-4400
    http://www.orangevillage.com

PARMA (city). Covers a land area of 19.960 square miles and a water area of 0.017 square miles. Located at 41.39° N. Lat.; 81.72° W. Long. Elevation is 880 feet.
History: Named for the Italian city of Parma. Population declined between 1970 and 1990, reflecting the pattern in conjunction with the greater Northern Ohio area. Settled 1816. Incorporated 1924.

Population: 87,876 (1990); 85,655 (2000); 83,038 (2005); 80,341 (2010 projected); Race: 94.9% White, 1.2% Black, 1.9% Asian, 1.7% Hispanic of any race (2005); Density: 4,160.1 persons per square mile (2005); Average household size: 2.41 (2005); Median age: 40.8 (2005); Males per 100 females: 91.5 (2005); Marriage status: 24.7% never married, 57.0% now married, 9.7% widowed, 8.7% divorced (2000); Foreign born: 9.1% (2000); Ancestry (includes multiple ancestries): 24.5% German, 18.1% Polish, 14.6% Irish, 13.5% Italian, 9.3% Slovak (2000).
Economy: Residential with a large industrial research center. Manufacturing: automobile parts, metal fabrication. Unemployment rate: 5.7% (2005); Total civilian labor force: 43,325 (2005); Single-family building permits issued: 31 (2005); Multi-family building permits issued: 7 (2005); Employment by occupation: 12.3% management, 17.7% professional, 14.2% services, 31.9% sales, 0.0% farming, 8.6% construction, 15.3% production (2000).
Income: Per capita income: $23,653 (2005); Median household income: $48,105 (2005); Average household income: $56,463 (2005); Percent of households with income of $100,000 or more: 11.0% (2005); Poverty rate: 4.9% (2000).
Taxes: Total city taxes per capita: $495 (2004); City property taxes per capita: $94 (2004).
Education: Percent of population age 25 and over with: High school diploma (including GED) or higher: 83.4% (2005); Bachelor's degree or higher: 17.9% (2005); Master's degree or higher: 5.2% (2005).

School District(s)
Lorain-Southside Community
  2003-04 Enrollment: n/a
Parma City SD (KG-12)
  2003-04 Enrollment: 13,427 . . . . (440) 842-5300
Parma Community (KG-07)
  2003-04 Enrollment: 231 . . . . (440) 888-5490
Summit Academy-Parma (02-08)
  2003-04 Enrollment: 65 . . . . (440) 888-5407

Four-year College(s)
Bryant and Stratton College-Parma (Private, For-profit)
  Fall 2004 Enrollment: 216 . . . . (216) 265-3151
  2005-06 Tuition: In-state $11,820; Out-of-state $11,820

Housing: Homeownership rate: 77.4% (2005); Median home value: $133,349 (2005); Median rent: $534 per month (2000); Median age of housing: 42 years (2000).
Safety: Violent crime rate: 16.5 per 10,000 population; Property crime rate: 207.3 per 10,000 population (2004).
Transportation: Commute to work: 93.3% car, 3.1% public transportation, 1.4% walk, 1.6% work from home (2000); Travel time to work: 22.8% less than 15 minutes, 43.1% 15 to 30 minutes, 23.9% 30 to 45 minutes, 6.5% 45 to 60 minutes, 3.7% 60 minutes or more (2000)

Additional Information Contacts
City of Parma . . . . (440) 885-8000
  http://www.cityofparma-oh.gov
Parma Area Chamber of Commerce . . . . (440) 886-1700
  http://www.parmaareachamber.org

PARMA HEIGHTS (city). Covers a land area of 4.199 square miles and a water area of 0 square miles. Located at 41.38° N. Lat.; 81.76° W. Long. Elevation is 870 feet.
History: Named for the city in Italy. Settled 1818; set off from Parma and incorporated 1912.
Population: 21,448 (1990); 21,659 (2000); 21,006 (2005); 20,348 (2010 projected); Race: 93.3% White, 1.5% Black, 3.1% Asian, 1.8% Hispanic of any race (2005); Density: 5,003.1 persons per square mile (2005); Average household size: 2.19 (2005); Median age: 43.7 (2005); Males per 100 females: 86.9 (2005); Marriage status: 23.6% never married, 53.1% now married, 12.3% widowed, 10.9% divorced (2000); Foreign born: 10.2% (2000); Ancestry (includes multiple ancestries): 25.0% German, 16.3% Irish, 13.1% Polish, 12.0% Italian, 7.8% Slovak (2000).
Economy: Single-family building permits issued: 12 (2005); Multi-family building permits issued: 0 (2005); Employment by occupation: 12.2% management, 18.3% professional, 12.2% services, 35.0% sales, 0.0% farming, 7.9% construction, 14.3% production (2000).
Income: Per capita income: $22,708 (2005); Median household income: $41,355 (2005); Average household income: $49,428 (2005); Percent of households with income of $100,000 or more: 8.5% (2005); Poverty rate: 7.6% (2000).
Education: Percent of population age 25 and over with: High school diploma (including GED) or higher: 82.8% (2005); Bachelor's degree or higher: 18.5% (2005); Master's degree or higher: 5.7% (2005).

School District(s)
Parma City SD (KG-12)
  2003-04 Enrollment: 13,427 . . . . (440) 842-5300

Two-year College(s)
Quest Career College (Private, For-profit)
  Fall 2004 Enrollment: 31 . . . . (440) 886-5544
  2005-06 Tuition: In-state $25,155; Out-of-state $25,155

Housing: Homeownership rate: 59.9% (2005); Median home value: $132,062 (2005); Median rent: $526 per month (2000); Median age of housing: 40 years (2000).
Safety: Violent crime rate: 19.8 per 10,000 population; Property crime rate: 231.0 per 10,000 population (2004).
Transportation: Commute to work: 93.1% car, 3.5% public transportation, 1.2% walk, 1.8% work from home (2000); Travel time to work: 25.7% less than 15 minutes, 41.2% 15 to 30 minutes, 22.2% 30 to 45 minutes, 7.1% 45 to 60 minutes, 3.8% 60 minutes or more (2000)

PEPPER PIKE (city). Covers a land area of 7.093 square miles and a water area of 0.007 square miles. Located at 41.47° N. Lat.; 81.46° W. Long. Elevation is 1,050 feet.
Population: 6,185 (1990); 6,040 (2000); 5,918 (2005); 5,799 (2010 projected); Race: 89.1% White, 5.4% Black, 4.3% Asian, 1.1% Hispanic of any race (2005); Density: 834.3 persons per square mile (2005); Average household size: 2.69 (2005); Median age: 49.7 (2005); Males per 100 females: 90.9 (2005); Marriage status: 17.0% never married, 73.6% now married, 5.4% widowed, 3.9% divorced (2000); Foreign born: 12.2% (2000); Ancestry (includes multiple ancestries): 13.3% German, 12.7% Other groups, 9.6% English, 9.3% Irish, 9.1% Russian (2000).
Economy: Single-family building permits issued: 20 (2005); Multi-family building permits issued: 0 (2005); Employment by occupation: 25.4% management, 38.5% professional, 5.9% services, 25.9% sales, 0.3% farming, 0.9% construction, 3.0% production (2000).
Income: Per capita income: $74,690 (2005); Median household income: $142,382 (2005); Average household income: $198,882 (2005); Percent of households with income of $100,000 or more: 63.0% (2005); Poverty rate: 3.7% (2000).
Education: Percent of population age 25 and over with: High school diploma (including GED) or higher: 97.3% (2005); Bachelor's degree or higher: 71.8% (2005); Master's degree or higher: 38.1% (2005).

School District(s)
Orange City School District (PK-12)
  2003-04 Enrollment: 2,368 . . . . (216) 831-8600

Four-year College(s)
Ursuline College (Private, Not-for-profit, Roman Catholic)
  Fall 2004 Enrollment: 1,462 . . . . (440) 449-4200
  2005-06 Tuition: In-state $19,090; Out-of-state $19,090

Housing: Homeownership rate: 95.6% (2005); Median home value: $399,914 (2005); Median rent: $523 per month (2000); Median age of housing: 34 years (2000).
Transportation: Commute to work: 91.1% car, 1.6% public transportation, 1.5% walk, 5.5% work from home (2000); Travel time to work: 28.2% less than 15 minutes, 40.7% 15 to 30 minutes, 27.4% 30 to 45 minutes, 1.9% 45 to 60 minutes, 1.8% 60 minutes or more (2000)

Additional Information Contacts
City of Pepper Pike . . . . (216) 831-8500
  http://www.pepperpike.org

RICHMOND HEIGHTS (city). Covers a land area of 4.370 square miles and a water area of 0.006 square miles. Located at 41.55° N. Lat.; 81.50° W. Long. Elevation is 880 feet.
Population: 9,611 (1990); 10,944 (2000); 10,805 (2005); 10,654 (2010 projected); Race: 60.8% White, 30.4% Black, 5.8% Asian, 1.8% Hispanic of any race (2005); Density: 2,472.6 persons per square mile (2005); Average household size: 2.24 (2005); Median age: 42.2 (2005); Males per 100 females: 89.7 (2005); Marriage status: 29.4% never married, 51.6% now married, 9.0% widowed, 10.0% divorced (2000); Foreign born: 17.4% (2000); Ancestry (includes multiple ancestries): 30.2% Other groups, 12.5% German, 11.6% Italian, 6.6% Polish, 6.3% Irish (2000).
Economy: Single-family building permits issued: 23 (2005); Multi-family building permits issued: 0 (2005); Employment by occupation: 16.6% management, 25.5% professional, 12.8% services, 26.8% sales, 0.2% farming, 4.6% construction, 13.5% production (2000).

Income: Per capita income: $28,543 (2005); Median household income: $47,026 (2005); Average household income: $63,141 (2005); Percent of households with income of $100,000 or more: 16.9% (2005); Poverty rate: 5.3% (2000).
Taxes: Total city taxes per capita: $707 (2004); City property taxes per capita: $267 (2004).
Education: Percent of population age 25 and over with: High school diploma (including GED) or higher: 89.4% (2005); Bachelor's degree or higher: 35.9% (2005); Master's degree or higher: 12.1% (2005).

School District(s)
Richmond Heights Local SD (PK-12)
 2003-04 Enrollment: 1,119 . . . . (216) 692-8485
Housing: Homeownership rate: 62.3% (2005); Median home value: $168,717 (2005); Median rent: $525 per month (2000); Median age of housing: 34 years (2000).
Hospitals: UHHS Richmond Heights Hospital (100 beds)
Transportation: Commute to work: 92.7% car, 2.6% public transportation, 1.1% walk, 3.0% work from home (2000); Travel time to work: 19.4% less than 15 minutes, 44.8% 15 to 30 minutes, 25.1% 30 to 45 minutes, 6.4% 45 to 60 minutes, 4.3% 60 minutes or more (2000)

ROCKY RIVER
ROCKY RIVER (city). Covers a land area of 4.755 square miles and a water area of 0.873 square miles. Located at 41.47° N. Lat.; 81.84° W. Long. Elevation is 680 feet.
History: Named for its location at the mouth of the Rocky River, so named because of its rocky river bed. The town of Rocky River was established in 1815 on Lake Erie at the mouth of the Rocky River.
Population: 20,410 (1990); 20,735 (2000); 19,942 (2005); 19,163 (2010 projected); Race: 96.3% White, 0.5% Black, 1.5% Asian, 1.3% Hispanic of any race (2005); Density: 4,194.0 persons per square mile (2005); Average household size: 2.10 (2005); Median age: 45.6 (2005); Males per 100 females: 82.8 (2005); Marriage status: 21.0% never married, 57.3% now married, 11.4% widowed, 10.3% divorced (2000); Foreign born: 7.0% (2000); Ancestry (includes multiple ancestries): 28.1% German, 26.9% Irish, 12.4% English, 9.4% Italian, 6.6% Polish (2000).
Economy: Single-family building permits issued: 38 (2005); Multi-family building permits issued: 0 (2005); Employment by occupation: 21.7% management, 27.3% professional, 9.6% services, 32.2% sales, 0.1% farming, 3.8% construction, 5.4% production (2000).
Income: Per capita income: $38,754 (2005); Median household income: $57,576 (2005); Average household income: $81,338 (2005); Percent of households with income of $100,000 or more: 23.6% (2005); Poverty rate: 2.3% (2000).
Education: Percent of population age 25 and over with: High school diploma (including GED) or higher: 93.3% (2005); Bachelor's degree or higher: 46.6% (2005); Master's degree or higher: 17.8% (2005).

School District(s)
Rocky River City SD (PK-12)
 2003-04 Enrollment: 2,598 . . . . (440) 333-6000
Housing: Homeownership rate: 71.7% (2005); Median home value: $208,358 (2005); Median rent: $614 per month (2000); Median age of housing: 41 years (2000).
Newspapers: Lorain County Times (General - Circulation 3,200)
Transportation: Commute to work: 88.7% car, 3.5% public transportation, 2.8% walk, 4.4% work from home (2000); Travel time to work: 27.7% less than 15 minutes, 44.4% 15 to 30 minutes, 21.2% 30 to 45 minutes, 4.5% 45 to 60 minutes, 2.2% 60 minutes or more (2000)
Additional Information Contacts
City of Rocky River . . . . (440) 331-0600
 http://www.rrcity.com
Rocky River Chamber of Commerce . . . . (440) 331-1140
 http://www.rockyriverchamber.com

SEVEN HILLS
SEVEN HILLS (city). Covers a land area of 5.009 square miles and a water area of 0 square miles. Located at 41.38° N. Lat.; 81.67° W. Long. Elevation is 900 feet.
History: Named for the seven hills of Rome. Incorporated as a city 1961. Part of its city hall is an old schoolhouse, built in 1861.
Population: 12,339 (1990); 12,080 (2000); 12,104 (2005); 12,122 (2010 projected); Race: 96.7% White, 0.2% Black, 2.5% Asian, 0.9% Hispanic of any race (2005); Density: 2,416.4 persons per square mile (2005); Average household size: 2.48 (2005); Median age: 48.8 (2005); Males per 100 females: 93.2 (2005); Marriage status: 19.5% never married, 65.5% now married, 9.5% widowed, 5.5% divorced (2000); Foreign born: 11.5% (2000); Ancestry (includes multiple ancestries): 22.6% Polish, 19.1% German, 16.4% Italian, 9.2% Irish, 8.9% Slovak (2000).
Economy: Single-family building permits issued: 44 (2005); Multi-family building permits issued: 0 (2005); Employment by occupation: 15.7% management, 23.0% professional, 11.2% services, 29.2% sales, 0.1% farming, 8.1% construction, 12.8% production (2000).
Income: Per capita income: $29,128 (2005); Median household income: $61,928 (2005); Average household income: $72,009 (2005); Percent of households with income of $100,000 or more: 21.6% (2005); Poverty rate: 2.6% (2000).
Education: Percent of population age 25 and over with: High school diploma (including GED) or higher: 85.0% (2005); Bachelor's degree or higher: 22.2% (2005); Master's degree or higher: 7.6% (2005).

School District(s)
Parma City SD (KG-12)
 2003-04 Enrollment: 13,427 . . . . (440) 842-5300
Housing: Homeownership rate: 96.6% (2005); Median home value: $187,257 (2005); Median rent: $643 per month (2000); Median age of housing: 34 years (2000).
Safety: Violent crime rate: 10.7 per 10,000 population; Property crime rate: 83.3 per 10,000 population (2004).
Transportation: Commute to work: 94.5% car, 2.0% public transportation, 0.1% walk, 2.9% work from home (2000); Travel time to work: 19.8% less than 15 minutes, 48.3% 15 to 30 minutes, 25.1% 30 to 45 minutes, 4.2% 45 to 60 minutes, 2.5% 60 minutes or more (2000)
Additional Information Contacts
City of Seven Hills . . . . (216) 524-4421
 http://www.sevenhillsohio.org

SHAKER HEIGHTS
SHAKER HEIGHTS (city). Covers a land area of 6.276 square miles and a water area of 0.043 square miles. Located at 41.47° N. Lat.; 81.55° W. Long. Elevation is 1,000 feet.
History: Named for a community of Shakers founded in the region in the early 1800s. The Shakers founded a religious community here in the early 1800's. The site was acquired in 1905 by O.P. and M.J. VanSweringen, railroad tycoons, who connected it with downtown Cleveland by a rapid transit line. Shaker Heights grew as a residential area.
Population: 30,831 (1990); 29,405 (2000); 28,029 (2005); 26,689 (2010 projected); Race: 57.3% White, 35.5% Black, 4.1% Asian, 1.1% Hispanic of any race (2005); Density: 4,465.7 persons per square mile (2005); Average household size: 2.40 (2005); Median age: 40.7 (2005); Males per 100 females: 84.3 (2005); Marriage status: 25.5% never married, 56.3% now married, 7.6% widowed, 10.6% divorced (2000); Foreign born: 7.2% (2000); Ancestry (includes multiple ancestries): 36.6% Other groups, 13.2% German, 9.4% Irish, 9.2% English, 5.1% Russian (2000).
Economy: Unemployment rate: 4.7% (2005); Total civilian labor force: 15,166 (2005); Single-family building permits issued: 34 (2005); Multi-family building permits issued: 0 (2005); Employment by occupation: 21.2% management, 42.1% professional, 7.7% services, 21.7% sales, 0.0% farming, 1.7% construction, 5.5% production (2000).
Income: Per capita income: $44,162 (2005); Median household income: $70,145 (2005); Average household income: $105,551 (2005); Percent of households with income of $100,000 or more: 33.7% (2005); Poverty rate: 6.9% (2000).
Taxes: Total city taxes per capita: $1,071 (2004); City property taxes per capita: $208 (2004).
Education: Percent of population age 25 and over with: High school diploma (including GED) or higher: 94.6% (2005); Bachelor's degree or higher: 61.5% (2005); Master's degree or higher: 35.6% (2005).

School District(s)
Shaker Heights City SD (PK-12)
 2003-04 Enrollment: 5,625 . . . . (216) 295-4000
Housing: Homeownership rate: 65.4% (2005); Median home value: $217,186 (2005); Median rent: $679 per month (2000); Median age of housing: 55 years (2000).
Transportation: Commute to work: 85.6% car, 8.1% public transportation, 1.4% walk, 4.1% work from home (2000); Travel time to work: 22.0% less than 15 minutes, 47.9% 15 to 30 minutes, 22.1% 30 to 45 minutes, 5.1% 45 to 60 minutes, 2.9% 60 minutes or more (2000)
Additional Information Contacts
City of Shaker Heights . . . . (216) 491-1400
 http://www.shakeronline.com

SOLON (city). Covers a land area of 20.552 square miles and a water area of 0.043 square miles. Located at 41.39° N. Lat.; 81.44° W. Long. Elevation is 1,036 feet.
History: Named for Solon Bull, one of the town's early settlers. Founded 1820. Incorporated as a city 1960.
Population: 18,548 (1990); 21,802 (2000); 22,422 (2005); 22,968 (2010 projected); Race: 85.1% White, 7.1% Black, 6.4% Asian, 0.8% Hispanic of any race (2005); Density: 1,091.0 persons per square mile (2005); Average household size: 2.89 (2005); Median age: 40.0 (2005); Males per 100 females: 95.8 (2005); Marriage status: 18.9% never married, 68.4% now married, 5.2% widowed, 7.5% divorced (2000); Foreign born: 8.6% (2000); Ancestry (includes multiple ancestries): 16.8% German, 14.5% Italian, 13.8% Other groups, 11.6% Irish, 10.0% Polish (2000).
Economy: Manufacturing includes metal products, machinery, electrical products and equipment, tools, and chemicals. Single-family building permits issued: 127 (2005); Multi-family building permits issued: 2 (2005); Employment by occupation: 22.8% management, 30.4% professional, 7.9% services, 28.5% sales, 0.0% farming, 3.9% construction, 6.4% production (2000).
Income: Per capita income: $41,394 (2005); Median household income: $91,198 (2005); Average household income: $119,683 (2005); Percent of households with income of $100,000 or more: 44.6% (2005); Poverty rate: 2.5% (2000).
Education: Percent of population age 25 and over with: High school diploma (including GED) or higher: 94.6% (2005); Bachelor's degree or higher: 50.7% (2005); Master's degree or higher: 22.1% (2005).

School District(s)
Solon City SD (PK-12)
    2003-04 Enrollment: 5,180 . . . . (440) 248-1600

Housing: Homeownership rate: 87.7% (2005); Median home value: $262,272 (2005); Median rent: $753 per month (2000); Median age of housing: 23 years (2000).
Safety: Violent crime rate: 6.7 per 10,000 population; Property crime rate: 118.4 per 10,000 population (2004).
Transportation: Commute to work: 94.7% car, 0.5% public transportation, 0.7% walk, 3.9% work from home (2000); Travel time to work: 28.1% less than 15 minutes, 36.7% 15 to 30 minutes, 25.2% 30 to 45 minutes, 7.2% 45 to 60 minutes, 2.8% 60 minutes or more (2000)

Additional Information Contacts
City of Solon. . . . . (440) 248-1155
http://www.solonohio.org

SOUTH EUCLID (city). Aka Bluestone. Covers a land area of 4.689 square miles and a water area of 0 square miles. Located at 41.52° N. Lat.; 81.52° W. Long. Elevation is 950 feet.
History: Named for Euclid, the mathematician of Alexandria. Site of Notre Dame College, a Roman Catholic school for women. Incorporated as a city 1940.
Population: 23,866 (1990); 23,537 (2000); 22,545 (2005); 21,555 (2010 projected); Race: 70.5% White, 25.6% Black, 1.7% Asian, 1.0% Hispanic of any race (2005); Density: 4,807.7 persons per square mile (2005); Average household size: 2.44 (2005); Median age: 39.4 (2005); Males per 100 females: 86.0 (2005); Marriage status: 26.1% never married, 55.2% now married, 8.0% widowed, 10.8% divorced (2000); Foreign born: 9.4% (2000); Ancestry (includes multiple ancestries): 25.6% Other groups, 15.4% Italian, 13.9% German, 13.7% Irish, 6.1% Russian (2000).
Economy: Unemployment rate: 5.1% (2005); Total civilian labor force: 12,691 (2005); Single-family building permits issued: 6 (2005); Multi-family building permits issued: 0 (2005); Employment by occupation: 13.1% management, 27.2% professional, 12.7% services, 31.4% sales, 0.0% farming, 5.1% construction, 10.4% production (2000).
Income: Per capita income: $25,064 (2005); Median household income: $53,009 (2005); Average household income: $60,936 (2005); Percent of households with income of $100,000 or more: 13.8% (2005); Poverty rate: 4.5% (2000).
Taxes: Total city taxes per capita: $485 (2004); City property taxes per capita: $206 (2004).
Education: Percent of population age 25 and over with: High school diploma (including GED) or higher: 90.1% (2005); Bachelor's degree or higher: 36.6% (2005); Master's degree or higher: 13.1% (2005).

School District(s)
South Euclid-Lyndhurst City SD (PK-12)
    2003-04 Enrollment: 4,583 . . . . (216) 691-2000

Housing: Homeownership rate: 84.0% (2005); Median home value: $127,761 (2005); Median rent: $614 per month (2000); Median age of housing: 47 years (2000).
Safety: Violent crime rate: 15.3 per 10,000 population; Property crime rate: 203.9 per 10,000 population (2004).
Transportation: Commute to work: 91.6% car, 3.3% public transportation, 1.3% walk, 3.3% work from home (2000); Travel time to work: 24.2% less than 15 minutes, 43.9% 15 to 30 minutes, 22.4% 30 to 45 minutes, 6.0% 45 to 60 minutes, 3.6% 60 minutes or more (2000)

Additional Information Contacts
City of South Euclid . . . . (216) 381-0400
http://www.cityofsoutheuclid.com

STRONGSVILLE (city). Covers a land area of 24.645 square miles and a water area of 0.007 square miles. Located at 41.31° N. Lat.; 81.83° W. Long. Elevation is 932 feet.
History: Named for Caleb Strong (1745-1819), a Massachusetts statesman. The city's population doubled between 1970 and 1990. Settled 1816. Incorporated 1927.
Population: 35,308 (1990); 43,858 (2000); 44,785 (2005); 45,592 (2010 projected); Race: 93.1% White, 1.5% Black, 3.9% Asian, 1.3% Hispanic of any race (2005); Density: 1,817.2 persons per square mile (2005); Average household size: 2.68 (2005); Median age: 40.3 (2005); Males per 100 females: 94.9 (2005); Marriage status: 20.7% never married, 66.9% now married, 5.3% widowed, 7.2% divorced (2000); Foreign born: 6.5% (2000); Ancestry (includes multiple ancestries): 29.1% German, 18.0% Irish, 13.4% Italian, 12.6% Polish, 10.7% English (2000).
Economy: Textbook publishing company and various light manufacturing. Unemployment rate: 3.7% (2005); Total civilian labor force: 24,977 (2005); Single-family building permits issued: 79 (2005); Multi-family building permits issued: 0 (2005); Employment by occupation: 19.9% management, 22.4% professional, 10.1% services, 30.8% sales, 0.1% farming, 6.3% construction, 10.4% production (2000).
Income: Per capita income: $34,635 (2005); Median household income: $76,641 (2005); Average household income: $92,415 (2005); Percent of households with income of $100,000 or more: 33.9% (2005); Poverty rate: 2.2% (2000).
Taxes: Total city taxes per capita: $627 (2004); City property taxes per capita: $164 (2004).
Education: Percent of population age 25 and over with: High school diploma (including GED) or higher: 93.0% (2005); Bachelor's degree or higher: 37.4% (2005); Master's degree or higher: 13.0% (2005).

School District(s)
Strongsville City SD (PK-12)
    2003-04 Enrollment: 7,340 . . . . (440) 572-7000

Two-year College(s)
ITT Technical Institute (Private, For-profit)
    Fall 2004 Enrollment: 711 . . . . (440) 234-9091
    2005-06 Tuition: In-state $14,196; Out-of-state $14,196

Housing: Homeownership rate: 82.7% (2005); Median home value: $198,266 (2005); Median rent: $573 per month (2000); Median age of housing: 21 years (2000).
Safety: Violent crime rate: 0.0 per 10,000 population; Property crime rate: 85.1 per 10,000 population (2004).
Transportation: Commute to work: 93.2% car, 2.2% public transportation, 0.7% walk, 3.4% work from home (2000); Travel time to work: 22.9% less than 15 minutes, 34.0% 15 to 30 minutes, 28.5% 30 to 45 minutes, 10.1% 45 to 60 minutes, 4.5% 60 minutes or more (2000)

Additional Information Contacts
City of Strongsville . . . . (440) 580-3100
http://www.strongsville.org/content
Strongsville Chamber of Commerce . . . . (440) 238-3366
http://strongsvillecofc.com

UNIVERSITY HEIGHTS (city). Covers a land area of 1.834 square miles and a water area of 0 square miles. Located at 41.49° N. Lat.; 81.53° W. Long. Elevation is 1,040 feet.
History: Named for it being home to John Carroll University. University Heights grew as a residential community. It took its name from John Carroll University, a liberal arts college founded here by the Jesuit Order in 1886.
Population: 14,790 (1990); 14,146 (2000); 13,581 (2005); 13,019 (2010 projected); Race: 73.6% White, 21.8% Black, 2.0% Asian, 1.7% Hispanic of any race (2005); Density: 7,405.5 persons per square mile (2005); Average household size: 2.72 (2005); Median age: 32.7 (2005); Males per 100 females: 90.1 (2005); Marriage status: 34.5% never married, 52.4% now

married, 6.0% widowed, 7.1% divorced (2000); Foreign born: 6.5% (2000); Ancestry (includes multiple ancestries): 27.2% Other groups, 16.1% German, 15.8% Irish, 10.4% Italian, 8.6% Polish (2000).
Economy: Single-family building permits issued: 0 (2005); Multi-family building permits issued: 0 (2005); Employment by occupation: 20.0% management, 33.7% professional, 10.3% services, 26.0% sales, 0.0% farming, 3.2% construction, 6.7% production (2000).
Income: Per capita income: $30,750 (2005); Median household income: $67,796 (2005); Average household income: $81,887 (2005); Percent of households with income of $100,000 or more: 26.2% (2005); Poverty rate: 5.8% (2000).
Education: Percent of population age 25 and over with: High school diploma (including GED) or higher: 93.9% (2005); Bachelor's degree or higher: 55.3% (2005); Master's degree or higher: 27.2% (2005).

School District(s)
Cleveland Hts-Univ Hts City SD (KG-12)
    2003-04 Enrollment: 6,887 . . . . (216) 371-7171

Housing: Homeownership rate: 75.0% (2005); Median home value: $165,866 (2005); Median rent: $653 per month (2000); Median age of housing: 50 years (2000).
Safety: Violent crime rate: 23.3 per 10,000 population; Property crime rate: 181.8 per 10,000 population (2004).
Transportation: Commute to work: 79.2% car, 6.2% public transportation, 9.2% walk, 4.8% work from home (2000); Travel time to work: 26.8% less than 15 minutes, 41.3% 15 to 30 minutes, 25.2% 30 to 45 minutes, 5.2% 45 to 60 minutes, 1.4% 60 minutes or more (2000)
Additional Information Contacts
City of University Heights . . . . (216) 932-7800
   http://www.universityheights.com

VALLEY VIEW (village).
Covers a land area of 5.631 square miles and a water area of 0.004 square miles. Located at 41.38° N. Lat.; 81.61° W. Long. Elevation is 645 feet.
Population: 2,137 (1990); 2,179 (2000); 2,144 (2005); 2,109 (2010 projected); Race: 98.4% White, 0.2% Black, 0.5% Asian, 0.5% Hispanic of any race (2005); Density: 380.7 persons per square mile (2005); Average household size: 2.74 (2005); Median age: 44.6 (2005); Males per 100 females: 98.3 (2005); Marriage status: 22.1% never married, 65.3% now married, 5.6% widowed, 7.0% divorced (2000); Foreign born: 3.8% (2000); Ancestry (includes multiple ancestries): 24.6% Polish, 19.5% German, 19.1% Italian, 16.6% Irish, 8.1% English (2000).
Economy: Single-family building permits issued: 2 (2005); Multi-family building permits issued: 0 (2005); Employment by occupation: 17.6% management, 20.3% professional, 13.1% services, 28.9% sales, 0.4% farming, 9.9% construction, 9.9% production (2000).
Income: Per capita income: $31,899 (2005); Median household income: $75,331 (2005); Average household income: $87,458 (2005); Percent of households with income of $100,000 or more: 30.9% (2005); Poverty rate: 3.1% (2000).
Education: Percent of population age 25 and over with: High school diploma (including GED) or higher: 87.0% (2005); Bachelor's degree or higher: 22.5% (2005); Master's degree or higher: 8.0% (2005).

Two-year College(s)
Ohio Center for Broadcasting (Private, For-profit)
    Fall 2004 Enrollment: 218 . . . . (216) 447-9117

Housing: Homeownership rate: 92.2% (2005); Median home value: $217,477 (2005); Median rent: $554 per month (2000); Median age of housing: 31 years (2000).
Newspapers: Brooklyn Sun Journal (General - Circulation 7,771); Garfield-Maple Sun (General - Circulation 8,549); Nordonia Hills Sun (General - Circulation 3,334); The Sun Courier (General - Circulation 7,372); The Twinsburg Sun (General - Circulation 3,334)
Transportation: Commute to work: 95.1% car, 0.7% public transportation, 0.6% walk, 3.3% work from home (2000); Travel time to work: 30.5% less than 15 minutes, 45.4% 15 to 30 minutes, 17.7% 30 to 45 minutes, 4.2% 45 to 60 minutes, 2.1% 60 minutes or more (2000)
Additional Information Contacts
Village of Valley View . . . . (216) 524-6511
   http://www.valleyview.net

WALTON HILLS (village).
Covers a land area of 6.876 square miles and a water area of 0 square miles. Located at 41.36° N. Lat.; 81.55° W. Long. Elevation is 989 feet.
Population: 2,278 (1990); 2,400 (2000); 2,389 (2005); 2,385 (2010 projected); Race: 95.7% White, 2.4% Black, 0.7% Asian, 1.2% Hispanic of any race (2005); Density: 347.4 persons per square mile (2005); Average household size: 2.61 (2005); Median age: 50.8 (2005); Males per 100 females: 91.6 (2005); Marriage status: 20.7% never married, 63.5% now married, 8.4% widowed, 7.5% divorced (2000); Foreign born: 4.0% (2000); Ancestry (includes multiple ancestries): 22.1% German, 20.0% Italian, 18.3% Polish, 10.0% Irish, 9.2% Slovak (2000).
Economy: Single-family building permits issued: 7 (2005); Multi-family building permits issued: 0 (2005); Employment by occupation: 17.9% management, 14.6% professional, 11.1% services, 31.6% sales, 0.0% farming, 12.1% construction, 12.6% production (2000).
Income: Per capita income: $30,436 (2005); Median household income: $66,211 (2005); Average household income: $77,009 (2005); Percent of households with income of $100,000 or more: 23.4% (2005); Poverty rate: 2.1% (2000).
Education: Percent of population age 25 and over with: High school diploma (including GED) or higher: 87.2% (2005); Bachelor's degree or higher: 19.5% (2005); Master's degree or higher: 5.0% (2005).
Housing: Homeownership rate: 96.9% (2005); Median home value: $219,737 (2005); Median rent: $450 per month (2000); Median age of housing: 35 years (2000).
Safety: Violent crime rate: 12.5 per 10,000 population; Property crime rate: 217.0 per 10,000 population (2004).
Transportation: Commute to work: 96.3% car, 0.2% public transportation, 0.0% walk, 3.5% work from home (2000); Travel time to work: 25.6% less than 15 minutes, 37.6% 15 to 30 minutes, 26.9% 30 to 45 minutes, 5.1% 45 to 60 minutes, 4.8% 60 minutes or more (2000)

WARRENSVILLE HEIGHTS (city).
Covers a land area of 4.127 square miles and a water area of 0 square miles. Located at 41.43° N. Lat.; 81.52° W. Long. Elevation is 1,039 feet.
History: Named for the David Warren family. Incorporated 1927.
Population: 16,002 (1990); 15,109 (2000); 14,552 (2005); 14,022 (2010 projected); Race: 5.7% White, 90.9% Black, 1.1% Asian, 0.8% Hispanic of any race (2005); Density: 3,526.4 persons per square mile (2005); Average household size: 2.35 (2005); Median age: 38.6 (2005); Males per 100 females: 73.9 (2005); Marriage status: 34.5% never married, 40.6% now married, 8.9% widowed, 16.0% divorced (2000); Foreign born: 3.3% (2000); Ancestry (includes multiple ancestries): 78.6% Other groups, 2.1% African, 1.3% Irish, 1.0% United States or American, 0.9% Polish (2000).
Economy: Chiefly residential, it has plants that manufacture machinery, automobile equipment and cardboard containers. The home of a summer stock musical theater-in-the-round. Single-family building permits issued: 5 (2005); Multi-family building permits issued: 0 (2005); Employment by occupation: 10.0% management, 20.0% professional, 18.6% services, 30.1% sales, 0.1% farming, 4.0% construction, 17.4% production (2000).
Income: Per capita income: $21,333 (2005); Median household income: $40,748 (2005); Average household income: $48,865 (2005); Percent of households with income of $100,000 or more: 8.5% (2005); Poverty rate: 11.4% (2000).
Education: Percent of population age 25 and over with: High school diploma (including GED) or higher: 83.5% (2005); Bachelor's degree or higher: 16.4% (2005); Master's degree or higher: 5.2% (2005).

School District(s)
Warrensville Heights City SD (PK-12)
    2003-04 Enrollment: 2,821 . . . . (216) 295-7710

Two-year College(s)
ITT Technical Institute (Private, For-profit)
    Fall 2004 Enrollment: n/a . . . . (216) 896-6500
    2005-06 Tuition: In-state $14,196; Out-of-state $14,196

Housing: Homeownership rate: 45.8% (2005); Median home value: $98,078 (2005); Median rent: $545 per month (2000); Median age of housing: 39 years (2000).
Hospitals: South Pointe Hospital (232 beds)
Safety: Violent crime rate: 34.6 per 10,000 population; Property crime rate: 239.3 per 10,000 population (2004).
Transportation: Commute to work: 86.3% car, 9.5% public transportation, 2.0% walk, 1.5% work from home (2000); Travel time to work: 20.9% less than 15 minutes, 39.2% 15 to 30 minutes, 25.4% 30 to 45 minutes, 7.3% 45 to 60 minutes, 7.2% 60 minutes or more (2000)
Additional Information Contacts
Tri-City Chamber of Commerce . . . . (216) 454-0199
   http://www.tricitychamber.com

WESTLAKE (city). Aka Dover. Covers a land area of 15.898 square miles and a water area of 0.004 square miles. Located at 41.45° N. Lat.; 81.92° W. Long. Elevation is 700 feet.
History: Named for its location southwest of Lakewood. Incorporated as a city 1956.
Population: 27,018 (1990); 31,719 (2000); 32,082 (2005); 32,402 (2010 projected); Race: 91.6% White, 1.1% Black, 5.1% Asian, 1.3% Hispanic of any race (2005); Density: 2,018.0 persons per square mile (2005); Average household size: 2.43 (2005); Median age: 43.8 (2005); Males per 100 females: 89.5 (2005); Marriage status: 21.4% never married, 61.0% now married, 9.1% widowed, 8.5% divorced (2000); Foreign born: 8.4% (2000); Ancestry (includes multiple ancestries): 26.2% German, 23.3% Irish, 11.6% Italian, 10.0% English, 8.2% Other groups (2000).
Economy: Manufacturing includes ink and plastics and chemicals. Unemployment rate: 4.4% (2005); Total civilian labor force: 16,715 (2005); Single-family building permits issued: 90 (2005); Multi-family building permits issued: 29 (2005); Employment by occupation: 26.5% management, 26.4% professional, 8.8% services, 27.8% sales, 0.0% farming, 4.7% construction, 5.8% production (2000).
Income: Per capita income: $44,475 (2005); Median household income: $73,366 (2005); Average household income: $106,718 (2005); Percent of households with income of $100,000 or more: 33.3% (2005); Poverty rate: 2.5% (2000).
Taxes: Total city taxes per capita: $847 (2004); City property taxes per capita: $349 (2004).
Education: Percent of population age 25 and over with: High school diploma (including GED) or higher: 92.1% (2005); Bachelor's degree or higher: 45.3% (2005); Master's degree or higher: 17.8% (2005).

School District(s)
Westlake City SD (PK-12)
    2003-04 Enrollment: 3,917 . . . . (440) 871-7300

Housing: Homeownership rate: 75.4% (2005); Median home value: $214,769 (2005); Median rent: $781 per month (2000); Median age of housing: 20 years (2000).
Hospitals: St. John West Shore Hospital (200 beds)
Safety: Violent crime rate: 0.3 per 10,000 population; Property crime rate: 8.1 per 10,000 population (2004).
Newspapers: The North Ridgeville Press And Light (General - Circulation 4,500); West Life (General - Circulation 15,000)
Transportation: Commute to work: 92.6% car, 2.3% public transportation, 0.6% walk, 3.9% work from home (2000); Travel time to work: 23.4% less than 15 minutes, 38.8% 15 to 30 minutes, 27.4% 30 to 45 minutes, 7.2% 45 to 60 minutes, 3.2% 60 minutes or more (2000)
Additional Information Contacts
City of Westlake . . . . (440) 871-3300
    http://www.cityofwestlake.org
West Shore Chamber of Commerce . . . . (440) 835-8787
    http://www.westshorechamber.org

WOODMERE (village). Covers a land area of 0.329 square miles and a water area of 0 square miles. Located at 41.45° N. Lat.; 81.48° W. Long. Elevation is 1,171 feet.
Population: 834 (1990); 828 (2000); 805 (2005); 782 (2010 projected); Race: 37.8% White, 49.4% Black, 9.8% Asian, 1.0% Hispanic of any race (2005); Density: 2,445.7 persons per square mile (2005); Average household size: 1.99 (2005); Median age: 37.3 (2005); Males per 100 females: 101.3 (2005); Marriage status: 40.6% never married, 38.8% now married, 6.2% widowed, 14.4% divorced (2000); Foreign born: 14.2% (2000); Ancestry (includes multiple ancestries): 63.3% Other groups, 5.5% German, 4.8% Polish, 4.5% Italian, 4.5% Irish (2000).
Economy: Single-family building permits issued: 1 (2005); Multi-family building permits issued: 0 (2005); Employment by occupation: 19.2% management, 22.8% professional, 12.4% services, 27.2% sales, 0.0% farming, 8.2% construction, 10.2% production (2000).
Income: Per capita income: $26,932 (2005); Median household income: $39,783 (2005); Average household income: $53,663 (2005); Percent of households with income of $100,000 or more: 14.9% (2005); Poverty rate: 10.7% (2000).
Education: Percent of population age 25 and over with: High school diploma (including GED) or higher: 87.1% (2005); Bachelor's degree or higher: 30.9% (2005); Master's degree or higher: 12.0% (2005).
Housing: Homeownership rate: 31.4% (2005); Median home value: $189,103 (2005); Median rent: $583 per month (2000); Median age of housing: 37 years (2000).

Transportation: Commute to work: 85.3% car, 5.5% public transportation, 3.8% walk, 5.1% work from home (2000); Travel time to work: 40.6% less than 15 minutes, 32.3% 15 to 30 minutes, 22.1% 30 to 45 minutes, 2.1% 45 to 60 minutes, 2.8% 60 minutes or more (2000)

Darke County

Located in western Ohio; bounded on the west by Indiana; drained by Greenville Creek and the Stillwater and Mississinewa Rivers. Covers a land area of 599.80 square miles, a water area of 0.49 square miles, and is located in the Eastern Time Zone. The county government was organized in 1809. County seat is Greenville.

Darke County is part of the Greenville, OH Micropolitan Statistical Area. The entire metro area includes: Darke County, OH

Weather Station: Greenville Water Plant   Elevation: 1,023 feet

	Jan	Feb	Mar	Apr	May	Jun	Jul	Aug	Sep	Oct	Nov	Dec
High	32	37	48	60	72	80	84	82	77	64	50	38
Low	15	18	28	38	48	58	61	58	50	39	31	21
Precip	2.2	2.1	2.9	3.6	4.0	4.0	4.2	3.2	2.5	2.7	3.1	2.7
Snow	8.3	5.6	3.0	0.5	tr	0.0	0.0	0.0	0.0	0.2	0.8	3.3

High and Low temperatures in degrees Fahrenheit; Precipitation and Snow in inches

Population: 53,597 (1990); 53,309 (2000); 52,911 (2005); 52,485 (2010 projected); Race: 98.1% White, 0.4% Black, 0.3% Asian, 1.0% Hispanic of any race (2005); Density: 88.2 persons per square mile (2005); Average household size: 2.57 (2005); Median age: 38.7 (2005); Males per 100 females: 96.8 (2005).
Religion: Five largest groups: 13.0% Catholic Church, 7.8% The United Methodist Church, 5.3% Evangelical Lutheran Church in America, 2.7% Southern Baptist Convention, 2.6% Church of the Brethren (2000).
Economy: Unemployment rate: 5.9% (2005); Total civilian labor force: 28,385 (2005); Leading industries: 28.9% manufacturing; 14.7% retail trade; 12.6% health care and social assistance (2004); Farms: 1,764 totaling 339,055 acres (2002); Companies that employ 500 or more persons: 3 (2004); Companies that employ 100 to 499 persons: 20 (2004); Companies that employ less than 100 persons: 1,233 (2004); Black-owned businesses: n/a (2002); Hispanic-owned businesses: n/a (2002); Women-owned businesses: 1,272 (2002); Retail sales per capita: $11,090 (2006). Single-family building permits issued: 103 (2005); Multi-family building permits issued: 66 (2005).
Income: Per capita income: $21,182 (2005); Median household income: $43,806 (2005); Average household income: $53,715 (2005); Percent of households with income of $100,000 or more: 9.6% (2005); Poverty rate: 7.9% (2003); Bankruptcy rate: 7.63% (2005).
Education: Percent of population age 25 and over with: High school diploma (including GED) or higher: 82.9% (2005); Bachelor's degree or higher: 10.1% (2005); Master's degree or higher: 3.6% (2005).
Housing: Homeownership rate: 76.7% (2005); Median home value: $118,092 (2005); Median rent: $346 per month (2000); Median age of housing: 43 years (2000).
Health: Birth rate: 135.6 per 10,000 population (2004); Death rate: 102.5 per 10,000 population (2004); Age-adjusted cancer mortality rate: 197.0 deaths per 100,000 population (2002); Number of physicians: 7.9 per 10,000 population (2004); Hospital beds: 13.8 per 10,000 population (2003); Hospital admissions: 497.7 per 10,000 population (2003).
Elections: 2004 Presidential election results: 69.6% Bush, 29.8% Kerry, 0.0% Nader, 0.3% Badnarik
National and State Parks: Fort Jefferson State Memorial; Treaty Of Greenville State Park
Additional Information Contacts
Darke County Government . . . . (937) 547-7370
    http://www.co.darke.oh.us/
City of Greenville . . . . (937) 548-1819
    http://www.cityofgreenville.org
Darke County Chamber of Commerce. . . . . (937) 548-2102
    http://www.darkecountyohio.com
Darke County Economic Development . . . . (937) 548-3250
    http://darkecounty.com
Darke County Visitors Bureau . . . . (937) 548-5158
    http://www.visitdarkecounty.org
Village of Versailles . . . . (937) 526-3294
    http://www.versaillesohio.cc

Darke County Communities

ANSONIA (village). Covers a land area of 0.667 square miles and a water area of 0.017 square miles. Located at 40.21° N. Lat.; 84.63° W. Long. Elevation is 1,009 feet.
Population: 1,279 (1990); 1,145 (2000); 1,148 (2005); 1,154 (2010 projected); Race: 99.1% White, 0.0% Black, 0.0% Asian, 1.7% Hispanic of any race (2005); Density: 1,721.5 persons per square mile (2005); Average household size: 2.48 (2005); Median age: 35.6 (2005); Males per 100 females: 99.3 (2005); Marriage status: 21.8% never married, 55.1% now married, 8.9% widowed, 14.2% divorced (2000); Foreign born: 0.0% (2000); Ancestry (includes multiple ancestries): 35.8% German, 18.5% United States or American, 12.9% Irish, 9.7% Other groups, 6.3% English (2000).
Economy: Employment by occupation: 6.3% management, 5.4% professional, 12.1% services, 21.4% sales, 3.7% farming, 10.2% construction, 40.9% production (2000).
Income: Per capita income: $19,233 (2005); Median household income: $40,236 (2005); Average household income: $47,792 (2005); Percent of households with income of $100,000 or more: 5.4% (2005); Poverty rate: 7.0% (2000).
Education: Percent of population age 25 and over with: High school diploma (including GED) or higher: 78.6% (2005); Bachelor's degree or higher: 2.8% (2005); Master's degree or higher: 0.8% (2005).
School District(s)
Ansonia Local SD (PK-12)
 2003-04 Enrollment: 803 . . . . (937) 337-4000
Housing: Homeownership rate: 74.2% (2005); Median home value: $83,152 (2005); Median rent: $345 per month (2000); Median age of housing: 48 years (2000).
Transportation: Commute to work: 93.2% car, 0.0% public transportation, 1.3% walk, 1.5% work from home (2000); Travel time to work: 30.2% less than 15 minutes, 46.5% 15 to 30 minutes, 14.8% 30 to 45 minutes, 5.0% 45 to 60 minutes, 3.5% 60 minutes or more (2000)

ARCANUM (village). Covers a land area of 1.160 square miles and a water area of 0 square miles. Located at 39.99° N. Lat.; 84.55° W. Long. Elevation is 1,051 feet.
Population: 2,059 (1990); 2,076 (2000); 2,103 (2005); 2,130 (2010 projected); Race: 98.9% White, 0.0% Black, 0.2% Asian, 0.5% Hispanic of any race (2005); Density: 1,813.1 persons per square mile (2005); Average household size: 2.38 (2005); Median age: 36.7 (2005); Males per 100 females: 91.9 (2005); Marriage status: 16.8% never married, 63.9% now married, 8.1% widowed, 11.2% divorced (2000); Foreign born: 1.2% (2000); Ancestry (includes multiple ancestries): 31.3% German, 9.3% United States or American, 9.1% English, 7.6% Irish, 7.1% Other groups (2000).
Economy: In diversified farming area. Employment by occupation: 10.2% management, 20.9% professional, 11.6% services, 23.8% sales, 1.0% farming, 11.9% construction, 20.5% production (2000).
Income: Per capita income: $23,718 (2005); Median household income: $46,656 (2005); Average household income: $56,553 (2005); Percent of households with income of $100,000 or more: 9.9% (2005); Poverty rate: 3.5% (2000).
Education: Percent of population age 25 and over with: High school diploma (including GED) or higher: 88.6% (2005); Bachelor's degree or higher: 13.9% (2005); Master's degree or higher: 5.2% (2005).
School District(s)
Arcanum Butler Local SD (KG-12)
 2003-04 Enrollment: 1,094 . . . . (937) 692-5174
Franklin Monroe Local SD (PK-12)
 2003-04 Enrollment: 743 . . . . (937) 692-8637
Housing: Homeownership rate: 73.6% (2005); Median home value: $125,955 (2005); Median rent: $363 per month (2000); Median age of housing: 46 years (2000).
Safety: Violent crime rate: 0.0 per 10,000 population; Property crime rate: 92.8 per 10,000 population (2004).
Transportation: Commute to work: 94.0% car, 0.4% public transportation, 2.9% walk, 1.5% work from home (2000); Travel time to work: 17.6% less than 15 minutes, 34.3% 15 to 30 minutes, 28.4% 30 to 45 minutes, 10.7% 45 to 60 minutes, 9.0% 60 minutes or more (2000)

CASTINE (village). Covers a land area of 0.076 square miles and a water area of 0 square miles. Located at 39.93° N. Lat.; 84.62° W. Long. Elevation is 1,080 feet.
Population: 163 (1990); 129 (2000); 140 (2005); 146 (2010 projected); Race: 99.3% White, 0.0% Black, 0.0% Asian, 0.7% Hispanic of any race (2005); Density: 1,845.1 persons per square mile (2005); Average household size: 2.98 (2005); Median age: 35.6 (2005); Males per 100 females: 122.2 (2005); Marriage status: 15.4% never married, 75.8% now married, 0.0% widowed, 8.8% divorced (2000); Foreign born: 0.0% (2000); Ancestry (includes multiple ancestries): 17.8% United States or American, 9.3% German, 3.9% Other groups, 3.1% Irish (2000).
Economy: In agricultural area. Employment by occupation: 13.9% management, 8.3% professional, 13.9% services, 18.1% sales, 0.0% farming, 22.2% construction, 23.6% production (2000).
Income: Per capita income: $13,696 (2005); Median household income: $36,250 (2005); Average household income: $40,798 (2005); Percent of households with income of $100,000 or more: 0.0% (2005); Poverty rate: 7.0% (2000).
Education: Percent of population age 25 and over with: High school diploma (including GED) or higher: 76.8% (2005); Bachelor's degree or higher: 4.9% (2005); Master's degree or higher: 4.9% (2005).
Housing: Homeownership rate: 70.2% (2005); Median home value: $97,273 (2005); Median rent: $325 per month (2000); Median age of housing: 48 years (2000).
Transportation: Commute to work: 100.0% car, 0.0% public transportation, 0.0% walk, 0.0% work from home (2000); Travel time to work: 29.4% less than 15 minutes, 25.0% 15 to 30 minutes, 23.5% 30 to 45 minutes, 8.8% 45 to 60 minutes, 13.2% 60 minutes or more (2000)

GETTYSBURG (village). Covers a land area of 0.440 square miles and a water area of <.001 square miles. Located at 40.11° N. Lat.; 84.49° W. Long. Elevation is 1,050 feet.
Population: 539 (1990); 558 (2000); 546 (2005); 538 (2010 projected); Race: 95.6% White, 0.9% Black, 1.3% Asian, 0.5% Hispanic of any race (2005); Density: 1,240.4 persons per square mile (2005); Average household size: 2.94 (2005); Median age: 30.3 (2005); Males per 100 females: 94.3 (2005); Marriage status: 23.2% never married, 60.5% now married, 4.7% widowed, 11.6% divorced (2000); Foreign born: 2.9% (2000); Ancestry (includes multiple ancestries): 37.3% German, 9.3% Other groups, 8.2% Irish, 8.0% United States or American, 7.3% French (except Basque) (2000).
Economy: Single-family building permits issued: 0 (2005); Multi-family building permits issued: 0 (2005); Employment by occupation: 7.7% management, 8.4% professional, 8.8% services, 21.5% sales, 0.8% farming, 11.1% construction, 41.8% production (2000).
Income: Per capita income: $16,891 (2005); Median household income: $41,923 (2005); Average household income: $49,583 (2005); Percent of households with income of $100,000 or more: 5.4% (2005); Poverty rate: 10.7% (2000).
Education: Percent of population age 25 and over with: High school diploma (including GED) or higher: 83.7% (2005); Bachelor's degree or higher: 9.4% (2005); Master's degree or higher: 4.2% (2005).
School District(s)
Greenville City School District (KG-12)
 2003-04 Enrollment: 3,419 . . . . (937) 548-3185
Housing: Homeownership rate: 78.0% (2005); Median home value: $93,902 (2005); Median rent: $333 per month (2000); Median age of housing: 49 years (2000).
Transportation: Commute to work: 88.6% car, 0.0% public transportation, 9.1% walk, 2.0% work from home (2000); Travel time to work: 28.5% less than 15 minutes, 50.2% 15 to 30 minutes, 13.7% 30 to 45 minutes, 5.6% 45 to 60 minutes, 2.0% 60 minutes or more (2000)

GORDON (village). Covers a land area of 0.164 square miles and a water area of 0 square miles. Located at 39.93° N. Lat.; 84.50° W. Long. Elevation is 1,045 feet.
Population: 206 (1990); 190 (2000); 193 (2005); 190 (2010 projected); Race: 100.0% White, 0.0% Black, 0.0% Asian, 0.0% Hispanic of any race (2005); Density: 1,177.9 persons per square mile (2005); Average household size: 2.54 (2005); Median age: 35.7 (2005); Males per 100 females: 94.9 (2005); Marriage status: 12.9% never married, 75.5% now married, 5.8% widowed, 5.8% divorced (2000); Foreign born: 0.0% (2000); Ancestry (includes multiple ancestries): 33.7% German, 23.2% United States or American, 14.2% Irish, 5.8% Scotch-Irish, 5.8% Other groups (2000).
Economy: In agricultural area. Employment by occupation: 4.4% management, 7.8% professional, 14.4% services, 22.2% sales, 0.0% farming, 21.1% construction, 30.0% production (2000).

Income: Per capita income: $21,166 (2005); Median household income: $45,588 (2005); Average household income: $53,750 (2005); Percent of households with income of $100,000 or more: 11.8% (2005); Poverty rate: 0.5% (2000).
Education: Percent of population age 25 and over with: High school diploma (including GED) or higher: 84.8% (2005); Bachelor's degree or higher: 1.6% (2005); Master's degree or higher: 0.0% (2005).
Housing: Homeownership rate: 88.2% (2005); Median home value: $97,308 (2005); Median rent: $325 per month (2000); Median age of housing: 60+ years (2000).
Transportation: Commute to work: 97.8% car, 0.0% public transportation, 0.0% walk, 2.2% work from home (2000); Travel time to work: 12.6% less than 15 minutes, 39.1% 15 to 30 minutes, 34.5% 30 to 45 minutes, 12.6% 45 to 60 minutes, 1.1% 60 minutes or more (2000)

GREENVILLE (city)

Covers a land area of 6.025 square miles and a water area of 0 square miles. Located at 40.10° N. Lat.; 84.62° W. Long. Elevation is 1,040 feet.
History: Fort Greenville, established here and named for General Nathanael Greene, was abandoned in 1795. A town was founded here in 1805 by the Swawnee chieftain, Tecumseh, and his brother, Tenakwatawa, known as The Prophet. After Prophet's Town was moved to Indiana, other settlers came and the town of Greenville was founded.
Population: 13,140 (1990); 13,294 (2000); 12,969 (2005); 12,609 (2010 projected); Race: 97.2% White, 0.5% Black, 0.7% Asian, 1.3% Hispanic of any race (2005); Density: 2,152.4 persons per square mile (2005); Average household size: 2.31 (2005); Median age: 41.7 (2005); Males per 100 females: 85.4 (2005); Marriage status: 20.3% never married, 53.3% now married, 13.3% widowed, 13.1% divorced (2000); Foreign born: 1.0% (2000); Ancestry (includes multiple ancestries): 30.9% German, 14.6% United States or American, 10.8% Irish, 10.0% English, 6.1% Other groups (2000).
Economy: Employment by occupation: 8.9% management, 15.1% professional, 16.1% services, 24.5% sales, 0.0% farming, 10.7% construction, 24.6% production (2000).
Income: Per capita income: $20,260 (2005); Median household income: $34,444 (2005); Average household income: $44,678 (2005); Percent of households with income of $100,000 or more: 6.4% (2005); Poverty rate: 13.4% (2000).
Education: Percent of population age 25 and over with: High school diploma (including GED) or higher: 80.9% (2005); Bachelor's degree or higher: 11.9% (2005); Master's degree or higher: 4.5% (2005).

School District(s)
Greenville City School District (KG-12)
   2003-04 Enrollment: 3,419 . . . . (937) 548-3185
Housing: Homeownership rate: 63.1% (2005); Median home value: $106,596 (2005); Median rent: $352 per month (2000); Median age of housing: 43 years (2000).
Hospitals: Wayne Hospital (92 beds)
Safety: Violent crime rate: 38.5 per 10,000 population; Property crime rate: 371.0 per 10,000 population (2004).
Newspapers: Daily Advocate (Circulation 6,600); The Early Bird (General - Circulation 26,625)
Transportation: Commute to work: 93.5% car, 0.3% public transportation, 2.9% walk, 2.3% work from home (2000); Travel time to work: 63.3% less than 15 minutes, 16.5% 15 to 30 minutes, 9.1% 30 to 45 minutes, 7.5% 45 to 60 minutes, 3.6% 60 minutes or more (2000)
Additional Information Contacts
City of Greenville . . . . (937) 548-1819
   http://www.cityofgreenville.org
Darke County Chamber of Commerce. . . . . (937) 548-2102
   http://www.darkecountyohio.com
Darke County Economic Development . . . . (937) 548-3250
   http://darkecounty.com
Darke County Visitors Bureau . . . . (937) 548-5158
   http://www.visitdarkecounty.org

HOLLANSBURG (village)

Covers a land area of 0.122 square miles and a water area of 0 square miles. Located at 39.99° N. Lat.; 84.79° W. Long. Elevation is 1,170 feet.
Population: 300 (1990); 214 (2000); 216 (2005); 212 (2010 projected); Race: 98.1% White, 0.0% Black, 0.0% Asian, 0.0% Hispanic of any race (2005); Density: 1,775.3 persons per square mile (2005); Average household size: 2.43 (2005); Median age: 34.4 (2005); Males per 100 females: 120.4 (2005); Marriage status: 29.2% never married, 48.5% now married, 10.5% widowed, 11.7% divorced (2000); Foreign born: 0.0% (2000); Ancestry (includes multiple ancestries): 21.3% German, 20.4% United States or American, 10.4% Irish, 8.7% Other groups, 5.2% French (except Basque) (2000).
Economy: Cheese. Employment by occupation: 7.1% management, 8.2% professional, 22.4% services, 9.2% sales, 0.0% farming, 16.3% construction, 36.7% production (2000).
Income: Per capita income: $16,470 (2005); Median household income: $37,019 (2005); Average household income: $39,972 (2005); Percent of households with income of $100,000 or more: 4.5% (2005); Poverty rate: 4.3% (2000).
Education: Percent of population age 25 and over with: High school diploma (including GED) or higher: 76.6% (2005); Bachelor's degree or higher: 3.5% (2005); Master's degree or higher: 0.0% (2005).
Housing: Homeownership rate: 80.9% (2005); Median home value: $51,176 (2005); Median rent: $350 per month (2000); Median age of housing: 60+ years (2000).
Transportation: Commute to work: 94.7% car, 0.0% public transportation, 5.3% walk, 0.0% work from home (2000); Travel time to work: 10.6% less than 15 minutes, 54.3% 15 to 30 minutes, 21.3% 30 to 45 minutes, 8.5% 45 to 60 minutes, 5.3% 60 minutes or more (2000)

ITHACA (village)

Covers a land area of 0.030 square miles and a water area of 0 square miles. Located at 39.93° N. Lat.; 84.55° W. Long. Elevation is 1,010 feet.
Population: 119 (1990); 102 (2000); 94 (2005); 90 (2010 projected); Race: 100.0% White, 0.0% Black, 0.0% Asian, 0.0% Hispanic of any race (2005); Density: 3,099.2 persons per square mile (2005); Average household size: 2.85 (2005); Median age: 35.5 (2005); Males per 100 females: 113.6 (2005); Marriage status: 24.5% never married, 62.8% now married, 10.6% widowed, 2.1% divorced (2000); Foreign born: 0.0% (2000); Ancestry (includes multiple ancestries): 25.2% English, 16.0% German, 14.3% United States or American, 3.4% Irish, 1.7% Other groups (2000).
Economy: In agricultural area. Employment by occupation: 0.0% management, 3.8% professional, 13.2% services, 26.4% sales, 0.0% farming, 7.5% construction, 49.1% production (2000).
Income: Per capita income: $16,649 (2005); Median household income: $48,269 (2005); Average household income: $47,424 (2005); Percent of households with income of $100,000 or more: 0.0% (2005); Poverty rate: 0.0% (2000).
Education: Percent of population age 25 and over with: High school diploma (including GED) or higher: 75.0% (2005); Bachelor's degree or higher: 0.0% (2005); Master's degree or higher: 0.0% (2005).
Housing: Homeownership rate: 69.7% (2005); Median home value: $81,429 (2005); Median rent: $458 per month (2000); Median age of housing: 49 years (2000).
Transportation: Commute to work: 100.0% car, 0.0% public transportation, 0.0% walk, 0.0% work from home (2000); Travel time to work: 14.0% less than 15 minutes, 42.0% 15 to 30 minutes, 40.0% 30 to 45 minutes, 0.0% 45 to 60 minutes, 4.0% 60 minutes or more (2000)

NEW MADISON (village)

Covers a land area of 0.372 square miles and a water area of 0 square miles. Located at 39.96° N. Lat.; 84.70° W. Long. Elevation is 1,113 feet.
Population: 928 (1990); 817 (2000); 844 (2005); 854 (2010 projected); Race: 97.5% White, 0.2% Black, 0.7% Asian, 0.0% Hispanic of any race (2005); Density: 2,269.0 persons per square mile (2005); Average household size: 2.32 (2005); Median age: 39.0 (2005); Males per 100 females: 96.7 (2005); Marriage status: 15.8% never married, 62.3% now married, 10.6% widowed, 11.3% divorced (2000); Foreign born: 1.8% (2000); Ancestry (includes multiple ancestries): 28.6% German, 17.8% United States or American, 9.1% Irish, 8.9% English, 6.6% Other groups (2000).
Economy: Canned foods; grain. Single-family building permits issued: 0 (2005); Multi-family building permits issued: 0 (2005); Employment by occupation: 6.3% management, 12.5% professional, 14.9% services, 24.0% sales, 0.0% farming, 6.5% construction, 35.8% production (2000).
Income: Per capita income: $20,441 (2005); Median household income: $37,679 (2005); Average household income: $47,397 (2005); Percent of households with income of $100,000 or more: 8.2% (2005); Poverty rate: 7.7% (2000).
Education: Percent of population age 25 and over with: High school diploma (including GED) or higher: 87.0% (2005); Bachelor's degree or higher: 7.4% (2005); Master's degree or higher: 3.2% (2005).

School District(s)
Tri-Village Local SD (PK-12)
   2003-04 Enrollment: 789 . . . . (937) 996-6261
Housing: Homeownership rate: 78.6% (2005); Median home value: $94,091 (2005); Median rent: $397 per month (2000); Median age of housing: 56 years (2000).
Transportation: Commute to work: 95.9% car, 0.5% public transportation, 2.4% walk, 1.2% work from home (2000); Travel time to work: 21.6% less than 15 minutes, 54.9% 15 to 30 minutes, 11.3% 30 to 45 minutes, 10.5% 45 to 60 minutes, 1.7% 60 minutes or more (2000)

NEW WESTON (village). Covers a land area of 0.256 square miles and a water area of 0 square miles. Located at 40.33° N. Lat.; 84.64° W. Long. Elevation is 1,015 feet.
Population: 148 (1990); 135 (2000); 138 (2005); 141 (2010 projected); Race: 97.8% White, 0.0% Black, 0.0% Asian, 0.0% Hispanic of any race (2005); Density: 539.7 persons per square mile (2005); Average household size: 2.76 (2005); Median age: 32.5 (2005); Males per 100 females: 115.6 (2005); Marriage status: 22.7% never married, 70.1% now married, 2.1% widowed, 5.2% divorced (2000); Foreign born: 1.6% (2000); Ancestry (includes multiple ancestries): 25.6% German, 23.3% United States or American, 6.2% French (except Basque), 4.7% Irish, 4.7% Other groups (2000).
Economy: In agricultural area; ceramics. Employment by occupation: 4.8% management, 3.2% professional, 19.0% services, 11.1% sales, 3.2% farming, 20.6% construction, 38.1% production (2000).
Income: Per capita income: $13,279 (2005); Median household income: $39,412 (2005); Average household income: $36,650 (2005); Percent of households with income of $100,000 or more: 0.0% (2005); Poverty rate: 12.6% (2000).
Education: Percent of population age 25 and over with: High school diploma (including GED) or higher: 53.6% (2005); Bachelor's degree or higher: 6.0% (2005); Master's degree or higher: 2.4% (2005).
Housing: Homeownership rate: 80.0% (2005); Median home value: $68,889 (2005); Median rent: $475 per month (2000); Median age of housing: 60+ years (2000).
Transportation: Commute to work: 91.8% car, 0.0% public transportation, 8.2% walk, 0.0% work from home (2000); Travel time to work: 14.8% less than 15 minutes, 62.3% 15 to 30 minutes, 16.4% 30 to 45 minutes, 6.6% 45 to 60 minutes, 0.0% 60 minutes or more (2000)

NORTH STAR (village). Covers a land area of 0.521 square miles and a water area of 0 square miles. Located at 40.32° N. Lat.; 84.56° W. Long. Elevation is 1,006 feet.
History: North Star was founded in 1844 by John Houston and Heronimus Star. This was the birthplace of Annie Oakley, born in 1860, who became an expert markswoman.
Population: 246 (1990); 209 (2000); 226 (2005); 243 (2010 projected); Race: 99.1% White, 0.0% Black, 0.9% Asian, 0.0% Hispanic of any race (2005); Density: 434.1 persons per square mile (2005); Average household size: 2.66 (2005); Median age: 40.9 (2005); Males per 100 females: 111.2 (2005); Marriage status: 19.7% never married, 66.9% now married, 12.1% widowed, 1.3% divorced (2000); Foreign born: 0.0% (2000); Ancestry (includes multiple ancestries): 61.5% German, 24.9% French (except Basque), 18.5% United States or American, 2.0% Other groups, 2.0% Dutch (2000).
Economy: Employment by occupation: 5.7% management, 10.5% professional, 18.1% services, 31.4% sales, 0.0% farming, 0.0% construction, 34.3% production (2000).
Income: Per capita income: $22,002 (2005); Median household income: $56,696 (2005); Average household income: $58,500 (2005); Percent of households with income of $100,000 or more: 7.1% (2005); Poverty rate: 5.4% (2000).
Education: Percent of population age 25 and over with: High school diploma (including GED) or higher: 91.3% (2005); Bachelor's degree or higher: 2.7% (2005); Master's degree or higher: 1.3% (2005).
School District(s)
Versailles Ex Vill SD (PK-12)
   2003-04 Enrollment: 1,413 . . . . (937) 526-4773
Housing: Homeownership rate: 89.4% (2005); Median home value: $121,795 (2005); Median rent: $306 per month (2000); Median age of housing: 38 years (2000).
Transportation: Commute to work: 85.4% car, 0.0% public transportation, 7.8% walk, 6.8% work from home (2000); Travel time to work: 24.0% less than 15 minutes, 65.6% 15 to 30 minutes, 8.3% 30 to 45 minutes, 0.0% 45 to 60 minutes, 2.1% 60 minutes or more (2000)

OSGOOD (village). Covers a land area of 0.344 square miles and a water area of 0 square miles. Located at 40.34° N. Lat.; 84.49° W. Long. Elevation is 961 feet.
Population: 289 (1990); 255 (2000); 252 (2005); 251 (2010 projected); Race: 100.0% White, 0.0% Black, 0.0% Asian, 0.0% Hispanic of any race (2005); Density: 733.4 persons per square mile (2005); Average household size: 2.42 (2005); Median age: 38.5 (2005); Males per 100 females: 98.4 (2005); Marriage status: 14.7% never married, 68.8% now married, 11.0% widowed, 5.5% divorced (2000); Foreign born: 1.1% (2000); Ancestry (includes multiple ancestries): 73.6% German, 18.2% French (except Basque), 6.7% United States or American, 3.0% Dutch, 1.9% Irish (2000).
Economy: In agricultural area. Employment by occupation: 8.6% management, 15.7% professional, 15.0% services, 15.0% sales, 0.0% farming, 6.4% construction, 39.3% production (2000).
Income: Per capita income: $20,218 (2005); Median household income: $46,111 (2005); Average household income: $48,990 (2005); Percent of households with income of $100,000 or more: 3.8% (2005); Poverty rate: 0.4% (2000).
Education: Percent of population age 25 and over with: High school diploma (including GED) or higher: 78.0% (2005); Bachelor's degree or higher: 11.0% (2005); Master's degree or higher: 6.4% (2005).
Housing: Homeownership rate: 88.5% (2005); Median home value: $125,000 (2005); Median rent: $381 per month (2000); Median age of housing: 33 years (2000).
Transportation: Commute to work: 89.0% car, 0.0% public transportation, 5.9% walk, 5.1% work from home (2000); Travel time to work: 46.5% less than 15 minutes, 38.0% 15 to 30 minutes, 7.8% 30 to 45 minutes, 6.2% 45 to 60 minutes, 1.6% 60 minutes or more (2000)

PALESTINE (village). Covers a land area of 0.147 square miles and a water area of 0 square miles. Located at 40.05° N. Lat.; 84.74° W. Long. Elevation is 1,105 feet.
Population: 219 (1990); 170 (2000); 178 (2005); 178 (2010 projected); Race: 93.8% White, 6.2% Black, 0.0% Asian, 0.0% Hispanic of any race (2005); Density: 1,207.2 persons per square mile (2005); Average household size: 2.92 (2005); Median age: 36.3 (2005); Males per 100 females: 100.0 (2005); Marriage status: 0.0% never married, 66.7% now married, 33.3% widowed, 0.0% divorced (2000); Foreign born: 0.0% (2000); Ancestry (includes multiple ancestries): 33.3% German (2000).
Economy: Employment by occupation: 0.0% management, 0.0% professional, 0.0% services, 100.0% sales, 0.0% farming, 0.0% construction, 0.0% production (2000).
Income: Per capita income: $10,913 (2005); Median household income: $35,703 (2005); Average household income: $31,844 (2005); Percent of households with income of $100,000 or more: 0.0% (2005); Poverty rate: 0.0% (2000).
Education: Percent of population age 25 and over with: High school diploma (including GED) or higher: 100.0% (2005); Bachelor's degree or higher: 0.0% (2005); Master's degree or higher: 0.0% (2005).
Housing: Homeownership rate: 86.9% (2005); Median home value: $73,250 (2005); Median rent: $n/a per month (2000); Median age of housing: 60+ years (2000).
Transportation: Commute to work: 100.0% car, 0.0% public transportation, 0.0% walk, 0.0% work from home (2000); Travel time to work: 100.0% less than 15 minutes, 0.0% 15 to 30 minutes, 0.0% 30 to 45 minutes, 0.0% 45 to 60 minutes, 0.0% 60 minutes or more (2000)

PITSBURG (village). Covers a land area of 0.190 square miles and a water area of 0 square miles. Located at 39.98° N. Lat.; 84.48° W. Long. Elevation is 1,025 feet.
History: Also spelled Pittsburg.
Population: 425 (1990); 392 (2000); 377 (2005); 364 (2010 projected); Race: 97.6% White, 0.0% Black, 0.0% Asian, 0.5% Hispanic of any race (2005); Density: 1,987.5 persons per square mile (2005); Average household size: 2.86 (2005); Median age: 29.4 (2005); Males per 100 females: 99.5 (2005); Marriage status: 9.9% never married, 81.5% now married, 6.0% widowed, 2.6% divorced (2000); Foreign born: 2.1% (2000); Ancestry (includes multiple ancestries): 37.0% German, 12.8% Irish, 12.8% English, 12.5% Other groups, 11.6% United States or American (2000).
Economy: Employment by occupation: 23.9% management, 17.4% professional, 11.0% services, 22.6% sales, 0.0% farming, 11.0% construction, 14.2% production (2000).

Income: Per capita income: $21,107 (2005); Median household income: $64,167 (2005); Average household income: $60,284 (2005); Percent of households with income of $100,000 or more: 14.4% (2005); Poverty rate: 4.0% (2000).
Education: Percent of population age 25 and over with: High school diploma (including GED) or higher: 98.1% (2005); Bachelor's degree or higher: 8.4% (2005); Master's degree or higher: 6.0% (2005).
Housing: Homeownership rate: 82.6% (2005); Median home value: $126,293 (2005); Median rent: $391 per month (2000); Median age of housing: 36 years (2000).
Transportation: Commute to work: 100.0% car, 0.0% public transportation, 0.0% walk, 0.0% work from home (2000); Travel time to work: 18.7% less than 15 minutes, 36.1% 15 to 30 minutes, 18.1% 30 to 45 minutes, 19.4% 45 to 60 minutes, 7.7% 60 minutes or more (2000)

ROSSBURG (village). Covers a land area of 0.140 square miles and a water area of 0 square miles. Located at 40.28° N. Lat.; 84.63° W. Long. Elevation is 1,036 feet.
Population: 268 (1990); 224 (2000); 230 (2005); 236 (2010 projected); Race: 99.1% White, 0.0% Black, 0.0% Asian, 0.9% Hispanic of any race (2005); Density: 1,643.1 persons per square mile (2005); Average household size: 2.56 (2005); Median age: 36.0 (2005); Males per 100 females: 91.7 (2005); Marriage status: 32.3% never married, 47.6% now married, 11.1% widowed, 9.0% divorced (2000); Foreign born: 1.4% (2000); Ancestry (includes multiple ancestries): 38.6% German, 11.9% Other groups, 11.4% Irish, 10.5% United States or American, 2.9% English (2000).
Economy: Employment by occupation: 9.3% management, 10.9% professional, 14.0% services, 14.7% sales, 3.9% farming, 13.2% construction, 34.1% production (2000).
Income: Per capita income: $14,533 (2005); Median household income: $32,059 (2005); Average household income: $37,139 (2005); Percent of households with income of $100,000 or more: 1.1% (2005); Poverty rate: 4.3% (2000).
Education: Percent of population age 25 and over with: High school diploma (including GED) or higher: 76.7% (2005); Bachelor's degree or higher: 1.4% (2005); Master's degree or higher: 0.0% (2005).
Housing: Homeownership rate: 81.1% (2005); Median home value: $70,000 (2005); Median rent: $339 per month (2000); Median age of housing: 60+ years (2000).
Transportation: Commute to work: 88.6% car, 0.0% public transportation, 9.8% walk, 1.6% work from home (2000); Travel time to work: 22.3% less than 15 minutes, 63.6% 15 to 30 minutes, 9.1% 30 to 45 minutes, 2.5% 45 to 60 minutes, 2.5% 60 minutes or more (2000)

UNION CITY (village). Covers a land area of 0.921 square miles and a water area of 0 square miles. Located at 40.20° N. Lat.; 84.80° W. Long. Elevation is 1,114 feet.
Population: 2,047 (1990); 1,767 (2000); 1,726 (2005); 1,712 (2010 projected); Race: 95.2% White, 1.3% Black, 0.2% Asian, 5.1% Hispanic of any race (2005); Density: 1,874.5 persons per square mile (2005); Average household size: 2.52 (2005); Median age: 35.7 (2005); Males per 100 females: 88.2 (2005); Marriage status: 21.2% never married, 56.1% now married, 9.2% widowed, 13.5% divorced (2000); Foreign born: 2.5% (2000); Ancestry (includes multiple ancestries): 25.1% German, 15.8% Other groups, 11.2% United States or American, 10.2% Irish, 6.3% English (2000).
Economy: Employment by occupation: 4.5% management, 4.1% professional, 18.6% services, 18.8% sales, 2.2% farming, 7.6% construction, 44.1% production (2000).
Income: Per capita income: $15,735 (2005); Median household income: $30,282 (2005); Average household income: $37,978 (2005); Percent of households with income of $100,000 or more: 2.8% (2005); Poverty rate: 20.8% (2000).
Education: Percent of population age 25 and over with: High school diploma (including GED) or higher: 62.7% (2005); Bachelor's degree or higher: 1.1% (2005); Master's degree or higher: 0.4% (2005).
School District(s)
Mississinawa Valley Local SD (PK-12)
    2003-04 Enrollment: 728 . . . . (937) 968-5656
Housing: Homeownership rate: 57.7% (2005); Median home value: $60,565 (2005); Median rent: $283 per month (2000); Median age of housing: 39 years (2000).
Transportation: Commute to work: 93.4% car, 0.6% public transportation, 3.5% walk, 1.7% work from home (2000); Travel time to work: 43.6% less than 15 minutes, 31.4% 15 to 30 minutes, 14.5% 30 to 45 minutes, 4.3% 45 to 60 minutes, 6.1% 60 minutes or more (2000)

VERSAILLES (village). Covers a land area of 1.746 square miles and a water area of 0 square miles. Located at 40.22° N. Lat.; 84.48° W. Long. Elevation is 978 feet.
History: Settled 1819, incorporated 1855.
Population: 2,446 (1990); 2,589 (2000); 2,557 (2005); 2,525 (2010 projected); Race: 99.3% White, 0.0% Black, 0.1% Asian, 0.2% Hispanic of any race (2005); Density: 1,464.2 persons per square mile (2005); Average household size: 2.41 (2005); Median age: 37.9 (2005); Males per 100 females: 93.6 (2005); Marriage status: 18.8% never married, 61.3% now married, 10.2% widowed, 9.7% divorced (2000); Foreign born: 0.1% (2000); Ancestry (includes multiple ancestries): 33.9% German, 21.4% French (except Basque), 9.8% Irish, 9.6% United States or American, 5.2% English (2000).
Economy: In agricultural area: poultry; grain, fruit, tobacco, vegetables. Single-family building permits issued: 11 (2005); Multi-family building permits issued: 0 (2005); Employment by occupation: 12.2% management, 11.3% professional, 14.0% services, 23.3% sales, 1.4% farming, 7.7% construction, 30.0% production (2000).
Income: Per capita income: $19,904 (2005); Median household income: $41,890 (2005); Average household income: $47,479 (2005); Percent of households with income of $100,000 or more: 7.6% (2005); Poverty rate: 5.3% (2000).
Education: Percent of population age 25 and over with: High school diploma (including GED) or higher: 84.1% (2005); Bachelor's degree or higher: 12.6% (2005); Master's degree or higher: 4.3% (2005).
School District(s)
Versailles Ex Vill SD (PK-12)
    2003-04 Enrollment: 1,413 . . . . (937) 526-4773
Housing: Homeownership rate: 71.1% (2005); Median home value: $124,613 (2005); Median rent: $327 per month (2000); Median age of housing: 47 years (2000).
Newspapers: The Versailles Policy (General - Circulation 2,200)
Transportation: Commute to work: 94.1% car, 0.3% public transportation, 2.4% walk, 2.8% work from home (2000); Travel time to work: 52.2% less than 15 minutes, 23.8% 15 to 30 minutes, 15.0% 30 to 45 minutes, 2.8% 45 to 60 minutes, 6.2% 60 minutes or more (2000)
Additional Information Contacts
Village of Versailles . . . . (937) 526-3294
  http://www.versaillesohio.cc

WAYNE LAKES (village). Aka Wayne Lakes Park. Covers a land area of 0.546 square miles and a water area of 0.108 square miles. Located at 40.02° N. Lat.; 84.66° W. Long.
Population: 671 (1990); 684 (2000); 645 (2005); 625 (2010 projected); Race: 98.4% White, 0.3% Black, 0.2% Asian, 0.9% Hispanic of any race (2005); Density: 1,181.2 persons per square mile (2005); Average household size: 2.37 (2005); Median age: 41.4 (2005); Males per 100 females: 99.1 (2005); Marriage status: 22.3% never married, 61.3% now married, 4.3% widowed, 12.1% divorced (2000); Foreign born: 1.2% (2000); Ancestry (includes multiple ancestries): 42.4% German, 14.3% Irish, 13.5% Other groups, 13.3% United States or American, 10.7% English (2000).
Economy: Single-family building permits issued: 1 (2005); Multi-family building permits issued: 0 (2005); Employment by occupation: 10.7% management, 9.9% professional, 9.0% services, 31.4% sales, 0.6% farming, 12.1% construction, 26.3% production (2000).
Income: Per capita income: $23,981 (2005); Median household income: $53,933 (2005); Average household income: $56,866 (2005); Percent of households with income of $100,000 or more: 7.0% (2005); Poverty rate: 2.5% (2000).
Education: Percent of population age 25 and over with: High school diploma (including GED) or higher: 89.3% (2005); Bachelor's degree or higher: 16.1% (2005); Master's degree or higher: 4.0% (2005).
Housing: Homeownership rate: 87.9% (2005); Median home value: $109,737 (2005); Median rent: $463 per month (2000); Median age of housing: 34 years (2000).
Transportation: Commute to work: 94.2% car, 0.3% public transportation, 0.0% walk, 4.6% work from home (2000); Travel time to work: 27.0% less than 15 minutes, 33.3% 15 to 30 minutes, 17.9% 30 to 45 minutes, 12.4% 45 to 60 minutes, 9.4% 60 minutes or more (2000)

PROFILES OF OHIO / Defiance County

YORKSHIRE (village). Covers a land area of 0.282 square miles and a water area of 0 square miles. Located at 40.32° N. Lat.; 84.49° W. Long. Elevation is 988 feet.
Population: 126 (1990); 110 (2000); 109 (2005); 109 (2010 projected); Race: 99.1% White, 0.0% Black, 0.0% Asian, 0.0% Hispanic of any race (2005); Density: 386.6 persons per square mile (2005); Average household size: 2.95 (2005); Median age: 32.9 (2005); Males per 100 females: 81.7 (2005); Marriage status: 38.0% never married, 40.5% now married, 6.3% widowed, 15.2% divorced (2000); Foreign born: 0.0% (2000); Ancestry (includes multiple ancestries): 69.9% German, 25.8% United States or American, 5.4% Scottish, 3.2% Other groups, 2.2% French (except Basque) (2000).
Economy: In agricultural area. Employment by occupation: 8.7% management, 4.3% professional, 15.2% services, 21.7% sales, 4.3% farming, 21.7% construction, 23.9% production (2000).
Income: Per capita income: $16,376 (2005); Median household income: $44,643 (2005); Average household income: $48,243 (2005); Percent of households with income of $100,000 or more: 8.1% (2005); Poverty rate: 3.2% (2000).
Education: Percent of population age 25 and over with: High school diploma (including GED) or higher: 73.5% (2005); Bachelor's degree or higher: 8.8% (2005); Master's degree or higher: 0.0% (2005).
Housing: Homeownership rate: 78.4% (2005); Median home value: $117,500 (2005); Median rent: $300 per month (2000); Median age of housing: 60+ years (2000).
Transportation: Commute to work: 87.0% car, 0.0% public transportation, 4.3% walk, 8.7% work from home (2000); Travel time to work: 23.8% less than 15 minutes, 54.8% 15 to 30 minutes, 7.1% 30 to 45 minutes, 9.5% 45 to 60 minutes, 4.8% 60 minutes or more (2000)

Defiance County

Located in northwestern Ohio; bounded on the west by Indiana; intersected by the Maumee, Auglize, and Tiffin Rivers. Covers a land area of 411.16 square miles, a water area of 3.03 square miles, and is located in the Eastern Time Zone. The county government was organized in 1845. County seat is Defiance.

Defiance County is part of the Defiance, OH Micropolitan Statistical Area. The entire metro area includes: Defiance County, OH

Weather Station: Defiance   Elevation: 698 feet

	Jan	Feb	Mar	Apr	May	Jun	Jul	Aug	Sep	Oct	Nov	Dec
High	31	35	46	59	71	81	85	82	76	63	49	37
Low	15	17	26	36	47	57	61	59	52	41	31	22
Precip	1.9	1.8	2.7	3.5	3.6	3.7	4.0	3.1	3.2	2.6	3.0	2.6
Snow	6.8	5.3	2.4	0.6	tr	0.0	0.0	0.0	0.0	tr	1.2	4.5

High and Low temperatures in degrees Fahrenheit; Precipitation and Snow in inches

Population: 39,350 (1990); 39,500 (2000); 38,848 (2005); 38,175 (2010 projected); Race: 93.0% White, 1.5% Black, 0.3% Asian, 7.1% Hispanic of any race (2005); Density: 94.5 persons per square mile (2005); Average household size: 2.56 (2005); Median age: 37.9 (2005); Males per 100 females: 97.1 (2005).
Religion: Five largest groups: 22.9% Catholic Church, 9.6% The United Methodist Church, 8.8% Lutheran Church—Missouri Synod, 6.3% Evangelical Lutheran Church in America, 2.9% Christian Churches and Churches of Christ (2000).
Economy: Unemployment rate: 6.2% (2005); Total civilian labor force: 20,574 (2005); Leading industries: 32.4% manufacturing; 17.6% retail trade; 12.6% health care and social assistance (2004); Farms: 982 totaling 208,994 acres (2002); Companies that employ 500 or more persons: 1 (2004); Companies that employ 100 to 499 persons: 23 (2004); Companies that employ less than 100 persons: 857 (2004); Black-owned businesses: n/a (2002); Hispanic-owned businesses: n/a (2002); Women-owned businesses: 573 (2002); Retail sales per capita: $18,103 (2006); Single-family building permits issued: 116 (2005); Multi-family building permits issued: 85 (2005).
Income: Per capita income: $22,147 (2005); Median household income: $48,428 (2005); Average household income: $56,373 (2005); Percent of households with income of $100,000 or more: 10.3% (2005); Poverty rate: 7.2% (2003); Bankruptcy rate: 9.64% (2005).
Education: Percent of population age 25 and over with: High school diploma (including GED) or higher: 84.6% (2005); Bachelor's degree or higher: 14.3% (2005); Master's degree or higher: 4.6% (2005).
Housing: Homeownership rate: 80.0% (2005); Median home value: $103,558 (2005); Median rent: $365 per month (2000); Median age of housing: 37 years (2000).
Health: Birth rate: 126.4 per 10,000 population (2004); Death rate: 81.4 per 10,000 population (2004); Age-adjusted cancer mortality rate: 203.9 deaths per 100,000 population (2002); Number of physicians: 15.9 per 10,000 population (2004); Hospital beds: 22.5 per 10,000 population (2003); Hospital admissions: 1,118.4 per 10,000 population (2003).
Elections: 2004 Presidential election results: 61.6% Bush, 37.7% Kerry, 0.0% Nader, 0.4% Badnarik
National and State Parks: Independence Dam State Park; Oxbow Lake State Wildlife Area
Additional Information Contacts
Defiance County Government . . . . (419) 782-4761
  http://www.defiance-county.com/
City of Defiance . . . . (419) 782-5756
  http://www.cityofdefiance.com
Defiance Area Chamber of Commerce . . . . (419) 782-7946
  http://www.defiancechamber.com
Hicksville Chamber of Commerce . . . . (419) 542-6337
  http://www.hicksville-chamber.com

Defiance County Communities

DEFIANCE (city). Covers a land area of 10.538 square miles and a water area of 0.488 square miles. Located at 41.28° N. Lat.; 84.36° W. Long. Elevation is 685 feet.
History: General Anthony Wayne built a fort here in 1794 and called it Fort Defiance. It was replaced in 1812 by General William Henry Harrison, who built Fort Winchester near Wayne's old fort. The town that developed after the War of 1812 was spurred by the Wabash & Erie Canal and the Miami & Erie Canal, which joined near here.
Population: 16,822 (1990); 16,465 (2000); 15,904 (2005); 15,356 (2010 projected); Race: 87.8% White, 3.0% Black, 0.3% Asian, 12.7% Hispanic of any race (2005); Density: 1,509.2 persons per square mile (2005); Average household size: 2.45 (2005); Median age: 36.6 (2005); Males per 100 females: 94.1 (2005); Marriage status: 26.2% never married, 55.1% now married, 7.8% widowed, 10.9% divorced (2000); Foreign born: 2.2% (2000); Ancestry (includes multiple ancestries): 34.9% German, 20.0% Other groups, 10.0% Irish, 9.6% United States or American, 6.4% English (2000).
Economy: Single-family building permits issued: 29 (2005); Multi-family building permits issued: 85 (2005); Employment by occupation: 8.0% management, 13.7% professional, 14.4% services, 22.5% sales, 0.3% farming, 7.2% construction, 33.8% production (2000).
Income: Per capita income: $22,376 (2005); Median household income: $44,958 (2005); Average household income: $54,346 (2005); Percent of households with income of $100,000 or more: 10.0% (2005); Poverty rate: 8.8% (2000).
Education: Percent of population age 25 and over with: High school diploma (including GED) or higher: 83.5% (2005); Bachelor's degree or higher: 17.1% (2005); Master's degree or higher: 5.1% (2005).
School District(s)
Ayersville Local School District (PK-12)
  2003-04 Enrollment: 908 . . . . (419) 395-1111
Defiance City SD (PK-12)
  2003-04 Enrollment: 2,541 . . . . (419) 782-0070
Northeastern Local SD (PK-12)
  2003-04 Enrollment: 1,187 . . . . (419) 497-3461
Four-year College(s)
Defiance College (Private, Not-for-profit, United Church of Christ)
  Fall 2004 Enrollment: 1,035 . . . . (419) 784-4010
  2005-06 Tuition: In-state $18,470; Out-of-state $18,470
Housing: Homeownership rate: 70.8% (2005); Median home value: $96,478 (2005); Median rent: $375 per month (2000); Median age of housing: 40 years (2000).
Hospitals: Defiance Regional Medical Center (61 beds)
Newspapers: The Crescent-News (Circulation 17,671)
Transportation: Commute to work: 94.5% car, 0.3% public transportation, 2.7% walk, 1.3% work from home (2000); Travel time to work: 59.2% less than 15 minutes, 21.7% 15 to 30 minutes, 12.7% 30 to 45 minutes, 2.9% 45 to 60 minutes, 3.5% 60 minutes or more (2000)
Additional Information Contacts
City of Defiance . . . . (419) 782-5756
  http://www.cityofdefiance.com

Defiance Area Chamber of Commerce . . . . (419) 782-7946
http://www.defiancechamber.com

HICKSVILLE (village). Covers a land area of 2.516 square miles and a water area of 0 square miles. Located at 41.29° N. Lat.; 84.76° W. Long. Elevation is 766 feet.
History: Hicksville was founded in 1836 by Henry Hicks, Isaac Smith, and John Bryan as a trading post dealing in furs. The town's industry passed from lumber, to mills and tanneries, and to canning and wood products.
Population: 3,772 (1990); 3,649 (2000); 3,504 (2005); 3,368 (2010 projected); Race: 97.1% White, 0.1% Black, 0.1% Asian, 3.5% Hispanic of any race (2005); Density: 1,392.8 persons per square mile (2005); Average household size: 2.43 (2005); Median age: 36.2 (2005); Males per 100 females: 89.0 (2005); Marriage status: 20.5% never married, 56.8% now married, 10.7% widowed, 12.0% divorced (2000); Foreign born: 0.4% (2000); Ancestry (includes multiple ancestries): 29.9% German, 17.0% United States or American, 8.2% Other groups, 7.7% Irish, 6.7% English (2000).
Economy: Single-family building permits issued: 4 (2005); Multi-family building permits issued: 0 (2005); Employment by occupation: 9.1% management, 11.1% professional, 10.9% services, 18.8% sales, 0.0% farming, 11.8% construction, 38.3% production (2000).
Income: Per capita income: $19,014 (2005); Median household income: $40,936 (2005); Average household income: $45,736 (2005); Percent of households with income of $100,000 or more: 4.3% (2005); Poverty rate: 3.2% (2000).
Education: Percent of population age 25 and over with: High school diploma (including GED) or higher: 82.3% (2005); Bachelor's degree or higher: 12.7% (2005); Master's degree or higher: 4.5% (2005).

School District(s)
Hicksville Ex Vill SD (PK-12)
    2003-04 Enrollment: 1,062 . . . . (419) 542-7665
Housing: Homeownership rate: 76.3% (2005); Median home value: $86,483 (2005); Median rent: $329 per month (2000); Median age of housing: 47 years (2000).
Hospitals: Community Memorial Hospital (25 beds)
Safety: Violent crime rate: 8.4 per 10,000 population; Property crime rate: 433.9 per 10,000 population (2004).
Newspapers: News Tribune (General - Circulation 2,350)
Transportation: Commute to work: 91.8% car, 0.0% public transportation, 5.6% walk, 2.6% work from home (2000); Travel time to work: 41.6% less than 15 minutes, 32.9% 15 to 30 minutes, 20.0% 30 to 45 minutes, 3.6% 45 to 60 minutes, 1.9% 60 minutes or more (2000)
Additional Information Contacts
Hicksville Chamber of Commerce . . . . (419) 542-6337
    http://www.hicksville-chamber.com

MARK CENTER (unincorporated postal area, zip code 43536). Aka Mark Centre. Covers a land area of 16.866 square miles and a water area of 0 square miles. Located at 41.29° N. Lat.; 84.63° W. Long. Elevation is 721 feet.
Population: 451 (2000); Race: 100.0% White, 0.0% Black, 0.0% Asian, 0.0% Hispanic of any race (2000); Density: 26.7 persons per square mile (2000); Age: 30.6% under 18, 3.1% over 64 (2000); Marriage status: 40.1% never married, 48.3% now married, 7.6% widowed, 4.0% divorced (2000); Foreign born: 0.0% (2000); Ancestry (includes multiple ancestries): 69.1% German, 11.9% Irish, 10.1% Hungarian, 10.1% French (except Basque), 4.0% English (2000).
Economy: Employment by occupation: 12.5% management, 7.3% professional, 14.7% services, 11.4% sales, 0.0% farming, 3.7% construction, 50.5% production (2000).
Income: Per capita income: $23,773 (2000); Median household income: $80,796 (2000); Poverty rate: 0.0% (2000).
Education: Percent of population age 25 and over with: High school diploma (including GED) or higher: 100.0% (2000); Bachelor's degree or higher: 8.6% (2000).
Housing: Homeownership rate: 75.6% (2000); Median home value: $82,100 (2000); Median rent: $240 per month (2000); Median age of housing: 60+ years (2000).
Transportation: Commute to work: 97.4% car, 0.0% public transportation, 0.0% walk, 2.6% work from home (2000); Travel time to work: 13.5% less than 15 minutes, 51.1% 15 to 30 minutes, 18.4% 30 to 45 minutes, 16.9% 45 to 60 minutes, 0.0% 60 minutes or more (2000)

NEY (village). Covers a land area of 0.412 square miles and a water area of 0 square miles. Located at 41.38° N. Lat.; 84.52° W. Long. Elevation is 714 feet.
Population: 331 (1990); 364 (2000); 381 (2005); 399 (2010 projected); Race: 98.2% White, 0.5% Black, 0.0% Asian, 0.3% Hispanic of any race (2005); Density: 925.7 persons per square mile (2005); Average household size: 2.61 (2005); Median age: 33.3 (2005); Males per 100 females: 96.4 (2005); Marriage status: 12.0% never married, 73.0% now married, 3.1% widowed, 12.0% divorced (2000); Foreign born: 0.0% (2000); Ancestry (includes multiple ancestries): 31.4% German, 11.9% United States or American, 10.5% Other groups, 8.1% Irish, 7.6% English (2000).
Economy: Grain and lumber mills. Single-family building permits issued: 0 (2005); Multi-family building permits issued: 0 (2005); Employment by occupation: 3.3% management, 6.0% professional, 9.3% services, 27.5% sales, 0.0% farming, 8.2% construction, 45.6% production (2000).
Income: Per capita income: $20,243 (2005); Median household income: $43,710 (2005); Average household income: $52,825 (2005); Percent of households with income of $100,000 or more: 6.8% (2005); Poverty rate: 4.3% (2000).
Education: Percent of population age 25 and over with: High school diploma (including GED) or higher: 80.6% (2005); Bachelor's degree or higher: 4.0% (2005); Master's degree or higher: 1.8% (2005).
Housing: Homeownership rate: 78.8% (2005); Median home value: $78,571 (2005); Median rent: $361 per month (2000); Median age of housing: 55 years (2000).
Transportation: Commute to work: 85.2% car, 2.2% public transportation, 10.4% walk, 2.2% work from home (2000); Travel time to work: 37.1% less than 15 minutes, 45.5% 15 to 30 minutes, 11.2% 30 to 45 minutes, 2.8% 45 to 60 minutes, 3.4% 60 minutes or more (2000)

SHERWOOD (village). Covers a land area of 1.445 square miles and a water area of 0.009 square miles. Located at 41.28° N. Lat.; 84.55° W. Long. Elevation is 709 feet.
Population: 828 (1990); 801 (2000); 760 (2005); 746 (2010 projected); Race: 96.3% White, 0.5% Black, 0.0% Asian, 3.2% Hispanic of any race (2005); Density: 526.0 persons per square mile (2005); Average household size: 2.60 (2005); Median age: 36.9 (2005); Males per 100 females: 90.0 (2005); Marriage status: 20.0% never married, 61.8% now married, 5.2% widowed, 12.9% divorced (2000); Foreign born: 0.0% (2000); Ancestry (includes multiple ancestries): 37.2% German, 15.3% Other groups, 11.6% Irish, 11.6% United States or American, 5.4% English (2000).
Economy: In farming area. Single-family building permits issued: 14 (2005); Multi-family building permits issued: 0 (2005); Employment by occupation: 2.4% management, 11.4% professional, 15.7% services, 15.7% sales, 0.0% farming, 10.9% construction, 43.9% production (2000).
Income: Per capita income: $17,536 (2005); Median household income: $42,727 (2005); Average household income: $45,642 (2005); Percent of households with income of $100,000 or more: 4.1% (2005); Poverty rate: 12.5% (2000).
Education: Percent of population age 25 and over with: High school diploma (including GED) or higher: 80.7% (2005); Bachelor's degree or higher: 8.6% (2005); Master's degree or higher: 4.3% (2005).

School District(s)
Central Local SD (PK-12)
    2003-04 Enrollment: 1,184 . . . . (419) 658-2808
Housing: Homeownership rate: 83.9% (2005); Median home value: $75,333 (2005); Median rent: $366 per month (2000); Median age of housing: 50 years (2000).
Transportation: Commute to work: 93.5% car, 0.5% public transportation, 1.3% walk, 3.0% work from home (2000); Travel time to work: 18.6% less than 15 minutes, 52.8% 15 to 30 minutes, 19.4% 30 to 45 minutes, 6.1% 45 to 60 minutes, 3.1% 60 minutes or more (2000)

Delaware County

Located in central Ohio; crossed by the Olentangy and Scioto Rivers. Covers a land area of 442.41 square miles, a water area of 13.56 square miles, and is located in the Eastern Time Zone. The county government was organized in 1808. County seat is Delaware.

Delaware County is part of the Columbus, OH Metropolitan Statistical Area. The entire metro area includes: Delaware County, OH; Fairfield County, OH; Franklin County, OH; Licking County, OH; Madison County, OH; Morrow County, OH; Pickaway County, OH; Union County, OH

Weather Station: Delaware   Elevation: 918 feet

	Jan	Feb	Mar	Apr	May	Jun	Jul	Aug	Sep	Oct	Nov	Dec
High	33	37	48	61	71	80	84	82	76	64	50	39
Low	16	19	28	37	48	57	61	59	51	40	31	23
Precip	2.3	1.9	2.5	3.4	4.0	4.2	4.1	3.5	2.8	2.5	3.5	2.7
Snow	8.1	4.3	2.9	0.9	0.0	0.0	0.0	0.0	0.0	tr	0.8	3.7

High and Low temperatures in degrees Fahrenheit; Precipitation and Snow in inches

Population: 66,929 (1990); 109,989 (2000); 142,926 (2005); 177,526 (2010 projected); Race: 91.0% White, 3.0% Black, 3.7% Asian, 1.2% Hispanic of any race (2005); Density: 323.1 persons per square mile (2005); Average household size: 2.73 (2005); Median age: 34.4 (2005); Males per 100 females: 98.1 (2005).
Religion: Five largest groups: 18.2% Catholic Church, 5.0% The United Methodist Church, 3.0% Presbyterian Church (U.S.A.), 1.0% American Baptist Churches in the USA, 1.0% Evangelical Lutheran Church in America (2000).
Economy: Unemployment rate: 3.8% (2005); Total civilian labor force: 79,285 (2005); Leading industries: 17.2% finance & insurance; 16.8% retail trade; 11.4% accommodation & food services (2004); Farms: 785 totaling 162,554 acres (2002); Companies that employ 500 or more persons: 10 (2004); Companies that employ 100 to 499 persons: 94 (2004); Companies that employ less than 100 persons: 3,255 (2004); Black-owned businesses: n/a (2002); Hispanic-owned businesses: n/a (2002); Women-owned businesses: 3,393 (2002); Retail sales per capita: $12,549 (2006); Single-family building permits issued: 1,851 (2005); Multi-family building permits issued: 106 (2005).
Income: Per capita income: $36,195 (2005); Median household income: $75,629 (2005); Average household income: $98,583 (2005); Percent of households with income of $100,000 or more: 34.3% (2005); Poverty rate: 4.6% (2003); Bankruptcy rate: 6.04% (2005).
Taxes: Total county taxes per capita: $348 (2004); County property taxes per capita: $98 (2004).
Education: Percent of population age 25 and over with: High school diploma (including GED) or higher: 92.8% (2005); Bachelor's degree or higher: 40.1% (2005); Master's degree or higher: 12.4% (2005).
Housing: Homeownership rate: 81.4% (2005); Median home value: $233,563 (2005); Median rent: $537 per month (2000); Median age of housing: 11 years (2000).
Health: Birth rate: 145.4 per 10,000 population (2004); Death rate: 46.7 per 10,000 population (2004); Age-adjusted cancer mortality rate: 178.0 deaths per 100,000 population (2002); Air Quality Index: 79.1% good, 20.0% moderate, 0.9% unhealthy for sensitive individuals, 0.0% unhealthy (percent of days in 2005); Number of physicians: 34.6 per 10,000 population (2004); Hospital beds: 5.5 per 10,000 population (2003); Hospital admissions: 179.7 per 10,000 population (2003).
Elections: 2004 Presidential election results: 66.1% Bush, 33.6% Kerry, 0.0% Nader, 0.2% Badnarik
National and State Parks: Alum Creek State Park
Additional Information Contacts
Delaware County Government . . . . (740) 833-2100
  http://www.co.delaware.oh.us/
Big Walnut Chamber of Commerce . . . . (740) 965-2860
  http://www.sunburybigwalnutchamber.com/index.htm
City of Delaware . . . . (740) 369-8696
  http://www.delawareohio.net
Delaware Area Chamber of Commerce . . . . (740) 369-6221
  http://www.delaware.org
Powell Chamber of Commerce . . . . (614) 888-1090
  http://www.powellchamber.com
Sunbury/Big Walnut Area Chamber of Commerce . . . . (740) 965-2860
  http://www.sunburybigwalnutchamber.com
Village of Powell . . . . (614) 885-5380
  http://www.cityofpowell.us
Village of Shawnee Hills . . . . (614) 889-2824
  http://www.shawneehillsoh.com

Delaware County Communities

ASHLEY (village). Covers a land area of 0.543 square miles and a water area of 0 square miles. Located at 40.40° N. Lat.; 82.95° W. Long. Elevation is 989 feet.
Population: 1,087 (1990); 1,216 (2000); 1,779 (2005); 2,340 (2010 projected); Race: 95.7% White, 1.4% Black, 0.0% Asian, 1.0% Hispanic of any race (2005); Density: 3,279.2 persons per square mile (2005); Average household size: 2.54 (2005); Median age: 32.7 (2005); Males per 100 females: 94.0 (2005); Marriage status: 17.2% never married, 59.4% now married, 9.5% widowed, 13.9% divorced (2000); Foreign born: 0.0% (2000); Ancestry (includes multiple ancestries): 22.8% German, 11.4% Irish, 10.0% United States or American, 8.2% English, 5.5% Other groups (2000).
Economy: Single-family building permits issued: 1 (2005); Multi-family building permits issued: 0 (2005); Employment by occupation: 7.9% management, 9.9% professional, 16.2% services, 26.3% sales, 0.0% farming, 14.9% construction, 24.9% production (2000).
Income: Per capita income: $19,141 (2005); Median household income: $43,217 (2005); Average household income: $47,943 (2005); Percent of households with income of $100,000 or more: 5.6% (2005); Poverty rate: 12.7% (2000).
Education: Percent of population age 25 and over with: High school diploma (including GED) or higher: 80.2% (2005); Bachelor's degree or higher: 8.0% (2005); Master's degree or higher: 2.4% (2005).
School District(s)
Buckeye Valley Local SD (PK-12)
  2003-04 Enrollment: 2,237 . . . . (740) 369-8735
Housing: Homeownership rate: 74.9% (2005); Median home value: $93,131 (2005); Median rent: $358 per month (2000); Median age of housing: 52 years (2000).
Transportation: Commute to work: 95.3% car, 1.0% public transportation, 1.9% walk, 1.4% work from home (2000); Travel time to work: 11.2% less than 15 minutes, 43.5% 15 to 30 minutes, 26.5% 30 to 45 minutes, 13.7% 45 to 60 minutes, 5.2% 60 minutes or more (2000)

DELAWARE (city). Covers a land area of 15.000 square miles and a water area of 0.100 square miles. Located at 40.29° N. Lat.; 83.07° W. Long. Elevation is 880 feet.
History: Named for Thomas West, Lord Delaware, first British governor of the colony of Virginia. Delaware was established around a sulphur spring, called Medicine Waters by the Mingo and Delaware tribes who lived here in the early 1800's. Joseph Barber settled on the present town site in 1807 and opened a tavern, and the town was platted in 1808. In 1833 a company, formed to exploit the local mineral springs, built a resort hotel. The resort was unsuccessful, but the hotel became the first building of Ohio Wesleyan University, chartered in 1842.
Population: 21,106 (1990); 25,243 (2000); 29,934 (2005); 35,088 (2010 projected); Race: 90.4% White, 4.2% Black, 1.9% Asian, 1.5% Hispanic of any race (2005); Density: 1,995.6 persons per square mile (2005); Average household size: 2.60 (2005); Median age: 31.2 (2005); Males per 100 females: 92.7 (2005); Marriage status: 25.3% never married, 57.4% now married, 5.8% widowed, 11.5% divorced (2000); Foreign born: 1.6% (2000); Ancestry (includes multiple ancestries): 25.7% German, 11.8% Irish, 11.4% English, 10.1% Other groups, 9.0% United States or American (2000).
Economy: Unemployment rate: 4.6% (2005); Total civilian labor force: 15,895 (2005); Single-family building permits issued: 348 (2005); Multi-family building permits issued: 67 (2005); Employment by occupation: 15.1% management, 22.3% professional, 13.1% services, 28.0% sales, 0.3% farming, 6.5% construction, 14.7% production (2000).
Income: Per capita income: $22,923 (2005); Median household income: $49,704 (2005); Average household income: $58,258 (2005); Percent of households with income of $100,000 or more: 12.4% (2005); Poverty rate: 7.3% (2000).
Education: Percent of population age 25 and over with: High school diploma (including GED) or higher: 88.2% (2005); Bachelor's degree or higher: 26.9% (2005); Master's degree or higher: 8.2% (2005).
School District(s)
Buckeye Valley Local SD (PK-12)
  2003-04 Enrollment: 2,237 . . . . (740) 369-8735
Delaware Area Career Center (09-12)
  2003-04 Enrollment: n/a . . . . (740) 548-0708
Delaware City SD (PK-12)
  2003-04 Enrollment: 4,498 . . . . (740) 833-1100
Delaware JVS
  2003-04 Enrollment: n/a . . . . (740) 548-0708
Department of Youth Services (06-12)
  2003-04 Enrollment: 1,333 . . . . (614) 728-2489
Vision Into Action, LLC
  2003-04 Enrollment: n/a

Four-year College(s)
Methodist Theological School-Ohio (Private, Not-for-profit, United Methodist)
  Fall 2004 Enrollment: 253 . . . . (740) 363-1146
Ohio Wesleyan University (Private, Not-for-profit, United Methodist)
  Fall 2004 Enrollment: 1,944. (740) 368-2000
  2005-06 Tuition: In-state $27,920; Out-of-state $27,920
Two-year College(s)
Delaware Area Career Center (Public)
  Fall 2004 Enrollment: 190 . . . . (740) 548-0708
Housing: Homeownership rate: 61.1% (2005); Median home value: $153,439 (2005); Median rent: $474 per month (2000); Median age of housing: 25 years (2000).
Hospitals: Grady Memorial Hospital (135 beds)
Safety: Violent crime rate: 26.0 per 10,000 population; Property crime rate: 367.8 per 10,000 population (2004).
Newspapers: The Delaware Gazette (Circulation 8,500)
Transportation: Commute to work: 91.2% car, 0.4% public transportation, 4.1% walk, 3.3% work from home (2000); Travel time to work: 31.5% less than 15 minutes, 27.1% 15 to 30 minutes, 23.2% 30 to 45 minutes, 11.4% 45 to 60 minutes, 6.7% 60 minutes or more (2000)
Additional Information Contacts
City of Delaware. . . . . (740) 369-8696
  http://www.delawareohio.net
Delaware Area Chamber of Commerce. . . . . (740) 369-6221
  http://www.delaware.org

GALENA (village). Covers a land area of 0.598 square miles and a water area of 0.046 square miles. Located at 40.21° N. Lat.; 82.88° W. Long. Elevation is 920 feet.
Population: 355 (1990); 305 (2000); 458 (2005); 615 (2010 projected); Race: 96.9% White, 0.0% Black, 0.0% Asian, 2.0% Hispanic of any race (2005); Density: 765.5 persons per square mile (2005); Average household size: 2.46 (2005); Median age: 37.2 (2005); Males per 100 females: 99.1 (2005); Marriage status: 20.3% never married, 68.5% now married, 2.5% widowed, 8.7% divorced (2000); Foreign born: 0.0% (2000); Ancestry (includes multiple ancestries): 27.2% German, 17.6% Other groups, 13.6% English, 7.0% Irish, 5.0% French (except Basque) (2000).
Economy: Employment by occupation: 16.7% management, 11.7% professional, 21.6% services, 28.4% sales, 0.0% farming, 14.2% construction, 7.4% production (2000).
Income: Per capita income: $25,278 (2005); Median household income: $57,386 (2005); Average household income: $62,245 (2005); Percent of households with income of $100,000 or more: 16.1% (2005); Poverty rate: 9.6% (2000).
Education: Percent of population age 25 and over with: High school diploma (including GED) or higher: 84.2% (2005); Bachelor's degree or higher: 21.1% (2005); Master's degree or higher: 9.1% (2005).
School District(s)
Big Walnut Local SD (PK-12)
  2003-04 Enrollment: 2,633 . . . . (740) 965-2706
Olentangy Local SD (PK-12)
  2003-04 Enrollment: 8,560 . . . . (740) 657-4050
Housing: Homeownership rate: 82.8% (2005); Median home value: $130,172 (2005); Median rent: $458 per month (2000); Median age of housing: 60+ years (2000).
Transportation: Commute to work: 95.1% car, 0.0% public transportation, 3.1% walk, 1.9% work from home (2000); Travel time to work: 24.5% less than 15 minutes, 25.8% 15 to 30 minutes, 28.9% 30 to 45 minutes, 10.7% 45 to 60 minutes, 10.1% 60 minutes or more (2000)
Additional Information Contacts
Sunbury/Big Walnut Area Chamber of Commerce . . . . (740) 965-2860
  http://www.sunburybigwalnutchamber.com

LEWIS CENTER (unincorporated postal area, zip code 43035). Covers a land area of 18.635 square miles and a water area of 0 square miles. Located at 40.18° N. Lat.; 82.98° W. Long. Elevation is 942 feet.
Population: 11,261 (2000); Race: 90.2% White, 3.9% Black, 3.1% Asian, 2.1% Hispanic of any race (2000); Density: 604.3 persons per square mile (2000); Age: 30.0% under 18, 3.9% over 64 (2000); Marriage status: 21.8% never married, 69.1% now married, 1.2% widowed, 8.0% divorced (2000); Foreign born: 3.6% (2000); Ancestry (includes multiple ancestries): 28.8% German, 17.4% Irish, 11.3% Other groups, 9.7% Italian, 9.3% English (2000).

Economy: Employment by occupation: 27.6% management, 25.3% professional, 10.4% services, 27.1% sales, 0.0% farming, 4.7% construction, 4.8% production (2000).
Income: Per capita income: $31,478 (2000); Median household income: $71,870 (2000); Poverty rate: 6.0% (2000).
Education: Percent of population age 25 and over with: High school diploma (including GED) or higher: 96.4% (2000); Bachelor's degree or higher: 50.6% (2000).
School District(s)
Olentangy Local SD (PK-12)
  2003-04 Enrollment: 8,560 . . . . (740) 657-4050
Housing: Homeownership rate: 74.3% (2000); Median home value: $216,400 (2000); Median rent: $577 per month (2000); Median age of housing: 3 years (2000).
Transportation: Commute to work: 94.8% car, 0.4% public transportation, 0.4% walk, 4.0% work from home (2000); Travel time to work: 19.4% less than 15 minutes, 50.7% 15 to 30 minutes, 21.2% 30 to 45 minutes, 4.9% 45 to 60 minutes, 3.8% 60 minutes or more (2000)

OSTRANDER (village). Covers a land area of 0.332 square miles and a water area of 0 square miles. Located at 40.26° N. Lat.; 83.21° W. Long. Elevation is 937 feet.
Population: 469 (1990); 405 (2000); 621 (2005); 837 (2010 projected); Race: 97.1% White, 0.3% Black, 0.0% Asian, 0.0% Hispanic of any race (2005); Density: 1,868.4 persons per square mile (2005); Average household size: 2.68 (2005); Median age: 33.7 (2005); Males per 100 females: 92.3 (2005); Marriage status: 15.4% never married, 65.1% now married, 7.7% widowed, 11.8% divorced (2000); Foreign born: 0.0% (2000); Ancestry (includes multiple ancestries): 29.4% German, 14.4% United States or American, 11.6% European, 11.1% Irish, 6.6% English (2000).
Economy: Employment by occupation: 12.6% management, 11.2% professional, 17.9% services, 26.5% sales, 0.0% farming, 13.0% construction, 18.8% production (2000).
Income: Per capita income: $24,827 (2005); Median household income: $56,944 (2005); Average household income: $66,455 (2005); Percent of households with income of $100,000 or more: 16.4% (2005); Poverty rate: 5.8% (2000).
Education: Percent of population age 25 and over with: High school diploma (including GED) or higher: 89.4% (2005); Bachelor's degree or higher: 11.1% (2005); Master's degree or higher: 2.5% (2005).
School District(s)
Buckeye Valley Local SD (PK-12)
  2003-04 Enrollment: 2,237 . . . . (740) 369-8735
Housing: Homeownership rate: 90.5% (2005); Median home value: $131,818 (2005); Median rent: $433 per month (2000); Median age of housing: 60+ years (2000).
Transportation: Commute to work: 97.3% car, 0.0% public transportation, 2.7% walk, 0.0% work from home (2000); Travel time to work: 11.3% less than 15 minutes, 52.5% 15 to 30 minutes, 18.6% 30 to 45 minutes, 11.3% 45 to 60 minutes, 6.3% 60 minutes or more (2000)

POWELL (village). Covers a land area of 3.036 square miles and a water area of 0 square miles. Located at 40.15° N. Lat.; 83.07° W. Long. Elevation is 922 feet.
Population: 2,776 (1990); 6,247 (2000); 8,495 (2005); 10,802 (2010 projected); Race: 89.2% White, 2.1% Black, 7.1% Asian, 1.3% Hispanic of any race (2005); Density: 2,797.7 persons per square mile (2005); Average household size: 3.21 (2005); Median age: 35.1 (2005); Males per 100 females: 99.5 (2005); Marriage status: 11.0% never married, 82.6% now married, 1.3% widowed, 5.0% divorced (2000); Foreign born: 3.3% (2000); Ancestry (includes multiple ancestries): 33.4% German, 19.8% Irish, 13.2% English, 9.1% Italian, 8.1% Other groups (2000).
Economy: Single-family building permits issued: 263 (2005); Multi-family building permits issued: 0 (2005); Employment by occupation: 32.4% management, 31.5% professional, 5.3% services, 25.6% sales, 0.0% farming, 3.5% construction, 1.7% production (2000).
Income: Per capita income: $48,048 (2005); Median household income: $126,809 (2005); Average household income: $154,317 (2005); Percent of households with income of $100,000 or more: 67.4% (2005); Poverty rate: 0.4% (2000).
Education: Percent of population age 25 and over with: High school diploma (including GED) or higher: 98.8% (2005); Bachelor's degree or higher: 68.7% (2005); Master's degree or higher: 25.6% (2005).

School District(s)

Dublin City SD (PK-12)
    2003-04 Enrollment: 12,376 .... (614) 764-5913
Olentangy Local SD (PK-12)
    2003-04 Enrollment: 8,560 .... (740) 657-4050
Worthington City SD (PK-12)
    2003-04 Enrollment: 9,754 .... (614) 883-3000

Housing: Homeownership rate: 97.8% (2005); Median home value: $295,983 (2005); Median rent: $1,333 per month (2000); Median age of housing: 6 years (2000).
Safety: Violent crime rate: 1.2 per 10,000 population; Property crime rate: 93.9 per 10,000 population (2004).
Transportation: Commute to work: 95.2% car, 0.3% public transportation, 0.3% walk, 4.2% work from home (2000); Travel time to work: 15.8% less than 15 minutes, 46.2% 15 to 30 minutes, 27.2% 30 to 45 minutes, 6.6% 45 to 60 minutes, 4.2% 60 minutes or more (2000)

Additional Information Contacts
Powell Chamber of Commerce .... (614) 888-1090
    http://www.powellchamber.com
Village of Powell .... (614) 885-5380
    http://www.cityofpowell.us

RADNOR (unincorporated postal area, zip code 43066). Aka Meredith. Covers a land area of 38.542 square miles and a water area of 0 square miles. Located at 40.40° N. Lat.; 83.15° W. Long. Elevation is 938 feet.
Population: 1,085 (2000); Race: 100.0% White, 0.0% Black, 0.0% Asian, 0.0% Hispanic of any race (2000); Density: 28.2 persons per square mile (2000); Age: 27.0% under 18, 5.7% over 64 (2000); Marriage status: 22.6% never married, 69.6% now married, 1.9% widowed, 5.8% divorced (2000); Foreign born: 0.0% (2000); Ancestry (includes multiple ancestries): 21.0% German, 15.4% Welsh, 11.7% United States or American, 9.8% Irish, 7.0% English (2000).
Economy: Employment by occupation: 11.7% management, 16.6% professional, 23.5% services, 20.0% sales, 1.7% farming, 7.8% construction, 18.8% production (2000).
Income: Per capita income: $16,057 (2000); Median household income: $41,570 (2000); Poverty rate: 8.5% (2000).
Education: Percent of population age 25 and over with: High school diploma (including GED) or higher: 90.3% (2000); Bachelor's degree or higher: 16.1% (2000).

School District(s)

Buckeye Valley Local SD (PK-12)
    2003-04 Enrollment: 2,237 .... (740) 369-8735

Housing: Homeownership rate: 76.5% (2000); Median home value: $106,900 (2000); Median rent: $507 per month (2000); Median age of housing: 60+ years (2000).
Transportation: Commute to work: 87.5% car, 1.4% public transportation, 0.0% walk, 9.9% work from home (2000); Travel time to work: 20.8% less than 15 minutes, 47.0% 15 to 30 minutes, 19.3% 30 to 45 minutes, 9.1% 45 to 60 minutes, 3.8% 60 minutes or more (2000)

SHAWNEE HILLS (village). Covers a land area of 0.388 square miles and a water area of 0 square miles. Located at 40.15° N. Lat.; 83.13° W. Long. Elevation is 900 feet.
Population: 423 (1990); 419 (2000); 429 (2005); 448 (2010 projected); Race: 91.4% White, 3.0% Black, 3.7% Asian, 2.6% Hispanic of any race (2005); Density: 1,107.1 persons per square mile (2005); Average household size: 2.27 (2005); Median age: 39.6 (2005); Males per 100 females: 90.7 (2005); Marriage status: 22.2% never married, 57.1% now married, 5.1% widowed, 15.6% divorced (2000); Foreign born: 2.9% (2000); Ancestry (includes multiple ancestries): 24.0% German, 13.2% Other groups, 12.0% Italian, 10.9% Irish, 10.8% English (2000).
Economy: Employment by occupation: 18.6% management, 20.2% professional, 20.7% services, 20.7% sales, 0.0% farming, 10.3% construction, 9.5% production (2000).
Income: Per capita income: $26,824 (2005); Median household income: $59,821 (2005); Average household income: $60,886 (2005); Percent of households with income of $100,000 or more: 15.3% (2005); Poverty rate: 7.8% (2000).
Education: Percent of population age 25 and over with: High school diploma (including GED) or higher: 87.3% (2005); Bachelor's degree or higher: 29.2% (2005); Master's degree or higher: 7.9% (2005).
Housing: Homeownership rate: 79.9% (2005); Median home value: $163,125 (2005); Median rent: $561 per month (2000); Median age of housing: 40 years (2000).
Transportation: Commute to work: 94.1% car, 0.0% public transportation, 5.0% walk, 0.8% work from home (2000); Travel time to work: 21.1% less than 15 minutes, 38.8% 15 to 30 minutes, 26.6% 30 to 45 minutes, 7.6% 45 to 60 minutes, 5.9% 60 minutes or more (2000)

Additional Information Contacts
Village of Shawnee Hills .... (614) 889-2824
    http://www.shawneehillsoh.com

SUNBURY (village). Covers a land area of 2.541 square miles and a water area of 0.001 square miles. Located at 40.24° N. Lat.; 82.86° W. Long. Elevation is 980 feet.
Population: 2,258 (1990); 2,630 (2000); 3,796 (2005); 4,979 (2010 projected); Race: 96.9% White, 0.5% Black, 0.5% Asian, 1.5% Hispanic of any race (2005); Density: 1,493.8 persons per square mile (2005); Average household size: 2.52 (2005); Median age: 34.0 (2005); Males per 100 females: 92.3 (2005); Marriage status: 20.3% never married, 58.7% now married, 8.3% widowed, 12.6% divorced (2000); Foreign born: 1.3% (2000); Ancestry (includes multiple ancestries): 25.6% German, 13.6% Irish, 12.4% English, 10.8% United States or American, 7.9% Other groups (2000).
Economy: Single-family building permits issued: 11 (2005); Multi-family building permits issued: 0 (2005); Employment by occupation: 13.0% management, 15.6% professional, 13.3% services, 29.8% sales, 0.5% farming, 13.0% construction, 14.9% production (2000).
Income: Per capita income: $23,469 (2005); Median household income: $51,648 (2005); Average household income: $58,728 (2005); Percent of households with income of $100,000 or more: 12.7% (2005); Poverty rate: 4.7% (2000).
Education: Percent of population age 25 and over with: High school diploma (including GED) or higher: 83.7% (2005); Bachelor's degree or higher: 18.9% (2005); Master's degree or higher: 4.5% (2005).

School District(s)

Big Walnut Local SD (PK-12)
    2003-04 Enrollment: 2,633 .... (740) 965-2706

Housing: Homeownership rate: 73.8% (2005); Median home value: $145,600 (2005); Median rent: $488 per month (2000); Median age of housing: 33 years (2000).
Safety: Violent crime rate: 6.5 per 10,000 population; Property crime rate: 261.7 per 10,000 population (2004).
Newspapers: The Sunbury News (General - Circulation 3,250)
Transportation: Commute to work: 93.5% car, 0.5% public transportation, 3.0% walk, 2.4% work from home (2000); Travel time to work: 22.9% less than 15 minutes, 34.7% 15 to 30 minutes, 29.1% 30 to 45 minutes, 10.0% 45 to 60 minutes, 3.5% 60 minutes or more (2000)

Additional Information Contacts
Big Walnut Chamber of Commerce .... (740) 965-2860
    http://www.sunburybigwalnutchamber.com/index.htm
Sunbury/Big Walnut Area Chamber of Commerce .... (740) 965-2860
    http://www.sunburybigwalnutchamber.com

Erie County

Located in northern Ohio; bounded on the north by Lake Erie; drained by the Huron and Vermilion Rivers; includes Kelleys Island. Covers a land area of 254.88 square miles, a water area of 371.27 square miles, and is located in the Eastern Time Zone. The county government was organized in 1838. County seat is Sandusky.

Erie County is part of the Sandusky, OH Metropolitan Statistical Area. The entire metro area includes: Erie County, OH

Weather Station: Sandusky   Elevation: 583 feet

	Jan	Feb	Mar	Apr	May	Jun	Jul	Aug	Sep	Oct	Nov	Dec
High	32	35	44	56	68	78	82	80	74	62	49	38
Low	18	20	29	39	51	61	65	63	56	45	35	25
Precip	1.9	1.7	2.5	3.1	3.3	4.1	3.4	3.6	3.1	2.3	2.8	2.5
Snow	8.7	6.0	3.0	0.6	tr	0.0	0.0	0.0	0.0	tr	0.3	4.3

High and Low temperatures in degrees Fahrenheit; Precipitation and Snow in inches

Population: 76,918 (1990); 79,551 (2000); 78,374 (2005); 77,155 (2010 projected); Race: 88.5% White, 8.4% Black, 0.5% Asian, 2.3% Hispanic of any race (2005); Density: 307.5 persons per square mile (2005); Average household size: 2.46 (2005); Median age: 40.7 (2005); Males per 100 females: 95.0 (2005).

Religion: Five largest groups: 27.8% Catholic Church, 7.3% Evangelical Lutheran Church in America, 5.4% United Church of Christ, 3.9% The United Methodist Church, 1.3% Assemblies of God (2000).
Economy: Unemployment rate: 6.4% (2005); Total civilian labor force: 43,055 (2005); Leading industries: 24.3% manufacturing; 15.6% retail trade; 15.0% accommodation & food services (2004); Farms: 392 totaling 94,681 acres (2002); Companies that employ 500 or more persons: 5 (2004); Companies that employ 100 to 499 persons: 41 (2004); Companies that employ less than 100 persons: 1,967 (2004); Black-owned businesses: n/a (2002); Hispanic-owned businesses: n/a (2002); Women-owned businesses: 1,627 (2002); Retail sales per capita: $14,544 (2006). Single-family building permits issued: 223 (2005); Multi-family building permits issued: 200 (2005).
Income: Per capita income: $24,387 (2005); Median household income: $47,287 (2005); Average household income: $59,190 (2005); Percent of households with income of $100,000 or more: 13.1% (2005); Poverty rate: 9.0% (2003); Bankruptcy rate: 12.17% (2005).
Taxes: Total county taxes per capita: $287 (2004); County property taxes per capita: $87 (2004).
Education: Percent of population age 25 and over with: High school diploma (including GED) or higher: 84.0% (2005); Bachelor's degree or higher: 16.7% (2005); Master's degree or higher: 5.7% (2005).
Housing: Homeownership rate: 72.5% (2005); Median home value: $131,412 (2005); Median rent: $409 per month (2000); Median age of housing: 39 years (2000).
Health: Birth rate: 114.5 per 10,000 population (2004); Death rate: 98.4 per 10,000 population (2004); Age-adjusted cancer mortality rate: 211.5 deaths per 100,000 population (2002); Number of physicians: 23.4 per 10,000 population (2004); Hospital beds: 47.3 per 10,000 population (2003); Hospital admissions: 1,722.6 per 10,000 population (2003).
Elections: 2004 Presidential election results: 46.4% Bush, 53.4% Kerry, 0.0% Nader, 0.1% Badnarik
National and State Parks: Glacial Grooves State Memorial; Kelleys Island State Park
Additional Information Contacts
Erie County Government . . . . (419) 627-7682
http://www.erie-county-ohio.net/
City of Huron . . . . (419) 433-5000
http://www.cityofhuron.org
City of Sandusky . . . . (419) 627-5844
http://www.ci.sandusky.oh.us
Huron Chamber of Commerce. . . . . (419) 433-5700
http://www.huron.net
Kelleys Island Chamber of Commerce . . . . (419) 746-2360
http://www.kelleysislandchamber.com
Sandusky Chamber of Commerce. . . . . (419) 625-6421
http://www.eriecountyohiocofc.com
Sandusky/Erie Co. Visitors & Convention Bureau . . . . (419) 625-2984
http://www.buckeyenorth.com

Erie County Communities

BAY VIEW (village). Covers a land area of 0.292 square miles and a water area of 0 square miles. Located at 41.46° N. Lat.; 82.82° W. Long. Elevation is 575 feet.
History: Bay View developed as a resort community with swimming, boating, and camping facilities.
Population: 739 (1990); 692 (2000); 625 (2005); 612 (2010 projected); Race: 97.8% White, 0.0% Black, 0.3% Asian, 2.1% Hispanic of any race (2005); Density: 2,142.9 persons per square mile (2005); Average household size: 2.31 (2005); Median age: 43.5 (2005); Males per 100 females: 97.8 (2005); Marriage status: 17.2% never married, 62.9% now married, 9.3% widowed, 10.6% divorced (2000); Foreign born: 0.7% (2000); Ancestry (includes multiple ancestries): 42.3% German, 16.3% Irish, 12.3% English, 8.2% United States or American, 7.7% Polish (2000).
Economy: Single-family building permits issued: 1 (2005); Multi-family building permits issued: 0 (2005); Employment by occupation: 12.8% management, 11.3% professional, 15.5% services, 21.6% sales, 0.0% farming, 11.9% construction, 26.8% production (2000).
Income: Per capita income: $22,704 (2005); Median household income: $45,313 (2005); Average household income: $52,556 (2005); Percent of households with income of $100,000 or more: 9.3% (2005); Poverty rate: 4.0% (2000).

Education: Percent of population age 25 and over with: High school diploma (including GED) or higher: 77.6% (2005); Bachelor's degree or higher: 13.2% (2005); Master's degree or higher: 2.5% (2005).
Housing: Homeownership rate: 87.4% (2005); Median home value: $109,406 (2005); Median rent: $414 per month (2000); Median age of housing: 46 years (2000).
Transportation: Commute to work: 97.5% car, 0.0% public transportation, 1.9% walk, 0.6% work from home (2000); Travel time to work: 26.2% less than 15 minutes, 55.8% 15 to 30 minutes, 10.4% 30 to 45 minutes, 2.2% 45 to 60 minutes, 5.4% 60 minutes or more (2000)

BERLIN HEIGHTS (village). Covers a land area of 1.563 square miles and a water area of 0 square miles. Located at 41.32° N. Lat.; 82.49° W. Long. Elevation is 777 feet.
History: Berlin Heights developed as the center of an apple and peach district, begun in 1812 when John Hoak and John Fleming brought from Canada a number of young fruit trees.
Population: 691 (1990); 685 (2000); 671 (2005); 665 (2010 projected); Race: 98.8% White, 0.0% Black, 0.0% Asian, 1.2% Hispanic of any race (2005); Density: 429.3 persons per square mile (2005); Average household size: 2.60 (2005); Median age: 39.2 (2005); Males per 100 females: 95.6 (2005); Marriage status: 24.2% never married, 62.4% now married, 4.9% widowed, 8.5% divorced (2000); Foreign born: 1.2% (2000); Ancestry (includes multiple ancestries): 38.9% German, 10.5% Irish, 9.8% English, 7.9% United States or American, 4.5% Other groups (2000).
Economy: Single-family building permits issued: 2 (2005); Multi-family building permits issued: 0 (2005); Employment by occupation: 7.6% management, 19.4% professional, 17.5% services, 19.1% sales, 1.9% farming, 11.5% construction, 22.9% production (2000).
Income: Per capita income: $22,981 (2005); Median household income: $54,167 (2005); Average household income: $59,767 (2005); Percent of households with income of $100,000 or more: 12.0% (2005); Poverty rate: 6.9% (2000).
Education: Percent of population age 25 and over with: High school diploma (including GED) or higher: 83.4% (2005); Bachelor's degree or higher: 20.0% (2005); Master's degree or higher: 7.8% (2005).
School District(s)
Berlin-Milan Local SD (PK-12)
    2003-04 Enrollment: 1,874 . . . . (419) 499-4272
Housing: Homeownership rate: 81.8% (2005); Median home value: $131,117 (2005); Median rent: $381 per month (2000); Median age of housing: 60+ years (2000).
Transportation: Commute to work: 91.9% car, 0.6% public transportation, 6.2% walk, 1.3% work from home (2000); Travel time to work: 28.0% less than 15 minutes, 37.2% 15 to 30 minutes, 19.1% 30 to 45 minutes, 10.9% 45 to 60 minutes, 4.9% 60 minutes or more (2000)

CASTALIA (village). Covers a land area of 1.044 square miles and a water area of 0.006 square miles. Located at 41.40° N. Lat.; 82.80° W. Long. Elevation is 635 feet.
Population: 915 (1990); 935 (2000); 903 (2005); 885 (2010 projected); Race: 96.6% White, 1.1% Black, 0.0% Asian, 3.8% Hispanic of any race (2005); Density: 865.0 persons per square mile (2005); Average household size: 2.55 (2005); Median age: 38.2 (2005); Males per 100 females: 93.8 (2005); Marriage status: 22.0% never married, 57.7% now married, 9.1% widowed, 11.2% divorced (2000); Foreign born: 1.0% (2000); Ancestry (includes multiple ancestries): 37.9% German, 14.1% English, 12.8% Irish, 9.1% Other groups, 7.9% United States or American (2000).
Economy: Blue Hole Spring here attracts tourists. Single-family building permits issued: 0 (2005); Multi-family building permits issued: 0 (2005); Employment by occupation: 7.8% management, 15.8% professional, 16.9% services, 21.2% sales, 0.5% farming, 8.7% construction, 29.2% production (2000).
Income: Per capita income: $21,146 (2005); Median household income: $46,695 (2005); Average household income: $53,941 (2005); Percent of households with income of $100,000 or more: 11.6% (2005); Poverty rate: 6.1% (2000).
Education: Percent of population age 25 and over with: High school diploma (including GED) or higher: 81.3% (2005); Bachelor's degree or higher: 7.7% (2005); Master's degree or higher: 2.4% (2005).
School District(s)
Margaretta Local SD (PK-12)
    2003-04 Enrollment: 1,467 . . . . (419) 684-5322

Housing: Homeownership rate: 70.3% (2005); Median home value: $130,357 (2005); Median rent: $418 per month (2000); Median age of housing: 51 years (2000).
Transportation: Commute to work: 96.9% car, 0.2% public transportation, 1.9% walk, 1.0% work from home (2000); Travel time to work: 31.6% less than 15 minutes, 47.8% 15 to 30 minutes, 10.2% 30 to 45 minutes, 1.9% 45 to 60 minutes, 8.5% 60 minutes or more (2000)

FAIRVIEW LANES (CDP).
Covers a land area of 0.365 square miles and a water area of 0 square miles. Located at 41.42° N. Lat.; 82.65° W. Long.
Population: 1,120 (1990); 1,015 (2000); 1,142 (2005); 1,260 (2010 projected); Race: 98.8% White, 0.8% Black, 0.3% Asian, 1.4% Hispanic of any race (2005); Density: 3,127.0 persons per square mile (2005); Average household size: 2.51 (2005); Median age: 41.9 (2005); Males per 100 females: 94.2 (2005); Marriage status: 16.6% never married, 68.7% now married, 6.7% widowed, 8.1% divorced (2000); Foreign born: 0.0% (2000); Ancestry (includes multiple ancestries): 49.4% German, 14.9% English, 12.3% Irish, 8.3% Italian, 4.4% Welsh (2000).
Economy: Employment by occupation: 8.7% management, 21.1% professional, 14.2% services, 31.6% sales, 0.0% farming, 7.1% construction, 17.3% production (2000).
Income: Per capita income: $29,505 (2005); Median household income: $63,365 (2005); Average household income: $74,055 (2005); Percent of households with income of $100,000 or more: 18.2% (2005); Poverty rate: 0.0% (2000).
Education: Percent of population age 25 and over with: High school diploma (including GED) or higher: 89.6% (2005); Bachelor's degree or higher: 24.2% (2005); Master's degree or higher: 8.8% (2005).
Housing: Homeownership rate: 94.7% (2005); Median home value: $133,235 (2005); Median rent: $625 per month (2000); Median age of housing: 38 years (2000).
Transportation: Commute to work: 98.5% car, 1.5% public transportation, 0.0% walk, 0.0% work from home (2000); Travel time to work: 52.4% less than 15 minutes, 34.2% 15 to 30 minutes, 6.5% 30 to 45 minutes, 2.4% 45 to 60 minutes, 4.5% 60 minutes or more (2000)

HURON (city).
Covers a land area of 4.886 square miles and a water area of 2.845 square miles. Located at 41.40° N. Lat.; 82.56° W. Long. Elevation is 580 feet.
History: A French trading post was established here about 1749. In 1805, trader B.F. Flemond arrived, and the town of Huron soon grew up around the harbor at the mouth of the Huron River. Shipping and shipbuilding supported the town.
Population: 7,074 (1990); 7,958 (2000); 7,858 (2005); 7,775 (2010 projected); Race: 96.7% White, 0.8% Black, 0.9% Asian, 1.9% Hispanic of any race (2005); Density: 1,608.1 persons per square mile (2005); Average household size: 2.36 (2005); Median age: 40.7 (2005); Males per 100 females: 91.9 (2005); Marriage status: 19.0% never married, 65.5% now married, 6.4% widowed, 9.1% divorced (2000); Foreign born: 1.7% (2000); Ancestry (includes multiple ancestries): 40.0% German, 16.5% Irish, 13.0% Italian, 10.6% English, 5.9% Other groups (2000).
Economy: Single-family building permits issued: 9 (2005); Multi-family building permits issued: 0 (2005); Employment by occupation: 14.5% management, 23.0% professional, 13.3% services, 24.3% sales, 0.2% farming, 6.1% construction, 18.6% production (2000).
Income: Per capita income: $30,162 (2005); Median household income: $58,578 (2005); Average household income: $70,538 (2005); Percent of households with income of $100,000 or more: 21.4% (2005); Poverty rate: 3.6% (2000).
Education: Percent of population age 25 and over with: High school diploma (including GED) or higher: 91.5% (2005); Bachelor's degree or higher: 28.8% (2005); Master's degree or higher: 11.0% (2005).
School District(s)
Huron City Schools (PK-12)
    2003-04 Enrollment: 1,664 . . . . (419) 433-3911
Two-year College(s)
Bowling Green State University-Firelands (Public)
    Fall 2004 Enrollment: 1,986. . . . . (419) 433-5560
    2005-06 Tuition: In-state $4,114; Out-of-state $11,422
Housing: Homeownership rate: 73.6% (2005); Median home value: $154,313 (2005); Median rent: $434 per month (2000); Median age of housing: 35 years (2000).
Safety: Violent crime rate: 0.0 per 10,000 population; Property crime rate: 237.9 per 10,000 population (2004).

Transportation: Commute to work: 95.7% car, 0.0% public transportation, 1.8% walk, 1.9% work from home (2000); Travel time to work: 39.2% less than 15 minutes, 40.8% 15 to 30 minutes, 12.8% 30 to 45 minutes, 2.6% 45 to 60 minutes, 4.6% 60 minutes or more (2000)
Additional Information Contacts
City of Huron . . . . (419) 433-5000
    http://www.cityofhuron.org
Huron Chamber of Commerce. . . . . (419) 433-5700
    http://www.huron.net

KELLEYS ISLAND (village).
Covers a land area of 4.559 square miles and a water area of 0.061 square miles. Located at 41.60° N. Lat.; 82.69° W. Long. Elevation is 598 feet.
History: In 1833 Irad and Datus Kelley acquired the island in Lake Erie, and settled here. They first harvested the forests of red cedar. In 1846 they planted an acre of grapes, and the island was soon known for its wine, as well as its peaches and grapes. Later, quarrying of the limestone became an important industry.
Population: 172 (1990); 367 (2000); 429 (2005); 482 (2010 projected); Race: 99.5% White, 0.5% Black, 0.0% Asian, 0.0% Hispanic of any race (2005); Density: 94.1 persons per square mile (2005); Average household size: 1.97 (2005); Median age: 53.3 (2005); Males per 100 females: 101.4 (2005); Marriage status: 9.8% never married, 69.5% now married, 9.5% widowed, 11.1% divorced (2000); Foreign born: 1.7% (2000); Ancestry (includes multiple ancestries): 28.0% German, 15.9% English, 15.3% Irish, 8.6% Polish, 7.2% Other groups (2000).
Economy: Single-family building permits issued: 14 (2005); Multi-family building permits issued: 0 (2005); Employment by occupation: 15.6% management, 7.5% professional, 14.3% services, 32.7% sales, 0.0% farming, 11.6% construction, 18.4% production (2000).
Income: Per capita income: $25,400 (2005); Median household income: $40,114 (2005); Average household income: $49,931 (2005); Percent of households with income of $100,000 or more: 11.9% (2005); Poverty rate: 9.8% (2000).
Education: Percent of population age 25 and over with: High school diploma (including GED) or higher: 94.5% (2005); Bachelor's degree or higher: 20.7% (2005); Master's degree or higher: 4.3% (2005).
School District(s)
Kelleys Island Local SD (PK-12)
    2003-04 Enrollment: 30 . . . . (419) 746-2730
Housing: Homeownership rate: 81.7% (2005); Median home value: $196,667 (2005); Median rent: $506 per month (2000); Median age of housing: 31 years (2000).
Transportation: Commute to work: 77.6% car, 2.7% public transportation, 3.4% walk, 16.3% work from home (2000); Travel time to work: 71.5% less than 15 minutes, 10.6% 15 to 30 minutes, 8.9% 30 to 45 minutes, 0.0% 45 to 60 minutes, 8.9% 60 minutes or more (2000)
Additional Information Contacts
Kelleys Island Chamber of Commerce . . . . (419) 746-2360
    http://www.kelleysislandchamber.com

MILAN (village).
Covers a land area of 1.175 square miles and a water area of 0 square miles. Located at 41.29° N. Lat.; 82.60° W. Long. Elevation is 667 feet.
History: Several villages occupied this site on the Huron River before the permanent settlement of Milan was laid out in 1816 by Ebenezer Merry. The town became a shipping port in 1839, when residents completed a canal to the Huron River, three miles away. Wheat was the principal cargo of the ships that left Milan. Milan prospered until the river became unnavigable for lake boats and the canal ceased to be used in the 1880's.
Population: 1,464 (1990); 1,445 (2000); 1,397 (2005); 1,366 (2010 projected); Race: 97.8% White, 0.6% Black, 0.6% Asian, 1.1% Hispanic of any race (2005); Density: 1,189.1 persons per square mile (2005); Average household size: 2.64 (2005); Median age: 42.7 (2005); Males per 100 females: 89.8 (2005); Marriage status: 21.4% never married, 62.0% now married, 7.7% widowed, 8.9% divorced (2000); Foreign born: 0.8% (2000); Ancestry (includes multiple ancestries): 45.7% German, 14.7% English, 13.3% Irish, 5.4% Other groups, 5.3% Polish (2000).
Economy: Single-family building permits issued: 4 (2005); Multi-family building permits issued: 0 (2005); Employment by occupation: 9.0% management, 21.8% professional, 12.4% services, 27.1% sales, 0.0% farming, 9.0% construction, 20.6% production (2000).
Income: Per capita income: $25,282 (2005); Median household income: $53,613 (2005); Average household income: $65,118 (2005); Percent of

households with income of $100,000 or more: 15.3% (2005); Poverty rate: 4.6% (2000).
Education: Percent of population age 25 and over with: High school diploma (including GED) or higher: 87.3% (2005); Bachelor's degree or higher: 23.1% (2005); Master's degree or higher: 7.9% (2005).

School District(s)
Berlin-Milan Local SD (PK-12)
    2003-04 Enrollment: 1,874 .... (419) 499-4272
Ehove Joint Vocational SD (09-12)
    2003-04 Enrollment: n/a .... (419) 499-4663

Two-year College(s)
Ehove Career Center (Public)
    Fall 2004 Enrollment: 294 .... (419) 499-4663

Housing: Homeownership rate: 79.2% (2005); Median home value: $145,670 (2005); Median rent: $432 per month (2000); Median age of housing: 46 years (2000).
Transportation: Commute to work: 92.4% car, 0.0% public transportation, 4.1% walk, 1.8% work from home (2000); Travel time to work: 49.2% less than 15 minutes, 29.3% 15 to 30 minutes, 12.5% 30 to 45 minutes, 3.4% 45 to 60 minutes, 5.7% 60 minutes or more (2000)

SANDUSKY (city). Covers a land area of 10.050 square miles and a water area of 11.937 square miles. Located at 41.44° N. Lat.; 82.70° W. Long. Elevation is 600 feet.
History: Sandusky was platted in 1818, replacing a smaller tract laid out in 1816 and called Portland. Its location on the southeastern corner of Sandusky Bay (named Lac Sandouske by French explorers, after the Wyandotte San-doos-tee) made the town a tourist and vacation destination, as well as an industrial community. The town was a port of entry and a shipping center, a stopping place for all vessels that sailed the Great Lakes. Sandusky became the seat of Erie County in 1838, but the 1840's brought epidemics of cholera that killed hundreds of people. In the 1850's Sandusky was an important station on the Underground Railroad.
Population: 29,764 (1990); 27,844 (2000); 26,654 (2005); 25,442 (2010 projected); Race: 73.9% White, 20.9% Black, 0.4% Asian, 3.4% Hispanic of any race (2005); Density: 2,652.2 persons per square mile (2005); Average household size: 2.30 (2005); Median age: 36.8 (2005); Males per 100 females: 89.7 (2005); Marriage status: 29.0% never married, 48.9% now married, 9.1% widowed, 13.0% divorced (2000); Foreign born: 1.7% (2000); Ancestry (includes multiple ancestries): 32.1% German, 24.7% Other groups, 12.4% Irish, 7.8% English, 7.4% Italian (2000).
Economy: Unemployment rate: 7.2% (2005); Total civilian labor force: 14,598 (2005); Single-family building permits issued: 29 (2005); Multi-family building permits issued: 0 (2005); Employment by occupation: 7.0% management, 12.0% professional, 21.1% services, 24.9% sales, 0.2% farming, 7.8% construction, 27.1% production (2000).
Income: Per capita income: $19,644 (2005); Median household income: $33,841 (2005); Average household income: $44,716 (2005); Percent of households with income of $100,000 or more: 6.1% (2005); Poverty rate: 15.3% (2000).
Taxes: Total city taxes per capita: $548 (2004); City property taxes per capita: $75 (2004).
Education: Percent of population age 25 and over with: High school diploma (including GED) or higher: 79.6% (2005); Bachelor's degree or higher: 11.2% (2005); Master's degree or higher: 3.2% (2005).

School District(s)
Perkins Local SD (PK-12)
    2003-04 Enrollment: 2,267 .... (419) 625-0484
Sandusky City SD (PK-12)
    2003-04 Enrollment: 4,227 .... (419) 626-6940

Two-year College(s)
Firelands Regional Medical Center School of Nursing (Private, Not-for-profit)
    Fall 2004 Enrollment: 117 .... (419) 557-7111
    2005-06 Tuition: In-state $13,364; Out-of-state $13,364
Ohio Business College (Private, For-profit)
    Fall 2004 Enrollment: 232 .... (419) 627-8345
    2005-06 Tuition: In-state $6,948; Out-of-state $6,948
Sandusky Adult Education (Public)
    Fall 2004 Enrollment: 354 .... (419) 625-9294

Housing: Homeownership rate: 56.8% (2005); Median home value: $87,812 (2005); Median rent: $387 per month (2000); Median age of housing: 50 years (2000).
Hospitals: Firelands Regional Medical Center (265 beds); Providence Hospital (270 beds)
Safety: Violent crime rate: 52.1 per 10,000 population; Property crime rate: 670.9 per 10,000 population (2004).
Newspapers: Sandusky Register (Circulation 23,141)
Transportation: Commute to work: 94.6% car, 0.6% public transportation, 2.3% walk, 1.4% work from home (2000); Travel time to work: 59.1% less than 15 minutes, 28.5% 15 to 30 minutes, 6.7% 30 to 45 minutes, 1.8% 45 to 60 minutes, 4.0% 60 minutes or more (2000); Amtrak: Service available.

Additional Information Contacts
City of Sandusky .... (419) 627-5844
    http://www.ci.sandusky.oh.us
Sandusky Chamber of Commerce .... (419) 625-6421
    http://www.eriecountyohiocofc.com
Sandusky/Erie Co. Visitors & Convention Bureau .... (419) 625-2984
    http://www.buckeyenorth.com

SANDUSKY SOUTH (CDP). Covers a land area of 4.266 square miles and a water area of 0.020 square miles. Located at 41.41° N. Lat.; 82.68° W. Long.
Population: 6,466 (1990); 6,599 (2000); 6,253 (2005); 5,978 (2010 projected); Race: 88.0% White, 9.1% Black, 0.9% Asian, 1.3% Hispanic of any race (2005); Density: 1,465.8 persons per square mile (2005); Average household size: 2.92 (2005); Median age: 46.9 (2005); Males per 100 females: 117.9 (2005); Marriage status: 20.0% never married, 60.8% now married, 9.3% widowed, 10.0% divorced (2000); Foreign born: 1.9% (2000); Ancestry (includes multiple ancestries): 39.4% German, 12.2% Irish, 11.0% Other groups, 10.4% English, 7.1% Italian (2000).
Economy: Employment by occupation: 8.9% management, 19.2% professional, 19.9% services, 22.7% sales, 0.3% farming, 6.8% construction, 22.2% production (2000).
Income: Per capita income: $24,470 (2005); Median household income: $55,141 (2005); Average household income: $66,014 (2005); Percent of households with income of $100,000 or more: 17.4% (2005); Poverty rate: 4.0% (2000).
Education: Percent of population age 25 and over with: High school diploma (including GED) or higher: 79.1% (2005); Bachelor's degree or higher: 15.2% (2005); Master's degree or higher: 5.4% (2005).
Housing: Homeownership rate: 87.9% (2005); Median home value: $133,590 (2005); Median rent: $390 per month (2000); Median age of housing: 36 years (2000).
Transportation: Commute to work: 96.4% car, 0.5% public transportation, 0.2% walk, 2.2% work from home (2000); Travel time to work: 70.1% less than 15 minutes, 19.7% 15 to 30 minutes, 4.6% 30 to 45 minutes, 2.7% 45 to 60 minutes, 2.9% 60 minutes or more (2000)

Fairfield County

Located in central Ohio; drained by the Hocking River; includes part of Buckeye Lake. Covers a land area of 505.11 square miles, a water area of 3.49 square miles, and is located in the Eastern Time Zone. The county government was organized in 1800. County seat is Lancaster.

Fairfield County is part of the Columbus, OH Metropolitan Statistical Area. The entire metro area includes: Delaware County, OH; Fairfield County, OH; Franklin County, OH; Licking County, OH; Madison County, OH; Morrow County, OH; Pickaway County, OH; Union County, OH

Weather Station: Lancaster 2 NW   Elevation: 859 feet

	Jan	Feb	Mar	Apr	May	Jun	Jul	Aug	Sep	Oct	Nov	Dec
High	35	39	50	62	72	80	84	83	77	65	52	41
Low	17	19	28	37	48	57	62	60	52	40	32	23
Precip	2.3	2.2	2.6	3.2	4.2	3.8	4.4	3.6	2.8	2.5	3.1	2.9
Snow	na	na	na	0.7	0.0	0.0	0.0	0.0	0.0	tr	0.3	na

High and Low temperatures in degrees Fahrenheit; Precipitation and Snow in inches

Population: 103,472 (1990); 122,759 (2000); 137,152 (2005); 152,242 (2010 projected); Race: 92.0% White, 5.2% Black, 1.1% Asian, 1.1% Hispanic of any race (2005); Density: 271.5 persons per square mile (2005); Average household size: 2.67 (2005); Median age: 36.4 (2005); Males per 100 females: 98.4 (2005).
Religion: Five largest groups: 11.7% Catholic Church, 8.3% The United Methodist Church, 4.2% Evangelical Lutheran Church in America, 2.4% Christian Churches and Churches of Christ, 1.3% Southern Baptist Convention (2000).
Economy: Unemployment rate: 5.2% (2005); Total civilian labor force: 72,199 (2005); Leading industries: 17.8% retail trade; 17.2% health care and social assistance; 16.0% manufacturing (2004); Farms: 1,173 totaling

196,128 acres (2002); Companies that employ 500 or more persons: 2 (2004); Companies that employ 100 to 499 persons: 38 (2004); Companies that employ less than 100 persons: 2,592 (2004); Black-owned businesses: n/a (2002); Hispanic-owned businesses: n/a (2002); Women-owned businesses: 2,935 (2002); Retail sales per capita: $10,142 (2006). Single-family building permits issued: 810 (2005); Multi-family building permits issued: 182 (2005).
Income: Per capita income: $25,170 (2005); Median household income: $54,404 (2005); Average household income: $66,674 (2005); Percent of households with income of $100,000 or more: 18.2% (2005); Poverty rate: 6.9% (2003); Bankruptcy rate: 9.63% (2005).
Taxes: Total county taxes per capita: $182 (2004); County property taxes per capita: $94 (2004).
Education: Percent of population age 25 and over with: High school diploma (including GED) or higher: 87.9% (2005); Bachelor's degree or higher: 21.3% (2005); Master's degree or higher: 6.5% (2005).
Housing: Homeownership rate: 77.1% (2005); Median home value: $157,675 (2005); Median rent: $442 per month (2000); Median age of housing: 28 years (2000).
Health: Birth rate: 116.6 per 10,000 population (2004); Death rate: 78.8 per 10,000 population (2004); Age-adjusted cancer mortality rate: 185.3 deaths per 100,000 population (2002); Number of physicians: 16.5 per 10,000 population (2004); Hospital beds: 16.7 per 10,000 population (2003); Hospital admissions: 979.9 per 10,000 population (2003).
Elections: 2004 Presidential election results: 62.9% Bush, 36.5% Kerry, 0.0% Nader, 0.3% Badnarik
National and State Parks: Rock Mill Dam State Wildlife Area; Shallenberger State Nature Reserve; Sherman House State Memorial; Tarlton State Park

Additional Information Contacts
Fairfield County Government . . . . (740) 687-7190
   http://www.co.fairfield.oh.us/
Baltimore Chamber of Commerce . . . . (740) 862-8199
   http://www.baltimoreohio.org
City of Lancaster . . . . (740) 687-6608
   http://www.ci.lancaster.oh.us
City of Pickerington . . . . (614) 837-3974
   http://www.ci.pickerington.oh.us
Lancaster Fairfield County Chamber of Commerce . . . . . . (740) 653-8251
   http://www.lancoc.org
Pickerington Chamber of Commerce . . . . (614) 837-1958
   http://www.pickeringtonchamber.com
Village of Baltimore . . . . (740) 862-4491
   http://www.baltimoreohio.org
Village of Thurston . . . . (740) 862-6003
   http://www.thurstonohio.com

Fairfield County Communities

AMANDA (village). Covers a land area of 0.327 square miles and a water area of 0 square miles. Located at 39.65° N. Lat.; 82.74° W. Long. Elevation is 930 feet.
Population: 774 (1990); 707 (2000); 770 (2005); 832 (2010 projected); Race: 98.4% White, 0.0% Black, 0.0% Asian, 1.0% Hispanic of any race (2005); Density: 2,353.2 persons per square mile (2005); Average household size: 2.70 (2005); Median age: 34.5 (2005); Males per 100 females: 89.7 (2005); Marriage status: 16.7% never married, 70.0% now married, 4.7% widowed, 8.6% divorced (2000); Foreign born: 0.8% (2000); Ancestry (includes multiple ancestries): 22.5% German, 17.0% United States or American, 10.6% English, 8.3% Irish, 6.8% Other groups (2000).
Economy: In agricultural area. Employment by occupation: 8.2% management, 9.8% professional, 18.6% services, 24.8% sales, 1.0% farming, 14.1% construction, 23.5% production (2000).
Income: Per capita income: $18,201 (2005); Median household income: $44,136 (2005); Average household income: $49,175 (2005); Percent of households with income of $100,000 or more: 6.3% (2005); Poverty rate: 3.6% (2000).
Education: Percent of population age 25 and over with: High school diploma (including GED) or higher: 81.9% (2005); Bachelor's degree or higher: 6.9% (2005); Master's degree or higher: 1.4% (2005).

School District(s)
Amanda Clearcreek Digital Academy
   2003-04 Enrollment: n/a . . . . (740) 969-4112
Amanda-Clearcreek Local SD (PK-12)
   2003-04 Enrollment: 1,653 . . . . (740) 969-7250

Housing: Homeownership rate: 73.0% (2005); Median home value: $111,650 (2005); Median rent: $381 per month (2000); Median age of housing: 56 years (2000).
Transportation: Commute to work: 93.6% car, 0.0% public transportation, 5.7% walk, 0.7% work from home (2000); Travel time to work: 15.8% less than 15 minutes, 34.7% 15 to 30 minutes, 19.9% 30 to 45 minutes, 19.2% 45 to 60 minutes, 10.4% 60 minutes or more (2000)

BALTIMORE (village). Covers a land area of 1.782 square miles and a water area of 0 square miles. Located at 39.84° N. Lat.; 82.60° W. Long. Elevation is 860 feet.
Population: 3,004 (1990); 2,881 (2000); 2,928 (2005); 3,026 (2010 projected); Race: 98.7% White, 0.1% Black, 0.3% Asian, 0.3% Hispanic of any race (2005); Density: 1,643.1 persons per square mile (2005); Average household size: 2.42 (2005); Median age: 35.6 (2005); Males per 100 females: 89.6 (2005); Marriage status: 20.1% never married, 56.1% now married, 11.2% widowed, 12.5% divorced (2000); Foreign born: 0.3% (2000); Ancestry (includes multiple ancestries): 31.9% German, 12.8% United States or American, 12.3% Irish, 8.8% English, 6.6% Other groups (2000).
Economy: Single-family building permits issued: 5 (2005); Multi-family building permits issued: 0 (2005); Employment by occupation: 9.8% management, 9.9% professional, 16.8% services, 30.1% sales, 0.3% farming, 19.1% construction, 13.9% production (2000).
Income: Per capita income: $21,557 (2005); Median household income: $44,889 (2005); Average household income: $52,026 (2005); Percent of households with income of $100,000 or more: 9.1% (2005); Poverty rate: 9.5% (2000).
Education: Percent of population age 25 and over with: High school diploma (including GED) or higher: 81.5% (2005); Bachelor's degree or higher: 8.4% (2005); Master's degree or higher: 2.4% (2005).

School District(s)
Liberty Union Thurston Digital
   2003-04 Enrollment: n/a . . . . (740) 862-4171
Liberty Union-Thurston Local SD (PK-12)
   2003-04 Enrollment: 1,430 . . . . (740) 862-4171

Housing: Homeownership rate: 63.1% (2005); Median home value: $124,574 (2005); Median rent: $363 per month (2000); Median age of housing: 47 years (2000).
Transportation: Commute to work: 95.5% car, 0.0% public transportation, 1.6% walk, 2.2% work from home (2000); Travel time to work: 22.9% less than 15 minutes, 26.2% 15 to 30 minutes, 29.0% 30 to 45 minutes, 15.3% 45 to 60 minutes, 6.5% 60 minutes or more (2000)

Additional Information Contacts
Baltimore Chamber of Commerce . . . . (740) 862-8199
   http://www.baltimoreohio.org
Village of Baltimore . . . . (740) 862-4491
   http://www.baltimoreohio.org

BREMEN (village). Covers a land area of 0.835 square miles and a water area of 0 square miles. Located at 39.70° N. Lat.; 82.43° W. Long. Elevation is 800 feet.
Population: 1,389 (1990); 1,265 (2000); 1,322 (2005); 1,396 (2010 projected); Race: 99.3% White, 0.0% Black, 0.0% Asian, 0.5% Hispanic of any race (2005); Density: 1,583.6 persons per square mile (2005); Average household size: 2.56 (2005); Median age: 33.2 (2005); Males per 100 females: 89.4 (2005); Marriage status: 21.8% never married, 59.9% now married, 8.8% widowed, 9.5% divorced (2000); Foreign born: 0.2% (2000); Ancestry (includes multiple ancestries): 30.9% German, 16.6% United States or American, 12.7% Irish, 6.3% English, 3.3% Other groups (2000).
Economy: In agricultural area. Manufacturing of glass products, building materials, cheese; lumber milling. Oil wells, molding sand pits; timber. Single-family building permits issued: 2 (2005); Multi-family building permits issued: 0 (2005); Employment by occupation: 8.6% management, 13.6% professional, 20.9% services, 25.1% sales, 0.0% farming, 10.8% construction, 21.0% production (2000).
Income: Per capita income: $18,565 (2005); Median household income: $41,890 (2005); Average household income: $47,471 (2005); Percent of households with income of $100,000 or more: 5.2% (2005); Poverty rate: 6.7% (2000).
Education: Percent of population age 25 and over with: High school diploma (including GED) or higher: 83.8% (2005); Bachelor's degree or higher: 7.8% (2005); Master's degree or higher: 2.6% (2005).

School District(s)
Fairfield Union Local SD (PK-12)
   2003-04 Enrollment: 1,958 . . . . (740) 536-7384
Housing: Homeownership rate: 74.5% (2005); Median home value: $112,151 (2005); Median rent: $356 per month (2000); Median age of housing: 60+ years (2000).
Transportation: Commute to work: 92.3% car, 0.0% public transportation, 4.6% walk, 2.9% work from home (2000); Travel time to work: 24.8% less than 15 minutes, 38.9% 15 to 30 minutes, 14.4% 30 to 45 minutes, 6.9% 45 to 60 minutes, 15.0% 60 minutes or more (2000)

CARROLL (village).
Covers a land area of 0.275 square miles and a water area of 0 square miles. Located at 39.79° N. Lat.; 82.70° W. Long. Elevation is 820 feet.
Population: 533 (1990); 488 (2000); 482 (2005); 487 (2010 projected); Race: 99.2% White, 0.0% Black, 0.4% Asian, 0.2% Hispanic of any race (2005); Density: 1,755.5 persons per square mile (2005); Average household size: 2.56 (2005); Median age: 35.4 (2005); Males per 100 females: 92.0 (2005); Marriage status: 35.7% never married, 47.2% now married, 3.2% widowed, 13.9% divorced (2000); Foreign born: 0.2% (2000); Ancestry (includes multiple ancestries): 32.3% German, 15.3% Irish, 13.7% United States or American, 10.9% English, 8.5% Other groups (2000).
Economy: In agricultural area. Single-family building permits issued: 0 (2005); Multi-family building permits issued: 0 (2005); Employment by occupation: 5.4% management, 8.3% professional, 10.9% services, 31.5% sales, 0.0% farming, 17.4% construction, 26.4% production (2000).
Income: Per capita income: $22,422 (2005); Median household income: $47,712 (2005); Average household income: $57,487 (2005); Percent of households with income of $100,000 or more: 10.1% (2005); Poverty rate: 5.7% (2000).
Education: Percent of population age 25 and over with: High school diploma (including GED) or higher: 91.5% (2005); Bachelor's degree or higher: 7.5% (2005); Master's degree or higher: 0.0% (2005).
School District(s)
Bloom-Carroll Digital Academy
   2003-04 Enrollment: n/a
Bloom-Carroll Local SD (PK-12)
   2003-04 Enrollment: 1,494 . . . . (614) 837-6560
Eastland-Fairfield Career/Tech (09-12)
   2003-04 Enrollment: n/a . . . . (614) 836-4530
Housing: Homeownership rate: 65.4% (2005); Median home value: $114,904 (2005); Median rent: $464 per month (2000); Median age of housing: 60+ years (2000).
Transportation: Commute to work: 94.9% car, 0.4% public transportation, 2.2% walk, 2.5% work from home (2000); Travel time to work: 25.4% less than 15 minutes, 32.5% 15 to 30 minutes, 26.1% 30 to 45 minutes, 11.9% 45 to 60 minutes, 4.1% 60 minutes or more (2000)

FAIRFIELD BEACH (CDP).
Covers a land area of 0.648 square miles and a water area of 0.318 square miles. Located at 39.91° N. Lat.; 82.47° W. Long. Elevation is 940 feet.
Population: 1,084 (1990); 1,163 (2000); 1,267 (2005); 1,376 (2010 projected); Race: 97.3% White, 0.2% Black, 0.0% Asian, 0.2% Hispanic of any race (2005); Density: 1,956.3 persons per square mile (2005); Average household size: 2.41 (2005); Median age: 39.1 (2005); Males per 100 females: 104.0 (2005); Marriage status: 17.1% never married, 66.0% now married, 8.3% widowed, 8.6% divorced (2000); Foreign born: 1.8% (2000); Ancestry (includes multiple ancestries): 22.7% United States or American, 20.7% German, 11.9% Irish, 10.2% English, 6.4% Other groups (2000).
Economy: Employment by occupation: 12.1% management, 11.7% professional, 12.1% services, 23.6% sales, 0.0% farming, 12.1% construction, 28.3% production (2000).
Income: Per capita income: $19,132 (2005); Median household income: $37,296 (2005); Average household income: $46,171 (2005); Percent of households with income of $100,000 or more: 5.0% (2005); Poverty rate: 6.3% (2000).
Education: Percent of population age 25 and over with: High school diploma (including GED) or higher: 75.8% (2005); Bachelor's degree or higher: 3.4% (2005); Master's degree or higher: 1.8% (2005).
Housing: Homeownership rate: 87.8% (2005); Median home value: $109,564 (2005); Median rent: $675 per month (2000); Median age of housing: 41 years (2000).
Transportation: Commute to work: 98.4% car, 0.0% public transportation, 0.0% walk, 1.6% work from home (2000); Travel time to work: 9.7% less than 15 minutes, 21.1% 15 to 30 minutes, 27.1% 30 to 45 minutes, 27.8% 45 to 60 minutes, 14.2% 60 minutes or more (2000)

LANCASTER (city).
Covers a land area of 18.066 square miles and a water area of 0.010 square miles. Located at 39.71° N. Lat.; 82.60° W. Long. Elevation is 860 feet.
History: Lancaster was established on one of the three sections of land given to Ebenezer Zane for his work in laying out Zane's Trace. In 1800 the settlement on the banks of the Hocking River was named New Lancaster, because settlers had come from Lancaster, Pennsylvania. The first newspaper was printed in German, which was the language used in the early schools.
Population: 35,664 (1990); 35,335 (2000); 36,150 (2005); 37,502 (2010 projected); Race: 96.4% White, 1.1% Black, 0.7% Asian, 1.1% Hispanic of any race (2005); Density: 2,001.0 persons per square mile (2005); Average household size: 2.34 (2005); Median age: 35.7 (2005); Males per 100 females: 89.5 (2005); Marriage status: 22.2% never married, 55.9% now married, 8.3% widowed, 13.6% divorced (2000); Foreign born: 0.9% (2000); Ancestry (includes multiple ancestries): 27.6% German, 15.2% United States or American, 13.4% Irish, 8.8% English, 8.2% Other groups (2000).
Economy: Unemployment rate: 6.3% (2005); Total civilian labor force: 18,286 (2005); Single-family building permits issued: 121 (2005); Multi-family building permits issued: 142 (2005); Employment by occupation: 9.1% management, 14.7% professional, 17.1% services, 29.2% sales, 0.1% farming, 11.4% construction, 18.5% production (2000).
Income: Per capita income: $20,021 (2005); Median household income: $36,782 (2005); Average household income: $46,533 (2005); Percent of households with income of $100,000 or more: 6.6% (2005); Poverty rate: 10.6% (2000).
Taxes: Total city taxes per capita: $415 (2004); City property taxes per capita: $48 (2004).
Education: Percent of population age 25 and over with: High school diploma (including GED) or higher: 83.5% (2005); Bachelor's degree or higher: 13.5% (2005); Master's degree or higher: 4.5% (2005).
School District(s)
Fairfield Union Local SD (PK-12)
   2003-04 Enrollment: 1,958 . . . . (740) 536-7384
Lancaster City SD (PK-12)
   2003-04 Enrollment: 6,104 . . . . (740) 687-7300
Lancaster Digital Academy (02-12)
   2003-04 Enrollment: 43 . . . . (740) 687-7300
Lancaster Fairfield Alternative School
   2003-04 Enrollment: n/a
Four-year College(s)
Ohio University-Lancaster Campus (Public)
   Fall 2004 Enrollment: 1,723 . . . . (740) 654-6711
   2005-06 Tuition: In-state $4,323; Out-of-state $8,646
Two-year College(s)
Southeastern Business College (Private, For-profit)
   Fall 2004 Enrollment: 75 . . . . (740) 687-6126
   2005-06 Tuition: In-state $9,330; Out-of-state $9,330
Housing: Homeownership rate: 59.8% (2005); Median home value: $116,390 (2005); Median rent: $414 per month (2000); Median age of housing: 43 years (2000).
Hospitals: Fairfield Medical Center (229 beds)
Safety: Violent crime rate: 27.5 per 10,000 population; Property crime rate: 458.5 per 10,000 population (2004).
Newspapers: Lancaster Eagle-Gazette (Circulation 15,344)
Transportation: Commute to work: 93.3% car, 0.5% public transportation, 3.2% walk, 2.1% work from home (2000); Travel time to work: 40.3% less than 15 minutes, 23.6% 15 to 30 minutes, 14.7% 30 to 45 minutes, 12.8% 45 to 60 minutes, 8.6% 60 minutes or more (2000)
Additional Information Contacts
City of Lancaster . . . . (740) 687-6608
   http://www.ci.lancaster.oh.us
Lancaster Fairfield County Chamber of Commerce . . . . . . (740) 653-8251
   http://www.lancoc.org

LITHOPOLIS (village).
Covers a land area of 0.401 square miles and a water area of 0 square miles. Located at 39.80° N. Lat.; 82.80° W. Long. Elevation is 930 feet.
History: The name of Lithopolis means "stone city" in the Greek, an appropriate name for a town that grew around sandstone quarries.

Population: 563 (1990); 600 (2000); 679 (2005); 766 (2010 projected); Race: 98.2% White, 0.4% Black, 0.0% Asian, 0.6% Hispanic of any race (2005); Density: 1,691.7 persons per square mile (2005); Average household size: 2.37 (2005); Median age: 39.3 (2005); Males per 100 females: 96.8 (2005); Marriage status: 25.2% never married, 60.3% now married, 3.8% widowed, 10.7% divorced (2000); Foreign born: 0.4% (2000); Ancestry (includes multiple ancestries): 29.7% German, 16.0% Irish, 11.0% Other groups, 10.3% United States or American, 8.1% English (2000).
Economy: Single-family building permits issued: 56 (2005); Multi-family building permits issued: 0 (2005); Employment by occupation: 12.5% management, 7.5% professional, 16.2% services, 28.7% sales, 1.1% farming, 17.7% construction, 16.2% production (2000).
Income: Per capita income: $23,487 (2005); Median household income: $45,821 (2005); Average household income: $55,566 (2005); Percent of households with income of $100,000 or more: 10.5% (2005); Poverty rate: 5.6% (2000).
Education: Percent of population age 25 and over with: High school diploma (including GED) or higher: 87.3% (2005); Bachelor's degree or higher: 16.0% (2005); Master's degree or higher: 4.8% (2005).
School District(s)
Bloom-Carroll Local SD (PK-12)
   2003-04 Enrollment: 1,494 . . . . (614) 837-6560
Housing: Homeownership rate: 64.5% (2005); Median home value: $148,239 (2005); Median rent: $410 per month (2000); Median age of housing: 45 years (2000).
Transportation: Commute to work: 90.5% car, 0.0% public transportation, 3.8% walk, 4.2% work from home (2000); Travel time to work: 15.1% less than 15 minutes, 38.2% 15 to 30 minutes, 35.1% 30 to 45 minutes, 5.2% 45 to 60 minutes, 6.4% 60 minutes or more (2000)

MILLERSPORT (village). Covers a land area of 0.995 square miles and a water area of 0.034 square miles. Located at 39.90° N. Lat.; 82.53° W. Long. Elevation is 904 feet.
Population: 1,048 (1990); 963 (2000); 944 (2005); 955 (2010 projected); Race: 98.1% White, 0.0% Black, 0.0% Asian, 1.0% Hispanic of any race (2005); Density: 948.5 persons per square mile (2005); Average household size: 2.34 (2005); Median age: 36.4 (2005); Males per 100 females: 81.9 (2005); Marriage status: 21.5% never married, 58.7% now married, 4.7% widowed, 15.1% divorced (2000); Foreign born: 0.3% (2000); Ancestry (includes multiple ancestries): 28.4% German, 17.7% English, 16.4% United States or American, 11.7% Irish, 7.5% Other groups (2000).
Economy: In agricultural area. Single-family building permits issued: 1 (2005); Multi-family building permits issued: 0 (2005); Employment by occupation: 14.7% management, 10.9% professional, 14.5% services, 26.8% sales, 0.8% farming, 9.2% construction, 23.1% production (2000).
Income: Per capita income: $22,262 (2005); Median household income: $44,706 (2005); Average household income: $52,017 (2005); Percent of households with income of $100,000 or more: 9.4% (2005); Poverty rate: 5.9% (2000).
Education: Percent of population age 25 and over with: High school diploma (including GED) or higher: 86.6% (2005); Bachelor's degree or higher: 13.5% (2005); Master's degree or higher: 4.3% (2005).
School District(s)
Walnut Township Local SD (PK-12)
   2003-04 Enrollment: 747 . . . . (740) 467-2802
Walnut Twp Digital Academy
   2003-04 Enrollment: n/a . . . . (740) 467-2802
Housing: Homeownership rate: 69.3% (2005); Median home value: $122,124 (2005); Median rent: $400 per month (2000); Median age of housing: 40 years (2000).
Transportation: Commute to work: 92.5% car, 0.6% public transportation, 1.9% walk, 3.2% work from home (2000); Travel time to work: 18.5% less than 15 minutes, 28.9% 15 to 30 minutes, 30.9% 30 to 45 minutes, 15.2% 45 to 60 minutes, 6.4% 60 minutes or more (2000)

PICKERINGTON (city). Covers a land area of 7.433 square miles and a water area of 0 square miles. Located at 39.89° N. Lat.; 82.76° W. Long. Elevation is 842 feet.
History: The first settlers in the community that is now Pickerington arrived in the area in 1808. In 1815, Abraham Pickering laid out the original plat of old Pickerington. One hundred fifty years later relatively few people lived in the area, and Pickerington slumbered as an agricultural and dairy community. As a result of reaching an official population of over 5,000 persons, Pickerington was certified as a city by the Ohio Secretary of State in 1991. In 1996 the city was designated by the Ohio Legislature as the "Violet Capital of Ohio." Pickerington is the home of the American Motorcyclist Association Motorcycle Heritage Museum and Motorcycle Hall of Fame.
Population: 6,400 (1990); 9,792 (2000); 13,662 (2005); 17,361 (2010 projected); Race: 88.5% White, 7.3% Black, 2.1% Asian, 1.8% Hispanic of any race (2005); Density: 1,838.0 persons per square mile (2005); Average household size: 2.79 (2005); Median age: 33.4 (2005); Males per 100 females: 96.5 (2005); Marriage status: 20.3% never married, 68.3% now married, 2.7% widowed, 8.7% divorced (2000); Foreign born: 2.3% (2000); Ancestry (includes multiple ancestries): 31.4% German, 17.8% Irish, 10.0% English, 9.6% Other groups, 8.3% Italian (2000).
Economy: Single-family building permits issued: 277 (2005); Multi-family building permits issued: 34 (2005); Employment by occupation: 22.3% management, 19.5% professional, 11.9% services, 31.6% sales, 0.0% farming, 6.4% construction, 8.2% production (2000).
Income: Per capita income: $28,685 (2005); Median household income: $70,091 (2005); Average household income: $79,849 (2005); Percent of households with income of $100,000 or more: 26.1% (2005); Poverty rate: 3.2% (2000).
Education: Percent of population age 25 and over with: High school diploma (including GED) or higher: 95.0% (2005); Bachelor's degree or higher: 31.1% (2005); Master's degree or higher: 6.9% (2005).
School District(s)
Pickerington Local SD (PK-12)
   2003-04 Enrollment: 8,917 . . . . (614) 833-2110
Housing: Homeownership rate: 77.1% (2005); Median home value: $165,987 (2005); Median rent: $595 per month (2000); Median age of housing: 12 years (2000).
Safety: Violent crime rate: 11.1 per 10,000 population; Property crime rate: 237.9 per 10,000 population (2004).
Transportation: Commute to work: 96.1% car, 0.4% public transportation, 0.6% walk, 2.4% work from home (2000); Travel time to work: 16.7% less than 15 minutes, 38.7% 15 to 30 minutes, 28.9% 30 to 45 minutes, 9.6% 45 to 60 minutes, 6.0% 60 minutes or more (2000)
Additional Information Contacts
City of Pickerington . . . . (614) 837-3974
   http://www.ci.pickerington.oh.us
Pickerington Chamber of Commerce. . . . . (614) 837-1958
   http://www.pickeringtonchamber.com

PLEASANTVILLE (village). Covers a land area of 0.278 square miles and a water area of 0 square miles. Located at 39.81° N. Lat.; 82.52° W. Long. Elevation is 912 feet.
Population: 945 (1990); 877 (2000); 878 (2005); 900 (2010 projected); Race: 96.8% White, 0.2% Black, 0.9% Asian, 1.0% Hispanic of any race (2005); Density: 3,159.1 persons per square mile (2005); Average household size: 2.75 (2005); Median age: 34.5 (2005); Males per 100 females: 88.4 (2005); Marriage status: 26.1% never married, 52.4% now married, 7.5% widowed, 14.0% divorced (2000); Foreign born: 0.2% (2000); Ancestry (includes multiple ancestries): 29.3% German, 18.5% Irish, 11.4% United States or American, 7.7% Other groups, 6.6% English (2000).
Economy: In agricultural area. Single-family building permits issued: 0 (2005); Multi-family building permits issued: 0 (2005); Employment by occupation: 6.8% management, 10.3% professional, 23.6% services, 21.2% sales, 0.5% farming, 13.9% construction, 23.6% production (2000).
Income: Per capita income: $14,825 (2005); Median household income: $36,449 (2005); Average household income: $40,729 (2005); Percent of households with income of $100,000 or more: 3.8% (2005); Poverty rate: 11.3% (2000).
Education: Percent of population age 25 and over with: High school diploma (including GED) or higher: 77.0% (2005); Bachelor's degree or higher: 4.6% (2005); Master's degree or higher: 1.1% (2005).
School District(s)
Fairfield Union Local SD (PK-12)
   2003-04 Enrollment: 1,958 . . . . (740) 536-7384
Housing: Homeownership rate: 68.7% (2005); Median home value: $105,220 (2005); Median rent: $317 per month (2000); Median age of housing: 53 years (2000).
Transportation: Commute to work: 95.5% car, 0.0% public transportation, 2.2% walk, 1.4% work from home (2000); Travel time to work: 19.5% less than 15 minutes, 43.1% 15 to 30 minutes, 16.1% 30 to 45 minutes, 15.0% 45 to 60 minutes, 6.2% 60 minutes or more (2000)

RUSHVILLE (village). Covers a land area of 0.226 square miles and a water area of 0 square miles. Located at 39.76° N. Lat.; 82.43° W. Long. Elevation is 1,050 feet.
History: Rushville was the birthplace of Benjamin Russell Hanby (1833-1867), who wrote the song "Darling Nellie Gray." Though it was published and became popular across the country, Hanby never received royalties for his work.
Population: 229 (1990); 268 (2000); 282 (2005); 298 (2010 projected); Race: 96.8% White, 0.0% Black, 0.0% Asian, 0.0% Hispanic of any race (2005); Density: 1,245.2 persons per square mile (2005); Average household size: 2.94 (2005); Median age: 31.0 (2005); Males per 100 females: 93.2 (2005); Marriage status: 25.1% never married, 56.8% now married, 4.9% widowed, 13.1% divorced (2000); Foreign born: 0.8% (2000); Ancestry (includes multiple ancestries): 26.6% German, 16.7% United States or American, 15.5% Irish, 11.9% Other groups, 7.5% English (2000).
Economy: Employment by occupation: 7.3% management, 4.1% professional, 12.2% services, 44.7% sales, 0.0% farming, 13.8% construction, 17.9% production (2000).
Income: Per capita income: $15,488 (2005); Median household income: $38,462 (2005); Average household income: $45,495 (2005); Percent of households with income of $100,000 or more: 5.2% (2005); Poverty rate: 14.7% (2000).
Education: Percent of population age 25 and over with: High school diploma (including GED) or higher: 92.7% (2005); Bachelor's degree or higher: 9.1% (2005); Master's degree or higher: 0.0% (2005).
School District(s)
Fairfield Union Local SD (PK-12)
    2003-04 Enrollment: 1,958 . . . . (740) 536-7384
Housing: Homeownership rate: 74.0% (2005); Median home value: $108,333 (2005); Median rent: $394 per month (2000); Median age of housing: 60+ years (2000).
Transportation: Commute to work: 97.5% car, 0.0% public transportation, 0.8% walk, 1.7% work from home (2000); Travel time to work: 6.0% less than 15 minutes, 27.6% 15 to 30 minutes, 16.4% 30 to 45 minutes, 35.3% 45 to 60 minutes, 14.7% 60 minutes or more (2000)

STOUTSVILLE (village). Covers a land area of 1.333 square miles and a water area of 0 square miles. Located at 39.60° N. Lat.; 82.82° W. Long. Elevation is 970 feet.
Population: 518 (1990); 581 (2000); 717 (2005); 853 (2010 projected); Race: 98.5% White, 0.4% Black, 0.0% Asian, 0.8% Hispanic of any race (2005); Density: 537.8 persons per square mile (2005); Average household size: 2.66 (2005); Median age: 36.2 (2005); Males per 100 females: 99.2 (2005); Marriage status: 19.8% never married, 62.8% now married, 5.8% widowed, 11.6% divorced (2000); Foreign born: 0.0% (2000); Ancestry (includes multiple ancestries): 32.3% German, 17.5% United States or American, 11.0% Irish, 11.0% English, 7.6% Other groups (2000).
Economy: Employment by occupation: 4.6% management, 15.2% professional, 7.8% services, 30.4% sales, 0.0% farming, 12.4% construction, 29.7% production (2000).
Income: Per capita income: $23,361 (2005); Median household income: $53,652 (2005); Average household income: $62,037 (2005); Percent of households with income of $100,000 or more: 12.2% (2005); Poverty rate: 3.8% (2000).
Education: Percent of population age 25 and over with: High school diploma (including GED) or higher: 83.2% (2005); Bachelor's degree or higher: 10.5% (2005); Master's degree or higher: 3.6% (2005).
Housing: Homeownership rate: 79.6% (2005); Median home value: $120,882 (2005); Median rent: $369 per month (2000); Median age of housing: 55 years (2000).
Transportation: Commute to work: 93.2% car, 0.0% public transportation, 3.6% walk, 3.2% work from home (2000); Travel time to work: 22.7% less than 15 minutes, 39.8% 15 to 30 minutes, 15.6% 30 to 45 minutes, 13.0% 45 to 60 minutes, 8.9% 60 minutes or more (2000)

SUGAR GROVE (village). Covers a land area of 0.205 square miles and a water area of 0 square miles. Located at 39.62° N. Lat.; 82.54° W. Long. Elevation is 780 feet.
Population: 465 (1990); 448 (2000); 468 (2005); 493 (2010 projected); Race: 99.6% White, 0.0% Black, 0.0% Asian, 0.9% Hispanic of any race (2005); Density: 2,279.6 persons per square mile (2005); Average household size: 2.71 (2005); Median age: 31.5 (2005); Males per 100 females: 89.5 (2005); Marriage status: 22.5% never married, 58.6% now married, 5.7% widowed, 13.2% divorced (2000); Foreign born: 0.0% (2000); Ancestry (includes multiple ancestries): 26.3% German, 9.9% Other groups, 8.0% Irish, 6.3% United States or American, 4.8% Welsh (2000).
Economy: In agricultural area. Single-family building permits issued: 0 (2005); Multi-family building permits issued: 0 (2005); Employment by occupation: 5.7% management, 13.0% professional, 15.1% services, 25.5% sales, 0.0% farming, 17.7% construction, 22.9% production (2000).
Income: Per capita income: $18,130 (2005); Median household income: $43,315 (2005); Average household income: $49,046 (2005); Percent of households with income of $100,000 or more: 4.0% (2005); Poverty rate: 6.0% (2000).
Education: Percent of population age 25 and over with: High school diploma (including GED) or higher: 93.6% (2005); Bachelor's degree or higher: 7.1% (2005); Master's degree or higher: 1.8% (2005).
School District(s)
Berne Union Local SD (PK-12)
    2003-04 Enrollment: 990 . . . . (740) 746-8341
Housing: Homeownership rate: 66.5% (2005); Median home value: $105,603 (2005); Median rent: $454 per month (2000); Median age of housing: 60+ years (2000).
Transportation: Commute to work: 89.9% car, 1.1% public transportation, 4.8% walk, 3.2% work from home (2000); Travel time to work: 15.8% less than 15 minutes, 37.2% 15 to 30 minutes, 7.1% 30 to 45 minutes, 13.7% 45 to 60 minutes, 26.2% 60 minutes or more (2000)

THURSTON (village). Covers a land area of 0.259 square miles and a water area of 0 square miles. Located at 39.84° N. Lat.; 82.54° W. Long. Elevation is 881 feet.
Population: 556 (1990); 555 (2000); 615 (2005); 683 (2010 projected); Race: 95.0% White, 0.3% Black, 0.8% Asian, 0.0% Hispanic of any race (2005); Density: 2,377.2 persons per square mile (2005); Average household size: 2.67 (2005); Median age: 33.3 (2005); Males per 100 females: 95.9 (2005); Marriage status: 21.2% never married, 59.0% now married, 6.8% widowed, 13.0% divorced (2000); Foreign born: 2.0% (2000); Ancestry (includes multiple ancestries): 27.9% United States or American, 22.7% German, 15.5% Irish, 10.3% Other groups, 8.8% English (2000).
Economy: In livestock raising and farming area. Employment by occupation: 6.7% management, 7.1% professional, 14.7% services, 28.0% sales, 0.0% farming, 19.6% construction, 24.0% production (2000).
Income: Per capita income: $14,065 (2005); Median household income: $32,391 (2005); Average household income: $37,609 (2005); Percent of households with income of $100,000 or more: 2.6% (2005); Poverty rate: 9.9% (2000).
Education: Percent of population age 25 and over with: High school diploma (including GED) or higher: 76.6% (2005); Bachelor's degree or higher: 4.7% (2005); Master's degree or higher: 1.3% (2005).
Housing: Homeownership rate: 78.7% (2005); Median home value: $98,684 (2005); Median rent: $381 per month (2000); Median age of housing: 49 years (2000).
Transportation: Commute to work: 95.3% car, 0.9% public transportation, 0.0% walk, 3.7% work from home (2000); Travel time to work: 15.5% less than 15 minutes, 31.9% 15 to 30 minutes, 27.5% 30 to 45 minutes, 18.4% 45 to 60 minutes, 6.8% 60 minutes or more (2000)
Additional Information Contacts
Village of Thurston . . . . (740) 862-6003
    http://www.thurstonohio.com

WEST RUSHVILLE (village). Covers a land area of 0.061 square miles and a water area of 0 square miles. Located at 39.76° N. Lat.; 82.44° W. Long. Elevation is 1,015 feet.
Population: 134 (1990); 132 (2000); 148 (2005); 166 (2010 projected); Race: 98.6% White, 0.0% Black, 0.0% Asian, 4.7% Hispanic of any race (2005); Density: 2,437.8 persons per square mile (2005); Average household size: 2.64 (2005); Median age: 34.4 (2005); Males per 100 females: 97.3 (2005); Marriage status: 34.0% never married, 50.5% now married, 10.7% widowed, 4.9% divorced (2000); Foreign born: 1.6% (2000); Ancestry (includes multiple ancestries): 22.5% United States or American, 20.9% German, 13.2% Other groups, 13.2% Irish, 3.1% French Canadian (2000).
Economy: Employment by occupation: 1.4% management, 2.8% professional, 15.5% services, 42.3% sales, 0.0% farming, 18.3% construction, 19.7% production (2000).

Income: Per capita income: $20,557 (2005); Median household income: $42,500 (2005); Average household income: $54,330 (2005); Percent of households with income of $100,000 or more: 12.5% (2005); Poverty rate: 6.2% (2000).
Education: Percent of population age 25 and over with: High school diploma (including GED) or higher: 84.4% (2005); Bachelor's degree or higher: 8.9% (2005); Master's degree or higher: 2.2% (2005).

School District(s)
Fairfield Union Digital Academy
    2003-04 Enrollment: n/a . . . . (740) 536-7384
Housing: Homeownership rate: 76.8% (2005); Median home value: $132,500 (2005); Median rent: $386 per month (2000); Median age of housing: 60+ years (2000).
Transportation: Commute to work: 100.0% car, 0.0% public transportation, 0.0% walk, 0.0% work from home (2000); Travel time to work: 24.2% less than 15 minutes, 33.9% 15 to 30 minutes, 16.1% 30 to 45 minutes, 12.9% 45 to 60 minutes, 12.9% 60 minutes or more (2000)

Fayette County

Located in south central Ohio; drained by Paint, Sugar, and Rattlesnakes Creeks. Covers a land area of 406.58 square miles, a water area of 0.50 square miles, and is located in the Eastern Time Zone. The county government was organized in 1810. County seat is Washington.

Fayette County is part of the Washington, OH Micropolitan Statistical Area. The entire metro area includes: Fayette County, OH

Weather Station: Washington Court House   Elevation: 958 feet

	Jan	Feb	Mar	Apr	May	Jun	Jul	Aug	Sep	Oct	Nov	Dec
High	36	40	51	63	72	79	83	82	76	66	52	41
Low	20	23	32	41	52	61	65	63	56	44	35	26
Precip	2.4	2.4	3.3	3.6	4.7	3.8	4.0	3.9	2.6	2.7	3.0	2.8
Snow	8.7	6.1	4.1	0.7	tr	0.0	0.0	0.0	0.0	0.2	1.0	3.5

High and Low temperatures in degrees Fahrenheit; Precipitation and Snow in inches

Population: 27,466 (1990); 28,433 (2000); 28,129 (2005); 27,810 (2010 projected); Race: 95.6% White, 2.2% Black, 0.5% Asian, 1.5% Hispanic of any race (2005); Density: 69.2 persons per square mile (2005); Average household size: 2.54 (2005); Median age: 38.5 (2005); Males per 100 females: 97.6 (2005).
Religion: Five largest groups: 8.3% The United Methodist Church, 5.8% Christian Churches and Churches of Christ, 2.4% Presbyterian Church (U.S.A.), 2.3% Catholic Church, 1.9% American Baptist Churches in the USA (2000).
Economy: Unemployment rate: 5.8% (2005); Total civilian labor force: 15,915 (2005); Leading industries: 26.7% manufacturing; 24.3% retail trade; 11.8% health care and social assistance (2004); Farms: 480 totaling 203,212 acres (2002); Companies that employ 500 or more persons: 2 (2004); Companies that employ 100 to 499 persons: 15 (2004); Companies that employ less than 100 persons: 664 (2004); Black-owned businesses: n/a (2002); Hispanic-owned businesses: n/a (2002); Women-owned businesses: 252 (2002); Retail sales per capita: $22,962 (2006). Single-family building permits issued: 131 (2005); Multi-family building permits issued: 50 (2005).
Income: Per capita income: $21,526 (2005); Median household income: $44,040 (2005); Average household income: $53,789 (2005); Percent of households with income of $100,000 or more: 9.3% (2005); Poverty rate: 10.6% (2003); Bankruptcy rate: 12.38% (2005).
Taxes: Total county taxes per capita: $262 (2004); County property taxes per capita: $107 (2004).
Education: Percent of population age 25 and over with: High school diploma (including GED) or higher: 78.8% (2005); Bachelor's degree or higher: 10.8% (2005); Master's degree or higher: 3.0% (2005).
Housing: Homeownership rate: 66.5% (2005); Median home value: $109,970 (2005); Median rent: $365 per month (2000); Median age of housing: 40 years (2000).
Health: Birth rate: 130.0 per 10,000 population (2004); Death rate: 137.2 per 10,000 population (2004); Age-adjusted cancer mortality rate: 199.6 deaths per 100,000 population (2002); Number of physicians: 6.8 per 10,000 population (2004); Hospital beds: 12.8 per 10,000 population (2003); Hospital admissions: 610.2 per 10,000 population (2003).
Elections: 2004 Presidential election results: 62.7% Bush, 36.9% Kerry, 0.0% Nader, 0.2% Badnarik
Additional Information Contacts

Fayette County Government . . . . (740) 335-0720
    http://www.fayette-co-oh.com/
City of Washington Court House . . . . (740) 636-2340
    http://www.ci.washington-court-house.oh.us
Fayette County Chamber of Commerce . . . . (740) 335-0761
    http://www.fayettecountychamberoh.com

Fayette County Communities

BLOOMINGBURG (village). Covers a land area of 0.697 square miles and a water area of 0 square miles. Located at 39.60° N. Lat.; 83.39° W. Long. Elevation is 998 feet.
Population: 769 (1990); 874 (2000); 934 (2005); 977 (2010 projected); Race: 93.3% White, 3.9% Black, 0.0% Asian, 4.6% Hispanic of any race (2005); Density: 1,339.6 persons per square mile (2005); Average household size: 2.77 (2005); Median age: 31.8 (2005); Males per 100 females: 101.7 (2005); Marriage status: 26.3% never married, 53.4% now married, 5.9% widowed, 14.3% divorced (2000); Foreign born: 0.3% (2000); Ancestry (includes multiple ancestries): 25.9% United States or American, 15.2% Other groups, 11.2% German, 8.0% English, 7.1% Irish (2000).
Economy: Employment by occupation: 1.3% management, 8.6% professional, 15.0% services, 18.7% sales, 2.7% farming, 14.2% construction, 39.6% production (2000).
Income: Per capita income: $14,111 (2005); Median household income: $35,547 (2005); Average household income: $37,856 (2005); Percent of households with income of $100,000 or more: 1.8% (2005); Poverty rate: 16.0% (2000).
Education: Percent of population age 25 and over with: High school diploma (including GED) or higher: 67.6% (2005); Bachelor's degree or higher: 2.0% (2005); Master's degree or higher: 0.5% (2005).

School District(s)
Miami Trace Local SD (PK-12)
    2003-04 Enrollment: 2,719 . . . . (740) 335-3010
Housing: Homeownership rate: 65.0% (2005); Median home value: $79,318 (2005); Median rent: $381 per month (2000); Median age of housing: 36 years (2000).
Transportation: Commute to work: 92.4% car, 2.7% public transportation, 3.8% walk, 0.5% work from home (2000); Travel time to work: 30.5% less than 15 minutes, 39.0% 15 to 30 minutes, 12.8% 30 to 45 minutes, 10.1% 45 to 60 minutes, 7.6% 60 minutes or more (2000)

JEFFERSONVILLE (village). Covers a land area of 1.703 square miles and a water area of 0.035 square miles. Located at 39.65° N. Lat.; 83.55° W. Long. Elevation is 1,049 feet.
Population: 1,318 (1990); 1,288 (2000); 1,291 (2005); 1,283 (2010 projected); Race: 90.0% White, 7.4% Black, 0.0% Asian, 0.5% Hispanic of any race (2005); Density: 758.0 persons per square mile (2005); Average household size: 2.45 (2005); Median age: 34.3 (2005); Males per 100 females: 93.8 (2005); Marriage status: 26.7% never married, 46.8% now married, 8.7% widowed, 17.9% divorced (2000); Foreign born: 0.2% (2000); Ancestry (includes multiple ancestries): 21.2% United States or American, 11.2% German, 10.9% Other groups, 9.8% Irish, 5.0% English (2000).
Economy: In livestock raising and farming area. Employment by occupation: 6.9% management, 7.1% professional, 16.6% services, 25.0% sales, 0.5% farming, 10.2% construction, 33.6% production (2000).
Income: Per capita income: $18,145 (2005); Median household income: $38,611 (2005); Average household income: $44,366 (2005); Percent of households with income of $100,000 or more: 5.9% (2005); Poverty rate: 17.1% (2000).
Education: Percent of population age 25 and over with: High school diploma (including GED) or higher: 79.2% (2005); Bachelor's degree or higher: 7.7% (2005); Master's degree or higher: 1.4% (2005).

School District(s)
Miami Trace Local SD (PK-12)
    2003-04 Enrollment: 2,719 . . . . (740) 335-3010
Housing: Homeownership rate: 57.6% (2005); Median home value: $94,000 (2005); Median rent: $360 per month (2000); Median age of housing: 28 years (2000).
Transportation: Commute to work: 95.1% car, 0.0% public transportation, 1.6% walk, 2.8% work from home (2000); Travel time to work: 31.9% less than 15 minutes, 34.6% 15 to 30 minutes, 16.3% 30 to 45 minutes, 10.2% 45 to 60 minutes, 7.1% 60 minutes or more (2000)

MILLEDGEVILLE (village). Covers a land area of 0.101 square miles and a water area of 0 square miles. Located at 39.59° N. Lat.; 83.58° W. Long. Elevation is 1,050 feet.
Population: 120 (1990); 122 (2000); 119 (2005); 118 (2010 projected); Race: 98.3% White, 1.7% Black, 0.0% Asian, 0.0% Hispanic of any race (2005); Density: 1,172.7 persons per square mile (2005); Average household size: 2.59 (2005); Median age: 40.0 (2005); Males per 100 females: 116.4 (2005); Marriage status: 22.8% never married, 64.1% now married, 2.2% widowed, 10.9% divorced (2000); Foreign born: 4.4% (2000); Ancestry (includes multiple ancestries): 21.1% Other groups, 7.9% German, 5.3% Irish, 3.5% Dutch, 3.5% United States or American (2000).
Economy: Employment by occupation: 6.0% management, 3.0% professional, 22.4% services, 17.9% sales, 0.0% farming, 6.0% construction, 44.8% production (2000).
Income: Per capita income: $21,471 (2005); Median household income: $48,929 (2005); Average household income: $55,543 (2005); Percent of households with income of $100,000 or more: 6.5% (2005); Poverty rate: 4.4% (2000).
Education: Percent of population age 25 and over with: High school diploma (including GED) or higher: 70.0% (2005); Bachelor's degree or higher: 10.0% (2005); Master's degree or higher: 3.3% (2005).
Housing: Homeownership rate: 80.4% (2005); Median home value: $85,000 (2005); Median rent: $406 per month (2000); Median age of housing: 60+ years (2000).
Transportation: Commute to work: 92.5% car, 0.0% public transportation, 0.0% walk, 7.5% work from home (2000); Travel time to work: 35.5% less than 15 minutes, 38.7% 15 to 30 minutes, 16.1% 30 to 45 minutes, 6.5% 45 to 60 minutes, 3.2% 60 minutes or more (2000)

OCTA (village). Covers a land area of 0.285 square miles and a water area of 0 square miles. Located at 39.60° N. Lat.; 83.61° W. Long. Elevation is 1,045 feet.
Population: 83 (1990); 83 (2000); 80 (2005); 77 (2010 projected); Race: 91.3% White, 8.8% Black, 0.0% Asian, 6.3% Hispanic of any race (2005); Density: 280.7 persons per square mile (2005); Average household size: 2.22 (2005); Median age: 44.2 (2005); Males per 100 females: 110.5 (2005); Marriage status: 18.9% never married, 64.2% now married, 3.8% widowed, 13.2% divorced (2000); Foreign born: 0.0% (2000); Ancestry (includes multiple ancestries): 24.3% German, 21.6% United States or American, 18.9% Dutch, 10.8% Irish, 8.1% Other groups (2000).
Economy: Employment by occupation: 0.0% management, 0.0% professional, 13.8% services, 34.5% sales, 0.0% farming, 13.8% construction, 37.9% production (2000).
Income: Per capita income: $20,406 (2005); Median household income: $35,119 (2005); Average household income: $45,347 (2005); Percent of households with income of $100,000 or more: 5.6% (2005); Poverty rate: 8.1% (2000).
Education: Percent of population age 25 and over with: High school diploma (including GED) or higher: 55.7% (2005); Bachelor's degree or higher: 0.0% (2005); Master's degree or higher: 0.0% (2005).
Housing: Homeownership rate: 63.9% (2005); Median home value: $73,750 (2005); Median rent: $313 per month (2000); Median age of housing: 52 years (2000).
Transportation: Commute to work: 81.5% car, 0.0% public transportation, 0.0% walk, 0.0% work from home (2000); Travel time to work: 25.9% less than 15 minutes, 29.6% 15 to 30 minutes, 25.9% 30 to 45 minutes, 0.0% 45 to 60 minutes, 18.5% 60 minutes or more (2000)

WASHINGTON COURT HOUSE (city). Aka City of Washington Court House; Washington C.H.. Covers a land area of 6.438 square miles and a water area of 0.066 square miles. Located at 39.53° N. Lat.; 83.43° W. Long.
History: Originally known as the City of Washington, the official name was changed in 2002 to the City of Washington Court House to avoid confusion with a municipality in Guernsey County with the name "Washington" (now known as Old Washington).
Population: 13,044 (1990); 13,524 (2000); 13,272 (2005); 13,065 (2010 projected); Race: 94.4% White, 2.8% Black, 0.9% Asian, 1.7% Hispanic of any race (2005); Density: 2,061.6 persons per square mile (2005); Average household size: 2.43 (2005); Median age: 37.9 (2005); Males per 100 females: 93.6 (2005); Marriage status: 22.3% never married, 54.2% now married, 10.0% widowed, 13.5% divorced (2000); Foreign born: 1.3% (2000); Ancestry (includes multiple ancestries): 19.1% German, 18.0% United States or American, 12.4% Irish, 9.5% English, 8.6% Other groups (2000).
Economy: Single-family building permits issued: 87 (2005); Multi-family building permits issued: 50 (2005); Employment by occupation: 10.2% management, 15.4% professional, 14.2% services, 25.3% sales, 0.7% farming, 7.6% construction, 26.7% production (2000).
Income: Per capita income: $21,624 (2005); Median household income: $39,649 (2005); Average household income: $51,335 (2005); Percent of households with income of $100,000 or more: 8.7% (2005); Poverty rate: 12.5% (2000).
Education: Percent of population age 25 and over with: High school diploma (including GED) or higher: 77.3% (2005); Bachelor's degree or higher: 13.1% (2005); Master's degree or higher: 3.8% (2005).
School District(s)
Miami Trace Local SD (PK-12)
    2003-04 Enrollment: 2,719 . . . . (740) 335-3010
Washington Court House City SD (PK-12)
    2003-04 Enrollment: 2,315 . . . . (740) 335-6620
Housing: Homeownership rate: 56.4% (2005); Median home value: $99,692 (2005); Median rent: $361 per month (2000); Median age of housing: 44 years (2000).
Hospitals: Fayette County Memorial Hospital (70 beds)
Safety: Violent crime rate: 15.7 per 10,000 population; Property crime rate: 460.9 per 10,000 population (2004).
Newspapers: Record-Herald (Circulation 6,000)
Transportation: Commute to work: 92.8% car, 0.3% public transportation, 3.1% walk, 2.5% work from home (2000); Travel time to work: 48.7% less than 15 minutes, 20.6% 15 to 30 minutes, 13.6% 30 to 45 minutes, 6.4% 45 to 60 minutes, 10.7% 60 minutes or more (2000)
Additional Information Contacts
City of Washington Court House . . . . (740) 636-2340
    http://www.ci.washington-court-house.oh.us
Fayette County Chamber of Commerce . . . . (740) 335-0761
    http://www.fayettecountychamberoh.com

Franklin County

Located in central Ohio; crossed by the Scioto and Olentangy Rivers. Covers a land area of 539.87 square miles, a water area of 3.45 square miles, and is located in the Eastern Time Zone. The county government was organized in 1803. County seat is Columbus.

Franklin County is part of the Columbus, OH Metropolitan Statistical Area. The entire metro area includes: Delaware County, OH; Fairfield County, OH; Franklin County, OH; Licking County, OH; Madison County, OH; Morrow County, OH; Pickaway County, OH; Union County, OH

Weather Station: Columbus Valley Crossing   Elevation: 734 feet

	Jan	Feb	Mar	Apr	May	Jun	Jul	Aug	Sep	Oct	Nov	Dec
High	36	41	52	64	74	82	85	84	78	66	53	42
Low	20	23	32	40	51	60	64	62	55	43	34	26
Precip	2.5	2.0	3.0	3.7	4.3	4.1	4.4	4.3	2.9	2.5	3.3	2.9
Snow	8.4	5.0	1.9	0.6	tr	0.0	0.0	0.0	0.0	tr	0.6	2.8

High and Low temperatures in degrees Fahrenheit; Precipitation and Snow in inches

Weather Station: Columbus-Port Columbus Int'l   Elevation: 807 feet

	Jan	Feb	Mar	Apr	May	Jun	Jul	Aug	Sep	Oct	Nov	Dec
High	35	39	51	62	73	81	85	83	76	65	52	41
Low	20	23	31	40	51	60	64	63	55	43	35	26
Precip	2.5	2.2	2.9	3.3	3.9	4.2	4.6	3.7	2.9	2.3	3.2	2.9
Snow	10.5	6.1	4.3	1.2	tr	tr	tr	0.0	tr	0.2	1.6	4.5

High and Low temperatures in degrees Fahrenheit; Precipitation and Snow in inches

Weather Station: Westerville   Elevation: 807 feet

	Jan	Feb	Mar	Apr	May	Jun	Jul	Aug	Sep	Oct	Nov	Dec
High	36	41	52	64	74	82	85	84	78	66	52	41
Low	18	21	30	39	49	58	62	61	54	42	34	25
Precip	2.5	2.2	2.8	3.6	4.0	4.6	4.0	3.5	2.9	2.6	3.4	2.9
Snow	7.7	5.1	2.3	0.7	tr	0.0	0.0	0.0	0.0	tr	0.5	3.3

High and Low temperatures in degrees Fahrenheit; Precipitation and Snow in inches

Population: 961,437 (1990); 1,068,978 (2000); 1,096,456 (2005); 1,124,931 (2010 projected); Race: 72.6% White, 19.0% Black, 3.9% Asian, 2.9% Hispanic of any race (2005); Density: 2,031.0 persons per square mile (2005); Average household size: 2.41 (2005); Median age: 34.1 (2005); Males per 100 females: 95.5 (2005).

Religion: Five largest groups: 13.7% Catholic Church, 4.1% The United Methodist Church, 2.8% Evangelical Lutheran Church in America, 2.1% Southern Baptist Convention, 1.5% Presbyterian Church (U.S.A.) (2000).
Economy: Unemployment rate: 5.3% (2005); Total civilian labor force: 604,384 (2005); Leading industries: 13.3% health care and social assistance; 12.1% retail trade; 9.6% finance & insurance (2004); Farms: 561 totaling 81,593 acres (2002); Companies that employ 500 or more persons: 112 (2004); Companies that employ 100 to 499 persons: 910 (2004); Companies that employ less than 100 persons: 27,542 (2004); Black-owned businesses: 7,888 (2002); Hispanic-owned businesses: 887 (2002); Women-owned businesses: 25,366 (2002); Retail sales per capita: $19,435 (2006). Single-family building permits issued: 4,446 (2005); Multi-family building permits issued: 2,838 (2005).
Income: Per capita income: $26,657 (2005); Median household income: $48,629 (2005); Average household income: $63,763 (2005); Percent of households with income of $100,000 or more: 16.2% (2005); Poverty rate: 12.0% (2003); Bankruptcy rate: 13.78% (2005).
Taxes: Total county taxes per capita: $382 (2004); County property taxes per capita: $286 (2004).
Education: Percent of population age 25 and over with: High school diploma (including GED) or higher: 86.1% (2005); Bachelor's degree or higher: 32.1% (2005); Master's degree or higher: 10.6% (2005).
Housing: Homeownership rate: 57.2% (2005); Median home value: $137,219 (2005); Median rent: $496 per month (2000); Median age of housing: 30 years (2000).
Health: Birth rate: 157.3 per 10,000 population (2004); Death rate: 77.5 per 10,000 population (2004); Age-adjusted cancer mortality rate: 229.9 deaths per 100,000 population (2002); Air Quality Index: 33.7% good, 59.7% moderate, 6.0% unhealthy for sensitive individuals, 0.5% unhealthy (percent of days in 2005); Number of physicians: 39.9 per 10,000 population (2004); Hospital beds: 37.0 per 10,000 population (2003); Hospital admissions: 1,657.7 per 10,000 population (2003).
Elections: 2004 Presidential election results: 45.1% Bush, 54.4% Kerry, 0.0% Nader, 0.3% Badnarik

Additional Information Contacts

Franklin County Government	(614) 462-3322
http://www.co.franklin.oh.us	
Bexley Area Chamber of Commerce	(614) 470-4500
http://www.bexleyareachamber.org	
Canal Winchester Chamber of Commerce	(614) 837-1556
http://www.canalwinchester.com	
Canal Winchester Convention & Visitors Bureau	(614) 920-0649
http://www.cwcvb.com	
City of Bexley	(614) 235-8694
http://www.bexley.org	
City of Columbus	(614) 645-8100
http://www.ci.columbus.oh.us	
City of Dublin	(614) 410-4400
http://www.dublin.oh.us	
City of Gahanna	(614) 342-4000
http://www.gahanna.gov	
City of Grandview Heights	(614) 481-6217
http://www.grandviewheights.org	
City of Grove City	(614) 277-3075
http://www.ci.grove-city.oh.us	
City of Hilliard	(614) 876-7361
http://www.cityofhilliard.com	
City of Reynoldsburg	(614) 322-6800
http://www.ci.reynoldsburg.oh.us	
City of Upper Arlington	(614) 583-5040
http://www.ua-ohio.net	
City of Westerville	(614) 901-6400
http://www.ci.westerville.oh.us	
City of Whitehall	(614) 338-3106
http://www.ci.whitehall.oh.us	
City of Worthington	(614) 436-3100
http://www.worthington.org	
Columbus Chamber of Commerce	(614) 221-1321
http://www.columbus-chamber.org	
Columbus Convention & Visitors Bureau	(614) 221-6623
http://www.experiencecolumbus.com	
Dublin Chamber of Commerce	(614) 889-2001
http://www.dublinchamber.org	
Dublin Convention and Visitors Bureau	(614) 792-7666
http://www.dublinvisit.org	
Gahanna Area Chamber of Commerce	(614) 471-0451
http://www.gahannaareachamber.com	
Grandview-Marble Cliff Chamber	(614) 486-0196
http://www.grandviewchamber.org	
Grove City Chamber of Commerce	(614) 875-9762
http://www.gcchamber.org	
Groveport Madison Chamber of Commerce	(614) 836-1138
http://www.groveport.org	
Hilliard Area Chamber of Commerce	(614) 876-7666
http://www.hilliardchamber.org	
Hilliard Convention & Visitors Bureau	(614) 876-6911
http://www.hilliardcvb.org	
New Albany Chamber of Commerce	(614) 855-4408
http://www.newalbanychamber.com	
Reynoldsburg Chamber of Commerce	(614) 866-4753
http://www.reynoldsburgchamber.com	
Upper Arlington Area Chamber of Commerce	(614) 481-5710
http://www.uachamber.org	
Village of Canal Winchester	(614) 837-7493
http://www.canalwinchester.org/index2.htm	
Village of Groveport	(614) 836-5301
http://www.groveport.org	
Village of New Albany	(614) 855-3913
http://www.villageofnewalbany.org	
Village of Obetz	(614) 491-1080
http://www.obetz.oh.us	
Westerville Chamber of Commerce	(614) 882-8917
http://www.westervillechamber.com	
Whitehall Chamber of Commerce	(614) 237-7792
http://www.whitehallchamber.org	
Worthington Chamber of Commerce	(614) 888-3040
http://www.worthington.org	
Worthington Convention & Visitors Bureau	(614) 841-2545
http://www.worthington.org/cvb	

Franklin County Communities

AMLIN (unincorporated postal area, zip code 43002). Covers a land area of 9.461 square miles and a water area of 0 square miles. Located at 40.06° N. Lat.; 83.18° W. Long. Elevation is 944 feet.
Population: 1,304 (2000); Race: 100.0% White, 0.0% Black, 0.0% Asian, 0.0% Hispanic of any race (2000); Density: 137.8 persons per square mile (2000); Age: 16.0% under 18, 11.9% over 64 (2000); Marriage status: 18.5% never married, 62.0% now married, 6.0% widowed, 13.4% divorced (2000); Foreign born: 1.3% (2000); Ancestry (includes multiple ancestries): 28.8% German, 28.7% United States or American, 16.4% Irish, 16.0% English, 6.9% French (except Basque) (2000).
Economy: Employment by occupation: 6.5% management, 15.6% professional, 17.8% services, 27.8% sales, 0.0% farming, 13.8% construction, 18.5% production (2000).
Income: Per capita income: $23,344 (2000); Median household income: $40,795 (2000); Poverty rate: 7.7% (2000).
Education: Percent of population age 25 and over with: High school diploma (including GED) or higher: 83.5% (2000); Bachelor's degree or higher: 20.2% (2000).
Housing: Homeownership rate: 89.0% (2000); Median home value: $136,700 (2000); Median rent: $364 per month (2000); Median age of housing: 23 years (2000).
Transportation: Commute to work: 96.2% car, 0.0% public transportation, 0.9% walk, 2.9% work from home (2000); Travel time to work: 35.8% less than 15 minutes, 38.7% 15 to 30 minutes, 13.4% 30 to 45 minutes, 6.0% 45 to 60 minutes, 6.0% 60 minutes or more (2000)

BEXLEY (city). Covers a land area of 2.446 square miles and a water area of 0 square miles. Located at 39.96° N. Lat.; 82.93° W. Long. Elevation is 790 feet.
History: Named for Bexley, England. Bexley developed as a residential suburb of Columbus, and as the location of Capital University, founded in 1830 as a Lutheran divinity school.
Population: 13,111 (1990); 13,203 (2000); 12,425 (2005); 11,753 (2010 projected); Race: 91.3% White, 4.8% Black, 1.2% Asian, 1.1% Hispanic of any race (2005); Density: 5,080.3 persons per square mile (2005); Average household size: 2.81 (2005); Median age: 36.5 (2005); Males per 100 females: 89.7 (2005); Marriage status: 29.5% never married, 56.6% now married, 6.1% widowed, 7.8% divorced (2000); Foreign born: 6.4% (2000);

Ancestry (includes multiple ancestries): 27.7% German, 14.8% Irish, 13.1% English, 12.9% Other groups, 7.3% Russian (2000).
Economy: Single-family building permits issued: 5 (2005); Multi-family building permits issued: 31 (2005); Employment by occupation: 20.0% management, 38.8% professional, 9.5% services, 26.2% sales, 0.1% farming, 1.9% construction, 3.5% production (2000).
Income: Per capita income: $40,963 (2005); Median household income: $76,382 (2005); Average household income: $113,460 (2005); Percent of households with income of $100,000 or more: 36.5% (2005); Poverty rate: 4.6% (2000).
Education: Percent of population age 25 and over with: High school diploma (including GED) or higher: 96.9% (2005); Bachelor's degree or higher: 66.8% (2005); Master's degree or higher: 31.8% (2005).

School District(s)
Bexley City SD (PK-12)
    2003-04 Enrollment: 2,211 . . . . (614) 231-7611

Housing: Homeownership rate: 77.3% (2005); Median home value: $235,314 (2005); Median rent: $534 per month (2000); Median age of housing: 57 years (2000).
Safety: Violent crime rate: 19.8 per 10,000 population; Property crime rate: 366.6 per 10,000 population (2004).
Transportation: Commute to work: 86.4% car, 1.6% public transportation, 7.0% walk, 4.4% work from home (2000); Travel time to work: 42.0% less than 15 minutes, 43.1% 15 to 30 minutes, 11.3% 30 to 45 minutes, 1.8% 45 to 60 minutes, 1.8% 60 minutes or more (2000)

Additional Information Contacts
Bexley Area Chamber of Commerce . . . . (614) 470-4500
    http://www.bexleyareachamber.org
City of Bexley . . . . (614) 235-8694
    http://www.bexley.org

BLACKLICK (unincorporated postal area, zip code 43004). Aka Black Lick. Covers a land area of 13.718 square miles and a water area of 0 square miles. Located at 39.99° N. Lat.; 82.80° W. Long. Elevation is 955 feet.
Population: 8,664 (2000); Race: 82.0% White, 13.4% Black, 1.9% Asian, 1.0% Hispanic of any race (2000); Density: 631.6 persons per square mile (2000); Age: 26.7% under 18, 6.5% over 64 (2000); Marriage status: 25.5% never married, 62.4% now married, 3.6% widowed, 8.4% divorced (2000); Foreign born: 3.7% (2000); Ancestry (includes multiple ancestries): 27.6% German, 20.1% Other groups, 17.5% Irish, 9.0% English, 8.2% United States or American (2000).
Economy: Employment by occupation: 20.3% management, 21.3% professional, 9.3% services, 28.9% sales, 0.0% farming, 8.4% construction, 11.8% production (2000).
Income: Per capita income: $30,748 (2000); Median household income: $55,406 (2000); Poverty rate: 7.0% (2000).
Education: Percent of population age 25 and over with: High school diploma (including GED) or higher: 91.9% (2000); Bachelor's degree or higher: 36.9% (2000).

School District(s)
Gahanna-Jefferson City SD (PK-12)
    2003-04 Enrollment: 6,806 . . . . (614) 471-7065

Housing: Homeownership rate: 73.3% (2000); Median home value: $152,500 (2000); Median rent: $539 per month (2000); Median age of housing: 4 years (2000).
Transportation: Commute to work: 96.4% car, 0.4% public transportation, 0.8% walk, 1.8% work from home (2000); Travel time to work: 22.8% less than 15 minutes, 42.8% 15 to 30 minutes, 23.3% 30 to 45 minutes, 6.4% 45 to 60 minutes, 4.6% 60 minutes or more (2000)

BLACKLICK ESTATES (CDP). Covers a land area of 1.993 square miles and a water area of 0 square miles. Located at 39.90° N. Lat.; 82.86° W. Long.
Population: 9,850 (1990); 9,518 (2000); 8,824 (2005); 8,239 (2010 projected); Race: 83.5% White, 11.3% Black, 1.3% Asian, 1.4% Hispanic of any race (2005); Density: 4,427.1 persons per square mile (2005); Average household size: 2.81 (2005); Median age: 34.9 (2005); Males per 100 females: 96.4 (2005); Marriage status: 25.2% never married, 59.0% now married, 4.0% widowed, 11.9% divorced (2000); Foreign born: 2.0% (2000); Ancestry (includes multiple ancestries): 26.4% German, 15.3% Other groups, 12.8% Irish, 12.1% United States or American, 9.5% English (2000).
Economy: Employment by occupation: 10.8% management, 10.3% professional, 13.4% services, 34.6% sales, 0.0% farming, 11.8% construction, 19.0% production (2000).
Income: Per capita income: $20,754 (2005); Median household income: $52,259 (2005); Average household income: $58,322 (2005); Percent of households with income of $100,000 or more: 9.6% (2005); Poverty rate: 5.5% (2000).
Education: Percent of population age 25 and over with: High school diploma (including GED) or higher: 82.8% (2005); Bachelor's degree or higher: 9.5% (2005); Master's degree or higher: 1.9% (2005).
Housing: Homeownership rate: 78.4% (2005); Median home value: $97,483 (2005); Median rent: $490 per month (2000); Median age of housing: 32 years (2000).
Transportation: Commute to work: 95.5% car, 1.6% public transportation, 0.4% walk, 1.8% work from home (2000); Travel time to work: 19.7% less than 15 minutes, 50.3% 15 to 30 minutes, 24.0% 30 to 45 minutes, 3.3% 45 to 60 minutes, 2.7% 60 minutes or more (2000)

BRICE (village). Covers a land area of 0.077 square miles and a water area of 0 square miles. Located at 39.91° N. Lat.; 82.83° W. Long. Elevation is 780 feet.
Population: 91 (1990); 70 (2000); 95 (2005); 118 (2010 projected); Race: 96.8% White, 0.0% Black, 0.0% Asian, 0.0% Hispanic of any race (2005); Density: 1,234.8 persons per square mile (2005); Average household size: 2.79 (2005); Median age: 31.5 (2005); Males per 100 females: 102.1 (2005); Marriage status: 26.7% never married, 66.7% now married, 0.0% widowed, 6.7% divorced (2000); Foreign born: 0.0% (2000); Ancestry (includes multiple ancestries): 40.0% Other groups, 27.7% Irish, 16.9% German, 13.8% English, 7.7% Scotch-Irish (2000).
Economy: Single-family building permits issued: 0 (2005); Multi-family building permits issued: 0 (2005); Employment by occupation: 10.5% management, 10.5% professional, 5.3% services, 21.1% sales, 0.0% farming, 21.1% construction, 31.6% production (2000).
Income: Per capita income: $21,737 (2005); Median household income: $42,500 (2005); Average household income: $60,735 (2005); Percent of households with income of $100,000 or more: 11.8% (2005); Poverty rate: 0.0% (2000).
Education: Percent of population age 25 and over with: High school diploma (including GED) or higher: 67.9% (2005); Bachelor's degree or higher: 0.0% (2005); Master's degree or higher: 0.0% (2005).
Housing: Homeownership rate: 79.4% (2005); Median home value: $117,500 (2005); Median rent: $388 per month (2000); Median age of housing: 60+ years (2000).
Transportation: Commute to work: 73.7% car, 0.0% public transportation, 5.3% walk, 21.1% work from home (2000); Travel time to work: 0.0% less than 15 minutes, 60.0% 15 to 30 minutes, 0.0% 30 to 45 minutes, 26.7% 45 to 60 minutes, 13.3% 60 minutes or more (2000)

CANAL WINCHESTER (village). Covers a land area of 6.371 square miles and a water area of 0 square miles. Located at 39.84° N. Lat.; 82.81° W. Long.
History: The town of Canal Winchester developed as a produce center on the Ohio & Erie Canal.
Population: 2,538 (1990); 4,478 (2000); 5,208 (2005); 5,880 (2010 projected); Race: 94.6% White, 2.7% Black, 0.9% Asian, 0.6% Hispanic of any race (2005); Density: 817.5 persons per square mile (2005); Average household size: 2.71 (2005); Median age: 39.7 (2005); Males per 100 females: 88.6 (2005); Marriage status: 15.3% never married, 67.2% now married, 8.7% widowed, 8.8% divorced (2000); Foreign born: 2.2% (2000); Ancestry (includes multiple ancestries): 32.7% German, 15.8% Irish, 15.1% English, 9.1% Other groups, 5.4% United States or American (2000).
Economy: Single-family building permits issued: 105 (2005); Multi-family building permits issued: 0 (2005); Employment by occupation: 22.8% management, 24.1% professional, 13.0% services, 24.1% sales, 0.0% farming, 6.1% construction, 9.9% production (2000).
Income: Per capita income: $28,516 (2005); Median household income: $66,366 (2005); Average household income: $75,804 (2005); Percent of households with income of $100,000 or more: 28.0% (2005); Poverty rate: 2.2% (2000).
Education: Percent of population age 25 and over with: High school diploma (including GED) or higher: 91.4% (2005); Bachelor's degree or higher: 32.4% (2005); Master's degree or higher: 8.9% (2005).

School District(s)
Canal Winchester Local SD (PK-12)
    2003-04 Enrollment: 2,622 . . . . (614) 837-4533

Housing: Homeownership rate: 84.8% (2005); Median home value: $166,482 (2005); Median rent: $485 per month (2000); Median age of housing: 23 years (2000).
Transportation: Commute to work: 94.3% car, 1.0% public transportation, 0.7% walk, 3.6% work from home (2000); Travel time to work: 23.3% less than 15 minutes, 41.4% 15 to 30 minutes, 26.6% 30 to 45 minutes, 6.2% 45 to 60 minutes, 2.6% 60 minutes or more (2000)
Additional Information Contacts
Canal Winchester Chamber of Commerce . . . . (614) 837-1556
  http://www.canalwinchester.com
Canal Winchester Convention & Visitors Bureau. . . . . (614) 920-0649
  http://www.cwcvb.com
Village of Canal Winchester. . . . . (614) 837-7493
  http://www.canalwinchester.org/index2.htm

COLUMBUS (city). Covers a land area of 210.268 square miles and a water area of 2.281 square miles. Located at 39.99° N. Lat.; 82.99° W. Long. Elevation is 800 feet.
History: The site of Columbus was selected for the capital of Ohio in 1812, and the town was laid out. Columbus' early problems of cholera and lack of transportation were solved by draining the nearby swamps, and by the the Ohio & Erie Canal connected to Columbus by a feeder canal. The National Road reached Columbus in 1833, with stagecoaches arriving daily from the east. By 1872 transportation was being provided by five rail lines, and in 1873 Ohio State University was founded in Columbus.
Population: 648,656 (1990); 711,470 (2000); 733,424 (2005); 755,812 (2010 projected); Race: 64.6% White, 25.9% Black, 4.4% Asian, 3.2% Hispanic of any race (2005); Density: 3,488.0 persons per square mile (2005); Average household size: 2.33 (2005); Median age: 32.5 (2005); Males per 100 females: 95.7 (2005); Marriage status: 38.3% never married, 44.0% now married, 5.4% widowed, 12.4% divorced (2000); Foreign born: 6.7% (2000); Ancestry (includes multiple ancestries): 30.0% Other groups, 19.4% German, 11.7% Irish, 7.9% English, 7.2% United States or American (2000).
Economy: Unemployment rate: 5.4% (2005); Total civilian labor force: 408,548 (2005); Single-family building permits issued: 2,360 (2005); Multi-family building permits issued: 2,224 (2005); Employment by occupation: 13.9% management, 21.5% professional, 15.2% services, 30.1% sales, 0.1% farming, 6.5% construction, 12.7% production (2000).
Income: Per capita income: $23,546 (2005); Median household income: $43,535 (2005); Average household income: $54,442 (2005); Percent of households with income of $100,000 or more: 11.3% (2005); Poverty rate: 14.8% (2000).
Taxes: Total city taxes per capita: $724 (2004); City property taxes per capita: $56 (2004).
Education: Percent of population age 25 and over with: High school diploma (including GED) or higher: 84.4% (2005); Bachelor's degree or higher: 29.8% (2005); Master's degree or higher: 9.3% (2005).

School District(s)
Arts & College Preparatory Academy (09-11)
  2003-04 Enrollment: 97
Chase Academy for Communication Arts
  2003-04 Enrollment: n/a
Cincinnati City SD (PK-12)
  2003-04 Enrollment: 40,374 . . . . (513) 363-0000
Columbus Global Academy
  2003-04 Enrollment: n/a
Columbus International Prep
  2003-04 Enrollment: n/a . . . . (614) 478-9943
Columbus Public Schools (PK-12)
  2003-04 Enrollment: 63,098 . . . . (614) 365-5000
Columbus Youth Entrepreneurship (09-10)
  2003-04 Enrollment: 35 . . . . (614) 523-2600
Cornerstone Academy Community (KG-03)
  2003-04 Enrollment: 53 . . . . (614) 225-8924
Crittenton Community School (06-09)
  2003-04 Enrollment: 14 . . . . (614) 294-2661
Crossroads Preparatory Academy - Columbus
  2003-04 Enrollment: n/a
Dublin City SD (PK-12)
  2003-04 Enrollment: 12,376 . . . . (614) 764-5913
Electronic Classrm of Tomorrow (KG-12)
  2003-04 Enrollment: 5,213 . . . . (614) 492-8884
Excel Institute (06-12)
  2003-04 Enrollment: 51 . . . . (614) 236-1396
Graham School, The (09-12)
  2003-04 Enrollment: 196 . . . . (614) 262-1111
Grandview Heights City SD (PK-12)
  2003-04 Enrollment: 1,139 . . . . (614) 481-3600
Granville T Woods Comm Shule (KG-04)
  2003-04 Enrollment: 68 . . . . (614) 252-3630
Great Western Academy (KG-02)
  2003-04 Enrollment: 133 . . . . (614) 276-1028
Groveport Madison Local SD (PK-12)
  2003-04 Enrollment: 6,440 . . . . (614) 836-5371
Hamilton Local Digital Academy (KG-12)
  2003-04 Enrollment: 26 . . . . (614) 491-8044
Hamilton Local SD (PK-12)
  2003-04 Enrollment: 2,989 . . . . (614) 491-8044
Hilliard City SD (PK-12)
  2003-04 Enrollment: 14,219 . . . . (614) 771-4273
Horizon Science Academy Columbus (06-12)
  2003-04 Enrollment: 274 . . . . (614) 457-2231
International Academy of Columbus (KG-07)
  2003-04 Enrollment: 245 . . . . (614) 844-5539
Life Skills Center of N. Columbus (09-12)
  2003-04 Enrollment: 511 . . . . (614) 891-9041
Life Skills Center of Se Columbus (09-12)
  2003-04 Enrollment: 395 . . . . (614) 863-9175
Millennium Community (KG-05)
  2003-04 Enrollment: 673 . . . . (614) 255-5585
Montessouri Renaissance Exp (KG-05)
  2003-04 Enrollment: 57 . . . . (614) 299-1126
Northland Preparatory and Fitness Academy
  2003-04 Enrollment: n/a
Ohio School for the Deaf (PK-12)
  2003-04 Enrollment: 118 . . . . (614) 728-4030
Ohio State School for the Blin (KG-12)
  2003-04 Enrollment: 126 . . . . (614) 752-1152
South-Western City SD (PK-12)
  2003-04 Enrollment: 21,230 . . . . (614) 801-3000
Summit Academy Columbus
  2003-04 Enrollment: n/a
The Harte School - Columbus
  2003-04 Enrollment: n/a
Upper Arlington International Baccalaureate High School
  2003-04 Enrollment: n/a
Virtual Community School of Ohio (KG-12)
  2003-04 Enrollment: 1,459 . . . . (614) 501-9473
W C Cupe Community School (KG-05)
  2003-04 Enrollment: 241 . . . . (614) 294-3020
W. C. Handy Community Middle (06-08)
  2003-04 Enrollment: 204 . . . . (614) 428-6013
Westerville City SD (PK-12)
  2003-04 Enrollment: 14,142 . . . . (614) 797-5700
Whitehall Prepartory and Fitness Academy
  2003-04 Enrollment: n/a
Worthington City SD (PK-12)
  2003-04 Enrollment: 9,754 . . . . (614) 883-3000
Youthbuild Columbus Community (09-12)
  2003-04 Enrollment: 85 . . . . (614) 291-0805

Four-year College(s)
Capital University (Private, Not-for-profit, Evangelical Lutheran Church)
  Fall 2004 Enrollment: 3,894. . . . . (614) 236-6011
  2005-06 Tuition: In-state $23,433; Out-of-state $23,433
Columbus College of Art and Design (Private, Not-for-profit)
  Fall 2004 Enrollment: 1,559. . . . . (614) 224-9101
  2005-06 Tuition: In-state $19,728; Out-of-state $19,728
DeVry University-Ohio (Private, For-profit)
  Fall 2004 Enrollment: 3,949. . . . . (614) 253-7291
  2005-06 Tuition: In-state $12,100; Out-of-state $12,100
Franklin University (Private, Not-for-profit)
  Fall 2004 Enrollment: 6,823. . . . . (614) 797-4700
  2005-06 Tuition: In-state $7,564; Out-of-state $7,564
Mount Carmel College of Nursing (Private, Not-for-profit, Roman Catholic)
  Fall 2004 Enrollment: 573. . . . . (614) 234-5800
  2005-06 Tuition: In-state $7,024; Out-of-state $7,024
Ohio Dominican University (Private, Not-for-profit, Roman Catholic)
  Fall 2004 Enrollment: 2,844. . . . . (614) 253-2741
  2005-06 Tuition: In-state $19,454; Out-of-state $19,454

Ohio State University-Main Campus (Public)
   Fall 2004 Enrollment: 50,995. . . . . (614) 292-6446
   2005-06 Tuition: In-state $8,082; Out-of-state $19,305
Pontifical College Josephinum (Private, Not-for-profit, Roman Catholic)
   Fall 2004 Enrollment: 140. . . . . (614) 885-5585
   2005-06 Tuition: In-state $14,000; Out-of-state $14,000
Trinity Lutheran Seminary (Private, Not-for-profit, Evangelical Lutheran Church)
   Fall 2004 Enrollment: 216. . . . . (614) 235-4136
University of Phoenix-Columbus Ohio Campus (Private, For-profit)
   Fall 2004 Enrollment: 310. . . . . (614) 473-9003
   2005-06 Tuition: In-state $11,550; Out-of-state $11,550

Two-year College(s)

Academy of Court Reporting-Columbus (Private, For-profit)
   Fall 2004 Enrollment: 337. . . . . (614) 221-7770
   2005-06 Tuition: In-state $8,000; Out-of-state $8,000
American Institute of Alternative Medicine
   Fall 2004 Enrollment: 293. . . . . (614) 825-6278
American School of Technology (Private, For-profit)
   Fall 2004 Enrollment: 686. . . . . (614) 436-4820
Bradford School (Private, For-profit)
   Fall 2004 Enrollment: 362. . . . . (614) 416-6200
   2005-06 Tuition: In-state $11,560; Out-of-state $11,560
Columbus State Community College (Public)
   Fall 2004 Enrollment: 21,941. . . . . (614) 287-5353
   2005-06 Tuition: In-state $2,736; Out-of-state $6,048
Nationwide Beauty Academy (Private, For-profit)
   Fall 2004 Enrollment: 100. . . . . (614) 252-5252
North Adult Education Center (Public)
   Fall 2004 Enrollment: 210. . . . . (614) 365-6000
Ohio Institute of Health Careers (Private, For-profit)
   Fall 2004 Enrollment: 220. . . . . (614) 891-5030
Ohio State College of Barber Styling (Private, For-profit)
   Fall 2004 Enrollment: 84. . . . . (614) 868-1015
Ohio State School of Cosmetology (Private, For-profit)
   Fall 2004 Enrollment: 62. . . . . (614) 252-5252
Ohio State School of Cosmetology & Experts Barber School (Private, For-profit)
   Fall 2004 Enrollment: 101. . . . . (614) 252-5252
Roadmaster Truck Driving Institute (Private, For-profit)
   Fall 2004 Enrollment: n/a. . . . . (614) 351-1748
Technology Education College (Private, For-profit)
   Fall 2004 Enrollment: 502. . . . . (614) 456-4600
   2005-06 Tuition: In-state $10,602; Out-of-state $10,602
The Spa School (Private, For-profit)
   Fall 2004 Enrollment: 76. . . . . (614) 252-5252

Housing: Homeownership rate: 49.5% (2005); Median home value: $121,834 (2005); Median rent: $490 per month (2000); Median age of housing: 30 years (2000).
Hospitals: Children's Hospital, Education Foundation (353 beds); Doctors Hospital (478 beds); Grant Medical Center (385 beds); James Cancer Hospital and Solove Research Institute (156 beds); Mount Carmel East Hospital (287 beds); Mount Carmel East-West Health & Saint Ann (523 beds); Orient Correctional Institution - Fraser Health Center (100 beds); Riverside Methodist Hospital (1049 beds); The Ohio State University (404 beds)
Safety: Violent crime rate: 81.2 per 10,000 population; Property crime rate: 780.0 per 10,000 population (2004).
Newspapers: Bexley News (General - Circulation 9,850); Big Walnut News (General - Circulation 5,470); Columbus Alive (Alternative, General - Circulation 30,000); Communicator News (Black - Circulation 90,000); Dayton Communicator (Black - Circulation 27,000); Dublin News (General - Circulation 18,450); Gahanna News (General - Circulation 13,136); German Village Gazette (General - Circulation 4,375); Grove City News (General - Circulation 10,539); Grove City Southwest Messenger (General - Circulation 17,664); Hilliard Northwest News (General - Circulation 20,964); Madison Messenger (General - Circulation 12,466); New Albany News (General - Circulation 3,277); Northland News (General - Circulation 19,641); Northwest Columbus News (General - Circulation 7,376); Olentangy Valley News (General - Circulation 11,758); Pickerington Times-Sun (General - Circulation 11,235); Reynoldsburg News (General - Circulation 14,083); The Booster (General - Circulation 18,200); The Catholic Times (Catholic, Religious - Circulation 28,000); The Columbus Dispatch (Circulation 261,566); The Columbus Federal Voice (General - Circulation 16,000); The Daily Reporter (Circulation 27,000); The Eastside Messenger (General - Circulation 51,432); The Other Paper (Alternative, General - Circulation 50,000); The Southeast Messenger (General - Circulation 33,137); The Times (General - Circulation 11,035); The Westside Messenger (General - Circulation 45,139); Tri-Village News (General - Circulation 5,950); Upper Arlington News (General - Circulation 15,693); Westerville News & Public Opinion (General - Circulation 21,185); Westland News (General - Circulation 11,063); Whitehall News (General - Circulation 10,225); Worthington News (General - Circulation 18,606)
Transportation: Commute to work: 89.7% car, 3.9% public transportation, 3.2% walk, 2.3% work from home (2000); Travel time to work: 26.1% less than 15 minutes, 49.1% 15 to 30 minutes, 17.7% 30 to 45 minutes, 3.6% 45 to 60 minutes, 3.4% 60 minutes or more (2000)
Additional Information Contacts
City of Columbus . . . . (614) 645-8100
   http://www.ci.columbus.oh.us
Columbus Chamber of Commerce . . . . (614) 221-1321
   http://www.columbus-chamber.org
Columbus Convention & Visitors Bureau. . . . . (614) 221-6623
   http://www.experiencecolumbus.com
Gahanna Area Chamber of Commerce . . . . (614) 471-0451
   http://www.gahannaareachamber.com
Korean America Association of Greater Cleveland . . . . . . (216) 689-2999
   http://www.kaagc.org

DUBLIN (city). Covers a land area of 21.123 square miles and a water area of 0.018 square miles. Located at 40.10° N. Lat.; 83.14° W. Long. Elevation is 850 feet.
History: Named for Dublin, Ireland. Dublin was laid out in 1818 by John Sells, whose descendants organized the Sells Brothers' Circus. At one time, Dublin was selected to be the state capital by a commission appointed for that purpose, but "political horse trading" changed the selection.
Population: 17,231 (1990); 31,392 (2000); 34,533 (2005); 37,711 (2010 projected); Race: 86.3% White, 2.2% Black, 9.9% Asian, 1.3% Hispanic of any race (2005); Density: 1,634.8 persons per square mile (2005); Average household size: 2.76 (2005); Median age: 36.0 (2005); Males per 100 females: 98.4 (2005); Marriage status: 18.9% never married, 72.2% now married, 2.9% widowed, 6.0% divorced (2000); Foreign born: 9.1% (2000); Ancestry (includes multiple ancestries): 31.3% German, 17.0% Irish, 12.9% Other groups, 12.3% English, 9.4% Italian (2000).
Economy: Unemployment rate: 3.6% (2005); Total civilian labor force: 18,067 (2005); Single-family building permits issued: 375 (2005); Multi-family building permits issued: 381 (2005); Employment by occupation: 29.9% management, 29.9% professional, 6.5% services, 28.3% sales, 0.1% farming, 2.0% construction, 3.3% production (2000).
Income: Per capita income: $46,334 (2005); Median household income: $100,490 (2005); Average household income: $127,531 (2005); Percent of households with income of $100,000 or more: 50.2% (2005); Poverty rate: 2.7% (2000).
Taxes: Total city taxes per capita: $1,801 (2004); City property taxes per capita: $88 (2004).
Education: Percent of population age 25 and over with: High school diploma (including GED) or higher: 97.2% (2005); Bachelor's degree or higher: 63.7% (2005); Master's degree or higher: 22.3% (2005).

School District(s)

Columbus Public Schools (PK-12)
   2003-04 Enrollment: 63,098 . . . . (614) 365-5000
Dublin City SD (PK-12)
   2003-04 Enrollment: 12,376 . . . . (614) 764-5913
Dublin Community High School
   2003-04 Enrollment: n/a
Dublin Community Middle School
   2003-04 Enrollment: n/a . . . . (614) 764-5913
Housing: Homeownership rate: 75.6% (2005); Median home value: $279,928 (2005); Median rent: $839 per month (2000); Median age of housing: 9 years (2000).
Safety: Violent crime rate: 7.4 per 10,000 population; Property crime rate: 190.1 per 10,000 population (2004).
Transportation: Commute to work: 93.3% car, 0.4% public transportation, 0.5% walk, 5.4% work from home (2000); Travel time to work: 28.2% less than 15 minutes, 37.4% 15 to 30 minutes, 26.3% 30 to 45 minutes, 4.4% 45 to 60 minutes, 3.7% 60 minutes or more (2000)
Additional Information Contacts
City of Dublin . . . . (614) 410-4400
   http://www.dublin.oh.us

Dublin Chamber of Commerce .... (614) 889-2001
   http://www.dublinchamber.org
Dublin Convention and Visitors Bureau .... (614) 792-7666
   http://www.dublinvisit.org

GAHANNA (city). Covers a land area of 12.396 square miles and a water area of 0 square miles. Located at 40.02° N. Lat.; 82.86° W. Long. Elevation is 798 feet.
History: Named for an Algonquian Indian translation of "stream". Incorporated 1881.
Population: 24,610 (1990); 32,636 (2000); 32,481 (2005); 32,409 (2010 projected); Race: 83.9% White, 9.1% Black, 4.5% Asian, 1.6% Hispanic of any race (2005); Density: 2,620.3 persons per square mile (2005); Average household size: 2.68 (2005); Median age: 37.7 (2005); Males per 100 females: 94.8 (2005); Marriage status: 21.6% never married, 63.5% now married, 4.8% widowed, 10.2% divorced (2000); Foreign born: 4.9% (2000); Ancestry (includes multiple ancestries): 26.3% German, 16.0% Other groups, 14.4% Irish, 12.9% English, 7.8% United States or American (2000).
Economy: Unemployment rate: 4.4% (2005); Total civilian labor force: 18,395 (2005); Single-family building permits issued: 113 (2005); Multi-family building permits issued: 0 (2005); Employment by occupation: 20.7% management, 25.7% professional, 10.1% services, 29.7% sales, 0.0% farming, 5.7% construction, 8.1% production (2000).
Income: Per capita income: $34,756 (2005); Median household income: $75,792 (2005); Average household income: $93,030 (2005); Percent of households with income of $100,000 or more: 33.9% (2005); Poverty rate: 3.7% (2000).
Education: Percent of population age 25 and over with: High school diploma (including GED) or higher: 93.6% (2005); Bachelor's degree or higher: 40.9% (2005); Master's degree or higher: 13.9% (2005).
School District(s)
Gahanna-Jefferson City SD (PK-12)
   2003-04 Enrollment: 6,806 .... (614) 471-7065
Two-year College(s)
Bryman College-Columbus (Private, For-profit)
   Fall 2004 Enrollment: n/a .... (614) 322-3414
Housing: Homeownership rate: 77.8% (2005); Median home value: $179,101 (2005); Median rent: $582 per month (2000); Median age of housing: 18 years (2000).
Hospitals: Woods at Parkside (44 beds)
Safety: Violent crime rate: 8.4 per 10,000 population; Property crime rate: 273.3 per 10,000 population (2004).
Transportation: Commute to work: 94.4% car, 0.9% public transportation, 0.7% walk, 3.7% work from home (2000); Travel time to work: 26.6% less than 15 minutes, 51.4% 15 to 30 minutes, 15.9% 30 to 45 minutes, 2.4% 45 to 60 minutes, 3.7% 60 minutes or more (2000)
Additional Information Contacts
City of Gahanna .... (614) 342-4000
   http://www.gahanna.gov

GALLOWAY (unincorporated postal area, zip code 43119). Covers a land area of 33.748 square miles and a water area of 0 square miles. Located at 39.94° N. Lat.; 83.16° W. Long. Elevation is 905 feet.
Population: 21,695 (2000); Race: 90.8% White, 4.1% Black, 1.6% Asian, 1.9% Hispanic of any race (2000); Density: 642.9 persons per square mile (2000); Age: 30.7% under 18, 3.8% over 64 (2000) Marriage status: 24.9% never married, 62.3% now married, 2.3% widowed, 10.6% divorced (2000); Foreign born: 2.6% (2000); Ancestry (includes multiple ancestries): 27.5% German, 16.0% Irish, 13.4% United States or American, 12.4% Other groups, 9.8% English (2000).
Economy: Employment by occupation: 14.2% management, 17.5% professional, 11.4% services, 32.1% sales, 0.0% farming, 7.7% construction, 17.0% production (2000).
Income: Per capita income: $22,164 (2000); Median household income: $54,978 (2000); Poverty rate: 5.5% (2000).
Education: Percent of population age 25 and over with: High school diploma (including GED) or higher: 89.2% (2000); Bachelor's degree or higher: 22.4% (2000).
School District(s)
South-Western City SD (PK-12)
   2003-04 Enrollment: 21,230 .... (614) 801-3000
Housing: Homeownership rate: 74.3% (2000); Median home value: $122,200 (2000); Median rent: $544 per month (2000); Median age of housing: 8 years (2000).

Transportation: Commute to work: 96.2% car, 0.3% public transportation, 0.5% walk, 2.8% work from home (2000); Travel time to work: 19.1% less than 15 minutes, 47.9% 15 to 30 minutes, 24.7% 30 to 45 minutes, 5.2% 45 to 60 minutes, 3.0% 60 minutes or more (2000)

GRANDVIEW HEIGHTS (city). Covers a land area of 1.347 square miles and a water area of 0 square miles. Located at 39.98° N. Lat.; 83.04° W. Long. Elevation is 770 feet.
Population: 7,041 (1990); 6,695 (2000); 6,394 (2005); 6,115 (2010 projected); Race: 95.0% White, 1.6% Black, 1.3% Asian, 1.7% Hispanic of any race (2005); Density: 4,748.6 persons per square mile (2005); Average household size: 2.21 (2005); Median age: 37.8 (2005); Males per 100 females: 93.3 (2005); Marriage status: 31.0% never married, 49.3% now married, 7.8% widowed, 11.8% divorced (2000); Foreign born: 3.0% (2000); Ancestry (includes multiple ancestries): 32.4% German, 20.4% Irish, 18.8% English, 9.6% Italian, 6.1% Other groups (2000).
Economy: Single-family building permits issued: 1 (2005); Multi-family building permits issued: 0 (2005); Employment by occupation: 19.1% management, 32.3% professional, 8.0% services, 29.4% sales, 0.0% farming, 3.1% construction, 8.0% production (2000).
Income: Per capita income: $32,746 (2005); Median household income: $59,375 (2005); Average household income: $72,374 (2005); Percent of households with income of $100,000 or more: 20.7% (2005); Poverty rate: 4.5% (2000).
Education: Percent of population age 25 and over with: High school diploma (including GED) or higher: 92.0% (2005); Bachelor's degree or higher: 47.5% (2005); Master's degree or higher: 16.2% (2005).
Housing: Homeownership rate: 60.3% (2005); Median home value: $191,405 (2005); Median rent: $553 per month (2000); Median age of housing: 59 years (2000).
Safety: Violent crime rate: 10.8 per 10,000 population; Property crime rate: 419.2 per 10,000 population (2004).
Transportation: Commute to work: 88.8% car, 4.7% public transportation, 3.3% walk, 1.4% work from home (2000); Travel time to work: 42.0% less than 15 minutes, 43.6% 15 to 30 minutes, 9.6% 30 to 45 minutes, 3.0% 45 to 60 minutes, 1.9% 60 minutes or more (2000)
Additional Information Contacts
City of Grandview Heights .... (614) 481-6217
   http://www.grandviewheights.org

GROVE CITY (city). Covers a land area of 13.948 square miles and a water area of 0.011 square miles. Located at 39.87° N. Lat.; 83.07° W. Long. Elevation is 835 feet.
History: Named for its many tree groves, by William F. Brock. Grove City developed around an agricultural and truck gardening region. Many of its early residents were of German ancestry.
Population: 21,241 (1990); 27,075 (2000); 28,463 (2005); 29,852 (2010 projected); Race: 95.1% White, 2.0% Black, 0.8% Asian, 1.5% Hispanic of any race (2005); Density: 2,040.7 persons per square mile (2005); Average household size: 2.63 (2005); Median age: 36.3 (2005); Males per 100 females: 95.6 (2005); Marriage status: 20.7% never married, 62.7% now married, 5.9% widowed, 10.7% divorced (2000); Foreign born: 1.2% (2000); Ancestry (includes multiple ancestries): 29.6% German, 16.8% Irish, 12.0% United States or American, 11.3% English, 7.4% Other groups (2000).
Economy: Unemployment rate: 4.7% (2005); Total civilian labor force: 16,710 (2005); Single-family building permits issued: 463 (2005); Multi-family building permits issued: 68 (2005); Employment by occupation: 15.8% management, 18.2% professional, 13.1% services, 32.6% sales, 0.0% farming, 8.6% construction, 11.6% production (2000).
Income: Per capita income: $27,376 (2005); Median household income: $62,611 (2005); Average household income: $71,489 (2005); Percent of households with income of $100,000 or more: 21.0% (2005); Poverty rate: 4.6% (2000).
Education: Percent of population age 25 and over with: High school diploma (including GED) or higher: 89.2% (2005); Bachelor's degree or higher: 23.2% (2005); Master's degree or higher: 5.6% (2005).
School District(s)
Life Skills Center of SW Columbus (09-12)
   2003-04 Enrollment: 328 .... (614) 801-1366
South-Western City SD (PK-12)
   2003-04 Enrollment: 21,230 .... (614) 801-3000
Housing: Homeownership rate: 74.5% (2005); Median home value: $145,867 (2005); Median rent: $517 per month (2000); Median age of housing: 23 years (2000).

Newspapers: The Grove City Record (General - Circulation 4,273)
Transportation: Commute to work: 95.1% car, 1.1% public transportation, 0.9% walk, 2.0% work from home (2000); Travel time to work: 26.3% less than 15 minutes, 44.3% 15 to 30 minutes, 22.8% 30 to 45 minutes, 3.9% 45 to 60 minutes, 2.7% 60 minutes or more (2000)
Additional Information Contacts
City of Grove City..................................(614) 277-3075
  http://www.ci.grove-city.oh.us
Grove City Chamber of Commerce................(614) 875-9762
  http://www.gcchamber.org

GROVEPORT (village).
Covers a land area of 8.004 square miles and a water area of 0.008 square miles. Located at 39.85° N. Lat.; 82.89° W. Long. Elevation is 745 feet.
Population: 3,192 (1990); 3,865 (2000); 4,442 (2005); 4,982 (2010 projected); Race: 89.3% White, 6.0% Black, 1.8% Asian, 1.6% Hispanic of any race (2005); Density: 554.9 persons per square mile (2005); Average household size: 2.42 (2005); Median age: 38.1 (2005); Males per 100 females: 92.6 (2005); Marriage status: 20.0% never married, 59.8% now married, 7.6% widowed, 12.6% divorced (2000); Foreign born: 1.4% (2000); Ancestry (includes multiple ancestries): 26.1% German, 16.3% Other groups, 14.1% Irish, 11.5% United States or American, 11.1% English (2000).
Economy: In agricultural area. Single-family building permits issued: 103 (2005); Multi-family building permits issued: 0 (2005); Employment by occupation: 11.9% management, 13.3% professional, 13.4% services, 34.0% sales, 0.2% farming, 10.6% construction, 16.6% production (2000).
Income: Per capita income: $23,661 (2005); Median household income: $49,979 (2005); Average household income: $57,090 (2005); Percent of households with income of $100,000 or more: 12.2% (2005); Poverty rate: 5.9% (2000).
Education: Percent of population age 25 and over with: High school diploma (including GED) or higher: 83.1% (2005); Bachelor's degree or higher: 12.7% (2005); Master's degree or higher: 2.8% (2005).
School District(s)
Eastland-Fairfield Career/Tech (09-12)
  2003-04 Enrollment: n/a ....(614) 836-4530
Groveport Madison Local SD (PK-12)
  2003-04 Enrollment: 6,440 ....(614) 836-5371
Two-year College(s)
Eastland-Fairfield Career and Technical Schools (Public)
  Fall 2004 Enrollment: 190 ....(614) 836-4541
Housing: Homeownership rate: 69.2% (2005); Median home value: $141,776 (2005); Median rent: $477 per month (2000); Median age of housing: 33 years (2000).
Transportation: Commute to work: 93.8% car, 0.7% public transportation, 2.9% walk, 1.7% work from home (2000); Travel time to work: 32.5% less than 15 minutes, 40.5% 15 to 30 minutes, 21.6% 30 to 45 minutes, 3.4% 45 to 60 minutes, 2.0% 60 minutes or more (2000)
Additional Information Contacts
Groveport Madison Chamber of Commerce ....(614) 836-1138
  http://www.groveport.org
Village of Groveport..............................(614) 836-5301
  http://www.groveport.org

HARRISBURG (village).
Covers a land area of 0.100 square miles and a water area of 0 square miles. Located at 39.81° N. Lat.; 83.17° W. Long. Elevation is 800 feet.
Population: 340 (1990); 332 (2000); 352 (2005); 371 (2010 projected); Race: 96.0% White, 0.6% Black, 0.6% Asian, 1.1% Hispanic of any race (2005); Density: 3,530.8 persons per square mile (2005); Average household size: 2.43 (2005); Median age: 41.0 (2005); Males per 100 females: 103.5 (2005); Marriage status: 24.2% never married, 61.2% now married, 5.7% widowed, 8.9% divorced (2000); Foreign born: 0.0% (2000); Ancestry (includes multiple ancestries): 33.1% German, 18.6% Irish, 13.4% Other groups, 12.5% United States or American, 10.8% English (2000).
Economy: Employment by occupation: 7.3% management, 11.5% professional, 19.9% services, 32.5% sales, 1.0% farming, 7.9% construction, 19.9% production (2000).
Income: Per capita income: $22,408 (2005); Median household income: $52,163 (2005); Average household income: $54,397 (2005); Percent of households with income of $100,000 or more: 6.9% (2005); Poverty rate: 3.2% (2000).

Education: Percent of population age 25 and over with: High school diploma (including GED) or higher: 85.0% (2005); Bachelor's degree or higher: 10.7% (2005); Master's degree or higher: 0.0% (2005).
School District(s)
South-Western City SD (PK-12)
  2003-04 Enrollment: 21,230 ....(614) 801-3000
Housing: Homeownership rate: 77.2% (2005); Median home value: $117,361 (2005); Median rent: $382 per month (2000); Median age of housing: 60+ years (2000).
Transportation: Commute to work: 90.9% car, 1.6% public transportation, 2.7% walk, 2.7% work from home (2000); Travel time to work: 17.7% less than 15 minutes, 51.9% 15 to 30 minutes, 24.3% 30 to 45 minutes, 3.3% 45 to 60 minutes, 2.8% 60 minutes or more (2000)

HILLIARD (city).
Aka Hilliards. Covers a land area of 11.141 square miles and a water area of 0 square miles. Located at 40.03° N. Lat.; 83.14° W. Long. Elevation is 935 feet.
History: Hilliard became a small farming community after a local farmer named John Hilliard set up a railroad station in 1886. The town grew around the stop, which became known as Hilliard's Station. If fact, most of the town's residents called the town Hilliards (with a pronounced "s" on the end) until the 1950s, when the city council decided to inform everybody that the town's name was actually Hilliard. This can still be seen today, as old maps of central Ohio sometimes call the town Hilliards.
Population: 12,516 (1990); 24,230 (2000); 26,610 (2005); 28,881 (2010 projected); Race: 90.2% White, 1.9% Black, 5.1% Asian, 2.2% Hispanic of any race (2005); Density: 2,388.5 persons per square mile (2005); Average household size: 2.85 (2005); Median age: 34.6 (2005); Males per 100 females: 97.1 (2005); Marriage status: 19.8% never married, 68.1% now married, 3.6% widowed, 8.4% divorced (2000); Foreign born: 4.2% (2000); Ancestry (includes multiple ancestries): 30.1% German, 17.2% Irish, 12.7% English, 8.4% Other groups, 8.3% United States or American (2000).
Economy: In agricultural area. Unemployment rate: 3.7% (2005); Total civilian labor force: 14,856 (2005); Single-family building permits issued: 156 (2005); Multi-family building permits issued: 0 (2005); Employment by occupation: 19.4% management, 27.3% professional, 10.9% services, 27.9% sales, 0.0% farming, 6.1% construction, 8.4% production (2000).
Income: Per capita income: $34,094 (2005); Median household income: $83,104 (2005); Average household income: $96,713 (2005); Percent of households with income of $100,000 or more: 37.4% (2005); Poverty rate: 2.2% (2000).
Taxes: Total city taxes per capita: $620 (2004); City property taxes per capita: $44 (2004).
Education: Percent of population age 25 and over with: High school diploma (including GED) or higher: 92.6% (2005); Bachelor's degree or higher: 46.2% (2005); Master's degree or higher: 14.5% (2005).
School District(s)
Hilliard City SD (PK-12)
  2003-04 Enrollment: 14,219 ....(614) 771-4273
Two-year College(s)
ITT Technical Institute (Private, For-profit)
  Fall 2004 Enrollment: 339 ....(614) 771-4888
  2005-06 Tuition: In-state $14,196; Out-of-state $14,196
Housing: Homeownership rate: 74.7% (2005); Median home value: $194,290 (2005); Median rent: $653 per month (2000); Median age of housing: 9 years (2000).
Safety: Violent crime rate: 7.0 per 10,000 population; Property crime rate: 314.4 per 10,000 population (2004).
Transportation: Commute to work: 93.8% car, 0.7% public transportation, 0.7% walk, 4.4% work from home (2000); Travel time to work: 28.8% less than 15 minutes, 43.7% 15 to 30 minutes, 19.4% 30 to 45 minutes, 4.4% 45 to 60 minutes, 3.7% 60 minutes or more (2000)
Additional Information Contacts
City of Hilliard...................................(614) 876-7361
  http://www.cityofhilliard.com
Hilliard Area Chamber of Commerce................(614) 876-7666
  http://www.hilliardchamber.org
Hilliard Convention & Visitors Bureau ....(614) 876-6911
  http://www.hilliardcvb.org

HUBER RIDGE (CDP).
Covers a land area of 1.087 square miles and a water area of 0 square miles. Located at 40.09° N. Lat.; 82.91° W. Long. Elevation is 820 feet.
Population: 5,242 (1990); 4,883 (2000); 4,501 (2005); 4,147 (2010 projected); Race: 89.6% White, 6.4% Black, 1.2% Asian, 1.2% Hispanic of

any race (2005); Density: 4,141.1 persons per square mile (2005); Average household size: 2.75 (2005); Median age: 33.8 (2005); Males per 100 females: 91.3 (2005); Marriage status: 22.2% never married, 62.9% now married, 3.9% widowed, 11.0% divorced (2000); Foreign born: 3.1% (2000); Ancestry (includes multiple ancestries): 30.7% German, 16.6% Irish, 12.3% English, 10.9% United States or American, 10.5% Other groups (2000).
Economy: Employment by occupation: 16.4% management, 18.3% professional, 13.2% services, 34.0% sales, 0.0% farming, 7.1% construction, 11.0% production (2000).
Income: Per capita income: $22,604 (2005); Median household income: $55,649 (2005); Average household income: $62,226 (2005); Percent of households with income of $100,000 or more: 11.1% (2005); Poverty rate: 3.8% (2000).
Education: Percent of population age 25 and over with: High school diploma (including GED) or higher: 91.6% (2005); Bachelor's degree or higher: 25.1% (2005); Master's degree or higher: 5.1% (2005).
Housing: Homeownership rate: 74.4% (2005); Median home value: $123,452 (2005); Median rent: $635 per month (2000); Median age of housing: 32 years (2000).
Transportation: Commute to work: 94.4% car, 0.8% public transportation, 1.4% walk, 3.1% work from home (2000); Travel time to work: 25.2% less than 15 minutes, 48.7% 15 to 30 minutes, 21.6% 30 to 45 minutes, 1.3% 45 to 60 minutes, 3.2% 60 minutes or more (2000)

LAKE DARBY (CDP). Covers a land area of 3.405 square miles and a water area of 0 square miles. Located at 39.96° N. Lat.; 83.23° W. Long.
Population: 2,798 (1990); 3,727 (2000); 3,778 (2005); 3,927 (2010 projected); Race: 92.8% White, 2.2% Black, 0.7% Asian, 1.9% Hispanic of any race (2005); Density: 1,109.4 persons per square mile (2005); Average household size: 3.05 (2005); Median age: 31.7 (2005); Males per 100 females: 96.9 (2005); Marriage status: 18.2% never married, 70.6% now married, 1.1% widowed, 10.1% divorced (2000); Foreign born: 2.8% (2000); Ancestry (includes multiple ancestries): 27.4% German, 14.4% Irish, 12.9% United States or American, 10.9% Other groups, 6.7% English (2000).
Economy: Employment by occupation: 11.4% management, 18.7% professional, 13.5% services, 28.5% sales, 0.0% farming, 9.2% construction, 18.7% production (2000).
Income: Per capita income: $27,107 (2005); Median household income: $73,052 (2005); Average household income: $82,375 (2005); Percent of households with income of $100,000 or more: 22.4% (2005); Poverty rate: 1.9% (2000).
Education: Percent of population age 25 and over with: High school diploma (including GED) or higher: 91.0% (2005); Bachelor's degree or higher: 22.1% (2005); Master's degree or higher: 6.0% (2005).
Housing: Homeownership rate: 95.8% (2005); Median home value: $131,629 (2005); Median rent: $708 per month (2000); Median age of housing: 19 years (2000).
Transportation: Commute to work: 98.2% car, 0.0% public transportation, 0.0% walk, 1.8% work from home (2000); Travel time to work: 12.2% less than 15 minutes, 47.2% 15 to 30 minutes, 30.7% 30 to 45 minutes, 8.3% 45 to 60 minutes, 1.5% 60 minutes or more (2000)

LINCOLN VILLAGE (CDP). Covers a land area of 1.869 square miles and a water area of 0 square miles. Located at 39.95° N. Lat.; 83.13° W. Long.
Population: 9,994 (1990); 9,482 (2000); 8,748 (2005); 8,206 (2010 projected); Race: 89.9% White, 3.9% Black, 0.6% Asian, 6.5% Hispanic of any race (2005); Density: 4,681.8 persons per square mile (2005); Average household size: 2.32 (2005); Median age: 38.7 (2005); Males per 100 females: 94.2 (2005); Marriage status: 23.5% never married, 52.4% now married, 8.9% widowed, 15.2% divorced (2000); Foreign born: 6.0% (2000); Ancestry (includes multiple ancestries): 17.9% German, 16.8% United States or American, 15.7% Other groups, 12.8% Irish, 10.3% English (2000).
Economy: Employment by occupation: 7.9% management, 11.1% professional, 13.7% services, 31.6% sales, 0.0% farming, 12.8% construction, 22.8% production (2000).
Income: Per capita income: $18,901 (2005); Median household income: $37,435 (2005); Average household income: $43,557 (2005); Percent of households with income of $100,000 or more: 5.1% (2005); Poverty rate: 12.0% (2000).

Education: Percent of population age 25 and over with: High school diploma (including GED) or higher: 76.4% (2005); Bachelor's degree or higher: 10.4% (2005); Master's degree or higher: 2.9% (2005).
Housing: Homeownership rate: 64.6% (2005); Median home value: $100,588 (2005); Median rent: $421 per month (2000); Median age of housing: 38 years (2000).
Transportation: Commute to work: 91.7% car, 2.4% public transportation, 3.9% walk, 1.6% work from home (2000); Travel time to work: 30.4% less than 15 minutes, 45.8% 15 to 30 minutes, 17.7% 30 to 45 minutes, 2.7% 45 to 60 minutes, 3.4% 60 minutes or more (2000)

LOCKBOURNE (village). Covers a land area of 0.095 square miles and a water area of 0 square miles. Located at 39.80° N. Lat.; 82.97° W. Long. Elevation is 710 feet.
Population: 179 (1990); 280 (2000); 297 (2005); 305 (2010 projected); Race: 99.3% White, 0.0% Black, 0.0% Asian, 0.3% Hispanic of any race (2005); Density: 3,129.6 persons per square mile (2005); Average household size: 2.56 (2005); Median age: 40.9 (2005); Males per 100 females: 103.4 (2005); Marriage status: 19.9% never married, 57.4% now married, 7.4% widowed, 15.3% divorced (2000); Foreign born: 0.0% (2000); Ancestry (includes multiple ancestries): 16.7% German, 12.8% English, 12.5% Irish, 11.0% Other groups, 3.2% Hungarian (2000).
Economy: Employment by occupation: 6.6% management, 3.3% professional, 24.6% services, 18.9% sales, 0.0% farming, 17.2% construction, 29.5% production (2000).
Income: Per capita income: $17,870 (2005); Median household income: $39,565 (2005); Average household income: $45,754 (2005); Percent of households with income of $100,000 or more: 6.9% (2005); Poverty rate: 9.5% (2000).
Education: Percent of population age 25 and over with: High school diploma (including GED) or higher: 68.0% (2005); Bachelor's degree or higher: 9.0% (2005); Master's degree or higher: 2.0% (2005).

School District(s)
Hamilton Local SD (PK-12)
    2003-04 Enrollment: 2,989 . . . . (614) 491-8044

Housing: Homeownership rate: 75.9% (2005); Median home value: $85,882 (2005); Median rent: $430 per month (2000); Median age of housing: 60+ years (2000).
Transportation: Commute to work: 97.5% car, 0.0% public transportation, 0.0% walk, 2.5% work from home (2000); Travel time to work: 29.3% less than 15 minutes, 44.0% 15 to 30 minutes, 19.0% 30 to 45 minutes, 3.4% 45 to 60 minutes, 4.3% 60 minutes or more (2000)

MARBLE CLIFF (village). Covers a land area of 0.248 square miles and a water area of 0 square miles. Located at 39.98° N. Lat.; 83.06° W. Long. Elevation is 770 feet.
History: Limestone quarry gave its name.
Population: 636 (1990); 646 (2000); 583 (2005); 543 (2010 projected); Race: 97.6% White, 0.9% Black, 1.2% Asian, 0.3% Hispanic of any race (2005); Density: 2,355.5 persons per square mile (2005); Average household size: 2.18 (2005); Median age: 52.8 (2005); Males per 100 females: 68.5 (2005); Marriage status: 28.3% never married, 48.4% now married, 12.4% widowed, 11.0% divorced (2000); Foreign born: 2.7% (2000); Ancestry (includes multiple ancestries): 34.3% German, 19.2% English, 14.2% Irish, 9.2% Italian, 3.6% Scotch-Irish (2000).
Economy: Single-family building permits issued: 1 (2005); Multi-family building permits issued: 0 (2005); Employment by occupation: 28.4% management, 40.3% professional, 3.8% services, 25.0% sales, 0.0% farming, 1.3% construction, 1.3% production (2000).
Income: Per capita income: $38,110 (2005); Median household income: $53,618 (2005); Average household income: $78,867 (2005); Percent of households with income of $100,000 or more: 26.6% (2005); Poverty rate: 3.4% (2000).
Education: Percent of population age 25 and over with: High school diploma (including GED) or higher: 87.7% (2005); Bachelor's degree or higher: 57.7% (2005); Master's degree or higher: 21.4% (2005).
Housing: Homeownership rate: 57.7% (2005); Median home value: $361,538 (2005); Median rent: $552 per month (2000); Median age of housing: 43 years (2000).
Transportation: Commute to work: 91.8% car, 0.6% public transportation, 1.9% walk, 5.7% work from home (2000); Travel time to work: 38.9% less than 15 minutes, 52.3% 15 to 30 minutes, 8.7% 30 to 45 minutes, 0.0% 45 to 60 minutes, 0.0% 60 minutes or more (2000)
Additional Information Contacts

Grandview-Marble Cliff Chamber. . . . . (614) 486-0196
http://www.grandviewchamber.org

MINERVA PARK (village). Covers a land area of 0.496 square miles and a water area of 0.007 square miles. Located at 40.07° N. Lat.; 82.94° W. Long. Elevation is 860 feet.
Population: 1,314 (1990); 1,288 (2000); 1,305 (2005); 1,322 (2010 projected); Race: 96.9% White, 0.5% Black, 0.5% Asian, 0.8% Hispanic of any race (2005); Density: 2,631.3 persons per square mile (2005); Average household size: 2.38 (2005); Median age: 47.0 (2005); Males per 100 females: 94.2 (2005); Marriage status: 16.6% never married, 70.7% now married, 6.5% widowed, 6.2% divorced (2000); Foreign born: 2.0% (2000); Ancestry (includes multiple ancestries): 31.1% German, 19.9% English, 18.8% Irish, 8.9% United States or American, 8.3% Italian (2000).
Economy: Employment by occupation: 15.4% management, 29.2% professional, 10.4% services, 30.8% sales, 0.0% farming, 6.3% construction, 7.9% production (2000).
Income: Per capita income: $34,297 (2005); Median household income: $70,060 (2005); Average household income: $81,526 (2005); Percent of households with income of $100,000 or more: 28.1% (2005); Poverty rate: 1.3% (2000).
Education: Percent of population age 25 and over with: High school diploma (including GED) or higher: 94.4% (2005); Bachelor's degree or higher: 37.0% (2005); Master's degree or higher: 13.3% (2005).
Housing: Homeownership rate: 96.2% (2005); Median home value: $163,934 (2005); Median rent: $683 per month (2000); Median age of housing: 43 years (2000).
Transportation: Commute to work: 94.0% car, 0.3% public transportation, 0.6% walk, 5.1% work from home (2000); Travel time to work: 22.2% less than 15 minutes, 47.3% 15 to 30 minutes, 24.0% 30 to 45 minutes, 2.0% 45 to 60 minutes, 4.5% 60 minutes or more (2000)

NEW ALBANY (village). Covers a land area of 8.928 square miles and a water area of 0 square miles. Located at 40.07° N. Lat.; 82.82° W. Long. Elevation is 1,018 feet.
Population: 1,879 (1990); 3,711 (2000); 4,965 (2005); 6,080 (2010 projected); Race: 92.2% White, 1.7% Black, 4.1% Asian, 1.0% Hispanic of any race (2005); Density: 556.1 persons per square mile (2005); Average household size: 2.88 (2005); Median age: 38.3 (2005); Males per 100 females: 97.7 (2005); Marriage status: 18.5% never married, 73.1% now married, 3.0% widowed, 5.4% divorced (2000); Foreign born: 5.8% (2000); Ancestry (includes multiple ancestries): 28.8% German, 15.0% Irish, 14.7% English, 11.4% Other groups, 10.3% Italian (2000).
Economy: In agricultural area. Single-family building permits issued: 155 (2005); Multi-family building permits issued: 0 (2005); Employment by occupation: 33.0% management, 28.4% professional, 5.5% services, 21.6% sales, 0.0% farming, 4.5% construction, 7.1% production (2000).
Income: Per capita income: $68,829 (2005); Median household income: $128,310 (2005); Average household income: $198,339 (2005); Percent of households with income of $100,000 or more: 59.4% (2005); Poverty rate: 1.2% (2000).
Education: Percent of population age 25 and over with: High school diploma (including GED) or higher: 95.6% (2005); Bachelor's degree or higher: 54.2% (2005); Master's degree or higher: 21.2% (2005).
School District(s)
Plain Local SD (PK-12)
    2003-04 Enrollment: 2,877 . . . . (614) 855-2040
Housing: Homeownership rate: 82.6% (2005); Median home value: $578,601 (2005); Median rent: $648 per month (2000); Median age of housing: 5 years (2000).
Safety: Violent crime rate: 5.7 per 10,000 population; Property crime rate: 139.8 per 10,000 population (2004).
Transportation: Commute to work: 91.8% car, 0.0% public transportation, 0.5% walk, 6.5% work from home (2000); Travel time to work: 19.2% less than 15 minutes, 45.0% 15 to 30 minutes, 26.6% 30 to 45 minutes, 4.9% 45 to 60 minutes, 4.3% 60 minutes or more (2000)
Additional Information Contacts
New Albany Chamber of Commerce . . . . (614) 855-4408
    http://www.newalbanychamber.com
Village of New Albany . . . . (614) 855-3913
    http://www.villageofnewalbany.org

NEW ROME (village). Covers a land area of 0.030 square miles and a water area of 0 square miles. Located at 39.95° N. Lat.; 83.14° W. Long. Elevation is 915 feet.
Population: 40 (1990); 60 (2000); 59 (2005); 59 (2010 projected); Race: 96.6% White, 0.0% Black, 3.4% Asian, 8.5% Hispanic of any race (2005); Density: 1,960.2 persons per square mile (2005); Average household size: 2.19 (2005); Median age: 39.6 (2005); Males per 100 females: 96.7 (2005); Marriage status: 29.3% never married, 41.5% now married, 12.2% widowed, 17.1% divorced (2000); Foreign born: 4.6% (2000); Ancestry (includes multiple ancestries): 24.6% German, 20.0% Other groups, 13.8% United States or American, 13.8% Yugoslavian, 13.8% Irish (2000).
Economy: Employment by occupation: 13.0% management, 17.4% professional, 43.5% services, 26.1% sales, 0.0% farming, 0.0% construction, 0.0% production (2000).
Income: Per capita income: $18,051 (2005); Median household income: $26,000 (2005); Average household income: $39,444 (2005); Percent of households with income of $100,000 or more: 3.7% (2005); Poverty rate: 18.5% (2000).
Education: Percent of population age 25 and over with: High school diploma (including GED) or higher: 60.5% (2005); Bachelor's degree or higher: 11.6% (2005); Master's degree or higher: 4.7% (2005).
Housing: Homeownership rate: 33.3% (2005); Median home value: $76,667 (2005); Median rent: $463 per month (2000); Median age of housing: 43 years (2000).
Transportation: Commute to work: 56.5% car, 8.7% public transportation, 8.7% walk, 26.1% work from home (2000); Travel time to work: 64.7% less than 15 minutes, 11.8% 15 to 30 minutes, 11.8% 30 to 45 minutes, 0.0% 45 to 60 minutes, 11.8% 60 minutes or more (2000)

OBETZ (village). Covers a land area of 3.769 square miles and a water area of 0 square miles. Located at 39.87° N. Lat.; 82.94° W. Long. Elevation is 755 feet.
Population: 3,339 (1990); 3,977 (2000); 4,138 (2005); 4,306 (2010 projected); Race: 93.1% White, 2.9% Black, 0.2% Asian, 1.9% Hispanic of any race (2005); Density: 1,098.0 persons per square mile (2005); Average household size: 2.62 (2005); Median age: 34.1 (2005); Males per 100 females: 96.0 (2005); Marriage status: 21.4% never married, 56.9% now married, 4.3% widowed, 17.3% divorced (2000); Foreign born: 2.2% (2000); Ancestry (includes multiple ancestries): 20.7% German, 20.5% Other groups, 12.8% English, 11.8% Irish, 11.1% United States or American (2000).
Economy: Single-family building permits issued: 10 (2005); Multi-family building permits issued: 0 (2005); Employment by occupation: 9.8% management, 9.9% professional, 16.5% services, 35.2% sales, 0.3% farming, 9.7% construction, 18.7% production (2000).
Income: Per capita income: $20,262 (2005); Median household income: $50,050 (2005); Average household income: $53,132 (2005); Percent of households with income of $100,000 or more: 6.7% (2005); Poverty rate: 6.4% (2000).
Education: Percent of population age 25 and over with: High school diploma (including GED) or higher: 76.7% (2005); Bachelor's degree or higher: 8.1% (2005); Master's degree or higher: 2.7% (2005).
Housing: Homeownership rate: 79.7% (2005); Median home value: $115,764 (2005); Median rent: $477 per month (2000); Median age of housing: 23 years (2000).
Transportation: Commute to work: 96.4% car, 0.0% public transportation, 0.7% walk, 2.2% work from home (2000); Travel time to work: 29.3% less than 15 minutes, 49.2% 15 to 30 minutes, 14.8% 30 to 45 minutes, 4.0% 45 to 60 minutes, 2.6% 60 minutes or more (2000)
Additional Information Contacts
Village of Obetz . . . . (614) 491-1080
    http://www.obetz.oh.us

REYNOLDSBURG (city). Covers a land area of 10.584 square miles and a water area of 0 square miles. Located at 39.96° N. Lat.; 82.80° W. Long. Elevation is 880 feet.
History: Reynoldsburg is known as "The Birthplace of the Tomato" and the "Tomato Festival" is held there every September.
Population: 26,344 (1990); 32,069 (2000); 33,597 (2005); 35,081 (2010 projected); Race: 81.5% White, 12.9% Black, 2.1% Asian, 2.2% Hispanic of any race (2005); Density: 3,174.4 persons per square mile (2005); Average household size: 2.46 (2005); Median age: 36.8 (2005); Males per 100 females: 91.9 (2005); Marriage status: 23.5% never married, 58.4% now married, 5.4% widowed, 12.8% divorced (2000); Foreign born: 3.6% (2000); Ancestry (includes multiple ancestries): 26.8% German, 17.1% Other groups, 14.5% Irish, 10.7% English, 8.6% United States or American (2000).

Economy: Unemployment rate: 5.1% (2005); Total civilian labor force: 18,680 (2005); Single-family building permits issued: 112 (2005); Multi-family building permits issued: 0 (2005); Employment by occupation: 15.9% management, 20.1% professional, 13.8% services, 31.7% sales, 0.0% farming, 6.6% construction, 11.8% production (2000).
Income: Per capita income: $26,472 (2005); Median household income: $56,207 (2005); Average household income: $65,054 (2005); Percent of households with income of $100,000 or more: 16.6% (2005); Poverty rate: 5.5% (2000).
Education: Percent of population age 25 and over with: High school diploma (including GED) or higher: 90.5% (2005); Bachelor's degree or higher: 27.3% (2005); Master's degree or higher: 7.7% (2005).

School District(s)

Pickerington Local SD (PK-12)
    2003-04 Enrollment: 8,917 . . . . (614) 833-2110
Reynoldsburg City SD (PK-12)
    2003-04 Enrollment: 6,607 . . . . (614) 501-1020

Two-year College(s)

Ohio State School of Cosmetology (Private, For-profit)
    Fall 2004 Enrollment: 94 . . . . (614) 252-5252

Housing: Homeownership rate: 65.8% (2005); Median home value: $142,809 (2005); Median rent: $559 per month (2000); Median age of housing: 22 years (2000).
Safety: Violent crime rate: 27.3 per 10,000 population; Property crime rate: 406.7 per 10,000 population (2004).
Transportation: Commute to work: 94.8% car, 1.3% public transportation, 1.2% walk, 2.2% work from home (2000); Travel time to work: 25.1% less than 15 minutes, 44.4% 15 to 30 minutes, 23.3% 30 to 45 minutes, 4.4% 45 to 60 minutes, 2.9% 60 minutes or more (2000)
Additional Information Contacts
City of Reynoldsburg . . . . (614) 322-6800
    http://www.ci.reynoldsburg.oh.us
Reynoldsburg Chamber of Commerce . . . . (614) 866-4753
    http://www.reynoldsburgchamber.com

RIVERLEA

RIVERLEA (village). Covers a land area of 0.161 square miles and a water area of 0 square miles. Located at 40.08° N. Lat.; 83.02° W. Long. Elevation is 800 feet.
Population: 503 (1990); 499 (2000); 475 (2005); 469 (2010 projected); Race: 94.9% White, 0.0% Black, 1.7% Asian, 1.9% Hispanic of any race (2005); Density: 2,951.0 persons per square mile (2005); Average household size: 2.13 (2005); Median age: 48.5 (2005); Males per 100 females: 84.8 (2005); Marriage status: 16.4% never married, 65.7% now married, 7.0% widowed, 11.0% divorced (2000); Foreign born: 3.0% (2000); Ancestry (includes multiple ancestries): 29.3% German, 23.6% English, 11.4% Irish, 7.2% Italian, 6.8% Scottish (2000).
Economy: Employment by occupation: 17.6% management, 45.2% professional, 5.5% services, 26.5% sales, 0.0% farming, 1.1% construction, 4.0% production (2000).
Income: Per capita income: $53,716 (2005); Median household income: $106,071 (2005); Average household income: $114,417 (2005); Percent of households with income of $100,000 or more: 53.8% (2005); Poverty rate: 0.8% (2000).
Education: Percent of population age 25 and over with: High school diploma (including GED) or higher: 98.0% (2005); Bachelor's degree or higher: 68.0% (2005); Master's degree or higher: 33.7% (2005).
Housing: Homeownership rate: 90.1% (2005); Median home value: $258,989 (2005); Median rent: $579 per month (2000); Median age of housing: 48 years (2000).
Transportation: Commute to work: 87.1% car, 3.3% public transportation, 0.7% walk, 7.7% work from home (2000); Travel time to work: 22.7% less than 15 minutes, 54.2% 15 to 30 minutes, 16.7% 30 to 45 minutes, 3.6% 45 to 60 minutes, 2.8% 60 minutes or more (2000)

UPPER ARLINGTON

UPPER ARLINGTON (city). Covers a land area of 9.764 square miles and a water area of 0.022 square miles. Located at 40.02° N. Lat.; 83.06° W. Long. Elevation is 820 feet.
History: Named for the Upper Arlington Company, a development organization. Incorporated 1918.
Population: 34,171 (1990); 33,686 (2000); 31,752 (2005); 29,966 (2010 projected); Race: 93.4% White, 0.7% Black, 4.4% Asian, 1.1% Hispanic of any race (2005); Density: 3,252.1 persons per square mile (2005); Average household size: 2.40 (2005); Median age: 44.2 (2005); Males per 100 females: 90.0 (2005); Marriage status: 20.2% never married, 63.8% now married, 7.7% widowed, 8.3% divorced (2000); Foreign born: 6.3% (2000); Ancestry (includes multiple ancestries): 30.6% German, 19.2% English, 15.1% Irish, 7.7% Other groups, 6.8% Italian (2000).
Economy: Unemployment rate: 4.2% (2005); Total civilian labor force: 16,584 (2005); Single-family building permits issued: 16 (2005); Multi-family building permits issued: 20 (2005); Employment by occupation: 24.2% management, 39.9% professional, 6.2% services, 24.7% sales, 0.0% farming, 2.0% construction, 2.9% production (2000).
Income: Per capita income: $47,098 (2005); Median household income: $83,413 (2005); Average household income: $112,471 (2005); Percent of households with income of $100,000 or more: 39.2% (2005); Poverty rate: 2.4% (2000).
Taxes: Total city taxes per capita: $772 (2004); City property taxes per capita: $236 (2004).
Education: Percent of population age 25 and over with: High school diploma (including GED) or higher: 97.9% (2005); Bachelor's degree or higher: 67.5% (2005); Master's degree or higher: 29.8% (2005).

School District(s)

Upper Arlington City SD (KG-12)
    2003-04 Enrollment: 5,597 . . . . (614) 487-5000

Housing: Homeownership rate: 81.4% (2005); Median home value: $258,642 (2005); Median rent: $661 per month (2000); Median age of housing: 42 years (2000).
Transportation: Commute to work: 90.3% car, 1.5% public transportation, 1.4% walk, 5.8% work from home (2000); Travel time to work: 30.7% less than 15 minutes, 55.4% 15 to 30 minutes, 10.1% 30 to 45 minutes, 1.4% 45 to 60 minutes, 2.4% 60 minutes or more (2000)
Additional Information Contacts
City of Upper Arlington . . . . (614) 583-5040
    http://www.ua-ohio.net
Upper Arlington Area Chamber of Commerce . . . . (614) 481-5710
    http://www.uachamber.org

URBANCREST

URBANCREST (village). Covers a land area of 0.442 square miles and a water area of 0 square miles. Located at 39.89° N. Lat.; 83.08° W. Long. Elevation is 840 feet.
Population: 875 (1990); 868 (2000); 1,002 (2005); 1,095 (2010 projected); Race: 33.3% White, 45.1% Black, 15.8% Asian, 2.3% Hispanic of any race (2005); Density: 2,264.9 persons per square mile (2005); Average household size: 2.69 (2005); Median age: 25.4 (2005); Males per 100 females: 75.2 (2005); Marriage status: 41.5% never married, 38.7% now married, 7.4% widowed, 12.4% divorced (2000); Foreign born: 4.1% (2000); Ancestry (includes multiple ancestries): 54.7% Other groups, 16.4% United States or American, 9.5% German, 2.6% Irish, 1.7% French (except Basque) (2000).
Economy: Employment by occupation: 5.6% management, 10.3% professional, 19.8% services, 37.5% sales, 0.0% farming, 3.0% construction, 23.7% production (2000).
Income: Per capita income: $13,258 (2005); Median household income: $25,345 (2005); Average household income: $35,712 (2005); Percent of households with income of $100,000 or more: 5.1% (2005); Poverty rate: 32.7% (2000).
Education: Percent of population age 25 and over with: High school diploma (including GED) or higher: 58.9% (2005); Bachelor's degree or higher: 2.8% (2005); Master's degree or higher: 1.4% (2005).
Housing: Homeownership rate: 44.9% (2005); Median home value: $81,316 (2005); Median rent: $255 per month (2000); Median age of housing: 38 years (2000).
Transportation: Commute to work: 87.4% car, 0.0% public transportation, 7.9% walk, 1.9% work from home (2000); Travel time to work: 49.0% less than 15 minutes, 30.5% 15 to 30 minutes, 10.5% 30 to 45 minutes, 8.6% 45 to 60 minutes, 1.4% 60 minutes or more (2000)

VALLEYVIEW

VALLEYVIEW (village). Covers a land area of 0.152 square miles and a water area of 0 square miles. Located at 39.96° N. Lat.; 83.07° W. Long.
Population: 604 (1990); 601 (2000); 543 (2005); 521 (2010 projected); Race: 94.8% White, 1.3% Black, 3.1% Asian, 0.4% Hispanic of any race (2005); Density: 3,575.7 persons per square mile (2005); Average household size: 2.28 (2005); Median age: 41.7 (2005); Males per 100 females: 90.5 (2005); Marriage status: 19.3% never married, 55.8% now married, 9.6% widowed, 15.3% divorced (2000); Foreign born: 0.7% (2000); Ancestry (includes multiple ancestries): 24.0% German, 19.5% English, 14.8% United States or American, 14.1% Irish, 5.5% Other groups (2000).

Economy: Employment by occupation: 10.2% management, 9.6% professional, 7.2% services, 35.8% sales, 0.0% farming, 17.1% construction, 20.1% production (2000).
Income: Per capita income: $22,316 (2005); Median household income: $43,125 (2005); Average household income: $50,914 (2005); Percent of households with income of $100,000 or more: 4.6% (2005); Poverty rate: 5.7% (2000).
Education: Percent of population age 25 and over with: High school diploma (including GED) or higher: 73.0% (2005); Bachelor's degree or higher: 11.1% (2005); Master's degree or higher: 3.0% (2005).
Housing: Homeownership rate: 90.8% (2005); Median home value: $96,579 (2005); Median rent: $425 per month (2000); Median age of housing: 53 years (2000).
Transportation: Commute to work: 95.2% car, 2.4% public transportation, 0.3% walk, 0.7% work from home (2000); Travel time to work: 27.9% less than 15 minutes, 52.4% 15 to 30 minutes, 12.1% 30 to 45 minutes, 4.1% 45 to 60 minutes, 3.4% 60 minutes or more (2000).

WESTERVILLE (city).
Covers a land area of 12.387 square miles and a water area of 0 square miles. Located at 40.12° N. Lat.; 82.92° W. Long. Elevation is 875 feet.
History: Named for the Westervelt family, prominent farmers in the area. Westerville was settled in 1813 by Virginia Cavalier families and Quakers from Pennsylvania, and became the headquarters of the Anti-Saloon League in 1909.
Population: 30,722 (1990); 35,318 (2000); 34,555 (2005); 34,167 (2010 projected); Race: 91.6% White, 3.9% Black, 2.4% Asian, 1.3% Hispanic of any race (2005); Density: 2,789.5 persons per square mile (2005); Average household size: 2.73 (2005); Median age: 38.5 (2005); Males per 100 females: 91.0 (2005); Marriage status: 24.6% never married, 63.2% now married, 4.7% widowed, 7.5% divorced (2000); Foreign born: 3.2% (2000); Ancestry (includes multiple ancestries): 29.6% German, 15.4% Irish, 14.3% English, 9.1% United States or American, 8.6% Other groups (2000).
Economy: Unemployment rate: 4.3% (2005); Total civilian labor force: 19,439 (2005); Single-family building permits issued: 68 (2005); Multi-family building permits issued: 114 (2005); Employment by occupation: 21.6% management, 26.0% professional, 10.8% services, 29.8% sales, 0.1% farming, 4.7% construction, 7.0% production (2000).
Income: Per capita income: $35,243 (2005); Median household income: $80,266 (2005); Average household income: $95,398 (2005); Percent of households with income of $100,000 or more: 37.5% (2005); Poverty rate: 3.5% (2000).
Taxes: Total city taxes per capita: $835 (2004); City property taxes per capita: $300 (2004).
Education: Percent of population age 25 and over with: High school diploma (including GED) or higher: 94.7% (2005); Bachelor's degree or higher: 45.0% (2005); Master's degree or higher: 13.8% (2005).

School District(s)
Westerville City SD (PK-12)
    2003-04 Enrollment: 14,142 .... (614) 797-5700
Worthington City SD (PK-12)
    2003-04 Enrollment: 9,754 .... (614) 883-3000

Four-year College(s)
Otterbein College (Private, Not-for-profit, United Methodist)
    Fall 2004 Enrollment: 3,089..................... (614) 890-3000
    2005-06 Tuition: In-state $22,518; Out-of-state $22,518

Two-year College(s)
Ohio State School of Cosmetology (Private, For-profit)
    Fall 2004 Enrollment: 89 .... (614) 252-5252

Housing: Homeownership rate: 79.2% (2005); Median home value: $185,276 (2005); Median rent: $530 per month (2000); Median age of housing: 22 years (2000).
Hospitals: Mt. Carmel - St. Ann's Hospital (180 beds)
Safety: Violent crime rate: 12.6 per 10,000 population; Property crime rate: 320.6 per 10,000 population (2004).
Transportation: Commute to work: 92.6% car, 1.0% public transportation, 2.1% walk, 3.9% work from home (2000); Travel time to work: 29.6% less than 15 minutes, 42.3% 15 to 30 minutes, 22.1% 30 to 45 minutes, 3.1% 45 to 60 minutes, 2.8% 60 minutes or more (2000).
Additional Information Contacts
City of Westerville .... (614) 901-6400
   http://www.ci.westerville.oh.us
Westerville Chamber of Commerce .... (614) 882-8917
   http://www.westervillechamber.com

WHITEHALL (city).
Covers a land area of 5.215 square miles and a water area of 0 square miles. Located at 39.96° N. Lat.; 82.88° W. Long. Elevation is 790 feet.
History: Named for Whitehall, site of government offices in London, England. Incorporated 1948.
Population: 20,645 (1990); 19,201 (2000); 18,205 (2005); 17,351 (2010 projected); Race: 68.0% White, 23.9% Black, 2.5% Asian, 4.0% Hispanic of any race (2005); Density: 3,490.9 persons per square mile (2005); Average household size: 2.27 (2005); Median age: 35.8 (2005); Males per 100 females: 94.5 (2005); Marriage status: 30.8% never married, 45.3% now married, 7.0% widowed, 16.9% divorced (2000); Foreign born: 5.9% (2000); Ancestry (includes multiple ancestries): 25.0% Other groups, 18.5% German, 12.5% Irish, 12.1% United States or American, 7.4% English (2000).
Economy: Manufacturing includes water coolers and packaged meats. A large Federal defense construction supply center is here. Single-family building permits issued: 1 (2005); Multi-family building permits issued: 0 (2005); Employment by occupation: 6.6% management, 10.1% professional, 19.9% services, 37.2% sales, 0.0% farming, 9.9% construction, 16.3% production (2000).
Income: Per capita income: $18,056 (2005); Median household income: $34,632 (2005); Average household income: $40,917 (2005); Percent of households with income of $100,000 or more: 3.6% (2005); Poverty rate: 14.9% (2000).
Education: Percent of population age 25 and over with: High school diploma (including GED) or higher: 78.7% (2005); Bachelor's degree or higher: 11.4% (2005); Master's degree or higher: 3.9% (2005).

School District(s)
Whitehall City SD (KG-12)
    2003-04 Enrollment: 3,064 .... (614) 417-5000

Housing: Homeownership rate: 44.2% (2005); Median home value: $89,956 (2005); Median rent: $412 per month (2000); Median age of housing: 41 years (2000).
Safety: Violent crime rate: 84.2 per 10,000 population; Property crime rate: 836.0 per 10,000 population (2004).
Transportation: Commute to work: 91.7% car, 4.9% public transportation, 2.2% walk, 0.7% work from home (2000); Travel time to work: 27.0% less than 15 minutes, 43.6% 15 to 30 minutes, 21.2% 30 to 45 minutes, 3.5% 45 to 60 minutes, 4.7% 60 minutes or more (2000).
Additional Information Contacts
City of Whitehall .... (614) 338-3106
   http://www.ci.whitehall.oh.us
Whitehall Chamber of Commerce .... (614) 237-7792
   http://www.whitehallchamber.org

WORTHINGTON (city).
Covers a land area of 5.662 square miles and a water area of 0 square miles. Located at 40.09° N. Lat.; 83.02° W. Long. Elevation is 866 feet.
History: Worthington was settled in 1803 by a group led by Colonel James Kilbourne, who named the place after a parish in Connecticut. A series of educational institutions opened and closed in Worthington over the next century.
Population: 15,085 (1990); 14,125 (2000); 13,443 (2005); 12,832 (2010 projected); Race: 93.6% White, 1.5% Black, 3.1% Asian, 1.1% Hispanic of any race (2005); Density: 2,374.1 persons per square mile (2005); Average household size: 2.44 (2005); Median age: 45.8 (2005); Males per 100 females: 88.6 (2005); Marriage status: 18.1% never married, 65.7% now married, 7.5% widowed, 8.8% divorced (2000); Foreign born: 4.7% (2000); Ancestry (includes multiple ancestries): 33.5% German, 19.1% English, 15.7% Irish, 9.7% Other groups, 6.9% United States or American (2000).
Economy: Single-family building permits issued: 0 (2005); Multi-family building permits issued: 0 (2005); Employment by occupation: 21.2% management, 37.6% professional, 8.6% services, 24.2% sales, 0.1% farming, 3.9% construction, 4.6% production (2000).
Income: Per capita income: $38,466 (2005); Median household income: $75,300 (2005); Average household income: $92,565 (2005); Percent of households with income of $100,000 or more: 34.3% (2005); Poverty rate: 2.5% (2000).
Education: Percent of population age 25 and over with: High school diploma (including GED) or higher: 96.1% (2005); Bachelor's degree or higher: 60.0% (2005); Master's degree or higher: 25.8% (2005).

School District(s)
Ohio Connections Academy, Inc (KG-08)
    2003-04 Enrollment: 138

Worthington City SD (PK-12)
    2003-04 Enrollment: 9,754 . . . . (614) 883-3000
Housing: Homeownership rate: 84.3% (2005); Median home value: $193,350 (2005); Median rent: $514 per month (2000); Median age of housing: 37 years (2000).
Safety: Violent crime rate: 6.6 per 10,000 population; Property crime rate: 264.9 per 10,000 population (2004).
Newspapers: Johnstown Independent (General - Circulation 2,245); Rocky Fork Enterprise (General - Circulation 13,231); The Dublin Villager (General - Circulation 21,417); This Week In Bexley (General - Circulation 9,311); This Week In Clintonville (General - Circulation 14,085); This Week In Delaware/Big Walnut/Sunbury (General - Circulation 16,295); This Week In Northland (General - Circulation 18,864); This Week In Pickerington (General - Circulation 12,794); This Week In Powell (General - Circulation 11,278); This Week In Reynoldsburg (General - Circulation 13,947); This Week In Southside (General - Circulation 20,613); This Week In Upper Arlington (General - Circulation 21,164); This Week In West Side (General - Circulation 21,529); This Week In Westerville (General - Circulation 24,031); This Week In Worthington (General - Circulation 22,043); This Week in Delaware (General - Circulation 12,358); This Week in Grandview (General - Circulation 5,815); This Week in Hilliard (General - Circulation 21,489); This Week in New Albany (General - Circulation 3,975)
Transportation: Commute to work: 91.6% car, 1.7% public transportation, 1.3% walk, 5.1% work from home (2000); Travel time to work: 29.4% less than 15 minutes, 51.2% 15 to 30 minutes, 14.6% 30 to 45 minutes, 2.8% 45 to 60 minutes, 1.9% 60 minutes or more (2000)
Additional Information Contacts
City of Worthington . . . . (614) 436-3100
    http://www.worthington.org
Worthington Chamber of Commerce . . . . (614) 888-3040
    http://www.worthington.org
Worthington Convention & Visitors Bureau . . . . (614) 841-2545
    http://www.worthington.org/cvb

Fulton County

Located in northwestern Ohio; bounded on the north by Michigan; drained by the Tiffin River. Covers a land area of 406.78 square miles, a water area of 0.54 square miles, and is located in the Eastern Time Zone. The county government was organized in 1850. County seat is Wauseon.

Fulton County is part of the Toledo, OH Metropolitan Statistical Area. The entire metro area includes: Fulton County, OH; Lucas County, OH; Ottawa County, OH; Wood County, OH

Weather Station: Wauseon Water Plant   Elevation: 748 feet

	Jan	Feb	Mar	Apr	May	Jun	Jul	Aug	Sep	Oct	Nov	Dec
High	31	35	46	60	72	81	84	82	76	63	49	36
Low	15	18	27	37	48	57	61	59	51	41	32	22
Precip	1.9	1.6	2.5	3.4	3.4	3.7	3.4	3.7	3.1	2.6	3.0	2.4
Snow	8.7	7.0	4.4	0.9	tr	0.0	0.0	0.0	0.0	tr	2.2	5.8

High and Low temperatures in degrees Fahrenheit; Precipitation and Snow in inches

Population: 38,498 (1990); 42,084 (2000); 42,639 (2005); 43,206 (2010 projected); Race: 95.3% White, 0.3% Black, 0.5% Asian, 6.1% Hispanic of any race (2005); Density: 104.8 persons per square mile (2005); Average household size: 2.68 (2005); Median age: 37.2 (2005); Males per 100 females: 95.9 (2005).
Religion: Five largest groups: 21.2% Catholic Church, 8.8% The United Methodist Church, 5.8% Evangelical Lutheran Church in America, 5.7% Mennonite Church USA, 3.8% Christian Church (Disciples of Christ) (2000).
Economy: Unemployment rate: 6.1% (2005); Total civilian labor force: 22,947 (2005); Leading industries: 49.7% manufacturing; 10.5% health care and social assistance; 9.8% retail trade (2004); Farms: 783 totaling 197,410 acres (2002); Companies that employ 500 or more persons: 3 (2004); Companies that employ 100 to 499 persons: 27 (2004); Companies that employ less than 100 persons: 1,076 (2004); Black-owned businesses: n/a (2002); Hispanic-owned businesses: n/a (2002); Women-owned businesses: n/a (2002); Retail sales per capita: $11,744 (2006). Single-family building permits issued: 163 (2005); Multi-family building permits issued: 0 (2005).
Income: Per capita income: $21,365 (2005); Median household income: $48,263 (2005); Average household income: $57,025 (2005); Percent of households with income of $100,000 or more: 10.7% (2005); Poverty rate: 6.6% (2003); Bankruptcy rate: 9.17% (2005).
Education: Percent of population age 25 and over with: High school diploma (including GED) or higher: 85.2% (2005); Bachelor's degree or higher: 13.1% (2005); Master's degree or higher: 3.8% (2005).
Housing: Homeownership rate: 80.0% (2005); Median home value: $127,216 (2005); Median rent: $368 per month (2000); Median age of housing: 37 years (2000).
Health: Birth rate: 116.1 per 10,000 population (2004); Death rate: 91.8 per 10,000 population (2004); Age-adjusted cancer mortality rate: 166.6 deaths per 100,000 population (2002); Number of physicians: 9.3 per 10,000 population (2004); Hospital beds: 40.6 per 10,000 population (2003); Hospital admissions: 688.7 per 10,000 population (2003).
Elections: 2004 Presidential election results: 62.1% Bush, 37.5% Kerry, 0.0% Nader, 0.2% Badnarik
National and State Parks: Harrison Lake State Reservation
Additional Information Contacts
Fulton County Government . . . . (419) 337-9255
    http://www.fultoncountyoh.com/
Archbold Chamber of Commerce . . . . (419) 445-2222
    http://www.archbold.com
City of Wauseon. . . . . (419) 335-1511
    http://www.wauseon.com
Delta Chamber of Commerce . . . . (419) 822-3089
    http://www.deltaohio.com
Swanton Chamber of Commerce. . . . . (419) 826-1941
    http://www.swantonareacoc.com
Village of Archbold. . . . . (419) 445-4726
    http://www.archbold.com
Village of Swanton . . . . (419) 826-9515
    http://www.village.swanton.oh.us
Wauseon Chamber of Commerce . . . . (419) 335-9966
    http://www.wauseonchamber.com

Fulton County Communities

ARCHBOLD (village). Covers a land area of 4.251 square miles and a water area of 0.093 square miles. Located at 41.51° N. Lat.; 84.30° W. Long. Elevation is 734 feet.
Population: 3,590 (1990); 4,290 (2000); 4,485 (2005); 4,665 (2010 projected); Race: 90.6% White, 0.8% Black, 0.4% Asian, 13.6% Hispanic of any race (2005); Density: 1,055.1 persons per square mile (2005); Average household size: 2.45 (2005); Median age: 39.1 (2005); Males per 100 females: 90.8 (2005); Marriage status: 18.8% never married, 63.3% now married, 9.8% widowed, 8.1% divorced (2000); Foreign born: 1.1% (2000); Ancestry (includes multiple ancestries): 44.0% German, 14.9% Other groups, 7.1% United States or American, 6.8% English, 6.7% Swiss (2000).
Economy: Hay, wheat. Manufactures agricultural machinery, furniture, wood products. Slaughterhouse. Single-family building permits issued: 12 (2005); Multi-family building permits issued: 0 (2005); Employment by occupation: 11.6% management, 15.5% professional, 13.5% services, 25.2% sales, 0.3% farming, 6.9% construction, 27.1% production (2000).
Income: Per capita income: $23,534 (2005); Median household income: $45,979 (2005); Average household income: $57,649 (2005); Percent of households with income of $100,000 or more: 11.6% (2005); Poverty rate: 4.4% (2000).
Education: Percent of population age 25 and over with: High school diploma (including GED) or higher: 83.0% (2005); Bachelor's degree or higher: 20.8% (2005); Master's degree or higher: 4.8% (2005).
School District(s)
Archbold-Area Local SD (PK-12)
    2003-04 Enrollment: 1,484 . . . . (419) 445-2583
Four County Joint Vocational SD (11-12)
    2003-04 Enrollment: n/a . . . . (419) 267-3331
Gorham Fayette Local SD (PK-12)
    2003-04 Enrollment: 526. . . . . (419) 237-2573
Two-year College(s)
Northwest State Community College (Public)
    Fall 2004 Enrollment: 3,145. . . . . (419) 267-5511
    2005-06 Tuition: In-state $3,660; Out-of-state $6,750
Housing: Homeownership rate: 72.7% (2005); Median home value: $122,026 (2005); Median rent: $356 per month (2000); Median age of housing: 32 years (2000).
Safety: Violent crime rate: 11.2 per 10,000 population; Property crime rate: 173.0 per 10,000 population (2004).
Newspapers: Farmland News (General - Circulation 7,000)

Transportation: Commute to work: 90.7% car, 0.0% public transportation, 4.5% walk, 2.6% work from home (2000); Travel time to work: 70.6% less than 15 minutes, 19.3% 15 to 30 minutes, 5.2% 30 to 45 minutes, 2.6% 45 to 60 minutes, 2.2% 60 minutes or more (2000)
Additional Information Contacts
Archbold Chamber of Commerce . . . . (419) 445-2222
http://www.archbold.com
Village of Archbold . . . . (419) 445-4726
http://www.archbold.com

DELTA
(village). Covers a land area of 2.601 square miles and a water area of 0 square miles. Located at 41.57° N. Lat.; 84.00° W. Long. Elevation is 725 feet.
Population: 2,916 (1990); 2,930 (2000); 2,904 (2005); 2,883 (2010 projected); Race: 95.8% White, 0.1% Black, 0.1% Asian, 5.5% Hispanic of any race (2005); Density: 1,116.7 persons per square mile (2005); Average household size: 2.53 (2005); Median age: 36.2 (2005); Males per 100 females: 95.6 (2005); Marriage status: 19.9% never married, 64.1% now married, 5.7% widowed, 10.3% divorced (2000); Foreign born: 1.3% (2000); Ancestry (includes multiple ancestries): 40.6% German, 12.1% Other groups, 12.1% English, 11.4% Irish, 7.1% United States or American (2000).
Economy: Single-family building permits issued: 16 (2005); Multi-family building permits issued: 0 (2005); Employment by occupation: 6.5% management, 14.9% professional, 15.4% services, 21.8% sales, 0.5% farming, 13.9% construction, 27.0% production (2000).
Income: Per capita income: $21,591 (2005); Median household income: $46,981 (2005); Average household income: $54,569 (2005); Percent of households with income of $100,000 or more: 8.9% (2005); Poverty rate: 9.2% (2000).
Education: Percent of population age 25 and over with: High school diploma (including GED) or higher: 84.5% (2005); Bachelor's degree or higher: 13.6% (2005); Master's degree or higher: 4.2% (2005).
School District(s)
Pike-Delta-York Local SD (PK-12)
    2003-04 Enrollment: 1,574 . . . . (419) 822-3391
Housing: Homeownership rate: 75.9% (2005); Median home value: $114,658 (2005); Median rent: $380 per month (2000); Median age of housing: 49 years (2000).
Safety: Violent crime rate: 3.4 per 10,000 population; Property crime rate: 345.1 per 10,000 population (2004).
Transportation: Commute to work: 95.0% car, 1.2% public transportation, 1.1% walk, 2.0% work from home (2000); Travel time to work: 28.6% less than 15 minutes, 35.0% 15 to 30 minutes, 21.9% 30 to 45 minutes, 9.6% 45 to 60 minutes, 4.9% 60 minutes or more (2000)
Additional Information Contacts
Delta Chamber of Commerce . . . . (419) 822-3089
http://www.deltaohio.com

FAYETTE
(village). Covers a land area of 0.912 square miles and a water area of 0 square miles. Located at 41.67° N. Lat.; 84.32° W. Long. Elevation is 795 feet.
History: Fayette developed as a grain and livestock shipping center.
Population: 1,268 (1990); 1,340 (2000); 1,364 (2005); 1,380 (2010 projected); Race: 94.2% White, 0.2% Black, 0.0% Asian, 9.2% Hispanic of any race (2005); Density: 1,495.4 persons per square mile (2005); Average household size: 2.47 (2005); Median age: 32.4 (2005); Males per 100 females: 95.1 (2005); Marriage status: 22.0% never married, 56.6% now married, 8.3% widowed, 13.0% divorced (2000); Foreign born: 2.4% (2000); Ancestry (includes multiple ancestries): 29.6% German, 16.3% United States or American, 11.2% Other groups, 8.7% English, 8.2% Irish (2000).
Economy: Single-family building permits issued: 0 (2005); Multi-family building permits issued: 0 (2005); Employment by occupation: 7.4% management, 7.3% professional, 12.1% services, 15.9% sales, 3.4% farming, 10.8% construction, 43.1% production (2000).
Income: Per capita income: $17,381 (2005); Median household income: $37,386 (2005); Average household income: $42,948 (2005); Percent of households with income of $100,000 or more: 3.8% (2005); Poverty rate: 9.7% (2000).
Education: Percent of population age 25 and over with: High school diploma (including GED) or higher: 80.2% (2005); Bachelor's degree or higher: 8.3% (2005); Master's degree or higher: 2.3% (2005).

School District(s)
Gorham Fayette Local SD (PK-12)
    2003-04 Enrollment: 526 . . . . (419) 237-2573
Housing: Homeownership rate: 60.0% (2005); Median home value: $78,713 (2005); Median rent: $347 per month (2000); Median age of housing: 53 years (2000).
Transportation: Commute to work: 93.2% car, 0.0% public transportation, 4.9% walk, 1.9% work from home (2000); Travel time to work: 32.3% less than 15 minutes, 42.4% 15 to 30 minutes, 15.8% 30 to 45 minutes, 4.3% 45 to 60 minutes, 5.1% 60 minutes or more (2000)

LYONS
(village). Covers a land area of 0.708 square miles and a water area of 0 square miles. Located at 41.70° N. Lat.; 84.07° W. Long. Elevation is 771 feet.
Population: 562 (1990); 559 (2000); 566 (2005); 562 (2010 projected); Race: 95.6% White, 0.0% Black, 0.0% Asian, 4.2% Hispanic of any race (2005); Density: 799.4 persons per square mile (2005); Average household size: 2.49 (2005); Median age: 36.6 (2005); Males per 100 females: 98.6 (2005); Marriage status: 21.7% never married, 58.9% now married, 11.9% widowed, 7.4% divorced (2000); Foreign born: 0.4% (2000); Ancestry (includes multiple ancestries): 31.6% German, 13.7% Irish, 11.4% Other groups, 10.7% United States or American, 5.6% French (except Basque) (2000).
Economy: Single-family building permits issued: 2 (2005); Multi-family building permits issued: 0 (2005); Employment by occupation: 6.9% management, 8.7% professional, 15.6% services, 25.4% sales, 0.7% farming, 17.0% construction, 25.7% production (2000).
Income: Per capita income: $19,081 (2005); Median household income: $43,963 (2005); Average household income: $47,577 (2005); Percent of households with income of $100,000 or more: 3.5% (2005); Poverty rate: 5.6% (2000).
Education: Percent of population age 25 and over with: High school diploma (including GED) or higher: 89.1% (2005); Bachelor's degree or higher: 9.2% (2005); Master's degree or higher: 1.1% (2005).
School District(s)
Evergreen Local SD (PK-12)
    2003-04 Enrollment: 1,340 . . . . (419) 644-3521
Housing: Homeownership rate: 77.1% (2005); Median home value: $98,444 (2005); Median rent: $368 per month (2000); Median age of housing: 55 years (2000).
Transportation: Commute to work: 90.5% car, 0.0% public transportation, 5.5% walk, 2.6% work from home (2000); Travel time to work: 26.3% less than 15 minutes, 31.6% 15 to 30 minutes, 21.8% 30 to 45 minutes, 15.8% 45 to 60 minutes, 4.5% 60 minutes or more (2000)

METAMORA
(village). Covers a land area of 0.425 square miles and a water area of 0 square miles. Located at 41.71° N. Lat.; 83.91° W. Long. Elevation is 720 feet.
Population: 641 (1990); 563 (2000); 570 (2005); 577 (2010 projected); Race: 96.8% White, 1.4% Black, 0.0% Asian, 3.3% Hispanic of any race (2005); Density: 1,339.9 persons per square mile (2005); Average household size: 2.78 (2005); Median age: 36.0 (2005); Males per 100 females: 100.7 (2005); Marriage status: 20.7% never married, 59.2% now married, 10.1% widowed, 10.1% divorced (2000); Foreign born: 1.2% (2000); Ancestry (includes multiple ancestries): 43.5% German, 10.4% French (except Basque), 10.1% English, 9.0% Other groups, 8.1% Irish (2000).
Economy: Agriculture: tomatoes, corn; poultry hatcheries. Single-family building permits issued: 1 (2005); Multi-family building permits issued: 0 (2005); Employment by occupation: 7.5% management, 13.8% professional, 16.5% services, 23.6% sales, 0.0% farming, 11.4% construction, 27.2% production (2000).
Income: Per capita income: $21,469 (2005); Median household income: $51,750 (2005); Average household income: $59,695 (2005); Percent of households with income of $100,000 or more: 14.6% (2005); Poverty rate: 8.5% (2000).
Education: Percent of population age 25 and over with: High school diploma (including GED) or higher: 87.1% (2005); Bachelor's degree or higher: 14.0% (2005); Master's degree or higher: 6.1% (2005).
School District(s)
Evergreen Local SD (PK-12)
    2003-04 Enrollment: 1,340 . . . . (419) 644-3521
Housing: Homeownership rate: 76.6% (2005); Median home value: $115,809 (2005); Median rent: $380 per month (2000); Median age of housing: 60+ years (2000).

Transportation: Commute to work: 93.0% car, 0.0% public transportation, 4.5% walk, 2.0% work from home (2000); Travel time to work: 24.7% less than 15 minutes, 23.4% 15 to 30 minutes, 34.7% 30 to 45 minutes, 11.7% 45 to 60 minutes, 5.4% 60 minutes or more (2000)

SWANTON
(village). Covers a land area of 2.382 square miles and a water area of 0 square miles. Located at 41.58° N. Lat.; 83.89° W. Long. Elevation is 685 feet.

Population: 3,687 (1990); 3,307 (2000); 3,295 (2005); 3,299 (2010 projected); Race: 98.1% White, 0.2% Black, 0.2% Asian, 1.6% Hispanic of any race (2005); Density: 1,383.0 persons per square mile (2005); Average household size: 2.62 (2005); Median age: 38.8 (2005); Males per 100 females: 90.6 (2005); Marriage status: 21.0% never married, 59.4% now married, 8.8% widowed, 10.8% divorced (2000); Foreign born: 1.3% (2000); Ancestry (includes multiple ancestries): 43.2% German, 13.9% Irish, 11.9% English, 8.1% Other groups, 7.8% Polish (2000).
Economy: Construction materials. Single-family building permits issued: 19 (2005); Multi-family building permits issued: 0 (2005); Employment by occupation: 11.9% management, 16.7% professional, 11.6% services, 24.8% sales, 2.2% farming, 10.1% construction, 22.8% production (2000).
Income: Per capita income: $21,853 (2005); Median household income: $47,455 (2005); Average household income: $56,095 (2005); Percent of households with income of $100,000 or more: 12.4% (2005); Poverty rate: 4.6% (2000).
Education: Percent of population age 25 and over with: High school diploma (including GED) or higher: 87.3% (2005); Bachelor's degree or higher: 17.0% (2005); Master's degree or higher: 4.4% (2005).

School District(s)
Evergreen Local SD (PK-12)
   2003-04 Enrollment: 1,340 . . . . (419) 644-3521
Swanton Local SD (PK-12)
   2003-04 Enrollment: 1,585 . . . . (419) 826-7085
Housing: Homeownership rate: 75.5% (2005); Median home value: $123,585 (2005); Median rent: $431 per month (2000); Median age of housing: 44 years (2000).
Safety: Violent crime rate: 59.9 per 10,000 population; Property crime rate: 368.5 per 10,000 population (2004).
Newspapers: Swanton Enterprise (General - Circulation 1,600)
Transportation: Commute to work: 94.9% car, 0.5% public transportation, 2.3% walk, 1.6% work from home (2000); Travel time to work: 34.1% less than 15 minutes, 31.8% 15 to 30 minutes, 22.4% 30 to 45 minutes, 9.2% 45 to 60 minutes, 2.5% 60 minutes or more (2000)
Additional Information Contacts
Swanton Chamber of Commerce. (419) 826-1941
   http://www.swantonareacoc.com
Village of Swanton . . . . (419) 826-9515
   http://www.village.swanton.oh.us

WAUSEON
(city). Covers a land area of 4.933 square miles and a water area of 0 square miles. Located at 41.55° N. Lat.; 84.13° W. Long. Elevation is 757 feet.
History: Settled 1835, incorporated 1852.
Population: 6,478 (1990); 7,091 (2000); 7,233 (2005); 7,375 (2010 projected); Race: 92.4% White, 0.8% Black, 1.0% Asian, 10.0% Hispanic of any race (2005); Density: 1,466.3 persons per square mile (2005); Average household size: 2.59 (2005); Median age: 34.9 (2005); Males per 100 females: 89.8 (2005); Marriage status: 21.9% never married, 59.6% now married, 8.2% widowed, 10.3% divorced (2000); Foreign born: 2.2% (2000); Ancestry (includes multiple ancestries): 43.6% German, 12.6% Other groups, 11.8% Irish, 9.9% English, 5.6% French (except Basque) (2000).
Economy: In farming and dairying area. Manufacturing of electrical equipment, food products, furniture, transportation equipment, machinery, construction materials. Single-family building permits issued: 45 (2005); Multi-family building permits issued: 8 (2005); Employment by occupation: 9.7% management, 13.9% professional, 13.3% services, 24.5% sales, 0.0% farming, 8.2% construction, 30.4% production (2000).
Income: Per capita income: $19,130 (2005); Median household income: $42,734 (2005); Average household income: $49,247 (2005); Percent of households with income of $100,000 or more: 5.4% (2005); Poverty rate: 5.2% (2000).
Education: Percent of population age 25 and over with: High school diploma (including GED) or higher: 87.6% (2005); Bachelor's degree or higher: 12.8% (2005); Master's degree or higher: 4.7% (2005).

School District(s)
Pettisville Local Schools (PK-12)
   2003-04 Enrollment: 564 . . . . (419) 446-2705
Pike-Delta-York Local SD (PK-12)
   2003-04 Enrollment: 1,574 . . . . (419) 822-3391
Wauseon Ex Vill SD (PK-12)
   2003-04 Enrollment: 2,133 . . . . (419) 335-6616
Housing: Homeownership rate: 70.3% (2005); Median home value: $112,135 (2005); Median rent: $343 per month (2000); Median age of housing: 36 years (2000).
Hospitals: Fulton County Health Center (119 beds)
Newspapers: Fulton County Expositor (General - Circulation 4,506)
Transportation: Commute to work: 94.5% car, 0.4% public transportation, 3.1% walk, 1.1% work from home (2000); Travel time to work: 50.0% less than 15 minutes, 34.4% 15 to 30 minutes, 8.2% 30 to 45 minutes, 3.7% 45 to 60 minutes, 3.7% 60 minutes or more (2000)
Additional Information Contacts
City of Wauseon. . . . . (419) 335-1511
   http://www.wauseon.com
Wauseon Chamber of Commerce . . . . (419) 335-9966
   http://www.wauseonchamber.com

Gallia County

Located in southern Ohio; bounded on the east by the Ohio River and the West Virginia border; crossed by Raccoon Creek. Covers a land area of 468.78 square miles, a water area of 2.36 square miles, and is located in the Eastern Time Zone. The county government was organized in 1803. County seat is Gallipolis.

Gallia County is part of the Point Pleasant, WV-OH Micropolitan Statistical Area. The entire metro area includes: Gallia County, OH; Mason County, WV

Weather Station: Gallipolis   Elevation: 567 feet

	Jan	Feb	Mar	Apr	May	Jun	Jul	Aug	Sep	Oct	Nov	Dec
High	42	47	57	68	77	84	87	86	80	69	57	47
Low	22	24	32	40	50	59	64	63	56	43	35	27
Precip	2.9	2.9	3.6	3.3	4.0	3.9	4.3	3.7	3.0	2.8	3.1	3.3
Snow	6.1	4.6	2.2	tr	0.0	0.0	0.0	0.0	0.0	tr	0.3	1.0

High and Low temperatures in degrees Fahrenheit; Precipitation and Snow in inches

Population: 30,954 (1990); 31,069 (2000); 31,544 (2005); 32,031 (2010 projected); Race: 95.4% White, 2.6% Black, 0.6% Asian, 0.6% Hispanic of any race (2005); Density: 67.3 persons per square mile (2005); Average household size: 2.54 (2005); Median age: 38.1 (2005); Males per 100 females: 95.7 (2005).
Religion: Five largest groups: 5.9% The United Methodist Church, 4.3% American Baptist Churches in the USA, 3.0% General Association of Regular Baptist Churches, 2.6% Christian Churches and Churches of Christ, 2.4% Southern Baptist Convention (2000
Economy: Unemployment rate: 7.3% (2005); Total civilian labor force: 13,967 (2005); Leading industries: 29.5% health care and social assistance; 17.3% retail trade; 9.1% accommodation & food services (2004); Farms: 936 totaling 117,944 acres (2002); Companies that employ 500 or more persons: 3 (2004); Companies that employ 100 to 499 persons: 10 (2004); Companies that employ less than 100 persons: 621 (2004); Black-owned businesses: n/a (2002); Hispanic-owned businesses: n/a (2002); Women-owned businesses: 810 (2002); Retail sales per capita: $14,679 (2006). Single-family building permits issued: 1 (2005); Multi-family building permits issued: 0 (2005).
Income: Per capita income: $17,746 (2005); Median household income: $34,357 (2005); Average household income: $44,546 (2005); Percent of households with income of $100,000 or more: 7.8% (2005); Poverty rate: 15.5% (2003); Bankruptcy rate: 7.01% (2005).
Education: Percent of population age 25 and over with: High school diploma (including GED) or higher: 73.5% (2005); Bachelor's degree or higher: 11.6% (2005); Master's degree or higher: 4.6% (2005).
Housing: Homeownership rate: 75.3% (2005); Median home value: $81,655 (2005); Median rent: $300 per month (2000); Median age of housing: 27 years (2000).
Health: Birth rate: 134.6 per 10,000 population (2004); Death rate: 113.8 per 10,000 population (2004); Age-adjusted cancer mortality rate: 237.0 deaths per 100,000 population (2002); Air Quality Index: 100.0% good, 0.0% moderate, 0.0% unhealthy for sensitive individuals, 0.0% unhealthy (percent of days in 2005); Number of physicians: 33.2 per 10,000

population (2004); Hospital beds: 55.3 per 10,000 population (2003); Hospital admissions: 2,454.6 per 10,000 population (2003).
Elections: 2004 Presidential election results: 61.3% Bush, 38.3% Kerry, 0.0% Nader, 0.2% Badnarik
National and State Parks: Tycoon Lake State Wildlife Area
Additional Information Contacts
Gallia County Government........................... (740) 446-4374
  http://www.gallianet.net/
City of Gallipolis.................................... (740) 446-1789
  http://www.gallianet.net/Gallipolis/index.htm
Gallipolis Chamber of Commerce .... (740) 446-0596
  http://www.galliacounty.org

Gallia County Communities

BIDWELL (unincorporated postal area, zip code 45614). Covers a land area of 69.546 square miles and a water area of 0.447 square miles. Located at 38.91° N. Lat.; 82.29° W. Long. Elevation is 690 feet.
Population: 4,427 (2000); Race: 91.5% White, 5.8% Black, 1.2% Asian, 0.9% Hispanic of any race (2000); Density: 63.7 persons per square mile (2000); Age: 24.4% under 18, 13.7% over 64 (2000); Marriage status: 20.7% never married, 59.0% now married, 10.0% widowed, 10.3% divorced (2000); Foreign born: 1.3% (2000); Ancestry (includes multiple ancestries): 19.2% United States or American, 14.2% Other groups, 11.3% German, 9.0% English, 6.7% Irish (2000).
Economy: Employment by occupation: 9.0% management, 18.8% professional, 12.3% services, 19.7% sales, 0.7% farming, 14.7% construction, 24.8% production (2000).
Income: Per capita income: $15,561 (2000); Median household income: $29,306 (2000); Poverty rate: 21.3% (2000).
Education: Percent of population age 25 and over with: High school diploma (including GED) or higher: 72.4% (2000); Bachelor's degree or higher: 11.1% (2000).
School District(s)
Gallia County Local SD (PK-12)
  2003-04 Enrollment: 2,544 .... (740) 446-7917
Housing: Homeownership rate: 77.3% (2000); Median home value: $78,200 (2000); Median rent: $269 per month (2000); Median age of housing: 25 years (2000).
Transportation: Commute to work: 93.9% car, 0.0% public transportation, 1.7% walk, 3.6% work from home (2000); Travel time to work: 26.1% less than 15 minutes, 46.8% 15 to 30 minutes, 8.9% 30 to 45 minutes, 5.0% 45 to 60 minutes, 13.1% 60 minutes or more (2000)

CENTERVILLE (village). Aka Thurman. Covers a land area of 0.099 square miles and a water area of 0 square miles. Located at 38.89° N. Lat.; 82.44° W. Long.
Population: 128 (1990); 134 (2000); 128 (2005); 127 (2010 projected); Race: 96.9% White, 1.6% Black, 0.0% Asian, 0.0% Hispanic of any race (2005); Density: 1,290.3 persons per square mile (2005); Average household size: 2.72 (2005); Median age: 39.7 (2005); Males per 100 females: 93.9 (2005); Marriage status: 25.5% never married, 68.2% now married, 2.7% widowed, 3.6% divorced (2000); Foreign born: 0.0% (2000); Ancestry (includes multiple ancestries): 16.8% German, 9.8% Irish, 8.4% Scotch-Irish, 8.4% Other groups, 7.0% United States or American (2000).
Economy: Employment by occupation: 6.6% management, 19.7% professional, 23.0% services, 3.3% sales, 0.0% farming, 18.0% construction, 29.5% production (2000).
Income: Per capita income: $19,570 (2005); Median household income: $45,313 (2005); Average household income: $53,298 (2005); Percent of households with income of $100,000 or more: 12.8% (2005); Poverty rate: 15.4% (2000).
Education: Percent of population age 25 and over with: High school diploma (including GED) or higher: 71.1% (2005); Bachelor's degree or higher: 8.4% (2005); Master's degree or higher: 7.2% (2005).
Two-year College(s)
David Curtis School of Floral Design (Private, For-profit)
  Fall 2004 Enrollment: 17 .... (937) 433-0566
RETS Tech Center (Private, For-profit)
  Fall 2004 Enrollment: 558 .... (937) 433-3410
  2005-06 Tuition: In-state $7,610; Out-of-state $7,610
Housing: Homeownership rate: 85.1% (2005); Median home value: $48,889 (2005); Median rent: $288 per month (2000); Median age of housing: 48 years (2000).

Safety: Violent crime rate: 6.9 per 10,000 population; Property crime rate: 258.0 per 10,000 population (2004).
Transportation: Commute to work: 93.2% car, 0.0% public transportation, 3.4% walk, 0.0% work from home (2000); Travel time to work: 33.9% less than 15 minutes, 42.4% 15 to 30 minutes, 13.6% 30 to 45 minutes, 5.1% 45 to 60 minutes, 5.1% 60 minutes or more (2000)

CHESHIRE (village). Covers a land area of 0.184 square miles and a water area of 0.009 square miles. Located at 38.94° N. Lat.; 82.11° W. Long. Elevation is 573 feet.
Population: 263 (1990); 221 (2000); 211 (2005); 206 (2010 projected); Race: 98.6% White, 1.4% Black, 0.0% Asian, 0.0% Hispanic of any race (2005); Density: 1,146.8 persons per square mile (2005); Average household size: 2.32 (2005); Median age: 41.0 (2005); Males per 100 females: 93.6 (2005); Marriage status: 20.7% never married, 66.3% now married, 6.0% widowed, 7.1% divorced (2000); Foreign born: 0.0% (2000); Ancestry (includes multiple ancestries): 23.1% German, 12.8% United States or American, 9.8% Other groups, 8.1% Irish, 3.8% Scotch-Irish (2000).
Economy: Single-family building permits issued: 1 (2005); Multi-family building permits issued: 0 (2005); Employment by occupation: 6.3% management, 15.6% professional, 19.8% services, 28.1% sales, 0.0% farming, 13.5% construction, 16.7% production (2000).
Income: Per capita income: $19,254 (2005); Median household income: $35,682 (2005); Average household income: $44,643 (2005); Percent of households with income of $100,000 or more: 5.5% (2005); Poverty rate: 12.4% (2000).
Education: Percent of population age 25 and over with: High school diploma (including GED) or higher: 75.2% (2005); Bachelor's degree or higher: 7.1% (2005); Master's degree or higher: 2.1% (2005).
School District(s)
Gallia County Local SD (PK-12)
  2003-04 Enrollment: 2,544 .... (740) 446-7917
Housing: Homeownership rate: 74.7% (2005); Median home value: $73,000 (2005); Median rent: $288 per month (2000); Median age of housing: 55 years (2000).
Transportation: Commute to work: 87.0% car, 0.0% public transportation, 2.2% walk, 9.8% work from home (2000); Travel time to work: 20.5% less than 15 minutes, 51.8% 15 to 30 minutes, 6.0% 30 to 45 minutes, 4.8% 45 to 60 minutes, 16.9% 60 minutes or more (2000)

CROWN CITY (village). Covers a land area of 1.094 square miles and a water area of 0.029 square miles. Located at 38.59° N. Lat.; 82.28° W. Long. Elevation is 575 feet.
Population: 445 (1990); 411 (2000); 419 (2005); 423 (2010 projected); Race: 98.1% White, 0.2% Black, 0.0% Asian, 1.0% Hispanic of any race (2005); Density: 383.0 persons per square mile (2005); Average household size: 2.44 (2005); Median age: 39.3 (2005); Males per 100 females: 87.1 (2005); Marriage status: 21.5% never married, 62.5% now married, 8.1% widowed, 7.8% divorced (2000); Foreign born: 0.5% (2000); Ancestry (includes multiple ancestries): 17.6% Other groups, 16.0% German, 15.8% Irish, 13.2% United States or American, 3.8% Polish (2000).
Economy: Employment by occupation: 3.8% management, 18.9% professional, 9.4% services, 38.4% sales, 0.0% farming, 15.1% construction, 14.5% production (2000).
Income: Per capita income: $18,866 (2005); Median household income: $28,889 (2005); Average household income: $45,959 (2005); Percent of households with income of $100,000 or more: 10.5% (2005); Poverty rate: 20.0% (2000).
Education: Percent of population age 25 and over with: High school diploma (including GED) or higher: 72.8% (2005); Bachelor's degree or higher: 4.8% (2005); Master's degree or higher: 3.8% (2005).
School District(s)
Gallia County Local SD (PK-12)
  2003-04 Enrollment: 2,544 .... (740) 446-7917
Housing: Homeownership rate: 79.7% (2005); Median home value: $79,524 (2005); Median rent: $270 per month (2000); Median age of housing: 32 years (2000).
Transportation: Commute to work: 92.4% car, 0.0% public transportation, 3.2% walk, 2.5% work from home (2000); Travel time to work: 15.0% less than 15 minutes, 11.8% 15 to 30 minutes, 46.4% 30 to 45 minutes, 17.0% 45 to 60 minutes, 9.8% 60 minutes or more (2000)

GALLIPOLIS (city). Covers a land area of 3.615 square miles and a water area of 0.224 square miles. Located at 38.81° N. Lat.; 82.19° W. Long. Elevation is 576 feet.
History: Gallipolis was settled in 1790 by French immigrants who had been induced to leave France and purchase land in Ohio. After their long journey, they found that the deeds they had purchased were worthless, and those who stayed in Gallipolis had to buy their land all over again.
Population: 4,944 (1990); 4,180 (2000); 4,078 (2005); 4,053 (2010 projected); Race: 90.0% White, 6.4% Black, 1.7% Asian, 0.5% Hispanic of any race (2005); Density: 1,128.0 persons per square mile (2005); Average household size: 2.23 (2005); Median age: 44.7 (2005); Males per 100 females: 86.2 (2005); Marriage status: 23.9% never married, 47.7% now married, 13.2% widowed, 15.1% divorced (2000); Foreign born: 2.3% (2000); Ancestry (includes multiple ancestries): 15.9% United States or American, 13.7% Other groups, 13.4% German, 10.6% Irish, 6.4% English (2000).
Economy: Single-family building permits issued: 0 (2005); Multi-family building permits issued: 0 (2005); Employment by occupation: 6.0% management, 27.1% professional, 19.8% services, 25.5% sales, 0.0% farming, 8.1% construction, 13.6% production (2000).
Income: Per capita income: $18,038 (2005); Median household income: $27,054 (2005); Average household income: $39,086 (2005); Percent of households with income of $100,000 or more: 6.0% (2005); Poverty rate: 21.5% (2000).
Education: Percent of population age 25 and over with: High school diploma (including GED) or higher: 70.5% (2005); Bachelor's degree or higher: 18.2% (2005); Master's degree or higher: 7.8% (2005).

School District(s)
Gallia County Local SD (PK-12)
    2003-04 Enrollment: 2,544 . . . . (740) 446-7917
Gallipolis City SD (PK-12)
    2003-04 Enrollment: 2,366 . . . . (740) 446-3211

Two-year College(s)
Gallipolis Career College (Private, For-profit)
    Fall 2004 Enrollment: 182 . . . . (740) 446-4367
    2005-06 Tuition: In-state $8,640; Out-of-state $8,640

Housing: Homeownership rate: 53.1% (2005); Median home value: $89,589 (2005); Median rent: $318 per month (2000); Median age of housing: 55 years (2000).
Hospitals: Holzer Medical Center (243 beds)
Newspapers: Gallipolis Daily Tribune (Circulation 4,767); The Tri-County News (General - Circulation 15,500)
Transportation: Commute to work: 92.1% car, 1.5% public transportation, 4.7% walk, 0.3% work from home (2000); Travel time to work: 54.8% less than 15 minutes, 22.9% 15 to 30 minutes, 10.0% 30 to 45 minutes, 1.6% 45 to 60 minutes, 10.7% 60 minutes or more (2000)
Additional Information Contacts
City of Gallipolis . . . . (740) 446-1789
    http://www.gallianet.net/Gallipolis/index.htm
Gallipolis Chamber of Commerce . . . . (740) 446-0596
    http://www.galliacounty.org

PATRIOT (unincorporated postal area, zip code 45658). Covers a land area of 91.886 square miles and a water area of 0.006 square miles. Located at 38.76° N. Lat.; 82.41° W. Long. Elevation is 730 feet.
Population: 2,315 (2000); Race: 98.4% White, 0.0% Black, 0.0% Asian, 0.0% Hispanic of any race (2000); Density: 25.2 persons per square mile (2000); Age: 33.3% under 18, 9.1% over 64 (2000); Marriage status: 22.3% never married, 63.6% now married, 5.1% widowed, 8.9% divorced (2000); Foreign born: 0.0% (2000); Ancestry (includes multiple ancestries): 13.5% German, 13.1% United States or American, 12.8% Irish, 7.9% English, 7.4% Other groups (2000).
Economy: Employment by occupation: 6.2% management, 10.7% professional, 17.1% services, 19.1% sales, 4.5% farming, 11.8% construction, 30.5% production (2000).
Income: Per capita income: $11,944 (2000); Median household income: $30,968 (2000); Poverty rate: 26.0% (2000).
Education: Percent of population age 25 and over with: High school diploma (including GED) or higher: 71.1% (2000); Bachelor's degree or higher: 8.4% (2000).

School District(s)
Gallia County Local SD (PK-12)
    2003-04 Enrollment: 2,544 . . . . (740) 446-7917

Housing: Homeownership rate: 83.8% (2000); Median home value: $82,000 (2000); Median rent: $293 per month (2000); Median age of housing: 23 years (2000).
Transportation: Commute to work: 91.9% car, 0.0% public transportation, 3.5% walk, 4.6% work from home (2000); Travel time to work: 9.0% less than 15 minutes, 34.6% 15 to 30 minutes, 32.5% 30 to 45 minutes, 11.0% 45 to 60 minutes, 12.9% 60 minutes or more (2000)

RIO GRANDE (village). Covers a land area of 1.198 square miles and a water area of 0.008 square miles. Located at 38.88° N. Lat.; 82.38° W. Long. Elevation is 630 feet.
History: Rio Grande was settled by Nehemiah Atwood, who served under General William Henry Harrison in the War of 1812 and, in 1818, opened a tavern at this site. Atwood provided the endowment for Rio Grande College, established in 1876 under the supervision of the Baptist church.
Population: 1,076 (1990); 915 (2000); 916 (2005); 919 (2010 projected); Race: 90.9% White, 3.9% Black, 2.6% Asian, 0.8% Hispanic of any race (2005); Density: 764.9 persons per square mile (2005); Average household size: 3.91 (2005); Median age: 21.4 (2005); Males per 100 females: 100.4 (2005); Marriage status: 62.1% never married, 29.3% now married, 0.3% widowed, 8.3% divorced (2000); Foreign born: 2.1% (2000); Ancestry (includes multiple ancestries): 14.8% German, 13.6% Other groups, 9.1% Irish, 5.5% English, 5.4% United States or American (2000).
Economy: Employment by occupation: 9.5% management, 14.3% professional, 20.3% services, 45.1% sales, 0.0% farming, 7.4% construction, 3.3% production (2000).
Income: Per capita income: $11,132 (2005); Median household income: $21,341 (2005); Average household income: $35,972 (2005); Percent of households with income of $100,000 or more: 6.4% (2005); Poverty rate: 35.9% (2000).
Education: Percent of population age 25 and over with: High school diploma (including GED) or higher: 87.0% (2005); Bachelor's degree or higher: 23.4% (2005); Master's degree or higher: 11.9% (2005).

School District(s)
Gallia-Jackson-Vinton Joint Vocational SD (07-12)
    2003-04 Enrollment: n/a . . . . (740) 245-5334
Gallipolis City SD (PK-12)
    2003-04 Enrollment: 2,366 . . . . (740) 446-3211

Four-year College(s)
University of Rio Grande (Private, Not-for-profit)
    Fall 2004 Enrollment: 2,530 . . . . (740) 245-7206
    2005-06 Tuition: In-state $13,392; Out-of-state $14,444

Two-year College(s)
Gallia Jackson Vinton Joint Vocational School District (Public)
    Fall 2004 Enrollment: 142 . . . . (740) 245-5334

Housing: Homeownership rate: 37.6% (2005); Median home value: $101,429 (2005); Median rent: $270 per month (2000); Median age of housing: 30 years (2000).
Transportation: Commute to work: 53.8% car, 0.0% public transportation, 44.0% walk, 1.9% work from home (2000); Travel time to work: 62.4% less than 15 minutes, 18.9% 15 to 30 minutes, 7.0% 30 to 45 minutes, 4.3% 45 to 60 minutes, 7.3% 60 minutes or more (2000)

THURMAN (unincorporated postal area, zip code 45685). Aka Centerville. Covers a land area of 26.138 square miles and a water area of 0 square miles. Located at 38.87° N. Lat.; 82.40° W. Long. Elevation is 691 feet.
Population: 918 (2000); Race: 98.7% White, 0.6% Black, 0.0% Asian, 0.1% Hispanic of any race (2000); Density: 35.1 persons per square mile (2000); Age: 25.9% under 18, 11.3% over 64 (2000); Marriage status: 21.5% never married, 66.8% now married, 5.7% widowed, 6.0% divorced (2000); Foreign born: 0.2% (2000); Ancestry (includes multiple ancestries): 20.2% German, 13.5% Welsh, 10.5% Other groups, 9.9% United States or American, 9.9% Irish (2000).
Economy: Employment by occupation: 10.2% management, 16.9% professional, 9.9% services, 20.3% sales, 0.0% farming, 7.9% construction, 34.7% production (2000).
Income: Per capita income: $15,330 (2000); Median household income: $30,938 (2000); Poverty rate: 20.6% (2000).
Education: Percent of population age 25 and over with: High school diploma (including GED) or higher: 81.7% (2000); Bachelor's degree or higher: 11.4% (2000).
Housing: Homeownership rate: 80.5% (2000); Median home value: $80,800 (2000); Median rent: $325 per month (2000); Median age of housing: 27 years (2000).

Transportation: Commute to work: 98.8% car, 0.0% public transportation, 0.6% walk, 0.0% work from home (2000); Travel time to work: 21.3% less than 15 minutes, 46.8% 15 to 30 minutes, 22.5% 30 to 45 minutes, 1.5% 45 to 60 minutes, 7.9% 60 minutes or more (2000)

VINTON (village). Covers a land area of 1.115 square miles and a water area of 0 square miles. Located at 38.97° N. Lat.; 82.34° W. Long. Elevation is 620 feet.
Population: 293 (1990); 324 (2000); 319 (2005); 312 (2010 projected); Race: 97.5% White, 1.6% Black, 0.3% Asian, 0.0% Hispanic of any race (2005); Density: 286.0 persons per square mile (2005); Average household size: 2.57 (2005); Median age: 38.2 (2005); Males per 100 females: 96.9 (2005); Marriage status: 14.2% never married, 65.3% now married, 9.9% widowed, 10.6% divorced (2000); Foreign born: 0.0% (2000); Ancestry (includes multiple ancestries): 22.9% United States or American, 13.2% German, 8.2% Irish, 7.3% English, 7.3% French (except Basque) (2000).
Economy: In agricultural area. Employment by occupation: 4.2% management, 12.6% professional, 10.1% services, 25.2% sales, 0.0% farming, 26.1% construction, 21.8% production (2000).
Income: Per capita income: $14,404 (2005); Median household income: $28,846 (2005); Average household income: $37,056 (2005); Percent of households with income of $100,000 or more: 6.5% (2005); Poverty rate: 16.4% (2000).
Education: Percent of population age 25 and over with: High school diploma (including GED) or higher: 63.2% (2005); Bachelor's degree or higher: 6.6% (2005); Master's degree or higher: 2.8% (2005).

School District(s)
Gallia County Local SD (PK-12)
　　2003-04 Enrollment: 2,544 . . . . (740) 446-7917
Housing: Homeownership rate: 79.8% (2005); Median home value: $70,455 (2005); Median rent: $271 per month (2000); Median age of housing: 45 years (2000).
Transportation: Commute to work: 86.2% car, 0.0% public transportation, 3.4% walk, 6.0% work from home (2000); Travel time to work: 32.1% less than 15 minutes, 47.7% 15 to 30 minutes, 6.4% 30 to 45 minutes, 3.7% 45 to 60 minutes, 10.1% 60 minutes or more (2000)

Geauga County

Located in northeastern Ohio; drained by the Cuyahoga, Chagrin, and Grand Rivers; includes several lakes. Covers a land area of 403.66 square miles, a water area of 4.63 square miles, and is located in the Eastern Time Zone. The county government was organized in 1805. County seat is Chardon.

Geauga County is part of the Cleveland-Elyria-Mentor, OH Metropolitan Statistical Area. The entire metro area includes: Cuyahoga County, OH; Geauga County, OH; Lake County, OH; Lorain County, OH; Medina County, OH

Weather Station: Chardon　　　　　　　　　　　Elevation: 1,128 feet

	Jan	Feb	Mar	Apr	May	Jun	Jul	Aug	Sep	Oct	Nov	Dec
High	31	34	44	56	68	76	80	79	72	60	48	37
Low	14	15	24	34	44	53	58	56	49	39	32	22
Precip	3.2	2.7	3.4	3.8	4.1	4.4	4.0	4.6	4.5	3.9	4.3	4.1
Snow	26.2	18.9	14.4	2.9	tr	0.0	0.0	0.0	0.0	0.9	10.1	23.6

High and Low temperatures in degrees Fahrenheit; Precipitation and Snow in inches

Population: 81,100 (1990); 90,895 (2000); 95,568 (2005); 100,447 (2010 projected); Race: 97.4% White, 1.3% Black, 0.5% Asian, 0.5% Hispanic of any race (2005); Density: 236.8 persons per square mile (2005); Average household size: 2.83 (2005); Median age: 39.5 (2005); Males per 100 females: 97.0 (2005).
Religion: Five largest groups: 28.1% Catholic Church, 4.4% Old Order Amish Church, 2.8% United Church of Christ, 2.6% The United Methodist Church, 1.7% Episcopal Church (2000).
Economy: Unemployment rate: 4.7% (2005); Total civilian labor force: 50,399 (2005); Leading industries: 33.6% manufacturing; 12.6% health care and social assistance; 11.8% retail trade (2004); Farms: 975 totaling 66,474 acres (2002); Companies that employ 500 or more persons: 2 (2004); Companies that employ 100 to 499 persons: 36 (2004); Companies that employ less than 100 persons: 2,695 (2004); Black-owned businesses: n/a (2002); Hispanic-owned businesses: n/a (2002); Women-owned businesses: 1,982 (2002); Retail sales per capita: $9,755 (2006). Single-family building permits issued: 365 (2005); Multi-family building permits issued: 0 (2005).

Income: Per capita income: $31,309 (2005); Median household income: $67,004 (2005); Average household income: $88,058 (2005); Percent of households with income of $100,000 or more: 28.1% (2005); Poverty rate: 5.7% (2003); Bankruptcy rate: 5.38% (2005).
Taxes: Total county taxes per capita: $276 (2004); County property taxes per capita: $219 (2004).
Education: Percent of population age 25 and over with: High school diploma (including GED) or higher: 86.0% (2005); Bachelor's degree or higher: 31.2% (2005); Master's degree or higher: 11.6% (2005).
Housing: Homeownership rate: 87.2% (2005); Median home value: $219,285 (2005); Median rent: $513 per month (2000); Median age of housing: 29 years (2000).
Health: Birth rate: 112.9 per 10,000 population (2004); Death rate: 77.8 per 10,000 population (2004); Age-adjusted cancer mortality rate: 185.2 deaths per 100,000 population (2002); Air Quality Index: 73.1% good, 23.6% moderate, 3.3% unhealthy for sensitive individuals, 0.0% unhealthy (percent of days in 2005); Number of physicians: 23.1 per 10,000 population (2004); Hospital beds: 47.4 per 10,000 population (2003); Hospital admissions: 1,177.2 per 10,000 population (2003).
Elections: 2004 Presidential election results: 60.2% Bush, 39.4% Kerry, 0.0% Nader, 0.2% Badnarik
National and State Parks: Auburn State Wildlife Area; Punderson State Park
Additional Information Contacts

Geauga County Government	(440) 285-2222
http://www.co.geauga.oh.us/	
Burton Chamber of Commerce	(440) 834-4891
http://www.burtonchamberofcommerce.org	
Chardon Chamber of Commerce	(440) 285-9050
http://www.chardonchamber.com	
Chesterland Chamber of Commerce	(440) 729-7297
http://www.ohio-usa.com/geauga/chester	
Geauga County Tourism Council	(800) 775-TOUR
http://www.tourgeauga.com	
Middlefield Chamber of Commerce	(440) 632-5705
http://www.middlefieldcc.com	
Village of Chardon	(440) 286-2600
http://www.chardon.cc	
Village of Middlefield	(440) 632-5248
http://www.middlefieldohio.com	
Village of South Russell	(440) 338-6700
http://www.southrussell.com	

Geauga County Communities

AQUILLA (village). Aka Lake Aquilla. Covers a land area of 0.140 square miles and a water area of 0 square miles. Located at 41.54° N. Lat.; 81.17° W. Long. Elevation is 1,070 feet.
Population: 360 (1990); 372 (2000); 360 (2005); 359 (2010 projected); Race: 97.8% White, 0.3% Black, 1.4% Asian, 0.3% Hispanic of any race (2005); Density: 2,572.7 persons per square mile (2005); Average household size: 2.61 (2005); Median age: 36.2 (2005); Males per 100 females: 83.7 (2005); Marriage status: 29.2% never married, 51.5% now married, 5.3% widowed, 14.0% divorced (2000); Foreign born: 1.4% (2000); Ancestry (includes multiple ancestries): 19.1% German, 15.5% English, 12.8% Irish, 9.8% Italian, 7.6% United States or American (2000).
Economy: Employment by occupation: 13.8% management, 12.3% professional, 16.7% services, 17.2% sales, 0.0% farming, 12.8% construction, 27.1% production (2000).
Income: Per capita income: $21,646 (2005); Median household income: $53,333 (2005); Average household income: $56,467 (2005); Percent of households with income of $100,000 or more: 7.2% (2005); Poverty rate: 1.6% (2000).
Education: Percent of population age 25 and over with: High school diploma (including GED) or higher: 77.8% (2005); Bachelor's degree or higher: 14.2% (2005); Master's degree or higher: 2.9% (2005).
Housing: Homeownership rate: 81.9% (2005); Median home value: $118,214 (2005); Median rent: $533 per month (2000); Median age of housing: 52 years (2000).
Transportation: Commute to work: 93.1% car, 1.0% public transportation, 0.0% walk, 4.4% work from home (2000); Travel time to work: 30.9% less than 15 minutes, 25.8% 15 to 30 minutes, 27.8% 30 to 45 minutes, 10.3% 45 to 60 minutes, 5.2% 60 minutes or more (2000)

BAINBRIDGE (CDP). Covers a land area of 3.371 square miles and a water area of 0.066 square miles. Located at 41.39° N. Lat.; 81.33° W. Long. Elevation is 1,160 feet.
Population: 3,602 (1990); 3,417 (2000); 3,394 (2005); 3,408 (2010 projected); Race: 97.1% White, 0.9% Black, 0.8% Asian, 0.4% Hispanic of any race (2005); Density: 1,006.7 persons per square mile (2005); Average household size: 2.65 (2005); Median age: 42.9 (2005); Males per 100 females: 92.2 (2005); Marriage status: 16.7% never married, 71.2% now married, 5.4% widowed, 6.7% divorced (2000); Foreign born: 3.4% (2000); Ancestry (includes multiple ancestries): 23.8% German, 19.0% Irish, 14.8% English, 12.7% Italian, 7.5% Polish (2000).
Economy: Employment by occupation: 28.3% management, 29.9% professional, 9.1% services, 24.6% sales, 0.0% farming, 2.9% construction, 5.3% production (2000).
Income: Per capita income: $42,783 (2005); Median household income: $94,620 (2005); Average household income: $112,807 (2005); Percent of households with income of $100,000 or more: 46.1% (2005); Poverty rate: 2.1% (2000).
Education: Percent of population age 25 and over with: High school diploma (including GED) or higher: 94.5% (2005); Bachelor's degree or higher: 62.9% (2005); Master's degree or higher: 22.3% (2005).
Housing: Homeownership rate: 93.0% (2005); Median home value: $244,565 (2005); Median rent: $1,208 per month (2000); Median age of housing: 31 years (2000).
Transportation: Commute to work: 88.5% car, 1.2% public transportation, 0.0% walk, 9.8% work from home (2000); Travel time to work: 27.5% less than 15 minutes, 33.8% 15 to 30 minutes, 26.8% 30 to 45 minutes, 8.4% 45 to 60 minutes, 3.5% 60 minutes or more (2000)

BURTON (village). Covers a land area of 1.109 square miles and a water area of 0 square miles. Located at 41.47° N. Lat.; 81.14° W. Long. Elevation is 1,320 feet.
Population: 1,349 (1990); 1,450 (2000); 1,510 (2005); 1,577 (2010 projected); Race: 97.1% White, 1.0% Black, 0.5% Asian, 0.7% Hispanic of any race (2005); Density: 1,362.2 persons per square mile (2005); Average household size: 2.44 (2005); Median age: 40.2 (2005); Males per 100 females: 88.8 (2005); Marriage status: 23.4% never married, 53.6% now married, 11.6% widowed, 11.4% divorced (2000); Foreign born: 1.3% (2000); Ancestry (includes multiple ancestries): 28.4% German, 18.4% English, 15.9% Irish, 8.9% Other groups, 8.8% Italian (2000).
Economy: Employment by occupation: 12.1% management, 18.5% professional, 17.4% services, 23.2% sales, 0.0% farming, 12.1% construction, 16.8% production (2000).
Income: Per capita income: $22,412 (2005); Median household income: $46,397 (2005); Average household income: $52,771 (2005); Percent of households with income of $100,000 or more: 8.6% (2005); Poverty rate: 7.2% (2000).
Education: Percent of population age 25 and over with: High school diploma (including GED) or higher: 86.2% (2005); Bachelor's degree or higher: 23.2% (2005); Master's degree or higher: 8.4% (2005).
School District(s)
Berkshire Local SD (PK-12)
    2003-04 Enrollment: 1,403 . . . . (440) 834-4123
Two-year College(s)
Kent State University-Geauga Campus (Public)
    Fall 2004 Enrollment: 875 . . . . (440) 834-4187
    2005-06 Tuition: In-state $4,586; Out-of-state $12,018
Housing: Homeownership rate: 51.7% (2005); Median home value: $166,312 (2005); Median rent: $471 per month (2000); Median age of housing: 41 years (2000).
Transportation: Commute to work: 90.9% car, 0.0% public transportation, 4.0% walk, 4.4% work from home (2000); Travel time to work: 39.9% less than 15 minutes, 30.4% 15 to 30 minutes, 16.3% 30 to 45 minutes, 9.8% 45 to 60 minutes, 3.5% 60 minutes or more (2000)
Additional Information Contacts
Burton Chamber of Commerce . . . . (440) 834-4891
    http://www.burtonchamberofcommerce.org

CHARDON (village). Covers a land area of 4.603 square miles and a water area of 0.007 square miles. Located at 41.57° N. Lat.; 81.20° W. Long. Elevation is 1,280 feet.
History: Chardon was named for Peter Chardon Brooks, first owner of the site. The town developed as the maple syrup and sugar center of Ohio, from its location on the crest of a hill, surrounded by maple groves.
Population: 4,600 (1990); 5,156 (2000); 5,309 (2005); 5,480 (2010 projected); Race: 97.8% White, 0.5% Black, 0.4% Asian, 0.3% Hispanic of any race (2005); Density: 1,153.3 persons per square mile (2005); Average household size: 2.35 (2005); Median age: 38.9 (2005); Males per 100 females: 86.6 (2005); Marriage status: 20.2% never married, 56.5% now married, 11.5% widowed, 11.9% divorced (2000); Foreign born: 1.5% (2000); Ancestry (includes multiple ancestries): 25.8% German, 21.1% Irish, 16.8% English, 9.9% Italian, 8.7% Polish (2000).
Economy: Employment by occupation: 11.5% management, 23.1% professional, 12.2% services, 32.1% sales, 0.0% farming, 7.2% construction, 13.9% production (2000).
Income: Per capita income: $23,819 (2005); Median household income: $48,232 (2005); Average household income: $55,476 (2005); Percent of households with income of $100,000 or more: 11.0% (2005); Poverty rate: 3.8% (2000).
Education: Percent of population age 25 and over with: High school diploma (including GED) or higher: 89.1% (2005); Bachelor's degree or higher: 27.3% (2005); Master's degree or higher: 8.8% (2005).
School District(s)
Chardon Local SD (KG-12)
    2003-04 Enrollment: 3,272 . . . . (440) 285-4052
Housing: Homeownership rate: 59.9% (2005); Median home value: $191,289 (2005); Median rent: $528 per month (2000); Median age of housing: 30 years (2000).
Hospitals: Heather Hill Hospital & Health Partnership (118 beds)
Safety: Violent crime rate: 11.4 per 10,000 population; Property crime rate: 159.1 per 10,000 population (2004).
Transportation: Commute to work: 95.0% car, 0.3% public transportation, 1.3% walk, 3.4% work from home (2000); Travel time to work: 39.9% less than 15 minutes, 26.2% 15 to 30 minutes, 20.5% 30 to 45 minutes, 8.9% 45 to 60 minutes, 4.5% 60 minutes or more (2000)
Additional Information Contacts
Chardon Chamber of Commerce . . . . (440) 285-9050
    http://www.chardonchamber.com
Village of Chardon . . . . (440) 286-2600
    http://www.chardon.cc

CHESTERLAND (CDP). Covers a land area of 4.398 square miles and a water area of 0.005 square miles. Located at 41.52° N. Lat.; 81.33° W. Long. Elevation is 1,213 feet.
Population: 2,750 (1990); 2,646 (2000); 2,592 (2005); 2,575 (2010 projected); Race: 98.8% White, 0.4% Black, 0.6% Asian, 0.6% Hispanic of any race (2005); Density: 589.4 persons per square mile (2005); Average household size: 2.56 (2005); Median age: 45.4 (2005); Males per 100 females: 96.7 (2005); Marriage status: 21.1% never married, 62.7% now married, 6.2% widowed, 10.0% divorced (2000); Foreign born: 7.7% (2000); Ancestry (includes multiple ancestries): 23.7% German, 21.2% Italian, 13.3% English, 12.5% Irish, 6.8% Hungarian (2000).
Economy: Employment by occupation: 10.0% management, 21.4% professional, 14.2% services, 27.5% sales, 0.0% farming, 12.3% construction, 14.5% production (2000).
Income: Per capita income: $31,240 (2005); Median household income: $64,828 (2005); Average household income: $77,801 (2005); Percent of households with income of $100,000 or more: 23.3% (2005); Poverty rate: 3.2% (2000).
Education: Percent of population age 25 and over with: High school diploma (including GED) or higher: 85.3% (2005); Bachelor's degree or higher: 23.5% (2005); Master's degree or higher: 8.1% (2005).
School District(s)
West Geauga Local SD (KG-12)
    2003-04 Enrollment: 2,550 . . . . (440) 729-5900
Housing: Homeownership rate: 89.9% (2005); Median home value: $179,706 (2005); Median rent: $519 per month (2000); Median age of housing: 37 years (2000).
Transportation: Commute to work: 95.5% car, 0.0% public transportation, 0.0% walk, 3.8% work from home (2000); Travel time to work: 22.0% less than 15 minutes, 34.8% 15 to 30 minutes, 27.1% 30 to 45 minutes, 10.8% 45 to 60 minutes, 5.2% 60 minutes or more (2000)
Additional Information Contacts
Chesterland Chamber of Commerce . . . . (440) 729-7297
    http://www.ohio-usa.com/geauga/chester

HUNTSBURG (unincorporated postal area, zip code 44046). Covers a land area of 17.711 square miles and a water area of 0.597 square miles. Located at 41.54° N. Lat.; 81.08° W. Long. Elevation is 1,280 feet.

PROFILES OF OHIO / Geauga County 113

Population: 2,023 (2000); Race: 97.9% White, 1.9% Black, 0.0% Asian, 0.1% Hispanic of any race (2000); Density: 114.2 persons per square mile (2000); Age: 31.1% under 18, 11.7% over 64 (2000); Marriage status: 17.9% never married, 65.6% now married, 8.7% widowed, 7.7% divorced (2000); Foreign born: 0.6% (2000); Ancestry (includes multiple ancestries): 26.5% German, 19.0% Irish, 14.0% English, 7.4% Italian, 7.1% Polish (2000).
Economy: Employment by occupation: 6.4% management, 15.0% professional, 9.1% services, 30.2% sales, 1.9% farming, 19.8% construction, 17.6% production (2000).
Income: Per capita income: $22,630 (2000); Median household income: $58,810 (2000); Poverty rate: 3.9% (2000).
Education: Percent of population age 25 and over with: High school diploma (including GED) or higher: 84.9% (2000); Bachelor's degree or higher: 14.9% (2000).

School District(s)
Cardinal Local SD (PK-12)
    2003-04 Enrollment: 1,467 . . . . (440) 632-0261

Housing: Homeownership rate: 88.4% (2000); Median home value: $157,300 (2000); Median rent: $475 per month (2000); Median age of housing: 28 years (2000).
Transportation: Commute to work: 93.1% car, 0.0% public transportation, 1.4% walk, 4.4% work from home (2000); Travel time to work: 21.0% less than 15 minutes, 31.3% 15 to 30 minutes, 23.0% 30 to 45 minutes, 15.2% 45 to 60 minutes, 9.4% 60 minutes or more (2000)

MIDDLEFIELD (village). Covers a land area of 3.005 square miles and a water area of 0 square miles. Located at 41.46° N. Lat.; 81.07° W. Long. Elevation is 1,126 feet.
Population: 2,257 (1990); 2,233 (2000); 2,347 (2005); 2,470 (2010 projected); Race: 98.0% White, 0.7% Black, 0.5% Asian, 0.5% Hispanic of any race (2005); Density: 781.1 persons per square mile (2005); Average household size: 2.28 (2005); Median age: 38.7 (2005); Males per 100 females: 88.4 (2005); Marriage status: 23.1% never married, 51.4% now married, 13.6% widowed, 11.9% divorced (2000); Foreign born: 1.1% (2000); Ancestry (includes multiple ancestries): 27.7% German, 15.7% Irish, 13.5% English, 8.2% Italian, 7.8% United States or American (2000).
Economy: In agricultural area; rubber, plastic and metal products, lumber, food products. Employment by occupation: 11.2% management, 13.0% professional, 14.9% services, 28.0% sales, 0.2% farming, 7.8% construction, 25.0% production (2000).
Income: Per capita income: $22,081 (2005); Median household income: $40,616 (2005); Average household income: $49,217 (2005); Percent of households with income of $100,000 or more: 7.6% (2005); Poverty rate: 9.0% (2000).
Taxes: Total city taxes per capita: $165 (2004); City property taxes per capita: $165 (2004).
Education: Percent of population age 25 and over with: High school diploma (including GED) or higher: 77.2% (2005); Bachelor's degree or higher: 13.7% (2005); Master's degree or higher: 2.4% (2005).

School District(s)
Cardinal Local SD (PK-12)
    2003-04 Enrollment: 1,467 . . . . (440) 632-0261

Housing: Homeownership rate: 50.9% (2005); Median home value: $143,313 (2005); Median rent: $471 per month (2000); Median age of housing: 29 years (2000).
Safety: Violent crime rate: 12.5 per 10,000 population; Property crime rate: 195.8 per 10,000 population (2004).
Transportation: Commute to work: 93.4% car, 0.0% public transportation, 4.2% walk, 1.6% work from home (2000); Travel time to work: 47.2% less than 15 minutes, 22.1% 15 to 30 minutes, 13.3% 30 to 45 minutes, 12.9% 45 to 60 minutes, 4.4% 60 minutes or more (2000)

Additional Information Contacts
Geauga County Tourism Council. . . . . (800) 775-TOUR
    http://www.tourgeauga.com
Middlefield Chamber of Commerce . . . . (440) 632-5705
    http://www.middlefieldcc.com
Village of Middlefield . . . . (440) 632-5248
    http://www.middlefieldohio.com

MONTVILLE (unincorporated postal area, zip code 44064). Covers a land area of 20.168 square miles and a water area of 0.026 square miles. Located at 41.61° N. Lat.; 81.05° W. Long. Elevation is 1,200 feet.
Population: 1,659 (2000); Race: 96.6% White, 0.3% Black, 0.8% Asian, 0.0% Hispanic of any race (2000); Density: 82.3 persons per square mile (2000); Age: 25.6% under 18, 14.9% over 64 (2000); Marriage status: 15.8% never married, 71.1% now married, 9.0% widowed, 4.1% divorced (2000); Foreign born: 1.7% (2000); Ancestry (includes multiple ancestries): 24.4% German, 14.1% Polish, 13.9% English, 12.0% Irish, 7.3% Hungarian (2000).
Economy: Employment by occupation: 14.7% management, 14.4% professional, 12.5% services, 25.5% sales, 2.3% farming, 14.1% construction, 16.5% production (2000).
Income: Per capita income: $22,160 (2000); Median household income: $52,134 (2000); Poverty rate: 1.7% (2000).
Education: Percent of population age 25 and over with: High school diploma (including GED) or higher: 83.6% (2000); Bachelor's degree or higher: 14.0% (2000).
Housing: Homeownership rate: 92.1% (2000); Median home value: $131,100 (2000); Median rent: $347 per month (2000); Median age of housing: 32 years (2000).
Transportation: Commute to work: 93.8% car, 1.0% public transportation, 0.0% walk, 4.5% work from home (2000); Travel time to work: 16.8% less than 15 minutes, 35.2% 15 to 30 minutes, 24.0% 30 to 45 minutes, 11.5% 45 to 60 minutes, 12.4% 60 minutes or more (2000)

NEWBURY (unincorporated postal area, zip code 44065). Aka Newbury Center. Covers a land area of 19.431 square miles and a water area of 0.173 square miles. Located at 41.47° N. Lat.; 81.24° W. Long.
Population: 4,135 (2000); Race: 97.0% White, 0.2% Black, 1.7% Asian, 0.0% Hispanic of any race (2000); Density: 212.8 persons per square mile (2000); Age: 27.0% under 18, 10.1% over 64 (2000); Marriage status: 24.4% never married, 61.4% now married, 5.3% widowed, 8.9% divorced (2000); Foreign born: 3.2% (2000); Ancestry (includes multiple ancestries): 26.5% German, 17.9% Irish, 14.8% English, 14.4% Italian, 6.5% Polish (2000).
Economy: Employment by occupation: 13.4% management, 18.3% professional, 13.3% services, 27.3% sales, 1.6% farming, 10.3% construction, 15.8% production (2000).
Income: Per capita income: $24,822 (2000); Median household income: $58,583 (2000); Poverty rate: 5.6% (2000).
Education: Percent of population age 25 and over with: High school diploma (including GED) or higher: 87.9% (2000); Bachelor's degree or higher: 23.2% (2000).

School District(s)
Newbury Local School District (KG-12)
    2003-04 Enrollment: 781 . . . . (440) 564-5501

Housing: Homeownership rate: 83.9% (2000); Median home value: $160,900 (2000); Median rent: $538 per month (2000); Median age of housing: 38 years (2000).
Transportation: Commute to work: 96.3% car, 0.2% public transportation, 1.0% walk, 2.6% work from home (2000); Travel time to work: 28.3% less than 15 minutes, 25.1% 15 to 30 minutes, 27.3% 30 to 45 minutes, 17.2% 45 to 60 minutes, 2.0% 60 minutes or more (2000)

SOUTH RUSSELL (village). Covers a land area of 3.854 square miles and a water area of 0.030 square miles. Located at 41.43° N. Lat.; 81.34° W. Long. Elevation is 1,120 feet.
Population: 3,402 (1990); 4,022 (2000); 4,032 (2005); 4,074 (2010 projected); Race: 98.1% White, 0.3% Black, 1.2% Asian, 0.6% Hispanic of any race (2005); Density: 1,046.2 persons per square mile (2005); Average household size: 2.94 (2005); Median age: 41.1 (2005); Males per 100 females: 96.3 (2005); Marriage status: 15.9% never married, 74.3% now married, 4.9% widowed, 4.9% divorced (2000); Foreign born: 4.5% (2000); Ancestry (includes multiple ancestries): 30.2% German, 23.5% English, 22.8% Irish, 6.4% Polish, 5.8% Italian (2000).
Economy: Single-family building permits issued: 5 (2005); Multi-family building permits issued: 0 (2005); Employment by occupation: 31.6% management, 30.0% professional, 6.6% services, 25.0% sales, 0.3% farming, 4.0% construction, 2.5% production (2000).
Income: Per capita income: $44,702 (2005); Median household income: $102,037 (2005); Average household income: $131,368 (2005); Percent of households with income of $100,000 or more: 50.8% (2005); Poverty rate: 0.6% (2000).
Education: Percent of population age 25 and over with: High school diploma (including GED) or higher: 97.2% (2005); Bachelor's degree or higher: 65.5% (2005); Master's degree or higher: 27.4% (2005).
Housing: Homeownership rate: 97.7% (2005); Median home value: $323,956 (2005); Median rent: $907 per month (2000); Median age of housing: 26 years (2000).

Safety: Violent crime rate: 0.0 per 10,000 population; Property crime rate: 29.8 per 10,000 population (2004).
Transportation: Commute to work: 91.0% car, 2.0% public transportation, 0.6% walk, 6.4% work from home (2000); Travel time to work: 28.6% less than 15 minutes, 27.1% 15 to 30 minutes, 28.1% 30 to 45 minutes, 12.3% 45 to 60 minutes, 3.9% 60 minutes or more (2000)
Additional Information Contacts
Village of South Russell . . . . (440) 338-6700
http://www.southrussell.com

THOMPSON (unincorporated postal area, zip code 44086). Covers a land area of 26.245 square miles and a water area of 0.083 square miles. Located at 41.67° N. Lat.; 81.05° W. Long. Elevation is 1,273 feet.
Population: 2,310 (2000); Race: 97.5% White, 1.1% Black, 0.0% Asian, 0.5% Hispanic of any race (2000); Density: 88.0 persons per square mile (2000); Age: 25.7% under 18, 7.1% over 64 (2000); Marriage status: 26.4% never married, 61.2% now married, 2.5% widowed, 9.8% divorced (2000); Foreign born: 0.4% (2000); Ancestry (includes multiple ancestries): 36.4% German, 24.4% English, 14.3% Irish, 7.5% Italian, 6.7% Other groups (2000).
Economy: Employment by occupation: 9.4% management, 16.4% professional, 14.7% services, 24.2% sales, 0.4% farming, 15.8% construction, 19.1% production (2000).
Income: Per capita income: $21,324 (2000); Median household income: $51,076 (2000); Poverty rate: 3.3% (2000).
Education: Percent of population age 25 and over with: High school diploma (including GED) or higher: 88.3% (2000); Bachelor's degree or higher: 14.2% (2000).

School District(s)
Ledgemont Local SD (PK-12)
   2003-04 Enrollment: 656 . . . . (440) 298-3341
Housing: Homeownership rate: 90.2% (2000); Median home value: $138,800 (2000); Median rent: $425 per month (2000); Median age of housing: 27 years (2000).
Transportation: Commute to work: 91.0% car, 0.6% public transportation, 3.6% walk, 3.8% work from home (2000); Travel time to work: 11.2% less than 15 minutes, 30.9% 15 to 30 minutes, 34.9% 30 to 45 minutes, 14.2% 45 to 60 minutes, 8.7% 60 minutes or more (2000)

Greene County

Located in southwest central Ohio; crossed by the Little Miami and Mad Rivers. Covers a land area of 414.88 square miles, a water area of 1.34 square miles, and is located in the Eastern Time Zone. The county government was organized in 1803. County seat is Xenia.

Greene County is part of the Dayton, OH Metropolitan Statistical Area. The entire metro area includes: Greene County, OH; Miami County, OH; Montgomery County, OH; Preble County, OH

Weather Station: Xenia 6 SSE   Elevation: 967 feet

	Jan	Feb	Mar	Apr	May	Jun	Jul	Aug	Sep	Oct	Nov	Dec
High	36	41	52	63	73	80	84	82	76	65	52	41
Low	19	22	32	40	51	59	63	60	53	42	34	25
Precip	2.5	2.2	3.2	3.9	4.4	3.9	4.1	3.7	2.7	2.8	3.2	3.0
Snow	8.8	5.6	3.5	0.4	tr	0.0	0.0	0.0	0.0	0.2	0.9	3.3

High and Low temperatures in degrees Fahrenheit; Precipitation and Snow in inches

Population: 136,731 (1990); 147,886 (2000); 152,859 (2005); 158,031 (2010 projected); Race: 88.8% White, 6.0% Black, 2.5% Asian, 1.3% Hispanic of any race (2005); Density: 368.4 persons per square mile (2005); Average household size: 2.62 (2005); Median age: 36.1 (2005); Males per 100 females: 95.1 (2005).
Religion: Five largest groups: 9.0% Catholic Church, 3.8% Southern Baptist Convention, 2.5% The United Methodist Church, 2.4% Christian Churches and Churches of Christ, 2.3% Independent, Non-Charismatic Churches (2000).
Economy: Unemployment rate: 5.5% (2005); Total civilian labor force: 76,983 (2005); Leading industries: 21.4% retail trade; 16.2% professional (2004); Farms: 819 totaling 168,568 acres (2002); Companies that employ 500 or more persons: 3 (2004); Companies that employ 100 to 499 persons: 85 (2004); Companies that employ less than 100 persons: 2,902 (2004); Black-owned businesses: 181 (2002); Hispanic-owned businesses: n/a (2002); Women-owned businesses: 3,371 (2002); Retail sales per capita: $14,558 (2006). Single-family building permits issued: 1,043 (2005); Multi-family building permits issued: 324 (2005).
Income: Per capita income: $26,366 (2005); Median household income: $54,721 (2005); Average household income: $67,907 (2005); Percent of households with income of $100,000 or more: 19.1% (2005); Poverty rate: 8.2% (2003); Bankruptcy rate: 7.80% (2005).
Taxes: Total county taxes per capita: $266 (2004); County property taxes per capita: $129 (2004).
Education: Percent of population age 25 and over with: High school diploma (including GED) or higher: 88.1% (2005); Bachelor's degree or higher: 31.5% (2005); Master's degree or higher: 14.1% (2005).
Housing: Homeownership rate: 69.7% (2005); Median home value: $141,549 (2005); Median rent: $492 per month (2000); Median age of housing: 31 years (2000).
Health: Birth rate: 118.0 per 10,000 population (2004); Death rate: 80.9 per 10,000 population (2004); Age-adjusted cancer mortality rate: 205.9 deaths per 100,000 population (2002); Air Quality Index: 66.2% good, 32.5% moderate, 1.3% unhealthy for sensitive individuals, 0.0% unhealthy (percent of days in 2005); Number of physicians: 25.4 per 10,000 population (2004); Hospital beds: 12.1 per 10,000 population (2003); Hospital admissions: 514.4 per 10,000 population (2003).
Elections: 2004 Presidential election results: 61.0% Bush, 38.5% Kerry, 0.0% Nader, 0.3% Badnarik
National and State Parks: Beaver Creek State Wildlife Area; Dayton Aviation Heritage National Historical Park; Glen Thompson State Reserve; Huffman Prairie National Historic Landmark; John Bryan State Park; Little Miami State Forest Preserve; The Narrows State Scenic River Reserve; Williamson Mound State Memorial

Additional Information Contacts
Greene County Government . . . . (937) 562-5006
  http://www.co.greene.oh.us/
Beavercreek Chamber of Commerce . . . . (937) 426-2202
  http://www.beavercreekchamber.org
Bellbrook Sugarcreek Chmbr of Commerce . . . . (937) 848-4930
  http://www.bellbrooksugarcreekchamber.com
City of Beavercreek . . . . (937) 427-5510
  http://www.ci.beavercreek.oh.us
City of Bellbrook . . . . (937) 848-4666
  http://www.cityofbellbrook.org
City of Fairborn . . . . (937) 754-3016
  http://www.ci.fairborn.oh.us
City of Xenia . . . . (937) 376-7232
  http://www.ci.xenia.oh.us
Fairborn Chamber of Commerce . . . . (937) 878-3191
  http://www.fairborn.com
Greene County Convention & Visitors Bureau . . . . (937) 429-9100
  http://www.greenecountyohio.org
Village of Yellow Springs . . . . (937) 767-7202
  http://www.yso.com
Xenia Chamber of Commerce . . . . (937) 372-3591
  http://www.xacc.com
Yellow Springs Chamber of Commerce . . . . (937) 767-2686
  http://www.yellowspringsohio.org

Greene County Communities

BEAVERCREEK (city). Covers a land area of 26.392 square miles and a water area of 0 square miles. Located at 39.72° N. Lat.; 84.06° W. Long. Elevation is 850 feet.
History: First settled in the early 1800s; incorporated as a city in 1980.
Population: 33,946 (1990); 37,984 (2000); 39,417 (2005); 40,947 (2010 projected); Race: 92.0% White, 1.6% Black, 4.5% Asian, 1.2% Hispanic of any race (2005); Density: 1,493.5 persons per square mile (2005); Average household size: 2.63 (2005); Median age: 41.6 (2005); Males per 100 females: 97.9 (2005); Marriage status: 19.1% never married, 69.3% now married, 4.8% widowed, 6.8% divorced (2000); Foreign born: 4.7% (2000); Ancestry (includes multiple ancestries): 30.2% German, 14.4% Irish, 14.3% English, 10.3% United States or American, 8.8% Other groups (2000).
Economy: Unemployment rate: 4.5% (2005); Total civilian labor force: 20,493 (2005); Employment by occupation: 18.9% management, 32.3% professional, 8.9% services, 25.4% sales, 0.2% farming, 5.4% construction, 9.0% production (2000).
Income: Per capita income: $34,589 (2005); Median household income: $77,078 (2005); Average household income: $90,082 (2005); Percent of households with income of $100,000 or more: 32.4% (2005); Poverty rate: 2.4% (2000).

Education: Percent of population age 25 and over with: High school diploma (including GED) or higher: 92.7% (2005); Bachelor's degree or higher: 43.8% (2005); Master's degree or higher: 21.2% (2005).

School District(s)

Beavercreek City SD (PK-12)
    2003-04 Enrollment: 7,184 . . . . (937) 426-1522

Housing: Homeownership rate: 83.3% (2005); Median home value: $166,023 (2005); Median rent: $705 per month (2000); Median age of housing: 27 years (2000).
Safety: Violent crime rate: 11.7 per 10,000 population; Property crime rate: 365.6 per 10,000 population (2004).
Transportation: Commute to work: 95.9% car, 0.1% public transportation, 0.6% walk, 3.2% work from home (2000); Travel time to work: 32.1% less than 15 minutes, 54.2% 15 to 30 minutes, 9.5% 30 to 45 minutes, 1.7% 45 to 60 minutes, 2.5% 60 minutes or more (2000)

Additional Information Contacts
Beavercreek Chamber of Commerce . . . . (937) 426-2202
    http://www.beavercreekchamber.org
City of Beavercreek . . . . (937) 427-5510
    http://www.ci.beavercreek.oh.us
Greene County Convention & Visitors Bureau . . . . (937) 429-9100
    http://www.greenecountyohio.org

BELLBROOK (city). Covers a land area of 3.123 square miles and a water area of 0 square miles. Located at 39.63° N. Lat.; 84.08° W. Long. Elevation is 796 feet.
Population: 6,520 (1990); 7,009 (2000); 6,846 (2005); 6,694 (2010 projected); Race: 96.6% White, 0.9% Black, 1.2% Asian, 1.4% Hispanic of any race (2005); Density: 2,192.2 persons per square mile (2005); Average household size: 2.65 (2005); Median age: 37.8 (2005); Males per 100 females: 97.6 (2005); Marriage status: 20.8% never married, 68.0% now married, 4.3% widowed, 6.9% divorced (2000); Foreign born: 3.9% (2000); Ancestry (includes multiple ancestries): 31.9% German, 15.3% English, 12.4% Irish, 10.7% United States or American, 6.8% Other groups (2000).
Economy: Employment by occupation: 17.2% management, 28.1% professional, 9.2% services, 29.2% sales, 0.4% farming, 5.3% construction, 10.6% production (2000).
Income: Per capita income: $28,901 (2005); Median household income: $69,715 (2005); Average household income: $76,689 (2005); Percent of households with income of $100,000 or more: 24.8% (2005); Poverty rate: 2.3% (2000).
Education: Percent of population age 25 and over with: High school diploma (including GED) or higher: 93.7% (2005); Bachelor's degree or higher: 40.1% (2005); Master's degree or higher: 16.2% (2005).

School District(s)

Sugarcreek Local SD (PK-12)
    2003-04 Enrollment: 2,761 . . . . (937) 848-6251

Housing: Homeownership rate: 82.6% (2005); Median home value: $149,091 (2005); Median rent: $663 per month (2000); Median age of housing: 32 years (2000).
Safety: Violent crime rate: 1.4 per 10,000 population; Property crime rate: 150.4 per 10,000 population (2004).
Transportation: Commute to work: 95.5% car, 0.2% public transportation, 0.6% walk, 3.2% work from home (2000); Travel time to work: 22.0% less than 15 minutes, 55.3% 15 to 30 minutes, 15.5% 30 to 45 minutes, 2.8% 45 to 60 minutes, 4.6% 60 minutes or more (2000)

Additional Information Contacts
Bellbrook Sugarcreek Chmbr of Commerce . . . . (937) 848-4930
    http://www.bellbrooksugarcreekchamber.com
City of Bellbrook . . . . (937) 848-4666
    http://www.cityofbellbrook.org

BOWERSVILLE (village). Covers a land area of 0.138 square miles and a water area of 0 square miles. Located at 39.58° N. Lat.; 83.72° W. Long. Elevation is 1,090 feet.
Population: 225 (1990); 290 (2000); 355 (2005); 416 (2010 projected); Race: 98.0% White, 0.0% Black, 0.3% Asian, 0.6% Hispanic of any race (2005); Density: 2,572.3 persons per square mile (2005); Average household size: 2.57 (2005); Median age: 39.1 (2005); Males per 100 females: 107.6 (2005); Marriage status: 20.6% never married, 58.3% now married, 6.1% widowed, 14.9% divorced (2000); Foreign born: 0.0% (2000); Ancestry (includes multiple ancestries): 16.7% Other groups, 14.4% United States or American, 11.9% Irish, 10.6% German, 5.1% English (2000).

Economy: In agricultural area. Employment by occupation: 6.1% management, 15.2% professional, 15.2% services, 26.5% sales, 3.0% farming, 6.1% construction, 28.0% production (2000).
Income: Per capita income: $18,549 (2005); Median household income: $42,059 (2005); Average household income: $47,717 (2005); Percent of households with income of $100,000 or more: 5.8% (2005); Poverty rate: 2.2% (2000).
Education: Percent of population age 25 and over with: High school diploma (including GED) or higher: 66.7% (2005); Bachelor's degree or higher: 6.1% (2005); Master's degree or higher: 0.0% (2005).
Housing: Homeownership rate: 82.6% (2005); Median home value: $78,261 (2005); Median rent: $341 per month (2000); Median age of housing: 60+ years (2000).
Transportation: Commute to work: 95.9% car, 0.0% public transportation, 4.1% walk, 0.0% work from home (2000); Travel time to work: 31.7% less than 15 minutes, 29.3% 15 to 30 minutes, 15.4% 30 to 45 minutes, 22.0% 45 to 60 minutes, 1.6% 60 minutes or more (2000)

CEDARVILLE (village). Covers a land area of 1.065 square miles and a water area of 0.012 square miles. Located at 39.74° N. Lat.; 83.80° W. Long. Elevation is 1,055 feet.
History: Cedarville was settled in 1805 and developed around Cedarville College, chartered in 1887 and opened in 1894 under the Reformed Presbyterian Church.
Population: 3,216 (1990); 3,828 (2000); 4,434 (2005); 4,817 (2010 projected); Race: 94.9% White, 1.4% Black, 1.1% Asian, 1.1% Hispanic of any race (2005); Density: 4,163.7 persons per square mile (2005); Average household size: 5.25 (2005); Median age: 21.2 (2005); Males per 100 females: 84.2 (2005); Marriage status: 62.6% never married, 33.2% now married, 2.3% widowed, 1.9% divorced (2000); Foreign born: 0.9% (2000); Ancestry (includes multiple ancestries): 30.2% German, 17.7% English, 10.1% Other groups, 10.0% Irish, 5.6% United States or American (2000).
Economy: Employment by occupation: 5.2% management, 22.5% professional, 32.6% services, 28.9% sales, 0.4% farming, 3.9% construction, 6.5% production (2000).
Income: Per capita income: $11,451 (2005); Median household income: $41,686 (2005); Average household income: $49,369 (2005); Percent of households with income of $100,000 or more: 8.6% (2005); Poverty rate: 13.8% (2000).
Education: Percent of population age 25 and over with: High school diploma (including GED) or higher: 89.6% (2005); Bachelor's degree or higher: 38.8% (2005); Master's degree or higher: 15.6% (2005).

School District(s)

Cedar Cliff Local SD (PK-12)
    2003-04 Enrollment: 663 . . . . (937) 766-6000

Four-year College(s)

Cedarville University (Private, Not-for-profit, Baptist)
    Fall 2004 Enrollment: 3,093 . . . . (937) 766-2211
    2005-06 Tuition: In-state $17,120; Out-of-state $17,120

Housing: Homeownership rate: 54.4% (2005); Median home value: $125,939 (2005); Median rent: $365 per month (2000); Median age of housing: 38 years (2000).
Transportation: Commute to work: 56.2% car, 0.2% public transportation, 38.6% walk, 3.9% work from home (2000); Travel time to work: 60.7% less than 15 minutes, 21.8% 15 to 30 minutes, 12.5% 30 to 45 minutes, 2.0% 45 to 60 minutes, 2.9% 60 minutes or more (2000)

CLIFTON (village). Covers a land area of 0.177 square miles and a water area of 0.001 square miles. Located at 39.79° N. Lat.; 83.82° W. Long.
History: Clifton was settled on the Little Miami River where water-power was plentiful. Isaac Kaufman Funk, who formed a partnership with college classmate Adam Willis Wagnalls, was born in Clifton in 1839. Funk was the editor of "A Standard Dictionary of the English Language."
Population: 165 (1990); 179 (2000); 202 (2005); 226 (2010 projected); Race: 87.1% White, 1.5% Black, 0.0% Asian, 0.0% Hispanic of any race (2005); Density: 1,141.9 persons per square mile (2005); Average household size: 2.49 (2005); Median age: 42.8 (2005); Males per 100 females: 102.0 (2005); Marriage status: 27.1% never married, 53.5% now married, 9.7% widowed, 9.7% divorced (2000); Foreign born: 0.0% (2000); Ancestry (includes multiple ancestries): 21.5% English, 18.3% United States or American, 14.5% German, 8.1% Other groups, 5.9% Scottish (2000).

Economy: Employment by occupation: 6.3% management, 32.3% professional, 28.1% services, 12.5% sales, 0.0% farming, 8.3% construction, 12.5% production (2000).
Income: Per capita income: $25,297 (2005); Median household income: $47,375 (2005); Average household income: $63,086 (2005); Percent of households with income of $100,000 or more: 17.3% (2005); Poverty rate: 5.4% (2000).
Education: Percent of population age 25 and over with: High school diploma (including GED) or higher: 82.7% (2005); Bachelor's degree or higher: 18.0% (2005); Master's degree or higher: 7.9% (2005).
Housing: Homeownership rate: 71.6% (2005); Median home value: $94,545 (2005); Median rent: $481 per month (2000); Median age of housing: 60+ years (2000).
Transportation: Commute to work: 96.8% car, 0.0% public transportation, 0.0% walk, 0.0% work from home (2000); Travel time to work: 22.6% less than 15 minutes, 34.4% 15 to 30 minutes, 20.4% 30 to 45 minutes, 4.3% 45 to 60 minutes, 18.3% 60 minutes or more (2000)

FAIRBORN (city). Aka Fairfield. Covers a land area of 13.064 square miles and a water area of 0 square miles. Located at 39.80° N. Lat.; 84.02° W. Long. Elevation is 845 feet.
History: Air Force Museum nearby. Settled 1799, incorporated 1950 with the merging of Osborn and Fairborn.
Population: 31,928 (1990); 32,052 (2000); 32,310 (2005); 32,806 (2010 projected); Race: 85.8% White, 6.6% Black, 4.0% Asian, 1.8% Hispanic of any race (2005); Density: 2,473.2 persons per square mile (2005); Average household size: 2.30 (2005); Median age: 32.9 (2005); Males per 100 females: 95.2 (2005); Marriage status: 33.1% never married, 48.8% now married, 5.7% widowed, 12.4% divorced (2000); Foreign born: 4.6% (2000); Ancestry (includes multiple ancestries): 21.1% German, 17.6% Other groups, 12.1% Irish, 10.4% United States or American, 10.2% English (2000).
Economy: Major employers are Wright State University in nearby Dayton and the huge Wright-Patterson Air Force Base. Cement production. Unemployment rate: 6.2% (2005); Total civilian labor force: 16,478 (2005); Single-family building permits issued: 96 (2005); Multi-family building permits issued: 60 (2005); Employment by occupation: 10.7% management, 20.1% professional, 18.9% services, 27.4% sales, 0.1% farming, 9.0% construction, 13.8% production (2000).
Income: Per capita income: $21,122 (2005); Median household income: $39,896 (2005); Average household income: $48,137 (2005); Percent of households with income of $100,000 or more: 8.4% (2005); Poverty rate: 14.1% (2000).
Taxes: Total city taxes per capita: $294 (2004); City property taxes per capita: $88 (2004).
Education: Percent of population age 25 and over with: High school diploma (including GED) or higher: 84.2% (2005); Bachelor's degree or higher: 22.8% (2005); Master's degree or higher: 9.2% (2005).

School District(s)
Fairborn City Schools (PK-12)
    2003-04 Enrollment: 5,427 . . . . (937) 878-3961
Fairborn Digital Academy (01-11)
    2003-04 Enrollment: 38 . . . . (937) 878-3961

Two-year College(s)
Creative Images-A Certified Matrix Design Academy (Private, For-profit)
    Fall 2004 Enrollment: 149 . . . . (937) 878-9555
Housing: Homeownership rate: 51.3% (2005); Median home value: $105,180 (2005); Median rent: $487 per month (2000); Median age of housing: 34 years (2000).
Safety: Violent crime rate: 24.0 per 10,000 population; Property crime rate: 481.9 per 10,000 population (2004).
Transportation: Commute to work: 94.5% car, 0.3% public transportation, 3.4% walk, 1.1% work from home (2000); Travel time to work: 40.3% less than 15 minutes, 42.5% 15 to 30 minutes, 12.3% 30 to 45 minutes, 1.9% 45 to 60 minutes, 2.9% 60 minutes or more (2000)
Additional Information Contacts
City of Fairborn . . . . (937) 754-3016
    http://www.ci.fairborn.oh.us
Fairborn Chamber of Commerce . . . . (937) 878-3191
    http://www.fairborn.com

JAMESTOWN (village). Covers a land area of 1.214 square miles and a water area of <.001 square miles. Located at 39.65° N. Lat.; 83.73° W. Long. Elevation is 1,057 feet.
History: Jamestown was settled near the old route of Chiuxso's Trail, a wagon road through the forest connecting Ripley on the Ohio River with the Mad River Valley. The town was rebuilt after a cyclone destroyed the buildings in 1844.
Population: 1,947 (1990); 1,917 (2000); 1,958 (2005); 2,010 (2010 projected); Race: 95.5% White, 3.0% Black, 0.6% Asian, 0.5% Hispanic of any race (2005); Density: 1,613.1 persons per square mile (2005); Average household size: 2.52 (2005); Median age: 33.5 (2005); Males per 100 females: 93.1 (2005); Marriage status: 21.6% never married, 55.1% now married, 8.0% widowed, 15.4% divorced (2000); Foreign born: 0.5% (2000); Ancestry (includes multiple ancestries): 19.2% United States or American, 17.4% German, 13.3% Irish, 11.1% Other groups, 8.2% English (2000).
Economy: Employment by occupation: 5.6% management, 12.9% professional, 17.4% services, 21.6% sales, 0.6% farming, 11.5% construction, 30.3% production (2000).
Income: Per capita income: $19,943 (2005); Median household income: $44,000 (2005); Average household income: $50,190 (2005); Percent of households with income of $100,000 or more: 7.8% (2005); Poverty rate: 11.2% (2000).
Education: Percent of population age 25 and over with: High school diploma (including GED) or higher: 81.4% (2005); Bachelor's degree or higher: 9.5% (2005); Master's degree or higher: 3.0% (2005).

School District(s)
Greeneview Local SD (PK-12)
    2003-04 Enrollment: 1,645 . . . . (937) 675-2728
Housing: Homeownership rate: 66.6% (2005); Median home value: $98,889 (2005); Median rent: $414 per month (2000); Median age of housing: 47 years (2000).
Transportation: Commute to work: 93.4% car, 0.9% public transportation, 2.6% walk, 2.5% work from home (2000); Travel time to work: 23.6% less than 15 minutes, 31.5% 15 to 30 minutes, 24.5% 30 to 45 minutes, 12.6% 45 to 60 minutes, 7.9% 60 minutes or more (2000)

SHAWNEE HILLS (CDP). Covers a land area of 2.661 square miles and a water area of 0.239 square miles. Located at 39.65° N. Lat.; 83.77° W. Long. Elevation is 1,050 feet.
Population: 2,199 (1990); 2,355 (2000); 2,535 (2005); 2,721 (2010 projected); Race: 96.6% White, 1.1% Black, 0.5% Asian, 0.7% Hispanic of any race (2005); Density: 952.6 persons per square mile (2005); Average household size: 2.81 (2005); Median age: 36.9 (2005); Males per 100 females: 99.9 (2005); Marriage status: 18.4% never married, 68.7% now married, 2.4% widowed, 10.5% divorced (2000); Foreign born: 1.9% (2000); Ancestry (includes multiple ancestries): 20.4% German, 16.3% Other groups, 15.5% English, 11.6% Irish, 7.2% United States or American (2000).
Economy: Employment by occupation: 13.1% management, 15.5% professional, 12.0% services, 31.2% sales, 0.3% farming, 8.2% construction, 19.7% production (2000).
Income: Per capita income: $24,836 (2005); Median household income: $62,205 (2005); Average household income: $69,800 (2005); Percent of households with income of $100,000 or more: 16.2% (2005); Poverty rate: 3.2% (2000).
Education: Percent of population age 25 and over with: High school diploma (including GED) or higher: 88.6% (2005); Bachelor's degree or higher: 15.6% (2005); Master's degree or higher: 3.4% (2005).
Housing: Homeownership rate: 95.0% (2005); Median home value: $129,402 (2005); Median rent: $457 per month (2000); Median age of housing: 25 years (2000).
Transportation: Commute to work: 97.7% car, 0.6% public transportation, 0.0% walk, 0.9% work from home (2000); Travel time to work: 12.8% less than 15 minutes, 42.5% 15 to 30 minutes, 33.1% 30 to 45 minutes, 6.8% 45 to 60 minutes, 4.7% 60 minutes or more (2000)

SPRING VALLEY (village). Covers a land area of 0.278 square miles and a water area of 0 square miles. Located at 39.60° N. Lat.; 84.00° W. Long. Elevation is 760 feet.
History: Spring Valley was named for the nearby springs, whose water was bottled and shipped from the town. Spring Valley developed as a farming community, with tobacco grown here as early as 1825.
Population: 507 (1990); 510 (2000); 565 (2005); 618 (2010 projected); Race: 95.2% White, 2.3% Black, 0.2% Asian, 0.0% Hispanic of any race (2005); Density: 2,030.5 persons per square mile (2005); Average household size: 2.56 (2005); Median age: 39.3 (2005); Males per 100 females: 103.2 (2005); Marriage status: 25.0% never married, 53.5% now

married, 6.7% widowed, 14.8% divorced (2000); Foreign born: 0.4% (2000); Ancestry (includes multiple ancestries): 30.5% German, 15.9% Irish, 13.7% United States or American, 12.7% English, 6.8% Other groups (2000).
Economy: Employment by occupation: 11.0% management, 20.3% professional, 14.1% services, 26.2% sales, 1.4% farming, 13.1% construction, 13.8% production (2000).
Income: Per capita income: $23,774 (2005); Median household income: $48,500 (2005); Average household income: $60,781 (2005); Percent of households with income of $100,000 or more: 10.9% (2005); Poverty rate: 2.8% (2000).
Education: Percent of population age 25 and over with: High school diploma (including GED) or higher: 91.5% (2005); Bachelor's degree or higher: 16.5% (2005); Master's degree or higher: 6.2% (2005).
Housing: Homeownership rate: 83.7% (2005); Median home value: $101,087 (2005); Median rent: $375 per month (2000); Median age of housing: 60+ years (2000).
Transportation: Commute to work: 93.8% car, 0.0% public transportation, 1.4% walk, 2.8% work from home (2000); Travel time to work: 15.7% less than 15 minutes, 46.4% 15 to 30 minutes, 28.2% 30 to 45 minutes, 3.2% 45 to 60 minutes, 6.4% 60 minutes or more (2000)

WILBERFORCE (CDP). Covers a land area of 3.092 square miles and a water area of 0.052 square miles. Located at 39.71° N. Lat.; 83.88° W. Long. Elevation is 1,000 feet.
History: Wilberforce was named for William Wilberforce, an English reformer. The town grew around Wilberforce University, opened in 1856 by the Methodist Episcopal Church and purchased in 1863 by the African M.E. Church.
Population: 2,639 (1990); 1,579 (2000); 1,636 (2005); 1,672 (2010 projected); Race: 18.8% White, 74.9% Black, 0.1% Asian, 1.3% Hispanic of any race (2005); Density: 529.1 persons per square mile (2005); Average household size: 8.35 (2005); Median age: 21.0 (2005); Males per 100 females: 94.1 (2005); Marriage status: 72.0% never married, 23.1% now married, 3.0% widowed, 2.0% divorced (2000); Foreign born: 5.1% (2000); Ancestry (includes multiple ancestries): 76.6% Other groups, 4.0% African, 2.3% German, 2.0% United States or American, 1.5% Nigerian (2000).
Economy: Employment by occupation: 7.2% management, 32.5% professional, 18.6% services, 36.9% sales, 2.8% farming, 0.0% construction, 2.1% production (2000).
Income: Per capita income: $10,264 (2005); Median household income: $34,444 (2005); Average household income: $52,793 (2005); Percent of households with income of $100,000 or more: 11.2% (2005); Poverty rate: 6.5% (2000).
Education: Percent of population age 25 and over with: High school diploma (including GED) or higher: 85.0% (2005); Bachelor's degree or higher: 56.2% (2005); Master's degree or higher: 21.1% (2005).
Four-year College(s)
Central State University (Public, Historically black)
    Fall 2004 Enrollment: 1,820 . . . . (937) 376-6011
    2005-06 Tuition: In-state $4,994; Out-of-state $10,814
Payne Theological Seminary (Private, Not-for-profit, African Methodist Episcopal)
    Fall 2004 Enrollment: 51 . . . . (937) 376-2946
Wilberforce University (Private, Not-for-profit, Historically black, African Methodist Episcopal)
    Fall 2004 Enrollment: 998 . . . . (937) 376-2911
    2005-06 Tuition: In-state $10,780; Out-of-state $10,780
Housing: Homeownership rate: 84.2% (2005); Median home value: $165,417 (2005); Median rent: $725 per month (2000); Median age of housing: 33 years (2000).
Transportation: Commute to work: 62.1% car, 0.0% public transportation, 28.6% walk, 7.8% work from home (2000); Travel time to work: 65.4% less than 15 minutes, 19.4% 15 to 30 minutes, 13.2% 30 to 45 minutes, 2.0% 45 to 60 minutes, 0.0% 60 minutes or more (2000)

XENIA (city). Covers a land area of 12.147 square miles and a water area of 0 square miles. Located at 39.68° N. Lat.; 83.93° W. Long. Elevation is 938 feet.
History: Xenia developed around an agricultural area. An early industry was the production of rope and twine.
Population: 25,481 (1990); 24,164 (2000); 23,946 (2005); 23,926 (2010 projected); Race: 84.1% White, 12.3% Black, 0.3% Asian, 1.3% Hispanic of any race (2005); Density: 1,971.3 persons per square mile (2005); Average household size: 2.52 (2005); Median age: 35.1 (2005); Males per 100 females: 91.2 (2005); Marriage status: 23.5% never married, 56.8% now married, 7.0% widowed, 12.7% divorced (2000); Foreign born: 1.9% (2000); Ancestry (includes multiple ancestries): 20.1% Other groups, 16.8% German, 14.3% United States or American, 10.4% Irish, 8.8% English (2000).
Economy: Unemployment rate: 6.9% (2005); Total civilian labor force: 11,375 (2005); Employment by occupation: 9.0% management, 16.3% professional, 17.9% services, 26.0% sales, 0.1% farming, 10.3% construction, 20.5% production (2000).
Income: Per capita income: $18,858 (2005); Median household income: $40,304 (2005); Average household income: $46,114 (2005); Percent of households with income of $100,000 or more: 6.0% (2005); Poverty rate: 11.6% (2000).
Taxes: Total city taxes per capita: $412 (2004); City property taxes per capita: $67 (2004).
Education: Percent of population age 25 and over with: High school diploma (including GED) or higher: 81.4% (2005); Bachelor's degree or higher: 15.2% (2005); Master's degree or higher: 5.5% (2005).
School District(s)
Greene County Joint Vocational SD (07-12)
    2003-04 Enrollment: n/a . . . . (937) 372-6941
Summit Academy-Xenia (02-08)
    2003-04 Enrollment: 36 . . . . (937) 372-5210
Xenia Community City SD (PK-12)
    2003-04 Enrollment: 5,202 . . . . (937) 376-2961
Two-year College(s)
Greene County Career Center (Public)
    Fall 2004 Enrollment: 74 . . . . (937) 372-6941
Housing: Homeownership rate: 66.7% (2005); Median home value: $94,555 (2005); Median rent: $398 per month (2000); Median age of housing: 35 years (2000).
Hospitals: Greene Memorial Hospital (231 beds)
Safety: Violent crime rate: 12.6 per 10,000 population; Property crime rate: 480.5 per 10,000 population (2004).
Newspapers: Fairborn Daily Herald (Circulation 4,350); The Xenia Daily Gazette (Circulation 9,921)
Transportation: Commute to work: 95.3% car, 0.5% public transportation, 2.2% walk, 1.5% work from home (2000); Travel time to work: 37.0% less than 15 minutes, 32.9% 15 to 30 minutes, 22.1% 30 to 45 minutes, 3.8% 45 to 60 minutes, 4.2% 60 minutes or more (2000)
Additional Information Contacts
City of Xenia . . . . (937) 376-7232
   http://www.ci.xenia.oh.us
Xenia Chamber of Commerce . . . . (937) 372-3591
   http://www.xacc.com

YELLOW SPRINGS (village). Covers a land area of 1.898 square miles and a water area of 0 square miles. Located at 39.80° N. Lat.; 83.89° W. Long. Elevation is 1,020 feet.
History: Yellow Springs was founded in 1804 and named for the yellowed water of the nearby iron springs. Antioch College was founded here in 1853 with Horace Mann as its first president.
Population: 4,008 (1990); 3,761 (2000); 3,709 (2005); 3,696 (2010 projected); Race: 79.0% White, 11.6% Black, 1.6% Asian, 2.2% Hispanic of any race (2005); Density: 1,953.9 persons per square mile (2005); Average household size: 2.31 (2005); Median age: 44.5 (2005); Males per 100 females: 79.2 (2005); Marriage status: 24.7% never married, 54.1% now married, 6.7% widowed, 14.6% divorced (2000); Foreign born: 3.9% (2000); Ancestry (includes multiple ancestries): 23.2% Other groups, 21.7% German, 13.7% English, 11.8% Irish, 4.2% Scottish (2000).
Economy: Employment by occupation: 16.1% management, 44.2% professional, 12.5% services, 14.6% sales, 0.6% farming, 3.8% construction, 8.3% production (2000).
Income: Per capita income: $31,242 (2005); Median household income: $56,721 (2005); Average household income: $70,756 (2005); Percent of households with income of $100,000 or more: 21.9% (2005); Poverty rate: 7.0% (2000).
Education: Percent of population age 25 and over with: High school diploma (including GED) or higher: 95.6% (2005); Bachelor's degree or higher: 58.7% (2005); Master's degree or higher: 31.8% (2005).
School District(s)
Yellow Springs Ex Vill SD (PK-12)
    2003-04 Enrollment: 705 . . . . (937) 767-7381

Four-year College(s)
Antioch College (Private, Not-for-profit)
    Fall 2004 Enrollment: 496 . . . . (937) 769-1000
    2005-06 Tuition: In-state $25,230; Out-of-state $25,230
Antioch University McGregor (Private, Not-for-profit)
    Fall 2004 Enrollment: 737 . . . . (937) 769-1800
Antioch University PhD Program in Leadership and Change (Private, Not-for-profit)
    Fall 2004 Enrollment: 85 . . . . (937) 769-1360

Housing: Homeownership rate: 62.7% (2005); Median home value: $179,341 (2005); Median rent: $459 per month (2000); Median age of housing: 43 years (2000).
Newspapers: Yellow Springs News (General - Circulation 1,850)
Transportation: Commute to work: 79.2% car, 0.3% public transportation, 12.5% walk, 5.6% work from home (2000); Travel time to work: 36.6% less than 15 minutes, 36.8% 15 to 30 minutes, 16.8% 30 to 45 minutes, 1.1% 45 to 60 minutes, 8.7% 60 minutes or more (2000)
Additional Information Contacts
Village of Yellow Springs . . . . (937) 767-7202
    http://www.yso.com
Yellow Springs Chamber of Commerce . . . . (937) 767-2686
    http://www.yellowspringsohio.org

Guernsey County

Located in eastern Ohio; drained by Wills Creek; includes Salt Fork Lake. Covers a land area of 521.90 square miles, a water area of 6.39 square miles, and is located in the Eastern Time Zone. The county government was organized in 1810. County seat is Cambridge.

Guernsey County is part of the Cambridge, OH Micropolitan Statistical Area. The entire metro area includes: Guernsey County, OH

Weather Station: Cambridge   Elevation: 797 feet

	Jan	Feb	Mar	Apr	May	Jun	Jul	Aug	Sep	Oct	Nov	Dec
High	37	42	53	65	74	82	85	84	77	66	53	42
Low	20	22	31	39	49	58	62	61	54	42	34	26
Precip	2.7	2.3	3.0	3.4	4.0	4.1	4.3	3.9	3.0	2.6	3.3	2.8
Snow	7.4	4.1	2.9	0.6	tr	0.0	0.0	0.0	0.0	tr	0.8	2.6

High and Low temperatures in degrees Fahrenheit; Precipitation and Snow in inches

Population: 39,024 (1990); 40,792 (2000); 41,672 (2005); 42,581 (2010 projected); Race: 96.2% White, 1.5% Black, 0.3% Asian, 0.9% Hispanic of any race (2005); Density: 79.8 persons per square mile (2005); Average household size: 2.52 (2005); Median age: 38.2 (2005); Males per 100 females: 94.8 (2005).
Religion: Five largest groups: 10.0% The United Methodist Church, 4.5% Catholic Church, 3.1% Presbyterian Church (U.S.A.), 2.1% Churches of Christ, 2.0% American Baptist Churches in the USA (2000).
Economy: Unemployment rate: 7.2% (2005); Total civilian labor force: 20,099 (2005); Leading industries: 24.4% manufacturing; 19.6% health care and social assistance; 15.7% retail trade (2004); Farms: 910 totaling 137,443 acres (2002); Companies that employ 500 or more persons: 2 (2004); Companies that employ 100 to 499 persons: 16 (2004); Companies that employ less than 100 persons: 940 (2004); Black-owned businesses: n/a (2002); Hispanic-owned businesses: n/a (2002); Women-owned businesses: 982 (2002); Retail sales per capita: $11,762 (2006); Single-family building permits issued: 72 (2005); Multi-family building permits issued: 2 (2005).
Income: Per capita income: $17,609 (2005); Median household income: $34,457 (2005); Average household income: $44,001 (2005); Percent of households with income of $100,000 or more: 6.0% (2005); Poverty rate: 14.0% (2003); Bankruptcy rate: 10.09% (2005).
Education: Percent of population age 25 and over with: High school diploma (including GED) or higher: 78.6% (2005); Bachelor's degree or higher: 10.1% (2005); Master's degree or higher: 4.0% (2005).
Housing: Homeownership rate: 73.7% (2005); Median home value: $79,777 (2005); Median rent: $303 per month (2000); Median age of housing: 35 years (2000).
Health: Birth rate: 125.2 per 10,000 population (2004); Death rate: 108.4 per 10,000 population (2004); Age-adjusted cancer mortality rate: 238.9 deaths per 100,000 population (2002); Number of physicians: 15.5 per 10,000 population (2004); Hospital beds: 88.1 per 10,000 population (2003); Hospital admissions: 1,574.5 per 10,000 population (2003).
Elections: 2004 Presidential election results: 55.8% Bush, 43.5% Kerry, 0.0% Nader, 0.3% Badnarik

National and State Parks: Salt Fork State Park and Wildlife Area
Additional Information Contacts
Guernsey County Government . . . . (740) 432-9200
    http://www.guernseycounty.org/
Cambridge Area Chamber of Commerce . . . . (740) 439-6688
    http://www.cambridgeohiochamber.com
City of Cambridge . . . . (740) 439-1050
    http://www.cambridgeoh.org
Guernsey County Visitors & Convention Bureau . . . . (740) 432-2022
    http://www.visitguernseycounty.com

Guernsey County Communities

BYESVILLE (village). Covers a land area of 0.974 square miles and a water area of 0 square miles. Located at 39.96° N. Lat.; 81.54° W. Long. Elevation is 820 feet.
History: Byesville was named for Jonathan Bye, who built a flour mill here in the early 1800's. Later, the town's economy depended on coal mining.
Population: 2,547 (1990); 2,574 (2000); 2,464 (2005); 2,414 (2010 projected); Race: 98.0% White, 0.3% Black, 0.3% Asian, 0.8% Hispanic of any race (2005); Density: 2,529.7 persons per square mile (2005); Average household size: 2.38 (2005); Median age: 35.5 (2005); Males per 100 females: 87.4 (2005); Marriage status: 22.0% never married, 57.6% now married, 7.8% widowed, 12.6% divorced (2000); Foreign born: 0.7% (2000); Ancestry (includes multiple ancestries): 18.3% German, 16.4% Irish, 10.6% English, 10.2% United States or American, 5.9% Other groups (2000).
Economy: Employment by occupation: 4.8% management, 10.4% professional, 16.4% services, 27.5% sales, 0.0% farming, 10.5% construction, 30.5% production (2000).
Income: Per capita income: $14,773 (2005); Median household income: $30,833 (2005); Average household income: $35,101 (2005); Percent of households with income of $100,000 or more: 2.3% (2005); Poverty rate: 15.2% (2000).
Education: Percent of population age 25 and over with: High school diploma (including GED) or higher: 82.6% (2005); Bachelor's degree or higher: 4.5% (2005); Master's degree or higher: 1.9% (2005).

School District(s)
Rolling Hills Local SD (PK-12)
    2003-04 Enrollment: 2,226 . . . . (740) 432-5370

Housing: Homeownership rate: 64.3% (2005); Median home value: $66,994 (2005); Median rent: $294 per month (2000); Median age of housing: 48 years (2000).
Transportation: Commute to work: 95.2% car, 0.4% public transportation, 2.8% walk, 0.0% work from home (2000); Travel time to work: 52.2% less than 15 minutes, 31.1% 15 to 30 minutes, 9.4% 30 to 45 minutes, 1.6% 45 to 60 minutes, 5.7% 60 minutes or more (2000)

CAMBRIDGE (city). Covers a land area of 5.606 square miles and a water area of 0.004 square miles. Located at 40.02° N. Lat.; 81.58° W. Long. Elevation is 806 feet.
History: Cambridge was laid out in 1806 by Jacob Gomber and Zacheus Beatty, and named for Cambridge, Maryland, the former home of many of the first settlers. Oil and gas discovered in the area in the 1880's led to industrial development, including a glass factory founded in 1901.
Population: 11,871 (1990); 11,520 (2000); 11,555 (2005); 11,681 (2010 projected); Race: 92.8% White, 3.8% Black, 0.4% Asian, 1.4% Hispanic of any race (2005); Density: 2,061.3 persons per square mile (2005); Average household size: 2.33 (2005); Median age: 36.6 (2005); Males per 100 females: 87.1 (2005); Marriage status: 26.6% never married, 48.5% now married, 10.3% widowed, 14.5% divorced (2000); Foreign born: 1.8% (2000); Ancestry (includes multiple ancestries): 17.0% German, 14.4% Irish, 12.0% English, 10.8% Other groups, 9.1% United States or American (2000).
Economy: Employment by occupation: 8.7% management, 12.7% professional, 22.7% services, 20.6% sales, 0.3% farming, 9.6% construction, 25.5% production (2000).
Income: Per capita income: $16,096 (2005); Median household income: $27,510 (2005); Average household income: $37,109 (2005); Percent of households with income of $100,000 or more: 4.7% (2005); Poverty rate: 21.2% (2000).
Education: Percent of population age 25 and over with: High school diploma (including GED) or higher: 75.2% (2005); Bachelor's degree or higher: 12.5% (2005); Master's degree or higher: 4.8% (2005).

School District(s)
Cambridge City SD (PK-12)
  2003-04 Enrollment: 2,739 .... (740) 439-5021
East Muskingum Local SD (PK-12)
  2003-04 Enrollment: 2,121 .... (740) 826-7655

Two-year College(s)
Valley Beauty School (Private, For-profit)
  Fall 2004 Enrollment: 33 .... (740) 439-5559

Housing: Homeownership rate: 53.5% (2005); Median home value: $66,897 (2005); Median rent: $301 per month (2000); Median age of housing: 53 years (2000).
Hospitals: Appalachian Psychiatric Health Care System (132 beds); Southeastern Ohio Regional Medical Center (209 beds)
Newspapers: New Concord Leader (General - Circulation 1,250); The Daily Jeffersonian (Circulation 12,812)
Transportation: Commute to work: 90.3% car, 1.5% public transportation, 5.2% walk, 1.9% work from home (2000); Travel time to work: 60.0% less than 15 minutes, 22.1% 15 to 30 minutes, 8.8% 30 to 45 minutes, 2.9% 45 to 60 minutes, 6.1% 60 minutes or more (2000)

Additional Information Contacts
Cambridge Area Chamber of Commerce .... (740) 439-6688
  http://www.cambridgeohiochamber.com
City of Cambridge .... (740) 439-1050
  http://www.cambridgeoh.org
Guernsey County Visitors & Convention Bureau .... (740) 432-2022
  http://www.visitguernseycounty.com

CUMBERLAND (village). Covers a land area of 0.483 square miles and a water area of 0 square miles. Located at 39.85° N. Lat.; 81.65° W. Long. Elevation is 857 feet.
Population: 318 (1990); 402 (2000); 408 (2005); 389 (2010 projected); Race: 99.0% White, 0.5% Black, 0.0% Asian, 0.0% Hispanic of any race (2005); Density: 844.4 persons per square mile (2005); Average household size: 2.76 (2005); Median age: 35.5 (2005); Males per 100 females: 100.0 (2005); Marriage status: 20.7% never married, 60.3% now married, 4.5% widowed, 14.5% divorced (2000); Foreign born: 0.5% (2000); Ancestry (includes multiple ancestries): 13.5% German, 12.3% United States or American, 11.0% Irish, 8.3% English, 7.8% Other groups (2000).
Economy: Employment by occupation: 9.6% management, 8.2% professional, 13.0% services, 20.5% sales, 2.7% farming, 13.7% construction, 32.2% production (2000).
Income: Per capita income: $13,235 (2005); Median household income: $35,375 (2005); Average household income: $36,486 (2005); Percent of households with income of $100,000 or more: 2.7% (2005); Poverty rate: 20.1% (2000).
Education: Percent of population age 25 and over with: High school diploma (including GED) or higher: 72.1% (2005); Bachelor's degree or higher: 2.8% (2005); Master's degree or higher: 0.0% (2005).
Housing: Homeownership rate: 79.7% (2005); Median home value: $46,667 (2005); Median rent: $275 per month (2000); Median age of housing: 60+ years (2000).
Transportation: Commute to work: 95.7% car, 0.0% public transportation, 0.0% walk, 4.3% work from home (2000); Travel time to work: 18.2% less than 15 minutes, 46.2% 15 to 30 minutes, 21.2% 30 to 45 minutes, 3.0% 45 to 60 minutes, 11.4% 60 minutes or more (2000)

FAIRVIEW (village). Covers a land area of 0.425 square miles and a water area of 0 square miles. Located at 40.05° N. Lat.; 81.23° W. Long. Elevation is 1,238 feet.
History: Fairview was once the leading U.S. producer of pennyroyal, an herb used in early medicines.
Population: 79 (1990); 81 (2000); 83 (2005); 81 (2010 projected); Race: 100.0% White, 0.0% Black, 0.0% Asian, 0.0% Hispanic of any race (2005); Density: 195.5 persons per square mile (2005); Average household size: 3.19 (2005); Median age: 37.5 (2005); Males per 100 females: 93.0 (2005); Marriage status: 15.9% never married, 74.6% now married, 3.2% widowed, 6.3% divorced (2000); Foreign born: 0.0% (2000); Ancestry (includes multiple ancestries): 26.1% Irish, 22.7% German, 14.8% Other groups, 11.4% United States or American, 10.2% English (2000).
Economy: Employment by occupation: 0.0% management, 0.0% professional, 21.4% services, 7.1% sales, 0.0% farming, 25.0% construction, 46.4% production (2000).
Income: Per capita income: $13,735 (2005); Median household income: $41,429 (2005); Average household income: $43,846 (2005); Percent of households with income of $100,000 or more: 0.0% (2005); Poverty rate: 9.1% (2000).
Education: Percent of population age 25 and over with: High school diploma (including GED) or higher: 73.1% (2005); Bachelor's degree or higher: 0.0% (2005); Master's degree or higher: 0.0% (2005).
Housing: Homeownership rate: 96.2% (2005); Median home value: $50,000 (2005); Median rent: $n/a per month (2000); Median age of housing: 60+ years (2000).
Transportation: Commute to work: 75.0% car, 17.9% public transportation, 0.0% walk, 0.0% work from home (2000); Travel time to work: 17.9% less than 15 minutes, 35.7% 15 to 30 minutes, 14.3% 30 to 45 minutes, 10.7% 45 to 60 minutes, 21.4% 60 minutes or more (2000)

KIMBOLTON (village). Covers a land area of 0.239 square miles and a water area of 0 square miles. Located at 40.15° N. Lat.; 81.57° W. Long. Elevation is 805 feet.
Population: 134 (1990); 190 (2000); 195 (2005); 195 (2010 projected); Race: 90.3% White, 3.6% Black, 0.0% Asian, 0.0% Hispanic of any race (2005); Density: 815.1 persons per square mile (2005); Average household size: 3.25 (2005); Median age: 46.1 (2005); Males per 100 females: 109.7 (2005); Marriage status: 30.6% never married, 48.6% now married, 12.5% widowed, 8.3% divorced (2000); Foreign born: 1.1% (2000); Ancestry (includes multiple ancestries): 14.5% United States or American, 10.2% English, 8.1% French (except Basque), 7.0% Irish, 5.4% European (2000).
Economy: Employment by occupation: 8.1% management, 11.3% professional, 14.5% services, 25.8% sales, 0.0% farming, 17.7% construction, 22.6% production (2000).
Income: Per capita income: $15,486 (2005); Median household income: $27,500 (2005); Average household income: $44,167 (2005); Percent of households with income of $100,000 or more: 3.3% (2005); Poverty rate: 30.5% (2000).
Education: Percent of population age 25 and over with: High school diploma (including GED) or higher: 68.6% (2005); Bachelor's degree or higher: 13.6% (2005); Master's degree or higher: 11.4% (2005).
Housing: Homeownership rate: 85.0% (2005); Median home value: $40,714 (2005); Median rent: $458 per month (2000); Median age of housing: 35 years (2000).
Transportation: Commute to work: 90.3% car, 0.0% public transportation, 6.5% walk, 3.2% work from home (2000); Travel time to work: 31.7% less than 15 minutes, 43.3% 15 to 30 minutes, 13.3% 30 to 45 minutes, 3.3% 45 to 60 minutes, 8.3% 60 minutes or more (2000)

LORE CITY (village). Covers a land area of 0.334 square miles and a water area of 0 square miles. Located at 39.98° N. Lat.; 81.45° W. Long. Elevation is 822 feet.
History: Lore City grew around the coal mines. Morgan's Confederate raiders burned buildings here on their flight across Ohio.
Population: 384 (1990); 305 (2000); 292 (2005); 290 (2010 projected); Race: 94.5% White, 0.0% Black, 0.0% Asian, 0.7% Hispanic of any race (2005); Density: 875.2 persons per square mile (2005); Average household size: 2.39 (2005); Median age: 39.0 (2005); Males per 100 females: 82.5 (2005); Marriage status: 22.8% never married, 65.3% now married, 7.8% widowed, 4.1% divorced (2000); Foreign born: 0.0% (2000); Ancestry (includes multiple ancestries): 15.6% German, 13.5% Irish, 12.8% United States or American, 12.8% English, 10.4% Dutch (2000).
Economy: Employment by occupation: 5.0% management, 17.1% professional, 23.6% services, 22.9% sales, 0.0% farming, 12.9% construction, 18.6% production (2000).
Income: Per capita income: $16,010 (2005); Median household income: $34,906 (2005); Average household income: $38,320 (2005); Percent of households with income of $100,000 or more: 1.6% (2005); Poverty rate: 14.2% (2000).
Education: Percent of population age 25 and over with: High school diploma (including GED) or higher: 81.4% (2005); Bachelor's degree or higher: 11.1% (2005); Master's degree or higher: 2.5% (2005).

School District(s)
East Guernsey Local SD (PK-12)
  2003-04 Enrollment: 1,243 .... (740) 489-5190

Housing: Homeownership rate: 84.4% (2005); Median home value: $55,882 (2005); Median rent: $368 per month (2000); Median age of housing: 60+ years (2000).
Transportation: Commute to work: 90.4% car, 0.0% public transportation, 3.0% walk, 6.7% work from home (2000); Travel time to work: 18.3% less than 15 minutes, 54.8% 15 to 30 minutes, 7.1% 30 to 45 minutes, 10.3% 45 to 60 minutes, 9.5% 60 minutes or more (2000)

OLD WASHINGTON (village). Aka Washington. Covers a land area of 0.657 square miles and a water area of 0 square miles. Located at 40.03° N. Lat.; 81.44° W. Long. Elevation is 1,008 feet.
History: Old Washington was a stagecoach stop on the National Road, with several inns providing rooms and meals for travelers.
Population: 281 (1990); 265 (2000); 257 (2005); 255 (2010 projected); Race: 95.7% White, 2.3% Black, 1.9% Asian, 0.4% Hispanic of any race (2005); Density: 391.0 persons per square mile (2005); Average household size: 2.32 (2005); Median age: 44.9 (2005); Males per 100 females: 82.3 (2005); Marriage status: 19.1% never married, 58.2% now married, 8.8% widowed, 13.9% divorced (2000); Foreign born: 0.0% (2000); Ancestry (includes multiple ancestries): 18.1% Irish, 17.8% German, 11.5% United States or American, 9.1% English, 8.0% Other groups (2000).
Economy: Employment by occupation: 3.4% management, 10.9% professional, 15.1% services, 25.2% sales, 0.0% farming, 16.0% construction, 29.4% production (2000).
Income: Per capita income: $22,189 (2005); Median household income: $30,625 (2005); Average household income: $51,374 (2005); Percent of households with income of $100,000 or more: 6.3% (2005); Poverty rate: 13.9% (2000).
Education: Percent of population age 25 and over with: High school diploma (including GED) or higher: 83.1% (2005); Bachelor's degree or higher: 5.1% (2005); Master's degree or higher: 2.8% (2005).
School District(s)
East Guernsey Local SD (PK-12)
    2003-04 Enrollment: 1,243 . . . . (740) 489-5190
Housing: Homeownership rate: 79.3% (2005); Median home value: $77,037 (2005); Median rent: $331 per month (2000); Median age of housing: 53 years (2000).
Transportation: Commute to work: 91.1% car, 0.0% public transportation, 8.0% walk, 0.9% work from home (2000); Travel time to work: 25.2% less than 15 minutes, 39.6% 15 to 30 minutes, 17.1% 30 to 45 minutes, 0.9% 45 to 60 minutes, 17.1% 60 minutes or more (2000)

PLEASANT CITY (village). Covers a land area of 0.186 square miles and a water area of 0 square miles. Located at 39.90° N. Lat.; 81.54° W. Long. Elevation is 860 feet.
History: Pleasant City, first called Point Pleasant, developed around the coal mines in the 1890's.
Population: 419 (1990); 439 (2000); 351 (2005); 331 (2010 projected); Race: 98.0% White, 0.6% Black, 0.0% Asian, 0.0% Hispanic of any race (2005); Density: 1,891.1 persons per square mile (2005); Average household size: 2.49 (2005); Median age: 37.2 (2005); Males per 100 females: 81.9 (2005); Marriage status: 22.0% never married, 59.1% now married, 8.7% widowed, 10.2% divorced (2000); Foreign born: 1.8% (2000); Ancestry (includes multiple ancestries): 19.5% German, 14.7% Irish, 12.7% United States or American, 11.3% Other groups, 7.7% English (2000).
Economy: Employment by occupation: 14.2% management, 9.7% professional, 21.6% services, 15.9% sales, 0.0% farming, 14.8% construction, 23.9% production (2000).
Income: Per capita income: $15,499 (2005); Median household income: $33,611 (2005); Average household income: $38,582 (2005); Percent of households with income of $100,000 or more: 2.1% (2005); Poverty rate: 17.2% (2000).
Education: Percent of population age 25 and over with: High school diploma (including GED) or higher: 76.8% (2005); Bachelor's degree or higher: 8.3% (2005); Master's degree or higher: 3.1% (2005).
Housing: Homeownership rate: 78.0% (2005); Median home value: $50,000 (2005); Median rent: $278 per month (2000); Median age of housing: 60+ years (2000).
Transportation: Commute to work: 95.4% car, 1.7% public transportation, 2.9% walk, 0.0% work from home (2000); Travel time to work: 28.9% less than 15 minutes, 53.2% 15 to 30 minutes, 7.5% 30 to 45 minutes, 2.3% 45 to 60 minutes, 8.1% 60 minutes or more (2000)

QUAKER CITY (village). Covers a land area of 0.529 square miles and a water area of 0 square miles. Located at 39.97° N. Lat.; 81.29° W. Long. Elevation is 860 feet.
Population: 560 (1990); 563 (2000); 475 (2005); 461 (2010 projected); Race: 98.9% White, 0.2% Black, 0.0% Asian, 0.6% Hispanic of any race (2005); Density: 897.4 persons per square mile (2005); Average household size: 2.57 (2005); Median age: 35.1 (2005); Males per 100 females: 95.5 (2005); Marriage status: 19.2% never married, 61.4% now married, 9.3% widowed, 10.1% divorced (2000); Foreign born: 0.3% (2000); Ancestry (includes multiple ancestries): 22.7% United States or American, 15.0% Irish, 9.9% German, 9.0% English, 3.9% Scotch-Irish (2000).
Economy: Employment by occupation: 6.1% management, 7.0% professional, 16.5% services, 23.9% sales, 0.0% farming, 13.5% construction, 33.0% production (2000).
Income: Per capita income: $12,337 (2005); Median household income: $26,897 (2005); Average household income: $31,676 (2005); Percent of households with income of $100,000 or more: 0.5% (2005); Poverty rate: 16.0% (2000).
Education: Percent of population age 25 and over with: High school diploma (including GED) or higher: 79.9% (2005); Bachelor's degree or higher: 8.1% (2005); Master's degree or higher: 3.2% (2005).
School District(s)
East Guernsey Local SD (PK-12)
    2003-04 Enrollment: 1,243 . . . . (740) 489-5190
Housing: Homeownership rate: 70.3% (2005); Median home value: $48,387 (2005); Median rent: $256 per month (2000); Median age of housing: 60+ years (2000).
Transportation: Commute to work: 92.4% car, 0.0% public transportation, 4.9% walk, 2.7% work from home (2000); Travel time to work: 18.3% less than 15 minutes, 22.9% 15 to 30 minutes, 39.4% 30 to 45 minutes, 11.9% 45 to 60 minutes, 7.3% 60 minutes or more (2000)

SALESVILLE (village). Covers a land area of 0.098 square miles and a water area of 0 square miles. Located at 39.97° N. Lat.; 81.33° W. Long. Elevation is 860 feet.
History: Salesville was established near Leatherwood Creek, and was the setting for William Dean Howells' novel "The Leatherwood God."
Population: 84 (1990); 154 (2000); 152 (2005); 147 (2010 projected); Race: 99.3% White, 0.0% Black, 0.0% Asian, 0.0% Hispanic of any race (2005); Density: 1,547.2 persons per square mile (2005); Average household size: 2.92 (2005); Median age: 38.2 (2005); Males per 100 females: 92.4 (2005); Marriage status: 14.7% never married, 63.8% now married, 8.6% widowed, 12.9% divorced (2000); Foreign born: 0.0% (2000); Ancestry (includes multiple ancestries): 33.6% German, 17.4% Irish, 14.8% United States or American, 6.0% Scottish, 4.7% French (except Basque) (2000).
Economy: Employment by occupation: 4.4% management, 0.0% professional, 4.4% services, 32.4% sales, 0.0% farming, 29.4% construction, 29.4% production (2000).
Income: Per capita income: $13,191 (2005); Median household income: $36,364 (2005); Average household income: $38,558 (2005); Percent of households with income of $100,000 or more: 0.0% (2005); Poverty rate: 12.3% (2000).
Education: Percent of population age 25 and over with: High school diploma (including GED) or higher: 84.4% (2005); Bachelor's degree or higher: 4.2% (2005); Master's degree or higher: 0.0% (2005).
Housing: Homeownership rate: 96.2% (2005); Median home value: $51,111 (2005); Median rent: $225 per month (2000); Median age of housing: 58 years (2000).
Transportation: Commute to work: 97.1% car, 0.0% public transportation, 2.9% walk, 0.0% work from home (2000); Travel time to work: 13.2% less than 15 minutes, 58.8% 15 to 30 minutes, 17.6% 30 to 45 minutes, 0.0% 45 to 60 minutes, 10.3% 60 minutes or more (2000)

SENECAVILLE (village). Covers a land area of 0.486 square miles and a water area of 0 square miles. Located at 39.93° N. Lat.; 81.46° W. Long. Elevation is 880 feet.
Population: 434 (1990); 453 (2000); 442 (2005); 440 (2010 projected); Race: 100.0% White, 0.0% Black, 0.0% Asian, 0.0% Hispanic of any race (2005); Density: 908.6 persons per square mile (2005); Average household size: 2.53 (2005); Median age: 37.2 (2005); Males per 100 females: 89.7 (2005); Marriage status: 22.3% never married, 55.6% now married, 7.4% widowed, 14.6% divorced (2000); Foreign born: 0.4% (2000); Ancestry (includes multiple ancestries): 17.4% English, 16.2% German, 13.4% Irish, 11.9% United States or American, 5.7% Slovak (2000).
Economy: Dam nearby impounds Senecaville Lake for flood control. Employment by occupation: 2.6% management, 17.2% professional, 23.4% services, 18.8% sales, 0.5% farming, 14.1% construction, 23.4% production (2000).
Income: Per capita income: $15,271 (2005); Median household income: $30,536 (2005); Average household income: $38,571 (2005); Percent of households with income of $100,000 or more: 8.0% (2005); Poverty rate: 17.2% (2000).

Education: Percent of population age 25 and over with: High school diploma (including GED) or higher: 83.5% (2005); Bachelor's degree or higher: 6.0% (2005); Master's degree or higher: 1.1% (2005).

School District(s)
Mid-East Career and Technology Centers (PK-12)
　2003-04 Enrollment: n/a . . . . (740) 454-0105
Rolling Hills Local SD (PK-12)
　2003-04 Enrollment: 2,226 . . . . (740) 432-5370

Housing: Homeownership rate: 76.6% (2005); Median home value: $57,222 (2005); Median rent: $311 per month (2000); Median age of housing: 60+ years (2000).

Transportation: Commute to work: 95.2% car, 0.0% public transportation, 3.8% walk, 0.0% work from home (2000); Travel time to work: 14.5% less than 15 minutes, 57.0% 15 to 30 minutes, 10.2% 30 to 45 minutes, 6.5% 45 to 60 minutes, 11.8% 60 minutes or more (2000)

Hamilton County

Located in southwestern Ohio; bounded on the west by Indiana, and on the south by the Ohio River and the Kentucky border; drained by Great Miami, Little Miami, and Whitewater Rivers. Covers a land area of 407.36 square miles, a water area of 5.42 square miles, and is located in the Eastern Time Zone. The county government was organized in 1790. County seat is Cincinnati.

Hamilton County is part of the Cincinnati-Middletown, OH-KY-IN Metropolitan Statistical Area. The entire metro area includes: Dearborn County, IN; Franklin County, IN; Ohio County, IN; Boone County, KY; Bracken County, KY; Campbell County, KY; Gallatin County, KY; Grant County, KY; Kenton County, KY; Pendleton County, KY; Brown County, OH; Butler County, OH; Clermont County, OH; Hamilton County, OH; Warren County, OH

Weather Station: Cincinnati Fernbank　　　　　Elevation: 498 feet

	Jan	Feb	Mar	Apr	May	Jun	Jul	Aug	Sep	Oct	Nov	Dec
High	38	44	54	65	75	82	87	85	79	67	55	44
Low	20	23	31	40	50	60	64	63	55	43	35	26
Precip	3.5	2.9	4.4	4.4	5.5	4.6	4.5	4.1	2.9	3.3	3.7	3.6
Snow	6.7	na	2.6	0.1	tr	0.0	0.0	0.0	0.0	tr	0.4	2.2

High and Low temperatures in degrees Fahrenheit; Precipitation and Snow in inches

Weather Station: Cincinnati Lunken Airport　　　Elevation: 488 feet

	Jan	Feb	Mar	Apr	May	Jun	Jul	Aug	Sep	Oct	Nov	Dec
High	38	43	54	65	75	83	87	85	79	67	55	44
Low	22	25	34	43	53	62	67	65	57	45	36	28
Precip	2.7	2.4	3.9	3.7	4.6	4.0	3.8	4.1	3.1	3.0	3.4	3.2
Snow	4.6	3.7	2.6	0.2	tr	tr	tr	0.0	0.0	0.1	0.4	1.6

High and Low temperatures in degrees Fahrenheit; Precipitation and Snow in inches

Population: 866,228 (1990); 845,303 (2000); 812,803 (2005); 780,398 (2010 projected); Race: 71.6% White, 24.1% Black, 1.9% Asian, 1.2% Hispanic of any race (2005); Density: 1,995.3 persons per square mile (2005); Average household size: 2.41 (2005); Median age: 36.9 (2005); Males per 100 females: 91.9 (2005).

Religion: Five largest groups: 26.8% Catholic Church, 3.6% The United Methodist Church, 2.7% Jewish Estimate, 2.3% Presbyterian Church (U.S.A.), 1.8% Southern Baptist Convention (2000).

Economy: Unemployment rate: 5.7% (2005); Total civilian labor force: 426,785 (2005); Leading industries: 16.1% health care and social assistance; 12.6% manufacturing; 11.3% retail trade (2004); Farms: 399 totaling 29,520 acres (2002); Companies that employ 500 or more persons: 86 (2004); Companies that employ 100 to 499 persons: 761 (2004); Companies that employ less than 100 persons: 22,734 (2004); Black-owned businesses: 6,000 (2002); Hispanic-owned businesses: 684 (2002); Women-owned businesses: 18,646 (2002); Retail sales per capita: $17,173 (2006); Single-family building permits issued: 1,236 (2005); Multi-family building permits issued: 871 (2005).

Income: Per capita income: $27,603 (2005); Median household income: $46,491 (2005); Average household income: $65,749 (2005); Percent of households with income of $100,000 or more: 17.1% (2005); Poverty rate: 11.5% (2003); Bankruptcy rate: 10.59% (2005).

Taxes: Total county taxes per capita: $457 (2004); County property taxes per capita: $305 (2004).

Education: Percent of population age 25 and over with: High school diploma (including GED) or higher: 82.9% (2005); Bachelor's degree or higher: 29.2% (2005); Master's degree or higher: 10.7% (2005).

Housing: Homeownership rate: 60.6% (2005); Median home value: $132,146 (2005); Median rent: $424 per month (2000); Median age of housing: 42 years (2000).

Health: Birth rate: 145.9 per 10,000 population (2004); Death rate: 104.0 per 10,000 population (2004); Age-adjusted cancer mortality rate: 224.8 deaths per 100,000 population (2002); Air Quality Index: 49.3% good, 45.5% moderate, 4.9% unhealthy for sensitive individuals, 0.3% unhealthy (percent of days in 2005); Number of physicians: 50.3 per 10,000 population (2004); Hospital beds: 44.7 per 10,000 population (2003); Hospital admissions: 2,070.9 per 10,000 population (2003).

Elections: 2004 Presidential election results: 52.5% Bush, 47.1% Kerry, 0.0% Nader, 0.2% Badnarik

National and State Parks: Harrison State Park; Kroger Hills State Reserve; LIttle Miami State Scenic River; Little Miami State Park; William Howard Taft National Historic Site

Additional Information Contacts

Hamilton County Government . . . . (513) 946-4400	
http://www.hamilton-co.org	
Anderson Chamber of Commerce . . . . (513) 474-4802	
http://www.andersonareachamber.org	
Cincinnati Chamber of Commerce . . . . (513) 579-3100	
http://www.gccc.com	
City of Blue Ash . . . . (513) 745-8500	
http://www.blueash.com	
City of Cheviot . . . . (513) 661-2700	
http://www.cheviot.org	
City of Cincinnati . . . . (513) 591-6000	
http://www.cincinnati-oh.gov/index.html	
City of Forest Park . . . . (513) 595-5200	
http://www.forestpark.org	
City of Harrison . . . . (513) 367-3730	
http://www.harrisonoh.org	
City of Loveland . . . . (513) 683-0150	
http://www.lovelandoh.com	
City of Madeira . . . . (513) 561-7228	
http://www.madeiracity.com	
City of Montgomery . . . . (513) 891-2424	
http://www.ci.montgomery.oh.us	
City of Mount Healthy. . . . . (513) 931-8840	
http://www.mthealthy.org	
City of North College Hill . . . . (513) 521-7413	
http://www.northcollegehill.org	
City of Norwood . . . . (513) 458-4501	
http://www.norwood-ohio.com	
City of Reading . . . . (513) 733-3725	
http://www.readingohio.org	
City of Sharonville . . . . (513) 563-1144	
http://www.sharonville.org	
City of Springdale . . . . (513) 346-5700	
http://www.springdale.org	
City of Wyoming. . . . . (513) 821-7600	
http://www.wyoming.oh.us	
Greater Cincinnati Convention & Visitors Bureau . . . . (513) 621-2142	
http://www.cincyusa.com	
Hamilton County Chamber of Commerce . . . . (513) 984-6555	
http://www.gccc.com	
Loveland Chamber of Commerce . . . . (513) 683-1544	
http://www.lovelandchamber.org	
Northern Cincinnati Convention & Visitors Bureau . . . . . . (513) 771-5353	
http://www.cincynorth.com	
Norwood Chamber of Commerce . . . . (513) 956-7935	
http://www.norwoodchamber.org	
Over-The-Rhine Chamber of Commerce. . . . . (513) 241-2690	
http://www.otrchamber.com	
Reading Chamber of Commerce . . . . (513) 786-7274	
http://www.readingohiochamber.org	
Sharonville Chamber of Commerce . . . . (513) 554-1722	
http://www.sharonvillechamber.com	
Southwestern Ohio Chamber of Commerce . . . . (513) 984-0909	
http://www.gccc.com	
Village of Cleves . . . . (513) 941-5127	
http://www.cleves.org	
Village of Fairfax . . . . (513) 527-6503	
http://www.fairfaxohio.org	
Village of Glendale. . . . . (513) 771-7200	
http://www.glendaleohio.org	

Village of Golf Manor . . . . (513) 531-7418
   http://www.golfmanor.org
Village of Greenhills . . . . (513) 825-2100
   http://www.greenhillsohio.org
Village of Lincoln Heights . . . . (513) 733-5900
   http://www.lincolnheightsohio.org
Village of Lockland . . . . (513) 761-1124
   http://www.lockland.com

Hamilton County Communities

ADDYSTON (village). Covers a land area of 0.867 square miles and a water area of 0.041 square miles. Located at 39.13° N. Lat.; 84.71° W. Long. Elevation is 492 feet.
History: Addyston became a town in 1871 when Matthew Addy of Cincinnati established a pipe foundry.
Population: 1,198 (1990); 1,010 (2000); 907 (2005); 844 (2010 projected); Race: 89.6% White, 6.1% Black, 0.6% Asian, 1.8% Hispanic of any race (2005); Density: 1,046.3 persons per square mile (2005); Average household size: 2.74 (2005); Median age: 32.6 (2005); Males per 100 females: 97.6 (2005); Marriage status: 30.3% never married, 49.1% now married, 7.1% widowed, 13.5% divorced (2000); Foreign born: 1.2% (2000); Ancestry (includes multiple ancestries): 26.5% Other groups, 25.2% German, 15.6% Irish, 14.2% United States or American, 8.1% English (2000).
Economy: Single-family building permits issued: 0 (2005); Multi-family building permits issued: 0 (2005); Employment by occupation: 11.2% management, 8.5% professional, 25.6% services, 18.4% sales, 0.0% farming, 22.1% construction, 14.1% production (2000).
Income: Per capita income: $16,996 (2005); Median household income: $40,648 (2005); Average household income: $46,571 (2005); Percent of households with income of $100,000 or more: 8.2% (2005); Poverty rate: 11.6% (2000).
Education: Percent of population age 25 and over with: High school diploma (including GED) or higher: 61.1% (2005); Bachelor's degree or higher: 2.4% (2005); Master's degree or higher: 0.6% (2005).
School District(s)
Three Rivers Local Schools (PK-12)
   2003-04 Enrollment: 2,164 . . . . (513) 941-6400
Housing: Homeownership rate: 55.3% (2005); Median home value: $64,750 (2005); Median rent: $423 per month (2000); Median age of housing: 60+ years (2000).
Transportation: Commute to work: 93.8% car, 3.0% public transportation, 2.2% walk, 0.5% work from home (2000); Travel time to work: 26.4% less than 15 minutes, 27.4% 15 to 30 minutes, 28.3% 30 to 45 minutes, 11.1% 45 to 60 minutes, 6.8% 60 minutes or more (2000)

AMBERLEY (village). Covers a land area of 3.476 square miles and a water area of 0 square miles. Located at 39.19° N. Lat.; 84.42° W. Long. Elevation is 803 feet.
Population: 3,108 (1990); 3,425 (2000); 3,387 (2005); 3,307 (2010 projected); Race: 85.1% White, 10.3% Black, 2.8% Asian, 0.5% Hispanic of any race (2005); Density: 974.4 persons per square mile (2005); Average household size: 2.58 (2005); Median age: 50.2 (2005); Males per 100 females: 96.0 (2005); Marriage status: 12.1% never married, 76.3% now married, 6.7% widowed, 4.8% divorced (2000); Foreign born: 6.7% (2000); Ancestry (includes multiple ancestries): 21.9% German, 16.6% Other groups, 9.8% Irish, 9.5% United States or American, 9.2% Polish (2000).
Economy: Suburb of Cincinnati. Employment by occupation: 26.9% management, 33.7% professional, 5.8% services, 27.3% sales, 0.0% farming, 2.3% construction, 3.9% production (2000).
Income: Per capita income: $49,165 (2005); Median household income: $88,462 (2005); Average household income: $126,729 (2005); Percent of households with income of $100,000 or more: 44.1% (2005); Poverty rate: 3.5% (2000).
Education: Percent of population age 25 and over with: High school diploma (including GED) or higher: 94.5% (2005); Bachelor's degree or higher: 63.0% (2005); Master's degree or higher: 31.5% (2005).
Housing: Homeownership rate: 97.9% (2005); Median home value: $254,610 (2005); Median rent: $1,500 per month (2000); Median age of housing: 42 years (2000).
Safety: Violent crime rate: 11.9 per 10,000 population; Property crime rate: 89.6 per 10,000 population (2004).
Transportation: Commute to work: 95.4% car, 1.9% public transportation, 0.0% walk, 2.6% work from home (2000); Travel time to work: 24.8% less than 15 minutes, 56.1% 15 to 30 minutes, 15.2% 30 to 45 minutes, 2.0% 45 to 60 minutes, 2.1% 60 minutes or more (2000)

ARLINGTON HEIGHTS (village). Covers a land area of 0.257 square miles and a water area of 0 square miles. Located at 39.21° N. Lat.; 84.45° W. Long. Elevation is 570 feet.
Population: 1,084 (1990); 899 (2000); 831 (2005); 765 (2010 projected); Race: 92.3% White, 2.6% Black, 0.0% Asian, 0.7% Hispanic of any race (2005); Density: 3,229.8 persons per square mile (2005); Average household size: 2.29 (2005); Median age: 36.0 (2005); Males per 100 females: 98.3 (2005); Marriage status: 27.4% never married, 46.1% now married, 8.0% widowed, 18.4% divorced (2000); Foreign born: 0.7% (2000); Ancestry (includes multiple ancestries): 26.7% German, 18.0% United States or American, 12.6% Irish, 10.7% Other groups, 7.0% English (2000).
Economy: Suburb of Cincinnati. Single-family building permits issued: 0 (2005); Multi-family building permits issued: 0 (2005); Employment by occupation: 8.1% management, 6.8% professional, 19.1% services, 26.3% sales, 0.0% farming, 15.9% construction, 23.8% production (2000).
Income: Per capita income: $20,505 (2005); Median household income: $34,732 (2005); Average household income: $46,942 (2005); Percent of households with income of $100,000 or more: 7.2% (2005); Poverty rate: 13.0% (2000).
Education: Percent of population age 25 and over with: High school diploma (including GED) or higher: 68.0% (2005); Bachelor's degree or higher: 4.5% (2005); Master's degree or higher: 0.7% (2005).
Housing: Homeownership rate: 56.5% (2005); Median home value: $82,911 (2005); Median rent: $388 per month (2000); Median age of housing: 60+ years (2000).
Transportation: Commute to work: 96.0% car, 0.9% public transportation, 1.3% walk, 0.9% work from home (2000); Travel time to work: 24.2% less than 15 minutes, 52.1% 15 to 30 minutes, 16.7% 30 to 45 minutes, 4.1% 45 to 60 minutes, 2.8% 60 minutes or more (2000)

BLUE ASH (city). Covers a land area of 7.655 square miles and a water area of 0.014 square miles. Located at 39.24° N. Lat.; 84.37° W. Long. Elevation is 850 feet.
History: Settled in 1791; incorporated as a village in 1955; incorporated as a city in 1961.
Population: 11,905 (1990); 12,513 (2000); 11,944 (2005); 11,364 (2010 projected); Race: 85.1% White, 5.1% Black, 8.1% Asian, 1.0% Hispanic of any race (2005); Density: 1,560.3 persons per square mile (2005); Average household size: 2.48 (2005); Median age: 41.0 (2005); Males per 100 females: 94.0 (2005); Marriage status: 24.0% never married, 60.4% now married, 6.3% widowed, 9.2% divorced (2000); Foreign born: 10.0% (2000); Ancestry (includes multiple ancestries): 29.8% German, 16.4% Other groups, 13.4% Irish, 11.5% English, 6.7% United States or American (2000).
Economy: Single-family building permits issued: 21 (2005); Multi-family building permits issued: 0 (2005); Employment by occupation: 18.2% management, 34.9% professional, 8.9% services, 25.2% sales, 0.2% farming, 4.3% construction, 8.2% production (2000).
Income: Per capita income: $41,593 (2005); Median household income: $71,937 (2005); Average household income: $102,627 (2005); Percent of households with income of $100,000 or more: 33.1% (2005); Poverty rate: 4.7% (2000).
Taxes: Total city taxes per capita: $1,849 (2004); City property taxes per capita: $183 (2004).
Education: Percent of population age 25 and over with: High school diploma (including GED) or higher: 90.8% (2005); Bachelor's degree or higher: 49.4% (2005); Master's degree or higher: 23.6% (2005).
Four-year College(s)
University of Cincinnati-Raymond Walters College (Public)
   Fall 2004 Enrollment: 4,421 . . . . (513) 745-5600
   2005-06 Tuition: In-state $4,938; Out-of-state $12,801
Housing: Homeownership rate: 74.2% (2005); Median home value: $177,161 (2005); Median rent: $724 per month (2000); Median age of housing: 25 years (2000).
Transportation: Commute to work: 92.9% car, 1.5% public transportation, 1.4% walk, 3.4% work from home (2000); Travel time to work: 30.3% less than 15 minutes, 49.1% 15 to 30 minutes, 16.6% 30 to 45 minutes, 2.6% 45 to 60 minutes, 1.4% 60 minutes or more (2000)
Additional Information Contacts
City of Blue Ash . . . . (513) 745-8500
   http://www.blueash.com

BRIDGETOWN NORTH (CDP). Covers a land area of 3.365 square miles and a water area of 0 square miles. Located at 39.15° N. Lat.; 84.63° W. Long.
Population: 11,760 (1990); 12,569 (2000); 12,379 (2005); 12,161 (2010 projected); Race: 98.0% White, 0.4% Black, 0.7% Asian, 0.6% Hispanic of any race (2005); Density: 3,678.6 persons per square mile (2005); Average household size: 2.43 (2005); Median age: 39.8 (2005); Males per 100 females: 89.7 (2005); Marriage status: 22.2% never married, 58.7% now married, 11.2% widowed, 8.0% divorced (2000); Foreign born: 1.7% (2000); Ancestry (includes multiple ancestries): 57.0% German, 18.0% Irish, 9.4% English, 7.4% Italian, 5.7% United States or American (2000).
Economy: Employment by occupation: 11.9% management, 18.7% professional, 14.3% services, 34.1% sales, 0.0% farming, 10.1% construction, 11.0% production (2000).
Income: Per capita income: $25,892 (2005); Median household income: $51,067 (2005); Average household income: $62,869 (2005); Percent of households with income of $100,000 or more: 13.8% (2005); Poverty rate: 3.3% (2000).
Education: Percent of population age 25 and over with: High school diploma (including GED) or higher: 86.3% (2005); Bachelor's degree or higher: 19.0% (2005); Master's degree or higher: 5.0% (2005).
Housing: Homeownership rate: 86.9% (2005); Median home value: $125,078 (2005); Median rent: $467 per month (2000); Median age of housing: 42 years (2000).
Transportation: Commute to work: 95.0% car, 1.8% public transportation, 1.0% walk, 1.7% work from home (2000); Travel time to work: 24.9% less than 15 minutes, 38.1% 15 to 30 minutes, 27.2% 30 to 45 minutes, 6.8% 45 to 60 minutes, 3.0% 60 minutes or more (2000)

CAMP DENNISON (unincorporated postal area, zip code 45111). Covers a land area of 1.636 square miles and a water area of 0 square miles. Located at 39.19° N. Lat.; 84.29° W. Long. Elevation is 580 feet.
Population: 430 (2000); Race: 71.6% White, 26.4% Black, 0.0% Asian, 13.1% Hispanic of any race (2000); Density: 262.9 persons per square mile (2000); Age: 13.1% under 18, 17.3% over 64 (2000); Marriage status: 29.2% never married, 40.3% now married, 13.3% widowed, 17.2% divorced (2000); Foreign born: 3.8% (2000); Ancestry (includes multiple ancestries): 39.4% Other groups, 26.6% Irish, 20.1% German, 17.1% English, 7.5% United States or American (2000).
Economy: Employment by occupation: 15.4% management, 9.4% professional, 7.7% services, 43.2% sales, 0.0% farming, 16.2% construction, 8.1% production (2000).
Income: Per capita income: $29,257 (2000); Median household income: $63,250 (2000); Poverty rate: 0.0% (2000).
Education: Percent of population age 25 and over with: High school diploma (including GED) or higher: 79.6% (2000); Bachelor's degree or higher: 32.2% (2000).
Housing: Homeownership rate: 81.3% (2000); Median home value: $89,000 (2000); Median rent: $529 per month (2000); Median age of housing: 51 years (2000).
Transportation: Commute to work: 93.2% car, 3.4% public transportation, 0.0% walk, 3.4% work from home (2000); Travel time to work: 20.4% less than 15 minutes, 55.3% 15 to 30 minutes, 18.1% 30 to 45 minutes, 0.0% 45 to 60 minutes, 6.2% 60 minutes or more (2000)

CHERRY GROVE (CDP). Covers a land area of 1.128 square miles and a water area of 0 square miles. Located at 39.08° N. Lat.; 84.31° W. Long. Elevation is 880 feet.
Population: 4,972 (1990); 4,555 (2000); 4,379 (2005); 4,183 (2010 projected); Race: 95.5% White, 1.3% Black, 1.9% Asian, 0.9% Hispanic of any race (2005); Density: 3,882.1 persons per square mile (2005); Average household size: 2.94 (2005); Median age: 38.1 (2005); Males per 100 females: 93.4 (2005); Marriage status: 17.3% never married, 71.2% now married, 4.0% widowed, 7.5% divorced (2000); Foreign born: 2.4% (2000); Ancestry (includes multiple ancestries): 41.8% German, 22.8% Irish, 12.7% English, 10.9% Italian, 6.2% Other groups (2000).
Economy: Suburb of Cincinnati. Employment by occupation: 15.3% management, 27.1% professional, 10.9% services, 32.2% sales, 0.0% farming, 4.3% construction, 10.2% production (2000).
Income: Per capita income: $26,923 (2005); Median household income: $73,247 (2005); Average household income: $79,071 (2005); Percent of households with income of $100,000 or more: 25.0% (2005); Poverty rate: 0.5% (2000).
Education: Percent of population age 25 and over with: High school diploma (including GED) or higher: 94.5% (2005); Bachelor's degree or higher: 33.0% (2005); Master's degree or higher: 9.8% (2005).
Housing: Homeownership rate: 95.6% (2005); Median home value: $151,612 (2005); Median rent: $813 per month (2000); Median age of housing: 31 years (2000).
Transportation: Commute to work: 90.3% car, 3.1% public transportation, 2.3% walk, 3.6% work from home (2000); Travel time to work: 22.6% less than 15 minutes, 35.0% 15 to 30 minutes, 32.1% 30 to 45 minutes, 7.2% 45 to 60 minutes, 3.1% 60 minutes or more (2000)

CHEVIOT (city). Covers a land area of 1.163 square miles and a water area of <.001 square miles. Located at 39.15° N. Lat.; 84.61° W. Long. Elevation is 900 feet.
History: Settled early 1800s; incorporated 1904.
Population: 9,629 (1990); 9,015 (2000); 8,327 (2005); 7,650 (2010 projected); Race: 96.6% White, 0.7% Black, 0.7% Asian, 1.2% Hispanic of any race (2005); Density: 7,161.8 persons per square mile (2005); Average household size: 2.17 (2005); Median age: 37.1 (2005); Males per 100 females: 90.6 (2005); Marriage status: 24.8% never married, 52.2% now married, 10.7% widowed, 12.3% divorced (2000); Foreign born: 1.6% (2000); Ancestry (includes multiple ancestries): 44.7% German, 15.4% Irish, 9.3% United States or American, 7.7% English, 5.2% Italian (2000).
Economy: Diverse light manufacturing. Single-family building permits issued: 0 (2005); Multi-family building permits issued: 0 (2005); Employment by occupation: 10.7% management, 16.7% professional, 15.7% services, 31.4% sales, 0.0% farming, 14.4% construction, 11.1% production (2000).
Income: Per capita income: $22,564 (2005); Median household income: $40,388 (2005); Average household income: $48,331 (2005); Percent of households with income of $100,000 or more: 6.6% (2005); Poverty rate: 7.6% (2000).
Education: Percent of population age 25 and over with: High school diploma (including GED) or higher: 77.2% (2005); Bachelor's degree or higher: 16.4% (2005); Master's degree or higher: 3.9% (2005).
Housing: Homeownership rate: 61.7% (2005); Median home value: $101,351 (2005); Median rent: $387 per month (2000); Median age of housing: 55 years (2000).
Safety: Violent crime rate: 14.0 per 10,000 population; Property crime rate: 202.1 per 10,000 population (2004).
Transportation: Commute to work: 91.9% car, 4.0% public transportation, 2.5% walk, 1.2% work from home (2000); Travel time to work: 22.0% less than 15 minutes, 46.1% 15 to 30 minutes, 26.4% 30 to 45 minutes, 4.2% 45 to 60 minutes, 1.4% 60 minutes or more (2000)
Additional Information Contacts
City of Cheviot . . . . (513) 661-2700
  http://www.cheviot.org

CINCINNATI (city). Covers a land area of 77.968 square miles and a water area of 1.599 square miles. Located at 39.13° N. Lat.; 84.50° W. Long. Elevation is 683 feet.
History: Cincinnati was settled at an Ohio River crossroads in 1788 when developers platted a village that they named Losantiville. In 1790 the name was changed to Cincinnati by General Arthur St. Clair, Governor of the Northwest Territory, in honor of the Revolutionary Officers' Society. The Ohio River was the avenue down which settlers came to find space to establish farms, and Cincinnati became the center of commerce. Immigrants from Germany and Ireland joined other Europeans who came straight to Cincinnati. Steamboat travel on the Ohio River and the opening of the Miami & Erie Canal spurred trading. When Charles Dickens visited Cincinnati in 1842, he described it as "a place that commends itself... favorably and pleasantly to a stranger." The Civil War tore Cincinnati apart. Its sympathies were with the North, but its trade was with the South, and there was great rejoicing when the war ended.
Population: 363,974 (1990); 331,285 (2000); 310,852 (2005); 291,613 (2010 projected); Race: 50.6% White, 44.5% Black, 1.9% Asian, 1.4% Hispanic of any race (2005); Density: 3,986.9 persons per square mile (2005); Average household size: 2.20 (2005); Median age: 33.9 (2005); Males per 100 females: 90.6 (2005); Marriage status: 42.4% never married, 37.9% now married, 7.6% widowed, 12.1% divorced (2000); Foreign born: 3.8% (2000); Ancestry (includes multiple ancestries): 40.7% Other groups, 19.9% German, 10.4% Irish, 5.4% English, 4.8% United States or American (2000).
Economy: Unemployment rate: 6.4% (2005); Total civilian labor force: 157,193 (2005); Single-family building permits issued: 190 (2005);

Multi-family building permits issued: 426 (2005); Employment by occupation: 12.6% management, 23.2% professional, 17.9% services, 26.3% sales, 0.1% farming, 6.4% construction, 13.5% production (2000).
Income: Per capita income: $22,688 (2005); Median household income: $32,947 (2005); Average household income: $48,891 (2005); Percent of households with income of $100,000 or more: 10.0% (2005); Poverty rate: 21.9% (2000).
Taxes: Total city taxes per capita: $1,012 (2004); City property taxes per capita: $203 (2004).
Education: Percent of population age 25 and over with: High school diploma (including GED) or higher: 77.0% (2005); Bachelor's degree or higher: 27.0% (2005); Master's degree or higher: 10.4% (2005).

School District(s)

A.B. Miree Fundamental Academy (KG-08)
   2003-04 Enrollment: 397 . . . . (513) 351-8034
Alliance Academy of Cincinnati (KG-05)
   2003-04 Enrollment: 342 . . . . (513) 751-5555
Children's Home of Cincinnati
   2003-04 Enrollment: n/a . . . . (513) 272-1725
Cincinnati City SD (PK-12)
   2003-04 Enrollment: 40,374 . . . . (513) 363-0000
Cincinnati College Prep Acad (KG-08)
   2003-04 Enrollment: 439 . . . . (513) 684-0777
Deer Park Community City SD (PK-12)
   2003-04 Enrollment: 1,444 . . . . (513) 891-0222
Dohn Community (09-12)
   2003-04 Enrollment: 43 . . . . (513) 281-6100
East End Comm Heritage School (KG-12)
   2003-04 Enrollment: 201 . . . . (513) 281-3900
Finneytown Local SD (PK-12)
   2003-04 Enrollment: 1,787 . . . . (513) 728-3700
Forest Hills Local SD (PK-12)
   2003-04 Enrollment: 7,621 . . . . (513) 231-3600
Great Oaks Inst of Technology Joint Vocational SD (07-12)
   2003-04 Enrollment: n/a . . . . (513) 771-8840
Greater Cincinnati Community (KG-08)
   2003-04 Enrollment: 371 . . . . (513) 541-9750
Harmony Community School (02-12)
   2003-04 Enrollment: 466 . . . . (513) 921-5260
Indian Hill Ex Vill SD (PK-12)
   2003-04 Enrollment: 2,260 . . . . (513) 272-4500
International College Preparatory Academy (KG-06)
   2003-04 Enrollment: 582
Isus Trade & Tech Prep-Cinci (11-12)
   2003-04 Enrollment: 152 . . . . (513) 723-1513
James Cecil Wynn Center of Excellence
   2003-04 Enrollment: n/a
Lakota Local SD (PK-12)
   2003-04 Enrollment: 16,358 . . . . (513) 874-5505
Life Skills Center of Cincinnati (09-12)
   2003-04 Enrollment: 635 . . . . (513) 475-0222
Life Skills Center of Hamilton Co (09-11)
   2003-04 Enrollment: 212 . . . . (513) 821-6695
Lighthouse Community School Inc (06-12)
   2003-04 Enrollment: 59 . . . . (513) 561-7888
M Booth Academy (KG-04)
   2003-04 Enrollment: 88 . . . . (513) 241-1121
Madeira City SD (PK-12)
   2003-04 Enrollment: 1,508 . . . . (513) 985-6070
Mariemont City SD (PK-12)
   2003-04 Enrollment: 1,708 . . . . (513) 272-7500
Mt Healthy City SD (PK-12)
   2003-04 Enrollment: 3,788 . . . . (513) 729-0077
Nation Bdg Auto Repair & Tech
   2003-04 Enrollment: n/a . . . . (513) 731-1527
New Richmond Ex Vill SD (PK-12)
   2003-04 Enrollment: 2,411 . . . . (513) 553-2616
North College Hill City School District (PK-12)
   2003-04 Enrollment: 1,538 . . . . (513) 728-4770
Northwest Local School District (PK-12)
   2003-04 Enrollment: 10,657 . . . . (513) 923-1000
Oak Hills Local SD (PK-12)
   2003-04 Enrollment: 8,132 . . . . (513) 574-3200
Oak Tree Montessori (PK-06)
   2003-04 Enrollment: 97 . . . . (513) 241-0448

P.A.C.E. High School
   2003-04 Enrollment: n/a
Phoenix Community Learning Ctr (KG-08)
   2003-04 Enrollment: 349 . . . . (513) 351-5801
Princeton City SD (PK-12)
   2003-04 Enrollment: 6,105 . . . . (513) 771-8560
Riverside Academy (KG-08)
   2003-04 Enrollment: 495 . . . . (513) 921-7777
Saint Bernard-Elmwood Place City SD (PK-12)
   2003-04 Enrollment: 1,160 . . . . (513) 482-7121
Scholarts
   2003-04 Enrollment: n/a
Scholarts Career Center for Children
   2003-04 Enrollment: n/a
Summit Academy Cincinnati
   2003-04 Enrollment: n/a
Sycamore Community City SD (PK-12)
   2003-04 Enrollment: 5,759 . . . . (513) 791-4848
T.C.P. World Academy (KG-07)
   2003-04 Enrollment: 315 . . . . (513) 531-9500
Three Rivers Local Schools (PK-12)
   2003-04 Enrollment: 2,164 . . . . (513) 941-6400
W.E.B. Dubois (01-08)
   2003-04 Enrollment: 269 . . . . (513) 651-9624
West Clermont Local SD (PK-12)
   2003-04 Enrollment: 9,189 . . . . (513) 943-5000
Winton Woods City SD (PK-12)
   2003-04 Enrollment: 4,156 . . . . (513) 619-2300

Four-year College(s)

Art Academy of Cincinnati (Private, Not-for-profit)
   Fall 2004 Enrollment: 221 . . . . (513) 562-6262
   2005-06 Tuition: In-state $18,500; Out-of-state $18,500
Athenaeum of Ohio (Private, Not-for-profit, Roman Catholic)
   Fall 2004 Enrollment: 267 . . . . (513) 231-2223
   2005-06 Tuition: In-state $15,180; Out-of-state $15,180
Cincinnati Christian University (Private, Not-for-profit, Christian Churches and Churches of Christ)
   Fall 2004 Enrollment: 924 . . . . (513) 244-8100
   2005-06 Tuition: In-state $9,820; Out-of-state $9,820
Cincinnati College of Mortuary Science (Private, Not-for-profit)
   Fall 2004 Enrollment: 159 . . . . (513) 761-2020
   2005-06 Tuition: In-state $13,275; Out-of-state $13,275
College of Mount St. Joseph (Private, Not-for-profit, Roman Catholic)
   Fall 2004 Enrollment: 2,158 . . . . (513) 244-4200
   2005-06 Tuition: In-state $18,790; Out-of-state $18,790
Gods Bible School and College (Private, Not-for-profit, Other Protestant)
   Fall 2004 Enrollment: 301 . . . . (513) 721-7944
   2005-06 Tuition: In-state $4,630; Out-of-state $4,630
Hebrew Union College-Jewish Institute of Religion (Private, Not-for-profit, Jewish)
   Fall 2004 Enrollment: 126 . . . . (513) 221-1875
Temple Baptist College (Private, Not-for-profit, Baptist)
   Fall 2004 Enrollment: 120 . . . . (513) 851-3800
   2005-06 Tuition: In-state $8,670; Out-of-state $8,670
Union Institute & University (Private, Not-for-profit)
   Fall 2004 Enrollment: 2,539 . . . . (800) 486-3116
   2005-06 Tuition: In-state $8,912; Out-of-state $8,912
University of Cincinnati-Main Campus (Public)
   Fall 2004 Enrollment: 27,178 . . . . (513) 556-6000
   2005-06 Tuition: In-state $8,877; Out-of-state $22,629
University of Phoenix-Cincinnati Campus (Private, For-profit)
   Fall 2004 Enrollment: 489 . . . . (513) 772-9600
   2005-06 Tuition: In-state $11,550; Out-of-state $11,550
Xavier University (Private, Not-for-profit, Roman Catholic)
   Fall 2004 Enrollment: 6,668 . . . . (513) 745-3000
   2005-06 Tuition: In-state $21,850; Out-of-state $21,850

Two-year College(s)

Academy of Court Reporting-Cincinnati (Private, For-profit)
   Fall 2004 Enrollment: 381 . . . . (513) 723-0551
   2005-06 Tuition: In-state $8,000; Out-of-state $8,000
Antonelli College (Private, For-profit)
   Fall 2004 Enrollment: 428 . . . . (513) 241-4338
   2005-06 Tuition: In-state $11,920; Out-of-state $11,920

Art Institute of Cincinnati (Private, For-profit)
  Fall 2004 Enrollment: 74 .... (513) 751-1206
  2005-06 Tuition: In-state $13,996; Out-of-state $13,996
Art Institute of Ohio-Cincinnati (Private, For-profit)
  Fall 2004 Enrollment: n/a .... (513) 771-2821
  2005-06 Tuition: In-state $11,844; Out-of-state $11,844
Brown Mackie College-Cincinnati (Private, For-profit)
  Fall 2004 Enrollment: 911 .... (513) 771-2424
  2005-06 Tuition: In-state $6,444; Out-of-state $6,444
Christ Hospital School of Nursing (Private, Not-for-profit)
  Fall 2004 Enrollment: 257 .... (513) 585-2498
  2005-06 Tuition: In-state $4,875; Out-of-state $4,875
Cincinnati State Technical and Community College (Public)
  Fall 2004 Enrollment: 8,472 .... (513) 569-1500
  2005-06 Tuition: In-state $4,388; Out-of-state $8,775
College of Art Advertising (Private, For-profit)
  Fall 2004 Enrollment: 27 .... (513) 574-1010
  2005-06 Tuition: In-state $10,780; Out-of-state $10,780
Eastern Hills Academy of Hair Design (Private, For-profit)
  Fall 2004 Enrollment: 133 .... (513) 231-8621
Good Samaritan College of Nursing & Health Science (Private, Not-for-profit, Roman Catholic)
  Fall 2004 Enrollment: 309 .... (513) 872-2631
  2005-06 Tuition: In-state $12,652; Out-of-state $12,652
Great Oaks Institute of Technology and Career Development (Public)
  Fall 2004 Enrollment: 519 .... (513) 771-8925
Institute of Medical-Dental Technology (Private, For-profit)
  Fall 2004 Enrollment: 106 .... (513) 851-8500
International Academy (Private, For-profit)
  Fall 2004 Enrollment: 96 .... (513) 741-4777
Moler Hollywood Beauty Academy (Private, For-profit)
  Fall 2004 Enrollment: 92 .... (513) 621-5262
Moore University of Hair Design (Private, For-profit)
  Fall 2004 Enrollment: 18 .... (513) 531-3100
Ohio Center for Broadcasting (Private, For-profit)
  Fall 2004 Enrollment: 85 .... (513) 271-6060
  2005-06 Tuition: In-state $11,717; Out-of-state $11,717
Southwestern College (Private, For-profit)
  Fall 2004 Enrollment: 212 .... (513) 874-0432
  2005-06 Tuition: In-state $11,760; Out-of-state $11,760
Southwestern College of Business (Private, For-profit)
  Fall 2004 Enrollment: 244 .... (513) 421-3212
  2005-06 Tuition: In-state $10,760; Out-of-state $10,760
Western Hills School of Beauty and Hair Design (Private, For-profit)
  Fall 2004 Enrollment: 181 .... (513) 574-3818

Housing: Homeownership rate: 39.3% (2005); Median home value: $113,074 (2005); Median rent: $392 per month (2000); Median age of housing: 52 years (2000).
Hospitals: Bethesda Hospital (412 beds); Bethesda North Hospital (314 beds); Christ Hospital; Cincinnati Children's Hospital Medical Center (450 beds); Deaconess Hospital (273 beds); Department of Veterans Affairs Medical Center (378 beds); Drake Center (356 beds); Franciscan Hospital-Western Hills (290 beds); Good Samaritan Hospital (1600 beds); Health Alliance of Greater Cincinnati (550 beds); Jewish Hospital of Cincinnati (175 beds); Mercy Franciscan Hospital - Mt. Airy (269 beds); Mercy Hospital Anderson (186 beds); Shriners Hospitals for Children (30 beds); St. Luke Hospital West/Health Alliance (177 beds); Summit Behavior Health Center (274 beds); University Hospital Health Alliance (650 beds)
Safety: Violent crime rate: 114.8 per 10,000 population; Property crime rate: 714.5 per 10,000 population (2004).
Newspapers: Catholic Telegraph (Catholic - Circulation 23,000); Christian Standard (Christian - Circulation 59,000); CiN Weekly (General - Circulation 60,000); Cincinnati City Beat (Alternative, General - Circulation 50,000); Cincinnati Court Index (Circulation 1,300); Cincinnati Herald (Black - Circulation 10,000); Delhi Press/Price Hill Press (General - Circulation 17,727); Hilltop Press (General - Circulation 17,565); Northwest Press (General - Circulation 17,160); The American Israelite (Jewish - Circulation 7,000); The Cincinnati Enquirer (Circulation 218,514); The Cincinnati Post (Circulation 44,410); The Kentucky Post (Circulation 33,000); Tri-County Press (General - Circulation 8,130); Valley Courier-Suburban Week (General - Circulation 5,400); Western Hills Press (General - Circulation 20,770)
Transportation: Commute to work: 80.9% car, 10.1% public transportation, 5.5% walk, 2.6% work from home (2000); Travel time to work: 26.0% less than 15 minutes, 46.5% 15 to 30 minutes, 18.3% 30 to 45 minutes, 4.7% 45 to 60 minutes, 4.6% 60 minutes or more (2000); Amtrak: Service available.
Additional Information Contacts
Anderson Chamber of Commerce .... (513) 474-4802
  http://www.andersonareachamber.org
Cincinnati Chamber of Commerce..................... (513) 579-3100
  http://www.gccc.com
City of Cincinnati .... (513) 591-6000
  http://www.cincinnati-oh.gov/index.html
Greater Cincinnati Convention & Visitors Bureau .... (513) 621-2142
  http://www.cincyusa.com
Hamilton County Chamber of Commerce .... (513) 984-6555
  http://www.gccc.com
Northern Cincinnati Convention & Visitors Bureau .... (513) 771-5353
  http://www.cincynorth.com
Over-The-Rhine Chamber of Commerce................ (513) 241-2690
  http://www.otrchamber.com
Southwestern Ohio Chamber of Commerce .... (513) 984-0909
  http://www.gccc.com

CLEVES
(village). Covers a land area of 1.590 square miles and a water area of 0.002 square miles. Located at 39.16° N. Lat.; 84.75° W. Long. Elevation is 496 feet.
History: Cleves was platted in 1818 and named for John Cleves Symmes, a pioneer who had founded North Bend.
Population: 2,122 (1990); 2,790 (2000); 2,675 (2005); 2,510 (2010 projected); Race: 98.0% White, 0.5% Black, 0.2% Asian, 0.3% Hispanic of any race (2005); Density: 1,682.4 persons per square mile (2005); Average household size: 2.90 (2005); Median age: 34.2 (2005); Males per 100 females: 100.7 (2005); Marriage status: 21.6% never married, 63.9% now married, 5.9% widowed, 8.6% divorced (2000); Foreign born: 0.8% (2000); Ancestry (includes multiple ancestries): 30.1% German, 16.0% English, 15.4% Irish, 12.3% United States or American, 6.7% Other groups (2000).
Economy: Single-family building permits issued: 0 (2005); Multi-family building permits issued: 3 (2005); Employment by occupation: 8.9% management, 12.7% professional, 19.3% services, 26.9% sales, 0.0% farming, 18.4% construction, 13.8% production (2000).
Income: Per capita income: $21,134 (2005); Median household income: $55,235 (2005); Average household income: $61,182 (2005); Percent of households with income of $100,000 or more: 13.9% (2005); Poverty rate: 7.6% (2000).
Education: Percent of population age 25 and over with: High school diploma (including GED) or higher: 78.8% (2005); Bachelor's degree or higher: 13.4% (2005); Master's degree or higher: 4.6% (2005).

School District(s)
Three Rivers Local Schools (PK-12)
  2003-04 Enrollment: 2,164 .... (513) 941-6400
Housing: Homeownership rate: 77.4% (2005); Median home value: $120,571 (2005); Median rent: $387 per month (2000); Median age of housing: 42 years (2000).
Transportation: Commute to work: 95.8% car, 1.1% public transportation, 1.1% walk, 1.5% work from home (2000); Travel time to work: 22.2% less than 15 minutes, 33.5% 15 to 30 minutes, 30.0% 30 to 45 minutes, 10.4% 45 to 60 minutes, 4.0% 60 minutes or more (2000)
Additional Information Contacts
Village of Cleves .... (513) 941-5127
  http://www.cleves.org

COVEDALE
(CDP). Covers a land area of 2.796 square miles and a water area of 0 square miles. Located at 39.12° N. Lat.; 84.62° W. Long. Elevation is 890 feet.
Population: 6,674 (1990); 6,360 (2000); 6,390 (2005); 6,376 (2010 projected); Race: 98.4% White, 0.4% Black, 0.3% Asian, 0.7% Hispanic of any race (2005); Density: 2,285.0 persons per square mile (2005); Average household size: 2.56 (2005); Median age: 41.4 (2005); Males per 100 females: 93.4 (2005); Marriage status: 21.9% never married, 64.5% now married, 8.4% widowed, 5.2% divorced (2000); Foreign born: 2.0% (2000); Ancestry (includes multiple ancestries): 54.1% German, 23.3% Irish, 9.4% English, 8.4% United States or American, 6.2% Italian (2000).
Economy: Employment by occupation: 19.8% management, 23.1% professional, 9.9% services, 29.8% sales, 0.0% farming, 8.1% construction, 9.3% production (2000).
Income: Per capita income: $32,531 (2005); Median household income: $64,431 (2005); Average household income: $83,290 (2005); Percent of

households with income of $100,000 or more: 24.9% (2005); Poverty rate: 1.9% (2000).
Education: Percent of population age 25 and over with: High school diploma (including GED) or higher: 91.5% (2005); Bachelor's degree or higher: 31.8% (2005); Master's degree or higher: 11.1% (2005).
Housing: Homeownership rate: 92.7% (2005); Median home value: $143,179 (2005); Median rent: $570 per month (2000); Median age of housing: 43 years (2000).
Transportation: Commute to work: 94.8% car, 2.3% public transportation, 0.3% walk, 2.3% work from home (2000); Travel time to work: 23.8% less than 15 minutes, 34.7% 15 to 30 minutes, 32.8% 30 to 45 minutes, 5.8% 45 to 60 minutes, 2.9% 60 minutes or more (2000)

DEER PARK (city). Covers a land area of 0.857 square miles and a water area of 0 square miles. Located at 39.20° N. Lat.; 84.39° W. Long. Elevation is 870 feet.
Population: 6,181 (1990); 5,982 (2000); 5,700 (2005); 5,434 (2010 projected); Race: 95.8% White, 2.1% Black, 0.8% Asian, 0.8% Hispanic of any race (2005); Density: 6,650.0 persons per square mile (2005); Average household size: 2.23 (2005); Median age: 40.0 (2005); Males per 100 females: 87.2 (2005); Marriage status: 24.2% never married, 51.8% now married, 10.9% widowed, 13.2% divorced (2000); Foreign born: 2.2% (2000); Ancestry (includes multiple ancestries): 38.2% German, 16.2% Irish, 10.6% United States or American, 9.3% English, 7.5% Other groups (2000).
Economy: Suburb of Cincinnati. Single-family building permits issued: 0 (2005); Multi-family building permits issued: 0 (2005); Employment by occupation: 11.1% management, 18.0% professional, 16.2% services, 31.4% sales, 0.0% farming, 10.0% construction, 13.4% production (2000).
Income: Per capita income: $24,500 (2005); Median household income: $44,274 (2005); Average household income: $54,224 (2005); Percent of households with income of $100,000 or more: 10.0% (2005); Poverty rate: 5.3% (2000).
Taxes: Total city taxes per capita: $270 (2004); City property taxes per capita: $82 (2004).
Education: Percent of population age 25 and over with: High school diploma (including GED) or higher: 79.8% (2005); Bachelor's degree or higher: 16.5% (2005); Master's degree or higher: 3.1% (2005).
Housing: Homeownership rate: 72.3% (2005); Median home value: $118,407 (2005); Median rent: $441 per month (2000); Median age of housing: 54 years (2000).
Safety: Violent crime rate: 8.6 per 10,000 population; Property crime rate: 203.0 per 10,000 population (2004).
Transportation: Commute to work: 94.6% car, 0.7% public transportation, 1.8% walk, 2.7% work from home (2000); Travel time to work: 31.3% less than 15 minutes, 50.9% 15 to 30 minutes, 13.3% 30 to 45 minutes, 3.7% 45 to 60 minutes, 0.7% 60 minutes or more (2000)

DENT (CDP). Covers a land area of 6.006 square miles and a water area of 0 square miles. Located at 39.19° N. Lat.; 84.66° W. Long. Elevation is 810 feet.
Population: 6,416 (1990); 7,612 (2000); 8,559 (2005); 9,423 (2010 projected); Race: 97.7% White, 0.9% Black, 0.3% Asian, 0.4% Hispanic of any race (2005); Density: 1,425.1 persons per square mile (2005); Average household size: 2.36 (2005); Median age: 40.9 (2005); Males per 100 females: 94.2 (2005); Marriage status: 23.9% never married, 59.3% now married, 6.5% widowed, 10.3% divorced (2000); Foreign born: 0.9% (2000); Ancestry (includes multiple ancestries): 53.9% German, 16.7% Irish, 10.8% English, 7.7% Italian, 5.3% United States or American (2000).
Economy: Employment by occupation: 15.0% management, 22.5% professional, 12.0% services, 30.4% sales, 0.0% farming, 9.2% construction, 10.9% production (2000).
Income: Per capita income: $28,377 (2005); Median household income: $55,956 (2005); Average household income: $66,947 (2005); Percent of households with income of $100,000 or more: 17.7% (2005); Poverty rate: 3.7% (2000).
Education: Percent of population age 25 and over with: High school diploma (including GED) or higher: 89.8% (2005); Bachelor's degree or higher: 24.5% (2005); Master's degree or higher: 8.6% (2005).
Housing: Homeownership rate: 73.0% (2005); Median home value: $141,332 (2005); Median rent: $553 per month (2000); Median age of housing: 19 years (2000).
Transportation: Commute to work: 95.3% car, 1.0% public transportation, 1.1% walk, 2.0% work from home (2000); Travel time to work: 22.2% less than 15 minutes, 47.1% 15 to 30 minutes, 25.0% 30 to 45 minutes, 3.2% 45 to 60 minutes, 2.4% 60 minutes or more (2000)

DILLONVALE (CDP). Covers a land area of 0.902 square miles and a water area of 0 square miles. Located at 39.21° N. Lat.; 84.40° W. Long.
Population: 4,209 (1990); 3,716 (2000); 3,431 (2005); 3,161 (2010 projected); Race: 95.5% White, 1.9% Black, 0.5% Asian, 1.1% Hispanic of any race (2005); Density: 3,802.4 persons per square mile (2005); Average household size: 2.26 (2005); Median age: 43.3 (2005); Males per 100 females: 88.3 (2005); Marriage status: 23.5% never married, 55.2% now married, 10.4% widowed, 11.0% divorced (2000); Foreign born: 3.0% (2000); Ancestry (includes multiple ancestries): 41.7% German, 18.0% Irish, 11.8% English, 9.7% United States or American, 7.6% Other groups (2000).
Economy: Employment by occupation: 16.3% management, 17.7% professional, 12.7% services, 30.7% sales, 0.0% farming, 9.5% construction, 13.1% production (2000).
Income: Per capita income: $25,297 (2005); Median household income: $49,350 (2005); Average household income: $57,100 (2005); Percent of households with income of $100,000 or more: 10.3% (2005); Poverty rate: 3.8% (2000).
Education: Percent of population age 25 and over with: High school diploma (including GED) or higher: 86.2% (2005); Bachelor's degree or higher: 20.4% (2005); Master's degree or higher: 5.5% (2005).
Housing: Homeownership rate: 87.0% (2005); Median home value: $125,496 (2005); Median rent: $519 per month (2000); Median age of housing: 45 years (2000).
Transportation: Commute to work: 94.8% car, 1.2% public transportation, 0.7% walk, 3.3% work from home (2000); Travel time to work: 29.5% less than 15 minutes, 50.5% 15 to 30 minutes, 17.5% 30 to 45 minutes, 1.3% 45 to 60 minutes, 1.2% 60 minutes or more (2000)

DRY RUN (CDP). Covers a land area of 4.754 square miles and a water area of 0 square miles. Located at 39.10° N. Lat.; 84.33° W. Long.
Population: 5,389 (1990); 6,553 (2000); 6,532 (2005); 6,501 (2010 projected); Race: 95.9% White, 0.8% Black, 2.2% Asian, 1.0% Hispanic of any race (2005); Density: 1,373.9 persons per square mile (2005); Average household size: 3.14 (2005); Median age: 37.9 (2005); Males per 100 females: 100.7 (2005); Marriage status: 18.3% never married, 75.2% now married, 2.6% widowed, 4.0% divorced (2000); Foreign born: 3.6% (2000); Ancestry (includes multiple ancestries): 42.8% German, 25.4% Irish, 15.1% English, 7.2% Italian, 5.9% United States or American (2000).
Economy: Employment by occupation: 28.1% management, 30.9% professional, 8.2% services, 23.3% sales, 0.1% farming, 3.7% construction, 5.8% production (2000).
Income: Per capita income: $49,099 (2005); Median household income: $118,354 (2005); Average household income: $153,968 (2005); Percent of households with income of $100,000 or more: 60.0% (2005); Poverty rate: 2.0% (2000).
Education: Percent of population age 25 and over with: High school diploma (including GED) or higher: 97.0% (2005); Bachelor's degree or higher: 62.6% (2005); Master's degree or higher: 22.1% (2005).
Housing: Homeownership rate: 97.3% (2005); Median home value: $225,923 (2005); Median rent: $738 per month (2000); Median age of housing: 22 years (2000).
Transportation: Commute to work: 92.6% car, 1.2% public transportation, 0.2% walk, 5.9% work from home (2000); Travel time to work: 23.5% less than 15 minutes, 40.8% 15 to 30 minutes, 27.9% 30 to 45 minutes, 3.7% 45 to 60 minutes, 4.1% 60 minutes or more (2000)

ELMWOOD PLACE (village). Covers a land area of 0.331 square miles and a water area of 0 square miles. Located at 39.18° N. Lat.; 84.48° W. Long. Elevation is 520 feet.
History: Settled 1875, incorporated 1890.
Population: 2,937 (1990); 2,681 (2000); 2,445 (2005); 2,217 (2010 projected); Race: 90.8% White, 6.1% Black, 0.3% Asian, 2.0% Hispanic of any race (2005); Density: 7,392.9 persons per square mile (2005); Average household size: 2.50 (2005); Median age: 34.3 (2005); Males per 100 females: 104.3 (2005); Marriage status: 29.9% never married, 45.5% now married, 8.0% widowed, 16.6% divorced (2000); Foreign born: 1.0% (2000); Ancestry (includes multiple ancestries): 21.2% United States or American, 14.2% Other groups, 12.1% German, 7.4% Irish, 5.9% English (2000).
Economy: Machinery, foundry products. Single-family building permits issued: 0 (2005); Multi-family building permits issued: 0 (2005);

Employment by occupation: 4.0% management, 6.0% professional, 17.0% services, 27.1% sales, 0.0% farming, 10.7% construction, 35.3% production (2000).
Income: Per capita income: $14,165 (2005); Median household income: $30,984 (2005); Average household income: $35,375 (2005); Percent of households with income of $100,000 or more: 1.5% (2005); Poverty rate: 19.0% (2000).
Education: Percent of population age 25 and over with: High school diploma (including GED) or higher: 54.0% (2005); Bachelor's degree or higher: 3.8% (2005); Master's degree or higher: 0.9% (2005).
Housing: Homeownership rate: 46.1% (2005); Median home value: $74,431 (2005); Median rent: $330 per month (2000); Median age of housing: 60+ years (2000).
Transportation: Commute to work: 85.5% car, 3.9% public transportation, 7.2% walk, 1.8% work from home (2000); Travel time to work: 35.6% less than 15 minutes, 42.2% 15 to 30 minutes, 15.5% 30 to 45 minutes, 2.1% 45 to 60 minutes, 4.6% 60 minutes or more (2000)

EVENDALE
(village). Covers a land area of 4.771 square miles and a water area of 0 square miles. Located at 39.24° N. Lat.; 84.43° W. Long. Elevation is 584 feet.
Population: 3,175 (1990); 3,090 (2000); 2,932 (2005); 2,764 (2010 projected); Race: 85.1% White, 7.9% Black, 5.7% Asian, 0.5% Hispanic of any race (2005); Density: 614.5 persons per square mile (2005); Average household size: 2.85 (2005); Median age: 45.3 (2005); Males per 100 females: 101.4 (2005); Marriage status: 18.9% never married, 72.7% now married, 2.3% widowed, 6.1% divorced (2000); Foreign born: 4.7% (2000); Ancestry (includes multiple ancestries): 34.8% German, 16.1% Irish, 13.7% English, 13.0% Other groups, 7.4% United States or American (2000).
Economy: Single-family building permits issued: 2 (2005); Multi-family building permits issued: 0 (2005); Employment by occupation: 22.8% management, 31.6% professional, 6.3% services, 29.1% sales, 0.0% farming, 4.4% construction, 5.9% production (2000).
Income: Per capita income: $49,041 (2005); Median household income: $105,290 (2005); Average household income: $139,735 (2005); Percent of households with income of $100,000 or more: 52.5% (2005); Poverty rate: 0.3% (2000).
Education: Percent of population age 25 and over with: High school diploma (including GED) or higher: 93.0% (2005); Bachelor's degree or higher: 55.7% (2005); Master's degree or higher: 25.2% (2005).
Housing: Homeownership rate: 95.5% (2005); Median home value: $248,723 (2005); Median rent: $531 per month (2000); Median age of housing: 21 years (2000).
Transportation: Commute to work: 93.6% car, 0.5% public transportation, 0.6% walk, 5.3% work from home (2000); Travel time to work: 31.1% less than 15 minutes, 47.9% 15 to 30 minutes, 15.7% 30 to 45 minutes, 3.2% 45 to 60 minutes, 2.1% 60 minutes or more (2000)

FAIRFAX
(village). Covers a land area of 0.756 square miles and a water area of 0 square miles. Located at 39.14° N. Lat.; 84.39° W. Long. Elevation is 570 feet.
Population: 1,990 (1990); 1,938 (2000); 1,809 (2005); 1,678 (2010 projected); Race: 95.7% White, 1.3% Black, 1.4% Asian, 0.2% Hispanic of any race (2005); Density: 2,393.3 persons per square mile (2005); Average household size: 2.51 (2005); Median age: 37.7 (2005); Males per 100 females: 89.4 (2005); Marriage status: 27.1% never married, 52.9% now married, 8.1% widowed, 11.9% divorced (2000); Foreign born: 0.2% (2000); Ancestry (includes multiple ancestries): 39.8% German, 16.0% Irish, 10.3% English, 6.9% United States or American, 6.7% Other groups (2000).
Economy: Single-family building permits issued: 7 (2005); Multi-family building permits issued: 0 (2005); Employment by occupation: 12.2% management, 19.6% professional, 20.8% services, 26.2% sales, 0.0% farming, 8.0% construction, 13.2% production (2000).
Income: Per capita income: $21,580 (2005); Median household income: $46,443 (2005); Average household income: $54,144 (2005); Percent of households with income of $100,000 or more: 8.5% (2005); Poverty rate: 5.1% (2000).
Education: Percent of population age 25 and over with: High school diploma (including GED) or higher: 74.0% (2005); Bachelor's degree or higher: 15.7% (2005); Master's degree or higher: 4.3% (2005).
Housing: Homeownership rate: 80.9% (2005); Median home value: $118,851 (2005); Median rent: $535 per month (2000); Median age of housing: 55 years (2000).

Safety: Violent crime rate: 0.0 per 10,000 population; Property crime rate: 43.0 per 10,000 population (2004).
Transportation: Commute to work: 88.6% car, 5.3% public transportation, 3.6% walk, 2.5% work from home (2000); Travel time to work: 32.5% less than 15 minutes, 42.0% 15 to 30 minutes, 16.3% 30 to 45 minutes, 5.6% 45 to 60 minutes, 3.6% 60 minutes or more (2000)
Additional Information Contacts
Village of Fairfax .... (513) 527-6503
http://www.fairfaxohio.org

FINNEYTOWN
(CDP). Covers a land area of 3.988 square miles and a water area of 0 square miles. Located at 39.21° N. Lat.; 84.52° W. Long. Elevation is 900 feet.
Population: 13,094 (1990); 13,492 (2000); 12,878 (2005); 12,208 (2010 projected); Race: 69.1% White, 27.4% Black, 1.1% Asian, 0.8% Hispanic of any race (2005); Density: 3,228.8 persons per square mile (2005); Average household size: 2.55 (2005); Median age: 39.6 (2005); Males per 100 females: 88.4 (2005); Marriage status: 23.3% never married, 59.8% now married, 7.1% widowed, 9.8% divorced (2000); Foreign born: 2.8% (2000); Ancestry (includes multiple ancestries): 33.0% German, 28.1% Other groups, 13.2% Irish, 10.1% English, 5.5% United States or American (2000).
Economy: Employment by occupation: 15.5% management, 26.4% professional, 12.5% services, 28.5% sales, 0.0% farming, 5.8% construction, 11.3% production (2000).
Income: Per capita income: $27,912 (2005); Median household income: $58,805 (2005); Average household income: $70,954 (2005); Percent of households with income of $100,000 or more: 17.9% (2005); Poverty rate: 5.9% (2000).
Education: Percent of population age 25 and over with: High school diploma (including GED) or higher: 88.3% (2005); Bachelor's degree or higher: 36.2% (2005); Master's degree or higher: 12.4% (2005).
Housing: Homeownership rate: 80.1% (2005); Median home value: $129,383 (2005); Median rent: $567 per month (2000); Median age of housing: 41 years (2000).
Transportation: Commute to work: 92.5% car, 1.9% public transportation, 1.7% walk, 3.6% work from home (2000); Travel time to work: 21.3% less than 15 minutes, 50.5% 15 to 30 minutes, 23.0% 30 to 45 minutes, 3.6% 45 to 60 minutes, 1.6% 60 minutes or more (2000)

FOREST PARK
(city). Covers a land area of 6.509 square miles and a water area of 0 square miles. Located at 39.28° N. Lat.; 84.52° W. Long. Elevation is 836 feet.
History: After the surge in economic growth following WWII, the Warner-Kanter Corporation set aside a portion of undeveloped land from neighboring Greenhills and began to plan and build this new city. Forest Park was incorporated as a village in 1961 and achieved city status in 1968.
Population: 18,625 (1990); 19,463 (2000); 18,376 (2005); 17,213 (2010 projected); Race: 30.3% White, 60.9% Black, 4.9% Asian, 1.6% Hispanic of any race (2005); Density: 2,823.4 persons per square mile (2005); Average household size: 2.54 (2005); Median age: 35.9 (2005); Males per 100 females: 92.6 (2005); Marriage status: 29.3% never married, 53.8% now married, 5.5% widowed, 11.4% divorced (2000); Foreign born: 5.7% (2000); Ancestry (includes multiple ancestries): 54.5% Other groups, 14.6% German, 6.6% Irish, 5.8% English, 3.7% United States or American (2000).
Economy: Single-family building permits issued: 10 (2005); Multi-family building permits issued: 0 (2005); Employment by occupation: 12.5% management, 21.8% professional, 14.3% services, 30.6% sales, 0.0% farming, 4.2% construction, 16.6% production (2000).
Income: Per capita income: $24,553 (2005); Median household income: $53,715 (2005); Average household income: $62,013 (2005); Percent of households with income of $100,000 or more: 13.2% (2005); Poverty rate: 6.0% (2000).
Taxes: Total city taxes per capita: $530 (2004); City property taxes per capita: $200 (2004).
Education: Percent of population age 25 and over with: High school diploma (including GED) or higher: 88.5% (2005); Bachelor's degree or higher: 26.5% (2005); Master's degree or higher: 7.5% (2005).
Housing: Homeownership rate: 62.2% (2005); Median home value: $121,582 (2005); Median rent: $613 per month (2000); Median age of housing: 29 years (2000).
Safety: Violent crime rate: 25.6 per 10,000 population; Property crime rate: 295.1 per 10,000 population (2004).

Transportation: Commute to work: 92.9% car, 2.7% public transportation, 1.2% walk, 2.2% work from home (2000); Travel time to work: 23.1% less than 15 minutes, 42.9% 15 to 30 minutes, 23.5% 30 to 45 minutes, 6.2% 45 to 60 minutes, 4.3% 60 minutes or more (2000)
Additional Information Contacts
City of Forest Park..................................(513) 595-5200
http://www.forestpark.org

FORESTVILLE (CDP).
Covers a land area of 3.682 square miles and a water area of 0 square miles. Located at 39.07° N. Lat.; 84.33° W. Long. Elevation is 822 feet.
Population: 9,185 (1990); 10,978 (2000); 10,401 (2005); 9,856 (2010 projected); Race: 94.8% White, 1.0% Black, 2.8% Asian, 1.2% Hispanic of any race (2005); Density: 2,825.0 persons per square mile (2005); Average household size: 2.46 (2005); Median age: 40.1 (2005); Males per 100 females: 87.9 (2005); Marriage status: 20.4% never married, 62.0% now married, 10.3% widowed, 7.3% divorced (2000); Foreign born: 4.4% (2000); Ancestry (includes multiple ancestries): 38.7% German, 22.2% Irish, 13.7% English, 6.9% Other groups, 5.9% United States or American (2000).
Economy: Employment by occupation: 25.9% management, 23.5% professional, 11.5% services, 26.4% sales, 0.0% farming, 4.5% construction, 8.3% production (2000).
Income: Per capita income: $34,278 (2005); Median household income: $67,911 (2005); Average household income: $84,285 (2005); Percent of households with income of $100,000 or more: 30.1% (2005); Poverty rate: 3.6% (2000).
Education: Percent of population age 25 and over with: High school diploma (including GED) or higher: 92.2% (2005); Bachelor's degree or higher: 45.4% (2005); Master's degree or higher: 17.2% (2005).
Housing: Homeownership rate: 73.6% (2005); Median home value: $172,571 (2005); Median rent: $710 per month (2000); Median age of housing: 20 years (2000).
Transportation: Commute to work: 93.0% car, 1.9% public transportation, 0.7% walk, 3.5% work from home (2000); Travel time to work: 23.5% less than 15 minutes, 39.4% 15 to 30 minutes, 29.4% 30 to 45 minutes, 4.4% 45 to 60 minutes, 3.2% 60 minutes or more (2000)

FRUIT HILL (CDP).
Covers a land area of 1.251 square miles and a water area of 0 square miles. Located at 39.07° N. Lat.; 84.36° W. Long. Elevation is 750 feet.
Population: 4,168 (1990); 3,945 (2000); 3,562 (2005); 3,222 (2010 projected); Race: 97.2% White, 1.0% Black, 1.2% Asian, 0.6% Hispanic of any race (2005); Density: 2,847.0 persons per square mile (2005); Average household size: 2.71 (2005); Median age: 40.6 (2005); Males per 100 females: 92.9 (2005); Marriage status: 18.6% never married, 71.5% now married, 4.8% widowed, 5.0% divorced (2000); Foreign born: 2.2% (2000); Ancestry (includes multiple ancestries): 51.3% German, 17.9% Irish, 16.5% English, 5.7% Other groups, 5.2% Italian (2000).
Economy: Employment by occupation: 17.5% management, 25.9% professional, 13.0% services, 33.7% sales, 0.0% farming, 5.8% construction, 4.1% production (2000).
Income: Per capita income: $34,197 (2005); Median household income: $68,922 (2005); Average household income: $92,099 (2005); Percent of households with income of $100,000 or more: 28.8% (2005); Poverty rate: 2.5% (2000).
Education: Percent of population age 25 and over with: High school diploma (including GED) or higher: 90.7% (2005); Bachelor's degree or higher: 40.4% (2005); Master's degree or higher: 16.6% (2005).
Housing: Homeownership rate: 91.2% (2005); Median home value: $141,151 (2005); Median rent: $631 per month (2000); Median age of housing: 37 years (2000).
Transportation: Commute to work: 90.3% car, 2.1% public transportation, 0.0% walk, 6.0% work from home (2000); Travel time to work: 22.2% less than 15 minutes, 40.6% 15 to 30 minutes, 24.8% 30 to 45 minutes, 5.5% 45 to 60 minutes, 7.0% 60 minutes or more (2000)

GLENDALE (village).
Covers a land area of 1.666 square miles and a water area of 0 square miles. Located at 39.27° N. Lat.; 84.46° W. Long. Elevation is 630 feet.
History: Incorporated 1855.
Population: 2,445 (1990); 2,188 (2000); 2,174 (2005); 2,159 (2010 projected); Race: 83.3% White, 13.2% Black, 0.8% Asian, 1.3% Hispanic of any race (2005); Density: 1,304.5 persons per square mile (2005); Average household size: 2.27 (2005); Median age: 47.3 (2005); Males per 100 females: 94.5 (2005); Marriage status: 20.0% never married, 59.6% now married, 8.5% widowed, 11.9% divorced (2000); Foreign born: 0.8% (2000); Ancestry (includes multiple ancestries): 25.7% German, 19.4% Other groups, 13.6% Irish, 12.9% English, 5.6% Italian (2000).
Economy: Single-family building permits issued: 6 (2005); Multi-family building permits issued: 0 (2005); Employment by occupation: 21.3% management, 31.8% professional, 8.6% services, 25.5% sales, 0.0% farming, 5.4% construction, 7.5% production (2000).
Income: Per capita income: $52,523 (2005); Median household income: $88,194 (2005); Average household income: $119,176 (2005); Percent of households with income of $100,000 or more: 44.7% (2005); Poverty rate: 2.1% (2000).
Education: Percent of population age 25 and over with: High school diploma (including GED) or higher: 90.6% (2005); Bachelor's degree or higher: 56.5% (2005); Master's degree or higher: 16.9% (2005).
Housing: Homeownership rate: 84.8% (2005); Median home value: $241,813 (2005); Median rent: $597 per month (2000); Median age of housing: 53 years (2000).
Safety: Violent crime rate: 13.7 per 10,000 population; Property crime rate: 87.0 per 10,000 population (2004).
Transportation: Commute to work: 90.4% car, 0.6% public transportation, 3.7% walk, 4.6% work from home (2000); Travel time to work: 36.9% less than 15 minutes, 37.0% 15 to 30 minutes, 19.3% 30 to 45 minutes, 3.1% 45 to 60 minutes, 3.7% 60 minutes or more (2000)
Additional Information Contacts
Village of Glendale.................................(513) 771-7200
http://www.glendaleohio.org

GOLF MANOR (village).
Covers a land area of 0.580 square miles and a water area of 0 square miles. Located at 39.18° N. Lat.; 84.44° W. Long. Elevation is 700 feet.
History: Incorporated 1947.
Population: 4,154 (1990); 3,999 (2000); 3,729 (2005); 3,456 (2010 projected); Race: 26.1% White, 70.5% Black, 0.9% Asian, 0.6% Hispanic of any race (2005); Density: 6,430.7 persons per square mile (2005); Average household size: 2.27 (2005); Median age: 39.4 (2005); Males per 100 females: 82.5 (2005); Marriage status: 32.7% never married, 46.5% now married, 7.5% widowed, 13.3% divorced (2000); Foreign born: 6.0% (2000); Ancestry (includes multiple ancestries): 58.3% Other groups, 11.2% German, 6.2% Irish, 3.7% English, 3.0% Italian (2000).
Economy: Single-family building permits issued: 0 (2005); Multi-family building permits issued: 0 (2005); Employment by occupation: 9.6% management, 22.8% professional, 18.7% services, 27.5% sales, 0.0% farming, 5.4% construction, 16.0% production (2000).
Income: Per capita income: $21,734 (2005); Median household income: $42,773 (2005); Average household income: $49,327 (2005); Percent of households with income of $100,000 or more: 6.7% (2005); Poverty rate: 10.7% (2000).
Education: Percent of population age 25 and over with: High school diploma (including GED) or higher: 81.9% (2005); Bachelor's degree or higher: 20.6% (2005); Master's degree or higher: 8.0% (2005).
Housing: Homeownership rate: 56.2% (2005); Median home value: $91,791 (2005); Median rent: $435 per month (2000); Median age of housing: 47 years (2000).
Transportation: Commute to work: 85.2% car, 8.4% public transportation, 1.9% walk, 3.1% work from home (2000); Travel time to work: 23.2% less than 15 minutes, 51.9% 15 to 30 minutes, 18.1% 30 to 45 minutes, 3.5% 45 to 60 minutes, 3.3% 60 minutes or more (2000)
Additional Information Contacts
Village of Golf Manor..............................(513) 531-7418
http://www.golfmanor.org

GRANDVIEW (CDP).
Covers a land area of 4.357 square miles and a water area of 0.342 square miles. Located at 39.19° N. Lat.; 84.72° W. Long.
Population: 1,301 (1990); 1,391 (2000); 1,474 (2005); 1,534 (2010 projected); Race: 98.0% White, 0.1% Black, 0.4% Asian, 0.3% Hispanic of any race (2005); Density: 338.3 persons per square mile (2005); Average household size: 2.74 (2005); Median age: 36.3 (2005); Males per 100 females: 107.3 (2005); Marriage status: 22.2% never married, 60.6% now married, 10.1% widowed, 7.1% divorced (2000); Foreign born: 0.4% (2000); Ancestry (includes multiple ancestries): 49.4% German, 15.2% United States or American, 11.9% Irish, 11.5% English, 7.5% Italian (2000).

Economy: Employment by occupation: 3.3% management, 19.3% professional, 6.7% services, 38.1% sales, 0.0% farming, 15.2% construction, 17.4% production (2000).
Income: Per capita income: $21,867 (2005); Median household income: $39,392 (2005); Average household income: $60,023 (2005); Percent of households with income of $100,000 or more: 18.1% (2005); Poverty rate: 14.9% (2000).
Education: Percent of population age 25 and over with: High school diploma (including GED) or higher: 74.3% (2005); Bachelor's degree or higher: 16.5% (2005); Master's degree or higher: 6.2% (2005).
Housing: Homeownership rate: 84.5% (2005); Median home value: $115,323 (2005); Median rent: $420 per month (2000); Median age of housing: 27 years (2000).
Transportation: Commute to work: 100.0% car, 0.0% public transportation, 0.0% walk, 0.0% work from home (2000); Travel time to work: 17.2% less than 15 minutes, 43.2% 15 to 30 minutes, 30.1% 30 to 45 minutes, 6.0% 45 to 60 minutes, 3.6% 60 minutes or more (2000).

GREENHILLS (village). Covers a land area of 1.232 square miles and a water area of 0 square miles. Located at 39.26° N. Lat.; 84.51° W. Long. Elevation is 800 feet.
History: Greenhills was completed in 1937 as a Resettlement Administration project to provide housing.
Population: 4,393 (1990); 4,103 (2000); 3,788 (2005); 3,480 (2010 projected); Race: 93.5% White, 3.4% Black, 0.3% Asian, 1.2% Hispanic of any race (2005); Density: 3,073.7 persons per square mile (2005); Average household size: 2.45 (2005); Median age: 37.2 (2005); Males per 100 females: 89.9 (2005); Marriage status: 24.2% never married, 56.1% now married, 6.3% widowed, 13.4% divorced (2000); Foreign born: 2.3% (2000); Ancestry (includes multiple ancestries): 40.7% German, 22.8% Irish, 9.6% Other groups, 9.1% English, 5.3% United States or American (2000).
Economy: Single-family building permits issued: 1 (2005); Multi-family building permits issued: 0 (2005); Employment by occupation: 15.2% management, 24.8% professional, 13.6% services, 28.5% sales, 1.0% farming, 7.5% construction, 9.4% production (2000).
Income: Per capita income: $27,018 (2005); Median household income: $50,635 (2005); Average household income: $65,444 (2005); Percent of households with income of $100,000 or more: 17.2% (2005); Poverty rate: 3.8% (2000).
Education: Percent of population age 25 and over with: High school diploma (including GED) or higher: 91.4% (2005); Bachelor's degree or higher: 31.1% (2005); Master's degree or higher: 10.2% (2005).
Housing: Homeownership rate: 69.1% (2005); Median home value: $120,685 (2005); Median rent: $503 per month (2000); Median age of housing: 48 years (2000).
Transportation: Commute to work: 92.1% car, 2.5% public transportation, 1.2% walk, 4.0% work from home (2000); Travel time to work: 28.0% less than 15 minutes, 42.7% 15 to 30 minutes, 20.1% 30 to 45 minutes, 7.3% 45 to 60 minutes, 1.9% 60 minutes or more (2000).
Additional Information Contacts
Village of Greenhills . . . . (513) 825-2100
http://www.greenhillsohio.org

GROESBECK (CDP). Covers a land area of 2.938 square miles and a water area of 0 square miles. Located at 39.22° N. Lat.; 84.59° W. Long. Elevation is 850 feet.
Population: 6,684 (1990); 7,202 (2000); 6,793 (2005); 6,445 (2010 projected); Race: 90.5% White, 6.7% Black, 0.6% Asian, 0.6% Hispanic of any race (2005); Density: 2,311.9 persons per square mile (2005); Average household size: 2.57 (2005); Median age: 36.9 (2005); Males per 100 females: 95.9 (2005); Marriage status: 24.6% never married, 59.3% now married, 8.6% widowed, 7.5% divorced (2000); Foreign born: 0.8% (2000); Ancestry (includes multiple ancestries): 46.6% German, 14.7% Irish, 10.5% Other groups, 8.9% United States or American, 7.5% English (2000).
Economy: Employment by occupation: 13.6% management, 17.7% professional, 11.3% services, 34.4% sales, 0.2% farming, 10.2% construction, 12.6% production (2000).
Income: Per capita income: $24,598 (2005); Median household income: $55,360 (2005); Average household income: $63,141 (2005); Percent of households with income of $100,000 or more: 14.8% (2005); Poverty rate: 5.6% (2000).
Education: Percent of population age 25 and over with: High school diploma (including GED) or higher: 85.4% (2005); Bachelor's degree or higher: 19.8% (2005); Master's degree or higher: 6.7% (2005).
Housing: Homeownership rate: 83.7% (2005); Median home value: $123,490 (2005); Median rent: $522 per month (2000); Median age of housing: 32 years (2000).
Transportation: Commute to work: 95.1% car, 2.5% public transportation, 0.3% walk, 1.8% work from home (2000); Travel time to work: 21.7% less than 15 minutes, 51.9% 15 to 30 minutes, 20.4% 30 to 45 minutes, 3.5% 45 to 60 minutes, 2.5% 60 minutes or more (2000).

HARRISON (city). Covers a land area of 3.698 square miles and a water area of 0.028 square miles. Located at 39.25° N. Lat.; 84.80° W. Long. Elevation is 528 feet.
History: Harrison was settled before 1800, and the town was laid out in 1813 on the Ohio-Indiana border. It was named for William Henry Harrison.
Population: 7,904 (1990); 7,487 (2000); 7,467 (2005); 7,433 (2010 projected); Race: 97.9% White, 0.2% Black, 0.5% Asian, 0.5% Hispanic of any race (2005); Density: 2,019.1 persons per square mile (2005); Average household size: 2.71 (2005); Median age: 33.8 (2005); Males per 100 females: 94.2 (2005); Marriage status: 24.0% never married, 60.0% now married, 6.9% widowed, 9.0% divorced (2000); Foreign born: 0.6% (2000); Ancestry (includes multiple ancestries): 37.6% German, 15.2% Irish, 11.1% United States or American, 11.0% English, 9.4% Other groups (2000).
Economy: Single-family building permits issued: 121 (2005); Multi-family building permits issued: 144 (2005); Employment by occupation: 7.8% management, 17.7% professional, 17.2% services, 31.7% sales, 0.0% farming, 11.2% construction, 14.3% production (2000).
Income: Per capita income: $19,975 (2005); Median household income: $50,114 (2005); Average household income: $53,964 (2005); Percent of households with income of $100,000 or more: 8.7% (2005); Poverty rate: 6.8% (2000).
Education: Percent of population age 25 and over with: High school diploma (including GED) or higher: 79.2% (2005); Bachelor's degree or higher: 12.6% (2005); Master's degree or higher: 3.6% (2005).
School District(s)
Southwest Local SD (PK-12)
    2003-04 Enrollment: 3,971 . . . . (513) 367-4139
Housing: Homeownership rate: 73.1% (2005); Median home value: $124,239 (2005); Median rent: $428 per month (2000); Median age of housing: 30 years (2000).
Safety: Violent crime rate: 10.7 per 10,000 population; Property crime rate: 525.8 per 10,000 population (2004).
Newspapers: The Harrison Press (General - Circulation 5,382)
Transportation: Commute to work: 96.6% car, 0.7% public transportation, 1.4% walk, 0.7% work from home (2000); Travel time to work: 29.8% less than 15 minutes, 23.7% 15 to 30 minutes, 34.1% 30 to 45 minutes, 9.5% 45 to 60 minutes, 2.9% 60 minutes or more (2000).
Additional Information Contacts
City of Harrison . . . . (513) 367-3730
http://www.harrisonoh.org

KENWOOD (CDP). Covers a land area of 2.333 square miles and a water area of 0 square miles. Located at 39.20° N. Lat.; 84.37° W. Long. Elevation is 800 feet.
Population: 7,437 (1990); 7,423 (2000); 6,961 (2005); 6,549 (2010 projected); Race: 87.5% White, 5.4% Black, 6.0% Asian, 2.0% Hispanic of any race (2005); Density: 2,984.2 persons per square mile (2005); Average household size: 2.22 (2005); Median age: 46.9 (2005); Males per 100 females: 80.8 (2005); Marriage status: 18.2% never married, 59.1% now married, 14.9% widowed, 7.8% divorced (2000); Foreign born: 9.0% (2000); Ancestry (includes multiple ancestries): 32.0% German, 15.0% Irish, 14.8% English, 13.3% Other groups, 7.0% United States or American (2000).
Economy: Employment by occupation: 20.5% management, 35.6% professional, 10.6% services, 25.3% sales, 0.0% farming, 2.4% construction, 5.5% production (2000).
Income: Per capita income: $36,402 (2005); Median household income: $58,186 (2005); Average household income: $79,332 (2005); Percent of households with income of $100,000 or more: 25.2% (2005); Poverty rate: 3.3% (2000).
Education: Percent of population age 25 and over with: High school diploma (including GED) or higher: 91.5% (2005); Bachelor's degree or higher: 49.9% (2005); Master's degree or higher: 19.8% (2005).
Housing: Homeownership rate: 63.7% (2005); Median home value: $208,664 (2005); Median rent: $882 per month (2000); Median age of housing: 34 years (2000).

Transportation: Commute to work: 89.1% car, 1.5% public transportation, 1.5% walk, 6.7% work from home (2000); Travel time to work: 24.3% less than 15 minutes, 51.6% 15 to 30 minutes, 20.2% 30 to 45 minutes, 2.0% 45 to 60 minutes, 2.0% 60 minutes or more (2000)

LINCOLN HEIGHTS (village).
Covers a land area of 0.739 square miles and a water area of 0 square miles. Located at 39.24° N. Lat.; 84.45° W. Long. Elevation is 680 feet.
History: Incorporated 1946.
Population: 4,805 (1990); 4,113 (2000); 3,858 (2005); 3,598 (2010 projected); Race: 1.2% White, 97.5% Black, 0.0% Asian, 1.2% Hispanic of any race (2005); Density: 5,221.0 persons per square mile (2005); Average household size: 2.52 (2005); Median age: 31.3 (2005); Males per 100 females: 75.9 (2005); Marriage status: 39.3% never married, 38.0% now married, 9.6% widowed, 13.1% divorced (2000); Foreign born: 0.7% (2000); Ancestry (includes multiple ancestries): 83.8% Other groups, 1.4% African, 1.2% Irish, 0.8% German, 0.6% United States or American (2000).
Economy: Single-family building permits issued: 8 (2005); Multi-family building permits issued: 0 (2005); Employment by occupation: 5.5% management, 9.7% professional, 29.1% services, 25.7% sales, 0.0% farming, 2.4% construction, 27.6% production (2000).
Income: Per capita income: $14,280 (2005); Median household income: $22,315 (2005); Average household income: $36,032 (2005); Percent of households with income of $100,000 or more: 4.9% (2005); Poverty rate: 29.9% (2000).
Education: Percent of population age 25 and over with: High school diploma (including GED) or higher: 67.2% (2005); Bachelor's degree or higher: 5.8% (2005); Master's degree or higher: 1.6% (2005).
Housing: Homeownership rate: 35.8% (2005); Median home value: $75,339 (2005); Median rent: $281 per month (2000); Median age of housing: 44 years (2000).
Transportation: Commute to work: 87.4% car, 5.6% public transportation, 5.4% walk, 1.6% work from home (2000); Travel time to work: 29.7% less than 15 minutes, 44.5% 15 to 30 minutes, 16.3% 30 to 45 minutes, 5.3% 45 to 60 minutes, 4.2% 60 minutes or more (2000)
Additional Information Contacts
Village of Lincoln Heights . . . . (513) 733-5900
http://www.lincolnheightsohio.org

LOCKLAND (village).
Covers a land area of 1.223 square miles and a water area of 0 square miles. Located at 39.22° N. Lat.; 84.45° W. Long. Elevation is 575 feet.
History: Plotted 1828, incorporated 1865.
Population: 4,357 (1990); 3,707 (2000); 3,404 (2005); 3,108 (2010 projected); Race: 69.6% White, 26.5% Black, 0.6% Asian, 1.9% Hispanic of any race (2005); Density: 2,783.1 persons per square mile (2005); Average household size: 2.26 (2005); Median age: 37.5 (2005); Males per 100 females: 102.4 (2005); Marriage status: 33.0% never married, 43.1% now married, 8.9% widowed, 15.0% divorced (2000); Foreign born: 4.9% (2000); Ancestry (includes multiple ancestries): 27.1% Other groups, 21.6% German, 9.7% Irish, 8.1% English, 6.9% United States or American (2000).
Economy: Single-family building permits issued: 4 (2005); Multi-family building permits issued: 0 (2005); Employment by occupation: 7.3% management, 10.4% professional, 20.4% services, 26.2% sales, 0.0% farming, 8.6% construction, 27.1% production (2000).
Income: Per capita income: $17,136 (2005); Median household income: $31,205 (2005); Average household income: $38,783 (2005); Percent of households with income of $100,000 or more: 4.7% (2005); Poverty rate: 17.1% (2000).
Education: Percent of population age 25 and over with: High school diploma (including GED) or higher: 71.2% (2005); Bachelor's degree or higher: 8.5% (2005); Master's degree or higher: 2.8% (2005).
School District(s)
Lockland Local SD (PK-12)
    2003-04 Enrollment: 631 . . . . (513) 563-5000
Housing: Homeownership rate: 48.9% (2005); Median home value: $83,952 (2005); Median rent: $361 per month (2000); Median age of housing: 57 years (2000).
Safety: Violent crime rate: 145.2 per 10,000 population; Property crime rate: 526.8 per 10,000 population (2004).
Transportation: Commute to work: 90.4% car, 5.8% public transportation, 1.7% walk, 1.7% work from home (2000); Travel time to work: 26.4% less than 15 minutes, 46.7% 15 to 30 minutes, 22.1% 30 to 45 minutes, 3.5% 45 to 60 minutes, 1.3% 60 minutes or more (2000)

Additional Information Contacts
Village of Lockland . . . . (513) 761-1124
http://www.lockland.com

LOVELAND (city).
Covers a land area of 4.646 square miles and a water area of 0.055 square miles. Located at 39.26° N. Lat.; 84.27° W. Long. Elevation is 584 feet.
History: Loveland was first settled in 1795 by Col. Thomas Paxton and is named after James Loveland, who operated a general store and post office near the railroad tracks downtown. It was incorporated as a village on May 12, 1878, and later incorporated as a chartered city in 1961. In its early days, Loveland was known as a resort town, with its summer homes for the wealthy, earning it the nickname "Little Switzerland of the Miami Valley." Notable residents included future Chief Justice Salmon P. Chase.
Population: 10,756 (1990); 11,677 (2000); 11,604 (2005); 11,682 (2010 projected); Race: 95.6% White, 1.3% Black, 1.2% Asian, 1.3% Hispanic of any race (2005); Density: 2,497.8 persons per square mile (2005); Average household size: 2.56 (2005); Median age: 37.2 (2005); Males per 100 females: 91.7 (2005); Marriage status: 22.8% never married, 61.8% now married, 6.1% widowed, 9.3% divorced (2000); Foreign born: 2.9% (2000); Ancestry (includes multiple ancestries): 31.5% German, 17.5% Irish, 12.4% English, 9.4% Other groups, 8.5% United States or American (2000).
Economy: Single-family building permits issued: 60 (2005); Multi-family building permits issued: 0 (2005); Employment by occupation: 18.3% management, 20.2% professional, 12.9% services, 30.7% sales, 0.1% farming, 6.9% construction, 10.9% production (2000).
Income: Per capita income: $31,847 (2005); Median household income: $63,575 (2005); Average household income: $81,163 (2005); Percent of households with income of $100,000 or more: 24.5% (2005); Poverty rate: 5.7% (2000).
Education: Percent of population age 25 and over with: High school diploma (including GED) or higher: 89.9% (2005); Bachelor's degree or higher: 35.2% (2005); Master's degree or higher: 12.2% (2005).
School District(s)
Loveland City SD (PK-12)
    2003-04 Enrollment: 4,278 . . . . (513) 683-5600
Milford Ex Vill SD (PK-12)
    2003-04 Enrollment: 6,225 . . . . (513) 831-1314
Sycamore Community City SD (PK-12)
    2003-04 Enrollment: 5,759 . . . . (513) 791-4848
Housing: Homeownership rate: 74.7% (2005); Median home value: $148,659 (2005); Median rent: $530 per month (2000); Median age of housing: 25 years (2000).
Newspapers: Bethel Journal (General - Circulation 2,035); Community Journal - Clermont Edition (General - Circulation 24,035); Community Journal - North Clermont Edition (General - Circulation 14,656); Community Press - Mason and Deerfield (General - Circulation 11,350); Eastern Hills Journal (General - Circulation 12,818); Forest Hills Journal (General - Circulation 14,110); Loveland Herald (General - Circulation 6,274); Northeast Suburban Life (General - Circulation 8,011); Suburban Life (General - Circulation 8,370)
Transportation: Commute to work: 95.3% car, 0.7% public transportation, 0.4% walk, 3.2% work from home (2000); Travel time to work: 25.6% less than 15 minutes, 43.0% 15 to 30 minutes, 22.2% 30 to 45 minutes, 6.1% 45 to 60 minutes, 3.1% 60 minutes or more (2000)
Additional Information Contacts
City of Loveland . . . . (513) 683-0150
http://www.lovelandoh.com
Loveland Chamber of Commerce . . . . (513) 683-1544
http://www.lovelandchamber.org

MACK NORTH (CDP).
Aka Mack. Covers a land area of 3.076 square miles and a water area of 0 square miles. Located at 39.16° N. Lat.; 84.66° W. Long.
Population: 2,816 (1990); 3,529 (2000); 3,816 (2005); 4,062 (2010 projected); Race: 97.6% White, 1.0% Black, 0.2% Asian, 0.8% Hispanic of any race (2005); Density: 1,240.5 persons per square mile (2005); Average household size: 3.11 (2005); Median age: 37.9 (2005); Males per 100 females: 102.1 (2005); Marriage status: 21.0% never married, 69.0% now married, 5.0% widowed, 4.9% divorced (2000); Foreign born: 1.4% (2000); Ancestry (includes multiple ancestries): 51.0% German, 18.6% Irish, 8.4% English, 7.5% Italian, 4.0% United States or American (2000).
Economy: Employment by occupation: 16.4% management, 18.9% professional, 9.7% services, 30.9% sales, 0.0% farming, 12.0% construction, 12.1% production (2000).

Income: Per capita income: $34,416 (2005); Median household income: $85,514 (2005); Average household income: $107,121 (2005); Percent of households with income of $100,000 or more: 39.9% (2005); Poverty rate: 4.0% (2000).
Education: Percent of population age 25 and over with: High school diploma (including GED) or higher: 88.8% (2005); Bachelor's degree or higher: 29.6% (2005); Master's degree or higher: 10.6% (2005).
Housing: Homeownership rate: 96.3% (2005); Median home value: $191,981 (2005); Median rent: $566 per month (2000); Median age of housing: 27 years (2000).
Transportation: Commute to work: 94.7% car, 2.1% public transportation, 1.0% walk, 2.3% work from home (2000); Travel time to work: 21.0% less than 15 minutes, 39.4% 15 to 30 minutes, 30.3% 30 to 45 minutes, 7.6% 45 to 60 minutes, 1.7% 60 minutes or more (2000)

MACK SOUTH (CDP).
Covers a land area of 3.696 square miles and a water area of 0 square miles. Located at 39.14° N. Lat.; 84.67° W. Long.
Population: 5,767 (1990); 5,837 (2000); 6,042 (2005); 6,224 (2010 projected); Race: 98.8% White, 0.0% Black, 0.5% Asian, 0.2% Hispanic of any race (2005); Density: 1,634.7 persons per square mile (2005); Average household size: 2.98 (2005); Median age: 41.9 (2005); Males per 100 females: 97.3 (2005); Marriage status: 23.3% never married, 70.7% now married, 3.8% widowed, 2.2% divorced (2000); Foreign born: 1.2% (2000); Ancestry (includes multiple ancestries): 63.8% German, 19.3% Irish, 9.1% Italian, 7.4% English, 7.3% United States or American (2000).
Economy: Employment by occupation: 20.5% management, 25.8% professional, 12.2% services, 30.1% sales, 0.0% farming, 6.4% construction, 5.1% production (2000).
Income: Per capita income: $40,139 (2005); Median household income: $95,741 (2005); Average household income: $119,646 (2005); Percent of households with income of $100,000 or more: 47.0% (2005); Poverty rate: 0.4% (2000).
Education: Percent of population age 25 and over with: High school diploma (including GED) or higher: 95.1% (2005); Bachelor's degree or higher: 38.5% (2005); Master's degree or higher: 11.3% (2005).
Housing: Homeownership rate: 98.1% (2005); Median home value: $202,326 (2005); Median rent: $435 per month (2000); Median age of housing: 29 years (2000).
Transportation: Commute to work: 94.0% car, 2.1% public transportation, 0.4% walk, 3.2% work from home (2000); Travel time to work: 19.7% less than 15 minutes, 36.2% 15 to 30 minutes, 33.1% 30 to 45 minutes, 6.3% 45 to 60 minutes, 4.7% 60 minutes or more (2000)

MADEIRA (city).
Covers a land area of 3.366 square miles and a water area of 0 square miles. Located at 39.18° N. Lat.; 84.36° W. Long. Elevation is 772 feet.
Population: 9,143 (1990); 8,923 (2000); 8,505 (2005); 8,063 (2010 projected); Race: 95.1% White, 1.3% Black, 2.2% Asian, 0.8% Hispanic of any race (2005); Density: 2,526.8 persons per square mile (2005); Average household size: 2.61 (2005); Median age: 43.1 (2005); Males per 100 females: 89.8 (2005); Marriage status: 18.2% never married, 66.2% now married, 8.4% widowed, 7.2% divorced (2000); Foreign born: 2.8% (2000); Ancestry (includes multiple ancestries): 43.0% German, 20.5% Irish, 14.3% English, 6.2% United States or American, 4.9% Italian (2000).
Economy: Single-family building permits issued: 3 (2005); Multi-family building permits issued: 0 (2005); Employment by occupation: 18.0% management, 33.3% professional, 9.9% services, 27.2% sales, 0.0% farming, 4.3% construction, 7.4% production (2000).
Income: Per capita income: $36,073 (2005); Median household income: $68,640 (2005); Average household income: $92,581 (2005); Percent of households with income of $100,000 or more: 30.7% (2005); Poverty rate: 1.3% (2000).
Education: Percent of population age 25 and over with: High school diploma (including GED) or higher: 92.1% (2005); Bachelor's degree or higher: 44.6% (2005); Master's degree or higher: 17.0% (2005).
Housing: Homeownership rate: 91.7% (2005); Median home value: $188,800 (2005); Median rent: $456 per month (2000); Median age of housing: 45 years (2000).
Safety: Violent crime rate: 3.5 per 10,000 population; Property crime rate: 118.3 per 10,000 population (2004).
Transportation: Commute to work: 92.5% car, 1.3% public transportation, 1.0% walk, 5.1% work from home (2000); Travel time to work: 27.9% less than 15 minutes, 54.8% 15 to 30 minutes, 14.0% 30 to 45 minutes, 1.2% 45 to 60 minutes, 2.2% 60 minutes or more (2000)
Additional Information Contacts

City of Madeira . . . . (513) 561-7228
http://www.madeiracity.com

MARIEMONT (village).
Covers a land area of 0.854 square miles and a water area of 0.009 square miles. Located at 39.14° N. Lat.; 84.37° W. Long. Elevation is 590 feet.
History: Mariemont was laid out in 1922 along the Little Miami River on land owned by Marie Emery of Cincinnati. A large stone tower on a knoll above the town housed the Bells of Mariemont, 23 bells weighing from 100 pounds to two tons.
Population: 3,169 (1990); 3,408 (2000); 3,166 (2005); 2,929 (2010 projected); Race: 96.1% White, 1.4% Black, 0.9% Asian, 1.2% Hispanic of any race (2005); Density: 3,708.2 persons per square mile (2005); Average household size: 2.37 (2005); Median age: 39.2 (2005); Males per 100 females: 79.6 (2005); Marriage status: 18.1% never married, 61.9% now married, 10.9% widowed, 9.1% divorced (2000); Foreign born: 3.9% (2000); Ancestry (includes multiple ancestries): 37.9% German, 20.2% English, 18.6% Irish, 6.3% Scottish, 4.9% Italian (2000).
Economy: Single-family building permits issued: 0 (2005); Multi-family building permits issued: 0 (2005); Employment by occupation: 20.9% management, 41.0% professional, 10.8% services, 23.7% sales, 0.0% farming, 1.4% construction, 2.2% production (2000).
Income: Per capita income: $35,963 (2005); Median household income: $67,083 (2005); Average household income: $84,319 (2005); Percent of households with income of $100,000 or more: 29.2% (2005); Poverty rate: 5.0% (2000).
Education: Percent of population age 25 and over with: High school diploma (including GED) or higher: 93.4% (2005); Bachelor's degree or higher: 63.2% (2005); Master's degree or higher: 27.9% (2005).
Housing: Homeownership rate: 61.6% (2005); Median home value: $251,672 (2005); Median rent: $644 per month (2000); Median age of housing: 55 years (2000).
Safety: Violent crime rate: 0.0 per 10,000 population; Property crime rate: 206.4 per 10,000 population (2004).
Transportation: Commute to work: 90.6% car, 3.1% public transportation, 1.8% walk, 4.5% work from home (2000); Travel time to work: 22.4% less than 15 minutes, 58.7% 15 to 30 minutes, 17.7% 30 to 45 minutes, 0.8% 45 to 60 minutes, 0.3% 60 minutes or more (2000)

MONFORT HEIGHTS EAST (CDP).
Covers a land area of 1.439 square miles and a water area of 0 square miles. Located at 39.18° N. Lat.; 84.58° W. Long.
Population: 3,645 (1990); 3,880 (2000); 3,939 (2005); 4,002 (2010 projected); Race: 89.9% White, 6.8% Black, 1.8% Asian, 0.6% Hispanic of any race (2005); Density: 2,737.2 persons per square mile (2005); Average household size: 2.48 (2005); Median age: 34.8 (2005); Males per 100 females: 95.3 (2005); Marriage status: 24.1% never married, 63.1% now married, 6.3% widowed, 6.6% divorced (2000); Foreign born: 1.7% (2000); Ancestry (includes multiple ancestries): 49.8% German, 13.9% Irish, 9.5% Other groups, 7.7% English, 6.8% Italian (2000).
Economy: Employment by occupation: 14.3% management, 25.3% professional, 10.9% services, 31.4% sales, 0.0% farming, 7.9% construction, 10.2% production (2000).
Income: Per capita income: $26,154 (2005); Median household income: $54,683 (2005); Average household income: $64,698 (2005); Percent of households with income of $100,000 or more: 14.6% (2005); Poverty rate: 7.5% (2000).
Education: Percent of population age 25 and over with: High school diploma (including GED) or higher: 92.3% (2005); Bachelor's degree or higher: 30.4% (2005); Master's degree or higher: 6.7% (2005).
Housing: Homeownership rate: 75.0% (2005); Median home value: $128,111 (2005); Median rent: $531 per month (2000); Median age of housing: 35 years (2000).
Transportation: Commute to work: 89.8% car, 2.6% public transportation, 2.6% walk, 4.7% work from home (2000); Travel time to work: 18.6% less than 15 minutes, 48.9% 15 to 30 minutes, 26.2% 30 to 45 minutes, 3.7% 45 to 60 minutes, 2.6% 60 minutes or more (2000)

MONFORT HEIGHTS SOUTH (CDP). Aka Monfort Heights.
Covers a land area of 3.108 square miles and a water area of <.001 square miles. Located at 39.17° N. Lat.; 84.60° W. Long.
Population: 4,399 (1990); 4,466 (2000); 4,657 (2005); 4,818 (2010 projected); Race: 97.5% White, 0.6% Black, 0.7% Asian, 0.5% Hispanic of any race (2005); Density: 1,498.5 persons per square mile (2005); Average household size: 2.61 (2005); Median age: 41.2 (2005); Males per 100

females: 98.3 (2005); Marriage status: 21.8% never married, 63.8% now married, 8.3% widowed, 6.1% divorced (2000); Foreign born: 1.9% (2000); Ancestry (includes multiple ancestries): 52.4% German, 17.3% Irish, 11.5% English, 11.4% United States or American, 6.6% Italian (2000).
Economy: Employment by occupation: 16.7% management, 20.9% professional, 13.3% services, 31.0% sales, 0.0% farming, 7.0% construction, 11.2% production (2000).
Income: Per capita income: $35,502 (2005); Median household income: $68,691 (2005); Average household income: $92,758 (2005); Percent of households with income of $100,000 or more: 27.7% (2005); Poverty rate: 5.6% (2000).
Education: Percent of population age 25 and over with: High school diploma (including GED) or higher: 89.4% (2005); Bachelor's degree or higher: 25.8% (2005); Master's degree or higher: 7.2% (2005).
Housing: Homeownership rate: 94.3% (2005); Median home value: $139,881 (2005); Median rent: $513 per month (2000); Median age of housing: 38 years (2000).
Transportation: Commute to work: 95.1% car, 2.5% public transportation, 0.0% walk, 2.2% work from home (2000); Travel time to work: 22.1% less than 15 minutes, 49.4% 15 to 30 minutes, 23.8% 30 to 45 minutes, 2.5% 45 to 60 minutes, 2.3% 60 minutes or more (2000)

MONTGOMERY (city).
Covers a land area of 5.325 square miles and a water area of 0 square miles. Located at 39.24° N. Lat.; 84.34° W. Long. Elevation is 840 feet.
Population: 9,896 (1990); 10,163 (2000); 9,530 (2005); 8,938 (2010 projected); Race: 93.5% White, 1.7% Black, 3.3% Asian, 0.8% Hispanic of any race (2005); Density: 1,789.8 persons per square mile (2005); Average household size: 2.77 (2005); Median age: 44.7 (2005); Males per 100 females: 93.4 (2005); Marriage status: 16.1% never married, 72.9% now married, 7.0% widowed, 4.0% divorced (2000); Foreign born: 7.0% (2000); Ancestry (includes multiple ancestries): 34.2% German, 16.7% Irish, 14.9% English, 7.4% Other groups, 5.9% United States or American (2000).
Economy: Single-family building permits issued: 23 (2005); Multi-family building permits issued: 0 (2005); Employment by occupation: 30.1% management, 33.4% professional, 6.6% services, 23.5% sales, 0.2% farming, 2.2% construction, 4.0% production (2000).
Income: Per capita income: $50,230 (2005); Median household income: $99,904 (2005); Average household income: $138,826 (2005); Percent of households with income of $100,000 or more: 49.9% (2005); Poverty rate: 2.8% (2000).
Taxes: Total city taxes per capita: $992 (2004); City property taxes per capita: $368 (2004).
Education: Percent of population age 25 and over with: High school diploma (including GED) or higher: 95.7% (2005); Bachelor's degree or higher: 62.8% (2005); Master's degree or higher: 26.0% (2005).
Housing: Homeownership rate: 91.0% (2005); Median home value: $255,688 (2005); Median rent: $841 per month (2000); Median age of housing: 27 years (2000).
Safety: Violent crime rate: 4.1 per 10,000 population; Property crime rate: 282.7 per 10,000 population (2004).
Transportation: Commute to work: 90.7% car, 0.9% public transportation, 1.6% walk, 6.4% work from home (2000); Travel time to work: 29.0% less than 15 minutes, 44.3% 15 to 30 minutes, 19.4% 30 to 45 minutes, 2.6% 45 to 60 minutes, 4.6% 60 minutes or more (2000)
Additional Information Contacts
City of Montgomery . . . . (513) 891-2424
http://www.ci.montgomery.oh.us

MOUNT HEALTHY (city).
Covers a land area of 1.423 square miles and a water area of 0 square miles. Located at 39.23° N. Lat.; 84.54° W. Long. Elevation is 855 feet.
History: Mount Healthy was founded in 1817 by John Laboyteaux and Samuel Hill. It was first called Mount Pleasant, but the name was later changed to reflect the village's escape from the cholera epidemic of the 1850's.
Population: 7,580 (1990); 7,149 (2000); 6,646 (2005); 6,182 (2010 projected); Race: 70.6% White, 26.0% Black, 0.6% Asian, 1.1% Hispanic of any race (2005); Density: 4,668.8 persons per square mile (2005); Average household size: 2.16 (2005); Median age: 38.0 (2005); Males per 100 females: 79.0 (2005); Marriage status: 28.7% never married, 46.8% now married, 12.7% widowed, 11.8% divorced (2000); Foreign born: 2.3% (2000); Ancestry (includes multiple ancestries): 32.0% German, 28.8% Other groups, 10.0% Irish, 8.0% English, 7.4% United States or American (2000).
Economy: Single-family building permits issued: 3 (2005); Multi-family building permits issued: 0 (2005); Employment by occupation: 11.1% management, 19.3% professional, 15.6% services, 30.3% sales, 0.0% farming, 6.2% construction, 17.5% production (2000).
Income: Per capita income: $20,988 (2005); Median household income: $36,124 (2005); Average household income: $44,039 (2005); Percent of households with income of $100,000 or more: 5.3% (2005); Poverty rate: 8.9% (2000).
Education: Percent of population age 25 and over with: High school diploma (including GED) or higher: 77.1% (2005); Bachelor's degree or higher: 16.3% (2005); Master's degree or higher: 5.1% (2005).
School District(s)
Hamilton County Math & Science (KG-02)
    2003-04 Enrollment: 156 . . . . (513) 728-8620
Housing: Homeownership rate: 48.2% (2005); Median home value: $98,108 (2005); Median rent: $466 per month (2000); Median age of housing: 43 years (2000).
Safety: Violent crime rate: 46.7 per 10,000 population; Property crime rate: 474.5 per 10,000 population (2004).
Transportation: Commute to work: 92.1% car, 2.5% public transportation, 2.0% walk, 2.6% work from home (2000); Travel time to work: 23.0% less than 15 minutes, 44.6% 15 to 30 minutes, 23.7% 30 to 45 minutes, 6.4% 45 to 60 minutes, 2.2% 60 minutes or more (2000)
Additional Information Contacts
City of Mount Healthy . . . . (513) 931-8840
http://www.mthealthy.org

MOUNT HEALTHY HEIGHTS (CDP).
Covers a land area of 0.768 square miles and a water area of 0 square miles. Located at 39.27° N. Lat.; 84.57° W. Long.
Population: 3,863 (1990); 3,450 (2000); 3,152 (2005); 2,888 (2010 projected); Race: 68.8% White, 27.0% Black, 1.7% Asian, 1.0% Hispanic of any race (2005); Density: 4,101.9 persons per square mile (2005); Average household size: 2.64 (2005); Median age: 32.7 (2005); Males per 100 females: 95.8 (2005); Marriage status: 30.3% never married, 56.8% now married, 3.4% widowed, 9.6% divorced (2000); Foreign born: 2.2% (2000); Ancestry (includes multiple ancestries): 36.5% German, 26.5% Other groups, 10.0% Irish, 4.5% United States or American, 4.0% English (2000).
Economy: Employment by occupation: 9.5% management, 17.1% professional, 11.6% services, 30.4% sales, 0.0% farming, 10.7% construction, 20.7% production (2000).
Income: Per capita income: $22,750 (2005); Median household income: $50,601 (2005); Average household income: $60,157 (2005); Percent of households with income of $100,000 or more: 11.0% (2005); Poverty rate: 4.2% (2000).
Education: Percent of population age 25 and over with: High school diploma (including GED) or higher: 84.5% (2005); Bachelor's degree or higher: 16.7% (2005); Master's degree or higher: 4.2% (2005).
Housing: Homeownership rate: 67.4% (2005); Median home value: $99,502 (2005); Median rent: $608 per month (2000); Median age of housing: 30 years (2000).
Transportation: Commute to work: 96.6% car, 1.9% public transportation, 0.0% walk, 1.5% work from home (2000); Travel time to work: 17.7% less than 15 minutes, 44.5% 15 to 30 minutes, 26.3% 30 to 45 minutes, 6.5% 45 to 60 minutes, 5.0% 60 minutes or more (2000)

NEWTOWN (village).
Covers a land area of 2.322 square miles and a water area of 0 square miles. Located at 39.12° N. Lat.; 84.35° W. Long. Elevation is 550 feet.
History: Laid out 1801.
Population: 1,589 (1990); 2,420 (2000); 2,333 (2005); 2,252 (2010 projected); Race: 95.4% White, 2.7% Black, 1.0% Asian, 1.5% Hispanic of any race (2005); Density: 1,005.0 persons per square mile (2005); Average household size: 2.56 (2005); Median age: 37.7 (2005); Males per 100 females: 96.1 (2005); Marriage status: 26.3% never married, 60.4% now married, 5.0% widowed, 8.2% divorced (2000); Foreign born: 2.0% (2000); Ancestry (includes multiple ancestries): 37.5% German, 16.3% Irish, 10.1% English, 8.4% United States or American, 6.5% Other groups (2000).
Economy: Concrete products, plastics, machinery. Single-family building permits issued: 32 (2005); Multi-family building permits issued: 0 (2005); Employment by occupation: 20.3% management, 15.4% professional, 14.0% services, 24.8% sales, 0.0% farming, 12.3% construction, 13.1% production (2000).
Income: Per capita income: $38,643 (2005); Median household income: $59,872 (2005); Average household income: $98,963 (2005); Percent of

households with income of $100,000 or more: 27.4% (2005); Poverty rate: 7.1% (2000).
Education: Percent of population age 25 and over with: High school diploma (including GED) or higher: 84.6% (2005); Bachelor's degree or higher: 33.6% (2005); Master's degree or higher: 12.6% (2005).
Housing: Homeownership rate: 70.1% (2005); Median home value: $134,259 (2005); Median rent: $689 per month (2000); Median age of housing: 36 years (2000).
Safety: Violent crime rate: 17.1 per 10,000 population; Property crime rate: 281.9 per 10,000 population (2004).
Transportation: Commute to work: 92.9% car, 0.4% public transportation, 5.2% walk, 0.7% work from home (2000); Travel time to work: 22.0% less than 15 minutes, 48.6% 15 to 30 minutes, 22.4% 30 to 45 minutes, 4.7% 45 to 60 minutes, 2.3% 60 minutes or more (2000)

NORTH BEND (village).
Covers a land area of 1.076 square miles and a water area of 0.092 square miles. Located at 39.15° N. Lat.; 84.74° W. Long. Elevation is 600 feet.
History: North Bend was founded in 1789 by John Cleves Symmes. William Henry Harrison lived here until he became the 9th President of the U.S. in 1841. This was the birthplace of his grandson, William Henry Harrison (1833-1901), the 23rd U.S. President.
Population: 541 (1990); 603 (2000); 565 (2005); 527 (2010 projected); Race: 99.8% White, 0.2% Black, 0.0% Asian, 0.0% Hispanic of any race (2005); Density: 525.0 persons per square mile (2005); Average household size: 2.37 (2005); Median age: 44.9 (2005); Males per 100 females: 94.2 (2005); Marriage status: 21.7% never married, 59.4% now married, 6.2% widowed, 12.6% divorced (2000); Foreign born: 0.3% (2000); Ancestry (includes multiple ancestries): 41.1% German, 22.6% Irish, 11.0% English, 8.0% United States or American, 6.8% Italian (2000).
Economy: Employment by occupation: 20.2% management, 17.3% professional, 15.8% services, 27.9% sales, 0.0% farming, 7.0% construction, 11.8% production (2000).
Income: Per capita income: $37,310 (2005); Median household income: $66,667 (2005); Average household income: $88,571 (2005); Percent of households with income of $100,000 or more: 29.0% (2005); Poverty rate: 6.5% (2000).
Education: Percent of population age 25 and over with: High school diploma (including GED) or higher: 85.8% (2005); Bachelor's degree or higher: 25.7% (2005); Master's degree or higher: 6.9% (2005).

School District(s)
Southwest Local SD (PK-12)
    2003-04 Enrollment: 3,971 . . . . (513) 367-4139
Three Rivers Local Schools (PK-12)
    2003-04 Enrollment: 2,164 . . . . (513) 941-6400

Housing: Homeownership rate: 67.2% (2005); Median home value: $145,000 (2005); Median rent: $400 per month (2000); Median age of housing: 43 years (2000).
Transportation: Commute to work: 89.2% car, 1.1% public transportation, 4.5% walk, 3.3% work from home (2000); Travel time to work: 26.5% less than 15 minutes, 36.9% 15 to 30 minutes, 28.8% 30 to 45 minutes, 6.5% 45 to 60 minutes, 1.2% 60 minutes or more (2000)

NORTH COLLEGE HILL (city).
Covers a land area of 1.836 square miles and a water area of 0.001 square miles. Located at 39.21° N. Lat.; 84.55° W. Long. Elevation is 840 feet.
History: Named for its location north of Cincinnati. Revolutionary War cemetery is in the city. Incorporated as a city 1940.
Population: 11,002 (1990); 10,082 (2000); 9,466 (2005); 8,879 (2010 projected); Race: 70.8% White, 26.7% Black, 0.3% Asian, 0.6% Hispanic of any race (2005); Density: 5,155.5 persons per square mile (2005); Average household size: 2.36 (2005); Median age: 37.6 (2005); Males per 100 females: 86.3 (2005); Marriage status: 30.3% never married, 49.7% now married, 9.7% widowed, 10.3% divorced (2000); Foreign born: 1.7% (2000); Ancestry (includes multiple ancestries): 34.9% German, 21.3% Other groups, 13.5% United States or American, 10.7% Irish, 7.2% English (2000).
Economy: Mostly residential. Clovernook Home for the Blind has a braille printing shop. Single-family building permits issued: 3 (2005); Multi-family building permits issued: 0 (2005); Employment by occupation: 9.3% management, 14.4% professional, 17.7% services, 33.2% sales, 0.3% farming, 10.3% construction, 14.8% production (2000).
Income: Per capita income: $20,922 (2005); Median household income: $41,275 (2005); Average household income: $48,610 (2005); Percent of households with income of $100,000 or more: 6.4% (2005); Poverty rate: 8.7% (2000).
Education: Percent of population age 25 and over with: High school diploma (including GED) or higher: 81.7% (2005); Bachelor's degree or higher: 13.8% (2005); Master's degree or higher: 4.6% (2005).
Housing: Homeownership rate: 68.8% (2005); Median home value: $97,885 (2005); Median rent: $476 per month (2000); Median age of housing: 48 years (2000).
Safety: Violent crime rate: 48.4 per 10,000 population; Property crime rate: 551.3 per 10,000 population (2004).
Transportation: Commute to work: 89.0% car, 6.0% public transportation, 2.5% walk, 2.5% work from home (2000); Travel time to work: 21.5% less than 15 minutes, 47.3% 15 to 30 minutes, 23.5% 30 to 45 minutes, 4.2% 45 to 60 minutes, 3.5% 60 minutes or more (2000)
Additional Information Contacts
City of North College Hill . . . . (513) 521-7413
   http://www.northcollegehill.org

NORTHBROOK (CDP).
Covers a land area of 1.939 square miles and a water area of 0 square miles. Located at 39.24° N. Lat.; 84.57° W. Long. Elevation is 820 feet.
Population: 11,471 (1990); 11,076 (2000); 10,216 (2005); 9,352 (2010 projected); Race: 79.3% White, 16.3% Black, 1.2% Asian, 1.7% Hispanic of any race (2005); Density: 5,269.5 persons per square mile (2005); Average household size: 2.60 (2005); Median age: 36.0 (2005); Males per 100 females: 90.4 (2005); Marriage status: 25.0% never married, 54.3% now married, 7.5% widowed, 13.2% divorced (2000); Foreign born: 0.9% (2000); Ancestry (includes multiple ancestries): 31.8% German, 18.1% Other groups, 12.8% Irish, 8.9% English, 8.8% United States or American (2000).
Economy: Employment by occupation: 9.2% management, 11.4% professional, 18.2% services, 34.5% sales, 0.0% farming, 10.3% construction, 16.4% production (2000).
Income: Per capita income: $21,692 (2005); Median household income: $49,233 (2005); Average household income: $56,330 (2005); Percent of households with income of $100,000 or more: 9.5% (2005); Poverty rate: 7.0% (2000).
Education: Percent of population age 25 and over with: High school diploma (including GED) or higher: 75.4% (2005); Bachelor's degree or higher: 11.1% (2005); Master's degree or higher: 3.0% (2005).
Housing: Homeownership rate: 79.0% (2005); Median home value: $92,224 (2005); Median rent: $593 per month (2000); Median age of housing: 33 years (2000).
Transportation: Commute to work: 95.1% car, 1.6% public transportation, 1.2% walk, 1.3% work from home (2000); Travel time to work: 22.4% less than 15 minutes, 44.5% 15 to 30 minutes, 26.4% 30 to 45 minutes, 4.4% 45 to 60 minutes, 2.3% 60 minutes or more (2000)

NORTHGATE (CDP).
Covers a land area of 2.522 square miles and a water area of 0.021 square miles. Located at 39.25° N. Lat.; 84.58° W. Long.
Population: 7,864 (1990); 8,016 (2000); 7,808 (2005); 7,531 (2010 projected); Race: 84.7% White, 11.2% Black, 1.6% Asian, 1.5% Hispanic of any race (2005); Density: 3,096.1 persons per square mile (2005); Average household size: 2.85 (2005); Median age: 37.6 (2005); Males per 100 females: 97.8 (2005); Marriage status: 26.4% never married, 60.0% now married, 6.5% widowed, 7.1% divorced (2000); Foreign born: 0.6% (2000); Ancestry (includes multiple ancestries): 40.6% German, 17.2% Other groups, 15.6% Irish, 8.4% United States or American, 6.4% English (2000).
Economy: Employment by occupation: 9.7% management, 12.4% professional, 16.8% services, 35.6% sales, 0.3% farming, 8.8% construction, 16.5% production (2000).
Income: Per capita income: $24,815 (2005); Median household income: $61,419 (2005); Average household income: $70,210 (2005); Percent of households with income of $100,000 or more: 17.8% (2005); Poverty rate: 3.7% (2000).
Education: Percent of population age 25 and over with: High school diploma (including GED) or higher: 81.8% (2005); Bachelor's degree or higher: 14.4% (2005); Master's degree or higher: 4.1% (2005).
Housing: Homeownership rate: 86.6% (2005); Median home value: $121,284 (2005); Median rent: $616 per month (2000); Median age of housing: 32 years (2000).
Transportation: Commute to work: 93.8% car, 1.1% public transportation, 1.6% walk, 2.2% work from home (2000); Travel time to work: 25.1% less

than 15 minutes, 47.8% 15 to 30 minutes, 18.4% 30 to 45 minutes, 3.9% 45 to 60 minutes, 4.8% 60 minutes or more (2000)

NORWOOD (city). Covers a land area of 3.116 square miles and a water area of 0 square miles. Located at 39.16° N. Lat.; 84.45° W. Long. Elevation is 660 feet.
History: Named for the shortened form of north woods. Norwood began in the early 1800's, and until 1888 was called Sharpsburg, for early settler John Sharp. The U.S. Playing Card Company was established here, and maintained a Playing Card Museum.
Population: 23,635 (1990); 21,675 (2000); 20,328 (2005); 18,991 (2010 projected); Race: 93.1% White, 2.9% Black, 0.9% Asian, 2.2% Hispanic of any race (2005); Density: 6,524.2 persons per square mile (2005); Average household size: 2.30 (2005); Median age: 36.0 (2005); Males per 100 females: 95.8 (2005); Marriage status: 34.0% never married, 44.5% now married, 8.1% widowed, 13.5% divorced (2000); Foreign born: 2.3% (2000); Ancestry (includes multiple ancestries): 28.2% German, 19.0% Irish, 11.7% Other groups, 10.5% United States or American, 9.8% English (2000).
Economy: Unemployment rate: 5.9% (2005); Total civilian labor force: 11,015 (2005); Single-family building permits issued: 0 (2005); Multi-family building permits issued: 0 (2005); Employment by occupation: 9.2% management, 14.6% professional, 17.3% services, 28.4% sales, 0.0% farming, 10.2% construction, 20.3% production (2000).
Income: Per capita income: $20,498 (2005); Median household income: $36,931 (2005); Average household income: $46,879 (2005); Percent of households with income of $100,000 or more: 8.0% (2005); Poverty rate: 12.9% (2000).
Education: Percent of population age 25 and over with: High school diploma (including GED) or higher: 70.8% (2005); Bachelor's degree or higher: 14.0% (2005); Master's degree or higher: 3.6% (2005).

School District(s)
Norwood City SD (PK-12)
    2003-04 Enrollment: 2,659 . . . . (513) 924-2500

Two-year College(s)
ITT Technical Institute (Private, For-profit)
    Fall 2004 Enrollment: 686 . . . . (513) 531-8300
    2005-06 Tuition: In-state $14,196; Out-of-state $14,196
Housing: Homeownership rate: 51.5% (2005); Median home value: $108,498 (2005); Median rent: $387 per month (2000); Median age of housing: 60+ years (2000).
Safety: Violent crime rate: 58.1 per 10,000 population; Property crime rate: 706.0 per 10,000 population (2004).
Transportation: Commute to work: 90.0% car, 3.5% public transportation, 4.0% walk, 1.6% work from home (2000); Travel time to work: 38.4% less than 15 minutes, 42.9% 15 to 30 minutes, 12.8% 30 to 45 minutes, 2.9% 45 to 60 minutes, 3.0% 60 minutes or more (2000)
Additional Information Contacts
City of Norwood . . . . (513) 458-4501
    http://www.norwood-ohio.com
Norwood Chamber of Commerce . . . . (513) 956-7935
    http://www.norwoodchamber.org

PLEASANT RUN (CDP). Covers a land area of 2.072 square miles and a water area of 0 square miles. Located at 39.29° N. Lat.; 84.56° W. Long. Elevation is 744 feet.
Population: 4,964 (1990); 5,267 (2000); 5,184 (2005); 5,145 (2010 projected); Race: 87.1% White, 8.4% Black, 2.5% Asian, 1.3% Hispanic of any race (2005); Density: 2,501.6 persons per square mile (2005); Average household size: 2.91 (2005); Median age: 36.1 (2005); Males per 100 females: 97.9 (2005); Marriage status: 21.8% never married, 64.6% now married, 6.8% widowed, 6.8% divorced (2000); Foreign born: 2.2% (2000); Ancestry (includes multiple ancestries): 33.9% German, 14.0% Other groups, 14.0% Irish, 10.7% United States or American, 10.6% English (2000).
Economy: Employment by occupation: 10.8% management, 17.0% professional, 12.7% services, 32.9% sales, 0.0% farming, 11.0% construction, 15.6% production (2000).
Income: Per capita income: $24,172 (2005); Median household income: $63,035 (2005); Average household income: $70,282 (2005); Percent of households with income of $100,000 or more: 16.2% (2005); Poverty rate: 3.0% (2000).
Education: Percent of population age 25 and over with: High school diploma (including GED) or higher: 87.8% (2005); Bachelor's degree or higher: 17.4% (2005); Master's degree or higher: 4.3% (2005).

Housing: Homeownership rate: 95.5% (2005); Median home value: $120,203 (2005); Median rent: $698 per month (2000); Median age of housing: 29 years (2000).
Transportation: Commute to work: 97.4% car, 0.2% public transportation, 0.2% walk, 1.8% work from home (2000); Travel time to work: 16.6% less than 15 minutes, 50.0% 15 to 30 minutes, 24.9% 30 to 45 minutes, 4.4% 45 to 60 minutes, 4.1% 60 minutes or more (2000)

PLEASANT RUN FARM (CDP). Covers a land area of 1.049 square miles and a water area of 0 square miles. Located at 39.29° N. Lat.; 84.55° W. Long.
Population: 4,529 (1990); 4,731 (2000); 4,595 (2005); 4,548 (2010 projected); Race: 68.8% White, 27.7% Black, 1.5% Asian, 0.7% Hispanic of any race (2005); Density: 4,381.8 persons per square mile (2005); Average household size: 2.82 (2005); Median age: 33.4 (2005); Males per 100 females: 91.5 (2005); Marriage status: 25.2% never married, 62.6% now married, 3.2% widowed, 9.0% divorced (2000); Foreign born: 2.0% (2000); Ancestry (includes multiple ancestries): 34.1% German, 21.0% Other groups, 12.5% Irish, 8.6% United States or American, 7.5% English (2000).
Economy: Employment by occupation: 15.8% management, 25.5% professional, 7.2% services, 29.8% sales, 0.0% farming, 6.4% construction, 15.3% production (2000).
Income: Per capita income: $25,400 (2005); Median household income: $67,733 (2005); Average household income: $71,736 (2005); Percent of households with income of $100,000 or more: 20.1% (2005); Poverty rate: 4.8% (2000).
Education: Percent of population age 25 and over with: High school diploma (including GED) or higher: 92.0% (2005); Bachelor's degree or higher: 30.4% (2005); Master's degree or higher: 11.5% (2005).
Housing: Homeownership rate: 83.3% (2005); Median home value: $136,383 (2005); Median rent: $533 per month (2000); Median age of housing: 25 years (2000).
Transportation: Commute to work: 93.6% car, 2.3% public transportation, 0.4% walk, 3.5% work from home (2000); Travel time to work: 19.7% less than 15 minutes, 45.3% 15 to 30 minutes, 24.9% 30 to 45 minutes, 5.2% 45 to 60 minutes, 5.0% 60 minutes or more (2000)

READING (city). Covers a land area of 2.920 square miles and a water area of 0 square miles. Located at 39.22° N. Lat.; 84.43° W. Long. Elevation is 560 feet.
History: Reading was platted in 1798 by Adam Vorhees, and named Vorheestown. The name was changed to honor Redingbo, William Penn's son-in-law.
Population: 12,038 (1990); 11,292 (2000); 10,489 (2005); 9,678 (2010 projected); Race: 92.3% White, 3.9% Black, 1.5% Asian, 0.9% Hispanic of any race (2005); Density: 3,592.6 persons per square mile (2005); Average household size: 2.26 (2005); Median age: 39.0 (2005); Males per 100 females: 95.0 (2005); Marriage status: 27.2% never married, 51.2% now married, 7.5% widowed, 14.0% divorced (2000); Foreign born: 2.7% (2000); Ancestry (includes multiple ancestries): 39.6% German, 17.8% Irish, 9.1% English, 8.6% Other groups, 8.5% United States or American (2000).
Economy: Single-family building permits issued: 0 (2005); Multi-family building permits issued: 0 (2005); Employment by occupation: 10.4% management, 14.7% professional, 15.6% services, 31.8% sales, 0.1% farming, 10.4% construction, 17.0% production (2000).
Income: Per capita income: $25,564 (2005); Median household income: $44,114 (2005); Average household income: $57,619 (2005); Percent of households with income of $100,000 or more: 12.3% (2005); Poverty rate: 7.3% (2000).
Taxes: Total city taxes per capita: $428 (2004); City property taxes per capita: $31 (2004).
Education: Percent of population age 25 and over with: High school diploma (including GED) or higher: 78.8% (2005); Bachelor's degree or higher: 16.0% (2005); Master's degree or higher: 5.8% (2005).

School District(s)
Reading Community City SD (PK-12)
    2003-04 Enrollment: 1,423 . . . . (513) 554-1800
Housing: Homeownership rate: 59.0% (2005); Median home value: $114,569 (2005); Median rent: $410 per month (2000); Median age of housing: 44 years (2000).
Safety: Violent crime rate: 58.5 per 10,000 population; Property crime rate: 416.0 per 10,000 population (2004).
Transportation: Commute to work: 95.4% car, 0.6% public transportation, 1.4% walk, 1.7% work from home (2000); Travel time to work: 30.5% less

than 15 minutes, 51.9% 15 to 30 minutes, 11.9% 30 to 45 minutes, 2.8% 45 to 60 minutes, 2.9% 60 minutes or more (2000)
Additional Information Contacts
City of Reading .... (513) 733-3725
  http://www.readingohio.org
Reading Chamber of Commerce .... (513) 786-7274
  http://www.readingohiochamber.org

SAINT BERNARD (city). Covers a land area of 1.541 square miles and a water area of 0 square miles. Located at 39.16° N. Lat.; 84.49° W. Long. Elevation is 537 feet.
Population: 5,344 (1990); 4,924 (2000); 4,499 (2005); 4,087 (2010 projected); Race: 90.2% White, 7.3% Black, 0.8% Asian, 0.7% Hispanic of any race (2005); Density: 2,920.2 persons per square mile (2005); Average household size: 2.36 (2005); Median age: 37.7 (2005); Males per 100 females: 91.9 (2005); Marriage status: 28.7% never married, 50.3% now married, 10.4% widowed, 10.6% divorced (2000); Foreign born: 2.5% (2000); Ancestry (includes multiple ancestries): 41.1% German, 17.1% Irish, 10.7% Other groups, 10.5% United States or American, 9.9% English (2000).
Economy: Single-family building permits issued: 0 (2005); Multi-family building permits issued: 0 (2005); Employment by occupation: 10.4% management, 15.7% professional, 15.5% services, 28.4% sales, 0.3% farming, 11.4% construction, 18.3% production (2000).
Income: Per capita income: $20,045 (2005); Median household income: $41,036 (2005); Average household income: $47,145 (2005); Percent of households with income of $100,000 or more: 6.1% (2005); Poverty rate: 8.7% (2000).
Education: Percent of population age 25 and over with: High school diploma (including GED) or higher: 80.9% (2005); Bachelor's degree or higher: 13.4% (2005); Master's degree or higher: 4.4% (2005).
School District(s)
Saint Bernard-Elmwood Place City SD (PK-12)
  2003-04 Enrollment: 1,160 .... (513) 482-7121
Housing: Homeownership rate: 64.0% (2005); Median home value: $108,048 (2005); Median rent: $391 per month (2000); Median age of housing: 60+ years (2000).
Safety: Violent crime rate: 51.6 per 10,000 population; Property crime rate: 406.5 per 10,000 population (2004).
Transportation: Commute to work: 89.2% car, 3.9% public transportation, 5.1% walk, 1.4% work from home (2000); Travel time to work: 35.7% less than 15 minutes, 48.0% 15 to 30 minutes, 9.8% 30 to 45 minutes, 3.8% 45 to 60 minutes, 2.8% 60 minutes or more (2000)

SHARONVILLE (city). Covers a land area of 9.806 square miles and a water area of 0.055 square miles. Located at 39.28° N. Lat.; 84.39° W. Long. Elevation is 589 feet.
History: Named for Sharon, Pennsylvania, which was named for the region in Palestine mentioned in the Bible. Sharonville was surveyed in 1796 by Simon Hegerman, and became a transportation center when the New York Central Lines built their freight yards and shops here.
Population: 13,092 (1990); 13,804 (2000); 13,307 (2005); 12,844 (2010 projected); Race: 86.1% White, 5.9% Black, 4.9% Asian, 2.7% Hispanic of any race (2005); Density: 1,357.0 persons per square mile (2005); Average household size: 2.17 (2005); Median age: 40.7 (2005); Males per 100 females: 93.0 (2005); Marriage status: 24.4% never married, 54.5% now married, 8.6% widowed, 12.6% divorced (2000); Foreign born: 6.4% (2000); Ancestry (includes multiple ancestries): 37.5% German, 14.8% Other groups, 12.7% Irish, 10.7% English, 8.9% United States or American (2000).
Economy: Single-family building permits issued: 9 (2005); Multi-family building permits issued: 0 (2005); Employment by occupation: 16.1% management, 24.8% professional, 13.7% services, 26.8% sales, 0.2% farming, 5.9% construction, 12.6% production (2000).
Income: Per capita income: $32,598 (2005); Median household income: $52,810 (2005); Average household income: $69,788 (2005); Percent of households with income of $100,000 or more: 19.3% (2005); Poverty rate: 4.0% (2000).
Education: Percent of population age 25 and over with: High school diploma (including GED) or higher: 88.0% (2005); Bachelor's degree or higher: 34.5% (2005); Master's degree or higher: 11.4% (2005).
Housing: Homeownership rate: 64.4% (2005); Median home value: $135,798 (2005); Median rent: $610 per month (2000); Median age of housing: 28 years (2000).
Safety: Violent crime rate: 36.9 per 10,000 population; Property crime rate: 523.2 per 10,000 population (2004).
Transportation: Commute to work: 95.2% car, 0.6% public transportation, 1.6% walk, 2.1% work from home (2000); Travel time to work: 36.5% less than 15 minutes, 41.1% 15 to 30 minutes, 16.4% 30 to 45 minutes, 4.0% 45 to 60 minutes, 2.1% 60 minutes or more (2000)
Additional Information Contacts
City of Sharonville .... (513) 563-1144
  http://www.sharonville.org
Sharonville Chamber of Commerce .... (513) 554-1722
  http://www.sharonvillechamber.com

SHERWOOD (CDP). Covers a land area of 1.109 square miles and a water area of 0 square miles. Located at 39.08° N. Lat.; 84.36° W. Long.
Population: 3,709 (1990); 3,907 (2000); 3,625 (2005); 3,370 (2010 projected); Race: 95.7% White, 0.7% Black, 2.0% Asian, 1.4% Hispanic of any race (2005); Density: 3,268.4 persons per square mile (2005); Average household size: 2.86 (2005); Median age: 37.3 (2005); Males per 100 females: 94.7 (2005); Marriage status: 18.1% never married, 74.9% now married, 3.5% widowed, 3.5% divorced (2000); Foreign born: 2.5% (2000); Ancestry (includes multiple ancestries): 44.6% German, 21.3% Irish, 15.3% English, 9.9% United States or American, 4.3% Italian (2000).
Economy: Employment by occupation: 19.7% management, 29.2% professional, 8.0% services, 28.6% sales, 0.0% farming, 5.8% construction, 8.6% production (2000).
Income: Per capita income: $35,366 (2005); Median household income: $85,330 (2005); Average household income: $101,026 (2005); Percent of households with income of $100,000 or more: 37.7% (2005); Poverty rate: 1.5% (2000).
Education: Percent of population age 25 and over with: High school diploma (including GED) or higher: 96.8% (2005); Bachelor's degree or higher: 54.0% (2005); Master's degree or higher: 17.9% (2005).
Housing: Homeownership rate: 95.7% (2005); Median home value: $162,140 (2005); Median rent: $844 per month (2000); Median age of housing: 32 years (2000).
Transportation: Commute to work: 90.7% car, 3.8% public transportation, 0.5% walk, 4.4% work from home (2000); Travel time to work: 24.6% less than 15 minutes, 36.7% 15 to 30 minutes, 30.2% 30 to 45 minutes, 6.1% 45 to 60 minutes, 2.4% 60 minutes or more (2000)

SILVERTON (city). Covers a land area of 1.114 square miles and a water area of 0 square miles. Located at 39.19° N. Lat.; 84.40° W. Long. Elevation is 840 feet.
History: Silverton developed as a residential community on the outskirts of Cincinnati.
Population: 5,859 (1990); 5,178 (2000); 4,814 (2005); 4,458 (2010 projected); Race: 44.5% White, 50.6% Black, 0.9% Asian, 1.4% Hispanic of any race (2005); Density: 4,321.1 persons per square mile (2005); Average household size: 2.00 (2005); Median age: 41.3 (2005); Males per 100 females: 81.7 (2005); Marriage status: 29.6% never married, 45.4% now married, 10.3% widowed, 14.6% divorced (2000); Foreign born: 0.2% (2000); Ancestry (includes multiple ancestries): 46.6% Other groups, 19.4% German, 9.9% Irish, 4.2% English, 3.6% United States or American (2000).
Economy: Single-family building permits issued: 0 (2005); Multi-family building permits issued: 0 (2005); Employment by occupation: 13.6% management, 16.8% professional, 17.4% services, 30.7% sales, 0.4% farming, 8.9% construction, 12.2% production (2000).
Income: Per capita income: $21,629 (2005); Median household income: $37,406 (2005); Average household income: $42,605 (2005); Percent of households with income of $100,000 or more: 5.1% (2005); Poverty rate: 9.5% (2000).
Education: Percent of population age 25 and over with: High school diploma (including GED) or higher: 78.8% (2005); Bachelor's degree or higher: 19.2% (2005); Master's degree or higher: 6.2% (2005).
Housing: Homeownership rate: 55.5% (2005); Median home value: $115,641 (2005); Median rent: $408 per month (2000); Median age of housing: 50 years (2000).
Safety: Violent crime rate: 20.2 per 10,000 population; Property crime rate: 422.6 per 10,000 population (2004).
Transportation: Commute to work: 90.0% car, 6.8% public transportation, 0.7% walk, 1.9% work from home (2000); Travel time to work: 22.5% less than 15 minutes, 48.1% 15 to 30 minutes, 19.5% 30 to 45 minutes, 3.7% 45 to 60 minutes, 6.2% 60 minutes or more (2000)

136   PROFILES OF OHIO / Hamilton County

SPRINGDALE (city). Covers a land area of 4.957 square miles and a water area of 0.012 square miles. Located at 39.29° N. Lat.; 84.48° W. Long. Elevation is 750 feet.
History: Springdale was the site in 1801-1802 of a meeting of the religious sect called the New Lights, who evidenced pronounced physical manifestations of jerking, rolling, whirling, falling, and barking.
Population: 10,601 (1990); 10,563 (2000); 9,912 (2005); 9,240 (2010 projected); Race: 62.8% White, 30.0% Black, 3.0% Asian, 4.5% Hispanic of any race (2005); Density: 1,999.7 persons per square mile (2005); Average household size: 2.35 (2005); Median age: 40.3 (2005); Males per 100 females: 84.0 (2005); Marriage status: 23.8% never married, 56.1% now married, 8.3% widowed, 11.7% divorced (2000); Foreign born: 5.7% (2000); Ancestry (includes multiple ancestries): 30.5% Other groups, 21.2% German, 9.4% Irish, 8.3% English, 7.9% United States or American (2000).
Economy: Single-family building permits issued: 1 (2005); Multi-family building permits issued: 19 (2005); Employment by occupation: 16.6% management, 22.1% professional, 12.5% services, 26.6% sales, 0.6% farming, 5.8% construction, 15.7% production (2000).
Income: Per capita income: $26,097 (2005); Median household income: $47,539 (2005); Average household income: $60,844 (2005); Percent of households with income of $100,000 or more: 14.4% (2005); Poverty rate: 8.9% (2000).
Education: Percent of population age 25 and over with: High school diploma (including GED) or higher: 85.6% (2005); Bachelor's degree or higher: 28.0% (2005); Master's degree or higher: 9.1% (2005).
Housing: Homeownership rate: 60.2% (2005); Median home value: $129,182 (2005); Median rent: $608 per month (2000); Median age of housing: 29 years (2000).
Safety: Violent crime rate: 34.5 per 10,000 population; Property crime rate: 1,097.5 per 10,000 population (2004).
Transportation: Commute to work: 94.7% car, 1.9% public transportation, 1.5% walk, 1.8% work from home (2000); Travel time to work: 30.7% less than 15 minutes, 36.2% 15 to 30 minutes, 22.8% 30 to 45 minutes, 6.6% 45 to 60 minutes, 3.7% 60 minutes or more (2000)
Additional Information Contacts
City of Springdale . . . . (513) 346-5700
http://www.springdale.org

TERRACE PARK (village). Covers a land area of 1.203 square miles and a water area of 0.063 square miles. Located at 39.16° N. Lat.; 84.30° W. Long. Elevation is 560 feet.
History: Terrace Park developed as a suburban community near Cincinnati.
Population: 2,133 (1990); 2,273 (2000); 2,156 (2005); 2,033 (2010 projected); Race: 98.5% White, 0.2% Black, 0.8% Asian, 1.0% Hispanic of any race (2005); Density: 1,792.5 persons per square mile (2005); Average household size: 3.05 (2005); Median age: 38.3 (2005); Males per 100 females: 99.8 (2005); Marriage status: 16.2% never married, 75.7% now married, 3.8% widowed, 4.3% divorced (2000); Foreign born: 2.6% (2000); Ancestry (includes multiple ancestries): 40.3% German, 20.6% English, 13.9% Irish, 4.1% Scotch-Irish, 4.0% United States or American (2000).
Economy: Single-family building permits issued: 5 (2005); Multi-family building permits issued: 0 (2005); Employment by occupation: 27.7% management, 32.2% professional, 6.6% services, 27.9% sales, 0.3% farming, 1.8% construction, 3.6% production (2000).
Income: Per capita income: $47,313 (2005); Median household income: $114,035 (2005); Average household income: $144,487 (2005); Percent of households with income of $100,000 or more: 56.8% (2005); Poverty rate: 2.0% (2000).
Education: Percent of population age 25 and over with: High school diploma (including GED) or higher: 98.6% (2005); Bachelor's degree or higher: 71.0% (2005); Master's degree or higher: 26.3% (2005).
School District(s)
Mariemont City SD (PK-12)
  2003-04 Enrollment: 1,708 . . . . (513) 272-7500
Housing: Homeownership rate: 95.0% (2005); Median home value: $362,977 (2005); Median rent: $1,028 per month (2000); Median age of housing: 49 years (2000).
Transportation: Commute to work: 88.3% car, 2.8% public transportation, 0.4% walk, 8.5% work from home (2000); Travel time to work: 23.0% less than 15 minutes, 43.8% 15 to 30 minutes, 25.9% 30 to 45 minutes, 4.8% 45 to 60 minutes, 2.4% 60 minutes or more (2000)

THE VILLAGE OF INDIAN HILL (city). Covers a land area of 18.534 square miles and a water area of 0.056 square miles. Located at 39.19° N. Lat.; 84.34° W. Long. Elevation is 750 feet.
Population: 5,382 (1990); 5,907 (2000); 5,689 (2005); 5,434 (2010 projected); Race: 93.9% White, 0.5% Black, 4.3% Asian, 0.7% Hispanic of any race (2005); Density: 306.9 persons per square mile (2005); Average household size: 2.84 (2005); Median age: 46.4 (2005); Males per 100 females: 96.1 (2005); Marriage status: 18.2% never married, 76.1% now married, 3.4% widowed, 2.3% divorced (2000); Foreign born: 7.9% (2000); Ancestry (includes multiple ancestries): 37.8% German, 23.3% English, 17.5% Irish, 7.9% Other groups, 5.8% Italian (2000).
Economy: Employment by occupation: 39.2% management, 29.1% professional, 3.1% services, 23.3% sales, 0.0% farming, 1.2% construction, 4.2% production (2000).
Income: Per capita income: $87,308 (2005); Median household income: $183,797 (2005); Average household income: $248,225 (2005); Percent of households with income of $100,000 or more: 73.5% (2005); Poverty rate: 2.4% (2000).
Education: Percent of population age 25 and over with: High school diploma (including GED) or higher: 97.8% (2005); Bachelor's degree or higher: 76.9% (2005); Master's degree or higher: 34.7% (2005).
Housing: Homeownership rate: 96.2% (2005); Median home value: $872,893 (2005); Median rent: $532 per month (2000); Median age of housing: 40 years (2000).
Transportation: Commute to work: 89.5% car, 0.0% public transportation, 1.0% walk, 7.8% work from home (2000); Travel time to work: 21.3% less than 15 minutes, 58.5% 15 to 30 minutes, 17.8% 30 to 45 minutes, 0.0% 45 to 60 minutes, 2.4% 60 minutes or more (2000)

TURPIN HILLS (CDP). Covers a land area of 2.973 square miles and a water area of <.001 square miles. Located at 39.10° N. Lat.; 84.37° W. Long. Elevation is 700 feet.
Population: 4,908 (1990); 4,960 (2000); 4,794 (2005); 4,662 (2010 projected); Race: 95.7% White, 0.7% Black, 2.2% Asian, 1.1% Hispanic of any race (2005); Density: 1,612.7 persons per square mile (2005); Average household size: 2.78 (2005); Median age: 40.0 (2005); Males per 100 females: 95.8 (2005); Marriage status: 17.8% never married, 75.1% now married, 3.6% widowed, 3.5% divorced (2000); Foreign born: 4.0% (2000); Ancestry (includes multiple ancestries): 35.8% German, 18.5% Irish, 12.8% English, 12.2% Italian, 6.9% United States or American (2000).
Economy: Employment by occupation: 28.2% management, 30.0% professional, 11.7% services, 22.3% sales, 0.0% farming, 2.4% construction, 5.4% production (2000).
Income: Per capita income: $46,174 (2005); Median household income: $96,442 (2005); Average household income: $128,547 (2005); Percent of households with income of $100,000 or more: 47.9% (2005); Poverty rate: 1.0% (2000).
Education: Percent of population age 25 and over with: High school diploma (including GED) or higher: 95.2% (2005); Bachelor's degree or higher: 62.3% (2005); Master's degree or higher: 22.6% (2005).
Housing: Homeownership rate: 86.5% (2005); Median home value: $242,236 (2005); Median rent: $578 per month (2000); Median age of housing: 26 years (2000).
Transportation: Commute to work: 93.2% car, 0.8% public transportation, 0.2% walk, 5.8% work from home (2000); Travel time to work: 23.3% less than 15 minutes, 52.7% 15 to 30 minutes, 17.9% 30 to 45 minutes, 2.8% 45 to 60 minutes, 3.3% 60 minutes or more (2000)

WHITE OAK (CDP). Covers a land area of 4.094 square miles and a water area of 0 square miles. Located at 39.21° N. Lat.; 84.59° W. Long. Elevation is 920 feet.
Population: 12,430 (1990); 13,277 (2000); 12,855 (2005); 12,436 (2010 projected); Race: 92.8% White, 4.3% Black, 1.2% Asian, 1.3% Hispanic of any race (2005); Density: 3,139.6 persons per square mile (2005); Average household size: 2.48 (2005); Median age: 37.6 (2005); Males per 100 females: 94.6 (2005); Marriage status: 23.6% never married, 58.5% now married, 7.7% widowed, 10.2% divorced (2000); Foreign born: 1.5% (2000); Ancestry (includes multiple ancestries): 48.1% German, 16.5% Irish, 8.8% United States or American, 7.6% Other groups, 7.1% English (2000).
Economy: Employment by occupation: 15.5% management, 17.6% professional, 14.9% services, 29.1% sales, 0.0% farming, 9.2% construction, 13.8% production (2000).

Income: Per capita income: $27,422 (2005); Median household income: $51,497 (2005); Average household income: $67,944 (2005); Percent of households with income of $100,000 or more: 19.3% (2005); Poverty rate: 5.1% (2000).
Education: Percent of population age 25 and over with: High school diploma (including GED) or higher: 84.3% (2005); Bachelor's degree or higher: 22.6% (2005); Master's degree or higher: 6.0% (2005).
Housing: Homeownership rate: 71.5% (2005); Median home value: $133,355 (2005); Median rent: $485 per month (2000); Median age of housing: 35 years (2000).
Transportation: Commute to work: 94.2% car, 2.1% public transportation, 1.0% walk, 2.1% work from home (2000); Travel time to work: 20.9% less than 15 minutes, 50.8% 15 to 30 minutes, 22.5% 30 to 45 minutes, 3.1% 45 to 60 minutes, 2.6% 60 minutes or more (2000)

WHITE OAK EAST (CDP). Covers a land area of 0.799 square miles and a water area of 0 square miles. Located at 39.20° N. Lat.; 84.59° W. Long.
Population: 3,544 (1990); 3,508 (2000); 3,429 (2005); 3,350 (2010 projected); Race: 96.4% White, 1.7% Black, 0.9% Asian, 0.6% Hispanic of any race (2005); Density: 4,294.2 persons per square mile (2005); Average household size: 2.39 (2005); Median age: 39.0 (2005); Males per 100 females: 91.2 (2005); Marriage status: 23.1% never married, 60.0% now married, 8.6% widowed, 8.3% divorced (2000); Foreign born: 1.6% (2000); Ancestry (includes multiple ancestries): 51.9% German, 23.8% Irish, 11.7% United States or American, 8.9% Other groups, 6.9% Italian (2000).
Economy: Employment by occupation: 15.4% management, 23.3% professional, 10.8% services, 30.6% sales, 0.0% farming, 7.7% construction, 12.2% production (2000).
Income: Per capita income: $30,247 (2005); Median household income: $62,612 (2005); Average household income: $72,428 (2005); Percent of households with income of $100,000 or more: 19.6% (2005); Poverty rate: 2.5% (2000).
Education: Percent of population age 25 and over with: High school diploma (including GED) or higher: 90.5% (2005); Bachelor's degree or higher: 31.1% (2005); Master's degree or higher: 10.1% (2005).
Housing: Homeownership rate: 79.5% (2005); Median home value: $131,149 (2005); Median rent: $387 per month (2000); Median age of housing: 38 years (2000).
Transportation: Commute to work: 96.4% car, 0.4% public transportation, 0.4% walk, 2.8% work from home (2000); Travel time to work: 15.9% less than 15 minutes, 55.6% 15 to 30 minutes, 19.8% 30 to 45 minutes, 5.8% 45 to 60 minutes, 2.9% 60 minutes or more (2000)

WHITE OAK WEST (CDP). Covers a land area of 1.342 square miles and a water area of 0 square miles. Located at 39.20° N. Lat.; 84.61° W. Long.
Population: 2,879 (1990); 2,932 (2000); 3,219 (2005); 3,474 (2010 projected); Race: 97.2% White, 1.4% Black, 0.6% Asian, 0.2% Hispanic of any race (2005); Density: 2,398.8 persons per square mile (2005); Average household size: 2.56 (2005); Median age: 42.9 (2005); Males per 100 females: 95.8 (2005); Marriage status: 23.3% never married, 65.7% now married, 5.5% widowed, 5.5% divorced (2000); Foreign born: 0.9% (2000); Ancestry (includes multiple ancestries): 54.9% German, 18.7% Irish, 10.5% English, 8.1% United States or American, 5.4% Other groups (2000).
Economy: Employment by occupation: 17.4% management, 23.2% professional, 13.0% services, 33.7% sales, 0.4% farming, 4.9% construction, 7.3% production (2000).
Income: Per capita income: $40,148 (2005); Median household income: $67,060 (2005); Average household income: $102,733 (2005); Percent of households with income of $100,000 or more: 32.3% (2005); Poverty rate: 3.0% (2000).
Education: Percent of population age 25 and over with: High school diploma (including GED) or higher: 94.0% (2005); Bachelor's degree or higher: 35.1% (2005); Master's degree or higher: 11.4% (2005).
Housing: Homeownership rate: 84.6% (2005); Median home value: $176,714 (2005); Median rent: $466 per month (2000); Median age of housing: 32 years (2000).
Transportation: Commute to work: 92.1% car, 1.3% public transportation, 2.2% walk, 4.4% work from home (2000); Travel time to work: 25.5% less than 15 minutes, 46.5% 15 to 30 minutes, 23.2% 30 to 45 minutes, 4.5% 45 to 60 minutes, 0.4% 60 minutes or more (2000)

WOODLAWN (village). Covers a land area of 2.585 square miles and a water area of 0 square miles. Located at 39.25° N. Lat.; 84.47° W. Long. Elevation is 586 feet.
Population: 2,674 (1990); 2,816 (2000); 2,660 (2005); 2,498 (2010 projected); Race: 29.5% White, 64.7% Black, 3.5% Asian, 1.5% Hispanic of any race (2005); Density: 1,028.9 persons per square mile (2005); Average household size: 2.21 (2005); Median age: 38.1 (2005); Males per 100 females: 94.4 (2005); Marriage status: 35.8% never married, 43.1% now married, 8.7% widowed, 12.3% divorced (2000); Foreign born: 4.9% (2000); Ancestry (includes multiple ancestries): 65.3% Other groups, 8.1% German, 4.4% Irish, 3.6% English, 1.4% Italian (2000).
Economy: Incorporated 1941. Single-family building permits issued: 1 (2005); Multi-family building permits issued: 0 (2005); Employment by occupation: 14.2% management, 28.1% professional, 15.5% services, 23.4% sales, 0.0% farming, 5.8% construction, 12.9% production (2000).
Income: Per capita income: $27,180 (2005); Median household income: $47,548 (2005); Average household income: $59,925 (2005); Percent of households with income of $100,000 or more: 12.5% (2005); Poverty rate: 10.4% (2000).
Education: Percent of population age 25 and over with: High school diploma (including GED) or higher: 89.3% (2005); Bachelor's degree or higher: 27.9% (2005); Master's degree or higher: 10.4% (2005).
Housing: Homeownership rate: 55.7% (2005); Median home value: $93,553 (2005); Median rent: $650 per month (2000); Median age of housing: 34 years (2000).
Safety: Violent crime rate: 44.6 per 10,000 population; Property crime rate: 617.3 per 10,000 population (2004).
Transportation: Commute to work: 93.6% car, 3.2% public transportation, 0.8% walk, 2.2% work from home (2000); Travel time to work: 28.1% less than 15 minutes, 44.5% 15 to 30 minutes, 18.5% 30 to 45 minutes, 4.8% 45 to 60 minutes, 4.0% 60 minutes or more (2000)

WYOMING (city). Covers a land area of 2.883 square miles and a water area of 0 square miles. Located at 39.22° N. Lat.; 84.47° W. Long. Elevation is 800 feet.
History: Settled 1865, incorporated 1874.
Population: 8,318 (1990); 8,261 (2000); 7,875 (2005); 7,468 (2010 projected); Race: 88.1% White, 8.7% Black, 1.5% Asian, 1.3% Hispanic of any race (2005); Density: 2,732.0 persons per square mile (2005); Average household size: 2.76 (2005); Median age: 41.0 (2005); Males per 100 females: 90.5 (2005); Marriage status: 19.6% never married, 68.0% now married, 5.2% widowed, 7.2% divorced (2000); Foreign born: 3.7% (2000); Ancestry (includes multiple ancestries): 33.8% German, 16.4% Other groups, 14.0% Irish, 13.6% English, 6.2% Italian (2000).
Economy: Single-family building permits issued: 14 (2005); Multi-family building permits issued: 0 (2005); Employment by occupation: 26.9% management, 38.5% professional, 7.2% services, 21.9% sales, 0.0% farming, 2.1% construction, 3.5% production (2000).
Income: Per capita income: $44,748 (2005); Median household income: $99,013 (2005); Average household income: $123,475 (2005); Percent of households with income of $100,000 or more: 49.6% (2005); Poverty rate: 1.4% (2000).
Education: Percent of population age 25 and over with: High school diploma (including GED) or higher: 96.7% (2005); Bachelor's degree or higher: 68.1% (2005); Master's degree or higher: 32.5% (2005).

School District(s)

Wyoming City SD (PK-12)
    2003-04 Enrollment: 1,984 . . . . (513) 772-2343
Housing: Homeownership rate: 86.7% (2005); Median home value: $288,868 (2005); Median rent: $508 per month (2000); Median age of housing: 49 years (2000).
Safety: Violent crime rate: 3.7 per 10,000 population; Property crime rate: 142.4 per 10,000 population (2004).
Transportation: Commute to work: 90.8% car, 0.7% public transportation, 1.1% walk, 7.1% work from home (2000); Travel time to work: 24.7% less than 15 minutes, 53.4% 15 to 30 minutes, 17.6% 30 to 45 minutes, 2.0% 45 to 60 minutes, 2.3% 60 minutes or more (2000)
Additional Information Contacts
City of Wyoming. . . . . (513) 821-7600
    http://www.wyoming.oh.us

Hancock County

Located in northwestern Ohio; crossed by the Blanchard River. Covers a land area of 531.35 square miles, a water area of 2.24 square miles, and is located in the Eastern Time Zone. The county government was organized in 1820. County seat is Findlay.

Hancock County is part of the Findlay, OH Micropolitan Statistical Area. The entire metro area includes: Hancock County, OH

Weather Station: Findlay Airport — Elevation: 797 feet

	Jan	Feb	Mar	Apr	May	Jun	Jul	Aug	Sep	Oct	Nov	Dec
High	31	35	46	59	70	79	83	81	74	62	48	37
Low	18	20	29	39	50	59	63	61	54	43	34	24
Precip	1.8	1.7	2.5	3.2	3.7	4.1	3.9	3.7	2.8	2.2	2.7	2.4
Snow	8.2	5.3	3.2	0.7	tr	tr	0.0	0.0	tr	0.1	1.2	5.5

High and Low temperatures in degrees Fahrenheit; Precipitation and Snow in inches

Weather Station: Findlay WPCC — Elevation: 767 feet

	Jan	Feb	Mar	Apr	May	Jun	Jul	Aug	Sep	Oct	Nov	Dec
High	31	35	46	59	71	80	84	81	75	62	48	36
Low	17	20	29	39	50	60	64	61	54	43	33	23
Precip	2.2	2.0	2.7	3.3	3.9	4.1	3.9	4.1	3.0	2.4	2.8	2.7
Snow	10.2	6.2	4.3	1.2	tr	0.0	0.0	0.0	0.0	0.2	1.4	6.0

High and Low temperatures in degrees Fahrenheit; Precipitation and Snow in inches

Population: 65,536 (1990); 71,295 (2000); 73,867 (2005); 76,544 (2010 projected); Race: 94.5% White, 1.3% Black, 1.6% Asian, 3.0% Hispanic of any race (2005); Density: 139.0 persons per square mile (2005); Average household size: 2.52 (2005); Median age: 36.8 (2005); Males per 100 females: 94.8 (2005).
Religion: Five largest groups: 12.3% The United Methodist Church, 12.0% Catholic Church, 6.4% Evangelical Lutheran Church in America, 3.1% Presbyterian Church (U.S.A.), 1.8% Christian Churches and Churches of Christ (2000).
Economy: Unemployment rate: 4.9% (2005); Total civilian labor force: 40,052 (2005); Leading industries: 27.9% manufacturing; 12.1% retail trade; 11.4% health care and social assistance (2004); Farms: 976 totaling 262,095 acres (2002); Companies that employ 500 or more persons: 10 (2004); Companies that employ 100 to 499 persons: 54 (2004); Companies that employ less than 100 persons: 1,774 (2004); Black-owned businesses: n/a (2002); Hispanic-owned businesses: n/a (2002); Women-owned businesses: 1,522 (2002); Retail sales per capita: $19,807 (2006). Single-family building permits issued: 981 (2005); Multi-family building permits issued: 0 (2005).
Income: Per capita income: $23,954 (2005); Median household income: $48,359 (2005); Average household income: $59,634 (2005); Percent of households with income of $100,000 or more: 12.9% (2005); Poverty rate: 7.5% (2003); Bankruptcy rate: 9.43% (2005).
Taxes: Total county taxes per capita: $188 (2004); County property taxes per capita: $107 (2004).
Education: Percent of population age 25 and over with: High school diploma (including GED) or higher: 88.5% (2005); Bachelor's degree or higher: 21.7% (2005); Master's degree or higher: 7.4% (2005).
Housing: Homeownership rate: 73.4% (2005); Median home value: $121,704 (2005); Median rent: $413 per month (2000); Median age of housing: 37 years (2000).
Health: Birth rate: 127.3 per 10,000 population (2004); Death rate: 78.8 per 10,000 population (2004); Age-adjusted cancer mortality rate: 164.4 deaths per 100,000 population (2002); Air Quality Index: 100.0% good, 0.0% moderate, 0.0% unhealthy for sensitive individuals, 0.0% unhealthy (percent of days in 2005); Number of physicians: 18.1 per 10,000 population (2004); Hospital beds: 14.2 per 10,000 population (2003); Hospital admissions: 1,098.2 per 10,000 population (2003).
Elections: 2004 Presidential election results: 70.5% Bush, 29.1% Kerry, 0.0% Nader, 0.2% Badnarik.
National and State Parks: Van Buren Lake State Park
Additional Information Contacts

Hancock County Government	(419) 424-7044
http://www.co.hancock.oh.us/	
City of Findlay	(419) 424-7137
http://www.ci.findlay.oh.us	
Findlay Hancock Co. Convention & Visitors Bureau	(419) 422-3315
http://www.visitfindlay.com	
Findlay Hancock Community Development	(419) 424-7095
http://www.findlayoh.com	
Findlay Hancock County Chamber	(419) 422-3313
http://www.findlayhancockchamber.com	

Hancock County Communities

ARCADIA (village). Covers a land area of 0.260 square miles and a water area of 0 square miles. Located at 41.11° N. Lat.; 83.51° W. Long. Elevation is 808 feet.
Population: 544 (1990); 537 (2000); 547 (2005); 550 (2010 projected); Race: 98.2% White, 0.0% Black, 0.0% Asian, 2.0% Hispanic of any race (2005); Density: 2,105.9 persons per square mile (2005); Average household size: 2.63 (2005); Median age: 33.0 (2005); Males per 100 females: 96.1 (2005); Marriage status: 23.6% never married, 61.7% now married, 3.9% widowed, 10.9% divorced (2000); Foreign born: 0.8% (2000); Ancestry (includes multiple ancestries): 50.3% German, 13.1% Other groups, 10.9% Irish, 9.2% English, 6.8% United States or American (2000).
Economy: Single-family building permits issued: 4 (2005); Multi-family building permits issued: 0 (2005); Employment by occupation: 4.6% management, 9.2% professional, 17.3% services, 21.2% sales, 0.0% farming, 14.5% construction, 33.2% production (2000).
Income: Per capita income: $22,665 (2005); Median household income: $51,724 (2005); Average household income: $59,603 (2005); Percent of households with income of $100,000 or more: 13.0% (2005); Poverty rate: 8.2% (2000).
Education: Percent of population age 25 and over with: High school diploma (including GED) or higher: 92.4% (2005); Bachelor's degree or higher: 5.8% (2005); Master's degree or higher: 0.0% (2005).

School District(s)

Arcadia Local SD (PK-12)
    2003-04 Enrollment: 629 . . . . (419) 894-6431
Housing: Homeownership rate: 85.1% (2005); Median home value: $76,667 (2005); Median rent: $336 per month (2000); Median age of housing: 54 years (2000).
Transportation: Commute to work: 94.3% car, 0.0% public transportation, 4.6% walk, 0.0% work from home (2000); Travel time to work: 39.4% less than 15 minutes, 50.7% 15 to 30 minutes, 7.1% 30 to 45 minutes, 1.4% 45 to 60 minutes, 1.4% 60 minutes or more (2000)

ARLINGTON (village). Covers a land area of 0.730 square miles and a water area of 0 square miles. Located at 40.89° N. Lat.; 83.65° W. Long. Elevation is 869 feet.
Population: 1,236 (1990); 1,351 (2000); 1,257 (2005); 1,242 (2010 projected); Race: 99.5% White, 0.2% Black, 0.0% Asian, 0.2% Hispanic of any race (2005); Density: 1,722.9 persons per square mile (2005); Average household size: 2.54 (2005); Median age: 38.2 (2005); Males per 100 females: 86.8 (2005); Marriage status: 22.5% never married, 57.2% now married, 13.9% widowed, 6.4% divorced (2000); Foreign born: 0.5% (2000); Ancestry (includes multiple ancestries): 45.5% German, 9.9% United States or American, 9.3% English, 9.0% Irish, 5.1% French (except Basque) (2000).
Economy: Limestone, concrete, plaster. Single-family building permits issued: 1 (2005); Multi-family building permits issued: 0 (2005); Employment by occupation: 9.3% management, 15.5% professional, 16.0% services, 24.2% sales, 0.3% farming, 10.3% construction, 24.5% production (2000).
Income: Per capita income: $21,294 (2005); Median household income: $44,423 (2005); Average household income: $52,621 (2005); Percent of households with income of $100,000 or more: 8.7% (2005); Poverty rate: 5.4% (2000).
Education: Percent of population age 25 and over with: High school diploma (including GED) or higher: 91.6% (2005); Bachelor's degree or higher: 15.9% (2005); Master's degree or higher: 3.6% (2005).

School District(s)

Arlington Local SD (PK-12)
    2003-04 Enrollment: 647 . . . . (419) 365-5121
Housing: Homeownership rate: 76.3% (2005); Median home value: $113,542 (2005); Median rent: $397 per month (2000); Median age of housing: 50 years (2000).
Transportation: Commute to work: 95.8% car, 0.0% public transportation, 2.2% walk, 1.6% work from home (2000); Travel time to work: 22.8% less than 15 minutes, 60.6% 15 to 30 minutes, 9.8% 30 to 45 minutes, 4.1% 45 to 60 minutes, 2.8% 60 minutes or more (2000)

BENTON RIDGE (village). Covers a land area of 0.464 square miles and a water area of 0 square miles. Located at 41.00° N. Lat.; 83.79° W. Long. Elevation is 778 feet.
Population: 351 (1990); 315 (2000); 339 (2005); 365 (2010 projected); Race: 98.8% White, 0.9% Black, 0.0% Asian, 0.6% Hispanic of any race (2005); Density: 730.3 persons per square mile (2005); Average household size: 2.63 (2005); Median age: 36.1 (2005); Males per 100 females: 104.2 (2005); Marriage status: 30.4% never married, 52.6% now married, 7.7% widowed, 9.3% divorced (2000); Foreign born: 0.0% (2000); Ancestry (includes multiple ancestries): 31.8% United States or American, 29.1% German, 9.9% English, 9.3% Irish, 6.6% Other groups (2000).
Economy: Employment by occupation: 5.9% management, 4.6% professional, 20.4% services, 15.8% sales, 0.0% farming, 20.4% construction, 32.9% production (2000).
Income: Per capita income: $23,805 (2005); Median household income: $55,903 (2005); Average household income: $62,558 (2005); Percent of households with income of $100,000 or more: 15.5% (2005); Poverty rate: 2.3% (2000).
Education: Percent of population age 25 and over with: High school diploma (including GED) or higher: 91.8% (2005); Bachelor's degree or higher: 6.8% (2005); Master's degree or higher: 0.5% (2005).
Housing: Homeownership rate: 89.1% (2005); Median home value: $104,245 (2005); Median rent: $285 per month (2000); Median age of housing: 60+ years (2000).
Transportation: Commute to work: 91.4% car, 0.0% public transportation, 4.6% walk, 3.9% work from home (2000); Travel time to work: 19.2% less than 15 minutes, 61.0% 15 to 30 minutes, 14.4% 30 to 45 minutes, 0.0% 45 to 60 minutes, 5.5% 60 minutes or more (2000)

FINDLAY (city). Covers a land area of 17.194 square miles and a water area of 0.110 square miles. Located at 41.04° N. Lat.; 83.64° W. Long. Elevation is 780 feet.
History: Findlay was laid out in 1821 by Joseph Vance and Elnathan Cory, and named for Fort Findlay, an outpost built under the direction of General Hull during the War of 1812. After the Civil War, the Findlay Natural Gas Company began to make commercial use of the gas and oil beneath the city. It was in the Findlay "Jeffersonian" in 1860 that Petroleum V. Nasby (pen name of David Ross Locke, the editor) wrote satirical letters attacking the institution of slavery.
Population: 36,546 (1990); 38,967 (2000); 39,608 (2005); 40,440 (2010 projected); Race: 92.9% White, 1.6% Black, 2.3% Asian, 3.8% Hispanic of any race (2005); Density: 2,303.6 persons per square mile (2005); Average household size: 2.41 (2005); Median age: 36.0 (2005); Males per 100 females: 92.0 (2005); Marriage status: 25.5% never married, 56.5% now married, 7.1% widowed, 10.9% divorced (2000); Foreign born: 2.7% (2000); Ancestry (includes multiple ancestries): 35.5% German, 10.7% Irish, 10.6% English, 9.5% United States or American, 9.5% Other groups (2000).
Economy: Unemployment rate: 4.8% (2005); Total civilian labor force: 22,138 (2005); Single-family building permits issued: 138 (2005); Multi-family building permits issued: 0 (2005); Employment by occupation: 12.5% management, 17.6% professional, 15.0% services, 22.7% sales, 0.2% farming, 8.0% construction, 24.0% production (2000).
Income: Per capita income: $23,985 (2005); Median household income: $44,380 (2005); Average household income: $56,815 (2005); Percent of households with income of $100,000 or more: 12.2% (2005); Poverty rate: 9.1% (2000).
Education: Percent of population age 25 and over with: High school diploma (including GED) or higher: 87.5% (2005); Bachelor's degree or higher: 23.9% (2005); Master's degree or higher: 8.0% (2005).

School District(s)
Findlay City SD (PK-12)
   2003-04 Enrollment: 6,479 . . . . (419) 425-8212
Findlay Digital Academy
   2003-04 Enrollment: n/a
Hancock Educational Service Center (08-12)
   2003-04 Enrollment: n/a . . . . (419) 422-7525
Liberty-Benton Local SD (PK-12)
   2003-04 Enrollment: 1,313 . . . . (419) 422-8526

Four-year College(s)
The University of Findlay (Private, Not-for-profit, Church of God)
   Fall 2004 Enrollment: 4,654 . . . . (419) 422-8313
   2005-06 Tuition: In-state $20,796; Out-of-state $20,796

Winebrenner Theological Seminary (Private, Not-for-profit, Other Protestant)
   Fall 2004 Enrollment: 92 . . . . (419) 434-4200

Two-year College(s)
Brown Mackie College-Findlay (Private, For-profit)
   Fall 2004 Enrollment: 411 . . . . (419) 423-2211
   2005-06 Tuition: In-state $11,180; Out-of-state $11,180

Housing: Homeownership rate: 65.0% (2005); Median home value: $118,021 (2005); Median rent: $416 per month (2000); Median age of housing: 39 years (2000).
Hospitals: Blanchard Valley Regional Health Center (150 beds)
Newspapers: The Courier (Circulation 22,617)
Transportation: Commute to work: 91.5% car, 1.1% public transportation, 3.7% walk, 2.6% work from home (2000); Travel time to work: 60.6% less than 15 minutes, 26.8% 15 to 30 minutes, 6.7% 30 to 45 minutes, 2.9% 45 to 60 minutes, 3.0% 60 minutes or more (2000)

Additional Information Contacts
City of Findlay . . . . (419) 424-7137
   http://www.ci.findlay.oh.us
Findlay Hancock Co. Convention & Visitors Bureau . . . . . . (419) 422-3315
   http://www.visitfindlay.com
Findlay Hancock Community Development . . . . (419) 424-7095
   http://www.findlayoh.com
Findlay Hancock County Chamber . . . . (419) 422-3313
   http://www.findlayhancockchamber.com

JENERA (village). Covers a land area of 0.376 square miles and a water area of 0 square miles. Located at 40.90° N. Lat.; 83.72° W. Long. Elevation is 859 feet.
Population: 285 (1990); 235 (2000); 251 (2005); 269 (2010 projected); Race: 96.4% White, 1.6% Black, 0.0% Asian, 0.8% Hispanic of any race (2005); Density: 668.0 persons per square mile (2005); Average household size: 2.41 (2005); Median age: 37.7 (2005); Males per 100 females: 94.6 (2005); Marriage status: 19.4% never married, 57.5% now married, 15.6% widowed, 7.5% divorced (2000); Foreign born: 0.0% (2000); Ancestry (includes multiple ancestries): 70.0% German, 9.3% English, 4.4% Swiss, 4.4% Other groups, 3.5% Irish (2000).
Economy: Employment by occupation: 13.6% management, 9.7% professional, 12.6% services, 26.2% sales, 0.0% farming, 12.6% construction, 25.2% production (2000).
Income: Per capita income: $21,594 (2005); Median household income: $44,130 (2005); Average household income: $52,115 (2005); Percent of households with income of $100,000 or more: 8.7% (2005); Poverty rate: 3.1% (2000).
Education: Percent of population age 25 and over with: High school diploma (including GED) or higher: 88.4% (2005); Bachelor's degree or higher: 10.4% (2005); Master's degree or higher: 3.0% (2005).
Housing: Homeownership rate: 85.6% (2005); Median home value: $79,545 (2005); Median rent: $438 per month (2000); Median age of housing: 60+ years (2000).
Transportation: Commute to work: 90.3% car, 0.0% public transportation, 7.8% walk, 1.9% work from home (2000); Travel time to work: 20.8% less than 15 minutes, 51.5% 15 to 30 minutes, 23.8% 30 to 45 minutes, 0.0% 45 to 60 minutes, 4.0% 60 minutes or more (2000)

MCCOMB (village). Covers a land area of 0.913 square miles and a water area of 0.036 square miles. Located at 41.10° N. Lat.; 83.79° W. Long. Elevation is 778 feet.
Population: 1,555 (1990); 1,676 (2000); 1,757 (2005); 1,840 (2010 projected); Race: 96.0% White, 0.3% Black, 0.9% Asian, 3.6% Hispanic of any race (2005); Density: 1,924.0 persons per square mile (2005); Average household size: 2.80 (2005); Median age: 31.1 (2005); Males per 100 females: 98.1 (2005); Marriage status: 22.1% never married, 60.7% now married, 5.1% widowed, 12.1% divorced (2000); Foreign born: 1.0% (2000); Ancestry (includes multiple ancestries): 36.0% German, 11.1% English, 10.1% Other groups, 8.7% Irish, 6.4% United States or American (2000).
Economy: Corn, wheat, oats; glass products. Single-family building permits issued: 3 (2005); Multi-family building permits issued: 0 (2005); Employment by occupation: 6.9% management, 11.7% professional, 13.4% services, 22.4% sales, 0.2% farming, 11.6% construction, 33.7% production (2000).
Income: Per capita income: $19,606 (2005); Median household income: $46,898 (2005); Average household income: $54,940 (2005); Percent of

households with income of $100,000 or more: 9.3% (2005); Poverty rate: 8.6% (2000).
Education: Percent of population age 25 and over with: High school diploma (including GED) or higher: 89.0% (2005); Bachelor's degree or higher: 14.4% (2005); Master's degree or higher: 4.3% (2005).

School District(s)
Mccomb Local SD (PK-12)
    2003-04 Enrollment: 862 . . . . (419) 293-3979

Housing: Homeownership rate: 77.4% (2005); Median home value: $99,120 (2005); Median rent: $439 per month (2000); Median age of housing: 45 years (2000).
Transportation: Commute to work: 93.1% car, 0.0% public transportation, 2.5% walk, 3.6% work from home (2000); Travel time to work: 28.3% less than 15 minutes, 55.4% 15 to 30 minutes, 7.8% 30 to 45 minutes, 3.7% 45 to 60 minutes, 4.9% 60 minutes or more (2000)

MOUNT BLANCHARD (village). Covers a land area of 0.540 square miles and a water area of 0 square miles. Located at 40.90° N. Lat.; 83.55° W. Long. Elevation is 835 feet.
Population: 491 (1990); 484 (2000); 530 (2005); 567 (2010 projected); Race: 97.9% White, 0.2% Black, 0.0% Asian, 1.5% Hispanic of any race (2005); Density: 980.9 persons per square mile (2005); Average household size: 2.48 (2005); Median age: 35.6 (2005); Males per 100 females: 92.7 (2005); Marriage status: 18.2% never married, 66.4% now married, 6.2% widowed, 9.2% divorced (2000); Foreign born: 0.0% (2000); Ancestry (includes multiple ancestries): 34.5% German, 12.6% English, 8.8% Irish, 8.4% United States or American, 4.8% Other groups (2000).
Economy: Single-family building permits issued: 1 (2005); Multi-family building permits issued: 0 (2005); Employment by occupation: 11.8% management, 11.8% professional, 12.7% services, 22.6% sales, 0.0% farming, 9.0% construction, 32.1% production (2000).
Income: Per capita income: $20,396 (2005); Median household income: $44,490 (2005); Average household income: $50,514 (2005); Percent of households with income of $100,000 or more: 7.9% (2005); Poverty rate: 4.8% (2000).
Education: Percent of population age 25 and over with: High school diploma (including GED) or higher: 84.3% (2005); Bachelor's degree or higher: 11.6% (2005); Master's degree or higher: 4.5% (2005).

School District(s)
Riverdale Local SD (PK-12)
    2003-04 Enrollment: 1,051 . . . . (419) 694-4994

Housing: Homeownership rate: 75.2% (2005); Median home value: $93,864 (2005); Median rent: $408 per month (2000); Median age of housing: 60+ years (2000).
Transportation: Commute to work: 90.0% car, 0.0% public transportation, 5.9% walk, 4.1% work from home (2000); Travel time to work: 18.4% less than 15 minutes, 56.1% 15 to 30 minutes, 21.2% 30 to 45 minutes, 1.9% 45 to 60 minutes, 2.4% 60 minutes or more (2000)

MOUNT CORY (village). Covers a land area of 0.384 square miles and a water area of 0 square miles. Located at 40.93° N. Lat.; 83.82° W. Long. Elevation is 820 feet.
Population: 245 (1990); 203 (2000); 207 (2005); 213 (2010 projected); Race: 96.1% White, 0.0% Black, 0.0% Asian, 1.4% Hispanic of any race (2005); Density: 538.5 persons per square mile (2005); Average household size: 2.49 (2005); Median age: 39.1 (2005); Males per 100 females: 101.0 (2005); Marriage status: 27.2% never married, 60.4% now married, 5.9% widowed, 6.5% divorced (2000); Foreign born: 0.0% (2000); Ancestry (includes multiple ancestries): 38.9% German, 10.9% Irish, 9.8% Dutch, 5.7% Swiss, 5.2% English (2000).
Economy: In agricultural area. Employment by occupation: 5.3% management, 8.4% professional, 17.9% services, 25.3% sales, 0.0% farming, 13.7% construction, 29.5% production (2000).
Income: Per capita income: $20,350 (2005); Median household income: $44,375 (2005); Average household income: $50,753 (2005); Percent of households with income of $100,000 or more: 4.8% (2005); Poverty rate: 1.0% (2000).
Education: Percent of population age 25 and over with: High school diploma (including GED) or higher: 88.0% (2005); Bachelor's degree or higher: 6.0% (2005); Master's degree or higher: 3.0% (2005).
Housing: Homeownership rate: 92.8% (2005); Median home value: $83,182 (2005); Median rent: $325 per month (2000); Median age of housing: 60+ years (2000).
Transportation: Commute to work: 91.4% car, 0.0% public transportation, 2.2% walk, 6.5% work from home (2000); Travel time to work: 25.3% less than 15 minutes, 52.9% 15 to 30 minutes, 18.4% 30 to 45 minutes, 0.0% 45 to 60 minutes, 3.4% 60 minutes or more (2000)

RAWSON (village). Covers a land area of 0.398 square miles and a water area of 0 square miles. Located at 40.95° N. Lat.; 83.78° W. Long. Elevation is 817 feet.
Population: 482 (1990); 465 (2000); 474 (2005); 485 (2010 projected); Race: 98.1% White, 0.0% Black, 0.0% Asian, 0.6% Hispanic of any race (2005); Density: 1,191.2 persons per square mile (2005); Average household size: 2.87 (2005); Median age: 34.3 (2005); Males per 100 females: 96.7 (2005); Marriage status: 24.8% never married, 64.0% now married, 1.8% widowed, 9.4% divorced (2000); Foreign born: 0.6% (2000); Ancestry (includes multiple ancestries): 26.6% German, 24.0% United States or American, 8.9% Irish, 7.1% English, 4.8% Other groups (2000).
Economy: In agricultural region. Employment by occupation: 6.1% management, 8.3% professional, 10.1% services, 24.1% sales, 0.0% farming, 14.9% construction, 36.4% production (2000).
Income: Per capita income: $17,421 (2005); Median household income: $48,176 (2005); Average household income: $50,045 (2005); Percent of households with income of $100,000 or more: 3.0% (2005); Poverty rate: 5.9% (2000).
Education: Percent of population age 25 and over with: High school diploma (including GED) or higher: 80.5% (2005); Bachelor's degree or higher: 5.2% (2005); Master's degree or higher: 0.0% (2005).

School District(s)
Cory-Rawson Local SD (PK-12)
    2003-04 Enrollment: 750 . . . . (419) 963-3415

Housing: Homeownership rate: 83.0% (2005); Median home value: $75,128 (2005); Median rent: $475 per month (2000); Median age of housing: 60+ years (2000).
Transportation: Commute to work: 93.9% car, 0.0% public transportation, 0.0% walk, 5.3% work from home (2000); Travel time to work: 18.5% less than 15 minutes, 58.8% 15 to 30 minutes, 13.9% 30 to 45 minutes, 2.8% 45 to 60 minutes, 6.0% 60 minutes or more (2000)

VAN BUREN (village). Covers a land area of 0.249 square miles and a water area of 0 square miles. Located at 41.13° N. Lat.; 83.64° W. Long. Elevation is 770 feet.
History: Van Buren was named for President Martin Van Buren. For a time, Van Buren was an oil center.
Population: 337 (1990); 313 (2000); 330 (2005); 347 (2010 projected); Race: 97.0% White, 0.3% Black, 0.0% Asian, 5.2% Hispanic of any race (2005); Density: 1,325.8 persons per square mile (2005); Average household size: 2.73 (2005); Median age: 37.9 (2005); Males per 100 females: 93.0 (2005); Marriage status: 14.2% never married, 69.8% now married, 6.5% widowed, 9.5% divorced (2000); Foreign born: 0.3% (2000); Ancestry (includes multiple ancestries): 45.6% German, 14.4% English, 8.4% French (except Basque), 8.4% Polish, 8.1% Dutch (2000).
Economy: Single-family building permits issued: 7 (2005); Multi-family building permits issued: 0 (2005); Employment by occupation: 10.4% management, 21.5% professional, 10.4% services, 16.0% sales, 0.0% farming, 6.7% construction, 35.0% production (2000).
Income: Per capita income: $22,341 (2005); Median household income: $58,224 (2005); Average household income: $60,930 (2005); Percent of households with income of $100,000 or more: 10.7% (2005); Poverty rate: 1.7% (2000).
Education: Percent of population age 25 and over with: High school diploma (including GED) or higher: 93.8% (2005); Bachelor's degree or higher: 15.2% (2005); Master's degree or higher: 6.2% (2005).

School District(s)
Van Buren Local SD (PK-12)
    2003-04 Enrollment: 945 . . . . (419) 299-3578

Housing: Homeownership rate: 96.7% (2005); Median home value: $116,803 (2005); Median rent: $n/a per month (2000); Median age of housing: 60+ years (2000).
Transportation: Commute to work: 95.0% car, 0.0% public transportation, 1.3% walk, 3.8% work from home (2000); Travel time to work: 32.5% less than 15 minutes, 52.6% 15 to 30 minutes, 7.8% 30 to 45 minutes, 2.6% 45 to 60 minutes, 4.5% 60 minutes or more (2000)

VANLUE (village). Covers a land area of 0.280 square miles and a water area of 0.007 square miles. Located at 40.97° N. Lat.; 83.48° W. Long. Elevation is 825 feet.
Population: 373 (1990); 371 (2000); 368 (2005); 364 (2010 projected); Race: 96.2% White, 0.3% Black, 0.0% Asian, 1.1% Hispanic of any race

(2005); Density: 1,315.1 persons per square mile (2005); Average household size: 2.59 (2005); Median age: 32.8 (2005); Males per 100 females: 95.7 (2005); Marriage status: 24.3% never married, 56.3% now married, 7.7% widowed, 11.6% divorced (2000); Foreign born: 0.0% (2000); Ancestry (includes multiple ancestries): 47.0% German, 11.4% Irish, 10.4% Other groups, 9.6% English, 5.7% French (except Basque) (2000).
Economy: In agricultural region. Single-family building permits issued: 0 (2005); Multi-family building permits issued: 0 (2005); Employment by occupation: 7.0% management, 7.6% professional, 16.8% services, 24.3% sales, 1.1% farming, 7.0% construction, 36.2% production (2000).
Income: Per capita income: $16,080 (2005); Median household income: $35,750 (2005); Average household income: $41,673 (2005); Percent of households with income of $100,000 or more: 2.8% (2005); Poverty rate: 3.7% (2000).
Education: Percent of population age 25 and over with: High school diploma (including GED) or higher: 84.7% (2005); Bachelor's degree or higher: 6.6% (2005); Master's degree or higher: 2.2% (2005).

School District(s)
Vanlue Local SD (PK-12)
    2003-04 Enrollment: 330 . . . . (419) 387-7724
Housing: Homeownership rate: 83.1% (2005); Median home value: $86,897 (2005); Median rent: $311 per month (2000); Median age of housing: 60+ years (2000).
Transportation: Commute to work: 89.5% car, 0.0% public transportation, 4.4% walk, 3.9% work from home (2000); Travel time to work: 20.7% less than 15 minutes, 65.5% 15 to 30 minutes, 6.9% 30 to 45 minutes, 2.3% 45 to 60 minutes, 4.6% 60 minutes or more (2000)

Hardin County

Located in west central Ohio; crossed by the Sciota, Blanchard, and Ottawa Rivers. Covers a land area of 470.29 square miles, a water area of 0.25 square miles, and is located in the Eastern Time Zone. The county government was organized in 1820. County seat is Kenton.

Weather Station: Kenton   Elevation: 994 feet

	Jan	Feb	Mar	Apr	May	Jun	Jul	Aug	Sep	Oct	Nov	Dec
High	32	37	47	60	72	81	85	83	76	64	50	38
Low	16	19	28	38	49	58	62	60	53	41	32	22
Precip	2.2	2.0	2.8	3.5	3.8	3.5	4.0	3.3	2.6	2.1	2.8	2.7
Snow	10.0	6.4	4.2	0.6	0.0	0.0	0.0	0.0	0.0	tr	1.2	5.4

High and Low temperatures in degrees Fahrenheit; Precipitation and Snow in inches

Population: 31,111 (1990); 31,945 (2000); 31,487 (2005); 31,013 (2010 projected); Race: 97.6% White, 0.8% Black, 0.3% Asian, 0.8% Hispanic of any race (2005); Density: 67.0 persons per square mile (2005); Average household size: 2.65 (2005); Median age: 34.3 (2005); Males per 100 females: 97.5 (2005).
Religion: Five largest groups: 12.5% The United Methodist Church, 5.6% Catholic Church, 4.4% Christian Churches and Churches of Christ, 4.1% United Church of Christ, 1.9% Christian Church (Disciples of Christ) (2000).
Economy: Unemployment rate: 5.8% (2005); Total civilian labor force: 16,161 (2005); Leading industries: 28.2% manufacturing; 13.4% retail trade; 11.3% health care and social assistance (2004); Farms: 842 totaling 246,393 acres (2002); Companies that employ 500 or more persons: 1 (2004); Companies that employ 100 to 499 persons: 10 (2004); Companies that employ less than 100 persons: 507 (2004); Black-owned businesses: n/a (2002); Hispanic-owned businesses: n/a (2002); Women-owned businesses: 306 (2002); Retail sales per capita: $8,262 (2006). Single-family building permits issued: 39 (2005); Multi-family building permits issued: 0 (2005).
Income: Per capita income: $17,787 (2005); Median household income: $37,779 (2005); Average household income: $46,026 (2005); Percent of households with income of $100,000 or more: 6.4% (2005); Poverty rate: 10.5% (2003); Bankruptcy rate: 9.55% (2005).
Education: Percent of population age 25 and over with: High school diploma (including GED) or higher: 80.7% (2005); Bachelor's degree or higher: 11.9% (2005); Master's degree or higher: 4.7% (2005).
Housing: Homeownership rate: 73.0% (2005); Median home value: $88,718 (2005); Median rent: $311 per month (2000); Median age of housing: 44 years (2000).
Health: Birth rate: 116.3 per 10,000 population (2004); Death rate: 107.0 per 10,000 population (2004); Age-adjusted cancer mortality rate: 271.1 deaths per 100,000 population (2002); Number of physicians: 6.5 per 10,000 population (2004); Hospital beds: 7.9 per 10,000 population (2003); Hospital admissions: 466.1 per 10,000 population (2003).
Elections: 2004 Presidential election results: 63.0% Bush, 36.5% Kerry, 0.0% Nader, 0.2% Badnarik
Additional Information Contacts
Hardin County Government . . . . (419) 674-2205
   http://www.co.hardin.oh.us/
Ada Chamber of Commerce . . . . (419) 634-0936
   http://www.hardinohio.org
Hardin County Tourist and Convention Bureau . . . . (419) 674-4591
   http://www.tourhardin.com
Kenton Chamber of Commerce . . . . (419) 673-4131
   http://chamber.hardinohio.org

Hardin County Communities

ADA (village). Covers a land area of 1.871 square miles and a water area of 0 square miles. Located at 40.76° N. Lat.; 83.82° W. Long. Elevation is 960 feet.
History: Ada grew up around Ohio Northern University, founded in 1871 as the Northwestern Ohio Normal School by Henry Solomon Lehr.
Population: 5,437 (1990); 5,582 (2000); 5,530 (2005); 5,507 (2010 projected); Race: 95.7% White, 2.0% Black, 0.9% Asian, 0.6% Hispanic of any race (2005); Density: 2,955.0 persons per square mile (2005); Average household size: 3.12 (2005); Median age: 23.2 (2005); Males per 100 females: 99.4 (2005); Marriage status: 53.5% never married, 35.3% now married, 3.3% widowed, 7.9% divorced (2000); Foreign born: 2.8% (2000); Ancestry (includes multiple ancestries): 31.8% German, 11.9% United States or American, 10.1% English, 10.0% Irish, 9.4% Other groups (2000).
Economy: Single-family building permits issued: 6 (2005); Multi-family building permits issued: 0 (2005); Employment by occupation: 5.3% management, 32.1% professional, 17.6% services, 25.5% sales, 0.0% farming, 4.5% construction, 14.9% production (2000).
Income: Per capita income: $13,752 (2005); Median household income: $27,701 (2005); Average household income: $38,895 (2005); Percent of households with income of $100,000 or more: 5.3% (2005); Poverty rate: 21.9% (2000).
Education: Percent of population age 25 and over with: High school diploma (including GED) or higher: 86.6% (2005); Bachelor's degree or higher: 33.0% (2005); Master's degree or higher: 13.5% (2005).

School District(s)
Ada Ex Vill SD (PK-12)
    2003-04 Enrollment: 887 . . . . (419) 634-6421

Four-year College(s)
Ohio Northern University (Private, Not-for-profit, United Methodist)
    Fall 2004 Enrollment: 3,495 . . . . (419) 772-2000
    2005-06 Tuition: In-state $27,045; Out-of-state $27,045
Housing: Homeownership rate: 49.1% (2005); Median home value: $80,585 (2005); Median rent: $339 per month (2000); Median age of housing: 38 years (2000).
Newspapers: Ada Herald (General - Circulation 2,700)
Transportation: Commute to work: 68.7% car, 0.5% public transportation, 27.2% walk, 2.3% work from home (2000); Travel time to work: 55.9% less than 15 minutes, 24.2% 15 to 30 minutes, 13.7% 30 to 45 minutes, 3.1% 45 to 60 minutes, 3.1% 60 minutes or more (2000)
Additional Information Contacts
Ada Chamber of Commerce . . . . (419) 634-0936
   http://www.hardinohio.org

ALGER (village). Covers a land area of 0.283 square miles and a water area of 0 square miles. Located at 40.70° N. Lat.; 83.84° W. Long. Elevation is 978 feet.
Population: 893 (1990); 888 (2000); 865 (2005); 838 (2010 projected); Race: 99.3% White, 0.0% Black, 0.0% Asian, 0.0% Hispanic of any race (2005); Density: 3,056.7 persons per square mile (2005); Average household size: 2.35 (2005); Median age: 34.6 (2005); Males per 100 females: 81.3 (2005); Marriage status: 18.9% never married, 57.6% now married, 9.5% widowed, 13.9% divorced (2000); Foreign born: 0.3% (2000); Ancestry (includes multiple ancestries): 25.9% United States or American, 12.3% German, 10.3% Irish, 5.2% Other groups, 4.4% English (2000).
Economy: In agricultural area. Employment by occupation: 1.9% management, 7.4% professional, 14.8% services, 19.2% sales, 0.0% farming, 11.5% construction, 45.2% production (2000).

Income: Per capita income: $15,564 (2005); Median household income: $28,276 (2005); Average household income: $36,583 (2005); Percent of households with income of $100,000 or more: 2.7% (2005); Poverty rate: 18.8% (2000).
Education: Percent of population age 25 and over with: High school diploma (including GED) or higher: 69.0% (2005); Bachelor's degree or higher: 4.0% (2005); Master's degree or higher: 0.3% (2005).
Housing: Homeownership rate: 66.6% (2005); Median home value: $60,185 (2005); Median rent: $252 per month (2000); Median age of housing: 39 years (2000).
Transportation: Commute to work: 91.2% car, 1.1% public transportation, 3.4% walk, 2.0% work from home (2000); Travel time to work: 22.8% less than 15 minutes, 42.9% 15 to 30 minutes, 25.1% 30 to 45 minutes, 6.1% 45 to 60 minutes, 3.2% 60 minutes or more (2000)

DOLA (unincorporated postal area, zip code 45835).
Covers a land area of 18.971 square miles and a water area of 0 square miles. Located at 40.76° N. Lat.; 83.70° W. Long. Elevation is 948 feet.
Population: 456 (2000); Race: 96.9% White, 0.0% Black, 1.8% Asian, 2.9% Hispanic of any race (2000); Density: 24.0 persons per square mile (2000); Age: 25.1% under 18, 14.2% over 64 (2000); Marriage status: 9.5% never married, 72.6% now married, 5.2% widowed, 12.7% divorced (2000); Foreign born: 0.0% (2000); Ancestry (includes multiple ancestries): 34.2% German, 11.6% Other groups, 10.4% English, 9.6% Irish, 7.1% Scottish (2000).
Economy: Employment by occupation: 23.9% management, 3.7% professional, 4.9% services, 17.8% sales, 0.0% farming, 4.3% construction, 45.4% production (2000).
Income: Per capita income: $21,228 (2000); Median household income: $46,023 (2000); Poverty rate: 20.4% (2000).
Education: Percent of population age 25 and over with: High school diploma (including GED) or higher: 84.0% (2000); Bachelor's degree or higher: 11.1% (2000).

School District(s)
Hardin Northern Local SD (PK-12)
    2003-04 Enrollment: 519 . . . . (419) 759-2331

Housing: Homeownership rate: 82.4% (2000); Median home value: $81,100 (2000); Median rent: $323 per month (2000); Median age of housing: 43 years (2000).
Transportation: Commute to work: 89.0% car, 0.0% public transportation, 3.1% walk, 8.0% work from home (2000); Travel time to work: 18.7% less than 15 minutes, 40.0% 15 to 30 minutes, 30.0% 30 to 45 minutes, 0.0% 45 to 60 minutes, 11.3% 60 minutes or more (2000)

DUNKIRK (village).
Covers a land area of 0.666 square miles and a water area of 0.059 square miles. Located at 40.78° N. Lat.; 83.64° W. Long. Elevation is 951 feet.
Population: 885 (1990); 952 (2000); 903 (2005); 884 (2010 projected); Race: 99.1% White, 0.0% Black, 0.1% Asian, 0.2% Hispanic of any race (2005); Density: 1,355.1 persons per square mile (2005); Average household size: 2.63 (2005); Median age: 34.4 (2005); Males per 100 females: 102.5 (2005); Marriage status: 22.1% never married, 63.7% now married, 5.0% widowed, 9.2% divorced (2000); Foreign born: 0.7% (2000); Ancestry (includes multiple ancestries): 21.1% German, 14.9% United States or American, 12.6% English, 5.1% Irish, 4.0% Other groups (2000).
Economy: In agricultural area; transportation equipment. Employment by occupation: 7.8% management, 8.9% professional, 20.2% services, 15.3% sales, 0.4% farming, 8.6% construction, 38.8% production (2000).
Income: Per capita income: $19,651 (2005); Median household income: $46,082 (2005); Average household income: $51,655 (2005); Percent of households with income of $100,000 or more: 6.7% (2005); Poverty rate: 9.3% (2000).
Education: Percent of population age 25 and over with: High school diploma (including GED) or higher: 78.8% (2005); Bachelor's degree or higher: 8.4% (2005); Master's degree or higher: 1.9% (2005).
Housing: Homeownership rate: 81.9% (2005); Median home value: $71,364 (2005); Median rent: $273 per month (2000); Median age of housing: 56 years (2000).
Transportation: Commute to work: 95.9% car, 0.7% public transportation, 1.6% walk, 1.8% work from home (2000); Travel time to work: 21.4% less than 15 minutes, 41.5% 15 to 30 minutes, 25.8% 30 to 45 minutes, 7.1% 45 to 60 minutes, 4.1% 60 minutes or more (2000)

FOREST (village).
Covers a land area of 1.187 square miles and a water area of 0 square miles. Located at 40.80° N. Lat.; 83.51° W. Long. Elevation is 930 feet.
Population: 1,594 (1990); 1,488 (2000); 1,372 (2005); 1,305 (2010 projected); Race: 98.8% White, 0.4% Black, 0.0% Asian, 0.7% Hispanic of any race (2005); Density: 1,155.7 persons per square mile (2005); Average household size: 2.47 (2005); Median age: 33.4 (2005); Males per 100 females: 95.2 (2005); Marriage status: 21.6% never married, 58.0% now married, 6.9% widowed, 13.5% divorced (2000); Foreign born: 0.0% (2000); Ancestry (includes multiple ancestries): 26.5% German, 14.9% United States or American, 9.5% Irish, 7.0% English, 5.8% Other groups (2000).
Economy: In agricultural area. Single-family building permits issued: 0 (2005); Multi-family building permits issued: 0 (2005); Employment by occupation: 5.5% management, 9.1% professional, 13.3% services, 20.9% sales, 0.4% farming, 6.1% construction, 44.7% production (2000).
Income: Per capita income: $17,555 (2005); Median household income: $37,805 (2005); Average household income: $43,318 (2005); Percent of households with income of $100,000 or more: 3.4% (2005); Poverty rate: 9.7% (2000).
Education: Percent of population age 25 and over with: High school diploma (including GED) or higher: 84.6% (2005); Bachelor's degree or higher: 6.5% (2005); Master's degree or higher: 2.0% (2005).
Housing: Homeownership rate: 79.9% (2005); Median home value: $79,796 (2005); Median rent: $290 per month (2000); Median age of housing: 47 years (2000).
Transportation: Commute to work: 93.3% car, 0.9% public transportation, 3.7% walk, 1.9% work from home (2000); Travel time to work: 24.9% less than 15 minutes, 36.0% 15 to 30 minutes, 25.1% 30 to 45 minutes, 6.4% 45 to 60 minutes, 7.6% 60 minutes or more (2000)

KENTON (city).
Covers a land area of 4.480 square miles and a water area of 0.094 square miles. Located at 40.64° N. Lat.; 83.60° W. Long. Elevation is 991 feet.
History: Kenton was platted in 1833 on the Scioto River, and named for pioneer Simon Kenton. The town's economic base moved from agriculture to ornamental iron fences and then back to agriculture.
Population: 8,777 (1990); 8,336 (2000); 8,103 (2005); 7,863 (2010 projected); Race: 97.2% White, 1.0% Black, 0.3% Asian, 0.9% Hispanic of any race (2005); Density: 1,808.6 persons per square mile (2005); Average household size: 2.35 (2005); Median age: 36.8 (2005); Males per 100 females: 89.1 (2005); Marriage status: 21.0% never married, 53.9% now married, 9.9% widowed, 15.1% divorced (2000); Foreign born: 0.8% (2000); Ancestry (includes multiple ancestries): 22.0% German, 16.4% United States or American, 11.9% Irish, 11.3% English, 9.1% Other groups (2000).
Economy: Single-family building permits issued: 6 (2005); Multi-family building permits issued: 0 (2005); Employment by occupation: 5.0% management, 9.4% professional, 17.5% services, 18.7% sales, 1.0% farming, 7.9% construction, 40.5% production (2000).
Income: Per capita income: $16,639 (2005); Median household income: $30,039 (2005); Average household income: $37,768 (2005); Percent of households with income of $100,000 or more: 3.2% (2005); Poverty rate: 16.2% (2000).
Education: Percent of population age 25 and over with: High school diploma (including GED) or higher: 76.9% (2005); Bachelor's degree or higher: 6.4% (2005); Master's degree or higher: 2.7% (2005).

School District(s)
Kenton City SD (PK-12)
    2003-04 Enrollment: 2,145 . . . . (419) 673-0775

Housing: Homeownership rate: 63.2% (2005); Median home value: $76,153 (2005); Median rent: $296 per month (2000); Median age of housing: 51 years (2000).
Hospitals: Hardin Memorial Hospital (103 beds)
Newspapers: Kenton Times (Circulation 7,000)
Transportation: Commute to work: 93.8% car, 0.4% public transportation, 3.5% walk, 2.0% work from home (2000); Travel time to work: 50.9% less than 15 minutes, 13.5% 15 to 30 minutes, 22.2% 30 to 45 minutes, 9.3% 45 to 60 minutes, 4.1% 60 minutes or more (2000)
Additional Information Contacts
Hardin County Tourist and Convention Bureau . . . . (419) 674-4591
    http://www.tourhardin.com
Kenton Chamber of Commerce . . . . (419) 673-4131
    http://chamber.hardinohio.org

MCGUFFEY (village). Covers a land area of 0.366 square miles and a water area of 0 square miles. Located at 40.69° N. Lat.; 83.78° W. Long. Elevation is 973 feet.
History: McGuffey was settled in a marshy region, and took to the growing of onions. Those who tended the onion fields were sometimes called "marsh rats."
Population: 550 (1990); 522 (2000); 527 (2005); 514 (2010 projected); Race: 97.7% White, 0.0% Black, 0.0% Asian, 0.9% Hispanic of any race (2005); Density: 1,440.3 persons per square mile (2005); Average household size: 2.47 (2005); Median age: 36.2 (2005); Males per 100 females: 98.1 (2005); Marriage status: 27.4% never married, 43.0% now married, 11.0% widowed, 18.7% divorced (2000); Foreign born: 0.0% (2000); Ancestry (includes multiple ancestries): 28.4% United States or American, 12.6% German, 10.0% English, 8.8% Irish, 8.4% Other groups (2000).
Economy: Employment by occupation: 6.8% management, 5.0% professional, 23.0% services, 13.0% sales, 0.0% farming, 11.2% construction, 41.0% production (2000).
Income: Per capita income: $12,642 (2005); Median household income: $24,896 (2005); Average household income: $31,279 (2005); Percent of households with income of $100,000 or more: 1.4% (2005); Poverty rate: 19.7% (2000).
Education: Percent of population age 25 and over with: High school diploma (including GED) or higher: 60.5% (2005); Bachelor's degree or higher: 1.5% (2005); Master's degree or higher: 0.0% (2005).
School District(s)
Upper Scioto Valley Local SD (PK-12)
    2003-04 Enrollment: 798 . . . . (419) 757-4451
Housing: Homeownership rate: 74.2% (2005); Median home value: $51,628 (2005); Median rent: $263 per month (2000); Median age of housing: 43 years (2000).
Transportation: Commute to work: 91.7% car, 1.3% public transportation, 7.0% walk, 0.0% work from home (2000); Travel time to work: 15.9% less than 15 minutes, 51.6% 15 to 30 minutes, 19.1% 30 to 45 minutes, 8.9% 45 to 60 minutes, 4.5% 60 minutes or more (2000)

MOUNT VICTORY (village). Covers a land area of 0.758 square miles and a water area of 0 square miles. Located at 40.53° N. Lat.; 83.52° W. Long. Elevation is 1,033 feet.
Population: 551 (1990); 600 (2000); 640 (2005); 665 (2010 projected); Race: 98.9% White, 0.0% Black, 0.0% Asian, 0.9% Hispanic of any race (2005); Density: 844.0 persons per square mile (2005); Average household size: 2.43 (2005); Median age: 35.5 (2005); Males per 100 females: 95.7 (2005); Marriage status: 23.1% never married, 54.9% now married, 9.4% widowed, 12.7% divorced (2000); Foreign born: 1.1% (2000); Ancestry (includes multiple ancestries): 23.6% United States or American, 21.1% German, 11.1% Other groups, 8.8% Irish, 7.7% English (2000).
Economy: In agricultural area. Employment by occupation: 8.1% management, 8.4% professional, 11.7% services, 18.1% sales, 0.3% farming, 14.1% construction, 39.3% production (2000).
Income: Per capita income: $18,383 (2005); Median household income: $43,088 (2005); Average household income: $44,734 (2005); Percent of households with income of $100,000 or more: 3.4% (2005); Poverty rate: 6.9% (2000).
Education: Percent of population age 25 and over with: High school diploma (including GED) or higher: 82.2% (2005); Bachelor's degree or higher: 6.1% (2005); Master's degree or higher: 1.6% (2005).
School District(s)
Ridgemont Local SD (PK-12)
    2003-04 Enrollment: 644 . . . . (937) 354-2441
Housing: Homeownership rate: 78.7% (2005); Median home value: $80,536 (2005); Median rent: $249 per month (2000); Median age of housing: 54 years (2000).
Transportation: Commute to work: 93.8% car, 1.0% public transportation, 2.1% walk, 2.4% work from home (2000); Travel time to work: 21.4% less than 15 minutes, 32.4% 15 to 30 minutes, 34.2% 30 to 45 minutes, 5.7% 45 to 60 minutes, 6.4% 60 minutes or more (2000)

PATTERSON (village). Covers a land area of 0.107 square miles and a water area of 0 square miles. Located at 40.78° N. Lat.; 83.52° W. Long. Elevation is 920 feet.
Population: 145 (1990); 138 (2000); 132 (2005); 125 (2010 projected); Race: 97.7% White, 0.0% Black, 0.0% Asian, 0.8% Hispanic of any race (2005); Density: 1,232.5 persons per square mile (2005); Average household size: 2.44 (2005); Median age: 43.8 (2005); Males per 100 females: 94.1 (2005); Marriage status: 15.8% never married, 65.8% now married, 13.2% widowed, 5.3% divorced (2000); Foreign born: 0.0% (2000); Ancestry (includes multiple ancestries): 20.4% German, 12.9% United States or American, 7.5% Irish, 6.8% Other groups, 4.1% Welsh (2000).
Economy: Employment by occupation: 0.0% management, 10.4% professional, 17.9% services, 7.5% sales, 0.0% farming, 3.0% construction, 61.2% production (2000).
Income: Per capita income: $26,193 (2005); Median household income: $48,500 (2005); Average household income: $64,028 (2005); Percent of households with income of $100,000 or more: 14.8% (2005); Poverty rate: 1.4% (2000).
Education: Percent of population age 25 and over with: High school diploma (including GED) or higher: 76.9% (2005); Bachelor's degree or higher: 4.4% (2005); Master's degree or higher: 0.0% (2005).
Housing: Homeownership rate: 90.7% (2005); Median home value: $56,500 (2005); Median rent: $344 per month (2000); Median age of housing: 60+ years (2000).
Transportation: Commute to work: 100.0% car, 0.0% public transportation, 0.0% walk, 0.0% work from home (2000); Travel time to work: 9.4% less than 15 minutes, 65.6% 15 to 30 minutes, 15.6% 30 to 45 minutes, 6.3% 45 to 60 minutes, 3.1% 60 minutes or more (2000)

RIDGEWAY (village). Covers a land area of 0.601 square miles and a water area of 0 square miles. Located at 40.51° N. Lat.; 83.57° W. Long. Elevation is 1,053 feet.
Population: 378 (1990); 354 (2000); 388 (2005); 413 (2010 projected); Race: 98.2% White, 1.5% Black, 0.0% Asian, 0.0% Hispanic of any race (2005); Density: 646.1 persons per square mile (2005); Average household size: 2.87 (2005); Median age: 33.5 (2005); Males per 100 females: 96.0 (2005); Marriage status: 23.8% never married, 64.7% now married, 6.7% widowed, 4.8% divorced (2000); Foreign born: 0.9% (2000); Ancestry (includes multiple ancestries): 27.3% German, 13.5% Irish, 7.8% United States or American, 7.2% English, 5.2% Dutch (2000).
Economy: Single-family building permits issued: 0 (2005); Multi-family building permits issued: 0 (2005); Employment by occupation: 8.7% management, 7.0% professional, 20.9% services, 9.3% sales, 1.2% farming, 12.2% construction, 40.7% production (2000).
Income: Per capita income: $19,987 (2005); Median household income: $47,404 (2005); Average household income: $57,444 (2005); Percent of households with income of $100,000 or more: 9.6% (2005); Poverty rate: 2.9% (2000).
Education: Percent of population age 25 and over with: High school diploma (including GED) or higher: 80.8% (2005); Bachelor's degree or higher: 4.6% (2005); Master's degree or higher: 0.8% (2005).
School District(s)
Ridgemont Local SD (PK-12)
    2003-04 Enrollment: 644 . . . . (937) 354-2441
Housing: Homeownership rate: 91.1% (2005); Median home value: $62,273 (2005); Median rent: $258 per month (2000); Median age of housing: 60+ years (2000).
Transportation: Commute to work: 95.3% car, 0.0% public transportation, 2.4% walk, 1.2% work from home (2000); Travel time to work: 17.4% less than 15 minutes, 42.5% 15 to 30 minutes, 30.5% 30 to 45 minutes, 3.6% 45 to 60 minutes, 6.0% 60 minutes or more (2000)

Harrison County

Located in eastern Ohio; drained by Stillwater and Conotton Creeks; includes Tappan and Clendening Lakes. Covers a land area of 403.53 square miles, a water area of 7.26 square miles, and is located in the Eastern Time Zone. The county government was organized in 1813. County seat is Cadiz.

Weather Station: Cadiz — Elevation: 1,259 feet

	Jan	Feb	Mar	Apr	May	Jun	Jul	Aug	Sep	Oct	Nov	Dec
High	35	39	50	62	71	79	83	82	76	64	51	40
Low	19	22	30	39	50	58	63	61	54	43	34	25
Precip	2.8	2.4	3.2	3.4	4.1	4.4	4.4	4.1	3.2	2.6	3.3	3.0
Snow	11.5	6.5	5.1	1.2	0.0	0.0	0.0	0.0	0.0	tr	1.7	6.3

High and Low temperatures in degrees Fahrenheit; Precipitation and Snow in inches

Population: 16,085 (1990); 15,856 (2000); 16,078 (2005); 16,305 (2010 projected); Race: 97.0% White, 1.9% Black, 0.1% Asian, 0.5% Hispanic of any race (2005); Density: 39.8 persons per square mile (2005); Average

household size: 2.43 (2005); Median age: 41.7 (2005); Males per 100 females: 95.3 (2005).
Religion: Five largest groups: 15.9% The United Methodist Church, 6.2% Presbyterian Church (U.S.A.), 3.5% Catholic Church, 2.6% Christian Churches and Churches of Christ, 1.1% Church of the Nazarene (2000).
Economy: Unemployment rate: 6.4% (2005); Total civilian labor force: 7,528 (2005); Leading industries: 22.9% health care and social assistance; 22.8% manufacturing; 10.9% mining (2004); Farms: 450 totaling 138,423 acres (2002); Companies that employ 500 or more persons: 0 (2004); Companies that employ 100 to 499 persons: 7 (2004); Companies that employ less than 100 persons: 292 (2004); Black-owned businesses: n/a (2002); Hispanic-owned businesses: n/a (2002); Women-owned businesses: 325 (2002); Retail sales per capita: $6,065 (2006). Single-family building permits issued: 3 (2005); Multi-family building permits issued: 0 (2005).
Income: Per capita income: $18,982 (2005); Median household income: $34,881 (2005); Average household income: $45,743 (2005); Percent of households with income of $100,000 or more: 6.7% (2005); Poverty rate: 12.1% (2003); Bankruptcy rate: 9.55% (2005).
Taxes: Total county taxes per capita: $174 (2004); County property taxes per capita: $102 (2004).
Education: Percent of population age 25 and over with: High school diploma (including GED) or higher: 79.8% (2005); Bachelor's degree or higher: 9.2% (2005); Master's degree or higher: 3.1% (2005).
Housing: Homeownership rate: 77.6% (2005); Median home value: $71,354 (2005); Median rent: $268 per month (2000); Median age of housing: 42 years (2000).
Health: Birth rate: 102.4 per 10,000 population (2004); Death rate: 141.3 per 10,000 population (2004); Age-adjusted cancer mortality rate: 237.3 deaths per 100,000 population (2002); Number of physicians: 7.5 per 10,000 population (2004); Hospital beds: 15.6 per 10,000 population (2003); Hospital admissions: 483.4 per 10,000 population (2003).
Elections: 2004 Presidential election results: 52.7% Bush, 46.6% Kerry, 0.0% Nader, 0.3% Badnarik
National and State Parks: Harrison County State Forest
Additional Information Contacts
Harrison County Government . . . . (740) 942-4623
  http://www.harrisoncountyohio.org/
Cadiz Chamber of Commerce . . . . (740) 942-3350
  http://pages.eohio.net/harrisonchamber

Harrison County Communities

BOWERSTON (village). Covers a land area of 0.507 square miles and a water area of 0 square miles. Located at 40.42° N. Lat.; 81.18° W. Long. Elevation is 960 feet.
Population: 343 (1990); 414 (2000); 417 (2005); 419 (2010 projected); Race: 100.0% White, 0.0% Black, 0.0% Asian, 0.0% Hispanic of any race (2005); Density: 822.8 persons per square mile (2005); Average household size: 2.76 (2005); Median age: 41.8 (2005); Males per 100 females: 87.8 (2005); Marriage status: 12.9% never married, 68.2% now married, 9.1% widowed, 9.7% divorced (2000); Foreign born: 1.7% (2000); Ancestry (includes multiple ancestries): 24.4% German, 17.3% Irish, 7.6% English, 7.3% United States or American, 4.4% Italian (2000).
Economy: Employment by occupation: 4.5% management, 15.6% professional, 15.6% services, 25.1% sales, 0.0% farming, 8.9% construction, 30.2% production (2000).
Income: Per capita income: $17,916 (2005); Median household income: $41,563 (2005); Average household income: $46,440 (2005); Percent of households with income of $100,000 or more: 6.0% (2005); Poverty rate: 6.5% (2000).
Education: Percent of population age 25 and over with: High school diploma (including GED) or higher: 81.2% (2005); Bachelor's degree or higher: 11.3% (2005); Master's degree or higher: 3.4% (2005).
School District(s)
Conotton Valley Union Local SD (PK-12)
  2003-04 Enrollment: 547 . . . . (740) 269-2000
Housing: Homeownership rate: 72.2% (2005); Median home value: $58,684 (2005); Median rent: $225 per month (2000); Median age of housing: 60+ years (2000).
Transportation: Commute to work: 94.9% car, 0.0% public transportation, 4.0% walk, 1.1% work from home (2000); Travel time to work: 34.5% less than 15 minutes, 23.0% 15 to 30 minutes, 27.6% 30 to 45 minutes, 8.6% 45 to 60 minutes, 6.3% 60 minutes or more (2000)

CADIZ (village). Covers a land area of 8.834 square miles and a water area of 0.099 square miles. Located at 40.27° N. Lat.; 80.99° W. Long. Elevation is 1,280 feet.
History: The town of Cadiz, settled at the junction of the Mingo and Moravian trails, was surveyed in 1803, and in 1830 became the seat of Harrison County.
Population: 3,468 (1990); 3,308 (2000); 3,391 (2005); 3,466 (2010 projected); Race: 89.8% White, 7.6% Black, 0.5% Asian, 0.3% Hispanic of any race (2005); Density: 383.9 persons per square mile (2005); Average household size: 2.34 (2005); Median age: 42.9 (2005); Males per 100 females: 84.4 (2005); Marriage status: 18.2% never married, 59.8% now married, 11.9% widowed, 10.1% divorced (2000); Foreign born: 1.0% (2000); Ancestry (includes multiple ancestries): 15.6% German, 12.4% United States or American, 12.0% English, 11.8% Other groups, 10.6% Irish (2000).
Economy: Employment by occupation: 5.6% management, 14.3% professional, 17.9% services, 25.7% sales, 1.1% farming, 13.4% construction, 21.9% production (2000).
Income: Per capita income: $20,063 (2005); Median household income: $33,311 (2005); Average household income: $46,385 (2005); Percent of households with income of $100,000 or more: 7.9% (2005); Poverty rate: 15.7% (2000).
Education: Percent of population age 25 and over with: High school diploma (including GED) or higher: 81.0% (2005); Bachelor's degree or higher: 10.5% (2005); Master's degree or higher: 4.5% (2005).
School District(s)
Belmont-Harrison Joint Vocational SD (09-12)
  2003-04 Enrollment: n/a . . . . (740) 695-9130
Harrison Hills City SD (PK-12)
  2003-04 Enrollment: 2,118 . . . . (740) 942-7800
Housing: Homeownership rate: 65.9% (2005); Median home value: $75,231 (2005); Median rent: $280 per month (2000); Median age of housing: 46 years (2000).
Hospitals: Harrison Community Hospital (48 beds)
Newspapers: Harrison News Herald (General - Circulation 24,000); Harrison News-Herald (General - Circulation 6,000)
Transportation: Commute to work: 92.8% car, 0.0% public transportation, 3.8% walk, 3.5% work from home (2000); Travel time to work: 54.3% less than 15 minutes, 11.7% 15 to 30 minutes, 15.8% 30 to 45 minutes, 9.3% 45 to 60 minutes, 9.0% 60 minutes or more (2000)
Additional Information Contacts
Cadiz Chamber of Commerce . . . . (740) 942-3350
  http://pages.eohio.net/harrisonchamber

DEERSVILLE (village). Covers a land area of 0.349 square miles and a water area of 0 square miles. Located at 40.30° N. Lat.; 81.18° W. Long. Elevation is 1,254 feet.
Population: 91 (1990); 82 (2000); 85 (2005); 88 (2010 projected); Race: 100.0% White, 0.0% Black, 0.0% Asian, 2.4% Hispanic of any race (2005); Density: 243.6 persons per square mile (2005); Average household size: 2.02 (2005); Median age: 46.5 (2005); Males per 100 females: 112.5 (2005); Marriage status: 24.1% never married, 57.8% now married, 10.8% widowed, 7.2% divorced (2000); Foreign born: 0.0% (2000); Ancestry (includes multiple ancestries): 23.3% United States or American, 18.9% Irish, 10.0% German, 8.9% English, 6.7% Scotch-Irish (2000).
Economy: Livestock. Employment by occupation: 13.5% management, 18.9% professional, 13.5% services, 32.4% sales, 0.0% farming, 0.0% construction, 21.6% production (2000).
Income: Per capita income: $18,059 (2005); Median household income: $29,167 (2005); Average household income: $36,548 (2005); Percent of households with income of $100,000 or more: 7.1% (2005); Poverty rate: 14.4% (2000).
Education: Percent of population age 25 and over with: High school diploma (including GED) or higher: 81.5% (2005); Bachelor's degree or higher: 6.2% (2005); Master's degree or higher: 3.1% (2005).
Housing: Homeownership rate: 73.8% (2005); Median home value: $72,857 (2005); Median rent: $125 per month (2000); Median age of housing: 47 years (2000).
Transportation: Commute to work: 78.4% car, 0.0% public transportation, 16.2% walk, 5.4% work from home (2000); Travel time to work: 31.4% less than 15 minutes, 25.7% 15 to 30 minutes, 22.9% 30 to 45 minutes, 5.7% 45 to 60 minutes, 14.3% 60 minutes or more (2000)

FREEPORT (village). Covers a land area of 0.599 square miles and a water area of 0 square miles. Located at 40.21° N. Lat.; 81.26° W. Long. Elevation is 1,000 feet.
Population: 475 (1990); 398 (2000); 391 (2005); 390 (2010 projected); Race: 99.0% White, 0.0% Black, 0.5% Asian, 0.0% Hispanic of any race (2005); Density: 652.8 persons per square mile (2005); Average household size: 2.31 (2005); Median age: 39.8 (2005); Males per 100 females: 85.3 (2005); Marriage status: 22.2% never married, 48.6% now married, 17.3% widowed, 11.9% divorced (2000); Foreign born: 0.0% (2000); Ancestry (includes multiple ancestries): 16.7% German, 10.7% United States or American, 8.5% Irish, 7.5% English, 7.5% Other groups (2000).
Economy: Employment by occupation: 2.9% management, 24.7% professional, 18.2% services, 13.5% sales, 0.0% farming, 14.7% construction, 25.9% production (2000).
Income: Per capita income: $14,668 (2005); Median household income: $21,778 (2005); Average household income: $33,935 (2005); Percent of households with income of $100,000 or more: 4.1% (2005); Poverty rate: 19.4% (2000).
Education: Percent of population age 25 and over with: High school diploma (including GED) or higher: 74.4% (2005); Bachelor's degree or higher: 10.7% (2005); Master's degree or higher: 5.9% (2005).
School District(s)
Harrison Hills City SD (PK-12)
   2003-04 Enrollment: 2,118 . . . . (740) 942-7800
Housing: Homeownership rate: 69.2% (2005); Median home value: $51,818 (2005); Median rent: $159 per month (2000); Median age of housing: 60+ years (2000).
Transportation: Commute to work: 72.4% car, 0.0% public transportation, 25.9% walk, 1.8% work from home (2000); Travel time to work: 39.5% less than 15 minutes, 21.0% 15 to 30 minutes, 23.4% 30 to 45 minutes, 10.8% 45 to 60 minutes, 5.4% 60 minutes or more (2000)

HARRISVILLE (village). Covers a land area of 0.151 square miles and a water area of 0 square miles. Located at 40.18° N. Lat.; 80.88° W. Long. Elevation is 1,250 feet.
Population: 308 (1990); 259 (2000); 261 (2005); 263 (2010 projected); Race: 99.6% White, 0.0% Black, 0.4% Asian, 0.0% Hispanic of any race (2005); Density: 1,726.6 persons per square mile (2005); Average household size: 2.35 (2005); Median age: 39.2 (2005); Males per 100 females: 110.5 (2005); Marriage status: 19.2% never married, 53.0% now married, 14.1% widowed, 13.6% divorced (2000); Foreign born: 0.0% (2000); Ancestry (includes multiple ancestries): 25.0% Irish, 18.9% Polish, 17.2% German, 13.9% Italian, 12.7% United States or American (2000).
Economy: In agriculture and coal-mining area. Employment by occupation: 10.6% management, 10.6% professional, 13.8% services, 26.6% sales, 0.0% farming, 19.1% construction, 19.1% production (2000).
Income: Per capita income: $18,803 (2005); Median household income: $31,739 (2005); Average household income: $44,212 (2005); Percent of households with income of $100,000 or more: 3.6% (2005); Poverty rate: 5.7% (2000).
Education: Percent of population age 25 and over with: High school diploma (including GED) or higher: 73.5% (2005); Bachelor's degree or higher: 8.3% (2005); Master's degree or higher: 0.0% (2005).
Housing: Homeownership rate: 81.1% (2005); Median home value: $45,714 (2005); Median rent: $238 per month (2000); Median age of housing: 60 years (2000).
Transportation: Commute to work: 100.0% car, 0.0% public transportation, 0.0% walk, 0.0% work from home (2000); Travel time to work: 11.7% less than 15 minutes, 26.6% 15 to 30 minutes, 28.7% 30 to 45 minutes, 10.6% 45 to 60 minutes, 22.3% 60 minutes or more (2000)

HOPEDALE (village). Covers a land area of 0.716 square miles and a water area of 0 square miles. Located at 40.32° N. Lat.; 80.89° W. Long. Elevation is 1,220 feet.
History: Hopedale was the home of motion picture actor Clark Gable, who spent part of his boyhood here. The town developed around the coal mines.
Population: 920 (1990); 984 (2000); 996 (2005); 1,009 (2010 projected); Race: 99.2% White, 0.3% Black, 0.0% Asian, 0.6% Hispanic of any race (2005); Density: 1,391.5 persons per square mile (2005); Average household size: 2.51 (2005); Median age: 44.9 (2005); Males per 100 females: 98.4 (2005); Marriage status: 16.0% never married, 63.9% now married, 11.0% widowed, 9.1% divorced (2000); Foreign born: 0.6% (2000); Ancestry (includes multiple ancestries): 18.6% German, 16.3%

Italian, 12.6% English, 12.6% Irish, 12.0% United States or American (2000).
Economy: Employment by occupation: 7.7% management, 12.9% professional, 16.8% services, 24.8% sales, 0.0% farming, 14.3% construction, 23.4% production (2000).
Income: Per capita income: $20,855 (2005); Median household income: $39,448 (2005); Average household income: $50,548 (2005); Percent of households with income of $100,000 or more: 9.8% (2005); Poverty rate: 11.8% (2000).
Education: Percent of population age 25 and over with: High school diploma (including GED) or higher: 80.6% (2005); Bachelor's degree or higher: 7.9% (2005); Master's degree or higher: 2.5% (2005).
School District(s)
Harrison Hills City SD (PK-12)
   2003-04 Enrollment: 2,118 . . . . (740) 942-7800
Housing: Homeownership rate: 77.6% (2005); Median home value: $70,196 (2005); Median rent: $288 per month (2000); Median age of housing: 45 years (2000).
Transportation: Commute to work: 96.3% car, 0.0% public transportation, 1.7% walk, 1.1% work from home (2000); Travel time to work: 26.7% less than 15 minutes, 39.7% 15 to 30 minutes, 16.1% 30 to 45 minutes, 6.6% 45 to 60 minutes, 10.9% 60 minutes or more (2000)

JEWETT (village). Covers a land area of 0.512 square miles and a water area of 0 square miles. Located at 40.36° N. Lat.; 81.00° W. Long. Elevation is 1,011 feet.
History: Laid out 1851, incorporated 1886.
Population: 778 (1990); 784 (2000); 797 (2005); 813 (2010 projected); Race: 98.9% White, 0.0% Black, 0.0% Asian, 0.3% Hispanic of any race (2005); Density: 1,557.6 persons per square mile (2005); Average household size: 2.58 (2005); Median age: 35.9 (2005); Males per 100 females: 92.5 (2005); Marriage status: 18.5% never married, 62.4% now married, 9.5% widowed, 9.7% divorced (2000); Foreign born: 0.4% (2000); Ancestry (includes multiple ancestries): 16.7% Irish, 15.3% German, 13.5% United States or American, 12.2% English, 10.2% Other groups (2000).
Economy: Coal mining; sawmilling. Single-family building permits issued: 3 (2005); Multi-family building permits issued: 0 (2005); Employment by occupation: 5.9% management, 9.5% professional, 22.7% services, 22.7% sales, 1.5% farming, 12.5% construction, 25.3% production (2000).
Income: Per capita income: $13,767 (2005); Median household income: $28,889 (2005); Average household income: $35,510 (2005); Percent of households with income of $100,000 or more: 3.2% (2005); Poverty rate: 21.7% (2000).
Education: Percent of population age 25 and over with: High school diploma (including GED) or higher: 76.8% (2005); Bachelor's degree or higher: 6.1% (2005); Master's degree or higher: 2.0% (2005).
School District(s)
Harrison Hills City SD (PK-12)
   2003-04 Enrollment: 2,118 . . . . (740) 942-7800
Housing: Homeownership rate: 72.2% (2005); Median home value: $54,507 (2005); Median rent: $313 per month (2000); Median age of housing: 60+ years (2000).
Transportation: Commute to work: 91.2% car, 0.8% public transportation, 5.4% walk, 2.7% work from home (2000); Travel time to work: 21.7% less than 15 minutes, 36.4% 15 to 30 minutes, 11.9% 30 to 45 minutes, 18.2% 45 to 60 minutes, 11.9% 60 minutes or more (2000)

NEW ATHENS (village). Covers a land area of 0.283 square miles and a water area of 0 square miles. Located at 40.18° N. Lat.; 80.99° W. Long. Elevation is 1,200 feet.
Population: 370 (1990); 342 (2000); 335 (2005); 333 (2010 projected); Race: 98.8% White, 0.6% Black, 0.0% Asian, 0.0% Hispanic of any race (2005); Density: 1,185.4 persons per square mile (2005); Average household size: 2.48 (2005); Median age: 40.5 (2005); Males per 100 females: 84.1 (2005); Marriage status: 23.5% never married, 55.7% now married, 10.4% widowed, 10.4% divorced (2000); Foreign born: 0.0% (2000); Ancestry (includes multiple ancestries): 23.7% German, 19.6% Irish, 14.2% English, 4.7% Scotch-Irish, 3.6% Other groups (2000).
Economy: In coal-mining area. Employment by occupation: 3.4% management, 12.2% professional, 15.0% services, 28.6% sales, 0.0% farming, 14.3% construction, 26.5% production (2000).
Income: Per capita income: $14,291 (2005); Median household income: $30,500 (2005); Average household income: $35,463 (2005); Percent of households with income of $100,000 or more: 0.7% (2005); Poverty rate: 19.6% (2000).

Education: Percent of population age 25 and over with: High school diploma (including GED) or higher: 81.0% (2005); Bachelor's degree or higher: 5.1% (2005); Master's degree or higher: 2.5% (2005).
Housing: Homeownership rate: 83.7% (2005); Median home value: $56,341 (2005); Median rent: $255 per month (2000); Median age of housing: 60+ years (2000).
Transportation: Commute to work: 96.6% car, 0.0% public transportation, 0.0% walk, 0.0% work from home (2000); Travel time to work: 11.7% less than 15 minutes, 53.8% 15 to 30 minutes, 14.5% 30 to 45 minutes, 6.9% 45 to 60 minutes, 13.1% 60 minutes or more (2000)

PIEDMONT (unincorporated postal area, zip code 43983). Covers a land area of 18.890 square miles and a water area of 0.010 square miles. Located at 40.14° N. Lat.; 81.20° W. Long. Elevation is 890 feet.
Population: 433 (2000); Race: 100.0% White, 0.0% Black, 0.0% Asian, 0.0% Hispanic of any race (2000); Density: 22.9 persons per square mile (2000); Age: 7.5% under 18, 20.1% over 64 (2000); Marriage status: 11.9% never married, 61.3% now married, 13.2% widowed, 13.6% divorced (2000); Foreign born: 0.0% (2000); Ancestry (includes multiple ancestries): 29.1% German, 15.0% English, 13.0% United States or American, 13.0% Irish, 9.4% French (except Basque) (2000).
Economy: Employment by occupation: 19.2% management, 25.0% professional, 19.2% services, 10.6% sales, 0.0% farming, 12.5% construction, 13.5% production (2000).
Income: Per capita income: $21,099 (2000); Median household income: $29,643 (2000); Poverty rate: 8.3% (2000).
Education: Percent of population age 25 and over with: High school diploma (including GED) or higher: 79.5% (2000); Bachelor's degree or higher: 16.0% (2000).
Housing: Homeownership rate: 100.0% (2000); Median home value: $49,800 (2000); Median rent: $n/a per month (2000); Median age of housing: 30 years (2000).
Transportation: Commute to work: 86.5% car, 0.0% public transportation, 5.8% walk, 0.0% work from home (2000); Travel time to work: 5.8% less than 15 minutes, 38.5% 15 to 30 minutes, 10.6% 30 to 45 minutes, 28.8% 45 to 60 minutes, 16.3% 60 minutes or more (2000)

SCIO (village). Covers a land area of 0.552 square miles and a water area of 0 square miles. Located at 40.39° N. Lat.; 81.08° W. Long. Elevation is 971 feet.
Population: 854 (1990); 799 (2000); 790 (2005); 788 (2010 projected); Race: 99.6% White, 0.1% Black, 0.0% Asian, 1.0% Hispanic of any race (2005); Density: 1,430.6 persons per square mile (2005); Average household size: 2.18 (2005); Median age: 40.2 (2005); Males per 100 females: 87.2 (2005); Marriage status: 21.6% never married, 50.9% now married, 12.0% widowed, 15.6% divorced (2000); Foreign born: 0.0% (2000); Ancestry (includes multiple ancestries): 19.3% German, 15.0% Irish, 12.3% United States or American, 8.2% Other groups, 7.7% English (2000).
Economy: Single-family building permits issued: 0 (2005); Multi-family building permits issued: 0 (2005); Employment by occupation: 5.9% management, 11.8% professional, 16.7% services, 24.1% sales, 0.0% farming, 5.9% construction, 35.6% production (2000).
Income: Per capita income: $17,525 (2005); Median household income: $28,519 (2005); Average household income: $38,246 (2005); Percent of households with income of $100,000 or more: 3.6% (2005); Poverty rate: 13.9% (2000).
Education: Percent of population age 25 and over with: High school diploma (including GED) or higher: 79.9% (2005); Bachelor's degree or higher: 8.1% (2005); Master's degree or higher: 3.3% (2005).
School District(s)
Harrison Hills City SD (PK-12)
    2003-04 Enrollment: 2,118 . . . . (740) 942-7800
Housing: Homeownership rate: 66.0% (2005); Median home value: $62,615 (2005); Median rent: $238 per month (2000); Median age of housing: 60+ years (2000).
Transportation: Commute to work: 92.6% car, 0.3% public transportation, 4.3% walk, 2.8% work from home (2000); Travel time to work: 29.0% less than 15 minutes, 24.8% 15 to 30 minutes, 18.2% 30 to 45 minutes, 9.2% 45 to 60 minutes, 18.8% 60 minutes or more (2000)

TIPPECANOE (unincorporated postal area, zip code 44699). Covers a land area of 51.622 square miles and a water area of 0.044 square miles. Located at 40.28° N. Lat.; 81.28° W. Long. Elevation is 875 feet.

Population: 987 (2000); Race: 100.0% White, 0.0% Black, 0.0% Asian, 0.8% Hispanic of any race (2000); Density: 19.1 persons per square mile (2000); Age: 23.7% under 18, 14.0% over 64 (2000); Marriage status: 16.8% never married, 69.2% now married, 6.1% widowed, 7.9% divorced (2000); Foreign born: 1.5% (2000); Ancestry (includes multiple ancestries): 23.1% German, 16.3% Irish, 6.8% Other groups, 6.4% English, 6.4% United States or American (2000).
Economy: Employment by occupation: 11.3% management, 13.1% professional, 15.6% services, 20.1% sales, 2.8% farming, 9.0% construction, 28.1% production (2000).
Income: Per capita income: $14,292 (2000); Median household income: $31,333 (2000); Poverty rate: 17.2% (2000).
Education: Percent of population age 25 and over with: High school diploma (including GED) or higher: 77.7% (2000); Bachelor's degree or higher: 8.2% (2000).
Housing: Homeownership rate: 77.0% (2000); Median home value: $45,500 (2000); Median rent: $283 per month (2000); Median age of housing: 34 years (2000).
Transportation: Commute to work: 91.0% car, 0.0% public transportation, 7.7% walk, 1.3% work from home (2000); Travel time to work: 10.9% less than 15 minutes, 29.8% 15 to 30 minutes, 36.0% 30 to 45 minutes, 9.3% 45 to 60 minutes, 14.0% 60 minutes or more (2000)

Henry County

Located in northwestern Ohio; crossed by the Maumee River. Covers a land area of 416.50 square miles, a water area of 3.47 square miles, and is located in the Eastern Time Zone. The county government was organized in 1820. County seat is Napoleon.

Weather Station: Napoleon   Elevation: 679 feet

	Jan	Feb	Mar	Apr	May	Jun	Jul	Aug	Sep	Oct	Nov	Dec
High	31	35	47	60	72	81	85	83	76	64	50	37
Low	15	18	27	37	48	57	62	59	52	41	33	22
Precip	2.0	1.7	2.7	3.6	3.5	3.4	3.9	3.4	2.7	2.5	2.9	2.5
Snow	8.7	5.8	2.8	1.1	0.0	0.0	0.0	0.0	0.0	0.1	0.9	5.2

High and Low temperatures in degrees Fahrenheit; Precipitation and Snow in inches

Population: 29,108 (1990); 29,210 (2000); 29,398 (2005); 29,584 (2010 projected); Race: 95.5% White, 0.4% Black, 0.6% Asian, 5.2% Hispanic of any race (2005); Density: 70.6 persons per square mile (2005); Average household size: 2.63 (2005); Median age: 37.4 (2005); Males per 100 females: 96.9 (2005).
Religion: Five largest groups: 19.9% Lutheran Church—Missouri Synod, 14.7% Evangelical Lutheran Church in America, 12.7% Catholic Church, 11.8% The United Methodist Church, 2.7% United Church of Christ (2000).
Economy: Unemployment rate: 6.2% (2005); Total civilian labor force: 15,892 (2005); Leading industries: 39.3% manufacturing; 13.3% health care and social assistance; 11.9% retail trade (2004); Farms: 844 totaling 236,273 acres (2002); Companies that employ 500 or more persons: 2 (2004); Companies that employ 100 to 499 persons: 10 (2004); Companies that employ less than 100 persons: 611 (2004); Black-owned businesses: n/a (2002); Hispanic-owned businesses: n/a (2002); Women-owned businesses: 724 (2002); Retail sales per capita: $10,728 (2006). Single-family building permits issued: 69 (2005); Multi-family building permits issued: 12 (2005).
Income: Per capita income: $20,832 (2005); Median household income: $46,849 (2005); Average household income: $54,481 (2005); Percent of households with income of $100,000 or more: 9.2% (2005); Poverty rate: 6.9% (2003); Bankruptcy rate: 8.62% (2005).
Education: Percent of population age 25 and over with: High school diploma (including GED) or higher: 83.5% (2005); Bachelor's degree or higher: 11.0% (2005); Master's degree or higher: 2.9% (2005).
Housing: Homeownership rate: 80.8% (2005); Median home value: $102,762 (2005); Median rent: $360 per month (2000); Median age of housing: 42 years (2000).
Health: Birth rate: 117.1 per 10,000 population (2004); Death rate: 96.6 per 10,000 population (2004); Age-adjusted cancer mortality rate: 203.8 deaths per 100,000 population (2002); Number of physicians: 6.1 per 10,000 population (2004); Hospital beds: 10.2 per 10,000 population (2003); Hospital admissions: 268.6 per 10,000 population (2003).
Elections: 2004 Presidential election results: 65.6% Bush, 33.8% Kerry, 0.0% Nader, 0.3% Badnarik
National and State Parks: Maumee State Forest; North Turkeyfoot State Park
Additional Information Contacts

Henry County Government .... (419) 592-4876
   http://www.henrycountyohio.com/
City of Napoleon .... (419) 592-4010
   http://www.napoleonohio.com
Napoleon Chamber of Commerce .... (419) 592-1786
   http://www.ohiohenrycounty.com

Henry County Communities

DESHLER (village). Covers a land area of 2.264 square miles and a water area of 0.027 square miles. Located at 41.20° N. Lat.; 83.90° W. Long. Elevation is 715 feet.
Population: 1,876 (1990); 1,831 (2000); 1,841 (2005); 1,852 (2010 projected); Race: 94.0% White, 0.1% Black, 0.8% Asian, 6.5% Hispanic of any race (2005); Density: 813.3 persons per square mile (2005); Average household size: 2.56 (2005); Median age: 35.8 (2005); Males per 100 females: 100.3 (2005); Marriage status: 20.0% never married, 60.2% now married, 9.8% widowed, 10.1% divorced (2000); Foreign born: 2.2% (2000); Ancestry (includes multiple ancestries): 43.5% German, 11.1% Other groups, 8.5% Irish, 6.5% English, 6.3% United States or American (2000).
Economy: Employment by occupation: 6.9% management, 12.1% professional, 14.2% services, 17.5% sales, 0.2% farming, 13.0% construction, 36.0% production (2000).
Income: Per capita income: $18,178 (2005); Median household income: $40,230 (2005); Average household income: $46,431 (2005); Percent of households with income of $100,000 or more: 5.7% (2005); Poverty rate: 7.5% (2000).
Education: Percent of population age 25 and over with: High school diploma (including GED) or higher: 77.4% (2005); Bachelor's degree or higher: 8.8% (2005); Master's degree or higher: 3.3% (2005).
School District(s)
Patrick Henry Local SD (PK-12)
   2003-04 Enrollment: 1,106 .... (419) 274-5451
Housing: Homeownership rate: 82.9% (2005); Median home value: $76,963 (2005); Median rent: $316 per month (2000); Median age of housing: 50 years (2000).
Newspapers: Deshler Flag (General - Circulation 1,500)
Transportation: Commute to work: 91.7% car, 0.4% public transportation, 5.4% walk, 1.1% work from home (2000); Travel time to work: 36.8% less than 15 minutes, 20.2% 15 to 30 minutes, 27.8% 30 to 45 minutes, 8.7% 45 to 60 minutes, 6.5% 60 minutes or more (2000)

FLORIDA (village). Covers a land area of 0.227 square miles and a water area of 0 square miles. Located at 41.32° N. Lat.; 84.20° W. Long. Elevation is 675 feet.
Population: 304 (1990); 246 (2000); 249 (2005); 250 (2010 projected); Race: 96.0% White, 0.0% Black, 0.8% Asian, 6.4% Hispanic of any race (2005); Density: 1,095.7 persons per square mile (2005); Average household size: 2.47 (2005); Median age: 39.4 (2005); Males per 100 females: 94.5 (2005); Marriage status: 19.0% never married, 62.0% now married, 5.5% widowed, 13.5% divorced (2000); Foreign born: 2.7% (2000); Ancestry (includes multiple ancestries): 49.0% German, 10.2% Other groups, 9.8% Irish, 8.6% United States or American, 5.1% English (2000).
Economy: Employment by occupation: 0.8% management, 12.3% professional, 9.8% services, 22.1% sales, 0.0% farming, 13.9% construction, 41.0% production (2000).
Income: Per capita income: $17,761 (2005); Median household income: $42,875 (2005); Average household income: $43,787 (2005); Percent of households with income of $100,000 or more: 1.0% (2005); Poverty rate: 9.0% (2000).
Education: Percent of population age 25 and over with: High school diploma (including GED) or higher: 72.3% (2005); Bachelor's degree or higher: 4.2% (2005); Master's degree or higher: 1.2% (2005).
Housing: Homeownership rate: 76.2% (2005); Median home value: $87,895 (2005); Median rent: $389 per month (2000); Median age of housing: 49 years (2000).
Transportation: Commute to work: 100.0% car, 0.0% public transportation, 0.0% walk, 0.0% work from home (2000); Travel time to work: 16.4% less than 15 minutes, 62.3% 15 to 30 minutes, 15.6% 30 to 45 minutes, 3.3% 45 to 60 minutes, 2.5% 60 minutes or more (2000)

HAMLER (village). Covers a land area of 0.572 square miles and a water area of 0.003 square miles. Located at 41.22° N. Lat.; 84.03° W. Long. Elevation is 714 feet.
Population: 627 (1990); 650 (2000); 671 (2005); 691 (2010 projected); Race: 88.8% White, 0.3% Black, 0.0% Asian, 20.6% Hispanic of any race (2005); Density: 1,173.9 persons per square mile (2005); Average household size: 2.71 (2005); Median age: 32.6 (2005); Males per 100 females: 91.2 (2005); Marriage status: 21.9% never married, 62.9% now married, 5.9% widowed, 9.3% divorced (2000); Foreign born: 1.9% (2000); Ancestry (includes multiple ancestries): 44.5% German, 25.0% Other groups, 4.8% Irish, 3.8% United States or American, 3.6% Dutch (2000).
Economy: Single-family building permits issued: 0 (2005); Multi-family building permits issued: 0 (2005); Employment by occupation: 7.6% management, 14.8% professional, 14.1% services, 13.1% sales, 0.7% farming, 10.7% construction, 39.2% production (2000).
Income: Per capita income: $17,038 (2005); Median household income: $41,429 (2005); Average household income: $46,099 (2005); Percent of households with income of $100,000 or more: 3.6% (2005); Poverty rate: 6.3% (2000).
Education: Percent of population age 25 and over with: High school diploma (including GED) or higher: 77.8% (2005); Bachelor's degree or higher: 10.4% (2005); Master's degree or higher: 4.0% (2005).
School District(s)
Patrick Henry Local SD (PK-12)
   2003-04 Enrollment: 1,106 .... (419) 274-5451
Housing: Homeownership rate: 80.2% (2005); Median home value: $77,755 (2005); Median rent: $360 per month (2000); Median age of housing: 48 years (2000).
Transportation: Commute to work: 95.1% car, 0.0% public transportation, 4.6% walk, 0.4% work from home (2000); Travel time to work: 24.5% less than 15 minutes, 42.9% 15 to 30 minutes, 16.3% 30 to 45 minutes, 11.7% 45 to 60 minutes, 4.6% 60 minutes or more (2000)

HOLGATE (village). Covers a land area of 0.980 square miles and a water area of 0 square miles. Located at 41.25° N. Lat.; 84.13° W. Long. Elevation is 714 feet.
Population: 1,290 (1990); 1,194 (2000); 1,242 (2005); 1,254 (2010 projected); Race: 94.4% White, 0.1% Black, 0.1% Asian, 15.1% Hispanic of any race (2005); Density: 1,267.7 persons per square mile (2005); Average household size: 2.65 (2005); Median age: 35.1 (2005); Males per 100 females: 93.2 (2005); Marriage status: 22.1% never married, 54.5% now married, 8.9% widowed, 14.5% divorced (2000); Foreign born: 3.5% (2000); Ancestry (includes multiple ancestries): 35.0% German, 24.1% Other groups, 8.2% United States or American, 6.5% Irish, 5.8% English (2000).
Economy: In dairying, poultry raising, and grain producing district. Single-family building permits issued: 0 (2005); Multi-family building permits issued: 0 (2005); Employment by occupation: 5.4% management, 11.7% professional, 15.4% services, 14.4% sales, 0.0% farming, 10.9% construction, 42.2% production (2000).
Income: Per capita income: $17,775 (2005); Median household income: $39,437 (2005); Average household income: $46,565 (2005); Percent of households with income of $100,000 or more: 6.0% (2005); Poverty rate: 10.5% (2000).
Education: Percent of population age 25 and over with: High school diploma (including GED) or higher: 74.8% (2005); Bachelor's degree or higher: 7.4% (2005); Master's degree or higher: 3.1% (2005).
School District(s)
Holgate Local SD (PK-12)
   2003-04 Enrollment: 504 .... (419) 264-5141
Housing: Homeownership rate: 77.8% (2005); Median home value: $71,500 (2005); Median rent: $377 per month (2000); Median age of housing: 51 years (2000).
Transportation: Commute to work: 95.6% car, 0.4% public transportation, 2.2% walk, 1.4% work from home (2000); Travel time to work: 19.3% less than 15 minutes, 49.3% 15 to 30 minutes, 20.1% 30 to 45 minutes, 7.2% 45 to 60 minutes, 4.0% 60 minutes or more (2000)

LIBERTY CENTER (village). Covers a land area of 1.045 square miles and a water area of 0 square miles. Located at 41.44° N. Lat.; 84.00° W. Long. Elevation is 685 feet.
Population: 1,084 (1990); 1,109 (2000); 1,147 (2005); 1,168 (2010 projected); Race: 98.4% White, 0.0% Black, 0.2% Asian, 1.4% Hispanic of any race (2005); Density: 1,097.3 persons per square mile (2005); Average

household size: 2.58 (2005); Median age: 35.3 (2005); Males per 100 females: 95.1 (2005); Marriage status: 21.4% never married, 61.4% now married, 6.3% widowed, 10.8% divorced (2000); Foreign born: 0.3% (2000); Ancestry (includes multiple ancestries): 43.2% German, 15.2% Irish, 9.1% United States or American, 8.4% Other groups, 7.3% French (except Basque) (2000).
Economy: Single-family building permits issued: 4 (2005); Multi-family building permits issued: 0 (2005); Employment by occupation: 6.0% management, 12.1% professional, 12.5% services, 15.3% sales, 0.6% farming, 11.5% construction, 42.1% production (2000).
Income: Per capita income: $19,017 (2005); Median household income: $44,732 (2005); Average household income: $49,017 (2005); Percent of households with income of $100,000 or more: 4.3% (2005); Poverty rate: 6.7% (2000).
Education: Percent of population age 25 and over with: High school diploma (including GED) or higher: 87.1% (2005); Bachelor's degree or higher: 10.9% (2005); Master's degree or higher: 2.7% (2005).
School District(s)
Liberty Center Local SD (PK-12)
   2003-04 Enrollment: 1,197 .... (419) 533-5011
Housing: Homeownership rate: 80.9% (2005); Median home value: $94,898 (2005); Median rent: $360 per month (2000); Median age of housing: 50 years (2000).
Newspapers: The Liberty Press (General - Circulation 1,300)
Transportation: Commute to work: 97.0% car, 0.0% public transportation, 1.4% walk, 1.2% work from home (2000); Travel time to work: 25.7% less than 15 minutes, 42.2% 15 to 30 minutes, 20.8% 30 to 45 minutes, 5.8% 45 to 60 minutes, 5.6% 60 minutes or more (2000)

MALINTA (village). Covers a land area of 0.771 square miles and a water area of 0 square miles. Located at 41.32° N. Lat.; 84.03° W. Long. Elevation is 686 feet.
Population: 295 (1990); 285 (2000); 277 (2005); 272 (2010 projected); Race: 97.5% White, 0.0% Black, 0.4% Asian, 4.7% Hispanic of any race (2005); Density: 359.5 persons per square mile (2005); Average household size: 2.47 (2005); Median age: 37.8 (2005); Males per 100 females: 97.9 (2005); Marriage status: 24.3% never married, 55.3% now married, 8.0% widowed, 12.4% divorced (2000); Foreign born: 0.0% (2000); Ancestry (includes multiple ancestries): 46.5% German, 11.1% Other groups, 9.4% Irish, 8.4% Dutch, 6.1% Belgian (2000).
Economy: Clay, concrete, and plaster products. Single-family building permits issued: 1 (2005); Multi-family building permits issued: 0 (2005); Employment by occupation: 9.2% management, 8.4% professional, 7.6% services, 16.8% sales, 0.0% farming, 14.5% construction, 43.5% production (2000).
Income: Per capita income: $19,305 (2005); Median household income: $43,276 (2005); Average household income: $47,746 (2005); Percent of households with income of $100,000 or more: 5.4% (2005); Poverty rate: 2.7% (2000).
Education: Percent of population age 25 and over with: High school diploma (including GED) or higher: 80.6% (2005); Bachelor's degree or higher: 6.1% (2005); Master's degree or higher: 1.1% (2005).
School District(s)
Patrick Henry Local SD (PK-12)
   2003-04 Enrollment: 1,106 .... (419) 274-5451
Housing: Homeownership rate: 84.8% (2005); Median home value: $81,154 (2005); Median rent: $311 per month (2000); Median age of housing: 60+ years (2000).
Transportation: Commute to work: 96.9% car, 0.0% public transportation, 2.3% walk, 0.0% work from home (2000); Travel time to work: 26.0% less than 15 minutes, 51.1% 15 to 30 minutes, 13.7% 30 to 45 minutes, 6.1% 45 to 60 minutes, 3.1% 60 minutes or more (2000)

MCCLURE (village). Covers a land area of 0.494 square miles and a water area of 0 square miles. Located at 41.37° N. Lat.; 83.94° W. Long. Elevation is 677 feet.
Population: 828 (1990); 761 (2000); 840 (2005); 901 (2010 projected); Race: 97.3% White, 0.0% Black, 0.4% Asian, 4.6% Hispanic of any race (2005); Density: 1,699.3 persons per square mile (2005); Average household size: 2.63 (2005); Median age: 36.5 (2005); Males per 100 females: 100.0 (2005); Marriage status: 20.8% never married, 66.3% now married, 5.6% widowed, 7.3% divorced (2000); Foreign born: 0.5% (2000); Ancestry (includes multiple ancestries): 35.0% German, 10.6% Other groups, 8.9% Irish, 8.5% English, 7.2% United States or American (2000).
Economy: Single-family building permits issued: 2 (2005); Multi-family building permits issued: 0 (2005); Employment by occupation: 7.1% management, 8.8% professional, 14.8% services, 19.2% sales, 0.8% farming, 13.7% construction, 35.6% production (2000).
Income: Per capita income: $20,182 (2005); Median household income: $47,643 (2005); Average household income: $52,977 (2005); Percent of households with income of $100,000 or more: 7.2% (2005); Poverty rate: 7.9% (2000).
Education: Percent of population age 25 and over with: High school diploma (including GED) or higher: 85.4% (2005); Bachelor's degree or higher: 5.8% (2005); Master's degree or higher: 1.1% (2005).
Housing: Homeownership rate: 85.0% (2005); Median home value: $76,508 (2005); Median rent: $313 per month (2000); Median age of housing: 48 years (2000).
Transportation: Commute to work: 96.4% car, 0.0% public transportation, 0.8% walk, 2.8% work from home (2000); Travel time to work: 14.0% less than 15 minutes, 48.9% 15 to 30 minutes, 24.6% 30 to 45 minutes, 8.3% 45 to 60 minutes, 4.3% 60 minutes or more (2000)

NAPOLEON (city). Covers a land area of 5.586 square miles and a water area of 0.382 square miles. Located at 41.39° N. Lat.; 84.12° W. Long. Elevation is 677 feet.
History: Napoleon was named by a group of Frenchmen who settled here in the midst of a predominantly German population. Napoleon developed as the seat of Henry County, and as the market center for a rural area.
Population: 9,127 (1990); 9,318 (2000); 9,247 (2005); 9,202 (2010 projected); Race: 93.5% White, 0.7% Black, 0.8% Asian, 6.5% Hispanic of any race (2005); Density: 1,655.4 persons per square mile (2005); Average household size: 2.41 (2005); Median age: 36.7 (2005); Males per 100 females: 89.3 (2005); Marriage status: 20.2% never married, 59.3% now married, 8.9% widowed, 11.6% divorced (2000); Foreign born: 1.5% (2000); Ancestry (includes multiple ancestries): 50.4% German, 12.8% Other groups, 8.7% Irish, 6.3% United States or American, 6.3% English (2000).
Economy: Single-family building permits issued: 10 (2005); Multi-family building permits issued: 12 (2005); Employment by occupation: 8.0% management, 14.3% professional, 14.0% services, 21.2% sales, 0.1% farming, 10.4% construction, 32.1% production (2000).
Income: Per capita income: $20,009 (2005); Median household income: $39,366 (2005); Average household income: $47,566 (2005); Percent of households with income of $100,000 or more: 6.9% (2005); Poverty rate: 10.1% (2000).
Education: Percent of population age 25 and over with: High school diploma (including GED) or higher: 83.0% (2005); Bachelor's degree or higher: 13.7% (2005); Master's degree or higher: 3.4% (2005).
School District(s)
Napoleon Area City SD (PK-12)
   2003-04 Enrollment: 2,387 .... (419) 599-7015
Housing: Homeownership rate: 69.6% (2005); Median home value: $100,089 (2005); Median rent: $363 per month (2000); Median age of housing: 36 years (2000).
Hospitals: Henry County Hospital (52 beds)
Newspapers: Northwest-Signal (Circulation 5,800)
Transportation: Commute to work: 94.6% car, 0.5% public transportation, 1.7% walk, 2.4% work from home (2000); Travel time to work: 51.1% less than 15 minutes, 32.7% 15 to 30 minutes, 9.6% 30 to 45 minutes, 2.9% 45 to 60 minutes, 3.7% 60 minutes or more (2000)
Additional Information Contacts
City of Napoleon .... (419) 592-4010
   http://www.napoleonohio.com
Napoleon Chamber of Commerce .... (419) 592-1786
   http://www.ohiohenrycounty.com

NEW BAVARIA (village). Covers a land area of 0.062 square miles and a water area of 0 square miles. Located at 41.20° N. Lat.; 84.16° W. Long. Elevation is 732 feet.
Population: 92 (1990); 78 (2000); 73 (2005); 71 (2010 projected); Race: 98.6% White, 0.0% Black, 1.4% Asian, 0.0% Hispanic of any race (2005); Density: 1,182.5 persons per square mile (2005); Average household size: 2.15 (2005); Median age: 40.8 (2005); Males per 100 females: 82.5 (2005); Marriage status: 25.4% never married, 71.2% now married, 0.0% widowed, 3.4% divorced (2000); Foreign born: 0.0% (2000); Ancestry (includes multiple ancestries): 40.8% German, 11.8% United States or American, 11.8% Swedish, 3.9% Italian, 2.6% Other groups (2000).

Economy: Employment by occupation: 8.1% management, 10.8% professional, 5.4% services, 8.1% sales, 8.1% farming, 16.2% construction, 43.2% production (2000).
Income: Per capita income: $22,466 (2005); Median household income: $41,667 (2005); Average household income: $48,235 (2005); Percent of households with income of $100,000 or more: 2.9% (2005); Poverty rate: 6.6% (2000).
Education: Percent of population age 25 and over with: High school diploma (including GED) or higher: 71.2% (2005); Bachelor's degree or higher: 3.8% (2005); Master's degree or higher: 3.8% (2005).
Housing: Homeownership rate: 82.4% (2005); Median home value: $63,333 (2005); Median rent: $<$100 per month (2000); Median age of housing: 56 years (2000).
Transportation: Commute to work: 100.0% car, 0.0% public transportation, 0.0% walk, 0.0% work from home (2000); Travel time to work: 21.6% less than 15 minutes, 56.8% 15 to 30 minutes, 18.9% 30 to 45 minutes, 0.0% 45 to 60 minutes, 2.7% 60 minutes or more (2000)

Highland County

Located in southwestern Ohio; drained by the East Fork of Little Miami River, and by several creeks. Covers a land area of 553.28 square miles, a water area of 4.56 square miles, and is located in the Eastern Time Zone. The county government was organized in 1805. County seat is Hillsboro.

Weather Station: Hillsboro — Elevation: 1,099 feet

	Jan	Feb	Mar	Apr	May	Jun	Jul	Aug	Sep	Oct	Nov	Dec
High	36	40	51	63	72	79	83	82	76	65	52	41
Low	20	23	32	41	51	60	64	62	56	44	35	26
Precip	2.9	2.7	3.8	4.1	4.7	4.2	4.0	4.3	3.4	2.9	3.2	3.1
Snow	7.3	5.0	3.8	0.6	tr	0.0	0.0	0.0	0.0	0.2	0.8	2.8

High and Low temperatures in degrees Fahrenheit; Precipitation and Snow in inches

Population: 35,728 (1990); 40,875 (2000); 42,380 (2005); 43,947 (2010 projected); Race: 96.8% White, 1.5% Black, 0.5% Asian, 0.7% Hispanic of any race (2005); Density: 76.6 persons per square mile (2005); Average household size: 2.60 (2005); Median age: 36.4 (2005); Males per 100 females: 95.5 (2005).
Religion: Five largest groups: 8.4% Christian Churches and Churches of Christ, 7.8% The United Methodist Church, 2.8% American Baptist Churches in the USA, 2.7% Catholic Church, 1.6% Church of God (Cleveland, Tennessee) (2000).
Economy: Unemployment rate: 5.9% (2005); Total civilian labor force: 20,901 (2005); Leading industries: 32.1% manufacturing; 17.7% retail trade; 16.7% health care and social assistance (2004); Farms: 1,381 totaling 273,263 acres (2002); Companies that employ 500 or more persons: 2 (2004); Companies that employ 100 to 499 persons: 16 (2004); Companies that employ less than 100 persons: 740 (2004); Black-owned businesses: n/a (2002); Hispanic-owned businesses: n/a (2002); Women-owned businesses: 950 (2002); Retail sales per capita: $9,431 (2006). Single-family building permits issued: 108 (2005); Multi-family building permits issued: 36 (2005).
Income: Per capita income: $19,085 (2005); Median household income: $40,336 (2005); Average household income: $49,383 (2005); Percent of households with income of $100,000 or more: 8.3% (2005); Poverty rate: 11.4% (2003); Bankruptcy rate: 10.60% (2005).
Education: Percent of population age 25 and over with: High school diploma (including GED) or higher: 76.3% (2005); Bachelor's degree or higher: 9.7% (2005); Master's degree or higher: 3.9% (2005).
Housing: Homeownership rate: 75.5% (2005); Median home value: $103,184 (2005); Median rent: $334 per month (2000); Median age of housing: 30 years (2000).
Health: Birth rate: 141.0 per 10,000 population (2004); Death rate: 103.9 per 10,000 population (2004); Age-adjusted cancer mortality rate: 184.9 deaths per 100,000 population (2002); Number of physicians: 8.4 per 10,000 population (2004); Hospital beds: 22.3 per 10,000 population (2003); Hospital admissions: 825.4 per 10,000 population (2003).
Elections: 2004 Presidential election results: 66.1% Bush, 33.5% Kerry, 0.0% Nader, 0.2% Badnarik
National and State Parks: Fallsville State Wildlife Area; Fort Hill State Memorial; Oldaker State Wildlife Area; Rocky Fork State Park
Additional Information Contacts
Highland County Government . . . . (937) 393-1911
  http://www.highlandcounty.com/
Highland County Chamber of Commerce . . . . (216) 491-6400
  http://www.tricitychamber.com
Highland County Convention & Visitors Bureau . . . . (937) 393-4883
  http://www.highlandcounty.com/modules/mypage

Highland County Communities

GREENFIELD (city). Covers a land area of 1.934 square miles and a water area of 0 square miles. Located at 39.35° N. Lat.; 83.38° W. Long. Elevation is 910 feet.
History: Platted 1798, incorporated 1841.
Population: 5,218 (1990); 4,906 (2000); 4,838 (2005); 4,809 (2010 projected); Race: 95.9% White, 2.1% Black, 0.1% Asian, 1.0% Hispanic of any race (2005); Density: 2,501.1 persons per square mile (2005); Average household size: 2.49 (2005); Median age: 36.0 (2005); Males per 100 females: 87.7 (2005); Marriage status: 22.0% never married, 56.2% now married, 9.4% widowed, 12.4% divorced (2000); Foreign born: 0.3% (2000); Ancestry (includes multiple ancestries): 23.0% United States or American, 16.3% German, 10.2% Irish, 9.9% Other groups, 6.1% English (2000).
Economy: In agricultural area. Manufacturing of footwear, leather products, consumer goods. Stone quarries. Single-family building permits issued: 7 (2005); Multi-family building permits issued: 2 (2005); Employment by occupation: 5.3% management, 11.4% professional, 14.7% services, 20.8% sales, 0.3% farming, 11.3% construction, 36.2% production (2000).
Income: Per capita income: $16,503 (2005); Median household income: $33,820 (2005); Average household income: $40,253 (2005); Percent of households with income of $100,000 or more: 4.8% (2005); Poverty rate: 15.1% (2000).
Education: Percent of population age 25 and over with: High school diploma (including GED) or higher: 70.9% (2005); Bachelor's degree or higher: 8.2% (2005); Master's degree or higher: 2.4% (2005).
School District(s)
Greenfield Ex Vill SD (PK-12)
  2003-04 Enrollment: 2,319 . . . . (937) 981-2152
Housing: Homeownership rate: 60.3% (2005); Median home value: $78,826 (2005); Median rent: $299 per month (2000); Median age of housing: 53 years (2000).
Hospitals: Greenfield Area Medical Center (46 beds)
Safety: Violent crime rate: 40.4 per 10,000 population; Property crime rate: 1,089.1 per 10,000 population (2004).
Transportation: Commute to work: 88.8% car, 0.6% public transportation, 5.6% walk, 4.7% work from home (2000); Travel time to work: 42.6% less than 15 minutes, 22.9% 15 to 30 minutes, 17.6% 30 to 45 minutes, 10.0% 45 to 60 minutes, 6.8% 60 minutes or more (2000)

HIGHLAND (village). Covers a land area of 0.165 square miles and a water area of 0 square miles. Located at 39.34° N. Lat.; 83.59° W. Long. Elevation is 1,065 feet.
Population: 234 (1990); 283 (2000); 285 (2005); 286 (2010 projected); Race: 96.5% White, 0.4% Black, 0.0% Asian, 1.1% Hispanic of any race (2005); Density: 1,725.6 persons per square mile (2005); Average household size: 2.59 (2005); Median age: 34.1 (2005); Males per 100 females: 106.5 (2005); Marriage status: 28.3% never married, 54.3% now married, 7.6% widowed, 9.9% divorced (2000); Foreign born: 1.0% (2000); Ancestry (includes multiple ancestries): 37.6% United States or American, 10.1% Other groups, 9.4% Irish, 9.1% English, 5.7% German (2000).
Economy: Employment by occupation: 6.9% management, 5.6% professional, 7.6% services, 20.1% sales, 0.0% farming, 18.1% construction, 41.7% production (2000).
Income: Per capita income: $19,930 (2005); Median household income: $53,472 (2005); Average household income: $51,636 (2005); Percent of households with income of $100,000 or more: 4.5% (2005); Poverty rate: 10.1% (2000).
Education: Percent of population age 25 and over with: High school diploma (including GED) or higher: 80.2% (2005); Bachelor's degree or higher: 5.3% (2005); Master's degree or higher: 4.3% (2005).
Housing: Homeownership rate: 79.1% (2005); Median home value: $76,087 (2005); Median rent: $314 per month (2000); Median age of housing: 56 years (2000).
Transportation: Commute to work: 99.3% car, 0.0% public transportation, 0.0% walk, 0.7% work from home (2000); Travel time to work: 23.7% less than 15 minutes, 51.8% 15 to 30 minutes, 11.5% 30 to 45 minutes, 4.3% 45 to 60 minutes, 8.6% 60 minutes or more (2000)

HILLSBORO (city). Covers a land area of 5.189 square miles and a water area of 0 square miles. Located at 39.20° N. Lat.; 83.61° W. Long. Elevation is 1,132 feet.
History: Hillsboro was platted in 1807, and developed around brickyards, tanneries, and grist and woolen mills. In 1873, The Women's Temperance Crusade was organized and managed to close all of the saloons in the town when the women marched into each in turn and held a prayer meeting.
Population: 6,441 (1990); 6,368 (2000); 6,618 (2005); 6,885 (2010 projected); Race: 90.5% White, 6.3% Black, 1.6% Asian, 1.2% Hispanic of any race (2005); Density: 1,275.3 persons per square mile (2005); Average household size: 2.34 (2005); Median age: 37.6 (2005); Males per 100 females: 84.2 (2005); Marriage status: 21.0% never married, 53.3% now married, 11.9% widowed, 13.8% divorced (2000); Foreign born: 1.9% (2000); Ancestry (includes multiple ancestries): 17.7% German, 17.5% United States or American, 16.8% Other groups, 11.1% English, 9.9% Irish (2000).
Economy: Single-family building permits issued: 22 (2005); Multi-family building permits issued: 3 (2005); Employment by occupation: 8.4% management, 17.2% professional, 14.0% services, 20.1% sales, 0.0% farming, 7.5% construction, 32.8% production (2000).
Income: Per capita income: $17,057 (2005); Median household income: $29,491 (2005); Average household income: $39,173 (2005); Percent of households with income of $100,000 or more: 5.6% (2005); Poverty rate: 18.1% (2000).
Education: Percent of population age 25 and over with: High school diploma (including GED) or higher: 73.6% (2005); Bachelor's degree or higher: 11.1% (2005); Master's degree or higher: 6.3% (2005).

School District(s)
Bright Local SD (PK-12)
   2003-04 Enrollment: 840 . . . . (937) 442-3114
Great Oaks Inst of Technology Joint Vocational SD (07-12)
   2003-04 Enrollment: n/a . . . . (513) 771-8840
Greenfield Ex Vill SD (PK-12)
   2003-04 Enrollment: 2,319 . . . . (937) 981-2152
Hillsboro City SD (PK-12)
   2003-04 Enrollment: 2,833 . . . . (937) 393-3475

Two-year College(s)
Southern State Community College (Public)
   Fall 2004 Enrollment: 2,346 . . . . (937) 393-3431
   2005-06 Tuition: In-state $3,213; Out-of-state $6,189

Housing: Homeownership rate: 56.3% (2005); Median home value: $98,825 (2005); Median rent: $324 per month (2000); Median age of housing: 35 years (2000).
Hospitals: Highland District Hospital (65 beds)
Safety: Violent crime rate: 10.5 per 10,000 population; Property crime rate: 436.4 per 10,000 population (2004).
Newspapers: Times Gazette (Circulation 7,000)
Transportation: Commute to work: 93.0% car, 0.2% public transportation, 2.5% walk, 3.7% work from home (2000); Travel time to work: 47.7% less than 15 minutes, 22.9% 15 to 30 minutes, 18.9% 30 to 45 minutes, 5.5% 45 to 60 minutes, 5.1% 60 minutes or more (2000).
Additional Information Contacts
Highland County Chamber of Commerce . . . . (216) 491-6400
   http://www.tricitychamber.com
Highland County Convention & Visitors Bureau . . . . (937) 393-4883
   http://www.highlandcounty.com/modules/mypage

LEESBURG (village). Covers a land area of 0.803 square miles and a water area of 0 square miles. Located at 39.34° N. Lat.; 83.55° W. Long. Elevation is 1,020 feet.
History: Shortly after Leesburg was founded in 1802, Quakers from Pennsylvania settled here. Prior to 1900, Leesburg hosted the annual meeting of the Society of Friends, attended by members from all parts of the United States.
Population: 1,194 (1990); 1,253 (2000); 1,267 (2005); 1,281 (2010 projected); Race: 98.7% White, 0.6% Black, 0.2% Asian, 0.1% Hispanic of any race (2005); Density: 1,577.5 persons per square mile (2005); Average household size: 2.47 (2005); Median age: 32.2 (2005); Males per 100 females: 97.0 (2005); Marriage status: 24.8% never married, 57.7% now married, 5.6% widowed, 11.8% divorced (2000); Foreign born: 0.5% (2000); Ancestry (includes multiple ancestries): 28.2% United States or American, 11.1% German, 9.2% Irish, 5.5% English, 4.6% Other groups (2000).
Economy: Employment by occupation: 6.5% management, 9.7% professional, 13.1% services, 17.9% sales, 0.0% farming, 15.3% construction, 37.5% production (2000).
Income: Per capita income: $20,710 (2005); Median household income: $41,204 (2005); Average household income: $51,150 (2005); Percent of households with income of $100,000 or more: 8.8% (2005); Poverty rate: 6.3% (2000).
Education: Percent of population age 25 and over with: High school diploma (including GED) or higher: 83.7% (2005); Bachelor's degree or higher: 8.6% (2005); Master's degree or higher: 3.0% (2005).

School District(s)
Fairfield Local SD (PK-12)
   2003-04 Enrollment: 913 . . . . (937) 780-2221

Housing: Homeownership rate: 65.1% (2005); Median home value: $90,882 (2005); Median rent: $350 per month (2000); Median age of housing: 36 years (2000).
Transportation: Commute to work: 93.0% car, 1.6% public transportation, 3.5% walk, 1.9% work from home (2000); Travel time to work: 32.6% less than 15 minutes, 35.9% 15 to 30 minutes, 16.6% 30 to 45 minutes, 5.1% 45 to 60 minutes, 9.8% 60 minutes or more (2000)

LYNCHBURG (village). Covers a land area of 0.878 square miles and a water area of 0 square miles. Located at 39.24° N. Lat.; 83.79° W. Long. Elevation is 1,009 feet.
Population: 1,322 (1990); 1,350 (2000); 1,294 (2005); 1,282 (2010 projected); Race: 98.6% White, 0.4% Black, 0.2% Asian, 0.2% Hispanic of any race (2005); Density: 1,474.5 persons per square mile (2005); Average household size: 2.57 (2005); Median age: 33.5 (2005); Males per 100 females: 93.1 (2005); Marriage status: 21.3% never married, 59.3% now married, 8.2% widowed, 11.2% divorced (2000); Foreign born: 0.6% (2000); Ancestry (includes multiple ancestries): 27.9% United States or American, 18.0% German, 17.2% Irish, 11.2% English, 7.5% Other groups (2000).
Economy: Employment by occupation: 6.8% management, 11.1% professional, 11.1% services, 26.7% sales, 0.0% farming, 12.2% construction, 32.0% production (2000).
Income: Per capita income: $19,405 (2005); Median household income: $41,108 (2005); Average household income: $49,920 (2005); Percent of households with income of $100,000 or more: 7.8% (2005); Poverty rate: 9.1% (2000).
Taxes: Total city taxes per capita: $122 (2004); City property taxes per capita: $100 (2004).
Education: Percent of population age 25 and over with: High school diploma (including GED) or higher: 78.4% (2005); Bachelor's degree or higher: 9.5% (2005); Master's degree or higher: 3.8% (2005).

School District(s)
Lynchburg-Clay Local SD (PK-12)
   2003-04 Enrollment: 1,302 . . . . (937) 364-6065

Housing: Homeownership rate: 69.4% (2005); Median home value: $96,813 (2005); Median rent: $371 per month (2000); Median age of housing: 45 years (2000).
Transportation: Commute to work: 95.6% car, 0.0% public transportation, 1.6% walk, 2.3% work from home (2000); Travel time to work: 20.1% less than 15 minutes, 39.2% 15 to 30 minutes, 17.8% 30 to 45 minutes, 9.6% 45 to 60 minutes, 13.3% 60 minutes or more (2000)

MOWRYSTOWN (village). Covers a land area of 0.483 square miles and a water area of 0.007 square miles. Located at 39.03° N. Lat.; 83.75° W. Long. Elevation is 997 feet.
Population: 460 (1990); 373 (2000); 397 (2005); 416 (2010 projected); Race: 99.0% White, 0.0% Black, 0.0% Asian, 0.0% Hispanic of any race (2005); Density: 822.5 persons per square mile (2005); Average household size: 2.58 (2005); Median age: 33.5 (2005); Males per 100 females: 107.9 (2005); Marriage status: 25.8% never married, 56.7% now married, 7.6% widowed, 9.8% divorced (2000); Foreign born: 0.0% (2000); Ancestry (includes multiple ancestries): 34.6% United States or American, 22.2% Other groups, 11.0% Irish, 10.1% German, 9.5% English (2000).
Economy: Employment by occupation: 2.5% management, 3.1% professional, 9.4% services, 19.4% sales, 0.0% farming, 21.9% construction, 43.8% production (2000).
Income: Per capita income: $17,047 (2005); Median household income: $41,765 (2005); Average household income: $43,945 (2005); Percent of households with income of $100,000 or more: 3.2% (2005); Poverty rate: 10.1% (2000).

Education: Percent of population age 25 and over with: High school diploma (including GED) or higher: 63.5% (2005); Bachelor's degree or higher: 1.2% (2005); Master's degree or higher: 0.0% (2005).

School District(s)

Bright Local SD (PK-12)
    2003-04 Enrollment: 840 . . . . (937) 442-3114

Housing: Homeownership rate: 79.2% (2005); Median home value: $73,171 (2005); Median rent: $338 per month (2000); Median age of housing: 60+ years (2000).
Transportation: Commute to work: 93.1% car, 0.0% public transportation, 2.5% walk, 1.3% work from home (2000); Travel time to work: 10.8% less than 15 minutes, 23.4% 15 to 30 minutes, 26.6% 30 to 45 minutes, 16.5% 45 to 60 minutes, 22.8% 60 minutes or more (2000)

SINKING SPRING (village). Covers a land area of 0.468 square miles and a water area of 0 square miles. Located at 39.07° N. Lat.; 83.38° W. Long. Elevation is 873 feet.
History: Nearby are Fort Hill and Serpent Mound, prehistoric earthworks.
Population: 189 (1990); 158 (2000); 139 (2005); 135 (2010 projected); Race: 97.1% White, 0.0% Black, 0.0% Asian, 0.0% Hispanic of any race (2005); Density: 297.0 persons per square mile (2005); Average household size: 2.73 (2005); Median age: 35.2 (2005); Males per 100 females: 93.1 (2005); Marriage status: 34.3% never married, 54.7% now married, 8.0% widowed, 2.9% divorced (2000); Foreign born: 0.0% (2000); Ancestry (includes multiple ancestries): 38.1% United States or American, 15.5% German, 15.5% Irish, 10.3% Other groups, 5.2% English (2000).
Economy: Employment by occupation: 1.5% management, 9.1% professional, 9.1% services, 25.8% sales, 1.5% farming, 12.1% construction, 40.9% production (2000).
Income: Per capita income: $17,950 (2005); Median household income: $43,750 (2005); Average household income: $48,922 (2005); Percent of households with income of $100,000 or more: 5.9% (2005); Poverty rate: 7.7% (2000).
Education: Percent of population age 25 and over with: High school diploma (including GED) or higher: 64.8% (2005); Bachelor's degree or higher: 4.4% (2005); Master's degree or higher: 0.0% (2005).
Housing: Homeownership rate: 76.5% (2005); Median home value: $79,000 (2005); Median rent: $188 per month (2000); Median age of housing: 48 years (2000).
Transportation: Commute to work: 89.1% car, 0.0% public transportation, 0.0% walk, 4.7% work from home (2000); Travel time to work: 3.3% less than 15 minutes, 24.6% 15 to 30 minutes, 27.9% 30 to 45 minutes, 9.8% 45 to 60 minutes, 34.4% 60 minutes or more (2000)

Hocking County

Located in south central Ohio; crossed by the Hocking River. Covers a land area of 422.75 square miles, a water area of 0.85 square miles, and is located in the Eastern Time Zone. The county government was organized in 1818. County seat is Logan.
Population: 25,533 (1990); 28,241 (2000); 28,838 (2005); 29,455 (2010 projected); Race: 97.3% White, 1.0% Black, 0.2% Asian, 0.5% Hispanic of any race (2005); Density: 68.2 persons per square mile (2005); Average household size: 2.57 (2005); Median age: 38.1 (2005); Males per 100 females: 99.0 (2005).
Religion: Five largest groups: 8.6% The United Methodist Church, 3.4% Catholic Church, 2.8% Southern Baptist Convention, 2.1% Evangelical Lutheran Church in America, 1.4% Christian Churches and Churches of Christ (2000).
Economy: Unemployment rate: 7.5% (2005); Total civilian labor force: 13,901 (2005); Leading industries: 22.2% manufacturing; 17.7% retail trade; 16.3% health care and social assistance (2004); Farms: 434 totaling 49,866 acres (2002); Companies that employ 500 or more persons: 0 (2004); Companies that employ 100 to 499 persons: 11 (2004); Companies that employ less than 100 persons: 532 (2004); Black-owned businesses: n/a (2002); Hispanic-owned businesses: n/a (2002); Women-owned businesses: 751 (2002); Retail sales per capita: $11,129 (2006).
Single-family building permits issued: 20 (2005); Multi-family building permits issued: 136 (2005).
Income: Per capita income: $18,294 (2005); Median household income: $38,386 (2005); Average household income: $46,395 (2005); Percent of households with income of $100,000 or more: 6.7% (2005); Poverty rate: 12.1% (2003); Bankruptcy rate: 9.62% (2005).
Taxes: Total county taxes per capita: $244 (2004); County property taxes per capita: $133 (2004).

Education: Percent of population age 25 and over with: High school diploma (including GED) or higher: 77.6% (2005); Bachelor's degree or higher: 9.7% (2005); Master's degree or higher: 3.6% (2005).
Housing: Homeownership rate: 76.0% (2005); Median home value: $99,978 (2005); Median rent: $295 per month (2000); Median age of housing: 30 years (2000).
Health: Birth rate: 134.0 per 10,000 population (2004); Death rate: 109.7 per 10,000 population (2004); Age-adjusted cancer mortality rate: 231.4 deaths per 100,000 population (2002); Number of physicians: 8.7 per 10,000 population (2004); Hospital beds: 32.0 per 10,000 population (2003); Hospital admissions: 615.3 per 10,000 population (2003).
Elections: 2004 Presidential election results: 52.5% Bush, 46.8% Kerry, 0.0% Nader, 0.3% Badnarik
National and State Parks: Hocking Hills State Park; Hocking State Forest; Lake Logan State Park; Sunday Creek State Wildlife Area; Wayne National Forest - Athens Ranger District
Additional Information Contacts
Hocking County Government. . . . . (740) 385-5195
    http://www.co.hocking.oh.us/
Logan Hocking Chamber of Commerce. . . . . (740) 385-6836
    http://www.logan-hockingchamber.com

Hocking County Communities

LAURELVILLE (village). Covers a land area of 0.205 square miles and a water area of 0 square miles. Located at 39.47° N. Lat.; 82.73° W. Long. Elevation is 741 feet.
Population: 605 (1990); 533 (2000); 502 (2005); 487 (2010 projected); Race: 98.4% White, 0.0% Black, 0.0% Asian, 0.6% Hispanic of any race (2005); Density: 2,453.5 persons per square mile (2005); Average household size: 2.03 (2005); Median age: 40.6 (2005); Males per 100 females: 88.7 (2005); Marriage status: 21.7% never married, 47.7% now married, 12.6% widowed, 18.0% divorced (2000); Foreign born: 0.0% (2000); Ancestry (includes multiple ancestries): 19.4% German, 12.7% United States or American, 11.0% Irish, 7.2% Other groups, 5.7% English (2000).
Economy: In agricultural area; grain products, lumber. Employment by occupation: 9.8% management, 10.7% professional, 27.7% services, 16.5% sales, 0.4% farming, 13.4% construction, 21.4% production (2000).
Income: Per capita income: $18,267 (2005); Median household income: $25,833 (2005); Average household income: $37,126 (2005); Percent of households with income of $100,000 or more: 3.6% (2005); Poverty rate: 13.5% (2000).
Education: Percent of population age 25 and over with: High school diploma (including GED) or higher: 64.0% (2005); Bachelor's degree or higher: 3.1% (2005); Master's degree or higher: 0.0% (2005).

School District(s)

Logan Elm Local SD (PK-12)
    2003-04 Enrollment: 2,323 . . . . (740) 474-7501

Housing: Homeownership rate: 51.8% (2005); Median home value: $90,968 (2005); Median rent: $294 per month (2000); Median age of housing: 54 years (2000).
Transportation: Commute to work: 88.7% car, 0.9% public transportation, 9.0% walk, 0.9% work from home (2000); Travel time to work: 23.6% less than 15 minutes, 27.3% 15 to 30 minutes, 17.7% 30 to 45 minutes, 9.1% 45 to 60 minutes, 22.3% 60 minutes or more (2000)

LOGAN (city). Covers a land area of 3.082 square miles and a water area of 0 square miles. Located at 39.53° N. Lat.; 82.40° W. Long. Elevation is 741 feet.
History: Logan was founded in 1816 by Governor Thomas Worthington, who purchased a tract near the Hocking Falls and set up mills. Logan flourished with the opening of the Hocking Canal in 1840, and the completion of the Hocking Valley Railroad in 1869.
Population: 6,799 (1990); 6,704 (2000); 6,759 (2005); 6,880 (2010 projected); Race: 97.8% White, 0.5% Black, 0.1% Asian, 0.5% Hispanic of any race (2005); Density: 2,193.0 persons per square mile (2005); Average household size: 2.37 (2005); Median age: 38.2 (2005); Males per 100 females: 86.4 (2005); Marriage status: 20.9% never married, 54.6% now married, 11.7% widowed, 12.8% divorced (2000); Foreign born: 0.6% (2000); Ancestry (includes multiple ancestries): 24.4% German, 14.7% United States or American, 14.5% Irish, 10.7% English, 6.4% Other groups (2000).
Economy: Single-family building permits issued: 20 (2005); Multi-family building permits issued: 72 (2005); Employment by occupation: 8.4%

management, 17.4% professional, 15.0% services, 24.5% sales, 0.2% farming, 12.3% construction, 22.2% production (2000).
Income: Per capita income: $16,933 (2005); Median household income: $31,526 (2005); Average household income: $39,457 (2005); Percent of households with income of $100,000 or more: 4.8% (2005); Poverty rate: 17.7% (2000).
Education: Percent of population age 25 and over with: High school diploma (including GED) or higher: 79.0% (2005); Bachelor's degree or higher: 10.2% (2005); Master's degree or higher: 4.3% (2005).

School District(s)
Logan-Hocking Local SD (PK-12)
    2003-04 Enrollment: 4,028 . . . . (740) 385-8517
Housing: Homeownership rate: 61.5% (2005); Median home value: $93,333 (2005); Median rent: $297 per month (2000); Median age of housing: 48 years (2000).
Hospitals: Hocking Valley Community Hospital (93 beds)
Safety: Violent crime rate: 13.1 per 10,000 population; Property crime rate: 759.7 per 10,000 population (2004).
Newspapers: Logan Daily News (Circulation 4,224)
Transportation: Commute to work: 94.0% car, 0.5% public transportation, 3.9% walk, 1.4% work from home (2000); Travel time to work: 50.7% less than 15 minutes, 16.1% 15 to 30 minutes, 11.5% 30 to 45 minutes, 4.1% 45 to 60 minutes, 17.6% 60 minutes or more (2000)
Additional Information Contacts
Logan Hocking Chamber of Commerce. . . . . (740) 385-6836
    http://www.logan-hockingchamber.com

MURRAY CITY (village).
Covers a land area of 0.299 square miles and a water area of 0 square miles. Located at 39.51° N. Lat.; 82.16° W. Long. Elevation is 712 feet.
Population: 513 (1990); 452 (2000); 483 (2005); 511 (2010 projected); Race: 97.5% White, 0.0% Black, 0.0% Asian, 0.0% Hispanic of any race (2005); Density: 1,612.9 persons per square mile (2005); Average household size: 2.34 (2005); Median age: 34.9 (2005); Males per 100 females: 98.8 (2005); Marriage status: 25.1% never married, 56.8% now married, 8.5% widowed, 9.6% divorced (2000); Foreign born: 0.0% (2000); Ancestry (includes multiple ancestries): 14.6% German, 12.6% Irish, 12.4% English, 9.0% Other groups, 7.0% United States or American (2000).
Economy: In coal-mining area. Employment by occupation: 3.0% management, 8.4% professional, 22.2% services, 24.0% sales, 0.0% farming, 18.6% construction, 24.0% production (2000).
Income: Per capita income: $13,861 (2005); Median household income: $29,063 (2005); Average household income: $32,500 (2005); Percent of households with income of $100,000 or more: 1.5% (2005); Poverty rate: 19.8% (2000).
Education: Percent of population age 25 and over with: High school diploma (including GED) or higher: 68.8% (2005); Bachelor's degree or higher: 4.2% (2005); Master's degree or higher: 0.6% (2005).
Housing: Homeownership rate: 67.5% (2005); Median home value: $50,513 (2005); Median rent: $258 per month (2000); Median age of housing: 60+ years (2000).
Transportation: Commute to work: 96.4% car, 0.0% public transportation, 2.4% walk, 1.2% work from home (2000); Travel time to work: 13.3% less than 15 minutes, 27.3% 15 to 30 minutes, 21.8% 30 to 45 minutes, 11.5% 45 to 60 minutes, 26.1% 60 minutes or more (2000)

ROCKBRIDGE (unincorporated postal area, zip code 43149).
Covers a land area of 56.031 square miles and a water area of 0.011 square miles. Located at 39.54° N. Lat.; 82.57° W. Long. Elevation is 760 feet.
Population: 2,596 (2000); Race: 99.3% White, 0.0% Black, 0.0% Asian, 0.3% Hispanic of any race (2000); Density: 46.3 persons per square mile (2000); Age: 24.7% under 18, 8.5% over 64 (2000); Marriage status: 21.0% never married, 63.6% now married, 4.3% widowed, 11.1% divorced (2000); Foreign born: 0.4% (2000); Ancestry (includes multiple ancestries): 22.2% German, 11.3% Irish, 9.6% United States or American, 9.5% English, 3.2% Other groups (2000).
Economy: Employment by occupation: 7.7% management, 10.5% professional, 14.9% services, 21.2% sales, 0.7% farming, 18.1% construction, 26.9% production (2000).
Income: Per capita income: $18,129 (2000); Median household income: $38,177 (2000); Poverty rate: 8.3% (2000).
Education: Percent of population age 25 and over with: High school diploma (including GED) or higher: 80.9% (2000); Bachelor's degree or higher: 14.4% (2000).

School District(s)
Logan-Hocking Local SD (PK-12)
    2003-04 Enrollment: 4,028 . . . . (740) 385-8517
Housing: Homeownership rate: 81.2% (2000); Median home value: $89,800 (2000); Median rent: $348 per month (2000); Median age of housing: 22 years (2000).
Transportation: Commute to work: 96.4% car, 0.6% public transportation, 0.3% walk, 2.1% work from home (2000); Travel time to work: 9.8% less than 15 minutes, 36.0% 15 to 30 minutes, 22.0% 30 to 45 minutes, 11.4% 45 to 60 minutes, 20.9% 60 minutes or more (2000)

SOUTH BLOOMINGVILLE (unincorporated postal area, zip code 43152).
Covers a land area of 55.684 square miles and a water area of 0 square miles. Located at 39.38° N. Lat.; 82.62° W. Long. Elevation is 696 feet.
Population: 1,098 (2000); Race: 99.4% White, 0.6% Black, 0.0% Asian, 0.0% Hispanic of any race (2000); Density: 19.7 persons per square mile (2000); Age: 24.6% under 18, 9.5% over 64 (2000); Marriage status: 21.1% never married, 65.6% now married, 4.5% widowed, 8.8% divorced (2000); Foreign born: 0.0% (2000); Ancestry (includes multiple ancestries): 30.3% United States or American, 16.0% German, 11.0% Irish, 6.1% Other groups, 5.8% English (2000).
Economy: Employment by occupation: 5.0% management, 8.2% professional, 23.5% services, 19.5% sales, 4.0% farming, 13.7% construction, 26.1% production (2000).
Income: Per capita income: $15,049 (2000); Median household income: $36,071 (2000); Poverty rate: 13.2% (2000).
Education: Percent of population age 25 and over with: High school diploma (including GED) or higher: 79.2% (2000); Bachelor's degree or higher: 10.4% (2000).

School District(s)
Logan-Hocking Local SD (PK-12)
    2003-04 Enrollment: 4,028 . . . . (740) 385-8517
Housing: Homeownership rate: 78.6% (2000); Median home value: $102,700 (2000); Median rent: $214 per month (2000); Median age of housing: 26 years (2000).
Transportation: Commute to work: 96.0% car, 0.0% public transportation, 0.0% walk, 4.0% work from home (2000); Travel time to work: 10.2% less than 15 minutes, 10.8% 15 to 30 minutes, 29.4% 30 to 45 minutes, 16.0% 45 to 60 minutes, 33.5% 60 minutes or more (2000)

Holmes County

Located in central Ohio; crossed by Killbuck Creek and Walhonding River. Covers a land area of 422.99 square miles, a water area of 1.03 square miles, and is located in the Eastern Time Zone. The county government was organized in 1824. County seat is Millersburg.
Population: 32,849 (1990); 38,943 (2000); 41,331 (2005); 43,827 (2010 projected); Race: 98.9% White, 0.4% Black, 0.1% Asian, 0.8% Hispanic of any race (2005); Density: 97.7 persons per square mile (2005); Average household size: 3.41 (2005); Median age: 29.0 (2005); Males per 100 females: 100.1 (2005).
Religion: Five largest groups: 15.9% Old Order Amish Church, 5.6% Christian Churches and Churches of Christ, 4.6% Mennonite Church USA, 3.9% The United Methodist Church, 3.1% Amish; Other Groups (2000).
Economy: Unemployment rate: 4.1% (2005); Total civilian labor force: 19,965 (2005); Leading industries: 36.9% manufacturing; 12.3% retail trade; 9.6% construction (2004); Farms: 1,809 totaling 206,603 acres (2002); Companies that employ 500 or more persons: 1 (2004); Companies that employ 100 to 499 persons: 26 (2004); Companies that employ less than 100 persons: 1,022 (2004); Black-owned businesses: n/a (2002); Hispanic-owned businesses: n/a (2002); Women-owned businesses: 932 (2002); Retail sales per capita: $10,097 (2006). Single-family building permits issued: 105 (2005); Multi-family building permits issued: 37 (2005).
Income: Per capita income: $16,214 (2005); Median household income: $42,552 (2005); Average household income: $54,179 (2005); Percent of households with income of $100,000 or more: 9.5% (2005); Poverty rate: 10.1% (2003); Bankruptcy rate: 3.15% (2005).
Taxes: Total county taxes per capita: $250 (2004); County property taxes per capita: $137 (2004).
Education: Percent of population age 25 and over with: High school diploma (including GED) or higher: 51.0% (2005); Bachelor's degree or higher: 8.0% (2005); Master's degree or higher: 2.4% (2005).

Housing: Homeownership rate: 76.9% (2005); Median home value: $139,300 (2005); Median rent: $331 per month (2000); Median age of housing: 27 years (2000).
Health: Birth rate: 211.8 per 10,000 population (2004); Death rate: 72.6 per 10,000 population (2004); Age-adjusted cancer mortality rate: 160.5 deaths per 100,000 population (2002); Number of physicians: 7.8 per 10,000 population (2004); Hospital beds: 9.8 per 10,000 population (2003); Hospital admissions: 523.0 per 10,000 population (2003).
Elections: 2004 Presidential election results: 75.5% Bush, 24.0% Kerry, 0.0% Nader, 0.2% Badnarik

Additional Information Contacts
Holmes County Government . . . . (330) 674-0286
  http://www.holmescounty.com/gov/
Holmes County Chamber of Commerce . . . . (330) 674-3975
  http://www.holmescountychamber.com
Village of Millersburg . . . . (330) 674-1886
  http://www.millersburgohio.com/villagehome

Holmes County Communities

BIG PRAIRIE (unincorporated postal area, zip code 44611). Covers a land area of 27.924 square miles and a water area of 0.010 square miles. Located at 40.63° N. Lat.; 82.08° W. Long. Elevation is 947 feet.
Population: 2,028 (2000); Race: 99.7% White, 0.0% Black, 0.0% Asian, 0.9% Hispanic of any race (2000); Density: 72.6 persons per square mile (2000); Age: 33.4% under 18, 6.5% over 64 (2000); Marriage status: 24.2% never married, 66.4% now married, 3.1% widowed, 6.2% divorced (2000); Foreign born: 0.1% (2000); Ancestry (includes multiple ancestries): 26.0% German, 18.9% United States or American, 9.1% Irish, 8.0% Other groups, 7.7% English (2000).
Economy: Employment by occupation: 7.0% management, 12.7% professional, 10.0% services, 17.9% sales, 1.9% farming, 8.0% construction, 42.4% production (2000).
Income: Per capita income: $13,305 (2000); Median household income: $35,814 (2000); Poverty rate: 10.3% (2000).
Education: Percent of population age 25 and over with: High school diploma (including GED) or higher: 77.9% (2000); Bachelor's degree or higher: 6.8% (2000).
Housing: Homeownership rate: 84.5% (2000); Median home value: $92,100 (2000); Median rent: $407 per month (2000); Median age of housing: 27 years (2000).
Transportation: Commute to work: 84.0% car, 0.0% public transportation, 3.4% walk, 11.6% work from home (2000); Travel time to work: 15.7% less than 15 minutes, 44.6% 15 to 30 minutes, 29.7% 30 to 45 minutes, 1.6% 45 to 60 minutes, 8.4% 60 minutes or more (2000)

GLENMONT (village). Covers a land area of 0.271 square miles and a water area of 0 square miles. Located at 40.51° N. Lat.; 82.09° W. Long. Elevation is 881 feet.
History: Glenmont grew up around the sandstone quarries that furnished the material for some of New York's brownstone houses.
Population: 246 (1990); 283 (2000); 306 (2005); 328 (2010 projected); Race: 99.0% White, 0.0% Black, 0.7% Asian, 0.3% Hispanic of any race (2005); Density: 1,128.8 persons per square mile (2005); Average household size: 2.45 (2005); Median age: 38.2 (2005); Males per 100 females: 98.7 (2005); Marriage status: 11.7% never married, 65.0% now married, 11.2% widowed, 12.1% divorced (2000); Foreign born: 0.7% (2000); Ancestry (includes multiple ancestries): 23.0% German, 21.3% Irish, 12.8% English, 12.1% United States or American, 7.1% Other groups (2000).
Economy: Employment by occupation: 3.6% management, 6.5% professional, 15.8% services, 15.8% sales, 0.0% farming, 19.4% construction, 38.8% production (2000).
Income: Per capita income: $18,301 (2005); Median household income: $39,167 (2005); Average household income: $44,800 (2005); Percent of households with income of $100,000 or more: 5.6% (2005); Poverty rate: 11.4% (2000).
Education: Percent of population age 25 and over with: High school diploma (including GED) or higher: 76.4% (2005); Bachelor's degree or higher: 7.5% (2005); Master's degree or higher: 2.5% (2005).
Housing: Homeownership rate: 74.4% (2005); Median home value: $66,800 (2005); Median rent: $300 per month (2000); Median age of housing: 49 years (2000).
Transportation: Commute to work: 94.9% car, 0.0% public transportation, 1.5% walk, 1.5% work from home (2000); Travel time to work: 23.7% less than 15 minutes, 25.9% 15 to 30 minutes, 34.1% 30 to 45 minutes, 11.1% 45 to 60 minutes, 5.2% 60 minutes or more (2000)

HOLMESVILLE (village). Covers a land area of 0.239 square miles and a water area of 0 square miles. Located at 40.62° N. Lat.; 81.92° W. Long. Elevation is 880 feet.
Population: 419 (1990); 386 (2000); 417 (2005); 453 (2010 projected); Race: 97.6% White, 0.0% Black, 0.0% Asian, 2.9% Hispanic of any race (2005); Density: 1,747.3 persons per square mile (2005); Average household size: 2.54 (2005); Median age: 36.7 (2005); Males per 100 females: 110.6 (2005); Marriage status: 29.7% never married, 53.4% now married, 4.8% widowed, 12.1% divorced (2000); Foreign born: 0.0% (2000); Ancestry (includes multiple ancestries): 20.6% German, 16.2% United States or American, 7.9% Other groups, 6.1% Irish, 4.4% English (2000).
Economy: Employment by occupation: 5.4% management, 5.9% professional, 12.3% services, 19.1% sales, 1.0% farming, 10.3% construction, 46.1% production (2000).
Income: Per capita income: $18,873 (2005); Median household income: $44,512 (2005); Average household income: $47,988 (2005); Percent of households with income of $100,000 or more: 4.3% (2005); Poverty rate: 6.4% (2000).
Education: Percent of population age 25 and over with: High school diploma (including GED) or higher: 71.7% (2005); Bachelor's degree or higher: 3.2% (2005); Master's degree or higher: 0.0% (2005).
School District(s)
Southeast Local SD (PK-12)
  2003-04 Enrollment: 1,718 . . . . (330) 698-3001
Housing: Homeownership rate: 74.4% (2005); Median home value: $87,027 (2005); Median rent: $346 per month (2000); Median age of housing: 60+ years (2000).
Transportation: Commute to work: 96.4% car, 0.0% public transportation, 0.0% walk, 1.0% work from home (2000); Travel time to work: 44.3% less than 15 minutes, 30.9% 15 to 30 minutes, 13.4% 30 to 45 minutes, 7.2% 45 to 60 minutes, 4.1% 60 minutes or more (2000)

KILLBUCK (village). Covers a land area of 0.283 square miles and a water area of 0 square miles. Located at 40.49° N. Lat.; 81.98° W. Long. Elevation is 810 feet.
History: Killbuck was settled in 1811, and named for the creek on which it was established.
Population: 809 (1990); 839 (2000); 970 (2005); 1,100 (2010 projected); Race: 99.7% White, 0.0% Black, 0.0% Asian, 0.6% Hispanic of any race (2005); Density: 3,423.9 persons per square mile (2005); Average household size: 2.32 (2005); Median age: 37.2 (2005); Males per 100 females: 91.3 (2005); Marriage status: 22.1% never married, 55.2% now married, 7.1% widowed, 15.6% divorced (2000); Foreign born: 0.0% (2000); Ancestry (includes multiple ancestries): 23.3% German, 13.4% United States or American, 12.2% Irish, 8.3% English, 6.8% Other groups (2000).
Economy: Employment by occupation: 4.9% management, 9.6% professional, 10.8% services, 19.1% sales, 0.9% farming, 7.5% construction, 47.1% production (2000).
Income: Per capita income: $17,853 (2005); Median household income: $34,577 (2005); Average household income: $41,429 (2005); Percent of households with income of $100,000 or more: 4.1% (2005); Poverty rate: 12.2% (2000).
Education: Percent of population age 25 and over with: High school diploma (including GED) or higher: 75.5% (2005); Bachelor's degree or higher: 4.2% (2005); Master's degree or higher: 1.9% (2005).
School District(s)
West Holmes Local SD (KG-12)
  2003-04 Enrollment: 2,805 . . . . (330) 674-3546
Housing: Homeownership rate: 64.4% (2005); Median home value: $82,297 (2005); Median rent: $319 per month (2000); Median age of housing: 52 years (2000).
Transportation: Commute to work: 93.7% car, 0.0% public transportation, 3.9% walk, 2.4% work from home (2000); Travel time to work: 39.5% less than 15 minutes, 36.7% 15 to 30 minutes, 15.4% 30 to 45 minutes, 5.7% 45 to 60 minutes, 2.7% 60 minutes or more (2000)

LAKEVILLE (unincorporated postal area, zip code 44638). Covers a land area of 29.839 square miles and a water area of 0.305 square miles. Located at 40.65° N. Lat.; 82.13° W. Long. Elevation is 988 feet.

Population: 1,533 (2000); Race: 97.2% White, 0.0% Black, 0.5% Asian, 2.6% Hispanic of any race (2000); Density: 51.4 persons per square mile (2000); Age: 31.2% under 18, 11.6% over 64 (2000); Marriage status: 23.7% never married, 60.6% now married, 6.1% widowed, 9.6% divorced (2000); Foreign born: 0.9% (2000); Ancestry (includes multiple ancestries): 28.4% German, 11.5% Irish, 10.0% United States or American, 7.9% Other groups, 5.1% English (2000).
Economy: Employment by occupation: 10.5% management, 10.3% professional, 14.7% services, 18.2% sales, 3.3% farming, 16.6% construction, 26.3% production (2000).
Income: Per capita income: $14,270 (2000); Median household income: $32,500 (2000); Poverty rate: 19.7% (2000).
Education: Percent of population age 25 and over with: High school diploma (including GED) or higher: 83.2% (2000); Bachelor's degree or higher: 14.8% (2000).

School District(s)
West Holmes Local SD (KG-12)
   2003-04 Enrollment: 2,805 . . . . (330) 674-3546

Housing: Homeownership rate: 77.1% (2000); Median home value: $88,300 (2000); Median rent: $325 per month (2000); Median age of housing: 35 years (2000).
Transportation: Commute to work: 89.4% car, 2.4% public transportation, 0.0% walk, 7.2% work from home (2000); Travel time to work: 25.7% less than 15 minutes, 37.4% 15 to 30 minutes, 26.6% 30 to 45 minutes, 4.3% 45 to 60 minutes, 6.0% 60 minutes or more (2000)

MILLERSBURG (village). Covers a land area of 2.017 square miles and a water area of 0 square miles. Located at 40.55° N. Lat.; 81.91° W. Long. Elevation is 906 feet.
History: Settlement in Millersburg began in 1816, when many "Pennsylvania Dutch" came here. The town has been the seat of Holmes County since 1824.
Population: 3,307 (1990); 3,326 (2000); 3,527 (2005); 3,702 (2010 projected); Race: 96.8% White, 1.8% Black, 0.1% Asian, 2.0% Hispanic of any race (2005); Density: 1,748.6 persons per square mile (2005); Average household size: 2.76 (2005); Median age: 37.9 (2005); Males per 100 females: 96.1 (2005); Marriage status: 26.0% never married, 50.5% now married, 8.3% widowed, 15.2% divorced (2000); Foreign born: 3.4% (2000); Ancestry (includes multiple ancestries): 25.9% German, 15.1% United States or American, 10.0% Irish, 9.9% English, 8.5% Other groups (2000).
Economy: Single-family building permits issued: 8 (2005); Multi-family building permits issued: 3 (2005); Employment by occupation: 7.3% management, 13.1% professional, 16.6% services, 25.6% sales, 0.9% farming, 9.7% construction, 26.8% production (2000).
Income: Per capita income: $16,461 (2005); Median household income: $37,196 (2005); Average household income: $43,104 (2005); Percent of households with income of $100,000 or more: 4.6% (2005); Poverty rate: 12.2% (2000).
Education: Percent of population age 25 and over with: High school diploma (including GED) or higher: 75.3% (2005); Bachelor's degree or higher: 16.0% (2005); Master's degree or higher: 5.7% (2005).

School District(s)
East Holmes Local Schools (KG-12)
   2003-04 Enrollment: 1,857 . . . . (330) 893-2610
West Holmes Digital Academy
   2003-04 Enrollment: n/a
West Holmes Local SD (KG-12)
   2003-04 Enrollment: 2,805 . . . . (330) 674-3546

Housing: Homeownership rate: 54.3% (2005); Median home value: $93,033 (2005); Median rent: $327 per month (2000); Median age of housing: 42 years (2000).
Hospitals: Joel Pomerene Memorial Hospital (55 beds)
Newspapers: The Holmes County Hub (General - Circulation 4,550)
Transportation: Commute to work: 93.9% car, 0.0% public transportation, 4.2% walk, 1.7% work from home (2000); Travel time to work: 54.0% less than 15 minutes, 25.3% 15 to 30 minutes, 12.5% 30 to 45 minutes, 5.3% 45 to 60 minutes, 2.9% 60 minutes or more (2000)
Additional Information Contacts
Holmes County Chamber of Commerce . . . . (330) 674-3975
   http://www.holmescountychamber.com
Village of Millersburg . . . . (330) 674-1886
   http://www.millersburgohio.com/villagehome

NASHVILLE (village). Covers a land area of 0.071 square miles and a water area of 0 square miles. Located at 40.59° N. Lat.; 82.11° W. Long. Elevation is 1,220 feet.
Population: 181 (1990); 172 (2000); 189 (2005); 207 (2010 projected); Race: 98.4% White, 0.0% Black, 0.0% Asian, 1.6% Hispanic of any race (2005); Density: 2,655.5 persons per square mile (2005); Average household size: 2.55 (2005); Median age: 37.3 (2005); Males per 100 females: 112.4 (2005); Marriage status: 20.3% never married, 66.2% now married, 6.8% widowed, 6.8% divorced (2000); Foreign born: 0.0% (2000); Ancestry (includes multiple ancestries): 33.5% German, 18.0% English, 16.8% Irish, 5.6% Other groups, 3.1% Dutch (2000).
Economy: Employment by occupation: 10.5% management, 9.3% professional, 19.8% services, 15.1% sales, 0.0% farming, 10.5% construction, 34.9% production (2000).
Income: Per capita income: $15,966 (2005); Median household income: $34,375 (2005); Average household income: $40,777 (2005); Percent of households with income of $100,000 or more: 2.7% (2005); Poverty rate: 11.2% (2000).
Education: Percent of population age 25 and over with: High school diploma (including GED) or higher: 77.9% (2005); Bachelor's degree or higher: 8.2% (2005); Master's degree or higher: 0.0% (2005).

School District(s)
West Holmes Local SD (KG-12)
   2003-04 Enrollment: 2,805 . . . . (330) 674-3546

Housing: Homeownership rate: 82.4% (2005); Median home value: $69,375 (2005); Median rent: $356 per month (2000); Median age of housing: 60+ years (2000).
Transportation: Commute to work: 90.7% car, 0.0% public transportation, 9.3% walk, 0.0% work from home (2000); Travel time to work: 12.8% less than 15 minutes, 33.7% 15 to 30 minutes, 48.8% 30 to 45 minutes, 4.7% 45 to 60 minutes, 0.0% 60 minutes or more (2000)

Huron County

Located in northern Ohio; drained by the Huron and Vermilion Rivers. Covers a land area of 492.69 square miles, a water area of 1.83 square miles, and is located in the Eastern Time Zone. The county government was organized in 1815. County seat is Norwalk.

Huron County is part of the Norwalk, OH Micropolitan Statistical Area. The entire metro area includes: Huron County, OH

Weather Station: Norwalk WWTP   Elevation: 669 feet

	Jan	Feb	Mar	Apr	May	Jun	Jul	Aug	Sep	Oct	Nov	Dec
High	32	35	45	58	69	79	83	81	74	62	49	38
Low	16	19	27	37	48	57	62	60	52	41	33	23
Precip	2.2	1.8	2.7	3.3	3.5	4.2	3.7	3.8	3.2	2.4	3.0	2.8
Snow	8.6	6.2	4.8	0.8	tr	0.0	0.0	tr	0.0	tr	0.9	5.4

High and Low temperatures in degrees Fahrenheit; Precipitation and Snow in inches

Population: 56,101 (1990); 59,487 (2000); 60,669 (2005); 61,888 (2010 projected); Race: 95.7% White, 0.8% Black, 0.4% Asian, 4.1% Hispanic of any race (2005); Density: 123.1 persons per square mile (2005); Average household size: 2.63 (2005); Median age: 36.0 (2005); Males per 100 females: 96.2 (2005).
Religion: Five largest groups: 25.1% Catholic Church, 6.6% The United Methodist Church, 4.9% Evangelical Lutheran Church in America, 1.9% The Christian and Missionary Alliance, 1.4% United Church of Christ (2000).
Economy: Unemployment rate: 7.7% (2005); Total civilian labor force: 30,354 (2005); Leading industries: 39.8% manufacturing; 12.2% retail trade; 11.0% health care and social assistance (2004); Farms: 865 totaling 228,346 acres (2002); Companies that employ 500 or more persons: 5 (2004); Companies that employ 100 to 499 persons: 26 (2004); Companies that employ less than 100 persons: 1,203 (2004); Black-owned businesses: n/a (2002); Hispanic-owned businesses: n/a (2002); Women-owned businesses: 1,141 (2002); Retail sales per capita: $10,977 (2006). Single-family building permits issued: 124 (2005); Multi-family building permits issued: 42 (2005).
Income: Per capita income: $20,032 (2005); Median household income: $44,494 (2005); Average household income: $52,450 (2005); Percent of households with income of $100,000 or more: 8.4% (2005); Poverty rate: 9.0% (2003); Bankruptcy rate: 12.65% (2005).
Taxes: Total county taxes per capita: $202 (2004); County property taxes per capita: $77 (2004).

Education: Percent of population age 25 and over with: High school diploma (including GED) or higher: 81.0% (2005); Bachelor's degree or higher: 10.8% (2005); Master's degree or higher: 3.3% (2005).
Housing: Homeownership rate: 72.4% (2005); Median home value: $118,433 (2005); Median rent: $370 per month (2000); Median age of housing: 40 years (2000).
Health: Birth rate: 145.1 per 10,000 population (2004); Death rate: 82.8 per 10,000 population (2004); Age-adjusted cancer mortality rate: 187.2 deaths per 100,000 population (2002); Number of physicians: 16.3 per 10,000 population (2004); Hospital beds: 35.4 per 10,000 population (2003); Hospital admissions: 1,263.6 per 10,000 population (2003).
Elections: 2004 Presidential election results: 58.0% Bush, 41.3% Kerry, 0.0% Nader, 0.3% Badnarik

Additional Information Contacts

Huron County Government	(419) 668-3092
http://www.hccommissioners.com/	
City of Norwalk	(419) 663-6700
http://www.norwalkoh.com	
City of Willard	(419) 933-2591
http://www.willardohio.com	
Norwalk Chamber of Commerce	(419) 668-4155
http://www.norwalkareachamber.com	
Village of Monroeville	(419) 465-4443
http://www.monroevilleohio.com	
Village of New London	(419) 929-4091
http://www.newlondonohio.com	
Willard Chamber of Commerce	(419) 935-1888
http://www.willardohio.com	

Huron County Communities

COLLINS (unincorporated postal area, zip code 44826). Covers a land area of 30.599 square miles and a water area of 0 square miles. Located at 41.22° N. Lat.; 82.48° W. Long. Elevation is 885 feet.
Population: 1,733 (2000); Race: 99.0% White, 0.0% Black, 0.3% Asian, 0.8% Hispanic of any race (2000); Density: 56.6 persons per square mile (2000); Age: 25.5% under 18, 15.2% over 64 (2000); Marriage status: 22.5% never married, 62.7% now married, 7.7% widowed, 7.1% divorced (2000); Foreign born: 1.6% (2000); Ancestry (includes multiple ancestries): 32.7% German, 15.1% English, 11.5% Irish, 7.6% United States or American, 6.5% Other groups (2000).
Economy: Employment by occupation: 11.2% management, 12.6% professional, 8.5% services, 21.3% sales, 0.0% farming, 19.6% construction, 26.9% production (2000).
Income: Per capita income: $18,648 (2000); Median household income: $40,573 (2000); Poverty rate: 7.2% (2000).
Education: Percent of population age 25 and over with: High school diploma (including GED) or higher: 83.1% (2000); Bachelor's degree or higher: 6.3% (2000).

School District(s)

Western Reserve Local SD (PK-12)
 2003-04 Enrollment: 1,404 . . . . (419) 660-8508

Housing: Homeownership rate: 91.4% (2000); Median home value: $112,500 (2000); Median rent: $350 per month (2000); Median age of housing: 40 years (2000).
Transportation: Commute to work: 98.6% car, 0.0% public transportation, 0.5% walk, 0.5% work from home (2000); Travel time to work: 30.9% less than 15 minutes, 30.1% 15 to 30 minutes, 23.2% 30 to 45 minutes, 12.5% 45 to 60 minutes, 3.3% 60 minutes or more (2000)

GREENWICH (village). Covers a land area of 1.357 square miles and a water area of 0.017 square miles. Located at 41.03° N. Lat.; 82.51° W. Long. Elevation is 1,030 feet.
History: Greenwich was incorporated in 1879 and named for the town in Connecticut.
Population: 1,442 (1990); 1,525 (2000); 1,538 (2005); 1,564 (2010 projected); Race: 98.2% White, 0.0% Black, 0.1% Asian, 0.8% Hispanic of any race (2005); Density: 1,133.6 persons per square mile (2005); Average household size: 2.59 (2005); Median age: 34.4 (2005); Males per 100 females: 91.5 (2005); Marriage status: 25.0% never married, 56.3% now married, 9.1% widowed, 9.7% divorced (2000); Foreign born: 0.3% (2000); Ancestry (includes multiple ancestries): 23.0% German, 14.5% English, 11.4% United States or American, 9.4% Other groups, 6.4% Irish (2000).
Economy: Single-family building permits issued: 2 (2005); Multi-family building permits issued: 0 (2005); Employment by occupation: 8.0% management, 10.1% professional, 11.3% services, 20.1% sales, 1.4% farming, 9.4% construction, 39.7% production (2000).
Income: Per capita income: $15,138 (2005); Median household income: $34,000 (2005); Average household income: $39,196 (2005); Percent of households with income of $100,000 or more: 2.7% (2005); Poverty rate: 10.1% (2000).
Education: Percent of population age 25 and over with: High school diploma (including GED) or higher: 75.5% (2005); Bachelor's degree or higher: 5.4% (2005); Master's degree or higher: 1.5% (2005).

School District(s)

South Central Local SD (PK-12)
 2003-04 Enrollment: 976 . . . . (419) 752-3815

Housing: Homeownership rate: 71.5% (2005); Median home value: $95,794 (2005); Median rent: $325 per month (2000); Median age of housing: 46 years (2000).
Transportation: Commute to work: 95.2% car, 0.7% public transportation, 1.6% walk, 2.4% work from home (2000); Travel time to work: 25.7% less than 15 minutes, 46.0% 15 to 30 minutes, 20.0% 30 to 45 minutes, 5.2% 45 to 60 minutes, 3.1% 60 minutes or more (2000)

MONROEVILLE (village). Covers a land area of 1.431 square miles and a water area of 0 square miles. Located at 41.24° N. Lat.; 82.69° W. Long. Elevation is 723 feet.
Population: 1,387 (1990); 1,433 (2000); 1,487 (2005); 1,543 (2010 projected); Race: 98.5% White, 0.1% Black, 0.0% Asian, 0.8% Hispanic of any race (2005); Density: 1,039.0 persons per square mile (2005); Average household size: 2.69 (2005); Median age: 33.5 (2005); Males per 100 females: 97.2 (2005); Marriage status: 27.2% never married, 55.9% now married, 6.4% widowed, 10.5% divorced (2000); Foreign born: 0.3% (2000); Ancestry (includes multiple ancestries): 43.7% German, 12.5% Irish, 10.8% United States or American, 8.6% English, 4.5% Other groups (2000).
Economy: Single-family building permits issued: 0 (2005); Multi-family building permits issued: 0 (2005); Employment by occupation: 7.0% management, 9.3% professional, 12.3% services, 19.2% sales, 0.0% farming, 11.7% construction, 40.5% production (2000).
Income: Per capita income: $19,919 (2005); Median household income: $48,109 (2005); Average household income: $52,807 (2005); Percent of households with income of $100,000 or more: 7.8% (2005); Poverty rate: 3.8% (2000).
Education: Percent of population age 25 and over with: High school diploma (including GED) or higher: 86.6% (2005); Bachelor's degree or higher: 9.1% (2005); Master's degree or higher: 2.6% (2005).

School District(s)

Monroeville Local SD (PK-12)
 2003-04 Enrollment: 775 . . . . (419) 465-2610
Willard City SD (PK-12)
 2003-04 Enrollment: 2,362 . . . . (419) 935-1541

Housing: Homeownership rate: 65.6% (2005); Median home value: $115,576 (2005); Median rent: $362 per month (2000); Median age of housing: 60+ years (2000).
Transportation: Commute to work: 95.0% car, 0.0% public transportation, 2.2% walk, 2.4% work from home (2000); Travel time to work: 47.8% less than 15 minutes, 36.3% 15 to 30 minutes, 10.1% 30 to 45 minutes, 2.7% 45 to 60 minutes, 3.1% 60 minutes or more (2000)

Additional Information Contacts

Village of Monroeville . . . . (419) 465-4443
 http://www.monroevilleohio.com

NEW LONDON (village). Covers a land area of 2.103 square miles and a water area of 0.404 square miles. Located at 41.08° N. Lat.; 82.39° W. Long. Elevation is 980 feet.
History: New London was settled in 1816 and developed as a rural trading and shipping center. The C.E. Ward Company was established here to produce band uniforms, graduation caps and gowns, church vestments, and other regalia for a worldwide market.
Population: 2,765 (1990); 2,696 (2000); 2,642 (2005); 2,608 (2010 projected); Race: 96.5% White, 2.0% Black, 0.2% Asian, 0.9% Hispanic of any race (2005); Density: 1,256.1 persons per square mile (2005); Average household size: 2.57 (2005); Median age: 35.0 (2005); Males per 100 females: 94.4 (2005); Marriage status: 22.9% never married, 57.8% now married, 7.9% widowed, 11.5% divorced (2000); Foreign born: 0.1% (2000); Ancestry (includes multiple ancestries): 22.1% German, 12.0% Other groups, 12.0% Irish, 11.6% English, 11.2% United States or American (2000).

Economy: Single-family building permits issued: 8 (2005); Multi-family building permits issued: 0 (2005); Employment by occupation: 6.2% management, 17.4% professional, 14.3% services, 17.2% sales, 0.3% farming, 13.3% construction, 31.2% production (2000).
Income: Per capita income: $16,539 (2005); Median household income: $36,071 (2005); Average household income: $41,670 (2005); Percent of households with income of $100,000 or more: 4.3% (2005); Poverty rate: 10.7% (2000).
Education: Percent of population age 25 and over with: High school diploma (including GED) or higher: 76.2% (2005); Bachelor's degree or higher: 10.5% (2005); Master's degree or higher: 4.5% (2005).

School District(s)
New London Local SD (PK-12)
   2003-04 Enrollment: 1,216 . . . . (419) 929-8433

Housing: Homeownership rate: 67.2% (2005); Median home value: $89,524 (2005); Median rent: $320 per month (2000); Median age of housing: 42 years (2000).
Newspapers: New London Record (General - Circulation 3,000)
Transportation: Commute to work: 91.0% car, 0.3% public transportation, 6.0% walk, 0.7% work from home (2000); Travel time to work: 38.4% less than 15 minutes, 24.1% 15 to 30 minutes, 16.3% 30 to 45 minutes, 10.9% 45 to 60 minutes, 10.2% 60 minutes or more (2000)

Additional Information Contacts
Village of New London . . . . (419) 929-4091
   http://www.newlondonohio.com

NORTH FAIRFIELD
(village). Covers a land area of 0.466 square miles and a water area of 0 square miles. Located at 41.10° N. Lat.; 82.61° W. Long. Elevation is 932 feet.

Population: 504 (1990); 573 (2000); 589 (2005); 594 (2010 projected); Race: 95.4% White, 0.0% Black, 0.7% Asian, 8.0% Hispanic of any race (2005); Density: 1,263.5 persons per square mile (2005); Average household size: 3.15 (2005); Median age: 30.1 (2005); Males per 100 females: 111.9 (2005); Marriage status: 24.3% never married, 64.1% now married, 3.9% widowed, 7.6% divorced (2000); Foreign born: 0.7% (2000); Ancestry (includes multiple ancestries): 22.4% German, 14.0% Irish, 12.0% Other groups, 7.7% English, 6.3% United States or American (2000).
Economy: Single-family building permits issued: 0 (2005); Multi-family building permits issued: 0 (2005); Employment by occupation: 3.4% management, 2.3% professional, 14.5% services, 22.1% sales, 0.0% farming, 9.5% construction, 48.1% production (2000).
Income: Per capita income: $18,471 (2005); Median household income: $48,500 (2005); Average household income: $56,270 (2005); Percent of households with income of $100,000 or more: 7.5% (2005); Poverty rate: 9.9% (2000).
Education: Percent of population age 25 and over with: High school diploma (including GED) or higher: 71.5% (2005); Bachelor's degree or higher: 2.6% (2005); Master's degree or higher: 0.6% (2005).
Housing: Homeownership rate: 87.2% (2005); Median home value: $85,152 (2005); Median rent: $331 per month (2000); Median age of housing: 60+ years (2000).
Transportation: Commute to work: 96.1% car, 0.0% public transportation, 0.8% walk, 2.3% work from home (2000); Travel time to work: 4.3% less than 15 minutes, 64.8% 15 to 30 minutes, 19.4% 30 to 45 minutes, 9.1% 45 to 60 minutes, 2.4% 60 minutes or more (2000)

NORWALK
(city). Covers a land area of 8.326 square miles and a water area of 0.248 square miles. Located at 41.24° N. Lat.; 82.61° W. Long. Elevation is 731 feet.

History: Norwalk was founded in 1816 by Platt Benedict, and named for the Connecticut town which had been the home of many of its first settlers.
Population: 14,920 (1990); 16,238 (2000); 16,330 (2005); 16,485 (2010 projected); Race: 94.2% White, 1.6% Black, 0.6% Asian, 4.5% Hispanic of any race (2005); Density: 1,961.3 persons per square mile (2005); Average household size: 2.52 (2005); Median age: 34.8 (2005); Males per 100 females: 92.6 (2005); Marriage status: 23.5% never married, 55.9% now married, 7.8% widowed, 12.8% divorced (2000); Foreign born: 2.4% (2000); Ancestry (includes multiple ancestries): 34.2% German, 11.2% English, 10.8% Irish, 10.4% Other groups, 9.2% United States or American (2000).
Economy: Single-family building permits issued: 35 (2005); Multi-family building permits issued: 42 (2005); Employment by occupation: 8.5% management, 14.4% professional, 14.4% services, 24.0% sales, 0.6% farming, 7.2% construction, 30.9% production (2000).
Income: Per capita income: $20,241 (2005); Median household income: $40,851 (2005); Average household income: $50,351 (2005); Percent of households with income of $100,000 or more: 8.2% (2005); Poverty rate: 8.8% (2000).
Education: Percent of population age 25 and over with: High school diploma (including GED) or higher: 81.0% (2005); Bachelor's degree or higher: 14.7% (2005); Master's degree or higher: 4.5% (2005).

School District(s)
Norwalk City SD (PK-12)
   2003-04 Enrollment: 2,952 . . . . (419) 668-2779

Housing: Homeownership rate: 61.9% (2005); Median home value: $117,068 (2005); Median rent: $391 per month (2000); Median age of housing: 40 years (2000).
Hospitals: Fisher-Titus Medical Center (112 beds)
Safety: Violent crime rate: 0.0 per 10,000 population; Property crime rate: 216.6 per 10,000 population (2004).
Newspapers: Norwalk Reflector (Circulation 8,713)
Transportation: Commute to work: 92.8% car, 0.5% public transportation, 3.2% walk, 1.9% work from home (2000); Travel time to work: 59.2% less than 15 minutes, 23.7% 15 to 30 minutes, 9.5% 30 to 45 minutes, 3.9% 45 to 60 minutes, 3.6% 60 minutes or more (2000)

Additional Information Contacts
City of Norwalk . . . . (419) 663-6700
   http://www.norwalkoh.com
Norwalk Chamber of Commerce . . . . (419) 668-4155
   http://www.norwalkareachamber.com

WAKEMAN
(village). Covers a land area of 0.795 square miles and a water area of 0.004 square miles. Located at 41.25° N. Lat.; 82.40° W. Long. Elevation is 856 feet.

History: Wakeman was the home of the C.S. Clark Seed Company, founded in 1878 and specializing in varieties of seed corn.
Population: 948 (1990); 951 (2000); 945 (2005); 950 (2010 projected); Race: 98.9% White, 0.0% Black, 0.0% Asian, 1.2% Hispanic of any race (2005); Density: 1,188.4 persons per square mile (2005); Average household size: 2.60 (2005); Median age: 37.4 (2005); Males per 100 females: 98.5 (2005); Marriage status: 19.5% never married, 60.6% now married, 6.6% widowed, 13.2% divorced (2000); Foreign born: 1.5% (2000); Ancestry (includes multiple ancestries): 30.8% German, 16.0% Irish, 13.7% English, 9.3% United States or American, 9.1% Other groups (2000).
Economy: Single-family building permits issued: 5 (2005); Multi-family building permits issued: 0 (2005); Employment by occupation: 6.6% management, 15.4% professional, 12.7% services, 17.4% sales, 1.0% farming, 14.1% construction, 32.8% production (2000).
Income: Per capita income: $20,942 (2005); Median household income: $51,225 (2005); Average household income: $54,368 (2005); Percent of households with income of $100,000 or more: 8.8% (2005); Poverty rate: 3.2% (2000).
Education: Percent of population age 25 and over with: High school diploma (including GED) or higher: 84.6% (2005); Bachelor's degree or higher: 10.0% (2005); Master's degree or higher: 3.9% (2005).
Housing: Homeownership rate: 78.3% (2005); Median home value: $121,154 (2005); Median rent: $431 per month (2000); Median age of housing: 51 years (2000).
Transportation: Commute to work: 93.3% car, 0.0% public transportation, 4.0% walk, 1.7% work from home (2000); Travel time to work: 18.2% less than 15 minutes, 38.1% 15 to 30 minutes, 26.1% 30 to 45 minutes, 9.4% 45 to 60 minutes, 8.1% 60 minutes or more (2000)

WILLARD
(city). Covers a land area of 3.467 square miles and a water area of 0.026 square miles. Located at 41.05° N. Lat.; 82.72° W. Long. Elevation is 955 feet.

Population: 6,263 (1990); 6,806 (2000); 6,864 (2005); 6,959 (2010 projected); Race: 89.5% White, 1.3% Black, 0.5% Asian, 14.5% Hispanic of any race (2005); Density: 1,979.8 persons per square mile (2005); Average household size: 2.65 (2005); Median age: 32.9 (2005); Males per 100 females: 90.7 (2005); Marriage status: 24.3% never married, 53.7% now married, 8.6% widowed, 13.4% divorced (2000); Foreign born: 4.8% (2000); Ancestry (includes multiple ancestries): 21.8% German, 16.6% Other groups, 13.9% United States or American, 10.7% English, 7.2% Irish (2000).
Economy: In fruit, vegetable, and grain area; makes rubber goods, food and dairy products, lumber, burial vaults. Single-family building permits issued: 5 (2005); Multi-family building permits issued: 0 (2005);

Employment by occupation: 4.7% management, 11.9% professional, 14.5% services, 20.2% sales, 1.8% farming, 5.9% construction, 40.9% production (2000).
Income: Per capita income: $14,943 (2005); Median household income: $31,454 (2005); Average household income: $39,306 (2005); Percent of households with income of $100,000 or more: 4.3% (2005); Poverty rate: 16.2% (2000).
Education: Percent of population age 25 and over with: High school diploma (including GED) or higher: 74.4% (2005); Bachelor's degree or higher: 7.7% (2005); Master's degree or higher: 2.4% (2005).

School District(s)

Willard City SD (PK-12)
    2003-04 Enrollment: 2,362 . . . . (419) 935-1541
Housing: Homeownership rate: 56.3% (2005); Median home value: $85,654 (2005); Median rent: $357 per month (2000); Median age of housing: 45 years (2000).
Hospitals: Mercy Hospital of Willard (25 beds)
Newspapers: Willard Times-Junction (General - Circulation 4,200)
Transportation: Commute to work: 92.9% car, 0.4% public transportation, 3.8% walk, 1.9% work from home (2000); Travel time to work: 62.3% less than 15 minutes, 18.8% 15 to 30 minutes, 12.1% 30 to 45 minutes, 4.9% 45 to 60 minutes, 1.8% 60 minutes or more (2000)
Additional Information Contacts
City of Willard. . . . . (419) 933-2591
    http://www.willardohio.com
Willard Chamber of Commerce . . . . (419) 935-1888
    http://www.willardohio.com

Jackson County

Located in southern Ohio; drained by the Little Scioto River. Covers a land area of 420.28 square miles, a water area of 1.22 square miles, and is located in the Eastern Time Zone. The county government was organized in 1816. County seat is Jackson.

Weather Station: Jackson 3 NW   Elevation: 797 feet

	Jan	Feb	Mar	Apr	May	Jun	Jul	Aug	Sep	Oct	Nov	Dec
High	38	43	53	65	74	81	85	83	77	66	54	43
Low	19	22	30	38	48	57	62	60	53	41	32	24
Precip	2.8	2.8	3.8	3.4	4.0	4.1	4.0	3.9	3.2	2.8	3.1	3.3
Snow	na	na	na	0.7	0.0	0.0	0.0	0.0	0.0	0.0	na	na

High and Low temperatures in degrees Fahrenheit; Precipitation and Snow in inches

Population: 30,230 (1990); 32,641 (2000); 33,271 (2005); 33,921 (2010 projected); Race: 97.8% White, 0.7% Black, 0.2% Asian, 0.9% Hispanic of any race (2005); Density: 79.2 persons per square mile (2005); Average household size: 2.56 (2005); Median age: 37.2 (2005); Males per 100 females: 94.0 (2005).
Religion: Five largest groups: 8.5% The United Methodist Church, 8.0% Church of God (Cleveland, Tennessee), 2.5% Church of the Nazarene, 2.0% The Wesleyan Church, 1.9% Presbyterian Church (U.S.A.) (2000).
Economy: Unemployment rate: 7.3% (2005); Total civilian labor force: 15,906 (2005); Leading industries: 33.5% manufacturing; 16.4% retail trade; 15.3% finance & insurance (2004); Farms: 458 totaling 73,800 acres (2002); Companies that employ 500 or more persons: 3 (2004); Companies that employ 100 to 499 persons: 8 (2004); Companies that employ less than 100 persons: 649 (2004); Black-owned businesses: n/a (2002); Hispanic-owned businesses: n/a (2002); Women-owned businesses: 368 (2002); Retail sales per capita: $11,043 (2006). Single-family building permits issued: 89 (2005); Multi-family building permits issued: 0 (2005).
Income: Per capita income: $16,685 (2005); Median household income: $34,322 (2005); Average household income: $42,096 (2005); Percent of households with income of $100,000 or more: 5.6% (2005); Poverty rate: 14.3% (2003); Bankruptcy rate: 8.50% (2005).
Taxes: Total county taxes per capita: $248 (2004); County property taxes per capita: $89 (2004).
Education: Percent of population age 25 and over with: High school diploma (including GED) or higher: 73.3% (2005); Bachelor's degree or higher: 11.0% (2005); Master's degree or higher: 3.9% (2005).
Housing: Homeownership rate: 73.9% (2005); Median home value: $79,605 (2005); Median rent: $284 per month (2000); Median age of housing: 32 years (2000).
Health: Birth rate: 146.7 per 10,000 population (2004); Death rate: 111.2 per 10,000 population (2004); Age-adjusted cancer mortality rate: 217.2 deaths per 100,000 population (2002); Number of physicians: 8.7 per 10,000 population (2004); Hospital beds: 0.0 per 10,000 population (2003); Hospital admissions: 0.0 per 10,000 population (2003).
Elections: 2004 Presidential election results: 59.9% Bush, 39.8% Kerry, 0.0% Nader, 0.2% Badnarik
National and State Parks: Buckeye Furnace State Memorial; Jackson Lake State Reserve; Leo Petroglyph State Memorial; Richland Furnace State Forest
Additional Information Contacts
Jackson County Government. . . . . (740) 286-3301
    http://www.jacksoncountyohio.org
Jackson Chamber of Commerce . . . . (740) 286-2722
    http://www.jacksonohio.org
Jackson-Belden Chamber of Commerce. . . . . (330) 833-4400
    http://www.jbcc.org
Wellston Chamber of Commerce. (740) 384-3051
    http://www.wellstonforum.com/wellston

Jackson County Communities

COALTON (village). Covers a land area of 0.549 square miles and a water area of 0 square miles. Located at 39.11° N. Lat.; 82.61° W. Long. Elevation is 720 feet.
History: During the 1880's, Coalton was a busy coal town.
Population: 553 (1990); 545 (2000); 599 (2005); 652 (2010 projected); Race: 97.0% White, 1.7% Black, 0.3% Asian, 1.3% Hispanic of any race (2005); Density: 1,090.2 persons per square mile (2005); Average household size: 2.57 (2005); Median age: 33.8 (2005); Males per 100 females: 94.5 (2005); Marriage status: 19.4% never married, 60.7% now married, 6.4% widowed, 13.5% divorced (2000); Foreign born: 0.5% (2000); Ancestry (includes multiple ancestries): 22.5% United States or American, 9.8% Other groups, 9.3% Irish, 8.0% German, 4.5% English (2000).
Economy: Single-family building permits issued: 1 (2005); Multi-family building permits issued: 0 (2005); Employment by occupation: 4.8% management, 10.8% professional, 18.3% services, 23.7% sales, 2.7% farming, 8.1% construction, 31.7% production (2000).
Income: Per capita income: $12,195 (2005); Median household income: $26,125 (2005); Average household income: $31,352 (2005); Percent of households with income of $100,000 or more: 3.0% (2005); Poverty rate: 27.5% (2000).
Education: Percent of population age 25 and over with: High school diploma (including GED) or higher: 67.0% (2005); Bachelor's degree or higher: 5.4% (2005); Master's degree or higher: 0.5% (2005).
Housing: Homeownership rate: 61.8% (2005); Median home value: $44,103 (2005); Median rent: $300 per month (2000); Median age of housing: 49 years (2000).
Transportation: Commute to work: 96.2% car, 0.0% public transportation, 1.6% walk, 2.2% work from home (2000); Travel time to work: 40.1% less than 15 minutes, 21.4% 15 to 30 minutes, 8.8% 30 to 45 minutes, 13.7% 45 to 60 minutes, 15.9% 60 minutes or more (2000)

JACKSON (city). Covers a land area of 7.511 square miles and a water area of 0.251 square miles. Located at 39.05° N. Lat.; 82.64° W. Long. Elevation is 680 feet.
History: Jackson was platted in 1817, and grew around the railroad that arrived in 1853. Many of Jackson's early settlers were Welsh who came to farm and later worked in the iron furnaces and coal mines.
Population: 6,351 (1990); 6,184 (2000); 6,204 (2005); 6,231 (2010 projected); Race: 98.1% White, 0.4% Black, 0.3% Asian, 1.4% Hispanic of any race (2005); Density: 826.0 persons per square mile (2005); Average household size: 2.29 (2005); Median age: 37.8 (2005); Males per 100 females: 86.4 (2005); Marriage status: 21.3% never married, 52.8% now married, 11.5% widowed, 14.4% divorced (2000); Foreign born: 2.2% (2000); Ancestry (includes multiple ancestries): 15.8% United States or American, 12.8% German, 8.4% Irish, 7.6% Other groups, 7.0% Welsh (2000).
Economy: Single-family building permits issued: 13 (2005); Multi-family building permits issued: 0 (2005); Employment by occupation: 9.9% management, 20.8% professional, 14.7% services, 25.6% sales, 0.4% farming, 8.1% construction, 20.4% production (2000).
Income: Per capita income: $16,745 (2005); Median household income: $29,840 (2005); Average household income: $38,249 (2005); Percent of households with income of $100,000 or more: 5.3% (2005); Poverty rate: 18.7% (2000).

Taxes: Total city taxes per capita: $281 (2004); City property taxes per capita: $84 (2004).
Education: Percent of population age 25 and over with: High school diploma (including GED) or higher: 72.5% (2005); Bachelor's degree or higher: 13.6% (2005); Master's degree or higher: 4.6% (2005).

School District(s)
Jackson City SD (PK-12)
    2003-04 Enrollment: 2,745 .... (740) 286-6442
Oak Hill Union Local SD (PK-12)
    2003-04 Enrollment: 1,261 .... (740) 682-7595

Two-year College(s)
Southeastern Business College (Private, For-profit)
    Fall 2004 Enrollment: 58 .... (740) 286-1554
    2005-06 Tuition: In-state $8,930; Out-of-state $8,930

Housing: Homeownership rate: 62.2% (2005); Median home value: $91,822 (2005); Median rent: $307 per month (2000); Median age of housing: 46 years (2000).
Newspapers: The Times-Journal (General - Circulation 9,200)
Transportation: Commute to work: 93.5% car, 0.0% public transportation, 3.9% walk, 1.6% work from home (2000); Travel time to work: 57.2% less than 15 minutes, 17.3% 15 to 30 minutes, 13.1% 30 to 45 minutes, 3.9% 45 to 60 minutes, 8.4% 60 minutes or more (2000)

Additional Information Contacts
Jackson Chamber of Commerce .... (740) 286-2722
    http://www.jacksonohio.org
Jackson-Belden Chamber of Commerce .... (330) 833-4400
    http://www.jbcc.org

OAK HILL (village). Covers a land area of 1.143 square miles and a water area of 0 square miles. Located at 38.89° N. Lat.; 82.57° W. Long. Elevation is 708 feet.
Population: 1,831 (1990); 1,685 (2000); 1,721 (2005); 1,758 (2010 projected); Race: 98.2% White, 0.2% Black, 0.3% Asian, 0.1% Hispanic of any race (2005); Density: 1,506.0 persons per square mile (2005); Average household size: 2.45 (2005); Median age: 36.1 (2005); Males per 100 females: 85.3 (2005); Marriage status: 22.2% never married, 54.0% now married, 11.3% widowed, 12.4% divorced (2000); Foreign born: 0.6% (2000); Ancestry (includes multiple ancestries): 19.4% United States or American, 15.4% German, 10.4% Welsh, 9.1% Irish, 7.5% Other groups (2000).
Economy: Forest area. Single-family building permits issued: 0 (2005); Multi-family building permits issued: 0 (2005); Employment by occupation: 7.9% management, 17.7% professional, 19.1% services, 19.8% sales, 2.4% farming, 8.6% construction, 24.4% production (2000).
Income: Per capita income: $16,331 (2005); Median household income: $31,318 (2005); Average household income: $39,481 (2005); Percent of households with income of $100,000 or more: 4.1% (2005); Poverty rate: 20.6% (2000).
Education: Percent of population age 25 and over with: High school diploma (including GED) or higher: 74.5% (2005); Bachelor's degree or higher: 13.5% (2005); Master's degree or higher: 4.8% (2005).

School District(s)
Oak Hill Union Local SD (PK-12)
    2003-04 Enrollment: 1,261 .... (740) 682-7595

Housing: Homeownership rate: 65.7% (2005); Median home value: $63,371 (2005); Median rent: $280 per month (2000); Median age of housing: 47 years (2000).
Transportation: Commute to work: 92.4% car, 1.1% public transportation, 4.5% walk, 1.4% work from home (2000); Travel time to work: 34.0% less than 15 minutes, 33.3% 15 to 30 minutes, 15.3% 30 to 45 minutes, 9.0% 45 to 60 minutes, 8.4% 60 minutes or more (2000)

WELLSTON (city). Covers a land area of 6.967 square miles and a water area of 0.083 square miles. Located at 39.12° N. Lat.; 82.53° W. Long. Elevation is 720 feet.
History: Wellston was named for Harvey Wells, who constructed a blast furnace in 1874 and platted a town around it.
Population: 6,062 (1990); 6,078 (2000); 5,998 (2005); 5,894 (2010 projected); Race: 97.9% White, 0.5% Black, 0.2% Asian, 0.9% Hispanic of any race (2005); Density: 860.9 persons per square mile (2005); Average household size: 2.55 (2005); Median age: 35.7 (2005); Males per 100 females: 90.6 (2005); Marriage status: 20.7% never married, 53.1% now married, 12.4% widowed, 13.8% divorced (2000); Foreign born: 0.8% (2000); Ancestry (includes multiple ancestries): 19.3% German, 14.7% United States or American, 12.1% Irish, 9.2% Other groups, 7.8% English (2000).
Economy: Single-family building permits issued: 6 (2005); Multi-family building permits issued: 0 (2005); Employment by occupation: 5.8% management, 14.2% professional, 16.8% services, 18.3% sales, 0.3% farming, 14.5% construction, 30.1% production (2000).
Income: Per capita income: $14,889 (2005); Median household income: $32,356 (2005); Average household income: $36,994 (2005); Percent of households with income of $100,000 or more: 3.2% (2005); Poverty rate: 18.8% (2000).
Education: Percent of population age 25 and over with: High school diploma (including GED) or higher: 72.3% (2005); Bachelor's degree or higher: 8.9% (2005); Master's degree or higher: 2.6% (2005).

School District(s)
Wellston City Schools (PK-12)
    2003-04 Enrollment: 1,854 .... (740) 384-2152

Housing: Homeownership rate: 66.1% (2005); Median home value: $65,511 (2005); Median rent: $259 per month (2000); Median age of housing: 43 years (2000).
Safety: Violent crime rate: 41.6 per 10,000 population; Property crime rate: 629.4 per 10,000 population (2004).
Newspapers: The Telegram (General - Circulation 6,200)
Transportation: Commute to work: 95.9% car, 0.0% public transportation, 1.0% walk, 3.1% work from home (2000); Travel time to work: 41.7% less than 15 minutes, 20.4% 15 to 30 minutes, 12.8% 30 to 45 minutes, 9.3% 45 to 60 minutes, 15.8% 60 minutes or more (2000)

Additional Information Contacts
Wellston Chamber of Commerce .... (740) 384-3051
    http://www.wellstonforum.com/wellston

Jefferson County

Located in eastern Ohio; bounded on the east by the Ohio River and the West Virginia border; drained by Yellow and Cross Creeks. Covers a land area of 409.61 square miles, a water area of 1.27 square miles, and is located in the Eastern Time Zone. The county government was organized in 1797. County seat is Steubenville.

Jefferson County is part of the Weirton-Steubenville, WV-OH Metropolitan Statistical Area. The entire metro area includes: Jefferson County, OH; Brooke County, WV; Hancock County, WV

Weather Station: Steubenville   Elevation: 990 feet

	Jan	Feb	Mar	Apr	May	Jun	Jul	Aug	Sep	Oct	Nov	Dec
High	36	40	51	62	72	80	83	82	76	64	52	42
Low	20	23	30	39	50	58	63	62	55	43	35	26
Precip	2.8	2.4	3.3	3.2	4.0	4.5	4.2	3.7	3.3	2.6	3.4	3.0
Snow	na	na	na	tr	0.0	0.0	0.0	0.0	0.0	0.2	0.3	na

High and Low temperatures in degrees Fahrenheit; Precipitation and Snow in inches

Population: 80,298 (1990); 73,894 (2000); 71,178 (2005); 68,466 (2010 projected); Race: 92.5% White, 5.6% Black, 0.5% Asian, 0.7% Hispanic of any race (2005); Density: 173.8 persons per square mile (2005); Average household size: 2.39 (2005); Median age: 42.6 (2005); Males per 100 females: 91.2 (2005).
Religion: Five largest groups: 19.9% Catholic Church, 9.2% The United Methodist Church, 3.3% Presbyterian Church (U.S.A.), 2.3% Christian Churches and Churches of Christ, 1.1% Serbian Orthodox Church in the USA (2000).
Economy: Unemployment rate: 7.6% (2005); Total civilian labor force: 31,522 (2005); Leading industries: 18.1% administration (2004); Farms: 461 totaling 67,231 acres (2002); Companies that employ 500 or more persons: 4 (2004); Companies that employ 100 to 499 persons: 20 (2004); Companies that employ less than 100 persons: 1,483 (2004); Black-owned businesses: n/a (2002); Hispanic-owned businesses: n/a (2002); Women-owned businesses: 848 (2002); Retail sales per capita: $11,685 (2006). Single-family building permits issued: 7 (2005); Multi-family building permits issued: 4 (2005).
Income: Per capita income: $18,871 (2005); Median household income: $34,611 (2005); Average household income: $44,385 (2005); Percent of households with income of $100,000 or more: 6.7% (2005); Poverty rate: 13.6% (2003); Bankruptcy rate: 12.25% (2005).
Taxes: Total county taxes per capita: $247 (2004); County property taxes per capita: $121 (2004).

Education: Percent of population age 25 and over with: High school diploma (including GED) or higher: 81.7% (2005); Bachelor's degree or higher: 11.9% (2005); Master's degree or higher: 4.2% (2005).
Housing: Homeownership rate: 74.6% (2005); Median home value: $74,740 (2005); Median rent: $281 per month (2000); Median age of housing: 45 years (2000).
Health: Birth rate: 98.5 per 10,000 population (2004); Death rate: 138.7 per 10,000 population (2004); Age-adjusted cancer mortality rate: 233.6 deaths per 100,000 population (2002); Air Quality Index: 41.1% good, 50.7% moderate, 7.7% unhealthy for sensitive individuals, 0.5% unhealthy (percent of days in 2005); Number of physicians: 15.1 per 10,000 population (2004); Hospital beds: 47.1 per 10,000 population (2003); Hospital admissions: 1,746.6 per 10,000 population (2003).
Elections: 2004 Presidential election results: 47.2% Bush, 52.3% Kerry, 0.0% Nader, 0.2% Badnarik
National and State Parks: Fernwood State Forest; Jefferson Lake State Park
Additional Information Contacts
Jefferson County Government . . . . (740) 283-8500
  http://www.jeffersoncountyoh.com/
City of Steubenville . . . . (740) 283-6000
  http://www.ci.steubenville.oh.us
Steubenville Chamber of Commerce . . . . (740) 282-6226
  http://www.jeffersoncountychamber.com

Jefferson County Communities

ADENA (village). Covers a land area of 0.538 square miles and a water area of 0 square miles. Located at 40.21° N. Lat.; 80.87° W. Long. Elevation is 884 feet.
Population: 842 (1990); 815 (2000); 755 (2005); 725 (2010 projected); Race: 98.1% White, 1.2% Black, 0.1% Asian, 0.0% Hispanic of any race (2005); Density: 1,403.4 persons per square mile (2005); Average household size: 2.29 (2005); Median age: 43.8 (2005); Males per 100 females: 89.2 (2005); Marriage status: 18.5% never married, 62.8% now married, 10.4% widowed, 8.2% divorced (2000); Foreign born: 1.1% (2000); Ancestry (includes multiple ancestries): 30.1% Polish, 13.1% German, 10.5% Italian, 10.4% Irish, 9.6% United States or American (2000).
Economy: Single-family building permits issued: 0 (2005); Multi-family building permits issued: 0 (2005); Employment by occupation: 7.6% management, 13.5% professional, 15.9% services, 32.7% sales, 0.0% farming, 16.5% construction, 13.8% production (2000).
Income: Per capita income: $18,358 (2005); Median household income: $31,290 (2005); Average household income: $42,000 (2005); Percent of households with income of $100,000 or more: 7.0% (2005); Poverty rate: 20.6% (2000).
Education: Percent of population age 25 and over with: High school diploma (including GED) or higher: 80.3% (2005); Bachelor's degree or higher: 6.9% (2005); Master's degree or higher: 2.4% (2005).
School District(s)
Buckeye Local SD (PK-12)
  2003-04 Enrollment: 2,415 . . . . (740) 769-7395
Housing: Homeownership rate: 82.1% (2005); Median home value: $48,830 (2005); Median rent: $217 per month (2000); Median age of housing: 60+ years (2000).
Transportation: Commute to work: 91.8% car, 0.0% public transportation, 5.4% walk, 1.6% work from home (2000); Travel time to work: 20.5% less than 15 minutes, 21.2% 15 to 30 minutes, 41.3% 30 to 45 minutes, 7.1% 45 to 60 minutes, 9.9% 60 minutes or more (2000)

AMSTERDAM (village). Covers a land area of 0.315 square miles and a water area of 0 square miles. Located at 40.47° N. Lat.; 80.92° W. Long. Elevation is 960 feet.
History: Settled 1830, incorporated 1904.
Population: 669 (1990); 568 (2000); 540 (2005); 512 (2010 projected); Race: 98.1% White, 0.2% Black, 0.0% Asian, 0.2% Hispanic of any race (2005); Density: 1,716.5 persons per square mile (2005); Average household size: 2.41 (2005); Median age: 35.5 (2005); Males per 100 females: 92.9 (2005); Marriage status: 19.3% never married, 63.1% now married, 8.9% widowed, 8.7% divorced (2000); Foreign born: 0.3% (2000); Ancestry (includes multiple ancestries): 22.8% German, 16.1% English, 15.9% Irish, 9.2% Polish, 7.0% Other groups (2000).
Economy: Employment by occupation: 1.6% management, 8.1% professional, 20.0% services, 16.8% sales, 1.1% farming, 18.4% construction, 34.1% production (2000).
Income: Per capita income: $14,273 (2005); Median household income: $28,043 (2005); Average household income: $34,408 (2005); Percent of households with income of $100,000 or more: 3.1% (2005); Poverty rate: 23.7% (2000).
Education: Percent of population age 25 and over with: High school diploma (including GED) or higher: 73.7% (2005); Bachelor's degree or higher: 4.1% (2005); Master's degree or higher: 0.9% (2005).
Housing: Homeownership rate: 69.2% (2005); Median home value: $50,339 (2005); Median rent: $258 per month (2000); Median age of housing: 60+ years (2000).
Transportation: Commute to work: 95.6% car, 0.0% public transportation, 1.1% walk, 3.3% work from home (2000); Travel time to work: 10.9% less than 15 minutes, 24.1% 15 to 30 minutes, 31.0% 30 to 45 minutes, 17.8% 45 to 60 minutes, 16.1% 60 minutes or more (2000)

BERGHOLZ (village). Covers a land area of 0.556 square miles and a water area of 0 square miles. Located at 40.52° N. Lat.; 80.88° W. Long. Elevation is 900 feet.
History: Settled 1885, incorporated 1906.
Population: 713 (1990); 769 (2000); 689 (2005); 663 (2010 projected); Race: 98.3% White, 0.4% Black, 0.4% Asian, 0.1% Hispanic of any race (2005); Density: 1,239.7 persons per square mile (2005); Average household size: 2.58 (2005); Median age: 38.5 (2005); Males per 100 females: 90.9 (2005); Marriage status: 27.4% never married, 56.9% now married, 7.9% widowed, 7.8% divorced (2000); Foreign born: 0.6% (2000); Ancestry (includes multiple ancestries): 14.3% Irish, 13.4% German, 10.3% United States or American, 7.8% English, 6.5% Italian (2000).
Economy: Lumber, metal stampings. Employment by occupation: 5.8% management, 10.8% professional, 19.8% services, 28.5% sales, 2.9% farming, 11.9% construction, 20.3% production (2000).
Income: Per capita income: $18,922 (2005); Median household income: $39,573 (2005); Average household income: $48,764 (2005); Percent of households with income of $100,000 or more: 10.1% (2005); Poverty rate: 16.2% (2000).
Education: Percent of population age 25 and over with: High school diploma (including GED) or higher: 75.9% (2005); Bachelor's degree or higher: 11.2% (2005); Master's degree or higher: 5.0% (2005).
School District(s)
Edison Local SD (PK-12)
  2003-04 Enrollment: 2,689 . . . . (330) 532-3199
Housing: Homeownership rate: 76.4% (2005); Median home value: $63,704 (2005); Median rent: $237 per month (2000); Median age of housing: 59 years (2000).
Transportation: Commute to work: 96.2% car, 0.0% public transportation, 2.3% walk, 0.6% work from home (2000); Travel time to work: 29.0% less than 15 minutes, 14.1% 15 to 30 minutes, 20.8% 30 to 45 minutes, 14.1% 45 to 60 minutes, 22.0% 60 minutes or more (2000)

BLOOMINGDALE (village). Covers a land area of 0.108 square miles and a water area of 0 square miles. Located at 40.34° N. Lat.; 80.81° W. Long. Elevation is 1,277 feet.
History: Laid out 1816. Also called Bloomfield.
Population: 227 (1990); 221 (2000); 222 (2005); 214 (2010 projected); Race: 97.7% White, 0.0% Black, 0.9% Asian, 0.0% Hispanic of any race (2005); Density: 2,064.2 persons per square mile (2005); Average household size: 2.64 (2005); Median age: 39.2 (2005); Males per 100 females: 88.1 (2005); Marriage status: 22.1% never married, 60.5% now married, 9.2% widowed, 8.2% divorced (2000); Foreign born: 0.0% (2000); Ancestry (includes multiple ancestries): 32.3% German, 23.7% Irish, 18.5% English, 9.5% United States or American, 7.3% Italian (2000).
Economy: Single-family building permits issued: 0 (2005); Multi-family building permits issued: 0 (2005); Employment by occupation: 2.6% management, 5.3% professional, 17.5% services, 22.8% sales, 0.0% farming, 18.4% construction, 33.3% production (2000).
Income: Per capita income: $19,764 (2005); Median household income: $54,286 (2005); Average household income: $52,232 (2005); Percent of households with income of $100,000 or more: 7.1% (2005); Poverty rate: 4.3% (2000).
Education: Percent of population age 25 and over with: High school diploma (including GED) or higher: 86.0% (2005); Bachelor's degree or higher: 12.7% (2005); Master's degree or higher: 3.3% (2005).

School District(s)
Indian Creek Local SD (PK-12)
　　2003-04 Enrollment: 2,322 . . . . (740) 264-3502
Jefferson County Joint Vocational SD (11-12)
　　2003-04 Enrollment: n/a . . . . (740) 264-5545
Housing: Homeownership rate: 79.8% (2005); Median home value: $72,105 (2005); Median rent: $250 per month (2000); Median age of housing: 60+ years (2000).
Transportation: Commute to work: 91.5% car, 0.0% public transportation, 1.9% walk, 0.9% work from home (2000); Travel time to work: 24.8% less than 15 minutes, 51.4% 15 to 30 minutes, 8.6% 30 to 45 minutes, 6.7% 45 to 60 minutes, 8.6% 60 minutes or more (2000)

BRILLIANT (unincorporated postal area, zip code 43913). Covers a land area of 4.858 square miles and a water area of 0.012 square miles. Located at 40.32° N. Lat.; 80.76° W. Long. Elevation is 700 feet.
Population: 1,728 (2000); Race: 99.5% White, 0.0% Black, 0.0% Asian, 0.0% Hispanic of any race (2000); Density: 355.7 persons per square mile (2000); Age: 22.8% under 18, 16.4% over 64 (2000); Marriage status: 17.7% never married, 62.3% now married, 10.5% widowed, 9.4% divorced (2000); Foreign born: 0.0% (2000); Ancestry (includes multiple ancestries): 17.7% German, 13.3% Irish, 12.4% United States or American, 8.7% English, 6.9% Italian (2000).
Economy: Employment by occupation: 6.8% management, 15.8% professional, 21.3% services, 27.7% sales, 0.0% farming, 9.3% construction, 19.1% production (2000).
Income: Per capita income: $13,091 (2000); Median household income: $26,450 (2000); Poverty rate: 13.1% (2000).
Education: Percent of population age 25 and over with: High school diploma (including GED) or higher: 83.0% (2000); Bachelor's degree or higher: 7.7% (2000).
School District(s)
Buckeye Local SD (PK-12)
　　2003-04 Enrollment: 2,415 . . . . (740) 769-7395
Housing: Homeownership rate: 72.7% (2000); Median home value: $51,800 (2000); Median rent: $241 per month (2000); Median age of housing: 45 years (2000).
Transportation: Commute to work: 91.9% car, 0.5% public transportation, 4.3% walk, 3.0% work from home (2000); Travel time to work: 30.0% less than 15 minutes, 50.9% 15 to 30 minutes, 11.5% 30 to 45 minutes, 3.0% 45 to 60 minutes, 4.7% 60 minutes or more (2000)

DILLONVALE (village). Covers a land area of 0.413 square miles and a water area of 0.009 square miles. Located at 40.19° N. Lat.; 80.77° W. Long. Elevation is 750 feet.
History: Dillonvale grew in the center of a large coal-mining region.
Population: 857 (1990); 781 (2000); 747 (2005); 706 (2010 projected); Race: 98.3% White, 0.7% Black, 0.3% Asian, 0.0% Hispanic of any race (2005); Density: 1,807.3 persons per square mile (2005); Average household size: 2.28 (2005); Median age: 43.1 (2005); Males per 100 females: 90.1 (2005); Marriage status: 24.4% never married, 49.0% now married, 13.6% widowed, 12.9% divorced (2000); Foreign born: 0.0% (2000); Ancestry (includes multiple ancestries): 19.9% Polish, 16.1% Irish, 12.3% Italian, 12.1% German, 7.0% Czech (2000).
Economy: Single-family building permits issued: 0 (2005); Multi-family building permits issued: 0 (2005); Employment by occupation: 5.1% management, 10.2% professional, 19.5% services, 22.2% sales, 0.0% farming, 13.2% construction, 29.7% production (2000).
Income: Per capita income: $19,418 (2005); Median household income: $34,512 (2005); Average household income: $44,223 (2005); Percent of households with income of $100,000 or more: 6.4% (2005); Poverty rate: 11.9% (2000).
Education: Percent of population age 25 and over with: High school diploma (including GED) or higher: 81.1% (2005); Bachelor's degree or higher: 3.9% (2005); Master's degree or higher: 1.7% (2005).
School District(s)
Martins Ferry City SD (PK-12)
　　2003-04 Enrollment: 1,522 . . . . (740) 633-1732
Housing: Homeownership rate: 86.9% (2005); Median home value: $41,444 (2005); Median rent: $268 per month (2000); Median age of housing: 60+ years (2000).
Transportation: Commute to work: 94.6% car, 0.0% public transportation, 4.7% walk, 0.6% work from home (2000); Travel time to work: 20.1% less than 15 minutes, 25.2% 15 to 30 minutes, 37.3% 30 to 45 minutes, 4.8% 45 to 60 minutes, 12.7% 60 minutes or more (2000)

EMPIRE (village). Covers a land area of 0.329 square miles and a water area of 0 square miles. Located at 40.51° N. Lat.; 80.62° W. Long. Elevation is 682 feet.
Population: 364 (1990); 300 (2000); 302 (2005); 303 (2010 projected); Race: 97.0% White, 1.0% Black, 0.0% Asian, 1.3% Hispanic of any race (2005); Density: 919.2 persons per square mile (2005); Average household size: 2.36 (2005); Median age: 34.8 (2005); Males per 100 females: 92.4 (2005); Marriage status: 24.4% never married, 48.7% now married, 10.7% widowed, 16.2% divorced (2000); Foreign born: 0.0% (2000); Ancestry (includes multiple ancestries): 24.3% Irish, 16.0% English, 15.3% German, 10.0% United States or American, 9.3% Other groups (2000).
Economy: Employment by occupation: 3.4% management, 7.6% professional, 18.6% services, 22.9% sales, 0.0% farming, 14.4% construction, 33.1% production (2000).
Income: Per capita income: $12,003 (2005); Median household income: $22,647 (2005); Average household income: $28,320 (2005); Percent of households with income of $100,000 or more: 1.6% (2005); Poverty rate: 16.3% (2000).
Education: Percent of population age 25 and over with: High school diploma (including GED) or higher: 82.3% (2005); Bachelor's degree or higher: 2.6% (2005); Master's degree or higher: 1.6% (2005).
Housing: Homeownership rate: 68.8% (2005); Median home value: $39,949 (2005); Median rent: $273 per month (2000); Median age of housing: 31 years (2000).
Transportation: Commute to work: 98.3% car, 0.0% public transportation, 1.7% walk, 0.0% work from home (2000); Travel time to work: 46.1% less than 15 minutes, 29.6% 15 to 30 minutes, 18.3% 30 to 45 minutes, 2.6% 45 to 60 minutes, 3.5% 60 minutes or more (2000)

HAMMONDSVILLE (unincorporated postal area, zip code 43930). Covers a land area of 27.112 square miles and a water area of 0.025 square miles. Located at 40.56° N. Lat.; 80.76° W. Long. Elevation is 687 feet.
Population: 743 (2000); Race: 100.0% White, 0.0% Black, 0.0% Asian, 0.0% Hispanic of any race (2000); Density: 27.4 persons per square mile (2000); Age: 27.4% under 18, 12.9% over 64 (2000); Marriage status: 21.3% never married, 63.0% now married, 6.9% widowed, 8.8% divorced (2000); Foreign born: 0.3% (2000); Ancestry (includes multiple ancestries): 17.4% German, 13.0% United States or American, 8.7% English, 8.6% Irish, 6.8% Polish (2000).
Economy: Employment by occupation: 6.1% management, 17.2% professional, 16.1% services, 17.7% sales, 1.1% farming, 11.6% construction, 30.2% production (2000).
Income: Per capita income: $15,401 (2000); Median household income: $38,500 (2000); Poverty rate: 8.8% (2000).
Education: Percent of population age 25 and over with: High school diploma (including GED) or higher: 82.4% (2000); Bachelor's degree or higher: 14.3% (2000).
School District(s)
Edison Local SD (PK-12)
　　2003-04 Enrollment: 2,689 . . . . (330) 532-3199
Housing: Homeownership rate: 90.6% (2000); Median home value: $88,800 (2000); Median rent: $n/a per month (2000); Median age of housing: 30 years (2000).
Transportation: Commute to work: 94.7% car, 0.0% public transportation, 0.0% walk, 5.3% work from home (2000); Travel time to work: 12.8% less than 15 minutes, 28.5% 15 to 30 minutes, 33.0% 30 to 45 minutes, 9.5% 45 to 60 minutes, 16.2% 60 minutes or more (2000)

IRONDALE (village). Covers a land area of 1.401 square miles and a water area of 0.024 square miles. Located at 40.57° N. Lat.; 80.72° W. Long. Elevation is 718 feet.
Population: 382 (1990); 418 (2000); 415 (2005); 403 (2010 projected); Race: 95.4% White, 3.1% Black, 0.5% Asian, 1.9% Hispanic of any race (2005); Density: 296.3 persons per square mile (2005); Average household size: 2.64 (2005); Median age: 35.7 (2005); Males per 100 females: 101.5 (2005); Marriage status: 22.1% never married, 57.7% now married, 13.5% widowed, 6.7% divorced (2000); Foreign born: 0.0% (2000); Ancestry (includes multiple ancestries): 28.5% German, 23.5% Irish, 12.7% English, 5.5% Other groups, 5.5% United States or American (2000).
Economy: Clay products, lumber. Employment by occupation: 4.0% management, 12.0% professional, 17.0% services, 17.0% sales, 0.0% farming, 15.0% construction, 35.0% production (2000).

Income: Per capita income: $15,880 (2005); Median household income: $34,138 (2005); Average household income: $41,975 (2005); Percent of households with income of $100,000 or more: 7.6% (2005); Poverty rate: 20.5% (2000).
Education: Percent of population age 25 and over with: High school diploma (including GED) or higher: 72.9% (2005); Bachelor's degree or higher: 4.2% (2005); Master's degree or higher: 0.0% (2005).

School District(s)
Edison Local SD (PK-12)
    2003-04 Enrollment: 2,689 . . . . (330) 532-3199

Housing: Homeownership rate: 84.7% (2005); Median home value: $34,561 (2005); Median rent: $278 per month (2000); Median age of housing: 60+ years (2000).
Transportation: Commute to work: 91.0% car, 0.0% public transportation, 5.0% walk, 4.0% work from home (2000); Travel time to work: 14.6% less than 15 minutes, 40.6% 15 to 30 minutes, 22.9% 30 to 45 minutes, 2.1% 45 to 60 minutes, 19.8% 60 minutes or more (2000)

MINGO JUNCTION (village).
Covers a land area of 2.538 square miles and a water area of 0 square miles. Located at 40.32° N. Lat.; 80.61° W. Long. Elevation is 675 feet.
History: Mingo Junction developed near Steubenville as a steel town.
Population: 4,406 (1990); 3,631 (2000); 3,398 (2005); 3,164 (2010 projected); Race: 95.6% White, 2.9% Black, 0.0% Asian, 0.7% Hispanic of any race (2005); Density: 1,338.9 persons per square mile (2005); Average household size: 2.31 (2005); Median age: 44.1 (2005); Males per 100 females: 87.9 (2005); Marriage status: 20.7% never married, 57.8% now married, 10.1% widowed, 11.4% divorced (2000); Foreign born: 0.4% (2000); Ancestry (includes multiple ancestries): 22.6% Italian, 21.2% German, 16.3% Irish, 8.0% Slovak, 7.6% English (2000).
Economy: Single-family building permits issued: 1 (2005); Multi-family building permits issued: 0 (2005); Employment by occupation: 5.3% management, 15.8% professional, 19.1% services, 30.2% sales, 0.0% farming, 7.5% construction, 22.0% production (2000).
Income: Per capita income: $18,646 (2005); Median household income: $33,428 (2005); Average household income: $43,013 (2005); Percent of households with income of $100,000 or more: 5.7% (2005); Poverty rate: 12.8% (2000).
Education: Percent of population age 25 and over with: High school diploma (including GED) or higher: 84.7% (2005); Bachelor's degree or higher: 8.9% (2005); Master's degree or higher: 1.8% (2005).

School District(s)
Indian Creek Local SD (PK-12)
    2003-04 Enrollment: 2,322 . . . . (740) 264-3502

Housing: Homeownership rate: 73.3% (2005); Median home value: $73,231 (2005); Median rent: $259 per month (2000); Median age of housing: 46 years (2000).
Safety: Violent crime rate: 43.1 per 10,000 population; Property crime rate: 204.1 per 10,000 population (2004).
Transportation: Commute to work: 93.2% car, 0.0% public transportation, 4.0% walk, 1.9% work from home (2000); Travel time to work: 43.8% less than 15 minutes, 41.3% 15 to 30 minutes, 6.4% 30 to 45 minutes, 4.2% 45 to 60 minutes, 4.4% 60 minutes or more (2000)

MOUNT PLEASANT (village).
Covers a land area of 0.250 square miles and a water area of 0 square miles. Located at 40.17° N. Lat.; 80.80° W. Long. Elevation is 1,200 feet.
History: Mount Pleasant began in the early 1800's as a Quaker community. The town was an abolitionist stronghold, and a refuge for fugitive slaves from the south long before the Civil War. The first abolitionist newspaper, the "Philanthopist," was published here in 1817 by Charles Osborn.
Population: 498 (1990); 535 (2000); 539 (2005); 515 (2010 projected); Race: 97.6% White, 0.7% Black, 0.9% Asian, 0.0% Hispanic of any race (2005); Density: 2,152.6 persons per square mile (2005); Average household size: 2.60 (2005); Median age: 41.3 (2005); Males per 100 females: 95.3 (2005); Marriage status: 23.1% never married, 63.8% now married, 7.5% widowed, 5.7% divorced (2000); Foreign born: 0.4% (2000); Ancestry (includes multiple ancestries): 20.1% Polish, 19.4% German, 16.9% Italian, 14.4% Irish, 10.0% English (2000).
Economy: Single-family building permits issued: 0 (2005); Multi-family building permits issued: 0 (2005); Employment by occupation: 6.6% management, 10.9% professional, 13.1% services, 28.4% sales, 0.0% farming, 17.9% construction, 23.1% production (2000).

Income: Per capita income: $21,702 (2005); Median household income: $52,724 (2005); Average household income: $56,510 (2005); Percent of households with income of $100,000 or more: 9.2% (2005); Poverty rate: 9.3% (2000).
Education: Percent of population age 25 and over with: High school diploma (including GED) or higher: 82.5% (2005); Bachelor's degree or higher: 5.2% (2005); Master's degree or higher: 4.1% (2005).
Housing: Homeownership rate: 87.4% (2005); Median home value: $59,750 (2005); Median rent: $294 per month (2000); Median age of housing: 60+ years (2000).
Transportation: Commute to work: 93.9% car, 0.0% public transportation, 3.5% walk, 0.9% work from home (2000); Travel time to work: 13.2% less than 15 minutes, 47.1% 15 to 30 minutes, 26.9% 30 to 45 minutes, 7.0% 45 to 60 minutes, 5.7% 60 minutes or more (2000)

NEW ALEXANDRIA (village).
Covers a land area of 0.361 square miles and a water area of 0 square miles. Located at 40.29° N. Lat.; 80.67° W. Long. Elevation is 1,250 feet.
Population: 257 (1990); 222 (2000); 220 (2005); 214 (2010 projected); Race: 97.7% White, 0.0% Black, 0.0% Asian, 0.0% Hispanic of any race (2005); Density: 609.1 persons per square mile (2005); Average household size: 2.39 (2005); Median age: 44.3 (2005); Males per 100 females: 91.3 (2005); Marriage status: 15.4% never married, 67.9% now married, 7.1% widowed, 9.6% divorced (2000); Foreign born: 0.0% (2000); Ancestry (includes multiple ancestries): 26.3% Irish, 17.0% German, 11.1% English, 9.4% Polish, 8.8% Other groups (2000).
Economy: In coal-mining area. Employment by occupation: 6.6% management, 13.1% professional, 32.8% services, 8.2% sales, 0.0% farming, 18.0% construction, 21.3% production (2000).
Income: Per capita income: $17,295 (2005); Median household income: $34,333 (2005); Average household income: $41,359 (2005); Percent of households with income of $100,000 or more: 7.6% (2005); Poverty rate: 15.8% (2000).
Education: Percent of population age 25 and over with: High school diploma (including GED) or higher: 71.4% (2005); Bachelor's degree or higher: 3.0% (2005); Master's degree or higher: 0.0% (2005).
Housing: Homeownership rate: 83.7% (2005); Median home value: $50,000 (2005); Median rent: $163 per month (2000); Median age of housing: 50 years (2000).
Transportation: Commute to work: 96.4% car, 0.0% public transportation, 0.0% walk, 0.0% work from home (2000); Travel time to work: 23.6% less than 15 minutes, 56.4% 15 to 30 minutes, 14.5% 30 to 45 minutes, 5.5% 45 to 60 minutes, 0.0% 60 minutes or more (2000)

RAYLAND (village).
Covers a land area of 0.434 square miles and a water area of 0 square miles. Located at 40.18° N. Lat.; 80.69° W. Long. Elevation is 680 feet.
Population: 490 (1990); 434 (2000); 399 (2005); 369 (2010 projected); Race: 98.2% White, 0.8% Black, 0.3% Asian, 0.5% Hispanic of any race (2005); Density: 918.3 persons per square mile (2005); Average household size: 2.45 (2005); Median age: 43.3 (2005); Males per 100 females: 81.4 (2005); Marriage status: 21.4% never married, 62.5% now married, 9.3% widowed, 6.8% divorced (2000); Foreign born: 0.0% (2000); Ancestry (includes multiple ancestries): 22.2% Italian, 20.6% German, 16.4% Irish, 10.9% Hungarian, 10.6% Polish (2000).
Economy: In coal-mining area. Employment by occupation: 1.3% management, 9.4% professional, 20.1% services, 28.9% sales, 0.0% farming, 14.5% construction, 25.8% production (2000).
Income: Per capita income: $15,777 (2005); Median household income: $32,069 (2005); Average household income: $38,620 (2005); Percent of households with income of $100,000 or more: 4.9% (2005); Poverty rate: 23.3% (2000).
Education: Percent of population age 25 and over with: High school diploma (including GED) or higher: 84.6% (2005); Bachelor's degree or higher: 8.4% (2005); Master's degree or higher: 2.8% (2005).

School District(s)
Buckeye Local SD (PK-12)
    2003-04 Enrollment: 2,415 . . . . (740) 769-7395

Housing: Homeownership rate: 81.6% (2005); Median home value: $60,278 (2005); Median rent: $236 per month (2000); Median age of housing: 60+ years (2000).
Transportation: Commute to work: 97.4% car, 0.0% public transportation, 1.3% walk, 0.0% work from home (2000); Travel time to work: 27.9% less than 15 minutes, 25.3% 15 to 30 minutes, 29.9% 30 to 45 minutes, 7.1% 45 to 60 minutes, 9.7% 60 minutes or more (2000)

RICHMOND (village). Covers a land area of 0.531 square miles and a water area of 0 square miles. Located at 40.43° N. Lat.; 80.77° W. Long. Elevation is 1,285 feet.
Population: 446 (1990); 471 (2000); 396 (2005); 378 (2010 projected); Race: 97.7% White, 0.0% Black, 1.8% Asian, 0.3% Hispanic of any race (2005); Density: 745.2 persons per square mile (2005); Average household size: 2.36 (2005); Median age: 42.7 (2005); Males per 100 females: 82.5 (2005); Marriage status: 17.6% never married, 59.3% now married, 11.0% widowed, 12.1% divorced (2000); Foreign born: 0.0% (2000); Ancestry (includes multiple ancestries): 24.4% Irish, 22.8% German, 11.5% English, 11.0% Italian, 6.5% French (except Basque) (2000).
Economy: In agricultural area. Employment by occupation: 2.6% management, 9.8% professional, 18.7% services, 21.2% sales, 0.0% farming, 15.0% construction, 32.6% production (2000).
Income: Per capita income: $16,187 (2005); Median household income: $31,250 (2005); Average household income: $38,155 (2005); Percent of households with income of $100,000 or more: 4.2% (2005); Poverty rate: 11.0% (2000).
Education: Percent of population age 25 and over with: High school diploma (including GED) or higher: 82.3% (2005); Bachelor's degree or higher: 6.0% (2005); Master's degree or higher: 2.1% (2005).
School District(s)
Edison Local SD (PK-12)
    2003-04 Enrollment: 2,689 . . . . (330) 532-3199
Housing: Homeownership rate: 82.7% (2005); Median home value: $70,000 (2005); Median rent: $291 per month (2000); Median age of housing: 47 years (2000).
Transportation: Commute to work: 96.9% car, 0.0% public transportation, 0.0% walk, 3.1% work from home (2000); Travel time to work: 18.7% less than 15 minutes, 55.6% 15 to 30 minutes, 17.6% 30 to 45 minutes, 2.7% 45 to 60 minutes, 5.3% 60 minutes or more (2000)

SMITHFIELD (village). Covers a land area of 0.959 square miles and a water area of 0 square miles. Located at 40.27° N. Lat.; 80.78° W. Long. Elevation is 1,220 feet.
Population: 957 (1990); 867 (2000); 816 (2005); 768 (2010 projected); Race: 89.5% White, 7.8% Black, 0.0% Asian, 0.2% Hispanic of any race (2005); Density: 851.3 persons per square mile (2005); Average household size: 2.40 (2005); Median age: 41.3 (2005); Males per 100 females: 91.1 (2005); Marriage status: 19.3% never married, 58.8% now married, 8.8% widowed, 13.1% divorced (2000); Foreign born: 0.8% (2000); Ancestry (includes multiple ancestries): 19.7% Irish, 18.7% Other groups, 15.3% German, 10.1% Italian, 8.5% United States or American (2000).
Economy: In coal-mining area. Single-family building permits issued: 0 (2005); Multi-family building permits issued: 0 (2005); Employment by occupation: 5.5% management, 15.4% professional, 16.5% services, 24.0% sales, 0.0% farming, 14.2% construction, 24.4% production (2000).
Income: Per capita income: $17,173 (2005); Median household income: $27,647 (2005); Average household income: $41,000 (2005); Percent of households with income of $100,000 or more: 7.9% (2005); Poverty rate: 28.8% (2000).
Education: Percent of population age 25 and over with: High school diploma (including GED) or higher: 72.2% (2005); Bachelor's degree or higher: 4.4% (2005); Master's degree or higher: 0.9% (2005).
Housing: Homeownership rate: 67.1% (2005); Median home value: $55,616 (2005); Median rent: $267 per month (2000); Median age of housing: 53 years (2000).
Transportation: Commute to work: 93.4% car, 0.0% public transportation, 6.6% walk, 0.0% work from home (2000); Travel time to work: 19.5% less than 15 minutes, 44.4% 15 to 30 minutes, 24.1% 30 to 45 minutes, 5.8% 45 to 60 minutes, 6.2% 60 minutes or more (2000)

STEUBENVILLE (city). Covers a land area of 10.322 square miles and a water area of 0.005 square miles. Located at 40.36° N. Lat.; 80.63° W. Long. Elevation is 1,060 feet.
History: Jacob Walker came to the Ohio River in 1765. He was followed in 1786 by government scouts who selected this site for a fort, called Fort Steuben for Baron Frederick William von Steuben, a Prussian drillmaster who aided the colonies in the Revolutionary War. A community called La Belle sprang up around the fort, and when the fort was destroyed in 1790, the settlement remained. Bezaleel Wells and James Ross laid out the town in 1797. It was named Steubenville, and became the seat of Jefferson County. Industries began in the early 1800's with a pottery, a drift coal mine, nail factory and foundry. As river traffic increased, Steubenville became an important port. The Frazier, Kilgore and Company rolling mill, using the labels of Wheeling Steel and Weirton Steel, was erected in 1856.
Population: 22,298 (1990); 19,015 (2000); 18,604 (2005); 18,167 (2010 projected); Race: 79.5% White, 17.0% Black, 1.1% Asian, 1.0% Hispanic of any race (2005); Density: 1,802.3 persons per square mile (2005); Average household size: 2.24 (2005); Median age: 43.5 (2005); Males per 100 females: 86.0 (2005); Marriage status: 26.6% never married, 51.4% now married, 11.3% widowed, 10.7% divorced (2000); Foreign born: 2.4% (2000); Ancestry (includes multiple ancestries): 18.9% Italian, 18.3% Other groups, 12.9% German, 12.7% Irish, 6.9% Polish (2000).
Economy: Single-family building permits issued: 4 (2005); Multi-family building permits issued: 0 (2005); Employment by occupation: 9.4% management, 21.5% professional, 19.9% services, 27.2% sales, 0.2% farming, 7.1% construction, 14.6% production (2000).
Income: Per capita income: $20,109 (2005); Median household income: $30,550 (2005); Average household income: $43,974 (2005); Percent of households with income of $100,000 or more: 8.5% (2005); Poverty rate: 20.4% (2000).
Education: Percent of population age 25 and over with: High school diploma (including GED) or higher: 79.5% (2005); Bachelor's degree or higher: 18.1% (2005); Master's degree or higher: 7.4% (2005).
School District(s)
Edison Local SD (PK-12)
    2003-04 Enrollment: 2,689 . . . . (330) 532-3199
Steubenville City SD (PK-12)
    2003-04 Enrollment: 2,391 . . . . (740) 283-3767
Four-year College(s)
Franciscan University of Steubenville (Private, Not-for-profit, Roman Catholic)
    Fall 2004 Enrollment: 2,374. . . . . (740) 283-3771
    2005-06 Tuition: In-state $16,450; Out-of-state $16,450
Two-year College(s)
Century School of Cosmetology (Private, For-profit)
    Fall 2004 Enrollment: 69 . . . . (740) 282-3312
Jefferson Community College (Public)
    Fall 2004 Enrollment: 1,658. . . . . (740) 264-5591
    2005-06 Tuition: In-state $2,730; Out-of-state $3,450
Trinity Health System School of Nursing (Private, Not-for-profit, Roman Catholic)
    Fall 2004 Enrollment: 148 . . . . (740) 283-7467
    2005-06 Tuition: In-state $4,716; Out-of-state $5,052
Housing: Homeownership rate: 59.9% (2005); Median home value: $79,576 (2005); Median rent: $282 per month (2000); Median age of housing: 50 years (2000).
Hospitals: Trinity Medical Center - East (401 beds); Trinity Medical Center - West (231 beds)
Safety: Violent crime rate: 53.0 per 10,000 population; Property crime rate: 495.7 per 10,000 population (2004).
Newspapers: Brooke Scene (General - Circulation 12,000); Herald-Star (Circulation 15,416); Steubenville Register (Catholic, Religious - Circulation 18,700)
Transportation: Commute to work: 93.2% car, 0.9% public transportation, 3.0% walk, 2.7% work from home (2000); Travel time to work: 55.9% less than 15 minutes, 27.4% 15 to 30 minutes, 8.4% 30 to 45 minutes, 4.1% 45 to 60 minutes, 4.3% 60 minutes or more (2000)
Additional Information Contacts
City of Steubenville . . . . (740) 283-6000
    http://www.ci.steubenville.oh.us
Steubenville Chamber of Commerce. . . . . (740) 282-6226
    http://www.jeffersoncountychamber.com

STRATTON (village). Covers a land area of 0.532 square miles and a water area of 0 square miles. Located at 40.52° N. Lat.; 80.62° W. Long. Elevation is 676 feet.
Population: 278 (1990); 277 (2000); 275 (2005); 274 (2010 projected); Race: 96.7% White, 0.0% Black, 3.3% Asian, 0.7% Hispanic of any race (2005); Density: 517.2 persons per square mile (2005); Average household size: 1.94 (2005); Median age: 46.0 (2005); Males per 100 females: 87.1 (2005); Marriage status: 23.0% never married, 40.9% now married, 22.1% widowed, 14.0% divorced (2000); Foreign born: 0.0% (2000); Ancestry (includes multiple ancestries): 19.8% German, 16.2% Irish, 15.8% English, 10.8% United States or American, 5.4% Slovak (2000).
Economy: Single-family building permits issued: 0 (2005); Multi-family building permits issued: 0 (2005); Employment by occupation: 10.8%

management, 14.4% professional, 19.8% services, 27.9% sales, 0.0% farming, 6.3% construction, 20.7% production (2000).
Income: Per capita income: $17,936 (2005); Median household income: $26,053 (2005); Average household income: $34,736 (2005); Percent of households with income of $100,000 or more: 4.2% (2005); Poverty rate: 7.6% (2000).
Education: Percent of population age 25 and over with: High school diploma (including GED) or higher: 81.6% (2005); Bachelor's degree or higher: 2.9% (2005); Master's degree or higher: 0.0% (2005).
Housing: Homeownership rate: 80.3% (2005); Median home value: $35,294 (2005); Median rent: $230 per month (2000); Median age of housing: 50 years (2000).
Transportation: Commute to work: 85.6% car, 0.0% public transportation, 11.7% walk, 2.7% work from home (2000); Travel time to work: 36.1% less than 15 minutes, 53.7% 15 to 30 minutes, 1.9% 30 to 45 minutes, 8.3% 45 to 60 minutes, 0.0% 60 minutes or more (2000)

TILTONSVILLE (village). Aka Tiltonville. Covers a land area of 0.556 square miles and a water area of 0 square miles. Located at 40.17° N. Lat.; 80.69° W. Long. Elevation is 675 feet.
Population: 1,517 (1990); 1,329 (2000); 1,238 (2005); 1,142 (2010 projected); Race: 98.9% White, 0.0% Black, 0.0% Asian, 0.2% Hispanic of any race (2005); Density: 2,228.4 persons per square mile (2005); Average household size: 2.15 (2005); Median age: 46.5 (2005); Males per 100 females: 82.3 (2005); Marriage status: 19.5% never married, 54.9% now married, 14.2% widowed, 11.5% divorced (2000); Foreign born: 1.6% (2000); Ancestry (includes multiple ancestries): 21.0% Italian, 20.9% German, 16.6% Irish, 15.9% Polish, 9.6% Hungarian (2000).
Economy: Single-family building permits issued: 0 (2005); Multi-family building permits issued: 0 (2005); Employment by occupation: 10.5% management, 14.3% professional, 16.7% services, 32.4% sales, 0.0% farming, 10.5% construction, 15.7% production (2000).
Income: Per capita income: $17,617 (2005); Median household income: $31,529 (2005); Average household income: $37,930 (2005); Percent of households with income of $100,000 or more: 4.5% (2005); Poverty rate: 13.9% (2000).
Education: Percent of population age 25 and over with: High school diploma (including GED) or higher: 81.6% (2005); Bachelor's degree or higher: 9.3% (2005); Master's degree or higher: 1.9% (2005).
School District(s)
Buckeye Local SD (PK-12)
   2003-04 Enrollment: 2,415 . . . . (740) 769-7395
Housing: Homeownership rate: 67.1% (2005); Median home value: $64,219 (2005); Median rent: $256 per month (2000); Median age of housing: 59 years (2000).
Transportation: Commute to work: 93.1% car, 0.0% public transportation, 4.8% walk, 1.7% work from home (2000); Travel time to work: 30.1% less than 15 minutes, 48.2% 15 to 30 minutes, 12.7% 30 to 45 minutes, 3.8% 45 to 60 minutes, 5.1% 60 minutes or more (2000)

TORONTO (city). Covers a land area of 1.883 square miles and a water area of 0.004 square miles. Located at 40.46° N. Lat.; 80.60° W. Long. Elevation is 700 feet.
History: Toronto was laid out in 1818 by John Depuy when it was called Newburg, and later Sloan's Station. In 1881 it was renamed Toronto for a prominent citizen who had come from Toronto, Canada.
Population: 6,127 (1990); 5,676 (2000); 5,450 (2005); 5,224 (2010 projected); Race: 97.7% White, 0.9% Black, 0.2% Asian, 0.6% Hispanic of any race (2005); Density: 2,894.6 persons per square mile (2005); Average household size: 2.27 (2005); Median age: 41.1 (2005); Males per 100 females: 85.3 (2005); Marriage status: 21.0% never married, 57.3% now married, 10.6% widowed, 11.1% divorced (2000); Foreign born: 0.6% (2000); Ancestry (includes multiple ancestries): 19.5% German, 19.2% Irish, 13.0% United States or American, 10.5% English, 9.1% Other groups (2000).
Economy: Single-family building permits issued: 0 (2005); Multi-family building permits issued: 0 (2005); Employment by occupation: 5.1% management, 11.4% professional, 17.4% services, 29.7% sales, 0.0% farming, 12.6% construction, 23.9% production (2000).
Income: Per capita income: $17,234 (2005); Median household income: $33,553 (2005); Average household income: $39,103 (2005); Percent of households with income of $100,000 or more: 3.2% (2005); Poverty rate: 13.4% (2000).

Education: Percent of population age 25 and over with: High school diploma (including GED) or higher: 84.2% (2005); Bachelor's degree or higher: 7.7% (2005); Master's degree or higher: 2.6% (2005).
School District(s)
Toronto City SD (PK-12)
   2003-04 Enrollment: 1,011 . . . . (740) 537-2456
Housing: Homeownership rate: 70.2% (2005); Median home value: $73,180 (2005); Median rent: $257 per month (2000); Median age of housing: 53 years (2000).
Safety: Violent crime rate: 9.0 per 10,000 population; Property crime rate: 167.6 per 10,000 population (2004).
Transportation: Commute to work: 92.3% car, 0.0% public transportation, 5.6% walk, 1.1% work from home (2000); Travel time to work: 41.6% less than 15 minutes, 42.5% 15 to 30 minutes, 7.9% 30 to 45 minutes, 3.9% 45 to 60 minutes, 4.1% 60 minutes or more (2000)

WINTERSVILLE (village). Covers a land area of 3.523 square miles and a water area of 0.004 square miles. Located at 40.37° N. Lat.; 80.70° W. Long. Elevation is 1,220 feet.
History: Land office here for first land sales in Northwest Territory. Incorporated 1947.
Population: 4,368 (1990); 4,067 (2000); 3,922 (2005); 3,764 (2010 projected); Race: 93.4% White, 5.5% Black, 0.2% Asian, 0.7% Hispanic of any race (2005); Density: 1,113.2 persons per square mile (2005); Average household size: 2.29 (2005); Median age: 46.0 (2005); Males per 100 females: 93.8 (2005); Marriage status: 20.5% never married, 60.4% now married, 9.5% widowed, 9.6% divorced (2000); Foreign born: 1.4% (2000); Ancestry (includes multiple ancestries): 24.0% Italian, 19.4% Irish, 19.0% German, 10.6% English, 8.6% Other groups (2000).
Economy: Single-family building permits issued: 2 (2005); Multi-family building permits issued: 0 (2005); Employment by occupation: 5.9% management, 18.5% professional, 15.4% services, 29.0% sales, 0.0% farming, 11.6% construction, 19.7% production (2000).
Income: Per capita income: $22,035 (2005); Median household income: $40,486 (2005); Average household income: $49,800 (2005); Percent of households with income of $100,000 or more: 8.4% (2005); Poverty rate: 6.9% (2000).
Education: Percent of population age 25 and over with: High school diploma (including GED) or higher: 86.8% (2005); Bachelor's degree or higher: 16.5% (2005); Master's degree or higher: 5.2% (2005).
School District(s)
Indian Creek Local SD (PK-12)
   2003-04 Enrollment: 2,322 . . . . (740) 264-3502
Housing: Homeownership rate: 71.7% (2005); Median home value: $91,385 (2005); Median rent: $377 per month (2000); Median age of housing: 39 years (2000).
Safety: Violent crime rate: 5.2 per 10,000 population; Property crime rate: 200.9 per 10,000 population (2004).
Transportation: Commute to work: 95.4% car, 0.4% public transportation, 0.5% walk, 3.0% work from home (2000); Travel time to work: 37.4% less than 15 minutes, 47.9% 15 to 30 minutes, 6.9% 30 to 45 minutes, 4.2% 45 to 60 minutes, 3.6% 60 minutes or more (2000)

YORKVILLE (village). Covers a land area of 0.611 square miles and a water area of 0 square miles. Located at 40.15° N. Lat.; 80.70° W. Long.
History: Yorkville grew around the Wheeling Steel Corporation's mill. It was named for York, Pennsylvania, the former home of many of the early settlers.
Population: 1,246 (1990); 1,230 (2000); 1,175 (2005); 1,122 (2010 projected); Race: 97.0% White, 1.5% Black, 0.0% Asian, 0.3% Hispanic of any race (2005); Density: 1,922.9 persons per square mile (2005); Average household size: 2.28 (2005); Median age: 42.6 (2005); Males per 100 females: 95.2 (2005); Marriage status: 22.2% never married, 51.5% now married, 12.0% widowed, 14.3% divorced (2000); Foreign born: 2.3% (2000); Ancestry (includes multiple ancestries): 25.4% Italian, 19.1% German, 16.4% Irish, 12.5% Polish, 7.8% Hungarian (2000).
Economy: Single-family building permits issued: 0 (2005); Multi-family building permits issued: 0 (2005); Employment by occupation: 7.1% management, 19.7% professional, 19.1% services, 24.1% sales, 0.0% farming, 6.6% construction, 23.4% production (2000).
Income: Per capita income: $17,825 (2005); Median household income: $33,214 (2005); Average household income: $40,203 (2005); Percent of households with income of $100,000 or more: 4.8% (2005); Poverty rate: 10.0% (2000).

Education: Percent of population age 25 and over with: High school diploma (including GED) or higher: 84.1% (2005); Bachelor's degree or higher: 13.9% (2005); Master's degree or higher: 4.3% (2005).

School District(s)

Buckeye Local SD (PK-12)
   2003-04 Enrollment: 2,415 . . . . (740) 769-7395

Housing: Homeownership rate: 60.5% (2005); Median home value: $66,078 (2005); Median rent: $290 per month (2000); Median age of housing: 49 years (2000).
Transportation: Commute to work: 88.2% car, 1.4% public transportation, 8.1% walk, 1.6% work from home (2000); Travel time to work: 32.1% less than 15 minutes, 47.1% 15 to 30 minutes, 13.0% 30 to 45 minutes, 3.8% 45 to 60 minutes, 4.0% 60 minutes or more (2000)

Knox County

Located in central Ohio; drained by the Kokosing and Mohican Rivers and the North Fork of the Licking River. Covers a land area of 527.12 square miles, a water area of 2.41 square miles, and is located in the Eastern Time Zone. The county government was organized in 1808. County seat is Mount Vernon.

Knox County is part of the Mount Vernon, OH Micropolitan Statistical Area. The entire metro area includes: Knox County, OH

Weather Station: Centerburg 2 SE   Elevation: 1,204 feet

	Jan	Feb	Mar	Apr	May	Jun	Jul	Aug	Sep	Oct	Nov	Dec
High	32	36	47	60	70	79	82	81	74	62	49	37
Low	16	19	28	38	48	57	61	60	52	40	32	22
Precip	2.5	2.1	3.0	3.7	4.0	4.6	4.6	3.9	3.2	2.8	3.6	3.0
Snow	na	3.2	na	0.3	tr	0.0	0.0	0.0	0.0	tr	0.9	na

High and Low temperatures in degrees Fahrenheit; Precipitation and Snow in inches

Weather Station: Danville 2 W   Elevation: 967 feet

	Jan	Feb	Mar	Apr	May	Jun	Jul	Aug	Sep	Oct	Nov	Dec
High	34	38	50	62	72	80	84	83	76	64	51	40
Low	16	18	27	35	45	54	58	57	49	38	30	22
Precip	2.6	2.4	3.1	3.7	4.2	4.7	4.3	3.8	3.3	2.7	3.4	3.1
Snow	12.4	8.4	4.6	1.3	tr	0.0	0.0	0.0	0.0	tr	1.8	7.0

High and Low temperatures in degrees Fahrenheit; Precipitation and Snow in inches

Weather Station: Fredericktown 4 S   Elevation: 1,049 feet

	Jan	Feb	Mar	Apr	May	Jun	Jul	Aug	Sep	Oct	Nov	Dec
High	32	37	47	60	70	79	83	81	75	63	50	39
Low	13	16	26	35	45	55	58	56	49	38	30	22
Precip	2.6	2.1	3.0	3.6	4.3	4.4	4.2	3.7	3.3	2.6	3.3	2.9
Snow	7.8	5.3	3.1	0.7	tr	0.0	0.0	0.0	0.0	0.0	1.0	3.5

High and Low temperatures in degrees Fahrenheit; Precipitation and Snow in inches

Population: 47,473 (1990); 54,500 (2000); 57,991 (2005); 61,641 (2010 projected); Race: 97.5% White, 0.7% Black, 0.5% Asian, 0.8% Hispanic of any race (2005); Density: 110.0 persons per square mile (2005); Average household size: 2.71 (2005); Median age: 36.8 (2005); Males per 100 females: 95.1 (2005).
Religion: Five largest groups: 7.7% The United Methodist Church, 5.7% Catholic Church, 5.6% Christian Churches and Churches of Christ, 3.6% Church of the Nazarene, 2.0% American Baptist Churches in the USA (2000).
Economy: Unemployment rate: 5.4% (2005); Total civilian labor force: 30,098 (2005); Leading industries: 23.5% manufacturing; 12.9% retail trade; 12.3% health care and social assistance (2004); Farms: 1,258 totaling 209,067 acres (2002); Companies that employ 500 or more persons: 6 (2004); Companies that employ 100 to 499 persons: 23 (2004); Companies that employ less than 100 persons: 1,119 (2004); Black-owned businesses: n/a (2002); Hispanic-owned businesses: n/a (2002); Women-owned businesses: 1,050 (2002); Retail sales per capita: $8,611 (2006); Single-family building permits issued: 365 (2005); Multi-family building permits issued: 8 (2005).
Income: Per capita income: $20,569 (2005); Median household income: $44,638 (2005); Average household income: $54,845 (2005); Percent of households with income of $100,000 or more: 10.9% (2005); Poverty rate: 10.0% (2003); Bankruptcy rate: 8.25% (2005).
Education: Percent of population age 25 and over with: High school diploma (including GED) or higher: 81.9% (2005); Bachelor's degree or higher: 16.6% (2005); Master's degree or higher: 6.1% (2005).

Housing: Homeownership rate: 76.3% (2005); Median home value: $121,868 (2005); Median rent: $360 per month (2000); Median age of housing: 37 years (2000).
Health: Birth rate: 123.1 per 10,000 population (2004); Death rate: 100.2 per 10,000 population (2004); Age-adjusted cancer mortality rate: 213.6 deaths per 100,000 population (2002); Air Quality Index: 81.9% good, 17.2% moderate, 0.9% unhealthy for sensitive individuals, 0.0% unhealthy (percent of days in 2005); Number of physicians: 12.3 per 10,000 population (2004); Hospital beds: 14.2 per 10,000 population (2003); Hospital admissions: 679.1 per 10,000 population (2003).
Elections: 2004 Presidential election results: 63.1% Bush, 36.3% Kerry, 0.0% Nader, 0.3% Badnarik
National and State Parks: Knox Lake State Wildlife Area
Additional Information Contacts

Knox County Government . . . . (740) 393-6703
   http://www.knoxcountyohio.org/
City of Mount Vernon . . . . (740) 393-9517
   http://www.mountvernonohio.org
Mount Vernon Knox County Chamber . . . . (740) 393-1111
   http://www.knoxchamber.com
Mount Vernon Visitors Bureau . . . . (740) 392-6102
   http://www.visitknoxohio.org

Knox County Communities

BRINKHAVEN (unincorporated postal area, zip code 43006). Aka Brink Haven. Covers a land area of 20.423 square miles and a water area of 0 square miles. Located at 40.47° N. Lat.; 82.19° W. Long. Elevation is 920 feet.
Population: 597 (2000); Race: 99.2% White, 0.0% Black, 0.0% Asian, 0.3% Hispanic of any race (2000); Density: 29.2 persons per square mile (2000); Age: 27.8% under 18, 12.3% over 64 (2000); Marriage status: 19.0% never married, 66.4% now married, 4.5% widowed, 10.1% divorced (2000); Foreign born: 0.0% (2000); Ancestry (includes multiple ancestries): 18.0% German, 17.5% United States or American, 11.7% English, 6.6% Other groups, 5.2% Irish (2000).
Economy: Employment by occupation: 6.6% management, 5.1% professional, 20.6% services, 12.9% sales, 5.1% farming, 9.6% construction, 40.1% production (2000).
Income: Per capita income: $13,105 (2000); Median household income: $37,885 (2000); Poverty rate: 16.0% (2000).
Education: Percent of population age 25 and over with: High school diploma (including GED) or higher: 77.2% (2000); Bachelor's degree or higher: 6.4% (2000).
Housing: Homeownership rate: 85.3% (2000); Median home value: $64,600 (2000); Median rent: $208 per month (2000); Median age of housing: 47 years (2000).
Transportation: Commute to work: 95.1% car, 0.0% public transportation, 1.9% walk, 3.0% work from home (2000); Travel time to work: 19.8% less than 15 minutes, 23.3% 15 to 30 minutes, 28.0% 30 to 45 minutes, 10.5% 45 to 60 minutes, 18.3% 60 minutes or more (2000)

CENTERBURG (village). Covers a land area of 0.643 square miles and a water area of 0 square miles. Located at 40.30° N. Lat.; 82.69° W. Long. Elevation is 1,210 feet.
History: Centerburg was settled in 1806 and named for its position near the geographical center of the state.
Population: 1,311 (1990); 1,432 (2000); 1,561 (2005); 1,683 (2010 projected); Race: 98.0% White, 0.4% Black, 0.3% Asian, 0.1% Hispanic of any race (2005); Density: 2,429.3 persons per square mile (2005); Average household size: 2.83 (2005); Median age: 36.0 (2005); Males per 100 females: 100.1 (2005); Marriage status: 21.7% never married, 61.2% now married, 7.2% widowed, 9.9% divorced (2000); Foreign born: 0.2% (2000); Ancestry (includes multiple ancestries): 20.0% German, 17.0% English, 13.1% United States or American, 13.0% Irish, 8.8% Other groups (2000).
Economy: Single-family building permits issued: 9 (2005); Multi-family building permits issued: 0 (2005); Employment by occupation: 10.2% management, 14.9% professional, 16.6% services, 27.2% sales, 1.3% farming, 14.7% construction, 15.2% production (2000).
Income: Per capita income: $19,540 (2005); Median household income: $47,076 (2005); Average household income: $53,800 (2005); Percent of households with income of $100,000 or more: 8.9% (2005); Poverty rate: 5.6% (2000).

Education: Percent of population age 25 and over with: High school diploma (including GED) or higher: 77.8% (2005); Bachelor's degree or higher: 11.4% (2005); Master's degree or higher: 3.6% (2005).

School District(s)
Centerburg Local SD (PK-12)
    2003-04 Enrollment: 1,141 .... (740) 625-6346
Housing: Homeownership rate: 62.1% (2005); Median home value: $122,337 (2005); Median rent: $409 per month (2000); Median age of housing: 56 years (2000).
Transportation: Commute to work: 92.8% car, 0.0% public transportation, 3.3% walk, 3.1% work from home (2000); Travel time to work: 17.5% less than 15 minutes, 21.6% 15 to 30 minutes, 30.0% 30 to 45 minutes, 23.3% 45 to 60 minutes, 7.6% 60 minutes or more (2000)

DANVILLE
(village). Covers a land area of 0.537 square miles and a water area of 0 square miles. Located at 40.44° N. Lat.; 82.26° W. Long. Elevation is 966 feet.
Population: 1,034 (1990); 1,104 (2000); 1,120 (2005); 1,164 (2010 projected); Race: 98.1% White, 0.1% Black, 0.3% Asian, 0.4% Hispanic of any race (2005); Density: 2,084.9 persons per square mile (2005); Average household size: 2.50 (2005); Median age: 33.6 (2005); Males per 100 females: 99.6 (2005); Marriage status: 18.6% never married, 59.1% now married, 9.1% widowed, 13.2% divorced (2000); Foreign born: 0.5% (2000); Ancestry (includes multiple ancestries): 19.7% United States or American, 16.8% German, 10.6% Irish, 9.9% English, 5.1% Other groups (2000).
Economy: In agricultural area. Single-family building permits issued: 1 (2005); Multi-family building permits issued: 0 (2005); Employment by occupation: 7.5% management, 12.8% professional, 15.3% services, 21.9% sales, 1.8% farming, 11.2% construction, 29.6% production (2000).
Income: Per capita income: $16,713 (2005); Median household income: $32,237 (2005); Average household income: $41,507 (2005); Percent of households with income of $100,000 or more: 5.8% (2005); Poverty rate: 15.2% (2000).
Education: Percent of population age 25 and over with: High school diploma (including GED) or higher: 77.0% (2005); Bachelor's degree or higher: 10.9% (2005); Master's degree or higher: 2.9% (2005).

School District(s)
Danville Digital Academy
    2003-04 Enrollment: n/a
Danville Local School District (PK-12)
    2003-04 Enrollment: 651 .... (740) 599-6116
Housing: Homeownership rate: 62.3% (2005); Median home value: $88,939 (2005); Median rent: $319 per month (2000); Median age of housing: 46 years (2000).
Transportation: Commute to work: 90.0% car, 0.2% public transportation, 7.0% walk, 2.1% work from home (2000); Travel time to work: 30.5% less than 15 minutes, 31.0% 15 to 30 minutes, 25.7% 30 to 45 minutes, 4.3% 45 to 60 minutes, 8.6% 60 minutes or more (2000)

FREDERICKTOWN
(village). Covers a land area of 1.412 square miles and a water area of 0.035 square miles. Located at 40.48° N. Lat.; 82.54° W. Long. Elevation is 1,130 feet.
Population: 2,541 (1990); 2,428 (2000); 2,324 (2005); 2,309 (2010 projected); Race: 98.7% White, 0.3% Black, 0.1% Asian, 0.5% Hispanic of any race (2005); Density: 1,645.7 persons per square mile (2005); Average household size: 2.32 (2005); Median age: 36.3 (2005); Males per 100 females: 94.8 (2005); Marriage status: 16.6% never married, 59.1% now married, 9.7% widowed, 14.6% divorced (2000); Foreign born: 0.6% (2000); Ancestry (includes multiple ancestries): 22.8% German, 15.9% United States or American, 11.5% Irish, 10.8% English, 4.6% Other groups (2000).
Economy: Single-family building permits issued: 1 (2005); Multi-family building permits issued: 0 (2005); Employment by occupation: 9.5% management, 17.0% professional, 14.6% services, 26.1% sales, 0.0% farming, 7.8% construction, 25.1% production (2000).
Income: Per capita income: $20,914 (2005); Median household income: $40,542 (2005); Average household income: $48,460 (2005); Percent of households with income of $100,000 or more: 8.5% (2005); Poverty rate: 7.1% (2000).
Education: Percent of population age 25 and over with: High school diploma (including GED) or higher: 82.2% (2005); Bachelor's degree or higher: 16.5% (2005); Master's degree or higher: 5.4% (2005).

School District(s)
Fredericktown Digital Academy
    2003-04 Enrollment: n/a .... (740) 694-2956
Fredericktown Local SD (PK-12)
    2003-04 Enrollment: 1,178 .... (740) 694-2956
Housing: Homeownership rate: 71.0% (2005); Median home value: $100,797 (2005); Median rent: $374 per month (2000); Median age of housing: 45 years (2000).
Safety: Violent crime rate: 15.6 per 10,000 population; Property crime rate: 176.0 per 10,000 population (2004).
Newspapers: Knox County Citizen (General - Circulation 1,500)
Transportation: Commute to work: 93.9% car, 0.0% public transportation, 2.2% walk, 2.9% work from home (2000); Travel time to work: 28.7% less than 15 minutes, 44.8% 15 to 30 minutes, 14.4% 30 to 45 minutes, 2.5% 45 to 60 minutes, 9.6% 60 minutes or more (2000)

GAMBIER
(village). Covers a land area of 0.936 square miles and a water area of 0 square miles. Located at 40.37° N. Lat.; 82.39° W. Long. Elevation is 1,080 feet.
History: Gambier was the site of the founding of Kenyon College, established in 1824 by Philander Chase, first Episcopal bishop of Ohio, as a Theological Seminary. The college was located on land donated by Lord Gambier, for whom the town was named.
Population: 2,073 (1990); 1,871 (2000); 1,831 (2005); 1,819 (2010 projected); Race: 94.0% White, 3.0% Black, 1.3% Asian, 1.9% Hispanic of any race (2005); Density: 1,955.8 persons per square mile (2005); Average household size: 6.38 (2005); Median age: 20.9 (2005); Males per 100 females: 83.3 (2005); Marriage status: 79.0% never married, 15.6% now married, 1.9% widowed, 3.5% divorced (2000); Foreign born: 1.2% (2000); Ancestry (includes multiple ancestries): 10.4% German, 7.4% English, 5.6% Irish, 2.3% Other groups, 2.0% United States or American (2000).
Economy: Single-family building permits issued: 0 (2005); Multi-family building permits issued: 0 (2005); Employment by occupation: 9.5% management, 41.9% professional, 9.1% services, 33.2% sales, 0.3% farming, 2.7% construction, 3.2% production (2000).
Income: Per capita income: $11,613 (2005); Median household income: $57,311 (2005); Average household income: $62,117 (2005); Percent of households with income of $100,000 or more: 17.1% (2005); Poverty rate: 8.0% (2000).
Education: Percent of population age 25 and over with: High school diploma (including GED) or higher: 89.8% (2005); Bachelor's degree or higher: 56.4% (2005); Master's degree or higher: 36.4% (2005).

School District(s)
Mount Vernon City SD (PK-12)
    2003-04 Enrollment: 4,301 .... (740) 397-7422
Four-year College(s)
Kenyon College (Private, Not-for-profit)
    Fall 2004 Enrollment: 1,634 .... (740) 427-5000
    2005-06 Tuition: In-state $33,930; Out-of-state $33,930
Housing: Homeownership rate: 57.1% (2005); Median home value: $144,565 (2005); Median rent: $429 per month (2000); Median age of housing: 41 years (2000).
Transportation: Commute to work: 48.7% car, 0.0% public transportation, 49.2% walk, 1.6% work from home (2000); Travel time to work: 80.9% less than 15 minutes, 13.2% 15 to 30 minutes, 1.0% 30 to 45 minutes, 1.0% 45 to 60 minutes, 3.9% 60 minutes or more (2000)

GANN
(village). Aka Brinkhaven. Covers a land area of 0.191 square miles and a water area of 0 square miles. Located at 40.46° N. Lat.; 82.19° W. Long.
Population: 179 (1990); 143 (2000); 145 (2005); 146 (2010 projected); Race: 100.0% White, 0.0% Black, 0.0% Asian, 1.4% Hispanic of any race (2005); Density: 760.0 persons per square mile (2005); Average household size: 2.79 (2005); Median age: 33.0 (2005); Males per 100 females: 93.3 (2005); Marriage status: 27.7% never married, 57.1% now married, 5.4% widowed, 9.8% divorced (2000); Foreign born: 0.0% (2000); Ancestry (includes multiple ancestries): 17.7% United States or American, 10.2% German, 8.2% Italian, 4.8% Canadian, 4.8% Irish (2000).
Economy: Employment by occupation: 0.0% management, 4.3% professional, 34.3% services, 7.1% sales, 12.9% farming, 0.0% construction, 41.4% production (2000).
Income: Per capita income: $14,655 (2005); Median household income: $40,625 (2005); Average household income: $40,865 (2005); Percent of households with income of $100,000 or more: 1.9% (2005); Poverty rate: 17.7% (2000).

Education: Percent of population age 25 and over with: High school diploma (including GED) or higher: 72.3% (2005); Bachelor's degree or higher: 2.1% (2005); Master's degree or higher: 0.0% (2005).
Housing: Homeownership rate: 78.8% (2005); Median home value: $55,000 (2005); Median rent: $125 per month (2000); Median age of housing: 60+ years (2000).
Transportation: Commute to work: 100.0% car, 0.0% public transportation, 0.0% walk, 0.0% work from home (2000); Travel time to work: 19.1% less than 15 minutes, 33.8% 15 to 30 minutes, 30.9% 30 to 45 minutes, 2.9% 45 to 60 minutes, 13.2% 60 minutes or more (2000)

HOWARD (unincorporated postal area, zip code 43028). Covers a land area of 51.489 square miles and a water area of 0.824 square miles. Located at 40.42° N. Lat.; 82.31° W. Long. Elevation is 930 feet.
Population: 5,564 (2000); Race: 98.7% White, 0.3% Black, 0.2% Asian, 0.0% Hispanic of any race (2000); Density: 108.1 persons per square mile (2000); Age: 22.8% under 18, 13.2% over 64 (2000); Marriage status: 15.4% never married, 70.8% now married, 4.8% widowed, 9.0% divorced (2000); Foreign born: 1.0% (2000); Ancestry (includes multiple ancestries): 27.9% German, 13.3% Irish, 12.4% United States or American, 11.1% English, 5.6% Other groups (2000).
Economy: Employment by occupation: 7.7% management, 20.0% professional, 11.6% services, 27.3% sales, 0.8% farming, 14.1% construction, 18.4% production (2000).
Income: Per capita income: $21,519 (2000); Median household income: $46,344 (2000); Poverty rate: 5.5% (2000).
Education: Percent of population age 25 and over with: High school diploma (including GED) or higher: 86.9% (2000); Bachelor's degree or higher: 18.3% (2000).

School District(s)
East Knox Local SD (PK-12)
　　2003-04 Enrollment: 1,161 . . . . (740) 599-7493

Housing: Homeownership rate: 91.7% (2000); Median home value: $104,200 (2000); Median rent: $422 per month (2000); Median age of housing: 14 years (2000).
Transportation: Commute to work: 94.3% car, 0.8% public transportation, 0.7% walk, 3.6% work from home (2000); Travel time to work: 16.0% less than 15 minutes, 48.7% 15 to 30 minutes, 10.8% 30 to 45 minutes, 4.8% 45 to 60 minutes, 19.8% 60 minutes or more (2000)

MARTINSBURG (village). Covers a land area of 0.180 square miles and a water area of 0 square miles. Located at 40.27° N. Lat.; 82.35° W. Long. Elevation is 1,167 feet.
Population: 213 (1990); 185 (2000); 197 (2005); 209 (2010 projected); Race: 100.0% White, 0.0% Black, 0.0% Asian, 0.0% Hispanic of any race (2005); Density: 1,092.8 persons per square mile (2005); Average household size: 2.43 (2005); Median age: 38.5 (2005); Males per 100 females: 80.7 (2005); Marriage status: 16.4% never married, 56.6% now married, 13.1% widowed, 13.9% divorced (2000); Foreign born: 0.0% (2000); Ancestry (includes multiple ancestries): 21.7% German, 14.0% English, 12.1% United States or American, 8.9% Other groups, 3.2% Dutch (2000).
Economy: Employment by occupation: 0.0% management, 12.7% professional, 9.5% services, 19.0% sales, 0.0% farming, 17.5% construction, 41.3% production (2000).
Income: Per capita income: $15,025 (2005); Median household income: $37,596 (2005); Average household income: $36,543 (2005); Percent of households with income of $100,000 or more: 1.2% (2005); Poverty rate: 14.0% (2000).
Education: Percent of population age 25 and over with: High school diploma (including GED) or higher: 66.2% (2005); Bachelor's degree or higher: 0.0% (2005); Master's degree or higher: 0.0% (2005).
Housing: Homeownership rate: 69.1% (2005); Median home value: $72,727 (2005); Median rent: $367 per month (2000); Median age of housing: 60+ years (2000).
Transportation: Commute to work: 100.0% car, 0.0% public transportation, 0.0% walk, 0.0% work from home (2000); Travel time to work: 4.8% less than 15 minutes, 33.9% 15 to 30 minutes, 30.6% 30 to 45 minutes, 4.8% 45 to 60 minutes, 25.8% 60 minutes or more (2000)

MOUNT VERNON (city). Covers a land area of 8.404 square miles and a water area of 0.040 square miles. Located at 40.39° N. Lat.; 82.48° W. Long. Elevation is 1,020 feet.
History: Mount Vernon was laid out in 1805 by Benjamin Butler, Thomas Patterson, and Joseph Walker, all of whom became prominent citizens here. The town developed as a rural commercial center, and later as a manufacturer of steam, diesel, and gas engines. John Chapman, known as Johnny Appleseed, owned lots in Mount Vernon. This was the birthplace of Daniel Decatur Emmett (1815-1904) who wrote the song "Dixie."
Population: 15,215 (1990); 14,375 (2000); 14,542 (2005); 14,877 (2010 projected); Race: 96.4% White, 1.1% Black, 0.8% Asian, 1.0% Hispanic of any race (2005); Density: 1,730.3 persons per square mile (2005); Average household size: 2.31 (2005); Median age: 37.2 (2005); Males per 100 females: 86.9 (2005); Marriage status: 23.3% never married, 52.7% now married, 9.4% widowed, 14.6% divorced (2000); Foreign born: 1.6% (2000); Ancestry (includes multiple ancestries): 19.7% German, 15.6% United States or American, 12.5% Irish, 10.3% English, 8.1% Other groups (2000).
Economy: Single-family building permits issued: 40 (2005); Multi-family building permits issued: 0 (2005); Employment by occupation: 9.3% management, 17.0% professional, 20.4% services, 23.1% sales, 0.9% farming, 7.8% construction, 21.5% production (2000).
Income: Per capita income: $18,492 (2005); Median household income: $32,817 (2005); Average household income: $42,212 (2005); Percent of households with income of $100,000 or more: 6.0% (2005); Poverty rate: 15.6% (2000).
Education: Percent of population age 25 and over with: High school diploma (including GED) or higher: 80.3% (2005); Bachelor's degree or higher: 18.2% (2005); Master's degree or higher: 7.2% (2005).

School District(s)
Knox Co Esc Digital Academy
　　2003-04 Enrollment: n/a . . . . (740) 393-6767
Knox County Joint Vocational SD (PK-12)
　　2003-04 Enrollment: n/a . . . . (740) 397-5820
Mount Vernon City SD (PK-12)
　　2003-04 Enrollment: 4,301 . . . . (740) 397-7422

Four-year College(s)
Mount Vernon Nazarene University (Private, Not-for-profit, Church of the Nazarene)
　　Fall 2004 Enrollment: 2,455 . . . . (740) 392-6868
　　2005-06 Tuition: In-state $15,886; Out-of-state $15,886

Two-year College(s)
Knox County Career Center (Public)
　　Fall 2004 Enrollment: 88 . . . . (740) 393-2933

Housing: Homeownership rate: 57.2% (2005); Median home value: $94,365 (2005); Median rent: $353 per month (2000); Median age of housing: 48 years (2000).
Hospitals: Knox Community Hospital (115 beds)
Newspapers: Mount Vernon News (Circulation 9,671)
Transportation: Commute to work: 91.2% car, 1.7% public transportation, 2.8% walk, 3.3% work from home (2000); Travel time to work: 58.5% less than 15 minutes, 18.2% 15 to 30 minutes, 7.0% 30 to 45 minutes, 7.2% 45 to 60 minutes, 9.2% 60 minutes or more (2000)
Additional Information Contacts
City of Mount Vernon . . . . (740) 393-9517
　　http://www.mountvernonohio.org
Mount Vernon Knox County Chamber . . . . (740) 393-1111
　　http://www.knoxchamber.com
Mount Vernon Visitors Bureau . . . . (740) 392-6102
　　http://www.visitknoxohio.org

Lake County

Located in northeastern Ohio; bounded on the north by Lake Erie; drained by the Grand and Chagrin Rivers. Covers a land area of 228.21 square miles, a water area of 750.65 square miles, and is located in the Eastern Time Zone. The county government was organized in 1840. County seat is Painesville.

Lake County is part of the Cleveland-Elyria-Mentor, OH Metropolitan Statistical Area. The entire metro area includes: Cuyahoga County, OH; Geauga County, OH; Lake County, OH; Lorain County, OH; Medina County, OH

Weather Station: Painesville 4 NW　　　　　　　　　　　　　Elevation: 597 feet

	Jan	Feb	Mar	Apr	May	Jun	Jul	Aug	Sep	Oct	Nov	Dec
High	34	37	46	56	68	77	81	80	74	63	51	40
Low	20	21	29	39	50	59	64	63	57	46	37	27
Precip	2.3	1.8	2.8	3.2	3.0	3.8	3.1	3.7	4.1	3.3	3.5	2.9
Snow	10.2	7.3	5.2	1.2	tr	0.0	0.0	0.0	0.0	tr	2.1	8.8

High and Low temperatures in degrees Fahrenheit; Precipitation and Snow in inches

Population: 215,499 (1990); 227,511 (2000); 229,367 (2005); 231,228 (2010 projected); Race: 94.4% White, 2.2% Black, 1.2% Asian, 2.2% Hispanic of any race (2005); Density: 1,005.1 persons per square mile (2005); Average household size: 2.49 (2005); Median age: 39.9 (2005); Males per 100 females: 95.0 (2005).
Religion: Five largest groups: 35.7% Catholic Church, 4.0% The United Methodist Church, 1.6% Lutheran Church—Missouri Synod, 1.3% Southern Baptist Convention, 1.3% United Church of Christ (2000).
Economy: Unemployment rate: 5.1% (2005); Total civilian labor force: 130,551 (2005); Leading industries: 24.5% manufacturing; 16.7% retail trade; 11.5% health care and social assistance (2004); Farms: 333 totaling 19,785 acres (2002); Companies that employ 500 or more persons: 9 (2004); Companies that employ 100 to 499 persons: 136 (2004); Companies that employ less than 100 persons: 6,402 (2004); Black-owned businesses: n/a (2002); Hispanic-owned businesses: n/a (2002); Women-owned businesses: 3,487 (2002); Retail sales per capita: $18,786 (2006). Single-family building permits issued: 817 (2005); Multi-family building permits issued: 116 (2005).
Income: Per capita income: $26,222 (2005); Median household income: $53,477 (2005); Average household income: $64,752 (2005); Percent of households with income of $100,000 or more: 15.7% (2005); Poverty rate: 6.3% (2003); Bankruptcy rate: 9.43% (2005).
Taxes: Total county taxes per capita: $291 (2004); County property taxes per capita: $190 (2004).
Education: Percent of population age 25 and over with: High school diploma (including GED) or higher: 86.4% (2005); Bachelor's degree or higher: 21.6% (2005); Master's degree or higher: 6.9% (2005).
Housing: Homeownership rate: 77.8% (2005); Median home value: $150,811 (2005); Median rent: $553 per month (2000); Median age of housing: 34 years (2000).
Health: Birth rate: 109.8 per 10,000 population (2004); Death rate: 95.6 per 10,000 population (2004); Age-adjusted cancer mortality rate: 205.9 deaths per 100,000 population (2002); Air Quality Index: 71.5% good, 24.4% moderate, 3.8% unhealthy for sensitive individuals, 0.3% unhealthy (percent of days in 2005); Number of physicians: 15.9 per 10,000 population (2004); Hospital beds: 19.6 per 10,000 population (2003); Hospital admissions: 830.1 per 10,000 population (2003).
Elections: 2004 Presidential election results: 51.1% Bush, 48.5% Kerry, 0.0% Nader, 0.3% Badnarik
National and State Parks: Chaplin State Forest; Headlands Beach State Park; James A Garfield National Historic Site; Mentor Marsh State Nature Preserve
Additional Information Contacts
Lake County Government . . . . (440) 350-2500
  http://www.lakecountyohio.org/
City of Eastlake . . . . (440) 951-1416
  http://www.eastlakeohio.com
City of Kirtland . . . . (440) 256-1234
  http://kirtlandohio.com
City of Mentor . . . . (440) 255-1100
  http://www.cityofmentor.com
City of Painesville . . . . (440) 392-5800
  http://www.painesville.com
City of Wickliffe . . . . (440) 943-7100
  http://www.cityofwickliffe.com
City of Willoughby . . . . (440) 951-2800
  http://www.willoughbyohio.com
Eastlake Chamber of Commerce . . . . (440) 951-3600
  http://www.eastlakechamber.org
Madison-Perry Area Chamber of Commerce . . . . (440) 428-3760
  http://www.mpacc.org
Mentor Area Chamber of Commerce . . . . (440) 946-2625
  http://www.mentorchamber.org
Painesville Area Chamber of Commerce . . . . (440) 357-7572
  http://www.painesvilleohchamber.org
Village of Madison . . . . (440) 428-7526
  http://www.madisonvillage.org
Village of North Perry . . . . (440) 259-4994
  http://www.northperry.org
Wickliffe Chamber of Commerce . . . . (440) 943-1134
  http://www.cityofwickliffe.com
Willoughby Chamber of Commerce . . . . (440) 942-1632
  http://www.wacoc.com
Willowick Chamber of Commerce . . . . (440) 585-5765
  http://www.willowickchamber.org

Lake County Communities

EASTLAKE (city). Covers a land area of 6.397 square miles and a water area of 0.121 square miles. Located at 41.66° N. Lat.; 81.43° W. Long. Elevation is 620 feet.
History: Eastlake is the site where FirstEnergy's Eastlake Generating Station shut down at 1:31 p.m. EDT on August 14, 2003, eventually leading to the infamous 2003 North America blackout a few hours later.
Population: 21,161 (1990); 20,255 (2000); 19,842 (2005); 19,449 (2010 projected); Race: 96.7% White, 0.7% Black, 1.3% Asian, 0.9% Hispanic of any race (2005); Density: 3,102.0 persons per square mile (2005); Average household size: 2.45 (2005); Median age: 39.3 (2005); Males per 100 females: 95.7 (2005); Marriage status: 25.3% never married, 57.6% now married, 6.8% widowed, 10.4% divorced (2000); Foreign born: 5.0% (2000); Ancestry (includes multiple ancestries): 24.3% German, 20.3% Irish, 17.0% Italian, 9.8% English, 9.6% Polish (2000).
Economy: Diversified light manufacturing industries. Single-family building permits issued: 24 (2005); Multi-family building permits issued: 0 (2005); Employment by occupation: 8.6% management, 15.2% professional, 14.4% services, 28.7% sales, 0.0% farming, 10.2% construction, 23.0% production (2000).
Income: Per capita income: $22,606 (2005); Median household income: $47,250 (2005); Average household income: $55,235 (2005); Percent of households with income of $100,000 or more: 10.1% (2005); Poverty rate: 5.0% (2000).
Taxes: Total city taxes per capita: $593 (2004); City property taxes per capita: $258 (2004).
Education: Percent of population age 25 and over with: High school diploma (including GED) or higher: 82.8% (2005); Bachelor's degree or higher: 12.5% (2005); Master's degree or higher: 3.3% (2005).
School District(s)
Willoughby-Eastlake City SD (PK-12)
  2003-04 Enrollment: 8,876 . . . . (440) 946-5000
Housing: Homeownership rate: 77.6% (2005); Median home value: $133,439 (2005); Median rent: $538 per month (2000); Median age of housing: 35 years (2000).
Safety: Violent crime rate: 7.0 per 10,000 population; Property crime rate: 159.3 per 10,000 population (2004).
Transportation: Commute to work: 95.6% car, 1.0% public transportation, 1.2% walk, 1.6% work from home (2000); Travel time to work: 31.1% less than 15 minutes, 45.2% 15 to 30 minutes, 15.9% 30 to 45 minutes, 4.4% 45 to 60 minutes, 3.4% 60 minutes or more (2000)
Additional Information Contacts
City of Eastlake . . . . (440) 951-1416
  http://www.eastlakeohio.com
Eastlake Chamber of Commerce . . . . (440) 951-3600
  http://www.eastlakechamber.org

FAIRPORT HARBOR (village). Aka Fairport. Covers a land area of 1.042 square miles and a water area of 0.078 square miles. Located at 41.75° N. Lat.; 81.27° W. Long. Elevation is 610 feet.
History: Fairport Harbor grew around fishing, salt-making, and the shipping of iron ore. Many of the early residents were Hungarians and Finns.
Population: 3,017 (1990); 3,180 (2000); 3,195 (2005); 3,224 (2010 projected); Race: 97.3% White, 0.7% Black, 0.3% Asian, 1.9% Hispanic of any race (2005); Density: 3,066.5 persons per square mile (2005); Average household size: 2.21 (2005); Median age: 38.0 (2005); Males per 100 females: 98.9 (2005); Marriage status: 28.5% never married, 48.5% now married, 8.3% widowed, 14.7% divorced (2000); Foreign born: 2.7% (2000); Ancestry (includes multiple ancestries): 18.8% German, 14.9% Irish, 14.1% Hungarian, 10.9% Finnish, 9.4% Italian (2000).
Economy: Single-family building permits issued: 0 (2005); Multi-family building permits issued: 0 (2005); Employment by occupation: 8.5% management, 13.7% professional, 19.6% services, 26.1% sales, 0.0% farming, 11.8% construction, 20.2% production (2000).
Income: Per capita income: $22,267 (2005); Median household income: $39,792 (2005); Average household income: $49,075 (2005); Percent of households with income of $100,000 or more: 7.1% (2005); Poverty rate: 7.4% (2000).
Education: Percent of population age 25 and over with: High school diploma (including GED) or higher: 83.5% (2005); Bachelor's degree or higher: 15.0% (2005); Master's degree or higher: 4.4% (2005).

School District(s)
Fairport Harbor Ex Vill SD (PK-12)
    2003-04 Enrollment: 625 . . . . (440) 354-5400
Housing: Homeownership rate: 60.8% (2005); Median home value: $120,811 (2005); Median rent: $444 per month (2000); Median age of housing: 60+ years (2000).
Safety: Violent crime rate: 25.0 per 10,000 population; Property crime rate: 487.8 per 10,000 population (2004).
Transportation: Commute to work: 92.9% car, 2.1% public transportation, 1.7% walk, 2.4% work from home (2000); Travel time to work: 34.6% less than 15 minutes, 42.4% 15 to 30 minutes, 14.3% 30 to 45 minutes, 5.6% 45 to 60 minutes, 3.0% 60 minutes or more (2000)

GRAND RIVER (village). Aka Richmond.
Covers a land area of 0.550 square miles and a water area of 0.100 square miles. Located at 41.73° N. Lat.; 81.28° W. Long. Elevation is 610 feet.
History: Formerly Richmond.
Population: 295 (1990); 345 (2000); 331 (2005); 317 (2010 projected); Race: 99.1% White, 0.0% Black, 0.9% Asian, 0.3% Hispanic of any race (2005); Density: 601.6 persons per square mile (2005); Average household size: 2.88 (2005); Median age: 39.2 (2005); Males per 100 females: 106.9 (2005); Marriage status: 16.0% never married, 63.1% now married, 5.2% widowed, 15.7% divorced (2000); Foreign born: 2.1% (2000); Ancestry (includes multiple ancestries): 31.7% German, 16.9% Irish, 16.3% Italian, 12.4% English, 11.5% Polish (2000).
Economy: Employment by occupation: 6.0% management, 8.4% professional, 25.3% services, 16.9% sales, 0.0% farming, 13.9% construction, 29.5% production (2000).
Income: Per capita income: $18,595 (2005); Median household income: $50,379 (2005); Average household income: $53,522 (2005); Percent of households with income of $100,000 or more: 8.7% (2005); Poverty rate: 5.9% (2000).
Education: Percent of population age 25 and over with: High school diploma (including GED) or higher: 90.7% (2005); Bachelor's degree or higher: 3.5% (2005); Master's degree or higher: 2.2% (2005).
Housing: Homeownership rate: 78.3% (2005); Median home value: $136,667 (2005); Median rent: $565 per month (2000); Median age of housing: 49 years (2000).
Transportation: Commute to work: 100.0% car, 0.0% public transportation, 0.0% walk, 0.0% work from home (2000); Travel time to work: 40.1% less than 15 minutes, 27.4% 15 to 30 minutes, 15.3% 30 to 45 minutes, 14.6% 45 to 60 minutes, 2.5% 60 minutes or more (2000)

KIRTLAND (city).
Covers a land area of 16.600 square miles and a water area of 0.111 square miles. Located at 41.60° N. Lat.; 81.34° W. Long. Elevation is 710 feet.
History: Kirtland was the location in 1831 where Joseph Smith led a group of his followers. The town flourished as a Mormon stronghold until 1838, when Smith moved on. The Kirtland Temple built by the group remained a dominant factor in the town.
Population: 5,881 (1990); 6,670 (2000); 7,089 (2005); 7,480 (2010 projected); Race: 98.0% White, 0.3% Black, 0.5% Asian, 0.7% Hispanic of any race (2005); Density: 427.1 persons per square mile (2005); Average household size: 2.69 (2005); Median age: 44.4 (2005); Males per 100 females: 97.5 (2005); Marriage status: 21.0% never married, 65.3% now married, 7.2% widowed, 6.5% divorced (2000); Foreign born: 6.4% (2000); Ancestry (includes multiple ancestries): 27.0% German, 18.9% Irish, 14.3% Italian, 12.0% English, 6.6% Slovene (2000).
Economy: Employment by occupation: 18.4% management, 24.0% professional, 10.8% services, 24.2% sales, 0.3% farming, 10.1% construction, 12.1% production (2000).
Income: Per capita income: $36,765 (2005); Median household income: $71,842 (2005); Average household income: $97,414 (2005); Percent of households with income of $100,000 or more: 32.0% (2005); Poverty rate: 2.3% (2000).
Education: Percent of population age 25 and over with: High school diploma (including GED) or higher: 87.9% (2005); Bachelor's degree or higher: 32.5% (2005); Master's degree or higher: 11.1% (2005).
School District(s)
Kirtland Local SD (PK-12)
    2003-04 Enrollment: 1,070 . . . . (440) 256-3311
Two-year College(s)
Lakeland Community College (Public)
    Fall 2004 Enrollment: 8,605. (440) 525-7000
    2005-06 Tuition: In-state $3,147; Out-of-state $6,698

Housing: Homeownership rate: 86.5% (2005); Median home value: $238,068 (2005); Median rent: $560 per month (2000); Median age of housing: 33 years (2000).
Safety: Violent crime rate: 4.3 per 10,000 population; Property crime rate: 80.2 per 10,000 population (2004).
Transportation: Commute to work: 95.3% car, 0.2% public transportation, 1.1% walk, 3.3% work from home (2000); Travel time to work: 22.2% less than 15 minutes, 51.3% 15 to 30 minutes, 18.3% 30 to 45 minutes, 5.8% 45 to 60 minutes, 2.3% 60 minutes or more (2000)
Additional Information Contacts
City of Kirtland . . . . (440) 256-1234
    http://kirtlandohio.com

KIRTLAND HILLS (village).
Covers a land area of 5.585 square miles and a water area of 0.072 square miles. Located at 41.64° N. Lat.; 81.31° W. Long. Elevation is 800 feet.
History: The first Mormon temple was built here (1833-1836) by Joseph Smith and his followers. Settled 1808, incorporated 1926.
Population: 628 (1990); 597 (2000); 707 (2005); 807 (2010 projected); Race: 97.9% White, 0.3% Black, 0.1% Asian, 0.7% Hispanic of any race (2005); Density: 126.6 persons per square mile (2005); Average household size: 2.61 (2005); Median age: 46.7 (2005); Males per 100 females: 92.1 (2005); Marriage status: 19.8% never married, 69.0% now married, 5.6% widowed, 5.6% divorced (2000); Foreign born: 2.3% (2000); Ancestry (includes multiple ancestries): 21.5% German, 20.9% Irish, 17.2% Italian, 9.7% English, 8.2% Slovene (2000).
Economy: Employment by occupation: 32.5% management, 27.4% professional, 2.9% services, 23.6% sales, 0.0% farming, 8.3% construction, 5.4% production (2000).
Income: Per capita income: $81,987 (2005); Median household income: $127,206 (2005); Average household income: $213,893 (2005); Percent of households with income of $100,000 or more: 56.8% (2005); Poverty rate: 3.2% (2000).
Education: Percent of population age 25 and over with: High school diploma (including GED) or higher: 93.8% (2005); Bachelor's degree or higher: 47.8% (2005); Master's degree or higher: 20.0% (2005).
Housing: Homeownership rate: 90.0% (2005); Median home value: $515,625 (2005); Median rent: $525 per month (2000); Median age of housing: 28 years (2000).
Safety: Violent crime rate: 15.0 per 10,000 population; Property crime rate: 164.7 per 10,000 population (2004).
Transportation: Commute to work: 90.5% car, 0.7% public transportation, 0.7% walk, 8.2% work from home (2000); Travel time to work: 22.5% less than 15 minutes, 51.4% 15 to 30 minutes, 16.1% 30 to 45 minutes, 5.0% 45 to 60 minutes, 5.0% 60 minutes or more (2000)

LAKELINE (village).
Covers a land area of 0.076 square miles and a water area of 0 square miles. Located at 41.65° N. Lat.; 81.45° W. Long. Elevation is 617 feet.
Population: 210 (1990); 165 (2000); 220 (2005); 269 (2010 projected); Race: 100.0% White, 0.0% Black, 0.0% Asian, 0.0% Hispanic of any race (2005); Density: 2,898.5 persons per square mile (2005); Average household size: 2.50 (2005); Median age: 42.7 (2005); Males per 100 females: 109.5 (2005); Marriage status: 23.6% never married, 52.8% now married, 10.2% widowed, 13.4% divorced (2000); Foreign born: 2.4% (2000); Ancestry (includes multiple ancestries): 28.3% Irish, 24.1% German, 19.9% Other groups, 8.4% Italian, 7.8% English (2000).
Economy: Single-family building permits issued: 0 (2005); Multi-family building permits issued: 0 (2005); Employment by occupation: 7.0% management, 8.5% professional, 16.9% services, 32.4% sales, 0.0% farming, 4.2% construction, 31.0% production (2000).
Income: Per capita income: $22,648 (2005); Median household income: $51,667 (2005); Average household income: $56,619 (2005); Percent of households with income of $100,000 or more: 10.2% (2005); Poverty rate: 5.0% (2000).
Education: Percent of population age 25 and over with: High school diploma (including GED) or higher: 74.8% (2005); Bachelor's degree or higher: 9.3% (2005); Master's degree or higher: 4.0% (2005).
Housing: Homeownership rate: 90.9% (2005); Median home value: $141,176 (2005); Median rent: $469 per month (2000); Median age of housing: 53 years (2000).
Transportation: Commute to work: 97.2% car, 0.0% public transportation, 2.8% walk, 0.0% work from home (2000); Travel time to work: 21.1% less than 15 minutes, 62.0% 15 to 30 minutes, 9.9% 30 to 45 minutes, 1.4% 45 to 60 minutes, 5.6% 60 minutes or more (2000)

MADISON (village). Covers a land area of 4.578 square miles and a water area of 0 square miles. Located at 41.77° N. Lat.; 81.05° W. Long. Elevation is 744 feet.
History: Madison grew around its orchards, nurseries, and potato fields. It was known for Madison Willowcraft, the product of its basket-making industry.
Population: 2,480 (1990); 2,921 (2000); 3,019 (2005); 3,118 (2010 projected); Race: 98.0% White, 0.6% Black, 0.2% Asian, 1.1% Hispanic of any race (2005); Density: 659.5 persons per square mile (2005); Average household size: 2.57 (2005); Median age: 38.6 (2005); Males per 100 females: 99.7 (2005); Marriage status: 21.1% never married, 64.0% now married, 5.7% widowed, 9.2% divorced (2000); Foreign born: 1.3% (2000); Ancestry (includes multiple ancestries): 27.0% German, 20.3% Irish, 13.5% English, 10.7% United States or American, 9.0% Italian (2000).
Economy: Employment by occupation: 11.9% management, 22.1% professional, 11.7% services, 29.6% sales, 0.3% farming, 7.5% construction, 16.9% production (2000).
Income: Per capita income: $24,753 (2005); Median household income: $57,515 (2005); Average household income: $63,112 (2005); Percent of households with income of $100,000 or more: 12.4% (2005); Poverty rate: 3.4% (2000).
Education: Percent of population age 25 and over with: High school diploma (including GED) or higher: 88.3% (2005); Bachelor's degree or higher: 22.9% (2005); Master's degree or higher: 7.4% (2005).
School District(s)
Madison Local SD (PK-12)
    2003-04 Enrollment: 3,739 . . . . (440) 428-2166
Housing: Homeownership rate: 76.2% (2005); Median home value: $152,983 (2005); Median rent: $476 per month (2000); Median age of housing: 28 years (2000).
Newspapers: Lake County Gazette (General - Circulation 5,000); The Free Enterprise (General - Circulation 17,500); The Lake County Tribune (General - Circulation 3,020)
Transportation: Commute to work: 96.2% car, 0.2% public transportation, 1.8% walk, 1.7% work from home (2000); Travel time to work: 24.2% less than 15 minutes, 31.4% 15 to 30 minutes, 29.3% 30 to 45 minutes, 9.9% 45 to 60 minutes, 5.2% 60 minutes or more (2000)
Additional Information Contacts
Madison-Perry Area Chamber of Commerce. . . . . (440) 428-3760
    http://www.mpacc.org
Village of Madison . . . . (440) 428-7526
    http://www.madisonvillage.org

MENTOR (city). Covers a land area of 26.769 square miles and a water area of 1.307 square miles. Located at 41.69° N. Lat.; 81.34° W. Long. Elevation is 690 feet.
History: Named, possibly, for Hiram Mentor, an early settler. Mentor was founded in 1799. James A. Garfield lived in Mentor prior to his time as president of the U.S.
Population: 47,358 (1990); 50,278 (2000); 49,836 (2005); 49,444 (2010 projected); Race: 96.5% White, 0.8% Black, 1.6% Asian, 0.8% Hispanic of any race (2005); Density: 1,861.7 persons per square mile (2005); Average household size: 2.62 (2005); Median age: 40.2 (2005); Males per 100 females: 94.5 (2005); Marriage status: 21.5% never married, 62.5% now married, 6.8% widowed, 9.2% divorced (2000); Foreign born: 3.8% (2000); Ancestry (includes multiple ancestries): 26.6% German, 19.5% Irish, 16.2% Italian, 12.8% English, 8.4% Polish (2000).
Economy: Unemployment rate: 4.5% (2005); Total civilian labor force: 29,968 (2005); Single-family building permits issued: 73 (2005); Multi-family building permits issued: 0 (2005); Employment by occupation: 15.3% management, 20.8% professional, 11.1% services, 28.7% sales, 0.2% farming, 7.0% construction, 16.9% production (2000).
Income: Per capita income: $28,146 (2005); Median household income: $63,664 (2005); Average household income: $72,932 (2005); Percent of households with income of $100,000 or more: 21.8% (2005); Poverty rate: 2.7% (2000).
Taxes: Total city taxes per capita: $634 (2004); City property taxes per capita: $71 (2004).
Education: Percent of population age 25 and over with: High school diploma (including GED) or higher: 89.3% (2005); Bachelor's degree or higher: 27.8% (2005); Master's degree or higher: 9.0% (2005).
School District(s)
Mentor Ex Vill SD (PK-12)
    2003-04 Enrollment: 9,777 . . . . (440) 255-4444

Two-year College(s)
Brown Aveda Institute
    Fall 2004 Enrollment: 119 . . . . (440) 255-9494
Cleveland Institute of Dental-Medical Assistants (Private, For-profit)
    Fall 2004 Enrollment: 187 . . . . (216) 241-2930
Housing: Homeownership rate: 87.7% (2005); Median home value: $172,138 (2005); Median rent: $614 per month (2000); Median age of housing: 28 years (2000).
Safety: Violent crime rate: 10.2 per 10,000 population; Property crime rate: 261.0 per 10,000 population (2004).
Transportation: Commute to work: 95.6% car, 0.9% public transportation, 1.0% walk, 2.2% work from home (2000); Travel time to work: 29.5% less than 15 minutes, 39.5% 15 to 30 minutes, 20.8% 30 to 45 minutes, 7.2% 45 to 60 minutes, 3.0% 60 minutes or more (2000)
Additional Information Contacts
City of Mentor. . . . . (440) 255-1100
    http://www.cityofmentor.com
Mentor Area Chamber of Commerce. . . . . (440) 946-2625
    http://www.mentorchamber.org

MENTOR-ON-THE-LAKE (city). Covers a land area of 1.633 square miles and a water area of 0.034 square miles. Located at 41.71° N. Lat.; 81.36° W. Long. Elevation is 606 feet.
Population: 8,271 (1990); 8,127 (2000); 8,239 (2005); 8,369 (2010 projected); Race: 96.5% White, 0.9% Black, 0.9% Asian, 1.5% Hispanic of any race (2005); Density: 5,044.9 persons per square mile (2005); Average household size: 2.40 (2005); Median age: 36.9 (2005); Males per 100 females: 95.5 (2005); Marriage status: 25.2% never married, 56.4% now married, 6.5% widowed, 11.9% divorced (2000); Foreign born: 1.1% (2000); Ancestry (includes multiple ancestries): 26.8% German, 21.2% Irish, 14.0% Italian, 10.3% English, 9.0% Polish (2000).
Economy: Employment by occupation: 12.2% management, 15.6% professional, 15.1% services, 30.2% sales, 0.0% farming, 8.9% construction, 18.0% production (2000).
Income: Per capita income: $23,345 (2005); Median household income: $48,766 (2005); Average household income: $55,929 (2005); Percent of households with income of $100,000 or more: 10.0% (2005); Poverty rate: 5.7% (2000).
Education: Percent of population age 25 and over with: High school diploma (including GED) or higher: 87.8% (2005); Bachelor's degree or higher: 14.5% (2005); Master's degree or higher: 5.1% (2005).
School District(s)
Mentor Ex Vill SD (PK-12)
    2003-04 Enrollment: 9,777 . . . . (440) 255-4444
Housing: Homeownership rate: 68.6% (2005); Median home value: $138,562 (2005); Median rent: $609 per month (2000); Median age of housing: 30 years (2000).
Safety: Violent crime rate: 4.9 per 10,000 population; Property crime rate: 64.4 per 10,000 population (2004).
Transportation: Commute to work: 96.7% car, 0.7% public transportation, 0.7% walk, 1.6% work from home (2000); Travel time to work: 27.0% less than 15 minutes, 42.3% 15 to 30 minutes, 19.4% 30 to 45 minutes, 5.9% 45 to 60 minutes, 5.3% 60 minutes or more (2000)

NORTH MADISON (CDP). Covers a land area of 4.010 square miles and a water area of 0 square miles. Located at 41.83° N. Lat.; 81.05° W. Long. Elevation is 676 feet.
Population: 8,695 (1990); 8,451 (2000); 9,002 (2005); 9,502 (2010 projected); Race: 97.5% White, 0.1% Black, 0.6% Asian, 1.9% Hispanic of any race (2005); Density: 2,245.1 persons per square mile (2005); Average household size: 2.68 (2005); Median age: 35.3 (2005); Males per 100 females: 98.2 (2005); Marriage status: 21.1% never married, 61.3% now married, 5.3% widowed, 12.3% divorced (2000); Foreign born: 1.2% (2000); Ancestry (includes multiple ancestries): 22.5% German, 18.4% Irish, 10.9% Italian, 10.2% English, 10.1% United States or American (2000).
Economy: Employment by occupation: 7.7% management, 11.2% professional, 13.6% services, 26.3% sales, 0.5% farming, 14.0% construction, 26.6% production (2000).
Income: Per capita income: $20,654 (2005); Median household income: $48,216 (2005); Average household income: $55,215 (2005); Percent of households with income of $100,000 or more: 7.4% (2005); Poverty rate: 5.9% (2000).

Education: Percent of population age 25 and over with: High school diploma (including GED) or higher: 82.6% (2005); Bachelor's degree or higher: 9.7% (2005); Master's degree or higher: 3.8% (2005).
Housing: Homeownership rate: 82.5% (2005); Median home value: $124,002 (2005); Median rent: $496 per month (2000); Median age of housing: 35 years (2000).
Transportation: Commute to work: 97.2% car, 0.2% public transportation, 0.6% walk, 1.6% work from home (2000); Travel time to work: 16.9% less than 15 minutes, 30.7% 15 to 30 minutes, 33.1% 30 to 45 minutes, 10.9% 45 to 60 minutes, 8.4% 60 minutes or more (2000)

NORTH PERRY (village). Covers a land area of 3.890 square miles and a water area of 0 square miles. Located at 41.80° N. Lat.; 81.12° W. Long. Elevation is 680 feet.
Population: 830 (1990); 838 (2000); 923 (2005); 1,000 (2010 projected); Race: 98.8% White, 0.1% Black, 0.1% Asian, 0.5% Hispanic of any race (2005); Density: 237.3 persons per square mile (2005); Average household size: 2.71 (2005); Median age: 42.2 (2005); Males per 100 females: 98.1 (2005); Marriage status: 22.8% never married, 63.5% now married, 6.8% widowed, 6.8% divorced (2000); Foreign born: 1.3% (2000); Ancestry (includes multiple ancestries): 29.6% German, 23.3% Irish, 18.0% English, 8.0% Italian, 7.0% United States or American (2000).
Economy: Employment by occupation: 15.2% management, 13.7% professional, 14.9% services, 28.4% sales, 0.0% farming, 8.9% construction, 18.8% production (2000).
Income: Per capita income: $21,687 (2005); Median household income: $47,170 (2005); Average household income: $58,875 (2005); Percent of households with income of $100,000 or more: 12.6% (2005); Poverty rate: 6.0% (2000).
Education: Percent of population age 25 and over with: High school diploma (including GED) or higher: 85.8% (2005); Bachelor's degree or higher: 16.2% (2005); Master's degree or higher: 5.4% (2005).
Housing: Homeownership rate: 87.9% (2005); Median home value: $173,707 (2005); Median rent: $606 per month (2000); Median age of housing: 40 years (2000).
Transportation: Commute to work: 92.7% car, 0.7% public transportation, 1.7% walk, 4.9% work from home (2000); Travel time to work: 30.6% less than 15 minutes, 36.0% 15 to 30 minutes, 17.2% 30 to 45 minutes, 9.5% 45 to 60 minutes, 6.7% 60 minutes or more (2000)
Additional Information Contacts
Village of North Perry.................................. (440) 259-4994
http://www.northperry.org

PAINESVILLE (city). Covers a land area of 5.977 square miles and a water area of 0.710 square miles. Located at 41.72° N. Lat.; 81.25° W. Long. Elevation is 677 feet.
History: Named for Edward Paine, first settler, who had been a general in the American Revolution. Painesville was settled in the early 1800's by pioneers from Connecticut. Architect-builder Jonathan Goldsmith lived in Painesville from 1811 until his death in 1847, and the town had several examples of Goldsmith's work.
Population: 15,712 (1990); 17,503 (2000); 17,220 (2005); 17,014 (2010 projected); Race: 73.4% White, 13.7% Black, 0.5% Asian, 17.9% Hispanic of any race (2005); Density: 2,881.3 persons per square mile (2005); Average household size: 2.69 (2005); Median age: 32.1 (2005); Males per 100 females: 97.7 (2005); Marriage status: 29.7% never married, 50.5% now married, 7.3% widowed, 12.5% divorced (2000); Foreign born: 10.1% (2000); Ancestry (includes multiple ancestries): 26.7% Other groups, 18.7% German, 13.7% Irish, 10.5% English, 9.3% Italian (2000).
Economy: Single-family building permits issued: 111 (2005); Multi-family building permits issued: 18 (2005); Employment by occupation: 7.2% management, 13.0% professional, 17.8% services, 25.7% sales, 2.6% farming, 9.2% construction, 24.5% production (2000).
Income: Per capita income: $16,651 (2005); Median household income: $37,379 (2005); Average household income: $43,491 (2005); Percent of households with income of $100,000 or more: 5.5% (2005); Poverty rate: 16.0% (2000).
Taxes: Total city taxes per capita: $471 (2004); City property taxes per capita: $36 (2004).
Education: Percent of population age 25 and over with: High school diploma (including GED) or higher: 74.1% (2005); Bachelor's degree or higher: 12.5% (2005); Master's degree or higher: 4.3% (2005).
School District(s)
Auburn Joint Vocational SD (10-12)
   2003-04 Enrollment: n/a .... (440) 357-7542
Painesville City Local SD (KG-12)
   2003-04 Enrollment: 2,845 .... (440) 392-5060
Painesville Township Local SD (PK-12)
   2003-04 Enrollment: 4,519 .... (440) 352-0668
Four-year College(s)
Lake Erie College (Private, Not-for-profit)
   Fall 2004 Enrollment: 1,043.................... (440) 375-7000
   2005-06 Tuition: In-state $21,390; Out-of-state $21,390
Two-year College(s)
Auburn Career Center (Public)
   Fall 2004 Enrollment: 323 .... (800) 544-9750
Housing: Homeownership rate: 52.5% (2005); Median home value: $113,377 (2005); Median rent: $462 per month (2000); Median age of housing: 46 years (2000).
Hospitals: Lake Hospital System - East (359 beds)
Transportation: Commute to work: 92.9% car, 0.9% public transportation, 3.8% walk, 1.3% work from home (2000); Travel time to work: 32.4% less than 15 minutes, 41.6% 15 to 30 minutes, 17.4% 30 to 45 minutes, 5.4% 45 to 60 minutes, 3.2% 60 minutes or more (2000)
Additional Information Contacts
City of Painesville...................................... (440) 392-5800
   http://www.painesville.com
Painesville Area Chamber of Commerce............... (440) 357-7572
   http://www.painesvilleohchamber.org

PERRY (village). Covers a land area of 2.180 square miles and a water area of 0 square miles. Located at 41.75° N. Lat.; 81.13° W. Long. Elevation is 706 feet.
Population: 1,036 (1990); 1,195 (2000); 1,237 (2005); 1,279 (2010 projected); Race: 97.7% White, 0.1% Black, 1.2% Asian, 0.4% Hispanic of any race (2005); Density: 567.4 persons per square mile (2005); Average household size: 2.73 (2005); Median age: 38.9 (2005); Males per 100 females: 94.5 (2005); Marriage status: 21.2% never married, 62.6% now married, 5.0% widowed, 11.2% divorced (2000); Foreign born: 2.9% (2000); Ancestry (includes multiple ancestries): 31.2% German, 18.7% Irish, 15.6% Italian, 15.1% English, 6.2% Other groups (2000).
Economy: Employment by occupation: 9.4% management, 21.6% professional, 16.6% services, 24.4% sales, 0.3% farming, 12.1% construction, 15.5% production (2000).
Income: Per capita income: $26,198 (2005); Median household income: $62,306 (2005); Average household income: $71,540 (2005); Percent of households with income of $100,000 or more: 19.2% (2005); Poverty rate: 2.7% (2000).
Education: Percent of population age 25 and over with: High school diploma (including GED) or higher: 91.8% (2005); Bachelor's degree or higher: 22.3% (2005); Master's degree or higher: 7.4% (2005).
School District(s)
Perry Local SD (KG-12)
   2003-04 Enrollment: 1,854 .... (440) 259-3881
Housing: Homeownership rate: 83.4% (2005); Median home value: $174,172 (2005); Median rent: $504 per month (2000); Median age of housing: 36 years (2000).
Transportation: Commute to work: 97.0% car, 0.3% public transportation, 1.2% walk, 1.5% work from home (2000); Travel time to work: 32.9% less than 15 minutes, 38.2% 15 to 30 minutes, 16.6% 30 to 45 minutes, 8.1% 45 to 60 minutes, 4.2% 60 minutes or more (2000)

TIMBERLAKE (village). Covers a land area of 0.214 square miles and a water area of 0 square miles. Located at 41.66° N. Lat.; 81.44° W. Long. Elevation is 615 feet.
Population: 833 (1990); 775 (2000); 750 (2005); 725 (2010 projected); Race: 98.7% White, 0.0% Black, 0.3% Asian, 1.9% Hispanic of any race (2005); Density: 3,497.5 persons per square mile (2005); Average household size: 2.44 (2005); Median age: 47.5 (2005); Males per 100 females: 100.0 (2005); Marriage status: 22.9% never married, 58.3% now married, 6.1% widowed, 12.7% divorced (2000); Foreign born: 3.4% (2000); Ancestry (includes multiple ancestries): 30.1% German, 18.9% Irish, 16.7% Italian, 13.4% English, 8.5% Slovene (2000).
Economy: Single-family building permits issued: 1 (2005); Multi-family building permits issued: 0 (2005); Employment by occupation: 12.9% management, 17.0% professional, 14.8% services, 33.7% sales, 0.0% farming, 8.0% construction, 13.6% production (2000).
Income: Per capita income: $25,600 (2005); Median household income: $56,162 (2005); Average household income: $62,541 (2005); Percent of

households with income of $100,000 or more: 19.5% (2005); Poverty rate: 1.4% (2000).
Education: Percent of population age 25 and over with: High school diploma (including GED) or higher: 87.8% (2005); Bachelor's degree or higher: 22.4% (2005); Master's degree or higher: 7.7% (2005).
Housing: Homeownership rate: 95.1% (2005); Median home value: $180,702 (2005); Median rent: $771 per month (2000); Median age of housing: 44 years (2000).
Transportation: Commute to work: 92.9% car, 1.5% public transportation, 0.7% walk, 3.9% work from home (2000); Travel time to work: 30.9% less than 15 minutes, 37.1% 15 to 30 minutes, 23.0% 30 to 45 minutes, 6.1% 45 to 60 minutes, 2.8% 60 minutes or more (2000)

WAITE HILL (village).
Covers a land area of 4.213 square miles and a water area of 0.059 square miles. Located at 41.61° N. Lat.; 81.38° W. Long. Elevation is 780 feet.
Population: 454 (1990); 446 (2000); 448 (2005); 452 (2010 projected); Race: 97.5% White, 0.0% Black, 1.1% Asian, 0.0% Hispanic of any race (2005); Density: 106.3 persons per square mile (2005); Average household size: 2.38 (2005); Median age: 54.3 (2005); Males per 100 females: 101.8 (2005); Marriage status: 11.6% never married, 78.7% now married, 4.3% widowed, 5.4% divorced (2000); Foreign born: 5.8% (2000); Ancestry (includes multiple ancestries): 19.7% English, 19.5% German, 11.3% Irish, 8.9% Italian, 6.7% Slovene (2000).
Economy: Employment by occupation: 35.3% management, 35.8% professional, 5.5% services, 15.6% sales, 0.0% farming, 0.9% construction, 6.9% production (2000).
Income: Per capita income: $70,352 (2005); Median household income: $105,556 (2005); Average household income: $167,646 (2005); Percent of households with income of $100,000 or more: 51.1% (2005); Poverty rate: 0.9% (2000).
Education: Percent of population age 25 and over with: High school diploma (including GED) or higher: 95.8% (2005); Bachelor's degree or higher: 57.0% (2005); Master's degree or higher: 26.4% (2005).
Housing: Homeownership rate: 86.2% (2005); Median home value: $496,429 (2005); Median rent: $833 per month (2000); Median age of housing: 56 years (2000).
Safety: Violent crime rate: 0.0 per 10,000 population; Property crime rate: 20.5 per 10,000 population (2004).
Transportation: Commute to work: 87.5% car, 0.9% public transportation, 2.8% walk, 7.9% work from home (2000); Travel time to work: 25.6% less than 15 minutes, 44.2% 15 to 30 minutes, 25.1% 30 to 45 minutes, 4.0% 45 to 60 minutes, 1.0% 60 minutes or more (2000)

WICKLIFFE (city).
Covers a land area of 4.653 square miles and a water area of 0.003 square miles. Located at 41.60° N. Lat.; 81.47° W. Long. Elevation is 700 feet.
History: Named for Charles A. Wickliffe, a Kentucky lawyer. Borromeo College of Ohio and the Rabbinical College of Telshe are here. Incorporated 1916.
Population: 14,558 (1990); 13,484 (2000); 13,221 (2005); 12,978 (2010 projected); Race: 94.7% White, 3.0% Black, 1.1% Asian, 0.6% Hispanic of any race (2005); Density: 2,841.6 persons per square mile (2005); Average household size: 2.35 (2005); Median age: 43.8 (2005); Males per 100 females: 94.9 (2005); Marriage status: 23.5% never married, 57.2% now married, 10.1% widowed, 9.2% divorced (2000); Foreign born: 4.6% (2000); Ancestry (includes multiple ancestries): 21.2% German, 20.3% Italian, 18.0% Irish, 10.8% Polish, 9.9% Slovene (2000).
Economy: Manufacturing includes chemicals, machinery, meters. Single-family building permits issued: 8 (2005); Multi-family building permits issued: 0 (2005); Employment by occupation: 12.3% management, 17.8% professional, 15.8% services, 27.7% sales, 0.0% farming, 10.3% construction, 16.1% production (2000).
Income: Per capita income: $23,384 (2005); Median household income: $46,926 (2005); Average household income: $53,977 (2005); Percent of households with income of $100,000 or more: 9.4% (2005); Poverty rate: 6.5% (2000).
Education: Percent of population age 25 and over with: High school diploma (including GED) or higher: 85.5% (2005); Bachelor's degree or higher: 16.3% (2005); Master's degree or higher: 6.0% (2005).

School District(s)
Wickliffe City SD (PK-12)
   2003-04 Enrollment: 1,570 . . . . (440) 943-6900

Four-year College(s)
Rabbinical College Telshe (Private, Not-for-profit, Jewish)
   Fall 2004 Enrollment: 57 . . . . (440) 943-5300
   2005-06 Tuition: In-state $6,700; Out-of-state $6,700
Saint Mary Seminary (Private, Not-for-profit, Roman Catholic)
   Fall 2004 Enrollment: 133 . . . . (440) 943-7600
Housing: Homeownership rate: 84.4% (2005); Median home value: $135,006 (2005); Median rent: $489 per month (2000); Median age of housing: 44 years (2000).
Transportation: Commute to work: 93.8% car, 2.1% public transportation, 1.6% walk, 1.9% work from home (2000); Travel time to work: 36.7% less than 15 minutes, 42.5% 15 to 30 minutes, 15.4% 30 to 45 minutes, 3.5% 45 to 60 minutes, 1.9% 60 minutes or more (2000)
Additional Information Contacts
City of Wickliffe . . . . (440) 943-7100
   http://www.cityofwickliffe.com
Wickliffe Chamber of Commerce . . . . (440) 943-1134
   http://www.cityofwickliffe.com

WILLOUGHBY (city).
Covers a land area of 10.166 square miles and a water area of 0.064 square miles. Located at 41.65° N. Lat.; 81.40° W. Long. Elevation is 665 feet.
History: Willoughby was first called Chagrin, but was renamed for an instructor in the Willoughby Medical College, established in 1834. The college had a good reputation until 1843, when a local resident discovered her newly-buried husband was missing from his grave. The medical school's method of acquiring cadavers for research soon brought about its own demise.
Population: 20,510 (1990); 22,621 (2000); 22,426 (2005); 22,260 (2010 projected); Race: 95.4% White, 1.4% Black, 1.6% Asian, 0.8% Hispanic of any race (2005); Density: 2,206.1 persons per square mile (2005); Average household size: 2.15 (2005); Median age: 40.3 (2005); Males per 100 females: 86.3 (2005); Marriage status: 26.0% never married, 49.9% now married, 9.8% widowed, 14.4% divorced (2000); Foreign born: 3.7% (2000); Ancestry (includes multiple ancestries): 26.4% German, 18.9% Irish, 15.6% Italian, 11.3% English, 6.5% Polish (2000).
Economy: Single-family building permits issued: 82 (2005); Multi-family building permits issued: 29 (2005); Employment by occupation: 15.0% management, 19.7% professional, 13.0% services, 28.1% sales, 0.1% farming, 7.9% construction, 16.1% production (2000).
Income: Per capita income: $26,807 (2005); Median household income: $47,007 (2005); Average household income: $57,177 (2005); Percent of households with income of $100,000 or more: 11.9% (2005); Poverty rate: 5.8% (2000).
Education: Percent of population age 25 and over with: High school diploma (including GED) or higher: 87.8% (2005); Bachelor's degree or higher: 23.7% (2005); Master's degree or higher: 6.3% (2005).

School District(s)
Lake Educational Service Center
   2003-04 Enrollment: n/a . . . . (440) 350-2563
Willoughby-Eastlake City SD (PK-12)
   2003-04 Enrollment: 8,876 . . . . (440) 946-5000

Two-year College(s)
Willoughby-Eastlake School of Practical Nursing (Public)
   Fall 2004 Enrollment: 71 . . . . (440) 946-7085
   2005-06 Tuition: In-state $7,569; Out-of-state $7,569
Housing: Homeownership rate: 59.8% (2005); Median home value: $147,670 (2005); Median rent: $600 per month (2000); Median age of housing: 30 years (2000).
Hospitals: Lake Hospital System - West (359 beds); Laurelwood Hospital and Counseling Centers (160 beds)
Safety: Violent crime rate: 17.3 per 10,000 population; Property crime rate: 192.2 per 10,000 population (2004).
Newspapers: The News-Herald (Circulation 49,000)
Transportation: Commute to work: 95.4% car, 0.8% public transportation, 1.6% walk, 1.5% work from home (2000); Travel time to work: 29.5% less than 15 minutes, 42.2% 15 to 30 minutes, 21.2% 30 to 45 minutes, 4.2% 45 to 60 minutes, 2.8% 60 minutes or more (2000)
Additional Information Contacts
City of Willoughby . . . . (440) 951-2800
   http://www.willoughbyohio.com
Willoughby Chamber of Commerce . . . . (440) 942-1632
   http://www.wacoc.com

WILLOUGHBY HILLS (city). Covers a land area of 10.765 square miles and a water area of 0.086 square miles. Located at 41.58° N. Lat.; 81.44° W. Long. Elevation is 801 feet.
Population: 8,427 (1990); 8,595 (2000); 8,418 (2005); 8,260 (2010 projected); Race: 85.4% White, 7.9% Black, 5.4% Asian, 0.8% Hispanic of any race (2005); Density: 782.0 persons per square mile (2005); Average household size: 2.18 (2005); Median age: 45.0 (2005); Males per 100 females: 92.2 (2005); Marriage status: 25.6% never married, 55.9% now married, 7.5% widowed, 11.0% divorced (2000); Foreign born: 11.3% (2000); Ancestry (includes multiple ancestries): 21.2% German, 16.3% Italian, 15.0% Irish, 12.2% Slovene, 10.9% Other groups (2000).
Economy: Single-family building permits issued: 35 (2005); Multi-family building permits issued: 0 (2005); Employment by occupation: 17.0% management, 24.5% professional, 13.2% services, 28.7% sales, 0.0% farming, 5.2% construction, 11.5% production (2000).
Income: Per capita income: $29,403 (2005); Median household income: $51,197 (2005); Average household income: $64,186 (2005); Percent of households with income of $100,000 or more: 16.0% (2005); Poverty rate: 3.4% (2000).
Education: Percent of population age 25 and over with: High school diploma (including GED) or higher: 87.6% (2005); Bachelor's degree or higher: 32.3% (2005); Master's degree or higher: 11.9% (2005).

Four-year College(s)
Bryant and Stratton College-Willoughby Hills (Private, For-profit)
    Fall 2004 Enrollment: 152 . . . . (440) 944-6800
    2005-06 Tuition: In-state $17,730; Out-of-state $17,730

Housing: Homeownership rate: 55.0% (2005); Median home value: $260,793 (2005); Median rent: $620 per month (2000); Median age of housing: 32 years (2000).
Transportation: Commute to work: 95.3% car, 0.9% public transportation, 1.5% walk, 1.7% work from home (2000); Travel time to work: 24.7% less than 15 minutes, 43.4% 15 to 30 minutes, 22.6% 30 to 45 minutes, 6.0% 45 to 60 minutes, 3.3% 60 minutes or more (2000)

WILLOWICK (city). Covers a land area of 2.515 square miles and a water area of 0 square miles. Located at 41.63° N. Lat.; 81.46° W. Long. Elevation is 622 feet.
History: Named for the Willoughby and Wickliff families. Incorporated 1924.
Population: 15,269 (1990); 14,361 (2000); 13,931 (2005); 13,511 (2010 projected); Race: 97.4% White, 0.9% Black, 0.7% Asian, 1.0% Hispanic of any race (2005); Density: 5,538.3 persons per square mile (2005); Average household size: 2.30 (2005); Median age: 42.6 (2005); Males per 100 females: 92.5 (2005); Marriage status: 21.3% never married, 56.7% now married, 12.1% widowed, 9.9% divorced (2000); Foreign born: 4.6% (2000); Ancestry (includes multiple ancestries): 23.8% German, 19.3% Italian, 17.6% Irish, 11.9% Polish, 9.6% Slovene (2000).
Economy: Single-family building permits issued: 0 (2005); Multi-family building permits issued: 0 (2005); Employment by occupation: 12.0% management, 16.7% professional, 12.9% services, 32.4% sales, 0.0% farming, 8.2% construction, 17.8% production (2000).
Income: Per capita income: $24,397 (2005); Median household income: $48,045 (2005); Average household income: $56,079 (2005); Percent of households with income of $100,000 or more: 9.7% (2005); Poverty rate: 4.5% (2000).
Education: Percent of population age 25 and over with: High school diploma (including GED) or higher: 84.0% (2005); Bachelor's degree or higher: 14.4% (2005); Master's degree or higher: 4.0% (2005).

School District(s)
Willoughby-Eastlake City SD (PK-12)
    2003-04 Enrollment: 8,876 . . . . (440) 946-5000

Housing: Homeownership rate: 83.0% (2005); Median home value: $128,714 (2005); Median rent: $596 per month (2000); Median age of housing: 44 years (2000).
Safety: Violent crime rate: 4.3 per 10,000 population; Property crime rate: 139.0 per 10,000 population (2004).
Transportation: Commute to work: 95.0% car, 1.7% public transportation, 1.0% walk, 1.8% work from home (2000); Travel time to work: 32.5% less than 15 minutes, 42.2% 15 to 30 minutes, 17.7% 30 to 45 minutes, 4.8% 45 to 60 minutes, 2.8% 60 minutes or more (2000)
Additional Information Contacts
Willowick Chamber of Commerce . . . . (440) 585-5765
    http://www.willowickchamber.org

Lawrence County

Located in southern Ohio; bounded on the south by the Ohio River and the Kentucky and West Virginia borders. Covers a land area of 454.96 square miles, a water area of 2.32 square miles, and is located in the Eastern Time Zone. The county government was organized in 1815. County seat is Ironton.

Lawrence County is part of the Huntington-Ashland, WV-KY-OH Metropolitan Statistical Area. The entire metro area includes: Boyd County, KY; Greenup County, KY; Lawrence County, OH; Cabell County, WV; Wayne County, WV

Population: 61,834 (1990); 62,319 (2000); 62,916 (2005); 63,519 (2010 projected); Race: 96.6% White, 1.9% Black, 0.3% Asian, 0.5% Hispanic of any race (2005); Density: 138.3 persons per square mile (2005); Average household size: 2.47 (2005); Median age: 38.4 (2005); Males per 100 females: 92.5 (2005).
Religion: Five largest groups: 4.7% The United Methodist Church, 3.3% Southern Baptist Convention, 3.1% Catholic Church, 2.9% Christian Churches and Churches of Christ, 2.3% Church of the Nazarene (2000).
Economy: Unemployment rate: 6.1% (2005); Total civilian labor force: 28,384 (2005); Leading industries: 23.5% health care and social assistance; 23.5% retail trade; 11.9% accommodation & food services (2004); Farms: 644 totaling 65,326 acres (2002); Companies that employ 500 or more persons: 0 (2004); Companies that employ 100 to 499 persons: 18 (2004); Companies that employ less than 100 persons: 841 (2004); Black-owned businesses: n/a (2002); Hispanic-owned businesses: n/a (2002); Women-owned businesses: 880 (2002); Retail sales per capita: $9,599 (2006). Single-family building permits issued: 27 (2005); Multi-family building permits issued: 8 (2005).
Income: Per capita income: $16,998 (2005); Median household income: $32,706 (2005); Average household income: $41,694 (2005); Percent of households with income of $100,000 or more: 6.0% (2005); Poverty rate: 16.5% (2003); Bankruptcy rate: 9.11% (2005).
Education: Percent of population age 25 and over with: High school diploma (including GED) or higher: 75.7% (2005); Bachelor's degree or higher: 10.3% (2005); Master's degree or higher: 3.9% (2005).
Housing: Homeownership rate: 74.8% (2005); Median home value: $77,137 (2005); Median rent: $314 per month (2000); Median age of housing: 31 years (2000).
Health: Birth rate: 121.3 per 10,000 population (2004); Death rate: 112.4 per 10,000 population (2004); Age-adjusted cancer mortality rate: 267.3 deaths per 100,000 population (2002); Air Quality Index: 77.1% good, 21.5% moderate, 1.1% unhealthy for sensitive individuals, 0.3% unhealthy (percent of days in 2005); Number of physicians: 8.3 per 10,000 population (2004); Hospital beds: 0.0 per 10,000 population (2003); Hospital admissions: 0.0 per 10,000 population (2003).
Elections: 2004 Presidential election results: 55.8% Bush, 43.7% Kerry, 0.0% Nader, 0.3% Badnarik
National and State Parks: Dean State Forest; Wayne National Forest - Ironton Ranger District
Additional Information Contacts
Lawrence County Government . . . . (740) 533-4300
    http://www.lawrencecountyohio.org
Greater Lawrence County Chamber . . . . (740) 377-4550
    http://www.lawrencecountyohio.org
Village of South Point. . . . . (740) 377-4838
    http://www.villageofsouthpoint.com

Lawrence County Communities

ATHALIA (village). Covers a land area of 0.688 square miles and a water area of 0 square miles. Located at 38.51° N. Lat.; 82.30° W. Long. Elevation is 560 feet.
Population: 346 (1990); 328 (2000); 328 (2005); 326 (2010 projected); Race: 98.2% White, 0.3% Black, 0.3% Asian, 0.3% Hispanic of any race (2005); Density: 476.7 persons per square mile (2005); Average household size: 2.31 (2005); Median age: 36.2 (2005); Males per 100 females: 89.6 (2005); Marriage status: 25.4% never married, 57.4% now married, 6.6% widowed, 10.5% divorced (2000); Foreign born: 0.0% (2000); Ancestry (includes multiple ancestries): 14.1% English, 12.6% Other groups, 8.3% German, 7.7% United States or American, 6.4% Irish (2000).
Economy: Employment by occupation: 6.8% management, 14.4% professional, 18.6% services, 28.0% sales, 0.0% farming, 16.9% construction, 15.3% production (2000).

Income: Per capita income: $14,352 (2005); Median household income: $28,462 (2005); Average household income: $33,151 (2005); Percent of households with income of $100,000 or more: 0.7% (2005); Poverty rate: 12.9% (2000).
Education: Percent of population age 25 and over with: High school diploma (including GED) or higher: 76.0% (2005); Bachelor's degree or higher: 10.9% (2005); Master's degree or higher: 7.9% (2005).
Housing: Homeownership rate: 78.2% (2005); Median home value: $64,375 (2005); Median rent: $329 per month (2000); Median age of housing: 30 years (2000).
Transportation: Commute to work: 92.2% car, 1.7% public transportation, 0.0% walk, 0.9% work from home (2000); Travel time to work: 20.9% less than 15 minutes, 33.0% 15 to 30 minutes, 21.7% 30 to 45 minutes, 12.2% 45 to 60 minutes, 12.2% 60 minutes or more (2000)

BURLINGTON (CDP).
Covers a land area of 1.425 square miles and a water area of 0 square miles. Located at 38.40° N. Lat.; 82.52° W. Long. Elevation is 560 feet.
History: Burlington was founded by Reverend Plymale, a Baptist minister in Virginia who had been a slave-holder. He purchased the land in Ohio and presented each of his former slaves with an equal portion of it. In 1817 Burlington became the first seat of Lawrence County.
Population: 3,003 (1990); 2,794 (2000); 2,800 (2005); 2,826 (2010 projected); Race: 89.6% White, 7.3% Black, 0.1% Asian, 1.6% Hispanic of any race (2005); Density: 1,965.3 persons per square mile (2005); Average household size: 2.41 (2005); Median age: 44.9 (2005); Males per 100 females: 83.7 (2005); Marriage status: 16.8% never married, 60.2% now married, 12.8% widowed, 10.2% divorced (2000); Foreign born: 0.4% (2000); Ancestry (includes multiple ancestries): 18.1% United States or American, 14.0% Other groups, 8.6% Irish, 7.5% English, 5.7% German (2000).
Economy: Employment by occupation: 9.6% management, 11.0% professional, 18.9% services, 32.3% sales, 0.9% farming, 13.4% construction, 13.8% production (2000).
Income: Per capita income: $17,826 (2005); Median household income: $27,771 (2005); Average household income: $40,744 (2005); Percent of households with income of $100,000 or more: 7.0% (2005); Poverty rate: 16.6% (2000).
Education: Percent of population age 25 and over with: High school diploma (including GED) or higher: 70.4% (2005); Bachelor's degree or higher: 8.9% (2005); Master's degree or higher: 4.4% (2005).
School District(s)
South Point Local SD (KG-12)
    2003-04 Enrollment: 1,866 . . . . (740) 377-4315
Housing: Homeownership rate: 70.1% (2005); Median home value: $68,145 (2005); Median rent: $336 per month (2000); Median age of housing: 29 years (2000).
Transportation: Commute to work: 93.0% car, 1.0% public transportation, 2.0% walk, 2.9% work from home (2000); Travel time to work: 29.0% less than 15 minutes, 58.1% 15 to 30 minutes, 8.4% 30 to 45 minutes, 2.1% 45 to 60 minutes, 2.4% 60 minutes or more (2000)

CHESAPEAKE (village).
Covers a land area of 0.553 square miles and a water area of 0.032 square miles. Located at 38.42° N. Lat.; 82.45° W. Long. Elevation is 567 feet.
History: Chesapeake developed as a residential community, with many of its citizens commuting to Huntington, across the Ohio River in West Virginia.
Population: 1,073 (1990); 842 (2000); 834 (2005); 829 (2010 projected); Race: 98.4% White, 0.1% Black, 0.1% Asian, 1.7% Hispanic of any race (2005); Density: 1,509.2 persons per square mile (2005); Average household size: 2.09 (2005); Median age: 40.7 (2005); Males per 100 females: 90.0 (2005); Marriage status: 21.0% never married, 54.7% now married, 12.4% widowed, 11.9% divorced (2000); Foreign born: 2.0% (2000); Ancestry (includes multiple ancestries): 29.2% United States or American, 9.2% German, 8.8% English, 7.7% Other groups, 6.7% Irish (2000).
Economy: Employment by occupation: 5.5% management, 21.8% professional, 23.9% services, 25.8% sales, 0.0% farming, 14.1% construction, 8.9% production (2000).
Income: Per capita income: $18,279 (2005); Median household income: $30,000 (2005); Average household income: $38,113 (2005); Percent of households with income of $100,000 or more: 3.3% (2005); Poverty rate: 15.5% (2000).
Education: Percent of population age 25 and over with: High school diploma (including GED) or higher: 72.4% (2005); Bachelor's degree or higher: 9.8% (2005); Master's degree or higher: 2.2% (2005).
School District(s)
Chesapeake Union Ex Vill SD (KG-12)
    2003-04 Enrollment: 1,301 . . . . (740) 867-3135
Lawrence County Joint Vocational SD (10-12)
    2003-04 Enrollment: n/a . . . . (740) 867-6641
Two-year College(s)
O C Collins Career Center (Public)
    Fall 2004 Enrollment: 619 . . . . (740) 867-6641
Housing: Homeownership rate: 61.8% (2005); Median home value: $77,609 (2005); Median rent: $331 per month (2000); Median age of housing: 43 years (2000).
Transportation: Commute to work: 92.8% car, 0.6% public transportation, 3.1% walk, 2.8% work from home (2000); Travel time to work: 52.8% less than 15 minutes, 28.2% 15 to 30 minutes, 14.6% 30 to 45 minutes, 1.9% 45 to 60 minutes, 2.6% 60 minutes or more (2000)

COAL GROVE (village).
Covers a land area of 1.972 square miles and a water area of 0.166 square miles. Located at 38.50° N. Lat.; 82.64° W. Long. Elevation is 560 feet.
Population: 2,251 (1990); 2,027 (2000); 2,076 (2005); 2,124 (2010 projected); Race: 98.7% White, 0.1% Black, 0.0% Asian, 0.6% Hispanic of any race (2005); Density: 1,053.0 persons per square mile (2005); Average household size: 2.45 (2005); Median age: 39.4 (2005); Males per 100 females: 90.5 (2005); Marriage status: 19.7% never married, 59.5% now married, 8.5% widowed, 12.3% divorced (2000); Foreign born: 0.0% (2000); Ancestry (includes multiple ancestries): 22.9% United States or American, 11.1% German, 10.2% English, 10.0% Irish, 6.3% Other groups (2000).
Economy: Single-family building permits issued: 3 (2005); Multi-family building permits issued: 0 (2005); Employment by occupation: 5.2% management, 12.0% professional, 17.8% services, 32.4% sales, 0.1% farming, 11.4% construction, 21.1% production (2000).
Income: Per capita income: $16,220 (2005); Median household income: $29,197 (2005); Average household income: $39,123 (2005); Percent of households with income of $100,000 or more: 5.1% (2005); Poverty rate: 18.6% (2000).
Education: Percent of population age 25 and over with: High school diploma (including GED) or higher: 73.5% (2005); Bachelor's degree or higher: 6.9% (2005); Master's degree or higher: 2.5% (2005).
School District(s)
Dawson-Bryant Local SD (KG-12)
    2003-04 Enrollment: 1,333 . . . . (740) 532-6451
Housing: Homeownership rate: 71.0% (2005); Median home value: $66,139 (2005); Median rent: $300 per month (2000); Median age of housing: 43 years (2000).
Transportation: Commute to work: 92.1% car, 1.7% public transportation, 1.7% walk, 3.4% work from home (2000); Travel time to work: 45.6% less than 15 minutes, 34.7% 15 to 30 minutes, 11.2% 30 to 45 minutes, 2.8% 45 to 60 minutes, 5.7% 60 minutes or more (2000)

HANGING ROCK (village).
Covers a land area of 0.620 square miles and a water area of 0.064 square miles. Located at 38.55° N. Lat.; 82.72° W. Long. Elevation is 560 feet.
History: Hanging Rock was named for the sandstone cliff, 400 feet high, which has an overhang at the top. Hanging Rock was founded in 1820 and developed around an iron furnace.
Population: 306 (1990); 279 (2000); 282 (2005); 282 (2010 projected); Race: 99.6% White, 0.0% Black, 0.0% Asian, 0.0% Hispanic of any race (2005); Density: 454.6 persons per square mile (2005); Average household size: 2.50 (2005); Median age: 40.0 (2005); Males per 100 females: 100.0 (2005); Marriage status: 24.0% never married, 61.1% now married, 9.2% widowed, 5.7% divorced (2000); Foreign born: 0.0% (2000); Ancestry (includes multiple ancestries): 28.0% United States or American, 9.7% German, 9.0% Other groups, 8.7% French (except Basque), 8.7% English (2000).
Economy: Employment by occupation: 5.5% management, 14.7% professional, 20.2% services, 25.7% sales, 0.0% farming, 11.9% construction, 22.0% production (2000).
Income: Per capita income: $16,082 (2005); Median household income: $31,786 (2005); Average household income: $40,133 (2005); Percent of households with income of $100,000 or more: 7.1% (2005); Poverty rate: 17.0% (2000).

Education: Percent of population age 25 and over with: High school diploma (including GED) or higher: 74.2% (2005); Bachelor's degree or higher: 6.2% (2005); Master's degree or higher: 3.6% (2005).
Housing: Homeownership rate: 85.8% (2005); Median home value: $70,556 (2005); Median rent: $311 per month (2000); Median age of housing: 29 years (2000).
Transportation: Commute to work: 98.2% car, 0.0% public transportation, 1.8% walk, 0.0% work from home (2000); Travel time to work: 57.8% less than 15 minutes, 34.9% 15 to 30 minutes, 3.7% 30 to 45 minutes, 0.0% 45 to 60 minutes, 3.7% 60 minutes or more (2000)

IRONTON (city).
Covers a land area of 4.135 square miles and a water area of 0.263 square miles. Located at 38.53° N. Lat.; 82.67° W. Long. Elevation is 560 feet.
History: Ironton was founded in 1848 by John Campbell, one of the first ironmasters of the region. The ore deposits in the Ironton district were discovered about 1826, and a charcoal furnace was set up to make pigiron. The iron industry supported Ironton for a century.
Population: 12,708 (1990); 11,211 (2000); 11,113 (2005); 10,999 (2010 projected); Race: 93.4% White, 5.0% Black, 0.4% Asian, 0.5% Hispanic of any race (2005); Density: 2,687.6 persons per square mile (2005); Average household size: 2.24 (2005); Median age: 42.6 (2005); Males per 100 females: 83.2 (2005); Marriage status: 20.6% never married, 51.3% now married, 13.0% widowed, 15.2% divorced (2000); Foreign born: 0.8% (2000); Ancestry (includes multiple ancestries): 18.1% United States or American, 13.8% German, 11.6% Irish, 9.6% English, 9.3% Other groups (2000).
Economy: Single-family building permits issued: 7 (2005); Multi-family building permits issued: 0 (2005); Employment by occupation: 7.6% management, 22.4% professional, 17.1% services, 27.8% sales, 0.4% farming, 6.8% construction, 17.9% production (2000).
Income: Per capita income: $17,363 (2005); Median household income: $25,889 (2005); Average household income: $38,460 (2005); Percent of households with income of $100,000 or more: 6.6% (2005); Poverty rate: 23.1% (2000).
Taxes: Total city taxes per capita: $238 (2004); City property taxes per capita: $47 (2004).
Education: Percent of population age 25 and over with: High school diploma (including GED) or higher: 75.3% (2005); Bachelor's degree or higher: 10.8% (2005); Master's degree or higher: 4.2% (2005).

School District(s)
Dawson-Bryant Local SD (KG-12)
  2003-04 Enrollment: 1,333 . . . . (740) 532-6451
Ironton City SD (PK-12)
  2003-04 Enrollment: 1,626 . . . . (740) 532-4133
Rock Hill Local SD (KG-12)
  2003-04 Enrollment: 1,926 . . . . (740) 532-7030

Four-year College(s)
Ohio University-Southern Campus (Public)
  Fall 2004 Enrollment: 1,860 . . . . (740) 533-4600
  2005-06 Tuition: In-state $4,146; Out-of-state $5,829

Housing: Homeownership rate: 62.7% (2005); Median home value: $74,559 (2005); Median rent: $289 per month (2000); Median age of housing: 50 years (2000).
Newspapers: The Ironton Tribune (Circulation 6,800)
Transportation: Commute to work: 92.6% car, 1.0% public transportation, 4.1% walk, 1.6% work from home (2000); Travel time to work: 51.4% less than 15 minutes, 31.4% 15 to 30 minutes, 9.6% 30 to 45 minutes, 2.4% 45 to 60 minutes, 5.2% 60 minutes or more (2000)

KITTS HILL (unincorporated postal area, zip code 45645).
Covers a land area of 46.166 square miles and a water area of 0.013 square miles. Located at 38.55° N. Lat.; 82.53° W. Long. Elevation is 897 feet.
Population: 2,911 (2000); Race: 98.2% White, 0.2% Black, 0.5% Asian, 1.3% Hispanic of any race (2000); Density: 63.1 persons per square mile (2000); Age: 26.5% under 18, 9.9% over 64 (2000); Marriage status: 16.5% never married, 71.2% now married, 6.2% widowed, 6.1% divorced (2000); Foreign born: 0.5% (2000); Ancestry (includes multiple ancestries): 23.8% United States or American, 7.6% German, 6.4% Other groups, 6.0% English, 5.8% Irish (2000).
Economy: Employment by occupation: 7.7% management, 18.5% professional, 8.9% services, 27.2% sales, 0.0% farming, 20.1% construction, 17.6% production (2000).
Income: Per capita income: $13,753 (2000); Median household income: $33,021 (2000); Poverty rate: 18.6% (2000).

Education: Percent of population age 25 and over with: High school diploma (including GED) or higher: 84.9% (2000); Bachelor's degree or higher: 12.7% (2000).
Housing: Homeownership rate: 88.1% (2000); Median home value: $59,500 (2000); Median rent: $315 per month (2000); Median age of housing: 27 years (2000).
Transportation: Commute to work: 96.3% car, 0.6% public transportation, 0.6% walk, 1.9% work from home (2000); Travel time to work: 14.8% less than 15 minutes, 38.2% 15 to 30 minutes, 25.6% 30 to 45 minutes, 10.3% 45 to 60 minutes, 11.2% 60 minutes or more (2000)

PEDRO (unincorporated postal area, zip code 45659).
Covers a land area of 101.909 square miles and a water area of 0.361 square miles. Located at 38.67° N. Lat.; 82.61° W. Long. Elevation is 615 feet.
Population: 3,154 (2000); Race: 98.9% White, 0.0% Black, 0.0% Asian, 0.5% Hispanic of any race (2000); Density: 30.9 persons per square mile (2000); Age: 30.1% under 18, 8.4% over 64 (2000); Marriage status: 18.7% never married, 62.6% now married, 7.4% widowed, 11.3% divorced (2000); Foreign born: 0.2% (2000); Ancestry (includes multiple ancestries): 20.5% United States or American, 13.0% Irish, 11.5% German, 5.0% Other groups, 3.3% English (2000).
Economy: Employment by occupation: 2.5% management, 10.2% professional, 21.7% services, 24.2% sales, 1.5% farming, 13.1% construction, 26.8% production (2000).
Income: Per capita income: $11,157 (2000); Median household income: $23,617 (2000); Poverty rate: 27.3% (2000).
Education: Percent of population age 25 and over with: High school diploma (including GED) or higher: 68.1% (2000); Bachelor's degree or higher: 4.8% (2000).
Housing: Homeownership rate: 76.9% (2000); Median home value: $62,200 (2000); Median rent: $266 per month (2000); Median age of housing: 24 years (2000).
Transportation: Commute to work: 96.7% car, 1.0% public transportation, 1.0% walk, 0.8% work from home (2000); Travel time to work: 7.6% less than 15 minutes, 22.8% 15 to 30 minutes, 38.1% 30 to 45 minutes, 19.3% 45 to 60 minutes, 12.2% 60 minutes or more (2000)

PROCTORVILLE (village).
Covers a land area of 0.241 square miles and a water area of 0.026 square miles. Located at 38.43° N. Lat.; 82.38° W. Long. Elevation is 560 feet.
Population: 798 (1990); 620 (2000); 580 (2005); 562 (2010 projected); Race: 98.3% White, 0.9% Black, 0.0% Asian, 0.0% Hispanic of any race (2005); Density: 2,411.2 persons per square mile (2005); Average household size: 2.20 (2005); Median age: 38.7 (2005); Males per 100 females: 90.8 (2005); Marriage status: 22.3% never married, 49.0% now married, 12.6% widowed, 16.2% divorced (2000); Foreign born: 0.0% (2000); Ancestry (includes multiple ancestries): 16.6% German, 12.2% Irish, 10.4% English, 9.1% United States or American, 6.8% Other groups (2000).
Economy: Employment by occupation: 7.9% management, 14.9% professional, 19.4% services, 29.3% sales, 0.0% farming, 9.1% construction, 19.4% production (2000).
Income: Per capita income: $15,530 (2005); Median household income: $24,296 (2005); Average household income: $34,119 (2005); Percent of households with income of $100,000 or more: 2.7% (2005); Poverty rate: 18.6% (2000).
Education: Percent of population age 25 and over with: High school diploma (including GED) or higher: 73.0% (2005); Bachelor's degree or higher: 5.6% (2005); Master's degree or higher: 1.8% (2005).

School District(s)
Fairland Local SD (KG-12)
  2003-04 Enrollment: 1,838 . . . . (740) 886-3100

Housing: Homeownership rate: 57.2% (2005); Median home value: $71,143 (2005); Median rent: $316 per month (2000); Median age of housing: 42 years (2000).
Transportation: Commute to work: 93.6% car, 0.0% public transportation, 3.4% walk, 0.0% work from home (2000); Travel time to work: 38.6% less than 15 minutes, 42.9% 15 to 30 minutes, 9.9% 30 to 45 minutes, 0.9% 45 to 60 minutes, 7.7% 60 minutes or more (2000)

SCOTTOWN (unincorporated postal area, zip code 45678).
Covers a land area of 39.858 square miles and a water area of 0.468 square miles. Located at 38.61° N. Lat.; 82.38° W. Long. Elevation is 595 feet.
Population: 1,078 (2000); Race: 95.9% White, 0.0% Black, 3.5% Asian, 0.0% Hispanic of any race (2000); Density: 27.0 persons per square mile

(2000); Age: 23.0% under 18, 12.6% over 64 (2000); Marriage status: 23.7% never married, 59.4% now married, 8.1% widowed, 8.8% divorced (2000); Foreign born: 1.4% (2000); Ancestry (includes multiple ancestries): 22.3% United States or American, 11.2% Other groups, 9.1% German, 5.5% English, 3.6% Irish (2000).
Economy: Employment by occupation: 7.9% management, 15.5% professional, 28.3% services, 15.2% sales, 0.0% farming, 0.0% construction, 33.1% production (2000).
Income: Per capita income: $14,233 (2000); Median household income: $32,250 (2000); Poverty rate: 16.8% (2000).
Education: Percent of population age 25 and over with: High school diploma (including GED) or higher: 58.9% (2000); Bachelor's degree or higher: 4.4% (2000).
Housing: Homeownership rate: 80.6% (2000); Median home value: $42,300 (2000); Median rent: $180 per month (2000); Median age of housing: 33 years (2000).
Transportation: Commute to work: 100.0% car, 0.0% public transportation, 0.0% walk, 0.0% work from home (2000); Travel time to work: 0.0% less than 15 minutes, 30.5% 15 to 30 minutes, 47.2% 30 to 45 minutes, 15.1% 45 to 60 minutes, 7.2% 60 minutes or more (2000)

SOUTH POINT (village). Covers a land area of 2.419 square miles and a water area of 0 square miles. Located at 38.41° N. Lat.; 82.58° W. Long. Elevation is 570 feet.
History: South Point was named for its location at the southern tip of Ohio. The residents of South Point enjoyed a view of three states: Kentucky, West Virginia, and Ohio.
Population: 3,902 (1990); 3,742 (2000); 3,881 (2005); 4,016 (2010 projected); Race: 95.7% White, 2.4% Black, 0.2% Asian, 0.3% Hispanic of any race (2005); Density: 1,604.5 persons per square mile (2005); Average household size: 2.47 (2005); Median age: 39.0 (2005); Males per 100 females: 90.1 (2005); Marriage status: 20.6% never married, 62.5% now married, 7.1% widowed, 9.8% divorced (2000); Foreign born: 0.3% (2000); Ancestry (includes multiple ancestries): 20.5% United States or American, 13.1% English, 12.9% Irish, 11.3% German, 7.9% Other groups (2000).
Economy: Single-family building permits issued: 17 (2005); Multi-family building permits issued: 4 (2005); Employment by occupation: 8.8% management, 20.1% professional, 17.9% services, 29.4% sales, 0.0% farming, 5.1% construction, 18.7% production (2000).
Income: Per capita income: $16,577 (2005); Median household income: $34,743 (2005); Average household income: $40,429 (2005); Percent of households with income of $100,000 or more: 4.8% (2005); Poverty rate: 11.3% (2000).
Education: Percent of population age 25 and over with: High school diploma (including GED) or higher: 81.8% (2005); Bachelor's degree or higher: 14.7% (2005); Master's degree or higher: 6.2% (2005).

School District(s)
South Point Local SD (KG-12)
    2003-04 Enrollment: 1,866 . . . . (740) 377-4315
Four-year College(s)
Tri-State Bible College (Private, Not-for-profit, Undenominational)
    Fall 2004 Enrollment: 13 . . . . (740) 377-2520
    2005-06 Tuition: In-state $4,800; Out-of-state $4,800

Housing: Homeownership rate: 72.0% (2005); Median home value: $92,943 (2005); Median rent: $348 per month (2000); Median age of housing: 30 years (2000).
Transportation: Commute to work: 95.5% car, 0.5% public transportation, 1.0% walk, 1.1% work from home (2000); Travel time to work: 33.3% less than 15 minutes, 52.7% 15 to 30 minutes, 6.1% 30 to 45 minutes, 2.0% 45 to 60 minutes, 5.9% 60 minutes or more (2000)

Additional Information Contacts
Greater Lawrence County Chamber . . . . (740) 377-4550
    http://www.lawrencecountyohio.org
Village of South Point . . . . (740) 377-4838
    http://www.villageofsouthpoint.com

WATERLOO (unincorporated postal area, zip code 45688). Covers a land area of 36.160 square miles and a water area of 0.010 square miles. Located at 38.73° N. Lat.; 82.52° W. Long. Elevation is 620 feet.
Population: 440 (2000); Race: 94.0% White, 0.0% Black, 0.0% Asian, 0.0% Hispanic of any race (2000); Density: 12.2 persons per square mile (2000); Age: 32.6% under 18, 9.4% over 64 (2000); Marriage status: 29.9% never married, 42.5% now married, 6.4% widowed, 21.1% divorced (2000); Foreign born: 0.0% (2000); Ancestry (includes multiple ancestries): 28.6% United States or American, 15.0% German, 12.5% Other groups, 5.8% Irish, 4.3% Dutch (2000).
Economy: Employment by occupation: 7.2% management, 4.2% professional, 25.3% services, 19.3% sales, 6.0% farming, 9.0% construction, 28.9% production (2000).
Income: Per capita income: $8,787 (2000); Median household income: $20,804 (2000); Poverty rate: 39.1% (2000).
Education: Percent of population age 25 and over with: High school diploma (including GED) or higher: 49.2% (2000); Bachelor's degree or higher: 3.8% (2000).
Housing: Homeownership rate: 75.0% (2000); Median home value: $42,000 (2000); Median rent: $279 per month (2000); Median age of housing: 30 years (2000).
Transportation: Commute to work: 100.0% car, 0.0% public transportation, 0.0% walk, 0.0% work from home (2000); Travel time to work: 0.0% less than 15 minutes, 3.0% 15 to 30 minutes, 42.8% 30 to 45 minutes, 36.7% 45 to 60 minutes, 17.5% 60 minutes or more (2000)

WILLOW WOOD (unincorporated postal area, zip code 45696). Covers a land area of 34.810 square miles and a water area of 0.040 square miles. Located at 38.59° N. Lat.; 82.46° W. Long. Elevation is 580 feet.
Population: 1,366 (2000); Race: 97.7% White, 0.5% Black, 0.0% Asian, 0.4% Hispanic of any race (2000); Density: 39.2 persons per square mile (2000); Age: 31.6% under 18, 8.2% over 64 (2000); Marriage status: 19.7% never married, 60.8% now married, 9.1% widowed, 10.4% divorced (2000); Foreign born: 0.4% (2000); Ancestry (includes multiple ancestries): 30.6% United States or American, 12.7% English, 9.2% Other groups, 6.9% German, 6.4% Irish (2000).
Economy: Employment by occupation: 2.7% management, 13.3% professional, 23.6% services, 18.9% sales, 0.0% farming, 17.9% construction, 23.6% production (2000).
Income: Per capita income: $10,968 (2000); Median household income: $25,179 (2000); Poverty rate: 27.9% (2000).
Education: Percent of population age 25 and over with: High school diploma (including GED) or higher: 74.1% (2000); Bachelor's degree or higher: 7.2% (2000).

School District(s)
Symmes Valley Local SD (KG-12)
    2003-04 Enrollment: 908 . . . . (740) 643-2451

Housing: Homeownership rate: 86.7% (2000); Median home value: $71,800 (2000); Median rent: $275 per month (2000); Median age of housing: 30 years (2000).
Transportation: Commute to work: 100.0% car, 0.0% public transportation, 0.0% walk, 0.0% work from home (2000); Travel time to work: 14.7% less than 15 minutes, 25.5% 15 to 30 minutes, 45.2% 30 to 45 minutes, 4.6% 45 to 60 minutes, 10.0% 60 minutes or more (2000)

Licking County

Located in central Ohio; drained by the Licking River and Raccoon Creek; includes part of Buckeye Lake. Covers a land area of 686.50 square miles, a water area of 1.88 square miles, and is located in the Eastern Time Zone. The county government was organized in 1808. County seat is Newark.

Licking County is part of the Columbus, OH Metropolitan Statistical Area. The entire metro area includes: Delaware County, OH; Fairfield County, OH; Franklin County, OH; Licking County, OH; Madison County, OH; Morrow County, OH; Pickaway County, OH; Union County, OH

Weather Station: Newark Water Works   Elevation: 833 feet

	Jan	Feb	Mar	Apr	May	Jun	Jul	Aug	Sep	Oct	Nov	Dec
High	35	40	51	63	73	81	85	83	77	65	52	41
Low	19	22	30	39	49	58	62	60	53	41	33	25
Precip	2.8	2.5	3.2	3.9	4.3	4.4	4.5	4.2	3.0	2.7	3.4	3.2
Snow	8.4	5.3	2.8	0.9	tr	0.0	0.0	0.0	0.0	tr	0.5	2.7

High and Low temperatures in degrees Fahrenheit; Precipitation and Snow in inches

Population: 128,300 (1990); 145,491 (2000); 153,110 (2005); 161,066 (2010 projected); Race: 95.2% White, 2.2% Black, 0.8% Asian, 0.7% Hispanic of any race (2005); Density: 223.0 persons per square mile (2005); Average household size: 2.59 (2005); Median age: 37.4 (2005); Males per 100 females: 95.5 (2005).
Religion: Five largest groups: 8.4% Catholic Church, 6.6% The United Methodist Church, 4.6% Southern Baptist Convention, 2.8% Christian

Churches and Churches of Christ, 2.0% Presbyterian Church (U.S.A.) (2000).
Economy: Unemployment rate: 5.8% (2005); Total civilian labor force: 81,124 (2005); Leading industries: 17.5% manufacturing; 15.1% retail trade; 12.3% health care and social assistance (2004); Farms: 1,482 totaling 237,285 acres (2002); Companies that employ 500 or more persons: 7 (2004); Companies that employ 100 to 499 persons: 78 (2004); Companies that employ less than 100 persons: 2,923 (2004); Black-owned businesses: n/a (2002); Hispanic-owned businesses: n/a (2002); Women-owned businesses: 3,551 (2002); Retail sales per capita: $11,480 (2006). Single-family building permits issued: 767 (2005); Multi-family building permits issued: 320 (2005).
Income: Per capita income: $23,683 (2005); Median household income: $49,475 (2005); Average household income: $60,865 (2005); Percent of households with income of $100,000 or more: 14.4% (2005); Poverty rate: 8.4% (2003); Bankruptcy rate: 9.76% (2005).
Taxes: Total county taxes per capita: $249 (2004); County property taxes per capita: $109 (2004).
Education: Percent of population age 25 and over with: High school diploma (including GED) or higher: 84.9% (2005); Bachelor's degree or higher: 18.8% (2005); Master's degree or higher: 5.9% (2005).
Housing: Homeownership rate: 74.9% (2005); Median home value: $136,160 (2005); Median rent: $405 per month (2000); Median age of housing: 31 years (2000).
Health: Birth rate: 136.2 per 10,000 population (2004); Death rate: 88.6 per 10,000 population (2004); Age-adjusted cancer mortality rate: 225.6 deaths per 100,000 population (2002); Air Quality Index: 82.3% good, 16.9% moderate, 0.8% unhealthy for sensitive individuals, 0.0% unhealthy (percent of days in 2005); Number of physicians: 11.6 per 10,000 population (2004); Hospital beds: 15.7 per 10,000 population (2003); Hospital admissions: 475.7 per 10,000 population (2003).
Elections: 2004 Presidential election results: 61.7% Bush, 37.8% Kerry, 0.0% Nader, 0.2% Badnarik
National and State Parks: Black Hand State Nature Preserve; Moundbuilders State Memorial; Octagon State Memorial
Additional Information Contacts

Licking County Government	(740) 349-6066
http://www.lcounty.com/	
City of Heath	(740) 522-1420
http://www.heathohio.org	
City of Newark	(740) 349-6600
http://www.ci.newark.oh.us	
City of Pataskala	(740) 927-2021
http://www.ci.pataskala.oh.us	
Granville Chamber of Commerce	(740) 587-4490
http://www.granville.oh.us/page.cfm?ID=53	
Greater Buckeye Lake Chamber of Commerce	(740) 928-2048
http://www.buckeyelakecc.com	
Greater Licking Co. Convention & Visitors Bureau	(740) 345-8224
http://www.lccvb.com	
Johnstown Area Chamber of Commerce	(740) 967-2334
http://www.johnstown.ws/villagegov.html	
Newark & Licking County Chamber	(740) 345-9757
http://www.newarkchamber.com	
Pataskala Area Chamber of Commerce	(740) 964-5503
http://www.ci.pataskala.oh.us	
Village of Granville	(740) 587-0707
http://www.granville.oh.us	
Village of Hebron	(740) 928-2261
http://www.hebronvillage.com	
Village of Johnstown	(740) 967-3177
http://www.villageofjohnstown.org	

Licking County Communities

ALEXANDRIA (village). Covers a land area of 0.162 square miles and a water area of 0 square miles. Located at 40.09° N. Lat.; 82.61° W. Long. Elevation is 970 feet.
Population: 468 (1990); 85 (2000); 83 (2005); 82 (2010 projected); Race: 97.6% White, 0.0% Black, 0.0% Asian, 0.0% Hispanic of any race (2005); Density: 510.8 persons per square mile (2005); Average household size: 2.86 (2005); Median age: 31.4 (2005); Males per 100 females: 112.8 (2005); Marriage status: 0.0% never married, 66.7% now married, 33.3% widowed, 0.0% divorced (2000); Foreign born: 0.0% (2000); Ancestry (includes multiple ancestries): 82.4% German, 23.5% Scotch-Irish, 17.6% Other groups (2000).
Economy: In agricultural area. Employment by occupation: 0.0% management, 0.0% professional, 100.0% services, 0.0% sales, 0.0% farming, 0.0% construction, 0.0% production (2000).
Income: Per capita income: $14,096 (2005); Median household income: $34,667 (2005); Average household income: $40,345 (2005); Percent of households with income of $100,000 or more: 0.0% (2005); Poverty rate: 0.0% (2000).
Education: Percent of population age 25 and over with: High school diploma (including GED) or higher: 100.0% (2005); Bachelor's degree or higher: 41.3% (2005); Master's degree or higher: 0.0% (2005).

School District(s)
Northridge Local SD (PK-12)
    2003-04 Enrollment: 1,451 . . . . (740) 967-6631
Housing: Homeownership rate: 96.6% (2005); Median home value: $185,000 (2005); Median rent: $n/a per month (2000); Median age of housing: 11 years (2000).
Transportation: Commute to work: 100.0% car, 0.0% public transportation, 0.0% walk, 0.0% work from home (2000); Travel time to work: 0.0% less than 15 minutes, 0.0% 15 to 30 minutes, 100.0% 30 to 45 minutes, 0.0% 45 to 60 minutes, 0.0% 60 minutes or more (2000)

BEECHWOOD TRAILS (CDP). Covers a land area of 3.453 square miles and a water area of 0 square miles. Located at 40.02° N. Lat.; 82.65° W. Long.
Population: 1,367 (1990); 2,258 (2000); 2,656 (2005); 3,040 (2010 projected); Race: 96.8% White, 1.0% Black, 0.4% Asian, 0.6% Hispanic of any race (2005); Density: 769.1 persons per square mile (2005); Average household size: 2.94 (2005); Median age: 38.7 (2005); Males per 100 females: 101.4 (2005); Marriage status: 18.3% never married, 73.1% now married, 1.3% widowed, 7.4% divorced (2000); Foreign born: 0.9% (2000); Ancestry (includes multiple ancestries): 27.9% German, 13.1% Irish, 10.9% English, 10.3% United States or American, 9.6% Other groups (2000).
Economy: Employment by occupation: 19.2% management, 23.3% professional, 11.1% services, 31.0% sales, 0.5% farming, 9.3% construction, 5.5% production (2000).
Income: Per capita income: $29,078 (2005); Median household income: $82,174 (2005); Average household income: $85,621 (2005); Percent of households with income of $100,000 or more: 31.8% (2005); Poverty rate: 1.2% (2000).
Education: Percent of population age 25 and over with: High school diploma (including GED) or higher: 96.9% (2005); Bachelor's degree or higher: 32.7% (2005); Master's degree or higher: 7.0% (2005).
Housing: Homeownership rate: 97.7% (2005); Median home value: $182,859 (2005); Median rent: $675 per month (2000); Median age of housing: 16 years (2000).
Transportation: Commute to work: 93.7% car, 0.0% public transportation, 0.0% walk, 6.3% work from home (2000); Travel time to work: 11.4% less than 15 minutes, 35.6% 15 to 30 minutes, 34.3% 30 to 45 minutes, 15.3% 45 to 60 minutes, 3.5% 60 minutes or more (2000)

BUCKEYE LAKE (village). Covers a land area of 2.036 square miles and a water area of 0.011 square miles. Located at 39.93° N. Lat.; 82.48° W. Long. Elevation is 900 feet.
History: Beside lake created for Ohio Canal c.1827.
Population: 2,989 (1990); 3,049 (2000); 3,129 (2005); 3,235 (2010 projected); Race: 96.7% White, 0.9% Black, 0.1% Asian, 0.6% Hispanic of any race (2005); Density: 1,537.1 persons per square mile (2005); Average household size: 2.42 (2005); Median age: 35.8 (2005); Males per 100 females: 96.4 (2005); Marriage status: 21.0% never married, 52.1% now married, 8.0% widowed, 18.8% divorced (2000); Foreign born: 0.7% (2000); Ancestry (includes multiple ancestries): 23.7% German, 15.8% Irish, 10.4% Other groups, 10.1% United States or American, 8.4% English (2000).
Economy: State park here; camping, recreational facilities. Single-family building permits issued: 3 (2005); Multi-family building permits issued: 0 (2005); Employment by occupation: 8.6% management, 6.0% professional, 18.3% services, 23.7% sales, 0.0% farming, 13.6% construction, 29.9% production (2000).
Income: Per capita income: $17,978 (2005); Median household income: $34,416 (2005); Average household income: $43,438 (2005); Percent of households with income of $100,000 or more: 5.3% (2005); Poverty rate: 16.1% (2000).

Education: Percent of population age 25 and over with: High school diploma (including GED) or higher: 72.3% (2005); Bachelor's degree or higher: 4.3% (2005); Master's degree or higher: 1.8% (2005).
Housing: Homeownership rate: 68.3% (2005); Median home value: $54,833 (2005); Median rent: $357 per month (2000); Median age of housing: 31 years (2000).
Safety: Violent crime rate: 170.6 per 10,000 population; Property crime rate: 273.7 per 10,000 population (2004).
Newspapers: Buckeye Lake Beacon (General - Circulation 13,500)
Transportation: Commute to work: 89.7% car, 0.4% public transportation, 4.8% walk, 3.0% work from home (2000); Travel time to work: 29.3% less than 15 minutes, 27.9% 15 to 30 minutes, 22.8% 30 to 45 minutes, 12.4% 45 to 60 minutes, 7.6% 60 minutes or more (2000)
Additional Information Contacts
Greater Buckeye Lake Chamber of Commerce .... (740) 928-2048
http://www.buckeyelakecc.com

CROTON (unincorporated postal area, zip code 43013). Aka Hartford.
Covers a land area of 19.844 square miles and a water area of 0 square miles. Located at 40.11° N. Lat.; 82.69° W. Long. Elevation is 1,168 feet.
Population: 979 (2000); Race: 99.4% White, 0.0% Black, 0.0% Asian, 1.4% Hispanic of any race (2000); Density: 49.3 persons per square mile (2000); Age: 28.6% under 18, 12.4% over 64 (2000); Marriage status: 17.4% never married, 66.2% now married, 8.1% widowed, 8.3% divorced (2000); Foreign born: 0.2% (2000); Ancestry (includes multiple ancestries): 23.4% German, 19.1% United States or American, 16.0% English, 11.1% Irish, 8.1% Other groups (2000).
Economy: Employment by occupation: 16.3% management, 13.8% professional, 15.1% services, 24.4% sales, 5.3% farming, 13.4% construction, 11.7% production (2000).
Income: Per capita income: $18,127 (2000); Median household income: $51,429 (2000); Poverty rate: 7.6% (2000).
Education: Percent of population age 25 and over with: High school diploma (including GED) or higher: 86.0% (2000); Bachelor's degree or higher: 16.8% (2000).
School District(s)
Northridge Local SD (PK-12)
    2003-04 Enrollment: 1,451 .... (740) 967-6631
Housing: Homeownership rate: 78.2% (2000); Median home value: $99,400 (2000); Median rent: $409 per month (2000); Median age of housing: 47 years (2000).
Transportation: Commute to work: 91.6% car, 0.0% public transportation, 0.2% walk, 8.1% work from home (2000); Travel time to work: 23.3% less than 15 minutes, 19.6% 15 to 30 minutes, 32.4% 30 to 45 minutes, 19.1% 45 to 60 minutes, 5.6% 60 minutes or more (2000)

GRANVILLE (village). Covers a land area of 4.007 square miles and a water area of 0 square miles. Located at 40.06° N. Lat.; 82.51° W. Long. Elevation is 975 feet.
History: Granville was laid out in 1806 and named for the Massachusetts home of its early settlers. In 1831 the Granville Literary and Theological Institute was established, becoming Denison University in 1856.
Population: 4,196 (1990); 3,167 (2000); 3,347 (2005); 3,536 (2010 projected); Race: 96.6% White, 0.6% Black, 1.1% Asian, 1.0% Hispanic of any race (2005); Density: 835.3 persons per square mile (2005); Average household size: 2.45 (2005); Median age: 43.5 (2005); Males per 100 females: 95.3 (2005); Marriage status: 17.5% never married, 66.8% now married, 8.1% widowed, 7.6% divorced (2000); Foreign born: 3.4% (2000); Ancestry (includes multiple ancestries): 29.7% German, 24.7% English, 21.3% Irish, 7.9% Polish, 6.1% Italian (2000).
Economy: Employment by occupation: 31.6% management, 40.0% professional, 7.5% services, 17.7% sales, 0.0% farming, 1.2% construction, 2.0% production (2000).
Income: Per capita income: $40,828 (2005); Median household income: $78,448 (2005); Average household income: $99,890 (2005); Percent of households with income of $100,000 or more: 37.2% (2005); Poverty rate: 3.8% (2000).
Education: Percent of population age 25 and over with: High school diploma (including GED) or higher: 98.1% (2005); Bachelor's degree or higher: 68.7% (2005); Master's degree or higher: 32.9% (2005).
School District(s)
Granville Ex Vill SD (PK-12)
    2003-04 Enrollment: 2,113 .... (740) 587-0332

Four-year College(s)
Denison University (Private, Not-for-profit)
    Fall 2004 Enrollment: 2,211 .... (740) 587-0810
    2005-06 Tuition: In-state $28,920; Out-of-state $28,920
Housing: Homeownership rate: 75.7% (2005); Median home value: $267,681 (2005); Median rent: $572 per month (2000); Median age of housing: 41 years (2000).
Safety: Violent crime rate: 3.9 per 10,000 population; Property crime rate: 103.2 per 10,000 population (2004).
Newspapers: Granville Sentinel (General - Circulation 2,000); The Community Booster (General - Circulation 13,000)
Transportation: Commute to work: 88.5% car, 1.4% public transportation, 4.0% walk, 6.1% work from home (2000); Travel time to work: 48.5% less than 15 minutes, 23.6% 15 to 30 minutes, 14.7% 30 to 45 minutes, 8.0% 45 to 60 minutes, 5.1% 60 minutes or more (2000)
Additional Information Contacts
Granville Chamber of Commerce .... (740) 587-4490
    http://www.granville.oh.us/page.cfm?ID=53
Village of Granville .... (740) 587-0707
    http://www.granville.oh.us

GRANVILLE SOUTH (CDP). Covers a land area of 6.110 square miles and a water area of 0.025 square miles. Located at 40.05° N. Lat.; 82.54° W. Long.
Population: 1,124 (1990); 1,194 (2000); 1,206 (2005); 1,237 (2010 projected); Race: 97.2% White, 0.0% Black, 1.2% Asian, 0.7% Hispanic of any race (2005); Density: 197.4 persons per square mile (2005); Average household size: 2.89 (2005); Median age: 45.7 (2005); Males per 100 females: 93.3 (2005); Marriage status: 16.7% never married, 76.2% now married, 2.9% widowed, 4.2% divorced (2000); Foreign born: 2.0% (2000); Ancestry (includes multiple ancestries): 41.3% German, 25.7% English, 11.6% Irish, 7.5% Italian, 6.7% Welsh (2000).
Economy: Employment by occupation: 14.5% management, 32.6% professional, 11.3% services, 27.5% sales, 0.0% farming, 3.9% construction, 10.2% production (2000).
Income: Per capita income: $27,724 (2005); Median household income: $76,263 (2005); Average household income: $79,988 (2005); Percent of households with income of $100,000 or more: 27.5% (2005); Poverty rate: 1.3% (2000).
Education: Percent of population age 25 and over with: High school diploma (including GED) or higher: 97.9% (2005); Bachelor's degree or higher: 46.4% (2005); Master's degree or higher: 14.4% (2005).
Housing: Homeownership rate: 93.1% (2005); Median home value: $208,993 (2005); Median rent: $433 per month (2000); Median age of housing: 27 years (2000).
Transportation: Commute to work: 91.0% car, 0.8% public transportation, 0.0% walk, 7.0% work from home (2000); Travel time to work: 43.2% less than 15 minutes, 21.3% 15 to 30 minutes, 23.4% 30 to 45 minutes, 4.0% 45 to 60 minutes, 8.1% 60 minutes or more (2000)

GRATIOT (village). Covers a land area of 0.119 square miles and a water area of 0 square miles. Located at 39.95° N. Lat.; 82.21° W. Long. Elevation is 988 feet.
Population: 195 (1990); 187 (2000); 206 (2005); 225 (2010 projected); Race: 97.6% White, 1.5% Black, 0.0% Asian, 0.0% Hispanic of any race (2005); Density: 1,724.5 persons per square mile (2005); Average household size: 2.40 (2005); Median age: 40.1 (2005); Males per 100 females: 102.0 (2005); Marriage status: 19.2% never married, 64.8% now married, 8.0% widowed, 8.0% divorced (2000); Foreign born: 0.0% (2000); Ancestry (includes multiple ancestries): 27.3% German, 16.3% Irish, 11.6% United States or American, 9.3% English, 5.8% Italian (2000).
Economy: Employment by occupation: 7.0% management, 11.6% professional, 15.1% services, 25.6% sales, 1.2% farming, 8.1% construction, 31.4% production (2000).
Income: Per capita income: $20,049 (2005); Median household income: $41,000 (2005); Average household income: $48,023 (2005); Percent of households with income of $100,000 or more: 8.1% (2005); Poverty rate: 9.3% (2000).
Education: Percent of population age 25 and over with: High school diploma (including GED) or higher: 85.3% (2005); Bachelor's degree or higher: 4.2% (2005); Master's degree or higher: 0.0% (2005).
Housing: Homeownership rate: 82.6% (2005); Median home value: $114,205 (2005); Median rent: $342 per month (2000); Median age of housing: 60+ years (2000).
Transportation: Commute to work: 91.8% car, 0.0% public transportation, 5.9% walk, 2.4% work from home (2000); Travel time to work: 15.7% less

than 15 minutes, 47.0% 15 to 30 minutes, 28.9% 30 to 45 minutes, 4.8% 45 to 60 minutes, 3.6% 60 minutes or more (2000)

HANOVER (village). Covers a land area of 1.000 square miles and a water area of 0 square miles. Located at 40.07° N. Lat.; 82.27° W. Long. Elevation is 820 feet.
Population: 853 (1990); 885 (2000); 936 (2005); 984 (2010 projected); Race: 98.6% White, 0.4% Black, 0.0% Asian, 0.2% Hispanic of any race (2005); Density: 936.2 persons per square mile (2005); Average household size: 2.79 (2005); Median age: 38.3 (2005); Males per 100 females: 101.7 (2005); Marriage status: 21.1% never married, 67.1% now married, 5.0% widowed, 6.7% divorced (2000); Foreign born: 1.0% (2000); Ancestry (includes multiple ancestries): 20.5% German, 12.9% Irish, 12.1% English, 11.3% United States or American, 8.1% Other groups (2000).
Economy: Single-family building permits issued: 7 (2005); Multi-family building permits issued: 0 (2005); Employment by occupation: 9.1% management, 15.6% professional, 15.4% services, 21.3% sales, 0.2% farming, 13.7% construction, 24.7% production (2000).
Income: Per capita income: $23,050 (2005); Median household income: $57,475 (2005); Average household income: $64,403 (2005); Percent of households with income of $100,000 or more: 11.9% (2005); Poverty rate: 4.4% (2000).
Education: Percent of population age 25 and over with: High school diploma (including GED) or higher: 82.7% (2005); Bachelor's degree or higher: 4.2% (2005); Master's degree or higher: 0.8% (2005).
Housing: Homeownership rate: 88.1% (2005); Median home value: $127,057 (2005); Median rent: $428 per month (2000); Median age of housing: 29 years (2000).
Transportation: Commute to work: 94.3% car, 0.0% public transportation, 2.1% walk, 3.4% work from home (2000); Travel time to work: 14.6% less than 15 minutes, 59.3% 15 to 30 minutes, 12.0% 30 to 45 minutes, 7.2% 45 to 60 minutes, 7.0% 60 minutes or more (2000)

HARBOR HILLS (CDP). Covers a land area of 2.725 square miles and a water area of 0.721 square miles. Located at 39.93° N. Lat.; 82.43° W. Long.
Population: 1,372 (1990); 1,303 (2000); 1,271 (2005); 1,269 (2010 projected); Race: 98.3% White, 0.2% Black, 0.1% Asian, 0.0% Hispanic of any race (2005); Density: 466.3 persons per square mile (2005); Average household size: 2.22 (2005); Median age: 50.1 (2005); Males per 100 females: 102.1 (2005); Marriage status: 13.5% never married, 70.0% now married, 7.5% widowed, 9.0% divorced (2000); Foreign born: 3.2% (2000); Ancestry (includes multiple ancestries): 28.2% German, 10.9% Irish, 10.4% United States or American, 9.1% English, 7.3% Italian (2000).
Economy: Employment by occupation: 14.8% management, 16.8% professional, 12.9% services, 32.2% sales, 0.0% farming, 9.8% construction, 13.5% production (2000).
Income: Per capita income: $32,179 (2005); Median household income: $59,709 (2005); Average household income: $71,503 (2005); Percent of households with income of $100,000 or more: 19.2% (2005); Poverty rate: 2.4% (2000).
Education: Percent of population age 25 and over with: High school diploma (including GED) or higher: 87.0% (2005); Bachelor's degree or higher: 14.1% (2005); Master's degree or higher: 3.4% (2005).
Housing: Homeownership rate: 90.0% (2005); Median home value: $167,045 (2005); Median rent: $425 per month (2000); Median age of housing: 41 years (2000).
Transportation: Commute to work: 93.9% car, 1.2% public transportation, 0.0% walk, 4.9% work from home (2000); Travel time to work: 22.3% less than 15 minutes, 28.1% 15 to 30 minutes, 21.5% 30 to 45 minutes, 19.7% 45 to 60 minutes, 8.4% 60 minutes or more (2000)

HARTFORD (village). Covers a land area of 0.536 square miles and a water area of 0 square miles. Located at 40.23° N. Lat.; 82.68° W. Long.
Population: 418 (1990); 412 (2000); 469 (2005); 526 (2010 projected); Race: 97.0% White, 0.0% Black, 0.4% Asian, 1.1% Hispanic of any race (2005); Density: 875.5 persons per square mile (2005); Average household size: 2.71 (2005); Median age: 33.8 (2005); Males per 100 females: 115.1 (2005); Marriage status: 22.0% never married, 61.5% now married, 7.2% widowed, 9.3% divorced (2000); Foreign born: 0.5% (2000); Ancestry (includes multiple ancestries): 29.9% United States or American, 14.3% German, 9.5% Irish, 6.8% English, 4.0% Other groups (2000).
Economy: Single-family building permits issued: 0 (2005); Multi-family building permits issued: 0 (2005); Employment by occupation: 7.1% management, 9.6% professional, 21.2% services, 22.7% sales, 2.5% farming, 14.6% construction, 22.2% production (2000).
Income: Per capita income: $19,638 (2005); Median household income: $47,228 (2005); Average household income: $53,237 (2005); Percent of households with income of $100,000 or more: 8.1% (2005); Poverty rate: 6.0% (2000).
Education: Percent of population age 25 and over with: High school diploma (including GED) or higher: 89.5% (2005); Bachelor's degree or higher: 12.5% (2005); Master's degree or higher: 2.6% (2005).
School District(s)
Joseph Badger Local SD (PK-12)
    2003-04 Enrollment: 1,108 . . . . (330) 876-1051
Housing: Homeownership rate: 74.0% (2005); Median home value: $98,605 (2005); Median rent: $407 per month (2000); Median age of housing: 60+ years (2000).
Transportation: Commute to work: 97.9% car, 0.0% public transportation, 0.5% walk, 1.5% work from home (2000); Travel time to work: 27.2% less than 15 minutes, 18.3% 15 to 30 minutes, 23.0% 30 to 45 minutes, 23.6% 45 to 60 minutes, 7.9% 60 minutes or more (2000)

HEATH (city). Aka Fourmile Lock. Covers a land area of 10.442 square miles and a water area of 0.007 square miles. Located at 40.03° N. Lat.; 82.43° W. Long. Elevation is 850 feet.
History: Former Newark Air Force Base nearby that specialized in guidance of navigation systems; closed base scheduled for privatization.
Population: 7,414 (1990); 8,527 (2000); 8,700 (2005); 8,934 (2010 projected); Race: 95.4% White, 2.1% Black, 0.9% Asian, 1.0% Hispanic of any race (2005); Density: 833.2 persons per square mile (2005); Average household size: 2.48 (2005); Median age: 38.3 (2005); Males per 100 females: 91.6 (2005); Marriage status: 20.5% never married, 58.1% now married, 7.5% widowed, 13.9% divorced (2000); Foreign born: 0.5% (2000); Ancestry (includes multiple ancestries): 25.8% German, 14.2% Irish, 13.0% United States or American, 10.6% English, 9.6% Other groups (2000).
Economy: Employment by occupation: 13.0% management, 13.4% professional, 17.1% services, 28.8% sales, 0.1% farming, 8.5% construction, 19.1% production (2000).
Income: Per capita income: $22,613 (2005); Median household income: $43,421 (2005); Average household income: $54,942 (2005); Percent of households with income of $100,000 or more: 9.3% (2005); Poverty rate: 8.5% (2000).
Education: Percent of population age 25 and over with: High school diploma (including GED) or higher: 82.7% (2005); Bachelor's degree or higher: 13.9% (2005); Master's degree or higher: 3.5% (2005).
School District(s)
Heath City SD (PK-12)
    2003-04 Enrollment: 1,707 . . . . (740) 522-2816
Housing: Homeownership rate: 69.8% (2005); Median home value: $124,164 (2005); Median rent: $422 per month (2000); Median age of housing: 29 years (2000).
Safety: Violent crime rate: 20.6 per 10,000 population; Property crime rate: 514.8 per 10,000 population (2004).
Newspapers: Heath News (General - Circulation 4,200)
Transportation: Commute to work: 95.6% car, 0.9% public transportation, 1.1% walk, 1.7% work from home (2000); Travel time to work: 44.4% less than 15 minutes, 31.1% 15 to 30 minutes, 9.1% 30 to 45 minutes, 8.9% 45 to 60 minutes, 6.5% 60 minutes or more (2000)
Additional Information Contacts
City of Heath . . . . (740) 522-1420
    http://www.heathohio.org

HEBRON (village). Covers a land area of 2.683 square miles and a water area of 0 square miles. Located at 39.96° N. Lat.; 82.49° W. Long. Elevation is 889 feet.
History: Hebron developed as a commercial center on the Ohio & Erie Canal and the old National Road.
Population: 2,216 (1990); 2,034 (2000); 2,068 (2005); 2,161 (2010 projected); Race: 97.0% White, 0.2% Black, 0.8% Asian, 1.3% Hispanic of any race (2005); Density: 770.9 persons per square mile (2005); Average household size: 2.25 (2005); Median age: 36.8 (2005); Males per 100 females: 87.8 (2005); Marriage status: 23.6% never married, 51.2% now married, 9.9% widowed, 15.3% divorced (2000); Foreign born: 1.0% (2000); Ancestry (includes multiple ancestries): 25.0% German, 15.8% Irish, 11.6% United States or American, 10.2% English, 6.9% Other groups (2000).

Economy: Employment by occupation: 12.1% management, 7.7% professional, 18.2% services, 30.6% sales, 0.2% farming, 10.9% construction, 20.4% production (2000).
Income: Per capita income: $19,695 (2005); Median household income: $37,627 (2005); Average household income: $44,320 (2005); Percent of households with income of $100,000 or more: 5.2% (2005); Poverty rate: 9.5% (2000).
Education: Percent of population age 25 and over with: High school diploma (including GED) or higher: 82.9% (2005); Bachelor's degree or higher: 6.7% (2005); Master's degree or higher: 1.3% (2005).

School District(s)
Lakewood Digital Academy (KG-12)
    2003-04 Enrollment: 31 .... (740) 928-5878
Lakewood Local SD (PK-12)
    2003-04 Enrollment: 2,265 .... (740) 928-5878

Housing: Homeownership rate: 62.7% (2005); Median home value: $94,744 (2005); Median rent: $344 per month (2000); Median age of housing: 35 years (2000).
Safety: Violent crime rate: 9.7 per 10,000 population; Property crime rate: 497.3 per 10,000 population (2004).
Transportation: Commute to work: 95.1% car, 0.3% public transportation, 2.4% walk, 1.2% work from home (2000); Travel time to work: 33.8% less than 15 minutes, 25.7% 15 to 30 minutes, 21.8% 30 to 45 minutes, 10.8% 45 to 60 minutes, 7.9% 60 minutes or more (2000)

Additional Information Contacts
Village of Hebron .... (740) 928-2261
    http://www.hebronvillage.com

JOHNSTOWN (village).
Covers a land area of 2.094 square miles and a water area of 0 square miles. Located at 40.14° N. Lat.; 82.68° W. Long. Elevation is 1,160 feet.
History: Johnstown was the site of the discovery in 1926 of the skeleton of a mastodon. A farmer digging in his garden uncovered the bones of an animal that had been 8 feet tall and 15 feet long. The skeleton was purchased by the Cleveland Museum of Natural History.
Population: 3,272 (1990); 3,440 (2000); 3,704 (2005); 3,985 (2010 projected); Race: 98.5% White, 0.1% Black, 0.1% Asian, 0.5% Hispanic of any race (2005); Density: 1,769.0 persons per square mile (2005); Average household size: 2.42 (2005); Median age: 35.8 (2005); Males per 100 females: 92.5 (2005); Marriage status: 21.2% never married, 59.5% now married, 9.6% widowed, 9.7% divorced (2000); Foreign born: 1.4% (2000); Ancestry (includes multiple ancestries): 28.6% German, 16.0% United States or American, 14.3% Irish, 11.5% English, 4.8% Other groups (2000).
Economy: Single-family building permits issued: 35 (2005); Multi-family building permits issued: 2 (2005); Employment by occupation: 12.2% management, 17.6% professional, 11.8% services, 27.8% sales, 0.6% farming, 12.8% construction, 17.2% production (2000).
Income: Per capita income: $23,949 (2005); Median household income: $47,862 (2005); Average household income: $57,608 (2005); Percent of households with income of $100,000 or more: 11.5% (2005); Poverty rate: 7.6% (2000).
Education: Percent of population age 25 and over with: High school diploma (including GED) or higher: 79.9% (2005); Bachelor's degree or higher: 15.4% (2005); Master's degree or higher: 3.8% (2005).

School District(s)
Johnstown-Monroe Local SD (PK-12)
    2003-04 Enrollment: 1,498 .... (740) 967-6846
Northridge Local SD (PK-12)
    2003-04 Enrollment: 1,451 .... (740) 967-6631

Housing: Homeownership rate: 63.7% (2005); Median home value: $122,373 (2005); Median rent: $359 per month (2000); Median age of housing: 40 years (2000).
Safety: Violent crime rate: 2.7 per 10,000 population; Property crime rate: 341.8 per 10,000 population (2004).
Transportation: Commute to work: 93.7% car, 0.6% public transportation, 2.1% walk, 3.6% work from home (2000); Travel time to work: 29.5% less than 15 minutes, 29.5% 15 to 30 minutes, 26.9% 30 to 45 minutes, 9.2% 45 to 60 minutes, 4.9% 60 minutes or more (2000)

Additional Information Contacts
Johnstown Area Chamber of Commerce.............. (740) 967-2334
    http://www.johnstown.ws/villagegov.html
Village of Johnstown .... (740) 967-3177
    http://www.villageofjohnstown.org

KIRKERSVILLE (village).
Covers a land area of 1.963 square miles and a water area of 0 square miles. Located at 39.95° N. Lat.; 82.59° W. Long. Elevation is 940 feet.
Population: 563 (1990); 520 (2000); 501 (2005); 497 (2010 projected); Race: 97.4% White, 1.6% Black, 0.2% Asian, 3.2% Hispanic of any race (2005); Density: 255.2 persons per square mile (2005); Average household size: 2.86 (2005); Median age: 38.4 (2005); Males per 100 females: 102.0 (2005); Marriage status: 23.8% never married, 59.6% now married, 4.6% widowed, 11.9% divorced (2000); Foreign born: 0.6% (2000); Ancestry (includes multiple ancestries): 29.0% German, 19.8% Irish, 10.1% English, 9.0% Other groups, 7.7% United States or American (2000).
Economy: Employment by occupation: 14.2% management, 10.8% professional, 11.5% services, 21.5% sales, 0.0% farming, 24.2% construction, 17.7% production (2000).
Income: Per capita income: $21,189 (2005); Median household income: $52,885 (2005); Average household income: $59,471 (2005); Percent of households with income of $100,000 or more: 13.7% (2005); Poverty rate: 8.0% (2000).
Education: Percent of population age 25 and over with: High school diploma (including GED) or higher: 74.5% (2005); Bachelor's degree or higher: 13.7% (2005); Master's degree or higher: 3.0% (2005).

School District(s)
Southwest Licking Local SD (PK-12)
    2003-04 Enrollment: 3,527 .... (740) 927-3941

Housing: Homeownership rate: 76.6% (2005); Median home value: $117,857 (2005); Median rent: $413 per month (2000); Median age of housing: 58 years (2000).
Transportation: Commute to work: 93.8% car, 0.4% public transportation, 2.3% walk, 0.8% work from home (2000); Travel time to work: 21.2% less than 15 minutes, 35.7% 15 to 30 minutes, 29.4% 30 to 45 minutes, 9.4% 45 to 60 minutes, 4.3% 60 minutes or more (2000)

NEWARK (city).
Covers a land area of 19.554 square miles and a water area of 0.245 square miles. Located at 40.06° N. Lat.; 82.41° W. Long. Elevation is 829 feet.
History: In 1802, near the ancient mounds of a vanished people, General William Schenck platted a settlement and named it for his hometown in New Jersey. When Newark became the seat of Licking County in 1808, its citizens hammered together a one-room log cabin, with slab benches on a sawdust floor, as the courthouse. The canal came to Newark in 1832, and the population tripled, only to be cut again by a cholera epidemic in 1849. Natural gas discovered here in 1887 attracted iron and glass industries with its cheap fuel, and Newark again grew.
Population: 45,070 (1990); 46,279 (2000); 46,727 (2005); 47,404 (2010 projected); Race: 93.9% White, 3.0% Black, 0.8% Asian, 0.7% Hispanic of any race (2005); Density: 2,389.7 persons per square mile (2005); Average household size: 2.37 (2005); Median age: 36.3 (2005); Males per 100 females: 91.0 (2005); Marriage status: 23.4% never married, 53.8% now married, 8.2% widowed, 14.6% divorced (2000); Foreign born: 1.1% (2000); Ancestry (includes multiple ancestries): 23.1% German, 14.4% Irish, 13.6% United States or American, 10.8% English, 8.5% Other groups (2000).
Economy: Unemployment rate: 6.2% (2005); Total civilian labor force: 23,373 (2005); Single-family building permits issued: 722 (2005); Multi-family building permits issued: 314 (2005); Employment by occupation: 9.6% management, 14.1% professional, 18.0% services, 28.3% sales, 0.1% farming, 9.0% construction, 20.9% production (2000).
Income: Per capita income: $20,144 (2005); Median household income: $37,685 (2005); Average household income: $47,125 (2005); Percent of households with income of $100,000 or more: 7.7% (2005); Poverty rate: 13.0% (2000).
Taxes: Total city taxes per capita: $472 (2004); City property taxes per capita: $61 (2004).
Education: Percent of population age 25 and over with: High school diploma (including GED) or higher: 81.1% (2005); Bachelor's degree or higher: 15.0% (2005); Master's degree or higher: 4.6% (2005).

School District(s)
Community School at Pime
    2003-04 Enrollment: n/a
Licking County Joint Vocational SD (PK-12)
    2003-04 Enrollment: n/a .... (740) 366-3351
Licking Valley Local Sd SD (PK-12)
    2003-04 Enrollment: 2,166 .... (740) 763-3525

Newark City SD (PK-12)
  2003-04 Enrollment: 6,969 . . . . (740) 345-9891
Newark Digital Academy (03-12)
  2003-04 Enrollment: 52 . . . . (740) 328-2029
North Fork Local SD (PK-12)
  2003-04 Enrollment: 1,908 . . . . (740) 892-3666

Four-year College(s)
Ohio State University-Newark Campus (Public)
  Fall 2004 Enrollment: 2,143 . . . . (740) 366-1351
  2005-06 Tuition: In-state $5,310; Out-of-state $16,533

Two-year College(s)
Career and Technology Education Centers of Licking County (Public)
  Fall 2004 Enrollment: 412 . . . . (614) 366-3351
Central Ohio Technical College (Public)
  Fall 2004 Enrollment: 2,784 . . . . (740) 366-1351
  2005-06 Tuition: In-state $3,384; Out-of-state $6,084

Housing: Homeownership rate: 58.2% (2005); Median home value: $101,508 (2005); Median rent: $394 per month (2000); Median age of housing: 42 years (2000).
Hospitals: Licking Memorial Hospital (195 beds)
Safety: Violent crime rate: 17.6 per 10,000 population; Property crime rate: 515.0 per 10,000 population (2004).
Newspapers: The Advocate (Circulation 21,891)
Transportation: Commute to work: 94.9% car, 1.0% public transportation, 1.5% walk, 1.9% work from home (2000); Travel time to work: 44.5% less than 15 minutes, 30.8% 15 to 30 minutes, 10.3% 30 to 45 minutes, 8.7% 45 to 60 minutes, 5.6% 60 minutes or more (2000)

Additional Information Contacts
City of Newark . . . . (740) 349-6600
  http://www.ci.newark.oh.us
Greater Licking Co. Convention & Visitors Bureau . . . . (740) 345-8224
  http://www.lccvb.com
Newark & Licking County Chamber . . . . (740) 345-9757
  http://newarkchamber.com

PATASKALA (city). Covers a land area of 28.507 square miles and a water area of 0.022 square miles. Located at 39.99° N. Lat.; 82.69° W. Long. Elevation is 1,005 feet.
Population: 7,698 (1990); 10,249 (2000); 12,218 (2005); 14,076 (2010 projected); Race: 94.5% White, 2.7% Black, 0.7% Asian, 1.0% Hispanic of any race (2005); Density: 428.6 persons per square mile (2005); Average household size: 2.58 (2005); Median age: 35.6 (2005); Males per 100 females: 96.4 (2005); Marriage status: 19.9% never married, 62.9% now married, 5.1% widowed, 12.1% divorced (2000); Foreign born: 1.2% (2000); Ancestry (includes multiple ancestries): 26.4% German, 16.9% Irish, 12.2% English, 10.5% Other groups, 9.9% United States or American (2000).
Economy: In fruit and dairy area. Employment by occupation: 15.2% management, 17.2% professional, 10.7% services, 29.6% sales, 0.1% farming, 10.9% construction, 16.3% production (2000).
Income: Per capita income: $25,764 (2005); Median household income: $58,163 (2005); Average household income: $65,865 (2005); Percent of households with income of $100,000 or more: 16.5% (2005); Poverty rate: 5.4% (2000).
Education: Percent of population age 25 and over with: High school diploma (including GED) or higher: 86.6% (2005); Bachelor's degree or higher: 20.8% (2005); Master's degree or higher: 7.0% (2005).

School District(s)
Licking Heights Local SD (PK-12)
  2003-04 Enrollment: 2,008 . . . . (740) 927-6926
Southwest Licking Local SD (PK-12)
  2003-04 Enrollment: 3,527 . . . . (740) 927-3941

Housing: Homeownership rate: 75.8% (2005); Median home value: $156,779 (2005); Median rent: $459 per month (2000); Median age of housing: 21 years (2000).
Safety: Violent crime rate: 13.5 per 10,000 population; Property crime rate: 313.3 per 10,000 population (2004).
Newspapers: Pataskala Post (General - Circulation 8,500); The Pataskala Standard (General - Circulation 5,200)
Transportation: Commute to work: 95.8% car, 0.6% public transportation, 0.8% walk, 2.4% work from home (2000); Travel time to work: 18.6% less than 15 minutes, 35.0% 15 to 30 minutes, 34.6% 30 to 45 minutes, 9.5% 45 to 60 minutes, 2.4% 60 minutes or more (2000)

Additional Information Contacts
City of Pataskala . . . . (740) 927-2021
  http://www.ci.pataskala.oh.us
Pataskala Area Chamber of Commerce . . . . (740) 964-5503
  http://www.ci.pataskala.oh.us

SAINT LOUISVILLE (village). Covers a land area of 0.247 square miles and a water area of 0 square miles. Located at 40.17° N. Lat.; 82.41° W. Long. Elevation is 905 feet.
Population: 372 (1990); 346 (2000); 326 (2005); 320 (2010 projected); Race: 98.2% White, 0.0% Black, 0.0% Asian, 0.0% Hispanic of any race (2005); Density: 1,321.0 persons per square mile (2005); Average household size: 2.86 (2005); Median age: 34.2 (2005); Males per 100 females: 98.8 (2005); Marriage status: 26.2% never married, 50.4% now married, 10.5% widowed, 12.9% divorced (2000); Foreign born: 0.0% (2000); Ancestry (includes multiple ancestries): 38.0% German, 14.9% Other groups, 11.4% English, 10.2% Irish, 6.1% United States or American (2000).
Economy: Single-family building permits issued: 0 (2005); Multi-family building permits issued: 0 (2005); Employment by occupation: 2.7% management, 9.6% professional, 17.1% services, 31.5% sales, 0.0% farming, 15.8% construction, 23.3% production (2000).
Income: Per capita income: $16,365 (2005); Median household income: $44,545 (2005); Average household income: $46,798 (2005); Percent of households with income of $100,000 or more: 4.4% (2005); Poverty rate: 7.5% (2000).
Education: Percent of population age 25 and over with: High school diploma (including GED) or higher: 89.4% (2005); Bachelor's degree or higher: 5.5% (2005); Master's degree or higher: 1.0% (2005).
Housing: Homeownership rate: 86.0% (2005); Median home value: $102,128 (2005); Median rent: $404 per month (2000); Median age of housing: 60+ years (2000).
Transportation: Commute to work: 96.6% car, 0.0% public transportation, 0.0% walk, 2.1% work from home (2000); Travel time to work: 11.2% less than 15 minutes, 46.9% 15 to 30 minutes, 20.3% 30 to 45 minutes, 7.7% 45 to 60 minutes, 14.0% 60 minutes or more (2000)

UTICA (village). Covers a land area of 1.697 square miles and a water area of 0 square miles. Located at 40.23° N. Lat.; 82.44° W. Long. Elevation is 967 feet.
Population: 2,148 (1990); 2,130 (2000); 2,030 (2005); 2,002 (2010 projected); Race: 98.5% White, 0.1% Black, 0.2% Asian, 0.8% Hispanic of any race (2005); Density: 1,196.0 persons per square mile (2005); Average household size: 2.56 (2005); Median age: 37.9 (2005); Males per 100 females: 97.7 (2005); Marriage status: 19.4% never married, 55.8% now married, 10.2% widowed, 14.6% divorced (2000); Foreign born: 1.2% (2000); Ancestry (includes multiple ancestries): 21.8% German, 15.3% Irish, 11.6% United States or American, 11.1% English, 7.5% Other groups (2000).
Economy: In rich agricultural area: fruit. Employment by occupation: 6.7% management, 12.9% professional, 14.1% services, 22.2% sales, 1.6% farming, 11.3% construction, 31.3% production (2000).
Income: Per capita income: $19,559 (2005); Median household income: $39,752 (2005); Average household income: $49,287 (2005); Percent of households with income of $100,000 or more: 7.3% (2005); Poverty rate: 6.2% (2000).
Education: Percent of population age 25 and over with: High school diploma (including GED) or higher: 79.9% (2005); Bachelor's degree or higher: 9.2% (2005); Master's degree or higher: 1.9% (2005).

School District(s)
North Fork Local SD (PK-12)
  2003-04 Enrollment: 1,908 . . . . (740) 892-3666

Housing: Homeownership rate: 68.8% (2005); Median home value: $91,087 (2005); Median rent: $346 per month (2000); Median age of housing: 50 years (2000).
Newspapers: The Utica Herald (General - Circulation 2,100)
Transportation: Commute to work: 94.4% car, 0.0% public transportation, 2.7% walk, 2.5% work from home (2000); Travel time to work: 21.5% less than 15 minutes, 35.7% 15 to 30 minutes, 20.9% 30 to 45 minutes, 12.7% 45 to 60 minutes, 9.2% 60 minutes or more (2000)

Logan County

Located in west central Ohio; drained by the Great Miami and Mad Rivers; includes Campbell Hill, the highest point in the state (1,550 ft). Covers a land area of 458.44 square miles, a water area of 8.34 square miles, and is located in the Eastern Time Zone. The county government was organized in 1817. County seat is Bellefontaine.

Logan County is part of the Bellefontaine, OH Micropolitan Statistical Area. The entire metro area includes: Logan County, OH

Weather Station: Bellefontaine — Elevation: 1,184 feet

	Jan	Feb	Mar	Apr	May	Jun	Jul	Aug	Sep	Oct	Nov	Dec
High	32	37	48	61	72	80	83	81	76	64	50	38
Low	17	20	29	39	50	59	63	61	54	43	33	23
Precip	2.3	2.0	2.8	3.6	4.0	4.0	3.9	3.4	2.7	2.4	3.1	3.0
Snow	6.9	4.1	1.7	0.4	tr	0.0	0.0	0.0	0.0	0.2	0.8	3.7

High and Low temperatures in degrees Fahrenheit; Precipitation and Snow in inches

Population: 42,310 (1990); 46,005 (2000); 46,659 (2005); 47,329 (2010 projected); Race: 96.3% White, 1.5% Black, 0.4% Asian, 0.8% Hispanic of any race (2005); Density: 101.8 persons per square mile (2005); Average household size: 2.53 (2005); Median age: 37.6 (2005); Males per 100 females: 96.8 (2005).
Religion: Five largest groups: 9.0% The United Methodist Church, 5.6% Catholic Church, 2.3% Christian Church (Disciples of Christ), 2.3% General Association of Regular Baptist Churches, 2.3% Presbyterian Church (U.S.A.) (2000).
Economy: Unemployment rate: 5.3% (2005); Total civilian labor force: 24,568 (2005); Leading industries: 31.9% manufacturing; 11.7% retail trade; 10.2% health care and social assistance (2004); Farms: 1,055 totaling 225,093 acres (2002); Companies that employ 500 or more persons: 6 (2004); Companies that employ 100 to 499 persons: 22 (2004); Companies that employ less than 100 persons: 922 (2004); Black-owned businesses: n/a (2002); Hispanic-owned businesses: n/a (2002); Women-owned businesses: 999 (2002); Retail sales per capita: $10,660 (2006). Single-family building permits issued: 173 (2005); Multi-family building permits issued: 18 (2005).
Income: Per capita income: $21,878 (2005); Median household income: $46,201 (2005); Average household income: $54,940 (2005); Percent of households with income of $100,000 or more: 11.2% (2005); Poverty rate: 9.3% (2003); Bankruptcy rate: 10.80% (2005).
Education: Percent of population age 25 and over with: High school diploma (including GED) or higher: 83.7% (2005); Bachelor's degree or higher: 11.6% (2005); Master's degree or higher: 4.6% (2005).
Housing: Homeownership rate: 75.8% (2005); Median home value: $105,912 (2005); Median rent: $377 per month (2000); Median age of housing: 38 years (2000).
Health: Birth rate: 124.6 per 10,000 population (2004); Death rate: 104.8 per 10,000 population (2004); Age-adjusted cancer mortality rate: 211.6 deaths per 100,000 population (2002); Number of physicians: 11.8 per 10,000 population (2004); Hospital beds: 23.7 per 10,000 population (2003); Hospital admissions: 759.2 per 10,000 population (2003).
Elections: 2004 Presidential election results: 67.6% Bush, 31.9% Kerry, 0.0% Nader, 0.2% Badnarik
National and State Parks: Fox Island State Park; Indian Lake State Park; Indian Lake State Wildlife Area
Additional Information Contacts
Logan County Government . . . . (937) 599-7283
  http://www.co.logan.oh.us/
Bellefontaine Chamber of Commerce . . . . (937) 599-5121
  http://www.logancountyohio.com
City of Bellefontaine . . . . (937) 599-5121
  http://ci.bellefontaine.oh.us
Russells Point Chamber of Commerce . . . . (937) 843-5392
  http://indianlake.com
Village of Huntsville . . . . (937) 686-4300
  http://huntsvilleohio.com

Logan County Communities

BELLE CENTER (village). Covers a land area of 0.689 square miles and a water area of 0.013 square miles. Located at 40.50° N. Lat.; 83.74° W. Long. Elevation is 1,045 feet.
History: Belle Center developed as a rural trading village. A large butter and cheese plant was established here.
Population: 816 (1990); 807 (2000); 822 (2005); 841 (2010 projected); Race: 99.9% White, 0.0% Black, 0.0% Asian, 0.6% Hispanic of any race (2005); Density: 1,192.7 persons per square mile (2005); Average household size: 2.44 (2005); Median age: 37.0 (2005); Males per 100 females: 93.4 (2005); Marriage status: 18.8% never married, 61.2% now married, 8.9% widowed, 11.1% divorced (2000); Foreign born: 0.6% (2000); Ancestry (includes multiple ancestries): 26.3% German, 17.4% United States or American, 11.5% English, 10.4% Irish, 7.6% Other groups (2000).
Economy: Single-family building permits issued: 3 (2005); Multi-family building permits issued: 0 (2005); Employment by occupation: 2.9% management, 14.4% professional, 12.5% services, 22.5% sales, 0.0% farming, 7.0% construction, 40.8% production (2000).
Income: Per capita income: $23,531 (2005); Median household income: $50,718 (2005); Average household income: $56,187 (2005); Percent of households with income of $100,000 or more: 10.7% (2005); Poverty rate: 8.5% (2000).
Education: Percent of population age 25 and over with: High school diploma (including GED) or higher: 83.9% (2005); Bachelor's degree or higher: 10.0% (2005); Master's degree or higher: 5.5% (2005).
Housing: Homeownership rate: 86.9% (2005); Median home value: $88,243 (2005); Median rent: $339 per month (2000); Median age of housing: 60+ years (2000).
Transportation: Commute to work: 97.0% car, 0.0% public transportation, 2.2% walk, 0.5% work from home (2000); Travel time to work: 13.3% less than 15 minutes, 60.3% 15 to 30 minutes, 18.8% 30 to 45 minutes, 4.3% 45 to 60 minutes, 3.5% 60 minutes or more (2000)

BELLEFONTAINE (city). Covers a land area of 8.764 square miles and a water area of 0 square miles. Located at 40.36° N. Lat.; 83.75° W. Long. Elevation is 1,251 feet.
History: Bellefontaine was settled in 1806, and became the seat of Logan County in 1820. The name means "beautiful fountain," referring to the natural springs at the site.
Population: 12,328 (1990); 13,069 (2000); 12,963 (2005); 12,834 (2010 projected); Race: 91.4% White, 4.5% Black, 0.9% Asian, 1.2% Hispanic of any race (2005); Density: 1,479.2 persons per square mile (2005); Average household size: 2.43 (2005); Median age: 33.7 (2005); Males per 100 females: 91.6 (2005); Marriage status: 24.0% never married, 52.6% now married, 8.3% widowed, 15.1% divorced (2000); Foreign born: 2.5% (2000); Ancestry (includes multiple ancestries): 22.4% German, 16.5% United States or American, 13.1% Other groups, 10.7% Irish, 8.3% English (2000).
Economy: Employment by occupation: 7.3% management, 12.4% professional, 16.5% services, 22.3% sales, 0.1% farming, 8.6% construction, 32.9% production (2000).
Income: Per capita income: $19,912 (2005); Median household income: $38,575 (2005); Average household income: $48,043 (2005); Percent of households with income of $100,000 or more: 8.3% (2005); Poverty rate: 14.6% (2000).
Education: Percent of population age 25 and over with: High school diploma (including GED) or higher: 84.5% (2005); Bachelor's degree or higher: 13.3% (2005); Master's degree or higher: 6.6% (2005).
School District(s)
Bellefontaine City Schools (KG-12)
  2003-04 Enrollment: 2,808 . . . . (937) 593-9060
Benjamin Logan Local SD (KG-12)
  2003-04 Enrollment: 1,966 . . . . (937) 593-9211
Ohio Hi-Point Career Center (10-12)
  2003-04 Enrollment: n/a . . . . (937) 599-3010
Two-year College(s)
Ohio Hi Point Joint Vocational School District (Public)
  Fall 2004 Enrollment: 82 . . . . (937) 599-6275
  2005-06 Tuition: In-state $5,782; Out-of-state $5,782
Housing: Homeownership rate: 58.0% (2005); Median home value: $95,592 (2005); Median rent: $381 per month (2000); Median age of housing: 44 years (2000).
Hospitals: Mary Rutan Hospital (105 beds)
Safety: Violent crime rate: 108.4 per 10,000 population; Property crime rate: 413.7 per 10,000 population (2004).
Newspapers: Bellefontaine Examiner (Circulation 8,931)
Transportation: Commute to work: 93.8% car, 0.1% public transportation, 3.2% walk, 2.0% work from home (2000); Travel time to work: 53.4% less than 15 minutes, 30.3% 15 to 30 minutes, 8.2% 30 to 45 minutes, 2.6% 45 to 60 minutes, 5.4% 60 minutes or more (2000)
Additional Information Contacts
Bellefontaine Chamber of Commerce . . . . (937) 599-5121
  http://www.logancountyohio.com
City of Bellefontaine . . . . (937) 599-5121
  http://ci.bellefontaine.oh.us

DE GRAFF (village). Aka Degraff. Covers a land area of 0.857 square miles and a water area of 0 square miles. Located at 40.31° N. Lat.; 83.91° W. Long. Elevation is 1,007 feet.
History: Sometimes spelled Degraff.
Population: 1,331 (1990); 1,212 (2000); 1,110 (2005); 1,092 (2010 projected); Race: 99.7% White, 0.2% Black, 0.1% Asian, 0.3% Hispanic of any race (2005); Density: 1,295.4 persons per square mile (2005); Average household size: 2.47 (2005); Median age: 35.1 (2005); Males per 100 females: 100.7 (2005); Marriage status: 23.2% never married, 57.0% now married, 9.2% widowed, 10.6% divorced (2000); Foreign born: 0.7% (2000); Ancestry (includes multiple ancestries): 22.9% German, 19.8% United States or American, 8.0% English, 6.6% Irish, 2.6% Other groups (2000).
Economy: Single-family building permits issued: 0 (2005); Multi-family building permits issued: 0 (2005); Employment by occupation: 7.9% management, 9.6% professional, 12.1% services, 19.5% sales, 0.9% farming, 11.8% construction, 38.3% production (2000).
Income: Per capita income: $20,691 (2005); Median household income: $39,324 (2005); Average household income: $51,153 (2005); Percent of households with income of $100,000 or more: 11.4% (2005); Poverty rate: 8.2% (2000).
Education: Percent of population age 25 and over with: High school diploma (including GED) or higher: 83.9% (2005); Bachelor's degree or higher: 8.4% (2005); Master's degree or higher: 2.7% (2005).
School District(s)
Riverside Local SD (KG-12)
　　2003-04 Enrollment: 809 . . . . (937) 585-5981
Housing: Homeownership rate: 79.7% (2005); Median home value: $92,233 (2005); Median rent: $342 per month (2000); Median age of housing: 53 years (2000).
Transportation: Commute to work: 93.7% car, 0.0% public transportation, 3.8% walk, 2.3% work from home (2000); Travel time to work: 19.1% less than 15 minutes, 43.7% 15 to 30 minutes, 26.6% 30 to 45 minutes, 5.2% 45 to 60 minutes, 5.5% 60 minutes or more (2000)

EAST LIBERTY (unincorporated postal area, zip code 43319). Covers a land area of 20.961 square miles and a water area of 0.012 square miles. Located at 40.30° N. Lat.; 83.56° W. Long. Elevation is 1,130 feet.
Population: 967 (2000); Race: 96.5% White, 0.5% Black, 1.4% Asian, 0.5% Hispanic of any race (2000); Density: 46.1 persons per square mile (2000); Age: 28.5% under 18, 10.6% over 64 (2000); Marriage status: 19.4% never married, 62.6% now married, 3.6% widowed, 14.4% divorced (2000); Foreign born: 2.3% (2000); Ancestry (includes multiple ancestries): 26.7% German, 16.9% United States or American, 13.0% English, 11.7% Irish, 9.7% Other groups (2000).
Economy: Employment by occupation: 11.9% management, 5.7% professional, 9.6% services, 23.4% sales, 3.0% farming, 9.8% construction, 36.6% production (2000).
Income: Per capita income: $21,140 (2000); Median household income: $55,625 (2000); Poverty rate: 2.8% (2000).
Education: Percent of population age 25 and over with: High school diploma (including GED) or higher: 85.5% (2000); Bachelor's degree or higher: 4.3% (2000).
Housing: Homeownership rate: 86.1% (2000); Median home value: $89,700 (2000); Median rent: $455 per month (2000); Median age of housing: 60+ years (2000).
Transportation: Commute to work: 91.1% car, 0.0% public transportation, 4.0% walk, 4.9% work from home (2000); Travel time to work: 46.6% less than 15 minutes, 27.7% 15 to 30 minutes, 15.5% 30 to 45 minutes, 4.2% 45 to 60 minutes, 6.1% 60 minutes or more (2000)

HUNTSVILLE (village). Covers a land area of 0.337 square miles and a water area of 0 square miles. Located at 40.44° N. Lat.; 83.80° W. Long. Elevation is 1,069 feet.
Population: 343 (1990); 454 (2000); 455 (2005); 456 (2010 projected); Race: 96.7% White, 0.2% Black, 0.4% Asian, 0.2% Hispanic of any race (2005); Density: 1,349.8 persons per square mile (2005); Average household size: 2.54 (2005); Median age: 35.6 (2005); Males per 100 females: 90.4 (2005); Marriage status: 18.8% never married, 65.0% now married, 4.7% widowed, 11.6% divorced (2000); Foreign born: 0.0% (2000); Ancestry (includes multiple ancestries): 32.2% German, 17.9% Irish, 11.9% English, 9.9% United States or American, 6.8% Other groups (2000).
Economy: In agricultural area. Single-family building permits issued: 0 (2005); Multi-family building permits issued: 0 (2005); Employment by occupation: 9.7% management, 6.5% professional, 24.1% services, 25.5% sales, 0.9% farming, 7.9% construction, 25.5% production (2000).
Income: Per capita income: $19,912 (2005); Median household income: $44,415 (2005); Average household income: $50,615 (2005); Percent of households with income of $100,000 or more: 8.4% (2005); Poverty rate: 8.4% (2000).
Taxes: Total city taxes per capita: $190 (2004); City property taxes per capita: $23 (2004).
Education: Percent of population age 25 and over with: High school diploma (including GED) or higher: 86.1% (2005); Bachelor's degree or higher: 2.8% (2005); Master's degree or higher: 0.0% (2005).
School District(s)
Indian Lake Local SD (KG-12)
　　2003-04 Enrollment: 1,992 . . . . (937) 686-8601
Housing: Homeownership rate: 73.2% (2005); Median home value: $91,552 (2005); Median rent: $423 per month (2000); Median age of housing: 51 years (2000).
Transportation: Commute to work: 91.7% car, 0.0% public transportation, 1.9% walk, 5.1% work from home (2000); Travel time to work: 43.9% less than 15 minutes, 39.5% 15 to 30 minutes, 10.2% 30 to 45 minutes, 1.0% 45 to 60 minutes, 5.4% 60 minutes or more (2000)
Additional Information Contacts
Village of Huntsville . . . . (937) 686-4300
　　http://huntsvilleohio.com

LAKEVIEW (village). Covers a land area of 0.684 square miles and a water area of 0.005 square miles. Located at 40.48° N. Lat.; 83.92° W. Long. Elevation is 997 feet.
History: Lakeview developed as a resort on Indian Lake.
Population: 1,083 (1990); 1,074 (2000); 1,116 (2005); 1,159 (2010 projected); Race: 96.9% White, 0.1% Black, 0.4% Asian, 0.5% Hispanic of any race (2005); Density: 1,631.6 persons per square mile (2005); Average household size: 2.45 (2005); Median age: 37.1 (2005); Males per 100 females: 95.8 (2005); Marriage status: 19.3% never married, 56.5% now married, 8.6% widowed, 15.6% divorced (2000); Foreign born: 1.3% (2000); Ancestry (includes multiple ancestries): 22.7% German, 17.6% United States or American, 11.0% English, 9.6% Irish, 5.6% Other groups (2000).
Economy: Single-family building permits issued: 2 (2005); Multi-family building permits issued: 0 (2005); Employment by occupation: 7.4% management, 13.9% professional, 14.1% services, 17.2% sales, 0.0% farming, 12.1% construction, 35.2% production (2000).
Income: Per capita income: $17,646 (2005); Median household income: $36,851 (2005); Average household income: $43,280 (2005); Percent of households with income of $100,000 or more: 5.7% (2005); Poverty rate: 10.9% (2000).
Education: Percent of population age 25 and over with: High school diploma (including GED) or higher: 70.8% (2005); Bachelor's degree or higher: 4.1% (2005); Master's degree or higher: 1.0% (2005).
School District(s)
Indian Lake Local SD (KG-12)
　　2003-04 Enrollment: 1,992 . . . . (937) 686-8601
Housing: Homeownership rate: 73.8% (2005); Median home value: $66,667 (2005); Median rent: $354 per month (2000); Median age of housing: 42 years (2000).
Transportation: Commute to work: 96.8% car, 0.0% public transportation, 1.3% walk, 1.5% work from home (2000); Travel time to work: 26.7% less than 15 minutes, 38.0% 15 to 30 minutes, 17.5% 30 to 45 minutes, 7.9% 45 to 60 minutes, 9.8% 60 minutes or more (2000)

LEWISTOWN (unincorporated postal area, zip code 43333). Covers a land area of 29.227 square miles and a water area of 0.016 square miles. Located at 40.43° N. Lat.; 83.92° W. Long. Elevation is 1,022 feet.
Population: 693 (2000); Race: 100.0% White, 0.0% Black, 0.0% Asian, 0.0% Hispanic of any race (2000); Density: 23.7 persons per square mile (2000); Age: 23.0% under 18, 10.2% over 64 (2000); Marriage status: 21.6% never married, 58.3% now married, 8.9% widowed, 11.2% divorced (2000); Foreign born: 0.0% (2000); Ancestry (includes multiple ancestries): 33.1% German, 29.1% United States or American, 16.4% Irish, 8.5% English, 3.0% Other groups (2000).
Economy: Employment by occupation: 16.7% management, 20.1% professional, 22.0% services, 8.5% sales, 0.0% farming, 7.5% construction, 25.2% production (2000).

Income: Per capita income: $20,187 (2000); Median household income: $36,534 (2000); Poverty rate: 8.9% (2000).
Education: Percent of population age 25 and over with: High school diploma (including GED) or higher: 83.1% (2000); Bachelor's degree or higher: 7.3% (2000).

School District(s)
Indian Lake Local SD (KG-12)
   2003-04 Enrollment: 1,992 . . . . (937) 686-8601
Housing: Homeownership rate: 78.4% (2000); Median home value: $87,800 (2000); Median rent: $407 per month (2000); Median age of housing: 60+ years (2000).
Transportation: Commute to work: 91.5% car, 0.0% public transportation, 0.0% walk, 8.5% work from home (2000); Travel time to work: 35.7% less than 15 minutes, 44.7% 15 to 30 minutes, 12.4% 30 to 45 minutes, 1.1% 45 to 60 minutes, 6.1% 60 minutes or more (2000)

QUINCY (village).
Covers a land area of 1.132 square miles and a water area of 0 square miles. Located at 40.29° N. Lat.; 83.97° W. Long. Elevation is 1,055 feet.
Population: 697 (1990); 734 (2000); 720 (2005); 705 (2010 projected); Race: 98.5% White, 0.0% Black, 0.0% Asian, 0.7% Hispanic of any race (2005); Density: 635.9 persons per square mile (2005); Average household size: 2.82 (2005); Median age: 30.1 (2005); Males per 100 females: 102.2 (2005); Marriage status: 24.1% never married, 60.0% now married, 5.8% widowed, 10.0% divorced (2000); Foreign born: 0.0% (2000); Ancestry (includes multiple ancestries): 17.0% German, 12.6% English, 10.6% United States or American, 9.8% Irish, 5.9% Other groups (2000).
Economy: Single-family building permits issued: 2 (2005); Multi-family building permits issued: 0 (2005); Employment by occupation: 5.8% management, 6.4% professional, 18.0% services, 18.6% sales, 1.0% farming, 7.7% construction, 42.4% production (2000).
Income: Per capita income: $15,743 (2005); Median household income: $35,174 (2005); Average household income: $44,451 (2005); Percent of households with income of $100,000 or more: 6.7% (2005); Poverty rate: 14.9% (2000).
Education: Percent of population age 25 and over with: High school diploma (including GED) or higher: 79.8% (2005); Bachelor's degree or higher: 7.6% (2005); Master's degree or higher: 3.4% (2005).
Housing: Homeownership rate: 71.4% (2005); Median home value: $70,508 (2005); Median rent: $375 per month (2000); Median age of housing: 58 years (2000).
Transportation: Commute to work: 93.8% car, 0.0% public transportation, 4.9% walk, 1.3% work from home (2000); Travel time to work: 15.6% less than 15 minutes, 45.4% 15 to 30 minutes, 23.8% 30 to 45 minutes, 6.3% 45 to 60 minutes, 8.9% 60 minutes or more (2000)

RUSHSYLVANIA (village).
Covers a land area of 0.758 square miles and a water area of 0 square miles. Located at 40.46° N. Lat.; 83.67° W. Long. Elevation is 1,238 feet.
Population: 573 (1990); 543 (2000); 537 (2005); 527 (2010 projected); Race: 97.4% White, 0.0% Black, 0.4% Asian, 0.7% Hispanic of any race (2005); Density: 708.7 persons per square mile (2005); Average household size: 2.67 (2005); Median age: 33.2 (2005); Males per 100 females: 101.1 (2005); Marriage status: 21.5% never married, 59.8% now married, 5.4% widowed, 13.3% divorced (2000); Foreign born: 0.2% (2000); Ancestry (includes multiple ancestries): 19.3% United States or American, 17.3% German, 10.1% Irish, 6.6% Other groups, 6.6% English (2000).
Economy: Limestone quarry nearby. Single-family building permits issued: 1 (2005); Multi-family building permits issued: 0 (2005); Employment by occupation: 9.7% management, 8.9% professional, 17.4% services, 14.7% sales, 1.2% farming, 11.2% construction, 36.8% production (2000).
Income: Per capita income: $20,182 (2005); Median household income: $48,929 (2005); Average household income: $53,918 (2005); Percent of households with income of $100,000 or more: 8.0% (2005); Poverty rate: 10.9% (2000).
Education: Percent of population age 25 and over with: High school diploma (including GED) or higher: 80.8% (2005); Bachelor's degree or higher: 9.3% (2005); Master's degree or higher: 2.7% (2005).
Housing: Homeownership rate: 83.6% (2005); Median home value: $76,786 (2005); Median rent: $288 per month (2000); Median age of housing: 60+ years (2000).
Transportation: Commute to work: 93.8% car, 0.8% public transportation, 0.0% walk, 5.4% work from home (2000); Travel time to work: 16.8% less than 15 minutes, 57.4% 15 to 30 minutes, 12.7% 30 to 45 minutes, 4.5% 45 to 60 minutes, 8.6% 60 minutes or more (2000)

RUSSELLS POINT (village).
Covers a land area of 0.934 square miles and a water area of 0.081 square miles. Located at 40.47° N. Lat.; 83.89° W. Long. Elevation is 1,008 feet.
History: Russells Point developed as a resort and vacation center on Indian Lake.
Population: 1,545 (1990); 1,619 (2000); 1,590 (2005); 1,578 (2010 projected); Race: 98.0% White, 0.1% Black, 0.7% Asian, 1.6% Hispanic of any race (2005); Density: 1,702.1 persons per square mile (2005); Average household size: 2.21 (2005); Median age: 36.2 (2005); Males per 100 females: 88.8 (2005); Marriage status: 21.6% never married, 48.7% now married, 8.4% widowed, 21.2% divorced (2000); Foreign born: 0.6% (2000); Ancestry (includes multiple ancestries): 22.2% German, 18.5% United States or American, 10.3% Other groups, 9.8% Irish, 6.8% English (2000).
Economy: Single-family building permits issued: 1 (2005); Multi-family building permits issued: 0 (2005); Employment by occupation: 3.7% management, 12.7% professional, 16.0% services, 22.2% sales, 0.0% farming, 10.0% construction, 35.5% production (2000).
Income: Per capita income: $17,965 (2005); Median household income: $30,966 (2005); Average household income: $39,729 (2005); Percent of households with income of $100,000 or more: 5.1% (2005); Poverty rate: 20.2% (2000).
Education: Percent of population age 25 and over with: High school diploma (including GED) or higher: 72.6% (2005); Bachelor's degree or higher: 6.6% (2005); Master's degree or higher: 2.2% (2005).
Housing: Homeownership rate: 58.6% (2005); Median home value: $72,660 (2005); Median rent: $316 per month (2000); Median age of housing: 32 years (2000).
Transportation: Commute to work: 93.2% car, 0.8% public transportation, 2.9% walk, 2.9% work from home (2000); Travel time to work: 33.6% less than 15 minutes, 31.1% 15 to 30 minutes, 23.0% 30 to 45 minutes, 5.8% 45 to 60 minutes, 6.4% 60 minutes or more (2000)

Additional Information Contacts
Russells Point Chamber of Commerce . . . . (937) 843-5392
   http://indianlake.com

VALLEY HI (village).
Covers a land area of 0.659 square miles and a water area of 0 square miles. Located at 40.31° N. Lat.; 83.68° W. Long. Elevation is 1,270 feet.
Population: 217 (1990); 244 (2000); 244 (2005); 243 (2010 projected); Race: 97.5% White, 0.0% Black, 0.0% Asian, 1.6% Hispanic of any race (2005); Density: 370.4 persons per square mile (2005); Average household size: 2.46 (2005); Median age: 32.9 (2005); Males per 100 females: 100.0 (2005); Marriage status: 24.6% never married, 52.1% now married, 3.5% widowed, 19.9% divorced (2000); Foreign born: 0.0% (2000); Ancestry (includes multiple ancestries): 29.8% German, 13.4% Other groups, 13.2% Irish, 8.8% English, 5.3% French (except Basque) (2000).
Economy: Single-family building permits issued: 0 (2005); Multi-family building permits issued: 0 (2005); Employment by occupation: 11.1% management, 3.2% professional, 15.1% services, 31.0% sales, 0.0% farming, 9.1% construction, 30.6% production (2000).
Income: Per capita income: $22,111 (2005); Median household income: $50,446 (2005); Average household income: $54,495 (2005); Percent of households with income of $100,000 or more: 9.1% (2005); Poverty rate: 4.7% (2000).
Education: Percent of population age 25 and over with: High school diploma (including GED) or higher: 87.6% (2005); Bachelor's degree or higher: 5.9% (2005); Master's degree or higher: 0.0% (2005).
Housing: Homeownership rate: 75.8% (2005); Median home value: $19,999 (2005); Median rent: $462 per month (2000); Median age of housing: 16 years (2000).
Transportation: Commute to work: 99.2% car, 0.0% public transportation, 0.0% walk, 0.8% work from home (2000); Travel time to work: 11.7% less than 15 minutes, 57.7% 15 to 30 minutes, 18.1% 30 to 45 minutes, 5.6% 45 to 60 minutes, 6.9% 60 minutes or more (2000)

WEST LIBERTY (village).
Covers a land area of 1.107 square miles and a water area of 0 square miles. Located at 40.25° N. Lat.; 83.75° W. Long. Elevation is 1,111 feet.
History: West Liberty developed as a rural trading center around a milk plant, a flour mill, and grain elevators.
Population: 1,947 (1990); 1,813 (2000); 1,788 (2005); 1,817 (2010 projected); Race: 98.6% White, 0.1% Black, 0.3% Asian, 0.1% Hispanic of any race (2005); Density: 1,615.1 persons per square mile (2005); Average

household size: 2.74 (2005); Median age: 45.3 (2005); Males per 100 females: 78.6 (2005); Marriage status: 20.1% never married, 53.4% now married, 17.4% widowed, 9.1% divorced (2000); Foreign born: 0.5% (2000); Ancestry (includes multiple ancestries): 27.1% German, 11.5% United States or American, 11.4% English, 8.2% Irish, 5.6% Other groups (2000).
Economy: Single-family building permits issued: 4 (2005); Multi-family building permits issued: 0 (2005); Employment by occupation: 7.8% management, 16.3% professional, 16.4% services, 28.9% sales, 0.0% farming, 9.0% construction, 21.6% production (2000).
Income: Per capita income: $22,918 (2005); Median household income: $45,254 (2005); Average household income: $54,613 (2005); Percent of households with income of $100,000 or more: 9.6% (2005); Poverty rate: 5.3% (2000).
Education: Percent of population age 25 and over with: High school diploma (including GED) or higher: 87.0% (2005); Bachelor's degree or higher: 18.2% (2005); Master's degree or higher: 5.2% (2005).

School District(s)
West Liberty-Salem Local SD (PK-12)
    2003-04 Enrollment: 1,160 . . . . (937) 465-1075

Housing: Homeownership rate: 72.7% (2005); Median home value: $110,266 (2005); Median rent: $354 per month (2000); Median age of housing: 60+ years (2000).
Transportation: Commute to work: 90.7% car, 0.2% public transportation, 3.4% walk, 5.2% work from home (2000); Travel time to work: 44.4% less than 15 minutes, 38.7% 15 to 30 minutes, 9.3% 30 to 45 minutes, 2.7% 45 to 60 minutes, 5.1% 60 minutes or more (2000)

WEST MANSFIELD (village). Covers a land area of 0.825 square miles and a water area of 0.025 square miles. Located at 40.40° N. Lat.; 83.54° W. Long. Elevation is 1,090 feet.
Population: 843 (1990); 700 (2000); 653 (2005); 643 (2010 projected); Race: 97.9% White, 0.2% Black, 0.2% Asian, 0.3% Hispanic of any race (2005); Density: 791.8 persons per square mile (2005); Average household size: 2.49 (2005); Median age: 36.4 (2005); Males per 100 females: 83.9 (2005); Marriage status: 19.8% never married, 60.5% now married, 8.0% widowed, 11.6% divorced (2000); Foreign born: 0.3% (2000); Ancestry (includes multiple ancestries): 23.2% United States or American, 19.3% German, 11.9% English, 11.2% Irish, 7.4% Other groups (2000).
Economy: In agricultural area. Single-family building permits issued: 0 (2005); Multi-family building permits issued: 0 (2005); Employment by occupation: 6.5% management, 7.3% professional, 15.6% services, 21.3% sales, 0.8% farming, 11.3% construction, 37.2% production (2000).
Income: Per capita income: $21,321 (2005); Median household income: $46,143 (2005); Average household income: $53,139 (2005); Percent of households with income of $100,000 or more: 10.3% (2005); Poverty rate: 3.4% (2000).
Education: Percent of population age 25 and over with: High school diploma (including GED) or higher: 85.7% (2005); Bachelor's degree or higher: 7.1% (2005); Master's degree or higher: 2.3% (2005).
Housing: Homeownership rate: 81.7% (2005); Median home value: $89,231 (2005); Median rent: $350 per month (2000); Median age of housing: 60+ years (2000).
Transportation: Commute to work: 92.4% car, 0.0% public transportation, 4.9% walk, 1.9% work from home (2000); Travel time to work: 23.6% less than 15 minutes, 49.2% 15 to 30 minutes, 19.4% 30 to 45 minutes, 5.8% 45 to 60 minutes, 1.9% 60 minutes or more (2000)

ZANESFIELD (village). Covers a land area of 0.118 square miles and a water area of 0 square miles. Located at 40.33° N. Lat.; 83.67° W. Long. Elevation is 1,175 feet.
History: Zanesfield was settled in 1819 on the site of a blockhouse built by the English during the French and Indian War. The land once belonged to Isaac Zane, who was adopted by the Wyandot tribe when he was nine years old, and married the daughter of Chief Tarhe. He was known as White Eagle.
Population: 183 (1990); 220 (2000); 222 (2005); 225 (2010 projected); Race: 99.1% White, 0.0% Black, 0.0% Asian, 0.0% Hispanic of any race (2005); Density: 1,884.6 persons per square mile (2005); Average household size: 2.24 (2005); Median age: 35.6 (2005); Males per 100 females: 93.0 (2005); Marriage status: 18.3% never married, 65.1% now married, 8.6% widowed, 8.0% divorced (2000); Foreign born: 1.4% (2000); Ancestry (includes multiple ancestries): 19.0% German, 18.5% English, 13.3% Irish, 12.3% Other groups, 9.5% United States or American (2000).

Economy: Single-family building permits issued: 0 (2005); Multi-family building permits issued: 0 (2005); Employment by occupation: 1.8% management, 17.9% professional, 11.6% services, 27.7% sales, 0.0% farming, 8.9% construction, 32.1% production (2000).
Income: Per capita income: $21,239 (2005); Median household income: $47,500 (2005); Average household income: $47,626 (2005); Percent of households with income of $100,000 or more: 2.0% (2005); Poverty rate: 0.9% (2000).
Education: Percent of population age 25 and over with: High school diploma (including GED) or higher: 94.1% (2005); Bachelor's degree or higher: 17.8% (2005); Master's degree or higher: 5.3% (2005).
Housing: Homeownership rate: 71.7% (2005); Median home value: $77,222 (2005); Median rent: $425 per month (2000); Median age of housing: 60+ years (2000).
Transportation: Commute to work: 90.6% car, 0.0% public transportation, 4.7% walk, 4.7% work from home (2000); Travel time to work: 37.6% less than 15 minutes, 36.6% 15 to 30 minutes, 10.9% 30 to 45 minutes, 4.0% 45 to 60 minutes, 10.9% 60 minutes or more (2000)

Lorain County

Located in northern Ohio; bounded on the north by Lake Erie; drained by the Black and Vermilion Rivers. Covers a land area of 492.50 square miles, a water area of 430.52 square miles, and is located in the Eastern Time Zone. The county government was organized in 1822. County seat is Elyria.

Lorain County is part of the Cleveland-Elyria-Mentor, OH Metropolitan Statistical Area. The entire metro area includes: Cuyahoga County, OH; Geauga County, OH; Lake County, OH; Lorain County, OH; Medina County, OH

Weather Station: Elyria 3 E   Elevation: 728 feet

	Jan	Feb	Mar	Apr	May	Jun	Jul	Aug	Sep	Oct	Nov	Dec
High	34	38	48	60	72	81	85	83	76	64	51	39
Low	19	21	29	38	49	58	63	61	55	44	35	25
Precip	2.4	2.2	2.7	3.2	3.4	4.0	3.7	3.8	3.5	2.7	3.2	3.1
Snow	12.0	10.2	7.2	1.7	tr	tr	0.0	0.0	0.0	0.1	3.2	9.2

High and Low temperatures in degrees Fahrenheit; Precipitation and Snow in inches

Weather Station: Oberlin   Elevation: 813 feet

	Jan	Feb	Mar	Apr	May	Jun	Jul	Aug	Sep	Oct	Nov	Dec
High	33	37	47	60	71	80	84	82	75	63	50	38
Low	16	18	27	36	47	56	60	58	51	40	32	22
Precip	2.2	2.0	2.7	3.2	3.6	3.9	3.7	3.4	3.3	2.5	3.2	2.8
Snow	11.9	9.7	7.1	1.6	tr	0.0	0.0	0.0	0.0	tr	2.5	8.6

High and Low temperatures in degrees Fahrenheit; Precipitation and Snow in inches

Population: 271,126 (1990); 284,664 (2000); 294,884 (2005); 305,520 (2010 projected); Race: 85.2% White, 8.2% Black, 0.8% Asian, 7.1% Hispanic of any race (2005); Density: 598.7 persons per square mile (2005); Average household size: 2.64 (2005); Median age: 37.2 (2005); Males per 100 females: 96.3 (2005).
Religion: Five largest groups: 25.6% Catholic Church, 3.5% The United Methodist Church, 3.3% United Church of Christ, 2.8% Southern Baptist Convention, 1.5% Lutheran Church—Missouri Synod (2000).
Economy: Unemployment rate: 5.8% (2005); Total civilian labor force: 152,191 (2005); Leading industries: 23.0% manufacturing; 15.9% retail trade; 14.0% health care and social assistance (2004); Farms: 975 totaling 161,918 acres (2002); Companies that employ 500 or more persons: 10 (2004); Companies that employ 100 to 499 persons: 114 (2004); Companies that employ less than 100 persons: 5,912 (2004); Black-owned businesses: 439 (2002); Hispanic-owned businesses: 427 (2002); Women-owned businesses: 6,198 (2002); Retail sales per capita: $12,942 (2006). Single-family building permits issued: 1,784 (2005); Multi-family building permits issued: 174 (2005).
Income: Per capita income: $23,999 (2005); Median household income: $49,965 (2005); Average household income: $62,491 (2005); Percent of households with income of $100,000 or more: 15.3% (2005); Poverty rate: 9.8% (2003); Bankruptcy rate: 11.96% (2005).
Taxes: Total county taxes per capita: $226 (2004); County property taxes per capita: $153 (2004).
Education: Percent of population age 25 and over with: High school diploma (including GED) or higher: 83.1% (2005); Bachelor's degree or higher: 17.0% (2005); Master's degree or higher: 5.8% (2005).

Housing: Homeownership rate: 74.7% (2005); Median home value: $138,543 (2005); Median rent: $435 per month (2000); Median age of housing: 37 years (2000).
Health: Birth rate: 122.4 per 10,000 population (2004); Death rate: 94.5 per 10,000 population (2004); Age-adjusted cancer mortality rate: 241.2 deaths per 100,000 population (2002); Air Quality Index: 73.5% good, 24.8% moderate, 1.7% unhealthy for sensitive individuals, 0.0% unhealthy (percent of days in 2005); Number of physicians: 16.6 per 10,000 population (2004); Hospital beds: 21.9 per 10,000 population (2003); Hospital admissions: 1,011.4 per 10,000 population (2003).
Elections: 2004 Presidential election results: 43.5% Bush, 56.1% Kerry, 0.0% Nader, 0.2% Badnarik
National and State Parks: Findley State Park
Additional Information Contacts

Lorain County Government	(440) 329-5000
http://www.loraincounty.us	
Avon Lake Chamber of Commerce	(440) 933-9311
http://www.avonlakeavoncc.com	
City of Avon	(440) 937-7800
http://www.cityofavon.com	
City of Avon Lake	(440) 933-6141
http://www.avonlake.org	
City of Elyria	(440) 326-1400
http://www.cityofelyria.org	
City of Lorain	(440) 204-2002
http://www.cityoflorain.org	
City of North Ridgeville	(440) 353-0819
http://www.ci.north-ridgeville.oh.us	
Columbia Station Chamber of Commerce	(440) 236-9054
http://chamberplace.ghiis.com/1002/index.cfm	
Lorain County Chamber of Commerce	(440) 233-6500
http://www.loraincountychamber.com	
North Ridgeville Chamber of Commerce	(440) 327-3737
http://www.nrchamber.com	
Oberlin Chamber of Commerce	(440) 774-6262
http://www.oberlin.org	
Vermilion Chamber of Commerce	(440) 967-4477
http://www.vermilionohio.com	
Wellington Chamber of Commerce	(440) 647-2222
http://www.wellingtonohio.net	

Lorain County Communities

AMHERST (city). Covers a land area of 7.167 square miles and a water area of 0.006 square miles. Located at 41.40° N. Lat.; 82.22° W. Long. Elevation is 676 feet.
History: Named for Baron Jeffrey Amherst (1717-1797), British general in the French and Indian Wars. Amherst grew around an extensive sandstone quarry.
Population: 10,723 (1990); 11,797 (2000); 11,812 (2005); 11,857 (2010 projected); Race: 96.2% White, 0.6% Black, 0.9% Asian, 3.1% Hispanic of any race (2005); Density: 1,648.2 persons per square mile (2005); Average household size: 2.61 (2005); Median age: 41.3 (2005); Males per 100 females: 92.5 (2005); Marriage status: 17.8% never married, 67.2% now married, 7.3% widowed, 7.7% divorced (2000); Foreign born: 2.1% (2000); Ancestry (includes multiple ancestries): 30.2% German, 15.0% English, 14.7% Irish, 13.1% Polish, 9.3% Italian (2000).
Economy: Single-family building permits issued: 40 (2005); Multi-family building permits issued: 0 (2005); Employment by occupation: 12.8% management, 20.9% professional, 10.7% services, 27.2% sales, 0.1% farming, 9.2% construction, 19.1% production (2000).
Income: Per capita income: $27,862 (2005); Median household income: $59,998 (2005); Average household income: $72,269 (2005); Percent of households with income of $100,000 or more: 20.4% (2005); Poverty rate: 2.1% (2000).
Education: Percent of population age 25 and over with: High school diploma (including GED) or higher: 88.8% (2005); Bachelor's degree or higher: 22.3% (2005); Master's degree or higher: 8.0% (2005).

School District(s)
Amherst Ex Vill SD (PK-12)
    2003-04 Enrollment: 4,190 . . . . (440) 988-4406
Housing: Homeownership rate: 85.2% (2005); Median home value: $164,473 (2005); Median rent: $485 per month (2000); Median age of housing: 35 years (2000).
Hospitals: Amherst Hospital (71 beds)

Safety: Violent crime rate: 10.2 per 10,000 population; Property crime rate: 157.3 per 10,000 population (2004).
Transportation: Commute to work: 95.9% car, 0.5% public transportation, 0.7% walk, 2.5% work from home (2000); Travel time to work: 35.4% less than 15 minutes, 37.9% 15 to 30 minutes, 17.4% 30 to 45 minutes, 5.0% 45 to 60 minutes, 4.3% 60 minutes or more (2000).

AVON (city). Covers a land area of 20.872 square miles and a water area of 0.016 square miles. Located at 41.45° N. Lat.; 82.02° W. Long. Elevation is 670 feet.
History: Named for Avon, New York. Settled c.1814. Incorporated 1918.
Population: 7,337 (1990); 11,446 (2000); 15,097 (2005); 18,446 (2010 projected); Race: 96.2% White, 0.8% Black, 1.5% Asian, 1.4% Hispanic of any race (2005); Density: 723.3 persons per square mile (2005); Average household size: 2.72 (2005); Median age: 38.7 (2005); Males per 100 females: 95.1 (2005); Marriage status: 18.4% never married, 67.6% now married, 6.9% widowed, 7.1% divorced (2000); Foreign born: 3.7% (2000); Ancestry (includes multiple ancestries): 35.0% German, 18.2% Irish, 10.8% Italian, 10.4% English, 9.7% Polish (2000).
Economy: In agricultural area. Single-family building permits issued: 353 (2005); Multi-family building permits issued: 6 (2005); Employment by occupation: 20.0% management, 24.5% professional, 8.9% services, 27.3% sales, 0.4% farming, 8.4% construction, 10.4% production (2000).
Income: Per capita income: $33,682 (2005); Median household income: $77,810 (2005); Average household income: $90,581 (2005); Percent of households with income of $100,000 or more: 34.3% (2005); Poverty rate: 1.9% (2000).
Education: Percent of population age 25 and over with: High school diploma (including GED) or higher: 90.7% (2005); Bachelor's degree or higher: 32.1% (2005); Master's degree or higher: 9.6% (2005).

School District(s)
Avon Local SD (KG-12)
    2003-04 Enrollment: 2,508 . . . . (440) 937-4680
Housing: Homeownership rate: 88.0% (2005); Median home value: $211,700 (2005); Median rent: $650 per month (2000); Median age of housing: 18 years (2000).
Safety: Violent crime rate: 10.1 per 10,000 population; Property crime rate: 147.4 per 10,000 population (2004).
Transportation: Commute to work: 93.6% car, 2.0% public transportation, 0.4% walk, 3.6% work from home (2000); Travel time to work: 22.9% less than 15 minutes, 45.1% 15 to 30 minutes, 20.4% 30 to 45 minutes, 8.7% 45 to 60 minutes, 3.0% 60 minutes or more (2000).
Additional Information Contacts
City of Avon . . . . (440) 937-7800
    http://www.cityofavon.com

AVON LAKE (city). Covers a land area of 11.132 square miles and a water area of 0 square miles. Located at 41.50° N. Lat.; 82.00° W. Long. Elevation is 600 feet.
History: Named for Avon New York, which was named for the river in England. Avon Lake developed as a vacation area, with beaches for water sports.
Population: 15,066 (1990); 18,145 (2000); 20,558 (2005); 22,858 (2010 projected); Race: 96.6% White, 0.5% Black, 1.2% Asian, 1.4% Hispanic of any race (2005); Density: 1,846.8 persons per square mile (2005); Average household size: 2.66 (2005); Median age: 39.1 (2005); Males per 100 females: 95.0 (2005); Marriage status: 18.2% never married, 68.7% now married, 5.3% widowed, 7.8% divorced (2000); Foreign born: 3.4% (2000); Ancestry (includes multiple ancestries): 36.2% German, 22.7% Irish, 13.9% English, 11.4% Italian, 7.3% Polish (2000).
Economy: Single-family building permits issued: 307 (2005); Multi-family building permits issued: 6 (2005); Employment by occupation: 20.6% management, 25.5% professional, 9.4% services, 27.1% sales, 0.2% farming, 7.1% construction, 10.2% production (2000).
Income: Per capita income: $36,802 (2005); Median household income: $73,894 (2005); Average household income: $97,687 (2005); Percent of households with income of $100,000 or more: 32.8% (2005); Poverty rate: 2.3% (2000).
Taxes: Total city taxes per capita: $668 (2004); City property taxes per capita: $269 (2004).
Education: Percent of population age 25 and over with: High school diploma (including GED) or higher: 94.8% (2005); Bachelor's degree or higher: 42.6% (2005); Master's degree or higher: 15.8% (2005).

School District(s)
Avon Lake City Schools (PK-12)
   2003-04 Enrollment: 3,343 . . . . (440) 933-6210
Housing: Homeownership rate: 86.3% (2005); Median home value: $204,622 (2005); Median rent: $572 per month (2000); Median age of housing: 29 years (2000).
Safety: Violent crime rate: 5.5 per 10,000 population; Property crime rate: 77.7 per 10,000 population (2004).
Newspapers: The Press (General - Circulation 8,700)
Transportation: Commute to work: 94.6% car, 1.0% public transportation, 0.3% walk, 3.3% work from home (2000); Travel time to work: 24.7% less than 15 minutes, 35.1% 15 to 30 minutes, 28.5% 30 to 45 minutes, 7.9% 45 to 60 minutes, 3.7% 60 minutes or more (2000)
Additional Information Contacts
Avon Lake Chamber of Commerce . . . . (440) 933-9311
   http://www.avonlakeavoncc.com
City of Avon Lake. . . . . (440) 933-6141
   http://www.avonlake.org

COLUMBIA STATION (unincorporated postal area, zip code 44028). Covers a land area of 34.113 square miles and a water area of 0.344 square miles. Located at 41.31° N. Lat.; 81.93° W. Long. Elevation is 804 feet.
Population: 10,199 (2000); Race: 88.2% White, 9.6% Black, 0.2% Asian, 1.5% Hispanic of any race (2000); Density: 299.0 persons per square mile (2000); Age: 20.7% under 18, 8.8% over 64 (2000); Marriage status: 30.2% never married, 56.3% now married, 4.2% widowed, 9.3% divorced (2000); Foreign born: 2.6% (2000); Ancestry (includes multiple ancestries): 29.2% German, 16.2% Irish, 11.6% English, 9.4% Polish, 8.7% Other groups (2000).
Economy: Employment by occupation: 11.2% management, 15.1% professional, 13.9% services, 27.4% sales, 0.9% farming, 16.2% construction, 15.3% production (2000).
Income: Per capita income: $23,015 (2000); Median household income: $57,596 (2000); Poverty rate: 2.8% (2000).
Education: Percent of population age 25 and over with: High school diploma (including GED) or higher: 85.4% (2000); Bachelor's degree or higher: 14.4% (2000).
School District(s)
Columbia Local SD (PK-12)
   2003-04 Enrollment: 1,143 . . . . (440) 236-5008
Housing: Homeownership rate: 90.2% (2000); Median home value: $148,100 (2000); Median rent: $541 per month (2000); Median age of housing: 36 years (2000).
Newspapers: Rural-Urban Record (General - Circulation 17,139)
Transportation: Commute to work: 95.1% car, 0.9% public transportation, 1.2% walk, 2.4% work from home (2000); Travel time to work: 20.1% less than 15 minutes, 42.0% 15 to 30 minutes, 22.5% 30 to 45 minutes, 9.6% 45 to 60 minutes, 5.7% 60 minutes or more (2000)
Additional Information Contacts
Columbia Station Chamber of Commerce . . . . (440) 236-9054
   http://chamberplace.ghiis.com/1002/index.cfm

EATON ESTATES (CDP). Covers a land area of 0.880 square miles and a water area of 0 square miles. Located at 41.30° N. Lat.; 82.00° W. Long. Elevation is 800 feet.
Population: 1,586 (1990); 1,409 (2000); 1,447 (2005); 1,499 (2010 projected); Race: 97.7% White, 0.6% Black, 0.3% Asian, 1.8% Hispanic of any race (2005); Density: 1,644.9 persons per square mile (2005); Average household size: 3.01 (2005); Median age: 35.0 (2005); Males per 100 females: 99.3 (2005); Marriage status: 24.3% never married, 61.6% now married, 3.2% widowed, 10.9% divorced (2000); Foreign born: 0.5% (2000); Ancestry (includes multiple ancestries): 36.2% German, 28.9% Irish, 9.3% Other groups, 8.5% United States or American, 7.8% English (2000).
Economy: Employment by occupation: 3.6% management, 3.5% professional, 12.6% services, 26.9% sales, 0.0% farming, 9.8% construction, 43.7% production (2000).
Income: Per capita income: $18,822 (2005); Median household income: $55,221 (2005); Average household income: $56,622 (2005); Percent of households with income of $100,000 or more: 8.1% (2005); Poverty rate: 7.0% (2000).
Education: Percent of population age 25 and over with: High school diploma (including GED) or higher: 70.0% (2005); Bachelor's degree or higher: 3.4% (2005); Master's degree or higher: 0.0% (2005).

Housing: Homeownership rate: 90.2% (2005); Median home value: $111,260 (2005); Median rent: $492 per month (2000); Median age of housing: 44 years (2000).
Transportation: Commute to work: 96.3% car, 1.1% public transportation, 0.0% walk, 1.7% work from home (2000); Travel time to work: 12.9% less than 15 minutes, 46.8% 15 to 30 minutes, 29.1% 30 to 45 minutes, 6.8% 45 to 60 minutes, 4.4% 60 minutes or more (2000)

ELYRIA (city). Covers a land area of 19.886 square miles and a water area of 0.026 square miles. Located at 41.37° N. Lat.; 82.10° W. Long. Elevation is 733 feet.
History: Named for Herman Ely (1775-1852), merchant and founder of the town. Settlement at Elyria began in 1817 when Heman Ely, a New Englander, acquired land around the falls of the Black River and built a dam, grist mill, sawmill, and house. Novelist Sherwood Anderson managed a paint factory in Elyria before he became a writer.
Population: 57,491 (1990); 55,953 (2000); 55,857 (2005); 56,007 (2010 projected); Race: 81.0% White, 13.6% Black, 0.8% Asian, 3.2% Hispanic of any race (2005); Density: 2,808.9 persons per square mile (2005); Average household size: 2.45 (2005); Median age: 35.5 (2005); Males per 100 females: 92.8 (2005); Marriage status: 26.6% never married, 52.9% now married, 7.0% widowed, 13.6% divorced (2000); Foreign born: 1.5% (2000); Ancestry (includes multiple ancestries): 23.8% German, 20.3% Other groups, 14.3% Irish, 10.9% English, 7.5% Polish (2000).
Economy: Unemployment rate: 5.8% (2005); Total civilian labor force: 29,371 (2005); Single-family building permits issued: 75 (2005); Multi-family building permits issued: 61 (2005); Employment by occupation: 8.3% management, 15.7% professional, 17.2% services, 24.9% sales, 0.3% farming, 9.4% construction, 24.3% production (2000).
Income: Per capita income: $21,038 (2005); Median household income: $41,380 (2005); Average household income: $50,920 (2005); Percent of households with income of $100,000 or more: 8.9% (2005); Poverty rate: 11.7% (2000).
Taxes: Total city taxes per capita: $435 (2004); City property taxes per capita: $63 (2004).
Education: Percent of population age 25 and over with: High school diploma (including GED) or higher: 82.1% (2005); Bachelor's degree or higher: 13.3% (2005); Master's degree or higher: 4.3% (2005).
School District(s)
Elyria City SD (KG-12)
   2003-04 Enrollment: 8,127 . . . . (440) 284-8000
Elyria Community School (KG-05)
   2003-04 Enrollment: 173. . . . . (440) 366-5225
Life Skills-Greater Cleveland (09-12)
   2003-04 Enrollment: 358
Midview Local SD (KG-12)
   2003-04 Enrollment: 3,464 . . . . (440) 926-3737
Two-year College(s)
Lorain County Community College (Public)
   Fall 2004 Enrollment: 9,729. . . . . (440) 366-5222
   2005-06 Tuition: In-state $2,779; Out-of-state $5,616
Housing: Homeownership rate: 64.7% (2005); Median home value: $114,331 (2005); Median rent: $430 per month (2000); Median age of housing: 38 years (2000).
Hospitals: EMH Regional Medical Center (348 beds)
Newspapers: The Chronicle-Telegram (Circulation 27,908)
Transportation: Commute to work: 94.1% car, 0.9% public transportation, 2.6% walk, 1.6% work from home (2000); Travel time to work: 38.3% less than 15 minutes, 37.3% 15 to 30 minutes, 16.1% 30 to 45 minutes, 5.1% 45 to 60 minutes, 3.1% 60 minutes or more (2000); Amtrak: Service available.
Additional Information Contacts
City of Elyria. . . . . (440) 326-1400
   http://www.cityofelyria.org

GRAFTON (village). Covers a land area of 4.514 square miles and a water area of 0 square miles. Located at 41.27° N. Lat.; 82.05° W. Long. Elevation is 810 feet.
Population: 3,593 (1990); 2,302 (2000); 2,271 (2005); 2,277 (2010 projected); Race: 97.1% White, 0.8% Black, 0.4% Asian, 1.0% Hispanic of any race (2005); Density: 503.1 persons per square mile (2005); Average household size: 2.70 (2005); Median age: 35.7 (2005); Males per 100 females: 93.4 (2005); Marriage status: 23.1% never married, 60.8% now married, 6.3% widowed, 9.8% divorced (2000); Foreign born: 0.8% (2000);

Ancestry (includes multiple ancestries): 29.4% German, 14.1% Irish, 13.6% Polish, 12.5% English, 10.2% Italian (2000).
Economy: Single-family building permits issued: 16 (2005); Multi-family building permits issued: 0 (2005); Employment by occupation: 9.4% management, 10.3% professional, 14.7% services, 26.3% sales, 0.0% farming, 10.1% construction, 29.2% production (2000).
Income: Per capita income: $23,068 (2005); Median household income: $57,652 (2005); Average household income: $62,283 (2005); Percent of households with income of $100,000 or more: 13.8% (2005); Poverty rate: 2.4% (2000).
Education: Percent of population age 25 and over with: High school diploma (including GED) or higher: 86.3% (2005); Bachelor's degree or higher: 9.5% (2005); Master's degree or higher: 3.0% (2005).
School District(s)
Midview Local SD (KG-12)
    2003-04 Enrollment: 3,464 . . . . (440) 926-3737
Housing: Homeownership rate: 81.9% (2005); Median home value: $143,576 (2005); Median rent: $425 per month (2000); Median age of housing: 36 years (2000).
Transportation: Commute to work: 94.5% car, 0.0% public transportation, 2.7% walk, 1.7% work from home (2000); Travel time to work: 28.9% less than 15 minutes, 42.7% 15 to 30 minutes, 21.2% 30 to 45 minutes, 4.6% 45 to 60 minutes, 2.7% 60 minutes or more (2000).

KIPTON (village). Covers a land area of 0.462 square miles and a water area of 0 square miles. Located at 41.26° N. Lat.; 82.30° W. Long. Elevation is 857 feet.
Population: 283 (1990); 265 (2000); 286 (2005); 309 (2010 projected); Race: 98.3% White, 1.0% Black, 0.0% Asian, 0.3% Hispanic of any race (2005); Density: 618.6 persons per square mile (2005); Average household size: 2.47 (2005); Median age: 38.2 (2005); Males per 100 females: 113.4 (2005); Marriage status: 25.2% never married, 57.5% now married, 2.8% widowed, 14.5% divorced (2000); Foreign born: 0.0% (2000); Ancestry (includes multiple ancestries): 31.7% German, 21.8% English, 11.4% Irish, 11.1% Italian, 8.5% Other groups (2000).
Economy: Single-family building permits issued: 0 (2005); Multi-family building permits issued: 0 (2005); Employment by occupation: 2.9% management, 14.3% professional, 5.7% services, 20.0% sales, 9.3% farming, 26.4% construction, 21.4% production (2000).
Income: Per capita income: $25,795 (2005); Median household income: $54,286 (2005); Average household income: $63,599 (2005); Percent of households with income of $100,000 or more: 10.3% (2005); Poverty rate: 4.5% (2000).
Education: Percent of population age 25 and over with: High school diploma (including GED) or higher: 90.8% (2005); Bachelor's degree or higher: 12.2% (2005); Master's degree or higher: 4.1% (2005).
Housing: Homeownership rate: 82.8% (2005); Median home value: $113,158 (2005); Median rent: $400 per month (2000); Median age of housing: 60+ years (2000).
Transportation: Commute to work: 100.0% car, 0.0% public transportation, 0.0% walk, 0.0% work from home (2000); Travel time to work: 36.8% less than 15 minutes, 33.1% 15 to 30 minutes, 18.4% 30 to 45 minutes, 5.9% 45 to 60 minutes, 5.9% 60 minutes or more (2000).

LAGRANGE (village). Covers a land area of 1.759 square miles and a water area of 0 square miles. Located at 41.23° N. Lat.; 82.12° W. Long. Elevation is 825 feet.
Population: 1,220 (1990); 1,815 (2000); 1,867 (2005); 1,902 (2010 projected); Race: 96.4% White, 0.9% Black, 0.2% Asian, 1.6% Hispanic of any race (2005); Density: 1,061.5 persons per square mile (2005); Average household size: 2.87 (2005); Median age: 33.9 (2005); Males per 100 females: 94.7 (2005); Marriage status: 24.8% never married, 61.6% now married, 4.4% widowed, 9.2% divorced (2000); Foreign born: 0.8% (2000); Ancestry (includes multiple ancestries): 33.9% German, 19.2% Irish, 15.3% English, 7.3% Other groups, 6.7% Polish (2000).
Economy: In agricultural area. Single-family building permits issued: 24 (2005); Multi-family building permits issued: 0 (2005); Employment by occupation: 10.2% management, 13.3% professional, 14.7% services, 26.2% sales, 0.5% farming, 15.1% construction, 20.1% production (2000).
Income: Per capita income: $24,541 (2005); Median household income: $58,159 (2005); Average household income: $70,380 (2005); Percent of households with income of $100,000 or more: 19.2% (2005); Poverty rate: 6.2% (2000).

Education: Percent of population age 25 and over with: High school diploma (including GED) or higher: 87.9% (2005); Bachelor's degree or higher: 11.8% (2005); Master's degree or higher: 3.4% (2005).
School District(s)
Keystone Local SD (KG-12)
    2003-04 Enrollment: 1,843 . . . . (440) 355-5131
Housing: Homeownership rate: 75.6% (2005); Median home value: $166,129 (2005); Median rent: $503 per month (2000); Median age of housing: 26 years (2000).
Transportation: Commute to work: 93.3% car, 0.6% public transportation, 2.7% walk, 3.2% work from home (2000); Travel time to work: 25.9% less than 15 minutes, 41.4% 15 to 30 minutes, 22.9% 30 to 45 minutes, 5.7% 45 to 60 minutes, 4.1% 60 minutes or more (2000).

LORAIN (city). Covers a land area of 24.016 square miles and a water area of 0.231 square miles. Located at 41.44° N. Lat.; 82.16° W. Long. Elevation is 620 feet.
History: Named for the province of Lorraine in France. Lorain had its beginnings in 1807 when Nathan Perry and the Azariah Beebes established a trading post on the south shore of Lake Erie, at the mouth of the Black River. In 1810 others arrived, including John Reid, whose home became the post office, justice's office, and tavern. By 1819 shipbuilding began in Lorain. The town had first been known as Mouth of Black River, but in 1836 it was incorporated as Charleston. When the Cleveland, Lorain & Wheeling Railroad arrived in 1872, a new charter was granted under the name of Lorain. The first steel company came to Lorain in 1894, and was later acquired by the United States Steel Corporation, bringing immigrants from many countries to work here.
Population: 71,245 (1990); 68,652 (2000); 67,758 (2005); 67,096 (2010 projected); Race: 68.3% White, 16.0% Black, 0.4% Asian, 22.0% Hispanic of any race (2005); Density: 2,821.4 persons per square mile (2005); Average household size: 2.55 (2005); Median age: 34.8 (2005); Males per 100 females: 90.4 (2005); Marriage status: 28.3% never married, 50.5% now married, 8.4% widowed, 12.8% divorced (2000); Foreign born: 3.6% (2000); Ancestry (includes multiple ancestries): 36.9% Other groups, 16.0% German, 11.0% Irish, 7.8% Polish, 6.7% Italian (2000).
Economy: Unemployment rate: 6.9% (2005); Total civilian labor force: 31,475 (2005); Single-family building permits issued: 150 (2005); Multi-family building permits issued: 0 (2005); Employment by occupation: 7.4% management, 13.0% professional, 16.7% services, 25.7% sales, 0.6% farming, 9.6% construction, 27.0% production (2000).
Income: Per capita income: $18,087 (2005); Median household income: $36,883 (2005); Average household income: $45,672 (2005); Percent of households with income of $100,000 or more: 7.4% (2005); Poverty rate: 17.1% (2000).
Taxes: Total city taxes per capita: $322 (2004); City property taxes per capita: $52 (2004).
Education: Percent of population age 25 and over with: High school diploma (including GED) or higher: 74.3% (2005); Bachelor's degree or higher: 10.0% (2005); Master's degree or higher: 3.5% (2005).
School District(s)
Clearview Local SD (PK-12)
    2003-04 Enrollment: 1,503 . . . . (440) 233-5412
Lorain Alternative Academy
    2003-04 Enrollment: n/a . . . . (440) 233-2271
Lorain City SD (PK-12)
    2003-04 Enrollment: 10,320 . . . . (440) 233-2271
Lorain Community School (KG-05)
    2003-04 Enrollment: 174 . . . . (440) 204-2130
Lorain Elementary Digital
    2003-04 Enrollment: n/a . . . . (440) 233-2271
Lorain High School Digital
    2003-04 Enrollment: n/a . . . . (440) 233-2271
Lorain Middle School Digital
    2003-04 Enrollment: n/a . . . . (440) 233-2271
Summit Academy High School Lorain
    2003-04 Enrollment: n/a
Summit Academy-Lorain (02-08)
    2003-04 Enrollment: 78 . . . . (440) 245-2593
Two-year College(s)
Northern Institute of Cosmetology (Private, For-profit)
    Fall 2004 Enrollment: 36 . . . . (440) 244-4282
Ohio Business College-Lorain (Private, For-profit)
    Fall 2004 Enrollment: 250 . . . . (440) 277-0021
    2005-06 Tuition: In-state $6,948; Out-of-state $6,948

Housing: Homeownership rate: 61.2% (2005); Median home value: $104,317 (2005); Median rent: $408 per month (2000); Median age of housing: 43 years (2000).
Hospitals: Community Health Partners (343 beds); Community Health Partners (328 beds)
Safety: Violent crime rate: 48.8 per 10,000 population; Property crime rate: 334.7 per 10,000 population (2004).
Newspapers: The Morning Journal (Circulation 31,418)
Transportation: Commute to work: 95.5% car, 0.7% public transportation, 1.7% walk, 1.3% work from home (2000); Travel time to work: 32.6% less than 15 minutes, 41.9% 15 to 30 minutes, 15.3% 30 to 45 minutes, 5.8% 45 to 60 minutes, 4.4% 60 minutes or more (2000)
Additional Information Contacts
City of Lorain . . . . (440) 204-2002
  http://www.cityoflorain.org
Lorain County Chamber of Commerce . . . . (440) 233-6500
  http://www.loraincountychamber.com

NORTH RIDGEVILLE (city).
Covers a land area of 23.370 square miles and a water area of 0.141 square miles. Located at 41.39° N. Lat.; 82.00° W. Long. Elevation is 725 feet.
History: Ridgeville Township was first settled in May 1810 by settlers from Waterbury, Connecticut. The township was organized in 1813, and remained "Ridgeville Township" until 1958. However, the local post office was first called "North Ridgeville" in 1829. At the end of 1958, Ridgeville Township was incorporated as a village. By August of 1960 the village's population was sufficient (over 5,000) to allow the incorporation of the City of North Ridgeville.
Population: 21,564 (1990); 22,338 (2000); 25,363 (2005); 28,233 (2010 projected); Race: 95.7% White, 0.9% Black, 1.2% Asian, 2.1% Hispanic of any race (2005); Density: 1,085.3 persons per square mile (2005); Average household size: 2.62 (2005); Median age: 39.7 (2005); Males per 100 females: 96.4 (2005); Marriage status: 21.7% never married, 63.8% now married, 6.4% widowed, 8.1% divorced (2000); Foreign born: 3.3% (2000); Ancestry (includes multiple ancestries): 32.9% German, 19.2% Irish, 12.6% English, 10.7% Polish, 9.0% Italian (2000).
Economy: Unemployment rate: 4.5% (2005); Total civilian labor force: 14,950 (2005); Single-family building permits issued: 539 (2005); Multi-family building permits issued: 22 (2005); Employment by occupation: 11.3% management, 16.2% professional, 12.8% services, 29.8% sales, 0.3% farming, 11.4% construction, 18.1% production (2000).
Income: Per capita income: $26,487 (2005); Median household income: $60,658 (2005); Average household income: $69,064 (2005); Percent of households with income of $100,000 or more: 18.4% (2005); Poverty rate: 3.2% (2000).
Education: Percent of population age 25 and over with: High school diploma (including GED) or higher: 86.0% (2005); Bachelor's degree or higher: 16.3% (2005); Master's degree or higher: 4.3% (2005).
School District(s)
North Ridgeville City SD (KG-12)
  2003-04 Enrollment: 3,550 . . . . (440) 327-4444
Housing: Homeownership rate: 88.8% (2005); Median home value: $152,071 (2005); Median rent: $463 per month (2000); Median age of housing: 27 years (2000).
Safety: Violent crime rate: 8.6 per 10,000 population; Property crime rate: 172.9 per 10,000 population (2004).
Transportation: Commute to work: 96.1% car, 1.0% public transportation, 0.6% walk, 1.9% work from home (2000); Travel time to work: 18.8% less than 15 minutes, 44.4% 15 to 30 minutes, 24.8% 30 to 45 minutes, 7.2% 45 to 60 minutes, 4.8% 60 minutes or more (2000)
Additional Information Contacts
City of North Ridgeville . . . . (440) 353-0819
  http://www.ci.north-ridgeville.oh.us
North Ridgeville Chamber of Commerce . . . . (440) 327-3737
  http://www.nrchamber.com

OBERLIN (city).
Covers a land area of 4.379 square miles and a water area of 0.026 square miles. Located at 41.28° N. Lat.; 82.21° W. Long. Elevation is 801 feet.
History: Oberlin College was founded in 1833 by John L. Shipherd, a Presbyterian minister from Elyria, and Philo P. Steward, a missionary. In 1837 four women applied for the regular college course. When they were accepted, Oberlin became the first coeducational college in the country.
Population: 8,327 (1990); 8,195 (2000); 8,212 (2005); 8,238 (2010 projected); Race: 73.1% White, 15.6% Black, 3.9% Asian, 3.3% Hispanic of any race (2005); Density: 1,875.4 persons per square mile (2005); Average household size: 3.06 (2005); Median age: 25.6 (2005); Males per 100 females: 77.6 (2005); Marriage status: 50.0% never married, 35.2% now married, 7.9% widowed, 6.9% divorced (2000); Foreign born: 5.3% (2000); Ancestry (includes multiple ancestries): 27.7% Other groups, 17.0% German, 15.6% English, 10.4% Irish, 4.9% Italian (2000).
Economy: Single-family building permits issued: 8 (2005); Multi-family building permits issued: 5 (2005); Employment by occupation: 9.0% management, 34.8% professional, 21.5% services, 20.6% sales, 0.0% farming, 5.4% construction, 8.7% production (2000).
Income: Per capita income: $21,167 (2005); Median household income: $46,487 (2005); Average household income: $60,391 (2005); Percent of households with income of $100,000 or more: 16.1% (2005); Poverty rate: 19.4% (2000).
Taxes: Total city taxes per capita: $804 (2004); City property taxes per capita: $135 (2004).
Education: Percent of population age 25 and over with: High school diploma (including GED) or higher: 86.3% (2005); Bachelor's degree or higher: 41.5% (2005); Master's degree or higher: 24.5% (2005).
School District(s)
Firelands Local SD (KG-12)
  2003-04 Enrollment: 2,239 . . . . (440) 965-5821
Lorain County Joint Vocational SD (08-12)
  2003-04 Enrollment: n/a . . . . (440) 774-1051
Oberlin City SD (PK-12)
  2003-04 Enrollment: 1,115 . . . . (440) 774-1458
Four-year College(s)
Oberlin College (Private, Not-for-profit)
  Fall 2004 Enrollment: 2,857 . . . . (440) 775-8411
  2005-06 Tuition: In-state $32,724; Out-of-state $32,724
Two-year College(s)
Lorain County Joint Vocational School District (Public)
  Fall 2004 Enrollment: 72 . . . . (440) 774-1051
Housing: Homeownership rate: 50.2% (2005); Median home value: $141,415 (2005); Median rent: $444 per month (2000); Median age of housing: 41 years (2000).
Hospitals: Allen Medical Center (25 beds)
Newspapers: Oberlin News-Tribune (General - Circulation 3,000)
Transportation: Commute to work: 52.9% car, 0.2% public transportation, 36.1% walk, 4.3% work from home (2000); Travel time to work: 65.9% less than 15 minutes, 20.9% 15 to 30 minutes, 7.4% 30 to 45 minutes, 3.1% 45 to 60 minutes, 2.7% 60 minutes or more (2000)
Additional Information Contacts
Oberlin Chamber of Commerce . . . . (440) 774-6262
  http://www.oberlin.org

ROCHESTER (village).
Covers a land area of 1.102 square miles and a water area of 0 square miles. Located at 41.12° N. Lat.; 82.30° W. Long. Elevation is 925 feet.
Population: 206 (1990); 190 (2000); 208 (2005); 226 (2010 projected); Race: 100.0% White, 0.0% Black, 0.0% Asian, 0.0% Hispanic of any race (2005); Density: 188.8 persons per square mile (2005); Average household size: 2.74 (2005); Median age: 35.7 (2005); Males per 100 females: 114.4 (2005); Marriage status: 28.9% never married, 55.5% now married, 5.2% widowed, 10.4% divorced (2000); Foreign born: 1.0% (2000); Ancestry (includes multiple ancestries): 22.8% German, 19.3% United States or American, 15.8% Irish, 9.9% English, 5.0% French (except Basque) (2000).
Economy: Single-family building permits issued: 0 (2005); Multi-family building permits issued: 0 (2005); Employment by occupation: 4.2% management, 13.3% professional, 8.3% services, 10.0% sales, 5.0% farming, 16.7% construction, 42.5% production (2000).
Income: Per capita income: $20,096 (2005); Median household income: $49,000 (2005); Average household income: $55,000 (2005); Percent of households with income of $100,000 or more: 13.2% (2005); Poverty rate: 7.4% (2000).
Education: Percent of population age 25 and over with: High school diploma (including GED) or higher: 72.4% (2005); Bachelor's degree or higher: 6.0% (2005); Master's degree or higher: 1.5% (2005).
Housing: Homeownership rate: 82.9% (2005); Median home value: $114,423 (2005); Median rent: $425 per month (2000); Median age of housing: 60+ years (2000).
Transportation: Commute to work: 92.0% car, 0.0% public transportation, 5.4% walk, 2.7% work from home (2000); Travel time to work: 24.8% less

than 15 minutes, 41.3% 15 to 30 minutes, 22.0% 30 to 45 minutes, 7.3% 45 to 60 minutes, 4.6% 60 minutes or more (2000)

SHEFFIELD (village). Aka Sheffield Village. Covers a land area of 10.817 square miles and a water area of 0.002 square miles. Located at 41.44° N. Lat.; 82.08° W. Long. Elevation is 673 feet.
History: Incorporated 1933.
Population: 1,943 (1990); 2,949 (2000); 3,433 (2005); 3,888 (2010 projected); Race: 89.6% White, 4.8% Black, 1.0% Asian, 6.2% Hispanic of any race (2005); Density: 317.4 persons per square mile (2005); Average household size: 2.65 (2005); Median age: 39.3 (2005); Males per 100 females: 94.5 (2005); Marriage status: 19.0% never married, 67.3% now married, 6.4% widowed, 7.3% divorced (2000); Foreign born: 4.3% (2000); Ancestry (includes multiple ancestries): 30.6% German, 14.3% Other groups, 13.9% Irish, 13.3% Polish, 10.1% English (2000).
Economy: Single-family building permits issued: 6 (2005); Multi-family building permits issued: 52 (2005); Employment by occupation: 19.7% management, 16.9% professional, 8.6% services, 22.0% sales, 0.9% farming, 11.2% construction, 20.6% production (2000).
Income: Per capita income: $29,712 (2005); Median household income: $68,554 (2005); Average household income: $78,706 (2005); Percent of households with income of $100,000 or more: 26.5% (2005); Poverty rate: 3.2% (2000).
Education: Percent of population age 25 and over with: High school diploma (including GED) or higher: 89.3% (2005); Bachelor's degree or higher: 22.8% (2005); Master's degree or higher: 5.5% (2005).
School District(s)
Sheffield-Sheffield Lake City SD (PK-12)
    2003-04 Enrollment: 2,084 . . . . (440) 949-6181
Housing: Homeownership rate: 87.7% (2005); Median home value: $188,085 (2005); Median rent: $375 per month (2000); Median age of housing: 17 years (2000).
Transportation: Commute to work: 95.1% car, 0.0% public transportation, 0.9% walk, 3.7% work from home (2000); Travel time to work: 31.9% less than 15 minutes, 36.5% 15 to 30 minutes, 19.5% 30 to 45 minutes, 7.8% 45 to 60 minutes, 4.3% 60 minutes or more (2000)

SHEFFIELD LAKE (city). Aka Sheffield Village. Covers a land area of 2.522 square miles and a water area of 0 square miles. Located at 41.48° N. Lat.; 82.10° W. Long. Elevation is 600 feet.
History: Incorporated 1920.
Population: 9,825 (1990); 9,371 (2000); 9,183 (2005); 9,052 (2010 projected); Race: 96.4% White, 1.0% Black, 0.3% Asian, 3.1% Hispanic of any race (2005); Density: 3,640.7 persons per square mile (2005); Average household size: 2.62 (2005); Median age: 36.8 (2005); Males per 100 females: 94.9 (2005); Marriage status: 25.8% never married, 60.6% now married, 4.8% widowed, 8.8% divorced (2000); Foreign born: 1.7% (2000); Ancestry (includes multiple ancestries): 30.2% German, 16.1% Irish, 10.4% Italian, 10.1% English, 9.4% Polish (2000).
Economy: Single-family building permits issued: 11 (2005); Multi-family building permits issued: 0 (2005); Employment by occupation: 9.7% management, 12.6% professional, 15.8% services, 27.3% sales, 0.3% farming, 12.2% construction, 22.1% production (2000).
Income: Per capita income: $22,860 (2005); Median household income: $52,634 (2005); Average household income: $59,840 (2005); Percent of households with income of $100,000 or more: 11.4% (2005); Poverty rate: 4.7% (2000).
Education: Percent of population age 25 and over with: High school diploma (including GED) or higher: 84.6% (2005); Bachelor's degree or higher: 13.2% (2005); Master's degree or higher: 3.3% (2005).
School District(s)
Sheffield-Sheffield Lake City SD (PK-12)
    2003-04 Enrollment: 2,084 . . . . (440) 949-6181
Housing: Homeownership rate: 80.3% (2005); Median home value: $125,118 (2005); Median rent: $486 per month (2000); Median age of housing: 36 years (2000).
Safety: Violent crime rate: 6.5 per 10,000 population; Property crime rate: 237.0 per 10,000 population (2004).
Transportation: Commute to work: 95.7% car, 0.8% public transportation, 1.0% walk, 2.0% work from home (2000); Travel time to work: 22.0% less than 15 minutes, 40.1% 15 to 30 minutes, 24.7% 30 to 45 minutes, 9.9% 45 to 60 minutes, 3.4% 60 minutes or more (2000)

SOUTH AMHERST (village). Covers a land area of 2.451 square miles and a water area of 0.008 square miles. Located at 41.35° N. Lat.; 82.24° W. Long. Elevation is 803 feet.
History: South Amherst was at one time called Podunk. The town developed as a quarrying center.
Population: 1,820 (1990); 1,863 (2000); 1,838 (2005); 1,783 (2010 projected); Race: 97.3% White, 0.4% Black, 0.3% Asian, 2.0% Hispanic of any race (2005); Density: 749.8 persons per square mile (2005); Average household size: 2.74 (2005); Median age: 39.9 (2005); Males per 100 females: 96.2 (2005); Marriage status: 21.7% never married, 65.5% now married, 5.9% widowed, 7.0% divorced (2000); Foreign born: 1.6% (2000); Ancestry (includes multiple ancestries): 27.4% German, 18.6% Irish, 15.1% English, 9.5% Other groups, 9.0% Polish (2000).
Economy: Single-family building permits issued: 0 (2005); Multi-family building permits issued: 0 (2005); Employment by occupation: 8.2% management, 16.8% professional, 16.1% services, 22.4% sales, 0.7% farming, 13.6% construction, 22.2% production (2000).
Income: Per capita income: $22,593 (2005); Median household income: $51,079 (2005); Average household income: $61,432 (2005); Percent of households with income of $100,000 or more: 15.0% (2005); Poverty rate: 4.2% (2000).
Education: Percent of population age 25 and over with: High school diploma (including GED) or higher: 83.3% (2005); Bachelor's degree or higher: 12.6% (2005); Master's degree or higher: 4.7% (2005).
School District(s)
Firelands Local SD (KG-12)
    2003-04 Enrollment: 2,239 . . . . (440) 965-5821
Housing: Homeownership rate: 87.2% (2005); Median home value: $141,729 (2005); Median rent: $465 per month (2000); Median age of housing: 46 years (2000).
Transportation: Commute to work: 94.9% car, 1.5% public transportation, 0.7% walk, 2.6% work from home (2000); Travel time to work: 32.4% less than 15 minutes, 46.2% 15 to 30 minutes, 12.8% 30 to 45 minutes, 3.9% 45 to 60 minutes, 4.7% 60 minutes or more (2000)

VERMILION (city). Covers a land area of 10.791 square miles and a water area of 0.052 square miles. Located at 41.41° N. Lat.; 82.34° W. Long.
History: Vermilion was settled in 1808 along the Vermilion River, named for the red clay found along the river bottom. Vermilion developed as a fishing center and a tourist resort.
Population: 11,133 (1990); 10,927 (2000); 10,869 (2005); 10,861 (2010 projected); Race: 97.8% White, 0.2% Black, 0.3% Asian, 1.8% Hispanic of any race (2005); Density: 1,007.2 persons per square mile (2005); Average household size: 2.51 (2005); Median age: 39.8 (2005); Males per 100 females: 93.7 (2005); Marriage status: 20.2% never married, 64.0% now married, 7.3% widowed, 8.5% divorced (2000); Foreign born: 1.8% (2000); Ancestry (includes multiple ancestries): 34.0% German, 17.1% Irish, 13.8% English, 7.5% Other groups, 7.4% Italian (2000).
Economy: Single-family building permits issued: 21 (2005); Multi-family building permits issued: 2 (2005); Employment by occupation: 12.5% management, 15.6% professional, 12.8% services, 25.2% sales, 0.0% farming, 12.1% construction, 21.9% production (2000).
Income: Per capita income: $26,222 (2005); Median household income: $55,214 (2005); Average household income: $65,560 (2005); Percent of households with income of $100,000 or more: 14.2% (2005); Poverty rate: 5.4% (2000).
Education: Percent of population age 25 and over with: High school diploma (including GED) or higher: 86.4% (2005); Bachelor's degree or higher: 18.3% (2005); Master's degree or higher: 5.6% (2005).
School District(s)
Vermilion Local SD (PK-12)
    2003-04 Enrollment: 2,525 . . . . (440) 967-5210
Housing: Homeownership rate: 75.5% (2005); Median home value: $133,486 (2005); Median rent: $501 per month (2000); Median age of housing: 36 years (2000).
Safety: Violent crime rate: 4.6 per 10,000 population; Property crime rate: 407.8 per 10,000 population (2004).
Newspapers: Vermilion Photojournal (General - Circulation 4,000)
Transportation: Commute to work: 95.4% car, 0.4% public transportation, 1.6% walk, 2.6% work from home (2000); Travel time to work: 30.7% less than 15 minutes, 35.1% 15 to 30 minutes, 22.9% 30 to 45 minutes, 8.6% 45 to 60 minutes, 2.8% 60 minutes or more (2000)
Additional Information Contacts

Vermilion Chamber of Commerce . . . . (440) 967-4477
http://www.vermilionohio.com

WELLINGTON (village). Covers a land area of 2.936 square miles and a water area of 0.032 square miles. Located at 41.16° N. Lat.; 82.22° W. Long. Elevation is 854 feet.
History: Wellington developed in the dairy and grain area of Lorain County. It was an abolitionist center, and in 1858, when a Federal marshal stopped in Wellington with a runaway slave, the residents rescued the slave. Many of them were then arrested and charged with aiding a fugitive slave.
Population: 4,172 (1990); 4,511 (2000); 4,595 (2005); 4,737 (2010 projected); Race: 97.0% White, 1.2% Black, 0.2% Asian, 1.1% Hispanic of any race (2005); Density: 1,564.8 persons per square mile (2005); Average household size: 2.58 (2005); Median age: 35.9 (2005); Males per 100 females: 93.5 (2005); Marriage status: 25.4% never married, 52.1% now married, 10.8% widowed, 11.8% divorced (2000); Foreign born: 1.1% (2000); Ancestry (includes multiple ancestries): 24.1% German, 15.4% Irish, 14.4% English, 13.1% United States or American, 6.2% Other groups (2000).
Economy: Single-family building permits issued: 21 (2005); Multi-family building permits issued: 12 (2005); Employment by occupation: 6.0% management, 13.6% professional, 13.8% services, 24.2% sales, 1.0% farming, 12.1% construction, 29.4% production (2000).
Income: Per capita income: $20,609 (2005); Median household income: $44,748 (2005); Average household income: $52,323 (2005); Percent of households with income of $100,000 or more: 8.5% (2005); Poverty rate: 8.1% (2000).
Education: Percent of population age 25 and over with: High school diploma (including GED) or higher: 82.0% (2005); Bachelor's degree or higher: 11.7% (2005); Master's degree or higher: 2.7% (2005).

School District(s)
Keystone Local SD (KG-12)
    2003-04 Enrollment: 1,843 . . . . (440) 355-5131
Wellington Ex Vill SD (KG-12)
    2003-04 Enrollment: 1,648 . . . . (440) 647-4286
Housing: Homeownership rate: 66.3% (2005); Median home value: $133,104 (2005); Median rent: $399 per month (2000); Median age of housing: 46 years (2000).
Transportation: Commute to work: 94.6% car, 2.5% public transportation, 1.2% walk, 0.5% work from home (2000); Travel time to work: 41.0% less than 15 minutes, 21.6% 15 to 30 minutes, 23.9% 30 to 45 minutes, 8.4% 45 to 60 minutes, 5.1% 60 minutes or more (2000)
Additional Information Contacts
Wellington Chamber of Commerce . . . . (440) 647-2222
http://www.wellingtonohio.net

Lucas County

Located in northwestern Ohio; bounded on the north by Michigan, on the southeast by the Maumee River, and on the northeast by the west end of Lake Erie. Covers a land area of 340.46 square miles, a water area of 255.42 square miles, and is located in the Eastern Time Zone. The county government was organized in 1835. County seat is Toledo.

Lucas County is part of the Toledo, OH Metropolitan Statistical Area. The entire metro area includes: Fulton County, OH; Lucas County, OH; Ottawa County, OH; Wood County, OH

Weather Station: Toledo Express Airport   Elevation: 666 feet

	Jan	Feb	Mar	Apr	May	Jun	Jul	Aug	Sep	Oct	Nov	Dec
High	31	34	46	59	71	80	84	82	75	62	48	36
Low	16	18	27	37	48	57	61	59	52	41	32	22
Precip	1.9	1.9	2.7	3.3	3.1	3.8	2.9	3.2	2.9	2.3	2.8	2.6
Snow	10.9	8.2	5.7	1.4	tr	tr	tr	tr	tr	0.2	2.7	8.1

High and Low temperatures in degrees Fahrenheit; Precipitation and Snow in inches

Population: 462,361 (1990); 455,054 (2000); 453,814 (2005); 452,369 (2010 projected); Race: 76.5% White, 17.2% Black, 1.4% Asian, 4.9% Hispanic of any race (2005); Density: 1,332.9 persons per square mile (2005); Average household size: 2.45 (2005); Median age: 35.8 (2005); Males per 100 females: 93.6 (2005).
Religion: Five largest groups: 25.0% Catholic Church, 6.6% Evangelical Lutheran Church in America, 3.0% The United Methodist Church, 1.3% Jewish Estimate, 1.0% The Christian and Missionary Alliance (2000).
Economy: Unemployment rate: 6.9% (2005); Total civilian labor force: 224,346 (2005); Leading industries: 19.1% health care and social assistance; 13.5% retail trade; 11.9% manufacturing (2004); Farms: 405 totaling 77,823 acres (2002); Companies that employ 500 or more persons: 24 (2004); Companies that employ 100 to 499 persons: 304 (2004); Companies that employ less than 100 persons: 10,570 (2004); Black-owned businesses: 1,623 (2002); Hispanic-owned businesses: 473 (2002); Women-owned businesses: 7,699 (2002); Retail sales per capita: $16,028 (2006). Single-family building permits issued: 1,297 (2005); Multi-family building permits issued: 210 (2005).
Income: Per capita income: $22,943 (2005); Median household income: $42,149 (2005); Average household income: $55,740 (2005); Percent of households with income of $100,000 or more: 12.5% (2005); Poverty rate: 12.8% (2003); Bankruptcy rate: 14.37% (2005).
Taxes: Total county taxes per capita: $389 (2004); County property taxes per capita: $223 (2004).
Education: Percent of population age 25 and over with: High school diploma (including GED) or higher: 83.2% (2005); Bachelor's degree or higher: 21.5% (2005); Master's degree or higher: 7.5% (2005).
Housing: Homeownership rate: 65.9% (2005); Median home value: $104,876 (2005); Median rent: $393 per month (2000); Median age of housing: 43 years (2000).
Health: Birth rate: 134.9 per 10,000 population (2004); Death rate: 102.2 per 10,000 population (2004); Age-adjusted cancer mortality rate: 221.6 deaths per 100,000 population (2002); Air Quality Index: 68.5% good, 28.8% moderate, 2.5% unhealthy for sensitive individuals, 0.3% unhealthy (percent of days in 2005); Number of physicians: 41.2 per 10,000 population (2004); Hospital beds: 54.8 per 10,000 population (2003); Hospital admissions: 2,090.3 per 10,000 population (2003).
Elections: 2004 Presidential election results: 39.5% Bush, 60.2% Kerry, 0.0% Nader, 0.1% Badnarik
National and State Parks: Cedar Point National Wildlife Refuge; Fallen Timbers State Memorial; Fort Miamis State Memorial; Mallard Club Marsh State Wildlife Area; Maumee Bay State Park; Missionary Island State Wildlife Area; West Sister Island National Wildlife Refuge
Additional Information Contacts
Lucas County Government . . . . (419) 213-4000
    http://www.co.lucas.oh.us/
City of Maumee . . . . (419) 897-7100
    http://www.maumee.org
City of Oregon . . . . (419) 698-7095
    http://www.ci.oregon.oh.us
City of Sylvania . . . . (419) 885-8925
    http://www.cityofsylvania.com
City of Toledo . . . . (419) 245-1001
    http://www.ci.toledo.oh.us
Eastern Maumee Bay Chamber . . . . (419) 693-5580
    http://www.toledochamber.com/chamber/NWO.asp
Greater Toledo Convention & Visitors Bureau . . . . (800) 243-4667
    http://www.dotoledo.org/gtcvb
Holland-Springfield Chamber . . . . (419) 865-2110
    http://www.hollandspringfieldcoc.org
Maumee Chamber of Commerce . . . . (419) 893-5805
    http://www.maumeechamber.com
Sylvania Area Chamber of Commerce . . . . (419) 882-2135
    http://www.sylvaniachamber.org
Toldeo Area Chamber of Commerce . . . . (419) 243-8191
    http://www.toledochamber.com
Village of Ottawa Hills . . . . (419) 536-1111
    http://www.ottawahills.org
Village of Waterville . . . . (419) 878-8100
    http://www.waterville.org
Village of Whitehouse . . . . (419) 877-5383
    http://www.whitehouseoh.com
Waterville Chamber of Commerce . . . . (419) 878-5188
    http://www.waterville.org
Whitehouse Chamber of Commerce . . . . (419) 877-2747
    http://www.whitehouse.oh.us/chamber

Lucas County Communities

BERKEY (village). Covers a land area of 4.176 square miles and a water area of 0 square miles. Located at 41.71° N. Lat.; 83.83° W. Long. Elevation is 700 feet.

Population: 264 (1990); 265 (2000); 342 (2005); 410 (2010 projected); Race: 97.4% White, 0.0% Black, 0.6% Asian, 0.6% Hispanic of any race (2005); Density: 81.9 persons per square mile (2005); Average household size: 2.65 (2005); Median age: 37.7 (2005); Males per 100 females: 93.2 (2005); Marriage status: 17.6% never married, 69.5% now married, 11.0% widowed, 1.9% divorced (2000); Foreign born: 1.1% (2000); Ancestry (includes multiple ancestries): 44.8% German, 16.1% Irish, 13.0% English, 5.7% French (except Basque), 5.4% United States or American (2000).
Economy: Fifteen miles West Northwest of Toledo. Single-family building permits issued: 0 (2005); Multi-family building permits issued: 0 (2005); Employment by occupation: 12.4% management, 24.2% professional, 3.9% services, 30.7% sales, 0.0% farming, 10.5% construction, 18.3% production (2000).
Income: Per capita income: $30,080 (2005); Median household income: $66,146 (2005); Average household income: $79,748 (2005); Percent of households with income of $100,000 or more: 27.9% (2005); Poverty rate: 0.0% (2000).
Education: Percent of population age 25 and over with: High school diploma (including GED) or higher: 94.4% (2005); Bachelor's degree or higher: 25.0% (2005); Master's degree or higher: 7.9% (2005).
Housing: Homeownership rate: 90.7% (2005); Median home value: $160,938 (2005); Median rent: $363 per month (2000); Median age of housing: 56 years (2000).
Transportation: Commute to work: 98.6% car, 0.0% public transportation, 1.4% walk, 0.0% work from home (2000); Travel time to work: 12.5% less than 15 minutes, 36.8% 15 to 30 minutes, 34.0% 30 to 45 minutes, 6.9% 45 to 60 minutes, 9.7% 60 minutes or more (2000)

CURTICE (unincorporated postal area, zip code 43412).
Covers a land area of 28.487 square miles and a water area of 0.105 square miles. Located at 41.63° N. Lat.; 83.30° W. Long. Elevation is 590 feet.
Population: 4,462 (2000); Race: 96.2% White, 0.5% Black, 0.3% Asian, 5.0% Hispanic of any race (2000); Density: 156.6 persons per square mile (2000); Age: 24.6% under 18, 11.5% over 64 (2000); Marriage status: 24.1% never married, 62.1% now married, 4.6% widowed, 9.2% divorced (2000); Foreign born: 1.3% (2000); Ancestry (includes multiple ancestries): 41.6% German, 11.9% Irish, 9.1% Other groups, 9.1% French (except Basque), 7.1% Polish (2000).
Economy: Employment by occupation: 9.3% management, 12.8% professional, 11.8% services, 23.3% sales, 1.7% farming, 14.3% construction, 26.8% production (2000).
Income: Per capita income: $20,778 (2000); Median household income: $53,393 (2000); Poverty rate: 7.5% (2000).
Education: Percent of population age 25 and over with: High school diploma (including GED) or higher: 85.2% (2000); Bachelor's degree or higher: 11.8% (2000).
School District(s)
Genoa Area Local SD (PK-12)
  2003-04 Enrollment: 1,737 . . . . (419) 855-7741
Oregon City SD (PK-12)
  2003-04 Enrollment: 3,862 . . . . (419) 693-0661
Housing: Homeownership rate: 89.0% (2000); Median home value: $117,500 (2000); Median rent: $356 per month (2000); Median age of housing: 41 years (2000).
Transportation: Commute to work: 95.7% car, 0.4% public transportation, 0.2% walk, 3.0% work from home (2000); Travel time to work: 17.6% less than 15 minutes, 50.7% 15 to 30 minutes, 17.7% 30 to 45 minutes, 7.3% 45 to 60 minutes, 6.6% 60 minutes or more (2000)

HARBOR VIEW (village).
Covers a land area of 0.029 square miles and a water area of 0 square miles. Located at 41.69° N. Lat.; 83.44° W. Long. Elevation is 575 feet.
Population: 122 (1990); 99 (2000); 94 (2005); 93 (2010 projected); Race: 94.7% White, 0.0% Black, 0.0% Asian, 7.4% Hispanic of any race (2005); Density: 3,226.9 persons per square mile (2005); Average household size: 2.61 (2005); Median age: 37.2 (2005); Males per 100 females: 108.9 (2005); Marriage status: 23.2% never married, 52.4% now married, 6.1% widowed, 18.3% divorced (2000); Foreign born: 0.0% (2000); Ancestry (includes multiple ancestries): 24.1% German, 22.2% Other groups, 19.4% Irish, 18.5% United States or American, 6.5% Swedish (2000).
Economy: Employment by occupation: 0.0% management, 8.7% professional, 32.6% services, 28.3% sales, 0.0% farming, 21.7% construction, 8.7% production (2000).
Income: Per capita income: $19,335 (2005); Median household income: $45,714 (2005); Average household income: $50,486 (2005); Percent of households with income of $100,000 or more: 2.8% (2005); Poverty rate: 16.7% (2000).
Education: Percent of population age 25 and over with: High school diploma (including GED) or higher: 71.4% (2005); Bachelor's degree or higher: 0.0% (2005); Master's degree or higher: 0.0% (2005).
Housing: Homeownership rate: 91.7% (2005); Median home value: $53,077 (2005); Median rent: $425 per month (2000); Median age of housing: 60+ years (2000).
Transportation: Commute to work: 91.1% car, 0.0% public transportation, 8.9% walk, 0.0% work from home (2000); Travel time to work: 22.2% less than 15 minutes, 26.7% 15 to 30 minutes, 15.6% 30 to 45 minutes, 0.0% 45 to 60 minutes, 35.6% 60 minutes or more (2000)

HOLLAND (village).
Covers a land area of 0.867 square miles and a water area of 0 square miles. Located at 41.61° N. Lat.; 83.71° W. Long. Elevation is 635 feet.
Population: 1,238 (1990); 1,306 (2000); 1,421 (2005); 1,517 (2010 projected); Race: 93.0% White, 2.2% Black, 3.0% Asian, 2.5% Hispanic of any race (2005); Density: 1,639.8 persons per square mile (2005); Average household size: 2.41 (2005); Median age: 41.7 (2005); Males per 100 females: 85.8 (2005); Marriage status: 18.5% never married, 46.9% now married, 21.7% widowed, 12.9% divorced (2000); Foreign born: 2.0% (2000); Ancestry (includes multiple ancestries): 27.7% German, 9.6% English, 9.3% Other groups, 9.1% United States or American, 9.1% Polish (2000).
Economy: Employment by occupation: 8.6% management, 11.7% professional, 15.7% services, 29.0% sales, 0.0% farming, 12.4% construction, 22.8% production (2000).
Income: Per capita income: $18,442 (2005); Median household income: $34,677 (2005); Average household income: $42,076 (2005); Percent of households with income of $100,000 or more: 6.1% (2005); Poverty rate: 7.9% (2000).
Education: Percent of population age 25 and over with: High school diploma (including GED) or higher: 74.7% (2005); Bachelor's degree or higher: 13.7% (2005); Master's degree or higher: 4.0% (2005).
School District(s)
Springfield Digital Academy
  2003-04 Enrollment: n/a
Springfield Local Schools (PK-12)
  2003-04 Enrollment: 3,779 . . . . (419) 867-5600
Housing: Homeownership rate: 54.1% (2005); Median home value: $104,600 (2005); Median rent: $448 per month (2000); Median age of housing: 41 years (2000).
Transportation: Commute to work: 95.1% car, 0.0% public transportation, 2.1% walk, 1.5% work from home (2000); Travel time to work: 35.3% less than 15 minutes, 40.8% 15 to 30 minutes, 13.5% 30 to 45 minutes, 3.8% 45 to 60 minutes, 6.6% 60 minutes or more (2000)
Additional Information Contacts
Holland-Springfield Chamber. . . . . (419) 865-2110
  http://www.hollandspringfieldcoc.org

MAUMEE (city).
Covers a land area of 9.935 square miles and a water area of 0.604 square miles. Located at 41.57° N. Lat.; 83.65° W. Long. Elevation is 631 feet.
History: A French-Canadian trading post was here from 1680 to 1693. In 1764 the British built Fort Miami. When a store opened in 1817, the town began to grow around it. Earlier names of Waynesville and South Toledo gave way to the name of Maumee, a corruption of the Indian name Miami.
Population: 15,569 (1990); 15,237 (2000); 14,689 (2005); 14,159 (2010 projected); Race: 95.9% White, 1.2% Black, 0.9% Asian, 2.0% Hispanic of any race (2005); Density: 1,478.5 persons per square mile (2005); Average household size: 2.35 (2005); Median age: 39.2 (2005); Males per 100 females: 93.8 (2005); Marriage status: 24.4% never married, 58.2% now married, 7.4% widowed, 10.0% divorced (2000); Foreign born: 2.2% (2000); Ancestry (includes multiple ancestries): 41.6% German, 15.5% Irish, 12.2% Polish, 10.0% English, 7.0% Other groups (2000).
Economy: Single-family building permits issued: 10 (2005); Multi-family building permits issued: 0 (2005); Employment by occupation: 13.4% management, 24.7% professional, 13.3% services, 28.4% sales, 0.1% farming, 7.9% construction, 12.2% production (2000).
Income: Per capita income: $26,328 (2005); Median household income: $51,226 (2005); Average household income: $61,878 (2005); Percent of households with income of $100,000 or more: 13.7% (2005); Poverty rate: 4.3% (2000).

Education: Percent of population age 25 and over with: High school diploma (including GED) or higher: 92.7% (2005); Bachelor's degree or higher: 29.0% (2005); Master's degree or higher: 8.5% (2005).

School District(s)
Autism Academy of Learning (KG-12)
   2003-04 Enrollment: 41 . . . . (419) 865-7487
BPCPS
   2003-04 Enrollment: n/a
M.O.D.E.L. Community School (01-09)
   2003-04 Enrollment: 48 . . . . (419) 897-4400
Maumee City SD (PK-12)
   2003-04 Enrollment: 2,847 . . . . (419) 893-3200
Maumee Digital Academy
   2003-04 Enrollment: n/a
Ohio Virtual Academy (KG-09)
   2003-04 Enrollment: 2,135 . . . . (419) 482-0948

Housing: Homeownership rate: 72.9% (2005); Median home value: $134,309 (2005); Median rent: $461 per month (2000); Median age of housing: 40 years (2000).
Hospitals: St. Luke's Hospital (314 beds)
Transportation: Commute to work: 96.5% car, 0.5% public transportation, 1.0% walk, 2.0% work from home (2000); Travel time to work: 37.8% less than 15 minutes, 46.4% 15 to 30 minutes, 10.0% 30 to 45 minutes, 2.5% 45 to 60 minutes, 3.3% 60 minutes or more (2000)

Additional Information Contacts
City of Maumee . . . . (419) 897-7100
   http://www.maumee.org
Maumee Chamber of Commerce. (419) 893-5805
   http://www.maumeechamber.com

MONCLOVA
(unincorporated postal area, zip code 43542). Covers a land area of 13.563 square miles and a water area of 0 square miles. Located at 41.57° N. Lat.; 83.76° W. Long. Elevation is 640 feet.
Population: 2,389 (2000); Race: 96.7% White, 0.0% Black, 0.2% Asian, 4.6% Hispanic of any race (2000); Density: 176.1 persons per square mile (2000); Age: 27.5% under 18, 10.5% over 64 (2000); Marriage status: 21.3% never married, 62.4% now married, 6.3% widowed, 10.0% divorced (2000); Foreign born: 0.3% (2000); Ancestry (includes multiple ancestries): 39.0% German, 15.5% English, 10.4% Other groups, 10.1% Irish, 8.5% Polish (2000).
Economy: Employment by occupation: 13.7% management, 20.9% professional, 13.9% services, 20.9% sales, 2.2% farming, 9.6% construction, 18.8% production (2000).
Income: Per capita income: $24,271 (2000); Median household income: $62,159 (2000); Poverty rate: 3.3% (2000).
Education: Percent of population age 25 and over with: High school diploma (including GED) or higher: 89.4% (2000); Bachelor's degree or higher: 20.2% (2000).

School District(s)
Anthony Wayne Local SD (PK-12)
   2003-04 Enrollment: 3,879 . . . . (419) 877-5377

Housing: Homeownership rate: 89.6% (2000); Median home value: $136,100 (2000); Median rent: $530 per month (2000); Median age of housing: 35 years (2000).
Transportation: Commute to work: 93.3% car, 0.0% public transportation, 2.6% walk, 4.1% work from home (2000); Travel time to work: 34.2% less than 15 minutes, 37.5% 15 to 30 minutes, 17.1% 30 to 45 minutes, 6.0% 45 to 60 minutes, 5.3% 60 minutes or more (2000)

OREGON
(city). Covers a land area of 29.379 square miles and a water area of 8.712 square miles. Located at 41.64° N. Lat.; 83.46° W. Long. Elevation is 605 feet.
History: Incorporated 1958.
Population: 18,371 (1990); 19,355 (2000); 19,444 (2005); 19,535 (2010 projected); Race: 94.3% White, 0.9% Black, 0.9% Asian, 5.2% Hispanic of any race (2005); Density: 661.8 persons per square mile (2005); Average household size: 2.48 (2005); Median age: 40.2 (2005); Males per 100 females: 92.7 (2005); Marriage status: 22.9% never married, 59.7% now married, 7.7% widowed, 9.7% divorced (2000); Foreign born: 2.3% (2000); Ancestry (includes multiple ancestries): 33.8% German, 10.9% Irish, 9.9% Other groups, 8.9% Polish, 7.8% English (2000).
Economy: Port with railroad-owned and -operated docks. Has industries producing oil, chemicals and fabricated metal products. The majority of the city's area is open farmland, where tomatoes, soybeans, greenhouse vegetables, fruits, and grains are grown. Single-family building permits issued: 63 (2005); Multi-family building permits issued: 0 (2005); Employment by occupation: 11.2% management, 17.5% professional, 13.3% services, 25.2% sales, 0.3% farming, 11.0% construction, 21.4% production (2000).
Income: Per capita income: $24,965 (2005); Median household income: $50,853 (2005); Average household income: $61,398 (2005); Percent of households with income of $100,000 or more: 15.5% (2005); Poverty rate: 4.8% (2000).
Education: Percent of population age 25 and over with: High school diploma (including GED) or higher: 84.9% (2005); Bachelor's degree or higher: 15.8% (2005); Master's degree or higher: 5.6% (2005).

School District(s)
Lucas Educational Service Center
   2003-04 Enrollment: n/a . . . . (419) 698-1501
Oregon City SD (PK-12)
   2003-04 Enrollment: 3,862 . . . . (419) 693-0661
Oregon Schools Virtual Academy
   2003-04 Enrollment: n/a

Two-year College(s)
Oregon Career Center (Public)
   Fall 2004 Enrollment: n/a. . . . . (419) 697-3450

Housing: Homeownership rate: 74.5% (2005); Median home value: $137,441 (2005); Median rent: $404 per month (2000); Median age of housing: 34 years (2000).
Hospitals: Bay Park Community Hospital (70 beds); St. Charles Hospital (386 beds)
Transportation: Commute to work: 96.3% car, 0.0% public transportation, 1.5% walk, 1.6% work from home (2000); Travel time to work: 35.3% less than 15 minutes, 44.4% 15 to 30 minutes, 13.5% 30 to 45 minutes, 2.9% 45 to 60 minutes, 3.9% 60 minutes or more (2000)

Additional Information Contacts
City of Oregon . . . . (419) 698-7095
   http://www.ci.oregon.oh.us
Eastern Maumee Bay Chamber. (419) 693-5580
   http://www.toledochamber.com/chamber/NWO.asp

OTTAWA HILLS
(village). Covers a land area of 1.864 square miles and a water area of 0.009 square miles. Located at 41.67° N. Lat.; 83.64° W. Long. Elevation is 610 feet.
History: Settled 1916, incorporated 1924.
Population: 4,543 (1990); 4,564 (2000); 4,623 (2005); 4,692 (2010 projected); Race: 93.3% White, 1.1% Black, 3.0% Asian, 1.4% Hispanic of any race (2005); Density: 2,480.2 persons per square mile (2005); Average household size: 2.68 (2005); Median age: 44.8 (2005); Males per 100 females: 94.8 (2005); Marriage status: 18.4% never married, 69.1% now married, 6.1% widowed, 6.4% divorced (2000); Foreign born: 7.9% (2000); Ancestry (includes multiple ancestries): 28.1% German, 16.6% English, 15.0% Irish, 9.6% Other groups, 8.9% Polish (2000).
Economy: Employment by occupation: 26.4% management, 41.7% professional, 5.7% services, 19.4% sales, 0.0% farming, 4.0% construction, 2.8% production (2000).
Income: Per capita income: $59,193 (2005); Median household income: $103,840 (2005); Average household income: $158,453 (2005); Percent of households with income of $100,000 or more: 51.5% (2005); Poverty rate: 2.1% (2000).
Education: Percent of population age 25 and over with: High school diploma (including GED) or higher: 97.7% (2005); Bachelor's degree or higher: 69.1% (2005); Master's degree or higher: 40.0% (2005).
Housing: Homeownership rate: 88.0% (2005); Median home value: $282,965 (2005); Median rent: $730 per month (2000); Median age of housing: 46 years (2000).
Safety: Violent crime rate: 2.2 per 10,000 population; Property crime rate: 88.8 per 10,000 population (2004).
Transportation: Commute to work: 95.6% car, 0.0% public transportation, 0.6% walk, 3.3% work from home (2000); Travel time to work: 42.0% less than 15 minutes, 49.2% 15 to 30 minutes, 3.6% 30 to 45 minutes, 1.5% 45 to 60 minutes, 3.6% 60 minutes or more (2000)

Additional Information Contacts
Village of Ottawa Hills . . . . (419) 536-1111
   http://www.ottawahills.org

SYLVANIA
(city). Covers a land area of 5.792 square miles and a water area of 0.045 square miles. Located at 41.71° N. Lat.; 83.70° W. Long. Elevation is 665 feet.
History: Incorporated 1867.

Population: 17,488 (1990); 18,670 (2000); 18,884 (2005); 19,161 (2010 projected); Race: 94.5% White, 1.0% Black, 2.6% Asian, 1.8% Hispanic of any race (2005); Density: 3,260.2 persons per square mile (2005); Average household size: 2.56 (2005); Median age: 38.8 (2005); Males per 100 females: 91.3 (2005); Marriage status: 20.9% never married, 63.1% now married, 7.8% widowed, 8.2% divorced (2000); Foreign born: 4.7% (2000); Ancestry (includes multiple ancestries): 32.8% German, 15.6% Irish, 11.4% English, 10.7% Polish, 6.7% Other groups (2000).
Economy: Building materials, cement, light manufacturing. Employment by occupation: 15.7% management, 30.8% professional, 10.9% services, 26.9% sales, 0.2% farming, 5.6% construction, 9.8% production (2000).
Income: Per capita income: $31,469 (2005); Median household income: $64,476 (2005); Average household income: $80,594 (2005); Percent of households with income of $100,000 or more: 27.6% (2005); Poverty rate: 4.2% (2000).
Education: Percent of population age 25 and over with: High school diploma (including GED) or higher: 94.1% (2005); Bachelor's degree or higher: 43.2% (2005); Master's degree or higher: 15.2% (2005).

School District(s)

Sylvania City SD (PK-12)
    2003-04 Enrollment: 7,832 . . . . (419) 824-8501

Four-year College(s)

Lourdes College (Private, Not-for-profit, Roman Catholic)
    Fall 2004 Enrollment: 1,491. . . . . (419) 885-3211
    2005-06 Tuition: In-state $9,816; Out-of-state $9,816

Housing: Homeownership rate: 75.5% (2005); Median home value: $170,713 (2005); Median rent: $445 per month (2000); Median age of housing: 28 years (2000).
Hospitals: Flower Hospital (279 beds)
Safety: Violent crime rate: 2.6 per 10,000 population; Property crime rate: 142.7 per 10,000 population (2004).
Newspapers: Sylvania Herald (General - Circulation 24,000); Toledo Jewish News (Jewish - Circulation 7,000); West Toledo Herald (General - Circulation 20,000)
Transportation: Commute to work: 94.3% car, 0.6% public transportation, 1.4% walk, 3.4% work from home (2000); Travel time to work: 30.6% less than 15 minutes, 49.6% 15 to 30 minutes, 11.8% 30 to 45 minutes, 2.5% 45 to 60 minutes, 5.5% 60 minutes or more (2000)

Additional Information Contacts
City of Sylvania . . . . (419) 885-8925
    http://www.cityofsylvania.com
Sylvania Area Chamber of Commerce . . . . (419) 882-2135
    http://www.sylvaniachamber.org

TOLEDO (city). Covers a land area of 80.622 square miles and a water area of 3.453 square miles. Located at 41.66° N. Lat.; 83.57° W. Long. Elevation is 615 feet.
History: Toledo was established along the Maumee River on the westernmost tip of Lake Erie. A stockade called Fort Industry was built here around 1800, but was short-lived. In 1833 two small settlements voted to consolidate, and the residents chose the name of Toledo for the new town. The early years were difficult for the town, with cholera, a drought, business failures, and the Toledo War of 1835, a protracted boundary dispute between Ohio and Michigan which ended with Michigan being given the Upper Peninsula in exchange for Ohio keeping the disputed territory. In the 1840's things improved, with Toledo the logical choice as terminus of the Wabash & Erie Canal, followed by the Miami & Erie Canal. When the 1850's came, Toledo was a station on the Underground Railroad for escaping slaves. Among the industries that developed after the Civil War was the Libby Glass Company, which revolutionized the glass industry, and the Owens Bottle Machine Company.
Population: 332,921 (1990); 313,619 (2000); 306,374 (2005); 299,292 (2010 projected); Race: 68.6% White, 24.3% Black, 1.2% Asian, 5.9% Hispanic of any race (2005); Density: 3,800.1 persons per square mile (2005); Average household size: 2.39 (2005); Median age: 34.2 (2005); Males per 100 females: 93.1 (2005); Marriage status: 33.0% never married, 45.9% now married, 7.8% widowed, 13.3% divorced (2000); Foreign born: 3.0% (2000); Ancestry (includes multiple ancestries): 29.0% Other groups, 23.4% German, 10.8% Irish, 10.1% Polish, 6.0% English (2000).
Economy: Unemployment rate: 7.5% (2005); Total civilian labor force: 146,455 (2005); Single-family building permits issued: 120 (2005); Multi-family building permits issued: 135 (2005); Employment by occupation: 9.0% management, 16.7% professional, 17.9% services, 26.7% sales, 0.1% farming, 8.3% construction, 21.3% production (2000).
Income: Per capita income: $19,095 (2005); Median household income: $35,639 (2005); Average household income: $45,127 (2005); Percent of households with income of $100,000 or more: 7.4% (2005); Poverty rate: 17.9% (2000).
Taxes: Total city taxes per capita: $573 (2004); City property taxes per capita: $49 (2004).
Education: Percent of population age 25 and over with: High school diploma (including GED) or higher: 80.0% (2005); Bachelor's degree or higher: 17.1% (2005); Master's degree or higher: 5.5% (2005).

School District(s)

Academy of Business & Tech (KG-08)
    2003-04 Enrollment: 392 . . . . (419) 243-5880
Alliance Academy of Toledo (07-12)
    2003-04 Enrollment: 279 . . . . (419) 418-5150
Alternative Education Academy (KG-12)
    2003-04 Enrollment: 1,438 . . . . (419) 897-7928
Aurora Academy (KG-09)
    2003-04 Enrollment: 134 . . . . (419) 693-6841
Autistic Choice for Education
    2003-04 Enrollment: n/a
Brigadoon Academy Community School (07-10)
    2003-04 Enrollment: 27
Eagle Academy (KG-05)
    2003-04 Enrollment: 260 . . . . (419) 245-9862
Englewood Peace Academy (KG-09)
    2003-04 Enrollment: 232 . . . . (419) 243-7260
George A. Phillips Academy (KG-08)
    2003-04 Enrollment: 230
Glass City Academy (11-12)
    2003-04 Enrollment: 103
House of Emmanuel
    2003-04 Enrollment: n/a
Lake Erie Academy (KG-08)
    2003-04 Enrollment: 218
Life Skills Center of Toledo (09-12)
    2003-04 Enrollment: 455 . . . . (419) 241-5504
Lucas Educational Service Center
    2003-04 Enrollment: n/a . . . . (419) 698-1501
Maumee Bay Academy
    2003-04 Enrollment: n/a
Meadows Choice Community (01-10)
    2003-04 Enrollment: 57 . . . . (419) 691-3805
Montessori Academy of Greater Toledo
    2003-04 Enrollment: n/a
New Horizons Academy
    2003-04 Enrollment: n/a
Ottawa Hills Local SD (PK-12)
    2003-04 Enrollment: 1,030 . . . . (419) 536-6371
Paul Laurence Dunbar Academy (KG-06)
    2003-04 Enrollment: 181 . . . . (419) 244-4202
Performing Arts School of Tol (07-12)
    2003-04 Enrollment: 144 . . . . (419) 534-2228
Phoenix Academy Community School (07-12)
    2003-04 Enrollment: 206 . . . . (419) 729-8372
Polly Fox Academy Community School (08-12)
    2003-04 Enrollment: 63
Springfield Local Schools (PK-12)
    2003-04 Enrollment: 3,779 . . . . (419) 867-5600
Summit Academy Toledo
    2003-04 Enrollment: n/a
Sylvania City SD (PK-12)
    2003-04 Enrollment: 7,832 . . . . (419) 824-8501
Toledo Academy of Learning (KG-08)
    2003-04 Enrollment: 319 . . . . (419) 255-0253
Toledo Accelerated Academy (06-10)
    2003-04 Enrollment: 233 . . . . (419) 242-6160
Toledo City SD (PK-12)
    2003-04 Enrollment: 34,486 . . . . (419) 729-8200
Toledo School for the Arts (06-12)
    2003-04 Enrollment: 328 . . . . (419) 246-8732
Victory Learning Center
    2003-04 Enrollment: n/a
Washington Local Schools (PK-12)
    2003-04 Enrollment: 6,942 . . . . (419) 473-8220

Wildwood Environmental Academy
 2003-04 Enrollment: n/a
Wilson Education Beginnings
 2003-04 Enrollment: n/a
Four-year College(s)
Medical University of Ohio at Toledo (Public)
 Fall 2004 Enrollment: 1,086. . . . . (419) 383-4457
Mercy College of Northwest Ohio (Private, Not-for-profit, Roman Catholic)
 Fall 2004 Enrollment: 688 . . . . (419) 251-1313
 2005-06 Tuition: In-state $8,160; Out-of-state $8,160
University of Toledo (Public)
 Fall 2004 Enrollment: 19,480. (419) 530-4636
 2005-06 Tuition: In-state $7,494; Out-of-state $16,305
Two-year College(s)
Davis College (Private, For-profit)
 Fall 2004 Enrollment: 403 . . . . (419) 473-2700
 2005-06 Tuition: In-state $7,920; Out-of-state $7,920
Professional Skills Institute (Private, For-profit)
 Fall 2004 Enrollment: 228 . . . . (419) 531-9610
 2005-06 Tuition: In-state $10,168; Out-of-state $10,168
Stautzenberger College (Private, For-profit)
 Fall 2004 Enrollment: 805 . . . . (419) 866-0261
 2005-06 Tuition: In-state $6,480; Out-of-state $6,480
Toledo Academy of Beauty Culture-North (Private, For-profit)
 Fall 2004 Enrollment: 78 . . . . (419) 478-5325
Toledo Academy of Beauty Culture-South (Private, For-profit)
 Fall 2004 Enrollment: 134 . . . . (419) 381-7218
Toledo School of Practical Nursing (Public)
 Fall 2004 Enrollment: 261 . . . . (419) 671-8706
 2005-06 Tuition: In-state $9,000; Out-of-state $9,400
Housing: Homeownership rate: 60.0% (2005); Median home value: $85,646 (2005); Median rent: $380 per month (2000); Median age of housing: 48 years (2000).
Hospitals: Medical College of Ohio Hospitals (319 beds); Northcoast Behavioral Healthcare Systems - Toledo Campus (96 beds); Saint Anne Mercy Hospital (88 beds); Saint Vincent Mercy Medical Center (588 beds); Toledo Hospital (774 beds)
Safety: Violent crime rate: 105.5 per 10,000 population; Property crime rate: 700.2 per 10,000 population (2004).
Newspapers: Ann Arbor Family Press (Alternative, General - Circulation 25,000); Catholic Chronicle (Catholic, Religious - Circulation 19,651); La Prensa Nacional (Hispanic - Circulation 20,000); Point-Shoreland Journal (General - Circulation 8,700); The Blade (Circulation 138,976); Toledo City Paper (Alternative, General - Circulation 30,000); Toledo Journal (General - Circulation 19,500); Toledo Legal News (Circulation 500)
Transportation: Commute to work: 92.9% car, 2.5% public transportation, 2.3% walk, 1.5% work from home (2000); Travel time to work: 35.1% less than 15 minutes, 47.2% 15 to 30 minutes, 10.7% 30 to 45 minutes, 2.8% 45 to 60 minutes, 4.1% 60 minutes or more (2000); Amtrak: Service available.
Additional Information Contacts
City of Toledo. . . . . (419) 245-1001
 http://www.ci.toledo.oh.us
Greater Toledo Convention & Visitors Bureau. . . . . (800) 243-4667
 http://www.dotoledo.org/gtcvb
Toldeo Area Chamber of Commerce. . . . . (419) 243-8191
 http://www.toledochamber.com

WATERVILLE (village). Covers a land area of 3.502 square miles and a water area of 0.115 square miles. Located at 41.50° N. Lat.; 83.72° W. Long. Elevation is 650 feet.
History: Waterville was platted in 1818 by John Pray. It grew as the center of a garden nursery region.
Population: 4,585 (1990); 4,828 (2000); 5,058 (2005); 5,279 (2010 projected); Race: 97.7% White, 0.1% Black, 0.3% Asian, 1.5% Hispanic of any race (2005); Density: 1,444.4 persons per square mile (2005); Average household size: 2.74 (2005); Median age: 39.5 (2005); Males per 100 females: 93.1 (2005); Marriage status: 20.5% never married, 67.8% now married, 5.4% widowed, 6.3% divorced (2000); Foreign born: 1.7% (2000); Ancestry (includes multiple ancestries): 34.6% German, 18.2% English, 14.6% Polish, 12.3% Irish, 5.5% Italian (2000).
Economy: Employment by occupation: 16.1% management, 30.2% professional, 11.2% services, 26.4% sales, 0.6% farming, 7.1% construction, 8.4% production (2000).
Income: Per capita income: $27,155 (2005); Median household income: $66,196 (2005); Average household income: $73,199 (2005); Percent of households with income of $100,000 or more: 23.5% (2005); Poverty rate: 1.8% (2000).
Education: Percent of population age 25 and over with: High school diploma (including GED) or higher: 94.7% (2005); Bachelor's degree or higher: 36.4% (2005); Master's degree or higher: 14.0% (2005).
School District(s)
Anthony Wayne Local SD (PK-12)
 2003-04 Enrollment: 3,879 . . . . (419) 877-5377
Lucas Educational Service Center
 2003-04 Enrollment: n/a . . . . (419) 698-1501
Housing: Homeownership rate: 84.9% (2005); Median home value: $169,015 (2005); Median rent: $463 per month (2000); Median age of housing: 28 years (2000).
Transportation: Commute to work: 96.5% car, 0.3% public transportation, 1.1% walk, 2.1% work from home (2000); Travel time to work: 26.9% less than 15 minutes, 51.2% 15 to 30 minutes, 18.6% 30 to 45 minutes, 2.0% 45 to 60 minutes, 1.3% 60 minutes or more (2000)
Additional Information Contacts
Village of Waterville. . . . . (419) 878-8100
 http://www.waterville.org
Waterville Chamber of Commerce. . . . . (419) 878-5188
 http://www.waterville.org

WHITEHOUSE (village). Covers a land area of 3.454 square miles and a water area of 0 square miles. Located at 41.52° N. Lat.; 83.80° W. Long. Elevation is 650 feet.
Population: 2,646 (1990); 2,733 (2000); 3,171 (2005); 3,568 (2010 projected); Race: 98.5% White, 0.1% Black, 0.3% Asian, 1.1% Hispanic of any race (2005); Density: 918.0 persons per square mile (2005); Average household size: 2.59 (2005); Median age: 40.1 (2005); Males per 100 females: 95.4 (2005); Marriage status: 24.4% never married, 58.6% now married, 8.2% widowed, 8.8% divorced (2000); Foreign born: 1.8% (2000); Ancestry (includes multiple ancestries): 41.0% German, 15.3% Irish, 13.0% English, 9.4% French (except Basque), 6.9% Polish (2000).
Economy: Dairy products, fruit; manufacturing of automotive parts, glass. Single-family building permits issued: 103 (2005); Multi-family building permits issued: 0 (2005); Employment by occupation: 14.5% management, 21.7% professional, 15.7% services, 19.5% sales, 0.4% farming, 9.1% construction, 19.0% production (2000).
Income: Per capita income: $27,983 (2005); Median household income: $60,692 (2005); Average household income: $72,145 (2005); Percent of households with income of $100,000 or more: 24.1% (2005); Poverty rate: 2.6% (2000).
Education: Percent of population age 25 and over with: High school diploma (including GED) or higher: 91.4% (2005); Bachelor's degree or higher: 24.6% (2005); Master's degree or higher: 9.0% (2005).
School District(s)
Anthony Wayne Local SD (PK-12)
 2003-04 Enrollment: 3,879 . . . . (419) 877-5377
Housing: Homeownership rate: 77.6% (2005); Median home value: $149,645 (2005); Median rent: $410 per month (2000); Median age of housing: 27 years (2000).
Transportation: Commute to work: 97.9% car, 0.2% public transportation, 0.3% walk, 1.1% work from home (2000); Travel time to work: 30.3% less than 15 minutes, 43.1% 15 to 30 minutes, 21.5% 30 to 45 minutes, 2.9% 45 to 60 minutes, 2.3% 60 minutes or more (2000)
Additional Information Contacts
Village of Whitehouse . . . . (419) 877-5383
 http://www.whitehouseoh.com
Whitehouse Chamber of Commerce . . . . (419) 877-2747
 http://www.whitehouse.oh.us/chamber

Madison County

Located in central Ohio; drained by Deer, Paint, and Darby Creeks. Covers a land area of 465.44 square miles, a water area of 0.74 square miles, and is located in the Eastern Time Zone. The county government was organized in 1810. County seat is London.

Madison County is part of the Columbus, OH Metropolitan Statistical Area. The entire metro area includes: Delaware County, OH; Fairfield County, OH; Franklin County, OH; Licking County, OH; Madison County, OH; Morrow County, OH; Pickaway County, OH; Union County, OH

Weather Station: London   Elevation: 1,017 feet

	Jan	Feb	Mar	Apr	May	Jun	Jul	Aug	Sep	Oct	Nov	Dec
High	34	39	50	63	73	81	85	83	77	65	51	40
Low	18	21	29	38	49	58	62	60	52	41	33	24
Precip	2.4	2.2	2.8	3.6	4.1	4.3	4.0	3.3	2.8	2.6	3.3	3.0
Snow	6.9	na	na	0.4	0.0	0.0	0.0	0.0	0.0	0.2	0.5	na

High and Low temperatures in degrees Fahrenheit; Precipitation and Snow in inches

Population: 37,076 (1990); 40,213 (2000); 40,909 (2005); 41,625 (2010 projected); Race: 91.5% White, 6.4% Black, 0.8% Asian, 0.8% Hispanic of any race (2005); Density: 87.9 persons per square mile (2005); Average household size: 2.90 (2005); Median age: 36.8 (2005); Males per 100 females: 117.5 (2005).
Religion: Five largest groups: 10.2% The United Methodist Church, 5.9% Catholic Church, 2.2% Presbyterian Church (U.S.A.), 2.0% Southern Baptist Convention, 1.9% Church of the Nazarene (2000).
Economy: Unemployment rate: 5.8% (2005); Total civilian labor force: 19,859 (2005); Leading industries: 27.9% manufacturing; 18.3% retail trade; 12.8% accommodation & food services (2004); Farms: 730 totaling 245,886 acres (2002); Companies that employ 500 or more persons: 2 (2004); Companies that employ 100 to 499 persons: 17 (2004); Companies that employ less than 100 persons: 774 (2004); Black-owned businesses: n/a (2002); Hispanic-owned businesses: n/a (2002); Women-owned businesses: 799 (2002); Retail sales per capita: $11,345 (2006). Single-family building permits issued: 147 (2005); Multi-family building permits issued: 16 (2005).
Income: Per capita income: $22,113 (2005); Median household income: $51,218 (2005); Average household income: $61,276 (2005); Percent of households with income of $100,000 or more: 14.3% (2005); Poverty rate: 8.3% (2003); Bankruptcy rate: 12.37% (2005).
Taxes: Total county taxes per capita: $210 (2004); County property taxes per capita: $105 (2004).
Education: Percent of population age 25 and over with: High school diploma (including GED) or higher: 79.0% (2005); Bachelor's degree or higher: 13.2% (2005); Master's degree or higher: 3.8% (2005).
Housing: Homeownership rate: 72.0% (2005); Median home value: $128,897 (2005); Median rent: $389 per month (2000); Median age of housing: 31 years (2000).
Health: Birth rate: 121.0 per 10,000 population (2004); Death rate: 90.0 per 10,000 population (2004); Age-adjusted cancer mortality rate: 214.7 deaths per 100,000 population (2002); Air Quality Index: 77.2% good, 21.4% moderate, 1.4% unhealthy for sensitive individuals, 0.0% unhealthy (percent of days in 2005); Number of physicians: 10.0 per 10,000 population (2004); Hospital beds: 16.5 per 10,000 population (2003); Hospital admissions: 400.0 per 10,000 population (2003).
Elections: 2004 Presidential election results: 63.9% Bush, 35.7% Kerry, 0.0% Nader, 0.2% Badnarik
National and State Parks: Madison Lake State Park; Madison Lake State Reserve
Additional Information Contacts
Madison County Government . . . . (740) 852-2972
    http://www.co.madison.oh.us/
City of London . . . . (740) 852-3243
    http://ci.london.oh.us
London Chamber of Commerce. (740) 852-2250
    http://www.madisoncountychamber.org
Village of West Jefferson . . . . (614) 879-7674
    http://www.villageofwestjefferson.com

Madison County Communities

CHOCTAW LAKE (CDP). Aka Chocktou Lake. Covers a land area of 0.803 square miles and a water area of 0.402 square miles. Located at 39.96° N. Lat.; 83.48° W. Long.
Population: 1,234 (1990); 1,562 (2000); 1,653 (2005); 1,734 (2010 projected); Race: 94.9% White, 0.2% Black, 3.8% Asian, 0.4% Hispanic of any race (2005); Density: 2,059.4 persons per square mile (2005); Average household size: 2.66 (2005); Median age: 41.5 (2005); Males per 100 females: 101.6 (2005); Marriage status: 18.7% never married, 69.9% now married, 4.7% widowed, 6.7% divorced (2000); Foreign born: 1.8% (2000); Ancestry (includes multiple ancestries): 31.9% German, 21.6% English, 11.8% Irish, 6.3% Other groups, 3.6% Scotch-Irish (2000).
Economy: Employment by occupation: 16.1% management, 26.2% professional, 10.6% services, 27.0% sales, 1.0% farming, 6.3% construction, 12.8% production (2000).

Income: Per capita income: $36,933 (2005); Median household income: $91,979 (2005); Average household income: $98,309 (2005); Percent of households with income of $100,000 or more: 43.8% (2005); Poverty rate: 6.9% (2000).
Education: Percent of population age 25 and over with: High school diploma (including GED) or higher: 94.2% (2005); Bachelor's degree or higher: 37.2% (2005); Master's degree or higher: 11.9% (2005).
Housing: Homeownership rate: 95.8% (2005); Median home value: $216,905 (2005); Median rent: $900 per month (2000); Median age of housing: 21 years (2000).
Transportation: Commute to work: 93.4% car, 0.0% public transportation, 0.0% walk, 5.2% work from home (2000); Travel time to work: 20.1% less than 15 minutes, 17.5% 15 to 30 minutes, 41.6% 30 to 45 minutes, 16.8% 45 to 60 minutes, 4.1% 60 minutes or more (2000)

LONDON (city). Covers a land area of 8.508 square miles and a water area of 0 square miles. Located at 39.88° N. Lat.; 83.44° W. Long. Elevation is 1,054 feet.
History: London was established on a site that had formerly been a swamp, known for malaria and ague. When the swamp was drained, the land was good for farming and livestock raising. The town was incorporated in 1831 and soon became a stockyard and trading center.
Population: 8,883 (1990); 8,771 (2000); 9,260 (2005); 9,711 (2010 projected); Race: 92.3% White, 4.5% Black, 0.9% Asian, 0.6% Hispanic of any race (2005); Density: 1,088.4 persons per square mile (2005); Average household size: 2.41 (2005); Median age: 36.8 (2005); Males per 100 females: 87.9 (2005); Marriage status: 19.2% never married, 58.2% now married, 9.7% widowed, 12.9% divorced (2000); Foreign born: 1.7% (2000); Ancestry (includes multiple ancestries): 20.7% German, 20.6% United States or American, 12.2% Other groups, 12.1% Irish, 9.3% English (2000).
Economy: Single-family building permits issued: 63 (2005); Multi-family building permits issued: 0 (2005); Employment by occupation: 12.2% management, 17.2% professional, 18.2% services, 23.6% sales, 0.0% farming, 8.6% construction, 20.2% production (2000).
Income: Per capita income: $21,861 (2005); Median household income: $41,198 (2005); Average household income: $51,457 (2005); Percent of households with income of $100,000 or more: 9.9% (2005); Poverty rate: 11.7% (2000).
Education: Percent of population age 25 and over with: High school diploma (including GED) or higher: 76.7% (2005); Bachelor's degree or higher: 15.1% (2005); Master's degree or higher: 5.0% (2005).
School District(s)
Jonathan Alder Local SD (PK-12)
    2003-04 Enrollment: 1,809 . . . . (614) 873-5621
London City SD (PK-12)
    2003-04 Enrollment: 2,081 . . . . (740) 852-5700
London Digital Academy (06-12)
    2003-04 Enrollment: 30 . . . . (740) 852-5700
Madison-Plains Local SD (KG-12)
    2003-04 Enrollment: 1,627 . . . . (740) 852-0290
Housing: Homeownership rate: 56.4% (2005); Median home value: $113,384 (2005); Median rent: $375 per month (2000); Median age of housing: 37 years (2000).
Hospitals: Madison County Hospital (102 beds)
Newspapers: Plain City Advocate (General - Circulation 1,900); The Madison Press (Circulation 6,500); The Telegram (General - Circulation 1,800); The Tribune (General - Circulation 6,924); The Weekly Review (General - Circulation 12,000)
Transportation: Commute to work: 91.7% car, 0.8% public transportation, 3.0% walk, 2.8% work from home (2000); Travel time to work: 48.2% less than 15 minutes, 17.3% 15 to 30 minutes, 18.9% 30 to 45 minutes, 11.6% 45 to 60 minutes, 4.0% 60 minutes or more (2000)
Additional Information Contacts
City of London . . . . (740) 852-3243
    http://ci.london.oh.us
London Chamber of Commerce. (740) 852-2250
    http://www.madisoncountychamber.org

MIDWAY (village). Aka Sedalia. Covers a land area of 0.278 square miles and a water area of 0 square miles. Located at 39.73° N. Lat.; 83.47° W. Long. Elevation is 1,070 feet.
History: Also called Sedalia.
Population: 289 (1990); 274 (2000); 265 (2005); 263 (2010 projected); Race: 100.0% White, 0.0% Black, 0.0% Asian, 1.9% Hispanic of any race

(2005); Density: 952.5 persons per square mile (2005); Average household size: 2.45 (2005); Median age: 39.8 (2005); Males per 100 females: 94.9 (2005); Marriage status: 17.6% never married, 63.0% now married, 9.3% widowed, 10.2% divorced (2000); Foreign born: 0.7% (2000); Ancestry (includes multiple ancestries): 25.8% United States or American, 17.0% German, 10.0% English, 8.9% Irish, 5.5% Scotch-Irish (2000).
Economy: Employment by occupation: 9.8% management, 7.6% professional, 21.2% services, 25.8% sales, 0.8% farming, 11.4% construction, 23.5% production (2000).
Income: Per capita income: $20,764 (2005); Median household income: $42,500 (2005); Average household income: $50,949 (2005); Percent of households with income of $100,000 or more: 8.3% (2005); Poverty rate: 3.0% (2000).
Education: Percent of population age 25 and over with: High school diploma (including GED) or higher: 70.3% (2005); Bachelor's degree or higher: 4.1% (2005); Master's degree or higher: 1.7% (2005).
Housing: Homeownership rate: 85.2% (2005); Median home value: $98,947 (2005); Median rent: $338 per month (2000); Median age of housing: 60+ years (2000).
Transportation: Commute to work: 96.2% car, 0.0% public transportation, 2.3% walk, 1.5% work from home (2000); Travel time to work: 21.5% less than 15 minutes, 37.7% 15 to 30 minutes, 16.9% 30 to 45 minutes, 20.8% 45 to 60 minutes, 3.1% 60 minutes or more (2000)

MOUNT STERLING (village). Covers a land area of 0.983 square miles and a water area of 0 square miles. Located at 39.72° N. Lat.; 83.26° W. Long. Elevation is 906 feet.
History: Mount Sterling was founded in 1828 by John J. Smith, who named the town after his former home in Kentucky. An early industry was the Ohio Willow Wood Company, manufacturers of artificial limbs, polo balls and mallets.
Population: 1,647 (1990); 1,865 (2000); 1,758 (2005); 1,689 (2010 projected); Race: 97.3% White, 0.2% Black, 0.2% Asian, 2.3% Hispanic of any race (2005); Density: 1,789.0 persons per square mile (2005); Average household size: 2.38 (2005); Median age: 33.7 (2005); Males per 100 females: 89.0 (2005); Marriage status: 23.4% never married, 53.6% now married, 9.5% widowed, 13.6% divorced (2000); Foreign born: 0.9% (2000); Ancestry (includes multiple ancestries): 22.9% German, 19.3% United States or American, 15.9% Irish, 11.2% Other groups, 9.6% English (2000).
Economy: Single-family building permits issued: 1 (2005); Multi-family building permits issued: 0 (2005); Employment by occupation: 8.1% management, 11.0% professional, 13.4% services, 31.1% sales, 0.2% farming, 12.5% construction, 23.7% production (2000).
Income: Per capita income: $18,221 (2005); Median household income: $36,752 (2005); Average household income: $43,404 (2005); Percent of households with income of $100,000 or more: 4.7% (2005); Poverty rate: 9.4% (2000).
Education: Percent of population age 25 and over with: High school diploma (including GED) or higher: 78.1% (2005); Bachelor's degree or higher: 8.8% (2005); Master's degree or higher: 2.1% (2005).
School District(s)
Madison-Plains Local SD (KG-12)
    2003-04 Enrollment: 1,627 . . . . (740) 852-0290
Miami Trace Local SD (PK-12)
    2003-04 Enrollment: 2,719 . . . . (740) 335-3010
Westfall Local SD (PK-12)
    2003-04 Enrollment: 1,655 . . . . (740) 986-3671
Housing: Homeownership rate: 53.1% (2005); Median home value: $110,526 (2005); Median rent: $356 per month (2000); Median age of housing: 45 years (2000).
Safety: Violent crime rate: 0.0 per 10,000 population; Property crime rate: 292.7 per 10,000 population (2004).
Transportation: Commute to work: 90.4% car, 0.0% public transportation, 6.1% walk, 2.8% work from home (2000); Travel time to work: 32.1% less than 15 minutes, 22.9% 15 to 30 minutes, 27.0% 30 to 45 minutes, 11.4% 45 to 60 minutes, 6.6% 60 minutes or more (2000)

PLAIN CITY (village). Covers a land area of 1.812 square miles and a water area of 0 square miles. Located at 40.10° N. Lat.; 83.26° W. Long. Elevation is 934 feet.
History: Plain City was laid out in 1818 by Isaac Bigelow. It was first called Westminster, then Pleasant Valley, and finally named Plain City in 1851 because of its location on Big Darby Plain.
Population: 2,360 (1990); 2,832 (2000); 3,080 (2005); 3,352 (2010 projected); Race: 97.0% White, 0.4% Black, 0.6% Asian, 1.3% Hispanic of any race (2005); Density: 1,700.1 persons per square mile (2005); Average household size: 2.47 (2005); Median age: 35.1 (2005); Males per 100 females: 94.3 (2005); Marriage status: 23.5% never married, 53.7% now married, 9.5% widowed, 13.3% divorced (2000); Foreign born: 2.4% (2000); Ancestry (includes multiple ancestries): 23.4% German, 21.6% United States or American, 12.2% Irish, 9.9% English, 7.9% Other groups (2000).
Economy: Single-family building permits issued: 18 (2005); Multi-family building permits issued: 16 (2005); Employment by occupation: 8.4% management, 11.2% professional, 19.9% services, 30.4% sales, 0.0% farming, 11.4% construction, 18.7% production (2000).
Income: Per capita income: $25,724 (2005); Median household income: $52,727 (2005); Average household income: $63,536 (2005); Percent of households with income of $100,000 or more: 14.7% (2005); Poverty rate: 6.1% (2000).
Education: Percent of population age 25 and over with: High school diploma (including GED) or higher: 78.7% (2005); Bachelor's degree or higher: 14.2% (2005); Master's degree or higher: 3.3% (2005).
School District(s)
Central Ohio Joint Vocational SD (09-12)
    2003-04 Enrollment: n/a . . . . (614) 873-4666
Jonathan Alder Local SD (PK-12)
    2003-04 Enrollment: 1,809 . . . . (614) 873-5621
Housing: Homeownership rate: 56.9% (2005); Median home value: $144,796 (2005); Median rent: $407 per month (2000); Median age of housing: 34 years (2000).
Safety: Violent crime rate: 3.2 per 10,000 population; Property crime rate: 91.4 per 10,000 population (2004).
Transportation: Commute to work: 95.6% car, 0.0% public transportation, 2.8% walk, 1.2% work from home (2000); Travel time to work: 30.7% less than 15 minutes, 40.1% 15 to 30 minutes, 21.4% 30 to 45 minutes, 5.3% 45 to 60 minutes, 2.5% 60 minutes or more (2000)

SOUTH SOLON (village). Covers a land area of 0.199 square miles and a water area of 0 square miles. Located at 39.73° N. Lat.; 83.61° W. Long. Elevation is 1,118 feet.
Population: 393 (1990); 405 (2000); 420 (2005); 428 (2010 projected); Race: 98.1% White, 0.0% Black, 1.0% Asian, 0.7% Hispanic of any race (2005); Density: 2,108.6 persons per square mile (2005); Average household size: 2.82 (2005); Median age: 32.5 (2005); Males per 100 females: 101.0 (2005); Marriage status: 23.2% never married, 58.4% now married, 7.5% widowed, 10.8% divorced (2000); Foreign born: 0.7% (2000); Ancestry (includes multiple ancestries): 28.0% United States or American, 14.6% German, 4.1% Other groups, 3.9% English, 3.9% French (except Basque) (2000).
Economy: In livestock-raising and farming area. Employment by occupation: 3.1% management, 12.2% professional, 16.3% services, 24.5% sales, 1.0% farming, 12.8% construction, 30.1% production (2000).
Income: Per capita income: $18,982 (2005); Median household income: $43,311 (2005); Average household income: $53,507 (2005); Percent of households with income of $100,000 or more: 8.1% (2005); Poverty rate: 10.0% (2000).
Education: Percent of population age 25 and over with: High school diploma (including GED) or higher: 75.7% (2005); Bachelor's degree or higher: 7.1% (2005); Master's degree or higher: 2.0% (2005).
Housing: Homeownership rate: 71.1% (2005); Median home value: $75,789 (2005); Median rent: $388 per month (2000); Median age of housing: 60+ years (2000).
Safety: Violent crime rate: 0.0 per 10,000 population; Property crime rate: 0.0 per 10,000 population (2004).
Transportation: Commute to work: 97.8% car, 0.0% public transportation, 1.1% walk, 1.1% work from home (2000); Travel time to work: 11.9% less than 15 minutes, 30.1% 15 to 30 minutes, 29.5% 30 to 45 minutes, 17.0% 45 to 60 minutes, 11.4% 60 minutes or more (2000)

WEST JEFFERSON (village). Aka Jefferson. Covers a land area of 3.316 square miles and a water area of 0.015 square miles. Located at 39.94° N. Lat.; 83.27° W. Long. Elevation is 920 feet.
Population: 4,623 (1990); 4,331 (2000); 4,094 (2005); 3,953 (2010 projected); Race: 99.0% White, 0.0% Black, 0.2% Asian, 0.6% Hispanic of any race (2005); Density: 1,234.5 persons per square mile (2005); Average household size: 2.61 (2005); Median age: 36.7 (2005); Males per 100 females: 96.5 (2005); Marriage status: 19.4% never married, 58.7% now

married, 10.3% widowed, 11.6% divorced (2000); Foreign born: 0.4% (2000); Ancestry (includes multiple ancestries): 21.2% German, 18.5% United States or American, 10.9% English, 10.6% Irish, 6.0% Other groups (2000).
Economy: Single-family building permits issued: 0 (2005); Multi-family building permits issued: 0 (2005); Employment by occupation: 9.1% management, 9.6% professional, 14.5% services, 28.9% sales, 0.2% farming, 12.8% construction, 24.9% production (2000).
Income: Per capita income: $23,302 (2005); Median household income: $48,156 (2005); Average household income: $59,367 (2005); Percent of households with income of $100,000 or more: 11.7% (2005); Poverty rate: 5.9% (2000).
Education: Percent of population age 25 and over with: High school diploma (including GED) or higher: 75.6% (2005); Bachelor's degree or higher: 8.6% (2005); Master's degree or higher: 2.8% (2005).

School District(s)
Jefferson Local SD (PK-12)
 2003-04 Enrollment: 1,327 . . . . (614) 879-7654
West Jefferson Digital Academy
 2003-04 Enrollment: n/a . . . . (614) 879-7654

Housing: Homeownership rate: 72.2% (2005); Median home value: $109,375 (2005); Median rent: $434 per month (2000); Median age of housing: 38 years (2000).
Safety: Violent crime rate: 2.3 per 10,000 population; Property crime rate: 292.4 per 10,000 population (2004).
Transportation: Commute to work: 96.2% car, 0.5% public transportation, 1.0% walk, 1.6% work from home (2000); Travel time to work: 24.8% less than 15 minutes, 40.8% 15 to 30 minutes, 23.8% 30 to 45 minutes, 7.3% 45 to 60 minutes, 3.3% 60 minutes or more (2000)

Additional Information Contacts
Village of West Jefferson . . . . (614) 879-7674
 http://www.villageofwestjefferson.com

Mahoning County

Located in eastern Ohio; bounded on the east by Pennsylvania; crossed by the Mahoning and Little Beaver Rivers. Covers a land area of 415.25 square miles, a water area of 8.14 square miles, and is located in the Eastern Time Zone. The county government was organized in 1846. County seat is Youngstown.

Mahoning County is part of the Youngstown-Warren-Boardman, OH-PA Metropolitan Statistical Area. The entire metro area includes: Mahoning County, OH; Trumbull County, OH; Mercer County, PA

Weather Station: Canfield 1 S Elevation: 1,138 feet

	Jan	Feb	Mar	Apr	May	Jun	Jul	Aug	Sep	Oct	Nov	Dec
High	34	37	49	60	71	79	83	82	74	63	50	39
Low	16	17	26	34	45	54	58	56	49	38	31	22
Precip	2.0	1.8	2.9	3.0	3.9	4.2	4.4	3.6	3.8	2.8	3.1	2.7
Snow	na	na	3.3	0.7	0.0	0.0	0.0	0.0	0.0	0.3	1.1	na

High and Low temperatures in degrees Fahrenheit; Precipitation and Snow in inches

Population: 264,806 (1990); 257,555 (2000); 249,517 (2005); 241,436 (2010 projected); Race: 80.8% White, 15.6% Black, 0.7% Asian, 3.0% Hispanic of any race (2005); Density: 600.9 persons per square mile (2005); Average household size: 2.47 (2005); Median age: 40.5 (2005); Males per 100 females: 91.9 (2005).
Religion: Five largest groups: 39.0% Catholic Church, 3.5% The United Methodist Church, 3.2% Evangelical Lutheran Church in America, 2.9% Assemblies of God, 2.7% Presbyterian Church (U.S.A.) (2000).
Economy: Unemployment rate: 6.9% (2005); Total civilian labor force: 118,217 (2005); Leading industries: 20.6% health care and social assistance; 16.4% retail trade; 11.1% manufacturing (2004); Farms: 652 totaling 76,543 acres (2002); Companies that employ 500 or more persons: 4 (2004); Companies that employ 100 to 499 persons: 125 (2004); Companies that employ less than 100 persons: 6,210 (2004); Black-owned businesses: 379 (2002); Hispanic-owned businesses: n/a (2002); Women-owned businesses: 4,231 (2002); Retail sales per capita: $15,280 (2006). Single-family building permits issued: 511 (2005); Multi-family building permits issued: 0 (2005).
Income: Per capita income: $21,189 (2005); Median household income: $39,680 (2005); Average household income: $51,584 (2005); Percent of households with income of $100,000 or more: 10.4% (2005); Poverty rate: 12.9% (2003); Bankruptcy rate: 15.79% (2005).
Taxes: Total county taxes per capita: $277 (2004); County property taxes per capita: $84 (2004).
Education: Percent of population age 25 and over with: High school diploma (including GED) or higher: 82.6% (2005); Bachelor's degree or higher: 17.6% (2005); Master's degree or higher: 5.7% (2005).
Housing: Homeownership rate: 73.2% (2005); Median home value: $95,309 (2005); Median rent: $372 per month (2000); Median age of housing: 43 years (2000).
Health: Birth rate: 90.3 per 10,000 population (2004); Death rate: 104.9 per 10,000 population (2004); Age-adjusted cancer mortality rate: 201.5 deaths per 100,000 population (2002); Air Quality Index: 63.0% good, 34.8% moderate, 2.2% unhealthy for sensitive individuals, 0.0% unhealthy (percent of days in 2005); Number of physicians: 34.6 per 10,000 population (2004); Hospital beds: 35.8 per 10,000 population (2003); Hospital admissions: 1,648.7 per 10,000 population (2003).
Elections: 2004 Presidential election results: 36.7% Bush, 62.6% Kerry, 0.0% Nader, 0.4% Badnarik

Additional Information Contacts
Mahoning County Government . . . . (330) 740-2130
 http://www.mahoningcountyoh.gov
City of Campbell . . . . (330) 755-1451
 http://cityofcampbellohio.org
City of Canfield . . . . (330) 533-1101
 http://www.ci.canfield.oh.us
City of Youngstown . . . . (330) 742-8701
 http://www.cityofyoungstownoh.org
Village of Sebring . . . . (330) 938-9340
 http://www.sebringohio.net
Youngstown Chamber of Commerce . . . . (330) 744-2131
 http://www.regionalchamber.com

Mahoning County Communities

AUSTINTOWN (CDP). Covers a land area of 11.673 square miles and a water area of 0 square miles. Located at 41.09° N. Lat.; 80.73° W. Long. Elevation is 1,030 feet.
Population: 32,371 (1990); 31,627 (2000); 29,963 (2005); 28,400 (2010 projected); Race: 91.8% White, 5.3% Black, 0.9% Asian, 1.9% Hispanic of any race (2005); Density: 2,566.8 persons per square mile (2005); Average household size: 2.32 (2005); Median age: 41.2 (2005); Males per 100 females: 90.9 (2005); Marriage status: 24.8% never married, 55.5% now married, 8.5% widowed, 11.2% divorced (2000); Foreign born: 2.3% (2000); Ancestry (includes multiple ancestries): 26.1% German, 19.3% Italian, 17.8% Irish, 9.3% Other groups, 9.2% English (2000).
Economy: Employment by occupation: 8.1% management, 16.8% professional, 15.3% services, 29.4% sales, 0.0% farming, 8.1% construction, 22.2% production (2000).
Income: Per capita income: $21,427 (2005); Median household income: $41,645 (2005); Average household income: $49,004 (2005); Percent of households with income of $100,000 or more: 7.7% (2005); Poverty rate: 8.8% (2000).
Education: Percent of population age 25 and over with: High school diploma (including GED) or higher: 85.3% (2005); Bachelor's degree or higher: 15.7% (2005); Master's degree or higher: 4.3% (2005).
Housing: Homeownership rate: 67.0% (2005); Median home value: $100,594 (2005); Median rent: $422 per month (2000); Median age of housing: 34 years (2000).
Transportation: Commute to work: 97.8% car, 0.4% public transportation, 0.7% walk, 0.7% work from home (2000); Travel time to work: 30.9% less than 15 minutes, 51.6% 15 to 30 minutes, 9.6% 30 to 45 minutes, 3.2% 45 to 60 minutes, 4.8% 60 minutes or more (2000)

BELOIT (village). Covers a land area of 0.768 square miles and a water area of 0 square miles. Located at 40.92° N. Lat.; 80.99° W. Long. Elevation is 1,132 feet.
Population: 1,037 (1990); 1,024 (2000); 987 (2005); 971 (2010 projected); Race: 98.3% White, 0.3% Black, 0.1% Asian, 0.3% Hispanic of any race (2005); Density: 1,284.8 persons per square mile (2005); Average household size: 2.35 (2005); Median age: 40.7 (2005); Males per 100 females: 85.2 (2005); Marriage status: 19.5% never married, 58.0% now married, 10.4% widowed, 12.1% divorced (2000); Foreign born: 0.0% (2000); Ancestry (includes multiple ancestries): 26.0% German, 16.3% English, 14.7% United States or American, 11.2% Irish, 6.0% Other groups (2000).

Economy: Fire-clay mines. Employment by occupation: 4.7% management, 16.7% professional, 18.2% services, 20.3% sales, 0.0% farming, 6.2% construction, 33.8% production (2000).
Income: Per capita income: $20,686 (2005); Median household income: $38,803 (2005); Average household income: $48,613 (2005); Percent of households with income of $100,000 or more: 6.7% (2005); Poverty rate: 10.6% (2000).
Education: Percent of population age 25 and over with: High school diploma (including GED) or higher: 78.9% (2005); Bachelor's degree or higher: 9.3% (2005); Master's degree or higher: 2.9% (2005).

School District(s)
West Branch Local SD (PK-12)
 2003-04 Enrollment: 2,443 . . . . (330) 938-9324
Housing: Homeownership rate: 73.8% (2005); Median home value: $70,417 (2005); Median rent: $281 per month (2000); Median age of housing: 47 years (2000).
Transportation: Commute to work: 94.2% car, 0.0% public transportation, 3.3% walk, 0.9% work from home (2000); Travel time to work: 35.5% less than 15 minutes, 41.5% 15 to 30 minutes, 12.3% 30 to 45 minutes, 7.4% 45 to 60 minutes, 3.3% 60 minutes or more (2000)

BERLIN CENTER (unincorporated postal area, zip code 44401).
Covers a land area of 33.918 square miles and a water area of 0.059 square miles. Located at 41.03° N. Lat.; 80.95° W. Long. Elevation is 1,075 feet.
Population: 3,175 (2000); Race: 98.5% White, 0.0% Black, 0.2% Asian, 0.6% Hispanic of any race (2000); Density: 93.6 persons per square mile (2000); Age: 23.3% under 18, 10.7% over 64 (2000); Marriage status: 21.8% never married, 67.5% now married, 3.2% widowed, 7.6% divorced (2000); Foreign born: 2.8% (2000); Ancestry (includes multiple ancestries): 28.6% German, 15.0% Irish, 12.1% English, 11.8% Italian, 8.6% United States or American (2000).
Economy: Employment by occupation: 7.6% management, 15.4% professional, 11.9% services, 25.2% sales, 0.0% farming, 14.6% construction, 25.4% production (2000).
Income: Per capita income: $21,577 (2000); Median household income: $50,868 (2000); Poverty rate: 4.8% (2000).
Education: Percent of population age 25 and over with: High school diploma (including GED) or higher: 84.5% (2000); Bachelor's degree or higher: 14.7% (2000).

School District(s)
Western Reserve Local SD (PK-12)
 2003-04 Enrollment: 820 . . . . (330) 547-4100
Housing: Homeownership rate: 89.1% (2000); Median home value: $119,700 (2000); Median rent: $343 per month (2000); Median age of housing: 30 years (2000).
Transportation: Commute to work: 95.7% car, 0.0% public transportation, 0.8% walk, 2.8% work from home (2000); Travel time to work: 19.3% less than 15 minutes, 41.6% 15 to 30 minutes, 25.9% 30 to 45 minutes, 6.1% 45 to 60 minutes, 7.1% 60 minutes or more (2000)

BOARDMAN (CDP). Covers a land area of 15.933 square miles and a water area of 0.101 square miles. Located at 41.03° N. Lat.; 80.66° W. Long. Elevation is 1,110 feet.
History: Though the northern areas of town are suburban spillover from Youngstown, Boardman was traditionally an agricultural community with grain crops and apple orchards. The Ohio Southern railroad cut through the township and around 1900 even led to Southern Park, a horse racing facility on Washington Boulevard. Thus, the area was an early draw for Youngstown urbanites. Because of its agricultural nature, Boardman was ripe for strip development starting as early as 1950. Boardman is also the birthplace of former Cleveland Browns quarterback Bernie Kosar, whose eight-year career with the Browns made him one of the most popular football players in Ohio history.
Population: 38,727 (1990); 37,215 (2000); 35,416 (2005); 33,806 (2010 projected); Race: 94.4% White, 2.8% Black, 1.2% Asian, 1.9% Hispanic of any race (2005); Density: 2,222.9 persons per square mile (2005); Average household size: 2.30 (2005); Median age: 43.3 (2005); Males per 100 females: 88.5 (2005); Marriage status: 23.7% never married, 55.6% now married, 10.7% widowed, 10.0% divorced (2000); Foreign born: 3.0% (2000); Ancestry (includes multiple ancestries): 26.5% Italian, 20.8% German, 17.7% Irish, 9.6% English, 9.5% Slovak (2000).
Economy: Employment by occupation: 14.0% management, 20.0% professional, 14.5% services, 30.5% sales, 0.0% farming, 7.0% construction, 14.0% production (2000).
Income: Per capita income: $25,074 (2005); Median household income: $45,326 (2005); Average household income: $56,963 (2005); Percent of households with income of $100,000 or more: 11.9% (2005); Poverty rate: 5.2% (2000).
Education: Percent of population age 25 and over with: High school diploma (including GED) or higher: 89.1% (2005); Bachelor's degree or higher: 24.4% (2005); Master's degree or higher: 7.7% (2005).

Two-year College(s)
Raphaels School of Beauty Culture Inc (Private, For-profit)
 Fall 2004 Enrollment: 63 . . . . (330) 782-3395
Housing: Homeownership rate: 71.2% (2005); Median home value: $116,592 (2005); Median rent: $423 per month (2000); Median age of housing: 36 years (2000).
Safety: Violent crime rate: 8.9 per 10,000 population; Property crime rate: 288.3 per 10,000 population (2004).
Newspapers: Boardman News (General - Circulation 10,000)
Transportation: Commute to work: 96.9% car, 0.3% public transportation, 0.6% walk, 2.1% work from home (2000); Travel time to work: 37.3% less than 15 minutes, 41.6% 15 to 30 minutes, 13.9% 30 to 45 minutes, 2.4% 45 to 60 minutes, 4.8% 60 minutes or more (2000)

CAMPBELL (city). Covers a land area of 3.729 square miles and a water area of 0 square miles. Located at 41.07° N. Lat.; 80.59° W. Long. Elevation is 1,100 feet.
History: Until 1926, called East Youngstown.
Population: 10,038 (1990); 9,460 (2000); 8,838 (2005); 8,226 (2010 projected); Race: 76.3% White, 17.1% Black, 0.4% Asian, 11.4% Hispanic of any race (2005); Density: 2,370.0 persons per square mile (2005); Average household size: 2.51 (2005); Median age: 39.7 (2005); Males per 100 females: 86.8 (2005); Marriage status: 28.8% never married, 51.4% now married, 11.4% widowed, 8.4% divorced (2000); Foreign born: 6.2% (2000); Ancestry (includes multiple ancestries): 26.6% Other groups, 18.8% Italian, 12.8% Slovak, 10.4% Greek, 9.9% Irish (2000).
Economy: Single-family building permits issued: 0 (2005); Multi-family building permits issued: 0 (2005); Employment by occupation: 5.6% management, 11.7% professional, 18.7% services, 27.3% sales, 0.2% farming, 10.6% construction, 25.9% production (2000).
Income: Per capita income: $18,359 (2005); Median household income: $34,025 (2005); Average household income: $46,134 (2005); Percent of households with income of $100,000 or more: 6.7% (2005); Poverty rate: 18.3% (2000).
Education: Percent of population age 25 and over with: High school diploma (including GED) or higher: 75.2% (2005); Bachelor's degree or higher: 9.8% (2005); Master's degree or higher: 3.8% (2005).

School District(s)
Campbell City SD (PK-12)
 2003-04 Enrollment: 1,579 . . . . (330) 799-8777
Housing: Homeownership rate: 75.2% (2005); Median home value: $70,351 (2005); Median rent: $330 per month (2000); Median age of housing: 46 years (2000).
Transportation: Commute to work: 97.0% car, 0.2% public transportation, 0.8% walk, 1.7% work from home (2000); Travel time to work: 33.8% less than 15 minutes, 45.9% 15 to 30 minutes, 13.7% 30 to 45 minutes, 2.7% 45 to 60 minutes, 3.9% 60 minutes or more (2000)
Additional Information Contacts
City of Campbell. . . . . (330) 755-1451
 http://cityofcampbellohio.org

CANFIELD (city). Covers a land area of 4.643 square miles and a water area of 0 square miles. Located at 41.03° N. Lat.; 80.76° W. Long. Elevation is 1,161 feet.
History: Canfield was surveyed in 1798. After a brief oil boom, the town turned to lumber, clay, coal, and farm products for its revenue source.
Population: 5,577 (1990); 7,374 (2000); 7,056 (2005); 6,713 (2010 projected); Race: 96.3% White, 0.5% Black, 2.1% Asian, 0.7% Hispanic of any race (2005); Density: 1,519.6 persons per square mile (2005); Average household size: 2.48 (2005); Median age: 43.5 (2005); Males per 100 females: 90.7 (2005); Marriage status: 19.1% never married, 66.9% now married, 8.3% widowed, 5.8% divorced (2000); Foreign born: 2.8% (2000); Ancestry (includes multiple ancestries): 27.0% German, 23.1% Italian, 17.3% Irish, 12.5% English, 9.9% Slovak (2000).
Economy: Employment by occupation: 20.3% management, 25.7% professional, 12.2% services, 28.2% sales, 0.0% farming, 4.6% construction, 9.1% production (2000).

Income: Per capita income: $35,666 (2005); Median household income: $67,551 (2005); Average household income: $88,458 (2005); Percent of households with income of $100,000 or more: 30.6% (2005); Poverty rate: 3.2% (2000).
Education: Percent of population age 25 and over with: High school diploma (including GED) or higher: 93.9% (2005); Bachelor's degree or higher: 40.6% (2005); Master's degree or higher: 16.5% (2005).

School District(s)
Canfield Local SD (PK-12)
　2003-04 Enrollment: 3,097 . . . . (330) 533-3303
Mahoning Cty Career & Tech Ctr (11-12)
　2003-04 Enrollment: n/a . . . . (330) 729-4000

Two-year College(s)
Mahoning County Career and Technical Center (Public)
　Fall 2004 Enrollment: 19 . . . . (330) 729-4100
　2005-06 Tuition: In-state $4,000; Out-of-state $4,000

Housing: Homeownership rate: 83.6% (2005); Median home value: $167,448 (2005); Median rent: $445 per month (2000); Median age of housing: 31 years (2000).
Safety: Violent crime rate: 2.8 per 10,000 population; Property crime rate: 145.8 per 10,000 population (2004).
Transportation: Commute to work: 94.2% car, 0.2% public transportation, 0.7% walk, 4.2% work from home (2000); Travel time to work: 29.1% less than 15 minutes, 47.7% 15 to 30 minutes, 14.7% 30 to 45 minutes, 4.4% 45 to 60 minutes, 4.1% 60 minutes or more (2000)

Additional Information Contacts
City of Canfield. . . . . (330) 533-1101
　http://www.ci.canfield.oh.us

CRAIG BEACH
(village). Covers a land area of 0.929 square miles and a water area of 0.758 square miles. Located at 41.11° N. Lat.; 80.98° W. Long. Elevation is 975 feet.
Population: 1,402 (1990); 1,254 (2000); 1,293 (2005); 1,331 (2010 projected); Race: 97.4% White, 0.2% Black, 0.6% Asian, 0.7% Hispanic of any race (2005); Density: 1,392.3 persons per square mile (2005); Average household size: 2.51 (2005); Median age: 38.4 (2005); Males per 100 females: 93.9 (2005); Marriage status: 26.9% never married, 51.5% now married, 7.9% widowed, 13.7% divorced (2000); Foreign born: 1.1% (2000); Ancestry (includes multiple ancestries): 24.4% German, 19.1% Irish, 9.7% English, 9.1% Italian, 7.1% United States or American (2000).
Economy: Employment by occupation: 7.3% management, 10.3% professional, 16.8% services, 22.4% sales, 0.3% farming, 14.1% construction, 28.8% production (2000).
Income: Per capita income: $20,895 (2005); Median household income: $44,919 (2005); Average household income: $52,340 (2005); Percent of households with income of $100,000 or more: 10.1% (2005); Poverty rate: 13.0% (2000).
Education: Percent of population age 25 and over with: High school diploma (including GED) or higher: 80.7% (2005); Bachelor's degree or higher: 8.3% (2005); Master's degree or higher: 2.1% (2005).
Housing: Homeownership rate: 75.9% (2005); Median home value: $93,049 (2005); Median rent: $400 per month (2000); Median age of housing: 41 years (2000).
Transportation: Commute to work: 96.1% car, 0.0% public transportation, 1.1% walk, 1.2% work from home (2000); Travel time to work: 15.3% less than 15 minutes, 32.7% 15 to 30 minutes, 30.1% 30 to 45 minutes, 14.1% 45 to 60 minutes, 7.8% 60 minutes or more (2000)

LAKE MILTON
(unincorporated postal area, zip code 44429). Covers a land area of 7.097 square miles and a water area of 0 square miles. Located at 41.10° N. Lat.; 80.98° W. Long. Elevation is 990 feet.
History: Incorporated 1930, disincorporated 1947.
Population: 2,884 (2000); Race: 98.1% White, 0.3% Black, 0.2% Asian, 1.2% Hispanic of any race (2000); Density: 406.4 persons per square mile (2000); Age: 23.9% under 18, 10.2% over 64 (2000); Marriage status: 25.5% never married, 57.0% now married, 6.7% widowed, 10.7% divorced (2000); Foreign born: 1.5% (2000); Ancestry (includes multiple ancestries): 23.3% German, 15.1% Irish, 12.4% United States or American, 11.2% English, 10.7% Italian (2000).
Economy: Employment by occupation: 6.8% management, 14.6% professional, 13.6% services, 26.2% sales, 0.1% farming, 12.8% construction, 25.9% production (2000).
Income: Per capita income: $17,000 (2000); Median household income: $39,816 (2000); Poverty rate: 12.2% (2000).

Education: Percent of population age 25 and over with: High school diploma (including GED) or higher: 82.5% (2000); Bachelor's degree or higher: 10.0% (2000).

Two-year College(s)
TDDS Technical Institute
　Fall 2004 Enrollment: 591 . . . . (330) 538-2216

Housing: Homeownership rate: 81.5% (2000); Median home value: $86,900 (2000); Median rent: $406 per month (2000); Median age of housing: 40 years (2000).
Transportation: Commute to work: 92.6% car, 0.2% public transportation, 3.8% walk, 2.7% work from home (2000); Travel time to work: 21.6% less than 15 minutes, 30.3% 15 to 30 minutes, 24.5% 30 to 45 minutes, 12.7% 45 to 60 minutes, 10.9% 60 minutes or more (2000)

LOWELLVILLE
(village). Covers a land area of 1.437 square miles and a water area of 0 square miles. Located at 41.04° N. Lat.; 80.54° W. Long. Elevation is 850 feet.
History: Lowellville was settled in 1800 and incorporated in 1836. First a coal town, after 1845 the economy depended more on iron and steel.
Population: 1,349 (1990); 1,281 (2000); 1,168 (2005); 1,058 (2010 projected); Race: 99.1% White, 0.1% Black, 0.0% Asian, 1.8% Hispanic of any race (2005); Density: 812.8 persons per square mile (2005); Average household size: 2.41 (2005); Median age: 39.2 (2005); Males per 100 females: 91.2 (2005); Marriage status: 21.7% never married, 56.3% now married, 12.0% widowed, 10.0% divorced (2000); Foreign born: 2.1% (2000); Ancestry (includes multiple ancestries): 48.0% Italian, 18.6% German, 17.9% Irish, 7.8% Slovak, 5.4% English (2000).
Economy: Single-family building permits issued: 0 (2005); Multi-family building permits issued: 0 (2005); Employment by occupation: 10.6% management, 11.0% professional, 17.7% services, 24.8% sales, 0.0% farming, 10.6% construction, 25.2% production (2000).
Income: Per capita income: $16,888 (2005); Median household income: $33,403 (2005); Average household income: $40,670 (2005); Percent of households with income of $100,000 or more: 3.7% (2005); Poverty rate: 9.4% (2000).
Education: Percent of population age 25 and over with: High school diploma (including GED) or higher: 79.3% (2005); Bachelor's degree or higher: 8.2% (2005); Master's degree or higher: 3.1% (2005).

School District(s)
Lowellville Local SD (PK-12)
　2003-04 Enrollment: 651 . . . . (330) 536-6318

Housing: Homeownership rate: 77.1% (2005); Median home value: $73,333 (2005); Median rent: $285 per month (2000); Median age of housing: 60+ years (2000).
Transportation: Commute to work: 92.2% car, 0.0% public transportation, 5.0% walk, 1.0% work from home (2000); Travel time to work: 33.9% less than 15 minutes, 40.0% 15 to 30 minutes, 17.9% 30 to 45 minutes, 2.8% 45 to 60 minutes, 5.3% 60 minutes or more (2000)

MAPLE RIDGE
(CDP). Covers a land area of 2.011 square miles and a water area of 0 square miles. Located at 40.91° N. Lat.; 81.04° W. Long. Elevation is 1,104 feet.
Population: 1,018 (1990); 910 (2000); 889 (2005); 871 (2010 projected); Race: 98.7% White, 0.8% Black, 0.4% Asian, 0.3% Hispanic of any race (2005); Density: 442.1 persons per square mile (2005); Average household size: 2.51 (2005); Median age: 41.2 (2005); Males per 100 females: 92.0 (2005); Marriage status: 18.6% never married, 58.6% now married, 7.5% widowed, 15.3% divorced (2000); Foreign born: 0.0% (2000); Ancestry (includes multiple ancestries): 29.0% German, 19.6% Irish, 12.0% Italian, 10.1% United States or American, 9.6% English (2000).
Economy: Employment by occupation: 1.4% management, 7.2% professional, 22.8% services, 15.6% sales, 0.0% farming, 11.1% construction, 41.9% production (2000).
Income: Per capita income: $17,714 (2005); Median household income: $32,885 (2005); Average household income: $44,484 (2005); Percent of households with income of $100,000 or more: 5.4% (2005); Poverty rate: 5.8% (2000).
Education: Percent of population age 25 and over with: High school diploma (including GED) or higher: 73.6% (2005); Bachelor's degree or higher: 1.8% (2005); Master's degree or higher: 1.8% (2005).
Housing: Homeownership rate: 90.1% (2005); Median home value: $59,041 (2005); Median rent: $n/a per month (2000); Median age of housing: 48 years (2000).
Transportation: Commute to work: 100.0% car, 0.0% public transportation, 0.0% walk, 0.0% work from home (2000); Travel time to

work: 53.2% less than 15 minutes, 33.4% 15 to 30 minutes, 7.8% 30 to 45 minutes, 2.9% 45 to 60 minutes, 2.6% 60 minutes or more (2000)

NEW MIDDLETOWN (village). Covers a land area of 0.871 square miles and a water area of 0 square miles. Located at 40.96° N. Lat.; 80.55° W. Long. Elevation is 1,253 feet.
Population: 1,966 (1990); 1,682 (2000); 1,727 (2005); 1,767 (2010 projected); Race: 99.2% White, 0.1% Black, 0.0% Asian, 0.8% Hispanic of any race (2005); Density: 1,983.7 persons per square mile (2005); Average household size: 2.39 (2005); Median age: 42.1 (2005); Males per 100 females: 84.1 (2005); Marriage status: 20.7% never married, 63.2% now married, 9.1% widowed, 7.0% divorced (2000); Foreign born: 1.1% (2000); Ancestry (includes multiple ancestries): 30.5% German, 16.6% Italian, 15.8% Irish, 11.7% English, 8.0% Slovak (2000).
Economy: Employment by occupation: 7.7% management, 15.1% professional, 17.9% services, 28.8% sales, 0.0% farming, 12.1% construction, 18.4% production (2000).
Income: Per capita income: $21,720 (2005); Median household income: $39,246 (2005); Average household income: $51,881 (2005); Percent of households with income of $100,000 or more: 10.2% (2005); Poverty rate: 7.7% (2000).
Education: Percent of population age 25 and over with: High school diploma (including GED) or higher: 85.8% (2005); Bachelor's degree or higher: 11.3% (2005); Master's degree or higher: 3.7% (2005).
School District(s)
Springfield Local SD (PK-12)
   2003-04 Enrollment: 1,233 . . . . (330) 542-2929
Housing: Homeownership rate: 76.5% (2005); Median home value: $115,214 (2005); Median rent: $358 per month (2000); Median age of housing: 35 years (2000).
Safety: Violent crime rate: 6.1 per 10,000 population; Property crime rate: 151.8 per 10,000 population (2004).
Transportation: Commute to work: 98.0% car, 0.0% public transportation, 0.6% walk, 1.1% work from home (2000); Travel time to work: 26.6% less than 15 minutes, 42.8% 15 to 30 minutes, 17.1% 30 to 45 minutes, 6.9% 45 to 60 minutes, 6.6% 60 minutes or more (2000)

NEW SPRINGFIELD (unincorporated postal area, zip code 44443). Covers a land area of 14.009 square miles and a water area of 0 square miles. Located at 40.91° N. Lat.; 80.60° W. Long. Elevation is 1,211 feet.
Population: 2,055 (2000); Race: 98.3% White, 1.3% Black, 0.0% Asian, 1.4% Hispanic of any race (2000); Density: 146.7 persons per square mile (2000); Age: 22.4% under 18, 17.4% over 64 (2000); Marriage status: 24.7% never married, 61.9% now married, 6.5% widowed, 6.9% divorced (2000); Foreign born: 0.0% (2000); Ancestry (includes multiple ancestries): 38.6% German, 12.3% English, 10.9% Irish, 9.6% Italian, 7.7% Slovak (2000).
Economy: Employment by occupation: 10.7% management, 16.9% professional, 11.0% services, 29.9% sales, 2.3% farming, 11.1% construction, 18.0% production (2000).
Income: Per capita income: $20,158 (2000); Median household income: $35,375 (2000); Poverty rate: 5.9% (2000).
Education: Percent of population age 25 and over with: High school diploma (including GED) or higher: 88.2% (2000); Bachelor's degree or higher: 14.7% (2000).
Housing: Homeownership rate: 82.9% (2000); Median home value: $106,100 (2000); Median rent: $345 per month (2000); Median age of housing: 35 years (2000).
Transportation: Commute to work: 86.7% car, 0.0% public transportation, 7.1% walk, 4.4% work from home (2000); Travel time to work: 30.9% less than 15 minutes, 41.4% 15 to 30 minutes, 17.6% 30 to 45 minutes, 6.1% 45 to 60 minutes, 4.0% 60 minutes or more (2000)

NORTH BENTON (unincorporated postal area, zip code 44449). Covers a land area of 11.222 square miles and a water area of 0.081 square miles. Located at 40.99° N. Lat.; 81.02° W. Long. Elevation is 1,080 feet.
Population: 1,305 (2000); Race: 100.0% White, 0.0% Black, 0.0% Asian, 0.6% Hispanic of any race (2000); Density: 116.3 persons per square mile (2000); Age: 25.2% under 18, 10.8% over 64 (2000); Marriage status: 19.2% never married, 62.7% now married, 4.1% widowed, 14.0% divorced (2000); Foreign born: 0.0% (2000); Ancestry (includes multiple ancestries): 19.6% United States or American, 19.4% German, 16.7% Irish, 7.4% English, 5.6% Other groups (2000).
Economy: Employment by occupation: 11.7% management, 14.7% professional, 10.8% services, 17.0% sales, 0.0% farming, 13.7% construction, 32.2% production (2000).
Income: Per capita income: $18,716 (2000); Median household income: $42,355 (2000); Poverty rate: 12.0% (2000).
Education: Percent of population age 25 and over with: High school diploma (including GED) or higher: 74.8% (2000); Bachelor's degree or higher: 11.1% (2000).
Housing: Homeownership rate: 84.5% (2000); Median home value: $115,100 (2000); Median rent: $289 per month (2000); Median age of housing: 35 years (2000).
Transportation: Commute to work: 97.6% car, 0.0% public transportation, 0.0% walk, 2.4% work from home (2000); Travel time to work: 11.4% less than 15 minutes, 36.4% 15 to 30 minutes, 33.0% 30 to 45 minutes, 16.0% 45 to 60 minutes, 3.2% 60 minutes or more (2000)

NORTH JACKSON (unincorporated postal area, zip code 44451). Covers a land area of 36.720 square miles and a water area of 0.152 square miles. Located at 41.09° N. Lat.; 80.86° W. Long. Elevation is 1,030 feet.
Population: 3,101 (2000); Race: 99.2% White, 0.3% Black, 0.2% Asian, 1.0% Hispanic of any race (2000); Density: 84.4 persons per square mile (2000); Age: 24.2% under 18, 10.1% over 64 (2000); Marriage status: 23.1% never married, 62.6% now married, 5.7% widowed, 8.6% divorced (2000); Foreign born: 1.8% (2000); Ancestry (includes multiple ancestries): 28.2% German, 20.3% Irish, 13.2% Italian, 9.2% United States or American, 9.0% English (2000).
Economy: Employment by occupation: 8.0% management, 15.1% professional, 9.7% services, 27.7% sales, 0.3% farming, 11.5% construction, 27.7% production (2000).
Income: Per capita income: $19,489 (2000); Median household income: $46,541 (2000); Poverty rate: 4.5% (2000).
Education: Percent of population age 25 and over with: High school diploma (including GED) or higher: 87.1% (2000); Bachelor's degree or higher: 15.9% (2000).
School District(s)
Jackson-Milton Local SD (PK-12)
   2003-04 Enrollment: 890 . . . . (330) 538-3232
Western Reserve Local SD (PK-12)
   2003-04 Enrollment: 820 . . . . (330) 547-4100
Housing: Homeownership rate: 83.2% (2000); Median home value: $120,300 (2000); Median rent: $357 per month (2000); Median age of housing: 37 years (2000).
Transportation: Commute to work: 93.3% car, 0.0% public transportation, 4.5% walk, 2.2% work from home (2000); Travel time to work: 29.5% less than 15 minutes, 39.2% 15 to 30 minutes, 20.9% 30 to 45 minutes, 4.7% 45 to 60 minutes, 5.7% 60 minutes or more (2000)

NORTH LIMA (unincorporated postal area, zip code 44452). Covers a land area of 14.674 square miles and a water area of 0 square miles. Located at 40.95° N. Lat.; 80.65° W. Long. Elevation is 1,103 feet.
Population: 2,724 (2000); Race: 97.9% White, 1.8% Black, 0.0% Asian, 2.6% Hispanic of any race (2000); Density: 185.6 persons per square mile (2000); Age: 26.1% under 18, 16.9% over 64 (2000); Marriage status: 24.4% never married, 60.3% now married, 6.5% widowed, 8.8% divorced (2000); Foreign born: 1.1% (2000); Ancestry (includes multiple ancestries): 30.2% German, 19.0% Irish, 17.9% Italian, 8.2% United States or American, 7.4% Polish (2000).
Economy: Employment by occupation: 9.2% management, 13.1% professional, 22.4% services, 23.8% sales, 1.1% farming, 12.9% construction, 17.4% production (2000).
Income: Per capita income: $16,355 (2000); Median household income: $43,232 (2000); Poverty rate: 4.3% (2000).
Education: Percent of population age 25 and over with: High school diploma (including GED) or higher: 80.9% (2000); Bachelor's degree or higher: 19.3% (2000).
School District(s)
South Range Local SD (PK-12)
   2003-04 Enrollment: 1,318 . . . . (330) 549-5226
Two-year College(s)
Tri-State College of Massotherapy
   Fall 2004 Enrollment: 65 . . . . (330) 629-9998
   2005-06 Tuition: In-state $7,500; Out-of-state $7,500

Housing: Homeownership rate: 85.5% (2000); Median home value: $104,600 (2000); Median rent: $331 per month (2000); Median age of housing: 40 years (2000).
Transportation: Commute to work: 95.7% car, 0.0% public transportation, 1.8% walk, 2.5% work from home (2000); Travel time to work: 41.1% less than 15 minutes, 39.0% 15 to 30 minutes, 13.8% 30 to 45 minutes, 2.8% 45 to 60 minutes, 3.3% 60 minutes or more (2000)

PETERSBURG
(unincorporated postal area, zip code 44454). Covers a land area of 7.133 square miles and a water area of 0 square miles. Located at 40.91° N. Lat.; 80.53° W. Long. Elevation is 1,130 feet.
Population: 1,277 (2000); Race: 100.0% White, 0.0% Black, 0.0% Asian, 0.0% Hispanic of any race (2000); Density: 179.0 persons per square mile (2000); Age: 29.8% under 18, 4.6% over 64 (2000); Marriage status: 22.6% never married, 66.6% now married, 3.5% widowed, 7.3% divorced (2000); Foreign born: 1.0% (2000); Ancestry (includes multiple ancestries): 28.3% German, 22.7% English, 15.5% Irish, 12.5% Italian, 6.7% Welsh (2000).
Economy: Employment by occupation: 5.5% management, 18.7% professional, 12.6% services, 22.0% sales, 0.0% farming, 14.0% construction, 27.1% production (2000).
Income: Per capita income: $18,497 (2000); Median household income: $43,967 (2000); Poverty rate: 4.6% (2000).
Education: Percent of population age 25 and over with: High school diploma (including GED) or higher: 86.5% (2000); Bachelor's degree or higher: 16.1% (2000).
Housing: Homeownership rate: 86.2% (2000); Median home value: $87,800 (2000); Median rent: $250 per month (2000); Median age of housing: 32 years (2000).
Transportation: Commute to work: 93.0% car, 0.0% public transportation, 2.1% walk, 4.9% work from home (2000); Travel time to work: 19.9% less than 15 minutes, 37.2% 15 to 30 minutes, 33.3% 30 to 45 minutes, 2.2% 45 to 60 minutes, 7.3% 60 minutes or more (2000)

POLAND
(village). Covers a land area of 1.244 square miles and a water area of 0 square miles. Located at 41.02° N. Lat.; 80.61° W. Long. Elevation is 1,050 feet.
History: Poland was settled in 1799 by Jonathan Fowler, and originally named for him. Fowler operated the Stone Tavern, a stop on the Pittsburgh to Cleveland stage route. The town became a residential suburb of Youngstown.
Population: 2,992 (1990); 2,866 (2000); 2,747 (2005); 2,627 (2010 projected); Race: 99.1% White, 0.3% Black, 0.1% Asian, 1.1% Hispanic of any race (2005); Density: 2,207.6 persons per square mile (2005); Average household size: 2.59 (2005); Median age: 43.7 (2005); Males per 100 females: 92.2 (2005); Marriage status: 18.9% never married, 61.8% now married, 10.8% widowed, 8.6% divorced (2000); Foreign born: 2.9% (2000); Ancestry (includes multiple ancestries): 26.8% Italian, 25.0% German, 21.7% Irish, 13.7% English, 13.0% Slovak (2000).
Economy: Employment by occupation: 13.7% management, 24.7% professional, 7.5% services, 34.5% sales, 0.0% farming, 11.0% construction, 8.6% production (2000).
Income: Per capita income: $27,066 (2005); Median household income: $52,007 (2005); Average household income: $68,857 (2005); Percent of households with income of $100,000 or more: 15.6% (2005); Poverty rate: 6.1% (2000).
Education: Percent of population age 25 and over with: High school diploma (including GED) or higher: 89.9% (2005); Bachelor's degree or higher: 32.6% (2005); Master's degree or higher: 11.5% (2005).
School District(s)
Poland Local SD (PK-12)
    2003-04 Enrollment: 2,514 . . . . (330) 757-7000
Housing: Homeownership rate: 88.5% (2005); Median home value: $136,148 (2005); Median rent: $479 per month (2000); Median age of housing: 47 years (2000).
Safety: Violent crime rate: 0.0 per 10,000 population; Property crime rate: 64.6 per 10,000 population (2004).
Transportation: Commute to work: 96.7% car, 0.0% public transportation, 0.4% walk, 2.3% work from home (2000); Travel time to work: 40.9% less than 15 minutes, 38.1% 15 to 30 minutes, 12.6% 30 to 45 minutes, 2.2% 45 to 60 minutes, 6.1% 60 minutes or more (2000)

SEBRING
(village). Covers a land area of 2.051 square miles and a water area of 0 square miles. Located at 40.92° N. Lat.; 81.02° W. Long. Elevation is 1,100 feet.
Population: 4,848 (1990); 4,912 (2000); 4,598 (2005); 4,292 (2010 projected); Race: 98.0% White, 0.5% Black, 0.3% Asian, 0.8% Hispanic of any race (2005); Density: 2,241.9 persons per square mile (2005); Average household size: 2.30 (2005); Median age: 43.9 (2005); Males per 100 females: 81.6 (2005); Marriage status: 17.0% never married, 54.6% now married, 16.5% widowed, 11.9% divorced (2000); Foreign born: 0.7% (2000); Ancestry (includes multiple ancestries): 21.8% German, 14.3% Irish, 13.0% English, 10.7% United States or American, 7.3% Italian (2000).
Economy: Single-family building permits issued: 4 (2005); Multi-family building permits issued: 0 (2005); Employment by occupation: 8.6% management, 9.4% professional, 14.0% services, 24.7% sales, 0.5% farming, 7.5% construction, 35.3% production (2000).
Income: Per capita income: $18,845 (2005); Median household income: $34,864 (2005); Average household income: $42,118 (2005); Percent of households with income of $100,000 or more: 4.9% (2005); Poverty rate: 10.9% (2000).
Education: Percent of population age 25 and over with: High school diploma (including GED) or higher: 81.8% (2005); Bachelor's degree or higher: 13.5% (2005); Master's degree or higher: 3.7% (2005).
School District(s)
Sebring Local SD (PK-12)
    2003-04 Enrollment: 760 . . . . (330) 938-6165
Housing: Homeownership rate: 54.3% (2005); Median home value: $91,985 (2005); Median rent: $434 per month (2000); Median age of housing: 48 years (2000).
Safety: Violent crime rate: 18.9 per 10,000 population; Property crime rate: 347.1 per 10,000 population (2004).
Transportation: Commute to work: 95.7% car, 0.0% public transportation, 2.4% walk, 0.6% work from home (2000); Travel time to work: 48.4% less than 15 minutes, 25.6% 15 to 30 minutes, 15.1% 30 to 45 minutes, 7.0% 45 to 60 minutes, 3.9% 60 minutes or more (2000)
Additional Information Contacts
Village of Sebring . . . . (330) 938-9340
    http://www.sebringohio.net

STRUTHERS
(city). Covers a land area of 3.732 square miles and a water area of 0.013 square miles. Located at 41.05° N. Lat.; 80.59° W. Long. Elevation is 1,000 feet.
History: Principal steel industry has declined. Founded 1800, incorporated 1922.
Population: 12,284 (1990); 11,756 (2000); 11,159 (2005); 10,543 (2010 projected); Race: 96.9% White, 1.3% Black, 0.3% Asian, 1.9% Hispanic of any race (2005); Density: 2,990.2 persons per square mile (2005); Average household size: 2.46 (2005); Median age: 40.4 (2005); Males per 100 females: 88.8 (2005); Marriage status: 25.3% never married, 54.8% now married, 10.7% widowed, 9.1% divorced (2000); Foreign born: 1.7% (2000); Ancestry (includes multiple ancestries): 28.3% Italian, 20.0% German, 16.1% Slovak, 15.8% Irish, 6.4% Polish (2000).
Economy: Metal manufacturing continues. Employment by occupation: 4.5% management, 14.6% professional, 16.5% services, 29.0% sales, 0.1% farming, 10.4% construction, 24.9% production (2000).
Income: Per capita income: $17,807 (2005); Median household income: $34,468 (2005); Average household income: $43,515 (2005); Percent of households with income of $100,000 or more: 5.4% (2005); Poverty rate: 12.0% (2000).
Education: Percent of population age 25 and over with: High school diploma (including GED) or higher: 80.4% (2005); Bachelor's degree or higher: 10.2% (2005); Master's degree or higher: 2.5% (2005).
School District(s)
Struthers City SD (PK-12)
    2003-04 Enrollment: 2,004 . . . . (330) 750-1061
Two-year College(s)
The Youngstown College of Massotherapy (Private, For-profit)
    Fall 2004 Enrollment: 121 . . . . (330) 755-1406
Housing: Homeownership rate: 77.5% (2005); Median home value: $74,662 (2005); Median rent: $336 per month (2000); Median age of housing: 50 years (2000).
Newspapers: The Journal (General - Circulation 4,100)
Transportation: Commute to work: 96.5% car, 0.4% public transportation, 1.9% walk, 0.7% work from home (2000); Travel time to work: 35.7% less than 15 minutes, 44.6% 15 to 30 minutes, 13.4% 30 to 45 minutes, 2.3% 45 to 60 minutes, 4.0% 60 minutes or more (2000)

YOUNGSTOWN (city). Covers a land area of 33.896 square miles and a water area of 0.350 square miles. Located at 41.09° N. Lat.; 80.64° W. Long. Elevation is 861 feet.

History: Youngstown, established along the Mahoning River, was shaped by the steel industry. In 1797 John Young of New York led a party of settlers to this site. By 1802 James and Daniel Heaton had set up a crude smelter on Yellow Creek, utilizing native bog ores and limestones. The first coal mine in the Mahoning Valley opened in 1826, and Mahoning coal was soon used in the reduction of iron ore. In 1892 the Union Iron & Steel Company built a plant in Youngstown, and the banks of the river were soon lined with Bessemer converters, open-hearth furnaces, strip and rolling mills, pipe plants, and manufactories of steel accessories and products.

Population: 95,732 (1990); 82,026 (2000); 78,288 (2005); 74,582 (2010 projected); Race: 50.4% White, 43.5% Black, 0.5% Asian, 5.4% Hispanic of any race (2005); Density: 2,309.6 persons per square mile (2005); Average household size: 2.52 (2005); Median age: 36.7 (2005); Males per 100 females: 92.9 (2005); Marriage status: 34.0% never married, 42.2% now married, 11.0% widowed, 12.8% divorced (2000); Foreign born: 2.0% (2000); Ancestry (includes multiple ancestries): 42.7% Other groups, 11.2% Italian, 10.3% German, 9.4% Irish, 5.3% Slovak (2000).

Economy: Unemployment rate: 8.7% (2005); Total civilian labor force: 30,249 (2005); Single-family building permits issued: 9 (2005); Multi-family building permits issued: 0 (2005); Employment by occupation: 5.7% management, 13.1% professional, 24.1% services, 25.5% sales, 0.2% farming, 7.2% construction, 24.2% production (2000).

Income: Per capita income: $14,478 (2005); Median household income: $26,488 (2005); Average household income: $34,904 (2005); Percent of households with income of $100,000 or more: 3.9% (2005); Poverty rate: 24.8% (2000).

Taxes: Total city taxes per capita: $529 (2004); City property taxes per capita: $28 (2004).

Education: Percent of population age 25 and over with: High school diploma (including GED) or higher: 73.5% (2005); Bachelor's degree or higher: 9.9% (2005); Master's degree or higher: 2.9% (2005).

School District(s)
Austintown Local SD (PK-12)
   2003-04 Enrollment: 5,046 . . . . (330) 797-3900
Boardman Local SD (PK-12)
   2003-04 Enrollment: 4,897 . . . . (330) 726-3404
Eagle Heights Academy (KG-08)
   2003-04 Enrollment: 898 . . . . (330) 742-9090
Legacy Academy for Leaders & Arts (KG-08)
   2003-04 Enrollment: 259 . . . . (330) 747-1620
Liberty Local SD (PK-12)
   2003-04 Enrollment: 1,819 . . . . (330) 759-0807
Life Skills Center of Youngstown (09-12)
   2003-04 Enrollment: 305 . . . . (330) 743-6698
Mahoning Educational Service Center (03-12)
   2003-04 Enrollment: n/a . . . . (330) 965-7828
Mahoning Unlimited Classroom (04-12)
   2003-04 Enrollment: 113 . . . . (330) 965-7828
Mollie Kessler (01-08)
   2003-04 Enrollment: 55 . . . . (330) 746-3095
Summit Academy High School Youngstown
   2003-04 Enrollment: n/a
Summit Academy-Youngstown (01-08)
   2003-04 Enrollment: 189 . . . . (330) 747-0950
Youngstown City SD (KG-12)
   2003-04 Enrollment: 9,748 . . . . (330) 744-6900
Youngstown Community (KG-05)
   2003-04 Enrollment: 288 . . . . (330) 746-2240

Four-year College(s)
Youngstown State University (Public)
   Fall 2004 Enrollment: 13,157 . . . . (877) 468-6978
   2005-06 Tuition: In-state $6,333; Out-of-state $8,805

Two-year College(s)
Casal Aveda Institute (Private, For-profit)
   Fall 2004 Enrollment: 70 . . . . (330) 792-6504
Choffin Career and Technical Center (Public)
   Fall 2004 Enrollment: 144 . . . . (330) 744-8710
   2005-06 Tuition: In-state $4,500; Out-of-state $4,500
ITT Technical Institute (Private, For-profit)
   Fall 2004 Enrollment: 511 . . . . (330) 270-1600
   2005-06 Tuition: In-state $14,196; Out-of-state $14,196

Housing: Homeownership rate: 64.3% (2005); Median home value: $48,616 (2005); Median rent: $296 per month (2000); Median age of housing: 53 years (2000).

Hospitals: Forum Health - Western Reserve Care System (830 beds); St. Elizabeth Health Center (350 beds)

Safety: Violent crime rate: 92.2 per 10,000 population; Property crime rate: 532.2 per 10,000 population (2004).

Newspapers: Buckeye Review (Black - Circulation 3,000); Catholic Exponent (Catholic, Religious - Circulation 41,300); Daily Legal News (Circulation 1,000); The Jewish Journal (Jewish - Circulation 5,000); The Vindicator (Circulation 67,365)

Transportation: Commute to work: 91.8% car, 2.7% public transportation, 2.6% walk, 1.7% work from home (2000); Travel time to work: 38.4% less than 15 minutes, 43.4% 15 to 30 minutes, 11.0% 30 to 45 minutes, 2.2% 45 to 60 minutes, 5.0% 60 minutes or more (2000)

Additional Information Contacts
City of Youngstown . . . . (330) 742-8701
   http://www.cityofyoungstownoh.org
Youngstown Chamber of Commerce. . . . . (330) 744-2131
   http://www.regionalchamber.com

Marion County

Located in central Ohio; crossed by the Scioto River; drained by the Olentangy and Little Scioto Rivers. Covers a land area of 403.84 square miles, a water area of 0.30 square miles, and is located in the Eastern Time Zone. The county government was organized in 1820. County seat is Marion.

Marion County is part of the Marion, OH Micropolitan Statistical Area. The entire metro area includes: Marion County, OH

Weather Station: Marion 2 N   Elevation: 964 feet

	Jan	Feb	Mar	Apr	May	Jun	Jul	Aug	Sep	Oct	Nov	Dec
High	32	37	47	60	71	80	84	82	76	63	50	38
Low	16	19	28	37	48	58	62	59	52	41	32	23
Precip	2.4	1.7	2.3	3.7	4.2	4.2	4.4	3.7	3.0	2.7	3.0	2.8
Snow	9.7	5.3	3.2	0.6	0.0	0.0	0.0	0.0	0.0	tr	0.8	4.4

High and Low temperatures in degrees Fahrenheit; Precipitation and Snow in inches

Population: 64,274 (1990); 66,217 (2000); 66,570 (2005); 66,915 (2010 projected); Race: 91.9% White, 5.9% Black, 0.6% Asian, 1.3% Hispanic of any race (2005); Density: 164.8 persons per square mile (2005); Average household size: 2.66 (2005); Median age: 37.9 (2005); Males per 100 females: 108.3 (2005).

Religion: Five largest groups: 8.6% The United Methodist Church, 5.7% Evangelical Lutheran Church in America, 4.3% Catholic Church, 2.8% Church of the Nazarene, 2.7% American Baptist Churches in the USA (2000).

Economy: Unemployment rate: 6.2% (2005); Total civilian labor force: 32,177 (2005); Leading industries: 28.5% manufacturing; 18.3% health care and social assistance; 13.0% retail trade (2004); Farms: 520 totaling 205,605 acres (2002); Companies that employ 500 or more persons: 4 (2004); Companies that employ 100 to 499 persons: 38 (2004); Companies that employ less than 100 persons: 1,289 (2004); Black-owned businesses: n/a (2002); Hispanic-owned businesses: n/a (2002); Women-owned businesses: 1,114 (2002); Retail sales per capita: $12,874 (2006). Single-family building permits issued: 182 (2005); Multi-family building permits issued: 60 (2005).

Income: Per capita income: $20,580 (2005); Median household income: $43,555 (2005); Average household income: $52,756 (2005); Percent of households with income of $100,000 or more: 9.4% (2005); Poverty rate: 11.0% (2003); Bankruptcy rate: 11.24% (2005).

Taxes: Total county taxes per capita: $213 (2004); County property taxes per capita: $117 (2004).

Education: Percent of population age 25 and over with: High school diploma (including GED) or higher: 80.4% (2005); Bachelor's degree or higher: 11.3% (2005); Master's degree or higher: 3.9% (2005).

Housing: Homeownership rate: 73.3% (2005); Median home value: $94,403 (2005); Median rent: $379 per month (2000); Median age of housing: 43 years (2000).

Health: Birth rate: 122.3 per 10,000 population (2004); Death rate: 102.2 per 10,000 population (2004); Age-adjusted cancer mortality rate: 224.1 deaths per 100,000 population (2002); Number of physicians: 16.5 per 10,000 population (2004); Hospital beds: 19.8 per 10,000 population (2003); Hospital admissions: 1,552.4 per 10,000 population (2003).

Elections: 2004 Presidential election results: 58.7% Bush, 40.8% Kerry, 0.0% Nader, 0.3% Badnarik

Additional Information Contacts
Marion County Government . . . . (740) 223-4001
  http://www.co.marion.oh.us/
City of Marion . . . . (740) 387-3591
  http://mariononline.com/cityofmarion
Marion Chamber of Commerce . . . . (740) 382-2181
  http://www.marion.net/chamber

Marion County Communities

CALEDONIA (village). Covers a land area of 0.225 square miles and a water area of 0 square miles. Located at 40.63° N. Lat.; 82.96° W. Long. Elevation is 998 feet.
History: Caledonia was the boyhood home of Warren G. Harding, 29th President of the United States.
Population: 644 (1990); 578 (2000); 569 (2005); 564 (2010 projected); Race: 99.5% White, 0.4% Black, 0.0% Asian, 0.5% Hispanic of any race (2005); Density: 2,528.0 persons per square mile (2005); Average household size: 2.46 (2005); Median age: 38.3 (2005); Males per 100 females: 97.6 (2005); Marriage status: 14.7% never married, 68.2% now married, 8.1% widowed, 9.0% divorced (2000); Foreign born: 0.0% (2000); Ancestry (includes multiple ancestries): 23.9% German, 18.1% United States or American, 6.3% English, 3.9% Irish, 2.7% Other groups (2000).
Economy: Single-family building permits issued: 0 (2005); Multi-family building permits issued: 0 (2005); Employment by occupation: 7.1% management, 8.9% professional, 20.8% services, 27.5% sales, 2.2% farming, 6.3% construction, 27.1% production (2000).
Income: Per capita income: $21,213 (2005); Median household income: $45,613 (2005); Average household income: $52,251 (2005); Percent of households with income of $100,000 or more: 11.3% (2005); Poverty rate: 4.9% (2000).
Taxes: Total city taxes per capita: $111 (2004); City property taxes per capita: $85 (2004).
Education: Percent of population age 25 and over with: High school diploma (including GED) or higher: 84.6% (2005); Bachelor's degree or higher: 5.2% (2005); Master's degree or higher: 2.3% (2005).
School District(s)
River Valley Local SD (PK-12)
  2003-04 Enrollment: 1,831 . . . . (740) 725-5400
Housing: Homeownership rate: 82.7% (2005); Median home value: $89,107 (2005); Median rent: $375 per month (2000); Median age of housing: 51 years (2000).
Transportation: Commute to work: 94.3% car, 0.0% public transportation, 3.0% walk, 2.6% work from home (2000); Travel time to work: 27.1% less than 15 minutes, 58.1% 15 to 30 minutes, 9.7% 30 to 45 minutes, 0.8% 45 to 60 minutes, 4.3% 60 minutes or more (2000)

GREEN CAMP (village). Covers a land area of 0.339 square miles and a water area of 0 square miles. Located at 40.53° N. Lat.; 83.20° W. Long. Elevation is 915 feet.
Population: 393 (1990); 342 (2000); 348 (2005); 341 (2010 projected); Race: 100.0% White, 0.0% Black, 0.0% Asian, 0.0% Hispanic of any race (2005); Density: 1,025.4 persons per square mile (2005); Average household size: 2.56 (2005); Median age: 37.0 (2005); Males per 100 females: 107.1 (2005); Marriage status: 21.4% never married, 63.0% now married, 7.5% widowed, 8.2% divorced (2000); Foreign born: 0.6% (2000); Ancestry (includes multiple ancestries): 32.7% United States or American, 26.8% German, 9.4% Irish, 8.8% English, 1.5% Welsh (2000).
Economy: Single-family building permits issued: 0 (2005); Multi-family building permits issued: 0 (2005); Employment by occupation: 5.9% management, 6.4% professional, 15.5% services, 16.0% sales, 1.1% farming, 10.2% construction, 44.9% production (2000).
Income: Per capita income: $19,842 (2005); Median household income: $46,087 (2005); Average household income: $50,772 (2005); Percent of households with income of $100,000 or more: 6.6% (2005); Poverty rate: 9.1% (2000).
Education: Percent of population age 25 and over with: High school diploma (including GED) or higher: 84.6% (2005); Bachelor's degree or higher: 5.3% (2005); Master's degree or higher: 3.1% (2005).
School District(s)
Elgin Local SD (PK-12)
  2003-04 Enrollment: 1,627 . . . . (740) 382-1101
Housing: Homeownership rate: 79.4% (2005); Median home value: $82,667 (2005); Median rent: $378 per month (2000); Median age of housing: 60+ years (2000).
Transportation: Commute to work: 90.0% car, 1.1% public transportation, 3.3% walk, 4.4% work from home (2000); Travel time to work: 30.8% less than 15 minutes, 47.1% 15 to 30 minutes, 9.9% 30 to 45 minutes, 8.7% 45 to 60 minutes, 3.5% 60 minutes or more (2000)

LA RUE (village). Covers a land area of 0.482 square miles and a water area of 0 square miles. Located at 40.57° N. Lat.; 83.38° W. Long. Elevation is 926 feet.
History: La Rue was the home of the Oorang Dog Kennels, which used Olympic athlete Jim Thorpe and other Indian athletes to play exhibition football games advertising their highly trained dogs.
Population: 818 (1990); 775 (2000); 742 (2005); 717 (2010 projected); Race: 99.3% White, 0.0% Black, 0.0% Asian, 0.1% Hispanic of any race (2005); Density: 1,540.0 persons per square mile (2005); Average household size: 2.49 (2005); Median age: 37.3 (2005); Males per 100 females: 98.9 (2005); Marriage status: 21.0% never married, 60.4% now married, 7.4% widowed, 11.2% divorced (2000); Foreign born: 0.3% (2000); Ancestry (includes multiple ancestries): 20.2% German, 13.4% United States or American, 10.4% English, 9.1% Irish, 6.4% Other groups (2000).
Economy: Single-family building permits issued: 0 (2005); Multi-family building permits issued: 0 (2005); Employment by occupation: 3.9% management, 11.8% professional, 14.9% services, 18.5% sales, 1.7% farming, 6.5% construction, 42.7% production (2000).
Income: Per capita income: $19,749 (2005); Median household income: $40,132 (2005); Average household income: $48,935 (2005); Percent of households with income of $100,000 or more: 9.7% (2005); Poverty rate: 7.8% (2000).
Education: Percent of population age 25 and over with: High school diploma (including GED) or higher: 81.5% (2005); Bachelor's degree or higher: 4.4% (2005); Master's degree or higher: 1.2% (2005).
School District(s)
Elgin Local SD (PK-12)
  2003-04 Enrollment: 1,627 . . . . (740) 382-1101
Housing: Homeownership rate: 70.5% (2005); Median home value: $68,800 (2005); Median rent: $255 per month (2000); Median age of housing: 54 years (2000).
Transportation: Commute to work: 91.9% car, 0.0% public transportation, 4.5% walk, 3.7% work from home (2000); Travel time to work: 16.3% less than 15 minutes, 27.7% 15 to 30 minutes, 38.2% 30 to 45 minutes, 11.7% 45 to 60 minutes, 6.1% 60 minutes or more (2000)

MARION (city). Covers a land area of 11.346 square miles and a water area of 0.044 square miles. Located at 40.58° N. Lat.; 83.12° W. Long. Elevation is 956 feet.
History: The site of Marion was selected as the seat of Marion County in 1824 because of the abundance of well water, discovered when some thirsty travelers stuck a wooden spade in the ground and named the spot Jacob's Well. The Marion Steam Shovel Company was organized in 1884, sending the name of Marion all over the world on its digging equipment.
Population: 36,526 (1990); 35,318 (2000); 35,210 (2005); 35,004 (2010 projected); Race: 90.9% White, 6.5% Black, 0.7% Asian, 1.6% Hispanic of any race (2005); Density: 3,103.3 persons per square mile (2005); Average household size: 2.58 (2005); Median age: 36.0 (2005); Males per 100 females: 104.7 (2005); Marriage status: 26.0% never married, 50.4% now married, 8.1% widowed, 15.5% divorced (2000); Foreign born: 1.5% (2000); Ancestry (includes multiple ancestries): 18.6% United States or American, 17.5% German, 13.1% Other groups, 9.5% Irish, 7.7% English (2000).
Economy: Unemployment rate: 6.2% (2005); Total civilian labor force: 17,407 (2005); Single-family building permits issued: 53 (2005); Multi-family building permits issued: 0 (2005); Employment by occupation: 7.3% management, 11.9% professional, 17.6% services, 25.9% sales, 0.4% farming, 8.0% construction, 28.9% production (2000).
Income: Per capita income: $18,167 (2005); Median household income: $37,231 (2005); Average household income: $45,523 (2005); Percent of households with income of $100,000 or more: 6.4% (2005); Poverty rate: 13.8% (2000).
Taxes: Total city taxes per capita: $367 (2004); City property taxes per capita: $32 (2004).

Education: Percent of population age 25 and over with: High school diploma (including GED) or higher: 75.9% (2005); Bachelor's degree or higher: 9.1% (2005); Master's degree or higher: 2.9% (2005).

School District(s)

Department of Youth Services (06-12)
   2003-04 Enrollment: 1,333 .... (614) 728-2489
Elgin Digital Academy
   2003-04 Enrollment: n/a .... (740) 392-1101
Elgin Local SD (PK-12)
   2003-04 Enrollment: 1,627 .... (740) 382-1101
Marion City Digital Academy (01-12)
   2003-04 Enrollment: 59 .... (740) 223-4417
Marion City SD (PK-12)
   2003-04 Enrollment: 5,592 .... (740) 387-3300
Pleasant Community Digital
   2003-04 Enrollment: n/a .... (740) 389-4476
Pleasant Local SD (PK-12)
   2003-04 Enrollment: 1,419 .... (740) 389-4476
River Valley Digital Academy
   2003-04 Enrollment: n/a .... (740) 387-4261
River Valley Local SD (PK-12)
   2003-04 Enrollment: 1,831 .... (740) 725-5400
Treca Digital Academy (KG-12)
   2003-04 Enrollment: 1,073 .... (888) 828-4798
Tri-Rivers Joint Vocational SD (09-12)
   2003-04 Enrollment: n/a .... (740) 389-4681

Four-year College(s)

Ohio State University-Marion Campus (Public)
   Fall 2004 Enrollment: 1,521 .... (740) 389-6786
   2005-06 Tuition: In-state $5,310; Out-of-state $16,533

Two-year College(s)

Marion Technical College (Public)
   Fall 2004 Enrollment: 2,240 .... (740) 389-4636
   2005-06 Tuition: In-state $3,456; Out-of-state $5,364
Tri-Rivers Career Center (Public)
   Fall 2004 Enrollment: 75 .... (740) 389-4681

Housing: Homeownership rate: 63.8% (2005); Median home value: $81,724 (2005); Median rent: $371 per month (2000); Median age of housing: 52 years (2000).
Hospitals: Marion General Hospital (257 beds)
Safety: Violent crime rate: 27.3 per 10,000 population; Property crime rate: 486.9 per 10,000 population (2004).
Newspapers: The Marion Star (Circulation 14,464)
Transportation: Commute to work: 94.7% car, 0.9% public transportation, 1.8% walk, 1.2% work from home (2000); Travel time to work: 53.3% less than 15 minutes, 25.5% 15 to 30 minutes, 9.3% 30 to 45 minutes, 5.7% 45 to 60 minutes, 6.2% 60 minutes or more (2000)
Additional Information Contacts
City of Marion.................................... (740) 387-3591
   http://mariononline.com/cityofmarion
Marion Chamber of Commerce .... (740) 382-2181
   http://www.marion.net/chamber

MORRAL (village). Covers a land area of 2.714 square miles and a water area of 0 square miles. Located at 40.68° N. Lat.; 83.21° W. Long. Elevation is 912 feet.
Population: 373 (1990); 388 (2000); 400 (2005); 413 (2010 projected); Race: 99.5% White, 0.0% Black, 0.0% Asian, 0.0% Hispanic of any race (2005); Density: 147.4 persons per square mile (2005); Average household size: 2.60 (2005); Median age: 39.3 (2005); Males per 100 females: 104.1 (2005); Marriage status: 20.8% never married, 64.5% now married, 3.9% widowed, 10.8% divorced (2000); Foreign born: 0.7% (2000); Ancestry (includes multiple ancestries): 15.1% German, 8.9% Irish, 7.9% English, 7.7% United States or American, 6.7% Other groups (2000).
Economy: Metal products, food products. Single-family building permits issued: 1 (2005); Multi-family building permits issued: 0 (2005); Employment by occupation: 4.5% management, 12.6% professional, 17.6% services, 29.6% sales, 0.0% farming, 8.0% construction, 27.6% production (2000).
Income: Per capita income: $17,850 (2005); Median household income: $42,308 (2005); Average household income: $46,364 (2005); Percent of households with income of $100,000 or more: 1.9% (2005); Poverty rate: 6.5% (2000).

Education: Percent of population age 25 and over with: High school diploma (including GED) or higher: 75.1% (2005); Bachelor's degree or higher: 3.1% (2005); Master's degree or higher: 2.3% (2005).

School District(s)

Ridgedale Community School (UG-UG)
   2003-04 Enrollment: n/a .... (740) 382-6065
Ridgedale Local Schools (PK-12)
   2003-04 Enrollment: 986 .... (740) 382-6065

Housing: Homeownership rate: 89.0% (2005); Median home value: $68,077 (2005); Median rent: $365 per month (2000); Median age of housing: 60+ years (2000).
Transportation: Commute to work: 95.9% car, 0.0% public transportation, 1.5% walk, 2.5% work from home (2000); Travel time to work: 22.9% less than 15 minutes, 55.7% 15 to 30 minutes, 8.9% 30 to 45 minutes, 4.2% 45 to 60 minutes, 8.3% 60 minutes or more (2000)

NEW BLOOMINGTON (village). Aka Agosta. Covers a land area of 0.439 square miles and a water area of 0 square miles. Located at 40.58° N. Lat.; 83.31° W. Long. Elevation is 945 feet.
Population: 429 (1990); 548 (2000); 536 (2005); 517 (2010 projected); Race: 97.4% White, 0.0% Black, 0.0% Asian, 3.0% Hispanic of any race (2005); Density: 1,219.6 persons per square mile (2005); Average household size: 2.87 (2005); Median age: 31.9 (2005); Males per 100 females: 99.3 (2005); Marriage status: 22.9% never married, 60.8% now married, 2.8% widowed, 13.4% divorced (2000); Foreign born: 2.0% (2000); Ancestry (includes multiple ancestries): 27.0% United States or American, 16.0% Other groups, 15.3% German, 6.5% Irish, 5.4% English (2000).
Economy: In agricultural area. Employment by occupation: 3.2% management, 3.2% professional, 14.1% services, 18.9% sales, 2.4% farming, 14.1% construction, 44.2% production (2000).
Income: Per capita income: $15,812 (2005); Median household income: $40,500 (2005); Average household income: $45,321 (2005); Percent of households with income of $100,000 or more: 3.2% (2005); Poverty rate: 11.7% (2000).
Education: Percent of population age 25 and over with: High school diploma (including GED) or higher: 71.0% (2005); Bachelor's degree or higher: 2.9% (2005); Master's degree or higher: 0.6% (2005).
Housing: Homeownership rate: 92.5% (2005); Median home value: $38,649 (2005); Median rent: $300 per month (2000); Median age of housing: 29 years (2000).
Transportation: Commute to work: 97.5% car, 0.8% public transportation, 0.8% walk, 0.0% work from home (2000); Travel time to work: 13.1% less than 15 minutes, 47.3% 15 to 30 minutes, 18.1% 30 to 45 minutes, 18.1% 45 to 60 minutes, 3.4% 60 minutes or more (2000)

PROSPECT (village). Covers a land area of 0.725 square miles and a water area of 0 square miles. Located at 40.45° N. Lat.; 83.18° W. Long. Elevation is 905 feet.
History: Settled 1832, incorporated as village 1876.
Population: 1,237 (1990); 1,191 (2000); 1,146 (2005); 1,127 (2010 projected); Race: 99.5% White, 0.0% Black, 0.0% Asian, 0.0% Hispanic of any race (2005); Density: 1,580.8 persons per square mile (2005); Average household size: 2.50 (2005); Median age: 36.4 (2005); Males per 100 females: 98.3 (2005); Marriage status: 22.4% never married, 61.1% now married, 5.8% widowed, 10.7% divorced (2000); Foreign born: 0.3% (2000); Ancestry (includes multiple ancestries): 26.5% German, 13.6% United States or American, 12.4% Irish, 9.9% English, 4.2% Dutch (2000).
Economy: Single-family building permits issued: 0 (2005); Multi-family building permits issued: 0 (2005); Employment by occupation: 7.5% management, 19.2% professional, 13.1% services, 17.8% sales, 0.6% farming, 8.7% construction, 33.0% production (2000).
Income: Per capita income: $22,808 (2005); Median household income: $52,319 (2005); Average household income: $56,944 (2005); Percent of households with income of $100,000 or more: 11.1% (2005); Poverty rate: 2.6% (2000).
Education: Percent of population age 25 and over with: High school diploma (including GED) or higher: 91.3% (2005); Bachelor's degree or higher: 15.5% (2005); Master's degree or higher: 6.0% (2005).

School District(s)

Elgin Local SD (PK-12)
   2003-04 Enrollment: 1,627 .... (740) 382-1101

Housing: Homeownership rate: 75.8% (2005); Median home value: $105,652 (2005); Median rent: $402 per month (2000); Median age of housing: 60+ years (2000).

Transportation: Commute to work: 95.1% car, 0.0% public transportation, 3.9% walk, 1.0% work from home (2000); Travel time to work: 16.1% less than 15 minutes, 45.3% 15 to 30 minutes, 23.0% 30 to 45 minutes, 8.0% 45 to 60 minutes, 7.6% 60 minutes or more (2000)

WALDO (village). Covers a land area of 0.650 square miles and a water area of 0 square miles. Located at 40.45° N. Lat.; 83.07° W. Long. Elevation is 940 feet.

Population: 340 (1990); 332 (2000); 318 (2005); 313 (2010 projected); Race: 99.4% White, 0.0% Black, 0.6% Asian, 0.0% Hispanic of any race (2005); Density: 488.9 persons per square mile (2005); Average household size: 2.27 (2005); Median age: 41.7 (2005); Males per 100 females: 82.8 (2005); Marriage status: 23.2% never married, 58.3% now married, 11.4% widowed, 7.0% divorced (2000); Foreign born: 0.9% (2000); Ancestry (includes multiple ancestries): 33.7% German, 22.2% Irish, 15.7% United States or American, 5.9% Scottish, 5.0% English (2000).
Economy: Single-family building permits issued: 0 (2005); Multi-family building permits issued: 0 (2005); Employment by occupation: 6.0% management, 14.7% professional, 17.4% services, 28.3% sales, 0.0% farming, 15.2% construction, 18.5% production (2000).
Income: Per capita income: $19,638 (2005); Median household income: $35,938 (2005); Average household income: $44,607 (2005); Percent of households with income of $100,000 or more: 5.7% (2005); Poverty rate: 10.4% (2000).
Education: Percent of population age 25 and over with: High school diploma (including GED) or higher: 94.9% (2005); Bachelor's degree or higher: 12.4% (2005); Master's degree or higher: 3.7% (2005).
Housing: Homeownership rate: 80.0% (2005); Median home value: $96,923 (2005); Median rent: $425 per month (2000); Median age of housing: 60+ years (2000).
Transportation: Commute to work: 97.2% car, 0.0% public transportation, 2.8% walk, 0.0% work from home (2000); Travel time to work: 32.0% less than 15 minutes, 45.9% 15 to 30 minutes, 13.3% 30 to 45 minutes, 6.6% 45 to 60 minutes, 2.2% 60 minutes or more (2000)

Medina County

Located in northern Ohio; drained by the Rocky and Black Rivers; includes Chippewa Lake. Covers a land area of 421.55 square miles, a water area of 1.57 square miles, and is located in the Eastern Time Zone. The county government was organized in 1812. County seat is Medina.

Medina County is part of the Cleveland-Elyria-Mentor, OH Metropolitan Statistical Area. The entire metro area includes: Cuyahoga County, OH; Geauga County, OH; Lake County, OH; Lorain County, OH; Medina County, OH

Weather Station: Chippewa Lake   Elevation: 1,177 feet

	Jan	Feb	Mar	Apr	May	Jun	Jul	Aug	Sep	Oct	Nov	Dec
High	33	37	47	60	71	79	83	81	75	63	50	38
Low	17	18	27	36	47	56	60	58	52	41	32	23
Precip	2.3	2.1	3.0	3.4	3.6	3.8	3.9	3.6	3.7	2.5	3.4	3.0
Snow	10.7	8.6	6.7	2.1	tr	0.0	0.0	0.0	0.0	0.2	3.3	8.2

High and Low temperatures in degrees Fahrenheit; Precipitation and Snow in inches

Population: 122,354 (1990); 151,095 (2000); 166,428 (2005); 182,495 (2010 projected); Race: 96.8% White, 0.9% Black, 0.9% Asian, 1.0% Hispanic of any race (2005); Density: 394.8 persons per square mile (2005); Average household size: 2.72 (2005); Median age: 37.4 (2005); Males per 100 females: 97.4 (2005).
Religion: Five largest groups: 18.0% Catholic Church, 5.4% The United Methodist Church, 3.4% Evangelical Lutheran Church in America, 1.6% United Church of Christ, 1.6% Lutheran Church—Missouri Synod (2000).
Economy: Unemployment rate: 4.7% (2005); Total civilian labor force: 91,257 (2005); Leading industries: 19.3% manufacturing; 15.3% retail trade; 10.6% health care and social assistance (2004); Farms: 1,188 totaling 122,682 acres (2002); Companies that employ 500 or more persons: 4 (2004); Companies that employ 100 to 499 persons: 73 (2004); Companies that employ less than 100 persons: 3,943 (2004); Black-owned businesses: n/a (2002); Hispanic-owned businesses: 132 (2002); Women-owned businesses: 3,466 (2002); Retail sales per capita: $14,148 (2006). Single-family building permits issued: 1,161 (2005); Multi-family building permits issued: 28 (2005).
Income: Per capita income: $27,270 (2005); Median household income: $62,286 (2005); Average household income: $73,696 (2005); Percent of households with income of $100,000 or more: 21.0% (2005); Poverty rate: 5.4% (2003); Bankruptcy rate: 9.53% (2005).
Taxes: Total county taxes per capita: $191 (2004); County property taxes per capita: $136 (2004).
Education: Percent of population age 25 and over with: High school diploma (including GED) or higher: 88.7% (2005); Bachelor's degree or higher: 24.7% (2005); Master's degree or higher: 7.0% (2005).
Housing: Homeownership rate: 82.0% (2005); Median home value: $177,758 (2005); Median rent: $521 per month (2000); Median age of housing: 25 years (2000).
Health: Birth rate: 127.1 per 10,000 population (2004); Death rate: 71.1 per 10,000 population (2004); Age-adjusted cancer mortality rate: 187.8 deaths per 10,000 population (2002); Air Quality Index: 55.3% good, 41.8% moderate, 2.9% unhealthy for sensitive individuals, 0.0% unhealthy (percent of days in 2005); Number of physicians: 15.7 per 10,000 population (2004); Hospital beds: 13.6 per 10,000 population (2003); Hospital admissions: 544.0 per 10,000 population (2003).
Elections: 2004 Presidential election results: 56.8% Bush, 42.7% Kerry, 0.0% Nader, 0.3% Badnarik
National and State Parks: Spencer Lake State Wildlife Area
Additional Information Contacts

Medina County Government	(330) 722-9208
http://www.co.medina.oh.us/	
Brunswick Chamber of Commerce	(330) 225-8411
http://www.brunswickareachamber.org	
City of Brunswick	(330) 225-9144
http://www.brunswick.oh.us	
City of Medina	(330) 725-8861
http://www.medinaoh.org/dynamic/default.aspx	
City of Wadsworth	(330) 335-1521
http://www.wadsworthcity.com	
Lodi Chamber of Commerce	(330) 948-8047
http://www.lodiohiochamber.com	
Medina Chamber of Commerce	(330) 723-8773
http://www.medinaohchamber.com	
Medina County Convention & Visitors Bureau	(330) 722-5502
http://www.visitmedinacounty.com	
Seville Chamber of Commerce	(330) 769-1522
http://www.visitmedinacounty.com	
Valley City Chamber of Commerce	(330) 483-1111
http://www.valleycity.org	
Village of Seville	(330) 769-4146
http://www.villageofseville.com	
Wadsworth Chamber of Commerce	(330) 336-6150
http://www.wadsworthcity.com	

Medina County Communities

BRUNSWICK (city). Covers a land area of 12.541 square miles and a water area of 0.042 square miles. Located at 41.24° N. Lat.; 81.82° W. Long. Elevation is 1,070 feet.
History: Named for its pleasing sound to early residents. Small farm community for many years; population burgeoned with the housing boom after World War II. Settled 1815 as part of the Conn. Western Reserve. Incorporated 1960.
Population: 28,743 (1990); 33,388 (2000); 34,918 (2005); 36,761 (2010 projected); Race: 96.4% White, 0.8% Black, 1.2% Asian, 1.5% Hispanic of any race (2005); Density: 2,784.3 persons per square mile (2005); Average household size: 2.75 (2005); Median age: 35.6 (2005); Males per 100 females: 96.4 (2005); Marriage status: 22.7% never married, 63.6% now married, 5.1% widowed, 8.7% divorced (2000); Foreign born: 4.3% (2000); Ancestry (includes multiple ancestries): 29.0% German, 18.7% Irish, 12.6% Polish, 11.7% Italian, 8.3% English (2000).
Economy: Light industrial plants. Unemployment rate: 4.9% (2005); Total civilian labor force: 19,710 (2005); Single-family building permits issued: 71 (2005); Multi-family building permits issued: 0 (2005); Employment by occupation: 13.0% management, 18.0% professional, 12.6% services, 28.1% sales, 0.1% farming, 11.1% construction, 17.0% production (2000).
Income: Per capita income: $24,913 (2005); Median household income: $61,520 (2005); Average household income: $67,839 (2005); Percent of households with income of $100,000 or more: 16.5% (2005); Poverty rate: 4.6% (2000).
Education: Percent of population age 25 and over with: High school diploma (including GED) or higher: 87.3% (2005); Bachelor's degree or higher: 19.4% (2005); Master's degree or higher: 4.2% (2005).

School District(s)
Brunswick City SD (PK-12)
  2003-04 Enrollment: 7,254 . . . . (330) 225-7731
Two-year College(s)
Raphaels School of Beauty Culture Inc (Private, For-profit)
  Fall 2004 Enrollment: 13 . . . . (330) 225-0195
Housing: Homeownership rate: 80.8% (2005); Median home value: $163,681 (2005); Median rent: $536 per month (2000); Median age of housing: 25 years (2000).
Transportation: Commute to work: 95.3% car, 1.0% public transportation, 0.5% walk, 2.4% work from home (2000); Travel time to work: 21.4% less than 15 minutes, 32.7% 15 to 30 minutes, 30.1% 30 to 45 minutes, 11.0% 45 to 60 minutes, 4.8% 60 minutes or more (2000)
Additional Information Contacts
Brunswick Chamber of Commerce . . . . (330) 225-8411
  http://www.brunswickareachamber.org
City of Brunswick . . . . (330) 225-9144
  http://www.brunswick.oh.us

CHIPPEWA LAKE (village). Aka Chippewa-on-the-Lake. Covers a land area of 0.271 square miles and a water area of 0.001 square miles. Located at 41.07° N. Lat.; 81.90° W. Long.
Population: 938 (1990); 823 (2000); 808 (2005); 813 (2010 projected); Race: 98.8% White, 0.2% Black, 0.4% Asian, 0.9% Hispanic of any race (2005); Density: 2,979.9 persons per square mile (2005); Average household size: 2.41 (2005); Median age: 38.0 (2005); Males per 100 females: 107.7 (2005); Marriage status: 29.7% never married, 50.9% now married, 6.6% widowed, 12.8% divorced (2000); Foreign born: 1.3% (2000); Ancestry (includes multiple ancestries): 33.7% German, 16.3% Irish, 15.6% English, 7.9% Other groups, 7.2% Italian (2000).
Economy: Employment by occupation: 8.8% management, 7.9% professional, 20.4% services, 27.7% sales, 0.0% farming, 17.8% construction, 17.4% production (2000).
Income: Per capita income: $22,605 (2005); Median household income: $46,655 (2005); Average household income: $54,522 (2005); Percent of households with income of $100,000 or more: 9.3% (2005); Poverty rate: 9.2% (2000).
Education: Percent of population age 25 and over with: High school diploma (including GED) or higher: 83.0% (2005); Bachelor's degree or higher: 14.2% (2005); Master's degree or higher: 4.3% (2005).
Housing: Homeownership rate: 82.7% (2005); Median home value: $128,876 (2005); Median rent: $433 per month (2000); Median age of housing: 43 years (2000).
Transportation: Commute to work: 94.3% car, 1.8% public transportation, 0.0% walk, 3.4% work from home (2000); Travel time to work: 29.5% less than 15 minutes, 32.1% 15 to 30 minutes, 25.5% 30 to 45 minutes, 7.5% 45 to 60 minutes, 5.4% 60 minutes or more (2000)

GLORIA GLENS PARK (village). Covers a land area of 0.114 square miles and a water area of 0 square miles. Located at 41.05° N. Lat.; 81.90° W. Long. Elevation is 1,010 feet.
Population: 484 (1990); 538 (2000); 608 (2005); 679 (2010 projected); Race: 99.3% White, 0.0% Black, 0.0% Asian, 0.2% Hispanic of any race (2005); Density: 5,346.2 persons per square mile (2005); Average household size: 2.63 (2005); Median age: 35.4 (2005); Males per 100 females: 104.7 (2005); Marriage status: 22.7% never married, 56.6% now married, 6.5% widowed, 14.2% divorced (2000); Foreign born: 0.4% (2000); Ancestry (includes multiple ancestries): 30.2% German, 19.8% Irish, 12.1% English, 11.2% Polish, 5.7% Italian (2000).
Economy: Resort village. Employment by occupation: 8.1% management, 13.0% professional, 18.5% services, 26.3% sales, 0.0% farming, 13.0% construction, 21.1% production (2000).
Income: Per capita income: $21,423 (2005); Median household income: $50,184 (2005); Average household income: $56,385 (2005); Percent of households with income of $100,000 or more: 7.8% (2005); Poverty rate: 1.3% (2000).
Education: Percent of population age 25 and over with: High school diploma (including GED) or higher: 87.8% (2005); Bachelor's degree or higher: 14.2% (2005); Master's degree or higher: 1.3% (2005).
Housing: Homeownership rate: 75.8% (2005); Median home value: $119,706 (2005); Median rent: $536 per month (2000); Median age of housing: 48 years (2000).
Transportation: Commute to work: 97.4% car, 0.3% public transportation, 0.3% walk, 1.6% work from home (2000); Travel time to work: 24.7% less than 15 minutes, 36.8% 15 to 30 minutes, 24.4% 30 to 45 minutes, 6.4% 45 to 60 minutes, 7.7% 60 minutes or more (2000)

HINCKLEY (unincorporated postal area, zip code 44233). Covers a land area of 26.816 square miles and a water area of 0.136 square miles. Located at 41.23° N. Lat.; 81.73° W. Long. Elevation is 1,100 feet.
Population: 6,777 (2000); Race: 99.8% White, 0.0% Black, 0.2% Asian, 1.0% Hispanic of any race (2000); Density: 252.7 persons per square mile (2000); Age: 25.3% under 18, 10.5% over 64 (2000); Marriage status: 19.7% never married, 70.7% now married, 4.6% widowed, 5.1% divorced (2000); Foreign born: 6.1% (2000); Ancestry (includes multiple ancestries): 28.6% German, 15.9% Polish, 15.1% Irish, 12.3% English, 12.0% Italian (2000).
Economy: Employment by occupation: 16.0% management, 20.0% professional, 12.4% services, 24.6% sales, 0.0% farming, 13.8% construction, 13.1% production (2000).
Income: Per capita income: $29,186 (2000); Median household income: $70,548 (2000); Poverty rate: 2.7% (2000).
Education: Percent of population age 25 and over with: High school diploma (including GED) or higher: 89.5% (2000); Bachelor's degree or higher: 26.2% (2000).
School District(s)
Highland Local SD (PK-12)
  2003-04 Enrollment: 2,780 . . . . (330) 239-1901
Housing: Homeownership rate: 95.1% (2000); Median home value: $208,800 (2000); Median rent: $547 per month (2000); Median age of housing: 28 years (2000).
Transportation: Commute to work: 94.3% car, 0.4% public transportation, 1.1% walk, 3.7% work from home (2000); Travel time to work: 14.6% less than 15 minutes, 38.1% 15 to 30 minutes, 32.8% 30 to 45 minutes, 10.3% 45 to 60 minutes, 4.3% 60 minutes or more (2000)

HOMERVILLE (unincorporated postal area, zip code 44235). Covers a land area of 26.255 square miles and a water area of 0.030 square miles. Located at 41.02° N. Lat.; 82.11° W. Long. Elevation is 1,083 feet.
Population: 1,873 (2000); Race: 96.9% White, 1.8% Black, 0.0% Asian, 0.0% Hispanic of any race (2000); Density: 71.3 persons per square mile (2000); Age: 34.0% under 18, 6.0% over 64 (2000); Marriage status: 25.2% never married, 67.7% now married, 4.9% widowed, 2.3% divorced (2000); Foreign born: 1.2% (2000); Ancestry (includes multiple ancestries): 29.5% German, 22.5% United States or American, 15.7% English, 10.3% Polish, 9.9% Irish (2000).
Economy: Employment by occupation: 14.7% management, 16.2% professional, 8.0% services, 17.7% sales, 1.7% farming, 17.0% construction, 24.7% production (2000).
Income: Per capita income: $15,437 (2000); Median household income: $47,760 (2000); Poverty rate: 21.3% (2000).
Education: Percent of population age 25 and over with: High school diploma (including GED) or higher: 72.8% (2000); Bachelor's degree or higher: 14.5% (2000).
Housing: Homeownership rate: 88.0% (2000); Median home value: $119,700 (2000); Median rent: $417 per month (2000); Median age of housing: 26 years (2000).
Transportation: Commute to work: 82.9% car, 2.5% public transportation, 2.6% walk, 9.1% work from home (2000); Travel time to work: 18.3% less than 15 minutes, 16.2% 15 to 30 minutes, 31.2% 30 to 45 minutes, 10.4% 45 to 60 minutes, 23.9% 60 minutes or more (2000)

LITCHFIELD (unincorporated postal area, zip code 44253). Covers a land area of 25.487 square miles and a water area of 0.018 square miles. Located at 41.16° N. Lat.; 82.03° W. Long. Elevation is 1,010 feet.
Population: 3,312 (2000); Race: 96.5% White, 0.2% Black, 0.5% Asian, 0.5% Hispanic of any race (2000); Density: 130.0 persons per square mile (2000); Age: 30.2% under 18, 8.2% over 64 (2000); Marriage status: 21.0% never married, 67.0% now married, 4.1% widowed, 7.8% divorced (2000); Foreign born: 1.2% (2000); Ancestry (includes multiple ancestries): 37.5% German, 13.9% Irish, 11.6% English, 10.8% United States or American, 10.1% Polish (2000).
Economy: Employment by occupation: 11.4% management, 12.4% professional, 13.9% services, 25.0% sales, 0.4% farming, 15.9% construction, 21.0% production (2000).
Income: Per capita income: $20,288 (2000); Median household income: $56,563 (2000); Poverty rate: 5.6% (2000).

Education: Percent of population age 25 and over with: High school diploma (including GED) or higher: 87.0% (2000); Bachelor's degree or higher: 13.3% (2000).
School District(s)
Buckeye Local SD (PK-12)
   2003-04 Enrollment: 2,456 .... (330) 722-8257
Housing: Homeownership rate: 92.9% (2000); Median home value: $150,800 (2000); Median rent: $658 per month (2000); Median age of housing: 24 years (2000).
Transportation: Commute to work: 95.3% car, 0.6% public transportation, 0.4% walk, 2.1% work from home (2000); Travel time to work: 14.8% less than 15 minutes, 42.9% 15 to 30 minutes, 18.3% 30 to 45 minutes, 12.3% 45 to 60 minutes, 11.6% 60 minutes or more (2000)

LODI (village). Covers a land area of 2.119 square miles and a water area of 0.008 square miles. Located at 41.03° N. Lat.; 82.01° W. Long. Elevation is 924 feet.
History: Lodi was founded in 1824 by Judge Joseph Harris, who built his house on an ancient Indian mound. The town developed as a distribution center for dairy products and fertilizers.
Population: 3,050 (1990); 3,061 (2000); 3,324 (2005); 3,610 (2010 projected); Race: 98.3% White, 0.0% Black, 0.2% Asian, 0.6% Hispanic of any race (2005); Density: 1,568.6 persons per square mile (2005); Average household size: 2.34 (2005); Median age: 36.6 (2005); Males per 100 females: 90.9 (2005); Marriage status: 21.6% never married, 52.8% now married, 8.1% widowed, 17.5% divorced (2000); Foreign born: 1.4% (2000); Ancestry (includes multiple ancestries): 29.4% German, 15.5% Irish, 10.4% English, 9.3% United States or American, 7.9% Other groups (2000).
Economy: Employment by occupation: 9.9% management, 4.3% professional, 18.5% services, 30.6% sales, 0.0% farming, 8.9% construction, 27.7% production (2000).
Income: Per capita income: $18,276 (2005); Median household income: $34,457 (2005); Average household income: $42,294 (2005); Percent of households with income of $100,000 or more: 4.2% (2005); Poverty rate: 10.1% (2000).
Education: Percent of population age 25 and over with: High school diploma (including GED) or higher: 78.0% (2005); Bachelor's degree or higher: 6.1% (2005); Master's degree or higher: 0.5% (2005).
School District(s)
Cloverleaf Local SD (PK-12)
   2003-04 Enrollment: 3,568 .... (330) 948-2500
Housing: Homeownership rate: 65.8% (2005); Median home value: $108,779 (2005); Median rent: $419 per month (2000); Median age of housing: 36 years (2000).
Hospitals: Lodi Community Hospital (25 beds)
Transportation: Commute to work: 94.3% car, 0.6% public transportation, 2.7% walk, 2.2% work from home (2000); Travel time to work: 31.2% less than 15 minutes, 37.8% 15 to 30 minutes, 13.2% 30 to 45 minutes, 11.4% 45 to 60 minutes, 6.4% 60 minutes or more (2000)
Additional Information Contacts
Lodi Chamber of Commerce .... (330) 948-8047
   http://www.lodiohiochamber.com

MEDINA (city). Covers a land area of 11.127 square miles and a water area of 0.194 square miles. Located at 41.13° N. Lat.; 81.86° W. Long. Elevation is 1,092 feet.
History: Named for the city of Hejaz, Saudi Arabia, to which Mohammed made his flight from Mecca in 622. Medina was platted in 1818 by a Captain Badger, who built a log cabin on the site. The town, first called Mecca, became known for its bee culture and honey products, calling itself the "sweetest town on earth."
Population: 19,807 (1990); 25,139 (2000); 26,899 (2005); 29,014 (2010 projected); Race: 94.2% White, 2.7% Black, 1.2% Asian, 1.1% Hispanic of any race (2005); Density: 2,417.6 persons per square mile (2005); Average household size: 2.63 (2005); Median age: 33.8 (2005); Males per 100 females: 92.8 (2005); Marriage status: 20.3% never married, 64.5% now married, 6.6% widowed, 8.7% divorced (2000); Foreign born: 2.7% (2000); Ancestry (includes multiple ancestries): 32.7% German, 16.7% Irish, 11.9% English, 9.6% Italian, 8.8% Polish (2000).
Economy: Unemployment rate: 4.5% (2005); Total civilian labor force: 14,123 (2005); Single-family building permits issued: 32 (2005); Multi-family building permits issued: 16 (2005); Employment by occupation: 15.0% management, 21.2% professional, 12.1% services, 29.8% sales, 0.1% farming, 7.4% construction, 14.3% production (2000).
Income: Per capita income: $24,975 (2005); Median household income: $54,397 (2005); Average household income: $64,382 (2005); Percent of households with income of $100,000 or more: 18.1% (2005); Poverty rate: 5.7% (2000).
Education: Percent of population age 25 and over with: High school diploma (including GED) or higher: 90.9% (2005); Bachelor's degree or higher: 33.0% (2005); Master's degree or higher: 8.4% (2005).
School District(s)
Buckeye Local SD (PK-12)
   2003-04 Enrollment: 2,456 .... (330) 722-8257
Cloverleaf Local SD (PK-12)
   2003-04 Enrollment: 3,568 .... (330) 948-2500
Highland Local SD (PK-12)
   2003-04 Enrollment: 2,780 .... (330) 239-1901
Medina City SD (PK-12)
   2003-04 Enrollment: 7,323 .... (330) 636-3000
Medina County Joint Vocational SD (PK-12)
   2003-04 Enrollment: n/a .... (330) 225-7111
Two-year College(s)
Hamrick Truck Driving School (Private, For-profit)
   Fall 2004 Enrollment: 152 .... (330) 239-2229
Medina County Career Center (Public)
   Fall 2004 Enrollment: 406 .... (330) 725-8461
Housing: Homeownership rate: 67.8% (2005); Median home value: $166,859 (2005); Median rent: $525 per month (2000); Median age of housing: 23 years (2000).
Hospitals: Medina General Hospital (118 beds)
Newspapers: Brunswick Sun Times (General - Circulation 6,076); Sun Banner Pride (General - Circulation 3,319); The Medina County Gazette (Circulation 16,500); The Medina Sun (General - Circulation 11,683); The Montrose Sun (General - Circulation 22,741)
Transportation: Commute to work: 93.8% car, 0.7% public transportation, 1.6% walk, 2.9% work from home (2000); Travel time to work: 35.2% less than 15 minutes, 25.5% 15 to 30 minutes, 21.6% 30 to 45 minutes, 11.6% 45 to 60 minutes, 6.0% 60 minutes or more (2000)
Additional Information Contacts
City of Medina .... (330) 725-8861
   http://www.medinaoh.org/dynamic/default.aspx
Medina Chamber of Commerce .... (330) 723-8773
   http://www.medinaohchamber.com
Medina County Convention & Visitors Bureau .... (330) 722-5502
   http://www.visitmedinacounty.com

SEVILLE (village). Covers a land area of 2.017 square miles and a water area of 0 square miles. Located at 41.01° N. Lat.; 81.86° W. Long. Elevation is 990 feet.
Population: 1,812 (1990); 2,160 (2000); 2,426 (2005); 2,693 (2010 projected); Race: 99.1% White, 0.2% Black, 0.2% Asian, 0.7% Hispanic of any race (2005); Density: 1,202.8 persons per square mile (2005); Average household size: 2.61 (2005); Median age: 38.6 (2005); Males per 100 females: 90.1 (2005); Marriage status: 17.1% never married, 65.2% now married, 8.3% widowed, 9.4% divorced (2000); Foreign born: 0.9% (2000); Ancestry (includes multiple ancestries): 29.9% German, 14.8% Irish, 13.1% English, 5.1% Italian, 4.7% Other groups (2000).
Economy: In agricultural area. Employment by occupation: 11.8% management, 13.2% professional, 14.0% services, 30.3% sales, 0.4% farming, 10.2% construction, 20.1% production (2000).
Income: Per capita income: $24,919 (2005); Median household income: $54,869 (2005); Average household income: $64,327 (2005); Percent of households with income of $100,000 or more: 15.3% (2005); Poverty rate: 3.7% (2000).
Education: Percent of population age 25 and over with: High school diploma (including GED) or higher: 89.0% (2005); Bachelor's degree or higher: 17.1% (2005); Master's degree or higher: 5.3% (2005).
School District(s)
Cloverleaf Local SD (PK-12)
   2003-04 Enrollment: 3,568 .... (330) 948-2500
Housing: Homeownership rate: 82.3% (2005); Median home value: $135,725 (2005); Median rent: $479 per month (2000); Median age of housing: 26 years (2000).
Transportation: Commute to work: 95.1% car, 0.0% public transportation, 2.3% walk, 2.3% work from home (2000); Travel time to work: 22.0% less than 15 minutes, 44.1% 15 to 30 minutes, 17.8% 30 to 45 minutes, 9.3% 45 to 60 minutes, 6.8% 60 minutes or more (2000)
Additional Information Contacts

Seville Chamber of Commerce . . . . (330) 769-1522
    http://www.visitmedinacounty.com
Village of Seville. . . . . (330) 769-4146
    http://www.villageofseville.com

SPENCER (village). Covers a land area of 0.988 square miles and a water area of 0.008 square miles. Located at 41.10° N. Lat.; 82.12° W. Long. Elevation is 910 feet.
Population: 726 (1990); 747 (2000); 947 (2005); 1,145 (2010 projected); Race: 98.6% White, 0.0% Black, 0.3% Asian, 1.1% Hispanic of any race (2005); Density: 958.2 persons per square mile (2005); Average household size: 2.53 (2005); Median age: 34.5 (2005); Males per 100 females: 96.9 (2005); Marriage status: 19.0% never married, 60.6% now married, 9.7% widowed, 10.7% divorced (2000); Foreign born: 1.5% (2000); Ancestry (includes multiple ancestries): 28.1% German, 24.8% United States or American, 12.4% Irish, 11.3% English, 6.1% Polish (2000).
Economy: In agricultural area. Employment by occupation: 7.0% management, 11.0% professional, 13.0% services, 25.6% sales, 3.4% farming, 17.5% construction, 22.5% production (2000).
Income: Per capita income: $19,469 (2005); Median household income: $41,833 (2005); Average household income: $49,298 (2005); Percent of households with income of $100,000 or more: 7.0% (2005); Poverty rate: 3.9% (2000).
Education: Percent of population age 25 and over with: High school diploma (including GED) or higher: 85.0% (2005); Bachelor's degree or higher: 7.8% (2005); Master's degree or higher: 2.8% (2005).
School District(s)
Cloverleaf Local SD (PK-12)
    2003-04 Enrollment: 3,568 . . . . (330) 948-2500
Housing: Homeownership rate: 69.8% (2005); Median home value: $118,393 (2005); Median rent: $470 per month (2000); Median age of housing: 60+ years (2000).
Transportation: Commute to work: 94.2% car, 0.0% public transportation, 1.7% walk, 2.0% work from home (2000); Travel time to work: 15.6% less than 15 minutes, 36.9% 15 to 30 minutes, 26.8% 30 to 45 minutes, 8.8% 45 to 60 minutes, 11.8% 60 minutes or more (2000)

VALLEY CITY (unincorporated postal area, zip code 44280). Covers a land area of 24.786 square miles and a water area of 0.010 square miles. Located at 41.23° N. Lat.; 81.92° W. Long. Elevation is 815 feet.
Population: 4,150 (2000); Race: 98.1% White, 0.0% Black, 0.0% Asian, 1.5% Hispanic of any race (2000); Density: 167.4 persons per square mile (2000); Age: 22.9% under 18, 14.1% over 64 (2000); Marriage status: 18.6% never married, 67.7% now married, 6.6% widowed, 7.2% divorced (2000); Foreign born: 2.5% (2000); Ancestry (includes multiple ancestries): 38.0% German, 15.1% Irish, 12.5% English, 10.4% Polish, 7.7% Italian (2000).
Economy: Employment by occupation: 12.3% management, 19.4% professional, 17.0% services, 23.7% sales, 0.0% farming, 15.2% construction, 12.4% production (2000).
Income: Per capita income: $25,583 (2000); Median household income: $59,972 (2000); Poverty rate: 3.5% (2000).
Education: Percent of population age 25 and over with: High school diploma (including GED) or higher: 86.1% (2000); Bachelor's degree or higher: 20.3% (2000).
Housing: Homeownership rate: 92.6% (2000); Median home value: $166,100 (2000); Median rent: $637 per month (2000); Median age of housing: 26 years (2000).
Transportation: Commute to work: 91.6% car, 0.8% public transportation, 0.4% walk, 7.2% work from home (2000); Travel time to work: 20.8% less than 15 minutes, 33.2% 15 to 30 minutes, 26.6% 30 to 45 minutes, 12.4% 45 to 60 minutes, 7.0% 60 minutes or more (2000)
Additional Information Contacts
Valley City Chamber of Commerce . . . . (330) 483-1111
    http://www.valleycity.org

WADSWORTH (city). Covers a land area of 9.501 square miles and a water area of 0 square miles. Located at 41.02° N. Lat.; 81.73° W. Long. Elevation is 1,200 feet.
History: Named for Colonel E. Wadsworth. Wadsworth developed as an industrial town, manufacturing matches, valves, locomotive appliances, and lubricators.
Population: 16,147 (1990); 18,437 (2000); 19,626 (2005); 20,996 (2010 projected); Race: 97.4% White, 0.3% Black, 1.0% Asian, 0.8% Hispanic of any race (2005); Density: 2,065.6 persons per square mile (2005); Average household size: 2.49 (2005); Median age: 38.0 (2005); Males per 100 females: 93.1 (2005); Marriage status: 17.9% never married, 65.0% now married, 8.3% widowed, 8.8% divorced (2000); Foreign born: 2.5% (2000); Ancestry (includes multiple ancestries): 34.5% German, 15.8% Irish, 11.7% English, 8.7% Italian, 7.5% United States or American (2000).
Economy: Single-family building permits issued: 146 (2005); Multi-family building permits issued: 0 (2005); Employment by occupation: 15.3% management, 19.7% professional, 14.2% services, 25.7% sales, 0.1% farming, 9.3% construction, 15.6% production (2000).
Income: Per capita income: $25,635 (2005); Median household income: $53,540 (2005); Average household income: $63,477 (2005); Percent of households with income of $100,000 or more: 15.4% (2005); Poverty rate: 5.4% (2000).
Taxes: Total city taxes per capita: $399 (2004); City property taxes per capita: $95 (2004).
Education: Percent of population age 25 and over with: High school diploma (including GED) or higher: 88.5% (2005); Bachelor's degree or higher: 27.3% (2005); Master's degree or higher: 7.2% (2005).
School District(s)
Wadsworth City SD (PK-12)
    2003-04 Enrollment: 4,695 . . . . (330) 336-3571
Housing: Homeownership rate: 74.5% (2005); Median home value: $155,849 (2005); Median rent: $470 per month (2000); Median age of housing: 35 years (2000).
Hospitals: Wadsworth-Rittman Hospital (113 beds)
Safety: Violent crime rate: 16.9 per 10,000 population; Property crime rate: 204.1 per 10,000 population (2004).
Transportation: Commute to work: 94.3% car, 0.2% public transportation, 1.3% walk, 3.5% work from home (2000); Travel time to work: 34.6% less than 15 minutes, 44.0% 15 to 30 minutes, 12.6% 30 to 45 minutes, 5.0% 45 to 60 minutes, 3.9% 60 minutes or more (2000)
Additional Information Contacts
City of Wadsworth . . . . (330) 335-1521
    http://www.wadsworthcity.com
Wadsworth Chamber of Commerce. . . . . (330) 336-6150
    http://www.wadsworthcity.com

WESTFIELD CENTER (village). Aka Leroy. Covers a land area of 2.113 square miles and a water area of 0 square miles. Located at 41.03° N. Lat.; 81.93° W. Long. Elevation is 1,100 feet.
Population: 915 (1990); 1,054 (2000); 1,184 (2005); 1,314 (2010 projected); Race: 98.7% White, 0.0% Black, 0.5% Asian, 0.4% Hispanic of any race (2005); Density: 560.3 persons per square mile (2005); Average household size: 2.57 (2005); Median age: 43.0 (2005); Males per 100 females: 99.7 (2005); Marriage status: 16.7% never married, 74.3% now married, 3.9% widowed, 5.2% divorced (2000); Foreign born: 1.3% (2000); Ancestry (includes multiple ancestries): 35.9% German, 21.8% English, 17.1% Irish, 7.8% Polish, 7.4% Italian (2000).
Economy: Employment by occupation: 22.2% management, 25.2% professional, 8.6% services, 33.6% sales, 0.0% farming, 4.7% construction, 5.7% production (2000).
Income: Per capita income: $36,852 (2005); Median household income: $73,611 (2005); Average household income: $94,648 (2005); Percent of households with income of $100,000 or more: 30.6% (2005); Poverty rate: 3.0% (2000).
Education: Percent of population age 25 and over with: High school diploma (including GED) or higher: 98.2% (2005); Bachelor's degree or higher: 47.1% (2005); Master's degree or higher: 12.8% (2005).
School District(s)
Cloverleaf Local SD (PK-12)
    2003-04 Enrollment: 3,568 . . . . (330) 948-2500
Housing: Homeownership rate: 90.7% (2005); Median home value: $212,987 (2005); Median rent: $563 per month (2000); Median age of housing: 27 years (2000).
Transportation: Commute to work: 90.4% car, 0.7% public transportation, 4.0% walk, 4.3% work from home (2000); Travel time to work: 40.3% less than 15 minutes, 26.1% 15 to 30 minutes, 20.6% 30 to 45 minutes, 7.6% 45 to 60 minutes, 5.5% 60 minutes or more (2000)

Meigs County

Located in southeastern Ohio; bounded on the southeast by the Ohio River and the West Virginia border; drained by the Shade River and Leading Creek. Covers a land area of 429.42 square miles, a water area of 2.95

square miles, and is located in the Eastern Time Zone. The county government was organized in 1819. County seat is Pomeroy.
Population: 22,987 (1990); 23,072 (2000); 23,359 (2005); 23,652 (2010 projected); Race: 97.6% White, 0.9% Black, 0.2% Asian, 0.4% Hispanic of any race (2005); Density: 54.4 persons per square mile (2005); Average household size: 2.45 (2005); Median age: 39.4 (2005); Males per 100 females: 94.7 (2005).
Religion: Five largest groups: 6.7% The United Methodist Church, 5.4% Christian Churches and Churches of Christ, 3.5% Church of the Nazarene, 1.7% Southern Baptist Convention, 1.5% Churches of Christ (2000).
Economy: Unemployment rate: 9.9% (2005); Total civilian labor force: 9,074 (2005); Leading industries: 24.7% retail trade; 19.8% health care and social assistance; 15.7% accommodation & food services (2004); Farms: 552 totaling 90,362 acres (2002); Companies that employ 500 or more persons: 0 (2004); Companies that employ 100 to 499 persons: 2 (2004); Companies that employ less than 100 persons: 337 (2004); Black-owned businesses: n/a (2002); Hispanic-owned businesses: n/a (2002); Women-owned businesses: n/a (2002); Retail sales per capita: $7,512 (2006). Single-family building permits issued: 12 (2005); Multi-family building permits issued: 0 (2005).
Income: Per capita income: $16,042 (2005); Median household income: $30,801 (2005); Average household income: $39,143 (2005); Percent of households with income of $100,000 or more: 4.6% (2005); Poverty rate: 16.8% (2003); Bankruptcy rate: 7.32% (2005).
Education: Percent of population age 25 and over with: High school diploma (including GED) or higher: 73.1% (2005); Bachelor's degree or higher: 7.4% (2005); Master's degree or higher: 2.4% (2005).
Housing: Homeownership rate: 79.5% (2005); Median home value: $66,447 (2005); Median rent: $263 per month (2000); Median age of housing: 30 years (2000).
Health: Birth rate: 126.1 per 10,000 population (2004); Death rate: 111.8 per 10,000 population (2004); Age-adjusted cancer mortality rate: 223.1 deaths per 100,000 population (2002); Air Quality Index: 100.0% good, 0.0% moderate, 0.0% unhealthy for sensitive individuals, 0.0% unhealthy (percent of days in 2005); Number of physicians: 2.6 per 10,000 population (2004); Hospital beds: 0.0 per 10,000 population (2003); Hospital admissions: 0.0 per 10,000 population (2003).
Elections: 2004 Presidential election results: 58.2% Bush, 41.2% Kerry, 0.0% Nader, 0.3% Badnarik
National and State Parks: Buffington Island State Memorial; Forked Run State Park
Additional Information Contacts
Meigs County Government . . . . (740) 992-2895
 http://www.meigscountyohio.com/
Meigs County Chamber of Commerce. . . . . (740) 992-5005
 http://www.meigscountychamber.com
Meigs County Economic Development . . . . (740) 992-3034
 http://www.meigscountyohio.com/econ_development/index.htm

Meigs County Communities

LANGSVILLE (unincorporated postal area, zip code 45741). Covers a land area of 46.721 square miles and a water area of 0.010 square miles. Located at 39.07° N. Lat.; 82.24° W. Long. Elevation is 590 feet.
Population: 918 (2000); Race: 95.5% White, 0.0% Black, 0.0% Asian, 0.0% Hispanic of any race (2000); Density: 19.6 persons per square mile (2000); Age: 25.5% under 18, 9.1% over 64 (2000); Marriage status: 24.7% never married, 63.6% now married, 4.0% widowed, 7.7% divorced (2000); Foreign born: 0.0% (2000); Ancestry (includes multiple ancestries): 29.2% United States or American, 13.1% German, 10.6% Other groups, 7.3% Irish, 6.4% English (2000).
Economy: Employment by occupation: 6.8% management, 17.5% professional, 14.5% services, 19.1% sales, 0.0% farming, 13.5% construction, 28.6% production (2000).
Income: Per capita income: $11,230 (2000); Median household income: $27,188 (2000); Poverty rate: 31.8% (2000).
Education: Percent of population age 25 and over with: High school diploma (including GED) or higher: 64.7% (2000); Bachelor's degree or higher: 4.5% (2000).
Housing: Homeownership rate: 80.3% (2000); Median home value: $53,600 (2000); Median rent: $225 per month (2000); Median age of housing: 29 years (2000).
Transportation: Commute to work: 93.1% car, 0.0% public transportation, 1.6% walk, 1.6% work from home (2000); Travel time to work: 13.4% less than 15 minutes, 38.2% 15 to 30 minutes, 32.2% 30 to 45 minutes, 7.6% 45 to 60 minutes, 8.6% 60 minutes or more (2000)

LONG BOTTOM (unincorporated postal area, zip code 45743). Covers a land area of 40.144 square miles and a water area of 0 square miles. Located at 39.07° N. Lat.; 81.84° W. Long. Elevation is 599 feet.
History: Long Bottom developed around a ferry that crossed the Ohio River to West Virginia.
Population: 1,593 (2000); Race: 97.5% White, 0.0% Black, 0.0% Asian, 1.8% Hispanic of any race (2000); Density: 39.7 persons per square mile (2000); Age: 21.9% under 18, 14.8% over 64 (2000); Marriage status: 19.0% never married, 62.8% now married, 6.7% widowed, 11.6% divorced (2000); Foreign born: 0.0% (2000); Ancestry (includes multiple ancestries): 29.4% United States or American, 15.6% German, 11.6% Irish, 8.2% English, 4.9% Other groups (2000).
Economy: Employment by occupation: 4.3% management, 9.4% professional, 22.8% services, 18.8% sales, 1.8% farming, 18.8% construction, 24.2% production (2000).
Income: Per capita income: $13,508 (2000); Median household income: $28,291 (2000); Poverty rate: 18.1% (2000).
Education: Percent of population age 25 and over with: High school diploma (including GED) or higher: 73.0% (2000); Bachelor's degree or higher: 6.3% (2000).
Housing: Homeownership rate: 83.7% (2000); Median home value: $58,300 (2000); Median rent: $239 per month (2000); Median age of housing: 26 years (2000).
Transportation: Commute to work: 94.0% car, 0.6% public transportation, 2.9% walk, 2.4% work from home (2000); Travel time to work: 11.8% less than 15 minutes, 34.8% 15 to 30 minutes, 21.0% 30 to 45 minutes, 18.1% 45 to 60 minutes, 14.3% 60 minutes or more (2000)

MIDDLEPORT (village). Covers a land area of 1.809 square miles and a water area of 0.093 square miles. Located at 38.99° N. Lat.; 82.05° W. Long. Elevation is 575 feet.
History: Middleport was an active river town along the Ohio River during the last half of the 1800's. The disastrous flooding of the river in 1937 destroyed Middleport's waterfront.
Population: 2,847 (1990); 2,525 (2000); 2,530 (2005); 2,543 (2010 projected); Race: 95.0% White, 3.2% Black, 0.3% Asian, 0.4% Hispanic of any race (2005); Density: 1,398.9 persons per square mile (2005); Average household size: 2.26 (2005); Median age: 40.8 (2005); Males per 100 females: 82.5 (2005); Marriage status: 20.4% never married, 54.1% now married, 12.0% widowed, 13.5% divorced (2000); Foreign born: 0.0% (2000); Ancestry (includes multiple ancestries): 23.7% United States or American, 17.4% German, 10.0% Irish, 8.4% English, 8.0% Other groups (2000).
Economy: Single-family building permits issued: 4 (2005); Multi-family building permits issued: 0 (2005); Employment by occupation: 2.8% management, 16.5% professional, 23.6% services, 20.0% sales, 1.6% farming, 12.5% construction, 23.0% production (2000).
Income: Per capita income: $14,753 (2005); Median household income: $24,707 (2005); Average household income: $32,569 (2005); Percent of households with income of $100,000 or more: 3.1% (2005); Poverty rate: 24.1% (2000).
Taxes: Total city taxes per capita: $137 (2004); City property taxes per capita: $36 (2004).
Education: Percent of population age 25 and over with: High school diploma (including GED) or higher: 67.9% (2005); Bachelor's degree or higher: 6.9% (2005); Master's degree or higher: 2.8% (2005).
School District(s)
Meigs Local SD (PK-12)
  2003-04 Enrollment: 2,092 . . . . (740) 992-2153
Housing: Homeownership rate: 64.3% (2005); Median home value: $52,857 (2005); Median rent: $257 per month (2000); Median age of housing: 54 years (2000).
Transportation: Commute to work: 95.8% car, 0.6% public transportation, 2.5% walk, 0.0% work from home (2000); Travel time to work: 39.4% less than 15 minutes, 26.8% 15 to 30 minutes, 19.6% 30 to 45 minutes, 6.7% 45 to 60 minutes, 7.5% 60 minutes or more (2000)

POMEROY (village). Covers a land area of 3.236 square miles and a water area of 0.047 square miles. Located at 39.02° N. Lat.; 82.03° W. Long. Elevation is 590 feet.
History: Pomeroy began in 1804 when Samuel Pomeroy, a Boston merchant, purchased land here. Coal mining began in Pomeroy in the early

1800's, making the town the primary shipper of coal in Ohio prior to 1850. Salt making was also a leading early industry.
Population: 2,259 (1990); 1,966 (2000); 1,918 (2005); 1,874 (2010 projected); Race: 95.3% White, 2.1% Black, 0.2% Asian, 0.1% Hispanic of any race (2005); Density: 592.7 persons per square mile (2005); Average household size: 2.31 (2005); Median age: 35.6 (2005); Males per 100 females: 78.9 (2005); Marriage status: 24.1% never married, 48.8% now married, 13.2% widowed, 13.9% divorced (2000); Foreign born: 0.2% (2000); Ancestry (includes multiple ancestries): 23.2% German, 21.8% United States or American, 13.2% Irish, 9.3% Other groups, 4.4% English (2000).
Economy: Single-family building permits issued: 1 (2005); Multi-family building permits issued: 0 (2005); Employment by occupation: 4.9% management, 20.2% professional, 21.2% services, 20.2% sales, 6.0% farming, 12.3% construction, 15.2% production (2000).
Income: Per capita income: $12,123 (2005); Median household income: $21,827 (2005); Average household income: $27,880 (2005); Percent of households with income of $100,000 or more: 1.9% (2005); Poverty rate: 39.2% (2000).
Education: Percent of population age 25 and over with: High school diploma (including GED) or higher: 67.9% (2005); Bachelor's degree or higher: 9.3% (2005); Master's degree or higher: 4.4% (2005).
School District(s)
Meigs Local SD (PK-12)
    2003-04 Enrollment: 2,092 . . . . (740) 992-2153
Housing: Homeownership rate: 61.8% (2005); Median home value: $46,260 (2005); Median rent: $246 per month (2000); Median age of housing: 57 years (2000).
Newspapers: The Daily Sentinel (Circulation 3,900)
Transportation: Commute to work: 91.6% car, 0.0% public transportation, 1.7% walk, 3.0% work from home (2000); Travel time to work: 45.5% less than 15 minutes, 27.5% 15 to 30 minutes, 10.6% 30 to 45 minutes, 9.6% 45 to 60 minutes, 6.8% 60 minutes or more (2000)
Additional Information Contacts
Meigs County Chamber of Commerce. . . . . (740) 992-5005
    http://www.meigscountychamber.com
Meigs County Economic Development . . . . (740) 992-3034
    http://www.meigscountyohio.com/econ_development/index.htm

PORTLAND (unincorporated postal area, zip code 45770). Covers a land area of 18.387 square miles and a water area of 0 square miles. Located at 38.98° N. Lat.; 81.80° W. Long. Elevation is 610 feet.
Population: 542 (2000); Race: 100.0% White, 0.0% Black, 0.0% Asian, 0.0% Hispanic of any race (2000); Density: 29.5 persons per square mile (2000); Age: 13.6% under 18, 19.6% over 64 (2000); Marriage status: 22.7% never married, 53.1% now married, 12.1% widowed, 12.1% divorced (2000); Foreign born: 1.4% (2000); Ancestry (includes multiple ancestries): 14.4% German, 13.6% English, 10.3% Irish, 9.1% United States or American, 7.5% French (except Basque) (2000).
Economy: Employment by occupation: 15.2% management, 6.8% professional, 16.2% services, 10.5% sales, 10.5% farming, 18.8% construction, 22.0% production (2000).
Income: Per capita income: $12,589 (2000); Median household income: $29,896 (2000); Poverty rate: 9.9% (2000).
Education: Percent of population age 25 and over with: High school diploma (including GED) or higher: 57.5% (2000); Bachelor's degree or higher: 4.7% (2000).
Housing: Homeownership rate: 76.8% (2000); Median home value: $34,600 (2000); Median rent: $263 per month (2000); Median age of housing: 33 years (2000).
Transportation: Commute to work: 78.0% car, 0.0% public transportation, 0.0% walk, 14.7% work from home (2000); Travel time to work: 23.3% less than 15 minutes, 43.6% 15 to 30 minutes, 20.9% 30 to 45 minutes, 0.0% 45 to 60 minutes, 12.3% 60 minutes or more (2000)

RACINE (village). Covers a land area of 0.416 square miles and a water area of 0 square miles. Located at 38.96° N. Lat.; 81.91° W. Long. Elevation is 601 feet.
Population: 775 (1990); 746 (2000); 739 (2005); 726 (2010 projected); Race: 99.3% White, 0.1% Black, 0.4% Asian, 0.1% Hispanic of any race (2005); Density: 1,776.1 persons per square mile (2005); Average household size: 2.42 (2005); Median age: 38.3 (2005); Males per 100 females: 89.0 (2005); Marriage status: 25.4% never married, 58.4% now married, 6.5% widowed, 9.7% divorced (2000); Foreign born: 0.1% (2000); Ancestry (includes multiple ancestries): 31.8% United States or American, 17.6% German, 16.9% English, 6.7% Other groups, 5.2% Irish (2000).
Economy: Employment by occupation: 8.0% management, 12.2% professional, 20.7% services, 24.1% sales, 2.1% farming, 19.4% construction, 13.5% production (2000).
Income: Per capita income: $15,301 (2005); Median household income: $27,436 (2005); Average household income: $37,074 (2005); Percent of households with income of $100,000 or more: 5.2% (2005); Poverty rate: 26.4% (2000).
Education: Percent of population age 25 and over with: High school diploma (including GED) or higher: 77.6% (2005); Bachelor's degree or higher: 6.1% (2005); Master's degree or higher: 2.2% (2005).
School District(s)
Southern Local SD (PK-12)
    2003-04 Enrollment: 749 . . . . (740) 949-2669
Housing: Homeownership rate: 72.5% (2005); Median home value: $67,288 (2005); Median rent: $289 per month (2000); Median age of housing: 45 years (2000).
Transportation: Commute to work: 97.0% car, 0.0% public transportation, 1.3% walk, 0.4% work from home (2000); Travel time to work: 25.8% less than 15 minutes, 37.8% 15 to 30 minutes, 16.7% 30 to 45 minutes, 10.7% 45 to 60 minutes, 9.0% 60 minutes or more (2000)

REEDSVILLE (unincorporated postal area, zip code 45772). Covers a land area of 41.108 square miles and a water area of 0.226 square miles. Located at 39.14° N. Lat.; 81.83° W. Long. Elevation is 640 feet.
Population: 2,083 (2000); Race: 97.3% White, 0.0% Black, 1.4% Asian, 1.1% Hispanic of any race (2000); Density: 50.7 persons per square mile (2000); Age: 25.5% under 18, 14.4% over 64 (2000); Marriage status: 16.8% never married, 69.2% now married, 7.1% widowed, 6.9% divorced (2000); Foreign born: 1.4% (2000); Ancestry (includes multiple ancestries): 20.3% United States or American, 12.6% German, 9.6% Irish, 8.5% English, 8.3% Other groups (2000).
Economy: Employment by occupation: 8.8% management, 8.3% professional, 16.5% services, 21.5% sales, 2.3% farming, 17.8% construction, 24.8% production (2000).
Income: Per capita income: $15,537 (2000); Median household income: $30,543 (2000); Poverty rate: 8.1% (2000).
Education: Percent of population age 25 and over with: High school diploma (including GED) or higher: 72.4% (2000); Bachelor's degree or higher: 6.4% (2000).
School District(s)
Eastern Local SD (PK-12)
    2003-04 Enrollment: 829 . . . . (740) 667-6079
Housing: Homeownership rate: 87.9% (2000); Median home value: $60,900 (2000); Median rent: $180 per month (2000); Median age of housing: 29 years (2000).
Transportation: Commute to work: 96.3% car, 0.0% public transportation, 0.0% walk, 3.7% work from home (2000); Travel time to work: 20.9% less than 15 minutes, 18.5% 15 to 30 minutes, 35.4% 30 to 45 minutes, 13.1% 45 to 60 minutes, 12.1% 60 minutes or more (2000)

RUTLAND (village). Covers a land area of 0.821 square miles and a water area of 0 square miles. Located at 39.04° N. Lat.; 82.12° W. Long. Elevation is 578 feet.
Population: 469 (1990); 401 (2000); 453 (2005); 495 (2010 projected); Race: 99.3% White, 0.0% Black, 0.0% Asian, 0.0% Hispanic of any race (2005); Density: 551.6 persons per square mile (2005); Average household size: 2.41 (2005); Median age: 38.4 (2005); Males per 100 females: 88.8 (2005); Marriage status: 22.6% never married, 55.4% now married, 13.9% widowed, 8.0% divorced (2000); Foreign born: 0.0% (2000); Ancestry (includes multiple ancestries): 32.4% United States or American, 14.6% German, 6.3% English, 6.0% Irish, 4.3% Other groups (2000).
Economy: In coal-mining area. Employment by occupation: 5.8% management, 14.9% professional, 13.0% services, 26.0% sales, 0.0% farming, 21.4% construction, 18.8% production (2000).
Income: Per capita income: $15,497 (2005); Median household income: $30,814 (2005); Average household income: $37,340 (2005); Percent of households with income of $100,000 or more: 4.3% (2005); Poverty rate: 11.9% (2000).
Education: Percent of population age 25 and over with: High school diploma (including GED) or higher: 76.2% (2005); Bachelor's degree or higher: 6.9% (2005); Master's degree or higher: 4.3% (2005).

School District(s)
Meigs Local SD (PK-12)
2003-04 Enrollment: 2,092 . . . . (740) 992-2153

Housing: Homeownership rate: 80.3% (2005); Median home value: $51,842 (2005); Median rent: $279 per month (2000); Median age of housing: 39 years (2000).
Transportation: Commute to work: 93.4% car, 0.0% public transportation, 1.3% walk, 3.3% work from home (2000); Travel time to work: 28.6% less than 15 minutes, 36.7% 15 to 30 minutes, 23.8% 30 to 45 minutes, 4.1% 45 to 60 minutes, 6.8% 60 minutes or more (2000)

SYRACUSE (village). Covers a land area of 0.923 square miles and a water area of 0.033 square miles. Located at 39.00° N. Lat.; 81.97° W. Long. Elevation is 580 feet.
Population: 866 (1990); 879 (2000); 907 (2005); 905 (2010 projected); Race: 97.5% White, 1.3% Black, 0.0% Asian, 0.1% Hispanic of any race (2005); Density: 983.2 persons per square mile (2005); Average household size: 2.26 (2005); Median age: 41.9 (2005); Males per 100 females: 91.8 (2005); Marriage status: 17.5% never married, 62.7% now married, 9.6% widowed, 10.3% divorced (2000); Foreign born: 0.0% (2000); Ancestry (includes multiple ancestries): 30.7% United States or American, 17.0% German, 8.4% Irish, 7.3% English, 3.7% Other groups (2000).
Economy: In coal-mining and livestock area. Employment by occupation: 10.4% management, 21.2% professional, 11.6% services, 27.2% sales, 1.0% farming, 13.0% construction, 15.7% production (2000).
Income: Per capita income: $20,358 (2005); Median household income: $33,281 (2005); Average household income: $45,933 (2005); Percent of households with income of $100,000 or more: 8.0% (2005); Poverty rate: 15.5% (2000).
Education: Percent of population age 25 and over with: High school diploma (including GED) or higher: 81.8% (2005); Bachelor's degree or higher: 14.0% (2005); Master's degree or higher: 4.3% (2005).
Housing: Homeownership rate: 76.6% (2005); Median home value: $74,937 (2005); Median rent: $262 per month (2000); Median age of housing: 31 years (2000).
Transportation: Commute to work: 94.6% car, 0.0% public transportation, 1.5% walk, 3.4% work from home (2000); Travel time to work: 28.0% less than 15 minutes, 38.0% 15 to 30 minutes, 21.7% 30 to 45 minutes, 7.1% 45 to 60 minutes, 5.3% 60 minutes or more (2000)

Mercer County

Located in western Ohio; bounded on the west by Indiana; drained by the Wabash and St. Marys Rivers; includes part of Grand Lake. Covers a land area of 463.27 square miles, a water area of 10.03 square miles, and is located in the Eastern Time Zone. The county government was organized in 1820. County seat is Celina.

Mercer County is part of the Celina, OH Micropolitan Statistical Area. The entire metro area includes: Mercer County, OH

Weather Station: Celina 3 NE — Elevation: 859 feet

	Jan	Feb	Mar	Apr	May	Jun	Jul	Aug	Sep	Oct	Nov	Dec
High	32	37	49	62	73	81	85	82	77	65	50	38
Low	18	21	30	40	51	60	64	61	55	44	34	24
Precip	2.1	2.1	2.8	3.5	3.6	3.8	4.5	3.5	2.7	2.3	3.0	2.6
Snow	11.4	7.7	4.7	1.1	0.0	0.0	0.0	0.0	0.0	0.3	1.6	6.3

High and Low temperatures in degrees Fahrenheit; Precipitation and Snow in inches

Population: 39,443 (1990); 40,924 (2000); 41,009 (2005); 41,082 (2010 projected); Race: 98.3% White, 0.2% Black, 0.5% Asian, 1.3% Hispanic of any race (2005); Density: 88.5 persons per square mile (2005); Average household size: 2.72 (2005); Median age: 36.7 (2005); Males per 100 females: 99.8 (2005).
Religion: Five largest groups: 61.2% Catholic Church, 8.6% The United Methodist Church, 5.5% Evangelical Lutheran Church in America, 2.5% Churches of God, General Conference, 1.1% The Missionary Church (2000).
Economy: Unemployment rate: 4.0% (2005); Total civilian labor force: 23,897 (2005); Leading industries: 24.4% manufacturing; 13.7% retail trade; 12.5% health care and social assistance (2004); Farms: 1,268 totaling 268,569 acres (2002); Companies that employ 500 or more persons: 1 (2004); Companies that employ 100 to 499 persons: 17 (2004); Companies that employ less than 100 persons: 995 (2004); Black-owned businesses: n/a (2002); Hispanic-owned businesses: n/a (2002); Women-owned businesses: n/a (2002); Retail sales per capita: $13,041 (2006). Single-family building permits issued: 117 (2005); Multi-family building permits issued: 28 (2005).
Income: Per capita income: $20,867 (2005); Median household income: $47,319 (2005); Average household income: $56,163 (2005); Percent of households with income of $100,000 or more: 10.2% (2005); Poverty rate: 6.8% (2003); Bankruptcy rate: 5.90% (2005).
Taxes: Total county taxes per capita: $187 (2004); County property taxes per capita: $94 (2004).
Education: Percent of population age 25 and over with: High school diploma (including GED) or higher: 84.0% (2005); Bachelor's degree or higher: 12.7% (2005); Master's degree or higher: 5.1% (2005).
Housing: Homeownership rate: 80.1% (2005); Median home value: $115,674 (2005); Median rent: $346 per month (2000); Median age of housing: 36 years (2000).
Health: Birth rate: 125.2 per 10,000 population (2004); Death rate: 82.6 per 10,000 population (2004); Age-adjusted cancer mortality rate: 166.3 deaths per 100,000 population (2002); Number of physicians: 9.7 per 10,000 population (2004); Hospital beds: 14.6 per 10,000 population (2003); Hospital admissions: 485.1 per 10,000 population (2003).
Elections: 2004 Presidential election results: 74.9% Bush, 24.5% Kerry, 0.0% Nader, 0.4% Badnarik
National and State Parks: Grand Lake State Park; Harbor Point State Park
Additional Information Contacts
Mercer County Government. . . . . (419) 586-3178
http://www.mercercountyohio.org/
Celina-Mercer Chamber of Commerce . . . . (419) 586-2219
http://www.celinamercer.com
City of Celina . . . . (419) 586-6464
http://www.ci.celina.oh.us
Coldwater Chamber of Commerce . . . . (419) 678-4881
http://www.villageofcoldwater.com

Mercer County Communities

BURKETTSVILLE (village). Aka Gilberts. Covers a land area of 0.166 square miles and a water area of 0 square miles. Located at 40.35° N. Lat.; 84.64° W. Long. Elevation is 975 feet.
Population: 287 (1990); 254 (2000); 260 (2005); 266 (2010 projected); Race: 98.8% White, 0.0% Black, 0.0% Asian, 0.0% Hispanic of any race (2005); Density: 1,567.7 persons per square mile (2005); Average household size: 2.68 (2005); Median age: 33.0 (2005); Males per 100 females: 106.3 (2005); Marriage status: 36.8% never married, 57.8% now married, 4.5% widowed, 0.9% divorced (2000); Foreign born: 0.0% (2000); Ancestry (includes multiple ancestries): 74.4% German, 3.9% French (except Basque), 3.5% United States or American, 1.6% European, 0.8% Other groups (2000).
Economy: Employment by occupation: 4.1% management, 6.9% professional, 10.3% services, 14.5% sales, 8.3% farming, 15.2% construction, 40.7% production (2000).
Income: Per capita income: $21,740 (2005); Median household income: $52,232 (2005); Average household income: $58,273 (2005); Percent of households with income of $100,000 or more: 12.4% (2005); Poverty rate: 0.8% (2000).
Education: Percent of population age 25 and over with: High school diploma (including GED) or higher: 75.3% (2005); Bachelor's degree or higher: 7.5% (2005); Master's degree or higher: 1.7% (2005).
Housing: Homeownership rate: 87.6% (2005); Median home value: $87,333 (2005); Median rent: $325 per month (2000); Median age of housing: 47 years (2000).
Transportation: Commute to work: 86.4% car, 0.0% public transportation, 7.9% walk, 4.3% work from home (2000); Travel time to work: 35.1% less than 15 minutes, 44.8% 15 to 30 minutes, 14.9% 30 to 45 minutes, 0.0% 45 to 60 minutes, 5.2% 60 minutes or more (2000)

CELINA (city). Covers a land area of 4.390 square miles and a water area of 0.045 square miles. Located at 40.55° N. Lat.; 84.57° W. Long. Elevation is 870 feet.
History: Celina was settled in 1834 in a densely forested area. Lumber mills soon attracted woodworkers and cabinet makers, and furniture manufacture became the leading industry.
Population: 9,851 (1990); 10,303 (2000); 10,164 (2005); 10,041 (2010 projected); Race: 96.7% White, 0.3% Black, 1.1% Asian, 2.2% Hispanic of any race (2005); Density: 2,315.2 persons per square mile (2005); Average household size: 2.41 (2005); Median age: 37.1 (2005); Males per 100

females: 92.4 (2005); Marriage status: 21.1% never married, 57.8% now married, 8.7% widowed, 12.4% divorced (2000); Foreign born: 1.0% (2000); Ancestry (includes multiple ancestries): 48.8% German, 8.5% United States or American, 7.2% Irish, 6.6% Other groups, 6.5% English (2000).
Economy: Single-family building permits issued: 28 (2005); Multi-family building permits issued: 18 (2005); Employment by occupation: 8.5% management, 18.0% professional, 18.3% services, 20.5% sales, 0.3% farming, 7.4% construction, 27.0% production (2000).
Income: Per capita income: $19,769 (2005); Median household income: $38,773 (2005); Average household income: $46,846 (2005); Percent of households with income of $100,000 or more: 6.8% (2005); Poverty rate: 11.7% (2000).
Taxes: Total city taxes per capita: $365 (2004); City property taxes per capita: $38 (2004).
Education: Percent of population age 25 and over with: High school diploma (including GED) or higher: 84.7% (2005); Bachelor's degree or higher: 16.2% (2005); Master's degree or higher: 7.4% (2005).

School District(s)
Celina City SD (KG-12)
    2003-04 Enrollment: 3,199 . . . . (419) 586-8300
Mercer Educational Service Center (09-12)
    2003-04 Enrollment: n/a . . . . (419) 586-6628

Two-year College(s)
Wright State University-Lake Campus (Public)
    Fall 2004 Enrollment: 996 . . . . (419) 586-0300
    2005-06 Tuition: In-state $4,617; Out-of-state $10,992

Housing: Homeownership rate: 66.2% (2005); Median home value: $99,971 (2005); Median rent: $355 per month (2000); Median age of housing: 35 years (2000).
Safety: Violent crime rate: 22.3 per 10,000 population; Property crime rate: 334.1 per 10,000 population (2004).
Newspapers: The Daily Standard (Circulation 10,400)
Transportation: Commute to work: 96.3% car, 0.1% public transportation, 1.7% walk, 1.5% work from home (2000); Travel time to work: 52.0% less than 15 minutes, 25.7% 15 to 30 minutes, 12.0% 30 to 45 minutes, 5.1% 45 to 60 minutes, 5.2% 60 minutes or more (2000)

Additional Information Contacts
Celina-Mercer Chamber of Commerce . . . . (419) 586-2219
    http://www.celinamercer.com
City of Celina . . . . (419) 586-6464
    http://www.ci.celina.oh.us

CHICKASAW (village). Covers a land area of 0.229 square miles and a water area of 0 square miles. Located at 40.43° N. Lat.; 84.49° W. Long. Elevation is 946 feet.
Population: 431 (1990); 364 (2000); 359 (2005); 355 (2010 projected); Race: 99.7% White, 0.0% Black, 0.0% Asian, 2.2% Hispanic of any race (2005); Density: 1,570.4 persons per square mile (2005); Average household size: 2.62 (2005); Median age: 37.5 (2005); Males per 100 females: 111.2 (2005); Marriage status: 24.7% never married, 64.2% now married, 8.2% widowed, 2.9% divorced (2000); Foreign born: 0.0% (2000); Ancestry (includes multiple ancestries): 70.8% German, 6.1% United States or American, 4.5% French (except Basque), 3.3% English, 2.5% Swedish (2000).
Economy: Single-family building permits issued: 1 (2005); Multi-family building permits issued: 0 (2005); Employment by occupation: 12.4% management, 13.0% professional, 9.9% services, 19.9% sales, 3.1% farming, 11.2% construction, 30.4% production (2000).
Income: Per capita income: $21,929 (2005); Median household income: $48,750 (2005); Average household income: $57,464 (2005); Percent of households with income of $100,000 or more: 9.5% (2005); Poverty rate: 5.0% (2000).
Education: Percent of population age 25 and over with: High school diploma (including GED) or higher: 87.1% (2005); Bachelor's degree or higher: 13.8% (2005); Master's degree or higher: 8.5% (2005).
Housing: Homeownership rate: 77.4% (2005); Median home value: $137,500 (2005); Median rent: $388 per month (2000); Median age of housing: 30 years (2000).
Transportation: Commute to work: 86.6% car, 0.0% public transportation, 7.6% walk, 5.7% work from home (2000); Travel time to work: 48.0% less than 15 minutes, 39.2% 15 to 30 minutes, 7.4% 30 to 45 minutes, 1.4% 45 to 60 minutes, 4.1% 60 minutes or more (2000)

COLDWATER (village). Covers a land area of 1.976 square miles and a water area of 0 square miles. Located at 40.48° N. Lat.; 84.62° W. Long. Elevation is 912 feet.
Population: 4,390 (1990); 4,482 (2000); 4,523 (2005); 4,576 (2010 projected); Race: 98.9% White, 0.1% Black, 0.2% Asian, 1.4% Hispanic of any race (2005); Density: 2,288.8 persons per square mile (2005); Average household size: 2.69 (2005); Median age: 36.7 (2005); Males per 100 females: 94.8 (2005); Marriage status: 20.1% never married, 64.9% now married, 9.2% widowed, 5.8% divorced (2000); Foreign born: 0.6% (2000); Ancestry (includes multiple ancestries): 73.5% German, 5.7% Irish, 4.2% United States or American, 3.6% Other groups, 2.9% French (except Basque) (2000).
Economy: In agricultural area. Manufacturing: agricultural machinery, apparel, food products. Single-family building permits issued: 17 (2005); Multi-family building permits issued: 0 (2005); Employment by occupation: 5.6% management, 13.8% professional, 15.7% services, 29.3% sales, 0.3% farming, 6.9% construction, 28.4% production (2000).
Income: Per capita income: $22,033 (2005); Median household income: $48,746 (2005); Average household income: $58,529 (2005); Percent of households with income of $100,000 or more: 10.6% (2005); Poverty rate: 5.4% (2000).
Education: Percent of population age 25 and over with: High school diploma (including GED) or higher: 85.2% (2005); Bachelor's degree or higher: 11.0% (2005); Master's degree or higher: 2.8% (2005).

School District(s)
Coldwater Ex Vill SD (PK-12)
    2003-04 Enrollment: 1,623 . . . . (419) 678-2611

Housing: Homeownership rate: 79.8% (2005); Median home value: $103,790 (2005); Median rent: $342 per month (2000); Median age of housing: 35 years (2000).
Hospitals: Mercer County Joint Township Community Hospital (76 beds)
Safety: Violent crime rate: 0.0 per 10,000 population; Property crime rate: 185.8 per 10,000 population (2004).
Newspapers: Mercer County Chronicle (General - Circulation 2,400)
Transportation: Commute to work: 94.5% car, 0.0% public transportation, 3.0% walk, 2.2% work from home (2000); Travel time to work: 52.8% less than 15 minutes, 29.7% 15 to 30 minutes, 11.5% 30 to 45 minutes, 3.3% 45 to 60 minutes, 2.7% 60 minutes or more (2000)

Additional Information Contacts
Coldwater Chamber of Commerce . . . . (419) 678-4881
    http://www.villageofcoldwater.com

FORT RECOVERY (village). Covers a land area of 0.961 square miles and a water area of 0.015 square miles. Located at 40.41° N. Lat.; 84.77° W. Long. Elevation is 948 feet.
History: The original Fort Recovery was built by General Anthony Wayne in 1793.
Population: 1,392 (1990); 1,273 (2000); 1,313 (2005); 1,358 (2010 projected); Race: 98.7% White, 0.2% Black, 0.3% Asian, 1.0% Hispanic of any race (2005); Density: 1,366.5 persons per square mile (2005); Average household size: 2.46 (2005); Median age: 36.6 (2005); Males per 100 females: 98.0 (2005); Marriage status: 24.9% never married, 60.8% now married, 9.0% widowed, 5.3% divorced (2000); Foreign born: 0.7% (2000); Ancestry (includes multiple ancestries): 60.7% German, 7.7% Irish, 7.2% United States or American, 6.2% Other groups, 5.6% English (2000).
Economy: Single-family building permits issued: 9 (2005); Multi-family building permits issued: 2 (2005); Employment by occupation: 8.7% management, 10.4% professional, 12.4% services, 22.6% sales, 2.3% farming, 11.9% construction, 31.6% production (2000).
Income: Per capita income: $22,509 (2005); Median household income: $46,005 (2005); Average household income: $54,953 (2005); Percent of households with income of $100,000 or more: 8.1% (2005); Poverty rate: 3.9% (2000).
Education: Percent of population age 25 and over with: High school diploma (including GED) or higher: 82.9% (2005); Bachelor's degree or higher: 9.6% (2005); Master's degree or higher: 4.0% (2005).

School District(s)
Fort Recovery Local SD (PK-12)
    2003-04 Enrollment: 1,083 . . . . (419) 375-4139

Housing: Homeownership rate: 79.4% (2005); Median home value: $93,780 (2005); Median rent: $313 per month (2000); Median age of housing: 51 years (2000).
Transportation: Commute to work: 89.7% car, 0.6% public transportation, 5.4% walk, 2.8% work from home (2000); Travel time to work: 49.2% less

than 15 minutes, 29.9% 15 to 30 minutes, 13.3% 30 to 45 minutes, 4.5% 45 to 60 minutes, 3.0% 60 minutes or more (2000)

MARIA STEIN (unincorporated postal area, zip code 45860). Covers a land area of 34.838 square miles and a water area of 0.012 square miles. Located at 40.40° N. Lat.; 84.51° W. Long. Elevation is 973 feet.
Population: 2,269 (2000); Race: 100.0% White, 0.0% Black, 0.0% Asian, 0.1% Hispanic of any race (2000); Density: 65.1 persons per square mile (2000); Age: 38.0% under 18, 12.4% over 64 (2000); Marriage status: 22.6% never married, 70.6% now married, 3.8% widowed, 3.0% divorced (2000); Foreign born: 0.0% (2000); Ancestry (includes multiple ancestries): 75.9% German, 9.2% United States or American, 6.1% French (except Basque), 1.7% Dutch, 1.7% Irish (2000).
Economy: Employment by occupation: 15.5% management, 16.6% professional, 7.8% services, 21.2% sales, 4.8% farming, 8.9% construction, 25.2% production (2000).
Income: Per capita income: $17,110 (2000); Median household income: $52,361 (2000); Poverty rate: 2.0% (2000).
Education: Percent of population age 25 and over with: High school diploma (including GED) or higher: 83.6% (2000); Bachelor's degree or higher: 10.5% (2000).
School District(s)
Marion Local SD (PK-12)
    2003-04 Enrollment: 997 . . . . (419) 925-4294
Housing: Homeownership rate: 86.2% (2000); Median home value: $133,500 (2000); Median rent: $334 per month (2000); Median age of housing: 38 years (2000).
Transportation: Commute to work: 89.7% car, 0.0% public transportation, 3.0% walk, 7.4% work from home (2000); Travel time to work: 51.1% less than 15 minutes, 41.6% 15 to 30 minutes, 4.4% 30 to 45 minutes, 1.0% 45 to 60 minutes, 1.9% 60 minutes or more (2000)

MENDON (village). Covers a land area of 0.379 square miles and a water area of 0 square miles. Located at 40.67° N. Lat.; 84.51° W. Long. Elevation is 825 feet.
Population: 772 (1990); 697 (2000); 677 (2005); 657 (2010 projected); Race: 99.3% White, 0.0% Black, 0.0% Asian, 1.0% Hispanic of any race (2005); Density: 1,784.6 persons per square mile (2005); Average household size: 2.61 (2005); Median age: 34.4 (2005); Males per 100 females: 100.3 (2005); Marriage status: 23.9% never married, 58.5% now married, 5.5% widowed, 12.1% divorced (2000); Foreign born: 0.1% (2000); Ancestry (includes multiple ancestries): 39.0% German, 8.1% United States or American, 6.6% Irish, 5.5% Other groups, 3.8% English (2000).
Economy: In agricultural area; cannery. Employment by occupation: 4.4% management, 7.3% professional, 18.8% services, 18.8% sales, 0.8% farming, 10.2% construction, 39.8% production (2000).
Income: Per capita income: $17,976 (2005); Median household income: $40,223 (2005); Average household income: $46,988 (2005); Percent of households with income of $100,000 or more: 6.2% (2005); Poverty rate: 5.3% (2000).
Education: Percent of population age 25 and over with: High school diploma (including GED) or higher: 82.3% (2005); Bachelor's degree or higher: 3.5% (2005); Master's degree or higher: 0.7% (2005).
School District(s)
Parkway Local SD (PK-12)
    2003-04 Enrollment: 1,237 . . . . (419) 363-3045
Housing: Homeownership rate: 78.4% (2005); Median home value: $62,391 (2005); Median rent: $320 per month (2000); Median age of housing: 50 years (2000).
Transportation: Commute to work: 97.6% car, 0.8% public transportation, 1.6% walk, 0.0% work from home (2000); Travel time to work: 22.9% less than 15 minutes, 51.3% 15 to 30 minutes, 16.5% 30 to 45 minutes, 5.1% 45 to 60 minutes, 4.3% 60 minutes or more (2000)

MONTEZUMA (village). Covers a land area of 0.115 square miles and a water area of <.001 square miles. Located at 40.48° N. Lat.; 84.54° W. Long. Elevation is 884 feet.
Population: 199 (1990); 191 (2000); 208 (2005); 224 (2010 projected); Race: 98.1% White, 0.0% Black, 0.0% Asian, 1.9% Hispanic of any race (2005); Density: 1,808.5 persons per square mile (2005); Average household size: 2.63 (2005); Median age: 37.3 (2005); Males per 100 females: 87.4 (2005); Marriage status: 31.3% never married, 53.7% now married, 4.5% widowed, 10.4% divorced (2000); Foreign born: 0.0% (2000); Ancestry (includes multiple ancestries): 55.1% German, 19.3%

Irish, 13.1% English, 10.8% United States or American, 6.8% Other groups (2000).
Economy: Single-family building permits issued: 0 (2005); Multi-family building permits issued: 0 (2005); Employment by occupation: 7.4% management, 3.2% professional, 9.6% services, 25.5% sales, 3.2% farming, 11.7% construction, 39.4% production (2000).
Income: Per capita income: $20,625 (2005); Median household income: $44,583 (2005); Average household income: $54,304 (2005); Percent of households with income of $100,000 or more: 6.3% (2005); Poverty rate: 10.3% (2000).
Education: Percent of population age 25 and over with: High school diploma (including GED) or higher: 84.0% (2005); Bachelor's degree or higher: 7.6% (2005); Master's degree or higher: 3.1% (2005).
Housing: Homeownership rate: 92.4% (2005); Median home value: $82,500 (2005); Median rent: $415 per month (2000); Median age of housing: 50 years (2000).
Transportation: Commute to work: 92.6% car, 0.0% public transportation, 2.1% walk, 1.1% work from home (2000); Travel time to work: 36.6% less than 15 minutes, 45.2% 15 to 30 minutes, 12.9% 30 to 45 minutes, 5.4% 45 to 60 minutes, 0.0% 60 minutes or more (2000)

ROCKFORD (village). Covers a land area of 0.644 square miles and a water area of 0 square miles. Located at 40.69° N. Lat.; 84.64° W. Long. Elevation is 813 feet.
History: Rockford was settled after the Treaty of 1818 on the site of a trading post operated by Anthony Shane. The town was first called Shane's Crossing.
Population: 1,163 (1990); 1,126 (2000); 1,154 (2005); 1,166 (2010 projected); Race: 99.0% White, 0.3% Black, 0.0% Asian, 1.6% Hispanic of any race (2005); Density: 1,791.4 persons per square mile (2005); Average household size: 2.44 (2005); Median age: 37.4 (2005); Males per 100 females: 87.0 (2005); Marriage status: 26.1% never married, 56.5% now married, 7.6% widowed, 9.8% divorced (2000); Foreign born: 0.2% (2000); Ancestry (includes multiple ancestries): 51.5% German, 11.9% Irish, 8.6% Other groups, 7.6% English, 4.4% United States or American (2000).
Economy: Single-family building permits issued: 5 (2005); Multi-family building permits issued: 0 (2005); Employment by occupation: 6.8% management, 11.0% professional, 14.2% services, 22.2% sales, 0.5% farming, 4.3% construction, 40.9% production (2000).
Income: Per capita income: $21,880 (2005); Median household income: $42,567 (2005); Average household income: $48,414 (2005); Percent of households with income of $100,000 or more: 6.1% (2005); Poverty rate: 6.7% (2000).
Education: Percent of population age 25 and over with: High school diploma (including GED) or higher: 79.2% (2005); Bachelor's degree or higher: 9.8% (2005); Master's degree or higher: 3.8% (2005).
School District(s)
Parkway Local SD (PK-12)
    2003-04 Enrollment: 1,237 . . . . (419) 363-3045
Housing: Homeownership rate: 76.7% (2005); Median home value: $75,263 (2005); Median rent: $289 per month (2000); Median age of housing: 51 years (2000).
Transportation: Commute to work: 92.3% car, 0.0% public transportation, 5.7% walk, 0.9% work from home (2000); Travel time to work: 30.8% less than 15 minutes, 43.7% 15 to 30 minutes, 17.6% 30 to 45 minutes, 4.3% 45 to 60 minutes, 3.6% 60 minutes or more (2000)

SAINT HENRY (village). Covers a land area of 1.439 square miles and a water area of 0 square miles. Located at 40.41° N. Lat.; 84.63° W. Long. Elevation is 967 feet.
Population: 2,121 (1990); 2,271 (2000); 2,392 (2005); 2,493 (2010 projected); Race: 99.1% White, 0.0% Black, 0.0% Asian, 1.5% Hispanic of any race (2005); Density: 1,662.3 persons per square mile (2005); Average household size: 3.06 (2005); Median age: 30.8 (2005); Males per 100 females: 104.1 (2005); Marriage status: 22.8% never married, 70.5% now married, 3.7% widowed, 2.9% divorced (2000); Foreign born: 1.1% (2000); Ancestry (includes multiple ancestries): 73.1% German, 6.0% United States or American, 4.3% Other groups, 3.6% Irish, 2.7% French (except Basque) (2000).
Economy: Single-family building permits issued: 11 (2005); Multi-family building permits issued: 0 (2005); Employment by occupation: 10.4% management, 16.7% professional, 13.4% services, 19.5% sales, 0.6% farming, 8.5% construction, 30.9% production (2000).
Income: Per capita income: $20,927 (2005); Median household income: $55,697 (2005); Average household income: $63,588 (2005); Percent of

households with income of $100,000 or more: 12.9% (2005); Poverty rate: 3.6% (2000).
Education: Percent of population age 25 and over with: High school diploma (including GED) or higher: 84.6% (2005); Bachelor's degree or higher: 13.3% (2005); Master's degree or higher: 5.2% (2005).

School District(s)
Saint Henry Consolidated Local SD (PK-12)
    2003-04 Enrollment: 1,157 . . . . (419) 678-4834
Housing: Homeownership rate: 82.3% (2005); Median home value: $129,118 (2005); Median rent: $368 per month (2000); Median age of housing: 30 years (2000).
Transportation: Commute to work: 94.3% car, 0.0% public transportation, 4.0% walk, 0.7% work from home (2000); Travel time to work: 48.1% less than 15 minutes, 35.0% 15 to 30 minutes, 11.9% 30 to 45 minutes, 2.6% 45 to 60 minutes, 2.4% 60 minutes or more (2000)

Miami County

Located in western Ohio; crossed by the Great Miami and Stillwater Rivers. Covers a land area of 407.04 square miles, a water area of 2.18 square miles, and is located in the Eastern Time Zone. The county government was organized in 1807. County seat is Troy.

Miami County is part of the Dayton, OH Metropolitan Statistical Area. The entire metro area includes: Greene County, OH; Miami County, OH; Montgomery County, OH; Preble County, OH

Population: 93,204 (1990); 98,868 (2000); 100,981 (2005); 103,164 (2010 projected); Race: 95.4% White, 1.8% Black, 1.1% Asian, 0.8% Hispanic of any race (2005); Density: 248.1 persons per square mile (2005); Average household size: 2.53 (2005); Median age: 38.5 (2005); Males per 100 females: 96.6 (2005).
Religion: Five largest groups: 12.9% Catholic Church, 6.6% The United Methodist Church, 4.2% United Church of Christ, 3.2% Church of the Brethren, 3.0% Evangelical Lutheran Church in America (2000).
Economy: Unemployment rate: 5.6% (2005); Total civilian labor force: 54,101 (2005); Leading industries: 32.5% manufacturing; 13.8% retail trade; 11.2% health care and social assistance (2004); Farms: 1,071 totaling 184,028 acres (2002); Companies that employ 500 or more persons: 6 (2004); Companies that employ 100 to 499 persons: 51 (2004); Companies that employ less than 100 persons: 2,201 (2004); Black-owned businesses: n/a (2002); Hispanic-owned businesses: n/a (2002); Women-owned businesses: 2,679 (2002); Retail sales per capita: $12,839 (2006). Single-family building permits issued: 307 (2005); Multi-family building permits issued: 0 (2005).
Income: Per capita income: $24,067 (2005); Median household income: $48,351 (2005); Average household income: $60,340 (2005); Percent of households with income of $100,000 or more: 13.2% (2005); Poverty rate: 8.1% (2003); Bankruptcy rate: 9.12% (2005).
Taxes: Total county taxes per capita: $213 (2004); County property taxes per capita: $111 (2004).
Education: Percent of population age 25 and over with: High school diploma (including GED) or higher: 82.9% (2005); Bachelor's degree or higher: 16.4% (2005); Master's degree or higher: 5.4% (2005).
Housing: Homeownership rate: 72.7% (2005); Median home value: $135,221 (2005); Median rent: $423 per month (2000); Median age of housing: 39 years (2000).
Health: Birth rate: 116.3 per 10,000 population (2004); Death rate: 97.1 per 10,000 population (2004); Age-adjusted cancer mortality rate: 193.8 deaths per 100,000 population (2002); Air Quality Index: 84.7% good, 14.9% moderate, 0.5% unhealthy for sensitive individuals, 0.0% unhealthy (percent of days in 2005); Number of physicians: 14.0 per 10,000 population (2004); Hospital beds: 16.4 per 10,000 population (2003); Hospital admissions: 965.2 per 10,000 population (2003).
Elections: 2004 Presidential election results: 65.7% Bush, 34.0% Kerry, 0.0% Nader, 0.2% Badnarik

Additional Information Contacts
Miami County Government . . . . (937) 332-7000
    http://www.co.miami.oh.us/
City of Piqua . . . . (937) 778-2051
    http://www.piquaoh.org
City of Tipp City . . . . (937) 669-8477
    http://www.tippcityohio.gov
City of Troy . . . . (937) 339-1221
    http://www.troyohio.gov
Piqua Chamber of Commerce . . . . (937) 773-2765
    http://www.piquaareachamber.com
Tipp City Chamber of Commerce . . . . (937) 667-8300
    http://www.tippcityohio.gov
Troy Area Chamber of Commerce . . . . (937) 339-8769
    http://www.troyohiochamber.com
West Milton Chamber of Commerce . . . . (937) 698-3055
    http://www.co.miami.oh.us

Miami County Communities

BRADFORD (village). Covers a land area of 0.772 square miles and a water area of 0 square miles. Located at 40.12° N. Lat.; 84.43° W. Long. Elevation is 989 feet.
Population: 2,039 (1990); 1,859 (2000); 1,899 (2005); 1,921 (2010 projected); Race: 98.5% White, 0.0% Black, 0.2% Asian, 0.3% Hispanic of any race (2005); Density: 2,459.1 persons per square mile (2005); Average household size: 2.63 (2005); Median age: 34.3 (2005); Males per 100 females: 96.8 (2005); Marriage status: 20.7% never married, 60.1% now married, 8.0% widowed, 11.3% divorced (2000); Foreign born: 0.3% (2000); Ancestry (includes multiple ancestries): 29.1% German, 14.5% United States or American, 9.6% Irish, 5.4% English, 4.7% Other groups (2000).
Economy: Employment by occupation: 4.1% management, 7.3% professional, 15.9% services, 21.9% sales, 0.0% farming, 9.0% construction, 41.9% production (2000).
Income: Per capita income: $17,122 (2005); Median household income: $41,755 (2005); Average household income: $45,035 (2005); Percent of households with income of $100,000 or more: 2.4% (2005); Poverty rate: 6.7% (2000).
Education: Percent of population age 25 and over with: High school diploma (including GED) or higher: 76.6% (2005); Bachelor's degree or higher: 3.7% (2005); Master's degree or higher: 0.6% (2005).

School District(s)
Bradford Ex Vill SD (PK-12)
    2003-04 Enrollment: 664 . . . . (937) 448-2770
Housing: Homeownership rate: 76.5% (2005); Median home value: $84,627 (2005); Median rent: $351 per month (2000); Median age of housing: 60+ years (2000).
Safety: Violent crime rate: 5.4 per 10,000 population; Property crime rate: 43.6 per 10,000 population (2004).
Transportation: Commute to work: 94.6% car, 0.6% public transportation, 2.4% walk, 1.5% work from home (2000); Travel time to work: 21.6% less than 15 minutes, 48.6% 15 to 30 minutes, 18.0% 30 to 45 minutes, 6.2% 45 to 60 minutes, 5.5% 60 minutes or more (2000)

CASSTOWN (village). Covers a land area of 0.107 square miles and a water area of 0 square miles. Located at 40.05° N. Lat.; 84.12° W. Long. Elevation is 937 feet.
Population: 271 (1990); 322 (2000); 354 (2005); 385 (2010 projected); Race: 100.0% White, 0.0% Black, 0.0% Asian, 0.0% Hispanic of any race (2005); Density: 3,316.8 persons per square mile (2005); Average household size: 2.48 (2005); Median age: 40.8 (2005); Males per 100 females: 94.5 (2005); Marriage status: 22.0% never married, 61.8% now married, 7.9% widowed, 8.3% divorced (2000); Foreign born: 0.6% (2000); Ancestry (includes multiple ancestries): 32.3% German, 30.0% United States or American, 10.6% Irish, 7.1% English, 6.5% French (except Basque) (2000).
Economy: In agricultural area. Employment by occupation: 6.3% management, 6.8% professional, 11.4% services, 25.0% sales, 1.7% farming, 14.8% construction, 34.1% production (2000).
Income: Per capita income: $18,891 (2005); Median household income: $42,734 (2005); Average household income: $46,766 (2005); Percent of households with income of $100,000 or more: 7.0% (2005); Poverty rate: 4.3% (2000).
Education: Percent of population age 25 and over with: High school diploma (including GED) or higher: 86.1% (2005); Bachelor's degree or higher: 5.9% (2005); Master's degree or higher: 0.4% (2005).

School District(s)
Miami East Local SD (PK-12)
    2003-04 Enrollment: 1,342 . . . . (937) 335-7505
Housing: Homeownership rate: 78.3% (2005); Median home value: $95,789 (2005); Median rent: $393 per month (2000); Median age of housing: 60+ years (2000).

Transportation: Commute to work: 92.5% car, 0.0% public transportation, 1.2% walk, 4.0% work from home (2000); Travel time to work: 24.7% less than 15 minutes, 40.4% 15 to 30 minutes, 24.1% 30 to 45 minutes, 2.4% 45 to 60 minutes, 8.4% 60 minutes or more (2000)

CONOVER (unincorporated postal area, zip code 45317). Covers a land area of 21.354 square miles and a water area of 0 square miles. Located at 40.17° N. Lat.; 84.02° W. Long. Elevation is 1,138 feet.
Population: 1,078 (2000); Race: 99.0% White, 0.0% Black, 0.0% Asian, 0.0% Hispanic of any race (2000); Density: 50.5 persons per square mile (2000); Age: 20.5% under 18, 18.1% over 64 (2000); Marriage status: 18.8% never married, 61.3% now married, 7.4% widowed, 12.4% divorced (2000); Foreign born: 0.7% (2000); Ancestry (includes multiple ancestries): 28.7% German, 13.4% English, 10.0% Irish, 8.3% United States or American, 4.8% Norwegian (2000).
Economy: Employment by occupation: 8.2% management, 11.1% professional, 15.8% services, 18.4% sales, 0.0% farming, 11.7% construction, 34.8% production (2000).
Income: Per capita income: $20,023 (2000); Median household income: $41,156 (2000); Poverty rate: 3.0% (2000).
Education: Percent of population age 25 and over with: High school diploma (including GED) or higher: 83.3% (2000); Bachelor's degree or higher: 8.1% (2000).
Housing: Homeownership rate: 82.7% (2000); Median home value: $100,300 (2000); Median rent: $333 per month (2000); Median age of housing: 50 years (2000).
Transportation: Commute to work: 95.6% car, 0.0% public transportation, 2.0% walk, 2.4% work from home (2000); Travel time to work: 32.3% less than 15 minutes, 43.3% 15 to 30 minutes, 16.4% 30 to 45 minutes, 4.2% 45 to 60 minutes, 3.8% 60 minutes or more (2000)

COVINGTON (village). Covers a land area of 1.152 square miles and a water area of 0.028 square miles. Located at 40.11° N. Lat.; 84.35° W. Long. Elevation is 930 feet.
History: Covington was settled in 1807 on the site of an outpost built by General Anthony Wayne.
Population: 2,690 (1990); 2,559 (2000); 2,571 (2005); 2,594 (2010 projected); Race: 98.5% White, 0.2% Black, 0.1% Asian, 0.9% Hispanic of any race (2005); Density: 2,231.3 persons per square mile (2005); Average household size: 2.49 (2005); Median age: 39.0 (2005); Males per 100 females: 92.6 (2005); Marriage status: 19.5% never married, 62.7% now married, 8.2% widowed, 9.5% divorced (2000); Foreign born: 1.0% (2000); Ancestry (includes multiple ancestries): 34.6% German, 13.7% United States or American, 11.0% Irish, 8.2% English, 3.6% Dutch (2000).
Economy: Employment by occupation: 12.8% management, 11.8% professional, 16.2% services, 25.8% sales, 0.0% farming, 8.2% construction, 25.2% production (2000).
Income: Per capita income: $21,924 (2005); Median household income: $44,308 (2005); Average household income: $54,050 (2005); Percent of households with income of $100,000 or more: 8.0% (2005); Poverty rate: 2.6% (2000).
Education: Percent of population age 25 and over with: High school diploma (including GED) or higher: 81.5% (2005); Bachelor's degree or higher: 9.9% (2005); Master's degree or higher: 3.2% (2005).
School District(s)
Covington Exempted Village School District (PK-12)
   2003-04 Enrollment: 867 . . . . (937) 473-2249
Housing: Homeownership rate: 76.0% (2005); Median home value: $112,640 (2005); Median rent: $383 per month (2000); Median age of housing: 56 years (2000).
Safety: Violent crime rate: 15.6 per 10,000 population; Property crime rate: 203.1 per 10,000 population (2004).
Transportation: Commute to work: 94.4% car, 0.4% public transportation, 4.0% walk, 1.0% work from home (2000); Travel time to work: 36.0% less than 15 minutes, 42.6% 15 to 30 minutes, 12.8% 30 to 45 minutes, 5.4% 45 to 60 minutes, 3.1% 60 minutes or more (2000)

FLETCHER (village). Covers a land area of 0.309 square miles and a water area of 0 square miles. Located at 40.14° N. Lat.; 84.11° W. Long. Elevation is 1,050 feet.
Population: 545 (1990); 510 (2000); 536 (2005); 560 (2010 projected); Race: 97.8% White, 0.7% Black, 0.0% Asian, 0.9% Hispanic of any race (2005); Density: 1,736.1 persons per square mile (2005); Average household size: 2.64 (2005); Median age: 33.1 (2005); Males per 100 females: 103.0 (2005); Marriage status: 20.9% never married, 64.8% now married, 6.9% widowed, 7.4% divorced (2000); Foreign born: 1.9% (2000); Ancestry (includes multiple ancestries): 16.7% German, 13.2% United States or American, 9.4% Irish, 5.6% Other groups, 4.2% English (2000).
Economy: In agricultural area. Employment by occupation: 6.4% management, 10.7% professional, 14.6% services, 25.3% sales, 1.7% farming, 12.4% construction, 28.8% production (2000).
Income: Per capita income: $21,390 (2005); Median household income: $47,885 (2005); Average household income: $56,478 (2005); Percent of households with income of $100,000 or more: 9.9% (2005); Poverty rate: 9.4% (2000).
Education: Percent of population age 25 and over with: High school diploma (including GED) or higher: 79.9% (2005); Bachelor's degree or higher: 2.4% (2005); Master's degree or higher: 0.0% (2005).
School District(s)
Miami East Local SD (PK-12)
   2003-04 Enrollment: 1,342 . . . . (937) 335-7505
Housing: Homeownership rate: 83.3% (2005); Median home value: $91,207 (2005); Median rent: $427 per month (2000); Median age of housing: 60+ years (2000).
Transportation: Commute to work: 94.2% car, 0.0% public transportation, 2.2% walk, 2.7% work from home (2000); Travel time to work: 28.6% less than 15 minutes, 56.4% 15 to 30 minutes, 8.6% 30 to 45 minutes, 3.6% 45 to 60 minutes, 2.7% 60 minutes or more (2000)

LAURA (village). Covers a land area of 0.284 square miles and a water area of 0 square miles. Located at 39.99° N. Lat.; 84.40° W. Long. Elevation is 990 feet.
Population: 531 (1990); 487 (2000); 513 (2005); 534 (2010 projected); Race: 97.1% White, 0.0% Black, 0.2% Asian, 3.1% Hispanic of any race (2005); Density: 1,806.1 persons per square mile (2005); Average household size: 2.73 (2005); Median age: 36.0 (2005); Males per 100 females: 110.2 (2005); Marriage status: 20.5% never married, 62.9% now married, 2.1% widowed, 14.5% divorced (2000); Foreign born: 1.8% (2000); Ancestry (includes multiple ancestries): 25.4% German, 13.9% Irish, 12.9% United States or American, 12.1% Other groups, 3.8% English (2000).
Economy: In agricultural area. Single-family building permits issued: 3 (2005); Multi-family building permits issued: 0 (2005); Employment by occupation: 3.9% management, 10.2% professional, 9.5% services, 25.4% sales, 4.6% farming, 16.6% construction, 29.7% production (2000).
Income: Per capita income: $20,936 (2005); Median household income: $48,750 (2005); Average household income: $57,128 (2005); Percent of households with income of $100,000 or more: 11.2% (2005); Poverty rate: 2.8% (2000).
Education: Percent of population age 25 and over with: High school diploma (including GED) or higher: 86.1% (2005); Bachelor's degree or higher: 7.0% (2005); Master's degree or higher: 2.1% (2005).
Housing: Homeownership rate: 83.5% (2005); Median home value: $96,939 (2005); Median rent: $375 per month (2000); Median age of housing: 60+ years (2000).
Transportation: Commute to work: 94.6% car, 0.7% public transportation, 2.9% walk, 1.1% work from home (2000); Travel time to work: 15.3% less than 15 minutes, 39.6% 15 to 30 minutes, 30.5% 30 to 45 minutes, 7.6% 45 to 60 minutes, 6.9% 60 minutes or more (2000)

LUDLOW FALLS (village). Covers a land area of 0.184 square miles and a water area of 0 square miles. Located at 39.99° N. Lat.; 84.34° W. Long. Elevation is 910 feet.
Population: 300 (1990); 210 (2000); 219 (2005); 225 (2010 projected); Race: 98.2% White, 0.0% Black, 0.0% Asian, 0.9% Hispanic of any race (2005); Density: 1,193.4 persons per square mile (2005); Average household size: 2.55 (2005); Median age: 35.1 (2005); Males per 100 females: 114.7 (2005); Marriage status: 26.3% never married, 51.5% now married, 5.3% widowed, 17.0% divorced (2000); Foreign born: 0.5% (2000); Ancestry (includes multiple ancestries): 38.6% United States or American, 33.2% German, 14.9% Irish, 7.9% English, 4.0% Swiss (2000).
Economy: Single-family building permits issued: 0 (2005); Multi-family building permits issued: 0 (2005); Employment by occupation: 9.2% management, 15.0% professional, 18.3% services, 11.7% sales, 0.0% farming, 18.3% construction, 27.5% production (2000).
Income: Per capita income: $18,836 (2005); Median household income: $44,167 (2005); Average household income: $47,965 (2005); Percent of households with income of $100,000 or more: 5.8% (2005); Poverty rate: 6.9% (2000).

Education: Percent of population age 25 and over with: High school diploma (including GED) or higher: 86.5% (2005); Bachelor's degree or higher: 5.7% (2005); Master's degree or higher: 0.0% (2005).
Housing: Homeownership rate: 73.3% (2005); Median home value: $94,706 (2005); Median rent: $350 per month (2000); Median age of housing: 60+ years (2000).
Transportation: Commute to work: 94.9% car, 0.0% public transportation, 2.5% walk, 2.5% work from home (2000); Travel time to work: 32.2% less than 15 minutes, 27.0% 15 to 30 minutes, 34.8% 30 to 45 minutes, 2.6% 45 to 60 minutes, 3.5% 60 minutes or more (2000)

PIQUA (city). Covers a land area of 10.694 square miles and a water area of 0.241 square miles. Located at 40.14° N. Lat.; 84.24° W. Long. Elevation is 869 feet.
History: Piqua was settled in 1797 and called Washington until 1816, when the legislature renamed it for a tribe of the Shawnee, who previously had villages near the site. The earlier fur trading was replaced by a flatboat business, as cargoes of lumber and farm products were sent to New Orleans. In 1815 Piqua became a producer of linseed oil. The Miami & Erie Canal and the railroads stimulated Piqua's growth in the later 1800's.
Population: 21,160 (1990); 20,738 (2000); 20,607 (2005); 20,513 (2010 projected); Race: 94.1% White, 3.1% Black, 0.6% Asian, 0.9% Hispanic of any race (2005); Density: 1,927.0 persons per square mile (2005); Average household size: 2.46 (2005); Median age: 36.0 (2005); Males per 100 females: 92.5 (2005); Marriage status: 22.6% never married, 55.1% now married, 8.7% widowed, 13.6% divorced (2000); Foreign born: 1.4% (2000); Ancestry (includes multiple ancestries): 28.1% German, 14.6% United States or American, 10.7% Irish, 10.4% Other groups, 8.2% English (2000).
Economy: Employment by occupation: 9.2% management, 10.0% professional, 15.1% services, 26.4% sales, 0.3% farming, 8.3% construction, 30.6% production (2000).
Income: Per capita income: $20,704 (2005); Median household income: $39,274 (2005); Average household income: $49,955 (2005); Percent of households with income of $100,000 or more: 7.8% (2005); Poverty rate: 12.2% (2000).
Taxes: Total city taxes per capita: $493 (2004); City property taxes per capita: $73 (2004).
Education: Percent of population age 25 and over with: High school diploma (including GED) or higher: 75.3% (2005); Bachelor's degree or higher: 10.3% (2005); Master's degree or higher: 3.4% (2005).

School District(s)
Piqua City SD (PK-12)
    2003-04 Enrollment: 3,954 . . . . (937) 773-4321
Upper Valley Joint Vocational SD (08-12)
    2003-04 Enrollment: n/a . . . . (937) 778-1980

Four-year College(s)
Edison State Community College (Public)
    Fall 2004 Enrollment: 3,139 . . . . (937) 778-8600
    2005-06 Tuition: In-state $3,270; Out-of-state $6,060

Two-year College(s)
Upper Valley Joint Vocational School (Public)
    Fall 2004 Enrollment: 56 . . . . (937) 778-1980
    2005-06 Tuition: In-state $4,950; Out-of-state $4,950

Housing: Homeownership rate: 63.5% (2005); Median home value: $99,393 (2005); Median rent: $415 per month (2000); Median age of housing: 49 years (2000).
Safety: Violent crime rate: 20.2 per 10,000 population; Property crime rate: 622.5 per 10,000 population (2004).
Newspapers: The Piqua Daily Call (Circulation 7,500)
Transportation: Commute to work: 93.1% car, 1.3% public transportation, 2.5% walk, 2.2% work from home (2000); Travel time to work: 49.9% less than 15 minutes, 33.5% 15 to 30 minutes, 10.2% 30 to 45 minutes, 3.6% 45 to 60 minutes, 2.7% 60 minutes or more (2000)
Additional Information Contacts
City of Piqua. . . . . (937) 778-2051
    http://www.piquaoh.org
Piqua Chamber of Commerce . . . . (937) 773-2765
    http://www.piquaareachamber.com

PLEASANT HILL (village). Covers a land area of 0.474 square miles and a water area of 0 square miles. Located at 40.05° N. Lat.; 84.34° W. Long. Elevation is 935 feet.
Population: 1,124 (1990); 1,134 (2000); 1,202 (2005); 1,269 (2010 projected); Race: 99.1% White, 0.0% Black, 0.4% Asian, 0.2% Hispanic of any race (2005); Density: 2,536.4 persons per square mile (2005); Average household size: 2.64 (2005); Median age: 35.6 (2005); Males per 100 females: 92.6 (2005); Marriage status: 20.4% never married, 67.5% now married, 6.0% widowed, 6.1% divorced (2000); Foreign born: 0.5% (2000); Ancestry (includes multiple ancestries): 33.9% German, 15.6% United States or American, 11.4% English, 7.6% Irish, 5.4% Dutch (2000).
Economy: In agricultural area. Employment by occupation: 10.8% management, 15.7% professional, 15.0% services, 23.0% sales, 0.0% farming, 9.1% construction, 26.3% production (2000).
Income: Per capita income: $23,074 (2005); Median household income: $53,931 (2005); Average household income: $60,956 (2005); Percent of households with income of $100,000 or more: 11.0% (2005); Poverty rate: 2.6% (2000).
Education: Percent of population age 25 and over with: High school diploma (including GED) or higher: 87.6% (2005); Bachelor's degree or higher: 12.7% (2005); Master's degree or higher: 4.7% (2005).

School District(s)
Newton Local SD (PK-12)
    2003-04 Enrollment: 567 . . . . (937) 676-3271

Housing: Homeownership rate: 81.1% (2005); Median home value: $124,531 (2005); Median rent: $376 per month (2000); Median age of housing: 57 years (2000).
Transportation: Commute to work: 94.8% car, 0.0% public transportation, 2.6% walk, 2.2% work from home (2000); Travel time to work: 33.8% less than 15 minutes, 44.2% 15 to 30 minutes, 14.8% 30 to 45 minutes, 3.6% 45 to 60 minutes, 3.6% 60 minutes or more (2000)

POTSDAM (village). Covers a land area of 0.459 square miles and a water area of 0 square miles. Located at 39.96° N. Lat.; 84.41° W. Long. Elevation is 1,010 feet.
Population: 250 (1990); 203 (2000); 213 (2005); 221 (2010 projected); Race: 99.5% White, 0.0% Black, 0.0% Asian, 0.5% Hispanic of any race (2005); Density: 463.9 persons per square mile (2005); Average household size: 3.00 (2005); Median age: 33.9 (2005); Males per 100 females: 108.8 (2005); Marriage status: 25.2% never married, 64.4% now married, 2.2% widowed, 8.1% divorced (2000); Foreign born: 0.0% (2000); Ancestry (includes multiple ancestries): 34.4% United States or American, 18.0% German, 10.6% Irish, 8.5% Other groups, 2.6% Dutch (2000).
Economy: Employment by occupation: 3.8% management, 12.5% professional, 12.5% services, 32.5% sales, 0.0% farming, 16.3% construction, 22.5% production (2000).
Income: Per capita income: $20,082 (2005); Median household income: $46,719 (2005); Average household income: $60,246 (2005); Percent of households with income of $100,000 or more: 9.9% (2005); Poverty rate: 6.9% (2000).
Education: Percent of population age 25 and over with: High school diploma (including GED) or higher: 77.3% (2005); Bachelor's degree or higher: 5.0% (2005); Master's degree or higher: 4.2% (2005).
Housing: Homeownership rate: 87.3% (2005); Median home value: $113,462 (2005); Median rent: $506 per month (2000); Median age of housing: 60+ years (2000).
Transportation: Commute to work: 90.0% car, 0.0% public transportation, 0.0% walk, 10.0% work from home (2000); Travel time to work: 44.4% less than 15 minutes, 31.9% 15 to 30 minutes, 22.2% 30 to 45 minutes, 0.0% 45 to 60 minutes, 1.4% 60 minutes or more (2000)

TIPP CITY (city). Aka Tippecanoe City. Covers a land area of 6.178 square miles and a water area of 0.041 square miles. Located at 39.96° N. Lat.; 84.18° W. Long. Elevation is 830 feet.
History: Formerly called Tippecanoe City.
Population: 6,857 (1990); 9,221 (2000); 9,307 (2005); 9,424 (2010 projected); Race: 96.8% White, 0.3% Black, 1.4% Asian, 1.4% Hispanic of any race (2005); Density: 1,506.6 persons per square mile (2005); Average household size: 2.50 (2005); Median age: 36.3 (2005); Males per 100 females: 94.9 (2005); Marriage status: 19.3% never married, 59.1% now married, 8.5% widowed, 13.1% divorced (2000); Foreign born: 1.4% (2000); Ancestry (includes multiple ancestries): 35.8% German, 13.7% Irish, 12.2% English, 10.8% United States or American, 7.5% Other groups (2000).
Economy: Pulp and paper products, furniture, transportation equipment, metal products. Employment by occupation: 14.3% management, 20.2% professional, 11.2% services, 28.1% sales, 0.2% farming, 6.2% construction, 19.8% production (2000).
Income: Per capita income: $27,327 (2005); Median household income: $54,309 (2005); Average household income: $67,951 (2005); Percent of

households with income of $100,000 or more: 19.5% (2005); Poverty rate: 5.2% (2000).
Education: Percent of population age 25 and over with: High school diploma (including GED) or higher: 89.7% (2005); Bachelor's degree or higher: 23.2% (2005); Master's degree or higher: 7.0% (2005).

School District(s)
Bethel Local SD (PK-12)
    2003-04 Enrollment: 954 .... (937) 845-9414
Tipp City Ex Vill SD (KG-12)
    2003-04 Enrollment: 2,638 .... (937) 667-8444
Housing: Homeownership rate: 66.2% (2005); Median home value: $147,917 (2005); Median rent: $436 per month (2000); Median age of housing: 27 years (2000).
Safety: Violent crime rate: 14.0 per 10,000 population; Property crime rate: 293.4 per 10,000 population (2004).
Newspapers: Tipp City Herald (General - Circulation 7,000); West Milton Record (General - Circulation 3,000)
Transportation: Commute to work: 96.2% car, 0.1% public transportation, 1.6% walk, 1.4% work from home (2000); Travel time to work: 38.8% less than 15 minutes, 35.2% 15 to 30 minutes, 20.4% 30 to 45 minutes, 2.1% 45 to 60 minutes, 3.5% 60 minutes or more (2000)
Additional Information Contacts
City of Tipp City .... (937) 669-8477
    http://www.tippcityohio.gov
Tipp City Chamber of Commerce .... (937) 667-8300
    http://www.tippcityohio.gov

TROY (city). Covers a land area of 9.701 square miles and a water area of 0.067 square miles. Located at 40.04° N. Lat.; 84.20° W. Long. Elevation is 835 feet.
History: Troy was settled in 1798 by Michael Garver, who built a cabin here and encouraged other settlers to follow him. The coming of the canal in 1837 and the railroad in 1850 brought industrial growth to Troy.
Population: 19,956 (1990); 21,999 (2000); 21,914 (2005); 21,985 (2010 projected); Race: 90.4% White, 4.6% Black, 0.2% Asian, 0.9% Hispanic of any race (2005); Density: 2,259.0 persons per square mile (2005); Average household size: 2.42 (2005); Median age: 36.3 (2005); Males per 100 females: 95.4 (2005); Marriage status: 21.0% never married, 57.6% now married, 7.2% widowed, 14.1% divorced (2000); Foreign born: 2.1% (2000); Ancestry (includes multiple ancestries): 25.3% German, 14.6% United States or American, 11.7% Other groups, 11.4% Irish, 8.0% English (2000).
Economy: Employment by occupation: 12.7% management, 18.5% professional, 13.5% services, 24.7% sales, 0.5% farming, 5.1% construction, 25.1% production (2000).
Income: Per capita income: $21,570 (2005); Median household income: $41,737 (2005); Average household income: $51,180 (2005); Percent of households with income of $100,000 or more: 8.6% (2005); Poverty rate: 8.2% (2000).
Taxes: Total city taxes per capita: $594 (2004); City property taxes per capita: $70 (2004).
Education: Percent of population age 25 and over with: High school diploma (including GED) or higher: 81.4% (2005); Bachelor's degree or higher: 17.1% (2005); Master's degree or higher: 5.8% (2005).

School District(s)
Miami East Local SD (PK-12)
    2003-04 Enrollment: 1,342 .... (937) 335-7505
Troy City SD (KG-12)
    2003-04 Enrollment: 4,538 .... (937) 332-6700

Two-year College(s)
Hobart Institute of Welding Technology (Private, Not-for-profit)
    Fall 2004 Enrollment: 97 .... (937) 332-5000
Housing: Homeownership rate: 60.3% (2005); Median home value: $123,090 (2005); Median rent: $435 per month (2000); Median age of housing: 37 years (2000).
Hospitals: Upper Valley Medical Center (128 beds)
Newspapers: Troy Daily News (Circulation 10,864)
Transportation: Commute to work: 95.9% car, 0.6% public transportation, 1.6% walk, 0.8% work from home (2000); Travel time to work: 49.5% less than 15 minutes, 33.8% 15 to 30 minutes, 11.3% 30 to 45 minutes, 2.9% 45 to 60 minutes, 2.4% 60 minutes or more (2000)
Additional Information Contacts
City of Troy .... (937) 339-1221
    http://www.troyohio.gov

Troy Area Chamber of Commerce .... (937) 339-8769
    http://www.troyohiochamber.com

WEST MILTON (village). Aka Milton. Covers a land area of 2.414 square miles and a water area of 0.056 square miles. Located at 39.95° N. Lat.; 84.32° W. Long. Elevation is 918 feet.
History: Settled 1807, incorporated 1835.
Population: 4,499 (1990); 4,645 (2000); 4,698 (2005); 4,767 (2010 projected); Race: 98.5% White, 0.3% Black, 0.3% Asian, 0.8% Hispanic of any race (2005); Density: 1,945.9 persons per square mile (2005); Average household size: 2.46 (2005); Median age: 36.5 (2005); Males per 100 females: 93.5 (2005); Marriage status: 18.8% never married, 59.7% now married, 6.4% widowed, 15.1% divorced (2000); Foreign born: 0.2% (2000); Ancestry (includes multiple ancestries): 27.5% German, 16.7% United States or American, 9.7% Other groups, 9.7% Irish, 7.5% English (2000).
Economy: In agricultural area; manufacturing. Employment by occupation: 8.7% management, 17.0% professional, 15.7% services, 25.1% sales, 1.4% farming, 9.0% construction, 23.2% production (2000).
Income: Per capita income: $21,178 (2005); Median household income: $44,863 (2005); Average household income: $52,010 (2005); Percent of households with income of $100,000 or more: 9.1% (2005); Poverty rate: 6.7% (2000).
Education: Percent of population age 25 and over with: High school diploma (including GED) or higher: 85.3% (2005); Bachelor's degree or higher: 14.3% (2005); Master's degree or higher: 4.8% (2005).

School District(s)
Milton-Union Exempted Village Schools (PK-12)
    2003-04 Enrollment: 1,806 .... (937) 884-7910
Housing: Homeownership rate: 65.9% (2005); Median home value: $121,109 (2005); Median rent: $402 per month (2000); Median age of housing: 39 years (2000).
Transportation: Commute to work: 96.4% car, 0.3% public transportation, 2.1% walk, 1.1% work from home (2000); Travel time to work: 19.1% less than 15 minutes, 44.6% 15 to 30 minutes, 27.1% 30 to 45 minutes, 4.7% 45 to 60 minutes, 4.4% 60 minutes or more (2000)
Additional Information Contacts
West Milton Chamber of Commerce .... (937) 698-3055
    http://www.co.miami.oh.us

Monroe County

Located in eastern Ohio; bounded on the southeast by the Ohio River and the West Virginia border; drained by Little Muskingum River and Sunfish Creek. Covers a land area of 455.54 square miles, a water area of 1.92 square miles, and is located in the Eastern Time Zone. The county government was organized in 1813. County seat is Woodsfield.

Weather Station: Hannibal Lock & Dam   Elevation: 620 feet

	Jan	Feb	Mar	Apr	May	Jun	Jul	Aug	Sep	Oct	Nov	Dec
High	37	42	51	63	73	81	84	83	76	65	54	42
Low	20	22	29	38	48	57	62	61	54	42	33	25
Precip	3.1	2.6	3.6	3.3	4.1	3.6	4.6	3.4	3.0	2.6	3.3	3.1
Snow	na	na	na	tr	0.0	0.0	0.0	0.0	0.0	0.0	tr	na

High and Low temperatures in degrees Fahrenheit; Precipitation and Snow in inches

Population: 15,497 (1990); 15,180 (2000); 14,817 (2005); 14,447 (2010 projected); Race: 98.8% White, 0.3% Black, 0.1% Asian, 0.5% Hispanic of any race (2005); Density: 32.5 persons per square mile (2005); Average household size: 2.47 (2005); Median age: 42.0 (2005); Males per 100 females: 98.1 (2005).
Religion: Five largest groups: 15.2% Churches of Christ, 10.5% The United Methodist Church, 6.1% Catholic Church, 6.0% United Church of Christ, 5.9% Southern Baptist Convention (2000).
Economy: Unemployment rate: 13.3% (2005); Total civilian labor force: 5,458 (2005); Leading industries: 10.6% retail trade; 5.2% transportation & warehousing; 4.0% other services (except public administration) (2004); Farms: 654 totaling 107,198 acres (2002); Companies that employ 500 or more persons: 2 (2004); Companies that employ 100 to 499 persons: 2 (2004); Companies that employ less than 100 persons: 282 (2004); Black-owned businesses: n/a (2002); Hispanic-owned businesses: n/a (2002); Women-owned businesses: 239 (2002); Retail sales per capita: $5,729 (2006). Single-family building permits issued: 0 (2005); Multi-family building permits issued: 0 (2005).
Income: Per capita income: $17,135 (2005); Median household income: $34,575 (2005); Average household income: $42,108 (2005); Percent of

households with income of $100,000 or more: 4.2% (2005); Poverty rate: 11.7% (2003); Bankruptcy rate: 7.08% (2005).
Education: Percent of population age 25 and over with: High school diploma (including GED) or higher: 78.7% (2005); Bachelor's degree or higher: 8.5% (2005); Master's degree or higher: 2.6% (2005).
Housing: Homeownership rate: 80.8% (2005); Median home value: $72,552 (2005); Median rent: $255 per month (2000); Median age of housing: 37 years (2000).
Health: Birth rate: 102.6 per 10,000 population (2004); Death rate: 77.1 per 10,000 population (2004); Age-adjusted cancer mortality rate: 193.7 deaths per 100,000 population (2002); Number of physicians: 4.0 per 10,000 population (2004); Hospital beds: 0.0 per 10,000 population (2003); Hospital admissions: 0.0 per 10,000 population (2003).
Elections: 2004 Presidential election results: 44.3% Bush, 54.9% Kerry, 0.0% Nader, 0.4% Badnarik
National and State Parks: Monroe Lake State Wildlife Area; Sunfish Creek State Forest; Wayne National Forest - Athens Ranger District
Additional Information Contacts
Monroe County Government . . . . (740) 472-1341
  http://www.monroecountyohio.net/
Monroe Chamber of Commerce . . . . (740) 472-5499
  http://www.monroechamber.com

Monroe County Communities

ANTIOCH (village). Covers a land area of 0.104 square miles and a water area of 0 square miles. Located at 39.66° N. Lat.; 81.06° W. Long. Elevation is 1,050 feet.
Population: 68 (1990); 89 (2000); 91 (2005); 91 (2010 projected); Race: 100.0% White, 0.0% Black, 0.0% Asian, 4.4% Hispanic of any race (2005); Density: 878.6 persons per square mile (2005); Average household size: 2.60 (2005); Median age: 40.0 (2005); Males per 100 females: 85.7 (2005); Marriage status: 12.9% never married, 67.1% now married, 18.6% widowed, 1.4% divorced (2000); Foreign born: 2.4% (2000); Ancestry (includes multiple ancestries): 54.2% German, 13.3% Irish, 12.0% English, 6.0% Dutch, 4.8% United States or American (2000).
Economy: In agricultural area. Employment by occupation: 7.1% management, 35.7% professional, 7.1% services, 17.9% sales, 0.0% farming, 21.4% construction, 10.7% production (2000).
Income: Per capita income: $15,137 (2005); Median household income: $30,625 (2005); Average household income: $39,357 (2005); Percent of households with income of $100,000 or more: 5.7% (2005); Poverty rate: 10.8% (2000).
Education: Percent of population age 25 and over with: High school diploma (including GED) or higher: 76.3% (2005); Bachelor's degree or higher: 5.1% (2005); Master's degree or higher: 1.7% (2005).
Housing: Homeownership rate: 85.7% (2005); Median home value: $55,714 (2005); Median rent: $288 per month (2000); Median age of housing: 60+ years (2000).
Transportation: Commute to work: 100.0% car, 0.0% public transportation, 0.0% walk, 0.0% work from home (2000); Travel time to work: 14.3% less than 15 minutes, 71.4% 15 to 30 minutes, 7.1% 30 to 45 minutes, 0.0% 45 to 60 minutes, 7.1% 60 minutes or more (2000)

BEALLSVILLE (village). Covers a land area of 0.369 square miles and a water area of 0 square miles. Located at 39.84° N. Lat.; 81.03° W. Long. Elevation is 1,263 feet.
Population: 464 (1990); 423 (2000); 432 (2005); 428 (2010 projected); Race: 98.6% White, 0.0% Black, 0.0% Asian, 0.2% Hispanic of any race (2005); Density: 1,169.9 persons per square mile (2005); Average household size: 2.43 (2005); Median age: 34.6 (2005); Males per 100 females: 90.3 (2005); Marriage status: 24.2% never married, 53.8% now married, 7.3% widowed, 14.7% divorced (2000); Foreign born: 1.0% (2000); Ancestry (includes multiple ancestries): 25.6% German, 14.8% Irish, 10.5% Other groups, 9.8% United States or American, 5.5% English (2000).
Economy: Sawmilling. Employment by occupation: 1.3% management, 12.5% professional, 16.3% services, 14.4% sales, 2.5% farming, 19.4% construction, 33.8% production (2000).
Income: Per capita income: $18,877 (2005); Median household income: $31,667 (2005); Average household income: $45,815 (2005); Percent of households with income of $100,000 or more: 3.4% (2005); Poverty rate: 18.1% (2000).
Education: Percent of population age 25 and over with: High school diploma (including GED) or higher: 79.5% (2005); Bachelor's degree or higher: 3.9% (2005); Master's degree or higher: 1.4% (2005).
School District(s)
Switzerland of Ohio Local SD (PK-12)
  2003-04 Enrollment: 2,764 . . . . (740) 472-5801
Housing: Homeownership rate: 67.4% (2005); Median home value: $50,400 (2005); Median rent: $150 per month (2000); Median age of housing: 54 years (2000).
Transportation: Commute to work: 88.0% car, 1.3% public transportation, 7.0% walk, 2.5% work from home (2000); Travel time to work: 22.1% less than 15 minutes, 23.4% 15 to 30 minutes, 31.8% 30 to 45 minutes, 12.3% 45 to 60 minutes, 10.4% 60 minutes or more (2000)

CLARINGTON (village). Covers a land area of 1.117 square miles and a water area of 0.141 square miles. Located at 39.77° N. Lat.; 80.86° W. Long. Elevation is 655 feet.
History: Clarington was originally settled by Swiss immigrants, who engaged in clock-making. Many of the later residents were of Slavic and Italian descent.
Population: 406 (1990); 444 (2000); 429 (2005); 418 (2010 projected); Race: 99.1% White, 0.9% Black, 0.0% Asian, 0.7% Hispanic of any race (2005); Density: 383.9 persons per square mile (2005); Average household size: 2.38 (2005); Median age: 42.5 (2005); Males per 100 females: 90.7 (2005); Marriage status: 21.8% never married, 52.5% now married, 7.5% widowed, 18.2% divorced (2000); Foreign born: 0.0% (2000); Ancestry (includes multiple ancestries): 28.4% German, 14.9% Irish, 14.9% United States or American, 10.1% English, 6.7% French (except Basque) (2000).
Economy: Employment by occupation: 6.6% management, 14.2% professional, 30.1% services, 17.5% sales, 0.0% farming, 8.7% construction, 23.0% production (2000).
Income: Per capita income: $14,773 (2005); Median household income: $28,478 (2005); Average household income: $35,208 (2005); Percent of households with income of $100,000 or more: 2.2% (2005); Poverty rate: 25.2% (2000).
Education: Percent of population age 25 and over with: High school diploma (including GED) or higher: 79.4% (2005); Bachelor's degree or higher: 6.4% (2005); Master's degree or higher: 1.0% (2005).
Housing: Homeownership rate: 78.9% (2005); Median home value: $60,036 (2005); Median rent: $230 per month (2000); Median age of housing: 51 years (2000).
Transportation: Commute to work: 93.6% car, 1.2% public transportation, 1.2% walk, 2.3% work from home (2000); Travel time to work: 15.0% less than 15 minutes, 36.5% 15 to 30 minutes, 19.8% 30 to 45 minutes, 16.8% 45 to 60 minutes, 12.0% 60 minutes or more (2000)

GRAYSVILLE (village). Covers a land area of 0.996 square miles and a water area of 0 square miles. Located at 39.66° N. Lat.; 81.17° W. Long. Elevation is 1,100 feet.
Population: 89 (1990); 113 (2000); 111 (2005); 109 (2010 projected); Race: 100.0% White, 0.0% Black, 0.0% Asian, 2.7% Hispanic of any race (2005); Density: 111.4 persons per square mile (2005); Average household size: 2.71 (2005); Median age: 36.5 (2005); Males per 100 females: 109.4 (2005); Marriage status: 7.7% never married, 76.9% now married, 2.6% widowed, 12.8% divorced (2000); Foreign born: 0.0% (2000); Ancestry (includes multiple ancestries): 11.2% Irish, 8.0% United States or American, 8.0% Other groups, 7.2% German, 5.6% English (2000).
Economy: In agricultural area. Employment by occupation: 0.0% management, 0.0% professional, 22.9% services, 25.7% sales, 0.0% farming, 22.9% construction, 28.6% production (2000).
Income: Per capita income: $14,910 (2005); Median household income: $32,500 (2005); Average household income: $40,366 (2005); Percent of households with income of $100,000 or more: 2.4% (2005); Poverty rate: 28.8% (2000).
Education: Percent of population age 25 and over with: High school diploma (including GED) or higher: 71.4% (2005); Bachelor's degree or higher: 2.9% (2005); Master's degree or higher: 2.9% (2005).
School District(s)
Switzerland of Ohio Local SD (PK-12)
  2003-04 Enrollment: 2,764 . . . . (740) 472-5801
Housing: Homeownership rate: 80.5% (2005); Median home value: $55,714 (2005); Median rent: $263 per month (2000); Median age of housing: 60+ years (2000).
Transportation: Commute to work: 94.1% car, 0.0% public transportation, 0.0% walk, 5.9% work from home (2000); Travel time to work: 6.3% less

than 15 minutes, 37.5% 15 to 30 minutes, 0.0% 30 to 45 minutes, 34.4% 45 to 60 minutes, 21.9% 60 minutes or more (2000)

JERUSALEM (village). Covers a land area of 0.251 square miles and a water area of 0 square miles. Located at 39.85° N. Lat.; 81.09° W. Long. Elevation is 1,260 feet.
Population: 144 (1990); 152 (2000); 159 (2005); 161 (2010 projected); Race: 100.0% White, 0.0% Black, 0.0% Asian, 0.0% Hispanic of any race (2005); Density: 633.5 persons per square mile (2005); Average household size: 2.18 (2005); Median age: 44.7 (2005); Males per 100 females: 87.1 (2005); Marriage status: 19.5% never married, 50.0% now married, 11.0% widowed, 19.5% divorced (2000); Foreign born: 0.0% (2000); Ancestry (includes multiple ancestries): 26.6% German, 17.7% United States or American, 14.1% Irish, 8.3% English, 2.1% Welsh (2000).
Economy: In agricultural area. Employment by occupation: 5.3% management, 5.3% professional, 14.7% services, 37.3% sales, 0.0% farming, 14.7% construction, 22.7% production (2000).
Income: Per capita income: $15,204 (2005); Median household income: $29,333 (2005); Average household income: $33,116 (2005); Percent of households with income of $100,000 or more: 1.4% (2005); Poverty rate: 13.5% (2000).
Education: Percent of population age 25 and over with: High school diploma (including GED) or higher: 86.6% (2005); Bachelor's degree or higher: 4.2% (2005); Master's degree or higher: 1.7% (2005).
Housing: Homeownership rate: 79.5% (2005); Median home value: $54,667 (2005); Median rent: $255 per month (2000); Median age of housing: 59 years (2000).
Transportation: Commute to work: 92.8% car, 4.3% public transportation, 2.9% walk, 0.0% work from home (2000); Travel time to work: 21.7% less than 15 minutes, 21.7% 15 to 30 minutes, 14.5% 30 to 45 minutes, 2.9% 45 to 60 minutes, 39.1% 60 minutes or more (2000)

LEWISVILLE (village). Covers a land area of 0.373 square miles and a water area of 0 square miles. Located at 39.76° N. Lat.; 81.21° W. Long. Elevation is 1,187 feet.
Population: 261 (1990); 233 (2000); 216 (2005); 204 (2010 projected); Race: 98.6% White, 0.0% Black, 0.9% Asian, 0.0% Hispanic of any race (2005); Density: 579.7 persons per square mile (2005); Average household size: 2.43 (2005); Median age: 40.8 (2005); Males per 100 females: 83.1 (2005); Marriage status: 19.9% never married, 59.7% now married, 13.4% widowed, 7.0% divorced (2000); Foreign born: 0.0% (2000); Ancestry (includes multiple ancestries): 42.3% German, 12.3% Irish, 5.7% United States or American, 4.4% English, 4.0% Other groups (2000).
Economy: In agricultural area. Employment by occupation: 0.0% management, 10.7% professional, 18.7% services, 22.7% sales, 0.0% farming, 17.3% construction, 30.7% production (2000).
Income: Per capita income: $12,136 (2005); Median household income: $26,471 (2005); Average household income: $28,511 (2005); Percent of households with income of $100,000 or more: 0.0% (2005); Poverty rate: 10.1% (2000).
Education: Percent of population age 25 and over with: High school diploma (including GED) or higher: 73.3% (2005); Bachelor's degree or higher: 6.0% (2005); Master's degree or higher: 1.3% (2005).
Housing: Homeownership rate: 89.9% (2005); Median home value: $67,200 (2005); Median rent: $250 per month (2000); Median age of housing: 60+ years (2000).
Transportation: Commute to work: 97.3% car, 2.7% public transportation, 0.0% walk, 0.0% work from home (2000); Travel time to work: 25.3% less than 15 minutes, 30.7% 15 to 30 minutes, 16.0% 30 to 45 minutes, 12.0% 45 to 60 minutes, 16.0% 60 minutes or more (2000)

MILTONSBURG (village). Covers a land area of 0.077 square miles and a water area of 0 square miles. Located at 39.83° N. Lat.; 81.16° W. Long. Elevation is 1,292 feet.
Population: 56 (1990); 29 (2000); 31 (2005); 32 (2010 projected); Race: 100.0% White, 0.0% Black, 0.0% Asian, 0.0% Hispanic of any race (2005); Density: 402.2 persons per square mile (2005); Average household size: 2.58 (2005); Median age: 38.8 (2005); Males per 100 females: 82.4 (2005); Marriage status: 18.8% never married, 81.3% now married, 0.0% widowed, 0.0% divorced (2000); Foreign born: 0.0% (2000); Ancestry (includes multiple ancestries): 70.0% English, 35.0% French (except Basque), 15.0% Irish, 10.0% Russian, 10.0% Other groups (2000).
Economy: In agricultural area. Limestone quarry. Employment by occupation: 0.0% management, 28.6% professional, 0.0% services, 0.0% sales, 0.0% farming, 0.0% construction, 71.4% production (2000).

Income: Per capita income: $20,323 (2005); Median household income: $50,417 (2005); Average household income: $52,500 (2005); Percent of households with income of $100,000 or more: 0.0% (2005); Poverty rate: 0.0% (2000).
Education: Percent of population age 25 and over with: High school diploma (including GED) or higher: 100.0% (2005); Bachelor's degree or higher: 9.1% (2005); Master's degree or higher: 9.1% (2005).
Housing: Homeownership rate: 100.0% (2005); Median home value: $53,333 (2005); Median rent: $n/a per month (2000); Median age of housing: 23 years (2000).
Transportation: Commute to work: 100.0% car, 0.0% public transportation, 0.0% walk, 0.0% work from home (2000); Travel time to work: 0.0% less than 15 minutes, 28.6% 15 to 30 minutes, 42.9% 30 to 45 minutes, 28.6% 45 to 60 minutes, 0.0% 60 minutes or more (2000)

SARDIS (unincorporated postal area, zip code 43946). Covers a land area of 56.186 square miles and a water area of 0.023 square miles. Located at 39.64° N. Lat.; 80.96° W. Long. Elevation is 668 feet.
Population: 2,057 (2000); Race: 97.4% White, 0.0% Black, 0.3% Asian, 0.0% Hispanic of any race (2000); Density: 36.6 persons per square mile (2000); Age: 18.1% under 18, 14.4% over 64 (2000); Marriage status: 22.6% never married, 65.8% now married, 5.5% widowed, 6.0% divorced (2000); Foreign born: 0.6% (2000); Ancestry (includes multiple ancestries): 24.1% German, 11.5% United States or American, 11.3% Irish, 11.1% English, 7.9% Other groups (2000).
Economy: Employment by occupation: 5.3% management, 9.8% professional, 10.2% services, 27.4% sales, 0.9% farming, 17.9% construction, 28.5% production (2000).
Income: Per capita income: $20,635 (2000); Median household income: $35,804 (2000); Poverty rate: 9.6% (2000).
Education: Percent of population age 25 and over with: High school diploma (including GED) or higher: 86.4% (2000); Bachelor's degree or higher: 8.2% (2000).

School District(s)
Switzerland of Ohio Local SD (PK-12)
    2003-04 Enrollment: 2,764 . . . . (740) 472-5801

Housing: Homeownership rate: 82.7% (2000); Median home value: $80,200 (2000); Median rent: $311 per month (2000); Median age of housing: 33 years (2000).
Transportation: Commute to work: 96.5% car, 0.8% public transportation, 1.2% walk, 1.5% work from home (2000); Travel time to work: 34.9% less than 15 minutes, 36.3% 15 to 30 minutes, 12.3% 30 to 45 minutes, 5.5% 45 to 60 minutes, 11.0% 60 minutes or more (2000)

STAFFORD (village). Covers a land area of 0.338 square miles and a water area of 0 square miles. Located at 39.71° N. Lat.; 81.27° W. Long. Elevation is 1,080 feet.
Population: 97 (1990); 86 (2000); 84 (2005); 83 (2010 projected); Race: 98.8% White, 0.0% Black, 0.0% Asian, 0.0% Hispanic of any race (2005); Density: 248.4 persons per square mile (2005); Average household size: 2.27 (2005); Median age: 44.2 (2005); Males per 100 females: 100.0 (2005); Marriage status: 28.1% never married, 51.6% now married, 4.7% widowed, 15.6% divorced (2000); Foreign born: 0.0% (2000); Ancestry (includes multiple ancestries): 55.7% German, 18.6% Dutch, 15.7% Irish, 7.1% United States or American, 5.7% Italian (2000).
Economy: Employment by occupation: 5.0% management, 0.0% professional, 15.0% services, 50.0% sales, 0.0% farming, 10.0% construction, 20.0% production (2000).
Income: Per capita income: $14,167 (2005); Median household income: $29,231 (2005); Average household income: $32,162 (2005); Percent of households with income of $100,000 or more: 0.0% (2005); Poverty rate: 11.4% (2000).
Education: Percent of population age 25 and over with: High school diploma (including GED) or higher: 61.0% (2005); Bachelor's degree or higher: 6.8% (2005); Master's degree or higher: 0.0% (2005).
Housing: Homeownership rate: 67.6% (2005); Median home value: $65,556 (2005); Median rent: $250 per month (2000); Median age of housing: 60+ years (2000).
Transportation: Commute to work: 100.0% car, 0.0% public transportation, 0.0% walk, 0.0% work from home (2000); Travel time to work: 10.0% less than 15 minutes, 20.0% 15 to 30 minutes, 15.0% 30 to 45 minutes, 55.0% 45 to 60 minutes, 0.0% 60 minutes or more (2000)

WILSON (village). Covers a land area of 0.418 square miles and a water area of 0.064 square miles. Located at 39.86° N. Lat.; 81.07° W. Long. Elevation is 1,247 feet.
Population: 136 (1990); 118 (2000); 127 (2005); 133 (2010 projected); Race: 98.4% White, 0.0% Black, 0.0% Asian, 0.0% Hispanic of any race (2005); Density: 304.2 persons per square mile (2005); Average household size: 2.23 (2005); Median age: 52.0 (2005); Males per 100 females: 119.0 (2005); Marriage status: 9.6% never married, 73.4% now married, 5.3% widowed, 11.7% divorced (2000); Foreign born: 0.0% (2000); Ancestry (includes multiple ancestries): 19.8% German, 12.1% United States or American, 10.3% English, 9.5% Irish, 5.2% Italian (2000).
Economy: Employment by occupation: 4.5% management, 22.4% professional, 7.5% services, 19.4% sales, 0.0% farming, 13.4% construction, 32.8% production (2000).
Income: Per capita income: $20,020 (2005); Median household income: $34,643 (2005); Average household income: $44,605 (2005); Percent of households with income of $100,000 or more: 3.5% (2005); Poverty rate: 4.3% (2000).
Education: Percent of population age 25 and over with: High school diploma (including GED) or higher: 96.0% (2005); Bachelor's degree or higher: 19.0% (2005); Master's degree or higher: 11.0% (2005).
Housing: Homeownership rate: 98.2% (2005); Median home value: $66,667 (2005); Median rent: $n/a per month (2000); Median age of housing: 40 years (2000).
Transportation: Commute to work: 95.5% car, 0.0% public transportation, 0.0% walk, 1.5% work from home (2000); Travel time to work: 21.2% less than 15 minutes, 13.6% 15 to 30 minutes, 43.9% 30 to 45 minutes, 7.6% 45 to 60 minutes, 13.6% 60 minutes or more (2000)

WOODSFIELD (village). Covers a land area of 2.043 square miles and a water area of 0 square miles. Located at 39.76° N. Lat.; 81.11° W. Long. Elevation is 1,213 feet.
History: Settled 1815, incorporated 1834.
Population: 2,960 (1990); 2,598 (2000); 2,472 (2005); 2,342 (2010 projected); Race: 98.7% White, 0.1% Black, 0.2% Asian, 0.6% Hispanic of any race (2005); Density: 1,209.7 persons per square mile (2005); Average household size: 2.26 (2005); Median age: 44.1 (2005); Males per 100 females: 82.7 (2005); Marriage status: 21.0% never married, 59.8% now married, 10.4% widowed, 8.8% divorced (2000); Foreign born: 0.1% (2000); Ancestry (includes multiple ancestries): 27.9% German, 10.6% Irish, 10.4% English, 7.9% United States or American, 6.5% Other groups (2000).
Economy: In agricultural area; coal mines, oil and gas wells; hardwood timber. Manufacturing tools. Single-family building permits issued: 0 (2005); Multi-family building permits issued: 0 (2005); Employment by occupation: 10.5% management, 14.2% professional, 19.4% services, 25.0% sales, 0.6% farming, 10.1% construction, 20.3% production (2000).
Income: Per capita income: $15,978 (2005); Median household income: $27,267 (2005); Average household income: $35,594 (2005); Percent of households with income of $100,000 or more: 2.8% (2005); Poverty rate: 17.3% (2000).
Education: Percent of population age 25 and over with: High school diploma (including GED) or higher: 76.3% (2005); Bachelor's degree or higher: 12.5% (2005); Master's degree or higher: 3.9% (2005).

School District(s)
Switzerland of Ohio Local SD (PK-12)
    2003-04 Enrollment: 2,764 . . . . (740) 472-5801

Housing: Homeownership rate: 65.5% (2005); Median home value: $66,576 (2005); Median rent: $238 per month (2000); Median age of housing: 47 years (2000).
Newspapers: Monroe County Beacon (General - Circulation 5,300); Monroe County Sentinel (General - Circulation 7,250)
Transportation: Commute to work: 89.1% car, 1.2% public transportation, 5.3% walk, 4.3% work from home (2000); Travel time to work: 53.5% less than 15 minutes, 9.5% 15 to 30 minutes, 18.3% 30 to 45 minutes, 9.4% 45 to 60 minutes, 9.5% 60 minutes or more (2000)
Additional Information Contacts
Monroe Chamber of Commerce . . . . (740) 472-5499
    http://www.monroechamber.com

Montgomery County

Located in western Ohio; crossed by the Great Miami, Stillwater, and Mad Rivers. Covers a land area of 461.68 square miles, a water area of 2.67 square miles, and is located in the Eastern Time Zone. The county government was organized in 1803. County seat is Dayton.

Montgomery County is part of the Dayton, OH Metropolitan Statistical Area. The entire metro area includes: Greene County, OH; Miami County, OH; Montgomery County, OH; Preble County, OH

Weather Station: Dayton Int'l Airport   Elevation: 997 feet

	Jan	Feb	Mar	Apr	May	Jun	Jul	Aug	Sep	Oct	Nov	Dec
High	34	39	50	62	72	81	85	83	76	64	51	40
Low	19	22	31	41	51	60	65	62	55	44	34	25
Precip	2.5	2.3	3.3	4.1	4.2	4.2	3.7	3.4	2.6	2.7	3.3	3.1
Snow	9.7	6.6	4.7	0.8	tr	0.0	tr	0.0	0.0	0.4	1.5	4.4

High and Low temperatures in degrees Fahrenheit; Precipitation and Snow in inches

Weather Station: Dayton MCD   Elevation: 744 feet

	Jan	Feb	Mar	Apr	May	Jun	Jul	Aug	Sep	Oct	Nov	Dec
High	35	40	50	63	74	83	87	85	79	66	52	41
Low	20	23	32	42	53	63	67	65	57	45	36	27
Precip	2.6	2.3	3.1	4.1	4.4	4.1	3.9	3.3	2.6	2.7	3.3	2.9
Snow	6.3	3.6	2.4	0.2	0.0	0.0	0.0	0.0	0.0	tr	0.4	2.8

High and Low temperatures in degrees Fahrenheit; Precipitation and Snow in inches

Population: 573,809 (1990); 559,062 (2000); 550,137 (2005); 540,921 (2010 projected); Race: 75.7% White, 20.1% Black, 1.6% Asian, 1.3% Hispanic of any race (2005); Density: 1,191.6 persons per square mile (2005); Average household size: 2.41 (2005); Median age: 37.5 (2005); Males per 100 females: 92.9 (2005).
Religion: Five largest groups: 16.0% Catholic Church, 4.9% Southern Baptist Convention, 4.5% The United Methodist Church, 2.3% Evangelical Lutheran Church in America, 1.9% American Baptist Churches in the USA (2000).
Economy: Unemployment rate: 6.4% (2005); Total civilian labor force: 272,178 (2005); Leading industries: 16.7% health care and social assistance; 15.5% manufacturing; 11.5% retail trade (2004); Farms: 832 totaling 101,912 acres (2002); Companies that employ 500 or more persons: 41 (2004); Companies that employ 100 to 499 persons: 349 (2004); Companies that employ less than 100 persons: 12,442 (2004); Black-owned businesses: 2,489 (2002); Hispanic-owned businesses: 239 (2002); Women-owned businesses: 11,002 (2002); Retail sales per capita: $14,798 (2006). Single-family building permits issued: 1,280 (2005); Multi-family building permits issued: 92 (2005).
Income: Per capita income: $24,525 (2005); Median household income: $44,797 (2005); Average household income: $58,325 (2005); Percent of households with income of $100,000 or more: 13.6% (2005); Poverty rate: 11.2% (2003); Bankruptcy rate: 13.29% (2005).
Taxes: Total county taxes per capita: $302 (2004); County property taxes per capita: $166 (2004).
Education: Percent of population age 25 and over with: High school diploma (including GED) or higher: 83.7% (2005); Bachelor's degree or higher: 23.1% (2005); Master's degree or higher: 8.5% (2005).
Housing: Homeownership rate: 65.0% (2005); Median home value: $112,600 (2005); Median rent: $427 per month (2000); Median age of housing: 38 years (2000).
Health: Birth rate: 131.7 per 10,000 population (2004); Death rate: 103.5 per 10,000 population (2004); Age-adjusted cancer mortality rate: 217.5 deaths per 100,000 population (2002); Air Quality Index: 39.7% good, 54.2% moderate, 6.0% unhealthy for sensitive individuals, 0.0% unhealthy (percent of days in 2005); Number of physicians: 36.0 per 10,000 population (2004); Hospital beds: 50.0 per 10,000 population (2003); Hospital admissions: 1,853.1 per 10,000 population (2003).
Elections: 2004 Presidential election results: 49.0% Bush, 50.6% Kerry, 0.0% Nader, 0.2% Badnarik
National and State Parks: Miamisburg Mound State Memorial; Sycamore State Park
Additional Information Contacts
Montgomery County Government . . . . (937) 225-4690
    http://www.co.montgomery.oh.us/
Brookville Chamber of Commerce . . . . (937) 833-2375
    http://www.brookvilleohio.com
City of Centerville . . . . (937) 433-7151
    http://www.ci.centerville.oh.us
City of Clayton . . . . (937) 836-3500
    http://www.clayton.oh.us
City of Dayton . . . . (937) 333-3333
    http://www.cityofdayton.org

PROFILES OF OHIO / Montgomery County

City of Englewood .... (937) 836-5106
http://www.ci.englewood.oh.us
City of Huber Heights........................... (937) 233-1423
http://www.ci.huber-heights.oh.us
City of Kettering .... (937) 296-2400
http://www.ketteringoh.org
City of Miamisburg .... (937) 866-3303
http://www.ci.miamisburg.oh.us
City of Moraine.................................. (937) 535-1000
http://www.ci.moraine.oh.us/index.php
City of Riverside................................. (937) 233-1801
http://www.riverside.oh.us
City of Trotwood................................. (937) 837-7771
http://www.trotwood.org/home.html
City of Union .... (937) 836-8624
http://www.ci.union.oh.us
City of Vandalia .... (937) 898-5891
http://www.ci.vandalia.oh.us
City of West Carrollton City .... (937) 859-5183
http://www.westcarrollton.org
Dayton Area Chamber of Commerce.............. (937) 226-1444
http://www.daytonchamber.org
Dayton/Montgomery Co. Convention & Visitors Bureau ... (800) 221-8235
http://www.daytoncvb.com
Engelwood Chamber of Commerce................ (937) 836-2550
http://www.englewood-northmontcoc.com
Huber Heights Chamber of Commerce .... (937) 233-5700
http://www.huberheightschamber.com
Kettering Moraine Chamber of Commerce .... (937) 299-3852
http://www.kmo-coc.org
South Metro Dayton Chamber of Commerce....... (937) 433-2032
http://www.smrcoc.org
Trotwood Chamber of Commerce .... (937) 837-1484
http://www.trotwoodchamber.com
Vandalia-Butler Chamber of Commerce .... (937) 898-5351
http://www.vandaliabutlerchamber.org
Village of Brookville .... (937) 833-2135
http://www.brookvilleohio.com
Village of Germantown........................... (937) 855-7255
http://www.ci.germantown.oh.us
Village of New Lebanon......................... (937) 687-1341
http://www.newlebanonoh.com

Montgomery County Communities

BROOKVILLE (village). Covers a land area of 3.368 square miles and a water area of 0 square miles. Located at 39.83° N. Lat.; 84.41° W. Long. Elevation is 1,033 feet.
Population: 5,087 (1990); 5,289 (2000); 5,385 (2005); 5,480 (2010 projected); Race: 98.4% White, 0.1% Black, 0.9% Asian, 0.4% Hispanic of any race (2005); Density: 1,599.1 persons per square mile (2005); Average household size: 2.35 (2005); Median age: 41.5 (2005); Males per 100 females: 88.8 (2005); Marriage status: 21.0% never married, 58.4% now married, 8.8% widowed, 11.8% divorced (2000); Foreign born: 0.5% (2000); Ancestry (includes multiple ancestries): 31.0% German, 13.3% United States or American, 10.2% Irish, 6.3% English, 4.8% Other groups (2000).
Economy: Furniture, transportation equip. Single-family building permits issued: 20 (2005); Multi-family building permits issued: 6 (2005); Employment by occupation: 8.3% management, 17.9% professional, 14.4% services, 26.5% sales, 0.0% farming, 11.2% construction, 21.7% production (2000).
Income: Per capita income: $23,649 (2005); Median household income: $44,669 (2005); Average household income: $54,602 (2005); Percent of households with income of $100,000 or more: 10.7% (2005); Poverty rate: 5.3% (2000).
Education: Percent of population age 25 and over with: High school diploma (including GED) or higher: 83.7% (2005); Bachelor's degree or higher: 18.5% (2005); Master's degree or higher: 7.7% (2005).
School District(s)
Brookville Local School District (PK-12)
 2003-04 Enrollment: 1,631 .... (937) 833-2181
Housing: Homeownership rate: 66.7% (2005); Median home value: $120,144 (2005); Median rent: $445 per month (2000); Median age of housing: 38 years (2000).
Safety: Violent crime rate: 11.3 per 10,000 population; Property crime rate: 232.5 per 10,000 population (2004).
Newspapers: Brookville Star (General - Circulation 6,300)
Transportation: Commute to work: 93.5% car, 0.3% public transportation, 3.1% walk, 1.6% work from home (2000); Travel time to work: 34.9% less than 15 minutes, 28.7% 15 to 30 minutes, 26.9% 30 to 45 minutes, 4.7% 45 to 60 minutes, 4.7% 60 minutes or more (2000)
Additional Information Contacts
Brookville Chamber of Commerce................... (937) 833-2375
http://www.brookvilleohio.com
Village of Brookville .... (937) 833-2135
http://www.brookvilleohio.com

CENTERVILLE (city). Covers a land area of 10.200 square miles and a water area of 0.019 square miles. Located at 39.63° N. Lat.; 84.14° W. Long. Elevation is 1,020 feet.
History: Incorporated 1879.
Population: 21,563 (1990); 23,024 (2000); 22,902 (2005); 22,894 (2010 projected); Race: 91.0% White, 3.3% Black, 3.9% Asian, 1.1% Hispanic of any race (2005); Density: 2,245.2 persons per square mile (2005); Average household size: 2.27 (2005); Median age: 43.6 (2005); Males per 100 females: 87.4 (2005); Marriage status: 20.2% never married, 61.7% now married, 7.9% widowed, 10.1% divorced (2000); Foreign born: 4.2% (2000); Ancestry (includes multiple ancestries): 34.1% German, 17.7% Irish, 14.9% English, 9.8% Other groups, 6.2% United States or American (2000).
Economy: Single-family building permits issued: 71 (2005); Multi-family building permits issued: 0 (2005); Employment by occupation: 18.8% management, 32.8% professional, 9.7% services, 28.3% sales, 0.0% farming, 3.9% construction, 6.6% production (2000).
Income: Per capita income: $34,677 (2005); Median household income: $62,855 (2005); Average household income: $77,514 (2005); Percent of households with income of $100,000 or more: 25.5% (2005); Poverty rate: 4.1% (2000).
Education: Percent of population age 25 and over with: High school diploma (including GED) or higher: 95.5% (2005); Bachelor's degree or higher: 45.7% (2005); Master's degree or higher: 17.8% (2005).
School District(s)
Centerville City SD (KG-12)
 2003-04 Enrollment: 8,120 .... (937) 433-8841
Housing: Homeownership rate: 74.4% (2005); Median home value: $158,286 (2005); Median rent: $556 per month (2000); Median age of housing: 24 years (2000).
Transportation: Commute to work: 95.5% car, 1.0% public transportation, 0.5% walk, 2.8% work from home (2000); Travel time to work: 29.7% less than 15 minutes, 49.3% 15 to 30 minutes, 13.5% 30 to 45 minutes, 3.7% 45 to 60 minutes, 3.8% 60 minutes or more (2000)
Additional Information Contacts
City of Centerville................................. (937) 433-7151
http://www.ci.centerville.oh.us

CLAYTON (city). Covers a land area of 18.444 square miles and a water area of 0.113 square miles. Located at 39.85° N. Lat.; 84.31° W. Long. Elevation is 1,000 feet.
Population: 13,159 (1990); 13,347 (2000); 13,215 (2005); 13,094 (2010 projected); Race: 85.1% White, 11.4% Black, 1.7% Asian, 0.9% Hispanic of any race (2005); Density: 716.5 persons per square mile (2005); Average household size: 2.64 (2005); Median age: 40.2 (2005); Males per 100 females: 97.4 (2005); Marriage status: 20.8% never married, 66.0% now married, 4.6% widowed, 8.6% divorced (2000); Foreign born: 2.1% (2000); Ancestry (includes multiple ancestries): 32.2% German, 14.7% Other groups, 14.2% Irish, 9.7% English, 8.7% United States or American (2000).
Economy: Employment by occupation: 18.4% management, 24.7% professional, 11.3% services, 28.1% sales, 0.0% farming, 7.3% construction, 10.2% production (2000).
Income: Per capita income: $30,597 (2005); Median household income: $65,757 (2005); Average household income: $80,747 (2005); Percent of households with income of $100,000 or more: 24.4% (2005); Poverty rate: 4.4% (2000).
Taxes: Total city taxes per capita: $178 (2004); City property taxes per capita: $30 (2004).
Education: Percent of population age 25 and over with: High school diploma (including GED) or higher: 91.5% (2005); Bachelor's degree or higher: 32.5% (2005); Master's degree or higher: 12.7% (2005).

School District(s)

Miami Valley Career Tech (09-12)
 2003-04 Enrollment: n/a .... (937) 837-7781
Northmont City SD (KG-12)
 2003-04 Enrollment: 5,933 .... (937) 832-5000

Two-year College(s)

Miami Valley Career Technology Center (Public)
 Fall 2004 Enrollment: 441 .... (800) 716-7161
 2005-06 Tuition: In-state $5,795; Out-of-state $5,795

Housing: Homeownership rate: 85.1% (2005); Median home value: $148,305 (2005); Median rent: $472 per month (2000); Median age of housing: 29 years (2000).

Transportation: Commute to work: 95.3% car, 0.7% public transportation, 1.1% walk, 2.5% work from home (2000); Travel time to work: 26.1% less than 15 minutes, 44.6% 15 to 30 minutes, 22.2% 30 to 45 minutes, 3.3% 45 to 60 minutes, 3.9% 60 minutes or more (2000)

Additional Information Contacts

City of Clayton .... (937) 836-3500
http://www.clayton.oh.us

DAYTON (city). Covers a land area of 55.777 square miles and a water area of 0.851 square miles. Located at 39.76° N. Lat.; 84.19° W. Long. Elevation is 750 feet.

History: Settlers began coming in 1795 to the site where the Great Miami River was joined by the Stillwater and Mad Rivers and Wolf Creek. When Ohio became a state in 1803, Dayton became the Montgomery County seat, and two years later the town was incorporated. The opening of the canal system in the 1830's increased Dayton's river traffic, augmented by the railroad traffic that began in 1851. Industries such as the railroad car works and the National Cash Register Company were founded between 1850 and 1890, and by the early 1900's locally-made Stoddard-Dayton, Speedwell, and Big Four automobiles were wheeling around Dayton. Wilbur and Orville Wright used the Dayton Public Library to learn about aerodynamics, and soon established an experimental airplane factory here. Charles F. Kettering came to Dayton to work at the cash register plant, invented a quick-starting electric motor, and started the Dayton Engineering Laboratories Company (Delco). Dayton suffered recurring floods until a system of levees and dams to restrain the rivers was completed in 1921.

Population: 182,920 (1990); 166,179 (2000); 159,845 (2005); 153,413 (2010 projected); Race: 52.7% White, 43.2% Black, 0.8% Asian, 1.7% Hispanic of any race (2005); Density: 2,865.8 persons per square mile (2005); Average household size: 2.44 (2005); Median age: 33.7 (2005); Males per 100 females: 94.4 (2005); Marriage status: 38.7% never married, 39.2% now married, 7.8% widowed, 14.3% divorced (2000); Foreign born: 2.0% (2000); Ancestry (includes multiple ancestries): 40.1% Other groups, 14.4% German, 8.3% Irish, 7.7% United States or American, 4.9% English (2000).

Economy: Unemployment rate: 7.6% (2005); Total civilian labor force: 71,169 (2005); Single-family building permits issued: 215 (2005); Multi-family building permits issued: 0 (2005); Employment by occupation: 8.6% management, 17.1% professional, 21.1% services, 25.3% sales, 0.1% farming, 7.8% construction, 20.0% production (2000).

Income: Per capita income: $17,218 (2005); Median household income: $30,864 (2005); Average household income: $40,766 (2005); Percent of households with income of $100,000 or more: 6.3% (2005); Poverty rate: 23.0% (2000).

Taxes: Total city taxes per capita: $802 (2004); City property taxes per capita: $127 (2004).

Education: Percent of population age 25 and over with: High school diploma (including GED) or higher: 75.5% (2005); Bachelor's degree or higher: 14.8% (2005); Master's degree or higher: 5.0% (2005).

School District(s)

Arise Academy
 2003-04 Enrollment: n/a
Centerville City SD (KG-12)
 2003-04 Enrollment: 8,120 .... (937) 433-8841
City Day Community School (KG-05)
 2003-04 Enrollment: 120 .... (937) 223-8130
Colin Powell Leadership Acad (KG-07)
 2003-04 Enrollment: 284 .... (937) 263-3937
Dayton Academy, The (KG-08)
 2003-04 Enrollment: 1,091 .... (937) 262-4080
Dayton City SD (PK-12)
 2003-04 Enrollment: 18,491 .... (937) 542-3000
Dayton View Academy (KG-08)
 2003-04 Enrollment: 1,113 .... (937) 567-9426
East End Community School (KG-03)
 2003-04 Enrollment: 106 .... (937) 222-7355
General Chappie James Military Academy
 2003-04 Enrollment: n/a
Jefferson Township Local SD (PK-12)
 2003-04 Enrollment: 814 .... (937) 835-5682
Kettering City SD (KG-12)
 2003-04 Enrollment: 7,747 .... (937) 499-1400
Mad River Local SD (KG-12)
 2003-04 Enrollment: 3,619 .... (937) 259-6606
Miami Valley Career Tech (09-12)
 2003-04 Enrollment: n/a .... (937) 837-7781
Miamisburg City SD (KG-12)
 2003-04 Enrollment: 5,306 .... (937) 866-3381
Moraine Community School (KG-10)
 2003-04 Enrollment: 182 .... (937) 294-4522
Mound Street Health Careers Acadmy (10-12)
 2003-04 Enrollment: 107 .... (937) 223-3041
Mound Street It Careers Academy (10-12)
 2003-04 Enrollment: 110 .... (937) 223-3041
Mound Street Military Careers Academy (10-12)
 2003-04 Enrollment: 109 .... (937) 223-3041
N. Dayton School of Science & Discovery (KG-06)
 2003-04 Enrollment: 485 .... (937) 278-6671
New Choices Community, The (07-08)
 2003-04 Enrollment: 109 .... (937) 224-8201
Northmont City SD (KG-12)
 2003-04 Enrollment: 5,933 .... (937) 832-5000
Northridge Local SD (KG-12)
 2003-04 Enrollment: 1,990 .... (937) 278-5885
Oakwood City SD (KG-12)
 2003-04 Enrollment: 2,042 .... (937) 297-5332
Omega School of Excellence (05-08)
 2003-04 Enrollment: 210 .... (937) 278-2372
Partnership Academy
 2003-04 Enrollment: n/a
Pathway School of Discovery (KG-05)
 2003-04 Enrollment: 265 .... (937) 235-5498
Pete Entrepreneurship Training Academy
 2003-04 Enrollment: n/a
Rhea Academy Inc (KG-08)
 2003-04 Enrollment: 117 .... (937) 461-7432
Richard Allen Academy II (KG-08)
 2003-04 Enrollment: 333 .... (937) 586-9756
Richard Allen Dayton View Camp (KG-08)
 2003-04 Enrollment: 218 .... (937) 567-9124
Richard Allen Edgemont Campus (KG-08)
 2003-04 Enrollment: 221 .... (937) 586-9815
Summit Academy Dayton
 2003-04 Enrollment: n/a
Techcon Institute
 2003-04 Enrollment: n/a
Trade & Technology Prep (10-12)
 2003-04 Enrollment: 245 .... (937) 223-2323
Trade & Technology Prep-Hamilton
 2003-04 Enrollment: n/a .... (937) 223-2323
Trotwood-Madison City Schools (PK-12)
 2003-04 Enrollment: 3,470 .... (937) 854-3050
Vandalia-Butler City SD (PK-12)
 2003-04 Enrollment: 3,518 .... (937) 415-6400
West Carrollton City SD (PK-12)
 2003-04 Enrollment: 3,898 .... (937) 859-5121
Wow Community School (KG-06)
 2003-04 Enrollment: 375 .... (937) 542-3600

Four-year College(s)

United Theological Seminary (Private, Not-for-profit, United Methodist)
 Fall 2004 Enrollment: 352 .... (937) 529-2201
University of Dayton (Private, Not-for-profit, Roman Catholic)
 Fall 2004 Enrollment: 10,495 .... (937) 229-1000
 2005-06 Tuition: In-state $22,046; Out-of-state $22,046
Wright State University-Main Campus (Public)
 Fall 2004 Enrollment: 15,985 .... (937) 775-3333
 2005-06 Tuition: In-state $6,619; Out-of-state $12,994

Two-year College(s)

Carousel Beauty College (Private, For-profit)
    Fall 2004 Enrollment: 37 . . . . (937) 223-3572
Creative Images-A Certified Matrix Design Academy (Private, For-profit)
    Fall 2004 Enrollment: 149 . . . . (937) 433-1944
Dayton Barber College (Private, For-profit)
    Fall 2004 Enrollment: 53 . . . . (937) 222-9101
ITT Technical Institute (Private, For-profit)
    Fall 2004 Enrollment: 514 . . . . (937) 264-7700
    2005-06 Tuition: In-state $14,196; Out-of-state $14,196
International College of Broadcasting (Private, For-profit)
    Fall 2004 Enrollment: 99 . . . . (937) 258-8251
    2005-06 Tuition: In-state $8,040; Out-of-state $8,040
Miami-Jacobs Career College (Private, For-profit)
    Fall 2004 Enrollment: 522 . . . . (937) 461-5174
    2005-06 Tuition: In-state $9,450; Out-of-state $9,450
Ohio Institute of Photography and Technology (Private, For-profit)
    Fall 2004 Enrollment: 713 . . . . (937) 294-6155
    2005-06 Tuition: In-state $10,683; Out-of-state $10,683
Sinclair Community College (Public)
    Fall 2004 Enrollment: 19,622 . . . . (937) 512-3000
    2005-06 Tuition: In-state $2,496; Out-of-state $4,503
Southwestern College (Private, For-profit)
    Fall 2004 Enrollment: 232 . . . . (937) 224-0061
    2005-06 Tuition: In-state $8,370; Out-of-state $8,370

Housing: Homeownership rate: 53.2% (2005); Median home value: $76,598 (2005); Median rent: $359 per month (2000); Median age of housing: 51 years (2000).
Hospitals: 74th Medical Group, Wright-Patterson Airforce Base (101 beds); Children's Medical Center (155 beds); Dayton Heart Hospital (47 beds); Good Samaritan Hospital and Health Center (560 beds); Grandview Hospital and Medical Center (452 beds); Kindred Hospital Dayton (67 beds); Miami Valley Hospital (848 beds); Twin Valley Behavioral Healthcare-Dayton Campus; Veterans Affairs Medical Center (539 beds)
Safety: Violent crime rate: 100.6 per 10,000 population; Property crime rate: 786.8 per 10,000 population (2004).
Newspapers: Daily Court Reporter (Circulation 750); Dayton City Paper (Alternative, General - Circulation 30,000); Dayton Daily News (Circulation 191,366); Down Towner (General - Circulation 24,500); Huber Heights Courier (General - Circulation 11,500); Oakwood Register (General - Circulation 6,900)
Transportation: Commute to work: 85.2% car, 7.0% public transportation, 5.3% walk, 1.6% work from home (2000); Travel time to work: 33.5% less than 15 minutes, 46.9% 15 to 30 minutes, 11.3% 30 to 45 minutes, 3.6% 45 to 60 minutes, 4.7% 60 minutes or more (2000)
Additional Information Contacts
City of Dayton . . . . (937) 333-3333
    http://www.cityofdayton.org
Dayton Area Chamber of Commerce. . . . . (937) 226-1444
    http://www.daytonchamber.org
Dayton/Montgomery Co. Convention & Visitors Bureau . . . (800) 221-8235
    http://www.daytoncvb.com
South Metro Dayton Chamber of Commerce. . . . . (937) 433-2032
    http://www.smrcoc.org

DREXEL (CDP). Covers a land area of 2.180 square miles and a water area of 0 square miles. Located at 39.74° N. Lat.; 84.29° W. Long. Elevation is 955 feet.
Population: 2,449 (1990); 2,057 (2000); 1,904 (2005); 1,770 (2010 projected); Race: 62.1% White, 33.9% Black, 0.2% Asian, 0.8% Hispanic of any race (2005); Density: 873.3 persons per square mile (2005); Average household size: 2.61 (2005); Median age: 32.4 (2005); Males per 100 females: 91.9 (2005); Marriage status: 37.6% never married, 38.8% now married, 12.2% widowed, 11.3% divorced (2000); Foreign born: 0.2% (2000); Ancestry (includes multiple ancestries): 38.2% Other groups, 14.5% United States or American, 13.1% Irish, 4.4% German, 2.4% Dutch (2000).
Economy: Employment by occupation: 2.2% management, 9.5% professional, 33.2% services, 16.6% sales, 0.0% farming, 12.6% construction, 25.9% production (2000).
Income: Per capita income: $10,584 (2005); Median household income: $21,295 (2005); Average household income: $27,099 (2005); Percent of households with income of $100,000 or more: 2.7% (2005); Poverty rate: 31.5% (2000).

Education: Percent of population age 25 and over with: High school diploma (including GED) or higher: 47.8% (2005); Bachelor's degree or higher: 5.7% (2005); Master's degree or higher: 1.3% (2005).
Housing: Homeownership rate: 61.0% (2005); Median home value: $55,000 (2005); Median rent: $297 per month (2000); Median age of housing: 50 years (2000).
Transportation: Commute to work: 87.0% car, 6.0% public transportation, 4.2% walk, 2.1% work from home (2000); Travel time to work: 21.4% less than 15 minutes, 48.7% 15 to 30 minutes, 17.9% 30 to 45 minutes, 6.9% 45 to 60 minutes, 5.0% 60 minutes or more (2000)

ENGLEWOOD (city). Covers a land area of 6.560 square miles and a water area of 0.045 square miles. Located at 39.86° N. Lat.; 84.30° W. Long. Elevation is 920 feet.
History: Englewood was established as a Mennonite community by descendants of a group that had been invited to Pennsylvania by William Penn.
Population: 11,620 (1990); 12,235 (2000); 12,618 (2005); 12,949 (2010 projected); Race: 91.1% White, 5.3% Black, 1.7% Asian, 0.9% Hispanic of any race (2005); Density: 1,923.5 persons per square mile (2005); Average household size: 2.37 (2005); Median age: 40.3 (2005); Males per 100 females: 90.2 (2005); Marriage status: 19.9% never married, 61.2% now married, 9.1% widowed, 9.8% divorced (2000); Foreign born: 2.5% (2000); Ancestry (includes multiple ancestries): 31.8% German, 11.4% Irish, 11.1% United States or American, 11.1% English, 10.8% Other groups (2000).
Economy: Single-family building permits issued: 105 (2005); Multi-family building permits issued: 4 (2005); Employment by occupation: 13.4% management, 22.6% professional, 13.6% services, 26.8% sales, 0.1% farming, 7.9% construction, 15.6% production (2000).
Income: Per capita income: $26,271 (2005); Median household income: $51,952 (2005); Average household income: $61,412 (2005); Percent of households with income of $100,000 or more: 15.9% (2005); Poverty rate: 5.1% (2000).
Education: Percent of population age 25 and over with: High school diploma (including GED) or higher: 88.0% (2005); Bachelor's degree or higher: 23.2% (2005); Master's degree or higher: 7.1% (2005).
School District(s)
Northmont City SD (KG-12)
    2003-04 Enrollment: 5,933 . . . . (937) 832-5000
Housing: Homeownership rate: 73.0% (2005); Median home value: $131,286 (2005); Median rent: $459 per month (2000); Median age of housing: 27 years (2000).
Safety: Violent crime rate: 17.6 per 10,000 population; Property crime rate: 382.1 per 10,000 population (2004).
Newspapers: Englewood Independent (General - Circulation 8,000)
Transportation: Commute to work: 94.6% car, 0.4% public transportation, 2.1% walk, 2.0% work from home (2000); Travel time to work: 28.2% less than 15 minutes, 41.5% 15 to 30 minutes, 24.3% 30 to 45 minutes, 2.5% 45 to 60 minutes, 3.6% 60 minutes or more (2000)
Additional Information Contacts
City of Englewood . . . . (937) 836-5106
    http://www.ci.englewood.oh.us
Englewood Chamber of Commerce. . . . . (937) 836-2550
    http://www.englewood-northmontcoc.com

FARMERSVILLE (village). Covers a land area of 0.705 square miles and a water area of 0 square miles. Located at 39.68° N. Lat.; 84.42° W. Long. Elevation is 882 feet.
Population: 934 (1990); 980 (2000); 980 (2005); 984 (2010 projected); Race: 98.8% White, 0.2% Black, 0.3% Asian, 0.4% Hispanic of any race (2005); Density: 1,389.7 persons per square mile (2005); Average household size: 2.72 (2005); Median age: 34.1 (2005); Males per 100 females: 96.0 (2005); Marriage status: 19.3% never married, 64.4% now married, 6.5% widowed, 9.8% divorced (2000); Foreign born: 0.2% (2000); Ancestry (includes multiple ancestries): 30.3% German, 24.7% United States or American, 6.8% Other groups, 6.8% Irish, 5.1% English (2000).
Economy: In agricultural area. Employment by occupation: 6.3% management, 11.6% professional, 18.9% services, 27.1% sales, 0.2% farming, 12.0% construction, 23.9% production (2000).
Income: Per capita income: $20,163 (2005); Median household income: $49,996 (2005); Average household income: $54,889 (2005); Percent of households with income of $100,000 or more: 11.4% (2005); Poverty rate: 3.5% (2000).

Education: Percent of population age 25 and over with: High school diploma (including GED) or higher: 84.1% (2005); Bachelor's degree or higher: 7.8% (2005); Master's degree or higher: 2.5% (2005).
School District(s)
Valley View Local SD (PK-12)
   2003-04 Enrollment: 2,056 . . . . (937) 855-6581
Housing: Homeownership rate: 80.0% (2005); Median home value: $107,083 (2005); Median rent: $400 per month (2000); Median age of housing: 47 years (2000).
Transportation: Commute to work: 93.4% car, 0.0% public transportation, 3.2% walk, 3.4% work from home (2000); Travel time to work: 23.7% less than 15 minutes, 39.6% 15 to 30 minutes, 29.2% 30 to 45 minutes, 4.6% 45 to 60 minutes, 2.9% 60 minutes or more (2000)

FORT MCKINLEY (CDP).
Covers a land area of 1.332 square miles and a water area of 0 square miles. Located at 39.79° N. Lat.; 84.24° W. Long. Elevation is 931 feet.
Population: 4,238 (1990); 3,989 (2000); 3,884 (2005); 3,760 (2010 projected); Race: 36.4% White, 59.6% Black, 0.5% Asian, 0.6% Hispanic of any race (2005); Density: 2,915.5 persons per square mile (2005); Average household size: 2.46 (2005); Median age: 37.6 (2005); Males per 100 females: 85.7 (2005); Marriage status: 34.3% never married, 42.7% now married, 9.2% widowed, 13.8% divorced (2000); Foreign born: 3.8% (2000); Ancestry (includes multiple ancestries): 52.0% Other groups, 11.0% German, 5.4% United States or American, 5.0% Irish, 2.9% English (2000).
Economy: Employment by occupation: 8.9% management, 10.7% professional, 18.8% services, 23.8% sales, 0.0% farming, 10.8% construction, 27.0% production (2000).
Income: Per capita income: $16,779 (2005); Median household income: $33,458 (2005); Average household income: $40,837 (2005); Percent of households with income of $100,000 or more: 4.7% (2005); Poverty rate: 15.4% (2000).
Education: Percent of population age 25 and over with: High school diploma (including GED) or higher: 74.6% (2005); Bachelor's degree or higher: 9.5% (2005); Master's degree or higher: 2.6% (2005).
Housing: Homeownership rate: 77.7% (2005); Median home value: $66,828 (2005); Median rent: $398 per month (2000); Median age of housing: 42 years (2000).
Transportation: Commute to work: 94.6% car, 3.0% public transportation, 1.0% walk, 1.5% work from home (2000); Travel time to work: 19.6% less than 15 minutes, 57.9% 15 to 30 minutes, 16.2% 30 to 45 minutes, 2.1% 45 to 60 minutes, 4.2% 60 minutes or more (2000)

GERMANTOWN (village).
Covers a land area of 3.588 square miles and a water area of 0 square miles. Located at 39.62° N. Lat.; 84.36° W. Long. Elevation is 730 feet.
History: Laid out 1814.
Population: 4,916 (1990); 4,884 (2000); 5,031 (2005); 5,177 (2010 projected); Race: 98.4% White, 0.3% Black, 0.4% Asian, 0.9% Hispanic of any race (2005); Density: 1,402.2 persons per square mile (2005); Average household size: 2.52 (2005); Median age: 37.9 (2005); Males per 100 females: 98.0 (2005); Marriage status: 18.4% never married, 63.1% now married, 6.2% widowed, 12.3% divorced (2000); Foreign born: 0.6% (2000); Ancestry (includes multiple ancestries): 25.3% German, 12.7% Irish, 11.2% Other groups, 8.5% United States or American, 7.9% English (2000).
Economy: Employment by occupation: 13.1% management, 16.0% professional, 12.4% services, 24.6% sales, 0.0% farming, 10.9% construction, 23.0% production (2000).
Income: Per capita income: $27,515 (2005); Median household income: $53,725 (2005); Average household income: $68,951 (2005); Percent of households with income of $100,000 or more: 18.0% (2005); Poverty rate: 5.8% (2000).
Education: Percent of population age 25 and over with: High school diploma (including GED) or higher: 86.1% (2005); Bachelor's degree or higher: 18.7% (2005); Master's degree or higher: 6.6% (2005).
School District(s)
Valley View Local SD (PK-12)
   2003-04 Enrollment: 2,056 . . . . (937) 855-6581
Housing: Homeownership rate: 74.3% (2005); Median home value: $125,828 (2005); Median rent: $424 per month (2000); Median age of housing: 40 years (2000).
Safety: Violent crime rate: 2.0 per 10,000 population; Property crime rate: 362.2 per 10,000 population (2004).
Newspapers: The Germantown Press (General - Circulation 2,500)
Transportation: Commute to work: 94.1% car, 1.0% public transportation, 2.9% walk, 1.2% work from home (2000); Travel time to work: 19.7% less than 15 minutes, 39.8% 15 to 30 minutes, 27.9% 30 to 45 minutes, 6.5% 45 to 60 minutes, 6.1% 60 minutes or more (2000)
Additional Information Contacts
Village of Germantown. . . . . (937) 855-7255
   http://www.ci.germantown.oh.us

HUBER HEIGHTS (city).
Covers a land area of 21.027 square miles and a water area of 0.095 square miles. Located at 39.85° N. Lat.; 84.12° W. Long. Elevation is 970 feet.
History: The City of Huber Heights was known as Wayne Township prior to incorporation in 1981. The year 1956 marked the start of the most major transformation to hit the township since its original founding. In that year, Charles H. Huber started the first privately owned utility company in Ohio and launched the construction of his first plat of brick, single-family homes. Over the period 1956-1992, Huber Homes built a total of 10,707 single-family homes and 2,258 multifamily units in the community. In November of 1981, the electors of the city voted for a city charter, which gave the city home rule powers and established a modified council-manager form of government.
Population: 38,478 (1990); 38,212 (2000); 38,300 (2005); 38,352 (2010 projected); Race: 83.8% White, 10.0% Black, 2.6% Asian, 1.5% Hispanic of any race (2005); Density: 1,821.4 persons per square mile (2005); Average household size: 2.60 (2005); Median age: 36.0 (2005); Males per 100 females: 95.1 (2005); Marriage status: 22.6% never married, 61.3% now married, 5.0% widowed, 11.1% divorced (2000); Foreign born: 3.2% (2000); Ancestry (includes multiple ancestries): 24.9% German, 18.0% Other groups, 11.5% Irish, 10.3% English, 9.7% United States or American (2000).
Economy: Unemployment rate: 5.7% (2005); Total civilian labor force: 19,889 (2005); Employment by occupation: 12.3% management, 17.8% professional, 13.9% services, 27.5% sales, 0.1% farming, 8.5% construction, 19.9% production (2000).
Income: Per capita income: $23,990 (2005); Median household income: $53,461 (2005); Average household income: $62,175 (2005); Percent of households with income of $100,000 or more: 13.2% (2005); Poverty rate: 5.9% (2000).
Taxes: Total city taxes per capita: $385 (2004); City property taxes per capita: $84 (2004).
Education: Percent of population age 25 and over with: High school diploma (including GED) or higher: 88.4% (2005); Bachelor's degree or higher: 19.1% (2005); Master's degree or higher: 6.7% (2005).
School District(s)
Huber Heights City SD (PK-12)
   2003-04 Enrollment: 6,821 . . . . (937) 237-6300
Two-year College(s)
Carousel of Miami Valley Beauty College (Private, For-profit)
   Fall 2004 Enrollment: 62 . . . . (937) 223-3572
Housing: Homeownership rate: 72.5% (2005); Median home value: $108,676 (2005); Median rent: $515 per month (2000); Median age of housing: 29 years (2000).
Safety: Violent crime rate: 18.0 per 10,000 population; Property crime rate: 408.7 per 10,000 population (2004).
Transportation: Commute to work: 96.2% car, 0.9% public transportation, 0.7% walk, 1.7% work from home (2000); Travel time to work: 25.3% less than 15 minutes, 51.7% 15 to 30 minutes, 16.4% 30 to 45 minutes, 3.1% 45 to 60 minutes, 3.5% 60 minutes or more (2000)
Additional Information Contacts
City of Huber Heights. . . . . (937) 233-1423
   http://www.ci.huber-heights.oh.us
Huber Heights Chamber of Commerce . . . . (937) 233-5700
   http://www.huberheightschamber.com

KETTERING (city).
Covers a land area of 18.685 square miles and a water area of 0 square miles. Located at 39.69° N. Lat.; 84.15° W. Long. Elevation is 1,005 feet.
History: Settled c.1812, incorporated 1952.
Population: 60,570 (1990); 57,502 (2000); 55,815 (2005); 54,191 (2010 projected); Race: 94.6% White, 1.8% Black, 1.6% Asian, 1.1% Hispanic of any race (2005); Density: 2,987.1 persons per square mile (2005); Average household size: 2.21 (2005); Median age: 40.4 (2005); Males per 100 females: 91.1 (2005); Marriage status: 23.7% never married, 56.9% now married, 8.1% widowed, 11.3% divorced (2000); Foreign born: 2.7%

(2000); Ancestry (includes multiple ancestries): 33.8% German, 15.5% Irish, 12.7% English, 8.6% United States or American, 8.6% Other groups (2000).
Economy: Manufacturing: electric motors, transportation equipment, machinery. Numerous testing laboratories for auto and electrical products. The city is the seat of the Kettering College of Medical Arts and two major hospitals and research centers. Unemployment rate: 5.4% (2005); Total civilian labor force: 29,632 (2005); Single-family building permits issued: 12 (2005); Multi-family building permits issued: 12 (2005); Employment by occupation: 15.3% management, 24.2% professional, 12.0% services, 28.8% sales, 0.2% farming, 6.5% construction, 13.0% production (2000).
Income: Per capita income: $29,788 (2005); Median household income: $49,717 (2005); Average household income: $65,677 (2005); Percent of households with income of $100,000 or more: 14.9% (2005); Poverty rate: 4.6% (2000).
Taxes: Total city taxes per capita: $614 (2004); City property taxes per capita: $144 (2004).
Education: Percent of population age 25 and over with: High school diploma (including GED) or higher: 91.0% (2005); Bachelor's degree or higher: 31.1% (2005); Master's degree or higher: 11.3% (2005).

School District(s)
Kettering City SD (KG-12)
    2003-04 Enrollment: 7,747 . . . . (937) 499-1400

Four-year College(s)
Kettering College of Medical Arts (Private, Not-for-profit, Seventh Day Adventists)
    Fall 2004 Enrollment: 722 . . . . (937) 395-8601
    2005-06 Tuition: In-state $6,770; Out-of-state $6,770

Two-year College(s)
Carousel Beauty College (Private, For-profit)
    Fall 2004 Enrollment: 54 . . . . (937) 223-3572
School of Advertising Art Inc (Private, For-profit)
    Fall 2004 Enrollment: 123 . . . . (937) 294-0592
    2005-06 Tuition: In-state $17,775; Out-of-state $17,775

Housing: Homeownership rate: 67.2% (2005); Median home value: $129,238 (2005); Median rent: $494 per month (2000); Median age of housing: 41 years (2000).
Hospitals: Keltering Medical Center (669 beds)
Safety: Violent crime rate: 16.6 per 10,000 population; Property crime rate: 377.3 per 10,000 population (2004).
Newspapers: Centerville-Bellebrook Times (General - Circulation 25,000); Kettering-Oakwood Times (General - Circulation 30,000)
Transportation: Commute to work: 93.9% car, 1.1% public transportation, 1.4% walk, 2.9% work from home (2000); Travel time to work: 33.6% less than 15 minutes, 50.2% 15 to 30 minutes, 10.5% 30 to 45 minutes, 2.7% 45 to 60 minutes, 3.0% 60 minutes or more (2000)
Additional Information Contacts
City of Kettering . . . . (937) 296-2400
    http://www.ketteringoh.org
Kettering Moraine Chamber of Commerce . . . . (937) 299-3852
    http://www.kmo-coc.org

MIAMISBURG (city).
Covers a land area of 11.190 square miles and a water area of 0.189 square miles. Located at 39.63° N. Lat.; 84.27° W. Long. Elevation is 710 feet.
History: Miamisburg was laid out in 1818 on the site of a blockhouse called Hole's Station, which had been built by Zachariah Hole about 1800. The Hoover and Gamble Company, manufacturer of reapers, was founded here in 1840. Tobacco warehouses were situated in Miamisburg in the late 1800's.
Population: 18,641 (1990); 19,489 (2000); 19,819 (2005); 20,089 (2010 projected); Race: 95.4% White, 1.7% Black, 0.8% Asian, 0.9% Hispanic of any race (2005); Density: 1,771.1 persons per square mile (2005); Average household size: 2.59 (2005); Median age: 38.6 (2005); Males per 100 females: 92.5 (2005); Marriage status: 19.9% never married, 64.0% now married, 5.7% widowed, 10.4% divorced (2000); Foreign born: 1.7% (2000); Ancestry (includes multiple ancestries): 26.5% German, 12.9% United States or American, 12.4% Irish, 11.0% English, 8.0% Other groups (2000).
Economy: Single-family building permits issued: 129 (2005); Multi-family building permits issued: 0 (2005); Employment by occupation: 11.9% management, 19.3% professional, 13.4% services, 30.2% sales, 0.0% farming, 8.5% construction, 16.7% production (2000).
Income: Per capita income: $26,265 (2005); Median household income: $55,059 (2005); Average household income: $67,316 (2005); Percent of households with income of $100,000 or more: 18.5% (2005); Poverty rate: 6.1% (2000).
Education: Percent of population age 25 and over with: High school diploma (including GED) or higher: 83.3% (2005); Bachelor's degree or higher: 18.9% (2005); Master's degree or higher: 5.4% (2005).

School District(s)
Miamisburg City SD (KG-12)
    2003-04 Enrollment: 5,306 . . . . (937) 866-3381
Miamisburg Elementary Digital Academy
    2003-04 Enrollment: n/a
Miamisburg Secondary Digital Academy
    2003-04 Enrollment: n/a

Housing: Homeownership rate: 72.2% (2005); Median home value: $136,610 (2005); Median rent: $419 per month (2000); Median age of housing: 33 years (2000).
Safety: Violent crime rate: 28.6 per 10,000 population; Property crime rate: 467.9 per 10,000 population (2004).
Newspapers: Miamisburg West Carrollton News (General - Circulation 6,500)
Transportation: Commute to work: 94.8% car, 1.0% public transportation, 1.8% walk, 2.1% work from home (2000); Travel time to work: 36.1% less than 15 minutes, 47.0% 15 to 30 minutes, 10.5% 30 to 45 minutes, 3.2% 45 to 60 minutes, 3.2% 60 minutes or more (2000)
Additional Information Contacts
City of Miamisburg . . . . (937) 866-3303
    http://www.ci.miamisburg.oh.us

MORAINE (city).
Covers a land area of 9.071 square miles and a water area of 0.273 square miles. Located at 39.69° N. Lat.; 84.22° W. Long. Elevation is 740 feet.
Population: 6,722 (1990); 6,897 (2000); 6,767 (2005); 6,677 (2010 projected); Race: 88.4% White, 6.5% Black, 2.6% Asian, 1.5% Hispanic of any race (2005); Density: 746.0 persons per square mile (2005); Average household size: 2.37 (2005); Median age: 34.3 (2005); Males per 100 females: 99.5 (2005); Marriage status: 24.8% never married, 54.2% now married, 5.2% widowed, 15.8% divorced (2000); Foreign born: 4.3% (2000); Ancestry (includes multiple ancestries): 17.3% Other groups, 17.2% German, 15.3% United States or American, 14.7% Irish, 13.3% English (2000).
Economy: Manufacturing: truck components, power-train systems. Single-family building permits issued: 7 (2005); Multi-family building permits issued: 0 (2005); Employment by occupation: 10.8% management, 10.9% professional, 15.6% services, 26.3% sales, 0.1% farming, 14.1% construction, 22.1% production (2000).
Income: Per capita income: $19,144 (2005); Median household income: $38,155 (2005); Average household income: $45,204 (2005); Percent of households with income of $100,000 or more: 6.6% (2005); Poverty rate: 9.6% (2000).
Education: Percent of population age 25 and over with: High school diploma (including GED) or higher: 74.8% (2005); Bachelor's degree or higher: 8.6% (2005); Master's degree or higher: 2.6% (2005).
Housing: Homeownership rate: 61.4% (2005); Median home value: $85,175 (2005); Median rent: $455 per month (2000); Median age of housing: 32 years (2000).
Transportation: Commute to work: 93.0% car, 1.7% public transportation, 0.8% walk, 3.2% work from home (2000); Travel time to work: 42.6% less than 15 minutes, 40.2% 15 to 30 minutes, 10.2% 30 to 45 minutes, 2.5% 45 to 60 minutes, 4.5% 60 minutes or more (2000)
Additional Information Contacts
City of Moraine . . . . (937) 535-1000
    http://www.ci.moraine.oh.us/index.php

NEW LEBANON (village).
Covers a land area of 1.999 square miles and a water area of 0 square miles. Located at 39.74° N. Lat.; 84.39° W. Long. Elevation is 910 feet.
History: New Lebanon was established as a community of Dunkards. A murder and the burning of the town in 1876 were attributed to a conflict between warring gangs.
Population: 4,501 (1990); 4,231 (2000); 4,195 (2005); 4,177 (2010 projected); Race: 98.3% White, 0.3% Black, 0.1% Asian, 0.8% Hispanic of any race (2005); Density: 2,099.0 persons per square mile (2005); Average household size: 2.64 (2005); Median age: 36.3 (2005); Males per 100 females: 90.4 (2005); Marriage status: 20.4% never married, 58.0% now married, 8.4% widowed, 13.2% divorced (2000); Foreign born: 0.7% (2000); Ancestry (includes multiple ancestries): 24.9% German, 22.7%

United States or American, 9.7% English, 9.2% Other groups, 8.5% Irish (2000).
Economy: Employment by occupation: 9.4% management, 10.8% professional, 12.9% services, 20.6% sales, 0.0% farming, 17.7% construction, 28.5% production (2000).
Income: Per capita income: $20,332 (2005); Median household income: $45,999 (2005); Average household income: $52,702 (2005); Percent of households with income of $100,000 or more: 7.2% (2005); Poverty rate: 5.4% (2000).
Education: Percent of population age 25 and over with: High school diploma (including GED) or higher: 78.8% (2005); Bachelor's degree or higher: 4.5% (2005); Master's degree or higher: 1.5% (2005).

School District(s)
New Lebanon Local SD (KG-12)
    2003-04 Enrollment: 1,319 . . . . (937) 687-1301
Housing: Homeownership rate: 74.8% (2005); Median home value: $99,667 (2005); Median rent: $370 per month (2000); Median age of housing: 35 years (2000).
Transportation: Commute to work: 99.1% car, 0.0% public transportation, 0.5% walk, 0.4% work from home (2000); Travel time to work: 16.3% less than 15 minutes, 41.8% 15 to 30 minutes, 33.4% 30 to 45 minutes, 2.6% 45 to 60 minutes, 5.9% 60 minutes or more (2000)
Additional Information Contacts
Village of New Lebanon. . . . . (937) 687-1341
    http://www.newlebanonoh.com

NORTHRIDGE (CDP). Covers a land area of 2.273 square miles and a water area of 0 square miles. Located at 39.80° N. Lat.; 84.19° W. Long. Elevation is 800 feet.
Population: 9,432 (1990); 8,487 (2000); 8,055 (2005); 7,695 (2010 projected); Race: 84.4% White, 13.2% Black, 0.1% Asian, 0.8% Hispanic of any race (2005); Density: 3,543.8 persons per square mile (2005); Average household size: 2.46 (2005); Median age: 34.0 (2005); Males per 100 females: 89.4 (2005); Marriage status: 31.4% never married, 46.0% now married, 6.9% widowed, 15.7% divorced (2000); Foreign born: 0.7% (2000); Ancestry (includes multiple ancestries): 18.8% Other groups, 14.8% United States or American, 12.7% German, 8.8% Irish, 6.5% English (2000).
Economy: Employment by occupation: 3.2% management, 7.1% professional, 14.3% services, 30.3% sales, 0.2% farming, 12.5% construction, 32.3% production (2000).
Income: Per capita income: $15,155 (2005); Median household income: $30,000 (2005); Average household income: $37,216 (2005); Percent of households with income of $100,000 or more: 3.7% (2005); Poverty rate: 21.9% (2000).
Education: Percent of population age 25 and over with: High school diploma (including GED) or higher: 64.4% (2005); Bachelor's degree or higher: 3.5% (2005); Master's degree or higher: 1.2% (2005).
Housing: Homeownership rate: 61.4% (2005); Median home value: $74,035 (2005); Median rent: $345 per month (2000); Median age of housing: 44 years (2000).
Transportation: Commute to work: 94.2% car, 3.7% public transportation, 1.0% walk, 0.3% work from home (2000); Travel time to work: 38.6% less than 15 minutes, 44.6% 15 to 30 minutes, 9.8% 30 to 45 minutes, 2.9% 45 to 60 minutes, 4.2% 60 minutes or more (2000)

OAKWOOD (city). Covers a land area of 2.189 square miles and a water area of 0 square miles. Located at 39.71° N. Lat.; 84.17° W. Long. Elevation is 970 feet.
History: Incorporated as village in 1907; became city after 1930.
Population: 8,957 (1990); 9,215 (2000); 8,780 (2005); 8,340 (2010 projected); Race: 96.9% White, 0.5% Black, 1.2% Asian, 1.3% Hispanic of any race (2005); Density: 4,010.3 persons per square mile (2005); Average household size: 2.57 (2005); Median age: 40.0 (2005); Males per 100 females: 89.6 (2005); Marriage status: 18.6% never married, 66.3% now married, 4.7% widowed, 10.4% divorced (2000); Foreign born: 2.5% (2000); Ancestry (includes multiple ancestries): 34.0% German, 19.3% English, 18.3% Irish, 5.9% United States or American, 5.3% Italian (2000).
Economy: Employment by occupation: 26.5% management, 38.5% professional, 6.6% services, 19.6% sales, 0.0% farming, 3.0% construction, 5.7% production (2000).
Income: Per capita income: $45,430 (2005); Median household income: $84,175 (2005); Average household income: $116,543 (2005); Percent of households with income of $100,000 or more: 40.2% (2005); Poverty rate: 3.3% (2000).

Education: Percent of population age 25 and over with: High school diploma (including GED) or higher: 95.6% (2005); Bachelor's degree or higher: 63.1% (2005); Master's degree or higher: 30.6% (2005).
Housing: Homeownership rate: 83.8% (2005); Median home value: $219,638 (2005); Median rent: $502 per month (2000); Median age of housing: 59 years (2000).
Transportation: Commute to work: 92.4% car, 0.9% public transportation, 3.0% walk, 3.5% work from home (2000); Travel time to work: 43.8% less than 15 minutes, 42.1% 15 to 30 minutes, 7.8% 30 to 45 minutes, 1.5% 45 to 60 minutes, 4.9% 60 minutes or more (2000)

PHILLIPSBURG (village). Covers a land area of 0.266 square miles and a water area of 0 square miles. Located at 39.90° N. Lat.; 84.40° W. Long. Elevation is 1,035 feet.
Population: 687 (1990); 628 (2000); 614 (2005); 588 (2010 projected); Race: 98.4% White, 1.1% Black, 0.0% Asian, 1.0% Hispanic of any race (2005); Density: 2,312.5 persons per square mile (2005); Average household size: 2.47 (2005); Median age: 36.9 (2005); Males per 100 females: 94.9 (2005); Marriage status: 23.7% never married, 60.8% now married, 5.8% widowed, 9.6% divorced (2000); Foreign born: 0.5% (2000); Ancestry (includes multiple ancestries): 40.4% German, 11.8% Irish, 8.0% United States or American, 5.1% English, 3.4% Other groups (2000).
Economy: Employment by occupation: 8.6% management, 8.6% professional, 16.6% services, 20.2% sales, 0.0% farming, 14.2% construction, 31.8% production (2000).
Income: Per capita income: $23,567 (2005); Median household income: $49,153 (2005); Average household income: $58,112 (2005); Percent of households with income of $100,000 or more: 9.2% (2005); Poverty rate: 6.1% (2000).
Education: Percent of population age 25 and over with: High school diploma (including GED) or higher: 85.1% (2005); Bachelor's degree or higher: 6.3% (2005); Master's degree or higher: 1.2% (2005).

School District(s)
Northmont City SD (KG-12)
    2003-04 Enrollment: 5,933 . . . . (937) 832-5000
Housing: Homeownership rate: 80.3% (2005); Median home value: $112,371 (2005); Median rent: $432 per month (2000); Median age of housing: 60+ years (2000).
Transportation: Commute to work: 93.9% car, 1.0% public transportation, 3.7% walk, 1.4% work from home (2000); Travel time to work: 24.7% less than 15 minutes, 44.9% 15 to 30 minutes, 19.9% 30 to 45 minutes, 5.5% 45 to 60 minutes, 5.1% 60 minutes or more (2000)

RIVERSIDE (city). Covers a land area of 7.857 square miles and a water area of 0.041 square miles. Located at 39.77° N. Lat.; 84.12° W. Long. Elevation is 770 feet.
Population: 25,374 (1990); 23,545 (2000); 23,134 (2005); 22,700 (2010 projected); Race: 90.5% White, 4.5% Black, 2.2% Asian, 1.5% Hispanic of any race (2005); Density: 2,944.3 persons per square mile (2005); Average household size: 2.38 (2005); Median age: 38.3 (2005); Males per 100 females: 94.6 (2005); Marriage status: 24.2% never married, 55.1% now married, 7.4% widowed, 13.3% divorced (2000); Foreign born: 2.9% (2000); Ancestry (includes multiple ancestries): 22.3% German, 15.8% Other groups, 14.4% United States or American, 13.4% Irish, 9.1% English (2000).
Economy: Unemployment rate: 7.2% (2005); Total civilian labor force: 11,087 (2005); Employment by occupation: 9.1% management, 15.2% professional, 15.8% services, 27.5% sales, 0.2% farming, 10.5% construction, 21.6% production (2000).
Income: Per capita income: $20,536 (2005); Median household income: $40,574 (2005); Average household income: $48,801 (2005); Percent of households with income of $100,000 or more: 7.6% (2005); Poverty rate: 10.1% (2000).
Education: Percent of population age 25 and over with: High school diploma (including GED) or higher: 78.5% (2005); Bachelor's degree or higher: 14.9% (2005); Master's degree or higher: 5.1% (2005).
Housing: Homeownership rate: 66.4% (2005); Median home value: $95,398 (2005); Median rent: $417 per month (2000); Median age of housing: 41 years (2000).
Safety: Violent crime rate: 30.3 per 10,000 population; Property crime rate: 475.0 per 10,000 population (2004).
Transportation: Commute to work: 95.7% car, 1.2% public transportation, 0.9% walk, 1.2% work from home (2000); Travel time to work: 33.9% less than 15 minutes, 50.7% 15 to 30 minutes, 8.0% 30 to 45 minutes, 2.9% 45 to 60 minutes, 4.6% 60 minutes or more (2000)

Additional Information Contacts
City of Riverside .... (937) 233-1801
http://www.riverside.oh.us

SHILOH (CDP). Covers a land area of 3.838 square miles and a water area of 0.052 square miles. Located at 39.80° N. Lat.; 84.22° W. Long. Elevation is 830 feet.
Population: 11,673 (1990); 11,272 (2000); 10,974 (2005); 10,647 (2010 projected); Race: 55.6% White, 40.5% Black, 0.7% Asian, 1.0% Hispanic of any race (2005); Density: 2,859.2 persons per square mile (2005); Average household size: 1.96 (2005); Median age: 44.7 (2005); Males per 100 females: 84.7 (2005); Marriage status: 26.9% never married, 47.2% now married, 10.5% widowed, 15.3% divorced (2000); Foreign born: 4.0% (2000); Ancestry (includes multiple ancestries): 36.1% Other groups, 18.6% German, 7.3% Irish, 6.9% English, 6.4% United States or American (2000).
Economy: Employment by occupation: 11.1% management, 25.1% professional, 12.2% services, 29.6% sales, 0.0% farming, 5.8% construction, 16.3% production (2000).
Income: Per capita income: $24,211 (2005); Median household income: $36,690 (2005); Average household income: $46,578 (2005); Percent of households with income of $100,000 or more: 8.7% (2005); Poverty rate: 10.0% (2000).
Education: Percent of population age 25 and over with: High school diploma (including GED) or higher: 84.4% (2005); Bachelor's degree or higher: 26.6% (2005); Master's degree or higher: 11.3% (2005).
Housing: Homeownership rate: 54.2% (2005); Median home value: $104,921 (2005); Median rent: $419 per month (2000); Median age of housing: 38 years (2000).
Transportation: Commute to work: 93.8% car, 2.2% public transportation, 1.2% walk, 2.1% work from home (2000); Travel time to work: 27.1% less than 15 minutes, 47.8% 15 to 30 minutes, 16.1% 30 to 45 minutes, 4.4% 45 to 60 minutes, 4.6% 60 minutes or more (2000)

TROTWOOD (city). Covers a land area of 30.530 square miles and a water area of 0.014 square miles. Located at 39.79° N. Lat.; 84.29° W. Long. Elevation is 850 feet.
History: In 1801, the first pioneer families to arrive in the area settled along Wolf Creek, and on November 2, 1802, its namesake Leonard Wolf made the area's first recorded land purchase near there. In 1807 a large colony of German Baptist Brethren and Old School Baptists from Pennsylvania also settled along Wolf Creek. The Village of Trotwood was incorporated in 1901. With its population having reached 6,997, the Village of Trotwood became eligible for city status, and on February 13, 1971, Trotwood was officially incorporated as a city. The City of Trotwood merged with Madison Township in 1996.
Population: 29,395 (1990); 27,420 (2000); 26,884 (2005); 26,415 (2010 projected); Race: 33.8% White, 62.8% Black, 0.3% Asian, 0.8% Hispanic of any race (2005); Density: 880.6 persons per square mile (2005); Average household size: 2.42 (2005); Median age: 39.3 (2005); Males per 100 females: 83.9 (2005); Marriage status: 27.9% never married, 49.4% now married, 8.9% widowed, 13.7% divorced (2000); Foreign born: 1.2% (2000); Ancestry (includes multiple ancestries): 53.5% Other groups, 8.2% German, 7.6% United States or American, 4.6% Irish, 3.4% English (2000).
Economy: Unemployment rate: 8.0% (2005); Total civilian labor force: 12,070 (2005); Single-family building permits issued: 93 (2005); Multi-family building permits issued: 0 (2005); Employment by occupation: 9.2% management, 15.5% professional, 15.8% services, 27.2% sales, 0.0% farming, 7.3% construction, 25.1% production (2000).
Income: Per capita income: $20,229 (2005); Median household income: $38,775 (2005); Average household income: $48,128 (2005); Percent of households with income of $100,000 or more: 9.4% (2005); Poverty rate: 15.3% (2000).
Education: Percent of population age 25 and over with: High school diploma (including GED) or higher: 78.3% (2005); Bachelor's degree or higher: 15.4% (2005); Master's degree or higher: 6.6% (2005).
School District(s)
Academy of Dayton (KG-08)
    2003-04 Enrollment: 202 .... (937) 567-1072
Main Street Automotive Magnet School
    2003-04 Enrollment: n/a
Trotwood Fitness & Prep Acad (KG-06)
    2003-04 Enrollment: 153
Trotwood-Madison City Schools (PK-12)
    2003-04 Enrollment: 3,470 .... (937) 854-3050
Housing: Homeownership rate: 62.2% (2005); Median home value: $92,286 (2005); Median rent: $449 per month (2000); Median age of housing: 35 years (2000).
Transportation: Commute to work: 93.4% car, 3.5% public transportation, 1.0% walk, 1.5% work from home (2000); Travel time to work: 20.4% less than 15 minutes, 48.7% 15 to 30 minutes, 20.7% 30 to 45 minutes, 5.2% 45 to 60 minutes, 5.0% 60 minutes or more (2000)
Additional Information Contacts
City of Trotwood .... (937) 837-7771
http://www.trotwood.org/home.html
Trotwood Chamber of Commerce .... (937) 837-1484
http://www.trotwoodchamber.com

UNION (city). Covers a land area of 4.281 square miles and a water area of 0.001 square miles. Located at 39.90° N. Lat.; 84.31° W. Long. Elevation is 930 feet.
Population: 5,736 (1990); 5,574 (2000); 5,381 (2005); 5,189 (2010 projected); Race: 96.6% White, 1.0% Black, 0.3% Asian, 1.2% Hispanic of any race (2005); Density: 1,256.9 persons per square mile (2005); Average household size: 2.62 (2005); Median age: 35.7 (2005); Males per 100 females: 93.4 (2005); Marriage status: 16.1% never married, 65.9% now married, 4.9% widowed, 13.1% divorced (2000); Foreign born: 0.5% (2000); Ancestry (includes multiple ancestries): 34.9% German, 16.5% Irish, 14.9% United States or American, 12.0% English, 10.5% Other groups (2000).
Economy: Single-family building permits issued: 51 (2005); Multi-family building permits issued: 14 (2005); Employment by occupation: 10.4% management, 17.2% professional, 13.6% services, 28.8% sales, 0.2% farming, 9.0% construction, 20.9% production (2000).
Income: Per capita income: $24,317 (2005); Median household income: $56,198 (2005); Average household income: $63,828 (2005); Percent of households with income of $100,000 or more: 12.1% (2005); Poverty rate: 3.7% (2000).
Education: Percent of population age 25 and over with: High school diploma (including GED) or higher: 85.4% (2005); Bachelor's degree or higher: 13.5% (2005); Master's degree or higher: 3.1% (2005).
School District(s)
Northmont City SD (KG-12)
    2003-04 Enrollment: 5,933 .... (937) 832-5000
Housing: Homeownership rate: 86.0% (2005); Median home value: $112,500 (2005); Median rent: $509 per month (2000); Median age of housing: 27 years (2000).
Transportation: Commute to work: 94.5% car, 0.8% public transportation, 2.6% walk, 2.1% work from home (2000); Travel time to work: 21.1% less than 15 minutes, 44.8% 15 to 30 minutes, 27.2% 30 to 45 minutes, 4.5% 45 to 60 minutes, 2.4% 60 minutes or more (2000)
Additional Information Contacts
City of Union .... (937) 836-8624
http://www.ci.union.oh.us

VANDALIA (city). Covers a land area of 11.810 square miles and a water area of 0.072 square miles. Located at 39.88° N. Lat.; 84.19° W. Long. Elevation is 970 feet.
History: Vandalia was settled in 1838 and named for Vandalia, Illinois. Vandalia was known as the site of the largest shotgun tournament in the world, held by the Amateur Trapshooters' Association.
Population: 14,297 (1990); 14,603 (2000); 14,483 (2005); 14,346 (2010 projected); Race: 95.2% White, 1.5% Black, 1.6% Asian, 1.0% Hispanic of any race (2005); Density: 1,226.4 persons per square mile (2005); Average household size: 2.32 (2005); Median age: 39.5 (2005); Males per 100 females: 93.9 (2005); Marriage status: 21.1% never married, 60.1% now married, 6.2% widowed, 12.6% divorced (2000); Foreign born: 2.2% (2000); Ancestry (includes multiple ancestries): 30.3% German, 12.8% Irish, 10.8% English, 9.8% United States or American, 7.4% Other groups (2000).
Economy: Single-family building permits issued: 68 (2005); Multi-family building permits issued: 0 (2005); Employment by occupation: 14.6% management, 20.1% professional, 12.1% services, 26.7% sales, 0.1% farming, 9.2% construction, 17.2% production (2000).
Income: Per capita income: $27,024 (2005); Median household income: $48,740 (2005); Average household income: $62,020 (2005); Percent of households with income of $100,000 or more: 15.0% (2005); Poverty rate: 5.2% (2000).

Education: Percent of population age 25 and over with: High school diploma (including GED) or higher: 87.2% (2005); Bachelor's degree or higher: 22.1% (2005); Master's degree or higher: 8.3% (2005).

School District(s)

Vandalia-Butler City SD (PK-12)
    2003-04 Enrollment: 3,518 . . . . (937) 415-6400

Housing: Homeownership rate: 65.4% (2005); Median home value: $136,467 (2005); Median rent: $428 per month (2000); Median age of housing: 30 years (2000).
Safety: Violent crime rate: 7.6 per 10,000 population; Property crime rate: 258.2 per 10,000 population (2004).
Newspapers: Vandalia Drummer News (General - Circulation 5,300)
Transportation: Commute to work: 95.1% car, 0.5% public transportation, 1.2% walk, 2.7% work from home (2000); Travel time to work: 38.5% less than 15 minutes, 41.5% 15 to 30 minutes, 14.6% 30 to 45 minutes, 2.2% 45 to 60 minutes, 3.3% 60 minutes or more (2000)

Additional Information Contacts

City of Vandalia . . . . (937) 898-5891
    http://www.ci.vandalia.oh.us
Vandalia-Butler Chamber of Commerce . . . . (937) 898-5351
    http://www.vandaliabutlerchamber.org

WEST CARROLLTON CITY (city). Aka West Carrollton. Covers a land area of 6.308 square miles and a water area of 0.197 square miles. Located at 39.66° N. Lat.; 84.24° W. Long. Elevation is 716 feet.

Population: 14,403 (1990); 13,818 (2000); 13,346 (2005); 12,879 (2010 projected); Race: 91.6% White, 4.7% Black, 1.3% Asian, 1.6% Hispanic of any race (2005); Density: 2,115.8 persons per square mile (2005); Average household size: 2.21 (2005); Median age: 36.4 (2005); Males per 100 females: 92.9 (2005); Marriage status: 24.8% never married, 54.6% now married, 6.0% widowed, 14.6% divorced (2000); Foreign born: 2.5% (2000); Ancestry (includes multiple ancestries): 22.8% German, 14.9% Other groups, 14.3% United States or American, 10.7% English, 10.5% Irish (2000).
Economy: Paper products. Sand and gravel pits nearby. Single-family building permits issued: 2 (2005); Multi-family building permits issued: 0 (2005); Employment by occupation: 12.7% management, 19.3% professional, 13.2% services, 26.1% sales, 0.2% farming, 7.3% construction, 21.2% production (2000).
Income: Per capita income: $22,935 (2005); Median household income: $44,063 (2005); Average household income: $50,418 (2005); Percent of households with income of $100,000 or more: 7.9% (2005); Poverty rate: 7.4% (2000).
Education: Percent of population age 25 and over with: High school diploma (including GED) or higher: 86.5% (2005); Bachelor's degree or higher: 17.0% (2005); Master's degree or higher: 5.0% (2005).

School District(s)

West Carrollton City SD (PK-12)
    2003-04 Enrollment: 3,898 . . . . (937) 859-5121
West Carrollton Community
    2003-04 Enrollment: n/a . . . . (937) 435-2211

Housing: Homeownership rate: 58.9% (2005); Median home value: $106,907 (2005); Median rent: $490 per month (2000); Median age of housing: 29 years (2000).
Safety: Violent crime rate: 22.9 per 10,000 population; Property crime rate: 370.7 per 10,000 population (2004).
Transportation: Commute to work: 96.0% car, 1.7% public transportation, 1.2% walk, 1.1% work from home (2000); Travel time to work: 38.2% less than 15 minutes, 42.8% 15 to 30 minutes, 12.9% 30 to 45 minutes, 2.5% 45 to 60 minutes, 3.6% 60 minutes or more (2000)

Additional Information Contacts

City of West Carrollton City . . . . (937) 859-5183
    http://www.westcarrollton.org

WOODBOURNE-HYDE PARK (CDP). Covers a land area of 4.582 square miles and a water area of 0 square miles. Located at 39.66° N. Lat.; 84.17° W. Long.

Population: 7,867 (1990); 7,910 (2000); 7,557 (2005); 7,249 (2010 projected); Race: 95.5% White, 1.2% Black, 2.1% Asian, 0.8% Hispanic of any race (2005); Density: 1,649.2 persons per square mile (2005); Average household size: 2.65 (2005); Median age: 50.2 (2005); Males per 100 females: 91.0 (2005); Marriage status: 13.8% never married, 74.3% now married, 7.1% widowed, 4.9% divorced (2000); Foreign born: 4.6% (2000); Ancestry (includes multiple ancestries): 34.0% German, 16.1% Irish, 15.1% English, 5.9% Other groups, 5.6% United States or American (2000).

Economy: Employment by occupation: 23.6% management, 37.1% professional, 5.7% services, 25.1% sales, 0.7% farming, 2.5% construction, 5.3% production (2000).
Income: Per capita income: $44,801 (2005); Median household income: $89,315 (2005); Average household income: $116,325 (2005); Percent of households with income of $100,000 or more: 42.7% (2005); Poverty rate: 2.1% (2000).
Education: Percent of population age 25 and over with: High school diploma (including GED) or higher: 95.6% (2005); Bachelor's degree or higher: 53.7% (2005); Master's degree or higher: 25.2% (2005).
Housing: Homeownership rate: 96.8% (2005); Median home value: $189,415 (2005); Median rent: $1,040 per month (2000); Median age of housing: 37 years (2000).
Transportation: Commute to work: 93.4% car, 0.5% public transportation, 0.3% walk, 5.2% work from home (2000); Travel time to work: 32.2% less than 15 minutes, 50.0% 15 to 30 minutes, 12.3% 30 to 45 minutes, 3.1% 45 to 60 minutes, 2.4% 60 minutes or more (2000)

WRIGHT-PATTERSON AFB (CDP). Covers a land area of 11.693 square miles and a water area of 0.087 square miles. Located at 39.79° N. Lat.; 84.08° W. Long.

Population: 8,447 (1990); 6,656 (2000); 6,907 (2005); 7,147 (2010 projected); Race: 76.6% White, 14.6% Black, 2.1% Asian, 4.2% Hispanic of any race (2005); Density: 590.7 persons per square mile (2005); Average household size: 3.74 (2005); Median age: 23.2 (2005); Males per 100 females: 104.1 (2005); Marriage status: 16.3% never married, 80.6% now married, 0.4% widowed, 2.7% divorced (2000); Foreign born: 8% (2000); Ancestry (includes multiple ancestries): 29.0% Other groups, 20.2% German, 11.6% Irish, 10.3% English, 8.1% United States or American (2000).
Economy: Employment by occupation: 9.3% management, 24.1% professional, 23.5% services, 34.1% sales, 0.0% farming, 4.4% construction, 4.6% production (2000).
Income: Per capita income: $15,287 (2005); Median household income: $47,634 (2005); Average household income: $54,976 (2005); Percent of households with income of $100,000 or more: 7.7% (2005); Poverty rate: 1.8% (2000).
Education: Percent of population age 25 and over with: High school diploma (including GED) or higher: 97.2% (2005); Bachelor's degree or higher: 33.5% (2005); Master's degree or higher: 16.5% (2005).
Housing: Homeownership rate: 4.2% (2005); Median home value: $42,857 (2005); Median rent: $620 per month (2000); Median age of housing: 39 years (2000).
Transportation: Commute to work: 94.1% car, 0.9% public transportation, 1.5% walk, 2.9% work from home (2000); Travel time to work: 60.0% less than 15 minutes, 33.4% 15 to 30 minutes, 4.8% 30 to 45 minutes, 0.8% 45 to 60 minutes, 1.0% 60 minutes or more (2000)

Morgan County

Located in east central Ohio; crossed by the Muskingum River, and Meigs and Wolf Creeks. Covers a land area of 417.66 square miles, a water area of 4.20 square miles, and is located in the Eastern Time Zone. The county government was organized in 1817. County seat is McConnelsville.

Weather Station: McConnelsville Lock 7   Elevation: 757 feet

	Jan	Feb	Mar	Apr	May	Jun	Jul	Aug	Sep	Oct	Nov	Dec
High	38	42	53	65	74	81	85	84	78	66	54	43
Low	18	19	28	37	47	56	61	60	52	39	32	24
Precip	3.0	2.5	3.5	3.6	4.4	4.1	4.9	4.4	3.2	2.8	3.4	3.2
Snow	7.9	5.7	3.4	0.9	0.0	0.0	0.0	0.0	0.0	0.0	0.7	2.6

High and Low temperatures in degrees Fahrenheit; Precipitation and Snow in inches

Population: 14,194 (1990); 14,897 (2000); 14,836 (2005); 14,768 (2010 projected); Race: 94.0% White, 3.1% Black, 0.1% Asian, 0.4% Hispanic of any race (2005); Density: 35.5 persons per square mile (2005); Average household size: 2.47 (2005); Median age: 39.4 (2005); Males per 100 females: 96.6 (2005).
Religion: Five largest groups: 12.5% The United Methodist Church, 7.4% Christian Churches and Churches of Christ, 2.8% Churches of Christ, 1.2% Southern Baptist Convention, 1.2% Catholic Church (2000).
Economy: Unemployment rate: 9.9% (2005); Total civilian labor force: 6,259 (2005); Leading industries: 20.2% health care and social assistance; 18.2% retail trade; 10.0% accommodation & food services (2004); Farms: 508 totaling 100,198 acres (2002); Companies that employ 500 or more persons: 0 (2004); Companies that employ 100 to 499 persons: 2 (2004);

Companies that employ less than 100 persons: 195 (2004); Black-owned businesses: n/a (2002); Hispanic-owned businesses: n/a (2002); Women-owned businesses: n/a (2002); Retail sales per capita: $5,025 (2006). Single-family building permits issued: 63 (2005); Multi-family building permits issued: 0 (2005).
Income: Per capita income: $15,902 (2005); Median household income: $31,951 (2005); Average household income: $38,954 (2005); Percent of households with income of $100,000 or more: 3.8% (2005); Poverty rate: 14.2% (2003); Bankruptcy rate: 6.22% (2005).
Taxes: Total county taxes per capita: $184 (2004); County property taxes per capita: $134 (2004).
Education: Percent of population age 25 and over with: High school diploma (including GED) or higher: 80.5% (2005); Bachelor's degree or higher: 9.0% (2005); Master's degree or higher: 3.9% (2005).
Housing: Homeownership rate: 78.7% (2005); Median home value: $80,285 (2005); Median rent: $266 per month (2000); Median age of housing: 35 years (2000).
Health: Birth rate: 129.7 per 10,000 population (2004); Death rate: 117.7 per 10,000 population (2004); Age-adjusted cancer mortality rate: 178.3 deaths per 100,000 population (2002); Air Quality Index: 99.1% good, 0.9% moderate, 0.0% unhealthy for sensitive individuals, 0.0% unhealthy (percent of days in 2005); Number of physicians: 1.3 per 10,000 population (2004); Hospital beds: 0.0 per 10,000 population (2003); Hospital admissions: 0.0 per 10,000 population (2003).
Elections: 2004 Presidential election results: 56.1% Bush, 42.9% Kerry, 0.0% Nader, 0.5% Badnarik.
National and State Parks: Burr Oak State Park; Muskingum River Parkway State Park
Additional Information Contacts
Morgan County Government . . . . (740) 962-3183
  http://www.morgancounty.org/
Morgan County Chamber of Commerce . . . . (740) 962-3200
  http://www.morgancounty.org

Morgan County Communities

CHESTERHILL (village). Covers a land area of 0.544 square miles and a water area of 0 square miles. Located at 39.48° N. Lat.; 81.86° W. Long. Elevation is 980 feet.
Population: 309 (1990); 305 (2000); 271 (2005); 255 (2010 projected); Race: 81.9% White, 12.5% Black, 0.0% Asian, 0.7% Hispanic of any race (2005); Density: 498.3 persons per square mile (2005); Average household size: 2.26 (2005); Median age: 37.2 (2005); Males per 100 females: 97.8 (2005); Marriage status: 21.0% never married, 54.8% now married, 12.1% widowed, 12.1% divorced (2000); Foreign born: 0.0% (2000); Ancestry (includes multiple ancestries): 18.9% United States or American, 14.0% German, 13.7% English, 11.0% Irish, 7.6% Other groups (2000).
Economy: Employment by occupation: 10.8% management, 13.4% professional, 12.7% services, 20.4% sales, 0.0% farming, 11.5% construction, 31.2% production (2000).
Income: Per capita income: $18,469 (2005); Median household income: $35,882 (2005); Average household income: $41,708 (2005); Percent of households with income of $100,000 or more: 5.8% (2005); Poverty rate: 19.8% (2000).
Education: Percent of population age 25 and over with: High school diploma (including GED) or higher: 84.7% (2005); Bachelor's degree or higher: 6.0% (2005); Master's degree or higher: 1.6% (2005).
Housing: Homeownership rate: 79.2% (2005); Median home value: $56,400 (2005); Median rent: $267 per month (2000); Median age of housing: 60+ years (2000).
Transportation: Commute to work: 93.0% car, 0.0% public transportation, 3.8% walk, 3.2% work from home (2000); Travel time to work: 19.7% less than 15 minutes, 23.0% 15 to 30 minutes, 29.6% 30 to 45 minutes, 10.5% 45 to 60 minutes, 17.1% 60 minutes or more (2000)

MALTA (village). Covers a land area of 0.311 square miles and a water area of 0.032 square miles. Located at 39.65° N. Lat.; 81.86° W. Long. Elevation is 671 feet.
History: Malta was founded in 1816 by Simeon Pool and John Bell, who owned the land. The town was named for the island of Malta in the Mediterranean where Pool had visited.
Population: 802 (1990); 696 (2000); 621 (2005); 565 (2010 projected); Race: 90.8% White, 5.8% Black, 0.2% Asian, 0.3% Hispanic of any race (2005); Density: 1,999.6 persons per square mile (2005); Average household size: 2.41 (2005); Median age: 39.0 (2005); Males per 100 females: 85.9 (2005); Marriage status: 32.5% never married, 44.6% now married, 7.7% widowed, 15.2% divorced (2000); Foreign born: 0.1% (2000); Ancestry (includes multiple ancestries): 21.8% United States or American, 15.2% German, 12.7% Irish, 9.9% English, 9.0% Other groups (2000).
Economy: Single-family building permits issued: 0 (2005); Multi-family building permits issued: 0 (2005); Employment by occupation: 6.2% management, 8.2% professional, 29.6% services, 16.2% sales, 0.7% farming, 9.6% construction, 29.6% production (2000).
Income: Per capita income: $12,051 (2005); Median household income: $24,455 (2005); Average household income: $28,246 (2005); Percent of households with income of $100,000 or more: 0.0% (2005); Poverty rate: 25.3% (2000).
Education: Percent of population age 25 and over with: High school diploma (including GED) or higher: 81.3% (2005); Bachelor's degree or higher: 4.9% (2005); Master's degree or higher: 3.0% (2005).
School District(s)
Morgan Local SD (PK-12)
  2003-04 Enrollment: 2,265 . . . . (740) 962-2782
Housing: Homeownership rate: 68.6% (2005); Median home value: $56,379 (2005); Median rent: $307 per month (2000); Median age of housing: 60+ years (2000).
Transportation: Commute to work: 88.0% car, 0.0% public transportation, 6.2% walk, 5.2% work from home (2000); Travel time to work: 48.6% less than 15 minutes, 20.7% 15 to 30 minutes, 8.3% 30 to 45 minutes, 6.5% 45 to 60 minutes, 15.9% 60 minutes or more (2000)

MCCONNELSVILLE (village). Covers a land area of 1.757 square miles and a water area of 0.067 square miles. Located at 39.64° N. Lat.; 81.85° W. Long. Elevation is 700 feet.
History: McConnelsville was platted in 1817 by General Robert McConnell, and became a Muskingum River shipping port for salt bound for Pittsburgh by keelboat.
Population: 1,824 (1990); 1,676 (2000); 1,590 (2005); 1,480 (2010 projected); Race: 95.6% White, 1.5% Black, 0.1% Asian, 0.2% Hispanic of any race (2005); Density: 904.7 persons per square mile (2005); Average household size: 2.03 (2005); Median age: 41.5 (2005); Males per 100 females: 80.5 (2005); Marriage status: 21.1% never married, 51.4% now married, 14.2% widowed, 13.4% divorced (2000); Foreign born: 0.2% (2000); Ancestry (includes multiple ancestries): 16.8% German, 14.2% United States or American, 11.1% Irish, 9.6% English, 6.6% Other groups (2000).
Economy: Single-family building permits issued: 2 (2005); Multi-family building permits issued: 0 (2005); Employment by occupation: 7.9% management, 17.9% professional, 15.1% services, 27.4% sales, 1.0% farming, 14.0% construction, 16.6% production (2000).
Income: Per capita income: $19,443 (2005); Median household income: $27,581 (2005); Average household income: $39,533 (2005); Percent of households with income of $100,000 or more: 6.0% (2005); Poverty rate: 18.1% (2000).
Education: Percent of population age 25 and over with: High school diploma (including GED) or higher: 85.3% (2005); Bachelor's degree or higher: 13.9% (2005); Master's degree or higher: 6.5% (2005).
School District(s)
Morgan Local SD (PK-12)
  2003-04 Enrollment: 2,265 . . . . (740) 962-2782
Housing: Homeownership rate: 57.0% (2005); Median home value: $78,814 (2005); Median rent: $273 per month (2000); Median age of housing: 58 years (2000).
Newspapers: Morgan County Herald (General - Circulation 4,936)
Transportation: Commute to work: 90.0% car, 0.0% public transportation, 4.8% walk, 3.2% work from home (2000); Travel time to work: 61.4% less than 15 minutes, 10.1% 15 to 30 minutes, 7.4% 30 to 45 minutes, 6.8% 45 to 60 minutes, 14.2% 60 minutes or more (2000)
Additional Information Contacts
Morgan County Chamber of Commerce . . . . (740) 962-3200
  http://www.morgancounty.org

STOCKPORT (village). Covers a land area of 0.334 square miles and a water area of 0 square miles. Located at 39.54° N. Lat.; 81.79° W. Long. Elevation is 700 feet.
Population: 450 (1990); 540 (2000); 501 (2005); 494 (2010 projected); Race: 94.0% White, 2.6% Black, 0.0% Asian, 0.8% Hispanic of any race (2005); Density: 1,498.2 persons per square mile (2005); Average household size: 2.32 (2005); Median age: 35.3 (2005); Males per 100

females: 82.8 (2005); Marriage status: 21.1% never married, 57.6% now married, 10.0% widowed, 11.3% divorced (2000); Foreign born: 0.2% (2000); Ancestry (includes multiple ancestries): 19.1% United States or American, 13.5% English, 10.7% German, 9.3% Irish, 5.4% Other groups (2000).
Economy: Employment by occupation: 6.3% management, 12.7% professional, 23.8% services, 19.0% sales, 2.1% farming, 8.5% construction, 27.5% production (2000).
Income: Per capita income: $12,809 (2005); Median household income: $22,931 (2005); Average household income: $29,711 (2005); Percent of households with income of $100,000 or more: 0.5% (2005); Poverty rate: 39.6% (2000).
Education: Percent of population age 25 and over with: High school diploma (including GED) or higher: 85.3% (2005); Bachelor's degree or higher: 8.9% (2005); Master's degree or higher: 0.0% (2005).

School District(s)

Morgan Local SD (PK-12)
    2003-04 Enrollment: 2,265 . . . . (740) 962-2782
Housing: Homeownership rate: 65.3% (2005); Median home value: $64,872 (2005); Median rent: $254 per month (2000); Median age of housing: 55 years (2000).
Transportation: Commute to work: 93.6% car, 0.0% public transportation, 3.2% walk, 3.2% work from home (2000); Travel time to work: 20.4% less than 15 minutes, 36.5% 15 to 30 minutes, 2.8% 30 to 45 minutes, 9.9% 45 to 60 minutes, 30.4% 60 minutes or more (2000)

Morrow County

Located in central Ohio; drained by the Kokosing River and Whetstone and Big Walnut Creeks. Covers a land area of 406.22 square miles, a water area of 1.13 square miles, and is located in the Eastern Time Zone. The county government was organized in 1848. County seat is Mount Gilead.

Morrow County is part of the Columbus, OH Metropolitan Statistical Area. The entire metro area includes: Delaware County, OH; Fairfield County, OH; Franklin County, OH; Licking County, OH; Madison County, OH; Morrow County, OH; Pickaway County, OH; Union County, OH

Population: 27,749 (1990); 31,628 (2000); 34,395 (2005); 37,293 (2010 projected); Race: 98.0% White, 0.5% Black, 0.4% Asian, 0.6% Hispanic of any race (2005); Density: 84.7 persons per square mile (2005); Average household size: 2.71 (2005); Median age: 37.1 (2005); Males per 100 females: 99.4 (2005).
Religion: Five largest groups: 10.2% The United Methodist Church, 2.5% Christian Churches and Churches of Christ, 2.0% The Christian and Missionary Alliance, 1.6% American Baptist Churches in the USA, 1.5% Church of the Nazarene (2000).
Economy: Unemployment rate: 6.1% (2005); Total civilian labor force: 17,765 (2005); Leading industries: 30.2% manufacturing; 19.3% health care and social assistance; 16.8% retail trade (2004); Farms: 863 totaling 179,051 acres (2002); Companies that employ 500 or more persons: 1 (2004); Companies that employ 100 to 499 persons: 7 (2004); Companies that employ less than 100 persons: 417 (2004); Black-owned businesses: n/a (2002); Hispanic-owned businesses: n/a (2002); Women-owned businesses: n/a (2002); Retail sales per capita: $5,870 (2006).
Single-family building permits issued: 171 (2005); Multi-family building permits issued: 0 (2005).
Income: Per capita income: $20,535 (2005); Median household income: $46,443 (2005); Average household income: $55,290 (2005); Percent of households with income of $100,000 or more: 9.5% (2005); Poverty rate: 9.1% (2003); Bankruptcy rate: 9.79% (2005).
Taxes: Total county taxes per capita: $174 (2004); County property taxes per capita: $96 (2004).
Education: Percent of population age 25 and over with: High school diploma (including GED) or higher: 78.5% (2005); Bachelor's degree or higher: 9.4% (2005); Master's degree or higher: 2.9% (2005).
Housing: Homeownership rate: 82.4% (2005); Median home value: $124,879 (2005); Median rent: $343 per month (2000); Median age of housing: 29 years (2000).
Health: Birth rate: 130.3 per 10,000 population (2004); Death rate: 86.0 per 10,000 population (2004); Age-adjusted cancer mortality rate: 243.5 deaths per 100,000 population (2002); Number of physicians: 3.2 per 10,000 population (2004); Hospital beds: 15.8 per 10,000 population (2003); Hospital admissions: 362.0 per 10,000 population (2003).
Elections: 2004 Presidential election results: 64.1% Bush, 35.4% Kerry, 0.0% Nader, 0.2% Badnarik

National and State Parks: Mount Gilead State Park
Additional Information Contacts
Morrow County Government . . . . (419) 947-4085
    http://www.morrowcounty.info/
Morrow County Chamber of Commerce . . . . (419) 946-2821
    http://www.morrowcochamber.com
Village of Mount Gilead . . . . (419) 946-8111
    http://www.mountgilead.net

Morrow County Communities

CARDINGTON
(village). Covers a land area of 1.864 square miles and a water area of 0 square miles. Located at 40.49° N. Lat.; 82.89° W. Long. Elevation is 1,014 feet.
History: Cardington was founded in 1822 and named for an old carding mill here. After the Civil War, Cardington became a lumber town.
Population: 1,847 (1990); 1,849 (2000); 1,982 (2005); 2,127 (2010 projected); Race: 98.1% White, 0.4% Black, 0.2% Asian, 0.3% Hispanic of any race (2005); Density: 1,063.6 persons per square mile (2005); Average household size: 2.40 (2005); Median age: 33.6 (2005); Males per 100 females: 90.9 (2005); Marriage status: 22.6% never married, 54.7% now married, 8.8% widowed, 13.8% divorced (2000); Foreign born: 0.7% (2000); Ancestry (includes multiple ancestries): 19.1% United States or American, 19.1% German, 10.7% English, 8.2% Irish, 7.7% Other groups (2000).
Economy: Single-family building permits issued: 6 (2005); Multi-family building permits issued: 0 (2005); Employment by occupation: 6.6% management, 12.4% professional, 23.6% services, 19.1% sales, 0.5% farming, 10.3% construction, 27.6% production (2000).
Income: Per capita income: $17,801 (2005); Median household income: $34,330 (2005); Average household income: $42,767 (2005); Percent of households with income of $100,000 or more: 4.5% (2005); Poverty rate: 16.7% (2000).
Education: Percent of population age 25 and over with: High school diploma (including GED) or higher: 77.3% (2005); Bachelor's degree or higher: 9.0% (2005); Master's degree or higher: 1.8% (2005).

School District(s)

Cardington Local Digital
    2003-04 Enrollment: n/a . . . . (419) 864-3691
Cardington-Lincoln Local SD (PK-12)
    2003-04 Enrollment: 1,258 . . . . (419) 864-3691
Housing: Homeownership rate: 61.1% (2005); Median home value: $96,379 (2005); Median rent: $326 per month (2000); Median age of housing: 42 years (2000).
Newspapers: Morrow County Independent (General - Circulation 1,100)
Transportation: Commute to work: 92.5% car, 0.4% public transportation, 3.7% walk, 3.1% work from home (2000); Travel time to work: 30.4% less than 15 minutes, 24.0% 15 to 30 minutes, 23.2% 30 to 45 minutes, 13.4% 45 to 60 minutes, 8.9% 60 minutes or more (2000)

CHESTERVILLE
(village). Covers a land area of 0.095 square miles and a water area of 0 square miles. Located at 40.48° N. Lat.; 82.68° W. Long. Elevation is 1,142 feet.
Population: 286 (1990); 193 (2000); 206 (2005); 217 (2010 projected); Race: 98.1% White, 0.0% Black, 0.0% Asian, 1.5% Hispanic of any race (2005); Density: 2,173.8 persons per square mile (2005); Average household size: 3.27 (2005); Median age: 42.5 (2005); Males per 100 females: 74.6 (2005); Marriage status: 19.3% never married, 50.0% now married, 23.9% widowed, 6.8% divorced (2000); Foreign born: 0.0% (2000); Ancestry (includes multiple ancestries): 26.2% German, 15.2% United States or American, 13.8% English, 9.5% Other groups, 7.1% Dutch (2000).
Economy: Single-family building permits issued: 3 (2005); Multi-family building permits issued: 0 (2005); Employment by occupation: 5.5% management, 16.4% professional, 17.3% services, 33.6% sales, 2.7% farming, 14.5% construction, 10.0% production (2000).
Income: Per capita income: $15,145 (2005); Median household income: $46,500 (2005); Average household income: $46,944 (2005); Percent of households with income of $100,000 or more: 4.8% (2005); Poverty rate: 9.9% (2000).
Education: Percent of population age 25 and over with: High school diploma (including GED) or higher: 79.0% (2005); Bachelor's degree or higher: 10.5% (2005); Master's degree or higher: 5.6% (2005).

School District(s)
Highland Local SD (PK-12)
  2003-04 Enrollment: 1,781 . . . . (419) 768-2206
Housing: Homeownership rate: 81.0% (2005); Median home value: $70,000 (2005); Median rent: $475 per month (2000); Median age of housing: 60+ years (2000).
Transportation: Commute to work: 86.9% car, 0.0% public transportation, 10.3% walk, 2.8% work from home (2000); Travel time to work: 28.8% less than 15 minutes, 26.9% 15 to 30 minutes, 24.0% 30 to 45 minutes, 7.7% 45 to 60 minutes, 12.5% 60 minutes or more (2000)

EDISON (village). Covers a land area of 0.288 square miles and a water area of 0 square miles. Located at 40.55° N. Lat.; 82.86° W. Long. Elevation is 1,062 feet.
Population: 488 (1990); 437 (2000); 477 (2005); 521 (2010 projected); Race: 97.9% White, 0.0% Black, 1.0% Asian, 0.6% Hispanic of any race (2005); Density: 1,655.0 persons per square mile (2005); Average household size: 2.61 (2005); Median age: 36.1 (2005); Males per 100 females: 97.9 (2005); Marriage status: 24.9% never married, 51.1% now married, 8.8% widowed, 15.1% divorced (2000); Foreign born: 0.0% (2000); Ancestry (includes multiple ancestries): 17.6% German, 13.2% United States or American, 13.0% Other groups, 8.8% English, 8.6% Irish (2000).
Economy: In agricultural area. Single-family building permits issued: 3 (2005); Multi-family building permits issued: 0 (2005); Employment by occupation: 3.8% management, 5.3% professional, 17.2% services, 31.6% sales, 0.0% farming, 19.6% construction, 22.5% production (2000).
Income: Per capita income: $20,278 (2005); Median household income: $44,808 (2005); Average household income: $52,855 (2005); Percent of households with income of $100,000 or more: 8.2% (2005); Poverty rate: 13.4% (2000).
Education: Percent of population age 25 and over with: High school diploma (including GED) or higher: 83.5% (2005); Bachelor's degree or higher: 10.8% (2005); Master's degree or higher: 2.2% (2005).
School District(s)
Goal Digital Academy (02-12)
  2003-04 Enrollment: 29 . . . . (419) 946-1903
Mount Gilead Exempted Village School District (PK-12)
  2003-04 Enrollment: 1,411 . . . . (419) 946-1646
Tomorrow Center (03-12)
  2003-04 Enrollment: 38 . . . . (419) 946-1903
Housing: Homeownership rate: 79.2% (2005); Median home value: $94,255 (2005); Median rent: $415 per month (2000); Median age of housing: 60+ years (2000).
Transportation: Commute to work: 99.0% car, 0.0% public transportation, 1.0% walk, 0.0% work from home (2000); Travel time to work: 27.6% less than 15 minutes, 20.7% 15 to 30 minutes, 17.7% 30 to 45 minutes, 22.7% 45 to 60 minutes, 11.3% 60 minutes or more (2000).

FULTON (village). Covers a land area of 0.150 square miles and a water area of 0 square miles. Located at 40.46° N. Lat.; 82.82° W. Long. Elevation is 1,057 feet.
Population: 325 (1990); 264 (2000); 290 (2005); 315 (2010 projected); Race: 99.0% White, 0.0% Black, 0.0% Asian, 1.0% Hispanic of any race (2005); Density: 1,929.2 persons per square mile (2005); Average household size: 2.74 (2005); Median age: 41.9 (2005); Males per 100 females: 100.0 (2005); Marriage status: 33.7% never married, 50.4% now married, 7.0% widowed, 8.9% divorced (2000); Foreign born: 0.0% (2000); Ancestry (includes multiple ancestries): 24.7% German, 17.8% Irish, 15.1% United States or American, 10.9% English, 7.6% Other groups (2000).
Economy: Employment by occupation: 5.7% management, 5.1% professional, 21.7% services, 12.1% sales, 0.0% farming, 15.3% construction, 40.1% production (2000).
Income: Per capita income: $17,457 (2005); Median household income: $35,789 (2005); Average household income: $44,693 (2005); Percent of households with income of $100,000 or more: 6.6% (2005); Poverty rate: 11.3% (2000).
Education: Percent of population age 25 and over with: High school diploma (including GED) or higher: 47.3% (2005); Bachelor's degree or higher: 2.3% (2005); Master's degree or higher: 0.9% (2005).
Housing: Homeownership rate: 69.8% (2005); Median home value: $77,391 (2005); Median rent: $325 per month (2000); Median age of housing: 58 years (2000).
Transportation: Commute to work: 73.7% car, 21.1% public transportation, 2.6% walk, 2.6% work from home (2000); Travel time to work: 16.2% less than 15 minutes, 34.5% 15 to 30 minutes, 26.4% 30 to 45 minutes, 16.9% 45 to 60 minutes, 6.1% 60 minutes or more (2000)

MARENGO (village). Covers a land area of 0.178 square miles and a water area of 0 square miles. Located at 40.40° N. Lat.; 82.81° W. Long. Elevation is 1,119 feet.
Population: 393 (1990); 297 (2000); 335 (2005); 376 (2010 projected); Race: 95.5% White, 0.0% Black, 1.2% Asian, 0.6% Hispanic of any race (2005); Density: 1,882.4 persons per square mile (2005); Average household size: 2.56 (2005); Median age: 32.2 (2005); Males per 100 females: 95.9 (2005); Marriage status: 21.6% never married, 54.4% now married, 9.1% widowed, 14.9% divorced (2000); Foreign born: 0.0% (2000); Ancestry (includes multiple ancestries): 14.7% Other groups, 12.5% United States or American, 12.5% German, 9.2% Irish, 7.0% English (2000).
Economy: Employment by occupation: 5.3% management, 13.0% professional, 13.6% services, 21.3% sales, 0.0% farming, 24.9% construction, 21.9% production (2000).
Income: Per capita income: $17,634 (2005); Median household income: $41,250 (2005); Average household income: $45,095 (2005); Percent of households with income of $100,000 or more: 4.6% (2005); Poverty rate: 9.2% (2000).
Education: Percent of population age 25 and over with: High school diploma (including GED) or higher: 78.8% (2005); Bachelor's degree or higher: 8.2% (2005); Master's degree or higher: 3.8% (2005).
School District(s)
Highland Local SD (PK-12)
  2003-04 Enrollment: 1,781 . . . . (419) 768-2206
Housing: Homeownership rate: 67.9% (2005); Median home value: $98,889 (2005); Median rent: $465 per month (2000); Median age of housing: 60+ years (2000).
Transportation: Commute to work: 89.2% car, 0.0% public transportation, 6.0% walk, 3.0% work from home (2000); Travel time to work: 21.6% less than 15 minutes, 27.2% 15 to 30 minutes, 37.0% 30 to 45 minutes, 9.9% 45 to 60 minutes, 4.3% 60 minutes or more (2000)

MOUNT GILEAD (village). Covers a land area of 3.176 square miles and a water area of 0.011 square miles. Located at 40.55° N. Lat.; 82.83° W. Long. Elevation is 1,125 feet.
History: Mount Gilead was settled in 1817 by Lewis and Ralph Hardenbrook, whose farm was in a tulip-tree forest. Until 1824 the settlement was called Whetstone, and later Youngstown. In 1832 the Ohio legislature changed the name again to honor Mount Gilead, Virginia.
Population: 3,216 (1990); 3,290 (2000); 3,394 (2005); 3,528 (2010 projected); Race: 96.1% White, 2.2% Black, 0.7% Asian, 1.2% Hispanic of any race (2005); Density: 1,068.5 persons per square mile (2005); Average household size: 2.50 (2005); Median age: 37.4 (2005); Males per 100 females: 92.8 (2005); Marriage status: 16.5% never married, 62.1% now married, 13.1% widowed, 8.3% divorced (2000); Foreign born: 1.4% (2000); Ancestry (includes multiple ancestries): 21.7% German, 16.3% United States or American, 11.9% Irish, 9.2% English, 9.0% Other groups (2000).
Economy: Single-family building permits issued: 1 (2005); Multi-family building permits issued: 0 (2005); Employment by occupation: 11.3% management, 13.4% professional, 14.8% services, 21.7% sales, 0.0% farming, 13.1% construction, 25.6% production (2000).
Income: Per capita income: $21,185 (2005); Median household income: $35,910 (2005); Average household income: $50,996 (2005); Percent of households with income of $100,000 or more: 11.1% (2005); Poverty rate: 13.2% (2000).
Education: Percent of population age 25 and over with: High school diploma (including GED) or higher: 76.0% (2005); Bachelor's degree or higher: 9.7% (2005); Master's degree or higher: 4.4% (2005).
School District(s)
Mount Gilead Exempted Village School District (PK-12)
  2003-04 Enrollment: 1,411 . . . . (419) 946-1646
Housing: Homeownership rate: 63.2% (2005); Median home value: $119,012 (2005); Median rent: $274 per month (2000); Median age of housing: 48 years (2000).
Hospitals: Morrow County Hospital (79 beds)
Safety: Violent crime rate: 11.5 per 10,000 population; Property crime rate: 290.5 per 10,000 population (2004).
Newspapers: The Morrow County Sentinel (General - Circulation 4,500)
Transportation: Commute to work: 93.4% car, 0.8% public transportation, 4.2% walk, 1.5% work from home (2000); Travel time to work: 39.3% less

than 15 minutes, 18.3% 15 to 30 minutes, 17.4% 30 to 45 minutes, 11.7% 45 to 60 minutes, 13.4% 60 minutes or more (2000)

Additional Information Contacts

Morrow County Chamber of Commerce . . . . (419) 946-2821
http://www.morrowcochamber.com
Village of Mount Gilead . . . . (419) 946-8111
http://www.mountgilead.net

SPARTA (village). Covers a land area of 0.088 square miles and a water area of 0 square miles. Located at 40.39° N. Lat.; 82.70° W. Long. Elevation is 1,350 feet.
Population: 201 (1990); 191 (2000); 205 (2005); 219 (2010 projected); Race: 96.1% White, 2.9% Black, 0.0% Asian, 0.5% Hispanic of any race (2005); Density: 2,317.8 persons per square mile (2005); Average household size: 2.70 (2005); Median age: 39.0 (2005); Males per 100 females: 99.0 (2005); Marriage status: 22.4% never married, 60.2% now married, 1.9% widowed, 15.5% divorced (2000); Foreign born: 2.8% (2000); Ancestry (includes multiple ancestries): 22.9% United States or American, 21.0% German, 15.4% Irish, 6.5% Other groups, 5.1% Welsh (2000).
Economy: Employment by occupation: 11.6% management, 11.6% professional, 23.3% services, 18.6% sales, 0.0% farming, 4.7% construction, 30.2% production (2000).
Income: Per capita income: $14,293 (2005); Median household income: $33,000 (2005); Average household income: $38,553 (2005); Percent of households with income of $100,000 or more: 3.9% (2005); Poverty rate: 16.4% (2000).
Education: Percent of population age 25 and over with: High school diploma (including GED) or higher: 76.3% (2005); Bachelor's degree or higher: 5.8% (2005); Master's degree or higher: 0.0% (2005).

School District(s)

Highland Digital
2003-04 Enrollment: n/a . . . . (419) 768-2206
Highland Local SD (PK-12)
2003-04 Enrollment: 1,781 . . . . (419) 768-2206

Housing: Homeownership rate: 65.8% (2005); Median home value: $83,333 (2005); Median rent: $282 per month (2000); Median age of housing: 60+ years (2000).
Transportation: Commute to work: 97.5% car, 0.0% public transportation, 0.0% walk, 2.5% work from home (2000); Travel time to work: 16.7% less than 15 minutes, 24.4% 15 to 30 minutes, 21.8% 30 to 45 minutes, 24.4% 45 to 60 minutes, 12.8% 60 minutes or more (2000)

Muskingum County

Located in central Ohio; crossed by the Muskingum and Licking Rivers, and Salt and Jonathan Creeks. Covers a land area of 664.63 square miles, a water area of 7.97 square miles, and is located in the Eastern Time Zone. The county government was organized in 1804. County seat is Zanesville.

Muskingum County is part of the Zanesville, OH Micropolitan Statistical Area. The entire metro area includes: Muskingum County, OH

Weather Station: Philo 3 SW   Elevation: 1,017 feet

	Jan	Feb	Mar	Apr	May	Jun	Jul	Aug	Sep	Oct	Nov	Dec
High	35	40	50	62	71	78	82	81	74	63	51	40
Low	20	22	30	40	49	57	61	60	53	42	34	25
Precip	2.1	2.1	2.7	3.1	4.1	4.2	4.2	3.8	2.8	2.5	3.0	2.5
Snow	9.4	5.3	4.3	1.1	tr	0.0	0.0	0.0	0.0	tr	1.1	3.6

High and Low temperatures in degrees Fahrenheit; Precipitation and Snow in inches

Weather Station: Zanesville Municipal Airport   Elevation: 879 feet

	Jan	Feb	Mar	Apr	May	Jun	Jul	Aug	Sep	Oct	Nov	Dec
High	36	41	51	62	72	80	84	82	76	64	52	41
Low	20	23	31	40	50	59	63	61	54	42	34	25
Precip	2.5	2.3	3.1	3.5	4.1	4.4	4.2	4.0	2.9	2.6	3.1	2.8
Snow	8.6	4.3	3.5	1.4	tr	tr	tr	0.0	tr	tr	1.2	3.5

High and Low temperatures in degrees Fahrenheit; Precipitation and Snow in inches

Population: 82,068 (1990); 84,585 (2000); 85,833 (2005); 87,112 (2010 projected); Race: 93.6% White, 4.0% Black, 0.3% Asian, 0.5% Hispanic of any race (2005); Density: 129.1 persons per square mile (2005); Average household size: 2.58 (2005); Median age: 37.5 (2005); Males per 100 females: 92.5 (2005).
Religion: Five largest groups: 11.4% The United Methodist Church, 6.3% Catholic Church, 5.1% American Baptist Churches in the USA, 3.0% Presbyterian Church (U.S.A.), 2.1% Evangelical Lutheran Church in America (2000).
Economy: Unemployment rate: 8.3% (2005); Total civilian labor force: 40,073 (2005); Leading industries: 22.4% manufacturing; 17.7% health care and social assistance; 16.0% retail trade (2004); Farms: 1,222 totaling 193,175 acres (2002); Companies that employ 500 or more persons: 8 (2004); Companies that employ 100 to 499 persons: 38 (2004); Companies that employ less than 100 persons: 1,970 (2004); Black-owned businesses: n/a (2002); Hispanic-owned businesses: n/a (2002); Women-owned businesses: 1,683 (2002); Retail sales per capita: $17,178 (2006). Single-family building permits issued: 2 (2005); Multi-family building permits issued: 80 (2005).
Income: Per capita income: $20,367 (2005); Median household income: $40,636 (2005); Average household income: $51,403 (2005); Percent of households with income of $100,000 or more: 8.6% (2005); Poverty rate: 13.1% (2003); Bankruptcy rate: 11.64% (2005).
Taxes: Total county taxes per capita: $300 (2004); County property taxes per capita: $133 (2004).
Education: Percent of population age 25 and over with: High school diploma (including GED) or higher: 80.9% (2005); Bachelor's degree or higher: 12.9% (2005); Master's degree or higher: 4.7% (2005).
Housing: Homeownership rate: 74.0% (2005); Median home value: $98,706 (2005); Median rent: $331 per month (2000); Median age of housing: 38 years (2000).
Health: Birth rate: 126.3 per 10,000 population (2004); Death rate: 106.4 per 10,000 population (2004); Age-adjusted cancer mortality rate: 228.8 deaths per 100,000 population (2002); Number of physicians: 19.0 per 10,000 population (2004); Hospital beds: 43.1 per 10,000 population (2003); Hospital admissions: 2,008.6 per 10,000 population (2003).
Elections: 2004 Presidential election results: 57.3% Bush, 42.3% Kerry, 0.0% Nader, 0.2% Badnarik
National and State Parks: Blue Rock State Forest; Blue Rock State Park; Dillon State Park; Dillon State Wildlife Area; Monroe Basin State Wildlife Area; Muskingum River Parkway State Park; Powelson State Wildlife Area

Additional Information Contacts

Muskingum County Government . . . . (740) 455-7100
http://www.muskingumcounty.org/
City of Zanesville . . . . (740) 455-0603
http://www.coz.org
Zanesfield-Muskingum County Chamber of Commerce . . . (740) 455-8282
http://www.zmchamber.com
Zanesville Chamber of Commerce . . . . (937) 599-3389
http://www.logancountyohio.com

Muskingum County Communities

ADAMSVILLE (village). Covers a land area of 0.051 square miles and a water area of 0 square miles. Located at 40.07° N. Lat.; 81.88° W. Long. Elevation is 1,020 feet.
Population: 151 (1990); 127 (2000); 128 (2005); 128 (2010 projected); Race: 100.0% White, 0.0% Black, 0.0% Asian, 0.0% Hispanic of any race (2005); Density: 2,503.2 persons per square mile (2005); Average household size: 2.67 (2005); Median age: 31.7 (2005); Males per 100 females: 93.9 (2005); Marriage status: 45.5% never married, 51.2% now married, 0.8% widowed, 2.5% divorced (2000); Foreign born: 0.0% (2000); Ancestry (includes multiple ancestries): 26.2% United States or American, 7.6% German, 4.8% Dutch, 4.8% Irish, 2.1% English (2000).
Economy: In agricultural area. Employment by occupation: 5.0% management, 2.5% professional, 8.8% services, 8.8% sales, 0.0% farming, 26.3% construction, 48.8% production (2000).
Income: Per capita income: $16,602 (2005); Median household income: $40,455 (2005); Average household income: $44,271 (2005); Percent of households with income of $100,000 or more: 6.3% (2005); Poverty rate: 4.8% (2000).
Education: Percent of population age 25 and over with: High school diploma (including GED) or higher: 71.3% (2005); Bachelor's degree or higher: 2.5% (2005); Master's degree or higher: 2.5% (2005).

School District(s)

Tri-Valley Local Schools (PK-12)
2003-04 Enrollment: 3,150 . . . . (740) 754-1572

Housing: Homeownership rate: 75.0% (2005); Median home value: $41,310 (2005); Median rent: $271 per month (2000); Median age of housing: 47 years (2000).
Transportation: Commute to work: 100.0% car, 0.0% public transportation, 0.0% walk, 0.0% work from home (2000); Travel time to

work: 8.8% less than 15 minutes, 47.5% 15 to 30 minutes, 42.5% 30 to 45 minutes, 0.0% 45 to 60 minutes, 1.3% 60 minutes or more (2000)

BLUE ROCK (unincorporated postal area, zip code 43720). Aka Gaysport. Covers a land area of 44.288 square miles and a water area of 0.054 square miles. Located at 39.80° N. Lat.; 81.88° W. Long. Elevation is 680 feet.
Population: 1,206 (2000); Race: 97.7% White, 0.6% Black, 1.1% Asian, 0.0% Hispanic of any race (2000); Density: 27.2 persons per square mile (2000); Age: 31.6% under 18, 9.7% over 64 (2000); Marriage status: 17.6% never married, 71.3% now married, 2.2% widowed, 8.9% divorced (2000); Foreign born: 1.4% (2000); Ancestry (includes multiple ancestries): 19.9% United States or American, 13.8% German, 12.0% Irish, 7.3% English, 3.1% Other groups (2000).
Economy: Employment by occupation: 6.6% management, 12.2% professional, 15.0% services, 16.3% sales, 0.0% farming, 16.5% construction, 33.5% production (2000).
Income: Per capita income: $13,848 (2000); Median household income: $35,200 (2000); Poverty rate: 2.5% (2000).
Education: Percent of population age 25 and over with: High school diploma (including GED) or higher: 83.3% (2000); Bachelor's degree or higher: 3.1% (2000).
Housing: Homeownership rate: 87.8% (2000); Median home value: $78,300 (2000); Median rent: $246 per month (2000); Median age of housing: 29 years (2000).
Transportation: Commute to work: 96.7% car, 0.0% public transportation, 3.3% walk, 0.0% work from home (2000); Travel time to work: 9.0% less than 15 minutes, 32.6% 15 to 30 minutes, 32.1% 30 to 45 minutes, 10.3% 45 to 60 minutes, 16.1% 60 minutes or more (2000)

CHANDLERSVILLE (unincorporated postal area, zip code 43727). Covers a land area of 72.662 square miles and a water area of 0.682 square miles. Located at 39.87° N. Lat.; 81.81° W. Long. Elevation is 730 feet.
Population: 1,300 (2000); Race: 99.7% White, 0.0% Black, 0.0% Asian, 0.0% Hispanic of any race (2000); Density: 17.9 persons per square mile (2000); Age: 24.5% under 18, 15.6% over 64 (2000); Marriage status: 19.0% never married, 65.2% now married, 3.3% widowed, 12.5% divorced (2000); Foreign born: 0.4% (2000); Ancestry (includes multiple ancestries): 23.3% German, 14.5% Irish, 10.9% United States or American, 10.2% English, 5.7% Other groups (2000).
Economy: Employment by occupation: 10.9% management, 17.2% professional, 12.0% services, 20.1% sales, 3.3% farming, 12.7% construction, 23.9% production (2000).
Income: Per capita income: $15,815 (2000); Median household income: $40,602 (2000); Poverty rate: 6.6% (2000).
Education: Percent of population age 25 and over with: High school diploma (including GED) or higher: 84.5% (2000); Bachelor's degree or higher: 9.6% (2000).
Housing: Homeownership rate: 91.0% (2000); Median home value: $82,100 (2000); Median rent: $269 per month (2000); Median age of housing: 34 years (2000).
Transportation: Commute to work: 94.4% car, 0.0% public transportation, 1.3% walk, 4.3% work from home (2000); Travel time to work: 20.1% less than 15 minutes, 42.0% 15 to 30 minutes, 16.7% 30 to 45 minutes, 10.6% 45 to 60 minutes, 10.6% 60 minutes or more (2000)

DRESDEN (village). Covers a land area of 1.167 square miles and a water area of 0.044 square miles. Located at 40.12° N. Lat.; 82.01° W. Long. Elevation is 750 feet.
Population: 1,588 (1990); 1,423 (2000); 1,407 (2005); 1,412 (2010 projected); Race: 99.3% White, 0.1% Black, 0.0% Asian, 0.5% Hispanic of any race (2005); Density: 1,205.6 persons per square mile (2005); Average household size: 2.32 (2005); Median age: 38.8 (2005); Males per 100 females: 84.9 (2005); Marriage status: 21.1% never married, 55.7% now married, 11.1% widowed, 12.1% divorced (2000); Foreign born: 0.1% (2000); Ancestry (includes multiple ancestries): 25.4% German, 16.2% United States or American, 12.7% Irish, 8.4% English, 4.0% Other groups (2000).
Economy: Tourism. Basket manufacturing. Single-family building permits issued: 0 (2005); Multi-family building permits issued: 0 (2005); Employment by occupation: 10.9% management, 11.5% professional, 16.7% services, 18.0% sales, 0.3% farming, 8.0% construction, 34.5% production (2000).
Income: Per capita income: $23,340 (2005); Median household income: $44,895 (2005); Average household income: $54,024 (2005); Percent of households with income of $100,000 or more: 9.1% (2005); Poverty rate: 5.8% (2000).
Education: Percent of population age 25 and over with: High school diploma (including GED) or higher: 84.4% (2005); Bachelor's degree or higher: 10.2% (2005); Master's degree or higher: 3.3% (2005).
School District(s)
Tri-Valley Local Schools (PK-12)
  2003-04 Enrollment: 3,150 . . . . (740) 754-1572
Housing: Homeownership rate: 69.0% (2005); Median home value: $97,195 (2005); Median rent: $333 per month (2000); Median age of housing: 39 years (2000).
Newspapers: Dresden Transcript (General - Circulation 5,100)
Transportation: Commute to work: 93.4% car, 0.4% public transportation, 3.1% walk, 3.0% work from home (2000); Travel time to work: 44.1% less than 15 minutes, 32.3% 15 to 30 minutes, 13.5% 30 to 45 minutes, 5.2% 45 to 60 minutes, 4.9% 60 minutes or more (2000)

DUNCAN FALLS (unincorporated postal area, zip code 43734). Covers a land area of 3.393 square miles and a water area of 0 square miles. Located at 39.87° N. Lat.; 81.90° W. Long. Elevation is 690 feet.
History: Duncan Falls may have been named for a trapper who lived in the valley during the 1790's, and for the falls on the Muskingum River, which disappeared when a dam was built.
Population: 1,055 (2000); Race: 97.8% White, 0.0% Black, 0.0% Asian, 0.0% Hispanic of any race (2000); Density: 311.0 persons per square mile (2000); Age: 22.8% under 18, 12.3% over 64 (2000); Marriage status: 24.2% never married, 57.9% now married, 9.0% widowed, 8.9% divorced (2000); Foreign born: 0.0% (2000); Ancestry (includes multiple ancestries): 25.9% German, 14.0% English, 9.2% United States or American, 8.1% Irish, 2.7% Scotch-Irish (2000).
Economy: Employment by occupation: 9.3% management, 30.6% professional, 5.6% services, 23.9% sales, 0.0% farming, 12.5% construction, 18.2% production (2000).
Income: Per capita income: $19,383 (2000); Median household income: $40,417 (2000); Poverty rate: 8.5% (2000).
Education: Percent of population age 25 and over with: High school diploma (including GED) or higher: 94.7% (2000); Bachelor's degree or higher: 20.8% (2000).
School District(s)
Franklin Local Digital Academy (06-12)
  2003-04 Enrollment: 27 . . . . (740) 674-5203
Franklin Local School District (PK-12)
  2003-04 Enrollment: 2,418 . . . . (740) 674-5203
Housing: Homeownership rate: 80.1% (2000); Median home value: $109,200 (2000); Median rent: $351 per month (2000); Median age of housing: 42 years (2000).
Transportation: Commute to work: 90.9% car, 0.0% public transportation, 1.0% walk, 3.3% work from home (2000); Travel time to work: 18.1% less than 15 minutes, 53.0% 15 to 30 minutes, 12.3% 30 to 45 minutes, 9.8% 45 to 60 minutes, 6.8% 60 minutes or more (2000)

FRAZEYSBURG (village). Covers a land area of 0.760 square miles and a water area of 0 square miles. Located at 40.11° N. Lat.; 82.11° W. Long. Elevation is 760 feet.
Population: 1,165 (1990); 1,201 (2000); 1,191 (2005); 1,200 (2010 projected); Race: 96.8% White, 1.3% Black, 0.5% Asian, 0.4% Hispanic of any race (2005); Density: 1,566.3 persons per square mile (2005); Average household size: 2.42 (2005); Median age: 33.2 (2005); Males per 100 females: 87.6 (2005); Marriage status: 24.6% never married, 52.1% now married, 8.8% widowed, 14.6% divorced (2000); Foreign born: 0.3% (2000); Ancestry (includes multiple ancestries): 25.2% German, 12.1% English, 11.7% United States or American, 9.7% Irish, 4.9% Other groups (2000).
Economy: Employment by occupation: 5.7% management, 10.7% professional, 14.8% services, 15.8% sales, 0.0% farming, 12.8% construction, 40.2% production (2000).
Income: Per capita income: $19,872 (2005); Median household income: $41,571 (2005); Average household income: $48,007 (2005); Percent of households with income of $100,000 or more: 6.3% (2005); Poverty rate: 6.6% (2000).
Education: Percent of population age 25 and over with: High school diploma (including GED) or higher: 78.4% (2005); Bachelor's degree or higher: 5.1% (2005); Master's degree or higher: 1.3% (2005).

School District(s)
Tri-Valley Local Schools (PK-12)
    2003-04 Enrollment: 3,150 . . . . (740) 754-1572
Housing: Homeownership rate: 66.3% (2005); Median home value: $82,436 (2005); Median rent: $353 per month (2000); Median age of housing: 32 years (2000).
Transportation: Commute to work: 95.8% car, 0.0% public transportation, 3.0% walk, 0.8% work from home (2000); Travel time to work: 45.4% less than 15 minutes, 26.6% 15 to 30 minutes, 17.1% 30 to 45 minutes, 3.4% 45 to 60 minutes, 7.5% 60 minutes or more (2000)

FULTONHAM (village). Aka Uniontown. Covers a land area of 0.156 square miles and a water area of 0 square miles. Located at 39.85° N. Lat.; 82.14° W. Long. Elevation is 950 feet.
History: Fultonham developed around the Columbia Cement Company plant, which used the local desposits of limestone.
Population: 178 (1990); 151 (2000); 157 (2005); 164 (2010 projected); Race: 97.5% White, 1.3% Black, 0.0% Asian, 0.0% Hispanic of any race (2005); Density: 1,003.3 persons per square mile (2005); Average household size: 2.57 (2005); Median age: 39.1 (2005); Males per 100 females: 96.3 (2005); Marriage status: 36.9% never married, 43.9% now married, 9.6% widowed, 9.6% divorced (2000); Foreign born: 0.0% (2000); Ancestry (includes multiple ancestries): 18.5% German, 11.6% Irish, 11.0% English, 11.0% Other groups, 6.4% United States or American (2000).
Economy: Employment by occupation: 4.6% management, 18.5% professional, 7.7% services, 16.9% sales, 1.5% farming, 13.8% construction, 36.9% production (2000).
Income: Per capita income: $12,834 (2005); Median household income: $29,333 (2005); Average household income: $33,033 (2005); Percent of households with income of $100,000 or more: 0.0% (2005); Poverty rate: 13.3% (2000).
Education: Percent of population age 25 and over with: High school diploma (including GED) or higher: 76.0% (2005); Bachelor's degree or higher: 9.0% (2005); Master's degree or higher: 3.0% (2005).
Housing: Homeownership rate: 75.4% (2005); Median home value: $57,895 (2005); Median rent: $314 per month (2000); Median age of housing: 55 years (2000).
Transportation: Commute to work: 100.0% car, 0.0% public transportation, 0.0% walk, 0.0% work from home (2000); Travel time to work: 16.9% less than 15 minutes, 52.3% 15 to 30 minutes, 16.9% 30 to 45 minutes, 13.8% 45 to 60 minutes, 0.0% 60 minutes or more (2000)

HOPEWELL (unincorporated postal area, zip code 43746). Aka Mount Sterling. Covers a land area of 21.564 square miles and a water area of 0.036 square miles. Located at 39.96° N. Lat.; 82.18° W. Long. Elevation is 1,100 feet.
Population: 1,345 (2000); Race: 97.5% White, 0.0% Black, 1.4% Asian, 0.0% Hispanic of any race (2000); Density: 62.4 persons per square mile (2000); Age: 23.0% under 18, 6.2% over 64 (2000); Marriage status: 22.4% never married, 58.0% now married, 4.2% widowed, 15.4% divorced (2000); Foreign born: 1.1% (2000); Ancestry (includes multiple ancestries): 17.8% United States or American, 16.1% German, 14.5% English, 11.1% Irish, 6.7% Other groups (2000).
Economy: Employment by occupation: 15.2% management, 8.1% professional, 20.0% services, 23.0% sales, 1.2% farming, 10.9% construction, 21.5% production (2000).
Income: Per capita income: $20,739 (2000); Median household income: $45,469 (2000); Poverty rate: 4.6% (2000).
Education: Percent of population age 25 and over with: High school diploma (including GED) or higher: 84.6% (2000); Bachelor's degree or higher: 11.3% (2000).
School District(s)
West Muskingum Local SD (PK-12)
    2003-04 Enrollment: 1,816 . . . . (740) 455-4052
Housing: Homeownership rate: 82.0% (2000); Median home value: $116,700 (2000); Median rent: $344 per month (2000); Median age of housing: 24 years (2000).
Transportation: Commute to work: 92.5% car, 1.2% public transportation, 1.5% walk, 4.8% work from home (2000); Travel time to work: 19.1% less than 15 minutes, 41.3% 15 to 30 minutes, 21.5% 30 to 45 minutes, 9.2% 45 to 60 minutes, 8.9% 60 minutes or more (2000)

NASHPORT (unincorporated postal area, zip code 43830). Covers a land area of 51.098 square miles and a water area of 0.030 square miles. Located at 40.06° N. Lat.; 82.16° W. Long. Elevation is 820 feet.
Population: 5,485 (2000); Race: 97.6% White, 1.5% Black, 0.2% Asian, 1.1% Hispanic of any race (2000); Density: 107.3 persons per square mile (2000); Age: 29.8% under 18, 8.2% over 64 (2000); Marriage status: 17.5% never married, 69.3% now married, 4.5% widowed, 8.7% divorced (2000); Foreign born: 0.4% (2000); Ancestry (includes multiple ancestries): 20.8% German, 13.6% United States or American, 13.6% English, 10.3% Irish, 6.4% Other groups (2000).
Economy: Employment by occupation: 10.8% management, 21.2% professional, 14.5% services, 19.7% sales, 0.3% farming, 8.0% construction, 25.6% production (2000).
Income: Per capita income: $20,546 (2000); Median household income: $48,464 (2000); Poverty rate: 6.3% (2000).
Education: Percent of population age 25 and over with: High school diploma (including GED) or higher: 87.9% (2000); Bachelor's degree or higher: 19.3% (2000).
School District(s)
Licking Valley Local Sd SD (PK-12)
    2003-04 Enrollment: 2,166 . . . . (740) 763-3525
Tri-Valley Local Schools (PK-12)
    2003-04 Enrollment: 3,150 . . . . (740) 754-1572
Housing: Homeownership rate: 81.2% (2000); Median home value: $109,500 (2000); Median rent: $386 per month (2000); Median age of housing: 23 years (2000).
Transportation: Commute to work: 94.0% car, 0.0% public transportation, 2.5% walk, 2.7% work from home (2000); Travel time to work: 20.6% less than 15 minutes, 50.1% 15 to 30 minutes, 14.8% 30 to 45 minutes, 5.2% 45 to 60 minutes, 9.4% 60 minutes or more (2000)

NEW CONCORD (village). Covers a land area of 1.497 square miles and a water area of 0 square miles. Located at 39.99° N. Lat.; 81.73° W. Long. Elevation is 900 feet.
History: New Concord began in 1807 when the National Road was opened. Muskingum College was founded here in 1836.
Population: 2,320 (1990); 2,651 (2000); 2,712 (2005); 2,770 (2010 projected); Race: 95.6% White, 1.8% Black, 1.7% Asian, 1.0% Hispanic of any race (2005); Density: 1,811.7 persons per square mile (2005); Average household size: 3.89 (2005); Median age: 22.8 (2005); Males per 100 females: 85.6 (2005); Marriage status: 58.9% never married, 31.7% now married, 4.8% widowed, 4.6% divorced (2000); Foreign born: 2.9% (2000); Ancestry (includes multiple ancestries): 29.7% German, 17.7% Irish, 12.1% English, 9.0% Other groups, 5.9% Italian (2000).
Economy: Single-family building permits issued: 0 (2005); Multi-family building permits issued: 0 (2005); Employment by occupation: 7.9% management, 23.8% professional, 21.9% services, 31.4% sales, 1.1% farming, 3.7% construction, 10.2% production (2000).
Income: Per capita income: $19,627 (2005); Median household income: $29,451 (2005); Average household income: $45,287 (2005); Percent of households with income of $100,000 or more: 8.9% (2005); Poverty rate: 24.6% (2000).
Education: Percent of population age 25 and over with: High school diploma (including GED) or higher: 87.2% (2005); Bachelor's degree or higher: 34.4% (2005); Master's degree or higher: 19.4% (2005).
School District(s)
East Muskingum Local SD (PK-12)
    2003-04 Enrollment: 2,121 . . . . (740) 826-7655
Four-year College(s)
Muskingum College (Private, Not-for-profit, Presbyterian Church (USA))
    Fall 2004 Enrollment: 2,176 . . . . (740) 826-8114
    2005-06 Tuition: In-state $16,175; Out-of-state $16,175
Housing: Homeownership rate: 56.1% (2005); Median home value: $109,318 (2005); Median rent: $307 per month (2000); Median age of housing: 43 years (2000).
Transportation: Commute to work: 60.2% car, 0.0% public transportation, 35.7% walk, 2.4% work from home (2000); Travel time to work: 61.0% less than 15 minutes, 24.3% 15 to 30 minutes, 7.2% 30 to 45 minutes, 3.3% 45 to 60 minutes, 4.2% 60 minutes or more (2000)

NORTH ZANESVILLE (CDP). Covers a land area of 3.592 square miles and a water area of 0.003 square miles. Located at 39.98° N. Lat.; 82.00° W. Long. Elevation is 820 feet.
Population: 2,964 (1990); 3,013 (2000); 3,095 (2005); 3,178 (2010 projected); Race: 94.7% White, 2.1% Black, 1.8% Asian, 0.4% Hispanic of any race (2005); Density: 861.7 persons per square mile (2005); Average household size: 2.44 (2005); Median age: 46.6 (2005); Males per 100 females: 88.6 (2005); Marriage status: 19.7% never married, 65.5% now

married, 5.6% widowed, 9.1% divorced (2000); Foreign born: 1.8% (2000); Ancestry (includes multiple ancestries): 25.7% German, 21.8% English, 11.9% Irish, 10.5% United States or American, 8.5% Other groups (2000).
Economy: Employment by occupation: 14.9% management, 30.3% professional, 12.0% services, 22.6% sales, 0.7% farming, 7.3% construction, 12.2% production (2000).
Income: Per capita income: $30,557 (2005); Median household income: $57,535 (2005); Average household income: $74,176 (2005); Percent of households with income of $100,000 or more: 19.4% (2005); Poverty rate: 5.2% (2000).
Education: Percent of population age 25 and over with: High school diploma (including GED) or higher: 89.0% (2005); Bachelor's degree or higher: 27.6% (2005); Master's degree or higher: 10.4% (2005).
Housing: Homeownership rate: 88.5% (2005); Median home value: $145,129 (2005); Median rent: $398 per month (2000); Median age of housing: 36 years (2000).
Transportation: Commute to work: 94.3% car, 1.8% public transportation, 0.4% walk, 3.5% work from home (2000); Travel time to work: 50.9% less than 15 minutes, 26.3% 15 to 30 minutes, 11.1% 30 to 45 minutes, 5.4% 45 to 60 minutes, 6.3% 60 minutes or more (2000)

NORWICH (village). Covers a land area of 0.096 square miles and a water area of 0 square miles. Located at 39.98° N. Lat.; 81.79° W. Long. Elevation is 980 feet.
History: The village of Norwich was reported in the 1800's to be the home of a headless creature which roamed Stumpy Hollow at night, frightening the residents and leaving them speechless.
Population: 133 (1990); 113 (2000); 119 (2005); 126 (2010 projected); Race: 98.3% White, 0.0% Black, 0.0% Asian, 0.0% Hispanic of any race (2005); Density: 1,237.4 persons per square mile (2005); Average household size: 2.77 (2005); Median age: 36.5 (2005); Males per 100 females: 77.6 (2005); Marriage status: 21.9% never married, 69.9% now married, 2.7% widowed, 5.5% divorced (2000); Foreign born: 0.0% (2000); Ancestry (includes multiple ancestries): 43.8% German, 30.5% Scotch-Irish, 11.4% Irish, 8.6% French (except Basque), 8.6% Other groups (2000).
Economy: Employment by occupation: 1.9% management, 15.4% professional, 21.2% services, 11.5% sales, 0.0% farming, 0.0% construction, 50.0% production (2000).
Income: Per capita income: $21,996 (2005); Median household income: $54,167 (2005); Average household income: $60,872 (2005); Percent of households with income of $100,000 or more: 18.6% (2005); Poverty rate: 36.2% (2000).
Education: Percent of population age 25 and over with: High school diploma (including GED) or higher: 67.9% (2005); Bachelor's degree or higher: 3.7% (2005); Master's degree or higher: 3.7% (2005).
Housing: Homeownership rate: 79.1% (2005); Median home value: $62,857 (2005); Median rent: $225 per month (2000); Median age of housing: 41 years (2000).
Transportation: Commute to work: 62.0% car, 0.0% public transportation, 20.0% walk, 4.0% work from home (2000); Travel time to work: 50.0% less than 15 minutes, 27.1% 15 to 30 minutes, 2.1% 30 to 45 minutes, 4.2% 45 to 60 minutes, 16.7% 60 minutes or more (2000)

PHILO (village). Aka Taylorsville. Covers a land area of 0.418 square miles and a water area of 0 square miles. Located at 39.86° N. Lat.; 81.90° W. Long. Elevation is 712 feet.
Population: 810 (1990); 769 (2000); 843 (2005); 898 (2010 projected); Race: 98.3% White, 0.4% Black, 0.1% Asian, 0.0% Hispanic of any race (2005); Density: 2,014.6 persons per square mile (2005); Average household size: 2.67 (2005); Median age: 33.9 (2005); Males per 100 females: 88.6 (2005); Marriage status: 19.1% never married, 58.1% now married, 12.0% widowed, 10.8% divorced (2000); Foreign born: 0.4% (2000); Ancestry (includes multiple ancestries): 25.8% United States or American, 13.6% German, 7.4% Irish, 5.0% Other groups, 4.3% English (2000).
Economy: Single-family building permits issued: 0 (2005); Multi-family building permits issued: 0 (2005); Employment by occupation: 8.6% management, 12.9% professional, 17.2% services, 19.5% sales, 0.0% farming, 13.5% construction, 28.4% production (2000).
Income: Per capita income: $15,896 (2005); Median household income: $35,652 (2005); Average household income: $42,405 (2005); Percent of households with income of $100,000 or more: 2.5% (2005); Poverty rate: 15.5% (2000).

Education: Percent of population age 25 and over with: High school diploma (including GED) or higher: 78.2% (2005); Bachelor's degree or higher: 4.2% (2005); Master's degree or higher: 1.2% (2005).

School District(s)
Franklin Local School District (PK-12)
    2003-04 Enrollment: 2,418 . . . . (740) 674-5203

Housing: Homeownership rate: 82.9% (2005); Median home value: $71,233 (2005); Median rent: $335 per month (2000); Median age of housing: 54 years (2000).
Transportation: Commute to work: 97.9% car, 0.0% public transportation, 1.0% walk, 1.0% work from home (2000); Travel time to work: 18.5% less than 15 minutes, 40.4% 15 to 30 minutes, 20.6% 30 to 45 minutes, 5.6% 45 to 60 minutes, 15.0% 60 minutes or more (2000)

PLEASANT GROVE (CDP). Covers a land area of 3.193 square miles and a water area of 0.007 square miles. Located at 39.94° N. Lat.; 81.96° W. Long. Elevation is 928 feet.
Population: 2,001 (1990); 2,016 (2000); 2,074 (2005); 2,120 (2010 projected); Race: 96.2% White, 2.3% Black, 0.2% Asian, 0.3% Hispanic of any race (2005); Density: 649.6 persons per square mile (2005); Average household size: 2.71 (2005); Median age: 45.7 (2005); Males per 100 females: 88.2 (2005); Marriage status: 19.2% never married, 56.7% now married, 13.5% widowed, 10.6% divorced (2000); Foreign born: 5.1% (2000); Ancestry (includes multiple ancestries): 18.7% German, 14.4% United States or American, 10.0% English, 7.7% Irish, 6.4% Other groups (2000).
Economy: Employment by occupation: 5.8% management, 16.6% professional, 18.3% services, 28.5% sales, 0.9% farming, 9.1% construction, 20.9% production (2000).
Income: Per capita income: $19,365 (2005); Median household income: $39,925 (2005); Average household income: $49,041 (2005); Percent of households with income of $100,000 or more: 7.3% (2005); Poverty rate: 11.3% (2000).
Education: Percent of population age 25 and over with: High school diploma (including GED) or higher: 80.8% (2005); Bachelor's degree or higher: 11.9% (2005); Master's degree or higher: 3.3% (2005).
Housing: Homeownership rate: 79.2% (2005); Median home value: $99,022 (2005); Median rent: $333 per month (2000); Median age of housing: 30 years (2000).
Transportation: Commute to work: 91.9% car, 1.2% public transportation, 2.1% walk, 3.8% work from home (2000); Travel time to work: 47.0% less than 15 minutes, 34.9% 15 to 30 minutes, 9.8% 30 to 45 minutes, 4.8% 45 to 60 minutes, 3.5% 60 minutes or more (2000)

SOUTH ZANESVILLE (village). Covers a land area of 0.730 square miles and a water area of 0 square miles. Located at 39.90° N. Lat.; 82.02° W. Long. Elevation is 740 feet.
Population: 2,056 (1990); 1,936 (2000); 1,980 (2005); 2,032 (2010 projected); Race: 97.5% White, 1.0% Black, 0.1% Asian, 0.3% Hispanic of any race (2005); Density: 2,713.5 persons per square mile (2005); Average household size: 2.40 (2005); Median age: 36.7 (2005); Males per 100 females: 90.4 (2005); Marriage status: 24.8% never married, 51.5% now married, 6.0% widowed, 17.7% divorced (2000); Foreign born: 0.7% (2000); Ancestry (includes multiple ancestries): 18.1% United States or American, 12.5% German, 9.6% Other groups, 6.6% Irish, 4.5% English (2000).
Economy: Lumber. Single-family building permits issued: 1 (2005); Multi-family building permits issued: 0 (2005); Employment by occupation: 5.7% management, 12.4% professional, 14.3% services, 25.1% sales, 0.3% farming, 10.7% construction, 31.4% production (2000).
Income: Per capita income: $17,039 (2005); Median household income: $36,236 (2005); Average household income: $40,844 (2005); Percent of households with income of $100,000 or more: 3.4% (2005); Poverty rate: 11.1% (2000).
Education: Percent of population age 25 and over with: High school diploma (including GED) or higher: 77.6% (2005); Bachelor's degree or higher: 6.0% (2005); Master's degree or higher: 1.7% (2005).
Housing: Homeownership rate: 78.7% (2005); Median home value: $57,021 (2005); Median rent: $329 per month (2000); Median age of housing: 35 years (2000).
Safety: Violent crime rate: 15.1 per 10,000 population; Property crime rate: 90.5 per 10,000 population (2004).
Transportation: Commute to work: 94.0% car, 0.5% public transportation, 1.1% walk, 3.3% work from home (2000); Travel time to work: 29.5% less

than 15 minutes, 33.3% 15 to 30 minutes, 15.6% 30 to 45 minutes, 9.7% 45 to 60 minutes, 11.9% 60 minutes or more (2000)

ZANESVILLE (city). Covers a land area of 11.238 square miles and a water area of 0.262 square miles. Located at 39.94° N. Lat.; 82.01° W. Long. Elevation is 710 feet.
History: Zanesville, situated at the confluence of the Licking and Muskingum Rivers, was established in the late 1790's. Clay suitable for pottery-making was discovered in the vicinity, and by 1808 dishes, stoneware, and bricks were bearing the Zanesville imprint. Local sands were used in the glass plant started in Zanesville in 1815, making goblets and water pitchers that became prized collectors items. Zanesville was named for Ebenezer Zane, who surveyed Zane's Trace, an overland route through Ohio, in 1797. A descendant of Zane was western writer Zane Grey, who was born in Zanesville in 1875.
Population: 27,058 (1990); 25,586 (2000); 24,695 (2005); 23,943 (2010 projected); Race: 84.7% White, 11.1% Black, 0.3% Asian, 0.8% Hispanic of any race (2005); Density: 2,197.5 persons per square mile (2005); Average household size: 2.39 (2005); Median age: 35.5 (2005); Males per 100 females: 86.6 (2005); Marriage status: 25.5% never married, 49.1% now married, 9.6% widowed, 15.8% divorced (2000); Foreign born: 0.9% (2000); Ancestry (includes multiple ancestries): 16.7% Other groups, 15.1% United States or American, 14.6% German, 10.4% Irish, 7.4% English (2000).
Economy: Unemployment rate: 8.5% (2005); Total civilian labor force: 10,717 (2005); Single-family building permits issued: 1 (2005); Multi-family building permits issued: 0 (2005); Employment by occupation: 5.4% management, 17.4% professional, 18.2% services, 25.4% sales, 0.4% farming, 7.5% construction, 25.7% production (2000).
Income: Per capita income: $16,617 (2005); Median household income: $29,863 (2005); Average household income: $39,281 (2005); Percent of households with income of $100,000 or more: 4.6% (2005); Poverty rate: 22.4% (2000).
Education: Percent of population age 25 and over with: High school diploma (including GED) or higher: 74.2% (2005); Bachelor's degree or higher: 11.7% (2005); Master's degree or higher: 4.5% (2005).

School District(s)
East Muskingum Local SD (PK-12)
   2003-04 Enrollment: 2,121 . . . . (740) 826-7655
Foxfire Alternative (10-12)
   2003-04 Enrollment: 55 . . . . (419) 293-3979
Maysville Local SD (PK-12)
   2003-04 Enrollment: 2,265 . . . . (740) 453-0754
Mid-East Career and Technology Centers (PK-12)
   2003-04 Enrollment: n/a . . . . (740) 454-0105
West Muskingum Local SD (PK-12)
   2003-04 Enrollment: 1,816 . . . . (740) 455-4052
Zanesville City SD (PK-12)
   2003-04 Enrollment: 4,251 . . . . (740) 454-9751
Zanesville Digital Academy
   2003-04 Enrollment: n/a . . . . (740) 454-9751

Four-year College(s)
Ohio University-Zanesville Campus (Public)
   Fall 2004 Enrollment: 1,877 . . . . (740) 453-0762
   2005-06 Tuition: In-state $4,323; Out-of-state $8,646

Two-year College(s)
Adult Center for Education (Public)
   Fall 2004 Enrollment: 238 . . . . (740) 455-3111
Valley Beauty School (Private, For-profit)
   Fall 2004 Enrollment: 34 . . . . (740) 452-6821
Zane State College (Public)
   Fall 2004 Enrollment: 1,789 . . . . (740) 454-2501
   2005-06 Tuition: In-state $3,647; Out-of-state $7,269

Housing: Homeownership rate: 54.7% (2005); Median home value: $72,386 (2005); Median rent: $318 per month (2000); Median age of housing: 55 years (2000).
Hospitals: Bethesda Hospital (352 beds); Good Samaritan Medical & Rehabilitation Center (368 beds)
Safety: Violent crime rate: 39.5 per 10,000 population; Property crime rate: 646.7 per 10,000 population (2004).
Newspapers: The Times Recorder (Circulation 21,123)
Transportation: Commute to work: 92.8% car, 1.3% public transportation, 2.9% walk, 2.0% work from home (2000); Travel time to work: 49.6% less than 15 minutes, 26.3% 15 to 30 minutes, 10.2% 30 to 45 minutes, 6.0% 45 to 60 minutes, 8.0% 60 minutes or more (2000)

Additional Information Contacts
City of Zanesville . . . . (740) 455-0603
   http://www.coz.org
Zanesfield-Muskingum County Chamber of Commerce . . . (740) 455-8282
   http://www.zmchamber.com
Zanesville Chamber of Commerce . . . . (937) 599-3389
   http://www.logancountyohio.com

Noble County

Located in eastern Ohio; drained by Wills, Duck, and Seneca Creeks. Covers a land area of 399.00 square miles, a water area of 5.59 square miles, and is located in the Eastern Time Zone. The county government was organized in 1851. County seat is Caldwell.
Population: 11,336 (1990); 14,058 (2000); 14,127 (2005); 14,194 (2010 projected); Race: 92.6% White, 6.7% Black, 0.1% Asian, 0.5% Hispanic of any race (2005); Density: 35.4 persons per square mile (2005); Average household size: 3.06 (2005); Median age: 36.6 (2005); Males per 100 females: 130.4 (2005).
Religion: Five largest groups: 11.3% Catholic Church, 8.4% The United Methodist Church, 4.8% Churches of Christ, 1.8% Southern Baptist Convention, 1.7% Christian Churches and Churches of Christ (2000).
Economy: Unemployment rate: 8.1% (2005); Total civilian labor force: 5,923 (2005); Leading industries: 26.8% manufacturing; 21.3% health care and social assistance; 19.0% retail trade (2004); Farms: 602 totaling 106,957 acres (2002); Companies that employ 500 or more persons: 0 (2004); Companies that employ 100 to 499 persons: 2 (2004); Companies that employ less than 100 persons: 188 (2004); Black-owned businesses: n/a (2002); Hispanic-owned businesses: n/a (2002); Women-owned businesses: n/a (2002); Retail sales per capita: $6,422 (2006). Single-family building permits issued: 27 (2005); Multi-family building permits issued: 0 (2005).
Income: Per capita income: $16,378 (2005); Median household income: $38,305 (2005); Average household income: $45,858 (2005); Percent of households with income of $100,000 or more: 5.6% (2005); Poverty rate: 12.2% (2003); Bankruptcy rate: 4.80% (2005).
Education: Percent of population age 25 and over with: High school diploma (including GED) or higher: 78.7% (2005); Bachelor's degree or higher: 8.2% (2005); Master's degree or higher: 2.4% (2005).
Housing: Homeownership rate: 80.2% (2005); Median home value: $80,019 (2005); Median rent: $273 per month (2000); Median age of housing: 34 years (2000).
Health: Birth rate: 108.5 per 10,000 population (2004); Death rate: 111.3 per 10,000 population (2004); Age-adjusted cancer mortality rate: 236.1 deaths per 100,000 population (2002); Number of physicians: 2.8 per 10,000 population (2004); Hospital beds: 0.0 per 10,000 population (2003); Hospital admissions: 0.0 per 10,000 population (2003).
Elections: 2004 Presidential election results: 58.7% Bush, 40.6% Kerry, 0.0% Nader, 0.4% Badnarik
National and State Parks: Wolf Run State Park

Additional Information Contacts
Noble County Government . . . . (740) 732-2969
   http://www.noblecountyohio.com/
Caldwell Chamber of Commerce . . . . (740) 732-5288
   http://www.noblecountyohio.com

Noble County Communities

BATESVILLE (village). Covers a land area of 0.248 square miles and a water area of 0 square miles. Located at 39.91° N. Lat.; 81.28° W. Long. Elevation is 892 feet.
Population: 95 (1990); 100 (2000); 108 (2005); 113 (2010 projected); Race: 100.0% White, 0.0% Black, 0.0% Asian, 0.0% Hispanic of any race (2005); Density: 434.9 persons per square mile (2005); Average household size: 2.51 (2005); Median age: 36.3 (2005); Males per 100 females: 86.2 (2005); Marriage status: 7.5% never married, 66.3% now married, 18.8% widowed, 7.5% divorced (2000); Foreign born: 0.0% (2000); Ancestry (includes multiple ancestries): 13.4% Irish, 10.9% German, 5.0% Other groups, 5.0% Russian, 1.7% Italian (2000).
Economy: Employment by occupation: 0.0% management, 10.8% professional, 37.8% services, 10.8% sales, 0.0% farming, 13.5% construction, 27.0% production (2000).
Income: Per capita income: $24,444 (2005); Median household income: $31,875 (2005); Average household income: $61,395 (2005); Percent of

households with income of $100,000 or more: 9.3% (2005); Poverty rate: 17.6% (2000).
Education: Percent of population age 25 and over with: High school diploma (including GED) or higher: 74.3% (2005); Bachelor's degree or higher: 5.7% (2005); Master's degree or higher: 0.0% (2005).
Housing: Homeownership rate: 88.4% (2005); Median home value: $46,667 (2005); Median rent: $338 per month (2000); Median age of housing: 60+ years (2000).
Transportation: Commute to work: 89.2% car, 0.0% public transportation, 5.4% walk, 5.4% work from home (2000); Travel time to work: 20.0% less than 15 minutes, 42.9% 15 to 30 minutes, 25.7% 30 to 45 minutes, 0.0% 45 to 60 minutes, 11.4% 60 minutes or more (2000)

BELLE VALLEY (village). Covers a land area of 0.416 square miles and a water area of 0 square miles. Located at 39.78° N. Lat.; 81.55° W. Long. Elevation is 760 feet.
History: Belle Valley developed around a large coal mine. In the early 1900's the mine attracted many Eastern European immigrants who found work here.
Population: 290 (1990); 263 (2000); 284 (2005); 287 (2010 projected); Race: 97.5% White, 0.7% Black, 0.0% Asian, 0.7% Hispanic of any race (2005); Density: 683.1 persons per square mile (2005); Average household size: 2.47 (2005); Median age: 41.2 (2005); Males per 100 females: 94.5 (2005); Marriage status: 29.1% never married, 48.4% now married, 8.5% widowed, 14.1% divorced (2000); Foreign born: 0.4% (2000); Ancestry (includes multiple ancestries): 10.9% German, 7.9% Slovak, 7.5% Irish, 7.5% United States or American, 6.7% English (2000).
Economy: Employment by occupation: 5.2% management, 14.7% professional, 15.5% services, 13.8% sales, 2.6% farming, 7.8% construction, 40.5% production (2000).
Income: Per capita income: $17,377 (2005); Median household income: $36,442 (2005); Average household income: $42,913 (2005); Percent of households with income of $100,000 or more: 5.2% (2005); Poverty rate: 19.9% (2000).
Education: Percent of population age 25 and over with: High school diploma (including GED) or higher: 80.5% (2005); Bachelor's degree or higher: 1.5% (2005); Master's degree or higher: 1.0% (2005).
Housing: Homeownership rate: 77.4% (2005); Median home value: $50,000 (2005); Median rent: $278 per month (2000); Median age of housing: 60+ years (2000).
Transportation: Commute to work: 96.5% car, 0.0% public transportation, 0.0% walk, 0.0% work from home (2000); Travel time to work: 24.8% less than 15 minutes, 45.1% 15 to 30 minutes, 14.2% 30 to 45 minutes, 4.4% 45 to 60 minutes, 11.5% 60 minutes or more (2000)

CALDWELL (village). Covers a land area of 0.979 square miles and a water area of 0 square miles. Located at 39.74° N. Lat.; 81.51° W. Long. Elevation is 744 feet.
History: Caldwell was founded in 1857 as the seat of Noble County, and named for the owners of the town site. Coal mining was Caldwell's primary industry.
Population: 1,797 (1990); 1,956 (2000); 1,857 (2005); 1,757 (2010 projected); Race: 99.1% White, 0.1% Black, 0.5% Asian, 0.2% Hispanic of any race (2005); Density: 1,897.1 persons per square mile (2005); Average household size: 2.29 (2005); Median age: 45.4 (2005); Males per 100 females: 81.5 (2005); Marriage status: 23.5% never married, 47.7% now married, 17.9% widowed, 11.0% divorced (2000); Foreign born: 0.0% (2000); Ancestry (includes multiple ancestries): 20.1% German, 11.5% Irish, 10.5% United States or American, 9.4% English, 4.8% Other groups (2000).
Economy: Employment by occupation: 9.8% management, 14.7% professional, 18.9% services, 25.6% sales, 1.3% farming, 8.2% construction, 21.6% production (2000).
Income: Per capita income: $17,361 (2005); Median household income: $29,653 (2005); Average household income: $37,491 (2005); Percent of households with income of $100,000 or more: 3.3% (2005); Poverty rate: 14.5% (2000).
Education: Percent of population age 25 and over with: High school diploma (including GED) or higher: 78.6% (2005); Bachelor's degree or higher: 10.4% (2005); Master's degree or higher: 2.0% (2005).
School District(s)
Caldwell Ex Vill SD (PK-12)
    2003-04 Enrollment: 1,042 . . . . (740) 732-5637

Housing: Homeownership rate: 61.2% (2005); Median home value: $76,000 (2005); Median rent: $304 per month (2000); Median age of housing: 57 years (2000).
Newspapers: The Journal & The Noble County Leader (General - Circulation 5,150)
Transportation: Commute to work: 90.6% car, 0.0% public transportation, 5.4% walk, 4.0% work from home (2000); Travel time to work: 67.7% less than 15 minutes, 11.9% 15 to 30 minutes, 9.1% 30 to 45 minutes, 5.1% 45 to 60 minutes, 6.2% 60 minutes or more (2000)
Additional Information Contacts
Caldwell Chamber of Commerce . . . . (740) 732-5288
    http://www.noblecountyohio.com

DEXTER CITY (village). Covers a land area of 0.175 square miles and a water area of 0 square miles. Located at 39.65° N. Lat.; 81.47° W. Long. Elevation is 740 feet.
Population: 161 (1990); 166 (2000); 162 (2005); 160 (2010 projected); Race: 100.0% White, 0.0% Black, 0.0% Asian, 0.0% Hispanic of any race (2005); Density: 925.6 persons per square mile (2005); Average household size: 2.61 (2005); Median age: 38.4 (2005); Males per 100 females: 100.0 (2005); Marriage status: 29.8% never married, 48.9% now married, 8.5% widowed, 12.8% divorced (2000); Foreign born: 0.0% (2000); Ancestry (includes multiple ancestries): 28.7% German, 20.5% English, 11.1% Irish, 7.0% Other groups, 5.8% United States or American (2000).
Economy: Employment by occupation: 0.0% management, 13.2% professional, 35.5% services, 9.2% sales, 0.0% farming, 10.5% construction, 31.6% production (2000).
Income: Per capita income: $13,781 (2005); Median household income: $32,500 (2005); Average household income: $36,008 (2005); Percent of households with income of $100,000 or more: 0.0% (2005); Poverty rate: 21.6% (2000).
Education: Percent of population age 25 and over with: High school diploma (including GED) or higher: 69.4% (2005); Bachelor's degree or higher: 9.3% (2005); Master's degree or higher: 0.0% (2005).
Housing: Homeownership rate: 74.2% (2005); Median home value: $43,333 (2005); Median rent: $175 per month (2000); Median age of housing: 60+ years (2000).
Transportation: Commute to work: 97.4% car, 0.0% public transportation, 0.0% walk, 2.6% work from home (2000); Travel time to work: 27.0% less than 15 minutes, 35.1% 15 to 30 minutes, 25.7% 30 to 45 minutes, 6.8% 45 to 60 minutes, 5.4% 60 minutes or more (2000)

SARAHSVILLE (village). Covers a land area of 0.168 square miles and a water area of 0 square miles. Located at 39.80° N. Lat.; 81.46° W. Long. Elevation is 980 feet.
Population: 162 (1990); 198 (2000); 219 (2005); 233 (2010 projected); Race: 99.1% White, 0.9% Black, 0.0% Asian, 4.1% Hispanic of any race (2005); Density: 1,302.2 persons per square mile (2005); Average household size: 3.17 (2005); Median age: 33.0 (2005); Males per 100 females: 106.6 (2005); Marriage status: 28.7% never married, 61.9% now married, 5.6% widowed, 3.8% divorced (2000); Foreign born: 0.0% (2000); Ancestry (includes multiple ancestries): 8.7% German, 8.7% Irish, 5.1% French (except Basque), 3.6% Dutch, 3.6% United States or American (2000).
Economy: In agricultural area. Employment by occupation: 10.0% management, 16.3% professional, 25.0% services, 10.0% sales, 2.5% farming, 16.3% construction, 20.0% production (2000).
Income: Per capita income: $14,258 (2005); Median household income: $42,969 (2005); Average household income: $45,254 (2005); Percent of households with income of $100,000 or more: 5.8% (2005); Poverty rate: 14.4% (2000).
Education: Percent of population age 25 and over with: High school diploma (including GED) or higher: 77.9% (2005); Bachelor's degree or higher: 0.0% (2005); Master's degree or higher: 0.0% (2005).
School District(s)
Noble Local SD (PK-12)
    2003-04 Enrollment: 1,259 . . . . (740) 732-2084
Housing: Homeownership rate: 87.0% (2005); Median home value: $62,000 (2005); Median rent: $263 per month (2000); Median age of housing: 57 years (2000).
Transportation: Commute to work: 88.8% car, 0.0% public transportation, 3.8% walk, 7.5% work from home (2000); Travel time to work: 18.9% less than 15 minutes, 39.2% 15 to 30 minutes, 31.1% 30 to 45 minutes, 8.1% 45 to 60 minutes, 2.7% 60 minutes or more (2000)

SUMMERFIELD (village). Covers a land area of 0.370 square miles and a water area of 0 square miles. Located at 39.79° N. Lat.; 81.33° W. Long. Elevation is 1,197 feet.
Population: 295 (1990); 296 (2000); 261 (2005); 256 (2010 projected); Race: 100.0% White, 0.0% Black, 0.0% Asian, 0.0% Hispanic of any race (2005); Density: 704.8 persons per square mile (2005); Average household size: 2.87 (2005); Median age: 29.3 (2005); Males per 100 females: 86.4 (2005); Marriage status: 22.2% never married, 61.5% now married, 10.3% widowed, 6.0% divorced (2000); Foreign born: 0.0% (2000); Ancestry (includes multiple ancestries): 32.2% German, 11.0% Irish, 9.5% English, 6.3% United States or American, 6.3% Other groups (2000).
Economy: Employment by occupation: 5.9% management, 11.9% professional, 27.7% services, 15.8% sales, 0.0% farming, 13.9% construction, 24.8% production (2000).
Income: Per capita income: $12,059 (2005); Median household income: $28,462 (2005); Average household income: $34,588 (2005); Percent of households with income of $100,000 or more: 1.1% (2005); Poverty rate: 16.7% (2000).
Education: Percent of population age 25 and over with: High school diploma (including GED) or higher: 74.0% (2005); Bachelor's degree or higher: 6.8% (2005); Master's degree or higher: 0.7% (2005).
Housing: Homeownership rate: 81.3% (2005); Median home value: $35,652 (2005); Median rent: $194 per month (2000); Median age of housing: 60 years (2000).
Transportation: Commute to work: 85.7% car, 1.0% public transportation, 3.1% walk, 10.2% work from home (2000); Travel time to work: 14.8% less than 15 minutes, 40.9% 15 to 30 minutes, 8.0% 30 to 45 minutes, 13.6% 45 to 60 minutes, 22.7% 60 minutes or more (2000)

Ottawa County

Located in northern Ohio; bounded on the northeast by Lake Erie; drained by Portage River; includes the Bass Islands. Covers a land area of 254.95 square miles, a water area of 330.17 square miles, and is located in the Eastern Time Zone. The county government was organized in 1840. County seat is Port Clinton.

Ottawa County is part of the Toledo, OH Metropolitan Statistical Area. The entire metro area includes: Fulton County, OH; Lucas County, OH; Ottawa County, OH; Wood County, OH

Weather Station: Put-In-Bay   Elevation: 577 feet

	Jan	Feb	Mar	Apr	May	Jun	Jul	Aug	Sep	Oct	Nov	Dec
High	31	34	43	55	67	77	82	81	74	61	48	37
Low	18	20	29	39	51	61	67	66	59	48	37	26
Precip	1.6	1.4	5.2	2.9	3.3	3.4	3.1	3.3	3.2	2.6	2.7	2.2
Snow	7.3	5.3	2.8	0.4	tr	0.0	0.0	0.0	0.0	tr	0.2	3.7

High and Low temperatures in degrees Fahrenheit; Precipitation and Snow in inches

Population: 40,029 (1990); 40,985 (2000); 41,398 (2005); 41,816 (2010 projected); Race: 96.7% White, 0.6% Black, 0.3% Asian, 3.8% Hispanic of any race (2005); Density: 162.4 persons per square mile (2005); Average household size: 2.44 (2005); Median age: 42.1 (2005); Males per 100 females: 97.7 (2005).
Religion: Five largest groups: 21.9% Catholic Church, 17.1% Evangelical Lutheran Church in America, 7.0% United Church of Christ, 6.1% The United Methodist Church, 1.0% Lutheran Church—Missouri Synod (2000).
Economy: Unemployment rate: 7.7% (2005); Total civilian labor force: 21,604 (2005); Leading industries: 24.1% manufacturing; 15.4% retail trade; 12.3% health care and social assistance (2004); Farms: 517 totaling 114,430 acres (2002); Companies that employ 500 or more persons: 3 (2004); Companies that employ 100 to 499 persons: 10 (2004); Companies that employ less than 100 persons: 1,108 (2004); Black-owned businesses: n/a (2002); Hispanic-owned businesses: n/a (2002); Women-owned businesses: 648 (2002); Retail sales per capita: $14,161 (2006); Single-family building permits issued: 328 (2005); Multi-family building permits issued: 8 (2005).
Income: Per capita income: $24,397 (2005); Median household income: $48,559 (2005); Average household income: $58,936 (2005); Percent of households with income of $100,000 or more: 13.4% (2005); Poverty rate: 6.9% (2003); Bankruptcy rate: 9.19% (2005).
Taxes: Total county taxes per capita: $272 (2004); County property taxes per capita: $156 (2004).
Education: Percent of population age 25 and over with: High school diploma (including GED) or higher: 84.1% (2005); Bachelor's degree or higher: 15.9% (2005); Master's degree or higher: 5.4% (2005).
Housing: Homeownership rate: 80.8% (2005); Median home value: $134,628 (2005); Median rent: $386 per month (2000); Median age of housing: 35 years (2000).
Health: Birth rate: 109.4 per 10,000 population (2004); Death rate: 109.9 per 10,000 population (2004); Age-adjusted cancer mortality rate: 207.1 deaths per 100,000 population (2002); Number of physicians: 12.8 per 10,000 population (2004); Hospital beds: 6.1 per 10,000 population (2003); Hospital admissions: 302.4 per 10,000 population (2003).
Elections: 2004 Presidential election results: 51.9% Bush, 47.8% Kerry, 0.0% Nader, 0.2% Badnarik
National and State Parks: Catawba Island State Park; Crane Creek State Park; East Harbor State Park; Ottawa National Wildlife Refuge; South Bass Island State Park

Additional Information Contacts

Ottawa County Government	(419) 734-6710
http://www.co.ottawa.oh.us/	
City of Port Clinton	(419) 734-5522
http://www.ci.port-clinton.oh.us	
Lakeside Marblhd Chamber of Commerce	(419) 798-9777
http://www.marbleheadpeninsula.com	
Oak Harbor Chamber of Commerce	(419) 898-0479
http://www.oakharborohio.net	
Ottawa County Visitors Bureau	(800) 441-1271
http://www.lake-erie.com	
Port Clinton Chamber of Commerce	(419) 734-5503
http://www.portclintonchamber.com	
Put-In-Bay Chamber of Commerce	(419) 285-2832
http://www.put-in-bay.com	
Village of Genoa	(419) 855-7791
http://www.genoaohio.org	
Village of Oak Harbor	(419) 898-5561
http://www.oakharbor.oh.us	

Ottawa County Communities

CLAY CENTER (village). Covers a land area of 0.903 square miles and a water area of 0 square miles. Located at 41.56° N. Lat.; 83.36° W. Long. Elevation is 610 feet.
Population: 303 (1990); 294 (2000); 299 (2005); 302 (2010 projected); Race: 98.7% White, 0.0% Black, 0.0% Asian, 4.7% Hispanic of any race (2005); Density: 331.2 persons per square mile (2005); Average household size: 2.62 (2005); Median age: 35.5 (2005); Males per 100 females: 100.7 (2005); Marriage status: 19.4% never married, 69.4% now married, 3.6% widowed, 7.7% divorced (2000); Foreign born: 0.0% (2000); Ancestry (includes multiple ancestries): 55.7% German, 10.1% Polish, 7.4% French (except Basque), 6.4% Other groups, 6.4% Irish (2000).
Economy: Eleven miles East Southeast of Toledo. Single-family building permits issued: 1 (2005); Multi-family building permits issued: 0 (2005); Employment by occupation: 7.3% management, 9.3% professional, 16.0% services, 20.0% sales, 0.0% farming, 16.7% construction, 30.7% production (2000).
Income: Per capita income: $27,642 (2005); Median household income: $62,500 (2005); Average household income: $72,500 (2005); Percent of households with income of $100,000 or more: 14.9% (2005); Poverty rate: 3.0% (2000).
Education: Percent of population age 25 and over with: High school diploma (including GED) or higher: 85.1% (2005); Bachelor's degree or higher: 8.7% (2005); Master's degree or higher: 4.6% (2005).
Housing: Homeownership rate: 83.3% (2005); Median home value: $91,364 (2005); Median rent: $317 per month (2000); Median age of housing: 60+ years (2000).
Transportation: Commute to work: 91.3% car, 0.0% public transportation, 8.0% walk, 0.0% work from home (2000); Travel time to work: 43.3% less than 15 minutes, 33.3% 15 to 30 minutes, 18.7% 30 to 45 minutes, 1.3% 45 to 60 minutes, 3.3% 60 minutes or more (2000)

ELMORE (village). Covers a land area of 0.831 square miles and a water area of 0 square miles. Located at 41.47° N. Lat.; 83.29° W. Long. Elevation is 615 feet.
Population: 1,411 (1990); 1,426 (2000); 1,574 (2005); 1,707 (2010 projected); Race: 97.6% White, 0.1% Black, 0.0% Asian, 5.0% Hispanic of any race (2005); Density: 1,894.7 persons per square mile (2005); Average

household size: 2.40 (2005); Median age: 36.9 (2005); Males per 100 females: 89.9 (2005); Marriage status: 17.5% never married, 64.5% now married, 9.7% widowed, 8.2% divorced (2000); Foreign born: 0.6% (2000); Ancestry (includes multiple ancestries): 48.1% German, 9.4% English, 9.4% Irish, 6.6% Other groups, 6.2% Hungarian (2000).
Economy: Employment by occupation: 11.9% management, 14.6% professional, 11.0% services, 29.7% sales, 1.2% farming, 7.9% construction, 23.7% production (2000).
Income: Per capita income: $21,279 (2005); Median household income: $43,858 (2005); Average household income: $51,056 (2005); Percent of households with income of $100,000 or more: 9.8% (2005); Poverty rate: 5.5% (2000).
Education: Percent of population age 25 and over with: High school diploma (including GED) or higher: 86.4% (2005); Bachelor's degree or higher: 18.1% (2005); Master's degree or higher: 5.2% (2005).

School District(s)
Woodmore Local SD (PK-12)
    2003-04 Enrollment: 1,190 . . . . (419) 849-2381
Housing: Homeownership rate: 73.2% (2005); Median home value: $120,946 (2005); Median rent: $267 per month (2000); Median age of housing: 60+ years (2000).
Transportation: Commute to work: 93.5% car, 0.5% public transportation, 3.0% walk, 1.7% work from home (2000); Travel time to work: 27.9% less than 15 minutes, 31.9% 15 to 30 minutes, 30.8% 30 to 45 minutes, 6.3% 45 to 60 minutes, 3.1% 60 minutes or more (2000)

GENOA (village). Covers a land area of 1.496 square miles and a water area of 0 square miles. Located at 41.52° N. Lat.; 83.36° W. Long. Elevation is 625 feet.
History: Settled 1835 as Stony Ridge Station.
Population: 2,381 (1990); 2,230 (2000); 2,218 (2005); 2,188 (2010 projected); Race: 96.0% White, 0.5% Black, 0.3% Asian, 6.4% Hispanic of any race (2005); Density: 1,482.2 persons per square mile (2005); Average household size: 2.56 (2005); Median age: 39.7 (2005); Males per 100 females: 91.5 (2005); Marriage status: 21.3% never married, 54.3% now married, 12.8% widowed, 11.6% divorced (2000); Foreign born: 0.8% (2000); Ancestry (includes multiple ancestries): 32.1% German, 11.5% Irish, 10.6% Other groups, 9.6% English, 6.3% United States or American (2000).
Economy: Employment by occupation: 11.4% management, 13.3% professional, 16.0% services, 24.7% sales, 0.0% farming, 13.3% construction, 21.2% production (2000).
Income: Per capita income: $22,365 (2005); Median household income: $47,528 (2005); Average household income: $55,237 (2005); Percent of households with income of $100,000 or more: 9.2% (2005); Poverty rate: 2.0% (2000).
Education: Percent of population age 25 and over with: High school diploma (including GED) or higher: 84.8% (2005); Bachelor's degree or higher: 10.8% (2005); Master's degree or higher: 2.2% (2005).

School District(s)
Genoa Area Local SD (PK-12)
    2003-04 Enrollment: 1,737 . . . . (419) 855-7741
Housing: Homeownership rate: 76.5% (2005); Median home value: $112,130 (2005); Median rent: $408 per month (2000); Median age of housing: 53 years (2000).
Transportation: Commute to work: 96.5% car, 0.0% public transportation, 2.7% walk, 0.0% work from home (2000); Travel time to work: 25.2% less than 15 minutes, 39.6% 15 to 30 minutes, 24.4% 30 to 45 minutes, 8.0% 45 to 60 minutes, 2.8% 60 minutes or more (2000)
Additional Information Contacts
Village of Genoa . . . . (419) 855-7791
    http://www.genoaohio.org

GRAYTOWN (unincorporated postal area, zip code 43432). Covers a land area of 24.748 square miles and a water area of 0.017 square miles. Located at 41.55° N. Lat.; 83.25° W. Long. Elevation is 595 feet.
Population: 1,357 (2000); Race: 97.1% White, 0.0% Black, 0.0% Asian, 6.4% Hispanic of any race (2000); Density: 54.8 persons per square mile (2000); Age: 29.5% under 18, 11.5% over 64 (2000); Marriage status: 20.6% never married, 70.9% now married, 2.9% widowed, 5.6% divorced (2000); Foreign born: 0.9% (2000); Ancestry (includes multiple ancestries): 52.2% German, 10.8% Irish, 6.9% Other groups, 3.8% Hungarian, 3.7% English (2000).
Economy: Employment by occupation: 10.9% management, 18.9% professional, 10.5% services, 20.9% sales, 1.4% farming, 8.9% construction, 28.5% production (2000).
Income: Per capita income: $20,032 (2000); Median household income: $61,750 (2000); Poverty rate: 4.6% (2000).
Education: Percent of population age 25 and over with: High school diploma (including GED) or higher: 88.9% (2000); Bachelor's degree or higher: 13.8% (2000).

School District(s)
Benton Carroll Salem Local SD (PK-12)
    2003-04 Enrollment: 2,024 . . . . (419) 898-6210
Housing: Homeownership rate: 93.1% (2000); Median home value: $120,700 (2000); Median rent: $917 per month (2000); Median age of housing: 49 years (2000).
Transportation: Commute to work: 92.9% car, 0.0% public transportation, 2.9% walk, 4.2% work from home (2000); Travel time to work: 24.9% less than 15 minutes, 38.3% 15 to 30 minutes, 26.8% 30 to 45 minutes, 4.8% 45 to 60 minutes, 5.2% 60 minutes or more (2000)

LACARNE (unincorporated postal area, zip code 43439). Aka La Carne. Covers a land area of 0.017 square miles and a water area of 0 square miles. Located at 41.51° N. Lat.; 83.04° W. Long. Elevation is 679 feet.
Population: 74 (2000); Race: 100.0% White, 0.0% Black, 0.0% Asian, 0.0% Hispanic of any race (2000); Density: 4,360.1 persons per square mile (2000); Age: 38.3% under 18, 13.3% over 64 (2000); Marriage status: 21.6% never married, 35.1% now married, 0.0% widowed, 43.2% divorced (2000); Foreign born: 11.7% (2000); Ancestry (includes multiple ancestries): 51.7% German, 23.3% United States or American, 11.7% Irish, 11.7% Lithuanian, 10.0% Dutch (2000).
Economy: Employment by occupation: 0.0% management, 0.0% professional, 0.0% services, 0.0% sales, 0.0% farming, 0.0% construction, 100.0% production (2000).
Income: Per capita income: $15,100 (2000); Median household income: $27,500 (2000); Poverty rate: 0.0% (2000).
Education: Percent of population age 25 and over with: High school diploma (including GED) or higher: 100.0% (2000); Bachelor's degree or higher: 0.0% (2000).
Housing: Homeownership rate: 100.0% (2000); Median home value: $79,300 (2000); Median rent: $n/a per month (2000); Median age of housing: 60+ years (2000).
Transportation: Commute to work: 100.0% car, 0.0% public transportation, 0.0% walk, 0.0% work from home (2000); Travel time to work: 53.8% less than 15 minutes, 0.0% 15 to 30 minutes, 46.2% 30 to 45 minutes, 0.0% 45 to 60 minutes, 0.0% 60 minutes or more (2000)

LAKESIDE MARBLEHEAD (unincorporated postal area, zip code 43440). Part of the Village of Marblehead. Covers a land area of 15.362 square miles and a water area of 0.846 square miles. Located at 41.53° N. Lat.; 82.75° W. Long.
Population: 4,319 (2000); Race: 97.2% White, 0.8% Black, 0.0% Asian, 2.0% Hispanic of any race (2000); Density: 281.1 persons per square mile (2000); Age: 17.6% under 18, 22.8% over 64 (2000); Marriage status: 17.4% never married, 61.2% now married, 9.4% widowed, 11.9% divorced (2000); Foreign born: 1.3% (2000); Ancestry (includes multiple ancestries): 31.7% German, 12.3% English, 10.8% Irish, 8.6% Slovak, 8.1% Polish (2000).
Economy: Employment by occupation: 11.8% management, 14.4% professional, 17.1% services, 25.1% sales, 0.0% farming, 12.2% construction, 19.5% production (2000).
Income: Per capita income: $28,563 (2000); Median household income: $42,007 (2000); Poverty rate: 3.7% (2000).
Education: Percent of population age 25 and over with: High school diploma (including GED) or higher: 86.1% (2000); Bachelor's degree or higher: 18.7% (2000).

School District(s)
Danbury Local SD (PK-12)
    2003-04 Enrollment: 620 . . . . (419) 798-5185
Housing: Homeownership rate: 82.5% (2000); Median home value: $127,900 (2000); Median rent: $416 per month (2000); Median age of housing: 33 years (2000).
Transportation: Commute to work: 89.0% car, 0.6% public transportation, 4.2% walk, 4.9% work from home (2000); Travel time to work: 33.1% less than 15 minutes, 36.8% 15 to 30 minutes, 14.7% 30 to 45 minutes, 5.0% 45 to 60 minutes, 10.4% 60 minutes or more (2000)

Additional Information Contacts
Lakeside Marblhd Chamber of Commerce .... (419) 798-9777
http://www.marbleheadpeninsula.com

MARBLEHEAD (village).
Covers a land area of 2.834 square miles and a water area of 0.979 square miles. Located at 41.53° N. Lat.; 82.72° W. Long. Elevation is 625 feet.
History: The Benajah Wolcott family settled here in 1809 and found three orchards which the French had planted earlier. Quarrying began in 1834 when John Clemens, a relative of Mark Twain, established himself here. Marblehead may have been called Marble Headland by an early visitor, who thought the white limestone cliffs were marble.
Population: 858 (1990); 762 (2000); 711 (2005); 697 (2010 projected); Race: 97.9% White, 0.4% Black, 0.1% Asian, 2.0% Hispanic of any race (2005); Density: 250.9 persons per square mile (2005); Average household size: 2.24 (2005); Median age: 51.1 (2005); Males per 100 females: 99.7 (2005); Marriage status: 20.5% never married, 67.2% now married, 6.9% widowed, 5.4% divorced (2000); Foreign born: 0.8% (2000); Ancestry (includes multiple ancestries): 30.3% German, 27.1% Slovak, 12.6% Irish, 11.6% English, 6.5% Polish (2000).
Economy: Employment by occupation: 12.2% management, 15.8% professional, 17.0% services, 23.3% sales, 0.0% farming, 14.3% construction, 17.3% production (2000).
Income: Per capita income: $31,711 (2005); Median household income: $53,333 (2005); Average household income: $69,135 (2005); Percent of households with income of $100,000 or more: 18.9% (2005); Poverty rate: 4.7% (2000).
Education: Percent of population age 25 and over with: High school diploma (including GED) or higher: 92.3% (2005); Bachelor's degree or higher: 24.6% (2005); Master's degree or higher: 11.5% (2005).
Housing: Homeownership rate: 85.5% (2005); Median home value: $161,818 (2005); Median rent: $411 per month (2000); Median age of housing: 30 years (2000).
Newspapers: Peninsula News (General - Circulation 1,800)
Transportation: Commute to work: 81.5% car, 0.9% public transportation, 4.3% walk, 10.1% work from home (2000); Travel time to work: 40.8% less than 15 minutes, 27.3% 15 to 30 minutes, 17.7% 30 to 45 minutes, 2.3% 45 to 60 minutes, 11.9% 60 minutes or more (2000)

MARTIN (unincorporated postal area, zip code 43445).
Covers a land area of 19.025 square miles and a water area of 0.129 square miles. Located at 41.59° N. Lat.; 83.29° W. Long. Elevation is 600 feet.
Population: 1,170 (2000); Race: 86.2% White, 0.0% Black, 0.0% Asian, 12.1% Hispanic of any race (2000); Density: 61.5 persons per square mile (2000); Age: 33.9% under 18, 7.9% over 64 (2000); Marriage status: 29.1% never married, 64.8% now married, 2.5% widowed, 3.7% divorced (2000); Foreign born: 2.0% (2000); Ancestry (includes multiple ancestries): 57.7% German, 15.3% Other groups, 11.1% Irish, 5.4% Hungarian, 5.2% Italian (2000).
Economy: Employment by occupation: 6.0% management, 10.1% professional, 15.3% services, 25.2% sales, 1.0% farming, 14.5% construction, 27.9% production (2000).
Income: Per capita income: $18,604 (2000); Median household income: $56,719 (2000); Poverty rate: 5.8% (2000).
Education: Percent of population age 25 and over with: High school diploma (including GED) or higher: 82.0% (2000); Bachelor's degree or higher: 12.7% (2000).
Housing: Homeownership rate: 87.1% (2000); Median home value: $109,600 (2000); Median rent: $375 per month (2000); Median age of housing: 44 years (2000).
Transportation: Commute to work: 95.2% car, 2.2% public transportation, 0.0% walk, 2.7% work from home (2000); Travel time to work: 23.7% less than 15 minutes, 40.6% 15 to 30 minutes, 29.5% 30 to 45 minutes, 4.8% 45 to 60 minutes, 1.4% 60 minutes or more (2000)

OAK HARBOR (village).
Covers a land area of 1.327 square miles and a water area of 0.140 square miles. Located at 41.51° N. Lat.; 83.14° W. Long. Elevation is 585 feet.
History: Sometimes spelled Oakharbor.
Population: 2,637 (1990); 2,841 (2000); 2,830 (2005); 2,824 (2010 projected); Race: 98.0% White, 0.1% Black, 0.6% Asian, 2.3% Hispanic of any race (2005); Density: 2,131.9 persons per square mile (2005); Average household size: 2.42 (2005); Median age: 38.0 (2005); Males per 100 females: 92.0 (2005); Marriage status: 23.8% never married, 57.7% now married, 7.5% widowed, 11.0% divorced (2000); Foreign born: 0.5% (2000); Ancestry (includes multiple ancestries): 51.6% German, 9.9% Irish, 8.2% English, 7.1% Other groups, 5.2% United States or American (2000).
Economy: Baskets, food products, building materials, barrels; ships fruit. Single-family building permits issued: 9 (2005); Multi-family building permits issued: 0 (2005); Employment by occupation: 9.7% management, 18.9% professional, 14.5% services, 21.0% sales, 0.0% farming, 8.1% construction, 27.9% production (2000).
Income: Per capita income: $25,604 (2005); Median household income: $49,043 (2005); Average household income: $61,879 (2005); Percent of households with income of $100,000 or more: 13.5% (2005); Poverty rate: 3.5% (2000).
Taxes: Total city taxes per capita: $343 (2004); City property taxes per capita: $81 (2004).
Education: Percent of population age 25 and over with: High school diploma (including GED) or higher: 89.0% (2005); Bachelor's degree or higher: 17.3% (2005); Master's degree or higher: 6.2% (2005).
School District(s)
Benton Carroll Salem Local SD (PK-12)
    2003-04 Enrollment: 2,024 .... (419) 898-6210
Housing: Homeownership rate: 71.4% (2005); Median home value: $121,350 (2005); Median rent: $346 per month (2000); Median age of housing: 55 years (2000).
Newspapers: The Ottawa County Exponent (General - Circulation 3,000)
Transportation: Commute to work: 95.4% car, 0.0% public transportation, 2.1% walk, 2.0% work from home (2000); Travel time to work: 38.7% less than 15 minutes, 36.3% 15 to 30 minutes, 16.2% 30 to 45 minutes, 5.7% 45 to 60 minutes, 3.1% 60 minutes or more (2000)
Additional Information Contacts
Oak Harbor Chamber of Commerce .... (419) 898-0479
    http://www.oakharborohio.net
Village of Oak Harbor............................. (419) 898-5561
    http://www.oakharbor.oh.us

PORT CLINTON (city).
Covers a land area of 2.106 square miles and a water area of 0.201 square miles. Located at 41.51° N. Lat.; 82.94° W. Long. Elevation is 592 feet.
History: Port Clinton was platted in 1828 and settled by some Scotch immigrants, bound for Chicago, who were shipwrecked at this point and settled here. The town was named for DeWitt Clinton.
Population: 7,170 (1990); 6,391 (2000); 6,325 (2005); 6,248 (2010 projected); Race: 93.6% White, 2.0% Black, 0.5% Asian, 6.0% Hispanic of any race (2005); Density: 3,002.7 persons per square mile (2005); Average household size: 2.25 (2005); Median age: 40.0 (2005); Males per 100 females: 95.0 (2005); Marriage status: 25.8% never married, 51.7% now married, 8.6% widowed, 13.9% divorced (2000); Foreign born: 1.2% (2000); Ancestry (includes multiple ancestries): 37.4% German, 12.3% Irish, 11.7% Other groups, 10.9% English, 6.5% United States or American (2000).
Economy: Employment by occupation: 10.0% management, 15.7% professional, 17.4% services, 26.4% sales, 0.4% farming, 9.6% construction, 20.5% production (2000).
Income: Per capita income: $20,299 (2005); Median household income: $37,106 (2005); Average household income: $45,102 (2005); Percent of households with income of $100,000 or more: 7.4% (2005); Poverty rate: 9.7% (2000).
Education: Percent of population age 25 and over with: High school diploma (including GED) or higher: 80.0% (2005); Bachelor's degree or higher: 11.9% (2005); Master's degree or higher: 5.2% (2005).
School District(s)
Port Clinton City SD (PK-12)
    2003-04 Enrollment: 1,971 .... (419) 732-2102
Housing: Homeownership rate: 67.6% (2005); Median home value: $111,374 (2005); Median rent: $389 per month (2000); Median age of housing: 44 years (2000).
Hospitals: Magruder Memorial Hospital (98 beds)
Safety: Violent crime rate: 7.9 per 10,000 population; Property crime rate: 470.8 per 10,000 population (2004).
Newspapers: News-Herald (Circulation 5,940); The Beacon (General - Circulation 17,000)
Transportation: Commute to work: 90.7% car, 1.3% public transportation, 3.8% walk, 2.8% work from home (2000); Travel time to work: 54.4% less than 15 minutes, 26.2% 15 to 30 minutes, 9.2% 30 to 45 minutes, 4.4% 45 to 60 minutes, 5.9% 60 minutes or more (2000)
Additional Information Contacts

City of Port Clinton............................... (419) 734-5522
http://www.ci.port-clinton.oh.us
Ottawa County Visitors Bureau .... (800) 441-1271
http://www.lake-erie.com
Port Clinton Chamber of Commerce .... (419) 734-5503
http://www.portclintonchamber.com

PUT-IN-BAY (village). Covers a land area of 0.458 square miles and a water area of 0.178 square miles. Located at 41.65° N. Lat.; 82.81° W. Long. Elevation is 587 feet.
History: Perry's Victory and International Peace Memorial national monument (est. 1936) is near here. A granite column 352 feet high commemorates battle of Lake Erie (1813), in which Admiral Perry's U.S. fleet defeated the British, and symbolizes century of peace between U.S. and Canada.
Population: 144 (1990); 128 (2000); 129 (2005); 131 (2010 projected); Race: 99.2% White, 0.0% Black, 0.0% Asian, 0.0% Hispanic of any race (2005); Density: 281.4 persons per square mile (2005); Average household size: 1.87 (2005); Median age: 47.5 (2005); Males per 100 females: 122.4 (2005); Marriage status: 23.1% never married, 62.3% now married, 8.5% widowed, 6.2% divorced (2000); Foreign born: 0.0% (2000); Ancestry (includes multiple ancestries): 54.4% German, 18.8% Irish, 11.4% Italian, 8.1% English, 6.7% Hungarian (2000).
Economy: Tourist resort. Has state and federal fish hatcheries, commercial fisheries. Employment by occupation: 20.7% management, 24.1% professional, 12.6% services, 27.6% sales, 2.3% farming, 3.4% construction, 9.2% production (2000).
Income: Per capita income: $46,647 (2005); Median household income: $69,853 (2005); Average household income: $87,210 (2005); Percent of households with income of $100,000 or more: 31.9% (2005); Poverty rate: 0.0% (2000).
Education: Percent of population age 25 and over with: High school diploma (including GED) or higher: 92.2% (2005); Bachelor's degree or higher: 44.1% (2005); Master's degree or higher: 16.7% (2005).
School District(s)
Put-In-Bay Local SD (KG-12)
2003-04 Enrollment: 77 .... (419) 285-3614
Housing: Homeownership rate: 72.5% (2005); Median home value: $352,941 (2005); Median rent: $425 per month (2000); Median age of housing: 60+ years (2000).
Transportation: Commute to work: 65.5% car, 3.4% public transportation, 14.9% walk, 13.8% work from home (2000); Travel time to work: 70.7% less than 15 minutes, 20.0% 15 to 30 minutes, 5.3% 30 to 45 minutes, 0.0% 45 to 60 minutes, 4.0% 60 minutes or more (2000)
Additional Information Contacts
Put-In-Bay Chamber of Commerce .... (419) 285-2832
http://www.put-in-bay.com

ROCKY RIDGE (village). Covers a land area of 1.018 square miles and a water area of 0.015 square miles. Located at 41.53° N. Lat.; 83.21° W. Long. Elevation is 608 feet.
Population: 425 (1990); 389 (2000); 379 (2005); 376 (2010 projected); Race: 99.2% White, 0.0% Black, 0.0% Asian, 5.8% Hispanic of any race (2005); Density: 372.4 persons per square mile (2005); Average household size: 2.92 (2005); Median age: 35.8 (2005); Males per 100 females: 101.6 (2005); Marriage status: 30.7% never married, 51.6% now married, 6.4% widowed, 11.3% divorced (2000); Foreign born: 1.0% (2000); Ancestry (includes multiple ancestries): 47.9% German, 12.2% Irish, 8.5% Other groups, 5.4% French (except Basque), 4.4% Polish (2000).
Economy: In agricultural area. Employment by occupation: 5.8% management, 9.1% professional, 16.2% services, 13.0% sales, 0.0% farming, 8.4% construction, 47.4% production (2000).
Income: Per capita income: $17,018 (2005); Median household income: $43,571 (2005); Average household income: $49,615 (2005); Percent of households with income of $100,000 or more: 7.7% (2005); Poverty rate: 13.8% (2000).
Education: Percent of population age 25 and over with: High school diploma (including GED) or higher: 73.5% (2005); Bachelor's degree or higher: 4.2% (2005); Master's degree or higher: 0.4% (2005).
School District(s)
Benton Carroll Salem Local SD (PK-12)
2003-04 Enrollment: 2,024 .... (419) 898-6210
Housing: Homeownership rate: 77.7% (2005); Median home value: $95,625 (2005); Median rent: $325 per month (2000); Median age of housing: 45 years (2000).
Transportation: Commute to work: 95.4% car, 0.0% public transportation, 0.0% walk, 4.6% work from home (2000); Travel time to work: 24.1% less than 15 minutes, 41.4% 15 to 30 minutes, 22.8% 30 to 45 minutes, 10.3% 45 to 60 minutes, 1.4% 60 minutes or more (2000)

Paulding County

Located in northwestern Ohio; bounded on the west by Indiana; drained by the Auglaize and Maumee Rivers. Covers a land area of 416.26 square miles, a water area of 2.64 square miles, and is located in the Eastern Time Zone. The county government was organized in 1820. County seat is Paulding.

Weather Station: Paulding   Elevation: 725 feet

	Jan	Feb	Mar	Apr	May	Jun	Jul	Aug	Sep	Oct	Nov	Dec
High	30	35	46	59	71	80	84	82	75	63	49	37
Low	14	17	26	36	47	57	61	58	50	39	30	21
Precip	1.9	1.7	2.7	3.4	3.8	3.4	3.4	3.0	3.0	2.5	3.0	2.6
Snow	5.5	5.3	3.2	0.4	0.0	0.0	0.0	0.0	0.0	tr	1.2	4.1

High and Low temperatures in degrees Fahrenheit; Precipitation and Snow in inches

Population: 20,488 (1990); 20,293 (2000); 19,364 (2005); 18,444 (2010 projected); Race: 95.9% White, 1.1% Black, 0.2% Asian, 3.0% Hispanic of any race (2005); Density: 46.5 persons per square mile (2005); Average household size: 2.55 (2005); Median age: 38.4 (2005); Males per 100 females: 96.7 (2005).
Religion: Five largest groups: 13.6% Catholic Church, 9.4% The United Methodist Church, 4.1% Church of the Nazarene, 3.9% Evangelical Lutheran Church in America, 2.5% Apostolic Christian Church of America, Inc. (2000).
Economy: Unemployment rate: 5.5% (2005); Total civilian labor force: 10,784 (2005); Leading industries: 35.3% manufacturing; 15.6% health care and social assistance; 14.1% retail trade (2004); Farms: 651 totaling 238,497 acres (2002); Companies that employ 500 or more persons: 0 (2004); Companies that employ 100 to 499 persons: 6 (2004); Companies that employ less than 100 persons: 317 (2004); Black-owned businesses: n/a (2002); Hispanic-owned businesses: n/a (2002); Women-owned businesses: n/a (2002); Retail sales per capita: $8,763 (2006). Single-family building permits issued: 25 (2005); Multi-family building permits issued: 18 (2005).
Income: Per capita income: $20,498 (2005); Median household income: $43,861 (2005); Average household income: $52,100 (2005); Percent of households with income of $100,000 or more: 8.0% (2005); Poverty rate: 8.4% (2003); Bankruptcy rate: 10.13% (2005).
Education: Percent of population age 25 and over with: High school diploma (including GED) or higher: 81.5% (2005); Bachelor's degree or higher: 7.8% (2005); Master's degree or higher: 3.3% (2005).
Housing: Homeownership rate: 83.9% (2005); Median home value: $87,102 (2005); Median rent: $305 per month (2000); Median age of housing: 36 years (2000).
Health: Birth rate: 96.3 per 10,000 population (2004); Death rate: 95.2 per 10,000 population (2004); Age-adjusted cancer mortality rate: 238.3 deaths per 100,000 population (2002); Number of physicians: 4.1 per 10,000 population (2004); Hospital beds: 12.7 per 10,000 population (2003); Hospital admissions: 290.2 per 10,000 population (2003).
Elections: 2004 Presidential election results: 62.8% Bush, 36.5% Kerry, 0.0% Nader, 0.3% Badnarik
Additional Information Contacts
Paulding County Government .... (419) 399-8215
http://www.pauldingcountycourt.com/
Paulding Chamber of Commerce.................... (419) 399-5215
http://www.pauldingchamber.com

Paulding County Communities

ANTWERP (village). Covers a land area of 1.160 square miles and a water area of 0 square miles. Located at 41.18° N. Lat.; 84.73° W. Long. Elevation is 732 feet.
Population: 1,870 (1990); 1,740 (2000); 1,652 (2005); 1,564 (2010 projected); Race: 97.9% White, 0.4% Black, 0.0% Asian, 2.2% Hispanic of any race (2005); Density: 1,424.3 persons per square mile (2005); Average household size: 2.30 (2005); Median age: 37.3 (2005); Males per 100 females: 91.0 (2005); Marriage status: 22.2% never married, 55.6% now married, 9.4% widowed, 12.8% divorced (2000); Foreign born: 0.1% (2000); Ancestry (includes multiple ancestries): 36.6% German, 11.2%

United States or American, 9.8% Irish, 7.7% English, 5.2% Other groups (2000).
Economy: Dairy, livestock, grain; cheese making. Single-family building permits issued: 4 (2005); Multi-family building permits issued: 0 (2005); Employment by occupation: 8.4% management, 14.6% professional, 12.9% services, 22.6% sales, 0.5% farming, 9.5% construction, 31.5% production (2000).
Income: Per capita income: $21,665 (2005); Median household income: $36,240 (2005); Average household income: $49,916 (2005); Percent of households with income of $100,000 or more: 7.4% (2005); Poverty rate: 8.9% (2000).
Education: Percent of population age 25 and over with: High school diploma (including GED) or higher: 84.3% (2005); Bachelor's degree or higher: 9.2% (2005); Master's degree or higher: 3.5% (2005).
School District(s)
Antwerp Local SD (PK-12)
    2003-04 Enrollment: 728 . . . . (419) 258-5421
Housing: Homeownership rate: 70.3% (2005); Median home value: $80,517 (2005); Median rent: $334 per month (2000); Median age of housing: 41 years (2000).
Newspapers: Antwerp Bee-Argus (General - Circulation 1,500)
Transportation: Commute to work: 93.6% car, 0.9% public transportation, 2.9% walk, 2.0% work from home (2000); Travel time to work: 40.7% less than 15 minutes, 24.7% 15 to 30 minutes, 24.8% 30 to 45 minutes, 3.8% 45 to 60 minutes, 6.0% 60 minutes or more (2000)

BROUGHTON
(village). Covers a land area of 0.216 square miles and a water area of 0 square miles. Located at 41.08° N. Lat.; 84.53° W. Long. Elevation is 726 feet.
Population: 151 (1990); 166 (2000); 172 (2005); 168 (2010 projected); Race: 97.1% White, 0.0% Black, 0.0% Asian, 2.3% Hispanic of any race (2005); Density: 795.9 persons per square mile (2005); Average household size: 2.82 (2005); Median age: 36.4 (2005); Males per 100 females: 115.0 (2005); Marriage status: 23.6% never married, 60.0% now married, 7.1% widowed, 9.3% divorced (2000); Foreign born: 0.0% (2000); Ancestry (includes multiple ancestries): 22.2% German, 10.6% Irish, 9.2% English, 5.8% United States or American, 3.4% Other groups (2000).
Economy: Employment by occupation: 6.6% management, 2.2% professional, 5.5% services, 20.9% sales, 0.0% farming, 2.2% construction, 62.6% production (2000).
Income: Per capita income: $16,512 (2005); Median household income: $42,500 (2005); Average household income: $46,557 (2005); Percent of households with income of $100,000 or more: 3.3% (2005); Poverty rate: 5.8% (2000).
Education: Percent of population age 25 and over with: High school diploma (including GED) or higher: 70.3% (2005); Bachelor's degree or higher: 1.8% (2005); Master's degree or higher: 1.8% (2005).
Housing: Homeownership rate: 95.1% (2005); Median home value: $63,333 (2005); Median rent: $225 per month (2000); Median age of housing: 36 years (2000).
Transportation: Commute to work: 94.0% car, 0.0% public transportation, 6.0% walk, 0.0% work from home (2000); Travel time to work: 47.6% less than 15 minutes, 17.9% 15 to 30 minutes, 27.4% 30 to 45 minutes, 4.8% 45 to 60 minutes, 2.4% 60 minutes or more (2000)

CECIL
(village). Covers a land area of 1.467 square miles and a water area of 0 square miles. Located at 41.21° N. Lat.; 84.60° W. Long. Elevation is 725 feet.
Population: 249 (1990); 216 (2000); 201 (2005); 190 (2010 projected); Race: 96.5% White, 0.0% Black, 0.0% Asian, 1.5% Hispanic of any race (2005); Density: 137.0 persons per square mile (2005); Average household size: 2.79 (2005); Median age: 38.8 (2005); Males per 100 females: 123.3 (2005); Marriage status: 24.4% never married, 41.9% now married, 10.0% widowed, 23.8% divorced (2000); Foreign born: 0.0% (2000); Ancestry (includes multiple ancestries): 32.5% German, 9.6% Other groups, 8.1% Irish, 4.3% United States or American, 3.8% Polish (2000).
Economy: Employment by occupation: 13.5% management, 5.6% professional, 19.1% services, 15.7% sales, 0.0% farming, 10.1% construction, 36.0% production (2000).
Income: Per capita income: $11,580 (2005); Median household income: $31,667 (2005); Average household income: $32,326 (2005); Percent of households with income of $100,000 or more: 0.0% (2005); Poverty rate: 23.4% (2000).
Education: Percent of population age 25 and over with: High school diploma (including GED) or higher: 76.9% (2005); Bachelor's degree or higher: 8.2% (2005); Master's degree or higher: 4.5% (2005).
Housing: Homeownership rate: 91.7% (2005); Median home value: $43,750 (2005); Median rent: $225 per month (2000); Median age of housing: 60+ years (2000).
Transportation: Commute to work: 93.3% car, 0.0% public transportation, 6.7% walk, 0.0% work from home (2000); Travel time to work: 28.1% less than 15 minutes, 38.2% 15 to 30 minutes, 25.8% 30 to 45 minutes, 6.7% 45 to 60 minutes, 1.1% 60 minutes or more (2000)

GROVER HILL
(village). Covers a land area of 0.290 square miles and a water area of 0 square miles. Located at 41.01° N. Lat.; 84.47° W. Long. Elevation is 727 feet.
Population: 498 (1990); 412 (2000); 366 (2005); 346 (2010 projected); Race: 96.2% White, 0.8% Black, 0.0% Asian, 3.0% Hispanic of any race (2005); Density: 1,261.8 persons per square mile (2005); Average household size: 2.42 (2005); Median age: 37.6 (2005); Males per 100 females: 94.7 (2005); Marriage status: 25.2% never married, 56.2% now married, 11.2% widowed, 7.3% divorced (2000); Foreign born: 0.7% (2000); Ancestry (includes multiple ancestries): 22.1% German, 19.2% Irish, 8.4% Other groups, 7.9% English, 4.7% United States or American (2000).
Economy: In agricultural area. Single-family building permits issued: 0 (2005); Multi-family building permits issued: 0 (2005); Employment by occupation: 8.6% management, 7.5% professional, 19.5% services, 12.1% sales, 2.3% farming, 8.0% construction, 42.0% production (2000).
Income: Per capita income: $18,245 (2005); Median household income: $37,019 (2005); Average household income: $44,222 (2005); Percent of households with income of $100,000 or more: 6.6% (2005); Poverty rate: 17.7% (2000).
Education: Percent of population age 25 and over with: High school diploma (including GED) or higher: 77.6% (2005); Bachelor's degree or higher: 2.0% (2005); Master's degree or higher: 0.4% (2005).
School District(s)
Wayne Trace Local SD (PK-12)
    2003-04 Enrollment: 1,155 . . . . (419) 263-2415
Housing: Homeownership rate: 88.7% (2005); Median home value: $50,154 (2005); Median rent: $406 per month (2000); Median age of housing: 56 years (2000).
Transportation: Commute to work: 95.8% car, 0.0% public transportation, 3.0% walk, 1.2% work from home (2000); Travel time to work: 11.5% less than 15 minutes, 44.8% 15 to 30 minutes, 18.8% 30 to 45 minutes, 9.7% 45 to 60 minutes, 15.2% 60 minutes or more (2000)

HAVILAND
(village). Covers a land area of 0.287 square miles and a water area of 0 square miles. Located at 41.01° N. Lat.; 84.58° W. Long. Elevation is 736 feet.
Population: 229 (1990); 180 (2000); 170 (2005); 160 (2010 projected); Race: 98.2% White, 0.0% Black, 0.0% Asian, 1.8% Hispanic of any race (2005); Density: 591.7 persons per square mile (2005); Average household size: 2.62 (2005); Median age: 34.3 (2005); Males per 100 females: 112.5 (2005); Marriage status: 28.2% never married, 53.2% now married, 5.6% widowed, 12.9% divorced (2000); Foreign born: 0.0% (2000); Ancestry (includes multiple ancestries): 21.5% German, 12.3% Other groups, 8.6% United States or American, 8.0% Irish, 5.5% Swiss (2000).
Economy: Employment by occupation: 4.9% management, 8.2% professional, 26.2% services, 3.3% sales, 0.0% farming, 9.8% construction, 47.5% production (2000).
Income: Per capita income: $17,206 (2005); Median household income: $38,587 (2005); Average household income: $45,000 (2005); Percent of households with income of $100,000 or more: 9.2% (2005); Poverty rate: 13.1% (2000).
Education: Percent of population age 25 and over with: High school diploma (including GED) or higher: 65.5% (2005); Bachelor's degree or higher: 3.6% (2005); Master's degree or higher: 0.0% (2005).
School District(s)
Wayne Trace Local SD (PK-12)
    2003-04 Enrollment: 1,155 . . . . (419) 263-2415
Housing: Homeownership rate: 80.0% (2005); Median home value: $61,538 (2005); Median rent: $219 per month (2000); Median age of housing: 60 years (2000).
Transportation: Commute to work: 98.4% car, 0.0% public transportation, 0.0% walk, 1.6% work from home (2000); Travel time to work: 31.7% less

than 15 minutes, 35.0% 15 to 30 minutes, 20.0% 30 to 45 minutes, 11.7% 45 to 60 minutes, 1.7% 60 minutes or more (2000)

LATTY (village). Covers a land area of 0.267 square miles and a water area of 0 square miles. Located at 41.08° N. Lat.; 84.58° W. Long. Elevation is 730 feet.
Population: 205 (1990); 200 (2000); 211 (2005); 212 (2010 projected); Race: 86.3% White, 6.6% Black, 0.5% Asian, 3.8% Hispanic of any race (2005); Density: 789.4 persons per square mile (2005); Average household size: 2.54 (2005); Median age: 36.0 (2005); Males per 100 females: 102.9 (2005); Marriage status: 23.3% never married, 66.3% now married, 3.1% widowed, 7.4% divorced (2000); Foreign born: 0.0% (2000); Ancestry (includes multiple ancestries): 36.7% German, 22.2% Other groups, 10.1% Swiss, 8.7% United States or American, 6.3% English (2000).
Economy: In agricultural area. Employment by occupation: 20.8% management, 6.5% professional, 7.8% services, 11.7% sales, 0.0% farming, 18.2% construction, 35.1% production (2000).
Income: Per capita income: $23,187 (2005); Median household income: $46,786 (2005); Average household income: $58,946 (2005); Percent of households with income of $100,000 or more: 10.8% (2005); Poverty rate: 12.6% (2000).
Education: Percent of population age 25 and over with: High school diploma (including GED) or higher: 80.0% (2005); Bachelor's degree or higher: 3.1% (2005); Master's degree or higher: 1.5% (2005).
Housing: Homeownership rate: 85.5% (2005); Median home value: $73,750 (2005); Median rent: $338 per month (2000); Median age of housing: 51 years (2000).
Transportation: Commute to work: 94.8% car, 0.0% public transportation, 2.6% walk, 2.6% work from home (2000); Travel time to work: 42.7% less than 15 minutes, 21.3% 15 to 30 minutes, 24.0% 30 to 45 minutes, 12.0% 45 to 60 minutes, 0.0% 60 minutes or more (2000)

MELROSE (village). Covers a land area of 0.860 square miles and a water area of 0 square miles. Located at 41.09° N. Lat.; 84.41° W. Long. Elevation is 715 feet.
Population: 307 (1990); 322 (2000); 313 (2005); 299 (2010 projected); Race: 97.1% White, 0.0% Black, 0.0% Asian, 2.9% Hispanic of any race (2005); Density: 363.9 persons per square mile (2005); Average household size: 2.82 (2005); Median age: 29.9 (2005); Males per 100 females: 96.9 (2005); Marriage status: 30.7% never married, 48.4% now married, 8.9% widowed, 12.0% divorced (2000); Foreign born: 0.0% (2000); Ancestry (includes multiple ancestries): 30.1% German, 12.8% Irish, 11.8% Other groups, 8.1% United States or American, 6.1% English (2000).
Economy: Employment by occupation: 9.2% management, 2.3% professional, 6.9% services, 20.8% sales, 0.0% farming, 10.0% construction, 50.8% production (2000).
Income: Per capita income: $15,335 (2005); Median household income: $41,944 (2005); Average household income: $43,243 (2005); Percent of households with income of $100,000 or more: 1.8% (2005); Poverty rate: 14.5% (2000).
Education: Percent of population age 25 and over with: High school diploma (including GED) or higher: 63.7% (2005); Bachelor's degree or higher: 0.0% (2005); Master's degree or higher: 0.0% (2005).
Housing: Homeownership rate: 75.7% (2005); Median home value: $57,778 (2005); Median rent: $267 per month (2000); Median age of housing: 36 years (2000).
Transportation: Commute to work: 97.7% car, 0.0% public transportation, 0.0% walk, 0.0% work from home (2000); Travel time to work: 12.3% less than 15 minutes, 39.2% 15 to 30 minutes, 33.1% 30 to 45 minutes, 10.0% 45 to 60 minutes, 5.4% 60 minutes or more (2000)

OAKWOOD (village). Covers a land area of 0.585 square miles and a water area of 0 square miles. Located at 41.09° N. Lat.; 84.37° W. Long. Elevation is 700 feet.
Population: 709 (1990); 607 (2000); 577 (2005); 545 (2010 projected); Race: 98.8% White, 0.0% Black, 0.3% Asian, 0.2% Hispanic of any race (2005); Density: 985.7 persons per square mile (2005); Average household size: 2.52 (2005); Median age: 37.2 (2005); Males per 100 females: 87.3 (2005); Marriage status: 17.9% never married, 62.3% now married, 9.8% widowed, 10.0% divorced (2000); Foreign born: 0.3% (2000); Ancestry (includes multiple ancestries): 21.0% United States or American, 20.2% German, 12.4% Other groups, 6.6% Irish, 5.8% English (2000).
Economy: Agricultural area. Single-family building permits issued: 0 (2005); Multi-family building permits issued: 0 (2005); Employment by occupation: 6.5% management, 11.4% professional, 14.6% services, 15.4% sales, 1.6% farming, 9.8% construction, 40.7% production (2000).
Income: Per capita income: $17,678 (2005); Median household income: $37,120 (2005); Average household income: $44,541 (2005); Percent of households with income of $100,000 or more: 4.4% (2005); Poverty rate: 10.9% (2000).
Education: Percent of population age 25 and over with: High school diploma (including GED) or higher: 78.8% (2005); Bachelor's degree or higher: 4.6% (2005); Master's degree or higher: 2.7% (2005).

School District(s)
Paulding Ex Vill SD (PK-12)
    2003-04 Enrollment: 1,809 . . . . (419) 399-4656
Housing: Homeownership rate: 78.6% (2005); Median home value: $65,000 (2005); Median rent: $278 per month (2000); Median age of housing: 45 years (2000).
Transportation: Commute to work: 93.4% car, 0.0% public transportation, 5.8% walk, 0.8% work from home (2000); Travel time to work: 33.5% less than 15 minutes, 40.2% 15 to 30 minutes, 12.6% 30 to 45 minutes, 7.5% 45 to 60 minutes, 6.3% 60 minutes or more (2000)

PAULDING (village). Covers a land area of 2.280 square miles and a water area of 0.098 square miles. Located at 41.14° N. Lat.; 84.58° W. Long. Elevation is 723 feet.
Population: 3,637 (1990); 3,595 (2000); 3,370 (2005); 3,145 (2010 projected); Race: 91.2% White, 2.7% Black, 0.3% Asian, 6.6% Hispanic of any race (2005); Density: 1,478.4 persons per square mile (2005); Average household size: 2.40 (2005); Median age: 38.1 (2005); Males per 100 females: 90.8 (2005); Marriage status: 23.8% never married, 57.9% now married, 8.3% widowed, 10.0% divorced (2000); Foreign born: 0.8% (2000); Ancestry (includes multiple ancestries): 34.3% German, 16.5% Other groups, 12.5% United States or American, 7.2% Irish, 5.0% English (2000).
Economy: Corn, wheat, oats; alfalfa milling. Manufacturing. Single-family building permits issued: 7 (2005); Multi-family building permits issued: 0 (2005); Employment by occupation: 7.3% management, 13.6% professional, 14.5% services, 22.6% sales, 0.5% farming, 8.9% construction, 32.6% production (2000).
Income: Per capita income: $18,877 (2005); Median household income: $37,720 (2005); Average household income: $44,749 (2005); Percent of households with income of $100,000 or more: 4.6% (2005); Poverty rate: 9.0% (2000).
Education: Percent of population age 25 and over with: High school diploma (including GED) or higher: 84.0% (2005); Bachelor's degree or higher: 9.4% (2005); Master's degree or higher: 5.1% (2005).

School District(s)
Paulding Ex Vill SD (PK-12)
    2003-04 Enrollment: 1,809 . . . . (419) 399-4656
Western Buckeye Educational Service Center
    2003-04 Enrollment: n/a . . . . (419) 238-4746
Housing: Homeownership rate: 74.4% (2005); Median home value: $80,156 (2005); Median rent: $293 per month (2000); Median age of housing: 41 years (2000).
Hospitals: Paulding County Hospital (25 beds)
Newspapers: Paulding Progress (General - Circulation 4,300)
Transportation: Commute to work: 92.0% car, 1.5% public transportation, 4.2% walk, 1.5% work from home (2000); Travel time to work: 54.2% less than 15 minutes, 13.6% 15 to 30 minutes, 17.7% 30 to 45 minutes, 8.8% 45 to 60 minutes, 5.7% 60 minutes or more (2000)
Additional Information Contacts
Paulding Chamber of Commerce. . . . . (419) 399-5215
    http://www.pauldingchamber.com

PAYNE (village). Covers a land area of 0.538 square miles and a water area of 0 square miles. Located at 41.07° N. Lat.; 84.72° W. Long. Elevation is 753 feet.
Population: 1,325 (1990); 1,166 (2000); 1,049 (2005); 1,003 (2010 projected); Race: 97.1% White, 0.6% Black, 0.0% Asian, 3.8% Hispanic of any race (2005); Density: 1,951.0 persons per square mile (2005); Average household size: 2.23 (2005); Median age: 38.0 (2005); Males per 100 females: 86.0 (2005); Marriage status: 22.9% never married, 54.7% now married, 11.3% widowed, 11.1% divorced (2000); Foreign born: 0.8% (2000); Ancestry (includes multiple ancestries): 39.8% German, 14.0% Irish, 9.8% United States or American, 6.8% English, 5.1% Other groups (2000).

Economy: Grain; livestock. Single-family building permits issued: 7 (2005); Multi-family building permits issued: 2 (2005); Employment by occupation: 7.3% management, 13.1% professional, 15.0% services, 20.8% sales, 1.2% farming, 5.4% construction, 37.2% production (2000).
Income: Per capita income: $20,022 (2005); Median household income: $39,146 (2005); Average household income: $44,660 (2005); Percent of households with income of $100,000 or more: 5.5% (2005); Poverty rate: 5.3% (2000).
Education: Percent of population age 25 and over with: High school diploma (including GED) or higher: 81.7% (2005); Bachelor's degree or higher: 10.4% (2005); Master's degree or higher: 3.5% (2005).

School District(s)
Wayne Trace Local SD (PK-12)
    2003-04 Enrollment: 1,155 . . . . (419) 263-2415

Housing: Homeownership rate: 74.0% (2005); Median home value: $74,565 (2005); Median rent: $264 per month (2000); Median age of housing: 44 years (2000).
Safety: Violent crime rate: 0.0 per 10,000 population; Property crime rate: 121.6 per 10,000 population (2004).
Transportation: Commute to work: 93.5% car, 0.4% public transportation, 3.8% walk, 1.1% work from home (2000); Travel time to work: 30.9% less than 15 minutes, 33.9% 15 to 30 minutes, 21.2% 30 to 45 minutes, 6.4% 45 to 60 minutes, 7.6% 60 minutes or more (2000)

Perry County

Located in central Ohio; drained by Rush, Sunday, Jonathan, and Moxahala Creeks; includes part of Buckeye Lake. Covers a land area of 409.78 square miles, a water area of 2.82 square miles, and is located in the Eastern Time Zone. The county government was organized in 1817. County seat is New Lexington.

Weather Station: New Lexington 2 NW   Elevation: 889 feet

	Jan	Feb	Mar	Apr	May	Jun	Jul	Aug	Sep	Oct	Nov	Dec
High	37	41	52	64	74	81	85	83	77	66	53	42
Low	18	20	28	37	47	56	60	59	52	40	31	23
Precip	2.9	2.6	3.4	3.8	4.3	4.3	4.7	3.9	2.8	2.7	3.4	3.1
Snow	9.2	5.9	3.6	0.5	tr	0.0	0.0	0.0	0.0	tr	0.7	3.0

High and Low temperatures in degrees Fahrenheit; Precipitation and Snow in inches

Population: 31,557 (1990); 34,078 (2000); 35,646 (2005); 37,282 (2010 projected); Race: 98.5% White, 0.3% Black, 0.1% Asian, 0.5% Hispanic of any race (2005); Density: 87.0 persons per square mile (2005); Average household size: 2.70 (2005); Median age: 36.2 (2005); Males per 100 females: 99.7 (2005).
Religion: Five largest groups: 8.8% The United Methodist Church, 8.8% Catholic Church, 4.2% Evangelical Lutheran Church in America, 1.2% Christian Church (Disciples of Christ), 1.0% United Church of Christ (2000).
Economy: Unemployment rate: 8.2% (2005); Total civilian labor force: 16,630 (2005); Leading industries: 23.3% manufacturing; 17.1% retail trade; 15.9% health care and social assistance (2004); Farms: 639 totaling 91,907 acres (2002); Companies that employ 500 or more persons: 0 (2004); Companies that employ 100 to 499 persons: 8 (2004); Companies that employ less than 100 persons: 502 (2004); Black-owned businesses: n/a (2002); Hispanic-owned businesses: n/a (2002); Women-owned businesses: 595 (2002); Retail sales per capita: $4,999 (2006). Single-family building permits issued: 80 (2005); Multi-family building permits issued: 37 (2005).
Income: Per capita income: $17,916 (2005); Median household income: $39,871 (2005); Average household income: $48,068 (2005); Percent of households with income of $100,000 or more: 6.9% (2005); Poverty rate: 12.2% (2003); Bankruptcy rate: 12.48% (2005).
Taxes: Total county taxes per capita: $126 (2004); County property taxes per capita: $78 (2004).
Education: Percent of population age 25 and over with: High school diploma (including GED) or higher: 78.7% (2005); Bachelor's degree or higher: 6.9% (2005); Master's degree or higher: 2.5% (2005).
Housing: Homeownership rate: 79.7% (2005); Median home value: $88,390 (2005); Median rent: $300 per month (2000); Median age of housing: 36 years (2000).
Health: Birth rate: 125.2 per 10,000 population (2004); Death rate: 99.8 per 10,000 population (2004); Age-adjusted cancer mortality rate: 263.0 deaths per 100,000 population (2002); Number of physicians: 4.6 per 10,000 population (2004); Hospital beds: 0.0 per 10,000 population (2003); Hospital admissions: 0.0 per 10,000 population (2003).
Elections: 2004 Presidential election results: 51.7% Bush, 47.8% Kerry, 0.0% Nader, 0.2% Badnarik
National and State Parks: Avondale State Wildlife Area; Perry State Forest
Additional Information Contacts
Perry County Government . . . . (740) 342-2045
    http://www.perrycountyohiocofc.com
Chamber of Commerce Perry County . . . . (740) 342-3547
    http://www.perrycountyohiocofc.com
City of New Lexington . . . . (740) 342-1633
    http://www.newlexington.org
Village of Crooksville . . . . (740) 982-2656
    http://www.crooksville.com

Perry County Communities

CORNING (village). Covers a land area of 0.436 square miles and a water area of 0 square miles. Located at 39.60° N. Lat.; 82.08° W. Long. Elevation is 732 feet.
Population: 703 (1990); 593 (2000); 609 (2005); 627 (2010 projected); Race: 97.7% White, 0.3% Black, 0.0% Asian, 0.2% Hispanic of any race (2005); Density: 1,396.8 persons per square mile (2005); Average household size: 2.47 (2005); Median age: 38.4 (2005); Males per 100 females: 88.0 (2005); Marriage status: 26.3% never married, 53.9% now married, 12.3% widowed, 7.5% divorced (2000); Foreign born: 0.0% (2000); Ancestry (includes multiple ancestries): 17.6% German, 15.1% English, 13.8% United States or American, 13.3% Irish, 5.6% Other groups (2000).
Economy: Employment by occupation: 4.6% management, 14.9% professional, 12.8% services, 25.6% sales, 0.0% farming, 14.9% construction, 27.2% production (2000).
Income: Per capita income: $16,782 (2005); Median household income: $33,333 (2005); Average household income: $41,377 (2005); Percent of households with income of $100,000 or more: 4.5% (2005); Poverty rate: 15.3% (2000).
Education: Percent of population age 25 and over with: High school diploma (including GED) or higher: 79.4% (2005); Bachelor's degree or higher: 7.1% (2005); Master's degree or higher: 3.7% (2005).

School District(s)
Southern Local SD (PK-12)
    2003-04 Enrollment: 1,042 . . . . (740) 394-2402

Housing: Homeownership rate: 78.1% (2005); Median home value: $50,217 (2005); Median rent: $300 per month (2000); Median age of housing: 60+ years (2000).
Transportation: Commute to work: 95.7% car, 0.0% public transportation, 1.1% walk, 3.2% work from home (2000); Travel time to work: 14.9% less than 15 minutes, 40.9% 15 to 30 minutes, 18.8% 30 to 45 minutes, 6.6% 45 to 60 minutes, 18.8% 60 minutes or more (2000)

CROOKSVILLE (village). Covers a land area of 1.526 square miles and a water area of 0 square miles. Located at 39.76° N. Lat.; 82.09° W. Long. Elevation is 780 feet.
Population: 2,643 (1990); 2,483 (2000); 2,429 (2005); 2,422 (2010 projected); Race: 98.5% White, 0.2% Black, 0.0% Asian, 0.4% Hispanic of any race (2005); Density: 1,592.2 persons per square mile (2005); Average household size: 2.56 (2005); Median age: 34.1 (2005); Males per 100 females: 91.4 (2005); Marriage status: 20.5% never married, 58.1% now married, 10.2% widowed, 11.1% divorced (2000); Foreign born: 0.6% (2000); Ancestry (includes multiple ancestries): 17.3% German, 12.9% United States or American, 10.1% English, 9.0% Irish, 7.0% Other groups (2000).
Economy: Single-family building permits issued: 1 (2005); Multi-family building permits issued: 0 (2005); Employment by occupation: 4.9% management, 13.4% professional, 12.2% services, 20.0% sales, 0.0% farming, 12.2% construction, 37.2% production (2000).
Income: Per capita income: $16,028 (2005); Median household income: $31,994 (2005); Average household income: $41,025 (2005); Percent of households with income of $100,000 or more: 4.6% (2005); Poverty rate: 13.6% (2000).
Education: Percent of population age 25 and over with: High school diploma (including GED) or higher: 77.4% (2005); Bachelor's degree or higher: 4.2% (2005); Master's degree or higher: 1.8% (2005).

School District(s)
Crooksville Digital Academy
    2003-04 Enrollment: n/a

Crooksville Ex Vill SD (PK-12)
    2003-04 Enrollment: 1,257 . . . . (740) 982-7040
Housing: Homeownership rate: 70.1% (2005); Median home value: $60,824 (2005); Median rent: $269 per month (2000); Median age of housing: 55 years (2000).
Transportation: Commute to work: 91.3% car, 0.0% public transportation, 3.4% walk, 3.0% work from home (2000); Travel time to work: 34.5% less than 15 minutes, 19.7% 15 to 30 minutes, 20.7% 30 to 45 minutes, 10.4% 45 to 60 minutes, 14.7% 60 minutes or more (2000)
Additional Information Contacts
Village of Crooksville . . . . (740) 982-2656
    http://www.crooksville.com

GLENFORD (village). Covers a land area of 0.130 square miles and a water area of 0 square miles. Located at 39.88° N. Lat.; 82.32° W. Long. Elevation is 844 feet.
History: Glenford was established near a prehistoric fortification known as Glenford Fort. A stone wall 7-10 feet high and 6,600 feet long enclosed an area with a central mound.
Population: 208 (1990); 198 (2000); 196 (2005); 194 (2010 projected); Race: 95.9% White, 1.0% Black, 0.0% Asian, 2.0% Hispanic of any race (2005); Density: 1,503.6 persons per square mile (2005); Average household size: 2.84 (2005); Median age: 34.6 (2005); Males per 100 females: 113.0 (2005); Marriage status: 27.7% never married, 62.8% now married, 4.7% widowed, 4.7% divorced (2000); Foreign born: 0.0% (2000); Ancestry (includes multiple ancestries): 28.6% German, 21.2% English, 10.6% Irish, 6.9% Other groups, 4.8% Italian (2000).
Economy: Single-family building permits issued: 0 (2005); Multi-family building permits issued: 0 (2005); Employment by occupation: 11.3% management, 8.5% professional, 11.3% services, 22.6% sales, 4.7% farming, 16.0% construction, 25.5% production (2000).
Income: Per capita income: $19,120 (2005); Median household income: $46,719 (2005); Average household income: $54,312 (2005); Percent of households with income of $100,000 or more: 10.1% (2005); Poverty rate: 1.6% (2000).
Education: Percent of population age 25 and over with: High school diploma (including GED) or higher: 86.2% (2005); Bachelor's degree or higher: 4.9% (2005); Master's degree or higher: 3.3% (2005).
School District(s)
Northern Local SD (PK-12)
    2003-04 Enrollment: 2,360 . . . . (740) 743-1303
Housing: Homeownership rate: 73.9% (2005); Median home value: $86,471 (2005); Median rent: $425 per month (2000); Median age of housing: 60+ years (2000).
Transportation: Commute to work: 83.0% car, 0.0% public transportation, 15.1% walk, 1.9% work from home (2000); Travel time to work: 17.3% less than 15 minutes, 26.9% 15 to 30 minutes, 18.3% 30 to 45 minutes, 22.1% 45 to 60 minutes, 15.4% 60 minutes or more (2000)

HEMLOCK (village). Covers a land area of 0.379 square miles and a water area of 0 square miles. Located at 39.59° N. Lat.; 82.15° W. Long. Elevation is 765 feet.
Population: 203 (1990); 142 (2000); 133 (2005); 132 (2010 projected); Race: 94.7% White, 0.0% Black, 2.3% Asian, 3.8% Hispanic of any race (2005); Density: 350.5 persons per square mile (2005); Average household size: 2.96 (2005); Median age: 29.6 (2005); Males per 100 females: 95.6 (2005); Marriage status: 22.5% never married, 67.5% now married, 10.0% widowed, 0.0% divorced (2000); Foreign born: 0.0% (2000); Ancestry (includes multiple ancestries): 21.4% German, 15.7% Irish, 11.4% English, 11.4% Other groups, 7.9% United States or American (2000).
Economy: Employment by occupation: 0.0% management, 0.0% professional, 35.5% services, 16.1% sales, 0.0% farming, 12.9% construction, 35.5% production (2000).
Income: Per capita income: $10,583 (2005); Median household income: $27,143 (2005); Average household income: $31,278 (2005); Percent of households with income of $100,000 or more: 0.0% (2005); Poverty rate: 24.3% (2000).
Education: Percent of population age 25 and over with: High school diploma (including GED) or higher: 59.7% (2005); Bachelor's degree or higher: 0.0% (2005); Master's degree or higher: 0.0% (2005).
Housing: Homeownership rate: 93.3% (2005); Median home value: $36,364 (2005); Median rent: $331 per month (2000); Median age of housing: 60+ years (2000).
Transportation: Commute to work: 100.0% car, 0.0% public transportation, 0.0% walk, 0.0% work from home (2000); Travel time to work: 12.9% less than 15 minutes, 12.9% 15 to 30 minutes, 25.8% 30 to 45 minutes, 25.8% 45 to 60 minutes, 22.6% 60 minutes or more (2000)

JUNCTION CITY (village). Covers a land area of 0.641 square miles and a water area of 0 square miles. Located at 39.72° N. Lat.; 82.29° W. Long. Elevation is 860 feet.
Population: 770 (1990); 818 (2000); 832 (2005); 834 (2010 projected); Race: 99.2% White, 0.0% Black, 0.0% Asian, 0.7% Hispanic of any race (2005); Density: 1,298.3 persons per square mile (2005); Average household size: 2.72 (2005); Median age: 32.2 (2005); Males per 100 females: 97.6 (2005); Marriage status: 22.1% never married, 55.6% now married, 6.3% widowed, 16.0% divorced (2000); Foreign born: 0.0% (2000); Ancestry (includes multiple ancestries): 27.3% German, 16.9% Irish, 12.8% United States or American, 12.5% Other groups, 5.8% English (2000).
Economy: Employment by occupation: 2.8% management, 11.4% professional, 15.9% services, 18.4% sales, 0.3% farming, 13.4% construction, 37.9% production (2000).
Income: Per capita income: $14,360 (2005); Median household income: $35,469 (2005); Average household income: $39,044 (2005); Percent of households with income of $100,000 or more: 2.6% (2005); Poverty rate: 22.8% (2000).
Education: Percent of population age 25 and over with: High school diploma (including GED) or higher: 78.0% (2005); Bachelor's degree or higher: 4.5% (2005); Master's degree or higher: 0.8% (2005).
School District(s)
New Lexington City SD (PK-12)
    2003-04 Enrollment: 1,966 . . . . (740) 342-4133
Housing: Homeownership rate: 66.3% (2005); Median home value: $72,619 (2005); Median rent: $339 per month (2000); Median age of housing: 48 years (2000).
Transportation: Commute to work: 94.6% car, 0.0% public transportation, 4.8% walk, 0.6% work from home (2000); Travel time to work: 26.6% less than 15 minutes, 26.6% 15 to 30 minutes, 14.2% 30 to 45 minutes, 8.8% 45 to 60 minutes, 23.8% 60 minutes or more (2000)

MOUNT PERRY (unincorporated postal area, zip code 43760). Covers a land area of 35.786 square miles and a water area of 0.093 square miles. Located at 39.88° N. Lat.; 82.19° W. Long. Elevation is 840 feet.
Population: 1,748 (2000); Race: 97.1% White, 0.0% Black, 0.6% Asian, 0.0% Hispanic of any race (2000); Density: 48.8 persons per square mile (2000); Age: 25.3% under 18, 11.3% over 64 (2000); Marriage status: 17.5% never married, 73.3% now married, 2.8% widowed, 6.4% divorced (2000); Foreign born: 1.3% (2000); Ancestry (includes multiple ancestries): 18.9% United States or American, 13.2% German, 11.5% English, 8.2% Irish, 4.9% Other groups (2000).
Economy: Employment by occupation: 7.3% management, 12.8% professional, 15.4% services, 16.6% sales, 1.5% farming, 19.5% construction, 26.9% production (2000).
Income: Per capita income: $20,616 (2000); Median household income: $40,476 (2000); Poverty rate: 5.5% (2000).
Education: Percent of population age 25 and over with: High school diploma (including GED) or higher: 74.0% (2000); Bachelor's degree or higher: 5.0% (2000).
Housing: Homeownership rate: 87.6% (2000); Median home value: $85,200 (2000); Median rent: $243 per month (2000); Median age of housing: 19 years (2000).
Transportation: Commute to work: 93.3% car, 1.6% public transportation, 0.0% walk, 5.1% work from home (2000); Travel time to work: 7.6% less than 15 minutes, 31.7% 15 to 30 minutes, 29.9% 30 to 45 minutes, 16.4% 45 to 60 minutes, 14.4% 60 minutes or more (2000)

NEW LEXINGTON (city). Covers a land area of 2.325 square miles and a water area of 0 square miles. Located at 39.71° N. Lat.; 82.21° W. Long. Elevation is 958 feet.
History: New Lexington developed around the tile and pottery works, which used the excellent clays found in the vicinity.
Population: 5,268 (1990); 4,689 (2000); 4,729 (2005); 4,797 (2010 projected); Race: 98.7% White, 0.2% Black, 0.2% Asian, 0.4% Hispanic of any race (2005); Density: 2,034.3 persons per square mile (2005); Average household size: 2.52 (2005); Median age: 33.4 (2005); Males per 100 females: 93.3 (2005); Marriage status: 24.7% never married, 54.5% now married, 10.3% widowed, 10.6% divorced (2000); Foreign born: 1.1% (2000); Ancestry (includes multiple ancestries): 22.3% United States or

American, 20.0% German, 12.3% Irish, 7.2% English, 7.1% Other groups (2000).
Economy: Single-family building permits issued: 4 (2005); Multi-family building permits issued: 0 (2005); Employment by occupation: 6.7% management, 12.6% professional, 17.1% services, 20.0% sales, 0.0% farming, 9.6% construction, 34.1% production (2000).
Income: Per capita income: $15,106 (2005); Median household income: $31,149 (2005); Average household income: $36,609 (2005); Percent of households with income of $100,000 or more: 2.9% (2005); Poverty rate: 17.6% (2000).
Education: Percent of population age 25 and over with: High school diploma (including GED) or higher: 77.3% (2005); Bachelor's degree or higher: 7.6% (2005); Master's degree or higher: 3.7% (2005).

School District(s)
New Lexington City SD (PK-12)
    2003-04 Enrollment: 1,966 . . . . (740) 342-4133

Housing: Homeownership rate: 62.9% (2005); Median home value: $78,419 (2005); Median rent: $289 per month (2000); Median age of housing: 48 years (2000).
Safety: Violent crime rate: 14.8 per 10,000 population; Property crime rate: 413.0 per 10,000 population (2004).
Newspapers: Perry County Tribune (General - Circulation 4,200)
Transportation: Commute to work: 91.9% car, 1.3% public transportation, 3.7% walk, 2.0% work from home (2000); Travel time to work: 43.2% less than 15 minutes, 13.9% 15 to 30 minutes, 16.9% 30 to 45 minutes, 9.4% 45 to 60 minutes, 16.6% 60 minutes or more (2000)
Additional Information Contacts
Chamber of Commerce Perry County . . . . (740) 342-3547
    http://www.perrycountyohiocofc.com
City of New Lexington . . . . (740) 342-1633
    http://www.newlexington.org

NEW STRAITSVILLE (village). Covers a land area of 1.313 square miles and a water area of 0 square miles. Located at 39.58° N. Lat.; 82.23° W. Long. Elevation is 862 feet.
History: New Straitsville was laid out in 1870 by a mining company. An undergound coal fire began to burn here in 1884, when some desperate miners set fire to loaded coal cars and pushed them down five mine shafts.
Population: 865 (1990); 774 (2000); 803 (2005); 824 (2010 projected); Race: 97.8% White, 0.1% Black, 0.0% Asian, 2.5% Hispanic of any race (2005); Density: 611.5 persons per square mile (2005); Average household size: 2.44 (2005); Median age: 36.4 (2005); Males per 100 females: 93.5 (2005); Marriage status: 23.3% never married, 52.9% now married, 10.7% widowed, 13.1% divorced (2000); Foreign born: 0.0% (2000); Ancestry (includes multiple ancestries): 16.8% German, 10.2% Irish, 10.0% English, 7.2% United States or American, 4.0% Other groups (2000).
Economy: Employment by occupation: 4.3% management, 5.6% professional, 11.3% services, 23.5% sales, 0.0% farming, 10.6% construction, 44.7% production (2000).
Income: Per capita income: $15,620 (2005); Median household income: $31,159 (2005); Average household income: $38,123 (2005); Percent of households with income of $100,000 or more: 3.6% (2005); Poverty rate: 16.6% (2000).
Education: Percent of population age 25 and over with: High school diploma (including GED) or higher: 72.9% (2005); Bachelor's degree or higher: 4.2% (2005); Master's degree or higher: 1.7% (2005).
Housing: Homeownership rate: 78.7% (2005); Median home value: $46,528 (2005); Median rent: $257 per month (2000); Median age of housing: 60+ years (2000).
Transportation: Commute to work: 97.4% car, 0.0% public transportation, 2.0% walk, 0.7% work from home (2000); Travel time to work: 9.7% less than 15 minutes, 39.0% 15 to 30 minutes, 11.3% 30 to 45 minutes, 16.3% 45 to 60 minutes, 23.7% 60 minutes or more (2000)

RENDVILLE (village). Covers a land area of 0.310 square miles and a water area of 0 square miles. Located at 39.61° N. Lat.; 82.08° W. Long. Elevation is 800 feet.
Population: 32 (1990); 46 (2000); 48 (2005); 51 (2010 projected); Race: 93.8% White, 4.2% Black, 0.0% Asian, 0.0% Hispanic of any race (2005); Density: 154.9 persons per square mile (2005); Average household size: 2.40 (2005); Median age: 33.9 (2005); Males per 100 females: 100.0 (2005); Marriage status: 31.9% never married, 27.7% now married, 25.5% widowed, 14.9% divorced (2000); Foreign born: 0.0% (2000); Ancestry (includes multiple ancestries): 30.2% United States or American, 18.9% Other groups, 7.5% Irish, 5.7% German (2000).
Economy: In coal-mining area. Employment by occupation: 0.0% management, 15.4% professional, 23.1% services, 19.2% sales, 0.0% farming, 0.0% construction, 42.3% production (2000).
Income: Per capita income: $15,885 (2005); Median household income: $21,000 (2005); Average household income: $38,125 (2005); Percent of households with income of $100,000 or more: 5.0% (2005); Poverty rate: 13.2% (2000).
Education: Percent of population age 25 and over with: High school diploma (including GED) or higher: 50.0% (2005); Bachelor's degree or higher: 0.0% (2005); Master's degree or higher: 0.0% (2005).
Housing: Homeownership rate: 80.0% (2005); Median home value: $25,000 (2005); Median rent: $325 per month (2000); Median age of housing: 59 years (2000).
Transportation: Commute to work: 100.0% car, 0.0% public transportation, 0.0% walk, 0.0% work from home (2000); Travel time to work: 11.5% less than 15 minutes, 3.8% 15 to 30 minutes, 23.1% 30 to 45 minutes, 38.5% 45 to 60 minutes, 23.1% 60 minutes or more (2000)

ROSEVILLE (village). Covers a land area of 0.696 square miles and a water area of 0 square miles. Located at 39.80° N. Lat.; 82.07° W. Long.
Population: 1,973 (1990); 1,936 (2000); 2,020 (2005); 2,092 (2010 projected); Race: 98.0% White, 0.4% Black, 0.0% Asian, 0.4% Hispanic of any race (2005); Density: 2,902.9 persons per square mile (2005); Average household size: 2.65 (2005); Median age: 31.2 (2005); Males per 100 females: 92.2 (2005); Marriage status: 25.9% never married, 54.0% now married, 6.8% widowed, 13.2% divorced (2000); Foreign born: 0.1% (2000); Ancestry (includes multiple ancestries): 15.1% United States or American, 12.5% German, 12.3% Irish, 8.7% Other groups, 7.9% English (2000).
Economy: Single-family building permits issued: 0 (2005); Multi-family building permits issued: 0 (2005); Employment by occupation: 4.1% management, 8.2% professional, 23.8% services, 18.8% sales, 0.3% farming, 12.7% construction, 32.2% production (2000).
Income: Per capita income: $13,395 (2005); Median household income: $27,802 (2005); Average household income: $35,555 (2005); Percent of households with income of $100,000 or more: 3.3% (2005); Poverty rate: 27.6% (2000).
Education: Percent of population age 25 and over with: High school diploma (including GED) or higher: 72.4% (2005); Bachelor's degree or higher: 3.9% (2005); Master's degree or higher: 0.9% (2005).

School District(s)
Franklin Local School District (PK-12)
    2003-04 Enrollment: 2,418 . . . . (740) 674-5203

Housing: Homeownership rate: 65.2% (2005); Median home value: $60,159 (2005); Median rent: $259 per month (2000); Median age of housing: 51 years (2000).
Transportation: Commute to work: 94.0% car, 0.8% public transportation, 1.0% walk, 2.4% work from home (2000); Travel time to work: 26.7% less than 15 minutes, 30.8% 15 to 30 minutes, 15.9% 30 to 45 minutes, 13.5% 45 to 60 minutes, 13.1% 60 minutes or more (2000)

SHAWNEE (village). Covers a land area of 1.993 square miles and a water area of 0.005 square miles. Located at 39.60° N. Lat.; 82.21° W. Long. Elevation is 840 feet.
Population: 742 (1990); 608 (2000); 575 (2005); 566 (2010 projected); Race: 99.5% White, 0.0% Black, 0.5% Asian, 0.0% Hispanic of any race (2005); Density: 288.6 persons per square mile (2005); Average household size: 2.89 (2005); Median age: 32.8 (2005); Males per 100 females: 99.7 (2005); Marriage status: 33.1% never married, 47.0% now married, 6.4% widowed, 13.5% divorced (2000); Foreign born: 0.0% (2000); Ancestry (includes multiple ancestries): 16.0% German, 15.2% United States or American, 14.3% Irish, 12.7% English, 5.4% Other groups (2000).
Economy: Employment by occupation: 5.2% management, 12.4% professional, 12.0% services, 17.2% sales, 0.0% farming, 21.0% construction, 32.2% production (2000).
Income: Per capita income: $15,243 (2005); Median household income: $40,625 (2005); Average household income: $44,045 (2005); Percent of households with income of $100,000 or more: 4.0% (2005); Poverty rate: 15.6% (2000).
Education: Percent of population age 25 and over with: High school diploma (including GED) or higher: 83.8% (2005); Bachelor's degree or higher: 1.7% (2005); Master's degree or higher: 0.6% (2005).
Housing: Homeownership rate: 82.9% (2005); Median home value: $51,087 (2005); Median rent: $275 per month (2000); Median age of housing: 60+ years (2000).

Transportation: Commute to work: 96.4% car, 0.0% public transportation, 0.9% walk, 1.8% work from home (2000); Travel time to work: 24.4% less than 15 minutes, 32.3% 15 to 30 minutes, 10.6% 30 to 45 minutes, 13.4% 45 to 60 minutes, 19.4% 60 minutes or more (2000)

SOMERSET (village).
Covers a land area of 1.166 square miles and a water area of 0 square miles. Located at 39.80° N. Lat.; 82.30° W. Long. Elevation is 1,065 feet.
History: Somerset was laid out in 1810 by John Fink and Jacob Miller, and served as the seat of Perry County from 1829 to 1857. Civil War general Philip Henry Sheridan spent his boyhood in Somerset.
Population: 1,450 (1990); 1,549 (2000); 1,602 (2005); 1,657 (2010 projected); Race: 98.9% White, 0.0% Black, 0.1% Asian, 0.3% Hispanic of any race (2005); Density: 1,373.7 persons per square mile (2005); Average household size: 2.50 (2005); Median age: 40.4 (2005); Males per 100 females: 85.2 (2005); Marriage status: 22.5% never married, 49.9% now married, 14.2% widowed, 13.4% divorced (2000); Foreign born: 0.3% (2000); Ancestry (includes multiple ancestries): 28.4% German, 19.9% United States or American, 17.5% Irish, 7.9% English, 6.1% Other groups (2000).
Economy: Single-family building permits issued: 2 (2005); Multi-family building permits issued: 0 (2005); Employment by occupation: 7.8% management, 18.2% professional, 12.3% services, 20.1% sales, 0.0% farming, 13.3% construction, 28.4% production (2000).
Income: Per capita income: $16,122 (2005); Median household income: $32,647 (2005); Average household income: $39,136 (2005); Percent of households with income of $100,000 or more: 4.8% (2005); Poverty rate: 12.8% (2000).
Education: Percent of population age 25 and over with: High school diploma (including GED) or higher: 81.8% (2005); Bachelor's degree or higher: 7.3% (2005); Master's degree or higher: 2.0% (2005).
School District(s)
Northern Local SD (PK-12)
  2003-04 Enrollment: 2,360 . . . . (740) 743-1303
Housing: Homeownership rate: 64.2% (2005); Median home value: $101,613 (2005); Median rent: $245 per month (2000); Median age of housing: 47 years (2000).
Transportation: Commute to work: 92.1% car, 1.2% public transportation, 4.5% walk, 1.3% work from home (2000); Travel time to work: 30.0% less than 15 minutes, 22.9% 15 to 30 minutes, 20.0% 30 to 45 minutes, 10.2% 45 to 60 minutes, 16.9% 60 minutes or more (2000)

THORNVILLE (village).
Covers a land area of 0.433 square miles and a water area of 0 square miles. Located at 39.89° N. Lat.; 82.42° W. Long. Elevation is 980 feet.
Population: 829 (1990); 731 (2000); 677 (2005); 673 (2010 projected); Race: 99.0% White, 0.0% Black, 0.0% Asian, 0.0% Hispanic of any race (2005); Density: 1,562.1 persons per square mile (2005); Average household size: 2.55 (2005); Median age: 39.0 (2005); Males per 100 females: 100.3 (2005); Marriage status: 18.5% never married, 67.3% now married, 6.4% widowed, 7.7% divorced (2000); Foreign born: 0.3% (2000); Ancestry (includes multiple ancestries): 36.0% German, 9.9% Irish, 8.5% English, 6.5% Other groups, 5.6% Italian (2000).
Economy: In agricultural area. Single-family building permits issued: 16 (2005); Multi-family building permits issued: 0 (2005); Employment by occupation: 8.6% management, 19.5% professional, 12.0% services, 29.1% sales, 0.5% farming, 11.2% construction, 19.0% production (2000).
Income: Per capita income: $24,653 (2005); Median household income: $56,250 (2005); Average household income: $62,981 (2005); Percent of households with income of $100,000 or more: 16.2% (2005); Poverty rate: 4.2% (2000).
Education: Percent of population age 25 and over with: High school diploma (including GED) or higher: 93.9% (2005); Bachelor's degree or higher: 15.3% (2005); Master's degree or higher: 4.1% (2005).
School District(s)
Northern Local SD (PK-12)
  2003-04 Enrollment: 2,360 . . . . (740) 743-1303
Housing: Homeownership rate: 80.0% (2005); Median home value: $127,320 (2005); Median rent: $409 per month (2000); Median age of housing: 57 years (2000).
Transportation: Commute to work: 95.2% car, 0.0% public transportation, 3.0% walk, 1.9% work from home (2000); Travel time to work: 15.1% less than 15 minutes, 31.5% 15 to 30 minutes, 19.7% 30 to 45 minutes, 23.0% 45 to 60 minutes, 10.7% 60 minutes or more (2000)

Pickaway County

Located in south central Ohio; crossed by the Scioto River. Covers a land area of 501.91 square miles, a water area of 4.88 square miles, and is located in the Eastern Time Zone. The county government was organized in 1810. County seat is Circleville.

Pickaway County is part of the Columbus, OH Metropolitan Statistical Area. The entire metro area includes: Delaware County, OH; Fairfield County, OH; Franklin County, OH; Licking County, OH; Madison County, OH; Morrow County, OH; Pickaway County, OH; Union County, OH

Weather Station: Circleville   Elevation: 672 feet

	Jan	Feb	Mar	Apr	May	Jun	Jul	Aug	Sep	Oct	Nov	Dec
High	37	41	52	64	74	82	86	84	78	67	53	42
Low	21	23	31	40	51	60	64	61	54	43	35	26
Precip	2.4	2.1	2.8	3.5	4.6	3.9	3.9	3.9	3.1	2.6	3.1	2.7
Snow	5.9	4.0	2.0	0.4	0.0	0.0	0.0	0.0	0.0	0.1	0.7	1.8

High and Low temperatures in degrees Fahrenheit; Precipitation and Snow in inches

Population: 48,244 (1990); 52,727 (2000); 51,461 (2005); 50,184 (2010 projected); Race: 93.7% White, 4.8% Black, 0.3% Asian, 0.7% Hispanic of any race (2005); Density: 102.5 persons per square mile (2005); Average household size: 2.98 (2005); Median age: 37.1 (2005); Males per 100 females: 117.6 (2005).
Religion: Five largest groups: 10.1% The United Methodist Church, 3.8% Catholic Church, 3.8% Evangelical Lutheran Church in America, 2.3% Southern Baptist Convention, 1.1% Church of the Nazarene (2000).
Economy: Unemployment rate: 7.0% (2005); Total civilian labor force: 24,484 (2005); Leading industries: 30.5% manufacturing; 17.8% health care and social assistance; 13.9% retail trade (2004); Farms: 791 totaling 275,029 acres (2002); Companies that employ 500 or more persons: 2 (2004); Companies that employ 100 to 499 persons: 24 (2004); Companies that employ less than 100 persons: 801 (2004); Black-owned businesses: n/a (2002); Hispanic-owned businesses: n/a (2002); Women-owned businesses: n/a (2002); Retail sales per capita: $9,049 (2006); Single-family building permits issued: 167 (2005); Multi-family building permits issued: 2 (2005).
Income: Per capita income: $20,409 (2005); Median household income: $49,042 (2005); Average household income: $57,917 (2005); Percent of households with income of $100,000 or more: 13.2% (2005); Poverty rate: 10.3% (2003); Bankruptcy rate: 10.66% (2005).
Taxes: Total county taxes per capita: $183 (2004); County property taxes per capita: $87 (2004).
Education: Percent of population age 25 and over with: High school diploma (including GED) or higher: 77.2% (2005); Bachelor's degree or higher: 11.4% (2005); Master's degree or higher: 3.8% (2005).
Housing: Homeownership rate: 74.9% (2005); Median home value: $131,535 (2005); Median rent: $381 per month (2000); Median age of housing: 30 years (2000).
Health: Birth rate: 98.7 per 10,000 population (2004); Death rate: 97.1 per 10,000 population (2004); Age-adjusted cancer mortality rate: 195.7 deaths per 100,000 population (2002); Number of physicians: 8.3 per 10,000 population (2004); Hospital beds: 16.4 per 10,000 population (2003); Hospital admissions: 786.6 per 10,000 population (2003).
Elections: 2004 Presidential election results: 62.0% Bush, 37.5% Kerry, 0.0% Nader, 0.3% Badnarik
National and State Parks: A W Marion State Park; Logan Elm State Memorial
Additional Information Contacts
Pickaway County Government. . . . . (740) 474-6093
  http://www.pickaway.org/
Circleville Chamber of Commerce . . . . (740) 474-4923
  http://www.pickaway.com

Pickaway County Communities

ASHVILLE (village).
Covers a land area of 1.559 square miles and a water area of 0 square miles. Located at 39.71° N. Lat.; 82.95° W. Long. Elevation is 709 feet.
Population: 2,728 (1990); 3,174 (2000); 3,127 (2005); 3,161 (2010 projected); Race: 98.0% White, 0.1% Black, 0.0% Asian, 1.2% Hispanic of any race (2005); Density: 2,005.6 persons per square mile (2005); Average household size: 2.52 (2005); Median age: 32.5 (2005); Males per 100 females: 89.6 (2005); Marriage status: 19.6% never married, 62.7% now married, 6.5% widowed, 11.1% divorced (2000); Foreign born: 0.0%

(2000); Ancestry (includes multiple ancestries): 21.0% German, 12.4% United States or American, 12.3% Irish, 9.7% English, 5.3% Other groups (2000).
Economy: Food products. Employment by occupation: 8.5% management, 12.6% professional, 19.2% services, 25.6% sales, 0.0% farming, 12.0% construction, 22.0% production (2000).
Income: Per capita income: $20,014 (2005); Median household income: $46,007 (2005); Average household income: $50,350 (2005); Percent of households with income of $100,000 or more: 7.8% (2005); Poverty rate: 9.5% (2000).
Education: Percent of population age 25 and over with: High school diploma (including GED) or higher: 81.2% (2005); Bachelor's degree or higher: 11.9% (2005); Master's degree or higher: 3.7% (2005).

School District(s)
Teays Valley Local SD (PK-12)
  2003-04 Enrollment: 3,233 . . . . (740) 983-4111

Housing: Homeownership rate: 57.2% (2005); Median home value: $143,099 (2005); Median rent: $369 per month (2000); Median age of housing: 27 years (2000).
Transportation: Commute to work: 94.1% car, 0.0% public transportation, 2.4% walk, 3.2% work from home (2000); Travel time to work: 26.4% less than 15 minutes, 29.3% 15 to 30 minutes, 28.7% 30 to 45 minutes, 11.1% 45 to 60 minutes, 4.4% 60 minutes or more (2000)

CIRCLEVILLE (city).
Covers a land area of 6.620 square miles and a water area of 0.117 square miles. Located at 39.60° N. Lat.; 82.93° W. Long. Elevation is 702 feet.
History: Named for local circular earthworks made by prehistoric mound builders. Circleville was settled in 1810 on the site of two ancient forts erected by the mound builders, one of them a round enclosure from which Circleville took its name.
Population: 12,743 (1990); 13,485 (2000); 12,912 (2005); 12,292 (2010 projected); Race: 96.1% White, 1.8% Black, 0.6% Asian, 0.9% Hispanic of any race (2005); Density: 1,950.6 persons per square mile (2005); Average household size: 2.50 (2005); Median age: 36.6 (2005); Males per 100 females: 90.9 (2005); Marriage status: 22.5% never married, 57.5% now married, 8.3% widowed, 11.7% divorced (2000); Foreign born: 0.9% (2000); Ancestry (includes multiple ancestries): 19.1% German, 16.3% United States or American, 9.7% Irish, 8.9% English, 7.4% Other groups (2000).
Economy: Single-family building permits issued: 26 (2005); Multi-family building permits issued: 2 (2005); Employment by occupation: 11.2% management, 14.8% professional, 16.3% services, 24.4% sales, 0.4% farming, 11.7% construction, 21.2% production (2000).
Income: Per capita income: $19,533 (2005); Median household income: $38,360 (2005); Average household income: $47,926 (2005); Percent of households with income of $100,000 or more: 9.0% (2005); Poverty rate: 13.3% (2000).
Taxes: Total city taxes per capita: $487 (2004); City property taxes per capita: $67 (2004).
Education: Percent of population age 25 and over with: High school diploma (including GED) or higher: 76.9% (2005); Bachelor's degree or higher: 13.2% (2005); Master's degree or higher: 4.1% (2005).

School District(s)
Circleville City SD (PK-12)
  2003-04 Enrollment: 2,490 . . . . (740) 474-4340
Department of Youth Services (06-12)
  2003-04 Enrollment: 1,333 . . . . (614) 728-2489
Logan Elm Local SD (PK-12)
  2003-04 Enrollment: 2,323 . . . . (740) 474-7501
Westfall Local SD (PK-12)
  2003-04 Enrollment: 1,655 . . . . (740) 986-3671

Four-year College(s)
Circleville Bible College (Private, Not-for-profit, Other Protestant)
  Fall 2004 Enrollment: 431 . . . . (740) 474-8896
  2005-06 Tuition: In-state $10,612; Out-of-state $10,612

Housing: Homeownership rate: 59.5% (2005); Median home value: $114,192 (2005); Median rent: $393 per month (2000); Median age of housing: 39 years (2000).
Hospitals: Berger Hospital (91 beds)
Safety: Violent crime rate: 24.6 per 10,000 population; Property crime rate: 784.2 per 10,000 population (2004).
Newspapers: The Circleville Herald (Circulation 6,693); The Pickaway Paper (General - Circulation 19,600)

Transportation: Commute to work: 95.1% car, 0.3% public transportation, 2.7% walk, 1.6% work from home (2000); Travel time to work: 45.7% less than 15 minutes, 18.4% 15 to 30 minutes, 18.6% 30 to 45 minutes, 11.8% 45 to 60 minutes, 5.6% 60 minutes or more (2000)
Additional Information Contacts
Circleville Chamber of Commerce . . . . (740) 474-4923
http://www.pickaway.com

COMMERCIAL POINT (village).
Covers a land area of 1.089 square miles and a water area of 0 square miles. Located at 39.77° N. Lat.; 83.06° W. Long. Elevation is 780 feet.
Population: 762 (1990); 776 (2000); 836 (2005); 785 (2010 projected); Race: 98.4% White, 0.0% Black, 0.2% Asian, 0.7% Hispanic of any race (2005); Density: 767.6 persons per square mile (2005); Average household size: 2.77 (2005); Median age: 34.8 (2005); Males per 100 females: 90.4 (2005); Marriage status: 23.6% never married, 64.6% now married, 3.1% widowed, 8.7% divorced (2000); Foreign born: 0.3% (2000); Ancestry (includes multiple ancestries): 18.6% German, 16.1% United States or American, 11.5% Irish, 7.9% Other groups, 6.9% English (2000).
Economy: Employment by occupation: 17.2% management, 9.7% professional, 9.2% services, 29.5% sales, 0.0% farming, 15.3% construction, 19.1% production (2000).
Income: Per capita income: $25,371 (2005); Median household income: $59,483 (2005); Average household income: $70,232 (2005); Percent of households with income of $100,000 or more: 14.9% (2005); Poverty rate: 9.0% (2000).
Education: Percent of population age 25 and over with: High school diploma (including GED) or higher: 75.0% (2005); Bachelor's degree or higher: 11.8% (2005); Master's degree or higher: 2.6% (2005).

School District(s)
Teays Valley Local SD (PK-12)
  2003-04 Enrollment: 3,233 . . . . (740) 983-4111

Housing: Homeownership rate: 85.1% (2005); Median home value: $149,490 (2005); Median rent: $348 per month (2000); Median age of housing: 19 years (2000).
Transportation: Commute to work: 96.7% car, 0.3% public transportation, 2.0% walk, 1.0% work from home (2000); Travel time to work: 13.9% less than 15 minutes, 38.7% 15 to 30 minutes, 37.5% 30 to 45 minutes, 4.6% 45 to 60 minutes, 5.3% 60 minutes or more (2000)

DARBYVILLE (village).
Covers a land area of 0.467 square miles and a water area of 0.016 square miles. Located at 39.69° N. Lat.; 83.11° W. Long. Elevation is 740 feet.
Population: 272 (1990); 293 (2000); 302 (2005); 312 (2010 projected); Race: 100.0% White, 0.0% Black, 0.0% Asian, 3.6% Hispanic of any race (2005); Density: 646.7 persons per square mile (2005); Average household size: 3.05 (2005); Median age: 34.7 (2005); Males per 100 females: 94.8 (2005); Marriage status: 20.1% never married, 52.6% now married, 7.7% widowed, 19.6% divorced (2000); Foreign born: 0.0% (2000); Ancestry (includes multiple ancestries): 33.9% United States or American, 12.1% German, 10.7% Irish, 10.4% Other groups, 5.9% English (2000).
Economy: In agricultural area. Employment by occupation: 4.9% management, 3.3% professional, 18.9% services, 32.8% sales, 0.0% farming, 11.5% construction, 28.7% production (2000).
Income: Per capita income: $15,331 (2005); Median household income: $44,609 (2005); Average household income: $46,768 (2005); Percent of households with income of $100,000 or more: 3.0% (2005); Poverty rate: 22.0% (2000).
Education: Percent of population age 25 and over with: High school diploma (including GED) or higher: 70.1% (2005); Bachelor's degree or higher: 1.1% (2005); Master's degree or higher: 0.0% (2005).
Housing: Homeownership rate: 67.7% (2005); Median home value: $59,000 (2005); Median rent: $292 per month (2000); Median age of housing: 37 years (2000).
Transportation: Commute to work: 94.1% car, 0.0% public transportation, 4.2% walk, 0.0% work from home (2000); Travel time to work: 12.7% less than 15 minutes, 33.1% 15 to 30 minutes, 36.4% 30 to 45 minutes, 13.6% 45 to 60 minutes, 4.2% 60 minutes or more (2000)

LOGAN ELM VILLAGE (CDP).
Covers a land area of 0.512 square miles and a water area of 0 square miles. Located at 39.57° N. Lat.; 82.95° W. Long. Elevation is 700 feet.
Population: 1,287 (1990); 1,062 (2000); 990 (2005); 924 (2010 projected); Race: 97.4% White, 1.2% Black, 0.9% Asian, 0.7% Hispanic of any race (2005); Density: 1,932.6 persons per square mile (2005); Average

household size: 2.49 (2005); Median age: 45.4 (2005); Males per 100 females: 78.7 (2005); Marriage status: 15.7% never married, 59.4% now married, 11.4% widowed, 13.5% divorced (2000); Foreign born: 0.6% (2000); Ancestry (includes multiple ancestries): 22.3% United States or American, 16.8% German, 7.5% English, 6.1% Irish, 5.9% Other groups (2000).
Economy: Employment by occupation: 11.6% management, 18.8% professional, 9.7% services, 28.8% sales, 0.0% farming, 13.5% construction, 17.6% production (2000).
Income: Per capita income: $19,571 (2005); Median household income: $42,500 (2005); Average household income: $45,955 (2005); Percent of households with income of $100,000 or more: 4.5% (2005); Poverty rate: 10.6% (2000).
Education: Percent of population age 25 and over with: High school diploma (including GED) or higher: 65.1% (2005); Bachelor's degree or higher: 3.5% (2005); Master's degree or higher: 0.0% (2005).
Housing: Homeownership rate: 80.2% (2005); Median home value: $112,204 (2005); Median rent: $290 per month (2000); Median age of housing: 26 years (2000).
Transportation: Commute to work: 94.0% car, 0.0% public transportation, 2.6% walk, 3.3% work from home (2000); Travel time to work: 46.6% less than 15 minutes, 20.2% 15 to 30 minutes, 18.2% 30 to 45 minutes, 5.7% 45 to 60 minutes, 9.4% 60 minutes or more (2000).

NEW HOLLAND (village). Covers a land area of 1.869 square miles and a water area of 0 square miles. Located at 39.55° N. Lat.; 83.25° W. Long. Elevation is 851 feet.
History: New Holland was founded in 1818, and grew as a center for poultry and hog raising.
Population: 844 (1990); 785 (2000); 723 (2005); 683 (2010 projected); Race: 97.9% White, 0.4% Black, 0.0% Asian, 0.1% Hispanic of any race (2005); Density: 386.9 persons per square mile (2005); Average household size: 2.49 (2005); Median age: 37.9 (2005); Males per 100 females: 93.3 (2005); Marriage status: 18.0% never married, 63.8% now married, 10.3% widowed, 7.9% divorced (2000); Foreign born: 0.0% (2000); Ancestry (includes multiple ancestries): 13.9% German, 12.3% Irish, 10.6% Other groups, 7.9% United States or American, 7.9% English (2000).
Economy: Single-family building permits issued: 1 (2005); Multi-family building permits issued: 0 (2005); Employment by occupation: 5.9% management, 12.4% professional, 16.6% services, 24.9% sales, 0.9% farming, 8.6% construction, 30.8% production (2000).
Income: Per capita income: $17,832 (2005); Median household income: $35,612 (2005); Average household income: $44,457 (2005); Percent of households with income of $100,000 or more: 6.9% (2005); Poverty rate: 7.9% (2000).
Education: Percent of population age 25 and over with: High school diploma (including GED) or higher: 74.8% (2005); Bachelor's degree or higher: 5.8% (2005); Master's degree or higher: 3.7% (2005).

School District(s)
Miami Trace Local SD (PK-12)
    2003-04 Enrollment: 2,719 . . . . (740) 335-3010
Housing: Homeownership rate: 76.9% (2005); Median home value: $89,762 (2005); Median rent: $326 per month (2000); Median age of housing: 56 years (2000).
Transportation: Commute to work: 93.5% car, 0.0% public transportation, 4.6% walk, 0.6% work from home (2000); Travel time to work: 14.3% less than 15 minutes, 40.4% 15 to 30 minutes, 23.9% 30 to 45 minutes, 12.4% 45 to 60 minutes, 9.0% 60 minutes or more (2000).

ORIENT (village). Aka Morgan. Covers a land area of 0.124 square miles and a water area of 0 square miles. Located at 39.80° N. Lat.; 83.15° W. Long. Elevation is 841 feet.
Population: 273 (1990); 269 (2000); 237 (2005); 205 (2010 projected); Race: 99.2% White, 0.0% Black, 0.0% Asian, 0.0% Hispanic of any race (2005); Density: 1,910.4 persons per square mile (2005); Average household size: 2.82 (2005); Median age: 33.2 (2005); Males per 100 females: 107.9 (2005); Marriage status: 26.5% never married, 59.1% now married, 4.8% widowed, 9.6% divorced (2000); Foreign born: 0.0% (2000); Ancestry (includes multiple ancestries): 39.4% United States or American, 17.2% Irish, 16.5% German, 9.0% English, 3.9% Other groups (2000).
Economy: Employment by occupation: 8.1% management, 8.1% professional, 14.1% services, 28.9% sales, 0.0% farming, 14.1% construction, 26.8% production (2000).
Income: Per capita income: $17,331 (2005); Median household income: $37,143 (2005); Average household income: $48,899 (2005); Percent of households with income of $100,000 or more: 13.1% (2005); Poverty rate: 11.5% (2000).
Education: Percent of population age 25 and over with: High school diploma (including GED) or higher: 46.2% (2005); Bachelor's degree or higher: 6.3% (2005); Master's degree or higher: 1.4% (2005).
Housing: Homeownership rate: 77.4% (2005); Median home value: $75,909 (2005); Median rent: $295 per month (2000); Median age of housing: 60+ years (2000).
Transportation: Commute to work: 100.0% car, 0.0% public transportation, 0.0% walk, 0.0% work from home (2000); Travel time to work: 15.4% less than 15 minutes, 25.5% 15 to 30 minutes, 28.2% 30 to 45 minutes, 26.8% 45 to 60 minutes, 4.0% 60 minutes or more (2000).

SOUTH BLOOMFIELD (village). Covers a land area of 1.149 square miles and a water area of 0 square miles. Located at 39.71° N. Lat.; 82.98° W. Long. Elevation is 695 feet.
Population: 1,031 (1990); 1,179 (2000); 1,277 (2005); 1,339 (2010 projected); Race: 99.0% White, 0.0% Black, 0.2% Asian, 1.3% Hispanic of any race (2005); Density: 1,111.6 persons per square mile (2005); Average household size: 2.44 (2005); Median age: 35.0 (2005); Males per 100 females: 90.6 (2005); Marriage status: 19.9% never married, 58.0% now married, 6.9% widowed, 15.3% divorced (2000); Foreign born: 0.9% (2000); Ancestry (includes multiple ancestries): 18.3% German, 15.2% United States or American, 9.3% Irish, 6.1% English, 5.3% Other groups (2000).
Economy: Single-family building permits issued: 39 (2005); Multi-family building permits issued: 0 (2005); Employment by occupation: 8.2% management, 5.8% professional, 19.2% services, 24.0% sales, 0.2% farming, 13.8% construction, 28.9% production (2000).
Income: Per capita income: $19,800 (2005); Median household income: $42,250 (2005); Average household income: $48,254 (2005); Percent of households with income of $100,000 or more: 6.1% (2005); Poverty rate: 7.8% (2000).
Education: Percent of population age 25 and over with: High school diploma (including GED) or higher: 74.1% (2005); Bachelor's degree or higher: 3.9% (2005); Master's degree or higher: 0.5% (2005).
Housing: Homeownership rate: 80.2% (2005); Median home value: $68,696 (2005); Median rent: $423 per month (2000); Median age of housing: 24 years (2000).
Transportation: Commute to work: 96.0% car, 0.0% public transportation, 2.5% walk, 1.6% work from home (2000); Travel time to work: 18.6% less than 15 minutes, 35.7% 15 to 30 minutes, 32.3% 30 to 45 minutes, 8.6% 45 to 60 minutes, 4.8% 60 minutes or more (2000).

TARLTON (village). Covers a land area of 0.420 square miles and a water area of 0 square miles. Located at 39.55° N. Lat.; 82.77° W. Long. Elevation is 892 feet.
History: Tarlton Cross Mound nearby.
Population: 315 (1990); 298 (2000); 293 (2005); 279 (2010 projected); Race: 100.0% White, 0.0% Black, 0.0% Asian, 0.0% Hispanic of any race (2005); Density: 698.2 persons per square mile (2005); Average household size: 2.90 (2005); Median age: 37.7 (2005); Males per 100 females: 96.6 (2005); Marriage status: 26.8% never married, 55.0% now married, 8.2% widowed, 10.0% divorced (2000); Foreign born: 0.0% (2000); Ancestry (includes multiple ancestries): 14.7% German, 12.9% United States or American, 9.8% English, 6.6% Dutch, 5.6% Irish (2000).
Economy: Employment by occupation: 3.1% management, 10.7% professional, 10.7% services, 18.3% sales, 0.0% farming, 16.0% construction, 41.2% production (2000).
Income: Per capita income: $15,845 (2005); Median household income: $39,821 (2005); Average household income: $45,965 (2005); Percent of households with income of $100,000 or more: 5.9% (2005); Poverty rate: 6.0% (2000).
Education: Percent of population age 25 and over with: High school diploma (including GED) or higher: 70.7% (2005); Bachelor's degree or higher: 1.1% (2005); Master's degree or higher: 0.0% (2005).
Housing: Homeownership rate: 83.2% (2005); Median home value: $90,000 (2005); Median rent: $300 per month (2000); Median age of housing: 59 years (2000).
Transportation: Commute to work: 89.8% car, 1.6% public transportation, 8.6% walk, 0.0% work from home (2000); Travel time to work: 26.6% less than 15 minutes, 33.6% 15 to 30 minutes, 18.0% 30 to 45 minutes, 10.2% 45 to 60 minutes, 11.7% 60 minutes or more (2000).

WILLIAMSPORT (village). Covers a land area of 1.341 square miles and a water area of 0 square miles. Located at 39.58° N. Lat.; 83.11° W. Long. Elevation is 771 feet.
Population: 851 (1990); 1,002 (2000); 961 (2005); 906 (2010 projected); Race: 98.9% White, 0.5% Black, 0.0% Asian, 0.0% Hispanic of any race (2005); Density: 716.7 persons per square mile (2005); Average household size: 2.83 (2005); Median age: 33.3 (2005); Males per 100 females: 80.3 (2005); Marriage status: 24.6% never married, 52.8% now married, 7.9% widowed, 14.7% divorced (2000); Foreign born: 0.5% (2000); Ancestry (includes multiple ancestries): 24.0% German, 19.7% United States or American, 11.1% English, 9.5% Irish, 8.3% Other groups (2000).
Economy: In agricultural area: grain, soybeans. Employment by occupation: 7.4% management, 9.1% professional, 17.9% services, 31.4% sales, 0.4% farming, 12.2% construction, 21.7% production (2000).
Income: Per capita income: $16,336 (2005); Median household income: $37,262 (2005); Average household income: $44,366 (2005); Percent of households with income of $100,000 or more: 5.9% (2005); Poverty rate: 22.7% (2000).
Education: Percent of population age 25 and over with: High school diploma (including GED) or higher: 72.2% (2005); Bachelor's degree or higher: 6.4% (2005); Master's degree or higher: 1.0% (2005).

School District(s)
Westfall Local SD (PK-12)
    2003-04 Enrollment: 1,655 . . . . (740) 986-3671

Housing: Homeownership rate: 69.9% (2005); Median home value: $99,538 (2005); Median rent: $336 per month (2000); Median age of housing: 43 years (2000).
Transportation: Commute to work: 93.8% car, 0.9% public transportation, 4.1% walk, 0.9% work from home (2000); Travel time to work: 19.4% less than 15 minutes, 35.8% 15 to 30 minutes, 13.6% 30 to 45 minutes, 20.5% 45 to 60 minutes, 10.8% 60 minutes or more (2000)

Pike County

Located in southern Ohio; crossed by the Scioto River. Covers a land area of 441.49 square miles, a water area of 2.46 square miles, and is located in the Eastern Time Zone. The county government was organized in 1815. County seat is Waverly City.

Weather Station: Waverly   Elevation: 557 feet

	Jan	Feb	Mar	Apr	May	Jun	Jul	Aug	Sep	Oct	Nov	Dec
High	39	44	55	67	75	83	86	85	79	68	56	45
Low	19	22	30	38	49	58	63	60	53	40	32	24
Precip	2.7	2.3	3.6	3.6	4.2	3.9	4.0	4.4	2.6	2.6	3.1	3.0
Snow	4.7	na	3.0	0.1	0.0	0.0	0.0	0.0	0.0	tr	0.1	1.5

High and Low temperatures in degrees Fahrenheit; Precipitation and Snow in inches

Population: 24,249 (1990); 27,695 (2000); 28,456 (2005); 29,245 (2010 projected); Race: 96.9% White, 0.7% Black, 0.3% Asian, 0.6% Hispanic of any race (2005); Density: 64.5 persons per square mile (2005); Average household size: 2.62 (2005); Median age: 36.1 (2005); Males per 100 females: 95.1 (2005).
Religion: Five largest groups: 5.6% Southern Baptist Convention, 4.2% The United Methodist Church, 1.5% Christian Churches and Churches of Christ, 1.2% Christian Union, 1.1% Catholic Church (2000).
Economy: Unemployment rate: 10.1% (2005); Total civilian labor force: 10,778 (2005); Leading industries: 46.6% manufacturing; 15.8% health care and social assistance; 12.8% retail trade (2000); Farms: 505 totaling 83,602 acres (2002); Companies that employ 500 or more persons: 2 (2004); Companies that employ 100 to 499 persons: 6 (2004); Companies that employ less than 100 persons: 460 (2004); Black-owned businesses: n/a (2002); Hispanic-owned businesses: n/a (2002); Women-owned businesses: 589 (2002); Retail sales per capita: $8,965 (2006). Single-family building permits issued: 101 (2005); Multi-family building permits issued: 54 (2005).
Income: Per capita income: $18,079 (2005); Median household income: $36,596 (2005); Average household income: $46,964 (2005); Percent of households with income of $100,000 or more: 8.3% (2005); Poverty rate: 15.7% (2003); Bankruptcy rate: 8.14% (2005).
Taxes: Total county taxes per capita: $202 (2004); County property taxes per capita: $201 (2004).
Education: Percent of population age 25 and over with: High school diploma (including GED) or higher: 69.8% (2005); Bachelor's degree or higher: 9.5% (2005); Master's degree or higher: 3.3% (2005).
Housing: Homeownership rate: 70.4% (2005); Median home value: $83,809 (2005); Median rent: $313 per month (2000); Median age of housing: 26 years (2000).
Health: Birth rate: 134.0 per 10,000 population (2004); Death rate: 114.2 per 10,000 population (2004); Age-adjusted cancer mortality rate: 277.4 deaths per 100,000 population (2002); Number of physicians: 9.2 per 10,000 population (2004); Hospital beds: 13.1 per 10,000 population (2003); Hospital admissions: 499.5 per 10,000 population (2003).
Elections: 2004 Presidential election results: 51.8% Bush, 47.6% Kerry, 0.0% Nader, 0.3% Badnarik.
National and State Parks: Lake White State Park
Additional Information Contacts
Pike County Government . . . . (740) 947-4817
   http://www.piketravel.com/
City of Waverly City . . . . (740) 947-5162
   http://www.cityofwaverly.net
Waverly Chamber of Commerce . . . . (740) 947-7715
   http://www.cityofwaverly.net

Pike County Communities

BEAVER (village). Covers a land area of 0.391 square miles and a water area of 0 square miles. Located at 39.03° N. Lat.; 82.82° W. Long. Elevation is 690 feet.
Population: 336 (1990); 464 (2000); 465 (2005); 468 (2010 projected); Race: 97.2% White, 0.0% Black, 0.2% Asian, 0.2% Hispanic of any race (2005); Density: 1,190.5 persons per square mile (2005); Average household size: 2.35 (2005); Median age: 32.2 (2005); Males per 100 females: 83.8 (2005); Marriage status: 20.1% never married, 57.7% now married, 8.7% widowed, 13.5% divorced (2000); Foreign born: 1.0% (2000); Ancestry (includes multiple ancestries): 13.7% United States or American, 12.9% German, 7.3% Irish, 6.3% Other groups, 3.9% Dutch (2000).
Economy: Sawmills. Employment by occupation: 5.6% management, 9.9% professional, 18.0% services, 18.6% sales, 1.2% farming, 26.1% construction, 20.5% production (2000).
Income: Per capita income: $13,392 (2005); Median household income: $23,947 (2005); Average household income: $31,452 (2005); Percent of households with income of $100,000 or more: 3.0% (2005); Poverty rate: 28.6% (2000).
Education: Percent of population age 25 and over with: High school diploma (including GED) or higher: 65.8% (2005); Bachelor's degree or higher: 5.8% (2005); Master's degree or higher: 1.1% (2005).

School District(s)
Eastern Local SD (PK-12)
    2003-04 Enrollment: 809 . . . . (740) 226-4851

Housing: Homeownership rate: 47.5% (2005); Median home value: $88,571 (2005); Median rent: $273 per month (2000); Median age of housing: 37 years (2000).
Transportation: Commute to work: 82.0% car, 5.0% public transportation, 8.7% walk, 0.0% work from home (2000); Travel time to work: 28.0% less than 15 minutes, 36.6% 15 to 30 minutes, 15.5% 30 to 45 minutes, 8.7% 45 to 60 minutes, 11.2% 60 minutes or more (2000)

LATHAM (unincorporated postal area, zip code 45646). Covers a land area of 12.529 square miles and a water area of 0.014 square miles. Located at 39.08° N. Lat.; 83.31° W. Long. Elevation is 634 feet.
Population: 295 (2000); Race: 100.0% White, 0.0% Black, 0.0% Asian, 0.0% Hispanic of any race (2000); Density: 23.5 persons per square mile (2000); Age: 18.4% under 18, 18.4% over 64 (2000); Marriage status: 18.6% never married, 60.6% now married, 10.4% widowed, 10.4% divorced (2000); Foreign born: 0.0% (2000); Ancestry (includes multiple ancestries): 40.0% United States or American, 4.1% Irish, 3.4% German, 2.2% Other groups, 1.9% English (2000).
Economy: Employment by occupation: 4.5% management, 3.8% professional, 14.4% services, 29.5% sales, 0.0% farming, 18.9% construction, 28.8% production (2000).
Income: Per capita income: $13,250 (2000); Median household income: $29,583 (2000); Poverty rate: 25.6% (2000).
Education: Percent of population age 25 and over with: High school diploma (including GED) or higher: 49.6% (2000); Bachelor's degree or higher: 0.0% (2000).

School District(s)
Western Local SD (PK-12)
    2003-04 Enrollment: 954 . . . . (740) 493-3113

Housing: Homeownership rate: 87.0% (2000); Median home value: $38,800 (2000); Median rent: $315 per month (2000); Median age of housing: 33 years (2000).
Transportation: Commute to work: 94.4% car, 0.0% public transportation, 0.0% walk, 5.6% work from home (2000); Travel time to work: 37.8% less than 15 minutes, 18.5% 15 to 30 minutes, 22.7% 30 to 45 minutes, 15.1% 45 to 60 minutes, 5.9% 60 minutes or more (2000)

PIKETON (village).
Covers a land area of 1.996 square miles and a water area of 0.040 square miles. Located at 39.06° N. Lat.; 83.00° W. Long. Elevation is 578 feet.
History: Piketon was settled in 1814, when it was called Jefferson. Piketon served as the seat of Pike County until 1861.
Population: 1,700 (1990); 1,907 (2000); 1,911 (2005); 1,947 (2010 projected); Race: 96.8% White, 0.6% Black, 0.4% Asian, 0.4% Hispanic of any race (2005); Density: 957.7 persons per square mile (2005); Average household size: 2.71 (2005); Median age: 40.0 (2005); Males per 100 females: 76.3 (2005); Marriage status: 18.8% never married, 58.8% now married, 7.6% widowed, 14.7% divorced (2000); Foreign born: 0.3% (2000); Ancestry (includes multiple ancestries): 18.7% United States or American, 10.5% German, 6.8% Irish, 6.1% English, 5.1% Other groups (2000).
Economy: Single-family building permits issued: 5 (2005); Multi-family building permits issued: 0 (2005); Employment by occupation: 8.3% management, 11.6% professional, 23.0% services, 20.2% sales, 1.5% farming, 8.6% construction, 26.9% production (2000).
Income: Per capita income: $14,185 (2005); Median household income: $24,270 (2005); Average household income: $36,933 (2005); Percent of households with income of $100,000 or more: 5.9% (2005); Poverty rate: 30.3% (2000).
Education: Percent of population age 25 and over with: High school diploma (including GED) or higher: 67.4% (2005); Bachelor's degree or higher: 7.9% (2005); Master's degree or higher: 2.8% (2005).

School District(s)
Pike County Area Joint Vocational SD (07-12)
 2003-04 Enrollment: n/a .... (740) 289-2721
Scioto Valley Local SD (PK-12)
 2003-04 Enrollment: 1,679 .... (740) 289-4456
Western Local SD (PK-12)
 2003-04 Enrollment: 954 .... (740) 493-3113

Two-year College(s)
Pike County Joint Vocational School District (Public)
 Fall 2004 Enrollment: 50 .... (740) 289-2282
Housing: Homeownership rate: 52.1% (2005); Median home value: $90,980 (2005); Median rent: $263 per month (2000); Median age of housing: 30 years (2000).
Transportation: Commute to work: 92.7% car, 0.0% public transportation, 4.5% walk, 1.7% work from home (2000); Travel time to work: 52.0% less than 15 minutes, 23.6% 15 to 30 minutes, 13.2% 30 to 45 minutes, 4.4% 45 to 60 minutes, 6.8% 60 minutes or more (2000)

WAVERLY CITY (city).
Aka Waverly. Covers a land area of 3.919 square miles and a water area of 0 square miles. Located at 39.12° N. Lat.; 82.98° W. Long.
History: Waverly City (also known as Waverly) was founded in 1829 by James Emmitt and called Uniontown. The name was changed to Waverly in 1830 at the suggestion of Captain Francis Cleveland, a canal engineer, who had been reading Walter Scott's Waverly novels. Waverly managed to take the county seat from Piketon in 1861.
Population: 4,296 (1990); 4,433 (2000); 4,337 (2005); 4,328 (2010 projected); Race: 96.4% White, 1.2% Black, 0.9% Asian, 0.5% Hispanic of any race (2005); Density: 1,106.8 persons per square mile (2005); Average household size: 2.15 (2005); Median age: 44.1 (2005); Males per 100 females: 81.6 (2005); Marriage status: 17.0% never married, 57.2% now married, 12.5% widowed, 13.4% divorced (2000); Foreign born: 1.4% (2000); Ancestry (includes multiple ancestries): 16.2% German, 15.8% English, 13.9% United States or American, 10.9% Irish, 7.6% Other groups (2000).
Economy: Single-family building permits issued: 25 (2005); Multi-family building permits issued: 0 (2005); Employment by occupation: 9.0% management, 24.4% professional, 11.2% services, 28.6% sales, 0.0% farming, 5.5% construction, 21.4% production (2000).
Income: Per capita income: $21,192 (2005); Median household income: $36,625 (2005); Average household income: $44,928 (2005); Percent of households with income of $100,000 or more: 6.3% (2005); Poverty rate: 12.2% (2000).
Education: Percent of population age 25 and over with: High school diploma (including GED) or higher: 81.3% (2005); Bachelor's degree or higher: 21.8% (2005); Master's degree or higher: 7.3% (2005).

School District(s)
Waverly City SD (PK-12)
 2003-04 Enrollment: 2,174 .... (740) 947-4770
Housing: Homeownership rate: 49.4% (2005); Median home value: $94,488 (2005); Median rent: $381 per month (2000); Median age of housing: 42 years (2000).
Hospitals: Pike Community Hospital (63 beds)
Safety: Violent crime rate: 4.5 per 10,000 population; Property crime rate: 962.5 per 10,000 population (2004).
Newspapers: The News-Watchman (General - Circulation 5,000); The Paper (General - Circulation 42,000)
Transportation: Commute to work: 93.0% car, 0.7% public transportation, 4.2% walk, 1.8% work from home (2000); Travel time to work: 54.3% less than 15 minutes, 26.3% 15 to 30 minutes, 10.4% 30 to 45 minutes, 3.6% 45 to 60 minutes, 5.5% 60 minutes or more (2000)
Additional Information Contacts
City of Waverly City .... (740) 947-5162
 http://www.cityofwaverly.net
Waverly Chamber of Commerce .... (740) 947-7715
 http://www.cityofwaverly.net

Portage County

Located in northeastern Ohio; crossed by the Cuyahoga River and tributaries of the Mahoning; includes many small lakes. Covers a land area of 492.39 square miles, a water area of 14.72 square miles, and is located in the Eastern Time Zone. The county government was organized in 1807. County seat is Ravenna.

Portage County is part of the Akron, OH Metropolitan Statistical Area. The entire metro area includes: Portage County, OH; Summit County, OH

Weather Station: Hiram   Elevation: 1,227 feet

	Jan	Feb	Mar	Apr	May	Jun	Jul	Aug	Sep	Oct	Nov	Dec
High	32	36	46	58	70	77	82	80	73	61	49	37
Low	16	19	27	37	48	56	61	60	53	42	33	23
Precip	2.7	2.3	3.4	3.6	3.8	4.1	3.9	3.8	4.2	3.2	3.7	3.5
Snow	16.1	12.4	10.2	1.5	tr	0.0	0.0	0.0	0.0	0.2	6.0	15.2

High and Low temperatures in degrees Fahrenheit; Precipitation and Snow in inches

Population: 142,585 (1990); 152,061 (2000); 156,171 (2005); 160,433 (2010 projected); Race: 93.6% White, 3.4% Black, 1.2% Asian, 0.8% Hispanic of any race (2005); Density: 317.2 persons per square mile (2005); Average household size: 2.64 (2005); Median age: 35.5 (2005); Males per 100 females: 95.3 (2005).
Religion: Five largest groups: 19.4% Catholic Church, 3.7% The United Methodist Church, 1.7% United Church of Christ, 1.6% Christian Church (Disciples of Christ), 1.0% Independent, Non-Charismatic Churches (2000).
Economy: Unemployment rate: 5.6% (2005); Total civilian labor force: 88,812 (2005); Leading industries: 25.5% manufacturing; 14.8% retail trade; 11.4% health care and social assistance (2004); Farms: 962 totaling 96,874 acres (2002); Companies that employ 500 or more persons: 3 (2004); Companies that employ 100 to 499 persons: 66 (2004); Companies that employ less than 100 persons: 3,146 (2004); Black-owned businesses: 215 (2002); Hispanic-owned businesses: n/a (2002); Women-owned businesses: 3,247 (2002); Retail sales per capita: $11,152 (2006). Single-family building permits issued: 625 (2005); Multi-family building permits issued: 131 (2005).
Income: Per capita income: $23,514 (2005); Median household income: $49,192 (2005); Average household income: $61,071 (2005); Percent of households with income of $100,000 or more: 14.2% (2005); Poverty rate: 8.6% (2003); Bankruptcy rate: 11.56% (2005).
Taxes: Total county taxes per capita: $231 (2004); County property taxes per capita: $145 (2004).
Education: Percent of population age 25 and over with: High school diploma (including GED) or higher: 86.0% (2005); Bachelor's degree or higher: 21.5% (2005); Master's degree or higher: 7.2% (2005).
Housing: Homeownership rate: 71.4% (2005); Median home value: $138,747 (2005); Median rent: $469 per month (2000); Median age of housing: 30 years (2000).

Health: Birth rate: 101.5 per 10,000 population (2004); Death rate: 75.2 per 10,000 population (2004); Age-adjusted cancer mortality rate: 231.2 deaths per 100,000 population (2002); Air Quality Index: 66.3% good, 29.1% moderate, 4.3% unhealthy for sensitive individuals, 0.4% unhealthy (percent of days in 2005); Number of physicians: 11.9 per 10,000 population (2004); Hospital beds: 7.6 per 10,000 population (2003); Hospital admissions: 530.4 per 10,000 population (2003).
Elections: 2004 Presidential election results: 46.4% Bush, 53.1% Kerry, 0.0% Nader, 0.3% Badnarik
National and State Parks: Nelson-Kennedy Ledges State Park; Tinkers Creek State Park; West Branch State Park
Additional Information Contacts
Portage County Government . . . . (330) 297-3600
   http://www.co.portage.oh.us/
Aurora Chamber of Commerce . . . . (330) 562-3355
   http://www.auroraohiochamber.com
Brimfield Area Chamber of Commerce . . . . (330) 554-2236
   http://www.brimfieldchamber.com
City of Aurora . . . . (330) 562-6131
   http://www.auroraoh.com/default.aspx
City of Kent . . . . (330) 678-8007
   http://www.kentohio.org
City of Ravenna . . . . (330) 296-3864
   http://www.ci.ravenna.oh.us
Garrettsville Chamber of Commerce . . . . (330) 527-2411
   http://www.garrettsvillehiramarea.com
Kent Chamber of Commerce . . . . (330) 673-9855
   http://www.kentbiz.com
Ravenna Chamber of Commerce . . . . (330) 296-3886
   http://www.ravennachamber.com
Rootstown Area Chamber of Commerce . . . . (330) 325-2379
   http://www.rootstownchamber.org
Streetsboro Chamber of Commerce . . . . (330) 626-4769
   http://www.streetsborochamber.org
Streetsboro Visitors and Convention Bureau . . . . (330) 422-1770
   http://www.streetsborovcb.com
Village of Garrettsville . . . . (330) 527-4424
   http://www.garrettsville.org

Portage County Communities

ATWATER (unincorporated postal area, zip code 44201). Covers a land area of 52.866 square miles and a water area of 0.112 square miles. Located at 41.02° N. Lat.; 81.20° W. Long. Elevation is 1,140 feet.
Population: 6,915 (2000); Race: 99.2% White, 0.2% Black, 0.1% Asian, 0.0% Hispanic of any race (2000); Density: 130.8 persons per square mile (2000); Age: 27.0% under 18, 11.3% over 64 (2000); Marriage status: 21.1% never married, 67.4% now married, 3.9% widowed, 7.5% divorced (2000); Foreign born: 0.5% (2000); Ancestry (includes multiple ancestries): 31.9% German, 12.6% Irish, 11.4% English, 9.6% United States or American, 5.8% Other groups (2000).
Economy: Employment by occupation: 8.0% management, 9.8% professional, 11.4% services, 30.3% sales, 0.7% farming, 14.8% construction, 25.2% production (2000).
Income: Per capita income: $19,060 (2000); Median household income: $47,665 (2000); Poverty rate: 5.2% (2000).
Education: Percent of population age 25 and over with: High school diploma (including GED) or higher: 86.9% (2000); Bachelor's degree or higher: 10.3% (2000).
School District(s)
Waterloo Local SD (PK-12)
   2003-04 Enrollment: 1,401 . . . . (330) 947-2664
Housing: Homeownership rate: 88.1% (2000); Median home value: $123,500 (2000); Median rent: $503 per month (2000); Median age of housing: 30 years (2000).
Transportation: Commute to work: 95.6% car, 0.0% public transportation, 1.1% walk, 2.3% work from home (2000); Travel time to work: 14.2% less than 15 minutes, 40.1% 15 to 30 minutes, 25.2% 30 to 45 minutes, 12.2% 45 to 60 minutes, 8.3% 60 minutes or more (2000)

AURORA (city). Covers a land area of 23.221 square miles and a water area of 0.872 square miles. Located at 41.31° N. Lat.; 81.35° W. Long. Elevation is 1,130 feet.
History: From its start as a pioneer town to a thriving suburb, Aurora has seen many changes in its 200 years. Before 1799, Aurora was merely a spot on the map of the Connecticut Western Reserve, a parcel of land drawn in a lottery by members of the Big Beaver Land Co. comprised of citizens of Suffield, Connecticut. The new landowners contracted Capt. Ebenezer Sheldon, a former Revolutionary War soldier, to settle their land and act as their agent. Having suffered business reversals, Sheldon at age 45 looked to the Western Reserve for a fresh start. Leaving his family behind, Sheldon traveled the south route to Ohio through Pittsburgh and had the distinction of being the first white man to enter the township for the purpose of settling. The site of Sheldon's first log cabin, built with the help of Elias Harmon, lies east on Pioneer Trail near the edge of the township on prime property straddling the Chagrin River. After carving out a bit of civilization in the wilderness, Sheldon retrieved his family from Connecticut and they became the first family in Aurora. The Golden Age of Cheese between 1855 and 1910 was responsible for developing Aurora into a well-established town. In 1929, the village of Aurora was founded in the center of the former Aurora Township. By 1971, Aurora took on city status after growing to more than 6,000 residents in the 1970 U.S. Census.
Population: 9,192 (1990); 13,556 (2000); 14,507 (2005); 15,448 (2010 projected); Race: 94.5% White, 2.5% Black, 1.9% Asian, 0.6% Hispanic of any race (2005); Density: 624.7 persons per square mile (2005); Average household size: 2.63 (2005); Median age: 42.0 (2005); Males per 100 females: 93.0 (2005); Marriage status: 17.3% never married, 70.0% now married, 5.5% widowed, 7.2% divorced (2000); Foreign born: 2.8% (2000); Ancestry (includes multiple ancestries): 26.1% German, 16.4% Irish, 13.9% Italian, 13.6% English, 9.8% Polish (2000).
Economy: Sandstone quarry. Sea World and Geauga Lake theme parks. Single-family building permits issued: 72 (2005); Multi-family building permits issued: 42 (2005); Employment by occupation: 26.0% management, 21.4% professional, 9.0% services, 28.4% sales, 0.1% farming, 5.9% construction, 9.1% production (2000).
Income: Per capita income: $41,063 (2005); Median household income: $81,705 (2005); Average household income: $107,234 (2005); Percent of households with income of $100,000 or more: 38.3% (2005); Poverty rate: 3.6% (2000).
Taxes: Total city taxes per capita: $1,104 (2004); City property taxes per capita: $272 (2004).
Education: Percent of population age 25 and over with: High school diploma (including GED) or higher: 93.1% (2005); Bachelor's degree or higher: 41.3% (2005); Master's degree or higher: 12.3% (2005).
School District(s)
Aurora City SD (PK-12)
   2003-04 Enrollment: 2,851 . . . . (330) 562-6106
Housing: Homeownership rate: 81.5% (2005); Median home value: $229,034 (2005); Median rent: $890 per month (2000); Median age of housing: 18 years (2000).
Safety: Violent crime rate: 3.5 per 10,000 population; Property crime rate: 108.4 per 10,000 population (2004).
Transportation: Commute to work: 93.5% car, 0.1% public transportation, 0.5% walk, 5.5% work from home (2000); Travel time to work: 22.7% less than 15 minutes, 31.6% 15 to 30 minutes, 30.5% 30 to 45 minutes, 10.8% 45 to 60 minutes, 4.5% 60 minutes or more (2000)
Additional Information Contacts
Aurora Chamber of Commerce . . . . (330) 562-3355
   http://www.auroraohiochamber.com
City of Aurora . . . . (330) 562-6131
   http://www.auroraoh.com/default.aspx

BRADY LAKE (village). Aka Bradys Lake. Covers a land area of 0.316 square miles and a water area of 0.105 square miles. Located at 41.16° N. Lat.; 81.31° W. Long. Elevation is 1,070 feet.
Population: 498 (1990); 513 (2000); 524 (2005); 528 (2010 projected); Race: 95.8% White, 2.1% Black, 0.0% Asian, 1.0% Hispanic of any race (2005); Density: 1,660.4 persons per square mile (2005); Average household size: 2.50 (2005); Median age: 39.5 (2005); Males per 100 females: 97.0 (2005); Marriage status: 23.1% never married, 59.8% now married, 6.7% widowed, 10.4% divorced (2000); Foreign born: 0.8% (2000); Ancestry (includes multiple ancestries): 29.3% German, 18.7% Irish, 14.3% English, 9.8% United States or American, 8.4% Italian (2000).
Economy: Employment by occupation: 8.6% management, 20.0% professional, 14.8% services, 25.2% sales, 0.0% farming, 10.0% construction, 21.4% production (2000).
Income: Per capita income: $22,853 (2005); Median household income: $45,200 (2005); Average household income: $57,024 (2005); Percent of households with income of $100,000 or more: 13.3% (2005); Poverty rate: 3.8% (2000).

Education: Percent of population age 25 and over with: High school diploma (including GED) or higher: 78.8% (2005); Bachelor's degree or higher: 17.3% (2005); Master's degree or higher: 6.9% (2005).
Housing: Homeownership rate: 73.8% (2005); Median home value: $113,889 (2005); Median rent: $493 per month (2000); Median age of housing: 50 years (2000).
Transportation: Commute to work: 96.9% car, 0.7% public transportation, 0.0% walk, 1.7% work from home (2000); Travel time to work: 38.3% less than 15 minutes, 33.7% 15 to 30 minutes, 14.5% 30 to 45 minutes, 8.5% 45 to 60 minutes, 5.0% 60 minutes or more (2000)

BRIMFIELD (CDP). Covers a land area of 3.975 square miles and a water area of 0.028 square miles. Located at 41.09° N. Lat.; 81.34° W. Long. Elevation is 1,110 feet.
Population: 3,223 (1990); 3,248 (2000); 3,204 (2005); 3,160 (2010 projected); Race: 96.3% White, 1.6% Black, 0.2% Asian, 0.5% Hispanic of any race (2005); Density: 806.1 persons per square mile (2005); Average household size: 2.79 (2005); Median age: 37.3 (2005); Males per 100 females: 96.2 (2005); Marriage status: 23.2% never married, 57.6% now married, 8.1% widowed, 11.2% divorced (2000); Foreign born: 1.1% (2000); Ancestry (includes multiple ancestries): 24.5% German, 19.6% Irish, 11.1% English, 8.9% Other groups, 8.2% Italian (2000).
Economy: Employment by occupation: 8.7% management, 13.5% professional, 23.3% services, 27.6% sales, 0.0% farming, 7.2% construction, 19.7% production (2000).
Income: Per capita income: $20,775 (2005); Median household income: $46,652 (2005); Average household income: $57,792 (2005); Percent of households with income of $100,000 or more: 10.5% (2005); Poverty rate: 9.1% (2000).
Education: Percent of population age 25 and over with: High school diploma (including GED) or higher: 83.2% (2005); Bachelor's degree or higher: 13.6% (2005); Master's degree or higher: 4.3% (2005).
Housing: Homeownership rate: 84.7% (2005); Median home value: $121,982 (2005); Median rent: $619 per month (2000); Median age of housing: 35 years (2000).
Transportation: Commute to work: 95.6% car, 2.0% public transportation, 0.0% walk, 0.3% work from home (2000); Travel time to work: 26.0% less than 15 minutes, 44.1% 15 to 30 minutes, 20.9% 30 to 45 minutes, 3.5% 45 to 60 minutes, 5.6% 60 minutes or more (2000)
Additional Information Contacts
Brimfield Area Chamber of Commerce . . . . (330) 554-2236
 http://www.brimfieldchamber.com

DEERFIELD (unincorporated postal area, zip code 44411). Covers a land area of 20.081 square miles and a water area of 0.561 square miles. Located at 41.02° N. Lat.; 81.05° W. Long. Elevation is 1,073 feet.
Population: 2,705 (2000); Race: 99.7% White, 0.3% Black, 0.0% Asian, 0.0% Hispanic of any race (2000); Density: 134.7 persons per square mile (2000); Age: 28.3% under 18, 9.6% over 64 (2000); Marriage status: 17.6% never married, 66.5% now married, 3.5% widowed, 12.4% divorced (2000); Foreign born: 0.0% (2000); Ancestry (includes multiple ancestries): 16.7% Irish, 16.6% German, 13.5% United States or American, 9.5% English, 5.6% Other groups (2000).
Economy: Employment by occupation: 9.4% management, 8.1% professional, 11.1% services, 22.9% sales, 0.4% farming, 15.8% construction, 32.4% production (2000).
Income: Per capita income: $17,585 (2000); Median household income: $46,920 (2000); Poverty rate: 4.1% (2000).
Education: Percent of population age 25 and over with: High school diploma (including GED) or higher: 81.3% (2000); Bachelor's degree or higher: 9.0% (2000).
School District(s)
Southeast Local School District (PK-12)
 2003-04 Enrollment: 2,210 . . . . (330) 654-5841
Housing: Homeownership rate: 87.2% (2000); Median home value: $111,600 (2000); Median rent: $324 per month (2000); Median age of housing: 28 years (2000).
Transportation: Commute to work: 92.8% car, 0.5% public transportation, 0.9% walk, 3.9% work from home (2000); Travel time to work: 11.3% less than 15 minutes, 28.9% 15 to 30 minutes, 33.4% 30 to 45 minutes, 13.5% 45 to 60 minutes, 12.9% 60 minutes or more (2000)

DIAMOND (unincorporated postal area, zip code 44412). Covers a land area of 24.964 square miles and a water area of 0 square miles. Located at 41.09° N. Lat.; 81.00° W. Long. Elevation is 990 feet.
Population: 2,702 (2000); Race: 99.3% White, 0.0% Black, 0.3% Asian, 0.1% Hispanic of any race (2000); Density: 108.2 persons per square mile (2000); Age: 25.5% under 18, 12.0% over 64 (2000); Marriage status: 20.3% never married, 63.4% now married, 5.7% widowed, 10.5% divorced (2000); Foreign born: 0.5% (2000); Ancestry (includes multiple ancestries): 34.1% German, 14.7% Irish, 8.2% United States or American, 7.7% Italian, 7.7% English (2000).
Economy: Employment by occupation: 10.4% management, 12.5% professional, 13.9% services, 20.8% sales, 0.0% farming, 13.4% construction, 29.1% production (2000).
Income: Per capita income: $19,020 (2000); Median household income: $50,045 (2000); Poverty rate: 6.3% (2000).
Education: Percent of population age 25 and over with: High school diploma (including GED) or higher: 85.5% (2000); Bachelor's degree or higher: 9.9% (2000).
School District(s)
Southeast Local School District (PK-12)
 2003-04 Enrollment: 2,210 . . . . (330) 654-5841
Housing: Homeownership rate: 86.4% (2000); Median home value: $116,400 (2000); Median rent: $433 per month (2000); Median age of housing: 26 years (2000).
Transportation: Commute to work: 97.5% car, 0.5% public transportation, 0.0% walk, 2.0% work from home (2000); Travel time to work: 9.1% less than 15 minutes, 40.3% 15 to 30 minutes, 25.2% 30 to 45 minutes, 12.5% 45 to 60 minutes, 13.0% 60 minutes or more (2000)

GARRETTSVILLE (village). Aka Garrettsville-Hiram. Covers a land area of 2.531 square miles and a water area of 0 square miles. Located at 41.28° N. Lat.; 81.09° W. Long. Elevation is 1,000 feet.
Population: 2,193 (1990); 2,262 (2000); 2,335 (2005); 2,406 (2010 projected); Race: 98.2% White, 0.3% Black, 0.1% Asian, 0.5% Hispanic of any race (2005); Density: 922.6 persons per square mile (2005); Average household size: 2.38 (2005); Median age: 37.4 (2005); Males per 100 females: 92.2 (2005); Marriage status: 21.1% never married, 63.3% now married, 6.8% widowed, 8.9% divorced (2000); Foreign born: 1.8% (2000); Ancestry (includes multiple ancestries): 31.7% German, 17.2% English, 15.2% Irish, 6.8% United States or American, 6.4% Polish (2000).
Economy: Employment by occupation: 13.4% management, 17.4% professional, 16.4% services, 22.5% sales, 0.4% farming, 9.9% construction, 20.0% production (2000).
Income: Per capita income: $24,118 (2005); Median household income: $53,009 (2005); Average household income: $57,406 (2005); Percent of households with income of $100,000 or more: 10.8% (2005); Poverty rate: 4.4% (2000).
Education: Percent of population age 25 and over with: High school diploma (including GED) or higher: 92.4% (2005); Bachelor's degree or higher: 21.8% (2005); Master's degree or higher: 6.4% (2005).
School District(s)
James A Garfield Local SD (PK-12)
 2003-04 Enrollment: 1,570 . . . . (330) 527-4336
Housing: Homeownership rate: 65.0% (2005); Median home value: $158,864 (2005); Median rent: $430 per month (2000); Median age of housing: 38 years (2000).
Transportation: Commute to work: 92.8% car, 0.0% public transportation, 4.7% walk, 1.4% work from home (2000); Travel time to work: 34.0% less than 15 minutes, 21.8% 15 to 30 minutes, 27.9% 30 to 45 minutes, 10.2% 45 to 60 minutes, 6.0% 60 minutes or more (2000)
Additional Information Contacts
Garrettsville Chamber of Commerce . . . . (330) 527-2411
 http://www.garrettsvillehiramarea.com
Village of Garrettsville . . . . (330) 527-4424
 http://www.garrettsville.org

HIRAM (village). Covers a land area of 0.908 square miles and a water area of 0 square miles. Located at 41.31° N. Lat.; 81.14° W. Long. Elevation is 1,250 feet.
History: Hiram grew up around Hiram College, founded in 1850 by the Disciples of Christ as the Western Reserve Eclectic Institute. President James A. Garfield was valedictorian of his class when he graduated from the Institute in 1853.
Population: 1,330 (1990); 1,242 (2000); 1,265 (2005); 1,292 (2010 projected); Race: 89.0% White, 6.4% Black, 2.1% Asian, 2.0% Hispanic of any race (2005); Density: 1,392.5 persons per square mile (2005); Average household size: 5.23 (2005); Median age: 20.9 (2005); Males per 100 females: 92.0 (2005); Marriage status: 71.4% never married, 23.6% now

married, 1.4% widowed, 3.5% divorced (2000); Foreign born: 3.9% (2000); Ancestry (includes multiple ancestries): 21.9% German, 17.9% Irish, 14.7% English, 13.1% Other groups, 11.3% Italian (2000).
Economy: Employment by occupation: 3.9% management, 19.3% professional, 36.2% services, 26.0% sales, 2.5% farming, 5.0% construction, 7.2% production (2000).
Income: Per capita income: $20,273 (2005); Median household income: $53,333 (2005); Average household income: $59,969 (2005); Percent of households with income of $100,000 or more: 13.2% (2005); Poverty rate: 4.3% (2000).
Education: Percent of population age 25 and over with: High school diploma (including GED) or higher: 93.9% (2005); Bachelor's degree or higher: 43.8% (2005); Master's degree or higher: 23.3% (2005).

School District(s)
Crestwood Local SD (PK-12)
    2003-04 Enrollment: 2,725 . . . . (330) 274-8511

Four-year College(s)
Hiram College (Private, Not-for-profit)
    Fall 2004 Enrollment: 1,125 . . . . (330) 569-3211
    2005-06 Tuition: In-state $24,180; Out-of-state $24,180

Housing: Homeownership rate: 46.3% (2005); Median home value: $171,429 (2005); Median rent: $414 per month (2000); Median age of housing: 43 years (2000).
Transportation: Commute to work: 59.0% car, 0.0% public transportation, 37.0% walk, 3.3% work from home (2000); Travel time to work: 50.1% less than 15 minutes, 30.5% 15 to 30 minutes, 7.2% 30 to 45 minutes, 7.6% 45 to 60 minutes, 4.6% 60 minutes or more (2000)

KENT (city).
Covers a land area of 8.687 square miles and a water area of 0.021 square miles. Located at 41.15° N. Lat.; 81.36° W. Long. Elevation is 1,097 feet.
History: Kent developed around Kent State University, founded in 1910 as a state normal school and accredited as a university in 1935.
Population: 28,879 (1990); 27,906 (2000); 27,850 (2005); 27,770 (2010 projected); Race: 84.1% White, 10.0% Black, 2.9% Asian, 1.4% Hispanic of any race (2005); Density: 3,205.9 persons per square mile (2005); Average household size: 2.82 (2005); Median age: 24.7 (2005); Males per 100 females: 85.1 (2005); Marriage status: 57.7% never married, 30.4% now married, 4.1% widowed, 7.8% divorced (2000); Foreign born: 4.4% (2000); Ancestry (includes multiple ancestries): 26.0% German, 15.2% Other groups, 15.0% Irish, 11.0% English, 10.8% Italian (2000).
Economy: Unemployment rate: 4.7% (2005); Total civilian labor force: 16,719 (2005); Single-family building permits issued: 52 (2005); Multi-family building permits issued: 27 (2005); Employment by occupation: 9.3% management, 22.9% professional, 20.9% services, 29.0% sales, 0.1% farming, 4.8% construction, 13.1% production (2000).
Income: Per capita income: $16,924 (2005); Median household income: $32,197 (2005); Average household income: $44,492 (2005); Percent of households with income of $100,000 or more: 9.6% (2005); Poverty rate: 25.2% (2000).
Education: Percent of population age 25 and over with: High school diploma (including GED) or higher: 91.6% (2005); Bachelor's degree or higher: 37.8% (2005); Master's degree or higher: 16.3% (2005).

School District(s)
Field Local SD (KG-12)
    2003-04 Enrollment: 2,310 . . . . (330) 673-2659
Kent City SD (PK-12)
    2003-04 Enrollment: 3,796 . . . . (330) 673-6515
Kent Digital Academy (03-12)
    2003-04 Enrollment: 26 . . . . (330) 676-7610

Four-year College(s)
Kent State University-Kent Campus (Public)
    Fall 2004 Enrollment: 24,347 . . . . (330) 672-3000
    2005-06 Tuition: In-state $7,954; Out-of-state $15,386

Housing: Homeownership rate: 37.7% (2005); Median home value: $129,289 (2005); Median rent: $458 per month (2000); Median age of housing: 35 years (2000).
Safety: Violent crime rate: 28.1 per 10,000 population; Property crime rate: 272.9 per 10,000 population (2004).
Transportation: Commute to work: 81.6% car, 2.2% public transportation, 13.1% walk, 2.3% work from home (2000); Travel time to work: 42.7% less than 15 minutes, 33.7% 15 to 30 minutes, 11.7% 30 to 45 minutes, 6.6% 45 to 60 minutes, 5.3% 60 minutes or more (2000)
Additional Information Contacts

City of Kent . . . . (330) 678-8007
    http://www.kentohio.org
Kent Chamber of Commerce . . . . (330) 673-9855
    http://www.kentbiz.com

MANTUA (village).
Covers a land area of 1.407 square miles and a water area of 0 square miles. Located at 41.28° N. Lat.; 81.22° W. Long. Elevation is 1,150 feet.
Population: 1,178 (1990); 1,046 (2000); 1,025 (2005); 1,034 (2010 projected); Race: 98.5% White, 0.5% Black, 0.3% Asian, 0.6% Hispanic of any race (2005); Density: 728.5 persons per square mile (2005); Average household size: 2.32 (2005); Median age: 37.1 (2005); Males per 100 females: 89.8 (2005); Marriage status: 22.6% never married, 55.8% now married, 7.1% widowed, 14.4% divorced (2000); Foreign born: 1.6% (2000); Ancestry (includes multiple ancestries): 29.1% German, 23.1% Irish, 16.8% English, 8.3% Italian, 7.8% Hungarian (2000).
Economy: In dairy, poultry, and vegetable area. Employment by occupation: 10.6% management, 15.4% professional, 13.3% services, 29.8% sales, 0.0% farming, 12.2% construction, 18.8% production (2000).
Income: Per capita income: $25,117 (2005); Median household income: $55,507 (2005); Average household income: $58,379 (2005); Percent of households with income of $100,000 or more: 10.7% (2005); Poverty rate: 3.4% (2000).
Education: Percent of population age 25 and over with: High school diploma (including GED) or higher: 90.1% (2005); Bachelor's degree or higher: 18.3% (2005); Master's degree or higher: 5.4% (2005).

School District(s)
Crestwood Local SD (PK-12)
    2003-04 Enrollment: 2,725 . . . . (330) 274-8511

Housing: Homeownership rate: 63.0% (2005); Median home value: $140,226 (2005); Median rent: $454 per month (2000); Median age of housing: 60+ years (2000).
Transportation: Commute to work: 92.1% car, 0.2% public transportation, 4.8% walk, 2.9% work from home (2000); Travel time to work: 30.7% less than 15 minutes, 35.2% 15 to 30 minutes, 23.8% 30 to 45 minutes, 7.8% 45 to 60 minutes, 2.5% 60 minutes or more (2000)

RAVENNA (city).
Covers a land area of 5.352 square miles and a water area of 0.012 square miles. Located at 41.15° N. Lat.; 81.24° W. Long. Elevation is 1,128 feet.
History: Ravenna was settled in 1799 by Benjamin Tappan, Jr., a New Englander and later U.S. senator from Ohio. The town was named for the Italian city.
Population: 12,237 (1990); 11,771 (2000); 11,360 (2005); 11,100 (2010 projected); Race: 92.4% White, 4.7% Black, 0.5% Asian, 1.0% Hispanic of any race (2005); Density: 2,122.4 persons per square mile (2005); Average household size: 2.33 (2005); Median age: 37.2 (2005); Males per 100 females: 90.2 (2005); Marriage status: 24.3% never married, 50.9% now married, 9.0% widowed, 15.8% divorced (2000); Foreign born: 1.0% (2000); Ancestry (includes multiple ancestries): 28.1% German, 17.2% Irish, 10.9% Italian, 10.5% English, 9.7% Other groups (2000).
Economy: Single-family building permits issued: 47 (2005); Multi-family building permits issued: 0 (2005); Employment by occupation: 8.3% management, 15.8% professional, 15.9% services, 25.6% sales, 0.5% farming, 8.2% construction, 25.8% production (2000).
Income: Per capita income: $19,758 (2005); Median household income: $38,012 (2005); Average household income: $44,711 (2005); Percent of households with income of $100,000 or more: 6.0% (2005); Poverty rate: 10.3% (2000).
Taxes: Total city taxes per capita: $599 (2004); City property taxes per capita: $53 (2004).
Education: Percent of population age 25 and over with: High school diploma (including GED) or higher: 80.4% (2005); Bachelor's degree or higher: 14.7% (2005); Master's degree or higher: 3.9% (2005).

School District(s)
Crestwood Local SD (PK-12)
    2003-04 Enrollment: 2,725 . . . . (330) 274-8511
Maplewood Career Center (11-12)
    2003-04 Enrollment: n/a . . . . (330) 296-2892
Ravenna City SD (PK-12)
    2003-04 Enrollment: 3,386 . . . . (330) 296-9679
Southeast Local School District (PK-12)
    2003-04 Enrollment: 2,210 . . . . (330) 654-5841

Two-year College(s)
Bohecker College (Private, For-profit)
 Fall 2004 Enrollment: 290 .... (330) 297-7319
 2005-06 Tuition: In-state $7,431; Out-of-state $7,431
Housing: Homeownership rate: 54.5% (2005); Median home value: $115,533 (2005); Median rent: $405 per month (2000); Median age of housing: 48 years (2000).
Hospitals: Robinson Memorial Hospital (285 beds)
Safety: Violent crime rate: 36.4 per 10,000 population; Property crime rate: 645.3 per 10,000 population (2004).
Newspapers: Record-Courier (Circulation 18,632)
Transportation: Commute to work: 93.8% car, 0.9% public transportation, 3.0% walk, 1.6% work from home (2000); Travel time to work: 36.2% less than 15 minutes, 32.3% 15 to 30 minutes, 19.5% 30 to 45 minutes, 7.9% 45 to 60 minutes, 4.2% 60 minutes or more (2000)
Additional Information Contacts
City of Ravenna .... (330) 296-3864
 http://www.ci.ravenna.oh.us
Ravenna Chamber of Commerce .... (330) 296-3886
 http://www.ravennachamber.com

ROOTSTOWN
(unincorporated postal area, zip code 44272). Covers a land area of 20.213 square miles and a water area of 0.049 square miles. Located at 41.09° N. Lat.; 81.19° W. Long. Elevation is 1,126 feet.
Population: 4,047 (2000); Race: 98.5% White, 0.0% Black, 0.2% Asian, 0.2% Hispanic of any race (2000); Density: 200.2 persons per square mile (2000); Age: 26.3% under 18, 13.3% over 64 (2000); Marriage status: 19.5% never married, 64.7% now married, 6.0% widowed, 9.8% divorced (2000); Foreign born: 1.4% (2000); Ancestry (includes multiple ancestries): 33.3% German, 17.2% Irish, 16.8% English, 11.9% United States or American, 7.2% Other groups (2000).
Economy: Employment by occupation: 11.6% management, 13.8% professional, 14.5% services, 26.6% sales, 0.4% farming, 10.2% construction, 22.8% production (2000).
Income: Per capita income: $20,199 (2000); Median household income: $48,373 (2000); Poverty rate: 3.3% (2000).
Education: Percent of population age 25 and over with: High school diploma (including GED) or higher: 88.7% (2000); Bachelor's degree or higher: 13.3% (2000).
School District(s)
Rootstown Local SD (PK-12)
 2003-04 Enrollment: 1,295 .... (330) 325-9911
Four-year College(s)
Northeastern Ohio Universities College of Medicine (Public)
 Fall 2004 Enrollment: 430 .... (330) 325-2511
Housing: Homeownership rate: 78.7% (2000); Median home value: $125,900 (2000); Median rent: $513 per month (2000); Median age of housing: 32 years (2000).
Transportation: Commute to work: 96.3% car, 0.0% public transportation, 0.6% walk, 3.1% work from home (2000); Travel time to work: 28.5% less than 15 minutes, 35.5% 15 to 30 minutes, 24.8% 30 to 45 minutes, 6.4% 45 to 60 minutes, 4.7% 60 minutes or more (2000)
Additional Information Contacts
Rootstown Area Chamber of Commerce .... (330) 325-2379
 http://www.rootstownchamber.org

STREETSBORO
(city). Covers a land area of 24.017 square miles and a water area of 0.362 square miles. Located at 41.24° N. Lat.; 81.34° W. Long. Elevation is 1,137 feet.
History: Streetsboro was settled in 1822 and named for Titus Street, original owner of the land.
Population: 9,932 (1990); 12,311 (2000); 14,559 (2005); 16,626 (2010 projected); Race: 93.7% White, 2.6% Black, 2.3% Asian, 0.9% Hispanic of any race (2005); Density: 606.2 persons per square mile (2005); Average household size: 2.45 (2005); Median age: 36.1 (2005); Males per 100 females: 96.7 (2005); Marriage status: 22.6% never married, 60.1% now married, 5.3% widowed, 12.0% divorced (2000); Foreign born: 2.3% (2000); Ancestry (includes multiple ancestries): 27.8% German, 15.9% Irish, 11.5% Italian, 9.6% Polish, 9.0% English (2000).
Economy: Single-family building permits issued: 89 (2005); Multi-family building permits issued: 0 (2005); Employment by occupation: 11.9% management, 17.2% professional, 11.5% services, 25.6% sales, 0.1% farming, 8.7% construction, 25.1% production (2000).
Income: Per capita income: $24,927 (2005); Median household income: $53,761 (2005); Average household income: $60,835 (2005); Percent of households with income of $100,000 or more: 12.3% (2005); Poverty rate: 5.3% (2000).
Education: Percent of population age 25 and over with: High school diploma (including GED) or higher: 86.7% (2005); Bachelor's degree or higher: 20.0% (2005); Master's degree or higher: 4.8% (2005).
School District(s)
Streetsboro City Schools (PK-12)
 2003-04 Enrollment: 2,087 .... (330) 626-4900
Housing: Homeownership rate: 69.5% (2005); Median home value: $135,976 (2005); Median rent: $580 per month (2000); Median age of housing: 20 years (2000).
Safety: Violent crime rate: 7.9 per 10,000 population; Property crime rate: 323.5 per 10,000 population (2004).
Transportation: Commute to work: 97.5% car, 0.3% public transportation, 0.9% walk, 1.2% work from home (2000); Travel time to work: 27.2% less than 15 minutes, 38.7% 15 to 30 minutes, 21.6% 30 to 45 minutes, 8.7% 45 to 60 minutes, 3.8% 60 minutes or more (2000)
Additional Information Contacts
Streetsboro Chamber of Commerce .... (330) 626-4769
 http://www.streetsborochamber.org
Streetsboro Visitors and Convention Bureau .... (330) 422-1770
 http://www.streetsborovcb.com

SUGAR BUSH KNOLLS
(village). Covers a land area of 0.228 square miles and a water area of 0.014 square miles. Located at 41.20° N. Lat.; 81.34° W. Long. Elevation is 1,100 feet.
Population: 211 (1990); 227 (2000); 302 (2005); 371 (2010 projected); Race: 98.7% White, 0.0% Black, 0.7% Asian, 0.7% Hispanic of any race (2005); Density: 1,324.5 persons per square mile (2005); Average household size: 2.82 (2005); Median age: 47.2 (2005); Males per 100 females: 102.7 (2005); Marriage status: 26.1% never married, 65.9% now married, 3.4% widowed, 4.5% divorced (2000); Foreign born: 6.2% (2000); Ancestry (includes multiple ancestries): 22.3% Irish, 21.3% German, 17.1% Italian, 13.7% English, 4.7% Slovene (2000).
Economy: Employment by occupation: 20.8% management, 31.7% professional, 2.5% services, 32.5% sales, 0.0% farming, 3.3% construction, 9.2% production (2000).
Income: Per capita income: $61,432 (2005); Median household income: $140,789 (2005); Average household income: $173,388 (2005); Percent of households with income of $100,000 or more: 64.5% (2005); Poverty rate: 2.8% (2000).
Education: Percent of population age 25 and over with: High school diploma (including GED) or higher: 96.6% (2005); Bachelor's degree or higher: 63.0% (2005); Master's degree or higher: 35.1% (2005).
Housing: Homeownership rate: 99.1% (2005); Median home value: $279,310 (2005); Median rent: $425 per month (2000); Median age of housing: 24 years (2000).
Transportation: Commute to work: 94.1% car, 0.0% public transportation, 0.0% walk, 3.4% work from home (2000); Travel time to work: 23.7% less than 15 minutes, 48.2% 15 to 30 minutes, 14.0% 30 to 45 minutes, 8.8% 45 to 60 minutes, 5.3% 60 minutes or more (2000)

WINDHAM
(village). Covers a land area of 2.124 square miles and a water area of 0 square miles. Located at 41.23° N. Lat.; 81.03° W. Long. Elevation is 970 feet.
Population: 2,943 (1990); 2,806 (2000); 2,780 (2005); 2,788 (2010 projected); Race: 91.8% White, 5.8% Black, 0.1% Asian, 0.4% Hispanic of any race (2005); Density: 1,309.1 persons per square mile (2005); Average household size: 2.86 (2005); Median age: 29.5 (2005); Males per 100 females: 89.4 (2005); Marriage status: 28.3% never married, 48.2% now married, 6.6% widowed, 16.9% divorced (2000); Foreign born: 0.3% (2000); Ancestry (includes multiple ancestries): 21.2% United States or American, 18.8% German, 14.9% Irish, 9.6% Other groups, 9.3% English (2000).
Economy: In agricultural area. Employment by occupation: 3.5% management, 8.0% professional, 16.9% services, 19.4% sales, 0.7% farming, 10.3% construction, 41.3% production (2000).
Income: Per capita income: $12,759 (2005); Median household income: $32,937 (2005); Average household income: $36,529 (2005); Percent of households with income of $100,000 or more: 3.5% (2005); Poverty rate: 23.8% (2000).
Education: Percent of population age 25 and over with: High school diploma (including GED) or higher: 75.4% (2005); Bachelor's degree or higher: 3.2% (2005); Master's degree or higher: 0.8% (2005).

School District(s)
Windham Ex Vill SD (PK-12)
  2003-04 Enrollment: 1,093 . . . . (330) 326-2711
Housing: Homeownership rate: 48.6% (2005); Median home value: $91,503 (2005); Median rent: $319 per month (2000); Median age of housing: 51 years (2000).
Safety: Violent crime rate: 43.3 per 10,000 population; Property crime rate: 613.3 per 10,000 population (2004).
Transportation: Commute to work: 95.7% car, 0.0% public transportation, 1.2% walk, 1.9% work from home (2000); Travel time to work: 19.9% less than 15 minutes, 26.6% 15 to 30 minutes, 32.1% 30 to 45 minutes, 12.4% 45 to 60 minutes, 9.0% 60 minutes or more (2000)

Preble County

Located in western Ohio; bounded on the west by Indiana; drained by the East Fork of the Whitewater River. Covers a land area of 424.80 square miles, a water area of 1.52 square miles, and is located in the Eastern Time Zone. The county government was organized in 1808. County seat is Eaton.

Preble County is part of the Dayton, OH Metropolitan Statistical Area. The entire metro area includes: Greene County, OH; Miami County, OH; Montgomery County, OH; Preble County, OH

Weather Station: Eaton   Elevation: 1,000 feet

	Jan	Feb	Mar	Apr	May	Jun	Jul	Aug	Sep	Oct	Nov	Dec
High	33	38	49	61	72	81	85	83	77	65	51	39
Low	15	18	28	37	48	57	61	59	52	39	31	22
Precip	2.5	2.2	3.3	4.1	4.6	3.8	3.7	3.4	2.6	2.7	3.4	3.0
Snow	na	na	na	0.5	0.0	0.0	0.0	0.0	0.0	0.0	tr	na

High and Low temperatures in degrees Fahrenheit; Precipitation and Snow in inches

Population: 40,113 (1990); 42,337 (2000); 42,412 (2005); 42,474 (2010 projected); Race: 98.3% White, 0.4% Black, 0.4% Asian, 0.5% Hispanic of any race (2005); Density: 99.8 persons per square mile (2005); Average household size: 2.60 (2005); Median age: 38.8 (2005); Males per 100 females: 99.2 (2005).
Religion: Five largest groups: 7.1% Southern Baptist Convention, 5.6% Catholic Church, 5.2% The United Methodist Church, 4.9% Evangelical Lutheran Church in America, 3.9% Church of the Brethren (2000).
Economy: Unemployment rate: 5.9% (2005); Total civilian labor force: 21,661 (2005); Leading industries: 37.3% manufacturing; 15.7% retail trade; 10.1% health care and social assistance (2004); Farms: 1,065 totaling 198,048 acres (2002); Companies that employ 500 or more persons: 1 (2004); Companies that employ 100 to 499 persons: 15 (2004); Companies that employ less than 100 persons: 711 (2004); Black-owned businesses: n/a (2002); Hispanic-owned businesses: n/a (2002); Women-owned businesses: n/a (2002); Retail sales per capita: $9,496 (2006). Single-family building permits issued: 97 (2005); Multi-family building permits issued: 12 (2005).
Income: Per capita income: $20,681 (2005); Median household income: $46,456 (2005); Average household income: $53,441 (2005); Percent of households with income of $100,000 or more: 8.9% (2005); Poverty rate: 7.5% (2003); Bankruptcy rate: 10.72% (2005).
Education: Percent of population age 25 and over with: High school diploma (including GED) or higher: 81.6% (2005); Bachelor's degree or higher: 10.0% (2005); Master's degree or higher: 3.5% (2005).
Housing: Homeownership rate: 79.1% (2005); Median home value: $121,201 (2005); Median rent: $368 per month (2000); Median age of housing: 37 years (2000).
Health: Birth rate: 107.0 per 10,000 population (2004); Death rate: 88.0 per 10,000 population (2004); Age-adjusted cancer mortality rate: 217.3 deaths per 100,000 population (2002); Air Quality Index: 63.0% good, 35.1% moderate, 1.9% unhealthy for sensitive individuals, 0.0% unhealthy (percent of days in 2005); Number of physicians: 4.7 per 10,000 population (2004); Hospital beds: 0.0 per 10,000 population (2003); Hospital admissions: 0.0 per 10,000 population (2003).
Elections: 2004 Presidential election results: 65.0% Bush, 34.4% Kerry, 0.0% Nader, 0.3% Badnarik.
National and State Parks: Fort Saint Clair State Park; Hueston Woods State Park
Additional Information Contacts
Preble County Government . . . . (937) 456-8143
  http://www.preblecounty.com/
Eaton-Preble County Chamber . . . . (937) 456-4949
  http://preblecountyohio.com

Preble County Communities

CAMDEN (village). Covers a land area of 1.231 square miles and a water area of 0 square miles. Located at 39.63° N. Lat.; 84.64° W. Long. Elevation is 840 feet.
Population: 2,210 (1990); 2,302 (2000); 2,209 (2005); 2,187 (2010 projected); Race: 98.1% White, 0.8% Black, 0.2% Asian, 0.6% Hispanic of any race (2005); Density: 1,794.5 persons per square mile (2005); Average household size: 2.50 (2005); Median age: 33.3 (2005); Males per 100 females: 91.1 (2005); Marriage status: 17.0% never married, 56.9% now married, 9.8% widowed, 16.2% divorced (2000); Foreign born: 0.0% (2000); Ancestry (includes multiple ancestries): 28.5% United States or American, 13.9% German, 6.6% Irish, 6.3% English, 5.8% Other groups (2000).
Economy: Employment by occupation: 8.1% management, 9.8% professional, 18.7% services, 21.6% sales, 0.6% farming, 12.0% construction, 29.1% production (2000).
Income: Per capita income: $16,029 (2005); Median household income: $34,305 (2005); Average household income: $40,099 (2005); Percent of households with income of $100,000 or more: 2.8% (2005); Poverty rate: 9.1% (2000).
Education: Percent of population age 25 and over with: High school diploma (including GED) or higher: 69.7% (2005); Bachelor's degree or higher: 4.7% (2005); Master's degree or higher: 1.4% (2005).
School District(s)
Preble Shawnee Local SD (PK-12)
  2003-04 Enrollment: 1,667 . . . . (937) 452-3323
Housing: Homeownership rate: 69.4% (2005); Median home value: $80,738 (2005); Median rent: $354 per month (2000); Median age of housing: 33 years (2000).
Transportation: Commute to work: 94.5% car, 0.0% public transportation, 1.6% walk, 3.9% work from home (2000); Travel time to work: 20.0% less than 15 minutes, 39.5% 15 to 30 minutes, 20.3% 30 to 45 minutes, 12.7% 45 to 60 minutes, 7.5% 60 minutes or more (2000)

COLLEGE CORNER (village). Covers a land area of 0.266 square miles and a water area of 0 square miles. Located at 39.56° N. Lat.; 84.81° W. Long. Elevation is 1,010 feet.
Population: 472 (1990); 424 (2000); 418 (2005); 420 (2010 projected); Race: 98.8% White, 0.2% Black, 0.0% Asian, 0.0% Hispanic of any race (2005); Density: 1,569.9 persons per square mile (2005); Average household size: 2.04 (2005); Median age: 34.4 (2005); Males per 100 females: 106.9 (2005); Marriage status: 23.8% never married, 63.0% now married, 5.1% widowed, 8.0% divorced (2000); Foreign born: 0.0% (2000); Ancestry (includes multiple ancestries): 21.7% German, 13.5% United States or American, 13.2% English, 11.8% Irish, 7.1% Other groups (2000).
Economy: Employment by occupation: 7.0% management, 11.4% professional, 23.1% services, 35.4% sales, 0.0% farming, 11.8% construction, 11.4% production (2000).
Income: Per capita income: $21,130 (2005); Median household income: $38,750 (2005); Average household income: $43,085 (2005); Percent of households with income of $100,000 or more: 4.4% (2005); Poverty rate: 8.8% (2000).
Education: Percent of population age 25 and over with: High school diploma (including GED) or higher: 83.3% (2005); Bachelor's degree or higher: 12.4% (2005); Master's degree or higher: 3.9% (2005).
School District(s)
College Corner Local SD (KG-12)
  2003-04 Enrollment: 136 . . . . (765) 732-3183
Housing: Homeownership rate: 55.1% (2005); Median home value: $89,459 (2005); Median rent: $413 per month (2000); Median age of housing: 60+ years (2000).
Transportation: Commute to work: 91.6% car, 0.0% public transportation, 1.4% walk, 5.6% work from home (2000); Travel time to work: 44.1% less than 15 minutes, 31.2% 15 to 30 minutes, 7.9% 30 to 45 minutes, 6.4% 45 to 60 minutes, 10.4% 60 minutes or more (2000)

EATON (city). Covers a land area of 5.671 square miles and a water area of 0.008 square miles. Located at 39.74° N. Lat.; 84.63° W. Long. Elevation is 1,046 feet.

History: Eaton was founded in 1806 and named for General William Eaton, who served in the Tripolitan War of 1805.
Population: 7,407 (1990); 8,133 (2000); 8,123 (2005); 8,140 (2010 projected); Race: 98.0% White, 0.4% Black, 0.7% Asian, 0.6% Hispanic of any race (2005); Density: 1,432.5 persons per square mile (2005); Average household size: 2.45 (2005); Median age: 38.9 (2005); Males per 100 females: 90.8 (2005); Marriage status: 21.4% never married, 55.0% now married, 9.2% widowed, 14.4% divorced (2000); Foreign born: 1.5% (2000); Ancestry (includes multiple ancestries): 26.0% German, 11.1% United States or American, 9.4% Irish, 8.7% English, 6.9% Other groups (2000).
Economy: Single-family building permits issued: 20 (2005); Multi-family building permits issued: 12 (2005); Employment by occupation: 11.1% management, 13.1% professional, 14.7% services, 20.7% sales, 0.5% farming, 10.1% construction, 29.8% production (2000).
Income: Per capita income: $18,505 (2005); Median household income: $39,875 (2005); Average household income: $44,265 (2005); Percent of households with income of $100,000 or more: 4.3% (2005); Poverty rate: 8.7% (2000).
Education: Percent of population age 25 and over with: High school diploma (including GED) or higher: 79.5% (2005); Bachelor's degree or higher: 10.4% (2005); Master's degree or higher: 3.8% (2005).

School District(s)
Eaton Community Schools (PK-12)
    2003-04 Enrollment: 2,334 . . . . (937) 456-1107

Housing: Homeownership rate: 67.4% (2005); Median home value: $99,877 (2005); Median rent: $367 per month (2000); Median age of housing: 37 years (2000).
Safety: Violent crime rate: 8.6 per 10,000 population; Property crime rate: 431.2 per 10,000 population (2004).
Newspapers: Register Herald (General - Circulation 6,800)
Transportation: Commute to work: 94.2% car, 1.1% public transportation, 2.5% walk, 2.2% work from home (2000); Travel time to work: 48.3% less than 15 minutes, 20.6% 15 to 30 minutes, 14.4% 30 to 45 minutes, 8.6% 45 to 60 minutes, 8.0% 60 minutes or more (2000)
Additional Information Contacts
Eaton-Preble County Chamber . . . . (937) 456-4949
    http://preblecountyohio.com

ELDORADO (village). Covers a land area of 0.229 square miles and a water area of 0 square miles. Located at 39.90° N. Lat.; 84.67° W. Long. Elevation is 1,143 feet.
Population: 549 (1990); 543 (2000); 530 (2005); 526 (2010 projected); Race: 99.8% White, 0.0% Black, 0.0% Asian, 0.4% Hispanic of any race (2005); Density: 2,318.9 persons per square mile (2005); Average household size: 2.52 (2005); Median age: 35.8 (2005); Males per 100 females: 94.9 (2005); Marriage status: 17.7% never married, 64.5% now married, 8.1% widowed, 9.6% divorced (2000); Foreign born: 0.0% (2000); Ancestry (includes multiple ancestries): 28.0% German, 14.1% United States or American, 11.2% Irish, 8.5% English, 6.0% Other groups (2000).
Economy: Employment by occupation: 8.3% management, 9.4% professional, 15.9% services, 24.6% sales, 1.4% farming, 3.3% construction, 37.0% production (2000).
Income: Per capita income: $19,580 (2005); Median household income: $44,796 (2005); Average household income: $49,417 (2005); Percent of households with income of $100,000 or more: 7.1% (2005); Poverty rate: 2.3% (2000).
Education: Percent of population age 25 and over with: High school diploma (including GED) or higher: 85.6% (2005); Bachelor's degree or higher: 7.3% (2005); Master's degree or higher: 2.3% (2005).
Housing: Homeownership rate: 81.9% (2005); Median home value: $88,571 (2005); Median rent: $375 per month (2000); Median age of housing: 47 years (2000).
Transportation: Commute to work: 98.9% car, 0.0% public transportation, 0.4% walk, 0.7% work from home (2000); Travel time to work: 21.5% less than 15 minutes, 42.6% 15 to 30 minutes, 23.0% 30 to 45 minutes, 10.0% 45 to 60 minutes, 3.0% 60 minutes or more (2000)

GRATIS (village). Covers a land area of 0.944 square miles and a water area of 0 square miles. Located at 39.64° N. Lat.; 84.52° W. Long. Elevation is 876 feet.
Population: 998 (1990); 934 (2000); 909 (2005); 896 (2010 projected); Race: 99.1% White, 0.1% Black, 0.0% Asian, 0.6% Hispanic of any race (2005); Density: 962.7 persons per square mile (2005); Average household size: 2.62 (2005); Median age: 35.2 (2005); Males per 100 females: 107.5

(2005); Marriage status: 21.5% never married, 65.8% now married, 5.2% widowed, 7.4% divorced (2000); Foreign born: 0.0% (2000); Ancestry (includes multiple ancestries): 20.0% German, 14.8% United States or American, 9.4% Irish, 6.1% English, 5.8% Other groups (2000).
Economy: Employment by occupation: 9.4% management, 8.5% professional, 16.3% services, 16.7% sales, 0.0% farming, 17.9% construction, 31.2% production (2000).
Income: Per capita income: $18,538 (2005); Median household income: $40,369 (2005); Average household income: $48,393 (2005); Percent of households with income of $100,000 or more: 7.8% (2005); Poverty rate: 11.0% (2000).
Education: Percent of population age 25 and over with: High school diploma (including GED) or higher: 77.7% (2005); Bachelor's degree or higher: 2.8% (2005); Master's degree or higher: 0.7% (2005).
Housing: Homeownership rate: 82.1% (2005); Median home value: $98,387 (2005); Median rent: $393 per month (2000); Median age of housing: 35 years (2000).
Transportation: Commute to work: 97.2% car, 0.0% public transportation, 0.5% walk, 1.9% work from home (2000); Travel time to work: 13.3% less than 15 minutes, 31.4% 15 to 30 minutes, 28.3% 30 to 45 minutes, 21.9% 45 to 60 minutes, 5.0% 60 minutes or more (2000)

LEWISBURG (village). Covers a land area of 1.078 square miles and a water area of 0 square miles. Located at 39.84° N. Lat.; 84.54° W. Long. Elevation is 1,000 feet.
History: Lewisburg developed as a rural trade center. Tobacco was once a leading crop here.
Population: 1,865 (1990); 1,798 (2000); 1,745 (2005); 1,726 (2010 projected); Race: 97.9% White, 0.2% Black, 0.8% Asian, 0.4% Hispanic of any race (2005); Density: 1,619.4 persons per square mile (2005); Average household size: 2.60 (2005); Median age: 34.8 (2005); Males per 100 females: 93.0 (2005); Marriage status: 22.0% never married, 61.0% now married, 7.6% widowed, 9.4% divorced (2000); Foreign born: 0.5% (2000); Ancestry (includes multiple ancestries): 30.1% German, 12.8% Irish, 10.3% United States or American, 7.7% English, 7.3% Other groups (2000).
Economy: Employment by occupation: 9.4% management, 12.2% professional, 15.9% services, 20.5% sales, 0.2% farming, 16.7% construction, 25.1% production (2000).
Income: Per capita income: $21,530 (2005); Median household income: $47,295 (2005); Average household income: $56,075 (2005); Percent of households with income of $100,000 or more: 9.4% (2005); Poverty rate: 6.5% (2000).
Education: Percent of population age 25 and over with: High school diploma (including GED) or higher: 84.3% (2005); Bachelor's degree or higher: 9.1% (2005); Master's degree or higher: 2.3% (2005).

School District(s)
Tri-County North Local SD (PK-12)
    2003-04 Enrollment: 1,178 . . . . (937) 962-2671

Housing: Homeownership rate: 72.4% (2005); Median home value: $110,791 (2005); Median rent: $386 per month (2000); Median age of housing: 57 years (2000).
Transportation: Commute to work: 91.1% car, 0.0% public transportation, 6.0% walk, 1.9% work from home (2000); Travel time to work: 38.7% less than 15 minutes, 27.3% 15 to 30 minutes, 23.5% 30 to 45 minutes, 6.8% 45 to 60 minutes, 3.6% 60 minutes or more (2000)

NEW PARIS (village). Covers a land area of 0.714 square miles and a water area of 0.016 square miles. Located at 39.85° N. Lat.; 84.79° W. Long. Elevation is 1,040 feet.
Population: 1,801 (1990); 1,623 (2000); 1,590 (2005); 1,560 (2010 projected); Race: 98.9% White, 0.6% Black, 0.2% Asian, 0.1% Hispanic of any race (2005); Density: 2,225.9 persons per square mile (2005); Average household size: 2.30 (2005); Median age: 37.0 (2005); Males per 100 females: 93.9 (2005); Marriage status: 19.9% never married, 55.1% now married, 8.4% widowed, 16.6% divorced (2000); Foreign born: 0.5% (2000); Ancestry (includes multiple ancestries): 23.0% German, 15.5% United States or American, 10.3% English, 9.8% Irish, 7.5% Other groups (2000).
Economy: Lumber. Employment by occupation: 9.6% management, 8.2% professional, 14.8% services, 24.7% sales, 0.0% farming, 12.0% construction, 30.7% production (2000).
Income: Per capita income: $16,197 (2005); Median household income: $33,387 (2005); Average household income: $37,215 (2005); Percent of households with income of $100,000 or more: 2.5% (2005); Poverty rate: 10.1% (2000).

Education: Percent of population age 25 and over with: High school diploma (including GED) or higher: 75.5% (2005); Bachelor's degree or higher: 3.5% (2005); Master's degree or higher: 1.2% (2005).

School District(s)
National Trail Local SD (PK-12)
    2003-04 Enrollment: 1,155 . . . . (937) 437-3333

Housing: Homeownership rate: 67.6% (2005); Median home value: $65,455 (2005); Median rent: $324 per month (2000); Median age of housing: 44 years (2000).

Transportation: Commute to work: 95.4% car, 0.3% public transportation, 2.6% walk, 0.3% work from home (2000); Travel time to work: 36.1% less than 15 minutes, 46.2% 15 to 30 minutes, 9.9% 30 to 45 minutes, 2.5% 45 to 60 minutes, 5.2% 60 minutes or more (2000)

VERONA (village). Covers a land area of 0.170 square miles and a water area of 0 square miles. Located at 39.90° N. Lat.; 84.48° W. Long. Elevation is 1,020 feet.

Population: 472 (1990); 430 (2000); 425 (2005); 407 (2010 projected); Race: 100.0% White, 0.0% Black, 0.0% Asian, 1.6% Hispanic of any race (2005); Density: 2,499.7 persons per square mile (2005); Average household size: 2.64 (2005); Median age: 34.5 (2005); Males per 100 females: 98.6 (2005); Marriage status: 19.0% never married, 62.7% now married, 5.1% widowed, 13.2% divorced (2000); Foreign born: 0.2% (2000); Ancestry (includes multiple ancestries): 24.7% German, 23.3% United States or American, 12.2% English, 11.1% Irish, 5.3% Dutch (2000).

Economy: Employment by occupation: 3.1% management, 15.5% professional, 10.4% services, 16.6% sales, 0.0% farming, 21.8% construction, 32.6% production (2000).

Income: Per capita income: $17,506 (2005); Median household income: $40,391 (2005); Average household income: $46,211 (2005); Percent of households with income of $100,000 or more: 4.3% (2005); Poverty rate: 8.4% (2000).

Education: Percent of population age 25 and over with: High school diploma (including GED) or higher: 79.4% (2005); Bachelor's degree or higher: 4.2% (2005); Master's degree or higher: 1.1% (2005).

Housing: Homeownership rate: 80.7% (2005); Median home value: $87,273 (2005); Median rent: $323 per month (2000); Median age of housing: 60+ years (2000).

Transportation: Commute to work: 98.4% car, 0.0% public transportation, 0.0% walk, 0.5% work from home (2000); Travel time to work: 17.7% less than 15 minutes, 42.5% 15 to 30 minutes, 24.2% 30 to 45 minutes, 11.3% 45 to 60 minutes, 4.3% 60 minutes or more (2000)

WEST ALEXANDRIA (village). Covers a land area of 0.723 square miles and a water area of 0 square miles. Located at 39.74° N. Lat.; 84.53° W. Long. Elevation is 900 feet.

Population: 1,488 (1990); 1,395 (2000); 1,397 (2005); 1,390 (2010 projected); Race: 98.8% White, 0.6% Black, 0.0% Asian, 0.5% Hispanic of any race (2005); Density: 1,931.8 persons per square mile (2005); Average household size: 2.37 (2005); Median age: 37.5 (2005); Males per 100 females: 100.4 (2005); Marriage status: 24.1% never married, 53.6% now married, 10.5% widowed, 11.8% divorced (2000); Foreign born: 0.4% (2000); Ancestry (includes multiple ancestries): 33.3% German, 15.1% United States or American, 9.4% Irish, 8.4% Other groups, 6.3% English (2000).

Economy: In agricultural area. Employment by occupation: 6.3% management, 14.5% professional, 17.8% services, 26.9% sales, 1.1% farming, 8.8% construction, 24.6% production (2000).

Income: Per capita income: $19,742 (2005); Median household income: $40,805 (2005); Average household income: $46,825 (2005); Percent of households with income of $100,000 or more: 6.5% (2005); Poverty rate: 7.4% (2000).

Education: Percent of population age 25 and over with: High school diploma (including GED) or higher: 83.1% (2005); Bachelor's degree or higher: 13.2% (2005); Master's degree or higher: 6.1% (2005).

School District(s)
Twin Valley Community Local SD (PK-12)
    2003-04 Enrollment: 1,064 . . . . (937) 839-4688

Housing: Homeownership rate: 64.0% (2005); Median home value: $104,215 (2005); Median rent: $404 per month (2000); Median age of housing: 56 years (2000).

Newspapers: The Lewisburg Leader (General - Circulation 1,000); Twin Valley News (General - Circulation 1,000)

Transportation: Commute to work: 93.5% car, 0.4% public transportation, 4.4% walk, 1.7% work from home (2000); Travel time to work: 29.8% less than 15 minutes, 27.6% 15 to 30 minutes, 27.3% 30 to 45 minutes, 10.1% 45 to 60 minutes, 5.2% 60 minutes or more (2000)

WEST ELKTON (village). Covers a land area of 0.506 square miles and a water area of 0 square miles. Located at 39.58° N. Lat.; 84.55° W. Long. Elevation is 1,040 feet.

Population: 154 (1990); 194 (2000); 192 (2005); 188 (2010 projected); Race: 99.0% White, 0.0% Black, 0.0% Asian, 0.5% Hispanic of any race (2005); Density: 379.3 persons per square mile (2005); Average household size: 2.67 (2005); Median age: 36.9 (2005); Males per 100 females: 115.7 (2005); Marriage status: 19.5% never married, 57.5% now married, 6.3% widowed, 16.7% divorced (2000); Foreign born: 0.9% (2000); Ancestry (includes multiple ancestries): 23.6% United States or American, 11.2% German, 7.3% Other groups, 5.6% Irish, 5.6% English (2000).

Economy: In agricultural area. Employment by occupation: 7.4% management, 11.6% professional, 20.0% services, 28.4% sales, 0.0% farming, 15.8% construction, 16.8% production (2000).

Income: Per capita income: $21,888 (2005); Median household income: $47,632 (2005); Average household income: $58,368 (2005); Percent of households with income of $100,000 or more: 16.7% (2005); Poverty rate: 8.2% (2000).

Education: Percent of population age 25 and over with: High school diploma (including GED) or higher: 77.3% (2005); Bachelor's degree or higher: 3.1% (2005); Master's degree or higher: 2.3% (2005).

School District(s)
Preble Shawnee Local SD (PK-12)
    2003-04 Enrollment: 1,667 . . . . (937) 452-3323

Housing: Homeownership rate: 81.9% (2005); Median home value: $113,000 (2005); Median rent: $420 per month (2000); Median age of housing: 60+ years (2000).

Transportation: Commute to work: 94.6% car, 0.0% public transportation, 3.3% walk, 2.2% work from home (2000); Travel time to work: 21.1% less than 15 minutes, 34.4% 15 to 30 minutes, 22.2% 30 to 45 minutes, 10.0% 45 to 60 minutes, 12.2% 60 minutes or more (2000)

WEST MANCHESTER (village). Covers a land area of 0.234 square miles and a water area of 0 square miles. Located at 39.90° N. Lat.; 84.62° W. Long. Elevation is 1,093 feet.

Population: 490 (1990); 433 (2000); 433 (2005); 426 (2010 projected); Race: 99.1% White, 0.0% Black, 0.0% Asian, 1.2% Hispanic of any race (2005); Density: 1,851.7 persons per square mile (2005); Average household size: 2.52 (2005); Median age: 33.2 (2005); Males per 100 females: 101.4 (2005); Marriage status: 21.0% never married, 63.9% now married, 7.2% widowed, 7.8% divorced (2000); Foreign born: 0.0% (2000); Ancestry (includes multiple ancestries): 15.6% Other groups, 14.6% United States or American, 14.3% Irish, 12.8% German, 10.1% English (2000).

Economy: In agricultural area. Employment by occupation: 7.3% management, 13.3% professional, 7.8% services, 22.9% sales, 0.0% farming, 13.8% construction, 34.9% production (2000).

Income: Per capita income: $17,841 (2005); Median household income: $35,051 (2005); Average household income: $44,913 (2005); Percent of households with income of $100,000 or more: 6.4% (2005); Poverty rate: 7.7% (2000).

Education: Percent of population age 25 and over with: High school diploma (including GED) or higher: 83.0% (2005); Bachelor's degree or higher: 8.5% (2005); Master's degree or higher: 3.5% (2005).

Housing: Homeownership rate: 76.2% (2005); Median home value: $83,947 (2005); Median rent: $447 per month (2000); Median age of housing: 60+ years (2000).

Transportation: Commute to work: 93.1% car, 0.0% public transportation, 1.8% walk, 1.8% work from home (2000); Travel time to work: 11.7% less than 15 minutes, 54.9% 15 to 30 minutes, 20.7% 30 to 45 minutes, 8.9% 45 to 60 minutes, 3.8% 60 minutes or more (2000)

Putnam County

Located in northwestern Ohio; crossed by the Auglize and Blanchard Rivers. Covers a land area of 483.87 square miles, a water area of 0.36 square miles, and is located in the Eastern Time Zone. The county government was organized in 1820. County seat is Ottawa.

Weather Station: Pandora — Elevation: 767 feet

	Jan	Feb	Mar	Apr	May	Jun	Jul	Aug	Sep	Oct	Nov	Dec
High	32	36	47	60	72	81	84	82	75	63	49	37
Low	17	20	28	38	49	59	62	60	53	42	33	23
Precip	2.0	1.9	2.7	3.3	3.7	4.0	3.9	3.4	3.0	2.3	2.9	2.7
Snow	9.5	7.1	4.2	1.2	tr	0.0	0.0	0.0	tr	0.1	2.0	6.6

High and Low temperatures in degrees Fahrenheit; Precipitation and Snow in inches

Population: 33,819 (1990); 34,726 (2000); 34,794 (2005); 34,852 (2010 projected); Race: 96.3% White, 0.2% Black, 0.2% Asian, 4.4% Hispanic of any race (2005); Density: 71.9 persons per square mile (2005); Average household size: 2.79 (2005); Median age: 36.3 (2005); Males per 100 females: 98.9 (2005).
Religion: Five largest groups: 62.7% Catholic Church, 7.8% The United Methodist Church, 3.7% Mennonite Church USA, 1.6% Church of the Brethren, 1.0% United Church of Christ (2000).
Economy: Unemployment rate: 5.3% (2005); Total civilian labor force: 17,819 (2005); Leading industries: 28.4% manufacturing; 14.2% health care and social assistance; 13.7% retail trade (2004); Farms: 1,348 totaling 331,517 acres (2002); Companies that employ 500 or more persons: 0 (2004); Companies that employ 100 to 499 persons: 15 (2004); Companies that employ less than 100 persons: 719 (2004); Black-owned businesses: n/a (2002); Hispanic-owned businesses: n/a (2002); Women-owned businesses: 730 (2002); Retail sales per capita: $8,749 (2006); Single-family building permits issued: 102 (2005); Multi-family building permits issued: 0 (2005).
Income: Per capita income: $21,161 (2005); Median household income: $51,009 (2005); Average household income: $58,309 (2005); Percent of households with income of $100,000 or more: 11.3% (2005); Poverty rate: 6.0% (2003); Bankruptcy rate: 4.84% (2005).
Education: Percent of population age 25 and over with: High school diploma (including GED) or higher: 86.2% (2005); Bachelor's degree or higher: 12.9% (2005); Master's degree or higher: 4.0% (2005).
Housing: Homeownership rate: 84.3% (2005); Median home value: $113,183 (2005); Median rent: $340 per month (2000); Median age of housing: 36 years (2000).
Health: Birth rate: 132.8 per 10,000 population (2004); Death rate: 91.0 per 10,000 population (2004); Age-adjusted cancer mortality rate: 169.2 deaths per 100,000 population (2002); Number of physicians: 5.5 per 10,000 population (2004); Hospital beds: 0.0 per 10,000 population (2003); Hospital admissions: 0.0 per 10,000 population (2003).
Elections: 2004 Presidential election results: 76.2% Bush, 23.3% Kerry, 0.0% Nader, 0.2% Badnarik

Additional Information Contacts
Putnam County Government . . . . (419) 523-3656
  http://www.putnamcountyohio.com/
Leipsic Area Chamber of Commerce . . . . (419) 943-2009
  http://www.leipsic.com
Ottawa Chamber of Commerce . . . . (419) 523-3141
  http://www.ottawaohio.us
Ottoville Chamber of Commerce . . . . (419) 453-2426
  http://www.villageofottoville.org
Village of Ottawa . . . . (419) 523-5020
  http://ottawaohio.us/ottawa
Village of Ottoville . . . . (419) 453-2426
  http://www.villageofottoville.org/general.htm

Putnam County Communities

BELMORE
(village). Covers a land area of 0.426 square miles and a water area of 0 square miles. Located at 41.15° N. Lat.; 83.94° W. Long. Elevation is 736 feet.
Population: 161 (1990); 171 (2000); 176 (2005); 176 (2010 projected); Race: 84.1% White, 0.0% Black, 0.6% Asian, 17.6% Hispanic of any race (2005); Density: 413.1 persons per square mile (2005); Average household size: 3.38 (2005); Median age: 30.3 (2005); Males per 100 females: 83.3 (2005); Marriage status: 34.6% never married, 49.6% now married, 9.4% widowed, 6.3% divorced (2000); Foreign born: 0.0% (2000); Ancestry (includes multiple ancestries): 52.0% Other groups, 14.3% German, 12.6% Irish, 4.6% United States or American, 2.9% Pennsylvania German (2000).
Economy: In agricultural region. Employment by occupation: 0.0% management, 2.1% professional, 14.9% services, 6.4% sales, 0.0% farming, 6.4% construction, 70.2% production (2000).
Income: Per capita income: $14,247 (2005); Median household income: $47,857 (2005); Average household income: $48,221 (2005); Percent of households with income of $100,000 or more: 5.8% (2005); Poverty rate: 34.3% (2000).
Education: Percent of population age 25 and over with: High school diploma (including GED) or higher: 68.0% (2005); Bachelor's degree or higher: 0.0% (2005); Master's degree or higher: 0.0% (2005).
Housing: Homeownership rate: 80.8% (2005); Median home value: $33,636 (2005); Median rent: $150 per month (2000); Median age of housing: 60+ years (2000).
Transportation: Commute to work: 95.3% car, 0.0% public transportation, 4.7% walk, 0.0% work from home (2000); Travel time to work: 27.9% less than 15 minutes, 41.9% 15 to 30 minutes, 30.2% 30 to 45 minutes, 0.0% 45 to 60 minutes, 0.0% 60 minutes or more (2000)

CLOVERDALE
(village). Covers a land area of 0.600 square miles and a water area of 0 square miles. Located at 41.02° N. Lat.; 84.30° W. Long. Elevation is 720 feet.
Population: 270 (1990); 201 (2000); 207 (2005); 215 (2010 projected); Race: 99.5% White, 0.0% Black, 0.0% Asian, 0.5% Hispanic of any race (2005); Density: 344.9 persons per square mile (2005); Average household size: 3.00 (2005); Median age: 51.0 (2005); Males per 100 females: 99.0 (2005); Marriage status: 31.6% never married, 50.6% now married, 4.0% widowed, 13.8% divorced (2000); Foreign born: 1.9% (2000); Ancestry (includes multiple ancestries): 30.4% German, 10.1% English, 9.2% United States or American, 5.8% Other groups, 3.4% Dutch (2000).
Economy: In agricultural region. Single-family building permits issued: 0 (2005); Multi-family building permits issued: 0 (2005); Employment by occupation: 0.0% management, 13.0% professional, 20.8% services, 22.1% sales, 0.0% farming, 0.0% construction, 44.2% production (2000).
Income: Per capita income: $18,947 (2005); Median household income: $35,536 (2005); Average household income: $40,109 (2005); Percent of households with income of $100,000 or more: 1.4% (2005); Poverty rate: 19.9% (2000).
Education: Percent of population age 25 and over with: High school diploma (including GED) or higher: 70.6% (2005); Bachelor's degree or higher: 11.8% (2005); Master's degree or higher: 3.3% (2005).
Housing: Homeownership rate: 91.3% (2005); Median home value: $73,529 (2005); Median rent: $n/a per month (2000); Median age of housing: 42 years (2000).
Transportation: Commute to work: 100.0% car, 0.0% public transportation, 0.0% walk, 0.0% work from home (2000); Travel time to work: 29.3% less than 15 minutes, 21.3% 15 to 30 minutes, 41.3% 30 to 45 minutes, 5.3% 45 to 60 minutes, 2.7% 60 minutes or more (2000)

COLUMBUS GROVE
(village). Covers a land area of 1.026 square miles and a water area of 0 square miles. Located at 40.91° N. Lat.; 84.06° W. Long. Elevation is 773 feet.
Population: 2,394 (1990); 2,200 (2000); 2,116 (2005); 2,040 (2010 projected); Race: 97.4% White, 0.0% Black, 0.0% Asian, 3.8% Hispanic of any race (2005); Density: 2,063.0 persons per square mile (2005); Average household size: 2.44 (2005); Median age: 36.0 (2005); Males per 100 females: 91.3 (2005); Marriage status: 23.7% never married, 60.3% now married, 6.8% widowed, 9.2% divorced (2000); Foreign born: 0.5% (2000); Ancestry (includes multiple ancestries): 45.2% German, 12.9% United States or American, 8.1% Irish, 5.8% English, 5.5% Other groups (2000).
Economy: In agricultural area. Single-family building permits issued: 5 (2005); Multi-family building permits issued: 0 (2005); Employment by occupation: 8.6% management, 12.3% professional, 17.5% services, 19.5% sales, 2.0% farming, 10.2% construction, 30.0% production (2000).
Income: Per capita income: $20,691 (2005); Median household income: $45,088 (2005); Average household income: $50,557 (2005); Percent of households with income of $100,000 or more: 6.8% (2005); Poverty rate: 5.3% (2000).
Education: Percent of population age 25 and over with: High school diploma (including GED) or higher: 90.3% (2005); Bachelor's degree or higher: 9.3% (2005); Master's degree or higher: 1.5% (2005).
School District(s)
Columbus Grove Local SD (PK-12)
  2003-04 Enrollment: 861 . . . . (419) 659-2639
Housing: Homeownership rate: 77.9% (2005); Median home value: $91,712 (2005); Median rent: $320 per month (2000); Median age of housing: 47 years (2000).
Newspapers: Putnam County Vidette (General - Circulation 1,400)
Transportation: Commute to work: 95.4% car, 0.0% public transportation, 2.7% walk, 1.3% work from home (2000); Travel time to work: 29.8% less

than 15 minutes, 48.7% 15 to 30 minutes, 16.0% 30 to 45 minutes, 2.2% 45 to 60 minutes, 3.2% 60 minutes or more (2000)

CONTINENTAL (village). Covers a land area of 0.709 square miles and a water area of 0.009 square miles. Located at 41.09° N. Lat.; 84.26° W. Long. Elevation is 723 feet.
Population: 1,239 (1990); 1,188 (2000); 1,199 (2005); 1,213 (2010 projected); Race: 98.3% White, 0.1% Black, 0.1% Asian, 2.3% Hispanic of any race (2005); Density: 1,690.6 persons per square mile (2005); Average household size: 2.41 (2005); Median age: 36.3 (2005); Males per 100 females: 91.2 (2005); Marriage status: 23.3% never married, 57.8% now married, 7.4% widowed, 11.5% divorced (2000); Foreign born: 0.5% (2000); Ancestry (includes multiple ancestries): 29.6% German, 16.2% United States or American, 7.5% Irish, 6.2% English, 5.3% Other groups (2000).
Economy: In diversified agricultural area; food products, tile. Single-family building permits issued: 3 (2005); Multi-family building permits issued: 0 (2005); Employment by occupation: 3.7% management, 11.6% professional, 16.6% services, 16.8% sales, 0.7% farming, 11.6% construction, 38.8% production (2000).
Income: Per capita income: $16,731 (2005); Median household income: $36,096 (2005); Average household income: $40,362 (2005); Percent of households with income of $100,000 or more: 2.0% (2005); Poverty rate: 9.3% (2000).
Education: Percent of population age 25 and over with: High school diploma (including GED) or higher: 79.6% (2005); Bachelor's degree or higher: 6.4% (2005); Master's degree or higher: 3.1% (2005).
School District(s)
Continental Local SD (PK-12)
    2003-04 Enrollment: 740 . . . . (419) 596-3671
Housing: Homeownership rate: 76.1% (2005); Median home value: $72,394 (2005); Median rent: $302 per month (2000); Median age of housing: 39 years (2000).
Newspapers: Continental News Review (General - Circulation 1,000)
Transportation: Commute to work: 96.8% car, 0.2% public transportation, 0.7% walk, 0.6% work from home (2000); Travel time to work: 31.6% less than 15 minutes, 45.8% 15 to 30 minutes, 13.0% 30 to 45 minutes, 5.3% 45 to 60 minutes, 4.3% 60 minutes or more (2000)

DUPONT (village). Covers a land area of 0.931 square miles and a water area of 0 square miles. Located at 41.05° N. Lat.; 84.30° W. Long. Elevation is 725 feet.
Population: 279 (1990); 268 (2000); 283 (2005); 299 (2010 projected); Race: 96.5% White, 2.8% Black, 0.0% Asian, 3.9% Hispanic of any race (2005); Density: 303.9 persons per square mile (2005); Average household size: 2.83 (2005); Median age: 31.4 (2005); Males per 100 females: 100.7 (2005); Marriage status: 27.6% never married, 57.5% now married, 5.0% widowed, 9.9% divorced (2000); Foreign born: 0.5% (2000); Ancestry (includes multiple ancestries): 25.9% German, 8.5% Irish, 7.3% United States or American, 5.4% English, 3.1% French (except Basque) (2000).
Economy: Employment by occupation: 7.7% management, 9.9% professional, 18.7% services, 6.6% sales, 2.2% farming, 8.8% construction, 46.2% production (2000).
Income: Per capita income: $14,859 (2005); Median household income: $36,731 (2005); Average household income: $42,050 (2005); Percent of households with income of $100,000 or more: 4.0% (2005); Poverty rate: 7.7% (2000).
Education: Percent of population age 25 and over with: High school diploma (including GED) or higher: 75.0% (2005); Bachelor's degree or higher: 5.5% (2005); Master's degree or higher: 1.8% (2005).
Housing: Homeownership rate: 82.0% (2005); Median home value: $59,702 (2005); Median rent: $265 per month (2000); Median age of housing: 39 years (2000).
Transportation: Commute to work: 98.9% car, 0.0% public transportation, 1.1% walk, 0.0% work from home (2000); Travel time to work: 29.7% less than 15 minutes, 46.2% 15 to 30 minutes, 19.8% 30 to 45 minutes, 4.4% 45 to 60 minutes, 0.0% 60 minutes or more (2000)

FORT JENNINGS (village). Covers a land area of 0.507 square miles and a water area of 0 square miles. Located at 40.90° N. Lat.; 84.29° W. Long. Elevation is 750 feet.
Population: 436 (1990); 432 (2000); 488 (2005); 536 (2010 projected); Race: 99.6% White, 0.4% Black, 0.0% Asian, 0.0% Hispanic of any race (2005); Density: 962.7 persons per square mile (2005); Average household size: 2.48 (2005); Median age: 39.3 (2005); Males per 100 females: 98.4 (2005); Marriage status: 18.2% never married, 66.6% now married, 8.9% widowed, 6.3% divorced (2000); Foreign born: 0.0% (2000); Ancestry (includes multiple ancestries): 75.2% German, 6.0% Irish, 5.0% United States or American, 3.2% French (except Basque), 1.3% Other groups (2000).
Economy: Single-family building permits issued: 1 (2005); Multi-family building permits issued: 0 (2005); Employment by occupation: 7.5% management, 20.5% professional, 10.5% services, 23.4% sales, 0.8% farming, 11.3% construction, 25.9% production (2000).
Income: Per capita income: $23,489 (2005); Median household income: $48,245 (2005); Average household income: $58,185 (2005); Percent of households with income of $100,000 or more: 10.7% (2005); Poverty rate: 1.5% (2000).
Education: Percent of population age 25 and over with: High school diploma (including GED) or higher: 90.9% (2005); Bachelor's degree or higher: 12.5% (2005); Master's degree or higher: 2.8% (2005).
School District(s)
Jennings Local SD (PK-12)
    2003-04 Enrollment: 461 . . . . (419) 286-2238
Housing: Homeownership rate: 89.8% (2005); Median home value: $92,295 (2005); Median rent: $404 per month (2000); Median age of housing: 37 years (2000).
Transportation: Commute to work: 97.0% car, 0.0% public transportation, 2.1% walk, 0.8% work from home (2000); Travel time to work: 33.8% less than 15 minutes, 31.2% 15 to 30 minutes, 25.6% 30 to 45 minutes, 6.0% 45 to 60 minutes, 3.4% 60 minutes or more (2000)

GILBOA (village). Covers a land area of 0.149 square miles and a water area of 0 square miles. Located at 41.01° N. Lat.; 83.92° W. Long. Elevation is 750 feet.
Population: 208 (1990); 170 (2000); 160 (2005); 157 (2010 projected); Race: 98.8% White, 0.0% Black, 0.0% Asian, 0.6% Hispanic of any race (2005); Density: 1,072.3 persons per square mile (2005); Average household size: 2.32 (2005); Median age: 38.7 (2005); Males per 100 females: 113.3 (2005); Marriage status: 28.0% never married, 53.0% now married, 9.1% widowed, 9.8% divorced (2000); Foreign born: 0.0% (2000); Ancestry (includes multiple ancestries): 46.2% German, 11.0% United States or American, 8.1% Irish, 8.1% Swiss, 7.5% English (2000).
Economy: Employment by occupation: 2.4% management, 10.8% professional, 8.4% services, 20.5% sales, 0.0% farming, 8.4% construction, 49.4% production (2000).
Income: Per capita income: $17,234 (2005); Median household income: $34,000 (2005); Average household income: $39,964 (2005); Percent of households with income of $100,000 or more: 1.4% (2005); Poverty rate: 5.2% (2000).
Education: Percent of population age 25 and over with: High school diploma (including GED) or higher: 75.0% (2005); Bachelor's degree or higher: 8.0% (2005); Master's degree or higher: 2.7% (2005).
School District(s)
Pandora-Gilboa Local SD (PK-12)
    2003-04 Enrollment: 599 . . . . (419) 384-3227
Housing: Homeownership rate: 75.4% (2005); Median home value: $65,333 (2005); Median rent: $363 per month (2000); Median age of housing: 60+ years (2000).
Transportation: Commute to work: 96.4% car, 0.0% public transportation, 0.0% walk, 0.0% work from home (2000); Travel time to work: 47.0% less than 15 minutes, 36.1% 15 to 30 minutes, 9.6% 30 to 45 minutes, 4.8% 45 to 60 minutes, 2.4% 60 minutes or more (2000)

GLANDORF (village). Covers a land area of 1.533 square miles and a water area of 0 square miles. Located at 41.03° N. Lat.; 84.07° W. Long. Elevation is 730 feet.
Population: 829 (1990); 919 (2000); 810 (2005); 780 (2010 projected); Race: 98.6% White, 0.0% Black, 0.2% Asian, 1.4% Hispanic of any race (2005); Density: 528.3 persons per square mile (2005); Average household size: 3.16 (2005); Median age: 40.5 (2005); Males per 100 females: 91.5 (2005); Marriage status: 18.8% never married, 70.5% now married, 7.4% widowed, 3.3% divorced (2000); Foreign born: 0.3% (2000); Ancestry (includes multiple ancestries): 77.5% German, 5.2% Irish, 4.6% United States or American, 3.4% English, 2.5% French (except Basque) (2000).
Economy: Single-family building permits issued: 7 (2005); Multi-family building permits issued: 0 (2005); Employment by occupation: 10.5% management, 14.9% professional, 13.3% services, 24.9% sales, 0.0% farming, 12.3% construction, 24.1% production (2000).

Income: Per capita income: $21,741 (2005); Median household income: $58,621 (2005); Average household income: $63,682 (2005); Percent of households with income of $100,000 or more: 14.1% (2005); Poverty rate: 0.4% (2000).
Education: Percent of population age 25 and over with: High school diploma (including GED) or higher: 82.7% (2005); Bachelor's degree or higher: 16.9% (2005); Master's degree or higher: 5.0% (2005).

School District(s)
Ottawa-Glandorf Local SD (PK-12)
  2003-04 Enrollment: 1,731 .... (419) 523-5261
Housing: Homeownership rate: 92.6% (2005); Median home value: $125,735 (2005); Median rent: $320 per month (2000); Median age of housing: 41 years (2000).
Transportation: Commute to work: 96.0% car, 0.7% public transportation, 2.4% walk, 0.9% work from home (2000); Travel time to work: 51.5% less than 15 minutes, 15.2% 15 to 30 minutes, 25.5% 30 to 45 minutes, 4.3% 45 to 60 minutes, 3.6% 60 minutes or more (2000).

KALIDA (village). Covers a land area of 1.115 square miles and a water area of 0 square miles. Located at 40.98° N. Lat.; 84.19° W. Long. Elevation is 727 feet.
Population: 1,044 (1990); 1,031 (2000); 1,101 (2005); 1,143 (2010 projected); Race: 99.1% White, 0.0% Black, 0.0% Asian, 0.9% Hispanic of any race (2005); Density: 987.2 persons per square mile (2005); Average household size: 2.61 (2005); Median age: 35.4 (2005); Males per 100 females: 102.8 (2005); Marriage status: 22.9% never married, 64.3% now married, 8.7% widowed, 4.1% divorced (2000); Foreign born: 0.4% (2000); Ancestry (includes multiple ancestries): 72.7% German, 7.7% United States or American, 5.1% Irish, 3.2% Other groups, 2.6% English (2000).
Economy: Livestock; grain. Single-family building permits issued: 10 (2005); Multi-family building permits issued: 0 (2005); Employment by occupation: 12.6% management, 19.8% professional, 11.4% services, 25.3% sales, 0.0% farming, 10.3% construction, 20.6% production (2000).
Income: Per capita income: $25,886 (2005); Median household income: $59,048 (2005); Average household income: $67,536 (2005); Percent of households with income of $100,000 or more: 17.1% (2005); Poverty rate: 4.4% (2000).
Education: Percent of population age 25 and over with: High school diploma (including GED) or higher: 87.2% (2005); Bachelor's degree or higher: 18.5% (2005); Master's degree or higher: 6.0% (2005).

School District(s)
Kalida Local SD (PK-12)
  2003-04 Enrollment: 740 .... (419) 532-3534
Housing: Homeownership rate: 79.9% (2005); Median home value: $119,444 (2005); Median rent: $433 per month (2000); Median age of housing: 31 years (2000).
Transportation: Commute to work: 95.5% car, 0.4% public transportation, 3.2% walk, 0.4% work from home (2000); Travel time to work: 41.4% less than 15 minutes, 26.3% 15 to 30 minutes, 22.9% 30 to 45 minutes, 4.3% 45 to 60 minutes, 5.0% 60 minutes or more (2000).

LEIPSIC (village). Covers a land area of 3.225 square miles and a water area of 0 square miles. Located at 41.10° N. Lat.; 83.98° W. Long. Elevation is 766 feet.
Population: 2,296 (1990); 2,236 (2000); 2,138 (2005); 2,100 (2010 projected); Race: 80.4% White, 0.5% Black, 0.5% Asian, 22.7% Hispanic of any race (2005); Density: 663.0 persons per square mile (2005); Average household size: 2.67 (2005); Median age: 39.0 (2005); Males per 100 females: 89.9 (2005); Marriage status: 23.6% never married, 54.6% now married, 14.4% widowed, 7.4% divorced (2000); Foreign born: 1.9% (2000); Ancestry (includes multiple ancestries): 32.1% German, 25.2% Other groups, 13.8% United States or American, 4.6% English, 4.3% French (except Basque) (2000).
Economy: In grain-growing area; food and dairy products, clay and cement products. Single-family building permits issued: 2 (2005); Multi-family building permits issued: 0 (2005); Employment by occupation: 3.0% management, 9.2% professional, 22.3% services, 20.2% sales, 1.4% farming, 7.4% construction, 36.5% production (2000).
Income: Per capita income: $18,517 (2005); Median household income: $40,534 (2005); Average household income: $47,843 (2005); Percent of households with income of $100,000 or more: 6.0% (2005); Poverty rate: 14.7% (2000).
Education: Percent of population age 25 and over with: High school diploma (including GED) or higher: 80.4% (2005); Bachelor's degree or higher: 7.8% (2005); Master's degree or higher: 3.1% (2005).

School District(s)
Leipsic Local SD (PK-12)
  2003-04 Enrollment: 686 .... (419) 943-2165
Housing: Homeownership rate: 74.2% (2005); Median home value: $83,243 (2005); Median rent: $377 per month (2000); Median age of housing: 53 years (2000).
Transportation: Commute to work: 92.5% car, 0.4% public transportation, 5.6% walk, 0.5% work from home (2000); Travel time to work: 41.5% less than 15 minutes, 31.2% 15 to 30 minutes, 17.7% 30 to 45 minutes, 7.3% 45 to 60 minutes, 2.3% 60 minutes or more (2000).
Additional Information Contacts
Leipsic Area Chamber of Commerce.................. (419) 943-2009
  http://www.leipsic.com

MILLER CITY (village). Aka Millers City. Covers a land area of 0.118 square miles and a water area of 0 square miles. Located at 41.10° N. Lat.; 84.13° W. Long. Elevation is 732 feet.
Population: 186 (1990); 136 (2000); 139 (2005); 141 (2010 projected); Race: 94.2% White, 0.0% Black, 0.0% Asian, 7.2% Hispanic of any race (2005); Density: 1,177.7 persons per square mile (2005); Average household size: 2.57 (2005); Median age: 34.8 (2005); Males per 100 females: 98.6 (2005); Marriage status: 28.4% never married, 53.4% now married, 9.1% widowed, 9.1% divorced (2000); Foreign born: 0.0% (2000); Ancestry (includes multiple ancestries): 52.4% German, 19.0% French (except Basque), 8.6% United States or American, 4.8% Irish (2000).
Economy: Single-family building permits issued: 0 (2005); Multi-family building permits issued: 0 (2005); Employment by occupation: 0.0% management, 8.5% professional, 8.5% services, 23.4% sales, 0.0% farming, 6.4% construction, 53.2% production (2000).
Income: Per capita income: $23,704 (2005); Median household income: $51,786 (2005); Average household income: $59,676 (2005); Percent of households with income of $100,000 or more: 5.6% (2005); Poverty rate: 1.0% (2000).
Education: Percent of population age 25 and over with: High school diploma (including GED) or higher: 91.0% (2005); Bachelor's degree or higher: 20.2% (2005); Master's degree or higher: 7.9% (2005).

School District(s)
Miller City-New Cleveland Local SD (PK-12)
  2003-04 Enrollment: 474 .... (419) 876-3172
Housing: Homeownership rate: 92.6% (2005); Median home value: $87,778 (2005); Median rent: $425 per month (2000); Median age of housing: 42 years (2000).
Transportation: Commute to work: 93.6% car, 0.0% public transportation, 6.4% walk, 0.0% work from home (2000); Travel time to work: 19.1% less than 15 minutes, 34.0% 15 to 30 minutes, 31.9% 30 to 45 minutes, 12.8% 45 to 60 minutes, 2.1% 60 minutes or more (2000).

OTTAWA (village). Covers a land area of 3.876 square miles and a water area of 0.028 square miles. Located at 41.02° N. Lat.; 84.04° W. Long. Elevation is 736 feet.
History: Ottawa was established in 1833, and named for the Ottawa Indians. The Ohio Sugar Company, a beet-sugar refinery, was built here.
Population: 4,521 (1990); 4,367 (2000); 4,302 (2005); 4,226 (2010 projected); Race: 94.2% White, 0.2% Black, 0.6% Asian, 7.3% Hispanic of any race (2005); Density: 1,109.9 persons per square mile (2005); Average household size: 2.43 (2005); Median age: 38.6 (2005); Males per 100 females: 97.6 (2005); Marriage status: 24.4% never married, 56.1% now married, 8.3% widowed, 11.2% divorced (2000); Foreign born: 1.3% (2000); Ancestry (includes multiple ancestries): 62.1% German, 10.7% Other groups, 6.8% Irish, 5.7% United States or American, 3.5% English (2000).
Economy: Single-family building permits issued: 13 (2005); Multi-family building permits issued: 0 (2005); Employment by occupation: 13.2% management, 17.1% professional, 11.4% services, 19.0% sales, 0.5% farming, 7.6% construction, 31.2% production (2000).
Income: Per capita income: $24,015 (2005); Median household income: $42,445 (2005); Average household income: $58,015 (2005); Percent of households with income of $100,000 or more: 12.8% (2005); Poverty rate: 5.3% (2000).
Education: Percent of population age 25 and over with: High school diploma (including GED) or higher: 85.4% (2005); Bachelor's degree or higher: 19.7% (2005); Master's degree or higher: 7.0% (2005).

School District(s)
Ottawa-Glandorf Local SD (PK-12)
  2003-04 Enrollment: 1,731 .... (419) 523-5261

Putnam Educational Service Center (07-12)
   2003-04 Enrollment: n/a .... (419) 523-5951
Housing: Homeownership rate: 72.3% (2005); Median home value: $101,825 (2005); Median rent: $331 per month (2000); Median age of housing: 36 years (2000).
Newspapers: Putnam County Sentinel (General - Circulation 8,000)
Transportation: Commute to work: 91.8% car, 1.0% public transportation, 4.2% walk, 1.7% work from home (2000); Travel time to work: 55.7% less than 15 minutes, 17.3% 15 to 30 minutes, 21.5% 30 to 45 minutes, 2.8% 45 to 60 minutes, 2.7% 60 minutes or more (2000)
Additional Information Contacts
Ottawa Chamber of Commerce .... (419) 523-3141
   http://www.ottawaohio.us
Village of Ottawa .... (419) 523-5020
   http://ottawaohio.us/ottawa

OTTOVILLE
(village). Covers a land area of 0.697 square miles and a water area of 0 square miles. Located at 40.93° N. Lat.; 84.33° W. Long. Elevation is 743 feet.
Population: 934 (1990); 873 (2000); 868 (2005); 858 (2010 projected); Race: 99.0% White, 0.0% Black, 0.6% Asian, 0.6% Hispanic of any race (2005); Density: 1,245.0 persons per square mile (2005); Average household size: 2.45 (2005); Median age: 38.3 (2005); Males per 100 females: 93.8 (2005); Marriage status: 19.6% never married, 65.1% now married, 8.4% widowed, 6.9% divorced (2000); Foreign born: 0.0% (2000); Ancestry (includes multiple ancestries): 77.9% German, 4.5% Irish, 3.8% United States or American, 2.2% Polish, 1.7% Other groups (2000).
Economy: Single-family building permits issued: 4 (2005); Multi-family building permits issued: 0 (2005); Employment by occupation: 11.4% management, 14.3% professional, 13.8% services, 27.2% sales, 0.4% farming, 9.6% construction, 23.2% production (2000).
Income: Per capita income: $23,259 (2005); Median household income: $51,263 (2005); Average household income: $55,960 (2005); Percent of households with income of $100,000 or more: 9.9% (2005); Poverty rate: 2.1% (2000).
Education: Percent of population age 25 and over with: High school diploma (including GED) or higher: 91.4% (2005); Bachelor's degree or higher: 12.6% (2005); Master's degree or higher: 4.5% (2005).
School District(s)
Ottoville Local SD (PK-12)
   2003-04 Enrollment: 623 .... (419) 453-3356
Housing: Homeownership rate: 81.9% (2005); Median home value: $109,000 (2005); Median rent: $350 per month (2000); Median age of housing: 42 years (2000).
Transportation: Commute to work: 94.7% car, 0.0% public transportation, 3.1% walk, 1.1% work from home (2000); Travel time to work: 44.8% less than 15 minutes, 25.8% 15 to 30 minutes, 23.1% 30 to 45 minutes, 4.7% 45 to 60 minutes, 1.6% 60 minutes or more (2000)
Additional Information Contacts
Ottoville Chamber of Commerce .... (419) 453-2426
   http://www.villageofottoville.org
Village of Ottoville .... (419) 453-2426
   http://www.villageofottoville.org/general.htm

PANDORA
(village). Covers a land area of 0.813 square miles and a water area of 0 square miles. Located at 40.94° N. Lat.; 83.96° W. Long. Elevation is 773 feet.
Population: 1,078 (1990); 1,188 (2000); 1,215 (2005); 1,222 (2010 projected); Race: 98.8% White, 0.4% Black, 0.0% Asian, 1.4% Hispanic of any race (2005); Density: 1,495.3 persons per square mile (2005); Average household size: 2.63 (2005); Median age: 38.3 (2005); Males per 100 females: 90.7 (2005); Marriage status: 15.1% never married, 71.2% now married, 7.2% widowed, 6.5% divorced (2000); Foreign born: 0.5% (2000); Ancestry (includes multiple ancestries): 37.3% German, 18.6% Swiss, 11.7% United States or American, 7.2% Irish, 7.0% English (2000).
Economy: Diversified farming area; stone quarries. Single-family building permits issued: 2 (2005); Multi-family building permits issued: 0 (2005); Employment by occupation: 12.2% management, 16.2% professional, 12.2% services, 22.1% sales, 0.4% farming, 7.4% construction, 29.7% production (2000).
Income: Per capita income: $20,020 (2005); Median household income: $47,031 (2005); Average household income: $50,925 (2005); Percent of households with income of $100,000 or more: 5.6% (2005); Poverty rate: 4.0% (2000).

Education: Percent of population age 25 and over with: High school diploma (including GED) or higher: 88.0% (2005); Bachelor's degree or higher: 26.2% (2005); Master's degree or higher: 7.0% (2005).
School District(s)
Pandora-Gilboa Local SD (PK-12)
   2003-04 Enrollment: 599 .... (419) 384-3227
Housing: Homeownership rate: 83.1% (2005); Median home value: $103,472 (2005); Median rent: $342 per month (2000); Median age of housing: 47 years (2000).
Transportation: Commute to work: 92.3% car, 1.7% public transportation, 1.9% walk, 3.7% work from home (2000); Travel time to work: 35.6% less than 15 minutes, 39.5% 15 to 30 minutes, 19.8% 30 to 45 minutes, 2.9% 45 to 60 minutes, 2.1% 60 minutes or more (2000)

WEST LEIPSIC
(village). Covers a land area of 0.239 square miles and a water area of 0 square miles. Located at 41.10° N. Lat.; 84.00° W. Long. Elevation is 770 feet.
Population: 234 (1990); 271 (2000); 285 (2005); 294 (2010 projected); Race: 73.0% White, 0.0% Black, 0.0% Asian, 33.3% Hispanic of any race (2005); Density: 1,194.4 persons per square mile (2005); Average household size: 2.71 (2005); Median age: 33.4 (2005); Males per 100 females: 117.6 (2005); Marriage status: 23.8% never married, 62.7% now married, 5.4% widowed, 8.1% divorced (2000); Foreign born: 1.9% (2000); Ancestry (includes multiple ancestries): 38.4% German, 35.3% Other groups, 6.2% United States or American, 5.0% French (except Basque), 5.0% Irish (2000).
Economy: Employment by occupation: 2.7% management, 11.6% professional, 9.8% services, 11.6% sales, 0.0% farming, 4.5% construction, 59.8% production (2000).
Income: Per capita income: $21,614 (2005); Median household income: $44,300 (2005); Average household income: $58,667 (2005); Percent of households with income of $100,000 or more: 7.6% (2005); Poverty rate: 8.5% (2000).
Education: Percent of population age 25 and over with: High school diploma (including GED) or higher: 70.9% (2005); Bachelor's degree or higher: 2.9% (2005); Master's degree or higher: 0.0% (2005).
Housing: Homeownership rate: 84.8% (2005); Median home value: $60,588 (2005); Median rent: $288 per month (2000); Median age of housing: 60+ years (2000).
Transportation: Commute to work: 89.7% car, 0.0% public transportation, 2.8% walk, 4.7% work from home (2000); Travel time to work: 41.2% less than 15 minutes, 41.2% 15 to 30 minutes, 3.9% 30 to 45 minutes, 9.8% 45 to 60 minutes, 3.9% 60 minutes or more (2000)

Richland County

Located in north central Ohio; drained by forks of the Mohican River. Covers a land area of 496.88 square miles, a water area of 3.45 square miles, and is located in the Eastern Time Zone. The county government was organized in 1813. County seat is Mansfield.

Richland County is part of the Mansfield, OH Metropolitan Statistical Area. The entire metro area includes: Richland County, OH

Weather Station: Mansfield 5 W — Elevation: 1,348 feet

	Jan	Feb	Mar	Apr	May	Jun	Jul	Aug	Sep	Oct	Nov	Dec
High	32	36	47	59	70	78	82	80	74	62	49	37
Low	15	18	27	36	47	56	60	58	52	41	32	22
Precip	2.1	1.7	2.7	3.5	4.1	4.2	3.9	3.6	3.3	2.5	2.9	2.6
Snow	na	na	na	0.3	tr	0.0	0.0	0.0	0.0	tr	1.0	na

High and Low temperatures in degrees Fahrenheit; Precipitation and Snow in inches

Weather Station: Mansfield Lahm Municipal Airport — Elevation: 1,292 feet

	Jan	Feb	Mar	Apr	May	Jun	Jul	Aug	Sep	Oct	Nov	Dec
High	32	36	46	59	69	78	82	80	73	62	49	38
Low	18	20	28	38	49	58	62	61	54	43	34	24
Precip	2.6	2.1	3.3	4.2	4.4	4.4	4.3	4.5	3.5	2.7	3.8	3.2
Snow	12.9	9.8	6.9	2.0	tr	tr	0.0	0.0	tr	0.6	2.5	8.6

High and Low temperatures in degrees Fahrenheit; Precipitation and Snow in inches

Population: 126,137 (1990); 128,852 (2000); 128,231 (2005); 127,550 (2010 projected); Race: 87.9% White, 9.4% Black, 0.7% Asian, 0.9% Hispanic of any race (2005); Density: 258.1 persons per square mile (2005); Average household size: 2.57 (2005); Median age: 38.6 (2005); Males per 100 females: 101.5 (2005).

Religion: Five largest groups: 9.3% Catholic Church, 5.1% Evangelical Lutheran Church in America, 4.6% The United Methodist Church, 1.7% Assemblies of God, 1.6% Independent, Non-Charismatic Churches (2000).
Economy: Unemployment rate: 6.6% (2005); Total civilian labor force: 62,709 (2005); Leading industries: 26.2% manufacturing; 14.7% retail trade; 14.5% health care and social assistance (2004); Farms: 1,086 totaling 158,653 acres (2002); Companies that employ 500 or more persons: 9 (2004); Companies that employ 100 to 499 persons: 72 (2004); Companies that employ less than 100 persons: 2,932 (2004); Black-owned businesses: 292 (2002); Hispanic-owned businesses: n/a (2002); Women-owned businesses: 2,304 (2002); Retail sales per capita: $16,248 (2006). Single-family building permits issued: 265 (2005); Multi-family building permits issued: 165 (2005).
Income: Per capita income: $21,038 (2005); Median household income: $42,081 (2005); Average household income: $52,730 (2005); Percent of households with income of $100,000 or more: 10.4% (2005); Poverty rate: 11.1% (2003); Bankruptcy rate: 11.58% (2005).
Taxes: Total county taxes per capita: $258 (2004); County property taxes per capita: $112 (2004).
Education: Percent of population age 25 and over with: High school diploma (including GED) or higher: 80.2% (2005); Bachelor's degree or higher: 12.7% (2005); Master's degree or higher: 4.0% (2005).
Housing: Homeownership rate: 71.9% (2005); Median home value: $110,327 (2005); Median rent: $353 per month (2000); Median age of housing: 41 years (2000).
Health: Birth rate: 118.9 per 10,000 population (2004); Death rate: 99.5 per 10,000 population (2004); Age-adjusted cancer mortality rate: 190.1 deaths per 100,000 population (2002); Number of physicians: 18.4 per 10,000 population (2004); Hospital beds: 28.5 per 10,000 population (2003); Hospital admissions: 1,421.3 per 10,000 population (2003).
Elections: 2004 Presidential election results: 59.6% Bush, 39.8% Kerry, 0.0% Nader, 0.2% Badnarik
National and State Parks: Malabar Farm State Park
Additional Information Contacts
Richland County Government . . . . (419) 774-5599
  http://www.richlandcountyoh.us
City of Mansfield . . . . (419) 755-9626
  http://www.ci.mansfield.oh.us
Mansfield Chamber of Commerce . . . . (419) 522-3211
  http://www.mrachamber.com
Shelby Chamber of Commerce . . . . (419) 342-2426
  http://www.shelbyoh.com
Village of Bellville. . . . . (419) 886-2245
  http://www.bellvilleohio.net/villageadmin.htm
Village of Lexington . . . . (419) 884-0765
  http://www.villageoflexington.org
Village of Ontario . . . . (419) 529-6333
  http://www.ontarioohio.org

Richland County Communities

BELLVILLE (village). Covers a land area of 2.879 square miles and a water area of 0 square miles. Located at 40.62° N. Lat.; 82.51° W. Long. Elevation is 1,150 feet.
History: Bellville grew as a farm community surrounded by apple and peach orchards. Twice, the town's hopes for fortune were dashed. In 1853 Dr. James C. Lee, a former California miner, found gold here, but the amount turned out to be very small. In the 1890's it was thought that a spring might be of therapeutic value and a sanitarium was built, but failed to become a popular health spa.
Population: 1,744 (1990); 1,773 (2000); 1,765 (2005); 1,789 (2010 projected); Race: 98.8% White, 0.2% Black, 0.2% Asian, 1.0% Hispanic of any race (2005); Density: 613.2 persons per square mile (2005); Average household size: 2.31 (2005); Median age: 39.0 (2005); Males per 100 females: 90.2 (2005); Marriage status: 18.5% never married, 59.2% now married, 9.2% widowed, 13.1% divorced (2000); Foreign born: 0.7% (2000); Ancestry (includes multiple ancestries): 31.9% German, 14.8% Irish, 12.0% United States or American, 11.0% English, 5.8% Other groups (2000).
Economy: Employment by occupation: 9.9% management, 15.6% professional, 18.2% services, 27.9% sales, 0.7% farming, 9.7% construction, 18.0% production (2000).
Income: Per capita income: $20,924 (2005); Median household income: $40,357 (2005); Average household income: $48,338 (2005); Percent of households with income of $100,000 or more: 7.7% (2005); Poverty rate: 9.3% (2000).
Education: Percent of population age 25 and over with: High school diploma (including GED) or higher: 85.2% (2005); Bachelor's degree or higher: 11.4% (2005); Master's degree or higher: 2.2% (2005).
School District(s)
Clear Fork Valley Local SD (KG-12)
    2003-04 Enrollment: 1,843 . . . . (419) 886-3855
Housing: Homeownership rate: 69.2% (2005); Median home value: $120,833 (2005); Median rent: $317 per month (2000); Median age of housing: 49 years (2000).
Safety: Violent crime rate: 11.4 per 10,000 population; Property crime rate: 332.0 per 10,000 population (2004).
Newspapers: Bellville Star & Tri-Forks Press (General - Circulation 1,900)
Transportation: Commute to work: 92.2% car, 0.0% public transportation, 3.7% walk, 3.2% work from home (2000); Travel time to work: 33.0% less than 15 minutes, 44.5% 15 to 30 minutes, 13.4% 30 to 45 minutes, 3.8% 45 to 60 minutes, 5.2% 60 minutes or more (2000)
Additional Information Contacts
Village of Bellville. . . . . (419) 886-2245
  http://www.bellvilleohio.net/villageadmin.htm

BUTLER (village). Covers a land area of 1.075 square miles and a water area of 0 square miles. Located at 40.58° N. Lat.; 82.42° W. Long. Elevation is 1,073 feet.
Population: 982 (1990); 921 (2000); 988 (2005); 1,047 (2010 projected); Race: 99.3% White, 0.2% Black, 0.2% Asian, 0.7% Hispanic of any race (2005); Density: 918.8 persons per square mile (2005); Average household size: 2.57 (2005); Median age: 36.6 (2005); Males per 100 females: 103.3 (2005); Marriage status: 18.8% never married, 64.9% now married, 6.2% widowed, 10.1% divorced (2000); Foreign born: 0.5% (2000); Ancestry (includes multiple ancestries): 30.7% German, 12.7% Irish, 10.1% United States or American, 10.0% English, 4.7% Other groups (2000).
Economy: Ski resort nearby. Employment by occupation: 10.2% management, 10.4% professional, 16.2% services, 22.6% sales, 0.0% farming, 12.6% construction, 28.1% production (2000).
Income: Per capita income: $21,791 (2005); Median household income: $46,500 (2005); Average household income: $56,068 (2005); Percent of households with income of $100,000 or more: 10.9% (2005); Poverty rate: 4.9% (2000).
Education: Percent of population age 25 and over with: High school diploma (including GED) or higher: 82.4% (2005); Bachelor's degree or higher: 11.6% (2005); Master's degree or higher: 3.1% (2005).
School District(s)
Clear Fork Valley Local SD (KG-12)
    2003-04 Enrollment: 1,843 . . . . (419) 886-3855
Housing: Homeownership rate: 80.2% (2005); Median home value: $110,638 (2005); Median rent: $346 per month (2000); Median age of housing: 60+ years (2000).
Transportation: Commute to work: 96.1% car, 0.0% public transportation, 2.8% walk, 1.1% work from home (2000); Travel time to work: 29.2% less than 15 minutes, 29.4% 15 to 30 minutes, 29.4% 30 to 45 minutes, 6.1% 45 to 60 minutes, 5.9% 60 minutes or more (2000)

LEXINGTON (village). Covers a land area of 3.671 square miles and a water area of 0 square miles. Located at 40.68° N. Lat.; 82.58° W. Long. Elevation is 1,200 feet.
Population: 4,228 (1990); 4,165 (2000); 4,047 (2005); 4,015 (2010 projected); Race: 96.6% White, 1.4% Black, 0.9% Asian, 0.9% Hispanic of any race (2005); Density: 1,102.5 persons per square mile (2005); Average household size: 2.51 (2005); Median age: 37.8 (2005); Males per 100 females: 93.6 (2005); Marriage status: 18.3% never married, 64.1% now married, 6.7% widowed, 10.8% divorced (2000); Foreign born: 1.4% (2000); Ancestry (includes multiple ancestries): 29.6% German, 15.6% English, 11.7% Irish, 7.4% United States or American, 6.6% Other groups (2000).
Economy: Employment by occupation: 17.9% management, 19.7% professional, 13.2% services, 27.0% sales, 0.0% farming, 4.9% construction, 17.2% production (2000).
Income: Per capita income: $28,008 (2005); Median household income: $56,098 (2005); Average household income: $70,186 (2005); Percent of households with income of $100,000 or more: 20.3% (2005); Poverty rate: 2.5% (2000).

Education: Percent of population age 25 and over with: High school diploma (including GED) or higher: 91.4% (2005); Bachelor's degree or higher: 25.9% (2005); Master's degree or higher: 6.8% (2005).

School District(s)

Lexington Local SD (PK-12)
   2003-04 Enrollment: 2,819 . . . . (419) 884-2132

Housing: Homeownership rate: 72.8% (2005); Median home value: $140,638 (2005); Median rent: $385 per month (2000); Median age of housing: 31 years (2000).

Safety: Violent crime rate: 7.3 per 10,000 population; Property crime rate: 206.1 per 10,000 population (2004).

Transportation: Commute to work: 93.3% car, 0.0% public transportation, 3.2% walk, 3.4% work from home (2000); Travel time to work: 33.6% less than 15 minutes, 43.7% 15 to 30 minutes, 10.2% 30 to 45 minutes, 3.8% 45 to 60 minutes, 8.6% 60 minutes or more (2000)

Additional Information Contacts

Village of Lexington . . . . (419) 884-0765
   http://www.villageoflexington.org

LUCAS (village). Covers a land area of 0.598 square miles and a water area of 0 square miles. Located at 40.70° N. Lat.; 82.42° W. Long. Elevation is 1,105 feet.

Population: 761 (1990); 620 (2000); 629 (2005); 634 (2010 projected); Race: 97.1% White, 1.1% Black, 0.0% Asian, 0.2% Hispanic of any race (2005); Density: 1,052.1 persons per square mile (2005); Average household size: 2.47 (2005); Median age: 36.9 (2005); Males per 100 females: 97.2 (2005); Marriage status: 13.2% never married, 65.6% now married, 10.4% widowed, 10.8% divorced (2000); Foreign born: 1.7% (2000); Ancestry (includes multiple ancestries): 26.7% German, 20.7% United States or American, 10.9% Irish, 9.3% Other groups, 6.0% English (2000).

Economy: Employment by occupation: 7.4% management, 18.5% professional, 14.8% services, 19.2% sales, 2.6% farming, 11.8% construction, 25.8% production (2000).

Income: Per capita income: $20,560 (2005); Median household income: $43,112 (2005); Average household income: $50,716 (2005); Percent of households with income of $100,000 or more: 9.8% (2005); Poverty rate: 6.2% (2000).

Education: Percent of population age 25 and over with: High school diploma (including GED) or higher: 81.0% (2005); Bachelor's degree or higher: 3.4% (2005); Master's degree or higher: 1.9% (2005).

School District(s)

Lucas Local School District (PK-12)
   2003-04 Enrollment: 594 . . . . (419) 892-2338

Housing: Homeownership rate: 70.6% (2005); Median home value: $91,220 (2005); Median rent: $409 per month (2000); Median age of housing: 49 years (2000).

Transportation: Commute to work: 96.2% car, 1.1% public transportation, 0.0% walk, 2.7% work from home (2000); Travel time to work: 25.0% less than 15 minutes, 63.3% 15 to 30 minutes, 6.6% 30 to 45 minutes, 2.3% 45 to 60 minutes, 2.7% 60 minutes or more (2000)

MANSFIELD (city). Covers a land area of 29.905 square miles and a water area of 0 square miles. Located at 40.75° N. Lat.; 82.52° W. Long. Elevation is 1,249 feet.

History: Mansfield was named for Jared Mansfield, U.S. Surveyor General, who directed the townsite to be laid out in 1808. Mansfield grew as the surrounding lands were cleared of timber and put under cultivation. During the War of 1812, Mansfield was threatened by British allies, but John Chapman (better known as Johnny Appleseed) made the 30-mile trip to bring troops from Mount Vernon, and Mansfield was saved. Mansfield's growth was slow, spurred only by the arrival of the railroad in 1846, until after the Civil War. By 1900 it was the home of the Ohio Brass Company, the Empire Sheet and Tin Plate Company, Tappan Stove Company, and a plant of the Westinghouse Electric and Manufacturing Company.

Population: 50,489 (1990); 49,346 (2000); 48,058 (2005); 46,855 (2010 projected); Race: 76.8% White, 19.3% Black, 0.8% Asian, 1.2% Hispanic of any race (2005); Density: 1,607.0 persons per square mile (2005); Average household size: 2.41 (2005); Median age: 37.6 (2005); Males per 100 females: 99.1 (2005); Marriage status: 27.2% never married, 49.2% now married, 9.1% widowed, 14.5% divorced (2000); Foreign born: 2.2% (2000); Ancestry (includes multiple ancestries): 22.4% German, 21.7% Other groups, 10.0% Irish, 9.0% United States or American, 7.9% English (2000).

Economy: Unemployment rate: 6.7% (2005); Total civilian labor force: 23,157 (2005); Single-family building permits issued: 57 (2005); Multi-family building permits issued: 47 (2005); Employment by occupation: 7.9% management, 15.3% professional, 19.1% services, 23.7% sales, 0.0% farming, 8.2% construction, 25.8% production (2000).

Income: Per capita income: $19,271 (2005); Median household income: $33,059 (2005); Average household income: $44,576 (2005); Percent of households with income of $100,000 or more: 7.3% (2005); Poverty rate: 16.3% (2000).

Taxes: Total city taxes per capita: $520 (2004); City property taxes per capita: $46 (2004).

Education: Percent of population age 25 and over with: High school diploma (including GED) or higher: 78.1% (2005); Bachelor's degree or higher: 13.7% (2005); Master's degree or higher: 4.7% (2005).

School District(s)

Madison Local SD (PK-12)
   2003-04 Enrollment: 3,601 . . . . (419) 589-2600
Mansfield City SD (PK-12)
   2003-04 Enrollment: 5,802 . . . . (419) 525-6400
Mansfield Community (KG-04)
   2003-04 Enrollment: 146 . . . . (419) 522-4578
Mansfield Elective Academy
   2003-04 Enrollment: n/a
Mansfield Enhancement Academy
   2003-04 Enrollment: n/a
Mansfield Enrichment Academy
   2003-04 Enrollment: n/a
Ontario Local SD (PK-12)
   2003-04 Enrollment: 1,781 . . . . (419) 747-4311

Four-year College(s)

MedCentral College of Nursing (Private, Not-for-profit)
   Fall 2004 Enrollment: 350 . . . . (419) 520-2600
   2005-06 Tuition: In-state $9,225; Out-of-state $9,225
Ohio State University-Mansfield Campus (Public)
   Fall 2004 Enrollment: 1,634 . . . . (419) 755-4011
   2005-06 Tuition: In-state $5,310; Out-of-state $16,533

Two-year College(s)

Madison Local Schools-Madison Adult Education (Public)
   Fall 2004 Enrollment: 39 . . . . (419) 589-6363
North Central State College (Public)
   Fall 2004 Enrollment: 4,389 . . . . (419) 755-4800
   2005-06 Tuition: In-state $3,431; Out-of-state $6,862

Housing: Homeownership rate: 58.0% (2005); Median home value: $86,680 (2005); Median rent: $347 per month (2000); Median age of housing: 47 years (2000).

Hospitals: MedCentral Health System/Mansfield Hospital (461 beds)

Safety: Violent crime rate: 28.4 per 10,000 population; Property crime rate: 668.4 per 10,000 population (2004).

Newspapers: News Journal (Circulation 33,697); Tribune-Courier (General - Circulation 2,565)

Transportation: Commute to work: 94.1% car, 1.3% public transportation, 2.4% walk, 1.6% work from home (2000); Travel time to work: 47.3% less than 15 minutes, 39.5% 15 to 30 minutes, 6.4% 30 to 45 minutes, 2.3% 45 to 60 minutes, 4.6% 60 minutes or more (2000)

Additional Information Contacts

City of Mansfield . . . . (419) 755-9626
   http://www.ci.mansfield.oh.us
Mansfield Chamber of Commerce . . . . (419) 522-3211
   http://www.mrachamber.com

ONTARIO (village). Covers a land area of 10.918 square miles and a water area of 0 square miles. Located at 40.76° N. Lat.; 82.60° W. Long. Elevation is 1,390 feet.

Population: 4,148 (1990); 5,303 (2000); 5,380 (2005); 5,449 (2010 projected); Race: 90.8% White, 4.8% Black, 2.3% Asian, 0.9% Hispanic of any race (2005); Density: 492.7 persons per square mile (2005); Average household size: 2.41 (2005); Median age: 40.4 (2005); Males per 100 females: 95.3 (2005); Marriage status: 16.6% never married, 64.9% now married, 9.1% widowed, 9.4% divorced (2000); Foreign born: 4.8% (2000); Ancestry (includes multiple ancestries): 33.7% German, 12.2% English, 12.1% Irish, 7.8% Other groups, 6.4% United States or American (2000).

Economy: Employment by occupation: 12.0% management, 16.7% professional, 14.5% services, 32.6% sales, 0.4% farming, 7.6% construction, 16.2% production (2000).

Income: Per capita income: $25,213 (2005); Median household income: $51,374 (2005); Average household income: $60,773 (2005); Percent of households with income of $100,000 or more: 13.3% (2005); Poverty rate: 6.2% (2000).
Education: Percent of population age 25 and over with: High school diploma (including GED) or higher: 84.6% (2005); Bachelor's degree or higher: 18.6% (2005); Master's degree or higher: 7.0% (2005).
Housing: Homeownership rate: 72.1% (2005); Median home value: $134,499 (2005); Median rent: $423 per month (2000); Median age of housing: 29 years (2000).
Safety: Violent crime rate: 17.0 per 10,000 population; Property crime rate: 1,058.3 per 10,000 population (2004).
Transportation: Commute to work: 93.2% car, 1.3% public transportation, 0.0% walk, 5.6% work from home (2000); Travel time to work: 54.5% less than 15 minutes, 31.7% 15 to 30 minutes, 7.1% 30 to 45 minutes, 2.9% 45 to 60 minutes, 3.7% 60 minutes or more (2000)
Additional Information Contacts
Village of Ontario . . . . (419) 529-6333
   http://www.ontarioohio.org

PLYMOUTH (village). Covers a land area of 2.219 square miles and a water area of 0.024 square miles. Located at 40.99° N. Lat.; 82.66° W. Long.
Population: 1,951 (1990); 1,852 (2000); 1,948 (2005); 2,036 (2010 projected); Race: 98.2% White, 0.2% Black, 0.0% Asian, 0.9% Hispanic of any race (2005); Density: 877.7 persons per square mile (2005); Average household size: 2.72 (2005); Median age: 33.4 (2005); Males per 100 females: 94.8 (2005); Marriage status: 20.7% never married, 62.5% now married, 5.9% widowed, 10.9% divorced (2000); Foreign born: 0.3% (2000); Ancestry (includes multiple ancestries): 26.7% United States or American, 19.2% German, 10.0% Irish, 8.4% English, 8.3% Other groups (2000).
Economy: Single-family building permits issued: 1 (2005); Multi-family building permits issued: 4 (2005); Employment by occupation: 8.0% management, 11.6% professional, 13.5% services, 19.3% sales, 0.5% farming, 6.0% construction, 41.2% production (2000).
Income: Per capita income: $17,609 (2005); Median household income: $42,270 (2005); Average household income: $47,909 (2005); Percent of households with income of $100,000 or more: 6.8% (2005); Poverty rate: 13.3% (2000).
Education: Percent of population age 25 and over with: High school diploma (including GED) or higher: 75.7% (2005); Bachelor's degree or higher: 6.6% (2005); Master's degree or higher: 2.3% (2005).
School District(s)
Plymouth-Shiloh Local SD (PK-12)
   2003-04 Enrollment: 963 . . . . (419) 687-4733
Housing: Homeownership rate: 66.6% (2005); Median home value: $92,178 (2005); Median rent: $365 per month (2000); Median age of housing: 52 years (2000).
Transportation: Commute to work: 95.5% car, 0.0% public transportation, 1.8% walk, 1.5% work from home (2000); Travel time to work: 39.8% less than 15 minutes, 35.7% 15 to 30 minutes, 18.8% 30 to 45 minutes, 3.1% 45 to 60 minutes, 2.6% 60 minutes or more (2000)

SHELBY (city). Covers a land area of 5.038 square miles and a water area of 0.068 square miles. Located at 40.88° N. Lat.; 82.66° W. Long. Elevation is 1,102 feet.
Population: 9,672 (1990); 9,821 (2000); 9,554 (2005); 9,294 (2010 projected); Race: 98.2% White, 0.1% Black, 0.4% Asian, 1.1% Hispanic of any race (2005); Density: 1,896.3 persons per square mile (2005); Average household size: 2.37 (2005); Median age: 37.8 (2005); Males per 100 females: 92.4 (2005); Marriage status: 22.0% never married, 57.7% now married, 8.9% widowed, 11.4% divorced (2000); Foreign born: 1.1% (2000); Ancestry (includes multiple ancestries): 33.7% German, 14.0% Irish, 10.1% English, 10.1% United States or American, 7.7% Other groups (2000).
Economy: In rich agricultural region: livestock, poultry; corn. Manufacturing: steel tubing, cutlery, bicycles. Single-family building permits issued: 8 (2005); Multi-family building permits issued: 38 (2005); Employment by occupation: 8.4% management, 10.8% professional, 16.3% services, 26.2% sales, 0.0% farming, 7.4% construction, 31.0% production (2000).
Income: Per capita income: $19,824 (2005); Median household income: $39,267 (2005); Average household income: $46,619 (2005); Percent of households with income of $100,000 or more: 6.7% (2005); Poverty rate: 10.2% (2000).
Education: Percent of population age 25 and over with: High school diploma (including GED) or higher: 81.6% (2005); Bachelor's degree or higher: 9.3% (2005); Master's degree or higher: 2.6% (2005).
School District(s)
Pioneer Career & Technology (PK-12)
   2003-04 Enrollment: n/a . . . . (419) 347-7926
Shelby City SD (KG-12)
   2003-04 Enrollment: 2,254 . . . . (419) 342-3520
Two-year College(s)
Pioneer Career and Technology Center (Public)
   Fall 2004 Enrollment: 44 . . . . (419) 347-7744
Housing: Homeownership rate: 65.3% (2005); Median home value: $96,707 (2005); Median rent: $318 per month (2000); Median age of housing: 46 years (2000).
Hospitals: MedCentral Health System/Shelby Hospital (68 beds)
Safety: Violent crime rate: 13.5 per 10,000 population; Property crime rate: 449.1 per 10,000 population (2004).
Newspapers: The Daily Globe (Circulation 4,058)
Transportation: Commute to work: 94.0% car, 0.6% public transportation, 2.2% walk, 2.4% work from home (2000); Travel time to work: 45.0% less than 15 minutes, 38.3% 15 to 30 minutes, 9.9% 30 to 45 minutes, 1.8% 45 to 60 minutes, 5.0% 60 minutes or more (2000)
Additional Information Contacts
Shelby Chamber of Commerce . . . . (419) 342-2426
   http://www.shelbyoh.com

SHILOH (village). Covers a land area of 0.912 square miles and a water area of 0 square miles. Located at 40.97° N. Lat.; 82.60° W. Long. Elevation is 1,083 feet.
Population: 778 (1990); 721 (2000); 744 (2005); 764 (2010 projected); Race: 98.8% White, 0.0% Black, 0.0% Asian, 0.8% Hispanic of any race (2005); Density: 816.1 persons per square mile (2005); Average household size: 2.95 (2005); Median age: 31.9 (2005); Males per 100 females: 96.8 (2005); Marriage status: 22.5% never married, 60.7% now married, 6.6% widowed, 10.1% divorced (2000); Foreign born: 0.0% (2000); Ancestry (includes multiple ancestries): 20.2% United States or American, 15.8% German, 13.7% English, 6.2% Irish, 6.2% Other groups (2000).
Economy: Employment by occupation: 6.1% management, 8.4% professional, 14.8% services, 19.4% sales, 0.4% farming, 1.1% construction, 49.8% production (2000).
Income: Per capita income: $14,116 (2005); Median household income: $34,574 (2005); Average household income: $41,677 (2005); Percent of households with income of $100,000 or more: 3.6% (2005); Poverty rate: 17.3% (2000).
Education: Percent of population age 25 and over with: High school diploma (including GED) or higher: 64.6% (2005); Bachelor's degree or higher: 5.9% (2005); Master's degree or higher: 0.5% (2005).
School District(s)
Plymouth-Shiloh Local SD (PK-12)
   2003-04 Enrollment: 963 . . . . (419) 687-4733
Housing: Homeownership rate: 78.2% (2005); Median home value: $61,750 (2005); Median rent: $333 per month (2000); Median age of housing: 60+ years (2000).
Transportation: Commute to work: 90.5% car, 0.0% public transportation, 4.4% walk, 4.4% work from home (2000); Travel time to work: 15.4% less than 15 minutes, 52.3% 15 to 30 minutes, 25.7% 30 to 45 minutes, 3.7% 45 to 60 minutes, 2.9% 60 minutes or more (2000)

Ross County

Located in southern Ohio; crossed by the Scioto River and several creeks. Covers a land area of 688.41 square miles, a water area of 4.55 square miles, and is located in the Eastern Time Zone. The county government was organized in 1798. County seat is Chillicothe.

Ross County is part of the Chillicothe, OH Micropolitan Statistical Area. The entire metro area includes: Ross County, OH

Weather Station: Chillicothe Mound City   Elevation: 649 feet

	Jan	Feb	Mar	Apr	May	Jun	Jul	Aug	Sep	Oct	Nov	Dec
High	38	42	53	64	74	82	86	85	79	67	54	43
Low	19	22	30	39	49	58	63	61	53	41	33	25
Precip	2.5	2.3	3.4	3.5	4.4	3.5	3.9	3.6	2.8	2.6	2.9	2.6
Snow	7.1	4.6	3.1	0.4	tr	0.0	0.0	0.0	0.0	0.1	0.4	2.2

High and Low temperatures in degrees Fahrenheit; Precipitation and Snow in inches

Population: 69,330 (1990); 73,345 (2000); 74,809 (2005); 76,320 (2010 projected); Race: 92.1% White, 6.0% Black, 0.4% Asian, 0.6% Hispanic of any race (2005); Density: 108.7 persons per square mile (2005); Average household size: 2.67 (2005); Median age: 37.8 (2005); Males per 100 females: 108.2 (2005).
Religion: Five largest groups: 6.4% The United Methodist Church, 3.9% Catholic Church, 2.5% Southern Baptist Convention, 1.7% American Baptist Churches in the USA, 1.6% The Wesleyan Church (2000).
Economy: Unemployment rate: 7.3% (2005); Total civilian labor force: 34,821 (2005); Leading industries: 18.3% health care and social assistance; 17.4% retail trade; 17.4% manufacturing (2004); Farms: 952 totaling 246,690 acres (2002); Companies that employ 500 or more persons: 3 (2004); Companies that employ 100 to 499 persons: 22 (2004); Companies that employ less than 100 persons: 1,322 (2004); Black-owned businesses: n/a (2002); Hispanic-owned businesses: n/a (2002); Women-owned businesses: 1,177 (2002); Retail sales per capita: $11,218 (2006). Single-family building permits issued: 39 (2005); Multi-family building permits issued: 0 (2005).
Income: Per capita income: $20,259 (2005); Median household income: $41,669 (2005); Average household income: $51,554 (2005); Percent of households with income of $100,000 or more: 9.7% (2005); Poverty rate: 12.0% (2003); Bankruptcy rate: 8.96% (2005).
Taxes: Total county taxes per capita: $308 (2004); County property taxes per capita: $117 (2004).
Education: Percent of population age 25 and over with: High school diploma (including GED) or higher: 76.2% (2005); Bachelor's degree or higher: 11.5% (2005); Master's degree or higher: 4.0% (2005).
Housing: Homeownership rate: 73.8% (2005); Median home value: $98,821 (2005); Median rent: $329 per month (2000); Median age of housing: 35 years (2000).
Health: Birth rate: 112.5 per 10,000 population (2004); Death rate: 108.6 per 10,000 population (2004); Age-adjusted cancer mortality rate: 255.4 deaths per 100,000 population (2002); Number of physicians: 17.1 per 10,000 population (2004); Hospital beds: 65.2 per 10,000 population (2003); Hospital admissions: 1,977.1 per 10,000 population (2003).
Elections: 2004 Presidential election results: 54.4% Bush, 44.1% Kerry, 0.0% Nader, 1.2% Badnarik
National and State Parks: Adena State Memorial; Great Seal State Park; Hopewell Culture National Historical Park; Hopewell Culture National Historical Park; Paint Creek State Park; Ross County Lake State Wildlife Area; Scioto River Canal Lands Access State Wildlife Area; Scioto Trail State Forest; Seip Mound State Memorial; Story Mound State Memorial; Tar Hollow State Forest
Additional Information Contacts
Ross County Government . . . . (740) 702-3085
  http://www.co.ross.oh.us/
Chillicothe Chamber of Commerce . . . . (740) 702-2722
  http://www.chillicotheohio.com
City of Chillicothe . . . . (740) 774-1185
  http://ci.chillicothe.oh.us

Ross County Communities

ADELPHI (village). Covers a land area of 0.276 square miles and a water area of 0 square miles. Located at 39.46° N. Lat.; 82.74° W. Long. Elevation is 838 feet.
Population: 398 (1990); 371 (2000); 357 (2005); 348 (2010 projected); Race: 96.1% White, 3.4% Black, 0.0% Asian, 0.6% Hispanic of any race (2005); Density: 1,292.6 persons per square mile (2005); Average household size: 2.33 (2005); Median age: 37.8 (2005); Males per 100 females: 107.6 (2005); Marriage status: 24.1% never married, 59.5% now married, 9.4% widowed, 7.0% divorced (2000); Foreign born: 0.0% (2000); Ancestry (includes multiple ancestries): 19.7% United States or American, 18.4% German, 10.3% Other groups, 8.7% Irish, 5.8% English (2000).
Economy: In agricultural area. Employment by occupation: 2.9% management, 6.3% professional, 13.7% services, 21.1% sales, 0.0% farming, 15.4% construction, 40.6% production (2000).

Income: Per capita income: $19,636 (2005); Median household income: $41,136 (2005); Average household income: $45,817 (2005); Percent of households with income of $100,000 or more: 6.5% (2005); Poverty rate: 13.6% (2000).
Education: Percent of population age 25 and over with: High school diploma (including GED) or higher: 66.3% (2005); Bachelor's degree or higher: 0.4% (2005); Master's degree or higher: 0.4% (2005).
Housing: Homeownership rate: 80.4% (2005); Median home value: $84,595 (2005); Median rent: $305 per month (2000); Median age of housing: 50 years (2000).
Transportation: Commute to work: 91.2% car, 2.9% public transportation, 2.9% walk, 1.8% work from home (2000); Travel time to work: 19.0% less than 15 minutes, 38.1% 15 to 30 minutes, 14.9% 30 to 45 minutes, 8.9% 45 to 60 minutes, 19.0% 60 minutes or more (2000)

BAINBRIDGE (village). Covers a land area of 0.512 square miles and a water area of 0 square miles. Located at 39.22° N. Lat.; 83.27° W. Long. Elevation is 740 feet.
History: Bainbridge was founded in 1805 by Nathaniel Massie, a landowner and surveyor. In 1826 Dr. John Harris established a school for teaching dentistry here, where Chapin A. Harris was trained. Harris later founded the dental college at Baltimore and the "American Journal of Dental Science."
Population: 968 (1990); 1,012 (2000); 935 (2005); 921 (2010 projected); Race: 99.5% White, 0.2% Black, 0.1% Asian, 0.1% Hispanic of any race (2005); Density: 1,825.5 persons per square mile (2005); Average household size: 2.51 (2005); Median age: 36.4 (2005); Males per 100 females: 85.1 (2005); Marriage status: 24.0% never married, 53.7% now married, 12.8% widowed, 9.6% divorced (2000); Foreign born: 0.3% (2000); Ancestry (includes multiple ancestries): 17.6% United States or American, 13.7% German, 10.7% Other groups, 7.7% Irish, 6.2% English (2000).
Economy: Employment by occupation: 5.1% management, 10.6% professional, 22.6% services, 19.6% sales, 2.3% farming, 6.5% construction, 33.3% production (2000).
Income: Per capita income: $16,508 (2005); Median household income: $31,020 (2005); Average household income: $40,389 (2005); Percent of households with income of $100,000 or more: 7.5% (2005); Poverty rate: 19.9% (2000).
Education: Percent of population age 25 and over with: High school diploma (including GED) or higher: 68.2% (2005); Bachelor's degree or higher: 6.4% (2005); Master's degree or higher: 2.5% (2005).
School District(s)
Paint Valley Local SD (PK-12)
  2003-04 Enrollment: 1,193 . . . . (740) 634-2826
Housing: Homeownership rate: 63.8% (2005); Median home value: $75,200 (2005); Median rent: $255 per month (2000); Median age of housing: 49 years (2000).
Transportation: Commute to work: 90.2% car, 0.0% public transportation, 8.8% walk, 1.0% work from home (2000); Travel time to work: 30.1% less than 15 minutes, 12.0% 15 to 30 minutes, 27.7% 30 to 45 minutes, 14.5% 45 to 60 minutes, 15.7% 60 minutes or more (2000)

CHILLICOTHE (city). Covers a land area of 9.544 square miles and a water area of 0.198 square miles. Located at 39.33° N. Lat.; 82.98° W. Long. Elevation is 625 feet.
History: In 1796 Nathaniel Massie established a community of settlers on the Scioto River at the mouth of Paint Creek. When Edward Tiffin and other young men came from Virginia in 1798, the town of Chillicothe was founded and became the capitol of the Northwest Territory. Ohio became a state in 1803, and Chillicothe continued as the capitol until 1810. Then industrial growth replaced the business of state, and the first paper mill was founded in 1812. By 1815 a flour mill was turning out 50 barrels daily, and by 1835, when the canal made agriculture profitable, cereal mills constructed along its banks shipped their products east and south. By 1890 the town had factories manufacturing a variety of items, including the Champion bed lounge, Mosher ratchet jack, Neely razor blade, Scioto grain elevator, and Crown baking powder and spices.
Population: 22,771 (1990); 21,796 (2000); 21,614 (2005); 21,422 (2010 projected); Race: 90.1% White, 6.9% Black, 0.6% Asian, 0.9% Hispanic of any race (2005); Density: 2,264.7 persons per square mile (2005); Average household size: 2.27 (2005); Median age: 40.7 (2005); Males per 100 females: 88.6 (2005); Marriage status: 23.2% never married, 51.3% now married, 11.2% widowed, 14.2% divorced (2000); Foreign born: 1.0% (2000); Ancestry (includes multiple ancestries): 22.0% German, 13.9%

United States or American, 13.4% Other groups, 11.8% Irish, 10.5% English (2000).
Economy: Single-family building permits issued: 30 (2005); Multi-family building permits issued: 0 (2005); Employment by occupation: 9.3% management, 21.5% professional, 17.3% services, 24.7% sales, 0.1% farming, 6.1% construction, 21.1% production (2000).
Income: Per capita income: $21,680 (2005); Median household income: $37,075 (2005); Average household income: $48,636 (2005); Percent of households with income of $100,000 or more: 8.6% (2005); Poverty rate: 12.4% (2000).
Taxes: Total city taxes per capita: $535 (2004); City property taxes per capita: $63 (2004).
Education: Percent of population age 25 and over with: High school diploma (including GED) or higher: 77.3% (2005); Bachelor's degree or higher: 17.1% (2005); Master's degree or higher: 6.9% (2005).

School District(s)
Chillicothe City SD (PK-12)
   2003-04 Enrollment: 3,520 ....(740) 775-4250
Huntington Local SD (PK-12)
   2003-04 Enrollment: 1,393 ....(740) 663-5892
Pickaway-Ross County Joint Vocational SD (07-12)
   2003-04 Enrollment: n/a ....(740) 642-1200
Southeastern Local SD (PK-12)
   2003-04 Enrollment: 1,259 ....(740) 774-2003
Union-Scioto Local SD (PK-12)
   2003-04 Enrollment: 1,954 ....(740) 773-4102
Zane Trace Local SD (PK-12)
   2003-04 Enrollment: 1,589 ....(740) 775-1355

Four-year College(s)
Ohio University-Chillicothe Campus (Public)
   Fall 2004 Enrollment: 2,048......................(740) 774-7200
   2005-06 Tuition: In-state $4,323; Out-of-state $8,646

Two-year College(s)
Pickaway Ross Joint Vocational School District (Public)
   Fall 2004 Enrollment: 265 ....(740) 642-1200
   2005-06 Tuition: In-state $4,500; Out-of-state $4,500
Southeastern Business College (Private, For-profit)
   Fall 2004 Enrollment: 98 ....(740) 774-6300
   2005-06 Tuition: In-state $9,330; Out-of-state $9,330

Housing: Homeownership rate: 61.7% (2005); Median home value: $95,788 (2005); Median rent: $345 per month (2000); Median age of housing: 50 years (2000).
Hospitals: Adena Regional Medical Center (238 beds); Veterans Affairs Medical Center (297 beds)
Safety: Violent crime rate: 25.7 per 10,000 population; Property crime rate: 995.7 per 10,000 population (2004).
Newspapers: Chillicothe Gazette (Circulation 16,265)
Transportation: Commute to work: 93.3% car, 0.7% public transportation, 3.0% walk, 1.7% work from home (2000); Travel time to work: 56.9% less than 15 minutes, 22.9% 15 to 30 minutes, 7.8% 30 to 45 minutes, 4.0% 45 to 60 minutes, 8.5% 60 minutes or more (2000)
Additional Information Contacts
Chillicothe Chamber of Commerce ....(740) 702-2722
   http://www.chillicotheohio.com
City of Chillicothe ....(740) 774-1185
   http://ci.chillicothe.oh.us

CLARKSBURG (village).
Covers a land area of 0.186 square miles and a water area of 0 square miles. Located at 39.50° N. Lat.; 83.15° W. Long. Elevation is 772 feet.
Population: 567 (1990); 516 (2000); 547 (2005); 576 (2010 projected); Race: 97.6% White, 1.6% Black, 0.0% Asian, 0.0% Hispanic of any race (2005); Density: 2,939.5 persons per square mile (2005); Average household size: 2.83 (2005); Median age: 33.3 (2005); Males per 100 females: 104.9 (2005); Marriage status: 25.9% never married, 50.9% now married, 10.7% widowed, 12.5% divorced (2000); Foreign born: 0.0% (2000); Ancestry (includes multiple ancestries): 23.9% German, 15.4% Irish, 14.2% United States or American, 11.7% English, 9.1% Other groups (2000).
Economy: In agricultural area. Employment by occupation: 5.0% management, 13.9% professional, 13.3% services, 20.6% sales, 1.7% farming, 15.0% construction, 30.6% production (2000).
Income: Per capita income: $13,926 (2005); Median household income: $38,088 (2005); Average household income: $38,977 (2005); Percent of households with income of $100,000 or more: 2.6% (2005); Poverty rate: 18.8% (2000).
Education: Percent of population age 25 and over with: High school diploma (including GED) or higher: 74.6% (2005); Bachelor's degree or higher: 5.5% (2005); Master's degree or higher: 2.0% (2005).
Housing: Homeownership rate: 71.5% (2005); Median home value: $76,800 (2005); Median rent: $318 per month (2000); Median age of housing: 60+ years (2000).
Transportation: Commute to work: 93.3% car, 0.0% public transportation, 5.6% walk, 1.1% work from home (2000); Travel time to work: 10.2% less than 15 minutes, 34.5% 15 to 30 minutes, 37.9% 30 to 45 minutes, 7.9% 45 to 60 minutes, 9.6% 60 minutes or more (2000)

FRANKFORT (village).
Covers a land area of 0.564 square miles and a water area of 0 square miles. Located at 39.40° N. Lat.; 83.18° W. Long. Elevation is 745 feet.
History: Frankfort was established on the site of a Shawnee village that was burned and plundered by Simon Kenton in 1787.
Population: 1,176 (1990); 1,011 (2000); 1,076 (2005); 1,154 (2010 projected); Race: 93.3% White, 3.4% Black, 0.3% Asian, 0.0% Hispanic of any race (2005); Density: 1,908.1 persons per square mile (2005); Average household size: 2.24 (2005); Median age: 39.5 (2005); Males per 100 females: 91.8 (2005); Marriage status: 21.6% never married, 52.2% now married, 14.6% widowed, 11.6% divorced (2000); Foreign born: 1.7% (2000); Ancestry (includes multiple ancestries): 24.8% German, 16.1% English, 11.7% United States or American, 10.7% Other groups, 9.3% Irish (2000).
Economy: Employment by occupation: 9.5% management, 20.4% professional, 20.4% services, 18.3% sales, 0.9% farming, 10.4% construction, 20.0% production (2000).
Income: Per capita income: $21,302 (2005); Median household income: $38,539 (2005); Average household income: $47,661 (2005); Percent of households with income of $100,000 or more: 10.6% (2005); Poverty rate: 16.7% (2000).
Taxes: Total city taxes per capita: $31 (2004); City property taxes per capita: $31 (2004).
Education: Percent of population age 25 and over with: High school diploma (including GED) or higher: 78.8% (2005); Bachelor's degree or higher: 12.1% (2005); Master's degree or higher: 4.4% (2005).

School District(s)
Adena Local SD (PK-12)
   2003-04 Enrollment: 1,248 ....(740) 998-4633

Housing: Homeownership rate: 68.1% (2005); Median home value: $93,704 (2005); Median rent: $287 per month (2000); Median age of housing: 46 years (2000).
Transportation: Commute to work: 92.7% car, 0.7% public transportation, 5.4% walk, 0.2% work from home (2000); Travel time to work: 23.8% less than 15 minutes, 51.2% 15 to 30 minutes, 14.9% 30 to 45 minutes, 4.0% 45 to 60 minutes, 6.1% 60 minutes or more (2000)

KINGSTON (village).
Covers a land area of 0.369 square miles and a water area of 0 square miles. Located at 39.47° N. Lat.; 82.91° W. Long. Elevation is 797 feet.
Population: 1,153 (1990); 1,032 (2000); 969 (2005); 983 (2010 projected); Race: 98.8% White, 0.5% Black, 0.2% Asian, 0.5% Hispanic of any race (2005); Density: 2,625.2 persons per square mile (2005); Average household size: 2.21 (2005); Median age: 44.7 (2005); Males per 100 females: 84.6 (2005); Marriage status: 12.5% never married, 61.3% now married, 10.0% widowed, 16.2% divorced (2000); Foreign born: 0.7% (2000); Ancestry (includes multiple ancestries): 24.3% German, 18.7% United States or American, 15.6% Irish, 9.3% English, 7.7% Other groups (2000).
Economy: Grain products; gas wells. Employment by occupation: 8.6% management, 20.0% professional, 11.8% services, 25.7% sales, 0.7% farming, 9.9% construction, 23.5% production (2000).
Income: Per capita income: $23,309 (2005); Median household income: $37,361 (2005); Average household income: $49,624 (2005); Percent of households with income of $100,000 or more: 9.1% (2005); Poverty rate: 10.1% (2000).
Education: Percent of population age 25 and over with: High school diploma (including GED) or higher: 75.5% (2005); Bachelor's degree or higher: 11.1% (2005); Master's degree or higher: 2.7% (2005).

School District(s)
Logan Elm Local SD (PK-12)
   2003-04 Enrollment: 2,323 ....(740) 474-7501

Housing: Homeownership rate: 72.9% (2005); Median home value: $104,444 (2005); Median rent: $281 per month (2000); Median age of housing: 57 years (2000).
Transportation: Commute to work: 95.9% car, 0.0% public transportation, 3.5% walk, 0.7% work from home (2000); Travel time to work: 21.6% less than 15 minutes, 45.9% 15 to 30 minutes, 9.5% 30 to 45 minutes, 10.4% 45 to 60 minutes, 12.5% 60 minutes or more (2000)

LONDONDERRY (unincorporated postal area, zip code 45647).
Covers a land area of 48.747 square miles and a water area of 0.007 square miles. Located at 39.28° N. Lat.; 82.76° W. Long. Elevation is 685 feet.
History: Londonderry was named by its early settlers for their home county in Ireland.
Population: 1,889 (2000); Race: 99.3% White, 0.0% Black, 0.0% Asian, 0.7% Hispanic of any race (2000); Density: 38.8 persons per square mile (2000); Age: 23.5% under 18, 17.2% over 64 (2000); Marriage status: 18.8% never married, 62.5% now married, 8.9% widowed, 9.8% divorced (2000); Foreign born: 0.0% (2000); Ancestry (includes multiple ancestries): 21.1% United States or American, 10.1% German, 9.2% English, 7.4% Other groups, 5.3% Irish (2000).
Economy: Employment by occupation: 5.6% management, 10.5% professional, 17.0% services, 14.9% sales, 0.0% farming, 15.1% construction, 36.9% production (2000).
Income: Per capita income: $17,250 (2000); Median household income: $40,758 (2000); Poverty rate: 6.6% (2000).
Education: Percent of population age 25 and over with: High school diploma (including GED) or higher: 72.1% (2000); Bachelor's degree or higher: 5.9% (2000).
Housing: Homeownership rate: 82.4% (2000); Median home value: $76,000 (2000); Median rent: $296 per month (2000); Median age of housing: 31 years (2000).
Transportation: Commute to work: 97.0% car, 1.8% public transportation, 0.5% walk, 0.8% work from home (2000); Travel time to work: 11.0% less than 15 minutes, 49.6% 15 to 30 minutes, 18.8% 30 to 45 minutes, 7.6% 45 to 60 minutes, 13.0% 60 minutes or more (2000)

NORTH FORK VILLAGE (CDP).
Covers a land area of 1.528 square miles and a water area of 0 square miles. Located at 39.33° N. Lat.; 83.02° W. Long. Elevation is 680 feet.
Population: 1,443 (1990); 1,726 (2000); 1,828 (2005); 1,919 (2010 projected); Race: 94.4% White, 4.5% Black, 0.7% Asian, 0.7% Hispanic of any race (2005); Density: 1,196.4 persons per square mile (2005); Average household size: 2.34 (2005); Median age: 38.7 (2005); Males per 100 females: 83.9 (2005); Marriage status: 16.9% never married, 67.6% now married, 5.0% widowed, 10.5% divorced (2000); Foreign born: 1.5% (2000); Ancestry (includes multiple ancestries): 21.6% German, 11.0% Other groups, 10.4% Irish, 9.9% English, 8.7% United States or American (2000).
Economy: Employment by occupation: 18.9% management, 20.7% professional, 17.5% services, 20.6% sales, 0.0% farming, 8.8% construction, 13.5% production (2000).
Income: Per capita income: $23,788 (2005); Median household income: $44,397 (2005); Average household income: $55,246 (2005); Percent of households with income of $100,000 or more: 10.7% (2005); Poverty rate: 4.4% (2000).
Education: Percent of population age 25 and over with: High school diploma (including GED) or higher: 86.1% (2005); Bachelor's degree or higher: 26.9% (2005); Master's degree or higher: 7.6% (2005).
Housing: Homeownership rate: 56.1% (2005); Median home value: $139,910 (2005); Median rent: $391 per month (2000); Median age of housing: 26 years (2000).
Transportation: Commute to work: 93.2% car, 0.0% public transportation, 3.7% walk, 3.1% work from home (2000); Travel time to work: 43.4% less than 15 minutes, 35.0% 15 to 30 minutes, 7.6% 30 to 45 minutes, 3.3% 45 to 60 minutes, 10.7% 60 minutes or more (2000)

RICHMOND DALE (unincorporated postal area, zip code 45673).
Aka Richmondale. Covers a land area of 0.518 square miles and a water area of 0 square miles. Located at 39.20° N. Lat.; 82.81° W. Long. Elevation is 610 feet.
Population: 405 (2000); Race: 100.0% White, 0.0% Black, 0.0% Asian, 0.0% Hispanic of any race (2000); Density: 781.1 persons per square mile (2000); Age: 13.3% under 18, 12.0% over 64 (2000); Marriage status: 23.7% never married, 57.5% now married, 11.8% widowed, 6.9% divorced (2000); Foreign born: 0.0% (2000); Ancestry (includes multiple ancestries): 22.1% German, 12.5% United States or American, 11.2% Other groups, 9.6% European, 6.1% English (2000).
Economy: Employment by occupation: 0.0% management, 8.3% professional, 6.4% services, 21.1% sales, 0.0% farming, 6.4% construction, 57.8% production (2000).
Income: Per capita income: $16,708 (2000); Median household income: $33,365 (2000); Poverty rate: 3.5% (2000).
Education: Percent of population age 25 and over with: High school diploma (including GED) or higher: 73.9% (2000); Bachelor's degree or higher: 10.7% (2000).

School District(s)
Southeastern Local SD (PK-12)
    2003-04 Enrollment: 1,259 . . . . (740) 774-2003
Housing: Homeownership rate: 74.0% (2000); Median home value: $58,300 (2000); Median rent: $315 per month (2000); Median age of housing: 56 years (2000).
Transportation: Commute to work: 92.5% car, 0.0% public transportation, 7.5% walk, 0.0% work from home (2000); Travel time to work: 23.1% less than 15 minutes, 57.3% 15 to 30 minutes, 7.5% 30 to 45 minutes, 4.0% 45 to 60 minutes, 8.0% 60 minutes or more (2000)

SOUTH SALEM (village).
Covers a land area of 0.207 square miles and a water area of 0 square miles. Located at 39.33° N. Lat.; 83.30° W. Long. Elevation is 920 feet.
Population: 227 (1990); 213 (2000); 214 (2005); 214 (2010 projected); Race: 95.8% White, 0.9% Black, 0.0% Asian, 1.4% Hispanic of any race (2005); Density: 1,032.6 persons per square mile (2005); Average household size: 2.74 (2005); Median age: 36.4 (2005); Males per 100 females: 116.2 (2005); Marriage status: 26.2% never married, 58.7% now married, 7.0% widowed, 8.1% divorced (2000); Foreign born: 0.0% (2000); Ancestry (includes multiple ancestries): 21.2% German, 18.0% United States or American, 13.5% Irish, 12.6% Other groups, 9.9% Dutch (2000).
Economy: Employment by occupation: 7.9% management, 21.3% professional, 18.0% services, 10.1% sales, 1.1% farming, 10.1% construction, 31.5% production (2000).
Income: Per capita income: $16,285 (2005); Median household income: $37,000 (2005); Average household income: $44,679 (2005); Percent of households with income of $100,000 or more: 6.4% (2005); Poverty rate: 14.0% (2000).
Education: Percent of population age 25 and over with: High school diploma (including GED) or higher: 82.8% (2005); Bachelor's degree or higher: 5.3% (2005); Master's degree or higher: 2.0% (2005).

School District(s)
Greenfield Ex Vill SD (PK-12)
    2003-04 Enrollment: 2,319 . . . . (937) 981-2152
Housing: Homeownership rate: 85.9% (2005); Median home value: $77,407 (2005); Median rent: $263 per month (2000); Median age of housing: 60+ years (2000).
Transportation: Commute to work: 100.0% car, 0.0% public transportation, 0.0% walk, 0.0% work from home (2000); Travel time to work: 28.1% less than 15 minutes, 30.3% 15 to 30 minutes, 30.3% 30 to 45 minutes, 9.0% 45 to 60 minutes, 2.2% 60 minutes or more (2000)

Sandusky County

Located in northern Ohio; bounded on the northeast by Sandusky Bay of Lake Erie; crossed by the Sandusky and Portage Rivers. Covers a land area of 409.18 square miles, a water area of 8.59 square miles, and is located in the Eastern Time Zone. The county government was organized in 1820. County seat is Fremont.

Sandusky County is part of the Fremont, OH Micropolitan Statistical Area. The entire metro area includes: Sandusky County, OH

Weather Station: Fremont   Elevation: 597 feet

	Jan	Feb	Mar	Apr	May	Jun	Jul	Aug	Sep	Oct	Nov	Dec
High	31	35	45	58	70	79	84	81	75	62	49	37
Low	16	18	27	38	49	58	63	60	53	41	33	22
Precip	2.1	1.9	2.7	3.3	3.7	4.3	3.4	3.3	3.1	2.6	2.9	2.7
Snow	6.7	5.2	3.6	0.3	tr	0.0	0.0	0.0	0.0	tr	0.6	na

High and Low temperatures in degrees Fahrenheit; Precipitation and Snow in inches

Population: 61,963 (1990); 61,792 (2000); 61,701 (2005); 61,584 (2010 projected); Race: 91.8% White, 2.8% Black, 0.3% Asian, 7.2% Hispanic of any race (2005); Density: 150.8 persons per square mile (2005); Average

household size: 2.56 (2005); Median age: 38.2 (2005); Males per 100 females: 96.3 (2005).
Religion: Five largest groups: 20.5% Catholic Church, 11.5% Evangelical Lutheran Church in America, 8.1% The United Methodist Church, 1.8% Independent, Charismatic Churches, 1.6% Southern Baptist Convention (2000).
Economy: Unemployment rate: 6.3% (2005); Total civilian labor force: 33,366 (2005); Leading industries: 39.0% manufacturing; 13.5% health care and social assistance; 12.0% retail trade (2004); Farms: 802 totaling 196,152 acres (2002); Companies that employ 500 or more persons: 3 (2004); Companies that employ 100 to 499 persons: 36 (2004); Companies that employ less than 100 persons: 1,445 (2004); Black-owned businesses: n/a (2002); Hispanic-owned businesses: n/a (2002); Women-owned businesses: 1,465 (2002); Retail sales per capita: $12,192 (2006). Single-family building permits issued: 128 (2005); Multi-family building permits issued: 4 (2005).
Income: Per capita income: $21,927 (2005); Median household income: $45,383 (2005); Average household income: $55,416 (2005); Percent of households with income of $100,000 or more: 10.1% (2005); Poverty rate: 8.2% (2003); Bankruptcy rate: 8.46% (2005).
Education: Percent of population age 25 and over with: High school diploma (including GED) or higher: 82.2% (2005); Bachelor's degree or higher: 11.9% (2005); Master's degree or higher: 4.1% (2005).
Housing: Homeownership rate: 75.6% (2005); Median home value: $108,133 (2005); Median rent: $365 per month (2000); Median age of housing: 46 years (2000).
Health: Birth rate: 135.8 per 10,000 population (2004); Death rate: 103.7 per 10,000 population (2004); Age-adjusted cancer mortality rate: 203.0 deaths per 100,000 population (2002); Number of physicians: 10.0 per 10,000 population (2004); Hospital beds: 49.3 per 10,000 population (2003); Hospital admissions: 664.1 per 10,000 population (2003).
Elections: 2004 Presidential election results: 55.9% Bush, 43.7% Kerry, 0.0% Nader, 0.2% Badnarik
National and State Parks: Pfizer State Park; Sandusky Scenic River State Access Area; Spiegel Grove State Park
Additional Information Contacts
Sandusky County Government . . . . (419) 334-6100
  http://www.sandusky-county.org/
Bellevue Chamber of Commerce. (419) 483-2182
  http://www.cityofbellevue.com
Bellevue Development Corp. . . . . (419) 483-9700
  http://www.bellevuedevelopment.org
City of Bellevue . . . . (419) 484-8400
  http://www.cityofbellevue.com
City of Clyde. . . . . (419) 547-6898
  http://www.clydeohio.org
City of Fremont . . . . (419) 334-5900
  http://www.fremontohio.org
Fremont Chamber of Commerce . . . . (419) 332-1591
  http://www.scchamber.org

Sandusky County Communities

BALLVILLE (CDP). Covers a land area of 2.742 square miles and a water area of 0.204 square miles. Located at 41.32° N. Lat.; 83.13° W. Long. Elevation is 615 feet.
Population: 3,059 (1990); 3,255 (2000); 3,332 (2005); 3,371 (2010 projected); Race: 93.7% White, 1.4% Black, 0.9% Asian, 4.4% Hispanic of any race (2005); Density: 1,215.1 persons per square mile (2005); Average household size: 2.40 (2005); Median age: 46.3 (2005); Males per 100 females: 91.3 (2005); Marriage status: 14.4% never married, 68.1% now married, 9.3% widowed, 8.2% divorced (2000); Foreign born: 2.0% (2000); Ancestry (includes multiple ancestries): 48.5% German, 12.7% Irish, 10.4% English, 8.3% Other groups, 5.9% United States or American (2000).
Economy: In agricultural area; tomatoes. Employment by occupation: 15.6% management, 23.7% professional, 10.8% services, 20.5% sales, 1.6% farming, 9.0% construction, 18.7% production (2000).
Income: Per capita income: $32,726 (2005); Median household income: $54,344 (2005); Average household income: $78,304 (2005); Percent of households with income of $100,000 or more: 19.2% (2005); Poverty rate: 5.1% (2000).
Education: Percent of population age 25 and over with: High school diploma (including GED) or higher: 91.3% (2005); Bachelor's degree or higher: 24.1% (2005); Master's degree or higher: 10.3% (2005).
Housing: Homeownership rate: 88.9% (2005); Median home value: $145,941 (2005); Median rent: $428 per month (2000); Median age of housing: 35 years (2000).
Transportation: Commute to work: 96.2% car, 0.0% public transportation, 0.0% walk, 2.8% work from home (2000); Travel time to work: 51.1% less than 15 minutes, 29.2% 15 to 30 minutes, 10.8% 30 to 45 minutes, 4.0% 45 to 60 minutes, 4.9% 60 minutes or more (2000)

BELLEVUE (city). Covers a land area of 5.058 square miles and a water area of 0.093 square miles. Located at 41.27° N. Lat.; 82.84° W. Long.
History: Bellevue was established as a railroad town in 1839 and named by James Bell, a railroad employee.
Population: 8,391 (1990); 8,193 (2000); 8,043 (2005); 7,900 (2010 projected); Race: 97.5% White, 0.3% Black, 0.3% Asian, 2.7% Hispanic of any race (2005); Density: 1,590.1 persons per square mile (2005); Average household size: 2.42 (2005); Median age: 36.7 (2005); Males per 100 females: 93.7 (2005); Marriage status: 21.7% never married, 56.8% now married, 8.7% widowed, 12.8% divorced (2000); Foreign born: 1.3% (2000); Ancestry (includes multiple ancestries): 38.0% German, 12.5% Irish, 11.6% United States or American, 9.6% Italian, 9.5% English (2000).
Economy: Single-family building permits issued: 9 (2005); Multi-family building permits issued: 2 (2005); Employment by occupation: 10.0% management, 14.6% professional, 14.4% services, 18.5% sales, 0.2% farming, 10.9% construction, 31.3% production (2000).
Income: Per capita income: $21,508 (2005); Median household income: $43,292 (2005); Average household income: $51,992 (2005); Percent of households with income of $100,000 or more: 8.5% (2005); Poverty rate: 5.8% (2000).
Education: Percent of population age 25 and over with: High school diploma (including GED) or higher: 82.8% (2005); Bachelor's degree or higher: 9.2% (2005); Master's degree or higher: 2.3% (2005).
School District(s)
Bellevue City SD (PK-12)
  2003-04 Enrollment: 2,388 . . . . (419) 484-5000
Seneca East Local SD (PK-12)
  2003-04 Enrollment: 1,075 . . . . (419) 426-7041
Housing: Homeownership rate: 70.1% (2005); Median home value: $104,486 (2005); Median rent: $375 per month (2000); Median age of housing: 50 years (2000).
Hospitals: Bellevue Hospital (64 beds)
Newspapers: Bellevue Gazette (Circulation 3,200)
Transportation: Commute to work: 94.1% car, 1.2% public transportation, 3.1% walk, 1.0% work from home (2000); Travel time to work: 49.1% less than 15 minutes, 28.4% 15 to 30 minutes, 13.8% 30 to 45 minutes, 2.0% 45 to 60 minutes, 6.6% 60 minutes or more (2000)
Additional Information Contacts
Bellevue Chamber of Commerce. (419) 483-2182
  http://www.cityofbellevue.com
Bellevue Development Corp. . . . . (419) 483-9700
  http://www.bellevuedevelopment.org
City of Bellevue . . . . (419) 484-8400
  http://www.cityofbellevue.com

BURGOON (village). Covers a land area of 0.090 square miles and a water area of 0 square miles. Located at 41.26° N. Lat.; 83.25° W. Long. Elevation is 708 feet.
Population: 224 (1990); 199 (2000); 207 (2005); 213 (2010 projected); Race: 94.7% White, 0.0% Black, 1.9% Asian, 4.3% Hispanic of any race (2005); Density: 2,299.5 persons per square mile (2005); Average household size: 2.88 (2005); Median age: 36.4 (2005); Males per 100 females: 113.4 (2005); Marriage status: 16.7% never married, 68.2% now married, 4.5% widowed, 10.6% divorced (2000); Foreign born: 1.1% (2000); Ancestry (includes multiple ancestries): 37.8% German, 14.1% United States or American, 13.5% English, 8.6% Dutch, 8.1% Irish (2000).
Economy: In agricultural area. Employment by occupation: 10.5% management, 20.0% professional, 15.8% services, 17.9% sales, 0.0% farming, 2.1% construction, 33.7% production (2000).
Income: Per capita income: $28,188 (2005); Median household income: $64,773 (2005); Average household income: $81,042 (2005); Percent of households with income of $100,000 or more: 11.1% (2005); Poverty rate: 1.1% (2000).
Taxes: Total city taxes per capita: $56 (2004); City property taxes per capita: $56 (2004).

Education: Percent of population age 25 and over with: High school diploma (including GED) or higher: 90.1% (2005); Bachelor's degree or higher: 9.9% (2005); Master's degree or higher: 3.8% (2005).

School District(s)

Lakota Local SD (PK-12)
    2003-04 Enrollment: 1,164 . . . . (419) 457-2911

Housing: Homeownership rate: 88.9% (2005); Median home value: $87,826 (2005); Median rent: $375 per month (2000); Median age of housing: 60+ years (2000).

Transportation: Commute to work: 94.9% car, 0.0% public transportation, 5.1% walk, 0.0% work from home (2000); Travel time to work: 26.3% less than 15 minutes, 45.5% 15 to 30 minutes, 14.1% 30 to 45 minutes, 10.1% 45 to 60 minutes, 4.0% 60 minutes or more (2000)

CLYDE (city). Covers a land area of 4.389 square miles and a water area of 0.052 square miles. Located at 41.30° N. Lat.; 82.97° W. Long. Elevation is 690 feet.

History: The story of Clyde's beginnings tells of an officer during the War of 1812 who drove a stake into the ground here and said: "At this spot I shall build my future home, which shall be the nucleus of a thriving town." It was 1820 when the soldier returned, recovered his chosen land, and the city of Clyde came into being. Writer Sherwood Anderson spent his boyhood in Clyde, and portrayed the town in the novel "Winesburg, Ohio."

Population: 6,207 (1990); 6,064 (2000); 6,017 (2005); 5,982 (2010 projected); Race: 95.6% White, 0.1% Black, 0.3% Asian, 4.7% Hispanic of any race (2005); Density: 1,370.8 persons per square mile (2005); Average household size: 2.58 (2005); Median age: 36.6 (2005); Males per 100 females: 92.6 (2005); Marriage status: 26.4% never married, 53.3% now married, 8.0% widowed, 12.4% divorced (2000); Foreign born: 0.3% (2000); Ancestry (includes multiple ancestries): 41.1% German, 13.0% Irish, 10.8% Other groups, 10.2% United States or American, 9.7% English (2000).

Economy: Single-family building permits issued: 24 (2005); Multi-family building permits issued: 0 (2005); Employment by occupation: 6.0% management, 12.9% professional, 13.6% services, 14.5% sales, 0.0% farming, 7.8% construction, 45.3% production (2000).

Income: Per capita income: $20,208 (2005); Median household income: $45,133 (2005); Average household income: $51,138 (2005); Percent of households with income of $100,000 or more: 8.3% (2005); Poverty rate: 8.6% (2000).

Education: Percent of population age 25 and over with: High school diploma (including GED) or higher: 76.8% (2005); Bachelor's degree or higher: 10.7% (2005); Master's degree or higher: 3.6% (2005).

School District(s)

Bellevue City SD (PK-12)
    2003-04 Enrollment: 2,388 . . . . (419) 484-5000
Clyde-Green Springs Ex Vill SD (PK-12)
    2003-04 Enrollment: 2,297 . . . . (419) 547-0588

Housing: Homeownership rate: 73.9% (2005); Median home value: $95,917 (2005); Median rent: $393 per month (2000); Median age of housing: 47 years (2000).

Safety: Violent crime rate: 5.0 per 10,000 population; Property crime rate: 264.1 per 10,000 population (2004).

Newspapers: Clyde Enterprise (General - Circulation 2,100)

Transportation: Commute to work: 90.4% car, 2.7% public transportation, 6.1% walk, 0.6% work from home (2000); Travel time to work: 51.5% less than 15 minutes, 27.6% 15 to 30 minutes, 13.5% 30 to 45 minutes, 1.7% 45 to 60 minutes, 5.7% 60 minutes or more (2000)

Additional Information Contacts
City of Clyde. . . . . (419) 547-6898
    http://www.clydeohio.org

FREMONT (city). Covers a land area of 7.511 square miles and a water area of 0.218 square miles. Located at 41.34° N. Lat.; 83.11° W. Long. Elevation is 636 feet.

History: Settlement began here after the War of 1812, when the two small towns of Croghansville and Lower Sandusky were established on the Sandusky River. In 1829 the two united, and in 1849 the name was changed to Fremont, for explorer John C. Fremont. Fremont grew as a sugar-beet and cannery center.

Population: 18,243 (1990); 17,375 (2000); 16,787 (2005); 16,278 (2010 projected); Race: 81.0% White, 8.7% Black, 0.2% Asian, 13.2% Hispanic of any race (2005); Density: 2,234.8 persons per square mile (2005); Average household size: 2.50 (2005); Median age: 34.6 (2005); Males per 100 females: 90.6 (2005); Marriage status: 29.0% never married, 49.2% now married, 9.1% widowed, 12.7% divorced (2000); Foreign born: 2.3% (2000); Ancestry (includes multiple ancestries): 33.9% German, 22.4% Other groups, 9.4% Irish, 6.2% English, 6.0% United States or American (2000).

Economy: Single-family building permits issued: 10 (2005); Multi-family building permits issued: 0 (2005); Employment by occupation: 6.5% management, 14.1% professional, 14.8% services, 19.3% sales, 0.3% farming, 8.3% construction, 36.8% production (2000).

Income: Per capita income: $17,155 (2005); Median household income: $36,184 (2005); Average household income: $41,737 (2005); Percent of households with income of $100,000 or more: 3.7% (2005); Poverty rate: 12.9% (2000).

Taxes: Total city taxes per capita: $477 (2004); City property taxes per capita: $53 (2004).

Education: Percent of population age 25 and over with: High school diploma (including GED) or higher: 77.6% (2005); Bachelor's degree or higher: 10.1% (2005); Master's degree or higher: 3.4% (2005).

School District(s)

Fremont City SD (PK-12)
    2003-04 Enrollment: 4,598 . . . . (419) 332-6454
Vanguard-Sentinel Joint Vocational SD (07-12)
    2003-04 Enrollment: n/a . . . . (419) 332-2626

Two-year College(s)

Terra State Community College (Public)
    Fall 2004 Enrollment: 2,634. . . . . (419) 334-8400
    2005-06 Tuition: In-state $3,612; Out-of-state $7,401
Vanguard Career Center (Public)
    Fall 2004 Enrollment: 29 . . . . (419) 334-6901

Housing: Homeownership rate: 58.4% (2005); Median home value: $85,286 (2005); Median rent: $359 per month (2000); Median age of housing: 58 years (2000).

Hospitals: Memorial Hospital (186 beds)

Safety: Violent crime rate: 26.6 per 10,000 population; Property crime rate: 689.6 per 10,000 population (2004).

Newspapers: The News-Messenger (Circulation 13,936)

Transportation: Commute to work: 94.6% car, 1.0% public transportation, 2.2% walk, 1.1% work from home (2000); Travel time to work: 57.2% less than 15 minutes, 26.8% 15 to 30 minutes, 9.7% 30 to 45 minutes, 3.3% 45 to 60 minutes, 2.9% 60 minutes or more (2000)

Additional Information Contacts
City of Fremont . . . . (419) 334-5900
    http://www.fremontohio.org
Fremont Chamber of Commerce . . . . (419) 332-1591
    http://www.scchamber.org

GIBSONBURG (village). Covers a land area of 2.494 square miles and a water area of 0.039 square miles. Located at 41.38° N. Lat.; 83.32° W. Long. Elevation is 680 feet.

History: Founded 1871.

Population: 2,616 (1990); 2,506 (2000); 2,457 (2005); 2,436 (2010 projected); Race: 93.0% White, 0.5% Black, 0.4% Asian, 8.9% Hispanic of any race (2005); Density: 985.0 persons per square mile (2005); Average household size: 2.59 (2005); Median age: 36.4 (2005); Males per 100 females: 97.0 (2005); Marriage status: 20.7% never married, 59.6% now married, 10.6% widowed, 9.2% divorced (2000); Foreign born: 1.0% (2000); Ancestry (includes multiple ancestries): 44.1% German, 12.4% Other groups, 8.5% Irish, 6.4% English, 5.9% United States or American (2000).

Economy: Single-family building permits issued: 12 (2005); Multi-family building permits issued: 2 (2005); Employment by occupation: 10.5% management, 13.8% professional, 10.6% services, 19.2% sales, 0.0% farming, 11.5% construction, 34.5% production (2000).

Income: Per capita income: $19,420 (2005); Median household income: $44,563 (2005); Average household income: $48,519 (2005); Percent of households with income of $100,000 or more: 6.5% (2005); Poverty rate: 6.5% (2000).

Education: Percent of population age 25 and over with: High school diploma (including GED) or higher: 83.3% (2005); Bachelor's degree or higher: 10.5% (2005); Master's degree or higher: 5.1% (2005).

School District(s)

Gibsonburg Ex Vill SD (PK-12)
    2003-04 Enrollment: 1,236 . . . . (419) 637-2479

Housing: Homeownership rate: 74.2% (2005); Median home value: $97,247 (2005); Median rent: $341 per month (2000); Median age of housing: 60+ years (2000).

Safety: Violent crime rate: 12.2 per 10,000 population; Property crime rate: 727.9 per 10,000 population (2004).
Transportation: Commute to work: 94.4% car, 0.0% public transportation, 3.5% walk, 1.0% work from home (2000); Travel time to work: 30.2% less than 15 minutes, 35.0% 15 to 30 minutes, 25.8% 30 to 45 minutes, 6.0% 45 to 60 minutes, 3.0% 60 minutes or more (2000)

HELENA (village). Covers a land area of 0.297 square miles and a water area of 0 square miles. Located at 41.34° N. Lat.; 83.29° W. Long. Elevation is 695 feet.
Population: 267 (1990); 236 (2000); 241 (2005); 247 (2010 projected); Race: 96.7% White, 0.0% Black, 0.0% Asian, 7.1% Hispanic of any race (2005); Density: 811.0 persons per square mile (2005); Average household size: 2.34 (2005); Median age: 42.0 (2005); Males per 100 females: 92.8 (2005); Marriage status: 16.6% never married, 66.3% now married, 5.2% widowed, 11.9% divorced (2000); Foreign born: 0.0% (2000); Ancestry (includes multiple ancestries): 47.7% German, 15.3% Irish, 9.4% United States or American, 7.7% Other groups, 7.2% English (2000).
Economy: In agricultural area. Employment by occupation: 2.7% management, 11.7% professional, 22.5% services, 16.2% sales, 0.0% farming, 12.6% construction, 34.2% production (2000).
Income: Per capita income: $17,137 (2005); Median household income: $37,946 (2005); Average household income: $40,097 (2005); Percent of households with income of $100,000 or more: 1.9% (2005); Poverty rate: 12.4% (2000).
Education: Percent of population age 25 and over with: High school diploma (including GED) or higher: 87.7% (2005); Bachelor's degree or higher: 4.9% (2005); Master's degree or higher: 4.3% (2005).
Housing: Homeownership rate: 83.5% (2005); Median home value: $80,021 (2005); Median rent: $354 per month (2000); Median age of housing: 60+ years (2000).
Transportation: Commute to work: 98.2% car, 0.0% public transportation, 0.9% walk, 0.9% work from home (2000); Travel time to work: 24.5% less than 15 minutes, 53.6% 15 to 30 minutes, 11.8% 30 to 45 minutes, 2.7% 45 to 60 minutes, 7.3% 60 minutes or more (2000)

LINDSEY (village). Covers a land area of 1.541 square miles and a water area of 0 square miles. Located at 41.42° N. Lat.; 83.22° W. Long. Elevation is 620 feet.
Population: 529 (1990); 504 (2000); 495 (2005); 491 (2010 projected); Race: 92.7% White, 0.4% Black, 0.2% Asian, 8.9% Hispanic of any race (2005); Density: 321.1 persons per square mile (2005); Average household size: 2.46 (2005); Median age: 37.7 (2005); Males per 100 females: 100.4 (2005); Marriage status: 18.4% never married, 67.5% now married, 5.6% widowed, 8.5% divorced (2000); Foreign born: 0.0% (2000); Ancestry (includes multiple ancestries): 45.5% German, 13.1% Irish, 10.7% United States or American, 10.3% English, 8.7% French (except Basque) (2000).
Economy: In agricultural area. Manufacturing of meat products. Single-family building permits issued: 0 (2005); Multi-family building permits issued: 0 (2005); Employment by occupation: 3.7% management, 18.0% professional, 9.2% services, 19.5% sales, 0.4% farming, 13.2% construction, 36.0% production (2000).
Income: Per capita income: $24,364 (2005); Median household income: $52,546 (2005); Average household income: $60,000 (2005); Percent of households with income of $100,000 or more: 11.4% (2005); Poverty rate: 5.7% (2000).
Education: Percent of population age 25 and over with: High school diploma (including GED) or higher: 88.6% (2005); Bachelor's degree or higher: 15.0% (2005); Master's degree or higher: 5.4% (2005).
School District(s)
Fremont City SD (PK-12)
    2003-04 Enrollment: 4,598 . . . . (419) 332-6454
Housing: Homeownership rate: 83.6% (2005); Median home value: $120,395 (2005); Median rent: $415 per month (2000); Median age of housing: 60+ years (2000).
Transportation: Commute to work: 97.4% car, 0.0% public transportation, 1.1% walk, 1.5% work from home (2000); Travel time to work: 16.8% less than 15 minutes, 53.1% 15 to 30 minutes, 16.4% 30 to 45 minutes, 10.3% 45 to 60 minutes, 3.4% 60 minutes or more (2000)

STONY PRAIRIE (CDP). Covers a land area of 1.542 square miles and a water area of 0 square miles. Located at 41.35° N. Lat.; 83.14° W. Long.
Population: 894 (1990); 836 (2000); 814 (2005); 784 (2010 projected); Race: 92.6% White, 0.9% Black, 0.1% Asian, 17.6% Hispanic of any race (2005); Density: 528.0 persons per square mile (2005); Average household size: 2.35 (2005); Median age: 41.2 (2005); Males per 100 females: 97.1 (2005); Marriage status: 18.0% never married, 63.1% now married, 10.7% widowed, 8.2% divorced (2000); Foreign born: 3.2% (2000); Ancestry (includes multiple ancestries): 36.4% German, 18.1% Other groups, 12.8% United States or American, 9.3% Polish, 7.9% English (2000).
Economy: Employment by occupation: 3.6% management, 8.7% professional, 12.5% services, 19.8% sales, 0.0% farming, 8.9% construction, 46.5% production (2000).
Income: Per capita income: $20,547 (2005); Median household income: $42,794 (2005); Average household income: $48,338 (2005); Percent of households with income of $100,000 or more: 4.9% (2005); Poverty rate: 6.6% (2000).
Education: Percent of population age 25 and over with: High school diploma (including GED) or higher: 66.3% (2005); Bachelor's degree or higher: 6.8% (2005); Master's degree or higher: 1.8% (2005).
Housing: Homeownership rate: 78.0% (2005); Median home value: $77,363 (2005); Median rent: $292 per month (2000); Median age of housing: 46 years (2000).
Transportation: Commute to work: 98.8% car, 0.0% public transportation, 1.2% walk, 0.0% work from home (2000); Travel time to work: 60.5% less than 15 minutes, 32.4% 15 to 30 minutes, 5.5% 30 to 45 minutes, 1.7% 45 to 60 minutes, 0.0% 60 minutes or more (2000)

VICKERY (unincorporated postal area, zip code 43464). Covers a land area of 29.217 square miles and a water area of 0.048 square miles. Located at 41.40° N. Lat.; 82.92° W. Long. Elevation is 604 feet.
Population: 1,544 (2000); Race: 94.5% White, 1.2% Black, 0.8% Asian, 2.6% Hispanic of any race (2000); Density: 52.8 persons per square mile (2000); Age: 27.1% under 18, 7.5% over 64 (2000); Marriage status: 22.1% never married, 58.8% now married, 7.3% widowed, 11.8% divorced (2000); Foreign born: 0.8% (2000); Ancestry (includes multiple ancestries): 41.8% German, 12.6% Irish, 11.2% United States or American, 10.7% English, 10.5% Other groups (2000).
Economy: Employment by occupation: 8.4% management, 5.6% professional, 12.6% services, 17.3% sales, 3.4% farming, 14.1% construction, 38.6% production (2000).
Income: Per capita income: $17,336 (2000); Median household income: $39,956 (2000); Poverty rate: 7.4% (2000).
Education: Percent of population age 25 and over with: High school diploma (including GED) or higher: 83.0% (2000); Bachelor's degree or higher: 4.7% (2000).
School District(s)
Margaretta Local SD (PK-12)
    2003-04 Enrollment: 1,467 . . . . (419) 684-5322
Housing: Homeownership rate: 86.5% (2000); Median home value: $82,000 (2000); Median rent: $252 per month (2000); Median age of housing: 41 years (2000).
Transportation: Commute to work: 91.2% car, 0.0% public transportation, 0.0% walk, 7.8% work from home (2000); Travel time to work: 21.4% less than 15 minutes, 54.4% 15 to 30 minutes, 15.8% 30 to 45 minutes, 2.8% 45 to 60 minutes, 5.7% 60 minutes or more (2000)

WOODVILLE (village). Covers a land area of 1.247 square miles and a water area of 0 square miles. Located at 41.45° N. Lat.; 83.36° W. Long. Elevation is 635 feet.
History: Woodville developed in the center of an extensive limestone area. The lime produced here was noted for its whiteness, plasticity, and sand-carrying qualities.
Population: 1,996 (1990); 1,977 (2000); 1,981 (2005); 2,013 (2010 projected); Race: 97.3% White, 0.2% Black, 0.0% Asian, 3.1% Hispanic of any race (2005); Density: 1,588.9 persons per square mile (2005); Average household size: 2.45 (2005); Median age: 38.1 (2005); Males per 100 females: 92.0 (2005); Marriage status: 19.2% never married, 63.4% now married, 7.7% widowed, 9.8% divorced (2000); Foreign born: 0.6% (2000); Ancestry (includes multiple ancestries): 54.4% German, 11.7% Irish, 10.2% English, 7.4% United States or American, 7.3% Other groups (2000).
Economy: Single-family building permits issued: 2 (2005); Multi-family building permits issued: 0 (2005); Employment by occupation: 10.5% management, 19.6% professional, 15.2% services, 21.2% sales, 0.5% farming, 12.6% construction, 20.5% production (2000).
Income: Per capita income: $24,016 (2005); Median household income: $50,486 (2005); Average household income: $58,953 (2005); Percent of households with income of $100,000 or more: 12.6% (2005); Poverty rate: 3.9% (2000).

Education: Percent of population age 25 and over with: High school diploma (including GED) or higher: 89.3% (2005); Bachelor's degree or higher: 18.7% (2005); Master's degree or higher: 5.7% (2005).

School District(s)

Woodmore Local SD (PK-12)
    2003-04 Enrollment: 1,190 . . . . (419) 849-2381

Housing: Homeownership rate: 77.4% (2005); Median home value: $127,788 (2005); Median rent: $341 per month (2000); Median age of housing: 50 years (2000).

Transportation: Commute to work: 92.6% car, 0.0% public transportation, 3.6% walk, 3.0% work from home (2000); Travel time to work: 31.0% less than 15 minutes, 34.6% 15 to 30 minutes, 27.8% 30 to 45 minutes, 4.3% 45 to 60 minutes, 2.3% 60 minutes or more (2000)

Scioto County

Located in southern Ohio; bounded on the south by the Ohio River and the Kentucky border; crossed by the Scioto and Little Scioto Rivers. Covers a land area of 612.27 square miles, a water area of 3.80 square miles, and is located in the Eastern Time Zone. The county government was organized in 1803. County seat is Portsmouth.

Scioto County is part of the Portsmouth, OH Micropolitan Statistical Area. The entire metro area includes: Scioto County, OH

Weather Station: Portsmouth Sciotoville   Elevation: 538 feet

	Jan	Feb	Mar	Apr	May	Jun	Jul	Aug	Sep	Oct	Nov	Dec
High	40	44	55	66	75	83	87	85	79	68	56	45
Low	22	25	33	42	51	60	64	62	55	43	35	27
Precip	3.2	2.8	3.7	3.4	4.4	3.9	4.1	4.0	3.1	2.6	3.0	3.3
Snow	5.5	3.7	2.3	0.3	tr	0.0	0.0	0.0	0.0	tr	0.3	1.2

High and Low temperatures in degrees Fahrenheit; Precipitation and Snow in inches

Population: 80,327 (1990); 79,195 (2000); 76,683 (2005); 74,161 (2010 projected); Race: 94.7% White, 2.8% Black, 0.4% Asian, 0.8% Hispanic of any race (2005); Density: 125.2 persons per square mile (2005); Average household size: 2.53 (2005); Median age: 37.5 (2005); Males per 100 females: 96.2 (2005).

Religion: Five largest groups: 5.9% The United Methodist Church, 4.3% Catholic Church, 2.7% Christian Churches and Churches of Christ, 2.2% General Association of Regular Baptist Churches, 2.2% National Association of Free Will Baptists (2000).

Economy: Unemployment rate: 8.8% (2005); Total civilian labor force: 32,254 (2005); Leading industries: 31.8% health care and social assistance; 17.5% retail trade; 13.6% accommodation & food services (2004); Farms: 709 totaling 96,449 acres (2002); Companies that employ 500 or more persons: 1 (2004); Companies that employ 100 to 499 persons: 25 (2004); Companies that employ less than 100 persons: 1,431 (2004); Black-owned businesses: n/a (2002); Hispanic-owned businesses: n/a (2002); Women-owned businesses: 1,381 (2002); Retail sales per capita: $11,153 (2006). Single-family building permits issued: 5 (2005); Multi-family building permits issued: 54 (2005).

Income: Per capita income: $17,500 (2005); Median household income: $32,108 (2005); Average household income: $43,335 (2005); Percent of households with income of $100,000 or more: 6.9% (2005); Poverty rate: 17.3% (2003); Bankruptcy rate: 10.40% (2005).

Taxes: Total county taxes per capita: $161 (2004); County property taxes per capita: $53 (2004).

Education: Percent of population age 25 and over with: High school diploma (including GED) or higher: 74.2% (2005); Bachelor's degree or higher: 10.1% (2005); Master's degree or higher: 3.7% (2005).

Housing: Homeownership rate: 70.4% (2005); Median home value: $73,234 (2005); Median rent: $295 per month (2000); Median age of housing: 41 years (2000).

Health: Birth rate: 128.0 per 10,000 population (2004); Death rate: 128.0 per 10,000 population (2004); Age-adjusted cancer mortality rate: 221.7 deaths per 100,000 population (2002); Air Quality Index: 75.3% good, 23.8% moderate, 0.8% unhealthy for sensitive individuals, 0.0% unhealthy (percent of days in 2005); Number of physicians: 18.3 per 10,000 population (2004); Hospital beds: 28.7 per 10,000 population (2003); Hospital admissions: 1,489.0 per 10,000 population (2003).

Elections: 2004 Presidential election results: 51.9% Bush, 47.8% Kerry, 0.0% Nader, 0.2% Badnarik.

National and State Parks: Brush Creek State Forest; Shawnee State Forest; Shawnee State Park

Additional Information Contacts

Scioto County Government . . . . (740) 355-8313
    http://www.sciotocountyohio.com/
City of Portsmouth . . . . (740) 354-8807
    http://www.ci.portsmouth.oh.us
Portsmouth Chamber of Commerce . . . . (740) 353-7647
    http://www.portsmouth.org

Scioto County Communities

FRANKLIN FURNACE (CDP). Covers a land area of 2.384 square miles and a water area of 0.357 square miles. Located at 38.62° N. Lat.; 82.84° W. Long. Elevation is 580 feet.

Population: 1,212 (1990); 1,537 (2000); 1,480 (2005); 1,443 (2010 projected); Race: 87.4% White, 10.8% Black, 0.2% Asian, 0.4% Hispanic of any race (2005); Density: 620.9 persons per square mile (2005); Average household size: 2.93 (2005); Median age: 30.3 (2005); Males per 100 females: 130.5 (2005); Marriage status: 22.8% never married, 55.6% now married, 5.8% widowed, 15.9% divorced (2000); Foreign born: 1.6% (2000); Ancestry (includes multiple ancestries): 16.5% United States or American, 14.7% German, 12.5% Other groups, 7.8% Irish, 6.1% English (2000).

Economy: Employment by occupation: 6.2% management, 10.9% professional, 24.9% services, 18.0% sales, 0.0% farming, 9.0% construction, 31.0% production (2000).

Income: Per capita income: $15,115 (2005); Median household income: $30,353 (2005); Average household income: $40,688 (2005); Percent of households with income of $100,000 or more: 6.7% (2005); Poverty rate: 12.5% (2000).

Education: Percent of population age 25 and over with: High school diploma (including GED) or higher: 69.8% (2005); Bachelor's degree or higher: 10.4% (2005); Master's degree or higher: 2.5% (2005).

School District(s)

Department of Youth Services (06-12)
    2003-04 Enrollment: 1,333 . . . . (614) 728-2489
Green Local SD (PK-12)
    2003-04 Enrollment: 733 . . . . (740) 354-9221

Housing: Homeownership rate: 75.0% (2005); Median home value: $86,727 (2005); Median rent: $355 per month (2000); Median age of housing: 23 years (2000).

Transportation: Commute to work: 93.7% car, 0.0% public transportation, 4.9% walk, 1.4% work from home (2000); Travel time to work: 29.7% less than 15 minutes, 34.0% 15 to 30 minutes, 17.4% 30 to 45 minutes, 8.4% 45 to 60 minutes, 10.5% 60 minutes or more (2000)

LUCASVILLE (CDP). Covers a land area of 2.515 square miles and a water area of 0.036 square miles. Located at 38.88° N. Lat.; 82.99° W. Long. Elevation is 557 feet.

History: Lucasville was founded in 1819 by John Lucas on land received by his father, William Lucas, for Revolutionary War service. The founder's son, Robert Lucas, was governor of Ohio (1832-1836) and territorial governor of Iowa (1838-1841).

Population: 1,575 (1990); 1,588 (2000); 1,530 (2005); 1,442 (2010 projected); Race: 97.1% White, 0.1% Black, 0.5% Asian, 0.5% Hispanic of any race (2005); Density: 608.3 persons per square mile (2005); Average household size: 2.65 (2005); Median age: 36.9 (2005); Males per 100 females: 90.8 (2005); Marriage status: 22.4% never married, 61.2% now married, 7.5% widowed, 9.0% divorced (2000); Foreign born: 0.0% (2000); Ancestry (includes multiple ancestries): 35.8% United States or American, 13.2% German, 10.4% English, 9.2% Irish, 8.3% Other groups (2000).

Economy: Employment by occupation: 6.8% management, 18.5% professional, 25.3% services, 18.5% sales, 0.0% farming, 9.7% construction, 21.2% production (2000).

Income: Per capita income: $15,235 (2005); Median household income: $32,216 (2005); Average household income: $40,399 (2005); Percent of households with income of $100,000 or more: 5.0% (2005); Poverty rate: 8.5% (2000).

Education: Percent of population age 25 and over with: High school diploma (including GED) or higher: 62.5% (2005); Bachelor's degree or higher: 13.8% (2005); Master's degree or higher: 6.3% (2005).

School District(s)

Scioto County Joint Vocational School (10-12)
    2003-04 Enrollment: n/a . . . . (740) 259-5522
Valley Local School District (PK-12)
    2003-04 Enrollment: 1,216 . . . . (740) 259-3115

Two-year College(s)
Scioto County Joint Vocational School District (Public)
  Fall 2004 Enrollment: 294 . . . . (740) 259-5522
Housing: Homeownership rate: 72.6% (2005); Median home value: $78,542 (2005); Median rent: $293 per month (2000); Median age of housing: 35 years (2000).
Transportation: Commute to work: 97.6% car, 0.0% public transportation, 1.0% walk, 0.0% work from home (2000); Travel time to work: 29.8% less than 15 minutes, 37.6% 15 to 30 minutes, 21.2% 30 to 45 minutes, 3.9% 45 to 60 minutes, 7.5% 60 minutes or more (2000)

MCDERMOTT (unincorporated postal area, zip code 45652). Covers a land area of 42.649 square miles and a water area of 0.028 square miles. Located at 38.83° N. Lat.; 83.07° W. Long. Elevation is 580 feet.
Population: 3,566 (2000); Race: 97.6% White, 0.0% Black, 1.0% Asian, 0.2% Hispanic of any race (2000); Density: 83.6 persons per square mile (2000); Age: 26.3% under 18, 13.7% over 64 (2000); Marriage status: 19.7% never married, 61.8% now married, 6.6% widowed, 11.8% divorced (2000); Foreign born: 0.3% (2000); Ancestry (includes multiple ancestries): 20.1% United States or American, 10.6% English, 10.0% German, 9.2% Other groups, 7.0% Irish (2000).
Economy: Employment by occupation: 10.1% management, 15.4% professional, 19.3% services, 20.4% sales, 2.3% farming, 12.0% construction, 20.5% production (2000).
Income: Per capita income: $16,655 (2000); Median household income: $28,468 (2000); Poverty rate: 18.7% (2000).
Education: Percent of population age 25 and over with: High school diploma (including GED) or higher: 76.6% (2000); Bachelor's degree or higher: 6.2% (2000).
School District(s)
Northwest Local SD (PK-12)
  2003-04 Enrollment: 1,780 . . . . (740) 259-5558
Housing: Homeownership rate: 82.0% (2000); Median home value: $63,500 (2000); Median rent: $253 per month (2000); Median age of housing: 28 years (2000).
Transportation: Commute to work: 94.6% car, 0.8% public transportation, 3.0% walk, 1.6% work from home (2000); Travel time to work: 18.4% less than 15 minutes, 40.5% 15 to 30 minutes, 24.9% 30 to 45 minutes, 1.4% 45 to 60 minutes, 14.7% 60 minutes or more (2000)

MINFORD (unincorporated postal area, zip code 45653). Covers a land area of 47.606 square miles and a water area of 0.010 square miles. Located at 38.87° N. Lat.; 82.84° W. Long. Elevation is 657 feet.
Population: 4,163 (2000); Race: 99.3% White, 0.0% Black, 0.0% Asian, 0.2% Hispanic of any race (2000); Density: 87.4 persons per square mile (2000); Age: 25.7% under 18, 13.4% over 64 (2000); Marriage status: 19.8% never married, 65.3% now married, 5.9% widowed, 9.0% divorced (2000); Foreign born: 0.0% (2000); Ancestry (includes multiple ancestries): 21.6% United States or American, 16.0% German, 9.5% English, 7.4% Irish, 5.3% Other groups (2000).
Economy: Employment by occupation: 7.1% management, 19.1% professional, 15.6% services, 21.9% sales, 0.6% farming, 13.8% construction, 21.9% production (2000).
Income: Per capita income: $16,354 (2000); Median household income: $37,281 (2000); Poverty rate: 14.6% (2000).
Education: Percent of population age 25 and over with: High school diploma (including GED) or higher: 77.8% (2000); Bachelor's degree or higher: 11.7% (2000).
School District(s)
Minford Local SD (PK-12)
  2003-04 Enrollment: 1,652 . . . . (740) 820-3896
Housing: Homeownership rate: 85.0% (2000); Median home value: $75,700 (2000); Median rent: $287 per month (2000); Median age of housing: 29 years (2000).
Transportation: Commute to work: 96.1% car, 0.0% public transportation, 0.7% walk, 3.0% work from home (2000); Travel time to work: 19.2% less than 15 minutes, 38.4% 15 to 30 minutes, 29.5% 30 to 45 minutes, 5.0% 45 to 60 minutes, 7.8% 60 minutes or more (2000)

NEW BOSTON (village). Covers a land area of 1.107 square miles and a water area of 0.052 square miles. Located at 38.75° N. Lat.; 82.93° W. Long. Elevation is 520 feet.
History: New Boston was founded in 1891 and named for Boston, whose capitalists financed a sawmill here. New Boston later became a river steel town.

Population: 2,717 (1990); 2,340 (2000); 2,227 (2005); 2,135 (2010 projected); Race: 97.6% White, 0.1% Black, 0.2% Asian, 0.7% Hispanic of any race (2005); Density: 2,012.3 persons per square mile (2005); Average household size: 2.08 (2005); Median age: 37.8 (2005); Males per 100 females: 72.0 (2005); Marriage status: 23.0% never married, 43.2% now married, 15.6% widowed, 18.2% divorced (2000); Foreign born: 0.0% (2000); Ancestry (includes multiple ancestries): 20.3% United States or American, 13.2% Other groups, 10.8% German, 9.5% Irish, 6.7% English (2000).
Economy: Single-family building permits issued: 0 (2005); Multi-family building permits issued: 0 (2005); Employment by occupation: 5.1% management, 10.3% professional, 23.2% services, 36.2% sales, 0.0% farming, 5.4% construction, 19.8% production (2000).
Income: Per capita income: $13,254 (2005); Median household income: $18,623 (2005); Average household income: $27,004 (2005); Percent of households with income of $100,000 or more: 1.7% (2005); Poverty rate: 32.2% (2000).
Education: Percent of population age 25 and over with: High school diploma (including GED) or higher: 58.1% (2005); Bachelor's degree or higher: 5.4% (2005); Master's degree or higher: 1.1% (2005).
School District(s)
New Boston Local SD (PK-12)
  2003-04 Enrollment: 439 . . . . (740) 456-4626
Two-year College(s)
Southeastern Business College (Private, For-profit)
  Fall 2004 Enrollment: 66 . . . . (740) 456-4124
  2005-06 Tuition: In-state $9,305; Out-of-state $9,305
Housing: Homeownership rate: 38.9% (2005); Median home value: $53,813 (2005); Median rent: $246 per month (2000); Median age of housing: 53 years (2000).
Transportation: Commute to work: 90.1% car, 0.9% public transportation, 5.7% walk, 1.0% work from home (2000); Travel time to work: 51.7% less than 15 minutes, 27.5% 15 to 30 minutes, 5.0% 30 to 45 minutes, 7.3% 45 to 60 minutes, 8.6% 60 minutes or more (2000)

OTWAY (village). Covers a land area of 0.222 square miles and a water area of 0 square miles. Located at 38.86° N. Lat.; 83.18° W. Long. Elevation is 588 feet.
Population: 105 (1990); 86 (2000); 80 (2005); 75 (2010 projected); Race: 96.3% White, 0.0% Black, 0.0% Asian, 3.8% Hispanic of any race (2005); Density: 361.0 persons per square mile (2005); Average household size: 2.11 (2005); Median age: 45.7 (2005); Males per 100 females: 81.8 (2005); Marriage status: 20.3% never married, 53.6% now married, 14.5% widowed, 11.6% divorced (2000); Foreign born: 0.0% (2000); Ancestry (includes multiple ancestries): 27.1% United States or American, 14.1% German, 7.1% Dutch, 7.1% Scotch-Irish, 4.7% Irish (2000).
Economy: Sawmills. Employment by occupation: 4.0% management, 0.0% professional, 12.0% services, 36.0% sales, 0.0% farming, 24.0% construction, 24.0% production (2000).
Income: Per capita income: $15,719 (2005); Median household income: $32,875 (2005); Average household income: $33,092 (2005); Percent of households with income of $100,000 or more: 0.0% (2005); Poverty rate: 14.1% (2000).
Education: Percent of population age 25 and over with: High school diploma (including GED) or higher: 65.1% (2005); Bachelor's degree or higher: 3.2% (2005); Master's degree or higher: 0.0% (2005).
Housing: Homeownership rate: 78.9% (2005); Median home value: $50,000 (2005); Median rent: $283 per month (2000); Median age of housing: 60+ years (2000).
Transportation: Commute to work: 92.0% car, 8.0% public transportation, 0.0% walk, 0.0% work from home (2000); Travel time to work: 8.0% less than 15 minutes, 36.0% 15 to 30 minutes, 44.0% 30 to 45 minutes, 0.0% 45 to 60 minutes, 12.0% 60 minutes or more (2000)

PORTSMOUTH (city). Covers a land area of 10.770 square miles and a water area of 0.288 square miles. Located at 38.74° N. Lat.; 82.96° W. Long. Elevation is 540 feet.
History: Portsmouth was founded in 1803 by Major Henry Massie, a Virginia land speculator. By 1815 Portsmouth was an incorporated town. Industry moved from lumbering and fur trading, to canal-boat center, to iron works and brickyards. In 1927, a suspension bridge was built across the Ohio River to connect the town with South Portsmouth in Kentucky.
Population: 22,676 (1990); 20,909 (2000); 19,392 (2005); 17,974 (2010 projected); Race: 90.8% White, 5.3% Black, 1.1% Asian, 1.2% Hispanic of any race (2005); Density: 1,800.6 persons per square mile (2005); Average

household size: 2.27 (2005); Median age: 38.4 (2005); Males per 100 females: 85.6 (2005); Marriage status: 24.4% never married, 48.8% now married, 11.5% widowed, 15.2% divorced (2000); Foreign born: 1.1% (2000); Ancestry (includes multiple ancestries): 16.7% German, 15.9% United States or American, 12.8% Other groups, 12.5% Irish, 10.0% English (2000).
Economy: Single-family building permits issued: 0 (2005); Multi-family building permits issued: 54 (2005); Employment by occupation: 8.8% management, 20.3% professional, 21.6% services, 24.3% sales, 0.7% farming, 8.9% construction, 15.3% production (2000).
Income: Per capita income: $16,667 (2005); Median household income: $25,501 (2005); Average household income: $37,189 (2005); Percent of households with income of $100,000 or more: 5.1% (2005); Poverty rate: 23.6% (2000).
Education: Percent of population age 25 and over with: High school diploma (including GED) or higher: 74.0% (2005); Bachelor's degree or higher: 12.4% (2005); Master's degree or higher: 5.2% (2005).

School District(s)
Clay Local SD (KG-12)
    2003-04 Enrollment: 566 . . . . (740) 354-6645
Portsmouth City SD (PK-12)
    2003-04 Enrollment: 2,166 . . . . (740) 354-4727
Sciotoville (07-12)
    2003-04 Enrollment: 299 . . . . (740) 776-6777

Four-year College(s)
Shawnee State University (Public)
    Fall 2004 Enrollment: 3,798 . . . . (740) 354-3205
    2005-06 Tuition: In-state $5,508; Out-of-state $9,396

Two-year College(s)
Paramount Beauty Academy (Private, For-profit)
    Fall 2004 Enrollment: 58 . . . . (740) 353-2436

Housing: Homeownership rate: 53.9% (2005); Median home value: $62,685 (2005); Median rent: $302 per month (2000); Median age of housing: 58 years (2005).
Hospitals: Southern Ohio Medical Center (488 beds)
Safety: Violent crime rate: 102.2 per 10,000 population; Property crime rate: 1,487.0 per 10,000 population (2004).
Newspapers: The Portsmouth Daily Times (Circulation 14,627)
Transportation: Commute to work: 90.5% car, 1.4% public transportation, 5.5% walk, 1.6% work from home (2000); Travel time to work: 55.2% less than 15 minutes, 26.3% 15 to 30 minutes, 9.3% 30 to 45 minutes, 2.2% 45 to 60 minutes, 7.0% 60 minutes or more (2000)

Additional Information Contacts
City of Portsmouth . . . . (740) 354-8807
    http://www.ci.portsmouth.oh.us
Portsmouth Chamber of Commerce . . . . (740) 353-7647
    http://www.portsmouth.org

RARDEN (village). Covers a land area of 0.204 square miles and a water area of 0 square miles. Located at 38.92° N. Lat.; 83.24° W. Long. Elevation is 613 feet.
Population: 184 (1990); 176 (2000); 172 (2005); 162 (2010 projected); Race: 93.0% White, 0.0% Black, 0.0% Asian, 0.0% Hispanic of any race (2005); Density: 841.3 persons per square mile (2005); Average household size: 2.53 (2005); Median age: 37.2 (2005); Males per 100 females: 102.4 (2005); Marriage status: 31.7% never married, 49.0% now married, 11.4% widowed, 7.9% divorced (2000); Foreign born: 0.0% (2000); Ancestry (includes multiple ancestries): 27.7% United States or American, 13.5% Other groups, 10.0% Irish, 9.6% German, 2.7% Italian (2000).
Economy: Employment by occupation: 7.0% management, 9.0% professional, 12.0% services, 18.0% sales, 2.0% farming, 20.0% construction, 32.0% production (2000).
Income: Per capita income: $19,535 (2005); Median household income: $41,316 (2005); Average household income: $49,412 (2005); Percent of households with income of $100,000 or more: 5.9% (2005); Poverty rate: 1.2% (2000).
Education: Percent of population age 25 and over with: High school diploma (including GED) or higher: 72.2% (2005); Bachelor's degree or higher: 3.5% (2005); Master's degree or higher: 3.5% (2005).
Housing: Homeownership rate: 63.2% (2005); Median home value: $66,923 (2005); Median rent: $264 per month (2000); Median age of housing: 49 years (2000).
Transportation: Commute to work: 89.0% car, 0.0% public transportation, 6.0% walk, 3.0% work from home (2000); Travel time to work: 25.8% less than 15 minutes, 18.6% 15 to 30 minutes, 18.6% 30 to 45 minutes, 7.2% 45 to 60 minutes, 29.9% 60 minutes or more (2000)

ROSEMOUNT (CDP). Covers a land area of 5.754 square miles and a water area of 0 square miles. Located at 38.78° N. Lat.; 82.97° W. Long. Elevation is 600 feet.
Population: 2,277 (1990); 2,043 (2000); 1,978 (2005); 1,915 (2010 projected); Race: 98.3% White, 0.3% Black, 0.1% Asian, 0.2% Hispanic of any race (2005); Density: 343.7 persons per square mile (2005); Average household size: 2.38 (2005); Median age: 42.0 (2005); Males per 100 females: 88.4 (2005); Marriage status: 16.5% never married, 68.9% now married, 8.0% widowed, 6.6% divorced (2000); Foreign born: 0.6% (2000); Ancestry (includes multiple ancestries): 19.0% German, 18.0% United States or American, 10.2% Irish, 10.2% English, 7.8% Other groups (2000).
Economy: Employment by occupation: 17.0% management, 12.4% professional, 19.7% services, 28.4% sales, 0.0% farming, 7.6% construction, 14.8% production (2000).
Income: Per capita income: $22,652 (2005); Median household income: $42,762 (2005); Average household income: $53,982 (2005); Percent of households with income of $100,000 or more: 10.0% (2005); Poverty rate: 8.3% (2000).
Education: Percent of population age 25 and over with: High school diploma (including GED) or higher: 92.1% (2005); Bachelor's degree or higher: 17.6% (2005); Master's degree or higher: 3.4% (2005).
Housing: Homeownership rate: 81.0% (2005); Median home value: $87,811 (2005); Median rent: $383 per month (2000); Median age of housing: 43 years (2000).
Transportation: Commute to work: 95.6% car, 1.0% public transportation, 0.0% walk, 3.4% work from home (2000); Travel time to work: 49.1% less than 15 minutes, 34.0% 15 to 30 minutes, 13.5% 30 to 45 minutes, 2.6% 45 to 60 minutes, 0.9% 60 minutes or more (2000)

SCIOTODALE (CDP). Covers a land area of 1.968 square miles and a water area of <.001 square miles. Located at 38.75° N. Lat.; 82.86° W. Long. Elevation is 660 feet.
Population: 1,128 (1990); 982 (2000); 975 (2005); 986 (2010 projected); Race: 97.5% White, 0.2% Black, 0.2% Asian, 0.4% Hispanic of any race (2005); Density: 495.4 persons per square mile (2005); Average household size: 2.57 (2005); Median age: 39.7 (2005); Males per 100 females: 95.0 (2005); Marriage status: 19.6% never married, 57.4% now married, 5.5% widowed, 17.6% divorced (2000); Foreign born: 0.0% (2000); Ancestry (includes multiple ancestries): 14.9% Irish, 14.1% United States or American, 13.2% German, 10.0% English, 7.5% Other groups (2000).
Economy: Employment by occupation: 7.8% management, 12.4% professional, 19.7% services, 18.7% sales, 0.0% farming, 17.4% construction, 24.1% production (2000).
Income: Per capita income: $25,326 (2005); Median household income: $44,244 (2005); Average household income: $65,152 (2005); Percent of households with income of $100,000 or more: 15.3% (2005); Poverty rate: 24.2% (2000).
Education: Percent of population age 25 and over with: High school diploma (including GED) or higher: 82.5% (2005); Bachelor's degree or higher: 3.2% (2005); Master's degree or higher: 0.6% (2005).
Housing: Homeownership rate: 83.6% (2005); Median home value: $87,400 (2005); Median rent: $311 per month (2000); Median age of housing: 45 years (2000).
Transportation: Commute to work: 96.9% car, 0.0% public transportation, 0.0% walk, 1.8% work from home (2000); Travel time to work: 28.5% less than 15 minutes, 33.5% 15 to 30 minutes, 18.1% 30 to 45 minutes, 4.3% 45 to 60 minutes, 15.7% 60 minutes or more (2000)

SOUTH WEBSTER (village). Covers a land area of 1.306 square miles and a water area of 0.018 square miles. Located at 38.81° N. Lat.; 82.72° W. Long. Elevation is 702 feet.
Population: 806 (1990); 764 (2000); 684 (2005); 643 (2010 projected); Race: 98.2% White, 0.0% Black, 0.0% Asian, 0.7% Hispanic of any race (2005); Density: 523.6 persons per square mile (2005); Average household size: 2.41 (2005); Median age: 38.3 (2005); Males per 100 females: 87.4 (2005); Marriage status: 23.4% never married, 55.0% now married, 10.3% widowed, 11.3% divorced (2000); Foreign born: 0.3% (2000); Ancestry (includes multiple ancestries): 20.3% German, 13.5% United States or American, 7.9% Other groups, 6.4% Irish, 6.3% English (2000).

Economy: In agricultural area; makes refractories. Employment by occupation: 4.3% management, 18.4% professional, 23.3% services, 23.1% sales, 1.7% farming, 12.7% construction, 16.4% production (2000).
Income: Per capita income: $17,478 (2005); Median household income: $32,353 (2005); Average household income: $42,095 (2005); Percent of households with income of $100,000 or more: 6.3% (2005); Poverty rate: 16.4% (2000).
Education: Percent of population age 25 and over with: High school diploma (including GED) or higher: 83.2% (2005); Bachelor's degree or higher: 12.5% (2005); Master's degree or higher: 6.2% (2005).

School District(s)
Bloom-Vernon Local School District (PK-12)
    2003-04 Enrollment: 1,017 . . . . (740) 778-2281

Housing: Homeownership rate: 74.3% (2005); Median home value: $84,146 (2005); Median rent: $259 per month (2000); Median age of housing: 44 years (2000).
Transportation: Commute to work: 93.5% car, 1.2% public transportation, 2.1% walk, 1.2% work from home (2000); Travel time to work: 21.8% less than 15 minutes, 27.5% 15 to 30 minutes, 33.7% 30 to 45 minutes, 10.1% 45 to 60 minutes, 6.9% 60 minutes or more (2000)

STOUT (unincorporated postal area, zip code 45684). Covers a land area of 75.384 square miles and a water area of 0.046 square miles. Located at 38.78° N. Lat.; 83.10° W. Long.
Population: 1,827 (2000); Race: 99.1% White, 0.0% Black, 0.0% Asian, 0.1% Hispanic of any race (2000); Density: 24.2 persons per square mile (2000); Age: 23.5% under 18, 12.2% over 64 (2000); Marriage status: 16.6% never married, 63.3% now married, 7.4% widowed, 12.7% divorced (2000); Foreign born: 0.1% (2000); Ancestry (includes multiple ancestries): 24.3% United States or American, 12.3% German, 8.0% Other groups, 7.1% Irish, 7.1% English (2000).
Economy: Employment by occupation: 4.8% management, 16.4% professional, 15.0% services, 19.3% sales, 1.3% farming, 21.5% construction, 21.7% production (2000).
Income: Per capita income: $14,269 (2000); Median household income: $30,000 (2000); Poverty rate: 17.9% (2000).
Education: Percent of population age 25 and over with: High school diploma (including GED) or higher: 65.0% (2000); Bachelor's degree or higher: 9.0% (2000).
Housing: Homeownership rate: 81.4% (2000); Median home value: $64,300 (2000); Median rent: $244 per month (2000); Median age of housing: 26 years (2000).
Transportation: Commute to work: 91.8% car, 0.0% public transportation, 5.6% walk, 2.5% work from home (2000); Travel time to work: 15.5% less than 15 minutes, 32.6% 15 to 30 minutes, 23.3% 30 to 45 minutes, 13.0% 45 to 60 minutes, 15.5% 60 minutes or more (2000)

WEST PORTSMOUTH (CDP). Covers a land area of 4.747 square miles and a water area of 0 square miles. Located at 38.75° N. Lat.; 83.03° W. Long. Elevation is 600 feet.
Population: 3,551 (1990); 3,458 (2000); 3,149 (2005); 2,844 (2010 projected); Race: 96.9% White, 0.1% Black, 0.1% Asian, 0.1% Hispanic of any race (2005); Density: 663.4 persons per square mile (2005); Average household size: 2.48 (2005); Median age: 36.8 (2005); Males per 100 females: 91.0 (2005); Marriage status: 20.1% never married, 59.6% now married, 7.8% widowed, 12.5% divorced (2000); Foreign born: 0.1% (2000); Ancestry (includes multiple ancestries): 17.0% United States or American, 13.4% Irish, 12.5% German, 9.8% Other groups, 5.6% English (2000).
Economy: Employment by occupation: 3.4% management, 12.1% professional, 28.8% services, 19.4% sales, 0.4% farming, 12.5% construction, 23.4% production (2000).
Income: Per capita income: $14,071 (2005); Median household income: $30,558 (2005); Average household income: $34,917 (2005); Percent of households with income of $100,000 or more: 3.0% (2005); Poverty rate: 22.1% (2000).
Education: Percent of population age 25 and over with: High school diploma (including GED) or higher: 70.0% (2005); Bachelor's degree or higher: 5.1% (2005); Master's degree or higher: 0.7% (2005).

School District(s)
Washington-Nile Local SD (PK-12)
    2003-04 Enrollment: 1,699 . . . . (740) 858-1111

Housing: Homeownership rate: 76.0% (2005); Median home value: $47,419 (2005); Median rent: $310 per month (2000); Median age of housing: 45 years (2000).
Transportation: Commute to work: 95.3% car, 1.4% public transportation, 0.5% walk, 2.4% work from home (2000); Travel time to work: 41.7% less than 15 minutes, 32.5% 15 to 30 minutes, 13.5% 30 to 45 minutes, 4.4% 45 to 60 minutes, 7.8% 60 minutes or more (2000)

WHEELERSBURG (CDP). Covers a land area of 5.815 square miles and a water area of 0.080 square miles. Located at 38.73° N. Lat.; 82.84° W. Long. Elevation is 550 feet.
Population: 6,252 (1990); 6,471 (2000); 7,419 (2005); 8,204 (2010 projected); Race: 97.5% White, 0.4% Black, 0.2% Asian, 0.6% Hispanic of any race (2005); Density: 1,275.9 persons per square mile (2005); Average household size: 2.48 (2005); Median age: 40.1 (2005); Males per 100 females: 83.8 (2005); Marriage status: 18.5% never married, 61.6% now married, 9.2% widowed, 10.6% divorced (2000); Foreign born: 0.0% (2000); Ancestry (includes multiple ancestries): 21.2% German, 15.0% United States or American, 11.3% Irish, 7.8% English, 7.3% Other groups (2000).
Economy: Employment by occupation: 12.4% management, 23.5% professional, 22.8% services, 20.5% sales, 0.3% farming, 8.9% construction, 11.7% production (2000).
Income: Per capita income: $21,140 (2005); Median household income: $39,000 (2005); Average household income: $50,840 (2005); Percent of households with income of $100,000 or more: 8.9% (2005); Poverty rate: 14.2% (2000).
Education: Percent of population age 25 and over with: High school diploma (including GED) or higher: 78.9% (2005); Bachelor's degree or higher: 16.5% (2005); Master's degree or higher: 6.4% (2005).

School District(s)
Wheelersburg Local SD (PK-12)
    2003-04 Enrollment: 1,482 . . . . (740) 574-8484

Housing: Homeownership rate: 68.1% (2005); Median home value: $99,135 (2005); Median rent: $322 per month (2000); Median age of housing: 30 years (2000).
Newspapers: The Scioto Voice (General - Circulation 3,000)
Transportation: Commute to work: 97.2% car, 0.0% public transportation, 1.3% walk, 1.1% work from home (2000); Travel time to work: 32.3% less than 15 minutes, 42.7% 15 to 30 minutes, 12.9% 30 to 45 minutes, 6.7% 45 to 60 minutes, 5.5% 60 minutes or more (2000)

Seneca County

Located in northern Ohio; drained by the Sandusky River and its tributaries. Covers a land area of 550.59 square miles, a water area of 1.78 square miles, and is located in the Eastern Time Zone. The county government was organized in 1820. County seat is Tiffin.

Seneca County is part of the Tiffin, OH Micropolitan Statistical Area. The entire metro area includes: Seneca County, OH

Weather Station: Tiffin   Elevation: 738 feet

	Jan	Feb	Mar	Apr	May	Jun	Jul	Aug	Sep	Oct	Nov	Dec
High	32	36	48	60	72	80	84	82	76	63	49	38
Low	17	20	29	39	50	59	63	61	54	42	34	24
Precip	2.3	2.0	2.7	3.4	3.7	4.2	3.3	3.8	3.1	2.4	3.0	2.9
Snow	8.8	6.2	3.7	1.2	tr	0.0	0.0	0.0	0.0	tr	1.2	6.7

High and Low temperatures in degrees Fahrenheit; Precipitation and Snow in inches

Population: 59,733 (1990); 58,683 (2000); 57,371 (2005); 56,034 (2010 projected); Race: 94.7% White, 1.7% Black, 0.6% Asian, 3.6% Hispanic of any race (2005); Density: 104.2 persons per square mile (2005); Average household size: 2.59 (2005); Median age: 37.3 (2005); Males per 100 females: 97.9 (2005).
Religion: Five largest groups: 38.3% Catholic Church, 8.9% The United Methodist Church, 6.3% United Church of Christ, 4.5% Evangelical Lutheran Church in America, 1.0% Church of the Nazarene (2000).
Economy: Unemployment rate: 6.1% (2005); Total civilian labor force: 31,411 (2005); Leading industries: 30.8% manufacturing; 13.8% health care and social assistance; 11.7% retail trade (2004); Farms: 1,185 totaling 280,449 acres (2002); Companies that employ 500 or more persons: 2 (2004); Companies that employ 100 to 499 persons: 33 (2004); Companies that employ less than 100 persons: 1,317 (2004); Black-owned businesses: n/a (2002); Hispanic-owned businesses: n/a (2002); Women-owned businesses: 779 (2002); Retail sales per capita: $10,730 (2006). Single-family building permits issued: 82 (2005); Multi-family building permits issued: 40 (2005).

Income: Per capita income: $19,255 (2005); Median household income: $41,888 (2005); Average household income: $49,192 (2005); Percent of households with income of $100,000 or more: 7.0% (2005); Poverty rate: 9.1% (2003); Bankruptcy rate: 9.72% (2005).
Taxes: Total county taxes per capita: $195 (2004); County property taxes per capita: $111 (2004).
Education: Percent of population age 25 and over with: High school diploma (including GED) or higher: 83.1% (2005); Bachelor's degree or higher: 12.4% (2005); Master's degree or higher: 4.3% (2005).
Housing: Homeownership rate: 75.6% (2005); Median home value: $97,798 (2005); Median rent: $339 per month (2000); Median age of housing: 49 years (2000).
Health: Birth rate: 120.8 per 10,000 population (2004); Death rate: 88.8 per 10,000 population (2004); Age-adjusted cancer mortality rate: 225.3 deaths per 100,000 population (2002); Number of physicians: 11.8 per 10,000 population (2004); Hospital beds: 18.3 per 10,000 population (2003); Hospital admissions: 630.7 per 10,000 population (2003).
Elections: 2004 Presidential election results: 58.9% Bush, 40.6% Kerry, 0.0% Nader, 0.3% Badnarik
National and State Parks: Sandusky Scenic River State Access Area; Springville Marsh State Natural Area
Additional Information Contacts
Seneca County Government . . . . (419) 447-4550
  http://www.senecacounty.com/
City of Fostoria . . . . (419) 435-8282
  http://www.ci.fostoria.oh.us
Fostoria Chamber of Commerce . . . . (419) 435-0486
  http://www.fostoriaoh.org
Seneca County Convention and Visitors Bureau . . . . (419) 447-5866
  http://www.senecacounty.com/visitor
Tiffin Chamber of Commerce . . . . (419) 447-4141
  http://www.tiffinchamber.com

Seneca County Communities

ALVADA (unincorporated postal area, zip code 44802). Aka Alveda. Covers a land area of 29.497 square miles and a water area of 0 square miles. Located at 41.05° N. Lat.; 83.41° W. Long. Elevation is 847 feet.
Population: 1,013 (2000); Race: 99.9% White, 0.0% Black, 0.0% Asian, 1.5% Hispanic of any race (2000); Density: 34.3 persons per square mile (2000); Age: 30.7% under 18, 12.0% over 64 (2000); Marriage status: 22.4% never married, 68.3% now married, 2.7% widowed, 6.5% divorced (2000); Foreign born: 0.2% (2000); Ancestry (includes multiple ancestries): 50.0% German, 12.1% English, 8.6% United States or American, 7.3% Irish, 4.9% French (except Basque) (2000).
Economy: Employment by occupation: 11.8% management, 9.6% professional, 10.0% services, 22.3% sales, 0.8% farming, 15.5% construction, 30.1% production (2000).
Income: Per capita income: $18,673 (2000); Median household income: $48,621 (2000); Poverty rate: 1.6% (2000).
Education: Percent of population age 25 and over with: High school diploma (including GED) or higher: 86.8% (2000); Bachelor's degree or higher: 8.8% (2000).
Housing: Homeownership rate: 87.5% (2000); Median home value: $108,100 (2000); Median rent: $331 per month (2000); Median age of housing: 44 years (2000).
Transportation: Commute to work: 90.3% car, 0.0% public transportation, 1.4% walk, 7.1% work from home (2000); Travel time to work: 27.0% less than 15 minutes, 58.4% 15 to 30 minutes, 10.0% 30 to 45 minutes, 0.9% 45 to 60 minutes, 3.7% 60 minutes or more (2000)

ATTICA (village). Covers a land area of 0.535 square miles and a water area of 0 square miles. Located at 41.06° N. Lat.; 82.88° W. Long. Elevation is 950 feet.
Population: 992 (1990); 955 (2000); 866 (2005); 834 (2010 projected); Race: 98.8% White, 0.0% Black, 0.0% Asian, 0.6% Hispanic of any race (2005); Density: 1,617.2 persons per square mile (2005); Average household size: 2.37 (2005); Median age: 38.5 (2005); Males per 100 females: 88.7 (2005); Marriage status: 21.0% never married, 61.9% now married, 5.7% widowed, 11.5% divorced (2000); Foreign born: 1.3% (2000); Ancestry (includes multiple ancestries): 44.9% German, 11.0% Irish, 9.0% United States or American, 8.5% English, 5.7% Other groups (2000).
Economy: Single-family building permits issued: 0 (2005); Multi-family building permits issued: 0 (2005); Employment by occupation: 7.6% management, 10.1% professional, 16.7% services, 16.5% sales, 0.4% farming, 9.3% construction, 39.3% production (2000).
Income: Per capita income: $19,948 (2005); Median household income: $42,043 (2005); Average household income: $47,329 (2005); Percent of households with income of $100,000 or more: 5.5% (2005); Poverty rate: 9.8% (2000).
Education: Percent of population age 25 and over with: High school diploma (including GED) or higher: 83.0% (2005); Bachelor's degree or higher: 11.3% (2005); Master's degree or higher: 5.7% (2005).
School District(s)
Seneca East Local SD (PK-12)
  2003-04 Enrollment: 1,075 . . . . (419) 426-7041
Housing: Homeownership rate: 77.0% (2005); Median home value: $92,817 (2005); Median rent: $317 per month (2000); Median age of housing: 60 years (2000).
Newspapers: Attica Hub (General - Circulation 3,000)
Transportation: Commute to work: 91.3% car, 0.0% public transportation, 5.7% walk, 3.0% work from home (2000); Travel time to work: 30.9% less than 15 minutes, 38.4% 15 to 30 minutes, 22.6% 30 to 45 minutes, 4.6% 45 to 60 minutes, 3.5% 60 minutes or more (2000)

BETTSVILLE (village). Covers a land area of 0.520 square miles and a water area of 0 square miles. Located at 41.24° N. Lat.; 83.23° W. Long. Elevation is 707 feet.
Population: 752 (1990); 784 (2000); 775 (2005); 770 (2010 projected); Race: 95.2% White, 0.1% Black, 0.6% Asian, 5.5% Hispanic of any race (2005); Density: 1,489.4 persons per square mile (2005); Average household size: 2.57 (2005); Median age: 34.9 (2005); Males per 100 females: 97.2 (2005); Marriage status: 23.0% never married, 61.0% now married, 4.3% widowed, 11.7% divorced (2000); Foreign born: 1.1% (2000); Ancestry (includes multiple ancestries): 44.7% German, 13.4% Other groups, 9.6% United States or American, 8.5% English, 8.3% Irish (2000).
Economy: In agricultural area; dolomite products. Employment by occupation: 5.9% management, 8.1% professional, 13.8% services, 18.9% sales, 0.0% farming, 9.7% construction, 43.5% production (2000).
Income: Per capita income: $18,339 (2005); Median household income: $42,875 (2005); Average household income: $47,061 (2005); Percent of households with income of $100,000 or more: 2.6% (2005); Poverty rate: 7.4% (2000).
Education: Percent of population age 25 and over with: High school diploma (including GED) or higher: 81.2% (2005); Bachelor's degree or higher: 6.0% (2005); Master's degree or higher: 2.9% (2005).
School District(s)
Bettsville Local SD (KG-12)
  2003-04 Enrollment: 278 . . . . (419) 986-5166
Housing: Homeownership rate: 80.5% (2005); Median home value: $81,373 (2005); Median rent: $288 per month (2000); Median age of housing: 58 years (2000).
Transportation: Commute to work: 91.1% car, 1.1% public transportation, 5.3% walk, 1.7% work from home (2000); Travel time to work: 18.9% less than 15 minutes, 59.0% 15 to 30 minutes, 11.3% 30 to 45 minutes, 6.5% 45 to 60 minutes, 4.2% 60 minutes or more (2000)

BLOOMVILLE (village). Covers a land area of 0.607 square miles and a water area of 0 square miles. Located at 41.05° N. Lat.; 83.01° W. Long. Elevation is 920 feet.
Population: 949 (1990); 1,045 (2000); 988 (2005); 949 (2010 projected); Race: 97.2% White, 0.5% Black, 0.0% Asian, 4.0% Hispanic of any race (2005); Density: 1,626.4 persons per square mile (2005); Average household size: 2.79 (2005); Median age: 33.0 (2005); Males per 100 females: 90.0 (2005); Marriage status: 21.1% never married, 62.6% now married, 5.5% widowed, 10.8% divorced (2000); Foreign born: 0.6% (2000); Ancestry (includes multiple ancestries): 39.9% German, 18.1% United States or American, 13.8% English, 11.7% Irish, 7.4% Other groups (2000).
Economy: In agricultural area; limestone quarry. Single-family building permits issued: 0 (2005); Multi-family building permits issued: 0 (2005); Employment by occupation: 5.0% management, 12.2% professional, 20.5% services, 17.9% sales, 0.0% farming, 12.4% construction, 32.0% production (2000).
Income: Per capita income: $15,468 (2005); Median household income: $39,747 (2005); Average household income: $42,733 (2005); Percent of households with income of $100,000 or more: 3.4% (2005); Poverty rate: 5.8% (2000).

Education: Percent of population age 25 and over with: High school diploma (including GED) or higher: 86.3% (2005); Bachelor's degree or higher: 13.3% (2005); Master's degree or higher: 4.3% (2005).

School District(s)

Buckeye Central Local SD (KG-12)
    2003-04 Enrollment: 708 . . . . (419) 492-2864

Housing: Homeownership rate: 72.6% (2005); Median home value: $81,061 (2005); Median rent: $305 per month (2000); Median age of housing: 60+ years (2000).

Transportation: Commute to work: 93.4% car, 1.8% public transportation, 3.1% walk, 1.8% work from home (2000); Travel time to work: 20.9% less than 15 minutes, 47.5% 15 to 30 minutes, 19.1% 30 to 45 minutes, 5.2% 45 to 60 minutes, 7.2% 60 minutes or more (2000)

FOSTORIA

FOSTORIA (city). Covers a land area of 7.265 square miles and a water area of 0.218 square miles. Located at 41.15° N. Lat.; 83.41° W. Long. Elevation is 780 feet.

History: Fostoria grew from the union in 1854 of two rival settlements, Rome and Risdon, which had been established in 1832. The town was named for C.W. Foster, a local real estate developer whose son, Charles, served as governor of Ohio (1880-1884).

Population: 14,774 (1990); 13,931 (2000); 13,578 (2005); 13,271 (2010 projected); Race: 87.2% White, 5.5% Black, 0.7% Asian, 8.2% Hispanic of any race (2005); Density: 1,869.0 persons per square mile (2005); Average household size: 2.46 (2005); Median age: 36.4 (2005); Males per 100 females: 91.0 (2005); Marriage status: 26.4% never married, 49.6% now married, 10.2% widowed, 13.8% divorced (2000); Foreign born: 2.0% (2000); Ancestry (includes multiple ancestries): 33.2% German, 18.2% Other groups, 9.6% Irish, 7.6% English, 6.5% United States or American (2000).

Economy: Single-family building permits issued: 38 (2005); Multi-family building permits issued: 28 (2005); Employment by occupation: 6.9% management, 10.3% professional, 14.6% services, 18.9% sales, 0.2% farming, 8.0% construction, 41.2% production (2000).

Income: Per capita income: $16,735 (2005); Median household income: $33,165 (2005); Average household income: $40,597 (2005); Percent of households with income of $100,000 or more: 4.1% (2005); Poverty rate: 11.2% (2000).

Education: Percent of population age 25 and over with: High school diploma (including GED) or higher: 78.1% (2005); Bachelor's degree or higher: 8.8% (2005); Master's degree or higher: 2.6% (2005).

School District(s)

Fostoria City SD (PK-12)
    2003-04 Enrollment: 2,339 . . . . (419) 288-8400
Lakota Local SD (PK-12)
    2003-04 Enrollment: 1,164 . . . . (419) 457-2911

Housing: Homeownership rate: 70.7% (2005); Median home value: $67,479 (2005); Median rent: $325 per month (2000); Median age of housing: 53 years (2000).

Hospitals: Fostoria Community Hospital (66 beds)

Newspapers: The Review Times (Circulation 42,060)

Transportation: Commute to work: 92.1% car, 1.1% public transportation, 3.5% walk, 1.4% work from home (2000); Travel time to work: 46.0% less than 15 minutes, 28.5% 15 to 30 minutes, 16.2% 30 to 45 minutes, 4.5% 45 to 60 minutes, 4.8% 60 minutes or more (2000)

Additional Information Contacts

City of Fostoria. . . . . (419) 435-8282
    http://www.ci.fostoria.oh.us
Fostoria Chamber of Commerce . . . . (419) 435-0486
    http://www.fostoriaoh.org

GREEN SPRINGS

GREEN SPRINGS (village). Covers a land area of 1.072 square miles and a water area of 0.002 square miles. Located at 41.25° N. Lat.; 83.05° W. Long.

History: Green Springs developed as a winter and summer resort and spa, attracting visitors for its waters.

Population: 1,446 (1990); 1,247 (2000); 1,282 (2005); 1,293 (2010 projected); Race: 94.5% White, 0.3% Black, 0.9% Asian, 4.8% Hispanic of any race (2005); Density: 1,195.8 persons per square mile (2005); Average household size: 2.76 (2005); Median age: 40.0 (2005); Males per 100 females: 92.8 (2005); Marriage status: 18.8% never married, 59.5% now married, 12.3% widowed, 9.4% divorced (2000); Foreign born: 0.5% (2000); Ancestry (includes multiple ancestries): 35.5% German, 12.3% Irish, 11.2% Other groups, 10.6% English, 9.1% United States or American (2000).

Economy: Employment by occupation: 5.6% management, 8.8% professional, 14.9% services, 22.8% sales, 0.0% farming, 13.0% construction, 35.0% production (2000).

Income: Per capita income: $17,607 (2005); Median household income: $38,920 (2005); Average household income: $46,342 (2005); Percent of households with income of $100,000 or more: 5.2% (2005); Poverty rate: 8.7% (2000).

Education: Percent of population age 25 and over with: High school diploma (including GED) or higher: 77.3% (2005); Bachelor's degree or higher: 6.3% (2005); Master's degree or higher: 1.7% (2005).

School District(s)

Clyde-Green Springs Ex Vill SD (PK-12)
    2003-04 Enrollment: 2,297 . . . . (419) 547-0588

Housing: Homeownership rate: 68.3% (2005); Median home value: $85,000 (2005); Median rent: $322 per month (2000); Median age of housing: 60+ years (2000).

Hospitals: St Francis Health Care Centre (186 beds)

Transportation: Commute to work: 92.3% car, 1.0% public transportation, 3.3% walk, 1.9% work from home (2000); Travel time to work: 34.4% less than 15 minutes, 45.7% 15 to 30 minutes, 10.6% 30 to 45 minutes, 2.4% 45 to 60 minutes, 6.8% 60 minutes or more (2000)

KANSAS

KANSAS (unincorporated postal area, zip code 44841). Covers a land area of 19.918 square miles and a water area of 0 square miles. Located at 41.25° N. Lat.; 83.29° W. Long. Elevation is 725 feet.

Population: 863 (2000); Race: 100.0% White, 0.0% Black, 0.0% Asian, 0.0% Hispanic of any race (2000); Density: 43.3 persons per square mile (2000); Age: 27.1% under 18, 7.5% over 64 (2000); Marriage status: 29.5% never married, 60.2% now married, 3.7% widowed, 6.6% divorced (2000); Foreign born: 1.9% (2000); Ancestry (includes multiple ancestries): 49.9% German, 16.3% United States or American, 10.1% Irish, 6.2% English, 2.7% French (except Basque) (2000).

Economy: Employment by occupation: 10.2% management, 12.9% professional, 8.9% services, 16.6% sales, 5.6% farming, 8.1% construction, 37.8% production (2000).

Income: Per capita income: $17,943 (2000); Median household income: $51,193 (2000); Poverty rate: 8.7% (2000).

Education: Percent of population age 25 and over with: High school diploma (including GED) or higher: 88.0% (2000); Bachelor's degree or higher: 5.6% (2000).

School District(s)

Lakota Local SD (PK-12)
    2003-04 Enrollment: 1,164 . . . . (419) 457-2911

Housing: Homeownership rate: 90.3% (2000); Median home value: $82,900 (2000); Median rent: $385 per month (2000); Median age of housing: 49 years (2000).

Transportation: Commute to work: 95.8% car, 0.0% public transportation, 1.3% walk, 2.8% work from home (2000); Travel time to work: 23.4% less than 15 minutes, 48.9% 15 to 30 minutes, 12.4% 30 to 45 minutes, 7.6% 45 to 60 minutes, 7.6% 60 minutes or more (2000)

NEW RIEGEL

NEW RIEGEL (village). Covers a land area of 0.198 square miles and a water area of 0 square miles. Located at 41.05° N. Lat.; 83.31° W. Long. Elevation is 824 feet.

Population: 298 (1990); 226 (2000); 231 (2005); 232 (2010 projected); Race: 99.6% White, 0.0% Black, 0.0% Asian, 0.9% Hispanic of any race (2005); Density: 1,166.5 persons per square mile (2005); Average household size: 2.20 (2005); Median age: 41.0 (2005); Males per 100 females: 86.3 (2005); Marriage status: 24.6% never married, 56.3% now married, 7.1% widowed, 12.0% divorced (2000); Foreign born: 0.0% (2000); Ancestry (includes multiple ancestries): 75.0% German, 8.6% Other groups, 4.5% Italian, 4.1% Dutch, 2.7% United States or American (2000).

Economy: Employment by occupation: 0.9% management, 21.7% professional, 13.0% services, 20.0% sales, 0.0% farming, 12.2% construction, 32.2% production (2000).

Income: Per capita income: $22,547 (2005); Median household income: $35,625 (2005); Average household income: $49,452 (2005); Percent of households with income of $100,000 or more: 6.7% (2005); Poverty rate: 4.1% (2000).

Education: Percent of population age 25 and over with: High school diploma (including GED) or higher: 89.0% (2005); Bachelor's degree or higher: 8.5% (2005); Master's degree or higher: 2.4% (2005).

School District(s)
New Riegel Local SD (PK-12)
  2003-04 Enrollment: 449 . . . . (419) 595-2265
Housing: Homeownership rate: 74.3% (2005); Median home value: $91,852 (2005); Median rent: $275 per month (2000); Median age of housing: 60+ years (2000).
Transportation: Commute to work: 77.5% car, 0.0% public transportation, 18.9% walk, 1.8% work from home (2000); Travel time to work: 33.9% less than 15 minutes, 45.0% 15 to 30 minutes, 13.8% 30 to 45 minutes, 5.5% 45 to 60 minutes, 1.8% 60 minutes or more (2000)

REPUBLIC (village). Covers a land area of 0.863 square miles and a water area of 0 square miles. Located at 41.12° N. Lat.; 83.01° W. Long. Elevation is 884 feet.
Population: 563 (1990); 614 (2000); 624 (2005); 622 (2010 projected); Race: 99.5% White, 0.0% Black, 0.0% Asian, 2.1% Hispanic of any race (2005); Density: 723.0 persons per square mile (2005); Average household size: 2.70 (2005); Median age: 33.3 (2005); Males per 100 females: 101.9 (2005); Marriage status: 22.6% never married, 62.8% now married, 8.3% widowed, 6.2% divorced (2000); Foreign born: 0.7% (2000); Ancestry (includes multiple ancestries): 43.8% German, 10.3% United States or American, 9.8% English, 9.3% Irish, 6.2% Other groups (2000).
Economy: In livestock and grain area. Employment by occupation: 6.1% management, 9.6% professional, 17.9% services, 22.1% sales, 0.0% farming, 16.1% construction, 28.2% production (2000).
Income: Per capita income: $18,580 (2005); Median household income: $45,613 (2005); Average household income: $50,141 (2005); Percent of households with income of $100,000 or more: 7.8% (2005); Poverty rate: 7.6% (2000).
Education: Percent of population age 25 and over with: High school diploma (including GED) or higher: 84.2% (2005); Bachelor's degree or higher: 6.6% (2005); Master's degree or higher: 2.6% (2005).
School District(s)
Seneca East Local SD (PK-12)
  2003-04 Enrollment: 1,075 . . . . (419) 426-7041
Housing: Homeownership rate: 77.9% (2005); Median home value: $70,909 (2005); Median rent: $331 per month (2000); Median age of housing: 60+ years (2000).
Transportation: Commute to work: 87.6% car, 2.5% public transportation, 6.2% walk, 1.8% work from home (2000); Travel time to work: 28.9% less than 15 minutes, 50.7% 15 to 30 minutes, 10.7% 30 to 45 minutes, 7.8% 45 to 60 minutes, 1.9% 60 minutes or more (2000)

TIFFIN (city). Covers a land area of 6.494 square miles and a water area of 0.142 square miles. Located at 41.11° N. Lat.; 83.17° W. Long. Elevation is 760 feet.
History: In 1817, Erastus Bowe built the Pan Yan Tavern on the north side of the Sandusky River, and a town called Oakley grew up around it. In 1820 Josiah Hedges established a settlement on the south side of the river opposite Oakley, calling it Tiffin after Edward Tiffin, the first governor of Ohio. The two villages were united as Tiffin in 1850.
Population: 19,009 (1990); 18,135 (2000); 16,953 (2005); 16,050 (2010 projected); Race: 95.8% White, 1.5% Black, 0.7% Asian, 2.4% Hispanic of any race (2005); Density: 2,610.4 persons per square mile (2005); Average household size: 2.43 (2005); Median age: 36.0 (2005); Males per 100 females: 95.8 (2005); Marriage status: 30.0% never married, 50.3% now married, 8.3% widowed, 11.4% divorced (2000); Foreign born: 1.3% (2000); Ancestry (includes multiple ancestries): 44.2% German, 11.0% Irish, 9.6% United States or American, 9.0% English, 8.4% Other groups (2000).
Economy: Single-family building permits issued: 8 (2005); Multi-family building permits issued: 8 (2005); Employment by occupation: 8.0% management, 16.0% professional, 17.0% services, 21.6% sales, 0.3% farming, 8.6% construction, 28.4% production (2000).
Income: Per capita income: $18,189 (2005); Median household income: $36,308 (2005); Average household income: $43,034 (2005); Percent of households with income of $100,000 or more: 4.1% (2005); Poverty rate: 11.1% (2000).
Taxes: Total city taxes per capita: $444 (2004); City property taxes per capita: $54 (2004).
Education: Percent of population age 25 and over with: High school diploma (including GED) or higher: 83.8% (2005); Bachelor's degree or higher: 17.3% (2005); Master's degree or higher: 6.2% (2005).

School District(s)
Bridges Community Academy
  2003-04 Enrollment: n/a
Tiffin City Digital Academy
  2003-04 Enrollment: n/a
Tiffin City SD (PK-12)
  2003-04 Enrollment: 3,022 . . . . (419) 447-2515
Vanguard-Sentinel Joint Vocational SD (07-12)
  2003-04 Enrollment: n/a . . . . (419) 332-2626
Four-year College(s)
Heidelberg College (Private, Not-for-profit, United Church of Christ)
  Fall 2004 Enrollment: 1,483 . . . . (419) 448-2000
  2005-06 Tuition: In-state $16,134; Out-of-state $16,134
Tiffin University (Private, Not-for-profit)
  Fall 2004 Enrollment: 1,562 . . . . (800) 968-6446
  2005-06 Tuition: In-state $15,000; Out-of-state $15,000
Two-year College(s)
Tiffin Academy of Hair Design (Private, For-profit)
  Fall 2004 Enrollment: 26 . . . . (419) 447-3117
  2005-06 Tuition: In-state $8,150; Out-of-state $8,150
Housing: Homeownership rate: 64.6% (2005); Median home value: $91,752 (2005); Median rent: $356 per month (2000); Median age of housing: 54 years (2000).
Hospitals: Mercy Hospital of Tiffin (105 beds)
Safety: Violent crime rate: 12.0 per 10,000 population; Property crime rate: 450.0 per 10,000 population (2004).
Newspapers: The Advertiser-Tribune (Circulation 11,118)
Transportation: Commute to work: 88.8% car, 1.7% public transportation, 6.4% walk, 1.8% work from home (2000); Travel time to work: 60.2% less than 15 minutes, 18.9% 15 to 30 minutes, 12.6% 30 to 45 minutes, 3.8% 45 to 60 minutes, 4.5% 60 minutes or more (2000)
Additional Information Contacts
Seneca County Convention and Visitors Bureau . . . . (419) 447-5866
  http://www.senecacounty.com/visitor
Tiffin Chamber of Commerce . . . . (419) 447-4141
  http://www.tiffinchamber.com

Shelby County

Located in western Ohio; crossed by the Great Miami River; includes Lake Loramie. Covers a land area of 409.27 square miles, a water area of 1.76 square miles, and is located in the Eastern Time Zone. The county government was organized in 1819. County seat is Sidney.

Shelby County is part of the Sidney, OH Micropolitan Statistical Area. The entire metro area includes: Shelby County, OH

Population: 44,915 (1990); 47,910 (2000); 48,816 (2005); 49,750 (2010 projected); Race: 95.5% White, 1.6% Black, 1.1% Asian, 1.1% Hispanic of any race (2005); Density: 119.3 persons per square mile (2005); Average household size: 2.67 (2005); Median age: 35.8 (2005); Males per 100 females: 99.1 (2005).
Religion: Five largest groups: 28.1% Catholic Church, 7.6% Evangelical Lutheran Church in America, 6.4% The United Methodist Church, 3.0% Southern Baptist Convention, 2.5% United Church of Christ (2000).
Economy: Unemployment rate: 4.8% (2005); Total civilian labor force: 27,598 (2005); Leading industries: 52.7% manufacturing; 8.2% retail trade; 7.5% health care and social assistance (2004); Farms: 1,022 totaling 207,329 acres (2002); Companies that employ 500 or more persons: 6 (2004); Companies that employ 100 to 499 persons: 35 (2004); Companies that employ less than 100 persons: 1,027 (2004); Black-owned businesses: n/a (2002); Hispanic-owned businesses: n/a (2002); Women-owned businesses: 689 (2002); Retail sales per capita: $11,562 (2006).
Single-family building permits issued: 215 (2005); Multi-family building permits issued: 80 (2005).
Income: Per capita income: $22,286 (2005); Median household income: $48,414 (2005); Average household income: $58,272 (2005); Percent of households with income of $100,000 or more: 11.7% (2005); Poverty rate: 7.2% (2003); Bankruptcy rate: 7.72% (2005).
Taxes: Total county taxes per capita: $311 (2004); County property taxes per capita: $156 (2004).
Education: Percent of population age 25 and over with: High school diploma (including GED) or higher: 81.6% (2005); Bachelor's degree or higher: 12.7% (2005); Master's degree or higher: 4.0% (2005).

Housing: Homeownership rate: 74.6% (2005); Median home value: $123,052 (2005); Median rent: $380 per month (2000); Median age of housing: 34 years (2000).
Health: Birth rate: 154.7 per 10,000 population (2004); Death rate: 97.8 per 10,000 population (2004); Age-adjusted cancer mortality rate: 213.8 deaths per 100,000 population (2002); Number of physicians: 10.5 per 10,000 population (2004); Hospital beds: 18.5 per 10,000 population (2003); Hospital admissions: 808.6 per 10,000 population (2003).
Elections: 2004 Presidential election results: 70.9% Bush, 28.6% Kerry, 0.0% Nader, 0.2% Badnarik
National and State Parks: Lake Loramie State Park
Additional Information Contacts
Shelby County Government . . . . (937) 498-7226
   http://www.co.shelby.oh.us/
City of Sidney . . . . (937) 498-2335
   http://www.sidneyoh.com
Sidney Chamber of Commerce . . . . (937) 492-9122
   http://www.sidneyshelbychamber.com

Shelby County Communities

ANNA (village). Covers a land area of 0.837 square miles and a water area of 0 square miles. Located at 40.39° N. Lat.; 84.17° W. Long. Elevation is 1,035 feet.
Population: 1,211 (1990); 1,319 (2000); 1,555 (2005); 1,760 (2010 projected); Race: 96.5% White, 0.3% Black, 1.5% Asian, 0.7% Hispanic of any race (2005); Density: 1,858.8 persons per square mile (2005); Average household size: 2.74 (2005); Median age: 32.2 (2005); Males per 100 females: 99.4 (2005); Marriage status: 22.2% never married, 63.5% now married, 4.1% widowed, 10.3% divorced (2000); Foreign born: 1.8% (2000); Ancestry (includes multiple ancestries): 48.7% German, 10.8% Irish, 8.8% United States or American, 7.9% Other groups, 6.1% English (2000).
Economy: Engine plant. Single-family building permits issued: 14 (2005); Multi-family building permits issued: 22 (2005); Employment by occupation: 7.7% management, 14.0% professional, 13.3% services, 18.3% sales, 0.3% farming, 11.9% construction, 34.4% production (2000).
Income: Per capita income: $21,695 (2005); Median household income: $53,485 (2005); Average household income: $59,393 (2005); Percent of households with income of $100,000 or more: 10.2% (2005); Poverty rate: 3.6% (2000).
Education: Percent of population age 25 and over with: High school diploma (including GED) or higher: 87.5% (2005); Bachelor's degree or higher: 11.1% (2005); Master's degree or higher: 3.5% (2005).
School District(s)
Anna Local SD (KG-12)
   2003-04 Enrollment: 1,241 . . . . (937) 394-2011
Housing: Homeownership rate: 78.0% (2005); Median home value: $105,874 (2005); Median rent: $438 per month (2000); Median age of housing: 31 years (2000).
Transportation: Commute to work: 95.4% car, 0.0% public transportation, 2.4% walk, 1.8% work from home (2000); Travel time to work: 44.4% less than 15 minutes, 43.9% 15 to 30 minutes, 5.7% 30 to 45 minutes, 3.0% 45 to 60 minutes, 3.0% 60 minutes or more (2000)

BOTKINS (village). Covers a land area of 0.919 square miles and a water area of 0 square miles. Located at 40.45° N. Lat.; 84.18° W. Long. Elevation is 1,011 feet.
Population: 1,390 (1990); 1,205 (2000); 1,211 (2005); 1,221 (2010 projected); Race: 99.3% White, 0.3% Black, 0.0% Asian, 0.7% Hispanic of any race (2005); Density: 1,317.6 persons per square mile (2005); Average household size: 2.57 (2005); Median age: 35.3 (2005); Males per 100 females: 103.2 (2005); Marriage status: 24.8% never married, 60.9% now married, 5.6% widowed, 8.7% divorced (2000); Foreign born: 0.7% (2000); Ancestry (includes multiple ancestries): 60.1% German, 9.7% United States or American, 9.0% Irish, 4.7% English, 2.4% Dutch (2000).
Economy: Grain products. Single-family building permits issued: 0 (2005); Multi-family building permits issued: 6 (2005); Employment by occupation: 9.9% management, 14.6% professional, 12.8% services, 24.2% sales, 1.7% farming, 10.8% construction, 26.1% production (2000).
Income: Per capita income: $20,822 (2005); Median household income: $44,796 (2005); Average household income: $53,422 (2005); Percent of households with income of $100,000 or more: 9.5% (2005); Poverty rate: 3.6% (2000).
Education: Percent of population age 25 and over with: High school diploma (including GED) or higher: 89.9% (2005); Bachelor's degree or higher: 13.1% (2005); Master's degree or higher: 5.5% (2005).
School District(s)
Botkins Local SD (KG-12)
   2003-04 Enrollment: 580 . . . . (937) 693-3756
Housing: Homeownership rate: 78.2% (2005); Median home value: $100,517 (2005); Median rent: $310 per month (2000); Median age of housing: 40 years (2000).
Transportation: Commute to work: 94.5% car, 0.0% public transportation, 4.8% walk, 0.3% work from home (2000); Travel time to work: 43.9% less than 15 minutes, 43.7% 15 to 30 minutes, 8.5% 30 to 45 minutes, 1.5% 45 to 60 minutes, 2.3% 60 minutes or more (2000)

FORT LORAMIE (village). Aka Loramie. Covers a land area of 0.727 square miles and a water area of 0 square miles. Located at 40.34° N. Lat.; 84.37° W. Long. Elevation is 953 feet.
History: Fort Loramie built here (1794) by Anthony Wayne.
Population: 1,191 (1990); 1,344 (2000); 1,325 (2005); 1,317 (2010 projected); Race: 99.7% White, 0.0% Black, 0.0% Asian, 0.3% Hispanic of any race (2005); Density: 1,822.6 persons per square mile (2005); Average household size: 2.74 (2005); Median age: 33.1 (2005); Males per 100 females: 94.6 (2005); Marriage status: 27.1% never married, 64.9% now married, 5.3% widowed, 2.8% divorced (2000); Foreign born: 0.2% (2000); Ancestry (includes multiple ancestries): 71.1% German, 10.2% French (except Basque), 8.5% Irish, 6.5% United States or American, 1.5% Other groups (2000).
Economy: Single-family building permits issued: 9 (2005); Multi-family building permits issued: 0 (2005); Employment by occupation: 9.8% management, 19.0% professional, 10.7% services, 24.9% sales, 0.0% farming, 8.4% construction, 27.2% production (2000).
Income: Per capita income: $23,500 (2005); Median household income: $58,601 (2005); Average household income: $64,467 (2005); Percent of households with income of $100,000 or more: 16.1% (2005); Poverty rate: 1.4% (2000).
Education: Percent of population age 25 and over with: High school diploma (including GED) or higher: 86.8% (2005); Bachelor's degree or higher: 15.9% (2005); Master's degree or higher: 4.6% (2005).
School District(s)
Fort Loramie Local SD (KG-12)
   2003-04 Enrollment: 817 . . . . (937) 295-3931
Housing: Homeownership rate: 80.3% (2005); Median home value: $147,794 (2005); Median rent: $369 per month (2000); Median age of housing: 35 years (2000).
Transportation: Commute to work: 95.8% car, 0.0% public transportation, 2.6% walk, 1.3% work from home (2000); Travel time to work: 44.5% less than 15 minutes, 39.6% 15 to 30 minutes, 8.7% 30 to 45 minutes, 3.0% 45 to 60 minutes, 4.1% 60 minutes or more (2000)

HOUSTON (unincorporated postal area, zip code 45333). Covers a land area of 27.168 square miles and a water area of 0.017 square miles. Located at 40.26° N. Lat.; 84.33° W. Long. Elevation is 952 feet.
Population: 1,490 (2000); Race: 97.2% White, 0.0% Black, 2.8% Asian, 0.0% Hispanic of any race (2000); Density: 54.8 persons per square mile (2000); Age: 27.5% under 18, 8.9% over 64 (2000); Marriage status: 23.3% never married, 75.7% now married, 6.3% widowed, 6.7% divorced (2000); Foreign born: 2.8% (2000); Ancestry (includes multiple ancestries): 30.4% German, 13.5% United States or American, 12.1% Irish, 8.9% French (except Basque), 6.6% Other groups (2000).
Economy: Employment by occupation: 6.7% management, 10.8% professional, 13.4% services, 24.7% sales, 0.2% farming, 11.7% construction, 32.4% production (2000).
Income: Per capita income: $18,607 (2000); Median household income: $46,395 (2000); Poverty rate: 2.9% (2000).
Education: Percent of population age 25 and over with: High school diploma (including GED) or higher: 81.5% (2000); Bachelor's degree or higher: 8.9% (2000).
School District(s)
Hardin-Houston Local SD (KG-12)
   2003-04 Enrollment: 924 . . . . (937) 295-3010
Housing: Homeownership rate: 90.3% (2000); Median home value: $98,300 (2000); Median rent: $338 per month (2000); Median age of housing: 27 years (2000).
Transportation: Commute to work: 97.5% car, 0.0% public transportation, 0.1% walk, 2.1% work from home (2000); Travel time to work: 19.7% less

than 15 minutes, 60.2% 15 to 30 minutes, 15.7% 30 to 45 minutes, 2.8% 45 to 60 minutes, 1.6% 60 minutes or more (2000)

JACKSON CENTER (village). Covers a land area of 1.257 square miles and a water area of 0 square miles. Located at 40.44° N. Lat.; 84.03° W. Long. Elevation is 1,025 feet.
Population: 1,497 (1990); 1,369 (2000); 1,427 (2005); 1,483 (2010 projected); Race: 98.8% White, 0.8% Black, 0.0% Asian, 0.4% Hispanic of any race (2005); Density: 1,135.1 persons per square mile (2005); Average household size: 2.48 (2005); Median age: 33.0 (2005); Males per 100 females: 95.7 (2005); Marriage status: 16.6% never married, 64.7% now married, 8.2% widowed, 10.4% divorced (2000); Foreign born: 0.8% (2000); Ancestry (includes multiple ancestries): 33.3% German, 18.8% United States or American, 12.8% Irish, 7.5% Other groups, 6.5% English (2000).
Economy: Single-family building permits issued: 4 (2005); Multi-family building permits issued: 0 (2005); Employment by occupation: 10.9% management, 13.3% professional, 10.9% services, 20.0% sales, 0.3% farming, 6.7% construction, 38.0% production (2000).
Income: Per capita income: $20,016 (2005); Median household income: $44,516 (2005); Average household income: $49,588 (2005); Percent of households with income of $100,000 or more: 8.2% (2005); Poverty rate: 7.6% (2000).
Education: Percent of population age 25 and over with: High school diploma (including GED) or higher: 85.3% (2005); Bachelor's degree or higher: 12.1% (2005); Master's degree or higher: 5.0% (2005).

School District(s)
Jackson Center Local SD (KG-12)
    2003-04 Enrollment: 564 . . . . (937) 596-6053
Housing: Homeownership rate: 74.3% (2005); Median home value: $100,932 (2005); Median rent: $343 per month (2000); Median age of housing: 31 years (2000).
Transportation: Commute to work: 94.6% car, 0.0% public transportation, 3.5% walk, 1.6% work from home (2000); Travel time to work: 43.8% less than 15 minutes, 33.2% 15 to 30 minutes, 15.4% 30 to 45 minutes, 4.6% 45 to 60 minutes, 3.0% 60 minutes or more (2000)

KETTLERSVILLE (village). Covers a land area of 1.020 square miles and a water area of 0.002 square miles. Located at 40.44° N. Lat.; 84.26° W. Long. Elevation is 980 feet.
History: Also spelled Kettlerville.
Population: 194 (1990); 175 (2000); 168 (2005); 166 (2010 projected); Race: 98.8% White, 0.6% Black, 0.0% Asian, 3.0% Hispanic of any race (2005); Density: 164.7 persons per square mile (2005); Average household size: 2.85 (2005); Median age: 27.2 (2005); Males per 100 females: 84.6 (2005); Marriage status: 26.6% never married, 61.2% now married, 5.0% widowed, 7.2% divorced (2000); Foreign born: 0.0% (2000); Ancestry (includes multiple ancestries): 66.1% German, 10.0% Irish, 6.7% English, 4.4% Dutch, 3.3% Other groups (2000).
Economy: Single-family building permits issued: 0 (2005); Multi-family building permits issued: 0 (2005); Employment by occupation: 5.1% management, 12.2% professional, 18.4% services, 13.3% sales, 2.0% farming, 7.1% construction, 41.8% production (2000).
Income: Per capita income: $19,211 (2005); Median household income: $50,781 (2005); Average household income: $54,703 (2005); Percent of households with income of $100,000 or more: 11.9% (2005); Poverty rate: 1.2% (2000).
Education: Percent of population age 25 and over with: High school diploma (including GED) or higher: 84.3% (2005); Bachelor's degree or higher: 7.9% (2005); Master's degree or higher: 2.2% (2005).
Housing: Homeownership rate: 88.1% (2005); Median home value: $114,706 (2005); Median rent: $325 per month (2000); Median age of housing: 52 years (2000).
Transportation: Commute to work: 85.7% car, 0.0% public transportation, 8.2% walk, 6.1% work from home (2000); Travel time to work: 37.0% less than 15 minutes, 40.2% 15 to 30 minutes, 5.4% 30 to 45 minutes, 3.3% 45 to 60 minutes, 14.1% 60 minutes or more (2000)

LOCKINGTON (village). Covers a land area of 0.083 square miles and a water area of 0 square miles. Located at 40.20° N. Lat.; 84.23° W. Long. Elevation is 950 feet.
Population: 214 (1990); 208 (2000); 207 (2005); 207 (2010 projected); Race: 96.1% White, 2.9% Black, 0.0% Asian, 2.4% Hispanic of any race (2005); Density: 2,482.0 persons per square mile (2005); Average household size: 2.72 (2005); Median age: 39.7 (2005); Males per 100 females: 95.3 (2005); Marriage status: 19.4% never married, 67.5% now married, 5.6% widowed, 7.5% divorced (2000); Foreign born: 3.8% (2000); Ancestry (includes multiple ancestries): 36.3% German, 11.3% Irish, 8.0% English, 5.2% Other groups, 5.2% United States or American (2000).
Economy: Lockington dam is just South. Single-family building permits issued: 0 (2005); Multi-family building permits issued: 0 (2005); Employment by occupation: 9.8% management, 6.9% professional, 8.8% services, 10.8% sales, 2.0% farming, 18.6% construction, 43.1% production (2000).
Income: Per capita income: $19,106 (2005); Median household income: $41,563 (2005); Average household income: $52,039 (2005); Percent of households with income of $100,000 or more: 9.2% (2005); Poverty rate: 7.5% (2000).
Education: Percent of population age 25 and over with: High school diploma (including GED) or higher: 80.3% (2005); Bachelor's degree or higher: 5.8% (2005); Master's degree or higher: 0.0% (2005).
Housing: Homeownership rate: 76.3% (2005); Median home value: $80,909 (2005); Median rent: $263 per month (2000); Median age of housing: 59 years (2000).
Transportation: Commute to work: 93.9% car, 0.0% public transportation, 4.0% walk, 2.0% work from home (2000); Travel time to work: 33.0% less than 15 minutes, 41.2% 15 to 30 minutes, 14.4% 30 to 45 minutes, 7.2% 45 to 60 minutes, 4.1% 60 minutes or more (2000)

MAPLEWOOD (unincorporated postal area, zip code 45340). Covers a land area of 22.895 square miles and a water area of 0 square miles. Located at 40.37° N. Lat.; 84.05° W. Long. Elevation is 1,035 feet.
Population: 739 (2000); Race: 99.0% White, 0.0% Black, 0.3% Asian, 0.0% Hispanic of any race (2000); Density: 32.3 persons per square mile (2000); Age: 24.0% under 18, 8.1% over 64 (2000); Marriage status: 15.1% never married, 77.5% now married, 3.6% widowed, 3.8% divorced (2000); Foreign born: 0.3% (2000); Ancestry (includes multiple ancestries): 46.4% German, 12.7% United States or American, 9.5% English, 8.8% French (except Basque), 7.9% Irish (2000).
Economy: Employment by occupation: 14.4% management, 15.6% professional, 11.7% services, 12.7% sales, 2.7% farming, 11.0% construction, 31.8% production (2000).
Income: Per capita income: $19,271 (2000); Median household income: $51,917 (2000); Poverty rate: 3.8% (2000).
Education: Percent of population age 25 and over with: High school diploma (including GED) or higher: 86.3% (2000); Bachelor's degree or higher: 9.1% (2000).
Housing: Homeownership rate: 95.1% (2000); Median home value: $104,000 (2000); Median rent: $288 per month (2000); Median age of housing: 32 years (2000).
Transportation: Commute to work: 94.7% car, 0.0% public transportation, 0.0% walk, 5.3% work from home (2000); Travel time to work: 14.5% less than 15 minutes, 56.8% 15 to 30 minutes, 17.7% 30 to 45 minutes, 9.7% 45 to 60 minutes, 1.3% 60 minutes or more (2000)

PORT JEFFERSON (village). Covers a land area of 0.154 square miles and a water area of 0 square miles. Located at 40.33° N. Lat.; 84.09° W. Long. Elevation is 974 feet.
Population: 381 (1990); 321 (2000); 340 (2005); 357 (2010 projected); Race: 99.4% White, 0.0% Black, 0.6% Asian, 0.0% Hispanic of any race (2005); Density: 2,208.2 persons per square mile (2005); Average household size: 2.60 (2005); Median age: 37.3 (2005); Males per 100 females: 102.4 (2005); Marriage status: 19.9% never married, 62.9% now married, 7.2% widowed, 10.0% divorced (2000); Foreign born: 0.0% (2000); Ancestry (includes multiple ancestries): 28.5% German, 18.6% United States or American, 13.1% Irish, 6.5% English, 3.4% Other groups (2000).
Economy: Single-family building permits issued: 1 (2005); Multi-family building permits issued: 0 (2005); Employment by occupation: 2.5% management, 6.3% professional, 7.6% services, 10.8% sales, 0.0% farming, 18.4% construction, 54.4% production (2000).
Income: Per capita income: $19,449 (2005); Median household income: $43,152 (2005); Average household income: $50,477 (2005); Percent of households with income of $100,000 or more: 6.9% (2005); Poverty rate: 8.3% (2000).
Education: Percent of population age 25 and over with: High school diploma (including GED) or higher: 66.2% (2005); Bachelor's degree or higher: 0.9% (2005); Master's degree or higher: 0.9% (2005).

Housing: Homeownership rate: 78.6% (2005); Median home value: $78,636 (2005); Median rent: $350 per month (2000); Median age of housing: 49 years (2000).
Transportation: Commute to work: 100.0% car, 0.0% public transportation, 0.0% walk, 0.0% work from home (2000); Travel time to work: 9.7% less than 15 minutes, 76.6% 15 to 30 minutes, 10.4% 30 to 45 minutes, 3.2% 45 to 60 minutes, 0.0% 60 minutes or more (2000)

RUSSIA (village). Covers a land area of 0.645 square miles and a water area of 0 square miles. Located at 40.23° N. Lat.; 84.41° W. Long. Elevation is 970 feet.
Population: 491 (1990); 551 (2000); 582 (2005); 611 (2010 projected); Race: 99.1% White, 0.0% Black, 0.5% Asian, 1.7% Hispanic of any race (2005); Density: 902.0 persons per square mile (2005); Average household size: 2.75 (2005); Median age: 29.9 (2005); Males per 100 females: 103.5 (2005); Marriage status: 17.6% never married, 72.6% now married, 5.6% widowed, 4.2% divorced (2000); Foreign born: 0.2% (2000); Ancestry (includes multiple ancestries): 45.2% German, 35.6% French (except Basque), 13.9% United States or American, 8.1% Irish, 4.4% Other groups (2000).
Economy: Single-family building permits issued: 6 (2005); Multi-family building permits issued: 0 (2005); Employment by occupation: 9.8% management, 22.6% professional, 8.3% services, 16.5% sales, 0.8% farming, 8.3% construction, 33.8% production (2000).
Income: Per capita income: $26,796 (2005); Median household income: $55,357 (2005); Average household income: $73,561 (2005); Percent of households with income of $100,000 or more: 19.3% (2005); Poverty rate: 0.0% (2000).
Education: Percent of population age 25 and over with: High school diploma (including GED) or higher: 82.2% (2005); Bachelor's degree or higher: 19.6% (2005); Master's degree or higher: 2.7% (2005).

School District(s)
Russia Local SD (KG-12)
2003-04 Enrollment: 443 . . . . (937) 295-3454
Housing: Homeownership rate: 73.6% (2005); Median home value: $128,889 (2005); Median rent: $481 per month (2000); Median age of housing: 34 years (2000).
Transportation: Commute to work: 95.8% car, 0.0% public transportation, 3.4% walk, 0.8% work from home (2000); Travel time to work: 43.8% less than 15 minutes, 33.1% 15 to 30 minutes, 16.5% 30 to 45 minutes, 4.6% 45 to 60 minutes, 1.9% 60 minutes or more (2000)

SIDNEY (city). Covers a land area of 10.426 square miles and a water area of 0.068 square miles. Located at 40.29° N. Lat.; 84.16° W. Long. Elevation is 1,003 feet.
History: Sidney was platted in 1820 and named for Sir Philip Sidney, the English poet. The town developed around sawmills and woodworking mills. In 1879, Benjamin Slusser built a factory to produce the sheet-steel road scraper that he had invented.
Population: 19,245 (1990); 20,211 (2000); 20,067 (2005); 19,970 (2010 projected); Race: 91.5% White, 3.4% Black, 2.2% Asian, 1.8% Hispanic of any race (2005); Density: 1,924.7 persons per square mile (2005); Average household size: 2.49 (2005); Median age: 35.0 (2005); Males per 100 females: 96.3 (2005); Marriage status: 22.1% never married, 57.8% now married, 8.0% widowed, 12.0% divorced (2000); Foreign born: 2.3% (2000); Ancestry (includes multiple ancestries): 31.4% German, 15.6% United States or American, 11.2% Other groups, 10.9% Irish, 9.1% English (2000).
Economy: Single-family building permits issued: 50 (2005); Multi-family building permits issued: 30 (2005); Employment by occupation: 10.9% management, 13.8% professional, 14.5% services, 19.2% sales, 0.3% farming, 8.1% construction, 33.3% production (2000).
Income: Per capita income: $21,108 (2005); Median household income: $41,493 (2005); Average household income: $51,970 (2005); Percent of households with income of $100,000 or more: 9.3% (2005); Poverty rate: 11.5% (2000).
Education: Percent of population age 25 and over with: High school diploma (including GED) or higher: 78.3% (2005); Bachelor's degree or higher: 13.7% (2005); Master's degree or higher: 4.2% (2005).

School District(s)
Fairlawn Local SD (KG-12)
2003-04 Enrollment: 533 . . . . (937) 492-1974
Hardin-Houston Local SD (KG-12)
2003-04 Enrollment: 924 . . . . (937) 295-3010
Sidney City SD (PK-12)
2003-04 Enrollment: 3,897 . . . . (937) 497-2200
Housing: Homeownership rate: 62.3% (2005); Median home value: $104,382 (2005); Median rent: $378 per month (2000); Median age of housing: 38 years (2000).
Hospitals: Wilson Memorial Hospital (112 beds)
Newspapers: The Sidney Daily News (Circulation 13,242)
Transportation: Commute to work: 94.7% car, 0.4% public transportation, 2.0% walk, 2.3% work from home (2000); Travel time to work: 65.5% less than 15 minutes, 21.6% 15 to 30 minutes, 8.2% 30 to 45 minutes, 3.0% 45 to 60 minutes, 1.7% 60 minutes or more (2000)
Additional Information Contacts
City of Sidney . . . . (937) 498-2335
http://www.sidneyoh.com
Sidney Chamber of Commerce . . . . (937) 492-9122
http://www.sidneyshelbychamber.com

Stark County

Located in east central Ohio; crossed by the Tuscarawas River. Covers a land area of 576.14 square miles, a water area of 4.77 square miles, and is located in the Eastern Time Zone. The county government was organized in 1808. County seat is Canton.

Stark County is part of the Canton-Massillon, OH Metropolitan Statistical Area. The entire metro area includes: Carroll County, OH; Stark County, OH

Population: 367,585 (1990); 378,098 (2000); 377,490 (2005); 376,721 (2010 projected); Race: 89.9% White, 7.1% Black, 0.7% Asian, 0.9% Hispanic of any race (2005); Density: 655.2 persons per square mile (2005); Average household size: 2.52 (2005); Median age: 39.2 (2005); Males per 100 females: 92.9 (2005).
Religion: Five largest groups: 20.5% Catholic Church, 6.1% The United Methodist Church, 4.3% Independent, Non-Charismatic Churches, 3.2% Evangelical Lutheran Church in America, 2.7% Christian Churches and Churches of Christ (2000).
Economy: Unemployment rate: 6.3% (2005); Total civilian labor force: 191,613 (2005); Leading industries: 20.3% manufacturing; 16.7% health care and social assistance; 14.7% retail trade (2004); Farms: 1,337 totaling 145,163 acres (2002); Companies that employ 500 or more persons: 22 (2004); Companies that employ 100 to 499 persons: 207 (2004); Companies that employ less than 100 persons: 9,162 (2004); Black-owned businesses: 607 (2002); Hispanic-owned businesses: n/a (2002); Women-owned businesses: 7,563 (2002); Retail sales per capita: $15,020 (2006). Single-family building permits issued: 1,252 (2005); Multi-family building permits issued: 152 (2005).
Income: Per capita income: $23,116 (2005); Median household income: $44,622 (2005); Average household income: $57,467 (2005); Percent of households with income of $100,000 or more: 12.3% (2005); Poverty rate: 9.8% (2003); Bankruptcy rate: 12.59% (2005).
Taxes: Total county taxes per capita: $120 (2004); County property taxes per capita: $110 (2004).
Education: Percent of population age 25 and over with: High school diploma (including GED) or higher: 83.5% (2005); Bachelor's degree or higher: 18.1% (2005); Master's degree or higher: 6.1% (2005).
Housing: Homeownership rate: 72.8% (2005); Median home value: $123,806 (2005); Median rent: $398 per month (2000); Median age of housing: 40 years (2000).
Health: Birth rate: 116.3 per 10,000 population (2004); Death rate: 102.7 per 10,000 population (2004); Age-adjusted cancer mortality rate: 195.0 deaths per 100,000 population (2002); Air Quality Index: 64.4% good, 33.2% moderate, 2.2% unhealthy for sensitive individuals, 0.3% unhealthy (percent of days in 2005); Number of physicians: 26.0 per 10,000 population (2004); Hospital beds: 42.8 per 10,000 population (2003); Hospital admissions: 1,519.8 per 10,000 population (2003).
Elections: 2004 Presidential election results: 48.9% Bush, 50.6% Kerry, 0.0% Nader, 0.3% Badnarik
National and State Parks: Quail Hollow State Park
Additional Information Contacts
Stark County Government . . . . (330) 451-7371
http://www.co.stark.oh.us/
Alliance Chamber of Commerce . . . . (330) 823-6260
http://www.allianceohiochamber.org
Canton Chamber of Commerce . . . . (330) 456-7253
http://www.cantonchamber.org

Canton Stark County Convention & Visitors Bureau . . . . . . (330) 452-0243
  http://www.visitcantonohio.com
City of Alliance . . . . (330) 821-3110
  http://www.cityofalliance.com
City of Canton . . . . (330) 789-3291
  http://www.ci.canton.oh.us
City of Louisville . . . . (330) 875-3321
  http://www.louisvilleohio.com
City of Massillon . . . . (330) 830-1700
  http://www.massillonohio.com
City of North Canton . . . . (330) 499-5081
  http://www.northcantonohio.com
Hartville Chamber of Commerce . . . . (330) 877-5500
  http://www.lakechamber.com
Louisville Chamber of Commerce . . . . (330) 875-7371
  http://www.louisvilleohchamber.com
Massillon Chamber of Commerce . . . . (330) 833-3146
  http://www.massillonohchamber.com
Minerva Area Chamber of Commerce . . . . (330) 868-7979
  http://www.minervachamber.com
North Canton Chamber of Commerce . . . . (330) 499-5100
  http://www.northcantonchamber.org
Village of Navarre . . . . (330) 879-5508
  http://www.navarreohio.net

Stark County Communities

ALLIANCE (city). Covers a land area of 8.612 square miles and a water area of 0.002 square miles. Located at 40.91° N. Lat.; 81.10° W. Long. Elevation is 1,174 feet.
History: Between 1805 and 1835, four small towns were established along the Mahoning River. In 1854 the four communities were united under the name of Alliance. Alliance was incorporated in 1889, and became known for its production of cranes and heavy mill machinery.
Population: 23,552 (1990); 23,253 (2000); 22,631 (2005); 22,030 (2010 projected); Race: 85.7% White, 10.5% Black, 1.0% Asian, 1.2% Hispanic of any race (2005); Density: 2,627.9 persons per square mile (2005); Average household size: 2.60 (2005); Median age: 34.7 (2005); Males per 100 females: 88.4 (2005); Marriage status: 31.4% never married, 48.1% now married, 8.4% widowed, 12.0% divorced (2000); Foreign born: 1.6% (2000); Ancestry (includes multiple ancestries): 22.5% German, 14.9% Other groups, 11.8% Irish, 9.9% Italian, 9.5% English (2000).
Economy: Single-family building permits issued: 65 (2005); Multi-family building permits issued: 0 (2005); Employment by occupation: 7.2% management, 13.6% professional, 17.7% services, 25.5% sales, 0.6% farming, 7.4% construction, 27.9% production (2000).
Income: Per capita income: $16,597 (2005); Median household income: $33,432 (2005); Average household income: $41,898 (2005); Percent of households with income of $100,000 or more: 5.7% (2005); Poverty rate: 18.0% (2000).
Taxes: Total city taxes per capita: $390 (2004); City property taxes per capita: $65 (2004).
Education: Percent of population age 25 and over with: High school diploma (including GED) or higher: 79.7% (2005); Bachelor's degree or higher: 13.7% (2005); Master's degree or higher: 5.3% (2005).
School District(s)
Alliance City SD (PK-12)
  2003-04 Enrollment: 3,323 . . . . (330) 821-2100
Alliance Digital Acdmy for Sa
  2003-04 Enrollment: n/a . . . . (330) 821-2100
Dukes Digital Academy, Inc
  2003-04 Enrollment: n/a . . . . (330) 823-7458
Marlington Local SD (PK-12)
  2003-04 Enrollment: 2,738 . . . . (330) 823-7458
West Branch Local SD (PK-12)
  2003-04 Enrollment: 2,443 . . . . (330) 938-9324
Four-year College(s)
Mount Union College (Private, Not-for-profit, United Methodist)
  Fall 2004 Enrollment: 2,333 . . . . (800) 992-6682
  2005-06 Tuition: In-state $19,850; Out-of-state $19,850
Two-year College(s)
Community Services Division-Alliance City (Public)
  Fall 2004 Enrollment: 110 . . . . (330) 821-2102
  2005-06 Tuition: In-state $4,030; Out-of-state $4,030

Raphaels School of Beauty Culture (Private, For-profit)
  Fall 2004 Enrollment: 52 . . . . (330) 823-3884
Housing: Homeownership rate: 60.7% (2005); Median home value: $84,962 (2005); Median rent: $337 per month (2000); Median age of housing: 53 years (2000).
Hospitals: Alliance Community Hospital (184 beds)
Safety: Violent crime rate: 34.9 per 10,000 population; Property crime rate: 506.1 per 10,000 population (2004).
Newspapers: Alliance Review (Circulation 12,527)
Transportation: Commute to work: 90.2% car, 1.0% public transportation, 6.5% walk, 1.6% work from home (2000); Travel time to work: 56.0% less than 15 minutes, 23.0% 15 to 30 minutes, 11.4% 30 to 45 minutes, 4.3% 45 to 60 minutes, 5.3% 60 minutes or more (2000); Amtrak: Service available.
Additional Information Contacts
Alliance Chamber of Commerce . . . . (330) 823-6260
  http://www.allianceohiochamber.org
City of Alliance . . . . (330) 821-3110
  http://www.cityofalliance.com

BEACH CITY (village). Covers a land area of 0.463 square miles and a water area of 0 square miles. Located at 40.65° N. Lat.; 81.58° W. Long. Elevation is 970 feet.
History: Flood control dam completed in 1937 nearby.
Population: 1,051 (1990); 1,137 (2000); 1,179 (2005); 1,221 (2010 projected); Race: 98.5% White, 0.1% Black, 0.4% Asian, 1.0% Hispanic of any race (2005); Density: 2,545.5 persons per square mile (2005); Average household size: 2.46 (2005); Median age: 38.9 (2005); Males per 100 females: 93.6 (2005); Marriage status: 17.1% never married, 60.7% now married, 13.4% widowed, 8.8% divorced (2000); Foreign born: 0.2% (2000); Ancestry (includes multiple ancestries): 28.2% German, 20.1% United States or American, 10.9% Irish, 9.4% English, 6.2% Other groups (2000).
Economy: Single-family building permits issued: 0 (2005); Multi-family building permits issued: 0 (2005); Employment by occupation: 7.2% management, 12.1% professional, 18.6% services, 14.8% sales, 0.4% farming, 9.5% construction, 37.3% production (2000).
Income: Per capita income: $18,034 (2005); Median household income: $41,144 (2005); Average household income: $44,389 (2005); Percent of households with income of $100,000 or more: 2.9% (2005); Poverty rate: 8.1% (2000).
Education: Percent of population age 25 and over with: High school diploma (including GED) or higher: 79.3% (2005); Bachelor's degree or higher: 5.2% (2005); Master's degree or higher: 1.3% (2005).
School District(s)
Fairless Local SD (PK-12)
  2003-04 Enrollment: 1,883 . . . . (330) 767-3577
Housing: Homeownership rate: 75.6% (2005); Median home value: $80,213 (2005); Median rent: $313 per month (2000); Median age of housing: 56 years (2000).
Transportation: Commute to work: 95.8% car, 0.0% public transportation, 2.6% walk, 1.3% work from home (2000); Travel time to work: 26.7% less than 15 minutes, 40.0% 15 to 30 minutes, 25.8% 30 to 45 minutes, 3.6% 45 to 60 minutes, 4.0% 60 minutes or more (2000)

BREWSTER (village). Covers a land area of 2.027 square miles and a water area of 0.008 square miles. Located at 40.71° N. Lat.; 81.59° W. Long. Elevation is 1,080 feet.
Population: 2,307 (1990); 2,324 (2000); 2,463 (2005); 2,578 (2010 projected); Race: 98.8% White, 0.0% Black, 0.3% Asian, 0.4% Hispanic of any race (2005); Density: 1,215.0 persons per square mile (2005); Average household size: 2.68 (2005); Median age: 38.8 (2005); Males per 100 females: 93.9 (2005); Marriage status: 18.2% never married, 60.5% now married, 11.7% widowed, 9.6% divorced (2000); Foreign born: 0.8% (2000); Ancestry (includes multiple ancestries): 38.5% German, 13.2% Irish, 10.9% United States or American, 8.6% Italian, 8.0% English (2000).
Economy: Dairy products. Employment by occupation: 8.9% management, 9.0% professional, 14.4% services, 23.3% sales, 0.2% farming, 7.8% construction, 36.5% production (2000).
Income: Per capita income: $20,438 (2005); Median household income: $43,481 (2005); Average household income: $52,682 (2005); Percent of households with income of $100,000 or more: 6.5% (2005); Poverty rate: 5.9% (2000).

Education: Percent of population age 25 and over with: High school diploma (including GED) or higher: 84.1% (2005); Bachelor's degree or higher: 6.5% (2005); Master's degree or higher: 1.8% (2005).

School District(s)
Fairless Local SD (PK-12)
   2003-04 Enrollment: 1,883 .... (330) 767-3577

Housing: Homeownership rate: 78.9% (2005); Median home value: $102,419 (2005); Median rent: $382 per month (2000); Median age of housing: 44 years (2000).

Transportation: Commute to work: 95.2% car, 0.0% public transportation, 4.1% walk, 0.3% work from home (2000); Travel time to work: 40.0% less than 15 minutes, 39.1% 15 to 30 minutes, 14.8% 30 to 45 minutes, 5.0% 45 to 60 minutes, 1.2% 60 minutes or more (2000)

CANAL FULTON (village).
Covers a land area of 2.421 square miles and a water area of 0.034 square miles. Located at 40.89° N. Lat.; 81.59° W. Long. Elevation is 970 feet.

History: Canal Fulton was first called Milan, but the name was changed during the construction of the Ohio & Erie Canal to honor Robert Fulton, inventor of the steamboat.

Population: 4,539 (1990); 5,061 (2000); 5,063 (2005); 5,080 (2010 projected); Race: 97.0% White, 0.9% Black, 0.5% Asian, 0.7% Hispanic of any race (2005); Density: 2,091.7 persons per square mile (2005); Average household size: 2.72 (2005); Median age: 35.7 (2005); Males per 100 females: 89.8 (2005); Marriage status: 22.1% never married, 64.4% now married, 4.7% widowed, 8.8% divorced (2000); Foreign born: 1.7% (2000); Ancestry (includes multiple ancestries): 34.2% German, 14.5% Irish, 14.0% English, 8.2% Italian, 6.8% United States or American (2000).

Economy: Employment by occupation: 11.9% management, 19.0% professional, 10.1% services, 32.8% sales, 0.0% farming, 9.3% construction, 16.8% production (2000).

Income: Per capita income: $23,903 (2005); Median household income: $53,559 (2005); Average household income: $63,350 (2005); Percent of households with income of $100,000 or more: 13.3% (2005); Poverty rate: 4.4% (2000).

Education: Percent of population age 25 and over with: High school diploma (including GED) or higher: 89.1% (2005); Bachelor's degree or higher: 17.2% (2005); Master's degree or higher: 3.5% (2005).

School District(s)
Northwest Digital Academy, Inc
   2003-04 Enrollment: n/a .... (330) 854-2991
Northwest Local SD (PK-12)
   2003-04 Enrollment: 2,447 .... (330) 854-2291

Housing: Homeownership rate: 65.0% (2005); Median home value: $137,500 (2005); Median rent: $467 per month (2000); Median age of housing: 25 years (2000).

Safety: Violent crime rate: 0.0 per 10,000 population; Property crime rate: 284.5 per 10,000 population (2004).

Transportation: Commute to work: 92.7% car, 2.4% public transportation, 1.5% walk, 3.1% work from home (2000); Travel time to work: 23.8% less than 15 minutes, 41.5% 15 to 30 minutes, 23.6% 30 to 45 minutes, 4.1% 45 to 60 minutes, 7.1% 60 minutes or more (2000)

CANTON (city).
Covers a land area of 20.546 square miles and a water area of 0.014 square miles. Located at 40.80° N. Lat.; 81.37° W. Long. Elevation is 1,100 feet.

History: Pioneer settlers from New England built homes along Nimishillen Creek in 1805. The town was platted in 1806 by Bezaleel Wells, the "Father of Canton," and incorporated in 1822. Canton's first major industry began in 1827 when Joshua Gibbs developed an improved metal plow. This was the start of Canton's future as a processor of steel, manufacturing reapers, roller bearings, and other products. German and Swiss artisans came to Canton to work in the Dueber-Hampden Watch Company. President William McKinley was a resident of Canton, and conducted his campaign for the presidency from his home here. After his assassination in Buffalo in 1901, his remains were brought back to Canton for burial.

Population: 84,082 (1990); 80,806 (2000); 78,174 (2005); 75,536 (2010 projected); Race: 73.1% White, 21.7% Black, 0.4% Asian, 1.1% Hispanic of any race (2005); Density: 3,804.9 persons per square mile (2005); Average household size: 2.48 (2005); Median age: 35.5 (2005); Males per 100 females: 88.5 (2005); Marriage status: 31.0% never married, 45.8% now married, 8.9% widowed, 14.2% divorced (2000); Foreign born: 1.7% (2000); Ancestry (includes multiple ancestries): 25.0% Other groups, 21.5% German, 11.4% Irish, 8.6% Italian, 6.9% English (2000).

Economy: Unemployment rate: 7.7% (2005); Total civilian labor force: 36,389 (2005); Single-family building permits issued: 80 (2005); Multi-family building permits issued: 0 (2005); Employment by occupation: 8.4% management, 13.1% professional, 20.0% services, 26.3% sales, 0.1% farming, 7.9% construction, 24.1% production (2005).

Income: Per capita income: $17,075 (2005); Median household income: $31,537 (2005); Average household income: $40,884 (2005); Percent of households with income of $100,000 or more: 5.9% (2005); Poverty rate: 19.2% (2000).

Taxes: Total city taxes per capita: $539 (2004); City property taxes per capita: $47 (2004).

Education: Percent of population age 25 and over with: High school diploma (including GED) or higher: 75.3% (2005); Bachelor's degree or higher: 12.2% (2005); Master's degree or higher: 4.1% (2005).

School District(s)
Canton City SD (PK-12)
   2003-04 Enrollment: 11,798 .... (330) 438-2500
Canton City School Digital Acdmy (UG-UG)
   2003-04 Enrollment: n/a .... (330) 438-2500
Canton Local Digital
   2003-04 Enrollment: n/a .... (330) 484-8010
Canton Local School District (PK-12)
   2003-04 Enrollment: 2,538 .... (330) 484-8010
Golden Eagle Digital Academy (02-12)
   2003-04 Enrollment: 21 .... (330) 492-3500
Hope Academy Canton Campus (KG-08)
   2003-04 Enrollment: 341 .... (330) 454-3128
Jackson Local SD (PK-12)
   2003-04 Enrollment: 5,561 .... (330) 830-8000
Life Skills Center Canton (09-12)
   2003-04 Enrollment: 343
Little Eagle Kindergarten Pgm (KG-KG)
   2003-04 Enrollment: 26 .... (330) 492-3500
Perry Local SD (PK-12)
   2003-04 Enrollment: 4,854 .... (330) 477-8121
Plain Local Admy of Tech, Inc (06-08)
   2003-04 Enrollment: 26 .... (330) 492-3500
Plain Local SD (PK-12)
   2003-04 Enrollment: 6,122 .... (330) 492-3500
Summit Academy High School Canton
   2003-04 Enrollment: n/a
Summit Academy-Canton (02-08)
   2003-04 Enrollment: 67 .... (330) 453-8547
The Canton Acdemy
   2003-04 Enrollment: n/a

Four-year College(s)
Malone College (Private, Not-for-profit, Friends)
   Fall 2004 Enrollment: 2,250 .... (330) 471-8100
   2005-06 Tuition: In-state $16,790; Out-of-state $16,790

Two-year College(s)
Aultman Hospital School of Nursing (Private, Not-for-profit)
   Fall 2004 Enrollment: 296 .... (330) 363-6347
   2005-06 Tuition: In-state $12,885; Out-of-state $12,885
Kent State University-Stark Campus (Public)
   Fall 2004 Enrollment: 3,881 .... (330) 499-9600
   2005-06 Tuition: In-state $4,586; Out-of-state $12,018
Mercy Medical Center School of Radiology (Private, Not-for-profit, Roman Catholic)
   Fall 2004 Enrollment: n/a .... (330) 489-1273
   2005-06 Tuition: In-state $9,000; Out-of-state $9,000
National Beauty College (Private, For-profit)
   Fall 2004 Enrollment: 83 .... (330) 499-5596
Practical Nurse Program Canton City Schools (Public)
   Fall 2004 Enrollment: 119 .... (330) 453-3271
Stark State College of Technology (Public)
   Fall 2004 Enrollment: 6,265 .... (330) 494-6170
   2005-06 Tuition: In-state $4,320; Out-of-state $6,120

Housing: Homeownership rate: 59.9% (2005); Median home value: $79,437 (2005); Median rent: $352 per month (2000); Median age of housing: 55 years (2000).

Hospitals: Aultman Hospital (682 beds); Mercy Medical Center (476 beds)

Safety: Violent crime rate: 149.3 per 10,000 population; Property crime rate: 766.6 per 10,000 population (2004).

Newspapers: The Repository (Circulation 65,404)

Transportation: Commute to work: 91.8% car, 2.7% public transportation, 3.2% walk, 1.4% work from home (2000); Travel time to work: 43.8% less than 15 minutes, 39.3% 15 to 30 minutes, 9.8% 30 to 45 minutes, 3.2% 45 to 60 minutes, 3.9% 60 minutes or more (2000)
Additional Information Contacts
Canton Chamber of Commerce .... (330) 456-7253
 http://www.cantonchamber.org
Canton Stark County Convention & Visitors Bureau ...... (330) 452-0243
 http://www.visitcantonohio.com
City of Canton .... (330) 789-3291
 http://www.ci.canton.oh.us

EAST CANTON (village).
Covers a land area of 1.326 square miles and a water area of 0 square miles. Located at 40.78° N. Lat.; 81.28° W. Long. Elevation is 1,146 feet.
History: East Canton was founded in 1805 as Osnaburg. The name was changed in 1821. The town developed as a residential suburb for Canton, and as a center for glazed brick making.
Population: 1,742 (1990); 1,629 (2000); 1,654 (2005); 1,679 (2010 projected); Race: 94.3% White, 4.1% Black, 0.1% Asian, 1.0% Hispanic of any race (2005); Density: 1,247.6 persons per square mile (2005); Average household size: 2.41 (2005); Median age: 39.0 (2005); Males per 100 females: 98.1 (2005); Marriage status: 27.0% never married, 54.3% now married, 6.5% widowed, 12.2% divorced (2000); Foreign born: 1.2% (2000); Ancestry (includes multiple ancestries): 32.8% German, 12.2% Irish, 10.5% United States or American, 9.5% English, 8.4% Other groups (2000).
Economy: Employment by occupation: 5.8% management, 13.7% professional, 16.6% services, 23.9% sales, 0.7% farming, 9.5% construction, 29.8% production (2000).
Income: Per capita income: $20,787 (2005); Median household income: $44,280 (2005); Average household income: $50,193 (2005); Percent of households with income of $100,000 or more: 6.4% (2005); Poverty rate: 8.1% (2000).
Education: Percent of population age 25 and over with: High school diploma (including GED) or higher: 83.9% (2005); Bachelor's degree or higher: 9.6% (2005); Master's degree or higher: 2.6% (2005).
School District(s)
East Canton Digital Acad, Inc
 2003-04 Enrollment: n/a
Osnaburg Local SD (PK-12)
 2003-04 Enrollment: 953 .... (330) 488-1609
Housing: Homeownership rate: 68.2% (2005); Median home value: $113,484 (2005); Median rent: $431 per month (2000); Median age of housing: 43 years (2000).
Safety: Violent crime rate: 12.4 per 10,000 population; Property crime rate: 204.5 per 10,000 population (2004).
Transportation: Commute to work: 93.5% car, 1.6% public transportation, 3.3% walk, 0.4% work from home (2000); Travel time to work: 29.6% less than 15 minutes, 51.7% 15 to 30 minutes, 12.0% 30 to 45 minutes, 3.2% 45 to 60 minutes, 3.5% 60 minutes or more (2000)

EAST SPARTA (village).
Covers a land area of 0.599 square miles and a water area of 0 square miles. Located at 40.67° N. Lat.; 81.35° W. Long. Elevation is 970 feet.
Population: 771 (1990); 806 (2000); 882 (2005); 953 (2010 projected); Race: 98.3% White, 0.2% Black, 0.0% Asian, 0.0% Hispanic of any race (2005); Density: 1,471.4 persons per square mile (2005); Average household size: 2.51 (2005); Median age: 40.0 (2005); Males per 100 females: 94.7 (2005); Marriage status: 18.8% never married, 64.4% now married, 6.7% widowed, 10.0% divorced (2000); Foreign born: 0.2% (2000); Ancestry (includes multiple ancestries): 30.3% German, 21.3% Irish, 8.6% United States or American, 8.4% English, 5.3% Other groups (2000).
Economy: Single-family building permits issued: 0 (2005); Multi-family building permits issued: 0 (2005); Employment by occupation: 6.2% management, 8.7% professional, 15.2% services, 26.7% sales, 0.0% farming, 13.5% construction, 29.7% production (2000).
Income: Per capita income: $20,332 (2005); Median household income: $43,934 (2005); Average household income: $51,090 (2005); Percent of households with income of $100,000 or more: 6.8% (2005); Poverty rate: 5.3% (2000).
Education: Percent of population age 25 and over with: High school diploma (including GED) or higher: 86.0% (2005); Bachelor's degree or higher: 4.4% (2005); Master's degree or higher: 0.5% (2005).

School District(s)
Sandy Valley Local SD (PK-12)
 2003-04 Enrollment: 1,568 .... (330) 866-3339
Housing: Homeownership rate: 83.5% (2005); Median home value: $94,337 (2005); Median rent: $365 per month (2000); Median age of housing: 56 years (2000).
Transportation: Commute to work: 98.7% car, 0.0% public transportation, 0.8% walk, 0.5% work from home (2000); Travel time to work: 21.3% less than 15 minutes, 49.1% 15 to 30 minutes, 21.3% 30 to 45 minutes, 4.1% 45 to 60 minutes, 4.3% 60 minutes or more (2000)

GREENTOWN (CDP).
Covers a land area of 2.744 square miles and a water area of 0 square miles. Located at 40.92° N. Lat.; 81.40° W. Long. Elevation is 1,200 feet.
Population: 1,856 (1990); 3,154 (2000); 3,190 (2005); 3,270 (2010 projected); Race: 96.5% White, 1.2% Black, 1.0% Asian, 1.0% Hispanic of any race (2005); Density: 1,162.4 persons per square mile (2005); Average household size: 3.02 (2005); Median age: 36.2 (2005); Males per 100 females: 99.9 (2005); Marriage status: 23.2% never married, 66.3% now married, 3.9% widowed, 6.6% divorced (2000); Foreign born: 1.3% (2000); Ancestry (includes multiple ancestries): 30.8% German, 17.2% Italian, 15.1% Irish, 11.2% English, 7.0% Other groups (2000).
Economy: Employment by occupation: 21.5% management, 20.8% professional, 12.1% services, 23.7% sales, 0.0% farming, 7.3% construction, 14.6% production (2000).
Income: Per capita income: $32,391 (2005); Median household income: $82,008 (2005); Average household income: $97,755 (2005); Percent of households with income of $100,000 or more: 36.5% (2005); Poverty rate: 0.9% (2000).
Education: Percent of population age 25 and over with: High school diploma (including GED) or higher: 94.7% (2005); Bachelor's degree or higher: 34.3% (2005); Master's degree or higher: 12.6% (2005).
Housing: Homeownership rate: 86.5% (2005); Median home value: $193,373 (2005); Median rent: $539 per month (2000); Median age of housing: 18 years (2000).
Transportation: Commute to work: 94.4% car, 1.1% public transportation, 0.0% walk, 3.1% work from home (2000); Travel time to work: 31.9% less than 15 minutes, 49.2% 15 to 30 minutes, 8.5% 30 to 45 minutes, 4.2% 45 to 60 minutes, 6.2% 60 minutes or more (2000)

HARTVILLE (village).
Covers a land area of 1.833 square miles and a water area of 0 square miles. Located at 40.96° N. Lat.; 81.34° W. Long. Elevation is 1,160 feet.
Population: 2,327 (1990); 2,174 (2000); 1,967 (2005); 1,829 (2010 projected); Race: 98.1% White, 0.3% Black, 0.4% Asian, 0.7% Hispanic of any race (2005); Density: 1,073.3 persons per square mile (2005); Average household size: 2.48 (2005); Median age: 35.1 (2005); Males per 100 females: 97.9 (2005); Marriage status: 26.1% never married, 58.5% now married, 5.5% widowed, 9.9% divorced (2000); Foreign born: 1.4% (2000); Ancestry (includes multiple ancestries): 35.8% German, 16.2% Irish, 10.2% English, 7.2% Italian, 6.7% United States or American (2000).
Economy: Rubber goods, plastic products. Single-family building permits issued: 18 (2005); Multi-family building permits issued: 40 (2005); Employment by occupation: 13.1% management, 17.1% professional, 16.4% services, 28.0% sales, 0.7% farming, 11.2% construction, 13.5% production (2000).
Income: Per capita income: $22,362 (2005); Median household income: $44,820 (2005); Average household income: $54,798 (2005); Percent of households with income of $100,000 or more: 11.8% (2005); Poverty rate: 9.2% (2000).
Education: Percent of population age 25 and over with: High school diploma (including GED) or higher: 83.7% (2005); Bachelor's degree or higher: 22.8% (2005); Master's degree or higher: 5.4% (2005).
School District(s)
Lake Digital Academy, Inc
 2003-04 Enrollment: n/a .... (330) 877-9383
Lake Local SD (PK-12)
 2003-04 Enrollment: 3,359 .... (330) 877-9383
Housing: Homeownership rate: 52.1% (2005); Median home value: $145,802 (2005); Median rent: $453 per month (2000); Median age of housing: 32 years (2000).
Safety: Violent crime rate: 8.9 per 10,000 population; Property crime rate: 379.3 per 10,000 population (2004).
Newspapers: The Hartville News (General - Circulation 2,900)

Transportation: Commute to work: 93.7% car, 0.2% public transportation, 2.0% walk, 3.6% work from home (2000); Travel time to work: 33.0% less than 15 minutes, 35.5% 15 to 30 minutes, 22.7% 30 to 45 minutes, 3.0% 45 to 60 minutes, 5.8% 60 minutes or more (2000)
Additional Information Contacts
Hartville Chamber of Commerce . . . . (330) 877-5500
   http://www.lakechamber.com

HILLS AND DALES (village).
Covers a land area of 0.321 square miles and a water area of 0 square miles. Located at 40.82° N. Lat.; 81.44° W. Long. Elevation is 1,100 feet.
Population: 297 (1990); 260 (2000); 270 (2005); 276 (2010 projected); Race: 95.9% White, 0.0% Black, 0.4% Asian, 3.0% Hispanic of any race (2005); Density: 841.0 persons per square mile (2005); Average household size: 2.39 (2005); Median age: 52.3 (2005); Males per 100 females: 87.5 (2005); Marriage status: 17.2% never married, 73.1% now married, 6.3% widowed, 3.4% divorced (2000); Foreign born: 4.5% (2000); Ancestry (includes multiple ancestries): 32.9% German, 19.2% English, 14.7% Irish, 7.9% Other groups, 6.8% French (except Basque) (2000).
Economy: Employment by occupation: 45.7% management, 27.1% professional, 0.0% services, 24.8% sales, 0.0% farming, 1.6% construction, 0.8% production (2000).
Income: Per capita income: $70,815 (2005); Median household income: $118,750 (2005); Average household income: $169,204 (2005); Percent of households with income of $100,000 or more: 59.3% (2005); Poverty rate: 3.4% (2000).
Education: Percent of population age 25 and over with: High school diploma (including GED) or higher: 99.0% (2005); Bachelor's degree or higher: 68.8% (2005); Master's degree or higher: 34.6% (2005).
Housing: Homeownership rate: 98.2% (2005); Median home value: $456,818 (2005); Median rent: $n/a per month (2000); Median age of housing: 46 years (2000).
Transportation: Commute to work: 89.1% car, 0.0% public transportation, 0.0% walk, 9.3% work from home (2000); Travel time to work: 44.4% less than 15 minutes, 37.6% 15 to 30 minutes, 12.8% 30 to 45 minutes, 0.0% 45 to 60 minutes, 5.1% 60 minutes or more (2000)

LIMAVILLE (village).
Covers a land area of 0.273 square miles and a water area of 0 square miles. Located at 40.98° N. Lat.; 81.14° W. Long. Elevation is 1,090 feet.
Population: 152 (1990); 193 (2000); 203 (2005); 212 (2010 projected); Race: 96.6% White, 0.0% Black, 0.0% Asian, 4.4% Hispanic of any race (2005); Density: 744.1 persons per square mile (2005); Average household size: 2.67 (2005); Median age: 37.8 (2005); Males per 100 females: 109.3 (2005); Marriage status: 24.3% never married, 60.1% now married, 2.3% widowed, 13.3% divorced (2000); Foreign born: 1.5% (2000); Ancestry (includes multiple ancestries): 18.9% Irish, 12.9% German, 10.4% English, 9.5% United States or American, 8.0% Other groups (2000).
Economy: Single-family building permits issued: 0 (2005); Multi-family building permits issued: 0 (2005); Employment by occupation: 5.8% management, 10.5% professional, 23.3% services, 16.3% sales, 0.0% farming, 16.3% construction, 27.9% production (2000).
Income: Per capita income: $17,562 (2005); Median household income: $43,684 (2005); Average household income: $46,908 (2005); Percent of households with income of $100,000 or more: 2.6% (2005); Poverty rate: 8.5% (2000).
Education: Percent of population age 25 and over with: High school diploma (including GED) or higher: 81.9% (2005); Bachelor's degree or higher: 5.1% (2005); Master's degree or higher: 2.9% (2005).
Housing: Homeownership rate: 86.8% (2005); Median home value: $98,571 (2005); Median rent: $365 per month (2000); Median age of housing: 60+ years (2000).
Transportation: Commute to work: 96.3% car, 0.0% public transportation, 0.0% walk, 3.7% work from home (2000); Travel time to work: 29.1% less than 15 minutes, 54.4% 15 to 30 minutes, 6.3% 30 to 45 minutes, 6.3% 45 to 60 minutes, 3.8% 60 minutes or more (2000)

LOUISVILLE (city).
Covers a land area of 5.157 square miles and a water area of 0 square miles. Located at 40.83° N. Lat.; 81.25° W. Long. Elevation is 1,120 feet.
Population: 8,350 (1990); 8,904 (2000); 9,254 (2005); 9,580 (2010 projected); Race: 98.2% White, 0.4% Black, 0.4% Asian, 0.8% Hispanic of any race (2005); Density: 1,794.5 persons per square mile (2005); Average household size: 2.56 (2005); Median age: 36.7 (2005); Males per 100 females: 89.8 (2005); Marriage status: 21.4% never married, 60.8% now married, 8.0% widowed, 9.7% divorced (2000); Foreign born: 0.9% (2000); Ancestry (includes multiple ancestries): 32.5% German, 14.9% Irish, 9.8% Italian, 8.7% English, 7.9% French (except Basque) (2000).
Economy: Single-family building permits issued: 60 (2005); Multi-family building permits issued: 6 (2005); Employment by occupation: 11.1% management, 17.1% professional, 13.6% services, 26.6% sales, 0.0% farming, 6.8% construction, 24.8% production (2000).
Income: Per capita income: $22,978 (2005); Median household income: $46,830 (2005); Average household income: $58,308 (2005); Percent of households with income of $100,000 or more: 9.6% (2005); Poverty rate: 4.0% (2000).
Taxes: Total city taxes per capita: $478 (2004); City property taxes per capita: $40 (2004).
Education: Percent of population age 25 and over with: High school diploma (including GED) or higher: 88.7% (2005); Bachelor's degree or higher: 15.8% (2005); Master's degree or higher: 4.6% (2005).
School District(s)
Louisville City SD (PK-12)
   2003-04 Enrollment: 3,274 . . . . (330) 875-1666
Louisville Digital Academy
   2003-04 Enrollment: n/a . . . . (330) 875-1666
Marlington Local SD (PK-12)
   2003-04 Enrollment: 2,738 . . . . (330) 823-7458
Housing: Homeownership rate: 64.4% (2005); Median home value: $135,609 (2005); Median rent: $416 per month (2000); Median age of housing: 31 years (2000).
Safety: Violent crime rate: 1.1 per 10,000 population; Property crime rate: 126.7 per 10,000 population (2004).
Newspapers: The Louisville Herald (General - Circulation 3,100)
Transportation: Commute to work: 93.4% car, 1.5% public transportation, 2.3% walk, 1.9% work from home (2000); Travel time to work: 27.3% less than 15 minutes, 45.5% 15 to 30 minutes, 17.7% 30 to 45 minutes, 5.0% 45 to 60 minutes, 4.5% 60 minutes or more (2000)
Additional Information Contacts
City of Louisville . . . . (330) 875-3321
   http://www.louisvilleohio.com
Louisville Chamber of Commerce . . . . (330) 875-7371
   http://www.louisvilleohchamber.com

MAGNOLIA (village).
Covers a land area of 0.890 square miles and a water area of 0 square miles. Located at 40.65° N. Lat.; 81.29° W. Long. Elevation is 960 feet.
Population: 937 (1990); 931 (2000); 932 (2005); 947 (2010 projected); Race: 99.0% White, 0.5% Black, 0.0% Asian, 2.1% Hispanic of any race (2005); Density: 1,047.6 persons per square mile (2005); Average household size: 2.49 (2005); Median age: 40.1 (2005); Males per 100 females: 99.6 (2005); Marriage status: 22.2% never married, 62.6% now married, 6.4% widowed, 8.9% divorced (2000); Foreign born: 0.5% (2000); Ancestry (includes multiple ancestries): 35.1% German, 17.6% Irish, 16.8% Italian, 8.9% English, 4.8% Other groups (2000).
Economy: Employment by occupation: 10.1% management, 17.2% professional, 15.0% services, 20.6% sales, 0.0% farming, 14.4% construction, 22.7% production (2000).
Income: Per capita income: $21,757 (2005); Median household income: $43,110 (2005); Average household income: $54,073 (2005); Percent of households with income of $100,000 or more: 10.9% (2005); Poverty rate: 4.3% (2000).
Education: Percent of population age 25 and over with: High school diploma (including GED) or higher: 88.6% (2005); Bachelor's degree or higher: 13.9% (2005); Master's degree or higher: 4.0% (2005).
School District(s)
Cardinal Digital Academy, Inc (UG-UG)
   2003-04 Enrollment: n/a
Sandy Valley Local SD (PK-12)
   2003-04 Enrollment: 1,568 . . . . (330) 866-3339
Housing: Homeownership rate: 78.7% (2005); Median home value: $117,609 (2005); Median rent: $327 per month (2000); Median age of housing: 57 years (2000).
Transportation: Commute to work: 95.4% car, 1.1% public transportation, 0.7% walk, 1.8% work from home (2000); Travel time to work: 27.5% less than 15 minutes, 45.3% 15 to 30 minutes, 20.7% 30 to 45 minutes, 2.7% 45 to 60 minutes, 3.8% 60 minutes or more (2000)

MASSILLON

MASSILLON (city). Covers a land area of 16.749 square miles and a water area of 0.144 square miles. Located at 40.79° N. Lat.; 81.52° W. Long. Elevation is 951 feet.

History: Massillon came into existence in 1826 when the Ohio & Erie Canal was planned. The town was laid out on both sides of the Tuscarawas River by James Duncan and Ferdinand Hurxthal, and named for Jean Baptiste Massillon, a French divine and Mrs. Duncan's favorite writer. Two years later the canal was completed, and Massillon became a marketing and industrial town.

Population: 31,955 (1990); 31,325 (2000); 31,317 (2005); 31,311 (2010 projected); Race: 88.4% White, 8.9% Black, 0.3% Asian, 0.9% Hispanic of any race (2005); Density: 1,869.8 persons per square mile (2005); Average household size: 2.45 (2005); Median age: 38.5 (2005); Males per 100 females: 93.4 (2005); Marriage status: 23.0% never married, 56.2% now married, 8.2% widowed, 12.7% divorced (2000); Foreign born: 1.3% (2000); Ancestry (includes multiple ancestries): 33.6% German, 13.5% Irish, 12.8% Other groups, 8.3% English, 7.1% Italian (2000).

Economy: Unemployment rate: 6.5% (2005); Total civilian labor force: 15,750 (2005); Single-family building permits issued: 164 (2005); Multi-family building permits issued: 54 (2005); Employment by occupation: 8.3% management, 13.9% professional, 16.5% services, 26.1% sales, 0.2% farming, 7.9% construction, 27.1% production (2000).

Income: Per capita income: $19,894 (2005); Median household income: $37,372 (2005); Average household income: $47,981 (2005); Percent of households with income of $100,000 or more: 7.9% (2005); Poverty rate: 10.7% (2000).

Taxes: Total city taxes per capita: $443 (2004); City property taxes per capita: $48 (2004).

Education: Percent of population age 25 and over with: High school diploma (including GED) or higher: 80.7% (2005); Bachelor's degree or higher: 12.5% (2005); Master's degree or higher: 3.6% (2005).

School District(s)

Department of Youth Services (06-12)
   2003-04 Enrollment: 1,333 . . . . (614) 728-2489
Jackson Alternative School, Inc
   2003-04 Enrollment: n/a . . . . (330) 830-8000
Jackson Digital Academy, Inc
   2003-04 Enrollment: n/a . . . . (330) 830-8000
Jackson Local SD (PK-12)
   2003-04 Enrollment: 5,561 . . . . (330) 830-8000
Jackson School for the Arts, Inc
   2003-04 Enrollment: n/a . . . . (330) 830-8000
Massillon City SD (PK-12)
   2003-04 Enrollment: 4,547 . . . . (330) 830-1810
Massillon Digital Academy, Inc (KG-12)
   2003-04 Enrollment: n/a
Perry Local SD (PK-12)
   2003-04 Enrollment: 4,854 . . . . (330) 477-8121
Perry Panther Digital Academy (02-12)
   2003-04 Enrollment: 30 . . . . (330) 477-8121
Stark County Area Joint Vocational SD (09-12)
   2003-04 Enrollment: n/a . . . . (330) 832-1591
Tuslaw Digital Academy, Inc
   2003-04 Enrollment: n/a . . . . (330) 837-7813
Tuslaw Local SD (PK-12)
   2003-04 Enrollment: 1,429 . . . . (330) 837-7813

Housing: Homeownership rate: 69.4% (2005); Median home value: $97,639 (2005); Median rent: $356 per month (2000); Median age of housing: 50 years (2000).

Hospitals: Heartland Behavioral Healthcare (130 beds); Massillon Community Hospital (268 beds); Massillon Health System (183 beds)

Newspapers: The Independent (Circulation 14,136)

Transportation: Commute to work: 94.3% car, 1.4% public transportation, 2.0% walk, 1.3% work from home (2000); Travel time to work: 39.1% less than 15 minutes, 40.2% 15 to 30 minutes, 12.8% 30 to 45 minutes, 3.9% 45 to 60 minutes, 4.0% 60 minutes or more (2000)

Additional Information Contacts

City of Massillon . . . . (330) 830-1700
   http://www.massillonohio.com
Massillon Chamber of Commerce . . . . (330) 833-3146
   http://www.massillonohchamber.com

MEYERS LAKE

MEYERS LAKE (village). Aka Myers Lake. Covers a land area of 0.222 square miles and a water area of 0.211 square miles. Located at 40.81° N. Lat.; 81.41° W. Long. Elevation is 1,110 feet.

History: Former site of amusement park at streetcar line terminus.

Population: 493 (1990); 565 (2000); 574 (2005); 565 (2010 projected); Race: 95.5% White, 3.1% Black, 0.3% Asian, 1.2% Hispanic of any race (2005); Density: 2,589.0 persons per square mile (2005); Average household size: 1.82 (2005); Median age: 55.7 (2005); Males per 100 females: 79.4 (2005); Marriage status: 19.6% never married, 57.9% now married, 6.8% widowed, 15.7% divorced (2000); Foreign born: 3.2% (2000); Ancestry (includes multiple ancestries): 35.3% German, 17.0% English, 13.1% Irish, 7.8% Italian, 7.6% Other groups (2000).

Economy: Employment by occupation: 18.8% management, 25.6% professional, 11.8% services, 27.2% sales, 0.0% farming, 7.3% construction, 9.3% production (2000).

Income: Per capita income: $40,559 (2005); Median household income: $51,136 (2005); Average household income: $73,172 (2005); Percent of households with income of $100,000 or more: 19.0% (2005); Poverty rate: 6.6% (2000).

Education: Percent of population age 25 and over with: High school diploma (including GED) or higher: 91.6% (2005); Bachelor's degree or higher: 36.4% (2005); Master's degree or higher: 13.4% (2005).

Housing: Homeownership rate: 77.8% (2005); Median home value: $160,526 (2005); Median rent: $656 per month (2000); Median age of housing: 17 years (2000).

Transportation: Commute to work: 93.6% car, 0.6% public transportation, 1.0% walk, 4.8% work from home (2000); Travel time to work: 50.7% less than 15 minutes, 34.8% 15 to 30 minutes, 12.2% 30 to 45 minutes, 2.4% 45 to 60 minutes, 0.0% 60 minutes or more (2000)

MINERVA

MINERVA (village). Covers a land area of 2.138 square miles and a water area of 0 square miles. Located at 40.72° N. Lat.; 81.10° W. Long. Elevation is 1,053 feet.

History: Minerva was established as a town in 1835, when the Sandy & Beaver Canal was under construction. The town was named for the niece of John Whitacre, the founder.

Population: 4,318 (1990); 3,934 (2000); 3,958 (2005); 4,019 (2010 projected); Race: 98.9% White, 0.0% Black, 0.3% Asian, 0.6% Hispanic of any race (2005); Density: 1,851.5 persons per square mile (2005); Average household size: 2.42 (2005); Median age: 40.1 (2005); Males per 100 females: 90.2 (2005); Marriage status: 22.1% never married, 57.0% now married, 10.5% widowed, 10.4% divorced (2000); Foreign born: 0.9% (2000); Ancestry (includes multiple ancestries): 34.6% German, 17.5% Irish, 14.5% English, 7.0% Italian, 5.4% United States or American (2000).

Economy: Employment by occupation: 6.1% management, 12.5% professional, 16.5% services, 24.2% sales, 0.0% farming, 7.0% construction, 33.8% production (2000).

Income: Per capita income: $18,541 (2005); Median household income: $36,959 (2005); Average household income: $43,453 (2005); Percent of households with income of $100,000 or more: 5.1% (2005); Poverty rate: 9.8% (2000).

Education: Percent of population age 25 and over with: High school diploma (including GED) or higher: 87.1% (2005); Bachelor's degree or higher: 9.4% (2005); Master's degree or higher: 2.2% (2005).

School District(s)

Lion Digital Academy, Inc
   2003-04 Enrollment: n/a . . . . (330) 868-4332
Minerva Local SD (PK-12)
   2003-04 Enrollment: 2,202 . . . . (330) 868-4332

Housing: Homeownership rate: 68.0% (2005); Median home value: $92,333 (2005); Median rent: $353 per month (2000); Median age of housing: 49 years (2000).

Newspapers: Press-News (General - Circulation 2,500); The News Leader (General - Circulation 4,400)

Transportation: Commute to work: 93.6% car, 0.0% public transportation, 5.1% walk, 0.6% work from home (2000); Travel time to work: 56.3% less than 15 minutes, 16.7% 15 to 30 minutes, 19.3% 30 to 45 minutes, 4.9% 45 to 60 minutes, 2.8% 60 minutes or more (2000)

Additional Information Contacts

Minerva Area Chamber of Commerce . . . . (330) 868-7979
   http://www.minervachamber.com

NAVARRE (village). Covers a land area of 1.503 square miles and a water area of 0.004 square miles. Located at 40.72° N. Lat.; 81.52° W. Long. Elevation is 960 feet.
History: Navarre was founded by James Duncan and named by his wife for a prince of Navarre. A lock of the Ohio & Erie Canal was located in Navarre, which became a shipping center for farm produce.
Population: 1,778 (1990); 1,440 (2000); 1,484 (2005); 1,524 (2010 projected); Race: 98.4% White, 0.4% Black, 0.0% Asian, 0.0% Hispanic of any race (2005); Density: 987.1 persons per square mile (2005); Average household size: 2.34 (2005); Median age: 47.1 (2005); Males per 100 females: 83.0 (2005); Marriage status: 18.3% never married, 53.2% now married, 14.6% widowed, 13.9% divorced (2000); Foreign born: 0.7% (2000); Ancestry (includes multiple ancestries): 37.4% German, 13.0% Irish, 9.9% English, 8.0% Italian, 4.4% United States or American (2000).
Economy: Single-family building permits issued: 2 (2005); Multi-family building permits issued: 0 (2005); Employment by occupation: 10.2% management, 14.2% professional, 16.8% services, 26.3% sales, 0.0% farming, 8.5% construction, 24.0% production (2000).
Income: Per capita income: $20,063 (2005); Median household income: $36,218 (2005); Average household income: $43,618 (2005); Percent of households with income of $100,000 or more: 5.7% (2005); Poverty rate: 5.7% (2000).
Education: Percent of population age 25 and over with: High school diploma (including GED) or higher: 78.2% (2005); Bachelor's degree or higher: 11.1% (2005); Master's degree or higher: 5.6% (2005).

School District(s)
Fairless Digital Academy
  2003-04 Enrollment: n/a .... (330) 767-3577
Fairless Local SD (PK-12)
  2003-04 Enrollment: 1,883 .... (330) 767-3577
Perry Local SD (PK-12)
  2003-04 Enrollment: 4,854 .... (330) 477-8121

Housing: Homeownership rate: 66.8% (2005); Median home value: $106,627 (2005); Median rent: $316 per month (2000); Median age of housing: 60+ years (2000).
Safety: Violent crime rate: 34.7 per 10,000 population; Property crime rate: 48.5 per 10,000 population (2004).
Transportation: Commute to work: 91.2% car, 0.0% public transportation, 6.0% walk, 2.4% work from home (2000); Travel time to work: 40.5% less than 15 minutes, 42.0% 15 to 30 minutes, 11.8% 30 to 45 minutes, 1.8% 45 to 60 minutes, 3.9% 60 minutes or more (2000)

Additional Information Contacts
Village of Navarre .... (330) 879-5508
  http://www.navarreohio.net

NORTH CANTON (city). Covers a land area of 6.069 square miles and a water area of 0 square miles. Located at 40.87° N. Lat.; 81.40° W. Long. Elevation is 1,160 feet.
History: Settled c.1815, incorporated as a city 1961.
Population: 15,556 (1990); 16,369 (2000); 16,257 (2005); 16,172 (2010 projected); Race: 96.4% White, 1.3% Black, 1.2% Asian, 0.8% Hispanic of any race (2005); Density: 2,678.7 persons per square mile (2005); Average household size: 2.27 (2005); Median age: 43.1 (2005); Males per 100 females: 88.3 (2005); Marriage status: 20.8% never married, 58.3% now married, 10.4% widowed, 10.5% divorced (2000); Foreign born: 2.7% (2000); Ancestry (includes multiple ancestries): 34.1% German, 13.8% Irish, 13.0% English, 10.4% Italian, 5.3% Other groups (2000).
Economy: Vacuum cleaners and industrial die castings are among the city's manufactures. Diversified light manufacturing. Single-family building permits issued: 18 (2005); Multi-family building permits issued: 0 (2005); Employment by occupation: 15.8% management, 26.9% professional, 10.2% services, 29.4% sales, 0.0% farming, 5.4% construction, 12.1% production (2000).
Income: Per capita income: $26,472 (2005); Median household income: $45,757 (2005); Average household income: $58,841 (2005); Percent of households with income of $100,000 or more: 13.2% (2005); Poverty rate: 5.7% (2000).
Education: Percent of population age 25 and over with: High school diploma (including GED) or higher: 91.5% (2005); Bachelor's degree or higher: 33.7% (2005); Master's degree or higher: 13.7% (2005).

School District(s)
Canton City SD (PK-12)
  2003-04 Enrollment: 11,798 .... (330) 438-2500
North Canton City SD (PK-12)
  2003-04 Enrollment: 4,924 .... (330) 497-5600
North Canton Digital Academy, Inc
  2003-04 Enrollment: n/a .... (330) 497-5600

Four-year College(s)
Walsh University (Private, Not-for-profit, Roman Catholic)
  Fall 2004 Enrollment: 1,951 .... (330) 499-7090
  2005-06 Tuition: In-state $16,540; Out-of-state $16,540

Two-year College(s)
Brown Mackie College-North Canton (Private, For-profit)
  Fall 2004 Enrollment: 876 .... (330) 494-1214
  2005-06 Tuition: In-state $8,592; Out-of-state $8,592

Housing: Homeownership rate: 68.4% (2005); Median home value: $140,997 (2005); Median rent: $506 per month (2000); Median age of housing: 34 years (2000).
Safety: Violent crime rate: 8.4 per 10,000 population; Property crime rate: 232.2 per 10,000 population (2004).
Transportation: Commute to work: 93.8% car, 0.1% public transportation, 2.7% walk, 2.8% work from home (2000); Travel time to work: 42.7% less than 15 minutes, 37.5% 15 to 30 minutes, 14.6% 30 to 45 minutes, 2.4% 45 to 60 minutes, 2.8% 60 minutes or more (2000)

Additional Information Contacts
City of North Canton .... (330) 499-5081
  http://www.northcantonohio.com
North Canton Chamber of Commerce .... (330) 499-5100
  http://www.northcantonchamber.org

NORTH LAWRENCE (unincorporated postal area, zip code 44666). Covers a land area of 22.425 square miles and a water area of 0.105 square miles. Located at 40.84° N. Lat.; 81.62° W. Long. Elevation is 1,039 feet.
Population: 2,764 (2000); Race: 97.7% White, 1.3% Black, 1.0% Asian, 0.5% Hispanic of any race (2000); Density: 123.3 persons per square mile (2000); Age: 25.9% under 18, 10.9% over 64 (2000); Marriage status: 24.6% never married, 60.4% now married, 3.8% widowed, 11.1% divorced (2000); Foreign born: 0.9% (2000); Ancestry (includes multiple ancestries): 42.3% German, 14.3% Irish, 9.6% English, 8.6% Other groups, 5.9% United States or American (2000).
Economy: Employment by occupation: 8.6% management, 15.6% professional, 13.4% services, 23.9% sales, 1.0% farming, 10.1% construction, 27.3% production (2000).
Income: Per capita income: $22,225 (2000); Median household income: $48,214 (2000); Poverty rate: 5.8% (2000).
Education: Percent of population age 25 and over with: High school diploma (including GED) or higher: 86.0% (2000); Bachelor's degree or higher: 10.7% (2000).
Housing: Homeownership rate: 89.4% (2000); Median home value: $111,600 (2000); Median rent: $385 per month (2000); Median age of housing: 46 years (2000).
Transportation: Commute to work: 94.1% car, 0.5% public transportation, 0.7% walk, 3.6% work from home (2000); Travel time to work: 25.1% less than 15 minutes, 51.2% 15 to 30 minutes, 13.7% 30 to 45 minutes, 9.0% 45 to 60 minutes, 0.9% 60 minutes or more (2000)

PARIS (unincorporated postal area, zip code 44669). Covers a land area of 18.160 square miles and a water area of 0.035 square miles. Located at 40.79° N. Lat.; 81.16° W. Long. Elevation is 1,235 feet.
Population: 1,564 (2000); Race: 97.9% White, 0.0% Black, 0.0% Asian, 0.0% Hispanic of any race (2000); Density: 86.1 persons per square mile (2000); Age: 34.3% under 18, 10.2% over 64 (2000); Marriage status: 21.6% never married, 66.8% now married, 2.8% widowed, 8.8% divorced (2000); Foreign born: 0.3% (2000); Ancestry (includes multiple ancestries): 33.5% German, 12.5% United States or American, 9.5% Irish, 8.6% English, 7.4% Italian (2000).
Economy: Employment by occupation: 13.9% management, 16.0% professional, 9.6% services, 19.1% sales, 2.8% farming, 13.6% construction, 24.9% production (2000).
Income: Per capita income: $16,669 (2000); Median household income: $47,292 (2000); Poverty rate: 9.6% (2000).
Education: Percent of population age 25 and over with: High school diploma (including GED) or higher: 84.5% (2000); Bachelor's degree or higher: 18.5% (2000).
Housing: Homeownership rate: 90.1% (2000); Median home value: $109,200 (2000); Median rent: $416 per month (2000); Median age of housing: 38 years (2000).

Transportation: Commute to work: 89.1% car, 0.0% public transportation, 1.1% walk, 9.7% work from home (2000); Travel time to work: 20.6% less than 15 minutes, 49.0% 15 to 30 minutes, 20.3% 30 to 45 minutes, 5.9% 45 to 60 minutes, 4.1% 60 minutes or more (2000)

PERRY HEIGHTS (CDP). Aka Genoa. Covers a land area of 2.917 square miles and a water area of 0.041 square miles. Located at 40.79° N. Lat.; 81.46° W. Long. Elevation is 1,100 feet.
Population: 9,418 (1990); 8,900 (2000); 8,702 (2005); 8,522 (2010 projected); Race: 94.5% White, 3.1% Black, 0.2% Asian, 1.5% Hispanic of any race (2005); Density: 2,983.0 persons per square mile (2005); Average household size: 2.47 (2005); Median age: 40.2 (2005); Males per 100 females: 91.6 (2005); Marriage status: 23.7% never married, 54.8% now married, 9.8% widowed, 11.8% divorced (2000); Foreign born: 1.7% (2000); Ancestry (includes multiple ancestries): 34.6% German, 14.9% Irish, 8.2% English, 7.9% Other groups, 7.6% Italian (2000).
Economy: Employment by occupation: 8.3% management, 15.4% professional, 13.8% services, 29.2% sales, 0.2% farming, 9.5% construction, 23.6% production (2000).
Income: Per capita income: $24,167 (2005); Median household income: $45,951 (2005); Average household income: $57,142 (2005); Percent of households with income of $100,000 or more: 11.0% (2005); Poverty rate: 6.9% (2000).
Education: Percent of population age 25 and over with: High school diploma (including GED) or higher: 85.8% (2005); Bachelor's degree or higher: 12.4% (2005); Master's degree or higher: 3.8% (2005).
Housing: Homeownership rate: 74.2% (2005); Median home value: $111,143 (2005); Median rent: $434 per month (2000); Median age of housing: 37 years (2000).
Transportation: Commute to work: 96.9% car, 0.8% public transportation, 0.4% walk, 1.5% work from home (2000); Travel time to work: 30.2% less than 15 minutes, 47.0% 15 to 30 minutes, 9.8% 30 to 45 minutes, 6.5% 45 to 60 minutes, 6.5% 60 minutes or more (2000)

UNIONTOWN (CDP). Covers a land area of 2.496 square miles and a water area of 0.025 square miles. Located at 40.97° N. Lat.; 81.40° W. Long. Elevation is 1,130 feet.
Population: 3,074 (1990); 2,802 (2000); 2,636 (2005); 2,624 (2010 projected); Race: 97.8% White, 0.4% Black, 0.7% Asian, 0.6% Hispanic of any race (2005); Density: 1,056.0 persons per square mile (2005); Average household size: 2.40 (2005); Median age: 45.3 (2005); Males per 100 females: 90.5 (2005); Marriage status: 22.2% never married, 63.9% now married, 5.2% widowed, 8.7% divorced (2000); Foreign born: 2.5% (2000); Ancestry (includes multiple ancestries): 29.6% German, 21.1% English, 14.9% Irish, 9.5% Italian, 8.4% Other groups (2000).
Economy: Employment by occupation: 13.6% management, 23.2% professional, 9.4% services, 28.6% sales, 0.0% farming, 12.8% construction, 12.3% production (2000).
Income: Per capita income: $27,873 (2005); Median household income: $52,872 (2005); Average household income: $66,976 (2005); Percent of households with income of $100,000 or more: 18.0% (2005); Poverty rate: 2.7% (2000).
Education: Percent of population age 25 and over with: High school diploma (including GED) or higher: 89.0% (2005); Bachelor's degree or higher: 20.4% (2005); Master's degree or higher: 5.2% (2005).
School District(s)
Green Local SD (PK-12)
  2003-04 Enrollment: 4,165 . . . . (330) 896-7500
Green Local SD (PK-12)
  2003-04 Enrollment: 1,396 . . . . (330) 669-3921
Lake Local SD (PK-12)
  2003-04 Enrollment: 3,359 . . . . (330) 877-9383
Housing: Homeownership rate: 85.4% (2005); Median home value: $160,255 (2005); Median rent: $484 per month (2000); Median age of housing: 31 years (2000).
Transportation: Commute to work: 97.1% car, 1.2% public transportation, 0.0% walk, 1.7% work from home (2000); Travel time to work: 24.5% less than 15 minutes, 42.7% 15 to 30 minutes, 22.6% 30 to 45 minutes, 2.7% 45 to 60 minutes, 7.4% 60 minutes or more (2000)

WAYNESBURG (village). Covers a land area of 0.516 square miles and a water area of 0 square miles. Located at 40.66° N. Lat.; 81.25° W. Long. Elevation is 1,000 feet.
Population: 1,068 (1990); 1,003 (2000); 1,023 (2005); 1,046 (2010 projected); Race: 95.5% White, 3.0% Black, 0.3% Asian, 0.7% Hispanic of any race (2005); Density: 1,983.3 persons per square mile (2005); Average household size: 2.53 (2005); Median age: 37.0 (2005); Males per 100 females: 97.1 (2005); Marriage status: 25.0% never married, 55.0% now married, 9.6% widowed, 10.4% divorced (2000); Foreign born: 2.4% (2000); Ancestry (includes multiple ancestries): 33.0% German, 23.3% Italian, 13.9% Irish, 10.3% Other groups, 8.0% United States or American (2000).
Economy: Makes tile, brick, refractories. Employment by occupation: 6.0% management, 10.8% professional, 21.6% services, 22.8% sales, 0.7% farming, 13.7% construction, 24.5% production (2000).
Income: Per capita income: $18,253 (2005); Median household income: $37,917 (2005); Average household income: $46,105 (2005); Percent of households with income of $100,000 or more: 6.7% (2005); Poverty rate: 16.4% (2000).
Education: Percent of population age 25 and over with: High school diploma (including GED) or higher: 80.6% (2005); Bachelor's degree or higher: 5.2% (2005); Master's degree or higher: 3.2% (2005).
School District(s)
Sandy Valley Local SD (PK-12)
  2003-04 Enrollment: 1,568 . . . . (330) 866-3339
Housing: Homeownership rate: 69.1% (2005); Median home value: $94,324 (2005); Median rent: $368 per month (2000); Median age of housing: 60+ years (2000).
Transportation: Commute to work: 93.2% car, 0.7% public transportation, 3.4% walk, 2.7% work from home (2000); Travel time to work: 24.5% less than 15 minutes, 41.0% 15 to 30 minutes, 27.5% 30 to 45 minutes, 4.0% 45 to 60 minutes, 3.0% 60 minutes or more (2000)

WILMOT (village). Covers a land area of 0.164 square miles and a water area of 0 square miles. Located at 40.65° N. Lat.; 81.63° W. Long. Elevation is 1,093 feet.
History: Wilmot was platted in 1836, and developed as a trading center in the midst of the Amish country.
Population: 261 (1990); 335 (2000); 341 (2005); 346 (2010 projected); Race: 98.8% White, 0.0% Black, 0.3% Asian, 0.0% Hispanic of any race (2005); Density: 2,075.0 persons per square mile (2005); Average household size: 2.66 (2005); Median age: 32.0 (2005); Males per 100 females: 98.3 (2005); Marriage status: 22.7% never married, 61.1% now married, 5.3% widowed, 10.9% divorced (2000); Foreign born: 1.1% (2000); Ancestry (includes multiple ancestries): 23.4% German, 20.5% Other groups, 16.0% Irish, 14.2% Swiss, 8.8% English (2000).
Economy: Employment by occupation: 8.6% management, 17.1% professional, 9.2% services, 28.9% sales, 0.0% farming, 7.2% construction, 28.9% production (2000).
Income: Per capita income: $18,834 (2005); Median household income: $42,800 (2005); Average household income: $50,176 (2005); Percent of households with income of $100,000 or more: 3.1% (2005); Poverty rate: 6.6% (2000).
Education: Percent of population age 25 and over with: High school diploma (including GED) or higher: 77.0% (2005); Bachelor's degree or higher: 8.3% (2005); Master's degree or higher: 1.0% (2005).
Housing: Homeownership rate: 71.1% (2005); Median home value: $92,857 (2005); Median rent: $385 per month (2000); Median age of housing: 60+ years (2000).
Transportation: Commute to work: 87.4% car, 0.0% public transportation, 1.3% walk, 11.3% work from home (2000); Travel time to work: 19.4% less than 15 minutes, 58.2% 15 to 30 minutes, 14.9% 30 to 45 minutes, 4.5% 45 to 60 minutes, 3.0% 60 minutes or more (2000)

Summit County

Located in northeastern Ohio; drained by the Cuyahoga and Tuscarawas Rivers; includes Portage Lakes. Covers a land area of 412.72 square miles, a water area of 7.34 square miles, and is located in the Eastern Time Zone. The county government was organized in 1840. County seat is Akron.

Summit County is part of the Akron, OH Metropolitan Statistical Area. The entire metro area includes: Portage County, OH; Summit County, OH

Weather Station: Akron-Canton Regional Airport   Elevation: 1,207 feet

	Jan	Feb	Mar	Apr	May	Jun	Jul	Aug	Sep	Oct	Nov	Dec
High	33	37	47	59	70	78	82	81	73	62	49	38
Low	18	20	28	38	49	58	62	61	53	43	34	25
Precip	2.5	2.3	3.1	3.3	3.9	3.6	3.9	3.5	3.4	2.6	3.1	3.0
Snow	12.9	9.5	9.0	2.6	tr	tr	0.0	0.0	tr	0.6	3.2	9.1

High and Low temperatures in degrees Fahrenheit; Precipitation and Snow in inches

Population: 514,990 (1990); 542,899 (2000); 548,117 (2005); 553,389 (2010 projected); Race: 82.7% White, 13.4% Black, 1.8% Asian, 1.0% Hispanic of any race (2005); Density: 1,328.0 persons per square mile (2005); Average household size: 2.47 (2005); Median age: 38.3 (2005); Males per 100 females: 93.4 (2005).
Religion: Five largest groups: 22.4% Catholic Church, 4.0% Independent, Non-Charismatic Churches, 3.9% The United Methodist Church, 2.1% United Church of Christ, 1.3% Evangelical Lutheran Church in America (2000).
Economy: Unemployment rate: 5.8% (2005); Total civilian labor force: 290,961 (2005); Leading industries: 15.1% health care and social assistance; 14.1% manufacturing; 12.6% retail trade (2004); Farms: 377 totaling 21,117 acres (2002); Companies that employ 500 or more persons: 36 (2004); Companies that employ 100 to 499 persons: 364 (2004); Companies that employ less than 100 persons: 14,135 (2004); Black-owned businesses: 1,648 (2002); Hispanic-owned businesses: 378 (2002); Women-owned businesses: 11,827 (2002); Retail sales per capita: $16,085 (2006). Single-family building permits issued: 1,685 (2005); Multi-family building permits issued: 283 (2005).
Income: Per capita income: $25,949 (2005); Median household income: $47,551 (2005); Average household income: $62,907 (2005); Percent of households with income of $100,000 or more: 15.5% (2005); Poverty rate: 11.1% (2003); Bankruptcy rate: 13.62% (2005).
Taxes: Total county taxes per capita: $292 (2004); County property taxes per capita: $205 (2004).
Education: Percent of population age 25 and over with: High school diploma (including GED) or higher: 85.9% (2005); Bachelor's degree or higher: 25.5% (2005); Master's degree or higher: 8.6% (2005).
Housing: Homeownership rate: 70.7% (2005); Median home value: $129,875 (2005); Median rent: $456 per month (2000); Median age of housing: 41 years (2000).
Health: Birth rate: 125.5 per 10,000 population (2004); Death rate: 102.1 per 10,000 population (2004); Age-adjusted cancer mortality rate: 214.8 deaths per 100,000 population (2002); Air Quality Index: 51.2% good, 44.4% moderate, 4.4% unhealthy for sensitive individuals, 0.0% unhealthy (percent of days in 2005); Number of physicians: 35.2 per 10,000 population (2004); Hospital beds: 38.1 per 10,000 population (2003); Hospital admissions: 1,546.9 per 10,000 population (2003).
Elections: 2004 Presidential election results: 42.9% Bush, 56.7% Kerry, 0.0% Nader, 0.2% Badnarik
National and State Parks: Cuyahoga Valley National Park; Portage Lakes State Park

Additional Information Contacts

Summit County Government	(330) 643-2510
http://www.co.summit.oh.us/	
Akron Regional Development Board	(330) 376-5550
http://www.greaterakronchamber.org	
Akron-Summit Convention Bureau	(330) 374-7560
http://www.visitakron-summit.org	
Barberton Area Chamber of Commerce	(330) 745-3141
http://www.southsummitchamber.org	
City of Akron	(330) 375-2345
http://www.ci.akron.oh.us	
City of Barberton	(330) 848-6662
http://www.cityofbarberton.com/index.shtml	
City of Cuyahoga Falls	(330) 971-8000
http://cfo.cityofcf.com/website/web2/view.do	
City of Fairlawn	(330) 668-9500
http://www.cityoffairlawn.com/default.cfm	
City of Green	(330) 896-5510
http://www.cityofgreen.org	
City of Hudson	(330) 650-1799
http://www.hudson.oh.us	
City of Macedonia	(330) 468-8300
http://www.macedonia.oh.us	
City of Munroe Falls	(330) 688-7491
http://www.munroefalls.com	
City of Norton	(330) 825-7815
http://www.cityofnorton.org	
City of Stow	(330) 689-2700
http://www.stow.oh.us	
City of Tallmadge	(330) 633-0857
http://www.tallmadge-ohio.org	
City of Twinsburg	(330) 425-7161
http://www.mytwinsburg.com	
Cuyahoga Falls Chamber of Commerce	(330) 929-6756
http://www.cuyahogafallschamberofcommerce.com	
Fairlawn Area Chamber of Commerce	(330) 849-0402
http://www.fairlawnareachamber.org	
Hudson Chamber of Commerce	(330) 650-0621
http://www.hudsoncoc.org	
Nordonia Hills Chamber of Commerce	(330) 467-8956
http://www.nhcoc.org	
Northern Summit Co. Tourist Info Center	(330) 468-8687
http://www.tbic.org	
Stow Chamber of Commerce	(330) 688-1579
http://www.smfcc.com	
Tallmadge Chamber of Commerce	(330) 633-5417
http://www.tallmadge-chamber.com	
Twinsburg Chamber of Commerce	(330) 963-6249
http://www.twinsburgchamber.com	
Village of Reminderville	(330) 562-1234
http://www.reminderville.com	
Village of Richfield	(330) 659-9201
http://www.richfieldvillageohio.org	

Summit County Communities

AKRON (city). Covers a land area of 62.069 square miles and a water area of 0.339 square miles. Located at 41.07° N. Lat.; 81.51° W. Long. Elevation is 1,050 feet.
History: The first settler in the Akron area was Captain Joseph Hart, who established Middlebury, now East Akron, in 1807. The city of Akron was laid out in 1825 by General Simon Perkins, commissioner of the Ohio Canal Fund, who saw a great future for a town on the summit of the course of the Ohio & Erie Canal. When the canal opened to traffic in 1827, the town grew rapidly. In 1840 trade was improved further with the opening of the Ohio & Pennsylvania Canal. In 1859, former resident John Brown was executed here for his raid at Harper's Ferry. Dr. Benjamin Franklin Goodrich came to Akron in 1870 and founded a plant for manufacturing fire hose and other articles from rubber. Around 1900 Akron was the national center for the manufacture of farm machinery, and the American Cereal Company (Quaker Oats) emerged as a leading cereal producer. But it was the rubber industry that by 1915 made Akron a boom town.
Population: 223,165 (1990); 217,074 (2000); 210,096 (2005); 203,592 (2010 projected); Race: 65.1% White, 29.9% Black, 1.8% Asian, 1.3% Hispanic of any race (2005); Density: 3,384.9 persons per square mile (2005); Average household size: 2.39 (2005); Median age: 35.3 (2005); Males per 100 females: 92.2 (2005); Marriage status: 33.0% never married, 45.2% now married, 8.0% widowed, 13.8% divorced (2000); Foreign born: 3.2% (2000); Ancestry (includes multiple ancestries): 29.9% Other groups, 18.1% German, 11.5% Irish, 7.2% English, 6.8% Italian (2000).
Economy: Unemployment rate: 6.6% (2005); Total civilian labor force: 107,195 (2005); Single-family building permits issued: 269 (2005); Multi-family building permits issued: 218 (2005); Employment by occupation: 9.0% management, 17.0% professional, 18.3% services, 28.3% sales, 0.1% farming, 7.7% construction, 19.6% production (2000).
Income: Per capita income: $19,328 (2005); Median household income: $35,014 (2005); Average household income: $45,262 (2005); Percent of households with income of $100,000 or more: 6.9% (2005); Poverty rate: 17.5% (2000).
Taxes: Total city taxes per capita: $680 (2004); City property taxes per capita: $118 (2004).
Education: Percent of population age 25 and over with: High school diploma (including GED) or higher: 80.1% (2005); Bachelor's degree or higher: 18.4% (2005); Master's degree or higher: 6.2% (2005).

School District(s)
Akron Community School (KG-06)
    2003-04 Enrollment: 26 . . . . (440) 888-5490
Akron Digital Academy (KG-12)
    2003-04 Enrollment: 217 . . . . (330) 761-1661

Akron Public Schools (PK-12)
    2003-04 Enrollment: 28,816 . . . . (330) 761-1661
Akron Teachers Electronic Clrm
    2003-04 Enrollment: n/a . . . . (330) 434-2181
Coventry Digital Academy
    2003-04 Enrollment: n/a . . . . (330) 644-8489
Coventry Local SD (PK-12)
    2003-04 Enrollment: 2,334 . . . . (330) 644-8489
East Cleveland Academy
    2003-04 Enrollment: n/a . . . . (330) 865-4774
Edge Academy, The (KG-07)
    2003-04 Enrollment: 235 . . . . (330) 525-4581
Hope Academy Brown St Campus (KG-08)
    2003-04 Enrollment: 243 . . . . (330) 785-0180
Hope Academy University (KG-08)
    2003-04 Enrollment: 193 . . . . (330) 535-7728
Ida B Wells Community Academy (KG-06)
    2003-04 Enrollment: 111 . . . . (330) 867-1085
Life Skills Center of Akron (09-12)
    2003-04 Enrollment: 583 . . . . (330) 376-8700
Life Skills Center of Summit Co (09-12)
    2003-04 Enrollment: 81 . . . . (330) 745-3678
Life Skills of Northeast Ohio (UG-UG)
    2003-04 Enrollment: n/a
Lighthouse Comm & Prof Dev (KG-07)
    2003-04 Enrollment: 138 . . . . (330) 374-9235
Manchester Digital School
    2003-04 Enrollment: n/a . . . . (330) 882-6926
Manchester Local SD (PK-12)
    2003-04 Enrollment: 1,520 . . . . (330) 882-6926
Revere Local SD (KG-12)
    2003-04 Enrollment: 2,835 . . . . (330) 666-4155
Springfield Local SD (PK-12)
    2003-04 Enrollment: 3,076 . . . . (330) 798-1111
Summit Academy Creative Arts (06-08)
    2003-04 Enrollment: 53 . . . . (330) 434-2343
Summit Academy El-Springfield
    2003-04 Enrollment: n/a
Summit Academy High School Akron
    2003-04 Enrollment: n/a
Summit Academy Warren
    2003-04 Enrollment: n/a
Summit Academy of Alt Learners (01-06)
    2003-04 Enrollment: 61 . . . . (330) 253-7441

Four-year College(s)
University of Akron Main Campus (Public)
    Fall 2004 Enrollment: 21,598 . . . . (330) 972-7111
    2005-06 Tuition: In-state $7,958; Out-of-state $16,682

Two-year College(s)
Academy of Court Reporting-Akron (Private, For-profit)
    Fall 2004 Enrollment: 258 . . . . (330) 867-4030
    2005-06 Tuition: In-state $8,000; Out-of-state $8,000
Akron Adult Vocational Services (Public)
    Fall 2004 Enrollment: 562 . . . . (330) 761-1385
Akron Institute-A Division of Herzing Ohio Inc (Private, For-profit)
    Fall 2004 Enrollment: 221 . . . . (330) 724-1600
    2005-06 Tuition: In-state $11,250; Out-of-state $11,250
Akron School of Practical Nursing (Public)
    Fall 2004 Enrollment: 109 . . . . (330) 761-3255
Brown Mackie College-Akron (Private, For-profit)
    Fall 2004 Enrollment: 521 . . . . (330) 733-8766
    2005-06 Tuition: In-state $6,804; Out-of-state $6,804
National Institute of Massotherapy (Private, For-profit)
    Fall 2004 Enrollment: 155 . . . . (330) 867-1996
Ohio College of Massotherapy Inc (Private, Not-for-profit)
    Fall 2004 Enrollment: 284 . . . . (330) 665-1084
    2005-06 Tuition: In-state $7,740; Out-of-state $7,740

Housing: Homeownership rate: 59.7% (2005); Median home value: $89,490 (2005); Median rent: $413 per month (2000); Median age of housing: 50 years (2000).
Hospitals: Akron City Hospital (505 beds); Akron General Medical Center (537 beds); Children's Hospital Medical Center of Akron (253 beds); Edwin Shaw Hospital for Rehabilitation (188 beds); Health & Wellness Center: Akron General; St. Thomas Hospital Summa Health System (306 beds)
Safety: Violent crime rate: 58.5 per 10,000 population; Property crime rate: 596.6 per 10,000 population (2004).
Newspapers: Akron Legal News (Circulation 1,000); Reporter (Black - Circulation 35,000); The Akron Beacon Journal (Circulation 137,975); The Suburbanite (General - Circulation 31,600); West Side Leader (General - Circulation 41,000)
Transportation: Commute to work: 91.7% car, 3.3% public transportation, 2.3% walk, 2.0% work from home (2000); Travel time to work: 34.3% less than 15 minutes, 43.0% 15 to 30 minutes, 13.2% 30 to 45 minutes, 4.7% 45 to 60 minutes, 4.9% 60 minutes or more (2000)

Additional Information Contacts
Akron Regional Development Board . . . . (330) 376-5550
    http://www.greaterakronchamber.org
Akron-Summit Convention Bureau . . . . (330) 374-7560
    http://www.visitakron-summit.org
City of Akron . . . . (330) 375-2345
    http://www.ci.akron.oh.us
Fairlawn Area Chamber of Commerce . . . . (330) 849-0402
    http://www.fairlawnareachamber.org

BARBERTON (city). Covers a land area of 9.014 square miles and a water area of 0.219 square miles. Located at 41.01° N. Lat.; 81.60° W. Long. Elevation is 969 feet.

History: Barberton was laid out in 1891 by Ohio Columbus Barber, the owner of the Diamond Match Company. Barber dominated the town until his death in 1920, spending millions of dollars on the Anna Dean Experimental Farm, known as Barber's Folly, where cows and horses lived in luxury.
Population: 27,931 (1990); 27,899 (2000); 27,235 (2005); 26,632 (2010 projected); Race: 91.9% White, 5.5% Black, 0.4% Asian, 0.7% Hispanic of any race (2005); Density: 3,021.5 persons per square mile (2005); Average household size: 2.39 (2005); Median age: 37.8 (2005); Males per 100 females: 88.2 (2005); Marriage status: 25.3% never married, 52.2% now married, 9.5% widowed, 13.0% divorced (2000); Foreign born: 1.9% (2000); Ancestry (includes multiple ancestries): 23.9% German, 13.1% Irish, 11.4% Other groups, 10.1% United States or American, 7.1% English (2000).
Economy: Unemployment rate: 6.8% (2005); Total civilian labor force: 13,565 (2005); Single-family building permits issued: 65 (2005); Multi-family building permits issued: 0 (2005); Employment by occupation: 8.0% management, 12.1% professional, 17.5% services, 27.4% sales, 0.2% farming, 10.7% construction, 24.1% production (2000).
Income: Per capita income: $19,704 (2005); Median household income: $35,821 (2005); Average household income: $46,491 (2005); Percent of households with income of $100,000 or more: 6.9% (2005); Poverty rate: 13.3% (2000).
Taxes: Total city taxes per capita: $416 (2004); City property taxes per capita: $54 (2004).
Education: Percent of population age 25 and over with: High school diploma (including GED) or higher: 79.1% (2005); Bachelor's degree or higher: 10.6% (2005); Master's degree or higher: 3.3% (2005).

School District(s)
Barberton City SD (PK-12)
    2003-04 Enrollment: 4,596 . . . . (330) 753-1025
Barberton HS Evng Alter Succes
    2003-04 Enrollment: n/a . . . . (330) 753-1025

Housing: Homeownership rate: 65.0% (2005); Median home value: $90,511 (2005); Median rent: $380 per month (2000); Median age of housing: 49 years (2000).
Hospitals: Barberton Citizens Hospital (311 beds)
Safety: Violent crime rate: 21.1 per 10,000 population; Property crime rate: 400.5 per 10,000 population (2004).
Newspapers: Barberton Herald (General - Circulation 7,500)
Transportation: Commute to work: 94.4% car, 1.1% public transportation, 2.8% walk, 1.3% work from home (2000); Travel time to work: 38.8% less than 15 minutes, 39.1% 15 to 30 minutes, 13.7% 30 to 45 minutes, 4.6% 45 to 60 minutes, 3.9% 60 minutes or more (2000)

Additional Information Contacts
Barberton Area Chamber of Commerce . . . . (330) 745-3141
    http://www.southsummitchamber.org
City of Barberton . . . . (330) 848-6662
    http://www.cityofbarberton.com/index.shtml

BOSTON HEIGHTS (village). Covers a land area of 6.897 square miles and a water area of 0.007 square miles. Located at 41.25° N. Lat.; 81.50° W. Long. Elevation is 1,064 feet.
Population: 733 (1990); 1,186 (2000); 1,400 (2005); 1,594 (2010 projected); Race: 95.9% White, 0.7% Black, 2.1% Asian, 1.1% Hispanic of any race (2005); Density: 203.0 persons per square mile (2005); Average household size: 2.97 (2005); Median age: 37.3 (2005); Males per 100 females: 102.3 (2005); Marriage status: 17.7% never married, 74.9% now married, 2.7% widowed, 4.7% divorced (2000); Foreign born: 3.0% (2000); Ancestry (includes multiple ancestries): 25.5% German, 18.8% Irish, 15.4% Polish, 13.7% Italian, 10.9% English (2000).
Economy: Single-family building permits issued: 10 (2005); Multi-family building permits issued: 0 (2005); Employment by occupation: 26.7% management, 22.0% professional, 12.2% services, 24.7% sales, 0.0% farming, 7.3% construction, 7.0% production (2000).
Income: Per capita income: $41,007 (2005); Median household income: $92,935 (2005); Average household income: $121,890 (2005); Percent of households with income of $100,000 or more: 45.9% (2005); Poverty rate: 1.6% (2000).
Education: Percent of population age 25 and over with: High school diploma (including GED) or higher: 93.5% (2005); Bachelor's degree or higher: 40.6% (2005); Master's degree or higher: 11.0% (2005).
Housing: Homeownership rate: 90.4% (2005); Median home value: $321,176 (2005); Median rent: $638 per month (2000); Median age of housing: 16 years (2000).
Transportation: Commute to work: 90.9% car, 0.0% public transportation, 0.4% walk, 7.7% work from home (2000); Travel time to work: 23.1% less than 15 minutes, 37.6% 15 to 30 minutes, 30.0% 30 to 45 minutes, 8.0% 45 to 60 minutes, 1.3% 60 minutes or more (2000)

CLINTON (village). Covers a land area of 3.554 square miles and a water area of 0.090 square miles. Located at 40.92° N. Lat.; 81.63° W. Long. Elevation is 950 feet.
Population: 1,175 (1990); 1,337 (2000); 1,460 (2005); 1,565 (2010 projected); Race: 97.3% White, 0.4% Black, 0.5% Asian, 0.5% Hispanic of any race (2005); Density: 410.8 persons per square mile (2005); Average household size: 2.65 (2005); Median age: 38.4 (2005); Males per 100 females: 103.3 (2005); Marriage status: 19.3% never married, 61.9% now married, 5.9% widowed, 12.8% divorced (2000); Foreign born: 1.5% (2000); Ancestry (includes multiple ancestries): 30.2% German, 15.7% Irish, 8.9% English, 7.7% Other groups, 6.3% Italian (2000).
Economy: Employment by occupation: 10.1% management, 15.7% professional, 16.0% services, 20.1% sales, 0.0% farming, 15.0% construction, 22.9% production (2000).
Income: Per capita income: $24,990 (2005); Median household income: $56,858 (2005); Average household income: $66,171 (2005); Percent of households with income of $100,000 or more: 14.9% (2005); Poverty rate: 4.9% (2000).
Education: Percent of population age 25 and over with: High school diploma (including GED) or higher: 87.0% (2005); Bachelor's degree or higher: 17.5% (2005); Master's degree or higher: 5.3% (2005).

School District(s)
Northwest Local SD (PK-12)
   2003-04 Enrollment: 2,447 . . . . (330) 854-2291
Norton City Schools (PK-12)
   2003-04 Enrollment: 2,558 . . . . (330) 825-0863

Housing: Homeownership rate: 89.1% (2005); Median home value: $118,586 (2005); Median rent: $408 per month (2000); Median age of housing: 53 years (2000).
Transportation: Commute to work: 96.9% car, 0.0% public transportation, 1.0% walk, 1.8% work from home (2000); Travel time to work: 16.2% less than 15 minutes, 44.0% 15 to 30 minutes, 27.6% 30 to 45 minutes, 7.3% 45 to 60 minutes, 4.9% 60 minutes or more (2000)

CUYAHOGA FALLS (city). Covers a land area of 25.544 square miles and a water area of 0.094 square miles. Located at 41.14° N. Lat.; 81.49° W. Long. Elevation is 1,050 feet.
History: The city greatly expanded its area by annexing Northampton township in the 1980s. Incorporated 1836.
Population: 48,814 (1990); 49,374 (2000); 50,702 (2005); 52,009 (2010 projected); Race: 94.9% White, 2.2% Black, 1.4% Asian, 0.7% Hispanic of any race (2005); Density: 1,984.9 persons per square mile (2005); Average household size: 2.25 (2005); Median age: 38.3 (2005); Males per 100 females: 91.1 (2005); Marriage status: 24.5% never married, 56.1% now married, 8.3% widowed, 11.2% divorced (2000); Foreign born: 3.1% (2000); Ancestry (includes multiple ancestries): 31.0% German, 17.4% Irish, 13.0% English, 12.4% Italian, 6.7% Other groups (2000).
Economy: It is both residential and industrial, with factories that manufacture metals, rubber, chemicals, pharmaceuticals and machinery. Unemployment rate: 5.2% (2005); Total civilian labor force: 28,425 (2005); Single-family building permits issued: 86 (2005); Multi-family building permits issued: 28 (2005); Employment by occupation: 13.3% management, 21.2% professional, 13.5% services, 30.6% sales, 0.0% farming, 7.5% construction, 13.9% production (2000).
Income: Per capita income: $24,759 (2005); Median household income: $46,583 (2005); Average household income: $55,238 (2005); Percent of households with income of $100,000 or more: 10.6% (2005); Poverty rate: 6.1% (2000).
Taxes: Total city taxes per capita: $557 (2004); City property taxes per capita: $189 (2004).
Education: Percent of population age 25 and over with: High school diploma (including GED) or higher: 90.9% (2005); Bachelor's degree or higher: 25.7% (2005); Master's degree or higher: 7.8% (2005).

School District(s)
Cuyahoga Falls City SD (PK-12)
   2003-04 Enrollment: 5,399 . . . . (330) 926-3800
Woodridge Local School District (PK-12)
   2003-04 Enrollment: 1,786 . . . . (330) 928-9074

Two-year College(s)
National Institute of Technology (Private, Not-for-profit)
   Fall 2004 Enrollment: 489 . . . . (330) 923-9959
   2005-06 Tuition: In-state $9,900; Out-of-state $9,900
Riggs Lemar Beauty College (Private, For-profit)
   Fall 2004 Enrollment: 170 . . . . (330) 945-4045

Housing: Homeownership rate: 65.4% (2005); Median home value: $125,999 (2005); Median rent: $527 per month (2000); Median age of housing: 43 years (2000).
Hospitals: Cuyahoga Falls General Hospital (257 beds)
Safety: Violent crime rate: 21.6 per 10,000 population; Property crime rate: 392.9 per 10,000 population (2004).
Transportation: Commute to work: 95.1% car, 1.0% public transportation, 1.4% walk, 2.2% work from home (2000); Travel time to work: 32.7% less than 15 minutes, 41.5% 15 to 30 minutes, 14.8% 30 to 45 minutes, 5.8% 45 to 60 minutes, 5.1% 60 minutes or more (2000)
Additional Information Contacts
City of Cuyahoga Falls . . . . (330) 971-8000
   http://cfo.cityofcf.com/website/web2/view.do
Cuyahoga Falls Chamber of Commerce . . . . (330) 929-6756
   http://www.cuyahogafallschamberofcommerce.com

FAIRLAWN (city). Covers a land area of 4.429 square miles and a water area of 0.011 square miles. Located at 41.13° N. Lat.; 81.61° W. Long. Elevation is 1,005 feet.
Population: 5,938 (1990); 7,307 (2000); 7,208 (2005); 7,102 (2010 projected); Race: 86.3% White, 7.1% Black, 4.4% Asian, 1.3% Hispanic of any race (2005); Density: 1,627.3 persons per square mile (2005); Average household size: 2.44 (2005); Median age: 45.5 (2005); Males per 100 females: 84.2 (2005); Marriage status: 20.1% never married, 58.1% now married, 11.9% widowed, 9.9% divorced (2000); Foreign born: 7.1% (2000); Ancestry (includes multiple ancestries): 22.6% German, 12.9% Irish, 11.7% Other groups, 10.2% Italian, 10.0% English (2000).
Economy: Single-family building permits issued: 9 (2005); Multi-family building permits issued: 0 (2005); Employment by occupation: 21.1% management, 34.5% professional, 6.8% services, 28.3% sales, 0.1% farming, 2.5% construction, 6.7% production (2000).
Income: Per capita income: $38,911 (2005); Median household income: $69,653 (2005); Average household income: $94,090 (2005); Percent of households with income of $100,000 or more: 29.8% (2005); Poverty rate: 1.5% (2000).
Education: Percent of population age 25 and over with: High school diploma (including GED) or higher: 92.5% (2005); Bachelor's degree or higher: 46.7% (2005); Master's degree or higher: 18.7% (2005).

School District(s)
Copley-Fairlawn City SD (PK-12)
   2003-04 Enrollment: 3,254 . . . . (330) 664-4800

Two-year College(s)
Gerbers Akron Beauty School (Private, For-profit)
   Fall 2004 Enrollment: 28 . . . . (330) 867-6200

Housing: Homeownership rate: 66.6% (2005); Median home value: $180,884 (2005); Median rent: $666 per month (2000); Median age of housing: 31 years (2000).
Safety: Violent crime rate: 8.2 per 10,000 population; Property crime rate: 640.9 per 10,000 population (2004).
Transportation: Commute to work: 94.7% car, 0.6% public transportation, 0.8% walk, 3.1% work from home (2000); Travel time to work: 31.7% less than 15 minutes, 42.0% 15 to 30 minutes, 16.6% 30 to 45 minutes, 6.1% 45 to 60 minutes, 3.6% 60 minutes or more (2000)
Additional Information Contacts
City of Fairlawn .... (330) 668-9500
http://www.cityoffairlawn.com/default.cfm

GREEN
GREEN (city). Covers a land area of 32.060 square miles and a water area of 1.471 square miles. Located at 40.95° N. Lat.; 81.48° W. Long. Elevation is 1,150 feet.
History: Green was incorporated in 1991 as a municipality. Prior to incorporation, Green was a township with several unincorporated hamlets, most notably Greensburg. A section of the township became the village of Green and later merged with the rest of the township. Fred Ravagnani was the first "mayor" of Green village. What is today Green was originally part of Stark County, although Green has been situated wholly within the County of Summit since 1840.
Population: 19,179 (1990); 22,817 (2000); 23,542 (2005); 24,299 (2010 projected); Race: 97.0% White, 0.9% Black, 1.0% Asian, 0.5% Hispanic of any race (2005); Density: 734.3 persons per square mile (2005); Average household size: 2.59 (2005); Median age: 40.1 (2005); Males per 100 females: 97.3 (2005); Marriage status: 20.8% never married, 63.0% now married, 6.5% widowed, 9.7% divorced (2000); Foreign born: 1.9% (2000); Ancestry (includes multiple ancestries): 28.3% German, 16.4% Irish, 10.9% English, 9.1% United States or American, 7.8% Italian (2000).
Economy: Employment by occupation: 14.7% management, 20.5% professional, 12.6% services, 27.4% sales, 0.2% farming, 9.2% construction, 15.4% production (2000).
Income: Per capita income: $29,922 (2005); Median household income: $62,036 (2005); Average household income: $76,973 (2005); Percent of households with income of $100,000 or more: 23.1% (2005); Poverty rate: 5.0% (2000).
Education: Percent of population age 25 and over with: High school diploma (including GED) or higher: 88.9% (2005); Bachelor's degree or higher: 26.3% (2005); Master's degree or higher: 7.6% (2005).
School District(s)
Green Local SD (PK-12)
    2003-04 Enrollment: 4,165 .... (330) 896-7500
Portage Lakes Joint Vocational SD (09-12)
    2003-04 Enrollment: n/a .... (330) 896-8200
Two-year College(s)
Portage Lakes Career Center (Public)
    Fall 2004 Enrollment: 109 .... (330) 896-8200
W Howard Nicol School of Practical Nursing (Public)
    Fall 2004 Enrollment: 34 .... (330) 896-8105
Housing: Homeownership rate: 80.3% (2005); Median home value: $164,055 (2005); Median rent: $544 per month (2000); Median age of housing: 26 years (2000).
Transportation: Commute to work: 96.4% car, 0.5% public transportation, 0.5% walk, 2.1% work from home (2000); Travel time to work: 23.0% less than 15 minutes, 49.4% 15 to 30 minutes, 17.9% 30 to 45 minutes, 5.5% 45 to 60 minutes, 4.3% 60 minutes or more (2000)
Additional Information Contacts
City of Green .... (330) 896-5510
http://www.cityofgreen.org

HUDSON
HUDSON (city). Aka Hudson Village. Covers a land area of 25.588 square miles and a water area of 0.266 square miles. Located at 41.24° N. Lat.; 81.43° W. Long. Elevation is 1,090 feet.
History: The city is named after its founder, David Hudson, who settled here from Goshen, Connecticut, in 1799. The Underground Railroad passed through Hudson, also the birthplace of abolitionist John Brown. From 1837 to 1994, the area that is now the City of Hudson was in two parts, the Village of Hudson and Hudson Township. In 1994, voters approved a merger uniting the city. Today, the city is governed by a seven-member city council. There are four council representatives representing the four wards in Hudson, and three representatives at large.
Population: 17,128 (1990); 22,439 (2000); 23,295 (2005); 24,097 (2010 projected); Race: 93.6% White, 1.5% Black, 3.7% Asian, 0.9% Hispanic of any race (2005); Density: 910.4 persons per square mile (2005); Average household size: 3.04 (2005); Median age: 39.1 (2005); Males per 100 females: 98.0 (2005); Marriage status: 17.7% never married, 73.6% now married, 4.6% widowed, 4.1% divorced (2000); Foreign born: 5.2% (2000); Ancestry (includes multiple ancestries): 30.1% German, 19.8% Irish, 17.4% English, 10.6% Italian, 7.3% Polish (2000).
Economy: Employment by occupation: 29.8% management, 28.9% professional, 7.2% services, 27.1% sales, 0.1% farming, 2.5% construction, 4.4% production (2000).
Income: Per capita income: $47,846 (2005); Median household income: $111,037 (2005); Average household income: $144,936 (2005); Percent of households with income of $100,000 or more: 55.4% (2005); Poverty rate: 1.7% (2000).
Taxes: Total city taxes per capita: $576 (2004); City property taxes per capita: $250 (2004).
Education: Percent of population age 25 and over with: High school diploma (including GED) or higher: 97.3% (2005); Bachelor's degree or higher: 66.6% (2005); Master's degree or higher: 26.0% (2005).
School District(s)
Cleveland Municipal City SD (PK-12)
    2003-04 Enrollment: 69,655 .... (216) 574-8000
Hudson City SD (PK-12)
    2003-04 Enrollment: 5,566 .... (330) 653-1200
Housing: Homeownership rate: 90.3% (2005); Median home value: $267,474 (2005); Median rent: $1,131 per month (2000); Median age of housing: 20 years (2000).
Safety: Violent crime rate: 1.7 per 10,000 population; Property crime rate: 103.9 per 10,000 population (2004).
Transportation: Commute to work: 91.8% car, 0.4% public transportation, 1.1% walk, 5.9% work from home (2000); Travel time to work: 27.8% less than 15 minutes, 31.0% 15 to 30 minutes, 22.8% 30 to 45 minutes, 13.3% 45 to 60 minutes, 5.2% 60 minutes or more (2000)
Additional Information Contacts
City of Hudson .... (330) 650-1799
http://www.hudson.oh.us
Hudson Chamber of Commerce .... (330) 650-0621
http://www.hudsoncoc.org

LAKEMORE
LAKEMORE (village). Covers a land area of 1.462 square miles and a water area of 0.191 square miles. Located at 41.02° N. Lat.; 81.43° W. Long. Elevation is 1,110 feet.
History: Incorporated 1920.
Population: 2,684 (1990); 2,561 (2000); 2,536 (2005); 2,496 (2010 projected); Race: 97.6% White, 0.4% Black, 0.1% Asian, 0.6% Hispanic of any race (2005); Density: 1,734.7 persons per square mile (2005); Average household size: 2.60 (2005); Median age: 37.1 (2005); Males per 100 females: 99.1 (2005); Marriage status: 26.0% never married, 52.1% now married, 7.5% widowed, 14.3% divorced (2000); Foreign born: 0.6% (2000); Ancestry (includes multiple ancestries): 27.7% German, 20.7% Irish, 15.9% English, 12.8% Other groups, 6.6% United States or American (2000).
Economy: Single-family building permits issued: 33 (2005); Multi-family building permits issued: 21 (2005); Employment by occupation: 6.5% management, 9.0% professional, 18.8% services, 23.1% sales, 0.4% farming, 16.6% construction, 25.6% production (2000).
Income: Per capita income: $17,422 (2005); Median household income: $37,512 (2005); Average household income: $44,335 (2005); Percent of households with income of $100,000 or more: 5.0% (2005); Poverty rate: 10.1% (2000).
Education: Percent of population age 25 and over with: High school diploma (including GED) or higher: 71.8% (2005); Bachelor's degree or higher: 8.2% (2005); Master's degree or higher: 2.1% (2005).
School District(s)
Springfield Local SD (PK-12)
    2003-04 Enrollment: 3,076 .... (330) 798-1111
Housing: Homeownership rate: 78.4% (2005); Median home value: $93,303 (2005); Median rent: $455 per month (2000); Median age of housing: 47 years (2000).
Safety: Violent crime rate: 16.0 per 10,000 population; Property crime rate: 437.2 per 10,000 population (2004).
Transportation: Commute to work: 93.5% car, 2.3% public transportation, 2.3% walk, 1.2% work from home (2000); Travel time to work: 30.2% less than 15 minutes, 43.0% 15 to 30 minutes, 17.3% 30 to 45 minutes, 5.3% 45 to 60 minutes, 4.2% 60 minutes or more (2000)

PROFILES OF OHIO / Summit County 293

MACEDONIA (city). Covers a land area of 9.676 square miles and a water area of 0.038 square miles. Located at 41.31° N. Lat.; 81.50° W. Long. Elevation is 989 feet.
History: The city's name is said to derive from a small joke among divinity students at Western Reserve College, which in the early 1800s was in Hudson, Ohio. The students, who were called upon to preach in the small hamlet six miles to the north, recalled Acts 16:10: "...we sought to go to Macedonia, concluding that the Lord had called us to preach the gospel to them."
Population: 7,589 (1990); 9,224 (2000); 10,511 (2005); 11,691 (2010 projected); Race: 90.3% White, 6.1% Black, 2.4% Asian, 0.9% Hispanic of any race (2005); Density: 1,086.3 persons per square mile (2005); Average household size: 2.75 (2005); Median age: 39.4 (2005); Males per 100 females: 98.0 (2005); Marriage status: 19.7% never married, 69.0% now married, 3.4% widowed, 7.9% divorced (2000); Foreign born: 4.8% (2000); Ancestry (includes multiple ancestries): 21.7% German, 19.8% Italian, 15.0% Irish, 13.7% Polish, 12.1% English (2000).
Economy: Primarily urban area. Single-family building permits issued: 77 (2005); Multi-family building permits issued: 0 (2005); Employment by occupation: 19.2% management, 19.0% professional, 11.1% services, 31.9% sales, 0.1% farming, 6.8% construction, 11.9% production (2000).
Income: Per capita income: $31,974 (2005); Median household income: $78,991 (2005); Average household income: $88,050 (2005); Percent of households with income of $100,000 or more: 33.3% (2005); Poverty rate: 1.5% (2000).
Taxes: Total city taxes per capita: $698 (2004); City property taxes per capita: $156 (2004).
Education: Percent of population age 25 and over with: High school diploma (including GED) or higher: 93.2% (2005); Bachelor's degree or higher: 31.2% (2005); Master's degree or higher: 7.5% (2005).

School District(s)
Nordonia Hills City SD (PK-12)
    2003-04 Enrollment: 3,887 .... (330) 467-0580

Housing: Homeownership rate: 95.6% (2005); Median home value: $186,391 (2005); Median rent: $653 per month (2000); Median age of housing: 26 years (2000).
Transportation: Commute to work: 96.5% car, 0.8% public transportation, 0.3% walk, 2.4% work from home (2000); Travel time to work: 30.0% less than 15 minutes, 38.0% 15 to 30 minutes, 22.6% 30 to 45 minutes, 5.4% 45 to 60 minutes, 4.0% 60 minutes or more (2000)

Additional Information Contacts
City of Macedonia .... (330) 468-8300
    http://www.macedonia.oh.us
Nordonia Hills Chamber of Commerce .... (330) 467-8956
    http://www.nhcoc.org
Northern Summit Co. Tourist Info Center .... (330) 468-8687
    http://www.tbic.org

MOGADORE (village). Covers a land area of 2.092 square miles and a water area of 0.017 square miles. Located at 41.05° N. Lat.; 81.39° W. Long. Elevation is 1,150 feet.
Population: 4,066 (1990); 3,893 (2000); 3,968 (2005); 4,045 (2010 projected); Race: 98.4% White, 0.2% Black, 0.2% Asian, 0.2% Hispanic of any race (2005); Density: 1,896.6 persons per square mile (2005); Average household size: 2.57 (2005); Median age: 40.2 (2005); Males per 100 females: 96.6 (2005); Marriage status: 19.5% never married, 67.2% now married, 6.1% widowed, 7.2% divorced (2000); Foreign born: 0.6% (2000); Ancestry (includes multiple ancestries): 31.3% German, 13.4% Irish, 13.0% United States or American, 12.1% English, 6.9% Italian (2000).
Economy: Tools, clay products, composites, plastic products. Single-family building permits issued: 7 (2005); Multi-family building permits issued: 0 (2005); Employment by occupation: 10.6% management, 17.2% professional, 16.0% services, 27.6% sales, 0.0% farming, 7.9% construction, 20.7% production (2000).
Income: Per capita income: $23,624 (2005); Median household income: $53,765 (2005); Average household income: $59,960 (2005); Percent of households with income of $100,000 or more: 11.3% (2005); Poverty rate: 3.6% (2000).
Education: Percent of population age 25 and over with: High school diploma (including GED) or higher: 91.0% (2005); Bachelor's degree or higher: 17.8% (2005); Master's degree or higher: 4.8% (2005).

School District(s)
Field Local SD (KG-12)
    2003-04 Enrollment: 2,310 .... (330) 673-2659

Mogadore Local SD (PK-12)
    2003-04 Enrollment: 901 .... (330) 628-9946
Perfection Digital Academy
    2003-04 Enrollment: n/a .... (330) 628-9946

Two-year College(s)
Carnegie Institute of Integrative Medicine and Massotherapy (Private, Not-for-profit)
    Fall 2004 Enrollment: 112 .... (330) 630-1132

Housing: Homeownership rate: 85.2% (2005); Median home value: $126,044 (2005); Median rent: $459 per month (2000); Median age of housing: 43 years (2000).
Safety: Violent crime rate: 2.5 per 10,000 population; Property crime rate: 181.7 per 10,000 population (2004).
Transportation: Commute to work: 97.4% car, 0.0% public transportation, 0.9% walk, 1.4% work from home (2000); Travel time to work: 30.1% less than 15 minutes, 46.5% 15 to 30 minutes, 14.3% 30 to 45 minutes, 6.5% 45 to 60 minutes, 2.5% 60 minutes or more (2000)

MONTROSE-GHENT (CDP). Covers a land area of 9.422 square miles and a water area of 0.091 square miles. Located at 41.15° N. Lat.; 81.63° W. Long.
Population: 4,855 (1990); 5,261 (2000); 5,575 (2005); 5,886 (2010 projected); Race: 96.1% White, 0.9% Black, 2.1% Asian, 0.6% Hispanic of any race (2005); Density: 591.7 persons per square mile (2005); Average household size: 2.70 (2005); Median age: 47.2 (2005); Males per 100 females: 99.5 (2005); Marriage status: 16.8% never married, 70.1% now married, 5.6% widowed, 7.5% divorced (2000); Foreign born: 6.2% (2000); Ancestry (includes multiple ancestries): 33.5% German, 14.2% English, 13.1% Irish, 7.6% Italian, 5.3% Polish (2000).
Economy: Large-scale retailing. Employment by occupation: 23.4% management, 36.3% professional, 9.3% services, 22.2% sales, 0.0% farming, 3.1% construction, 5.7% production (2000).
Income: Per capita income: $55,465 (2005); Median household income: $104,116 (2005); Average household income: $149,007 (2005); Percent of households with income of $100,000 or more: 51.3% (2005); Poverty rate: 0.7% (2000).
Education: Percent of population age 25 and over with: High school diploma (including GED) or higher: 96.3% (2005); Bachelor's degree or higher: 61.1% (2005); Master's degree or higher: 27.8% (2005).
Housing: Homeownership rate: 96.2% (2005); Median home value: $324,484 (2005); Median rent: $911 per month (2000); Median age of housing: 30 years (2000).
Transportation: Commute to work: 92.2% car, 0.3% public transportation, 0.4% walk, 6.9% work from home (2000); Travel time to work: 27.4% less than 15 minutes, 52.5% 15 to 30 minutes, 14.0% 30 to 45 minutes, 4.2% 45 to 60 minutes, 1.8% 60 minutes or more (2000)

MUNROE FALLS (city). Covers a land area of 2.739 square miles and a water area of 0.091 square miles. Located at 41.13° N. Lat.; 81.43° W. Long. Elevation is 1,100 feet.
Population: 5,359 (1990); 5,314 (2000); 5,335 (2005); 5,382 (2010 projected); Race: 96.8% White, 1.0% Black, 1.2% Asian, 0.8% Hispanic of any race (2005); Density: 1,947.5 persons per square mile (2005); Average household size: 2.67 (2005); Median age: 42.9 (2005); Males per 100 females: 94.4 (2005); Marriage status: 20.2% never married, 68.7% now married, 4.1% widowed, 7.0% divorced (2000); Foreign born: 2.3% (2000); Ancestry (includes multiple ancestries): 26.5% German, 15.0% Irish, 12.9% English, 12.8% Italian, 5.5% United States or American (2000).
Economy: Paper products. Single-family building permits issued: 3 (2005); Multi-family building permits issued: 0 (2005); Employment by occupation: 20.4% management, 27.1% professional, 9.4% services, 25.4% sales, 0.0% farming, 5.9% construction, 11.8% production (2000).
Income: Per capita income: $31,250 (2005); Median household income: $67,759 (2005); Average household income: $81,414 (2005); Percent of households with income of $100,000 or more: 25.8% (2005); Poverty rate: 1.5% (2000).
Taxes: Total city taxes per capita: $374 (2004); City property taxes per capita: $142 (2004).
Education: Percent of population age 25 and over with: High school diploma (including GED) or higher: 89.3% (2005); Bachelor's degree or higher: 33.6% (2005); Master's degree or higher: 13.4% (2005).

School District(s)
Stow-Munroe Falls City SD (PK-12)
    2003-04 Enrollment: 6,080 .... (330) 689-5445

Housing: Homeownership rate: 85.5% (2005); Median home value: $156,885 (2005); Median rent: $467 per month (2000); Median age of housing: 30 years (2000).
Safety: Violent crime rate: 3.8 per 10,000 population; Property crime rate: 106.9 per 10,000 population (2004).
Transportation: Commute to work: 97.3% car, 1.0% public transportation, 0.0% walk, 1.7% work from home (2000); Travel time to work: 28.7% less than 15 minutes, 47.2% 15 to 30 minutes, 13.9% 30 to 45 minutes, 4.8% 45 to 60 minutes, 5.5% 60 minutes or more (2000)
Additional Information Contacts
City of Munroe Falls.................................(330) 688-7491
http://www.munroefalls.com

NEW FRANKLIN (village).
Covers a land area of 2.224 square miles and a water area of 0.071 square miles. Located at 40.95° N. Lat.; 81.53° W. Long.
Population: 2,317 (1990); 2,191 (2000); 2,267 (2005); 2,346 (2010 projected); Race: 98.2% White, 0.5% Black, 0.4% Asian, 0.2% Hispanic of any race (2005); Density: 1,019.4 persons per square mile (2005); Average household size: 2.48 (2005); Median age: 42.6 (2005); Males per 100 females: 98.2 (2005); Marriage status: 18.5% never married, 68.1% now married, 7.6% widowed, 5.8% divorced (2000); Foreign born: 2.7% (2000); Ancestry (includes multiple ancestries): 35.2% German, 15.8% English, 13.0% Irish, 9.5% United States or American, 6.4% Other groups (2000).
Economy: Employment by occupation: 10.1% management, 17.4% professional, 15.5% services, 24.9% sales, 0.0% farming, 11.4% construction, 20.8% production (2000).
Income: Per capita income: $25,656 (2005); Median household income: $55,974 (2005); Average household income: $63,705 (2005); Percent of households with income of $100,000 or more: 14.8% (2005); Poverty rate: 4.8% (2000).
Education: Percent of population age 25 and over with: High school diploma (including GED) or higher: 89.4% (2005); Bachelor's degree or higher: 16.2% (2005); Master's degree or higher: 4.9% (2005).
Housing: Homeownership rate: 86.0% (2005); Median home value: $146,101 (2005); Median rent: $446 per month (2000); Median age of housing: 39 years (2000).
Transportation: Commute to work: 96.5% car, 1.0% public transportation, 0.5% walk, 1.9% work from home (2000); Travel time to work: 16.3% less than 15 minutes, 49.3% 15 to 30 minutes, 20.8% 30 to 45 minutes, 8.0% 45 to 60 minutes, 5.7% 60 minutes or more (2000)

NORTHFIELD (village).
Covers a land area of 1.073 square miles and a water area of 0 square miles. Located at 41.34° N. Lat.; 81.53° W. Long. Elevation is 1,044 feet.
Population: 3,437 (1990); 3,827 (2000); 3,739 (2005); 3,658 (2010 projected); Race: 90.8% White, 3.9% Black, 3.1% Asian, 0.6% Hispanic of any race (2005); Density: 3,486.1 persons per square mile (2005); Average household size: 2.38 (2005); Median age: 37.2 (2005); Males per 100 females: 98.7 (2005); Marriage status: 27.2% never married, 55.4% now married, 5.0% widowed, 12.3% divorced (2000); Foreign born: 3.1% (2000); Ancestry (includes multiple ancestries): 26.5% German, 17.8% Irish, 17.7% Italian, 15.0% Polish, 8.1% Other groups (2000).
Economy: Furnace Run Reservation (recreation) is nearby. Single-family building permits issued: 13 (2005); Multi-family building permits issued: 0 (2005); Employment by occupation: 8.8% management, 15.5% professional, 18.0% services, 28.3% sales, 0.4% farming, 8.5% construction, 20.5% production (2000).
Income: Per capita income: $20,065 (2005); Median household income: $41,943 (2005); Average household income: $47,535 (2005); Percent of households with income of $100,000 or more: 5.2% (2005); Poverty rate: 4.3% (2000).
Education: Percent of population age 25 and over with: High school diploma (including GED) or higher: 83.0% (2005); Bachelor's degree or higher: 13.2% (2005); Master's degree or higher: 2.8% (2005).
School District(s)
Nordonia Hills City SD (PK-12)
   2003-04 Enrollment: 3,887.....................(330) 467-0580
Housing: Homeownership rate: 66.6% (2005); Median home value: $132,735 (2005); Median rent: $487 per month (2000); Median age of housing: 34 years (2000).
Hospitals: Northcoast Behavioral Healthcare Systems (272 beds)
Transportation: Commute to work: 91.4% car, 1.0% public transportation, 3.2% walk, 2.3% work from home (2000); Travel time to work: 30.2% less than 15 minutes, 41.1% 15 to 30 minutes, 21.1% 30 to 45 minutes, 4.3% 45 to 60 minutes, 3.2% 60 minutes or more (2000)
Additional Information Contacts
Nordonia Hills Chamber of Commerce................(330) 467-8956
http://www.nhcoc.org

NORTON (city).
Covers a land area of 20.117 square miles and a water area of 0.330 square miles. Located at 41.02° N. Lat.; 81.64° W. Long. Elevation is 1,050 feet.
History: Norton Township became a village in 1961 and a city in 1969. As a township, and prior to the establishment of the City of Barberton in 1892, Norton consisted of seven little hamlets: Norton Center, Loyal Oak, Western Star, Sherman, Hametown, Johnson's Corners, and New Portage. There were few settlers until after the War of 1812. Then the New Englanders came, followed shortly by persons of German descent from Pennsylvania. Norton derived its name from Birdseye Norton, the chief landowner and a cousin of David Hudson, founder of Hudson Township. Norton was known throughout the area for its fertile land and prosperous farms. Coal was prevalent in the southwestern portion of the township.
Population: 11,487 (1990); 11,523 (2000); 11,722 (2005); 11,924 (2010 projected); Race: 97.0% White, 1.5% Black, 0.3% Asian, 0.4% Hispanic of any race (2005); Density: 582.7 persons per square mile (2005); Average household size: 2.60 (2005); Median age: 41.5 (2005); Males per 100 females: 96.4 (2005); Marriage status: 20.7% never married, 64.4% now married, 6.0% widowed, 8.9% divorced (2000); Foreign born: 1.9% (2000); Ancestry (includes multiple ancestries): 28.8% German, 13.7% English, 13.6% Irish, 8.6% United States or American, 7.3% Italian (2000).
Economy: Single-family building permits issued: 40 (2005); Multi-family building permits issued: 2 (2005); Employment by occupation: 10.3% management, 17.4% professional, 14.1% services, 28.2% sales, 0.6% farming, 11.6% construction, 18.0% production (2000).
Income: Per capita income: $24,028 (2005); Median household income: $54,418 (2005); Average household income: $62,164 (2005); Percent of households with income of $100,000 or more: 13.8% (2005); Poverty rate: 5.9% (2000).
Education: Percent of population age 25 and over with: High school diploma (including GED) or higher: 85.6% (2005); Bachelor's degree or higher: 17.3% (2005); Master's degree or higher: 4.8% (2005).
School District(s)
Norton City Schools (PK-12)
   2003-04 Enrollment: 2,558........................(330) 825-0863
Norton Digital Academy
   2003-04 Enrollment: n/a..........................(330) 825-0863
Norton Learning Academy
   2003-04 Enrollment: n/a..........................(330) 825-0863
Two-year College(s)
Akron Machining Institute Inc (Private, Not-for-profit)
   Fall 2004 Enrollment: 71.........................(330) 745-1111
Housing: Homeownership rate: 89.0% (2005); Median home value: $129,807 (2005); Median rent: $515 per month (2000); Median age of housing: 41 years (2000).
Safety: Violent crime rate: 20.6 per 10,000 population; Property crime rate: 371.8 per 10,000 population (2004).
Transportation: Commute to work: 96.1% car, 0.1% public transportation, 0.7% walk, 2.9% work from home (2000); Travel time to work: 29.1% less than 15 minutes, 47.5% 15 to 30 minutes, 17.1% 30 to 45 minutes, 4.0% 45 to 60 minutes, 2.2% 60 minutes or more (2000)
Additional Information Contacts
City of Norton..(330) 825-7815
http://www.cityofnorton.org

PENINSULA (village).
Covers a land area of 4.674 square miles and a water area of 0.010 square miles. Located at 41.24° N. Lat.; 81.55° W. Long. Elevation is 805 feet.
Population: 562 (1990); 602 (2000); 680 (2005); 748 (2010 projected); Race: 97.4% White, 0.7% Black, 0.6% Asian, 0.1% Hispanic of any race (2005); Density: 145.5 persons per square mile (2005); Average household size: 2.48 (2005); Median age: 46.1 (2005); Males per 100 females: 97.7 (2005); Marriage status: 20.4% never married, 59.4% now married, 6.7% widowed, 13.5% divorced (2000); Foreign born: 2.3% (2000); Ancestry (includes multiple ancestries): 37.3% German, 17.6% Irish, 11.0% English, 9.5% Polish, 7.7% Other groups (2000).
Economy: Employment by occupation: 18.3% management, 22.4% professional, 9.8% services, 27.5% sales, 0.0% farming, 11.2% construction, 10.8% production (2000).

Income: Per capita income: $34,245 (2005); Median household income: $71,698 (2005); Average household income: $82,847 (2005); Percent of households with income of $100,000 or more: 27.7% (2005); Poverty rate: 1.2% (2000).
Education: Percent of population age 25 and over with: High school diploma (including GED) or higher: 88.8% (2005); Bachelor's degree or higher: 38.6% (2005); Master's degree or higher: 17.5% (2005).

School District(s)

Woodridge Local School District (PK-12)
   2003-04 Enrollment: 1,786 . . . . (330) 928-9074

Housing: Homeownership rate: 79.2% (2005); Median home value: $248,305 (2005); Median rent: $606 per month (2000); Median age of housing: 58 years (2000).
Transportation: Commute to work: 89.7% car, 0.0% public transportation, 1.1% walk, 9.2% work from home (2000); Travel time to work: 22.7% less than 15 minutes, 43.8% 15 to 30 minutes, 22.7% 30 to 45 minutes, 9.0% 45 to 60 minutes, 2.0% 60 minutes or more (2000)

PIGEON CREEK (CDP).
Covers a land area of 0.893 square miles and a water area of 0 square miles. Located at 41.11° N. Lat.; 81.67° W. Long.
Population: 1,008 (1990); 945 (2000); 949 (2005); 938 (2010 projected); Race: 95.4% White, 2.3% Black, 1.6% Asian, 0.1% Hispanic of any race (2005); Density: 1,063.0 persons per square mile (2005); Average household size: 2.88 (2005); Median age: 45.3 (2005); Males per 100 females: 96.5 (2005); Marriage status: 21.5% never married, 74.0% now married, 0.9% widowed, 3.6% divorced (2000); Foreign born: 5.6% (2000); Ancestry (includes multiple ancestries): 41.7% German, 10.7% English, 10.0% Other groups, 8.3% Italian, 7.8% Irish (2000).
Economy: Employment by occupation: 23.1% management, 34.0% professional, 8.6% services, 25.2% sales, 0.0% farming, 5.3% construction, 3.7% production (2000).
Income: Per capita income: $46,012 (2005); Median household income: $88,225 (2005); Average household income: $132,720 (2005); Percent of households with income of $100,000 or more: 40.1% (2005); Poverty rate: 0.0% (2000).
Education: Percent of population age 25 and over with: High school diploma (including GED) or higher: 98.7% (2005); Bachelor's degree or higher: 56.0% (2005); Master's degree or higher: 23.7% (2005).
Housing: Homeownership rate: 98.8% (2005); Median home value: $225,540 (2005); Median rent: $n/a per month (2000); Median age of housing: 27 years (2000).
Transportation: Commute to work: 95.8% car, 0.0% public transportation, 0.0% walk, 4.2% work from home (2000); Travel time to work: 26.5% less than 15 minutes, 32.8% 15 to 30 minutes, 22.5% 30 to 45 minutes, 14.7% 45 to 60 minutes, 3.4% 60 minutes or more (2000)

PORTAGE LAKES (CDP).
Covers a land area of 6.571 square miles and a water area of 1.586 square miles. Located at 40.99° N. Lat.; 81.53° W. Long. Elevation is 1,050 feet.
Population: 10,288 (1990); 9,870 (2000); 9,791 (2005); 9,732 (2010 projected); Race: 97.4% White, 0.7% Black, 0.4% Asian, 0.6% Hispanic of any race (2005); Density: 1,489.9 persons per square mile (2005); Average household size: 2.32 (2005); Median age: 42.7 (2005); Males per 100 females: 98.8 (2005); Marriage status: 21.4% never married, 56.9% now married, 7.7% widowed, 14.0% divorced (2000); Foreign born: 1.5% (2000); Ancestry (includes multiple ancestries): 27.5% German, 15.5% Irish, 12.4% English, 9.9% United States or American, 5.5% Italian (2000).
Economy: Employment by occupation: 12.7% management, 20.2% professional, 13.4% services, 25.4% sales, 0.0% farming, 11.5% construction, 16.8% production (2000).
Income: Per capita income: $25,471 (2005); Median household income: $49,175 (2005); Average household income: $58,727 (2005); Percent of households with income of $100,000 or more: 11.9% (2005); Poverty rate: 5.0% (2000).
Education: Percent of population age 25 and over with: High school diploma (including GED) or higher: 86.9% (2005); Bachelor's degree or higher: 20.1% (2005); Master's degree or higher: 6.4% (2005).
Housing: Homeownership rate: 77.9% (2005); Median home value: $123,082 (2005); Median rent: $495 per month (2000); Median age of housing: 44 years (2000).
Transportation: Commute to work: 94.9% car, 0.1% public transportation, 1.3% walk, 3.2% work from home (2000); Travel time to work: 27.2% less than 15 minutes, 49.6% 15 to 30 minutes, 15.4% 30 to 45 minutes, 3.6% 45 to 60 minutes, 4.2% 60 minutes or more (2000)

REMINDERVILLE (village).
Covers a land area of 1.992 square miles and a water area of 0.023 square miles. Located at 41.33° N. Lat.; 81.40° W. Long. Elevation is 1,010 feet.
Population: 2,163 (1990); 2,347 (2000); 2,151 (2005); 2,079 (2010 projected); Race: 94.6% White, 2.8% Black, 0.7% Asian, 1.1% Hispanic of any race (2005); Density: 1,079.8 persons per square mile (2005); Average household size: 2.53 (2005); Median age: 37.3 (2005); Males per 100 females: 99.7 (2005); Marriage status: 21.2% never married, 62.2% now married, 3.9% widowed, 12.7% divorced (2000); Foreign born: 5.0% (2000); Ancestry (includes multiple ancestries): 20.9% German, 16.0% Irish, 14.8% Italian, 11.7% Polish, 11.6% English (2000).
Economy: Single-family building permits issued: 44 (2005); Multi-family building permits issued: 0 (2005); Employment by occupation: 17.2% management, 21.8% professional, 12.1% services, 28.5% sales, 0.0% farming, 7.2% construction, 13.2% production (2000).
Income: Per capita income: $28,229 (2005); Median household income: $62,138 (2005); Average household income: $71,351 (2005); Percent of households with income of $100,000 or more: 18.9% (2005); Poverty rate: 4.4% (2000).
Education: Percent of population age 25 and over with: High school diploma (including GED) or higher: 95.6% (2005); Bachelor's degree or higher: 30.1% (2005); Master's degree or higher: 7.3% (2005).
Housing: Homeownership rate: 92.5% (2005); Median home value: $153,340 (2005); Median rent: $726 per month (2000); Median age of housing: 23 years (2000).
Transportation: Commute to work: 95.8% car, 0.0% public transportation, 0.6% walk, 3.3% work from home (2000); Travel time to work: 15.7% less than 15 minutes, 40.9% 15 to 30 minutes, 29.0% 30 to 45 minutes, 10.9% 45 to 60 minutes, 3.5% 60 minutes or more (2000)

Additional Information Contacts
Village of Reminderville . . . . (330) 562-1234
   http://www.reminderville.com

RICHFIELD (village).
Covers a land area of 8.489 square miles and a water area of 0.003 square miles. Located at 41.23° N. Lat.; 81.63° W. Long. Elevation is 1,139 feet.
History: Richfield was the home of John Brown (1800-1859) during the 1840's, when he was a sheep raiser and wool broker. Brown became a symbol of the Northern sympathies in the Civil War after his raid on the arsenal at Harpers Ferry in 1859, for which he was convicted of treason and hung.
Population: 3,256 (1990); 3,286 (2000); 3,623 (2005); 3,932 (2010 projected); Race: 96.5% White, 0.6% Black, 1.9% Asian, 0.2% Hispanic of any race (2005); Density: 426.8 persons per square mile (2005); Average household size: 2.64 (2005); Median age: 44.6 (2005); Males per 100 females: 98.1 (2005); Marriage status: 17.3% never married, 64.6% now married, 9.5% widowed, 8.7% divorced (2000); Foreign born: 5.7% (2000); Ancestry (includes multiple ancestries): 32.3% German, 14.3% Polish, 13.7% Irish, 13.1% English, 9.5% Italian (2000).
Economy: Employment by occupation: 18.5% management, 21.4% professional, 12.9% services, 25.2% sales, 0.5% farming, 9.5% construction, 12.0% production (2000).
Income: Per capita income: $37,383 (2005); Median household income: $76,274 (2005); Average household income: $96,196 (2005); Percent of households with income of $100,000 or more: 31.7% (2005); Poverty rate: 3.5% (2000).
Education: Percent of population age 25 and over with: High school diploma (including GED) or higher: 92.5% (2005); Bachelor's degree or higher: 24.6% (2005); Master's degree or higher: 8.3% (2005).

School District(s)

Akros Middle School
   2003-04 Enrollment: n/a
Revere Local SD (KG-12)
   2003-04 Enrollment: 2,835 . . . . (330) 666-4155

Housing: Homeownership rate: 89.4% (2005); Median home value: $197,195 (2005); Median rent: $648 per month (2000); Median age of housing: 39 years (2000).
Transportation: Commute to work: 93.4% car, 0.9% public transportation, 1.4% walk, 4.0% work from home (2000); Travel time to work: 22.0% less than 15 minutes, 33.0% 15 to 30 minutes, 32.2% 30 to 45 minutes, 10.8% 45 to 60 minutes, 2.1% 60 minutes or more (2000)

Additional Information Contacts
Village of Richfield . . . . (330) 659-9201
   http://www.richfieldvillageohio.org

SILVER LAKE (village). Covers a land area of 1.418 square miles and a water area of 0.181 square miles. Located at 41.15° N. Lat.; 81.46° W. Long. Elevation is 1,060 feet.
Population: 3,052 (1990); 3,019 (2000); 3,245 (2005); 3,459 (2010 projected); Race: 98.1% White, 0.2% Black, 0.6% Asian, 0.9% Hispanic of any race (2005); Density: 2,288.6 persons per square mile (2005); Average household size: 2.43 (2005); Median age: 49.3 (2005); Males per 100 females: 90.8 (2005); Marriage status: 13.7% never married, 73.4% now married, 7.9% widowed, 5.0% divorced (2000); Foreign born: 2.5% (2000); Ancestry (includes multiple ancestries): 32.3% German, 18.8% English, 15.0% Irish, 12.8% Italian, 6.4% Other groups (2000).
Economy: Employment by occupation: 22.5% management, 32.9% professional, 6.7% services, 30.7% sales, 0.0% farming, 3.7% construction, 3.4% production (2000).
Income: Per capita income: $39,545 (2005); Median household income: $76,966 (2005); Average household income: $95,533 (2005); Percent of households with income of $100,000 or more: 32.9% (2005); Poverty rate: 2.8% (2000).
Education: Percent of population age 25 and over with: High school diploma (including GED) or higher: 94.9% (2005); Bachelor's degree or higher: 50.2% (2005); Master's degree or higher: 19.6% (2005).
School District(s)
Cuyahoga Falls City SD (PK-12)
    2003-04 Enrollment: 5,399 . . . . (330) 926-3800
Housing: Homeownership rate: 96.0% (2005); Median home value: $204,956 (2005); Median rent: $739 per month (2000); Median age of housing: 44 years (2000).
Transportation: Commute to work: 93.4% car, 0.8% public transportation, 1.3% walk, 4.6% work from home (2000); Travel time to work: 36.6% less than 15 minutes, 34.2% 15 to 30 minutes, 15.7% 30 to 45 minutes, 7.3% 45 to 60 minutes, 6.2% 60 minutes or more (2000)

STOW (city). Covers a land area of 17.112 square miles and a water area of 0.230 square miles. Located at 41.17° N. Lat.; 81.43° W. Long. Elevation is 1,091 feet.
History: Settled 1802, incorporated as a city 1960.
Population: 27,702 (1990); 32,139 (2000); 35,044 (2005); 37,755 (2010 projected); Race: 94.4% White, 1.7% Black, 2.3% Asian, 1.0% Hispanic of any race (2005); Density: 2,047.9 persons per square mile (2005); Average household size: 2.58 (2005); Median age: 37.9 (2005); Males per 100 females: 94.1 (2005); Marriage status: 21.8% never married, 63.5% now married, 5.5% widowed, 9.3% divorced (2000); Foreign born: 3.7% (2000); Ancestry (includes multiple ancestries): 29.7% German, 17.7% Irish, 14.3% English, 12.0% Italian, 7.5% Other groups (2000).
Economy: Chiefly residential; some light industry. Unemployment rate: 4.5% (2005); Total civilian labor force: 19,586 (2005); Single-family building permits issued: 106 (2005); Multi-family building permits issued: 6 (2005); Employment by occupation: 15.8% management, 26.5% professional, 11.9% services, 27.2% sales, 0.0% farming, 6.1% construction, 12.5% production (2000).
Income: Per capita income: $29,342 (2005); Median household income: $64,394 (2005); Average household income: $74,898 (2005); Percent of households with income of $100,000 or more: 22.3% (2005); Poverty rate: 4.0% (2000).
Taxes: Total city taxes per capita: $601 (2004); City property taxes per capita: $195 (2004).
Education: Percent of population age 25 and over with: High school diploma (including GED) or higher: 93.2% (2005); Bachelor's degree or higher: 36.6% (2005); Master's degree or higher: 12.5% (2005).
School District(s)
Stow-Munroe Falls City SD (PK-12)
    2003-04 Enrollment: 6,080 . . . . (330) 689-5445
Two-year College(s)
Edutek College (Private, Not-for-profit)
    Fall 2004 Enrollment: 42 . . . . (330) 667-4667
    2005-06 Tuition: In-state $8,500; Out-of-state $8,500
Housing: Homeownership rate: 71.7% (2005); Median home value: $163,763 (2005); Median rent: $603 per month (2000); Median age of housing: 25 years (2000).
Safety: Violent crime rate: 3.8 per 10,000 population; Property crime rate: 203.7 per 10,000 population (2004).
Newspapers: Aurora Advocate (General - Circulation 6,900); Cuyahoga Falls News-Press (General - Circulation 25,500); Gateway News (General - Circulation 11,000); Hudson Hub-Times (General - Circulation 9,100); Stow Sentry (General - Circulation 14,280); Tallmadge Express (General - Circulation 6,700); Twinsburg Bulletin (General - Circulation 8,000)
Transportation: Commute to work: 95.6% car, 0.4% public transportation, 0.6% walk, 2.9% work from home (2000); Travel time to work: 27.1% less than 15 minutes, 42.0% 15 to 30 minutes, 19.1% 30 to 45 minutes, 7.5% 45 to 60 minutes, 4.3% 60 minutes or more (2000)
Additional Information Contacts
City of Stow . . . . (330) 689-2700
    http://www.stow.oh.us
Stow Chamber of Commerce . . . . (330) 688-1579
    http://www.smfcc.com

TALLMADGE (city). Covers a land area of 13.962 square miles and a water area of 0.023 square miles. Located at 41.09° N. Lat.; 81.42° W. Long. Elevation is 1,114 feet.
History: Settled 1807, incorporated 1950. Its historic architecture includes a 19th-century Congregational church near the city's center.
Population: 15,094 (1990); 16,390 (2000); 17,462 (2005); 18,488 (2010 projected); Race: 95.1% White, 2.4% Black, 1.0% Asian, 0.6% Hispanic of any race (2005); Density: 1,250.7 persons per square mile (2005); Average household size: 2.57 (2005); Median age: 42.8 (2005); Males per 100 females: 93.0 (2005); Marriage status: 21.0% never married, 63.7% now married, 7.4% widowed, 8.0% divorced (2000); Foreign born: 3.5% (2000); Ancestry (includes multiple ancestries): 29.0% German, 16.4% Irish, 13.1% English, 12.0% Italian, 8.0% United States or American (2000).
Economy: Industrial suburb. Single-family building permits issued: 46 (2005); Multi-family building permits issued: 8 (2005); Employment by occupation: 11.6% management, 22.6% professional, 12.2% services, 29.7% sales, 0.1% farming, 10.6% construction, 13.2% production (2000).
Income: Per capita income: $29,850 (2005); Median household income: $53,946 (2005); Average household income: $62,192 (2005); Percent of households with income of $100,000 or more: 15.1% (2005); Poverty rate: 4.7% (2000).
Taxes: Total city taxes per capita: $562 (2004); City property taxes per capita: $111 (2004).
Education: Percent of population age 25 and over with: High school diploma (including GED) or higher: 86.7% (2005); Bachelor's degree or higher: 24.3% (2005); Master's degree or higher: 8.0% (2005).
School District(s)
Tallmadge City Schools (PK-12)
    2003-04 Enrollment: 2,760 . . . . (330) 633-3291
Housing: Homeownership rate: 80.2% (2005); Median home value: $160,489 (2005); Median rent: $514 per month (2000); Median age of housing: 33 years (2000).
Safety: Violent crime rate: 16.3 per 10,000 population; Property crime rate: 257.6 per 10,000 population (2004).
Transportation: Commute to work: 96.0% car, 0.6% public transportation, 0.5% walk, 2.4% work from home (2000); Travel time to work: 32.9% less than 15 minutes, 46.4% 15 to 30 minutes, 12.6% 30 to 45 minutes, 3.0% 45 to 60 minutes, 5.0% 60 minutes or more (2000)
Additional Information Contacts
City of Tallmadge . . . . (330) 633-0857
    http://www.tallmadge-ohio.org
Tallmadge Chamber of Commerce . . . . (330) 633-5417
    http://www.tallmadge-chamber.com

TWINSBURG (city). Covers a land area of 12.443 square miles and a water area of 0.032 square miles. Located at 41.32° N. Lat.; 81.45° W. Long. Elevation is 1,004 feet.
History: Twinsburg was named for Moses and Aaron Wilcox, twins who built adjacent houses here in 1818.
Population: 9,759 (1990); 17,006 (2000); 17,760 (2005); 18,335 (2010 projected); Race: 84.4% White, 9.9% Black, 4.1% Asian, 1.2% Hispanic of any race (2005); Density: 1,427.3 persons per square mile (2005); Average household size: 2.53 (2005); Median age: 37.9 (2005); Males per 100 females: 92.5 (2005); Marriage status: 18.8% never married, 67.2% now married, 6.8% widowed, 7.2% divorced (2000); Foreign born: 4.1% (2000); Ancestry (includes multiple ancestries): 23.1% German, 15.0% Other groups, 15.0% Italian, 14.1% Irish, 11.4% Polish (2000).
Economy: Single-family building permits issued: 110 (2005); Multi-family building permits issued: 0 (2005); Employment by occupation: 21.1% management, 23.0% professional, 10.4% services, 28.9% sales, 0.0% farming, 6.0% construction, 10.6% production (2000).
Income: Per capita income: $32,852 (2005); Median household income: $70,750 (2005); Average household income: $82,330 (2005); Percent of

households with income of $100,000 or more: 29.2% (2005); Poverty rate: 2.1% (2000).
Taxes: Total city taxes per capita: $1,140 (2004); City property taxes per capita: $67 (2004).
Education: Percent of population age 25 and over with: High school diploma (including GED) or higher: 92.4% (2005); Bachelor's degree or higher: 38.8% (2005); Master's degree or higher: 12.5% (2005).

School District(s)
Twinsburg City SD (PK-12)
    2003-04 Enrollment: 3,953 . . . . (330) 486-2000
Housing: Homeownership rate: 77.1% (2005); Median home value: $196,871 (2005); Median rent: $687 per month (2000); Median age of housing: 12 years (2000).
Safety: Violent crime rate: 11.0 per 10,000 population; Property crime rate: 110.0 per 10,000 population (2004).
Transportation: Commute to work: 96.0% car, 0.4% public transportation, 0.4% walk, 2.7% work from home (2000); Travel time to work: 22.8% less than 15 minutes, 36.9% 15 to 30 minutes, 27.7% 30 to 45 minutes, 9.2% 45 to 60 minutes, 3.5% 60 minutes or more (2000)

Additional Information Contacts
City of Twinsburg . . . . (330) 425-7161
    http://www.mytwinsburg.com
Twinsburg Chamber of Commerce . . . . (330) 963-6249
    http://www.twinsburgchamber.com

Trumbull County

Located in northeastern Ohio; bounded on the east by Pennsylvania; drained by the Mahoning and Grand Rivers. Covers a land area of 616.48 square miles, a water area of 18.24 square miles, and is located in the Eastern Time Zone. The county government was organized in 1800. County seat is Warren.

Trumbull County is part of the Youngstown-Warren-Boardman, OH-PA Metropolitan Statistical Area. The entire metro area includes: Mahoning County, OH; Trumbull County, OH; Mercer County, PA

Weather Station: Mineral Ridge Water Works   Elevation: 889 feet

	Jan	Feb	Mar	Apr	May	Jun	Jul	Aug	Sep	Oct	Nov	Dec
High	35	40	50	62	74	82	86	84	77	65	52	41
Low	18	20	28	37	47	56	61	59	53	42	34	25
Precip	2.2	1.8	2.7	3.1	3.4	4.3	4.2	3.3	4.0	2.6	3.0	2.7
Snow	9.8	6.9	7.1	1.1	tr	0.0	0.0	0.0	0.0	tr	1.8	7.8

High and Low temperatures in degrees Fahrenheit; Precipitation and Snow in inches

Weather Station: Warren 3 S   Elevation: 898 feet

	Jan	Feb	Mar	Apr	May	Jun	Jul	Aug	Sep	Oct	Nov	Dec
High	34	38	48	60	71	79	83	81	74	63	50	39
Low	16	18	26	34	44	54	58	57	50	39	31	23
Precip	2.2	1.7	3.0	3.3	3.6	4.0	4.2	3.3	3.9	2.7	3.1	2.8
Snow	11.1	8.2	5.5	0.5	tr	0.0	0.0	0.0	0.0	tr	1.3	7.3

High and Low temperatures in degrees Fahrenheit; Precipitation and Snow in inches

Weather Station: Youngstown Municipal Airport   Elevation: 1,177 feet

	Jan	Feb	Mar	Apr	May	Jun	Jul	Aug	Sep	Oct	Nov	Dec
High	32	35	46	58	69	78	82	80	73	61	48	37
Low	17	19	27	37	47	55	60	58	51	41	33	24
Precip	2.3	2.0	3.1	3.3	3.4	3.9	4.1	3.4	3.9	2.5	3.2	3.0
Snow	14.1	10.5	10.7	2.2	tr	tr	tr	0.0	tr	0.6	4.5	12.1

High and Low temperatures in degrees Fahrenheit; Precipitation and Snow in inches

Population: 227,842 (1990); 225,116 (2000); 220,130 (2005); 215,042 (2010 projected); Race: 90.0% White, 7.9% Black, 0.5% Asian, 0.9% Hispanic of any race (2005); Density: 357.1 persons per square mile (2005); Average household size: 2.49 (2005); Median age: 40.1 (2005); Males per 100 females: 94.2 (2005).
Religion: Five largest groups: 23.1% Catholic Church, 5.1% The United Methodist Church, 2.5% Christian Church (Disciples of Christ), 1.9% Evangelical Lutheran Church in America, 1.3% Presbyterian Church (U.S.A.) (2000).
Economy: Unemployment rate: 6.8% (2005); Total civilian labor force: 106,583 (2005); Leading industries: 29.3% manufacturing; 14.4% retail trade; 13.1% health care and social assistance (2004); Farms: 1,016 totaling 125,962 acres (2002); Companies that employ 500 or more persons: 9 (2004); Companies that employ 100 to 499 persons: 96 (2004); Companies that employ less than 100 persons: 4,589 (2004); Black-owned businesses: 303 (2002); Hispanic-owned businesses: n/a (2002);

Women-owned businesses: 4,176 (2002); Retail sales per capita: $13,164 (2006). Single-family building permits issued: 350 (2005); Multi-family building permits issued: 99 (2005).
Income: Per capita income: $20,837 (2005); Median household income: $41,389 (2005); Average household income: $51,349 (2005); Percent of households with income of $100,000 or more: 9.5% (2005); Poverty rate: 11.0% (2003); Bankruptcy rate: 5.15% (2005).
Taxes: Total county taxes per capita: $209 (2004); County property taxes per capita: $112 (2004).
Education: Percent of population age 25 and over with: High school diploma (including GED) or higher: 82.5% (2005); Bachelor's degree or higher: 14.6% (2005); Master's degree or higher: 4.5% (2005).
Housing: Homeownership rate: 74.6% (2005); Median home value: $100,387 (2005); Median rent: $381 per month (2000); Median age of housing: 40 years (2000).
Health: Birth rate: 103.1 per 10,000 population (2004); Death rate: 112.4 per 10,000 population (2004); Age-adjusted cancer mortality rate: 205.0 deaths per 100,000 population (2002); Air Quality Index: 68.5% good, 28.9% moderate, 2.6% unhealthy for sensitive individuals, 0.0% unhealthy (percent of days in 2005); Number of physicians: 15.5 per 10,000 population (2004); Hospital beds: 22.4 per 10,000 population (2003); Hospital admissions: 998.3 per 10,000 population (2003).
Elections: 2004 Presidential election results: 37.9% Bush, 61.7% Kerry, 0.0% Nader, 0.2% Badnarik
National and State Parks: Grand River State Wildlife Area; Mosquito Creek State Park; Mosquito Creek State Wildlife Area

Additional Information Contacts
Trumbull County Government . . . . (330) 675-2451
    http://www.co.trumbull.oh.us/
City of Cortland . . . . (330) 638-0142
    http://www.cityofcortland.org
City of Girard . . . . (330) 545-3879
    http://www.cityofgirard.com
City of Hubbard . . . . (330) 534-3090
    http://www.cityofhubbard.com
City of Niles . . . . (330) 544-9000
    http://www.thecityofniles.com
Girard Chamber of Commerce . . . . (330) 545-8616
    http://www.girardchamber.org
Hubbard Chamber of Commerce . . . . (330) 534-5120
    http://www.cityofhubbard.com
Newton Falls Chamber of Commerce . . . . (330) 872-3223
    http://www.ci.newtonfalls.oh.us
Trumbull County Convention & Visitors Bureau. . . . . (330) 544-3468
Youngstown/Warren Regional Chamber of Commerce . . . . (330) 744-2131
    http://www.regionalchamber.com

Trumbull County Communities

BOLINDALE (CDP). Covers a land area of 0.959 square miles and a water area of 0 square miles. Located at 41.20° N. Lat.; 80.77° W. Long.
Population: 2,827 (1990); 2,489 (2000); 2,280 (2005); 2,034 (2010 projected); Race: 93.2% White, 4.9% Black, 0.4% Asian, 1.5% Hispanic of any race (2005); Density: 2,377.3 persons per square mile (2005); Average household size: 2.46 (2005); Median age: 40.1 (2005); Males per 100 females: 94.7 (2005); Marriage status: 23.4% never married, 52.4% now married, 9.5% widowed, 14.7% divorced (2000); Foreign born: 2.7% (2000); Ancestry (includes multiple ancestries): 20.0% German, 18.4% Irish, 12.7% Italian, 7.9% Other groups, 7.8% United States or American (2000).
Economy: Employment by occupation: 7.5% management, 10.3% professional, 17.7% services, 17.5% sales, 1.0% farming, 10.3% construction, 35.7% production (2000).
Income: Per capita income: $17,478 (2005); Median household income: $37,267 (2005); Average household income: $43,081 (2005); Percent of households with income of $100,000 or more: 4.9% (2005); Poverty rate: 10.0% (2000).
Education: Percent of population age 25 and over with: High school diploma (including GED) or higher: 79.0% (2005); Bachelor's degree or higher: 8.6% (2005); Master's degree or higher: 1.9% (2005).
Housing: Homeownership rate: 79.2% (2005); Median home value: $85,509 (2005); Median rent: $347 per month (2000); Median age of housing: 40 years (2000).
Transportation: Commute to work: 97.1% car, 1.1% public transportation, 1.8% walk, 0.0% work from home (2000); Travel time to work: 37.1% less

than 15 minutes, 47.1% 15 to 30 minutes, 6.1% 30 to 45 minutes, 5.1% 45 to 60 minutes, 4.7% 60 minutes or more (2000)

BRISTOLVILLE (unincorporated postal area, zip code 44402).
Covers a land area of 33.696 square miles and a water area of 0 square miles. Located at 41.38° N. Lat.; 80.87° W. Long. Elevation is 902 feet.
Population: 3,325 (2000); Race: 98.4% White, 0.9% Black, 0.2% Asian, 0.0% Hispanic of any race (2000); Density: 98.7 persons per square mile (2000); Age: 25.0% under 18, 11.5% over 64 (2000); Marriage status: 18.8% never married, 66.7% now married, 5.1% widowed, 9.4% divorced (2000); Foreign born: 0.5% (2000); Ancestry (includes multiple ancestries): 23.1% German, 14.3% English, 13.3% Irish, 10.9% United States or American, 9.2% Italian (2000).
Economy: Employment by occupation: 5.1% management, 9.3% professional, 14.5% services, 21.5% sales, 1.1% farming, 10.6% construction, 37.9% production (2000).
Income: Per capita income: $18,059 (2000); Median household income: $48,316 (2000); Poverty rate: 4.6% (2000).
Education: Percent of population age 25 and over with: High school diploma (including GED) or higher: 81.1% (2000); Bachelor's degree or higher: 8.0% (2000).

School District(s)
Bristol Local SD (PK-12)
    2003-04 Enrollment: 913 . . . . (330) 889-3882

Housing: Homeownership rate: 84.3% (2000); Median home value: $99,100 (2000); Median rent: $389 per month (2000); Median age of housing: 35 years (2000).
Transportation: Commute to work: 93.6% car, 0.2% public transportation, 2.1% walk, 2.6% work from home (2000); Travel time to work: 15.9% less than 15 minutes, 55.8% 15 to 30 minutes, 18.1% 30 to 45 minutes, 5.6% 45 to 60 minutes, 4.6% 60 minutes or more (2000)

BROOKFIELD (unincorporated postal area, zip code 44403).
Covers a land area of 12.936 square miles and a water area of 0 square miles. Located at 41.23° N. Lat.; 80.57° W. Long. Elevation is 1,160 feet.
Population: 4,161 (2000); Race: 97.2% White, 1.8% Black, 0.9% Asian, 0.2% Hispanic of any race (2000); Density: 321.7 persons per square mile (2000); Age: 20.8% under 18, 22.8% over 64 (2000); Marriage status: 17.5% never married, 64.2% now married, 9.9% widowed, 8.5% divorced (2000); Foreign born: 2.2% (2000); Ancestry (includes multiple ancestries): 20.5% German, 14.8% Italian, 13.2% Irish, 10.8% English, 10.0% Polish (2000).
Economy: Employment by occupation: 11.0% management, 19.8% professional, 12.2% services, 24.6% sales, 0.3% farming, 14.4% construction, 17.8% production (2000).
Income: Per capita income: $20,059 (2000); Median household income: $38,131 (2000); Poverty rate: 10.0% (2000).
Education: Percent of population age 25 and over with: High school diploma (including GED) or higher: 83.8% (2000); Bachelor's degree or higher: 15.7% (2000).

School District(s)
Brookfield Local SD (PK-12)
    2003-04 Enrollment: 1,475 . . . . (330) 448-4930

Housing: Homeownership rate: 86.1% (2000); Median home value: $111,400 (2000); Median rent: $389 per month (2000); Median age of housing: 28 years (2000).
Transportation: Commute to work: 96.8% car, 0.5% public transportation, 0.6% walk, 1.7% work from home (2000); Travel time to work: 29.3% less than 15 minutes, 53.0% 15 to 30 minutes, 9.2% 30 to 45 minutes, 4.1% 45 to 60 minutes, 4.3% 60 minutes or more (2000)

BROOKFIELD CENTER (CDP).
Covers a land area of 2.858 square miles and a water area of 0 square miles. Located at 41.24° N. Lat.; 80.56° W. Long.
Population: 1,396 (1990); 1,288 (2000); 1,317 (2005); 1,325 (2010 projected); Race: 98.7% White, 0.6% Black, 0.0% Asian, 1.0% Hispanic of any race (2005); Density: 460.9 persons per square mile (2005); Average household size: 2.32 (2005); Median age: 49.6 (2005); Males per 100 females: 96.3 (2005); Marriage status: 22.9% never married, 58.4% now married, 13.5% widowed, 5.2% divorced (2000); Foreign born: 3.0% (2000); Ancestry (includes multiple ancestries): 19.0% Italian, 16.3% Polish, 15.5% German, 13.1% Irish, 8.6% Slovak (2000).
Economy: Employment by occupation: 19.0% management, 21.6% professional, 11.0% services, 22.7% sales, 1.0% farming, 8.2% construction, 16.5% production (2000).
Income: Per capita income: $23,926 (2005); Median household income: $47,837 (2005); Average household income: $54,974 (2005); Percent of households with income of $100,000 or more: 13.2% (2005); Poverty rate: 6.2% (2000).
Education: Percent of population age 25 and over with: High school diploma (including GED) or higher: 80.5% (2005); Bachelor's degree or higher: 20.2% (2005); Master's degree or higher: 5.2% (2005).
Housing: Homeownership rate: 84.8% (2005); Median home value: $145,617 (2005); Median rent: $451 per month (2000); Median age of housing: 39 years (2000).
Transportation: Commute to work: 95.1% car, 1.6% public transportation, 2.0% walk, 0.0% work from home (2000); Travel time to work: 36.9% less than 15 minutes, 43.9% 15 to 30 minutes, 8.0% 30 to 45 minutes, 4.7% 45 to 60 minutes, 6.5% 60 minutes or more (2000)

BURGHILL (unincorporated postal area, zip code 44404).
Covers a land area of 18.814 square miles and a water area of 0 square miles. Located at 41.34° N. Lat.; 80.53° W. Long. Elevation is 1,033 feet.
Population: 1,703 (2000); Race: 98.9% White, 0.0% Black, 0.1% Asian, 0.6% Hispanic of any race (2000); Density: 90.5 persons per square mile (2000); Age: 26.9% under 18, 11.2% over 64 (2000); Marriage status: 16.7% never married, 67.8% now married, 7.3% widowed, 8.2% divorced (2000); Foreign born: 0.1% (2000); Ancestry (includes multiple ancestries): 26.9% German, 15.6% Irish, 10.0% Italian, 9.8% United States or American, 8.6% English (2000).
Economy: Employment by occupation: 8.0% management, 11.1% professional, 13.4% services, 20.6% sales, 0.0% farming, 7.5% construction, 39.5% production (2000).
Income: Per capita income: $18,829 (2000); Median household income: $50,278 (2000); Poverty rate: 7.0% (2000).
Education: Percent of population age 25 and over with: High school diploma (including GED) or higher: 85.2% (2000); Bachelor's degree or higher: 8.3% (2000).
Housing: Homeownership rate: 87.1% (2000); Median home value: $87,700 (2000); Median rent: $336 per month (2000); Median age of housing: 43 years (2000).
Transportation: Commute to work: 90.8% car, 0.0% public transportation, 4.2% walk, 3.4% work from home (2000); Travel time to work: 21.9% less than 15 minutes, 40.3% 15 to 30 minutes, 21.2% 30 to 45 minutes, 10.4% 45 to 60 minutes, 6.2% 60 minutes or more (2000)

CHAMPION HEIGHTS (CDP). Aka Champion.
Covers a land area of 3.401 square miles and a water area of 0 square miles. Located at 41.29° N. Lat.; 80.85° W. Long.
Population: 4,425 (1990); 4,727 (2000); 4,491 (2005); 4,269 (2010 projected); Race: 98.4% White, 0.5% Black, 0.1% Asian, 0.6% Hispanic of any race (2005); Density: 1,320.6 persons per square mile (2005); Average household size: 2.50 (2005); Median age: 41.0 (2005); Males per 100 females: 89.8 (2005); Marriage status: 18.4% never married, 62.6% now married, 10.8% widowed, 8.3% divorced (2000); Foreign born: 0.7% (2000); Ancestry (includes multiple ancestries): 27.5% German, 16.1% Irish, 15.8% English, 11.2% Italian, 8.9% United States or American (2000).
Economy: Employment by occupation: 10.3% management, 17.2% professional, 12.8% services, 28.0% sales, 0.3% farming, 8.3% construction, 23.2% production (2000).
Income: Per capita income: $22,085 (2005); Median household income: $45,169 (2005); Average household income: $54,531 (2005); Percent of households with income of $100,000 or more: 11.4% (2005); Poverty rate: 5.3% (2000).
Education: Percent of population age 25 and over with: High school diploma (including GED) or higher: 87.3% (2005); Bachelor's degree or higher: 13.5% (2005); Master's degree or higher: 3.4% (2005).
Housing: Homeownership rate: 83.6% (2005); Median home value: $114,813 (2005); Median rent: $415 per month (2000); Median age of housing: 42 years (2000).
Transportation: Commute to work: 96.2% car, 0.0% public transportation, 1.2% walk, 2.2% work from home (2000); Travel time to work: 35.2% less than 15 minutes, 42.6% 15 to 30 minutes, 13.1% 30 to 45 minutes, 5.0% 45 to 60 minutes, 4.1% 60 minutes or more (2000)

CHURCHILL (CDP).
Covers a land area of 2.494 square miles and a water area of 0 square miles. Located at 41.17° N. Lat.; 80.67° W. Long. Elevation is 1,060 feet.

Population: 2,683 (1990); 2,601 (2000); 2,536 (2005); 2,478 (2010 projected); Race: 87.9% White, 9.8% Black, 0.3% Asian, 1.3% Hispanic of any race (2005); Density: 1,017.0 persons per square mile (2005); Average household size: 2.42 (2005); Median age: 42.9 (2005); Males per 100 females: 97.7 (2005); Marriage status: 22.8% never married, 51.8% now married, 9.8% widowed, 15.5% divorced (2000); Foreign born: 3.3% (2000); Ancestry (includes multiple ancestries): 21.5% German, 19.8% Irish, 19.0% Italian, 15.5% Other groups, 10.8% English (2000).
Economy: Employment by occupation: 11.8% management, 13.5% professional, 19.2% services, 25.1% sales, 0.0% farming, 8.7% construction, 21.7% production (2000).
Income: Per capita income: $22,575 (2005); Median household income: $40,579 (2005); Average household income: $54,628 (2005); Percent of households with income of $100,000 or more: 12.4% (2005); Poverty rate: 11.2% (2000).
Education: Percent of population age 25 and over with: High school diploma (including GED) or higher: 85.7% (2005); Bachelor's degree or higher: 15.4% (2005); Master's degree or higher: 3.9% (2005).
Housing: Homeownership rate: 77.6% (2005); Median home value: $94,023 (2005); Median rent: $347 per month (2000); Median age of housing: 35 years (2000).
Transportation: Commute to work: 95.4% car, 0.0% public transportation, 3.8% walk, 0.0% work from home (2000); Travel time to work: 37.2% less than 15 minutes, 55.9% 15 to 30 minutes, 4.4% 30 to 45 minutes, 2.0% 45 to 60 minutes, 0.6% 60 minutes or more (2000)

CORTLAND (city). Covers a land area of 4.479 square miles and a water area of 0 square miles. Located at 41.33° N. Lat.; 80.72° W. Long. Elevation is 1,020 feet.
Population: 5,841 (1990); 6,830 (2000); 6,651 (2005); 6,467 (2010 projected); Race: 97.5% White, 1.1% Black, 0.3% Asian, 0.8% Hispanic of any race (2005); Density: 1,484.8 persons per square mile (2005); Average household size: 2.44 (2005); Median age: 40.9 (2005); Males per 100 females: 90.6 (2005); Marriage status: 21.3% never married, 61.6% now married, 7.7% widowed, 9.3% divorced (2000); Foreign born: 1.2% (2000); Ancestry (includes multiple ancestries): 20.3% German, 18.3% English, 17.8% Irish, 14.4% Italian, 7.4% Slovak (2000).
Economy: Employment by occupation: 12.9% management, 22.3% professional, 14.1% services, 25.3% sales, 0.0% farming, 5.9% construction, 19.4% production (2000).
Income: Per capita income: $25,222 (2005); Median household income: $53,221 (2005); Average household income: $61,361 (2005); Percent of households with income of $100,000 or more: 16.1% (2005); Poverty rate: 5.3% (2000).
Taxes: Total city taxes per capita: $289 (2004); City property taxes per capita: $270 (2004).
Education: Percent of population age 25 and over with: High school diploma (including GED) or higher: 91.8% (2005); Bachelor's degree or higher: 29.6% (2005); Master's degree or higher: 9.7% (2005).

School District(s)
Lakeview Local SD (PK-12)
    2003-04 Enrollment: 2,234 . . . . (330) 637-8741
Maplewood Local SD (PK-12)
    2003-04 Enrollment: 1,094 . . . . (330) 637-7506
Mathews Local SD (PK-12)
    2003-04 Enrollment: 993 . . . . (330) 394-1800
Housing: Homeownership rate: 73.9% (2005); Median home value: $150,002 (2005); Median rent: $427 per month (2000); Median age of housing: 23 years (2000).
Transportation: Commute to work: 94.8% car, 0.1% public transportation, 1.0% walk, 3.3% work from home (2000); Travel time to work: 23.2% less than 15 minutes, 55.5% 15 to 30 minutes, 13.6% 30 to 45 minutes, 3.8% 45 to 60 minutes, 3.8% 60 minutes or more (2000)
Additional Information Contacts
City of Cortland . . . . (330) 638-0142
    http://www.cityofcortland.org

FARMDALE (unincorporated postal area, zip code 44417). Covers a land area of 31.877 square miles and a water area of 0 square miles. Located at 41.42° N. Lat.; 80.65° W. Long. Elevation is 936 feet.
Population: 1,768 (2000); Race: 99.1% White, 0.9% Black, 0.0% Asian, 0.3% Hispanic of any race (2000); Density: 55.5 persons per square mile (2000); Age: 26.4% under 18, 11.6% over 64 (2000); Marriage status: 22.0% never married, 68.1% now married, 3.4% widowed, 6.5% divorced (2000); Foreign born: 0.7% (2000); Ancestry (includes multiple ancestries): 19.1% United States or American, 17.7% German, 16.1% English, 8.1% Italian, 7.5% Irish (2000).
Economy: Employment by occupation: 5.8% management, 11.9% professional, 17.4% services, 19.8% sales, 0.0% farming, 14.7% construction, 30.4% production (2000).
Income: Per capita income: $20,808 (2000); Median household income: $50,335 (2000); Poverty rate: 6.4% (2000).
Education: Percent of population age 25 and over with: High school diploma (including GED) or higher: 82.2% (2000); Bachelor's degree or higher: 7.4% (2000).

School District(s)
Joseph Badger Local SD (PK-12)
    2003-04 Enrollment: 1,108 . . . . (330) 876-1051
Housing: Homeownership rate: 88.5% (2000); Median home value: $104,000 (2000); Median rent: $445 per month (2000); Median age of housing: 34 years (2000).
Transportation: Commute to work: 98.7% car, 0.0% public transportation, 0.0% walk, 0.7% work from home (2000); Travel time to work: 15.3% less than 15 minutes, 34.5% 15 to 30 minutes, 32.7% 30 to 45 minutes, 10.7% 45 to 60 minutes, 6.8% 60 minutes or more (2000)

FOWLER (unincorporated postal area, zip code 44418). Covers a land area of 17.112 square miles and a water area of 0 square miles. Located at 41.30° N. Lat.; 80.60° W. Long. Elevation is 1,140 feet.
Population: 1,237 (2000); Race: 97.0% White, 1.4% Black, 1.1% Asian, 0.9% Hispanic of any race (2000); Density: 72.3 persons per square mile (2000); Age: 23.4% under 18, 13.1% over 64 (2000); Marriage status: 19.6% never married, 63.8% now married, 6.1% widowed, 10.4% divorced (2000); Foreign born: 1.7% (2000); Ancestry (includes multiple ancestries): 21.6% German, 11.8% English, 10.4% Irish, 8.5% Italian, 7.9% Polish (2000).
Economy: Employment by occupation: 12.3% management, 19.0% professional, 12.3% services, 28.5% sales, 0.0% farming, 7.8% construction, 20.1% production (2000).
Income: Per capita income: $19,340 (2000); Median household income: $46,818 (2000); Poverty rate: 4.1% (2000).
Education: Percent of population age 25 and over with: High school diploma (including GED) or higher: 89.6% (2000); Bachelor's degree or higher: 17.5% (2000).

School District(s)
Mathews Local SD (PK-12)
    2003-04 Enrollment: 993 . . . . (330) 394-1800
Housing: Homeownership rate: 85.2% (2000); Median home value: $105,600 (2000); Median rent: $396 per month (2000); Median age of housing: 34 years (2000).
Transportation: Commute to work: 93.9% car, 0.0% public transportation, 1.0% walk, 5.2% work from home (2000); Travel time to work: 17.3% less than 15 minutes, 54.6% 15 to 30 minutes, 18.7% 30 to 45 minutes, 4.1% 45 to 60 minutes, 5.3% 60 minutes or more (2000)

GIRARD (city). Covers a land area of 6.113 square miles and a water area of 0.485 square miles. Located at 41.15° N. Lat.; 80.69° W. Long. Elevation is 950 feet.
History: Girard was settled about 1800, but growth was slow until the Ohio & Erie Canal was completed. The town was probably named for Stephen Girard, philanthropist and founder of Girard College in Philadelphia, Pennsylvania.
Population: 11,550 (1990); 10,902 (2000); 10,510 (2005); 10,114 (2010 projected); Race: 95.3% White, 2.5% Black, 0.4% Asian, 0.8% Hispanic of any race (2005); Density: 1,719.4 persons per square mile (2005); Average household size: 2.32 (2005); Median age: 40.5 (2005); Males per 100 females: 89.1 (2005); Marriage status: 23.6% never married, 54.2% now married, 9.2% widowed, 13.0% divorced (2000); Foreign born: 2.0% (2000); Ancestry (includes multiple ancestries): 29.5% Italian, 21.8% German, 20.4% Irish, 8.6% English, 6.1% Other groups (2000).
Economy: Single-family building permits issued: 0 (2005); Multi-family building permits issued: 0 (2005); Employment by occupation: 7.1% management, 17.6% professional, 16.1% services, 24.8% sales, 0.0% farming, 9.6% construction, 24.8% production (2000).
Income: Per capita income: $18,963 (2005); Median household income: $34,449 (2005); Average household income: $43,967 (2005); Percent of households with income of $100,000 or more: 7.1% (2005); Poverty rate: 12.5% (2000).

Education: Percent of population age 25 and over with: High school diploma (including GED) or higher: 79.6% (2005); Bachelor's degree or higher: 16.2% (2005); Master's degree or higher: 5.1% (2005).

School District(s)

Girard City SD (PK-12)
   2003-04 Enrollment: 1,769 . . . . (330) 545-2596

Housing: Homeownership rate: 67.8% (2005); Median home value: $88,647 (2005); Median rent: $373 per month (2000); Median age of housing: 46 years (2000).
Safety: Violent crime rate: 16.9 per 10,000 population; Property crime rate: 458.0 per 10,000 population (2004).
Transportation: Commute to work: 95.2% car, 0.2% public transportation, 1.4% walk, 1.9% work from home (2000); Travel time to work: 38.4% less than 15 minutes, 46.8% 15 to 30 minutes, 10.7% 30 to 45 minutes, 1.5% 45 to 60 minutes, 2.6% 60 minutes or more (2000)

Additional Information Contacts
City of Girard . . . . (330) 545-3879
   http://www.cityofgirard.com
Girard Chamber of Commerce. . . . . (330) 545-8616
   http://www.girardchamber.org

HILLTOP (CDP). Covers a land area of 0.568 square miles and a water area of 0 square miles. Located at 41.16° N. Lat.; 80.73° W. Long.
Population: 576 (1990); 534 (2000); 529 (2005); 514 (2010 projected); Race: 96.4% White, 0.6% Black, 0.0% Asian, 1.5% Hispanic of any race (2005); Density: 931.6 persons per square mile (2005); Average household size: 2.62 (2005); Median age: 38.1 (2005); Males per 100 females: 98.9 (2005); Marriage status: 20.8% never married, 65.9% now married, 9.8% widowed, 3.5% divorced (2000); Foreign born: 0.0% (2000); Ancestry (includes multiple ancestries): 22.0% German, 18.8% Polish, 11.8% Slovak, 11.1% United States or American, 8.5% English (2000).
Economy: Employment by occupation: 3.6% management, 6.8% professional, 22.3% services, 21.4% sales, 0.0% farming, 17.3% construction, 28.6% production (2000).
Income: Per capita income: $18,894 (2005); Median household income: $48,605 (2005); Average household income: $49,480 (2005); Percent of households with income of $100,000 or more: 4.5% (2005); Poverty rate: 4.9% (2000).
Education: Percent of population age 25 and over with: High school diploma (including GED) or higher: 70.6% (2005); Bachelor's degree or higher: 2.2% (2005); Master's degree or higher: 0.0% (2005).
Housing: Homeownership rate: 88.1% (2005); Median home value: $69,730 (2005); Median rent: $325 per month (2000); Median age of housing: 55 years (2000).
Transportation: Commute to work: 100.0% car, 0.0% public transportation, 0.0% walk, 0.0% work from home (2000); Travel time to work: 35.9% less than 15 minutes, 22.7% 15 to 30 minutes, 10.9% 30 to 45 minutes, 13.6% 45 to 60 minutes, 16.8% 60 minutes or more (2000)

HOWLAND CENTER (CDP). Covers a land area of 4.036 square miles and a water area of 0 square miles. Located at 41.24° N. Lat.; 80.74° W. Long.
Population: 6,805 (1990); 6,481 (2000); 6,488 (2005); 6,559 (2010 projected); Race: 95.3% White, 1.6% Black, 1.7% Asian, 0.8% Hispanic of any race (2005); Density: 1,607.6 persons per square mile (2005); Average household size: 2.57 (2005); Median age: 43.3 (2005); Males per 100 females: 95.4 (2005); Marriage status: 20.0% never married, 64.6% now married, 6.7% widowed, 8.6% divorced (2000); Foreign born: 2.7% (2000); Ancestry (includes multiple ancestries): 22.3% German, 18.4% Italian, 14.7% Irish, 14.4% English, 7.2% Slovak (2000).
Economy: Employment by occupation: 13.5% management, 24.0% professional, 12.6% services, 23.9% sales, 0.0% farming, 8.2% construction, 17.8% production (2000).
Income: Per capita income: $23,716 (2005); Median household income: $53,148 (2005); Average household income: $60,430 (2005); Percent of households with income of $100,000 or more: 9.8% (2005); Poverty rate: 2.0% (2000).
Education: Percent of population age 25 and over with: High school diploma (including GED) or higher: 92.2% (2005); Bachelor's degree or higher: 26.3% (2005); Master's degree or higher: 10.0% (2005).
Housing: Homeownership rate: 88.3% (2005); Median home value: $129,919 (2005); Median rent: $509 per month (2000); Median age of housing: 30 years (2000).
Transportation: Commute to work: 96.7% car, 0.4% public transportation, 1.1% walk, 1.7% work from home (2000); Travel time to work: 40.3% less than 15 minutes, 44.4% 15 to 30 minutes, 8.7% 30 to 45 minutes, 2.3% 45 to 60 minutes, 4.3% 60 minutes or more (2000)

HUBBARD (city). Covers a land area of 3.448 square miles and a water area of 0.007 square miles. Located at 41.15° N. Lat.; 80.56° W. Long. Elevation is 970 feet.
History: Hubbard was named for Nehemiah Hubbard, who purchased the land on which the town was founded in 1801. Until 1880, coal mining was the principal industry.
Population: 8,444 (1990); 8,284 (2000); 8,023 (2005); 7,747 (2010 projected); Race: 97.9% White, 1.0% Black, 0.1% Asian, 0.4% Hispanic of any race (2005); Density: 2,326.6 persons per square mile (2005); Average household size: 2.35 (2005); Median age: 41.5 (2005); Males per 100 females: 90.1 (2005); Marriage status: 22.9% never married, 59.1% now married, 9.8% widowed, 8.2% divorced (2000); Foreign born: 2.4% (2000); Ancestry (includes multiple ancestries): 24.4% German, 23.4% Italian, 18.3% Irish, 12.4% Slovak, 8.4% English (2000).
Economy: Employment by occupation: 8.3% management, 21.3% professional, 12.6% services, 32.1% sales, 0.2% farming, 8.8% construction, 16.7% production (2000).
Income: Per capita income: $20,374 (2005); Median household income: $37,584 (2005); Average household income: $47,803 (2005); Percent of households with income of $100,000 or more: 7.7% (2005); Poverty rate: 8.6% (2000).
Taxes: Total city taxes per capita: $175 (2004); City property taxes per capita: $40 (2004).
Education: Percent of population age 25 and over with: High school diploma (including GED) or higher: 85.9% (2005); Bachelor's degree or higher: 18.1% (2005); Master's degree or higher: 4.7% (2005).

School District(s)

Hubbard Ex Vill SD (KG-12)
   2003-04 Enrollment: 2,305 . . . . (330) 534-1921

Housing: Homeownership rate: 72.2% (2005); Median home value: $98,167 (2005); Median rent: $376 per month (2000); Median age of housing: 42 years (2000).
Transportation: Commute to work: 96.4% car, 0.1% public transportation, 1.0% walk, 2.1% work from home (2000); Travel time to work: 31.0% less than 15 minutes, 46.4% 15 to 30 minutes, 15.3% 30 to 45 minutes, 2.8% 45 to 60 minutes, 4.5% 60 minutes or more (2000)

Additional Information Contacts
City of Hubbard . . . . (330) 534-3090
   http://www.cityofhubbard.com
Hubbard Chamber of Commerce. (330) 534-5120
   http://www.cityofhubbard.com

KINSMAN (unincorporated postal area, zip code 44428). Covers a land area of 52.479 square miles and a water area of 0.035 square miles. Located at 41.44° N. Lat.; 80.58° W. Long. Elevation is 927 feet.
History: Kinsman was settled in 1799 by John Kinsman. Clarence Darrow (1857-1938), noted criminal lawyer, was born in Kinsman, and described the village in his novel "Farmington" (1904).
Population: 3,487 (2000); Race: 100.0% White, 0.0% Black, 0.0% Asian, 0.0% Hispanic of any race (2000); Density: 66.4 persons per square mile (2000); Age: 23.1% under 18, 15.3% over 64 (2000); Marriage status: 21.6% never married, 61.7% now married, 7.2% widowed, 9.5% divorced (2000); Foreign born: 0.6% (2000); Ancestry (includes multiple ancestries): 23.5% German, 19.8% United States or American, 14.4% English, 14.0% Irish, 5.1% Italian (2000).
Economy: Employment by occupation: 10.4% management, 13.6% professional, 11.4% services, 19.1% sales, 0.6% farming, 7.0% construction, 37.9% production (2000).
Income: Per capita income: $15,885 (2000); Median household income: $37,089 (2000); Poverty rate: 7.9% (2000).
Education: Percent of population age 25 and over with: High school diploma (including GED) or higher: 82.5% (2000); Bachelor's degree or higher: 13.3% (2000).

School District(s)

Joseph Badger Local SD (PK-12)
   2003-04 Enrollment: 1,108 . . . . (330) 876-1051

Housing: Homeownership rate: 84.4% (2000); Median home value: $90,300 (2000); Median rent: $320 per month (2000); Median age of housing: 40 years (2000).
Transportation: Commute to work: 90.1% car, 0.3% public transportation, 2.1% walk, 6.1% work from home (2000); Travel time to work: 26.0% less

than 15 minutes, 24.5% 15 to 30 minutes, 32.7% 30 to 45 minutes, 10.2% 45 to 60 minutes, 6.5% 60 minutes or more (2000)

LEAVITTSBURG (CDP). Covers a land area of 1.668 square miles and a water area of 0.060 square miles. Located at 41.24° N. Lat.; 80.87° W. Long. Elevation is 900 feet.
Population: 2,112 (1990); 2,200 (2000); 2,172 (2005); 2,118 (2010 projected); Race: 98.9% White, 0.3% Black, 0.0% Asian, 1.1% Hispanic of any race (2005); Density: 1,302.4 persons per square mile (2005); Average household size: 2.66 (2005); Median age: 38.6 (2005); Males per 100 females: 96.7 (2005); Marriage status: 25.6% never married, 57.0% now married, 4.8% widowed, 12.7% divorced (2000); Foreign born: 1.1% (2000); Ancestry (includes multiple ancestries): 23.6% German, 18.8% United States or American, 18.0% Irish, 8.4% English, 7.6% Italian (2000).
Economy: Employment by occupation: 5.3% management, 9.2% professional, 18.9% services, 21.8% sales, 0.0% farming, 12.9% construction, 31.9% production (2000).
Income: Per capita income: $18,315 (2005); Median household income: $39,533 (2005); Average household income: $48,750 (2005); Percent of households with income of $100,000 or more: 8.1% (2005); Poverty rate: 8.9% (2000).
Education: Percent of population age 25 and over with: High school diploma (including GED) or higher: 73.8% (2005); Bachelor's degree or higher: 5.4% (2005); Master's degree or higher: 2.2% (2005).
School District(s)
Labrae Local SD (PK-12)
    2003-04 Enrollment: 1,497 . . . . (330) 898-1393
Housing: Homeownership rate: 83.7% (2005); Median home value: $66,194 (2005); Median rent: $352 per month (2000); Median age of housing: 50 years (2000).
Transportation: Commute to work: 97.7% car, 0.0% public transportation, 0.0% walk, 1.3% work from home (2000); Travel time to work: 29.7% less than 15 minutes, 40.7% 15 to 30 minutes, 19.1% 30 to 45 minutes, 3.1% 45 to 60 minutes, 7.5% 60 minutes or more (2000)

LORDSTOWN (village). Covers a land area of 23.133 square miles and a water area of 0.001 square miles. Located at 41.17° N. Lat.; 80.86° W. Long. Elevation is 957 feet.
Population: 3,404 (1990); 3,633 (2000); 3,668 (2005); 3,704 (2010 projected); Race: 96.0% White, 2.6% Black, 0.4% Asian, 0.4% Hispanic of any race (2005); Density: 158.6 persons per square mile (2005); Average household size: 2.52 (2005); Median age: 41.1 (2005); Males per 100 females: 97.7 (2005); Marriage status: 19.2% never married, 64.0% now married, 6.4% widowed, 10.4% divorced (2000); Foreign born: 1.0% (2000); Ancestry (includes multiple ancestries): 21.7% German, 16.1% English, 13.0% Irish, 9.3% United States or American, 7.6% Other groups (2000).
Economy: Employment by occupation: 9.2% management, 11.5% professional, 14.0% services, 30.2% sales, 0.7% farming, 9.5% construction, 24.9% production (2000).
Income: Per capita income: $26,145 (2005); Median household income: $56,234 (2005); Average household income: $65,911 (2005); Percent of households with income of $100,000 or more: 13.5% (2005); Poverty rate: 4.4% (2000).
Education: Percent of population age 25 and over with: High school diploma (including GED) or higher: 87.7% (2005); Bachelor's degree or higher: 14.3% (2005); Master's degree or higher: 4.1% (2005).
Housing: Homeownership rate: 85.8% (2005); Median home value: $126,484 (2005); Median rent: $410 per month (2000); Median age of housing: 26 years (2000).
Safety: Violent crime rate: 13.6 per 10,000 population; Property crime rate: 171.8 per 10,000 population (2004).
Transportation: Commute to work: 93.1% car, 0.0% public transportation, 2.2% walk, 4.0% work from home (2000); Travel time to work: 40.7% less than 15 minutes, 37.7% 15 to 30 minutes, 16.4% 30 to 45 minutes, 3.8% 45 to 60 minutes, 1.4% 60 minutes or more (2000)

MAPLEWOOD PARK (CDP). Covers a land area of 0.750 square miles and a water area of 0 square miles. Located at 41.13° N. Lat.; 80.58° W. Long.
Population: 390 (1990); 321 (2000); 295 (2005); 283 (2010 projected); Race: 46.4% White, 51.9% Black, 0.0% Asian, 0.0% Hispanic of any race (2005); Density: 393.3 persons per square mile (2005); Average household size: 2.54 (2005); Median age: 43.8 (2005); Males per 100 females: 99.3 (2005); Marriage status: 21.9% never married, 69.7% now married, 8.3% widowed, 0.0% divorced (2000); Foreign born: 0.0% (2000); Ancestry (includes multiple ancestries): 80.1% Other groups, 2.6% Slovak, 2.6% English, 2.6% Italian, 2.6% United States or American (2000).
Economy: Employment by occupation: 6.0% management, 20.7% professional, 12.1% services, 25.0% sales, 0.0% farming, 28.4% construction, 7.8% production (2000).
Income: Per capita income: $11,932 (2005); Median household income: $25,092 (2005); Average household income: $30,345 (2005); Percent of households with income of $100,000 or more: 1.7% (2005); Poverty rate: 19.1% (2000).
Education: Percent of population age 25 and over with: High school diploma (including GED) or higher: 72.1% (2005); Bachelor's degree or higher: 20.7% (2005); Master's degree or higher: 3.4% (2005).
Housing: Homeownership rate: 82.8% (2005); Median home value: $59,412 (2005); Median rent: $375 per month (2000); Median age of housing: 46 years (2000).
Transportation: Commute to work: 100.0% car, 0.0% public transportation, 0.0% walk, 0.0% work from home (2000); Travel time to work: 49.5% less than 15 minutes, 42.1% 15 to 30 minutes, 0.0% 30 to 45 minutes, 0.0% 45 to 60 minutes, 8.4% 60 minutes or more (2000)

MASURY (CDP). Covers a land area of 3.617 square miles and a water area of 0.034 square miles. Located at 41.20° N. Lat.; 80.53° W. Long. Elevation is 880 feet.
Population: 2,621 (1990); 2,618 (2000); 2,680 (2005); 2,665 (2010 projected); Race: 93.9% White, 3.7% Black, 0.2% Asian, 1.1% Hispanic of any race (2005); Density: 741.0 persons per square mile (2005); Average household size: 2.46 (2005); Median age: 41.4 (2005); Males per 100 females: 85.0 (2005); Marriage status: 21.4% never married, 60.0% now married, 7.6% widowed, 11.1% divorced (2000); Foreign born: 2.2% (2000); Ancestry (includes multiple ancestries): 26.0% German, 18.0% Italian, 16.4% Irish, 10.7% English, 6.9% Slovak (2000).
Economy: Employment by occupation: 8.3% management, 14.3% professional, 17.7% services, 25.1% sales, 0.7% farming, 10.2% construction, 23.7% production (2000).
Income: Per capita income: $20,826 (2005); Median household income: $41,781 (2005); Average household income: $49,819 (2005); Percent of households with income of $100,000 or more: 9.1% (2005); Poverty rate: 12.9% (2000).
Education: Percent of population age 25 and over with: High school diploma (including GED) or higher: 79.7% (2005); Bachelor's degree or higher: 13.4% (2005); Master's degree or higher: 5.0% (2005).
School District(s)
Brookfield Local SD (PK-12)
    2003-04 Enrollment: 1,475 . . . . (330) 448-4930
Housing: Homeownership rate: 71.1% (2005); Median home value: $75,432 (2005); Median rent: $372 per month (2000); Median age of housing: 49 years (2000).
Transportation: Commute to work: 95.5% car, 0.0% public transportation, 0.9% walk, 2.5% work from home (2000); Travel time to work: 38.7% less than 15 minutes, 38.2% 15 to 30 minutes, 13.6% 30 to 45 minutes, 2.7% 45 to 60 minutes, 6.7% 60 minutes or more (2000)

MCDONALD (village). Covers a land area of 1.680 square miles and a water area of 0 square miles. Located at 41.16° N. Lat.; 80.72° W. Long. Elevation is 980 feet.
Population: 3,526 (1990); 3,481 (2000); 3,368 (2005); 3,246 (2010 projected); Race: 97.6% White, 1.0% Black, 0.1% Asian, 1.1% Hispanic of any race (2005); Density: 2,005.1 persons per square mile (2005); Average household size: 2.61 (2005); Median age: 39.4 (2005); Males per 100 females: 91.1 (2005); Marriage status: 22.0% never married, 62.2% now married, 9.4% widowed, 6.4% divorced (2000); Foreign born: 0.5% (2000); Ancestry (includes multiple ancestries): 24.0% German, 20.4% Irish, 17.2% Italian, 9.6% Slovak, 9.2% English (2000).
Economy: Single-family building permits issued: 3 (2005); Multi-family building permits issued: 0 (2005); Employment by occupation: 9.5% management, 18.4% professional, 13.1% services, 25.7% sales, 0.0% farming, 6.4% construction, 26.9% production (2000).
Income: Per capita income: $20,010 (2005); Median household income: $45,199 (2005); Average household income: $52,204 (2005); Percent of households with income of $100,000 or more: 9.2% (2005); Poverty rate: 4.0% (2000).
Education: Percent of population age 25 and over with: High school diploma (including GED) or higher: 88.0% (2005); Bachelor's degree or higher: 20.6% (2005); Master's degree or higher: 4.6% (2005).

School District(s)
Mcdonald Local SD (PK-12)
  2003-04 Enrollment: 864 . . . . (330) 530-8051
Housing: Homeownership rate: 87.0% (2005); Median home value: $107,349 (2005); Median rent: $430 per month (2000); Median age of housing: 41 years (2000).
Transportation: Commute to work: 96.9% car, 0.0% public transportation, 1.7% walk, 1.4% work from home (2000); Travel time to work: 32.1% less than 15 minutes, 54.0% 15 to 30 minutes, 8.3% 30 to 45 minutes, 2.2% 45 to 60 minutes, 3.5% 60 minutes or more (2000)

MINERAL RIDGE (CDP).
Covers a land area of 3.295 square miles and a water area of 0.013 square miles. Located at 41.14° N. Lat.; 80.76° W. Long. Elevation is 1,020 feet.
Population: 3,928 (1990); 3,900 (2000); 3,945 (2005); 3,949 (2010 projected); Race: 96.6% White, 1.6% Black, 0.2% Asian, 1.6% Hispanic of any race (2005); Density: 1,197.1 persons per square mile (2005); Average household size: 2.77 (2005); Median age: 40.7 (2005); Males per 100 females: 92.3 (2005); Marriage status: 25.3% never married, 61.4% now married, 6.1% widowed, 7.2% divorced (2000); Foreign born: 1.0% (2000); Ancestry (includes multiple ancestries): 28.4% German, 21.4% Irish, 15.3% Italian, 12.3% English, 6.4% Other groups (2000).
Economy: Steel products, canned foods. Employment by occupation: 6.9% management, 20.1% professional, 13.7% services, 21.9% sales, 0.0% farming, 13.4% construction, 24.1% production (2000).
Income: Per capita income: $21,943 (2005); Median household income: $51,157 (2005); Average household income: $58,800 (2005); Percent of households with income of $100,000 or more: 14.4% (2005); Poverty rate: 9.2% (2000).
Education: Percent of population age 25 and over with: High school diploma (including GED) or higher: 89.3% (2005); Bachelor's degree or higher: 17.0% (2005); Master's degree or higher: 6.7% (2005).
School District(s)
Weathersfield Local SD (PK-12)
  2003-04 Enrollment: 1,068 . . . . (330) 652-0287
Housing: Homeownership rate: 76.4% (2005); Median home value: $119,464 (2005); Median rent: $370 per month (2000); Median age of housing: 28 years (2000).
Transportation: Commute to work: 98.0% car, 0.0% public transportation, 1.6% walk, 0.5% work from home (2000); Travel time to work: 35.0% less than 15 minutes, 49.5% 15 to 30 minutes, 12.5% 30 to 45 minutes, 1.4% 45 to 60 minutes, 1.6% 60 minutes or more (2000)

NEWTON FALLS (village).
Covers a land area of 2.281 square miles and a water area of 0.075 square miles. Located at 41.18° N. Lat.; 80.97° W. Long. Elevation is 924 feet.
Population: 5,088 (1990); 5,002 (2000); 4,830 (2005); 4,653 (2010 projected); Race: 98.0% White, 0.4% Black, 0.0% Asian, 0.7% Hispanic of any race (2005); Density: 2,117.7 persons per square mile (2005); Average household size: 2.25 (2005); Median age: 38.1 (2005); Males per 100 females: 89.6 (2005); Marriage status: 21.8% never married, 53.4% now married, 9.7% widowed, 15.0% divorced (2000); Foreign born: 0.7% (2000); Ancestry (includes multiple ancestries): 23.7% German, 15.3% Irish, 11.4% English, 10.4% Other groups, 7.4% Italian (2000).
Economy: Manufacturing of structural steel and tubing; also motor vehicles, machinery. Employment by occupation: 6.8% management, 15.1% professional, 11.4% services, 24.3% sales, 0.3% farming, 11.1% construction, 31.0% production (2000).
Income: Per capita income: $17,413 (2005); Median household income: $34,000 (2005); Average household income: $39,229 (2005); Percent of households with income of $100,000 or more: 3.7% (2005); Poverty rate: 10.5% (2000).
Education: Percent of population age 25 and over with: High school diploma (including GED) or higher: 80.3% (2005); Bachelor's degree or higher: 12.7% (2005); Master's degree or higher: 2.9% (2005).
School District(s)
Labrae Local SD (PK-12)
  2003-04 Enrollment: 1,497 . . . . (330) 898-1393
Newton Falls Ex Vill SD (PK-12)
  2003-04 Enrollment: 1,520 . . . . (330) 872-5445
Housing: Homeownership rate: 54.9% (2005); Median home value: $98,623 (2005); Median rent: $383 per month (2000); Median age of housing: 44 years (2000).
Transportation: Commute to work: 97.1% car, 0.0% public transportation, 2.2% walk, 0.7% work from home (2000); Travel time to work: 27.7% less than 15 minutes, 37.3% 15 to 30 minutes, 20.8% 30 to 45 minutes, 6.6% 45 to 60 minutes, 7.6% 60 minutes or more (2000)
Additional Information Contacts
Newton Falls Chamber of Commerce . . . . (330) 872-3223
  http://www.ci.newtonfalls.oh.us

NILES (city).
Covers a land area of 8.552 square miles and a water area of 0.018 square miles. Located at 41.18° N. Lat.; 80.75° W. Long. Elevation is 890 feet.
History: Niles was settled in 1806 by James Heaton, who built a gristmill and blast furnace in the area. It was known as Heaton's Furnace until 1834, when the name was changed to Nilestown for a Baltimore newspaper editor whom Heaton admired. The post office later shortened the name. William McKinley, the 25th president of the United States, was born in Niles in 1843.
Population: 21,353 (1990); 20,932 (2000); 20,041 (2005); 19,159 (2010 projected); Race: 95.8% White, 2.3% Black, 0.4% Asian, 0.9% Hispanic of any race (2005); Density: 2,343.3 persons per square mile (2005); Average household size: 2.31 (2005); Median age: 40.8 (2005); Males per 100 females: 89.9 (2005); Marriage status: 22.7% never married, 55.7% now married, 9.1% widowed, 12.6% divorced (2000); Foreign born: 1.9% (2000); Ancestry (includes multiple ancestries): 23.9% Italian, 21.4% German, 17.5% Irish, 10.6% English, 7.4% Other groups (2000).
Economy: Single-family building permits issued: 7 (2005); Multi-family building permits issued: 0 (2005); Employment by occupation: 7.7% management, 13.9% professional, 17.9% services, 26.7% sales, 0.1% farming, 7.8% construction, 25.9% production (2000).
Income: Per capita income: $21,586 (2005); Median household income: $38,234 (2005); Average household income: $49,289 (2005); Percent of households with income of $100,000 or more: 7.5% (2005); Poverty rate: 9.6% (2000).
Education: Percent of population age 25 and over with: High school diploma (including GED) or higher: 82.8% (2005); Bachelor's degree or higher: 11.7% (2005); Master's degree or higher: 2.8% (2005).
School District(s)
Niles City SD (PK-12)
  2003-04 Enrollment: 2,861 . . . . (330) 652-2509
Two-year College(s)
ETI Technical College (Private, For-profit)
  Fall 2004 Enrollment: 321 . . . . (330) 652-9919
  2005-06 Tuition: In-state $6,001; Out-of-state $6,001
Raphaels School of Beauty Culture (Private, For-profit)
  Fall 2004 Enrollment: 116 . . . . (330) 652-1559
Housing: Homeownership rate: 63.5% (2005); Median home value: $95,269 (2005); Median rent: $419 per month (2000); Median age of housing: 41 years (2000).
Newspapers: The Niles Times (General - Circulation 7,700)
Transportation: Commute to work: 96.3% car, 0.4% public transportation, 1.4% walk, 1.2% work from home (2000); Travel time to work: 40.4% less than 15 minutes, 46.0% 15 to 30 minutes, 7.8% 30 to 45 minutes, 2.2% 45 to 60 minutes, 3.6% 60 minutes or more (2000)
Additional Information Contacts
City of Niles . . . . (330) 544-9000
  http://www.thecityofniles.com
Trumbull County Convention & Visitors Bureau. . . . . (330) 544-3468

NORTH BLOOMFIELD (unincorporated postal area, zip code 44450).
Covers a land area of 48.401 square miles and a water area of 0.579 square miles. Located at 41.44° N. Lat.; 80.81° W. Long. Elevation is 900 feet.
Population: 2,115 (2000); Race: 96.5% White, 2.3% Black, 0.0% Asian, 0.7% Hispanic of any race (2000); Density: 43.7 persons per square mile (2000); Age: 31.8% under 18, 11.1% over 64 (2000); Marriage status: 25.1% never married, 57.5% now married, 8.2% widowed, 9.1% divorced (2000); Foreign born: 1.1% (2000); Ancestry (includes multiple ancestries): 23.6% German, 16.2% English, 11.1% United States or American, 10.0% Irish, 6.9% Other groups (2000).
Economy: Employment by occupation: 9.3% management, 10.2% professional, 10.4% services, 18.3% sales, 1.3% farming, 14.0% construction, 36.3% production (2000).
Income: Per capita income: $15,353 (2000); Median household income: $40,549 (2000); Poverty rate: 9.5% (2000).
Education: Percent of population age 25 and over with: High school diploma (including GED) or higher: 77.6% (2000); Bachelor's degree or higher: 8.4% (2000).

School District(s)
Bloomfield-Mespo Local SD (KG-12)
 2003-04 Enrollment: 351 . . . . (440) 685-4752
Maplewood Local SD (PK-12)
 2003-04 Enrollment: 1,094 . . . . (330) 637-7506
Housing: Homeownership rate: 78.4% (2000); Median home value: $87,300 (2000); Median rent: $345 per month (2000); Median age of housing: 39 years (2000).
Transportation: Commute to work: 90.8% car, 1.4% public transportation, 2.3% walk, 5.0% work from home (2000); Travel time to work: 17.9% less than 15 minutes, 39.9% 15 to 30 minutes, 26.4% 30 to 45 minutes, 9.6% 45 to 60 minutes, 6.2% 60 minutes or more (2000)

ORANGEVILLE (village).
Covers a land area of 0.793 square miles and a water area of 0.322 square miles. Located at 41.34° N. Lat.; 80.52° W. Long. Elevation is 940 feet.
Population: 253 (1990); 189 (2000); 181 (2005); 178 (2010 projected); Race: 97.2% White, 0.0% Black, 0.0% Asian, 0.0% Hispanic of any race (2005); Density: 228.3 persons per square mile (2005); Average household size: 2.45 (2005); Median age: 40.5 (2005); Males per 100 females: 98.9 (2005); Marriage status: 18.1% never married, 69.8% now married, 4.0% widowed, 8.1% divorced (2000); Foreign born: 0.0% (2000); Ancestry (includes multiple ancestries): 42.4% German, 15.2% English, 13.6% United States or American, 13.1% Dutch, 9.4% Irish (2000).
Economy: Employment by occupation: 6.1% management, 9.1% professional, 12.1% services, 33.3% sales, 0.0% farming, 14.1% construction, 25.3% production (2000).
Income: Per capita income: $19,599 (2005); Median household income: $47,414 (2005); Average household income: $47,939 (2005); Percent of households with income of $100,000 or more: 0.0% (2005); Poverty rate: 0.0% (2000).
Education: Percent of population age 25 and over with: High school diploma (including GED) or higher: 89.0% (2005); Bachelor's degree or higher: 10.2% (2005); Master's degree or higher: 2.4% (2005).
Housing: Homeownership rate: 78.4% (2005); Median home value: $102,083 (2005); Median rent: $279 per month (2000); Median age of housing: 60+ years (2000).
Transportation: Commute to work: 93.9% car, 0.0% public transportation, 6.1% walk, 0.0% work from home (2000); Travel time to work: 18.2% less than 15 minutes, 40.4% 15 to 30 minutes, 34.3% 30 to 45 minutes, 6.1% 45 to 60 minutes, 1.0% 60 minutes or more (2000)

SOUTH CANAL (CDP).
Covers a land area of 1.620 square miles and a water area of 0.038 square miles. Located at 41.17° N. Lat.; 80.98° W. Long.
Population: 1,319 (1990); 1,346 (2000); 1,316 (2005); 1,304 (2010 projected); Race: 98.6% White, 0.2% Black, 0.1% Asian, 0.7% Hispanic of any race (2005); Density: 812.4 persons per square mile (2005); Average household size: 2.77 (2005); Median age: 45.8 (2005); Males per 100 females: 92.1 (2005); Marriage status: 19.8% never married, 61.1% now married, 9.0% widowed, 10.1% divorced (2000); Foreign born: 1.3% (2000); Ancestry (includes multiple ancestries): 16.6% German, 13.4% Slovak, 9.6% Italian, 9.4% English, 7.1% Irish (2000).
Economy: Employment by occupation: 3.0% management, 10.4% professional, 13.4% services, 37.4% sales, 0.0% farming, 15.2% construction, 20.6% production (2000).
Income: Per capita income: $21,877 (2005); Median household income: $50,128 (2005); Average household income: $58,853 (2005); Percent of households with income of $100,000 or more: 14.1% (2005); Poverty rate: 3.9% (2000).
Education: Percent of population age 25 and over with: High school diploma (including GED) or higher: 82.9% (2005); Bachelor's degree or higher: 7.5% (2005); Master's degree or higher: 2.5% (2005).
Housing: Homeownership rate: 90.9% (2005); Median home value: $125,287 (2005); Median rent: $465 per month (2000); Median age of housing: 36 years (2000).
Transportation: Commute to work: 98.4% car, 0.0% public transportation, 0.7% walk, 0.0% work from home (2000); Travel time to work: 25.9% less than 15 minutes, 43.5% 15 to 30 minutes, 17.6% 30 to 45 minutes, 7.2% 45 to 60 minutes, 5.9% 60 minutes or more (2000)

SOUTHINGTON (unincorporated postal area, zip code 44470).
Covers a land area of 24.247 square miles and a water area of 0.030 square miles. Located at 41.29° N. Lat.; 80.95° W. Long. Elevation is 891 feet.
Population: 3,554 (2000); Race: 98.4% White, 1.1% Black, 0.0% Asian, 0.5% Hispanic of any race (2000); Density: 146.6 persons per square mile (2000); Age: 21.9% under 18, 13.6% over 64 (2000); Marriage status: 20.1% never married, 64.8% now married, 6.8% widowed, 8.3% divorced (2000); Foreign born: 0.7% (2000); Ancestry (includes multiple ancestries): 27.6% German, 18.0% English, 13.4% Irish, 8.7% United States or American, 5.2% Italian (2000).
Economy: Employment by occupation: 7.2% management, 12.1% professional, 11.7% services, 18.4% sales, 0.6% farming, 12.0% construction, 37.9% production (2000).
Income: Per capita income: $20,031 (2000); Median household income: $49,044 (2000); Poverty rate: 6.4% (2000).
Education: Percent of population age 25 and over with: High school diploma (including GED) or higher: 84.8% (2000); Bachelor's degree or higher: 10.0% (2000).
School District(s)
Southington Local SD (KG-12)
 2003-04 Enrollment: 661 . . . . (330) 898-7480
Housing: Homeownership rate: 92.0% (2000); Median home value: $102,500 (2000); Median rent: $416 per month (2000); Median age of housing: 35 years (2000).
Transportation: Commute to work: 97.1% car, 0.0% public transportation, 1.0% walk, 1.5% work from home (2000); Travel time to work: 13.7% less than 15 minutes, 51.2% 15 to 30 minutes, 17.6% 30 to 45 minutes, 8.3% 45 to 60 minutes, 9.1% 60 minutes or more (2000)

VIENNA (unincorporated postal area, zip code 44473).
Aka Vienna Center. Covers a land area of 25.220 square miles and a water area of 0.019 square miles. Located at 41.26° N. Lat.; 80.70° W. Long. Elevation is 1,050 feet.
Population: 4,215 (2000); Race: 97.4% White, 0.7% Black, 0.3% Asian, 0.2% Hispanic of any race (2000); Density: 167.1 persons per square mile (2000); Age: 22.7% under 18, 16.0% over 64 (2000); Marriage status: 19.4% never married, 64.0% now married, 7.7% widowed, 8.9% divorced (2000); Foreign born: 0.2% (2000); Ancestry (includes multiple ancestries): 23.0% German, 15.5% Irish, 12.3% English, 9.9% Italian, 5.8% United States or American (2000).
Economy: Employment by occupation: 9.4% management, 15.3% professional, 14.2% services, 23.8% sales, 1.0% farming, 12.2% construction, 24.0% production (2000).
Income: Per capita income: $19,652 (2000); Median household income: $45,556 (2000); Poverty rate: 4.4% (2000).
Education: Percent of population age 25 and over with: High school diploma (including GED) or higher: 88.4% (2000); Bachelor's degree or higher: 14.4% (2000).
School District(s)
Mathews Local SD (PK-12)
 2003-04 Enrollment: 993 . . . . (330) 394-1800
Housing: Homeownership rate: 87.9% (2000); Median home value: $97,900 (2000); Median rent: $369 per month (2000); Median age of housing: 31 years (2000).
Transportation: Commute to work: 94.1% car, 0.6% public transportation, 1.7% walk, 3.1% work from home (2000); Travel time to work: 30.9% less than 15 minutes, 49.3% 15 to 30 minutes, 11.5% 30 to 45 minutes, 3.1% 45 to 60 minutes, 5.1% 60 minutes or more (2000)

VIENNA CENTER (CDP).
Covers a land area of 4.236 square miles and a water area of 0 square miles. Located at 41.23° N. Lat.; 80.66° W. Long.
Population: 1,066 (1990); 994 (2000); 982 (2005); 973 (2010 projected); Race: 98.4% White, 0.9% Black, 0.3% Asian, 0.5% Hispanic of any race (2005); Density: 231.8 persons per square mile (2005); Average household size: 2.62 (2005); Median age: 41.1 (2005); Males per 100 females: 105.0 (2005); Marriage status: 24.1% never married, 66.4% now married, 6.3% widowed, 3.2% divorced (2000); Foreign born: 0.0% (2000); Ancestry (includes multiple ancestries): 16.4% Irish, 16.3% German, 14.8% English, 9.1% Italian, 8.8% Other groups (2000).
Economy: Employment by occupation: 7.5% management, 21.6% professional, 12.9% services, 25.3% sales, 0.0% farming, 7.9% construction, 24.8% production (2000).
Income: Per capita income: $23,469 (2005); Median household income: $52,827 (2005); Average household income: $61,147 (2005); Percent of households with income of $100,000 or more: 16.5% (2005); Poverty rate: 3.1% (2000).

Education: Percent of population age 25 and over with: High school diploma (including GED) or higher: 88.9% (2005); Bachelor's degree or higher: 15.7% (2005); Master's degree or higher: 6.2% (2005).
Housing: Homeownership rate: 83.7% (2005); Median home value: $115,351 (2005); Median rent: $430 per month (2000); Median age of housing: 41 years (2000).
Transportation: Commute to work: 93.9% car, 0.0% public transportation, 4.3% walk, 1.8% work from home (2000); Travel time to work: 34.3% less than 15 minutes, 51.7% 15 to 30 minutes, 5.2% 30 to 45 minutes, 3.7% 45 to 60 minutes, 5.2% 60 minutes or more (2000)

WARREN (city).
Covers a land area of 16.085 square miles and a water area of 0.027 square miles. Located at 41.23° N. Lat.; 80.81° W. Long. Elevation is 893 feet.
History: Warren was settled in 1798 when Ephraim Quinby and Richard Storr of the Connecticut Land Company came from Pennsylvania. In 1800 the settlement was made the seat of the newly formed Trumbull County. Warren, named for a surveyor, grew slowly, and was incorporated as a village in 1834. The opening of the canal brought a shipping industry, and manufacturing developed. In 1899 J. Ward Packard made the first Packard automobiles in Warren, as well as founding the forerunner of the Peerless Electric Company and other lamp manufacturing companies.
Population: 51,151 (1990); 46,832 (2000); 44,380 (2005); 42,102 (2010 projected); Race: 71.3% White, 25.6% Black, 0.4% Asian, 1.2% Hispanic of any race (2005); Density: 2,759.1 persons per square mile (2005); Average household size: 2.39 (2005); Median age: 37.1 (2005); Males per 100 females: 87.3 (2005); Marriage status: 26.7% never married, 49.5% now married, 9.0% widowed, 14.8% divorced (2000); Foreign born: 1.9% (2000); Ancestry (includes multiple ancestries): 25.3% Other groups, 15.2% German, 11.6% Irish, 10.3% Italian, 7.5% English (2000).
Economy: Unemployment rate: 7.4% (2005); Total civilian labor force: 19,786 (2005); Single-family building permits issued: 19 (2005); Multi-family building permits issued: 12 (2005); Employment by occupation: 7.8% management, 13.4% professional, 19.0% services, 23.3% sales, 0.2% farming, 8.3% construction, 28.1% production (2000).
Income: Per capita income: $17,225 (2005); Median household income: $31,618 (2005); Average household income: $40,580 (2005); Percent of households with income of $100,000 or more: 5.2% (2005); Poverty rate: 19.4% (2000).
Taxes: Total city taxes per capita: $463 (2004); City property taxes per capita: $31 (2004).
Education: Percent of population age 25 and over with: High school diploma (including GED) or higher: 77.4% (2005); Bachelor's degree or higher: 11.0% (2005); Master's degree or higher: 3.3% (2005).

School District(s)
Champion Local SD (PK-12)
   2003-04 Enrollment: 1,722 . . . . (330) 847-2330
Howland Local SD (PK-12)
   2003-04 Enrollment: 3,228 . . . . (330) 856-8200
Lakeview Local SD (PK-12)
   2003-04 Enrollment: 2,234 . . . . (330) 637-8741
Life Skills of Trumbull County (09-12)
   2003-04 Enrollment: 313 . . . . (330) 392-0231
Lordstown Local SD (PK-12)
   2003-04 Enrollment: 546 . . . . (330) 824-2534
Trumbull Career & Tech Ctr (11-12)
   2003-04 Enrollment: n/a . . . . (330) 847-0503
Warren City SD (KG-12)
   2003-04 Enrollment: 6,901 . . . . (330) 841-2321

Two-year College(s)
Kent State University-Trumbull Campus (Public)
   Fall 2004 Enrollment: 2,172 . . . . (330) 847-0571
   2005-06 Tuition: In-state $4,586; Out-of-state $12,018
TCTC Adult Training Center (Public)
   Fall 2004 Enrollment: 151 . . . . (330) 824-2588
Trumbull Business College (Private, For-profit)
   Fall 2004 Enrollment: 407 . . . . (330) 369-3200
   2005-06 Tuition: In-state $9,598; Out-of-state $9,598

Housing: Homeownership rate: 58.8% (2005); Median home value: $73,233 (2005); Median rent: $355 per month (2000); Median age of housing: 47 years (2000).
Hospitals: Hillside Rehabilitation Hospital (93 beds); St. Joseph Health Center (237 beds); Trumbull Memorial Hospital (350 beds)
Safety: Violent crime rate: 87.8 per 10,000 population; Property crime rate: 598.2 per 10,000 population (2004).

Newspapers: Tribune Chronicle (Circulation 34,036)
Transportation: Commute to work: 94.7% car, 0.2% public transportation, 1.8% walk, 1.7% work from home (2000); Travel time to work: 49.7% less than 15 minutes, 32.4% 15 to 30 minutes, 8.4% 30 to 45 minutes, 5.3% 45 to 60 minutes, 4.1% 60 minutes or more (2000)
Additional Information Contacts
Youngstown/Warren Regional Chamber of Commerce . . . . (330) 744-2131
   http://www.regionalchamber.com

WEST FARMINGTON (village).
Covers a land area of 0.878 square miles and a water area of 0 square miles. Located at 41.39° N. Lat.; 80.97° W. Long. Elevation is 887 feet.
Population: 542 (1990); 519 (2000); 537 (2005); 552 (2010 projected); Race: 99.1% White, 0.6% Black, 0.0% Asian, 0.0% Hispanic of any race (2005); Density: 611.8 persons per square mile (2005); Average household size: 2.78 (2005); Median age: 32.9 (2005); Males per 100 females: 96.7 (2005); Marriage status: 19.9% never married, 58.8% now married, 9.7% widowed, 11.6% divorced (2000); Foreign born: 0.4% (2000); Ancestry (includes multiple ancestries): 30.4% German, 13.3% English, 13.1% Irish, 9.9% United States or American, 8.7% Dutch (2000).
Economy: In agricultural area. Employment by occupation: 8.4% management, 14.9% professional, 7.4% services, 18.6% sales, 0.9% farming, 16.3% construction, 33.5% production (2000).
Income: Per capita income: $17,765 (2005); Median household income: $44,188 (2005); Average household income: $49,430 (2005); Percent of households with income of $100,000 or more: 6.2% (2005); Poverty rate: 8.9% (2000).
Education: Percent of population age 25 and over with: High school diploma (including GED) or higher: 78.2% (2005); Bachelor's degree or higher: 9.2% (2005); Master's degree or higher: 2.8% (2005).

School District(s)
Bristol Local SD (PK-12)
   2003-04 Enrollment: 913 . . . . (330) 889-3882

Housing: Homeownership rate: 76.7% (2005); Median home value: $94,400 (2005); Median rent: $390 per month (2000); Median age of housing: 60+ years (2000).
Transportation: Commute to work: 93.4% car, 0.5% public transportation, 4.3% walk, 1.9% work from home (2000); Travel time to work: 13.5% less than 15 minutes, 47.3% 15 to 30 minutes, 23.7% 30 to 45 minutes, 9.7% 45 to 60 minutes, 5.8% 60 minutes or more (2000)

WEST HILL (CDP).
Covers a land area of 1.634 square miles and a water area of 0 square miles. Located at 41.23° N. Lat.; 80.52° W. Long. Elevation is 1,050 feet.
Population: 2,954 (1990); 2,523 (2000); 2,337 (2005); 2,254 (2010 projected); Race: 89.1% White, 8.7% Black, 0.5% Asian, 0.9% Hispanic of any race (2005); Density: 1,429.9 persons per square mile (2005); Average household size: 2.38 (2005); Median age: 40.1 (2005); Males per 100 females: 93.5 (2005); Marriage status: 23.1% never married, 56.8% now married, 8.2% widowed, 11.9% divorced (2000); Foreign born: 3.6% (2000); Ancestry (includes multiple ancestries): 23.0% German, 17.9% Other groups, 14.1% Irish, 13.0% English, 11.5% Italian (2000).
Economy: Employment by occupation: 2.9% management, 7.9% professional, 22.5% services, 22.0% sales, 0.0% farming, 13.3% construction, 31.4% production (2000).
Income: Per capita income: $19,027 (2005); Median household income: $31,229 (2005); Average household income: $44,332 (2005); Percent of households with income of $100,000 or more: 5.2% (2005); Poverty rate: 13.3% (2000).
Education: Percent of population age 25 and over with: High school diploma (including GED) or higher: 78.1% (2005); Bachelor's degree or higher: 6.8% (2005); Master's degree or higher: 1.5% (2005).
Housing: Homeownership rate: 63.5% (2005); Median home value: $57,846 (2005); Median rent: $306 per month (2000); Median age of housing: 52 years (2000).
Transportation: Commute to work: 95.7% car, 0.0% public transportation, 0.0% walk, 0.9% work from home (2000); Travel time to work: 42.7% less than 15 minutes, 39.7% 15 to 30 minutes, 13.7% 30 to 45 minutes, 2.3% 45 to 60 minutes, 1.5% 60 minutes or more (2000)

YANKEE LAKE (village).
Covers a land area of 0.549 square miles and a water area of 0 square miles. Located at 41.26° N. Lat.; 80.56° W. Long. Elevation is 1,010 feet.
Population: 88 (1990); 99 (2000); 100 (2005); 99 (2010 projected); Race: 100.0% White, 0.0% Black, 0.0% Asian, 0.0% Hispanic of any race (2005);

Density: 182.3 persons per square mile (2005); Average household size: 2.38 (2005); Median age: 46.7 (2005); Males per 100 females: 122.2 (2005); Marriage status: 21.1% never married, 64.5% now married, 2.6% widowed, 11.8% divorced (2000); Foreign born: 0.0% (2000); Ancestry (includes multiple ancestries): 28.1% German, 19.1% English, 16.9% Slovak, 14.6% Croatian, 11.2% Italian (2000).
Economy: Employment by occupation: 10.2% management, 22.4% professional, 4.1% services, 14.3% sales, 0.0% farming, 30.6% construction, 18.4% production (2000).
Income: Per capita income: $22,350 (2005); Median household income: $48,750 (2005); Average household income: $53,214 (2005); Percent of households with income of $100,000 or more: 4.8% (2005); Poverty rate: 6.7% (2000).
Education: Percent of population age 25 and over with: High school diploma (including GED) or higher: 95.9% (2005); Bachelor's degree or higher: 16.2% (2005); Master's degree or higher: 4.1% (2005).
Housing: Homeownership rate: 88.1% (2005); Median home value: $126,042 (2005); Median rent: $288 per month (2000); Median age of housing: 36 years (2000).
Transportation: Commute to work: 100.0% car, 0.0% public transportation, 0.0% walk, 0.0% work from home (2000); Travel time to work: 10.2% less than 15 minutes, 51.0% 15 to 30 minutes, 30.6% 30 to 45 minutes, 4.1% 45 to 60 minutes, 4.1% 60 minutes or more (2000)

Tuscarawas County

Located in eastern Ohio; crossed by the Tuscarawas River. Covers a land area of 567.58 square miles, a water area of 3.91 square miles, and is located in the Eastern Time Zone. The county government was organized in 1808. County seat is New Philadelphia.

Tuscarawas County is part of the New Philadelphia-Dover, OH Micropolitan Statistical Area. The entire metro area includes: Tuscarawas County, OH

Weather Station: New Philadelphia   Elevation: 892 feet

	Jan	Feb	Mar	Apr	May	Jun	Jul	Aug	Sep	Oct	Nov	Dec
High	35	39	49	61	72	80	84	83	76	64	51	40
Low	18	19	27	36	46	56	60	59	52	40	32	24
Precip	2.7	2.4	3.2	3.5	4.1	4.4	4.1	4.2	3.2	2.6	3.3	3.0
Snow	9.9	6.6	5.1	1.5	tr	0.0	0.0	0.0	0.0	tr	1.4	5.2

High and Low temperatures in degrees Fahrenheit; Precipitation and Snow in inches

Population: 84,090 (1990); 90,914 (2000); 92,018 (2005); 93,143 (2010 projected); Race: 97.6% White, 0.8% Black, 0.3% Asian, 1.0% Hispanic of any race (2005); Density: 162.1 persons per square mile (2005); Average household size: 2.53 (2005); Median age: 38.9 (2005); Males per 100 females: 95.8 (2005).
Religion: Five largest groups: 9.5% The United Methodist Church, 9.3% Catholic Church, 6.7% Evangelical Lutheran Church in America, 5.8% United Church of Christ, 3.4% Old Order Amish Church (2000).
Economy: Unemployment rate: 5.7% (2005); Total civilian labor force: 47,477 (2005); Leading industries: 25.4% manufacturing; 14.8% retail trade; 14.6% health care and social assistance (2004); Farms: 1,076 totaling 159,665 acres (2002); Companies that employ 500 or more persons: 5 (2004); Companies that employ 100 to 499 persons: 45 (2004); Companies that employ less than 100 persons: 2,348 (2004); Black-owned businesses: n/a (2002); Hispanic-owned businesses: n/a (2002); Women-owned businesses: 1,707 (2002); Retail sales per capita: $12,654 (2006). Single-family building permits issued: 146 (2005); Multi-family building permits issued: 18 (2005).
Income: Per capita income: $19,336 (2005); Median household income: $39,670 (2005); Average household income: $48,488 (2005); Percent of households with income of $100,000 or more: 7.4% (2005); Poverty rate: 9.7% (2003); Bankruptcy rate: 8.92% (2005).
Taxes: Total county taxes per capita: $207 (2004); County property taxes per capita: $110 (2004).
Education: Percent of population age 25 and over with: High school diploma (including GED) or higher: 80.3% (2005); Bachelor's degree or higher: 12.2% (2005); Master's degree or higher: 4.1% (2005).
Housing: Homeownership rate: 75.3% (2005); Median home value: $106,809 (2005); Median rent: $354 per month (2000); Median age of housing: 41 years (2000).
Health: Birth rate: 133.2 per 10,000 population (2004); Death rate: 107.4 per 10,000 population (2004); Age-adjusted cancer mortality rate: 187.4 deaths per 100,000 population (2002); Air Quality Index: 99.7% good, 0.3% moderate, 0.0% unhealthy for sensitive individuals, 0.0% unhealthy (percent of days in 2005); Number of physicians: 12.2 per 10,000 population (2004); Hospital beds: 17.1 per 10,000 population (2003); Hospital admissions: 776.7 per 10,000 population (2003).
Elections: 2004 Presidential election results: 55.5% Bush, 43.9% Kerry, 0.0% Nader, 0.3% Badnarik
National and State Parks: Fort Laurens State Memorial
Additional Information Contacts

Tuscarawas County Government	(330) 364-8811
http://www.co.tuscarawas.oh.us/	
City of Dover	(330) 343-6726
http://www.doverohio.com	
City of New Philadelphia	(330) 364-4491
http://www.newphilaoh.com	
Newcomerstown Chamber of Commerce	(740) 498-7244
http://www.newcomerstown.com	
Tuscarawas County Chamber of Commerce	(330) 343-4474
http://www.tuschamber.com	
Uhrichsville Chamber of Commerce	(740) 922-5623
http://www.twincitychamber.org	
Village of Newcomerstown	(740) 492-0797
http://www.newcomerstown.com	

Tuscarawas County Communities

BALTIC (village). Covers a land area of 0.834 square miles and a water area of 0 square miles. Located at 40.44° N. Lat.; 81.70° W. Long. Elevation is 1,041 feet.
Population: 755 (1990); 743 (2000); 827 (2005); 879 (2010 projected); Race: 98.4% White, 0.1% Black, 0.4% Asian, 0.0% Hispanic of any race (2005); Density: 991.7 persons per square mile (2005); Average household size: 2.67 (2005); Median age: 40.4 (2005); Males per 100 females: 101.7 (2005); Marriage status: 20.3% never married, 55.0% now married, 12.6% widowed, 12.0% divorced (2000); Foreign born: 0.0% (2000); Ancestry (includes multiple ancestries): 44.4% German, 11.7% Swiss, 7.1% Irish, 5.6% United States or American, 5.2% English (2000).
Economy: Single-family building permits issued: 0 (2005); Multi-family building permits issued: 0 (2005); Employment by occupation: 9.8% management, 8.0% professional, 13.2% services, 16.9% sales, 1.5% farming, 14.7% construction, 35.9% production (2000).
Income: Per capita income: $17,318 (2005); Median household income: $35,294 (2005); Average household income: $41,315 (2005); Percent of households with income of $100,000 or more: 1.9% (2005); Poverty rate: 5.7% (2000).
Education: Percent of population age 25 and over with: High school diploma (including GED) or higher: 69.8% (2005); Bachelor's degree or higher: 5.9% (2005); Master's degree or higher: 2.2% (2005).

School District(s)
Garaway Local SD (PK-12)
    2003-04 Enrollment: 1,238 . . . . (330) 852-2421
Housing: Homeownership rate: 73.9% (2005); Median home value: $100,305 (2005); Median rent: $351 per month (2000); Median age of housing: 55 years (2000).
Transportation: Commute to work: 94.4% car, 0.0% public transportation, 2.2% walk, 1.9% work from home (2000); Travel time to work: 43.2% less than 15 minutes, 27.0% 15 to 30 minutes, 21.6% 30 to 45 minutes, 6.7% 45 to 60 minutes, 1.6% 60 minutes or more (2000)

BARNHILL (village). Covers a land area of 0.370 square miles and a water area of 0 square miles. Located at 40.44° N. Lat.; 81.36° W. Long. Elevation is 920 feet.
Population: 313 (1990); 364 (2000); 398 (2005); 430 (2010 projected); Race: 98.0% White, 0.8% Black, 0.0% Asian, 0.3% Hispanic of any race (2005); Density: 1,076.8 persons per square mile (2005); Average household size: 2.67 (2005); Median age: 34.1 (2005); Males per 100 females: 93.2 (2005); Marriage status: 24.2% never married, 56.3% now married, 8.7% widowed, 10.8% divorced (2000); Foreign born: 0.0% (2000); Ancestry (includes multiple ancestries): 19.2% German, 13.1% United States or American, 11.1% Other groups, 6.4% English, 6.4% Irish (2000).
Economy: Employment by occupation: 5.3% management, 7.3% professional, 18.7% services, 10.7% sales, 0.0% farming, 7.3% construction, 50.7% production (2000).
Income: Per capita income: $13,078 (2005); Median household income: $30,370 (2005); Average household income: $34,933 (2005); Percent of

households with income of $100,000 or more: 1.3% (2005); Poverty rate: 19.5% (2000).
Education: Percent of population age 25 and over with: High school diploma (including GED) or higher: 71.2% (2005); Bachelor's degree or higher: 4.7% (2005); Master's degree or higher: 1.6% (2005).
Housing: Homeownership rate: 86.6% (2005); Median home value: $54,186 (2005); Median rent: $360 per month (2000); Median age of housing: 28 years (2000).
Transportation: Commute to work: 97.3% car, 0.0% public transportation, 0.0% walk, 0.0% work from home (2000); Travel time to work: 37.2% less than 15 minutes, 36.5% 15 to 30 minutes, 16.2% 30 to 45 minutes, 6.1% 45 to 60 minutes, 4.1% 60 minutes or more (2000)

BOLIVAR (village). Covers a land area of 0.505 square miles and a water area of 0.006 square miles. Located at 40.65° N. Lat.; 81.45° W. Long. Elevation is 940 feet.
History: Bolivar was an important grain market during the boom days of the Ohio & Erie and the Sandy & Beaver Canals. Near Bolivar was the site of the cabin built in 1761 by Christian Frederick Post, a Moravian missionary.
Population: 953 (1990); 894 (2000); 892 (2005); 893 (2010 projected); Race: 98.4% White, 0.0% Black, 0.9% Asian, 0.1% Hispanic of any race (2005); Density: 1,765.8 persons per square mile (2005); Average household size: 2.34 (2005); Median age: 40.2 (2005); Males per 100 females: 95.6 (2005); Marriage status: 16.8% never married, 66.3% now married, 10.4% widowed, 6.5% divorced (2000); Foreign born: 0.3% (2000); Ancestry (includes multiple ancestries): 40.4% German, 12.3% Irish, 12.2% English, 5.8% United States or American, 5.4% Other groups (2000).
Economy: Single-family building permits issued: 0 (2005); Multi-family building permits issued: 0 (2005); Employment by occupation: 15.9% management, 10.8% professional, 15.6% services, 20.3% sales, 0.0% farming, 12.5% construction, 24.9% production (2000).
Income: Per capita income: $21,780 (2005); Median household income: $44,519 (2005); Average household income: $50,991 (2005); Percent of households with income of $100,000 or more: 7.6% (2005); Poverty rate: 3.9% (2000).
Education: Percent of population age 25 and over with: High school diploma (including GED) or higher: 82.2% (2005); Bachelor's degree or higher: 13.9% (2005); Master's degree or higher: 3.7% (2005).
School District(s)
Tuscarawas Valley Local SD (PK-12)
    2003-04 Enrollment: 1,744 . . . . (330) 859-2213
Housing: Homeownership rate: 84.5% (2005); Median home value: $114,685 (2005); Median rent: $373 per month (2000); Median age of housing: 49 years (2000).
Transportation: Commute to work: 92.4% car, 0.5% public transportation, 3.2% walk, 3.4% work from home (2000); Travel time to work: 32.4% less than 15 minutes, 47.7% 15 to 30 minutes, 12.2% 30 to 45 minutes, 3.8% 45 to 60 minutes, 3.8% 60 minutes or more (2000)

DENNISON (village). Covers a land area of 1.376 square miles and a water area of 0 square miles. Located at 40.39° N. Lat.; 81.33° W. Long. Elevation is 862 feet.
History: The site of Dennison was selected in 1864 by the Pittsburgh, Columbus & St. Louis Railroad for its division shops. The town was named for William Dennison, a Civil War governor of Ohio.
Population: 3,282 (1990); 2,992 (2000); 2,865 (2005); 2,788 (2010 projected); Race: 95.7% White, 1.8% Black, 0.1% Asian, 1.3% Hispanic of any race (2005); Density: 2,082.2 persons per square mile (2005); Average household size: 2.61 (2005); Median age: 35.0 (2005); Males per 100 females: 96.8 (2005); Marriage status: 24.1% never married, 56.8% now married, 8.7% widowed, 10.4% divorced (2000); Foreign born: 0.5% (2000); Ancestry (includes multiple ancestries): 22.8% German, 18.4% Irish, 10.0% Italian, 9.1% English, 8.6% United States or American (2000).
Economy: Single-family building permits issued: 0 (2005); Multi-family building permits issued: 0 (2005); Employment by occupation: 4.4% management, 11.0% professional, 19.1% services, 21.6% sales, 0.3% farming, 6.4% construction, 37.2% production (2000).
Income: Per capita income: $15,428 (2005); Median household income: $32,399 (2005); Average household income: $40,135 (2005); Percent of households with income of $100,000 or more: 4.3% (2005); Poverty rate: 17.2% (2000).
Education: Percent of population age 25 and over with: High school diploma (including GED) or higher: 75.6% (2005); Bachelor's degree or higher: 6.2% (2005); Master's degree or higher: 3.3% (2005).
School District(s)
Claymont City SD (PK-12)
    2003-04 Enrollment: 2,346 . . . . (740) 922-5478
Housing: Homeownership rate: 67.3% (2005); Median home value: $71,620 (2005); Median rent: $340 per month (2000); Median age of housing: 60+ years (2000).
Hospitals: Twin City Hospital (25 beds)
Transportation: Commute to work: 93.7% car, 0.0% public transportation, 2.8% walk, 2.1% work from home (2000); Travel time to work: 39.7% less than 15 minutes, 36.6% 15 to 30 minutes, 13.3% 30 to 45 minutes, 6.1% 45 to 60 minutes, 4.2% 60 minutes or more (2000)

DOVER (city). Covers a land area of 5.264 square miles and a water area of 0.069 square miles. Located at 40.52° N. Lat.; 81.47° W. Long. Elevation is 898 feet.
History: Dover was laid out in 1807 on land owned by Jesse Slingluff and Christian Deardorff, and settled by German immigrants from Pennsylvania. For a time it was known as Canal Dover, and was the collector's port for the Ohio & Erie Canal in Tuscarawas County.
Population: 11,544 (1990); 12,210 (2000); 12,124 (2005); 12,044 (2010 projected); Race: 96.8% White, 1.3% Black, 0.6% Asian, 0.8% Hispanic of any race (2005); Density: 2,303.3 persons per square mile (2005); Average household size: 2.43 (2005); Median age: 41.3 (2005); Males per 100 females: 87.7 (2005); Marriage status: 20.8% never married, 58.0% now married, 10.0% widowed, 11.2% divorced (2000); Foreign born: 0.7% (2000); Ancestry (includes multiple ancestries): 33.4% German, 12.3% Irish, 11.7% English, 11.2% Italian, 6.1% Other groups (2000).
Economy: Single-family building permits issued: 20 (2005); Multi-family building permits issued: 0 (2005); Employment by occupation: 10.8% management, 18.0% professional, 17.8% services, 25.2% sales, 0.1% farming, 6.4% construction, 21.6% production (2000).
Income: Per capita income: $20,641 (2005); Median household income: $40,365 (2005); Average household income: $49,649 (2005); Percent of households with income of $100,000 or more: 8.1% (2005); Poverty rate: 9.2% (2000).
Education: Percent of population age 25 and over with: High school diploma (including GED) or higher: 84.3% (2005); Bachelor's degree or higher: 17.8% (2005); Master's degree or higher: 6.1% (2005).
School District(s)
Dover City SD (PK-12)
    2003-04 Enrollment: 2,598 . . . . (330) 364-1906
Housing: Homeownership rate: 72.2% (2005); Median home value: $120,060 (2005); Median rent: $383 per month (2000); Median age of housing: 47 years (2000).
Hospitals: Union Hospital (105 beds)
Safety: Violent crime rate: 6.5 per 10,000 population; Property crime rate: 68.7 per 10,000 population (2004).
Transportation: Commute to work: 95.7% car, 0.1% public transportation, 1.6% walk, 1.8% work from home (2000); Travel time to work: 52.3% less than 15 minutes, 29.3% 15 to 30 minutes, 12.1% 30 to 45 minutes, 2.9% 45 to 60 minutes, 3.3% 60 minutes or more (2000)
Additional Information Contacts
City of Dover . . . . (330) 343-6726
    http://www.doverohio.com

DUNDEE (unincorporated postal area, zip code 44624). Covers a land area of 51.959 square miles and a water area of 0.025 square miles. Located at 40.60° N. Lat.; 81.65° W. Long. Elevation is 1,032 feet.
Population: 4,522 (2000); Race: 98.9% White, 0.0% Black, 0.0% Asian, 0.0% Hispanic of any race (2000); Density: 87.0 persons per square mile (2000); Age: 36.9% under 18, 6.2% over 64 (2000); Marriage status: 25.4% never married, 66.5% now married, 4.8% widowed, 3.3% divorced (2000); Foreign born: 0.0% (2000); Ancestry (includes multiple ancestries): 27.2% German, 13.8% United States or American, 6.6% Swiss, 5.2% Pennsylvania German, 3.4% Irish (2000).
Economy: Employment by occupation: 11.4% management, 4.8% professional, 13.1% services, 15.7% sales, 3.2% farming, 18.0% construction, 33.7% production (2000).
Income: Per capita income: $13,508 (2000); Median household income: $39,936 (2000); Poverty rate: 13.6% (2000).

Education: Percent of population age 25 and over with: High school diploma (including GED) or higher: 39.0% (2000); Bachelor's degree or higher: 2.1% (2000).

School District(s)
Garaway Local SD (PK-12)
    2003-04 Enrollment: 1,238 . . . . (330) 852-2421

Housing: Homeownership rate: 84.5% (2000); Median home value: $112,800 (2000); Median rent: $379 per month (2000); Median age of housing: 25 years (2000).

Transportation: Commute to work: 71.5% car, 1.6% public transportation, 5.6% walk, 17.6% work from home (2000); Travel time to work: 33.4% less than 15 minutes, 41.3% 15 to 30 minutes, 15.7% 30 to 45 minutes, 5.1% 45 to 60 minutes, 4.6% 60 minutes or more (2000)

GNADENHUTTEN (village).
Covers a land area of 0.999 square miles and a water area of <.001 square miles. Located at 40.36° N. Lat.; 81.43° W. Long. Elevation is 840 feet.

History: The name of Gnadenhutten is of German origin, meaning "tents of grace." A community was established here in 1772 by Joshua, a Mohican elder of a group of Indians from the Moravian mission founded by David Zeisberger at Schoenbrunn. The group was massacred by militiamen from Pennsylvania in 1782.

Population: 1,250 (1990); 1,280 (2000); 1,309 (2005); 1,339 (2010 projected); Race: 99.4% White, 0.1% Black, 0.0% Asian, 0.2% Hispanic of any race (2005); Density: 1,310.8 persons per square mile (2005); Average household size: 2.46 (2005); Median age: 39.0 (2005); Males per 100 females: 89.2 (2005); Marriage status: 18.0% never married, 65.1% now married, 8.2% widowed, 8.7% divorced (2000); Foreign born: 0.2% (2000); Ancestry (includes multiple ancestries): 29.3% German, 14.8% Irish, 11.5% United States or American, 10.0% English, 4.8% Italian (2000).

Economy: Single-family building permits issued: 3 (2005); Multi-family building permits issued: 0 (2005); Employment by occupation: 6.8% management, 12.0% professional, 19.8% services, 27.4% sales, 0.5% farming, 8.3% construction, 25.2% production (2000).

Income: Per capita income: $19,505 (2005); Median household income: $37,905 (2005); Average household income: $47,702 (2005); Percent of households with income of $100,000 or more: 5.6% (2005); Poverty rate: 8.8% (2000).

Education: Percent of population age 25 and over with: High school diploma (including GED) or higher: 84.8% (2005); Bachelor's degree or higher: 8.1% (2005); Master's degree or higher: 2.8% (2005).

School District(s)
Indian Valley Digital Academy
    2003-04 Enrollment: n/a
Indian Valley Local SD (PK-12)
    2003-04 Enrollment: 1,916 . . . . (740) 254-4334

Housing: Homeownership rate: 85.0% (2005); Median home value: $92,105 (2005); Median rent: $377 per month (2000); Median age of housing: 49 years (2000).

Transportation: Commute to work: 93.6% car, 0.7% public transportation, 3.5% walk, 2.2% work from home (2000); Travel time to work: 30.9% less than 15 minutes, 42.8% 15 to 30 minutes, 15.2% 30 to 45 minutes, 4.6% 45 to 60 minutes, 6.5% 60 minutes or more (2000)

MIDVALE (village).
Covers a land area of 0.610 square miles and a water area of 0 square miles. Located at 40.43° N. Lat.; 81.37° W. Long. Elevation is 870 feet.

Population: 573 (1990); 547 (2000); 582 (2005); 616 (2010 projected); Race: 98.6% White, 0.0% Black, 0.0% Asian, 0.7% Hispanic of any race (2005); Density: 954.9 persons per square mile (2005); Average household size: 2.53 (2005); Median age: 38.0 (2005); Males per 100 females: 101.4 (2005); Marriage status: 21.4% never married, 59.5% now married, 9.2% widowed, 9.9% divorced (2000); Foreign born: 0.8% (2000); Ancestry (includes multiple ancestries): 23.0% German, 11.5% Italian, 10.0% Irish, 9.0% English, 8.8% Other groups (2000).

Economy: Single-family building permits issued: 0 (2005); Multi-family building permits issued: 0 (2005); Employment by occupation: 7.4% management, 5.8% professional, 21.8% services, 25.5% sales, 1.6% farming, 10.7% construction, 27.2% production (2000).

Income: Per capita income: $15,339 (2005); Median household income: $30,278 (2005); Average household income: $38,815 (2005); Percent of households with income of $100,000 or more: 3.9% (2005); Poverty rate: 12.2% (2000).

Education: Percent of population age 25 and over with: High school diploma (including GED) or higher: 70.4% (2005); Bachelor's degree or higher: 2.9% (2005); Master's degree or higher: 1.3% (2005).

School District(s)
Indian Valley Local SD (PK-12)
    2003-04 Enrollment: 1,916 . . . . (740) 254-4334

Housing: Homeownership rate: 76.1% (2005); Median home value: $74,848 (2005); Median rent: $369 per month (2000); Median age of housing: 60+ years (2000).

Transportation: Commute to work: 96.7% car, 0.0% public transportation, 0.8% walk, 1.6% work from home (2000); Travel time to work: 34.7% less than 15 minutes, 47.7% 15 to 30 minutes, 9.2% 30 to 45 minutes, 0.0% 45 to 60 minutes, 8.4% 60 minutes or more (2000)

MINERAL CITY (village).
Covers a land area of 0.811 square miles and a water area of 0 square miles. Located at 40.60° N. Lat.; 81.36° W. Long. Elevation is 960 feet.

Population: 755 (1990); 841 (2000); 844 (2005); 848 (2010 projected); Race: 97.6% White, 0.0% Black, 0.0% Asian, 2.0% Hispanic of any race (2005); Density: 1,040.3 persons per square mile (2005); Average household size: 2.70 (2005); Median age: 35.3 (2005); Males per 100 females: 100.5 (2005); Marriage status: 20.6% never married, 59.6% now married, 6.6% widowed, 13.3% divorced (2000); Foreign born: 1.1% (2000); Ancestry (includes multiple ancestries): 26.8% German, 14.0% United States or American, 12.1% Irish, 7.6% Italian, 4.7% English (2000).

Economy: In coal mining area. Single-family building permits issued: 0 (2005); Multi-family building permits issued: 0 (2005); Employment by occupation: 2.9% management, 8.0% professional, 15.3% services, 21.7% sales, 0.8% farming, 12.6% construction, 38.6% production (2000).

Income: Per capita income: $15,471 (2005); Median household income: $39,554 (2005); Average household income: $41,717 (2005); Percent of households with income of $100,000 or more: 1.9% (2005); Poverty rate: 8.9% (2000).

Education: Percent of population age 25 and over with: High school diploma (including GED) or higher: 76.8% (2005); Bachelor's degree or higher: 4.6% (2005); Master's degree or higher: 1.0% (2005).

School District(s)
Tuscarawas Valley Local SD (PK-12)
    2003-04 Enrollment: 1,744 . . . . (330) 859-2213

Housing: Homeownership rate: 72.8% (2005); Median home value: $73,333 (2005); Median rent: $295 per month (2000); Median age of housing: 60+ years (2000).

Transportation: Commute to work: 96.9% car, 0.0% public transportation, 1.7% walk, 1.4% work from home (2000); Travel time to work: 15.7% less than 15 minutes, 43.4% 15 to 30 minutes, 26.3% 30 to 45 minutes, 3.4% 45 to 60 minutes, 11.1% 60 minutes or more (2000)

NEW PHILADELPHIA (city).
Covers a land area of 7.795 square miles and a water area of 0.140 square miles. Located at 40.48° N. Lat.; 81.44° W. Long. Elevation is 910 feet.

History: New Philadelphia was founded in 1804 by John Knisely, and settled by many Swiss-German immigrants from Pennsylvania.

Population: 16,617 (1990); 17,056 (2000); 17,060 (2005); 17,113 (2010 projected); Race: 96.4% White, 1.2% Black, 0.5% Asian, 1.9% Hispanic of any race (2005); Density: 2,188.5 persons per square mile (2005); Average household size: 2.31 (2005); Median age: 38.9 (2005); Males per 100 females: 92.0 (2005); Marriage status: 22.2% never married, 54.9% now married, 9.8% widowed, 13.1% divorced (2000); Foreign born: 1.9% (2000); Ancestry (includes multiple ancestries): 29.8% German, 14.3% Irish, 10.7% English, 7.9% United States or American, 7.8% Italian (2000).

Economy: Single-family building permits issued: 31 (2005); Multi-family building permits issued: 14 (2005); Employment by occupation: 9.7% management, 15.1% professional, 15.8% services, 25.8% sales, 0.4% farming, 8.0% construction, 25.1% production (2000).

Income: Per capita income: $20,616 (2005); Median household income: $36,165 (2005); Average household income: $47,314 (2005); Percent of households with income of $100,000 or more: 6.9% (2005); Poverty rate: 10.2% (2000).

Education: Percent of population age 25 and over with: High school diploma (including GED) or higher: 83.4% (2005); Bachelor's degree or higher: 14.9% (2005); Master's degree or higher: 4.7% (2005).

School District(s)
Buckeye Joint Vocational SD (07-12)
    2003-04 Enrollment: n/a . . . . (330) 339-2288

New Philadelphia City SD (PK-12)
2003-04 Enrollment: 3,307 . . . . (330) 364-0600
Quaker Digital Academy
2003-04 Enrollment: n/a . . . . (330) 364-0600
Two-year College(s)
Buckeye Joint Vocational School (Public)
Fall 2004 Enrollment: 151 . . . . (330) 308-5720
Kent State University-Tuscarawas Campus (Public)
Fall 2004 Enrollment: 1,935. . . . . (330) 339-3391
2005-06 Tuition: In-state $4,586; Out-of-state $12,018

Housing: Homeownership rate: 66.4% (2005); Median home value: $101,135 (2005); Median rent: $350 per month (2000); Median age of housing: 44 years (2000).
Safety: Violent crime rate: 6.9 per 10,000 population; Property crime rate: 104.0 per 10,000 population (2004).
Newspapers: The Times-Reporter (Circulation 23,693)
Transportation: Commute to work: 94.3% car, 0.1% public transportation, 1.2% walk, 2.0% work from home (2000); Travel time to work: 54.5% less than 15 minutes, 23.6% 15 to 30 minutes, 14.1% 30 to 45 minutes, 3.7% 45 to 60 minutes, 4.1% 60 minutes or more (2000)
Additional Information Contacts
City of New Philadelphia . . . . (330) 364-4491
http://www.newphilaoh.com
Tuscarawas County Chamber of Commerce. . . . . (330) 343-4474
http://www.tuschamber.com

NEWCOMERSTOWN (village).
Covers a land area of 2.475 square miles and a water area of 0.061 square miles. Located at 40.27° N. Lat.; 81.60° W. Long. Elevation is 806 feet.
History: First called Neighbor Town when it was settled in 1815 by the Neighbor brothers from New Jersey, the town became Newcomerstown in remembrance of Chief Eagle Feather who was called "the newcomer."
Population: 4,012 (1990); 4,008 (2000); 3,805 (2005); 3,667 (2010 projected); Race: 95.7% White, 2.6% Black, 0.1% Asian, 1.1% Hispanic of any race (2005); Density: 1,537.6 persons per square mile (2005); Average household size: 2.38 (2005); Median age: 38.8 (2005); Males per 100 females: 88.3 (2005); Marriage status: 19.6% never married, 55.7% now married, 12.7% widowed, 11.9% divorced (2000); Foreign born: 0.5% (2000); Ancestry (includes multiple ancestries): 19.8% German, 12.8% Irish, 10.8% Other groups, 10.6% English, 7.7% United States or American (2000).
Economy: Single-family building permits issued: 0 (2005); Multi-family building permits issued: 0 (2005); Employment by occupation: 5.8% management, 11.7% professional, 17.0% services, 20.0% sales, 1.4% farming, 9.7% construction, 34.4% production (2000).
Income: Per capita income: $17,418 (2005); Median household income: $32,438 (2005); Average household income: $40,523 (2005); Percent of households with income of $100,000 or more: 4.4% (2005); Poverty rate: 16.0% (2000).
Education: Percent of population age 25 and over with: High school diploma (including GED) or higher: 69.5% (2005); Bachelor's degree or higher: 5.9% (2005); Master's degree or higher: 2.1% (2005).
School District(s)
Newcomerstown Digital Academy
2003-04 Enrollment: n/a
Newcomerstown Ex Vill SD (PK-12)
2003-04 Enrollment: 1,308 . . . . (740) 498-8373
Housing: Homeownership rate: 67.2% (2005); Median home value: $66,920 (2005); Median rent: $280 per month (2000); Median age of housing: 56 years (2000).
Safety: Violent crime rate: 30.1 per 10,000 population; Property crime rate: 288.9 per 10,000 population (2004).
Newspapers: Newcomerstown News (General - Circulation 3,500)
Transportation: Commute to work: 93.4% car, 0.0% public transportation, 4.1% walk, 1.1% work from home (2000); Travel time to work: 47.9% less than 15 minutes, 18.5% 15 to 30 minutes, 20.5% 30 to 45 minutes, 6.0% 45 to 60 minutes, 7.0% 60 minutes or more (2000)
Additional Information Contacts
Newcomerstown Chamber of Commerce . . . . (740) 498-7244
http://www.newcomerstown.com
Village of Newcomerstown. . . . . (740) 492-0797
http://www.newcomerstown.com

PARRAL (village).
Covers a land area of 0.181 square miles and a water area of 0 square miles. Located at 40.56° N. Lat.; 81.49° W. Long. Elevation is 880 feet.
Population: 255 (1990); 241 (2000); 264 (2005); 284 (2010 projected); Race: 99.2% White, 0.0% Black, 0.0% Asian, 0.0% Hispanic of any race (2005); Density: 1,459.3 persons per square mile (2005); Average household size: 2.26 (2005); Median age: 43.1 (2005); Males per 100 females: 114.6 (2005); Marriage status: 14.0% never married, 67.4% now married, 4.7% widowed, 14.0% divorced (2000); Foreign born: 0.0% (2000); Ancestry (includes multiple ancestries): 32.2% German, 12.0% Italian, 12.0% Irish, 11.6% United States or American, 10.7% Swiss (2000).
Economy: Clay products. Single-family building permits issued: 0 (2005); Multi-family building permits issued: 0 (2005); Employment by occupation: 4.0% management, 12.8% professional, 13.6% services, 24.0% sales, 3.2% farming, 20.8% construction, 21.6% production (2000).
Income: Per capita income: $20,161 (2005); Median household income: $39,327 (2005); Average household income: $45,491 (2005); Percent of households with income of $100,000 or more: 4.3% (2005); Poverty rate: 7.0% (2000).
Education: Percent of population age 25 and over with: High school diploma (including GED) or higher: 90.0% (2005); Bachelor's degree or higher: 8.9% (2005); Master's degree or higher: 3.2% (2005).
Housing: Homeownership rate: 81.2% (2005); Median home value: $102,841 (2005); Median rent: $455 per month (2000); Median age of housing: 47 years (2000).
Transportation: Commute to work: 98.4% car, 0.0% public transportation, 0.0% walk, 0.0% work from home (2000); Travel time to work: 36.8% less than 15 minutes, 36.8% 15 to 30 minutes, 22.4% 30 to 45 minutes, 1.6% 45 to 60 minutes, 2.4% 60 minutes or more (2000)

PORT WASHINGTON (village).
Covers a land area of 0.506 square miles and a water area of 0 square miles. Located at 40.32° N. Lat.; 81.52° W. Long. Elevation is 820 feet.
History: Port Washington was once a shipping center on the Ohio & Erie Canal. Nearby was the settlement of Salem, established in 1780 for members of the Lichtenau community.
Population: 513 (1990); 552 (2000); 590 (2005); 628 (2010 projected); Race: 97.5% White, 0.2% Black, 0.0% Asian, 1.5% Hispanic of any race (2005); Density: 1,166.3 persons per square mile (2005); Average household size: 2.73 (2005); Median age: 38.4 (2005); Males per 100 females: 95.4 (2005); Marriage status: 19.0% never married, 66.4% now married, 4.2% widowed, 10.4% divorced (2000); Foreign born: 0.4% (2000); Ancestry (includes multiple ancestries): 29.8% German, 10.2% United States or American, 9.5% Irish, 7.5% Other groups, 5.5% English (2000).
Economy: Single-family building permits issued: 3 (2005); Multi-family building permits issued: 0 (2005); Employment by occupation: 2.9% management, 13.2% professional, 11.8% services, 23.9% sales, 1.1% farming, 11.0% construction, 36.0% production (2000).
Income: Per capita income: $14,928 (2005); Median household income: $39,792 (2005); Average household income: $40,775 (2005); Percent of households with income of $100,000 or more: 1.4% (2005); Poverty rate: 6.1% (2000).
Education: Percent of population age 25 and over with: High school diploma (including GED) or higher: 77.9% (2005); Bachelor's degree or higher: 5.9% (2005); Master's degree or higher: 1.3% (2005).
School District(s)
Indian Valley Local SD (PK-12)
2003-04 Enrollment: 1,916 . . . . (740) 254-4334
Housing: Homeownership rate: 80.6% (2005); Median home value: $74,043 (2005); Median rent: $332 per month (2000); Median age of housing: 60+ years (2000).
Transportation: Commute to work: 92.5% car, 1.1% public transportation, 1.5% walk, 1.5% work from home (2000); Travel time to work: 31.4% less than 15 minutes, 29.5% 15 to 30 minutes, 27.3% 30 to 45 minutes, 3.4% 45 to 60 minutes, 8.3% 60 minutes or more (2000)

ROSWELL (village).
Covers a land area of 0.272 square miles and a water area of 0 square miles. Located at 40.47° N. Lat.; 81.35° W. Long. Elevation is 960 feet.
Population: 257 (1990); 276 (2000); 309 (2005); 339 (2010 projected); Race: 98.7% White, 0.0% Black, 0.0% Asian, 0.0% Hispanic of any race (2005); Density: 1,135.4 persons per square mile (2005); Average household size: 2.94 (2005); Median age: 32.7 (2005); Males per 100

females: 102.0 (2005); Marriage status: 26.5% never married, 62.1% now married, 2.4% widowed, 9.0% divorced (2000); Foreign born: 0.0% (2000); Ancestry (includes multiple ancestries): 23.7% German, 17.3% Italian, 14.8% English, 12.7% Irish, 11.7% United States or American (2000).
Economy: In agricultural area. Employment by occupation: 6.7% management, 5.7% professional, 17.1% services, 17.1% sales, 0.0% farming, 8.6% construction, 44.8% production (2000).
Income: Per capita income: $12,087 (2005); Median household income: $28,667 (2005); Average household income: $35,571 (2005); Percent of households with income of $100,000 or more: 2.9% (2005); Poverty rate: 21.6% (2000).
Education: Percent of population age 25 and over with: High school diploma (including GED) or higher: 57.8% (2005); Bachelor's degree or higher: 2.8% (2005); Master's degree or higher: 1.1% (2005).
Housing: Homeownership rate: 81.0% (2005); Median home value: $57,826 (2005); Median rent: $329 per month (2000); Median age of housing: 59 years (2000).
Transportation: Commute to work: 95.2% car, 0.0% public transportation, 2.9% walk, 1.9% work from home (2000); Travel time to work: 10.7% less than 15 minutes, 64.1% 15 to 30 minutes, 8.7% 30 to 45 minutes, 16.5% 45 to 60 minutes, 0.0% 60 minutes or more (2000)

STONE CREEK (village).
Covers a land area of 0.431 square miles and a water area of <.001 square miles. Located at 40.39° N. Lat.; 81.55° W. Long. Elevation is 960 feet.
History: Stone Creek was laid out in 1854 by Phillip Leonard, and first called Phillipsburg. Settlers had come here as early as 1837 from Pennsylvania. The town grew around the iron ore mined in the area, and the clay used in brick plants. Early Swiss settlers also started a Swiss cheese industry.
Population: 181 (1990); 184 (2000); 184 (2005); 179 (2010 projected); Race: 100.0% White, 0.0% Black, 0.0% Asian, 0.0% Hispanic of any race (2005); Density: 426.9 persons per square mile (2005); Average household size: 2.75 (2005); Median age: 34.1 (2005); Males per 100 females: 93.7 (2005); Marriage status: 16.4% never married, 59.0% now married, 15.6% widowed, 9.0% divorced (2000); Foreign born: 0.0% (2000); Ancestry (includes multiple ancestries): 40.6% German, 15.0% United States or American, 10.0% English, 9.4% Irish, 4.4% Other groups (2000).
Economy: Single-family building permits issued: 0 (2005); Multi-family building permits issued: 0 (2005); Employment by occupation: 6.0% management, 7.5% professional, 19.4% services, 28.4% sales, 0.0% farming, 20.9% construction, 17.9% production (2000).
Income: Per capita income: $16,223 (2005); Median household income: $32,308 (2005); Average household income: $44,552 (2005); Percent of households with income of $100,000 or more: 7.5% (2005); Poverty rate: 8.8% (2000).
Education: Percent of population age 25 and over with: High school diploma (including GED) or higher: 76.8% (2005); Bachelor's degree or higher: 11.6% (2005); Master's degree or higher: 0.0% (2005).
Housing: Homeownership rate: 77.6% (2005); Median home value: $78,333 (2005); Median rent: $342 per month (2000); Median age of housing: 60+ years (2000).
Transportation: Commute to work: 97.0% car, 0.0% public transportation, 0.0% walk, 0.0% work from home (2000); Travel time to work: 14.9% less than 15 minutes, 53.7% 15 to 30 minutes, 9.0% 30 to 45 minutes, 17.9% 45 to 60 minutes, 4.5% 60 minutes or more (2000)

STRASBURG (village).
Covers a land area of 1.193 square miles and a water area of 0 square miles. Located at 40.59° N. Lat.; 81.52° W. Long. Elevation is 920 feet.
History: Strasburg was notable as the location of the Garver Brothers Store, founded in 1866 by Phillip A. Garver. When his sons, Rudolph and Albert, took over the store in the 1880's, they made it the focal point of the community by keeping a card index record of every man, woman, and child living within 18 miles of Strasburg, and anticipating their needs.
Population: 2,032 (1990); 2,310 (2000); 2,352 (2005); 2,403 (2010 projected); Race: 97.3% White, 0.1% Black, 0.1% Asian, 2.9% Hispanic of any race (2005); Density: 1,972.0 persons per square mile (2005); Average household size: 2.42 (2005); Median age: 37.5 (2005); Males per 100 females: 96.2 (2005); Marriage status: 20.6% never married, 62.2% now married, 6.1% widowed, 11.1% divorced (2000); Foreign born: 1.3% (2000); Ancestry (includes multiple ancestries): 38.7% German, 11.9% Irish, 10.3% English, 8.1% United States or American, 6.0% Italian (2000).
Economy: Single-family building permits issued: 27 (2005); Multi-family building permits issued: 0 (2005); Employment by occupation: 8.7% management, 14.7% professional, 16.8% services, 23.5% sales, 0.3% farming, 8.1% construction, 28.1% production (2000).
Income: Per capita income: $18,310 (2005); Median household income: $39,492 (2005); Average household income: $44,349 (2005); Percent of households with income of $100,000 or more: 4.8% (2005); Poverty rate: 8.2% (2000).
Education: Percent of population age 25 and over with: High school diploma (including GED) or higher: 83.5% (2005); Bachelor's degree or higher: 11.3% (2005); Master's degree or higher: 3.7% (2005).
School District(s)
Strasburg-Franklin Local SD (PK-12)
    2003-04 Enrollment: 721 . . . . (330) 878-5571
Housing: Homeownership rate: 63.1% (2005); Median home value: $105,682 (2005); Median rent: $360 per month (2000); Median age of housing: 41 years (2000).
Transportation: Commute to work: 95.0% car, 0.0% public transportation, 2.1% walk, 2.4% work from home (2000); Travel time to work: 31.5% less than 15 minutes, 41.5% 15 to 30 minutes, 19.0% 30 to 45 minutes, 3.9% 45 to 60 minutes, 4.1% 60 minutes or more (2000)

SUGARCREEK (village).
Aka Sugar Creek Station. Covers a land area of 3.799 square miles and a water area of 0 square miles. Located at 40.50° N. Lat.; 81.64° W. Long. Elevation is 1,000 feet.
Population: 2,296 (1990); 2,174 (2000); 2,001 (2005); 1,921 (2010 projected); Race: 99.1% White, 0.1% Black, 0.5% Asian, 0.1% Hispanic of any race (2005); Density: 526.7 persons per square mile (2005); Average household size: 2.48 (2005); Median age: 37.6 (2005); Males per 100 females: 95.0 (2005); Marriage status: 19.9% never married, 68.2% now married, 8.9% widowed, 2.9% divorced (2000); Foreign born: 0.0% (2000); Ancestry (includes multiple ancestries): 40.4% German, 16.7% Swiss, 10.2% United States or American, 7.2% Irish, 6.4% English (2000).
Economy: Single-family building permits issued: 10 (2005); Multi-family building permits issued: 0 (2005); Employment by occupation: 9.7% management, 12.0% professional, 12.8% services, 32.5% sales, 0.5% farming, 9.0% construction, 23.5% production (2000).
Income: Per capita income: $18,093 (2005); Median household income: $40,625 (2005); Average household income: $44,864 (2005); Percent of households with income of $100,000 or more: 6.4% (2005); Poverty rate: 7.2% (2000).
Education: Percent of population age 25 and over with: High school diploma (including GED) or higher: 69.9% (2005); Bachelor's degree or higher: 12.7% (2005); Master's degree or higher: 4.9% (2005).
School District(s)
Garaway Local SD (PK-12)
    2003-04 Enrollment: 1,238 . . . . (330) 852-2421
Housing: Homeownership rate: 72.2% (2005); Median home value: $120,429 (2005); Median rent: $346 per month (2000); Median age of housing: 39 years (2000).
Newspapers: The Budget (General - Circulation 20,000)
Transportation: Commute to work: 92.7% car, 0.0% public transportation, 4.2% walk, 2.0% work from home (2000); Travel time to work: 51.7% less than 15 minutes, 31.2% 15 to 30 minutes, 6.1% 30 to 45 minutes, 5.7% 45 to 60 minutes, 5.2% 60 minutes or more (2000)

TUSCARAWAS (village).
Covers a land area of 0.709 square miles and a water area of 0.020 square miles. Located at 40.39° N. Lat.; 81.40° W. Long. Elevation is 850 feet.
Population: 879 (1990); 934 (2000); 999 (2005); 1,061 (2010 projected); Race: 98.7% White, 0.0% Black, 0.3% Asian, 0.0% Hispanic of any race (2005); Density: 1,409.9 persons per square mile (2005); Average household size: 2.47 (2005); Median age: 40.3 (2005); Males per 100 females: 94.4 (2005); Marriage status: 19.5% never married, 61.1% now married, 9.0% widowed, 10.4% divorced (2000); Foreign born: 0.4% (2000); Ancestry (includes multiple ancestries): 32.0% German, 11.8% Irish, 11.7% English, 8.1% United States or American, 6.9% Italian (2000).
Economy: Single-family building permits issued: 2 (2005); Multi-family building permits issued: 0 (2005); Employment by occupation: 7.2% management, 9.6% professional, 19.2% services, 24.0% sales, 0.0% farming, 9.6% construction, 30.5% production (2000).
Income: Per capita income: $17,125 (2005); Median household income: $36,791 (2005); Average household income: $42,345 (2005); Percent of households with income of $100,000 or more: 2.2% (2005); Poverty rate: 7.4% (2000).

Education: Percent of population age 25 and over with: High school diploma (including GED) or higher: 81.0% (2005); Bachelor's degree or higher: 7.8% (2005); Master's degree or higher: 1.8% (2005).

School District(s)

Indian Valley Local SD (PK-12)
    2003-04 Enrollment: 1,916 . . . . (740) 254-4334

Housing: Homeownership rate: 84.2% (2005); Median home value: $97,681 (2005); Median rent: $338 per month (2000); Median age of housing: 47 years (2000).

Transportation: Commute to work: 94.7% car, 0.4% public transportation, 1.3% walk, 2.9% work from home (2000); Travel time to work: 36.0% less than 15 minutes, 45.4% 15 to 30 minutes, 8.7% 30 to 45 minutes, 4.8% 45 to 60 minutes, 5.0% 60 minutes or more (2000)

UHRICHSVILLE (city). Covers a land area of 2.858 square miles and a water area of 0.007 square miles. Located at 40.39° N. Lat.; 81.34° W. Long. Elevation is 860 feet.

History: Uhrichsville was settled in 1804 by Michael Uhrich of Pennsylvania, who purchased land in the area and built a flour mill. The town was platted in 1833 and became a center for the manufacture of vitrified clay products.

Population: 5,616 (1990); 5,662 (2000); 5,582 (2005); 5,513 (2010 projected); Race: 97.5% White, 0.9% Black, 0.2% Asian, 1.0% Hispanic of any race (2005); Density: 1,952.9 persons per square mile (2005); Average household size: 2.49 (2005); Median age: 35.3 (2005); Males per 100 females: 92.7 (2005); Marriage status: 21.1% never married, 55.3% now married, 9.9% widowed, 13.7% divorced (2000); Foreign born: 1.0% (2000); Ancestry (includes multiple ancestries): 22.3% German, 13.6% Irish, 10.0% United States or American, 9.9% Other groups, 8.7% English (2000).

Economy: Single-family building permits issued: 0 (2005); Multi-family building permits issued: 0 (2005); Employment by occupation: 6.5% management, 8.9% professional, 18.5% services, 21.8% sales, 0.0% farming, 9.9% construction, 34.5% production (2000).

Income: Per capita income: $13,964 (2005); Median household income: $29,230 (2005); Average household income: $34,684 (2005); Percent of households with income of $100,000 or more: 2.9% (2005); Poverty rate: 14.6% (2000).

Education: Percent of population age 25 and over with: High school diploma (including GED) or higher: 76.5% (2005); Bachelor's degree or higher: 6.2% (2005); Master's degree or higher: 3.7% (2005).

School District(s)

Claymont City SD (PK-12)
    2003-04 Enrollment: 2,346 . . . . (740) 922-5478

Housing: Homeownership rate: 65.8% (2005); Median home value: $72,178 (2005); Median rent: $319 per month (2000); Median age of housing: 59 years (2000).

Safety: Violent crime rate: 10.5 per 10,000 population; Property crime rate: 390.7 per 10,000 population (2004).

Transportation: Commute to work: 96.2% car, 0.2% public transportation, 3.3% walk, 0.3% work from home (2000); Travel time to work: 40.0% less than 15 minutes, 32.3% 15 to 30 minutes, 10.9% 30 to 45 minutes, 9.8% 45 to 60 minutes, 7.0% 60 minutes or more (2000)

Additional Information Contacts

Uhrichsville Chamber of Commerce . . . . (740) 922-5623
http://www.twincitychamber.org

ZOAR (village). Covers a land area of 0.550 square miles and a water area of 0.091 square miles. Located at 40.61° N. Lat.; 81.42° W. Long. Elevation is 930 feet.

History: Named for the biblical city to which Lot fled after leaving Sodom, Zoar was settled in 1817 by a group of Separatists from southern Germany who came seeking religious freedom. They established a communal corporation, chartered in 1832 as the Separatist Society of Zoar, which prospered for 80 years.

Population: 177 (1990); 193 (2000); 187 (2005); 185 (2010 projected); Race: 97.3% White, 0.0% Black, 1.6% Asian, 1.1% Hispanic of any race (2005); Density: 339.9 persons per square mile (2005); Average household size: 2.43 (2005); Median age: 50.1 (2005); Males per 100 females: 88.9 (2005); Marriage status: 15.2% never married, 62.9% now married, 9.9% widowed, 11.9% divorced (2000); Foreign born: 1.0% (2000); Ancestry (includes multiple ancestries): 39.1% German, 16.2% Irish, 11.7% English, 6.6% United States or American, 6.6% Italian (2000).

Economy: Single-family building permits issued: 1 (2005); Multi-family building permits issued: 0 (2005); Employment by occupation: 15.1% management, 26.7% professional, 16.3% services, 15.1% sales, 0.0% farming, 3.5% construction, 23.3% production (2000).

Income: Per capita income: $28,623 (2005); Median household income: $58,594 (2005); Average household income: $69,513 (2005); Percent of households with income of $100,000 or more: 19.5% (2005); Poverty rate: 3.6% (2000).

Education: Percent of population age 25 and over with: High school diploma (including GED) or higher: 92.9% (2005); Bachelor's degree or higher: 25.5% (2005); Master's degree or higher: 9.2% (2005).

Housing: Homeownership rate: 88.3% (2005); Median home value: $175,000 (2005); Median rent: $400 per month (2000); Median age of housing: 44 years (2000).

Transportation: Commute to work: 96.4% car, 0.0% public transportation, 0.0% walk, 0.0% work from home (2000); Travel time to work: 27.4% less than 15 minutes, 52.4% 15 to 30 minutes, 16.7% 30 to 45 minutes, 1.2% 45 to 60 minutes, 2.4% 60 minutes or more (2000)

Union County

Located in central Ohio; drained by Darby Creek. Covers a land area of 436.65 square miles, a water area of 0.33 square miles, and is located in the Eastern Time Zone. The county government was organized in 1820. County seat is Marysville.

Union County is part of the Columbus, OH Metropolitan Statistical Area. The entire metro area includes: Delaware County, OH; Fairfield County, OH; Franklin County, OH; Licking County, OH; Madison County, OH; Morrow County, OH; Pickaway County, OH; Union County, OH

Weather Station: Irwin   Elevation: 1,007 feet

	Jan	Feb	Mar	Apr	May	Jun	Jul	Aug	Sep	Oct	Nov	Dec
High	35	40	52	64	74	82	86	84	78	67	52	40
Low	17	20	29	38	49	58	61	59	52	41	33	23
Precip	2.3	1.9	2.6	3.5	4.1	4.3	4.7	3.7	2.9	2.6	3.1	2.7
Snow	6.8	4.5	2.5	0.8	tr	0.0	0.0	0.0	0.0	tr	1.0	na

High and Low temperatures in degrees Fahrenheit; Precipitation and Snow in inches

Weather Station: Marysville   Elevation: 997 feet

	Jan	Feb	Mar	Apr	May	Jun	Jul	Aug	Sep	Oct	Nov	Dec
High	34	38	49	61	72	80	84	82	76	63	50	39
Low	18	21	29	39	50	59	63	61	54	42	33	24
Precip	2.3	1.9	2.6	3.4	3.9	4.3	4.1	3.3	2.6	2.4	3.0	2.7
Snow	6.5	4.8	3.3	0.9	0.0	0.0	0.0	0.0	0.0	tr	1.1	3.6

High and Low temperatures in degrees Fahrenheit; Precipitation and Snow in inches

Population: 31,969 (1990); 40,909 (2000); 44,857 (2005); 48,993 (2010 projected); Race: 94.9% White, 2.8% Black, 0.9% Asian, 0.9% Hispanic of any race (2005); Density: 102.7 persons per square mile (2005); Average household size: 2.83 (2005); Median age: 35.5 (2005); Males per 100 females: 93.3 (2005).

Religion: Five largest groups: 8.8% The United Methodist Church, 4.8% Lutheran Church—Missouri Synod, 4.6% Evangelical Lutheran Church in America, 3.8% Catholic Church, 2.4% Presbyterian Church (U.S.A.) (2000).

Economy: Unemployment rate: 4.9% (2005); Total civilian labor force: 23,920 (2005); Leading industries: 35.9% manufacturing; 12.1% administration (2004); Farms: 1,021 totaling 256,024 acres (2002); Companies that employ 500 or more persons: 6 (2004); Companies that employ 100 to 499 persons: 23 (2004); Companies that employ less than 100 persons: 880 (2004); Black-owned businesses: n/a (2002); Hispanic-owned businesses: n/a (2002); Women-owned businesses: 798 (2002); Retail sales per capita: $11,098 (2006). Single-family building permits issued: 440 (2005); Multi-family building permits issued: 0 (2005).

Income: Per capita income: $23,651 (2005); Median household income: $58,732 (2005); Average household income: $65,806 (2005); Percent of households with income of $100,000 or more: 17.2% (2005); Poverty rate: 6.0% (2003); Bankruptcy rate: 9.92% (2005).

Taxes: Total county taxes per capita: $436 (2004); County property taxes per capita: $232 (2004).

Education: Percent of population age 25 and over with: High school diploma (including GED) or higher: 86.5% (2005); Bachelor's degree or higher: 16.5% (2005); Master's degree or higher: 4.2% (2005).

Housing: Homeownership rate: 78.5% (2005); Median home value: $154,399 (2005); Median rent: $455 per month (2000); Median age of housing: 27 years (2000).

Health: Birth rate: 133.7 per 10,000 population (2004); Death rate: 67.5 per 10,000 population (2004); Age-adjusted cancer mortality rate: 205.7 deaths per 100,000 population (2002); Number of physicians: 9.8 per 10,000 population (2004); Hospital beds: 18.5 per 10,000 population (2003); Hospital admissions: 665.7 per 10,000 population (2003).
Elections: 2004 Presidential election results: 70.1% Bush, 29.5% Kerry, 0.0% Nader, 0.3% Badnarik
Additional Information Contacts
Union County Government . . . . (937) 645-3012
http://www.co.union.oh.us/
Marysville Chamber of Commerce. . . . . (937) 642-6279
http://www.unioncounty.org

Union County Communities

IRWIN (unincorporated postal area, zip code 43029). Covers a land area of 23.353 square miles and a water area of 0 square miles. Located at 40.10° N. Lat.; 83.44° W. Long. Elevation is 1,012 feet.
Population: 621 (2000); **Race:** 99.2% White, 0.0% Black, 0.0% Asian, 0.0% Hispanic of any race (2000); **Density:** 26.6 persons per square mile (2000); **Age:** 32.9% under 18, 3.4% over 64 (2000); **Marriage status:** 38.9% never married, 57.3% now married, 1.7% widowed, 2.1% divorced (2000); **Foreign born:** 0.0% (2000); **Ancestry** (includes multiple ancestries): 37.5% German, 9.5% United States or American, 9.3% Hungarian, 8.3% Swiss, 6.6% English (2000).
Economy: Employment by occupation: 21.2% management, 4.3% professional, 12.2% services, 36.5% sales, 0.0% farming, 7.8% construction, 18.0% production (2000).
Income: Per capita income: $14,205 (2000); Median household income: $44,583 (2000); Poverty rate: 0.0% (2000).
Education: Percent of population age 25 and over with: High school diploma (including GED) or higher: 82.6% (2000); Bachelor's degree or higher: 21.8% (2000).
Two-year College(s)
Rosedale Bible College
  Fall 2004 Enrollment: 83 . . . . (740) 857-1311
  2005-06 Tuition: In-state $4,635; Out-of-state $4,635
Housing: Homeownership rate: 65.3% (2000); Median home value: $133,000 (2000); Median rent: $321 per month (2000); Median age of housing: 44 years (2000).
Transportation: Commute to work: 85.4% car, 0.0% public transportation, 6.5% walk, 6.8% work from home (2000); Travel time to work: 22.4% less than 15 minutes, 45.4% 15 to 30 minutes, 12.1% 30 to 45 minutes, 18.5% 45 to 60 minutes, 1.6% 60 minutes or more (2000)

MAGNETIC SPRINGS (village). Covers a land area of 0.244 square miles and a water area of 0 square miles. Located at 40.35° N. Lat.; 83.26° W. Long. Elevation is 944 feet.
Population: 373 (1990); 323 (2000); 327 (2005); 333 (2010 projected); **Race:** 97.2% White, 0.0% Black, 0.9% Asian, 0.0% Hispanic of any race (2005); **Density:** 1,341.4 persons per square mile (2005); Average household size: 2.73 (2005); Median age: 33.1 (2005); Males per 100 females: 105.7 (2005); Marriage status: 30.1% never married, 51.0% now married, 6.4% widowed, 12.4% divorced (2000); Foreign born: 0.3% (2000); Ancestry (includes multiple ancestries): 13.8% English, 13.8% German, 11.5% United States or American, 8.2% Irish, 5.6% Italian (2000).
Economy: Employment by occupation: 7.2% management, 10.5% professional, 21.6% services, 7.8% sales, 1.3% farming, 13.7% construction, 37.9% production (2000).
Income: Per capita income: $18,937 (2005); Median household income: $42,778 (2005); Average household income: $51,604 (2005); Percent of households with income of $100,000 or more: 7.5% (2005); Poverty rate: 6.0% (2000).
Education: Percent of population age 25 and over with: High school diploma (including GED) or higher: 72.9% (2005); Bachelor's degree or higher: 4.9% (2005); Master's degree or higher: 0.0% (2005).
School District(s)
North Union Local SD (PK-12)
  2003-04 Enrollment: 1,476 . . . . (740) 943-2509
Housing: Homeownership rate: 59.2% (2005); Median home value: $95,625 (2005); Median rent: $370 per month (2000); Median age of housing: 60+ years (2000).
Transportation: Commute to work: 96.0% car, 0.0% public transportation, 4.0% walk, 0.0% work from home (2000); Travel time to work: 16.8% less than 15 minutes, 53.0% 15 to 30 minutes, 13.4% 30 to 45 minutes, 13.4% 45 to 60 minutes, 3.4% 60 minutes or more (2000)

MARYSVILLE (city). Covers a land area of 15.526 square miles and a water area of 0.076 square miles. Located at 40.23° N. Lat.; 83.36° W. Long. Elevation is 991 feet.
History: Marysville was settled in 1816 by Jonathan Summers, and platted in 1820 by Samuel Culbertson, who named the town for his daughter. The log cabin that became a symbol of William Henry Harrison's presidential campaign of 1840 came from Marysville.
Population: 11,003 (1990); 15,942 (2000); 16,828 (2005); 17,862 (2010 projected); **Race:** 90.5% White, 6.3% Black, 1.6% Asian, 1.2% Hispanic of any race (2005); **Density:** 1,083.8 persons per square mile (2005); Average household size: 2.86 (2005); Median age: 32.5 (2005); Males per 100 females: 79.1 (2005); Marriage status: 24.0% never married, 56.4% now married, 6.1% widowed, 13.6% divorced (2000); Foreign born: 1.3% (2000); Ancestry (includes multiple ancestries): 28.2% German, 13.3% Irish, 12.8% Other groups, 10.3% English, 10.2% United States or American (2000).
Economy: Employment by occupation: 10.9% management, 17.0% professional, 12.4% services, 28.1% sales, 0.3% farming, 7.0% construction, 24.3% production (2000).
Income: Per capita income: $21,313 (2005); Median household income: $52,813 (2005); Average household income: $58,250 (2005); Percent of households with income of $100,000 or more: 12.6% (2005); Poverty rate: 5.7% (2000).
Education: Percent of population age 25 and over with: High school diploma (including GED) or higher: 84.4% (2005); Bachelor's degree or higher: 17.7% (2005); Master's degree or higher: 3.3% (2005).
School District(s)
Marysville Digital Academy
  2003-04 Enrollment: n/a . . . . (937) 644-8105
Marysville Exempted Village School District (PK-12)
  2003-04 Enrollment: 4,721 . . . . (937) 644-8105
Housing: Homeownership rate: 65.6% (2005); Median home value: $148,466 (2005); Median rent: $471 per month (2000); Median age of housing: 20 years (2000).
Hospitals: Memorial Hospital (82 beds)
Safety: Violent crime rate: 8.6 per 10,000 population; Property crime rate: 324.4 per 10,000 population (2004).
Newspapers: Marysville Journal-Tribune (Circulation 63,000)
Transportation: Commute to work: 95.2% car, 0.2% public transportation, 1.8% walk, 2.1% work from home (2000); Travel time to work: 41.0% less than 15 minutes, 33.7% 15 to 30 minutes, 16.4% 30 to 45 minutes, 5.3% 45 to 60 minutes, 3.7% 60 minutes or more (2000)
Additional Information Contacts
Marysville Chamber of Commerce. . . . . (937) 642-6279
http://www.unioncounty.org

MILFORD CENTER (village). Covers a land area of 0.354 square miles and a water area of 0 square miles. Located at 40.17° N. Lat.; 83.43° W. Long. Elevation is 990 feet.
Population: 651 (1990); 626 (2000); 694 (2005); 764 (2010 projected); **Race:** 98.8% White, 0.0% Black, 0.0% Asian, 0.7% Hispanic of any race (2005); **Density:** 1,963.2 persons per square mile (2005); Average household size: 2.65 (2005); Median age: 35.1 (2005); Males per 100 females: 100.0 (2005); Marriage status: 22.2% never married, 57.6% now married, 10.1% widowed, 10.1% divorced (2000); Foreign born: 0.0% (2000); Ancestry (includes multiple ancestries): 29.4% German, 19.2% United States or American, 11.9% English, 9.0% Irish, 8.5% Other groups (2000).
Economy: In agricultural area. Employment by occupation: 7.3% management, 6.4% professional, 22.4% services, 23.6% sales, 0.0% farming, 10.5% construction, 29.7% production (2000).
Income: Per capita income: $20,551 (2005); Median household income: $46,875 (2005); Average household income: $54,437 (2005); Percent of households with income of $100,000 or more: 10.3% (2005); Poverty rate: 1.0% (2000).
Education: Percent of population age 25 and over with: High school diploma (including GED) or higher: 79.1% (2005); Bachelor's degree or higher: 5.1% (2005); Master's degree or higher: 2.0% (2005).
School District(s)
Fairbanks Local SD (PK-12)
  2003-04 Enrollment: 928 . . . . (937) 349-3731

Housing: Homeownership rate: 82.8% (2005); Median home value: $92,449 (2005); Median rent: $486 per month (2000); Median age of housing: 60+ years (2000).
Transportation: Commute to work: 91.8% car, 0.7% public transportation, 2.9% walk, 2.6% work from home (2000); Travel time to work: 27.2% less than 15 minutes, 44.6% 15 to 30 minutes, 17.4% 30 to 45 minutes, 7.0% 45 to 60 minutes, 3.7% 60 minutes or more (2000)

RAYMOND (unincorporated postal area, zip code 43067). Aka Raymonds. Covers a land area of 30.775 square miles and a water area of 0.036 square miles. Located at 40.35° N. Lat.; 83.46° W. Long. Elevation is 1,030 feet.
Population: 1,537 (2000); Race: 100.0% White, 0.0% Black, 0.0% Asian, 0.0% Hispanic of any race (2000); Density: 49.9 persons per square mile (2000); Age: 31.6% under 18, 6.9% over 64 (2000); Marriage status: 16.1% never married, 69.8% now married, 2.7% widowed, 11.4% divorced (2000); Foreign born: 0.9% (2000); Ancestry (includes multiple ancestries): 20.8% United States or American, 16.7% German, 7.1% Irish, 6.5% Other groups, 4.4% Scottish (2000).
Economy: Employment by occupation: 4.8% management, 10.5% professional, 13.0% services, 25.9% sales, 1.5% farming, 11.6% construction, 32.6% production (2000).
Income: Per capita income: $18,194 (2000); Median household income: $52,138 (2000); Poverty rate: 5.4% (2000).
Education: Percent of population age 25 and over with: High school diploma (including GED) or higher: 87.6% (2000); Bachelor's degree or higher: 6.4% (2000).

School District(s)
Marysville Exempted Village School District (PK-12)
    2003-04 Enrollment: 4,721 . . . . (937) 644-8105
Housing: Homeownership rate: 89.9% (2000); Median home value: $99,500 (2000); Median rent: $521 per month (2000); Median age of housing: 39 years (2000).
Transportation: Commute to work: 97.8% car, 0.0% public transportation, 1.3% walk, 0.9% work from home (2000); Travel time to work: 26.9% less than 15 minutes, 50.9% 15 to 30 minutes, 10.0% 30 to 45 minutes, 6.9% 45 to 60 minutes, 5.4% 60 minutes or more (2000)

RICHWOOD (village). Covers a land area of 1.201 square miles and a water area of 0.019 square miles. Located at 40.42° N. Lat.; 83.29° W. Long. Elevation is 952 feet.
Population: 2,232 (1990); 2,156 (2000); 2,251 (2005); 2,360 (2010 projected); Race: 98.0% White, 0.2% Black, 0.1% Asian, 0.4% Hispanic of any race (2005); Density: 1,874.3 persons per square mile (2005); Average household size: 2.54 (2005); Median age: 33.4 (2005); Males per 100 females: 92.6 (2005); Marriage status: 21.0% never married, 57.7% now married, 10.7% widowed, 10.6% divorced (2000); Foreign born: 0.5% (2000); Ancestry (includes multiple ancestries): 19.5% German, 15.6% United States or American, 12.5% Irish, 7.7% Other groups, 6.8% English (2000).
Economy: In agricultural area. Food processing; metal products. Employment by occupation: 7.2% management, 11.7% professional, 20.1% services, 21.4% sales, 0.6% farming, 10.2% construction, 29.0% production (2000).
Income: Per capita income: $18,502 (2005); Median household income: $41,737 (2005); Average household income: $47,006 (2005); Percent of households with income of $100,000 or more: 6.1% (2005); Poverty rate: 8.4% (2000).
Education: Percent of population age 25 and over with: High school diploma (including GED) or higher: 81.7% (2005); Bachelor's degree or higher: 6.8% (2005); Master's degree or higher: 2.1% (2005).

School District(s)
North Union Local SD (PK-12)
    2003-04 Enrollment: 1,476 . . . . (740) 943-2509
Housing: Homeownership rate: 68.2% (2005); Median home value: $98,968 (2005); Median rent: $340 per month (2000); Median age of housing: 55 years (2000).
Newspapers: Richwood Gazette (General - Circulation 3,050)
Transportation: Commute to work: 94.7% car, 0.2% public transportation, 3.7% walk, 1.4% work from home (2000); Travel time to work: 22.6% less than 15 minutes, 41.0% 15 to 30 minutes, 22.9% 30 to 45 minutes, 7.9% 45 to 60 minutes, 5.6% 60 minutes or more (2000)

UNIONVILLE CENTER (village). Aka Unionville. Covers a land area of 0.160 square miles and a water area of 0 square miles. Located at 40.13° N. Lat.; 83.34° W. Long. Elevation is 970 feet.
Population: 238 (1990); 299 (2000); 321 (2005); 343 (2010 projected); Race: 99.4% White, 0.0% Black, 0.0% Asian, 0.9% Hispanic of any race (2005); Density: 2,012.4 persons per square mile (2005); Average household size: 2.68 (2005); Median age: 39.6 (2005); Males per 100 females: 108.4 (2005); Marriage status: 13.0% never married, 72.5% now married, 6.7% widowed, 7.8% divorced (2000); Foreign born: 0.0% (2000); Ancestry (includes multiple ancestries): 25.3% German, 20.8% Irish, 13.0% Other groups, 6.3% Dutch, 5.9% United States or American (2000).
Economy: Employment by occupation: 7.2% management, 2.9% professional, 15.1% services, 30.9% sales, 0.0% farming, 15.1% construction, 28.8% production (2000).
Income: Per capita income: $20,615 (2005); Median household income: $53,378 (2005); Average household income: $55,146 (2005); Percent of households with income of $100,000 or more: 5.8% (2005); Poverty rate: 6.3% (2000).
Education: Percent of population age 25 and over with: High school diploma (including GED) or higher: 85.0% (2005); Bachelor's degree or higher: 3.3% (2005); Master's degree or higher: 0.9% (2005).
Housing: Homeownership rate: 84.2% (2005); Median home value: $99,211 (2005); Median rent: $317 per month (2000); Median age of housing: 60+ years (2000).
Transportation: Commute to work: 97.0% car, 0.0% public transportation, 1.5% walk, 0.0% work from home (2000); Travel time to work: 18.5% less than 15 minutes, 31.9% 15 to 30 minutes, 35.6% 30 to 45 minutes, 11.9% 45 to 60 minutes, 2.2% 60 minutes or more (2000)

Van Wert County

Located in western Ohio; bounded on the west by Indiana; drained by the Little Auglaize River. Covers a land area of 410.09 square miles, a water area of 0.40 square miles, and is located in the Eastern Time Zone. The county government was organized in 1820. County seat is Van Wert.

Van Wert County is part of the Van Wert, OH Micropolitan Statistical Area. The entire metro area includes: Van Wert County, OH

Weather Station: Van Wert 1 S   Elevation: 787 feet

	Jan	Feb	Mar	Apr	May	Jun	Jul	Aug	Sep	Oct	Nov	Dec
High	32	36	48	61	73	81	85	83	77	64	50	38
Low	17	19	28	38	50	59	63	61	53	42	33	23
Precip	2.0	1.8	2.7	3.6	3.8	4.2	3.9	3.3	2.9	2.6	3.1	2.7
Snow	9.3	6.8	2.8	1.2	0.0	0.0	0.0	0.0	0.0	0.2	1.8	7.7

High and Low temperatures in degrees Fahrenheit; Precipitation and Snow in inches

Population: 30,464 (1990); 29,659 (2000); 29,186 (2005); 28,697 (2010 projected); Race: 97.3% White, 0.8% Black, 0.3% Asian, 1.7% Hispanic of any race (2005); Density: 71.2 persons per square mile (2005); Average household size: 2.52 (2005); Median age: 38.6 (2005); Males per 100 females: 95.3 (2005).
Religion: Five largest groups: 13.9% The United Methodist Church, 9.0% Catholic Church, 4.8% Lutheran Church—Missouri Synod, 4.1% Evangelical Lutheran Church in America, 2.9% Presbyterian Church (U.S.A.) (2000).
Economy: Unemployment rate: 5.2% (2005); Total civilian labor force: 15,242 (2005); Leading industries: 39.3% manufacturing; 15.2% health care and social assistance; 13.4% retail trade (2004); Farms: 681 totaling 250,224 acres (2002); Companies that employ 500 or more persons: 4 (2004); Companies that employ 100 to 499 persons: 11 (2004); Companies that employ less than 100 persons: 583 (2004); Black-owned businesses: n/a (2002); Hispanic-owned businesses: n/a (2002); Women-owned businesses: 411 (2002); Retail sales per capita: $12,595 (2006); Single-family building permits issued: 67 (2005); Multi-family building permits issued: 0 (2005).
Income: Per capita income: $20,296 (2005); Median household income: $42,892 (2005); Average household income: $50,607 (2005); Percent of households with income of $100,000 or more: 6.9% (2005); Poverty rate: 6.6% (2003); Bankruptcy rate: 10.60% (2005).
Education: Percent of population age 25 and over with: High school diploma (including GED) or higher: 86.7% (2005); Bachelor's degree or higher: 11.9% (2005); Master's degree or higher: 4.1% (2005).

Housing: Homeownership rate: 81.9% (2005); Median home value: $89,835 (2005); Median rent: $315 per month (2000); Median age of housing: 49 years (2000).
Health: Birth rate: 123.0 per 10,000 population (2004); Death rate: 112.4 per 10,000 population (2004); Age-adjusted cancer mortality rate: 221.5 deaths per 100,000 population (2002); Number of physicians: 9.2 per 10,000 population (2004); Hospital beds: 27.3 per 10,000 population (2003); Hospital admissions: 583.5 per 10,000 population (2003).
Elections: 2004 Presidential election results: 72.0% Bush, 27.6% Kerry, 0.0% Nader, 0.2% Badnarik

Additional Information Contacts
Van Wert County Government. . . . . (419) 238-6159
   http://www.vanwertcounty.org/
City of Van Wert. . . . . (419) 238-1237
   http://vanwert.org
Van Wert Chamber of Commerce . . . . (419) 238-4390
   http://www.vanwertchamber.com
Van Wert County Convention and Visitors Bureau . . . . (877) 989-2282
   http://www.vanwertcounty.org/cvb

Van Wert County Communities

CONVOY (village). Covers a land area of 0.557 square miles and a water area of 0 square miles. Located at 40.91° N. Lat.; 84.70° W. Long. Elevation is 787 feet.
Population: 1,205 (1990); 1,110 (2000); 1,111 (2005); 1,113 (2010 projected); Race: 97.1% White, 0.2% Black, 0.1% Asian, 1.5% Hispanic of any race (2005); Density: 1,995.0 persons per square mile (2005); Average household size: 2.55 (2005); Median age: 35.9 (2005); Males per 100 females: 93.6 (2005); Marriage status: 21.8% never married, 55.6% now married, 8.2% widowed, 14.3% divorced (2000); Foreign born: 0.8% (2000); Ancestry (includes multiple ancestries): 43.0% German, 15.1% Irish, 10.9% United States or American, 8.7% English, 6.9% Other groups (2000).
Economy: Single-family building permits issued: 5 (2005); Multi-family building permits issued: 0 (2005); Employment by occupation: 7.4% management, 8.7% professional, 20.0% services, 17.3% sales, 0.0% farming, 10.8% construction, 35.7% production (2000).
Income: Per capita income: $21,183 (2005); Median household income: $45,619 (2005); Average household income: $53,960 (2005); Percent of households with income of $100,000 or more: 8.7% (2005); Poverty rate: 6.3% (2000).
Education: Percent of population age 25 and over with: High school diploma (including GED) or higher: 85.1% (2005); Bachelor's degree or higher: 5.7% (2005); Master's degree or higher: 2.5% (2005).
School District(s)
Crestview Local SD (PK-12)
   2003-04 Enrollment: 1,065 . . . . (419) 749-9100
Housing: Homeownership rate: 85.5% (2005); Median home value: $72,468 (2005); Median rent: $354 per month (2000); Median age of housing: 60 years (2000).
Transportation: Commute to work: 94.8% car, 0.4% public transportation, 3.5% walk, 1.3% work from home (2000); Travel time to work: 31.0% less than 15 minutes, 39.8% 15 to 30 minutes, 16.4% 30 to 45 minutes, 11.3% 45 to 60 minutes, 1.6% 60 minutes or more (2000)

ELGIN (village). Covers a land area of 0.226 square miles and a water area of 0 square miles. Located at 40.74° N. Lat.; 84.47° W. Long. Elevation is 819 feet.
Population: 71 (1990); 50 (2000); 53 (2005); 52 (2010 projected); Race: 100.0% White, 0.0% Black, 0.0% Asian, 0.0% Hispanic of any race (2005); Density: 234.3 persons per square mile (2005); Average household size: 2.52 (2005); Median age: 39.6 (2005); Males per 100 females: 71.0 (2005); Marriage status: 15.6% never married, 62.5% now married, 9.4% widowed, 12.5% divorced (2000); Foreign born: 0.0% (2000); Ancestry (includes multiple ancestries): 24.0% German, 16.0% English, 12.0% Other groups, 4.0% Swiss, 4.0% Welsh (2000).
Economy: Employment by occupation: 5.3% management, 0.0% professional, 0.0% services, 42.1% sales, 0.0% farming, 15.8% construction, 36.8% production (2000).
Income: Per capita income: $13,962 (2005); Median household income: $24,000 (2005); Average household income: $35,238 (2005); Percent of households with income of $100,000 or more: 4.8% (2005); Poverty rate: 22.0% (2000).

Education: Percent of population age 25 and over with: High school diploma (including GED) or higher: 100.0% (2005); Bachelor's degree or higher: 0.0% (2005); Master's degree or higher: 0.0% (2005).
Housing: Homeownership rate: 95.2% (2005); Median home value: $71,429 (2005); Median rent: $n/a per month (2000); Median age of housing: 57 years (2000).
Transportation: Commute to work: 94.7% car, 0.0% public transportation, 5.3% walk, 0.0% work from home (2000); Travel time to work: 15.8% less than 15 minutes, 63.2% 15 to 30 minutes, 21.1% 30 to 45 minutes, 0.0% 45 to 60 minutes, 0.0% 60 minutes or more (2000)

MIDDLE POINT (village). Aka Middlepoint. Covers a land area of 0.556 square miles and a water area of 0 square miles. Located at 40.85° N. Lat.; 84.44° W. Long. Elevation is 780 feet.
Population: 641 (1990); 593 (2000); 609 (2005); 625 (2010 projected); Race: 97.7% White, 0.0% Black, 0.0% Asian, 2.0% Hispanic of any race (2005); Density: 1,094.9 persons per square mile (2005); Average household size: 2.50 (2005); Median age: 38.5 (2005); Males per 100 females: 95.8 (2005); Marriage status: 24.2% never married, 56.9% now married, 7.1% widowed, 11.7% divorced (2000); Foreign born: 0.3% (2000); Ancestry (includes multiple ancestries): 46.3% German, 15.4% United States or American, 8.0% Other groups, 7.9% English, 6.7% Irish (2000).
Economy: In agricultural area. Single-family building permits issued: 0 (2005); Multi-family building permits issued: 0 (2005); Employment by occupation: 7.4% management, 9.1% professional, 18.9% services, 15.8% sales, 1.0% farming, 8.8% construction, 39.1% production (2000).
Income: Per capita income: $17,607 (2005); Median household income: $37,632 (2005); Average household income: $43,945 (2005); Percent of households with income of $100,000 or more: 4.5% (2005); Poverty rate: 4.9% (2000).
Education: Percent of population age 25 and over with: High school diploma (including GED) or higher: 86.8% (2005); Bachelor's degree or higher: 4.2% (2005); Master's degree or higher: 2.2% (2005).
Housing: Homeownership rate: 89.8% (2005); Median home value: $60,943 (2005); Median rent: $370 per month (2000); Median age of housing: 59 years (2000).
Transportation: Commute to work: 95.2% car, 0.0% public transportation, 2.4% walk, 2.4% work from home (2000); Travel time to work: 31.3% less than 15 minutes, 46.5% 15 to 30 minutes, 12.0% 30 to 45 minutes, 6.0% 45 to 60 minutes, 4.2% 60 minutes or more (2000)

OHIO CITY (village). Covers a land area of 0.460 square miles and a water area of 0 square miles. Located at 40.77° N. Lat.; 84.61° W. Long. Elevation is 822 feet.
Population: 899 (1990); 784 (2000); 766 (2005); 730 (2010 projected); Race: 97.5% White, 0.3% Black, 0.0% Asian, 1.7% Hispanic of any race (2005); Density: 1,666.8 persons per square mile (2005); Average household size: 2.46 (2005); Median age: 35.4 (2005); Males per 100 females: 99.0 (2005); Marriage status: 20.5% never married, 63.7% now married, 5.6% widowed, 10.2% divorced (2000); Foreign born: 0.5% (2000); Ancestry (includes multiple ancestries): 34.7% German, 11.5% United States or American, 8.0% Irish, 5.6% English, 5.4% Other groups (2000).
Economy: Dairy products, canned foods, grain products. Single-family building permits issued: 1 (2005); Multi-family building permits issued: 0 (2005); Employment by occupation: 4.9% management, 7.9% professional, 13.3% services, 15.1% sales, 0.0% farming, 9.5% construction, 49.4% production (2000).
Income: Per capita income: $19,752 (2005); Median household income: $42,054 (2005); Average household income: $48,650 (2005); Percent of households with income of $100,000 or more: 4.2% (2005); Poverty rate: 3.6% (2000).
Education: Percent of population age 25 and over with: High school diploma (including GED) or higher: 83.8% (2005); Bachelor's degree or higher: 5.5% (2005); Master's degree or higher: 1.8% (2005).
School District(s)
Van Wert City SD (PK-12)
   2003-04 Enrollment: 2,290 . . . . (419) 238-0648
Housing: Homeownership rate: 83.0% (2005); Median home value: $63,711 (2005); Median rent: $271 per month (2000); Median age of housing: 52 years (2000).
Transportation: Commute to work: 89.6% car, 0.5% public transportation, 7.3% walk, 2.6% work from home (2000); Travel time to work: 43.6% less

than 15 minutes, 37.0% 15 to 30 minutes, 9.0% 30 to 45 minutes, 6.1% 45 to 60 minutes, 4.3% 60 minutes or more (2000)

SCOTT (village).
Covers a land area of 0.807 square miles and a water area of 0 square miles. Located at 40.98° N. Lat.; 84.58° W. Long. Elevation is 742 feet.

Population: 339 (1990); 322 (2000); 330 (2005); 334 (2010 projected); Race: 94.2% White, 4.2% Black, 0.0% Asian, 2.1% Hispanic of any race (2005); Density: 409.0 persons per square mile (2005); Average household size: 2.60 (2005); Median age: 34.4 (2005); Males per 100 females: 95.3 (2005); Marriage status: 20.3% never married, 70.3% now married, 2.6% widowed, 6.9% divorced (2000); Foreign born: 0.0% (2000); Ancestry (includes multiple ancestries): 39.8% German, 12.7% Other groups, 12.0% Irish, 8.6% United States or American, 5.6% English (2000).

Economy: Single-family building permits issued: 0 (2005); Multi-family building permits issued: 0 (2005); Employment by occupation: 3.5% management, 7.5% professional, 15.0% services, 21.4% sales, 1.2% farming, 6.4% construction, 45.1% production (2000).

Income: Per capita income: $20,765 (2005); Median household income: $42,500 (2005); Average household income: $53,957 (2005); Percent of households with income of $100,000 or more: 11.0% (2005); Poverty rate: 13.3% (2000).

Education: Percent of population age 25 and over with: High school diploma (including GED) or higher: 79.9% (2005); Bachelor's degree or higher: 4.3% (2005); Master's degree or higher: 0.0% (2005).

Housing: Homeownership rate: 88.2% (2005); Median home value: $58,621 (2005); Median rent: $258 per month (2000); Median age of housing: 47 years (2000).

Transportation: Commute to work: 97.5% car, 0.0% public transportation, 0.0% walk, 0.0% work from home (2000); Travel time to work: 19.9% less than 15 minutes, 52.2% 15 to 30 minutes, 21.7% 30 to 45 minutes, 5.0% 45 to 60 minutes, 1.2% 60 minutes or more (2000)

VAN WERT (city).
Covers a land area of 5.926 square miles and a water area of 0.182 square miles. Located at 40.86° N. Lat.; 84.58° W. Long. Elevation is 788 feet.

History: The site of Van Wert was chosen in 1835 by Captain James Watson Riley, who correctly foresaw that the location would make it a thoroughfare. The town developed into the peony center of Ohio, raising many flowers.

Population: 11,092 (1990); 10,690 (2000); 10,267 (2005); 9,848 (2010 projected); Race: 95.9% White, 1.5% Black, 0.5% Asian, 2.5% Hispanic of any race (2005); Density: 1,732.4 persons per square mile (2005); Average household size: 2.31 (2005); Median age: 38.6 (2005); Males per 100 females: 89.1 (2005); Marriage status: 22.0% never married, 56.6% now married, 9.1% widowed, 12.4% divorced (2000); Foreign born: 0.9% (2000); Ancestry (includes multiple ancestries): 33.5% German, 11.2% Irish, 10.6% United States or American, 8.5% Other groups, 7.5% English (2000).

Economy: Single-family building permits issued: 9 (2005); Multi-family building permits issued: 0 (2005); Employment by occupation: 10.2% management, 12.3% professional, 14.8% services, 22.1% sales, 0.0% farming, 7.9% construction, 32.7% production (2000).

Income: Per capita income: $18,422 (2005); Median household income: $34,715 (2005); Average household income: $41,896 (2005); Percent of households with income of $100,000 or more: 4.2% (2005); Poverty rate: 7.1% (2000).

Education: Percent of population age 25 and over with: High school diploma (including GED) or higher: 85.1% (2005); Bachelor's degree or higher: 14.0% (2005); Master's degree or higher: 4.7% (2005).

School District(s)
Lincolnview Local SD (PK-12)
    2003-04 Enrollment: 933 . . . . (419) 968-2226
Van Wert City SD (PK-12)
    2003-04 Enrollment: 2,290 . . . . (419) 238-0648
Vantage Joint Vocational SD (11-12)
    2003-04 Enrollment: n/a . . . . (419) 238-5411
Western Buckeye Educational Service Center
    2003-04 Enrollment: n/a . . . . (419) 238-4746

Two-year College(s)
Vantage Career Center (Public)
    Fall 2004 Enrollment: 54 . . . . (419) 238-5411

Housing: Homeownership rate: 71.8% (2005); Median home value: $82,753 (2005); Median rent: $314 per month (2000); Median age of housing: 52 years (2000).

Hospitals: Van Wert County Hospital (100 beds)

Safety: Violent crime rate: 23.5 per 10,000 population; Property crime rate: 467.9 per 10,000 population (2004).

Newspapers: Times-Bulletin (Circulation 6,600)

Transportation: Commute to work: 93.9% car, 0.1% public transportation, 3.0% walk, 2.0% work from home (2000); Travel time to work: 67.2% less than 15 minutes, 15.6% 15 to 30 minutes, 8.6% 30 to 45 minutes, 5.8% 45 to 60 minutes, 2.8% 60 minutes or more (2000)

Additional Information Contacts
City of Van Wert . . . . (419) 238-1237
    http://vanwert.org
Van Wert Chamber of Commerce . . . . (419) 238-4390
    http://www.vanwertchamber.com
Van Wert County Convention and Visitors Bureau . . . . . . (877) 989-2282
    http://www.vanwertcounty.org/cvb

VENEDOCIA (village).
Covers a land area of 0.134 square miles and a water area of 0 square miles. Located at 40.78° N. Lat.; 84.45° W. Long. Elevation is 805 feet.

Population: 158 (1990); 160 (2000); 167 (2005); 166 (2010 projected); Race: 98.8% White, 0.0% Black, 0.0% Asian, 1.2% Hispanic of any race (2005); Density: 1,249.1 persons per square mile (2005); Average household size: 2.69 (2005); Median age: 40.9 (2005); Males per 100 females: 79.6 (2005); Marriage status: 19.4% never married, 56.5% now married, 11.3% widowed, 12.9% divorced (2000); Foreign born: 0.0% (2000); Ancestry (includes multiple ancestries): 42.9% German, 19.0% Welsh, 14.1% United States or American, 12.9% Other groups, 11.7% Irish (2000).

Economy: Single-family building permits issued: 0 (2005); Multi-family building permits issued: 0 (2005); Employment by occupation: 4.5% management, 7.6% professional, 13.6% services, 10.6% sales, 0.0% farming, 15.2% construction, 48.5% production (2000).

Income: Per capita income: $13,503 (2005); Median household income: $32,778 (2005); Average household income: $36,371 (2005); Percent of households with income of $100,000 or more: 0.0% (2005); Poverty rate: 13.0% (2000).

Education: Percent of population age 25 and over with: High school diploma (including GED) or higher: 68.4% (2005); Bachelor's degree or higher: 4.3% (2005); Master's degree or higher: 0.9% (2005).

Housing: Homeownership rate: 82.3% (2005); Median home value: $64,545 (2005); Median rent: $279 per month (2000); Median age of housing: 60+ years (2000).

Transportation: Commute to work: 90.9% car, 0.0% public transportation, 6.1% walk, 0.0% work from home (2000); Travel time to work: 25.8% less than 15 minutes, 47.0% 15 to 30 minutes, 22.7% 30 to 45 minutes, 3.0% 45 to 60 minutes, 1.5% 60 minutes or more (2000)

WILLSHIRE (village).
Covers a land area of 0.379 square miles and a water area of 0 square miles. Located at 40.74° N. Lat.; 84.79° W. Long. Elevation is 798 feet.

Population: 541 (1990); 463 (2000); 443 (2005); 435 (2010 projected); Race: 99.1% White, 0.0% Black, 0.2% Asian, 0.9% Hispanic of any race (2005); Density: 1,168.4 persons per square mile (2005); Average household size: 2.38 (2005); Median age: 37.9 (2005); Males per 100 females: 108.0 (2005); Marriage status: 20.3% never married, 57.5% now married, 10.0% widowed, 12.2% divorced (2000); Foreign born: 1.1% (2000); Ancestry (includes multiple ancestries): 38.9% German, 7.9% Other groups, 7.5% English, 7.5% Dutch, 6.8% Irish (2000).

Economy: Sawmills. Single-family building permits issued: 0 (2005); Multi-family building permits issued: 0 (2005); Employment by occupation: 4.4% management, 3.9% professional, 15.3% services, 14.8% sales, 0.9% farming, 12.7% construction, 48.0% production (2000).

Income: Per capita income: $20,034 (2005); Median household income: $45,714 (2005); Average household income: $47,715 (2005); Percent of households with income of $100,000 or more: 3.8% (2005); Poverty rate: 5.9% (2000).

Education: Percent of population age 25 and over with: High school diploma (including GED) or higher: 79.1% (2005); Bachelor's degree or higher: 3.6% (2005); Master's degree or higher: 1.3% (2005).

School District(s)
Parkway Local SD (PK-12)
    2003-04 Enrollment: 1,237 . . . . (419) 363-3045

Housing: Homeownership rate: 81.2% (2005); Median home value: $59,189 (2005); Median rent: $329 per month (2000); Median age of housing: 54 years (2000).

Newspapers: Photo Star (General - Circulation 11,000)
Transportation: Commute to work: 96.4% car, 0.0% public transportation, 0.0% walk, 2.7% work from home (2000); Travel time to work: 24.8% less than 15 minutes, 51.8% 15 to 30 minutes, 14.7% 30 to 45 minutes, 6.9% 45 to 60 minutes, 1.8% 60 minutes or more (2000)

WREN (village). Covers a land area of 0.310 square miles and a water area of 0 square miles. Located at 40.80° N. Lat.; 84.77° W. Long. Elevation is 813 feet.
Population: 190 (1990); 199 (2000); 193 (2005); 190 (2010 projected); Race: 98.4% White, 0.0% Black, 0.0% Asian, 2.6% Hispanic of any race (2005); Density: 622.9 persons per square mile (2005); Average household size: 2.30 (2005); Median age: 39.2 (2005); Males per 100 females: 83.8 (2005); Marriage status: 26.8% never married, 48.8% now married, 7.9% widowed, 16.5% divorced (2000); Foreign born: 0.0% (2000); Ancestry (includes multiple ancestries): 32.0% German, 14.9% United States or American, 9.8% Irish, 7.2% Other groups, 6.7% English (2000).
Economy: In agricultural area. Single-family building permits issued: 0 (2005); Multi-family building permits issued: 0 (2005); Employment by occupation: 2.0% management, 11.9% professional, 10.9% services, 24.8% sales, 2.0% farming, 7.9% construction, 40.6% production (2000).
Income: Per capita income: $17,720 (2005); Median household income: $35,833 (2005); Average household income: $40,714 (2005); Percent of households with income of $100,000 or more: 1.2% (2005); Poverty rate: 6.7% (2000).
Education: Percent of population age 25 and over with: High school diploma (including GED) or higher: 91.2% (2005); Bachelor's degree or higher: 5.8% (2005); Master's degree or higher: 0.0% (2005).
Housing: Homeownership rate: 88.1% (2005); Median home value: $59,981 (2005); Median rent: $318 per month (2000); Median age of housing: 60+ years (2000).
Transportation: Commute to work: 100.0% car, 0.0% public transportation, 0.0% walk, 0.0% work from home (2000); Travel time to work: 7.1% less than 15 minutes, 60.2% 15 to 30 minutes, 15.3% 30 to 45 minutes, 9.2% 45 to 60 minutes, 8.2% 60 minutes or more (2000)

Vinton County

Located in southern Ohio; drained by Raccoon Creek. Covers a land area of 414.08 square miles, a water area of 0.88 square miles, and is located in the Eastern Time Zone. The county government was organized in 1850. County seat is McArthur.
Population: 11,098 (1990); 12,806 (2000); 13,395 (2005); 14,009 (2010 projected); Race: 98.4% White, 0.3% Black, 0.1% Asian, 0.5% Hispanic of any race (2005); Density: 32.3 persons per square mile (2005); Average household size: 2.58 (2005); Median age: 36.5 (2005); Males per 100 females: 99.1 (2005).
Religion: Five largest groups: 4.0% The United Methodist Church, 3.3% Christian Church (Disciples of Christ), 2.1% Southern Baptist Convention, 1.8% National Association of Free Will Baptists, 1.5% Catholic Church (2000).
Economy: Unemployment rate: 8.2% (2005); Total civilian labor force: 5,625 (2005); Leading industries: 38.5% manufacturing; 16.4% health care and social assistance; 9.3% nursing care facilities (2004); Farms: 237 totaling 43,651 acres (2002); Companies that employ 500 or more persons: 0 (2004); Companies that employ 100 to 499 persons: 3 (2004); Companies that employ less than 100 persons: 156 (2004); Black-owned businesses: n/a (2002); Hispanic-owned businesses: n/a (2002); Women-owned businesses: n/a (2002); Retail sales per capita: $3,512 (2006). Single-family building permits issued: 0 (2005); Multi-family building permits issued: 4 (2005).
Income: Per capita income: $15,863 (2005); Median household income: $33,166 (2005); Average household income: $40,726 (2005); Percent of households with income of $100,000 or more: 5.1% (2005); Poverty rate: 15.0% (2003); Bankruptcy rate: 6.48% (2005).
Education: Percent of population age 25 and over with: High school diploma (including GED) or higher: 71.2% (2005); Bachelor's degree or higher: 6.1% (2005); Master's degree or higher: 2.2% (2005).
Housing: Homeownership rate: 77.9% (2005); Median home value: $73,621 (2005); Median rent: $272 per month (2000); Median age of housing: 26 years (2000).
Health: Birth rate: 145.0 per 10,000 population (2004); Death rate: 90.9 per 10,000 population (2004); Age-adjusted cancer mortality rate: 164.9 deaths per 100,000 population (2002); Number of physicians: 0.0 per 10,000 population (2004); Hospital beds: 0.0 per 10,000 population (2003); Hospital admissions: 0.0 per 10,000 population (2003).
Elections: 2004 Presidential election results: 54.8% Bush, 44.7% Kerry, 0.0% Nader, 0.3% Badnarik
National and State Parks: Lake Alma State Reserve; Lake Hope State Park; Wayne National Forest; Zaleski State Forest
Additional Information Contacts
Vinton County Government . . . . (740) 596-4571
  http://www.vintoncounty.com/
Vinton Chamber of Commerce . . . . (740) 596-5033
  http://www.vintoncountytravel.com

Vinton County Communities

CREOLA (unincorporated postal area, zip code 45622). Covers a land area of 21.246 square miles and a water area of 0 square miles. Located at 39.36° N. Lat.; 82.49° W. Long. Elevation is 760 feet.
Population: 435 (2000); Race: 100.0% White, 0.0% Black, 0.0% Asian, 0.0% Hispanic of any race (2000); Density: 20.5 persons per square mile (2000); Age: 25.2% under 18, 11.1% over 64 (2000); Marriage status: 20.3% never married, 52.2% now married, 6.2% widowed, 21.4% divorced (2000); Foreign born: 0.0% (2000); Ancestry (includes multiple ancestries): 20.5% English, 17.0% United States or American, 14.1% Dutch, 10.9% Irish, 8.8% German (2000).
Economy: Employment by occupation: 4.7% management, 22.8% professional, 4.7% services, 6.3% sales, 6.3% farming, 24.4% construction, 30.7% production (2000).
Income: Per capita income: $17,312 (2000); Median household income: $33,977 (2000); Poverty rate: 18.5% (2000).
Education: Percent of population age 25 and over with: High school diploma (including GED) or higher: 67.2% (2000); Bachelor's degree or higher: 9.8% (2000).
Housing: Homeownership rate: 84.9% (2000); Median home value: $97,500 (2000); Median rent: $247 per month (2000); Median age of housing: 24 years (2000).
Transportation: Commute to work: 100.0% car, 0.0% public transportation, 0.0% walk, 0.0% work from home (2000); Travel time to work: 32.3% less than 15 minutes, 15.7% 15 to 30 minutes, 22.8% 30 to 45 minutes, 5.5% 45 to 60 minutes, 23.6% 60 minutes or more (2000)

HAMDEN (village). Covers a land area of 0.570 square miles and a water area of 0 square miles. Located at 39.16° N. Lat.; 82.52° W. Long. Elevation is 720 feet.
Population: 877 (1990); 871 (2000); 879 (2005); 887 (2010 projected); Race: 97.4% White, 0.0% Black, 0.0% Asian, 1.0% Hispanic of any race (2005); Density: 1,542.1 persons per square mile (2005); Average household size: 2.50 (2005); Median age: 37.3 (2005); Males per 100 females: 93.2 (2005); Marriage status: 20.1% never married, 60.5% now married, 8.9% widowed, 10.5% divorced (2000); Foreign born: 0.0% (2000); Ancestry (includes multiple ancestries): 34.3% United States or American, 11.3% German, 8.7% Other groups, 7.5% Irish, 4.4% English (2000).
Economy: In agricultural area. Employment by occupation: 8.7% management, 13.8% professional, 12.8% services, 14.1% sales, 2.2% farming, 14.7% construction, 33.7% production (2000).
Income: Per capita income: $15,623 (2005); Median household income: $31,017 (2005); Average household income: $39,124 (2005); Percent of households with income of $100,000 or more: 4.8% (2005); Poverty rate: 18.9% (2000).
Education: Percent of population age 25 and over with: High school diploma (including GED) or higher: 73.3% (2005); Bachelor's degree or higher: 6.8% (2005); Master's degree or higher: 3.9% (2005).
School District(s)
Vinton County Local SD (PK-12)
  2003-04 Enrollment: 2,633 . . . . (740) 596-5218
Housing: Homeownership rate: 76.4% (2005); Median home value: $59,394 (2005); Median rent: $316 per month (2000); Median age of housing: 45 years (2000).
Transportation: Commute to work: 90.9% car, 0.0% public transportation, 5.0% walk, 4.0% work from home (2000); Travel time to work: 33.6% less than 15 minutes, 31.1% 15 to 30 minutes, 10.5% 30 to 45 minutes, 9.8% 45 to 60 minutes, 15.0% 60 minutes or more (2000)

MCARTHUR (village). Covers a land area of 1.333 square miles and a water area of 0 square miles. Located at 39.24° N. Lat.; 82.48° W. Long. Elevation is 767 feet.
History: McArthur was platted in 1815 and named McArthurstown for Duncan McArthur, later governor of Ohio. It was sited at the junction of two wilderness roads. Local clays were used in brickmaking, the town's early industry.
Population: 1,541 (1990); 1,888 (2000); 1,972 (2005); 2,056 (2010 projected); Race: 98.7% White, 0.1% Black, 0.0% Asian, 0.5% Hispanic of any race (2005); Density: 1,479.2 persons per square mile (2005); Average household size: 2.40 (2005); Median age: 32.7 (2005); Males per 100 females: 85.2 (2005); Marriage status: 24.0% never married, 52.2% now married, 10.6% widowed, 13.2% divorced (2000); Foreign born: 0.3% (2000); Ancestry (includes multiple ancestries): 26.0% United States or American, 13.0% Other groups, 10.8% Irish, 10.7% German, 9.4% English (2000).
Economy: Employment by occupation: 10.9% management, 13.9% professional, 14.0% services, 21.0% sales, 1.4% farming, 15.3% construction, 23.4% production (2000).
Income: Per capita income: $16,083 (2005); Median household income: $28,793 (2005); Average household income: $38,561 (2005); Percent of households with income of $100,000 or more: 6.5% (2005); Poverty rate: 27.8% (2000).
Education: Percent of population age 25 and over with: High school diploma (including GED) or higher: 79.9% (2005); Bachelor's degree or higher: 10.4% (2005); Master's degree or higher: 3.6% (2005).
School District(s)
Vinton County Local SD (PK-12)
    2003-04 Enrollment: 2,633 . . . . (740) 596-5218
Housing: Homeownership rate: 60.7% (2005); Median home value: $75,873 (2005); Median rent: $275 per month (2000); Median age of housing: 39 years (2000).
Transportation: Commute to work: 91.2% car, 0.1% public transportation, 5.0% walk, 3.3% work from home (2000); Travel time to work: 44.9% less than 15 minutes, 13.5% 15 to 30 minutes, 20.5% 30 to 45 minutes, 8.9% 45 to 60 minutes, 12.2% 60 minutes or more (2000)
Additional Information Contacts
Vinton Chamber of Commerce . . . . (740) 596-5033
    http://www.vintoncountytravel.com

NEW PLYMOUTH (unincorporated postal area, zip code 45654). Covers a land area of 53.669 square miles and a water area of 0.009 square miles. Located at 39.37° N. Lat.; 82.39° W. Long. Elevation is 774 feet.
Population: 1,026 (2000); Race: 95.3% White, 0.0% Black, 0.0% Asian, 0.0% Hispanic of any race (2000); Density: 19.1 persons per square mile (2000); Age: 26.2% under 18, 12.2% over 64 (2000); Marriage status: 20.2% never married, 56.2% now married, 9.0% widowed, 14.6% divorced (2000); Foreign born: 0.0% (2000); Ancestry (includes multiple ancestries): 13.9% United States or American, 12.2% German, 8.1% Other groups, 6.1% Irish, 5.7% English (2000).
Economy: Employment by occupation: 11.1% management, 9.9% professional, 11.8% services, 21.9% sales, 0.0% farming, 15.4% construction, 30.0% production (2000).
Income: Per capita income: $13,501 (2000); Median household income: $33,080 (2000); Poverty rate: 16.4% (2000).
Education: Percent of population age 25 and over with: High school diploma (including GED) or higher: 75.5% (2000); Bachelor's degree or higher: 3.7% (2000).
Housing: Homeownership rate: 85.9% (2000); Median home value: $70,800 (2000); Median rent: $325 per month (2000); Median age of housing: 28 years (2000).
Transportation: Commute to work: 94.5% car, 0.0% public transportation, 1.8% walk, 1.5% work from home (2000); Travel time to work: 14.8% less than 15 minutes, 37.2% 15 to 30 minutes, 26.0% 30 to 45 minutes, 1.8% 45 to 60 minutes, 20.2% 60 minutes or more (2000)

RAY (unincorporated postal area, zip code 45672). Covers a land area of 62.631 square miles and a water area of 0.022 square miles. Located at 39.20° N. Lat.; 82.69° W. Long. Elevation is 615 feet.
Population: 1,782 (2000); Race: 97.3% White, 2.3% Black, 0.0% Asian, 0.0% Hispanic of any race (2000); Density: 28.5 persons per square mile (2000); Age: 29.0% under 18, 10.8% over 64 (2000); Marriage status: 17.4% never married, 67.7% now married, 4.2% widowed, 10.6% divorced (2000); Foreign born: 0.0% (2000); Ancestry (includes multiple ancestries): 33.8% United States or American, 10.7% Irish, 9.9% English, 8.9% German, 6.8% Other groups (2000).
Economy: Employment by occupation: 8.1% management, 9.5% professional, 13.5% services, 17.5% sales, 1.7% farming, 14.7% construction, 34.9% production (2000).
Income: Per capita income: $15,479 (2000); Median household income: $30,553 (2000); Poverty rate: 17.3% (2000).
Education: Percent of population age 25 and over with: High school diploma (including GED) or higher: 74.2% (2000); Bachelor's degree or higher: 6.9% (2000).
Housing: Homeownership rate: 85.0% (2000); Median home value: $64,300 (2000); Median rent: $318 per month (2000); Median age of housing: 25 years (2000).
Transportation: Commute to work: 95.0% car, 0.0% public transportation, 2.5% walk, 1.4% work from home (2000); Travel time to work: 10.7% less than 15 minutes, 25.7% 15 to 30 minutes, 35.8% 30 to 45 minutes, 1.3% 45 to 60 minutes, 26.6% 60 minutes or more (2000)

WILKESVILLE (village). Covers a land area of 0.294 square miles and a water area of 0 square miles. Located at 39.07° N. Lat.; 82.32° W. Long. Elevation is 706 feet.
Population: 151 (1990); 151 (2000); 144 (2005); 145 (2010 projected); Race: 95.8% White, 0.0% Black, 0.0% Asian, 0.0% Hispanic of any race (2005); Density: 489.8 persons per square mile (2005); Average household size: 2.12 (2005); Median age: 47.9 (2005); Males per 100 females: 100.0 (2005); Marriage status: 13.9% never married, 61.6% now married, 13.9% widowed, 10.6% divorced (2000); Foreign born: 1.2% (2000); Ancestry (includes multiple ancestries): 30.3% United States or American, 23.6% German, 20.0% Irish, 4.8% English, 3.6% Dutch (2000).
Economy: Employment by occupation: 7.1% management, 2.4% professional, 12.9% services, 23.5% sales, 4.7% farming, 18.8% construction, 30.6% production (2000).
Income: Per capita income: $18,247 (2005); Median household income: $25,224 (2005); Average household income: $38,640 (2005); Percent of households with income of $100,000 or more: 4.4% (2005); Poverty rate: 18.8% (2000).
Education: Percent of population age 25 and over with: High school diploma (including GED) or higher: 68.2% (2005); Bachelor's degree or higher: 6.4% (2005); Master's degree or higher: 1.8% (2005).
School District(s)
Vinton County Local SD (PK-12)
    2003-04 Enrollment: 2,633 . . . . (740) 596-5218
Housing: Homeownership rate: 92.6% (2005); Median home value: $61,429 (2005); Median rent: $125 per month (2000); Median age of housing: 39 years (2000).
Transportation: Commute to work: 94.1% car, 0.0% public transportation, 0.0% walk, 3.5% work from home (2000); Travel time to work: 19.5% less than 15 minutes, 25.6% 15 to 30 minutes, 39.0% 30 to 45 minutes, 1.2% 45 to 60 minutes, 14.6% 60 minutes or more (2000)

ZALESKI (village). Covers a land area of 0.477 square miles and a water area of 0 square miles. Located at 39.28° N. Lat.; 82.39° W. Long. Elevation is 713 feet.
History: Zaleski was settled in a forested area, the site of the Zaleski Resettlement Project that sought to rehabilitate timberlands.
Population: 294 (1990); 375 (2000); 403 (2005); 428 (2010 projected); Race: 98.0% White, 0.2% Black, 0.0% Asian, 0.0% Hispanic of any race (2005); Density: 845.0 persons per square mile (2005); Average household size: 2.49 (2005); Median age: 37.2 (2005); Males per 100 females: 92.8 (2005); Marriage status: 21.3% never married, 61.1% now married, 8.4% widowed, 9.1% divorced (2000); Foreign born: 0.0% (2000); Ancestry (includes multiple ancestries): 26.9% United States or American, 5.7% German, 5.4% Other groups, 3.6% Irish, 3.6% English (2000).
Economy: Employment by occupation: 3.1% management, 16.9% professional, 18.1% services, 17.5% sales, 0.6% farming, 28.7% construction, 15.0% production (2000).
Income: Per capita income: $15,043 (2005); Median household income: $32,600 (2005); Average household income: $37,423 (2005); Percent of households with income of $100,000 or more: 2.5% (2005); Poverty rate: 16.7% (2000).
Education: Percent of population age 25 and over with: High school diploma (including GED) or higher: 77.9% (2005); Bachelor's degree or higher: 3.9% (2005); Master's degree or higher: 2.9% (2005).

Housing: Homeownership rate: 81.5% (2005); Median home value: $47,143 (2005); Median rent: $290 per month (2000); Median age of housing: 40 years (2000).
Transportation: Commute to work: 92.5% car, 0.0% public transportation, 6.3% walk, 1.3% work from home (2000); Travel time to work: 25.9% less than 15 minutes, 28.5% 15 to 30 minutes, 29.7% 30 to 45 minutes, 6.3% 45 to 60 minutes, 9.5% 60 minutes or more (2000)

Warren County

Located in southwestern Ohio; crossed by the Little Miami River. Covers a land area of 399.63 square miles, a water area of 7.51 square miles, and is located in the Eastern Time Zone. The county government was organized in 1803. County seat is Lebanon.

Warren County is part of the Cincinnati-Middletown, OH-KY-IN Metropolitan Statistical Area. The entire metro area includes: Dearborn County, IN; Franklin County, IN; Ohio County, IN; Boone County, KY; Bracken County, KY; Campbell County, KY; Gallatin County, KY; Grant County, KY; Kenton County, KY; Pendleton County, KY; Brown County, OH; Butler County, OH; Clermont County, OH; Hamilton County, OH; Warren County, OH

Weather Station: Franklin   Elevation: 669 feet

	Jan	Feb	Mar	Apr	May	Jun	Jul	Aug	Sep	Oct	Nov	Dec
High	36	40	51	63	73	82	85	84	78	66	53	42
Low	18	21	30	39	49	59	63	60	52	40	33	24
Precip	2.5	2.3	3.2	3.9	4.4	3.7	4.2	3.3	2.7	3.0	3.3	3.0
Snow	na	2.4	1.6	tr	0.0	0.0	0.0	0.0	0.0	0.0	0.5	1.4

High and Low temperatures in degrees Fahrenheit; Precipitation and Snow in inches

Population: 113,967 (1990); 158,383 (2000); 192,092 (2005); 227,484 (2010 projected); Race: 92.8% White, 2.9% Black, 2.6% Asian, 1.3% Hispanic of any race (2005); Density: 480.7 persons per square mile (2005); Average household size: 2.78 (2005); Median age: 35.5 (2005); Males per 100 females: 101.0 (2005).
Religion: Five largest groups: 11.2% Catholic Church, 6.0% Southern Baptist Convention, 3.2% The United Methodist Church, 2.5% Christian Churches and Churches of Christ, 1.6% Presbyterian Church (U.S.A.) (2000).
Economy: Unemployment rate: 4.4% (2005); Total civilian labor force: 100,201 (2005); Leading industries: 20.8% manufacturing; 11.8% retail trade; 10.3% accommodation & food services (2004); Farms: 1,036 totaling 126,168 acres (2002); Companies that employ 500 or more persons: 13 (2004); Companies that employ 100 to 499 persons: 107 (2004); Companies that employ less than 100 persons: 3,350 (2004); Black-owned businesses: n/a (2002); Hispanic-owned businesses: 104 (2002); Women-owned businesses: 4,235 (2002); Retail sales per capita: $10,959 (2006). Single-family building permits issued: 2,241 (2005); Multi-family building permits issued: 236 (2005).
Income: Per capita income: $29,662 (2005); Median household income: $66,627 (2005); Average household income: $81,722 (2005); Percent of households with income of $100,000 or more: 26.6% (2005); Poverty rate: 5.1% (2003); Bankruptcy rate: 8.30% (2005).
Taxes: Total county taxes per capita: $268 (2004); County property taxes per capita: $134 (2004).
Education: Percent of population age 25 and over with: High school diploma (including GED) or higher: 86.7% (2005); Bachelor's degree or higher: 29.4% (2005); Master's degree or higher: 9.5% (2005).
Housing: Homeownership rate: 79.8% (2005); Median home value: $171,076 (2005); Median rent: $504 per month (2000); Median age of housing: 20 years (2000).
Health: Birth rate: 133.5 per 10,000 population (2004); Death rate: 60.0 per 10,000 population (2004); Age-adjusted cancer mortality rate: 202.6 deaths per 100,000 population (2002); Air Quality Index: 74.4% good, 22.8% moderate, 2.8% unhealthy for sensitive individuals, 0.0% unhealthy (percent of days in 2005); Number of physicians: 22.6 per 10,000 population (2004); Hospital beds: 0.0 per 10,000 population (2003); Hospital admissions: 0.0 per 10,000 population (2003).
Elections: 2004 Presidential election results: 72.1% Bush, 27.6% Kerry, 0.0% Nader, 0.2% Badnarik
National and State Parks: Caesar Creek Gorge State Natural Area; Fort Ancient State Memorial
Additional Information Contacts
Warren County Government . . . . (513) 695-1250
http://www.co.warren.oh.us/
City of Franklin. . . . . (937) 746-9921
http://www.franklinohio.org
City of Lebanon . . . . (513) 932-3060
http://www.ci.lebanon.oh.us
City of Mason. . . . . (513) 229-8500
http://www.imaginemason.org
City of Springboro . . . . (937) 748-4343
http://www.ci.springboro.oh.us
Franklin Area Chamber of Commerce . . . . (513) 746-8457
http://www.franklinohio.org
Lebanon Chamber of Commerce. . . . . (513) 932-1100
http://www.lebanonchamber.org
Mason Chamber of Commerce . . . . (513) 336-0125
http://www.necchamber.org
Morrow Area Chamber of Commerce . . . . (513) 899-4466
http://www.morrow-today.org
Springboro Chamber of Commerce. . . . . (513) 748-0074
http://www.springboroohio.org
Village of Carlisle . . . . (937) 746-0555
http://www.ci.carlisle.oh.us
Waynesville Chamber of Commerce . . . . (513) 897-8855
http://www.waynesvilleohio.com

Warren County Communities

BUTLERVILLE (village). Covers a land area of 0.148 square miles and a water area of 0 square miles. Located at 39.30° N. Lat.; 84.08° W. Long. Elevation is 856 feet.
Population: 188 (1990); 231 (2000); 260 (2005); 292 (2010 projected); Race: 98.5% White, 0.0% Black, 0.0% Asian, 0.0% Hispanic of any race (2005); Density: 1,759.8 persons per square mile (2005); Average household size: 2.83 (2005); Median age: 33.0 (2005); Males per 100 females: 108.0 (2005); Marriage status: 25.7% never married, 70.3% now married, 1.1% widowed, 2.9% divorced (2000); Foreign born: 0.0% (2000); Ancestry (includes multiple ancestries): 20.9% United States or American, 20.5% German, 18.4% English, 7.7% Irish, 4.3% Italian (2000).
Economy: In agricultural area. Single-family building permits issued: 0 (2005); Multi-family building permits issued: 0 (2005); Employment by occupation: 5.7% management, 3.3% professional, 14.6% services, 27.6% sales, 2.4% farming, 18.7% construction, 27.6% production (2000).
Income: Per capita income: $21,250 (2005); Median household income: $54,310 (2005); Average household income: $60,054 (2005); Percent of households with income of $100,000 or more: 9.8% (2005); Poverty rate: 0.9% (2000).
Education: Percent of population age 25 and over with: High school diploma (including GED) or higher: 84.6% (2005); Bachelor's degree or higher: 4.9% (2005); Master's degree or higher: 0.0% (2005).
Housing: Homeownership rate: 85.9% (2005); Median home value: $97,500 (2005); Median rent: $488 per month (2000); Median age of housing: 43 years (2000).
Transportation: Commute to work: 100.0% car, 0.0% public transportation, 0.0% walk, 0.0% work from home (2000); Travel time to work: 5.9% less than 15 minutes, 26.3% 15 to 30 minutes, 41.5% 30 to 45 minutes, 16.1% 45 to 60 minutes, 10.2% 60 minutes or more (2000)

CARLISLE (village). Covers a land area of 3.403 square miles and a water area of 0.161 square miles. Located at 39.58° N. Lat.; 84.31° W. Long. Elevation is 700 feet.
Population: 5,032 (1990); 5,121 (2000); 5,357 (2005); 5,669 (2010 projected); Race: 97.7% White, 0.2% Black, 0.6% Asian, 0.7% Hispanic of any race (2005); Density: 1,574.1 persons per square mile (2005); Average household size: 2.71 (2005); Median age: 35.8 (2005); Males per 100 females: 101.2 (2005); Marriage status: 16.8% never married, 69.4% now married, 5.0% widowed, 8.9% divorced (2000); Foreign born: 1.1% (2000); Ancestry (includes multiple ancestries): 18.9% United States or American, 17.7% German, 12.9% English, 10.7% Other groups, 10.4% Irish (2000).
Economy: Single-family building permits issued: 38 (2005); Multi-family building permits issued: 0 (2005); Employment by occupation: 6.0% management, 14.1% professional, 16.2% services, 23.6% sales, 0.0% farming, 11.2% construction, 28.8% production (2000).
Income: Per capita income: $20,881 (2005); Median household income: $49,137 (2005); Average household income: $55,813 (2005); Percent of households with income of $100,000 or more: 13.3% (2005); Poverty rate: 8.4% (2000).

Education: Percent of population age 25 and over with: High school diploma (including GED) or higher: 75.3% (2005); Bachelor's degree or higher: 7.0% (2005); Master's degree or higher: 2.1% (2005).

School District(s)
Carlisle Local SD (KG-12)
    2003-04 Enrollment: 1,775 . . . . (937) 746-0710

Housing: Homeownership rate: 76.6% (2005); Median home value: $131,727 (2005); Median rent: $359 per month (2000); Median age of housing: 33 years (2000).
Safety: Violent crime rate: 14.5 per 10,000 population; Property crime rate: 166.3 per 10,000 population (2004).
Transportation: Commute to work: 96.1% car, 0.0% public transportation, 1.2% walk, 1.8% work from home (2000); Travel time to work: 24.1% less than 15 minutes, 42.3% 15 to 30 minutes, 20.6% 30 to 45 minutes, 5.7% 45 to 60 minutes, 7.3% 60 minutes or more (2000)

Additional Information Contacts
Village of Carlisle . . . . (937) 746-0555
    http://www.ci.carlisle.oh.us

CORWIN
(village). Covers a land area of 0.299 square miles and a water area of 0 square miles. Located at 39.52° N. Lat.; 84.07° W. Long. Elevation is 732 feet.

Population: 263 (1990); 256 (2000); 289 (2005); 325 (2010 projected); Race: 99.3% White, 0.0% Black, 0.7% Asian, 0.0% Hispanic of any race (2005); Density: 965.9 persons per square mile (2005); Average household size: 2.49 (2005); Median age: 37.8 (2005); Males per 100 females: 99.3 (2005); Marriage status: 30.6% never married, 60.4% now married, 6.3% widowed, 2.7% divorced (2000); Foreign born: 0.0% (2000); Ancestry (includes multiple ancestries): 19.3% Irish, 15.8% German, 14.3% United States or American, 9.7% English, 5.4% Other groups (2000).
Economy: Employment by occupation: 7.0% management, 10.1% professional, 28.7% services, 13.2% sales, 1.6% farming, 17.1% construction, 22.5% production (2000).
Income: Per capita income: $24,135 (2005); Median household income: $54,605 (2005); Average household income: $60,129 (2005); Percent of households with income of $100,000 or more: 12.9% (2005); Poverty rate: 11.2% (2000).
Education: Percent of population age 25 and over with: High school diploma (including GED) or higher: 59.4% (2005); Bachelor's degree or higher: 6.9% (2005); Master's degree or higher: 0.0% (2005).
Housing: Homeownership rate: 75.9% (2005); Median home value: $125,000 (2005); Median rent: $458 per month (2000); Median age of housing: 50 years (2000).
Transportation: Commute to work: 87.4% car, 0.0% public transportation, 6.3% walk, 1.6% work from home (2000); Travel time to work: 34.4% less than 15 minutes, 36.8% 15 to 30 minutes, 23.2% 30 to 45 minutes, 1.6% 45 to 60 minutes, 4.0% 60 minutes or more (2000)

FIVE POINTS
(CDP). Covers a land area of 2.886 square miles and a water area of 0.011 square miles. Located at 39.56° N. Lat.; 84.21° W. Long. Elevation is 993 feet.

Population: 1,503 (1990); 2,191 (2000); 3,188 (2005); 4,168 (2010 projected); Race: 97.7% White, 0.4% Black, 1.2% Asian, 1.3% Hispanic of any race (2005); Density: 1,104.5 persons per square mile (2005); Average household size: 2.95 (2005); Median age: 40.1 (2005); Males per 100 females: 106.6 (2005); Marriage status: 17.4% never married, 78.6% now married, 2.1% widowed, 1.9% divorced (2000); Foreign born: 1.8% (2000); Ancestry (includes multiple ancestries): 33.9% German, 16.9% Irish, 15.1% English, 10.6% Italian, 8.1% United States or American (2000).
Economy: Employment by occupation: 24.1% management, 31.2% professional, 6.0% services, 28.8% sales, 0.0% farming, 3.1% construction, 6.8% production (2000).
Income: Per capita income: $45,969 (2005); Median household income: $119,068 (2005); Average household income: $135,694 (2005); Percent of households with income of $100,000 or more: 62.5% (2005); Poverty rate: 0.3% (2000).
Education: Percent of population age 25 and over with: High school diploma (including GED) or higher: 94.9% (2005); Bachelor's degree or higher: 51.9% (2005); Master's degree or higher: 22.9% (2005).
Housing: Homeownership rate: 98.3% (2005); Median home value: $262,193 (2005); Median rent: $1,179 per month (2000); Median age of housing: 14 years (2000).
Transportation: Commute to work: 96.1% car, 0.6% public transportation, 1.0% walk, 2.3% work from home (2000); Travel time to work: 27.6% less than 15 minutes, 41.2% 15 to 30 minutes, 19.7% 30 to 45 minutes, 5.5% 45 to 60 minutes, 6.1% 60 minutes or more (2000)

FRANKLIN
(city). Covers a land area of 9.110 square miles and a water area of 0.214 square miles. Located at 39.56° N. Lat.; 84.30° W. Long. Elevation is 700 feet.

History: Named for Benjamin Franklin, American statesman and inventor. Franklin was founded in 1796 by William Schenck, an officer in Harrison's Army in the War of 1812. The town was a port on the Great Miami River after the Miami & Erie Canal was built. Later, paper mills were established here.

Population: 11,274 (1990); 11,396 (2000); 12,229 (2005); 13,315 (2010 projected); Race: 96.9% White, 0.8% Black, 0.7% Asian, 0.9% Hispanic of any race (2005); Density: 1,342.4 persons per square mile (2005); Average household size: 2.43 (2005); Median age: 33.8 (2005); Males per 100 females: 90.2 (2005); Marriage status: 21.2% never married, 59.5% now married, 7.1% widowed, 12.2% divorced (2000); Foreign born: 1.1% (2000); Ancestry (includes multiple ancestries): 21.5% United States or American, 15.0% German, 10.4% Irish, 10.2% Other groups, 9.0% English (2000).
Economy: Single-family building permits issued: 48 (2005); Multi-family building permits issued: 0 (2005); Employment by occupation: 7.6% management, 13.2% professional, 15.5% services, 25.7% sales, 0.2% farming, 11.1% construction, 26.8% production (2000).
Income: Per capita income: $20,325 (2005); Median household income: $41,180 (2005); Average household income: $49,124 (2005); Percent of households with income of $100,000 or more: 8.9% (2005); Poverty rate: 10.1% (2000).
Education: Percent of population age 25 and over with: High school diploma (including GED) or higher: 74.1% (2005); Bachelor's degree or higher: 9.1% (2005); Master's degree or higher: 2.5% (2005).

School District(s)
Franklin City SD (KG-12)
    2003-04 Enrollment: 3,094 . . . . (937) 746-1699

Two-year College(s)
Southwestern College (Private, For-profit)
    Fall 2004 Enrollment: 183 . . . . (937) 746-6633
    2005-06 Tuition: In-state $8,170; Out-of-state $8,170

Housing: Homeownership rate: 60.4% (2005); Median home value: $113,071 (2005); Median rent: $406 per month (2000); Median age of housing: 35 years (2000).
Safety: Violent crime rate: 24.8 per 10,000 population; Property crime rate: 584.0 per 10,000 population (2004).
Newspapers: The Star Press (General - Circulation 14,500)
Transportation: Commute to work: 97.2% car, 0.2% public transportation, 1.2% walk, 1.2% work from home (2000); Travel time to work: 33.0% less than 15 minutes, 45.7% 15 to 30 minutes, 14.9% 30 to 45 minutes, 2.9% 45 to 60 minutes, 3.6% 60 minutes or more (2000)

Additional Information Contacts
City of Franklin . . . . (937) 746-9921
    http://www.franklinohio.org
Franklin Area Chamber of Commerce . . . . (513) 746-8457
    http://www.franklinohio.org

HARVEYSBURG
(village). Covers a land area of 0.657 square miles and a water area of 0 square miles. Located at 39.50° N. Lat.; 84.00° W. Long. Elevation is 930 feet.

Population: 471 (1990); 563 (2000); 640 (2005); 724 (2010 projected); Race: 96.4% White, 1.7% Black, 0.2% Asian, 2.7% Hispanic of any race (2005); Density: 974.4 persons per square mile (2005); Average household size: 2.90 (2005); Median age: 31.4 (2005); Males per 100 females: 95.1 (2005); Marriage status: 23.0% never married, 57.7% now married, 7.8% widowed, 11.5% divorced (2000); Foreign born: 0.3% (2000); Ancestry (includes multiple ancestries): 20.3% German, 17.1% English, 16.1% United States or American, 9.6% Other groups, 8.4% Irish (2000).
Economy: Single-family building permits issued: 1 (2005); Multi-family building permits issued: 0 (2005); Employment by occupation: 12.5% management, 7.5% professional, 15.4% services, 27.5% sales, 1.1% farming, 17.1% construction, 18.9% production (2000).
Income: Per capita income: $21,273 (2005); Median household income: $49,847 (2005); Average household income: $61,606 (2005); Percent of households with income of $100,000 or more: 12.2% (2005); Poverty rate: 8.6% (2000).

Education: Percent of population age 25 and over with: High school diploma (including GED) or higher: 81.5% (2005); Bachelor's degree or higher: 14.1% (2005); Master's degree or higher: 2.9% (2005).
Housing: Homeownership rate: 74.7% (2005); Median home value: $122,170 (2005); Median rent: $497 per month (2000); Median age of housing: 42 years (2000).
Transportation: Commute to work: 93.8% car, 1.1% public transportation, 0.7% walk, 3.6% work from home (2000); Travel time to work: 22.3% less than 15 minutes, 25.3% 15 to 30 minutes, 35.1% 30 to 45 minutes, 14.0% 45 to 60 minutes, 3.4% 60 minutes or more (2000)

HUNTER
(CDP). Covers a land area of 1.606 square miles and a water area of 0 square miles. Located at 39.49° N. Lat.; 84.29° W. Long.
Population: 1,950 (1990); 1,737 (2000); 1,640 (2005); 1,650 (2010 projected); Race: 98.5% White, 0.2% Black, 0.1% Asian, 0.6% Hispanic of any race (2005); Density: 1,021.3 persons per square mile (2005); Average household size: 2.49 (2005); Median age: 42.2 (2005); Males per 100 females: 100.5 (2005); Marriage status: 19.4% never married, 62.5% now married, 5.8% widowed, 12.2% divorced (2000); Foreign born: 1.7% (2000); Ancestry (includes multiple ancestries): 19.9% United States or American, 15.5% German, 14.9% Other groups, 14.4% English, 11.6% Irish (2000).
Economy: Employment by occupation: 11.0% management, 17.8% professional, 16.5% services, 18.6% sales, 0.0% farming, 16.5% construction, 19.7% production (2000).
Income: Per capita income: $26,348 (2005); Median household income: $49,829 (2005); Average household income: $65,669 (2005); Percent of households with income of $100,000 or more: 13.1% (2005); Poverty rate: 1.0% (2000).
Education: Percent of population age 25 and over with: High school diploma (including GED) or higher: 85.8% (2005); Bachelor's degree or higher: 13.7% (2005); Master's degree or higher: 2.7% (2005).
Housing: Homeownership rate: 92.1% (2005); Median home value: $132,620 (2005); Median rent: $454 per month (2000); Median age of housing: 36 years (2000).
Transportation: Commute to work: 99.2% car, 0.0% public transportation, 0.0% walk, 0.0% work from home (2000); Travel time to work: 34.0% less than 15 minutes, 50.1% 15 to 30 minutes, 9.9% 30 to 45 minutes, 4.5% 45 to 60 minutes, 1.5% 60 minutes or more (2000)

KINGS MILLS
(unincorporated postal area, zip code 45034). Covers a land area of 0.671 square miles and a water area of 0 square miles. Located at 39.35° N. Lat.; 84.24° W. Long. Elevation is 784 feet.
Population: 794 (2000); Race: 98.6% White, 0.0% Black, 0.0% Asian, 0.0% Hispanic of any race (2000); Density: 1,183.3 persons per square mile (2000); Age: 24.9% under 18, 4.5% over 64 (2000); Marriage status: 26.6% never married, 61.5% now married, 3.2% widowed, 8.7% divorced (2000); Foreign born: 0.0% (2000); Ancestry (includes multiple ancestries): 36.9% German, 19.7% Irish, 13.1% Other groups, 12.8% English, 8.0% United States or American (2000).
Economy: Employment by occupation: 11.9% management, 28.3% professional, 17.1% services, 17.7% sales, 0.0% farming, 11.9% construction, 13.2% production (2000).
Income: Per capita income: $26,323 (2000); Median household income: $59,038 (2000); Poverty rate: 0.9% (2000).
Education: Percent of population age 25 and over with: High school diploma (including GED) or higher: 93.7% (2000); Bachelor's degree or higher: 25.4% (2000).

School District(s)
Kings Local SD (PK-12)
   2003-04 Enrollment: 3,849 . . . . (513) 398-8050

Housing: Homeownership rate: 84.2% (2000); Median home value: $178,700 (2000); Median rent: $343 per month (2000); Median age of housing: 5 years (2000).
Transportation: Commute to work: 92.5% car, 0.0% public transportation, 1.3% walk, 6.2% work from home (2000); Travel time to work: 24.6% less than 15 minutes, 47.2% 15 to 30 minutes, 28.2% 30 to 45 minutes, 0.0% 45 to 60 minutes, 0.0% 60 minutes or more (2000)

LANDEN
(CDP). Covers a land area of 4.677 square miles and a water area of 0.083 square miles. Located at 39.30° N. Lat.; 84.28° W. Long. Elevation is 810 feet.
Population: 9,204 (1990); 12,766 (2000); 13,319 (2005); 14,201 (2010 projected); Race: 91.0% White, 1.4% Black, 5.1% Asian, 2.9% Hispanic of any race (2005); Density: 2,848.0 persons per square mile (2005); Average household size: 2.56 (2005); Median age: 34.2 (2005); Males per 100 females: 98.3 (2005); Marriage status: 22.0% never married, 65.3% now married, 3.0% widowed, 9.7% divorced (2000); Foreign born: 4.5% (2000); Ancestry (includes multiple ancestries): 36.4% German, 18.5% Irish, 12.4% English, 9.7% Other groups, 6.7% Italian (2000).
Economy: Employment by occupation: 24.8% management, 28.2% professional, 7.2% services, 28.0% sales, 0.0% farming, 5.3% construction, 6.6% production (2000).
Income: Per capita income: $34,496 (2005); Median household income: $72,162 (2005); Average household income: $88,475 (2005); Percent of households with income of $100,000 or more: 27.6% (2005); Poverty rate: 2.5% (2000).
Education: Percent of population age 25 and over with: High school diploma (including GED) or higher: 96.1% (2005); Bachelor's degree or higher: 50.6% (2005); Master's degree or higher: 15.1% (2005).
Housing: Homeownership rate: 68.5% (2005); Median home value: $172,149 (2005); Median rent: $742 per month (2000); Median age of housing: 13 years (2000).
Transportation: Commute to work: 92.7% car, 2.2% public transportation, 0.5% walk, 4.2% work from home (2000); Travel time to work: 25.1% less than 15 minutes, 38.7% 15 to 30 minutes, 23.8% 30 to 45 minutes, 7.0% 45 to 60 minutes, 5.4% 60 minutes or more (2000)

LEBANON
(city). Covers a land area of 11.774 square miles and a water area of 0.005 square miles. Located at 39.42° N. Lat.; 84.21° W. Long. Elevation is 769 feet.
History: Named for the Semitic translation of "to be white". Lebanon was founded in 1803 and grew as the commercial center for the region between the two Miami Rivers. This was the home of Thomas Corwin (1794-1865) who was governor of Ohio, a U.S. senator, Secretary of the Treasury, and Minister to Mexico under Abraham Lincoln.
Population: 11,282 (1990); 16,962 (2000); 19,110 (2005); 21,337 (2010 projected); Race: 88.7% White, 7.5% Black, 1.2% Asian, 1.5% Hispanic of any race (2005); Density: 1,623.1 persons per square mile (2005); Average household size: 2.83 (2005); Median age: 31.9 (2005); Males per 100 females: 109.7 (2005); Marriage status: 19.8% never married, 59.3% now married, 5.7% widowed, 15.2% divorced (2000); Foreign born: 1.8% (2000); Ancestry (includes multiple ancestries): 20.5% German, 15.5% United States or American, 11.5% Irish, 9.0% English, 7.6% Other groups (2000).
Economy: Single-family building permits issued: 142 (2005); Multi-family building permits issued: 57 (2005); Employment by occupation: 13.5% management, 20.1% professional, 12.1% services, 27.8% sales, 0.1% farming, 8.9% construction, 17.6% production (2000).
Income: Per capita income: $23,409 (2005); Median household income: $52,613 (2005); Average household income: $63,947 (2005); Percent of households with income of $100,000 or more: 17.2% (2005); Poverty rate: 6.4% (2000).
Taxes: Total city taxes per capita: $491 (2004); City property taxes per capita: $126 (2004).
Education: Percent of population age 25 and over with: High school diploma (including GED) or higher: 86.0% (2005); Bachelor's degree or higher: 25.2% (2005); Master's degree or higher: 6.2% (2005).

School District(s)
Lebanon City SD (PK-12)
   2003-04 Enrollment: 4,780 . . . . (513) 934-5770
Warren County Educational Service Center (07-10)
   2003-04 Enrollment: n/a . . . . (513) 695-2900
Warren County Joint Vocational SD (09-12)
   2003-04 Enrollment: n/a . . . . (513) 932-5677
Warren County Virtual Community School, Inc.
   2003-04 Enrollment: n/a

Two-year College(s)
Warren County Career Center (Public)
   Fall 2004 Enrollment: 74 . . . . (513) 932-8145

Housing: Homeownership rate: 60.0% (2005); Median home value: $151,906 (2005); Median rent: $495 per month (2000); Median age of housing: 22 years (2000).
Safety: Violent crime rate: 11.7 per 10,000 population; Property crime rate: 311.1 per 10,000 population (2004).
Newspapers: Sunday Western Star (General - Circulation 16,300); The Western Star (General - Circulation 12,500)
Transportation: Commute to work: 94.9% car, 0.7% public transportation, 1.3% walk, 2.5% work from home (2000); Travel time to work: 31.9% less

than 15 minutes, 32.5% 15 to 30 minutes, 25.3% 30 to 45 minutes, 8.2% 45 to 60 minutes, 2.2% 60 minutes or more (2000)
Additional Information Contacts
City of Lebanon . . . . (513) 932-3060
http://www.ci.lebanon.oh.us
Lebanon Chamber of Commerce. . . . . (513) 932-1100
http://www.lebanonchamber.org

LOVELAND PARK (CDP). Covers a land area of 1.473 square miles and a water area of 0.068 square miles. Located at 39.29° N. Lat.; 84.26° W. Long. Elevation is 728 feet.
Population: 1,406 (1990); 1,799 (2000); 1,824 (2005); 1,857 (2010 projected); Race: 95.3% White, 0.8% Black, 2.3% Asian, 0.9% Hispanic of any race (2005); Density: 1,238.1 persons per square mile (2005); Average household size: 2.76 (2005); Median age: 38.0 (2005); Males per 100 females: 99.3 (2005); Marriage status: 21.0% never married, 63.0% now married, 3.6% widowed, 12.4% divorced (2000); Foreign born: 1.3% (2000); Ancestry (includes multiple ancestries): 29.1% German, 23.8% Irish, 14.6% United States or American, 9.4% English, 8.6% Other groups (2000).
Economy: Employment by occupation: 19.7% management, 14.3% professional, 16.3% services, 18.3% sales, 0.0% farming, 15.9% construction, 15.4% production (2000).
Income: Per capita income: $28,507 (2005); Median household income: $49,719 (2005); Average household income: $78,665 (2005); Percent of households with income of $100,000 or more: 20.0% (2005); Poverty rate: 1.8% (2000).
Education: Percent of population age 25 and over with: High school diploma (including GED) or higher: 80.8% (2005); Bachelor's degree or higher: 19.9% (2005); Master's degree or higher: 6.6% (2005).
Housing: Homeownership rate: 87.0% (2005); Median home value: $136,951 (2005); Median rent: $489 per month (2000); Median age of housing: 38 years (2000).
Transportation: Commute to work: 91.6% car, 1.0% public transportation, 1.0% walk, 6.3% work from home (2000); Travel time to work: 27.9% less than 15 minutes, 35.0% 15 to 30 minutes, 23.3% 30 to 45 minutes, 6.7% 45 to 60 minutes, 7.1% 60 minutes or more (2000)

MAINEVILLE (village). Covers a land area of 0.243 square miles and a water area of 0 square miles. Located at 39.31° N. Lat.; 84.22° W. Long. Elevation is 805 feet.
Population: 366 (1990); 885 (2000); 1,624 (2005); 2,336 (2010 projected); Race: 98.0% White, 0.3% Black, 0.1% Asian, 1.2% Hispanic of any race (2005); Density: 6,674.2 persons per square mile (2005); Average household size: 2.39 (2005); Median age: 37.7 (2005); Males per 100 females: 88.4 (2005); Marriage status: 20.8% never married, 58.6% now married, 7.7% widowed, 12.9% divorced (2000); Foreign born: 1.6% (2000); Ancestry (includes multiple ancestries): 30.3% German, 18.4% English, 18.2% Irish, 14.8% United States or American, 7.0% Other groups (2000).
Economy: In agricultural area. Employment by occupation: 16.1% management, 20.0% professional, 11.2% services, 28.3% sales, 0.2% farming, 8.8% construction, 15.3% production (2000).
Income: Per capita income: $32,651 (2005); Median household income: $69,318 (2005); Average household income: $77,978 (2005); Percent of households with income of $100,000 or more: 23.8% (2005); Poverty rate: 3.2% (2000).
Education: Percent of population age 25 and over with: High school diploma (including GED) or higher: 85.4% (2005); Bachelor's degree or higher: 19.4% (2005); Master's degree or higher: 6.5% (2005).
School District(s)
Kings Local SD (PK-12)
    2003-04 Enrollment: 3,849 . . . . (513) 398-8050
Little Miami Local School District (KG-12)
    2003-04 Enrollment: 3,201 . . . . (513) 899-2264
Housing: Homeownership rate: 76.6% (2005); Median home value: $163,192 (2005); Median rent: $354 per month (2000); Median age of housing: 12 years (2000).
Transportation: Commute to work: 94.3% car, 0.6% public transportation, 0.0% walk, 4.3% work from home (2000); Travel time to work: 28.5% less than 15 minutes, 33.5% 15 to 30 minutes, 25.1% 30 to 45 minutes, 8.8% 45 to 60 minutes, 4.1% 60 minutes or more (2000)

MASON (city). Covers a land area of 17.613 square miles and a water area of 0.037 square miles. Located at 39.35° N. Lat.; 84.31° W. Long. Elevation is 810 feet.
History: On June 1, 1803, Revolutionary War veteran William Mason paid $1,700 at auction to purchase 640 acres of land in what is now downtown Mason. In 1815, he platted 16 lots on this land and named the village Palmira. In 1832, two years after the death of William Mason and according to his will, over 40 more lots were platted on the north, south, and west of Palmira. When the plat was officially recorded, the name of the village was listed as Palmyra. In 1835, a petition was sent to the federal post office to correct the name of the town. It had been listed as Kirkwood, possibly an error because the postmaster at the time was William Kirkwood. When village officials were informed that there was another Palmyra in Ohio, the name was officially changed to Mason. Mason remained a small farming community for another 125 years. In 1970, a year before the town was incorporated to become a city, there were fewer than 5,700 residents.
Population: 12,046 (1990); 22,016 (2000); 29,379 (2005); 36,797 (2010 projected); Race: 91.8% White, 1.9% Black, 4.6% Asian, 1.2% Hispanic of any race (2005); Density: 1,668.0 persons per square mile (2005); Average household size: 2.82 (2005); Median age: 35.0 (2005); Males per 100 females: 95.4 (2005); Marriage status: 18.1% never married, 69.2% now married, 4.5% widowed, 8.1% divorced (2000); Foreign born: 4.0% (2000); Ancestry (includes multiple ancestries): 33.5% German, 18.3% Irish, 14.0% English, 9.3% Other groups, 8.2% United States or American (2000).
Economy: Unemployment rate: 3.5% (2005); Total civilian labor force: 15,001 (2005); Single-family building permits issued: 305 (2005); Multi-family building permits issued: 0 (2005); Employment by occupation: 20.8% management, 23.2% professional, 9.5% services, 29.7% sales, 0.1% farming, 5.0% construction, 11.7% production (2000).
Income: Per capita income: $35,200 (2005); Median household income: $79,620 (2005); Average household income: $98,999 (2005); Percent of households with income of $100,000 or more: 36.1% (2005); Poverty rate: 2.8% (2000).
Taxes: Total city taxes per capita: $864 (2004); City property taxes per capita: $232 (2004).
Education: Percent of population age 25 and over with: High school diploma (including GED) or higher: 93.9% (2005); Bachelor's degree or higher: 41.1% (2005); Master's degree or higher: 12.8% (2005).
School District(s)
Kings Local SD (PK-12)
    2003-04 Enrollment: 3,849 . . . . (513) 398-8050
Mason City SD (PK-12)
    2003-04 Enrollment: 8,635 . . . . (513) 398-0474
Housing: Homeownership rate: 85.9% (2005); Median home value: $187,711 (2005); Median rent: $527 per month (2000); Median age of housing: 12 years (2000).
Newspapers: Pulse Journal (General - Circulation 34,000); Pulse Journal - Mason Edition (General - Circulation 12,000)
Transportation: Commute to work: 93.9% car, 1.0% public transportation, 0.3% walk, 4.5% work from home (2000); Travel time to work: 25.6% less than 15 minutes, 42.9% 15 to 30 minutes, 23.6% 30 to 45 minutes, 5.6% 45 to 60 minutes, 2.2% 60 minutes or more (2000)
Additional Information Contacts
City of Mason. . . . . (513) 229-8500
http://www.imaginemason.org
Mason Chamber of Commerce . . . . (513) 336-0125
http://www.necchamber.org

MORROW (village). Covers a land area of 1.691 square miles and a water area of 0.031 square miles. Located at 39.35° N. Lat.; 84.13° W. Long. Elevation is 650 feet.
History: Morrow was settled in 1844 and named for Jeremiah Morrow, Governor of Ohio from 1822 to 1826.
Population: 1,206 (1990); 1,286 (2000); 1,437 (2005); 1,600 (2010 projected); Race: 97.6% White, 0.7% Black, 0.1% Asian, 3.0% Hispanic of any race (2005); Density: 850.0 persons per square mile (2005); Average household size: 2.70 (2005); Median age: 39.0 (2005); Males per 100 females: 88.8 (2005); Marriage status: 17.2% never married, 59.3% now married, 8.4% widowed, 15.1% divorced (2000); Foreign born: 0.4% (2000); Ancestry (includes multiple ancestries): 20.0% German, 9.7% Irish, 9.5% United States or American, 9.0% English, 7.8% Other groups (2000).
Economy: Employment by occupation: 8.6% management, 10.9% professional, 16.0% services, 22.8% sales, 0.4% farming, 17.7% construction, 23.5% production (2000).

Income: Per capita income: $17,915 (2005); Median household income: $36,774 (2005); Average household income: $47,589 (2005); Percent of households with income of $100,000 or more: 9.6% (2005); Poverty rate: 15.5% (2000).
Education: Percent of population age 25 and over with: High school diploma (including GED) or higher: 70.3% (2005); Bachelor's degree or higher: 10.4% (2005); Master's degree or higher: 4.9% (2005).

School District(s)
Little Miami Local School District (KG-12)
   2003-04 Enrollment: 3,201 . . . . (513) 899-2264

Housing: Homeownership rate: 57.5% (2005); Median home value: $118,276 (2005); Median rent: $394 per month (2000); Median age of housing: 49 years (2000).
Transportation: Commute to work: 91.0% car, 0.0% public transportation, 4.6% walk, 3.5% work from home (2000); Travel time to work: 24.0% less than 15 minutes, 37.0% 15 to 30 minutes, 23.2% 30 to 45 minutes, 9.7% 45 to 60 minutes, 6.1% 60 minutes or more (2000)

Additional Information Contacts
Morrow Area Chamber of Commerce . . . . (513) 899-4466
  http://www.morrow-today.org

OREGONIA (unincorporated postal area, zip code 45054).
Covers a land area of 31.745 square miles and a water area of 0.006 square miles. Located at 39.44° N. Lat.; 84.06° W. Long. Elevation is 690 feet.
Population: 1,689 (2000); Race: 99.7% White, 0.0% Black, 0.0% Asian, 0.4% Hispanic of any race (2000); Density: 53.2 persons per square mile (2000); Age: 27.3% under 18, 8.1% over 64 (2000); Marriage status: 15.5% never married, 66.0% now married, 4.0% widowed, 14.5% divorced (2000); Foreign born: 0.7% (2000); Ancestry (includes multiple ancestries): 23.5% German, 18.3% United States or American, 12.2% English, 11.5% Irish, 3.9% Dutch (2000).
Economy: Employment by occupation: 18.4% management, 18.8% professional, 15.9% services, 21.6% sales, 0.0% farming, 13.1% construction, 12.3% production (2000).
Income: Per capita income: $25,329 (2000); Median household income: $56,136 (2000); Poverty rate: 4.8% (2000).
Education: Percent of population age 25 and over with: High school diploma (including GED) or higher: 85.2% (2000); Bachelor's degree or higher: 23.6% (2000).
Housing: Homeownership rate: 87.5% (2000); Median home value: $141,700 (2000); Median rent: $421 per month (2000); Median age of housing: 25 years (2000).
Transportation: Commute to work: 95.7% car, 0.0% public transportation, 0.7% walk, 3.6% work from home (2000); Travel time to work: 12.7% less than 15 minutes, 35.5% 15 to 30 minutes, 35.4% 30 to 45 minutes, 10.5% 45 to 60 minutes, 5.9% 60 minutes or more (2000)

PLEASANT PLAIN (village).
Covers a land area of 0.108 square miles and a water area of 0 square miles. Located at 39.28° N. Lat.; 84.10° W. Long. Elevation is 886 feet.
Population: 138 (1990); 156 (2000); 160 (2005); 168 (2010 projected); Race: 98.1% White, 0.0% Black, 1.9% Asian, 0.0% Hispanic of any race (2005); Density: 1,478.9 persons per square mile (2005); Average household size: 2.76 (2005); Median age: 36.3 (2005); Males per 100 females: 113.3 (2005); Marriage status: 18.9% never married, 60.4% now married, 5.7% widowed, 15.1% divorced (2000); Foreign born: 7.3% (2000); Ancestry (includes multiple ancestries): 35.1% German, 11.3% Other groups, 9.9% Italian, 8.6% Irish, 5.3% English (2000).
Economy: Employment by occupation: 17.4% management, 11.6% professional, 7.2% services, 33.3% sales, 0.0% farming, 21.7% construction, 8.7% production (2000).
Income: Per capita income: $18,719 (2005); Median household income: $52,174 (2005); Average household income: $51,638 (2005); Percent of households with income of $100,000 or more: 1.7% (2005); Poverty rate: 7.3% (2000).
Education: Percent of population age 25 and over with: High school diploma (including GED) or higher: 88.3% (2005); Bachelor's degree or higher: 18.4% (2005); Master's degree or higher: 1.0% (2005).
Housing: Homeownership rate: 81.0% (2005); Median home value: $89,200 (2005); Median rent: $575 per month (2000); Median age of housing: 60+ years (2000).
Transportation: Commute to work: 100.0% car, 0.0% public transportation, 0.0% walk, 0.0% work from home (2000); Travel time to work: 13.4% less than 15 minutes, 40.3% 15 to 30 minutes, 25.4% 30 to 45 minutes, 20.9% 45 to 60 minutes, 0.0% 60 minutes or more (2000)

SOUTH LEBANON (village).
Covers a land area of 1.668 square miles and a water area of 0.030 square miles. Located at 39.37° N. Lat.; 84.21° W. Long. Elevation is 630 feet.
Population: 2,786 (1990); 2,538 (2000); 2,885 (2005); 3,271 (2010 projected); Race: 98.1% White, 0.0% Black, 0.4% Asian, 1.5% Hispanic of any race (2005); Density: 1,729.2 persons per square mile (2005); Average household size: 2.46 (2005); Median age: 33.3 (2005); Males per 100 females: 98.4 (2005); Marriage status: 20.1% never married, 61.7% now married, 7.9% widowed, 10.3% divorced (2000); Foreign born: 0.4% (2000); Ancestry (includes multiple ancestries): 31.5% United States or American, 10.0% Irish, 9.6% German, 9.1% Other groups, 5.7% English (2000).
Economy: Chemicals. Single-family building permits issued: 72 (2005); Multi-family building permits issued: 0 (2005); Employment by occupation: 3.4% management, 4.7% professional, 22.7% services, 16.4% sales, 0.0% farming, 19.1% construction, 33.7% production (2000).
Income: Per capita income: $18,296 (2005); Median household income: $40,754 (2005); Average household income: $44,923 (2005); Percent of households with income of $100,000 or more: 3.7% (2005); Poverty rate: 12.7% (2000).
Education: Percent of population age 25 and over with: High school diploma (including GED) or higher: 52.0% (2005); Bachelor's degree or higher: 2.0% (2005); Master's degree or higher: 0.8% (2005).
Housing: Homeownership rate: 68.8% (2005); Median home value: $81,624 (2005); Median rent: $396 per month (2000); Median age of housing: 38 years (2000).
Transportation: Commute to work: 96.4% car, 0.4% public transportation, 1.7% walk, 0.5% work from home (2000); Travel time to work: 31.6% less than 15 minutes, 41.7% 15 to 30 minutes, 18.1% 30 to 45 minutes, 3.6% 45 to 60 minutes, 5.0% 60 minutes or more (2000)

SPRINGBORO (city).
Covers a land area of 8.810 square miles and a water area of 0 square miles. Located at 39.56° N. Lat.; 84.22° W. Long. Elevation is 780 feet.
History: Settled as early as 1796, Springboro was "founded" in 1815 by Jonathan Wright. Springboro was predominantly Quaker during its earlier years. It is known largely for its historical significance because slaves were hidden through the system of the Underground Railroad due to a large portion of its residents holding an anti-slavery opinion. Achilles Pugh, in fact, published a local paper during this time called "The Philanthropist" to enrich the belief of abolishing slavery.
Population: 7,772 (1990); 12,380 (2000); 15,693 (2005); 19,103 (2010 projected); Race: 93.8% White, 1.1% Black, 3.4% Asian, 1.2% Hispanic of any race (2005); Density: 1,781.2 persons per square mile (2005); Average household size: 2.89 (2005); Median age: 34.6 (2005); Males per 100 females: 95.6 (2005); Marriage status: 14.2% never married, 76.7% now married, 2.5% widowed, 6.6% divorced (2000); Foreign born: 2.1% (2000); Ancestry (includes multiple ancestries): 31.1% German, 17.4% Irish, 15.3% English, 11.0% United States or American, 8.9% Other groups (2000).
Economy: Single-family building permits issued: 137 (2005); Multi-family building permits issued: 0 (2005); Employment by occupation: 21.7% management, 26.2% professional, 8.6% services, 26.7% sales, 0.0% farming, 4.8% construction, 12.1% production (2000).
Income: Per capita income: $34,909 (2005); Median household income: $82,304 (2005); Average household income: $100,792 (2005); Percent of households with income of $100,000 or more: 38.8% (2005); Poverty rate: 3.0% (2000).
Taxes: Total city taxes per capita: $546 (2004); City property taxes per capita: $47 (2004).
Education: Percent of population age 25 and over with: High school diploma (including GED) or higher: 94.0% (2005); Bachelor's degree or higher: 43.2% (2005); Master's degree or higher: 16.0% (2005).

School District(s)
Springboro Community City SD (KG-12)
   2003-04 Enrollment: 4,320 . . . . (937) 748-3960

Housing: Homeownership rate: 87.5% (2005); Median home value: $203,698 (2005); Median rent: $476 per month (2000); Median age of housing: 11 years (2000).
Safety: Violent crime rate: 11.9 per 10,000 population; Property crime rate: 151.2 per 10,000 population (2004).
Transportation: Commute to work: 94.4% car, 0.2% public transportation, 0.7% walk, 3.9% work from home (2000); Travel time to work: 26.9% less than 15 minutes, 44.2% 15 to 30 minutes, 20.0% 30 to 45 minutes, 4.9% 45 to 60 minutes, 4.0% 60 minutes or more (2000)

Additional Information Contacts
City of Springboro .... (937) 748-4343
http://www.ci.springboro.oh.us
Springboro Chamber of Commerce .... (513) 748-0074
http://www.springboroohio.org

WAYNESVILLE (village).
Covers a land area of 2.274 square miles and a water area of 0.066 square miles. Located at 39.53° N. Lat.; 84.08° W. Long. Elevation is 754 feet.

History: Waynesville was laid out in 1796 by Samuel Highway and Dr. Evan Banes, and was named for General Anthony Wayne. Many of the early residents were Quakers from Carolina and Pennsylvania.

Population: 1,954 (1990); 2,558 (2000); 2,805 (2005); 3,093 (2010 projected); Race: 98.0% White, 0.0% Black, 0.1% Asian, 1.0% Hispanic of any race (2005); Density: 1,233.4 persons per square mile (2005); Average household size: 2.47 (2005); Median age: 36.8 (2005); Males per 100 females: 89.9 (2005); Marriage status: 20.1% never married, 61.0% now married, 9.2% widowed, 9.8% divorced (2000); Foreign born: 0.3% (2000); Ancestry (includes multiple ancestries): 23.0% German, 15.8% United States or American, 14.1% English, 13.2% Irish, 5.9% Other groups (2000).

Economy: Employment by occupation: 15.2% management, 23.5% professional, 13.5% services, 22.3% sales, 0.5% farming, 9.1% construction, 15.9% production (2000).

Income: Per capita income: $26,252 (2005); Median household income: $53,882 (2005); Average household income: $63,742 (2005); Percent of households with income of $100,000 or more: 15.2% (2005); Poverty rate: 3.9% (2000).

Education: Percent of population age 25 and over with: High school diploma (including GED) or higher: 82.5% (2005); Bachelor's degree or higher: 22.6% (2005); Master's degree or higher: 8.5% (2005).

School District(s)
Wayne Local SD (KG-12)
2003-04 Enrollment: 1,422 .... (513) 897-6971

Housing: Homeownership rate: 69.0% (2005); Median home value: $149,288 (2005); Median rent: $429 per month (2000); Median age of housing: 25 years (2000).

Safety: Violent crime rate: 14.1 per 10,000 population; Property crime rate: 179.6 per 10,000 population (2004).

Transportation: Commute to work: 94.7% car, 0.0% public transportation, 1.6% walk, 3.2% work from home (2000); Travel time to work: 22.0% less than 15 minutes, 36.3% 15 to 30 minutes, 30.8% 30 to 45 minutes, 7.1% 45 to 60 minutes, 3.7% 60 minutes or more (2000).

Additional Information Contacts
Waynesville Chamber of Commerce .... (513) 897-8855
http://www.waynesvilleohio.com

Washington County

Located in southeastern Ohio; bounded on the southeast by the Ohio River and the West Virginia border; crossed by the Muskingum and Little Muskingum Rivers. Covers a land area of 635.15 square miles, a water area of 5.00 square miles, and is located in the Eastern Time Zone. The county government was organized in 1788. County seat is Marietta.

Washington County is part of the Parkersburg-Marietta-Vienna, WV-OH Metropolitan Statistical Area. The entire metro area includes: Washington County, OH; Pleasants County, WV; Wirt County, WV; Wood County, WV

Weather Station: Marietta WWTP Elevation: 577 feet

	Jan	Feb	Mar	Apr	May	Jun	Jul	Aug	Sep	Oct	Nov	Dec
High	40	44	54	65	75	82	86	85	78	67	55	45
Low	22	24	32	41	50	59	64	62	55	43	35	27
Precip	3.1	2.8	3.7	3.1	4.0	4.4	4.2	4.2	3.3	2.9	3.2	3.4
Snow	7.2	na	3.4	0.5	0.0	0.0	0.0	0.0	0.0	tr	0.6	2.6

High and Low temperatures in degrees Fahrenheit; Precipitation and Snow in inches

Population: 62,254 (1990); 63,251 (2000); 62,332 (2005); 61,379 (2010 projected); Race: 97.2% White, 1.0% Black, 0.6% Asian, 0.5% Hispanic of any race (2005); Density: 98.1 persons per square mile (2005); Average household size: 2.48 (2005); Median age: 40.1 (2005); Males per 100 females: 94.9 (2005).

Religion: Five largest groups: 8.2% The United Methodist Church, 8.1% Catholic Church, 5.9% American Baptist Churches in the USA, 3.6% Churches of Christ, 2.0% Christian Churches and Churches of Christ (2000).

Economy: Unemployment rate: 6.0% (2005); Total civilian labor force: 32,646 (2005); Leading industries: 19.9% manufacturing; 17.4% health care and social assistance; 14.8% retail trade (2004); Farms: 952 totaling 141,455 acres (2002); Companies that employ 500 or more persons: 4 (2004); Companies that employ 100 to 499 persons: 26 (2004); Companies that employ less than 100 persons: 1,528 (2004); Black-owned businesses: n/a (2002); Hispanic-owned businesses: n/a (2002); Women-owned businesses: 1,544 (2002); Retail sales per capita: $12,734 (2006); Single-family building permits issued: 39 (2005); Multi-family building permits issued: 0 (2005).

Income: Per capita income: $21,020 (2005); Median household income: $39,879 (2005); Average household income: $51,152 (2005); Percent of households with income of $100,000 or more: 9.5% (2005); Poverty rate: 11.2% (2003); Bankruptcy rate: 7.17% (2005).

Taxes: Total county taxes per capita: $270 (2004); County property taxes per capita: $122 (2004).

Education: Percent of population age 25 and over with: High school diploma (including GED) or higher: 84.4% (2005); Bachelor's degree or higher: 14.9% (2005); Master's degree or higher: 5.6% (2005).

Housing: Homeownership rate: 76.6% (2005); Median home value: $89,994 (2005); Median rent: $319 per month (2000); Median age of housing: 33 years (2000).

Health: Birth rate: 108.6 per 10,000 population (2004); Death rate: 113.0 per 10,000 population (2004); Age-adjusted cancer mortality rate: 195.4 deaths per 100,000 population (2002); Air Quality Index: 80.0% good, 17.4% moderate, 2.6% unhealthy for sensitive individuals, 0.0% unhealthy (percent of days in 2005); Number of physicians: 18.2 per 10,000 population (2004); Hospital beds: 35.5 per 10,000 population (2003); Hospital admissions: 1,337.1 per 10,000 population (2003).

Elections: 2004 Presidential election results: 58.0% Bush, 41.5% Kerry, 0.0% Nader, 0.3% Badnarik.

National and State Parks: Howes State Park; Marietta State Forest Nursery

Additional Information Contacts
Washington County Government .... (740) 373-6623
http://www.co.washington.oh.us/
Belpre Chamber of Commerce .... (740) 423-8934
http://www.belprechamber.com
Beverly Chamber of Commerce .... (740) 984-8259
http://www.greatlakesonline.com/coc/oh/washington_county.htm
Marietta Chamber of Commerce .... (740) 373-5176
http://www.mariettachamber.com

Washington County Communities

BELPRE (city).
Covers a land area of 3.524 square miles and a water area of 0.027 square miles. Located at 39.28° N. Lat.; 81.58° W. Long. Elevation is 610 feet.

History: Belpre was established in 1789 by Captain Jonathan Stone who led a group of Revolutionary War veterans here from Marietta.

Population: 6,866 (1990); 6,660 (2000); 6,453 (2005); 6,247 (2010 projected); Race: 95.9% White, 2.2% Black, 0.6% Asian, 0.5% Hispanic of any race (2005); Density: 1,830.9 persons per square mile (2005); Average household size: 2.15 (2005); Median age: 42.1 (2005); Males per 100 females: 85.0 (2005); Marriage status: 20.3% never married, 55.4% now married, 9.9% widowed, 14.4% divorced (2000); Foreign born: 0.6% (2000); Ancestry (includes multiple ancestries): 18.3% German, 17.4% United States or American, 11.7% Irish, 10.1% English, 9.6% Other groups (2000).

Economy: Single-family building permits issued: 10 (2005); Multi-family building permits issued: 0 (2005); Employment by occupation: 10.6% management, 16.5% professional, 15.4% services, 32.4% sales, 0.0% farming, 8.1% construction, 17.1% production (2000).

Income: Per capita income: $20,421 (2005); Median household income: $33,550 (2005); Average household income: $43,469 (2005); Percent of households with income of $100,000 or more: 7.9% (2005); Poverty rate: 15.2% (2000).

Education: Percent of population age 25 and over with: High school diploma (including GED) or higher: 82.6% (2005); Bachelor's degree or higher: 13.5% (2005); Master's degree or higher: 4.1% (2005).

School District(s)
Belpre City SD (PK-12)
2003-04 Enrollment: 1,321 .... (740) 423-9511
Washington Educational Service Center (PK-PK)
2003-04 Enrollment: n/a .... (740) 373-6669

Housing: Homeownership rate: 66.2% (2005); Median home value: $87,311 (2005); Median rent: $334 per month (2000); Median age of housing: 34 years (2000).
Safety: Violent crime rate: 7.6 per 10,000 population; Property crime rate: 199.0 per 10,000 population (2004).
Transportation: Commute to work: 94.0% car, 0.4% public transportation, 2.4% walk, 1.9% work from home (2000); Travel time to work: 48.2% less than 15 minutes, 39.8% 15 to 30 minutes, 6.5% 30 to 45 minutes, 1.8% 45 to 60 minutes, 3.8% 60 minutes or more (2000)
Additional Information Contacts
Belpre Chamber of Commerce . . . . (740) 423-8934
   http://www.belprechamber.com

BEVERLY (village). Covers a land area of 0.729 square miles and a water area of 0.055 square miles. Located at 39.54° N. Lat.; 81.63° W. Long. Elevation is 700 feet.
History: Beverly was settled in 1789 by a group of adventurers from Marietta. Fort Frye was erected, but it was abandoned in 1794 and a new community was established on the Muskingum River at the mouth of Olive Green Creek.
Population: 1,511 (1990); 1,282 (2000); 1,248 (2005); 1,227 (2010 projected); Race: 99.4% White, 0.3% Black, 0.1% Asian, 0.3% Hispanic of any race (2005); Density: 1,711.0 persons per square mile (2005); Average household size: 2.26 (2005); Median age: 44.7 (2005); Males per 100 females: 85.7 (2005); Marriage status: 19.1% never married, 63.0% now married, 9.3% widowed, 8.5% divorced (2000); Foreign born: 0.4% (2000); Ancestry (includes multiple ancestries): 28.4% German, 13.0% Irish, 9.6% English, 9.6% United States or American, 4.1% Italian (2000).
Economy: Single-family building permits issued: 22 (2005); Multi-family building permits issued: 0 (2005); Employment by occupation: 8.5% management, 14.9% professional, 18.2% services, 27.5% sales, 0.8% farming, 11.0% construction, 19.2% production (2000).
Income: Per capita income: $23,952 (2005); Median household income: $40,135 (2005); Average household income: $51,585 (2005); Percent of households with income of $100,000 or more: 10.1% (2005); Poverty rate: 9.8% (2000).
Education: Percent of population age 25 and over with: High school diploma (including GED) or higher: 84.9% (2005); Bachelor's degree or higher: 17.7% (2005); Master's degree or higher: 5.8% (2005).
School District(s)
Fort Frye Local SD (PK-12)
   2003-04 Enrollment: 1,229 . . . . (740) 984-2497
Housing: Homeownership rate: 71.4% (2005); Median home value: $78,500 (2005); Median rent: $317 per month (2000); Median age of housing: 35 years (2000).
Transportation: Commute to work: 92.8% car, 0.0% public transportation, 4.5% walk, 2.1% work from home (2000); Travel time to work: 40.8% less than 15 minutes, 16.6% 15 to 30 minutes, 32.6% 30 to 45 minutes, 4.0% 45 to 60 minutes, 6.1% 60 minutes or more (2000)
Additional Information Contacts
Beverly Chamber of Commerce. . . . . (740) 984-8259
   http://www.greatlakesonline.com/coc/oh/washington_county.htm

CUTLER (unincorporated postal area, zip code 45724). Covers a land area of 52.092 square miles and a water area of 0.010 square miles. Located at 39.54° N. Lat.; 81.78° W. Long. Elevation is 780 feet.
Population: 1,547 (2000); Race: 91.2% White, 5.1% Black, 0.0% Asian, 0.0% Hispanic of any race (2000); Density: 29.7 persons per square mile (2000); Age: 25.1% under 18, 15.3% over 64 (2000); Marriage status: 17.1% never married, 66.4% now married, 7.4% widowed, 9.0% divorced (2000); Foreign born: 0.6% (2000); Ancestry (includes multiple ancestries): 13.7% German, 13.0% English, 12.5% United States or American, 8.5% Other groups, 7.8% Irish (2000).
Economy: Employment by occupation: 5.2% management, 18.3% professional, 17.9% services, 16.3% sales, 0.0% farming, 9.9% construction, 32.3% production (2000).
Income: Per capita income: $15,518 (2000); Median household income: $35,357 (2000); Poverty rate: 5.9% (2000).
Education: Percent of population age 25 and over with: High school diploma (including GED) or higher: 77.8% (2000); Bachelor's degree or higher: 9.7% (2000).
School District(s)
Warren Local SD (PK-12)
   2003-04 Enrollment: 2,692 . . . . (740) 678-2366

Housing: Homeownership rate: 90.6% (2000); Median home value: $82,000 (2000); Median rent: $293 per month (2000); Median age of housing: 25 years (2000).
Transportation: Commute to work: 91.8% car, 0.0% public transportation, 2.3% walk, 3.4% work from home (2000); Travel time to work: 8.5% less than 15 minutes, 15.1% 15 to 30 minutes, 44.7% 30 to 45 minutes, 24.1% 45 to 60 minutes, 7.7% 60 minutes or more (2000)

DEVOLA (CDP). Covers a land area of 5.132 square miles and a water area of 0.223 square miles. Located at 39.47° N. Lat.; 81.47° W. Long. Elevation is 680 feet.
History: Also spelled De Vola.
Population: 2,736 (1990); 2,771 (2000); 2,680 (2005); 2,557 (2010 projected); Race: 97.0% White, 0.0% Black, 2.5% Asian, 0.1% Hispanic of any race (2005); Density: 522.2 persons per square mile (2005); Average household size: 2.56 (2005); Median age: 46.2 (2005); Males per 100 females: 93.9 (2005); Marriage status: 16.2% never married, 66.5% now married, 10.9% widowed, 6.4% divorced (2000); Foreign born: 0.0% (2000); Ancestry (includes multiple ancestries): 33.2% German, 13.5% English, 11.6% Irish, 8.3% United States or American, 5.0% Scottish (2000).
Economy: Employment by occupation: 15.4% management, 28.6% professional, 10.7% services, 24.3% sales, 1.5% farming, 10.3% construction, 9.2% production (2000).
Income: Per capita income: $26,316 (2005); Median household income: $52,327 (2005); Average household income: $66,785 (2005); Percent of households with income of $100,000 or more: 18.3% (2005); Poverty rate: 4.5% (2000).
Education: Percent of population age 25 and over with: High school diploma (including GED) or higher: 92.8% (2005); Bachelor's degree or higher: 28.8% (2005); Master's degree or higher: 11.3% (2005).
Housing: Homeownership rate: 90.4% (2005); Median home value: $123,680 (2005); Median rent: $468 per month (2000); Median age of housing: 35 years (2000).
Transportation: Commute to work: 96.9% car, 0.0% public transportation, 1.4% walk, 1.7% work from home (2000); Travel time to work: 38.2% less than 15 minutes, 42.2% 15 to 30 minutes, 10.9% 30 to 45 minutes, 2.4% 45 to 60 minutes, 6.3% 60 minutes or more (2000)

FLEMING (unincorporated postal area, zip code 45729). Covers a land area of 27.516 square miles and a water area of 0.049 square miles. Located at 39.42° N. Lat.; 81.59° W. Long. Elevation is 797 feet.
Population: 1,410 (2000); Race: 97.4% White, 0.6% Black, 0.0% Asian, 0.0% Hispanic of any race (2000); Density: 51.2 persons per square mile (2000); Age: 22.6% under 18, 12.6% over 64 (2000); Marriage status: 12.4% never married, 74.6% now married, 8.0% widowed, 5.0% divorced (2000); Foreign born: 0.0% (2000); Ancestry (includes multiple ancestries): 25.9% German, 18.5% United States or American, 16.8% Irish, 10.2% English, 4.6% Other groups (2000).
Economy: Employment by occupation: 5.6% management, 16.1% professional, 9.0% services, 33.1% sales, 0.0% farming, 12.5% construction, 23.6% production (2000).
Income: Per capita income: $19,008 (2000); Median household income: $40,667 (2000); Poverty rate: 8.3% (2000).
Education: Percent of population age 25 and over with: High school diploma (including GED) or higher: 85.8% (2000); Bachelor's degree or higher: 14.4% (2000).
Housing: Homeownership rate: 92.6% (2000); Median home value: $85,000 (2000); Median rent: $331 per month (2000); Median age of housing: 25 years (2000).
Transportation: Commute to work: 94.4% car, 0.0% public transportation, 2.4% walk, 2.6% work from home (2000); Travel time to work: 11.9% less than 15 minutes, 52.0% 15 to 30 minutes, 26.2% 30 to 45 minutes, 7.5% 45 to 60 minutes, 2.4% 60 minutes or more (2000)

LITTLE HOCKING (unincorporated postal area, zip code 45742). Covers a land area of 26.393 square miles and a water area of 0 square miles. Located at 39.27° N. Lat.; 81.70° W. Long. Elevation is 660 feet.
History: George Washington camped near the site of Little Hocking, on the river of the same name, while making a tour of the Ohio Valley in 1770. At that time the river was called the Little Hockhocking.
Population: 3,217 (2000); Race: 97.8% White, 0.3% Black, 0.0% Asian, 1.0% Hispanic of any race (2000); Density: 121.9 persons per square mile (2000); Age: 27.6% under 18, 11.0% over 64 (2000); Marriage status: 18.6% never married, 68.0% now married, 4.5% widowed, 8.9% divorced

(2000); Foreign born: 0.8% (2000); Ancestry (includes multiple ancestries): 21.3% German, 19.4% United States or American, 10.3% English, 10.3% Irish, 5.7% Other groups (2000).
Economy: Employment by occupation: 5.9% management, 21.1% professional, 11.8% services, 30.1% sales, 0.0% farming, 9.1% construction, 22.0% production (2000).
Income: Per capita income: $16,633 (2000); Median household income: $39,583 (2000); Poverty rate: 5.5% (2000).
Education: Percent of population age 25 and over with: High school diploma (including GED) or higher: 83.4% (2000); Bachelor's degree or higher: 15.9% (2000).

School District(s)
Warren Local SD (PK-12)
    2003-04 Enrollment: 2,692 . . . . (740) 678-2366
Housing: Homeownership rate: 87.1% (2000); Median home value: $73,100 (2000); Median rent: $308 per month (2000); Median age of housing: 26 years (2000).
Transportation: Commute to work: 90.6% car, 0.0% public transportation, 1.1% walk, 5.6% work from home (2000); Travel time to work: 18.9% less than 15 minutes, 50.6% 15 to 30 minutes, 21.4% 30 to 45 minutes, 1.4% 45 to 60 minutes, 7.8% 60 minutes or more (2000)

LOWELL (village). Covers a land area of 0.254 square miles and a water area of 0 square miles. Located at 39.52° N. Lat.; 81.50° W. Long. Elevation is 618 feet.
History: Lowell was founded in 1822 and grew around woolen mills. It was named for the textile town in Massachusetts.
Population: 614 (1990); 628 (2000); 628 (2005); 616 (2010 projected); Race: 99.5% White, 0.0% Black, 0.0% Asian, 0.5% Hispanic of any race (2005); Density: 2,476.3 persons per square mile (2005); Average household size: 2.40 (2005); Median age: 39.7 (2005); Males per 100 females: 101.3 (2005); Marriage status: 19.2% never married, 54.5% now married, 14.6% widowed, 11.6% divorced (2000); Foreign born: 0.7% (2000); Ancestry (includes multiple ancestries): 33.4% German, 19.2% United States or American, 12.7% Irish, 9.3% English, 6.3% Other groups (2000).
Economy: Single-family building permits issued: 1 (2005); Multi-family building permits issued: 0 (2005); Employment by occupation: 3.1% management, 10.0% professional, 21.2% services, 21.9% sales, 0.8% farming, 13.5% construction, 29.6% production (2000).
Income: Per capita income: $18,806 (2005); Median household income: $39,426 (2005); Average household income: $45,076 (2005); Percent of households with income of $100,000 or more: 4.6% (2005); Poverty rate: 14.5% (2000).
Education: Percent of population age 25 and over with: High school diploma (including GED) or higher: 84.6% (2005); Bachelor's degree or higher: 6.2% (2005); Master's degree or higher: 2.6% (2005).

School District(s)
Fort Frye Local SD (PK-12)
    2003-04 Enrollment: 1,229 . . . . (740) 984-2497
Housing: Homeownership rate: 78.2% (2005); Median home value: $55,246 (2005); Median rent: $329 per month (2000); Median age of housing: 60+ years (2000).
Transportation: Commute to work: 93.3% car, 0.0% public transportation, 2.4% walk, 2.4% work from home (2000); Travel time to work: 14.6% less than 15 minutes, 63.6% 15 to 30 minutes, 15.4% 30 to 45 minutes, 3.2% 45 to 60 minutes, 3.2% 60 minutes or more (2000)

LOWER SALEM (village). Covers a land area of 0.079 square miles and a water area of 0 square miles. Located at 39.56° N. Lat.; 81.39° W. Long. Elevation is 653 feet.
History: Lower Salem was platted in 1850 by James Stanley.
Population: 103 (1990); 109 (2000); 108 (2005); 104 (2010 projected); Race: 93.5% White, 1.9% Black, 0.0% Asian, 0.0% Hispanic of any race (2005); Density: 1,360.6 persons per square mile (2005); Average household size: 3.00 (2005); Median age: 32.9 (2005); Males per 100 females: 74.2 (2005); Marriage status: 11.4% never married, 64.8% now married, 5.7% widowed, 18.2% divorced (2000); Foreign born: 0.0% (2000); Ancestry (includes multiple ancestries): 55.4% German, 21.6% Irish, 17.3% United States or American, 14.4% Swiss, 7.9% Dutch (2000).
Economy: Single-family building permits issued: 0 (2005); Multi-family building permits issued: 0 (2005); Employment by occupation: 15.7% management, 7.8% professional, 15.7% services, 27.5% sales, 0.0% farming, 11.8% construction, 21.6% production (2000).

Income: Per capita income: $17,153 (2005); Median household income: $41,667 (2005); Average household income: $51,458 (2005); Percent of households with income of $100,000 or more: 19.4% (2005); Poverty rate: 5.0% (2000).
Education: Percent of population age 25 and over with: High school diploma (including GED) or higher: 92.3% (2005); Bachelor's degree or higher: 6.2% (2005); Master's degree or higher: 1.5% (2005).

School District(s)
Fort Frye Local SD (PK-12)
    2003-04 Enrollment: 1,229 . . . . (740) 984-2497
Housing: Homeownership rate: 83.3% (2005); Median home value: $48,333 (2005); Median rent: $225 per month (2000); Median age of housing: 60+ years (2000).
Transportation: Commute to work: 80.4% car, 3.9% public transportation, 5.9% walk, 9.8% work from home (2000); Travel time to work: 6.5% less than 15 minutes, 52.2% 15 to 30 minutes, 23.9% 30 to 45 minutes, 4.3% 45 to 60 minutes, 13.0% 60 minutes or more (2000)

MACKSBURG (village). Covers a land area of 0.233 square miles and a water area of 0 square miles. Located at 39.63° N. Lat.; 81.45° W. Long. Elevation is 700 feet.
Population: 218 (1990); 202 (2000); 198 (2005); 195 (2010 projected); Race: 100.0% White, 0.0% Black, 0.0% Asian, 2.0% Hispanic of any race (2005); Density: 849.3 persons per square mile (2005); Average household size: 2.48 (2005); Median age: 37.2 (2005); Males per 100 females: 130.2 (2005); Marriage status: 16.1% never married, 51.7% now married, 14.7% widowed, 17.5% divorced (2000); Foreign born: 0.0% (2000); Ancestry (includes multiple ancestries): 49.5% United States or American, 8.4% Irish, 8.4% German, 4.2% English, 3.2% Dutch (2000).
Economy: Employment by occupation: 0.0% management, 14.1% professional, 33.8% services, 8.5% sales, 8.5% farming, 12.7% construction, 22.5% production (2000).
Income: Per capita income: $10,960 (2005); Median household income: $23,333 (2005); Average household income: $27,125 (2005); Percent of households with income of $100,000 or more: 3.8% (2005); Poverty rate: 45.3% (2000).
Education: Percent of population age 25 and over with: High school diploma (including GED) or higher: 46.5% (2005); Bachelor's degree or higher: 1.6% (2005); Master's degree or higher: 1.6% (2005).
Housing: Homeownership rate: 77.5% (2005); Median home value: $37,273 (2005); Median rent: $225 per month (2000); Median age of housing: 58 years (2000).
Transportation: Commute to work: 93.7% car, 0.0% public transportation, 4.8% walk, 1.6% work from home (2000); Travel time to work: 30.6% less than 15 minutes, 22.6% 15 to 30 minutes, 30.6% 30 to 45 minutes, 9.7% 45 to 60 minutes, 6.5% 60 minutes or more (2000)

MARIETTA (city). Covers a land area of 8.309 square miles and a water area of 0.264 square miles. Located at 39.42° N. Lat.; 81.45° W. Long. Elevation is 616 feet.
History: Marietta was settled at the confluence of the Muskingum and Ohio Rivers in 1788 by the Ohio Company of Associates, a group of New Englanders looking for land to the west. At first they called the settlement Muskingum, but soon the name was officially declared to be Marietta, a tribute to Queen Marie Antoinette of France for her help in the American Revolution.
Population: 15,187 (1990); 14,515 (2000); 13,892 (2005); 13,265 (2010 projected); Race: 95.9% White, 1.2% Black, 1.0% Asian, 0.8% Hispanic of any race (2005); Density: 1,672.0 persons per square mile (2005); Average household size: 2.44 (2005); Median age: 38.9 (2005); Males per 100 females: 88.0 (2005); Marriage status: 26.2% never married, 49.3% now married, 10.6% widowed, 13.9% divorced (2000); Foreign born: 1.2% (2000); Ancestry (includes multiple ancestries): 26.7% German, 14.0% English, 14.0% Irish, 9.8% United States or American, 6.9% Other groups (2000).
Economy: Single-family building permits issued: 4 (2005); Multi-family building permits issued: 0 (2005); Employment by occupation: 12.1% management, 22.4% professional, 18.1% services, 26.1% sales, 0.1% farming, 6.5% construction, 14.8% production (2000).
Income: Per capita income: $20,451 (2005); Median household income: $32,534 (2005); Average household income: $46,375 (2005); Percent of households with income of $100,000 or more: 8.7% (2005); Poverty rate: 16.9% (2000).
Taxes: Total city taxes per capita: $606 (2004); City property taxes per capita: $44 (2004).

Education: Percent of population age 25 and over with: High school diploma (including GED) or higher: 83.9% (2005); Bachelor's degree or higher: 23.1% (2005); Master's degree or higher: 10.5% (2005).

School District(s)

Frontier Local SD (PK-12)
    2003-04 Enrollment: 966 . . . . (740) 865-3473
Marietta City Schools (PK-12)
    2003-04 Enrollment: 3,202 . . . . (740) 374-6500
Warren Local SD (PK-12)
    2003-04 Enrollment: 2,692 . . . . (740) 678-2366
Washington County Joint Vocational SD (11-12)
    2003-04 Enrollment: n/a . . . . (740) 373-2766
Washington Educational Service Center (PK-PK)
    2003-04 Enrollment: n/a . . . . (740) 373-6669

Four-year College(s)

Marietta College (Private, Not-for-profit)
    Fall 2004 Enrollment: 1,480 . . . . (740) 376-4643
    2005-06 Tuition: In-state $22,656; Out-of-state $22,656

Two-year College(s)

Washington County Career Center-Adult Technical Training (Public)
    Fall 2004 Enrollment: 195 . . . . (740) 373-6283
Washington State Community College (Public)
    Fall 2004 Enrollment: 2,183 . . . . (740) 374-8716
    2005-06 Tuition: In-state $3,321; Out-of-state $6,513

Housing: Homeownership rate: 59.3% (2005); Median home value: $86,700 (2005); Median rent: $328 per month (2000); Median age of housing: 52 years (2000).
Hospitals: Marietta Memorial Hospital (204 beds); Selby General Hospital (80 beds)
Safety: Violent crime rate: 28.4 per 10,000 population; Property crime rate: 359.8 per 10,000 population (2004).
Newspapers: The Marietta Times (Circulation 11,000)
Transportation: Commute to work: 89.1% car, 0.4% public transportation, 7.7% walk, 2.1% work from home (2000); Travel time to work: 57.3% less than 15 minutes, 28.3% 15 to 30 minutes, 7.8% 30 to 45 minutes, 1.9% 45 to 60 minutes, 4.7% 60 minutes or more (2000)

Additional Information Contacts
Marietta Chamber of Commerce . . . . (740) 373-5176
    http://www.mariettachamber.com

MATAMORAS (village). Aka New Matamoras. Covers a land area of 0.360 square miles and a water area of 0.025 square miles. Located at 39.52° N. Lat.; 81.06° W. Long.
History: Matamoras, known as New Matamoras, was the center of a gas and oil boom during the latter decades of the 19th century.
Population: 1,007 (1990); 957 (2000); 919 (2005); 910 (2010 projected); Race: 99.2% White, 0.4% Black, 0.0% Asian, 0.3% Hispanic of any race (2005); Density: 2,551.0 persons per square mile (2005); Average household size: 2.26 (2005); Median age: 36.9 (2005); Males per 100 females: 84.5 (2005); Marriage status: 26.8% never married, 56.0% now married, 6.5% widowed, 10.6% divorced (2000); Foreign born: 0.2% (2000); Ancestry (includes multiple ancestries): 18.9% United States or American, 15.3% German, 14.3% Irish, 9.2% Other groups, 6.3% English (2000).
Economy: Single-family building permits issued: 0 (2005); Multi-family building permits issued: 0 (2005); Employment by occupation: 3.4% management, 9.1% professional, 27.2% services, 23.8% sales, 2.3% farming, 10.4% construction, 23.8% production (2000).
Income: Per capita income: $17,873 (2005); Median household income: $30,435 (2005); Average household income: $40,456 (2005); Percent of households with income of $100,000 or more: 8.9% (2005); Poverty rate: 29.3% (2000).
Education: Percent of population age 25 and over with: High school diploma (including GED) or higher: 74.7% (2005); Bachelor's degree or higher: 7.3% (2005); Master's degree or higher: 1.5% (2005).
Housing: Homeownership rate: 54.2% (2005); Median home value: $56,000 (2005); Median rent: $144 per month (2000); Median age of housing: 46 years (2000).
Transportation: Commute to work: 90.8% car, 0.0% public transportation, 6.5% walk, 1.1% work from home (2000); Travel time to work: 24.4% less than 15 minutes, 24.9% 15 to 30 minutes, 20.3% 30 to 45 minutes, 22.5% 45 to 60 minutes, 7.9% 60 minutes or more (2000)

NEW MATAMORAS (unincorporated postal area, zip code 45767). Aka Matamoras. Covers a land area of 102.833 square miles and a water area of 0.345 square miles. Located at 39.52° N. Lat.; 81.06° W. Long. Elevation is 637 feet.
Population: 2,840 (2000); Race: 97.4% White, 0.4% Black, 0.0% Asian, 0.1% Hispanic of any race (2000); Density: 27.6 persons per square mile (2000); Age: 22.5% under 18, 15.2% over 64 (2000); Marriage status: 18.0% never married, 65.3% now married, 8.4% widowed, 8.3% divorced (2000); Foreign born: 0.1% (2000); Ancestry (includes multiple ancestries): 19.0% German, 18.4% United States or American, 14.1% Irish, 9.7% English, 6.7% Other groups (2000).
Economy: Employment by occupation: 2.9% management, 8.8% professional, 25.9% services, 21.3% sales, 0.9% farming, 10.9% construction, 29.2% production (2000).
Income: Per capita income: $15,070 (2000); Median household income: $27,042 (2000); Poverty rate: 20.2% (2000).
Education: Percent of population age 25 and over with: High school diploma (including GED) or higher: 77.2% (2000); Bachelor's degree or higher: 6.0% (2000).

School District(s)

Frontier Local SD (PK-12)
    2003-04 Enrollment: 966 . . . . (740) 865-3473

Housing: Homeownership rate: 75.6% (2000); Median home value: $59,600 (2000); Median rent: $169 per month (2000); Median age of housing: 41 years (2000).
Transportation: Commute to work: 95.5% car, 0.0% public transportation, 2.5% walk, 0.6% work from home (2000); Travel time to work: 20.1% less than 15 minutes, 21.6% 15 to 30 minutes, 31.7% 30 to 45 minutes, 18.7% 45 to 60 minutes, 7.9% 60 minutes or more (2000)

NEWPORT (unincorporated postal area, zip code 45768). Covers a land area of 31.197 square miles and a water area of 0.080 square miles. Located at 39.39° N. Lat.; 81.25° W. Long. Elevation is 651 feet.
Population: 1,926 (2000); Race: 100.0% White, 0.0% Black, 0.0% Asian, 0.0% Hispanic of any race (2000); Density: 61.7 persons per square mile (2000); Age: 25.1% under 18, 12.4% over 64 (2000); Marriage status: 19.6% never married, 69.3% now married, 2.8% widowed, 8.4% divorced (2000); Foreign born: 0.6% (2000); Ancestry (includes multiple ancestries): 26.7% United States or American, 14.9% German, 9.0% Irish, 7.4% English, 6.5% Other groups (2000).
Economy: Employment by occupation: 10.3% management, 9.1% professional, 23.5% services, 26.9% sales, 0.3% farming, 9.3% construction, 20.6% production (2000).
Income: Per capita income: $17,073 (2000); Median household income: $39,329 (2000); Poverty rate: 9.1% (2000).
Education: Percent of population age 25 and over with: High school diploma (including GED) or higher: 85.0% (2000); Bachelor's degree or higher: 6.5% (2000).

School District(s)

Frontier Local SD (PK-12)
    2003-04 Enrollment: 966 . . . . (740) 865-3473

Housing: Homeownership rate: 79.7% (2000); Median home value: $75,400 (2000); Median rent: $253 per month (2000); Median age of housing: 28 years (2000).
Transportation: Commute to work: 92.7% car, 1.0% public transportation, 3.1% walk, 3.3% work from home (2000); Travel time to work: 19.2% less than 15 minutes, 40.9% 15 to 30 minutes, 25.7% 30 to 45 minutes, 12.4% 45 to 60 minutes, 1.8% 60 minutes or more (2000)

RENO (unincorporated postal area, zip code 45773). Covers a land area of 11.677 square miles and a water area of 0 square miles. Located at 39.47° N. Lat.; 81.28° W. Long. Elevation is 660 feet.
Population: 278 (2000); Race: 100.0% White, 0.0% Black, 0.0% Asian, 0.0% Hispanic of any race (2000); Density: 23.8 persons per square mile (2000); Age: 24.0% under 18, 7.8% over 64 (2000); Marriage status: 9.9% never married, 80.1% now married, 1.2% widowed, 8.8% divorced (2000); Foreign born: 8.3% (2000); Ancestry (includes multiple ancestries): 24.0% German, 16.6% United States or American, 11.1% Irish, 8.3% Canadian, 8.3% Italian (2000).
Economy: Employment by occupation: 3.6% management, 21.4% professional, 11.9% services, 36.9% sales, 0.0% farming, 6.0% construction, 20.2% production (2000).
Income: Per capita income: $10,268 (2000); Median household income: $31,250 (2000); Poverty rate: 20.7% (2000).
Education: Percent of population age 25 and over with: High school diploma (including GED) or higher: 70.7% (2000); Bachelor's degree or higher: 0.0% (2000).

School District(s)

Marietta City Schools (PK-12)
    2003-04 Enrollment: 3,202 . . . . (740) 374-6500

Housing: Homeownership rate: 100.0% (2000); Median home value: $32,500 (2000); Median rent: $n/a per month (2000); Median age of housing: 32 years (2000).

Transportation: Commute to work: 100.0% car, 0.0% public transportation, 0.0% walk, 0.0% work from home (2000); Travel time to work: 0.0% less than 15 minutes, 56.0% 15 to 30 minutes, 29.8% 30 to 45 minutes, 0.0% 45 to 60 minutes, 14.3% 60 minutes or more (2000)

VINCENT (unincorporated postal area, zip code 45784). Covers a land area of 38.733 square miles and a water area of 0.212 square miles. Located at 39.38° N. Lat.; 81.68° W. Long. Elevation is 770 feet.

Population: 2,833 (2000); Race: 97.9% White, 0.0% Black, 0.0% Asian, 0.0% Hispanic of any race (2000); Density: 73.1 persons per square mile (2000); Age: 26.8% under 18, 10.8% over 64 (2000); Marriage status: 19.1% never married, 67.3% now married, 3.8% widowed, 9.8% divorced (2000); Foreign born: 0.3% (2000); Ancestry (includes multiple ancestries): 20.2% United States or American, 18.6% German, 11.2% English, 8.6% Irish, 5.1% Other groups (2000).

Economy: Employment by occupation: 13.3% management, 15.3% professional, 12.2% services, 27.1% sales, 1.3% farming, 10.2% construction, 20.7% production (2000).

Income: Per capita income: $18,320 (2000); Median household income: $41,964 (2000); Poverty rate: 8.3% (2000).

Education: Percent of population age 25 and over with: High school diploma (including GED) or higher: 90.7% (2000); Bachelor's degree or higher: 13.6% (2000).

School District(s)

Warren Local SD (PK-12)
    2003-04 Enrollment: 2,692 . . . . (740) 678-2366

Housing: Homeownership rate: 89.3% (2000); Median home value: $96,900 (2000); Median rent: $298 per month (2000); Median age of housing: 24 years (2000).

Transportation: Commute to work: 93.4% car, 0.0% public transportation, 4.4% walk, 2.2% work from home (2000); Travel time to work: 16.3% less than 15 minutes, 41.1% 15 to 30 minutes, 31.4% 30 to 45 minutes, 6.0% 45 to 60 minutes, 5.2% 60 minutes or more (2000)

WATERFORD (unincorporated postal area, zip code 45786). Covers a land area of 56.396 square miles and a water area of 0.466 square miles. Located at 39.52° N. Lat.; 81.66° W. Long. Elevation is 675 feet.

Population: 2,989 (2000); Race: 97.4% White, 0.4% Black, 0.8% Asian, 0.0% Hispanic of any race (2000); Density: 53.0 persons per square mile (2000); Age: 28.1% under 18, 12.5% over 64 (2000); Marriage status: 16.5% never married, 67.1% now married, 5.1% widowed, 11.2% divorced (2000); Foreign born: 0.2% (2000); Ancestry (includes multiple ancestries): 32.5% German, 11.3% United States or American, 9.6% English, 9.6% Irish, 5.1% Other groups (2000).

Economy: Employment by occupation: 9.5% management, 12.1% professional, 16.2% services, 17.5% sales, 2.7% farming, 15.9% construction, 26.0% production (2000).

Income: Per capita income: $15,471 (2000); Median household income: $36,860 (2000); Poverty rate: 10.3% (2000).

Education: Percent of population age 25 and over with: High school diploma (including GED) or higher: 87.2% (2000); Bachelor's degree or higher: 7.5% (2000).

School District(s)

Wolf Creek Local SD (PK-12)
    2003-04 Enrollment: 685 . . . . (740) 984-2373

Housing: Homeownership rate: 87.6% (2000); Median home value: $77,300 (2000); Median rent: $276 per month (2000); Median age of housing: 26 years (2000).

Transportation: Commute to work: 92.7% car, 0.0% public transportation, 2.7% walk, 3.4% work from home (2000); Travel time to work: 31.7% less than 15 minutes, 19.7% 15 to 30 minutes, 30.7% 30 to 45 minutes, 11.8% 45 to 60 minutes, 6.1% 60 minutes or more (2000)

WHIPPLE (unincorporated postal area, zip code 45788). Covers a land area of 33.202 square miles and a water area of 0.005 square miles. Located at 39.51° N. Lat.; 81.37° W. Long. Elevation is 646 feet.

Population: 1,001 (2000); Race: 98.4% White, 0.0% Black, 0.0% Asian, 0.8% Hispanic of any race (2000); Density: 30.1 persons per square mile (2000); Age: 22.8% under 18, 11.3% over 64 (2000); Marriage status: 21.9% never married, 65.8% now married, 6.1% widowed, 6.2% divorced (2000); Foreign born: 0.8% (2000); Ancestry (includes multiple ancestries): 26.1% German, 11.7% Irish, 11.6% United States or American, 8.5% Other groups, 2.4% English (2000).

Economy: Employment by occupation: 8.3% management, 6.5% professional, 13.9% services, 25.0% sales, 3.4% farming, 14.6% construction, 28.3% production (2000).

Income: Per capita income: $16,281 (2000); Median household income: $36,071 (2000); Poverty rate: 9.3% (2000).

Education: Percent of population age 25 and over with: High school diploma (including GED) or higher: 85.9% (2000); Bachelor's degree or higher: 3.4% (2000).

Housing: Homeownership rate: 85.1% (2000); Median home value: $61,600 (2000); Median rent: $168 per month (2000); Median age of housing: 30 years (2000).

Transportation: Commute to work: 83.9% car, 0.0% public transportation, 0.0% walk, 7.4% work from home (2000); Travel time to work: 16.0% less than 15 minutes, 49.0% 15 to 30 minutes, 29.1% 30 to 45 minutes, 4.9% 45 to 60 minutes, 1.0% 60 minutes or more (2000)

WINGETT RUN (unincorporated postal area, zip code 45789). Covers a land area of 16.651 square miles and a water area of 0 square miles. Located at 39.55° N. Lat.; 81.25° W. Long. Elevation is 660 feet.

Population: 308 (2000); Race: 100.0% White, 0.0% Black, 0.0% Asian, 0.0% Hispanic of any race (2000); Density: 18.5 persons per square mile (2000); Age: 29.3% under 18, 9.1% over 64 (2000); Marriage status: 28.4% never married, 41.9% now married, 2.3% widowed, 27.5% divorced (2000); Foreign born: 0.0% (2000); Ancestry (includes multiple ancestries): 45.1% United States or American, 19.5% Other groups, 13.1% English, 9.4% Scotch-Irish, 5.7% German (2000).

Economy: Employment by occupation: 0.0% management, 6.3% professional, 33.1% services, 15.0% sales, 0.0% farming, 22.0% construction, 23.6% production (2000).

Income: Per capita income: $10,017 (2000); Median household income: $27,050 (2000); Poverty rate: 23.0% (2000).

Education: Percent of population age 25 and over with: High school diploma (including GED) or higher: 72.7% (2000); Bachelor's degree or higher: 5.0% (2000).

Housing: Homeownership rate: 74.5% (2000); Median home value: $14,400 (2000); Median rent: $225 per month (2000); Median age of housing: 34 years (2000).

Transportation: Commute to work: 100.0% car, 0.0% public transportation, 0.0% walk, 0.0% work from home (2000); Travel time to work: 7.1% less than 15 minutes, 0.0% 15 to 30 minutes, 56.7% 30 to 45 minutes, 29.9% 45 to 60 minutes, 6.3% 60 minutes or more (2000)

Wayne County

Located in north central Ohio; crossed by the Lake Fork of the Mohican River. Covers a land area of 555.36 square miles, a water area of 0.96 square miles, and is located in the Eastern Time Zone. The county government was organized in 1786. County seat is Wooster.

Wayne County is part of the Wooster, OH Micropolitan Statistical Area. The entire metro area includes: Wayne County, OH

Weather Station: Wooster Exp. Station   Elevation: 1,017 feet

	Jan	Feb	Mar	Apr	May	Jun	Jul	Aug	Sep	Oct	Nov	Dec
High	32	36	47	59	69	78	82	80	73	61	49	38
Low	18	20	28	37	48	57	61	59	52	41	33	24
Precip	2.2	1.9	2.8	3.4	3.9	4.0	4.0	3.9	3.4	2.6	3.1	2.7
Snow	10.0	7.2	5.1	1.2	tr	0.0	0.0	tr	0.0	tr	1.9	6.3

High and Low temperatures in degrees Fahrenheit; Precipitation and Snow in inches

Population: 101,461 (1990); 111,564 (2000); 113,733 (2005); 115,970 (2010 projected); Race: 96.2% White, 1.5% Black, 0.9% Asian, 0.9% Hispanic of any race (2005); Density: 204.8 persons per square mile (2005); Average household size: 2.73 (2005); Median age: 36.2 (2005); Males per 100 females: 98.1 (2005).

Religion: Five largest groups: 7.8% Catholic Church, 7.0% The United Methodist Church, 4.4% Presbyterian Church (U.S.A.), 4.2% Evangelical Lutheran Church in America, 4.1% Old Order Amish Church (2000).

Economy: Unemployment rate: 5.0% (2005); Total civilian labor force: 61,206 (2005); Leading industries: 32.6% manufacturing; 12.8% retail trade; 11.5% health care and social assistance (2004); Farms: 1,894 totaling 267,169 acres (2002); Companies that employ 500 or more

persons: 8 (2004); Companies that employ 100 to 499 persons: 64 (2004); Companies that employ less than 100 persons: 2,550 (2004); Black-owned businesses: n/a (2002); Hispanic-owned businesses: n/a (2002); Women-owned businesses: 2,275 (2002); Retail sales per capita: $10,487 (2006). Single-family building permits issued: 368 (2005); Multi-family building permits issued: 98 (2005).
Income: Per capita income: $20,518 (2005); Median household income: $45,651 (2005); Average household income: $55,508 (2005); Percent of households with income of $100,000 or more: 10.5% (2005); Poverty rate: 8.6% (2003); Bankruptcy rate: 7.51% (2005).
Taxes: Total county taxes per capita: $191 (2004); County property taxes per capita: $109 (2004).
Education: Percent of population age 25 and over with: High school diploma (including GED) or higher: 80.0% (2005); Bachelor's degree or higher: 17.3% (2005); Master's degree or higher: 5.6% (2005).
Housing: Homeownership rate: 73.8% (2005); Median home value: $129,242 (2005); Median rent: $403 per month (2000); Median age of housing: 33 years (2000).
Health: Birth rate: 145.5 per 10,000 population (2004); Death rate: 85.7 per 10,000 population (2004); Age-adjusted cancer mortality rate: 185.3 deaths per 100,000 population (2002); Number of physicians: 14.0 per 10,000 population (2004); Hospital beds: 14.6 per 10,000 population (2003); Hospital admissions: 572.7 per 10,000 population (2003).
Elections: 2004 Presidential election results: 61.5% Bush, 38.2% Kerry, 0.0% Nader, 0.2% Badnarik
National and State Parks: Killbuck Marsh State Wildlife Area
Additional Information Contacts
Wayne County Government. . . . . (330) 287-5400
  http://www.wayneohio.org/
Apple Creek Area Chamber of Commerce . . . . (330) 698-2631
  http://www.woosterchamber.com
City of Orrville . . . . (330) 684-5000
  http://www.orrville.com
City of Rittman . . . . (330) 925-2045
  http://www.rittman.com
Dalton Chamber of Commerce . . . . (330) 828-2444
  http://www.daltonohchamber.com
Orrville Area Chamber of Commerce. . . . . (330) 682-8881
  http://www.orrvillecc.com
Rittman Chamber of Commerce . . . . (330) 925-4828
  http://www.rittman.com
Wayne County Convention Bureau . . . . (330) 264-1800
  http://www.waynecountycvb.org
Wooster Chamber of Commerce . . . . (330) 262-5735
  http://www.wooster-wayne.com

Wayne County Communities

APPLE CREEK (village). Covers a land area of 0.606 square miles and a water area of 0 square miles. Located at 40.75° N. Lat.; 81.83° W. Long. Elevation is 1,060 feet.
Population: 863 (1990); 999 (2000); 985 (2005); 982 (2010 projected); Race: 97.7% White, 0.0% Black, 0.8% Asian, 0.6% Hispanic of any race (2005); Density: 1,625.2 persons per square mile (2005); Average household size: 2.47 (2005); Median age: 35.6 (2005); Males per 100 females: 90.5 (2005); Marriage status: 21.0% never married, 65.3% now married, 4.8% widowed, 8.9% divorced (2000); Foreign born: 1.6% (2000); Ancestry (includes multiple ancestries): 32.8% German, 11.6% Irish, 9.3% Other groups, 7.2% United States or American, 6.9% English (2000).
Economy: Grain products and lumber. Employment by occupation: 9.9% management, 17.4% professional, 12.8% services, 25.2% sales, 0.7% farming, 9.7% construction, 24.3% production (2000).
Income: Per capita income: $20,462 (2005); Median household income: $44,217 (2005); Average household income: $50,641 (2005); Percent of households with income of $100,000 or more: 6.8% (2005); Poverty rate: 5.5% (2000).
Education: Percent of population age 25 and over with: High school diploma (including GED) or higher: 81.0% (2005); Bachelor's degree or higher: 14.0% (2005); Master's degree or higher: 2.3% (2005).
School District(s)
Southeast Local SD (PK-12)
  2003-04 Enrollment: 1,718 . . . . (330) 698-3001
Housing: Homeownership rate: 72.9% (2005); Median home value: $105,455 (2005); Median rent: $394 per month (2000); Median age of housing: 43 years (2000).
Transportation: Commute to work: 89.8% car, 0.0% public transportation, 3.4% walk, 6.7% work from home (2000); Travel time to work: 32.7% less than 15 minutes, 53.7% 15 to 30 minutes, 5.0% 30 to 45 minutes, 3.4% 45 to 60 minutes, 5.2% 60 minutes or more (2000)
Additional Information Contacts
Apple Creek Area Chamber of Commerce . . . . (330) 698-2631
  http://www.woosterchamber.com

BURBANK (village). Covers a land area of 0.331 square miles and a water area of 0 square miles. Located at 40.98° N. Lat.; 81.99° W. Long. Elevation is 970 feet.
Population: 289 (1990); 279 (2000); 299 (2005); 318 (2010 projected); Race: 97.7% White, 0.0% Black, 1.7% Asian, 1.3% Hispanic of any race (2005); Density: 902.7 persons per square mile (2005); Average household size: 2.67 (2005); Median age: 36.4 (2005); Males per 100 females: 107.6 (2005); Marriage status: 25.9% never married, 55.2% now married, 6.0% widowed, 12.9% divorced (2000); Foreign born: 1.4% (2000); Ancestry (includes multiple ancestries): 30.5% German, 17.0% United States or American, 16.7% Other groups, 5.7% English, 3.9% Welsh (2000).
Economy: In agricultural area. Employment by occupation: 4.1% management, 6.9% professional, 14.5% services, 25.5% sales, 0.0% farming, 17.2% construction, 31.7% production (2000).
Income: Per capita income: $21,012 (2005); Median household income: $50,045 (2005); Average household income: $56,094 (2005); Percent of households with income of $100,000 or more: 6.3% (2005); Poverty rate: 7.2% (2000).
Education: Percent of population age 25 and over with: High school diploma (including GED) or higher: 82.4% (2005); Bachelor's degree or higher: 2.5% (2005); Master's degree or higher: 0.0% (2005).
School District(s)
North Central Local SD (PK-12)
  2003-04 Enrollment: 1,468 . . . . (330) 435-6382
Housing: Homeownership rate: 80.4% (2005); Median home value: $95,455 (2005); Median rent: $367 per month (2000); Median age of housing: 60+ years (2000).
Transportation: Commute to work: 96.4% car, 0.0% public transportation, 1.4% walk, 0.0% work from home (2000); Travel time to work: 23.0% less than 15 minutes, 46.8% 15 to 30 minutes, 15.8% 30 to 45 minutes, 2.9% 45 to 60 minutes, 11.5% 60 minutes or more (2000)

CONGRESS (village). Covers a land area of 0.166 square miles and a water area of 0 square miles. Located at 40.92° N. Lat.; 82.05° W. Long. Elevation is 1,160 feet.
History: Congress was established in 1827.
Population: 162 (1990); 192 (2000); 207 (2005); 218 (2010 projected); Race: 96.6% White, 0.0% Black, 0.0% Asian, 0.0% Hispanic of any race (2005); Density: 1,244.4 persons per square mile (2005); Average household size: 2.96 (2005); Median age: 38.1 (2005); Males per 100 females: 109.1 (2005); Marriage status: 23.0% never married, 64.5% now married, 4.6% widowed, 7.9% divorced (2000); Foreign born: 0.0% (2000); Ancestry (includes multiple ancestries): 29.9% German, 18.3% Irish, 16.2% Other groups, 10.7% English, 3.6% Italian (2000).
Economy: Employment by occupation: 7.2% management, 7.2% professional, 15.5% services, 23.7% sales, 7.2% farming, 14.4% construction, 24.7% production (2000).
Income: Per capita income: $16,377 (2005); Median household income: $44,000 (2005); Average household income: $48,429 (2005); Percent of households with income of $100,000 or more: 2.9% (2005); Poverty rate: 4.1% (2000).
Education: Percent of population age 25 and over with: High school diploma (including GED) or higher: 60.6% (2005); Bachelor's degree or higher: 5.6% (2005); Master's degree or higher: 0.0% (2005).
Housing: Homeownership rate: 88.6% (2005); Median home value: $95,000 (2005); Median rent: $483 per month (2000); Median age of housing: 60+ years (2000).
Transportation: Commute to work: 96.9% car, 0.0% public transportation, 0.0% walk, 3.1% work from home (2000); Travel time to work: 12.8% less than 15 minutes, 54.3% 15 to 30 minutes, 23.4% 30 to 45 minutes, 2.1% 45 to 60 minutes, 7.4% 60 minutes or more (2000)

CRESTON (village). Covers a land area of 2.207 square miles and a water area of 0 square miles. Located at 40.98° N. Lat.; 81.89° W. Long. Elevation is 985 feet.
Population: 1,931 (1990); 2,161 (2000); 2,100 (2005); 2,078 (2010 projected); Race: 98.7% White, 0.3% Black, 0.0% Asian, 0.2% Hispanic of

any race (2005); Density: 951.4 persons per square mile (2005); Average household size: 2.59 (2005); Median age: 37.9 (2005); Males per 100 females: 101.1 (2005); Marriage status: 17.7% never married, 64.8% now married, 8.1% widowed, 9.4% divorced (2000); Foreign born: 0.4% (2000); Ancestry (includes multiple ancestries): 28.4% German, 11.4% Irish, 11.3% English, 7.9% United States or American, 4.6% Other groups (2000).
Economy: Basket making. Employment by occupation: 6.7% management, 13.5% professional, 16.3% services, 26.7% sales, 0.3% farming, 9.9% construction, 26.6% production (2000).
Income: Per capita income: $18,000 (2005); Median household income: $42,841 (2005); Average household income: $46,667 (2005); Percent of households with income of $100,000 or more: 4.9% (2005); Poverty rate: 4.9% (2000).
Education: Percent of population age 25 and over with: High school diploma (including GED) or higher: 72.8% (2005); Bachelor's degree or higher: 7.9% (2005); Master's degree or higher: 1.7% (2005).

School District(s)
North Central Local SD (PK-12)
   2003-04 Enrollment: 1,468 . . . . (330) 435-6382
Housing: Homeownership rate: 79.4% (2005); Median home value: $113,213 (2005); Median rent: $381 per month (2000); Median age of housing: 34 years (2000).
Transportation: Commute to work: 95.5% car, 0.8% public transportation, 1.5% walk, 1.4% work from home (2000); Travel time to work: 31.5% less than 15 minutes, 40.6% 15 to 30 minutes, 16.7% 30 to 45 minutes, 8.8% 45 to 60 minutes, 2.4% 60 minutes or more (2000)

DALTON (village). Covers a land area of 1.222 square miles and a water area of 0 square miles. Located at 40.79° N. Lat.; 81.69° W. Long. Elevation is 1,100 feet.
Population: 1,381 (1990); 1,605 (2000); 1,606 (2005); 1,615 (2010 projected); Race: 98.0% White, 0.1% Black, 0.4% Asian, 1.3% Hispanic of any race (2005); Density: 1,314.7 persons per square mile (2005); Average household size: 2.60 (2005); Median age: 35.6 (2005); Males per 100 females: 96.1 (2005); Marriage status: 22.6% never married, 62.2% now married, 5.2% widowed, 10.0% divorced (2000); Foreign born: 0.3% (2000); Ancestry (includes multiple ancestries): 39.9% German, 15.3% Irish, 11.4% Swiss, 7.3% English, 6.1% United States or American (2000).
Economy: In agricultural area. Employment by occupation: 10.0% management, 16.7% professional, 15.2% services, 21.1% sales, 0.7% farming, 8.6% construction, 27.7% production (2000).
Income: Per capita income: $23,023 (2005); Median household income: $50,084 (2005); Average household income: $59,927 (2005); Percent of households with income of $100,000 or more: 10.7% (2005); Poverty rate: 4.5% (2000).
Education: Percent of population age 25 and over with: High school diploma (including GED) or higher: 87.7% (2005); Bachelor's degree or higher: 17.2% (2005); Master's degree or higher: 5.0% (2005).

School District(s)
Dalton Local SD (PK-12)
   2003-04 Enrollment: 1,004 . . . . (330) 828-2267
Housing: Homeownership rate: 78.3% (2005); Median home value: $123,522 (2005); Median rent: $407 per month (2000); Median age of housing: 34 years (2000).
Newspapers: The Dalton Gazette & Kidron News (General - Circulation 1,450)
Transportation: Commute to work: 93.9% car, 0.2% public transportation, 3.7% walk, 1.5% work from home (2000); Travel time to work: 44.5% less than 15 minutes, 40.5% 15 to 30 minutes, 10.0% 30 to 45 minutes, 3.4% 45 to 60 minutes, 1.7% 60 minutes or more (2000)
Additional Information Contacts
Dalton Chamber of Commerce . . . . (330) 828-2444
http://www.daltonohchamber.com

DOYLESTOWN (village). Covers a land area of 1.760 square miles and a water area of 0 square miles. Located at 40.97° N. Lat.; 81.69° W. Long. Elevation is 1,260 feet.
Population: 2,876 (1990); 2,799 (2000); 2,815 (2005); 2,844 (2010 projected); Race: 98.7% White, 0.2% Black, 0.2% Asian, 0.7% Hispanic of any race (2005); Density: 1,599.4 persons per square mile (2005); Average household size: 2.46 (2005); Median age: 40.5 (2005); Males per 100 females: 90.8 (2005); Marriage status: 21.5% never married, 62.2% now married, 6.8% widowed, 9.5% divorced (2000); Foreign born: 0.1% (2000); Ancestry (includes multiple ancestries): 33.0% German, 15.3% Irish, 13.0% English, 6.7% Italian, 6.5% United States or American (2000).
Economy: Single-family building permits issued: 14 (2005); Multi-family building permits issued: 0 (2005); Employment by occupation: 14.6% management, 21.9% professional, 12.5% services, 26.0% sales, 0.8% farming, 10.1% construction, 14.0% production (2000).
Income: Per capita income: $24,654 (2005); Median household income: $52,360 (2005); Average household income: $60,118 (2005); Percent of households with income of $100,000 or more: 14.2% (2005); Poverty rate: 5.2% (2000).
Education: Percent of population age 25 and over with: High school diploma (including GED) or higher: 88.6% (2005); Bachelor's degree or higher: 21.9% (2005); Master's degree or higher: 7.2% (2005).

School District(s)
Chippewa Local SD (PK-12)
   2003-04 Enrollment: 1,444 . . . . (330) 658-6368
Housing: Homeownership rate: 69.5% (2005); Median home value: $145,985 (2005); Median rent: $482 per month (2000); Median age of housing: 35 years (2000).
Transportation: Commute to work: 96.9% car, 0.4% public transportation, 1.9% walk, 0.8% work from home (2000); Travel time to work: 24.8% less than 15 minutes, 50.4% 15 to 30 minutes, 17.7% 30 to 45 minutes, 4.1% 45 to 60 minutes, 2.9% 60 minutes or more (2000)

FREDERICKSBURG (village). Covers a land area of 0.330 square miles and a water area of 0 square miles. Located at 40.67° N. Lat.; 81.87° W. Long. Elevation is 972 feet.
Population: 464 (1990); 487 (2000); 479 (2005); 477 (2010 projected); Race: 97.9% White, 0.0% Black, 0.0% Asian, 0.4% Hispanic of any race (2005); Density: 1,450.3 persons per square mile (2005); Average household size: 2.62 (2005); Median age: 35.7 (2005); Males per 100 females: 97.9 (2005); Marriage status: 28.1% never married, 57.8% now married, 8.1% widowed, 6.1% divorced (2000); Foreign born: 0.2% (2000); Ancestry (includes multiple ancestries): 24.8% German, 11.2% Irish, 9.6% Other groups, 7.7% English, 6.9% French (except Basque) (2000).
Economy: Employment by occupation: 4.5% management, 14.8% professional, 23.0% services, 19.8% sales, 0.0% farming, 10.3% construction, 27.6% production (2000).
Income: Per capita income: $14,828 (2005); Median household income: $35,750 (2005); Average household income: $38,661 (2005); Percent of households with income of $100,000 or more: 1.1% (2005); Poverty rate: 7.9% (2000).
Education: Percent of population age 25 and over with: High school diploma (including GED) or higher: 75.4% (2005); Bachelor's degree or higher: 10.6% (2005); Master's degree or higher: 2.0% (2005).

School District(s)
Southeast Local SD (PK-12)
   2003-04 Enrollment: 1,718 . . . . (330) 698-3001
Housing: Homeownership rate: 72.7% (2005); Median home value: $86,774 (2005); Median rent: $356 per month (2000); Median age of housing: 60+ years (2000).
Transportation: Commute to work: 87.8% car, 3.0% public transportation, 5.5% walk, 3.8% work from home (2000); Travel time to work: 29.4% less than 15 minutes, 61.8% 15 to 30 minutes, 3.1% 30 to 45 minutes, 2.2% 45 to 60 minutes, 3.5% 60 minutes or more (2000)

MARSHALLVILLE (village). Covers a land area of 0.561 square miles and a water area of 0 square miles. Located at 40.90° N. Lat.; 81.73° W. Long. Elevation is 1,110 feet.
Population: 807 (1990); 826 (2000); 780 (2005); 757 (2010 projected); Race: 96.9% White, 0.1% Black, 0.0% Asian, 1.5% Hispanic of any race (2005); Density: 1,389.5 persons per square mile (2005); Average household size: 2.68 (2005); Median age: 36.8 (2005); Males per 100 females: 103.1 (2005); Marriage status: 18.8% never married, 66.7% now married, 4.6% widowed, 9.8% divorced (2000); Foreign born: 1.6% (2000); Ancestry (includes multiple ancestries): 28.6% German, 16.4% Irish, 11.6% United States or American, 9.8% Other groups, 7.2% Swiss (2000).
Economy: In agricultural area; meat products. Employment by occupation: 6.5% management, 8.5% professional, 16.7% services, 24.9% sales, 0.5% farming, 15.0% construction, 28.0% production (2000).
Income: Per capita income: $18,462 (2005); Median household income: $46,679 (2005); Average household income: $49,485 (2005); Percent of households with income of $100,000 or more: 3.1% (2005); Poverty rate: 5.9% (2000).
Education: Percent of population age 25 and over with: High school diploma (including GED) or higher: 83.5% (2005); Bachelor's degree or higher: 6.5% (2005); Master's degree or higher: 1.4% (2005).

School District(s)
Green Local SD (PK-12)
 2003-04 Enrollment: 1,396 . . . . (330) 669-3921
Housing: Homeownership rate: 73.5% (2005); Median home value: $115,254 (2005); Median rent: $360 per month (2000); Median age of housing: 41 years (2000).
Transportation: Commute to work: 95.6% car, 0.5% public transportation, 2.2% walk, 1.2% work from home (2000); Travel time to work: 26.0% less than 15 minutes, 45.0% 15 to 30 minutes, 18.6% 30 to 45 minutes, 5.9% 45 to 60 minutes, 4.5% 60 minutes or more (2000)

MOUNT EATON (village). Covers a land area of 0.164 square miles and a water area of 0 square miles. Located at 40.69° N. Lat.; 81.70° W. Long. Elevation is 1,240 feet.
Population: 232 (1990); 246 (2000); 272 (2005); 298 (2010 projected); Race: 98.5% White, 0.7% Black, 0.0% Asian, 0.0% Hispanic of any race (2005); Density: 1,661.3 persons per square mile (2005); Average household size: 2.75 (2005); Median age: 33.0 (2005); Males per 100 females: 103.0 (2005); Marriage status: 27.7% never married, 60.9% now married, 2.7% widowed, 8.7% divorced (2000); Foreign born: 0.0% (2000); Ancestry (includes multiple ancestries): 33.2% German, 10.8% United States or American, 10.0% Swiss, 8.7% Other groups, 8.3% Irish (2000).
Economy: In agricultural area. Employment by occupation: 8.1% management, 6.5% professional, 20.2% services, 18.5% sales, 0.0% farming, 9.7% construction, 37.1% production (2000).
Income: Per capita income: $19,807 (2005); Median household income: $46,625 (2005); Average household income: $54,419 (2005); Percent of households with income of $100,000 or more: 10.1% (2005); Poverty rate: 0.4% (2000).
Education: Percent of population age 25 and over with: High school diploma (including GED) or higher: 67.5% (2005); Bachelor's degree or higher: 7.7% (2005); Master's degree or higher: 4.7% (2005).
School District(s)
Southeast Local SD (PK-12)
 2003-04 Enrollment: 1,718 . . . . (330) 698-3001
Housing: Homeownership rate: 73.7% (2005); Median home value: $92,857 (2005); Median rent: $373 per month (2000); Median age of housing: 60+ years (2000).
Transportation: Commute to work: 84.7% car, 0.0% public transportation, 6.5% walk, 7.3% work from home (2000); Travel time to work: 50.4% less than 15 minutes, 31.3% 15 to 30 minutes, 10.4% 30 to 45 minutes, 3.5% 45 to 60 minutes, 4.3% 60 minutes or more (2000)

ORRVILLE (city). Covers a land area of 5.342 square miles and a water area of 0.008 square miles. Located at 40.84° N. Lat.; 81.77° W. Long. Elevation is 1,064 feet.
History: Settled c.1850, incorporated 1864.
Population: 8,058 (1990); 8,551 (2000); 8,471 (2005); 8,407 (2010 projected); Race: 90.6% White, 5.6% Black, 1.4% Asian, 1.6% Hispanic of any race (2005); Density: 1,585.9 persons per square mile (2005); Average household size: 2.57 (2005); Median age: 36.4 (2005); Males per 100 females: 95.3 (2005); Marriage status: 21.1% never married, 61.8% now married, 5.6% widowed, 11.5% divorced (2000); Foreign born: 2.7% (2000); Ancestry (includes multiple ancestries): 30.2% German, 12.9% Other groups, 12.7% Irish, 9.3% English, 8.2% United States or American (2000).
Economy: In agricultural area; food and dairy products. Manufacturing: transportation equipment, machinery, chemicals, wood products, leather goods, mattresses. Employment by occupation: 10.5% management, 13.4% professional, 16.5% services, 23.1% sales, 0.8% farming, 7.1% construction, 28.6% production (2000).
Income: Per capita income: $18,933 (2005); Median household income: $40,064 (2005); Average household income: $47,903 (2005); Percent of households with income of $100,000 or more: 7.7% (2005); Poverty rate: 7.7% (2000).
Education: Percent of population age 25 and over with: High school diploma (including GED) or higher: 83.8% (2005); Bachelor's degree or higher: 16.9% (2005); Master's degree or higher: 5.2% (2005).
School District(s)
Orrville City SD (PK-12)
 2003-04 Enrollment: 1,863 . . . . (330) 682-4651
Two-year College(s)
University of Akron Wayne College (Public)
 Fall 2004 Enrollment: 1,691 . . . . (800) 221-8308
 2005-06 Tuition: In-state $5,053; Out-of-state $12,151
Housing: Homeownership rate: 62.2% (2005); Median home value: $126,459 (2005); Median rent: $411 per month (2000); Median age of housing: 41 years (2000).
Hospitals: Dunlap Memorial Hospital (51 beds)
Safety: Violent crime rate: 18.8 per 10,000 population; Property crime rate: 193.6 per 10,000 population (2004).
Transportation: Commute to work: 91.7% car, 0.0% public transportation, 3.4% walk, 2.5% work from home (2000); Travel time to work: 51.2% less than 15 minutes, 32.1% 15 to 30 minutes, 12.0% 30 to 45 minutes, 2.6% 45 to 60 minutes, 2.2% 60 minutes or more (2000)
Additional Information Contacts
City of Orrville . . . . (330) 684-5000
 http://www.orrville.com
Orrville Area Chamber of Commerce. . . . . (330) 682-8881
 http://www.orrvillecc.com

RITTMAN (city). Covers a land area of 6.031 square miles and a water area of 0.208 square miles. Located at 40.97° N. Lat.; 81.78° W. Long. Elevation is 979 feet.
Population: 6,155 (1990); 6,314 (2000); 6,275 (2005); 6,242 (2010 projected); Race: 97.8% White, 0.1% Black, 0.6% Asian, 1.1% Hispanic of any race (2005); Density: 1,040.4 persons per square mile (2005); Average household size: 2.57 (2005); Median age: 37.0 (2005); Males per 100 females: 96.2 (2005); Marriage status: 22.7% never married, 58.2% now married, 8.4% widowed, 10.8% divorced (2000); Foreign born: 2.5% (2000); Ancestry (includes multiple ancestries): 26.6% German, 14.6% Irish, 10.9% United States or American, 9.0% English, 7.1% Other groups (2000).
Economy: In agricultural area: fruits; livestock; dairying. Manufacturing of paper products. Employment by occupation: 7.6% management, 13.1% professional, 16.1% services, 21.5% sales, 1.1% farming, 11.4% construction, 29.2% production (2000).
Income: Per capita income: $17,437 (2005); Median household income: $37,364 (2005); Average household income: $44,654 (2005); Percent of households with income of $100,000 or more: 5.7% (2005); Poverty rate: 8.3% (2000).
Education: Percent of population age 25 and over with: High school diploma (including GED) or higher: 76.2% (2005); Bachelor's degree or higher: 9.5% (2005); Master's degree or higher: 2.6% (2005).
School District(s)
Rittman Ex Vill SD (PK-12)
 2003-04 Enrollment: 1,207 . . . . (330) 927-7401
Housing: Homeownership rate: 68.1% (2005); Median home value: $113,111 (2005); Median rent: $377 per month (2000); Median age of housing: 43 years (2000).
Transportation: Commute to work: 96.2% car, 0.0% public transportation, 1.9% walk, 1.7% work from home (2000); Travel time to work: 40.8% less than 15 minutes, 30.7% 15 to 30 minutes, 19.3% 30 to 45 minutes, 5.4% 45 to 60 minutes, 3.7% 60 minutes or more (2000)
Additional Information Contacts
City of Rittman . . . . (330) 925-2045
 http://www.rittman.com
Rittman Chamber of Commerce . . . . (330) 925-4828
 http://www.rittman.com

SHREVE (village). Covers a land area of 0.846 square miles and a water area of 0 square miles. Located at 40.68° N. Lat.; 82.02° W. Long. Elevation is 914 feet.
Population: 1,584 (1990); 1,582 (2000); 1,514 (2005); 1,485 (2010 projected); Race: 98.3% White, 0.5% Black, 0.1% Asian, 0.5% Hispanic of any race (2005); Density: 1,790.0 persons per square mile (2005); Average household size: 2.38 (2005); Median age: 34.5 (2005); Males per 100 females: 92.1 (2005); Marriage status: 16.7% never married, 59.0% now married, 7.4% widowed, 16.9% divorced (2000); Foreign born: 0.4% (2000); Ancestry (includes multiple ancestries): 25.3% German, 17.8% United States or American, 11.8% Irish, 10.4% English, 8.5% Other groups (2000).
Economy: In gas and oil producing area. Single-family building permits issued: 3 (2005); Multi-family building permits issued: 0 (2005); Employment by occupation: 5.4% management, 12.0% professional, 14.0% services, 22.2% sales, 0.8% farming, 10.3% construction, 35.3% production (2000).
Income: Per capita income: $17,267 (2005); Median household income: $35,004 (2005); Average household income: $41,105 (2005); Percent of

households with income of $100,000 or more: 5.2% (2005); Poverty rate: 10.4% (2000).
Education: Percent of population age 25 and over with: High school diploma (including GED) or higher: 80.3% (2005); Bachelor's degree or higher: 7.9% (2005); Master's degree or higher: 3.4% (2005).

School District(s)
Triway Local SD (PK-12)
   2003-04 Enrollment: 2,150 . . . . (330) 264-9491
Housing: Homeownership rate: 67.1% (2005); Median home value: $89,758 (2005); Median rent: $282 per month (2000); Median age of housing: 44 years (2000).
Transportation: Commute to work: 90.7% car, 0.1% public transportation, 5.8% walk, 3.0% work from home (2000); Travel time to work: 37.2% less than 15 minutes, 43.8% 15 to 30 minutes, 12.1% 30 to 45 minutes, 2.6% 45 to 60 minutes, 4.2% 60 minutes or more (2000)

SMITHVILLE (village).
Covers a land area of 1.235 square miles and a water area of 0 square miles. Located at 40.86° N. Lat.; 81.85° W. Long. Elevation is 1,060 feet.
Population: 1,387 (1990); 1,333 (2000); 1,256 (2005); 1,220 (2010 projected); Race: 98.1% White, 0.2% Black, 0.8% Asian, 0.6% Hispanic of any race (2005); Density: 1,017.1 persons per square mile (2005); Average household size: 2.39 (2005); Median age: 38.6 (2005); Males per 100 females: 91.8 (2005); Marriage status: 21.3% never married, 61.7% now married, 6.8% widowed, 10.2% divorced (2000); Foreign born: 1.0% (2000); Ancestry (includes multiple ancestries): 34.2% German, 11.1% English, 9.0% Irish, 8.7% Swiss, 6.6% United States or American (2000).
Economy: Employment by occupation: 8.9% management, 18.8% professional, 15.9% services, 23.4% sales, 0.7% farming, 8.4% construction, 23.8% production (2000).
Income: Per capita income: $19,984 (2005); Median household income: $43,250 (2005); Average household income: $47,719 (2005); Percent of households with income of $100,000 or more: 5.1% (2005); Poverty rate: 5.9% (2000).
Education: Percent of population age 25 and over with: High school diploma (including GED) or higher: 91.3% (2005); Bachelor's degree or higher: 18.9% (2005); Master's degree or higher: 7.2% (2005).

School District(s)
Green Local SD (PK-12)
   2003-04 Enrollment: 1,396 . . . . (330) 669-3921
Wayne County Joint Vocational SD (07-12)
   2003-04 Enrollment: n/a . . . . (330) 669-2134
Wooster City SD (PK-12)
   2003-04 Enrollment: 4,144 . . . . (330) 264-0869

Two-year College(s)
Wayne County Schools Career Center (Public)
   Fall 2004 Enrollment: 576 . . . . (330) 669-9611
Housing: Homeownership rate: 63.3% (2005); Median home value: $128,243 (2005); Median rent: $431 per month (2000); Median age of housing: 38 years (2000).
Transportation: Commute to work: 92.0% car, 0.3% public transportation, 2.5% walk, 4.3% work from home (2000); Travel time to work: 43.0% less than 15 minutes, 40.4% 15 to 30 minutes, 7.5% 30 to 45 minutes, 5.0% 45 to 60 minutes, 4.2% 60 minutes or more (2000)

STERLING (unincorporated postal area, zip code 44276).
Covers a land area of 19.953 square miles and a water area of 0 square miles. Located at 40.95° N. Lat.; 81.82° W. Long. Elevation is 973 feet.
Population: 1,881 (2000); Race: 98.9% White, 0.0% Black, 0.0% Asian, 2.3% Hispanic of any race (2000); Density: 94.3 persons per square mile (2000); Age: 29.2% under 18, 9.2% over 64 (2000); Marriage status: 20.8% never married, 71.3% now married, 3.2% widowed, 4.6% divorced (2000); Foreign born: 0.5% (2000); Ancestry (includes multiple ancestries): 29.6% German, 15.7% Irish, 14.2% Swiss, 9.6% English, 6.3% United States or American (2000).
Economy: Employment by occupation: 10.8% management, 14.4% professional, 13.0% services, 22.5% sales, 3.7% farming, 14.0% construction, 21.7% production (2000).
Income: Per capita income: $17,370 (2000); Median household income: $51,215 (2000); Poverty rate: 2.5% (2000).
Education: Percent of population age 25 and over with: High school diploma (including GED) or higher: 83.3% (2000); Bachelor's degree or higher: 10.8% (2000).

School District(s)
North Central Local SD (PK-12)
   2003-04 Enrollment: 1,468 . . . . (330) 435-6382
Housing: Homeownership rate: 81.1% (2000); Median home value: $108,500 (2000); Median rent: $468 per month (2000); Median age of housing: 36 years (2000).
Transportation: Commute to work: 89.7% car, 0.0% public transportation, 0.5% walk, 9.4% work from home (2000); Travel time to work: 28.8% less than 15 minutes, 43.9% 15 to 30 minutes, 15.0% 30 to 45 minutes, 3.5% 45 to 60 minutes, 8.9% 60 minutes or more (2000)

WEST SALEM (village).
Covers a land area of 1.033 square miles and a water area of 0 square miles. Located at 40.97° N. Lat.; 82.11° W. Long. Elevation is 1,120 feet.
History: West Salem was laid out in 1834 by the Rickel brothers, who came from Wooster.
Population: 1,555 (1990); 1,501 (2000); 1,469 (2005); 1,469 (2010 projected); Race: 96.7% White, 0.1% Black, 0.6% Asian, 1.3% Hispanic of any race (2005); Density: 1,422.1 persons per square mile (2005); Average household size: 2.56 (2005); Median age: 33.2 (2005); Males per 100 females: 101.8 (2005); Marriage status: 24.2% never married, 56.9% now married, 7.0% widowed, 11.9% divorced (2000); Foreign born: 0.0% (2000); Ancestry (includes multiple ancestries): 29.0% German, 11.9% Irish, 11.4% English, 10.0% United States or American, 8.5% Other groups (2000).
Economy: Employment by occupation: 2.9% management, 7.8% professional, 13.8% services, 23.7% sales, 0.0% farming, 13.5% construction, 38.4% production (2000).
Income: Per capita income: $17,444 (2005); Median household income: $40,976 (2005); Average household income: $44,643 (2005); Percent of households with income of $100,000 or more: 4.0% (2005); Poverty rate: 7.9% (2000).
Education: Percent of population age 25 and over with: High school diploma (including GED) or higher: 74.9% (2005); Bachelor's degree or higher: 5.0% (2005); Master's degree or higher: 1.1% (2005).

School District(s)
Northwestern Local SD (KG-12)
   2003-04 Enrollment: 1,443 . . . . (419) 846-3151
Housing: Homeownership rate: 76.7% (2005); Median home value: $88,205 (2005); Median rent: $389 per month (2000); Median age of housing: 31 years (2000).
Transportation: Commute to work: 93.3% car, 0.1% public transportation, 4.5% walk, 1.8% work from home (2000); Travel time to work: 24.6% less than 15 minutes, 29.0% 15 to 30 minutes, 29.1% 30 to 45 minutes, 8.7% 45 to 60 minutes, 8.7% 60 minutes or more (2000)

WOOSTER (city).
Covers a land area of 14.374 square miles and a water area of 0.017 square miles. Located at 40.80° N. Lat.; 81.93° W. Long. Elevation is 950 feet.
History: Wooster was settled in 1807 by the Larwill family. The town that grew after the War of 1812 was named for Revolutionary War general David Wooster. Wooster claims to have had America's first Christmas tree in 1847, when a young German immigrant, August Imgard, cut and decorated a small spruce tree.
Population: 23,108 (1990); 24,811 (2000); 25,075 (2005); 25,452 (2010 projected); Race: 92.0% White, 3.7% Black, 2.0% Asian, 1.3% Hispanic of any race (2005); Density: 1,744.5 persons per square mile (2005); Average household size: 2.44 (2005); Median age: 36.4 (2005); Males per 100 females: 92.2 (2005); Marriage status: 29.3% never married, 51.5% now married, 6.7% widowed, 12.5% divorced (2000); Foreign born: 3.3% (2000); Ancestry (includes multiple ancestries): 30.4% German, 13.6% Irish, 11.9% English, 9.5% Other groups, 8.1% United States or American (2000).
Economy: Unemployment rate: 4.9% (2005); Total civilian labor force: 14,138 (2005); Single-family building permits issued: 87 (2005); Multi-family building permits issued: 62 (2005); Employment by occupation: 11.4% management, 21.4% professional, 14.6% services, 25.5% sales, 0.4% farming, 5.6% construction, 21.2% production (2000).
Income: Per capita income: $23,374 (2005); Median household income: $40,860 (2005); Average household income: $55,862 (2005); Percent of households with income of $100,000 or more: 11.3% (2005); Poverty rate: 10.4% (2000).
Taxes: Total city taxes per capita: $476 (2004); City property taxes per capita: $98 (2004).

Education: Percent of population age 25 and over with: High school diploma (including GED) or higher: 84.7% (2005); Bachelor's degree or higher: 27.6% (2005); Master's degree or higher: 10.5% (2005).

School District(s)

Northwestern Local SD (KG-12)
   2003-04 Enrollment: 1,443 .... (419) 846-3151
Triway Local SD (PK-12)
   2003-04 Enrollment: 2,150 .... (330) 264-9491
Wooster City SD (PK-12)
   2003-04 Enrollment: 4,144 .... (330) 264-0869

Four-year College(s)

The College of Wooster (Private, Not-for-profit)
   Fall 2004 Enrollment: 1,827 .... (330) 263-2000
   2005-06 Tuition: In-state $28,230; Out-of-state $28,230

Two-year College(s)

Ohio State University Agricultural Technical Institute (Public)
   Fall 2004 Enrollment: 791 .... (330) 287-1331
   2005-06 Tuition: In-state $5,478; Out-of-state $16,701

Housing: Homeownership rate: 60.8% (2005); Median home value: $123,147 (2005); Median rent: $418 per month (2000); Median age of housing: 35 years (2000).
Hospitals: Wooster Community Hospital (130 beds)
Newspapers: The Daily Record (Circulation 23,357)
Transportation: Commute to work: 86.9% car, 0.9% public transportation, 9.2% walk, 2.6% work from home (2000); Travel time to work: 64.7% less than 15 minutes, 21.1% 15 to 30 minutes, 6.7% 30 to 45 minutes, 4.0% 45 to 60 minutes, 3.5% 60 minutes or more (2000)
Additional Information Contacts
Wayne County Convention Bureau .... (330) 264-1800
   http://www.waynecountycvb.org
Wooster Chamber of Commerce .... (330) 262-5735
   http://www.wooster-wayne.com

Williams County

Located in northwestern Ohio; bounded on the north by Michigan, and on the west by Indiana; crossed by the St. Joseph and Tiffin Rivers. Covers a land area of 421.74 square miles, a water area of 1.31 square miles, and is located in the Eastern Time Zone. The county government was organized in 1820. County seat is Bryan.

Weather Station: Montpelier   Elevation: 859 feet

	Jan	Feb	Mar	Apr	May	Jun	Jul	Aug	Sep	Oct	Nov	Dec
High	30	34	45	58	71	80	84	82	75	62	48	36
Low	13	16	25	35	46	55	60	57	49	38	30	20
Precip	1.9	1.9	2.9	3.6	3.5	3.5	3.5	3.6	3.2	2.6	3.1	2.5
Snow	9.9	8.5	4.5	0.8	0.0	0.0	0.0	0.0	0.0	0.2	1.9	8.1

High and Low temperatures in degrees Fahrenheit; Precipitation and Snow in inches

Population: 36,956 (1990); 39,188 (2000); 38,606 (2005); 38,003 (2010 projected); Race: 96.1% White, 0.9% Black, 0.7% Asian, 3.0% Hispanic of any race (2005); Density: 91.5 persons per square mile (2005); Average household size: 2.56 (2005); Median age: 38.2 (2005); Males per 100 females: 99.1 (2005).
Religion: Five largest groups: 11.6% Catholic Church, 10.5% The United Methodist Church, 6.6% Evangelical Lutheran Church in America, 3.8% Christian Churches and Churches of Christ, 2.9% Presbyterian Church (U.S.A.) (2000).
Economy: Unemployment rate: 6.2% (2005); Total civilian labor force: 19,592 (2005); Leading industries: 50.8% manufacturing; 10.0% retail trade; 9.7% health care and social assistance (2004); Farms: 1,099 totaling 213,265 acres (2002); Companies that employ 500 or more persons: 1 (2004); Companies that employ 100 to 499 persons: 30 (2004); Companies that employ less than 100 persons: 872 (2004); Black-owned businesses: n/a (2002); Hispanic-owned businesses: n/a (2002); Women-owned businesses: 746 (2002); Retail sales per capita: $9,994 (2006). Single-family building permits issued: 119 (2005); Multi-family building permits issued: 2 (2005).
Income: Per capita income: $20,590 (2005); Median household income: $44,245 (2005); Average household income: $51,693 (2005); Percent of households with income of $100,000 or more: 7.3% (2005); Poverty rate: 7.7% (2003); Bankruptcy rate: 10.83% (2005).
Taxes: Total county taxes per capita: $174 (2004); County property taxes per capita: $95 (2004).

Education: Percent of population age 25 and over with: High school diploma (including GED) or higher: 82.9% (2005); Bachelor's degree or higher: 10.7% (2005); Master's degree or higher: 3.5% (2005).
Housing: Homeownership rate: 76.9% (2005); Median home value: $104,176 (2005); Median rent: $375 per month (2000); Median age of housing: 39 years (2000).
Health: Birth rate: 112.3 per 10,000 population (2004); Death rate: 81.4 per 10,000 population (2004); Age-adjusted cancer mortality rate: 196.3 deaths per 100,000 population (2002); Number of physicians: 11.1 per 10,000 population (2004); Hospital beds: 29.1 per 10,000 population (2003); Hospital admissions: 967.0 per 10,000 population (2003).
Elections: 2004 Presidential election results: 64.6% Bush, 34.8% Kerry, 0.0% Nader, 0.3% Badnarik
Additional Information Contacts
Williams County Government .... (419) 636-2059
   http://www.co.williams.oh.us/
Bryan Chamber of Commerce .... (419) 636-2247
   http://www.bryanchamber.org
Montpelier Chamber of Commerce .... (419) 485-4416
   http://www.montpelierchamber.com
West Unity Chamber of Commerce .... (419) 924-2952
   http://www.westunity.net/2004

Williams County Communities

ALVORDTON (village). Covers a land area of 0.258 square miles and a water area of 0 square miles. Located at 41.66° N. Lat.; 84.43° W. Long. Elevation is 847 feet.
Population: 298 (1990); 305 (2000); 288 (2005); 284 (2010 projected); Race: 95.1% White, 1.4% Black, 0.0% Asian, 3.5% Hispanic of any race (2005); Density: 1,117.6 persons per square mile (2005); Average household size: 2.94 (2005); Median age: 39.3 (2005); Males per 100 females: 119.8 (2005); Marriage status: 25.8% never married, 46.5% now married, 4.2% widowed, 23.5% divorced (2000); Foreign born: 1.7% (2000); Ancestry (includes multiple ancestries): 25.9% German, 14.1% United States or American, 13.3% Other groups, 6.9% Irish, 3.7% French (except Basque) (2000).
Economy: Employment by occupation: 4.8% management, 1.8% professional, 11.4% services, 9.6% sales, 2.4% farming, 4.2% construction, 65.7% production (2000).
Income: Per capita income: $19,570 (2005); Median household income: $37,500 (2005); Average household income: $38,546 (2005); Percent of households with income of $100,000 or more: 0.0% (2005); Poverty rate: 11.5% (2000).
Education: Percent of population age 25 and over with: High school diploma (including GED) or higher: 77.0% (2005); Bachelor's degree or higher: 4.4% (2005); Master's degree or higher: 1.5% (2005).
Housing: Homeownership rate: 73.5% (2005); Median home value: $44,000 (2005); Median rent: $275 per month (2000); Median age of housing: 60+ years (2000).
Transportation: Commute to work: 95.8% car, 0.0% public transportation, 1.2% walk, 3.0% work from home (2000); Travel time to work: 26.7% less than 15 minutes, 57.8% 15 to 30 minutes, 6.2% 30 to 45 minutes, 6.2% 45 to 60 minutes, 3.1% 60 minutes or more (2000)

BLAKESLEE (village). Aka Blakesley. Covers a land area of 0.106 square miles and a water area of 0 square miles. Located at 41.52° N. Lat.; 84.73° W. Long. Elevation is 870 feet.
Population: 128 (1990); 130 (2000); 131 (2005); 130 (2010 projected); Race: 100.0% White, 0.0% Black, 0.0% Asian, 0.8% Hispanic of any race (2005); Density: 1,236.2 persons per square mile (2005); Average household size: 2.67 (2005); Median age: 30.5 (2005); Males per 100 females: 95.5 (2005); Marriage status: 8.8% never married, 75.0% now married, 6.3% widowed, 10.0% divorced (2000); Foreign born: 0.0% (2000); Ancestry (includes multiple ancestries): 38.0% German, 16.5% United States or American, 8.3% Syrian, 8.3% Other groups, 7.4% Irish (2000).
Economy: Employment by occupation: 22.6% management, 0.0% professional, 15.1% services, 13.2% sales, 0.0% farming, 13.2% construction, 35.8% production (2000).
Income: Per capita income: $18,626 (2005); Median household income: $44,808 (2005); Average household income: $49,796 (2005); Percent of households with income of $100,000 or more: 8.2% (2005); Poverty rate: 1.7% (2000).

Education: Percent of population age 25 and over with: High school diploma (including GED) or higher: 87.0% (2005); Bachelor's degree or higher: 2.6% (2005); Master's degree or higher: 0.0% (2005).
Housing: Homeownership rate: 67.3% (2005); Median home value: $90,000 (2005); Median rent: $300 per month (2000); Median age of housing: 57 years (2000).
Transportation: Commute to work: 94.3% car, 0.0% public transportation, 1.9% walk, 3.8% work from home (2000); Travel time to work: 13.7% less than 15 minutes, 51.0% 15 to 30 minutes, 25.5% 30 to 45 minutes, 9.8% 45 to 60 minutes, 0.0% 60 minutes or more (2000)

BRYAN (city). Covers a land area of 4.574 square miles and a water area of 0 square miles. Located at 41.47° N. Lat.; 84.55° W. Long. Elevation is 755 feet.
History: Bryan's early growth was attributed to its artesian wells, their supposed medicinal value creating a temporary business for the town, which became a trading and industrial center and the seat of Williams County.
Population: 8,575 (1990); 8,333 (2000); 8,080 (2005); 7,840 (2010 projected); Race: 95.9% White, 0.4% Black, 0.9% Asian, 4.1% Hispanic of any race (2005); Density: 1,766.4 persons per square mile (2005); Average household size: 2.33 (2005); Median age: 38.7 (2005); Males per 100 females: 91.5 (2005); Marriage status: 20.2% never married, 56.1% now married, 9.4% widowed, 14.3% divorced (2000); Foreign born: 1.5% (2000); Ancestry (includes multiple ancestries): 34.9% German, 11.7% United States or American, 11.2% Irish, 11.0% Other groups, 9.7% English (2000).
Economy: Single-family building permits issued: 23 (2005); Multi-family building permits issued: 0 (2005); Employment by occupation: 9.5% management, 14.4% professional, 12.3% services, 19.4% sales, 0.2% farming, 7.1% construction, 37.0% production (2000).
Income: Per capita income: $20,828 (2005); Median household income: $40,019 (2005); Average household income: $47,817 (2005); Percent of households with income of $100,000 or more: 6.7% (2005); Poverty rate: 6.0% (2000).
Education: Percent of population age 25 and over with: High school diploma (including GED) or higher: 82.8% (2005); Bachelor's degree or higher: 14.7% (2005); Master's degree or higher: 3.6% (2005).
School District(s)
Bryan City SD (PK-12)
    2003-04 Enrollment: 2,288 . . . . (419) 636-6973
Housing: Homeownership rate: 63.4% (2005); Median home value: $112,086 (2005); Median rent: $399 per month (2000); Median age of housing: 41 years (2000).
Hospitals: Community Hospitals of Williams County (131 beds)
Safety: Violent crime rate: 15.7 per 10,000 population; Property crime rate: 288.2 per 10,000 population (2004).
Newspapers: The Bryan Times (Circulation 10,591); The County Line (General - Circulation 24,135)
Transportation: Commute to work: 91.8% car, 0.6% public transportation, 3.9% walk, 3.0% work from home (2000); Travel time to work: 56.3% less than 15 minutes, 29.3% 15 to 30 minutes, 9.5% 30 to 45 minutes, 2.5% 45 to 60 minutes, 2.4% 60 minutes or more (2000); Amtrak: Service available.
Additional Information Contacts
Bryan Chamber of Commerce . . . . (419) 636-2247
    http://www.bryanchamber.org

EDGERTON (village). Covers a land area of 1.861 square miles and a water area of 0 square miles. Located at 41.44° N. Lat.; 84.74° W. Long. Elevation is 835 feet.
Population: 2,167 (1990); 2,117 (2000); 2,002 (2005); 1,925 (2010 projected); Race: 97.2% White, 0.1% Black, 0.1% Asian, 2.4% Hispanic of any race (2005); Density: 1,075.9 persons per square mile (2005); Average household size: 2.58 (2005); Median age: 37.4 (2005); Males per 100 females: 91.0 (2005); Marriage status: 20.2% never married, 56.6% now married, 11.0% widowed, 12.3% divorced (2000); Foreign born: 0.4% (2000); Ancestry (includes multiple ancestries): 43.2% German, 12.8% United States or American, 8.5% Other groups, 7.4% Irish, 6.8% English (2000).
Economy: Single-family building permits issued: 4 (2005); Multi-family building permits issued: 0 (2005); Employment by occupation: 6.9% management, 13.1% professional, 10.0% services, 21.8% sales, 0.4% farming, 8.8% construction, 39.1% production (2000).
Income: Per capita income: $19,180 (2005); Median household income: $42,664 (2005); Average household income: $48,998 (2005); Percent of households with income of $100,000 or more: 6.6% (2005); Poverty rate: 8.9% (2000).
Education: Percent of population age 25 and over with: High school diploma (including GED) or higher: 80.9% (2005); Bachelor's degree or higher: 9.9% (2005); Master's degree or higher: 3.7% (2005).
School District(s)
Edgerton Local Schools (PK-12)
    2003-04 Enrollment: 740 . . . . (419) 298-2112
Housing: Homeownership rate: 76.9% (2005); Median home value: $90,800 (2005); Median rent: $381 per month (2000); Median age of housing: 43 years (2000).
Newspapers: The Edgerton Earth (General - Circulation 1,475)
Transportation: Commute to work: 93.1% car, 0.2% public transportation, 3.5% walk, 1.9% work from home (2000); Travel time to work: 48.9% less than 15 minutes, 34.2% 15 to 30 minutes, 11.4% 30 to 45 minutes, 2.5% 45 to 60 minutes, 3.0% 60 minutes or more (2000).

EDON (village). Covers a land area of 1.040 square miles and a water area of 0 square miles. Located at 41.55° N. Lat.; 84.76° W. Long. Elevation is 900 feet.
Population: 911 (1990); 898 (2000); 936 (2005); 962 (2010 projected); Race: 98.7% White, 0.0% Black, 0.6% Asian, 0.2% Hispanic of any race (2005); Density: 899.7 persons per square mile (2005); Average household size: 2.46 (2005); Median age: 37.9 (2005); Males per 100 females: 90.6 (2005); Marriage status: 21.3% never married, 62.2% now married, 7.8% widowed, 8.7% divorced (2000); Foreign born: 0.2% (2000); Ancestry (includes multiple ancestries): 45.5% German, 14.1% United States or American, 10.7% Irish, 6.3% English, 5.1% French (except Basque) (2000).
Economy: Machine tools, poultry equipment, food products. Single-family building permits issued: 1 (2005); Multi-family building permits issued: 0 (2005); Employment by occupation: 9.4% management, 9.6% professional, 13.3% services, 19.3% sales, 0.5% farming, 4.1% construction, 43.8% production (2000).
Income: Per capita income: $23,504 (2005); Median household income: $47,672 (2005); Average household income: $57,743 (2005); Percent of households with income of $100,000 or more: 7.1% (2005); Poverty rate: 5.2% (2000).
Education: Percent of population age 25 and over with: High school diploma (including GED) or higher: 88.1% (2005); Bachelor's degree or higher: 9.6% (2005); Master's degree or higher: 3.1% (2005).
School District(s)
Edon-Northwest Local SD (PK-12)
    2003-04 Enrollment: 725 . . . . (419) 272-3213
Housing: Homeownership rate: 79.5% (2005); Median home value: $81,467 (2005); Median rent: $335 per month (2000); Median age of housing: 59 years (2000).
Newspapers: Edon Commercial (General - Circulation 5,100)
Transportation: Commute to work: 94.7% car, 0.0% public transportation, 3.0% walk, 2.1% work from home (2000); Travel time to work: 44.7% less than 15 minutes, 34.4% 15 to 30 minutes, 13.8% 30 to 45 minutes, 2.1% 45 to 60 minutes, 5.0% 60 minutes or more (2000)

HOLIDAY CITY (village). Covers a land area of 1.328 square miles and a water area of 0.022 square miles. Located at 41.61° N. Lat.; 84.55° W. Long.
Population: 45 (1990); 49 (2000); 46 (2005); 44 (2010 projected); Race: 91.3% White, 0.0% Black, 6.5% Asian, 0.0% Hispanic of any race (2005); Density: 34.6 persons per square mile (2005); Average household size: 3.07 (2005); Median age: 25.0 (2005); Males per 100 females: 70.4 (2005); Marriage status: 13.3% never married, 76.7% now married, 10.0% widowed, 0.0% divorced (2000); Foreign born: 0.0% (2000); Ancestry (includes multiple ancestries): 58.8% United States or American, 17.6% Other groups, 9.8% German, 3.9% Polish, 3.9% Lebanese (2000).
Economy: Employment by occupation: 15.8% management, 15.8% professional, 0.0% services, 10.5% sales, 0.0% farming, 10.5% construction, 47.4% production (2000).
Income: Per capita income: $10,489 (2005); Median household income: $30,000 (2005); Average household income: $32,167 (2005); Percent of households with income of $100,000 or more: 0.0% (2005); Poverty rate: 6.3% (2000).
Education: Percent of population age 25 and over with: High school diploma (including GED) or higher: 65.2% (2005); Bachelor's degree or higher: 17.4% (2005); Master's degree or higher: 0.0% (2005).

Housing: Homeownership rate: 73.3% (2005); Median home value: $78,333 (2005); Median rent: $408 per month (2000); Median age of housing: 29 years (2000).
Transportation: Commute to work: 100.0% car, 0.0% public transportation, 0.0% walk, 0.0% work from home (2000); Travel time to work: 12.5% less than 15 minutes, 87.5% 15 to 30 minutes, 0.0% 30 to 45 minutes, 0.0% 45 to 60 minutes, 0.0% 60 minutes or more (2000)

MONTPELIER
(village). Covers a land area of 2.698 square miles and a water area of 0 square miles. Located at 41.58° N. Lat.; 84.60° W. Long. Elevation is 850 feet.
History: Settled 1855, incorporated 1875.
Population: 4,254 (1990); 4,320 (2000); 4,094 (2005); 3,869 (2010 projected); Race: 96.0% White, 0.4% Black, 2.1% Asian, 1.7% Hispanic of any race (2005); Density: 1,517.2 persons per square mile (2005); Average household size: 2.43 (2005); Median age: 35.3 (2005); Males per 100 females: 91.4 (2005); Marriage status: 21.3% never married, 57.7% now married, 7.8% widowed, 13.2% divorced (2000); Foreign born: 1.0% (2000); Ancestry (includes multiple ancestries): 30.2% German, 17.8% United States or American, 9.6% English, 9.1% Irish, 7.4% Other groups (2000).
Economy: Wood fixtures, metal stampings, truck bodies. Single-family building permits issued: 1 (2005); Multi-family building permits issued: 0 (2005); Employment by occupation: 4.0% management, 7.4% professional, 14.4% services, 18.8% sales, 0.0% farming, 6.4% construction, 48.9% production (2000).
Income: Per capita income: $16,260 (2005); Median household income: $33,654 (2005); Average household income: $39,216 (2005); Percent of households with income of $100,000 or more: 1.7% (2005); Poverty rate: 6.2% (2000).
Education: Percent of population age 25 and over with: High school diploma (including GED) or higher: 83.1% (2005); Bachelor's degree or higher: 6.6% (2005); Master's degree or higher: 3.0% (2005).
School District(s)
Montpelier Ex Vill SD (PK-12)
 2003-04 Enrollment: 1,175 . . . . (419) 485-3676
Housing: Homeownership rate: 67.4% (2005); Median home value: $77,413 (2005); Median rent: $341 per month (2000); Median age of housing: 56 years (2000).
Safety: Violent crime rate: 54.9 per 10,000 population; Property crime rate: 491.6 per 10,000 population (2004).
Newspapers: Montpelier Leader-Enterprise (General - Circulation 1,700)
Transportation: Commute to work: 90.7% car, 0.6% public transportation, 5.5% walk, 2.6% work from home (2000); Travel time to work: 54.8% less than 15 minutes, 31.7% 15 to 30 minutes, 8.6% 30 to 45 minutes, 2.0% 45 to 60 minutes, 2.8% 60 minutes or more (2000)
Additional Information Contacts
Montpelier Chamber of Commerce . . . . (419) 485-4416
http://www.montpelierchamber.com

PIONEER
(village). Covers a land area of 1.601 square miles and a water area of 0.063 square miles. Located at 41.68° N. Lat.; 84.55° W. Long. Elevation is 874 feet.
Population: 1,328 (1990); 1,460 (2000); 1,460 (2005); 1,448 (2010 projected); Race: 97.0% White, 0.3% Black, 0.3% Asian, 2.1% Hispanic of any race (2005); Density: 911.8 persons per square mile (2005); Average household size: 2.41 (2005); Median age: 37.4 (2005); Males per 100 females: 96.0 (2005); Marriage status: 21.0% never married, 60.1% now married, 5.5% widowed, 13.4% divorced (2000); Foreign born: 0.5% (2000); Ancestry (includes multiple ancestries): 32.4% German, 13.0% United States or American, 8.5% Other groups, 7.6% English, 7.5% Irish (2000).
Economy: Light manufacturing. Employment by occupation: 8.5% management, 14.1% professional, 12.3% services, 17.2% sales, 0.1% farming, 9.9% construction, 37.9% production (2000).
Income: Per capita income: $21,274 (2005); Median household income: $41,855 (2005); Average household income: $51,339 (2005); Percent of households with income of $100,000 or more: 6.8% (2005); Poverty rate: 6.5% (2000).
Education: Percent of population age 25 and over with: High school diploma (including GED) or higher: 82.3% (2005); Bachelor's degree or higher: 10.6% (2005); Master's degree or higher: 3.5% (2005).
School District(s)
North Central Local SD (PK-12)
 2003-04 Enrollment: 704 . . . . (419) 737-2392

Housing: Homeownership rate: 69.8% (2005); Median home value: $106,711 (2005); Median rent: $378 per month (2000); Median age of housing: 26 years (2000).
Transportation: Commute to work: 93.1% car, 0.3% public transportation, 4.3% walk, 1.6% work from home (2000); Travel time to work: 47.3% less than 15 minutes, 32.1% 15 to 30 minutes, 14.2% 30 to 45 minutes, 3.0% 45 to 60 minutes, 3.4% 60 minutes or more (2000)

STRYKER
(village). Covers a land area of 0.810 square miles and a water area of 0 square miles. Located at 41.50° N. Lat.; 84.41° W. Long. Elevation is 719 feet.
Population: 1,468 (1990); 1,406 (2000); 1,390 (2005); 1,398 (2010 projected); Race: 95.9% White, 0.1% Black, 0.1% Asian, 8.8% Hispanic of any race (2005); Density: 1,716.4 persons per square mile (2005); Average household size: 2.55 (2005); Median age: 34.1 (2005); Males per 100 females: 92.0 (2005); Marriage status: 23.0% never married, 61.8% now married, 4.2% widowed, 11.1% divorced (2000); Foreign born: 1.3% (2000); Ancestry (includes multiple ancestries): 34.4% German, 13.9% Other groups, 9.0% English, 8.1% French (except Basque), 7.3% Irish (2000).
Economy: Corn, wheat, hay; manufacturing of ceramics. Single-family building permits issued: 1 (2005); Multi-family building permits issued: 0 (2005); Employment by occupation: 4.8% management, 9.1% professional, 11.4% services, 17.6% sales, 0.7% farming, 9.7% construction, 46.7% production (2000).
Income: Per capita income: $19,390 (2005); Median household income: $44,744 (2005); Average household income: $49,364 (2005); Percent of households with income of $100,000 or more: 5.7% (2005); Poverty rate: 5.4% (2000).
Education: Percent of population age 25 and over with: High school diploma (including GED) or higher: 82.1% (2005); Bachelor's degree or higher: 9.1% (2005); Master's degree or higher: 2.7% (2005).
School District(s)
Stryker Local SD (KG-12)
 2003-04 Enrollment: 524 . . . . (419) 682-6961
Housing: Homeownership rate: 78.0% (2005); Median home value: $79,615 (2005); Median rent: $318 per month (2000); Median age of housing: 53 years (2000).
Transportation: Commute to work: 93.2% car, 0.0% public transportation, 2.9% walk, 1.5% work from home (2000); Travel time to work: 50.0% less than 15 minutes, 37.3% 15 to 30 minutes, 5.9% 30 to 45 minutes, 1.9% 45 to 60 minutes, 4.9% 60 minutes or more (2000)

WEST UNITY
(village). Covers a land area of 1.033 square miles and a water area of 0 square miles. Located at 41.58° N. Lat.; 84.43° W. Long. Elevation is 788 feet.
Population: 1,731 (1990); 1,790 (2000); 1,860 (2005); 1,862 (2010 projected); Race: 97.2% White, 0.4% Black, 0.2% Asian, 3.2% Hispanic of any race (2005); Density: 1,800.7 persons per square mile (2005); Average household size: 2.41 (2005); Median age: 34.0 (2005); Males per 100 females: 95.6 (2005); Marriage status: 25.7% never married, 56.3% now married, 6.8% widowed, 11.2% divorced (2000); Foreign born: 0.6% (2000); Ancestry (includes multiple ancestries): 37.6% German, 9.8% English, 8.2% Other groups, 8.1% United States or American, 8.0% Irish (2000).
Economy: Electrical apparatus, furniture. Single-family building permits issued: 1 (2005); Multi-family building permits issued: 0 (2005); Employment by occupation: 6.2% management, 10.1% professional, 11.6% services, 21.1% sales, 0.4% farming, 8.6% construction, 41.9% production (2000).
Income: Per capita income: $18,184 (2005); Median household income: $37,843 (2005); Average household income: $43,235 (2005); Percent of households with income of $100,000 or more: 3.0% (2005); Poverty rate: 8.0% (2000).
Education: Percent of population age 25 and over with: High school diploma (including GED) or higher: 82.0% (2005); Bachelor's degree or higher: 8.2% (2005); Master's degree or higher: 3.2% (2005).
School District(s)
Millcreek-West Unity Local SD (PK-12)
 2003-04 Enrollment: 771 . . . . (419) 924-2365
Housing: Homeownership rate: 67.5% (2005); Median home value: $97,402 (2005); Median rent: $320 per month (2000); Median age of housing: 38 years (2000).
Newspapers: Advance Reporter (General - Circulation 1,975)

Transportation: Commute to work: 95.0% car, 0.0% public transportation, 2.3% walk, 2.2% work from home (2000); Travel time to work: 35.7% less than 15 minutes, 49.1% 15 to 30 minutes, 9.3% 30 to 45 minutes, 1.6% 45 to 60 minutes, 4.4% 60 minutes or more (2000)
Additional Information Contacts
West Unity Chamber of Commerce .... (419) 924-2952
http://www.westunity.net/2004

Wood County

Located in northwestern Ohio; bounded on the northwest by the Maumee River; crossed by the Portage River. Covers a land area of 617.32 square miles, a water area of 3.22 square miles, and is located in the Eastern Time Zone. The county government was organized in 1820. County seat is Bowling Green.

Wood County is part of the Toledo, OH Metropolitan Statistical Area. The entire metro area includes: Fulton County, OH; Lucas County, OH; Ottawa County, OH; Wood County, OH

Weather Station: Bowling Green WWTP   Elevation: 672 feet

	Jan	Feb	Mar	Apr	May	Jun	Jul	Aug	Sep	Oct	Nov	Dec
High	31	35	47	60	72	81	85	82	76	63	49	37
Low	16	19	28	37	48	58	62	59	52	41	32	23
Precip	1.7	1.6	2.4	3.3	3.5	3.5	3.7	3.3	2.6	2.5	2.7	2.3
Snow	7.2	5.4	3.1	0.7	tr	0.0	0.0	0.0	0.0	tr	0.7	4.8

High and Low temperatures in degrees Fahrenheit; Precipitation and Snow in inches

Weather Station: Hoytville 2 NE   Elevation: 698 feet

	Jan	Feb	Mar	Apr	May	Jun	Jul	Aug	Sep	Oct	Nov	Dec
High	31	35	46	59	71	80	84	81	75	63	49	37
Low	15	18	27	36	48	57	61	58	51	40	32	22
Precip	1.8	1.7	2.5	3.3	3.4	3.6	3.9	3.5	2.6	2.4	2.8	2.4
Snow	7.5	5.5	3.4	1.0	tr	0.0	0.0	0.0	0.0	tr	1.3	5.2

High and Low temperatures in degrees Fahrenheit; Precipitation and Snow in inches

Population: 113,269 (1990); 121,065 (2000); 123,889 (2005); 126,811 (2010 projected); Race: 94.6% White, 1.2% Black, 1.3% Asian, 3.5% Hispanic of any race (2005); Density: 200.7 persons per square mile (2005); Average household size: 2.64 (2005); Median age: 33.8 (2005); Males per 100 females: 94.4 (2005).
Religion: Five largest groups: 18.2% Catholic Church, 9.2% Evangelical Lutheran Church in America, 6.7% The United Methodist Church, 3.3% Muslim Estimate, 1.7% Assemblies of God (2000).
Economy: Unemployment rate: 5.6% (2005); Total civilian labor force: 67,025 (2005); Leading industries: 28.8% manufacturing; 12.9% retail trade; 10.9% accommodation & food services (2004); Farms: 1,066 totaling 305,834 acres (2002); Companies that employ 500 or more persons: 9 (2004); Companies that employ 100 to 499 persons: 82 (2004); Companies that employ less than 100 persons: 2,705 (2004); Black-owned businesses: n/a (2002); Hispanic-owned businesses: 169 (2002); Women-owned businesses: 2,283 (2002); Retail sales per capita: $13,312 (2006). Single-family building permits issued: 609 (2005); Multi-family building permits issued: 543 (2005).
Income: Per capita income: $23,965 (2005); Median household income: $48,642 (2005); Average household income: $62,108 (2005); Percent of households with income of $100,000 or more: 15.0% (2005); Poverty rate: 7.7% (2003); Bankruptcy rate: 8.76% (2005).
Taxes: Total county taxes per capita: $312 (2004); County property taxes per capita: $189 (2004).
Education: Percent of population age 25 and over with: High school diploma (including GED) or higher: 88.7% (2005); Bachelor's degree or higher: 26.2% (2005); Master's degree or higher: 10.4% (2005).
Housing: Homeownership rate: 71.2% (2005); Median home value: $132,068 (2005); Median rent: $427 per month (2000); Median age of housing: 29 years (2000).
Health: Birth rate: 114.0 per 10,000 population (2004); Death rate: 78.1 per 10,000 population (2004); Age-adjusted cancer mortality rate: 194.2 deaths per 100,000 population (2002); Air Quality Index: 81.4% good, 17.2% moderate, 1.4% unhealthy for sensitive individuals, 0.0% unhealthy (percent of days in 2005); Number of physicians: 18.6 per 10,000 population (2004); Hospital beds: 7.9 per 10,000 population (2003); Hospital admissions: 263.5 per 10,000 population (2003).
Elections: 2004 Presidential election results: 53.0% Bush, 46.4% Kerry, 0.0% Nader, 0.3% Badnarik.

National and State Parks: Fort Meigs State Memorial; Thurston State Park
Additional Information Contacts
Wood County Government .... (419) 354-9100
http://www.co.wood.oh.us/
Bowling Green Chamber of Commerce .... (419) 353-7945
http://www.bgchamber.net
Bowling Green Convention & Visitors Bureau .... (419) 353-7945
http://www.visitbgohio.org
City of Bowling Green .... (419) 354-6204
http://www.bgohio.org
City of Northwood .... (419) 693-9320
http://www.ci.northwood.oh.us
City of Perrysburg .... (419) 872-8010
http://www.ci.perrysburg.oh.us
City of Rossford .... (419) 666-0210
http://www.rossfordohio.com
Grand Rapids Chamber of Commerce .... (419) 832-1106
http://www.grandrapidsohio.com
Perrysburg Area Chamber .... (419) 874-9147
http://www.perrysburgchamber.com
Village of Grand Rapids .... (419) 832-5305
http://www.grandrapidsohio.com
Village of Pemberville .... (419) 287-3832
http://pembervillelibrary.org/pemberville

Wood County Communities

BAIRDSTOWN (village). Covers a land area of 0.267 square miles and a water area of 0 square miles. Located at 41.17° N. Lat.; 83.60° W. Long. Elevation is 735 feet.
Population: 133 (1990); 130 (2000); 154 (2005); 177 (2010 projected); Race: 95.5% White, 0.0% Black, 0.0% Asian, 1.9% Hispanic of any race (2005); Density: 576.6 persons per square mile (2005); Average household size: 2.61 (2005); Median age: 40.8 (2005); Males per 100 females: 102.6 (2005); Marriage status: 24.6% never married, 60.7% now married, 9.8% widowed, 4.9% divorced (2000); Foreign born: 2.3% (2000); Ancestry (includes multiple ancestries): 42.7% United States or American, 17.6% German, 9.9% Other groups, 3.1% Scottish, 3.1% Pennsylvania German (2000).
Economy: Single-family building permits issued: 0 (2005); Multi-family building permits issued: 0 (2005); Employment by occupation: 0.0% management, 0.0% professional, 18.3% services, 11.7% sales, 0.0% farming, 23.3% construction, 46.7% production (2000).
Income: Per capita income: $17,305 (2005); Median household income: $44,808 (2005); Average household income: $45,169 (2005); Percent of households with income of $100,000 or more: 1.7% (2005); Poverty rate: 7.6% (2000).
Education: Percent of population age 25 and over with: High school diploma (including GED) or higher: 76.5% (2005); Bachelor's degree or higher: 2.6% (2005); Master's degree or higher: 2.6% (2005).
Housing: Homeownership rate: 83.1% (2005); Median home value: $63,125 (2005); Median rent: $281 per month (2000); Median age of housing: 37 years (2000).
Transportation: Commute to work: 100.0% car, 0.0% public transportation, 0.0% walk, 0.0% work from home (2000); Travel time to work: 29.3% less than 15 minutes, 48.3% 15 to 30 minutes, 12.1% 30 to 45 minutes, 0.0% 45 to 60 minutes, 10.3% 60 minutes or more (2000)

BLOOMDALE (village). Covers a land area of 0.669 square miles and a water area of 0.004 square miles. Located at 41.17° N. Lat.; 83.55° W. Long. Elevation is 750 feet.
Population: 632 (1990); 724 (2000); 866 (2005); 996 (2010 projected); Race: 98.0% White, 0.0% Black, 0.3% Asian, 1.2% Hispanic of any race (2005); Density: 1,295.0 persons per square mile (2005); Average household size: 2.78 (2005); Median age: 33.3 (2005); Males per 100 females: 100.5 (2005); Marriage status: 20.7% never married, 63.7% now married, 8.5% widowed, 7.2% divorced (2000); Foreign born: 1.2% (2000); Ancestry (includes multiple ancestries): 38.4% German, 14.4% English, 11.5% Irish, 7.8% United States or American, 5.3% Other groups (2000).
Economy: Food products. Single-family building permits issued: 0 (2005); Multi-family building permits issued: 0 (2005); Employment by occupation: 11.2% management, 5.5% professional, 12.4% services, 17.0% sales, 0.0% farming, 8.9% construction, 45.1% production (2000).

Income: Per capita income: $18,346 (2005); Median household income: $44,857 (2005); Average household income: $50,921 (2005); Percent of households with income of $100,000 or more: 6.4% (2005); Poverty rate: 3.7% (2000).
Education: Percent of population age 25 and over with: High school diploma (including GED) or higher: 89.0% (2005); Bachelor's degree or higher: 14.2% (2005); Master's degree or higher: 2.9% (2005).

School District(s)
Elmwood Local SD (PK-12)
   2003-04 Enrollment: 1,312 . . . . (419) 655-2583

Housing: Homeownership rate: 87.5% (2005); Median home value: $91,379 (2005); Median rent: $354 per month (2000); Median age of housing: 60+ years (2000).
Transportation: Commute to work: 96.4% car, 0.0% public transportation, 1.2% walk, 2.4% work from home (2000); Travel time to work: 20.6% less than 15 minutes, 55.2% 15 to 30 minutes, 15.8% 30 to 45 minutes, 4.2% 45 to 60 minutes, 4.2% 60 minutes or more (2000)

BOWLING GREEN (city).
Covers a land area of 10.153 square miles and a water area of 0.033 square miles. Located at 41.37° N. Lat.; 83.65° W. Long. Elevation is 700 feet.
History: Bowling Green was laid out in 1835 and named by Joseph Gordon for his home town in Kentucky. Oil was found here in 1886, bringing an industrial boom. In 1914 the H.J. Heinz Company established a tomato-products plant in Bowling Green, and the same year Bowling Green State University opened as a normal school.
Population: 29,038 (1990); 29,636 (2000); 29,953 (2005); 30,315 (2010 projected); Race: 91.6% White, 2.6% Black, 2.0% Asian, 3.8% Hispanic of any race (2005); Density: 2,950.2 persons per square mile (2005); Average household size: 2.82 (2005); Median age: 24.4 (2005); Males per 100 females: 87.6 (2005); Marriage status: 54.7% never married, 35.8% now married, 3.7% widowed, 5.8% divorced (2000); Foreign born: 3.6% (2000); Ancestry (includes multiple ancestries): 31.4% German, 11.7% Irish, 10.6% English, 10.2% Other groups, 5.1% United States or American (2000).
Economy: Unemployment rate: 4.4% (2005); Total civilian labor force: 16,089 (2005); Employment by occupation: 9.9% management, 26.1% professional, 21.2% services, 24.6% sales, 0.2% farming, 3.7% construction, 14.2% production (2000).
Income: Per capita income: $17,149 (2005); Median household income: $32,946 (2005); Average household income: $45,422 (2005); Percent of households with income of $100,000 or more: 8.4% (2005); Poverty rate: 25.3% (2000).
Taxes: Total city taxes per capita: $538 (2004); City property taxes per capita: $64 (2004).
Education: Percent of population age 25 and over with: High school diploma (including GED) or higher: 91.0% (2005); Bachelor's degree or higher: 43.8% (2005); Master's degree or higher: 21.8% (2005).

School District(s)
Bowling Green City SD (PK-12)
   2003-04 Enrollment: 3,203 . . . . (419) 352-3576

Four-year College(s)
Bowling Green State University-Main Campus (Public)
   Fall 2004 Enrollment: 18,989. . . . . (419) 372-2531
   2005-06 Tuition: In-state $8,560; Out-of-state $15,868

Housing: Homeownership rate: 43.1% (2005); Median home value: $142,981 (2005); Median rent: $434 per month (2000); Median age of housing: 28 years (2000).
Hospitals: Wood County Hospital (162 beds)
Safety: Violent crime rate: 12.6 per 10,000 population; Property crime rate: 355.6 per 10,000 population (2004).
Newspapers: Sentinel-Tribune (Circulation 12,020)
Transportation: Commute to work: 83.7% car, 0.6% public transportation, 11.9% walk, 1.7% work from home (2000); Travel time to work: 62.2% less than 15 minutes, 19.0% 15 to 30 minutes, 14.3% 30 to 45 minutes, 2.6% 45 to 60 minutes, 1.9% 60 minutes or more (2000)

Additional Information Contacts
Bowling Green Chamber of Commerce. . . . . (419) 353-7945
   http://www.bgchamber.net
Bowling Green Convention & Visitors Bureau . . . . (419) 353-7945
   http://www.visitbgohio.com
City of Bowling Green . . . . (419) 354-6204
   http://www.bgohio.org

BRADNER (village).
Covers a land area of 0.611 square miles and a water area of 0 square miles. Located at 41.32° N. Lat.; 83.43° W. Long. Elevation is 700 feet.
Population: 1,076 (1990); 1,171 (2000); 1,224 (2005); 1,272 (2010 projected); Race: 98.8% White, 0.0% Black, 0.1% Asian, 3.1% Hispanic of any race (2005); Density: 2,002.2 persons per square mile (2005); Average household size: 2.57 (2005); Median age: 35.1 (2005); Males per 100 females: 99.0 (2005); Marriage status: 24.9% never married, 57.7% now married, 7.1% widowed, 10.3% divorced (2000); Foreign born: 0.3% (2000); Ancestry (includes multiple ancestries): 34.6% German, 16.9% United States or American, 9.9% Irish, 7.6% Other groups, 7.5% English (2000).
Economy: In agricultural area. Manufacturing of oil well machinery, feed milling; stone quarries; poultry hatcheries. Employment by occupation: 5.0% management, 8.5% professional, 13.1% services, 20.4% sales, 1.1% farming, 13.6% construction, 38.3% production (2000).
Income: Per capita income: $18,182 (2005); Median household income: $39,947 (2005); Average household income: $46,754 (2005); Percent of households with income of $100,000 or more: 4.8% (2005); Poverty rate: 12.2% (2000).
Education: Percent of population age 25 and over with: High school diploma (including GED) or higher: 78.2% (2005); Bachelor's degree or higher: 4.7% (2005); Master's degree or higher: 1.3% (2005).

School District(s)
Lakota Local SD (PK-12)
   2003-04 Enrollment: 1,164 . . . . (419) 457-2911

Housing: Homeownership rate: 72.5% (2005); Median home value: $90,349 (2005); Median rent: $371 per month (2000); Median age of housing: 60+ years (2000).
Transportation: Commute to work: 92.8% car, 0.4% public transportation, 3.4% walk, 2.3% work from home (2000); Travel time to work: 22.7% less than 15 minutes, 44.9% 15 to 30 minutes, 22.2% 30 to 45 minutes, 5.0% 45 to 60 minutes, 5.2% 60 minutes or more (2000)

CUSTAR (village).
Covers a land area of 0.251 square miles and a water area of 0 square miles. Located at 41.28° N. Lat.; 83.84° W. Long. Elevation is 693 feet.
Population: 209 (1990); 208 (2000); 213 (2005); 217 (2010 projected); Race: 98.1% White, 0.0% Black, 0.0% Asian, 4.2% Hispanic of any race (2005); Density: 850.2 persons per square mile (2005); Average household size: 2.84 (2005); Median age: 36.2 (2005); Males per 100 females: 93.6 (2005); Marriage status: 26.4% never married, 57.1% now married, 6.7% widowed, 9.8% divorced (2000); Foreign born: 0.5% (2000); Ancestry (includes multiple ancestries): 32.2% German, 10.9% Other groups, 5.4% English, 5.4% Dutch, 5.4% Irish (2000).
Economy: In agricultural area. Employment by occupation: 12.0% management, 12.0% professional, 18.0% services, 15.0% sales, 0.0% farming, 8.0% construction, 35.0% production (2000).
Income: Per capita income: $17,421 (2005); Median household income: $44,868 (2005); Average household income: $46,667 (2005); Percent of households with income of $100,000 or more: 5.3% (2005); Poverty rate: 12.9% (2000).
Education: Percent of population age 25 and over with: High school diploma (including GED) or higher: 89.4% (2005); Bachelor's degree or higher: 1.4% (2005); Master's degree or higher: 1.4% (2005).

School District(s)
Bowling Green City SD (PK-12)
   2003-04 Enrollment: 3,203 . . . . (419) 352-3576

Housing: Homeownership rate: 88.0% (2005); Median home value: $90,833 (2005); Median rent: $275 per month (2000); Median age of housing: 60+ years (2000).
Transportation: Commute to work: 85.9% car, 0.0% public transportation, 9.1% walk, 5.1% work from home (2000); Travel time to work: 16.0% less than 15 minutes, 27.7% 15 to 30 minutes, 26.6% 30 to 45 minutes, 12.8% 45 to 60 minutes, 17.0% 60 minutes or more (2000)

CYGNET (village).
Covers a land area of 0.337 square miles and a water area of 0.001 square miles. Located at 41.24° N. Lat.; 83.64° W. Long. Elevation is 705 feet.
Population: 560 (1990); 564 (2000); 673 (2005); 774 (2010 projected); Race: 97.0% White, 0.3% Black, 0.0% Asian, 2.8% Hispanic of any race (2005); Density: 1,995.2 persons per square mile (2005); Average household size: 2.63 (2005); Median age: 36.2 (2005); Males per 100 females: 102.7 (2005); Marriage status: 19.1% never married, 58.6% now

married, 8.0% widowed, 14.3% divorced (2000); Foreign born: 0.2% (2000); Ancestry (includes multiple ancestries): 35.6% German, 10.8% United States or American, 10.6% Irish, 9.5% English, 4.0% Other groups (2000).
Economy: In agricultural area. Employment by occupation: 9.5% management, 7.6% professional, 15.6% services, 22.5% sales, 1.1% farming, 13.4% construction, 30.2% production (2000).
Income: Per capita income: $17,303 (2005); Median household income: $43,226 (2005); Average household income: $45,488 (2005); Percent of households with income of $100,000 or more: 3.9% (2005); Poverty rate: 4.6% (2000).
Education: Percent of population age 25 and over with: High school diploma (including GED) or higher: 83.1% (2005); Bachelor's degree or higher: 6.4% (2005); Master's degree or higher: 2.8% (2005).

School District(s)
Elmwood Local SD (PK-12)
    2003-04 Enrollment: 1,312 . . . . (419) 655-2583

Housing: Homeownership rate: 86.7% (2005); Median home value: $84,528 (2005); Median rent: $347 per month (2000); Median age of housing: 60+ years (2000).
Transportation: Commute to work: 93.9% car, 1.9% public transportation, 3.4% walk, 0.8% work from home (2000); Travel time to work: 15.0% less than 15 minutes, 64.2% 15 to 30 minutes, 13.5% 30 to 45 minutes, 1.9% 45 to 60 minutes, 5.4% 60 minutes or more (2000)

GRAND RAPIDS
(village). Covers a land area of 0.503 square miles and a water area of 0.088 square miles. Located at 41.41° N. Lat.; 83.86° W. Long. Elevation is 654 feet.
History: Grand Rapids developed as a rural trading center. It was the location of locks on the Miami & Erie Canal.
Population: 1,042 (1990); 1,002 (2000); 1,052 (2005); 1,103 (2010 projected); Race: 96.8% White, 0.3% Black, 0.5% Asian, 3.5% Hispanic of any race (2005); Density: 2,090.1 persons per square mile (2005); Average household size: 2.43 (2005); Median age: 36.7 (2005); Males per 100 females: 90.6 (2005); Marriage status: 19.3% never married, 60.6% now married, 8.1% widowed, 12.0% divorced (2000); Foreign born: 2.2% (2000); Ancestry (includes multiple ancestries): 36.2% German, 14.0% English, 11.0% Irish, 9.9% United States or American, 9.7% Other groups (2000).
Economy: Employment by occupation: 10.7% management, 15.8% professional, 14.1% services, 20.4% sales, 0.8% farming, 13.9% construction, 24.4% production (2000).
Income: Per capita income: $24,305 (2005); Median household income: $47,773 (2005); Average household income: $57,702 (2005); Percent of households with income of $100,000 or more: 9.5% (2005); Poverty rate: 5.7% (2000).
Education: Percent of population age 25 and over with: High school diploma (including GED) or higher: 85.1% (2005); Bachelor's degree or higher: 15.5% (2005); Master's degree or higher: 3.8% (2005).

School District(s)
Otsego Local SD (PK-12)
    2003-04 Enrollment: 1,689 . . . . (419) 823-4381

Housing: Homeownership rate: 80.4% (2005); Median home value: $100,971 (2005); Median rent: $382 per month (2000); Median age of housing: 39 years (2000).
Transportation: Commute to work: 91.9% car, 0.0% public transportation, 6.1% walk, 1.2% work from home (2000); Travel time to work: 22.1% less than 15 minutes, 34.8% 15 to 30 minutes, 26.8% 30 to 45 minutes, 11.1% 45 to 60 minutes, 5.1% 60 minutes or more (2000)

Additional Information Contacts
Grand Rapids Chamber of Commerce . . . . (419) 832-1106
    http://www.grandrapidsohio.com
Village of Grand Rapids. . . . . (419) 832-5305
    http://www.grandrapidsohio.com

HASKINS
(village). Covers a land area of 1.527 square miles and a water area of 0 square miles. Located at 41.46° N. Lat.; 83.70° W. Long. Elevation is 660 feet.
Population: 549 (1990); 638 (2000); 721 (2005); 798 (2010 projected); Race: 97.4% White, 0.0% Black, 1.0% Asian, 3.1% Hispanic of any race (2005); Density: 472.0 persons per square mile (2005); Average household size: 2.59 (2005); Median age: 35.0 (2005); Males per 100 females: 102.5 (2005); Marriage status: 25.1% never married, 61.0% now married, 7.0% widowed, 7.0% divorced (2000); Foreign born: 0.3% (2000); Ancestry (includes multiple ancestries): 40.9% German, 12.8% English, 10.3% Irish, 8.8% United States or American, 7.9% French (except Basque) (2000).
Economy: In agricultural area. Employment by occupation: 13.3% management, 22.1% professional, 13.9% services, 15.9% sales, 0.0% farming, 13.6% construction, 21.2% production (2000).
Income: Per capita income: $22,933 (2005); Median household income: $51,415 (2005); Average household income: $59,478 (2005); Percent of households with income of $100,000 or more: 13.7% (2005); Poverty rate: 4.8% (2000).
Education: Percent of population age 25 and over with: High school diploma (including GED) or higher: 93.8% (2005); Bachelor's degree or higher: 20.3% (2005); Master's degree or higher: 5.3% (2005).

School District(s)
Otsego Local SD (PK-12)
    2003-04 Enrollment: 1,689 . . . . (419) 823-4381

Housing: Homeownership rate: 82.0% (2005); Median home value: $120,482 (2005); Median rent: $391 per month (2000); Median age of housing: 60+ years (2000).
Transportation: Commute to work: 95.8% car, 0.0% public transportation, 2.7% walk, 1.2% work from home (2000); Travel time to work: 30.2% less than 15 minutes, 50.8% 15 to 30 minutes, 13.6% 30 to 45 minutes, 3.3% 45 to 60 minutes, 2.1% 60 minutes or more (2000)

HOYTVILLE
(village). Covers a land area of 0.744 square miles and a water area of 0.012 square miles. Located at 41.19° N. Lat.; 83.78° W. Long. Elevation is 714 feet.
Population: 301 (1990); 296 (2000); 336 (2005); 372 (2010 projected); Race: 82.7% White, 0.0% Black, 2.4% Asian, 14.6% Hispanic of any race (2005); Density: 451.7 persons per square mile (2005); Average household size: 3.26 (2005); Median age: 28.5 (2005); Males per 100 females: 92.0 (2005); Marriage status: 27.5% never married, 49.4% now married, 8.6% widowed, 14.6% divorced (2000); Foreign born: 0.0% (2000); Ancestry (includes multiple ancestries): 46.7% German, 22.6% Other groups, 10.3% Irish, 9.1% United States or American, 8.5% English (2000).
Economy: Single-family building permits issued: 0 (2005); Multi-family building permits issued: 0 (2005); Employment by occupation: 4.3% management, 2.5% professional, 9.3% services, 13.0% sales, 6.2% farming, 9.9% construction, 54.9% production (2000).
Income: Per capita income: $14,457 (2005); Median household income: $45,208 (2005); Average household income: $47,160 (2005); Percent of households with income of $100,000 or more: 2.9% (2005); Poverty rate: 10.7% (2000).
Education: Percent of population age 25 and over with: High school diploma (including GED) or higher: 72.9% (2005); Bachelor's degree or higher: 1.1% (2005); Master's degree or higher: 1.1% (2005).

School District(s)
Mccomb Local SD (PK-12)
    2003-04 Enrollment: 862 . . . . (419) 293-3979

Housing: Homeownership rate: 85.4% (2005); Median home value: $49,474 (2005); Median rent: $311 per month (2000); Median age of housing: 60+ years (2000).
Transportation: Commute to work: 94.9% car, 0.0% public transportation, 5.1% walk, 0.0% work from home (2000); Travel time to work: 21.0% less than 15 minutes, 38.2% 15 to 30 minutes, 29.9% 30 to 45 minutes, 9.6% 45 to 60 minutes, 1.3% 60 minutes or more (2000)

JERRY CITY
(village). Covers a land area of 1.007 square miles and a water area of 0 square miles. Located at 41.25° N. Lat.; 83.60° W. Long. Elevation is 695 feet.
Population: 517 (1990); 453 (2000); 522 (2005); 584 (2010 projected); Race: 99.6% White, 0.0% Black, 0.0% Asian, 2.1% Hispanic of any race (2005); Density: 518.5 persons per square mile (2005); Average household size: 2.78 (2005); Median age: 34.1 (2005); Males per 100 females: 105.5 (2005); Marriage status: 23.8% never married, 57.5% now married, 5.1% widowed, 13.6% divorced (2000); Foreign born: 0.0% (2000); Ancestry (includes multiple ancestries): 28.1% German, 19.6% United States or American, 14.9% Other groups, 8.4% English, 3.7% Irish (2000).
Economy: In agricultural area. Single-family building permits issued: 3 (2005); Multi-family building permits issued: 0 (2005); Employment by occupation: 9.9% management, 8.5% professional, 9.0% services, 15.7% sales, 1.8% farming, 16.6% construction, 38.6% production (2000).
Income: Per capita income: $18,764 (2005); Median household income: $45,769 (2005); Average household income: $52,101 (2005); Percent of households with income of $100,000 or more: 8.5% (2005); Poverty rate: 9.8% (2000).

Education: Percent of population age 25 and over with: High school diploma (including GED) or higher: 76.3% (2005); Bachelor's degree or higher: 2.7% (2005); Master's degree or higher: 0.0% (2005).
Housing: Homeownership rate: 88.3% (2005); Median home value: $79,574 (2005); Median rent: $403 per month (2000); Median age of housing: 47 years (2000).
Transportation: Commute to work: 98.6% car, 0.0% public transportation, 0.0% walk, 1.4% work from home (2000); Travel time to work: 12.9% less than 15 minutes, 53.1% 15 to 30 minutes, 26.8% 30 to 45 minutes, 4.3% 45 to 60 minutes, 2.9% 60 minutes or more (2000)

LUCKEY (village).
Covers a land area of 0.677 square miles and a water area of 0.001 square miles. Located at 41.45° N. Lat.; 83.48° W. Long. Elevation is 665 feet.
Population: 848 (1990); 998 (2000); 1,065 (2005); 1,131 (2010 projected); Race: 96.1% White, 0.1% Black, 0.0% Asian, 3.9% Hispanic of any race (2005); Density: 1,574.1 persons per square mile (2005); Average household size: 2.77 (2005); Median age: 34.4 (2005); Males per 100 females: 93.6 (2005); Marriage status: 18.3% never married, 64.9% now married, 6.8% widowed, 10.0% divorced (2000); Foreign born: 1.9% (2000); Ancestry (includes multiple ancestries): 45.8% German, 11.6% Irish, 8.5% English, 8.4% United States or American, 5.7% Polish (2000).
Economy: Limestone quarries. Employment by occupation: 9.7% management, 15.9% professional, 15.9% services, 23.9% sales, 0.4% farming, 10.1% construction, 23.9% production (2000).
Income: Per capita income: $20,117 (2005); Median household income: $51,285 (2005); Average household income: $55,649 (2005); Percent of households with income of $100,000 or more: 8.3% (2005); Poverty rate: 5.4% (2000).
Education: Percent of population age 25 and over with: High school diploma (including GED) or higher: 89.3% (2005); Bachelor's degree or higher: 12.1% (2005); Master's degree or higher: 3.8% (2005).
School District(s)
Eastwood Local SD (PK-12)
    2003-04 Enrollment: 1,978 . . . . (419) 833-6411
Housing: Homeownership rate: 85.2% (2005); Median home value: $125,568 (2005); Median rent: $393 per month (2000); Median age of housing: 56 years (2000).
Transportation: Commute to work: 94.7% car, 0.7% public transportation, 1.8% walk, 1.8% work from home (2000); Travel time to work: 20.8% less than 15 minutes, 48.8% 15 to 30 minutes, 22.1% 30 to 45 minutes, 4.7% 45 to 60 minutes, 3.6% 60 minutes or more (2000)

MILLBURY (village).
Covers a land area of 0.983 square miles and a water area of 0 square miles. Located at 41.56° N. Lat.; 83.42° W. Long. Elevation is 615 feet.
Population: 1,111 (1990); 1,161 (2000); 1,262 (2005); 1,354 (2010 projected); Race: 99.2% White, 0.0% Black, 0.2% Asian, 0.6% Hispanic of any race (2005); Density: 1,283.9 persons per square mile (2005); Average household size: 2.70 (2005); Median age: 37.9 (2005); Males per 100 females: 95.4 (2005); Marriage status: 19.2% never married, 68.5% now married, 5.1% widowed, 7.3% divorced (2000); Foreign born: 1.8% (2000); Ancestry (includes multiple ancestries): 44.8% German, 11.8% English, 9.9% Irish, 8.9% United States or American, 7.5% French (except Basque) (2000).
Economy: Employment by occupation: 8.1% management, 15.3% professional, 13.3% services, 36.9% sales, 0.3% farming, 9.6% construction, 16.5% production (2000).
Income: Per capita income: $25,359 (2005); Median household income: $62,386 (2005); Average household income: $68,528 (2005); Percent of households with income of $100,000 or more: 19.5% (2005); Poverty rate: 2.6% (2000).
Education: Percent of population age 25 and over with: High school diploma (including GED) or higher: 88.5% (2005); Bachelor's degree or higher: 13.2% (2005); Master's degree or higher: 3.2% (2005).
School District(s)
Lake Local SD (KG-12)
    2003-04 Enrollment: 1,795 . . . . (419) 836-2552
Housing: Homeownership rate: 82.9% (2005); Median home value: $146,379 (2005); Median rent: $494 per month (2000); Median age of housing: 32 years (2000).
Newspapers: The Press - Metro Edition (General - Circulation 20,102); The Press - Suburban Edition (General - Circulation 17,096)
Transportation: Commute to work: 98.1% car, 0.3% public transportation, 0.3% walk, 0.9% work from home (2000); Travel time to work: 26.2% less than 15 minutes, 51.9% 15 to 30 minutes, 17.7% 30 to 45 minutes, 1.6% 45 to 60 minutes, 2.6% 60 minutes or more (2000)

MILTON CENTER (village). Aka Milton.
Covers a land area of 0.399 square miles and a water area of 0 square miles. Located at 41.30° N. Lat.; 83.82° W. Long. Elevation is 685 feet.
Population: 200 (1990); 195 (2000); 198 (2005); 199 (2010 projected); Race: 93.4% White, 0.0% Black, 0.0% Asian, 16.7% Hispanic of any race (2005); Density: 495.9 persons per square mile (2005); Average household size: 2.87 (2005); Median age: 35.0 (2005); Males per 100 females: 96.0 (2005); Marriage status: 25.3% never married, 51.9% now married, 7.8% widowed, 14.9% divorced (2000); Foreign born: 1.0% (2000); Ancestry (includes multiple ancestries): 27.6% German, 21.2% Other groups, 10.8% United States or American, 7.9% Irish, 6.9% Italian (2000).
Economy: In agricultural area. Employment by occupation: 3.8% management, 9.0% professional, 14.1% services, 19.2% sales, 0.0% farming, 21.8% construction, 32.1% production (2000).
Income: Per capita income: $13,838 (2005); Median household income: $33,333 (2005); Average household income: $39,710 (2005); Percent of households with income of $100,000 or more: 5.8% (2005); Poverty rate: 9.7% (2000).
Education: Percent of population age 25 and over with: High school diploma (including GED) or higher: 66.9% (2005); Bachelor's degree or higher: 7.9% (2005); Master's degree or higher: 1.6% (2005).
Housing: Homeownership rate: 84.1% (2005); Median home value: $66,667 (2005); Median rent: $292 per month (2000); Median age of housing: 60+ years (2000).
Transportation: Commute to work: 100.0% car, 0.0% public transportation, 0.0% walk, 0.0% work from home (2000); Travel time to work: 24.4% less than 15 minutes, 37.2% 15 to 30 minutes, 14.1% 30 to 45 minutes, 17.9% 45 to 60 minutes, 6.4% 60 minutes or more (2000)

NORTH BALTIMORE (village).
Covers a land area of 2.223 square miles and a water area of 0.028 square miles. Located at 41.18° N. Lat.; 83.67° W. Long. Elevation is 732 feet.
History: Settled 1834.
Population: 3,169 (1990); 3,361 (2000); 3,359 (2005); 3,374 (2010 projected); Race: 96.9% White, 0.0% Black, 0.4% Asian, 3.2% Hispanic of any race (2005); Density: 1,511.3 persons per square mile (2005); Average household size: 2.59 (2005); Median age: 34.8 (2005); Males per 100 females: 92.8 (2005); Marriage status: 21.7% never married, 57.1% now married, 9.0% widowed, 12.2% divorced (2000); Foreign born: 0.6% (2000); Ancestry (includes multiple ancestries): 31.3% German, 15.8% United States or American, 11.8% Irish, 11.2% Other groups, 7.4% English (2000).
Economy: In diversified farming area: corn, wheat. Leather goods, machine shop products, rubber products. Stone quarries nearby. Employment by occupation: 7.7% management, 7.9% professional, 14.2% services, 25.4% sales, 0.0% farming, 9.6% construction, 35.2% production (2000).
Income: Per capita income: $18,908 (2005); Median household income: $42,362 (2005); Average household income: $48,059 (2005); Percent of households with income of $100,000 or more: 6.5% (2005); Poverty rate: 8.8% (2000).
Education: Percent of population age 25 and over with: High school diploma (including GED) or higher: 81.0% (2005); Bachelor's degree or higher: 10.6% (2005); Master's degree or higher: 3.6% (2005).
School District(s)
North Baltimore Local SD (PK-12)
    2003-04 Enrollment: 856 . . . . (419) 257-3531
Housing: Homeownership rate: 73.9% (2005); Median home value: $86,630 (2005); Median rent: $299 per month (2000); Median age of housing: 50 years (2000).
Safety: Violent crime rate: 12.0 per 10,000 population; Property crime rate: 176.8 per 10,000 population (2004).
Newspapers: North Baltimore News (General - Circulation 1,200)
Transportation: Commute to work: 95.8% car, 0.0% public transportation, 2.3% walk, 1.9% work from home (2000); Travel time to work: 42.5% less than 15 minutes, 41.7% 15 to 30 minutes, 12.6% 30 to 45 minutes, 2.3% 45 to 60 minutes, 0.9% 60 minutes or more (2000)

NORTHWOOD (city).
Covers a land area of 8.403 square miles and a water area of 0.013 square miles. Located at 41.61° N. Lat.; 83.49° W. Long. Elevation is 613 feet.

Population: 5,506 (1990); 5,471 (2000); 5,440 (2005); 5,425 (2010 projected); Race: 94.6% White, 0.6% Black, 1.2% Asian, 4.6% Hispanic of any race (2005); Density: 647.4 persons per square mile (2005); Average household size: 2.64 (2005); Median age: 36.8 (2005); Males per 100 females: 96.4 (2005); Marriage status: 26.5% never married, 56.5% now married, 5.7% widowed, 11.2% divorced (2000); Foreign born: 2.6% (2000); Ancestry (includes multiple ancestries): 34.0% German, 11.5% Irish, 11.4% Other groups, 9.7% English, 8.7% United States or American (2000).
Economy: Employment by occupation: 14.6% management, 14.2% professional, 13.9% services, 26.9% sales, 0.0% farming, 7.9% construction, 22.5% production (2000).
Income: Per capita income: $23,748 (2005); Median household income: $56,197 (2005); Average household income: $62,462 (2005); Percent of households with income of $100,000 or more: 15.3% (2005); Poverty rate: 10.2% (2000).
Education: Percent of population age 25 and over with: High school diploma (including GED) or higher: 84.3% (2005); Bachelor's degree or higher: 12.9% (2005); Master's degree or higher: 2.4% (2005).

School District(s)
Northwood Local SD (PK-12)
  2003-04 Enrollment: 1,026 . . . . (419) 691-3888

Two-year College(s)
Toledo Academy of Beauty Culture-East (Private, For-profit)
  Fall 2004 Enrollment: 71 . . . . (419) 693-7257

Housing: Homeownership rate: 87.4% (2005); Median home value: $116,170 (2005); Median rent: $355 per month (2000); Median age of housing: 29 years (2000).
Safety: Violent crime rate: 30.9 per 10,000 population; Property crime rate: 788.0 per 10,000 population (2004).
Transportation: Commute to work: 98.2% car, 0.0% public transportation, 1.1% walk, 0.4% work from home (2000); Travel time to work: 33.9% less than 15 minutes, 47.7% 15 to 30 minutes, 11.3% 30 to 45 minutes, 1.9% 45 to 60 minutes, 5.3% 60 minutes or more (2000)
Additional Information Contacts
City of Northwood . . . . (419) 693-9320
  http://www.ci.northwood.oh.us

PEMBERVILLE (village).
Covers a land area of 1.107 square miles and a water area of 0 square miles. Located at 41.41° N. Lat.; 83.45° W. Long. Elevation is 650 feet.
History: Settled 1834, incorporated 1876.
Population: 1,304 (1990); 1,365 (2000); 1,433 (2005); 1,496 (2010 projected); Race: 95.3% White, 0.0% Black, 0.0% Asian, 5.2% Hispanic of any race (2005); Density: 1,294.1 persons per square mile (2005); Average household size: 2.47 (2005); Median age: 38.7 (2005); Males per 100 females: 90.3 (2005); Marriage status: 22.7% never married, 62.8% now married, 6.4% widowed, 8.2% divorced (2000); Foreign born: 1.6% (2000); Ancestry (includes multiple ancestries): 51.9% German, 9.2% English, 7.6% Irish, 7.1% Other groups, 3.0% United States or American (2000).
Economy: Grain, food products. Employment by occupation: 10.8% management, 20.7% professional, 12.9% services, 27.1% sales, 0.6% farming, 9.3% construction, 18.7% production (2000).
Income: Per capita income: $25,010 (2005); Median household income: $57,556 (2005); Average household income: $61,687 (2005); Percent of households with income of $100,000 or more: 12.9% (2005); Poverty rate: 3.4% (2000).
Education: Percent of population age 25 and over with: High school diploma (including GED) or higher: 89.4% (2005); Bachelor's degree or higher: 22.4% (2005); Master's degree or higher: 9.1% (2005).

School District(s)
Eastwood Local SD (PK-12)
  2003-04 Enrollment: 1,978 . . . . (419) 833-6411

Housing: Homeownership rate: 76.8% (2005); Median home value: $129,437 (2005); Median rent: $411 per month (2000); Median age of housing: 60+ years (2000).
Transportation: Commute to work: 90.2% car, 0.3% public transportation, 5.4% walk, 3.1% work from home (2000); Travel time to work: 32.9% less than 15 minutes, 41.0% 15 to 30 minutes, 18.6% 30 to 45 minutes, 4.2% 45 to 60 minutes, 3.3% 60 minutes or more (2000)
Additional Information Contacts
Village of Pemberville . . . . (419) 287-3832
  http://pembervillelibrary.org/pemberville

PERRYSBURG (city).
Covers a land area of 8.922 square miles and a water area of 0.212 square miles. Located at 41.55° N. Lat.; 83.63° W. Long. Elevation is 632 feet.
History: Perrysburg was settled in 1816 and named for Oliver Hazard Perry. Its site on the Maumee River made it a shipping and shipbuilding center. From 1822 to 1866, Perrysburg served as the seat of Wood County.
Population: 14,412 (1990); 16,945 (2000); 16,629 (2005); 16,376 (2010 projected); Race: 94.3% White, 1.1% Black, 2.6% Asian, 2.1% Hispanic of any race (2005); Density: 1,863.8 persons per square mile (2005); Average household size: 2.57 (2005); Median age: 38.5 (2005); Males per 100 females: 94.1 (2005); Marriage status: 19.3% never married, 65.7% now married, 6.9% widowed, 8.2% divorced (2000); Foreign born: 3.8% (2000); Ancestry (includes multiple ancestries): 39.6% German, 14.1% English, 13.5% Irish, 8.0% Polish, 6.5% Other groups (2000).
Economy: Employment by occupation: 20.4% management, 31.3% professional, 9.1% services, 25.2% sales, 0.0% farming, 4.2% construction, 9.8% production (2000).
Income: Per capita income: $33,747 (2005); Median household income: $67,607 (2005); Average household income: $86,384 (2005); Percent of households with income of $100,000 or more: 28.8% (2005); Poverty rate: 2.8% (2000).
Education: Percent of population age 25 and over with: High school diploma (including GED) or higher: 94.8% (2005); Bachelor's degree or higher: 47.4% (2005); Master's degree or higher: 19.0% (2005).

School District(s)
Eastwood Local SD (PK-12)
  2003-04 Enrollment: 1,978 . . . . (419) 833-6411
Penta Career Center (07-12)
  2003-04 Enrollment: n/a . . . . (419) 666-1120
Perrysburg Digital Academy (KG-12)
  2003-04 Enrollment: 66 . . . . (419) 874-9131
Perrysburg Exempted Village (PK-12)
  2003-04 Enrollment: 4,348 . . . . (419) 874-9131
Rossford Ex Vill SD (PK-12)
  2003-04 Enrollment: 2,020 . . . . (419) 666-2010

Two-year College(s)
Healing Arts Institute (Private, For-profit)
  Fall 2004 Enrollment: 42 . . . . (419) 874-4496
Owens Community College (Public)
  Fall 2004 Enrollment: 19,671 . . . . (567) 661-7000
  2005-06 Tuition: In-state $2,824; Out-of-state $5,248
Penta County Joint Vocational School (Public)
  Fall 2004 Enrollment: 262 . . . . (418) 661-6555

Housing: Homeownership rate: 75.0% (2005); Median home value: $181,955 (2005); Median rent: $516 per month (2000); Median age of housing: 24 years (2000).
Safety: Violent crime rate: 11.3 per 10,000 population; Property crime rate: 241.8 per 10,000 population (2004).
Newspapers: Perrysburg Messenger-Journal (General - Circulation 13,500)
Transportation: Commute to work: 94.8% car, 0.5% public transportation, 1.1% walk, 3.0% work from home (2000); Travel time to work: 32.7% less than 15 minutes, 52.6% 15 to 30 minutes, 9.1% 30 to 45 minutes, 2.0% 45 to 60 minutes, 3.6% 60 minutes or more (2000)
Additional Information Contacts
City of Perrysburg . . . . (419) 872-8010
  http://www.ci.perrysburg.oh.us
Perrysburg Area Chamber . . . . (419) 874-9147
  http://www.perrysburgchamber.com

PORTAGE (village).
Covers a land area of 1.497 square miles and a water area of 0 square miles. Located at 41.32° N. Lat.; 83.65° W. Long. Elevation is 685 feet.
History: Portage began as a trading post in 1824 and grew during the oil and gas boom of the 1880's and 1890's.
Population: 501 (1990); 428 (2000); 484 (2005); 537 (2010 projected); Race: 91.1% White, 1.2% Black, 0.0% Asian, 10.5% Hispanic of any race (2005); Density: 323.4 persons per square mile (2005); Average household size: 2.73 (2005); Median age: 38.2 (2005); Males per 100 females: 105.1 (2005); Marriage status: 29.6% never married, 53.8% now married, 7.4% widowed, 9.2% divorced (2000); Foreign born: 2.5% (2000); Ancestry (includes multiple ancestries): 36.0% German, 11.3% Other groups, 9.7% English, 9.7% Irish, 5.5% Scottish (2000).

Economy: Single-family building permits issued: 2 (2005); Multi-family building permits issued: 0 (2005); Employment by occupation: 8.7% management, 13.5% professional, 11.3% services, 21.7% sales, 0.0% farming, 7.4% construction, 37.4% production (2000).
Income: Per capita income: $17,789 (2005); Median household income: $41,750 (2005); Average household income: $47,472 (2005); Percent of households with income of $100,000 or more: 6.2% (2005); Poverty rate: 10.4% (2000).
Education: Percent of population age 25 and over with: High school diploma (including GED) or higher: 77.4% (2005); Bachelor's degree or higher: 15.8% (2005); Master's degree or higher: 5.4% (2005).

School District(s)

Elmwood Local SD (PK-12)
    2003-04 Enrollment: 1,312 . . . . (419) 655-2583

Housing: Homeownership rate: 70.6% (2005); Median home value: $99,565 (2005); Median rent: $431 per month (2000); Median age of housing: 60+ years (2000).
Transportation: Commute to work: 85.2% car, 12.2% public transportation, 0.0% walk, 1.7% work from home (2000); Travel time to work: 41.6% less than 15 minutes, 34.5% 15 to 30 minutes, 16.4% 30 to 45 minutes, 3.5% 45 to 60 minutes, 4.0% 60 minutes or more (2000)

RISINGSUN (village). Aka Rising Sun. Covers a land area of 0.577 square miles and a water area of 0 square miles. Located at 41.26° N. Lat.; 83.42° W. Long. Elevation is 720 feet.

Population: 659 (1990); 620 (2000); 603 (2005); 602 (2010 projected); Race: 97.3% White, 0.0% Black, 0.2% Asian, 2.3% Hispanic of any race (2005); Density: 1,044.3 persons per square mile (2005); Average household size: 2.61 (2005); Median age: 34.7 (2005); Males per 100 females: 85.0 (2005); Marriage status: 28.4% never married, 57.6% now married, 5.6% widowed, 8.4% divorced (2000); Foreign born: 0.8% (2000); Ancestry (includes multiple ancestries): 33.9% German, 20.1% United States or American, 9.0% Other groups, 6.6% Irish, 5.8% English (2000).
Economy: In agricultural area. Employment by occupation: 5.3% management, 6.7% professional, 16.0% services, 25.7% sales, 0.0% farming, 8.0% construction, 38.3% production (2000).
Income: Per capita income: $18,955 (2005); Median household income: $41,167 (2005); Average household income: $49,481 (2005); Percent of households with income of $100,000 or more: 9.5% (2005); Poverty rate: 7.2% (2000).
Education: Percent of population age 25 and over with: High school diploma (including GED) or higher: 83.5% (2005); Bachelor's degree or higher: 4.0% (2005); Master's degree or higher: 1.9% (2005).

School District(s)

Lakota Local SD (PK-12)
    2003-04 Enrollment: 1,164 . . . . (419) 457-2911

Housing: Homeownership rate: 73.2% (2005); Median home value: $77,955 (2005); Median rent: $362 per month (2000); Median age of housing: 60+ years (2000).
Transportation: Commute to work: 96.6% car, 0.0% public transportation, 1.0% walk, 1.0% work from home (2000); Travel time to work: 22.9% less than 15 minutes, 41.7% 15 to 30 minutes, 28.5% 30 to 45 minutes, 3.1% 45 to 60 minutes, 3.8% 60 minutes or more (2000)

ROSSFORD (city). Covers a land area of 4.300 square miles and a water area of 0.285 square miles. Located at 41.59° N. Lat.; 83.56° W. Long. Elevation is 620 feet.

History: Rossford began in 1896 when Edward Ford established a glass company that later merged with the Libbey-Owens corporation.
Population: 5,996 (1990); 6,406 (2000); 6,121 (2005); 5,912 (2010 projected); Race: 96.4% White, 1.0% Black, 0.9% Asian, 1.7% Hispanic of any race (2005); Density: 1,423.4 persons per square mile (2005); Average household size: 2.42 (2005); Median age: 37.8 (2005); Males per 100 females: 93.5 (2005); Marriage status: 24.7% never married, 57.7% now married, 8.8% widowed, 8.9% divorced (2000); Foreign born: 3.4% (2000); Ancestry (includes multiple ancestries): 35.3% German, 19.6% Polish, 11.8% Irish, 8.6% English, 6.6% Slovak (2000).
Economy: Employment by occupation: 11.5% management, 20.3% professional, 15.7% services, 24.4% sales, 0.0% farming, 9.7% construction, 18.3% production (2000).
Income: Per capita income: $25,624 (2005); Median household income: $47,432 (2005); Average household income: $62,091 (2005); Percent of households with income of $100,000 or more: 12.9% (2005); Poverty rate: 3.7% (2000).
Education: Percent of population age 25 and over with: High school diploma (including GED) or higher: 89.1% (2005); Bachelor's degree or higher: 20.9% (2005); Master's degree or higher: 5.9% (2005).

School District(s)

Rossford Ex Vill SD (PK-12)
    2003-04 Enrollment: 2,020 . . . . (419) 666-2010

Housing: Homeownership rate: 71.0% (2005); Median home value: $131,692 (2005); Median rent: $383 per month (2000); Median age of housing: 41 years (2000).
Safety: Violent crime rate: 11.0 per 10,000 population; Property crime rate: 401.9 per 10,000 population (2004).
Newspapers: The Rossford Record Journal (General - Circulation 1,714)
Transportation: Commute to work: 95.8% car, 0.7% public transportation, 1.6% walk, 1.5% work from home (2000); Travel time to work: 38.0% less than 15 minutes, 50.5% 15 to 30 minutes, 4.3% 30 to 45 minutes, 2.2% 45 to 60 minutes, 5.0% 60 minutes or more (2000)
Additional Information Contacts
City of Rossford . . . . (419) 666-0210
    http://www.rossfordohio.com

RUDOLPH (unincorporated postal area, zip code 43462). Covers a land area of 24.956 square miles and a water area of 0.025 square miles. Located at 41.28° N. Lat.; 83.69° W. Long. Elevation is 690 feet.

Population: 1,247 (2000); Race: 94.8% White, 0.0% Black, 0.0% Asian, 9.7% Hispanic of any race (2000); Density: 50.0 persons per square mile (2000); Age: 25.6% under 18, 11.1% over 64 (2000); Marriage status: 26.8% never married, 51.5% now married, 6.7% widowed, 14.9% divorced (2000); Foreign born: 0.0% (2000); Ancestry (includes multiple ancestries): 29.0% German, 15.3% Other groups, 13.1% United States or American, 12.3% Irish, 6.8% French (except Basque) (2000).
Economy: Employment by occupation: 9.6% management, 8.3% professional, 17.9% services, 20.6% sales, 1.6% farming, 7.8% construction, 34.2% production (2000).
Income: Per capita income: $17,684 (2000); Median household income: $40,066 (2000); Poverty rate: 4.5% (2000).
Education: Percent of population age 25 and over with: High school diploma (including GED) or higher: 75.8% (2000); Bachelor's degree or higher: 9.6% (2000).
Housing: Homeownership rate: 82.9% (2000); Median home value: $87,100 (2000); Median rent: $387 per month (2000); Median age of housing: 31 years (2000).
Transportation: Commute to work: 99.1% car, 0.0% public transportation, 0.0% walk, 0.9% work from home (2000); Travel time to work: 16.3% less than 15 minutes, 62.2% 15 to 30 minutes, 5.9% 30 to 45 minutes, 10.6% 45 to 60 minutes, 4.9% 60 minutes or more (2000)

TONTOGANY (village). Covers a land area of 0.182 square miles and a water area of 0 square miles. Located at 41.42° N. Lat.; 83.74° W. Long. Elevation is 665 feet.

Population: 364 (1990); 364 (2000); 383 (2005); 402 (2010 projected); Race: 98.7% White, 0.0% Black, 0.0% Asian, 4.2% Hispanic of any race (2005); Density: 2,100.3 persons per square mile (2005); Average household size: 2.62 (2005); Median age: 34.3 (2005); Males per 100 females: 101.6 (2005); Marriage status: 20.7% never married, 63.2% now married, 8.1% widowed, 8.1% divorced (2000); Foreign born: 0.0% (2000); Ancestry (includes multiple ancestries): 49.5% German, 24.2% English, 10.2% Other groups, 7.5% Irish, 5.9% Polish (2000).
Economy: Employment by occupation: 11.4% management, 12.9% professional, 15.8% services, 33.7% sales, 0.0% farming, 8.9% construction, 17.3% production (2000).
Income: Per capita income: $19,569 (2005); Median household income: $46,250 (2005); Average household income: $51,336 (2005); Percent of households with income of $100,000 or more: 8.2% (2005); Poverty rate: 5.1% (2000).
Education: Percent of population age 25 and over with: High school diploma (including GED) or higher: 92.1% (2005); Bachelor's degree or higher: 14.6% (2005); Master's degree or higher: 5.4% (2005).

School District(s)

Otsego Local SD (PK-12)
    2003-04 Enrollment: 1,689 . . . . (419) 823-4381

Housing: Homeownership rate: 78.1% (2005); Median home value: $111,864 (2005); Median rent: $435 per month (2000); Median age of housing: 60+ years (2000).
Transportation: Commute to work: 95.0% car, 0.0% public transportation, 2.5% walk, 2.5% work from home (2000); Travel time to work: 34.9% less

than 15 minutes, 44.6% 15 to 30 minutes, 16.9% 30 to 45 minutes, 0.0% 45 to 60 minutes, 3.6% 60 minutes or more (2000)

WALBRIDGE (village). Covers a land area of 1.662 square miles and a water area of 0.015 square miles. Located at 41.58° N. Lat.; 83.49° W. Long. Elevation is 617 feet.
Population: 2,736 (1990); 2,546 (2000); 2,531 (2005); 2,531 (2010 projected); Race: 97.4% White, 0.6% Black, 0.2% Asian, 2.7% Hispanic of any race (2005); Density: 1,523.0 persons per square mile (2005); Average household size: 2.31 (2005); Median age: 39.4 (2005); Males per 100 females: 89.9 (2005); Marriage status: 19.5% never married, 58.4% now married, 10.0% widowed, 12.0% divorced (2000); Foreign born: 1.3% (2000); Ancestry (includes multiple ancestries): 33.1% German, 16.9% United States or American, 12.9% Irish, 11.0% English, 9.3% Other groups (2000).
Economy: Employment by occupation: 9.3% management, 13.5% professional, 11.8% services, 27.6% sales, 0.0% farming, 12.3% construction, 25.5% production (2000).
Income: Per capita income: $22,717 (2005); Median household income: $44,597 (2005); Average household income: $52,318 (2005); Percent of households with income of $100,000 or more: 11.1% (2005); Poverty rate: 4.7% (2000).
Education: Percent of population age 25 and over with: High school diploma (including GED) or higher: 84.4% (2005); Bachelor's degree or higher: 7.1% (2005); Master's degree or higher: 3.1% (2005).
School District(s)
Lake Local SD (KG-12)
    2003-04 Enrollment: 1,795 . . . . (419) 836-2552
Housing: Homeownership rate: 72.2% (2005); Median home value: $116,458 (2005); Median rent: $397 per month (2000); Median age of housing: 40 years (2000).
Safety: Violent crime rate: 12.8 per 10,000 population; Property crime rate: 172.9 per 10,000 population (2004).
Transportation: Commute to work: 98.1% car, 0.6% public transportation, 0.0% walk, 1.2% work from home (2000); Travel time to work: 25.9% less than 15 minutes, 49.3% 15 to 30 minutes, 16.0% 30 to 45 minutes, 3.6% 45 to 60 minutes, 5.2% 60 minutes or more (2000)

WAYNE (village). Covers a land area of 0.322 square miles and a water area of 0 square miles. Located at 41.30° N. Lat.; 83.47° W. Long. Elevation is 700 feet.
History: Wayne was known as strongly abolitionist in sentiment prior to the Civil War. In the winter of 1858, Wayne was a transfer point for several hundred rifles headed for John Brown's hide-out in Maryland.
Population: 803 (1990); 842 (2000); 876 (2005); 905 (2010 projected); Race: 94.6% White, 0.3% Black, 0.1% Asian, 3.9% Hispanic of any race (2005); Density: 2,719.3 persons per square mile (2005); Average household size: 2.62 (2005); Median age: 36.0 (2005); Males per 100 females: 99.5 (2005); Marriage status: 26.5% never married, 59.8% now married, 6.2% widowed, 7.4% divorced (2000); Foreign born: 1.4% (2000); Ancestry (includes multiple ancestries): 35.2% German, 13.4% Other groups, 9.3% English, 8.9% Irish, 7.8% United States or American (2000).
Economy: Single-family building permits issued: 2 (2005); Multi-family building permits issued: 0 (2005); Employment by occupation: 5.9% management, 12.3% professional, 14.6% services, 19.5% sales, 0.0% farming, 13.6% construction, 34.0% production (2000).
Income: Per capita income: $21,233 (2005); Median household income: $51,667 (2005); Average household income: $55,689 (2005); Percent of households with income of $100,000 or more: 9.3% (2005); Poverty rate: 7.6% (2000).
Education: Percent of population age 25 and over with: High school diploma (including GED) or higher: 85.1% (2005); Bachelor's degree or higher: 11.3% (2005); Master's degree or higher: 2.8% (2005).
School District(s)
Elmwood Local SD (PK-12)
    2003-04 Enrollment: 1,312 . . . . (419) 655-2583
Housing: Homeownership rate: 78.7% (2005); Median home value: $89,516 (2005); Median rent: $410 per month (2000); Median age of housing: 60+ years (2000).
Transportation: Commute to work: 96.8% car, 0.0% public transportation, 1.3% walk, 1.9% work from home (2000); Travel time to work: 17.6% less than 15 minutes, 53.0% 15 to 30 minutes, 20.0% 30 to 45 minutes, 5.7% 45 to 60 minutes, 3.7% 60 minutes or more (2000)

WEST MILLGROVE (village). Covers a land area of 0.260 square miles and a water area of 0 square miles. Located at 41.24° N. Lat.; 83.49° W. Long. Elevation is 710 feet.
Population: 171 (1990); 78 (2000); 83 (2005); 87 (2010 projected); Race: 100.0% White, 0.0% Black, 0.0% Asian, 0.0% Hispanic of any race (2005); Density: 319.7 persons per square mile (2005); Average household size: 3.07 (2005); Median age: 31.8 (2005); Males per 100 females: 93.0 (2005); Marriage status: 31.1% never married, 55.4% now married, 5.4% widowed, 8.1% divorced (2000); Foreign born: 0.0% (2000); Ancestry (includes multiple ancestries): 38.8% Irish, 28.2% German, 21.4% English, 17.5% United States or American, 6.8% Other groups (2000).
Economy: Limestone quarry. Single-family building permits issued: 0 (2005); Multi-family building permits issued: 0 (2005); Employment by occupation: 0.0% management, 8.6% professional, 2.9% services, 25.7% sales, 0.0% farming, 37.1% construction, 25.7% production (2000).
Income: Per capita income: $15,512 (2005); Median household income: $55,147 (2005); Average household income: $47,685 (2005); Percent of households with income of $100,000 or more: 0.0% (2005); Poverty rate: 10.1% (2000).
Education: Percent of population age 25 and over with: High school diploma (including GED) or higher: 87.8% (2005); Bachelor's degree or higher: 6.1% (2005); Master's degree or higher: 6.1% (2005).
Housing: Homeownership rate: 74.1% (2005); Median home value: $57,500 (2005); Median rent: $367 per month (2000); Median age of housing: 60+ years (2000).
Transportation: Commute to work: 100.0% car, 0.0% public transportation, 0.0% walk, 0.0% work from home (2000); Travel time to work: 11.4% less than 15 minutes, 34.3% 15 to 30 minutes, 22.9% 30 to 45 minutes, 31.4% 45 to 60 minutes, 0.0% 60 minutes or more (2000)

WESTON (village). Covers a land area of 1.124 square miles and a water area of 0.003 square miles. Located at 41.34° N. Lat.; 83.79° W. Long. Elevation is 684 feet.
Population: 1,754 (1990); 1,659 (2000); 1,819 (2005); 1,973 (2010 projected); Race: 93.7% White, 0.1% Black, 0.0% Asian, 9.1% Hispanic of any race (2005); Density: 1,618.6 persons per square mile (2005); Average household size: 2.54 (2005); Median age: 33.0 (2005); Males per 100 females: 96.9 (2005); Marriage status: 26.5% never married, 55.9% now married, 4.8% widowed, 12.8% divorced (2000); Foreign born: 0.6% (2000); Ancestry (includes multiple ancestries): 30.1% German, 18.1% Other groups, 17.9% United States or American, 6.8% English, 6.7% Irish (2000).
Economy: Corn, wheat; hogs; food processing. Employment by occupation: 7.3% management, 11.5% professional, 15.7% services, 16.9% sales, 0.0% farming, 11.5% construction, 37.2% production (2000).
Income: Per capita income: $19,707 (2005); Median household income: $42,883 (2005); Average household income: $50,066 (2005); Percent of households with income of $100,000 or more: 8.1% (2005); Poverty rate: 9.9% (2000).
Education: Percent of population age 25 and over with: High school diploma (including GED) or higher: 82.5% (2005); Bachelor's degree or higher: 7.0% (2005); Master's degree or higher: 2.4% (2005).
School District(s)
Otsego Local SD (PK-12)
    2003-04 Enrollment: 1,689 . . . . (419) 823-4381
Housing: Homeownership rate: 75.7% (2005); Median home value: $73,086 (2005); Median rent: $337 per month (2000); Median age of housing: 39 years (2000).
Transportation: Commute to work: 96.6% car, 0.0% public transportation, 1.4% walk, 1.3% work from home (2000); Travel time to work: 16.1% less than 15 minutes, 52.2% 15 to 30 minutes, 17.4% 30 to 45 minutes, 9.8% 45 to 60 minutes, 4.4% 60 minutes or more (2000)

Wyandot County

Located in north central Ohio; drained by the Sandusky River. Covers a land area of 405.61 square miles, a water area of 2.01 square miles, and is located in the Eastern Time Zone. The county government was organized in 1845. County seat is Upper Sandusky.

Weather Station: Upper Sandusky   Elevation: 853 feet

	Jan	Feb	Mar	Apr	May	Jun	Jul	Aug	Sep	Oct	Nov	Dec
High	32	37	48	60	72	81	84	83	76	64	50	38
Low	17	20	29	38	49	58	62	60	53	42	33	24
Precip	2.1	1.8	2.6	3.5	4.0	3.7	3.2	3.2	3.0	2.2	3.1	2.6
Snow	8.3	5.8	3.6	1.2	tr	0.0	0.0	0.0	0.0	tr	1.4	6.3

High and Low temperatures in degrees Fahrenheit; Precipitation and Snow in inches

Population: 22,254 (1990); 22,908 (2000); 22,865 (2005); 22,812 (2010 projected); Race: 97.8% White, 0.2% Black, 0.6% Asian, 1.5% Hispanic of any race (2005); Density: 56.4 persons per square mile (2005); Average household size: 2.54 (2005); Median age: 38.8 (2005); Males per 100 females: 95.6 (2005).
Religion: Five largest groups: 20.5% Catholic Church, 12.5% The United Methodist Church, 11.5% Evangelical Lutheran Church in America, 4.8% United Church of Christ, 1.6% Church of the Nazarene (2000).
Economy: Unemployment rate: 5.8% (2005); Total civilian labor force: 13,068 (2005); Leading industries: 48.4% manufacturing; 12.9% all other plastics product mfg; 9.0% health care and social assistance (2004); Farms: 607 totaling 201,146 acres (2002); Companies that employ 500 or more persons: 3 (2004); Companies that employ 100 to 499 persons: 14 (2004); Companies that employ less than 100 persons: 567 (2004); Black-owned businesses: n/a (2002); Hispanic-owned businesses: n/a (2002); Women-owned businesses: 565 (2002); Retail sales per capita: $7,496 (2002). Single-family building permits issued: 55 (2005); Multi-family building permits issued: 8 (2005).
Income: Per capita income: $19,979 (2005); Median household income: $43,559 (2005); Average household income: $50,312 (2005); Percent of households with income of $100,000 or more: 6.7% (2005); Poverty rate: 6.3% (2003); Bankruptcy rate: 7.89% (2003).
Education: Percent of population age 25 and over with: High school diploma (including GED) or higher: 82.2% (2005); Bachelor's degree or higher: 9.7% (2005); Master's degree or higher: 2.8% (2005).
Housing: Homeownership rate: 74.9% (2005); Median home value: $99,265 (2005); Median rent: $313 per month (2000); Median age of housing: 48 years (2000).
Health: Birth rate: 123.6 per 10,000 population (2004); Death rate: 110.4 per 10,000 population (2004); Age-adjusted cancer mortality rate: 183.2 deaths per 100,000 population (2002); Air Quality Index: 97.9% good, 2.1% moderate, 0.0% unhealthy for sensitive individuals, 0.0% unhealthy (percent of days in 2005); Number of physicians: 7.0 per 10,000 population (2004); Hospital beds: 13.6 per 10,000 population (2003); Hospital admissions: 472.4 per 10,000 population (2003).
Elections: 2004 Presidential election results: 65.7% Bush, 33.6% Kerry, 0.0% Nader, 0.5% Badnarik
Additional Information Contacts
Wyandot County Government . . . . (419) 294-3836
   http://www.co.wyandot.oh.us/
Carey Chamber of Commerce . . . . (419) 396-7856
   http://www.wyandotonline.com/careychamber
Upper Sandusky Chamber of Commerce . . . . (419) 294-3349
   http://www.uppersanduskychamber.com

Wyandot County Communities

CAREY (village). Covers a land area of 1.973 square miles and a water area of 0.007 square miles. Located at 40.95° N. Lat.; 83.38° W. Long. Elevation is 825 feet.
History: Carey was platted in 1843, and grew as a trading and shipping center for onions and celery. The Shrine of Our Lady of Consolation was established here in 1875 by Father Joseph P. Gloden.
Population: 3,756 (1990); 3,901 (2000); 3,860 (2005); 3,809 (2010 projected); Race: 96.2% White, 0.2% Black, 2.1% Asian, 1.2% Hispanic of any race (2005); Density: 1,956.8 persons per square mile (2005); Average household size: 2.48 (2005); Median age: 35.8 (2005); Males per 100 females: 94.6 (2005); Marriage status: 27.6% never married, 53.4% now married, 9.2% widowed, 9.9% divorced (2000); Foreign born: 1.4% (2000); Ancestry (includes multiple ancestries): 32.3% German, 10.7% United States or American, 10.6% Other groups, 10.0% Irish, 4.6% Italian (2000).
Economy: Single-family building permits issued: 10 (2005); Multi-family building permits issued: 0 (2005); Employment by occupation: 6.1% management, 12.1% professional, 14.0% services, 18.1% sales, 0.8% farming, 14.2% construction, 34.8% production (2000).
Income: Per capita income: $17,695 (2005); Median household income: $37,258 (2005); Average household income: $43,634 (2005); Percent of households with income of $100,000 or more: 4.6% (2005); Poverty rate: 8.6% (2000).
Education: Percent of population age 25 and over with: High school diploma (including GED) or higher: 75.4% (2005); Bachelor's degree or higher: 9.1% (2005); Master's degree or higher: 1.6% (2005).

School District(s)
Carey Digital Academy
   2003-04 Enrollment: n/a . . . . (419) 396-7922
Carey Ex Vill SD (PK-12)
   2003-04 Enrollment: 892 . . . . (419) 396-7922
Housing: Homeownership rate: 69.9% (2005); Median home value: $94,706 (2005); Median rent: $297 per month (2000); Median age of housing: 49 years (2000).
Newspapers: Mohawk Leader (General - Circulation 800); The Progressor Times (General - Circulation 4,000)
Transportation: Commute to work: 93.3% car, 0.6% public transportation, 2.1% walk, 1.6% work from home (2000); Travel time to work: 40.3% less than 15 minutes, 43.3% 15 to 30 minutes, 7.6% 30 to 45 minutes, 2.8% 45 to 60 minutes, 6.0% 60 minutes or more (2000)
Additional Information Contacts
Carey Chamber of Commerce . . . . (419) 396-7856
   http://www.wyandotonline.com/careychamber

HARPSTER (village). Covers a land area of 1.947 square miles and a water area of 0 square miles. Located at 40.73° N. Lat.; 83.25° W. Long. Elevation is 905 feet.
Population: 233 (1990); 203 (2000); 197 (2005); 194 (2010 projected); Race: 98.0% White, 2.0% Black, 0.0% Asian, 0.0% Hispanic of any race (2005); Density: 101.2 persons per square mile (2005); Average household size: 2.35 (2005); Median age: 46.4 (2005); Males per 100 females: 101.0 (2005); Marriage status: 14.1% never married, 64.7% now married, 7.1% widowed, 14.1% divorced (2000); Foreign born: 0.0% (2000); Ancestry (includes multiple ancestries): 24.6% German, 18.8% United States or American, 12.9% English, 6.3% Other groups, 4.9% Irish (2000).
Economy: Employment by occupation: 15.6% management, 4.6% professional, 14.7% services, 28.4% sales, 0.0% farming, 9.2% construction, 27.5% production (2000).
Income: Per capita income: $20,647 (2005); Median household income: $41,964 (2005); Average household income: $48,423 (2005); Percent of households with income of $100,000 or more: 7.1% (2005); Poverty rate: 2.2% (2000).
Education: Percent of population age 25 and over with: High school diploma (including GED) or higher: 80.0% (2005); Bachelor's degree or higher: 3.6% (2005); Master's degree or higher: 0.0% (2005).
Housing: Homeownership rate: 86.9% (2005); Median home value: $70,833 (2005); Median rent: $455 per month (2000); Median age of housing: 60+ years (2000).
Transportation: Commute to work: 93.6% car, 0.0% public transportation, 0.0% walk, 2.8% work from home (2000); Travel time to work: 41.5% less than 15 minutes, 51.9% 15 to 30 minutes, 4.7% 30 to 45 minutes, 1.9% 45 to 60 minutes, 0.0% 60 minutes or more (2000)

KIRBY (village). Covers a land area of 0.107 square miles and a water area of 0 square miles. Located at 40.81° N. Lat.; 83.41° W. Long. Elevation is 875 feet.
Population: 155 (1990); 132 (2000); 140 (2005); 147 (2010 projected); Race: 100.0% White, 0.0% Black, 0.0% Asian, 0.0% Hispanic of any race (2005); Density: 1,307.1 persons per square mile (2005); Average household size: 2.55 (2005); Median age: 36.9 (2005); Males per 100 females: 105.9 (2005); Marriage status: 18.7% never married, 52.7% now married, 8.8% widowed, 19.8% divorced (2000); Foreign born: 0.0% (2000); Ancestry (includes multiple ancestries): 70.3% German, 6.3% United States or American, 3.6% Irish, 2.7% English, 1.8% French (except Basque) (2000).
Economy: Employment by occupation: 3.4% management, 8.6% professional, 6.9% services, 24.1% sales, 0.0% farming, 10.3% construction, 46.6% production (2000).
Income: Per capita income: $22,179 (2005); Median household income: $41,250 (2005); Average household income: $56,455 (2005); Percent of households with income of $100,000 or more: 5.5% (2005); Poverty rate: 9.0% (2000).
Education: Percent of population age 25 and over with: High school diploma (including GED) or higher: 85.9% (2005); Bachelor's degree or higher: 12.0% (2005); Master's degree or higher: 0.0% (2005).

Housing: Homeownership rate: 74.5% (2005); Median home value: $67,857 (2005); Median rent: $363 per month (2000); Median age of housing: 60+ years (2000).
Transportation: Commute to work: 94.0% car, 0.0% public transportation, 6.0% walk, 0.0% work from home (2000); Travel time to work: 18.0% less than 15 minutes, 50.0% 15 to 30 minutes, 32.0% 30 to 45 minutes, 0.0% 45 to 60 minutes, 0.0% 60 minutes or more (2000)

MARSEILLES (village).
Covers a land area of 0.096 square miles and a water area of 0 square miles. Located at 40.70° N. Lat.; 83.39° W. Long. Elevation is 880 feet.
Population: 130 (1990); 124 (2000); 131 (2005); 136 (2010 projected); Race: 98.5% White, 1.5% Black, 0.0% Asian, 0.0% Hispanic of any race (2005); Density: 1,368.0 persons per square mile (2005); Average household size: 2.52 (2005); Median age: 38.1 (2005); Males per 100 females: 95.5 (2005); Marriage status: 20.0% never married, 51.4% now married, 7.6% widowed, 21.0% divorced (2000); Foreign born: 0.0% (2000); Ancestry (includes multiple ancestries): 30.9% Other groups, 14.0% United States or American, 14.0% German, 7.4% Pennsylvania German, 6.6% Irish (2000).
Economy: Employment by occupation: 6.0% management, 13.4% professional, 19.4% services, 11.9% sales, 0.0% farming, 6.0% construction, 43.3% production (2000).
Income: Per capita income: $19,828 (2005); Median household income: $53,125 (2005); Average household income: $49,952 (2005); Percent of households with income of $100,000 or more: 3.8% (2005); Poverty rate: 5.9% (2000).
Education: Percent of population age 25 and over with: High school diploma (including GED) or higher: 72.5% (2005); Bachelor's degree or higher: 7.7% (2005); Master's degree or higher: 4.4% (2005).
Housing: Homeownership rate: 82.7% (2005); Median home value: $59,000 (2005); Median rent: $295 per month (2000); Median age of housing: 53 years (2000).
Transportation: Commute to work: 93.8% car, 0.0% public transportation, 6.3% walk, 0.0% work from home (2000); Travel time to work: 20.3% less than 15 minutes, 43.8% 15 to 30 minutes, 28.1% 30 to 45 minutes, 4.7% 45 to 60 minutes, 3.1% 60 minutes or more (2000)

MCCUTCHENVILLE (unincorporated postal area, zip code 44844).
Covers a land area of 16.280 square miles and a water area of 0.015 square miles. Located at 40.99° N. Lat.; 83.26° W. Long. Elevation is 790 feet.
Population: 759 (2000); Race: 98.5% White, 0.0% Black, 0.0% Asian, 0.0% Hispanic of any race (2000); Density: 46.6 persons per square mile (2000); Age: 28.7% under 18, 10.5% over 64 (2000); Marriage status: 27.1% never married, 62.2% now married, 5.6% widowed, 5.1% divorced (2000); Foreign born: 0.0% (2000); Ancestry (includes multiple ancestries): 50.2% German, 11.5% English, 8.4% United States or American, 4.3% Irish, 3.2% Other groups (2000).
Economy: Employment by occupation: 7.1% management, 13.1% professional, 17.2% services, 19.5% sales, 0.0% farming, 9.9% construction, 33.1% production (2000).
Income: Per capita income: $15,501 (2000); Median household income: $48,750 (2000); Poverty rate: 6.4% (2000).
Education: Percent of population age 25 and over with: High school diploma (including GED) or higher: 79.4% (2000); Bachelor's degree or higher: 7.2% (2000).
School District(s)
Mohawk Local SD (PK-12)
    2003-04 Enrollment: 1,114 . . . . (419) 927-2414
Housing: Homeownership rate: 89.6% (2000); Median home value: $74,600 (2000); Median rent: $325 per month (2000); Median age of housing: 46 years (2000).
Transportation: Commute to work: 89.3% car, 1.9% public transportation, 1.4% walk, 7.3% work from home (2000); Travel time to work: 22.3% less than 15 minutes, 63.2% 15 to 30 minutes, 9.0% 30 to 45 minutes, 2.3% 45 to 60 minutes, 3.3% 60 minutes or more (2000)

NEVADA (village).
Covers a land area of 1.032 square miles and a water area of 0.001 square miles. Located at 40.81° N. Lat.; 83.13° W. Long. Elevation is 925 feet.
Population: 849 (1990); 814 (2000); 868 (2005); 914 (2010 projected); Race: 97.2% White, 0.8% Black, 0.3% Asian, 1.3% Hispanic of any race (2005); Density: 841.1 persons per square mile (2005); Average household size: 2.55 (2005); Median age: 36.8 (2005); Males per 100 females: 98.2 (2005); Marriage status: 22.8% never married, 58.6% now married, 7.8% widowed, 10.8% divorced (2000); Foreign born: 1.5% (2000); Ancestry (includes multiple ancestries): 31.6% German, 17.8% United States or American, 11.2% Irish, 8.3% English, 6.2% Other groups (2000).
Economy: Manufacturing of food products, building materials. Single-family building permits issued: 2 (2005); Multi-family building permits issued: 0 (2005); Employment by occupation: 5.5% management, 11.8% professional, 11.8% services, 17.3% sales, 0.8% farming, 8.3% construction, 44.6% production (2000).
Income: Per capita income: $17,140 (2005); Median household income: $41,917 (2005); Average household income: $43,629 (2005); Percent of households with income of $100,000 or more: 1.5% (2005); Poverty rate: 4.9% (2000).
Education: Percent of population age 25 and over with: High school diploma (including GED) or higher: 73.2% (2005); Bachelor's degree or higher: 4.3% (2005); Master's degree or higher: 2.5% (2005).
Housing: Homeownership rate: 75.7% (2005); Median home value: $76,364 (2005); Median rent: $345 per month (2000); Median age of housing: 60+ years (2000).
Transportation: Commute to work: 93.6% car, 1.0% public transportation, 2.6% walk, 1.0% work from home (2000); Travel time to work: 23.5% less than 15 minutes, 51.8% 15 to 30 minutes, 11.9% 30 to 45 minutes, 6.4% 45 to 60 minutes, 6.4% 60 minutes or more (2000)

SYCAMORE (village).
Covers a land area of 0.588 square miles and a water area of 0 square miles. Located at 40.95° N. Lat.; 83.17° W. Long. Elevation is 855 feet.
Population: 919 (1990); 914 (2000); 907 (2005); 910 (2010 projected); Race: 99.6% White, 0.0% Black, 0.0% Asian, 0.3% Hispanic of any race (2005); Density: 1,542.5 persons per square mile (2005); Average household size: 2.30 (2005); Median age: 38.7 (2005); Males per 100 females: 84.3 (2005); Marriage status: 20.1% never married, 58.1% now married, 12.2% widowed, 9.6% divorced (2000); Foreign born: 0.4% (2000); Ancestry (includes multiple ancestries): 39.9% German, 13.6% Irish, 12.6% Other groups, 12.5% United States or American, 8.4% English (2000).
Economy: Grain, fruit; livestock, poultry; dairy products. Single-family building permits issued: 1 (2005); Multi-family building permits issued: 0 (2005); Employment by occupation: 5.0% management, 9.7% professional, 15.6% services, 22.5% sales, 0.0% farming, 10.4% construction, 36.9% production (2000).
Income: Per capita income: $20,336 (2005); Median household income: $40,707 (2005); Average household income: $46,815 (2005); Percent of households with income of $100,000 or more: 4.8% (2005); Poverty rate: 4.9% (2000).
Education: Percent of population age 25 and over with: High school diploma (including GED) or higher: 81.9% (2005); Bachelor's degree or higher: 9.0% (2005); Master's degree or higher: 3.8% (2005).
School District(s)
Mohawk Local SD (PK-12)
    2003-04 Enrollment: 1,114 . . . . (419) 927-2414
Housing: Homeownership rate: 76.1% (2005); Median home value: $75,789 (2005); Median rent: $329 per month (2000); Median age of housing: 60+ years (2000).
Transportation: Commute to work: 92.1% car, 0.0% public transportation, 7.5% walk, 0.4% work from home (2000); Travel time to work: 29.0% less than 15 minutes, 51.4% 15 to 30 minutes, 10.9% 30 to 45 minutes, 4.2% 45 to 60 minutes, 4.4% 60 minutes or more (2000)

UPPER SANDUSKY (city).
Covers a land area of 5.242 square miles and a water area of 0.053 square miles. Located at 40.83° N. Lat.; 83.27° W. Long. Elevation is 861 feet.
History: Upper Sandusky was laid out in 1843 on land that had belonged to the Wyandot tribe. The town of Upper Sandusky was preceded by Fort Ferree, built during the War of 1812 by General William Henry Harrison.
Population: 6,197 (1990); 6,533 (2000); 6,386 (2005); 6,250 (2010 projected); Race: 96.8% White, 0.4% Black, 0.7% Asian, 3.0% Hispanic of any race (2005); Density: 1,218.2 persons per square mile (2005); Average household size: 2.35 (2005); Median age: 40.4 (2005); Males per 100 females: 87.3 (2005); Marriage status: 20.1% never married, 57.7% now married, 10.9% widowed, 11.2% divorced (2000); Foreign born: 1.0% (2000); Ancestry (includes multiple ancestries): 38.6% German, 14.6% United States or American, 9.0% Other groups, 8.8% English, 7.9% Irish (2000).

Economy: Single-family building permits issued: 18 (2005); Multi-family building permits issued: 8 (2005); Employment by occupation: 9.9% management, 12.7% professional, 17.5% services, 19.9% sales, 0.3% farming, 7.8% construction, 31.9% production (2000).
Income: Per capita income: $19,649 (2005); Median household income: $38,674 (2005); Average household income: $45,571 (2005); Percent of households with income of $100,000 or more: 4.6% (2005); Poverty rate: 4.7% (2000).
Education: Percent of population age 25 and over with: High school diploma (including GED) or higher: 82.3% (2005); Bachelor's degree or higher: 12.4% (2005); Master's degree or higher: 3.8% (2005).

School District(s)

Upper Sandusky Ex Vill SD (PK-12)
   2003-04 Enrollment: 1,807 . . . . (419) 294-2307
Housing: Homeownership rate: 61.0% (2005); Median home value: $97,135 (2005); Median rent: $309 per month (2000); Median age of housing: 42 years (2000).
Hospitals: Wyandot Memorial Hospital (45 beds)
Newspapers: The Daily Chief-Union (Circulation 4,400)
Transportation: Commute to work: 94.4% car, 0.2% public transportation, 2.5% walk, 2.1% work from home (2000); Travel time to work: 59.9% less than 15 minutes, 21.4% 15 to 30 minutes, 10.0% 30 to 45 minutes, 1.8% 45 to 60 minutes, 7.0% 60 minutes or more (2000)

Additional Information Contacts
Upper Sandusky Chamber of Commerce . . . . (419) 294-3349
   http://www.uppersanduskychamber.com

WHARTON (village). Covers a land area of 1.257 square miles and a water area of 0 square miles. Located at 40.86° N. Lat.; 83.46° W. Long. Elevation is 880 feet.
Population: 378 (1990); 409 (2000); 427 (2005); 438 (2010 projected); Race: 99.3% White, 0.0% Black, 0.2% Asian, 0.5% Hispanic of any race (2005); Density: 339.6 persons per square mile (2005); Average household size: 2.77 (2005); Median age: 34.9 (2005); Males per 100 females: 100.5 (2005); Marriage status: 19.4% never married, 65.0% now married, 2.5% widowed, 13.1% divorced (2000); Foreign born: 0.3% (2000); Ancestry (includes multiple ancestries): 33.3% German, 12.5% United States or American, 12.0% Other groups, 10.9% English, 6.9% Irish (2000).
Economy: Cannery. Employment by occupation: 6.0% management, 8.8% professional, 8.2% services, 12.1% sales, 1.1% farming, 14.8% construction, 48.9% production (2000).
Income: Per capita income: $17,477 (2005); Median household income: $44,286 (2005); Average household income: $48,458 (2005); Percent of households with income of $100,000 or more: 7.8% (2005); Poverty rate: 2.6% (2000).
Education: Percent of population age 25 and over with: High school diploma (including GED) or higher: 88.0% (2005); Bachelor's degree or higher: 1.5% (2005); Master's degree or higher: 1.5% (2005).
Housing: Homeownership rate: 78.6% (2005); Median home value: $72,581 (2005); Median rent: $295 per month (2000); Median age of housing: 60+ years (2000).
Transportation: Commute to work: 96.6% car, 0.0% public transportation, 1.1% walk, 0.6% work from home (2000); Travel time to work: 23.3% less than 15 minutes, 55.1% 15 to 30 minutes, 15.3% 30 to 45 minutes, 4.0% 45 to 60 minutes, 2.3% 60 minutes or more (2000);

A

Aberdeen village (Brown County), 25
Ada village (Hardin County), 141
Adams County, 1 - 2
Adamsville village (Muskingum County), 232
Addyston village (Hamilton County), 122
Adelphi village (Ross County), 266
Adena village (Jefferson County), 159
Akron city (Summit County), 289
Albany village (Athens County), 14
Alexandria village (Licking County), 176
Alger village (Hardin County), 141
Alledonia postal area (Belmont County), 21
Allen County, 3 - 5
Alliance city (Stark County), 282
Alvada postal area (Seneca County), 276
Alvordton village (Williams County), 331
Amanda village (Fairfield County), 90
Amberley village (Hamilton County), 122
Amelia village (Clermont County), 42
Amesville village (Athens County), 14
Amherst city (Lorain County), 185
Amlin postal area (Franklin County), 96
Amsterdam village (Jefferson County), 159
Andover village (Ashtabula County), 10
Anna village (Shelby County), 279
Ansonia village (Darke County), 78
Antioch village (Monroe County), 218
Antwerp village (Paulding County), 241
Apple Creek village (Wayne County), 327
Aquilla village (Geauga County), 111
Arcadia village (Hancock County), 138
Arcanum village (Darke County), 78
Archbold village (Fulton County), 106
Arlington Heights village (Hamilton County), 122
Arlington village (Hancock County), 138
Ashland County, 6 - 8
Ashland city (Ashland County), 6
Ashley village (Delaware County), 84
Ashtabula County, 9 - 13
Ashtabula city (Ashtabula County), 10
Ashville village (Pickaway County), 247
Athalia village (Lawrence County), 172
Athens County, 14 - 17
Athens city (Athens County), 15
Attica village (Seneca County), 276
Atwater postal area (Portage County), 252
Auglaize County, 18 - 20
Aurora city (Portage County), 252
Austinburg postal area (Ashtabula County), 10
Austintown CDP (Mahoning County), 197
Avon Lake city (Lorain County), 185
Avon city (Lorain County), 185

B

Bailey Lakes village (Ashland County), 7
Bainbridge CDP (Geauga County), 112
Bainbridge village (Ross County), 266
Bairdstown village (Wood County), 334
Ballville CDP (Sandusky County), 269
Baltic village (Tuscarawas County), 305
Baltimore village (Fairfield County), 90
Barberton city (Summit County), 290
Barnesville village (Belmont County), 21
Barnhill village (Tuscarawas County), 305
Batavia village (Clermont County), 42
Batesville village (Noble County), 236
Bay View village (Erie County), 87
Bay Village city (Cuyahoga County), 60
Beach City village (Stark County), 282
Beachwood city (Cuyahoga County), 60
Beallsville village (Monroe County), 218

Beaver village (Pike County), 250
Beavercreek city (Greene County), 114
Beaverdam village (Allen County), 3
Beckett Ridge CDP (Butler County), 28
Bedford Heights city (Cuyahoga County), 61
Bedford city (Cuyahoga County), 60
Beechwood Trails CDP (Licking County), 176
Bellaire city (Belmont County), 22
Bellbrook city (Greene County), 115
Belle Center village (Logan County), 181
Belle Valley village (Noble County), 237
Bellefontaine city (Logan County), 181
Bellevue city (Sandusky County), 269
Bellville village (Richland County), 263
Belmont County, 21 - 24
Belmont village (Belmont County), 22
Belmore village (Putnam County), 259
Beloit village (Mahoning County), 197
Belpre city (Washington County), 322
Bentleyville village (Cuyahoga County), 61
Benton Ridge village (Hancock County), 139
Berea city (Cuyahoga County), 61
Bergholz village (Jefferson County), 159
Berkey village (Lucas County), 190
Berlin Center postal area (Mahoning County), 198
Berlin Heights village (Erie County), 87
Bethel village (Clermont County), 42
Bethesda village (Belmont County), 22
Bettsville village (Seneca County), 276
Beverly village (Washington County), 323
Bexley city (Franklin County), 96
Bidwell postal area (Gallia County), 109
Big Prairie postal area (Holmes County), 153
Blacklick Estates CDP (Franklin County), 97
Blacklick postal area (Franklin County), 97
Blakeslee village (Williams County), 331
Blanchester village (Clinton County), 46
Bloomdale village (Wood County), 334
Bloomingburg village (Fayette County), 94
Bloomingdale village (Jefferson County), 159
Bloomville village (Seneca County), 276
Blue Ash city (Hamilton County), 122
Blue Creek postal area (Adams County), 1
Blue Rock postal area (Muskingum County), 233
Bluffton village (Allen County), 3
Boardman CDP (Mahoning County), 198
Bolindale CDP (Trumbull County), 297
Bolivar village (Tuscarawas County), 306
Boston Heights village (Summit County), 291
Botkins village (Shelby County), 279
Bowerston village (Harrison County), 144
Bowersville village (Greene County), 115
Bowling Green city (Wood County), 335
Bradford village (Miami County), 214
Bradner village (Wood County), 335
Brady Lake village (Portage County), 252
Bratenahl village (Cuyahoga County), 62
Brecksville city (Cuyahoga County), 62
Bremen village (Fairfield County), 90
Brewster village (Stark County), 282
Brice village (Franklin County), 97
Bridgeport village (Belmont County), 22
Bridgetown North CDP (Hamilton County), 123
Brilliant postal area (Jefferson County), 160
Brimfield CDP (Portage County), 253
Brinkhaven postal area (Knox County), 164
Bristolville postal area (Trumbull County), 298
Broadview Heights city (Cuyahoga County), 62
Brook Park city (Cuyahoga County), 62
Brookfield Center CDP (Trumbull County), 298

Brookfield postal area (Trumbull County), 298
Brooklyn Heights village (Cuyahoga County), 63
Brooklyn city (Cuyahoga County), 63
Brookpark postal area (Cuyahoga County), 63
Brookside village (Belmont County), 23
Brookville village (Montgomery County), 221
Broughton village (Paulding County), 242
Brown County, 25 - 27
Brunswick city (Medina County), 205
Bryan city (Williams County), 332
Buchtel village (Athens County), 15
Buckeye Lake village (Licking County), 176
Buckland village (Auglaize County), 18
Bucyrus city (Crawford County), 57
Burbank village (Wayne County), 327
Burghill postal area (Trumbull County), 298
Burgoon village (Sandusky County), 269
Burkettsville village (Mercer County), 211
Burlington CDP (Lawrence County), 173
Burton village (Geauga County), 112
Butler County, 28 - 32
Butler village (Richland County), 263
Butlerville village (Warren County), 317
Byesville village (Guernsey County), 118

C

Cable postal area (Champaign County), 35
Cadiz village (Harrison County), 144
Cairo village (Allen County), 4
Calcutta CDP (Columbiana County), 49
Caldwell village (Noble County), 237
Caledonia village (Marion County), 203
Cambridge city (Guernsey County), 118
Camden village (Preble County), 256
Camp Dennison postal area (Hamilton County), 123
Campbell city (Mahoning County), 198
Canal Fulton village (Stark County), 283
Canal Winchester village (Franklin County), 97
Canfield city (Mahoning County), 198
Canton city (Stark County), 283
Cardington village (Morrow County), 230
Carey village (Wyandot County), 341
Carlisle village (Warren County), 317
Carroll County, 33 - 34
Carroll village (Fairfield County), 91
Carrollton village (Carroll County), 33
Casstown village (Miami County), 214
Castalia village (Erie County), 87
Castine village (Darke County), 78
Catawba village (Clark County), 37
Cecil village (Paulding County), 242
Cedarville village (Greene County), 115
Celina city (Mercer County), 211
Centerburg village (Knox County), 164
Centerville city (Montgomery County), 221
Centerville village (Gallia County), 109
Chagrin Falls village (Cuyahoga County), 64
Champaign County, 35 - 36
Champion Heights CDP (Trumbull County), 298
Chandlersville postal area (Muskingum County), 233
Chardon village (Geauga County), 112
Chatfield village (Crawford County), 57
Chauncey village (Athens County), 15
Cherry Fork village (Adams County), 1
Cherry Grove CDP (Hamilton County), 123
Chesapeake village (Lawrence County), 173
Cheshire village (Gallia County), 109
Chesterhill village (Morgan County), 229
Chesterland CDP (Geauga County), 112

CDP = Census Designated Place

Chesterville village (Morrow County), 230
Cheviot city (Hamilton County), 123
Chickasaw village (Mercer County), 212
Chillicothe city (Ross County), 266
Chilo village (Clermont County), 43
Chippewa Lake village (Medina County), 206
Choctaw Lake CDP (Madison County), 195
Christiansburg village (Champaign County), 35
Churchill CDP (Trumbull County), 298
Cincinnati city (Hamilton County), 123
Circleville city (Pickaway County), 248
Clarington village (Monroe County), 218
Clark County, 37 - 40
Clarksburg village (Ross County), 267
Clarksville village (Clinton County), 47
Clay Center village (Ottawa County), 238
Clayton city (Montgomery County), 221
Clermont County, 41 - 45
Cleveland Heights city (Cuyahoga County), 65
Cleveland city (Cuyahoga County), 64
Cleves village (Hamilton County), 125
Clifton village (Greene County), 115
Clinton County, 46 - 47
Clinton village (Summit County), 291
Cloverdale village (Putnam County), 259
Clyde city (Sandusky County), 270
Coal Grove village (Lawrence County), 173
Coalton village (Jackson County), 157
Coldwater village (Mercer County), 212
College Corner village (Preble County), 256
Collins postal area (Huron County), 155
Columbia Station postal area (Lorain County), 186
Columbiana County, 48 - 53
Columbiana village (Columbiana County), 49
Columbus Grove village (Putnam County), 259
Columbus city (Franklin County), 98
Commercial Point village (Pickaway County), 248
Conesville village (Coshocton County), 54
Congress village (Wayne County), 327
Conneaut city (Ashtabula County), 11
Conover postal area (Miami County), 215
Continental village (Putnam County), 260
Convoy village (Van Wert County), 313
Coolville village (Athens County), 15
Corning village (Perry County), 244
Cortland city (Trumbull County), 299
Corwin village (Warren County), 318
Coshocton County, 54 - 55
Coshocton city (Coshocton County), 55
Covedale CDP (Hamilton County), 125
Covington village (Miami County), 215
Craig Beach village (Mahoning County), 199
Crawford County, 56 - 58
Creola postal area (Vinton County), 315
Crestline village (Crawford County), 57
Creston village (Wayne County), 327
Cridersville village (Auglaize County), 18
Crooksville village (Perry County), 244
Croton postal area (Licking County), 177
Crown City village (Gallia County), 109
Crystal Lakes CDP (Clark County), 38
Cumberland village (Guernsey County), 119
Curtice postal area (Lucas County), 191
Custar village (Wood County), 335
Cutler postal area (Washington County), 323
Cuyahoga County, 59 - 76
Cuyahoga Falls city (Summit County), 291
Cuyahoga Heights village (Cuyahoga County), 66
Cygnet village (Wood County), 335

D

Dalton village (Wayne County), 328
Danville village (Knox County), 165
Darbyville village (Pickaway County), 248
Darke County, 77 - 81
Day Heights CDP (Clermont County), 43
Dayton city (Montgomery County), 222
De Graff village (Logan County), 182
Deer Park city (Hamilton County), 126
Deerfield postal area (Portage County), 253
Deersville village (Harrison County), 144
Defiance County, 82
Defiance city (Defiance County), 82
Delaware County, 83 - 85
Delaware city (Delaware County), 84
Dellroy village (Carroll County), 34
Delphos city (Allen County), 4
Delta village (Fulton County), 107
Dennison village (Tuscarawas County), 306
Dent CDP (Hamilton County), 126
Deshler village (Henry County), 147
Devola CDP (Washington County), 323
Dexter City village (Noble County), 237
Diamond postal area (Portage County), 253
Dillonvale CDP (Hamilton County), 126
Dillonvale village (Jefferson County), 160
Dola postal area (Hardin County), 142
Donnelsville village (Clark County), 38
Dorset postal area (Ashtabula County), 11
Dover city (Tuscarawas County), 306
Doylestown village (Wayne County), 328
Dresden village (Muskingum County), 233
Drexel CDP (Montgomery County), 223
Dry Run CDP (Hamilton County), 126
Dublin city (Franklin County), 99
Duncan Falls postal area (Muskingum County), 233
Dundee postal area (Tuscarawas County), 306
Dunkirk village (Hardin County), 142
Dupont village (Putnam County), 260

E

East Canton village (Stark County), 284
East Cleveland city (Cuyahoga County), 66
East Liberty postal area (Logan County), 182
East Liverpool city (Columbiana County), 50
East Palestine city (Columbiana County), 50
East Rochester postal area (Columbiana County), 50
East Sparta village (Stark County), 284
Eastlake city (Lake County), 167
Eaton Estates CDP (Lorain County), 186
Eaton city (Preble County), 256
Edgerton village (Williams County), 332
Edgewood CDP (Ashtabula County), 11
Edison village (Morrow County), 231
Edon village (Williams County), 332
Eldorado village (Preble County), 257
Elgin village (Van Wert County), 313
Elida village (Allen County), 4
Elmore village (Ottawa County), 238
Elmwood Place village (Hamilton County), 126
Elyria city (Lorain County), 186
Empire village (Jefferson County), 160
Englewood city (Montgomery County), 223
Enon village (Clark County), 38
Erie County, 86 - 88
Euclid city (Cuyahoga County), 66
Evendale village (Hamilton County), 127

F

Fairborn city (Greene County), 116

Fairfax village (Hamilton County), 127
Fairfield Beach CDP (Fairfield County), 91
Fairfield County, 89 - 93
Fairfield city (Butler County), 29
Fairlawn city (Summit County), 291
Fairport Harbor village (Lake County), 167
Fairview Lanes CDP (Erie County), 88
Fairview Park city (Cuyahoga County), 66
Fairview village (Guernsey County), 119
Farmdale postal area (Trumbull County), 299
Farmersville village (Montgomery County), 223
Fayette County, 94
Fayette village (Fulton County), 107
Fayetteville village (Brown County), 26
Felicity village (Clermont County), 43
Findlay city (Hancock County), 139
Finneytown CDP (Hamilton County), 127
Five Points CDP (Warren County), 318
Fleming postal area (Washington County), 323
Fletcher village (Miami County), 215
Florida village (Henry County), 147
Flushing village (Belmont County), 23
Forest Park city (Hamilton County), 127
Forest village (Hardin County), 142
Forestville CDP (Hamilton County), 128
Fort Jennings village (Putnam County), 260
Fort Loramie village (Shelby County), 279
Fort McKinley CDP (Montgomery County), 224
Fort Recovery village (Mercer County), 212
Fort Shawnee village (Allen County), 4
Fostoria city (Seneca County), 277
Fowler postal area (Trumbull County), 299
Frankfort village (Ross County), 267
Franklin County, 95 - 105
Franklin Furnace CDP (Scioto County), 272
Franklin city (Warren County), 318
Frazeysburg village (Muskingum County), 233
Fredericksburg village (Wayne County), 328
Fredericktown village (Knox County), 165
Freeport village (Harrison County), 145
Fremont city (Sandusky County), 270
Fresno postal area (Coshocton County), 55
Fruit Hill CDP (Hamilton County), 128
Fulton County, 106 - 107
Fulton village (Morrow County), 231
Fultonham village (Muskingum County), 234

G

Gahanna city (Franklin County), 100
Galena village (Delaware County), 85
Galion city (Crawford County), 58
Gallia County, 108 - 110
Gallipolis city (Gallia County), 110
Galloway postal area (Franklin County), 100
Gambier village (Knox County), 165
Gann village (Knox County), 165
Garfield Heights city (Cuyahoga County), 67
Garrettsville village (Portage County), 253
Gates Mills village (Cuyahoga County), 67
Geauga County, 111 - 113
Geneva city (Ashtabula County), 11
Geneva-on-the-Lake village (Ashtabula County), 11
Genoa village (Ottawa County), 239
Georgetown village (Brown County), 26
Germantown village (Montgomery County), 224
Gettysburg village (Darke County), 78
Gibsonburg village (Sandusky County), 270
Gilboa village (Putnam County), 260
Girard city (Trumbull County), 299

CDP = Census Designated Place

PROFILES OF OHIO / Alphabetical Place Index 347

Glandorf village (Putnam County), 260
Glendale village (Hamilton County), 128
Glenford village (Perry County), 245
Glenmont village (Holmes County), 153
Glenmoor CDP (Columbiana County), 50
Glenwillow village (Cuyahoga County), 67
Gloria Glens Park village (Medina County), 206
Glouster village (Athens County), 16
Gnadenhutten village (Tuscarawas County), 307
Golf Manor village (Hamilton County), 128
Gomer postal area (Allen County), 5
Gordon village (Darke County), 78
Goshen postal area (Clermont County), 43
Grafton village (Lorain County), 186
Grand Rapids village (Wood County), 336
Grand River village (Lake County), 168
Grandview Heights city (Franklin County), 100
Grandview CDP (Hamilton County), 128
Granville South CDP (Licking County), 177
Granville village (Licking County), 177
Gratiot village (Licking County), 177
Gratis village (Preble County), 257
Graysville village (Monroe County), 218
Graytown postal area (Ottawa County), 239
Green Camp village (Marion County), 203
Green Meadows CDP (Clark County), 38
Green Springs village (Seneca County), 277
Green city (Summit County), 292
Greene County, 114 - 117
Greenfield city (Highland County), 149
Greenhills village (Hamilton County), 129
Greentown CDP (Stark County), 284
Greenville city (Darke County), 79
Greenwich village (Huron County), 155
Groesbeck CDP (Hamilton County), 129
Grove City city (Franklin County), 100
Groveport village (Franklin County), 101
Grover Hill village (Paulding County), 242
Guernsey County, 118 - 120
Guysville postal area (Athens County), 16

H

Hamden village (Vinton County), 315
Hamersville village (Brown County), 26
Hamilton County, 121 - 137
Hamilton city (Butler County), 29
Hamler village (Henry County), 147
Hammondsville postal area (Jefferson County), 160
Hancock County, 138 - 140
Hanging Rock village (Lawrence County), 173
Hanover village (Licking County), 178
Hanoverton village (Columbiana County), 51
Harbor Hills CDP (Licking County), 178
Harbor View village (Lucas County), 191
Hardin County, 141 - 142
Harpster village (Wyandot County), 341
Harrisburg village (Franklin County), 101
Harrison County, 143 - 145
Harrison city (Hamilton County), 129
Harrisville village (Harrison County), 145
Harrod village (Allen County), 5
Hartford village (Licking County), 178
Hartville village (Stark County), 284
Harveysburg village (Warren County), 318
Haskins village (Wood County), 336
Haviland village (Paulding County), 242
Hayesville village (Ashland County), 7
Heath city (Licking County), 178
Hebron village (Licking County), 178
Helena village (Sandusky County), 271

Hemlock village (Perry County), 245
Henry County, 146 - 148
Hicksville village (Defiance County), 83
Higginsport village (Brown County), 26
Highland County, 149 - 150
Highland Heights city (Cuyahoga County), 68
Highland Hills village (Cuyahoga County), 68
Highland village (Highland County), 149
Hilliard city (Franklin County), 101
Hills and Dales village (Stark County), 285
Hillsboro city (Highland County), 150
Hilltop CDP (Trumbull County), 300
Hinckley postal area (Medina County), 206
Hiram village (Portage County), 253
Hocking County, 151
Holgate village (Henry County), 147
Holiday City village (Williams County), 332
Holiday Valley CDP (Clark County), 38
Holland village (Lucas County), 191
Hollansburg village (Darke County), 79
Holloway village (Belmont County), 23
Holmes County, 152 - 153
Holmesville village (Holmes County), 153
Homerville postal area (Medina County), 206
Homeworth postal area (Columbiana County), 51
Hopedale village (Harrison County), 145
Hopewell postal area (Muskingum County), 234
Houston postal area (Shelby County), 279
Howard postal area (Knox County), 166
Howland Center CDP (Trumbull County), 300
Hoytville village (Wood County), 336
Hubbard city (Trumbull County), 300
Huber Heights city (Montgomery County), 224
Huber Ridge CDP (Franklin County), 101
Hudson city (Summit County), 292
Hunter CDP (Warren County), 319
Hunting Valley village (Cuyahoga County), 68
Huntsburg postal area (Geauga County), 112
Huntsville village (Logan County), 182
Huron County, 154 - 156
Huron city (Erie County), 88

I

Independence city (Cuyahoga County), 68
Irondale village (Jefferson County), 160
Ironton city (Lawrence County), 174
Irwin postal area (Union County), 311
Ithaca village (Darke County), 79

J

Jackson Center village (Shelby County), 280
Jackson County, 157
Jackson city (Jackson County), 157
Jacksonburg village (Butler County), 29
Jacksonville village (Athens County), 16
Jacobsburg postal area (Belmont County), 23
Jamestown village (Greene County), 116
Jefferson County, 158 - 163
Jefferson village (Ashtabula County), 12
Jeffersonville village (Fayette County), 94
Jenera village (Hancock County), 139
Jeromesville village (Ashland County), 7
Jerry City village (Wood County), 336
Jerusalem village (Monroe County), 219
Jewett village (Harrison County), 145
Johnstown village (Licking County), 179
Junction City village (Perry County), 245

K

Kalida village (Putnam County), 261
Kansas postal area (Seneca County), 277

Kelleys Island village (Erie County), 88
Kensington postal area (Columbiana County), 51
Kent city (Portage County), 254
Kenton city (Hardin County), 142
Kenwood CDP (Hamilton County), 129
Kettering city (Montgomery County), 224
Kettlersville village (Shelby County), 280
Killbuck village (Holmes County), 153
Kimbolton village (Guernsey County), 119
Kings Mills postal area (Warren County), 319
Kingston village (Ross County), 267
Kingsville postal area (Ashtabula County), 12
Kinsman postal area (Trumbull County), 300
Kipton village (Lorain County), 187
Kirby village (Wyandot County), 341
Kirkersville village (Licking County), 179
Kirtland Hills village (Lake County), 168
Kirtland city (Lake County), 168
Kitts Hill postal area (Lawrence County), 174
Knox County, 164 - 165

L

La Croft CDP (Columbiana County), 51
La Rue village (Marion County), 203
Lacarne postal area (Ottawa County), 239
Lafayette village (Allen County), 5
Lagrange village (Lorain County), 187
Lake County, 166 - 171
Lake Darby CDP (Franklin County), 102
Lake Milton postal area (Mahoning County), 199
Lakeline village (Lake County), 168
Lakemore village (Summit County), 292
Lakeside Marblehead postal area (Ottawa County), 239
Lakeview village (Logan County), 182
Lakeville postal area (Holmes County), 153
Lakewood city (Cuyahoga County), 69
Lancaster city (Fairfield County), 91
Landen CDP (Warren County), 319
Langsville postal area (Meigs County), 209
Latham postal area (Pike County), 250
Latty village (Paulding County), 243
Laura village (Miami County), 215
Laurelville village (Hocking County), 151
Lawrence County, 172 - 174
Lawrenceville village (Clark County), 39
Leavittsburg CDP (Trumbull County), 301
Lebanon city (Warren County), 319
Leesburg village (Highland County), 150
Leesville village (Carroll County), 34
Leetonia village (Columbiana County), 51
Leipsic village (Putnam County), 261
Lewis Center postal area (Delaware County), 85
Lewisburg village (Preble County), 257
Lewistown postal area (Logan County), 182
Lewisville village (Monroe County), 219
Lexington village (Richland County), 263
Liberty Center village (Henry County), 147
Licking County, 175 - 179
Lima city (Allen County), 5
Limaville village (Stark County), 285
Lincoln Heights village (Hamilton County), 130
Lincoln Village CDP (Franklin County), 102
Lindsey village (Sandusky County), 271
Linndale village (Cuyahoga County), 69
Lisbon village (Columbiana County), 52
Litchfield postal area (Medina County), 206
Lithopolis village (Fairfield County), 91
Little Hocking postal area (Washington County), 323
Lockbourne village (Franklin County), 102

CDP = Census Designated Place

Lockington village (Shelby County), 280
Lockland village (Hamilton County), 130
Lodi village (Medina County), 207
Logan County, 180 - 183
Logan Elm Village CDP (Pickaway County), 248
Logan city (Hocking County), 151
London city (Madison County), 195
Londonderry postal area (Ross County), 268
Long Bottom postal area (Meigs County), 209
Lorain County, 184 - 189
Lorain city (Lorain County), 187
Lordstown village (Trumbull County), 301
Lore City village (Guernsey County), 119
Loudonville village (Ashland County), 8
Louisville city (Stark County), 285
Loveland Park CDP (Warren County), 320
Loveland city (Hamilton County), 130
Lowell village (Washington County), 324
Lowellville village (Mahoning County), 199
Lower Salem village (Washington County), 324
Lucas County, 190 - 193
Lucas village (Richland County), 264
Lucasville CDP (Scioto County), 272
Luckey village (Wood County), 337
Ludlow Falls village (Miami County), 215
Lynchburg village (Highland County), 150
Lyndhurst city (Cuyahoga County), 69
Lyons village (Fulton County), 107

M

Macedonia city (Summit County), 293
Mack North CDP (Hamilton County), 130
Mack South CDP (Hamilton County), 131
Macksburg village (Washington County), 324
Madeira city (Hamilton County), 131
Madison County, 194 - 196
Madison village (Lake County), 169
Magnetic Springs village (Union County), 311
Magnolia village (Stark County), 285
Mahoning County, 197 - 201
Maineville village (Warren County), 320
Malinta village (Henry County), 148
Malta village (Morgan County), 229
Malvern village (Carroll County), 34
Manchester village (Adams County), 1
Mansfield city (Richland County), 264
Mantua village (Portage County), 254
Maple Heights city (Cuyahoga County), 69
Maple Ridge CDP (Mahoning County), 199
Maplewood Park CDP (Trumbull County), 301
Maplewood postal area (Shelby County), 280
Marble Cliff village (Franklin County), 102
Marblehead village (Ottawa County), 240
Marengo village (Morrow County), 231
Maria Stein postal area (Mercer County), 213
Mariemont village (Hamilton County), 131
Marietta city (Washington County), 324
Marion County, 202 - 204
Marion city (Marion County), 203
Mark Center postal area (Defiance County), 83
Marseilles village (Wyandot County), 342
Marshallville village (Wayne County), 328
Martin postal area (Ottawa County), 240
Martins Ferry city (Belmont County), 23
Martinsburg village (Knox County), 166
Martinsville village (Clinton County), 47
Marysville city (Union County), 311
Mason city (Warren County), 320
Massillon city (Stark County), 286
Masury CDP (Trumbull County), 301
Matamoras village (Washington County), 325

Maumee city (Lucas County), 191
Mayfield Heights city (Cuyahoga County), 70
Mayfield village (Cuyahoga County), 70
McArthur village (Vinton County), 316
McClure village (Henry County), 148
McComb village (Hancock County), 139
McConnelsville village (Morgan County), 229
McCutchenville postal area (Wyandot County), 342
McDermott postal area (Scioto County), 273
McDonald village (Trumbull County), 301
McGuffey village (Hardin County), 143
Mechanicsburg village (Champaign County), 35
Mechanicstown postal area (Carroll County), 34
Medina County, 205 - 207
Medina city (Medina County), 207
Medway postal area (Clark County), 39
Meigs County, 208 - 210
Melrose village (Paulding County), 243
Mendon village (Mercer County), 213
Mentor city (Lake County), 169
Mentor-on-the-Lake city (Lake County), 169
Mercer County, 211 - 213
Metamora village (Fulton County), 107
Meyers Lake village (Stark County), 286
Miami County, 214 - 216
Miamisburg city (Montgomery County), 225
Middle Point village (Van Wert County), 313
Middleburg Heights city (Cuyahoga County), 70
Middlefield village (Geauga County), 113
Middleport village (Meigs County), 209
Middletown city (Butler County), 30
Midland village (Clinton County), 47
Midvale village (Tuscarawas County), 307
Midway village (Madison County), 195
Mifflin village (Ashland County), 8
Milan village (Erie County), 88
Milford Center village (Union County), 311
Milford city (Clermont County), 43
Millbury village (Wood County), 337
Milledgeville village (Fayette County), 95
Miller City village (Putnam County), 261
Millersburg village (Holmes County), 154
Millersport village (Fairfield County), 92
Millfield postal area (Athens County), 16
Millville village (Butler County), 30
Milton Center village (Wood County), 337
Miltonsburg village (Monroe County), 219
Mineral City village (Tuscarawas County), 307
Mineral Ridge CDP (Trumbull County), 302
Minerva Park village (Franklin County), 103
Minerva village (Stark County), 286
Minford postal area (Scioto County), 273
Mingo Junction village (Jefferson County), 161
Minster village (Auglaize County), 19
Mogadore village (Summit County), 293
Monclova postal area (Lucas County), 192
Monfort Heights East CDP (Hamilton County), 131
Monfort Heights South CDP (Hamilton County), 131
Monroe County, 217 - 219
Monroe city (Butler County), 30
Monroeville village (Huron County), 155
Montezuma village (Mercer County), 213
Montgomery County, 220 - 227
Montgomery city (Hamilton County), 132
Montpelier village (Williams County), 333
Montrose-Ghent CDP (Summit County), 293
Montville postal area (Geauga County), 113
Moraine city (Montgomery County), 225

Moreland Hills village (Cuyahoga County), 70
Morgan County, 228 - 229
Morral village (Marion County), 204
Morristown village (Belmont County), 24
Morrow County, 230 - 231
Morrow village (Warren County), 320
Moscow village (Clermont County), 44
Mount Blanchard village (Hancock County), 140
Mount Carmel CDP (Clermont County), 44
Mount Cory village (Hancock County), 140
Mount Eaton village (Wayne County), 329
Mount Gilead village (Morrow County), 231
Mount Healthy Heights CDP (Hamilton County), 132
Mount Healthy city (Hamilton County), 132
Mount Orab village (Brown County), 27
Mount Perry postal area (Perry County), 245
Mount Pleasant village (Jefferson County), 161
Mount Repose CDP (Clermont County), 44
Mount Sterling village (Madison County), 196
Mount Vernon city (Knox County), 166
Mount Victory village (Hardin County), 143
Mowrystown village (Highland County), 150
Mulberry CDP (Clermont County), 44
Munroe Falls city (Summit County), 293
Murray City village (Hocking County), 152
Muskingum County, 232 - 235
Mutual village (Champaign County), 36

N

Napoleon city (Henry County), 148
Nashport postal area (Muskingum County), 234
Nashville village (Holmes County), 154
Navarre village (Stark County), 287
Neffs CDP (Belmont County), 24
Negley postal area (Columbiana County), 52
Nellie village (Coshocton County), 55
Nelsonville city (Athens County), 16
Nevada village (Wyandot County), 342
Neville village (Clermont County), 44
New Albany village (Franklin County), 103
New Alexandria village (Jefferson County), 161
New Athens village (Harrison County), 145
New Bavaria village (Henry County), 148
New Bloomington village (Marion County), 204
New Boston village (Scioto County), 273
New Bremen village (Auglaize County), 19
New Carlisle city (Clark County), 39
New Concord village (Muskingum County), 234
New Franklin village (Summit County), 294
New Holland village (Pickaway County), 249
New Knoxville village (Auglaize County), 19
New Lebanon village (Montgomery County), 225
New Lexington city (Perry County), 245
New London village (Huron County), 155
New Madison village (Darke County), 79
New Marshfield postal area (Athens County), 17
New Matamoras postal area (Washington County), 325
New Miami village (Butler County), 31
New Middletown village (Mahoning County), 200
New Paris village (Preble County), 257
New Philadelphia city (Tuscarawas County), 307
New Plymouth postal area (Vinton County), 316

CDP = Census Designated Place

PROFILES OF OHIO / Alphabetical Place Index

New Richmond village (Clermont County), 45
New Riegel village (Seneca County), 277
New Rome village (Franklin County), 103
New Springfield postal area (Mahoning County), 200
New Straitsville village (Perry County), 246
New Vienna village (Clinton County), 47
New Washington village (Crawford County), 58
New Waterford village (Columbiana County), 52
New Weston village (Darke County), 80
Newark city (Licking County), 179
Newburgh Heights village (Cuyahoga County), 71
Newbury postal area (Geauga County), 113
Newcomerstown village (Tuscarawas County), 308
Newport postal area (Washington County), 325
Newton Falls village (Trumbull County), 302
Newtonsville village (Clermont County), 45
Newtown village (Hamilton County), 132
Ney village (Defiance County), 83
Niles city (Trumbull County), 302
Noble County, 236 - 237
North Baltimore village (Wood County), 337
North Bend village (Hamilton County), 133
North Benton postal area (Mahoning County), 200
North Bloomfield postal area (Trumbull County), 302
North Canton city (Stark County), 287
North College Hill city (Hamilton County), 133
North Fairfield village (Huron County), 156
North Fork Village CDP (Ross County), 268
North Hampton village (Clark County), 39
North Jackson postal area (Mahoning County), 200
North Kingsville village (Ashtabula County), 12
North Lawrence postal area (Stark County), 287
North Lewisburg village (Champaign County), 36
North Lima postal area (Mahoning County), 200
North Madison CDP (Lake County), 169
North Olmsted city (Cuyahoga County), 71
North Perry village (Lake County), 170
North Randall village (Cuyahoga County), 71
North Ridgeville city (Lorain County), 188
North Robinson village (Crawford County), 58
North Royalton city (Cuyahoga County), 71
North Star village (Darke County), 80
North Zanesville CDP (Muskingum County), 234
Northbrook CDP (Hamilton County), 133
Northfield village (Summit County), 294
Northgate CDP (Hamilton County), 133
Northridge CDP (Clark County), 40
Northridge CDP (Montgomery County), 226
Northwood city (Wood County), 337
Norton city (Summit County), 294
Norwalk city (Huron County), 156
Norwich village (Muskingum County), 235
Norwood city (Hamilton County), 134
Nova postal area (Ashland County), 8

O

Oak Harbor village (Ottawa County), 240
Oak Hill village (Jackson County), 158
Oakwood city (Montgomery County), 226
Oakwood village (Cuyahoga County), 72

Oakwood village (Paulding County), 243
Oberlin city (Lorain County), 188
Obetz village (Franklin County), 103
Octa village (Fayette County), 95
Ohio City village (Van Wert County), 313
Okeana postal area (Butler County), 31
Old Washington village (Guernsey County), 120
Olde West Chester CDP (Butler County), 31
Olmsted Falls city (Cuyahoga County), 72
Ontario village (Richland County), 264
Orange village (Cuyahoga County), 72
Orangeville village (Trumbull County), 303
Oregon city (Lucas County), 192
Oregonia postal area (Warren County), 321
Orient village (Pickaway County), 249
Orrville city (Wayne County), 329
Orwell village (Ashtabula County), 12
Osgood village (Darke County), 80
Ostrander village (Delaware County), 85
Ottawa County, 238 - 240
Ottawa Hills village (Lucas County), 192
Ottawa village (Putnam County), 261
Ottoville village (Putnam County), 262
Otway village (Scioto County), 273
Owensville village (Clermont County), 45
Oxford city (Butler County), 31

P

Painesville city (Lake County), 170
Palestine village (Darke County), 80
Pandora village (Putnam County), 262
Paris postal area (Stark County), 287
Park Layne CDP (Clark County), 40
Parma Heights city (Cuyahoga County), 73
Parma city (Cuyahoga County), 72
Parral village (Tuscarawas County), 308
Pataskala city (Licking County), 180
Patriot postal area (Gallia County), 110
Patterson village (Hardin County), 143
Paulding County, 241 - 243
Paulding village (Paulding County), 243
Payne village (Paulding County), 243
Pedro postal area (Lawrence County), 174
Peebles village (Adams County), 2
Pemberville village (Wood County), 338
Peninsula village (Summit County), 294
Pepper Pike city (Cuyahoga County), 73
Perry County, 244 - 246
Perry Heights CDP (Stark County), 288
Perry village (Lake County), 170
Perrysburg city (Wood County), 338
Perrysville village (Ashland County), 8
Petersburg postal area (Mahoning County), 201
Phillipsburg village (Montgomery County), 226
Philo village (Muskingum County), 235
Pickaway County, 247 - 249
Pickerington city (Fairfield County), 92
Piedmont postal area (Harrison County), 146
Pierpont postal area (Ashtabula County), 13
Pigeon Creek CDP (Summit County), 295
Pike County, 250
Piketon village (Pike County), 251
Pioneer village (Williams County), 333
Piqua city (Miami County), 216
Pitsburg village (Darke County), 80
Plain City village (Madison County), 196
Plainfield village (Coshocton County), 55
Pleasant City village (Guernsey County), 120
Pleasant Grove CDP (Muskingum County), 235
Pleasant Hill village (Miami County), 216
Pleasant Plain village (Warren County), 321

Pleasant Run Farm CDP (Hamilton County), 134
Pleasant Run CDP (Hamilton County), 134
Pleasantville village (Fairfield County), 92
Plymouth village (Richland County), 265
Poland village (Mahoning County), 201
Polk village (Ashland County), 9
Pomeroy village (Meigs County), 209
Port Clinton city (Ottawa County), 240
Port Jefferson village (Shelby County), 280
Port Washington village (Tuscarawas County), 308
Port William village (Clinton County), 48
Portage County, 251 - 255
Portage Lakes CDP (Summit County), 295
Portage village (Wood County), 338
Portland postal area (Meigs County), 210
Portsmouth city (Scioto County), 273
Potsdam village (Miami County), 216
Powell village (Delaware County), 85
Powhatan Point village (Belmont County), 24
Preble County, 256 - 257
Proctorville village (Lawrence County), 174
Prospect village (Marion County), 204
Put-in-Bay village (Ottawa County), 241
Putnam County, 258 - 261

Q

Quaker City village (Guernsey County), 120
Quincy village (Logan County), 183

R

Racine village (Meigs County), 210
Radnor postal area (Delaware County), 86
Rarden village (Scioto County), 274
Ravenna city (Portage County), 254
Rawson village (Hancock County), 140
Ray postal area (Vinton County), 316
Rayland village (Jefferson County), 161
Raymond postal area (Union County), 312
Reading city (Hamilton County), 134
Reedsville postal area (Meigs County), 210
Reminderville village (Summit County), 295
Rendville village (Perry County), 246
Reno postal area (Washington County), 325
Republic village (Seneca County), 278
Reynoldsburg city (Franklin County), 103
Richfield village (Summit County), 295
Richland County, 262 - 264
Richmond Dale postal area (Ross County), 268
Richmond Heights city (Cuyahoga County), 73
Richmond village (Jefferson County), 162
Richwood village (Union County), 312
Ridgeway village (Hardin County), 143
Rio Grande village (Gallia County), 110
Ripley village (Brown County), 27
Risingsun village (Wood County), 339
Rittman city (Wayne County), 329
Riverlea village (Franklin County), 104
Riverside city (Montgomery County), 226
Roaming Shores village (Ashtabula County), 13
Rochester village (Lorain County), 188
Rock Creek village (Ashtabula County), 13
Rockbridge postal area (Hocking County), 152
Rockford village (Mercer County), 213
Rocky Ridge village (Ottawa County), 241
Rocky River city (Cuyahoga County), 74
Rogers village (Columbiana County), 52
Rome postal area (Ashtabula County), 13
Rome village (Adams County), 2
Rootstown postal area (Portage County), 255

CDP = Census Designated Place

Rosemount CDP (Scioto County), 274
Roseville village (Perry County), 246
Ross County, 265 - 267
Ross CDP (Butler County), 32
Rossburg village (Darke County), 81
Rossford city (Wood County), 339
Roswell village (Tuscarawas County), 308
Rudolph postal area (Wood County), 339
Rushsylvania village (Logan County), 183
Rushville village (Fairfield County), 93
Russells Point village (Logan County), 183
Russellville village (Brown County), 27
Russia village (Shelby County), 281
Rutland village (Meigs County), 210

S

Sabina village (Clinton County), 48
Saint Bernard city (Hamilton County), 135
Saint Clairsville city (Belmont County), 24
Saint Henry village (Mercer County), 213
Saint Louisville village (Licking County), 180
Saint Martin village (Brown County), 27
Saint Marys city (Auglaize County), 19
Saint Paris village (Champaign County), 36
Salem city (Columbiana County), 53
Salesville village (Guernsey County), 120
Salineville village (Columbiana County), 53
Sandusky County, 268 - 271
Sandusky South CDP (Erie County), 89
Sandusky city (Erie County), 89
Sarahsville village (Noble County), 237
Sardinia village (Brown County), 28
Sardis postal area (Monroe County), 219
Savannah village (Ashland County), 9
Scio village (Harrison County), 146
Scioto County, 272 - 274
Sciotodale CDP (Scioto County), 274
Scott village (Van Wert County), 314
Scottown postal area (Lawrence County), 174
Seaman village (Adams County), 2
Sebring village (Mahoning County), 201
Seneca County, 275 - 277
Senecaville village (Guernsey County), 120
Seven Hills city (Cuyahoga County), 74
Seven Mile village (Butler County), 32
Seville village (Medina County), 207
Shade postal area (Athens County), 17
Shadyside village (Belmont County), 25
Shaker Heights city (Cuyahoga County), 74
Sharonville city (Hamilton County), 135
Shawnee Hills CDP (Greene County), 116
Shawnee Hills village (Delaware County), 86
Shawnee village (Perry County), 246
Sheffield Lake city (Lorain County), 189
Sheffield village (Lorain County), 189
Shelby County, 278 - 280
Shelby city (Richland County), 265
Sherrodsville village (Carroll County), 34
Sherwood CDP (Hamilton County), 135
Sherwood village (Defiance County), 83
Shiloh CDP (Montgomery County), 227
Shiloh village (Richland County), 265
Shreve village (Wayne County), 329
Sidney city (Shelby County), 281
Silver Lake village (Summit County), 296
Silverton city (Hamilton County), 135
Sinking Spring village (Highland County), 151
Smithfield village (Jefferson County), 162
Smithville village (Wayne County), 330
Solon city (Cuyahoga County), 75
Somerset village (Perry County), 247
Somerville village (Butler County), 32
South Amherst village (Lorain County), 189
South Bloomfield village (Pickaway County), 249

South Bloomingville postal area (Hocking County), 152
South Canal CDP (Trumbull County), 303
South Charleston village (Clark County), 40
South Euclid city (Cuyahoga County), 75
South Lebanon village (Warren County), 321
South Middletown CDP (Butler County), 32
South Point village (Lawrence County), 175
South Russell village (Geauga County), 113
South Salem village (Ross County), 268
South Solon village (Madison County), 196
South Vienna village (Clark County), 40
South Webster village (Scioto County), 274
South Zanesville village (Muskingum County), 235
Southington postal area (Trumbull County), 303
Sparta village (Morrow County), 232
Spencer village (Medina County), 208
Spencerville village (Allen County), 6
Spring Valley village (Greene County), 116
Springboro city (Warren County), 321
Springdale city (Hamilton County), 136
Springfield city (Clark County), 40
Stafford village (Monroe County), 219
Stark County, 281 - 287
Sterling postal area (Wayne County), 330
Steubenville city (Jefferson County), 162
Stewart postal area (Athens County), 17
Stockport village (Morgan County), 229
Stone Creek village (Tuscarawas County), 309
Stony Prairie CDP (Sandusky County), 271
Stout postal area (Scioto County), 275
Stoutsville village (Fairfield County), 93
Stow city (Summit County), 296
Strasburg village (Tuscarawas County), 309
Stratton village (Jefferson County), 162
Streetsboro city (Portage County), 255
Strongsville city (Cuyahoga County), 75
Struthers city (Mahoning County), 201
Stryker village (Williams County), 333
Sugar Bush Knolls village (Portage County), 255
Sugar Grove village (Fairfield County), 93
Sugarcreek village (Tuscarawas County), 309
Sullivan postal area (Ashland County), 9
Summerfield village (Noble County), 238
Summerside CDP (Clermont County), 45
Summit County, 288 - 296
Summitville village (Columbiana County), 53
Sunbury village (Delaware County), 86
Swanton village (Fulton County), 108
Sycamore village (Wyandot County), 342
Sylvania city (Lucas County), 192
Syracuse village (Meigs County), 211

T

Tallmadge city (Summit County), 296
Tarlton village (Pickaway County), 249
Terrace Park village (Hamilton County), 136
The Plains CDP (Athens County), 17
The Village of Indian Hill city (Hamilton County), 136
Thompson postal area (Geauga County), 114
Thornville village (Perry County), 247
Thurman postal area (Gallia County), 110
Thurston village (Fairfield County), 93
Tiffin city (Seneca County), 278
Tiltonsville village (Jefferson County), 163
Timberlake village (Lake County), 170
Tipp City city (Miami County), 216
Tippecanoe postal area (Harrison County), 146
Tiro village (Crawford County), 58

Toledo city (Lucas County), 193
Tontogany village (Wood County), 339
Toronto city (Jefferson County), 163
Tremont City village (Clark County), 41
Trenton city (Butler County), 32
Trimble village (Athens County), 18
Trotwood city (Montgomery County), 227
Troy city (Miami County), 217
Trumbull County, 297 - 304
Turpin Hills CDP (Hamilton County), 136
Tuscarawas County, 305 - 309
Tuscarawas village (Tuscarawas County), 309
Twinsburg city (Summit County), 296

U

Uhrichsville city (Tuscarawas County), 310
Union City village (Darke County), 81
Union County, 310 - 311
Union city (Montgomery County), 227
Uniontown CDP (Stark County), 288
Unionville Center village (Union County), 312
Uniopolis village (Auglaize County), 20
University Heights city (Cuyahoga County), 75
Upper Arlington city (Franklin County), 104
Upper Sandusky city (Wyandot County), 342
Urbana city (Champaign County), 36
Urbancrest village (Franklin County), 104
Utica village (Licking County), 180

V

Valley City postal area (Medina County), 208
Valley Hi village (Logan County), 183
Valley View village (Cuyahoga County), 76
Valleyview village (Franklin County), 104
Van Buren village (Hancock County), 140
Van Wert County, 312 - 314
Van Wert city (Van Wert County), 314
Vandalia city (Montgomery County), 227
Vanlue village (Hancock County), 140
Venedocia village (Van Wert County), 314
Vermilion city (Lorain County), 189
Verona village (Preble County), 258
Versailles village (Darke County), 81
Vickery postal area (Sandusky County), 271
Vienna Center CDP (Trumbull County), 303
Vienna postal area (Trumbull County), 303
Vincent postal area (Washington County), 326
Vinton County, 315 - 316
Vinton village (Gallia County), 111

W

Wadsworth city (Medina County), 208
Waite Hill village (Lake County), 171
Wakeman village (Huron County), 156
Walbridge village (Wood County), 340
Waldo village (Marion County), 205
Walhonding postal area (Coshocton County), 56
Walton Hills village (Cuyahoga County), 76
Wapakoneta city (Auglaize County), 20
Warren County, 317 - 321
Warren city (Trumbull County), 304
Warrensville Heights city (Cuyahoga County), 76
Warsaw village (Coshocton County), 56
Washington County, 322 - 325
Washington Court House city (Fayette County), 95
Washingtonville village (Columbiana County), 53
Waterford postal area (Washington County), 326

CDP = Census Designated Place

Waterloo postal area (Lawrence County), 175
Waterville village (Lucas County), 194
Wauseon city (Fulton County), 108
Waverly City city (Pike County), 251
Wayne County, 326 - 330
Wayne Lakes village (Darke County), 81
Wayne village (Wood County), 340
Waynesburg village (Stark County), 288
Waynesfield village (Auglaize County), 20
Waynesville village (Warren County), 322
Wellington village (Lorain County), 190
Wellston city (Jackson County), 158
Wellsville village (Columbiana County), 54
West Alexandria village (Preble County), 258
West Carrollton City city (Montgomery County), 228
West Elkton village (Preble County), 258
West Farmington village (Trumbull County), 304
West Hill CDP (Trumbull County), 304
West Jefferson village (Madison County), 196
West Lafayette village (Coshocton County), 56
West Leipsic village (Putnam County), 262
West Liberty village (Logan County), 183
West Manchester village (Preble County), 258
West Mansfield village (Logan County), 184
West Millgrove village (Wood County), 340
West Milton village (Miami County), 217
West Portsmouth CDP (Scioto County), 275
West Rushville village (Fairfield County), 93
West Salem village (Wayne County), 330
West Union village (Adams County), 2
West Unity village (Williams County), 333
Westerville city (Franklin County), 105
Westfield Center village (Medina County), 208

Westlake city (Cuyahoga County), 77
Weston village (Wood County), 340
Wetherington CDP (Butler County), 33
Wharton village (Wyandot County), 343
Wheelersburg CDP (Scioto County), 275
Whipple postal area (Washington County), 326
White Oak East CDP (Hamilton County), 137
White Oak West CDP (Hamilton County), 137
White Oak CDP (Hamilton County), 136
Whitehall city (Franklin County), 105
Whitehouse village (Lucas County), 194
Wickliffe city (Lake County), 171
Wilberforce CDP (Greene County), 117
Wilkesville village (Vinton County), 316
Willard city (Huron County), 156
Williams County, 331 - 333
Williamsburg village (Clermont County), 46
Williamsfield postal area (Ashtabula County), 13
Williamsport village (Pickaway County), 250
Willoughby Hills city (Lake County), 172
Willoughby city (Lake County), 171
Willow Wood postal area (Lawrence County), 175
Willowick city (Lake County), 172
Willshire village (Van Wert County), 314
Wilmington city (Clinton County), 48
Wilmot village (Stark County), 288
Wilson village (Monroe County), 220
Winchester village (Adams County), 2
Windham village (Portage County), 255
Windsor postal area (Ashtabula County), 14
Wingett Run postal area (Washington County), 326
Wintersville village (Jefferson County), 163
Withamsville CDP (Clermont County), 46
Wood County, 334 - 339

Woodbourne-Hyde Park CDP (Montgomery County), 228
Woodlawn village (Hamilton County), 137
Woodmere village (Cuyahoga County), 77
Woodsfield village (Monroe County), 220
Woodstock village (Champaign County), 37
Woodville village (Sandusky County), 271
Wooster city (Wayne County), 330
Worthington city (Franklin County), 105
Wren village (Van Wert County), 315
Wright-Patterson AFB CDP (Montgomery County), 228
Wyandot County, 340 - 343
Wyoming city (Hamilton County), 137

X

Xenia city (Greene County), 117

Y

Yankee Lake village (Trumbull County), 304
Yellow Springs village (Greene County), 117
Yorkshire village (Darke County), 82
Yorkville village (Jefferson County), 163
Youngstown city (Mahoning County), 202

Z

Zaleski village (Vinton County), 316
Zanesfield village (Logan County), 184
Zanesville city (Muskingum County), 236
Zoar village (Tuscarawas County), 310

CDP = Census Designated Place

COMPARATIVE STATISTICS

Population

Place	1990	2000	2005 Estimate	2010 Projection
Akron (city)	223,165	217,074	210,096	203,592
Alliance (city)	23,552	23,253	22,631	22,030
Ashland (city)	20,355	21,249	21,362	21,638
Ashtabula (city)	21,626	20,962	20,138	19,353
Athens (city)	21,362	21,342	22,292	23,320
Austintown (CDP)	32,371	31,627	29,963	28,400
Avon Lake (city)	15,066	18,145	20,558	22,858
Barberton (city)	27,931	27,899	27,235	26,632
Beavercreek (city)	33,946	37,984	39,417	40,947
Berea (city)	19,045	18,970	18,333	17,728
Boardman (CDP)	38,727	37,215	35,416	33,806
Bowling Green (city)	29,038	29,636	29,953	30,315
Brook Park (city)	22,961	21,218	20,434	19,658
Brunswick (city)	28,743	33,388	34,918	36,761
Canton (city)	84,082	80,806	78,174	75,536
Centerville (city)	21,563	23,024	22,902	22,894
Chillicothe (city)	22,771	21,796	21,614	21,422
Cincinnati (city)	363,974	331,285	310,852	291,613
Cleveland (city)	505,333	478,403	455,038	432,022
Cleveland Heights (city)	54,052	49,958	47,431	44,980
Columbus (city)	648,656	711,470	733,424	755,812
Cuyahoga Falls (city)	48,814	49,374	50,702	52,009
Dayton (city)	182,920	166,179	159,845	153,413
Delaware (city)	21,106	25,243	29,934	35,088
Dublin (city)	17,231	31,392	34,533	37,711
East Cleveland (city)	33,096	27,217	25,814	24,428
Eastlake (city)	21,161	20,255	19,842	19,449
Elyria (city)	57,491	55,953	55,857	56,007
Euclid (city)	54,875	52,717	50,579	48,413
Fairborn (city)	31,928	32,052	32,310	32,806
Fairfield (city)	40,084	42,097	42,564	43,263
Findlay (city)	36,546	38,967	39,608	40,440
Forest Park (city)	18,625	19,463	18,376	17,213
Gahanna (city)	24,610	32,636	32,481	32,409
Garfield Heights (city)	31,739	30,734	29,471	28,215
Green (city)	19,179	22,817	23,542	24,299
Grove City (city)	21,241	27,075	28,463	29,852
Hamilton (city)	61,618	60,690	60,873	61,383
Hilliard (city)	12,516	24,230	26,610	28,881
Huber Heights (city)	38,478	38,212	38,300	38,352
Hudson (city)	17,128	22,439	23,295	24,097
Kent (city)	28,879	27,906	27,850	27,770
Kettering (city)	60,570	57,502	55,815	54,191
Lakewood (city)	59,718	56,646	53,350	50,144
Lancaster (city)	35,664	35,335	36,150	37,502
Lebanon (city)	11,282	16,962	19,110	21,337
Lima (city)	45,620	40,081	38,585	37,150
Lorain (city)	71,245	68,652	67,758	67,096
Mansfield (city)	50,489	49,346	48,058	46,855
Maple Heights (city)	27,089	26,156	25,175	24,157

Place	1990	2000	2005 Estimate	2010 Projection
Marion (city)	36,526	35,318	35,210	35,004
Mason (city)	12,046	22,016	29,379	36,797
Massillon (city)	31,955	31,325	31,317	31,311
Mayfield Heights (city)	19,847	19,386	18,721	18,045
Medina (city)	19,807	25,139	26,899	29,014
Mentor (city)	47,358	50,278	49,836	49,444
Miamisburg (city)	18,641	19,489	19,819	20,089
Middletown (city)	52,003	51,605	51,958	52,598
Newark (city)	45,070	46,279	46,727	47,404
Niles (city)	21,353	20,932	20,041	19,159
North Olmsted (city)	34,240	34,113	33,153	32,193
North Ridgeville (city)	21,564	22,338	25,363	28,233
North Royalton (city)	23,197	28,648	30,102	31,448
Norwood (city)	23,635	21,675	20,328	18,991
Oregon (city)	18,371	19,355	19,444	19,535
Oxford (city)	21,307	21,943	22,509	23,193
Painesville (city)	15,712	17,503	17,220	17,014
Parma (city)	87,876	85,655	83,038	80,341
Parma Heights (city)	21,448	21,659	21,006	20,348
Piqua (city)	21,160	20,738	20,607	20,513
Portsmouth (city)	22,676	20,909	19,392	17,974
Reynoldsburg (city)	26,344	32,069	33,597	35,081
Riverside (city)	25,374	23,545	23,134	22,700
Rocky River (city)	20,410	20,735	19,942	19,163
Sandusky (city)	29,764	27,844	26,654	25,442
Shaker Heights (city)	30,831	29,405	28,029	26,689
Sidney (city)	19,245	20,211	20,067	19,970
Solon (city)	18,548	21,802	22,422	22,968
South Euclid (city)	23,866	23,537	22,545	21,555
Springfield (city)	71,064	65,358	62,899	60,477
Steubenville (city)	22,298	19,015	18,604	18,167
Stow (city)	27,702	32,139	35,044	37,755
Strongsville (city)	35,308	43,858	44,785	45,592
Sylvania (city)	17,488	18,670	18,884	19,161
Tallmadge (city)	15,094	16,390	17,462	18,488
Toledo (city)	332,921	313,619	306,374	299,292
Trotwood (city)	29,395	27,420	26,884	26,415
Troy (city)	19,956	21,999	21,914	21,985
Twinsburg (city)	9,759	17,006	17,760	18,335
Upper Arlington (city)	34,171	33,686	31,752	29,966
Wadsworth (city)	16,147	18,437	19,626	20,996
Warren (city)	51,151	46,832	44,380	42,102
Westerville (city)	30,722	35,318	34,555	34,167
Westlake (city)	27,018	31,719	32,082	32,402
Whitehall (city)	20,645	19,201	18,205	17,351
Willoughby (city)	20,510	22,621	22,426	22,260
Wooster (city)	23,108	24,811	25,075	25,452
Xenia (city)	25,481	24,164	23,946	23,926
Youngstown (city)	95,732	82,026	78,288	74,582
Zanesville (city)	27,058	25,586	24,695	23,943

Physical Characteristics

Place	Density (persons per square mile)	Land Area (square miles)	Water Area (square miles)	Elevation (feet)
Akron (city)	3,384.9	62.07	0.34	1,050
Alliance (city)	2,627.9	8.61	0.00	1,174
Ashland (city)	2,062.5	10.36	0.04	1,080
Ashtabula (city)	2,666.8	7.55	0.17	680
Athens (city)	2,674.4	8.34	0.00	723
Austintown (CDP)	2,566.8	11.67	0.00	1,030
Avon Lake (city)	1,846.8	11.13	0.00	600
Barberton (city)	3,021.5	9.01	0.22	969
Beavercreek (city)	1,493.5	26.39	0.00	850
Berea (city)	3,359.2	5.46	0.11	800
Boardman (CDP)	2,222.9	15.93	0.10	1,110
Bowling Green (city)	2,950.2	10.15	0.03	700
Brook Park (city)	2,711.0	7.54	0.00	790
Brunswick (city)	2,784.3	12.54	0.04	1,070
Canton (city)	3,804.9	20.55	0.01	1,100
Centerville (city)	2,245.2	10.20	0.02	1,020
Chillicothe (city)	2,264.7	9.54	0.20	625
Cincinnati (city)	3,986.9	77.97	1.60	683
Cleveland (city)	5,865.4	77.58	4.84	690
Cleveland Heights (city)	5,848.6	8.11	0.02	950
Columbus (city)	3,488.0	210.27	2.28	800
Cuyahoga Falls (city)	1,984.9	25.54	0.09	1,050
Dayton (city)	2,865.8	55.78	0.85	750
Delaware (city)	1,995.6	15.00	0.10	880
Dublin (city)	1,634.8	21.12	0.02	850
East Cleveland (city)	8,310.2	3.11	0.00	820
Eastlake (city)	3,102.0	6.40	0.12	620
Elyria (city)	2,808.9	19.89	0.03	733
Euclid (city)	4,723.5	10.71	0.86	618
Fairborn (city)	2,473.2	13.06	0.00	845
Fairfield (city)	2,027.8	20.99	0.09	590
Findlay (city)	2,303.6	17.19	0.11	780
Forest Park (city)	2,823.4	6.51	0.00	836
Gahanna (city)	2,620.3	12.40	0.00	798
Garfield Heights (city)	4,078.2	7.23	0.08	900
Green (city)	734.3	32.06	1.47	1,150
Grove City (city)	2,040.7	13.95	0.01	835
Hamilton (city)	2,816.7	21.61	0.47	600
Hilliard (city)	2,388.5	11.14	0.00	935
Huber Heights (city)	1,821.4	21.03	0.09	970
Hudson (city)	910.4	25.59	0.27	1,090
Kent (city)	3,205.9	8.69	0.02	1,097
Kettering (city)	2,987.1	18.69	0.00	1,005
Lakewood (city)	9,614.5	5.55	1.15	710
Lancaster (city)	2,001.0	18.07	0.01	860
Lebanon (city)	1,623.1	11.77	0.00	769
Lima (city)	3,018.0	12.78	0.10	875
Lorain (city)	2,821.4	24.02	0.23	620
Mansfield (city)	1,607.0	29.91	0.00	1,249
Maple Heights (city)	4,850.1	5.19	0.00	936

Place	Density (persons per square mile)	Land Area (square miles)	Water Area (square miles)	Elevation (feet)
Marion (city)	3,103.3	11.35	0.04	956
Mason (city)	1,668.0	17.61	0.04	810
Massillon (city)	1,869.8	16.75	0.14	951
Mayfield Heights (city)	4,438.4	4.22	0.00	1,080
Medina (city)	2,417.6	11.13	0.19	1,092
Mentor (city)	1,861.7	26.77	1.31	690
Miamisburg (city)	1,771.1	11.19	0.19	710
Middletown (city)	2,025.1	25.66	0.14	665
Newark (city)	2,389.7	19.55	0.24	829
Niles (city)	2,343.3	8.55	0.02	890
North Olmsted (city)	2,850.4	11.63	0.00	756
North Ridgeville (city)	1,085.3	23.37	0.14	725
North Royalton (city)	1,414.2	21.29	0.00	1,197
Norwood (city)	6,524.2	3.12	0.00	660
Oregon (city)	661.8	29.38	8.71	605
Oxford (city)	3,830.7	5.88	0.00	972
Painesville (city)	2,881.3	5.98	0.71	677
Parma (city)	4,160.1	19.96	0.02	880
Parma Heights (city)	5,003.1	4.20	0.00	870
Piqua (city)	1,927.0	10.69	0.24	869
Portsmouth (city)	1,800.6	10.77	0.29	540
Reynoldsburg (city)	3,174.4	10.58	0.00	880
Riverside (city)	2,944.3	7.86	0.04	770
Rocky River (city)	4,194.0	4.75	0.87	680
Sandusky (city)	2,652.2	10.05	11.94	600
Shaker Heights (city)	4,465.7	6.28	0.04	1,000
Sidney (city)	1,924.7	10.43	0.07	1,003
Solon (city)	1,091.0	20.55	0.04	1,036
South Euclid (city)	4,807.7	4.69	0.00	950
Springfield (city)	2,798.8	22.47	0.04	1,000
Steubenville (city)	1,802.3	10.32	0.00	1,060
Stow (city)	2,047.9	17.11	0.23	1,091
Strongsville (city)	1,817.2	24.64	0.01	932
Sylvania (city)	3,260.2	5.79	0.04	665
Tallmadge (city)	1,250.7	13.96	0.02	1,114
Toledo (city)	3,800.1	80.62	3.45	615
Trotwood (city)	880.6	30.53	0.01	850
Troy (city)	2,259.0	9.70	0.07	835
Twinsburg (city)	1,427.3	12.44	0.03	1,004
Upper Arlington (city)	3,252.1	9.76	0.02	820
Wadsworth (city)	2,065.6	9.50	0.00	1,200
Warren (city)	2,759.1	16.08	0.03	893
Westerville (city)	2,789.5	12.39	0.00	875
Westlake (city)	2,018.0	15.90	0.00	700
Whitehall (city)	3,490.9	5.22	0.00	790
Willoughby (city)	2,206.1	10.17	0.06	665
Wooster (city)	1,744.5	14.37	0.02	950
Xenia (city)	1,971.3	12.15	0.00	938
Youngstown (city)	2,309.6	33.90	0.35	861
Zanesville (city)	2,197.5	11.24	0.26	710

NOTE: Population Density figures as of 2005; Land Area and Water Area figures as of 2000.

Population by Race/Hispanic Origin

Place	White Alone[1] (%)	Black Alone[1] (%)	Asian Alone[1] (%)	Hispanic[2] (%)
Akron (city)	65.1	29.9	1.8	1.3
Alliance (city)	85.7	10.5	1.0	1.2
Ashland (city)	96.5	1.1	1.2	0.7
Ashtabula (city)	83.2	10.5	0.4	6.6
Athens (city)	89.3	3.4	4.9	1.2
Austintown (CDP)	91.8	5.3	0.9	1.9
Avon Lake (city)	96.6	0.5	1.2	1.4
Barberton (city)	91.9	5.5	0.4	0.7
Beavercreek (city)	92.0	1.6	4.5	1.2
Berea (city)	91.0	5.1	1.1	1.6
Boardman (CDP)	94.4	2.8	1.2	1.9
Bowling Green (city)	91.6	2.6	2.0	3.8
Brook Park (city)	93.6	2.2	1.6	2.0
Brunswick (city)	96.4	0.8	1.2	1.5
Canton (city)	73.1	21.7	0.4	1.1
Centerville (city)	91.0	3.3	3.9	1.1
Chillicothe (city)	90.1	6.9	0.6	0.9
Cincinnati (city)	50.6	44.5	1.9	1.4
Cleveland (city)	39.2	52.3	1.7	7.9
Cleveland Heights (city)	49.8	43.6	3.0	1.7
Columbus (city)	64.6	25.9	4.4	3.2
Cuyahoga Falls (city)	94.9	2.2	1.4	0.7
Dayton (city)	52.7	43.2	0.8	1.7
Delaware (city)	90.4	4.2	1.9	1.5
Dublin (city)	86.3	2.2	9.9	1.3
East Cleveland (city)	4.6	93.0	0.2	0.8
Eastlake (city)	96.7	0.7	1.3	0.9
Elyria (city)	81.0	13.6	0.8	3.2
Euclid (city)	60.3	36.1	1.1	1.2
Fairborn (city)	85.8	6.6	4.0	1.8
Fairfield (city)	87.3	7.6	2.9	1.8
Findlay (city)	92.9	1.6	2.3	3.8
Forest Park (city)	30.3	60.9	4.9	1.6
Gahanna (city)	83.9	9.1	4.5	1.6
Garfield Heights (city)	79.7	17.3	1.2	1.3
Green (city)	97.0	0.9	1.0	0.5
Grove City (city)	95.1	2.0	0.8	1.5
Hamilton (city)	87.9	7.8	0.6	3.2
Hilliard (city)	90.2	1.9	5.1	2.2
Huber Heights (city)	83.8	10.0	2.6	1.5
Hudson (city)	93.6	1.5	3.7	0.9
Kent (city)	84.1	10.0	2.9	1.4
Kettering (city)	94.6	1.8	1.6	1.1
Lakewood (city)	91.7	2.4	1.7	2.3
Lancaster (city)	96.4	1.1	0.7	1.1
Lebanon (city)	88.7	7.5	1.2	1.5
Lima (city)	68.6	26.4	0.8	2.1
Lorain (city)	68.3	16.0	0.4	22.0
Mansfield (city)	76.8	19.3	0.8	1.2
Maple Heights (city)	43.7	51.5	2.2	1.3

PROFILES OF OHIO / Comparative Statistics

Place	White Alone[1] (%)	Black Alone[1] (%)	Asian Alone[1] (%)	Hispanic[2] (%)
Marion (city)	90.9	6.5	0.7	1.6
Mason (city)	91.8	1.9	4.6	1.2
Massillon (city)	88.4	8.9	0.3	0.9
Mayfield Heights (city)	90.1	3.4	5.2	1.1
Medina (city)	94.2	2.7	1.2	1.1
Mentor (city)	96.5	0.8	1.6	0.8
Miamisburg (city)	95.4	1.7	0.8	0.9
Middletown (city)	85.5	11.5	0.5	1.1
Newark (city)	93.9	3.0	0.8	0.7
Niles (city)	95.8	2.3	0.4	0.9
North Olmsted (city)	92.8	1.1	3.5	1.7
North Ridgeville (city)	95.7	0.9	1.2	2.1
North Royalton (city)	95.5	0.8	2.3	1.0
Norwood (city)	93.1	2.9	0.9	2.2
Oregon (city)	94.3	0.9	0.9	5.2
Oxford (city)	90.0	4.7	2.8	1.7
Painesville (city)	73.4	13.7	0.5	17.9
Parma (city)	94.9	1.2	1.9	1.7
Parma Heights (city)	93.3	1.5	3.1	1.8
Piqua (city)	94.1	3.1	0.6	0.9
Portsmouth (city)	90.8	5.3	1.1	1.2
Reynoldsburg (city)	81.5	12.9	2.1	2.2
Riverside (city)	90.5	4.5	2.2	1.5
Rocky River (city)	96.3	0.5	1.5	1.3
Sandusky (city)	73.9	20.9	0.4	3.4
Shaker Heights (city)	57.3	35.5	4.1	1.1
Sidney (city)	91.5	3.4	2.2	1.8
Solon (city)	85.1	7.1	6.4	0.8
South Euclid (city)	70.5	25.6	1.7	1.0
Springfield (city)	77.6	17.9	0.9	1.4
Steubenville (city)	79.5	17.0	1.1	1.0
Stow (city)	94.4	1.7	2.3	1.0
Strongsville (city)	93.1	1.5	3.9	1.3
Sylvania (city)	94.5	1.0	2.6	1.8
Tallmadge (city)	95.1	2.4	1.0	0.6
Toledo (city)	68.6	24.3	1.2	5.9
Trotwood (city)	33.8	62.8	0.3	0.8
Troy (city)	90.4	4.6	2.8	0.9
Twinsburg (city)	84.4	9.9	4.1	1.2
Upper Arlington (city)	93.4	0.7	4.4	1.1
Wadsworth (city)	97.4	0.3	1.0	0.8
Warren (city)	71.3	25.6	0.4	1.2
Westerville (city)	91.6	3.9	2.4	1.3
Westlake (city)	91.6	1.1	5.1	1.3
Whitehall (city)	68.0	23.9	2.5	4.0
Willoughby (city)	95.4	1.4	1.6	0.8
Wooster (city)	92.0	3.7	2.0	1.3
Xenia (city)	84.1	12.3	0.3	1.3
Youngstown (city)	50.4	43.5	0.5	5.4
Zanesville (city)	84.7	11.1	0.3	0.8

NOTE: Data as of 2005; (1) Figures are not in combination with any other race; (2) Persons of Hispanic Origin may be of any race

Average Household Size, Median Age, Male/Female Ratio, and Foreign Born

Place	Average Household Size (persons)	Median Age (years)	Male/Female Ratio (males per 100 females)	Foreign Born (%)
Akron (city)	2.39	35.3	92.2	3.2
Alliance (city)	2.60	34.7	88.4	1.6
Ashland (city)	2.52	35.1	88.1	1.5
Ashtabula (city)	2.47	35.4	89.7	2.7
Athens (city)	3.32	22.6	88.6	6.3
Austintown (CDP)	2.32	41.2	90.9	2.3
Avon Lake (city)	2.66	39.1	95.0	3.4
Barberton (city)	2.39	37.8	88.2	1.9
Beavercreek (city)	2.63	41.6	97.9	4.7
Berea (city)	2.62	37.1	90.8	3.2
Boardman (CDP)	2.30	43.3	88.5	3.0
Bowling Green (city)	2.82	24.4	87.6	3.6
Brook Park (city)	2.54	41.9	95.1	4.3
Brunswick (city)	2.75	35.6	96.4	4.3
Canton (city)	2.48	35.5	88.5	1.7
Centerville (city)	2.27	43.6	87.4	4.2
Chillicothe (city)	2.27	40.7	88.6	1.0
Cincinnati (city)	2.20	33.9	90.6	3.8
Cleveland (city)	2.50	34.2	90.8	4.5
Cleveland Heights (city)	2.35	37.0	87.7	8.3
Columbus (city)	2.33	32.5	95.7	6.7
Cuyahoga Falls (city)	2.25	38.3	91.1	3.1
Dayton (city)	2.44	33.7	94.4	2.0
Delaware (city)	2.60	31.2	92.7	1.6
Dublin (city)	2.76	36.0	98.4	9.1
East Cleveland (city)	2.40	35.0	80.4	2.9
Eastlake (city)	2.45	39.3	95.7	5.0
Elyria (city)	2.45	35.5	92.8	1.5
Euclid (city)	2.15	40.5	84.8	5.3
Fairborn (city)	2.30	32.9	95.2	4.6
Fairfield (city)	2.45	36.2	95.2	3.6
Findlay (city)	2.41	36.0	92.0	2.7
Forest Park (city)	2.54	35.9	92.6	5.7
Gahanna (city)	2.68	37.7	94.8	4.9
Garfield Heights (city)	2.44	39.5	88.3	4.4
Green (city)	2.59	40.1	97.3	1.9
Grove City (city)	2.63	36.3	95.6	1.2
Hamilton (city)	2.48	35.4	93.7	2.2
Hilliard (city)	2.85	34.6	97.1	4.2
Huber Heights (city)	2.60	36.0	95.1	3.2
Hudson (city)	3.04	39.1	98.0	5.2
Kent (city)	2.82	24.7	85.1	4.4
Kettering (city)	2.21	40.4	91.1	2.7
Lakewood (city)	2.09	36.5	93.0	8.7
Lancaster (city)	2.34	35.7	89.5	0.9
Lebanon (city)	2.83	31.9	109.7	1.8
Lima (city)	2.57	33.3	101.8	1.1
Lorain (city)	2.55	34.8	90.4	3.6
Mansfield (city)	2.41	37.6	99.1	2.2
Maple Heights (city)	2.48	38.8	88.2	2.9

PROFILES OF OHIO / Comparative Statistics

Place	Average Household Size (persons)	Median Age (years)	Male/Female Ratio (males per 100 females)	Foreign Born (%)
Marion (city)	2.58	36.0	104.7	1.5
Mason (city)	2.82	35.0	95.4	4.0
Massillon (city)	2.45	38.5	93.4	1.3
Mayfield Heights (city)	1.95	45.3	82.8	18.1
Medina (city)	2.63	33.8	92.8	2.7
Mentor (city)	2.62	40.2	94.5	3.8
Miamisburg (city)	2.59	38.6	92.5	1.7
Middletown (city)	2.37	36.6	92.3	1.0
Newark (city)	2.37	36.3	91.0	1.1
Niles (city)	2.31	40.8	89.9	1.9
North Olmsted (city)	2.47	41.3	93.3	7.8
North Ridgeville (city)	2.62	39.7	96.4	3.3
North Royalton (city)	2.52	39.9	94.8	6.8
Norwood (city)	2.30	36.0	95.8	2.3
Oregon (city)	2.48	40.2	92.7	2.3
Oxford (city)	3.69	22.0	89.7	3.7
Painesville (city)	2.69	32.1	97.7	10.1
Parma (city)	2.41	40.8	91.5	9.1
Parma Heights (city)	2.19	43.7	86.9	10.2
Piqua (city)	2.46	36.0	92.5	1.4
Portsmouth (city)	2.27	38.4	85.6	1.1
Reynoldsburg (city)	2.46	36.8	91.9	3.6
Riverside (city)	2.38	38.3	94.6	2.9
Rocky River (city)	2.10	45.6	82.8	7.0
Sandusky (city)	2.30	36.8	89.7	1.7
Shaker Heights (city)	2.40	40.7	84.3	7.2
Sidney (city)	2.49	35.0	96.3	2.3
Solon (city)	2.89	40.0	95.8	8.6
South Euclid (city)	2.44	39.4	86.0	9.4
Springfield (city)	2.46	35.2	90.1	1.2
Steubenville (city)	2.24	43.5	86.0	2.4
Stow (city)	2.58	37.9	94.1	3.7
Strongsville (city)	2.68	40.3	94.9	6.5
Sylvania (city)	2.56	38.8	91.3	4.7
Tallmadge (city)	2.57	42.8	93.0	3.5
Toledo (city)	2.39	34.2	93.1	3.0
Trotwood (city)	2.42	39.3	83.9	1.2
Troy (city)	2.42	36.3	95.4	2.1
Twinsburg (city)	2.53	37.9	92.5	4.1
Upper Arlington (city)	2.40	44.2	90.0	6.3
Wadsworth (city)	2.49	38.0	93.1	2.5
Warren (city)	2.39	37.1	87.3	1.9
Westerville (city)	2.73	38.5	91.0	3.2
Westlake (city)	2.43	43.8	89.5	8.4
Whitehall (city)	2.27	35.8	94.5	5.9
Willoughby (city)	2.15	40.3	86.3	3.7
Wooster (city)	2.44	36.4	92.2	3.3
Xenia (city)	2.52	35.1	91.2	1.9
Youngstown (city)	2.52	36.7	92.9	2.0
Zanesville (city)	2.39	35.5	86.6	0.9

NOTE: Average Household Size, Median Age, and Male/Female Ratio figures as of 2005. Foreign Born figures as of 2000.

Five Largest Ancestry Groups

Place	Group 1	Group 2	Group 3	Group 4	Group 5
Akron (city)	Other (29.9%)	German (18.1%)	Irish (11.5%)	English (7.2%)	Italian (6.8%)
Alliance (city)	German (22.5%)	Other (14.9%)	Irish (11.8%)	Italian (9.9%)	English (9.5%)
Ashland (city)	German (31.5%)	Irish (11.7%)	American (11.3%)	English (10.8%)	Other (7.0%)
Ashtabula (city)	Other (18.7%)	German (16.9%)	Italian (15.0%)	Irish (11.5%)	English (9.2%)
Athens (city)	German (28.3%)	Irish (17.1%)	Other (12.6%)	English (10.6%)	Italian (8.3%)
Austintown (CDP)	German (26.1%)	Italian (19.3%)	Irish (17.8%)	Other (9.3%)	English (9.2%)
Avon Lake (city)	German (36.2%)	Irish (22.7%)	English (13.9%)	Italian (11.4%)	Polish (7.3%)
Barberton (city)	German (23.9%)	Irish (13.1%)	Other (11.4%)	American (10.1%)	English (7.1%)
Beavercreek (city)	German (30.2%)	Irish (14.4%)	English (14.3%)	American (10.3%)	Other (8.8%)
Berea (city)	German (27.8%)	Irish (17.8%)	English (13.5%)	Polish (10.7%)	Italian (9.8%)
Boardman (CDP)	Italian (26.5%)	German (20.8%)	Irish (17.7%)	English (9.6%)	Slovak (9.5%)
Bowling Green (city)	German (31.4%)	Irish (11.7%)	English (10.6%)	Other (10.2%)	American (5.1%)
Brook Park (city)	German (26.5%)	Irish (18.5%)	Polish (14.1%)	Italian (13.2%)	English (7.2%)
Brunswick (city)	German (29.0%)	Irish (18.7%)	Polish (12.6%)	Italian (11.7%)	English (8.3%)
Canton (city)	Other (25.0%)	German (21.5%)	Irish (11.4%)	Italian (8.6%)	English (6.9%)
Centerville (city)	German (34.1%)	Irish (17.7%)	English (14.9%)	Other (9.8%)	American (6.2%)
Chillicothe (city)	German (22.0%)	American (13.9%)	Other (13.4%)	Irish (11.8%)	English (10.5%)
Cincinnati (city)	Other (40.7%)	German (19.9%)	Irish (10.4%)	English (5.4%)	American (4.8%)
Cleveland (city)	Other (50.9%)	German (9.2%)	Irish (8.1%)	Polish (4.8%)	Italian (4.6%)
Cleveland Heights (city)	Other (44.5%)	German (12.1%)	Irish (10.3%)	English (7.5%)	Italian (5.8%)
Columbus (city)	Other (30.0%)	German (19.4%)	Irish (11.7%)	English (7.9%)	American (7.2%)
Cuyahoga Falls (city)	German (31.0%)	Irish (17.4%)	English (13.0%)	Italian (12.4%)	Other (6.7%)
Dayton (city)	Other (40.1%)	German (14.4%)	Irish (8.3%)	American (7.7%)	English (4.9%)
Delaware (city)	German (25.7%)	Irish (11.8%)	English (11.4%)	Other (10.1%)	American (9.0%)
Dublin (city)	German (31.3%)	Irish (17.0%)	Other (12.9%)	English (12.3%)	Italian (9.4%)
East Cleveland (city)	Other (80.1%)	African (1.1%)	American (1.1%)	German (0.7%)	Italian (0.6%)
Eastlake (city)	German (24.3%)	Irish (20.3%)	Italian (17.0%)	English (9.8%)	Polish (9.6%)
Elyria (city)	German (23.8%)	Other (20.3%)	Irish (14.3%)	English (10.9%)	Polish (7.5%)
Euclid (city)	Other (29.9%)	German (15.2%)	Irish (12.6%)	Italian (9.6%)	Slovene (8.8%)
Fairborn (city)	German (21.1%)	Other (17.6%)	Irish (12.1%)	American (10.4%)	English (10.2%)
Fairfield (city)	German (31.7%)	Irish (14.4%)	Other (12.9%)	English (11.2%)	American (9.0%)
Findlay (city)	German (35.5%)	Irish (10.7%)	English (10.6%)	American (9.5%)	Other (9.5%)
Forest Park (city)	Other (54.5%)	German (14.6%)	Irish (6.6%)	English (5.8%)	American (3.7%)
Gahanna (city)	German (26.3%)	Other (16.0%)	Irish (14.4%)	English (12.9%)	American (7.8%)
Garfield Heights (city)	Polish (26.1%)	Other (17.4%)	German (14.9%)	Italian (14.0%)	Irish (10.2%)
Green (city)	German (28.3%)	Irish (16.4%)	English (10.9%)	American (9.1%)	Italian (7.8%)
Grove City (city)	German (29.6%)	Irish (16.8%)	American (12.0%)	English (11.3%)	Other (7.4%)
Hamilton (city)	German (21.6%)	American (15.0%)	Other (14.7%)	Irish (11.8%)	English (8.6%)
Hilliard (city)	German (30.1%)	Irish (17.2%)	English (12.7%)	Other (8.4%)	American (8.3%)
Huber Heights (city)	German (24.9%)	Other (18.0%)	Irish (11.5%)	English (10.3%)	American (9.7%)
Hudson (city)	German (30.1%)	Irish (19.8%)	English (17.4%)	Italian (10.6%)	Polish (7.3%)
Kent (city)	German (26.0%)	Other (15.2%)	Irish (15.0%)	English (11.0%)	Italian (10.8%)
Kettering (city)	German (33.8%)	Irish (15.5%)	English (12.7%)	American (8.6%)	Other (8.6%)
Lakewood (city)	German (25.2%)	Irish (23.6%)	English (9.8%)	Italian (8.9%)	Polish (7.8%)
Lancaster (city)	German (27.6%)	American (15.2%)	Irish (13.4%)	English (8.8%)	Other (8.2%)
Lebanon (city)	German (20.5%)	American (15.5%)	Irish (11.5%)	English (9.0%)	Other (7.6%)
Lima (city)	Other (27.6%)	German (20.9%)	Irish (11.0%)	American (9.6%)	English (5.2%)
Lorain (city)	Other (36.9%)	German (16.0%)	Irish (11.0%)	Polish (7.8%)	Italian (6.7%)
Mansfield (city)	German (22.4%)	Other (21.7%)	Irish (10.0%)	American (9.0%)	English (7.9%)
Maple Heights (city)	Other (42.4%)	Italian (10.0%)	Polish (9.9%)	German (8.6%)	Irish (6.4%)

PROFILES OF OHIO / Comparative Statistics

Place	Group 1	Group 2	Group 3	Group 4	Group 5
Marion (city)	American (18.6%)	German (17.5%)	Other (13.1%)	Irish (9.5%)	English (7.7%)
Mason (city)	German (33.5%)	Irish (18.3%)	English (14.0%)	Other (9.3%)	American (8.2%)
Massillon (city)	German (33.6%)	Irish (13.5%)	Other (12.8%)	English (8.3%)	Italian (7.1%)
Mayfield Heights (city)	Italian (26.1%)	German (15.4%)	Other (12.6%)	Irish (9.0%)	Russian (6.8%)
Medina (city)	German (32.7%)	Irish (16.7%)	English (11.9%)	Italian (9.6%)	Polish (8.8%)
Mentor (city)	German (26.6%)	Irish (19.5%)	Italian (16.2%)	English (12.8%)	Polish (8.4%)
Miamisburg (city)	German (26.5%)	American (12.9%)	Irish (12.4%)	English (11.0%)	Other (8.0%)
Middletown (city)	Other (17.2%)	German (16.9%)	American (15.4%)	Irish (11.5%)	English (10.0%)
Newark (city)	German (23.1%)	Irish (14.4%)	American (13.6%)	English (10.8%)	Other (8.5%)
Niles (city)	Italian (23.9%)	German (21.4%)	Irish (17.5%)	English (10.6%)	Other (7.4%)
North Olmsted (city)	German (29.9%)	Irish (22.8%)	Italian (10.7%)	Polish (9.9%)	English (9.6%)
North Ridgeville (city)	German (32.9%)	Irish (19.2%)	English (12.6%)	Polish (10.7%)	Italian (9.0%)
North Royalton (city)	German (25.4%)	Polish (18.4%)	Irish (14.0%)	Italian (12.3%)	English (8.3%)
Norwood (city)	German (28.2%)	Irish (19.0%)	Other (11.7%)	American (10.5%)	English (9.8%)
Oregon (city)	German (33.8%)	Irish (10.9%)	Other (9.9%)	Polish (8.9%)	English (7.8%)
Oxford (city)	German (31.6%)	Irish (15.9%)	Other (11.1%)	English (10.8%)	Italian (8.2%)
Painesville (city)	Other (26.7%)	German (18.7%)	Irish (13.7%)	English (10.5%)	Italian (9.3%)
Parma (city)	German (24.5%)	Polish (18.1%)	Irish (14.6%)	Italian (13.5%)	Slovak (9.3%)
Parma Heights (city)	German (25.0%)	Irish (16.3%)	Polish (13.1%)	Italian (12.0%)	Slovak (7.8%)
Piqua (city)	German (28.1%)	American (14.6%)	Irish (10.7%)	Other (10.4%)	English (8.2%)
Portsmouth (city)	German (16.7%)	American (15.9%)	Other (12.8%)	Irish (12.5%)	English (10.0%)
Reynoldsburg (city)	German (26.8%)	Other (17.1%)	Irish (14.5%)	English (10.7%)	American (8.6%)
Riverside (city)	German (22.3%)	Other (15.8%)	American (14.4%)	Irish (13.4%)	English (9.1%)
Rocky River (city)	German (28.1%)	Irish (26.9%)	English (12.4%)	Italian (9.4%)	Polish (6.6%)
Sandusky (city)	German (32.1%)	Other (24.7%)	Irish (12.4%)	English (7.8%)	Italian (7.4%)
Shaker Heights (city)	Other (36.6%)	German (13.2%)	Irish (9.4%)	English (9.2%)	Russian (5.1%)
Sidney (city)	German (31.4%)	American (15.6%)	Other (11.2%)	Irish (10.9%)	English (9.1%)
Solon (city)	German (16.8%)	Italian (14.5%)	Other (13.8%)	Irish (11.6%)	Polish (10.0%)
South Euclid (city)	Other (25.6%)	Italian (15.4%)	German (13.9%)	Irish (13.7%)	Russian (6.1%)
Springfield (city)	Other (21.9%)	German (17.9%)	American (13.8%)	Irish (10.4%)	English (6.5%)
Steubenville (city)	Italian (18.9%)	Other (18.3%)	German (12.9%)	Irish (12.7%)	Polish (6.9%)
Stow (city)	German (29.7%)	Irish (17.7%)	English (14.3%)	Italian (12.0%)	Other (7.5%)
Strongsville (city)	German (29.1%)	Irish (18.0%)	Italian (13.4%)	Polish (12.6%)	English (10.7%)
Sylvania (city)	German (32.8%)	Irish (15.6%)	English (11.4%)	Polish (10.7%)	Other (6.7%)
Tallmadge (city)	German (29.0%)	Irish (16.4%)	English (13.1%)	Italian (12.0%)	American (8.0%)
Toledo (city)	Other (29.0%)	German (23.4%)	Irish (10.8%)	Polish (10.1%)	English (6.0%)
Trotwood (city)	Other (53.5%)	German (8.2%)	American (7.6%)	Irish (4.6%)	English (3.4%)
Troy (city)	German (25.3%)	American (14.6%)	Other (11.7%)	Irish (11.4%)	English (8.0%)
Twinsburg (city)	German (23.1%)	Other (15.0%)	Italian (15.0%)	Irish (14.1%)	Polish (11.4%)
Upper Arlington (city)	German (30.6%)	English (19.2%)	Irish (15.1%)	Other (7.7%)	Italian (6.8%)
Wadsworth (city)	German (34.5%)	Irish (15.8%)	English (11.7%)	Italian (8.7%)	American (7.5%)
Warren (city)	Other (25.3%)	German (15.2%)	Irish (11.6%)	Italian (10.3%)	English (7.5%)
Westerville (city)	German (29.6%)	Irish (15.4%)	English (14.3%)	American (9.1%)	Other (8.6%)
Westlake (city)	German (26.2%)	Irish (23.3%)	Italian (11.6%)	English (10.0%)	Other (8.2%)
Whitehall (city)	Other (25.0%)	German (18.5%)	Irish (12.5%)	American (12.1%)	English (7.4%)
Willoughby (city)	German (26.4%)	Irish (18.9%)	Italian (15.6%)	English (11.3%)	Polish (6.5%)
Wooster (city)	German (30.4%)	Irish (13.6%)	English (11.9%)	Other (9.5%)	American (8.1%)
Xenia (city)	Other (20.1%)	German (16.8%)	American (14.3%)	Irish (10.4%)	English (8.8%)
Youngstown (city)	Other (42.7%)	Italian (11.2%)	German (10.3%)	Irish (9.4%)	Slovak (5.3%)
Zanesville (city)	Other (16.7%)	American (15.1%)	German (14.6%)	Irish (10.4%)	English (7.4%)

NOTE: Data as of 2000; "Other" includes Hispanic and race groups. Please refer to the Explanation of Data for more information.

Marriage Status

Place	Never Married (%)	Now Married (%)	Widowed (%)	Divorced (%)
Akron (city)	33.0	45.2	8.0	13.8
Alliance (city)	31.4	48.1	8.4	12.0
Ashland (city)	26.6	54.8	8.1	10.5
Ashtabula (city)	27.4	49.1	9.8	13.8
Athens (city)	70.0	24.6	2.3	3.1
Austintown (CDP)	24.8	55.5	8.5	11.2
Avon Lake (city)	18.2	68.7	5.3	7.8
Barberton (city)	25.3	52.2	9.5	13.0
Beavercreek (city)	19.1	69.3	4.8	6.8
Berea (city)	33.1	48.7	7.3	10.9
Boardman (CDP)	23.7	55.6	10.7	10.0
Bowling Green (city)	54.7	35.8	3.7	5.8
Brook Park (city)	23.8	58.2	8.4	9.5
Brunswick (city)	22.7	63.6	5.1	8.7
Canton (city)	31.0	45.8	8.9	14.2
Centerville (city)	20.2	61.7	7.9	10.1
Chillicothe (city)	23.2	51.3	11.2	14.2
Cincinnati (city)	42.4	37.9	7.6	12.1
Cleveland (city)	38.9	38.2	9.0	13.9
Cleveland Heights (city)	36.7	47.5	6.1	9.7
Columbus (city)	38.3	44.0	5.4	12.4
Cuyahoga Falls (city)	24.5	56.1	8.3	11.2
Dayton (city)	38.7	39.2	7.8	14.3
Delaware (city)	25.3	57.4	5.8	11.5
Dublin (city)	18.9	72.2	2.9	6.0
East Cleveland (city)	42.3	32.0	10.5	15.3
Eastlake (city)	25.3	57.6	6.8	10.4
Elyria (city)	26.6	52.9	7.0	13.6
Euclid (city)	30.3	45.8	10.4	13.5
Fairborn (city)	33.1	48.8	5.7	12.4
Fairfield (city)	25.3	59.1	5.0	10.6
Findlay (city)	25.5	56.5	7.1	10.9
Forest Park (city)	29.3	53.8	5.5	11.4
Gahanna (city)	21.6	63.5	4.8	10.2
Garfield Heights (city)	26.6	52.8	10.4	10.2
Green (city)	20.8	63.0	6.5	9.7
Grove City (city)	20.7	62.7	5.9	10.7
Hamilton (city)	24.7	52.5	8.6	14.2
Hilliard (city)	19.8	68.1	3.6	8.4
Huber Heights (city)	22.6	61.3	5.0	11.1
Hudson (city)	17.7	73.6	4.6	4.1
Kent (city)	57.7	30.4	4.1	7.8
Kettering (city)	23.7	56.9	8.1	11.3
Lakewood (city)	38.3	43.1	6.5	12.1
Lancaster (city)	22.2	55.9	8.3	13.6
Lebanon (city)	19.8	59.3	5.7	15.2
Lima (city)	33.6	43.0	8.5	14.9
Lorain (city)	28.3	50.5	8.4	12.8
Mansfield (city)	27.2	49.2	9.1	14.5
Maple Heights (city)	27.4	52.1	10.0	10.6

PROFILES OF OHIO / Comparative Statistics

Place	Never Married (%)	Now Married (%)	Widowed (%)	Divorced (%)
Marion (city)	26.0	50.4	8.1	15.5
Mason (city)	18.1	69.2	4.5	8.1
Massillon (city)	23.0	56.2	8.2	12.7
Mayfield Heights (city)	24.4	50.7	14.0	10.9
Medina (city)	20.3	64.5	6.6	8.7
Mentor (city)	21.5	62.5	6.8	9.2
Miamisburg (city)	19.9	64.0	5.7	10.4
Middletown (city)	23.7	53.5	8.3	14.6
Newark (city)	23.4	53.8	8.2	14.6
Niles (city)	22.7	55.7	9.1	12.6
North Olmsted (city)	23.9	59.6	7.3	9.2
North Ridgeville (city)	21.7	63.8	6.4	8.1
North Royalton (city)	24.8	59.8	6.9	8.5
Norwood (city)	34.0	44.5	8.1	13.5
Oregon (city)	22.9	59.7	7.7	9.7
Oxford (city)	70.4	24.1	2.4	3.2
Painesville (city)	29.7	50.5	7.3	12.5
Parma (city)	24.7	57.0	9.7	8.7
Parma Heights (city)	23.6	53.1	12.3	10.9
Piqua (city)	22.6	55.1	8.7	13.6
Portsmouth (city)	24.4	48.8	11.5	15.2
Reynoldsburg (city)	23.5	58.4	5.4	12.8
Riverside (city)	24.2	55.1	7.4	13.3
Rocky River (city)	21.0	57.3	11.4	10.3
Sandusky (city)	29.0	48.9	9.1	13.0
Shaker Heights (city)	25.5	56.3	7.6	10.6
Sidney (city)	22.1	57.8	8.0	12.0
Solon (city)	18.9	68.4	5.2	7.5
South Euclid (city)	26.1	55.2	8.0	10.8
Springfield (city)	29.0	47.6	9.7	13.6
Steubenville (city)	26.6	51.4	11.3	10.7
Stow (city)	21.8	63.5	5.5	9.3
Strongsville (city)	20.7	66.9	5.3	7.2
Sylvania (city)	20.9	63.1	7.8	8.2
Tallmadge (city)	21.0	63.7	7.4	8.0
Toledo (city)	33.0	45.9	7.8	13.3
Trotwood (city)	27.9	49.4	8.9	13.7
Troy (city)	21.0	57.6	7.2	14.1
Twinsburg (city)	18.8	67.2	6.8	7.2
Upper Arlington (city)	20.2	63.8	7.7	8.3
Wadsworth (city)	17.9	65.0	8.3	8.8
Warren (city)	26.7	49.5	9.0	14.8
Westerville (city)	24.6	63.2	4.7	7.5
Westlake (city)	21.4	61.0	9.1	8.5
Whitehall (city)	30.8	45.3	7.0	16.9
Willoughby (city)	26.0	49.9	9.8	14.4
Wooster (city)	29.3	51.5	6.7	12.5
Xenia (city)	23.5	56.8	7.0	12.7
Youngstown (city)	34.0	42.2	11.0	12.8
Zanesville (city)	25.5	49.1	9.6	15.8

NOTE: Data as of 2000

Employment and Building Permits Issued

Place	Unemployment Rate (%)	Total Civilian Labor Force	Single-Family Building Permits	Multi-Family Building Permits
Akron (city)	6.6	107,195	269	218
Alliance (city)	n/a	n/a	65	0
Ashland (city)	n/a	n/a	41	128
Ashtabula (city)	n/a	n/a	3	0
Athens (city)	n/a	n/a	15	5
Austintown (CDP)	n/a	n/a	n/a	n/a
Avon Lake (city)	n/a	n/a	307	6
Barberton (city)	6.8	13,565	65	0
Beavercreek (city)	4.5	20,493	n/a	n/a
Berea (city)	n/a	n/a	100	0
Boardman (CDP)	n/a	n/a	n/a	n/a
Bowling Green (city)	4.4	16,089	n/a	n/a
Brook Park (city)	5.9	10,778	8	0
Brunswick (city)	4.9	19,710	71	0
Canton (city)	7.7	36,389	80	0
Centerville (city)	n/a	n/a	71	0
Chillicothe (city)	n/a	n/a	30	0
Cincinnati (city)	6.4	157,193	190	426
Cleveland (city)	7.9	191,940	345	98
Cleveland Heights (city)	4.6	27,735	6	0
Columbus (city)	5.4	408,548	2,360	2,224
Cuyahoga Falls (city)	5.2	28,425	86	28
Dayton (city)	7.6	71,169	215	0
Delaware (city)	4.6	15,895	348	67
Dublin (city)	3.6	18,067	375	381
East Cleveland (city)	8.3	9,959	2	0
Eastlake (city)	n/a	n/a	24	0
Elyria (city)	5.8	29,371	75	61
Euclid (city)	6.2	26,000	9	0
Fairborn (city)	6.2	16,478	96	60
Fairfield (city)	4.8	25,057	93	0
Findlay (city)	4.8	22,138	138	0
Forest Park (city)	n/a	n/a	10	0
Gahanna (city)	4.4	18,395	113	0
Garfield Heights (city)	6.5	15,007	18	0
Green (city)	n/a	n/a	n/a	n/a
Grove City (city)	4.7	16,710	463	68
Hamilton (city)	6.0	29,771	171	119
Hilliard (city)	3.7	14,856	156	0
Huber Heights (city)	5.7	19,889	n/a	n/a
Hudson (city)	n/a	n/a	n/a	n/a
Kent (city)	4.7	16,719	52	27
Kettering (city)	5.4	29,632	12	12
Lakewood (city)	5.0	32,809	1	0
Lancaster (city)	6.3	18,286	121	142
Lebanon (city)	n/a	n/a	142	57
Lima (city)	7.1	17,558	6	3
Lorain (city)	6.9	31,475	150	0
Mansfield (city)	6.7	23,157	57	47
Maple Heights (city)	6.4	12,872	14	0

PROFILES OF OHIO / Comparative Statistics

Place	Unemployment Rate (%)	Total Civilian Labor Force	Single-Family Building Permits	Multi-Family Building Permits
Marion (city)	6.2	17,407	53	0
Mason (city)	3.5	15,001	305	0
Massillon (city)	6.5	15,750	164	54
Mayfield Heights (city)	n/a	n/a	44	0
Medina (city)	4.5	14,123	32	16
Mentor (city)	4.5	29,968	73	0
Miamisburg (city)	n/a	n/a	129	0
Middletown (city)	6.1	26,152	34	22
Newark (city)	6.2	23,373	722	314
Niles (city)	n/a	n/a	7	0
North Olmsted (city)	4.8	18,683	36	0
North Ridgeville (city)	4.5	14,950	539	22
North Royalton (city)	4.6	17,397	174	35
Norwood (city)	5.9	11,015	0	0
Oregon (city)	n/a	n/a	63	0
Oxford (city)	n/a	n/a	38	17
Painesville (city)	n/a	n/a	111	18
Parma (city)	5.7	43,325	31	7
Parma Heights (city)	n/a	n/a	12	0
Piqua (city)	n/a	n/a	n/a	n/a
Portsmouth (city)	n/a	n/a	0	54
Reynoldsburg (city)	5.1	18,680	112	0
Riverside (city)	7.2	11,087	n/a	n/a
Rocky River (city)	n/a	n/a	38	0
Sandusky (city)	7.2	14,598	29	0
Shaker Heights (city)	4.7	15,166	34	0
Sidney (city)	n/a	n/a	50	30
Solon (city)	n/a	n/a	127	2
South Euclid (city)	5.1	12,691	6	0
Springfield (city)	7.1	29,055	20	6
Steubenville (city)	n/a	n/a	4	0
Stow (city)	4.5	19,586	106	6
Strongsville (city)	3.7	24,977	79	0
Sylvania (city)	n/a	n/a	n/a	n/a
Tallmadge (city)	n/a	n/a	46	8
Toledo (city)	7.5	146,455	120	135
Trotwood (city)	8.0	12,070	93	0
Troy (city)	n/a	n/a	n/a	n/a
Twinsburg (city)	n/a	n/a	110	0
Upper Arlington (city)	4.2	16,584	16	20
Wadsworth (city)	n/a	n/a	146	0
Warren (city)	7.4	19,786	19	12
Westerville (city)	4.3	19,439	68	114
Westlake (city)	4.4	16,715	90	29
Whitehall (city)	n/a	n/a	1	0
Willoughby (city)	n/a	n/a	82	29
Wooster (city)	4.9	14,138	87	62
Xenia (city)	6.9	11,375	n/a	n/a
Youngstown (city)	8.7	30,249	9	0
Zanesville (city)	8.5	10,717	1	0

NOTE: Unemployment Rate and Civilian Labor Force are 2005 annual averages; Building permit data covers 2005; n/a not available.

Employment by Occupation

Place	Sales	Professional	Management	Services	Production	Construction
Akron (city)	28.3	17.0	9.0	18.3	19.6	7.7
Alliance (city)	25.5	13.6	7.2	17.7	27.9	7.4
Ashland (city)	24.8	17.9	9.6	15.5	24.9	6.8
Ashtabula (city)	23.7	13.1	6.6	19.4	28.5	8.4
Athens (city)	24.8	37.4	8.2	22.5	4.7	2.3
Austintown (CDP)	29.4	16.8	8.1	15.3	22.2	8.1
Avon Lake (city)	27.1	25.5	20.6	9.4	10.2	7.1
Barberton (city)	27.4	12.1	8.0	17.5	24.1	10.7
Beavercreek (city)	25.4	32.3	18.9	8.9	9.0	5.4
Berea (city)	33.5	21.4	12.1	13.3	12.8	6.7
Boardman (CDP)	30.5	20.0	14.0	14.5	14.0	7.0
Bowling Green (city)	24.6	26.1	9.9	21.2	14.2	3.7
Brook Park (city)	30.1	12.3	9.7	16.0	20.6	11.3
Brunswick (city)	28.1	18.0	13.0	12.6	17.0	11.1
Canton (city)	26.3	13.1	8.4	20.0	24.1	7.9
Centerville (city)	28.3	32.8	18.8	9.7	6.6	3.9
Chillicothe (city)	24.7	21.5	9.3	17.3	21.1	6.1
Cincinnati (city)	26.3	23.2	12.6	17.9	13.5	6.4
Cleveland (city)	26.7	14.3	8.2	20.9	22.3	7.5
Cleveland Heights (city)	22.6	38.2	15.3	12.0	8.6	3.3
Columbus (city)	30.1	21.5	13.9	15.2	12.7	6.5
Cuyahoga Falls (city)	30.6	21.2	13.3	13.5	13.9	7.5
Dayton (city)	25.3	17.1	8.6	21.1	20.0	7.8
Delaware (city)	28.0	22.3	15.1	13.1	14.7	6.5
Dublin (city)	28.3	29.9	29.9	6.5	3.3	2.0
East Cleveland (city)	27.2	13.8	6.6	27.4	19.0	6.0
Eastlake (city)	28.7	15.2	8.6	14.4	23.0	10.2
Elyria (city)	24.9	15.7	8.3	17.2	24.3	9.4
Euclid (city)	30.8	18.7	11.9	15.2	16.5	6.8
Fairborn (city)	27.4	20.1	10.7	18.9	13.8	9.0
Fairfield (city)	30.6	23.5	15.9	10.4	12.4	7.1
Findlay (city)	22.7	17.6	12.5	15.0	24.0	8.0
Forest Park (city)	30.6	21.8	12.5	14.3	16.6	4.2
Gahanna (city)	29.7	25.7	20.7	10.1	8.1	5.7
Garfield Heights (city)	34.6	14.2	9.7	15.1	18.3	8.0
Green (city)	27.4	20.5	14.7	12.6	15.4	9.2
Grove City (city)	32.6	18.2	15.8	13.1	11.6	8.6
Hamilton (city)	28.0	13.7	8.8	16.7	21.8	10.8
Hilliard (city)	27.9	27.3	19.4	10.9	8.4	6.1
Huber Heights (city)	27.5	17.8	12.3	13.9	19.9	8.5
Hudson (city)	27.1	28.9	29.8	7.2	4.4	2.5
Kent (city)	29.0	22.9	9.3	20.9	13.1	4.8
Kettering (city)	28.8	24.2	15.3	12.0	13.0	6.5
Lakewood (city)	28.0	25.1	15.9	13.8	10.4	6.7
Lancaster (city)	29.2	14.7	9.1	17.1	18.5	11.4
Lebanon (city)	27.8	20.1	13.5	12.1	17.6	8.9
Lima (city)	22.0	12.0	6.4	20.8	29.9	8.5
Lorain (city)	25.7	13.0	7.4	16.7	27.0	9.6
Mansfield (city)	23.7	15.3	7.9	19.1	25.8	8.2
Maple Heights (city)	30.6	15.5	9.7	14.8	21.9	7.2

Place	Sales	Professional	Management	Services	Production	Construction
Marion (city)	25.9	11.9	7.3	17.6	28.9	8.0
Mason (city)	29.7	23.2	20.8	9.5	11.7	5.0
Massillon (city)	26.1	13.9	8.3	16.5	27.1	7.9
Mayfield Heights (city)	31.5	23.5	14.5	14.0	9.3	7.1
Medina (city)	29.8	21.2	15.0	12.1	14.3	7.4
Mentor (city)	28.7	20.8	15.3	11.1	16.9	7.0
Miamisburg (city)	30.2	19.3	11.9	13.4	16.7	8.5
Middletown (city)	25.5	16.0	8.3	16.3	24.2	9.6
Newark (city)	28.3	14.1	9.6	18.0	20.9	9.0
Niles (city)	26.7	13.9	7.7	17.9	25.9	7.8
North Olmsted (city)	30.6	21.6	16.1	12.4	11.8	7.3
North Ridgeville (city)	29.8	16.2	11.3	12.8	18.1	11.4
North Royalton (city)	30.1	19.9	17.2	11.6	12.7	8.4
Norwood (city)	28.4	14.6	9.2	17.3	20.3	10.2
Oregon (city)	25.2	17.5	11.2	13.3	21.4	11.0
Oxford (city)	24.1	31.3	8.3	25.6	7.0	3.7
Painesville (city)	25.7	13.0	7.2	17.8	24.5	9.2
Parma (city)	31.9	17.7	12.3	14.2	15.3	8.6
Parma Heights (city)	35.0	18.3	12.2	12.2	14.3	7.9
Piqua (city)	26.4	10.0	9.2	15.1	30.6	8.3
Portsmouth (city)	24.3	20.3	8.8	21.6	15.3	8.9
Reynoldsburg (city)	31.7	20.1	15.9	13.8	11.8	6.6
Riverside (city)	27.5	15.2	9.1	15.8	21.6	10.5
Rocky River (city)	32.2	27.3	21.7	9.6	5.4	3.8
Sandusky (city)	24.9	12.0	7.0	21.1	27.1	7.8
Shaker Heights (city)	21.7	42.1	21.2	7.7	5.5	1.7
Sidney (city)	19.2	13.8	10.9	14.5	33.3	8.1
Solon (city)	28.5	30.4	22.8	7.9	6.4	3.9
South Euclid (city)	31.4	27.2	13.1	12.7	10.4	5.1
Springfield (city)	25.2	16.0	8.5	17.9	24.1	8.1
Steubenville (city)	27.2	21.5	9.4	19.9	14.6	7.1
Stow (city)	27.2	26.5	15.8	11.9	12.5	6.1
Strongsville (city)	30.8	22.4	19.9	10.1	10.4	6.3
Sylvania (city)	26.9	30.8	15.7	10.9	9.8	5.6
Tallmadge (city)	29.7	22.6	11.6	12.2	13.2	10.6
Toledo (city)	26.7	16.7	9.0	17.9	21.3	8.3
Trotwood (city)	27.2	15.5	9.2	15.8	25.1	7.3
Troy (city)	24.7	18.5	12.7	13.5	25.1	5.1
Twinsburg (city)	28.9	23.0	21.1	10.4	10.6	6.0
Upper Arlington (city)	24.7	39.9	24.2	6.2	2.9	2.0
Wadsworth (city)	25.7	19.7	15.3	14.2	15.6	9.3
Warren (city)	23.3	13.4	7.8	19.0	28.1	8.3
Westerville (city)	29.8	26.0	21.6	10.8	7.0	4.7
Westlake (city)	27.8	26.4	26.5	8.8	5.8	4.7
Whitehall (city)	37.2	10.1	6.6	19.9	16.3	9.9
Willoughby (city)	28.1	19.7	15.0	13.0	16.1	7.9
Wooster (city)	25.5	21.4	11.4	14.6	21.2	5.6
Xenia (city)	26.0	16.3	9.0	17.9	20.5	10.3
Youngstown (city)	25.5	13.1	5.7	24.1	24.2	7.2
Zanesville (city)	25.4	17.4	5.4	18.2	25.7	7.5

NOTE: Data as of 2000

Educational Attainment

Place	Percent of Population 25 Years and Over with: High School Diploma including Equivalency	Bachelor's Degree or Higher	Masters's Degree or Higher
Akron (city)	80.1	18.4	6.2
Alliance (city)	79.7	13.7	5.3
Ashland (city)	83.6	19.7	6.8
Ashtabula (city)	77.5	10.4	3.1
Athens (city)	92.9	61.4	35.1
Austintown (CDP)	85.3	15.7	4.3
Avon Lake (city)	94.8	42.6	15.8
Barberton (city)	79.1	10.6	3.3
Beavercreek (city)	92.7	43.8	21.2
Berea (city)	89.1	28.9	9.7
Boardman (CDP)	89.1	24.4	7.7
Bowling Green (city)	91.0	43.8	21.8
Brook Park (city)	80.7	9.8	2.5
Brunswick (city)	87.3	19.4	4.2
Canton (city)	75.3	12.2	4.1
Centerville (city)	95.5	45.7	17.8
Chillicothe (city)	77.3	17.1	6.9
Cincinnati (city)	77.0	27.0	10.4
Cleveland (city)	69.1	11.7	3.9
Cleveland Heights (city)	91.6	50.0	25.3
Columbus (city)	84.4	29.8	9.3
Cuyahoga Falls (city)	90.9	25.7	7.8
Dayton (city)	75.5	14.8	5.0
Delaware (city)	88.2	26.9	8.2
Dublin (city)	97.2	63.7	22.3
East Cleveland (city)	69.1	8.9	3.7
Eastlake (city)	82.8	12.5	3.3
Elyria (city)	82.1	13.3	4.3
Euclid (city)	82.1	19.7	5.8
Fairborn (city)	84.2	22.8	9.2
Fairfield (city)	89.1	27.6	8.3
Findlay (city)	87.5	23.9	8.0
Forest Park (city)	88.5	26.5	7.5
Gahanna (city)	93.6	40.9	13.9
Garfield Heights (city)	80.1	11.9	3.3
Green (city)	88.9	26.3	7.6
Grove City (city)	89.2	23.2	5.6
Hamilton (city)	73.6	12.4	3.7
Hilliard (city)	92.6	46.2	14.5
Huber Heights (city)	88.4	19.1	6.7
Hudson (city)	97.3	66.6	26.0
Kent (city)	91.6	37.8	16.3
Kettering (city)	91.0	31.1	11.3
Lakewood (city)	88.7	35.8	12.1
Lancaster (city)	83.5	13.5	4.5
Lebanon (city)	86.0	25.2	6.2
Lima (city)	75.8	9.8	3.1
Lorain (city)	74.3	10.0	3.5
Mansfield (city)	78.1	13.7	4.7
Maple Heights (city)	82.2	12.9	3.0

	Percent of Population 25 Years and Over with:		
Place	High School Diploma including Equivalency	Bachelor's Degree or Higher	Masters's Degree or Higher
Marion (city)	75.9	9.1	2.9
Mason (city)	93.9	41.1	12.8
Massillon (city)	80.7	12.5	3.6
Mayfield Heights (city)	85.7	27.7	10.7
Medina (city)	90.9	33.0	8.4
Mentor (city)	89.3	27.8	9.0
Miamisburg (city)	83.3	18.9	5.4
Middletown (city)	77.2	13.2	5.0
Newark (city)	81.1	15.0	4.6
Niles (city)	82.8	11.7	2.8
North Olmsted (city)	90.4	27.2	9.2
North Ridgeville (city)	86.0	16.3	4.3
North Royalton (city)	88.0	29.4	8.4
Norwood (city)	70.8	14.0	3.6
Oregon (city)	84.9	15.8	5.6
Oxford (city)	90.0	54.2	29.5
Painesville (city)	74.1	12.5	4.3
Parma (city)	83.4	17.9	5.2
Parma Heights (city)	82.8	18.5	5.7
Piqua (city)	75.3	10.3	3.4
Portsmouth (city)	74.0	12.4	5.2
Reynoldsburg (city)	90.5	27.3	7.7
Riverside (city)	78.5	14.9	5.1
Rocky River (city)	93.3	46.6	17.8
Sandusky (city)	79.6	11.2	3.2
Shaker Heights (city)	94.6	61.5	35.6
Sidney (city)	78.3	13.7	4.2
Solon (city)	94.6	50.7	22.1
South Euclid (city)	90.1	36.6	13.1
Springfield (city)	77.0	13.1	4.9
Steubenville (city)	79.5	18.1	7.4
Stow (city)	93.2	36.6	12.5
Strongsville (city)	93.0	37.4	13.0
Sylvania (city)	94.1	43.2	15.2
Tallmadge (city)	86.7	24.3	8.0
Toledo (city)	80.0	17.1	5.5
Trotwood (city)	78.3	15.4	6.6
Troy (city)	81.4	17.1	5.8
Twinsburg (city)	92.4	38.8	12.5
Upper Arlington (city)	97.9	67.5	29.8
Wadsworth (city)	88.5	27.3	7.2
Warren (city)	77.4	11.0	3.3
Westerville (city)	94.7	45.0	13.8
Westlake (city)	92.1	45.3	17.8
Whitehall (city)	78.7	11.4	3.9
Willoughby (city)	87.8	23.7	6.3
Wooster (city)	84.7	27.6	10.5
Xenia (city)	81.4	15.2	5.5
Youngstown (city)	73.5	9.9	2.9
Zanesville (city)	74.2	11.7	4.5

NOTE: Data as of 2005

Income and Poverty

Place	Average Household Income ($)	Median Household Income ($)	Per Capita Income ($)	Households with income of $100,000+ (%)	Poverty Rate[1] (%)
Akron (city)	45,262	35,014	19,328	6.9	17.5
Alliance (city)	41,898	33,432	16,597	5.7	18.0
Ashland (city)	45,292	36,311	18,518	7.0	10.5
Ashtabula (city)	37,328	29,914	15,252	3.7	21.4
Athens (city)	35,625	18,625	12,107	8.0	51.9
Austintown (CDP)	49,004	41,645	21,427	7.7	8.8
Avon Lake (city)	97,687	73,894	36,802	32.8	2.3
Barberton (city)	46,491	35,821	19,704	6.9	13.3
Beavercreek (city)	90,082	77,078	34,589	32.4	2.4
Berea (city)	61,592	50,164	24,047	15.4	5.5
Boardman (CDP)	56,963	45,326	25,074	11.9	5.2
Bowling Green (city)	45,422	32,946	17,149	8.4	25.3
Brook Park (city)	58,842	50,791	23,328	11.4	4.6
Brunswick (city)	67,839	61,520	24,913	16.5	4.6
Canton (city)	40,884	31,537	17,075	5.9	19.2
Centerville (city)	77,514	62,855	34,677	25.5	4.1
Chillicothe (city)	48,636	37,075	21,680	8.6	12.4
Cincinnati (city)	48,891	32,947	22,688	10.0	21.9
Cleveland (city)	38,551	28,802	15,729	5.3	26.3
Cleveland Heights (city)	69,604	51,138	29,789	18.7	10.6
Columbus (city)	54,442	43,535	23,546	11.3	14.8
Cuyahoga Falls (city)	55,238	46,583	24,759	10.6	6.1
Dayton (city)	40,766	30,864	17,218	6.3	23.0
Delaware (city)	58,258	49,704	22,923	12.4	7.3
Dublin (city)	127,531	100,490	46,334	50.2	2.7
East Cleveland (city)	31,864	22,123	13,488	3.5	32.0
Eastlake (city)	55,235	47,250	22,606	10.1	5.0
Elyria (city)	50,920	41,380	21,038	8.9	11.7
Euclid (city)	45,894	37,719	21,440	6.6	9.7
Fairborn (city)	48,137	39,896	21,122	8.4	14.1
Fairfield (city)	66,299	56,022	27,178	16.2	4.2
Findlay (city)	56,815	44,380	23,985	12.2	9.1
Forest Park (city)	62,013	53,715	24,553	13.2	6.0
Gahanna (city)	93,030	75,792	34,756	33.9	3.7
Garfield Heights (city)	51,376	43,949	21,232	7.6	8.5
Green (city)	76,973	62,036	29,922	23.1	5.0
Grove City (city)	71,489	62,611	27,376	21.0	4.6
Hamilton (city)	47,559	38,957	19,467	7.1	13.4
Hilliard (city)	96,713	83,104	34,094	37.4	2.2
Huber Heights (city)	62,175	53,461	23,990	13.2	5.9
Hudson (city)	144,936	111,037	47,846	55.4	1.7
Kent (city)	44,492	32,197	16,924	9.6	25.2
Kettering (city)	65,677	49,717	29,788	14.9	4.6
Lakewood (city)	55,969	43,940	26,934	12.0	8.9
Lancaster (city)	46,533	36,782	20,021	6.6	10.6
Lebanon (city)	63,947	52,613	23,409	17.2	6.4
Lima (city)	37,337	29,353	14,977	4.2	22.7
Lorain (city)	45,672	36,883	18,087	7.4	17.1
Mansfield (city)	44,576	33,059	19,271	7.3	16.3
Maple Heights (city)	50,170	43,831	20,351	7.0	5.9

Place	Average Household Income ($)	Median Household Income ($)	Per Capita Income ($)	Households with income of $100,000+ (%)	Poverty Rate[1] (%)
Marion (city)	45,523	37,231	18,167	6.4	13.8
Mason (city)	98,999	79,620	35,200	36.1	2.8
Massillon (city)	47,981	37,372	19,894	7.9	10.7
Mayfield Heights (city)	53,964	42,308	27,825	10.0	6.3
Medina (city)	64,382	54,397	24,975	18.1	5.7
Mentor (city)	72,932	63,664	28,146	21.8	2.7
Miamisburg (city)	67,316	55,059	26,265	18.5	6.1
Middletown (city)	50,344	39,851	21,409	9.2	12.6
Newark (city)	47,125	37,685	20,144	7.7	13.0
Niles (city)	49,289	38,234	21,586	7.5	9.6
North Olmsted (city)	68,164	59,354	27,719	19.0	4.1
North Ridgeville (city)	69,064	60,658	26,487	18.4	3.2
North Royalton (city)	77,734	64,674	30,991	25.1	2.3
Norwood (city)	46,879	36,931	20,498	8.0	12.9
Oregon (city)	61,398	50,853	24,965	15.5	4.8
Oxford (city)	46,638	27,850	13,934	12.8	43.7
Painesville (city)	43,491	37,379	16,651	5.5	16.0
Parma (city)	56,463	48,105	23,653	11.0	4.9
Parma Heights (city)	49,428	41,355	22,708	8.5	7.6
Piqua (city)	49,955	39,274	20,704	7.8	12.2
Portsmouth (city)	37,189	25,501	16,667	5.1	23.6
Reynoldsburg (city)	65,054	56,207	26,472	16.6	5.5
Riverside (city)	48,801	40,574	20,536	7.6	10.1
Rocky River (city)	81,338	57,576	38,754	23.6	2.3
Sandusky (city)	44,716	33,841	19,644	6.1	15.3
Shaker Heights (city)	105,551	70,145	44,162	33.7	6.9
Sidney (city)	51,970	41,493	21,108	9.3	11.5
Solon (city)	119,683	91,198	41,394	44.6	2.5
South Euclid (city)	60,936	53,009	25,064	13.8	4.5
Springfield (city)	44,850	34,713	18,549	7.1	16.9
Steubenville (city)	43,974	30,550	20,109	8.5	20.4
Stow (city)	74,898	64,394	29,342	22.3	4.0
Strongsville (city)	92,415	76,641	34,635	33.9	2.2
Sylvania (city)	80,594	64,476	31,469	27.6	4.2
Tallmadge (city)	62,192	53,946	29,850	15.1	4.7
Toledo (city)	45,127	35,639	19,095	7.4	17.9
Trotwood (city)	48,128	38,775	20,229	9.4	15.3
Troy (city)	51,180	41,737	21,570	8.6	8.2
Twinsburg (city)	82,330	70,750	32,852	29.2	2.1
Upper Arlington (city)	112,471	83,413	47,098	39.2	2.4
Wadsworth (city)	63,477	53,540	25,635	15.4	5.4
Warren (city)	40,580	31,618	17,225	5.2	19.4
Westerville (city)	95,398	80,266	35,243	37.5	3.5
Westlake (city)	106,718	73,366	44,475	33.3	2.5
Whitehall (city)	40,917	34,632	18,056	3.6	14.9
Willoughby (city)	57,177	47,007	26,807	11.9	5.8
Wooster (city)	55,862	40,860	23,374	11.3	10.4
Xenia (city)	46,114	40,304	18,858	6.0	11.6
Youngstown (city)	34,904	26,488	14,478	3.9	24.8
Zanesville (city)	39,281	29,863	16,617	4.6	22.4

NOTE: Data as of 2005 except for Poverty Rate which is from 2000; (1) Percentage of population with income below the poverty level

Taxes

Place	Total City Taxes Per Capita ($)	City Property Taxes Per Capita ($)
Akron (city)	680	118
Alliance (city)	390	65
Ashland (city)	n/a	n/a
Ashtabula (city)	n/a	n/a
Athens (city)	460	28
Austintown (CDP)	n/a	n/a
Avon Lake (city)	668	269
Barberton (city)	416	54
Beavercreek (city)	n/a	n/a
Berea (city)	700	225
Boardman (CDP)	n/a	n/a
Bowling Green (city)	538	64
Brook Park (city)	1,196	114
Brunswick (city)	n/a	n/a
Canton (city)	539	47
Centerville (city)	n/a	n/a
Chillicothe (city)	535	63
Cincinnati (city)	1,012	203
Cleveland (city)	822	135
Cleveland Heights (city)	640	218
Columbus (city)	724	56
Cuyahoga Falls (city)	557	189
Dayton (city)	802	127
Delaware (city)	n/a	n/a
Dublin (city)	1,801	88
East Cleveland (city)	386	72
Eastlake (city)	593	258
Elyria (city)	435	63
Euclid (city)	544	185
Fairborn (city)	294	88
Fairfield (city)	556	107
Findlay (city)	n/a	n/a
Forest Park (city)	530	200
Gahanna (city)	n/a	n/a
Garfield Heights (city)	559	251
Green (city)	n/a	n/a
Grove City (city)	n/a	n/a
Hamilton (city)	468	109
Hilliard (city)	620	44
Huber Heights (city)	385	84
Hudson (city)	576	250
Kent (city)	n/a	n/a
Kettering (city)	614	144
Lakewood (city)	537	224
Lancaster (city)	415	48
Lebanon (city)	491	126
Lima (city)	406	27
Lorain (city)	322	52
Mansfield (city)	520	46
Maple Heights (city)	472	186

Place	Total City Taxes Per Capita ($)	City Property Taxes Per Capita ($)
Marion (city)	367	32
Mason (city)	864	232
Massillon (city)	443	48
Mayfield Heights (city)	n/a	n/a
Medina (city)	n/a	n/a
Mentor (city)	634	71
Miamisburg (city)	n/a	n/a
Middletown (city)	489	133
Newark (city)	472	61
Niles (city)	n/a	n/a
North Olmsted (city)	674	296
North Ridgeville (city)	n/a	n/a
North Royalton (city)	411	134
Norwood (city)	n/a	n/a
Oregon (city)	n/a	n/a
Oxford (city)	n/a	n/a
Painesville (city)	471	36
Parma (city)	495	94
Parma Heights (city)	n/a	n/a
Piqua (city)	493	73
Portsmouth (city)	n/a	n/a
Reynoldsburg (city)	n/a	n/a
Riverside (city)	n/a	n/a
Rocky River (city)	n/a	n/a
Sandusky (city)	548	75
Shaker Heights (city)	1,071	208
Sidney (city)	n/a	n/a
Solon (city)	n/a	n/a
South Euclid (city)	485	206
Springfield (city)	482	40
Steubenville (city)	n/a	n/a
Stow (city)	601	195
Strongsville (city)	627	164
Sylvania (city)	n/a	n/a
Tallmadge (city)	562	111
Toledo (city)	573	49
Trotwood (city)	n/a	n/a
Troy (city)	594	70
Twinsburg (city)	1,140	67
Upper Arlington (city)	772	236
Wadsworth (city)	399	95
Warren (city)	463	31
Westerville (city)	835	300
Westlake (city)	847	349
Whitehall (city)	n/a	n/a
Willoughby (city)	n/a	n/a
Wooster (city)	476	98
Xenia (city)	412	67
Youngstown (city)	529	28
Zanesville (city)	n/a	n/a

NOTE: Data as of 2004.

Housing

Place	Homeownership Rate (%)	Median Home Value ($)	Median Age of Housing (years)	Median Rent ($/month)
Akron (city)	59.7	89,490	50	413
Alliance (city)	60.7	84,962	53	337
Ashland (city)	64.6	107,516	45	370
Ashtabula (city)	58.3	81,612	52	369
Athens (city)	29.6	138,848	37	423
Austintown (CDP)	67.0	100,594	34	422
Avon Lake (city)	86.3	204,622	29	572
Barberton (city)	65.0	90,511	49	380
Beavercreek (city)	83.3	166,023	27	705
Berea (city)	70.9	139,582	42	508
Boardman (CDP)	71.2	116,592	36	423
Bowling Green (city)	43.1	142,981	28	434
Brook Park (city)	83.5	129,948	38	565
Brunswick (city)	80.8	163,681	25	536
Canton (city)	59.9	79,437	55	352
Centerville (city)	74.4	158,286	24	556
Chillicothe (city)	61.7	95,788	50	345
Cincinnati (city)	39.3	113,074	52	392
Cleveland (city)	48.5	84,970	60	379
Cleveland Heights (city)	62.8	134,303	60+	580
Columbus (city)	49.5	121,834	30	490
Cuyahoga Falls (city)	65.4	125,999	43	527
Dayton (city)	53.2	76,598	51	359
Delaware (city)	61.1	153,439	25	474
Dublin (city)	75.6	279,928	9	839
East Cleveland (city)	34.9	79,053	56	397
Eastlake (city)	77.6	133,439	35	538
Elyria (city)	64.7	114,331	38	430
Euclid (city)	59.2	109,599	45	483
Fairborn (city)	51.3	105,180	34	487
Fairfield (city)	65.8	141,031	23	593
Findlay (city)	65.0	118,021	39	416
Forest Park (city)	62.2	121,582	29	613
Gahanna (city)	77.8	179,101	18	582
Garfield Heights (city)	79.7	107,963	47	483
Green (city)	80.3	164,055	26	544
Grove City (city)	74.5	145,867	23	517
Hamilton (city)	61.0	101,323	47	402
Hilliard (city)	74.7	194,290	9	653
Huber Heights (city)	72.5	108,676	29	515
Hudson (city)	90.3	267,474	20	1,131
Kent (city)	37.7	129,289	35	458
Kettering (city)	67.2	129,238	41	494
Lakewood (city)	45.1	138,852	60+	492
Lancaster (city)	59.8	116,390	43	414
Lebanon (city)	60.0	151,906	22	495
Lima (city)	57.4	64,297	51	344
Lorain (city)	61.2	104,317	43	408
Mansfield (city)	58.0	86,680	47	347
Maple Heights (city)	83.7	98,297	45	462

PROFILES OF OHIO / Comparative Statistics

Place	Homeownership Rate (%)	Median Home Value ($)	Median Age of Housing (years)	Median Rent ($/month)
Marion (city)	63.8	81,724	52	371
Mason (city)	85.9	187,711	12	527
Massillon (city)	69.4	97,639	50	356
Mayfield Heights (city)	50.5	147,058	36	624
Medina (city)	67.8	166,859	23	525
Mentor (city)	87.7	172,138	28	614
Miamisburg (city)	72.2	136,610	33	419
Middletown (city)	60.0	109,145	41	414
Newark (city)	58.2	101,508	42	394
Niles (city)	63.5	95,269	41	419
North Olmsted (city)	79.8	164,723	34	577
North Ridgeville (city)	88.8	152,071	27	463
North Royalton (city)	74.7	198,126	21	587
Norwood (city)	51.5	108,498	60+	387
Oregon (city)	74.5	137,441	34	404
Oxford (city)	34.0	153,865	27	443
Painesville (city)	52.5	113,377	46	462
Parma (city)	77.4	133,349	42	534
Parma Heights (city)	59.9	132,062	40	526
Piqua (city)	63.5	99,393	49	415
Portsmouth (city)	53.9	62,685	58	302
Reynoldsburg (city)	65.8	142,809	22	559
Riverside (city)	66.4	95,398	41	417
Rocky River (city)	71.7	208,358	41	614
Sandusky (city)	56.8	87,812	50	387
Shaker Heights (city)	65.4	217,186	55	679
Sidney (city)	62.3	104,382	38	378
Solon (city)	87.7	262,272	23	753
South Euclid (city)	84.0	127,761	47	614
Springfield (city)	57.8	81,498	50	364
Steubenville (city)	59.9	79,576	50	282
Stow (city)	71.7	163,763	25	603
Strongsville (city)	82.7	198,266	21	573
Sylvania (city)	75.5	170,713	28	445
Tallmadge (city)	80.2	160,489	33	514
Toledo (city)	60.0	85,646	48	380
Trotwood (city)	62.2	92,286	35	449
Troy (city)	60.3	123,090	37	435
Twinsburg (city)	77.1	196,871	12	687
Upper Arlington (city)	81.4	258,642	42	661
Wadsworth (city)	74.5	155,849	35	470
Warren (city)	58.8	73,233	47	355
Westerville (city)	79.2	185,276	22	530
Westlake (city)	75.4	214,769	20	781
Whitehall (city)	44.2	89,956	41	412
Willoughby (city)	59.8	147,670	30	600
Wooster (city)	60.8	123,147	35	418
Xenia (city)	66.7	94,555	35	398
Youngstown (city)	64.3	48,616	53	296
Zanesville (city)	54.7	72,386	55	318

NOTE: Homeownership Rate and Median Home Value as of 2005; Median Rent and Median Age of Housing as of 2000.

Commute to Work

Place	Automobile (%)	Public Transportation (%)	Walk (%)	Work from Home (%)
Akron (city)	91.7	3.3	2.3	2.0
Alliance (city)	90.2	1.0	6.5	1.6
Ashland (city)	90.3	0.6	5.7	2.4
Ashtabula (city)	92.6	2.1	2.9	1.6
Athens (city)	51.1	1.0	40.6	4.2
Austintown (CDP)	97.8	0.4	0.7	0.7
Avon Lake (city)	94.6	1.0	0.3	3.3
Barberton (city)	94.4	1.1	2.8	1.3
Beavercreek (city)	95.9	0.1	0.6	3.2
Berea (city)	86.6	2.8	7.1	2.7
Boardman (CDP)	96.9	0.3	0.6	2.1
Bowling Green (city)	83.7	0.6	11.9	1.7
Brook Park (city)	94.1	2.5	0.9	1.3
Brunswick (city)	95.3	1.0	0.5	2.4
Canton (city)	91.8	2.7	3.2	1.4
Centerville (city)	95.5	1.0	0.5	2.8
Chillicothe (city)	93.3	0.7	3.0	1.7
Cincinnati (city)	80.9	10.1	5.5	2.6
Cleveland (city)	81.3	12.0	4.0	1.6
Cleveland Heights (city)	85.7	5.8	3.6	3.8
Columbus (city)	89.7	3.9	3.2	2.3
Cuyahoga Falls (city)	95.1	1.0	1.4	2.2
Dayton (city)	85.2	7.0	5.3	1.6
Delaware (city)	91.2	0.4	4.1	3.3
Dublin (city)	93.3	0.4	0.5	5.4
East Cleveland (city)	75.5	17.9	3.9	1.9
Eastlake (city)	95.6	1.0	1.2	1.6
Elyria (city)	94.1	0.9	2.6	1.6
Euclid (city)	90.6	5.7	1.7	1.5
Fairborn (city)	94.5	0.3	3.4	1.1
Fairfield (city)	95.7	1.1	0.5	2.3
Findlay (city)	91.5	1.1	3.7	2.6
Forest Park (city)	92.9	2.7	1.2	2.2
Gahanna (city)	94.4	0.9	0.7	3.7
Garfield Heights (city)	92.5	3.2	2.0	1.6
Green (city)	96.4	0.5	0.5	2.1
Grove City (city)	95.1	1.1	0.9	2.0
Hamilton (city)	94.2	1.0	2.5	1.5
Hilliard (city)	93.8	0.7	0.7	4.4
Huber Heights (city)	96.2	0.9	0.7	1.7
Hudson (city)	91.8	0.4	1.1	5.9
Kent (city)	81.6	2.2	13.1	2.3
Kettering (city)	93.9	1.1	1.4	2.9
Lakewood (city)	85.1	7.8	3.6	2.6
Lancaster (city)	93.3	0.5	3.2	2.1
Lebanon (city)	94.9	0.7	1.3	2.5
Lima (city)	94.0	1.7	1.7	1.6
Lorain (city)	95.5	0.7	1.7	1.3
Mansfield (city)	94.1	1.3	2.4	1.6
Maple Heights (city)	92.8	4.1	1.5	1.0

Place	Automobile (%)	Public Transportation (%)	Walk (%)	Work from Home (%)
Marion (city)	94.7	0.9	1.8	1.2
Mason (city)	93.9	1.0	0.3	4.5
Massillon (city)	94.3	1.4	2.0	1.3
Mayfield Heights (city)	91.5	2.1	2.5	3.1
Medina (city)	93.8	0.7	1.6	2.9
Mentor (city)	95.6	0.9	1.0	2.2
Miamisburg (city)	94.8	1.0	1.8	2.1
Middletown (city)	94.7	1.1	1.8	1.7
Newark (city)	94.9	1.0	1.5	1.9
Niles (city)	96.3	0.4	1.4	1.2
North Olmsted (city)	92.4	2.7	1.5	2.9
North Ridgeville (city)	96.1	1.0	0.6	1.9
North Royalton (city)	92.8	1.7	1.0	3.9
Norwood (city)	90.0	3.5	4.0	1.6
Oregon (city)	96.3	0.0	1.5	1.6
Oxford (city)	63.5	2.0	27.7	3.9
Painesville (city)	92.9	0.9	3.8	1.3
Parma (city)	93.3	3.1	1.4	1.6
Parma Heights (city)	93.1	3.5	1.2	1.8
Piqua (city)	93.1	1.3	2.5	2.2
Portsmouth (city)	90.5	1.4	5.5	1.6
Reynoldsburg (city)	94.8	1.3	1.2	2.2
Riverside (city)	95.7	1.2	0.9	1.2
Rocky River (city)	88.7	3.5	2.8	4.4
Sandusky (city)	94.6	0.6	2.3	1.4
Shaker Heights (city)	85.6	8.1	1.4	4.1
Sidney (city)	94.7	0.4	2.0	2.3
Solon (city)	94.7	0.5	0.7	3.9
South Euclid (city)	91.6	3.3	1.3	3.3
Springfield (city)	91.7	1.5	4.2	1.6
Steubenville (city)	93.2	0.9	3.0	2.7
Stow (city)	95.6	0.4	0.6	2.9
Strongsville (city)	93.2	2.2	0.7	3.4
Sylvania (city)	94.3	0.6	1.4	3.4
Tallmadge (city)	96.0	0.6	0.5	2.4
Toledo (city)	92.9	2.5	2.3	1.5
Trotwood (city)	93.4	3.5	1.0	1.5
Troy (city)	95.9	0.6	1.6	0.8
Twinsburg (city)	96.0	0.4	0.4	2.7
Upper Arlington (city)	90.3	1.5	1.4	5.8
Wadsworth (city)	94.3	0.2	1.3	3.5
Warren (city)	94.7	0.2	1.8	1.7
Westerville (city)	92.6	1.0	2.1	3.9
Westlake (city)	92.6	2.3	0.6	3.9
Whitehall (city)	91.7	4.9	2.2	0.7
Willoughby (city)	95.4	0.8	1.6	1.5
Wooster (city)	86.9	0.9	9.2	2.6
Xenia (city)	95.3	0.5	2.2	1.5
Youngstown (city)	91.8	2.7	2.6	1.7
Zanesville (city)	92.8	1.3	2.9	2.0

NOTE: Data as of 2000

Travel Time to Work

Place	Less than 15 Minutes (%)	15 to 30 Minutes (%)	30 to 45 Minutes (%)	45 to 60 Minutes (%)	60 Minutes or More (%)
Akron (city)	34.3	43.0	13.2	4.7	4.9
Alliance (city)	56.0	23.0	11.4	4.3	5.3
Ashland (city)	64.9	17.9	10.1	2.7	4.4
Ashtabula (city)	50.1	27.5	9.8	6.7	5.9
Athens (city)	74.2	20.0	3.3	0.6	1.8
Austintown (CDP)	30.9	51.6	9.6	3.2	4.8
Avon Lake (city)	24.7	35.1	28.5	7.9	3.7
Barberton (city)	38.8	39.1	13.7	4.6	3.9
Beavercreek (city)	32.1	54.2	9.5	1.7	2.5
Berea (city)	33.0	36.4	21.3	6.0	3.3
Boardman (CDP)	37.3	41.6	13.9	2.4	4.8
Bowling Green (city)	62.2	19.0	14.3	2.6	1.9
Brook Park (city)	30.8	43.0	18.6	4.5	3.1
Brunswick (city)	21.4	32.7	30.1	11.0	4.8
Canton (city)	43.8	39.3	9.8	3.2	3.9
Centerville (city)	29.7	49.3	13.5	3.7	3.8
Chillicothe (city)	56.9	22.9	7.8	4.0	8.5
Cincinnati (city)	26.0	46.5	18.3	4.7	4.6
Cleveland (city)	22.0	45.0	20.7	5.6	6.7
Cleveland Heights (city)	22.3	44.3	23.8	4.9	4.7
Columbus (city)	26.1	49.1	17.7	3.6	3.4
Cuyahoga Falls (city)	32.7	41.5	14.8	5.8	5.1
Dayton (city)	33.5	46.9	11.3	3.6	4.7
Delaware (city)	31.5	27.1	23.2	11.4	6.7
Dublin (city)	28.2	37.4	26.3	4.4	3.7
East Cleveland (city)	17.8	37.6	26.8	8.1	9.7
Eastlake (city)	31.1	45.2	15.9	4.4	3.4
Elyria (city)	38.3	37.3	16.1	5.1	3.1
Euclid (city)	25.1	43.3	22.7	4.2	4.8
Fairborn (city)	40.3	42.5	12.3	1.9	2.9
Fairfield (city)	27.1	43.9	20.5	6.1	2.4
Findlay (city)	60.6	26.8	6.7	2.9	3.0
Forest Park (city)	23.1	42.9	23.5	6.2	4.3
Gahanna (city)	26.6	51.4	15.9	2.4	3.7
Garfield Heights (city)	25.5	47.0	20.5	3.2	3.9
Green (city)	23.0	49.4	17.9	5.5	4.3
Grove City (city)	26.3	44.3	22.8	3.9	2.7
Hamilton (city)	32.2	36.9	20.0	6.5	4.4
Hilliard (city)	28.8	43.7	19.4	4.4	3.7
Huber Heights (city)	25.3	51.7	16.4	3.1	3.5
Hudson (city)	27.8	31.0	22.8	13.3	5.2
Kent (city)	42.7	33.7	11.7	6.6	5.3
Kettering (city)	33.6	50.2	10.5	2.7	3.0
Lakewood (city)	26.4	45.9	20.4	4.3	2.9
Lancaster (city)	40.3	23.6	14.7	12.8	8.6
Lebanon (city)	31.9	32.5	25.3	8.2	2.2
Lima (city)	50.7	34.3	8.1	3.3	3.5
Lorain (city)	32.6	41.9	15.3	5.8	4.4
Mansfield (city)	47.3	39.5	6.4	2.3	4.6
Maple Heights (city)	24.9	43.6	21.7	5.9	3.9

Place	Less than 15 Minutes (%)	15 to 30 Minutes (%)	30 to 45 Minutes (%)	45 to 60 Minutes (%)	60 Minutes or More (%)
Marion (city)	53.3	25.5	9.3	5.7	6.2
Mason (city)	25.6	42.9	23.6	5.6	2.2
Massillon (city)	39.1	40.2	12.8	3.9	4.0
Mayfield Heights (city)	32.4	40.3	20.3	4.3	2.7
Medina (city)	35.2	25.5	21.6	11.6	6.0
Mentor (city)	29.5	39.5	20.8	7.2	3.0
Miamisburg (city)	36.1	47.0	10.5	3.2	3.2
Middletown (city)	42.5	32.4	17.0	4.7	3.3
Newark (city)	44.5	30.8	10.3	8.7	5.6
Niles (city)	40.4	46.0	7.8	2.2	3.6
North Olmsted (city)	25.5	41.2	23.3	6.6	3.5
North Ridgeville (city)	18.8	44.4	24.8	7.2	4.8
North Royalton (city)	18.3	37.6	28.6	10.4	5.1
Norwood (city)	38.4	42.9	12.8	2.9	3.0
Oregon (city)	35.3	44.4	13.5	2.9	3.9
Oxford (city)	63.9	17.9	8.4	6.1	3.7
Painesville (city)	32.4	41.6	17.4	5.4	3.2
Parma (city)	22.8	43.1	23.9	6.5	3.7
Parma Heights (city)	25.7	41.2	22.2	7.1	3.8
Piqua (city)	49.9	33.5	10.2	3.6	2.7
Portsmouth (city)	55.2	26.3	9.3	2.2	7.0
Reynoldsburg (city)	25.1	44.4	23.3	4.4	2.9
Riverside (city)	33.9	50.7	8.0	2.9	4.6
Rocky River (city)	27.7	44.4	21.2	4.5	2.2
Sandusky (city)	59.1	28.5	6.7	1.8	4.0
Shaker Heights (city)	22.0	47.9	22.1	5.1	2.9
Sidney (city)	65.5	21.6	8.2	3.0	1.7
Solon (city)	28.1	36.7	25.2	7.2	2.8
South Euclid (city)	24.2	43.9	22.4	6.0	3.6
Springfield (city)	45.8	33.3	11.3	5.4	4.2
Steubenville (city)	55.9	27.4	8.4	4.1	4.3
Stow (city)	27.1	42.0	19.1	7.5	4.3
Strongsville (city)	22.9	34.0	28.5	10.1	4.5
Sylvania (city)	30.6	49.6	11.8	2.5	5.5
Tallmadge (city)	32.9	46.4	12.6	3.0	5.0
Toledo (city)	35.1	47.2	10.7	2.8	4.1
Trotwood (city)	20.4	48.7	20.7	5.2	5.0
Troy (city)	49.5	33.8	11.3	2.9	2.4
Twinsburg (city)	22.8	36.9	27.7	9.2	3.5
Upper Arlington (city)	30.7	55.4	10.1	1.4	2.4
Wadsworth (city)	34.6	44.0	12.6	5.0	3.9
Warren (city)	49.7	32.4	8.4	5.3	4.1
Westerville (city)	29.6	42.3	22.1	3.1	2.8
Westlake (city)	23.4	38.8	27.4	7.2	3.2
Whitehall (city)	27.0	43.6	21.2	3.5	4.7
Willoughby (city)	29.5	42.2	21.2	4.2	2.8
Wooster (city)	64.7	21.1	6.7	4.0	3.5
Xenia (city)	37.0	32.9	22.1	3.8	4.2
Youngstown (city)	38.4	43.4	11.0	2.2	5.0
Zanesville (city)	49.6	26.3	10.2	6.0	8.0

NOTE: Data as of 2000

Crime

Place	Violent Crime Rate (crimes per 10,000 population)	Property Crime Rate (crimes per 10,000 population)
Akron (city)	58.5	596.6
Alliance (city)	34.9	506.1
Ashland (city)	9.8	272.6
Ashtabula (city)	n/a	n/a
Athens (city)	17.1	238.5
Austintown (CDP)	n/a	n/a
Avon Lake (city)	5.5	77.7
Barberton (city)	21.1	400.5
Beavercreek (city)	11.7	365.6
Berea (city)	18.3	197.4
Boardman (CDP)	8.9	288.3
Bowling Green (city)	12.6	355.6
Brook Park (city)	9.2	37.2
Brunswick (city)	n/a	n/a
Canton (city)	149.3	766.6
Centerville (city)	n/a	n/a
Chillicothe (city)	25.7	995.7
Cincinnati (city)	114.8	714.5
Cleveland (city)	129.4	584.3
Cleveland Heights (city)	2.6	136.2
Columbus (city)	81.2	780.0
Cuyahoga Falls (city)	21.6	392.9
Dayton (city)	100.6	786.8
Delaware (city)	26.0	367.8
Dublin (city)	7.4	190.1
East Cleveland (city)	23.9	2.7
Eastlake (city)	7.0	159.3
Elyria (city)	n/a	n/a
Euclid (city)	38.0	344.4
Fairborn (city)	24.0	481.9
Fairfield (city)	28.4	358.9
Findlay (city)	n/a	n/a
Forest Park (city)	25.6	295.1
Gahanna (city)	8.4	273.3
Garfield Heights (city)	31.4	279.9
Green (city)	n/a	n/a
Grove City (city)	n/a	n/a
Hamilton (city)	88.7	856.8
Hilliard (city)	7.0	314.4
Huber Heights (city)	18.0	408.7
Hudson (city)	1.7	103.9
Kent (city)	28.1	272.9
Kettering (city)	16.6	377.3
Lakewood (city)	22.9	215.5
Lancaster (city)	27.5	458.5
Lebanon (city)	11.7	311.1
Lima (city)	114.4	697.0
Lorain (city)	48.8	334.7
Mansfield (city)	28.4	668.4
Maple Heights (city)	n/a	n/a

Place	Violent Crime Rate (crimes per 10,000 population)	Property Crime Rate (crimes per 10,000 population)
Marion (city)	27.3	486.9
Mason (city)	n/a	n/a
Massillon (city)	n/a	n/a
Mayfield Heights (city)	n/a	n/a
Medina (city)	n/a	n/a
Mentor (city)	10.2	261.0
Miamisburg (city)	28.6	467.9
Middletown (city)	29.6	660.0
Newark (city)	17.6	515.0
Niles (city)	n/a	n/a
North Olmsted (city)	9.5	149.6
North Ridgeville (city)	8.6	172.9
North Royalton (city)	8.8	43.5
Norwood (city)	58.1	706.0
Oregon (city)	n/a	n/a
Oxford (city)	37.6	329.6
Painesville (city)	n/a	n/a
Parma (city)	16.5	207.3
Parma Heights (city)	19.8	231.0
Piqua (city)	20.2	622.5
Portsmouth (city)	102.2	1,487.0
Reynoldsburg (city)	27.3	406.7
Riverside (city)	30.3	475.0
Rocky River (city)	n/a	n/a
Sandusky (city)	52.1	670.9
Shaker Heights (city)	n/a	n/a
Sidney (city)	n/a	n/a
Solon (city)	6.7	118.4
South Euclid (city)	15.3	203.9
Springfield (city)	75.8	954.4
Steubenville (city)	53.0	495.7
Stow (city)	3.8	203.7
Strongsville (city)	0.0	85.1
Sylvania (city)	2.6	142.7
Tallmadge (city)	16.3	257.6
Toledo (city)	105.5	700.2
Trotwood (city)	n/a	n/a
Troy (city)	n/a	n/a
Twinsburg (city)	11.0	110.0
Upper Arlington (city)	n/a	n/a
Wadsworth (city)	16.9	204.1
Warren (city)	87.8	598.2
Westerville (city)	12.6	320.6
Westlake (city)	0.3	8.1
Whitehall (city)	84.2	836.0
Willoughby (city)	17.3	192.2
Wooster (city)	n/a	n/a
Xenia (city)	12.6	480.5
Youngstown (city)	92.2	532.2
Zanesville (city)	39.5	646.7

NOTE: Data as of 2004.

EDUCATION

Ohio Public School Educational Profile

Category	Value	Category	Value
Schools *(2003-2004)*	3,988	**Diploma Recipients** *(2002-2003)*	110,608
Instructional Level		White, Non-Hispanic	95,036
Primary	2,187	Black, Non-Hispanic	11,945
Middle	744	Asian/Pacific Islander	1,568
High	802	American Indian/Alaskan Native	100
Other Level	209	Hispanic	1,441
Curriculum		**High School Drop-out Rate** (%) *(2001-2002)*	3.1
Regular	3,797	White, Non-Hispanic	2.4
Special Education	61	Black, Non-Hispanic	7.2
Vocational	75	Asian/Pacific Islander	2.0
Alternative	9	American Indian/Alaskan Native	7.1
Type		Hispanic	6.6
Magnet	0	**Staff** *(2003-2004)*	
Charter	165	Teachers	121,734.7
Title I Eligible	2,659	Average Salary ($)	47,791
School-wide Title I	1,000	Librarians/Media Specialists	1,669.4
Students *(2003-2004)*	1,845,428	Guidance Counselors	3,694.1
Gender (%)		**Ratios** *(2003-2004)*	
Male	51.5	Student/Teacher Ratio	15.2 to 1
Female	48.5	Student/Librarian Ratio	1,105.4 to 1
Race/Ethnicity (%)		Student/Counselor Ratio	499.6 to 1
White, Non-Hispanic	77.8	**College Entrance Exam Scores** *(2005)*	
Black, Non-Hispanic	16.7	Scholastic Aptitude Test (SAT)	
Asian/Pacific Islander	1.3	Participation Rate (%)	29
American Indian/Alaskan Native	0.1	Mean SAT Reasoning Test Verbal Score	539
Hispanic	2.1	Mean SAT Reasoning Test Math Score	543
Classification (%)		American College Testing Program (ACT)	
Individual Education Program (IEP)	13.9	Participation Rate (%)	66
Migrant *(2002-2003)*	0.1	Average Composite Score	21.4
English Language Learner (ELL)	1.3	Average English Score	20.7
Eligible for Free Lunch Program	24.0	Average Math Score	21.2
Eligible for Reduced-Price Lunch Program	5.5	Average Reading Score	21.9
Current Spending *($ per student in FY 2003)*	8,027	Average Science Score	21.5
Instruction	4,693		
Support Services	3,049		

Note: For an explanation of data, please refer to the User's Guide in the front of the book

Number of Schools

Rank	Number	District Name	City
1	153	Columbus Public Schools	Columbus
2	122	Cleveland Municipal City SD	Cleveland
3	86	Cincinnati City SD	Cincinnati
4	67	Toledo City SD	Toledo
5	63	Akron Public Schools	Akron
6	39	Dayton City SD	Dayton
7	36	South-Western City SD	Grove City
8	30	Canton City SD	Canton
9	26	Youngstown City SD	Youngstown
10	23	Westerville City SD	Westerville
11	21	Parma City SD	Parma
12	20	Hamilton City SD	Hamilton
12	20	Hilliard City SD	Hilliard
14	19	Lakota Local SD	Liberty Twp
14	19	Marion City SD	Marion
14	19	Springfield City SD	Springfield
17	18	Dublin City SD	Dublin
17	18	Worthington City SD	Worthington
19	17	Elyria City SD	Elyria
20	16	Findlay City SD	Findlay
20	16	Lorain City SD	Lorain
20	16	Mentor Ex Vill SD	Mentor
20	16	Newark City SD	Newark
24	15	Warren City SD	Warren
25	14	Lakewood City SD	Lakewood
25	14	Lima City SD	Lima
25	14	Logan-Hocking Local SD	Logan
25	14	Mansfield City SD	Mansfield
25	14	Middletown City SD	Middletown
25	14	Northwest Local SD	Cincinnati
25	14	Olentangy Local SD	Lewis Center
25	14	Willoughby-Eastlake City SD	Willoughby
33	13	Berea City SD	Berea
33	13	Cleveland Hts-Univ Hts City SD	University Hgts
35	12	Ashtabula Area City SD	Ashtabula
35	12	Cuyahoga Falls City SD	Cuyahoga Falls
35	12	Kettering City SD	Kettering
35	12	Lancaster City SD	Lancaster
35	12	Sandusky City SD	Sandusky
35	12	Sylvania City SD	Sylvania
35	12	Washington Local Schools	Toledo
35	12	West Clermont Local SD	Cincinnati
35	12	Zanesville City SD	Zanesville
44	11	Brunswick City SD	Brunswick
44	11	Centerville City SD	Centerville
44	11	Gahanna-Jefferson City SD	Gahanna
44	11	Pickerington Local SD	Pickerington
44	11	Princeton City SD	Cincinnati
44	11	Strongsville City SD	Strongsville
44	11	Wooster City SD	Wooster
51	10	Adams County/Ohio Valley LSD	West Union
51	10	Barberton City SD	Barberton
51	10	East Holmes Local Schools	Berlin
51	10	Euclid City SD	Euclid
51	10	Fairfield City SD	Fairfield
51	10	Groveport Madison Local SD	Groveport
51	10	Huber Heights City SD	Huber Heights
51	10	Massillon City SD	Massillon
51	10	Miami Trace Local SD	Wash Ct House
51	10	Plain Local SD	Canton
51	10	Switzerland of Ohio Local SD	Woodsfield
51	10	Xenia Community City SD	Xenia
63	9	Carrollton Ex Vill SD	Carrollton
63	9	Crestwood Local SD	Mantua
63	9	Delaware City SD	Delaware
63	9	Forest Hills Local SD	Cincinnati
63	9	Fremont City SD	Fremont
63	9	Medina City SD	Medina
63	9	Miamisburg City SD	Miamisburg
63	9	Mount Vernon City SD	Mount Vernon
63	9	Mt Healthy City SD	Cincinnati
63	9	North Olmsted City Schools	North Olmsted
63	9	Northmont City SD	Englewood
63	9	Oak Hills Local SD	Cincinnati
63	9	Perry Local SD	Massillon
63	9	Piqua City SD	Piqua
63	9	Shaker Heights City SD	Shaker Heights
63	9	Sidney City SD	Sidney
63	9	South Euclid-Lyndhurst City SD	Lyndhurst
63	9	Stow-Munroe Falls City SD	Stow
63	9	Troy City SD	Troy
82	8	Ashland City SD	Ashland
82	8	Austintown Local SD	Youngstown
82	8	Beavercreek City SD	Beavercreek
82	8	Bowling Green City SD	Bowling Green
82	8	Conneaut Area City SD	Conneaut
82	8	East Cleveland City SD	East Cleveland
82	8	Franklin City SD	Franklin
82	8	Gallia County Local SD	Gallipolis
82	8	Kenton City SD	Kenton
82	8	Marysville Exempted Village SD	Marysville
82	8	Milford Ex Vill SD	Milford
82	8	New Philadelphia City SD	New Philadelphia
82	8	Painesville Township Local SD	Painesville
82	8	Ravenna City SD	Ravenna
82	8	Reynoldsburg City SD	Reynoldsburg
82	8	Southwest Local SD	Harrison
82	8	Steubenville City SD	Steubenville
82	8	Tecumseh Local SD	New Carlisle
82	8	Upper Arlington City SD	Upper Arlington
82	8	Wadsworth City SD	Wadsworth
102	7	Athens City SD	The Plains
102	7	Avon Lake City Schools	Avon Lake
102	7	Bedford City SD	Bedford
102	7	Bellevue City SD	Bellevue
102	7	Boardman Local SD	Youngstown
102	7	Buckeye Local SD	Rayland
102	7	Bucyrus City SD	Bucyrus
102	7	Cloverleaf Local SD	Lodi
102	7	Defiance City SD	Defiance
102	7	Edison Local SD	Hammondsville
102	7	Fairborn City Schools	Fairborn
102	7	Geneva Area City Schools	Geneva
102	7	Greenville City SD	Greenville
102	7	Jackson City SD	Jackson
102	7	Kent City SD	Kent
102	7	Mad River Local SD	Dayton
102	7	Mayfield City SD	Highland Hgts
102	7	North Canton City SD	North Canton
102	7	Northeastern Local SD	Springfield
102	7	Norwood City SD	Norwood
102	7	Oregon City SD	Oregon
102	7	Painesville City Local SD	Painesville
102	7	River View Local SD	Warsaw
102	7	Solon City SD	Solon
102	7	Springfield Local SD	Akron
102	7	Sycamore Community City SD	Cincinnati
102	7	Tiffin City SD	Tiffin
102	7	Tri-Valley Local Schools	Dresden
102	7	Trotwood-Madison City Schools	Trotwood
102	7	Van Wert City SD	Van Wert
102	7	Vinton County Local SD	Mc Arthur
102	7	Washington Court House City SD	Wash Ct House
102	7	West Carrollton City SD	West Carrollton
102	7	West Holmes Local SD	Millersburg
102	7	Westlake City SD	Westlake
102	7	Winton Woods City SD	Cincinnati
138	6	Alliance City SD	Alliance
138	6	Amherst Ex Vill SD	Amherst
138	6	Anthony Wayne Local SD	Whitehouse
138	6	Bellefontaine City Schools	Bellefontaine
138	6	Benton Carroll Salem Local SD	Oak Harbor
138	6	Brecksville-Broadview Hgts City	Brecksville
138	6	Buckeye Local SD	Ashtabula
138	6	Chardon Local SD	Chardon
138	6	Chillicothe City SD	Chillicothe
138	6	Circleville City SD	Circleville
138	6	Claymont City SD	Dennison
138	6	Coventry Local SD	Akron
138	6	East Liverpool City SD	East Liverpool
138	6	East Muskingum Local SD	New Concord
138	6	Eastwood Local SD	Pemberville
138	6	Galion City SD	Galion
138	6	Harrison Hills City SD	Hopedale
138	6	Hillsboro City SD	Hillsboro
138	6	Howland Local SD	Warren
138	6	Hudson City SD	Hudson
138	6	Indian Creek Local SD	Wintersville
138	6	Ironton City SD	Ironton
138	6	Jackson Local SD	Massillon
138	6	Kings Local SD	Kings Mills
138	6	Lebanon City SD	Lebanon
138	6	Licking Valley Local SD Sd	Newark
138	6	Little Miami Local SD	Morrow
138	6	Logan Elm Local SD	Circleville
138	6	London City SD	London
138	6	Louisville City SD	Louisville
138	6	Loveland City SD	Loveland
138	6	Madison Local SD	Mansfield
138	6	Madison-Plains Local SD	London
138	6	Maple Heights City SD	Maple Heights
138	6	Marietta City Schools	Marietta
138	6	Mason City SD	Mason
138	6	Maumee City SD	Maumee
138	6	Niles City SD	Niles
138	6	Nordonia Hills City SD	Northfield
138	6	North Ridgeville City SD	N Ridgeville
138	6	North Royalton City SD	N Royalton
138	6	Norton City Schools	Norton
138	6	Norwalk City SD	Norwalk
138	6	Perrysburg Exempted Village	Perrysburg
138	6	Poland Local SD	Poland
138	6	Port Clinton City SD	Port Clinton
138	6	Portsmouth City SD	Portsmouth
138	6	Salem City SD	Salem
138	6	Sheffield-Sheffield Lake City SD	Sheffield Vlg
138	6	Shelby City SD	Shelby
138	6	Southeast Local SD	Apple Creek
138	6	Southwest Licking Local SD	Etna
138	6	Springfield Local Schools	Holland
138	6	St Marys City SD	Saint Marys
138	6	Urbana City SD	Urbana
138	6	Vandalia-Butler City SD	Vandalia
138	6	Wapakoneta City City SD	Wapakoneta
138	6	Warren Local SD	Vincent
138	6	Warrensville Heights City SD	Warrensville Hgts
138	6	West Branch Local SD	Beloit
138	6	Willard City SD	Willard
199	5	Avon Local SD	Avon
199	5	Beachwood City SD	Beachwood
199	5	Beaver Local SD	Lisbon
199	5	Bexley City SD	Bexley
199	5	Big Walnut Local SD	Galena
199	5	Buckeye Local SD	Medina
199	5	Buckeye Valley Local SD	Delaware
199	5	Cambridge City SD	Cambridge
199	5	Canal Winchester Local SD	Canal Winchester
199	5	Canton Local SD	Canton
199	5	Celina City SD	Celina
199	5	Clark-Shawnee Local SD	Springfield
199	5	Clyde-Green Springs Ex Vill SD	Clyde
199	5	Copley-Fairlawn City SD	Copley
199	5	Coshocton City SD	Coshocton
199	5	Dover City SD	Dover
199	5	Edgewood City SD	Trenton
199	5	Fairfield Union Local SD	W Rushville
199	5	Fairless Local SD	Navarre
199	5	Fairview Park City SD	Fairview Park
199	5	Field Local SD	Mogadore
199	5	Finneytown Local SD	Cincinnati
199	5	Fostoria City SD	Fostoria
199	5	Franklin Local SD	Duncan Falls
199	5	Gallipolis City SD	Gallipolis
199	5	Garfield Heights City SD	Garfield Hgts
199	5	Green Local SD	Green
199	5	Greeneview Local SD	Jamestown
199	5	Greenfield Ex Vill SD	Greenfield
199	5	Hamilton Local SD	Columbus
199	5	Highland Local SD	Sparta
199	5	Highland Local SD	Medina
199	5	Kenston Local SD	Chagrin Falls
199	5	Lake Local SD	Hartville
199	5	Lakewood Local SD	Hebron
199	5	Lexington Local SD	Lexington
199	5	Madison Local SD	Madison
199	5	Mariemont City SD	Cincinnati
199	5	Marlington Local SD	Alliance
199	5	Martins Ferry City SD	Martins Ferry
199	5	Midview Local SD	Grafton
199	5	Morgan Local SD	McConnelsville
199	5	Napoleon Area City SD	Napoleon
199	5	New Richmond Ex Vill SD	New Richmond
199	5	Northern Local SD	Thornville
199	5	Northridge Local SD	Dayton
199	5	Northwest Local SD	Canal Fulton
199	5	Oakwood City SD	Dayton
199	5	Orrville City SD	Orrville
199	5	Otsego Local SD	Tontogany
199	5	Ridgewood Local SD	West Lafayette
199	5	Rolling Hills Local SD	Cambridge
199	5	Rossford Ex Vill SD	Rossford
199	5	Southeast Local SD	Ravenna
199	5	Springboro Community City SD	Springboro
199	5	Streetsboro City Schools	Streetsboro
199	5	Sugarcreek Local SD	Bellbrook
199	5	Tallmadge City Schools	Tallmadge
199	5	Teays Valley Local SD	Ashville
199	5	Three Rivers Local Schools	Cleves
199	5	Tipp City Ex Vill SD	Tipp City
199	5	Triway Local SD	Wooster
199	5	Tuscarawas Valley Local SD	Zoarville
199	5	Twinsburg City SD	Twinsburg
199	5	Upper Sandusky Ex Vill SD	Upper Sandusky
199	5	West Muskingum Local SD	Zanesville
199	5	Whitehall City SD	Whitehall
199	5	Wilmington City SD	Wilmington
199	5	Wyoming City SD	Wyoming
268	4	Alexander Local SD	Albany
268	4	Amanda-Clearcreek Local SD	Amanda
268	4	Aurora City SD	Aurora
268	4	Bay Village City SD	Bay Village
268	4	Berlin-Milan Local SD	Milan
268	4	Bethel-Tate Local SD	Bethel
268	4	Bryan City SD	Bryan
268	4	Canfield Local SD	Canfield

268	4	Carlisle Local SD	Carlisle
268	4	Chagrin Falls Ex Vill SD	Chagrin Falls
268	4	Clear Fork Valley Local SD	Bellville
268	4	Clermont Northeastern Local SD	Batavia
268	4	East Clinton Local SD	Lees Creek
268	4	Eastern Local SD	Sardinia
268	4	Eaton Community Schools	Eaton
268	4	Elgin Local SD	Marion
268	4	Elida Local SD	Elida
268	4	Fairland Local SD	Proctorville
268	4	Genoa Area Local SD	Genoa
268	4	Girard City SD	Girard
268	4	Goshen Local SD	Goshen
268	4	Graham Local SD	Saint Paris
268	4	Granville Ex Vill SD	Granville
268	4	Greenon Local SD	Springfield
268	4	Heath City SD	Heath
268	4	Indian Hill Ex Vill SD	Cincinnati
268	4	Indian Lake Local SD	Lewistown
268	4	Indian Valley Local SD	Gnadenhutten
268	4	James A Garfield Local SD	Garrettsville
268	4	Jonathan Alder Local SD	Plain City
268	4	Keystone Local SD	Lagrange
268	4	Lake Local SD	Millbury
268	4	Lakeview Local SD	Cortland
268	4	Meigs Local SD	Pomeroy
268	4	Minerva Local SD	Minerva
268	4	New Lexington City SD	New Lexington
268	4	Newton Falls Ex Vill SD	Newton Falls
268	4	North College Hill City SD	Cincinnati
268	4	North Fork Local SD	Utica
268	4	Olmsted Falls City SD	Olmsted Falls
268	4	Ontario Local SD	Mansfield
268	4	Orange City SD	Cleveland
268	4	Ottawa-Glandorf Local SD	Ottawa
268	4	Paulding Ex Vill SD	Paulding
268	4	Perkins Local SD	Sandusky
268	4	Pike-Delta-York Local SD	Delta
268	4	Plain Local SD	New Albany
268	4	Preble Shawnee Local SD	Camden
268	4	Revere Local SD	Bath
268	4	River Valley Local SD	Caledonia
268	4	Rocky River City SD	Rocky River
268	4	Ross Local SD	Hamilton
268	4	Sandy Valley Local SD	Magnolia
268	4	Shawnee Local SD	Lima
268	4	South Point Local SD	South Point
268	4	Swanton Local SD	Swanton
268	4	Talawanda City SD	Oxford
268	4	Valley View Local SD	Germantown
268	4	Vermilion Local SD	Vermilion
268	4	Wauseon Ex Vill SD	Wauseon
268	4	Waverly City SD	Waverly
268	4	Wellston City Schools	Wellston
268	4	West Geauga Local SD	Chesterland
268	4	Western Brown Local SD	Mount Orab
268	4	Woodridge Local SD	Peninsula
333	3	Batavia Local SD	Batavia
333	3	Bath Local SD	Lima
333	3	Bellaire Local SD	Bellaire
333	3	Benjamin Logan Local SD	Bellefontaine
333	3	Black River Local SD	Sullivan
333	3	Blanchester Local SD	Blanchester
333	3	Brookville Local SD	Brookville
333	3	Campbell City SD	Campbell
333	3	Champion Local SD	Warren
333	3	Clearview Local SD	Lorain
333	3	Clinton-Massie Local SD	Clarksville
333	3	Coldwater Ex Vill SD	Coldwater
333	3	Firelands Local SD	Oberlin
333	3	Hubbard Ex Vill SD	Hubbard
333	3	Huron City Schools	Huron
333	3	Jefferson Area Local SD	Jefferson
333	3	Liberty Local SD	Youngstown
333	3	Licking Heights Local SD	Summit Station
333	3	Madeira City SD	Cincinnati
333	3	Madison Local SD	Middletown
333	3	Manchester Local SD	Akron
333	3	Maysville Local SD	Zanesville
333	3	Milton-Union Exempted Vill Schls	West Milton
333	3	Minford Local SD	Minford
333	3	Monroe Local SD	Monroe
333	3	Northwest Local SD	Mc Dermott
333	3	Northwestern Local SD	Springfield
333	3	Perry Local SD	Perry
333	3	Rock Hill Local SD	Ironton
333	3	Scioto Valley Local SD	Piketon
333	3	St Clairsville-Richland City SD	St Clairsville
333	3	Struthers City SD	Struthers
333	3	Union Local SD	Morristown
333	3	Union-Scioto Local SD	Chillicothe
333	3	Washington-Nile Local SD	West Portsmouth
333	3	Wellington Ex Vill SD	Wellington
333	3	Westfall Local SD	Williamsport
333	3	Wickliffe City SD	Wickliffe
333	3	Zane Trace Local SD	Chillicothe
372	2	United Local SD	Hanoverton
373	1	Electronic Classrm of Tomorrow	Columbus
373	1	Ohio Virtual Academy	Maumee

Number of Teachers

Rank	Number	District Name	City
1	5,108	Cleveland Municipal City SD	Cleveland
2	3,838	Columbus Public Schools	Columbus
3	3,133	Akron Public Schools	Akron
4	3,132	Cincinnati City SD	Cincinnati
5	2,538	Toledo City SD	Toledo
6	1,417	Dayton City SD	Dayton
7	1,326	South-Western City SD	Grove City
8	964	Lakota Local SD	Liberty Twp
9	921	Hilliard City SD	Hilliard
10	792	Dublin City SD	Dublin
11	787	Parma City SD	Parma
12	784	Westerville City SD	Westerville
13	755	Canton City SD	Canton
14	717	Youngstown City SD	Youngstown
15	657	Worthington City SD	Worthington
16	628	Lorain City SD	Lorain
17	627	Mentor Ex Vill SD	Mentor
18	626	Huber Heights City SD	Huber Heights
19	617	Springfield City SD	Springfield
20	615	Northwest Local SD	Cincinnati
21	569	Hamilton City SD	Hamilton
22	549	Elyria City SD	Elyria
23	535	Centerville City SD	Centerville
24	518	Willoughby-Eastlake City SD	Willoughby
25	517	Olentangy Local SD	Lewis Center
26	508	Gahanna-Jefferson City SD	Gahanna
27	505	West Clermont Local SD	Cincinnati
28	504	Fairfield City SD	Fairfield
29	499	Pickerington Local SD	Pickerington
30	499	Sylvania City SD	Sylvania
31	494	Kettering City SD	Kettering
32	492	Middletown City SD	Middletown
33	489	Berea City SD	Berea
34	487	Warren City SD	Warren
35	485	Princeton City SD	Cincinnati
36	482	Mason City SD	Mason
37	477	Cleveland Hts-Univ Hts City SD	University Hgts
38	470	Medina City SD	Medina
39	455	Washington Local Schools	Toledo
40	445	Oak Hills Local SD	Cincinnati
41	437	Findlay City SD	Findlay
42	434	Forest Hills Local SD	Cincinnati
43	428	Mansfield City SD	Mansfield
44	423	Lakewood City SD	Lakewood
45	417	Newark City SD	Newark
46	413	Shaker Heights City SD	Shaker Heights
47	409	Strongsville City SD	Strongsville
48	404	Brunswick City SD	Brunswick
49	400	Upper Arlington City SD	Upper Arlington
50	398	Sycamore Community City SD	Cincinnati
51	387	Plain Local SD	Canton
52	383	Euclid City SD	Euclid
53	369	Beavercreek City SD	Beavercreek
54	365	Lima City SD	Lima
55	364	Groveport Madison Local SD	Groveport
56	359	Cuyahoga Falls City SD	Cuyahoga Falls
57	357	Hudson City SD	Hudson
58	351	Marion City SD	Marion
59	346	Lancaster City SD	Lancaster
60	338	Milford Ex Vill SD	Milford
61	336	Reynoldsburg City SD	Reynoldsburg
62	336	Adams County/Ohio Valley LSD	West Union
63	335	Stow-Munroe Falls City SD	Stow
64	333	Solon City SD	Solon
65	330	Mayfield City SD	Highland Hgts
66	329	Xenia Community City SD	Xenia
67	326	Massillon City SD	Massillon
68	316	Northmont City SD	Englewood
69	313	North Olmsted City Schools	North Olmsted
70	311	Jackson Local SD	Massillon
71	310	Fairborn City Schools	Fairborn
72	306	Miamisburg City SD	Miamisburg
73	303	South Euclid-Lyndhurst City SD	Lyndhurst
74	298	Boardman Local SD	Youngstown
75	298	Marysville Exempted Village SD	Marysville
76	298	Kent City SD	Kent
77	297	Sandusky City SD	Sandusky
78	295	East Cleveland City SD	East Cleveland
79	293	Wooster City SD	Wooster
80	292	North Canton City SD	North Canton
81	291	Barberton City SD	Barberton
82	291	Austintown Local SD	Youngstown
83	290	Zanesville City SD	Zanesville
84	283	Winton Woods City SD	Cincinnati
85	282	Ashtabula Area City SD	Ashtabula
86	282	Delaware City SD	Delaware
87	275	Perrysburg Exempted Village	Perrysburg
88	269	Brecksville-Broadview Hgts City	Brecksville
89	260	Mt Healthy City SD	Cincinnati
90	256	Perry Local SD	Massillon
91	256	Oregon City SD	Oregon
92	252	Mount Vernon City SD	Mount Vernon
93	252	Bedford City SD	Bedford
94	251	West Carrollton City SD	West Carrollton
95	250	North Royalton City SD	N Royalton
96	249	Fremont City SD	Fremont
97	249	Madison Local SD	Mansfield
98	244	Westlake City SD	Westlake
99	239	Lebanon City SD	Lebanon
100	238	Mad River Local SD	Dayton
101	237	Wadsworth City SD	Wadsworth
102	234	Troy City SD	Troy
103	234	Vandalia-Butler City SD	Vandalia
104	233	Painesville Township Local SD	Painesville
105	232	Green Local SD	Green
106	232	Northeastern Local SD	Springfield
107	231	Loveland City SD	Loveland
108	229	Greenville City SD	Greenville
109	229	Springfield Local Schools	Holland
110	229	Twinsburg City SD	Twinsburg
111	227	Logan-Hocking Local SD	Logan
112	225	Ashland City SD	Ashland
113	225	Springboro Community City SD	Springboro
114	223	North Ridgeville City SD	N Ridgeville
115	223	Alliance City SD	Alliance
116	222	Athens City SD	The Plains
117	221	Maple Heights City SD	Maple Heights
118	221	East Liverpool City SD	East Liverpool
119	219	Sidney City SD	Sidney
120	219	Amherst Ex Vill SD	Amherst
121	218	Tecumseh Local SD	New Carlisle
122	215	Kings Local SD	Kings Mills
123	214	Anthony Wayne Local SD	Whitehouse
124	212	Ravenna City SD	Ravenna
125	212	New Philadelphia City SD	New Philadelphia
126	209	Avon Lake City Schools	Avon Lake
127	208	Southwest Local SD	Harrison
128	206	Bowling Green City SD	Bowling Green
129	206	Southwest Licking Local SD	Etna
130	205	Kenston Local SD	Chagrin Falls
131	203	Edgewood City SD	Trenton
132	203	Trotwood-Madison City Schools	Trotwood
133	200	Springfield Local SD	Akron
134	200	Copley-Fairlawn City SD	Copley
135	200	Nordonia Hills City SD	Northfield
136	197	Garfield Heights City SD	Garfield Hgts
136	197	Talawanda City SD	Oxford
138	197	Maumee City SD	Maumee
139	197	Teays Valley Local SD	Ashville
140	196	Cloverleaf Local SD	Lodi
141	196	Olmsted Falls City SD	Olmsted Falls
142	196	Switzerland of Ohio Local SD	Woodsfield
143	194	Madison Local SD	Madison
144	193	Howland Local SD	Warren
145	193	Chardon Local SD	Chardon
146	193	Orange City SD	Cleveland
147	193	Louisville City SD	Louisville
148	192	Warrensville Heights City SD	Warrensville Hgts
149	191	Celina City SD	Celina
150	191	Whitehall City SD	Whitehall
151	190	Lake Local SD	Hartville
152	186	Bellefontaine City Schools	Bellefontaine
153	186	Western Brown Local SD	Mount Orab
154	185	Hillsboro City SD	Hillsboro
155	183	Hamilton Local SD	Columbus
156	183	Wilmington City SD	Wilmington
157	182	Piqua City SD	Piqua
158	182	Painesville City Local SD	Painesville
159	181	Chillicothe City SD	Chillicothe
160	181	Canfield Local SD	Canfield
161	179	Cambridge City SD	Cambridge
162	179	Little Miami Local SD	Morrow
163	179	Plain Local SD	New Albany
164	178	Norwood City SD	Norwood
165	178	Marietta City Schools	Marietta
165	178	Tallmadge City Schools	Tallmadge
167	177	Franklin City SD	Franklin
167	177	Revere Local SD	Bath
169	177	Tiffin City SD	Tiffin
170	175	Midview Local SD	Grafton
171	173	West Holmes Local SD	Millersburg
172	169	Gallia County Local SD	Gallipolis
173	169	Canton Local SD	Canton
174	169	Big Walnut Local SD	Galena

PROFILES OF OHIO / School District Rankings 389

175	168	Carrollton Ex Vill SD	Carrollton
175	168	Niles City SD	Niles
177	167	Edison Local SD	Hammondsville
178	167	Vinton County Local SD	Mc Arthur
179	165	Defiance City SD	Defiance
180	164	Tri-Valley Local Schools	Dresden
181	164	Bay Village City SD	Bay Village
182	164	Dover City SD	Dover
183	163	Warren Local SD	Vincent
184	163	Aurora City SD	Aurora
184	163	Buckeye Local SD	Rayland
186	161	Canal Winchester Local SD	Canal Winchester
187	161	Wapakoneta City City SD	Wapakoneta
188	160	Miami Trace Local SD	Wash Ct House
189	159	Marlington Local SD	Alliance
190	159	Bexley City SD	Bexley
191	158	Salem City SD	Salem
192	158	Meigs Local SD	Pomeroy
193	157	Rocky River City SD	Rocky River
194	156	Crestwood Local SD	Mantua
194	156	New Richmond Ex Vill SD	New Richmond
196	156	Lexington Local SD	Lexington
197	156	Conneaut Area City SD	Conneaut
198	155	Geneva Area City Schools	Geneva
199	155	Highland Local SD	Medina
200	154	River View Local SD	Warsaw
201	154	Washington Court House City SD	Wash Ct House
202	153	Indian Hill Ex Vill SD	Cincinnati
203	153	West Geauga Local SD	Chesterland
204	153	Lakewood Local SD	Hebron
205	152	Morgan Local SD	McConnelsville
206	152	Steubenville City SD	Steubenville
207	151	Gallipolis City SD	Gallipolis
208	151	Beachwood City SD	Beachwood
209	151	Napoleon Area City SD	Napoleon
210	150	Streetsboro City Schools	Streetsboro
211	149	Norton City Schools	Norton
212	148	Northwest Local SD	Canal Fulton
213	148	Avon Local SD	Avon
214	147	Van Wert City SD	Van Wert
215	147	Greenfield Ex Vill SD	Greenfield
216	147	Tipp City Ex Vill SD	Tipp City
217	147	St Marys City SD	Saint Marys
218	146	Oakwood City SD	Dayton
219	146	Ross Local SD	Hamilton
220	145	Circleville City SD	Circleville
220	145	Vermilion Local SD	Vermilion
222	145	Norwalk City SD	Norwalk
223	144	Urbana City SD	Urbana
224	144	Bellevue City SD	Bellevue
225	144	Jackson City SD	Jackson
226	143	Portsmouth City SD	Portsmouth
227	143	Buckeye Local SD	Medina
228	143	Bryan City SD	Bryan
229	142	Galion City SD	Galion
230	142	Franklin Local SD	Duncan Falls
231	142	Electronic Classrm of Tomorrow	Columbus
232	140	Shelby City SD	Shelby
233	140	Logan Elm Local SD	Circleville
234	140	Elida Local SD	Elida
235	139	Claymont City SD	Dennison
235	139	Shawnee Local SD	Lima
237	139	Clark-Shawnee Local SD	Springfield
238	139	Beaver Local SD	Lisbon
238	139	Buckeye Local SD	Ashtabula
238	139	Perkins Local SD	Sandusky
241	138	Sugarcreek Local SD	Bellbrook
242	138	Goshen Local SD	Goshen
243	136	Kenton City SD	Kenton
244	136	Chagrin Falls Ex Vill SD	Chagrin Falls
245	136	Willard City SD	Willard
246	135	Northern Local SD	Thornville
247	134	London City SD	London
248	133	Wyoming City SD	Wyoming
249	133	Harrison Hills City SD	Hopedale
250	133	Indian Creek Local SD	Wintersville
251	132	Field Local SD	Mogadore
252	131	Rossford Ex Vill SD	Rossford
253	131	West Branch Local SD	Beloit
254	131	Fairview Park City SD	Fairview Park
254	131	Rock Hill Local SD	Ironton
256	130	Licking Valley Local SD Sd	Newark
257	130	Buckeye Valley Local SD	Delaware
258	130	Clyde-Green Springs Ex Vill SD	Clyde
259	130	Eaton Community Schools	Eaton
259	130	Hubbard Ex Vill SD	Hubbard
259	130	Indian Valley Local SD	Gnadenhutten
262	129	Minerva Local SD	Minerva
263	128	Graham Local SD	Saint Paris
264	127	Woodridge Local SD	Peninsula
265	127	Port Clinton City SD	Port Clinton
266	126	Coventry Local SD	Akron
267	126	Triway Local SD	Wooster
268	126	Three Rivers Local Schools	Cleves
269	126	Indian Lake Local SD	Lewistown
269	126	Northridge Local SD	Dayton
271	126	Southeast Local SD	Ravenna
272	124	Jefferson Area Local SD	Jefferson
273	124	Paulding Ex Vill SD	Paulding
274	123	Coshocton City SD	Coshocton
274	123	East Holmes Local Schools	Berlin
276	123	Fairless Local SD	Navarre
276	123	Fostoria City SD	Fostoria
278	122	Mariemont City SD	Cincinnati
278	122	Poland Local SD	Poland
280	122	East Muskingum Local SD	New Concord
281	122	Waverly City SD	Waverly
282	121	Sheffield-Sheffield Lake City SD	Sheffield Vlg
283	120	Firelands Local SD	Oberlin
284	119	Maysville Local SD	Zanesville
285	119	Upper Sandusky Ex Vill SD	Upper Sandusky
286	118	Wellston City Schools	Wellston
287	118	Perry Local SD	Perry
288	117	Valley View Local SD	Germantown
289	117	Struthers City SD	Struthers
290	117	Orrville City SD	Orrville
291	117	Finneytown Local SD	Cincinnati
292	116	Wauseon Ex Vill SD	Wauseon
293	116	Lakeview Local SD	Cortland
294	116	Alexander Local SD	Albany
294	116	Greenon Local SD	Springfield
296	115	Preble Shawnee Local SD	Camden
297	114	Blanchester Local SD	Blanchester
297	114	Bucyrus City SD	Bucyrus
299	114	Berlin-Milan Local SD	Milan
299	114	Southeast Local SD	Apple Creek
301	114	Granville Ex Vill SD	Granville
302	113	Benjamin Logan Local SD	Bellefontaine
302	113	South Point Local SD	South Point
302	113	Union Local SD	Morristown
305	112	Wickliffe City SD	Wickliffe
306	112	Benton Carroll Salem Local SD	Oak Harbor
307	112	Rolling Hills Local SD	Cambridge
308	111	Batavia Local SD	Batavia
309	111	Licking Heights Local SD	Summit Station
310	111	New Lexington City SD	New Lexington
311	110	Ironton City SD	Ironton
312	108	Champion Local SD	Warren
312	108	Elgin Local SD	Marion
314	106	Bellaire Local SD	Bellaire
314	106	Union-Scioto Local SD	Chillicothe
314	106	Washington-Nile Local SD	West Portsmouth
317	106	Milton-Union Exempted Vill Schls	West Milton
318	106	Northwest Local SD	Mc Dermott
319	105	Northwestern Local SD	Springfield
320	105	Clear Fork Valley Local SD	Bellville
320	105	North Fork Local SD	Utica
322	105	River Valley Local SD	Caledonia
323	105	St Clairsville-Richland City SD	St Clairsville
324	104	Carlisle Local SD	Carlisle
325	104	West Muskingum Local SD	Zanesville
326	104	Sandy Valley Local SD	Magnolia
327	103	Fairfield Union Local SD	W Rushville
328	103	Clermont Northeastern Local SD	Batavia
329	102	Bath Local SD	Lima
330	101	Liberty Local SD	Youngstown
331	101	Highland Local SD	Sparta
332	101	Tuscarawas Valley Local SD	Zoarville
333	100	Bethel-Tate Local SD	Bethel
333	100	Madeira City SD	Cincinnati
335	100	Campbell City SD	Campbell
335	100	Girard City SD	Girard
337	99	Fairland Local SD	Proctorville
338	99	Westfall Local SD	Williamsport
339	98	Monroe Local SD	Monroe
340	98	Clearview Local SD	Lorain
341	97	Madison Local SD	Middletown
342	96	Keystone Local SD	Lagrange
343	95	Coldwater Ex Vill SD	Coldwater
344	95	Huron City Schools	Huron
344	95	Ottawa-Glandorf Local SD	Ottawa
346	95	Black River Local SD	Sullivan
346	95	Madison-Plains Local SD	London
348	94	Wellington Ex Vill SD	Wellington
349	94	Otsego Local SD	Tontogany
350	94	Eastwood Local SD	Pemberville
351	94	James A Garfield Local SD	Garrettsville
352	93	Heath City SD	Heath
353	93	Minford Local SD	Minford
354	92	Ontario Local SD	Mansfield
355	91	Clinton-Massie Local SD	Clarksville
356	91	Amanda-Clearcreek Local SD	Amanda
356	91	East Clinton Local SD	Lees Creek
356	91	Martins Ferry City SD	Martins Ferry
356	91	Newton Falls Ex Vill SD	Newton Falls
356	91	Scioto Valley Local SD	Piketon
361	90	Eastern Local SD	Sardinia
361	90	Greeneview Local SD	Jamestown
361	90	Jonathan Alder Local SD	Plain City
364	89	Swanton Local SD	Swanton
365	89	Genoa Area Local SD	Genoa
366	87	Pike-Delta-York Local SD	Delta
367	87	North College Hill City SD	Cincinnati
368	85	Brookville Local SD	Brookville
369	84	Ridgewood Local SD	West Lafayette
370	84	Zane Trace Local SD	Chillicothe
371	83	United Local SD	Hanoverton
372	80	Manchester Local SD	Akron
373	79	Lake Local SD	Millbury
374	53	Ohio Virtual Academy	Maumee

Number of Students

Rank	Number	District Name	City
1	69,655	Cleveland Municipal City SD	Cleveland
2	63,098	Columbus Public Schools	Columbus
3	40,374	Cincinnati City SD	Cincinnati
4	34,486	Toledo City SD	Toledo
5	28,816	Akron Public Schools	Akron
6	21,230	South-Western City SD	Grove City
7	18,491	Dayton City SD	Dayton
8	16,358	Lakota Local SD	Liberty Twp
9	14,219	Hilliard City SD	Hilliard
10	14,142	Westerville City SD	Westerville
11	13,427	Parma City SD	Parma
12	12,376	Dublin City SD	Dublin
13	11,798	Canton City SD	Canton
14	10,657	Northwest Local SD	Cincinnati
15	10,320	Lorain City SD	Lorain
16	9,777	Mentor Ex Vill SD	Mentor
17	9,754	Worthington City SD	Worthington
18	9,748	Youngstown City SD	Youngstown
19	9,607	Hamilton City SD	Hamilton
20	9,547	Fairfield City SD	Fairfield
21	9,358	Springfield City SD	Springfield
22	9,189	West Clermont Local SD	Cincinnati
23	8,917	Pickerington Local SD	Pickerington
24	8,876	Willoughby-Eastlake City SD	Willoughby
25	8,635	Mason City SD	Mason
26	8,560	Olentangy Local SD	Lewis Center
27	8,132	Oak Hills Local SD	Cincinnati
28	8,127	Elyria City SD	Elyria
29	8,120	Centerville City SD	Centerville
30	8,027	Berea City SD	Berea
31	7,832	Sylvania City SD	Sylvania
32	7,747	Kettering City SD	Kettering
33	7,621	Forest Hills Local SD	Cincinnati
34	7,340	Strongsville City SD	Strongsville
35	7,323	Medina City SD	Medina
36	7,296	Middletown City SD	Middletown
37	7,254	Brunswick City SD	Brunswick
38	7,184	Beavercreek City SD	Beavercreek
39	7,083	Lakewood City SD	Lakewood
40	6,969	Newark City SD	Newark
41	6,942	Washington Local Schools	Toledo
42	6,901	Warren City SD	Warren
43	6,887	Cleveland Hts-Univ Hts City SD	University Hgts
44	6,821	Huber Heights City SD	Huber Heights
45	6,806	Gahanna-Jefferson City SD	Gahanna
46	6,607	Reynoldsburg City SD	Reynoldsburg
47	6,479	Findlay City SD	Findlay
48	6,440	Groveport Madison Local SD	Groveport
49	6,420	Euclid City SD	Euclid
50	6,225	Milford Ex Vill SD	Milford
51	6,122	Plain Local SD	Canton
52	6,105	Princeton City SD	Cincinnati
53	6,104	Lancaster City SD	Lancaster
54	6,080	Stow-Munroe Falls City SD	Stow
55	5,933	Northmont City SD	Englewood
56	5,802	Mansfield City SD	Mansfield
57	5,759	Sycamore Community City SD	Cincinnati
58	5,625	Shaker Heights City SD	Shaker Heights
59	5,597	Upper Arlington City SD	Upper Arlington
60	5,592	Marion City SD	Marion
61	5,566	Hudson City SD	Hudson
62	5,561	Jackson Local SD	Massillon
63	5,427	Fairborn City Schools	Fairborn
64	5,399	Cuyahoga Falls City SD	Cuyahoga Falls
65	5,306	Miamisburg City SD	Miamisburg
66	5,213	Electronic Classrm of Tomorrow	Columbus
67	5,202	Xenia Community City SD	Xenia
68	5,180	Solon City SD	Solon
69	5,098	Adams County/Ohio Valley LSD	West Union
70	5,092	East Cleveland City SD	East Cleveland
71	5,046	Austintown Local SD	Youngstown
72	4,994	Lima City SD	Lima
73	4,924	North Canton City SD	North Canton
74	4,897	Boardman Local SD	Youngstown

75	4,854	Perry Local SD	Massillon
76	4,780	Lebanon City SD	Lebanon
77	4,721	Marysville Exempted Village SD	Marysville
78	4,695	Wadsworth City SD	Wadsworth
79	4,666	Brecksville-Broadview Hgts City	Brecksville
80	4,661	Ashtabula Area City SD	Ashtabula
81	4,598	Fremont City SD	Fremont
82	4,596	Barberton City SD	Barberton
83	4,583	South Euclid-Lyndhurst City SD	Lyndhurst
84	4,573	North Olmsted City Schools	North Olmsted
85	4,547	Massillon City SD	Massillon
86	4,538	Troy City SD	Troy
87	4,519	Painesville Township Local SD	Painesville
88	4,498	Delaware City SD	Delaware
89	4,496	North Royalton City SD	N Royalton
90	4,348	Perrysburg Exempted Village	Perrysburg
91	4,331	Mayfield City SD	Highland Hgts
92	4,320	Springboro Community City SD	Springboro
93	4,301	Mount Vernon City SD	Mount Vernon
94	4,278	Loveland City SD	Loveland
95	4,251	Zanesville City SD	Zanesville
96	4,227	Sandusky City SD	Sandusky
97	4,190	Amherst Ex Vill SD	Amherst
98	4,165	Green Local SD	Green
99	4,156	Winton Woods City SD	Cincinnati
100	4,144	Wooster City SD	Wooster
101	4,028	Logan-Hocking Local SD	Logan
102	3,971	Southwest Local SD	Harrison
103	3,954	Piqua City SD	Piqua
104	3,953	Twinsburg City SD	Twinsburg
105	3,917	Westlake City SD	Westlake
106	3,898	West Carrollton City SD	West Carrollton
107	3,897	Sidney City SD	Sidney
108	3,890	Bedford City SD	Bedford
109	3,887	Nordonia Hills City SD	Northfield
110	3,879	Anthony Wayne Local SD	Whitehouse
111	3,862	Oregon City SD	Oregon
112	3,859	Garfield Heights City SD	Garfield Hgts
113	3,849	Kings Local SD	Kings Mills
114	3,817	Ashland City SD	Ashland
115	3,796	Kent City SD	Kent
116	3,788	Mt Healthy City SD	Cincinnati
117	3,779	Springfield Local Schools	Holland
118	3,739	Madison Local SD	Madison
119	3,686	Maple Heights City SD	Maple Heights
120	3,628	Northeastern Local SD	Springfield
121	3,619	Mad River Local SD	Dayton
122	3,601	Madison Local SD	Mansfield
123	3,595	Edgewood City SD	Trenton
124	3,578	Tecumseh Local SD	New Carlisle
125	3,568	Cloverleaf Local SD	Lodi
126	3,550	North Ridgeville City SD	N Ridgeville
127	3,527	Southwest Licking Local SD	Etna
128	3,520	Chillicothe City SD	Chillicothe
129	3,518	Vandalia-Butler City SD	Vandalia
130	3,470	Trotwood-Madison City Schools	Trotwood
131	3,464	Midview Local SD	Grafton
132	3,419	Greenville City SD	Greenville
133	3,418	Western Brown Local SD	Mount Orab
134	3,386	Ravenna City SD	Ravenna
135	3,359	Lake Local SD	Hartville
136	3,343	Avon Lake City Schools	Avon Lake
137	3,342	Olmsted Falls City SD	Olmsted Falls
138	3,323	Alliance City SD	Alliance
139	3,307	New Philadelphia City SD	New Philadelphia
140	3,274	Louisville City SD	Louisville
141	3,272	Chardon Local SD	Chardon
142	3,254	Copley-Fairlawn City SD	Copley
143	3,233	Teays Valley Local SD	Ashville
144	3,228	Howland Local SD	Warren
145	3,203	Bowling Green City SD	Bowling Green
146	3,202	Marietta City Schools	Marietta
147	3,201	Little Miami Local SD	Morrow
148	3,199	Celina City SD	Celina
149	3,195	Wilmington City SD	Wilmington
150	3,160	Wapakoneta City City SD	Wapakoneta
151	3,150	Tri-Valley Local Schools	Dresden
152	3,134	Kenston Local SD	Chagrin Falls
153	3,104	Talawanda City SD	Oxford
154	3,097	Canfield Local SD	Canfield
155	3,094	Franklin City SD	Franklin
156	3,082	East Liverpool City SD	East Liverpool
157	3,076	Springfield Local SD	Akron
158	3,064	Whitehall City SD	Whitehall
159	3,022	Tiffin City SD	Tiffin
160	3,011	Geneva Area City Schools	Geneva
161	2,989	Hamilton Local SD	Columbus
162	2,975	Athens City SD	The Plains
163	2,952	Norwalk City SD	Norwalk
164	2,932	Carrollton Ex Vill SD	Carrollton
165	2,877	Plain Local SD	New Albany
166	2,861	Niles City SD	Niles
167	2,851	Aurora City SD	Aurora
168	2,847	Maumee City SD	Maumee
169	2,845	Painesville City Local SD	Painesville
170	2,835	Revere Local SD	Bath
171	2,833	Hillsboro City SD	Hillsboro
172	2,821	Warrensville Heights City SD	Warrensville Hgts
173	2,819	Lexington Local SD	Lexington
174	2,808	Bellefontaine City Schools	Bellefontaine
175	2,805	West Holmes Local SD	Millersburg
176	2,780	Highland Local SD	Medina
177	2,764	Switzerland of Ohio Local SD	Woodsfield
178	2,761	Sugarcreek Local SD	Bellbrook
179	2,760	Tallmadge City Schools	Tallmadge
180	2,745	Jackson City SD	Jackson
181	2,739	Cambridge City SD	Cambridge
182	2,738	Marlington Local SD	Alliance
183	2,725	Crestwood Local SD	Mantua
184	2,719	Miami Trace Local SD	Wash Ct House
185	2,692	Warren Local SD	Vincent
186	2,689	Edison Local SD	Hammondsville
187	2,659	Norwood City SD	Norwood
188	2,657	Shawnee Local SD	Lima
189	2,638	Tipp City Ex Vill SD	Tipp City
190	2,633	Big Walnut Local SD	Galena
190	2,633	Vinton County Local SD	Mc Arthur
192	2,622	Canal Winchester Local SD	Canal Winchester
193	2,598	Dover City SD	Dover
193	2,598	Rocky River City SD	Rocky River
195	2,591	Elida Local SD	Elida
195	2,591	St Marys City SD	Saint Marys
197	2,586	River View Local SD	Warsaw
198	2,580	Ross Local SD	Hamilton
199	2,558	Norton City Schools	Norton
200	2,550	West Geauga Local SD	Chesterland
201	2,547	Clark-Shawnee Local SD	Springfield
202	2,544	Gallia County Local SD	Gallipolis
203	2,541	Defiance City SD	Defiance
204	2,538	Canton Local SD	Canton
205	2,527	Conneaut Area City SD	Conneaut
206	2,525	Goshen Local SD	Goshen
206	2,525	Vermilion Local SD	Vermilion
208	2,514	Poland Local SD	Poland
209	2,508	Avon Local SD	Avon
210	2,490	Circleville City SD	Circleville
211	2,456	Buckeye Local SD	Medina
212	2,455	Bay Village City SD	Bay Village
212	2,455	Beaver Local SD	Lisbon
214	2,447	Northwest Local SD	Canal Fulton
215	2,445	Salem City SD	Salem
216	2,443	West Branch Local SD	Beloit
217	2,418	Franklin Local SD	Duncan Falls
218	2,415	Buckeye Local SD	Rayland
219	2,411	New Richmond Ex Vill SD	New Richmond
220	2,391	Steubenville City SD	Steubenville
221	2,388	Bellevue City SD	Bellevue
222	2,387	Napoleon Area City SD	Napoleon
223	2,368	Orange City SD	Cleveland
224	2,366	Gallipolis City SD	Gallipolis
225	2,362	Willard City SD	Willard
226	2,360	Northern Local SD	Thornville
227	2,353	Urbana City SD	Urbana
228	2,346	Claymont City SD	Dennison
229	2,339	Fostoria City SD	Fostoria
230	2,334	Coventry Local SD	Akron
230	2,334	Eaton Community Schools	Eaton
232	2,323	Logan Elm Local SD	Circleville
233	2,322	Indian Creek Local SD	Wintersville
234	2,319	Greenfield Ex Vill SD	Greenfield
235	2,315	Washington Court House City SD	Wash Ct House
236	2,310	Field Local SD	Mogadore
237	2,305	Hubbard Ex Vill SD	Hubbard
238	2,297	Clyde-Green Springs Ex Vill SD	Clyde
239	2,290	Van Wert City SD	Van Wert
240	2,288	Bryan City SD	Bryan
241	2,287	Buckeye Local SD	Ashtabula
242	2,267	Perkins Local SD	Sandusky
243	2,265	Lakewood Local SD	Hebron
243	2,265	Maysville Local SD	Zanesville
243	2,265	Morgan Local SD	McConnelsville
246	2,260	Indian Hill Ex Vill SD	Cincinnati
247	2,257	Jefferson Area Local SD	Jefferson
248	2,254	Shelby City SD	Shelby
249	2,239	Firelands Local SD	Oberlin
250	2,238	Galion City SD	Galion
251	2,237	Buckeye Valley Local SD	Delaware
252	2,234	Lakeview Local SD	Cortland
253	2,226	Rolling Hills Local SD	Cambridge
254	2,211	Bexley City SD	Bexley
255	2,210	Southeast Local SD	Ravenna
256	2,202	Minerva Local SD	Minerva
257	2,189	Graham Local SD	Saint Paris
258	2,174	Waverly City SD	Waverly
259	2,166	Licking Valley Local SD Sd	Newark
259	2,166	Portsmouth City SD	Portsmouth
261	2,164	Three Rivers Local Schools	Cleves
262	2,150	Triway Local SD	Wooster
263	2,145	Kenton City SD	Kenton
264	2,135	Ohio Virtual Academy	Maumee
265	2,133	Wauseon Ex Vill SD	Wauseon
266	2,121	East Muskingum Local SD	New Concord
267	2,118	Harrison Hills City SD	Hopedale
268	2,113	Granville Ex Vill SD	Granville
269	2,092	Meigs Local SD	Pomeroy
270	2,087	Streetsboro City Schools	Streetsboro
271	2,085	Bath Local SD	Lima
272	2,084	Sheffield-Sheffield Lake City SD	Sheffield Vlg
273	2,081	London City SD	London
274	2,056	Valley View Local SD	Germantown
275	2,042	Oakwood City SD	Dayton
276	2,024	Benton Carroll Salem Local SD	Oak Harbor
277	2,020	Rossford Ex Vill SD	Rossford
278	2,008	Licking Heights Local SD	Summit Station
279	2,004	Struthers City SD	Struthers
280	1,992	Indian Lake Local SD	Lewistown
281	1,990	Northridge Local SD	Dayton
282	1,984	Wyoming City SD	Wyoming
283	1,980	Greenon Local SD	Springfield
284	1,978	Coshocton City SD	Coshocton
284	1,978	Eastwood Local SD	Pemberville
286	1,972	Clermont Northeastern Local SD	Batavia
287	1,971	Port Clinton City SD	Port Clinton
288	1,970	Bethel-Tate Local SD	Bethel
288	1,970	Chagrin Falls Ex Vill SD	Chagrin Falls
290	1,966	Benjamin Logan Local SD	Bellefontaine
290	1,966	New Lexington City SD	New Lexington
292	1,958	Fairfield Union Local SD	W Rushville
293	1,954	Union-Scioto Local SD	Chillicothe
294	1,951	Northwestern Local SD	Springfield
295	1,926	Rock Hill Local SD	Ironton
296	1,924	Batavia Local SD	Batavia
297	1,916	Indian Valley Local SD	Gnadenhutten
298	1,908	North Fork Local SD	Utica
299	1,891	Bucyrus City SD	Bucyrus
300	1,883	Fairless Local SD	Navarre
301	1,874	Berlin-Milan Local SD	Milan
302	1,866	South Point Local SD	South Point
303	1,863	Orrville City SD	Orrville
304	1,857	East Holmes Local Schools	Berlin
305	1,854	Perry Local SD	Perry
305	1,854	Wellston City Schools	Wellston
307	1,843	Clear Fork Valley Local SD	Bellville
307	1,843	Keystone Local SD	Lagrange
309	1,838	Fairland Local SD	Proctorville
310	1,831	Fairview Park City SD	Fairview Park
310	1,831	River Valley Local SD	Caledonia
312	1,819	Liberty Local SD	Youngstown
313	1,816	West Muskingum Local SD	Zanesville
314	1,809	Jonathan Alder Local SD	Plain City
314	1,809	Paulding Ex Vill SD	Paulding
316	1,807	Upper Sandusky Ex Vill SD	Upper Sandusky
317	1,806	Milton-Union Exempted Vill Schls	West Milton
318	1,795	Lake Local SD	Millbury
319	1,787	Finneytown Local SD	Cincinnati
320	1,786	Woodridge Local SD	Peninsula
321	1,781	Highland Local SD	Sparta
321	1,781	Ontario Local SD	Mansfield
323	1,780	Northwest Local SD	Mc Dermott
324	1,775	Carlisle Local SD	Carlisle
325	1,774	Clinton-Massie Local SD	Clarksville
326	1,771	Blanchester Local SD	Blanchester
327	1,769	Girard City SD	Girard
328	1,744	Tuscarawas Valley Local SD	Zoarville
329	1,737	Genoa Area Local SD	Genoa
330	1,731	Ottawa-Glandorf Local SD	Ottawa
331	1,722	Champion Local SD	Warren
332	1,718	Southeast Local SD	Apple Creek
333	1,708	Mariemont City SD	Cincinnati
334	1,707	Heath City SD	Heath
335	1,699	Washington-Nile Local SD	West Portsmouth
336	1,689	Otsego Local SD	Tontogany
337	1,679	Alexander Local SD	Albany
337	1,679	Scioto Valley Local SD	Piketon
339	1,669	Black River Local SD	Sullivan
340	1,667	Preble Shawnee Local SD	Camden
341	1,664	Huron City Schools	Huron
342	1,655	Westfall Local SD	Williamsport
343	1,653	Amanda-Clearcreek Local SD	Amanda
344	1,652	Minford Local SD	Minford
345	1,648	Wellington Ex Vill SD	Wellington
346	1,645	Greeneview Local SD	Jamestown
347	1,631	Brookville Local SD	Brookville
348	1,627	Elgin Local SD	Marion
348	1,627	Madison-Plains Local SD	London
350	1,626	Ironton City SD	Ironton
351	1,623	Coldwater Ex Vill SD	Coldwater
352	1,596	Beachwood City SD	Beachwood

353	1,590	Madison Local SD	Middletown
354	1,589	Zane Trace Local SD	Chillicothe
355	1,585	Swanton Local SD	Swanton
356	1,579	Campbell City SD	Campbell
356	1,579	St Clairsville-Richland City SD	St Clairsville
358	1,574	Pike-Delta-York Local SD	Delta
359	1,571	East Clinton Locai SD	Lees Creek
360	1,570	James A Garfield Local SD	Garrettsville
360	1,570	Wickliffe City SD	Wickliffe
362	1,568	Sandy Valley Local SD	Magnolia
363	1,553	Union Local SD	Morristown
364	1,549	Bellaire Local SD	Bellaire
365	1,543	Eastern Local SD	Sardinia
366	1,538	North College Hill City SD	Cincinnati
367	1,537	United Local SD	Hanoverton
368	1,522	Martins Ferry City SD	Martins Ferry
369	1,521	Monroe Local SD	Monroe
370	1,520	Manchester Local SD	Akron
370	1,520	Newton Falls Ex Vill SD	Newton Falls
372	1,508	Madeira City SD	Cincinnati
373	1,503	Clearview Local SD	Lorain
374	1,501	Ridgewood Local SD	West Lafayette

Male Students

Rank	Percent	District Name	City
1	54.6	Harrison Hills City SD	Hopedale
2	54.6	Orange City SD	Cleveland
3	54.4	Southeast Local SD	Apple Creek
4	54.3	St Marys City SD	Saint Marys
5	54.3	Orrville City SD	Orrville
6	54.3	Tallmadge City Schools	Tallmadge
7	54.2	Genoa Area Local SD	Genoa
8	54.1	Union Local SD	Morristown
9	53.9	Beachwood City SD	Beachwood
10	53.9	Canton Local SD	Canton
11	53.9	Wickliffe City SD	Wickliffe
12	53.8	Tuscarawas Valley Local SD	Zoarville
13	53.8	Mayfield City SD	Highland Hgts
14	53.8	Berlin-Milan Local SD	Milan
15	53.7	Minerva Local SD	Minerva
16	53.7	Maumee City SD	Maumee
17	53.6	Ross Local SD	Hamilton
18	53.5	Brookville Local SD	Brookville
19	53.5	West Carrollton City SD	West Carrollton
20	53.4	Portsmouth City SD	Portsmouth
21	53.4	Buckeye Valley Local SD	Delaware
22	53.4	East Muskingum Local SD	New Concord
23	53.4	Claymont City SD	Dennison
24	53.4	Coldwater Ex Vill SD	Coldwater
25	53.3	North College Hill City SD	Cincinnati
26	53.2	Finneytown Local SD	Cincinnati
27	53.2	Madison Local SD	Mansfield
28	53.2	Hudson City SD	Hudson
29	53.2	Preble Shawnee Local SD	Camden
30	53.2	Piqua City SD	Piqua
31	53.2	Ashland City SD	Ashland
32	53.1	Black River Local SD	Sullivan
33	53.1	Northwest Local SD	Mc Dermott
34	53.0	Wooster City SD	Wooster
35	53.0	River Valley Local SD	Caledonia
36	53.0	Greenfield Ex Vill SD	Greenfield
37	53.0	Vandalia-Butler City SD	Vandalia
38	53.0	Indian Hill Ex Vill SD	Cincinnati
39	52.9	Euclid City SD	Euclid
40	52.9	Field Local SD	Mogadore
41	52.9	Massillon City SD	Massillon
42	52.8	Mt Healthy City SD	Cincinnati
43	52.8	Painesville City Local SD	Painesville
44	52.8	Berea City SD	Berea
45	52.8	Highland Local SD	Sparta
46	52.8	Garfield Heights City SD	Garfield Hgts
47	52.7	Lakewood Local SD	Hebron
48	52.7	Liberty Local SD	Youngstown
49	52.7	New Lexington City SD	New Lexington
50	52.7	Fairborn City Schools	Fairborn
51	52.7	Wadsworth City SD	Wadsworth
52	52.7	Bexley City SD	Bexley
53	52.6	Avon Lake City Schools	Avon Lake
54	52.6	Milton-Union Exempted Vill Schls	West Milton
55	52.6	Edgewood City SD	Trenton
56	52.6	Ironton City SD	Ironton
57	52.6	Jackson City SD	Jackson
58	52.6	Springfield Local Schools	Holland
59	52.6	Celina City SD	Celina
60	52.6	Amanda-Clearcreek Local SD	Amanda
61	52.6	Oregon City SD	Oregon
62	52.5	Vinton County Local SD	Mc Arthur
63	52.5	Oak Hills Local SD	Cincinnati
64	52.5	Green Local SD	Green
65	52.5	Kenton City SD	Kenton
66	52.5	Northwest Local SD	Cincinnati
67	52.5	Lancaster City SD	Lancaster
68	52.5	Perry Local SD	Massillon
69	52.5	Winton Woods City SD	Cincinnati
70	52.5	Jefferson Area Local SD	Jefferson
71	52.4	Carlisle Local SD	Carlisle
72	52.4	Lima City SD	Lima
73	52.4	Madeira City SD	Cincinnati
74	52.4	Warren Local SD	Vincent
75	52.4	Crestwood Local SD	Mantua
76	52.4	Logan Elm Local SD	Circleville
77	52.4	Perrysburg Exempted Village	Perrysburg
78	52.4	Bryan City SD	Bryan
79	52.4	Conneaut Area City SD	Conneaut
80	52.4	Cambridge City SD	Cambridge
81	52.4	Strongsville City SD	Strongsville
82	52.4	Kettering City SD	Kettering
83	52.3	Lake Local SD	Hartville
84	52.3	Lakewood City SD	Lakewood
85	52.3	Washington Court House City SD	Wash Ct House
86	52.3	Pickerington Local SD	Pickerington
87	52.3	Miami Trace Local SD	Wash Ct House
88	52.3	Gahanna-Jefferson City SD	Gahanna
89	52.3	Springfield City SD	Springfield
90	52.3	Chagrin Falls Ex Vill SD	Chagrin Falls
91	52.2	Washington Local Schools	Toledo
92	52.2	Geneva Area City Schools	Geneva
93	52.2	Southwest Local SD	Harrison
94	52.2	Tiffin City SD	Tiffin
95	52.2	Campbell City SD	Campbell
96	52.2	East Holmes Local Schools	Berlin
97	52.2	Port Clinton City SD	Port Clinton
98	52.2	North Olmsted City Schools	North Olmsted
99	52.2	Valley View Local SD	Germantown
100	52.2	Champion Local SD	Warren
101	52.2	Urbana City SD	Urbana
102	52.2	Lexington Local SD	Lexington
103	52.2	Teays Valley Local SD	Ashville
104	52.2	Kings Local SD	Kings Mills
105	52.2	Clermont Northeastern Local SD	Batavia
106	52.2	Sandy Valley Local SD	Magnolia
107	52.2	North Ridgeville City SD	N Ridgeville
108	52.1	Ontario Local SD	Mansfield
109	52.1	Worthington City SD	Worthington
110	52.1	Norwood City SD	Norwood
111	52.1	Maple Heights City SD	Maple Heights
112	52.1	Rossford Ex Vill SD	Rossford
113	52.1	Logan-Hocking Local SD	Logan
114	52.1	Bellaire Local SD	Bellaire
115	52.1	Marysville Exempted Village SD	Marysville
116	52.1	Switzerland of Ohio Local SD	Woodsfield
117	52.1	St Clairsville-Richland City SD	St Clairsville
118	52.1	River View Local SD	Warsaw
119	52.1	Kent City SD	Kent
120	52.1	Fairview Park City SD	Fairview Park
121	52.1	Three Rivers Local Schools	Cleves
122	52.1	Rock Hill Local SD	Ironton
123	52.1	Huber Heights City SD	Huber Heights
124	52.1	West Geauga Local SD	Chesterland
125	52.0	Madison Local SD	Madison
126	52.0	Wyoming City SD	Wyoming
127	52.0	Miamisburg City SD	Miamisburg
128	52.0	Beaver Local SD	Lisbon
129	52.0	Ohio Virtual Academy	Maumee
130	52.0	Ashtabula Area City SD	Ashtabula
131	52.0	Southeast Local SD	Ravenna
132	52.0	South Euclid-Lyndhurst City SD	Lyndhurst
133	52.0	Mariemont City SD	Cincinnati
134	52.0	Wilmington City SD	Wilmington
135	52.0	West Branch Local SD	Beloit
136	51.9	Marion City SD	Marion
137	51.9	Batavia Local SD	Batavia
138	51.9	Shelby City SD	Shelby
139	51.9	Waverly City SD	Waverly
140	51.9	North Fork Local SD	Utica
141	51.9	Bucyrus City SD	Bucyrus
142	51.9	Martins Ferry City SD	Martins Ferry
143	51.9	Lakota Local SD	Liberty Twp
144	51.9	Fairfield Union Local SD	W Rushville
145	51.9	Firelands Local SD	Oberlin
146	51.8	Twinsburg City SD	Twinsburg
147	51.8	Clinton-Massie Local SD	Clarksville
148	51.8	Willoughby-Eastlake City SD	Willoughby
149	51.8	Northeastern Local SD	Springfield
150	51.8	Boardman Local SD	Youngstown
151	51.8	Mount Vernon City SD	Mount Vernon
152	51.8	Shaker Heights City SD	Shaker Heights
153	51.8	Woodridge Local SD	Peninsula
154	51.8	Fostoria City SD	Fostoria
155	51.8	Stow-Munroe Falls City SD	Stow
156	51.8	Indian Creek Local SD	Wintersville
157	51.8	Toledo City SD	Toledo
158	51.8	Trotwood-Madison City Schools	Trotwood
159	51.8	Mansfield City SD	Mansfield
160	51.7	Barberton City SD	Barberton
161	51.7	Centerville City SD	Centerville
162	51.7	Swanton Local SD	Swanton
163	51.7	Bellevue City SD	Bellevue
164	51.7	Dover City SD	Dover
165	51.7	Franklin Local SD	Duncan Falls
166	51.7	Huron City Schools	Huron
167	51.7	Scioto Valley Local SD	Piketon
168	51.7	Fairland Local SD	Proctorville
169	51.7	New Richmond Ex Vill SD	New Richmond
170	51.7	Princeton City SD	Cincinnati
171	51.7	Eaton Community Schools	Eaton
172	51.7	Coshocton City SD	Coshocton
173	51.7	West Clermont Local SD	Cincinnati
174	51.7	Troy City SD	Troy
175	51.7	Elida Local SD	Elida
176	51.7	Defiance City SD	Defiance
177	51.6	Delaware City SD	Delaware
178	51.6	Poland Local SD	Poland
178	51.6	Steubenville City SD	Steubenville
180	51.6	Xenia Community City SD	Xenia
181	51.6	Lorain City SD	Lorain
182	51.6	Monroe Local SD	Monroe
183	51.6	Milford Ex Vill SD	Milford
184	51.6	Sidney City SD	Sidney
185	51.6	Hilliard City SD	Hilliard
186	51.6	Midview Local SD	Grafton
187	51.6	Buckeye Local SD	Rayland
188	51.6	Revere Local SD	Bath
189	51.6	Hillsboro City SD	Hillsboro
190	51.6	Eastern Local SD	Sardinia
191	51.5	Fremont City SD	Fremont
192	51.5	Licking Heights Local SD	Summit Station
193	51.5	Cloverleaf Local SD	Lodi
194	51.5	Nordonia Hills City SD	Northfield
195	51.5	East Liverpool City SD	East Liverpool
196	51.5	Greeneview Local SD	Jamestown
197	51.5	Girard City SD	Girard
198	51.5	Shawnee Local SD	Lima
199	51.5	Dublin City SD	Dublin
200	51.5	Middletown City SD	Middletown
201	51.5	Ravenna City SD	Ravenna
202	51.5	Norwalk City SD	Norwalk
203	51.5	Sugarcreek Local SD	Bellbrook
204	51.5	Northwest Local SD	Canal Fulton
205	51.5	Marietta City Schools	Marietta
206	51.4	New Philadelphia City SD	New Philadelphia
207	51.4	Bowling Green City SD	Bowling Green
208	51.4	Austintown Local SD	Youngstown
209	51.4	Washington-Nile Local SD	West Portsmouth
210	51.4	Streetsboro City Schools	Streetsboro
211	51.4	Mason City SD	Mason
212	51.4	Hamilton City SD	Hamilton
213	51.4	Tipp City Ex Vill SD	Tipp City
214	51.4	Painesville Township Local SD	Painesville
215	51.4	Findlay City SD	Findlay
216	51.4	Edison Local SD	Hammondsville
217	51.4	Sycamore Community City SD	Cincinnati
218	51.4	Kenston Local SD	Chagrin Falls
219	51.4	Granville Ex Vill SD	Granville
220	51.4	Cleveland Municipal City SD	Cleveland
221	51.4	Westerville City SD	Westerville
222	51.3	South-Western City SD	Grove City
223	51.3	Dayton City SD	Dayton
224	51.3	Highland Local SD	Medina
225	51.3	West Muskingum Local SD	Zanesville
226	51.3	Akron Public Schools	Akron
227	51.3	Northern Local SD	Thornville
228	51.3	Western Brown Local SD	Mount Orab
229	51.3	Gallia County Local SD	Gallipolis
230	51.2	Canfield Local SD	Canfield
231	51.2	Alexander Local SD	Albany
232	51.2	Gallipolis City SD	Gallipolis
233	51.2	Eastwood Local SD	Pemberville
234	51.2	Ridgewood Local SD	West Lafayette
235	51.2	Youngstown City SD	Youngstown
236	51.2	Westlake City SD	Westlake
237	51.2	Lake Local SD	Millbury
238	51.2	Big Walnut Local SD	Galena
239	51.2	Newton Falls Ex Vill SD	Newton Falls
240	51.2	Madison-Plains Local SD	London
241	51.2	Tecumseh Local SD	New Carlisle
242	51.2	Paulding Ex Vill SD	Paulding
243	51.2	Benton Carroll Salem Local SD	Oak Harbor
244	51.2	Wellington Ex Vill SD	Wellington
245	51.2	Napoleon Area City SD	Napoleon
246	51.2	Franklin City SD	Franklin
247	51.2	Tri-Valley Local Schools	Dresden
248	51.2	Copley-Fairlawn City SD	Copley
249	51.2	Solon City SD	Solon
250	51.1	Wapakoneta City City SD	Wapakoneta
251	51.1	Clark-Shawnee Local SD	Springfield
252	51.1	London City SD	London

253	51.1	Canton City SD	Canton
254	51.1	Morgan Local SD	McConnelsville
255	51.1	Talawanda City SD	Oxford
256	51.1	Chardon Local SD	Chardon
257	51.1	Licking Valley Local SD Sd	Newark
258	51.1	Graham Local SD	Saint Paris
259	51.1	Sylvania City SD	Sylvania
260	51.1	Beavercreek City SD	Beavercreek
261	51.1	Bellefontaine City Schools	Bellefontaine
262	51.1	Westfall Local SD	Williamsport
263	51.1	Alliance City SD	Alliance
264	51.0	Northmont City SD	Englewood
265	51.0	Vermilion Local SD	Vermilion
266	51.0	Springfield Local SD	Akron
267	51.0	Whitehall City SD	Whitehall
268	51.0	Niles City SD	Niles
269	51.0	Groveport Madison Local SD	Groveport
270	51.0	Chillicothe City SD	Chillicothe
271	51.0	Upper Arlington City SD	Upper Arlington
272	51.0	Upper Sandusky Ex Vill SD	Upper Sandusky
273	50.9	Medina City SD	Medina
274	50.9	Jonathan Alder Local SD	Plain City
275	50.9	Clyde-Green Springs Ex Vill SD	Clyde
276	50.9	Bethel-Tate Local SD	Bethel
277	50.9	Cuyahoga Falls City SD	Cuyahoga Falls
278	50.9	Clear Fork Valley Local SD	Bellville
279	50.9	Columbus Public Schools	Columbus
280	50.9	Elyria City SD	Elyria
281	50.9	Greenville City SD	Greenville
282	50.9	Reynoldsburg City SD	Reynoldsburg
283	50.9	Pike-Delta-York Local SD	Delta
284	50.9	Newark City SD	Newark
285	50.8	Springboro Community City SD	Springboro
286	50.8	Benjamin Logan Local SD	Bellefontaine
287	50.8	Elgin Local SD	Marion
288	50.8	Indian Lake Local SD	Lewistown
289	50.8	Lebanon City SD	Lebanon
290	50.8	Aurora City SD	Aurora
291	50.8	Athens City SD	The Plains
292	50.8	Howland Local SD	Warren
293	50.8	Wellston City Schools	Wellston
294	50.8	Van Wert City SD	Van Wert
295	50.8	Plain Local SD	Canton
296	50.8	Fairless Local SD	Navarre
297	50.7	Blanchester Local SD	Blanchester
298	50.7	Forest Hills Local SD	Cincinnati
299	50.7	Sandusky City SD	Sandusky
300	50.7	Otsego Local SD	Tontogany
301	50.7	Indian Valley Local SD	Gnadenhutten
302	50.7	Struthers City SD	Struthers
303	50.7	Canal Winchester Local SD	Canal Winchester
304	50.7	Mentor Ex Vill SD	Mentor
305	50.7	Brecksville-Broadview Hgts City	Brecksville
306	50.7	Bedford City SD	Bedford
307	50.7	Meigs Local SD	Pomeroy
308	50.7	West Holmes Local SD	Millersburg
309	50.7	North Canton City SD	North Canton
310	50.7	Buckeye Local SD	Medina
311	50.7	Goshen Local SD	Goshen
312	50.7	North Royalton City SD	N Royalton
313	50.7	Southwest Licking Local SD	Etna
314	50.7	Willard City SD	Willard
315	50.7	Minford Local SD	Minford
316	50.6	Bath Local SD	Lima
317	50.6	Hubbard Ex Vill SD	Hubbard
318	50.6	Olmsted Falls City SD	Olmsted Falls
319	50.6	Amherst Ex Vill SD	Amherst
320	50.6	Olentangy Local SD	Lewis Center
321	50.6	Parma City SD	Parma
322	50.6	Plain Local SD	New Albany
323	50.6	Heath City SD	Heath
324	50.5	Hamilton Local SD	Columbus
325	50.5	United Local SD	Hanoverton
326	50.5	Circleville City SD	Circleville
327	50.5	Loveland City SD	Loveland
328	50.5	Cleveland Hts-Univ Hts City SD	University Hgts
329	50.5	Brunswick City SD	Brunswick
330	50.5	Greenon Local SD	Springfield
331	50.4	Salem City SD	Salem
332	50.4	Wauseon Ex Vill SD	Wauseon
333	50.4	Fairfield City SD	Fairfield
334	50.4	Triway Local SD	Wooster
335	50.3	Mad River Local SD	Dayton
336	50.3	Jackson Local SD	Massillon
337	50.3	Warren City SD	Warren
338	50.3	Perry Local SD	Perry
339	50.3	James A Garfield Local SD	Garrettsville
340	50.3	Rocky River City SD	Rocky River
341	50.2	Keystone Local SD	Lagrange
342	50.1	Bay Village City SD	Bay Village
343	50.1	Maysville Local SD	Zanesville
344	50.1	East Clinton Local SD	Lees Creek
345	50.1	Carrollton Ex Vill SD	Carrollton
346	50.0	Norton City Schools	Norton
347	50.0	Adams County/Ohio Valley LSD	West Union
348	50.0	Lakeview Local SD	Cortland
349	49.9	Avon Local SD	Avon
350	49.9	Union-Scioto Local SD	Chillicothe
351	49.8	Little Miami Local SD	Morrow
352	49.8	Anthony Wayne Local SD	Whitehouse
353	49.7	Madison Local SD	Middletown
354	49.7	Northwestern Local SD	Springfield
355	49.7	Coventry Local SD	Akron
356	49.6	Northridge Local SD	Dayton
357	49.5	Perkins Local SD	Sandusky
358	49.5	Ottawa-Glandorf Local SD	Ottawa
359	49.4	Marlington Local SD	Alliance
360	49.3	Louisville City SD	Louisville
361	49.3	South Point Local SD	South Point
362	49.3	Manchester Local SD	Akron
363	49.3	Rolling Hills Local SD	Cambridge
364	49.3	Zanesville City SD	Zanesville
365	49.2	Oakwood City SD	Dayton
366	49.1	Cincinnati City SD	Cincinnati
367	49.1	Clearview Local SD	Lorain
368	49.1	Buckeye Local SD	Ashtabula
369	49.1	Warrensville Heights City SD	Warrensville Hgts
370	48.9	East Cleveland City SD	East Cleveland
371	48.6	Zane Trace Local SD	Chillicothe
372	48.1	Galion City SD	Galion
373	48.0	Sheffield-Sheffield Lake City SD	Sheffield Vlg
374	45.7	Electronic Classrm of Tomorrow	Columbus

Female Students

Rank	Percent	District Name	City
1	54.2	Electronic Classrm of Tomorrow	Columbus
2	51.9	Sheffield-Sheffield Lake City SD	Sheffield Vlg
3	51.8	Galion City SD	Galion
4	51.3	Zane Trace Local SD	Chillicothe
5	51.0	East Cleveland City SD	East Cleveland
6	50.8	Warrensville Heights City SD	Warrensville Hgts
7	50.8	Buckeye Local SD	Ashtabula
8	50.8	Clearview Local SD	Lorain
9	50.8	Cincinnati City SD	Cincinnati
10	50.7	Oakwood City SD	Dayton
11	50.6	Zanesville City SD	Zanesville
12	50.6	Rolling Hills Local SD	Cambridge
13	50.6	Manchester Local SD	Akron
14	50.6	South Point Local SD	South Point
15	50.6	Louisville City SD	Louisville
16	50.5	Marlington Local SD	Alliance
17	50.4	Ottawa-Glandorf Local SD	Ottawa
18	50.4	Perkins Local SD	Sandusky
19	50.3	Northridge Local SD	Dayton
20	50.2	Coventry Local SD	Akron
21	50.2	Northwestern Local SD	Springfield
22	50.2	Madison Local SD	Middletown
23	50.1	Anthony Wayne Local SD	Whitehouse
24	50.1	Little Miami Local SD	Morrow
25	50.0	Union-Scioto Local SD	Chillicothe
26	50.0	Avon Local SD	Avon
27	50.0	Lakeview Local SD	Cortland
28	49.9	Adams County/Ohio Valley LSD	West Union
29	49.9	Norton City Schools	Norton
30	49.8	Carrollton Ex Vill SD	Carrollton
31	49.8	East Clinton Local SD	Lees Creek
32	49.8	Maysville Local SD	Zanesville
33	49.8	Bay Village City SD	Bay Village
34	49.7	Keystone Local SD	Lagrange
35	49.6	Rocky River City SD	Rocky River
36	49.6	James A Garfield Local SD	Garrettsville
37	49.6	Perry Local SD	Perry
38	49.6	Warren City SD	Warren
39	49.6	Jackson Local SD	Massillon
40	49.6	Mad River Local SD	Dayton
41	49.5	Triway Local SD	Wooster
42	49.5	Fairfield City SD	Fairfield
43	49.5	Wauseon Ex Vill SD	Wauseon
44	49.5	Salem City SD	Salem
45	49.4	Greenon Local SD	Springfield
46	49.4	Brunswick City SD	Brunswick
47	49.4	Cleveland Hts-Univ Hts City SD	University Hgts
48	49.4	Loveland City SD	Loveland
49	49.4	Circleville City SD	Circleville
50	49.4	United Local SD	Hanoverton
51	49.4	Hamilton Local SD	Columbus
52	49.3	Heath City SD	Heath
53	49.3	Plain Local SD	New Albany
54	49.3	Parma City SD	Parma
55	49.3	Olentangy Local SD	Lewis Center
56	49.3	Amherst Ex Vill SD	Amherst
57	49.3	Olmsted Falls City SD	Olmsted Falls
58	49.3	Hubbard Ex Vill SD	Hubbard
59	49.3	Bath Local SD	Lima
60	49.2	Minford Local SD	Minford
61	49.2	Willard City SD	Willard
62	49.2	Southwest Licking Local SD	Etna
63	49.2	North Royalton City SD	N Royalton
64	49.2	Goshen Local SD	Goshen
65	49.2	Buckeye Local SD	Medina
66	49.2	North Canton City SD	North Canton
67	49.2	West Holmes Local SD	Millersburg
68	49.2	Meigs Local SD	Pomeroy
69	49.2	Bedford City SD	Bedford
70	49.2	Brecksville-Broadview Hgts City	Brecksville
71	49.2	Mentor Ex Vill SD	Mentor
72	49.2	Canal Winchester Local SD	Canal Winchester
73	49.2	Struthers City SD	Struthers
74	49.2	Indian Valley Local SD	Gnadenhutten
75	49.2	Otsego Local SD	Tontogany
76	49.2	Sandusky City SD	Sandusky
77	49.2	Forest Hills Local SD	Cincinnati
78	49.2	Blanchester Local SD	Blanchester
79	49.1	Fairless Local SD	Navarre
80	49.1	Plain Local SD	Canton
81	49.1	Van Wert City SD	Van Wert
82	49.1	Wellston City Schools	Wellston
83	49.1	Howland Local SD	Warren
84	49.1	Athens City SD	The Plains
85	49.1	Aurora City SD	Aurora
86	49.1	Lebanon City SD	Lebanon
87	49.1	Indian Lake Local SD	Lewistown
88	49.1	Elgin Local SD	Marion
89	49.1	Benjamin Logan Local SD	Bellefontaine
90	49.1	Springboro Community City SD	Springboro
91	49.0	Newark City SD	Newark
92	49.0	Pike-Delta-York Local SD	Delta
93	49.0	Reynoldsburg City SD	Reynoldsburg
94	49.0	Greenville City SD	Greenville
95	49.0	Elyria City SD	Elyria
96	49.0	Columbus Public Schools	Columbus
97	49.0	Clear Fork Valley Local SD	Bellville
98	49.0	Cuyahoga Falls City SD	Cuyahoga Falls
99	49.0	Bethel-Tate Local SD	Bethel
100	49.0	Clyde-Green Springs Ex Vill SD	Clyde
101	49.0	Jonathan Alder Local SD	Plain City
102	49.0	Medina City SD	Medina
103	48.9	Upper Sandusky Ex Vill SD	Upper Sandusky
104	48.9	Upper Arlington City SD	Upper Arlington
105	48.9	Chillicothe City SD	Chillicothe
106	48.9	Groveport Madison Local SD	Groveport
107	48.9	Niles City SD	Niles
108	48.9	Whitehall City SD	Whitehall
109	48.9	Springfield Local SD	Akron
110	48.9	Vermilion Local SD	Vermilion
111	48.9	Northmont City SD	Englewood
112	48.8	Alliance City SD	Alliance
113	48.8	Westfall Local SD	Williamsport
114	48.8	Bellefontaine City Schools	Bellefontaine
115	48.8	Beavercreek City SD	Beavercreek
116	48.8	Sylvania City SD	Sylvania
117	48.8	Graham Local SD	Saint Paris
118	48.8	Licking Valley Local SD Sd	Newark
119	48.8	Chardon Local SD	Chardon
120	48.8	Talawanda City SD	Oxford
121	48.8	Morgan Local SD	McConnelsville
122	48.8	Canton City SD	Canton
123	48.8	London City SD	London
124	48.8	Clark-Shawnee Local SD	Springfield
125	48.8	Wapakoneta City City SD	Wapakoneta
126	48.7	Solon City SD	Solon
127	48.7	Copley-Fairlawn City SD	Copley
128	48.7	Tri-Valley Local Schools	Dresden
129	48.7	Franklin City SD	Franklin
130	48.7	Napoleon Area City SD	Napoleon
131	48.7	Wellington Ex Vill SD	Wellington
132	48.7	Benton Carroll Salem Local SD	Oak Harbor
133	48.7	Paulding Ex Vill SD	Paulding
134	48.7	Tecumseh Local SD	New Carlisle
135	48.7	Madison-Plains Local SD	London
136	48.7	Newton Falls Ex Vill SD	Newton Falls
137	48.7	Big Walnut Local SD	Galena
138	48.7	Lake Local SD	Millbury
139	48.7	Westlake City SD	Westlake
140	48.7	Youngstown City SD	Youngstown
141	48.7	Ridgewood Local SD	West Lafayette
142	48.7	Eastwood Local SD	Pemberville
143	48.7	Gallipolis City SD	Gallipolis
144	48.7	Alexander Local SD	Albany
145	48.7	Canfield Local SD	Canfield
146	48.6	Gallia County Local SD	Gallipolis
147	48.6	Western Brown Local SD	Mount Orab
148	48.6	Northern Local SD	Thornville
149	48.6	Akron Public Schools	Akron
150	48.6	West Muskingum Local SD	Zanesville
151	48.6	Highland Local SD	Medina

152	48.6	Dayton City SD	Dayton
153	48.6	South-Western City SD	Grove City
154	48.5	Westerville City SD	Westerville
155	48.5	Cleveland Municipal City SD	Cleveland
156	48.5	Granville Ex Vill SD	Granville
157	48.5	Kenston Local SD	Chagrin Falls
158	48.5	Sycamore Community City SD	Cincinnati
159	48.5	Edison Local SD	Hammondsville
160	48.5	Findlay City SD	Findlay
161	48.5	Painesville Township Local SD	Painesville
162	48.5	Tipp City Ex Vill SD	Tipp City
163	48.5	Hamilton City SD	Hamilton
164	48.5	Mason City SD	Mason
165	48.5	Streetsboro City Schools	Streetsboro
166	48.5	Washington-Nile Local SD	West Portsmouth
167	48.5	Austintown Local SD	Youngstown
168	48.5	Bowling Green City SD	Bowling Green
169	48.5	New Philadelphia City SD	New Philadelphia
170	48.4	Marietta City Schools	Marietta
171	48.4	Northwest Local SD	Canal Fulton
172	48.4	Sugarcreek Local SD	Bellbrook
173	48.4	Norwalk City SD	Norwalk
174	48.4	Ravenna City SD	Ravenna
175	48.4	Middletown City SD	Middletown
176	48.4	Dublin City SD	Dublin
177	48.4	Shawnee Local SD	Lima
178	48.4	Girard City SD	Girard
179	48.4	Greeneview Local SD	Jamestown
180	48.4	East Liverpool City SD	East Liverpool
181	48.4	Nordonia Hills City SD	Northfield
182	48.4	Cloverleaf Local SD	Lodi
183	48.4	Licking Heights Local SD	Summit Station
184	48.4	Fremont City SD	Fremont
185	48.3	Eastern Local SD	Sardinia
186	48.3	Hillsboro City SD	Hillsboro
187	48.3	Revere Local SD	Bath
188	48.3	Buckeye Local SD	Rayland
189	48.3	Midview Local SD	Grafton
190	48.3	Hilliard City SD	Hilliard
191	48.3	Sidney City SD	Sidney
192	48.3	Milford Ex Vill SD	Milford
193	48.3	Monroe Local SD	Monroe
194	48.3	Lorain City SD	Lorain
195	48.3	Xenia Community City SD	Xenia
196	48.3	Poland Local SD	Poland
196	48.3	Steubenville City SD	Steubenville
198	48.3	Delaware City SD	Delaware
199	48.2	Defiance City SD	Defiance
200	48.2	Elida Local SD	Elida
201	48.2	Troy City SD	Troy
202	48.2	West Clermont Local SD	Cincinnati
203	48.2	Coshocton City SD	Coshocton
204	48.2	Eaton Community Schools	Eaton
205	48.2	Princeton City SD	Cincinnati
206	48.2	New Richmond Ex Vill SD	New Richmond
207	48.2	Fairland Local SD	Proctorville
208	48.2	Scioto Valley Local SD	Piketon
209	48.2	Huron City Schools	Huron
210	48.2	Franklin Local SD	Duncan Falls
211	48.2	Dover City SD	Dover
212	48.2	Bellevue City SD	Bellevue
213	48.2	Swanton Local SD	Swanton
214	48.2	Centerville City SD	Centerville
215	48.2	Barberton City SD	Barberton
216	48.1	Mansfield City SD	Mansfield
217	48.1	Trotwood-Madison City Schools	Trotwood
218	48.1	Toledo City SD	Toledo
219	48.1	Indian Creek Local SD	Wintersville
220	48.1	Stow-Munroe Falls City SD	Stow
221	48.1	Fostoria City SD	Fostoria
222	48.1	Woodridge Local SD	Peninsula
223	48.1	Shaker Heights City SD	Shaker Heights
224	48.1	Mount Vernon City SD	Mount Vernon
225	48.1	Boardman Local SD	Youngstown
226	48.1	Northeastern Local SD	Springfield
227	48.1	Willoughby-Eastlake City SD	Willoughby
228	48.1	Clinton-Massie Local SD	Clarksville
229	48.1	Twinsburg City SD	Twinsburg
230	48.0	Firelands Local SD	Oberlin
231	48.0	Fairfield Union Local SD	W Rushville
232	48.0	Lakota Local SD	Liberty Twp
233	48.0	Martins Ferry City SD	Martins Ferry
234	48.0	Bucyrus City SD	Bucyrus
235	48.0	North Fork Local SD	Utica
236	48.0	Waverly City SD	Waverly
237	48.0	Shelby City SD	Shelby
238	48.0	Batavia Local SD	Batavia
239	48.0	Marion City SD	Marion
240	47.9	West Branch Local SD	Beloit
241	47.9	Wilmington City SD	Wilmington
242	47.9	Mariemont City SD	Cincinnati
243	47.9	South Euclid-Lyndhurst City SD	Lyndhurst
244	47.9	Southeast Local SD	Ravenna
245	47.9	Ashtabula Area City SD	Ashtabula
246	47.9	Ohio Virtual Academy	Maumee
247	47.9	Beaver Local SD	Lisbon
248	47.9	Miamisburg City SD	Miamisburg
249	47.9	Wyoming City SD	Wyoming
250	47.9	Madison Local SD	Madison
251	47.8	West Geauga Local SD	Chesterland
252	47.8	Huber Heights City SD	Huber Heights
253	47.8	Rock Hill Local SD	Ironton
254	47.8	Three Rivers Local Schools	Cleves
255	47.8	Fairview Park City SD	Fairview Park
256	47.8	Kent City SD	Kent
257	47.8	River View Local SD	Warsaw
258	47.8	St Clairsville-Richland City SD	St Clairsville
259	47.8	Switzerland of Ohio Local SD	Woodsfield
260	47.8	Marysville Exempted Village SD	Marysville
261	47.8	Bellaire Local SD	Bellaire
262	47.8	Logan-Hocking Local SD	Logan
263	47.8	Rossford Ex Vill SD	Rossford
264	47.8	Maple Heights City SD	Maple Heights
265	47.8	Norwood City SD	Norwood
266	47.8	Worthington City SD	Worthington
267	47.8	Ontario Local SD	Mansfield
268	47.7	North Ridgeville City SD	N Ridgeville
269	47.7	Sandy Valley Local SD	Magnolia
270	47.7	Clermont Northeastern Local SD	Batavia
271	47.7	Kings Local SD	Kings Mills
272	47.7	Teays Valley Local SD	Ashville
273	47.7	Lexington Local SD	Lexington
274	47.7	Urbana City SD	Urbana
275	47.7	Champion Local SD	Warren
276	47.7	Valley View Local SD	Germantown
277	47.7	North Olmsted City Schools	North Olmsted
278	47.7	Port Clinton City SD	Port Clinton
279	47.7	East Holmes Local Schools	Berlin
280	47.7	Campbell City SD	Campbell
281	47.7	Tiffin City SD	Tiffin
282	47.7	Southwest Local SD	Harrison
283	47.7	Geneva Area City Schools	Geneva
284	47.7	Washington Local Schools	Toledo
285	47.6	Chagrin Falls Ex Vill SD	Chagrin Falls
286	47.6	Springfield City SD	Springfield
287	47.6	Gahanna-Jefferson City SD	Gahanna
288	47.6	Miami Trace Local SD	Wash Ct House
289	47.6	Pickerington Local SD	Pickerington
290	47.6	Washington Court House City SD	Wash Ct House
291	47.6	Lakewood City SD	Lakewood
292	47.6	Lake Local SD	Hartville
293	47.5	Kettering City SD	Kettering
294	47.5	Strongsville City SD	Strongsville
295	47.5	Cambridge City SD	Cambridge
296	47.5	Conneaut Area City SD	Conneaut
297	47.5	Bryan City SD	Bryan
298	47.5	Perrysburg Exempted Village	Perrysburg
299	47.5	Logan Elm Local SD	Circleville
300	47.5	Crestwood Local SD	Mantua
301	47.5	Warren Local SD	Vincent
302	47.5	Madeira City SD	Cincinnati
303	47.5	Lima City SD	Lima
304	47.5	Carlisle Local SD	Carlisle
305	47.4	Jefferson Area Local SD	Jefferson
306	47.4	Winton Woods City SD	Cincinnati
307	47.4	Perry Local SD	Massillon
308	47.4	Lancaster City SD	Lancaster
309	47.4	Northwest Local SD	Cincinnati
310	47.4	Kenton City SD	Kenton
311	47.4	Green Local SD	Green
312	47.4	Oak Hills Local SD	Cincinnati
313	47.4	Vinton County Local SD	Mc Arthur
314	47.3	Oregon City SD	Oregon
315	47.3	Amanda-Clearcreek Local SD	Amanda
316	47.3	Celina City SD	Celina
317	47.3	Springfield Local Schools	Holland
318	47.3	Jackson City SD	Jackson
319	47.3	Ironton City SD	Ironton
320	47.3	Edgewood City SD	Trenton
321	47.3	Milton-Union Exempted Vill Schls	West Milton
322	47.3	Avon Lake City Schools	Avon Lake
323	47.2	Bexley City SD	Bexley
324	47.2	Wadsworth City SD	Wadsworth
325	47.2	Fairborn City Schools	Fairborn
326	47.2	New Lexington City SD	New Lexington
327	47.2	Liberty Local SD	Youngstown
328	47.2	Lakewood Local SD	Hebron
329	47.1	Garfield Heights City SD	Garfield Hgts
330	47.1	Highland Local SD	Sparta
331	47.1	Berea City SD	Berea
332	47.1	Painesville City Local SD	Painesville
333	47.1	Mt Healthy City SD	Cincinnati
334	47.0	Massillon City SD	Massillon
335	47.0	Field Local SD	Mogadore
336	47.0	Euclid City SD	Euclid
337	46.9	Indian Hill Ex Vill SD	Cincinnati
338	46.9	Vandalia-Butler City SD	Vandalia
339	46.9	Greenfield Ex Vill SD	Greenfield
340	46.9	River Valley Local SD	Caledonia
341	46.9	Wooster City SD	Wooster
342	46.8	Northwest Local SD	Mc Dermott
343	46.8	Black River Local SD	Sullivan
344	46.7	Ashland City SD	Ashland
345	46.7	Piqua City SD	Piqua
346	46.7	Preble Shawnee Local SD	Camden
347	46.7	Hudson City SD	Hudson
348	46.7	Madison Local SD	Mansfield
349	46.7	Finneytown Local SD	Cincinnati
350	46.6	North College Hill City SD	Cincinnati
351	46.5	Coldwater Ex Vill SD	Coldwater
352	46.5	Claymont City SD	Dennison
353	46.5	East Muskingum Local SD	New Concord
354	46.5	Buckeye Valley Local SD	Delaware
355	46.5	Portsmouth City SD	Portsmouth
356	46.4	West Carrollton City SD	West Carrollton
357	46.4	Brookville Local SD	Brookville
358	46.3	Ross Local SD	Hamilton
359	46.2	Maumee City SD	Maumee
360	46.2	Minerva Local SD	Minerva
361	46.1	Berlin-Milan Local SD	Milan
362	46.1	Mayfield City SD	Highland Hgts
363	46.1	Tuscarawas Valley Local SD	Zoarville
364	46.0	Wickliffe City SD	Wickliffe
365	46.0	Canton Local SD	Canton
366	46.0	Beachwood City SD	Beachwood
367	45.8	Union Local SD	Morristown
368	45.7	Genoa Area Local SD	Genoa
369	45.6	Tallmadge City Schools	Tallmadge
370	45.6	Orrville City SD	Orrville
371	45.6	St Marys City SD	Saint Marys
372	45.5	Southeast Local SD	Apple Creek
373	45.3	Orange City SD	Cleveland
374	45.3	Harrison Hills City SD	Hopedale

Individual Education Program Students

Rank	Percent	District Name	City
1	29.6	Harrison Hills City SD	Hopedale
2	23.5	Dayton City SD	Dayton
3	22.8	Zanesville City SD	Zanesville
4	22.1	Coshocton City SD	Coshocton
5	22.0	Bellaire Local SD	Bellaire
6	21.8	Claymont City SD	Dennison
7	21.7	Gallipolis City SD	Gallipolis
8	21.5	South Point Local SD	South Point
9	20.8	Mount Vernon City SD	Mount Vernon
10	20.4	Lima City SD	Lima
10	20.4	Napoleon Area City SD	Napoleon
12	20.3	Youngstown City SD	Youngstown
13	20.0	Sandusky City SD	Sandusky
14	19.8	Mansfield City SD	Mansfield
15	19.6	Bellefontaine City Schools	Bellefontaine
15	19.6	Meigs Local SD	Pomeroy
17	19.5	Alexander Local SD	Albany
17	19.5	Bucyrus City SD	Bucyrus
19	19.4	East Liverpool City SD	East Liverpool
20	19.2	Marion City SD	Marion
21	19.0	Hamilton City SD	Hamilton
22	18.9	Cincinnati City SD	Cincinnati
22	18.9	Springfield Local Schools	Holland
22	18.9	Urbana City SD	Urbana
22	18.9	Warren City SD	Warren
26	18.8	Sidney City SD	Sidney
27	18.7	Ashtabula Area City SD	Ashtabula
28	18.6	Fostoria City SD	Fostoria
28	18.6	Gallia County Local SD	Gallipolis
30	18.5	Celina City SD	Celina
31	18.3	St Marys City SD	Saint Marys
32	18.2	Buckeye Local SD	Rayland
32	18.2	Cleveland Municipal City SD	Cleveland
32	18.2	Paulding Ex Vill SD	Paulding
35	18.0	Indian Lake Local SD	Lewistown
36	17.8	Findlay City SD	Findlay
36	17.8	Ironton City SD	Ironton
36	17.8	Middletown City SD	Middletown
39	17.7	Euclid City SD	Euclid
40	17.6	Port Clinton City SD	Port Clinton
40	17.6	Springfield Local SD	Akron
42	17.5	Marietta City Schools	Marietta
43	17.4	Defiance City SD	Defiance
43	17.4	Tiffin City SD	Tiffin
45	17.3	Alliance City SD	Alliance
45	17.3	Bellevue City SD	Bellevue
45	17.3	Mt Healthy City SD	Cincinnati
45	17.3	Vinton County Local SD	Mc Arthur
49	17.2	Austintown Local SD	Youngstown
49	17.2	Toledo City SD	Toledo
49	17.2	Winton Woods City SD	Cincinnati

394 PROFILES OF OHIO / School District Rankings

52	17.1	Delaware City SD	Delaware
53	17.0	Logan-Hocking Local SD	Logan
53	17.0	Wellston City Schools	Wellston
55	16.9	Canton City SD	Canton
56	16.8	Edgewood City SD	Trenton
56	16.8	Galion City SD	Galion
56	16.8	New Philadelphia City SD	New Philadelphia
56	16.8	Piqua City SD	Piqua
60	16.7	Goshen Local SD	Goshen
60	16.7	Switzerland of Ohio Local SD	Woodsfield
62	16.6	North College Hill City SD	Cincinnati
62	16.6	Ravenna City SD	Ravenna
62	16.6	Upper Sandusky Ex Vill SD	Upper Sandusky
65	16.5	Akron Public Schools	Akron
65	16.5	Cambridge City SD	Cambridge
65	16.5	Perkins Local SD	Sandusky
68	16.2	Kenton City SD	Kenton
68	16.2	River View Local SD	Warsaw
68	16.2	Union Local SD	Morristown
71	15.9	Groveport Madison Local SD	Groveport
71	15.9	Mayfield City SD	Highland Hgts
71	15.9	Norwalk City SD	Norwalk
74	15.8	Whitehall City SD	Whitehall
75	15.7	Wapakoneta City City SD	Wapakoneta
76	15.6	Fairless Local SD	Navarre
76	15.6	London City SD	London
76	15.6	Parma City SD	Parma
76	15.6	Springfield City SD	Springfield
76	15.6	Van Wert City SD	Van Wert
81	15.5	Marysville Exempted Village SD	Marysville
81	15.5	West Muskingum Local SD	Zanesville
83	15.4	Graham Local SD	Saint Paris
83	15.4	Indian Creek Local SD	Wintersville
83	15.4	North Ridgeville City SD	N Ridgeville
83	15.4	Rock Hill Local SD	Ironton
87	15.3	Ashland City SD	Ashland
87	15.3	Circleville City SD	Circleville
87	15.3	Indian Valley Local SD	Gnadenhutten
87	15.3	Jackson City SD	Jackson
87	15.3	Marlington Local SD	Alliance
87	15.3	South Euclid-Lyndhurst City SD	Lyndhurst
87	15.3	Warrensville Heights City SD	Warrensville Hgts
94	15.2	Barberton City SD	Barberton
94	15.2	Benton Carroll Salem Local SD	Oak Harbor
94	15.2	Cleveland Hts-Univ Hts City SD	University Hgts
94	15.2	Fairview Park City SD	Fairview Park
94	15.2	Westlake City SD	Westlake
94	15.2	Wickliffe City SD	Wickliffe
100	15.1	Adams County/Ohio Valley LSD	West Union
100	15.1	Campbell City SD	Campbell
100	15.1	Dover City SD	Dover
100	15.1	Greenville City SD	Greenville
100	15.1	Mad River Local SD	Dayton
100	15.1	West Holmes Local SD	Millersburg
106	15.0	Franklin City SD	Franklin
106	15.0	Shaker Heights City SD	Shaker Heights
106	15.0	Shelby City SD	Shelby
109	14.9	Clyde-Green Springs Ex Vill SD	Clyde
109	14.9	Elyria City SD	Elyria
109	14.9	Fremont City SD	Fremont
109	14.9	Massillon City SD	Massillon
109	14.9	Maumee City SD	Maumee
109	14.9	Medina City SD	Medina
109	14.9	New Richmond Ex Vill SD	New Richmond
109	14.9	Rossford Ex Vill SD	Rossford
109	14.9	Vermilion Local SD	Vermilion
109	14.9	Waverly City SD	Waverly
119	14.8	Benjamin Logan Local SD	Bellefontaine
119	14.8	Brookville Local SD	Brookville
119	14.8	Field Local SD	Mogadore
119	14.8	Gahanna-Jefferson City SD	Gahanna
119	14.8	Kettering City SD	Kettering
119	14.8	Martins Ferry City SD	Martins Ferry
119	14.8	Pike-Delta-York Local SD	Delta
126	14.7	Girard City SD	Girard
126	14.7	Highland Local SD	Sparta
126	14.7	Perry Local SD	Massillon
126	14.7	Scioto Valley Local SD	Piketon
130	14.6	Blanchester Local SD	Blanchester
130	14.6	Columbus Public Schools	Columbus
130	14.6	Conneaut Area City SD	Conneaut
130	14.6	Painesville City Local SD	Painesville
130	14.6	Xenia Community City SD	Xenia
135	14.5	Athens City SD	The Plains
135	14.5	Berea City SD	Berea
135	14.5	Canton Local SD	Canton
138	14.4	Garfield Heights City SD	Garfield Hgts
138	14.4	Geneva Area City Schools	Geneva
138	14.4	Lorain City SD	Lorain
138	14.4	Otsego Local SD	Tontogany
138	14.4	Willoughby-Eastlake City SD	Willoughby
143	14.3	Madison Local SD	Mansfield
143	14.3	Three Rivers Local Schools	Cleves
145	14.2	Berlin-Milan Local SD	Milan
146	14.1	Buckeye Valley Local SD	Delaware
146	14.1	Lakewood City SD	Lakewood
146	14.1	Northwest Local SD	Mc Dermott
146	14.1	Southeast Local SD	Apple Creek
146	14.1	Southwest Local SD	Harrison
146	14.1	Woodridge Local SD	Peninsula
146	14.1	Wooster City SD	Wooster
153	14.0	Rolling Hills Local SD	Cambridge
153	14.0	West Geauga Local SD	Chesterland
153	14.0	Willard City SD	Willard
156	13.9	Franklin Local SD	Duncan Falls
156	13.9	Northwest Local SD	Canal Fulton
156	13.9	Washington Court House City SD	Wash Ct House
159	13.8	Bay Village City SD	Bay Village
159	13.8	Clearview Local SD	Lorain
159	13.8	Cuyahoga Falls City SD	Cuyahoga Falls
159	13.8	Southwest Licking Local SD	Etna
159	13.8	Streetsboro City Schools	Streetsboro
159	13.8	Swanton Local SD	Swanton
165	13.7	Avon Local SD	Avon
165	13.7	Carrollton Ex Vill SD	Carrollton
165	13.7	Clermont Northeastern Local SD	Batavia
165	13.7	East Clinton Local SD	Lees Creek
165	13.7	Logan Elm Local SD	Circleville
165	13.7	Northern Local SD	Thornville
165	13.7	Ross Local SD	Hamilton
165	13.7	South-Western City SD	Grove City
165	13.7	United Local SD	Hanoverton
165	13.7	Washington Local Schools	Toledo
175	13.6	Big Walnut Local SD	Galena
175	13.6	Kings Local SD	Kings Mills
175	13.6	Minerva Local SD	Minerva
175	13.6	New Lexington City SD	New Lexington
175	13.6	Southeast Local SD	Ravenna
180	13.5	Bedford City SD	Bedford
180	13.5	Maple Heights City SD	Maple Heights
180	13.5	Sandy Valley Local SD	Magnolia
180	13.5	Triway Local SD	Wooster
180	13.5	Warren Local SD	Vincent
185	13.4	North Fork Local SD	Utica
185	13.4	Reynoldsburg City SD	Reynoldsburg
185	13.4	Rocky River City SD	Rocky River
185	13.4	Teays Valley Local SD	Ashville
189	13.3	Crestwood Local SD	Mantua
189	13.3	Newark City SD	Newark
189	13.3	Plain Local SD	Canton
192	13.2	Beaver Local SD	Lisbon
192	13.2	Bowling Green City SD	Bowling Green
192	13.2	Chillicothe City SD	Chillicothe
192	13.2	Howland Local SD	Warren
192	13.2	Miami Trace Local SD	Wash Ct House
192	13.2	Morgan Local SD	McConnelsville
198	13.1	Clear Fork Valley Local SD	Bellville
198	13.1	East Muskingum Local SD	New Concord
198	13.1	Lakewood Local SD	Hebron
198	13.1	Northridge Local SD	Dayton
198	13.1	Ridgewood Local SD	West Lafayette
198	13.1	Sylvania City SD	Sylvania
204	13.0	Fairland Local SD	Proctorville
204	13.0	Hillsboro City SD	Hillsboro
206	12.9	Amanda-Clearcreek Local SD	Amanda
206	12.9	Coldwater Ex Vill SD	Coldwater
206	12.9	Huron City Schools	Huron
206	12.9	Niles City SD	Niles
206	12.9	Oak Hills Local SD	Cincinnati
206	12.9	Princeton City SD	Cincinnati
206	12.9	Vandalia-Butler City SD	Vandalia
213	12.8	Madison Local SD	Middletown
213	12.8	Maysville Local SD	Zanesville
213	12.8	Steubenville City SD	Steubenville
213	12.8	Tuscarawas Valley Local SD	Zoarville
217	12.7	Beavercreek City SD	Beavercreek
217	12.7	East Holmes Local Schools	Berlin
217	12.7	Lancaster City SD	Lancaster
217	12.7	Licking Valley Local SD Sd	Newark
217	12.7	Newton Falls Ex Vill SD	Newton Falls
217	12.7	Orrville City SD	Orrville
217	12.7	Strongsville City SD	Strongsville
217	12.7	Trotwood-Madison City Schools	Trotwood
225	12.6	Fairborn City Schools	Fairborn
225	12.6	North Olmsted City Schools	North Olmsted
225	12.6	Sheffield-Sheffield Lake City SD	Sheffield Vlg
228	12.5	Edison Local SD	Hammondsville
228	12.5	Ottawa-Glandorf Local SD	Ottawa
230	12.4	Centerville City SD	Centerville
230	12.4	Miamisburg City SD	Miamisburg
230	12.4	Norwood City SD	Norwood
230	12.4	Salem City SD	Salem
234	12.3	Lexington Local SD	Lexington
234	12.3	Northwest Local SD	Cincinnati
234	12.3	St Clairsville-Richland City SD	St Clairsville
237	12.2	Amherst Ex Vill SD	Amherst
237	12.2	Canal Winchester Local SD	Canal Winchester
237	12.2	Struthers City SD	Struthers
240	12.1	Kent City SD	Kent
240	12.1	Orange City SD	Cleveland
240	12.1	Zane Trace Local SD	Chillicothe
243	12.0	Cloverleaf Local SD	Lodi
243	12.0	Green Local SD	Green
243	12.0	Greenfield Ex Vill SD	Greenfield
243	12.0	Huber Heights City SD	Huber Heights
243	12.0	Mentor Ex Vill SD	Mentor
243	12.0	Preble Shawnee Local SD	Camden
249	11.9	Elgin Local SD	Marion
249	11.9	West Carrollton City SD	West Carrollton
251	11.8	Finneytown Local SD	Cincinnati
251	11.8	Greeneview Local SD	Jamestown
251	11.8	Hamilton Local SD	Columbus
251	11.8	James A Garfield Local SD	Garrettsville
251	11.8	Jefferson Area Local SD	Jefferson
251	11.8	Solon City SD	Solon
257	11.7	Bryan City SD	Bryan
257	11.7	Madeira City SD	Cincinnati
257	11.7	Troy City SD	Troy
257	11.7	West Clermont Local SD	Cincinnati
261	11.6	Buckeye Local SD	Medina
261	11.6	Chardon Local SD	Chardon
261	11.6	Lakeview Local SD	Cortland
261	11.6	Madison-Plains Local SD	London
261	11.6	Portsmouth City SD	Portsmouth
261	11.6	River Valley Local SD	Caledonia
261	11.6	Westfall Local SD	Williamsport
268	11.5	Chagrin Falls Ex Vill SD	Chagrin Falls
268	11.5	Hilliard City SD	Hilliard
268	11.5	Madison Local SD	Madison
268	11.5	Nordonia Hills City SD	Northfield
268	11.5	Tecumseh Local SD	New Carlisle
273	11.4	Carlisle Local SD	Carlisle
273	11.4	Firelands Local SD	Oberlin
273	11.4	Northwestern Local SD	Springfield
273	11.4	Poland Local SD	Poland
273	11.4	Westerville City SD	Westerville
278	11.3	Monroe Local SD	Monroe
278	11.3	Northmont City SD	Englewood
280	11.2	Fairfield City SD	Fairfield
280	11.2	Licking Heights Local SD	Summit Station
280	11.2	Midview Local SD	Grafton
280	11.2	Minford Local SD	Minford
280	11.2	Tallmadge City Schools	Tallmadge
285	11.1	Bexley City SD	Bexley
285	11.1	East Cleveland City SD	East Cleveland
285	11.1	Hudson City SD	Hudson
285	11.1	Milton-Union Exempted Vill Schls	West Milton
285	11.1	Oregon City SD	Oregon
290	11.0	Eaton Community Schools	Eaton
290	11.0	Tri-Valley Local Schools	Dresden
290	11.0	Valley View Local SD	Germantown
293	10.9	Brunswick City SD	Brunswick
293	10.9	Jonathan Alder Local SD	Plain City
293	10.9	Lake Local SD	Millbury
293	10.9	Lake Local SD	Hartville
293	10.9	Wauseon Ex Vill SD	Wauseon
293	10.9	Wilmington City SD	Wilmington
299	10.8	Clinton-Massie Local SD	Clarksville
299	10.8	Hubbard Ex Vill SD	Hubbard
299	10.8	Louisville City SD	Louisville
299	10.8	Milford Ex Vill SD	Milford
299	10.8	North Canton City SD	North Canton
299	10.8	North Royalton City SD	N Royalton
299	10.8	Springboro Community City SD	Springboro
299	10.8	Talawanda City SD	Oxford
299	10.8	West Branch Local SD	Beloit
308	10.7	Buckeye Local SD	Ashtabula
308	10.7	Stow-Munroe Falls City SD	Stow
310	10.6	Bath Local SD	Lima
310	10.6	Black River Local SD	Sullivan
310	10.6	Granville Ex Vill SD	Granville
310	10.6	Little Miami Local SD	Morrow
310	10.6	Painesville Township Local SD	Painesville
315	10.5	Batavia Local SD	Batavia
315	10.5	Brecksville-Broadview Hgts City	Brecksville
315	10.5	Eastern Local SD	Sardinia
315	10.5	Forest Hills Local SD	Cincinnati
315	10.5	Genoa Area Local SD	Genoa
315	10.5	Greenon Local SD	Springfield
315	10.5	Twinsburg City SD	Twinsburg
322	10.4	Elida Local SD	Elida
322	10.4	Heath City SD	Heath
322	10.4	Olmsted Falls City SD	Olmsted Falls
325	10.3	Beachwood City SD	Beachwood
325	10.3	Coventry Local SD	Akron
325	10.3	Union-Scioto Local SD	Chillicothe
325	10.3	Worthington City SD	Worthington
329	10.2	Canfield Local SD	Canfield

PROFILES OF OHIO / School District Rankings 395

329	10.2	Copley-Fairlawn City SD	Copley
329	10.2	Olentangy Local SD	Lewis Center
332	10.1	Sugarcreek Local SD	Bellbrook
333	10.0	Kenston Local SD	Chagrin Falls
333	10.0	Washington-Nile Local SD	West Portsmouth
333	10.0	Wellington Ex Vill SD	Wellington
336	9.9	Dublin City SD	Dublin
336	9.9	Keystone Local SD	Lagrange
338	9.8	Highland Local SD	Medina
338	9.8	Wadsworth City SD	Wadsworth
340	9.7	Wyoming City SD	Wyoming
341	9.6	Upper Arlington City SD	Upper Arlington
342	9.5	Electronic Classrm of Tomorrow	Columbus
343	9.4	Mariemont City SD	Cincinnati
343	9.4	Pickerington Local SD	Pickerington
343	9.4	Sycamore Community City SD	Cincinnati
346	9.2	Boardman Local SD	Youngstown
347	9.1	Avon Lake City Schools	Avon Lake
348	9.0	Lebanon City SD	Lebanon
348	9.0	Shawnee Local SD	Lima
348	9.0	Western Brown Local SD	Mount Orab
351	8.8	Eastwood Local SD	Pemberville
351	8.8	Loveland City SD	Loveland
353	8.7	Aurora City SD	Aurora
353	8.7	Mason City SD	Mason
353	8.7	Tipp City Ex Vill SD	Tipp City
356	8.6	Manchester Local SD	Akron
357	8.5	Clark-Shawnee Local SD	Springfield
357	8.5	Northeastern Local SD	Springfield
357	8.5	Plain Local SD	New Albany
360	8.4	Indian Hill Ex Vill SD	Cincinnati
361	8.3	Lakota Local SD	Liberty Twp
362	8.2	Norton City Schools	Norton
362	8.2	Revere Local SD	Bath
364	8.1	Ontario Local SD	Mansfield
364	8.1	Perrysburg Exempted Village	Perrysburg
366	8.0	Fairfield Union Local SD	W Rushville
366	8.0	Liberty Local SD	Youngstown
368	7.7	Oakwood City SD	Dayton
369	7.6	Jackson Local SD	Massillon
369	7.6	Perry Local SD	Perry
371	7.4	Bethel-Tate Local SD	Bethel
372	6.9	Anthony Wayne Local SD	Whitehouse
373	5.4	Ohio Virtual Academy	Maumee
374	4.4	Champion Local SD	Warren

English Language Learner Students

Rank	Percent	District Name	City
1	59.0	East Holmes Local Schools	Berlin
2	23.8	Painesville City Local SD	Painesville
3	8.1	Lakewood City SD	Lakewood
4	7.6	Whitehall City SD	Whitehall
5	6.9	Columbus Public Schools	Columbus
6	5.9	North Olmsted City Schools	North Olmsted
7	5.7	Copley-Fairlawn City SD	Copley
7	5.7	Fremont City SD	Fremont
9	5.2	South-Western City SD	Grove City
10	5.1	Dublin City SD	Dublin
11	4.8	Mayfield City SD	Highland Hgts
12	4.5	Tecumseh Local SD	New Carlisle
13	4.3	Sycamore Community City SD	Cincinnati
14	4.0	Cleveland Municipal City SD	Cleveland
15	3.8	Fairview Park City SD	Fairview Park
15	3.8	Princeton City SD	Cincinnati
17	3.7	Hamilton City SD	Hamilton
17	3.7	West Carrollton City SD	West Carrollton
19	3.4	Hilliard City SD	Hilliard
20	3.3	Fostoria City SD	Fostoria
21	3.1	Athens City SD	The Plains
21	3.1	Westerville City SD	Westerville
23	3.0	Ashtabula Area City SD	Ashtabula
24	2.9	Wauseon Ex Vill SD	Wauseon
25	2.8	Worthington City SD	Worthington
26	2.5	Huber Heights City SD	Huber Heights
26	2.5	Parma City SD	Parma
28	2.4	Centerville City SD	Centerville
29	2.3	Shaker Heights City SD	Shaker Heights
30	2.2	Lorain City SD	Lorain
31	2.1	Fairfield City SD	Fairfield
31	2.1	Nordonia Hills City SD	Northfield
33	2.0	Reynoldsburg City SD	Reynoldsburg
34	1.9	Willoughby-Eastlake City SD	Willoughby
35	1.8	Campbell City SD	Campbell
35	1.8	Madeira City SD	Cincinnati
35	1.8	Napoleon Area City SD	Napoleon
35	1.8	Solon City SD	Solon
35	1.8	Woodridge Local SD	Peninsula
40	1.7	Lake Local SD	Hartville
40	1.7	Tipp City Ex Vill SD	Tipp City
40	1.7	Willard City SD	Willard
43	1.6	Orange City SD	Cleveland
43	1.6	Sidney City SD	Sidney
45	1.5	Brecksville-Broadview Hgts City	Brecksville
45	1.5	Licking Heights Local SD	Summit Station
45	1.5	London City SD	London
45	1.5	Middletown City SD	Middletown
45	1.5	Norwood City SD	Norwood
45	1.5	Upper Arlington City SD	Upper Arlington
51	1.4	Berea City SD	Berea
51	1.4	Marlington Local SD	Alliance
51	1.4	North Royalton City SD	N Royalton
51	1.4	Toledo City SD	Toledo
51	1.4	Winton Woods City SD	Cincinnati
56	1.3	Akron Public Schools	Akron
56	1.3	Clearview Local SD	Lorain
56	1.3	Groveport Madison Local SD	Groveport
56	1.3	Lakota Local SD	Liberty Twp
56	1.3	Northmont City SD	Englewood
56	1.3	Troy City SD	Troy
62	1.2	Cuyahoga Falls City SD	Cuyahoga Falls
62	1.2	Jackson Local SD	Massillon
62	1.2	Mason City SD	Mason
62	1.2	Olentangy Local SD	Lewis Center
62	1.2	Strongsville City SD	Strongsville
62	1.2	Washington Local Schools	Toledo
68	1.1	Boardman Local SD	Youngstown
68	1.1	Delaware City SD	Delaware
68	1.1	West Clermont Local SD	Cincinnati
71	1.0	Dayton City SD	Dayton
71	1.0	Gahanna-Jefferson City SD	Gahanna
71	1.0	Rocky River City SD	Rocky River
71	1.0	Twinsburg City SD	Twinsburg
75	0.9	Bellefontaine City Schools	Bellefontaine
75	0.9	Cincinnati City SD	Cincinnati
75	0.9	Loveland City SD	Loveland
75	0.9	Mad River Local SD	Dayton
75	0.9	Mt Healthy City SD	Cincinnati
75	0.9	Springfield Local Schools	Holland
81	0.8	Bay Village City SD	Bay Village
81	0.8	Cleveland Hts-Univ Hts City SD	University Hgts
81	0.8	Geneva Area City Schools	Geneva
81	0.8	Green Local SD	Green
81	0.8	Kent City SD	Kent
81	0.8	Lebanon City SD	Lebanon
81	0.8	Maple Heights City SD	Maple Heights
81	0.8	Northwest Local SD	Cincinnati
81	0.8	Oregon City SD	Oregon
81	0.8	Plain Local SD	New Albany
81	0.8	Stow-Munroe Falls City SD	Stow
92	0.7	Bucyrus City SD	Bucyrus
92	0.7	Chagrin Falls Ex Vill SD	Chagrin Falls
92	0.7	Finneytown Local SD	Cincinnati
92	0.7	Indian Hill Ex Vill SD	Cincinnati
92	0.7	Kings Local SD	Kings Mills
92	0.7	Mentor Ex Vill SD	Mentor
92	0.7	Perry Local SD	Massillon
99	0.6	Avon Lake City Schools	Avon Lake
99	0.6	Barberton City SD	Barberton
99	0.6	Bexley City SD	Bexley
99	0.6	Elida Local SD	Elida
99	0.6	Fairborn City Schools	Fairborn
99	0.6	Findlay City SD	Findlay
99	0.6	Girard City SD	Girard
99	0.6	Hillsboro City SD	Hillsboro
99	0.6	Kettering City SD	Kettering
99	0.6	Pickerington Local SD	Pickerington
99	0.6	Wyoming City SD	Wyoming
110	0.5	Bowling Green City SD	Bowling Green
110	0.5	Canal Winchester Local SD	Canal Winchester
110	0.5	Electronic Classrm of Tomorrow	Columbus
110	0.5	Euclid City SD	Euclid
110	0.5	Field Local SD	Mogadore
110	0.5	Garfield Heights City SD	Garfield Hgts
110	0.5	Howland Local SD	Warren
110	0.5	Hudson City SD	Hudson
110	0.5	Lake Local SD	Millbury
110	0.5	Madison-Plains Local SD	London
110	0.5	North Canton City SD	North Canton
110	0.5	Norton City Schools	Norton
110	0.5	Oakwood City SD	Dayton
110	0.5	St Marys City SD	Saint Marys
110	0.5	Sugarcreek Local SD	Bellbrook
125	0.4	Beavercreek City SD	Beavercreek
125	0.4	Bedford City SD	Bedford
125	0.4	Brunswick City SD	Brunswick
125	0.4	Dover City SD	Dover
125	0.4	Eaton Community Schools	Eaton
125	0.4	Elgin Local SD	Marion
125	0.4	Midview Local SD	Grafton
125	0.4	New Philadelphia City SD	New Philadelphia
125	0.4	Perrysburg Exempted Village	Perrysburg
125	0.4	Pike-Delta-York Local SD	Delta
125	0.4	Southeast Local SD	Apple Creek
125	0.4	Talawanda City SD	Oxford
125	0.4	Vandalia-Butler City SD	Vandalia
138	0.3	Beachwood City SD	Beachwood
138	0.3	Berlin-Milan Local SD	Milan
138	0.3	Buckeye Local SD	Ashtabula
138	0.3	Defiance City SD	Defiance
138	0.3	Elyria City SD	Elyria
138	0.3	Forest Hills Local SD	Cincinnati
138	0.3	Lakewood Local SD	Hebron
138	0.3	Little Miami Local SD	Morrow
138	0.3	Maumee City SD	Maumee
138	0.3	Miamisburg City SD	Miamisburg
138	0.3	Newark City SD	Newark
138	0.3	Northeastern Local SD	Springfield
138	0.3	Northridge Local SD	Dayton
138	0.3	Northwestern Local SD	Springfield
138	0.3	Piqua City SD	Piqua
138	0.3	Plain Local SD	Canton
138	0.3	Revere Local SD	Bath
138	0.3	South Euclid-Lyndhurst City SD	Lyndhurst
138	0.3	Southeast Local SD	Ravenna
138	0.3	Springboro Community City SD	Springboro
138	0.3	St Clairsville-Richland City SD	St Clairsville
138	0.3	Sylvania City SD	Sylvania
138	0.3	Youngstown City SD	Youngstown
161	0.2	Alliance City SD	Alliance
161	0.2	Ashland City SD	Ashland
161	0.2	Aurora City SD	Aurora
161	0.2	Big Walnut Local SD	Galena
161	0.2	Brookville Local SD	Brookville
161	0.2	Bryan City SD	Bryan
161	0.2	Canfield Local SD	Canfield
161	0.2	Canton City SD	Canton
161	0.2	Fairless Local SD	Navarre
161	0.2	Granville Ex Vill SD	Granville
161	0.2	Greeneview Local SD	Jamestown
161	0.2	Huron City Schools	Huron
161	0.2	Kenston Local SD	Chagrin Falls
161	0.2	Lima City SD	Lima
161	0.2	Louisville City SD	Louisville
161	0.2	Marion City SD	Marion
161	0.2	Marysville Exempted Village SD	Marysville
161	0.2	Massillon City SD	Massillon
161	0.2	Medina City SD	Medina
161	0.2	Mount Vernon City SD	Mount Vernon
161	0.2	Painesville Township Local SD	Painesville
161	0.2	Rolling Hills Local SD	Cambridge
161	0.2	Springfield City SD	Springfield
161	0.2	Streetsboro City Schools	Streetsboro
161	0.2	West Holmes Local SD	Millersburg
161	0.2	West Muskingum Local SD	Zanesville
161	0.2	Westlake City SD	Westlake
161	0.2	Xenia Community City SD	Xenia
189	0.1	Alexander Local SD	Albany
189	0.1	Austintown Local SD	Youngstown
189	0.1	Avon Local SD	Avon
189	0.1	Batavia Local SD	Batavia
189	0.1	Carlisle Local SD	Carlisle
189	0.1	Chardon Local SD	Chardon
189	0.1	Clyde-Green Springs Ex Vill SD	Clyde
189	0.1	Franklin City SD	Franklin
189	0.1	Gallia County Local SD	Gallipolis
189	0.1	Greenon Local SD	Springfield
189	0.1	Greenville City SD	Greenville
189	0.1	Hamilton Local SD	Columbus
189	0.1	Hubbard Ex Vill SD	Hubbard
189	0.1	Jefferson Area Local SD	Jefferson
189	0.1	Kenton City SD	Kenton
189	0.1	Milford Ex Vill SD	Milford
189	0.1	Minerva Local SD	Minerva
189	0.1	Monroe Local SD	Monroe
189	0.1	North Fork Local SD	Utica
189	0.1	Olmsted Falls City SD	Olmsted Falls
189	0.1	Ontario Local SD	Mansfield
189	0.1	Ottawa-Glandorf Local SD	Ottawa
189	0.1	Perkins Local SD	Sandusky
189	0.1	Southwest Licking Local SD	Etna
189	0.1	Southwest Local SD	Harrison
189	0.1	Tallmadge City Schools	Tallmadge
189	0.1	Tiffin City SD	Tiffin
189	0.1	Triway Local SD	Wooster
189	0.1	Wadsworth City SD	Wadsworth
189	0.1	Washington Court House City SD	Wash Ct House
189	0.1	Washington-Nile Local SD	West Portsmouth
189	0.1	Wellington Ex Vill SD	Wellington
189	0.1	West Branch Local SD	Beloit
189	0.1	Wickliffe City SD	Wickliffe
223	0.0	Adams County/Ohio Valley LSD	West Union
223	0.0	Bath Local SD	Lima
223	0.0	Bellevue City SD	Bellevue
223	0.0	Canton Local SD	Canton
223	0.0	Circleville City SD	Circleville
223	0.0	Crestwood Local SD	Mantua
223	0.0	Edgewood City SD	Trenton

396 PROFILES OF OHIO / School District Rankings

223	0.0	Gallipolis City SD	Gallipolis
223	0.0	Highland Local SD	Medina
223	0.0	Jackson City SD	Jackson
223	0.0	Lakeview Local SD	Cortland
223	0.0	Lancaster City SD	Lancaster
223	0.0	Marietta City Schools	Marietta
223	0.0	Maysville Local SD	Zanesville
223	0.0	New Richmond Ex Vill SD	New Richmond
223	0.0	Oak Hills Local SD	Cincinnati
223	0.0	Rossford Ex Vill SD	Rossford
223	0.0	Salem City SD	Salem
223	0.0	Sandusky City SD	Sandusky
223	0.0	Teays Valley Local SD	Ashville
223	0.0	Wapakoneta City City SD	Wapakoneta
223	0.0	Warren City SD	Warren
223	0.0	Wilmington City SD	Wilmington
223	0.0	Wooster City SD	Wooster
247	0.0	Amanda-Clearcreek Local SD	Amanda
247	0.0	Amherst Ex Vill SD	Amherst
247	0.0	Anthony Wayne Local SD	Whitehouse
247	0.0	Beaver Local SD	Lisbon
247	0.0	Bellaire Local SD	Bellaire
247	0.0	Benjamin Logan Local SD	Bellefontaine
247	0.0	Benton Carroll Salem Local SD	Oak Harbor
247	0.0	Bethel-Tate Local SD	Bethel
247	0.0	Black River Local SD	Sullivan
247	0.0	Blanchester Local SD	Blanchester
247	0.0	Buckeye Local SD	Medina
247	0.0	Buckeye Local SD	Rayland
247	0.0	Buckeye Valley Local SD	Delaware
247	0.0	Cambridge City SD	Cambridge
247	0.0	Carrollton Ex Vill SD	Carrollton
247	0.0	Celina City SD	Celina
247	0.0	Champion Local SD	Warren
247	0.0	Chillicothe City SD	Chillicothe
247	0.0	Clark-Shawnee Local SD	Springfield
247	0.0	Claymont City SD	Dennison
247	0.0	Clear Fork Valley Local SD	Bellville
247	0.0	Clermont Northeastern Local SD	Batavia
247	0.0	Clinton-Massie Local SD	Clarksville
247	0.0	Cloverleaf Local SD	Lodi
247	0.0	Coldwater Ex Vill SD	Coldwater
247	0.0	Conneaut Area City SD	Conneaut
247	0.0	Coshocton City SD	Coshocton
247	0.0	Coventry Local SD	Akron
247	0.0	East Cleveland City SD	East Cleveland
247	0.0	East Clinton Local SD	Lees Creek
247	0.0	East Liverpool City SD	East Liverpool
247	0.0	East Muskingum Local SD	New Concord
247	0.0	Eastern Local SD	Sardinia
247	0.0	Eastwood Local SD	Pemberville
247	0.0	Edison Local SD	Hammondsville
247	0.0	Fairfield Union Local SD	W Rushville
247	0.0	Fairland Local SD	Proctorville
247	0.0	Firelands Local SD	Oberlin
247	0.0	Franklin Local SD	Duncan Falls
247	0.0	Galion City SD	Galion
247	0.0	Genoa Area Local SD	Genoa
247	0.0	Goshen Local SD	Goshen
247	0.0	Graham Local SD	Saint Paris
247	0.0	Greenfield Ex Vill SD	Greenfield
247	0.0	Harrison Hills City SD	Hopedale
247	0.0	Heath City SD	Heath
247	0.0	Highland Local SD	Sparta
247	0.0	Indian Creek Local SD	Wintersville
247	0.0	Indian Lake Local SD	Lewistown
247	0.0	Indian Valley Local SD	Gnadenhutten
247	0.0	Ironton City SD	Ironton
247	0.0	James A Garfield Local SD	Garrettsville
247	0.0	Jonathan Alder Local SD	Plain City
247	0.0	Keystone Local SD	Lagrange
247	0.0	Lexington Local SD	Lexington
247	0.0	Liberty Local SD	Youngstown
247	0.0	Licking Valley Local SD Sd	Newark
247	0.0	Logan Elm Local SD	Circleville
247	0.0	Logan-Hocking Local SD	Logan
247	0.0	Madison Local SD	Mansfield
247	0.0	Madison Local SD	Middletown
247	0.0	Madison Local SD	Madison
247	0.0	Manchester Local SD	Akron
247	0.0	Mansfield City SD	Mansfield
247	0.0	Mariemont City SD	Cincinnati
247	0.0	Martins Ferry City SD	Martins Ferry
247	0.0	Meigs Local SD	Pomeroy
247	0.0	Miami Trace Local SD	Wash Ct House
247	0.0	Milton-Union Exempted Vill Schls	West Milton
247	0.0	Minford Local SD	Minford
247	0.0	Morgan Local SD	McConnelsville
247	0.0	New Lexington City SD	New Lexington
247	0.0	Newton Falls Ex Vill SD	Newton Falls
247	0.0	Niles City SD	Niles
247	0.0	North College Hill City SD	Cincinnati
247	0.0	North Ridgeville City SD	N Ridgeville
247	0.0	Northern Local SD	Thornville
247	0.0	Northwest Local SD	Mc Dermott
247	0.0	Northwest Local SD	Canal Fulton
247	0.0	Norwalk City SD	Norwalk
247	0.0	Ohio Virtual Academy	Maumee
247	0.0	Orrville City SD	Orrville
247	0.0	Otsego Local SD	Tontogany
247	0.0	Paulding Ex Vill SD	Paulding
247	0.0	Perry Local SD	Perry
247	0.0	Poland Local SD	Poland
247	0.0	Port Clinton City SD	Port Clinton
247	0.0	Portsmouth City SD	Portsmouth
247	0.0	Preble Shawnee Local SD	Camden
247	0.0	Ravenna City SD	Ravenna
247	0.0	Ridgewood Local SD	West Lafayette
247	0.0	River Valley Local SD	Caledonia
247	0.0	River View Local SD	Warsaw
247	0.0	Rock Hill Local SD	Ironton
247	0.0	Ross Local SD	Hamilton
247	0.0	Sandy Valley Local SD	Magnolia
247	0.0	Scioto Valley Local SD	Piketon
247	0.0	Shawnee Local SD	Lima
247	0.0	Sheffield-Sheffield Lake City SD	Sheffield Vlg
247	0.0	Shelby City SD	Shelby
247	0.0	South Point Local SD	South Point
247	0.0	Springfield Local SD	Akron
247	0.0	Steubenville City SD	Steubenville
247	0.0	Struthers City SD	Struthers
247	0.0	Swanton Local SD	Swanton
247	0.0	Switzerland of Ohio Local SD	Woodsfield
247	0.0	Three Rivers Local Schools	Cleves
247	0.0	Tri-Valley Local Schools	Dresden
247	0.0	Trotwood-Madison City Schools	Trotwood
247	0.0	Tuscarawas Valley Local SD	Zoarville
247	0.0	Union Local SD	Morristown
247	0.0	Union-Scioto Local SD	Chillicothe
247	0.0	United Local SD	Hanoverton
247	0.0	Upper Sandusky Ex Vill SD	Upper Sandusky
247	0.0	Urbana City SD	Urbana
247	0.0	Valley View Local SD	Germantown
247	0.0	Van Wert City SD	Van Wert
247	0.0	Vermilion Local SD	Vermilion
247	0.0	Vinton County Local SD	Mc Arthur
247	0.0	Warren Local SD	Vincent
247	0.0	Warrensville Heights City SD	Warrensville Hgts
247	0.0	Waverly City SD	Waverly
247	0.0	Wellston City Schools	Wellston
247	0.0	West Geauga Local SD	Chesterland
247	0.0	Western Brown Local SD	Mount Orab
247	0.0	Westfall Local SD	Williamsport
247	0.0	Zane Trace Local SD	Chillicothe
247	0.0	Zanesville City SD	Zanesville

Migrant Students

Rank	Percent	District Name	City
1	14.2	Painesville City Local SD	Painesville
2	6.1	Willard City SD	Willard
3	3.3	Woodridge Local SD	Peninsula
4	3.1	Tecumseh Local SD	New Carlisle
5	2.2	Wauseon Ex Vill SD	Wauseon
6	1.7	South-Western City SD	Grove City
7	1.6	Fremont City SD	Fremont
7	1.6	Napoleon Area City SD	Napoleon
9	1.0	Benton Carroll Salem Local SD	Oak Harbor
9	1.0	Marlington Local SD	Alliance
9	1.0	Sycamore Community City SD	Cincinnati
12	0.9	Tipp City Ex Vill SD	Tipp City
13	0.7	Berlin-Milan Local SD	Milan
13	0.7	Reynoldsburg City SD	Reynoldsburg
15	0.6	Ottawa-Glandorf Local SD	Ottawa
16	0.3	Perrysburg Exempted Village	Perrysburg
16	0.3	Urbana City SD	Urbana
18	0.2	Alliance City SD	Alliance
18	0.2	Bowling Green City SD	Bowling Green
18	0.2	Columbus Public Schools	Columbus
18	0.2	North Royalton City SD	N Royalton
18	0.2	Wellington Ex Vill SD	Wellington
23	0.1	Bellevue City SD	Bellevue
23	0.1	Black River Local SD	Sullivan
23	0.1	Clearview Local SD	Lorain
23	0.1	Cloverleaf Local SD	Lodi
23	0.1	Clyde-Green Springs Ex Vill SD	Clyde
23	0.1	Eastwood Local SD	Pemberville
23	0.1	Elyria City SD	Elyria
23	0.1	Fairborn City Schools	Fairborn
23	0.1	Fairview Park City SD	Fairview Park
23	0.1	Field Local SD	Mogadore
23	0.1	Firelands Local SD	Oberlin
23	0.1	Highland Local SD	Medina
23	0.1	Keystone Local SD	Lagrange
23	0.1	Lorain City SD	Lorain
23	0.1	Marion City SD	Marion
23	0.1	North Ridgeville City SD	N Ridgeville
23	0.1	Painesville Township Local SD	Painesville
23	0.1	Pike-Delta-York Local SD	Delta
23	0.1	Springfield City SD	Springfield
23	0.1	Sylvania City SD	Sylvania
23	0.1	Tiffin City SD	Tiffin
23	0.1	Warrensville Heights City SD	Warrensville Hgts
23	0.1	Willoughby-Eastlake City SD	Willoughby
46	0.0	Amherst Ex Vill SD	Amherst
46	0.0	Ashtabula Area City SD	Ashtabula
46	0.0	Avon Lake City Schools	Avon Lake
46	0.0	Bay Village City SD	Bay Village
46	0.0	Bexley City SD	Bexley
46	0.0	Canfield Local SD	Canfield
46	0.0	Centerville City SD	Centerville
46	0.0	Cincinnati City SD	Cincinnati
46	0.0	Findlay City SD	Findlay
46	0.0	Gahanna-Jefferson City SD	Gahanna
46	0.0	Geneva Area City Schools	Geneva
46	0.0	Greenville City SD	Greenville
46	0.0	Hamilton City SD	Hamilton
46	0.0	Hudson City SD	Hudson
46	0.0	Kenston Local SD	Chagrin Falls
46	0.0	Lakota Local SD	Liberty Twp
46	0.0	Mad River Local SD	Dayton
46	0.0	Madison Local SD	Madison
46	0.0	Medina City SD	Medina
46	0.0	Nordonia Hills City SD	Northfield
46	0.0	North Olmsted City Schools	North Olmsted
46	0.0	Olmsted Falls City SD	Olmsted Falls
46	0.0	Southwest Licking Local SD	Etna
46	0.0	Strongsville City SD	Strongsville
46	0.0	Vandalia-Butler City SD	Vandalia
46	0.0	Vermilion Local SD	Vermilion
72	n/a	Adams County/Ohio Valley LSD	West Union
72	n/a	Akron Public Schools	Akron
72	n/a	Alexander Local SD	Albany
72	n/a	Amanda-Clearcreek Local SD	Amanda
72	n/a	Anthony Wayne Local SD	Whitehouse
72	n/a	Ashland City SD	Ashland
72	n/a	Athens City SD	The Plains
72	n/a	Aurora City SD	Aurora
72	n/a	Austintown Local SD	Youngstown
72	n/a	Avon Local SD	Avon
72	n/a	Barberton City SD	Barberton
72	n/a	Batavia Local SD	Batavia
72	n/a	Bath Local SD	Lima
72	n/a	Beachwood City SD	Beachwood
72	n/a	Beaver Local SD	Lisbon
72	n/a	Beavercreek City SD	Beavercreek
72	n/a	Bedford City SD	Bedford
72	n/a	Bellaire Local SD	Bellaire
72	n/a	Bellefontaine City Schools	Bellefontaine
72	n/a	Benjamin Logan Local SD	Bellefontaine
72	n/a	Berea City SD	Berea
72	n/a	Bethel-Tate Local SD	Bethel
72	n/a	Big Walnut Local SD	Galena
72	n/a	Blanchester Local SD	Blanchester
72	n/a	Boardman Local SD	Youngstown
72	n/a	Brecksville-Broadview Hgts City	Brecksville
72	n/a	Brookville Local SD	Brookville
72	n/a	Brunswick City SD	Brunswick
72	n/a	Bryan City SD	Bryan
72	n/a	Buckeye Local SD	Rayland
72	n/a	Buckeye Local SD	Ashtabula
72	n/a	Buckeye Local SD	Medina
72	n/a	Buckeye Valley Local SD	Delaware
72	n/a	Bucyrus City SD	Bucyrus
72	n/a	Cambridge City SD	Cambridge
72	n/a	Campbell City SD	Campbell
72	n/a	Canal Winchester Local SD	Canal Winchester
72	n/a	Canton City SD	Canton
72	n/a	Canton Local SD	Canton
72	n/a	Carlisle Local SD	Carlisle
72	n/a	Carrollton Ex Vill SD	Carrollton
72	n/a	Celina City SD	Celina
72	n/a	Chagrin Falls Ex Vill SD	Chagrin Falls
72	n/a	Champion Local SD	Warren
72	n/a	Chardon Local SD	Chardon
72	n/a	Chillicothe City SD	Chillicothe
72	n/a	Circleville City SD	Circleville
72	n/a	Clark-Shawnee Local SD	Springfield
72	n/a	Claymont City SD	Dennison
72	n/a	Clear Fork Valley Local SD	Bellville
72	n/a	Clermont Northeastern Local SD	Batavia
72	n/a	Cleveland Hts-Univ Hts City SD	University Hgts
72	n/a	Cleveland Municipal City SD	Cleveland
72	n/a	Clinton-Massie Local SD	Clarksville
72	n/a	Coldwater Ex Vill SD	Coldwater
72	n/a	Conneaut Area City SD	Conneaut
72	n/a	Copley-Fairlawn City SD	Copley
72	n/a	Coshocton City SD	Coshocton
72	n/a	Coventry Local SD	Akron

72	n/a	Crestwood Local SD	Mantua
72	n/a	Cuyahoga Falls City SD	Cuyahoga Falls
72	n/a	Dayton City SD	Dayton
72	n/a	Defiance City SD	Defiance
72	n/a	Delaware City SD	Delaware
72	n/a	Dover City SD	Dover
72	n/a	Dublin City SD	Dublin
72	n/a	East Cleveland City SD	East Cleveland
72	n/a	East Clinton Local SD	Lees Creek
72	n/a	East Holmes Local Schools	Berlin
72	n/a	East Liverpool City SD	East Liverpool
72	n/a	East Muskingum Local SD	New Concord
72	n/a	Eastern Local SD	Sardinia
72	n/a	Eaton Community Schools	Eaton
72	n/a	Edgewood City SD	Trenton
72	n/a	Edison Local SD	Hammondsville
72	n/a	Electronic Classrm of Tomorrow	Columbus
72	n/a	Elgin Local SD	Marion
72	n/a	Elida Local SD	Elida
72	n/a	Euclid City SD	Euclid
72	n/a	Fairfield City SD	Fairfield
72	n/a	Fairfield Union Local SD	W Rushville
72	n/a	Fairland Local SD	Proctorville
72	n/a	Fairless Local SD	Navarre
72	n/a	Finneytown Local SD	Cincinnati
72	n/a	Forest Hills Local SD	Cincinnati
72	n/a	Fostoria City SD	Fostoria
72	n/a	Franklin City SD	Franklin
72	n/a	Franklin Local SD	Duncan Falls
72	n/a	Galion City SD	Galion
72	n/a	Gallia County Local SD	Gallipolis
72	n/a	Gallipolis City SD	Gallipolis
72	n/a	Garfield Heights City SD	Garfield Hgts
72	n/a	Genoa Area Local SD	Genoa
72	n/a	Girard City SD	Girard
72	n/a	Goshen Local SD	Goshen
72	n/a	Graham Local SD	Saint Paris
72	n/a	Granville Ex Vill SD	Granville
72	n/a	Green Local SD	Green
72	n/a	Greeneview Local SD	Jamestown
72	n/a	Greenfield Ex Vill SD	Greenfield
72	n/a	Greenon Local SD	Springfield
72	n/a	Groveport Madison Local SD	Groveport
72	n/a	Hamilton Local SD	Columbus
72	n/a	Harrison Hills City SD	Hopedale
72	n/a	Heath City SD	Heath
72	n/a	Highland Local SD	Sparta
72	n/a	Hilliard City SD	Hilliard
72	n/a	Hillsboro City SD	Hillsboro
72	n/a	Howland Local SD	Warren
72	n/a	Hubbard Ex Vill SD	Hubbard
72	n/a	Huber Heights City SD	Huber Heights
72	n/a	Huron City Schools	Huron
72	n/a	Indian Creek Local SD	Wintersville
72	n/a	Indian Hill Ex Vill SD	Cincinnati
72	n/a	Indian Lake Local SD	Lewistown
72	n/a	Indian Valley Local SD	Gnadenhutten
72	n/a	Ironton City SD	Ironton
72	n/a	Jackson City SD	Jackson
72	n/a	Jackson Local SD	Massillon
72	n/a	James A Garfield Local SD	Garrettsville
72	n/a	Jefferson Area Local SD	Jefferson
72	n/a	Jonathan Alder Local SD	Plain City
72	n/a	Kent City SD	Kent
72	n/a	Kenton City SD	Kenton
72	n/a	Kettering City SD	Kettering
72	n/a	Kings Local SD	Kings Mills
72	n/a	Lake Local SD	Millbury
72	n/a	Lake Local SD	Hartville
72	n/a	Lakeview Local SD	Cortland
72	n/a	Lakewood City SD	Lakewood
72	n/a	Lakewood Local SD	Hebron
72	n/a	Lancaster City SD	Lancaster
72	n/a	Lebanon City SD	Lebanon
72	n/a	Lexington Local SD	Lexington
72	n/a	Liberty Local SD	Youngstown
72	n/a	Licking Heights Local SD	Summit Station
72	n/a	Licking Valley Local SD Sd	Newark
72	n/a	Lima City SD	Lima
72	n/a	Little Miami Local SD	Morrow
72	n/a	Logan Elm Local SD	Circleville
72	n/a	Logan-Hocking Local SD	Logan
72	n/a	London City SD	London
72	n/a	Louisville City SD	Louisville
72	n/a	Loveland City SD	Loveland
72	n/a	Madeira City SD	Cincinnati
72	n/a	Madison Local SD	Middletown
72	n/a	Madison Local SD	Mansfield
72	n/a	Madison-Plains Local SD	London
72	n/a	Manchester Local SD	Akron
72	n/a	Mansfield City SD	Mansfield
72	n/a	Maple Heights City SD	Maple Heights
72	n/a	Mariemont City SD	Cincinnati
72	n/a	Marietta City Schools	Marietta
72	n/a	Martins Ferry City SD	Martins Ferry
72	n/a	Marysville Exempted Village SD	Marysville
72	n/a	Mason City SD	Mason
72	n/a	Massillon City SD	Massillon
72	n/a	Maumee City SD	Maumee
72	n/a	Mayfield City SD	Highland Hgts
72	n/a	Maysville Local SD	Zanesville
72	n/a	Meigs Local SD	Pomeroy
72	n/a	Mentor Ex Vill SD	Mentor
72	n/a	Miami Trace Local SD	Wash Ct House
72	n/a	Miamisburg City SD	Miamisburg
72	n/a	Middletown City SD	Middletown
72	n/a	Midview Local SD	Grafton
72	n/a	Milford Ex Vill SD	Milford
72	n/a	Milton-Union Exempted Vill Schls	West Milton
72	n/a	Minerva Local SD	Minerva
72	n/a	Minford Local SD	Minford
72	n/a	Monroe Local SD	Monroe
72	n/a	Morgan Local SD	McConnelsville
72	n/a	Mount Vernon City SD	Mount Vernon
72	n/a	Mt Healthy City SD	Cincinnati
72	n/a	New Lexington City SD	New Lexington
72	n/a	New Philadelphia City SD	New Philadelphia
72	n/a	New Richmond Ex Vill SD	New Richmond
72	n/a	Newark City SD	Newark
72	n/a	Newton Falls Ex Vill SD	Newton Falls
72	n/a	Niles City SD	Niles
72	n/a	North Canton City SD	North Canton
72	n/a	North College Hill City SD	Cincinnati
72	n/a	North Fork Local SD	Utica
72	n/a	Northeastern Local SD	Springfield
72	n/a	Northern Local SD	Thornville
72	n/a	Northmont City SD	Englewood
72	n/a	Northridge Local SD	Dayton
72	n/a	Northwest Local SD	Cincinnati
72	n/a	Northwest Local SD	Mc Dermott
72	n/a	Northwest Local SD	Canal Fulton
72	n/a	Northwestern Local SD	Springfield
72	n/a	Norton City Schools	Norton
72	n/a	Norwalk City SD	Norwalk
72	n/a	Norwood City SD	Norwood
72	n/a	Oak Hills Local SD	Cincinnati
72	n/a	Oakwood City SD	Dayton
72	n/a	Ohio Virtual Academy	Maumee
72	n/a	Olentangy Local SD	Lewis Center
72	n/a	Ontario Local SD	Mansfield
72	n/a	Orange City SD	Cleveland
72	n/a	Oregon City SD	Oregon
72	n/a	Orrville City SD	Orrville
72	n/a	Otsego Local SD	Tontogany
72	n/a	Parma City SD	Parma
72	n/a	Paulding Ex Vill SD	Paulding
72	n/a	Perkins Local SD	Sandusky
72	n/a	Perry Local SD	Perry
72	n/a	Perry Local SD	Massillon
72	n/a	Pickerington Local SD	Pickerington
72	n/a	Piqua City SD	Piqua
72	n/a	Plain Local SD	New Albany
72	n/a	Plain Local SD	Canton
72	n/a	Poland Local SD	Poland
72	n/a	Port Clinton City SD	Port Clinton
72	n/a	Portsmouth City SD	Portsmouth
72	n/a	Preble Shawnee Local SD	Camden
72	n/a	Princeton City SD	Cincinnati
72	n/a	Ravenna City SD	Ravenna
72	n/a	Revere Local SD	Bath
72	n/a	Ridgewood Local SD	West Lafayette
72	n/a	River Valley Local SD	Caledonia
72	n/a	River View Local SD	Warsaw
72	n/a	Rock Hill Local SD	Ironton
72	n/a	Rocky River City SD	Rocky River
72	n/a	Rolling Hills Local SD	Cambridge
72	n/a	Ross Local SD	Hamilton
72	n/a	Rossford Ex Vill SD	Rossford
72	n/a	Salem City SD	Salem
72	n/a	Sandusky City SD	Sandusky
72	n/a	Sandy Valley Local SD	Magnolia
72	n/a	Scioto Valley Local SD	Piketon
72	n/a	Shaker Heights City SD	Shaker Heights
72	n/a	Shawnee Local SD	Lima
72	n/a	Sheffield-Sheffield Lake City SD	Sheffield Vlg
72	n/a	Shelby City SD	Shelby
72	n/a	Sidney City SD	Sidney
72	n/a	Solon City SD	Solon
72	n/a	South Euclid-Lyndhurst City SD	Lyndhurst
72	n/a	South Point Local SD	South Point
72	n/a	Southeast Local SD	Ravenna
72	n/a	Southeast Local SD	Apple Creek
72	n/a	Southwest Local SD	Harrison
72	n/a	Springboro Community City SD	Springboro
72	n/a	Springfield Local SD	Akron
72	n/a	Springfield Local Schools	Holland
72	n/a	St Clairsville-Richland City SD	St Clairsville
72	n/a	St Marys City SD	Saint Marys
72	n/a	Steubenville City SD	Steubenville
72	n/a	Stow-Munroe Falls City SD	Stow
72	n/a	Streetsboro City Schools	Streetsboro
72	n/a	Struthers City SD	Struthers
72	n/a	Sugarcreek Local SD	Bellbrook
72	n/a	Swanton Local SD	Swanton
72	n/a	Switzerland of Ohio Local SD	Woodsfield
72	n/a	Talawanda City SD	Oxford
72	n/a	Tallmadge City Schools	Tallmadge
72	n/a	Teays Valley Local SD	Ashville
72	n/a	Three Rivers Local Schools	Cleves
72	n/a	Toledo City SD	Toledo
72	n/a	Tri-Valley Local Schools	Dresden
72	n/a	Triway Local SD	Wooster
72	n/a	Trotwood-Madison City Schools	Trotwood
72	n/a	Troy City SD	Troy
72	n/a	Tuscarawas Valley Local SD	Zoarville
72	n/a	Twinsburg City SD	Twinsburg
72	n/a	Union Local SD	Morristown
72	n/a	Union-Scioto Local SD	Chillicothe
72	n/a	United Local SD	Hanoverton
72	n/a	Upper Arlington City SD	Upper Arlington
72	n/a	Upper Sandusky Ex Vill SD	Upper Sandusky
72	n/a	Valley View Local SD	Germantown
72	n/a	Van Wert City SD	Van Wert
72	n/a	Vinton County Local SD	Mc Arthur
72	n/a	Wadsworth City SD	Wadsworth
72	n/a	Wapakoneta City City SD	Wapakoneta
72	n/a	Warren City SD	Warren
72	n/a	Warren Local SD	Vincent
72	n/a	Washington Court House City SD	Wash Ct House
72	n/a	Washington Local Schools	Toledo
72	n/a	Washington-Nile Local SD	West Portsmouth
72	n/a	Waverly City SD	Waverly
72	n/a	Wellston City Schools	Wellston
72	n/a	West Branch Local SD	Beloit
72	n/a	West Carrollton City SD	West Carrollton
72	n/a	West Clermont Local SD	Cincinnati
72	n/a	West Geauga Local SD	Chesterland
72	n/a	West Holmes Local SD	Millersburg
72	n/a	West Muskingum Local SD	Zanesville
72	n/a	Western Brown Local SD	Mount Orab
72	n/a	Westerville City SD	Westerville
72	n/a	Westfall Local SD	Williamsport
72	n/a	Westlake City SD	Westlake
72	n/a	Whitehall City SD	Whitehall
72	n/a	Wickliffe City SD	Wickliffe
72	n/a	Wilmington City SD	Wilmington
72	n/a	Winton Woods City SD	Cincinnati
72	n/a	Wooster City SD	Wooster
72	n/a	Worthington City SD	Worthington
72	n/a	Wyoming City SD	Wyoming
72	n/a	Xenia Community City SD	Xenia
72	n/a	Youngstown City SD	Youngstown
72	n/a	Zane Trace Local SD	Chillicothe
72	n/a	Zanesville City SD	Zanesville

Students Eligible for Free Lunch

Rank	Percent	District Name	City
1	72.9	Cleveland Municipal City SD	Cleveland
2	72.0	Painesville City Local SD	Painesville
3	66.8	Youngstown City SD	Youngstown
4	66.2	Dayton City SD	Dayton
5	62.8	East Cleveland City SD	East Cleveland
5	62.8	Lima City SD	Lima
7	61.7	Mansfield City SD	Mansfield
8	57.3	Cincinnati City SD	Cincinnati
9	55.8	Warrensville Heights City SD	Warrensville Hgts
10	55.1	Canton City SD	Canton
11	54.7	Sandusky City SD	Sandusky
12	53.5	Lorain City SD	Lorain
12	53.5	Zanesville City SD	Zanesville
14	51.9	Toledo City SD	Toledo
15	50.7	Bellaire Local SD	Bellaire
16	50.4	Alliance City SD	Alliance
17	50.2	Columbus Public Schools	Columbus
18	48.9	Trotwood-Madison City Schools	Trotwood
18	48.9	Warren City SD	Warren
20	48.2	Clearview Local SD	Lorain
21	48.0	Springfield City SD	Springfield
22	46.5	Steubenville City SD	Steubenville
23	46.4	Portsmouth City SD	Portsmouth
23	46.4	Rock Hill Local SD	Ironton
25	46.0	Northwest Local SD	Mc Dermott
26	45.6	Ashtabula Area City SD	Ashtabula
27	44.4	Vinton County Local SD	Mc Arthur
28	43.8	East Liverpool City SD	East Liverpool
29	43.3	New Lexington City SD	New Lexington

398 PROFILES OF OHIO / School District Rankings

30	42.9	Campbell City SD	Campbell
31	42.8	Meigs Local SD	Pomeroy
32	42.2	Hamilton City SD	Hamilton
33	41.9	Northridge Local SD	Dayton
34	41.8	Mt Healthy City SD	Cincinnati
35	41.5	Fostoria City SD	Fostoria
36	40.8	Whitehall City SD	Whitehall
37	40.2	Adams County/Ohio Valley LSD	West Union
38	39.3	Struthers City SD	Struthers
39	39.2	Conneaut Area City SD	Conneaut
39	39.2	Norwood City SD	Norwood
41	37.6	Euclid City SD	Euclid
41	37.6	Washington-Nile Local SD	West Portsmouth
43	37.3	Scioto Valley Local SD	Piketon
44	37.2	Barberton City SD	Barberton
44	37.2	Gallia County Local SD	Gallipolis
46	36.9	Massillon City SD	Massillon
47	36.8	South Point Local SD	South Point
48	36.7	Elyria City SD	Elyria
49	36.2	Cambridge City SD	Cambridge
50	35.9	Ironton City SD	Ironton
51	35.8	Maple Heights City SD	Maple Heights
51	35.8	North College Hill City SD	Cincinnati
53	35.6	Coshocton City SD	Coshocton
54	35.4	Morgan Local SD	McConnelsville
55	35.2	Wellston City Schools	Wellston
56	35.0	Princeton City SD	Cincinnati
57	34.0	Bucyrus City SD	Bucyrus
58	33.4	Martins Ferry City SD	Martins Ferry
59	32.9	Cleveland Hts-Univ Hts City SD	University Hgts
60	32.7	Buckeye Local SD	Rayland
60	32.7	Middletown City SD	Middletown
62	32.0	Maysville Local SD	Zanesville
63	31.6	Marion City SD	Marion
64	31.4	Minford Local SD	Minford
64	31.4	Rolling Hills Local SD	Cambridge
64	31.4	Union Local SD	Morristown
67	30.9	Waverly City SD	Waverly
68	30.7	Harrison Hills City SD	Hopedale
69	30.5	Indian Creek Local SD	Wintersville
69	30.5	Niles City SD	Niles
71	30.2	Franklin Local SD	Duncan Falls
71	30.2	Fremont City SD	Fremont
73	29.7	Switzerland of Ohio Local SD	Woodsfield
74	28.9	South-Western City SD	Grove City
75	28.6	Bedford City SD	Bedford
75	28.6	Lancaster City SD	Lancaster
75	28.6	Piqua City SD	Piqua
78	28.4	Athens City SD	The Plains
78	28.4	Ravenna City SD	Ravenna
80	28.3	Chillicothe City SD	Chillicothe
81	28.0	Gallipolis City SD	Gallipolis
82	27.9	Girard City SD	Girard
82	27.9	Sidney City SD	Sidney
82	27.9	Willard City SD	Willard
85	27.6	New Richmond Ex Vill SD	New Richmond
86	27.5	Logan-Hocking Local SD	Logan
87	27.2	Claymont City SD	Dennison
87	27.2	Newark City SD	Newark
89	27.1	Jackson City SD	Jackson
90	27.0	Xenia Community City SD	Xenia
91	26.9	Edison Local SD	Hammondsville
92	26.8	Geneva Area City Schools	Geneva
93	26.7	Beaver Local SD	Lisbon
94	26.1	Hillsboro City SD	Hillsboro
95	25.7	Mad River Local SD	Dayton
96	25.6	Carrollton Ex Vill SD	Carrollton
96	25.6	Wooster City SD	Wooster
98	25.5	Garfield Heights City SD	Garfield Hgts
99	25.1	Washington Court House City SD	Wash Ct House
100	24.7	Akron Public Schools	Akron
100	24.7	Urbana City SD	Urbana
102	24.3	Alexander Local SD	Albany
103	24.2	Indian Valley Local SD	Gnadenhutten
103	24.2	Minerva Local SD	Minerva
103	24.2	West Holmes Local SD	Millersburg
106	24.0	Buckeye Local SD	Ashtabula
106	24.0	Canton Local SD	Canton
106	24.0	Circleville City SD	Circleville
106	24.0	Groveport Madison Local SD	Groveport
110	23.9	Port Clinton City SD	Port Clinton
111	23.8	Bellefontaine City Schools	Bellefontaine
112	23.7	Lakewood City SD	Lakewood
112	23.7	Mount Vernon City SD	Mount Vernon
114	23.6	Fairborn City Schools	Fairborn
114	23.6	Madison Local SD	Mansfield
116	23.0	Galion City SD	Galion
116	23.0	Lakewood Local SD	Hebron
118	22.8	Springfield Local SD	Akron
119	22.6	Eastern Local SD	Sardinia
119	22.6	Fairland Local SD	Proctorville
119	22.6	Greenfield Ex Vill SD	Greenfield
122	22.3	Fairless Local SD	Navarre
123	22.2	Norwalk City SD	Norwalk
124	22.1	Kenton City SD	Kenton
125	22.0	Ridgewood Local SD	West Lafayette
126	21.6	Batavia Local SD	Batavia
126	21.6	Salem City SD	Salem
128	21.5	Hubbard Ex Vill SD	Hubbard
129	21.4	Kent City SD	Kent
129	21.4	United Local SD	Hanoverton
131	21.3	Winton Woods City SD	Cincinnati
132	21.2	Liberty Local SD	Youngstown
133	21.1	Woodridge Local SD	Peninsula
134	20.8	Elida Local SD	Elida
135	20.7	Ashland City SD	Ashland
135	20.7	Springfield Local Schools	Holland
137	20.6	Tecumseh Local SD	New Carlisle
138	20.5	Western Brown Local SD	Mount Orab
139	20.2	Hamilton Local SD	Columbus
139	20.2	Westfall Local SD	Williamsport
141	20.1	Marietta City Schools	Marietta
142	20.0	Jefferson Area Local SD	Jefferson
143	19.9	Indian Lake Local SD	Lewistown
144	19.8	Wilmington City SD	Wilmington
145	19.7	Findlay City SD	Findlay
145	19.7	Newton Falls Ex Vill SD	Newton Falls
145	19.7	Washington Local Schools	Toledo
148	19.6	Greenville City SD	Greenville
149	19.3	Goshen Local SD	Goshen
149	19.3	West Muskingum Local SD	Zanesville
151	19.2	Austintown Local SD	Youngstown
151	19.2	Orrville City SD	Orrville
151	19.2	Southeast Local SD	Apple Creek
151	19.2	St Clairsville-Richland City SD	St Clairsville
151	19.2	West Branch Local SD	Beloit
156	19.1	Blanchester Local SD	Blanchester
157	18.8	Elgin Local SD	Marion
158	18.6	Highland Local SD	Sparta
158	18.6	Shelby City SD	Shelby
160	18.5	Celina City SD	Celina
161	18.4	Plain Local SD	Canton
162	18.3	Napoleon Area City SD	Napoleon
163	18.2	Sandy Valley Local SD	Magnolia
164	18.0	Northern Local SD	Thornville
165	17.9	Van Wert City SD	Van Wert
166	17.8	Defiance City SD	Defiance
167	17.7	Wapakoneta City City SD	Wapakoneta
168	17.6	Madison Local SD	Madison
168	17.6	Vermilion Local SD	Vermilion
170	17.5	Northwest Local SD	Cincinnati
171	17.2	Miami Trace Local SD	Wash Ct House
172	17.0	London City SD	London
173	16.9	Milton-Union Exempted Vill Schls	West Milton
174	16.6	Bath Local SD	Lima
174	16.6	Tiffin City SD	Tiffin
176	16.5	Franklin City SD	Franklin
176	16.5	River View Local SD	Warsaw
178	16.2	Three Rivers Local Schools	Cleves
179	15.9	Sheffield-Sheffield Lake City SD	Sheffield Vlg
179	15.9	Wellington Ex Vill SD	Wellington
181	15.7	Bethel-Tate Local SD	Bethel
182	15.6	Clear Fork Valley Local SD	Bellville
182	15.6	Clyde-Green Springs Ex Vill SD	Clyde
184	15.5	Streetsboro City Schools	Streetsboro
185	15.4	East Muskingum Local SD	New Concord
185	15.4	St Marys City SD	Saint Marys
185	15.4	Tri-Valley Local Schools	Dresden
188	15.2	Delaware City SD	Delaware
188	15.2	Wauseon Ex Vill SD	Wauseon
188	15.2	West Carrollton City SD	West Carrollton
191	15.0	Lake Local SD	Millbury
192	14.9	Black River Local SD	Sullivan
192	14.9	East Clinton Local SD	Lees Creek
192	14.9	Upper Sandusky Ex Vill SD	Upper Sandusky
192	14.9	Warren Local SD	Vincent
196	14.8	Kettering City SD	Kettering
196	14.8	Miamisburg City SD	Miamisburg
196	14.8	Preble Shawnee Local SD	Camden
196	14.8	Troy City SD	Troy
200	14.6	Logan Elm Local SD	Circleville
200	14.6	Triway Local SD	Wooster
202	14.5	Clermont Northeastern Local SD	Batavia
202	14.5	Field Local SD	Mogadore
202	14.5	Licking Valley Local SD Sd	Newark
202	14.5	Perry Local SD	Massillon
202	14.5	Pike-Delta-York Local SD	Delta
202	14.5	Southeast Local SD	Ravenna
208	14.4	Bellevue City SD	Bellevue
208	14.4	South Euclid-Lyndhurst City SD	Lyndhurst
208	14.4	Tuscarawas Valley Local SD	Zoarville
211	14.3	Parma City SD	Parma
211	14.3	River Valley Local SD	Caledonia
213	14.2	Paulding Ex Vill SD	Paulding
213	14.2	Willoughby-Eastlake City SD	Willoughby
215	14.1	Rossford Ex Vill SD	Rossford
215	14.1	Talawanda City SD	Oxford
217	14.0	James A Garfield Local SD	Garrettsville
218	13.9	Huber Heights City SD	Huber Heights
219	13.8	Amanda-Clearcreek Local SD	Amanda
220	13.6	Fairfield Union Local SD	W Rushville
221	13.5	Fairview Park City SD	Fairview Park
221	13.5	Licking Heights Local SD	Summit Station
223	13.4	East Holmes Local Schools	Berlin
224	13.3	Louisville City SD	Louisville
224	13.3	Southwest Local SD	Harrison
226	13.2	New Philadelphia City SD	New Philadelphia
227	13.1	Marlington Local SD	Alliance
227	13.1	North Fork Local SD	Utica
229	13.0	Cuyahoga Falls City SD	Cuyahoga Falls
229	13.0	Finneytown Local SD	Cincinnati
229	13.0	Oregon City SD	Oregon
232	12.8	Benton Carroll Salem Local SD	Oak Harbor
233	12.7	Teays Valley Local SD	Ashville
234	12.6	Bowling Green City SD	Bowling Green
234	12.6	Heath City SD	Heath
234	12.6	Shawnee Local SD	Lima
237	12.4	Boardman Local SD	Youngstown
237	12.4	Cloverleaf Local SD	Lodi
237	12.4	Eaton Community Schools	Eaton
237	12.4	Norton City Schools	Norton
241	12.3	Midview Local SD	Grafton
242	12.2	Swanton Local SD	Swanton
243	12.1	Berea City SD	Berea
243	12.1	Zane Trace Local SD	Chillicothe
245	12.0	Monroe Local SD	Monroe
246	11.9	Bryan City SD	Bryan
247	11.8	Madison Local SD	Middletown
248	11.5	Genoa Area Local SD	Genoa
249	11.3	Edgewood City SD	Trenton
249	11.3	Madison-Plains Local SD	London
251	11.1	Canal Winchester Local SD	Canal Winchester
252	11.0	Buckeye Local SD	Medina
252	11.0	Northwestern Local SD	Springfield
254	10.9	Huron City Schools	Huron
255	10.8	Carlisle Local SD	Carlisle
256	10.7	Brookville Local SD	Brookville
257	10.5	Champion Local SD	Warren
257	10.5	Clark-Shawnee Local SD	Springfield
257	10.5	Crestwood Local SD	Mantua
260	10.4	Greeneview Local SD	Jamestown
260	10.4	Northwest Local SD	Canal Fulton
260	10.4	West Clermont Local SD	Cincinnati
263	10.3	North Olmsted City Schools	North Olmsted
264	10.1	Howland Local SD	Warren
264	10.1	North Ridgeville City SD	N Ridgeville
264	10.1	Wickliffe City SD	Wickliffe
267	10.0	Lebanon City SD	Lebanon
268	9.9	Benjamin Logan Local SD	Bellefontaine
268	9.9	Firelands Local SD	Oberlin
270	9.8	Painesville Township Local SD	Painesville
270	9.8	Perkins Local SD	Sandusky
272	9.6	Reynoldsburg City SD	Reynoldsburg
273	9.5	Graham Local SD	Saint Paris
273	9.5	Jonathan Alder Local SD	Plain City
275	9.3	Berlin-Milan Local SD	Milan
276	9.0	Dover City SD	Dover
277	8.9	Otsego Local SD	Tontogany
278	8.8	Northmont City SD	Englewood
279	8.7	Clinton-Massie Local SD	Clarksville
279	8.7	Milford Ex Vill SD	Milford
281	8.6	Tallmadge City Schools	Tallmadge
282	8.5	Fairfield City SD	Fairfield
282	8.5	Lakeview Local SD	Cortland
282	8.5	Marysville Exempted Village SD	Marysville
282	8.5	Westerville City SD	Westerville
286	8.4	Southwest Licking Local SD	Etna
287	8.3	Eastwood Local SD	Pemberville
288	8.2	Shaker Heights City SD	Shaker Heights
288	8.2	Twinsburg City SD	Twinsburg
290	8.1	Green Local SD	Green
291	8.0	Brunswick City SD	Brunswick
291	8.0	Perry Local SD	Perry
293	7.8	Big Walnut Local SD	Galena
294	7.5	Vandalia-Butler City SD	Vandalia
295	7.4	Lexington Local SD	Lexington
296	7.3	Maumee City SD	Maumee
297	7.2	Keystone Local SD	Lagrange
297	7.2	Manchester Local SD	Akron
299	7.1	Coldwater Ex Vill SD	Coldwater
299	7.1	Hilliard City SD	Hilliard
299	7.1	Wadsworth City SD	Wadsworth
302	7.0	Mentor Ex Vill SD	Mentor
303	6.9	Chardon Local SD	Chardon
303	6.9	Greenon Local SD	Springfield
303	6.9	Olmsted Falls City SD	Olmsted Falls
303	6.9	Ontario Local SD	Mansfield

303	6.9	Ross Local SD	Hamilton
308	6.7	Avon Local SD	Avon
308	6.7	Buckeye Valley Local SD	Delaware
308	6.7	Gahanna-Jefferson City SD	Gahanna
308	6.7	Kings Local SD	Kings Mills
312	6.6	Little Miami Local SD	Morrow
313	6.4	Amherst Ex Vill SD	Amherst
313	6.4	Northeastern Local SD	Springfield
313	6.4	Ottawa-Glandorf Local SD	Ottawa
316	6.1	Sylvania City SD	Sylvania
316	6.1	Union-Scioto Local SD	Chillicothe
318	6.0	Nordonia Hills City SD	Northfield
319	5.9	Mayfield City SD	Highland Hgts
320	5.8	Lake Local SD	Hartville
321	5.5	Copley-Fairlawn City SD	Copley
322	5.4	North Canton City SD	North Canton
322	5.4	Pickerington Local SD	Pickerington
324	5.3	Sycamore Community City SD	Cincinnati
325	5.2	Loveland City SD	Loveland
325	5.2	Medina City SD	Medina
325	5.2	North Royalton City SD	N Royalton
328	5.0	Tipp City Ex Vill SD	Tipp City
328	5.0	Worthington City SD	Worthington
330	4.8	Jackson Local SD	Massillon
331	4.7	Sugarcreek Local SD	Bellbrook
331	4.7	Valley View Local SD	Germantown
333	4.5	Bexley City SD	Bexley
334	4.4	Strongsville City SD	Strongsville
335	4.3	Centerville City SD	Centerville
335	4.3	Kenston Local SD	Chagrin Falls
335	4.3	Lakota Local SD	Liberty Twp
335	4.3	Mariemont City SD	Cincinnati
339	4.2	Anthony Wayne Local SD	Whitehouse
340	3.9	Olentangy Local SD	Lewis Center
341	3.7	Beavercreek City SD	Beavercreek
341	3.7	Perrysburg Exempted Village	Perrysburg
343	3.6	Stow-Munroe Falls City SD	Stow
344	3.5	Brecksville-Broadview Hgts City	Brecksville
344	3.5	Poland Local SD	Poland
346	3.4	Aurora City SD	Aurora
347	3.2	Bay Village City SD	Bay Village
347	3.2	Highland Local SD	Medina
349	3.1	Avon Lake City Schools	Avon Lake
349	3.1	Beachwood City SD	Beachwood
351	3.0	Canfield Local SD	Canfield
351	3.0	Dublin City SD	Dublin
351	3.0	Westlake City SD	Westlake
354	2.8	Springboro Community City SD	Springboro
355	2.7	Forest Hills Local SD	Cincinnati
355	2.7	Rocky River City SD	Rocky River
357	2.5	Plain Local SD	New Albany
358	2.4	Madeira City SD	Cincinnati
358	2.4	Wyoming City SD	Wyoming
360	2.2	West Geauga Local SD	Chesterland
361	2.0	Revere Local SD	Bath
362	1.8	Solon City SD	Solon
363	1.7	Orange City SD	Cleveland
364	1.6	Mason City SD	Mason
364	1.6	Oak Hills Local SD	Cincinnati
366	1.3	Hudson City SD	Hudson
367	0.8	Indian Hill Ex Vill SD	Cincinnati
367	0.8	Upper Arlington City SD	Upper Arlington
369	0.6	Granville Ex Vill SD	Granville
369	0.6	Oakwood City SD	Dayton
371	0.5	Chagrin Falls Ex Vill SD	Chagrin Falls
372	n/a	Coventry Local SD	Akron
372	n/a	Electronic Classrm of Tomorrow	Columbus
372	n/a	Ohio Virtual Academy	Maumee

Students Eligible for Reduced-Price Lunch

Rank	Percent	District Name	City
1	14.3	Southeast Local SD	Apple Creek
2	14.1	Struthers City SD	Struthers
3	14.0	Rock Hill Local SD	Ironton
4	13.2	Euclid City SD	Euclid
4	13.2	Mad River Local SD	Dayton
6	13.0	Bucyrus City SD	Bucyrus
7	11.6	North College Hill City SD	Cincinnati
8	11.5	Warrensville Heights City SD	Warrensville Hgts
9	11.2	Buckeye Local SD	Ashtabula
9	11.2	Geneva Area City Schools	Geneva
11	11.1	Carrollton Ex Vill SD	Carrollton
11	11.1	Clearview Local SD	Lorain
13	10.7	Fostoria City SD	Fostoria
14	10.5	Maple Heights City SD	Maple Heights
15	10.3	Canton City SD	Canton
15	10.3	Northwest Local SD	Mc Dermott
17	10.2	Hubbard Ex Vill SD	Hubbard
18	10.1	Barberton City SD	Barberton
18	10.1	Dayton City SD	Dayton
18	10.1	Edison Local SD	Hammondsville
18	10.1	Sandusky City SD	Sandusky
22	10.0	Mt Healthy City SD	Cincinnati
22	10.0	New Lexington City SD	New Lexington
24	9.9	Wellington Ex Vill SD	Wellington
24	9.9	Whitehall City SD	Whitehall
26	9.8	Switzerland of Ohio Local SD	Woodsfield
27	9.7	Orrville City SD	Orrville
27	9.7	Ravenna City SD	Ravenna
27	9.7	West Holmes Local SD	Millersburg
30	9.6	Conneaut Area City SD	Conneaut
31	9.5	Clyde-Green Springs Ex Vill SD	Clyde
31	9.5	Fremont City SD	Fremont
31	9.5	Garfield Heights City SD	Garfield Hgts
31	9.5	Piqua City SD	Piqua
35	9.4	Alliance City SD	Alliance
35	9.4	Indian Valley Local SD	Gnadenhutten
35	9.4	Lorain City SD	Lorain
35	9.4	Sandy Valley Local SD	Magnolia
39	9.3	Elyria City SD	Elyria
39	9.3	Girard City SD	Girard
39	9.3	Vinton County Local SD	Mc Arthur
42	9.2	Minford Local SD	Minford
43	9.1	Canton Local SD	Canton
44	9.0	Massillon City SD	Massillon
45	8.9	Eastern Local SD	Sardinia
45	8.9	Minerva Local SD	Minerva
45	8.9	Newton Falls Ex Vill SD	Newton Falls
45	8.9	South-Western City SD	Grove City
49	8.8	Mansfield City SD	Mansfield
49	8.8	Meigs Local SD	Pomeroy
51	8.7	Adams County/Ohio Valley LSD	West Union
51	8.7	Blanchester Local SD	Blanchester
51	8.7	Rolling Hills Local SD	Cambridge
54	8.6	Bellevue City SD	Bellevue
55	8.5	Beaver Local SD	Lisbon
56	8.4	Marion City SD	Marion
56	8.4	Niles City SD	Niles
58	8.3	Benton Carroll Salem Local SD	Oak Harbor
58	8.3	Cleveland Hts-Univ Hts City SD	University Hgts
58	8.3	Fairless Local SD	Navarre
58	8.3	Norwood City SD	Norwood
62	8.2	East Holmes Local Schools	Berlin
62	8.2	Tiffin City SD	Tiffin
62	8.2	Urbana City SD	Urbana
65	8.1	Jefferson Area Local SD	Jefferson
65	8.1	Lancaster City SD	Lancaster
65	8.1	Madison Local SD	Mansfield
68	8.0	Bath Local SD	Lima
68	8.0	Coshocton City SD	Coshocton
68	8.0	Franklin Local SD	Duncan Falls
68	8.0	Harrison Hills City SD	Hopedale
68	8.0	Springfield Local SD	Akron
73	7.9	Logan-Hocking Local SD	Logan
73	7.9	Maysville Local SD	Zanesville
73	7.9	North Fork Local SD	Utica
73	7.9	Pike-Delta-York Local SD	Delta
73	7.9	Van Wert City SD	Van Wert
73	7.9	Warren City SD	Warren
73	7.9	Washington-Nile Local SD	West Portsmouth
80	7.8	Ashtabula Area City SD	Ashtabula
80	7.8	Kenton City SD	Kenton
80	7.8	Lake Local SD	Millbury
80	7.8	Painesville City Local SD	Painesville
80	7.8	Shelby City SD	Shelby
85	7.7	Greenfield Ex Vill SD	Greenfield
85	7.7	Trotwood-Madison City Schools	Trotwood
87	7.6	Sheffield-Sheffield Lake City SD	Sheffield Vlg
88	7.5	Louisville City SD	Louisville
88	7.5	Morgan Local SD	McConnelsville
88	7.5	Norwalk City SD	Norwalk
88	7.5	Ridgewood Local SD	West Lafayette
88	7.5	Westfall Local SD	Williamsport
93	7.4	Goshen Local SD	Goshen
93	7.4	Groveport Madison Local SD	Groveport
93	7.4	Northridge Local SD	Dayton
93	7.4	Sidney City SD	Sidney
93	7.4	Tecumseh Local SD	New Carlisle
98	7.3	Cambridge City SD	Cambridge
98	7.3	Hamilton City SD	Hamilton
98	7.3	Northwest Local SD	Cincinnati
98	7.3	Preble Shawnee Local SD	Camden
98	7.3	Streetsboro City Schools	Streetsboro
103	7.2	Austintown Local SD	Youngstown
103	7.2	Cloverleaf Local SD	Lodi
103	7.2	Middletown City SD	Middletown
103	7.2	Newark City SD	Newark
103	7.2	Parma City SD	Parma
103	7.2	River View Local SD	Warsaw
103	7.2	Western Brown Local SD	Mount Orab
110	7.1	Ashland City SD	Ashland
110	7.1	Cincinnati City SD	Cincinnati
110	7.1	Claymont City SD	Dennison
110	7.1	Cleveland Municipal City SD	Cleveland
110	7.1	Elgin Local SD	Marion
110	7.1	James A Garfield Local SD	Garrettsville
110	7.1	Liberty Local SD	Youngstown
117	7.0	Batavia Local SD	Batavia
117	7.0	Berea City SD	Berea
117	7.0	Cuyahoga Falls City SD	Cuyahoga Falls
117	7.0	Hamilton Local SD	Columbus
117	7.0	Martins Ferry City SD	Martins Ferry
122	6.9	Bedford City SD	Bedford
122	6.9	Rossford Ex Vill SD	Rossford
124	6.8	Campbell City SD	Campbell
124	6.8	East Cleveland City SD	East Cleveland
124	6.8	River Valley Local SD	Caledonia
124	6.8	Wooster City SD	Wooster
128	6.7	Columbus Public Schools	Columbus
128	6.7	Kettering City SD	Kettering
128	6.7	New Richmond Ex Vill SD	New Richmond
128	6.7	Princeton City SD	Cincinnati
128	6.7	Southeast Local SD	Ravenna
128	6.7	United Local SD	Hanoverton
128	6.7	Vermilion Local SD	Vermilion
128	6.7	Wauseon Ex Vill SD	Wauseon
136	6.6	Indian Creek Local SD	Wintersville
136	6.6	Madison Local SD	Madison
136	6.6	Union Local SD	Morristown
136	6.6	Wellston City Schools	Wellston
136	6.6	West Branch Local SD	Beloit
136	6.6	Wickliffe City SD	Wickliffe
142	6.5	Buckeye Local SD	Rayland
142	6.5	Hillsboro City SD	Hillsboro
142	6.5	Springfield Local Schools	Holland
145	6.4	Fairborn City Schools	Fairborn
145	6.4	Lima City SD	Lima
147	6.3	Galion City SD	Galion
147	6.3	Gallia County Local SD	Gallipolis
147	6.3	Greenville City SD	Greenville
147	6.3	Huber Heights City SD	Huber Heights
147	6.3	Northmont City SD	Englewood
147	6.3	Perry Local SD	Massillon
147	6.3	Scioto Valley Local SD	Piketon
147	6.3	Tuscarawas Valley Local SD	Zoarville
147	6.3	Warren Local SD	Vincent
156	6.2	Northern Local SD	Thornville
156	6.2	Zane Trace Local SD	Chillicothe
158	6.1	Oregon City SD	Oregon
158	6.1	Willoughby-Eastlake City SD	Willoughby
158	6.1	Wilmington City SD	Wilmington
158	6.1	Winton Woods City SD	Cincinnati
162	6.0	Bellaire Local SD	Bellaire
162	6.0	Eastwood Local SD	Pemberville
162	6.0	Elida Local SD	Elida
162	6.0	Jackson City SD	Jackson
162	6.0	Wapakoneta City City SD	Wapakoneta
162	6.0	Willard City SD	Willard
168	5.8	Findlay City SD	Findlay
168	5.8	Lakewood City SD	Lakewood
168	5.8	Miami Trace Local SD	Wash Ct House
168	5.8	Perry Local SD	Perry
168	5.8	Portsmouth City SD	Portsmouth
168	5.8	South Point Local SD	South Point
168	5.8	Washington Court House City SD	Wash Ct House
168	5.8	Washington Local Schools	Toledo
176	5.7	Zanesville City SD	Zanesville
177	5.6	Bryan City SD	Bryan
177	5.6	Celina City SD	Celina
177	5.6	Edgewood City SD	Trenton
177	5.6	Madison-Plains Local SD	London
177	5.6	Marlington Local SD	Alliance
177	5.6	Northwest Local SD	Canal Fulton
177	5.6	St Clairsville-Richland City SD	St Clairsville
184	5.5	Black River Local SD	Sullivan
184	5.5	Chillicothe City SD	Chillicothe
184	5.5	Defiance City SD	Defiance
184	5.5	East Liverpool City SD	East Liverpool
184	5.5	Plain Local SD	Canton
184	5.5	South Euclid-Lyndhurst City SD	Lyndhurst
190	5.4	Clear Fork Valley Local SD	Bellville
190	5.4	Fairview Park City SD	Fairview Park
190	5.4	St Marys City SD	Saint Marys
190	5.4	West Carrollton City SD	West Carrollton
194	5.3	Bellefontaine City Schools	Bellefontaine
194	5.3	Boardman Local SD	Youngstown
194	5.3	North Olmsted City Schools	North Olmsted
194	5.3	Triway Local SD	Wooster
194	5.3	Xenia Community City SD	Xenia
199	5.2	Athens City SD	The Plains
199	5.2	East Muskingum Local SD	New Concord
199	5.2	Logan Elm Local SD	Circleville
199	5.2	Mount Vernon City SD	Mount Vernon
199	5.2	Norton City Schools	Norton
199	5.2	Springfield City SD	Springfield

199	5.2	Steubenville City SD	Steubenville
199	5.2	Swanton Local SD	Swanton
199	5.2	Youngstown City SD	Youngstown
208	5.1	Bethel-Tate Local SD	Bethel
208	5.1	Clermont Northeastern Local SD	Batavia
208	5.1	Highland Local SD	Sparta
208	5.1	Howland Local SD	Warren
208	5.1	Indian Lake Local SD	Lewistown
208	5.1	Licking Valley Local SD Sd	Newark
214	5.0	Amanda-Clearcreek Local SD	Amanda
214	5.0	Champion Local SD	Warren
214	5.0	Circleville City SD	Circleville
214	5.0	East Clinton Local SD	Lees Creek
214	5.0	Keystone Local SD	Lagrange
214	5.0	Miamisburg City SD	Miamisburg
214	5.0	Napoleon Area City SD	Napoleon
221	4.9	Field Local SD	Mogadore
221	4.9	Graham Local SD	Saint Paris
221	4.9	Kent City SD	Kent
221	4.9	Milton-Union Exempted Vill Schls	West Milton
221	4.9	Three Rivers Local Schools	Cleves
221	4.9	Toledo City SD	Toledo
221	4.9	Woodridge Local SD	Peninsula
228	4.8	Delaware City SD	Delaware
228	4.8	Midview Local SD	Grafton
228	4.8	Monroe Local SD	Monroe
228	4.8	Paulding Ex Vill SD	Paulding
228	4.8	Troy City SD	Troy
233	4.7	Fairland Local SD	Proctorville
233	4.7	Heath City SD	Heath
233	4.7	Shawnee Local SD	Lima
236	4.6	Alexander Local SD	Albany
236	4.6	Ironton City SD	Ironton
236	4.6	Lakewood Local SD	Hebron
236	4.6	Upper Sandusky Ex Vill SD	Upper Sandusky
236	4.6	Waverly City SD	Waverly
241	4.5	Eaton Community Schools	Eaton
241	4.5	Lexington Local SD	Lexington
241	4.5	Marysville Exempted Village SD	Marysville
241	4.5	Port Clinton City SD	Port Clinton
241	4.5	Tri-Valley Local Schools	Dresden
246	4.4	Franklin City SD	Franklin
246	4.4	London City SD	London
246	4.4	Salem City SD	Salem
249	4.3	Brunswick City SD	Brunswick
249	4.3	Southwest Local SD	Harrison
249	4.3	Vandalia-Butler City SD	Vandalia
252	4.2	Nordonia Hills City SD	Northfield
253	4.1	Berlin-Milan Local SD	Milan
253	4.1	Brookville Local SD	Brookville
253	4.1	Jonathan Alder Local SD	Plain City
253	4.1	Licking Heights Local SD	Summit Station
253	4.1	Maumee City SD	Maumee
253	4.1	Perkins Local SD	Sandusky
253	4.1	Teays Valley Local SD	Ashville
260	4.0	Clark-Shawnee Local SD	Springfield
260	4.0	Fairfield Union Local SD	W Rushville
262	3.9	Amherst Ex Vill SD	Amherst
262	3.9	Clinton-Massie Local SD	Clarksville
262	3.9	Marietta City Schools	Marietta
265	3.8	Coldwater Ex Vill SD	Coldwater
265	3.8	Firelands Local SD	Oberlin
265	3.8	Southwest Licking Local SD	Etna
268	3.7	Gallipolis City SD	Gallipolis
268	3.7	Madison Local SD	Middletown
268	3.7	New Philadelphia City SD	New Philadelphia
271	3.6	Crestwood Local SD	Mantua
272	3.5	Painesville Township Local SD	Painesville
273	3.4	Chardon Local SD	Chardon
273	3.4	North Canton City SD	North Canton
273	3.4	Olmsted Falls City SD	Olmsted Falls
276	3.3	Canal Winchester Local SD	Canal Winchester
276	3.3	Carlisle Local SD	Carlisle
276	3.3	Finneytown Local SD	Cincinnati
276	3.3	Genoa Area Local SD	Genoa
276	3.3	Lebanon City SD	Lebanon
276	3.3	Mentor Ex Vill SD	Mentor
282	3.2	Akron Public Schools	Akron
282	3.2	Big Walnut Local SD	Galena
282	3.2	North Ridgeville City SD	N Ridgeville
282	3.2	Wadsworth City SD	Wadsworth
282	3.2	West Clermont Local SD	Cincinnati
287	3.1	Fairfield City SD	Fairfield
287	3.1	Manchester Local SD	Akron
287	3.1	Milford Ex Vill SD	Milford
287	3.1	West Muskingum Local SD	Zanesville
291	3.0	Bowling Green City SD	Bowling Green
291	3.0	Copley-Fairlawn City SD	Copley
291	3.0	Lake Local SD	Hartville
291	3.0	Northwestern Local SD	Springfield
291	3.0	Talawanda City SD	Oxford
291	3.0	Twinsburg City SD	Twinsburg
297	2.9	Green Local SD	Green
297	2.9	Greeneview Local SD	Jamestown
299	2.8	Benjamin Logan Local SD	Bellefontaine
299	2.8	Huron City Schools	Huron
299	2.8	North Royalton City SD	N Royalton
299	2.8	Ontario Local SD	Mansfield
299	2.8	Tallmadge City Schools	Tallmadge
304	2.7	Greenon Local SD	Springfield
305	2.6	Dover City SD	Dover
305	2.6	Worthington City SD	Worthington
307	2.5	Lakeview Local SD	Cortland
307	2.5	Northeastern Local SD	Springfield
307	2.5	Otsego Local SD	Tontogany
307	2.5	Ottawa-Glandorf Local SD	Ottawa
311	2.4	Jackson Local SD	Massillon
311	2.4	Pickerington Local SD	Pickerington
311	2.4	Valley View Local SD	Germantown
314	2.3	Beavercreek City SD	Beavercreek
314	2.3	Gahanna-Jefferson City SD	Gahanna
314	2.3	Reynoldsburg City SD	Reynoldsburg
314	2.3	Ross Local SD	Hamilton
314	2.3	Westerville City SD	Westerville
319	2.2	Bexley City SD	Bexley
319	2.2	Hilliard City SD	Hilliard
321	2.1	Buckeye Valley Local SD	Delaware
321	2.1	Highland Local SD	Medina
321	2.1	Medina City SD	Medina
321	2.1	Perrysburg Exempted Village	Perrysburg
321	2.1	Strongsville City SD	Strongsville
321	2.1	Sycamore Community City SD	Cincinnati
327	2.0	Avon Lake City Schools	Avon Lake
327	2.0	Avon Local SD	Avon
327	2.0	Canfield Local SD	Canfield
327	2.0	Kenston Local SD	Chagrin Falls
327	2.0	Loveland City SD	Loveland
327	2.0	Poland Local SD	Poland
327	2.0	Stow-Munroe Falls City SD	Stow
334	1.9	Mariemont City SD	Cincinnati
334	1.9	Plain Local SD	New Albany
334	1.9	Shaker Heights City SD	Shaker Heights
334	1.9	Tipp City Ex Vill SD	Tipp City
338	1.8	Bay Village City SD	Bay Village
338	1.8	Brecksville-Broadview Hgts City	Brecksville
338	1.8	Kings Local SD	Kings Mills
338	1.8	Sylvania City SD	Sylvania
342	1.7	Buckeye Local SD	Medina
342	1.7	Little Miami Local SD	Morrow
342	1.7	West Geauga Local SD	Chesterland
342	1.7	Westlake City SD	Westlake
346	1.6	Mayfield City SD	Highland Hgts
346	1.6	Union-Scioto Local SD	Chillicothe
348	1.4	Aurora City SD	Aurora
348	1.4	Solon City SD	Solon
350	1.3	Beachwood City SD	Beachwood
350	1.3	Mason City SD	Mason
350	1.3	Olentangy Local SD	Lewis Center
353	1.2	Forest Hills Local SD	Cincinnati
353	1.2	Lakota Local SD	Liberty Twp
353	1.2	Sugarcreek Local SD	Bellbrook
356	1.1	Anthony Wayne Local SD	Whitehouse
356	1.1	Springboro Community City SD	Springboro
356	1.1	Wyoming City SD	Wyoming
359	1.0	Centerville City SD	Centerville
359	1.0	Dublin City SD	Dublin
359	1.0	Rocky River City SD	Rocky River
362	0.6	Granville Ex Vill SD	Granville
362	0.6	Madeira City SD	Cincinnati
362	0.6	Oak Hills Local SD	Cincinnati
362	0.6	Revere Local SD	Bath
366	0.5	Hudson City SD	Hudson
366	0.5	Orange City SD	Cleveland
366	0.5	Upper Arlington City SD	Upper Arlington
369	0.4	Oakwood City SD	Dayton
370	0.2	Indian Hill Ex Vill SD	Cincinnati
371	0.1	Chagrin Falls Ex Vill SD	Chagrin Falls
372	n/a	Coventry Local SD	Akron
372	n/a	Electronic Classrm of Tomorrow	Columbus
372	n/a	Ohio Virtual Academy	Maumee

Student/Teacher Ratio

Rank	Ratio	District Name	City
1	39.6	Ohio Virtual Academy	Maumee
2	36.6	Electronic Classrm of Tomorrow	Columbus
3	21.6	Lake Local SD	Millbury
3	21.6	Piqua City SD	Piqua
5	21.0	Eastwood Local SD	Pemberville
6	20.5	Poland Local SD	Poland
7	20.3	Bath Local SD	Lima
7	20.3	Norwalk City SD	Norwalk
9	20.0	Jonathan Alder Local SD	Plain City
9	20.0	Lebanon City SD	Lebanon
11	19.9	Rolling Hills Local SD	Cambridge
11	19.9	Sugarcreek Local SD	Bellbrook
13	19.8	Wadsworth City SD	Wadsworth
14	19.6	Bethel-Tate Local SD	Bethel
14	19.6	Midview Local SD	Grafton
14	19.6	Reynoldsburg City SD	Reynoldsburg
14	19.6	Wapakoneta City City SD	Wapakoneta
18	19.5	Garfield Heights City SD	Garfield Hgts
19	19.4	Clinton-Massie Local SD	Clarksville
19	19.4	Geneva Area City Schools	Geneva
19	19.4	Genoa Area Local SD	Genoa
19	19.4	Nordonia Hills City SD	Northfield
23	19.3	Beavercreek City SD	Beavercreek
23	19.3	Ontario Local SD	Mansfield
25	19.2	Lakeview Local SD	Cortland
25	19.2	Madison Local SD	Madison
25	19.2	Painesville Township Local SD	Painesville
28	19.1	Amherst Ex Vill SD	Amherst
28	19.1	Brookville Local SD	Brookville
28	19.1	Clermont Northeastern Local SD	Batavia
28	19.1	Jackson City SD	Jackson
28	19.1	Southwest Local SD	Harrison
28	19.1	Springboro Community City SD	Springboro
28	19.1	Tri-Valley Local Schools	Dresden
35	19.0	Keystone Local SD	Lagrange
35	19.0	Manchester Local SD	Akron
35	19.0	Shawnee Local SD	Lima
35	19.0	Troy City SD	Troy
39	18.9	Fairfield City SD	Fairfield
39	18.9	Fairfield Union Local SD	W Rushville
39	18.9	Fostoria City SD	Fostoria
39	18.9	Maysville Local SD	Zanesville
39	18.9	Perry Local SD	Massillon
39	18.9	Zane Trace Local SD	Chillicothe
45	18.7	Northmont City SD	Englewood
46	18.6	Chillicothe City SD	Chillicothe
46	18.6	West Branch Local SD	Beloit
48	18.5	Elida Local SD	Elida
48	18.5	Fairland Local SD	Proctorville
48	18.5	Granville Ex Vill SD	Granville
48	18.5	Loveland City SD	Loveland
48	18.5	Scioto Valley Local SD	Piketon
48	18.5	United Local SD	Hanoverton
54	18.4	Coventry Local SD	Akron
54	18.4	Firelands Local SD	Oberlin
54	18.4	Fremont City SD	Fremont
54	18.4	Milford Ex Vill SD	Milford
54	18.4	Northwestern Local SD	Springfield
59	18.3	Clark-Shawnee Local SD	Springfield
59	18.3	Goshen Local SD	Goshen
59	18.3	Oak Hills Local SD	Cincinnati
59	18.3	Union-Scioto Local SD	Chillicothe
59	18.3	Wauseon Ex Vill SD	Wauseon
59	18.3	Western Brown Local SD	Mount Orab
65	18.2	Amanda-Clearcreek Local SD	Amanda
65	18.2	Greeneview Local SD	Jamestown
65	18.2	Heath City SD	Heath
68	18.1	Anthony Wayne Local SD	Whitehouse
68	18.1	Benton Carroll Salem Local SD	Oak Harbor
68	18.1	Cloverleaf Local SD	Lodi
68	18.1	Jefferson Area Local SD	Jefferson
68	18.1	North Fork Local SD	Utica
68	18.1	Ottawa-Glandorf Local SD	Ottawa
68	18.1	Pike-Delta-York Local SD	Delta
68	18.1	Stow-Munroe Falls City SD	Stow
68	18.1	West Clermont Local SD	Cincinnati
77	18.0	Eaton Community Schools	Eaton
77	18.0	Lexington Local SD	Lexington
77	18.0	Licking Heights Local SD	Summit Station
77	18.0	Westerville City SD	Westerville
81	17.9	Brunswick City SD	Brunswick
81	17.9	Green Local SD	Green
81	17.9	Highland Local SD	Medina
81	17.9	Jackson Local SD	Massillon
81	17.9	Kings Local SD	Kings Mills
81	17.9	Liberty Local SD	Youngstown
81	17.9	Marietta City Schools	Marietta
81	17.9	Mason City SD	Mason
81	17.9	North Royalton City SD	N Royalton
81	17.9	Otsego Local SD	Tontogany
81	17.9	Strongsville City SD	Strongsville
92	17.8	Little Miami Local SD	Morrow
92	17.8	Pickerington Local SD	Pickerington
92	17.8	Waverly City SD	Waverly
95	17.7	Beaver Local SD	Lisbon
95	17.7	Edgewood City SD	Trenton
95	17.7	Girard City SD	Girard
95	17.7	Groveport Madison Local SD	Groveport
95	17.7	Hubbard Ex Vill SD	Hubbard
95	17.7	Logan-Hocking Local SD	Logan
95	17.7	Minford Local SD	Minford
95	17.7	North College Hill City SD	Cincinnati
95	17.7	Ridgewood Local SD	West Lafayette

PROFILES OF OHIO / School District Rankings 401

95	17.7	Ross Local SD	Hamilton
95	17.7	Swanton Local SD	Swanton
95	17.7	Tipp City Ex Vill SD	Tipp City
107	17.6	Black River Local SD	Sullivan
107	17.6	Clyde-Green Springs Ex Vill SD	Clyde
107	17.6	Lake Local SD	Hartville
107	17.6	Lancaster City SD	Lancaster
107	17.6	New Lexington City SD	New Lexington
107	17.6	Sidney City SD	Sidney
107	17.6	St Marys City SD	Saint Marys
114	17.5	Aurora City SD	Aurora
114	17.5	Carrollton Ex Vill SD	Carrollton
114	17.5	Clear Fork Valley Local SD	Bellville
114	17.5	Fairborn City Schools	Fairborn
114	17.5	Forest Hills Local SD	Cincinnati
114	17.5	Highland Local SD	Sparta
114	17.5	Indian Creek Local SD	Wintersville
114	17.5	Southeast Local SD	Ravenna
114	17.5	Wilmington City SD	Wilmington
123	17.4	Crestwood Local SD	Mantua
123	17.4	East Muskingum Local SD	New Concord
123	17.4	Field Local SD	Mogadore
123	17.4	Franklin City SD	Franklin
123	17.4	Huron City Schools	Huron
123	17.4	River Valley Local SD	Caledonia
123	17.4	Valley View Local SD	Germantown
123	17.4	West Muskingum Local SD	Zanesville
123	17.4	Willard City SD	Willard
132	17.3	Austintown Local SD	Youngstown
132	17.3	Benjamin Logan Local SD	Bellefontaine
132	17.3	Brecksville-Broadview Hgts City	Brecksville
132	17.3	East Cleveland City SD	East Cleveland
132	17.3	East Clinton Local SD	Lees Creek
132	17.3	Miamisburg City SD	Miamisburg
132	17.3	Northern Local SD	Thornville
132	17.3	Northwest Local SD	Cincinnati
132	17.3	Twinsburg City SD	Twinsburg
141	17.2	Batavia Local SD	Batavia
141	17.2	Marlington Local SD	Alliance
141	17.2	Tuscarawas Valley Local SD	Zoarville
141	17.2	Wellington Ex Vill SD	Wellington
145	17.1	Buckeye Local SD	Medina
145	17.1	Buckeye Valley Local SD	Delaware
145	17.1	Canfield Local SD	Canfield
145	17.1	Circleville City SD	Circleville
145	17.1	Graham Local SD	Saint Paris
145	17.1	Greenon Local SD	Springfield
145	17.1	Madison-Plains Local SD	London
145	17.1	Norton City Schools	Norton
145	17.1	Sheffield-Sheffield Lake City SD	Sheffield Vlg
145	17.1	Southwest Licking Local SD	Etna
145	17.1	Three Rivers Local Schools	Cleves
145	17.1	Vermilion Local SD	Vermilion
145	17.1	Willoughby-Eastlake City SD	Willoughby
158	17.0	Carlisle Local SD	Carlisle
158	17.0	Eastern Local SD	Sardinia
158	17.0	Franklin Local SD	Duncan Falls
158	17.0	Louisville City SD	Louisville
158	17.0	Miami Trace Local SD	Wash Ct House
158	17.0	Milton-Union Exempted Vill Schls	West Milton
158	17.0	Minerva Local SD	Minerva
158	17.0	Mount Vernon City SD	Mount Vernon
158	17.0	Niles City SD	Niles
158	17.0	Olmsted Falls City SD	Olmsted Falls
158	17.0	Struthers City SD	Struthers
158	17.0	Tiffin City SD	Tiffin
158	17.0	Triway Local SD	Wooster
171	16.9	Ashland City SD	Ashland
171	16.9	Coldwater Ex Vill SD	Coldwater
171	16.9	Hamilton City SD	Hamilton
171	16.9	Lakota Local SD	Liberty Twp
171	16.9	Trotwood-Madison City Schools	Trotwood
176	16.8	Chardon Local SD	Chardon
176	16.8	Claymont City SD	Dennison
176	16.8	Euclid City SD	Euclid
176	16.8	North Canton City SD	North Canton
176	16.8	Northwest Local SD	Mc Dermott
181	16.7	Howland Local SD	Warren
181	16.7	James A Garfield Local SD	Garrettsville
181	16.7	Martins Ferry City SD	Martins Ferry
181	16.7	Newark City SD	Newark
181	16.7	Newton Falls Ex Vill SD	Newton Falls
181	16.7	Parma City SD	Parma
181	16.7	Westfall Local SD	Williamsport
188	16.6	Avon Local SD	Avon
188	16.6	Licking Valley Local SD Sd	Newark
188	16.6	Logan Elm Local SD	Circleville
188	16.6	Olentangy Local SD	Lewis Center
192	16.5	Bellevue City SD	Bellevue
192	16.5	Buckeye Local SD	Ashtabula
192	16.5	Bucyrus City SD	Bucyrus
192	16.5	Maple Heights City SD	Maple Heights
192	16.5	Rocky River City SD	Rocky River
192	16.5	Springfield Local Schools	Holland
192	16.5	Warren Local SD	Vincent
192	16.5	West Geauga Local SD	Chesterland
200	16.4	Berea City SD	Berea
200	16.4	Berlin-Milan Local SD	Milan
200	16.4	Boardman Local SD	Youngstown
200	16.4	Columbus Public Schools	Columbus
200	16.4	Lakewood City SD	Lakewood
200	16.4	Lorain City SD	Lorain
200	16.4	Madison Local SD	Middletown
200	16.4	Northwest Local SD	Canal Fulton
200	16.4	River View Local SD	Warsaw
200	16.4	South Point Local SD	South Point
200	16.4	Teays Valley Local SD	Ashville
200	16.4	Tecumseh Local SD	New Carlisle
212	16.3	Hamilton Local SD	Columbus
212	16.3	Perkins Local SD	Sandusky
212	16.3	Urbana City SD	Urbana
215	16.2	Ashtabula Area City SD	Ashtabula
215	16.2	Canal Winchester Local SD	Canal Winchester
215	16.2	Celina City SD	Celina
215	16.2	Copley-Fairlawn City SD	Copley
215	16.2	West Holmes Local SD	Millersburg
220	16.1	Conneaut Area City SD	Conneaut
221	16.0	Coshocton City SD	Coshocton
221	16.0	Edison Local SD	Hammondsville
221	16.0	Plain Local SD	New Albany
221	16.0	Shelby City SD	Shelby
221	16.0	Westlake City SD	Westlake
226	15.9	Avon Lake City Schools	Avon Lake
226	15.9	Bryan City SD	Bryan
226	15.9	Delaware City SD	Delaware
226	15.9	Harrison Hills City SD	Hopedale
226	15.9	Marion City SD	Marion
226	15.9	Orrville City SD	Orrville
226	15.9	South-Western City SD	Grove City
226	15.9	Washington-Nile Local SD	West Portsmouth
234	15.8	Campbell City SD	Campbell
234	15.8	Champion Local SD	Warren
234	15.8	Dover City SD	Dover
234	15.8	Indian Lake Local SD	Lewistown
234	15.8	Marysville Exempted Village SD	Marysville
234	15.8	Napoleon Area City SD	Napoleon
234	15.8	Perrysburg Exempted Village	Perrysburg
234	15.8	Plain Local SD	Canton
234	15.8	Revere Local SD	Bath
234	15.8	Vinton County Local SD	Mc Arthur
234	15.8	Xenia Community City SD	Xenia
245	15.7	Galion City SD	Galion
245	15.7	Greenfield Ex Vill SD	Greenfield
245	15.7	Kenton City SD	Kenton
245	15.7	North Ridgeville City SD	N Ridgeville
245	15.7	Perry Local SD	Perry
245	15.7	Steubenville City SD	Steubenville
245	15.7	Sylvania City SD	Sylvania
245	15.7	Talawanda City SD	Oxford
253	15.6	Big Walnut Local SD	Galena
253	15.6	Gallipolis City SD	Gallipolis
253	15.6	Hudson City SD	Hudson
253	15.6	Medina City SD	Medina
253	15.6	Mentor Ex Vill SD	Mentor
253	15.6	New Philadelphia City SD	New Philadelphia
253	15.6	Northeastern Local SD	Springfield
253	15.6	Solon City SD	Solon
253	15.6	Wellston City Schools	Wellston
253	15.6	Whitehall City SD	Whitehall
263	15.5	Bowling Green City SD	Bowling Green
263	15.5	Canton City SD	Canton
263	15.5	Dublin City SD	Dublin
263	15.5	London City SD	London
263	15.5	Port Clinton City SD	Port Clinton
263	15.5	Tallmadge City Schools	Tallmadge
263	15.5	Van Wert City SD	Van Wert
263	15.5	West Carrollton City SD	West Carrollton
271	15.4	Bedford City SD	Bedford
271	15.4	Blanchester Local SD	Blanchester
271	15.4	Hilliard City SD	Hilliard
271	15.4	Kettering City SD	Kettering
271	15.4	Monroe Local SD	Monroe
271	15.4	New Richmond Ex Vill SD	New Richmond
271	15.4	Salem City SD	Salem
278	15.3	Clearview Local SD	Lorain
278	15.3	Defiance City SD	Defiance
278	15.3	Finneytown Local SD	Cincinnati
278	15.3	Hillsboro City SD	Hillsboro
278	15.3	Rossford Ex Vill SD	Rossford
278	15.3	Springfield Local SD	Akron
284	15.2	Adams County/Ohio Valley LSD	West Union
284	15.2	Cambridge City SD	Cambridge
284	15.2	Fairless Local SD	Navarre
284	15.2	Ravenna City SD	Ravenna
284	15.2	Upper Sandusky Ex Vill SD	Upper Sandusky
284	15.2	Washington Local Schools	Toledo
290	15.1	Kenston Local SD	Chagrin Falls
290	15.1	Oregon City SD	Oregon
290	15.1	Portsmouth City SD	Portsmouth
290	15.1	Sandy Valley Local SD	Magnolia
290	15.1	South Euclid-Lyndhurst City SD	Lyndhurst
290	15.1	Springfield City SD	Springfield
296	15.0	Bellefontaine City Schools	Bellefontaine
296	15.0	Canton Local SD	Canton
296	15.0	Centerville City SD	Centerville
296	15.0	Cuyahoga Falls City SD	Cuyahoga Falls
296	15.0	East Holmes Local Schools	Berlin
296	15.0	Elgin Local SD	Marion
296	15.0	Gallia County Local SD	Gallipolis
296	15.0	Mad River Local SD	Dayton
296	15.0	Madeira City SD	Cincinnati
296	15.0	Southeast Local SD	Apple Creek
296	15.0	St Clairsville-Richland City SD	St Clairsville
296	15.0	Vandalia-Butler City SD	Vandalia
296	15.0	Washington Court House City SD	Wash Ct House
309	14.9	Alliance City SD	Alliance
309	14.9	Bay Village City SD	Bay Village
309	14.9	Norwood City SD	Norwood
309	14.9	Painesville City Local SD	Painesville
313	14.8	Buckeye Local SD	Rayland
313	14.8	Findlay City SD	Findlay
313	14.8	Greenville City SD	Greenville
313	14.8	Lakewood Local SD	Hebron
313	14.8	Middletown City SD	Middletown
313	14.8	Morgan Local SD	McConnelsville
313	14.8	Worthington City SD	Worthington
313	14.8	Wyoming City SD	Wyoming
321	14.7	Indian Hill Ex Vill SD	Cincinnati
321	14.7	Indian Valley Local SD	Gnadenhutten
321	14.7	Ironton City SD	Ironton
321	14.7	Rock Hill Local SD	Ironton
321	14.7	Warrensville Heights City SD	Warrensville Hgts
326	14.6	Barberton City SD	Barberton
326	14.6	Mt Healthy City SD	Cincinnati
326	14.6	North Olmsted City Schools	North Olmsted
326	14.6	Paulding Ex Vill SD	Paulding
326	14.6	Winton Woods City SD	Cincinnati
326	14.6	Zanesville City SD	Zanesville
332	14.5	Alexander Local SD	Albany
332	14.5	Bellaire Local SD	Bellaire
332	14.5	Preble Shawnee Local SD	Camden
335	14.4	Chagrin Falls Ex Vill SD	Chagrin Falls
335	14.4	Elyria City SD	Elyria
335	14.4	Maumee City SD	Maumee
335	14.4	Northridge Local SD	Dayton
335	14.4	Sycamore Community City SD	Cincinnati
340	14.2	Cleveland Hts-Univ Hts City SD	University Hgts
340	14.2	Madison Local SD	Mansfield
340	14.2	Sandusky City SD	Sandusky
343	14.1	Switzerland of Ohio Local SD	Woodsfield
343	14.1	Warren City SD	Warren
343	14.1	Wooster City SD	Wooster
346	14.0	Woodridge Local SD	Peninsula
347	13.9	Bexley City SD	Bexley
347	13.9	East Liverpool City SD	East Liverpool
347	13.9	Fairview Park City SD	Fairview Park
347	13.9	Mariemont City SD	Cincinnati
347	13.9	Massillon City SD	Massillon
347	13.9	Oakwood City SD	Dayton
347	13.9	Streetsboro City Schools	Streetsboro
347	13.9	Upper Arlington City SD	Upper Arlington
347	13.9	Wickliffe City SD	Wickliffe
356	13.7	Lima City SD	Lima
356	13.7	Union Local SD	Morristown
358	13.6	Shaker Heights City SD	Shaker Heights
358	13.6	Toledo City SD	Toledo
360	13.5	Cleveland Municipal City SD	Cleveland
360	13.5	Mansfield City SD	Mansfield
362	13.4	Gahanna-Jefferson City SD	Gahanna
363	13.3	Athens City SD	The Plains
363	13.3	Youngstown City SD	Youngstown
365	13.2	Meigs Local SD	Pomeroy
366	13.1	Mayfield City SD	Highland Hgts
367	13.0	Dayton City SD	Dayton
368	12.8	Cincinnati City SD	Cincinnati
369	12.7	Kent City SD	Kent
370	12.6	Princeton City SD	Cincinnati
371	12.2	Orange City SD	Cleveland
372	10.8	Huber Heights City SD	Huber Heights
373	10.5	Beachwood City SD	Beachwood
374	9.2	Akron Public Schools	Akron

Student/Librarian Ratio

Rank	Ratio	District Name	City
1	13,963.3	Amherst Ex Vill SD	Amherst
2	9,580.0	Indian Valley Local SD	Gnadenhutten
3	5,903.0	Northmont City SD	Englewood

402 PROFILES OF OHIO / School District Rankings

4	5,259.5	South-Western City SD	Grove City
5	4,568.0	Ashtabula Area City SD	Ashtabula
5	4,568.0	West Clermont Local SD	Cincinnati
7	4,498.0	Delaware City SD	Delaware
8	3,739.0	Madison Local SD	Madison
9	3,518.0	Vandalia-Butler City SD	Vandalia
10	3,345.6	Geneva Area City Schools	Geneva
11	3,307.0	New Philadelphia City SD	New Philadelphia
12	3,303.5	Reynoldsburg City SD	Reynoldsburg
13	3,254.0	Copley-Fairlawn City SD	Copley
14	3,239.5	Findlay City SD	Findlay
15	3,160.0	Wapakoneta City City SD	Wapakoneta
16	3,116.0	Celina City SD	Celina
17	3,093.0	Kenston Local SD	Chagrin Falls
18	2,975.0	Athens City SD	The Plains
19	2,932.0	Carrollton Ex Vill SD	Carrollton
20	2,924.0	Canton City SD	Canton
21	2,878.3	Mason City SD	Mason
22	2,745.0	Jackson City SD	Jackson
23	2,738.0	Marlington Local SD	Alliance
24	2,713.5	Fairborn City Schools	Fairborn
25	2,689.0	Edison Local SD	Hammondsville
26	2,659.0	Norwood City SD	Norwood
27	2,657.0	Shawnee Local SD	Lima
28	2,647.5	Miamisburg City SD	Miamisburg
29	2,633.0	Big Walnut Local SD	Galena
29	2,633.0	Vinton County Local SD	Mc Arthur
31	2,598.0	Dover City SD	Dover
32	2,591.0	Elida Local SD	Elida
33	2,580.0	Ross Local SD	Hamilton
34	2,558.0	Norton City Schools	Norton
35	2,541.0	River View Local SD	Warsaw
36	2,538.0	Canton Local SD	Canton
37	2,529.0	Kettering City SD	Kettering
38	2,527.0	Conneaut Area City SD	Conneaut
39	2,462.0	North Canton City SD	North Canton
40	2,453.0	Buckeye Local SD	Medina
41	2,443.0	West Branch Local SD	Beloit
42	2,433.0	Middletown City SD	Middletown
43	2,418.0	Franklin Local SD	Duncan Falls
44	2,415.0	Buckeye Local SD	Rayland
45	2,411.0	New Richmond Ex Vill SD	New Richmond
46	2,401.8	Hamilton City SD	Hamilton
47	2,366.0	Gallipolis City SD	Gallipolis
48	2,362.0	Willard City SD	Willard
49	2,360.5	Marysville Exempted Village SD	Marysville
50	2,356.0	Urbana City SD	Urbana
51	2,347.5	Wadsworth City SD	Wadsworth
52	2,339.0	Fostoria City SD	Fostoria
53	2,334.0	Eaton Community Schools	Eaton
54	2,323.0	Logan Elm Local SD	Circleville
55	2,319.0	Greenfield Ex Vill SD	Greenfield
56	2,297.0	Clyde-Green Springs Ex Vill SD	Clyde
57	2,290.0	Van Wert City SD	Van Wert
58	2,287.0	Buckeye Local SD	Ashtabula
59	2,285.0	North Olmsted City Schools	North Olmsted
60	2,266.7	Huber Heights City SD	Huber Heights
61	2,257.0	Jefferson Area Local SD	Jefferson
62	2,244.0	Painesville Township Local SD	Painesville
63	2,238.0	Galion City SD	Galion
64	2,230.5	Troy City SD	Troy
65	2,226.0	Rolling Hills Local SD	Cambridge
66	2,222.0	Firelands Local SD	Oberlin
67	2,202.0	Minerva Local SD	Minerva
68	2,174.0	Perrysburg Exempted Village	Perrysburg
68	2,174.0	Waverly City SD	Waverly
70	2,160.0	Springboro Community City SD	Springboro
71	2,150.0	Triway Local SD	Wooster
72	2,145.0	Kenton City SD	Kenton
73	2,140.0	Euclid City SD	Euclid
74	2,133.0	Wauseon Ex Vill SD	Wauseon
75	2,131.4	Northwest Local SD	Cincinnati
76	2,087.0	Streetsboro City Schools	Streetsboro
77	2,064.0	Lorain City SD	Lorain
78	2,020.0	Rossford Ex Vill SD	Rossford
79	2,014.0	Logan-Hocking Local SD	Logan
80	2,008.0	Licking Heights Local SD	Summit Station
81	2,004.0	Struthers City SD	Struthers
82	1,992.0	Indian Lake Local SD	Lewistown
83	1,980.0	Greenon Local SD	Springfield
84	1,978.0	Eastwood Local SD	Pemberville
85	1,977.5	Piqua City SD	Piqua
86	1,971.0	Port Clinton City SD	Port Clinton
87	1,970.3	Washington Local Schools	Toledo
88	1,958.0	Fairfield Union Local SD	W Rushville
89	1,954.0	Union-Scioto Local SD	Chillicothe
90	1,943.5	Nordonia Hills City SD	Northfield
91	1,943.0	West Carrollton City SD	West Carrollton
92	1,939.5	Anthony Wayne Local SD	Whitehouse
93	1,883.0	Fairless Local SD	Navarre
94	1,874.0	Berlin-Milan Local SD	Milan
95	1,866.0	South Point Local SD	South Point
96	1,857.0	East Holmes Local Schools	Berlin
97	1,853.7	Jackson Local SD	Massillon
98	1,843.0	Clear Fork Valley Local SD	Bellville
99	1,834.0	Maple Heights City SD	Maple Heights
100	1,831.0	Keystone Local SD	Lagrange
100	1,831.0	River Valley Local SD	Caledonia
102	1,819.0	Liberty Local SD	Youngstown
103	1,814.0	Northridge Local SD	Dayton
104	1,813.5	Brunswick City SD	Brunswick
105	1,812.7	Miami Trace Local SD	Wash Ct House
106	1,809.0	Jonathan Alder Local SD	Plain City
106	1,809.0	Paulding Ex Vill SD	Paulding
108	1,789.0	Tecumseh Local SD	New Carlisle
109	1,787.0	Finneytown Local SD	Cincinnati
110	1,785.5	Mad River Local SD	Dayton
111	1,782.5	Cloverleaf Local SD	Lodi
112	1,781.0	Highland Local SD	Sparta
113	1,775.2	Willoughby-Eastlake City SD	Willoughby
114	1,774.0	Clinton-Massie Local SD	Clarksville
115	1,771.0	Blanchester Local SD	Blanchester
116	1,769.0	Girard City SD	Girard
117	1,766.5	Madison Local SD	Mansfield
118	1,763.5	Southwest Licking Local SD	Etna
119	1,744.0	Tuscarawas Valley Local SD	Zoarville
120	1,737.0	Genoa Area Local SD	Genoa
121	1,721.3	Warren City SD	Warren
122	1,718.0	Trotwood-Madison City Schools	Trotwood
123	1,717.5	Midview Local SD	Grafton
124	1,716.0	Lake Local SD	Millbury
125	1,701.0	Greenville City SD	Greenville
126	1,699.3	Adams County/Ohio Valley LSD	West Union
127	1,694.5	Akron Public Schools	Akron
128	1,682.0	Austintown Local SD	Youngstown
129	1,679.5	Lake Local SD	Hartville
130	1,679.0	Scioto Valley Local SD	Piketon
131	1,664.7	Lima City SD	Lima
132	1,664.0	Huron City Schools	Huron
133	1,655.0	Westfall Local SD	Williamsport
134	1,653.0	Amanda-Clearcreek Local SD	Amanda
135	1,645.0	Greeneview Local SD	Jamestown
136	1,637.0	Louisville City SD	Louisville
137	1,632.3	Boardman Local SD	Youngstown
138	1,627.0	Madison-Plains Local SD	London
139	1,623.0	Coldwater Ex Vill SD	Coldwater
140	1,618.0	Perry Local SD	Massillon
141	1,617.5	Ravenna City SD	Ravenna
142	1,616.5	Teays Valley Local SD	Ashville
143	1,601.0	Marietta City Schools	Marietta
144	1,600.5	Little Miami Local SD	Morrow
145	1,597.5	Wilmington City SD	Wilmington
146	1,592.3	Youngstown City SD	Youngstown
147	1,590.0	Madison Local SD	Middletown
148	1,589.0	Zane Trace Local SD	Chillicothe
149	1,588.4	Southwest Local SD	Harrison
150	1,579.0	St Clairsville-Richland City SD	St Clairsville
151	1,575.0	Tri-Valley Local Schools	Dresden
152	1,574.0	Pike-Delta-York Local SD	Delta
153	1,571.0	East Clinton Local SD	Lees Creek
154	1,570.0	Wickliffe City SD	Wickliffe
155	1,568.0	Sandy Valley Local SD	Magnolia
156	1,566.4	Sylvania City SD	Sylvania
157	1,552.0	Talawanda City SD	Oxford
158	1,548.5	Canfield Local SD	Canfield
159	1,543.0	Eastern Local SD	Sardinia
160	1,541.0	Dayton City SD	Dayton
161	1,538.0	North College Hill City SD	Cincinnati
161	1,538.0	Springfield Local SD	Akron
163	1,532.3	Fremont City SD	Fremont
164	1,530.5	Plain Local SD	Canton
165	1,520.0	Manchester Local SD	Akron
165	1,520.0	Newton Falls Ex Vill SD	Newton Falls
167	1,515.7	Massillon City SD	Massillon
168	1,512.0	Tiffin City SD	Tiffin
169	1,503.0	Clearview Local SD	Lorain
170	1,501.0	Ridgewood Local SD	West Lafayette
171	1,494.5	Hamilton Local SD	Columbus
172	1,461.6	Parma City SD	Parma
173	1,444.7	Mayfield City SD	Highland Hgts
174	1,436.9	Toledo City SD	Toledo
175	1,433.7	Mount Vernon City SD	Mount Vernon
176	1,430.5	Niles City SD	Niles
177	1,426.0	Loveland City SD	Loveland
178	1,425.8	Beavercreek City SD	Beavercreek
179	1,424.7	Barberton City SD	Barberton
180	1,417.0	Zanesville City SD	Zanesville
181	1,409.0	Sandusky City SD	Sandusky
182	1,403.5	Revere Local SD	Bath
183	1,400.5	Bellefontaine City Schools	Bellefontaine
184	1,398.0	Marion City SD	Marion
185	1,393.8	Newark City SD	Newark
186	1,388.3	Green Local SD	Green
187	1,381.3	Wooster City SD	Wooster
188	1,380.0	Tallmadge City Schools	Tallmadge
189	1,369.5	Cambridge City SD	Cambridge
190	1,364.0	Fairfield City SD	Fairfield
191	1,358.5	Painesville City Local SD	Painesville
192	1,355.3	Oak Hills Local SD	Cincinnati
193	1,349.8	Cuyahoga Falls City SD	Cuyahoga Falls
194	1,349.6	Springfield Local Schools	Holland
195	1,346.0	Warren Local SD	Vincent
196	1,333.1	Springfield City SD	Springfield
197	1,329.6	Alliance City SD	Alliance
198	1,304.5	Tipp City Ex Vill SD	Tipp City
199	1,300.5	Xenia Community City SD	Xenia
200	1,296.7	Bedford City SD	Bedford
201	1,287.3	Sidney City SD	Sidney
202	1,284.6	North Royalton City SD	N Royalton
203	1,283.0	Kings Local SD	Kings Mills
204	1,273.5	Clark-Shawnee Local SD	Springfield
205	1,272.3	Ashland City SD	Ashland
206	1,272.0	Gallia County Local SD	Gallipolis
207	1,270.5	Defiance City SD	Defiance
208	1,268.5	West Geauga Local SD	Chesterland
209	1,262.7	Mt Healthy City SD	Cincinnati
210	1,262.5	Goshen Local SD	Goshen
211	1,257.0	Poland Local SD	Poland
212	1,246.0	Vermilion Local SD	Vermilion
213	1,235.0	Avon Local SD	Avon
214	1,227.5	Beaver Local SD	Lisbon
215	1,223.5	Northwest Local SD	Canal Fulton
216	1,222.8	Strongsville City SD	Strongsville
217	1,222.5	Salem City SD	Salem
218	1,220.8	Lancaster City SD	Lancaster
219	1,216.0	Stow-Munroe Falls City SD	Stow
220	1,210.7	West Muskingum Local SD	Zanesville
221	1,195.0	Lebanon City SD	Lebanon
222	1,194.0	Bellevue City SD	Bellevue
223	1,193.5	Napoleon Area City SD	Napoleon
224	1,188.9	Pickerington Local SD	Pickerington
225	1,173.0	Claymont City SD	Dennison
226	1,169.5	Northern Local SD	Thornville
227	1,167.0	Coventry Local SD	Akron
228	1,166.5	Brecksville-Broadview Hgts City	Brecksville
229	1,161.0	Indian Creek Local SD	Wintersville
230	1,160.4	Mansfield City SD	Mansfield
231	1,157.5	Washington Court House City SD	Wash Ct House
232	1,144.0	Bryan City SD	Bryan
233	1,133.5	Perkins Local SD	Sandusky
234	1,132.5	Maysville Local SD	Zanesville
235	1,127.0	Shelby City SD	Shelby
236	1,125.3	Chillicothe City SD	Chillicothe
237	1,118.5	Buckeye Valley Local SD	Delaware
238	1,113.3	Olmsted Falls City SD	Olmsted Falls
239	1,105.0	Southeast Local SD	Ravenna
240	1,088.7	Forest Hills Local SD	Cincinnati
241	1,083.0	Portsmouth City SD	Portsmouth
242	1,082.0	Three Rivers Local Schools	Cleves
243	1,076.3	Howland Local SD	Warren
244	1,060.5	East Muskingum Local SD	New Concord
245	1,059.0	Harrison Hills City SD	Hopedale
246	1,046.1	Medina City SD	Medina
247	1,042.5	Bath Local SD	Lima
248	1,040.5	London City SD	London
249	1,039.0	Winton Woods City SD	Cincinnati
250	1,037.5	Milford Ex Vill SD	Milford
251	1,031.3	Franklin City SD	Franklin
252	1,028.0	Valley View Local SD	Germantown
253	1,024.7	United Local SD	Hanoverton
254	1,012.0	Benton Carroll Salem Local SD	Oak Harbor
255	992.0	Wyoming City SD	Wyoming
256	990.0	Lakewood City SD	Lakewood
257	989.0	Coshocton City SD	Coshocton
258	986.0	Clermont Northeastern Local SD	Batavia
259	985.0	Bethel-Tate Local SD	Bethel
259	985.0	Chagrin Falls Ex Vill SD	Chagrin Falls
261	984.0	Norwalk City SD	Norwalk
262	983.0	Benjamin Logan Local SD	Bellefontaine
263	975.5	Northwestern Local SD	Springfield
264	965.5	Oregon City SD	Oregon
265	963.0	Rock Hill Local SD	Ironton
266	962.0	Batavia Local SD	Batavia
267	954.0	North Fork Local SD	Utica
268	950.3	Aurora City SD	Aurora
269	949.0	Maumee City SD	Maumee
270	945.5	Bucyrus City SD	Bucyrus
271	944.3	Hillsboro City SD	Hillsboro
272	939.7	Lexington Local SD	Lexington
273	931.5	Orrville City SD	Orrville
274	927.0	Wellston City Schools	Wellston
275	926.3	Highland Local SD	Medina
276	921.3	Switzerland of Ohio Local SD	Woodsfield
277	908.3	Crestwood Local SD	Mantua
278	907.6	Lakota Local SD	Liberty Twp
279	907.3	Northeastern Local SD	Springfield
280	903.5	Upper Sandusky Ex Vill SD	Upper Sandusky
281	903.0	Milton-Union Exempted Vill Schls	West Milton

PROFILES OF OHIO / School District Rankings 403

282	891.2	Columbus Public Schools	Columbus
283	890.5	Ontario Local SD	Mansfield
284	890.0	Northwest Local SD	Mc Dermott
285	889.6	Berea City SD	Berea
286	887.5	Carlisle Local SD	Carlisle
287	883.5	Westerville City SD	Westerville
288	881.2	Elyria City SD	Elyria
289	874.8	North Ridgeville City SD	N Ridgeville
290	866.0	Rocky River City SD	Rocky River
291	863.7	St Marys City SD	Saint Marys
292	853.5	Heath City SD	Heath
293	844.9	Cincinnati City SD	Cincinnati
294	844.5	Otsego Local SD	Tontogany
295	835.8	Avon Lake City Schools	Avon Lake
296	834.5	Black River Local SD	Sullivan
297	833.7	Western Brown Local SD	Mount Orab
298	833.5	Preble Shawnee Local SD	Camden
299	830.0	Circleville City SD	Circleville
300	822.7	Sycamore Community City SD	Cincinnati
301	818.3	Bay Village City SD	Bay Village
302	815.5	Wellington Ex Vill SD	Wellington
303	813.5	Elgin Local SD	Marion
304	813.0	Ironton City SD	Ironton
305	812.0	Chardon Local SD	Chardon
306	800.8	Bowling Green City SD	Bowling Green
307	799.1	Fairland Local SD	Proctorville
308	792.5	Swanton Local SD	Swanton
309	790.6	Twinsburg City SD	Twinsburg
310	789.5	Campbell City SD	Campbell
311	785.0	James A Garfield Local SD	Garrettsville
312	776.5	Union Local SD	Morristown
313	771.8	Garfield Heights City SD	Garfield Hgts
314	770.5	East Liverpool City SD	East Liverpool
315	770.0	Field Local SD	Mogadore
316	768.3	Hubbard Ex Vill SD	Hubbard
317	761.8	South Euclid-Lyndhurst City SD	Lyndhurst
318	761.0	Martins Ferry City SD	Martins Ferry
319	760.5	Monroe Local SD	Monroe
320	755.0	Lakewood Local SD	Hebron
321	744.7	Lakeview Local SD	Cortland
322	740.0	Solon City SD	Solon
323	727.4	East Cleveland City SD	East Cleveland
324	722.0	Licking Valley Local SD Sd	Newark
325	713.3	Olentangy Local SD	Lewis Center
326	704.3	Granville Ex Vill SD	Granville
327	704.0	Warrensville Heights City SD	Warrensville Hgts
328	695.8	Hudson City SD	Hudson
329	682.2	Dublin City SD	Dublin
330	680.7	Oakwood City SD	Dayton
331	667.3	Hilliard City SD	Hilliard
332	655.3	New Lexington City SD	New Lexington
333	651.5	Westlake City SD	Westlake
334	650.8	Cleveland Municipal City SD	Cleveland
335	644.0	Groveport Madison Local SD	Groveport
336	632.7	Kent City SD	Kent
337	618.9	Centerville City SD	Centerville
338	618.0	Perry Local SD	Perry
339	610.3	Princeton City SD	Cincinnati
340	607.3	Fairview Park City SD	Fairview Park
341	599.2	Edgewood City SD	Trenton
342	596.4	Whitehall City SD	Whitehall
343	592.0	Orange City SD	Cleveland
344	575.4	Plain Local SD	New Albany
345	573.9	Mentor Ex Vill SD	Mentor
346	569.3	Mariemont City SD	Cincinnati
347	567.2	Gahanna-Jefferson City SD	Gahanna
348	566.3	Washington-Nile Local SD	West Portsmouth
349	565.0	Indian Hill Ex Vill SD	Cincinnati
350	562.4	Shaker Heights City SD	Shaker Heights
351	557.9	Upper Arlington City SD	Upper Arlington
352	550.7	Minford Local SD	Minford
353	547.3	Graham Local SD	Saint Paris
354	543.7	Brookville Local SD	Brookville
355	540.4	Worthington City SD	Worthington
356	536.7	Cleveland Hts-Univ Hts City SD	University Hgts
357	524.4	Canal Winchester Local SD	Canal Winchester
358	523.0	Meigs Local SD	Pomeroy
359	519.4	West Holmes Local SD	Millersburg
360	502.7	Madeira City SD	Cincinnati
361	453.0	Morgan Local SD	McConnelsville
362	446.5	Woodridge Local SD	Peninsula
363	442.2	Bexley City SD	Bexley
364	430.5	Champion Local SD	Warren
365	399.0	Beachwood City SD	Beachwood
366	n/a	Alexander Local SD	Albany
366	n/a	Bellaire Local SD	Bellaire
366	n/a	Electronic Classrm of Tomorrow	Columbus
366	n/a	Ohio Virtual Academy	Maumee
366	n/a	Ottawa-Glandorf Local SD	Ottawa
366	n/a	Sheffield-Sheffield Lake City SD	Sheffield Vlg
366	n/a	Southeast Local SD	Apple Creek
366	n/a	Steubenville City SD	Steubenville
366	n/a	Sugarcreek Local SD	Bellbrook

Student/Counselor Ratio

Rank	Ratio	District Name	City
1	5,213.0	Electronic Classrm of Tomorrow	Columbus
2	1,925.3	Cincinnati City SD	Cincinnati
3	1,891.0	Bucyrus City SD	Bucyrus
4	1,883.0	Fairless Local SD	Navarre
5	1,638.3	New Lexington City SD	New Lexington
6	1,571.0	East Clinton Local SD	Lees Creek
7	1,316.5	Vinton County Local SD	Mc Arthur
8	1,270.5	River View Local SD	Warsaw
9	1,183.0	Gallipolis City SD	Gallipolis
10	1,181.1	New Philadelphia City SD	New Philadelphia
11	1,145.3	Trotwood-Madison City Schools	Trotwood
12	1,118.5	Buckeye Valley Local SD	Delaware
13	1,027.3	Dayton City SD	Dayton
14	994.0	Whitehall City SD	Whitehall
15	990.0	Greenon Local SD	Springfield
16	985.5	Port Clinton City SD	Port Clinton
17	977.3	Carrollton Ex Vill SD	Carrollton
18	963.0	Rock Hill Local SD	Ironton
19	943.9	Reynoldsburg City SD	Reynoldsburg
20	939.7	Lexington Local SD	Lexington
21	937.0	Berlin-Milan Local SD	Milan
22	933.0	South Point Local SD	South Point
23	928.5	East Holmes Local Schools	Berlin
24	908.0	West Muskingum Local SD	Zanesville
25	890.5	Highland Local SD	Sparta
26	876.6	South-Western City SD	Grove City
27	860.2	Mount Vernon City SD	Mount Vernon
28	852.7	Norton City Schools	Norton
29	848.7	East Cleveland City SD	East Cleveland
30	832.0	Huron City Schools	Huron
31	830.5	West Clermont Local SD	Cincinnati
32	826.5	Amanda-Clearcreek Local SD	Amanda
33	813.5	Madison-Plains Local SD	London
34	811.5	Coldwater Ex Vill SD	Coldwater
35	810.3	Newark City SD	Newark
36	808.3	Teays Valley Local SD	Ashville
37	789.5	Campbell City SD	Campbell
38	787.5	Tri-Valley Local Schools	Dresden
39	784.0	Sandy Valley Local SD	Magnolia
40	780.0	Franklin Local SD	Duncan Falls
41	779.7	Northern Local SD	Thornville
42	778.0	Coventry Local SD	Akron
43	777.2	West Carrollton City SD	West Carrollton
44	776.5	Union Local SD	Morristown
45	774.3	Canfield Local SD	Canfield
46	771.5	Eastern Local SD	Sardinia
47	763.0	Lancaster City SD	Lancaster
48	762.3	Buckeye Local SD	Ashtabula
49	761.3	Ashtabula Area City SD	Ashtabula
50	757.8	Fairfield City SD	Fairfield
51	755.0	Morgan Local SD	McConnelsville
52	753.1	Fairfield Union Local SD	W Rushville
53	752.3	Jefferson Area Local SD	Jefferson
54	750.5	Ridgewood Local SD	West Lafayette
55	747.8	Madison Local SD	Madison
56	746.0	Galion City SD	Galion
57	736.7	Southeast Local SD	Ravenna
58	715.0	Kenton City SD	Kenton
59	707.0	East Muskingum Local SD	New Concord
60	706.0	Harrison Hills City SD	Hopedale
61	703.6	Vandalia-Butler City SD	Vandalia
62	701.3	West Holmes Local SD	Millersburg
63	698.2	Amherst Ex Vill SD	Amherst
64	695.7	Streetsboro City Schools	Streetsboro
65	693.7	London City SD	London
66	691.0	Switzerland of Ohio Local SD	Woodsfield
67	686.3	Jackson City SD	Jackson
68	685.3	Valley View Local SD	Germantown
69	683.2	Clearview Local SD	Lorain
70	682.8	Willoughby-Eastlake City SD	Willoughby
71	681.3	Crestwood Local SD	Mantua
72	678.4	Fairborn City Schools	Fairborn
73	672.3	Edison Local SD	Hammondsville
74	672.1	Oak Hills Local SD	Cincinnati
75	671.3	Logan-Hocking Local SD	Logan
76	667.0	Strongsville City SD	Strongsville
77	664.8	Norwood City SD	Norwood
78	663.5	Middletown City SD	Middletown
79	663.3	Cleveland Municipal City SD	Cleveland
80	659.3	Coshocton City SD	Coshocton
81	658.2	Loveland City SD	Loveland
82	657.7	Parma City SD	Parma
83	657.3	Clermont Northeastern Local SD	Batavia
84	656.7	Bethel-Tate Local SD	Bethel
85	651.3	Union-Scioto Local SD	Chillicothe
86	650.5	Mentor Ex Vill SD	Mentor
87	650.3	Northwestern Local SD	Springfield
88	649.5	Dover City SD	Dover
89	645.0	Lorain City SD	Lorain
90	641.3	Batavia Local SD	Batavia
91	640.4	Marietta City Schools	Marietta
92	640.2	Little Miami Local SD	Morrow
93	636.0	Gallia County Local SD	Gallipolis
94	631.8	Conneaut Area City SD	Conneaut
95	629.7	Winton Woods City SD	Cincinnati
96	628.5	Poland Local SD	Poland
97	625.9	Warren City SD	Warren
98	623.2	Celina City SD	Celina
99	622.5	Circleville City SD	Circleville
100	622.3	Marlington Local SD	Alliance
101	618.8	Franklin City SD	Franklin
102	618.0	Wellston City Schools	Wellston
103	617.5	Avon Local SD	Avon
104	613.8	Beaver Local SD	Lisbon
105	611.3	Maple Heights City SD	Maple Heights
105	611.3	Salem City SD	Salem
107	610.3	Medina City SD	Medina
107	610.3	River Valley Local SD	Caledonia
109	604.7	Northridge Local SD	Dayton
110	603.8	Buckeye Local SD	Rayland
111	603.0	Paulding Ex Vill SD	Paulding
112	602.0	Milton-Union Exempted Vill Schls	West Milton
113	599.5	Brunswick City SD	Brunswick
114	597.8	Hamilton Local SD	Columbus
114	597.8	Steubenville City SD	Steubenville
116	596.1	Stow-Munroe Falls City SD	Stow
117	595.0	Athens City SD	The Plains
118	593.7	Ontario Local SD	Mansfield
119	590.4	Norwalk City SD	Norwalk
120	590.3	Blanchester Local SD	Blanchester
121	589.7	Girard City SD	Girard
122	586.9	Wadsworth City SD	Wadsworth
123	585.5	Groveport Madison Local SD	Groveport
124	582.5	Marion City SD	Marion
125	581.3	Tuscarawas Valley Local SD	Zoarville
126	580.8	Logan Elm Local SD	Circleville
127	580.7	Lima City SD	Lima
128	580.5	Indian Creek Local SD	Wintersville
129	579.8	Greenfield Ex Vill SD	Greenfield
130	579.0	Genoa Area Local SD	Genoa
131	577.5	Field Local SD	Mogadore
132	576.3	Hubbard Ex Vill SD	Hubbard
133	575.4	Plain Local SD	New Albany
134	574.6	Fremont City SD	Fremont
135	574.3	Clyde-Green Springs Ex Vill SD	Clyde
136	573.7	Licking Heights Local SD	Summit Station
137	572.5	Midview Local SD	Grafton
137	572.5	Van Wert City SD	Van Wert
139	572.2	Niles City SD	Niles
140	571.4	South Euclid-Lyndhurst City SD	Lyndhurst
141	569.0	Heath City SD	Heath
142	567.0	Greenville City SD	Greenville
143	566.4	Adams County/Ohio Valley LSD	West Union
144	566.3	Lakewood Local SD	Hebron
144	566.3	Maysville Local SD	Zanesville
146	563.0	Otsego Local SD	Tontogany
147	562.7	Chillicothe City SD	Chillicothe
148	560.9	Northwest Local SD	Cincinnati
149	559.7	Alexander Local SD	Albany
149	559.7	Scioto Valley Local SD	Piketon
151	556.5	Rolling Hills Local SD	Cambridge
152	555.8	Highland Local SD	Medina
153	555.5	Firelands Local SD	Oberlin
154	554.0	Alliance City SD	Alliance
155	551.7	Canton Local SD	Canton
155	551.7	Westfall Local SD	Williamsport
157	551.3	Garfield Heights City SD	Garfield Hgts
158	550.7	Minford Local SD	Minford
159	550.5	Minerva Local SD	Minerva
159	550.5	Tecumseh Local SD	New Carlisle
161	546.4	Lakota Local SD	Liberty Twp
162	545.3	Ashland City SD	Ashland
163	545.0	Zanesville City SD	Zanesville
164	543.7	Brookville Local SD	Brookville
165	543.5	Waverly City SD	Waverly
166	541.5	Licking Valley Local SD Sd	Newark
167	541.3	Chardon Local SD	Chardon
167	541.3	Massillon City SD	Massillon
169	540.0	Springboro Community City SD	Springboro
170	539.9	Cuyahoga Falls City SD	Cuyahoga Falls
170	539.9	Findlay City SD	Findlay
170	539.9	Springfield Local Schools	Holland
173	538.7	Olmsted Falls City SD	Olmsted Falls
174	537.5	Triway Local SD	Wooster
175	535.0	Euclid City SD	Euclid
176	533.3	Wauseon Ex Vill SD	Wauseon
177	533.1	Lakewood City SD	Lakewood
178	532.5	Wilmington City SD	Wilmington
179	532.2	Indian Valley Local SD	Gnadenhutten
180	532.0	Northwest Local SD	Canal Fulton

404 PROFILES OF OHIO / School District Rankings

181	531.1	Lebanon City SD	Lebanon
182	529.7	Zane Trace Local SD	Chillicothe
183	528.3	Swanton Local SD	Swanton
184	526.6	Big Walnut Local SD	Galena
185	526.3	St Clairsville-Richland City SD	St Clairsville
186	524.8	Troy City SD	Troy
187	524.7	Pike-Delta-York Local SD	Delta
188	523.6	Westerville City SD	Westerville
189	521.3	Bath Local SD	Lima
190	520.2	Mason City SD	Mason
191	520.0	Sheffield-Sheffield Lake City SD	Sheffield Vlg
192	518.2	Elida Local SD	Elida
192	518.2	St Marys City SD	Saint Marys
194	518.0	Wapakoneta City City SD	Wapakoneta
195	516.3	Bellaire Local SD	Bellaire
196	514.7	Toledo City SD	Toledo
197	512.7	North College Hill City SD	Cincinnati
198	512.3	United Local SD	Hanoverton
199	511.3	Shaker Heights City SD	Shaker Heights
200	510.5	Oakwood City SD	Dayton
201	509.9	Akron Public Schools	Akron
202	509.4	Clark-Shawnee Local SD	Springfield
203	509.3	Cloverleaf Local SD	Lodi
204	507.0	Monroe Local SD	Monroe
205	506.7	Manchester Local SD	Akron
205	506.7	Newton Falls Ex Vill SD	Newton Falls
207	506.5	James A Garfield Local SD	Garrettsville
208	505.0	Goshen Local SD	Goshen
209	504.3	Miamisburg City SD	Miamisburg
210	502.7	Madeira City SD	Cincinnati
211	501.8	Geneva Area City Schools	Geneva
212	501.0	Struthers City SD	Struthers
213	498.4	Vermilion Local SD	Vermilion
214	498.0	Indian Lake Local SD	Lewistown
215	497.6	Columbus Public Schools	Columbus
216	494.5	Eastwood Local SD	Pemberville
217	494.4	Piqua City SD	Piqua
218	493.0	Copley-Fairlawn City SD	Copley
218	493.0	Sugarcreek Local SD	Bellbrook
220	491.5	Benjamin Logan Local SD	Bellefontaine
221	490.6	Buckeye Local SD	Medina
222	489.1	Olentangy Local SD	Lewis Center
223	488.6	West Branch Local SD	Beloit
224	485.7	Huber Heights City SD	Huber Heights
225	482.9	Bellefontaine City Schools	Bellefontaine
226	482.8	Oregon City SD	Oregon
227	482.2	New Richmond Ex Vill SD	New Richmond
228	481.9	Wooster City SD	Wooster
229	480.9	Three Rivers Local Schools	Cleves
230	479.3	Forest Hills Local SD	Cincinnati
231	477.6	Bellevue City SD	Bellevue
232	477.5	Northeastern Local SD	Springfield
233	477.0	North Fork Local SD	Utica
234	474.5	Kent City SD	Kent
235	472.2	Hillsboro City SD	Hillsboro
236	471.2	Urbana City SD	Urbana
237	469.2	Claymont City SD	Dennison
238	467.8	Canton City SD	Canton
239	467.2	Southwest Local SD	Harrison
240	466.8	Eaton Community Schools	Eaton
241	466.6	Brecksville-Broadview Hgts City	Brecksville
242	465.8	Orrville City SD	Orrville
243	465.4	Worthington City SD	Worthington
244	463.5	Perry Local SD	Perry
245	463.4	Jackson Local SD	Massillon
246	462.1	Ravenna City SD	Ravenna
247	461.9	Western Brown Local SD	Mount Orab
248	461.3	Howland Local SD	Warren
249	460.8	Clear Fork Valley Local SD	Bellville
250	460.0	Tallmadge City Schools	Tallmadge
251	459.7	Twinsburg City SD	Twinsburg
251	459.7	Washington Local Schools	Toledo
253	457.3	Nordonia Hills City SD	Northfield
254	456.5	Cambridge City SD	Cambridge
255	455.9	North Canton City SD	North Canton
256	455.5	Fairview Park City SD	Fairview Park
257	454.9	Kenston Local SD	Chagrin Falls
258	454.8	Liberty Local SD	Youngstown
259	454.1	Northmont City SD	Englewood
260	453.2	Miami Trace Local SD	Wash Ct House
261	452.8	Painesville City Local SD	Painesville
262	452.7	Green Local SD	Green
263	452.3	Jonathan Alder Local SD	Plain City
264	451.8	Upper Sandusky Ex Vill SD	Upper Sandusky
265	450.8	Shelby City SD	Shelby
266	449.8	Delaware City SD	Delaware
266	449.8	Hilliard City SD	Hilliard
268	449.4	Edgewood City SD	Trenton
269	447.6	Kings Local SD	Kings Mills
270	446.8	Lakeview Local SD	Cortland
271	445.9	Pickerington Local SD	Pickerington
272	445.2	Boardman Local SD	Youngstown
273	445.0	Northwest Local SD	Mc Dermott
274	444.6	Milford Ex Vill SD	Milford
275	443.5	Clinton-Massie Local SD	Clarksville
276	443.4	Talawanda City SD	Oxford
277	441.6	Madison Local SD	Mansfield
278	440.3	East Liverpool City SD	East Liverpool
279	439.9	Berea City SD	Berea
280	438.6	Aurora City SD	Aurora
281	437.8	Graham Local SD	Saint Paris
282	437.0	Canal Winchester Local SD	Canal Winchester
283	435.9	Princeton City SD	Cincinnati
284	434.8	Perrysburg Exempted Village	Perrysburg
284	434.8	Tipp City Ex Vill SD	Tipp City
286	433.4	Mayfield City SD	Highland Hgts
287	432.9	Carlisle Local SD	Carlisle
288	432.8	Ottawa-Glandorf Local SD	Ottawa
289	430.5	Champion Local SD	Warren
290	430.1	Southwest Licking Local SD	Etna
291	430.0	Ross Local SD	Hamilton
292	429.5	Southeast Local SD	Apple Creek
293	429.2	Marysville Exempted Village SD	Marysville
294	429.0	Lake Local SD	Millbury
295	427.4	Barberton City SD	Barberton
296	427.0	Mariemont City SD	Cincinnati
297	426.3	Anthony Wayne Local SD	Whitehouse
298	422.7	Sandusky City SD	Sandusky
299	420.9	Mt Healthy City SD	Cincinnati
300	420.5	Austintown Local SD	Youngstown
301	419.9	Lake Local SD	Hartville
302	419.5	Xenia Community City SD	Xenia
303	419.1	Centerville City SD	Centerville
304	418.4	Meigs Local SD	Pomeroy
305	416.8	Preble Shawnee Local SD	Camden
306	414.4	Mansfield City SD	Mansfield
307	412.3	Hudson City SD	Hudson
308	412.2	Sylvania City SD	Sylvania
309	411.3	Greeneview Local SD	Jamestown
310	408.7	North Royalton City SD	N Royalton
311	408.4	Fairland Local SD	Proctorville
312	407.8	Wellington Ex Vill SD	Wellington
313	404.8	Benton Carroll Salem Local SD	Oak Harbor
314	404.0	Rossford Ex Vill SD	Rossford
315	403.3	Fostoria City SD	Fostoria
316	402.3	Warrensville Heights City SD	Warrensville Hgts
317	401.0	Revere Local SD	Bath
318	400.4	Bowling Green City SD	Bowling Green
319	400.3	Hamilton City SD	Hamilton
320	398.5	Solon City SD	Solon
321	397.8	Napoleon Area City SD	Napoleon
322	396.8	Wyoming City SD	Wyoming
323	396.1	Beavercreek City SD	Beavercreek
323	396.1	Dublin City SD	Dublin
325	394.0	Chagrin Falls Ex Vill SD	Chagrin Falls
326	393.7	Willard City SD	Willard
327	393.3	Avon Lake City Schools	Avon Lake
328	392.5	Wickliffe City SD	Wickliffe
329	390.9	Westlake City SD	Westlake
330	389.8	Louisville City SD	Louisville
331	389.0	Bedford City SD	Bedford
332	384.5	Springfield Local SD	Akron
333	382.4	Gahanna-Jefferson City SD	Gahanna
334	381.3	Bryan City SD	Bryan
335	380.8	North Olmsted City Schools	North Olmsted
336	379.6	Shawnee Local SD	Lima
337	378.0	Tiffin City SD	Tiffin
338	377.7	Elyria City SD	Elyria
339	374.0	Painesville Township Local SD	Painesville
340	371.1	Rocky River City SD	Rocky River
341	367.5	Youngstown City SD	Youngstown
342	366.2	Keystone Local SD	Lagrange
343	364.4	Plain Local SD	Canton
344	363.0	Defiance City SD	Defiance
345	361.0	Portsmouth City SD	Portsmouth
346	357.2	Woodridge Local SD	Peninsula
347	352.2	Granville Ex Vill SD	Granville
348	349.0	Sycamore Community City SD	Cincinnati
349	346.5	Upper Arlington City SD	Upper Arlington
350	343.4	Mad River Local SD	Dayton
351	339.8	Washington-Nile Local SD	West Portsmouth
352	335.7	Springfield City SD	Springfield
353	323.9	Perkins Local SD	Sandusky
354	323.6	Perry Local SD	Massillon
355	321.8	Sidney City SD	Sidney
356	318.1	North Ridgeville City SD	N Ridgeville
357	316.3	Maumee City SD	Maumee
358	306.9	Bay Village City SD	Bay Village
359	304.4	Martins Ferry City SD	Martins Ferry
360	299.1	Warren Local SD	Vincent
361	296.0	Orange City SD	Cleveland
362	295.0	West Geauga Local SD	Chesterland
363	289.6	Kettering City SD	Kettering
364	289.4	Washington Court House City SD	Wash Ct House
365	279.2	Finneytown Local SD	Cincinnati
366	266.0	Beachwood City SD	Beachwood
367	265.0	Madison Local SD	Middletown
368	257.1	Bexley City SD	Bexley
369	249.5	Cleveland Hts-Univ Hts City SD	University Hgts
370	238.4	Black River Local SD	Sullivan
371	232.4	Elgin Local SD	Marion
372	232.3	Ironton City SD	Ironton
373	230.6	Indian Hill Ex Vill SD	Cincinnati
374	n/a	Ohio Virtual Academy	Maumee

Current Spending per Student in FY2003

Rank	Dollars	District Name	City
1	16,952	Beachwood City SD	Beachwood
2	14,304	Orange City SD	Cleveland
3	13,555	Perry Local SD	Perry
4	12,683	Shaker Heights City SD	Shaker Heights
5	12,002	Cleveland Hts-Univ Hts City SD	University Hgts
6	11,616	Sycamore Community City SD	Cincinnati
7	11,064	Youngstown City SD	Youngstown
8	10,866	Princeton City SD	Cincinnati
9	10,821	Warrensville Heights City SD	Warrensville Hgts
10	10,734	East Cleveland City SD	East Cleveland
11	10,491	Dayton City SD	Dayton
12	10,439	South Euclid-Lyndhurst City SD	Lyndhurst
13	10,402	Upper Arlington City SD	Upper Arlington
14	10,300	Cincinnati City SD	Cincinnati
15	10,281	Bexley City SD	Bexley
16	10,255	Bedford City SD	Bedford
17	10,199	Cleveland Municipal City SD	Cleveland
18	10,188	Columbus Public Schools	Columbus
19	10,168	Indian Hill Ex Vill SD	Cincinnati
20	10,156	Toledo City SD	Toledo
21	10,146	Worthington City SD	Worthington
22	10,019	Mayfield City SD	Highland Hgts
23	9,917	Solon City SD	Solon
24	9,901	Kent City SD	Kent
25	9,880	Fairview Park City SD	Fairview Park
26	9,760	Mansfield City SD	Mansfield
27	9,505	Canton City SD	Canton
28	9,498	Akron Public Schools	Akron
29	9,469	Portsmouth City SD	Portsmouth
30	9,405	Euclid City SD	Euclid
31	9,388	Westlake City SD	Westlake
32	9,298	Chagrin Falls Ex Vill SD	Chagrin Falls
33	9,274	Lakewood City SD	Lakewood
34	9,258	New Richmond Ex Vill SD	New Richmond
35	9,198	Wickliffe City SD	Wickliffe
36	9,150	Wooster City SD	Wooster
37	9,131	Bay Village City SD	Bay Village
38	9,059	Northridge Local SD	Dayton
39	9,008	Warren City SD	Warren
40	8,989	Hudson City SD	Hudson
41	8,964	Parma City SD	Parma
42	8,957	Maumee City SD	Maumee
43	8,949	Springfield City SD	Springfield
44	8,941	Dublin City SD	Dublin
45	8,917	Rocky River City SD	Rocky River
46	8,914	Medina City SD	Medina
47	8,902	Monroe Local SD	Monroe
48	8,869	Port Clinton City SD	Port Clinton
49	8,859	Sandusky City SD	Sandusky
50	8,832	North Olmsted City Schools	North Olmsted
51	8,737	Berea City SD	Berea
51	8,737	Plain Local SD	New Albany
53	8,729	Bellaire Local SD	Bellaire
53	8,729	Olmsted Falls City SD	Olmsted Falls
53	8,729	Wyoming City SD	Wyoming
56	8,698	Lima City SD	Lima
57	8,617	Mentor Ex Vill SD	Mentor
58	8,614	Sylvania City SD	Sylvania
59	8,598	Mariemont City SD	Cincinnati
60	8,594	Twinsburg City SD	Twinsburg
61	8,579	Finneytown Local SD	Cincinnati
62	8,548	Woodridge Local SD	Peninsula
63	8,528	East Liverpool City SD	East Liverpool
64	8,501	Norwood City SD	Norwood
65	8,494	Oakwood City SD	Dayton
66	8,491	Zanesville City SD	Zanesville
67	8,474	Trotwood-Madison City Schools	Trotwood
68	8,458	Winton Woods City SD	Cincinnati
69	8,437	Madeira City SD	Cincinnati
70	8,406	Oregon City SD	Oregon
71	8,403	Benton Carroll Salem Local SD	Oak Harbor
72	8,392	Washington Local Schools	Toledo
73	8,391	Lorain City SD	Lorain
74	8,376	Middletown City SD	Middletown
75	8,373	Groveport Madison Local SD	Groveport
76	8,364	Madison Local SD	Mansfield
77	8,350	Marysville Exempted Village SD	Marysville
78	8,349	Massillon City SD	Massillon
79	8,325	Brecksville-Broadview Hgts City	Brecksville
80	8,316	Springfield Local Schools	Holland

PROFILES OF OHIO / School District Rankings 405

81	8,299	Mt Healthy City SD	Cincinnati
82	8,288	Perkins Local SD	Sandusky
83	8,277	Strongsville City SD	Strongsville
84	8,268	Revere Local SD	Bath
85	8,246	Kenston Local SD	Chagrin Falls
86	8,241	Nordonia Hills City SD	Northfield
87	8,236	Elyria City SD	Elyria
88	8,230	Painesville City Local SD	Painesville
89	8,221	Barberton City SD	Barberton
90	8,188	Copley-Fairlawn City SD	Copley
91	8,183	Rossford Ex Vill SD	Rossford
92	8,166	Avon Lake City Schools	Avon Lake
93	8,127	Hilliard City SD	Hilliard
94	8,096	Athens City SD	The Plains
95	8,090	Bowling Green City SD	Bowling Green
96	8,065	Salem City SD	Salem
97	8,032	Gahanna-Jefferson City SD	Gahanna
98	8,028	Eastwood Local SD	Pemberville
99	7,996	Canal Winchester Local SD	Canal Winchester
100	7,973	Southeast Local SD	Apple Creek
101	7,962	Aurora City SD	Aurora
102	7,944	Centerville City SD	Centerville
103	7,943	Kettering City SD	Kettering
103	7,943	Morgan Local SD	McConnelsville
105	7,942	Mad River Local SD	Dayton
106	7,933	Ravenna City SD	Ravenna
107	7,918	Willoughby-Eastlake City SD	Willoughby
108	7,913	Alliance City SD	Alliance
109	7,883	South-Western City SD	Grove City
110	7,882	Campbell City SD	Campbell
110	7,882	Findlay City SD	Findlay
112	7,881	Delaware City SD	Delaware
113	7,857	Vandalia-Butler City SD	Vandalia
114	7,852	West Carrollton City SD	West Carrollton
115	7,838	Canton Local SD	Canton
115	7,838	Xenia Community City SD	Xenia
117	7,817	Pike-Delta-York Local SD	Delta
118	7,811	Whitehall City SD	Whitehall
119	7,795	Liberty Local SD	Youngstown
120	7,787	Celina City SD	Celina
121	7,785	Meigs Local SD	Pomeroy
122	7,781	Streetsboro City Schools	Streetsboro
123	7,766	Carlisle Local SD	Carlisle
124	7,756	Garfield Heights City SD	Garfield Hgts
125	7,744	Lancaster City SD	Lancaster
126	7,739	Ashtabula Area City SD	Ashtabula
127	7,733	Clearview Local SD	Lorain
128	7,719	Sheffield-Sheffield Lake City SD	Sheffield Vlg
129	7,713	Buckeye Local SD	Medina
130	7,711	North Royalton City SD	N Royalton
131	7,701	Westerville City SD	Westerville
132	7,695	Olentangy Local SD	Lewis Center
133	7,681	Buckeye Valley Local SD	Delaware
134	7,665	Fairborn City Schools	Fairborn
135	7,653	Buckeye Local SD	Ashtabula
136	7,636	Kings Local SD	Kings Mills
137	7,633	Champion Local SD	Warren
138	7,632	Austintown Local SD	Youngstown
139	7,622	Three Rivers Local Schools	Cleves
140	7,614	Boardman Local SD	Youngstown
141	7,599	St Clairsville-Richland City SD	St Clairsville
142	7,598	Fostoria City SD	Fostoria
143	7,593	Tecumseh Local SD	New Carlisle
144	7,581	Circleville City SD	Circleville
145	7,576	Switzerland of Ohio Local SD	Woodsfield
146	7,573	Cuyahoga Falls City SD	Cuyahoga Falls
147	7,543	Struthers City SD	Struthers
148	7,532	Southwest Licking Local SD	Etna
149	7,527	Huron City Schools	Huron
150	7,491	Granville Ex Vill SD	Granville
151	7,471	Tallmadge City Schools	Tallmadge
152	7,470	Paulding Ex Vill SD	Paulding
153	7,468	Shelby City SD	Shelby
154	7,461	Springfield Local SD	Akron
155	7,456	Miami Trace Local SD	Wash Ct House
156	7,439	Marion City SD	Marion
157	7,438	Howland Local SD	Warren
158	7,429	Talawanda City SD	Oxford
159	7,423	Orrville City SD	Orrville
160	7,413	Chardon Local SD	Chardon
161	7,410	Coshocton City SD	Coshocton
162	7,401	Jackson Local SD	Massillon
162	7,401	Northwest Local SD	Mc Dermott
164	7,396	Niles City SD	Niles
165	7,395	West Geauga Local SD	Chesterland
166	7,383	Mason City SD	Mason
167	7,380	Valley View Local SD	Germantown
168	7,376	Brunswick City SD	Brunswick
169	7,358	Ironton City SD	Ironton
170	7,357	Goshen Local SD	Goshen
171	7,356	Bucyrus City SD	Bucyrus
172	7,355	Forest Hills Local SD	Cincinnati
173	7,353	Huber Heights City SD	Huber Heights
174	7,349	Hamilton City SD	Hamilton
175	7,348	Logan Elm Local SD	Circleville
176	7,346	Cambridge City SD	Cambridge
177	7,335	Urbana City SD	Urbana
178	7,326	Northwest Local SD	Cincinnati
179	7,319	Kenton City SD	Kenton
180	7,311	Newark City SD	Newark
181	7,307	Vinton County Local SD	Mc Arthur
182	7,298	Vermilion Local SD	Vermilion
183	7,295	Union Local SD	Morristown
184	7,293	Perrysburg Exempted Village	Perrysburg
185	7,291	Painesville Township Local SD	Painesville
186	7,279	Maple Heights City SD	Maple Heights
187	7,273	Miamisburg City SD	Miamisburg
187	7,273	Ridgewood Local SD	West Lafayette
189	7,257	Steubenville City SD	Steubenville
190	7,245	Swanton Local SD	Swanton
191	7,227	Norton City Schools	Norton
192	7,194	Milford Ex Vill SD	Milford
193	7,189	Beavercreek City SD	Beavercreek
194	7,171	Loveland City SD	Loveland
195	7,169	Hamilton Local SD	Columbus
196	7,167	Scioto Valley Local SD	Piketon
197	7,149	Adams County/Ohio Valley LSD	West Union
197	7,149	Galion City SD	Galion
199	7,139	Franklin City SD	Franklin
200	7,138	Field Local SD	Mogadore
201	7,137	Washington-Nile Local SD	West Portsmouth
202	7,130	Pickerington Local SD	Pickerington
203	7,127	Girard City SD	Girard
204	7,126	Big Walnut Local SD	Galena
205	7,123	Gallia County Local SD	Gallipolis
206	7,122	Lakota Local SD	Liberty Twp
207	7,116	Crestwood Local SD	Mantua
208	7,110	Ashland City SD	Ashland
208	7,110	Rock Hill Local SD	Ironton
208	7,110	Stow-Munroe Falls City SD	Stow
211	7,096	Greenfield Ex Vill SD	Greenfield
212	7,094	Madison-Plains Local SD	London
213	7,087	Newton Falls Ex Vill SD	Newton Falls
214	7,076	Minerva Local SD	Minerva
215	7,070	Southeast Local SD	Ravenna
216	7,061	North Ridgeville City SD	N Ridgeville
217	7,054	Fairfield Union Local SD	W Rushville
218	7,051	Napoleon Area City SD	Napoleon
219	7,049	North College Hill City SD	Cincinnati
220	7,047	Fremont City SD	Fremont
221	7,042	Batavia Local SD	Batavia
222	7,041	London City SD	London
223	7,036	Triway Local SD	Wooster
224	7,033	Dover City SD	Dover
225	7,020	Wellington Ex Vill SD	Wellington
225	7,020	Wellston City Schools	Wellston
227	7,014	Buckeye Local SD	Rayland
227	7,014	Lakewood Local SD	Hebron
229	7,011	Anthony Wayne Local SD	Whitehouse
229	7,011	Northmont City SD	Englewood
231	7,010	Troy City SD	Troy
232	7,005	North Canton City SD	North Canton
233	7,003	Preble Shawnee Local SD	Camden
234	6,999	River Valley Local SD	Caledonia
235	6,997	Berlin-Milan Local SD	Milan
236	6,991	Fairfield City SD	Fairfield
237	6,986	Licking Valley Local SD Sd	Newark
238	6,984	Plain Local SD	Canton
239	6,983	Chillicothe City SD	Chillicothe
240	6,979	East Holmes Local Schools	Berlin
241	6,972	Southwest Local SD	Harrison
242	6,971	Ontario Local SD	Mansfield
243	6,966	Bellefontaine City Schools	Bellefontaine
244	6,935	Minford Local SD	Minford
245	6,934	Marietta City Schools	Marietta
246	6,920	Green Local SD	Green
247	6,914	Madison Local SD	Middletown
248	6,908	Shawnee Local SD	Lima
249	6,884	Greenville City SD	Greenville
250	6,881	Clyde-Green Springs Ex Vill SD	Clyde
251	6,874	Hubbard Ex Vill SD	Hubbard
251	6,874	Milton-Union Exempted Vill Schls	West Milton
253	6,860	Indian Lake Local SD	Lewistown
254	6,855	Lakeview Local SD	Cortland
255	6,848	Conneaut Area City SD	Conneaut
256	6,845	Highland Local SD	Sparta
256	6,845	Manchester Local SD	Akron
258	6,844	Bellevue City SD	Bellevue
259	6,843	Gallipolis City SD	Gallipolis
259	6,843	Otsego Local SD	Tontogany
261	6,842	Genoa Area Local SD	Genoa
262	6,840	Edgewood City SD	Trenton
263	6,830	James A Garfield Local SD	Garrettsville
264	6,823	River View Local SD	Warsaw
265	6,821	Fairless Local SD	Navarre
266	6,818	Logan-Hocking Local SD	Logan
266	6,818	Van Wert City SD	Van Wert
268	6,815	South Point Local SD	South Point
269	6,811	Harrison Hills City SD	Hopedale
269	6,811	Westfall Local SD	Williamsport
271	6,807	Perry Local SD	Massillon
271	6,807	Teays Valley Local SD	Ashville
273	6,804	Hillsboro City SD	Hillsboro
274	6,785	Coldwater Ex Vill SD	Coldwater
275	6,784	Poland Local SD	Poland
276	6,779	Edison Local SD	Hammondsville
277	6,765	Defiance City SD	Defiance
278	6,760	Brookville Local SD	Brookville
279	6,751	Bath Local SD	Lima
279	6,751	Piqua City SD	Piqua
281	6,743	West Clermont Local SD	Cincinnati
282	6,731	Sandy Valley Local SD	Magnolia
283	6,714	Sugarcreek Local SD	Bellbrook
284	6,702	Northwest Local SD	Canal Fulton
285	6,695	Canfield Local SD	Canfield
286	6,694	New Lexington City SD	New Lexington
287	6,691	Upper Sandusky Ex Vill SD	Upper Sandusky
288	6,684	Rolling Hills Local SD	Cambridge
289	6,669	Wadsworth City SD	Wadsworth
290	6,651	Indian Creek Local SD	Wintersville
291	6,649	Highland Local SD	Medina
292	6,643	Jefferson Area Local SD	Jefferson
293	6,642	Alexander Local SD	Albany
293	6,642	Heath City SD	Heath
295	6,640	East Muskingum Local SD	New Concord
296	6,637	Amherst Ex Vill SD	Amherst
297	6,623	Eastern Local SD	Sardinia
298	6,617	Sidney City SD	Sidney
299	6,611	Oak Hills Local SD	Cincinnati
300	6,608	Warren Local SD	Vincent
301	6,607	Licking Heights Local SD	Summit Station
302	6,603	Martins Ferry City SD	Martins Ferry
303	6,601	Elgin Local SD	Marion
304	6,599	Cloverleaf Local SD	Lodi
305	6,594	Ross Local SD	Hamilton
306	6,586	Tiffin City SD	Tiffin
307	6,577	Bryan City SD	Bryan
308	6,574	Firelands Local SD	Oberlin
308	6,574	Midview Local SD	Grafton
310	6,571	West Holmes Local SD	Millersburg
311	6,567	Geneva Area City Schools	Geneva
312	6,555	Willard City SD	Willard
313	6,554	Franklin Local SD	Duncan Falls
313	6,554	Graham Local SD	Saint Paris
315	6,552	Elida Local SD	Elida
316	6,548	Union-Scioto Local SD	Chillicothe
317	6,543	Coventry Local SD	Akron
317	6,543	Marlington Local SD	Alliance
319	6,541	Wapakoneta City City SD	Wapakoneta
320	6,522	Blanchester Local SD	Blanchester
321	6,519	Jackson City SD	Jackson
322	6,503	Madison Local SD	Madison
323	6,500	Claymont City SD	Dennison
324	6,499	Lebanon City SD	Lebanon
324	6,499	Little Miami Local SD	Morrow
326	6,491	Clark-Shawnee Local SD	Springfield
327	6,487	Greeneview Local SD	Jamestown
328	6,485	West Branch Local SD	Beloit
329	6,483	Lexington Local SD	Lexington
330	6,478	United Local SD	Hanoverton
331	6,475	Mount Vernon City SD	Mount Vernon
332	6,474	Eaton Community Schools	Eaton
333	6,458	West Muskingum Local SD	Zanesville
334	6,451	North Fork Local SD	Utica
335	6,447	Northwestern Local SD	Springfield
336	6,445	Benjamin Logan Local SD	Bellefontaine
337	6,444	Northeastern Local SD	Springfield
338	6,430	Clear Fork Valley Local SD	Bellville
339	6,428	Springboro Community City SD	Springboro
340	6,426	New Philadelphia City SD	New Philadelphia
341	6,419	Indian Valley Local SD	Gnadenhutten
342	6,414	St Marys City SD	Saint Marys
343	6,409	Tipp City Ex Vill SD	Tipp City
344	6,403	Carrollton Ex Vill SD	Carrollton
345	6,399	Washington Court House City SD	Wash Ct House
346	6,386	Maysville Local SD	Zanesville
347	6,378	Ottawa-Glandorf Local SD	Ottawa
348	6,373	Keystone Local SD	Lagrange
349	6,353	Fairland Local SD	Proctorville
350	6,342	Tuscarawas Valley Local SD	Zoarville
351	6,323	East Clinton Local SD	Lees Creek
352	6,319	Louisville City SD	Louisville
353	6,311	Jonathan Alder Local SD	Plain City
354	6,302	Black River Local SD	Sullivan
355	6,292	Greenon Local SD	Springfield
356	6,266	Amanda-Clearcreek Local SD	Amanda
357	6,261	Reynoldsburg City SD	Reynoldsburg
358	6,254	Waverly City SD	Waverly

359	6,249	Avon Local SD	Avon
360	6,231	Western Brown Local SD	Mount Orab
361	6,178	Wilmington City SD	Wilmington
362	6,177	Lake Local SD	Hartville
363	6,168	Northern Local SD	Thornville
364	6,161	Lake Local SD	Millbury
365	6,129	Beaver Local SD	Lisbon
366	6,020	Tri-Valley Local Schools	Dresden
367	6,017	Wauseon Ex Vill SD	Wauseon
368	5,890	Zane Trace Local SD	Chillicothe
369	5,828	Bethel-Tate Local SD	Bethel
370	5,825	Clinton-Massie Local SD	Clarksville
371	5,770	Norwalk City SD	Norwalk
372	5,735	Clermont Northeastern Local SD	Batavia
373	4,819	Electronic Classrm of Tomorrow	Columbus
374	4,285	Ohio Virtual Academy	Maumee

Number of Diploma Recipients

Rank	Number	District Name	City
1	2,600	Columbus Public Schools	Columbus
2	2,443	Cleveland Municipal City SD	Cleveland
3	1,526	Akron Public Schools	Akron
4	1,478	Toledo City SD	Toledo
5	1,305	Cincinnati City SD	Cincinnati
6	1,003	South-Western City SD	Grove City
7	970	Westerville City SD	Westerville
8	963	Lakota Local SD	Liberty Twp
9	886	Parma City SD	Parma
10	858	Dayton City SD	Dayton
11	803	Worthington City SD	Worthington
12	785	Hilliard City SD	Hilliard
13	767	Dublin City SD	Dublin
14	730	Mentor Ex Vill SD	Mentor
15	656	Northwest Local SD	Cincinnati
16	637	Willoughby-Eastlake City SD	Willoughby
17	633	Oak Hills Local SD	Cincinnati
18	611	Berea City SD	Berea
19	608	Fairfield City SD	Fairfield
20	599	Sylvania City SD	Sylvania
21	590	Centerville City SD	Centerville
22	585	Forest Hills Local SD	Cincinnati
23	534	Kettering City SD	Kettering
24	524	Hamilton City SD	Hamilton
25	520	West Clermont Local SD	Cincinnati
26	518	Lakewood City SD	Lakewood
27	508	Strongsville City SD	Strongsville
28	501	Medina City SD	Medina
29	495	Beavercreek City SD	Beavercreek
29	495	Canton City SD	Canton
31	494	Pickerington Local SD	Pickerington
32	476	Lorain City SD	Lorain
33	475	Brunswick City SD	Brunswick
34	458	Reynoldsburg City SD	Reynoldsburg
35	448	Washington Local Schools	Toledo
36	437	Huber Heights City SD	Huber Heights
37	426	Findlay City SD	Findlay
38	425	Sycamore Community City SD	Cincinnati
39	424	Gahanna-Jefferson City SD	Gahanna
40	422	Jackson Local SD	Massillon
41	421	Upper Arlington City SD	Upper Arlington
41	421	Youngstown City SD	Youngstown
43	420	Stow-Munroe Falls City SD	Stow
44	417	Milford Ex Vill SD	Milford
45	411	Springfield City SD	Springfield
46	403	Princeton City SD	Cincinnati
47	393	Northmont City SD	Englewood
48	390	Plain Local SD	Canton
48	390	Solon City SD	Solon
50	389	Newark City SD	Newark
51	381	Hudson City SD	Hudson
52	380	Boardman Local SD	Youngstown
53	368	North Olmsted City Schools	North Olmsted
54	367	Mason City SD	Mason
55	363	Euclid City SD	Euclid
56	362	Elyria City SD	Elyria
56	362	Shaker Heights City SD	Shaker Heights
58	360	Cuyahoga Falls City SD	Cuyahoga Falls
58	360	Middletown City SD	Middletown
60	358	Lancaster City SD	Lancaster
61	352	Warren City SD	Warren
62	351	Austintown Local SD	Youngstown
63	349	Fairborn City Schools	Fairborn
64	346	Cleveland Hts-Univ Hts City SD	University Hgts
65	342	Perry Local SD	Massillon
65	342	South Euclid-Lyndhurst City SD	Lyndhurst
67	341	Mayfield City SD	Highland Hgts
68	340	Brecksville-Broadview Hgts City	Brecksville
69	335	North Royalton City SD	N Royalton
70	330	Miamisburg City SD	Miamisburg
71	328	Perrysburg Exempted Village	Perrysburg
72	327	Wadsworth City SD	Wadsworth
73	325	Fremont City SD	Fremont
74	319	North Canton City SD	North Canton
75	315	Olentangy Local SD	Lewis Center
76	314	Groveport Madison Local SD	Groveport
76	314	Xenia Community City SD	Xenia
78	309	Nordonia Hills City SD	Northfield
79	308	Kent City SD	Kent
80	306	Adams County/Ohio Valley LSD	West Union
80	306	Painesville Township Local SD	Painesville
82	294	Troy City SD	Troy
83	288	Ashland City SD	Ashland
84	285	Chillicothe City SD	Chillicothe
84	285	Loveland City SD	Loveland
86	284	Mount Vernon City SD	Mount Vernon
87	282	Celina City SD	Celina
88	281	Amherst Ex Vill SD	Amherst
88	281	Wooster City SD	Wooster
90	280	Marion City SD	Marion
91	279	Lebanon City SD	Lebanon
92	277	Southwest Local SD	Harrison
93	276	Westlake City SD	Westlake
94	273	Cloverleaf Local SD	Lodi
95	267	Greenville City SD	Greenville
96	264	Barberton City SD	Barberton
97	263	Garfield Heights City SD	Garfield Hgts
98	261	Delaware City SD	Delaware
99	260	Talawanda City SD	Oxford
100	258	Mansfield City SD	Mansfield
101	257	Marysville Exempted Village SD	Marysville
102	256	Bowling Green City SD	Bowling Green
103	255	Massillon City SD	Massillon
104	254	Madison Local SD	Madison
104	254	West Carrollton City SD	West Carrollton
106	252	East Cleveland City SD	East Cleveland
107	248	Lake Local SD	Hartville
108	247	Green Local SD	Green
108	247	Tiffin City SD	Tiffin
110	244	Lima City SD	Lima
110	244	Vandalia-Butler City SD	Vandalia
112	243	Avon Lake City Schools	Avon Lake
113	242	Maumee City SD	Maumee
114	240	Ashtabula Area City SD	Ashtabula
114	240	Dover City SD	Dover
116	238	New Philadelphia City SD	New Philadelphia
117	236	Springfield Local Schools	Holland
118	233	Anthony Wayne Local SD	Whitehouse
118	233	Sidney City SD	Sidney
118	233	Southwest Licking Local SD	Etna
121	232	Chardon Local SD	Chardon
122	231	Bedford City SD	Bedford
122	231	Sandusky City SD	Sandusky
122	231	Springboro Community City SD	Springboro
122	231	Wapakoneta City City SD	Wapakoneta
122	231	Wilmington City SD	Wilmington
127	230	Howland Local SD	Warren
128	228	Piqua City SD	Piqua
129	227	Logan-Hocking Local SD	Logan
130	225	Canfield Local SD	Canfield
130	225	Oregon City SD	Oregon
130	225	Revere Local SD	Bath
133	224	Geneva Area City Schools	Geneva
133	224	Madison Local SD	Mansfield
133	224	Tecumseh Local SD	New Carlisle
136	223	Kings Local SD	Kings Mills
137	219	Olmsted Falls City SD	Olmsted Falls
138	218	Winton Woods City SD	Cincinnati
139	216	Marietta City Schools	Marietta
140	215	Lexington Local SD	Lexington
141	214	Kenston Local SD	Chagrin Falls
142	213	Alliance City SD	Alliance
143	211	Copley-Fairlawn City SD	Copley
144	210	Niles City SD	Niles
145	208	Midview Local SD	Grafton
146	207	Defiance City SD	Defiance
147	206	Twinsburg City SD	Twinsburg
148	203	Clark-Shawnee Local SD	Springfield
148	203	Jackson City SD	Jackson
150	202	Switzerland of Ohio Local SD	Woodsfield
151	199	Bellefontaine City Schools	Bellefontaine
151	199	Carrollton Ex Vill SD	Carrollton
151	199	Hubbard Ex Vill SD	Hubbard
151	199	Louisville City SD	Louisville
155	198	Mt Healthy City SD	Cincinnati
155	198	North Ridgeville City SD	N Ridgeville
155	198	Northeastern Local SD	Springfield
155	198	Poland Local SD	Poland
159	196	Crestwood Local SD	Mantua
159	196	Highland Local SD	Medina
161	195	West Geauga Local SD	Chesterland
162	194	Napoleon Area City SD	Napoleon
162	194	Tri-Valley Local Schools	Dresden
164	193	Orange City SD	Cleveland
164	193	St Marys City SD	Saint Marys
166	192	Trotwood-Madison City Schools	Trotwood
166	192	Whitehall City SD	Whitehall
168	191	Big Walnut Local SD	Galena
168	191	Springfield Local SD	Akron
170	190	Franklin City SD	Franklin
170	190	Warren Local SD	Vincent
172	189	Maple Heights City SD	Maple Heights
173	187	Elida Local SD	Elida
173	187	West Branch Local SD	Beloit
175	185	East Liverpool City SD	East Liverpool
175	185	Tallmadge City Schools	Tallmadge
177	184	River View Local SD	Warsaw
177	184	Sugarcreek Local SD	Bellbrook
179	183	Buckeye Local SD	Rayland
179	183	Norton City Schools	Norton
179	183	Salem City SD	Salem
182	182	Buckeye Local SD	Medina
182	182	Edgewood City SD	Trenton
182	182	Hillsboro City SD	Hillsboro
182	182	Mad River Local SD	Dayton
186	181	Zanesville City SD	Zanesville
187	180	Bellevue City SD	Bellevue
188	178	Coventry Local SD	Akron
189	177	Bexley City SD	Bexley
189	177	East Muskingum Local SD	New Concord
189	177	Edison Local SD	Hammondsville
192	175	Field Local SD	Mogadore
192	175	Lakeview Local SD	Cortland
192	175	Tipp City Ex Vill SD	Tipp City
195	174	Ravenna City SD	Ravenna
196	171	Clyde-Green Springs Ex Vill SD	Clyde
196	171	Marlington Local SD	Alliance
196	171	Shawnee Local SD	Lima
196	171	Shelby City SD	Shelby
196	171	Southeast Local SD	Ravenna
196	171	Steubenville City SD	Steubenville
196	171	Vermilion Local SD	Vermilion
203	170	Galion City SD	Galion
203	170	Miami Trace Local SD	Wash Ct House
205	169	Little Miami Local SD	Morrow
205	169	Port Clinton City SD	Port Clinton
205	169	Ross Local SD	Hamilton
208	168	Bay Village City SD	Bay Village
208	168	Teays Valley Local SD	Ashville
210	167	Fairview Park City SD	Fairview Park
210	167	Logan Elm Local SD	Circleville
212	165	Franklin Local SD	Duncan Falls
212	165	Gallia County Local SD	Gallipolis
214	164	Ottawa-Glandorf Local SD	Ottawa
215	162	Canton Local SD	Canton
215	162	Conneaut Area City SD	Conneaut
217	161	Beaver Local SD	Lisbon
218	160	Buckeye Local SD	Ashtabula
218	160	Maysville Local SD	Zanesville
218	160	Norwalk City SD	Norwalk
218	160	Warrensville Heights City SD	Warrensville Hgts
222	157	Buckeye Valley Local SD	Delaware
222	157	Morgan Local SD	McConnelsville
224	155	Lakewood Local SD	Hebron
224	155	New Richmond Ex Vill SD	New Richmond
226	154	Cambridge City SD	Cambridge
227	153	Upper Sandusky Ex Vill SD	Upper Sandusky
227	153	Van Wert City SD	Van Wert
229	152	Bath Local SD	Lima
229	152	Benton Carroll Salem Local SD	Oak Harbor
229	152	Granville Ex Vill SD	Granville
232	151	Indian Hill Ex Vill SD	Cincinnati
232	151	Northern Local SD	Thornville
232	151	Northwest Local SD	Canal Fulton
235	150	Liberty Local SD	Youngstown
235	150	Perkins Local SD	Sandusky
235	150	West Holmes Local SD	Millersburg
238	149	Aurora City SD	Aurora
238	149	Bryan City SD	Bryan
238	149	Gallipolis City SD	Gallipolis
238	149	Union Local SD	Morristown
242	148	Champion Local SD	Warren
243	147	Kenton City SD	Kenton
243	147	Monroe Local SD	Monroe
245	146	Chagrin Falls Ex Vill SD	Chagrin Falls
245	146	Goshen Local SD	Goshen
245	146	Greenon Local SD	Springfield
245	146	Triway Local SD	Wooster
249	145	Claymont City SD	Dennison
249	145	Minerva Local SD	Minerva
249	145	Rocky River City SD	Rocky River
249	145	Wauseon Ex Vill SD	Wauseon
253	144	Vinton County Local SD	Mc Arthur
253	144	Washington Court House City SD	Wash Ct House
253	144	Willard City SD	Willard
256	143	Western Brown Local SD	Mount Orab
256	143	Wyoming City SD	Wyoming
258	142	Beachwood City SD	Beachwood

PROFILES OF OHIO / School District Rankings 407

258	142	Circleville City SD	Circleville
258	142	Fairfield Union Local SD	W Rushville
258	142	West Muskingum Local SD	Zanesville
262	141	Finneytown Local SD	Cincinnati
262	141	Swanton Local SD	Swanton
264	140	Eastwood Local SD	Pemberville
264	140	Firelands Local SD	Oberlin
264	140	Oakwood City SD	Dayton
267	139	Clear Fork Valley Local SD	Bellville
267	139	Jefferson Area Local SD	Jefferson
267	139	River Valley Local SD	Caledonia
270	138	Bethel-Tate Local SD	Bethel
270	138	Harrison Hills City SD	Hopedale
270	138	Valley View Local SD	Germantown
273	137	Lake Local SD	Millbury
273	137	Norwood City SD	Norwood
273	137	Rossford Ex Vill SD	Rossford
276	136	Huron City Schools	Huron
276	136	Three Rivers Local Schools	Cleves
278	135	Canal Winchester Local SD	Canal Winchester
278	135	Eaton Community Schools	Eaton
278	135	Northwestern Local SD	Springfield
281	134	London City SD	London
281	134	Paulding Ex Vill SD	Paulding
283	133	Hamilton Local SD	Columbus
283	133	Manchester Local SD	Akron
283	133	Union-Scioto Local SD	Chillicothe
286	132	Berlin-Milan Local SD	Milan
286	132	Graham Local SD	Saint Paris
286	132	Greenfield Ex Vill SD	Greenfield
286	132	Indian Creek Local SD	Wintersville
286	132	Perry Local SD	Perry
291	131	Benjamin Logan Local SD	Bellefontaine
292	130	Indian Lake Local SD	Lewistown
292	130	Sheffield-Sheffield Lake City SD	Sheffield Vlg
294	129	Martins Ferry City SD	Martins Ferry
295	128	Ironton City SD	Ironton
296	127	Genoa Area Local SD	Genoa
296	127	Madison-Plains Local SD	London
296	127	Orrville City SD	Orrville
299	125	Elgin Local SD	Marion
299	125	Meigs Local SD	Pomeroy
301	124	Coldwater Ex Vill SD	Coldwater
301	124	Rolling Hills Local SD	Cambridge
303	123	Struthers City SD	Struthers
304	122	Coshocton City SD	Coshocton
304	122	Indian Valley Local SD	Gnadenhutten
306	121	Clermont Northeastern Local SD	Batavia
307	120	Alexander Local SD	Albany
307	120	St Clairsville-Richland City SD	St Clairsville
309	119	Fairless Local SD	Navarre
309	119	Girard City SD	Girard
309	119	Ontario Local SD	Mansfield
309	119	Streetsboro City Schools	Streetsboro
313	118	Bucyrus City SD	Bucyrus
313	118	Northwest Local SD	Mc Dermott
313	118	Urbana City SD	Urbana
316	117	Avon Local SD	Avon
316	117	Clinton-Massie Local SD	Clarksville
316	117	North Fork Local SD	Utica
316	117	Otsego Local SD	Tontogany
316	117	Wickliffe City SD	Wickliffe
321	116	Milton-Union Exempted Vill Schls	West Milton
321	116	Pike-Delta-York Local SD	Delta
321	116	Preble Shawnee Local SD	Camden
324	115	Fairland Local SD	Proctorville
324	115	Fostoria City SD	Fostoria
324	115	Licking Valley Local SD Sd	Newark
327	114	Waverly City SD	Waverly
328	113	Keystone Local SD	Lagrange
328	113	Mariemont City SD	Cincinnati
328	113	Minford Local SD	Minford
328	113	Sandy Valley Local SD	Magnolia
328	113	Washington-Nile Local SD	West Portsmouth
333	111	Carlisle Local SD	Carlisle
334	110	Bellaire Local SD	Bellaire
334	110	Ridgewood Local SD	West Lafayette
336	109	Jonathan Alder Local SD	Plain City
336	109	Madeira City SD	Cincinnati
336	109	Wellington Ex Vill SD	Wellington
339	108	Plain Local SD	New Albany
339	108	Tuscarawas Valley Local SD	Zoarville
341	106	Highland Local SD	Sparta
342	105	South Point Local SD	South Point
343	104	Brookville Local SD	Brookville
343	104	Heath City SD	Heath
345	102	Greeneview Local SD	Jamestown
345	102	Portsmouth City SD	Portsmouth
347	101	James A Garfield Local SD	Garrettsville
348	100	Campbell City SD	Campbell
348	100	New Lexington City SD	New Lexington
348	100	Rock Hill Local SD	Ironton
351	99	United Local SD	Hanoverton
352	98	Black River Local SD	Sullivan
353	97	Clearview Local SD	Lorain
353	97	Westfall Local SD	Williamsport
355	96	Southeast Local SD	Apple Creek
355	96	Woodridge Local SD	Peninsula
357	95	Eastern Local SD	Sardinia
357	95	Madison Local SD	Middletown
357	95	Zane Trace Local SD	Chillicothe
360	93	Blanchester Local SD	Blanchester
360	93	East Clinton Local SD	Lees Creek
360	93	Northridge Local SD	Dayton
363	92	Batavia Local SD	Batavia
363	92	Licking Heights Local SD	Summit Station
363	92	North College Hill City SD	Cincinnati
366	89	Newton Falls Ex Vill SD	Newton Falls
366	89	Scioto Valley Local SD	Piketon
368	88	Painesville City Local SD	Painesville
369	87	Amanda-Clearcreek Local SD	Amanda
369	87	Athens City SD	The Plains
371	78	Wellston City Schools	Wellston
372	63	East Holmes Local Schools	Berlin
373	31	Electronic Classrm of Tomorrow	Columbus
374	n/a	Ohio Virtual Academy	Maumee

High School Drop-out Rate

Rank	Percent	District Name	City
1	16.0	Canton City SD	Canton
2	15.1	Cleveland Municipal City SD	Cleveland
3	12.2	Lima City SD	Lima
4	10.7	East Cleveland City SD	East Cleveland
5	9.0	Newark City SD	Newark
6	8.7	Columbus Public Schools	Columbus
6	8.7	Youngstown City SD	Youngstown
8	8.5	Zanesville City SD	Zanesville
9	8.4	Dayton City SD	Dayton
10	8.2	Cincinnati City SD	Cincinnati
11	8.1	Norwood City SD	Norwood
12	7.8	Bedford City SD	Bedford
13	7.6	Portsmouth City SD	Portsmouth
14	7.2	Mad River Local SD	Dayton
15	6.9	Trotwood-Madison City Schools	Trotwood
16	6.8	Hamilton City SD	Hamilton
16	6.8	Lorain City SD	Lorain
16	6.8	Marion City SD	Marion
16	6.8	New Lexington City SD	New Lexington
20	6.7	Toledo City SD	Toledo
21	6.2	Logan-Hocking Local SD	Logan
21	6.2	Springfield City SD	Springfield
23	6.1	Ashtabula Area City SD	Ashtabula
23	6.1	Washington Local Schools	Toledo
25	6.0	Elyria City SD	Elyria
26	5.9	Alliance City SD	Alliance
26	5.9	Maple Heights City SD	Maple Heights
26	5.9	Painesville City Local SD	Painesville
26	5.9	South-Western City SD	Grove City
26	5.9	Whitehall City SD	Whitehall
31	5.8	Mansfield City SD	Mansfield
31	5.8	New Richmond Ex Vill SD	New Richmond
33	5.7	Northridge Local SD	Dayton
34	5.6	West Clermont Local SD	Cincinnati
35	5.5	Fairborn City Schools	Fairborn
36	5.4	Madison Local SD	Mansfield
37	5.3	Fostoria City SD	Fostoria
37	5.3	Franklin City SD	Franklin
37	5.3	Huber Heights City SD	Huber Heights
37	5.3	Warren City SD	Warren
41	5.2	Middletown City SD	Middletown
41	5.2	Northwest Local SD	Cincinnati
41	5.2	Norwalk City SD	Norwalk
41	5.2	Scioto Valley Local SD	Piketon
41	5.2	Steubenville City SD	Steubenville
41	5.2	Western Brown Local SD	Mount Orab
47	5.1	Massillon City SD	Massillon
48	5.0	Akron Public Schools	Akron
48	5.0	Morgan Local SD	McConnelsville
48	5.0	Parma City SD	Parma
48	5.0	Southwest Local SD	Harrison
48	5.0	Vinton County Local SD	Mc Arthur
53	4.9	Ravenna City SD	Ravenna
53	4.9	Tiffin City SD	Tiffin
53	4.9	Xenia Community City SD	Xenia
56	4.8	Barberton City SD	Barberton
56	4.8	Defiance City SD	Defiance
58	4.7	Ironton City SD	Ironton
59	4.6	Fremont City SD	Fremont
59	4.6	Tecumseh Local SD	New Carlisle
59	4.6	Tuscarawas Valley Local SD	Zoarville
62	4.5	Bucyrus City SD	Bucyrus
62	4.5	Eaton Community Schools	Eaton
62	4.5	Goshen Local SD	Goshen
62	4.5	London City SD	London
66	4.4	Indian Lake Local SD	Lewistown
66	4.4	Lancaster City SD	Lancaster
66	4.4	Mt Healthy City SD	Cincinnati
69	4.3	Gallipolis City SD	Gallipolis
69	4.3	Groveport Madison Local SD	Groveport
71	4.2	Bethel-Tate Local SD	Bethel
71	4.2	Clermont Northeastern Local SD	Batavia
71	4.2	Rolling Hills Local SD	Cambridge
74	4.1	North Fork Local SD	Utica
75	4.0	Circleville City SD	Circleville
75	4.0	Princeton City SD	Cincinnati
75	4.0	Talawanda City SD	Oxford
78	3.9	Alexander Local SD	Albany
78	3.9	Batavia Local SD	Batavia
78	3.9	Delaware City SD	Delaware
78	3.9	Greenfield Ex Vill SD	Greenfield
78	3.9	Greenon Local SD	Springfield
78	3.9	Hamilton Local SD	Columbus
78	3.9	Teays Valley Local SD	Ashville
78	3.9	Three Rivers Local Schools	Cleves
78	3.9	Waverly City SD	Waverly
87	3.8	Fairland Local SD	Proctorville
88	3.7	Cambridge City SD	Cambridge
88	3.7	Gallia County Local SD	Gallipolis
88	3.7	Sandusky City SD	Sandusky
91	3.6	Bellaire Local SD	Bellaire
91	3.6	Minerva Local SD	Minerva
91	3.6	Napoleon Area City SD	Napoleon
91	3.6	Washington-Nile Local SD	West Portsmouth
95	3.5	Cleveland Hts-Univ Hts City SD	University Hgts
95	3.5	Harrison Hills City SD	Hopedale
95	3.5	Mariemont City SD	Cincinnati
95	3.5	Washington Court House City SD	Wash Ct House
99	3.4	Edgewood City SD	Trenton
99	3.4	Lakewood City SD	Lakewood
99	3.4	Madison Local SD	Madison
99	3.4	Rock Hill Local SD	Ironton
99	3.4	Willard City SD	Willard
104	3.3	Chillicothe City SD	Chillicothe
104	3.3	East Clinton Local SD	Lees Creek
104	3.3	Galion City SD	Galion
104	3.3	James A Garfield Local SD	Garrettsville
104	3.3	Miami Trace Local SD	Wash Ct House
104	3.3	Piqua City SD	Piqua
110	3.2	Adams County/Ohio Valley LSD	West Union
110	3.2	Niles City SD	Niles
110	3.2	Port Clinton City SD	Port Clinton
110	3.2	Ross Local SD	Hamilton
110	3.2	Shelby City SD	Shelby
110	3.2	Union-Scioto Local SD	Chillicothe
110	3.2	Winton Woods City SD	Cincinnati
117	3.1	Kenton City SD	Kenton
117	3.1	Troy City SD	Troy
119	3.0	Buckeye Local SD	Ashtabula
119	3.0	Franklin Local SD	Duncan Falls
119	3.0	Garfield Heights City SD	Garfield Hgts
119	3.0	Oregon City SD	Oregon
119	3.0	Willoughby-Eastlake City SD	Willoughby
124	2.9	Ashland City SD	Ashland
124	2.9	Bellefontaine City Schools	Bellefontaine
124	2.9	Madison Local SD	Middletown
124	2.9	North College Hill City SD	Cincinnati
124	2.9	Orrville City SD	Orrville
124	2.9	Sidney City SD	Sidney
124	2.9	Valley View Local SD	Germantown
124	2.9	Van Wert City SD	Van Wert
132	2.8	Midview Local SD	Grafton
132	2.8	Mount Vernon City SD	Mount Vernon
132	2.8	Springfield Local Schools	Holland
132	2.8	Urbana City SD	Urbana
132	2.8	Wickliffe City SD	Wickliffe
137	2.7	Bryan City SD	Bryan
137	2.7	Gahanna-Jefferson City SD	Gahanna
137	2.7	Heath City SD	Heath
137	2.7	Licking Valley Local SD Sd	Newark
137	2.7	Switzerland of Ohio Local SD	Woodsfield
142	2.6	Canal Winchester Local SD	Canal Winchester
142	2.6	Findlay City SD	Findlay
142	2.6	Plain Local SD	Canton
142	2.6	River View Local SD	Warsaw
142	2.6	Rossford Ex Vill SD	Rossford
147	2.5	Brookville Local SD	Brookville
147	2.5	Finneytown Local SD	Cincinnati
147	2.5	Jackson City SD	Jackson
147	2.5	Licking Heights Local SD	Summit Station
147	2.5	Milton-Union Exempted Vill Schls	West Milton
147	2.5	Northwest Local SD	Mc Dermott
147	2.5	Struthers City SD	Struthers
147	2.5	Warren Local SD	Vincent
155	2.4	Conneaut Area City SD	Conneaut
155	2.4	Madison-Plains Local SD	London
155	2.4	Monroe Local SD	Monroe

408 PROFILES OF OHIO / School District Rankings

Rank	Score	District	City
155	2.4	Preble Shawnee Local SD	Camden
155	2.4	Southwest Licking Local SD	Etna
155	2.4	United Local SD	Hanoverton
155	2.4	Woodridge Local SD	Peninsula
162	2.3	Beavercreek City SD	Beavercreek
162	2.3	Big Walnut Local SD	Galena
162	2.3	Clinton-Massie Local SD	Clarksville
162	2.3	Milford Ex Vill SD	Milford
162	2.3	South Point Local SD	South Point
162	2.3	Southeast Local SD	Ravenna
162	2.3	Upper Sandusky Ex Vill SD	Upper Sandusky
169	2.2	Benjamin Logan Local SD	Bellefontaine
169	2.2	East Liverpool City SD	East Liverpool
169	2.2	Eastern Local SD	Sardinia
169	2.2	Greeneview Local SD	Jamestown
169	2.2	Jonathan Alder Local SD	Plain City
169	2.2	Kent City SD	Kent
169	2.2	Ridgewood Local SD	West Lafayette
169	2.2	Tri-Valley Local Schools	Dresden
169	2.2	Westerville City SD	Westerville
178	2.1	Athens City SD	The Plains
178	2.1	Clyde-Green Springs Ex Vill SD	Clyde
178	2.1	Elida Local SD	Elida
178	2.1	New Philadelphia City SD	New Philadelphia
178	2.1	Nordonia Hills City SD	Northfield
178	2.1	Otsego Local SD	Tontogany
178	2.1	Wellston City Schools	Wellston
178	2.1	Zane Trace Local SD	Chillicothe
186	2.0	Anthony Wayne Local SD	Whitehouse
186	2.0	Cuyahoga Falls City SD	Cuyahoga Falls
186	2.0	Greenville City SD	Greenville
186	2.0	Salem City SD	Salem
186	2.0	Sandy Valley Local SD	Magnolia
186	2.0	Shawnee Local SD	Lima
186	2.0	Springfield Local SD	Akron
186	2.0	Triway Local SD	Wooster
186	2.0	Vermilion Local SD	Vermilion
186	2.0	West Holmes Local SD	Millersburg
196	1.9	Beaver Local SD	Lisbon
196	1.9	Blanchester Local SD	Blanchester
196	1.9	Carlisle Local SD	Carlisle
196	1.9	East Muskingum Local SD	New Concord
196	1.9	Geneva Area City Schools	Geneva
196	1.9	Little Miami Local SD	Morrow
196	1.9	Painesville Township Local SD	Painesville
196	1.9	Pike-Delta-York Local SD	Delta
196	1.9	St Clairsville-Richland City SD	St Clairsville
196	1.9	Union Local SD	Morristown
196	1.9	Wadsworth City SD	Wadsworth
196	1.9	Wellington Ex Vill SD	Wellington
208	1.8	Bath Local SD	Lima
208	1.8	Bellevue City SD	Bellevue
208	1.8	Celina City SD	Celina
208	1.8	Clark-Shawnee Local SD	Springfield
208	1.8	Genoa Area Local SD	Genoa
208	1.8	Northwestern Local SD	Springfield
208	1.8	Sylvania City SD	Sylvania
208	1.8	Westfall Local SD	Williamsport
216	1.7	Avon Lake City Schools	Avon Lake
216	1.7	Clear Fork Valley Local SD	Bellville
216	1.7	Field Local SD	Mogadore
216	1.7	Hilliard City SD	Hilliard
216	1.7	Lebanon City SD	Lebanon
216	1.7	Loveland City SD	Loveland
216	1.7	Northeastern Local SD	Springfield
216	1.7	Rocky River City SD	Rocky River
216	1.7	Southeast Local SD	Apple Creek
225	1.6	Berea City SD	Berea
225	1.6	Cloverleaf Local SD	Lodi
225	1.6	Fairless Local SD	Navarre
225	1.6	Highland Local SD	Medina
225	1.6	Jefferson Area Local SD	Jefferson
225	1.6	Marietta City Schools	Marietta
225	1.6	Miamisburg City SD	Miamisburg
225	1.6	North Ridgeville City SD	N Ridgeville
225	1.6	Olmsted Falls City SD	Olmsted Falls
225	1.6	Plain Local SD	New Albany
225	1.6	Reynoldsburg City SD	Reynoldsburg
225	1.6	Sheffield-Sheffield Lake City SD	Sheffield Vlg
225	1.6	Twinsburg City SD	Twinsburg
225	1.6	Wapakoneta City SD	Wapakoneta
225	1.6	Wauseon Ex Vill SD	Wauseon
240	1.5	Amanda-Clearcreek Local SD	Amanda
240	1.5	Buckeye Local SD	Medina
240	1.5	Forest Hills Local SD	Cincinnati
240	1.5	Girard City SD	Girard
240	1.5	Highland Local SD	Sparta
240	1.5	Mason City SD	Mason
240	1.5	Swanton Local SD	Swanton
240	1.5	West Carrollton City SD	West Carrollton
248	1.4	Coventry Local SD	Akron
248	1.4	Elgin Local SD	Marion
248	1.4	Firelands Local SD	Oberlin
248	1.4	Graham Local SD	Saint Paris
248	1.4	Hubbard Ex Vill SD	Hubbard
248	1.4	Logan Elm Local SD	Circleville
248	1.4	Maumee City SD	Maumee
248	1.4	Maysville Local SD	Zanesville
256	1.3	Berlin-Milan Local SD	Milan
256	1.3	Crestwood Local SD	Mantua
256	1.3	Dover City SD	Dover
256	1.3	Fairview Park City SD	Fairview Park
256	1.3	Manchester Local SD	Akron
256	1.3	Northern Local SD	Thornville
256	1.3	River Valley Local SD	Caledonia
256	1.3	Strongsville Local SD	Strongsville
256	1.3	Wilmington City SD	Wilmington
265	1.2	Bay Village City SD	Bay Village
265	1.2	Boardman Local SD	Youngstown
265	1.2	Buckeye Local SD	Rayland
265	1.2	Champion Local SD	Warren
265	1.2	Chardon Local SD	Chardon
265	1.2	Fairfield City SD	Fairfield
265	1.2	Hillsboro City SD	Hillsboro
265	1.2	Lake Local SD	Millbury
265	1.2	Minford Local SD	Minford
265	1.2	North Olmsted City Schools	North Olmsted
265	1.2	Ontario Local SD	Mansfield
265	1.2	Ottawa-Glandorf Local SD	Ottawa
265	1.2	Paulding Ex Vill SD	Paulding
265	1.2	Westlake City SD	Westlake
279	1.1	Brunswick City SD	Brunswick
279	1.1	Carrollton Ex Vill SD	Carrollton
279	1.1	Clearview Local SD	Lorain
279	1.1	Edison Local SD	Hammondsville
279	1.1	Indian Creek Local SD	Wintersville
279	1.1	Keystone Local SD	Lagrange
279	1.1	Kings Local SD	Kings Mills
279	1.1	Louisville City SD	Louisville
279	1.1	Newton Falls Ex Vill SD	Newton Falls
279	1.1	Oakwood City SD	Dayton
279	1.1	Springboro Community City SD	Springboro
279	1.1	Stow-Munroe Falls City SD	Stow
291	1.0	Aurora City SD	Aurora
291	1.0	Bowling Green City SD	Bowling Green
291	1.0	Dublin City SD	Dublin
291	1.0	Mayfield City SD	Highland Hgts
291	1.0	Orange City SD	Cleveland
291	1.0	Perrysburg Exempted Village	Perrysburg
291	1.0	Sugarcreek Local SD	Bellbrook
298	0.9	Centerville City SD	Centerville
298	0.9	Coldwater Ex Vill SD	Coldwater
298	0.9	Lakota Local SD	Liberty Twp
298	0.9	Liberty Local SD	Youngstown
298	0.9	Meigs Local SD	Pomeroy
298	0.9	Mentor Ex Vill SD	Mentor
298	0.9	Pickerington Local SD	Pickerington
298	0.9	Streetsboro City Schools	Streetsboro
298	0.9	Sycamore Community City SD	Cincinnati
298	0.9	Vandalia-Butler City SD	Vandalia
298	0.9	Worthington City SD	Worthington
309	0.8	Black River Local SD	Sullivan
309	0.8	Lake Local SD	Hartville
309	0.8	Lakewood Local SD	Hebron
309	0.8	Lexington Local SD	Lexington
309	0.8	Revere Local SD	Bath
309	0.8	Wooster City SD	Wooster
315	0.7	Benton Carroll Salem Local SD	Oak Harbor
315	0.7	Brecksville-Broadview Hgts City	Brecksville
315	0.7	Buckeye Valley Local SD	Delaware
315	0.7	Coshocton City SD	Coshocton
315	0.7	Fairfield Union Local SD	W Rushville
315	0.7	Hudson City SD	Hudson
315	0.7	Huron City Schools	Huron
315	0.7	Marysville Exempted Village SD	Marysville
315	0.7	Northmont City SD	Englewood
315	0.7	Northwest Local SD	Canal Fulton
315	0.7	Perry Local SD	Perry
315	0.7	Solon City SD	Solon
315	0.7	Tallmadge City Schools	Tallmadge
328	0.6	Beachwood City SD	Beachwood
328	0.6	Copley-Fairlawn City SD	Copley
328	0.6	Indian Hill Ex Vill SD	Cincinnati
328	0.6	Jackson Local SD	Massillon
328	0.6	North Canton City SD	North Canton
328	0.6	South Euclid-Lyndhurst City SD	Lyndhurst
334	0.5	Bexley City SD	Bexley
334	0.5	Chagrin Falls Ex Vill SD	Chagrin Falls
334	0.5	Claymont City SD	Dennison
334	0.5	Eastwood Local SD	Pemberville
334	0.5	Howland Local SD	Warren
334	0.5	Indian Valley Local SD	Gnadenhutten
334	0.5	Kettering City SD	Kettering
334	0.5	North Royalton City SD	N Royalton
334	0.5	Norton City Schools	Norton
334	0.5	Oak Hills Local SD	Cincinnati
334	0.5	Perkins Local SD	Sandusky
345	0.4	Avon Local SD	Avon
345	0.4	Green Local SD	Green
345	0.4	Kenston Local SD	Chagrin Falls
345	0.4	Madeira City SD	Cincinnati
345	0.4	Martins Ferry City SD	Martins Ferry
345	0.4	Olentangy Local SD	Lewis Center
345	0.4	Perry Local SD	Massillon
345	0.4	Tipp City Ex Vill SD	Tipp City
345	0.4	West Branch Local SD	Beloit
345	0.4	West Geauga Local SD	Chesterland
355	0.3	Austintown Local SD	Youngstown
355	0.3	Canfield Local SD	Canfield
355	0.3	Granville Ex Vill SD	Granville
355	0.3	Lakeview Local SD	Cortland
355	0.3	Marlington Local SD	Alliance
355	0.3	Medina City SD	Medina
355	0.3	St Marys City SD	Saint Marys
355	0.3	Upper Arlington City SD	Upper Arlington
363	0.2	Amherst Ex Vill SD	Amherst
363	0.2	Campbell City SD	Campbell
363	0.2	Canton Local SD	Canton
363	0.2	Poland Local SD	Poland
363	0.2	West Muskingum Local SD	Zanesville
368	0.1	Euclid City SD	Euclid
368	0.1	Warrensville Heights City SD	Warrensville Hgts
370	0.0	East Holmes Local Schools	Berlin
370	0.0	Electronic Classrm of Tomorrow	Columbus
370	0.0	Shaker Heights City SD	Shaker Heights
370	0.0	Wyoming City SD	Wyoming
374	n/a	Ohio Virtual Academy	Maumee

2005 Ohio NAEP Public School Snapshot
Grade 4 Mathematics

The National Assessment of Educational Progress (NAEP) assesses mathematics in five content areas: number properties and operations; measurement; geometry; data analysis and probability; and algebra. The NAEP mathematics scale ranges from 0 to 500.

Overall Mathematics Results for Ohio

- In 2005, the average scale score for fourth-grade students in Ohio was 242. This was higher[1] than their average score in 2003 (238), and was higher than their average score in 1992 (219).
- Ohio's average score (242) in 2005 was higher than that of the Nation's public schools (237).
- Of the 52 states and other jurisdictions[2] that participated in the 2005 fourth-grade assessment, students' average scale scores in Ohio were higher than those in 29 jurisdictions, not significantly different from those in 18 jurisdictions, and lower than those in 4 jurisdictions.
- The percentage of students in Ohio who performed at or above the NAEP *Proficient* level was 43 percent in 2005. This percentage was greater than that in 2003 (36 percent), and was greater than that in 1992 (16 percent).
- The percentage of students in Ohio who performed at or above the NAEP *Basic* level was 84 percent in 2005. This percentage was not significantly different from that in 2003 (81 percent), and was greater than that in 1992 (57 percent).

Student Percentage at NAEP Achievement Levels

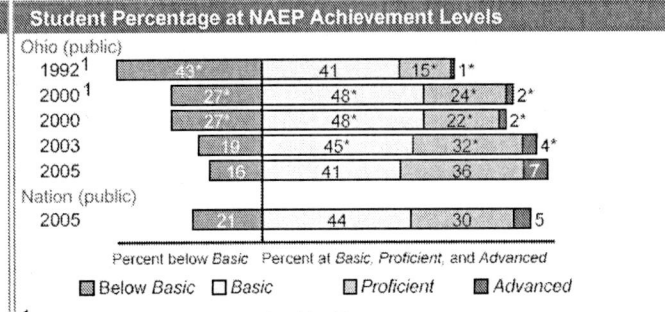

Ohio (public)

Year	Below Basic	Basic	Proficient	Advanced
1992[1]	43*	41	15*	1*
2000[1]	27*	48*	24*	2*
2000	27*	48*	22*	2*
2003	19	45*	32*	4*
2005	16	41	36	7

Nation (public)

Year	Below Basic	Basic	Proficient	Advanced
2005	21	44	30	5

Percent below *Basic* | Percent at *Basic*, *Proficient*, and *Advanced*

■ Below *Basic*   □ *Basic*   □ *Proficient*   ■ *Advanced*

[1] Accommodations were not permitted for this assessment.

NOTE: The NAEP mathematics achievement levels correspond to the following scale points: Below *Basic*, 213 or lower; *Basic*, 214–248; *Proficient*, 249–281; *Advanced*, 282 or above.

Performance of NAEP Reporting Groups in Ohio

Reporting groups	Percent of students	Average score	Percent below Basic	Basic	Proficient	Percent Advanced
Male	51	243↑	16	84	45↑	7↑
Female	49	241↑	16	84	40↑	6↑
White	72	248↑	9	91	51↑	8↑
Black	21	221	41	59	16	1
Hispanic	2	231	24	76	21	2
Asian/Pacific Islander	1	‡	‡	‡	‡	‡
American Indian/Alaska Native	#	‡	‡	‡	‡	‡
Eligible for free/reduced-price school lunch	38	227	31	69	21	1
Not eligible for free/reduced-price school lunch	59	252↑	7	93	56↑	10↑

Average Score Gaps Between Selected Groups

- In 2005, male students in Ohio had an average score that was not found to be significantly different from that of female students. In 1992, there was no significant difference between the average score of male and female students.
- In 2005, Black students had an average score that was lower than that of White students by 28 points. In 1992, the average score for Black students was lower than that of White students by 28 points.
- In 2005, Hispanic students had an average score that was lower than that of White students by 18 points. Data are not reported for Hispanic students in 1992, because reporting standards were not met. Therefore, the performance gap data are not reported.
- In 2005, students who were eligible for free/reduced-price school lunch, an indicator of poverty, had an average score that was lower than that of students who were not eligible for free/reduced-price school lunch by 25 points. In 2000, the average score for students who were eligible for free/reduced-price school lunch was lower than the score of those not eligible by 22 points.
- In 2005, the score gap between students at the 75th percentile and students at the 25th percentile was 37 points. In 1992, the score gap between students at the 75th percentile and students at the 25th percentile was 42 points.

Mathematics Scale Scores at Selected Percentiles

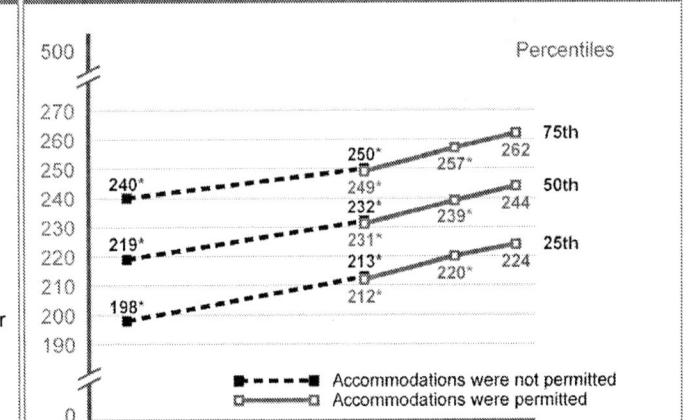

Percentile	'92	'00	'03	'05
75th	240*	250*	257*	262
50th	219*	232*/231*	239*	244
25th	198*	213*/212*	220*	224

■---■ Accommodations were not permitted
□—□ Accommodations were permitted

Scores at selected percentiles on the NAEP mathematics scale indicate how well students at lower, middle, and higher levels of the distribution performed.

\# The estimate rounds to zero.   ‡ Reporting standards not met.
* Significantly different from 2005.   ↑ Significantly higher than 2003.   ↓ Significantly lower than 2003.

[1] Comparisons (higher/lower/not different) are based on statistical tests. The .05 level was used for testing statistical significance. Performance comparisons may be affected by differences in exclusion rates across years for students with disabilities (2% nationally in 2005) and English language learners (1% nationally in 2005) in the NAEP samples. Statistical comparisons are calculated on the basis of unrounded scale scores or percentages.
[2] "Other Jurisdictions" refers to the District of Columbia and the Department of Defense Education Activity schools.

NOTE: Detail may not sum to totals because of rounding and because the "Information not available" category for free/reduced-price lunch and the "Unclassifed" category for race/ethnicity are not displayed. Visit http://nces.ed.gov/nationsreportcard/states/ for additional results and detailed information.

SOURCE: U.S. Department of Education, Institute of Education Sciences, National Center for Education Statistics, National Assessment of Educational Progress (NAEP), selected years, 1992–2005 Mathematics Assessments.

2005 Ohio NAEP Public School Snapshot
Grade 4 Reading

The National Assessment of Educational Progress (NAEP) assesses reading in two content areas: reading for literary experience and to gain information. The NAEP reading scale ranges from 0 to 500.

Overall Reading Results for Ohio

- In 2005, the average scale score for fourth-grade students in Ohio was 223. This was not significantly different from[1] their average score in 2003 (222), and was higher than their average score in 1992 (217).
- Ohio's average score (223) in 2005 was higher than that of the Nation's public schools (217).
- Of the 52 states and other jurisdictions[2] that participated in the 2005 fourth-grade assessment, students' average scale scores in Ohio were higher than those in 22 jurisdictions, not significantly different from those in 25 jurisdictions, and lower than those in 4 jurisdictions.
- The percentage of students in Ohio who performed at or above the NAEP Proficient level was 34 percent in 2005. This percentage was not significantly different from that in 2003 (34 percent), and was greater than that in 1992 (27 percent).
- The percentage of students in Ohio who performed at or above the NAEP Basic level was 69 percent in 2005. This percentage was not significantly different from that in 2003 (69 percent), and was greater than that in 1992 (63 percent).

Student Percentage at NAEP Achievement Levels

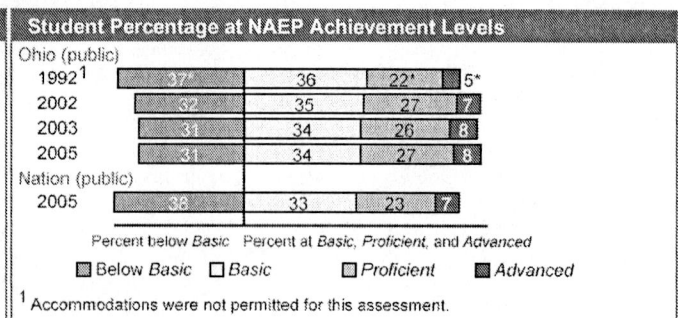

Ohio (public)
Year	Below Basic	Basic	Proficient	Advanced
1992[1]	37*	36	22*	5*
2002	32	35	27	7
2003	31	34	26	8
2005	31	34	27	8

Nation (public)
Year	Below Basic	Basic	Proficient	Advanced
2005	38	33	23	7

Percent below *Basic*   Percent at *Basic*, *Proficient*, and *Advanced*

[1] Accommodations were not permitted for this assessment.

NOTE: The NAEP reading achievement levels correspond to the following scale points: Below *Basic*, 207 or lower; *Basic*, 208–237; *Proficient*, 238–267; *Advanced*, 268 or above.

Performance of NAEP Reporting Groups in Ohio

Reporting groups	Percent of students	Average score	Percent below *Basic*	Percent at or above *Basic*	Percent at or above *Proficient*	Percent *Advanced*
Male	50	219	35	65	31	7
Female	50	226	28	72	37	8
White	74	230	23	77	41	10
Black	20	197	62	38	10	#
Hispanic	2	211	43	57	24	7
Asian/Pacific Islander	1	‡	‡	‡	‡	‡
American Indian/Alaska Native	#	‡	‡	‡	‡	‡
Eligible for free/reduced-price school lunch	37	206	50	50	17	2
Not eligible for free/reduced-price school lunch	60	233	20	80	45	11

Average Score Gaps Between Selected Groups

- In 2005, male students in Ohio had an average score that was lower than that of female students by 6 points. In 1992, the average score for male students was lower than that of female students by 7 points.
- In 2005, Black students had an average score that was lower than that of White students by 33 points. This performance gap was wider than that of 1992 (23 points).
- In 2005, Hispanic students had an average score that was lower than that of White students by 19 points. Data are not reported for Hispanic students in 1992, because reporting standards were not met. Therefore, the performance gap data are not reported.
- In 2005, students who were eligible for free/reduced-price school lunch, an indicator of poverty, had an average score that was lower than that of students who were not eligible for free/reduced-price school lunch by 27 points. In 2002, the average score for students who were eligible for free/reduced-price school lunch was lower than the score of those not eligible by 24 points.
- In 2005, the score gap between students at the 75th percentile and students at the 25th percentile was 45 points. In 1992, the score gap between students at the 75th percentile and students at the 25th percentile was 43 points.

Reading Scale Scores at Selected Percentiles

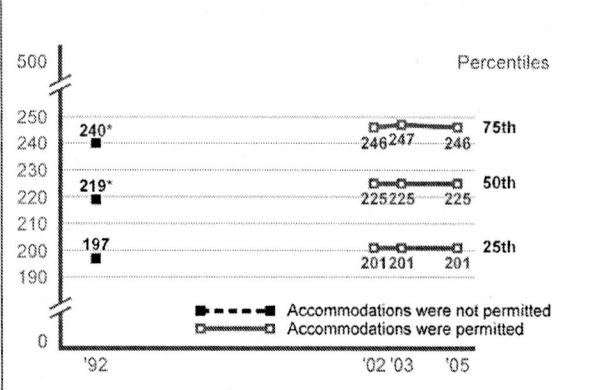

Percentile	'92	'02	'03	'05
75th	240*	246	247	246
50th	219*	225	225	225
25th	197	201	201	201

Accommodations were not permitted
Accommodations were permitted

Scores at selected percentiles on the NAEP reading scale indicate how well students at lower, middle, and higher levels of the distribution performed.

\# The estimate rounds to zero.   ‡ Reporting standards not met.
* Significantly different from 2005.   ↑ Significantly higher than 2003.   ↓ Significantly lower than 2003.

[1] Comparisons (higher/lower/not different) are based on statistical tests. The .05 level was used for testing statistical significance. Performance comparisons may be affected by differences in exclusion rates across years for students with disabilities (5% nationally in 2005) and English language learners (2% nationally in 2005) in the NAEP samples. Statistical comparisons are calculated on the basis of unrounded scale scores or percentages.
[2] "Other Jurisdictions" refers to the District of Columbia and the Department of Defense Education Activity schools.
NOTE: Detail may not sum to totals because of rounding and because the "Information not available" category for free/reduced-price lunch and the "Unclassifed" category for race/ethnicity are not displayed. Visit http://nces.ed.gov/nationsreportcard/states/ for additional results and detailed information.
SOURCE: U.S. Department of Education, Institute of Education Sciences, National Center for Education Statistics, National Assessment of Educational Progress (NAEP), selected years, 1992–2005 Reading Assessments.

2005 Ohio NAEP Public School Snapshot
Grade 4 Writing

The writing assessment of the National Assessment of Educational Progress (NAEP) measures narrative, informative, and persuasive writing–three purposes identified in the NAEP framework. The NAEP writing scale ranges from 0 to 300.

Overall Writing Results for Ohio

- The average scale score for fourth-grade students in Ohio was 157.
- Ohio's average score (157) was higher[1] than that of the nation's public schools (153).
- Students' average scale scores in Ohio were higher than those in 26 jurisdictions[2], not significantly different from those in 17 jurisdictions, and lower than those in 4 jurisdictions.
- The percentage of students who performed at or above the NAEP *Proficient* level was 28 percent. The percentage of students who performed at or above the *Basic* level was 90 percent.

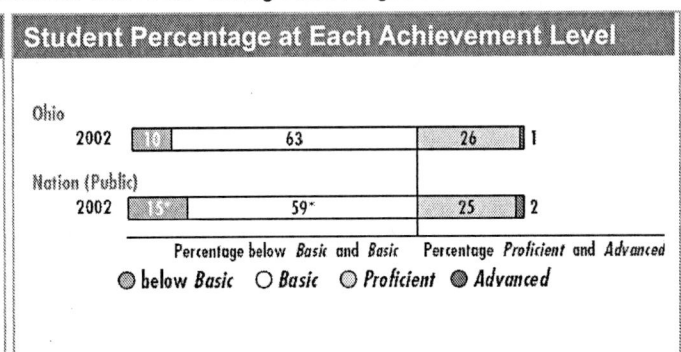

Student Percentage at Each Achievement Level

Ohio 2002: below Basic 10, Basic 63, Proficient 26, Advanced 1
Nation (Public) 2002: below Basic 15*, Basic 59*, Proficient 25, Advanced 2

● below *Basic*   ○ *Basic*   ○ *Proficient*   ● *Advanced*

Performance of NAEP Reporting Groups in Ohio

Reporting groups	Percentage of students	Average Score	Below Basic	Basic	Proficient	Advanced
Male	50	150 ↑	13 ↓	67 ↑	19	1
Female	50	164	6 ↓	59	33	2
White	76	162	7 ↓	61 ↑	31	2
Black	20	140	20	68	11	#
Hispanic	2	---	---	---	---	---
Asian/Pacific Islander	1	---	---	---	---	---
American Indian/Alaska Native	#	---	---	---	---	---
Free/reduced-priced school lunch						
Eligible	32	143	18 ↓	69 ↑	14	#
Not eligible	61	164	5 ↓	60	33	2
Information not available	7	158	8	64	26	2

Average Score Gaps Between Selected Groups

- Female students in Ohio had an average score that was higher than that of male students (14 points). This performance gap was not significantly different from that of the Nation (18 points).
- White students had an average score that was higher than that of Black students (22 points). This performance gap was not significantly different from that of the Nation (20 points).
- The sample size was not sufficient to permit a reliable estimate for Hispanic students in Ohio.
- Students who were not eligible for free/reduced-price school lunch had an average score that was higher than that of students who were eligible (21 points). This performance gap was not significantly different from that of the Nation (22 points).

Writing Scale Scores at Selected Percentiles

Scale Score Distribution

	25th Percentile	50th Percentile	75th Percentile
Ohio	135 ↑	157 ↑	179
Nation (Public)	128	153	178

An examination of scores at different percentiles on the 0-300 NAEP writing scale at each grade indicates how well students at lower, middle, and higher levels of the distribution performed. For example, the data above shows that 75 percent of students in public schools nationally scored below *178*, while 75 percent of students in Ohio scored below *179*.

\# Percentage rounds to zero.
--- Reporting standards not met; sample size insufficient to permit a reliable estimate.
* Significantly different from Ohio.   ↑ Significantly higher than, ↓ lower than appropriate subgroup in the nation (public).
[1] Comparisons (higher/lower/not different) are based on statistical tests. The .05 level was used for testing statistical significance.
[2] "Jurisdictions" includes participating states and other jurisdictions (such as Guam or the District of Columbia).
NOTE: Detail may not sum to totals because of rounding. Score gaps are calculated based on differences between unrounded average scale scores.
Visit http://nces.ed.gov/nationsreportcard/states/ for additional results and detailed information.
SOURCE: U.S. Department of Education, Institute of Education Sciences, National Center for Education Statistics, National Assessment of Educational Progress (NAEP), 2002 Writing Assessment.

2005 Ohio NAEP Public School Snapshot
Grade 4 Science

The National Assessment of Educational Progress (NAEP) assesses science in two major dimensions: Fields of Science (Earth, Physical, and Life) and Knowing and Doing Science (Conceptual Understanding, Scientific Investigation, and Practical Reasoning). The NAEP science scale ranges from 0 to 300. Scales are created separately for each grade.

Overall Science Results for Ohio

- In 2005, the average scale score for fourth-grade students in Ohio was 157. This was not significantly different from their average score in 2000 (155).[1]
- Ohio's average score (157) in 2005 was higher than that of the nation's public schools (149).
- Of the 44 states and one jurisdiction that participated in the 2005 fourth-grade assessment, students' average scale score in Ohio was higher than those in 25 jurisdictions, not significantly different from those in 12 jurisdictions, and lower than those in 7 jurisdictions.[2]
- The percentage of students in Ohio who performed at or above the NAEP *Proficient* level was 35 percent in 2005. This percentage was not significantly different from that in 2000 (31 percent).
- The percentage of students in Ohio who performed at or above the NAEP *Basic* level was 75 percent in 2005. This percentage was not significantly different from that in 2000 (73 percent).

Student Percentages at NAEP Achievement Levels

Year	Below Basic	Basic	Proficient	Advanced
Ohio (public) 2000[1]	28	40	28	4
Ohio (public) 2000	27	42	28	3
Ohio (public) 2005	25	40	31	3
Nation (public) 2005	34	39	25	2

[1] Accommodations were not permitted for this assessment.

NOTE: The NAEP grade 4 science achievement levels correspond to the following scale points: Below *Basic*, 137 or lower; *Basic*, 138–169; *Proficient*, 170–204; *Advanced*, 205 or above.

Performance of NAEP Reporting Groups in Ohio: 2005

Reporting groups	Percent of students	Average score	Percent below *Basic*	Percent at or above *Basic*	Percent at or above *Proficient*	Percent *Advanced*
Male	53	159	23	77	39	4
Female	47	154	27	73	30	2
White	74	164	14	86	43	4
Black	20	130	61	39	7	#
Hispanic	2	146	39	61	22	1
Asian/Pacific Islander	1	‡	‡	‡	‡	‡
American Indian/Alaska Native	#	‡	‡	‡	‡	‡
Eligible for free/reduced-price school lunch	37	139	47	53	15	1
Not eligible for free/reduced-price school lunch	60	167	12	88	47	5

Average Score Gaps Between Selected Groups

- In 2005, male students in Ohio had an average score that was higher than that of female students by 5 points. In 2000, there was no significant difference between the average score of male and female students.
- In 2005, Black students had an average score that was lower than that of White students by 34 points. In 2000, the average score for Black students was lower than that of White students by 31 points.
- In 2005, Hispanic students had an average score that was lower than that of White students by 18 points. Data are not reported for Hispanic students in 2000, because reporting standards were not met. Therefore, the performance gap results are not reported.
- In 2005, students who were eligible for free/reduced-price school lunch, an indicator of poverty, had an average score that was lower than that of students who were not eligible for free/reduced-price school lunch by 28 points. In 2000, the average score for students who were eligible for free/reduced-price school lunch was lower than the score of those not eligible by 27 points.
- In 2005, the score gap between students at the 75th percentile and students at the 25th percentile was 39 points. In 2000, the score gap between students at the 75th percentile and students at the 25th percentile was 39 points.

Science Scale Scores at Selected Percentiles

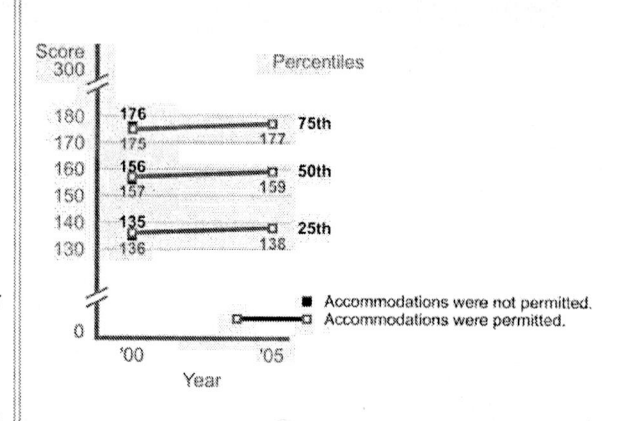

Percentile	'00	'05
75th	176	177
75th (accom.)	175	
50th	156	159
50th (accom.)	157	
25th	135	138
25th (accom.)	136	

Scores at selected percentiles on the NAEP science scale indicate how well students at lower, middle, and higher levels performed.

\# The estimate rounds to zero.   ‡ Reporting standards not met.
* Significantly different from 2005.   ↑ Significantly higher than 2000.   ↓ Significantly lower than 2000.

[1] Comparisons (higher/lower/not different) are based on statistical tests. The .05 level was used for testing statistical significance. Comparisons across jurisdictions and comparisons with the nation or within a jurisdiction across years may be affected by differences in exclusion rates for students with disabilities (SD) and English language learners (ELL). The exclusion rates for SD and ELL in Ohio were 3 percent and percentage rounds to zero in 2005, respectively. Statistical comparisons are calculated on the basis of unrounded scale scores or percentages.
[2] "Jurisdiction" refers to states and the Department of Defense Education Activity schools.

NOTE: Detail may not sum to totals because of rounding and because the "Information not available" category for free/reduced-price school lunch and the "Unclassifed" category for race/ethnicity are not displayed. Visit http://nces.ed.gov/nationsreportcard/states/ for additional results and detailed information.
SOURCE: U.S. Department of Education, Institute of Education Sciences, National Center for Education Statistics, National Assessment of Educational Progress (NAEP), 2000 and 2005 Science Assessments.

2005 Ohio NAEP Public School Snapshot
Grade 8 Mathematics

The National Assessment of Educational Progress (NAEP) assesses mathematics in five content areas: number properties and operations; measurement; geometry; data analysis and probability; and algebra. The NAEP mathematics scale ranges from 0 to 500.

Overall Mathematics Results for Ohio

- In 2005, the average scale score for eighth-grade students in Ohio was 283. This was not significantly different from[1] their average score in 2003 (282), and was higher than their average score in 1990 (264).
- Ohio's average score (283) in 2005 was higher than that of the Nation's public schools (278).
- Of the 52 states and other jurisdictions[2] that participated in the 2005 eighth-grade assessment, students' average scale scores in Ohio were higher than those in 24 jurisdictions, not significantly different from those in 21 jurisdictions, and lower than those in 6 jurisdictions.
- The percentage of students in Ohio who performed at or above the NAEP *Proficient* level was 33 percent in 2005. This percentage was not significantly different from that in 2003 (30 percent), and was greater than that in 1990 (15 percent).
- The percentage of students in Ohio who performed at or above the NAEP *Basic* level was 74 percent in 2005. This percentage was not significantly different from that in 2003 (74 percent), and was greater than that in 1990 (53 percent).

Student Percentage at NAEP Achievement Levels

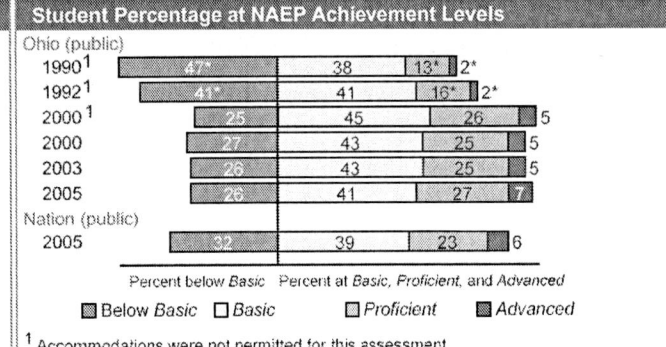

Ohio (public)
Year	Below Basic	Basic	Proficient	Advanced
1990[1]	47*	38	13*	2*
1992[1]	41*	41	16*	2*
2000[1]	25	45	26	5
2000	27	43	25	5
2003	26	43	25	5
2005	26	41	27	7

Nation (public)
Year	Below Basic	Basic	Proficient	Advanced
2005	32	39	23	6

Percent below *Basic* Percent at *Basic*, *Proficient*, and *Advanced*
■ Below *Basic* □ *Basic* □ *Proficient* ■ *Advanced*

[1] Accommodations were not permitted for this assessment.

NOTE: The NAEP mathematics achievement levels correspond to the following scale points: Below *Basic*, 261 or lower; *Basic*, 262–298; *Proficient*, 299–332; *Advanced*, 333 or above.

Performance of NAEP Reporting Groups in Ohio

Reporting groups	Percent of students	Average score	Percent below *Basic*	Percent at or above *Basic*	Percent at or above *Proficient*	Percent *Advanced*
Male	50	284	25	75	34	7
Female	50	282	26	74	32	6
White	80	289	19	81	38	8
Black	15	255	58	42	7	#
Hispanic	1	259	47	53	11	2
Asian/Pacific Islander	2	‡	‡	‡	‡	‡
American Indian/Alaska Native	#	‡	‡	‡	‡	‡
Eligible for free/reduced-price school lunch	30 ↑	265	45	55	16	1
Not eligible for free/reduced-price school lunch	64	290	18	82	39	8

Average Score Gaps Between Selected Groups

- In 2005, male students in Ohio had an average score that was not found to be significantly different from that of female students. In 1990, the average score for male students was higher than that of female students by 5 points.
- In 2005, Black students had an average score that was lower than that of White students by 34 points. In 1990, the average score for Black students was lower than that of White students by 35 points.
- In 2005, Hispanic students had an average score that was lower than that of White students by 30 points. Data are not reported for Hispanic students in 1990, because reporting standards were not met. Therefore, the performance gap data are not reported.
- In 2005, students who were eligible for free/reduced-price school lunch, an indicator of poverty, had an average score that was lower than that of students who were not eligible for free/reduced-price school lunch by 25 points. In 2000, the average score for students who were eligible for free/reduced-price school lunch was lower than the score of those not eligible by 30 points.
- In 2005, the score gap between students at the 75th percentile and students at the 25th percentile was 45 points. In 1990, the score gap between students at the 75th percentile and students at the 25th percentile was 45 points.

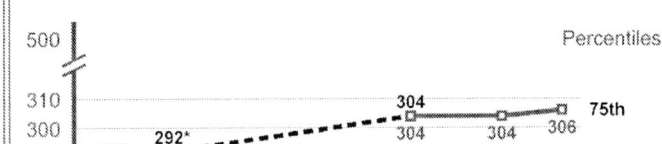

Mathematics Scale Scores at Selected Percentiles

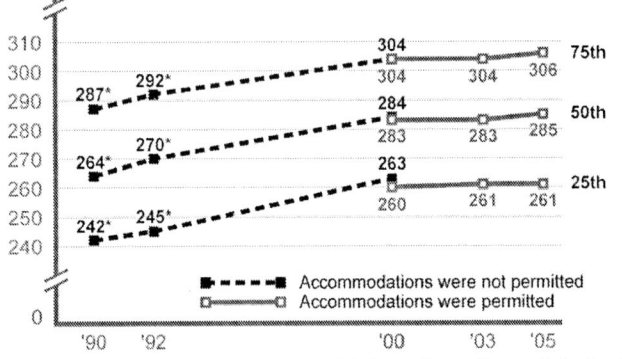

Percentile	'90	'92	'00	'03	'05
75th	287*	292*	304	304	306
50th	264*	270*	284	283	285
25th	242*	245*	263	260	261

■--■ Accommodations were not permitted
□—□ Accommodations were permitted

Scores at selected percentiles on the NAEP mathematics scale indicate how well students at lower, middle, and higher levels of the distribution performed.

\# The estimate rounds to zero.
* Significantly different from 2005.
‡ Reporting standards not met.
↑ Significantly higher than 2003. ↓ Significantly lower than 2003.

[1] Comparisons (higher/lower/not different) are based on statistical tests. The .05 level was used for testing statistical significance. Performance comparisons may be affected by differences in exclusion rates across years for students with disabilities (3% nationally in 2005) and English language learners (1% nationally in 2005) in the NAEP samples. Statistical comparisons are calculated on the basis of unrounded scale scores or percentages.
[2] "Other Jurisdictions" refers to the District of Columbia and the Department of Defense Education Activity schools.
NOTE: Detail may not sum to totals because of rounding and because the "Information not available" category for free/reduced-price lunch and the "Unclassified" category for race/ethnicity are not displayed. Visit http://nces.ed.gov/nationsreportcard/states/ for additional results and detailed information.
SOURCE: U.S. Department of Education, Institute of Education Sciences, National Center for Education Statistics, National Assessment of Educational Progress (NAEP), selected years, 1990–2005 Mathematics Assessments.

PROFILES OF OHIO / National Assessment of Educational Progress (NAEP)

2005 Ohio NAEP Public School Snapshot
Grade 8 Reading

The National Assessment of Educational Progress (NAEP) assesses reading in three content areas: reading for literary experience, to gain information, and to perform a task. The NAEP reading scale ranges from 0 to 500.

Overall Reading Results for Ohio

- In 2005, the average scale score for eighth-grade students in Ohio was 267. This was not significantly different from[1] their average score in 2003 (267), and was not significantly different from their average score in 2002 (268).
- Ohio's average score (267) in 2005 was higher than that of the Nation's public schools (260).
- Of the 52 states and other jurisdictions[2] that participated in the 2005 eighth-grade assessment, students' average scale scores in Ohio were higher than those in 25 jurisdictions, not significantly different from those in 23 jurisdictions, and lower than those in 3 jurisdictions.
- The percentage of students in Ohio who performed at or above the NAEP *Proficient* level was 36 percent in 2005. This percentage was not significantly different from that in 2003 (34 percent), and was not significantly different from that in 2002 (35 percent).
- The percentage of students in Ohio who performed at or above the NAEP *Basic* level was 78 percent in 2005. This percentage was not significantly different from that in 2003 (78 percent), and was not significantly different from that in 2002 (82 percent).

Student Percentage at NAEP Achievement Levels

Ohio (public)
- 2002: 18 | 46 | 33 | 3
- 2003: 22 | 44 | 31 | 3
- 2005: 22 | 42 | 32 | 4

Nation (public)
- 2005: 29 | 42 | 26 | 3

Percent below *Basic* | Percent at *Basic*, *Proficient*, and *Advanced*

■ Below *Basic* □ *Basic* ▨ *Proficient* ■ *Advanced*

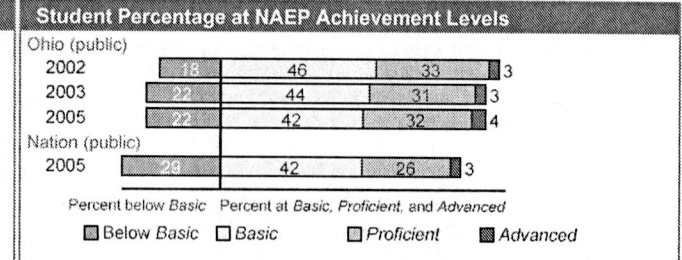

NOTE: The NAEP reading achievement levels correspond to the following scale points: Below *Basic*, 242 or lower; *Basic*, 243–280; *Proficient*, 281–322; *Advanced*, 323 or above.

Performance of NAEP Reporting Groups in Ohio

Reporting groups	Percent of students	Average score	Percent below *Basic*	Percent of students at or above *Basic*	Percent of students at or above *Proficient*	Percent *Advanced*
Male	49	261	27	73	30	3
Female	51	272	18	82	41	5
White	78	272	17	83	41	4
Black	17	243	46	54	10	#
Hispanic	2	245	47	53	14	#
Asian/Pacific Islander	1	‡	‡	‡	‡	‡
American Indian/Alaska Native	#	‡	‡	‡	‡	‡
Eligible for free/reduced-price school lunch	32↑	251	37	63	18	1
Not eligible for free/reduced-price school lunch	61	274	16	84	43	5

Average Score Gaps Between Selected Groups

- In 2005, male students in Ohio had an average score that was lower than that of female students by 11 points. In 2002, the average score for male students was lower than that of female students by 6 points.
- In 2005, Black students had an average score that was lower than that of White students by 29 points. Data are not reported for Black students in 2002, because reporting standards were not met. Therefore, the performance gap data are not reported.
- In 2005, Hispanic students had an average score that was lower than that of White students by 27 points. Data are not reported for Hispanic students in 2002, because reporting standards were not met. Therefore, the performance gap data are not reported.
- In 2005, students who were eligible for free/reduced-price school lunch, an indicator of poverty, had an average score that was lower than that of students who were not eligible for free/reduced-price school lunch by 23 points. In 2002, the average score for students who were eligible for free/reduced-price school lunch was lower than the score of those not eligible by 16 points.
- In 2005, the score gap between students at the 75th percentile and students at the 25th percentile was 45 points. This performance gap was wider than that of 2002 (39 points).

Reading Scale Scores at Selected Percentiles

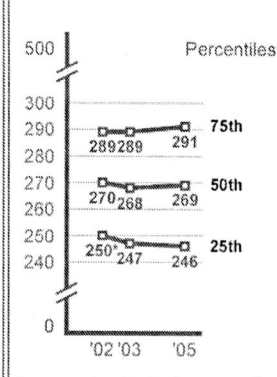

Percentiles:
- 75th: '02: 289, '03: 289, '05: 291
- 50th: '02: 270, '03: 268, '05: 269
- 25th: '02: 250*, '03: 247, '05: 246

Scores at selected percentiles on the NAEP reading scale indicate how well students at lower, middle, and higher levels of the distribution performed.

\# The estimate rounds to zero. ‡ Reporting standards not met.
* Significantly different from 2005. † Significantly higher than 2003. ↓ Significantly lower than 2003.

[1] Comparisons (higher/lower/not different) are based on statistical tests. The .05 level was used for testing statistical significance. Performance comparisons may be affected by differences in exclusion rates across years for students with disabilities (4% nationally in 2005) and English language learners (1% nationally in 2005) in the NAEP samples. Statistical comparisons are calculated on the basis of unrounded scale scores or percentages.
[2] "Other Jurisdictions" refers to the District of Columbia and the Department of Defense Education Activity schools.
NOTE: Detail may not sum to totals because of rounding and because the "Information not available" category for free/reduced-price lunch and the "Unclassifed" category for race/ethnicity are not displayed. Visit http://nces.ed.gov/nationsreportcard/states/ for additional results and detailed information.
SOURCE: U.S. Department of Education, Institute of Education Sciences, National Center for Education Statistics, National Assessment of Educational Progress (NAEP), selected years, 2002–2005 Reading Assessments.

2005 Ohio NAEP Public School Snapshot
Grade 8 Writing

The writing assessment of the National Assessment of Educational Progress (NAEP) measures narrative, informative, and persuasive writing–three purposes identified in the NAEP framework. The NAEP writing scale ranges from 0 to 300.

Overall Writing Results for Ohio

- The average scale score for eighth-grade students in Ohio was 160.
- Ohio's average score (160) was higher[1] than that of the nation's public schools (152).
- Students' average scale scores in Ohio were higher than those in 33 jurisdictions[2], and not significantly different from those in 13 jurisdictions.
- The percentage of students who performed at or above the NAEP *Proficient* level was 38 percent. The percentage of students who performed at or above the *Basic* level was 89 percent.

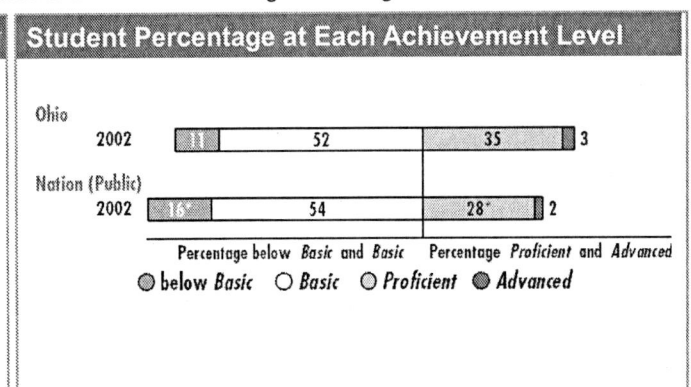

Student Percentage at Each Achievement Level

Ohio 2002: 11 | 52 | 35 | 3
Nation (Public) 2002: 16 | 54 | 28* | 2

Percentage below *Basic* and *Basic*   Percentage *Proficient* and *Advanced*
● below *Basic*   ○ *Basic*   ○ *Proficient*   ● *Advanced*

Performance of NAEP Reporting Groups in Ohio

Reporting groups	Percentage of students	Average Score	Below Basic	Basic	Proficient	Advanced
Male	50	150 ↑	15 ↓	59	25 ↑	1
Female	50	170 ↑	6 ↓	45	45 ↑	5
White	80	165 ↑	7 ↓	51	39 ↑	3
Black	15	133	29	57	14	1
Hispanic	2	---	---	---	---	---
Asian/Pacific Islander	1	---	---	---	---	---
American Indian/Alaska Native	#	---	---	---	---	---
Free/reduced-priced school lunch						
Eligible	24	144	22	55	22	1
Not eligible	65	167 ↑	6 ↓	50	41 ↑	3
Information not available	11	155	11	59	29	1

Average Score Gaps Between Selected Groups

- Female students in Ohio had an average score that was higher than that of male students (20 points). This performance gap was not significantly different from that of the Nation (21 points).
- White students had an average score that was higher than that of Black students (33 points). This performance gap was not significantly different from that of the Nation (25 points).
- The sample size was not sufficient to permit a reliable estimate for Hispanic students in Ohio.
- Students who were not eligible for free/reduced-price school lunch had an average score that was higher than that of students who were eligible (23 points). This performance gap was not significantly different from that of the Nation (25 points).

Writing Scale Scores at Selected Percentiles

Scale Score Distribution

	25th Percentile	50th Percentile	75th Percentile
Ohio	138 ↑	162 ↑	185 ↑
Nation (Public)	127	153	178

An examination of scores at different percentiles on the 0-300 NAEP writing scale at each grade indicates how well students at lower, middle, and higher levels of the distribution performed. For example, the data above shows that 75 percent of students in public schools nationally scored below *178*, while 75 percent of students in Ohio scored below *185*.

\# Percentage rounds to zero.
* Significantly different from Ohio.   ↑ Significantly higher than, ↓ lower than appropriate subgroup in the nation (public).
--- Reporting standards not met; sample size insufficient to permit a reliable estimate.
[1] Comparisons (higher/lower/not different) are based on statistical tests. The .05 level was used for testing statistical significance.
[2] "Jurisdictions" includes participating states and other jurisdictions (such as Guam or the District of Columbia).
NOTE: Detail may not sum to totals because of rounding. Score gaps are calculated based on differences between unrounded average scale scores. Performance changes across years should be interpreted in the context of changes in rates of exclusion of special-needs students, which occurred in some states. See *The Nation's Report Card: Writing 2002* for additional information.
Visit http://nces.ed.gov/nationsreportcard/states/ for additional results and detailed information.
SOURCE: U.S. Department of Education, Institute of Education Sciences, National Center for Education Statistics, National Assessment of Educational Progress (NAEP), 2002 Writing Assessment.

2005 Ohio NAEP Public School Snapshot
Grade 8 Science

The National Assessment of Educational Progress (NAEP) assesses science in two major dimensions: Fields of Science (Earth, Physical, and Life) and Knowing and Doing Science (Conceptual Understanding, Scientific Investigation, and Practical Reasoning). The NAEP science scale ranges from 0 to 300. Scales are created separately for each grade.

Overall Science Results for Ohio

- In 2005, the average scale score for eighth-grade students in Ohio was 155. This was not significantly different from their average score in 2000 (159).[1]
- Ohio's average score (155) in 2005 was higher than that of the nation's public schools (147).
- Of the 44 states and one jurisdiction that participated in the 2005 eighth-grade assessment, students' average scale score in Ohio was higher than those in 23 jurisdictions, not significantly different from those in 13 jurisdictions, and lower than those in 8 jurisdictions.[2]
- The percentage of students in Ohio who performed at or above the NAEP *Proficient* level was 35 percent in 2005. This percentage was not significantly different from that in 2000 (39 percent).
- The percentage of students in Ohio who performed at or above the NAEP *Basic* level was 67 percent in 2005. This percentage was not significantly different from that in 2000 (72 percent).

Student Percentages at NAEP Achievement Levels

	Below Basic	Basic	Proficient	Advanced
Ohio (public) 2000[1]	27*	32	35	6
Ohio (public) 2000	28	33	34	5
Ohio (public) 2005	33	32	31	4
Nation (public) 2005	43	30	24	3

[1] Accommodations were not permitted for this assessment.

NOTE: The NAEP grade 8 science achievement levels correspond to the following scale points: Below *Basic*, 142 or lower; *Basic*, 143–169; *Proficient*, 170–207; *Advanced*, 208 or above.

Performance of NAEP Reporting Groups in Ohio: 2005

Reporting groups	Percent of students	Average score	Percent below *Basic*	Percent of students at or above *Basic*	Percent of students at or above *Proficient*	Percent *Advanced*
Male	48	157	31	69	38	5
Female	52	154	34	66	33	3
White	79↓	162	25	75	41	5
Black	16↑	124	71	29	7	#
Hispanic	1	142	48	52	24	#
Asian/Pacific Islander	1	‡	‡	‡	‡	‡
American Indian/Alaska Native	#	‡	‡	‡	‡	‡
Eligible for free/reduced-price school lunch	31↑	134	59	41	13	#
Not eligible for free/reduced-price school lunch	62↓	165	21	79	45	6

Average Score Gaps Between Selected Groups

- In 2005, male students in Ohio had an average score that was not significantly different from that of female students. In 2000, the average score for male students was higher than that of female students by 5 points.
- In 2005, Black students had an average score that was lower than that of White students by 38 points. In 2000, the average score for Black students was lower than that of White students by 36 points.
- In 2005, Hispanic students had an average score that was lower than that of White students by 20 points. Data are not reported for Hispanic students in 2000, because reporting standards were not met. Therefore, the performance gap results are not reported.
- In 2005, students who were eligible for free/reduced-price school lunch, an indicator of poverty, had an average score that was lower than that of students who were not eligible for free/reduced-price school lunch by 31 points. In 2000, the average score for students who were eligible for free/reduced-price school lunch was lower than the score of those not eligible by 22 points.
- In 2005, the score gap between students at the 75th percentile and students at the 25th percentile was 43 points. In 2000, the score gap between students at the 75th percentile and students at the 25th percentile was 42 points.

Science Scale Scores at Selected Percentiles

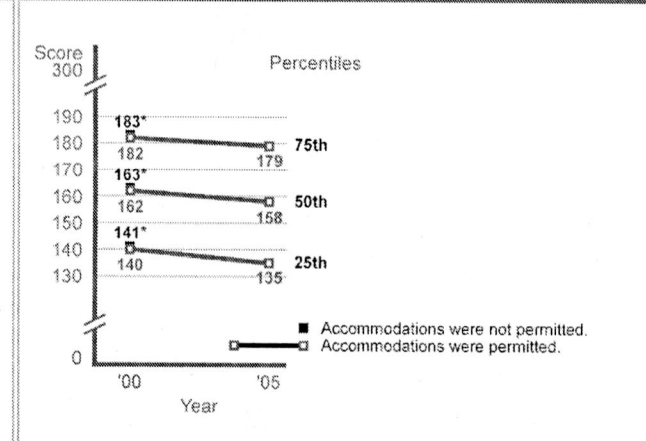

Percentile	'00	'05
75th	183* / 182	179
50th	163* / 162	158
25th	141* / 140	135

- Accommodations were not permitted.
- Accommodations were permitted.

Scores at selected percentiles on the NAEP science scale indicate how well students at lower, middle, and higher levels performed.

\# The estimate rounds to zero. ‡ Reporting standards not met.
* Significantly different from 2005. ↑ Significantly higher than 2000. ↓ Significantly lower than 2000.

[1] Comparisons (higher/lower/not different) are based on statistical tests. The .05 level was used for testing statistical significance. Comparisons across jurisdictions and comparisons with the nation or within a jurisdiction across years may be affected by differences in exclusion rates for students with disabilities (SD) and English language learners (ELL). The exclusion rates for SD and ELL in Ohio were 4 percent and percentage rounds to zero in 2005, respectively. Statistical comparisons are calculated on the basis of unrounded scale scores or percentages.
[2] "Jurisdiction" refers to states and the Department of Defense Education Activity schools.
NOTE: Detail may not sum to totals because of rounding and because the "Information not available" category for free/reduced-price school lunch and the "Unclassifed" category for race/ethnicity are not displayed. Visit http://nces.ed.gov/nationsreportcard/states/ for additional results and detailed information.
SOURCE: U.S. Department of Education, Institute of Education Sciences, National Center for Education Statistics, National Assessment of Educational Progress (NAEP), 2000 and 2005 Science Assessments.

March 2006 Ohio Achievement Tests
Summary of Parameters for Grades 3, 4 and 5

Parameter	Grade 3 Reading	Grade 3 Math	Grade 4 Reading	Grade 4 Math	Grade 4 Writing	Grade 5 Reading	Grade 5 Math
N-count	122,249	128,911	129,131	129,087	128,960	132,191	132,254
Max Raw Score	49	52	49	52	39	49	52
Max Scaled Score	520	520	525	549	516	542	547
Min Scaled Score	250	239	262	249	216	250	247
Raw Score Mean	34.57	38.26	32.29	32.51	24.04	31.38	27.12
Raw Score Standard Deviation	8.33	8.38	9.70	10.25	6.01	10.04	10.13
Raw Score SEM	3.02	3.04	3.23	3.44	3.82	3.18	3.44
Scaled Score Mean	415.07	418.43	419.72	421.70	423.70	422.04	407.38
Scaled Score Standard Deviation	27.99	29.28	29.94	32.70	24.99	34.85	30.94
Scaled Score SEM	10.15	10.61	9.98	10.99	15.90	11.04	10.51
Reliability	0.87	0.87	0.89	0.89	0.60	0.90	0.88

March 2006 Ohio Achievement Tests
Percentage of Students at Each Performance Level for Grades 3, 4 and 5

Standard	Grade 3 Reading Percent	Grade 3 Math Percent	Grade 4 Reading Percent	Grade 4 Math Percent	Grade 4 Writing Percent	Grade 5 Reading Percent	Grade 5 Math Percent
Advanced	28.4	20.2	6.1	18.4	3.0	16.4	17.7
Accelerated	23.9	17.4	25.2	21.4	26.7	16.8	15.2
Proficient	18.9	37.2	45.4	37.1	56.3	42.0	29.5
Basic	15.3	18.3	12.1	15.0	10.2	11.5	17.4
Limited	13.5	6.9	11.2	8.1	3.8	13.4	20.2

March 2006 Ohio Achievement Tests
Summary of Parameters for Grades 6, 7 and 8

	Grade 6		Grade 7		Grade 8	
Parameter	Reading	Math	Reading	Math	Reading	Math
N-count	135,582	135,645	141,190	141,030	141,369	141,290
Max Raw Score	49	50	47	50	48	46
Max Scaled Score	558	579	541	560	548	534
Min Scaled Score	274	233	274	271	267	290
Raw Score Mean	26.76	25.37	28.10	20.48	26.46	21.30
Raw Score Standard Deviation	9.30	9.91	9.70	9.59	9.58	9.35
Raw Score SEM	3.33	3.45	3.27	3.27	3.16	3.23
Scaled Score Mean	426.63	416.15	421.43	410.29	421.09	412.51
Scaled Score Standard Deviation	28.42	34.98	30.33	30.07	31.18	26.75
Scaled Score SEM	10.16	12.19	10.22	10.24	10.30	9.25
Reliability	0.87	0.88	0.89	0.88	0.89	0.88

March 2006 Ohio Achievement Tests
Percentage of Students at Each Performance Level for Grades 6, 7 and 8

	Grade 6		Grade 7		Grade 8	
	Reading	Math	Reading	Math	Reading	Math
Standard	Percent	Percent	Percent	Percent	Percent	Percent
Advanced	15.8	18.3	15.0	7.6	19.6	5.7
Accelerated	26.7	20.6	23.6	13.6	26.1	18.2
Proficient	41.2	29.4	40.3	41.8	31.4	44.5
Basic	11.2	18.6	13.1	26.6	13.1	21.9
Limited	5.1	13.2	8.1	10.4	9.9	9.7

March 2005 Proficiency Tests
Grade 4 Summary Statistics

	Mathematics	Citizenship	Science
N-Count	132,199	131,979	131,920
Reliability (Cronbach's alpha)	0.89	0.89	0.85
Raw Score Mean	39.05	43.12	36.15
Raw Score Standard Deviation	9.61	8.77	8.98
Raw Score SEM	3.19	2.91	3.48
Scaled Score Mean	228.47	230.68	223.36
Scaled Score Standard Deviation	31.17	28.44	40.62
Scaled Score SEM	10.34	9.43	15.73

March 2005 Proficiency Tests
Grade 6 Summary Statistics

	Writing	Reading	Mathematics	Citizenship	Science
N-Count	139,504	139,577	139,584	139,439	139,309
Reliability (Cronbach's alpha)	0.63*	0.87	0.92	0.92	0.89
Raw Score Mean	5.63	36.09	33.90	44.18	34.38
Raw Score Standard Deviation	1.59	8.65	13.07	12.39	10.97
Raw Score SEM	0.97	3.12	3.70	3.50	3.64
Scaled Score Mean	NA	233.80	211.36	219.17	211.44
Scaled Score Standard Deviation	NA	32.97	36.61	31.14	31.42
Scaled Score SEM	NA	11.89	10.35	8.81	10.42

*Taken from Generalizability study.

March 2005 Ohio Graduation Tests
Summary Statistics for Public and Non-Public Schools

	Reading	Math.	Writing	Science	Social Studies
N-count	148,518	148,614	147,751	147,790	147,306
Raw Score Minimum	0	0	0	0	0
Raw Score Maximum	48	46	48	48	48
Raw Score Mean	33.26	27.30	32.05	28.39	30.12
Raw Score Standard Deviation	9.37	9.56	7.42	9.20	10.13
Raw Score SEM	2.90	2.88	2.56	3.02	3.04
Scaled Score Minimum	268	260	250	211	231
Scaled Score Maximum	545	568	611	591	565
Scaled Score Mean	434.17	426.41	427.61	415.90	423.58
Scaled Score Standard Deviation	24.34	29.88	31.27	31.89	31.28
Scaled Score SEM	7.54	9.01	10.79	10.48	9.38
Reliability (Cronbach alpha)	0.904	0.909	0.881	0.892	0.910
Public Students	134,698	134,799	133,936	134,003	133,520
Non-public Students	13,820	13,815	13,815	13,787	13,786

March 2005 Ohio Graduation Tests
Summary Statistics for Public Schools

Reading

	Performance Level	Number	Percent	
Proficient or above:	Advanced	36,469	27.1	90.7
	Accelerated	46,790	34.7	
	Proficient	38,886	28.9	
Below proficient:	Basic	7,644	5.7	9.3
	Limited	4,909	3.6	

Mathematics

	Performance Level	Number	Percent	
Proficient or above:	Advanced	35,329	26.2	79.6
	Accelerated	33,434	24.8	
	Proficient	38,495	28.6	
Below proficient:	Basic	15,844	11.8	20.4
	Limited	11,697	8.7	

Writing

	Performance Level	Number	Percent	
Proficient or above:	Advanced	7,405	5.5	82.1
	Accelerated	56,254	42.0	
	Proficient	46,276	34.6	
Below proficient:	Basic	16,404	12.2	17.9
	Limited	7,597	5.7	

Science

	Performance Level	Number	Percent	
Proficient or above:	Advanced	22,115	16.5	70.9
	Accelerated	30,000	22.4	
	Proficient	42,844	32.0	
Below proficient:	Basic	25,212	18.8	29.1
	Limited	13,832	10.3	

Social Studies

	Performance Level	Number	Percent	
Proficient or above:	Advanced	29,924	22.4	77.5
	Accelerated	28,544	21.4	
	Proficient	44,947	33.7	
Below proficient:	Basic	16,297	12.2	22.5
	Limited	13,808	10.3	

Note: Percents may not add up to 100 percent due to rounding

PROFILES OF OHIO / Ancestry Rankings 423

Acadian/Cajun

Top 10 Places Sorted by Number
Based on all places, regardless of population

Place	Number	%
Cincinnati (city) Hamilton County	60	0.02
Columbus (city) Franklin County	41	0.01
Loveland (city) Hamilton County	29	0.24
Mansfield (city) Richland County	27	0.05
Barberton (city) Summit County	23	0.08
Beavercreek (city) Greene County	22	0.06
Hamilton (city) Butler County	20	0.03
Norwood (city) Hamilton County	15	0.07
Toledo (city) Lucas County	12	0.00
Chardon (village) Geauga County	11	0.21

Top 10 Places Sorted by Percent
Based on all places, regardless of population

Place	Number	%
Pioneer (village) Williams County	5	0.34
Loveland (city) Hamilton County	29	0.24
Chardon (village) Geauga County	11	0.21
Luckey (village) Wood County	2	0.20
Waynesville (village) Warren County	3	0.11
Wapakoneta (city) Auglaize County	9	0.10
Cortland (city) Trumbull County	7	0.10
New Carlisle (city) Clark County	6	0.10
Sebring (village) Mahoning County	5	0.10
Barberton (city) Summit County	23	0.08

Top 10 Places Sorted by Percent
Based on places with populations of 10,000 or more

Place	Number	%
Loveland (city) Hamilton County	29	0.24
Barberton (city) Summit County	23	0.08
Norwood (city) Hamilton County	15	0.07
Beavercreek (city) Greene County	22	0.06
Steubenville (city) Jefferson County	11	0.06
Mansfield (city) Richland County	27	0.05
Vandalia (city) Montgomery County	8	0.05
Shiloh (cdp) Montgomery County	6	0.05
Lebanon (city) Warren County	7	0.04
Mount Vernon (city) Knox County	6	0.04

Afghan

Top 10 Places Sorted by Number
Based on all places, regardless of population

Place	Number	%
Columbus (city) Franklin County	98	0.01
Upper Arlington (city) Franklin County	26	0.08
Cleveland (city) Cuyahoga County	18	0.00
Canton (city) Stark County	12	0.01
Mansfield (city) Richland County	7	0.01
Lakewood (city) Cuyahoga County	6	0.01
Cincinnati (city) Hamilton County	5	0.00
Turpin Hills (cdp) Hamilton County	4	0.08

Top 10 Places Sorted by Percent
Based on all places, regardless of population

Place	Number	%
Upper Arlington (city) Franklin County	26	0.08
Turpin Hills (cdp) Hamilton County	4	0.08
Columbus (city) Franklin County	98	0.01
Canton (city) Stark County	12	0.01
Mansfield (city) Richland County	7	0.01
Lakewood (city) Cuyahoga County	6	0.01
Cleveland (city) Cuyahoga County	18	0.00
Cincinnati (city) Hamilton County	5	0.00

Top 10 Places Sorted by Percent
Based on places with populations of 10,000 or more

Place	Number	%
Upper Arlington (city) Franklin County	26	0.08
Columbus (city) Franklin County	98	0.01
Canton (city) Stark County	12	0.01
Mansfield (city) Richland County	7	0.01
Lakewood (city) Cuyahoga County	6	0.01
Cleveland (city) Cuyahoga County	18	0.00
Cincinnati (city) Hamilton County	5	0.00

African American/Black

Top 10 Places Sorted by Number
Based on all places, regardless of population

Place	Number	%
Cleveland (city) Cuyahoga County	249,192	52.09
Columbus (city) Franklin County	185,173	26.03
Cincinnati (city) Hamilton County	145,615	43.95
Toledo (city) Lucas County	77,765	24.80
Dayton (city) Montgomery County	73,552	44.26
Akron (city) Summit County	64,530	29.73
Youngstown (city) Mahoning County	37,301	45.47
East Cleveland (city) Cuyahoga County	25,752	94.62
Cleveland Heights (city) Cuyahoga County	21,649	43.33
Canton (city) Stark County	18,537	22.94

Top 10 Places Sorted by Percent
Based on all places, regardless of population

Place	Number	%
Lincoln Heights (village) Hamilton County	4,058	98.66
East Cleveland (city) Cuyahoga County	25,752	94.62
Warrensville Heights (city) Cuyahoga County	13,863	91.75
Wilberforce (cdp) Greene County	1,391	88.09
North Randall (village) Cuyahoga County	668	73.73
Woodlawn (village) Hamilton County	1,951	69.28
Bedford Heights (city) Cuyahoga County	7,855	69.05
Highland Hills (village) Cuyahoga County	1,090	67.37
Golf Manor (village) Hamilton County	2,578	64.47
Trotwood (city) Montgomery County	16,405	59.83

Top 10 Places Sorted by Percent
Based on places with populations of 10,000 or more

Place	Number	%
East Cleveland (city) Cuyahoga County	25,752	94.62
Warrensville Heights (city) Cuyahoga County	13,863	91.75
Bedford Heights (city) Cuyahoga County	7,855	69.05
Trotwood (city) Montgomery County	16,405	59.83
Forest Park (city) Hamilton County	11,269	57.90
Cleveland (city) Cuyahoga County	249,192	52.09
Youngstown (city) Mahoning County	37,301	45.47
Maple Heights (city) Cuyahoga County	11,879	45.42
Dayton (city) Montgomery County	73,552	44.26
Cincinnati (city) Hamilton County	145,615	43.95

African American/Black: Not Hispanic

Top 10 Places Sorted by Number
Based on all places, regardless of population

Place	Number	%
Cleveland (city) Cuyahoga County	245,890	51.40
Columbus (city) Franklin County	183,224	25.75
Cincinnati (city) Hamilton County	144,770	43.70
Toledo (city) Lucas County	76,563	24.41
Dayton (city) Montgomery County	73,073	43.97
Akron (city) Summit County	64,073	29.52
Youngstown (city) Mahoning County	36,561	44.57
East Cleveland (city) Cuyahoga County	25,596	94.04
Cleveland Heights (city) Cuyahoga County	21,460	42.96
Canton (city) Stark County	18,353	22.71

Top 10 Places Sorted by Percent
Based on all places, regardless of population

Place	Number	%
Lincoln Heights (village) Hamilton County	4,043	98.30
East Cleveland (city) Cuyahoga County	25,596	94.04
Warrensville Heights (city) Cuyahoga County	13,799	91.33
Wilberforce (cdp) Greene County	1,376	87.14
North Randall (village) Cuyahoga County	663	73.18
Woodlawn (village) Hamilton County	1,945	69.07
Bedford Heights (city) Cuyahoga County	7,793	68.51
Highland Hills (village) Cuyahoga County	1,085	67.06
Golf Manor (village) Hamilton County	2,567	64.19
Trotwood (city) Montgomery County	16,342	59.60

Top 10 Places Sorted by Percent
Based on places with populations of 10,000 or more

Place	Number	%
East Cleveland (city) Cuyahoga County	25,596	94.04
Warrensville Heights (city) Cuyahoga County	13,799	91.33
Bedford Heights (city) Cuyahoga County	7,793	68.51
Trotwood (city) Montgomery County	16,342	59.60
Forest Park (city) Hamilton County	11,216	57.63
Cleveland (city) Cuyahoga County	245,890	51.40
Maple Heights (city) Cuyahoga County	11,798	45.11
Youngstown (city) Mahoning County	36,561	44.57
Dayton (city) Montgomery County	73,073	43.97
Cincinnati (city) Hamilton County	144,770	43.70

African American/Black: Hispanic

Top 10 Places Sorted by Number
Based on all places, regardless of population

Place	Number	%
Cleveland (city) Cuyahoga County	3,302	0.69
Columbus (city) Franklin County	1,949	0.27
Toledo (city) Lucas County	1,202	0.38
Lorain (city) Lorain County	1,039	1.51
Cincinnati (city) Hamilton County	845	0.26
Youngstown (city) Mahoning County	740	0.90
Dayton (city) Montgomery County	479	0.29
Akron (city) Summit County	457	0.21
Cleveland Heights (city) Cuyahoga County	189	0.38
Elyria (city) Lorain County	185	0.33

Top 10 Places Sorted by Percent
Based on all places, regardless of population

Place	Number	%
Linndale (village) Cuyahoga County	4	3.42
Lorain (city) Lorain County	1,039	1.51
Van Buren (village) Hancock County	4	1.28
Jeromesville (village) Ashland County	6	1.26
Latty (village) Paulding County	2	1.00
Wilberforce (cdp) Greene County	15	0.95
Belmont (village) Belmont County	5	0.94
Bloomingburg (village) Fayette County	8	0.92
Youngstown (city) Mahoning County	740	0.90
Campbell (city) Mahoning County	74	0.78

Top 10 Places Sorted by Percent
Based on places with populations of 10,000 or more

Place	Number	%
Lorain (city) Lorain County	1,039	1.51
Youngstown (city) Mahoning County	740	0.90
Cleveland (city) Cuyahoga County	3,302	0.69
East Cleveland (city) Cuyahoga County	156	0.57
Painesville (city) Lake County	97	0.55
Bedford Heights (city) Cuyahoga County	62	0.55
Warrensville Heights (city) Cuyahoga County	64	0.42
Fremont (city) Sandusky County	72	0.41
Defiance (city) Defiance County	65	0.39
Toledo (city) Lucas County	1,202	0.38

Notes: (cdp) census designated place; Refer to the User's Guide in the front of the book for more detailed information.

African, sub-Saharan

Top 10 Places Sorted by Number
Based on all places, regardless of population

Place	Number	%
Columbus (city) Franklin County	15,914	2.24
Cincinnati (city) Hamilton County	7,196	2.18
Cleveland (city) Cuyahoga County	6,075	1.27
Akron (city) Summit County	3,687	1.70
Toledo (city) Lucas County	2,947	0.94
Dayton (city) Montgomery County	2,179	1.31
Youngstown (city) Mahoning County	1,031	1.26
Canton (city) Stark County	978	1.21
Trotwood (city) Montgomery County	638	2.32
Mansfield (city) Richland County	613	1.24

Top 10 Places Sorted by Percent
Based on all places, regardless of population

Place	Number	%
Wilberforce (cdp) Greene County	89	6.24
Lockland (village) Hamilton County	134	3.61
North Randall (village) Cuyahoga County	33	3.61
Forest Park (city) Hamilton County	539	2.78
Whitehall (city) Franklin County	514	2.67
Golf Manor (village) Hamilton County	95	2.38
Warrensville Heights (city) Cuyahoga County	363	2.36
Trotwood (city) Montgomery County	638	2.32
Columbus (city) Franklin County	15,914	2.24
North Robinson (village) Crawford County	5	2.23

Top 10 Places Sorted by Percent
Based on places with populations of 10,000 or more

Place	Number	%
Forest Park (city) Hamilton County	539	2.78
Whitehall (city) Franklin County	514	2.67
Warrensville Heights (city) Cuyahoga County	363	2.36
Trotwood (city) Montgomery County	638	2.32
Columbus (city) Franklin County	15,914	2.24
Cincinnati (city) Hamilton County	7,196	2.18
Akron (city) Summit County	3,687	1.70
Springdale (city) Hamilton County	178	1.68
Sandusky (city) Erie County	447	1.60
Shiloh (cdp) Montgomery County	178	1.58

African, Subsaharan: African

Top 10 Places Sorted by Number
Based on all places, regardless of population

Place	Number	%
Columbus (city) Franklin County	8,924	1.25
Cincinnati (city) Hamilton County	6,339	1.92
Cleveland (city) Cuyahoga County	5,696	1.19
Akron (city) Summit County	3,525	1.62
Toledo (city) Lucas County	2,668	0.85
Dayton (city) Montgomery County	1,766	1.06
Youngstown (city) Mahoning County	960	1.17
Canton (city) Stark County	914	1.13
Lima (city) Allen County	575	1.43
Mansfield (city) Richland County	543	1.10

Top 10 Places Sorted by Percent
Based on all places, regardless of population

Place	Number	%
Wilberforce (cdp) Greene County	57	4.00
North Randall (village) Cuyahoga County	27	2.95
Golf Manor (village) Hamilton County	95	2.38
North Robinson (village) Crawford County	5	2.23
Warrensville Heights (city) Cuyahoga County	329	2.13
Cincinnati (city) Hamilton County	6,339	1.92
Sugar Bush Knolls (village) Portage County	4	1.90
Athalia (village) Lawrence County	6	1.84
Bainbridge (cdp) Geauga County	63	1.81
Fort McKinley (cdp) Montgomery County	68	1.76

Top 10 Places Sorted by Percent
Based on places with populations of 10,000 or more

Place	Number	%
Warrensville Heights (city) Cuyahoga County	329	2.13
Cincinnati (city) Hamilton County	6,339	1.92
Trotwood (city) Montgomery County	478	1.74
Akron (city) Summit County	3,525	1.62
Sandusky (city) Erie County	447	1.60
Forest Park (city) Hamilton County	299	1.54
Springdale (city) Hamilton County	158	1.49
Lima (city) Allen County	575	1.43
Shiloh (cdp) Montgomery County	142	1.26
Columbus (city) Franklin County	8,924	1.25

African, Subsaharan: Cape Verdean

Top 10 Places Sorted by Number
Based on all places, regardless of population

Place	Number	%
Columbus (city) Franklin County	59	0.01
Cincinnati (city) Hamilton County	27	0.01
Cleveland (city) Cuyahoga County	25	0.01
Alliance (city) Stark County	22	0.09
Athens (city) Athens County	16	0.08
Canton (city) Stark County	15	0.02
Bowling Green (city) Wood County	12	0.04
Pleasant Run Farm (cdp) Hamilton County	11	0.24
Euclid (city) Cuyahoga County	11	0.02
Akron (city) Summit County	11	0.01

Top 10 Places Sorted by Percent
Based on all places, regardless of population

Place	Number	%
Pleasant Run Farm (cdp) Hamilton County	11	0.24
East Canton (village) Stark County	3	0.18
Alliance (city) Stark County	22	0.09
Athens (city) Athens County	16	0.08
Lincoln Village (cdp) Franklin County	7	0.07
Bedford (city) Cuyahoga County	8	0.06
Bowling Green (city) Wood County	12	0.04
Troy (city) Miami County	9	0.04
Struthers (city) Mahoning County	4	0.03
Canton (city) Stark County	15	0.02

Top 10 Places Sorted by Percent
Based on places with populations of 10,000 or more

Place	Number	%
Alliance (city) Stark County	22	0.09
Athens (city) Athens County	16	0.08
Bedford (city) Cuyahoga County	8	0.06
Bowling Green (city) Wood County	12	0.04
Troy (city) Miami County	9	0.04
Struthers (city) Mahoning County	4	0.03
Canton (city) Stark County	15	0.02
Euclid (city) Cuyahoga County	11	0.02
Cleveland Heights (city) Cuyahoga County	9	0.02
Columbus (city) Franklin County	59	0.01

African, Subsaharan: Ethiopian

Top 10 Places Sorted by Number
Based on all places, regardless of population

Place	Number	%
Columbus (city) Franklin County	1,241	0.17
Whitehall (city) Franklin County	162	0.84
Cincinnati (city) Hamilton County	143	0.04
Dayton (city) Montgomery County	65	0.04
Cleveland (city) Cuyahoga County	43	0.01
Mansfield (city) Richland County	35	0.07
University Heights (city) Cuyahoga County	33	0.23
Grandview Heights (city) Franklin County	20	0.30
Oberlin (city) Lorain County	19	0.23
Shaker Heights (city) Cuyahoga County	18	0.06

Top 10 Places Sorted by Percent
Based on all places, regardless of population

Place	Number	%
Whitehall (city) Franklin County	162	0.84
Yellow Springs (village) Greene County	12	0.33
Grandview Heights (city) Franklin County	20	0.30
Sardinia (village) Brown County	2	0.24
University Heights (city) Cuyahoga County	33	0.23
Oberlin (city) Lorain County	19	0.23
North Randall (village) Cuyahoga County	2	0.22
Columbus (city) Franklin County	1,241	0.17
Mount Healthy Heights (cdp) Hamilton County	5	0.14
Aurora (city) Portage County	16	0.12

Top 10 Places Sorted by Percent
Based on places with populations of 10,000 or more

Place	Number	%
Whitehall (city) Franklin County	162	0.84
University Heights (city) Cuyahoga County	33	0.23
Columbus (city) Franklin County	1,241	0.17
Aurora (city) Portage County	16	0.12
Shiloh (cdp) Montgomery County	14	0.12
Mayfield Heights (city) Cuyahoga County	15	0.08
Mansfield (city) Richland County	35	0.07
Shaker Heights (city) Cuyahoga County	18	0.06
Cincinnati (city) Hamilton County	143	0.04
Dayton (city) Montgomery County	65	0.04

African, Subsaharan: Ghanian

Top 10 Places Sorted by Number
Based on all places, regardless of population

Place	Number	%
Columbus (city) Franklin County	731	0.10
Cincinnati (city) Hamilton County	54	0.02
Dayton (city) Montgomery County	43	0.03
Akron (city) Summit County	39	0.02
Fairfield (city) Butler County	28	0.07
Cleveland (city) Cuyahoga County	28	0.01
Fairlawn (city) Summit County	26	0.35
Cleveland Heights (city) Cuyahoga County	26	0.05
Wooster (city) Wayne County	25	0.10
Moreland Hills (village) Cuyahoga County	17	0.51

Top 10 Places Sorted by Percent
Based on all places, regardless of population

Place	Number	%
Berkey (village) Lucas County	3	1.15
Moreland Hills (village) Cuyahoga County	17	0.51
Fairlawn (city) Summit County	26	0.35
Columbus (city) Franklin County	731	0.10
Wooster (city) Wayne County	25	0.10
Wyoming (city) Hamilton County	8	0.10
Fairfield (city) Butler County	28	0.07
Blacklick Estates (cdp) Franklin County	7	0.07
Cleveland Heights (city) Cuyahoga County	26	0.05
Shaker Heights (city) Cuyahoga County	12	0.04

Top 10 Places Sorted by Percent
Based on places with populations of 10,000 or more

Place	Number	%
Columbus (city) Franklin County	731	0.10
Wooster (city) Wayne County	25	0.10
Fairfield (city) Butler County	28	0.07
Cleveland Heights (city) Cuyahoga County	26	0.05
Shaker Heights (city) Cuyahoga County	12	0.04
Bedford (city) Cuyahoga County	6	0.04
Dayton (city) Montgomery County	43	0.03

Notes: (cdp) census designated place; Refer to the User's Guide in the front of the book for more detailed information.

Place	Number	%
Mansfield (city) Richland County	15	0.03
North Olmsted (city) Cuyahoga County	11	0.03
Bowling Green (city) Wood County	8	0.03

African, Subsaharan: Kenyan

Top 10 Places Sorted by Number
Based on all places, regardless of population

Place	Number	%
Columbus (city) Franklin County	86	0.01
Cincinnati (city) Hamilton County	65	0.02
Reynoldsburg (city) Franklin County	45	0.14
Shaker Heights (city) Cuyahoga County	41	0.14
Pepper Pike (city) Cuyahoga County	31	0.51
Dayton (city) Montgomery County	23	0.01
Elyria (city) Lorain County	22	0.04
Toledo (city) Lucas County	19	0.01
Oberlin (city) Lorain County	18	0.22
Sylvania (city) Lucas County	15	0.08

Top 10 Places Sorted by Percent
Based on all places, regardless of population

Place	Number	%
Pepper Pike (city) Cuyahoga County	31	0.51
Oberlin (city) Lorain County	18	0.22
Jefferson (village) Ashtabula County	6	0.17
Reynoldsburg (city) Franklin County	45	0.14
Shaker Heights (city) Cuyahoga County	41	0.14
Ottawa Hills (village) Lucas County	5	0.11
Sylvania (city) Lucas County	15	0.08
Shiloh (cdp) Montgomery County	9	0.08
Elyria (city) Lorain County	22	0.04
Kent (city) Portage County	11	0.04

Top 10 Places Sorted by Percent
Based on places with populations of 10,000 or more

Place	Number	%
Reynoldsburg (city) Franklin County	45	0.14
Shaker Heights (city) Cuyahoga County	41	0.14
Sylvania (city) Lucas County	15	0.08
Shiloh (cdp) Montgomery County	9	0.08
Elyria (city) Lorain County	22	0.04
Kent (city) Portage County	11	0.04
Cincinnati (city) Hamilton County	65	0.02
Bowling Green (city) Wood County	6	0.02
Columbus (city) Franklin County	86	0.01
Dayton (city) Montgomery County	23	0.01

African, Subsaharan: Liberian

Top 10 Places Sorted by Number
Based on all places, regardless of population

Place	Number	%
Columbus (city) Franklin County	166	0.02
Toledo (city) Lucas County	64	0.02
Cleveland Heights (city) Cuyahoga County	52	0.10
Cleveland (city) Cuyahoga County	40	0.01
Kent (city) Portage County	37	0.13
Lakewood (city) Cuyahoga County	37	0.07
Trotwood (city) Montgomery County	27	0.10
Akron (city) Summit County	14	0.01
Warrensville Heights (city) Cuyahoga County	13	0.08
Euclid (city) Cuyahoga County	13	0.02

Top 10 Places Sorted by Percent
Based on all places, regardless of population

Place	Number	%
North Randall (village) Cuyahoga County	4	0.44
Ottawa Hills (village) Lucas County	11	0.24
Kent (city) Portage County	37	0.13
Harrison (city) Hamilton County	9	0.12
Cleveland Heights (city) Cuyahoga County	52	0.10
Trotwood (city) Montgomery County	27	0.10
Warrensville Heights (city) Cuyahoga County	13	0.08
Lakewood (city) Cuyahoga County	37	0.07
Green (city) Summit County	7	0.03
Columbus (city) Franklin County	166	0.02

Top 10 Places Sorted by Percent
Based on places with populations of 10,000 or more

Place	Number	%
Kent (city) Portage County	37	0.13
Cleveland Heights (city) Cuyahoga County	52	0.10
Trotwood (city) Montgomery County	27	0.10
Warrensville Heights (city) Cuyahoga County	13	0.08
Lakewood (city) Cuyahoga County	37	0.07
Green (city) Summit County	7	0.03
Columbus (city) Franklin County	166	0.02
Toledo (city) Lucas County	64	0.02
Euclid (city) Cuyahoga County	13	0.02
North Olmsted (city) Cuyahoga County	7	0.02

African, Subsaharan: Nigerian

Top 10 Places Sorted by Number
Based on all places, regardless of population

Place	Number	%
Columbus (city) Franklin County	813	0.11
Cincinnati (city) Hamilton County	232	0.07
Cleveland (city) Cuyahoga County	159	0.03
Dayton (city) Montgomery County	147	0.09
Toledo (city) Lucas County	135	0.04
Trotwood (city) Montgomery County	133	0.48
Forest Park (city) Hamilton County	132	0.68
University Heights (city) Cuyahoga County	93	0.66
Solon (city) Cuyahoga County	82	0.38
Youngstown (city) Mahoning County	71	0.09

Top 10 Places Sorted by Percent
Based on all places, regardless of population

Place	Number	%
Wilberforce (cdp) Greene County	22	1.54
Orange (village) Cuyahoga County	39	1.21
Ontario (village) Richland County	51	0.98
Albany (village) Athens County	7	0.85
Forest Park (city) Hamilton County	132	0.68
University Heights (city) Cuyahoga County	93	0.66
Forestville (cdp) Hamilton County	55	0.50
Trotwood (city) Montgomery County	133	0.48
Sebring (village) Mahoning County	20	0.41
The Plains (cdp) Athens County	12	0.41

Top 10 Places Sorted by Percent
Based on places with populations of 10,000 or more

Place	Number	%
Forest Park (city) Hamilton County	132	0.68
University Heights (city) Cuyahoga County	93	0.66
Forestville (cdp) Hamilton County	55	0.50
Trotwood (city) Montgomery County	133	0.48
Solon (city) Cuyahoga County	82	0.38
Sidney (city) Shelby County	63	0.31
Sharonville (city) Hamilton County	25	0.18
Sylvania (city) Lucas County	31	0.17
North College Hill (city) Hamilton County	13	0.13
Shiloh (cdp) Montgomery County	13	0.12

African, Subsaharan: Senegalese

Top 10 Places Sorted by Number
Based on all places, regardless of population

Place	Number	%
Columbus (city) Franklin County	95	0.01
Cincinnati (city) Hamilton County	26	0.01
Beachwood (city) Cuyahoga County	20	0.16
Fairborn (city) Greene County	20	0.06
Mansfield (city) Richland County	12	0.02
Wilberforce (cdp) Greene County	10	0.70
Lockland (village) Hamilton County	8	0.22
Upper Arlington (city) Franklin County	7	0.02
Cleveland (city) Cuyahoga County	5	0.00

Top 10 Places Sorted by Percent
Based on all places, regardless of population

Place	Number	%
Wilberforce (cdp) Greene County	10	0.70
Lockland (village) Hamilton County	8	0.22
Beachwood (city) Cuyahoga County	20	0.16
Fairborn (city) Greene County	20	0.06
Mansfield (city) Richland County	12	0.02
Upper Arlington (city) Franklin County	7	0.02
Columbus (city) Franklin County	95	0.01
Cincinnati (city) Hamilton County	26	0.01
Cleveland (city) Cuyahoga County	5	0.00

Top 10 Places Sorted by Percent
Based on places with populations of 10,000 or more

Place	Number	%
Beachwood (city) Cuyahoga County	20	0.16
Fairborn (city) Greene County	20	0.06
Mansfield (city) Richland County	12	0.02
Upper Arlington (city) Franklin County	7	0.02
Columbus (city) Franklin County	95	0.01
Cincinnati (city) Hamilton County	26	0.01
Cleveland (city) Cuyahoga County	5	0.00

African, Subsaharan: Sierra Leonean

Top 10 Places Sorted by Number
Based on all places, regardless of population

Place	Number	%
Columbus (city) Franklin County	88	0.01
Cincinnati (city) Hamilton County	32	0.01
Toledo (city) Lucas County	5	0.00
Willshire (village) Van Wert County	2	0.45

Top 10 Places Sorted by Percent
Based on all places, regardless of population

Place	Number	%
Willshire (village) Van Wert County	2	0.45
Columbus (city) Franklin County	88	0.01
Cincinnati (city) Hamilton County	32	0.01
Toledo (city) Lucas County	5	0.00

Top 10 Places Sorted by Percent
Based on places with populations of 10,000 or more

Place	Number	%
Columbus (city) Franklin County	88	0.01
Cincinnati (city) Hamilton County	32	0.01
Toledo (city) Lucas County	5	0.00

African, Subsaharan: Somalian

Top 10 Places Sorted by Number
Based on all places, regardless of population

Place	Number	%
Columbus (city) Franklin County	2,839	0.40
Blue Ash (city) Hamilton County	16	0.13
Toledo (city) Lucas County	12	0.00
Reynoldsburg (city) Franklin County	9	0.03
Bexley (city) Franklin County	7	0.05
Wooster (city) Wayne County	7	0.03
Urbancrest (village) Franklin County	4	0.48

Notes: (cdp) census designated place; Refer to the User's Guide in the front of the book for more detailed information.

426 PROFILES OF OHIO / Ancestry Rankings

Top 10 Places Sorted by Percent
Based on all places, regardless of population

Place	Number	%
Urbancrest (village) Franklin County	4	0.48
Columbus (city) Franklin County	2,839	0.40
Blue Ash (city) Hamilton County	16	0.13
Bexley (city) Franklin County	7	0.05
Reynoldsburg (city) Franklin County	9	0.03
Wooster (city) Wayne County	7	0.03
Toledo (city) Lucas County	12	0.00

Top 10 Places Sorted by Percent
Based on places with populations of 10,000 or more

Place	Number	%
Columbus (city) Franklin County	2,839	0.40
Blue Ash (city) Hamilton County	16	0.13
Bexley (city) Franklin County	7	0.05
Reynoldsburg (city) Franklin County	9	0.03
Wooster (city) Wayne County	7	0.03
Toledo (city) Lucas County	12	0.00

African, Subsaharan: South African

Top 10 Places Sorted by Number
Based on all places, regardless of population

Place	Number	%
Reynoldsburg (city) Franklin County	108	0.34
Beachwood (city) Cuyahoga County	55	0.45
Forest Park (city) Hamilton County	51	0.26
Columbus (city) Franklin County	50	0.01
Dublin (city) Franklin County	47	0.15
Loveland (city) Hamilton County	34	0.28
Landen (cdp) Warren County	31	0.25
Solon (city) Cuyahoga County	28	0.13
Richmond Heights (city) Cuyahoga County	27	0.25
Fostoria (city) Seneca County	27	0.19

Top 10 Places Sorted by Percent
Based on all places, regardless of population

Place	Number	%
Amelia (village) Clermont County	16	0.59
Peninsula (village) Summit County	3	0.58
Beachwood (city) Cuyahoga County	55	0.45
Moreland Hills (village) Cuyahoga County	13	0.39
Reynoldsburg (city) Franklin County	108	0.34
Loveland (city) Hamilton County	34	0.28
Turpin Hills (cdp) Hamilton County	14	0.28
Forest Park (city) Hamilton County	51	0.26
Landen (cdp) Warren County	31	0.25
Richmond Heights (city) Cuyahoga County	27	0.25

Top 10 Places Sorted by Percent
Based on places with populations of 10,000 or more

Place	Number	%
Beachwood (city) Cuyahoga County	55	0.45
Reynoldsburg (city) Franklin County	108	0.34
Loveland (city) Hamilton County	34	0.28
Forest Park (city) Hamilton County	51	0.26
Landen (cdp) Warren County	31	0.25
Richmond Heights (city) Cuyahoga County	27	0.25
Fostoria (city) Seneca County	27	0.19
Dublin (city) Franklin County	47	0.15
Solon (city) Cuyahoga County	28	0.13
Montgomery (city) Hamilton County	10	0.10

African, Subsaharan: Sudanese

Top 10 Places Sorted by Number
Based on all places, regardless of population

Place	Number	%
Whitehall (city) Franklin County	97	0.50
Brooklyn (city) Cuyahoga County	38	0.33
Cincinnati (city) Hamilton County	36	0.01
Cleveland Heights (city) Cuyahoga County	33	0.07
Xenia (city) Greene County	24	0.10
Columbus (city) Franklin County	22	0.00
Cleveland (city) Cuyahoga County	15	0.00
Euclid (city) Cuyahoga County	11	0.02
Wooster (city) Wayne County	8	0.03
Lima (city) Allen County	7	0.02

Top 10 Places Sorted by Percent
Based on all places, regardless of population

Place	Number	%
Whitehall (city) Franklin County	97	0.50
Woodmere (village) Cuyahoga County	3	0.36
Brooklyn (city) Cuyahoga County	38	0.33
Xenia (city) Greene County	24	0.10
Cleveland Heights (city) Cuyahoga County	33	0.07
Wooster (city) Wayne County	8	0.03
Euclid (city) Cuyahoga County	11	0.02
Lima (city) Allen County	7	0.02
Cincinnati (city) Hamilton County	36	0.01
Columbus (city) Franklin County	22	0.00

Top 10 Places Sorted by Percent
Based on places with populations of 10,000 or more

Place	Number	%
Whitehall (city) Franklin County	97	0.50
Brooklyn (city) Cuyahoga County	38	0.33
Xenia (city) Greene County	24	0.10
Cleveland Heights (city) Cuyahoga County	33	0.07
Wooster (city) Wayne County	8	0.03
Euclid (city) Cuyahoga County	11	0.02
Lima (city) Allen County	7	0.02
Cincinnati (city) Hamilton County	36	0.01
Columbus (city) Franklin County	22	0.00
Cleveland (city) Cuyahoga County	15	0.00

African, Subsaharan: Ugandan

Top 10 Places Sorted by Number
Based on all places, regardless of population

Place	Number	%
Cleveland Heights (city) Cuyahoga County	23	0.05
Groesbeck (cdp) Hamilton County	20	0.28
Hamilton (city) Butler County	19	0.03
Columbus (city) Franklin County	19	0.00
Cincinnati (city) Hamilton County	8	0.00
Lancaster (city) Fairfield County	7	0.02
Pepper Pike (city) Cuyahoga County	2	0.03

Top 10 Places Sorted by Percent
Based on all places, regardless of population

Place	Number	%
Groesbeck (cdp) Hamilton County	20	0.28
Cleveland Heights (city) Cuyahoga County	23	0.05
Hamilton (city) Butler County	19	0.03
Pepper Pike (city) Cuyahoga County	2	0.03
Lancaster (city) Fairfield County	7	0.02
Columbus (city) Franklin County	19	0.00
Cincinnati (city) Hamilton County	8	0.00

Top 10 Places Sorted by Percent
Based on places with populations of 10,000 or more

Place	Number	%
Cleveland Heights (city) Cuyahoga County	23	0.05
Hamilton (city) Butler County	19	0.03
Lancaster (city) Fairfield County	7	0.02
Columbus (city) Franklin County	19	0.00
Cincinnati (city) Hamilton County	8	0.00

African, Subsaharan: Zairian

Top 10 Places Sorted by Number
Based on all places, regardless of population

Place	Number	%

Top 10 Places Sorted by Percent
Based on all places, regardless of population

Place	Number	%

Top 10 Places Sorted by Percent
Based on places with populations of 10,000 or more

Place	Number	%

African, Subsaharan: Zimbabwean

Top 10 Places Sorted by Number
Based on all places, regardless of population

Place	Number	%
Columbus (city) Franklin County	82	0.01
Cincinnati (city) Hamilton County	19	0.01
Akron (city) Summit County	15	0.01
Cleveland Heights (city) Cuyahoga County	13	0.03
Kent (city) Portage County	8	0.03
Cleveland (city) Cuyahoga County	4	0.00
Waynesville (village) Warren County	2	0.08

Top 10 Places Sorted by Percent
Based on all places, regardless of population

Place	Number	%
Waynesville (village) Warren County	2	0.08
Cleveland Heights (city) Cuyahoga County	13	0.03
Kent (city) Portage County	8	0.03
Columbus (city) Franklin County	82	0.01
Cincinnati (city) Hamilton County	19	0.01
Akron (city) Summit County	15	0.01
Cleveland (city) Cuyahoga County	4	0.00

Top 10 Places Sorted by Percent
Based on places with populations of 10,000 or more

Place	Number	%
Cleveland Heights (city) Cuyahoga County	13	0.03
Kent (city) Portage County	8	0.03
Columbus (city) Franklin County	82	0.01
Cincinnati (city) Hamilton County	19	0.01
Akron (city) Summit County	15	0.01
Cleveland (city) Cuyahoga County	4	0.00

African, Subsaharan: Other

Top 10 Places Sorted by Number
Based on all places, regardless of population

Place	Number	%
Columbus (city) Franklin County	699	0.10
Cincinnati (city) Hamilton County	193	0.06
Dayton (city) Montgomery County	104	0.06
Lockland (village) Hamilton County	99	2.67
Sidney (city) Shelby County	54	0.27
Forest Park (city) Hamilton County	49	0.25
Whitehall (city) Franklin County	38	0.20
Cleveland (city) Cuyahoga County	29	0.01
Mount Carmel (cdp) Clermont County	19	0.44
Akron (city) Summit County	19	0.01

Top 10 Places Sorted by Percent
Based on all places, regardless of population

Place	Number	%
Lockland (village) Hamilton County	99	2.67
Vienna Center (cdp) Trumbull County	8	0.68

Notes: (cdp) census designated place; Refer to the User's Guide in the front of the book for more detailed information.

PROFILES OF OHIO / Ancestry Rankings

Place	Number	%
North Fork Village (cdp) Ross County	8	0.50
Mount Carmel (cdp) Clermont County	19	0.44
Mineral Ridge (cdp) Trumbull County	13	0.36
Sidney (city) Shelby County	54	0.27
Forest Park (city) Hamilton County	49	0.25
Moraine (city) Montgomery County	16	0.23
Oberlin (city) Lorain County	18	0.22
Whitehall (city) Franklin County	38	0.20

Top 10 Places Sorted by Percent
Based on places with populations of 10,000 or more

Place	Number	%
Sidney (city) Shelby County	54	0.27
Forest Park (city) Hamilton County	49	0.25
Whitehall (city) Franklin County	38	0.20
Springdale (city) Hamilton County	12	0.11
Columbus (city) Franklin County	699	0.10
Fremont (city) Sandusky County	17	0.10
Warrensville Heights (city) Cuyahoga County	12	0.08
Worthington (city) Franklin County	10	0.07
Cincinnati (city) Hamilton County	193	0.06
Dayton (city) Montgomery County	104	0.06

Alaska Native tribes, specified

Top 10 Places Sorted by Number
Based on all places, regardless of population

Place	Number	%
Columbus (city) Franklin County	44	0.01
Cleveland (city) Cuyahoga County	21	0.00
Cincinnati (city) Hamilton County	17	0.01
Akron (city) Summit County	14	0.01
Norwood (city) Hamilton County	13	0.06
Toledo (city) Lucas County	11	0.00
Parma (city) Cuyahoga County	10	0.01
Dayton (city) Montgomery County	8	0.00
Hamilton (city) Butler County	6	0.01
Ross (cdp) Butler County	5	0.25

Top 10 Places Sorted by Percent
Based on all places, regardless of population

Place	Number	%
West Manchester (village) Preble County	2	0.46
Cheshire (village) Gallia County	1	0.45
Eldorado (village) Preble County	2	0.37
Ross (cdp) Butler County	5	0.25
Brady Lake (village) Portage County	1	0.19
Lucas (village) Richland County	1	0.16
Bratenahl (village) Cuyahoga County	2	0.15
New Carlisle (city) Clark County	5	0.09
Fayette (village) Fulton County	1	0.07
Franklin Furnace (cdp) Scioto County	1	0.07

Top 10 Places Sorted by Percent
Based on places with populations of 10,000 or more

Place	Number	%
Norwood (city) Hamilton County	13	0.06
Bellefontaine (city) Logan County	4	0.03
Avon Lake (city) Lorain County	4	0.02
Bedford (city) Cuyahoga County	3	0.02
Columbus (city) Franklin County	44	0.01
Cincinnati (city) Hamilton County	17	0.01
Akron (city) Summit County	14	0.01
Parma (city) Cuyahoga County	10	0.01
Hamilton (city) Butler County	6	0.01
Fairborn (city) Greene County	4	0.01

Alaska Native: Alaska Athabascan

Top 10 Places Sorted by Number
Based on all places, regardless of population

Place	Number	%
Columbus (city) Franklin County	10	0.00
Cincinnati (city) Hamilton County	7	0.00
New Carlisle (city) Clark County	5	0.09
Cleveland (city) Cuyahoga County	5	0.00
Toledo (city) Lucas County	5	0.00
Trotwood (city) Montgomery County	3	0.01
Troy (city) Miami County	3	0.01
Northgate (cdp) Hamilton County	2	0.02
Dublin (city) Franklin County	2	0.01
Massillon (city) Stark County	2	0.01

Top 10 Places Sorted by Percent
Based on all places, regardless of population

Place	Number	%
Brady Lake (village) Portage County	1	0.19
Lucas (village) Richland County	1	0.16
New Carlisle (city) Clark County	5	0.09
Northgate (cdp) Hamilton County	2	0.02
Ada (village) Hardin County	1	0.02
Blanchester (village) Clinton County	1	0.02
Trotwood (city) Montgomery County	3	0.01
Troy (city) Miami County	3	0.01
Dublin (city) Franklin County	2	0.01
Massillon (city) Stark County	2	0.01

Top 10 Places Sorted by Percent
Based on places with populations of 10,000 or more

Place	Number	%
Trotwood (city) Montgomery County	3	0.01
Troy (city) Miami County	3	0.01
Dublin (city) Franklin County	2	0.01
Massillon (city) Stark County	2	0.01
Portsmouth (city) Scioto County	2	0.01
Aurora (city) Portage County	1	0.01
Coshocton (city) Coshocton County	1	0.01
Fostoria (city) Seneca County	1	0.01
Reading (city) Hamilton County	1	0.01
Columbus (city) Franklin County	10	0.00

Alaska Native: Aleut

Top 10 Places Sorted by Number
Based on all places, regardless of population

Place	Number	%
Norwood (city) Hamilton County	11	0.05
Akron (city) Summit County	8	0.00
Cincinnati (city) Hamilton County	6	0.00
Columbus (city) Franklin County	6	0.00
Bellefontaine (city) Logan County	4	0.03
Toledo (city) Lucas County	4	0.00
Fairborn (city) Greene County	3	0.01
Sidney (city) Shelby County	3	0.01
Dayton (city) Montgomery County	3	0.00
Cleveland (city) Cuyahoga County	2	0.00

Top 10 Places Sorted by Percent
Based on all places, regardless of population

Place	Number	%
Franklin Furnace (cdp) Scioto County	1	0.07
Norwood (city) Hamilton County	11	0.05
Lakemore (village) Summit County	1	0.04
Bellefontaine (city) Logan County	4	0.03
West Milton (village) Miami County	1	0.02
Wright-Patterson AFB (cdp) Montgomery County	1	0.02
Fairborn (city) Greene County	3	0.01
Sidney (city) Shelby County	3	0.01
Bedford (city) Cuyahoga County	1	0.01

Top 10 Places Sorted by Percent
Based on places with populations of 10,000 or more

Place	Number	%
Marietta (city) Washington County	1	0.01
Norwood (city) Hamilton County	11	0.05
Bellefontaine (city) Logan County	4	0.03
Fairborn (city) Greene County	3	0.01
Sidney (city) Shelby County	3	0.01
Bedford (city) Cuyahoga County	1	0.01
Marietta (city) Washington County	1	0.01
Miamisburg (city) Montgomery County	1	0.01
Akron (city) Summit County	8	0.00
Cincinnati (city) Hamilton County	6	0.00
Columbus (city) Franklin County	6	0.00

Alaska Native: Eskimo

Top 10 Places Sorted by Number
Based on all places, regardless of population

Place	Number	%
Columbus (city) Franklin County	16	0.00
Cleveland (city) Cuyahoga County	11	0.00
Ross (cdp) Butler County	5	0.25
Akron (city) Summit County	5	0.00
Delphos (city) Allen County	3	0.04
Dayton (city) Montgomery County	3	0.00
Youngstown (city) Mahoning County	3	0.00
Bratenahl (village) Cuyahoga County	2	0.15
Newton Falls (village) Trumbull County	2	0.04
Bedford (city) Cuyahoga County	2	0.01

Top 10 Places Sorted by Percent
Based on all places, regardless of population

Place	Number	%
Ross (cdp) Butler County	5	0.25
Bratenahl (village) Cuyahoga County	2	0.15
Glendale (village) Hamilton County	1	0.05
South Charleston (village) Clark County	1	0.05
Delphos (city) Allen County	3	0.04
Newton Falls (village) Trumbull County	2	0.04
North Kingsville (village) Ashtabula County	1	0.04
Obetz (village) Franklin County	1	0.03
Brookville (village) Montgomery County	1	0.02
West Milton (village) Miami County	1	0.02

Top 10 Places Sorted by Percent
Based on places with populations of 10,000 or more

Place	Number	%
Bedford (city) Cuyahoga County	2	0.01
North Olmsted (city) Cuyahoga County	2	0.01
Shaker Heights (city) Cuyahoga County	2	0.01
Berea (city) Cuyahoga County	1	0.01
Dover (city) Tuscarawas County	1	0.01
Maumee (city) Lucas County	1	0.01
Willowick (city) Lake County	1	0.01
Columbus (city) Franklin County	16	0.00
Cleveland (city) Cuyahoga County	11	0.00
Akron (city) Summit County	5	0.00

Alaska Native: Tlingit-Haida

Top 10 Places Sorted by Number
Based on all places, regardless of population

Place	Number	%
Columbus (city) Franklin County	11	0.00
Parma (city) Cuyahoga County	6	0.01
Avon Lake (city) Lorain County	4	0.02
Highland Heights (city) Cuyahoga County	3	0.04
Lakewood (city) Cuyahoga County	3	0.01
Cincinnati (city) Hamilton County	3	0.00
Cleveland (city) Cuyahoga County	3	0.00

Notes: (cdp) census designated place; Refer to the User's Guide in the front of the book for more detailed information.

PROFILES OF OHIO / Ancestry Rankings

Place	Number	%
North Ridgeville (city) Lorain County	2	0.01
Elyria (city) Lorain County	2	0.00
Hamilton (city) Butler County	2	0.00

Top 10 Places Sorted by Percent
Based on all places, regardless of population

Place	Number	%
Cheshire (village) Gallia County	1	0.45
Fayette (village) Fulton County	1	0.07
Highland Heights (city) Cuyahoga County	3	0.04
Amelia (village) Clermont County	1	0.04
Yellow Springs (village) Greene County	1	0.03
Avon Lake (city) Lorain County	4	0.02
Ada (village) Hardin County	1	0.02
Parma (city) Cuyahoga County	6	0.01
Lakewood (city) Cuyahoga County	3	0.01
North Ridgeville (city) Lorain County	2	0.01

Top 10 Places Sorted by Percent
Based on places with populations of 10,000 or more

Place	Number	%
Avon Lake (city) Lorain County	4	0.02
Parma (city) Cuyahoga County	6	0.01
Lakewood (city) Cuyahoga County	3	0.01
North Ridgeville (city) Lorain County	2	0.01
Columbus (city) Franklin County	11	0.00
Cincinnati (city) Hamilton County	3	0.00
Cleveland (city) Cuyahoga County	3	0.00
Elyria (city) Lorain County	2	0.00
Hamilton (city) Butler County	2	0.00
Middletown (city) Butler County	2	0.00

Alaska Native: All other tribes

Top 10 Places Sorted by Number
Based on all places, regardless of population

Place	Number	%
Hamilton (city) Butler County	3	0.00
Parma (city) Cuyahoga County	3	0.00
West Manchester (village) Preble County	2	0.46
Eldorado (village) Preble County	2	0.37
Brookville (village) Montgomery County	1	0.02
Columbus (city) Franklin County	1	0.00
Grove City (city) Franklin County	1	0.00
Norwood (city) Hamilton County	1	0.00
Springfield (city) Clark County	1	0.00

Top 10 Places Sorted by Percent
Based on all places, regardless of population

Place	Number	%
West Manchester (village) Preble County	2	0.46
Eldorado (village) Preble County	2	0.37
Brookville (village) Montgomery County	1	0.02
Hamilton (city) Butler County	3	0.00
Parma (city) Cuyahoga County	3	0.00
Columbus (city) Franklin County	1	0.00
Grove City (city) Franklin County	1	0.00
Norwood (city) Hamilton County	1	0.00
Springfield (city) Clark County	1	0.00

Top 10 Places Sorted by Percent
Based on places with populations of 10,000 or more

Place	Number	%
Hamilton (city) Butler County	3	0.00
Parma (city) Cuyahoga County	3	0.00
Columbus (city) Franklin County	1	0.00
Grove City (city) Franklin County	1	0.00
Norwood (city) Hamilton County	1	0.00
Springfield (city) Clark County	1	0.00

Alaska Native tribes, not specified

Top 10 Places Sorted by Number
Based on all places, regardless of population

Place	Number	%
Dayton (city) Montgomery County	4	0.00
Toledo (city) Lucas County	4	0.00
Masury (cdp) Trumbull County	3	0.11
Monfort Heights South (cdp) Hamilton County	3	0.07
Cambridge (city) Guernsey County	3	0.03
Akron (city) Summit County	3	0.00
Portsmouth (city) Scioto County	2	0.01
Lakewood (city) Cuyahoga County	2	0.00
Mount Gilead (village) Morrow County	1	0.03
Ontario (village) Richland County	1	0.02

Top 10 Places Sorted by Percent
Based on all places, regardless of population

Place	Number	%
Masury (cdp) Trumbull County	3	0.11
Monfort Heights South (cdp) Hamilton County	3	0.07
Cambridge (city) Guernsey County	3	0.03
Mount Gilead (village) Morrow County	1	0.03
Ontario (village) Richland County	1	0.02
Portsmouth (city) Scioto County	2	0.01
Broadview Heights (city) Cuyahoga County	1	0.01
Conneaut (city) Ashtabula County	1	0.01
Grandview Heights (city) Franklin County	1	0.01
Marietta (city) Washington County	1	0.01

Top 10 Places Sorted by Percent
Based on places with populations of 10,000 or more

Place	Number	%
Cambridge (city) Guernsey County	3	0.03
Portsmouth (city) Scioto County	2	0.01
Broadview Heights (city) Cuyahoga County	1	0.01
Conneaut (city) Ashtabula County	1	0.01
Marietta (city) Washington County	1	0.01
Vandalia (city) Montgomery County	1	0.01
Dayton (city) Montgomery County	4	0.00
Toledo (city) Lucas County	4	0.00
Akron (city) Summit County	3	0.00
Lakewood (city) Cuyahoga County	2	0.00

American Indian or Alaska Native, not specified

Top 10 Places Sorted by Number
Based on all places, regardless of population

Place	Number	%
Columbus (city) Franklin County	2,805	0.39
Cleveland (city) Cuyahoga County	1,858	0.39
Toledo (city) Lucas County	1,213	0.39
Cincinnati (city) Hamilton County	1,033	0.31
Akron (city) Summit County	792	0.36
Dayton (city) Montgomery County	677	0.41
Canton (city) Stark County	431	0.53
Youngstown (city) Mahoning County	361	0.44
Lorain (city) Lorain County	308	0.45
Springfield (city) Clark County	299	0.46

Top 10 Places Sorted by Percent
Based on all places, regardless of population

Place	Number	%
Clifton (village) Greene County	8	4.47
Rome (village) Adams County	5	4.27
Jacksonburg (village) Butler County	2	2.99
Rarden (village) Scioto County	5	2.84
Kimbolton (village) Guernsey County	5	2.63
Milton Center (village) Wood County	5	2.56
Port William (village) Clinton County	6	2.33
Catawba (village) Clark County	7	2.24

Place	Number	%
Jeromesville (village) Ashland County	8	1.67
North Fairfield (village) Huron County	9	1.57

Top 10 Places Sorted by Percent
Based on places with populations of 10,000 or more

Place	Number	%
Portsmouth (city) Scioto County	132	0.63
Zanesville (city) Muskingum County	149	0.58
Canton (city) Stark County	431	0.53
Whitehall (city) Franklin County	97	0.51
Chillicothe (city) Ross County	108	0.50
Warrensville Heights (city) Cuyahoga County	74	0.49
Cambridge (city) Guernsey County	57	0.49
Springfield (city) Clark County	299	0.46
East Cleveland (city) Cuyahoga County	125	0.46
Lorain (city) Lorain County	308	0.45

Albanian

Top 10 Places Sorted by Number
Based on all places, regardless of population

Place	Number	%
Lakewood (city) Cuyahoga County	593	1.05
Cleveland (city) Cuyahoga County	225	0.05
Akron (city) Summit County	160	0.07
Cincinnati (city) Hamilton County	155	0.05
Mansfield (city) Richland County	149	0.30
Columbus (city) Franklin County	133	0.02
Massillon (city) Stark County	87	0.28
Niles (city) Trumbull County	74	0.35
Parma (city) Cuyahoga County	70	0.08
Mason (city) Warren County	58	0.26

Top 10 Places Sorted by Percent
Based on all places, regardless of population

Place	Number	%
Lakewood (city) Cuyahoga County	593	1.05
Enon (village) Clark County	26	0.98
Harbor Hills (cdp) Licking County	9	0.73
New Franklin (village) Summit County	13	0.62
Kelleys Island (village) Erie County	2	0.58
Ottawa Hills (village) Lucas County	22	0.48
Peninsula (village) Summit County	2	0.39
Tipp City (city) Miami County	35	0.38
Gloria Glens Park (village) Medina County	2	0.38
Midvale (village) Tuscarawas County	2	0.38

Top 10 Places Sorted by Percent
Based on places with populations of 10,000 or more

Place	Number	%
Lakewood (city) Cuyahoga County	593	1.05
Niles (city) Trumbull County	74	0.35
Avon (city) Lorain County	35	0.31
Reading (city) Hamilton County	35	0.31
Mansfield (city) Richland County	149	0.30
Massillon (city) Stark County	87	0.28
Mason (city) Warren County	58	0.26
Rocky River (city) Cuyahoga County	51	0.25
Berea (city) Cuyahoga County	32	0.17
Wickliffe (city) Lake County	16	0.12

Alsatian

Top 10 Places Sorted by Number
Based on all places, regardless of population

Place	Number	%
Cleveland (city) Cuyahoga County	41	0.01
Akron (city) Summit County	35	0.02
Cincinnati (city) Hamilton County	31	0.01
Toledo (city) Lucas County	28	0.01
Columbus (city) Franklin County	23	0.00
Hudson (city) Summit County	22	0.10

Notes: (cdp) census designated place; Refer to the User's Guide in the front of the book for more detailed information.

PROFILES OF OHIO / Ancestry Rankings 429

Place	Number	%
Wauseon (city) Fulton County	21	0.30
Centerville (city) Montgomery County	18	0.08
Worthington (city) Franklin County	16	0.11
Cuyahoga Falls (city) Summit County	14	0.03

Top 10 Places Sorted by Percent
Based on all places, regardless of population

Place	Number	%
Kirtland Hills (village) Lake County	5	0.83
Bay View (village) Erie County	3	0.43
Wauseon (city) Fulton County	21	0.30
Groveport (village) Franklin County	9	0.23
Silver Lake (village) Summit County	7	0.23
Clinton (village) Summit County	3	0.23
Fairfax (village) Hamilton County	4	0.21
Canal Fulton (village) Stark County	9	0.18
Beach City (village) Stark County	2	0.18
White Oak West (cdp) Hamilton County	5	0.17

Top 10 Places Sorted by Percent
Based on places with populations of 10,000 or more

Place	Number	%
Worthington (city) Franklin County	16	0.11
Hudson (city) Summit County	22	0.10
Washington (city) Fayette County	13	0.10
Montgomery (city) Hamilton County	10	0.10
Centerville (city) Montgomery County	18	0.08
Loveland (city) Hamilton County	10	0.08
Coshocton (city) Coshocton County	8	0.07
Fremont (city) Sandusky County	10	0.06
Seven Hills (city) Cuyahoga County	7	0.06
South Euclid (city) Cuyahoga County	11	0.05

American Indian tribes, specified

Top 10 Places Sorted by Number
Based on all places, regardless of population

Place	Number	%
Columbus (city) Franklin County	4,012	0.56
Cleveland (city) Cuyahoga County	2,235	0.47
Toledo (city) Lucas County	1,665	0.53
Cincinnati (city) Hamilton County	1,458	0.44
Akron (city) Summit County	1,187	0.55
Dayton (city) Montgomery County	869	0.52
Canton (city) Stark County	812	1.00
Lorain (city) Lorain County	504	0.73
Youngstown (city) Mahoning County	484	0.59
Springfield (city) Clark County	430	0.66

Top 10 Places Sorted by Percent
Based on all places, regardless of population

Place	Number	%
Wilkesville (village) Vinton County	7	4.64
Congress (village) Wayne County	8	4.17
Linndale (village) Cuyahoga County	4	3.42
Rarden (village) Scioto County	6	3.41
Bairdstown (village) Wood County	4	3.08
Latty (village) Paulding County	6	3.00
Nellie (village) Coshocton County	4	2.99
West Leipsic (village) Putnam County	8	2.95
Hamden (village) Vinton County	25	2.87
Amesville (village) Athens County	5	2.72

Top 10 Places Sorted by Percent
Based on places with populations of 10,000 or more

Place	Number	%
Portsmouth (city) Scioto County	225	1.08
Canton (city) Stark County	812	1.00
Celina (city) Mercer County	88	0.85
Chillicothe (city) Ross County	184	0.84
Fairborn (city) Greene County	241	0.75
Lorain (city) Lorain County	504	0.73
Elyria (city) Lorain County	408	0.73
Zanesville (city) Muskingum County	180	0.70
Xenia (city) Greene County	167	0.69
Norwood (city) Hamilton County	149	0.69

American Indian: Apache

Top 10 Places Sorted by Number
Based on all places, regardless of population

Place	Number	%
Columbus (city) Franklin County	121	0.02
Cleveland (city) Cuyahoga County	56	0.01
Toledo (city) Lucas County	53	0.02
Cincinnati (city) Hamilton County	36	0.01
Canton (city) Stark County	33	0.04
Akron (city) Summit County	20	0.01
Dayton (city) Montgomery County	18	0.01
Lorain (city) Lorain County	15	0.02
Springfield (city) Clark County	15	0.02
Parma (city) Cuyahoga County	14	0.02

Top 10 Places Sorted by Percent
Based on all places, regardless of population

Place	Number	%
Lyons (village) Fulton County	4	0.72
Thurston (village) Fairfield County	3	0.54
Belle Valley (village) Noble County	1	0.38
Jamestown (village) Greene County	7	0.37
Wayne (village) Wood County	3	0.36
Lore City (village) Guernsey County	1	0.33
Lucasville (cdp) Scioto County	5	0.31
Edison (village) Morrow County	1	0.23
Fayette (village) Fulton County	3	0.22
Pemberville (village) Wood County	3	0.22

Top 10 Places Sorted by Percent
Based on places with populations of 10,000 or more

Place	Number	%
Celina (city) Mercer County	7	0.07
Sandusky (city) Erie County	13	0.05
Urbana (city) Champaign County	6	0.05
Canton (city) Stark County	33	0.04
Zanesville (city) Muskingum County	11	0.04
Tiffin (city) Seneca County	7	0.04
Fostoria (city) Seneca County	5	0.04
Northbrook (cdp) Hamilton County	4	0.04
Shiloh (cdp) Montgomery County	4	0.04
Huber Heights (city) Montgomery County	10	0.03

American Indian: Blackfeet

Top 10 Places Sorted by Number
Based on all places, regardless of population

Place	Number	%
Columbus (city) Franklin County	407	0.06
Cleveland (city) Cuyahoga County	271	0.06
Toledo (city) Lucas County	175	0.06
Akron (city) Summit County	155	0.07
Cincinnati (city) Hamilton County	143	0.04
Dayton (city) Montgomery County	70	0.04
Elyria (city) Lorain County	58	0.10
Canton (city) Stark County	49	0.06
Lorain (city) Lorain County	48	0.07
Cleveland Heights (city) Cuyahoga County	40	0.08

Top 10 Places Sorted by Percent
Based on all places, regardless of population

Place	Number	%
Kimbolton (village) Guernsey County	3	1.58
Congress (village) Wayne County	3	1.56
Galena (village) Delaware County	4	1.31
Butlerville (village) Warren County	3	1.30

Place	Number	%
Marshallville (village) Wayne County	7	0.85
Beallsville (village) Monroe County	3	0.71
Hamden (village) Vinton County	6	0.69
Byesville (village) Guernsey County	14	0.54
Lyons (village) Fulton County	3	0.54
Mowrystown (village) Highland County	2	0.54

Top 10 Places Sorted by Percent
Based on places with populations of 10,000 or more

Place	Number	%
Bellefontaine (city) Logan County	18	0.14
Painesville (city) Lake County	21	0.12
Conneaut (city) Ashtabula County	14	0.11
Elyria (city) Lorain County	58	0.10
Ashtabula (city) Ashtabula County	20	0.10
Portsmouth (city) Scioto County	20	0.10
East Cleveland (city) Cuyahoga County	24	0.09
Sandusky (city) Erie County	24	0.09
Cleveland Heights (city) Cuyahoga County	40	0.08
Bucyrus (city) Crawford County	11	0.08

American Indian: Cherokee

Top 10 Places Sorted by Number
Based on all places, regardless of population

Place	Number	%
Columbus (city) Franklin County	2,100	0.30
Cleveland (city) Cuyahoga County	984	0.21
Toledo (city) Lucas County	763	0.24
Cincinnati (city) Hamilton County	756	0.23
Akron (city) Summit County	662	0.30
Dayton (city) Montgomery County	490	0.29
Canton (city) Stark County	389	0.48
Youngstown (city) Mahoning County	295	0.36
Lorain (city) Lorain County	262	0.38
Springfield (city) Clark County	249	0.38

Top 10 Places Sorted by Percent
Based on all places, regardless of population

Place	Number	%
Bairdstown (village) Wood County	4	3.08
Nellie (village) Coshocton County	4	2.99
Wilkesville (village) Vinton County	4	2.65
Congress (village) Wayne County	5	2.60
Alvordton (village) Williams County	7	2.30
Rarden (village) Scioto County	4	2.27
Rendville (village) Perry County	1	2.17
Beaver (village) Pike County	10	2.16
Hemlock (village) Perry County	3	2.11
Chesterville (village) Morrow County	4	2.07

Top 10 Places Sorted by Percent
Based on places with populations of 10,000 or more

Place	Number	%
Portsmouth (city) Scioto County	126	0.60
Canton (city) Stark County	389	0.48
Chillicothe (city) Ross County	102	0.47
Fairborn (city) Greene County	145	0.45
Celina (city) Mercer County	46	0.45
Norwood (city) Hamilton County	95	0.44
Mansfield (city) Richland County	206	0.42
Zanesville (city) Muskingum County	103	0.40
Lorain (city) Lorain County	262	0.38
Springfield (city) Clark County	249	0.38

American Indian: Cheyenne

Top 10 Places Sorted by Number
Based on all places, regardless of population

Place	Number	%
Columbus (city) Franklin County	32	0.00
Cleveland (city) Cuyahoga County	19	0.00

Notes: (cdp) census designated place; Refer to the User's Guide in the front of the book for more detailed information.

Place	Number	%
Akron (city) Summit County	11	0.01
Youngstown (city) Mahoning County	10	0.01
Toledo (city) Lucas County	10	0.00
Cincinnati (city) Hamilton County	9	0.00
Norwood (city) Hamilton County	6	0.03
Lorain (city) Lorain County	6	0.01
New Vienna (village) Clinton County	5	0.39
Brook Park (city) Cuyahoga County	5	0.02

Top 10 Places Sorted by Percent
Based on all places, regardless of population

Place	Number	%
Gettysburg (village) Darke County	4	0.72
New Vienna (village) Clinton County	5	0.39
Anna (village) Shelby County	3	0.23
Piketon (village) Pike County	3	0.16
Stony Prairie (cdp) Sandusky County	1	0.12
Lakemore (village) Summit County	2	0.08
Wellsville (village) Columbiana County	3	0.07
Martins Ferry (city) Belmont County	4	0.06
Granville (village) Licking County	2	0.06
New Middletown (village) Mahoning County	1	0.06

Top 10 Places Sorted by Percent
Based on places with populations of 10,000 or more

Place	Number	%
Springdale (city) Hamilton County	4	0.04
Norwood (city) Hamilton County	6	0.03
Norton (city) Summit County	4	0.03
Brook Park (city) Cuyahoga County	5	0.02
Portsmouth (city) Scioto County	4	0.02
Marietta (city) Washington County	3	0.02
Whitehall (city) Franklin County	3	0.02
Amherst (city) Lorain County	2	0.02
Bedford Heights (city) Cuyahoga County	2	0.02
Akron (city) Summit County	11	0.01

American Indian: Chickasaw

Top 10 Places Sorted by Number
Based on all places, regardless of population

Place	Number	%
Columbus (city) Franklin County	16	0.00
Cleveland (city) Cuyahoga County	11	0.00
Cincinnati (city) Hamilton County	10	0.00
Akron (city) Summit County	7	0.00
Galion (city) Crawford County	5	0.04
Hamilton (city) Butler County	5	0.01
Dillonvale (cdp) Hamilton County	4	0.11
Oxford (city) Butler County	4	0.02
Canton (city) Stark County	4	0.00
Amanda (village) Fairfield County	3	0.42

Top 10 Places Sorted by Percent
Based on all places, regardless of population

Place	Number	%
Latty (village) Paulding County	2	1.00
Donnelsville (village) Clark County	2	0.68
Amanda (village) Fairfield County	3	0.42
Midland (village) Clinton County	1	0.38
Clarksville (village) Clinton County	1	0.20
Manchester (village) Adams County	3	0.15
Dillonvale (cdp) Hamilton County	4	0.11
Fruit Hill (cdp) Hamilton County	3	0.08
North Baltimore (village) Wood County	2	0.06
Carey (village) Wyandot County	2	0.05

Top 10 Places Sorted by Percent
Based on places with populations of 10,000 or more

Place	Number	%
Galion (city) Crawford County	5	0.04
Brooklyn (city) Cuyahoga County	3	0.03

Place	Number	%
Oxford (city) Butler County	4	0.02
Hamilton (city) Butler County	5	0.01
Barberton (city) Summit County	3	0.01
Centerville (city) Montgomery County	3	0.01
East Cleveland (city) Cuyahoga County	3	0.01
Fairfield (city) Butler County	3	0.01
Garfield Heights (city) Cuyahoga County	3	0.01
Kent (city) Portage County	3	0.01

American Indian: Chippewa

Top 10 Places Sorted by Number
Based on all places, regardless of population

Place	Number	%
Toledo (city) Lucas County	105	0.03
Columbus (city) Franklin County	90	0.01
Cleveland (city) Cuyahoga County	77	0.02
Akron (city) Summit County	34	0.02
Cincinnati (city) Hamilton County	29	0.01
Canton (city) Stark County	19	0.02
Dayton (city) Montgomery County	18	0.01
Cuyahoga Falls (city) Summit County	14	0.03
Ashtabula (city) Ashtabula County	13	0.06
Hamilton (city) Butler County	12	0.02

Top 10 Places Sorted by Percent
Based on all places, regardless of population

Place	Number	%
Port William (village) Clinton County	3	1.16
Rushville (village) Fairfield County	2	0.75
Rushsylvania (village) Logan County	3	0.55
Orangeville (village) Trumbull County	1	0.53
Cecil (village) Paulding County	1	0.46
Kingston (village) Ross County	3	0.29
Shiloh (village) Richland County	2	0.28
Aquilla (village) Geauga County	1	0.27
Elmwood Place (village) Hamilton County	7	0.26
Shawnee Hills (cdp) Greene County	6	0.25

Top 10 Places Sorted by Percent
Based on places with populations of 10,000 or more

Place	Number	%
Ashtabula (city) Ashtabula County	13	0.06
Conneaut (city) Ashtabula County	8	0.06
Marietta (city) Washington County	8	0.06
Greenville (city) Darke County	7	0.05
North College Hill (city) Hamilton County	5	0.05
Parma Heights (city) Cuyahoga County	8	0.04
Wadsworth (city) Medina County	8	0.04
Defiance (city) Defiance County	7	0.04
Washington (city) Fayette County	6	0.04
Springdale (city) Hamilton County	4	0.04

American Indian: Choctaw

Top 10 Places Sorted by Number
Based on all places, regardless of population

Place	Number	%
Cleveland (city) Cuyahoga County	68	0.01
Columbus (city) Franklin County	65	0.01
Toledo (city) Lucas County	40	0.01
Dayton (city) Montgomery County	28	0.02
Cincinnati (city) Hamilton County	28	0.01
Akron (city) Summit County	24	0.01
Elyria (city) Lorain County	18	0.03
East Cleveland (city) Cuyahoga County	14	0.05
Parma (city) Cuyahoga County	14	0.02
Canton (city) Stark County	10	0.01

Top 10 Places Sorted by Percent
Based on all places, regardless of population

Place	Number	%
Woodstock (village) Champaign County	3	0.95
Hartford (village) Licking County	2	0.49
Valley Hi (village) Logan County	1	0.41
New Holland (village) Pickaway County	3	0.38
Berkey (village) Lucas County	1	0.38
Wilmot (village) Stark County	1	0.30
Clarksville (village) Clinton County	1	0.20
Lindsey (village) Sandusky County	1	0.20
Beechwood Trails (cdp) Licking County	4	0.18
Thurston (village) Fairfield County	1	0.18

Top 10 Places Sorted by Percent
Based on places with populations of 10,000 or more

Place	Number	%
East Cleveland (city) Cuyahoga County	14	0.05
Englewood (city) Montgomery County	5	0.04
Elyria (city) Lorain County	18	0.03
Athens (city) Athens County	6	0.03
Wadsworth (city) Medina County	5	0.03
Whitehall (city) Franklin County	5	0.03
Brecksville (city) Cuyahoga County	4	0.03
Landen (cdp) Warren County	4	0.03
Springboro (city) Warren County	4	0.03
Amherst (city) Lorain County	3	0.03

American Indian: Colville

Top 10 Places Sorted by Number
Based on all places, regardless of population

Place	Number	%
Springboro (city) Warren County	1	0.01
Centerville (city) Montgomery County	1	0.00
Cleveland (city) Cuyahoga County	1	0.00
Cuyahoga Falls (city) Summit County	1	0.00
Fairborn (city) Greene County	1	0.00
Stow (city) Summit County	1	0.00
Wooster (city) Wayne County	1	0.00

Top 10 Places Sorted by Percent
Based on all places, regardless of population

Place	Number	%
Springboro (city) Warren County	1	0.01
Centerville (city) Montgomery County	1	0.00
Cleveland (city) Cuyahoga County	1	0.00
Cuyahoga Falls (city) Summit County	1	0.00
Fairborn (city) Greene County	1	0.00
Stow (city) Summit County	1	0.00
Wooster (city) Wayne County	1	0.00

Top 10 Places Sorted by Percent
Based on places with populations of 10,000 or more

Place	Number	%
Springboro (city) Warren County	1	0.01
Centerville (city) Montgomery County	1	0.00
Cleveland (city) Cuyahoga County	1	0.00
Cuyahoga Falls (city) Summit County	1	0.00
Fairborn (city) Greene County	1	0.00
Stow (city) Summit County	1	0.00
Wooster (city) Wayne County	1	0.00

American Indian: Comanche

Top 10 Places Sorted by Number
Based on all places, regardless of population

Place	Number	%
Columbus (city) Franklin County	19	0.00
Cleveland (city) Cuyahoga County	10	0.00
Urbana (city) Champaign County	7	0.06

Notes: (cdp) census designated place; Refer to the User's Guide in the front of the book for more detailed information.

PROFILES OF OHIO / Ancestry Rankings

Place	Number	%
Findlay (city) Hancock County	6	0.02
Cincinnati (city) Hamilton County	6	0.00
Toledo (city) Lucas County	6	0.00
Celina (city) Mercer County	5	0.05
Akron (city) Summit County	5	0.00
Warsaw (village) Coshocton County	4	0.51
Heath (city) Licking County	4	0.05

Top 10 Places Sorted by Percent
Based on all places, regardless of population

Place	Number	%
Warsaw (village) Coshocton County	4	0.51
Fairfield Beach (cdp) Fairfield County	2	0.17
Dalton (village) Wayne County	2	0.12
Chesapeake (village) Lawrence County	1	0.12
Millersport (village) Fairfield County	1	0.10
Roaming Shores (village) Ashtabula County	1	0.08
White Oak West (cdp) Hamilton County	2	0.07
Urbana (city) Champaign County	7	0.06
New Lexington (city) Perry County	3	0.06
Oak Hill (village) Jackson County	1	0.06

Top 10 Places Sorted by Percent
Based on places with populations of 10,000 or more

Place	Number	%
Urbana (city) Champaign County	7	0.06
Celina (city) Mercer County	5	0.05
Circleville (city) Pickaway County	4	0.03
Findlay (city) Hancock County	6	0.02
Chillicothe (city) Ross County	4	0.02
Englewood (city) Montgomery County	3	0.02
Ravenna (city) Portage County	2	0.02
Fairborn (city) Greene County	3	0.01
Lakewood (city) Cuyahoga County	3	0.01
Massillon (city) Stark County	3	0.01

American Indian: Cree

Top 10 Places Sorted by Number
Based on all places, regardless of population

Place	Number	%
Columbus (city) Franklin County	14	0.00
Cleveland (city) Cuyahoga County	13	0.00
Akron (city) Summit County	9	0.00
Toledo (city) Lucas County	7	0.00
North Royalton (city) Cuyahoga County	6	0.02
Lakewood (city) Cuyahoga County	5	0.01
Dayton (city) Montgomery County	5	0.00
Bridgetown North (cdp) Hamilton County	4	0.03
Conneaut (city) Ashtabula County	4	0.03
Alliance (city) Stark County	4	0.02

Top 10 Places Sorted by Percent
Based on all places, regardless of population

Place	Number	%
Rawson (village) Hancock County	1	0.22
North Fairfield (village) Huron County	1	0.17
Clinton (village) Summit County	1	0.07
West Salem (village) Wayne County	1	0.07
Gallipolis (city) Gallia County	2	0.05
Huber Ridge (cdp) Franklin County	2	0.04
Enon (village) Clark County	1	0.04
Bridgetown North (cdp) Hamilton County	4	0.03
Conneaut (city) Ashtabula County	4	0.03
Portage Lakes (cdp) Summit County	3	0.03

Top 10 Places Sorted by Percent
Based on places with populations of 10,000 or more

Place	Number	%
Bridgetown North (cdp) Hamilton County	4	0.03
Conneaut (city) Ashtabula County	4	0.03
North Royalton (city) Cuyahoga County	6	0.02

Place	Number	%
Alliance (city) Stark County	4	0.02
Northbrook (cdp) Hamilton County	2	0.02
Lakewood (city) Cuyahoga County	5	0.01
Beavercreek (city) Greene County	4	0.01
Elyria (city) Lorain County	4	0.01
Lorain (city) Lorain County	4	0.01
Sandusky (city) Erie County	4	0.01

American Indian: Creek

Top 10 Places Sorted by Number
Based on all places, regardless of population

Place	Number	%
Columbus (city) Franklin County	29	0.00
Cincinnati (city) Hamilton County	25	0.01
Dayton (city) Montgomery County	22	0.01
Cleveland (city) Cuyahoga County	18	0.00
Cleveland Heights (city) Cuyahoga County	9	0.02
Centerville (city) Montgomery County	8	0.03
Fairborn (city) Greene County	7	0.02
Akron (city) Summit County	7	0.00
Toledo (city) Lucas County	7	0.00
Forest Park (city) Hamilton County	6	0.03

Top 10 Places Sorted by Percent
Based on all places, regardless of population

Place	Number	%
Clifton (village) Greene County	2	1.12
Jacksonville (village) Athens County	2	0.37
New Bremen (village) Auglaize County	5	0.17
Caldwell (village) Noble County	3	0.15
Mack North (cdp) Hamilton County	5	0.14
Centerburg (village) Knox County	2	0.14
North Perry (village) Lake County	1	0.12
Blanchester (village) Clinton County	4	0.09
Richwood (village) Union County	2	0.09
Gnadenhutten (village) Tuscarawas County	1	0.08

Top 10 Places Sorted by Percent
Based on places with populations of 10,000 or more

Place	Number	%
Clayton (city) Montgomery County	5	0.04
Centerville (city) Montgomery County	8	0.03
Forest Park (city) Hamilton County	6	0.03
Avon (city) Lorain County	4	0.03
Norton (city) Summit County	3	0.03
Cleveland Heights (city) Cuyahoga County	9	0.02
Fairborn (city) Greene County	7	0.02
Massillon (city) Stark County	6	0.02
Xenia (city) Greene County	6	0.02
Zanesville (city) Muskingum County	6	0.02

American Indian: Crow

Top 10 Places Sorted by Number
Based on all places, regardless of population

Place	Number	%
Toledo (city) Lucas County	17	0.01
Columbus (city) Franklin County	11	0.00
Cleveland Heights (city) Cuyahoga County	9	0.02
Akron (city) Summit County	8	0.00
Cleveland (city) Cuyahoga County	8	0.00
New Philadelphia (city) Tuscarawas County	7	0.04
Cincinnati (city) Hamilton County	7	0.00
North Ridgeville (city) Lorain County	5	0.02
Dayton (city) Montgomery County	5	0.00
Thurston (village) Fairfield County	4	0.72

Top 10 Places Sorted by Percent
Based on all places, regardless of population

Place	Number	%
Thurston (village) Fairfield County	4	0.72

Place	Number	%
Tuscarawas (village) Tuscarawas County	3	0.32
Sherrodsville (village) Carroll County	1	0.32
Wharton (village) Wyandot County	1	0.24
Wayne Lakes (village) Darke County	1	0.15
Pleasantville (village) Fairfield County	1	0.11
Syracuse (village) Meigs County	1	0.11
Greentown (cdp) Stark County	3	0.10
Caldwell (village) Noble County	2	0.10
Edgerton (village) Williams County	2	0.09

Top 10 Places Sorted by Percent
Based on places with populations of 10,000 or more

Place	Number	%
New Philadelphia (city) Tuscarawas County	7	0.04
Cleveland Heights (city) Cuyahoga County	9	0.02
North Ridgeville (city) Lorain County	5	0.02
Sidney (city) Shelby County	4	0.02
Steubenville (city) Jefferson County	4	0.02
Miamisburg (city) Montgomery County	3	0.02
Sylvania (city) Lucas County	3	0.02
Vandalia (city) Montgomery County	3	0.02
Whitehall (city) Franklin County	3	0.02
Springdale (city) Hamilton County	2	0.02

American Indian: Delaware

Top 10 Places Sorted by Number
Based on all places, regardless of population

Place	Number	%
Canton (city) Stark County	86	0.11
Columbus (city) Franklin County	32	0.00
Lorain (city) Lorain County	9	0.01
Cleveland (city) Cuyahoga County	9	0.00
Zanesville (city) Muskingum County	8	0.03
Akron (city) Summit County	8	0.00
Cincinnati (city) Hamilton County	8	0.00
Alliance (city) Stark County	7	0.03
Canal Winchester (village) Franklin County	6	0.13
Celina (city) Mercer County	6	0.06

Top 10 Places Sorted by Percent
Based on all places, regardless of population

Place	Number	%
Plainfield (village) Coshocton County	1	0.63
Bolivar (village) Tuscarawas County	3	0.34
Galena (village) Delaware County	1	0.33
East Canton (village) Stark County	5	0.31
Aquilla (village) Geauga County	1	0.27
Irondale (village) Jefferson County	1	0.24
Glenmoor (cdp) Columbiana County	3	0.14
Canal Winchester (village) Franklin County	6	0.13
Mineral City (village) Tuscarawas County	1	0.12
Canton (city) Stark County	86	0.11

Top 10 Places Sorted by Percent
Based on places with populations of 10,000 or more

Place	Number	%
Canton (city) Stark County	86	0.11
Celina (city) Mercer County	6	0.06
Dover (city) Tuscarawas County	5	0.04
Pataskala (city) Licking County	4	0.04
Zanesville (city) Muskingum County	8	0.03
Alliance (city) Stark County	7	0.03
New Philadelphia (city) Tuscarawas County	5	0.03
Kent (city) Portage County	6	0.02
Coshocton (city) Coshocton County	2	0.02
Galion (city) Crawford County	2	0.02

Notes: (cdp) census designated place; Refer to the User's Guide in the front of the book for more detailed information.

American Indian: Houma

Top 10 Places Sorted by Number
Based on all places, regardless of population

Place	Number	%
Lake Darby (cdp) Franklin County	4	0.11
Canton (city) Stark County	4	0.00
Struthers (city) Mahoning County	3	0.03
Columbus (city) Franklin County	3	0.00
Risingsun (village) Wood County	2	0.32
Mentor (city) Lake County	2	0.00
Berea (city) Cuyahoga County	1	0.01
Ravenna (city) Portage County	1	0.01
Akron (city) Summit County	1	0.00
Cuyahoga Falls (city) Summit County	1	0.00

Top 10 Places Sorted by Percent
Based on all places, regardless of population

Place	Number	%
Risingsun (village) Wood County	2	0.32
Lake Darby (cdp) Franklin County	4	0.11
Struthers (city) Mahoning County	3	0.03
Berea (city) Cuyahoga County	1	0.01
Ravenna (city) Portage County	1	0.01
Canton (city) Stark County	4	0.00
Columbus (city) Franklin County	3	0.00
Mentor (city) Lake County	2	0.00
Akron (city) Summit County	1	0.00
Cuyahoga Falls (city) Summit County	1	0.00

Top 10 Places Sorted by Percent
Based on places with populations of 10,000 or more

Place	Number	%
Struthers (city) Mahoning County	3	0.03
Berea (city) Cuyahoga County	1	0.01
Ravenna (city) Portage County	1	0.01
Canton (city) Stark County	4	0.00
Columbus (city) Franklin County	3	0.00
Mentor (city) Lake County	2	0.00
Akron (city) Summit County	1	0.00
Cuyahoga Falls (city) Summit County	1	0.00
Reynoldsburg (city) Franklin County	1	0.00
Toledo (city) Lucas County	1	0.00

American Indian: Iroquois

Top 10 Places Sorted by Number
Based on all places, regardless of population

Place	Number	%
Columbus (city) Franklin County	118	0.02
Cleveland (city) Cuyahoga County	91	0.02
Canton (city) Stark County	89	0.11
Toledo (city) Lucas County	41	0.01
Lorain (city) Lorain County	38	0.06
Akron (city) Summit County	38	0.02
Cincinnati (city) Hamilton County	28	0.01
Dayton (city) Montgomery County	21	0.01
Bowling Green (city) Wood County	19	0.06
Lakewood (city) Cuyahoga County	18	0.03

Top 10 Places Sorted by Percent
Based on all places, regardless of population

Place	Number	%
West Leipsic (village) Putnam County	5	1.85
Polk (village) Ashland County	2	0.56
Freeport (village) Harrison County	2	0.50
Cloverdale (village) Putnam County	1	0.50
Urbancrest (village) Franklin County	4	0.46
Galena (village) Delaware County	1	0.33
Hunter (cdp) Warren County	5	0.29
Vanlue (village) Hancock County	1	0.27
Morrow (village) Warren County	3	0.23

| Pleasant City (village) Guernsey County | 1 | 0.23 |

Top 10 Places Sorted by Percent
Based on places with populations of 10,000 or more

Place	Number	%
Canton (city) Stark County	89	0.11
Maumee (city) Lucas County	10	0.07
Lorain (city) Lorain County	38	0.06
Bowling Green (city) Wood County	19	0.06
University Heights (city) Cuyahoga County	9	0.06
Marietta (city) Washington County	8	0.06
Delaware (city) Delaware County	13	0.05
Willoughby (city) Lake County	11	0.05
Middleburg Heights (city) Cuyahoga County	8	0.05
Aurora (city) Portage County	7	0.05

American Indian: Kiowa

Top 10 Places Sorted by Number
Based on all places, regardless of population

Place	Number	%
Columbus (city) Franklin County	10	0.00
Cleveland (city) Cuyahoga County	7	0.00
Dennison (village) Tuscarawas County	6	0.20
North Ridgeville (city) Lorain County	6	0.03
Akron (city) Summit County	5	0.00
Wheelersburg (cdp) Scioto County	3	0.05
Coshocton (city) Coshocton County	3	0.03
Middleburg Heights (city) Cuyahoga County	3	0.02
Toledo (city) Lucas County	3	0.00
Piketon (village) Pike County	2	0.10

Top 10 Places Sorted by Percent
Based on all places, regardless of population

Place	Number	%
Dennison (village) Tuscarawas County	6	0.20
Piketon (village) Pike County	2	0.10
Wheelersburg (cdp) Scioto County	3	0.05
North Ridgeville (city) Lorain County	6	0.03
Coshocton (city) Coshocton County	3	0.03
Middleburg Heights (city) Cuyahoga County	3	0.02
Blue Ash (city) Hamilton County	2	0.02
Finneytown (cdp) Hamilton County	2	0.01
Lebanon (city) Warren County	2	0.01
Circleville (city) Pickaway County	1	0.01

Top 10 Places Sorted by Percent
Based on places with populations of 10,000 or more

Place	Number	%
North Ridgeville (city) Lorain County	6	0.03
Coshocton (city) Coshocton County	3	0.03
Middleburg Heights (city) Cuyahoga County	3	0.02
Blue Ash (city) Hamilton County	2	0.02
Finneytown (cdp) Hamilton County	2	0.01
Lebanon (city) Warren County	2	0.01
Circleville (city) Pickaway County	1	0.01
West Carrollton City (city) Montgomery County	1	0.01
Columbus (city) Franklin County	10	0.00
Cleveland (city) Cuyahoga County	7	0.00

American Indian: Latin American Indians

Top 10 Places Sorted by Number
Based on all places, regardless of population

Place	Number	%
Columbus (city) Franklin County	160	0.02
Cleveland (city) Cuyahoga County	155	0.03
Cincinnati (city) Hamilton County	136	0.04
Toledo (city) Lucas County	118	0.04
Lorain (city) Lorain County	46	0.07
Cleveland Heights (city) Cuyahoga County	17	0.03
Dover (city) Tuscarawas County	15	0.12

Youngstown (city) Mahoning County	15	0.02
Norwood (city) Hamilton County	14	0.06
Akron (city) Summit County	14	0.01

Top 10 Places Sorted by Percent
Based on all places, regardless of population

Place	Number	%
Summitville (village) Columbiana County	1	0.93
Latty (village) Paulding County	1	0.50
Aberdeen (village) Brown County	7	0.44
West Leipsic (village) Putnam County	1	0.37
Castalia (village) Erie County	3	0.32
Waynesville (village) Warren County	8	0.31
West Unity (village) Williams County	5	0.28
Strasburg (village) Tuscarawas County	6	0.26
Rockford (village) Mercer County	2	0.18
Cridersville (village) Auglaize County	3	0.17

Top 10 Places Sorted by Percent
Based on places with populations of 10,000 or more

Place	Number	%
Dover (city) Tuscarawas County	15	0.12
Lorain (city) Lorain County	46	0.07
Norwood (city) Hamilton County	14	0.06
Struthers (city) Mahoning County	7	0.06
Fremont (city) Sandusky County	9	0.05
Celina (city) Mercer County	5	0.05
Cincinnati (city) Hamilton County	136	0.04
Toledo (city) Lucas County	118	0.04
Brunswick (city) Medina County	13	0.04
Sandusky (city) Erie County	10	0.04

American Indian: Lumbee

Top 10 Places Sorted by Number
Based on all places, regardless of population

Place	Number	%
Columbus (city) Franklin County	45	0.01
Parma (city) Cuyahoga County	17	0.02
Toledo (city) Lucas County	12	0.00
Elyria (city) Lorain County	11	0.02
Fostoria (city) Seneca County	8	0.06
Cleveland (city) Cuyahoga County	7	0.00
Reynoldsburg (city) Franklin County	6	0.02
Hilltop (cdp) Trumbull County	5	0.94
Walbridge (village) Wood County	5	0.20
Pleasant Run (cdp) Hamilton County	5	0.09

Top 10 Places Sorted by Percent
Based on all places, regardless of population

Place	Number	%
Hilltop (cdp) Trumbull County	5	0.94
Walbridge (village) Wood County	5	0.20
West Salem (village) Wayne County	3	0.20
Sunbury (village) Delaware County	3	0.11
Gratis (village) Preble County	1	0.11
Pleasant Run (cdp) Hamilton County	5	0.09
Logan (city) Hocking County	5	0.07
Lodi (village) Medina County	2	0.07
Navarre (village) Stark County	1	0.07
Fostoria (city) Seneca County	8	0.06

Top 10 Places Sorted by Percent
Based on places with populations of 10,000 or more

Place	Number	%
Fostoria (city) Seneca County	8	0.06
Landen (cdp) Warren County	4	0.03
Parma (city) Cuyahoga County	17	0.02
Elyria (city) Lorain County	11	0.02
Reynoldsburg (city) Franklin County	6	0.02
Delaware (city) Delaware County	5	0.02
Alliance (city) Stark County	4	0.02

Notes: (cdp) census designated place; Refer to the User's Guide in the front of the book for more detailed information.

PROFILES OF OHIO / Ancestry Rankings

Place	Number	%
Tallmadge (city) Summit County	4	0.02
Columbus (city) Franklin County	45	0.01
Westlake (city) Cuyahoga County	4	0.01

American Indian: Menominee

Top 10 Places Sorted by Number
Based on all places, regardless of population

Place	Number	%
Columbus (city) Franklin County	9	0.00
Lima (city) Allen County	6	0.01
Toledo (city) Lucas County	6	0.01
Fostoria (city) Seneca County	3	0.02
Norwalk (city) Huron County	3	0.02
Cambridge (city) Guernsey County	2	0.02
Dublin (city) Franklin County	2	0.01
Norwood (city) Hamilton County	2	0.01
Cincinnati (city) Hamilton County	2	0.01
Dayton (city) Montgomery County	2	0.00

Top 10 Places Sorted by Percent
Based on all places, regardless of population

Place	Number	%
Sugarcreek (village) Tuscarawas County	1	0.05
Fostoria (city) Seneca County	3	0.02
Norwalk (city) Huron County	3	0.02
Cambridge (city) Guernsey County	2	0.02
Lima (city) Allen County	6	0.01
Dublin (city) Franklin County	2	0.01
Norwood (city) Hamilton County	2	0.01
Bedford Heights (city) Cuyahoga County	1	0.01
Bryan (city) Williams County	1	0.01
Columbus (city) Franklin County	9	0.00

Top 10 Places Sorted by Percent
Based on places with populations of 10,000 or more

Place	Number	%
Fostoria (city) Seneca County	3	0.02
Norwalk (city) Huron County	3	0.02
Cambridge (city) Guernsey County	2	0.02
Lima (city) Allen County	6	0.01
Dublin (city) Franklin County	2	0.01
Norwood (city) Hamilton County	2	0.01
Bedford Heights (city) Cuyahoga County	1	0.01
Columbus (city) Franklin County	9	0.00
Toledo (city) Lucas County	6	0.00
Cincinnati (city) Hamilton County	2	0.00

American Indian: Navajo

Top 10 Places Sorted by Number
Based on all places, regardless of population

Place	Number	%
Columbus (city) Franklin County	73	0.01
Cleveland (city) Cuyahoga County	38	0.01
Cincinnati (city) Hamilton County	26	0.01
Toledo (city) Lucas County	22	0.01
Akron (city) Summit County	18	0.01
Dayton (city) Montgomery County	11	0.01
Lancaster (city) Fairfield County	9	0.03
Canton (city) Stark County	9	0.01
Northbrook (cdp) Hamilton County	7	0.06
Berea (city) Cuyahoga County	7	0.04

Top 10 Places Sorted by Percent
Based on all places, regardless of population

Place	Number	%
South Salem (village) Ross County	1	0.47
Marengo (village) Morrow County	1	0.34
Smithville (village) Wayne County	3	0.23
South Amherst (village) Lorain County	4	0.21
Pioneer (village) Williams County	3	0.21

Place	Number	%
Somerset (village) Perry County	3	0.19
Roseville (village) Perry County	3	0.15
Malta (village) Morgan County	1	0.14
Woodmere (village) Cuyahoga County	1	0.12
Bellville (village) Richland County	2	0.11

Top 10 Places Sorted by Percent
Based on places with populations of 10,000 or more

Place	Number	%
Northbrook (cdp) Hamilton County	7	0.06
Pataskala (city) Licking County	6	0.06
Berea (city) Cuyahoga County	7	0.04
Franklin (city) Warren County	5	0.04
Reading (city) Hamilton County	4	0.04
Lancaster (city) Fairfield County	9	0.03
Conneaut (city) Ashtabula County	4	0.03
Middleburg Heights (city) Cuyahoga County	4	0.03
Ravenna (city) Portage County	3	0.03
Huber Heights (city) Montgomery County	7	0.02

American Indian: Osage

Top 10 Places Sorted by Number
Based on all places, regardless of population

Place	Number	%
Columbus (city) Franklin County	15	0.00
Toledo (city) Lucas County	6	0.00
Zanesville (city) Muskingum County	5	0.02
Cleves (village) Hamilton County	4	0.14
Edgerton (village) Williams County	3	0.14
Lincoln Village (cdp) Franklin County	3	0.03
Ashtabula (city) Ashtabula County	3	0.01
Chillicothe (city) Ross County	3	0.01
Middletown (city) Butler County	3	0.01
Uhrichsville (city) Tuscarawas County	2	0.04

Top 10 Places Sorted by Percent
Based on all places, regardless of population

Place	Number	%
Jeromesville (village) Ashland County	1	0.21
Cleves (village) Hamilton County	4	0.14
Edgerton (village) Williams County	3	0.14
Clinton (village) Summit County	1	0.07
Uhrichsville (city) Tuscarawas County	2	0.04
Waterville (village) Lucas County	2	0.04
Lincoln Village (cdp) Franklin County	3	0.03
The Plains (cdp) Athens County	1	0.03
Zanesville (city) Muskingum County	5	0.02
Geneva (city) Ashtabula County	1	0.02

Top 10 Places Sorted by Percent
Based on places with populations of 10,000 or more

Place	Number	%
Zanesville (city) Muskingum County	5	0.02
Ashtabula (city) Ashtabula County	3	0.01
Chillicothe (city) Ross County	3	0.01
Middletown (city) Butler County	3	0.01
Trotwood (city) Montgomery County	2	0.01
Lyndhurst (city) Cuyahoga County	1	0.01
Marietta (city) Washington County	1	0.01
Mount Vernon (city) Knox County	1	0.01
Vandalia (city) Montgomery County	1	0.01
Columbus (city) Franklin County	15	0.00

American Indian: Ottawa

Top 10 Places Sorted by Number
Based on all places, regardless of population

Place	Number	%
Toledo (city) Lucas County	20	0.01
Cleveland (city) Cuyahoga County	16	0.00
Columbus (city) Franklin County	9	0.00

Place	Number	%
Canton (city) Stark County	8	0.01
Sylvania (city) Lucas County	6	0.03
Sandusky (city) Erie County	5	0.02
Bellbrook (city) Greene County	4	0.06
Lorain (city) Lorain County	4	0.01
Fairport Harbor (village) Lake County	3	0.09
Oregon (city) Lucas County	3	0.02

Top 10 Places Sorted by Percent
Based on all places, regardless of population

Place	Number	%
Convoy (village) Van Wert County	2	0.18
Wayne Lakes (village) Darke County	1	0.15
Fairport Harbor (village) Lake County	3	0.09
Fairfield Beach (cdp) Fairfield County	1	0.09
Bellbrook (city) Greene County	4	0.06
Amelia (village) Clermont County	1	0.04
Burlington (cdp) Lawrence County	1	0.04
Sylvania (city) Lucas County	6	0.03
Port Clinton (city) Ottawa County	2	0.03
Silver Lake (village) Summit County	1	0.03

Top 10 Places Sorted by Percent
Based on places with populations of 10,000 or more

Place	Number	%
Sylvania (city) Lucas County	6	0.03
Sandusky (city) Erie County	5	0.02
Oregon (city) Lucas County	3	0.02
Urbana (city) Champaign County	2	0.02
Toledo (city) Lucas County	20	0.01
Canton (city) Stark County	8	0.01
Lorain (city) Lorain County	4	0.01
Cuyahoga Falls (city) Summit County	3	0.01
Portsmouth (city) Scioto County	3	0.01
Massillon (city) Stark County	2	0.01

American Indian: Paiute

Top 10 Places Sorted by Number
Based on all places, regardless of population

Place	Number	%
East Cleveland (city) Cuyahoga County	15	0.06
Columbus (city) Franklin County	5	0.00
Forest Park (city) Hamilton County	4	0.02
Johnstown (village) Licking County	3	0.09
Avon (city) Lorain County	3	0.03
Cincinnati (city) Hamilton County	3	0.00
Cleveland (city) Cuyahoga County	3	0.00
Newark (city) Licking County	2	0.00
Toledo (city) Lucas County	2	0.00
Canal Winchester (village) Franklin County	1	0.02

Top 10 Places Sorted by Percent
Based on all places, regardless of population

Place	Number	%
Johnstown (village) Licking County	3	0.09
East Cleveland (city) Cuyahoga County	15	0.06
Avon (city) Lorain County	3	0.03
Forest Park (city) Hamilton County	4	0.02
Canal Winchester (village) Franklin County	1	0.02
Uhrichsville (city) Tuscarawas County	1	0.02
Columbus (city) Franklin County	5	0.00
Cincinnati (city) Hamilton County	3	0.00
Cleveland (city) Cuyahoga County	3	0.00
Newark (city) Licking County	2	0.00

Top 10 Places Sorted by Percent
Based on places with populations of 10,000 or more

Place	Number	%
East Cleveland (city) Cuyahoga County	15	0.06
Avon (city) Lorain County	3	0.03
Forest Park (city) Hamilton County	4	0.02

Notes: (cdp) census designated place; Refer to the User's Guide in the front of the book for more detailed information.

434 PROFILES OF OHIO / Ancestry Rankings

Place	Number	%
Columbus (city) Franklin County	5	0.00
Cincinnati (city) Hamilton County	3	0.00
Cleveland (city) Cuyahoga County	3	0.00
Newark (city) Licking County	2	0.00
Toledo (city) Lucas County	2	0.00
Elyria (city) Lorain County	1	0.00
Massillon (city) Stark County	1	0.00

American Indian: Pima

Top 10 Places Sorted by Number
Based on all places, regardless of population

Place	Number	%
Cleveland (city) Cuyahoga County	8	0.00
Columbus (city) Franklin County	7	0.00
Dayton (city) Montgomery County	4	0.00
Streetsboro (city) Portage County	3	0.02
Bryan (city) Williams County	2	0.02
Cincinnati (city) Hamilton County	2	0.00
South Amherst (village) Lorain County	1	0.05
Monfort Heights East (cdp) Hamilton County	1	0.03
Kettering (city) Montgomery County	1	0.00
Newark (city) Licking County	1	0.00

Top 10 Places Sorted by Percent
Based on all places, regardless of population

Place	Number	%
South Amherst (village) Lorain County	1	0.05
Monfort Heights East (cdp) Hamilton County	1	0.03
Streetsboro (city) Portage County	3	0.02
Bryan (city) Williams County	2	0.02
Cleveland (city) Cuyahoga County	8	0.00
Columbus (city) Franklin County	7	0.00
Dayton (city) Montgomery County	4	0.00
Cincinnati (city) Hamilton County	2	0.00
Kettering (city) Montgomery County	1	0.00
Newark (city) Licking County	1	0.00

Top 10 Places Sorted by Percent
Based on places with populations of 10,000 or more

Place	Number	%
Streetsboro (city) Portage County	3	0.02
Cleveland (city) Cuyahoga County	8	0.00
Columbus (city) Franklin County	7	0.00
Dayton (city) Montgomery County	4	0.00
Cincinnati (city) Hamilton County	2	0.00
Kettering (city) Montgomery County	1	0.00
Newark (city) Licking County	1	0.00
Riverside (city) Montgomery County	1	0.00

American Indian: Potawatomi

Top 10 Places Sorted by Number
Based on all places, regardless of population

Place	Number	%
Toledo (city) Lucas County	18	0.01
Columbus (city) Franklin County	12	0.00
Springfield (city) Clark County	8	0.01
Massillon (city) Stark County	6	0.02
Cincinnati (city) Hamilton County	6	0.00
Yellow Springs (village) Greene County	5	0.13
Xenia (city) Greene County	5	0.02
Cleveland (city) Cuyahoga County	5	0.00
Groveport (village) Franklin County	4	0.10
Austintown (cdp) Mahoning County	4	0.01

Top 10 Places Sorted by Percent
Based on all places, regardless of population

Place	Number	%
Port Washington (village) Tuscarawas County	1	0.18
Stryker (village) Williams County	2	0.14
Yellow Springs (village) Greene County	5	0.13
Reminderville (village) Summit County	3	0.13
McClure (village) Henry County	1	0.13
Lakemore (village) Summit County	3	0.12
Millville (village) Butler County	1	0.12
Groveport (village) Franklin County	4	0.10
Montpelier (village) Williams County	3	0.07
Huron (city) Erie County	3	0.04

Top 10 Places Sorted by Percent
Based on places with populations of 10,000 or more

Place	Number	%
Massillon (city) Stark County	6	0.02
Xenia (city) Greene County	5	0.02
Toledo (city) Lucas County	18	0.01
Springfield (city) Clark County	8	0.01
Austintown (cdp) Mahoning County	4	0.01
Kent (city) Portage County	3	0.01
Solon (city) Cuyahoga County	3	0.01
Westlake (city) Cuyahoga County	3	0.01
Ashland (city) Ashland County	2	0.01
Beavercreek (city) Greene County	2	0.01

American Indian: Pueblo

Top 10 Places Sorted by Number
Based on all places, regardless of population

Place	Number	%
Columbus (city) Franklin County	23	0.00
Toledo (city) Lucas County	17	0.01
Cleveland (city) Cuyahoga County	16	0.00
Akron (city) Summit County	10	0.00
Lorain (city) Lorain County	7	0.01
Cincinnati (city) Hamilton County	6	0.00
Dayton (city) Montgomery County	6	0.00
University Heights (city) Cuyahoga County	5	0.04
Northbrook (cdp) Hamilton County	4	0.04
Niles (city) Trumbull County	4	0.02

Top 10 Places Sorted by Percent
Based on all places, regardless of population

Place	Number	%
Holmesville (village) Holmes County	1	0.26
Rock Creek (village) Ashtabula County	1	0.17
Wayne Lakes (village) Darke County	1	0.15
Eaton Estates (cdp) Lorain County	2	0.14
Amanda (village) Fairfield County	1	0.14
Urbancrest (village) Franklin County	1	0.12
Alger (village) Hardin County	1	0.11
North Randall (village) Cuyahoga County	1	0.11
Addyston (village) Hamilton County	1	0.10
McDonald (village) Trumbull County	3	0.09

Top 10 Places Sorted by Percent
Based on places with populations of 10,000 or more

Place	Number	%
University Heights (city) Cuyahoga County	5	0.04
Northbrook (cdp) Hamilton County	4	0.04
Niles (city) Trumbull County	4	0.02
Riverside (city) Montgomery County	4	0.02
Rocky River (city) Cuyahoga County	4	0.02
Steubenville (city) Jefferson County	4	0.02
Toledo (city) Lucas County	17	0.01
Lorain (city) Lorain County	7	0.01
Garfield Heights (city) Cuyahoga County	4	0.01
Elyria (city) Lorain County	3	0.01

American Indian: Puget Sound Salish

Top 10 Places Sorted by Number
Based on all places, regardless of population

Place	Number	%
Dayton (city) Montgomery County	5	0.00
Summerside (cdp) Clermont County	3	0.05
Canton (city) Stark County	3	0.00
Gates Mills (village) Cuyahoga County	2	0.08
Rossford (city) Wood County	2	0.03
Bowling Green (city) Wood County	2	0.01
Heath (city) Licking County	1	0.01
Oberlin (city) Lorain County	1	0.01
Wauseon (city) Fulton County	1	0.01
Columbus (city) Franklin County	1	0.00

Top 10 Places Sorted by Percent
Based on all places, regardless of population

Place	Number	%
Gates Mills (village) Cuyahoga County	2	0.08
Summerside (cdp) Clermont County	3	0.05
Rossford (city) Wood County	2	0.03
Bowling Green (city) Wood County	2	0.01
Heath (city) Licking County	1	0.01
Oberlin (city) Lorain County	1	0.01
Wauseon (city) Fulton County	1	0.01
Dayton (city) Montgomery County	5	0.00
Canton (city) Stark County	3	0.00
Columbus (city) Franklin County	1	0.00

Top 10 Places Sorted by Percent
Based on places with populations of 10,000 or more

Place	Number	%
Bowling Green (city) Wood County	2	0.01
Dayton (city) Montgomery County	5	0.00
Canton (city) Stark County	3	0.00
Columbus (city) Franklin County	1	0.00
Findlay (city) Hancock County	1	0.00

American Indian: Seminole

Top 10 Places Sorted by Number
Based on all places, regardless of population

Place	Number	%
Cleveland (city) Cuyahoga County	41	0.01
Columbus (city) Franklin County	35	0.00
Toledo (city) Lucas County	27	0.01
Cincinnati (city) Hamilton County	18	0.01
Dayton (city) Montgomery County	16	0.01
Youngstown (city) Mahoning County	14	0.02
Akron (city) Summit County	14	0.01
Cleveland Heights (city) Cuyahoga County	11	0.02
Canton (city) Stark County	11	0.01
Elyria (city) Lorain County	7	0.01

Top 10 Places Sorted by Percent
Based on all places, regardless of population

Place	Number	%
New Bremen (village) Auglaize County	5	0.17
Bay View (village) Erie County	1	0.14
Philo (village) Muskingum County	1	0.13
Bethesda (village) Belmont County	1	0.07
West Salem (village) Wayne County	1	0.07
Choctaw Lake (cdp) Madison County	1	0.06
Mineral Ridge (cdp) Trumbull County	2	0.05
Harrison (city) Hamilton County	3	0.04
Northridge (cdp) Montgomery County	3	0.04
Huber Ridge (cdp) Franklin County	2	0.04

Top 10 Places Sorted by Percent
Based on places with populations of 10,000 or more

Place	Number	%
Steubenville (city) Jefferson County	6	0.03
Youngstown (city) Mahoning County	14	0.02
Cleveland Heights (city) Cuyahoga County	11	0.02
Lancaster (city) Fairfield County	6	0.02
Kent (city) Portage County	5	0.02
Shaker Heights (city) Cuyahoga County	5	0.02

Notes: (cdp) census designated place; Refer to the User's Guide in the front of the book for more detailed information.

Place	Number	%
Mason (city) Warren County	4	0.02
Portsmouth (city) Scioto County	4	0.02
Fostoria (city) Seneca County	3	0.02
Fremont (city) Sandusky County	3	0.02

American Indian: Shoshone

Top 10 Places Sorted by Number
Based on all places, regardless of population

Place	Number	%
Akron (city) Summit County	6	0.00
Forestville (cdp) Hamilton County	3	0.03
Columbus (city) Franklin County	3	0.00
Lorain (city) Lorain County	3	0.00
Minerva (village) Stark County	2	0.05
South Point (village) Lawrence County	2	0.05
Port Clinton (city) Ottawa County	2	0.03
Sheffield Lake (city) Lorain County	2	0.02
Bedford (city) Cuyahoga County	2	0.01
East Cleveland (city) Cuyahoga County	2	0.01

Top 10 Places Sorted by Percent
Based on all places, regardless of population

Place	Number	%
Seaman (village) Adams County	1	0.10
Neffs (cdp) Belmont County	1	0.09
Minerva (village) Stark County	2	0.05
South Point (village) Lawrence County	2	0.05
Drexel (cdp) Montgomery County	1	0.05
Devola (cdp) Washington County	1	0.04
Woodsfield (village) Monroe County	1	0.04
Forestville (cdp) Hamilton County	3	0.03
Port Clinton (city) Ottawa County	2	0.03
Delta (village) Fulton County	1	0.03

Top 10 Places Sorted by Percent
Based on places with populations of 10,000 or more

Place	Number	%
Forestville (cdp) Hamilton County	3	0.03
Bedford (city) Cuyahoga County	2	0.01
East Cleveland (city) Cuyahoga County	2	0.01
Findlay (city) Hancock County	2	0.01
Garfield Heights (city) Cuyahoga County	2	0.01
Avon (city) Lorain County	1	0.01
Avon Lake (city) Lorain County	1	0.01
Greenville (city) Darke County	1	0.01
North Canton (city) Stark County	1	0.01
Norwalk (city) Huron County	1	0.01

American Indian: Sioux

Top 10 Places Sorted by Number
Based on all places, regardless of population

Place	Number	%
Columbus (city) Franklin County	178	0.03
Cleveland (city) Cuyahoga County	140	0.03
Akron (city) Summit County	63	0.03
Toledo (city) Lucas County	60	0.02
Dayton (city) Montgomery County	50	0.03
Cincinnati (city) Hamilton County	47	0.01
Lakewood (city) Cuyahoga County	26	0.05
Canton (city) Stark County	26	0.03
Newark (city) Licking County	20	0.04
Elyria (city) Lorain County	18	0.03

Top 10 Places Sorted by Percent
Based on all places, regardless of population

Place	Number	%
Rarden (village) Scioto County	2	1.14
Norwich (village) Muskingum County	1	0.88
Lore City (village) Guernsey County	2	0.66
Tremont City (village) Clark County	2	0.57
Orangeville (village) Trumbull County	1	0.53
Waynesfield (village) Auglaize County	4	0.50
Andover (village) Ashtabula County	5	0.39
West Leipsic (village) Putnam County	1	0.37
New Bloomington (village) Marion County	2	0.36
Phillipsburg (village) Montgomery County	2	0.32

Top 10 Places Sorted by Percent
Based on places with populations of 10,000 or more

Place	Number	%
Marysville (city) Union County	14	0.09
Bellefontaine (city) Logan County	9	0.07
Blue Ash (city) Hamilton County	7	0.06
Lakewood (city) Cuyahoga County	26	0.05
Kent (city) Portage County	15	0.05
Portsmouth (city) Scioto County	10	0.05
Cambridge (city) Guernsey County	6	0.05
Salem (city) Columbiana County	6	0.05
Newark (city) Licking County	20	0.04
Reynoldsburg (city) Franklin County	12	0.04

American Indian: Tohono O'Odham

Top 10 Places Sorted by Number
Based on all places, regardless of population

Place	Number	%
Cleveland (city) Cuyahoga County	9	0.00
Columbus (city) Franklin County	7	0.00
Cincinnati (city) Hamilton County	4	0.00
Dayton (city) Montgomery County	3	0.00
Youngstown (city) Mahoning County	2	0.00
Westfield Center (village) Medina County	1	0.09
Clinton (village) Summit County	1	0.07
Holiday Valley (cdp) Clark County	1	0.06
Sabina (village) Clinton County	1	0.04
Bedford Heights (city) Cuyahoga County	1	0.01

Top 10 Places Sorted by Percent
Based on all places, regardless of population

Place	Number	%
Westfield Center (village) Medina County	1	0.09
Clinton (village) Summit County	1	0.07
Holiday Valley (cdp) Clark County	1	0.06
Sabina (village) Clinton County	1	0.04
Bedford Heights (city) Cuyahoga County	1	0.01
Norton (city) Summit County	1	0.01
Orrville (city) Wayne County	1	0.01
Willowick (city) Lake County	1	0.01
Wilmington (city) Clinton County	1	0.01
Cleveland (city) Cuyahoga County	9	0.00

Top 10 Places Sorted by Percent
Based on places with populations of 10,000 or more

Place	Number	%
Bedford Heights (city) Cuyahoga County	1	0.01
Norton (city) Summit County	1	0.01
Willowick (city) Lake County	1	0.01
Wilmington (city) Clinton County	1	0.01
Cleveland (city) Cuyahoga County	9	0.00
Columbus (city) Franklin County	7	0.00
Cincinnati (city) Hamilton County	4	0.00
Dayton (city) Montgomery County	3	0.00
Youngstown (city) Mahoning County	2	0.00
Elyria (city) Lorain County	1	0.00

American Indian: Ute

Top 10 Places Sorted by Number
Based on all places, regardless of population

Place	Number	%
Brook Park (city) Cuyahoga County	4	0.02
Lancaster (city) Fairfield County	4	0.01
Hamden (village) Vinton County	3	0.34
Streetsboro (city) Portage County	3	0.02
Hudson (city) Summit County	3	0.01
Canton (city) Stark County	3	0.00
Woodsfield (village) Monroe County	2	0.08
Cleveland (city) Cuyahoga County	2	0.00
The Plains (cdp) Athens County	1	0.03
Berea (city) Cuyahoga County	1	0.01

Top 10 Places Sorted by Percent
Based on all places, regardless of population

Place	Number	%
Hamden (village) Vinton County	3	0.34
Woodsfield (village) Monroe County	2	0.08
The Plains (cdp) Athens County	1	0.03
Brook Park (city) Cuyahoga County	4	0.02
Streetsboro (city) Portage County	3	0.02
Lancaster (city) Fairfield County	4	0.01
Hudson (city) Summit County	3	0.01
Berea (city) Cuyahoga County	1	0.01
Marietta (city) Washington County	1	0.01
Mount Vernon (city) Knox County	1	0.01

Top 10 Places Sorted by Percent
Based on places with populations of 10,000 or more

Place	Number	%
Brook Park (city) Cuyahoga County	4	0.02
Streetsboro (city) Portage County	3	0.02
Lancaster (city) Fairfield County	4	0.01
Hudson (city) Summit County	3	0.01
Berea (city) Cuyahoga County	1	0.01
Marietta (city) Washington County	1	0.01
Mount Vernon (city) Knox County	1	0.01
Norwalk (city) Huron County	1	0.01
Canton (city) Stark County	3	0.00
Cleveland (city) Cuyahoga County	2	0.00

American Indian: Yakama

Top 10 Places Sorted by Number
Based on all places, regardless of population

Place	Number	%
Wellsville (village) Columbiana County	2	0.05
Cleveland (city) Cuyahoga County	2	0.00
Oberlin (city) Lorain County	1	0.01
Canton (city) Stark County	1	0.00
Toledo (city) Lucas County	1	0.00
Westerville (city) Franklin County	1	0.00

Top 10 Places Sorted by Percent
Based on all places, regardless of population

Place	Number	%
Wellsville (village) Columbiana County	2	0.05
Oberlin (city) Lorain County	1	0.01
Cleveland (city) Cuyahoga County	2	0.00
Canton (city) Stark County	1	0.00
Toledo (city) Lucas County	1	0.00
Westerville (city) Franklin County	1	0.00

Top 10 Places Sorted by Percent
Based on places with populations of 10,000 or more

Place	Number	%
Cleveland (city) Cuyahoga County	2	0.00
Canton (city) Stark County	1	0.00
Toledo (city) Lucas County	1	0.00
Westerville (city) Franklin County	1	0.00

Notes: (cdp) census designated place; Refer to the User's Guide in the front of the book for more detailed information.

American Indian: Yaqui

Top 10 Places Sorted by Number
Based on all places, regardless of population

Place	Number	%
Columbus (city) Franklin County	9	0.00
Belpre (city) Washington County	3	0.05
Cheviot (city) Hamilton County	3	0.03
Springfield (city) Clark County	3	0.00
Addyston (village) Hamilton County	2	0.20
Bryan (city) Williams County	2	0.02
Dover (city) Tuscarawas County	2	0.02
Ashtabula (city) Ashtabula County	2	0.01
Akron (city) Summit County	2	0.00
Euclid (city) Cuyahoga County	2	0.00

Top 10 Places Sorted by Percent
Based on all places, regardless of population

Place	Number	%
Addyston (village) Hamilton County	2	0.20
Forest (village) Hardin County	1	0.07
Belpre (city) Washington County	3	0.05
Bolindale (cdp) Trumbull County	1	0.04
Grafton (village) Lorain County	1	0.04
Cheviot (city) Hamilton County	3	0.03
Bryan (city) Williams County	2	0.02
Dover (city) Tuscarawas County	2	0.02
Uhrichsville (city) Tuscarawas County	1	0.02
Ashtabula (city) Ashtabula County	2	0.01

Top 10 Places Sorted by Percent
Based on places with populations of 10,000 or more

Place	Number	%
Dover (city) Tuscarawas County	2	0.02
Ashtabula (city) Ashtabula County	2	0.01
Avon Lake (city) Lorain County	1	0.01
Fremont (city) Sandusky County	1	0.01
Mount Vernon (city) Knox County	1	0.01
Tiffin (city) Seneca County	1	0.01
Columbus (city) Franklin County	9	0.00
Springfield (city) Clark County	3	0.00
Akron (city) Summit County	2	0.00
Euclid (city) Cuyahoga County	2	0.00

American Indian: Yuman

Top 10 Places Sorted by Number
Based on all places, regardless of population

Place	Number	%
Seaman (village) Adams County	2	0.19
Bowling Green (city) Wood County	2	0.01
Cleveland (city) Cuyahoga County	2	0.00
Portage (village) Wood County	1	0.23
Forest Park (city) Hamilton County	1	0.01
Martins Ferry (city) Belmont County	1	0.01
Richmond Heights (city) Cuyahoga County	1	0.01
Worthington (city) Franklin County	1	0.01
Canton (city) Stark County	1	0.00
Eastlake (city) Lake County	1	0.00

Top 10 Places Sorted by Percent
Based on all places, regardless of population

Place	Number	%
Portage (village) Wood County	1	0.23
Seaman (village) Adams County	2	0.19
Bowling Green (city) Wood County	2	0.01
Forest Park (city) Hamilton County	1	0.01
Martins Ferry (city) Belmont County	1	0.01
Richmond Heights (city) Cuyahoga County	1	0.01
Worthington (city) Franklin County	1	0.01
Cleveland (city) Cuyahoga County	2	0.00
Canton (city) Stark County	1	0.00
Eastlake (city) Lake County	1	0.00

Top 10 Places Sorted by Percent
Based on places with populations of 10,000 or more

Place	Number	%
Bowling Green (city) Wood County	2	0.01
Forest Park (city) Hamilton County	1	0.01
Richmond Heights (city) Cuyahoga County	1	0.01
Worthington (city) Franklin County	1	0.01
Cleveland (city) Cuyahoga County	2	0.00
Canton (city) Stark County	1	0.00
Eastlake (city) Lake County	1	0.00
Kettering (city) Montgomery County	1	0.00
Mansfield (city) Richland County	1	0.00
Massillon (city) Stark County	1	0.00

American Indian: All other tribes

Top 10 Places Sorted by Number
Based on all places, regardless of population

Place	Number	%
Columbus (city) Franklin County	353	0.05
Cleveland (city) Cuyahoga County	143	0.03
Toledo (city) Lucas County	117	0.04
Cincinnati (city) Hamilton County	108	0.03
Dayton (city) Montgomery County	64	0.04
Springfield (city) Clark County	58	0.09
Akron (city) Summit County	57	0.03
Canton (city) Stark County	37	0.05
Youngstown (city) Mahoning County	36	0.04
Urbana (city) Champaign County	28	0.24

Top 10 Places Sorted by Percent
Based on all places, regardless of population

Place	Number	%
Linndale (village) Cuyahoga County	3	2.56
Wilkesville (village) Vinton County	3	1.99
Rome (village) Adams County	2	1.71
Amesville (village) Athens County	3	1.63
Alexandria (village) Licking County	1	1.18
Harbor View (village) Lucas County	1	1.01
Hollansburg (village) Darke County	2	0.93
Rio Grande (village) Gallia County	7	0.77
McGuffey (village) Hardin County	4	0.77
Corning (village) Perry County	4	0.67

Top 10 Places Sorted by Percent
Based on places with populations of 10,000 or more

Place	Number	%
Urbana (city) Champaign County	28	0.24
Portsmouth (city) Scioto County	28	0.13
Chillicothe (city) Ross County	27	0.12
Xenia (city) Greene County	24	0.10
West Carrollton City (city) Montgomery County	14	0.10
Springfield (city) Clark County	58	0.09
Shiloh (cdp) Montgomery County	10	0.09
Celina (city) Mercer County	9	0.09
Oxford (city) Butler County	18	0.08
Troy (city) Miami County	18	0.08

American Indian tribes, not specified

Top 10 Places Sorted by Number
Based on all places, regardless of population

Place	Number	%
Columbus (city) Franklin County	329	0.05
Cleveland (city) Cuyahoga County	238	0.05
Toledo (city) Lucas County	179	0.06
Cincinnati (city) Hamilton County	135	0.04
Dayton (city) Montgomery County	91	0.05
Akron (city) Summit County	85	0.04
Canton (city) Stark County	59	0.07
Lorain (city) Lorain County	44	0.06
Youngstown (city) Mahoning County	42	0.05
Mansfield (city) Richland County	39	0.08

Top 10 Places Sorted by Percent
Based on all places, regardless of population

Place	Number	%
Pitsburg (village) Darke County	5	1.28
Moscow (village) Clermont County	3	1.23
Fredericksburg (village) Wayne County	5	1.03
Vanlue (village) Hancock County	3	0.81
Beallsville (village) Monroe County	3	0.71
Sinking Spring (village) Highland County	1	0.63
New Athens (village) Harrison County	2	0.58
Belmore (village) Putnam County	1	0.58
Zaleski (village) Vinton County	2	0.53
Sparta (village) Morrow County	1	0.52

Top 10 Places Sorted by Percent
Based on places with populations of 10,000 or more

Place	Number	%
Ravenna (city) Portage County	13	0.11
Troy (city) Miami County	22	0.10
Defiance (city) Defiance County	17	0.10
Lebanon (city) Warren County	16	0.09
Brooklyn (city) Cuyahoga County	11	0.09
Mansfield (city) Richland County	39	0.08
Bowling Green (city) Wood County	23	0.08
Canton (city) Stark County	59	0.07
Huber Heights (city) Montgomery County	26	0.07
Barberton (city) Summit County	19	0.07

Arab

Top 10 Places Sorted by Number
Based on all places, regardless of population

Place	Number	%
Columbus (city) Franklin County	4,512	0.63
Toledo (city) Lucas County	3,668	1.17
Cleveland (city) Cuyahoga County	2,916	0.61
Lakewood (city) Cuyahoga County	2,371	4.19
Akron (city) Summit County	1,453	0.67
Parma (city) Cuyahoga County	1,381	1.61
North Olmsted (city) Cuyahoga County	1,050	3.08
Cincinnati (city) Hamilton County	981	0.30
Westlake (city) Cuyahoga County	926	2.91
Strongsville (city) Cuyahoga County	623	1.42

Top 10 Places Sorted by Percent
Based on all places, regardless of population

Place	Number	%
Blakeslee (village) Williams County	10	8.26
Masury (cdp) Trumbull County	161	5.85
Fairlawn (city) Summit County	356	4.86
Lakewood (city) Cuyahoga County	2,371	4.19
Holiday City (village) Williams County	2	3.92
Gates Mills (village) Cuyahoga County	95	3.88
Moreland Hills (village) Cuyahoga County	126	3.82
Clay Center (village) Ottawa County	11	3.72
Sugar Bush Knolls (village) Portage County	7	3.32
Ottawa Hills (village) Lucas County	150	3.30

Top 10 Places Sorted by Percent
Based on places with populations of 10,000 or more

Place	Number	%
Lakewood (city) Cuyahoga County	2,371	4.19
North Olmsted (city) Cuyahoga County	1,050	3.08
Westlake (city) Cuyahoga County	926	2.91
Brooklyn (city) Cuyahoga County	317	2.74
Rocky River (city) Cuyahoga County	444	2.14
Fairview Park (city) Cuyahoga County	333	1.90
Brecksville (city) Cuyahoga County	245	1.84

Notes: (cdp) census designated place; Refer to the User's Guide in the front of the book for more detailed information.

PROFILES OF OHIO / Ancestry Rankings 437

Place	Number	%
Parma Heights (city) Cuyahoga County	389	1.80
Montgomery (city) Hamilton County	165	1.64
Parma (city) Cuyahoga County	1,381	1.61

Arab: Arab/Arabic

Top 10 Places Sorted by Number
Based on all places, regardless of population

Place	Number	%
Columbus (city) Franklin County	921	0.13
Cleveland (city) Cuyahoga County	805	0.17
Lakewood (city) Cuyahoga County	721	1.27
Toledo (city) Lucas County	359	0.11
North Olmsted (city) Cuyahoga County	335	0.98
Akron (city) Summit County	248	0.11
Westlake (city) Cuyahoga County	237	0.74
Westerville (city) Franklin County	159	0.45
Dayton (city) Montgomery County	144	0.09
Parma (city) Cuyahoga County	120	0.14

Top 10 Places Sorted by Percent
Based on all places, regardless of population

Place	Number	%
Chauncey (village) Athens County	19	1.77
Lakewood (city) Cuyahoga County	721	1.27
Richfield (village) Summit County	36	1.09
North Olmsted (city) Cuyahoga County	335	0.98
Saint Louisville (village) Licking County	3	0.88
Moreland Hills (village) Cuyahoga County	27	0.82
Rossford (city) Wood County	48	0.76
Westlake (city) Cuyahoga County	237	0.74
Mount Carmel (cdp) Clermont County	32	0.74
Marshallville (village) Wayne County	6	0.72

Top 10 Places Sorted by Percent
Based on places with populations of 10,000 or more

Place	Number	%
Lakewood (city) Cuyahoga County	721	1.27
North Olmsted (city) Cuyahoga County	335	0.98
Westlake (city) Cuyahoga County	237	0.74
West Carrollton City (city) Montgomery County	92	0.66
Westerville (city) Franklin County	159	0.45
Middleburg Heights (city) Cuyahoga County	66	0.42
Kent (city) Portage County	108	0.39
Bellefontaine (city) Logan County	51	0.39
Fairview Park (city) Cuyahoga County	64	0.36
Northbrook (cdp) Hamilton County	38	0.34

Arab: Egyptian

Top 10 Places Sorted by Number
Based on all places, regardless of population

Place	Number	%
Columbus (city) Franklin County	491	0.07
Cleveland (city) Cuyahoga County	329	0.07
Lakewood (city) Cuyahoga County	118	0.21
Parma (city) Cuyahoga County	103	0.12
Upper Arlington (city) Franklin County	101	0.30
Parma Heights (city) Cuyahoga County	98	0.45
Toledo (city) Lucas County	95	0.03
Cincinnati (city) Hamilton County	82	0.02
Mayfield Heights (city) Cuyahoga County	71	0.37
Westlake (city) Cuyahoga County	70	0.22

Top 10 Places Sorted by Percent
Based on all places, regardless of population

Place	Number	%
South Russell (village) Geauga County	46	1.14
Ottawa Hills (village) Lucas County	48	1.06
Rio Grande (village) Gallia County	9	1.01
Pepper Pike (city) Cuyahoga County	60	0.99
Woodmere (village) Cuyahoga County	6	0.72
The Village of Indian Hill (city) Hamilton County	40	0.69
Orange (village) Cuyahoga County	19	0.59
Parma Heights (city) Cuyahoga County	98	0.45
Mayfield Heights (city) Cuyahoga County	71	0.37
Marshallville (village) Wayne County	3	0.36

Top 10 Places Sorted by Percent
Based on places with populations of 10,000 or more

Place	Number	%
Parma Heights (city) Cuyahoga County	98	0.45
Mayfield Heights (city) Cuyahoga County	71	0.37
Upper Arlington (city) Franklin County	101	0.30
Worthington (city) Franklin County	37	0.26
Richmond Heights (city) Cuyahoga County	27	0.25
Westlake (city) Cuyahoga County	70	0.22
Lakewood (city) Cuyahoga County	118	0.21
Brooklyn (city) Cuyahoga County	22	0.19
Lyndhurst (city) Cuyahoga County	28	0.18
Blue Ash (city) Hamilton County	22	0.17

Arab: Iraqi

Top 10 Places Sorted by Number
Based on all places, regardless of population

Place	Number	%
Toledo (city) Lucas County	121	0.04
Columbus (city) Franklin County	111	0.02
Mayfield Heights (city) Cuyahoga County	46	0.24
Olmsted Falls (city) Cuyahoga County	40	0.51
Parma Heights (city) Cuyahoga County	31	0.14
Cleveland (city) Cuyahoga County	27	0.01
Clayton (city) Montgomery County	20	0.15
Solon (city) Cuyahoga County	20	0.09
Beachwood (city) Cuyahoga County	18	0.15
Brecksville (city) Cuyahoga County	13	0.10

Top 10 Places Sorted by Percent
Based on all places, regardless of population

Place	Number	%
Olmsted Falls (city) Cuyahoga County	40	0.51
Oakwood (village) Cuyahoga County	9	0.25
Mayfield Heights (city) Cuyahoga County	46	0.24
Golf Manor (village) Hamilton County	8	0.20
Clayton (city) Montgomery County	20	0.15
Beachwood (city) Cuyahoga County	18	0.15
Logan (city) Hocking County	10	0.15
Parma Heights (city) Cuyahoga County	31	0.14
Monfort Heights South (cdp) Hamilton County	6	0.13
Brecksville (city) Cuyahoga County	13	0.10

Top 10 Places Sorted by Percent
Based on places with populations of 10,000 or more

Place	Number	%
Mayfield Heights (city) Cuyahoga County	46	0.24
Clayton (city) Montgomery County	20	0.15
Beachwood (city) Cuyahoga County	18	0.15
Parma Heights (city) Cuyahoga County	31	0.14
Brecksville (city) Cuyahoga County	13	0.10
Solon (city) Cuyahoga County	20	0.09
Toledo (city) Lucas County	121	0.04
Shiloh (city) Montgomery County	4	0.04
Brunswick (city) Medina County	9	0.03
Riverside (city) Montgomery County	7	0.03

Arab: Jordanian

Top 10 Places Sorted by Number
Based on all places, regardless of population

Place	Number	%
Toledo (city) Lucas County	174	0.06
Akron (city) Summit County	150	0.07
Columbus (city) Franklin County	146	0.02
Cleveland (city) Cuyahoga County	135	0.03
Lakewood (city) Cuyahoga County	106	0.19
Miamisburg (city) Montgomery County	91	0.46
Fairfield (city) Butler County	77	0.18
Huber Heights (city) Montgomery County	46	0.12
Avon (city) Lorain County	37	0.32
Kettering (city) Montgomery County	37	0.06

Top 10 Places Sorted by Percent
Based on all places, regardless of population

Place	Number	%
Greenhills (village) Hamilton County	28	0.69
Miamisburg (city) Montgomery County	91	0.46
Mulberry (cdp) Clermont County	12	0.38
Montgomery (city) Hamilton County	35	0.35
Avon (city) Lorain County	37	0.32
Magnolia (village) Stark County	3	0.30
Landen (cdp) Warren County	35	0.28
Brooklyn (city) Cuyahoga County	30	0.26
Bay Village (city) Cuyahoga County	33	0.21
Lakewood (city) Cuyahoga County	106	0.19

Top 10 Places Sorted by Percent
Based on places with populations of 10,000 or more

Place	Number	%
Miamisburg (city) Montgomery County	91	0.46
Montgomery (city) Hamilton County	35	0.35
Avon (city) Lorain County	37	0.32
Landen (cdp) Warren County	35	0.28
Brooklyn (city) Cuyahoga County	30	0.26
Bay Village (city) Cuyahoga County	33	0.21
Lakewood (city) Cuyahoga County	106	0.19
Fairfield (city) Butler County	77	0.18
Fairview Park (city) Cuyahoga County	28	0.16
Huber Heights (city) Montgomery County	46	0.12

Arab: Lebanese

Top 10 Places Sorted by Number
Based on all places, regardless of population

Place	Number	%
Toledo (city) Lucas County	2,048	0.65
Columbus (city) Franklin County	1,291	0.18
Cleveland (city) Cuyahoga County	1,004	0.21
Parma (city) Cuyahoga County	958	1.12
Akron (city) Summit County	834	0.38
Lakewood (city) Cuyahoga County	645	1.14
Cincinnati (city) Hamilton County	559	0.17
Strongsville (city) Cuyahoga County	478	1.09
Boardman (cdp) Mahoning County	441	1.18
Westlake (city) Cuyahoga County	304	0.95

Top 10 Places Sorted by Percent
Based on all places, regardless of population

Place	Number	%
Holiday City (village) Williams County	2	3.92
Fairlawn (city) Summit County	255	3.48
Montrose-Ghent (cdp) Summit County	105	2.10
Gates Mills (village) Cuyahoga County	48	1.96
Sherwood (cdp) Hamilton County	57	1.47
Higginsport (village) Brown County	5	1.44
Loveland Park (cdp) Warren County	25	1.40
Hills and Dales (village) Stark County	4	1.37
Brooklyn (city) Cuyahoga County	154	1.33
North Randall (village) Cuyahoga County	12	1.31

Top 10 Places Sorted by Percent
Based on places with populations of 10,000 or more

Place	Number	%
Brooklyn (city) Cuyahoga County	154	1.33
Brecksville (city) Cuyahoga County	161	1.21
Boardman (cdp) Mahoning County	441	1.18

Notes: (cdp) census designated place; Refer to the User's Guide in the front of the book for more detailed information.

Place	Number	%
Lakewood (city) Cuyahoga County	645	1.14
Parma (city) Cuyahoga County	958	1.12
Strongsville (city) Cuyahoga County	478	1.09
Parma Heights (city) Cuyahoga County	233	1.08
Sylvania (city) Lucas County	201	1.07
Westlake (city) Cuyahoga County	304	0.95
Broadview Heights (city) Cuyahoga County	148	0.93

Arab: Moroccan

Top 10 Places Sorted by Number
Based on all places, regardless of population

Place	Number	%
Cleveland (city) Cuyahoga County	133	0.03
Columbus (city) Franklin County	121	0.02
Youngstown (city) Mahoning County	92	0.11
Bexley (city) Franklin County	69	0.52
South Euclid (city) Cuyahoga County	35	0.15
Cincinnati (city) Hamilton County	30	0.01
Lakewood (city) Cuyahoga County	26	0.05
Fairfield (city) Butler County	22	0.05
Fairview Park (city) Cuyahoga County	20	0.11
Englewood (city) Montgomery County	19	0.16

Top 10 Places Sorted by Percent
Based on all places, regardless of population

Place	Number	%
Bexley (city) Franklin County	69	0.52
Brookside (village) Belmont County	2	0.31
Englewood (city) Montgomery County	19	0.16
South Euclid (city) Cuyahoga County	35	0.15
Gallipolis (city) Gallia County	5	0.12
Youngstown (city) Mahoning County	92	0.11
Fairview Park (city) Cuyahoga County	20	0.11
Highland Heights (city) Cuyahoga County	9	0.11
Riverside (city) Montgomery County	18	0.08
Wilmington (city) Clinton County	9	0.08

Top 10 Places Sorted by Percent
Based on places with populations of 10,000 or more

Place	Number	%
Bexley (city) Franklin County	69	0.52
Englewood (city) Montgomery County	19	0.16
South Euclid (city) Cuyahoga County	35	0.15
Youngstown (city) Mahoning County	92	0.11
Fairview Park (city) Cuyahoga County	20	0.11
Riverside (city) Montgomery County	18	0.08
Wilmington (city) Clinton County	9	0.08
Vermilion (city) Lorain County	8	0.07
West Carrollton City (city) Montgomery County	9	0.06
Lakewood (city) Cuyahoga County	26	0.05

Arab: Palestinian

Top 10 Places Sorted by Number
Based on all places, regardless of population

Place	Number	%
Columbus (city) Franklin County	510	0.07
Lakewood (city) Cuyahoga County	473	0.84
North Olmsted (city) Cuyahoga County	354	1.04
Toledo (city) Lucas County	322	0.10
Cleveland (city) Cuyahoga County	244	0.05
Rocky River (city) Cuyahoga County	106	0.51
Westlake (city) Cuyahoga County	98	0.31
Parma (city) Cuyahoga County	87	0.10
Akron (city) Summit County	82	0.04
Cincinnati (city) Hamilton County	67	0.02

Top 10 Places Sorted by Percent
Based on all places, regardless of population

Place	Number	%
North Olmsted (city) Cuyahoga County	354	1.04

Lakewood (city) Cuyahoga County	473	0.84
Ottawa Hills (village) Lucas County	31	0.68
Rocky River (city) Cuyahoga County	106	0.51
Campbell (city) Mahoning County	47	0.50
Lowellville (village) Mahoning County	6	0.47
Brooklyn (city) Cuyahoga County	49	0.42
Montgomery (city) Hamilton County	35	0.35
Westlake (city) Cuyahoga County	98	0.31
Landen (cdp) Warren County	30	0.24

Top 10 Places Sorted by Percent
Based on places with populations of 10,000 or more

Place	Number	%
North Olmsted (city) Cuyahoga County	354	1.04
Lakewood (city) Cuyahoga County	473	0.84
Rocky River (city) Cuyahoga County	106	0.51
Brooklyn (city) Cuyahoga County	49	0.42
Montgomery (city) Hamilton County	35	0.35
Westlake (city) Cuyahoga County	98	0.31
Landen (cdp) Warren County	30	0.24
Tallmadge (city) Summit County	35	0.21
Fairview Park (city) Cuyahoga County	36	0.20
Middleburg Heights (city) Cuyahoga County	26	0.17

Arab: Syrian

Top 10 Places Sorted by Number
Based on all places, regardless of population

Place	Number	%
Columbus (city) Franklin County	381	0.05
Toledo (city) Lucas County	304	0.10
Canton (city) Stark County	278	0.34
Lakewood (city) Cuyahoga County	213	0.38
Cleveland (city) Cuyahoga County	187	0.04
Westlake (city) Cuyahoga County	156	0.49
Akron (city) Summit County	123	0.06
Cincinnati (city) Hamilton County	100	0.03
Amherst (city) Lorain County	88	0.74
Parma (city) Cuyahoga County	74	0.09

Top 10 Places Sorted by Percent
Based on all places, regardless of population

Place	Number	%
Blakeslee (village) Williams County	10	8.26
Clay Center (village) Ottawa County	11	3.72
Sugar Bush Knolls (village) Portage County	6	2.84
Stony Prairie (cdp) Sandusky County	24	2.68
Moreland Hills (village) Cuyahoga County	67	2.03
Gates Mills (village) Cuyahoga County	47	1.92
Waldo (village) Marion County	6	1.78
Sherwood (cdp) Hamilton County	41	1.06
Ottawa Hills (village) Lucas County	43	0.95
Meyers Lake (village) Stark County	5	0.88

Top 10 Places Sorted by Percent
Based on places with populations of 10,000 or more

Place	Number	%
Amherst (city) Lorain County	88	0.74
Westlake (city) Cuyahoga County	156	0.49
Lakewood (city) Cuyahoga County	213	0.38
Brecksville (city) Cuyahoga County	50	0.38
Montgomery (city) Hamilton County	38	0.38
Canton (city) Stark County	278	0.34
Fairview Park (city) Cuyahoga County	60	0.34
Sylvania (city) Lucas County	62	0.33
Brook Park (city) Cuyahoga County	65	0.31
Springboro (city) Warren County	37	0.30

Arab: Other

Top 10 Places Sorted by Number
Based on all places, regardless of population

Place	Number	%
Columbus (city) Franklin County	540	0.08
Toledo (city) Lucas County	228	0.07
Masury (cdp) Trumbull County	157	5.70
Dayton (city) Montgomery County	118	0.07
Youngstown (city) Mahoning County	81	0.10
Athens (city) Athens County	69	0.33
Fairlawn (city) Summit County	63	0.86
Brooklyn (city) Cuyahoga County	62	0.54
Lakewood (city) Cuyahoga County	62	0.11
Westlake (city) Cuyahoga County	61	0.19

Top 10 Places Sorted by Percent
Based on all places, regardless of population

Place	Number	%
Masury (cdp) Trumbull County	157	5.70
Woodmere (village) Cuyahoga County	11	1.33
Fairlawn (city) Summit County	63	0.86
North Lewisburg (village) Champaign County	11	0.69
Brooklyn (city) Cuyahoga County	62	0.54
Athens (city) Athens County	69	0.33
Sheffield Lake (city) Lorain County	31	0.33
Jeffersonville (village) Fayette County	4	0.31
Yellow Springs (village) Greene County	11	0.30
Middleport (village) Meigs County	7	0.28

Top 10 Places Sorted by Percent
Based on places with populations of 10,000 or more

Place	Number	%
Brooklyn (city) Cuyahoga County	62	0.54
Athens (city) Athens County	69	0.33
Blue Ash (city) Hamilton County	25	0.20
Westlake (city) Cuyahoga County	61	0.19
Miamisburg (city) Montgomery County	28	0.14
Lakewood (city) Cuyahoga County	62	0.11
Fairview Park (city) Cuyahoga County	20	0.11
Washington (city) Fayette County	15	0.11
Youngstown (city) Mahoning County	81	0.10
North Canton (city) Stark County	17	0.10

Armenian

Top 10 Places Sorted by Number
Based on all places, regardless of population

Place	Number	%
Columbus (city) Franklin County	216	0.03
Toledo (city) Lucas County	102	0.03
Westlake (city) Cuyahoga County	94	0.30
Upper Arlington (city) Franklin County	90	0.27
Akron (city) Summit County	88	0.04
North Royalton (city) Cuyahoga County	87	0.30
Cincinnati (city) Hamilton County	83	0.03
Westerville (city) Franklin County	81	0.23
Dayton (city) Montgomery County	62	0.04
Cleveland Heights (city) Cuyahoga County	60	0.12

Top 10 Places Sorted by Percent
Based on all places, regardless of population

Place	Number	%
West Leipsic (village) Putnam County	9	3.49
Hamler (village) Henry County	8	1.27
Riverlea (village) Franklin County	6	1.20
Bainbridge (cdp) Geauga County	38	1.09
Moreland Hills (village) Cuyahoga County	24	0.73
Granville (village) Licking County	21	0.72
Sebring (village) Mahoning County	31	0.63
Cherry Grove (cdp) Hamilton County	25	0.56
Beloit (village) Mahoning County	5	0.49

Notes: (cdp) census designated place; Refer to the User's Guide in the front of the book for more detailed information.

Place	Number	%
Glendale (village) Hamilton County	10	0.46

Top 10 Places Sorted by Percent
Based on places with populations of 10,000 or more

Place	Number	%
Westlake (city) Cuyahoga County	94	0.30
North Royalton (city) Cuyahoga County	87	0.30
Middleburg Heights (city) Cuyahoga County	47	0.30
Upper Arlington (city) Franklin County	90	0.27
Avon Lake (city) Lorain County	46	0.25
Sharonville (city) Hamilton County	34	0.25
Brecksville (city) Cuyahoga County	33	0.25
Broadview Heights (city) Cuyahoga County	39	0.24
Westerville (city) Franklin County	81	0.23
Tallmadge (city) Summit County	34	0.21

Asian

Top 10 Places Sorted by Number
Based on all places, regardless of population

Place	Number	%
Columbus (city) Franklin County	28,624	4.02
Cleveland (city) Cuyahoga County	7,910	1.65
Cincinnati (city) Hamilton County	6,187	1.87
Toledo (city) Lucas County	4,293	1.37
Akron (city) Summit County	3,919	1.81
Dublin (city) Franklin County	2,527	8.05
Parma (city) Cuyahoga County	1,634	1.91
Strongsville (city) Cuyahoga County	1,594	3.63
Dayton (city) Montgomery County	1,561	0.94
Beavercreek (city) Greene County	1,549	4.08

Top 10 Places Sorted by Percent
Based on all places, regardless of population

Place	Number	%
Urbancrest (village) Franklin County	129	14.86
Dublin (city) Franklin County	2,527	8.05
Woodmere (village) Cuyahoga County	64	7.73
Blue Ash (city) Hamilton County	845	6.75
Beckett Ridge (cdp) Butler County	522	6.03
Evendale (village) Hamilton County	179	5.79
Lower Salem (village) Washington County	6	5.50
Solon (city) Cuyahoga County	1,168	5.36
Richmond Heights (city) Cuyahoga County	582	5.32
Highland Heights (city) Cuyahoga County	410	5.07

Top 10 Places Sorted by Percent
Based on places with populations of 10,000 or more

Place	Number	%
Dublin (city) Franklin County	2,527	8.05
Blue Ash (city) Hamilton County	845	6.75
Solon (city) Cuyahoga County	1,168	5.36
Richmond Heights (city) Cuyahoga County	582	5.32
Athens (city) Athens County	1,080	5.06
Westlake (city) Cuyahoga County	1,506	4.75
Mayfield Heights (city) Cuyahoga County	878	4.53
Sharonville (city) Hamilton County	579	4.19
Forest Park (city) Hamilton County	802	4.12
Beavercreek (city) Greene County	1,549	4.08

Asian: Bangladeshi

Top 10 Places Sorted by Number
Based on all places, regardless of population

Place	Number	%
Columbus (city) Franklin County	194	0.03
Dayton (city) Montgomery County	22	0.01
Cincinnati (city) Hamilton County	17	0.01
Akron (city) Summit County	16	0.01
Strongsville (city) Cuyahoga County	14	0.03
Toledo (city) Lucas County	14	0.00
Dublin (city) Franklin County	13	0.04
Brecksville (city) Cuyahoga County	10	0.07
Beavercreek (city) Greene County	10	0.03
Moraine (city) Montgomery County	9	0.13

Top 10 Places Sorted by Percent
Based on all places, regardless of population

Place	Number	%
Lucasville (cdp) Scioto County	4	0.25
Holland (village) Lucas County	3	0.23
Moraine (city) Montgomery County	9	0.13
Powell (village) Delaware County	8	0.13
Ada (village) Hardin County	5	0.09
Willoughby Hills (city) Lake County	7	0.08
Groveport (village) Franklin County	3	0.08
Brecksville (city) Cuyahoga County	10	0.07
Bedford Heights (city) Cuyahoga County	8	0.07
Twinsburg (city) Summit County	9	0.05

Top 10 Places Sorted by Percent
Based on places with populations of 10,000 or more

Place	Number	%
Brecksville (city) Cuyahoga County	10	0.07
Bedford Heights (city) Cuyahoga County	8	0.07
Twinsburg (city) Summit County	9	0.05
Dublin (city) Franklin County	13	0.04
Riverside (city) Montgomery County	9	0.04
Forest Park (city) Hamilton County	8	0.04
Columbus (city) Franklin County	194	0.03
Strongsville (city) Cuyahoga County	14	0.03
Beavercreek (city) Greene County	10	0.03
Parma Heights (city) Cuyahoga County	7	0.03

Asian: Cambodian

Top 10 Places Sorted by Number
Based on all places, regardless of population

Place	Number	%
Columbus (city) Franklin County	1,366	0.19
Cleveland (city) Cuyahoga County	391	0.08
Cincinnati (city) Hamilton County	229	0.07
Dayton (city) Montgomery County	81	0.05
Urbancrest (village) Franklin County	58	6.68
Fairfield (city) Butler County	42	0.10
Parma (city) Cuyahoga County	40	0.05
Forest Park (city) Hamilton County	39	0.20
Gahanna (city) Franklin County	38	0.12
Akron (city) Summit County	37	0.02

Top 10 Places Sorted by Percent
Based on all places, regardless of population

Place	Number	%
Urbancrest (village) Franklin County	58	6.68
Valleyview (village) Franklin County	11	1.83
Madeira (city) Hamilton County	36	0.40
Lockland (village) Hamilton County	13	0.35
Pleasant Run (cdp) Hamilton County	17	0.32
Fairfax (village) Hamilton County	6	0.31
Harrisburg (village) Franklin County	1	0.30
New Richmond (village) Clermont County	6	0.27
Northgate (cdp) Hamilton County	20	0.25
Kenwood (cdp) Hamilton County	18	0.24

Top 10 Places Sorted by Percent
Based on places with populations of 10,000 or more

Place	Number	%
Forest Park (city) Hamilton County	39	0.20
Columbus (city) Franklin County	1,366	0.19
Brooklyn (city) Cuyahoga County	20	0.17
Celina (city) Mercer County	13	0.13
Gahanna (city) Franklin County	38	0.12
Fairfield (city) Butler County	42	0.10
Norwood (city) Hamilton County	19	0.09

Place	Number	%
Cleveland (city) Cuyahoga County	391	0.08
Hilliard (city) Franklin County	19	0.08
Oxford (city) Butler County	17	0.08

Asian: Chinese, except Taiwanese

Top 10 Places Sorted by Number
Based on all places, regardless of population

Place	Number	%
Columbus (city) Franklin County	5,977	0.84
Cleveland (city) Cuyahoga County	2,231	0.47
Cincinnati (city) Hamilton County	1,521	0.46
Toledo (city) Lucas County	1,040	0.33
Akron (city) Summit County	656	0.30
Upper Arlington (city) Franklin County	502	1.49
Dublin (city) Franklin County	476	1.52
Cleveland Heights (city) Cuyahoga County	465	0.93
Shaker Heights (city) Cuyahoga County	371	1.26
Solon (city) Cuyahoga County	355	1.63

Top 10 Places Sorted by Percent
Based on all places, regardless of population

Place	Number	%
Highland Heights (city) Cuyahoga County	141	1.74
Solon (city) Cuyahoga County	355	1.63
Athens (city) Athens County	339	1.59
Dublin (city) Franklin County	476	1.52
Upper Arlington (city) Franklin County	502	1.49
Riverlea (village) Franklin County	7	1.40
Richmond Heights (city) Cuyahoga County	144	1.32
Oberlin (city) Lorain County	107	1.31
Shaker Heights (city) Cuyahoga County	371	1.26
Jeromesville (village) Ashland County	6	1.26

Top 10 Places Sorted by Percent
Based on places with populations of 10,000 or more

Place	Number	%
Solon (city) Cuyahoga County	355	1.63
Athens (city) Athens County	339	1.59
Dublin (city) Franklin County	476	1.52
Upper Arlington (city) Franklin County	502	1.49
Richmond Heights (city) Cuyahoga County	144	1.32
Shaker Heights (city) Cuyahoga County	371	1.26
Hudson (city) Summit County	263	1.17
Blue Ash (city) Hamilton County	141	1.13
Mayfield Heights (city) Cuyahoga County	210	1.08
Worthington (city) Franklin County	138	0.98

Asian: Filipino

Top 10 Places Sorted by Number
Based on all places, regardless of population

Place	Number	%
Columbus (city) Franklin County	1,851	0.26
Cleveland (city) Cuyahoga County	955	0.20
Cincinnati (city) Hamilton County	598	0.18
Toledo (city) Lucas County	529	0.17
Parma (city) Cuyahoga County	340	0.40
Akron (city) Summit County	252	0.12
Dayton (city) Montgomery County	242	0.15
Huber Heights (city) Montgomery County	218	0.57
Strongsville (city) Cuyahoga County	211	0.48
Elyria (city) Lorain County	197	0.35

Top 10 Places Sorted by Percent
Based on all places, regardless of population

Place	Number	%
Hemlock (village) Perry County	4	2.82
Wright-Patterson AFB (cdp) Montgomery County	116	1.74
New Rome (village) Franklin County	1	1.67
Devola (cdp) Washington County	42	1.52
Hills and Dales (village) Stark County	3	1.15

Notes: (cdp) census designated place; Refer to the User's Guide in the front of the book for more detailed information.

Place	Number	%
Aquilla (village) Geauga County	4	1.08
Tiro (village) Crawford County	3	1.07
Holland (village) Lucas County	12	0.92
Gettysburg (village) Darke County	5	0.90
Trimble (village) Athens County	4	0.86

Top 10 Places Sorted by Percent
Based on places with populations of 10,000 or more

Place	Number	%
Seven Hills (city) Cuyahoga County	81	0.67
North Royalton (city) Cuyahoga County	170	0.59
Forest Park (city) Hamilton County	112	0.58
Huber Heights (city) Montgomery County	218	0.57
Fairborn (city) Greene County	171	0.53
Northbrook (cdp) Hamilton County	58	0.52
Brecksville (city) Cuyahoga County	68	0.51
Strongsville (city) Cuyahoga County	211	0.48
Broadview Heights (city) Cuyahoga County	76	0.48
Bedford Heights (city) Cuyahoga County	52	0.46

Asian: Hmong

Top 10 Places Sorted by Number
Based on all places, regardless of population

Place	Number	%
Akron (city) Summit County	280	0.13
Columbus (city) Franklin County	13	0.00
Toledo (city) Lucas County	8	0.00
Medina (city) Medina County	6	0.02
Cuyahoga Falls (city) Summit County	5	0.01
Canton (city) Stark County	3	0.00
Cincinnati (city) Hamilton County	3	0.00
Shaker Heights (city) Cuyahoga County	2	0.01
Sharonville (city) Hamilton County	1	0.01
Euclid (city) Cuyahoga County	1	0.00

Top 10 Places Sorted by Percent
Based on all places, regardless of population

Place	Number	%
Akron (city) Summit County	280	0.13
Medina (city) Medina County	6	0.02
Cuyahoga Falls (city) Summit County	5	0.01
Shaker Heights (city) Cuyahoga County	2	0.01
Sharonville (city) Hamilton County	1	0.01
Columbus (city) Franklin County	13	0.00
Toledo (city) Lucas County	8	0.00
Canton (city) Stark County	3	0.00
Cincinnati (city) Hamilton County	3	0.00
Euclid (city) Cuyahoga County	1	0.00

Top 10 Places Sorted by Percent
Based on places with populations of 10,000 or more

Place	Number	%
Akron (city) Summit County	280	0.13
Medina (city) Medina County	6	0.02
Cuyahoga Falls (city) Summit County	5	0.01
Shaker Heights (city) Cuyahoga County	2	0.01
Sharonville (city) Hamilton County	1	0.01
Columbus (city) Franklin County	13	0.00
Toledo (city) Lucas County	8	0.00
Canton (city) Stark County	3	0.00
Cincinnati (city) Hamilton County	3	0.00
Euclid (city) Cuyahoga County	1	0.00

Asian: Indian

Top 10 Places Sorted by Number
Based on all places, regardless of population

Place	Number	%
Columbus (city) Franklin County	7,025	0.99
Cincinnati (city) Hamilton County	1,633	0.49
Cleveland (city) Cuyahoga County	1,445	0.30
Toledo (city) Lucas County	908	0.29
Akron (city) Summit County	756	0.35
Strongsville (city) Cuyahoga County	738	1.68
Dublin (city) Franklin County	678	2.16
Westlake (city) Cuyahoga County	611	1.93
Parma (city) Cuyahoga County	603	0.70
Solon (city) Cuyahoga County	510	2.34

Top 10 Places Sorted by Percent
Based on all places, regardless of population

Place	Number	%
Lower Salem (village) Washington County	6	5.50
Holiday City (village) Williams County	2	4.08
Urbancrest (village) Franklin County	29	3.34
Blue Ash (city) Hamilton County	379	3.03
Evendale (village) Hamilton County	90	2.91
Woodmere (village) Cuyahoga County	20	2.42
Solon (city) Cuyahoga County	510	2.34
Beckett Ridge (cdp) Butler County	203	2.34
The Village of Indian Hill (city) Hamilton County	136	2.30
Pepper Pike (city) Cuyahoga County	136	2.25

Top 10 Places Sorted by Percent
Based on places with populations of 10,000 or more

Place	Number	%
Blue Ash (city) Hamilton County	379	3.03
Solon (city) Cuyahoga County	510	2.34
Richmond Heights (city) Cuyahoga County	240	2.19
Dublin (city) Franklin County	678	2.16
Sharonville (city) Hamilton County	290	2.10
Westlake (city) Cuyahoga County	611	1.93
Forest Park (city) Hamilton County	364	1.87
Mayfield Heights (city) Cuyahoga County	346	1.78
Strongsville (city) Cuyahoga County	738	1.68
Twinsburg (city) Summit County	265	1.56

Asian: Indonesian

Top 10 Places Sorted by Number
Based on all places, regardless of population

Place	Number	%
Columbus (city) Franklin County	490	0.07
Cleveland (city) Cuyahoga County	67	0.01
Lakewood (city) Cuyahoga County	46	0.08
Toledo (city) Lucas County	39	0.01
Cincinnati (city) Hamilton County	38	0.01
Athens (city) Athens County	22	0.10
Kettering (city) Montgomery County	18	0.03
Cleveland Heights (city) Cuyahoga County	16	0.03
Dayton (city) Montgomery County	15	0.01
Upper Arlington (city) Franklin County	13	0.04

Top 10 Places Sorted by Percent
Based on all places, regardless of population

Place	Number	%
Gates Mills (village) Cuyahoga County	4	0.16
Hiram (village) Portage County	2	0.16
Athens (city) Athens County	22	0.10
Lakewood (city) Cuyahoga County	46	0.08
Columbus (city) Franklin County	490	0.07
Fairview Park (city) Cuyahoga County	12	0.07
Pepper Pike (city) Cuyahoga County	4	0.07
Oberlin (city) Lorain County	5	0.06
White Oak East (cdp) Hamilton County	2	0.06
Hilliard (city) Franklin County	12	0.05

Top 10 Places Sorted by Percent
Based on places with populations of 10,000 or more

Place	Number	%
Athens (city) Athens County	22	0.10
Lakewood (city) Cuyahoga County	46	0.08
Columbus (city) Franklin County	490	0.07
Fairview Park (city) Cuyahoga County	12	0.07
Hilliard (city) Franklin County	12	0.05
Upper Arlington (city) Franklin County	13	0.04
Twinsburg (city) Summit County	6	0.04
Kettering (city) Montgomery County	18	0.03
Cleveland Heights (city) Cuyahoga County	16	0.03
Stow (city) Summit County	10	0.03

Asian: Japanese

Top 10 Places Sorted by Number
Based on all places, regardless of population

Place	Number	%
Columbus (city) Franklin County	2,458	0.35
Dublin (city) Franklin County	855	2.72
Cleveland (city) Cuyahoga County	343	0.07
Cincinnati (city) Hamilton County	336	0.10
Toledo (city) Lucas County	291	0.09
Findlay (city) Hancock County	285	0.73
Sidney (city) Shelby County	239	1.18
Hilliard (city) Franklin County	174	0.72
Troy (city) Miami County	172	0.78
Huber Heights (city) Montgomery County	169	0.44

Top 10 Places Sorted by Percent
Based on all places, regardless of population

Place	Number	%
Dublin (city) Franklin County	855	2.72
Choctaw Lake (cdp) Madison County	19	1.22
Sidney (city) Shelby County	239	1.18
Yellow Springs (village) Greene County	37	0.98
Gambier (village) Knox County	17	0.91
Mayfield (village) Cuyahoga County	29	0.84
Cuyahoga Heights (village) Cuyahoga County	5	0.83
Troy (city) Miami County	172	0.78
Montgomery (city) Hamilton County	77	0.76
Fairlawn (city) Summit County	55	0.75

Top 10 Places Sorted by Percent
Based on places with populations of 10,000 or more

Place	Number	%
Dublin (city) Franklin County	855	2.72
Sidney (city) Shelby County	239	1.18
Troy (city) Miami County	172	0.78
Montgomery (city) Hamilton County	77	0.76
Blue Ash (city) Hamilton County	92	0.74
Findlay (city) Hancock County	285	0.73
Hilliard (city) Franklin County	174	0.72
Mayfield Heights (city) Cuyahoga County	136	0.70
Athens (city) Athens County	146	0.68
Landen (cdp) Warren County	78	0.61

Asian: Korean

Top 10 Places Sorted by Number
Based on all places, regardless of population

Place	Number	%
Columbus (city) Franklin County	2,930	0.41
Cincinnati (city) Hamilton County	464	0.14
Cleveland (city) Cuyahoga County	380	0.08
Toledo (city) Lucas County	370	0.12
Akron (city) Summit County	366	0.17
Beavercreek (city) Greene County	284	0.75
Fairborn (city) Greene County	206	0.64
Westlake (city) Cuyahoga County	193	0.61
Dublin (city) Franklin County	191	0.61
Dayton (city) Montgomery County	161	0.10

Top 10 Places Sorted by Percent
Based on all places, regardless of population

Place	Number	%
Woodmere (village) Cuyahoga County	22	2.66

Notes: (cdp) census designated place; Refer to the User's Guide in the front of the book for more detailed information.

Place	Number	%
North Hampton (village) Clark County	8	2.16
Burgoon (village) Sandusky County	3	1.51
Chauncey (village) Athens County	15	1.41
Hoytville (village) Wood County	4	1.35
Pepper Pike (city) Cuyahoga County	65	1.08
Highland (village) Highland County	3	1.06
Zoar (village) Tuscarawas County	2	1.04
Blue Ash (city) Hamilton County	118	0.94
Belmont (village) Belmont County	5	0.94

Top 10 Places Sorted by Percent
Based on places with populations of 10,000 or more

Place	Number	%
Blue Ash (city) Hamilton County	118	0.94
Beavercreek (city) Greene County	284	0.75
Broadview Heights (city) Cuyahoga County	108	0.68
Fairborn (city) Greene County	206	0.64
Westlake (city) Cuyahoga County	193	0.61
Dublin (city) Franklin County	191	0.61
Beachwood (city) Cuyahoga County	69	0.57
Montgomery (city) Hamilton County	55	0.54
Athens (city) Athens County	106	0.50
Worthington (city) Franklin County	70	0.50

Asian: Laotian

Top 10 Places Sorted by Number
Based on all places, regardless of population

Place	Number	%
Columbus (city) Franklin County	1,290	0.18
Akron (city) Summit County	516	0.24
Toledo (city) Lucas County	146	0.05
Whitehall (city) Franklin County	75	0.39
Cleveland (city) Cuyahoga County	70	0.01
Orrville (city) Wayne County	67	0.78
Findlay (city) Hancock County	67	0.17
Carey (village) Wyandot County	59	1.51
Euclid (city) Cuyahoga County	50	0.09
Montpelier (village) Williams County	48	1.11

Top 10 Places Sorted by Percent
Based on all places, regardless of population

Place	Number	%
Carey (village) Wyandot County	59	1.51
Montpelier (village) Williams County	48	1.11
Orrville (city) Wayne County	67	0.78
Buckland (village) Auglaize County	2	0.78
Deshler (village) Henry County	13	0.71
Groveport (village) Franklin County	19	0.49
Whitehall (city) Franklin County	75	0.39
Sugarcreek (village) Tuscarawas County	8	0.37
Wauseon (city) Fulton County	21	0.30
Smithville (village) Wayne County	4	0.30

Top 10 Places Sorted by Percent
Based on places with populations of 10,000 or more

Place	Number	%
Whitehall (city) Franklin County	75	0.39
Akron (city) Summit County	516	0.24
Columbus (city) Franklin County	1,290	0.18
Findlay (city) Hancock County	67	0.17
Fostoria (city) Seneca County	18	0.13
Euclid (city) Cuyahoga County	50	0.09
Richmond Heights (city) Cuyahoga County	10	0.09
Oregon (city) Lucas County	15	0.08
Bexley (city) Franklin County	10	0.08
Wadsworth (city) Medina County	11	0.06

Asian: Malaysian

Top 10 Places Sorted by Number
Based on all places, regardless of population

Place	Number	%
Columbus (city) Franklin County	66	0.01
Toledo (city) Lucas County	43	0.01
Athens (city) Athens County	25	0.12
Cleveland (city) Cuyahoga County	18	0.00
Findlay (city) Hancock County	9	0.02
Akron (city) Summit County	8	0.00
Lakewood (city) Cuyahoga County	7	0.01
Monfort Heights East (cdp) Hamilton County	6	0.15
Maumee (city) Lucas County	6	0.04
Dublin (city) Franklin County	6	0.02

Top 10 Places Sorted by Percent
Based on all places, regardless of population

Place	Number	%
Woodmere (village) Cuyahoga County	2	0.24
Monfort Heights East (cdp) Hamilton County	6	0.15
Greentown (cdp) Stark County	4	0.13
Athens (city) Athens County	25	0.12
Gates Mills (village) Cuyahoga County	2	0.08
Boston Heights (village) Summit County	1	0.08
The Plains (cdp) Athens County	2	0.07
Ripley (village) Brown County	1	0.06
New Albany (village) Franklin County	2	0.05
South Russell (village) Geauga County	2	0.05

Top 10 Places Sorted by Percent
Based on places with populations of 10,000 or more

Place	Number	%
Athens (city) Athens County	25	0.12
Maumee (city) Lucas County	6	0.04
Reading (city) Hamilton County	3	0.03
Findlay (city) Hancock County	9	0.02
Dublin (city) Franklin County	6	0.02
Fairborn (city) Greene County	6	0.02
Riverside (city) Montgomery County	4	0.02
Clayton (city) Montgomery County	3	0.02
Fremont (city) Sandusky County	3	0.02
Urbana (city) Champaign County	2	0.02

Asian: Pakistani

Top 10 Places Sorted by Number
Based on all places, regardless of population

Place	Number	%
Columbus (city) Franklin County	434	0.06
Cincinnati (city) Hamilton County	85	0.03
Cleveland (city) Cuyahoga County	70	0.01
Toledo (city) Lucas County	68	0.02
Akron (city) Summit County	59	0.03
Westlake (city) Cuyahoga County	50	0.16
Lakewood (city) Cuyahoga County	48	0.08
Strongsville (city) Cuyahoga County	46	0.10
Forest Park (city) Hamilton County	42	0.22
Austintown (cdp) Mahoning County	31	0.10

Top 10 Places Sorted by Percent
Based on all places, regardless of population

Place	Number	%
Mount Cory (village) Hancock County	3	1.48
Orange (village) Cuyahoga County	13	0.40
Oak Hill (village) Jackson County	4	0.24
Woodmere (village) Cuyahoga County	2	0.24
Forest Park (city) Hamilton County	42	0.22
Richmond Heights (city) Cuyahoga County	20	0.18
Dry Run (cdp) Hamilton County	12	0.18
Westlake (city) Cuyahoga County	50	0.16
Amberley (village) Hamilton County	5	0.15
Marble Cliff (village) Franklin County	1	0.15

Top 10 Places Sorted by Percent
Based on places with populations of 10,000 or more

Place	Number	%
Forest Park (city) Hamilton County	42	0.22
Richmond Heights (city) Cuyahoga County	20	0.18
Westlake (city) Cuyahoga County	50	0.16
Middleburg Heights (city) Cuyahoga County	20	0.13
Brecksville (city) Cuyahoga County	17	0.13
Strongsville (city) Cuyahoga County	46	0.10
Austintown (cdp) Mahoning County	31	0.10
Mason (city) Warren County	19	0.09
Forestville (cdp) Hamilton County	10	0.09
Lakewood (city) Cuyahoga County	48	0.08

Asian: Sri Lankan

Top 10 Places Sorted by Number
Based on all places, regardless of population

Place	Number	%
Columbus (city) Franklin County	116	0.02
Cincinnati (city) Hamilton County	65	0.02
Hilliard (city) Franklin County	15	0.06
Fairborn (city) Greene County	14	0.04
Upper Arlington (city) Franklin County	12	0.04
Shaker Heights (city) Cuyahoga County	11	0.04
Akron (city) Summit County	11	0.01
Toledo (city) Lucas County	10	0.00
Solon (city) Cuyahoga County	9	0.04
Bowling Green (city) Wood County	9	0.03

Top 10 Places Sorted by Percent
Based on all places, regardless of population

Place	Number	%
Fairfax (village) Hamilton County	7	0.36
Gates Mills (village) Cuyahoga County	6	0.24
Mount Repose (cdp) Clermont County	5	0.12
Hilliard (city) Franklin County	15	0.06
Blue Ash (city) Hamilton County	7	0.06
Deer Park (city) Hamilton County	3	0.05
Glendale (village) Hamilton County	1	0.05
Fairborn (city) Greene County	14	0.04
Upper Arlington (city) Franklin County	12	0.04
Shaker Heights (city) Cuyahoga County	11	0.04

Top 10 Places Sorted by Percent
Based on places with populations of 10,000 or more

Place	Number	%
Hilliard (city) Franklin County	15	0.06
Blue Ash (city) Hamilton County	7	0.06
Fairborn (city) Greene County	14	0.04
Upper Arlington (city) Franklin County	12	0.04
Shaker Heights (city) Cuyahoga County	11	0.04
Solon (city) Cuyahoga County	9	0.04
Aurora (city) Portage County	6	0.04
Bowling Green (city) Wood County	9	0.03
Kent (city) Portage County	9	0.03
Athens (city) Athens County	7	0.03

Asian: Taiwanese

Top 10 Places Sorted by Number
Based on all places, regardless of population

Place	Number	%
Columbus (city) Franklin County	435	0.06
Upper Arlington (city) Franklin County	103	0.31
Cincinnati (city) Hamilton County	87	0.03
Dublin (city) Franklin County	80	0.25
Cleveland (city) Cuyahoga County	56	0.01
Athens (city) Athens County	47	0.22
Beavercreek (city) Greene County	46	0.12

Notes: (cdp) census designated place; Refer to the User's Guide in the front of the book for more detailed information.

442 PROFILES OF OHIO / Ancestry Rankings

Place	Number	%
Solon (city) Cuyahoga County	39	0.18
Westlake (city) Cuyahoga County	37	0.12
Hilliard (city) Franklin County	32	0.13

Top 10 Places Sorted by Percent
Based on all places, regardless of population

Place	Number	%
Evendale (village) Hamilton County	16	0.52
Shawnee Hills (village) Delaware County	2	0.48
Pigeon Creek (cdp) Summit County	4	0.42
Five Points (cdp) Warren County	7	0.32
Upper Arlington (city) Franklin County	103	0.31
Highland Heights (city) Cuyahoga County	25	0.31
Dublin (city) Franklin County	80	0.25
Athens (city) Athens County	47	0.22
Cherry Grove (cdp) Hamilton County	10	0.22
The Village of Indian Hill (city) Hamilton County	12	0.20

Top 10 Places Sorted by Percent
Based on places with populations of 10,000 or more

Place	Number	%
Upper Arlington (city) Franklin County	103	0.31
Dublin (city) Franklin County	80	0.25
Athens (city) Athens County	47	0.22
Solon (city) Cuyahoga County	39	0.18
Springdale (city) Hamilton County	19	0.18
Montgomery (city) Hamilton County	16	0.16
Sharonville (city) Hamilton County	21	0.15
Hilliard (city) Franklin County	32	0.13
Centerville (city) Montgomery County	29	0.13
Beavercreek (city) Greene County	46	0.12

Asian: Thai

Top 10 Places Sorted by Number
Based on all places, regardless of population

Place	Number	%
Columbus (city) Franklin County	472	0.07
Cleveland (city) Cuyahoga County	121	0.03
Cincinnati (city) Hamilton County	88	0.03
Akron (city) Summit County	79	0.04
Toledo (city) Lucas County	76	0.02
Dayton (city) Montgomery County	48	0.03
Fairborn (city) Greene County	41	0.13
Huber Heights (city) Montgomery County	40	0.10
Cleveland Heights (city) Cuyahoga County	37	0.07
Lakewood (city) Cuyahoga County	30	0.05

Top 10 Places Sorted by Percent
Based on all places, regardless of population

Place	Number	%
Riverlea (village) Franklin County	3	0.60
Kirtland Hills (village) Lake County	3	0.50
Richmond (village) Jefferson County	2	0.42
Hills and Dales (village) Stark County	1	0.38
Pigeon Creek (cdp) Summit County	3	0.32
Enon (village) Clark County	8	0.30
Wilmot (village) Stark County	1	0.30
Wright-Patterson AFB (cdp) Montgomery County	17	0.26
Green Springs (village) Seneca County	3	0.24
Rawson (village) Hancock County	1	0.22

Top 10 Places Sorted by Percent
Based on places with populations of 10,000 or more

Place	Number	%
Fairborn (city) Greene County	41	0.13
Athens (city) Athens County	28	0.13
Huber Heights (city) Montgomery County	40	0.10
Riverside (city) Montgomery County	22	0.09
Columbus (city) Franklin County	472	0.07
Cleveland Heights (city) Cuyahoga County	37	0.07
Gahanna (city) Franklin County	23	0.07

Place	Number	%
Whitehall (city) Franklin County	13	0.07
Ashland (city) Ashland County	12	0.06
Berea (city) Cuyahoga County	11	0.06

Asian: Vietnamese

Top 10 Places Sorted by Number
Based on all places, regardless of population

Place	Number	%
Columbus (city) Franklin County	2,089	0.29
Cleveland (city) Cuyahoga County	1,186	0.25
Cincinnati (city) Hamilton County	620	0.19
Akron (city) Summit County	434	0.20
Toledo (city) Lucas County	298	0.10
Huber Heights (city) Montgomery County	245	0.64
Dayton (city) Montgomery County	179	0.11
Fairborn (city) Greene County	145	0.45
Fairfield (city) Butler County	120	0.29
Kettering (city) Montgomery County	120	0.21

Top 10 Places Sorted by Percent
Based on all places, regardless of population

Place	Number	%
Moraine (city) Montgomery County	64	0.93
Olde West Chester (cdp) Butler County	2	0.86
Beckett Ridge (cdp) Butler County	66	0.76
Springdale (city) Hamilton County	74	0.70
Urbancrest (village) Franklin County	6	0.69
Huber Heights (city) Montgomery County	245	0.64
Magnetic Springs (village) Union County	2	0.62
Pleasant Run Farm (cdp) Hamilton County	28	0.59
Brooklyn (city) Cuyahoga County	67	0.58
Northgate (cdp) Hamilton County	46	0.57

Top 10 Places Sorted by Percent
Based on places with populations of 10,000 or more

Place	Number	%
Springdale (city) Hamilton County	74	0.70
Huber Heights (city) Montgomery County	245	0.64
Brooklyn (city) Cuyahoga County	67	0.58
Forest Park (city) Hamilton County	93	0.48
Fairborn (city) Greene County	145	0.45
Sharonville (city) Hamilton County	47	0.34
Columbus (city) Franklin County	2,089	0.29
Fairfield (city) Butler County	120	0.29
Riverside (city) Montgomery County	68	0.29
Parma Heights (city) Cuyahoga County	59	0.27

Asian: Other Asian, specified

Top 10 Places Sorted by Number
Based on all places, regardless of population

Place	Number	%
Columbus (city) Franklin County	103	0.01
Cincinnati (city) Hamilton County	44	0.01
Cleveland (city) Cuyahoga County	44	0.01
Akron (city) Summit County	39	0.02
Toledo (city) Lucas County	22	0.01
Hamilton (city) Butler County	15	0.02
Cleveland Heights (city) Cuyahoga County	14	0.03
Dayton (city) Montgomery County	13	0.01
Frankfort (village) Ross County	12	1.19
Franklin (city) Warren County	11	0.10

Top 10 Places Sorted by Percent
Based on all places, regardless of population

Place	Number	%
Frankfort (village) Ross County	12	1.19
Seven Mile (village) Butler County	5	0.74
Corning (village) Perry County	2	0.34
Rio Grande (village) Gallia County	3	0.33
Woodmere (village) Cuyahoga County	2	0.24

Place	Number	%
Crown City (village) Gallia County	1	0.24
Lucasville (cdp) Scioto County	3	0.19
Hiram (village) Portage County	2	0.16
Roseville (village) Perry County	3	0.15
Fort Loramie (village) Shelby County	2	0.15

Top 10 Places Sorted by Percent
Based on places with populations of 10,000 or more

Place	Number	%
Franklin (city) Warren County	11	0.10
Springboro (city) Warren County	11	0.09
University Heights (city) Cuyahoga County	10	0.07
Landen (cdp) Warren County	8	0.06
Oxford (city) Butler County	10	0.05
Richmond Heights (city) Cuyahoga County	5	0.05
Athens (city) Athens County	8	0.04
Blue Ash (city) Hamilton County	5	0.04
Finneytown (cdp) Hamilton County	5	0.04
Cleveland Heights (city) Cuyahoga County	14	0.03

Asian: Other Asian, not specified

Top 10 Places Sorted by Number
Based on all places, regardless of population

Place	Number	%
Columbus (city) Franklin County	1,315	0.18
Cleveland (city) Cuyahoga County	518	0.11
Toledo (city) Lucas County	399	0.13
Cincinnati (city) Hamilton County	341	0.10
Akron (city) Summit County	239	0.11
Dayton (city) Montgomery County	129	0.08
Parma (city) Cuyahoga County	107	0.12
North Olmsted (city) Cuyahoga County	91	0.27
Lakewood (city) Cuyahoga County	85	0.15
Westlake (city) Cuyahoga County	75	0.24

Top 10 Places Sorted by Percent
Based on all places, regardless of population

Place	Number	%
Urbancrest (village) Franklin County	34	3.92
Chauncey (village) Athens County	11	1.03
Put-in-Bay (village) Ottawa County	1	0.78
Old Washington (village) Guernsey County	2	0.75
Potsdam (village) Miami County	1	0.49
Powhatan Point (village) Belmont County	8	0.46
North Randall (village) Cuyahoga County	4	0.44
Pigeon Creek (cdp) Summit County	3	0.32
Fairlawn (city) Summit County	23	0.31
McComb (village) Hancock County	5	0.30

Top 10 Places Sorted by Percent
Based on places with populations of 10,000 or more

Place	Number	%
North Olmsted (city) Cuyahoga County	91	0.27
Westlake (city) Cuyahoga County	75	0.24
Miamisburg (city) Montgomery County	46	0.24
Athens (city) Athens County	46	0.22
Fairview Park (city) Cuyahoga County	35	0.20
Forestville (cdp) Hamilton County	22	0.20
Columbus (city) Franklin County	1,315	0.18
Bowling Green (city) Wood County	53	0.18
Centerville (city) Montgomery County	42	0.18
Fairborn (city) Greene County	54	0.17

Assyrian/Chaldean/Syriac

Top 10 Places Sorted by Number
Based on all places, regardless of population

Place	Number	%
Rocky River (city) Cuyahoga County	39	0.19
Defiance (city) Defiance County	20	0.12
Toledo (city) Lucas County	15	0.00

Notes: (cdp) census designated place; Refer to the User's Guide in the front of the book for more detailed information.

PROFILES OF OHIO / Ancestry Rankings

Place	Number	%
Middlefield (village) Geauga County	7	0.32
Aurora (city) Portage County	7	0.05
Dayton (city) Montgomery County	7	0.00
Cedarville (village) Greene County	6	0.16
Oregon (city) Lucas County	6	0.03
Gahanna (city) Franklin County	6	0.02
Kettering (city) Montgomery County	6	0.01

Top 10 Places Sorted by Percent
Based on all places, regardless of population

Place	Number	%
Middlefield (village) Geauga County	7	0.32
Rocky River (city) Cuyahoga County	39	0.19
Cedarville (village) Greene County	6	0.16
Defiance (city) Defiance County	20	0.12
Aurora (city) Portage County	7	0.05
Oregon (city) Lucas County	6	0.03
Gahanna (city) Franklin County	6	0.02
Parma Heights (city) Cuyahoga County	5	0.02
Kettering (city) Montgomery County	6	0.01
Lakewood (city) Cuyahoga County	6	0.01

Top 10 Places Sorted by Percent
Based on places with populations of 10,000 or more

Place	Number	%
Rocky River (city) Cuyahoga County	39	0.19
Defiance (city) Defiance County	20	0.12
Aurora (city) Portage County	7	0.05
Oregon (city) Lucas County	6	0.03
Gahanna (city) Franklin County	6	0.02
Parma Heights (city) Cuyahoga County	5	0.02
Kettering (city) Montgomery County	6	0.01
Lakewood (city) Cuyahoga County	6	0.01
Huber Heights (city) Montgomery County	5	0.01
Toledo (city) Lucas County	15	0.00

Australian

Top 10 Places Sorted by Number
Based on all places, regardless of population

Place	Number	%
Columbus (city) Franklin County	262	0.04
Toledo (city) Lucas County	107	0.03
Cincinnati (city) Hamilton County	65	0.02
Shaker Heights (city) Cuyahoga County	54	0.18
Solon (city) Cuyahoga County	51	0.23
Beachwood (city) Cuyahoga County	50	0.41
Mount Vernon (city) Knox County	50	0.34
Akron (city) Summit County	50	0.02
Elyria (city) Lorain County	46	0.08
Cleveland (city) Cuyahoga County	40	0.01

Top 10 Places Sorted by Percent
Based on all places, regardless of population

Place	Number	%
Carrollton (village) Carroll County	19	0.61
Germantown (village) Montgomery County	29	0.60
Lake Darby (cdp) Franklin County	20	0.55
New Riegel (village) Seneca County	1	0.45
Beachwood (city) Cuyahoga County	50	0.41
Timberlake (village) Lake County	3	0.39
Peninsula (village) Summit County	2	0.39
Wright-Patterson AFB (cdp) Montgomery County	25	0.38
Fort Shawnee (village) Allen County	14	0.35
Mount Vernon (city) Knox County	50	0.34

Top 10 Places Sorted by Percent
Based on places with populations of 10,000 or more

Place	Number	%
Beachwood (city) Cuyahoga County	50	0.41
Mount Vernon (city) Knox County	50	0.34
Loveland (city) Hamilton County	29	0.24
Solon (city) Cuyahoga County	51	0.23
Worthington (city) Franklin County	30	0.21
Shaker Heights (city) Cuyahoga County	54	0.18
Bexley (city) Franklin County	20	0.15
Hudson (city) Summit County	26	0.12
Dublin (city) Franklin County	35	0.11
Montgomery (city) Hamilton County	10	0.10

Austrian

Top 10 Places Sorted by Number
Based on all places, regardless of population

Place	Number	%
Columbus (city) Franklin County	1,483	0.21
Cincinnati (city) Hamilton County	804	0.24
Cleveland (city) Cuyahoga County	749	0.16
Akron (city) Summit County	602	0.28
Parma (city) Cuyahoga County	473	0.55
Toledo (city) Lucas County	396	0.13
Lakewood (city) Cuyahoga County	385	0.68
Strongsville (city) Cuyahoga County	312	0.71
Euclid (city) Cuyahoga County	310	0.59
Westlake (city) Cuyahoga County	269	0.84

Top 10 Places Sorted by Percent
Based on all places, regardless of population

Place	Number	%
Tuscarawas (village) Tuscarawas County	36	3.75
Peninsula (village) Summit County	14	2.70
Pepper Pike (city) Cuyahoga County	117	1.94
Orange (village) Cuyahoga County	58	1.79
Newton Falls (village) Trumbull County	90	1.78
Turpin Hills (cdp) Hamilton County	84	1.68
Aquilla (village) Geauga County	6	1.63
Beachwood (city) Cuyahoga County	198	1.62
New Concord (village) Muskingum County	42	1.56
North Perry (village) Lake County	13	1.55

Top 10 Places Sorted by Percent
Based on places with populations of 10,000 or more

Place	Number	%
Beachwood (city) Cuyahoga County	198	1.62
Mayfield Heights (city) Cuyahoga County	203	1.05
Lyndhurst (city) Cuyahoga County	159	1.04
Brecksville (city) Cuyahoga County	120	0.90
Avon (city) Lorain County	103	0.90
Rocky River (city) Cuyahoga County	176	0.85
New Philadelphia (city) Tuscarawas County	143	0.85
Westlake (city) Cuyahoga County	269	0.84
University Heights (city) Cuyahoga County	114	0.81
South Euclid (city) Cuyahoga County	187	0.79

Basque

Top 10 Places Sorted by Number
Based on all places, regardless of population

Place	Number	%
Columbus (city) Franklin County	37	0.01
Cleveland Heights (city) Cuyahoga County	19	0.04
Cleveland (city) Cuyahoga County	16	0.00
Reading (city) Hamilton County	15	0.13
Centerville (city) Montgomery County	13	0.06
Bowling Green (city) Wood County	12	0.04
Willoughby Hills (city) Lake County	11	0.13
Toledo (city) Lucas County	10	0.00
Westlake (city) Cuyahoga County	9	0.03
Hilliard (city) Franklin County	8	0.03

Top 10 Places Sorted by Percent
Based on all places, regardless of population

Place	Number	%
New Albany (village) Franklin County	6	0.16
Reading (city) Hamilton County	15	0.13
Willoughby Hills (city) Lake County	11	0.13
Centerville (city) Montgomery County	13	0.06
Chagrin Falls (village) Cuyahoga County	2	0.05
Cleveland Heights (city) Cuyahoga County	19	0.04
Bowling Green (city) Wood County	12	0.04
Bedford (city) Cuyahoga County	5	0.04
Westlake (city) Cuyahoga County	9	0.03
Hilliard (city) Franklin County	8	0.03

Top 10 Places Sorted by Percent
Based on places with populations of 10,000 or more

Place	Number	%
Reading (city) Hamilton County	15	0.13
Centerville (city) Montgomery County	13	0.06
Cleveland Heights (city) Cuyahoga County	19	0.04
Bowling Green (city) Wood County	12	0.04
Bedford (city) Cuyahoga County	5	0.04
Westlake (city) Cuyahoga County	9	0.03
Hilliard (city) Franklin County	8	0.03
Fairview Park (city) Cuyahoga County	5	0.03
Shaker Heights (city) Cuyahoga County	6	0.02
Rocky River (city) Cuyahoga County	5	0.02

Belgian

Top 10 Places Sorted by Number
Based on all places, regardless of population

Place	Number	%
Columbus (city) Franklin County	510	0.07
Toledo (city) Lucas County	458	0.15
Cincinnati (city) Hamilton County	167	0.05
Akron (city) Summit County	117	0.05
Cleveland (city) Cuyahoga County	98	0.02
Cleveland Heights (city) Cuyahoga County	95	0.19
Gahanna (city) Franklin County	92	0.28
Springfield (city) Clark County	91	0.14
Findlay (city) Hancock County	83	0.21
Sylvania (city) Lucas County	82	0.44

Top 10 Places Sorted by Percent
Based on all places, regardless of population

Place	Number	%
Malinta (village) Henry County	18	6.06
Vanlue (village) Hancock County	7	1.82
New Riegel (village) Seneca County	3	1.36
Lyons (village) Fulton County	7	1.27
Tiltonsville (village) Jefferson County	16	1.23
Granville (village) Licking County	35	1.20
Magnolia (village) Stark County	11	1.12
Cairo (village) Allen County	5	1.01
Montpelier (village) Williams County	41	0.95
Montrose-Ghent (cdp) Summit County	47	0.94

Top 10 Places Sorted by Percent
Based on places with populations of 10,000 or more

Place	Number	%
Maumee (city) Lucas County	72	0.47
Montgomery (city) Hamilton County	46	0.46
Mount Vernon (city) Knox County	65	0.45
Sylvania (city) Lucas County	82	0.44
Marietta (city) Washington County	51	0.35
Perrysburg (city) Wood County	55	0.32
Loveland (city) Hamilton County	38	0.32
Gahanna (city) Franklin County	92	0.28
Centerville (city) Montgomery County	63	0.27
Springboro (city) Warren County	33	0.27

Notes: (cdp) census designated place; Refer to the User's Guide in the front of the book for more detailed information.

PROFILES OF OHIO / Ancestry Rankings

Brazilian

Top 10 Places Sorted by Number
Based on all places, regardless of population

Place	Number	%
Columbus (city) Franklin County	272	0.04
Canton (city) Stark County	79	0.10
Cleveland (city) Cuyahoga County	69	0.01
Granville South (cdp) Licking County	64	5.26
Cincinnati (city) Hamilton County	54	0.02
Dayton (city) Montgomery County	42	0.03
Westlake (city) Cuyahoga County	35	0.11
Bowling Green (city) Wood County	32	0.11
North Canton (city) Stark County	31	0.19
Fairlawn (city) Summit County	30	0.41

Top 10 Places Sorted by Percent
Based on all places, regardless of population

Place	Number	%
Granville South (cdp) Licking County	64	5.26
Ridgeway (village) Hardin County	12	3.45
Fairlawn (city) Summit County	30	0.41
Cedarville (village) Greene County	14	0.37
Beckett Ridge (cdp) Butler County	30	0.35
Mulberry (cdp) Clermont County	11	0.35
North Canton (city) Stark County	31	0.19
Gloria Glens Park (village) Medina County	1	0.19
Loveland (city) Hamilton County	21	0.18
Amelia (village) Clermont County	5	0.18

Top 10 Places Sorted by Percent
Based on places with populations of 10,000 or more

Place	Number	%
North Canton (city) Stark County	31	0.19
Loveland (city) Hamilton County	21	0.18
Celina (city) Mercer County	16	0.15
Marietta (city) Washington County	21	0.14
Mayfield Heights (city) Cuyahoga County	26	0.13
Marysville (city) Union County	21	0.13
Westlake (city) Cuyahoga County	35	0.11
Bowling Green (city) Wood County	32	0.11
Canton (city) Stark County	79	0.10
North Ridgeville (city) Lorain County	20	0.09

British

Top 10 Places Sorted by Number
Based on all places, regardless of population

Place	Number	%
Columbus (city) Franklin County	3,186	0.45
Cincinnati (city) Hamilton County	1,188	0.36
Toledo (city) Lucas County	689	0.22
Akron (city) Summit County	663	0.31
Cleveland (city) Cuyahoga County	492	0.10
Dayton (city) Montgomery County	483	0.29
Upper Arlington (city) Franklin County	346	1.03
Cuyahoga Falls (city) Summit County	307	0.62
Hudson (city) Summit County	285	1.27
Canton (city) Stark County	280	0.35

Top 10 Places Sorted by Percent
Based on all places, regardless of population

Place	Number	%
Old Washington (village) Guernsey County	10	3.48
Chilo (village) Clermont County	3	3.30
Terrace Park (village) Hamilton County	66	2.90
Germantown (village) Montgomery County	126	2.63
Riverlea (village) Franklin County	12	2.40
Lindsey (village) Sandusky County	12	2.38
Beverly (village) Washington County	26	2.07
Hunting Valley (village) Cuyahoga County	15	2.04
Lucas (village) Richland County	12	2.00

| College Corner (village) Preble County | 8 | 1.89 |

Top 10 Places Sorted by Percent
Based on places with populations of 10,000 or more

Place	Number	%
Hudson (city) Summit County	285	1.27
Montgomery (city) Hamilton County	121	1.20
Worthington (city) Franklin County	157	1.10
Bay Village (city) Cuyahoga County	176	1.09
Rocky River (city) Cuyahoga County	220	1.06
Sharonville (city) Hamilton County	144	1.05
Upper Arlington (city) Franklin County	346	1.03
Oxford (city) Butler County	223	1.01
Vandalia (city) Montgomery County	143	0.98
Kent (city) Portage County	239	0.85

Bulgarian

Top 10 Places Sorted by Number
Based on all places, regardless of population

Place	Number	%
Columbus (city) Franklin County	217	0.03
Toledo (city) Lucas County	167	0.05
Cincinnati (city) Hamilton County	106	0.03
Cleveland (city) Cuyahoga County	79	0.02
Akron (city) Summit County	67	0.03
Oregon (city) Lucas County	63	0.33
Massillon (city) Stark County	56	0.18
Youngstown (city) Mahoning County	54	0.07
Rocky River (city) Cuyahoga County	51	0.25
Lebanon (city) Warren County	45	0.27

Top 10 Places Sorted by Percent
Based on all places, regardless of population

Place	Number	%
Burbank (village) Wayne County	7	2.48
Linndale (village) Cuyahoga County	3	2.48
Lyons (village) Fulton County	5	0.90
Sherwood (cdp) Hamilton County	34	0.88
New London (village) Huron County	17	0.63
Fruit Hill (cdp) Hamilton County	24	0.62
Waterville (village) Lucas County	27	0.57
Uniontown (cdp) Stark County	16	0.56
Willard (city) Huron County	35	0.51
Ada (village) Hardin County	28	0.51

Top 10 Places Sorted by Percent
Based on places with populations of 10,000 or more

Place	Number	%
Oregon (city) Lucas County	63	0.33
Lebanon (city) Warren County	45	0.27
Rocky River (city) Cuyahoga County	51	0.25
Fairview Park (city) Cuyahoga County	43	0.24
Mount Vernon (city) Knox County	34	0.23
Sylvania (city) Lucas County	42	0.22
Massillon (city) Stark County	56	0.18
Avon (city) Lorain County	19	0.17
Blue Ash (city) Hamilton County	19	0.15
Defiance (city) Defiance County	23	0.14

Canadian

Top 10 Places Sorted by Number
Based on all places, regardless of population

Place	Number	%
Columbus (city) Franklin County	1,034	0.15
Toledo (city) Lucas County	682	0.22
Cincinnati (city) Hamilton County	398	0.12
Cleveland (city) Cuyahoga County	359	0.08
Akron (city) Summit County	218	0.10
Dublin (city) Franklin County	214	0.68
Cleveland Heights (city) Cuyahoga County	198	0.40

Westerville (city) Franklin County	170	0.48
Upper Arlington (city) Franklin County	156	0.46
Mentor (city) Lake County	154	0.31

Top 10 Places Sorted by Percent
Based on all places, regardless of population

Place	Number	%
Gann (village) Knox County	7	4.76
Broughton (village) Paulding County	6	2.90
Hartford (village) Licking County	11	2.76
Huntsville (village) Logan County	10	2.21
Sciotodale (cdp) Scioto County	19	1.82
Gates Mills (village) Cuyahoga County	40	1.63
Reminderville (village) Summit County	34	1.45
Shawnee Hills (cdp) Greene County	34	1.44
Bentleyville (village) Cuyahoga County	13	1.37
The Village of Indian Hill (city) Hamilton County	75	1.29

Top 10 Places Sorted by Percent
Based on places with populations of 10,000 or more

Place	Number	%
Brecksville (city) Cuyahoga County	96	0.72
Dublin (city) Franklin County	214	0.68
Troy (city) Miami County	138	0.62
Rocky River (city) Cuyahoga County	118	0.57
Bay Village (city) Cuyahoga County	91	0.57
Twinsburg (city) Summit County	87	0.52
Hudson (city) Summit County	114	0.51
Defiance (city) Defiance County	80	0.49
Westerville (city) Franklin County	170	0.48
Upper Arlington (city) Franklin County	156	0.46

Carpatho Rusyn

Top 10 Places Sorted by Number
Based on all places, regardless of population

Place	Number	%
Akron (city) Summit County	51	0.02
Cleveland (city) Cuyahoga County	48	0.01
Columbus (city) Franklin County	41	0.01
North Royalton (city) Cuyahoga County	34	0.12
Parma (city) Cuyahoga County	34	0.04
Brooklyn (city) Cuyahoga County	30	0.26
Amherst (city) Lorain County	30	0.25
Perrysburg (city) Wood County	21	0.12
Parma Heights (city) Cuyahoga County	21	0.10
Warren (city) Trumbull County	21	0.04

Top 10 Places Sorted by Percent
Based on all places, regardless of population

Place	Number	%
Belle Valley (village) Noble County	1	0.37
Brooklyn (city) Cuyahoga County	30	0.26
Washingtonville (village) Columbiana County	2	0.26
Amherst (city) Lorain County	30	0.25
Shawnee Hills (village) Delaware County	1	0.24
Macedonia (city) Summit County	19	0.21
Newburgh Heights (village) Cuyahoga County	5	0.21
Campbell (city) Mahoning County	15	0.16
Bedford (city) Cuyahoga County	18	0.13
Geneva-on-the-Lake (village) Ashtabula County	2	0.13

Top 10 Places Sorted by Percent
Based on places with populations of 10,000 or more

Place	Number	%
Brooklyn (city) Cuyahoga County	30	0.26
Amherst (city) Lorain County	30	0.25
Bedford (city) Cuyahoga County	18	0.13
North Royalton (city) Cuyahoga County	34	0.12
Perrysburg (city) Wood County	21	0.12
Parma Heights (city) Cuyahoga County	21	0.10
Willoughby (city) Lake County	15	0.07

Notes: (cdp) census designated place; Refer to the User's Guide in the front of the book for more detailed information.

PROFILES OF OHIO / Ancestry Rankings 445

Place	Number	%
Solon (city) Cuyahoga County	14	0.06
Bay Village (city) Cuyahoga County	9	0.06
Vermilion (city) Lorain County	7	0.06

Celtic

Top 10 Places Sorted by Number
Based on all places, regardless of population

Place	Number	%
Columbus (city) Franklin County	222	0.03
Cincinnati (city) Hamilton County	67	0.02
Toledo (city) Lucas County	46	0.01
Sherwood (cdp) Hamilton County	45	1.16
Cleveland Heights (city) Cuyahoga County	44	0.09
Pickerington (city) Fairfield County	42	0.43
Akron (city) Summit County	38	0.02
Alliance (city) Stark County	32	0.14
Newark (city) Licking County	29	0.06
Steubenville (city) Jefferson County	26	0.14

Top 10 Places Sorted by Percent
Based on all places, regardless of population

Place	Number	%
Bowersville (village) Greene County	8	2.56
Belle Valley (village) Noble County	5	1.87
Sherwood (cdp) Hamilton County	45	1.16
Proctorville (village) Lawrence County	6	0.98
Casstown (village) Miami County	3	0.97
Harbor Hills (cdp) Licking County	11	0.89
Quincy (village) Logan County	5	0.71
Addyston (village) Hamilton County	6	0.60
Stoutsville (village) Fairfield County	3	0.56
Navarre (village) Stark County	8	0.55

Top 10 Places Sorted by Percent
Based on places with populations of 10,000 or more

Place	Number	%
Van Wert (city) Van Wert County	22	0.21
Aurora (city) Portage County	25	0.18
Alliance (city) Stark County	32	0.14
Steubenville (city) Jefferson County	26	0.14
Bay Village (city) Cuyahoga County	17	0.11
Forestville (cdp) Hamilton County	12	0.11
Cleveland Heights (city) Cuyahoga County	44	0.09
Centerville (city) Montgomery County	20	0.09
Montgomery (city) Hamilton County	9	0.09
Fairborn (city) Greene County	26	0.08

Croatian

Top 10 Places Sorted by Number
Based on all places, regardless of population

Place	Number	%
Cleveland (city) Cuyahoga County	2,219	0.46
Euclid (city) Cuyahoga County	1,705	3.23
Mentor (city) Lake County	1,173	2.33
Columbus (city) Franklin County	1,117	0.16
Youngstown (city) Mahoning County	1,013	1.23
Eastlake (city) Lake County	901	4.47
Boardman (cdp) Mahoning County	864	2.32
Akron (city) Summit County	856	0.39
Parma (city) Cuyahoga County	851	0.99
Lorain (city) Lorain County	830	1.21

Top 10 Places Sorted by Percent
Based on all places, regardless of population

Place	Number	%
Yankee Lake (village) Trumbull County	13	14.61
Aquilla (village) Geauga County	22	5.99
Eastlake (city) Lake County	901	4.47
Willoughby Hills (city) Lake County	383	4.42
Struthers (city) Mahoning County	506	4.30
Masury (cdp) Trumbull County	117	4.25
Hubbard (city) Trumbull County	326	3.95
Willowick (city) Lake County	555	3.85
Poland (village) Mahoning County	110	3.84
McDonald (village) Trumbull County	126	3.64

Top 10 Places Sorted by Percent
Based on places with populations of 10,000 or more

Place	Number	%
Eastlake (city) Lake County	901	4.47
Struthers (city) Mahoning County	506	4.30
Willowick (city) Lake County	555	3.85
Euclid (city) Cuyahoga County	1,705	3.23
Seven Hills (city) Cuyahoga County	329	2.72
Mentor (city) Lake County	1,173	2.33
Boardman (cdp) Mahoning County	864	2.32
Richmond Heights (city) Cuyahoga County	252	2.30
Wickliffe (city) Lake County	260	1.93
Amherst (city) Lorain County	226	1.90

Cypriot

Top 10 Places Sorted by Number
Based on all places, regardless of population

Place	Number	%
Akron (city) Summit County	51	0.02
Columbus (city) Franklin County	27	0.00
Toledo (city) Lucas County	24	0.01
Brecksville (city) Cuyahoga County	20	0.15
Boardman (cdp) Mahoning County	18	0.05
Bowling Green (city) Wood County	12	0.04
Elyria (city) Lorain County	9	0.02
Cuyahoga Falls (city) Summit County	8	0.02
Lakewood (city) Cuyahoga County	7	0.01

Top 10 Places Sorted by Percent
Based on all places, regardless of population

Place	Number	%
Brecksville (city) Cuyahoga County	20	0.15
Boardman (cdp) Mahoning County	18	0.05
Bowling Green (city) Wood County	12	0.04
Akron (city) Summit County	51	0.02
Elyria (city) Lorain County	9	0.02
Cuyahoga Falls (city) Summit County	8	0.02
Toledo (city) Lucas County	24	0.01
Lakewood (city) Cuyahoga County	7	0.01
Columbus (city) Franklin County	27	0.00

Top 10 Places Sorted by Percent
Based on places with populations of 10,000 or more

Place	Number	%
Brecksville (city) Cuyahoga County	20	0.15
Boardman (cdp) Mahoning County	18	0.05
Bowling Green (city) Wood County	12	0.04
Akron (city) Summit County	51	0.02
Elyria (city) Lorain County	9	0.02
Cuyahoga Falls (city) Summit County	8	0.02
Toledo (city) Lucas County	24	0.01
Lakewood (city) Cuyahoga County	7	0.01
Columbus (city) Franklin County	27	0.00

Czech

Top 10 Places Sorted by Number
Based on all places, regardless of population

Place	Number	%
Cleveland (city) Cuyahoga County	3,580	0.75
Parma (city) Cuyahoga County	2,554	2.98
Columbus (city) Franklin County	2,232	0.31
Garfield Heights (city) Cuyahoga County	1,445	4.72
Strongsville (city) Cuyahoga County	1,180	2.69
Lakewood (city) Cuyahoga County	1,014	1.79
Mentor (city) Lake County	990	1.97
Maple Heights (city) Cuyahoga County	964	3.69
North Royalton (city) Cuyahoga County	949	3.31
Solon (city) Cuyahoga County	757	3.47

Top 10 Places Sorted by Percent
Based on all places, regardless of population

Place	Number	%
Valley View (village) Cuyahoga County	157	7.22
Dillonvale (village) Jefferson County	54	6.97
Glenwillow (village) Cuyahoga County	31	6.97
Newburgh Heights (village) Cuyahoga County	155	6.49
Brooklyn Heights (village) Cuyahoga County	94	5.96
Seven Hills (city) Cuyahoga County	704	5.83
Independence (city) Cuyahoga County	347	4.82
Pigeon Creek (cdp) Summit County	43	4.81
Walton Hills (village) Cuyahoga County	114	4.77
Garfield Heights (city) Cuyahoga County	1,445	4.72

Top 10 Places Sorted by Percent
Based on places with populations of 10,000 or more

Place	Number	%
Seven Hills (city) Cuyahoga County	704	5.83
Garfield Heights (city) Cuyahoga County	1,445	4.72
Brecksville (city) Cuyahoga County	568	4.26
Broadview Heights (city) Cuyahoga County	610	3.82
Maple Heights (city) Cuyahoga County	964	3.69
Solon (city) Cuyahoga County	757	3.47
North Royalton (city) Cuyahoga County	949	3.31
Middleburg Heights (city) Cuyahoga County	484	3.11
Aurora (city) Portage County	412	3.04
Brooklyn (city) Cuyahoga County	350	3.02

Czechoslovakian

Top 10 Places Sorted by Number
Based on all places, regardless of population

Place	Number	%
Columbus (city) Franklin County	1,125	0.16
Cleveland (city) Cuyahoga County	1,096	0.23
Parma (city) Cuyahoga County	766	0.89
Toledo (city) Lucas County	569	0.18
Akron (city) Summit County	563	0.26
Lakewood (city) Cuyahoga County	446	0.79
Strongsville (city) Cuyahoga County	334	0.76
Westlake (city) Cuyahoga County	281	0.88
Cincinnati (city) Hamilton County	232	0.07
Mentor (city) Lake County	218	0.43

Top 10 Places Sorted by Percent
Based on all places, regardless of population

Place	Number	%
Morristown (village) Belmont County	16	5.25
Metamora (village) Fulton County	23	4.07
South Canal (cdp) Trumbull County	50	3.71
Rochester (village) Lorain County	5	2.48
Donnelsville (village) Clark County	6	2.47
Antioch (village) Monroe County	2	2.41
West Rushville (village) Fairfield County	3	2.33
Brooklyn Heights (village) Cuyahoga County	31	1.97
Fairport Harbor (village) Lake County	58	1.82
Riverlea (village) Franklin County	9	1.80

Top 10 Places Sorted by Percent
Based on places with populations of 10,000 or more

Place	Number	%
Brecksville (city) Cuyahoga County	184	1.38
Brooklyn (city) Cuyahoga County	140	1.21
Seven Hills (city) Cuyahoga County	127	1.05
Broadview Heights (city) Cuyahoga County	153	0.96
Bedford (city) Cuyahoga County	130	0.91
Parma (city) Cuyahoga County	766	0.89

Notes: (cdp) census designated place; Refer to the User's Guide in the front of the book for more detailed information.

PROFILES OF OHIO / Ancestry Rankings

Place	Number	%
Vermilion (city) Lorain County	97	0.89
Westlake (city) Cuyahoga County	281	0.88
Avon (city) Lorain County	96	0.84
Lakewood (city) Cuyahoga County	446	0.79

Danish

Top 10 Places Sorted by Number
Based on all places, regardless of population

Place	Number	%
Columbus (city) Franklin County	938	0.13
Toledo (city) Lucas County	467	0.15
Cincinnati (city) Hamilton County	374	0.11
Cleveland (city) Cuyahoga County	333	0.07
Mentor (city) Lake County	215	0.43
Akron (city) Summit County	209	0.10
Sandusky (city) Erie County	186	0.66
Strongsville (city) Cuyahoga County	184	0.42
Cuyahoga Falls (city) Summit County	177	0.36
Westerville (city) Franklin County	170	0.48

Top 10 Places Sorted by Percent
Based on all places, regardless of population

Place	Number	%
Peninsula (village) Summit County	12	2.32
Fulton (village) Morrow County	7	2.30
Zoar (village) Tuscarawas County	4	2.03
Castalia (village) Erie County	17	1.73
Port William (village) Clinton County	4	1.65
Port Clinton (city) Ottawa County	101	1.59
Waite Hill (village) Lake County	7	1.55
Newtown (village) Hamilton County	31	1.26
Cedarville (village) Greene County	47	1.23
Marblehead (village) Ottawa County	9	1.19

Top 10 Places Sorted by Percent
Based on places with populations of 10,000 or more

Place	Number	%
Fairview Park (city) Cuyahoga County	159	0.90
Lebanon (city) Warren County	128	0.76
Sandusky (city) Erie County	186	0.66
Bay Village (city) Cuyahoga County	101	0.63
Hudson (city) Summit County	132	0.59
Avon (city) Lorain County	66	0.58
Oxford (city) Butler County	115	0.52
Perrysburg (city) Wood County	88	0.51
Landen (cdp) Warren County	65	0.51
Lyndhurst (city) Cuyahoga County	77	0.50

Dutch

Top 10 Places Sorted by Number
Based on all places, regardless of population

Place	Number	%
Columbus (city) Franklin County	9,831	1.38
Toledo (city) Lucas County	4,309	1.37
Akron (city) Summit County	3,053	1.41
Cincinnati (city) Hamilton County	3,032	0.92
Cleveland (city) Cuyahoga County	2,847	0.60
Dayton (city) Montgomery County	1,802	1.08
Canton (city) Stark County	1,445	1.78
Springfield (city) Clark County	1,414	2.16
Kettering (city) Montgomery County	1,366	2.37
Mansfield (city) Richland County	1,082	2.19

Top 10 Places Sorted by Percent
Based on all places, regardless of population

Place	Number	%
Octa (village) Fayette County	14	18.92
Stafford (village) Monroe County	13	18.57
Catawba (village) Clark County	29	15.03
Uniopolis (village) Auglaize County	32	13.56
Orangeville (village) Trumbull County	25	13.09
Lore City (village) Guernsey County	34	10.40
South Salem (village) Ross County	22	9.91
Mount Cory (village) Hancock County	19	9.84
Lawrenceville (village) Clark County	28	9.52
Amesville (village) Athens County	18	9.47

Top 10 Places Sorted by Percent
Based on places with populations of 10,000 or more

Place	Number	%
Bellefontaine (city) Logan County	483	3.70
Greenville (city) Darke County	444	3.36
Norwalk (city) Huron County	509	3.13
Vermilion (city) Lorain County	335	3.08
Cambridge (city) Guernsey County	355	3.07
Englewood (city) Montgomery County	374	3.06
Lancaster (city) Fairfield County	1,025	2.91
Tallmadge (city) Summit County	474	2.90
Salem (city) Columbiana County	350	2.90
Piqua (city) Miami County	586	2.81

Eastern European

Top 10 Places Sorted by Number
Based on all places, regardless of population

Place	Number	%
Columbus (city) Franklin County	428	0.06
Beachwood (city) Cuyahoga County	391	3.21
Shaker Heights (city) Cuyahoga County	372	1.26
Cleveland Heights (city) Cuyahoga County	323	0.65
Cincinnati (city) Hamilton County	262	0.08
Bexley (city) Franklin County	223	1.69
University Heights (city) Cuyahoga County	198	1.40
Solon (city) Cuyahoga County	198	0.91
Gahanna (city) Franklin County	140	0.43
South Euclid (city) Cuyahoga County	124	0.53

Top 10 Places Sorted by Percent
Based on all places, regardless of population

Place	Number	%
Hills and Dales (village) Stark County	16	5.48
Beachwood (city) Cuyahoga County	391	3.21
Orange (village) Cuyahoga County	92	2.84
Amberley (village) Hamilton County	79	2.32
Bexley (city) Franklin County	223	1.69
Gates Mills (village) Cuyahoga County	41	1.67
Moreland Hills (village) Cuyahoga County	54	1.64
University Heights (city) Cuyahoga County	198	1.40
Shaker Heights (city) Cuyahoga County	372	1.26
Pepper Pike (city) Cuyahoga County	70	1.16

Top 10 Places Sorted by Percent
Based on places with populations of 10,000 or more

Place	Number	%
Beachwood (city) Cuyahoga County	391	3.21
Bexley (city) Franklin County	223	1.69
University Heights (city) Cuyahoga County	198	1.40
Shaker Heights (city) Cuyahoga County	372	1.26
Solon (city) Cuyahoga County	198	0.91
Blue Ash (city) Hamilton County	92	0.72
Cleveland Heights (city) Cuyahoga County	323	0.65
South Euclid (city) Cuyahoga County	124	0.53
Montgomery (city) Hamilton County	47	0.47
Gahanna (city) Franklin County	140	0.43

English

Top 10 Places Sorted by Number
Based on all places, regardless of population

Place	Number	%
Columbus (city) Franklin County	55,990	7.87
Toledo (city) Lucas County	18,854	6.01
Cincinnati (city) Hamilton County	18,016	5.45
Akron (city) Summit County	15,720	7.24
Cleveland (city) Cuyahoga County	13,169	2.75
Dayton (city) Montgomery County	8,170	4.92
Kettering (city) Montgomery County	7,303	12.69
Upper Arlington (city) Franklin County	6,462	19.23
Mentor (city) Lake County	6,457	12.84
Cuyahoga Falls (city) Summit County	6,410	12.99

Top 10 Places Sorted by Percent
Based on all places, regardless of population

Place	Number	%
Miltonsburg (village) Monroe County	14	70.00
La Croft (cdp) Columbiana County	373	26.16
Granville South (cdp) Licking County	313	25.74
Ithaca (village) Darke County	30	25.21
Granville (village) Licking County	721	24.72
Neville (village) Clermont County	33	24.63
Nellie (village) Coshocton County	33	24.44
Tontogany (village) Wood County	90	24.19
Riverlea (village) Franklin County	118	23.55
South Russell (village) Geauga County	946	23.52

Top 10 Places Sorted by Percent
Based on places with populations of 10,000 or more

Place	Number	%
Upper Arlington (city) Franklin County	6,462	19.23
Worthington (city) Franklin County	2,728	19.05
Hudson (city) Summit County	3,899	17.42
Bay Village (city) Cuyahoga County	2,493	15.50
Springboro (city) Warren County	1,870	15.32
Amherst (city) Lorain County	1,784	15.02
Centerville (city) Montgomery County	3,462	14.93
Montgomery (city) Hamilton County	1,494	14.88
Beavercreek (city) Greene County	5,470	14.33
Westerville (city) Franklin County	5,075	14.33

Estonian

Top 10 Places Sorted by Number
Based on all places, regardless of population

Place	Number	%
Broadview Heights (city) Cuyahoga County	44	0.28
Lakewood (city) Cuyahoga County	39	0.07
Parma (city) Cuyahoga County	34	0.04
Wetherington (cdp) Butler County	33	3.24
Sherwood (cdp) Hamilton County	28	0.72
Columbus (city) Franklin County	27	0.00
Parma Heights (city) Cuyahoga County	19	0.09
Mentor (city) Lake County	18	0.04
Stow (city) Summit County	16	0.05
Cleveland Heights (city) Cuyahoga County	15	0.03

Top 10 Places Sorted by Percent
Based on all places, regardless of population

Place	Number	%
Wetherington (cdp) Butler County	33	3.24
Sherwood (cdp) Hamilton County	28	0.72
Wakeman (village) Huron County	7	0.72
Maineville (village) Warren County	4	0.44
Bentleyville (village) Cuyahoga County	4	0.42
Newtown (village) Hamilton County	10	0.41
Lordstown (village) Trumbull County	12	0.33
Attica (village) Seneca County	3	0.31
Broadview Heights (city) Cuyahoga County	44	0.28
Dry Run (cdp) Hamilton County	13	0.20

Top 10 Places Sorted by Percent
Based on places with populations of 10,000 or more

Place	Number	%
Broadview Heights (city) Cuyahoga County	44	0.28
Parma Heights (city) Cuyahoga County	19	0.09

Notes: (cdp) census designated place; Refer to the User's Guide in the front of the book for more detailed information.

Place	Number	%
Painesville (city) Lake County	14	0.08
Lakewood (city) Cuyahoga County	39	0.07
Oregon (city) Lucas County	14	0.07
Ashland (city) Ashland County	13	0.06
Bridgetown North (cdp) Hamilton County	7	0.06
Stow (city) Summit County	16	0.05
Athens (city) Athens County	11	0.05
Centerville (city) Montgomery County	11	0.05

European

Top 10 Places Sorted by Number
Based on all places, regardless of population

Place	Number	%
Columbus (city) Franklin County	5,217	0.73
Cincinnati (city) Hamilton County	2,175	0.66
Cleveland (city) Cuyahoga County	949	0.20
Akron (city) Summit County	933	0.43
Dayton (city) Montgomery County	894	0.54
Toledo (city) Lucas County	785	0.25
Fairborn (city) Greene County	709	2.22
Cleveland Heights (city) Cuyahoga County	670	1.34
Kettering (city) Montgomery County	627	1.09
Fairfield (city) Butler County	503	1.20

Top 10 Places Sorted by Percent
Based on all places, regardless of population

Place	Number	%
Ostrander (village) Delaware County	42	11.63
Marseilles (village) Wyandot County	9	6.62
Donnelsville (village) Clark County	15	6.17
Kimbolton (village) Guernsey County	10	5.38
Lowell (village) Washington County	28	4.67
Gilboa (village) Putnam County	8	4.62
Clifton (village) Greene County	8	4.30
Chesterville (village) Morrow County	8	3.81
Beechwood Trails (cdp) Licking County	84	3.62
Murray City (village) Hocking County	15	3.38

Top 10 Places Sorted by Percent
Based on places with populations of 10,000 or more

Place	Number	%
Fairborn (city) Greene County	709	2.22
Montgomery (city) Hamilton County	191	1.90
Bexley (city) Franklin County	236	1.79
Athens (city) Athens County	374	1.76
Worthington (city) Franklin County	239	1.67
University Heights (city) Cuyahoga County	236	1.67
Pataskala (city) Licking County	169	1.65
Blue Ash (city) Hamilton County	192	1.51
Delaware (city) Delaware County	376	1.49
Shiloh (cdp) Montgomery County	160	1.42

Finnish

Top 10 Places Sorted by Number
Based on all places, regardless of population

Place	Number	%
Ashtabula (city) Ashtabula County	878	4.21
Columbus (city) Franklin County	822	0.12
Conneaut (city) Ashtabula County	741	5.92
Mentor (city) Lake County	508	1.01
Cleveland (city) Cuyahoga County	475	0.10
Fairport Harbor (village) Lake County	348	10.94
Painesville (city) Lake County	289	1.65
Edgewood (cdp) Ashtabula County	259	5.41
Toledo (city) Lucas County	215	0.07
Lakewood (city) Cuyahoga County	214	0.38

Top 10 Places Sorted by Percent
Based on all places, regardless of population

Place	Number	%
Fairport Harbor (village) Lake County	348	10.94
Conneaut (city) Ashtabula County	741	5.92
Edgewood (cdp) Ashtabula County	259	5.41
Grand River (village) Lake County	17	5.03
North Kingsville (village) Ashtabula County	125	4.71
Ashtabula (city) Ashtabula County	878	4.21
Cheshire (village) Gallia County	8	3.42
New Riegel (village) Seneca County	6	2.73
Andover (village) Ashtabula County	35	2.64
Logan Elm Village (cdp) Pickaway County	26	2.58

Top 10 Places Sorted by Percent
Based on places with populations of 10,000 or more

Place	Number	%
Conneaut (city) Ashtabula County	741	5.92
Ashtabula (city) Ashtabula County	878	4.21
Painesville (city) Lake County	289	1.65
Mentor (city) Lake County	508	1.01
Avon (city) Lorain County	92	0.80
Bay Village (city) Cuyahoga County	104	0.65
Niles (city) Trumbull County	134	0.64
Amherst (city) Lorain County	59	0.50
Solon (city) Cuyahoga County	105	0.48
Girard (city) Trumbull County	51	0.46

French, except Basque

Top 10 Places Sorted by Number
Based on all places, regardless of population

Place	Number	%
Toledo (city) Lucas County	14,382	4.59
Columbus (city) Franklin County	13,588	1.91
Cincinnati (city) Hamilton County	5,602	1.69
Cleveland (city) Cuyahoga County	4,106	0.86
Akron (city) Summit County	3,799	1.75
Dayton (city) Montgomery County	2,446	1.47
Kettering (city) Montgomery County	2,086	3.63
Canton (city) Stark County	1,988	2.45
Cuyahoga Falls (city) Summit County	1,586	3.21
Lakewood (city) Cuyahoga County	1,574	2.78

Top 10 Places Sorted by Percent
Based on all places, regardless of population

Place	Number	%
Russia (village) Shelby County	202	35.56
Miltonsburg (village) Monroe County	7	35.00
North Star (village) Darke County	51	24.88
Versailles (village) Darke County	567	21.40
Miller City (village) Putnam County	20	19.05
Osgood (village) Darke County	49	18.22
Fayetteville (village) Brown County	51	13.21
Olde West Chester (cdp) Butler County	32	12.03
Metamora (village) Fulton County	59	10.44
Fort Loramie (village) Shelby County	140	10.21

Top 10 Places Sorted by Percent
Based on places with populations of 10,000 or more

Place	Number	%
Oregon (city) Lucas County	1,445	7.47
Maumee (city) Lucas County	814	5.35
Montgomery (city) Hamilton County	535	5.33
Perrysburg (city) Wood County	832	4.86
Toledo (city) Lucas County	14,382	4.59
Sylvania (city) Lucas County	805	4.30
Piqua (city) Miami County	880	4.23
Clayton (city) Montgomery County	528	3.95
Centerville (city) Montgomery County	900	3.88
Mason (city) Warren County	822	3.75

French Canadian

Top 10 Places Sorted by Number
Based on all places, regardless of population

Place	Number	%
Toledo (city) Lucas County	2,604	0.83
Columbus (city) Franklin County	2,010	0.28
Cleveland (city) Cuyahoga County	873	0.18
Cincinnati (city) Hamilton County	768	0.23
Dayton (city) Montgomery County	505	0.30
Akron (city) Summit County	469	0.22
Kettering (city) Montgomery County	365	0.63
Lakewood (city) Cuyahoga County	339	0.60
Parma (city) Cuyahoga County	277	0.32
Elyria (city) Lorain County	259	0.46

Top 10 Places Sorted by Percent
Based on all places, regardless of population

Place	Number	%
Ney (village) Defiance County	15	4.05
Clay Center (village) Ottawa County	12	4.05
Swanton (village) Fulton County	120	3.59
West Rushville (village) Fairfield County	4	3.10
Olde West Chester (cdp) Butler County	8	3.01
Custar (village) Wood County	6	2.97
Berkey (village) Lucas County	7	2.68
Benton Ridge (village) Hancock County	7	2.32
Alvordton (village) Williams County	8	2.31
Saint Martin (village) Brown County	2	2.27

Top 10 Places Sorted by Percent
Based on places with populations of 10,000 or more

Place	Number	%
Sylvania (city) Lucas County	249	1.33
Maumee (city) Lucas County	174	1.14
Vermilion (city) Lorain County	114	1.05
Perrysburg (city) Wood County	176	1.03
Northbrook (cdp) Hamilton County	106	0.94
Oregon (city) Lucas County	178	0.92
Toledo (city) Lucas County	2,604	0.83
Eastlake (city) Lake County	158	0.78
Englewood (city) Montgomery County	95	0.78
Marietta (city) Washington County	100	0.69

German

Top 10 Places Sorted by Number
Based on all places, regardless of population

Place	Number	%
Columbus (city) Franklin County	137,761	19.36
Toledo (city) Lucas County	73,482	23.43
Cincinnati (city) Hamilton County	65,659	19.86
Cleveland (city) Cuyahoga County	44,172	9.23
Akron (city) Summit County	39,203	18.06
Dayton (city) Montgomery County	23,990	14.44
Parma (city) Cuyahoga County	21,013	24.53
Kettering (city) Montgomery County	19,450	33.81
Canton (city) Stark County	17,447	21.51
Cuyahoga Falls (city) Summit County	15,305	31.01

Top 10 Places Sorted by Percent
Based on all places, regardless of population

Place	Number	%
Alexandria (village) Licking County	14	82.35
Ottoville (village) Putnam County	677	77.91
Glandorf (village) Putnam County	719	77.48
Minster (village) Auglaize County	2,131	75.43
Fort Jennings (village) Putnam County	349	75.22
New Riegel (village) Seneca County	165	75.00
Burkettsville (village) Mercer County	189	74.41
Osgood (village) Darke County	198	73.61
Coldwater (village) Mercer County	3,392	73.55

Notes: (cdp) census designated place; Refer to the User's Guide in the front of the book for more detailed information.

Saint Henry (village) Mercer County	1,683	73.14

Top 10 Places Sorted by Percent
Based on places with populations of 10,000 or more

Place	Number	%
Bridgetown North (cdp) Hamilton County	7,249	56.98
Celina (city) Mercer County	5,089	48.85
White Oak (cdp) Hamilton County	6,375	48.11
Tiffin (city) Seneca County	8,025	44.25
Maumee (city) Lucas County	6,330	41.57
Perrysburg (city) Wood County	6,774	39.59
Reading (city) Hamilton County	4,432	39.56
Forestville (cdp) Hamilton County	4,281	38.70
Sharonville (city) Hamilton County	5,145	37.55
Landen (cdp) Warren County	4,604	36.41

German Russian

Top 10 Places Sorted by Number
Based on all places, regardless of population

Place	Number	%
Columbus (city) Franklin County	23	0.00
Euclid (city) Cuyahoga County	20	0.04
Lorain (city) Lorain County	18	0.03
Canfield (city) Mahoning County	16	0.21
Middletown (city) Butler County	16	0.03
Akron (city) Summit County	16	0.01
Clyde (city) Sandusky County	15	0.25
Cleveland (city) Cuyahoga County	13	0.00
Springfield (city) Clark County	12	0.02
Huber Heights (city) Montgomery County	11	0.03

Top 10 Places Sorted by Percent
Based on all places, regardless of population

Place	Number	%
Clyde (city) Sandusky County	15	0.25
Canfield (city) Mahoning County	16	0.21
Windham (village) Portage County	4	0.14
Geneva-on-the-Lake (village) Ashtabula County	2	0.13
McConnelsville (village) Morgan County	2	0.12
Willowick (city) Lake County	7	0.05
Euclid (city) Cuyahoga County	20	0.04
Lorain (city) Lorain County	18	0.03
Middletown (city) Butler County	16	0.03
Huber Heights (city) Montgomery County	11	0.03

Top 10 Places Sorted by Percent
Based on places with populations of 10,000 or more

Place	Number	%
Willowick (city) Lake County	7	0.05
Euclid (city) Cuyahoga County	20	0.04
Lorain (city) Lorain County	18	0.03
Middletown (city) Butler County	16	0.03
Huber Heights (city) Montgomery County	11	0.03
Beavercreek (city) Greene County	10	0.03
Sandusky (city) Erie County	7	0.03
Springfield (city) Clark County	12	0.02
Warren (city) Trumbull County	11	0.02
Akron (city) Summit County	16	0.01

Greek

Top 10 Places Sorted by Number
Based on all places, regardless of population

Place	Number	%
Columbus (city) Franklin County	2,702	0.38
Toledo (city) Lucas County	1,554	0.50
Cleveland (city) Cuyahoga County	1,385	0.29
Akron (city) Summit County	1,267	0.58
Canton (city) Stark County	1,059	1.31
Cincinnati (city) Hamilton County	1,040	0.31
Warren (city) Trumbull County	1,033	2.20
Campbell (city) Mahoning County	981	10.37
Parma (city) Cuyahoga County	867	1.01
Lakewood (city) Cuyahoga County	703	1.24

Top 10 Places Sorted by Percent
Based on all places, regardless of population

Place	Number	%
Campbell (city) Mahoning County	981	10.37
Yorkville (village) Jefferson County	55	4.40
Vienna Center (cdp) Trumbull County	35	2.95
Gratiot (village) Licking County	5	2.91
Wetherington (cdp) Butler County	28	2.75
Seven Hills (city) Cuyahoga County	310	2.57
Fairlawn (city) Summit County	172	2.35
Brimfield (cdp) Portage County	70	2.24
Ostrander (village) Delaware County	8	2.22
Warren (city) Trumbull County	1,033	2.20

Top 10 Places Sorted by Percent
Based on places with populations of 10,000 or more

Place	Number	%
Seven Hills (city) Cuyahoga County	310	2.57
Warren (city) Trumbull County	1,033	2.20
Westlake (city) Cuyahoga County	647	2.03
Brooklyn (city) Cuyahoga County	208	1.80
Upper Arlington (city) Franklin County	588	1.75
North Canton (city) Stark County	260	1.59
Middleburg Heights (city) Cuyahoga County	236	1.52
Fairview Park (city) Cuyahoga County	266	1.51
North Royalton (city) Cuyahoga County	406	1.42
Boardman (cdp) Mahoning County	508	1.36

Guyanese

Top 10 Places Sorted by Number
Based on all places, regardless of population

Place	Number	%
Cleveland (city) Cuyahoga County	159	0.03
Toledo (city) Lucas County	77	0.02
Columbus (city) Franklin County	61	0.01
Parma (city) Cuyahoga County	35	0.04
Euclid (city) Cuyahoga County	26	0.05
Cincinnati (city) Hamilton County	21	0.01
Shiloh (cdp) Montgomery County	19	0.17
Westlake (city) Cuyahoga County	18	0.06
Cleveland Heights (city) Cuyahoga County	18	0.04
North Ridgeville (city) Lorain County	16	0.07

Top 10 Places Sorted by Percent
Based on all places, regardless of population

Place	Number	%
Highland Hills (village) Cuyahoga County	5	0.38
Shiloh (cdp) Montgomery County	19	0.17
Sheffield (village) Lorain County	5	0.17
Richmond Heights (city) Cuyahoga County	14	0.13
North Ridgeville (city) Lorain County	16	0.07
Athens (city) Athens County	14	0.07
Westlake (city) Cuyahoga County	18	0.06
Bedford Heights (city) Cuyahoga County	7	0.06
Euclid (city) Cuyahoga County	26	0.05
Miamisburg (city) Montgomery County	10	0.05

Top 10 Places Sorted by Percent
Based on places with populations of 10,000 or more

Place	Number	%
Shiloh (cdp) Montgomery County	19	0.17
Richmond Heights (city) Cuyahoga County	14	0.13
North Ridgeville (city) Lorain County	16	0.07
Athens (city) Athens County	14	0.07
Westlake (city) Cuyahoga County	18	0.06
Bedford Heights (city) Cuyahoga County	7	0.06
Euclid (city) Cuyahoga County	26	0.05
Miamisburg (city) Montgomery County	10	0.05
Warrensville Heights (city) Cuyahoga County	8	0.05
Parma (city) Cuyahoga County	35	0.04

Hawaii Native/Pacific Islander

Top 10 Places Sorted by Number
Based on all places, regardless of population

Place	Number	%
Columbus (city) Franklin County	974	0.14
Cleveland (city) Cuyahoga County	514	0.11
Cincinnati (city) Hamilton County	338	0.10
Toledo (city) Lucas County	197	0.06
Akron (city) Summit County	178	0.08
Dayton (city) Montgomery County	149	0.09
Canton (city) Stark County	71	0.09
Youngstown (city) Mahoning County	63	0.08
Lorain (city) Lorain County	61	0.09
Hamilton (city) Butler County	57	0.09

Top 10 Places Sorted by Percent
Based on all places, regardless of population

Place	Number	%
Belmont (village) Belmont County	20	3.76
Frankfort (village) Ross County	12	1.19
Glenford (village) Perry County	2	1.01
Lore City (village) Guernsey County	3	0.98
Summitville (village) Columbiana County	1	0.93
Valley Hi (village) Logan County	2	0.82
Mowrystown (village) Highland County	3	0.80
Buckland (village) Auglaize County	2	0.78
Roswell (village) Tuscarawas County	2	0.72
Patterson (village) Hardin County	1	0.72

Top 10 Places Sorted by Percent
Based on places with populations of 10,000 or more

Place	Number	%
Landen (cdp) Warren County	30	0.23
University Heights (city) Cuyahoga County	28	0.20
Marietta (city) Washington County	27	0.19
Girard (city) Trumbull County	21	0.19
Sidney (city) Shelby County	31	0.15
Sharonville (city) Hamilton County	21	0.15
Columbus (city) Franklin County	974	0.14
Fairborn (city) Greene County	45	0.14
Delaware (city) Delaware County	36	0.14
Middleburg Heights (city) Cuyahoga County	21	0.14

Hawaii Native/Pacific Islander: Melanesian

Top 10 Places Sorted by Number
Based on all places, regardless of population

Place	Number	%
Cincinnati (city) Hamilton County	11	0.00
Columbus (city) Franklin County	5	0.00
Lore City (village) Guernsey County	2	0.66
Geneva (city) Ashtabula County	2	0.03
Dublin (city) Franklin County	2	0.01
Akron (city) Summit County	2	0.00
Urbana (city) Champaign County	1	0.01
Willard (city) Huron County	1	0.01
Chillicothe (city) Ross County	1	0.00
Dayton (city) Montgomery County	1	0.00

Top 10 Places Sorted by Percent
Based on all places, regardless of population

Place	Number	%
Lore City (village) Guernsey County	2	0.66
Geneva (city) Ashtabula County	2	0.03
Dublin (city) Franklin County	2	0.01
Urbana (city) Champaign County	1	0.01
Willard (city) Huron County	1	0.01

Notes: (cdp) census designated place; Refer to the User's Guide in the front of the book for more detailed information.

PROFILES OF OHIO / Ancestry Rankings

Place	Number	%
Cincinnati (city) Hamilton County	11	0.00
Columbus (city) Franklin County	5	0.00
Akron (city) Summit County	2	0.00
Chillicothe (city) Ross County	1	0.00
Dayton (city) Montgomery County	1	0.00

Top 10 Places Sorted by Percent
Based on places with populations of 10,000 or more

Place	Number	%
Dublin (city) Franklin County	2	0.01
Urbana (city) Champaign County	1	0.01
Cincinnati (city) Hamilton County	11	0.00
Columbus (city) Franklin County	5	0.00
Akron (city) Summit County	2	0.00
Chillicothe (city) Ross County	1	0.00
Dayton (city) Montgomery County	1	0.00
Mansfield (city) Richland County	1	0.00
Norwood (city) Hamilton County	1	0.00

Hawaii Native/Pacific Islander: Fijian

Top 10 Places Sorted by Number
Based on all places, regardless of population

Place	Number	%
Columbus (city) Franklin County	5	0.00
Lore City (village) Guernsey County	2	0.66
Geneva (city) Ashtabula County	2	0.03
Akron (city) Summit County	2	0.00
Urbana (city) Champaign County	1	0.01
Willard (city) Huron County	1	0.01
Dayton (city) Montgomery County	1	0.00
Mansfield (city) Richland County	1	0.00

Top 10 Places Sorted by Percent
Based on all places, regardless of population

Place	Number	%
Lore City (village) Guernsey County	2	0.66
Geneva (city) Ashtabula County	2	0.03
Urbana (city) Champaign County	1	0.01
Willard (city) Huron County	1	0.01
Columbus (city) Franklin County	5	0.00
Akron (city) Summit County	2	0.00
Dayton (city) Montgomery County	1	0.00
Mansfield (city) Richland County	1	0.00

Top 10 Places Sorted by Percent
Based on places with populations of 10,000 or more

Place	Number	%
Urbana (city) Champaign County	1	0.01
Columbus (city) Franklin County	5	0.00
Akron (city) Summit County	2	0.00
Dayton (city) Montgomery County	1	0.00
Mansfield (city) Richland County	1	0.00

Hawaii Native/Pacific Islander: Other Melanesian

Top 10 Places Sorted by Number
Based on all places, regardless of population

Place	Number	%
Cincinnati (city) Hamilton County	11	0.00
Dublin (city) Franklin County	2	0.01
Chillicothe (city) Ross County	1	0.00
Norwood (city) Hamilton County	1	0.00

Top 10 Places Sorted by Percent
Based on all places, regardless of population

Place	Number	%
Dublin (city) Franklin County	2	0.01
Cincinnati (city) Hamilton County	11	0.00
Chillicothe (city) Ross County	1	0.00
Norwood (city) Hamilton County	1	0.00

Top 10 Places Sorted by Percent
Based on places with populations of 10,000 or more

Place	Number	%
Dublin (city) Franklin County	2	0.01
Cincinnati (city) Hamilton County	11	0.00
Chillicothe (city) Ross County	1	0.00
Norwood (city) Hamilton County	1	0.00

Hawaii Native/Pacific Islander: Micronesian

Top 10 Places Sorted by Number
Based on all places, regardless of population

Place	Number	%
Columbus (city) Franklin County	126	0.02
Cleveland (city) Cuyahoga County	83	0.02
Cincinnati (city) Hamilton County	62	0.02
Dayton (city) Montgomery County	29	0.02
Akron (city) Summit County	23	0.01
Sidney (city) Shelby County	21	0.10
Toledo (city) Lucas County	19	0.01
Mansfield (city) Richland County	18	0.04
Canton (city) Stark County	17	0.02
Oberlin (city) Lorain County	14	0.17

Top 10 Places Sorted by Percent
Based on all places, regardless of population

Place	Number	%
Glenford (village) Perry County	2	1.01
Valley Hi (village) Logan County	2	0.82
North Robinson (village) Crawford County	1	0.47
Donnelsville (village) Clark County	1	0.34
Strasburg (village) Tuscarawas County	7	0.30
Perrysville (village) Ashland County	2	0.25
Waynesfield (village) Auglaize County	2	0.25
Anna (village) Shelby County	3	0.23
Crooksville (village) Perry County	5	0.20
Oberlin (city) Lorain County	14	0.17

Top 10 Places Sorted by Percent
Based on places with populations of 10,000 or more

Place	Number	%
Sidney (city) Shelby County	21	0.10
Springdale (city) Hamilton County	8	0.08
East Liverpool (city) Columbiana County	9	0.07
Girard (city) Trumbull County	8	0.07
Centerville (city) Montgomery County	13	0.06
Landen (cdp) Warren County	8	0.06
Ashland (city) Ashland County	10	0.05
Avon Lake (city) Lorain County	9	0.05
Northbrook (cdp) Hamilton County	5	0.05
Mansfield (city) Richland County	18	0.04

Hawaii Native/Pacific Islander: Guamanian or Chamorro

Top 10 Places Sorted by Number
Based on all places, regardless of population

Place	Number	%
Columbus (city) Franklin County	116	0.02
Cleveland (city) Cuyahoga County	78	0.02
Cincinnati (city) Hamilton County	59	0.02
Dayton (city) Montgomery County	27	0.02
Akron (city) Summit County	22	0.01
Toledo (city) Lucas County	19	0.01
Sidney (city) Shelby County	18	0.09
Mansfield (city) Richland County	18	0.04
Canton (city) Stark County	17	0.02
Oberlin (city) Lorain County	14	0.17

Top 10 Places Sorted by Percent
Based on all places, regardless of population

Place	Number	%
Glenford (village) Perry County	2	1.01
North Robinson (village) Crawford County	1	0.47
Strasburg (village) Tuscarawas County	7	0.30
Perrysville (village) Ashland County	2	0.25
Waynesfield (village) Auglaize County	2	0.25
Anna (village) Shelby County	3	0.23
Oberlin (city) Lorain County	14	0.17
Burton (village) Geauga County	2	0.14
Silver Lake (village) Summit County	4	0.13
Albany (village) Athens County	1	0.12

Top 10 Places Sorted by Percent
Based on places with populations of 10,000 or more

Place	Number	%
Sidney (city) Shelby County	18	0.09
Springdale (city) Hamilton County	8	0.08
Girard (city) Trumbull County	8	0.07
Landen (cdp) Warren County	8	0.06
Centerville (city) Montgomery County	12	0.05
Ashland (city) Ashland County	10	0.05
East Liverpool (city) Columbiana County	7	0.05
Northbrook (cdp) Hamilton County	5	0.05
Mansfield (city) Richland County	18	0.04
Fairborn (city) Greene County	13	0.04

Hawaii Native/Pacific Islander: Other Micronesian

Top 10 Places Sorted by Number
Based on all places, regardless of population

Place	Number	%
Columbus (city) Franklin County	10	0.00
Crooksville (village) Perry County	5	0.20
Medina (city) Medina County	5	0.02
Cleveland (city) Cuyahoga County	5	0.00
Mulberry (cdp) Clermont County	4	0.13
Parma (city) Cuyahoga County	4	0.00
West Liberty (village) Logan County	3	0.17
Bellefontaine (city) Logan County	3	0.02
Mayfield Heights (city) Cuyahoga County	3	0.02
Huber Heights (city) Montgomery County	3	0.01

Top 10 Places Sorted by Percent
Based on all places, regardless of population

Place	Number	%
Valley Hi (village) Logan County	2	0.82
Donnelsville (village) Clark County	1	0.34
Crooksville (village) Perry County	5	0.20
West Liberty (village) Logan County	3	0.17
Quincy (village) Logan County	1	0.14
Mulberry (cdp) Clermont County	4	0.13
Edgerton (village) Williams County	2	0.09
Bremen (village) Fairfield County	1	0.08
Amberley (village) Hamilton County	1	0.03
Cedarville (village) Greene County	1	0.03

Top 10 Places Sorted by Percent
Based on places with populations of 10,000 or more

Place	Number	%
Medina (city) Medina County	5	0.02
Bellefontaine (city) Logan County	3	0.02
Mayfield Heights (city) Cuyahoga County	3	0.02
Celina (city) Mercer County	2	0.02
East Liverpool (city) Columbiana County	2	0.02
Huber Heights (city) Montgomery County	3	0.01
Sidney (city) Shelby County	3	0.01
Avon Lake (city) Lorain County	2	0.01
Forest Park (city) Hamilton County	2	0.01
Perrysburg (city) Wood County	2	0.01

Notes: (cdp) census designated place; Refer to the User's Guide in the front of the book for more detailed information.

Hawaii Native/Pacific Islander: Polynesian

Top 10 Places Sorted by Number
Based on all places, regardless of population

Place	Number	%
Columbus (city) Franklin County	381	0.05
Cleveland (city) Cuyahoga County	169	0.04
Cincinnati (city) Hamilton County	114	0.03
Toledo (city) Lucas County	110	0.04
Akron (city) Summit County	81	0.04
Dayton (city) Montgomery County	57	0.03
Canton (city) Stark County	40	0.05
Delaware (city) Delaware County	29	0.11
Hamilton (city) Butler County	28	0.05
Parma (city) Cuyahoga County	27	0.03

Top 10 Places Sorted by Percent
Based on all places, regardless of population

Place	Number	%
Belmont (village) Belmont County	10	1.88
Mowrystown (village) Highland County	3	0.80
Roswell (village) Tuscarawas County	2	0.72
Patterson (village) Hardin County	1	0.72
Empire (village) Jefferson County	2	0.67
Fort Recovery (village) Mercer County	7	0.55
Pitsburg (village) Darke County	2	0.51
Hartford (village) Licking County	2	0.49
South Salem (village) Ross County	1	0.47
Dellroy (village) Carroll County	1	0.34

Top 10 Places Sorted by Percent
Based on places with populations of 10,000 or more

Place	Number	%
Tallmadge (city) Summit County	22	0.13
Delaware (city) Delaware County	29	0.11
Middleburg Heights (city) Cuyahoga County	17	0.11
Landen (cdp) Warren County	14	0.11
Bexley (city) Franklin County	12	0.09
Circleville (city) Pickaway County	11	0.08
Forest Park (city) Hamilton County	13	0.07
Miamisburg (city) Montgomery County	13	0.07
Warrensville Heights (city) Cuyahoga County	10	0.07
Finneytown (cdp) Hamilton County	9	0.07

Hawaii Native/Pacific Islander: Native Hawaiian

Top 10 Places Sorted by Number
Based on all places, regardless of population

Place	Number	%
Columbus (city) Franklin County	187	0.03
Cleveland (city) Cuyahoga County	105	0.02
Cincinnati (city) Hamilton County	66	0.02
Akron (city) Summit County	52	0.02
Toledo (city) Lucas County	51	0.02
Canton (city) Stark County	30	0.04
Delaware (city) Delaware County	26	0.10
Dayton (city) Montgomery County	24	0.01
Tallmadge (city) Summit County	22	0.13
Beavercreek (city) Greene County	21	0.06

Top 10 Places Sorted by Percent
Based on all places, regardless of population

Place	Number	%
Belmont (village) Belmont County	5	0.94
Mowrystown (village) Highland County	3	0.80
Patterson (village) Hardin County	1	0.72
Fort Recovery (village) Mercer County	7	0.55
Hartford (village) Licking County	2	0.49
South Salem (village) Ross County	1	0.47
Roaming Shores (village) Ashtabula County	4	0.32
Wetherington (cdp) Butler County	3	0.30

Place	Number	%
Quincy (village) Logan County	2	0.27
Pitsburg (village) Darke County	1	0.26

Top 10 Places Sorted by Percent
Based on places with populations of 10,000 or more

Place	Number	%
Tallmadge (city) Summit County	22	0.13
Delaware (city) Delaware County	26	0.10
Circleville (city) Pickaway County	11	0.08
Landen (cdp) Warren County	9	0.07
Beavercreek (city) Greene County	21	0.06
Finneytown (cdp) Hamilton County	8	0.06
Huber Heights (city) Montgomery County	18	0.05
Lancaster (city) Fairfield County	16	0.05
Chillicothe (city) Ross County	10	0.05
Painesville (city) Lake County	9	0.05

Hawaii Native/Pacific Islander: Samoan

Top 10 Places Sorted by Number
Based on all places, regardless of population

Place	Number	%
Columbus (city) Franklin County	186	0.03
Cleveland (city) Cuyahoga County	61	0.01
Toledo (city) Lucas County	49	0.02
Cincinnati (city) Hamilton County	42	0.01
Dayton (city) Montgomery County	30	0.02
Akron (city) Summit County	21	0.01
Hamilton (city) Butler County	17	0.03
Elyria (city) Lorain County	12	0.02
Willoughby (city) Lake County	11	0.05
Springfield (city) Clark County	11	0.02

Top 10 Places Sorted by Percent
Based on all places, regardless of population

Place	Number	%
Belmont (village) Belmont County	5	0.94
Roswell (village) Tuscarawas County	2	0.72
Empire (village) Jefferson County	2	0.67
Dellroy (village) Carroll County	1	0.34
Pitsburg (village) Darke County	1	0.26
Beallsville (village) Monroe County	1	0.24
Delta (village) Fulton County	6	0.20
West Salem (village) Wayne County	3	0.20
Drexel (cdp) Montgomery County	4	0.19
Genoa (village) Ottawa County	4	0.18

Top 10 Places Sorted by Percent
Based on places with populations of 10,000 or more

Place	Number	%
Willoughby (city) Lake County	11	0.05
Bexley (city) Franklin County	7	0.05
Landen (cdp) Warren County	5	0.04
Shiloh (cdp) Montgomery County	4	0.04
Columbus (city) Franklin County	186	0.03
Hamilton (city) Butler County	17	0.03
Miamisburg (city) Montgomery County	6	0.03
Rocky River (city) Cuyahoga County	6	0.03
Whitehall (city) Franklin County	6	0.03
Forest Park (city) Hamilton County	5	0.03

Hawaii Native/Pacific Islander: Tongan

Top 10 Places Sorted by Number
Based on all places, regardless of population

Place	Number	%
Middleburg Heights (city) Cuyahoga County	7	0.05
Toledo (city) Lucas County	5	0.00
Newark (city) Licking County	4	0.01
Strongsville (city) Cuyahoga County	4	0.01
Sidney (city) Shelby County	2	0.01
Parma (city) Cuyahoga County	2	0.00

Place	Number	%
Milford (city) Clermont County	1	0.02
Berea (city) Cuyahoga County	1	0.01
Cleveland Heights (city) Cuyahoga County	1	0.00
Columbus (city) Franklin County	1	0.00

Top 10 Places Sorted by Percent
Based on all places, regardless of population

Place	Number	%
Middleburg Heights (city) Cuyahoga County	7	0.05
Milford (city) Clermont County	1	0.02
Newark (city) Licking County	4	0.01
Strongsville (city) Cuyahoga County	4	0.01
Sidney (city) Shelby County	2	0.01
Berea (city) Cuyahoga County	1	0.01
Toledo (city) Lucas County	5	0.00
Parma (city) Cuyahoga County	2	0.00
Cleveland Heights (city) Cuyahoga County	1	0.00
Columbus (city) Franklin County	1	0.00

Top 10 Places Sorted by Percent
Based on places with populations of 10,000 or more

Place	Number	%
Middleburg Heights (city) Cuyahoga County	7	0.05
Newark (city) Licking County	4	0.01
Strongsville (city) Cuyahoga County	4	0.01
Sidney (city) Shelby County	2	0.01
Berea (city) Cuyahoga County	1	0.01
Toledo (city) Lucas County	5	0.00
Parma (city) Cuyahoga County	2	0.00
Cleveland Heights (city) Cuyahoga County	1	0.00
Columbus (city) Franklin County	1	0.00
Dayton (city) Montgomery County	1	0.00

Hawaii Native/Pacific Islander: Other Polynesian

Top 10 Places Sorted by Number
Based on all places, regardless of population

Place	Number	%
Akron (city) Summit County	8	0.00
Xenia (city) Greene County	7	0.03
Columbus (city) Franklin County	7	0.00
Cincinnati (city) Hamilton County	6	0.00
Warrensville Heights (city) Cuyahoga County	5	0.03
Toledo (city) Lucas County	5	0.00
Middleburg Heights (city) Cuyahoga County	4	0.03
Ashland (city) Ashland County	4	0.02
Austintown (cdp) Mahoning County	3	0.01
Boardman (cdp) Mahoning County	3	0.01

Top 10 Places Sorted by Percent
Based on all places, regardless of population

Place	Number	%
Hartville (village) Stark County	1	0.05
Xenia (city) Greene County	7	0.03
Warrensville Heights (city) Cuyahoga County	5	0.03
Middleburg Heights (city) Cuyahoga County	4	0.03
West Portsmouth (cdp) Scioto County	1	0.03
Ashland (city) Ashland County	4	0.02
Wellington (village) Lorain County	1	0.02
West Milton (village) Miami County	1	0.02
Austintown (cdp) Mahoning County	3	0.01
Boardman (cdp) Mahoning County	3	0.01

Top 10 Places Sorted by Percent
Based on places with populations of 10,000 or more

Place	Number	%
Xenia (city) Greene County	7	0.03
Warrensville Heights (city) Cuyahoga County	5	0.03
Middleburg Heights (city) Cuyahoga County	4	0.03
Ashland (city) Ashland County	4	0.02
Austintown (cdp) Mahoning County	3	0.01

Notes: (cdp) census designated place; Refer to the User's Guide in the front of the book for more detailed information.

Place	Number	%
Boardman (cdp) Mahoning County	3	0.01
Fairborn (city) Greene County	3	0.01
Mansfield (city) Richland County	3	0.01
Whitehall (city) Franklin County	1	0.01
Wilmington (city) Clinton County	1	0.01

Hawaii Native/Pacific Islander: Other Pacific Islander, specified

Top 10 Places Sorted by Number
Based on all places, regardless of population

Place	Number	%
Cleveland (city) Cuyahoga County	34	0.01
Columbus (city) Franklin County	26	0.00
Akron (city) Summit County	18	0.01
Cincinnati (city) Hamilton County	18	0.01
Toledo (city) Lucas County	15	0.00
Hamilton (city) Butler County	12	0.02
Dayton (city) Montgomery County	11	0.01
Frankfort (village) Ross County	10	0.99
East Cleveland (city) Cuyahoga County	9	0.03
Springboro (city) Warren County	8	0.06

Top 10 Places Sorted by Percent
Based on all places, regardless of population

Place	Number	%
Frankfort (village) Ross County	10	0.99
Crown City (village) Gallia County	1	0.24
Lucasville (cdp) Scioto County	3	0.19
Fort Loramie (village) Shelby County	2	0.15
Doylestown (village) Wayne County	3	0.11
Monfort Heights East (cdp) Hamilton County	4	0.10
Roseville (village) Perry County	2	0.10
Springboro (city) Warren County	8	0.06
University Heights (city) Cuyahoga County	7	0.05
Middlefield (village) Geauga County	1	0.04

Top 10 Places Sorted by Percent
Based on places with populations of 10,000 or more

Place	Number	%
Springboro (city) Warren County	8	0.06
University Heights (city) Cuyahoga County	7	0.05
East Cleveland (city) Cuyahoga County	9	0.03
Bedford Heights (city) Cuyahoga County	3	0.03
Cambridge (city) Guernsey County	3	0.03
Hamilton (city) Butler County	12	0.02
Stow (city) Summit County	5	0.02
Worthington (city) Franklin County	3	0.02
Shiloh (cdp) Montgomery County	2	0.02
Cleveland (city) Cuyahoga County	34	0.01

Hawaii Native/Pacific Islander: Other Pacific Islander, not specified

Top 10 Places Sorted by Number
Based on all places, regardless of population

Place	Number	%
Columbus (city) Franklin County	436	0.06
Cleveland (city) Cuyahoga County	228	0.05
Cincinnati (city) Hamilton County	133	0.04
Akron (city) Summit County	54	0.02
Toledo (city) Lucas County	53	0.02
Dayton (city) Montgomery County	51	0.03
Lorain (city) Lorain County	38	0.06
Youngstown (city) Mahoning County	29	0.04
Parma (city) Cuyahoga County	21	0.02
Dublin (city) Franklin County	20	0.06

Top 10 Places Sorted by Percent
Based on all places, regardless of population

Place	Number	%
Belmont (village) Belmont County	10	1.88
Summitville (village) Columbiana County	1	0.93
Buckland (village) Auglaize County	2	0.78
Kirkersville (village) Licking County	3	0.58
Bloomingdale (village) Jefferson County	1	0.45
Philo (village) Muskingum County	3	0.39
South Webster (village) Scioto County	3	0.39
Corning (village) Perry County	2	0.34
Lore City (village) Guernsey County	1	0.33
Jeffersonville (village) Fayette County	3	0.23

Top 10 Places Sorted by Percent
Based on places with populations of 10,000 or more

Place	Number	%
University Heights (city) Cuyahoga County	18	0.13
Marietta (city) Washington County	16	0.11
Lebanon (city) Warren County	15	0.09
Girard (city) Trumbull County	10	0.09
Montgomery (city) Hamilton County	9	0.09
Broadview Heights (city) Cuyahoga County	11	0.07
Sharonville (city) Hamilton County	10	0.07
Richmond Heights (city) Cuyahoga County	8	0.07
Columbus (city) Franklin County	436	0.06
Lorain (city) Lorain County	38	0.06

Hispanic or Latino

Top 10 Places Sorted by Number
Based on all places, regardless of population

Place	Number	%
Cleveland (city) Cuyahoga County	34,728	7.26
Columbus (city) Franklin County	17,471	2.46
Toledo (city) Lucas County	17,141	5.47
Lorain (city) Lorain County	14,438	21.03
Youngstown (city) Mahoning County	4,282	5.22
Cincinnati (city) Hamilton County	4,230	1.28
Dayton (city) Montgomery County	2,626	1.58
Akron (city) Summit County	2,513	1.16
Painesville (city) Lake County	2,256	12.89
Fremont (city) Sandusky County	2,140	12.32

Top 10 Places Sorted by Percent
Based on all places, regardless of population

Place	Number	%
West Leipsic (village) Putnam County	88	32.47
Belmore (village) Putnam County	44	25.73
Leipsic (village) Putnam County	535	23.93
Lorain (city) Lorain County	14,438	21.03
Hamler (village) Henry County	134	20.62
Holgate (village) Henry County	222	18.59
Milton Center (village) Wood County	34	17.44
Stony Prairie (cdp) Sandusky County	138	16.51
Hoytville (village) Wood County	48	16.22
Painesville (city) Lake County	2,256	12.89

Top 10 Places Sorted by Percent
Based on places with populations of 10,000 or more

Place	Number	%
Lorain (city) Lorain County	14,438	21.03
Painesville (city) Lake County	2,256	12.89
Defiance (city) Defiance County	2,100	12.75
Fremont (city) Sandusky County	2,140	12.32
Fostoria (city) Seneca County	1,104	7.92
Cleveland (city) Cuyahoga County	34,728	7.26
Toledo (city) Lucas County	17,141	5.47
Ashtabula (city) Ashtabula County	1,115	5.32
Youngstown (city) Mahoning County	4,282	5.22
Oregon (city) Lucas County	922	4.76

Hispanic: Central American

Top 10 Places Sorted by Number
Based on all places, regardless of population

Place	Number	%
Cleveland (city) Cuyahoga County	1,166	0.24
Columbus (city) Franklin County	1,040	0.15
Cincinnati (city) Hamilton County	397	0.12
Toledo (city) Lucas County	151	0.05
Akron (city) Summit County	134	0.06
Dayton (city) Montgomery County	72	0.04
New Philadelphia (city) Tuscarawas County	67	0.39
Canton (city) Stark County	62	0.08
Cleveland Heights (city) Cuyahoga County	60	0.12
Youngstown (city) Mahoning County	58	0.07

Top 10 Places Sorted by Percent
Based on all places, regardless of population

Place	Number	%
Harveysburg (village) Warren County	11	1.95
Milton Center (village) Wood County	3	1.54
Strasburg (village) Tuscarawas County	29	1.26
Shawnee Hills (village) Delaware County	5	1.19
Holgate (village) Henry County	7	0.59
Millersburg (village) Holmes County	18	0.54
Willard (city) Huron County	34	0.50
Sugar Bush Knolls (village) Portage County	1	0.44
Holiday Valley (cdp) Clark County	7	0.41
Riverlea (village) Franklin County	2	0.40

Top 10 Places Sorted by Percent
Based on places with populations of 10,000 or more

Place	Number	%
New Philadelphia (city) Tuscarawas County	67	0.39
Springdale (city) Hamilton County	27	0.26
Cleveland (city) Cuyahoga County	1,166	0.24
Sharonville (city) Hamilton County	32	0.23
Whitehall (city) Franklin County	40	0.21
Dover (city) Tuscarawas County	22	0.18
Landen (cdp) Warren County	20	0.16
Columbus (city) Franklin County	1,040	0.15
Norwood (city) Hamilton County	31	0.14
Painesville (city) Lake County	22	0.13

Hispanic: Costa Rican

Top 10 Places Sorted by Number
Based on all places, regardless of population

Place	Number	%
Columbus (city) Franklin County	67	0.01
Cleveland (city) Cuyahoga County	39	0.01
Cincinnati (city) Hamilton County	38	0.01
Dayton (city) Montgomery County	17	0.01
Lebanon (city) Warren County	12	0.07
Sharonville (city) Hamilton County	11	0.08
Bellefontaine (city) Logan County	8	0.06
Austintown (cdp) Mahoning County	8	0.03
Kettering (city) Montgomery County	8	0.01
Shelby (city) Richland County	7	0.07

Top 10 Places Sorted by Percent
Based on all places, regardless of population

Place	Number	%
Anna (village) Shelby County	3	0.23
Fredericksburg (village) Wayne County	1	0.21
Plain City (village) Madison County	5	0.18
Risingsun (village) Wood County	1	0.16
South Russell (village) Geauga County	5	0.12
Cherry Grove (cdp) Hamilton County	4	0.09
Sharonville (city) Hamilton County	11	0.08
Kenwood (cdp) Hamilton County	6	0.08
Lebanon (city) Warren County	12	0.07

Notes: (cdp) census designated place; Refer to the User's Guide in the front of the book for more detailed information.

Place	Number	%
Shelby (city) Richland County	7	0.07

Top 10 Places Sorted by Percent
Based on places with populations of 10,000 or more

Place	Number	%
Sharonville (city) Hamilton County	11	0.08
Lebanon (city) Warren County	12	0.07
Bellefontaine (city) Logan County	8	0.06
Perrysburg (city) Wood County	7	0.04
Marysville (city) Union County	6	0.04
Austintown (cdp) Mahoning County	8	0.03
North Olmsted (city) Cuyahoga County	6	0.02
Oxford (city) Butler County	5	0.02
Athens (city) Athens County	4	0.02
Painesville (city) Lake County	4	0.02

Hispanic: Guatemalan

Top 10 Places Sorted by Number
Based on all places, regardless of population

Place	Number	%
Cleveland (city) Cuyahoga County	431	0.09
Cincinnati (city) Hamilton County	211	0.06
Columbus (city) Franklin County	115	0.02
New Philadelphia (city) Tuscarawas County	65	0.38
Strasburg (village) Tuscarawas County	26	1.13
Toledo (city) Lucas County	23	0.01
Lakewood (city) Cuyahoga County	21	0.04
Akron (city) Summit County	21	0.01
Dover (city) Tuscarawas County	19	0.16
Lorain (city) Lorain County	15	0.02

Top 10 Places Sorted by Percent
Based on all places, regardless of population

Place	Number	%
Strasburg (village) Tuscarawas County	26	1.13
Holgate (village) Henry County	7	0.59
New Philadelphia (city) Tuscarawas County	65	0.38
Minerva Park (village) Franklin County	3	0.23
Moraine (city) Montgomery County	12	0.17
Dover (city) Tuscarawas County	19	0.16
Utica (village) Licking County	3	0.14
Burton (village) Geauga County	2	0.14
Monroeville (village) Huron County	2	0.14
Dennison (village) Tuscarawas County	4	0.13

Top 10 Places Sorted by Percent
Based on places with populations of 10,000 or more

Place	Number	%
New Philadelphia (city) Tuscarawas County	65	0.38
Dover (city) Tuscarawas County	19	0.16
Springdale (city) Hamilton County	13	0.12
Cleveland (city) Cuyahoga County	431	0.09
Cincinnati (city) Hamilton County	211	0.06
Lakewood (city) Cuyahoga County	21	0.04
Hilliard (city) Franklin County	10	0.04
South Euclid (city) Cuyahoga County	10	0.04
Athens (city) Athens County	9	0.04
Amherst (city) Lorain County	5	0.04

Hispanic: Honduran

Top 10 Places Sorted by Number
Based on all places, regardless of population

Place	Number	%
Cleveland (city) Cuyahoga County	170	0.04
Columbus (city) Franklin County	108	0.02
Akron (city) Summit County	48	0.02
Cincinnati (city) Hamilton County	47	0.01
Canton (city) Stark County	34	0.04
Norwood (city) Hamilton County	17	0.08
Toledo (city) Lucas County	15	0.00
North Canton (city) Stark County	13	0.08
Mount Carmel (cdp) Clermont County	10	0.23
Parma (city) Cuyahoga County	10	0.01

Top 10 Places Sorted by Percent
Based on all places, regardless of population

Place	Number	%
Milton Center (village) Wood County	3	1.54
Shawnee Hills (village) Delaware County	5	1.19
Sugar Bush Knolls (village) Portage County	1	0.44
Riverlea (village) Franklin County	2	0.40
Fairport Harbor (village) Lake County	9	0.28
Mount Carmel (cdp) Clermont County	10	0.23
Holiday Valley (cdp) Clark County	4	0.23
Jeffersonville (village) Fayette County	3	0.23
Millersburg (village) Holmes County	7	0.21
Hartville (village) Stark County	4	0.18

Top 10 Places Sorted by Percent
Based on places with populations of 10,000 or more

Place	Number	%
Norwood (city) Hamilton County	17	0.08
North Canton (city) Stark County	13	0.08
Sharonville (city) Hamilton County	8	0.06
Cleveland (city) Cuyahoga County	170	0.04
Canton (city) Stark County	34	0.04
Painesville (city) Lake County	6	0.03
Whitehall (city) Franklin County	6	0.03
Berea (city) Cuyahoga County	5	0.03
Columbus (city) Franklin County	108	0.02
Akron (city) Summit County	48	0.02

Hispanic: Nicaraguan

Top 10 Places Sorted by Number
Based on all places, regardless of population

Place	Number	%
Cleveland (city) Cuyahoga County	91	0.02
Columbus (city) Franklin County	73	0.01
Toledo (city) Lucas County	69	0.02
Cincinnati (city) Hamilton County	23	0.01
Painesville (city) Lake County	11	0.06
Bowling Green (city) Wood County	10	0.03
Middletown (city) Butler County	9	0.02
Akron (city) Summit County	9	0.00
Mentor (city) Lake County	8	0.02
Springdale (city) Hamilton County	7	0.07

Top 10 Places Sorted by Percent
Based on all places, regardless of population

Place	Number	%
Harveysburg (village) Warren County	6	1.07
Gambier (village) Knox County	6	0.32
Lucasville (cdp) Scioto County	3	0.19
Fayette (village) Fulton County	2	0.15
Grandview Heights (city) Franklin County	6	0.09
Summerside (cdp) Clermont County	5	0.09
Springdale (city) Hamilton County	7	0.07
Northridge (cdp) Clark County	5	0.07
Willard (city) Huron County	5	0.07
Navarre (village) Stark County	1	0.07

Top 10 Places Sorted by Percent
Based on places with populations of 10,000 or more

Place	Number	%
Springdale (city) Hamilton County	7	0.07
Painesville (city) Lake County	11	0.06
University Heights (city) Cuyahoga County	5	0.04
Wilmington (city) Clinton County	5	0.04
Bowling Green (city) Wood County	10	0.03
Loveland (city) Hamilton County	4	0.03
Cleveland (city) Cuyahoga County	91	0.02
Toledo (city) Lucas County	69	0.02
Middletown (city) Butler County	9	0.02
Mentor (city) Lake County	8	0.02

Hispanic: Panamanian

Top 10 Places Sorted by Number
Based on all places, regardless of population

Place	Number	%
Columbus (city) Franklin County	173	0.02
Cleveland (city) Cuyahoga County	47	0.01
Cincinnati (city) Hamilton County	45	0.01
Toledo (city) Lucas County	33	0.01
Dayton (city) Montgomery County	27	0.02
Youngstown (city) Mahoning County	20	0.02
Huber Heights (city) Montgomery County	18	0.05
Akron (city) Summit County	18	0.01
Mansfield (city) Richland County	17	0.03
Lorain (city) Lorain County	13	0.02

Top 10 Places Sorted by Percent
Based on all places, regardless of population

Place	Number	%
North Randall (village) Cuyahoga County	2	0.22
Gloria Glens Park (village) Medina County	1	0.19
Sherwood (cdp) Hamilton County	7	0.18
Hartville (village) Stark County	4	0.18
Holiday Valley (cdp) Clark County	3	0.18
Russia (village) Shelby County	1	0.18
Botkins (village) Shelby County	2	0.17
Lithopolis (village) Fairfield County	1	0.17
Wright-Patterson AFB (cdp) Montgomery County	7	0.11
Lockland (village) Hamilton County	4	0.11

Top 10 Places Sorted by Percent
Based on places with populations of 10,000 or more

Place	Number	%
Huber Heights (city) Montgomery County	18	0.05
Pataskala (city) Licking County	5	0.05
Forest Park (city) Hamilton County	7	0.04
Marysville (city) Union County	6	0.04
Finneytown (cdp) Hamilton County	5	0.04
Shiloh (cdp) Montgomery County	5	0.04
Bedford Heights (city) Cuyahoga County	4	0.04
Richmond Heights (city) Cuyahoga County	4	0.04
Mansfield (city) Richland County	17	0.03
Fairborn (city) Greene County	11	0.03

Hispanic: Salvadoran

Top 10 Places Sorted by Number
Based on all places, regardless of population

Place	Number	%
Columbus (city) Franklin County	455	0.06
Cleveland (city) Cuyahoga County	324	0.07
Akron (city) Summit County	30	0.01
Whitehall (city) Franklin County	28	0.15
Willard (city) Huron County	27	0.40
Cincinnati (city) Hamilton County	27	0.01
Cleveland Heights (city) Cuyahoga County	24	0.05
Youngstown (city) Mahoning County	20	0.02
Middletown (city) Butler County	14	0.03
North Olmsted (city) Cuyahoga County	12	0.04

Top 10 Places Sorted by Percent
Based on places with populations of 10,000 or more

Place	Number	%
Harveysburg (village) Warren County	5	0.89
Willard (city) Huron County	27	0.40
Arlington Heights (village) Hamilton County	2	0.40
Millersburg (village) Holmes County	7	0.21
Whitehall (city) Franklin County	28	0.15

Notes: (cdp) census designated place; Refer to the User's Guide in the front of the book for more detailed information.

PROFILES OF OHIO / Ancestry Rankings 453

Place	Number	%
Northgate (cdp) Hamilton County	11	0.14
Lincoln Village (cdp) Franklin County	11	0.12
Five Points (cdp) Warren County	2	0.09
Sharonville (city) Hamilton County	11	0.08
Bolindale (cdp) Trumbull County	2	0.08

Top 10 Places Sorted by Percent
Based on places with populations of 10,000 or more

Place	Number	%
Whitehall (city) Franklin County	28	0.15
Sharonville (city) Hamilton County	11	0.08
Cleveland (city) Cuyahoga County	324	0.07
University Heights (city) Cuyahoga County	10	0.07
Bellefontaine (city) Logan County	9	0.07
Columbus (city) Franklin County	455	0.06
Cleveland Heights (city) Cuyahoga County	24	0.05
Brooklyn (city) Cuyahoga County	6	0.05
Springdale (city) Hamilton County	5	0.05
North Olmsted (city) Cuyahoga County	12	0.04

Hispanic: Other Central American

Top 10 Places Sorted by Number
Based on all places, regardless of population

Place	Number	%
Cleveland (city) Cuyahoga County	64	0.01
Columbus (city) Franklin County	49	0.01
Tiffin (city) Seneca County	6	0.03
Cincinnati (city) Hamilton County	6	0.00
Finneytown (cdp) Hamilton County	5	0.04
Landen (cdp) Warren County	5	0.04
Millersburg (village) Holmes County	4	0.12
Cambridge (city) Guernsey County	4	0.03
Warrensville Heights (city) Cuyahoga County	4	0.03
Berea (city) Cuyahoga County	4	0.02

Top 10 Places Sorted by Percent
Based on all places, regardless of population

Place	Number	%
Marshallville (village) Wayne County	2	0.24
Grandview (cdp) Hamilton County	3	0.22
Strasburg (village) Tuscarawas County	3	0.13
Millersburg (village) Holmes County	4	0.12
Hiram (village) Portage County	1	0.08
Finneytown (cdp) Hamilton County	5	0.04
Landen (cdp) Warren County	5	0.04
Wyoming (city) Hamilton County	3	0.04
Tiffin (city) Seneca County	6	0.03
Cambridge (city) Guernsey County	4	0.03

Top 10 Places Sorted by Percent
Based on places with populations of 10,000 or more

Place	Number	%
Finneytown (cdp) Hamilton County	5	0.04
Landen (cdp) Warren County	5	0.04
Tiffin (city) Seneca County	6	0.03
Cambridge (city) Guernsey County	4	0.03
Warrensville Heights (city) Cuyahoga County	4	0.03
Berea (city) Cuyahoga County	4	0.02
Fairview Park (city) Cuyahoga County	4	0.02
Whitehall (city) Franklin County	3	0.02
Cleveland (city) Cuyahoga County	64	0.01
Columbus (city) Franklin County	49	0.01

Hispanic: Cuban

Top 10 Places Sorted by Number
Based on all places, regardless of population

Place	Number	%
Columbus (city) Franklin County	627	0.09
Cleveland (city) Cuyahoga County	512	0.11
Cincinnati (city) Hamilton County	220	0.07
Toledo (city) Lucas County	181	0.06
Dayton (city) Montgomery County	117	0.07
Akron (city) Summit County	74	0.03
Youngstown (city) Mahoning County	68	0.08
Lorain (city) Lorain County	64	0.09
Kettering (city) Montgomery County	61	0.11
Hamilton (city) Butler County	56	0.09

Top 10 Places Sorted by Percent
Based on all places, regardless of population

Place	Number	%
Glenford (village) Perry County	2	1.01
Sarahsville (village) Noble County	2	1.01
Kalida (village) Putnam County	5	0.48
Chauncey (village) Athens County	5	0.47
Sugar Grove (village) Fairfield County	2	0.45
Wetherington (cdp) Butler County	4	0.40
West Leipsic (village) Putnam County	1	0.37
North Randall (village) Cuyahoga County	3	0.33
Empire (village) Jefferson County	1	0.33
West Mansfield (village) Logan County	2	0.29

Top 10 Places Sorted by Percent
Based on places with populations of 10,000 or more

Place	Number	%
Landen (cdp) Warren County	30	0.23
Oxford (city) Butler County	34	0.15
Blue Ash (city) Hamilton County	19	0.15
Washington (city) Fayette County	18	0.13
Montgomery (city) Hamilton County	13	0.13
Rocky River (city) Cuyahoga County	24	0.12
Clayton (city) Montgomery County	16	0.12
Cleveland (city) Cuyahoga County	512	0.11
Kettering (city) Montgomery County	61	0.11
Brecksville (city) Cuyahoga County	15	0.11

Hispanic: Dominican Republic

Top 10 Places Sorted by Number
Based on all places, regardless of population

Place	Number	%
Cleveland (city) Cuyahoga County	542	0.11
Columbus (city) Franklin County	298	0.04
Hamilton (city) Butler County	91	0.15
Lorain (city) Lorain County	69	0.10
Cincinnati (city) Hamilton County	51	0.02
Dayton (city) Montgomery County	29	0.02
Lincoln Village (cdp) Franklin County	26	0.27
Toledo (city) Lucas County	23	0.01
Whitehall (city) Franklin County	22	0.11
Lakewood (city) Cuyahoga County	20	0.04

Top 10 Places Sorted by Percent
Based on all places, regardless of population

Place	Number	%
Phillipsburg (village) Montgomery County	5	0.80
Van Buren (village) Hancock County	2	0.64
Lincoln Village (cdp) Franklin County	26	0.27
Washingtonville (village) Columbiana County	2	0.25
Willard (city) Huron County	15	0.22
Genoa (village) Ottawa County	5	0.22
Gambier (village) Knox County	3	0.16
Hamilton (city) Butler County	91	0.15
Lake Darby (cdp) Franklin County	5	0.13
Green Meadows (cdp) Clark County	3	0.13

Top 10 Places Sorted by Percent
Based on places with populations of 10,000 or more

Place	Number	%
Hamilton (city) Butler County	91	0.15
Cleveland (city) Cuyahoga County	542	0.11
Whitehall (city) Franklin County	22	0.11

Place	Number	%
Lorain (city) Lorain County	69	0.10
Reading (city) Hamilton County	9	0.08
West Carrollton City (city) Montgomery County	10	0.07
Sharonville (city) Hamilton County	8	0.06
Pataskala (city) Licking County	6	0.06
Reynoldsburg (city) Franklin County	17	0.05
Austintown (cdp) Mahoning County	15	0.05

Hispanic: Mexican

Top 10 Places Sorted by Number
Based on all places, regardless of population

Place	Number	%
Toledo (city) Lucas County	13,320	4.25
Columbus (city) Franklin County	8,686	1.22
Cleveland (city) Cuyahoga County	2,973	0.62
Lorain (city) Lorain County	2,437	3.55
Painesville (city) Lake County	1,869	10.68
Fremont (city) Sandusky County	1,584	9.12
Cincinnati (city) Hamilton County	1,542	0.47
Defiance (city) Defiance County	1,371	8.33
Dayton (city) Montgomery County	1,360	0.82
Findlay (city) Hancock County	1,215	3.12

Top 10 Places Sorted by Percent
Based on all places, regardless of population

Place	Number	%
West Leipsic (village) Putnam County	60	22.14
Leipsic (village) Putnam County	441	19.72
Belmore (village) Putnam County	32	18.71
Hamler (village) Henry County	108	16.62
Hoytville (village) Wood County	45	15.20
Holgate (village) Henry County	168	14.07
Stony Prairie (cdp) Sandusky County	116	13.88
Milton Center (village) Wood County	24	12.31
Painesville (city) Lake County	1,869	10.68
Willard (city) Huron County	636	9.34

Top 10 Places Sorted by Percent
Based on places with populations of 10,000 or more

Place	Number	%
Painesville (city) Lake County	1,869	10.68
Fremont (city) Sandusky County	1,584	9.12
Defiance (city) Defiance County	1,371	8.33
Fostoria (city) Seneca County	948	6.80
Toledo (city) Lucas County	13,320	4.25
Oregon (city) Lucas County	689	3.56
Lorain (city) Lorain County	2,437	3.55
Findlay (city) Hancock County	1,215	3.12
Norwalk (city) Huron County	469	2.89
Springdale (city) Hamilton County	255	2.41

Hispanic: Puerto Rican

Top 10 Places Sorted by Number
Based on all places, regardless of population

Place	Number	%
Cleveland (city) Cuyahoga County	25,385	5.31
Lorain (city) Lorain County	10,536	15.35
Youngstown (city) Mahoning County	3,222	3.93
Columbus (city) Franklin County	2,790	0.39
Campbell (city) Mahoning County	873	9.23
Elyria (city) Lorain County	853	1.52
Toledo (city) Lucas County	742	0.24
Ashtabula (city) Ashtabula County	727	3.47
Parma (city) Cuyahoga County	695	0.81
Akron (city) Summit County	654	0.30

Top 10 Places Sorted by Percent
Based on all places, regardless of population

Place	Number	%
Lorain (city) Lorain County	10,536	15.35

Notes: (cdp) census designated place; Refer to the User's Guide in the front of the book for more detailed information.

Place	Number	%
Campbell (city) Mahoning County	873	9.23
Linndale (village) Cuyahoga County	9	7.69
Cleveland (city) Cuyahoga County	25,385	5.31
New Rome (village) Franklin County	3	5.00
Geneva (city) Ashtabula County	269	4.08
Youngstown (city) Mahoning County	3,222	3.93
Sheffield (village) Lorain County	108	3.66
Ashtabula (city) Ashtabula County	727	3.47
Brooklyn (city) Cuyahoga County	300	2.59

Top 10 Places Sorted by Percent
Based on places with populations of 10,000 or more

Place	Number	%
Lorain (city) Lorain County	10,536	15.35
Cleveland (city) Cuyahoga County	25,385	5.31
Youngstown (city) Mahoning County	3,222	3.93
Ashtabula (city) Ashtabula County	727	3.47
Brooklyn (city) Cuyahoga County	300	2.59
Elyria (city) Lorain County	853	1.52
Amherst (city) Lorain County	169	1.43
Painesville (city) Lake County	245	1.40
Defiance (city) Defiance County	193	1.17
Boardman (cdp) Mahoning County	422	1.13

Hispanic: South American

Top 10 Places Sorted by Number
Based on all places, regardless of population

Place	Number	%
Columbus (city) Franklin County	944	0.13
Cleveland (city) Cuyahoga County	557	0.12
Cincinnati (city) Hamilton County	320	0.10
Toledo (city) Lucas County	159	0.05
Lakewood (city) Cuyahoga County	116	0.20
Akron (city) Summit County	115	0.05
Cleveland Heights (city) Cuyahoga County	89	0.18
Shaker Heights (city) Cuyahoga County	78	0.27
Parma (city) Cuyahoga County	77	0.09
Upper Arlington (city) Franklin County	69	0.20

Top 10 Places Sorted by Percent
Based on all places, regardless of population

Place	Number	%
Urbancrest (village) Franklin County	9	1.04
Meyers Lake (village) Stark County	5	0.88
Albany (village) Athens County	7	0.87
Burlington (cdp) Lawrence County	22	0.79
Bratenahl (village) Cuyahoga County	9	0.67
Timberlake (village) Lake County	5	0.65
Hilltop (cdp) Trumbull County	3	0.56
Hunting Valley (village) Cuyahoga County	4	0.54
Bentleyville (village) Cuyahoga County	5	0.53
Kenwood (cdp) Hamilton County	33	0.44

Top 10 Places Sorted by Percent
Based on places with populations of 10,000 or more

Place	Number	%
Oxford (city) Butler County	66	0.30
Worthington (city) Franklin County	42	0.30
University Heights (city) Cuyahoga County	41	0.29
Athens (city) Athens County	60	0.28
Shaker Heights (city) Cuyahoga County	78	0.27
Richmond Heights (city) Cuyahoga County	30	0.27
Brecksville (city) Cuyahoga County	33	0.25
Gahanna (city) Franklin County	67	0.21
Landen (cdp) Warren County	27	0.21
Lakewood (city) Cuyahoga County	116	0.20

Hispanic: Argentinean

Top 10 Places Sorted by Number
Based on all places, regardless of population

Place	Number	%
Columbus (city) Franklin County	72	0.01
Cincinnati (city) Hamilton County	49	0.01
Cleveland (city) Cuyahoga County	43	0.01
Gahanna (city) Franklin County	24	0.07
Akron (city) Summit County	20	0.01
Shaker Heights (city) Cuyahoga County	18	0.06
Oberlin (city) Lorain County	16	0.20
Cleveland Heights (city) Cuyahoga County	16	0.03
Lakewood (city) Cuyahoga County	16	0.03
Toledo (city) Lucas County	11	0.00

Top 10 Places Sorted by Percent
Based on all places, regardless of population

Place	Number	%
Hunting Valley (village) Cuyahoga County	4	0.54
Bentleyville (village) Cuyahoga County	4	0.42
Hiram (village) Portage County	5	0.40
Oberlin (city) Lorain County	16	0.20
Yellow Springs (village) Greene County	5	0.13
Ottawa Hills (village) Lucas County	5	0.11
Gahanna (city) Franklin County	24	0.07
Pepper Pike (city) Cuyahoga County	4	0.07
Chagrin Falls (village) Cuyahoga County	3	0.07
South Russell (village) Geauga County	3	0.07

Top 10 Places Sorted by Percent
Based on places with populations of 10,000 or more

Place	Number	%
Gahanna (city) Franklin County	24	0.07
Shaker Heights (city) Cuyahoga County	18	0.06
Defiance (city) Defiance County	10	0.06
Beachwood (city) Cuyahoga County	7	0.06
University Heights (city) Cuyahoga County	7	0.05
Brooklyn (city) Cuyahoga County	6	0.05
Richmond Heights (city) Cuyahoga County	6	0.05
Kent (city) Portage County	10	0.04
Avon Lake (city) Lorain County	7	0.04
Twinsburg (city) Summit County	7	0.04

Hispanic: Bolivian

Top 10 Places Sorted by Number
Based on all places, regardless of population

Place	Number	%
Columbus (city) Franklin County	34	0.00
Burlington (cdp) Lawrence County	21	0.75
Cincinnati (city) Hamilton County	12	0.00
Cleveland (city) Cuyahoga County	10	0.00
Urbancrest (village) Franklin County	9	1.04
Kettering (city) Montgomery County	9	0.02
Miamisburg (city) Montgomery County	8	0.04
Centerville (city) Montgomery County	8	0.03
Toledo (city) Lucas County	8	0.00
Wauseon (city) Fulton County	6	0.08

Top 10 Places Sorted by Percent
Based on all places, regardless of population

Place	Number	%
Urbancrest (village) Franklin County	9	1.04
Burlington (cdp) Lawrence County	21	0.75
Fletcher (village) Miami County	2	0.39
Payne (village) Paulding County	1	0.09
Wauseon (city) Fulton County	6	0.08
Pandora (village) Putnam County	1	0.08
Mount Carmel (cdp) Clermont County	3	0.07
Bratenahl (village) Cuyahoga County	1	0.07
Pickerington (city) Fairfield County	6	0.06

Place	Number	%
Granville (village) Licking County	2	0.06

Top 10 Places Sorted by Percent
Based on places with populations of 10,000 or more

Place	Number	%
Miamisburg (city) Montgomery County	8	0.04
Centerville (city) Montgomery County	8	0.03
Brooklyn (city) Cuyahoga County	3	0.03
Kettering (city) Montgomery County	9	0.02
Tallmadge (city) Summit County	4	0.02
Fairview Park (city) Cuyahoga County	3	0.02
Worthington (city) Franklin County	3	0.02
Dover (city) Tuscarawas County	2	0.02
Upper Arlington (city) Franklin County	5	0.01
Lima (city) Allen County	4	0.01

Hispanic: Chilean

Top 10 Places Sorted by Number
Based on all places, regardless of population

Place	Number	%
Cleveland (city) Cuyahoga County	61	0.01
Columbus (city) Franklin County	51	0.01
Cincinnati (city) Hamilton County	21	0.01
Toledo (city) Lucas County	17	0.01
Westerville (city) Franklin County	15	0.04
Lakewood (city) Cuyahoga County	11	0.02
Wyoming (city) Hamilton County	10	0.12
Shaker Heights (city) Cuyahoga County	10	0.03
Wooster (city) Wayne County	9	0.04
University Heights (city) Cuyahoga County	8	0.06

Top 10 Places Sorted by Percent
Based on all places, regardless of population

Place	Number	%
Timberlake (village) Lake County	5	0.65
Elida (village) Allen County	3	0.16
Wyoming (city) Hamilton County	10	0.12
Hunter (cdp) Warren County	2	0.12
Woodlawn (village) Hamilton County	3	0.11
The Village of Indian Hill (city) Hamilton County	6	0.10
New Boston (village) Scioto County	2	0.09
Kenwood (cdp) Hamilton County	6	0.08
Fairlawn (city) Summit County	5	0.07
University Heights (city) Cuyahoga County	8	0.06

Top 10 Places Sorted by Percent
Based on places with populations of 10,000 or more

Place	Number	%
University Heights (city) Cuyahoga County	8	0.06
Worthington (city) Franklin County	7	0.05
Celina (city) Mercer County	5	0.05
Westerville (city) Franklin County	15	0.04
Wooster (city) Wayne County	9	0.04
Sylvania (city) Lucas County	7	0.04
Shaker Heights (city) Cuyahoga County	10	0.03
Kent (city) Portage County	8	0.03
South Euclid (city) Cuyahoga County	8	0.03
Westlake (city) Cuyahoga County	8	0.03

Hispanic: Colombian

Top 10 Places Sorted by Number
Based on all places, regardless of population

Place	Number	%
Columbus (city) Franklin County	289	0.04
Cleveland (city) Cuyahoga County	162	0.03
Cincinnati (city) Hamilton County	96	0.03
Toledo (city) Lucas County	44	0.01
Lakewood (city) Cuyahoga County	32	0.06
Dayton (city) Montgomery County	27	0.02
Oxford (city) Butler County	26	0.12

Notes: (cdp) census designated place; Refer to the User's Guide in the front of the book for more detailed information.

Place	Number	%
North Olmsted (city) Cuyahoga County	24	0.07
Cleveland Heights (city) Cuyahoga County	24	0.05
Kettering (city) Montgomery County	24	0.04

Top 10 Places Sorted by Percent
Based on all places, regardless of population

Place	Number	%
Meyers Lake (village) Stark County	5	0.88
Hilltop (cdp) Trumbull County	3	0.56
Albany (village) Athens County	3	0.37
Galena (village) Delaware County	1	0.33
New Straitsville (village) Perry County	2	0.26
Dillonvale (cdp) Hamilton County	9	0.24
Weston (village) Wood County	4	0.24
Bratenahl (village) Cuyahoga County	3	0.22
Granville (village) Licking County	6	0.19
North Lewisburg (village) Champaign County	3	0.19

Top 10 Places Sorted by Percent
Based on places with populations of 10,000 or more

Place	Number	%
Oxford (city) Butler County	26	0.12
Perrysburg (city) Wood County	16	0.09
Richmond Heights (city) Cuyahoga County	10	0.09
University Heights (city) Cuyahoga County	12	0.08
Worthington (city) Franklin County	12	0.08
North Olmsted (city) Cuyahoga County	24	0.07
Fairview Park (city) Cuyahoga County	12	0.07
Twinsburg (city) Summit County	12	0.07
Brecksville (city) Cuyahoga County	10	0.07
Landen (cdp) Warren County	9	0.07

Hispanic: Ecuadorian

Top 10 Places Sorted by Number
Based on all places, regardless of population

Place	Number	%
Columbus (city) Franklin County	97	0.01
Cleveland (city) Cuyahoga County	58	0.01
Cincinnati (city) Hamilton County	30	0.01
Dayton (city) Montgomery County	22	0.01
Akron (city) Summit County	20	0.01
Moraine (city) Montgomery County	17	0.25
Lorain (city) Lorain County	17	0.02
Hamilton (city) Butler County	15	0.02
Oxford (city) Butler County	11	0.05
Toledo (city) Lucas County	11	0.00

Top 10 Places Sorted by Percent
Based on all places, regardless of population

Place	Number	%
Sherrodsville (village) Carroll County	1	0.32
Moraine (city) Montgomery County	17	0.25
Jeromesville (village) Ashland County	1	0.21
Burton (village) Geauga County	2	0.14
Lincoln Village (cdp) Franklin County	10	0.11
South Amherst (village) Lorain County	2	0.11
Chagrin Falls (village) Cuyahoga County	4	0.10
University Heights (city) Cuyahoga County	9	0.06
Finneytown (cdp) Hamilton County	8	0.06
Orrville (city) Wayne County	5	0.06

Top 10 Places Sorted by Percent
Based on places with populations of 10,000 or more

Place	Number	%
University Heights (city) Cuyahoga County	9	0.06
Finneytown (cdp) Hamilton County	8	0.06
Oxford (city) Butler County	11	0.05
Athens (city) Athens County	10	0.05
Worthington (city) Franklin County	7	0.05
Avon Lake (city) Lorain County	7	0.04
Washington (city) Fayette County	6	0.04

Place	Number	%
Franklin (city) Warren County	5	0.04
Greenville (city) Darke County	4	0.03
Reading (city) Hamilton County	3	0.03

Hispanic: Paraguayan

Top 10 Places Sorted by Number
Based on all places, regardless of population

Place	Number	%
Toledo (city) Lucas County	7	0.00
Columbus (city) Franklin County	5	0.00
Brimfield (cdp) Portage County	4	0.12
Mayfield Heights (city) Cuyahoga County	4	0.02
Rocky River (city) Cuyahoga County	4	0.02
Cincinnati (city) Hamilton County	4	0.00
Sylvania (city) Lucas County	3	0.02
University Heights (city) Cuyahoga County	3	0.02
Cuyahoga Falls (city) Summit County	3	0.01
Cleveland (city) Cuyahoga County	3	0.00

Top 10 Places Sorted by Percent
Based on all places, regardless of population

Place	Number	%
Brimfield (cdp) Portage County	4	0.12
Sunbury (village) Delaware County	1	0.04
Mariemont (village) Hamilton County	1	0.03
Mayfield (village) Cuyahoga County	1	0.03
Mulberry (village) Clermont County	1	0.03
White Oak West (cdp) Hamilton County	1	0.03
Mayfield Heights (city) Cuyahoga County	4	0.02
Rocky River (city) Cuyahoga County	4	0.02
Sylvania (city) Lucas County	3	0.02
University Heights (city) Cuyahoga County	3	0.02

Top 10 Places Sorted by Percent
Based on places with populations of 10,000 or more

Place	Number	%
Mayfield Heights (city) Cuyahoga County	4	0.02
Rocky River (city) Cuyahoga County	4	0.02
Sylvania (city) Lucas County	3	0.02
University Heights (city) Cuyahoga County	3	0.02
Cuyahoga Falls (city) Summit County	3	0.01
Fairview Park (city) Cuyahoga County	2	0.01
Miamisburg (city) Montgomery County	2	0.01
Perrysburg (city) Wood County	2	0.01
Avon Lake (city) Lorain County	1	0.01
Bexley (city) Franklin County	1	0.01

Hispanic: Peruvian

Top 10 Places Sorted by Number
Based on all places, regardless of population

Place	Number	%
Columbus (city) Franklin County	179	0.03
Cleveland (city) Cuyahoga County	142	0.03
Cincinnati (city) Hamilton County	57	0.02
Parma (city) Cuyahoga County	44	0.05
Lakewood (city) Cuyahoga County	21	0.04
Maple Heights (city) Cuyahoga County	19	0.07
Gahanna (city) Franklin County	19	0.06
Toledo (city) Lucas County	18	0.01
Upper Arlington (city) Franklin County	17	0.05
Lorain (city) Lorain County	17	0.02

Top 10 Places Sorted by Percent
Based on all places, regardless of population

Place	Number	%
South Webster (village) Scioto County	2	0.26
Nevada (village) Wyandot County	2	0.25
Rayland (village) Jefferson County	1	0.23
Bratenahl (village) Cuyahoga County	3	0.22
Gambier (village) Knox County	3	0.16

Place	Number	%
Mount Sterling (village) Madison County	3	0.16
Amelia (village) Clermont County	4	0.15
Mount Healthy (city) Hamilton County	10	0.14
Fairfax (village) Hamilton County	2	0.10
Landen (cdp) Warren County	11	0.09

Top 10 Places Sorted by Percent
Based on places with populations of 10,000 or more

Place	Number	%
Landen (cdp) Warren County	11	0.09
Maple Heights (city) Cuyahoga County	19	0.07
Gahanna (city) Franklin County	19	0.06
Montgomery (city) Hamilton County	6	0.06
Parma (city) Cuyahoga County	44	0.05
Upper Arlington (city) Franklin County	17	0.05
North Olmsted (city) Cuyahoga County	16	0.05
South Euclid (city) Cuyahoga County	12	0.05
Athens (city) Athens County	10	0.05
Mayfield Heights (city) Cuyahoga County	9	0.05

Hispanic: Uruguayan

Top 10 Places Sorted by Number
Based on all places, regardless of population

Place	Number	%
Richmond Heights (city) Cuyahoga County	7	0.06
Massillon (city) Stark County	5	0.02
Cleveland (city) Cuyahoga County	5	0.00
Huber Heights (city) Montgomery County	4	0.01
Cleveland Heights (city) Cuyahoga County	3	0.01
Oxford (city) Butler County	3	0.01
Shaker Heights (city) Cuyahoga County	3	0.01
Columbus (city) Franklin County	3	0.00
Kenwood (cdp) Hamilton County	2	0.03
Stow (city) Summit County	2	0.01

Top 10 Places Sorted by Percent
Based on all places, regardless of population

Place	Number	%
Richmond Heights (city) Cuyahoga County	7	0.06
Day Heights (cdp) Clermont County	1	0.04
Kenwood (cdp) Hamilton County	2	0.03
Mogadore (village) Summit County	1	0.03
Massillon (city) Stark County	5	0.02
Huber Heights (city) Montgomery County	4	0.01
Cleveland Heights (city) Cuyahoga County	3	0.01
Oxford (city) Butler County	3	0.01
Shaker Heights (city) Cuyahoga County	3	0.01
Stow (city) Summit County	2	0.01

Top 10 Places Sorted by Percent
Based on places with populations of 10,000 or more

Place	Number	%
Richmond Heights (city) Cuyahoga County	7	0.06
Massillon (city) Stark County	5	0.02
Huber Heights (city) Montgomery County	4	0.01
Cleveland Heights (city) Cuyahoga County	3	0.01
Oxford (city) Butler County	3	0.01
Shaker Heights (city) Cuyahoga County	3	0.01
Stow (city) Summit County	2	0.01
Avon (city) Lorain County	1	0.01
Landen (cdp) Warren County	1	0.01
Loveland (city) Hamilton County	1	0.01

Hispanic: Venezuelan

Top 10 Places Sorted by Number
Based on all places, regardless of population

Place	Number	%
Columbus (city) Franklin County	180	0.03
Cleveland (city) Cuyahoga County	47	0.01
Cincinnati (city) Hamilton County	36	0.01

Notes: (cdp) census designated place; Refer to the User's Guide in the front of the book for more detailed information.

456 PROFILES OF OHIO / Ancestry Rankings

Place	Number	%
Toledo (city) Lucas County	27	0.01
Lakewood (city) Cuyahoga County	24	0.04
Upper Arlington (city) Franklin County	22	0.07
Akron (city) Summit County	20	0.01
Shaker Heights (city) Cuyahoga County	17	0.06
Cleveland Heights (city) Cuyahoga County	17	0.03
Dublin (city) Franklin County	16	0.05

Top 10 Places Sorted by Percent
Based on all places, regardless of population

Place	Number	%
Laurelville (village) Hocking County	2	0.38
Albany (village) Athens County	3	0.37
Nelsonville (city) Athens County	13	0.25
Bolindale (cdp) Trumbull County	6	0.24
South Canal (cdp) Trumbull County	3	0.22
Kenwood (cdp) Hamilton County	14	0.19
Lakemore (village) Summit County	4	0.16
Woodmere (village) Cuyahoga County	1	0.12
Bentleyville (village) Cuyahoga County	1	0.11
Greentown (cdp) Stark County	3	0.10

Top 10 Places Sorted by Percent
Based on places with populations of 10,000 or more

Place	Number	%
Upper Arlington (city) Franklin County	22	0.07
Athens (city) Athens County	14	0.07
Blue Ash (city) Hamilton County	9	0.07
Shaker Heights (city) Cuyahoga County	17	0.06
Rocky River (city) Cuyahoga County	13	0.06
Dublin (city) Franklin County	16	0.05
Fairborn (city) Greene County	15	0.05
Hudson (city) Summit County	12	0.05
Lakewood (city) Cuyahoga County	24	0.04
Riverside (city) Montgomery County	10	0.04

Hispanic: Other South American

Top 10 Places Sorted by Number
Based on all places, regardless of population

Place	Number	%
Columbus (city) Franklin County	34	0.00
Cleveland (city) Cuyahoga County	26	0.01
Toledo (city) Lucas County	16	0.01
Cincinnati (city) Hamilton County	14	0.01
Brecksville (city) Cuyahoga County	10	0.07
Akron (city) Summit County	8	0.00
Willowick (city) Lake County	7	0.05
Gahanna (city) Franklin County	7	0.02
Middleburg Heights (city) Cuyahoga County	5	0.03
Bowling Green (city) Wood County	5	0.02

Top 10 Places Sorted by Percent
Based on all places, regardless of population

Place	Number	%
Wharton (village) Wyandot County	1	0.24
Albany (village) Athens County	1	0.12
Wetherington (cdp) Butler County	1	0.10
Brecksville (city) Cuyahoga County	10	0.07
Mount Carmel (cdp) Clermont County	3	0.07
Bratenahl (village) Cuyahoga County	1	0.07
Willowick (city) Lake County	7	0.05
Powell (village) Delaware County	3	0.05
Yellow Springs (village) Greene County	2	0.05
Seville (village) Medina County	1	0.05

Top 10 Places Sorted by Percent
Based on places with populations of 10,000 or more

Place	Number	%
Brecksville (city) Cuyahoga County	10	0.07
Willowick (city) Lake County	7	0.05
Middleburg Heights (city) Cuyahoga County	5	0.03

Place	Number	%
Gahanna (city) Franklin County	7	0.02
Bowling Green (city) Wood County	5	0.02
Hilliard (city) Franklin County	5	0.02
Brook Park (city) Cuyahoga County	4	0.02
South Euclid (city) Cuyahoga County	4	0.02
Forest Park (city) Hamilton County	3	0.02
Lyndhurst (city) Cuyahoga County	3	0.02

Hispanic: Other

Top 10 Places Sorted by Number
Based on all places, regardless of population

Place	Number	%
Cleveland (city) Cuyahoga County	3,593	0.75
Columbus (city) Franklin County	3,086	0.43
Toledo (city) Lucas County	2,565	0.82
Lorain (city) Lorain County	1,229	1.79
Cincinnati (city) Hamilton County	1,052	0.32
Akron (city) Summit County	577	0.27
Dayton (city) Montgomery County	525	0.32
Defiance (city) Defiance County	508	3.09
Youngstown (city) Mahoning County	441	0.54
Fremont (city) Sandusky County	406	2.34

Top 10 Places Sorted by Percent
Based on all places, regardless of population

Place	Number	%
West Leipsic (village) Putnam County	26	9.59
Belmore (village) Putnam County	12	7.02
Leipsic (village) Putnam County	90	4.03
Holgate (village) Henry County	47	3.94
Hamler (village) Henry County	25	3.85
Antioch (village) Monroe County	3	3.37
Archbold (village) Fulton County	142	3.31
Defiance (city) Defiance County	508	3.09
Milton Center (village) Wood County	6	3.08
West Rushville (village) Fairfield County	4	3.03

Top 10 Places Sorted by Percent
Based on places with populations of 10,000 or more

Place	Number	%
Defiance (city) Defiance County	508	3.09
Fremont (city) Sandusky County	406	2.34
Lorain (city) Lorain County	1,229	1.79
Fostoria (city) Seneca County	140	1.00
Oregon (city) Lucas County	163	0.84
Toledo (city) Lucas County	2,565	0.82
Washington (city) Fayette County	108	0.80
Cleveland (city) Cuyahoga County	3,593	0.75
Bowling Green (city) Wood County	211	0.71
Sandusky (city) Erie County	169	0.61

Hungarian

Top 10 Places Sorted by Number
Based on all places, regardless of population

Place	Number	%
Cleveland (city) Cuyahoga County	8,385	1.75
Toledo (city) Lucas County	6,188	1.97
Columbus (city) Franklin County	5,889	0.83
Parma (city) Cuyahoga County	4,514	5.27
Akron (city) Summit County	4,025	1.85
Lorain (city) Lorain County	3,078	4.48
Lakewood (city) Cuyahoga County	2,674	4.72
Elyria (city) Lorain County	2,342	4.19
Mentor (city) Lake County	2,253	4.48
Strongsville (city) Cuyahoga County	1,885	4.30

Top 10 Places Sorted by Percent
Based on all places, regardless of population

Place	Number	%
Fairport Harbor (village) Lake County	448	14.09

Place	Number	%
Grand River (village) Lake County	38	11.24
Rayland (village) Jefferson County	49	10.86
Tiltonsville (village) Jefferson County	124	9.55
Reminderville (village) Summit County	193	8.25
Yankee Lake (village) Trumbull County	7	7.87
Yorkville (village) Jefferson County	98	7.83
Mantua (village) Portage County	85	7.79
Pepper Pike (city) Cuyahoga County	458	7.58
Sheffield (village) Lorain County	221	7.49

Top 10 Places Sorted by Percent
Based on places with populations of 10,000 or more

Place	Number	%
Lyndhurst (city) Cuyahoga County	1,127	7.38
Oregon (city) Lucas County	1,412	7.29
Beachwood (city) Cuyahoga County	830	6.81
Avon (city) Lorain County	708	6.19
Solon (city) Cuyahoga County	1,325	6.08
Twinsburg (city) Summit County	1,012	5.99
Amherst (city) Lorain County	711	5.98
Bedford (city) Cuyahoga County	841	5.92
Streetsboro (city) Portage County	721	5.85
Middleburg Heights (city) Cuyahoga County	875	5.63

Icelander

Top 10 Places Sorted by Number
Based on all places, regardless of population

Place	Number	%
Cuyahoga Falls (city) Summit County	36	0.07
Columbus (city) Franklin County	36	0.01
Dublin (city) Franklin County	32	0.10
Vermilion (city) Lorain County	31	0.29
Mariemont (village) Hamilton County	30	0.86
Cleveland (city) Cuyahoga County	25	0.01
Toledo (city) Lucas County	25	0.01
Cincinnati (city) Hamilton County	22	0.01
Terrace Park (village) Hamilton County	19	0.84
Parma (city) Cuyahoga County	18	0.02

Top 10 Places Sorted by Percent
Based on all places, regardless of population

Place	Number	%
Mariemont (village) Hamilton County	30	0.86
Terrace Park (village) Hamilton County	19	0.84
Stoutsville (village) Fairfield County	3	0.56
Enon (village) Clark County	12	0.45
Waite Hill (village) Lake County	2	0.44
Roseville (village) Perry County	7	0.36
Beechwood Trails (cdp) Licking County	8	0.34
Vermilion (city) Lorain County	31	0.29
Fruit Hill (cdp) Hamilton County	8	0.21
Dry Run (cdp) Hamilton County	9	0.14

Top 10 Places Sorted by Percent
Based on places with populations of 10,000 or more

Place	Number	%
Vermilion (city) Lorain County	31	0.29
North College Hill (city) Hamilton County	11	0.11
Dublin (city) Franklin County	32	0.10
Landen (cdp) Warren County	11	0.09
Streetsboro (city) Portage County	10	0.08
Cuyahoga Falls (city) Summit County	36	0.07
Maple Heights (city) Cuyahoga County	17	0.06
Middleburg Heights (city) Cuyahoga County	9	0.06
Sandusky (city) Erie County	13	0.05
Sharonville (city) Hamilton County	7	0.05

Notes: (cdp) census designated place; Refer to the User's Guide in the front of the book for more detailed information.

Iranian

Top 10 Places Sorted by Number
Based on all places, regardless of population

Place	Number	%
Columbus (city) Franklin County	725	0.10
Cincinnati (city) Hamilton County	159	0.05
Akron (city) Summit County	121	0.06
Mayfield Heights (city) Cuyahoga County	117	0.60
Upper Arlington (city) Franklin County	105	0.31
Cleveland Heights (city) Cuyahoga County	87	0.17
Dublin (city) Franklin County	82	0.26
Strongsville (city) Cuyahoga County	64	0.15
Westlake (city) Cuyahoga County	56	0.18
Pepper Pike (city) Cuyahoga County	54	0.89

Top 10 Places Sorted by Percent
Based on all places, regardless of population

Place	Number	%
Hunting Valley (village) Cuyahoga County	20	2.71
Waite Hill (village) Lake County	7	1.55
Riverlea (village) Franklin County	5	1.00
Montrose-Ghent (cdp) Summit County	47	0.94
Moreland Hills (village) Cuyahoga County	30	0.91
Pepper Pike (city) Cuyahoga County	54	0.89
Seven Mile (village) Butler County	6	0.85
Wetherington (cdp) Butler County	8	0.78
South Russell (village) Geauga County	28	0.70
Mulberry (cdp) Clermont County	20	0.64

Top 10 Places Sorted by Percent
Based on places with populations of 10,000 or more

Place	Number	%
Mayfield Heights (city) Cuyahoga County	117	0.60
Bexley (city) Franklin County	51	0.39
Upper Arlington (city) Franklin County	105	0.31
Beachwood (city) Cuyahoga County	37	0.30
Marietta (city) Washington County	42	0.29
Cambridge (city) Guernsey County	31	0.27
Forestville (cdp) Hamilton County	30	0.27
Dublin (city) Franklin County	82	0.26
Springboro (city) Warren County	26	0.21
Westlake (city) Cuyahoga County	56	0.18

Irish

Top 10 Places Sorted by Number
Based on all places, regardless of population

Place	Number	%
Columbus (city) Franklin County	83,226	11.69
Cleveland (city) Cuyahoga County	38,986	8.15
Cincinnati (city) Hamilton County	34,226	10.35
Toledo (city) Lucas County	33,738	10.76
Akron (city) Summit County	24,889	11.46
Dayton (city) Montgomery County	13,825	8.32
Lakewood (city) Cuyahoga County	13,379	23.62
Parma (city) Cuyahoga County	12,466	14.55
Mentor (city) Lake County	9,804	19.50
Canton (city) Stark County	9,213	11.36

Top 10 Places Sorted by Percent
Based on all places, regardless of population

Place	Number	%
West Millgrove (village) Wood County	40	38.83
Neffs (cdp) Belmont County	356	31.09
Eaton Estates (cdp) Lorain County	385	28.95
Lakeline (village) Lake County	47	28.31
Brice (village) Franklin County	18	27.69
Rocky River (city) Cuyahoga County	5,580	26.91
Bay Village (city) Cuyahoga County	4,310	26.79
Fairview Park (city) Cuyahoga County	4,694	26.71
New Alexandria (village) Jefferson County	45	26.32
Fairview (village) Guernsey County	23	26.14

Top 10 Places Sorted by Percent
Based on places with populations of 10,000 or more

Place	Number	%
Rocky River (city) Cuyahoga County	5,580	26.91
Bay Village (city) Cuyahoga County	4,310	26.79
Fairview Park (city) Cuyahoga County	4,694	26.71
Lakewood (city) Cuyahoga County	13,379	23.62
Westlake (city) Cuyahoga County	7,433	23.33
North Olmsted (city) Cuyahoga County	7,761	22.75
Avon Lake (city) Lorain County	4,116	22.68
Forestville (cdp) Hamilton County	2,455	22.20
Girard (city) Trumbull County	2,273	20.39
Eastlake (city) Lake County	4,104	20.35

Israeli

Top 10 Places Sorted by Number
Based on all places, regardless of population

Place	Number	%
Columbus (city) Franklin County	226	0.03
Beachwood (city) Cuyahoga County	178	1.46
South Euclid (city) Cuyahoga County	119	0.51
Pepper Pike (city) Cuyahoga County	98	1.62
Cincinnati (city) Hamilton County	91	0.03
Toledo (city) Lucas County	69	0.02
Cleveland Heights (city) Cuyahoga County	49	0.10
Orange (village) Cuyahoga County	40	1.24
Woodbourne-Hyde Park (cdp) Montgomery County	35	0.43
Bexley (city) Franklin County	33	0.25

Top 10 Places Sorted by Percent
Based on all places, regardless of population

Place	Number	%
Pepper Pike (city) Cuyahoga County	98	1.62
Beachwood (city) Cuyahoga County	178	1.46
Orange (village) Cuyahoga County	40	1.24
Peninsula (village) Summit County	3	0.58
South Euclid (city) Cuyahoga County	119	0.51
Woodbourne-Hyde Park (cdp) Montgomery County	35	0.43
Eldorado (village) Preble County	2	0.39
Mayfield (village) Cuyahoga County	12	0.34
Bexley (city) Franklin County	33	0.25
Clayton (city) Montgomery County	32	0.24

Top 10 Places Sorted by Percent
Based on places with populations of 10,000 or more

Place	Number	%
Beachwood (city) Cuyahoga County	178	1.46
South Euclid (city) Cuyahoga County	119	0.51
Bexley (city) Franklin County	33	0.25
Clayton (city) Montgomery County	32	0.24
Montgomery (city) Hamilton County	24	0.24
University Heights (city) Cuyahoga County	33	0.23
Blue Ash (city) Hamilton County	23	0.18
Mayfield Heights (city) Cuyahoga County	23	0.12
Cleveland Heights (city) Cuyahoga County	49	0.10
Brecksville (city) Cuyahoga County	12	0.09

Italian

Top 10 Places Sorted by Number
Based on all places, regardless of population

Place	Number	%
Columbus (city) Franklin County	35,236	4.95
Cleveland (city) Cuyahoga County	22,053	4.61
Akron (city) Summit County	14,705	6.77
Parma (city) Cuyahoga County	11,603	13.55
Cincinnati (city) Hamilton County	10,877	3.29
Boardman (cdp) Mahoning County	9,888	26.53
Toledo (city) Lucas County	9,383	2.99
Youngstown (city) Mahoning County	9,210	11.23
Mentor (city) Lake County	8,167	16.24
Canton (city) Stark County	6,940	8.56

Top 10 Places Sorted by Percent
Based on all places, regardless of population

Place	Number	%
Lowellville (village) Mahoning County	615	48.01
Highland Heights (city) Cuyahoga County	2,528	31.28
Girard (city) Trumbull County	3,285	29.46
Struthers (city) Mahoning County	3,332	28.34
Poland (village) Mahoning County	767	26.76
Boardman (cdp) Mahoning County	9,888	26.53
Mayfield Heights (city) Cuyahoga County	5,061	26.11
Yorkville (village) Jefferson County	318	25.42
Mayfield (village) Cuyahoga County	873	25.09
Wintersville (village) Jefferson County	966	24.02

Top 10 Places Sorted by Percent
Based on places with populations of 10,000 or more

Place	Number	%
Girard (city) Trumbull County	3,285	29.46
Struthers (city) Mahoning County	3,332	28.34
Boardman (cdp) Mahoning County	9,888	26.53
Mayfield Heights (city) Cuyahoga County	5,061	26.11
Niles (city) Trumbull County	5,011	23.94
Lyndhurst (city) Cuyahoga County	3,646	23.86
Wickliffe (city) Lake County	2,741	20.33
Willowick (city) Lake County	2,780	19.30
Austintown (cdp) Mahoning County	6,098	19.27
Steubenville (city) Jefferson County	3,613	18.92

Latvian

Top 10 Places Sorted by Number
Based on all places, regardless of population

Place	Number	%
Columbus (city) Franklin County	290	0.04
Cleveland (city) Cuyahoga County	213	0.04
Lakewood (city) Cuyahoga County	141	0.25
Parma (city) Cuyahoga County	131	0.15
Cincinnati (city) Hamilton County	102	0.03
Brook Park (city) Cuyahoga County	65	0.31
Toledo (city) Lucas County	65	0.02
Strongsville (city) Cuyahoga County	60	0.14
Cuyahoga Falls (city) Summit County	53	0.11
Cleveland Heights (city) Cuyahoga County	52	0.10

Top 10 Places Sorted by Percent
Based on all places, regardless of population

Place	Number	%
Wetherington (cdp) Butler County	33	3.24
Mifflin (village) Ashland County	2	1.52
Bentleyville (village) Cuyahoga County	8	0.84
Hiram (village) Portage County	9	0.74
Evendale (village) Hamilton County	19	0.61
McDonald (village) Trumbull County	20	0.58
South Russell (village) Geauga County	21	0.52
Bratenahl (village) Cuyahoga County	7	0.52
Cuyahoga Heights (village) Cuyahoga County	3	0.50
Highland Heights (city) Cuyahoga County	38	0.47

Top 10 Places Sorted by Percent
Based on places with populations of 10,000 or more

Place	Number	%
Broadview Heights (city) Cuyahoga County	51	0.32
Brook Park (city) Cuyahoga County	65	0.31
Lakewood (city) Cuyahoga County	141	0.25
Beachwood (city) Cuyahoga County	31	0.25
Mayfield Heights (city) Cuyahoga County	38	0.20
Norton (city) Summit County	23	0.20
North Royalton (city) Cuyahoga County	50	0.17

Notes: (cdp) census designated place; Refer to the User's Guide in the front of the book for more detailed information.

458 PROFILES OF OHIO / Ancestry Rankings

Place	Number	%
Worthington (city) Franklin County	23	0.16
Parma (city) Cuyahoga County	131	0.15
Fairview Park (city) Cuyahoga County	26	0.15

Lithuanian

Top 10 Places Sorted by Number
Based on all places, regardless of population

Place	Number	%
Cleveland (city) Cuyahoga County	1,444	0.30
Columbus (city) Franklin County	1,028	0.14
Euclid (city) Cuyahoga County	811	1.54
Parma (city) Cuyahoga County	527	0.62
Cincinnati (city) Hamilton County	496	0.15
Mentor (city) Lake County	426	0.85
Akron (city) Summit County	423	0.19
Beachwood (city) Cuyahoga County	308	2.53
Lakewood (city) Cuyahoga County	299	0.53
Cleveland Heights (city) Cuyahoga County	296	0.59

Top 10 Places Sorted by Percent
Based on all places, regardless of population

Place	Number	%
Donnelsville (village) Clark County	10	4.12
Salesville (village) Guernsey County	6	4.03
Grand River (village) Lake County	13	3.85
Beachwood (city) Cuyahoga County	308	2.53
Moscow (village) Clermont County	6	2.30
South Canal (cdp) Trumbull County	30	2.23
Willowick (city) Lake County	270	1.87
Brady Lake (village) Portage County	9	1.79
Waite Hill (village) Lake County	8	1.77
Amberley (village) Hamilton County	60	1.76

Top 10 Places Sorted by Percent
Based on places with populations of 10,000 or more

Place	Number	%
Beachwood (city) Cuyahoga County	308	2.53
Willowick (city) Lake County	270	1.87
Richmond Heights (city) Cuyahoga County	173	1.58
Euclid (city) Cuyahoga County	811	1.54
Eastlake (city) Lake County	262	1.30
Bexley (city) Franklin County	172	1.30
Lyndhurst (city) Cuyahoga County	167	1.09
Wickliffe (city) Lake County	147	1.09
Willoughby (city) Lake County	228	1.01
Bucyrus (city) Crawford County	125	0.95

Luxemburger

Top 10 Places Sorted by Number
Based on all places, regardless of population

Place	Number	%
Cincinnati (city) Hamilton County	66	0.02
Toledo (city) Lucas County	40	0.01
Dover (city) Tuscarawas County	29	0.24
Landen (cdp) Warren County	23	0.18
Vermilion (city) Lorain County	21	0.19
Fostoria (city) Seneca County	21	0.15
Mason (city) Warren County	19	0.09
Centerville (city) Montgomery County	19	0.08
Perrysburg (city) Wood County	18	0.11
Delaware (city) Delaware County	15	0.06

Top 10 Places Sorted by Percent
Based on all places, regardless of population

Place	Number	%
Bentleyville (village) Cuyahoga County	8	0.84
Milan (village) Erie County	5	0.34
South Russell (village) Geauga County	13	0.32
Doylestown (village) Wayne County	8	0.29
Five Points (cdp) Warren County	6	0.26
Timberlake (village) Lake County	2	0.26
Dover (city) Tuscarawas County	29	0.24
Pleasantville (village) Fairfield County	2	0.23
Mariemont (village) Hamilton County	7	0.20
Vermilion (city) Lorain County	21	0.19

Top 10 Places Sorted by Percent
Based on places with populations of 10,000 or more

Place	Number	%
Dover (city) Tuscarawas County	29	0.24
Vermilion (city) Lorain County	21	0.19
Landen (cdp) Warren County	23	0.18
Fostoria (city) Seneca County	21	0.15
Perrysburg (city) Wood County	18	0.11
Mason (city) Warren County	19	0.09
Centerville (city) Montgomery County	19	0.08
Aurora (city) Portage County	9	0.07
Delaware (city) Delaware County	15	0.06
Reading (city) Hamilton County	7	0.06

Macedonian

Top 10 Places Sorted by Number
Based on all places, regardless of population

Place	Number	%
Columbus (city) Franklin County	471	0.07
Gahanna (city) Franklin County	284	0.87
Akron (city) Summit County	214	0.10
Lorain (city) Lorain County	105	0.15
Cleveland (city) Cuyahoga County	101	0.02
Massillon (city) Stark County	92	0.29
Lakewood (city) Cuyahoga County	92	0.16
Green (city) Summit County	79	0.35
Whitehall (city) Franklin County	75	0.39
Cincinnati (city) Hamilton County	70	0.02

Top 10 Places Sorted by Percent
Based on all places, regardless of population

Place	Number	%
Brookfield Center (cdp) Trumbull County	17	1.46
Bloomingdale (village) Jefferson County	3	1.29
Ontario (village) Richland County	66	1.26
Gahanna (city) Franklin County	284	0.87
Fairlawn (city) Summit County	63	0.86
Mount Eaton (village) Wayne County	2	0.83
Mogadore (village) Summit County	30	0.81
Obetz (village) Franklin County	27	0.71
Meyers Lake (village) Stark County	3	0.53
Lexington (village) Richland County	21	0.50

Top 10 Places Sorted by Percent
Based on places with populations of 10,000 or more

Place	Number	%
Gahanna (city) Franklin County	284	0.87
Amherst (city) Lorain County	52	0.44
Whitehall (city) Franklin County	75	0.39
Green (city) Summit County	79	0.35
Broadview Heights (city) Cuyahoga County	50	0.31
Massillon (city) Stark County	92	0.29
Parma Heights (city) Cuyahoga County	57	0.26
Barberton (city) Summit County	59	0.21
North Canton (city) Stark County	35	0.21
Forestville (cdp) Hamilton County	20	0.18

Maltese

Top 10 Places Sorted by Number
Based on all places, regardless of population

Place	Number	%
Columbus (city) Franklin County	29	0.00
Moraine (city) Montgomery County	23	0.33
Hudson (city) Summit County	23	0.10
Beavercreek (city) Greene County	22	0.06
Cincinnati (city) Hamilton County	20	0.01
Silver Lake (village) Summit County	17	0.56
Gahanna (city) Franklin County	16	0.05
Garfield Heights (city) Cuyahoga County	16	0.05
Norwalk (city) Huron County	12	0.07
Toledo (city) Lucas County	11	0.00

Top 10 Places Sorted by Percent
Based on all places, regardless of population

Place	Number	%
Silver Lake (village) Summit County	17	0.56
Orwell (village) Ashtabula County	7	0.46
Felicity (village) Clermont County	3	0.34
Moraine (city) Montgomery County	23	0.33
Canal Winchester (village) Franklin County	10	0.22
South Russell (village) Geauga County	8	0.20
Gates Mills (village) Cuyahoga County	5	0.20
Plymouth (village) Richland County	3	0.16
De Graff (village) Logan County	2	0.16
Hudson (city) Summit County	23	0.10

Top 10 Places Sorted by Percent
Based on places with populations of 10,000 or more

Place	Number	%
Hudson (city) Summit County	23	0.10
Norwalk (city) Huron County	12	0.07
Beavercreek (city) Greene County	22	0.06
Gahanna (city) Franklin County	16	0.05
Garfield Heights (city) Cuyahoga County	16	0.05
Urbana (city) Champaign County	6	0.05
Wadsworth (city) Medina County	8	0.04
Sylvania (city) Lucas County	7	0.04
Delaware (city) Delaware County	8	0.03
Eastlake (city) Lake County	6	0.03

New Zealander

Top 10 Places Sorted by Number
Based on all places, regardless of population

Place	Number	%
Toledo (city) Lucas County	27	0.01
Cuyahoga Falls (city) Summit County	14	0.03
Delaware (city) Delaware County	10	0.04
New Albany (village) Franklin County	9	0.25
Kent (city) Portage County	7	0.03
Fairborn (city) Greene County	7	0.02
Brunswick (city) Medina County	6	0.02
Cleveland (city) Cuyahoga County	6	0.00
Winchester (village) Adams County	2	0.20

Top 10 Places Sorted by Percent
Based on all places, regardless of population

Place	Number	%
New Albany (village) Franklin County	9	0.25
Winchester (village) Adams County	2	0.20
Delaware (city) Delaware County	10	0.04
Cuyahoga Falls (city) Summit County	14	0.03
Kent (city) Portage County	7	0.03
Fairborn (city) Greene County	7	0.02
Brunswick (city) Medina County	6	0.02
Toledo (city) Lucas County	27	0.01
Cleveland (city) Cuyahoga County	6	0.00

Top 10 Places Sorted by Percent
Based on places with populations of 10,000 or more

Place	Number	%
Delaware (city) Delaware County	10	0.04
Cuyahoga Falls (city) Summit County	14	0.03
Kent (city) Portage County	7	0.03
Fairborn (city) Greene County	7	0.02
Brunswick (city) Medina County	6	0.02

Notes: (cdp) census designated place; Refer to the User's Guide in the front of the book for more detailed information.

Place	Number	%
Toledo (city) Lucas County	27	0.01
Cleveland (city) Cuyahoga County	6	0.00

Northern European

Top 10 Places Sorted by Number
Based on all places, regardless of population

Place	Number	%
Columbus (city) Franklin County	293	0.04
Cincinnati (city) Hamilton County	167	0.05
Shaker Heights (city) Cuyahoga County	71	0.24
Toledo (city) Lucas County	71	0.02
Kettering (city) Montgomery County	66	0.11
Mentor (city) Lake County	55	0.11
Centerville (city) Montgomery County	46	0.20
Dublin (city) Franklin County	46	0.15
Cleveland Heights (city) Cuyahoga County	45	0.09
Aurora (city) Portage County	43	0.32

Top 10 Places Sorted by Percent
Based on all places, regardless of population

Place	Number	%
South Solon (village) Madison County	10	2.43
Harrisburg (village) Franklin County	5	1.45
Granville South (cdp) Licking County	14	1.15
Granville (village) Licking County	33	1.13
Yellow Springs (village) Greene County	32	0.87
Newcomerstown (village) Tuscarawas County	33	0.83
Mariemont (village) Hamilton County	29	0.83
Swanton (village) Fulton County	20	0.60
Kirkersville (village) Licking County	3	0.56
Minerva Park (village) Franklin County	7	0.55

Top 10 Places Sorted by Percent
Based on places with populations of 10,000 or more

Place	Number	%
Aurora (city) Portage County	43	0.32
Bexley (city) Franklin County	36	0.27
Shaker Heights (city) Cuyahoga County	71	0.24
Marysville (city) Union County	33	0.21
Centerville (city) Montgomery County	46	0.20
Maumee (city) Lucas County	29	0.19
Pataskala (city) Licking County	19	0.19
Springdale (city) Hamilton County	19	0.18
White Oak (cdp) Hamilton County	22	0.17
Dublin (city) Franklin County	46	0.15

Norwegian

Top 10 Places Sorted by Number
Based on all places, regardless of population

Place	Number	%
Columbus (city) Franklin County	3,027	0.43
Cincinnati (city) Hamilton County	983	0.30
Toledo (city) Lucas County	961	0.31
Akron (city) Summit County	783	0.36
Cleveland (city) Cuyahoga County	570	0.12
Dayton (city) Montgomery County	494	0.30
Beavercreek (city) Greene County	465	1.22
Cuyahoga Falls (city) Summit County	447	0.91
Lakewood (city) Cuyahoga County	366	0.65
Kettering (city) Montgomery County	366	0.64

Top 10 Places Sorted by Percent
Based on all places, regardless of population

Place	Number	%
Wetherington (cdp) Butler County	47	4.61
Van Buren (village) Hancock County	13	4.36
Bentleyville (village) Cuyahoga County	34	3.59
Lawrenceville (village) Clark County	10	3.40
Helena (village) Sandusky County	8	3.40
Cedarville (village) Greene County	119	3.11

Place	Number	%
Wright-Patterson AFB (cdp) Montgomery County	174	2.63
Ottawa Hills (village) Lucas County	114	2.51
Lakeline (village) Lake County	4	2.41
Corwin (village) Warren County	6	2.32

Top 10 Places Sorted by Percent
Based on places with populations of 10,000 or more

Place	Number	%
Montgomery (city) Hamilton County	160	1.59
Hudson (city) Summit County	339	1.51
Beavercreek (city) Greene County	465	1.22
Worthington (city) Franklin County	170	1.19
Avon Lake (city) Lorain County	212	1.17
Oxford (city) Butler County	242	1.10
Springdale (city) Hamilton County	115	1.09
Perrysburg (city) Wood County	178	1.04
Upper Arlington (city) Franklin County	342	1.02
Berea (city) Cuyahoga County	189	0.99

Pennsylvania German

Top 10 Places Sorted by Number
Based on all places, regardless of population

Place	Number	%
Columbus (city) Franklin County	487	0.07
Akron (city) Summit County	405	0.19
Canton (city) Stark County	224	0.28
Toledo (city) Lucas County	223	0.07
Cleveland (city) Cuyahoga County	192	0.04
Warren (city) Trumbull County	181	0.39
Austintown (cdp) Mahoning County	179	0.57
Youngstown (city) Mahoning County	175	0.21
Wadsworth (city) Medina County	154	0.83
Cincinnati (city) Hamilton County	114	0.03

Top 10 Places Sorted by Percent
Based on all places, regardless of population

Place	Number	%
Marseilles (village) Wyandot County	10	7.35
Hoytville (village) Wood County	13	4.08
Glenford (village) Perry County	7	3.70
Bairdstown (village) Wood County	4	3.05
Mount Eaton (village) Wayne County	7	2.90
Vienna Center (cdp) Trumbull County	34	2.87
Belmore (village) Putnam County	5	2.86
Sugar Bush Knolls (village) Portage County	6	2.84
North Hampton (village) Clark County	5	2.67
Wharton (village) Wyandot County	9	2.29

Top 10 Places Sorted by Percent
Based on places with populations of 10,000 or more

Place	Number	%
Wadsworth (city) Medina County	154	0.83
Austintown (cdp) Mahoning County	179	0.57
Dover (city) Tuscarawas County	59	0.48
Ashland (city) Ashland County	100	0.47
Salem (city) Columbiana County	54	0.45
Galion (city) Crawford County	52	0.45
Wooster (city) Wayne County	100	0.40
Warren (city) Trumbull County	181	0.39
Alliance (city) Stark County	87	0.37
Ashtabula (city) Ashtabula County	78	0.37

Polish

Top 10 Places Sorted by Number
Based on all places, regardless of population

Place	Number	%
Toledo (city) Lucas County	31,802	10.14
Cleveland (city) Cuyahoga County	22,978	4.80
Parma (city) Cuyahoga County	15,503	18.10
Columbus (city) Franklin County	14,510	2.04

Place	Number	%
Garfield Heights (city) Cuyahoga County	7,983	26.07
Strongsville (city) Cuyahoga County	5,536	12.62
Lorain (city) Lorain County	5,386	7.85
North Royalton (city) Cuyahoga County	5,278	18.42
Akron (city) Summit County	5,200	2.40
Lakewood (city) Cuyahoga County	4,406	7.78

Top 10 Places Sorted by Percent
Based on all places, regardless of population

Place	Number	%
Cuyahoga Heights (village) Cuyahoga County	239	39.90
Independence (city) Cuyahoga County	2,323	32.28
Adena (village) Jefferson County	249	30.11
Newburgh Heights (village) Cuyahoga County	706	29.55
Garfield Heights (city) Cuyahoga County	7,983	26.07
Valley View (village) Cuyahoga County	536	24.64
Brooklyn Heights (village) Cuyahoga County	368	23.34
Seven Hills (city) Cuyahoga County	2,732	22.62
Mount Pleasant (village) Jefferson County	113	20.14
Dillonvale (village) Jefferson County	154	19.87

Top 10 Places Sorted by Percent
Based on places with populations of 10,000 or more

Place	Number	%
Garfield Heights (city) Cuyahoga County	7,983	26.07
Seven Hills (city) Cuyahoga County	2,732	22.62
North Royalton (city) Cuyahoga County	5,278	18.42
Brecksville (city) Cuyahoga County	2,436	18.27
Parma (city) Cuyahoga County	15,503	18.10
Broadview Heights (city) Cuyahoga County	2,565	16.06
Brook Park (city) Cuyahoga County	2,998	14.13
Brooklyn (city) Cuyahoga County	1,629	14.06
Amherst (city) Lorain County	1,557	13.10
Parma Heights (city) Cuyahoga County	2,827	13.05

Portuguese

Top 10 Places Sorted by Number
Based on all places, regardless of population

Place	Number	%
Columbus (city) Franklin County	549	0.08
Cincinnati (city) Hamilton County	158	0.05
Toledo (city) Lucas County	157	0.05
Ashtabula (city) Ashtabula County	133	0.64
Cleveland (city) Cuyahoga County	115	0.02
Canton (city) Stark County	113	0.14
Kettering (city) Montgomery County	84	0.15
Akron (city) Summit County	70	0.03
Beavercreek (city) Greene County	65	0.17
North Olmsted (city) Cuyahoga County	64	0.19

Top 10 Places Sorted by Percent
Based on all places, regardless of population

Place	Number	%
Kipton (village) Lorain County	14	5.17
Wilson (village) Monroe County	3	2.59
Burgoon (village) Sandusky County	4	2.16
North Perry (village) Lake County	16	1.91
Granville South (cdp) Licking County	18	1.48
Buchtel (village) Athens County	8	1.43
Rossburg (village) Darke County	3	1.43
Arcadia (village) Hancock County	7	1.31
Ludlow Falls (village) Miami County	2	0.99
Rushsylvania (village) Logan County	5	0.92

Top 10 Places Sorted by Percent
Based on places with populations of 10,000 or more

Place	Number	%
Ashtabula (city) Ashtabula County	133	0.64
Forestville (cdp) Hamilton County	34	0.31
Conneaut (city) Ashtabula County	34	0.27
Perrysburg (city) Wood County	41	0.24

Notes: (cdp) census designated place; Refer to the User's Guide in the front of the book for more detailed information.

Place	Number	%
Landen (cdp) Warren County	30	0.24
Worthington (city) Franklin County	33	0.23
Streetsboro (city) Portage County	28	0.23
Avon Lake (city) Lorain County	40	0.22
Norton (city) Summit County	24	0.21
Mason (city) Warren County	44	0.20

Romanian

Top 10 Places Sorted by Number
Based on all places, regardless of population

Place	Number	%
Cleveland (city) Cuyahoga County	1,461	0.31
Columbus (city) Franklin County	954	0.13
Akron (city) Summit County	623	0.29
Lakewood (city) Cuyahoga County	582	1.03
Canton (city) Stark County	517	0.64
Parma (city) Cuyahoga County	506	0.59
Warren (city) Trumbull County	487	1.04
North Olmsted (city) Cuyahoga County	453	1.33
Boardman (cdp) Mahoning County	414	1.11
Alliance (city) Stark County	406	1.75

Top 10 Places Sorted by Percent
Based on all places, regardless of population

Place	Number	%
Yankee Lake (village) Trumbull County	6	6.74
Brookfield Center (cdp) Trumbull County	43	3.69
Limaville (village) Stark County	5	2.49
Sheffield (village) Lorain County	61	2.07
Perry Heights (cdp) Stark County	175	1.95
Alliance (city) Stark County	406	1.75
Howland Center (cdp) Trumbull County	108	1.64
Middleburg Heights (city) Cuyahoga County	249	1.60
Bolindale (cdp) Trumbull County	38	1.55
West Leipsic (village) Putnam County	4	1.55

Top 10 Places Sorted by Percent
Based on places with populations of 10,000 or more

Place	Number	%
Alliance (city) Stark County	406	1.75
Middleburg Heights (city) Cuyahoga County	249	1.60
Parma Heights (city) Cuyahoga County	327	1.51
North Olmsted (city) Cuyahoga County	453	1.33
Beachwood (city) Cuyahoga County	154	1.26
Rocky River (city) Cuyahoga County	237	1.14
Boardman (cdp) Mahoning County	414	1.11
North Canton (city) Stark County	177	1.08
Niles (city) Trumbull County	220	1.05
Warren (city) Trumbull County	487	1.04

Russian

Top 10 Places Sorted by Number
Based on all places, regardless of population

Place	Number	%
Columbus (city) Franklin County	4,333	0.61
Cleveland (city) Cuyahoga County	2,429	0.51
Cincinnati (city) Hamilton County	1,948	0.59
Beachwood (city) Cuyahoga County	1,894	15.54
Shaker Heights (city) Cuyahoga County	1,509	5.13
Akron (city) Summit County	1,469	0.68
Solon (city) Cuyahoga County	1,464	6.71
South Euclid (city) Cuyahoga County	1,439	6.11
Cleveland Heights (city) Cuyahoga County	1,438	2.88
Mayfield Heights (city) Cuyahoga County	1,318	6.80

Top 10 Places Sorted by Percent
Based on all places, regardless of population

Place	Number	%
Beachwood (city) Cuyahoga County	1,894	15.54
Moreland Hills (village) Cuyahoga County	331	10.02
Miltonsburg (village) Monroe County	2	10.00
Orange (village) Cuyahoga County	319	9.86
Pepper Pike (city) Cuyahoga County	552	9.14
Amberley (village) Hamilton County	295	8.67
Bexley (city) Franklin County	967	7.33
Mayfield Heights (city) Cuyahoga County	1,318	6.80
Solon (city) Cuyahoga County	1,464	6.71
Hunting Valley (village) Cuyahoga County	48	6.51

Top 10 Places Sorted by Percent
Based on places with populations of 10,000 or more

Place	Number	%
Beachwood (city) Cuyahoga County	1,894	15.54
Bexley (city) Franklin County	967	7.33
Mayfield Heights (city) Cuyahoga County	1,318	6.80
Solon (city) Cuyahoga County	1,464	6.71
University Heights (city) Cuyahoga County	880	6.22
South Euclid (city) Cuyahoga County	1,439	6.11
Lyndhurst (city) Cuyahoga County	893	5.84
Shaker Heights (city) Cuyahoga County	1,509	5.13
Richmond Heights (city) Cuyahoga County	496	4.53
Blue Ash (city) Hamilton County	454	3.56

Scandinavian

Top 10 Places Sorted by Number
Based on all places, regardless of population

Place	Number	%
Columbus (city) Franklin County	596	0.08
Cincinnati (city) Hamilton County	168	0.05
Toledo (city) Lucas County	122	0.04
Beavercreek (city) Greene County	108	0.28
Fairborn (city) Greene County	79	0.25
Cleveland Heights (city) Cuyahoga County	76	0.15
Huber Heights (city) Montgomery County	74	0.19
Cleveland (city) Cuyahoga County	72	0.02
Hudson (city) Summit County	71	0.32
Upper Arlington (city) Franklin County	62	0.18

Top 10 Places Sorted by Percent
Based on all places, regardless of population

Place	Number	%
Waldo (village) Marion County	7	2.07
Wilson (village) Monroe County	2	1.72
Saint Louisville (village) Licking County	5	1.46
Cloverdale (village) Putnam County	2	0.97
Westfield Center (village) Medina County	10	0.94
Sparta (village) Morrow County	2	0.93
North Fork Village (cdp) Ross County	14	0.87
Ross (cdp) Butler County	15	0.82
Granville South (cdp) Licking County	10	0.82
Saint Bernard (city) Hamilton County	34	0.69

Top 10 Places Sorted by Percent
Based on places with populations of 10,000 or more

Place	Number	%
Amherst (city) Lorain County	46	0.39
Springboro (city) Warren County	43	0.35
Hudson (city) Summit County	71	0.32
Perrysburg (city) Wood County	53	0.31
Bay Village (city) Cuyahoga County	48	0.30
Beavercreek (city) Greene County	108	0.28
Lebanon (city) Warren County	47	0.28
Maumee (city) Lucas County	41	0.27
Fairborn (city) Greene County	79	0.25
Norwood (city) Hamilton County	52	0.24

Scotch-Irish

Top 10 Places Sorted by Number
Based on all places, regardless of population

Place	Number	%
Columbus (city) Franklin County	9,675	1.36
Akron (city) Summit County	2,991	1.38
Cincinnati (city) Hamilton County	2,970	0.90
Toledo (city) Lucas County	2,923	0.93
Cleveland (city) Cuyahoga County	2,319	0.48
Dayton (city) Montgomery County	1,659	1.00
Cuyahoga Falls (city) Summit County	1,446	2.93
Kettering (city) Montgomery County	1,267	2.20
Upper Arlington (city) Franklin County	1,153	3.43
Canton (city) Stark County	1,114	1.37

Top 10 Places Sorted by Percent
Based on all places, regardless of population

Place	Number	%
Norwich (village) Muskingum County	32	30.48
Alexandria (village) Licking County	4	23.53
Holiday Valley (cdp) Clark County	224	12.33
Centerville (village) Gallia County	12	8.39
Brice (village) Franklin County	5	7.69
Otway (village) Scioto County	6	7.06
Lithopolis (village) Fairfield County	39	7.01
Freeport (village) Harrison County	28	6.97
Riverlea (village) Franklin County	34	6.79
Summitville (village) Columbiana County	6	6.74

Top 10 Places Sorted by Percent
Based on places with populations of 10,000 or more

Place	Number	%
Avon Lake (city) Lorain County	638	3.52
Upper Arlington (city) Franklin County	1,153	3.43
Worthington (city) Franklin County	443	3.09
Aurora (city) Portage County	414	3.05
Cuyahoga Falls (city) Summit County	1,446	2.93
Steubenville (city) Jefferson County	491	2.57
Hudson (city) Summit County	554	2.48
Mason (city) Warren County	535	2.44
Centerville (city) Montgomery County	550	2.37
Westerville (city) Franklin County	835	2.36

Scottish

Top 10 Places Sorted by Number
Based on all places, regardless of population

Place	Number	%
Columbus (city) Franklin County	11,819	1.66
Cincinnati (city) Hamilton County	4,086	1.24
Toledo (city) Lucas County	3,419	1.09
Akron (city) Summit County	3,134	1.44
Cleveland (city) Cuyahoga County	2,475	0.52
Dayton (city) Montgomery County	1,965	1.18
Kettering (city) Montgomery County	1,563	2.72
Lakewood (city) Cuyahoga County	1,393	2.46
Westerville (city) Franklin County	1,368	3.86
Cuyahoga Falls (city) Summit County	1,357	2.75

Top 10 Places Sorted by Percent
Based on all places, regardless of population

Place	Number	%
Zanesfield (village) Logan County	20	9.48
Summitville (village) Columbiana County	7	7.87
Riverlea (village) Franklin County	34	6.79
Waite Hill (village) Lake County	29	6.43
Mariemont (village) Hamilton County	220	6.29
South Vienna (village) Clark County	31	6.26
West Mansfield (village) Logan County	43	6.11
Salesville (village) Guernsey County	9	6.04
Waldo (village) Marion County	20	5.92

Notes: (cdp) census designated place; Refer to the User's Guide in the front of the book for more detailed information.

Clifton (village) Greene County — 11 — 5.91

Top 10 Places Sorted by Percent
Based on places with populations of 10,000 or more

Place	Number	%
Avon Lake (city) Lorain County	794	4.38
Upper Arlington (city) Franklin County	1,326	3.95
Bay Village (city) Cuyahoga County	633	3.93
Westerville (city) Franklin County	1,368	3.86
Worthington (city) Franklin County	511	3.57
Wadsworth (city) Medina County	658	3.55
Aurora (city) Portage County	481	3.55
Bexley (city) Franklin County	463	3.51
North Canton (city) Stark County	557	3.40
Perrysburg (city) Wood County	573	3.35

Serbian

Top 10 Places Sorted by Number
Based on all places, regardless of population

Place	Number	%
Akron (city) Summit County	1,135	0.52
Parma (city) Cuyahoga County	941	1.10
Cleveland (city) Cuyahoga County	721	0.15
Columbus (city) Franklin County	651	0.09
Barberton (city) Summit County	334	1.19
Lorain (city) Lorain County	324	0.47
Broadview Heights (city) Cuyahoga County	314	1.97
Lakewood (city) Cuyahoga County	296	0.52
Strongsville (city) Cuyahoga County	266	0.61
Brunswick (city) Medina County	255	0.76

Top 10 Places Sorted by Percent
Based on all places, regardless of population

Place	Number	%
Maple Ridge (cdp) Mahoning County	34	3.71
Mingo Junction (village) Jefferson County	97	2.65
Burbank (village) Wayne County	7	2.48
Yankee Lake (village) Trumbull County	2	2.25
Broadview Heights (city) Cuyahoga County	314	1.97
Shadyside (village) Belmont County	68	1.87
Bellaire (city) Belmont County	88	1.78
Bloomingdale (village) Jefferson County	4	1.72
McDonald (village) Trumbull County	58	1.68
Morristown (village) Belmont County	5	1.64

Top 10 Places Sorted by Percent
Based on places with populations of 10,000 or more

Place	Number	%
Broadview Heights (city) Cuyahoga County	314	1.97
Norton (city) Summit County	158	1.37
Barberton (city) Summit County	334	1.19
Seven Hills (city) Cuyahoga County	135	1.12
Parma (city) Cuyahoga County	941	1.10
Steubenville (city) Jefferson County	192	1.01
Brooklyn (city) Cuyahoga County	105	0.91
North Royalton (city) Cuyahoga County	229	0.80
Brunswick (city) Medina County	255	0.76
Massillon (city) Stark County	222	0.71

Slavic

Top 10 Places Sorted by Number
Based on all places, regardless of population

Place	Number	%
Columbus (city) Franklin County	374	0.05
Cleveland (city) Cuyahoga County	189	0.04
North Royalton (city) Cuyahoga County	126	0.44
Parma (city) Cuyahoga County	112	0.13
Cincinnati (city) Hamilton County	106	0.03
Akron (city) Summit County	100	0.05
Lakewood (city) Cuyahoga County	91	0.16
Toledo (city) Lucas County	87	0.03
Youngstown (city) Mahoning County	80	0.10
Steubenville (city) Jefferson County	69	0.36

Top 10 Places Sorted by Percent
Based on all places, regardless of population

Place	Number	%
Brookfield Center (cdp) Trumbull County	52	4.47
Deersville (village) Harrison County	2	2.22
Sugar Bush Knolls (village) Portage County	3	1.42
Amsterdam (village) Jefferson County	7	1.20
Saint Louisville (village) Licking County	4	1.17
Pleasant City (village) Guernsey County	5	1.13
Chesterland (cdp) Geauga County	27	0.98
Powhatan Point (village) Belmont County	16	0.92
Willshire (village) Van Wert County	4	0.90
Stony Prairie (cdp) Sandusky County	8	0.89

Top 10 Places Sorted by Percent
Based on places with populations of 10,000 or more

Place	Number	%
North Royalton (city) Cuyahoga County	126	0.44
Brooklyn (city) Cuyahoga County	46	0.40
Steubenville (city) Jefferson County	69	0.36
Painesville (city) Lake County	59	0.34
Loveland (city) Hamilton County	39	0.33
Parma Heights (city) Cuyahoga County	66	0.30
Avon Lake (city) Lorain County	55	0.30
Willowick (city) Lake County	37	0.26
Barberton (city) Summit County	66	0.24
Worthington (city) Franklin County	35	0.24

Slovak

Top 10 Places Sorted by Number
Based on all places, regardless of population

Place	Number	%
Cleveland (city) Cuyahoga County	8,402	1.76
Parma (city) Cuyahoga County	7,940	9.27
Youngstown (city) Mahoning County	4,345	5.30
Boardman (cdp) Mahoning County	3,552	9.53
Lakewood (city) Cuyahoga County	3,006	5.31
Lorain (city) Lorain County	2,618	3.81
Columbus (city) Franklin County	2,491	0.35
Akron (city) Summit County	2,479	1.14
Strongsville (city) Cuyahoga County	2,467	5.62
Austintown (cdp) Mahoning County	2,411	7.62

Top 10 Places Sorted by Percent
Based on all places, regardless of population

Place	Number	%
Marblehead (village) Ottawa County	206	27.14
Yankee Lake (village) Trumbull County	15	16.85
Struthers (city) Mahoning County	1,887	16.05
South Canal (cdp) Trumbull County	181	13.44
Poland (village) Mahoning County	372	12.98
Campbell (city) Mahoning County	1,207	12.76
Hubbard (city) Trumbull County	1,024	12.42
Hilltop (cdp) Trumbull County	67	11.80
Canfield (city) Mahoning County	741	9.89
McDonald (village) Trumbull County	333	9.62

Top 10 Places Sorted by Percent
Based on places with populations of 10,000 or more

Place	Number	%
Struthers (city) Mahoning County	1,887	16.05
Boardman (cdp) Mahoning County	3,552	9.53
Brooklyn (city) Cuyahoga County	1,090	9.41
Parma (city) Cuyahoga County	7,940	9.27
Seven Hills (city) Cuyahoga County	1,081	8.95
North Royalton (city) Cuyahoga County	2,276	7.94
Middleburg Heights (city) Cuyahoga County	1,226	7.89
Parma Heights (city) Cuyahoga County	1,690	7.80
Austintown (cdp) Mahoning County	2,411	7.62
Broadview Heights (city) Cuyahoga County	1,177	7.37

Slovene

Top 10 Places Sorted by Number
Based on all places, regardless of population

Place	Number	%
Euclid (city) Cuyahoga County	4,640	8.80
Cleveland (city) Cuyahoga County	3,828	0.80
Mentor (city) Lake County	3,652	7.26
Eastlake (city) Lake County	1,558	7.72
Parma (city) Cuyahoga County	1,477	1.72
Willowick (city) Lake County	1,387	9.63
Willoughby (city) Lake County	1,346	5.96
Wickliffe (city) Lake County	1,336	9.91
Willoughby Hills (city) Lake County	1,060	12.23
Strongsville (city) Cuyahoga County	979	2.23

Top 10 Places Sorted by Percent
Based on all places, regardless of population

Place	Number	%
Willoughby Hills (city) Lake County	1,060	12.23
Wickliffe (city) Lake County	1,336	9.91
Willowick (city) Lake County	1,387	9.63
Euclid (city) Cuyahoga County	4,640	8.80
Timberlake (village) Lake County	65	8.46
Kirtland Hills (village) Lake County	49	8.18
Eastlake (city) Lake County	1,558	7.72
Highland Heights (city) Cuyahoga County	591	7.31
Mentor (city) Lake County	3,652	7.26
Waite Hill (village) Lake County	30	6.65

Top 10 Places Sorted by Percent
Based on places with populations of 10,000 or more

Place	Number	%
Wickliffe (city) Lake County	1,336	9.91
Willowick (city) Lake County	1,387	9.63
Euclid (city) Cuyahoga County	4,640	8.80
Eastlake (city) Lake County	1,558	7.72
Mentor (city) Lake County	3,652	7.26
Willoughby (city) Lake County	1,346	5.96
Richmond Heights (city) Cuyahoga County	613	5.60
Lyndhurst (city) Cuyahoga County	583	3.82
Broadview Heights (city) Cuyahoga County	515	3.23
Mayfield Heights (city) Cuyahoga County	507	2.62

Soviet Union

Top 10 Places Sorted by Number
Based on all places, regardless of population

Place	Number	%
Beachwood (city) Cuyahoga County	9	0.07
Columbus (city) Franklin County	6	0.00

Top 10 Places Sorted by Percent
Based on all places, regardless of population

Place	Number	%
Beachwood (city) Cuyahoga County	9	0.07
Columbus (city) Franklin County	6	0.00

Top 10 Places Sorted by Percent
Based on places with populations of 10,000 or more

Place	Number	%
Beachwood (city) Cuyahoga County	9	0.07
Columbus (city) Franklin County	6	0.00

Notes: (cdp) census designated place; Refer to the User's Guide in the front of the book for more detailed information.

Swedish

Top 10 Places Sorted by Number
Based on all places, regardless of population

Place	Number	%
Columbus (city) Franklin County	4,254	0.60
Toledo (city) Lucas County	1,640	0.52
Akron (city) Summit County	1,629	0.75
Cleveland (city) Cuyahoga County	1,331	0.28
Cincinnati (city) Hamilton County	1,318	0.40
Dublin (city) Franklin County	720	2.29
Beavercreek (city) Greene County	604	1.58
Cuyahoga Falls (city) Summit County	597	1.21
Parma (city) Cuyahoga County	597	0.70
Boardman (cdp) Mahoning County	592	1.59

Top 10 Places Sorted by Percent
Based on all places, regardless of population

Place	Number	%
New Bavaria (village) Henry County	9	11.84
Harbor View (village) Lucas County	7	6.48
South Middletown (cdp) Butler County	9	5.17
Blakeslee (village) Williams County	6	4.96
Put-in-Bay (village) Ottawa County	6	4.03
Granville (village) Licking County	110	3.77
South Russell (village) Geauga County	141	3.51
Edgewood (cdp) Ashtabula County	156	3.26
Pigeon Creek (cdp) Summit County	28	3.13
Hartville (village) Stark County	69	3.10

Top 10 Places Sorted by Percent
Based on places with populations of 10,000 or more

Place	Number	%
Dublin (city) Franklin County	720	2.29
Ashtabula (city) Ashtabula County	478	2.29
Hudson (city) Summit County	485	2.17
Bexley (city) Franklin County	282	2.14
Conneaut (city) Ashtabula County	244	1.95
Struthers (city) Mahoning County	205	1.74
Bay Village (city) Cuyahoga County	278	1.73
Springboro (city) Warren County	199	1.63
Boardman (cdp) Mahoning County	592	1.59
Beavercreek (city) Greene County	604	1.58

Swiss

Top 10 Places Sorted by Number
Based on all places, regardless of population

Place	Number	%
Columbus (city) Franklin County	2,640	0.37
Toledo (city) Lucas County	1,245	0.40
Akron (city) Summit County	976	0.45
Cincinnati (city) Hamilton County	800	0.24
Canton (city) Stark County	775	0.96
Orrville (city) Wayne County	654	7.66
Dover (city) Tuscarawas County	625	5.10
Wooster (city) Wayne County	573	2.29
Cleveland (city) Cuyahoga County	541	0.11
Alliance (city) Stark County	537	2.31

Top 10 Places Sorted by Percent
Based on all places, regardless of population

Place	Number	%
Pandora (village) Putnam County	227	18.64
Sugarcreek (village) Tuscarawas County	366	16.70
Lower Salem (village) Washington County	20	14.39
Wilmot (village) Stark County	50	14.25
Baltic (village) Tuscarawas County	86	11.75
Dalton (village) Wayne County	179	11.44
Parral (village) Tuscarawas County	26	10.74
Bluffton (village) Allen County	385	10.39
Olde West Chester (cdp) Butler County	27	10.15

| Latty (village) Paulding County | 21 | 10.14 |

Top 10 Places Sorted by Percent
Based on places with populations of 10,000 or more

Place	Number	%
Dover (city) Tuscarawas County	625	5.10
New Philadelphia (city) Tuscarawas County	418	2.48
Wadsworth (city) Medina County	432	2.33
Alliance (city) Stark County	537	2.31
Wooster (city) Wayne County	573	2.29
North Canton (city) Stark County	291	1.78
Massillon (city) Stark County	495	1.58
Maumee (city) Lucas County	179	1.18
Findlay (city) Hancock County	431	1.10
Upper Arlington (city) Franklin County	365	1.09

Turkish

Top 10 Places Sorted by Number
Based on all places, regardless of population

Place	Number	%
Columbus (city) Franklin County	454	0.06
Cleveland (city) Cuyahoga County	151	0.03
Cincinnati (city) Hamilton County	119	0.04
Upper Arlington (city) Franklin County	97	0.29
Kent (city) Portage County	81	0.29
Dublin (city) Franklin County	79	0.25
Toledo (city) Lucas County	66	0.02
Montgomery (city) Hamilton County	59	0.59
Solon (city) Cuyahoga County	49	0.22
Akron (city) Summit County	48	0.02

Top 10 Places Sorted by Percent
Based on all places, regardless of population

Place	Number	%
Fairport Harbor (village) Lake County	20	0.63
Montgomery (city) Hamilton County	59	0.59
Amelia (village) Clermont County	16	0.59
Pepper Pike (city) Cuyahoga County	27	0.45
Enon (village) Clark County	11	0.42
Bainbridge (cdp) Geauga County	13	0.37
Forestville (cdp) Hamilton County	37	0.33
Ottawa Hills (village) Lucas County	15	0.33
Cleves (village) Hamilton County	9	0.32
New Vienna (village) Clinton County	4	0.31

Top 10 Places Sorted by Percent
Based on places with populations of 10,000 or more

Place	Number	%
Montgomery (city) Hamilton County	59	0.59
Forestville (cdp) Hamilton County	37	0.33
Upper Arlington (city) Franklin County	97	0.29
Kent (city) Portage County	81	0.29
Dublin (city) Franklin County	79	0.25
Springboro (city) Warren County	29	0.24
Solon (city) Cuyahoga County	49	0.22
Loveland (city) Hamilton County	23	0.19
South Euclid (city) Cuyahoga County	43	0.18
Sylvania (city) Lucas County	32	0.17

Ukrainian

Top 10 Places Sorted by Number
Based on all places, regardless of population

Place	Number	%
Parma (city) Cuyahoga County	3,692	4.31
Cleveland (city) Cuyahoga County	3,224	0.67
Columbus (city) Franklin County	1,955	0.27
Youngstown (city) Mahoning County	1,111	1.35
Strongsville (city) Cuyahoga County	1,019	2.32
Akron (city) Summit County	844	0.39
North Royalton (city) Cuyahoga County	836	2.92

Lakewood (city) Cuyahoga County	663	1.17
Austintown (cdp) Mahoning County	651	2.06
Parma Heights (city) Cuyahoga County	622	2.87

Top 10 Places Sorted by Percent
Based on all places, regardless of population

Place	Number	%
Parma (city) Cuyahoga County	3,692	4.31
Wetherington (cdp) Butler County	44	4.31
Glenwillow (village) Cuyahoga County	19	4.27
Seven Hills (city) Cuyahoga County	501	4.15
Chatfield (village) Crawford County	9	4.02
Brooklyn Heights (village) Cuyahoga County	55	3.49
Middleburg Heights (city) Cuyahoga County	473	3.04
Olde West Chester (cdp) Butler County	8	3.01
North Royalton (city) Cuyahoga County	836	2.92
Peninsula (village) Summit County	15	2.90

Top 10 Places Sorted by Percent
Based on places with populations of 10,000 or more

Place	Number	%
Parma (city) Cuyahoga County	3,692	4.31
Seven Hills (city) Cuyahoga County	501	4.15
Middleburg Heights (city) Cuyahoga County	473	3.04
North Royalton (city) Cuyahoga County	836	2.92
Parma Heights (city) Cuyahoga County	622	2.87
Broadview Heights (city) Cuyahoga County	393	2.46
Strongsville (city) Cuyahoga County	1,019	2.32
Mayfield Heights (city) Cuyahoga County	416	2.15
Girard (city) Trumbull County	233	2.09
Austintown (cdp) Mahoning County	651	2.06

United States or American

Top 10 Places Sorted by Number
Based on all places, regardless of population

Place	Number	%
Columbus (city) Franklin County	51,427	7.23
Cincinnati (city) Hamilton County	15,919	4.81
Akron (city) Summit County	13,911	6.41
Cleveland (city) Cuyahoga County	13,063	2.73
Dayton (city) Montgomery County	12,783	7.69
Toledo (city) Lucas County	12,242	3.92
Hamilton (city) Butler County	9,129	15.05
Springfield (city) Clark County	9,036	13.83
Middletown (city) Butler County	7,955	15.36
Marion (city) Marion County	6,571	18.62

Top 10 Places Sorted by Percent
Based on all places, regardless of population

Place	Number	%
Holiday City (village) Williams County	30	58.82
South Middletown (cdp) Butler County	91	52.30
Macksburg (village) Washington County	94	49.47
Bairdstown (village) Wood County	56	42.75
Orient (village) Pickaway County	110	39.43
Ludlow Falls (village) Miami County	78	38.61
Sinking Spring (village) Highland County	59	38.06
Cherry Fork (village) Adams County	56	37.84
Highland (village) Highland County	112	37.58
Lucasville (cdp) Scioto County	587	35.81

Top 10 Places Sorted by Percent
Based on places with populations of 10,000 or more

Place	Number	%
Franklin (city) Warren County	2,482	21.51
Marion (city) Marion County	6,571	18.62
Ironton (city) Lawrence County	2,042	18.09
Washington (city) Fayette County	2,420	18.00
Bellefontaine (city) Logan County	2,155	16.51
Galion (city) Crawford County	1,879	16.35
Circleville (city) Pickaway County	2,206	16.26

Notes: (cdp) census designated place; Refer to the User's Guide in the front of the book for more detailed information.

PROFILES OF OHIO / Ancestry Rankings 463

Place	Number	%
Urbana (city) Champaign County	1,889	16.26
Portsmouth (city) Scioto County	3,315	15.91
Mount Vernon (city) Knox County	2,275	15.62

Welsh

Top 10 Places Sorted by Number
Based on all places, regardless of population

Place	Number	%
Columbus (city) Franklin County	9,969	1.40
Akron (city) Summit County	2,390	1.10
Cincinnati (city) Hamilton County	1,745	0.53
Toledo (city) Lucas County	1,611	0.51
Cleveland (city) Cuyahoga County	1,309	0.27
Cuyahoga Falls (city) Summit County	1,064	2.16
Upper Arlington (city) Franklin County	1,060	3.15
Canton (city) Stark County	1,012	1.25
Austintown (cdp) Mahoning County	990	3.13
Youngstown (city) Mahoning County	983	1.20

Top 10 Places Sorted by Percent
Based on all places, regardless of population

Place	Number	%
Venedocia (village) Van Wert County	31	19.02
Oak Hill (village) Jackson County	177	10.41
Catawba (village) Clark County	15	7.77
Cairo (village) Allen County	35	7.09
Jackson (city) Jackson County	417	6.97
Yankee Lake (village) Trumbull County	6	6.74
Granville South (cdp) Licking County	81	6.66
La Croft (cdp) Columbiana County	84	5.89
Rogers (village) Columbiana County	15	5.86
Washingtonville (village) Columbiana County	45	5.84

Top 10 Places Sorted by Percent
Based on places with populations of 10,000 or more

Place	Number	%
Niles (city) Trumbull County	819	3.91
Dover (city) Tuscarawas County	395	3.22
Grove City (city) Franklin County	856	3.17
Upper Arlington (city) Franklin County	1,060	3.15
Austintown (cdp) Mahoning County	990	3.13
Worthington (city) Franklin County	448	3.13
Girard (city) Trumbull County	303	2.72
Westerville (city) Franklin County	956	2.70
Boardman (cdp) Mahoning County	950	2.55
North Canton (city) Stark County	406	2.48

West Indian, excluding Hispanic

Top 10 Places Sorted by Number
Based on all places, regardless of population

Place	Number	%
Columbus (city) Franklin County	1,726	0.24
Cleveland (city) Cuyahoga County	1,651	0.35
Cincinnati (city) Hamilton County	634	0.19
Toledo (city) Lucas County	562	0.18
Dayton (city) Montgomery County	392	0.24
Akron (city) Summit County	378	0.17
Cleveland Heights (city) Cuyahoga County	322	0.64
Warrensville Heights (city) Cuyahoga County	194	1.26
Euclid (city) Cuyahoga County	175	0.33
South Euclid (city) Cuyahoga County	156	0.66

Top 10 Places Sorted by Percent
Based on all places, regardless of population

Place	Number	%
Warrensville Heights (city) Cuyahoga County	194	1.26
Mount Healthy (city) Hamilton County	87	1.20
The Plains (cdp) Athens County	34	1.15
Nelsonville (city) Athens County	51	1.00
Woodmere (village) Cuyahoga County	8	0.96
Woodlawn (village) Hamilton County	26	0.91
Golf Manor (village) Hamilton County	34	0.85
Shiloh (cdp) Montgomery County	88	0.78
Wilberforce (cdp) Greene County	11	0.77
Gettysburg (village) Darke County	4	0.73

Top 10 Places Sorted by Percent
Based on places with populations of 10,000 or more

Place	Number	%
Warrensville Heights (city) Cuyahoga County	194	1.26
Shiloh (cdp) Montgomery County	88	0.78
South Euclid (city) Cuyahoga County	156	0.66
Cleveland Heights (city) Cuyahoga County	322	0.64
University Heights (city) Cuyahoga County	82	0.58
Springdale (city) Hamilton County	58	0.55
Forest Park (city) Hamilton County	104	0.54
East Cleveland (city) Cuyahoga County	145	0.53
Bedford Heights (city) Cuyahoga County	52	0.46
Bedford (city) Cuyahoga County	57	0.40

West Indian: Bahamian, excluding Hispanic

Top 10 Places Sorted by Number
Based on all places, regardless of population

Place	Number	%
Dayton (city) Montgomery County	49	0.03
Strongsville (city) Cuyahoga County	33	0.08
Columbus (city) Franklin County	25	0.00
Cleveland (city) Cuyahoga County	21	0.00
Youngstown (city) Mahoning County	14	0.02
Findlay (city) Hancock County	10	0.03
Mayfield Heights (city) Cuyahoga County	9	0.05
Steubenville (city) Jefferson County	8	0.04
Cleveland Heights (city) Cuyahoga County	7	0.01
Toledo (city) Lucas County	6	0.00

Top 10 Places Sorted by Percent
Based on all places, regardless of population

Place	Number	%
Woodlawn (village) Hamilton County	4	0.14
Strongsville (city) Cuyahoga County	33	0.08
Mount Healthy (city) Hamilton County	4	0.06
Mayfield Heights (city) Cuyahoga County	9	0.05
Steubenville (city) Jefferson County	8	0.04
Dayton (city) Montgomery County	49	0.03
Findlay (city) Hancock County	10	0.03
Maumee (city) Lucas County	5	0.03
Youngstown (city) Mahoning County	14	0.02
Cleveland Heights (city) Cuyahoga County	7	0.01

Top 10 Places Sorted by Percent
Based on places with populations of 10,000 or more

Place	Number	%
Strongsville (city) Cuyahoga County	33	0.08
Mayfield Heights (city) Cuyahoga County	9	0.05
Steubenville (city) Jefferson County	8	0.04
Dayton (city) Montgomery County	49	0.03
Findlay (city) Hancock County	10	0.03
Maumee (city) Lucas County	5	0.03
Youngstown (city) Mahoning County	14	0.02
Cleveland Heights (city) Cuyahoga County	7	0.01
Columbus (city) Franklin County	25	0.00
Cleveland (city) Cuyahoga County	21	0.00

West Indian: Barbadian, excluding Hispanic

Top 10 Places Sorted by Number
Based on all places, regardless of population

Place	Number	%
Columbus (city) Franklin County	32	0.00
Forest Park (city) Hamilton County	22	0.11
Euclid (city) Cuyahoga County	19	0.04
Youngstown (city) Mahoning County	14	0.02
Clayton (city) Montgomery County	12	0.09
Piqua (city) Miami County	12	0.06
Austintown (cdp) Mahoning County	11	0.03
Kettering (city) Montgomery County	11	0.02
East Cleveland (city) Cuyahoga County	9	0.03
Mount Healthy (city) Hamilton County	6	0.08

Top 10 Places Sorted by Percent
Based on all places, regardless of population

Place	Number	%
Forest Park (city) Hamilton County	22	0.11
Clayton (city) Montgomery County	12	0.09
Mount Healthy (city) Hamilton County	6	0.08
Piqua (city) Miami County	12	0.06
Euclid (city) Cuyahoga County	19	0.04
Austintown (cdp) Mahoning County	11	0.03
East Cleveland (city) Cuyahoga County	9	0.03
Warrensville Heights (city) Cuyahoga County	5	0.03
Youngstown (city) Mahoning County	14	0.02
Kettering (city) Montgomery County	11	0.02

Top 10 Places Sorted by Percent
Based on places with populations of 10,000 or more

Place	Number	%
Forest Park (city) Hamilton County	22	0.11
Clayton (city) Montgomery County	12	0.09
Piqua (city) Miami County	12	0.06
Euclid (city) Cuyahoga County	19	0.04
Austintown (cdp) Mahoning County	11	0.03
East Cleveland (city) Cuyahoga County	9	0.03
Warrensville Heights (city) Cuyahoga County	5	0.03
Youngstown (city) Mahoning County	14	0.02
Kettering (city) Montgomery County	11	0.02
Maple Heights (city) Cuyahoga County	6	0.02

West Indian: Belizean, excluding Hispanic

Top 10 Places Sorted by Number
Based on all places, regardless of population

Place	Number	%
Columbus (city) Franklin County	25	0.00
Dayton (city) Montgomery County	21	0.01
Cleveland (city) Cuyahoga County	16	0.00
Mount Healthy Heights (cdp) Hamilton County	9	0.26
Euclid (city) Cuyahoga County	7	0.01
Chillicothe (city) Ross County	6	0.03
Shaker Heights (city) Cuyahoga County	6	0.02
Parma (city) Cuyahoga County	6	0.01
Gambier (village) Knox County	5	0.26
Bedford Heights (city) Cuyahoga County	5	0.04

Top 10 Places Sorted by Percent
Based on all places, regardless of population

Place	Number	%
Mount Healthy Heights (cdp) Hamilton County	9	0.26
Gambier (village) Knox County	5	0.26
Bedford Heights (city) Cuyahoga County	5	0.04
Chillicothe (city) Ross County	6	0.03
Shaker Heights (city) Cuyahoga County	6	0.02
Dayton (city) Montgomery County	21	0.01
Euclid (city) Cuyahoga County	7	0.01
Parma (city) Cuyahoga County	6	0.01
Columbus (city) Franklin County	25	0.00
Cleveland (city) Cuyahoga County	16	0.00

Top 10 Places Sorted by Percent
Based on places with populations of 10,000 or more

Place	Number	%
Bedford Heights (city) Cuyahoga County	5	0.04

Notes: (cdp) census designated place; Refer to the User's Guide in the front of the book for more detailed information.

Place	Number	%
Chillicothe (city) Ross County	6	0.03
Shaker Heights (city) Cuyahoga County	6	0.02
Dayton (city) Montgomery County	21	0.01
Euclid (city) Cuyahoga County	7	0.01
Parma (city) Cuyahoga County	6	0.01
Columbus (city) Franklin County	25	0.00
Cleveland (city) Cuyahoga County	16	0.00

West Indian: Bermudan, excluding Hispanic

Top 10 Places Sorted by Number
Based on all places, regardless of population

Place	Number	%
Columbus (city) Franklin County	28	0.00
Dayton (city) Montgomery County	15	0.01
Toledo (city) Lucas County	15	0.00
Pepper Pike (city) Cuyahoga County	12	0.20
Mount Healthy (city) Hamilton County	12	0.17
Warrensville Heights (city) Cuyahoga County	11	0.07
Akron (city) Summit County	9	0.00
Xenia (city) Greene County	7	0.03
Lakewood (city) Cuyahoga County	6	0.01
Cincinnati (city) Hamilton County	4	0.00

Top 10 Places Sorted by Percent
Based on all places, regardless of population

Place	Number	%
Pepper Pike (city) Cuyahoga County	12	0.20
Mount Healthy (city) Hamilton County	12	0.17
Warrensville Heights (city) Cuyahoga County	11	0.07
Xenia (city) Greene County	7	0.03
Dayton (city) Montgomery County	15	0.01
Lakewood (city) Cuyahoga County	6	0.01
Columbus (city) Franklin County	28	0.00
Toledo (city) Lucas County	15	0.00
Akron (city) Summit County	9	0.00
Cincinnati (city) Hamilton County	4	0.00

Top 10 Places Sorted by Percent
Based on places with populations of 10,000 or more

Place	Number	%
Warrensville Heights (city) Cuyahoga County	11	0.07
Xenia (city) Greene County	7	0.03
Dayton (city) Montgomery County	15	0.01
Lakewood (city) Cuyahoga County	6	0.01
Columbus (city) Franklin County	28	0.00
Toledo (city) Lucas County	15	0.00
Akron (city) Summit County	9	0.00
Cincinnati (city) Hamilton County	4	0.00

West Indian: British West Indian, excluding Hispanic

Top 10 Places Sorted by Number
Based on all places, regardless of population

Place	Number	%
Columbus (city) Franklin County	44	0.01
Fairview Park (city) Cuyahoga County	27	0.15
Cincinnati (city) Hamilton County	16	0.00
University Heights (city) Cuyahoga County	15	0.11
Gahanna (city) Franklin County	14	0.04
Akron (city) Summit County	14	0.01
Fairfield (city) Butler County	12	0.03
Toledo (city) Lucas County	11	0.00
Athens (city) Athens County	8	0.04
Clayton (city) Montgomery County	7	0.05

Top 10 Places Sorted by Percent
Based on all places, regardless of population

Place	Number	%
Fairview Park (city) Cuyahoga County	27	0.15
University Heights (city) Cuyahoga County	15	0.11
Clayton (city) Montgomery County	7	0.05
Gahanna (city) Franklin County	14	0.04
Athens (city) Athens County	8	0.04
Fairfield (city) Butler County	12	0.03
Fremont (city) Sandusky County	5	0.03
Ravenna (city) Portage County	4	0.03
Huber Heights (city) Montgomery County	7	0.02
Westlake (city) Cuyahoga County	6	0.02

Top 10 Places Sorted by Percent
Based on places with populations of 10,000 or more

Place	Number	%
Fairview Park (city) Cuyahoga County	27	0.15
University Heights (city) Cuyahoga County	15	0.11
Clayton (city) Montgomery County	7	0.05
Gahanna (city) Franklin County	14	0.04
Athens (city) Athens County	8	0.04
Fairfield (city) Butler County	12	0.03
Fremont (city) Sandusky County	5	0.03
Ravenna (city) Portage County	4	0.03
Huber Heights (city) Montgomery County	7	0.02
Westlake (city) Cuyahoga County	6	0.02

West Indian: Dutch West Indian, excluding Hispanic

Top 10 Places Sorted by Number
Based on all places, regardless of population

Place	Number	%
Lorain (city) Lorain County	44	0.06
Akron (city) Summit County	36	0.02
Columbus (city) Franklin County	33	0.00
Austintown (cdp) Mahoning County	18	0.06
Dayton (city) Montgomery County	16	0.01
Medina (city) Medina County	13	0.05
Crooksville (village) Perry County	11	0.45
Norwood (city) Hamilton County	11	0.05
Whitehall (city) Franklin County	10	0.05
Greenfield (city) Highland County	9	0.18

Top 10 Places Sorted by Percent
Based on all places, regardless of population

Place	Number	%
Crooksville (village) Perry County	11	0.45
Meyers Lake (village) Stark County	2	0.35
Fulton (village) Morrow County	1	0.33
Centerburg (village) Knox County	4	0.28
New Straitsville (village) Perry County	2	0.26
Mechanicsburg (village) Champaign County	4	0.22
Greenfield (city) Highland County	9	0.18
McArthur (village) Vinton County	3	0.16
New Waterford (village) Columbiana County	2	0.15
McComb (village) Hancock County	2	0.12

Top 10 Places Sorted by Percent
Based on places with populations of 10,000 or more

Place	Number	%
Lorain (city) Lorain County	44	0.06
Austintown (cdp) Mahoning County	18	0.06
Ravenna (city) Portage County	7	0.06
Medina (city) Medina County	13	0.05
Norwood (city) Hamilton County	11	0.05
Whitehall (city) Franklin County	10	0.05
Mayfield Heights (city) Cuyahoga County	7	0.04
Centerville (city) Montgomery County	7	0.03
Green (city) Summit County	6	0.03
Steubenville (city) Jefferson County	6	0.03

West Indian: Haitian, excluding Hispanic

Top 10 Places Sorted by Number
Based on all places, regardless of population

Place	Number	%
Columbus (city) Franklin County	131	0.02
Cincinnati (city) Hamilton County	70	0.02
Dayton (city) Montgomery County	52	0.03
Akron (city) Summit County	45	0.02
Cleveland (city) Cuyahoga County	43	0.01
The Plains (cdp) Athens County	34	1.15
Springdale (city) Hamilton County	31	0.29
Sidney (city) Shelby County	28	0.14
Northgate (cdp) Hamilton County	26	0.33
Wilmington (city) Clinton County	24	0.20

Top 10 Places Sorted by Percent
Based on all places, regardless of population

Place	Number	%
The Plains (cdp) Athens County	34	1.15
Northgate (cdp) Hamilton County	26	0.33
Springdale (city) Hamilton County	31	0.29
Wilmington (city) Clinton County	24	0.20
Sidney (city) Shelby County	28	0.14
Woodlawn (village) Hamilton County	4	0.14
Utica (village) Licking County	3	0.14
Mentor-on-the-Lake (city) Lake County	8	0.10
Portsmouth (city) Scioto County	14	0.07
Chillicothe (city) Ross County	14	0.06

Top 10 Places Sorted by Percent
Based on places with populations of 10,000 or more

Place	Number	%
Springdale (city) Hamilton County	31	0.29
Wilmington (city) Clinton County	24	0.20
Sidney (city) Shelby County	28	0.14
Portsmouth (city) Scioto County	14	0.07
Chillicothe (city) Ross County	14	0.06
Westerville (city) Franklin County	16	0.05
Barberton (city) Summit County	14	0.05
Warrensville Heights (city) Cuyahoga County	8	0.05
Centerville (city) Montgomery County	10	0.04
Rocky River (city) Cuyahoga County	9	0.04

West Indian: Jamaican, excluding Hispanic

Top 10 Places Sorted by Number
Based on all places, regardless of population

Place	Number	%
Cleveland (city) Cuyahoga County	1,194	0.25
Columbus (city) Franklin County	1,058	0.15
Toledo (city) Lucas County	480	0.15
Cincinnati (city) Hamilton County	437	0.13
Akron (city) Summit County	235	0.11
Cleveland Heights (city) Cuyahoga County	209	0.42
Dayton (city) Montgomery County	170	0.10
Euclid (city) Cuyahoga County	140	0.27
South Euclid (city) Cuyahoga County	124	0.53
East Cleveland (city) Cuyahoga County	118	0.43

Top 10 Places Sorted by Percent
Based on all places, regardless of population

Place	Number	%
Nelsonville (city) Athens County	51	1.00
Woodmere (village) Cuyahoga County	8	0.96
Golf Manor (village) Hamilton County	34	0.85
Shiloh (cdp) Montgomery County	88	0.78
Wilberforce (cdp) Greene County	11	0.77
Warrensville Heights (city) Cuyahoga County	108	0.70
North Bend (village) Hamilton County	4	0.65
Woodlawn (village) Hamilton County	18	0.63

Notes: (cdp) census designated place; Refer to the User's Guide in the front of the book for more detailed information.

PROFILES OF OHIO / Ancestry Rankings 465

Place	Number	%
Mount Healthy (city) Hamilton County	39	0.54
South Euclid (city) Cuyahoga County	124	0.53

Top 10 Places Sorted by Percent
Based on places with populations of 10,000 or more

Place	Number	%
Shiloh (cdp) Montgomery County	88	0.78
Warrensville Heights (city) Cuyahoga County	108	0.70
South Euclid (city) Cuyahoga County	124	0.53
University Heights (city) Cuyahoga County	67	0.47
East Cleveland (city) Cuyahoga County	118	0.43
Cleveland Heights (city) Cuyahoga County	209	0.42
Bedford Heights (city) Cuyahoga County	42	0.37
Bedford (city) Cuyahoga County	49	0.34
Forest Park (city) Hamilton County	57	0.29
Euclid (city) Cuyahoga County	140	0.27

West Indian: Trinidadian and Tobagonian, excluding Hispanic

Top 10 Places Sorted by Number
Based on all places, regardless of population

Place	Number	%
Cleveland (city) Cuyahoga County	184	0.04
Columbus (city) Franklin County	106	0.01
Warrensville Heights (city) Cuyahoga County	51	0.33
Huber Heights (city) Montgomery County	44	0.11
Middleburg Heights (city) Cuyahoga County	33	0.21
South Euclid (city) Cuyahoga County	29	0.12
The Village of Indian Hill (city) Hamilton County	20	0.34
Vandalia (city) Montgomery County	19	0.13
Edgewood (cdp) Ashtabula County	17	0.36
Toledo (city) Lucas County	17	0.01

Top 10 Places Sorted by Percent
Based on all places, regardless of population

Place	Number	%
Edgewood (cdp) Ashtabula County	17	0.36
The Village of Indian Hill (city) Hamilton County	20	0.34
Warrensville Heights (city) Cuyahoga County	51	0.33
Newtown (village) Hamilton County	8	0.33
Middleburg Heights (city) Cuyahoga County	33	0.21
Vandalia (city) Montgomery County	19	0.13
Northwood (city) Wood County	7	0.13
South Euclid (city) Cuyahoga County	29	0.12
Huber Heights (city) Montgomery County	44	0.11
Mount Healthy (city) Hamilton County	8	0.11

Top 10 Places Sorted by Percent
Based on places with populations of 10,000 or more

Place	Number	%
Warrensville Heights (city) Cuyahoga County	51	0.33
Middleburg Heights (city) Cuyahoga County	33	0.21
Vandalia (city) Montgomery County	19	0.13
South Euclid (city) Cuyahoga County	29	0.12
Huber Heights (city) Montgomery County	44	0.11
Bedford (city) Cuyahoga County	8	0.06
White Oak (cdp) Hamilton County	7	0.05
Cleveland (city) Cuyahoga County	184	0.04
Shaker Heights (city) Cuyahoga County	12	0.04
Kent (city) Portage County	11	0.04

West Indian: U.S. Virgin Islander, excluding Hispanic

Top 10 Places Sorted by Number
Based on all places, regardless of population

Place	Number	%
Columbus (city) Franklin County	43	0.01
Cleveland (city) Cuyahoga County	30	0.01
Dayton (city) Montgomery County	15	0.01
Akron (city) Summit County	11	0.01

Place	Number	%
Fairlawn (city) Summit County	9	0.12
Chillicothe (city) Ross County	6	0.03
Murray City (village) Hocking County	2	0.45

Top 10 Places Sorted by Percent
Based on all places, regardless of population

Place	Number	%
Murray City (village) Hocking County	2	0.45
Fairlawn (city) Summit County	9	0.12
Chillicothe (city) Ross County	6	0.03
Columbus (city) Franklin County	43	0.01
Cleveland (city) Cuyahoga County	30	0.01
Dayton (city) Montgomery County	15	0.01
Akron (city) Summit County	11	0.01

Top 10 Places Sorted by Percent
Based on places with populations of 10,000 or more

Place	Number	%
Chillicothe (city) Ross County	6	0.03
Columbus (city) Franklin County	43	0.01
Cleveland (city) Cuyahoga County	30	0.01
Dayton (city) Montgomery County	15	0.01
Akron (city) Summit County	11	0.01

West Indian: West Indian, excluding Hispanic

Top 10 Places Sorted by Number
Based on all places, regardless of population

Place	Number	%
Columbus (city) Franklin County	201	0.03
Cleveland (city) Cuyahoga County	154	0.03
Cincinnati (city) Hamilton County	93	0.03
Cleveland Heights (city) Cuyahoga County	85	0.17
Dayton (city) Montgomery County	32	0.02
Huber Ridge (cdp) Franklin County	31	0.63
Reynoldsburg (city) Franklin County	30	0.09
Painesville (city) Lake County	22	0.13
Lorain (city) Lorain County	21	0.03
Gahanna (city) Franklin County	20	0.06

Top 10 Places Sorted by Percent
Based on all places, regardless of population

Place	Number	%
Gettysburg (village) Darke County	4	0.73
Huber Ridge (cdp) Franklin County	31	0.63
Cridersville (village) Auglaize County	7	0.39
Sandusky South (cdp) Erie County	17	0.26
Mount Healthy (city) Hamilton County	18	0.25
Oakwood (village) Cuyahoga County	9	0.25
Edgewood (cdp) Ashtabula County	9	0.19
Oberlin (city) Lorain County	15	0.18
Amelia (village) Clermont County	5	0.18
Terrace Park (village) Hamilton County	4	0.18

Top 10 Places Sorted by Percent
Based on places with populations of 10,000 or more

Place	Number	%
Cleveland Heights (city) Cuyahoga County	85	0.17
Painesville (city) Lake County	22	0.13
Reynoldsburg (city) Franklin County	30	0.09
Forest Park (city) Hamilton County	18	0.09
Bridgetown North (cdp) Hamilton County	12	0.09
North College Hill (city) Hamilton County	9	0.09
Berea (city) Cuyahoga County	15	0.08
East Cleveland (city) Cuyahoga County	18	0.07
Warrensville Heights (city) Cuyahoga County	11	0.07
Gahanna (city) Franklin County	20	0.06

West Indian: Other, excluding Hispanic

Top 10 Places Sorted by Number
Based on all places, regardless of population

Place	Number	%
Mansfield (city) Richland County	19	0.04
Ripley (village) Brown County	2	0.11

Top 10 Places Sorted by Percent
Based on all places, regardless of population

Place	Number	%
Ripley (village) Brown County	2	0.11
Mansfield (city) Richland County	19	0.04

Top 10 Places Sorted by Percent
Based on places with populations of 10,000 or more

Place	Number	%
Mansfield (city) Richland County	19	0.04

White

Top 10 Places Sorted by Number
Based on all places, regardless of population

Place	Number	%
Columbus (city) Franklin County	496,425	69.77
Toledo (city) Lucas County	227,094	72.41
Cleveland (city) Cuyahoga County	206,487	43.16
Cincinnati (city) Hamilton County	179,453	54.17
Akron (city) Summit County	149,577	68.91
Dayton (city) Montgomery County	91,049	54.79
Parma (city) Cuyahoga County	82,806	96.67
Canton (city) Stark County	62,328	77.13
Kettering (city) Montgomery County	55,389	96.33
Hamilton (city) Butler County	54,699	90.13

Top 10 Places Sorted by Percent
Based on all places, regardless of population

Place	Number	%
Fort Loramie (village) Shelby County	1,344	100.00
Bremen (village) Fairfield County	1,265	100.00
Junction City (village) Perry County	818	100.00
Lowell (village) Washington County	628	100.00
Milford Center (village) Union County	626	100.00
Midvale (village) Tuscarawas County	547	100.00
Fredericksburg (village) Wayne County	487	100.00
Jerry City (village) Wood County	453	100.00
Senecaville (village) Guernsey County	453	100.00
Sugar Grove (village) Fairfield County	448	100.00

Top 10 Places Sorted by Percent
Based on places with populations of 10,000 or more

Place	Number	%
Vermilion (city) Lorain County	10,831	99.12
Salem (city) Columbiana County	12,068	98.94
Bridgetown North (cdp) Hamilton County	12,426	98.86
Galion (city) Crawford County	11,206	98.81
Bay Village (city) Cuyahoga County	15,875	98.68
Wadsworth (city) Medina County	18,164	98.52
Willowick (city) Lake County	14,147	98.51
Lancaster (city) Fairfield County	34,748	98.34
Franklin (city) Warren County	11,204	98.32
Greenville (city) Darke County	13,064	98.27

White: Not Hispanic

Top 10 Places Sorted by Number
Based on all places, regardless of population

Place	Number	%
Columbus (city) Franklin County	487,638	68.54
Toledo (city) Lucas County	217,906	69.48

Notes: (cdp) census designated place; Refer to the User's Guide in the front of the book for more detailed information.

Place	Number	%
Cleveland (city) Cuyahoga County	191,741	40.08
Cincinnati (city) Hamilton County	177,483	53.57
Akron (city) Summit County	148,161	68.25
Dayton (city) Montgomery County	89,683	53.97
Parma (city) Cuyahoga County	81,853	95.56
Canton (city) Stark County	61,720	76.38
Kettering (city) Montgomery County	54,906	95.49
Hamilton (city) Butler County	53,999	88.98

Top 10 Places Sorted by Percent
Based on all places, regardless of population

Place	Number	%
Senecaville (village) Guernsey County	453	100.00
Bowerston (village) Harrison County	414	100.00
Green Camp (village) Marion County	342	100.00
Casstown (village) Miami County	322	100.00
Tarlton (village) Pickaway County	298	100.00
Summerfield (village) Noble County	296	100.00
Hanging Rock (village) Lawrence County	279	100.00
Osgood (village) Darke County	255	100.00
Parral (village) Tuscarawas County	241	100.00
Butlerville (village) Warren County	231	100.00

Top 10 Places Sorted by Percent
Based on places with populations of 10,000 or more

Place	Number	%
Bridgetown North (cdp) Hamilton County	12,390	98.58
Salem (city) Columbiana County	12,015	98.51
Galion (city) Crawford County	11,130	98.14
Wadsworth (city) Medina County	18,072	98.02
Franklin (city) Warren County	11,156	97.89
Bay Village (city) Cuyahoga County	15,740	97.84
Willowick (city) Lake County	14,050	97.83
Green (city) Summit County	22,305	97.76
Norton (city) Summit County	11,260	97.72
Lancaster (city) Fairfield County	34,522	97.70

White: Hispanic

Top 10 Places Sorted by Number
Based on all places, regardless of population

Place	Number	%
Cleveland (city) Cuyahoga County	14,746	3.08
Toledo (city) Lucas County	9,188	2.93
Columbus (city) Franklin County	8,787	1.24
Lorain (city) Lorain County	6,929	10.09
Cincinnati (city) Hamilton County	1,970	0.59
Youngstown (city) Mahoning County	1,908	2.33
Akron (city) Summit County	1,416	0.65
Dayton (city) Montgomery County	1,366	0.82
Fremont (city) Sandusky County	1,090	6.27
Painesville (city) Lake County	1,052	6.01

Top 10 Places Sorted by Percent
Based on all places, regardless of population

Place	Number	%
Holgate (village) Henry County	134	11.22
Stony Prairie (cdp) Sandusky County	92	11.00
Milton Center (village) Wood County	21	10.77
Lorain (city) Lorain County	6,929	10.09
Hamler (village) Henry County	65	10.00
West Leipsic (village) Putnam County	25	9.23
Leipsic (village) Putnam County	177	7.92
Campbell (city) Mahoning County	660	6.98
Fremont (city) Sandusky County	1,090	6.27
Willard (city) Huron County	424	6.23

Top 10 Places Sorted by Percent
Based on places with populations of 10,000 or more

Place	Number	%
Lorain (city) Lorain County	6,929	10.09
Fremont (city) Sandusky County	1,090	6.27
Painesville (city) Lake County	1,052	6.01
Defiance (city) Defiance County	956	5.81
Fostoria (city) Seneca County	592	4.25
Cleveland (city) Cuyahoga County	14,746	3.08
Oregon (city) Lucas County	575	2.97
Toledo (city) Lucas County	9,188	2.93
Ashtabula (city) Ashtabula County	549	2.62
Youngstown (city) Mahoning County	1,908	2.33

Yugoslavian

Top 10 Places Sorted by Number
Based on all places, regardless of population

Place	Number	%
Columbus (city) Franklin County	631	0.09
Akron (city) Summit County	626	0.29
Cleveland (city) Cuyahoga County	599	0.13
Parma (city) Cuyahoga County	383	0.45
Lakewood (city) Cuyahoga County	254	0.45
Euclid (city) Cuyahoga County	226	0.43
Cincinnati (city) Hamilton County	213	0.06
Parma Heights (city) Cuyahoga County	182	0.84
Green (city) Summit County	168	0.74
Mansfield (city) Richland County	164	0.33

Top 10 Places Sorted by Percent
Based on all places, regardless of population

Place	Number	%
New Rome (village) Franklin County	9	13.85
Fultonham (village) Muskingum County	3	1.73
Ontario (village) Richland County	51	0.98
Peninsula (village) Summit County	5	0.97
Harrisburg (village) Franklin County	3	0.87
Parma Heights (city) Cuyahoga County	182	0.84
Apple Creek (village) Wayne County	8	0.82
Doylestown (village) Wayne County	21	0.77
Lexington (village) Richland County	32	0.76
Green (city) Summit County	168	0.74

Top 10 Places Sorted by Percent
Based on places with populations of 10,000 or more

Place	Number	%
Parma Heights (city) Cuyahoga County	182	0.84
Green (city) Summit County	168	0.74
Mayfield Heights (city) Cuyahoga County	131	0.68
North Royalton (city) Cuyahoga County	155	0.54
Eastlake (city) Lake County	104	0.52
Seven Hills (city) Cuyahoga County	57	0.47
Avon (city) Lorain County	54	0.47
Parma (city) Cuyahoga County	383	0.45
Lakewood (city) Cuyahoga County	254	0.45
Brecksville (city) Cuyahoga County	60	0.45

Notes: (cdp) census designated place; Refer to the User's Guide in the front of the book for more detailed information.

Population

Total Population
Top 10 Places Sorted by Number

Place	Number
Columbus, OH (city) Franklin County	711,644
Cleveland, OH (city) Cuyahoga County	478,393
Cincinnati, OH (city) Hamilton County	330,662
Toledo, OH (city) Lucas County	313,587
Akron, OH (city) Summit County	217,088
Dayton, OH (city) Montgomery County	166,193
Parma, OH (city) Cuyahoga County	85,655
Youngstown, OH (city) Mahoning County	82,026
Canton, OH (city) Stark County	81,118
Lorain, OH (city) Lorain County	68,655

Hispanic
Top 10 Places Sorted by Number

Place	Number
Cleveland, OH (city) Cuyahoga County	34,554
Columbus, OH (city) Franklin County	17,368
Toledo, OH (city) Lucas County	17,241
Lorain, OH (city) Lorain County	14,189
Cincinnati, OH (city) Hamilton County	4,089
Youngstown, OH (city) Mahoning County	4,088
Akron, OH (city) Summit County	2,367
Painesville, OH (city) Lake County	2,312
Defiance, OH (city) Defiance County	2,126
Dayton, OH (city) Montgomery County	2,079

Hispanic
Top 10 Places Sorted by Percent of Total Population

Place	Percent
Lorain, OH (city) Lorain County	20.67
Painesville, OH (city) Lake County	13.22
Defiance, OH (city) Defiance County	13.04
Fremont, OH (city) Sandusky County	11.73
Fostoria, OH (city) Seneca County	7.97
Cleveland, OH (city) Cuyahoga County	7.22
Ashtabula, OH (city) Ashtabula County	5.98
Toledo, OH (city) Lucas County	5.50
Youngstown, OH (city) Mahoning County	4.98
Oregon, OH (city) Lucas County	4.49

Argentinian
Top 10 Places Sorted by Number

Place	Number
No places met population threshold.	

Argentinian
Top 10 Places Sorted by Percent of Hispanic Population

Place	Percent
No places met population threshold.	

Argentinian
Top 10 Places Sorted by Percent of Total Population

Place	Percent
No places met population threshold.	

Bolivian
Top 10 Places Sorted by Number

Place	Number
No places met population threshold.	

Bolivian
Top 10 Places Sorted by Percent of Hispanic Population

Place	Percent
No places met population threshold.	

Bolivian
Top 10 Places Sorted by Percent of Total Population

Place	Percent
No places met population threshold.	

Central American
Top 10 Places Sorted by Number

Place	Number
Cleveland, OH (city) Cuyahoga County	1,677
Columbus, OH (city) Franklin County	784
Cincinnati, OH (city) Hamilton County	503

Central American
Top 10 Places Sorted by Percent of Hispanic Population

Place	Percent
Cincinnati, OH (city) Hamilton County	12.30
Cleveland, OH (city) Cuyahoga County	4.85
Columbus, OH (city) Franklin County	4.51

Central American
Top 10 Places Sorted by Percent of Total Population

Place	Percent
Cleveland, OH (city) Cuyahoga County	0.35
Cincinnati, OH (city) Hamilton County	0.15
Columbus, OH (city) Franklin County	0.11

Chilean
Top 10 Places Sorted by Number

Place	Number
No places met population threshold.	

Chilean
Top 10 Places Sorted by Percent of Hispanic Population

Place	Percent
No places met population threshold.	

Chilean
Top 10 Places Sorted by Percent of Total Population

Place	Percent
No places met population threshold.	

Colombian
Top 10 Places Sorted by Number

Place	Number
No places met population threshold.	

Colombian
Top 10 Places Sorted by Percent of Hispanic Population

Place	Percent
No places met population threshold.	

Colombian
Top 10 Places Sorted by Percent of Total Population

Place	Percent
No places met population threshold.	

Costa Rican
Top 10 Places Sorted by Number

Place	Number
No places met population threshold.	

Costa Rican
Top 10 Places Sorted by Percent of Hispanic Population

Place	Percent
No places met population threshold.	

Costa Rican
Top 10 Places Sorted by Percent of Total Population

Place	Percent
No places met population threshold.	

Cuban
Top 10 Places Sorted by Number

Place	Number
Columbus, OH (city) Franklin County	700
Cleveland, OH (city) Cuyahoga County	436

Cuban
Top 10 Places Sorted by Percent of Hispanic Population

Place	Percent
Columbus, OH (city) Franklin County	4.03
Cleveland, OH (city) Cuyahoga County	1.26

Cuban
Top 10 Places Sorted by Percent of Total Population

Place	Percent
Columbus, OH (city) Franklin County	0.10
Cleveland, OH (city) Cuyahoga County	0.09

Dominican
Top 10 Places Sorted by Number

Place	Number
Cleveland, OH (city) Cuyahoga County	619

Dominican
Top 10 Places Sorted by Percent of Hispanic Population

Place	Percent
Cleveland, OH (city) Cuyahoga County	1.79

Dominican
Top 10 Places Sorted by Percent of Total Population

Place	Percent
Cleveland, OH (city) Cuyahoga County	0.13

Ecuadorian
Top 10 Places Sorted by Number

Place	Number
No places met population threshold.	

Ecuadorian
Top 10 Places Sorted by Percent of Hispanic Population

Place	Percent
No places met population threshold.	

Ecuadorian
Top 10 Places Sorted by Percent of Total Population

Place	Percent
No places met population threshold.	

Guatelmalan
Top 10 Places Sorted by Number

Place	Number
Cleveland, OH (city) Cuyahoga County	452

Guatelmalan
Top 10 Places Sorted by Percent of Hispanic Population

Place	Percent
Cleveland, OH (city) Cuyahoga County	1.31

Notes: Please refer to the User's Guide for an explanation of data; tables include places with populations > 9,999 and reflect only those areas that meet Summary File 4 population thresholds, therefore there may be less than 10 places listed

PROFILES OF OHIO / Hispanic Rankings: Population

Guatemalan
Top 10 Places Sorted by Percent of Total Population

Place	Percent
Cleveland, OH (city) Cuyahoga County	0.09

Honduran
Top 10 Places Sorted by Number

Place	Number
No places met population threshold.	

Honduran
Top 10 Places Sorted by Percent of Hispanic Population

Place	Percent
No places met population threshold.	

Honduran
Top 10 Places Sorted by Percent of Total Population

Place	Percent
No places met population threshold.	

Mexican
Top 10 Places Sorted by Number

Place	Number
Toledo, OH (city) Lucas County	12,901
Columbus, OH (city) Franklin County	8,496
Cleveland, OH (city) Cuyahoga County	3,351
Lorain, OH (city) Lorain County	2,327
Painesville, OH (city) Lake County	1,863
Cincinnati, OH (city) Hamilton County	1,554
Fremont, OH (city) Sandusky County	1,376
Defiance, OH (city) Defiance County	1,307
Findlay, OH (city) Hancock County	1,137
Dayton, OH (city) Montgomery County	984

Mexican
Top 10 Places Sorted by Percent of Hispanic Population

Place	Percent
Fostoria, OH (city) Seneca County	83.32
Painesville, OH (city) Lake County	80.58
Norwalk, OH (city) Huron County	75.88
Toledo, OH (city) Lucas County	74.83
Findlay, OH (city) Hancock County	74.56
Oregon, OH (city) Lucas County	72.53
Sandusky, OH (city) Erie County	72.25
Bowling Green, OH (city) Wood County	69.95
Fremont, OH (city) Sandusky County	67.62
Hamilton, OH (city) Butler County	65.29

Mexican
Top 10 Places Sorted by Percent of Total Population

Place	Percent
Painesville, OH (city) Lake County	10.65
Defiance, OH (city) Defiance County	8.02
Fremont, OH (city) Sandusky County	7.93
Fostoria, OH (city) Seneca County	6.64
Toledo, OH (city) Lucas County	4.11
Lorain, OH (city) Lorain County	3.39
Oregon, OH (city) Lucas County	3.26
Norwalk, OH (city) Huron County	3.17
Findlay, OH (city) Hancock County	2.90
Bowling Green, OH (city) Wood County	2.28

Nicaraguan
Top 10 Places Sorted by Number

Place	Number
No places met population threshold.	

Nicaraguan
Top 10 Places Sorted by Percent of Hispanic Population

Place	Percent
No places met population threshold.	

Nicaraguan
Top 10 Places Sorted by Percent of Total Population

Place	Percent
No places met population threshold.	

Panamanian
Top 10 Places Sorted by Number

Place	Number
No places met population threshold.	

Panamanian
Top 10 Places Sorted by Percent of Hispanic Population

Place	Percent
No places met population threshold.	

Panamanian
Top 10 Places Sorted by Percent of Total Population

Place	Percent
No places met population threshold.	

Paraguayan
Top 10 Places Sorted by Number

Place	Number
No places met population threshold.	

Paraguayan
Top 10 Places Sorted by Percent of Hispanic Population

Place	Percent
No places met population threshold.	

Paraguayan
Top 10 Places Sorted by Percent of Total Population

Place	Percent
No places met population threshold.	

Peruvian
Top 10 Places Sorted by Number

Place	Number
No places met population threshold.	

Peruvian
Top 10 Places Sorted by Percent of Hispanic Population

Place	Percent
No places met population threshold.	

Peruvian
Top 10 Places Sorted by Percent of Total Population

Place	Percent
No places met population threshold.	

Puerto Rican
Top 10 Places Sorted by Number

Place	Number
Cleveland, OH (city) Cuyahoga County	24,293
Lorain, OH (city) Lorain County	10,050
Columbus, OH (city) Franklin County	3,069
Youngstown, OH (city) Mahoning County	2,976
Toledo, OH (city) Lucas County	1,043
Elyria, OH (city) Lorain County	689
Ashtabula, OH (city) Ashtabula County	637
Akron, OH (city) Summit County	614
Boardman, OH (cdp) Mahoning County	584
Cincinnati, OH (city) Hamilton County	566

Puerto Rican
Top 10 Places Sorted by Percent of Hispanic Population

Place	Percent
Youngstown, OH (city) Mahoning County	72.80
Lorain, OH (city) Lorain County	70.83
Cleveland, OH (city) Cuyahoga County	70.30
Boardman, OH (cdp) Mahoning County	66.59
Ashtabula, OH (city) Ashtabula County	51.04
Elyria, OH (city) Lorain County	49.36
Lakewood, OH (city) Cuyahoga County	44.71
Parma, OH (city) Cuyahoga County	43.53
Akron, OH (city) Summit County	25.94
Columbus, OH (city) Franklin County	17.67

Puerto Rican
Top 10 Places Sorted by Percent of Total Population

Place	Percent
Lorain, OH (city) Lorain County	14.64
Cleveland, OH (city) Cuyahoga County	5.08
Youngstown, OH (city) Mahoning County	3.63
Ashtabula, OH (city) Ashtabula County	3.05
Boardman, OH (cdp) Mahoning County	1.57
Elyria, OH (city) Lorain County	1.23
Lakewood, OH (city) Cuyahoga County	0.99
Parma, OH (city) Cuyahoga County	0.64
Columbus, OH (city) Franklin County	0.43
Toledo, OH (city) Lucas County	0.33

Salvadoran
Top 10 Places Sorted by Number

Place	Number
Cleveland, OH (city) Cuyahoga County	454
Columbus, OH (city) Franklin County	404

Salvadoran
Top 10 Places Sorted by Percent of Hispanic Population

Place	Percent
Columbus, OH (city) Franklin County	2.33
Cleveland, OH (city) Cuyahoga County	1.31

Salvadoran
Top 10 Places Sorted by Percent of Total Population

Place	Percent
Cleveland, OH (city) Cuyahoga County	0.09
Columbus, OH (city) Franklin County	0.06

South American
Top 10 Places Sorted by Number

Place	Number
Columbus, OH (city) Franklin County	1,020
Cleveland, OH (city) Cuyahoga County	553
Cincinnati, OH (city) Hamilton County	473

South American
Top 10 Places Sorted by Percent of Hispanic Population

Place	Percent
Cincinnati, OH (city) Hamilton County	11.57
Columbus, OH (city) Franklin County	5.87
Cleveland, OH (city) Cuyahoga County	1.60

South American
Top 10 Places Sorted by Percent of Total Population

Place	Percent
Cincinnati, OH (city) Hamilton County	0.14
Columbus, OH (city) Franklin County	0.14
Cleveland, OH (city) Cuyahoga County	0.12

Notes: Please refer to the User's Guide for an explanation of data; tables include places with populations > 9,999 and reflect only those areas that meet Summary File 4 population thresholds, therefore there may be less than 10 places listed

PROFILES OF OHIO / Hispanic Rankings: Median Age

Spaniard
Top 10 Places Sorted by Number

Place	Number
No places met population threshold.	

Spaniard
Top 10 Places Sorted by Percent of Hispanic Population

Place	Percent
No places met population threshold.	

Spaniard
Top 10 Places Sorted by Percent of Total Population

Place	Percent
No places met population threshold.	

Uruguayan
Top 10 Places Sorted by Number

Place	Number
No places met population threshold.	

Uruguayan
Top 10 Places Sorted by Percent of Hispanic Population

Place	Percent
No places met population threshold.	

Uruguayan
Top 10 Places Sorted by Percent of Total Population

Place	Percent
No places met population threshold.	

Venezuelan
Top 10 Places Sorted by Number

Place	Number
No places met population threshold.	

Venezuelan
Top 10 Places Sorted by Percent of Hispanic Population

Place	Percent
No places met population threshold.	

Venezuelan
Top 10 Places Sorted by Percent of Total Population

Place	Percent
No places met population threshold.	

Other Hispanic
Top 10 Places Sorted by Number

Place	Number
Cleveland, OH (city) Cuyahoga County	3,529
Columbus, OH (city) Franklin County	2,953
Toledo, OH (city) Lucas County	2,688
Lorain, OH (city) Lorain County	1,399
Cincinnati, OH (city) Hamilton County	712
Fremont, OH (city) Sandusky County	554
Defiance, OH (city) Defiance County	526
Akron, OH (city) Summit County	493
Youngstown, OH (city) Mahoning County	470
Dayton, OH (city) Montgomery County	445

Other Hispanic
Top 10 Places Sorted by Percent of Hispanic Population

Place	Percent
Fremont, OH (city) Sandusky County	27.22
Defiance, OH (city) Defiance County	24.74
Dayton, OH (city) Montgomery County	21.40
Akron, OH (city) Summit County	20.83
Cincinnati, OH (city) Hamilton County	17.41
Columbus, OH (city) Franklin County	17.00

Place	
Toledo, OH (city) Lucas County	15.59
Youngstown, OH (city) Mahoning County	11.50
Cleveland, OH (city) Cuyahoga County	10.21
Lorain, OH (city) Lorain County	9.86

Other Hispanic
Top 10 Places Sorted by Percent of Total Population

Place	Percent
Defiance, OH (city) Defiance County	3.23
Fremont, OH (city) Sandusky County	3.19
Lorain, OH (city) Lorain County	2.04
Toledo, OH (city) Lucas County	0.86
Cleveland, OH (city) Cuyahoga County	0.74
Youngstown, OH (city) Mahoning County	0.57
Columbus, OH (city) Franklin County	0.41
Dayton, OH (city) Montgomery County	0.27
Akron, OH (city) Summit County	0.23
Cincinnati, OH (city) Hamilton County	0.22

Median Age

Total Population
Top 10 Places Sorted by Number

Place	Years
Upper Arlington, OH (city) Franklin County	42.5
Parma Heights, OH (city) Cuyahoga County	42.1
Brooklyn, OH (city) Cuyahoga County	42.0
Westlake, OH (city) Cuyahoga County	41.9
Boardman, OH (cdp) Mahoning County	41.8
Beavercreek, OH (city) Greene County	40.6
Austintown, OH (cdp) Mahoning County	40.1
North Olmsted, OH (city) Cuyahoga County	39.8
Brook Park, OH (city) Cuyahoga County	39.6
Oregon, OH (city) Lucas County	39.5

Hispanic
Top 10 Places Sorted by Number

Place	Years
Parma Heights, OH (city) Cuyahoga County	38.9
Boardman, OH (cdp) Mahoning County	33.0
Riverside, OH (city) Montgomery County	32.0
Austintown, OH (cdp) Mahoning County	31.5
Kettering, OH (city) Montgomery County	31.0
Perrysburg, OH (city) Wood County	30.8
Brooklyn, OH (city) Cuyahoga County	30.2
Cleveland Heights, OH (city) Cuyahoga County	29.8
Parma, OH (city) Cuyahoga County	29.2
Upper Arlington, OH (city) Franklin County	29.2

Argentinian
Top 10 Places Sorted by Number

Place	Years
No places met population threshold.	

Bolivian
Top 10 Places Sorted by Number

Place	Years
No places met population threshold.	

Central American
Top 10 Places Sorted by Number

Place	Years
Columbus, OH (city) Franklin County	26.7
Cleveland, OH (city) Cuyahoga County	26.4
Cincinnati, OH (city) Hamilton County	25.0

Chilean
Top 10 Places Sorted by Number

Place	Years
No places met population threshold.	

Colombian
Top 10 Places Sorted by Number

Place	Years
No places met population threshold.	

Costa Rican
Top 10 Places Sorted by Number

Place	Years
No places met population threshold.	

Cuban
Top 10 Places Sorted by Number

Place	Years
Cleveland, OH (city) Cuyahoga County	31.3
Columbus, OH (city) Franklin County	27.1

Dominican
Top 10 Places Sorted by Number

Place	Years
Cleveland, OH (city) Cuyahoga County	26.8

Ecuadorian
Top 10 Places Sorted by Number

Place	Years
No places met population threshold.	

Guatemalan
Top 10 Places Sorted by Number

Place	Years
Cleveland, OH (city) Cuyahoga County	26.5

Honduran
Top 10 Places Sorted by Number

Place	Years
No places met population threshold.	

Mexican
Top 10 Places Sorted by Number

Place	Years
Youngstown, OH (city) Mahoning County	30.8
Lorain, OH (city) Lorain County	27.2
Cleveland, OH (city) Cuyahoga County	27.0
Oregon, OH (city) Lucas County	26.5
Sandusky, OH (city) Erie County	25.8
Lakewood, OH (city) Cuyahoga County	25.7
Defiance, OH (city) Defiance County	25.4
Lima, OH (city) Allen County	25.1
Dayton, OH (city) Montgomery County	24.9
Hamilton, OH (city) Butler County	24.6

Nicaraguan
Top 10 Places Sorted by Number

Place	Years
No places met population threshold.	

Panamanian
Top 10 Places Sorted by Number

Place	Years
No places met population threshold.	

Paraguayan
Top 10 Places Sorted by Number

Place	Years
No places met population threshold.	

Notes: Please refer to the User's Guide for an explanation of data; tables include places with populations > 9,999 and reflect only those areas that meet Summary File 4 population thresholds, therefore there may be less than 10 places listed

PROFILES OF OHIO / Hispanic Rankings: Average Household Size

Peruvian
Top 10 Places Sorted by Number

Place	Years
No places met population threshold.	

Puerto Rican
Top 10 Places Sorted by Number

Place	Years
Boardman, OH (cdp) Mahoning County	31.9
Parma, OH (city) Cuyahoga County	27.5
Lorain, OH (city) Lorain County	24.8
Cincinnati, OH (city) Hamilton County	24.4
Lakewood, OH (city) Cuyahoga County	24.2
Youngstown, OH (city) Mahoning County	24.2
Cleveland, OH (city) Cuyahoga County	24.1
Columbus, OH (city) Franklin County	23.7
Akron, OH (city) Summit County	22.3
Ashtabula, OH (city) Ashtabula County	22.1

Salvadoran
Top 10 Places Sorted by Number

Place	Years
Columbus, OH (city) Franklin County	25.0
Cleveland, OH (city) Cuyahoga County	23.8

South American
Top 10 Places Sorted by Number

Place	Years
Cincinnati, OH (city) Hamilton County	30.8
Cleveland, OH (city) Cuyahoga County	30.7
Columbus, OH (city) Franklin County	30.2

Spaniard
Top 10 Places Sorted by Number

Place	Years
No places met population threshold.	

Uruguayan
Top 10 Places Sorted by Number

Place	Years
No places met population threshold.	

Venezuelan
Top 10 Places Sorted by Number

Place	Years
No places met population threshold.	

Other Hispanic
Top 10 Places Sorted by Number

Place	Years
Akron, OH (city) Summit County	33.5
Cincinnati, OH (city) Hamilton County	30.1
Dayton, OH (city) Montgomery County	28.8
Columbus, OH (city) Franklin County	25.2
Defiance, OH (city) Defiance County	22.8
Youngstown, OH (city) Mahoning County	21.8
Toledo, OH (city) Lucas County	21.3
Fremont, OH (city) Sandusky County	20.5
Cleveland, OH (city) Cuyahoga County	18.6
Lorain, OH (city) Lorain County	15.4

Average Household Size

Total Population
Top 10 Places Sorted by Number

Place	Number
Brunswick, OH (city) Medina County	2.79
Strongsville, OH (city) Cuyahoga County	2.69
Westerville, OH (city) Franklin County	2.67
Beavercreek, OH (city) Greene County	2.66
Huber Heights, OH (city) Montgomery County	2.64
Perrysburg, OH (city) Wood County	2.61
Brook Park, OH (city) Cuyahoga County	2.58
Lorain, OH (city) Lorain County	2.57
Painesville, OH (city) Lake County	2.55
Xenia, OH (city) Greene County	2.52

Hispanic
Top 10 Places Sorted by Number

Place	Number
Painesville, OH (city) Lake County	4.97
Norwalk, OH (city) Huron County	3.62
Xenia, OH (city) Greene County	3.58
Ashtabula, OH (city) Ashtabula County	3.55
Hamilton, OH (city) Butler County	3.48
Strongsville, OH (city) Cuyahoga County	3.47
Maple Heights, OH (city) Cuyahoga County	3.25
Riverside, OH (city) Montgomery County	3.14
Brook Park, OH (city) Cuyahoga County	3.12
Lorain, OH (city) Lorain County	3.12

Argentinian
Top 10 Places Sorted by Number

Place	Number
No places met population threshold.	

Bolivian
Top 10 Places Sorted by Number

Place	Number
No places met population threshold.	

Central American
Top 10 Places Sorted by Number

Place	Number
Cincinnati, OH (city) Hamilton County	3.81
Cleveland, OH (city) Cuyahoga County	3.79
Columbus, OH (city) Franklin County	2.87

Chilean
Top 10 Places Sorted by Number

Place	Number
No places met population threshold.	

Colombian
Top 10 Places Sorted by Number

Place	Number
No places met population threshold.	

Costa Rican
Top 10 Places Sorted by Number

Place	Number
No places met population threshold.	

Cuban
Top 10 Places Sorted by Number

Place	Number
Columbus, OH (city) Franklin County	3.25
Cleveland, OH (city) Cuyahoga County	2.04

Dominican
Top 10 Places Sorted by Number

Place	Number
Cleveland, OH (city) Cuyahoga County	2.99

Ecuadorian
Top 10 Places Sorted by Number

Place	Number
No places met population threshold.	

Guatemalan
Top 10 Places Sorted by Number

Place	Number
Cleveland, OH (city) Cuyahoga County	3.71

Honduran
Top 10 Places Sorted by Number

Place	Number
No places met population threshold.	

Mexican
Top 10 Places Sorted by Number

Place	Number
Painesville, OH (city) Lake County	5.51
Ashtabula, OH (city) Ashtabula County	4.80
Hamilton, OH (city) Butler County	4.39
Dayton, OH (city) Montgomery County	3.87
Norwalk, OH (city) Huron County	3.70
Canton, OH (city) Stark County	3.22
Columbus, OH (city) Franklin County	3.18
Oregon, OH (city) Lucas County	3.17
Lorain, OH (city) Lorain County	3.14
Lakewood, OH (city) Cuyahoga County	3.02

Nicaraguan
Top 10 Places Sorted by Number

Place	Number
No places met population threshold.	

Panamanian
Top 10 Places Sorted by Number

Place	Number
No places met population threshold.	

Paraguayan
Top 10 Places Sorted by Number

Place	Number
No places met population threshold.	

Peruvian
Top 10 Places Sorted by Number

Place	Number
No places met population threshold.	

Puerto Rican
Top 10 Places Sorted by Number

Place	Number
Toledo, OH (city) Lucas County	3.79
Lorain, OH (city) Lorain County	3.11
Cleveland, OH (city) Cuyahoga County	3.10
Ashtabula, OH (city) Ashtabula County	3.08
Boardman, OH (cdp) Mahoning County	2.93
Youngstown, OH (city) Mahoning County	2.88
Akron, OH (city) Summit County	2.63
Columbus, OH (city) Franklin County	2.59
Lakewood, OH (city) Cuyahoga County	2.43
Parma, OH (city) Cuyahoga County	2.36

Salvadoran
Top 10 Places Sorted by Number

Place	Number
Cleveland, OH (city) Cuyahoga County	4.11
Columbus, OH (city) Franklin County	3.54

Notes: Please refer to the User's Guide for an explanation of data; tables include places with populations > 9,999 and reflect only those areas that meet Summary File 4 population thresholds, therefore there may be less than 10 places listed

PROFILES OF OHIO / Hispanic Rankings: Language Spoken at Home: English Only 471

South American
Top 10 Places Sorted by Number

Place	Number
Cleveland, OH (city) Cuyahoga County	3.05
Columbus, OH (city) Franklin County	2.41
Cincinnati, OH (city) Hamilton County	2.15

Spaniard
Top 10 Places Sorted by Number

Place	Number
No places met population threshold.	

Uruguayan
Top 10 Places Sorted by Number

Place	Number
No places met population threshold.	

Venezuelan
Top 10 Places Sorted by Number

Place	Number
No places met population threshold.	

Other Hispanic
Top 10 Places Sorted by Number

Place	Number
Youngstown, OH (city) Mahoning County	3.60
Cleveland, OH (city) Cuyahoga County	3.20
Fremont, OH (city) Sandusky County	3.17
Defiance, OH (city) Defiance County	3.12
Lorain, OH (city) Lorain County	3.05
Toledo, OH (city) Lucas County	3.00
Akron, OH (city) Summit County	2.71
Columbus, OH (city) Franklin County	2.55
Dayton, OH (city) Montgomery County	2.34
Cincinnati, OH (city) Hamilton County	1.65

Language Spoken at Home: English Only

Total Population 5 Years and Over Who Speak English-Only at Home
Top 10 Places Sorted by Number

Place	Number
Columbus, OH (city) Franklin County	593,275
Cleveland, OH (city) Cuyahoga County	387,438
Cincinnati, OH (city) Hamilton County	286,454
Toledo, OH (city) Lucas County	269,728
Akron, OH (city) Summit County	189,917
Dayton, OH (city) Montgomery County	147,790
Canton, OH (city) Stark County	71,291
Parma, OH (city) Cuyahoga County	69,839
Youngstown, OH (city) Mahoning County	69,647
Springfield, OH (city) Clark County	58,165

Total Population 5 Years and Over Who Speak English-Only at Home
Top 10 Places Sorted by Percent

Place	Percent
Middletown, OH (city) Butler County	96.74
Springfield, OH (city) Clark County	96.52
Tiffin, OH (city) Seneca County	96.46
Marion, OH (city) Marion County	96.22
Elyria, OH (city) Lorain County	96.15
Lima, OH (city) Allen County	96.12
Xenia, OH (city) Greene County	95.99
Sandusky, OH (city) Erie County	95.77
Dayton, OH (city) Montgomery County	95.64
Norwood, OH (city) Hamilton County	95.39

Hispanics 5 Years and Over Who Speak English-Only at Home
Top 10 Places Sorted by Number

Place	Number
Toledo, OH (city) Lucas County	8,574
Cleveland, OH (city) Cuyahoga County	7,066
Columbus, OH (city) Franklin County	5,079
Lorain, OH (city) Lorain County	4,246
Cincinnati, OH (city) Hamilton County	1,493
Youngstown, OH (city) Mahoning County	1,155
Akron, OH (city) Summit County	1,149
Dayton, OH (city) Montgomery County	754
Findlay, OH (city) Hancock County	750
Elyria, OH (city) Lorain County	725

Hispanics 5 Years and Over Who Speak English-Only at Home
Top 10 Places Sorted by Percent

Place	Percent
Oregon, OH (city) Lucas County	67.78
Warren, OH (city) Trumbull County	66.30
Elyria, OH (city) Lorain County	65.08
Springfield, OH (city) Clark County	64.37
Austintown, OH (cdp) Mahoning County	63.12
Fostoria, OH (city) Seneca County	59.96
Riverside, OH (city) Montgomery County	59.10
Tiffin, OH (city) Seneca County	58.92
Findlay, OH (city) Hancock County	57.96
Mansfield, OH (city) Richland County	57.80

Argentinians 5 Years and Over Who Speak English-Only at Home
Top 10 Places Sorted by Number

Place	Number
No places met population threshold.	

Argentinians 5 Years and Over Who Speak English-Only at Home
Top 10 Places Sorted by Percent

Place	Percent
No places met population threshold.	

Bolivians 5 Years and Over Who Speak English-Only at Home
Top 10 Places Sorted by Number

Place	Number
No places met population threshold.	

Bolivians 5 Years and Over Who Speak English-Only at Home
Top 10 Places Sorted by Percent

Place	Percent
No places met population threshold.	

Central Americans 5 Years and Over Who Speak English-Only at Home
Top 10 Places Sorted by Number

Place	Number
Cleveland, OH (city) Cuyahoga County	157
Columbus, OH (city) Franklin County	114
Cincinnati, OH (city) Hamilton County	30

Central Americans 5 Years and Over Who Speak English-Only at Home
Top 10 Places Sorted by Percent

Place	Percent
Columbus, OH (city) Franklin County	15.51
Cleveland, OH (city) Cuyahoga County	10.20
Cincinnati, OH (city) Hamilton County	6.22

Chileans 5 Years and Over Who Speak English-Only at Home
Top 10 Places Sorted by Number

Place	Number
No places met population threshold.	

Chileans 5 Years and Over Who Speak English-Only at Home
Top 10 Places Sorted by Percent

Place	Percent
No places met population threshold.	

Colombians 5 Years and Over Who Speak English-Only at Home
Top 10 Places Sorted by Number

Place	Number
No places met population threshold.	

Colombians 5 Years and Over Who Speak English-Only at Home
Top 10 Places Sorted by Percent

Place	Percent
No places met population threshold.	

Costa Ricans 5 Years and Over Who Speak English-Only at Home
Top 10 Places Sorted by Number

Place	Number
No places met population threshold.	

Costa Ricans 5 Years and Over Who Speak English-Only at Home
Top 10 Places Sorted by Percent

Place	Percent
No places met population threshold.	

Cubans 5 Years and Over Who Speak English-Only at Home
Top 10 Places Sorted by Number

Place	Number
Columbus, OH (city) Franklin County	274
Cleveland, OH (city) Cuyahoga County	102

Cubans 5 Years and Over Who Speak English-Only at Home
Top 10 Places Sorted by Percent

Place	Percent
Columbus, OH (city) Franklin County	42.35
Cleveland, OH (city) Cuyahoga County	26.36

Dominicans 5 Years and Over Who Speak English-Only at Home
Top 10 Places Sorted by Number

Place	Number
Cleveland, OH (city) Cuyahoga County	29

Dominicans 5 Years and Over Who Speak English-Only at Home
Top 10 Places Sorted by Percent

Place	Percent
Cleveland, OH (city) Cuyahoga County	5.00

Ecuadorians 5 Years and Over Who Speak English-Only at Home
Top 10 Places Sorted by Number

Place	Number
No places met population threshold.	

Notes: Please refer to the User's Guide for an explanation of data; tables include places with populations > 9,999 and reflect only those areas that meet Summary File 4 population thresholds, therefore there may be less than 10 places listed

PROFILES OF OHIO / Hispanic Rankings: Language Spoken at Home: English Only

Ecuadorians 5 Years and Over Who Speak English-Only at Home
Top 10 Places Sorted by Percent

Place	Percent
No places met population threshold.	

Guatemalans 5 Years and Over Who Speak English-Only at Home
Top 10 Places Sorted by Number

Place	Number
Cleveland, OH (city) Cuyahoga County	35

Guatemalans 5 Years and Over Who Speak English-Only at Home
Top 10 Places Sorted by Percent

Place	Percent
Cleveland, OH (city) Cuyahoga County	8.41

Hondurans 5 Years and Over Who Speak English-Only at Home
Top 10 Places Sorted by Number

Place	Number
No places met population threshold.	

Hondurans 5 Years and Over Who Speak English-Only at Home
Top 10 Places Sorted by Percent

Place	Percent
No places met population threshold.	

Mexicans 5 Years and Over Who Speak English-Only at Home
Top 10 Places Sorted by Number

Place	Number
Toledo, OH (city) Lucas County	6,533
Columbus, OH (city) Franklin County	1,993
Cleveland, OH (city) Cuyahoga County	1,569
Lorain, OH (city) Lorain County	1,048
Cincinnati, OH (city) Hamilton County	676
Findlay, OH (city) Hancock County	600
Defiance, OH (city) Defiance County	493
Fremont, OH (city) Sandusky County	469
Fostoria, OH (city) Seneca County	465
Akron, OH (city) Summit County	448

Mexicans 5 Years and Over Who Speak English-Only at Home
Top 10 Places Sorted by Percent

Place	Percent
Elyria, OH (city) Lorain County	82.39
Oregon, OH (city) Lucas County	73.27
Findlay, OH (city) Hancock County	61.29
Fostoria, OH (city) Seneca County	58.94
Toledo, OH (city) Lucas County	58.13
Akron, OH (city) Summit County	55.72
Springfield, OH (city) Clark County	55.19
Cleveland, OH (city) Cuyahoga County	53.11
Lima, OH (city) Allen County	52.23
Cincinnati, OH (city) Hamilton County	51.64

Nicaraguans 5 Years and Over Who Speak English-Only at Home
Top 10 Places Sorted by Number

Place	Number
No places met population threshold.	

Nicaraguans 5 Years and Over Who Speak English-Only at Home
Top 10 Places Sorted by Percent

Place	Percent
No places met population threshold.	

Panamanians 5 Years and Over Who Speak English-Only at Home
Top 10 Places Sorted by Number

Place	Number
No places met population threshold.	

Panamanians 5 Years and Over Who Speak English-Only at Home
Top 10 Places Sorted by Percent

Place	Percent
No places met population threshold.	

Paraguayans 5 Years and Over Who Speak English-Only at Home
Top 10 Places Sorted by Number

Place	Number
No places met population threshold.	

Paraguayans 5 Years and Over Who Speak English-Only at Home
Top 10 Places Sorted by Percent

Place	Percent
No places met population threshold.	

Peruvians 5 Years and Over Who Speak English-Only at Home
Top 10 Places Sorted by Number

Place	Number
No places met population threshold.	

Peruvians 5 Years and Over Who Speak English-Only at Home
Top 10 Places Sorted by Percent

Place	Percent
No places met population threshold.	

Puerto Ricans 5 Years and Over Who Speak English-Only at Home
Top 10 Places Sorted by Number

Place	Number
Cleveland, OH (city) Cuyahoga County	4,055
Lorain, OH (city) Lorain County	2,498
Columbus, OH (city) Franklin County	1,171
Youngstown, OH (city) Mahoning County	661
Toledo, OH (city) Lucas County	429
Elyria, OH (city) Lorain County	328
Lakewood, OH (city) Cuyahoga County	296
Akron, OH (city) Summit County	257
Boardman, OH (cdp) Mahoning County	205
Cincinnati, OH (city) Hamilton County	171

Puerto Ricans 5 Years and Over Who Speak English-Only at Home
Top 10 Places Sorted by Percent

Place	Percent
Lakewood, OH (city) Cuyahoga County	64.21
Elyria, OH (city) Lorain County	57.64
Akron, OH (city) Summit County	48.95
Toledo, OH (city) Lucas County	45.54
Columbus, OH (city) Franklin County	42.17
Boardman, OH (cdp) Mahoning County	38.75
Cincinnati, OH (city) Hamilton County	35.19
Parma, OH (city) Cuyahoga County	31.72
Lorain, OH (city) Lorain County	27.81
Ashtabula, OH (city) Ashtabula County	25.73

Salvadorans 5 Years and Over Who Speak English-Only at Home
Top 10 Places Sorted by Number

Place	Number
Columbus, OH (city) Franklin County	32
Cleveland, OH (city) Cuyahoga County	10

Salvadorans 5 Years and Over Who Speak English-Only at Home
Top 10 Places Sorted by Percent

Place	Percent
Columbus, OH (city) Franklin County	9.01
Cleveland, OH (city) Cuyahoga County	2.45

South Americans 5 Years and Over Who Speak English-Only at Home
Top 10 Places Sorted by Number

Place	Number
Columbus, OH (city) Franklin County	215
Cincinnati, OH (city) Hamilton County	99
Cleveland, OH (city) Cuyahoga County	61

South Americans 5 Years and Over Who Speak English-Only at Home
Top 10 Places Sorted by Percent

Place	Percent
Cincinnati, OH (city) Hamilton County	23.08
Columbus, OH (city) Franklin County	22.44
Cleveland, OH (city) Cuyahoga County	12.25

Spaniards 5 Years and Over Who Speak English-Only at Home
Top 10 Places Sorted by Number

Place	Number
No places met population threshold.	

Spaniards 5 Years and Over Who Speak English-Only at Home
Top 10 Places Sorted by Percent

Place	Percent
No places met population threshold.	

Uruguayans 5 Years and Over Who Speak English-Only at Home
Top 10 Places Sorted by Number

Place	Number
No places met population threshold.	

Uruguayans 5 Years and Over Who Speak English-Only at Home
Top 10 Places Sorted by Percent

Place	Percent
No places met population threshold.	

Venezuelans 5 Years and Over Who Speak English-Only at Home
Top 10 Places Sorted by Number

Place	Number
No places met population threshold.	

Venezuelans 5 Years and Over Who Speak English-Only at Home
Top 10 Places Sorted by Percent

Place	Percent
No places met population threshold.	

Notes: Please refer to the User's Guide for an explanation of data; tables include places with populations > 9,999 and reflect only those areas that meet Summary File 4 population thresholds, therefore there may be less than 10 places listed

PROFILES OF OHIO / Hispanic Rankings: Language Spoken at Home: Spanish

Other Hispanics 5 Years and Over Who Speak English-Only at Home
Top 10 Places Sorted by Number

Place	Number
Toledo, OH (city) Lucas County	1,489
Columbus, OH (city) Franklin County	1,293
Cleveland, OH (city) Cuyahoga County	1,043
Lorain, OH (city) Lorain County	645
Cincinnati, OH (city) Hamilton County	372
Akron, OH (city) Summit County	343
Youngstown, OH (city) Mahoning County	274
Dayton, OH (city) Montgomery County	257
Fremont, OH (city) Sandusky County	136
Defiance, OH (city) Defiance County	100

Other Hispanics 5 Years and Over Who Speak English-Only at Home
Top 10 Places Sorted by Percent

Place	Percent
Akron, OH (city) Summit County	79.77
Toledo, OH (city) Lucas County	63.07
Youngstown, OH (city) Mahoning County	61.99
Dayton, OH (city) Montgomery County	61.93
Lorain, OH (city) Lorain County	56.73
Cincinnati, OH (city) Hamilton County	55.19
Columbus, OH (city) Franklin County	50.10
Cleveland, OH (city) Cuyahoga County	37.20
Fremont, OH (city) Sandusky County	28.69
Defiance, OH (city) Defiance County	21.14

Language Spoken at Home: Spanish

Total Population 5 Years and Over Who Speak Spanish at Home
Top 10 Places Sorted by Number

Place	Number
Cleveland, OH (city) Cuyahoga County	28,564
Columbus, OH (city) Franklin County	19,275
Toledo, OH (city) Lucas County	9,992
Lorain, OH (city) Lorain County	9,113
Cincinnati, OH (city) Hamilton County	6,720
Youngstown, OH (city) Mahoning County	3,546
Akron, OH (city) Summit County	3,122
Dayton, OH (city) Montgomery County	3,062
Painesville, OH (city) Lake County	2,069
Hamilton, OH (city) Butler County	1,701

Total Population 5 Years and Over Who Speak Spanish at Home
Top 10 Places Sorted by Percent

Place	Percent
Lorain, OH (city) Lorain County	14.40
Painesville, OH (city) Lake County	13.05
Defiance, OH (city) Defiance County	9.01
Fremont, OH (city) Sandusky County	8.70
Cleveland, OH (city) Cuyahoga County	6.50
Ashtabula, OH (city) Ashtabula County	5.42
Youngstown, OH (city) Mahoning County	4.65
Bowling Green, OH (city) Wood County	4.24
Whitehall, OH (city) Franklin County	4.23
Fostoria, OH (city) Seneca County	3.62

Hispanics 5 Years and Over Who Speak Spanish at Home
Top 10 Places Sorted by Number

Place	Number
Cleveland, OH (city) Cuyahoga County	23,081
Columbus, OH (city) Franklin County	10,201
Lorain, OH (city) Lorain County	8,318
Toledo, OH (city) Lucas County	6,372
Youngstown, OH (city) Mahoning County	2,486
Cincinnati, OH (city) Hamilton County	2,050
Painesville, OH (city) Lake County	1,826
Defiance, OH (city) Defiance County	1,162
Fremont, OH (city) Sandusky County	1,130
Dayton, OH (city) Montgomery County	1,056

Hispanics 5 Years and Over Who Speak Spanish at Home
Top 10 Places Sorted by Percent

Place	Percent
Painesville, OH (city) Lake County	91.39
Hamilton, OH (city) Butler County	80.15
Whitehall, OH (city) Franklin County	79.80
Ashtabula, OH (city) Ashtabula County	77.65
Cleveland, OH (city) Cuyahoga County	76.11
Youngstown, OH (city) Mahoning County	68.28
Lorain, OH (city) Lorain County	66.14
Columbus, OH (city) Franklin County	65.88
Fremont, OH (city) Sandusky County	64.02
Defiance, OH (city) Defiance County	62.74

Argentinians 5 Years and Over Who Speak Spanish at Home
Top 10 Places Sorted by Number

Place	Number
No places met population threshold.	

Argentinians 5 Years and Over Who Speak Spanish at Home
Top 10 Places Sorted by Percent

Place	Percent
No places met population threshold.	

Bolivians 5 Years and Over Who Speak Spanish at Home
Top 10 Places Sorted by Number

Place	Number
No places met population threshold.	

Bolivians 5 Years and Over Who Speak Spanish at Home
Top 10 Places Sorted by Percent

Place	Percent
No places met population threshold.	

Central Americans 5 Years and Over Who Speak Spanish at Home
Top 10 Places Sorted by Number

Place	Number
Cleveland, OH (city) Cuyahoga County	1,362
Columbus, OH (city) Franklin County	621
Cincinnati, OH (city) Hamilton County	441

Central Americans 5 Years and Over Who Speak Spanish at Home
Top 10 Places Sorted by Percent

Place	Percent
Cincinnati, OH (city) Hamilton County	91.49
Cleveland, OH (city) Cuyahoga County	88.50
Columbus, OH (city) Franklin County	84.49

Chileans 5 Years and Over Who Speak Spanish at Home
Top 10 Places Sorted by Number

Place	Number
No places met population threshold.	

Chileans 5 Years and Over Who Speak Spanish at Home
Top 10 Places Sorted by Percent

Place	Percent
No places met population threshold.	

Colombians 5 Years and Over Who Speak Spanish at Home
Top 10 Places Sorted by Number

Place	Number
No places met population threshold.	

Colombians 5 Years and Over Who Speak Spanish at Home
Top 10 Places Sorted by Percent

Place	Percent
No places met population threshold.	

Costa Ricans 5 Years and Over Who Speak Spanish at Home
Top 10 Places Sorted by Number

Place	Number
No places met population threshold.	

Costa Ricans 5 Years and Over Who Speak Spanish at Home
Top 10 Places Sorted by Percent

Place	Percent
No places met population threshold.	

Cubans 5 Years and Over Who Speak Spanish at Home
Top 10 Places Sorted by Number

Place	Number
Columbus, OH (city) Franklin County	368
Cleveland, OH (city) Cuyahoga County	285

Cubans 5 Years and Over Who Speak Spanish at Home
Top 10 Places Sorted by Percent

Place	Percent
Cleveland, OH (city) Cuyahoga County	73.64
Columbus, OH (city) Franklin County	56.88

Dominicans 5 Years and Over Who Speak Spanish at Home
Top 10 Places Sorted by Number

Place	Number
Cleveland, OH (city) Cuyahoga County	551

Dominicans 5 Years and Over Who Speak Spanish at Home
Top 10 Places Sorted by Percent

Place	Percent
Cleveland, OH (city) Cuyahoga County	95.00

Ecuadorians 5 Years and Over Who Speak Spanish at Home
Top 10 Places Sorted by Number

Place	Number
No places met population threshold.	

Ecuadorians 5 Years and Over Who Speak Spanish at Home
Top 10 Places Sorted by Percent

Place	Percent
No places met population threshold.	

Notes: Please refer to the User's Guide for an explanation of data; tables include places with populations > 9,999 and reflect only those areas that meet Summary File 4 population thresholds, therefore there may be less than 10 places listed

474 PROFILES OF OHIO / Hispanic Rankings: Language Spoken at Home: Spanish

Guatemalans 5 Years and Over Who Speak Spanish at Home
Top 10 Places Sorted by Number

Place	Number
Cleveland, OH (city) Cuyahoga County	381

Guatemalans 5 Years and Over Who Speak Spanish at Home
Top 10 Places Sorted by Percent

Place	Percent
Cleveland, OH (city) Cuyahoga County	91.59

Hondurans 5 Years and Over Who Speak Spanish at Home
Top 10 Places Sorted by Number

Place	Number
No places met population threshold.	

Hondurans 5 Years and Over Who Speak Spanish at Home
Top 10 Places Sorted by Percent

Place	Percent
No places met population threshold.	

Mexicans 5 Years and Over Who Speak Spanish at Home
Top 10 Places Sorted by Number

Place	Number
Columbus, OH (city) Franklin County	5,430
Toledo, OH (city) Lucas County	4,679
Painesville, OH (city) Lake County	1,533
Cleveland, OH (city) Cuyahoga County	1,368
Lorain, OH (city) Lorain County	1,007
Fremont, OH (city) Sandusky County	734
Hamilton, OH (city) Butler County	672
Defiance, OH (city) Defiance County	618
Cincinnati, OH (city) Hamilton County	594
Dayton, OH (city) Montgomery County	550

Mexicans 5 Years and Over Who Speak Spanish at Home
Top 10 Places Sorted by Percent

Place	Percent
Painesville, OH (city) Lake County	95.16
Ashtabula, OH (city) Ashtabula County	86.13
Hamilton, OH (city) Butler County	84.00
Columbus, OH (city) Franklin County	72.59
Dayton, OH (city) Montgomery County	68.32
Fremont, OH (city) Sandusky County	61.01
Defiance, OH (city) Defiance County	55.63
Youngstown, OH (city) Mahoning County	54.99
Bowling Green, OH (city) Wood County	52.57
Lakewood, OH (city) Cuyahoga County	50.55

Nicaraguans 5 Years and Over Who Speak Spanish at Home
Top 10 Places Sorted by Number

Place	Number
No places met population threshold.	

Nicaraguans 5 Years and Over Who Speak Spanish at Home
Top 10 Places Sorted by Percent

Place	Percent
No places met population threshold.	

Panamanians 5 Years and Over Who Speak Spanish at Home
Top 10 Places Sorted by Number

Place	Number
No places met population threshold.	

Panamanians 5 Years and Over Who Speak Spanish at Home
Top 10 Places Sorted by Percent

Place	Percent
No places met population threshold.	

Paraguayans 5 Years and Over Who Speak Spanish at Home
Top 10 Places Sorted by Number

Place	Number
No places met population threshold.	

Paraguayans 5 Years and Over Who Speak Spanish at Home
Top 10 Places Sorted by Percent

Place	Percent
No places met population threshold.	

Peruvians 5 Years and Over Who Speak Spanish at Home
Top 10 Places Sorted by Number

Place	Number
No places met population threshold.	

Peruvians 5 Years and Over Who Speak Spanish at Home
Top 10 Places Sorted by Percent

Place	Percent
No places met population threshold.	

Puerto Ricans 5 Years and Over Who Speak Spanish at Home
Top 10 Places Sorted by Number

Place	Number
Cleveland, OH (city) Cuyahoga County	17,373
Lorain, OH (city) Lorain County	6,479
Youngstown, OH (city) Mahoning County	1,994
Columbus, OH (city) Franklin County	1,579
Toledo, OH (city) Lucas County	450
Ashtabula, OH (city) Ashtabula County	407
Parma, OH (city) Cuyahoga County	325
Boardman, OH (cdp) Mahoning County	324
Cincinnati, OH (city) Hamilton County	308
Akron, OH (city) Summit County	250

Puerto Ricans 5 Years and Over Who Speak Spanish at Home
Top 10 Places Sorted by Percent

Place	Percent
Cleveland, OH (city) Cuyahoga County	80.85
Youngstown, OH (city) Mahoning County	75.10
Ashtabula, OH (city) Ashtabula County	74.27
Lorain, OH (city) Lorain County	72.13
Parma, OH (city) Cuyahoga County	68.28
Cincinnati, OH (city) Hamilton County	63.37
Boardman, OH (cdp) Mahoning County	61.25
Columbus, OH (city) Franklin County	56.86
Toledo, OH (city) Lucas County	47.77
Akron, OH (city) Summit County	47.62

Salvadorans 5 Years and Over Who Speak Spanish at Home
Top 10 Places Sorted by Number

Place	Number
Cleveland, OH (city) Cuyahoga County	392
Columbus, OH (city) Franklin County	323

Salvadorans 5 Years and Over Who Speak Spanish at Home
Top 10 Places Sorted by Percent

Place	Percent
Cleveland, OH (city) Cuyahoga County	96.08
Columbus, OH (city) Franklin County	90.99

South Americans 5 Years and Over Who Speak Spanish at Home
Top 10 Places Sorted by Number

Place	Number
Columbus, OH (city) Franklin County	734
Cleveland, OH (city) Cuyahoga County	437
Cincinnati, OH (city) Hamilton County	330

South Americans 5 Years and Over Who Speak Spanish at Home
Top 10 Places Sorted by Percent

Place	Percent
Cleveland, OH (city) Cuyahoga County	87.75
Cincinnati, OH (city) Hamilton County	76.92
Columbus, OH (city) Franklin County	76.62

Spaniards 5 Years and Over Who Speak Spanish at Home
Top 10 Places Sorted by Number

Place	Number
No places met population threshold.	

Spaniards 5 Years and Over Who Speak Spanish at Home
Top 10 Places Sorted by Percent

Place	Percent
No places met population threshold.	

Uruguayans 5 Years and Over Who Speak Spanish at Home
Top 10 Places Sorted by Number

Place	Number
No places met population threshold.	

Uruguayans 5 Years and Over Who Speak Spanish at Home
Top 10 Places Sorted by Percent

Place	Percent
No places met population threshold.	

Venezuelans 5 Years and Over Who Speak Spanish at Home
Top 10 Places Sorted by Number

Place	Number
No places met population threshold.	

Venezuelans 5 Years and Over Who Speak Spanish at Home
Top 10 Places Sorted by Percent

Place	Percent
No places met population threshold.	

Notes: Please refer to the User's Guide for an explanation of data; tables include places with populations > 9,999 and reflect only those areas that meet Summary File 4 population thresholds, therefore there may be less than 10 places listed

Other Hispanics 5 Years and Over Who Speak Spanish at Home
Top 10 Places Sorted by Number

Place	Number
Cleveland, OH (city) Cuyahoga County	1,679
Columbus, OH (city) Franklin County	1,182
Toledo, OH (city) Lucas County	847
Lorain, OH (city) Lorain County	492
Defiance, OH (city) Defiance County	373
Fremont, OH (city) Sandusky County	338
Cincinnati, OH (city) Hamilton County	280
Youngstown, OH (city) Mahoning County	168
Dayton, OH (city) Montgomery County	153
Akron, OH (city) Summit County	84

Other Hispanics 5 Years and Over Who Speak Spanish at Home
Top 10 Places Sorted by Percent

Place	Percent
Defiance, OH (city) Defiance County	78.86
Fremont, OH (city) Sandusky County	71.31
Cleveland, OH (city) Cuyahoga County	59.88
Columbus, OH (city) Franklin County	45.80
Lorain, OH (city) Lorain County	43.27
Cincinnati, OH (city) Hamilton County	41.54
Youngstown, OH (city) Mahoning County	38.01
Dayton, OH (city) Montgomery County	36.87
Toledo, OH (city) Lucas County	35.87
Akron, OH (city) Summit County	19.53

Foreign Born

Total Population
Top 10 Places Sorted by Number

Place	Number
Columbus, OH (city) Franklin County	47,713
Cleveland, OH (city) Cuyahoga County	21,372
Cincinnati, OH (city) Hamilton County	12,461
Toledo, OH (city) Lucas County	9,475
Parma, OH (city) Cuyahoga County	7,797
Akron, OH (city) Summit County	6,911
Lakewood, OH (city) Cuyahoga County	4,945
Cleveland Heights, OH (city) Cuyahoga County	4,130
Dayton, OH (city) Montgomery County	3,245
Strongsville, OH (city) Cuyahoga County	2,841

Total Population
Top 10 Places Sorted by Percent

Place	Percent
Parma Heights, OH (city) Cuyahoga County	10.17
Painesville, OH (city) Lake County	10.07
Parma, OH (city) Cuyahoga County	9.10
Brooklyn, OH (city) Cuyahoga County	8.97
Lakewood, OH (city) Cuyahoga County	8.73
Westlake, OH (city) Cuyahoga County	8.39
Cleveland Heights, OH (city) Cuyahoga County	8.26
North Olmsted, OH (city) Cuyahoga County	7.85
Columbus, OH (city) Franklin County	6.70
Strongsville, OH (city) Cuyahoga County	6.48

Hispanic
Top 10 Places Sorted by Number

Place	Number
Columbus, OH (city) Franklin County	6,389
Cleveland, OH (city) Cuyahoga County	3,456
Toledo, OH (city) Lucas County	1,775
Painesville, OH (city) Lake County	1,611
Cincinnati, OH (city) Hamilton County	1,544
Lorain, OH (city) Lorain County	921
Hamilton, OH (city) Butler County	814
Dayton, OH (city) Montgomery County	618
Akron, OH (city) Summit County	469
Ashtabula, OH (city) Ashtabula County	271

Hispanic
Top 10 Places Sorted by Percent

Place	Percent
Painesville, OH (city) Lake County	69.68
Hamilton, OH (city) Butler County	58.02
Upper Arlington, OH (city) Franklin County	43.09
Norwood, OH (city) Hamilton County	41.93
Cincinnati, OH (city) Hamilton County	37.76
Columbus, OH (city) Franklin County	36.79
Middletown, OH (city) Butler County	35.91
Fairfield, OH (city) Butler County	34.69
Whitehall, OH (city) Franklin County	33.19
Dayton, OH (city) Montgomery County	29.73

Argentinian
Top 10 Places Sorted by Number

Place	Number
No places met population threshold.	

Argentinian
Top 10 Places Sorted by Percent

Place	Percent
No places met population threshold.	

Bolivian
Top 10 Places Sorted by Number

Place	Number
No places met population threshold.	

Bolivian
Top 10 Places Sorted by Percent

Place	Percent
No places met population threshold.	

Central American
Top 10 Places Sorted by Number

Place	Number
Cleveland, OH (city) Cuyahoga County	1,257
Columbus, OH (city) Franklin County	564
Cincinnati, OH (city) Hamilton County	466

Central American
Top 10 Places Sorted by Percent

Place	Percent
Cincinnati, OH (city) Hamilton County	92.64
Cleveland, OH (city) Cuyahoga County	74.96
Columbus, OH (city) Franklin County	71.94

Chilean
Top 10 Places Sorted by Number

Place	Number
No places met population threshold.	

Chilean
Top 10 Places Sorted by Percent

Place	Percent
No places met population threshold.	

Colombian
Top 10 Places Sorted by Number

Place	Number
No places met population threshold.	

Colombian
Top 10 Places Sorted by Percent

Place	Percent
No places met population threshold.	

Costa Rican
Top 10 Places Sorted by Number

Place	Number
No places met population threshold.	

Costa Rican
Top 10 Places Sorted by Percent

Place	Percent
No places met population threshold.	

Cuban
Top 10 Places Sorted by Number

Place	Number
Columbus, OH (city) Franklin County	202
Cleveland, OH (city) Cuyahoga County	162

Cuban
Top 10 Places Sorted by Percent

Place	Percent
Cleveland, OH (city) Cuyahoga County	37.16
Columbus, OH (city) Franklin County	28.86

Dominican
Top 10 Places Sorted by Number

Place	Number
Cleveland, OH (city) Cuyahoga County	369

Dominican
Top 10 Places Sorted by Percent

Place	Percent
Cleveland, OH (city) Cuyahoga County	59.61

Ecuadorian
Top 10 Places Sorted by Number

Place	Number
No places met population threshold.	

Ecuadorian
Top 10 Places Sorted by Percent

Place	Percent
No places met population threshold.	

Guatelmalan
Top 10 Places Sorted by Number

Place	Number
Cleveland, OH (city) Cuyahoga County	345

Guatelmalan
Top 10 Places Sorted by Percent

Place	Percent
Cleveland, OH (city) Cuyahoga County	76.33

Honduran
Top 10 Places Sorted by Number

Place	Number
No places met population threshold.	

Honduran
Top 10 Places Sorted by Percent

Place	Percent
No places met population threshold.	

Notes: Please refer to the User's Guide for an explanation of data; tables include places with populations > 9,999 and reflect only those areas that meet Summary File 4 population thresholds, therefore there may be less than 10 places listed

PROFILES OF OHIO / Hispanic Rankings: Foreign-Born Naturalized Citizens

Mexican
Top 10 Places Sorted by Number

Place	Number
Columbus, OH (city) Franklin County	4,100
Painesville, OH (city) Lake County	1,572
Toledo, OH (city) Lucas County	1,205
Hamilton, OH (city) Butler County	669
Cleveland, OH (city) Cuyahoga County	597
Cincinnati, OH (city) Hamilton County	486
Lorain, OH (city) Lorain County	476
Dayton, OH (city) Montgomery County	363
Akron, OH (city) Summit County	233
Ashtabula, OH (city) Ashtabula County	217

Mexican
Top 10 Places Sorted by Percent

Place	Percent
Painesville, OH (city) Lake County	84.38
Hamilton, OH (city) Butler County	73.03
Ashtabula, OH (city) Ashtabula County	51.91
Columbus, OH (city) Franklin County	48.26
Dayton, OH (city) Montgomery County	36.89
Cincinnati, OH (city) Hamilton County	31.27
Norwalk, OH (city) Huron County	30.62
Lakewood, OH (city) Cuyahoga County	26.54
Akron, OH (city) Summit County	26.06
Canton, OH (city) Stark County	24.53

Nicaraguan
Top 10 Places Sorted by Number

Place	Number
No places met population threshold.	

Nicaraguan
Top 10 Places Sorted by Percent

Place	Percent
No places met population threshold.	

Panamanian
Top 10 Places Sorted by Number

Place	Number
No places met population threshold.	

Panamanian
Top 10 Places Sorted by Percent

Place	Percent
No places met population threshold.	

Paraguayan
Top 10 Places Sorted by Number

Place	Number
No places met population threshold.	

Paraguayan
Top 10 Places Sorted by Percent

Place	Percent
No places met population threshold.	

Peruvian
Top 10 Places Sorted by Number

Place	Number
No places met population threshold.	

Peruvian
Top 10 Places Sorted by Percent

Place	Percent
No places met population threshold.	

Puerto Rican
Top 10 Places Sorted by Number

Place	Number
Cleveland, OH (city) Cuyahoga County	136
Columbus, OH (city) Franklin County	36
Toledo, OH (city) Lucas County	25
Lorain, OH (city) Lorain County	21
Cincinnati, OH (city) Hamilton County	16
Akron, OH (city) Summit County	8
Parma, OH (city) Cuyahoga County	8
Ashtabula, OH (city) Ashtabula County	0
Boardman, OH (cdp) Mahoning County	0
Elyria, OH (city) Lorain County	0

Puerto Rican
Top 10 Places Sorted by Percent

Place	Percent
Cincinnati, OH (city) Hamilton County	2.83
Toledo, OH (city) Lucas County	2.40
Parma, OH (city) Cuyahoga County	1.45
Akron, OH (city) Summit County	1.30
Columbus, OH (city) Franklin County	1.17
Cleveland, OH (city) Cuyahoga County	0.56
Lorain, OH (city) Lorain County	0.21
Ashtabula, OH (city) Ashtabula County	0.00
Boardman, OH (cdp) Mahoning County	0.00
Elyria, OH (city) Lorain County	0.00

Salvadoran
Top 10 Places Sorted by Number

Place	Number
Cleveland, OH (city) Cuyahoga County	361
Columbus, OH (city) Franklin County	318

Salvadoran
Top 10 Places Sorted by Percent

Place	Percent
Cleveland, OH (city) Cuyahoga County	79.52
Columbus, OH (city) Franklin County	78.71

South American
Top 10 Places Sorted by Number

Place	Number
Columbus, OH (city) Franklin County	674
Cleveland, OH (city) Cuyahoga County	371
Cincinnati, OH (city) Hamilton County	326

South American
Top 10 Places Sorted by Percent

Place	Percent
Cincinnati, OH (city) Hamilton County	68.92
Cleveland, OH (city) Cuyahoga County	67.09
Columbus, OH (city) Franklin County	66.08

Spaniard
Top 10 Places Sorted by Number

Place	Number
No places met population threshold.	

Spaniard
Top 10 Places Sorted by Percent

Place	Percent
No places met population threshold.	

Uruguayan
Top 10 Places Sorted by Number

Place	Number
No places met population threshold.	

Uruguayan
Top 10 Places Sorted by Percent

Place	Percent
No places met population threshold.	

Venezuelan
Top 10 Places Sorted by Number

Place	Number
No places met population threshold.	

Venezuelan
Top 10 Places Sorted by Percent

Place	Percent
No places met population threshold.	

Other Hispanic
Top 10 Places Sorted by Number

Place	Number
Columbus, OH (city) Franklin County	571
Cleveland, OH (city) Cuyahoga County	538
Toledo, OH (city) Lucas County	239
Cincinnati, OH (city) Hamilton County	186
Lorain, OH (city) Lorain County	122
Dayton, OH (city) Montgomery County	85
Defiance, OH (city) Defiance County	65
Youngstown, OH (city) Mahoning County	52
Fremont, OH (city) Sandusky County	31
Akron, OH (city) Summit County	26

Other Hispanic
Top 10 Places Sorted by Percent

Place	Percent
Cincinnati, OH (city) Hamilton County	26.12
Columbus, OH (city) Franklin County	19.34
Dayton, OH (city) Montgomery County	19.10
Cleveland, OH (city) Cuyahoga County	15.25
Defiance, OH (city) Defiance County	12.36
Youngstown, OH (city) Mahoning County	11.06
Toledo, OH (city) Lucas County	8.89
Lorain, OH (city) Lorain County	8.72
Fremont, OH (city) Sandusky County	5.60
Akron, OH (city) Summit County	5.27

Foreign-Born Naturalized Citizens

Total Population
Top 10 Places Sorted by Number

Place	Number
Columbus, OH (city) Franklin County	14,197
Cleveland, OH (city) Cuyahoga County	9,755
Parma, OH (city) Cuyahoga County	4,567
Toledo, OH (city) Lucas County	4,487
Cincinnati, OH (city) Hamilton County	4,139
Akron, OH (city) Summit County	3,181
Lakewood, OH (city) Cuyahoga County	2,603
Cleveland Heights, OH (city) Cuyahoga County	1,926
Westlake, OH (city) Cuyahoga County	1,905
Strongsville, OH (city) Cuyahoga County	1,760

Total Population
Top 10 Places Sorted by Percent

Place	Percent
Westlake, OH (city) Cuyahoga County	5.98
Parma Heights, OH (city) Cuyahoga County	5.38
Parma, OH (city) Cuyahoga County	5.33
Brooklyn, OH (city) Cuyahoga County	5.26
North Olmsted, OH (city) Cuyahoga County	4.95
Lakewood, OH (city) Cuyahoga County	4.60
Strongsville, OH (city) Cuyahoga County	4.01
Cleveland Heights, OH (city) Cuyahoga County	3.85
Upper Arlington, OH (city) Franklin County	3.30

Notes: Please refer to the User's Guide for an explanation of data; tables include places with populations > 9,999 and reflect only those areas that meet Summary File 4 population thresholds, therefore there may be less than 10 places listed

Euclid, OH (city) Cuyahoga County 3.26

Hispanic
Top 10 Places Sorted by Number

Place	Number
Columbus, OH (city) Franklin County	1,504
Cleveland, OH (city) Cuyahoga County	1,425
Toledo, OH (city) Lucas County	644
Cincinnati, OH (city) Hamilton County	426
Lorain, OH (city) Lorain County	340
Akron, OH (city) Summit County	217
Painesville, OH (city) Lake County	185
Parma, OH (city) Cuyahoga County	153
Fremont, OH (city) Sandusky County	138
Dayton, OH (city) Montgomery County	127

Hispanic
Top 10 Places Sorted by Percent

Place	Percent
Upper Arlington, OH (city) Franklin County	25.00
Fairfield, OH (city) Butler County	24.03
Middletown, OH (city) Butler County	21.55
Cleveland Heights, OH (city) Cuyahoga County	17.11
Brunswick, OH (city) Medina County	16.99
Beavercreek, OH (city) Greene County	14.86
Kettering, OH (city) Montgomery County	13.68
Xenia, OH (city) Greene County	13.26
Parma, OH (city) Cuyahoga County	12.07
North Olmsted, OH (city) Cuyahoga County	11.29

Argentinian
Top 10 Places Sorted by Number

Place	Number
No places met population threshold.	

Argentinian
Top 10 Places Sorted by Percent

Place	Percent
No places met population threshold.	

Bolivian
Top 10 Places Sorted by Number

Place	Number
No places met population threshold.	

Bolivian
Top 10 Places Sorted by Percent

Place	Percent
No places met population threshold.	

Central American
Top 10 Places Sorted by Number

Place	Number
Cleveland, OH (city) Cuyahoga County	462
Columbus, OH (city) Franklin County	134
Cincinnati, OH (city) Hamilton County	79

Central American
Top 10 Places Sorted by Percent

Place	Percent
Cleveland, OH (city) Cuyahoga County	27.55
Columbus, OH (city) Franklin County	17.09
Cincinnati, OH (city) Hamilton County	15.71

Chilean
Top 10 Places Sorted by Number

Place	Number
No places met population threshold.	

Chilean
Top 10 Places Sorted by Percent

Place	Percent
No places met population threshold.	

Colombian
Top 10 Places Sorted by Number

Place	Number
No places met population threshold.	

Colombian
Top 10 Places Sorted by Percent

Place	Percent
No places met population threshold.	

Costa Rican
Top 10 Places Sorted by Number

Place	Number
No places met population threshold.	

Costa Rican
Top 10 Places Sorted by Percent

Place	Percent
No places met population threshold.	

Cuban
Top 10 Places Sorted by Number

Place	Number
Columbus, OH (city) Franklin County	120
Cleveland, OH (city) Cuyahoga County	90

Cuban
Top 10 Places Sorted by Percent

Place	Percent
Cleveland, OH (city) Cuyahoga County	20.64
Columbus, OH (city) Franklin County	17.14

Dominican
Top 10 Places Sorted by Number

Place	Number
Cleveland, OH (city) Cuyahoga County	129

Dominican
Top 10 Places Sorted by Percent

Place	Percent
Cleveland, OH (city) Cuyahoga County	20.84

Ecuadorian
Top 10 Places Sorted by Number

Place	Number
No places met population threshold.	

Ecuadorian
Top 10 Places Sorted by Percent

Place	Percent
No places met population threshold.	

Guatemalan
Top 10 Places Sorted by Number

Place	Number
Cleveland, OH (city) Cuyahoga County	98

Guatemalan
Top 10 Places Sorted by Percent

Place	Percent
Cleveland, OH (city) Cuyahoga County	21.68

Honduran
Top 10 Places Sorted by Number

Place	Number
No places met population threshold.	

Honduran
Top 10 Places Sorted by Percent

Place	Percent
No places met population threshold.	

Mexican
Top 10 Places Sorted by Number

Place	Number
Columbus, OH (city) Franklin County	694
Toledo, OH (city) Lucas County	418
Cleveland, OH (city) Cuyahoga County	267
Painesville, OH (city) Lake County	177
Lorain, OH (city) Lorain County	131
Fremont, OH (city) Sandusky County	111
Cincinnati, OH (city) Hamilton County	89
Akron, OH (city) Summit County	72
Youngstown, OH (city) Mahoning County	65
Dayton, OH (city) Montgomery County	56

Mexican
Top 10 Places Sorted by Percent

Place	Percent
Youngstown, OH (city) Mahoning County	12.70
Lakewood, OH (city) Cuyahoga County	11.42
Canton, OH (city) Stark County	10.14
Painesville, OH (city) Lake County	9.50
Columbus, OH (city) Franklin County	8.17
Fremont, OH (city) Sandusky County	8.07
Akron, OH (city) Summit County	8.05
Cleveland, OH (city) Cuyahoga County	7.97
Ashtabula, OH (city) Ashtabula County	7.18
Cincinnati, OH (city) Hamilton County	5.73

Nicaraguan
Top 10 Places Sorted by Number

Place	Number
No places met population threshold.	

Nicaraguan
Top 10 Places Sorted by Percent

Place	Percent
No places met population threshold.	

Panamanian
Top 10 Places Sorted by Number

Place	Number
No places met population threshold.	

Panamanian
Top 10 Places Sorted by Percent

Place	Percent
No places met population threshold.	

Paraguayan
Top 10 Places Sorted by Number

Place	Number
No places met population threshold.	

Notes: Please refer to the User's Guide for an explanation of data; tables include places with populations > 9,999 and reflect only those areas that meet Summary File 4 population thresholds, therefore there may be less than 10 places listed

478 PROFILES OF OHIO / Hispanic Rankings: Educational Attainment: H.S. Graduates

Paraguayan
Top 10 Places Sorted by Percent
Place	Percent
No places met population threshold.	

Peruvian
Top 10 Places Sorted by Number
Place	Number
No places met population threshold.	

Peruvian
Top 10 Places Sorted by Percent
Place	Percent
No places met population threshold.	

Puerto Rican
Top 10 Places Sorted by Number
Place	Number
Cleveland, OH (city) Cuyahoga County	47
Columbus, OH (city) Franklin County	36
Toledo, OH (city) Lucas County	12
Cincinnati, OH (city) Hamilton County	8
Akron, OH (city) Summit County	0
Ashtabula, OH (city) Ashtabula County	0
Boardman, OH (cdp) Mahoning County	0
Elyria, OH (city) Lorain County	0
Lakewood, OH (city) Cuyahoga County	0
Lorain, OH (city) Lorain County	0

Puerto Rican
Top 10 Places Sorted by Percent
Place	Percent
Cincinnati, OH (city) Hamilton County	1.41
Columbus, OH (city) Franklin County	1.17
Toledo, OH (city) Lucas County	1.15
Cleveland, OH (city) Cuyahoga County	0.19
Akron, OH (city) Summit County	0.00
Ashtabula, OH (city) Ashtabula County	0.00
Boardman, OH (cdp) Mahoning County	0.00
Elyria, OH (city) Lorain County	0.00
Lakewood, OH (city) Cuyahoga County	0.00
Lorain, OH (city) Lorain County	0.00

Salvadoran
Top 10 Places Sorted by Number
Place	Number
Cleveland, OH (city) Cuyahoga County	180
Columbus, OH (city) Franklin County	22

Salvadoran
Top 10 Places Sorted by Percent
Place	Percent
Cleveland, OH (city) Cuyahoga County	39.65
Columbus, OH (city) Franklin County	5.45

South American
Top 10 Places Sorted by Number
Place	Number
Columbus, OH (city) Franklin County	272
Cleveland, OH (city) Cuyahoga County	204
Cincinnati, OH (city) Hamilton County	107

South American
Top 10 Places Sorted by Percent
Place	Percent
Cleveland, OH (city) Cuyahoga County	36.89
Columbus, OH (city) Franklin County	26.67
Cincinnati, OH (city) Hamilton County	22.62

Spaniard
Top 10 Places Sorted by Number
Place	Number
No places met population threshold.	

Spaniard
Top 10 Places Sorted by Percent
Place	Percent
No places met population threshold.	

Uruguayan
Top 10 Places Sorted by Number
Place	Number
No places met population threshold.	

Uruguayan
Top 10 Places Sorted by Percent
Place	Percent
No places met population threshold.	

Venezuelan
Top 10 Places Sorted by Number
Place	Number
No places met population threshold.	

Venezuelan
Top 10 Places Sorted by Percent
Place	Percent
No places met population threshold.	

Other Hispanic
Top 10 Places Sorted by Number
Place	Number
Cleveland, OH (city) Cuyahoga County	216
Columbus, OH (city) Franklin County	179
Toledo, OH (city) Lucas County	119
Cincinnati, OH (city) Hamilton County	97
Lorain, OH (city) Lorain County	40
Defiance, OH (city) Defiance County	34
Fremont, OH (city) Sandusky County	27
Youngstown, OH (city) Mahoning County	26
Akron, OH (city) Summit County	20
Dayton, OH (city) Montgomery County	5

Other Hispanic
Top 10 Places Sorted by Percent
Place	Percent
Cincinnati, OH (city) Hamilton County	13.62
Defiance, OH (city) Defiance County	6.46
Cleveland, OH (city) Cuyahoga County	6.12
Columbus, OH (city) Franklin County	6.06
Youngstown, OH (city) Mahoning County	5.53
Fremont, OH (city) Sandusky County	4.87
Toledo, OH (city) Lucas County	4.43
Akron, OH (city) Summit County	4.06
Lorain, OH (city) Lorain County	2.86
Dayton, OH (city) Montgomery County	1.12

Educational Attainment: H.S. Graduates

Total Populations 25 Years and Over Who are High School Graduates
Top 10 Places Sorted by Number
Place	Number
Columbus, OH (city) Franklin County	369,376
Cleveland, OH (city) Cuyahoga County	204,829
Cincinnati, OH (city) Hamilton County	159,012
Toledo, OH (city) Lucas County	157,014
Akron, OH (city) Summit County	111,556
Dayton, OH (city) Montgomery County	75,651
Parma, OH (city) Cuyahoga County	50,540
Canton, OH (city) Stark County	38,747
Youngstown, OH (city) Mahoning County	38,543
Kettering, OH (city) Montgomery County	36,547

Total Populations 25 Years and Over Who are High School Graduates
Top 10 Places Sorted by Percent
Place	Percent
Upper Arlington, OH (city) Franklin County	97.93
Perrysburg, OH (city) Wood County	94.74
Westerville, OH (city) Franklin County	94.55
Strongsville, OH (city) Cuyahoga County	92.99
Beavercreek, OH (city) Greene County	92.38
Westlake, OH (city) Cuyahoga County	92.14
Cleveland Heights, OH (city) Cuyahoga County	91.58
Bowling Green, OH (city) Wood County	91.20
Kettering, OH (city) Montgomery County	90.97
North Olmsted, OH (city) Cuyahoga County	90.41

Hispanics 25 Years and Over Who are High School Graduates
Top 10 Places Sorted by Number
Place	Number
Cleveland, OH (city) Cuyahoga County	9,165
Columbus, OH (city) Franklin County	5,818
Toledo, OH (city) Lucas County	4,920
Lorain, OH (city) Lorain County	4,066
Cincinnati, OH (city) Hamilton County	1,671
Youngstown, OH (city) Mahoning County	1,159
Akron, OH (city) Summit County	824
Dayton, OH (city) Montgomery County	739
Defiance, OH (city) Defiance County	714
Parma, OH (city) Cuyahoga County	675

Hispanics 25 Years and Over Who are High School Graduates
Top 10 Places Sorted by Percent
Place	Percent
Beavercreek, OH (city) Greene County	98.05
Upper Arlington, OH (city) Franklin County	97.12
Reynoldsburg, OH (city) Franklin County	96.83
Perrysburg, OH (city) Wood County	95.83
Westlake, OH (city) Cuyahoga County	94.39
Berea, OH (city) Cuyahoga County	93.81
Fairborn, OH (city) Greene County	92.45
Huber Heights, OH (city) Montgomery County	91.23
North Olmsted, OH (city) Cuyahoga County	89.51
Austintown, OH (cdp) Mahoning County	89.38

Argentinians 25 Years and Over Who are High School Graduates
Top 10 Places Sorted by Number
Place	Number
No places met population threshold.	

Argentinians 25 Years and Over Who are High School Graduates
Top 10 Places Sorted by Percent
Place	Percent
No places met population threshold.	

Bolivians 25 Years and Over Who are High School Graduates
Top 10 Places Sorted by Number
Place	Number
No places met population threshold.	

Notes: Please refer to the User's Guide for an explanation of data; tables include places with populations > 9,999 and reflect only those areas that meet Summary File 4 population thresholds, therefore there may be less than 10 places listed

PROFILES OF OHIO / Hispanic Rankings: Educational Attainment: H.S. Graduates

Bolivians 25 Years and Over Who are High School Graduates
Top 10 Places Sorted by Percent

Place	Percent
No places met population threshold.	

Central Americans 25 Years and Over Who are High School Graduates
Top 10 Places Sorted by Number

Place	Number
Cleveland, OH (city) Cuyahoga County	404
Columbus, OH (city) Franklin County	284
Cincinnati, OH (city) Hamilton County	126

Central Americans 25 Years and Over Who are High School Graduates
Top 10 Places Sorted by Percent

Place	Percent
Columbus, OH (city) Franklin County	64.40
Cincinnati, OH (city) Hamilton County	49.61
Cleveland, OH (city) Cuyahoga County	46.38

Chileans 25 Years and Over Who are High School Graduates
Top 10 Places Sorted by Number

Place	Number
No places met population threshold.	

Chileans 25 Years and Over Who are High School Graduates
Top 10 Places Sorted by Percent

Place	Percent
No places met population threshold.	

Colombians 25 Years and Over Who are High School Graduates
Top 10 Places Sorted by Number

Place	Number
No places met population threshold.	

Colombians 25 Years and Over Who are High School Graduates
Top 10 Places Sorted by Percent

Place	Percent
No places met population threshold.	

Costa Ricans 25 Years and Over Who are High School Graduates
Top 10 Places Sorted by Number

Place	Number
No places met population threshold.	

Costa Ricans 25 Years and Over Who are High School Graduates
Top 10 Places Sorted by Percent

Place	Percent
No places met population threshold.	

Cubans 25 Years and Over Who are High School Graduates
Top 10 Places Sorted by Number

Place	Number
Columbus, OH (city) Franklin County	309
Cleveland, OH (city) Cuyahoga County	151

Cubans 25 Years and Over Who are High School Graduates
Top 10 Places Sorted by Percent

Place	Percent
Columbus, OH (city) Franklin County	82.40
Cleveland, OH (city) Cuyahoga County	59.92

Dominicans 25 Years and Over Who are High School Graduates
Top 10 Places Sorted by Number

Place	Number
Cleveland, OH (city) Cuyahoga County	185

Dominicans 25 Years and Over Who are High School Graduates
Top 10 Places Sorted by Percent

Place	Percent
Cleveland, OH (city) Cuyahoga County	55.39

Ecuadorians 25 Years and Over Who are High School Graduates
Top 10 Places Sorted by Number

Place	Number
No places met population threshold.	

Ecuadorians 25 Years and Over Who are High School Graduates
Top 10 Places Sorted by Percent

Place	Percent
No places met population threshold.	

Guatemalans 25 Years and Over Who are High School Graduates
Top 10 Places Sorted by Number

Place	Number
Cleveland, OH (city) Cuyahoga County	110

Guatemalans 25 Years and Over Who are High School Graduates
Top 10 Places Sorted by Percent

Place	Percent
Cleveland, OH (city) Cuyahoga County	44.53

Hondurans 25 Years and Over Who are High School Graduates
Top 10 Places Sorted by Number

Place	Number
No places met population threshold.	

Hondurans 25 Years and Over Who are High School Graduates
Top 10 Places Sorted by Percent

Place	Percent
No places met population threshold.	

Mexicans 25 Years and Over Who are High School Graduates
Top 10 Places Sorted by Number

Place	Number
Toledo, OH (city) Lucas County	3,692
Columbus, OH (city) Franklin County	2,345
Cleveland, OH (city) Cuyahoga County	1,055
Lorain, OH (city) Lorain County	804
Cincinnati, OH (city) Hamilton County	503
Defiance, OH (city) Defiance County	465
Fremont, OH (city) Sandusky County	342
Findlay, OH (city) Hancock County	317
Akron, OH (city) Summit County	313
Dayton, OH (city) Montgomery County	283

Mexicans 25 Years and Over Who are High School Graduates
Top 10 Places Sorted by Percent

Place	Percent
Lakewood, OH (city) Cuyahoga County	81.67
Oregon, OH (city) Lucas County	76.00
Elyria, OH (city) Lorain County	74.56
Akron, OH (city) Summit County	71.79
Sandusky, OH (city) Erie County	70.32
Defiance, OH (city) Defiance County	69.72
Cincinnati, OH (city) Hamilton County	68.62
Bowling Green, OH (city) Wood County	67.60
Norwalk, OH (city) Huron County	66.99
Findlay, OH (city) Hancock County	63.27

Nicaraguans 25 Years and Over Who are High School Graduates
Top 10 Places Sorted by Number

Place	Number
No places met population threshold.	

Nicaraguans 25 Years and Over Who are High School Graduates
Top 10 Places Sorted by Percent

Place	Percent
No places met population threshold.	

Panamanians 25 Years and Over Who are High School Graduates
Top 10 Places Sorted by Number

Place	Number
No places met population threshold.	

Panamanians 25 Years and Over Who are High School Graduates
Top 10 Places Sorted by Percent

Place	Percent
No places met population threshold.	

Paraguayans 25 Years and Over Who are High School Graduates
Top 10 Places Sorted by Number

Place	Number
No places met population threshold.	

Paraguayans 25 Years and Over Who are High School Graduates
Top 10 Places Sorted by Percent

Place	Percent
No places met population threshold.	

Peruvians 25 Years and Over Who are High School Graduates
Top 10 Places Sorted by Number

Place	Number
No places met population threshold.	

Peruvians 25 Years and Over Who are High School Graduates
Top 10 Places Sorted by Percent

Place	Percent
No places met population threshold.	

Notes: Please refer to the User's Guide for an explanation of data; tables include places with populations > 9,999 and reflect only those areas that meet Summary File 4 population thresholds, therefore there may be less than 10 places listed

PROFILES OF OHIO / Hispanic Rankings: Educational Attainment: College Graduates

Puerto Ricans 25 Years and Over Who are High School Graduates
Top 10 Places Sorted by Number

Place	Number
Cleveland, OH (city) Cuyahoga County	6,255
Lorain, OH (city) Lorain County	2,819
Columbus, OH (city) Franklin County	1,131
Youngstown, OH (city) Mahoning County	819
Toledo, OH (city) Lucas County	303
Parma, OH (city) Cuyahoga County	259
Boardman, OH (cdp) Mahoning County	257
Lakewood, OH (city) Cuyahoga County	249
Cincinnati, OH (city) Hamilton County	233
Elyria, OH (city) Lorain County	202

Puerto Ricans 25 Years and Over Who are High School Graduates
Top 10 Places Sorted by Percent

Place	Percent
Lakewood, OH (city) Cuyahoga County	91.54
Parma, OH (city) Cuyahoga County	85.76
Cincinnati, OH (city) Hamilton County	85.66
Boardman, OH (cdp) Mahoning County	79.57
Toledo, OH (city) Lucas County	79.11
Columbus, OH (city) Franklin County	78.54
Akron, OH (city) Summit County	73.13
Elyria, OH (city) Lorain County	68.24
Youngstown, OH (city) Mahoning County	56.52
Lorain, OH (city) Lorain County	56.40

Salvadorans 25 Years and Over Who are High School Graduates
Top 10 Places Sorted by Number

Place	Number
Columbus, OH (city) Franklin County	89
Cleveland, OH (city) Cuyahoga County	46

Salvadorans 25 Years and Over Who are High School Graduates
Top 10 Places Sorted by Percent

Place	Percent
Columbus, OH (city) Franklin County	44.06
Cleveland, OH (city) Cuyahoga County	22.33

South Americans 25 Years and Over Who are High School Graduates
Top 10 Places Sorted by Number

Place	Number
Columbus, OH (city) Franklin County	560
Cleveland, OH (city) Cuyahoga County	318
Cincinnati, OH (city) Hamilton County	315

South Americans 25 Years and Over Who are High School Graduates
Top 10 Places Sorted by Percent

Place	Percent
Cincinnati, OH (city) Hamilton County	98.44
Columbus, OH (city) Franklin County	88.89
Cleveland, OH (city) Cuyahoga County	84.80

Spaniards 25 Years and Over Who are High School Graduates
Top 10 Places Sorted by Number

Place	Number
No places met population threshold.	

Spaniards 25 Years and Over Who are High School Graduates
Top 10 Places Sorted by Percent

Place	Percent
No places met population threshold.	

Uruguayans 25 Years and Over Who are High School Graduates
Top 10 Places Sorted by Number

Place	Number
No places met population threshold.	

Uruguayans 25 Years and Over Who are High School Graduates
Top 10 Places Sorted by Percent

Place	Percent
No places met population threshold.	

Venezuelans 25 Years and Over Who are High School Graduates
Top 10 Places Sorted by Number

Place	Number
No places met population threshold.	

Venezuelans 25 Years and Over Who are High School Graduates
Top 10 Places Sorted by Percent

Place	Percent
No places met population threshold.	

Other Hispanics 25 Years and Over Who are High School Graduates
Top 10 Places Sorted by Number

Place	Number
Columbus, OH (city) Franklin County	1,022
Cleveland, OH (city) Cuyahoga County	763
Toledo, OH (city) Lucas County	753
Cincinnati, OH (city) Hamilton County	349
Lorain, OH (city) Lorain County	293
Akron, OH (city) Summit County	203
Dayton, OH (city) Montgomery County	203
Defiance, OH (city) Defiance County	185
Youngstown, OH (city) Mahoning County	125
Fremont, OH (city) Sandusky County	113

Other Hispanics 25 Years and Over Who are High School Graduates
Top 10 Places Sorted by Percent

Place	Percent
Dayton, OH (city) Montgomery County	79.30
Cincinnati, OH (city) Hamilton County	76.37
Defiance, OH (city) Defiance County	74.00
Akron, OH (city) Summit County	70.73
Columbus, OH (city) Franklin County	68.22
Toledo, OH (city) Lucas County	62.49
Lorain, OH (city) Lorain County	61.43
Youngstown, OH (city) Mahoning County	58.14
Cleveland, OH (city) Cuyahoga County	52.73
Fremont, OH (city) Sandusky County	47.68

Educational Attainment: College Graduates

Total Populations 25 Years and Over Who are Four-Year College Graduates
Top 10 Places Sorted by Number

Place	Number
Columbus, OH (city) Franklin County	128,058
Cincinnati, OH (city) Hamilton County	55,215
Cleveland, OH (city) Cuyahoga County	33,949
Toledo, OH (city) Lucas County	33,091
Akron, OH (city) Summit County	25,110
Cleveland Heights, OH (city) Cuyahoga County	16,760
Upper Arlington, OH (city) Franklin County	16,063
Dayton, OH (city) Montgomery County	14,477
Lakewood, OH (city) Cuyahoga County	14,193
Kettering, OH (city) Montgomery County	12,458

Total Populations 25 Years and Over Who are Four-Year College Graduates
Top 10 Places Sorted by Percent

Place	Percent
Upper Arlington, OH (city) Franklin County	67.46
Cleveland Heights, OH (city) Cuyahoga County	50.00
Perrysburg, OH (city) Wood County	46.92
Westlake, OH (city) Cuyahoga County	45.31
Westerville, OH (city) Franklin County	44.58
Bowling Green, OH (city) Wood County	44.16
Beavercreek, OH (city) Greene County	42.94
Strongsville, OH (city) Cuyahoga County	36.99
Lakewood, OH (city) Cuyahoga County	35.92
Kettering, OH (city) Montgomery County	31.01

Hispanics 25 Years and Over Who are Four-Year College Graduates
Top 10 Places Sorted by Number

Place	Number
Columbus, OH (city) Franklin County	1,656
Cleveland, OH (city) Cuyahoga County	1,327
Cincinnati, OH (city) Hamilton County	857
Toledo, OH (city) Lucas County	677
Lorain, OH (city) Lorain County	326
Lakewood, OH (city) Cuyahoga County	216
Akron, OH (city) Summit County	204
Dayton, OH (city) Montgomery County	178
Cleveland Heights, OH (city) Cuyahoga County	167
Boardman, OH (cdp) Mahoning County	151

Hispanics 25 Years and Over Who are Four-Year College Graduates
Top 10 Places Sorted by Percent

Place	Percent
Upper Arlington, OH (city) Franklin County	65.87
Beavercreek, OH (city) Greene County	59.02
Westlake, OH (city) Cuyahoga County	50.93
Cleveland Heights, OH (city) Cuyahoga County	42.93
Riverside, OH (city) Montgomery County	41.49
Westerville, OH (city) Franklin County	39.13
Cincinnati, OH (city) Hamilton County	38.97
Fairborn, OH (city) Greene County	36.33
Fairfield, OH (city) Butler County	33.61
Berea, OH (city) Cuyahoga County	31.86

Argentinians 25 Years and Over Who are Four-Year College Graduates
Top 10 Places Sorted by Number

Place	Number
No places met population threshold.	

Argentinians 25 Years and Over Who are Four-Year College Graduates
Top 10 Places Sorted by Percent

Place	Percent
No places met population threshold.	

Bolivians 25 Years and Over Who are Four-Year College Graduates
Top 10 Places Sorted by Number

Place	Number
No places met population threshold.	

Notes: Please refer to the User's Guide for an explanation of data; tables include places with populations > 9,999 and reflect only those areas that meet Summary File 4 population thresholds, therefore there may be less than 10 places listed

PROFILES OF OHIO / Hispanic Rankings: Educational Attainment: College Graduates

Bolivians 25 Years and Over Who are Four-Year College Graduates
Top 10 Places Sorted by Percent

Place	Percent
No places met population threshold.	

Central Americans 25 Years and Over Who are Four-Year College Graduates
Top 10 Places Sorted by Number

Place	Number
Columbus, OH (city) Franklin County	111
Cleveland, OH (city) Cuyahoga County	105
Cincinnati, OH (city) Hamilton County	71

Central Americans 25 Years and Over Who are Four-Year College Graduates
Top 10 Places Sorted by Percent

Place	Percent
Cincinnati, OH (city) Hamilton County	27.95
Columbus, OH (city) Franklin County	25.17
Cleveland, OH (city) Cuyahoga County	12.06

Chileans 25 Years and Over Who are Four-Year College Graduates
Top 10 Places Sorted by Number

Place	Number
No places met population threshold.	

Chileans 25 Years and Over Who are Four-Year College Graduates
Top 10 Places Sorted by Percent

Place	Percent
No places met population threshold.	

Colombians 25 Years and Over Who are Four-Year College Graduates
Top 10 Places Sorted by Number

Place	Number
No places met population threshold.	

Colombians 25 Years and Over Who are Four-Year College Graduates
Top 10 Places Sorted by Percent

Place	Percent
No places met population threshold.	

Costa Ricans 25 Years and Over Who are Four-Year College Graduates
Top 10 Places Sorted by Number

Place	Number
No places met population threshold.	

Costa Ricans 25 Years and Over Who are Four-Year College Graduates
Top 10 Places Sorted by Percent

Place	Percent
No places met population threshold.	

Cubans 25 Years and Over Who are Four-Year College Graduates
Top 10 Places Sorted by Number

Place	Number
Columbus, OH (city) Franklin County	122
Cleveland, OH (city) Cuyahoga County	42

Cubans 25 Years and Over Who are Four-Year College Graduates
Top 10 Places Sorted by Percent

Place	Percent
Columbus, OH (city) Franklin County	32.53
Cleveland, OH (city) Cuyahoga County	16.67

Dominicans 25 Years and Over Who are Four-Year College Graduates
Top 10 Places Sorted by Number

Place	Number
Cleveland, OH (city) Cuyahoga County	24

Dominicans 25 Years and Over Who are Four-Year College Graduates
Top 10 Places Sorted by Percent

Place	Percent
Cleveland, OH (city) Cuyahoga County	7.19

Ecuadorians 25 Years and Over Who are Four-Year College Graduates
Top 10 Places Sorted by Number

Place	Number
No places met population threshold.	

Ecuadorians 25 Years and Over Who are Four-Year College Graduates
Top 10 Places Sorted by Percent

Place	Percent
No places met population threshold.	

Guatemalans 25 Years and Over Who are Four-Year College Graduates
Top 10 Places Sorted by Number

Place	Number
Cleveland, OH (city) Cuyahoga County	7

Guatemalans 25 Years and Over Who are Four-Year College Graduates
Top 10 Places Sorted by Percent

Place	Percent
Cleveland, OH (city) Cuyahoga County	2.83

Hondurans 25 Years and Over Who are Four-Year College Graduates
Top 10 Places Sorted by Number

Place	Number
No places met population threshold.	

Hondurans 25 Years and Over Who are Four-Year College Graduates
Top 10 Places Sorted by Percent

Place	Percent
No places met population threshold.	

Mexicans 25 Years and Over Who are Four-Year College Graduates
Top 10 Places Sorted by Number

Place	Number
Columbus, OH (city) Franklin County	508
Toledo, OH (city) Lucas County	426
Cincinnati, OH (city) Hamilton County	249
Cleveland, OH (city) Cuyahoga County	192
Akron, OH (city) Summit County	87
Lakewood, OH (city) Cuyahoga County	72
Findlay, OH (city) Hancock County	53
Lorain, OH (city) Lorain County	51
Defiance, OH (city) Defiance County	47
Dayton, OH (city) Montgomery County	33

Mexicans 25 Years and Over Who are Four-Year College Graduates
Top 10 Places Sorted by Percent

Place	Percent
Lakewood, OH (city) Cuyahoga County	40.00
Cincinnati, OH (city) Hamilton County	33.97
Akron, OH (city) Summit County	19.95
Columbus, OH (city) Franklin County	12.76
Cleveland, OH (city) Cuyahoga County	10.87
Findlay, OH (city) Hancock County	10.58
Norwalk, OH (city) Huron County	9.71
Toledo, OH (city) Lucas County	7.15
Defiance, OH (city) Defiance County	7.05
Dayton, OH (city) Montgomery County	6.73

Nicaraguans 25 Years and Over Who are Four-Year College Graduates
Top 10 Places Sorted by Number

Place	Number
No places met population threshold.	

Nicaraguans 25 Years and Over Who are Four-Year College Graduates
Top 10 Places Sorted by Percent

Place	Percent
No places met population threshold.	

Panamanians 25 Years and Over Who are Four-Year College Graduates
Top 10 Places Sorted by Number

Place	Number
No places met population threshold.	

Panamanians 25 Years and Over Who are Four-Year College Graduates
Top 10 Places Sorted by Percent

Place	Percent
No places met population threshold.	

Paraguayans 25 Years and Over Who are Four-Year College Graduates
Top 10 Places Sorted by Number

Place	Number
No places met population threshold.	

Paraguayans 25 Years and Over Who are Four-Year College Graduates
Top 10 Places Sorted by Percent

Place	Percent
No places met population threshold.	

Peruvians 25 Years and Over Who are Four-Year College Graduates
Top 10 Places Sorted by Number

Place	Number
No places met population threshold.	

Peruvians 25 Years and Over Who are Four-Year College Graduates
Top 10 Places Sorted by Percent

Place	Percent
No places met population threshold.	

Notes: Please refer to the User's Guide for an explanation of data; tables include places with populations > 9,999 and reflect only those areas that meet Summary File 4 population thresholds, therefore there may be less than 10 places listed

Puerto Ricans 25 Years and Over Who are Four-Year College Graduates
Top 10 Places Sorted by Number

Place	Number
Cleveland, OH (city) Cuyahoga County	699
Columbus, OH (city) Franklin County	349
Lorain, OH (city) Lorain County	198
Cincinnati, OH (city) Hamilton County	107
Boardman, OH (cdp) Mahoning County	82
Youngstown, OH (city) Mahoning County	71
Lakewood, OH (city) Cuyahoga County	62
Toledo, OH (city) Lucas County	51
Parma, OH (city) Cuyahoga County	32
Akron, OH (city) Summit County	29

Puerto Ricans 25 Years and Over Who are Four-Year College Graduates
Top 10 Places Sorted by Percent

Place	Percent
Cincinnati, OH (city) Hamilton County	39.34
Boardman, OH (cdp) Mahoning County	25.39
Columbus, OH (city) Franklin County	24.24
Lakewood, OH (city) Cuyahoga County	22.79
Toledo, OH (city) Lucas County	13.32
Akron, OH (city) Summit County	10.82
Parma, OH (city) Cuyahoga County	10.60
Elyria, OH (city) Lorain County	8.45
Cleveland, OH (city) Cuyahoga County	5.92
Youngstown, OH (city) Mahoning County	4.90

Salvadorans 25 Years and Over Who are Four-Year College Graduates
Top 10 Places Sorted by Number

Place	Number
Columbus, OH (city) Franklin County	18
Cleveland, OH (city) Cuyahoga County	5

Salvadorans 25 Years and Over Who are Four-Year College Graduates
Top 10 Places Sorted by Percent

Place	Percent
Columbus, OH (city) Franklin County	8.91
Cleveland, OH (city) Cuyahoga County	2.43

South Americans 25 Years and Over Who are Four-Year College Graduates
Top 10 Places Sorted by Number

Place	Number
Columbus, OH (city) Franklin County	296
Cincinnati, OH (city) Hamilton County	219
Cleveland, OH (city) Cuyahoga County	98

South Americans 25 Years and Over Who are Four-Year College Graduates
Top 10 Places Sorted by Percent

Place	Percent
Cincinnati, OH (city) Hamilton County	68.44
Columbus, OH (city) Franklin County	46.98
Cleveland, OH (city) Cuyahoga County	26.13

Spaniards 25 Years and Over Who are Four-Year College Graduates
Top 10 Places Sorted by Number

Place	Number
No places met population threshold.	

Spaniards 25 Years and Over Who are Four-Year College Graduates
Top 10 Places Sorted by Percent

Place	Percent
No places met population threshold.	

Uruguayans 25 Years and Over Who are Four-Year College Graduates
Top 10 Places Sorted by Number

Place	Number
No places met population threshold.	

Uruguayans 25 Years and Over Who are Four-Year College Graduates
Top 10 Places Sorted by Percent

Place	Percent
No places met population threshold.	

Venezuelans 25 Years and Over Who are Four-Year College Graduates
Top 10 Places Sorted by Number

Place	Number
No places met population threshold.	

Venezuelans 25 Years and Over Who are Four-Year College Graduates
Top 10 Places Sorted by Percent

Place	Percent
No places met population threshold.	

Other Hispanics 25 Years and Over Who are Four-Year College Graduates
Top 10 Places Sorted by Number

Place	Number
Columbus, OH (city) Franklin County	194
Cleveland, OH (city) Cuyahoga County	145
Cincinnati, OH (city) Hamilton County	118
Toledo, OH (city) Lucas County	104
Akron, OH (city) Summit County	44
Lorain, OH (city) Lorain County	37
Dayton, OH (city) Montgomery County	36
Youngstown, OH (city) Mahoning County	15
Defiance, OH (city) Defiance County	11
Fremont, OH (city) Sandusky County	9

Other Hispanics 25 Years and Over Who are Four-Year College Graduates
Top 10 Places Sorted by Percent

Place	Percent
Cincinnati, OH (city) Hamilton County	25.82
Akron, OH (city) Summit County	15.33
Dayton, OH (city) Montgomery County	14.06
Columbus, OH (city) Franklin County	12.95
Cleveland, OH (city) Cuyahoga County	10.02
Toledo, OH (city) Lucas County	8.63
Lorain, OH (city) Lorain County	7.76
Youngstown, OH (city) Mahoning County	6.98
Defiance, OH (city) Defiance County	4.40
Fremont, OH (city) Sandusky County	3.80

Median Household Income

Total Population
Top 10 Places Sorted by Number

Place	Dollars
Upper Arlington, OH (city) Franklin County	72,116
Westerville, OH (city) Franklin County	69,135
Beavercreek, OH (city) Greene County	68,801
Strongsville, OH (city) Cuyahoga County	68,660
Westlake, OH (city) Cuyahoga County	64,963
Perrysburg, OH (city) Wood County	62,237
Brunswick, OH (city) Medina County	56,288
North Olmsted, OH (city) Cuyahoga County	52,542
Reynoldsburg, OH (city) Franklin County	51,108
Fairfield, OH (city) Butler County	50,316

Hispanic
Top 10 Places Sorted by Number

Place	Dollars
Strongsville, OH (city) Cuyahoga County	77,700
Upper Arlington, OH (city) Franklin County	73,977
Beavercreek, OH (city) Greene County	70,208
Brunswick, OH (city) Medina County	65,208
Westerville, OH (city) Franklin County	56,125
Riverside, OH (city) Montgomery County	55,431
Perrysburg, OH (city) Wood County	52,865
Fairfield, OH (city) Butler County	50,156
Reynoldsburg, OH (city) Franklin County	49,444
Huber Heights, OH (city) Montgomery County	48,897

Argentinian
Top 10 Places Sorted by Number

Place	Dollars
No places met population threshold.	

Bolivian
Top 10 Places Sorted by Number

Place	Dollars
No places met population threshold.	

Central American
Top 10 Places Sorted by Number

Place	Dollars
Columbus, OH (city) Franklin County	32,384
Cleveland, OH (city) Cuyahoga County	29,817
Cincinnati, OH (city) Hamilton County	24,318

Chilean
Top 10 Places Sorted by Number

Place	Dollars
No places met population threshold.	

Colombian
Top 10 Places Sorted by Number

Place	Dollars
No places met population threshold.	

Costa Rican
Top 10 Places Sorted by Number

Place	Dollars
No places met population threshold.	

Cuban
Top 10 Places Sorted by Number

Place	Dollars
Columbus, OH (city) Franklin County	46,146
Cleveland, OH (city) Cuyahoga County	38,167

Dominican
Top 10 Places Sorted by Number

Place	Dollars
Cleveland, OH (city) Cuyahoga County	23,750

Ecuadorian
Top 10 Places Sorted by Number

Place	Dollars
No places met population threshold.	

Notes: Please refer to the User's Guide for an explanation of data; tables include places with populations > 9,999 and reflect only those areas that meet Summary File 4 population thresholds, therefore there may be less than 10 places listed

PROFILES OF OHIO / Hispanic Rankings: Per Capita Income

Guatemalan
Top 10 Places Sorted by Number

Place	Dollars
Cleveland, OH (city) Cuyahoga County	25,938

Honduran
Top 10 Places Sorted by Number

Place	Dollars
No places met population threshold.	

Mexican
Top 10 Places Sorted by Number

Place	Dollars
Lakewood, OH (city) Cuyahoga County	61,250
Oregon, OH (city) Lucas County	41,417
Defiance, OH (city) Defiance County	41,210
Akron, OH (city) Summit County	39,489
Ashtabula, OH (city) Ashtabula County	37,500
Hamilton, OH (city) Butler County	35,795
Painesville, OH (city) Lake County	34,524
Lorain, OH (city) Lorain County	33,401
Columbus, OH (city) Franklin County	33,333
Toledo, OH (city) Lucas County	32,064

Nicaraguan
Top 10 Places Sorted by Number

Place	Dollars
No places met population threshold.	

Panamanian
Top 10 Places Sorted by Number

Place	Dollars
No places met population threshold.	

Paraguayan
Top 10 Places Sorted by Number

Place	Dollars
No places met population threshold.	

Peruvian
Top 10 Places Sorted by Number

Place	Dollars
No places met population threshold.	

Puerto Rican
Top 10 Places Sorted by Number

Place	Dollars
Lakewood, OH (city) Cuyahoga County	50,000
Parma, OH (city) Cuyahoga County	41,490
Boardman, OH (cdp) Mahoning County	36,500
Columbus, OH (city) Franklin County	29,972
Toledo, OH (city) Lucas County	27,083
Cincinnati, OH (city) Hamilton County	26,953
Elyria, OH (city) Lorain County	26,953
Lorain, OH (city) Lorain County	26,681
Cleveland, OH (city) Cuyahoga County	24,315
Akron, OH (city) Summit County	21,382

Salvadoran
Top 10 Places Sorted by Number

Place	Dollars
Columbus, OH (city) Franklin County	36,447
Cleveland, OH (city) Cuyahoga County	28,958

South American
Top 10 Places Sorted by Number

Place	Dollars
Cleveland, OH (city) Cuyahoga County	37,625
Columbus, OH (city) Franklin County	37,383

Cincinnati, OH (city) Hamilton County	34,750

Spaniard
Top 10 Places Sorted by Number

Place	Dollars
No places met population threshold.	

Uruguayan
Top 10 Places Sorted by Number

Place	Dollars
No places met population threshold.	

Venezuelan
Top 10 Places Sorted by Number

Place	Dollars
No places met population threshold.	

Other Hispanic
Top 10 Places Sorted by Number

Place	Dollars
Lorain, OH (city) Lorain County	45,938
Defiance, OH (city) Defiance County	43,438
Columbus, OH (city) Franklin County	29,485
Cleveland, OH (city) Cuyahoga County	25,804
Cincinnati, OH (city) Hamilton County	24,844
Akron, OH (city) Summit County	23,750
Toledo, OH (city) Lucas County	22,258
Fremont, OH (city) Sandusky County	21,023
Dayton, OH (city) Montgomery County	19,000
Youngstown, OH (city) Mahoning County	18,917

Per Capita Income

Total Population
Top 10 Places Sorted by Number

Place	Dollars
Upper Arlington, OH (city) Franklin County	42,025
Westlake, OH (city) Cuyahoga County	37,142
Beavercreek, OH (city) Greene County	30,298
Strongsville, OH (city) Cuyahoga County	29,722
Perrysburg, OH (city) Wood County	29,652
Westerville, OH (city) Franklin County	29,401
Kettering, OH (city) Montgomery County	27,009
Cleveland Heights, OH (city) Cuyahoga County	25,804
Fairfield, OH (city) Butler County	24,556
North Olmsted, OH (city) Cuyahoga County	24,329

Hispanic
Top 10 Places Sorted by Number

Place	Dollars
Beavercreek, OH (city) Greene County	25,348
Strongsville, OH (city) Cuyahoga County	25,068
Upper Arlington, OH (city) Franklin County	22,260
Perrysburg, OH (city) Wood County	22,129
Brooklyn, OH (city) Cuyahoga County	21,291
Tiffin, OH (city) Seneca County	20,467
Kettering, OH (city) Montgomery County	20,046
Westlake, OH (city) Cuyahoga County	19,786
Austintown, OH (cdp) Mahoning County	19,734
Parma, OH (city) Cuyahoga County	19,491

Argentinian
Top 10 Places Sorted by Number

Place	Dollars
No places met population threshold.	

Bolivian
Top 10 Places Sorted by Number

Place	Dollars
No places met population threshold.	

Central American
Top 10 Places Sorted by Number

Place	Dollars
Columbus, OH (city) Franklin County	13,998
Cincinnati, OH (city) Hamilton County	10,708
Cleveland, OH (city) Cuyahoga County	9,358

Chilean
Top 10 Places Sorted by Number

Place	Dollars
No places met population threshold.	

Colombian
Top 10 Places Sorted by Number

Place	Dollars
No places met population threshold.	

Costa Rican
Top 10 Places Sorted by Number

Place	Dollars
No places met population threshold.	

Cuban
Top 10 Places Sorted by Number

Place	Dollars
Columbus, OH (city) Franklin County	14,827
Cleveland, OH (city) Cuyahoga County	13,147

Dominican
Top 10 Places Sorted by Number

Place	Dollars
Cleveland, OH (city) Cuyahoga County	12,898

Ecuadorian
Top 10 Places Sorted by Number

Place	Dollars
No places met population threshold.	

Guatemalan
Top 10 Places Sorted by Number

Place	Dollars
Cleveland, OH (city) Cuyahoga County	8,042

Honduran
Top 10 Places Sorted by Number

Place	Dollars
No places met population threshold.	

Mexican
Top 10 Places Sorted by Number

Place	Dollars
Lakewood, OH (city) Cuyahoga County	17,623
Youngstown, OH (city) Mahoning County	16,488
Akron, OH (city) Summit County	15,485
Defiance, OH (city) Defiance County	15,084
Cincinnati, OH (city) Hamilton County	14,457
Oregon, OH (city) Lucas County	14,447
Lorain, OH (city) Lorain County	13,123
Columbus, OH (city) Franklin County	12,776
Cleveland, OH (city) Cuyahoga County	12,633
Sandusky, OH (city) Erie County	12,290

Nicaraguan
Top 10 Places Sorted by Number

Place	Dollars
No places met population threshold.	

Notes: Please refer to the User's Guide for an explanation of data; tables include places with populations > 9,999 and reflect only those areas that meet Summary File 4 population thresholds, therefore there may be less than 10 places listed

PROFILES OF OHIO / Hispanic Rankings: Poverty Status

Panamanian
Top 10 Places Sorted by Number

Place	Dollars
No places met population threshold.	

Paraguayan
Top 10 Places Sorted by Number

Place	Dollars
No places met population threshold.	

Peruvian
Top 10 Places Sorted by Number

Place	Dollars
No places met population threshold.	

Puerto Rican
Top 10 Places Sorted by Number

Place	Dollars
Cincinnati, OH (city) Hamilton County	16,874
Boardman, OH (cdp) Mahoning County	16,306
Parma, OH (city) Cuyahoga County	15,514
Lakewood, OH (city) Cuyahoga County	14,449
Columbus, OH (city) Franklin County	13,984
Lorain, OH (city) Lorain County	10,790
Akron, OH (city) Summit County	10,339
Elyria, OH (city) Lorain County	10,028
Cleveland, OH (city) Cuyahoga County	9,718
Ashtabula, OH (city) Ashtabula County	9,522

Salvadoran
Top 10 Places Sorted by Number

Place	Dollars
Columbus, OH (city) Franklin County	13,382
Cleveland, OH (city) Cuyahoga County	8,782

South American
Top 10 Places Sorted by Number

Place	Dollars
Cincinnati, OH (city) Hamilton County	25,630
Columbus, OH (city) Franklin County	18,062
Cleveland, OH (city) Cuyahoga County	16,626

Spaniard
Top 10 Places Sorted by Number

Place	Dollars
No places met population threshold.	

Uruguayan
Top 10 Places Sorted by Number

Place	Dollars
No places met population threshold.	

Venezuelan
Top 10 Places Sorted by Number

Place	Dollars
No places met population threshold.	

Other Hispanic
Top 10 Places Sorted by Number

Place	Dollars
Akron, OH (city) Summit County	18,483
Defiance, OH (city) Defiance County	18,007
Cincinnati, OH (city) Hamilton County	16,210
Columbus, OH (city) Franklin County	14,694
Toledo, OH (city) Lucas County	14,608
Dayton, OH (city) Montgomery County	11,299
Lorain, OH (city) Lorain County	10,254
Cleveland, OH (city) Cuyahoga County	8,702
Fremont, OH (city) Sandusky County	8,527

Youngstown, OH (city) Mahoning County	8,149

Poverty Status

Total Populations with Income Below Poverty Level
Top 10 Places Sorted by Number

Place	Number
Cleveland, OH (city) Cuyahoga County	122,479
Columbus, OH (city) Franklin County	102,723
Cincinnati, OH (city) Hamilton County	69,722
Toledo, OH (city) Lucas County	54,903
Akron, OH (city) Summit County	36,975
Dayton, OH (city) Montgomery County	35,756
Youngstown, OH (city) Mahoning County	19,127
Canton, OH (city) Stark County	14,957
Lorain, OH (city) Lorain County	11,582
Springfield, OH (city) Clark County	10,577

Total Populations with Income Below Poverty Level
Top 10 Places Sorted by Percent

Place	Percent
Cleveland, OH (city) Cuyahoga County	26.27
Bowling Green, OH (city) Wood County	25.27
Youngstown, OH (city) Mahoning County	24.78
Dayton, OH (city) Montgomery County	22.99
Lima, OH (city) Allen County	22.67
Cincinnati, OH (city) Hamilton County	21.91
Ashtabula, OH (city) Ashtabula County	21.35
Warren, OH (city) Trumbull County	19.38
Canton, OH (city) Stark County	19.16
Toledo, OH (city) Lucas County	17.89

Hispanics with Income Below Poverty Level
Top 10 Places Sorted by Number

Place	Number
Cleveland, OH (city) Cuyahoga County	11,110
Toledo, OH (city) Lucas County	4,355
Lorain, OH (city) Lorain County	3,180
Columbus, OH (city) Franklin County	3,166
Youngstown, OH (city) Mahoning County	1,273
Cincinnati, OH (city) Hamilton County	909
Painesville, OH (city) Lake County	662
Dayton, OH (city) Montgomery County	592
Akron, OH (city) Summit County	471
Fremont, OH (city) Sandusky County	440

Hispanics with Income Below Poverty Level
Top 10 Places Sorted by Percent

Place	Percent
Warren, OH (city) Trumbull County	43.82
Cleveland, OH (city) Cuyahoga County	32.57
Youngstown, OH (city) Mahoning County	32.22
Ashtabula, OH (city) Ashtabula County	32.21
Marion, OH (city) Marion County	31.53
Dayton, OH (city) Montgomery County	31.04
Hamilton, OH (city) Butler County	30.17
Painesville, OH (city) Lake County	29.50
Canton, OH (city) Stark County	26.89
Lima, OH (city) Allen County	26.82

Argentinians with Income Below Poverty Level
Top 10 Places Sorted by Number

Place	Number
No places met population threshold.	

Argentinians with Income Below Poverty Level
Top 10 Places Sorted by Percent

Place	Percent
No places met population threshold.	

Bolivians with Income Below Poverty Level
Top 10 Places Sorted by Number

Place	Number
No places met population threshold.	

Bolivians with Income Below Poverty Level
Top 10 Places Sorted by Percent

Place	Percent
No places met population threshold.	

Central Americans with Income Below Poverty Level
Top 10 Places Sorted by Number

Place	Number
Cleveland, OH (city) Cuyahoga County	318
Columbus, OH (city) Franklin County	165
Cincinnati, OH (city) Hamilton County	116

Central Americans with Income Below Poverty Level
Top 10 Places Sorted by Percent

Place	Percent
Cincinnati, OH (city) Hamilton County	23.06
Columbus, OH (city) Franklin County	21.26
Cleveland, OH (city) Cuyahoga County	19.21

Chileans with Income Below Poverty Level
Top 10 Places Sorted by Number

Place	Number
No places met population threshold.	

Chileans with Income Below Poverty Level
Top 10 Places Sorted by Percent

Place	Percent
No places met population threshold.	

Colombians with Income Below Poverty Level
Top 10 Places Sorted by Number

Place	Number
No places met population threshold.	

Colombians with Income Below Poverty Level
Top 10 Places Sorted by Percent

Place	Percent
No places met population threshold.	

Costa Ricans with Income Below Poverty Level
Top 10 Places Sorted by Number

Place	Number
No places met population threshold.	

Costa Ricans with Income Below Poverty Level
Top 10 Places Sorted by Percent

Place	Percent
No places met population threshold.	

Cubans with Income Below Poverty Level
Top 10 Places Sorted by Number

Place	Number
Cleveland, OH (city) Cuyahoga County	178
Columbus, OH (city) Franklin County	59

Cubans with Income Below Poverty Level
Top 10 Places Sorted by Percent

Place	Percent
Cleveland, OH (city) Cuyahoga County	42.38
Columbus, OH (city) Franklin County	8.51

Notes: Please refer to the User's Guide for an explanation of data; tables include places with populations > 9,999 and reflect only those areas that meet Summary File 4 population thresholds, therefore there may be less than 10 places listed

Dominicans with Income Below Poverty Level
Top 10 Places Sorted by Number

Place	Number
Cleveland, OH (city) Cuyahoga County	171

Dominicans with Income Below Poverty Level
Top 10 Places Sorted by Percent

Place	Percent
Cleveland, OH (city) Cuyahoga County	27.63

Ecuadorians with Income Below Poverty Level
Top 10 Places Sorted by Number

Place	Number
No places met population threshold.	

Ecuadorians with Income Below Poverty Level
Top 10 Places Sorted by Percent

Place	Percent
No places met population threshold.	

Guatemalans with Income Below Poverty Level
Top 10 Places Sorted by Number

Place	Number
Cleveland, OH (city) Cuyahoga County	118

Guatemalans with Income Below Poverty Level
Top 10 Places Sorted by Percent

Place	Percent
Cleveland, OH (city) Cuyahoga County	27.00

Hondurans with Income Below Poverty Level
Top 10 Places Sorted by Number

Place	Number
No places met population threshold.	

Hondurans with Income Below Poverty Level
Top 10 Places Sorted by Percent

Place	Percent
No places met population threshold.	

Mexicans with Income Below Poverty Level
Top 10 Places Sorted by Number

Place	Number
Toledo, OH (city) Lucas County	3,057
Columbus, OH (city) Franklin County	1,836
Cleveland, OH (city) Cuyahoga County	960
Painesville, OH (city) Lake County	591
Lorain, OH (city) Lorain County	419
Cincinnati, OH (city) Hamilton County	354
Dayton, OH (city) Montgomery County	349
Hamilton, OH (city) Butler County	247
Defiance, OH (city) Defiance County	218
Fostoria, OH (city) Seneca County	214

Mexicans with Income Below Poverty Level
Top 10 Places Sorted by Percent

Place	Percent
Youngstown, OH (city) Mahoning County	39.75
Dayton, OH (city) Montgomery County	36.89
Canton, OH (city) Stark County	36.23
Painesville, OH (city) Lake County	31.95
Cleveland, OH (city) Cuyahoga County	29.34
Hamilton, OH (city) Butler County	27.78
Springfield, OH (city) Clark County	26.59
Lima, OH (city) Allen County	25.77
Ashtabula, OH (city) Ashtabula County	25.12
Toledo, OH (city) Lucas County	24.00

Nicaraguans with Income Below Poverty Level
Top 10 Places Sorted by Number

Place	Number
No places met population threshold.	

Nicaraguans with Income Below Poverty Level
Top 10 Places Sorted by Percent

Place	Percent
No places met population threshold.	

Panamanians with Income Below Poverty Level
Top 10 Places Sorted by Number

Place	Number
No places met population threshold.	

Panamanians with Income Below Poverty Level
Top 10 Places Sorted by Percent

Place	Percent
No places met population threshold.	

Paraguayans with Income Below Poverty Level
Top 10 Places Sorted by Number

Place	Number
No places met population threshold.	

Paraguayans with Income Below Poverty Level
Top 10 Places Sorted by Percent

Place	Percent
No places met population threshold.	

Peruvians with Income Below Poverty Level
Top 10 Places Sorted by Number

Place	Number
No places met population threshold.	

Peruvians with Income Below Poverty Level
Top 10 Places Sorted by Percent

Place	Percent
No places met population threshold.	

Puerto Ricans with Income Below Poverty Level
Top 10 Places Sorted by Number

Place	Number
Cleveland, OH (city) Cuyahoga County	8,433
Lorain, OH (city) Lorain County	2,300
Youngstown, OH (city) Mahoning County	874
Columbus, OH (city) Franklin County	404
Toledo, OH (city) Lucas County	374
Ashtabula, OH (city) Ashtabula County	294
Akron, OH (city) Summit County	145
Elyria, OH (city) Lorain County	113
Lakewood, OH (city) Cuyahoga County	68
Cincinnati, OH (city) Hamilton County	53

Puerto Ricans with Income Below Poverty Level
Top 10 Places Sorted by Percent

Place	Percent
Ashtabula, OH (city) Ashtabula County	46.15
Toledo, OH (city) Lucas County	36.52
Cleveland, OH (city) Cuyahoga County	35.04
Youngstown, OH (city) Mahoning County	29.83
Akron, OH (city) Summit County	23.62
Lorain, OH (city) Lorain County	22.96
Elyria, OH (city) Lorain County	16.99
Columbus, OH (city) Franklin County	13.85
Lakewood, OH (city) Cuyahoga County	12.19
Cincinnati, OH (city) Hamilton County	9.48

Salvadorans with Income Below Poverty Level
Top 10 Places Sorted by Number

Place	Number
Columbus, OH (city) Franklin County	73
Cleveland, OH (city) Cuyahoga County	53

Salvadorans with Income Below Poverty Level
Top 10 Places Sorted by Percent

Place	Percent
Columbus, OH (city) Franklin County	18.07
Cleveland, OH (city) Cuyahoga County	11.86

South Americans with Income Below Poverty Level
Top 10 Places Sorted by Number

Place	Number
Columbus, OH (city) Franklin County	150
Cincinnati, OH (city) Hamilton County	118
Cleveland, OH (city) Cuyahoga County	56

South Americans with Income Below Poverty Level
Top 10 Places Sorted by Percent

Place	Percent
Cincinnati, OH (city) Hamilton County	24.95
Columbus, OH (city) Franklin County	14.88
Cleveland, OH (city) Cuyahoga County	10.41

Spaniards with Income Below Poverty Level
Top 10 Places Sorted by Number

Place	Number
No places met population threshold.	

Spaniards with Income Below Poverty Level
Top 10 Places Sorted by Percent

Place	Percent
No places met population threshold.	

Uruguayans with Income Below Poverty Level
Top 10 Places Sorted by Number

Place	Number
No places met population threshold.	

Uruguayans with Income Below Poverty Level
Top 10 Places Sorted by Percent

Place	Percent
No places met population threshold.	

Venezuelans with Income Below Poverty Level
Top 10 Places Sorted by Number

Place	Number
No places met population threshold.	

Venezuelans with Income Below Poverty Level
Top 10 Places Sorted by Percent

Place	Percent
No places met population threshold.	

Other Hispanics with Income Below Poverty Level
Top 10 Places Sorted by Number

Place	Number
Cleveland, OH (city) Cuyahoga County	982
Toledo, OH (city) Lucas County	713
Columbus, OH (city) Franklin County	448
Lorain, OH (city) Lorain County	379
Fremont, OH (city) Sandusky County	244
Cincinnati, OH (city) Hamilton County	217
Youngstown, OH (city) Mahoning County	166
Dayton, OH (city) Montgomery County	133
Akron, OH (city) Summit County	111

Notes: Please refer to the User's Guide for an explanation of data; tables include places with populations > 9,999 and reflect only those areas that meet Summary File 4 population thresholds, therefore there may be less than 10 places listed

Defiance, OH (city) Defiance County   24

Other Hispanics with Income Below Poverty Level
Top 10 Places Sorted by Percent

Place	Percent
Fremont, OH (city) Sandusky County	44.04
Youngstown, OH (city) Mahoning County	39.24
Cincinnati, OH (city) Hamilton County	32.10
Dayton, OH (city) Montgomery County	31.52
Cleveland, OH (city) Cuyahoga County	28.51
Lorain, OH (city) Lorain County	27.58
Toledo, OH (city) Lucas County	26.82
Akron, OH (city) Summit County	24.89
Columbus, OH (city) Franklin County	15.44
Defiance, OH (city) Defiance County	4.71

Homeownership

Total Populations Who Own Their Own Homes
Top 10 Places Sorted by Number

Place	Number
Columbus, OH (city) Franklin County	148,315
Cleveland, OH (city) Cuyahoga County	92,498
Toledo, OH (city) Lucas County	77,028
Cincinnati, OH (city) Hamilton County	57,655
Akron, OH (city) Summit County	53,441
Dayton, OH (city) Montgomery County	35,536
Parma, OH (city) Cuyahoga County	27,222
Youngstown, OH (city) Mahoning County	20,600
Canton, OH (city) Stark County	19,375
Kettering, OH (city) Montgomery County	17,082

Total Populations Who Own Their Own Homes
Top 10 Places Sorted by Percent

Place	Percent
Beavercreek, OH (city) Greene County	84.21
Maple Heights, OH (city) Cuyahoga County	83.82
Brook Park, OH (city) Cuyahoga County	83.61
Strongsville, OH (city) Cuyahoga County	82.73
Upper Arlington, OH (city) Franklin County	81.11
Brunswick, OH (city) Medina County	80.90
Garfield Heights, OH (city) Cuyahoga County	80.12
North Olmsted, OH (city) Cuyahoga County	79.71
Westerville, OH (city) Franklin County	79.01
Parma, OH (city) Cuyahoga County	77.50

Hispanics Who Own Their Own Homes
Top 10 Places Sorted by Number

Place	Number
Cleveland, OH (city) Cuyahoga County	4,272
Toledo, OH (city) Lucas County	2,422
Lorain, OH (city) Lorain County	2,129
Columbus, OH (city) Franklin County	1,419
Youngstown, OH (city) Mahoning County	737
Defiance, OH (city) Defiance County	372
Akron, OH (city) Summit County	354
Cincinnati, OH (city) Hamilton County	338
Fremont, OH (city) Sandusky County	280
Dayton, OH (city) Montgomery County	236

Hispanics Who Own Their Own Homes
Top 10 Places Sorted by Percent

Place	Percent
Beavercreek, OH (city) Greene County	84.76
Brook Park, OH (city) Cuyahoga County	84.62
Strongsville, OH (city) Cuyahoga County	76.58
Maple Heights, OH (city) Cuyahoga County	74.34
Perrysburg, OH (city) Wood County	73.79
Garfield Heights, OH (city) Cuyahoga County	73.33
Brunswick, OH (city) Medina County	67.86
Westlake, OH (city) Cuyahoga County	67.24
Fostoria, OH (city) Seneca County	63.04
Xenia, OH (city) Greene County	62.14

Argentinians Who Own Their Own Homes
Top 10 Places Sorted by Number

Place	Number
No places met population threshold.

Argentinians Who Own Their Own Homes
Top 10 Places Sorted by Percent

Place	Percent
No places met population threshold.

Bolivians Who Own Their Own Homes
Top 10 Places Sorted by Number

Place	Number
No places met population threshold.

Bolivians Who Own Their Own Homes
Top 10 Places Sorted by Percent

Place	Percent
No places met population threshold.

Central Americans Who Own Their Own Homes
Top 10 Places Sorted by Number

Place	Number
Cleveland, OH (city) Cuyahoga County	196
Columbus, OH (city) Franklin County	43
Cincinnati, OH (city) Hamilton County	6

Central Americans Who Own Their Own Homes
Top 10 Places Sorted by Percent

Place	Percent
Cleveland, OH (city) Cuyahoga County	44.75
Columbus, OH (city) Franklin County	17.62
Cincinnati, OH (city) Hamilton County	4.92

Chileans Who Own Their Own Homes
Top 10 Places Sorted by Number

Place	Number
No places met population threshold.

Chileans Who Own Their Own Homes
Top 10 Places Sorted by Percent

Place	Percent
No places met population threshold.

Colombians Who Own Their Own Homes
Top 10 Places Sorted by Number

Place	Number
No places met population threshold.

Colombians Who Own Their Own Homes
Top 10 Places Sorted by Percent

Place	Percent
No places met population threshold.

Costa Ricans Who Own Their Own Homes
Top 10 Places Sorted by Number

Place	Number
No places met population threshold.

Costa Ricans Who Own Their Own Homes
Top 10 Places Sorted by Percent

Place	Percent
No places met population threshold.

Cubans Who Own Their Own Homes
Top 10 Places Sorted by Number

Place	Number
Columbus, OH (city) Franklin County	128
Cleveland, OH (city) Cuyahoga County	70

Cubans Who Own Their Own Homes
Top 10 Places Sorted by Percent

Place	Percent
Columbus, OH (city) Franklin County	57.40
Cleveland, OH (city) Cuyahoga County	41.92

Dominicans Who Own Their Own Homes
Top 10 Places Sorted by Number

Place	Number
Cleveland, OH (city) Cuyahoga County	85

Dominicans Who Own Their Own Homes
Top 10 Places Sorted by Percent

Place	Percent
Cleveland, OH (city) Cuyahoga County	34.69

Ecuadorians Who Own Their Own Homes
Top 10 Places Sorted by Number

Place	Number
No places met population threshold.

Ecuadorians Who Own Their Own Homes
Top 10 Places Sorted by Percent

Place	Percent
No places met population threshold.

Guatemalans Who Own Their Own Homes
Top 10 Places Sorted by Number

Place	Number
Cleveland, OH (city) Cuyahoga County	39

Guatemalans Who Own Their Own Homes
Top 10 Places Sorted by Percent

Place	Percent
Cleveland, OH (city) Cuyahoga County	33.05

Hondurans Who Own Their Own Homes
Top 10 Places Sorted by Number

Place	Number
No places met population threshold.

Hondurans Who Own Their Own Homes
Top 10 Places Sorted by Percent

Place	Percent
No places met population threshold.

Mexicans Who Own Their Own Homes
Top 10 Places Sorted by Number

Place	Number
Toledo, OH (city) Lucas County	1,849
Columbus, OH (city) Franklin County	516
Lorain, OH (city) Lorain County	481
Cleveland, OH (city) Cuyahoga County	426
Defiance, OH (city) Defiance County	254
Fremont, OH (city) Sandusky County	190
Fostoria, OH (city) Seneca County	168
Oregon, OH (city) Lucas County	134
Akron, OH (city) Summit County	123
Findlay, OH (city) Hancock County	100

Notes: Please refer to the User's Guide for an explanation of data; tables include places with populations > 9,999 and reflect only those areas that meet Summary File 4 population thresholds, therefore there may be less than 10 places listed

Mexicans Who Own Their Own Homes
Top 10 Places Sorted by Percent

Place	Percent
Lorain, OH (city) Lorain County	63.96
Fostoria, OH (city) Seneca County	61.31
Oregon, OH (city) Lucas County	60.91
Defiance, OH (city) Defiance County	55.82
Youngstown, OH (city) Mahoning County	55.19
Lakewood, OH (city) Cuyahoga County	52.94
Norwalk, OH (city) Huron County	52.04
Toledo, OH (city) Lucas County	51.45
Fremont, OH (city) Sandusky County	48.10
Sandusky, OH (city) Erie County	41.27

Nicaraguans Who Own Their Own Homes
Top 10 Places Sorted by Number

Place	Number
No places met population threshold.	

Nicaraguans Who Own Their Own Homes
Top 10 Places Sorted by Percent

Place	Percent
No places met population threshold.	

Panamanians Who Own Their Own Homes
Top 10 Places Sorted by Number

Place	Number
No places met population threshold.	

Panamanians Who Own Their Own Homes
Top 10 Places Sorted by Percent

Place	Percent
No places met population threshold.	

Paraguayans Who Own Their Own Homes
Top 10 Places Sorted by Number

Place	Number
No places met population threshold.	

Paraguayans Who Own Their Own Homes
Top 10 Places Sorted by Percent

Place	Percent
No places met population threshold.	

Peruvians Who Own Their Own Homes
Top 10 Places Sorted by Number

Place	Number
No places met population threshold.	

Peruvians Who Own Their Own Homes
Top 10 Places Sorted by Percent

Place	Percent
No places met population threshold.	

Puerto Ricans Who Own Their Own Homes
Top 10 Places Sorted by Number

Place	Number
Cleveland, OH (city) Cuyahoga County	2,987
Lorain, OH (city) Lorain County	1,483
Youngstown, OH (city) Mahoning County	590
Columbus, OH (city) Franklin County	284
Toledo, OH (city) Lucas County	122
Boardman, OH (cdp) Mahoning County	97
Parma, OH (city) Cuyahoga County	78
Akron, OH (city) Summit County	77
Cincinnati, OH (city) Hamilton County	63
Elyria, OH (city) Lorain County	50

Puerto Ricans Who Own Their Own Homes
Top 10 Places Sorted by Percent

Place	Percent
Youngstown, OH (city) Mahoning County	64.34
Boardman, OH (cdp) Mahoning County	59.88
Toledo, OH (city) Lucas County	48.61
Lorain, OH (city) Lorain County	46.93
Akron, OH (city) Summit County	42.31
Cleveland, OH (city) Cuyahoga County	40.39
Parma, OH (city) Cuyahoga County	38.05
Cincinnati, OH (city) Hamilton County	28.77
Columbus, OH (city) Franklin County	27.20
Elyria, OH (city) Lorain County	26.74

Salvadorans Who Own Their Own Homes
Top 10 Places Sorted by Number

Place	Number
Cleveland, OH (city) Cuyahoga County	80
Columbus, OH (city) Franklin County	19

Salvadorans Who Own Their Own Homes
Top 10 Places Sorted by Percent

Place	Percent
Cleveland, OH (city) Cuyahoga County	72.07
Columbus, OH (city) Franklin County	14.96

South Americans Who Own Their Own Homes
Top 10 Places Sorted by Number

Place	Number
Cleveland, OH (city) Cuyahoga County	118
Columbus, OH (city) Franklin County	115
Cincinnati, OH (city) Hamilton County	49

South Americans Who Own Their Own Homes
Top 10 Places Sorted by Percent

Place	Percent
Cleveland, OH (city) Cuyahoga County	45.56
Columbus, OH (city) Franklin County	32.49
Cincinnati, OH (city) Hamilton County	22.27

Spaniards Who Own Their Own Homes
Top 10 Places Sorted by Number

Place	Number
No places met population threshold.	

Spaniards Who Own Their Own Homes
Top 10 Places Sorted by Percent

Place	Percent
No places met population threshold.	

Uruguayans Who Own Their Own Homes
Top 10 Places Sorted by Number

Place	Number
No places met population threshold.	

Uruguayans Who Own Their Own Homes
Top 10 Places Sorted by Percent

Place	Percent
No places met population threshold.	

Venezuelans Who Own Their Own Homes
Top 10 Places Sorted by Number

Place	Number
No places met population threshold.	

Venezuelans Who Own Their Own Homes
Top 10 Places Sorted by Percent

Place	Percent
No places met population threshold.	

Other Hispanics Who Own Their Own Homes
Top 10 Places Sorted by Number

Place	Number
Cleveland, OH (city) Cuyahoga County	375
Toledo, OH (city) Lucas County	372
Columbus, OH (city) Franklin County	302
Akron, OH (city) Summit County	128
Lorain, OH (city) Lorain County	123
Cincinnati, OH (city) Hamilton County	96
Defiance, OH (city) Defiance County	79
Fremont, OH (city) Sandusky County	74
Dayton, OH (city) Montgomery County	57
Youngstown, OH (city) Mahoning County	53

Other Hispanics Who Own Their Own Homes
Top 10 Places Sorted by Percent

Place	Percent
Akron, OH (city) Summit County	60.09
Defiance, OH (city) Defiance County	57.66
Toledo, OH (city) Lucas County	50.47
Youngstown, OH (city) Mahoning County	48.62
Cleveland, OH (city) Cuyahoga County	45.79
Fremont, OH (city) Sandusky County	45.12
Lorain, OH (city) Lorain County	38.56
Columbus, OH (city) Franklin County	33.86
Cincinnati, OH (city) Hamilton County	30.09
Dayton, OH (city) Montgomery County	27.80

Median Gross Rent

All Specified Renter-Occupied Housing Units
Top 10 Places Sorted by Number

Place	Dollars/Month
Westlake, OH (city) Cuyahoga County	866
Beavercreek, OH (city) Greene County	821
Upper Arlington, OH (city) Franklin County	776
Fairfield, OH (city) Butler County	667
Brook Park, OH (city) Cuyahoga County	659
Reynoldsburg, OH (city) Franklin County	653
Huber Heights, OH (city) Montgomery County	651
Cleveland Heights, OH (city) Cuyahoga County	640
North Olmsted, OH (city) Cuyahoga County	634
Brunswick, OH (city) Medina County	630

Specified Housing Units Rented by Hispanics
Top 10 Places Sorted by Number

Place	Dollars/Month
Beavercreek, OH (city) Greene County	1,028
Westlake, OH (city) Cuyahoga County	775
Reynoldsburg, OH (city) Franklin County	699
Brunswick, OH (city) Medina County	681
Upper Arlington, OH (city) Franklin County	667
Fairfield, OH (city) Butler County	638
Parma, OH (city) Cuyahoga County	633
Huber Heights, OH (city) Montgomery County	619
North Olmsted, OH (city) Cuyahoga County	618
Parma Heights, OH (city) Cuyahoga County	600

Specified Housing Units Rented by Argentinians
Top 10 Places Sorted by Number

Place	Dollars/Month
No places met population threshold.	

Notes: Please refer to the User's Guide for an explanation of data; tables include places with populations > 9,999 and reflect only those areas that meet Summary File 4 population thresholds, therefore there may be less than 10 places listed

PROFILES OF OHIO / Hispanic Rankings: Median Home Value

Specified Housing Units Rented by Bolivians
Top 10 Places Sorted by Number

Place	Dollars/Month
No places met population threshold.	

Specified Housing Units Rented by Central Americans
Top 10 Places Sorted by Number

Place	Dollars/Month
Columbus, OH (city) Franklin County	599
Cleveland, OH (city) Cuyahoga County	486
Cincinnati, OH (city) Hamilton County	397

Specified Housing Units Rented by Chileans
Top 10 Places Sorted by Number

Place	Dollars/Month
No places met population threshold.	

Specified Housing Units Rented by Colombians
Top 10 Places Sorted by Number

Place	Dollars/Month
No places met population threshold.	

Specified Housing Units Rented by Costa Ricans
Top 10 Places Sorted by Number

Place	Dollars/Month
No places met population threshold.	

Specified Housing Units Rented by Cubans
Top 10 Places Sorted by Number

Place	Dollars/Month
Columbus, OH (city) Franklin County	599
Cleveland, OH (city) Cuyahoga County	479

Specified Housing Units Rented by Dominicans
Top 10 Places Sorted by Number

Place	Dollars/Month
Cleveland, OH (city) Cuyahoga County	460

Specified Housing Units Rented by Ecuadorians
Top 10 Places Sorted by Number

Place	Dollars/Month
No places met population threshold.	

Specified Housing Units Rented by Guatelmalans
Top 10 Places Sorted by Number

Place	Dollars/Month
Cleveland, OH (city) Cuyahoga County	498

Specified Housing Units Rented by Hondurans
Top 10 Places Sorted by Number

Place	Dollars/Month
No places met population threshold.	

Specified Housing Units Rented by Mexicans
Top 10 Places Sorted by Number

Place	Dollars/Month
Painesville, OH (city) Lake County	599
Lakewood, OH (city) Cuyahoga County	590
Hamilton, OH (city) Butler County	572
Dayton, OH (city) Montgomery County	555
Columbus, OH (city) Franklin County	541
Bowling Green, OH (city) Wood County	538
Elyria, OH (city) Lorain County	538
Canton, OH (city) Stark County	531
Lorain, OH (city) Lorain County	531
Akron, OH (city) Summit County	508

Specified Housing Units Rented by Nicaraguans
Top 10 Places Sorted by Number

Place	Dollars/Month
No places met population threshold.	

Specified Housing Units Rented by Panamanians
Top 10 Places Sorted by Number

Place	Dollars/Month
No places met population threshold.	

Specified Housing Units Rented by Paraguayans
Top 10 Places Sorted by Number

Place	Dollars/Month
No places met population threshold.	

Specified Housing Units Rented by Peruvians
Top 10 Places Sorted by Number

Place	Dollars/Month
No places met population threshold.	

Specified Housing Units Rented by Puerto Ricans
Top 10 Places Sorted by Number

Place	Dollars/Month
Parma, OH (city) Cuyahoga County	620
Columbus, OH (city) Franklin County	571
Boardman, OH (cdp) Mahoning County	563
Lakewood, OH (city) Cuyahoga County	554
Cincinnati, OH (city) Hamilton County	544
Elyria, OH (city) Lorain County	490
Toledo, OH (city) Lucas County	482
Cleveland, OH (city) Cuyahoga County	467
Lorain, OH (city) Lorain County	452
Akron, OH (city) Summit County	448

Specified Housing Units Rented by Salvadorans
Top 10 Places Sorted by Number

Place	Dollars/Month
Columbus, OH (city) Franklin County	584
Cleveland, OH (city) Cuyahoga County	442

Specified Housing Units Rented by South Americans
Top 10 Places Sorted by Number

Place	Dollars/Month
Columbus, OH (city) Franklin County	623
Cleveland, OH (city) Cuyahoga County	578
Cincinnati, OH (city) Hamilton County	534

Specified Housing Units Rented by Spaniards
Top 10 Places Sorted by Number

Place	Dollars/Month
No places met population threshold.	

Specified Housing Units Rented by Uruguayans
Top 10 Places Sorted by Number

Place	Dollars/Month
No places met population threshold.	

Specified Housing Units Rented by Venezuelans
Top 10 Places Sorted by Number

Place	Dollars/Month
No places met population threshold.	

Specified Housing Units Rented by Other Hispanics
Top 10 Places Sorted by Number

Place	Dollars/Month
Columbus, OH (city) Franklin County	580
Lorain, OH (city) Lorain County	525
Youngstown, OH (city) Mahoning County	524
Cincinnati, OH (city) Hamilton County	496
Akron, OH (city) Summit County	491
Defiance, OH (city) Defiance County	489
Cleveland, OH (city) Cuyahoga County	448
Toledo, OH (city) Lucas County	445
Fremont, OH (city) Sandusky County	424
Dayton, OH (city) Montgomery County	405

Median Home Value

All Specified Owner-Occupied Housing Units
Top 10 Places Sorted by Number

Place	Dollars
Upper Arlington, OH (city) Franklin County	214,700
Westlake, OH (city) Cuyahoga County	201,000
Strongsville, OH (city) Cuyahoga County	170,200
Westerville, OH (city) Franklin County	161,500
Perrysburg, OH (city) Wood County	158,700
Beavercreek, OH (city) Greene County	143,300
North Olmsted, OH (city) Cuyahoga County	142,300
Brunswick, OH (city) Medina County	136,000
Bowling Green, OH (city) Wood County	130,300
Fairfield, OH (city) Butler County	125,000

Specified Housing Units Owned and Occupied by Hispanics
Top 10 Places Sorted by Number

Place	Dollars
Upper Arlington, OH (city) Franklin County	186,500
Westerville, OH (city) Franklin County	180,000
Beavercreek, OH (city) Greene County	164,800
Westlake, OH (city) Cuyahoga County	161,900
Reynoldsburg, OH (city) Franklin County	160,200
Brunswick, OH (city) Medina County	158,000
Strongsville, OH (city) Cuyahoga County	148,800
North Olmsted, OH (city) Cuyahoga County	144,500
Huber Heights, OH (city) Montgomery County	140,000
Brooklyn, OH (city) Cuyahoga County	133,000

Specified Housing Units Owned and Occupied by Argentinians
Top 10 Places Sorted by Number

Place	Dollars
No places met population threshold.	

Specified Housing Units Owned and Occupied by Bolivians
Top 10 Places Sorted by Number

Place	Dollars
No places met population threshold.	

Specified Housing Units Owned and Occupied by Central Americans
Top 10 Places Sorted by Number

Place	Dollars
Columbus, OH (city) Franklin County	108,900
Cleveland, OH (city) Cuyahoga County	76,300
Cincinnati, OH (city) Hamilton County	55,000

Specified Housing Units Owned and Occupied by Chileans
Top 10 Places Sorted by Number

Place	Dollars
No places met population threshold.	

Specified Housing Units Owned and Occupied by Colombians
Top 10 Places Sorted by Number

Place	Dollars
No places met population threshold.	

Notes: Please refer to the User's Guide for an explanation of data; tables include places with populations > 9,999 and reflect only those areas that meet Summary File 4 population thresholds, therefore there may be less than 10 places listed

Specified Housing Units Owned and Occupied by Costa Ricans
Top 10 Places Sorted by Number

Place	Dollars
No places met population threshold.	

Specified Housing Units Owned and Occupied by Cubans
Top 10 Places Sorted by Number

Place	Dollars
Columbus, OH (city) Franklin County	112,500
Cleveland, OH (city) Cuyahoga County	81,900

Specified Housing Units Owned and Occupied by Dominicans
Top 10 Places Sorted by Number

Place	Dollars
Cleveland, OH (city) Cuyahoga County	62,900

Specified Housing Units Owned and Occupied by Ecuadorians
Top 10 Places Sorted by Number

Place	Dollars
No places met population threshold.	

Specified Housing Units Owned and Occupied by Guatemalans
Top 10 Places Sorted by Number

Place	Dollars
Cleveland, OH (city) Cuyahoga County	79,500

Specified Housing Units Owned and Occupied by Hondurans
Top 10 Places Sorted by Number

Place	Dollars
No places met population threshold.	

Specified Housing Units Owned and Occupied by Mexicans
Top 10 Places Sorted by Number

Place	Dollars
Oregon, OH (city) Lucas County	115,800
Cincinnati, OH (city) Hamilton County	115,400
Lakewood, OH (city) Cuyahoga County	111,900
Bowling Green, OH (city) Wood County	104,400
Columbus, OH (city) Franklin County	101,800
Akron, OH (city) Summit County	99,300
Springfield, OH (city) Clark County	91,400
Elyria, OH (city) Lorain County	85,000
Lorain, OH (city) Lorain County	78,000
Norwalk, OH (city) Huron County	75,600

Specified Housing Units Owned and Occupied by Nicaraguans
Top 10 Places Sorted by Number

Place	Dollars
No places met population threshold.	

Specified Housing Units Owned and Occupied by Panamanians
Top 10 Places Sorted by Number

Place	Dollars
No places met population threshold.	

Specified Housing Units Owned and Occupied by Paraguayans
Top 10 Places Sorted by Number

Place	Dollars
No places met population threshold.	

Specified Housing Units Owned and Occupied by Peruvians
Top 10 Places Sorted by Number

Place	Dollars
No places met population threshold.	

Specified Housing Units Owned and Occupied by Puerto Ricans
Top 10 Places Sorted by Number

Place	Dollars
Columbus, OH (city) Franklin County	133,300
Parma, OH (city) Cuyahoga County	117,300
Lakewood, OH (city) Cuyahoga County	107,300
Cincinnati, OH (city) Hamilton County	106,000
Lorain, OH (city) Lorain County	79,900
Boardman, OH (cdp) Mahoning County	76,600
Toledo, OH (city) Lucas County	74,400
Cleveland, OH (city) Cuyahoga County	72,000
Akron, OH (city) Summit County	65,800
Elyria, OH (city) Lorain County	65,800

Specified Housing Units Owned and Occupied by Salvadorans
Top 10 Places Sorted by Number

Place	Dollars
Columbus, OH (city) Franklin County	112,500
Cleveland, OH (city) Cuyahoga County	68,600

Specified Housing Units Owned and Occupied by South Americans
Top 10 Places Sorted by Number

Place	Dollars
Cincinnati, OH (city) Hamilton County	344,400
Columbus, OH (city) Franklin County	133,900
Cleveland, OH (city) Cuyahoga County	104,700

Specified Housing Units Owned and Occupied by Spaniards
Top 10 Places Sorted by Number

Place	Dollars
No places met population threshold.	

Specified Housing Units Owned and Occupied by Uruguayans
Top 10 Places Sorted by Number

Place	Dollars
No places met population threshold.	

Specified Housing Units Owned and Occupied by Venezuelans
Top 10 Places Sorted by Number

Place	Dollars
No places met population threshold.	

Specified Housing Units Owned and Occupied by Other Hispanics
Top 10 Places Sorted by Number

Place	Dollars
Columbus, OH (city) Franklin County	100,800
Lorain, OH (city) Lorain County	96,700
Akron, OH (city) Summit County	89,200
Defiance, OH (city) Defiance County	82,300
Cincinnati, OH (city) Hamilton County	80,800
Cleveland, OH (city) Cuyahoga County	74,300
Dayton, OH (city) Montgomery County	63,200
Fremont, OH (city) Sandusky County	63,100
Toledo, OH (city) Lucas County	54,600
Youngstown, OH (city) Mahoning County	40,000

Notes: Please refer to the User's Guide for an explanation of data; tables include places with populations > 9,999 and reflect only those areas that meet Summary File 4 population thresholds, therefore there may be less than 10 places listed

PROFILES OF OHIO / Asian Rankings: Population

Population

Total Population
Top 10 Places Sorted by Number

Place	Number
Columbus, OH (city) Franklin County	711,644
Cleveland, OH (city) Cuyahoga County	478,393
Cincinnati, OH (city) Hamilton County	330,662
Toledo, OH (city) Lucas County	313,587
Akron, OH (city) Summit County	217,088
Dayton, OH (city) Montgomery County	166,193
Parma, OH (city) Cuyahoga County	85,655
Kettering, OH (city) Montgomery County	57,531
Lakewood, OH (city) Cuyahoga County	56,646
Mentor, OH (city) Lake County	50,278

Asian
Top 10 Places Sorted by Number

Place	Number
Columbus, OH (city) Franklin County	24,743
Cleveland, OH (city) Cuyahoga County	6,878
Cincinnati, OH (city) Hamilton County	4,962
Akron, OH (city) Summit County	3,148
Toledo, OH (city) Lucas County	2,994
Dublin, OH (city) Franklin County	2,497
Strongsville, OH (city) Cuyahoga County	1,470
Parma, OH (city) Cuyahoga County	1,410
Cleveland Heights, OH (city) Cuyahoga County	1,358
Westlake, OH (city) Cuyahoga County	1,354

Asian
Top 10 Places Sorted by Percent of Total Population

Place	Percent
Dublin, OH (city) Franklin County	7.93
Beckett Ridge, OH (cdp) Butler County	7.32
Blue Ash, OH (city) Hamilton County	7.04
Highland Heights, OH (city) Cuyahoga County	5.09
Kenwood, OH (cdp) Hamilton County	4.98
Solon, OH (city) Cuyahoga County	4.91
Richmond Heights, OH (city) Cuyahoga County	4.71
Westlake, OH (city) Cuyahoga County	4.25
Hilliard, OH (city) Franklin County	4.16
Athens, OH (city) Athens County	4.13

Native Hawaiian and Other Pacific Islander
Top 10 Places Sorted by Number

Place	Number
No places met population threshold.	

Native Hawaiian and Other Pacific Islander
Top 10 Places Sorted by Percent of Asian Population

Place	Percent
No places met population threshold.	

Native Hawaiian and Other Pacific Islander
Top 10 Places Sorted by Percent of Total Population

Place	Percent
No places met population threshold.	

Asian Indian
Top 10 Places Sorted by Number

Place	Number
Columbus, OH (city) Franklin County	6,413
Cincinnati, OH (city) Hamilton County	1,541
Cleveland, OH (city) Cuyahoga County	1,206
Toledo, OH (city) Lucas County	865
Strongsville, OH (city) Cuyahoga County	727
Dublin, OH (city) Franklin County	666
Parma, OH (city) Cuyahoga County	635
Akron, OH (city) Summit County	599
Cleveland Heights, OH (city) Cuyahoga County	553
Westlake, OH (city) Cuyahoga County	541

Asian Indian
Top 10 Places Sorted by Percent of Asian Population

Place	Percent
Sharonville, OH (city) Hamilton County	70.68
North Royalton, OH (city) Cuyahoga County	55.92
Strongsville, OH (city) Cuyahoga County	49.46
Mayfield Heights, OH (city) Cuyahoga County	48.62
North Olmsted, OH (city) Cuyahoga County	45.14
Blue Ash, OH (city) Hamilton County	45.10
Parma, OH (city) Cuyahoga County	45.04
Fairfield, OH (city) Butler County	44.41
Solon, OH (city) Cuyahoga County	43.93
Cleveland Heights, OH (city) Cuyahoga County	40.72

Asian Indian
Top 10 Places Sorted by Percent of Total Population

Place	Percent
Blue Ash, OH (city) Hamilton County	3.18
Sharonville, OH (city) Hamilton County	2.87
Solon, OH (city) Cuyahoga County	2.16
Dublin, OH (city) Franklin County	2.12
Mayfield Heights, OH (city) Cuyahoga County	2.00
Westlake, OH (city) Cuyahoga County	1.70
Strongsville, OH (city) Cuyahoga County	1.66
North Olmsted, OH (city) Cuyahoga County	1.25
Beavercreek, OH (city) Greene County	1.24
Cleveland Heights, OH (city) Cuyahoga County	1.11

Bangladeshi
Top 10 Places Sorted by Number

Place	Number
No places met population threshold.	

Bangladeshi
Top 10 Places Sorted by Percent of Asian Population

Place	Percent
No places met population threshold.	

Bangladeshi
Top 10 Places Sorted by Percent of Total Population

Place	Percent
No places met population threshold.	

Cambodian
Top 10 Places Sorted by Number

Place	Number
Columbus, OH (city) Franklin County	1,192

Cambodian
Top 10 Places Sorted by Percent of Asian Population

Place	Percent
Columbus, OH (city) Franklin County	4.82

Cambodian
Top 10 Places Sorted by Percent of Total Population

Place	Percent
Columbus, OH (city) Franklin County	0.17

Chinese (except Taiwanese)
Top 10 Places Sorted by Number

Place	Number
Columbus, OH (city) Franklin County	5,147
Cleveland, OH (city) Cuyahoga County	2,029
Cincinnati, OH (city) Hamilton County	1,322
Toledo, OH (city) Lucas County	774
Akron, OH (city) Summit County	535
Dublin, OH (city) Franklin County	510
Cleveland Heights, OH (city) Cuyahoga County	394
Hudson, OH (city) Summit County	359
Solon, OH (city) Cuyahoga County	346
Upper Arlington, OH (city) Franklin County	339

Chinese (except Taiwanese)
Top 10 Places Sorted by Percent of Asian Population

Place	Percent
Hudson, OH (city) Summit County	49.11
Upper Arlington, OH (city) Franklin County	33.43
Solon, OH (city) Cuyahoga County	32.34
Cleveland, OH (city) Cuyahoga County	29.50
Cleveland Heights, OH (city) Cuyahoga County	29.01
Cincinnati, OH (city) Hamilton County	26.64
Toledo, OH (city) Lucas County	25.85
Columbus, OH (city) Franklin County	20.80
Dublin, OH (city) Franklin County	20.42
Akron, OH (city) Summit County	16.99

Chinese (except Taiwanese)
Top 10 Places Sorted by Percent of Total Population

Place	Percent
Dublin, OH (city) Franklin County	1.62
Hudson, OH (city) Summit County	1.60
Solon, OH (city) Cuyahoga County	1.59
Upper Arlington, OH (city) Franklin County	1.01
Cleveland Heights, OH (city) Cuyahoga County	0.79
Columbus, OH (city) Franklin County	0.72
Cleveland, OH (city) Cuyahoga County	0.42
Cincinnati, OH (city) Hamilton County	0.40
Akron, OH (city) Summit County	0.25
Toledo, OH (city) Lucas County	0.25

Fijian
Top 10 Places Sorted by Number

Place	Number
No places met population threshold.	

Fijian
Top 10 Places Sorted by Percent of Asian Population

Place	Percent
No places met population threshold.	

Fijian
Top 10 Places Sorted by Percent of Total Population

Place	Percent
No places met population threshold.	

Filipino
Top 10 Places Sorted by Number

Place	Number
Columbus, OH (city) Franklin County	1,379
Cleveland, OH (city) Cuyahoga County	837
Cincinnati, OH (city) Hamilton County	480
Toledo, OH (city) Lucas County	372

Filipino
Top 10 Places Sorted by Percent of Asian Population

Place	Percent
Toledo, OH (city) Lucas County	12.42
Cleveland, OH (city) Cuyahoga County	12.17
Cincinnati, OH (city) Hamilton County	9.67
Columbus, OH (city) Franklin County	5.57

Filipino
Top 10 Places Sorted by Percent of Total Population

Place	Percent
Columbus, OH (city) Franklin County	0.19
Cleveland, OH (city) Cuyahoga County	0.17
Cincinnati, OH (city) Hamilton County	0.15
Toledo, OH (city) Lucas County	0.12

Guamanian or Chamorro
Top 10 Places Sorted by Number

Place	Number
No places met population threshold.	

Notes: Please refer to the User's Guide for an explanation of data; tables reflect only those areas that meet Summary File 4 population thresholds, therefore there may be less than 10 places listed

PROFILES OF OHIO / Asian Rankings: Population

Guamanian or Chamorro
Top 10 Places Sorted by Percent of Asian Population

Place	Percent
No places met population threshold.	

Guamanian or Chamorro
Top 10 Places Sorted by Percent of Total Population

Place	Percent
No places met population threshold.	

Hawaiian, Native
Top 10 Places Sorted by Number

Place	Number
No places met population threshold.	

Hawaiian, Native
Top 10 Places Sorted by Percent of Asian Population

Place	Percent
No places met population threshold.	

Hawaiian, Native
Top 10 Places Sorted by Percent of Total Population

Place	Percent
No places met population threshold.	

Hmong
Top 10 Places Sorted by Number

Place	Number
No places met population threshold.	

Hmong
Top 10 Places Sorted by Percent of Asian Population

Place	Percent
No places met population threshold.	

Hmong
Top 10 Places Sorted by Percent of Total Population

Place	Percent
No places met population threshold.	

Indonesian
Top 10 Places Sorted by Number

Place	Number
Columbus, OH (city) Franklin County	514

Indonesian
Top 10 Places Sorted by Percent of Asian Population

Place	Percent
Columbus, OH (city) Franklin County	2.08

Indonesian
Top 10 Places Sorted by Percent of Total Population

Place	Percent
Columbus, OH (city) Franklin County	0.07

Japanese
Top 10 Places Sorted by Number

Place	Number
Columbus, OH (city) Franklin County	1,845
Dublin, OH (city) Franklin County	820

Japanese
Top 10 Places Sorted by Percent of Asian Population

Place	Percent
Dublin, OH (city) Franklin County	32.84
Columbus, OH (city) Franklin County	7.46

Japanese
Top 10 Places Sorted by Percent of Total Population

Place	Percent
Dublin, OH (city) Franklin County	2.60
Columbus, OH (city) Franklin County	0.26

Korean
Top 10 Places Sorted by Number

Place	Number
Columbus, OH (city) Franklin County	2,524

Korean
Top 10 Places Sorted by Percent of Asian Population

Place	Percent
Columbus, OH (city) Franklin County	10.20

Korean
Top 10 Places Sorted by Percent of Total Population

Place	Percent
Columbus, OH (city) Franklin County	0.35

Laotian
Top 10 Places Sorted by Number

Place	Number
Columbus, OH (city) Franklin County	979
Akron, OH (city) Summit County	572

Laotian
Top 10 Places Sorted by Percent of Asian Population

Place	Percent
Akron, OH (city) Summit County	18.17
Columbus, OH (city) Franklin County	3.96

Laotian
Top 10 Places Sorted by Percent of Total Population

Place	Percent
Akron, OH (city) Summit County	0.26
Columbus, OH (city) Franklin County	0.14

Malaysian
Top 10 Places Sorted by Number

Place	Number
No places met population threshold.	

Malaysian
Top 10 Places Sorted by Percent of Asian Population

Place	Percent
No places met population threshold.	

Malaysian
Top 10 Places Sorted by Percent of Total Population

Place	Percent
No places met population threshold.	

Pakistani
Top 10 Places Sorted by Number

Place	Number
No places met population threshold.	

Pakistani
Top 10 Places Sorted by Percent of Asian Population

Place	Percent
No places met population threshold.	

Pakistani
Top 10 Places Sorted by Percent of Total Population

Place	Percent
No places met population threshold.	

Samoan
Top 10 Places Sorted by Number

Place	Number
No places met population threshold.	

Samoan
Top 10 Places Sorted by Percent of Asian Population

Place	Percent
No places met population threshold.	

Samoan
Top 10 Places Sorted by Percent of Total Population

Place	Percent
No places met population threshold.	

Sri Lankan
Top 10 Places Sorted by Number

Place	Number
No places met population threshold.	

Sri Lankan
Top 10 Places Sorted by Percent of Asian Population

Place	Percent
No places met population threshold.	

Sri Lankan
Top 10 Places Sorted by Percent of Total Population

Place	Percent
No places met population threshold.	

Taiwanese
Top 10 Places Sorted by Number

Place	Number
Columbus, OH (city) Franklin County	463

Taiwanese
Top 10 Places Sorted by Percent of Asian Population

Place	Percent
Columbus, OH (city) Franklin County	1.87

Taiwanese
Top 10 Places Sorted by Percent of Total Population

Place	Percent
Columbus, OH (city) Franklin County	0.07

Thai
Top 10 Places Sorted by Number

Place	Number
Columbus, OH (city) Franklin County	389

Thai
Top 10 Places Sorted by Percent of Asian Population

Place	Percent
Columbus, OH (city) Franklin County	1.57

Thai
Top 10 Places Sorted by Percent of Total Population

Place	Percent
Columbus, OH (city) Franklin County	0.05

Notes: Please refer to the User's Guide for an explanation of data; tables reflect only those areas that meet Summary File 4 population thresholds, therefore there may be less than 10 places listed.

PROFILES OF OHIO / Asian Rankings: Median Age

Tongan
Top 10 Places Sorted by Number

Place	Number
No places met population threshold.	

Tongan
Top 10 Places Sorted by Percent of Asian Population

Place	Percent
No places met population threshold.	

Tongan
Top 10 Places Sorted by Percent of Total Population

Place	Percent
No places met population threshold.	

Vietnamese
Top 10 Places Sorted by Number

Place	Number
Columbus, OH (city) Franklin County	2,181
Cleveland, OH (city) Cuyahoga County	1,107
Akron, OH (city) Summit County	571

Vietnamese
Top 10 Places Sorted by Percent of Asian Population

Place	Percent
Akron, OH (city) Summit County	18.14
Cleveland, OH (city) Cuyahoga County	16.09
Columbus, OH (city) Franklin County	8.81

Vietnamese
Top 10 Places Sorted by Percent of Total Population

Place	Percent
Columbus, OH (city) Franklin County	0.31
Akron, OH (city) Summit County	0.26
Cleveland, OH (city) Cuyahoga County	0.23

Median Age

Total Population
Top 10 Places Sorted by Number

Place	Years
Beachwood, OH (city) Cuyahoga County	51.6
Kenwood, OH (cdp) Hamilton County	45.2
Worthington, OH (city) Franklin County	44.0
Mayfield Heights, OH (city) Cuyahoga County	43.9
Middleburg Heights, OH (city) Cuyahoga County	43.0
Upper Arlington, OH (city) Franklin County	42.5
Centerville, OH (city) Montgomery County	42.2
Highland Heights, OH (city) Cuyahoga County	42.2
Parma Heights, OH (city) Cuyahoga County	42.1
Westlake, OH (city) Cuyahoga County	41.9

Asian
Top 10 Places Sorted by Number

Place	Years
Westlake, OH (city) Cuyahoga County	43.2
Worthington, OH (city) Franklin County	40.6
Solon, OH (city) Cuyahoga County	39.7
Beavercreek, OH (city) Greene County	38.9
Highland Heights, OH (city) Cuyahoga County	38.6
Mentor, OH (city) Lake County	37.6
Westerville, OH (city) Franklin County	37.4
North Royalton, OH (city) Cuyahoga County	37.3
Hudson, OH (city) Summit County	37.0
Kenwood, OH (cdp) Hamilton County	36.7

Native Hawaiian and Other Pacific Islander
Top 10 Places Sorted by Number

Place	Years
No places met population threshold.	

Asian Indian
Top 10 Places Sorted by Number

Place	Years
Beavercreek, OH (city) Greene County	44.5
Westlake, OH (city) Cuyahoga County	41.2
Solon, OH (city) Cuyahoga County	41.0
North Royalton, OH (city) Cuyahoga County	32.5
North Olmsted, OH (city) Cuyahoga County	31.8
Strongsville, OH (city) Cuyahoga County	31.7
Fairfield, OH (city) Butler County	30.0
Parma, OH (city) Cuyahoga County	29.9
Mayfield Heights, OH (city) Cuyahoga County	29.8
Blue Ash, OH (city) Hamilton County	29.4

Bangladeshi
Top 10 Places Sorted by Number

Place	Years
No places met population threshold.	

Cambodian
Top 10 Places Sorted by Number

Place	Years
Columbus, OH (city) Franklin County	23.7

Chinese (except Taiwanese)
Top 10 Places Sorted by Number

Place	Years
Upper Arlington, OH (city) Franklin County	37.7
Solon, OH (city) Cuyahoga County	37.4
Hudson, OH (city) Summit County	35.8
Dublin, OH (city) Franklin County	35.1
Cleveland, OH (city) Cuyahoga County	32.1
Akron, OH (city) Summit County	31.7
Toledo, OH (city) Lucas County	31.5
Cincinnati, OH (city) Hamilton County	30.8
Columbus, OH (city) Franklin County	29.9
Cleveland Heights, OH (city) Cuyahoga County	28.2

Fijian
Top 10 Places Sorted by Number

Place	Years
No places met population threshold.	

Filipino
Top 10 Places Sorted by Number

Place	Years
Toledo, OH (city) Lucas County	37.1
Cleveland, OH (city) Cuyahoga County	35.5
Columbus, OH (city) Franklin County	33.6
Cincinnati, OH (city) Hamilton County	28.4

Guamanian or Chamorro
Top 10 Places Sorted by Number

Place	Years
No places met population threshold.	

Hawaiian, Native
Top 10 Places Sorted by Number

Place	Years
No places met population threshold.	

Hmong
Top 10 Places Sorted by Number

Place	Years
No places met population threshold.	

Indonesian
Top 10 Places Sorted by Number

Place	Years
Columbus, OH (city) Franklin County	21.9

Japanese
Top 10 Places Sorted by Number

Place	Years
Dublin, OH (city) Franklin County	33.4
Columbus, OH (city) Franklin County	30.3

Korean
Top 10 Places Sorted by Number

Place	Years
Columbus, OH (city) Franklin County	27.9

Laotian
Top 10 Places Sorted by Number

Place	Years
Columbus, OH (city) Franklin County	27.4
Akron, OH (city) Summit County	20.5

Malaysian
Top 10 Places Sorted by Number

Place	Years
No places met population threshold.	

Pakistani
Top 10 Places Sorted by Number

Place	Years
No places met population threshold.	

Samoan
Top 10 Places Sorted by Number

Place	Years
No places met population threshold.	

Sri Lankan
Top 10 Places Sorted by Number

Place	Years
No places met population threshold.	

Taiwanese
Top 10 Places Sorted by Number

Place	Years
Columbus, OH (city) Franklin County	26.9

Thai
Top 10 Places Sorted by Number

Place	Years
Columbus, OH (city) Franklin County	29.7

Tongan
Top 10 Places Sorted by Number

Place	Years
No places met population threshold.	

Vietnamese
Top 10 Places Sorted by Number

Place	Years
Cleveland, OH (city) Cuyahoga County	31.1
Columbus, OH (city) Franklin County	28.4
Akron, OH (city) Summit County	26.8

Average Household Size

Total Population
Top 10 Places Sorted by Number

Place	Number
Hudson, OH (city) Summit County	3.01
Highland Heights, OH (city) Cuyahoga County	2.90
Solon, OH (city) Cuyahoga County	2.88

Notes: Please refer to the User's Guide for an explanation of data; tables reflect only those areas that meet Summary File 4 population thresholds, therefore there may be less than 10 places listed

PROFILES OF OHIO / Asian Rankings: Language Spoken at Home: English Only

Place	Number
Beckett Ridge, OH (cdp) Butler County	2.80
Dublin, OH (city) Franklin County	2.80
Hilliard, OH (city) Franklin County	2.80
Brunswick, OH (city) Medina County	2.79
Mason, OH (city) Warren County	2.79
Gahanna, OH (city) Franklin County	2.70
Strongsville, OH (city) Cuyahoga County	2.69

Asian
Top 10 Places Sorted by Number

Place	Number
Beckett Ridge, OH (cdp) Butler County	4.27
Kenwood, OH (cdp) Hamilton County	4.26
North Royalton, OH (city) Cuyahoga County	3.76
Worthington, OH (city) Franklin County	3.68
Maple Heights, OH (city) Cuyahoga County	3.57
Hudson, OH (city) Summit County	3.54
Highland Heights, OH (city) Cuyahoga County	3.49
Twinsburg, OH (city) Summit County	3.47
Strongsville, OH (city) Cuyahoga County	3.46
Middleburg Heights, OH (city) Cuyahoga County	3.45

Native Hawaiian and Other Pacific Islander
Top 10 Places Sorted by Number

Place	Number
No places met population threshold.	

Asian Indian
Top 10 Places Sorted by Number

Place	Number
North Royalton, OH (city) Cuyahoga County	4.17
Strongsville, OH (city) Cuyahoga County	3.48
North Olmsted, OH (city) Cuyahoga County	3.21
Solon, OH (city) Cuyahoga County	3.21
Beavercreek, OH (city) Greene County	3.19
Dublin, OH (city) Franklin County	3.14
Blue Ash, OH (city) Hamilton County	3.12
Fairfield, OH (city) Butler County	2.73
Sharonville, OH (city) Hamilton County	2.73
Westlake, OH (city) Cuyahoga County	2.69

Bangladeshi
Top 10 Places Sorted by Number

Place	Number
No places met population threshold.	

Cambodian
Top 10 Places Sorted by Number

Place	Number
Columbus, OH (city) Franklin County	3.84

Chinese (except Taiwanese)
Top 10 Places Sorted by Number

Place	Number
Hudson, OH (city) Summit County	3.92
Dublin, OH (city) Franklin County	3.24
Solon, OH (city) Cuyahoga County	3.02
Upper Arlington, OH (city) Franklin County	2.59
Cleveland, OH (city) Cuyahoga County	2.47
Columbus, OH (city) Franklin County	2.30
Akron, OH (city) Summit County	2.28
Cincinnati, OH (city) Hamilton County	1.97
Toledo, OH (city) Lucas County	1.93
Cleveland Heights, OH (city) Cuyahoga County	1.81

Fijian
Top 10 Places Sorted by Number

Place	Number
No places met population threshold.	

Filipino
Top 10 Places Sorted by Number

Place	Number
Cleveland, OH (city) Cuyahoga County	2.87
Cincinnati, OH (city) Hamilton County	2.55
Toledo, OH (city) Lucas County	2.41
Columbus, OH (city) Franklin County	2.25

Guamanian or Chamorro
Top 10 Places Sorted by Number

Place	Number
No places met population threshold.	

Hawaiian, Native
Top 10 Places Sorted by Number

Place	Number
No places met population threshold.	

Hmong
Top 10 Places Sorted by Number

Place	Number
No places met population threshold.	

Indonesian
Top 10 Places Sorted by Number

Place	Number
Columbus, OH (city) Franklin County	2.04

Japanese
Top 10 Places Sorted by Number

Place	Number
Dublin, OH (city) Franklin County	3.20
Columbus, OH (city) Franklin County	2.17

Korean
Top 10 Places Sorted by Number

Place	Number
Columbus, OH (city) Franklin County	1.97

Laotian
Top 10 Places Sorted by Number

Place	Number
Akron, OH (city) Summit County	5.45
Columbus, OH (city) Franklin County	3.45

Malaysian
Top 10 Places Sorted by Number

Place	Number
No places met population threshold.	

Pakistani
Top 10 Places Sorted by Number

Place	Number
No places met population threshold.	

Samoan
Top 10 Places Sorted by Number

Place	Number
No places met population threshold.	

Sri Lankan
Top 10 Places Sorted by Number

Place	Number
No places met population threshold.	

Taiwanese
Top 10 Places Sorted by Number

Place	Number
Columbus, OH (city) Franklin County	2.17

Thai
Top 10 Places Sorted by Number

Place	Number
Columbus, OH (city) Franklin County	2.96

Tongan
Top 10 Places Sorted by Number

Place	Number
No places met population threshold.	

Vietnamese
Top 10 Places Sorted by Number

Place	Number
Akron, OH (city) Summit County	4.35
Cleveland, OH (city) Cuyahoga County	3.28
Columbus, OH (city) Franklin County	3.07

Language Spoken at Home: English Only

Total Population 5 Years and Over Who Speak English-Only at Home
Top 10 Places Sorted by Number

Place	Number
Columbus, OH (city) Franklin County	593,275
Cleveland, OH (city) Cuyahoga County	387,438
Cincinnati, OH (city) Hamilton County	286,454
Toledo, OH (city) Lucas County	269,728
Akron, OH (city) Summit County	189,917
Dayton, OH (city) Montgomery County	147,790
Parma, OH (city) Cuyahoga County	69,839
Kettering, OH (city) Montgomery County	51,686
Lakewood, OH (city) Cuyahoga County	46,390
Mentor, OH (city) Lake County	44,752

Total Population 5 Years and Over Who Speak English-Only at Home
Top 10 Places Sorted by Percent

Place	Percent
Dayton, OH (city) Montgomery County	95.64
Kettering, OH (city) Montgomery County	95.35
Westerville, OH (city) Franklin County	95.27
Cuyahoga Falls, OH (city) Summit County	95.23
Riverside, OH (city) Montgomery County	94.83
Sylvania, OH (city) Lucas County	94.71
Mentor, OH (city) Lake County	94.70
Findlay, OH (city) Hancock County	94.67
Reynoldsburg, OH (city) Franklin County	94.31
Mason, OH (city) Warren County	94.28

Asians 5 Years and Over Who Speak English-Only at Home
Top 10 Places Sorted by Number

Place	Number
Columbus, OH (city) Franklin County	3,508
Cincinnati, OH (city) Hamilton County	975
Cleveland, OH (city) Cuyahoga County	934
Toledo, OH (city) Lucas County	509
Akron, OH (city) Summit County	440
Cleveland Heights, OH (city) Cuyahoga County	344
Westlake, OH (city) Cuyahoga County	267
Dublin, OH (city) Franklin County	254
Kettering, OH (city) Montgomery County	240
Beavercreek, OH (city) Greene County	238

Notes: Please refer to the User's Guide for an explanation of data; tables reflect only those areas that meet Summary File 4 population thresholds, therefore there may be less than 10 places listed.

PROFILES OF OHIO / Asian Rankings: Language Spoken at Home: English Only

Asians 5 Years and Over Who Speak English-Only at Home
Top 10 Places Sorted by Percent

Place	Percent
Reynoldsburg, OH (city) Franklin County	39.58
Sylvania, OH (city) Lucas County	37.30
Mentor, OH (city) Lake County	36.22
South Euclid, OH (city) Cuyahoga County	34.65
Highland Heights, OH (city) Cuyahoga County	33.50
Kettering, OH (city) Montgomery County	32.92
Oxford, OH (city) Butler County	29.19
Wooster, OH (city) Wayne County	28.72
Lakewood, OH (city) Cuyahoga County	28.57
Fairview Park, OH (city) Cuyahoga County	28.21

Native Hawaiian and Other Pacific Islanders 5 Years and Over Who Speak English-Only at Home
Top 10 Places Sorted by Number

Place	Number
No places met population threshold.	

Native Hawaiian and Other Pacific Islanders 5 Years and Over Who Speak English-Only at Home
Top 10 Places Sorted by Percent

Place	Percent
No places met population threshold.	

Asian Indians 5 Years and Over Who Speak English-Only at Home
Top 10 Places Sorted by Number

Place	Number
Columbus, OH (city) Franklin County	1,043
Cleveland, OH (city) Cuyahoga County	210
Toledo, OH (city) Lucas County	175
Cincinnati, OH (city) Hamilton County	174
Cleveland Heights, OH (city) Cuyahoga County	136
Westlake, OH (city) Cuyahoga County	134
Dublin, OH (city) Franklin County	117
Fairfield, OH (city) Butler County	107
Blue Ash, OH (city) Hamilton County	92
Beavercreek, OH (city) Greene County	87

Asian Indians 5 Years and Over Who Speak English-Only at Home
Top 10 Places Sorted by Percent

Place	Percent
Fairfield, OH (city) Butler County	25.85
Westlake, OH (city) Cuyahoga County	25.82
Cleveland Heights, OH (city) Cuyahoga County	25.76
Blue Ash, OH (city) Hamilton County	24.86
Toledo, OH (city) Lucas County	21.34
Dublin, OH (city) Franklin County	19.44
Beavercreek, OH (city) Greene County	19.29
Cleveland, OH (city) Cuyahoga County	18.55
Columbus, OH (city) Franklin County	17.64
Akron, OH (city) Summit County	13.87

Bangladeshis 5 Years and Over Who Speak English-Only at Home
Top 10 Places Sorted by Number

Place	Number
No places met population threshold.	

Bangladeshis 5 Years and Over Who Speak English-Only at Home
Top 10 Places Sorted by Percent

Place	Percent
No places met population threshold.	

Cambodians 5 Years and Over Who Speak English-Only at Home
Top 10 Places Sorted by Number

Place	Number
Columbus, OH (city) Franklin County	79

Cambodians 5 Years and Over Who Speak English-Only at Home
Top 10 Places Sorted by Percent

Place	Percent
Columbus, OH (city) Franklin County	7.41

Chinese (except Taiwanese) 5 Years and Over Who Speak English-Only at Home
Top 10 Places Sorted by Number

Place	Number
Columbus, OH (city) Franklin County	468
Cleveland, OH (city) Cuyahoga County	203
Cincinnati, OH (city) Hamilton County	186
Akron, OH (city) Summit County	86
Cleveland Heights, OH (city) Cuyahoga County	79
Toledo, OH (city) Lucas County	54
Solon, OH (city) Cuyahoga County	49
Hudson, OH (city) Summit County	30
Upper Arlington, OH (city) Franklin County	22
Dublin, OH (city) Franklin County	5

Chinese (except Taiwanese) 5 Years and Over Who Speak English-Only at Home
Top 10 Places Sorted by Percent

Place	Percent
Cleveland Heights, OH (city) Cuyahoga County	22.44
Akron, OH (city) Summit County	17.03
Cincinnati, OH (city) Hamilton County	15.53
Solon, OH (city) Cuyahoga County	15.51
Cleveland, OH (city) Cuyahoga County	11.10
Columbus, OH (city) Franklin County	9.66
Hudson, OH (city) Summit County	9.01
Toledo, OH (city) Lucas County	7.01
Upper Arlington, OH (city) Franklin County	6.98
Dublin, OH (city) Franklin County	1.14

Fijians 5 Years and Over Who Speak English-Only at Home
Top 10 Places Sorted by Number

Place	Number
No places met population threshold.	

Fijians 5 Years and Over Who Speak English-Only at Home
Top 10 Places Sorted by Percent

Place	Percent
No places met population threshold.	

Filipinos 5 Years and Over Who Speak English-Only at Home
Top 10 Places Sorted by Number

Place	Number
Columbus, OH (city) Franklin County	546
Cincinnati, OH (city) Hamilton County	214
Toledo, OH (city) Lucas County	143
Cleveland, OH (city) Cuyahoga County	134

Filipinos 5 Years and Over Who Speak English-Only at Home
Top 10 Places Sorted by Percent

Place	Percent
Cincinnati, OH (city) Hamilton County	47.03
Columbus, OH (city) Franklin County	41.52
Toledo, OH (city) Lucas County	40.74
Cleveland, OH (city) Cuyahoga County	17.59

Guamanians or Chamorros 5 Years and Over Who Speak English-Only at Home
Top 10 Places Sorted by Number

Place	Number
No places met population threshold.	

Guamanians or Chamorros 5 Years and Over Who Speak English-Only at Home
Top 10 Places Sorted by Percent

Place	Percent
No places met population threshold.	

Hawaiian Natives 5 Years and Over Who Speak English-Only at Home
Top 10 Places Sorted by Number

Place	Number
No places met population threshold.	

Hawaiian Natives 5 Years and Over Who Speak English-Only at Home
Top 10 Places Sorted by Percent

Place	Percent
No places met population threshold.	

Hmongs 5 Years and Over Who Speak English-Only at Home
Top 10 Places Sorted by Number

Place	Number
No places met population threshold.	

Hmongs 5 Years and Over Who Speak English-Only at Home
Top 10 Places Sorted by Percent

Place	Percent
No places met population threshold.	

Indonesians 5 Years and Over Who Speak English-Only at Home
Top 10 Places Sorted by Number

Place	Number
Columbus, OH (city) Franklin County	24

Indonesians 5 Years and Over Who Speak English-Only at Home
Top 10 Places Sorted by Percent

Place	Percent
Columbus, OH (city) Franklin County	4.79

Japanese 5 Years and Over Who Speak English-Only at Home
Top 10 Places Sorted by Number

Place	Number
Columbus, OH (city) Franklin County	340
Dublin, OH (city) Franklin County	31

Japanese 5 Years and Over Who Speak English-Only at Home
Top 10 Places Sorted by Percent

Place	Percent
Columbus, OH (city) Franklin County	20.04
Dublin, OH (city) Franklin County	4.30

Koreans 5 Years and Over Who Speak English-Only at Home
Top 10 Places Sorted by Number

Place	Number
Columbus, OH (city) Franklin County	519

Notes: Please refer to the User's Guide for an explanation of data; tables reflect only those areas that meet Summary File 4 population thresholds, therefore there may be less than 10 places listed

PROFILES OF OHIO / Asian Rankings: Foreign Born

Koreans 5 Years and Over Who Speak English-Only at Home
Top 10 Places Sorted by Percent

Place	Percent
Columbus, OH (city) Franklin County	21.60

Laotians 5 Years and Over Who Speak English-Only at Home
Top 10 Places Sorted by Number

Place	Number
Akron, OH (city) Summit County	48
Columbus, OH (city) Franklin County	32

Laotians 5 Years and Over Who Speak English-Only at Home
Top 10 Places Sorted by Percent

Place	Percent
Akron, OH (city) Summit County	9.90
Columbus, OH (city) Franklin County	3.64

Malaysians 5 Years and Over Who Speak English-Only at Home
Top 10 Places Sorted by Number

Place	Number
No places met population threshold.	

Malaysians 5 Years and Over Who Speak English-Only at Home
Top 10 Places Sorted by Percent

Place	Percent
No places met population threshold.	

Pakistanis 5 Years and Over Who Speak English-Only at Home
Top 10 Places Sorted by Number

Place	Number
No places met population threshold.	

Pakistanis 5 Years and Over Who Speak English-Only at Home
Top 10 Places Sorted by Percent

Place	Percent
No places met population threshold.	

Samoans 5 Years and Over Who Speak English-Only at Home
Top 10 Places Sorted by Number

Place	Number
No places met population threshold.	

Samoans 5 Years and Over Who Speak English-Only at Home
Top 10 Places Sorted by Percent

Place	Percent
No places met population threshold.	

Sri Lankans 5 Years and Over Who Speak English-Only at Home
Top 10 Places Sorted by Number

Place	Number
No places met population threshold.	

Sri Lankans 5 Years and Over Who Speak English-Only at Home
Top 10 Places Sorted by Percent

Place	Percent
No places met population threshold.	

Taiwanese 5 Years and Over Who Speak English-Only at Home
Top 10 Places Sorted by Number

Place	Number
Columbus, OH (city) Franklin County	16

Taiwanese 5 Years and Over Who Speak English-Only at Home
Top 10 Places Sorted by Percent

Place	Percent
Columbus, OH (city) Franklin County	3.48

Thais 5 Years and Over Who Speak English-Only at Home
Top 10 Places Sorted by Number

Place	Number
Columbus, OH (city) Franklin County	38

Thais 5 Years and Over Who Speak English-Only at Home
Top 10 Places Sorted by Percent

Place	Percent
Columbus, OH (city) Franklin County	10.30

Tongans 5 Years and Over Who Speak English-Only at Home
Top 10 Places Sorted by Number

Place	Number
No places met population threshold.	

Tongans 5 Years and Over Who Speak English-Only at Home
Top 10 Places Sorted by Percent

Place	Percent
No places met population threshold.	

Vietnamese 5 Years and Over Who Speak English-Only at Home
Top 10 Places Sorted by Number

Place	Number
Columbus, OH (city) Franklin County	226
Cleveland, OH (city) Cuyahoga County	99
Akron, OH (city) Summit County	25

Vietnamese 5 Years and Over Who Speak English-Only at Home
Top 10 Places Sorted by Percent

Place	Percent
Columbus, OH (city) Franklin County	11.35
Cleveland, OH (city) Cuyahoga County	9.86
Akron, OH (city) Summit County	4.79

Foreign Born

Total Population
Top 10 Places Sorted by Number

Place	Number
Columbus, OH (city) Franklin County	47,713
Cleveland, OH (city) Cuyahoga County	21,372
Cincinnati, OH (city) Hamilton County	12,461
Toledo, OH (city) Lucas County	9,475
Parma, OH (city) Cuyahoga County	7,797
Akron, OH (city) Summit County	6,911
Lakewood, OH (city) Cuyahoga County	4,945
Cleveland Heights, OH (city) Cuyahoga County	4,130
Mayfield Heights, OH (city) Cuyahoga County	3,506
Dayton, OH (city) Montgomery County	3,245

Total Population
Top 10 Places Sorted by Percent

Place	Percent
Mayfield Heights, OH (city) Cuyahoga County	18.09
Richmond Heights, OH (city) Cuyahoga County	17.36
Beachwood, OH (city) Cuyahoga County	15.47
Highland Heights, OH (city) Cuyahoga County	11.14
Parma Heights, OH (city) Cuyahoga County	10.17
Blue Ash, OH (city) Hamilton County	9.98
South Euclid, OH (city) Cuyahoga County	9.43
Dublin, OH (city) Franklin County	9.11
Parma, OH (city) Cuyahoga County	9.10
Kenwood, OH (cdp) Hamilton County	9.00

Asian
Top 10 Places Sorted by Number

Place	Number
Columbus, OH (city) Franklin County	19,183
Cleveland, OH (city) Cuyahoga County	4,996
Cincinnati, OH (city) Hamilton County	3,806
Akron, OH (city) Summit County	2,437
Toledo, OH (city) Lucas County	2,370
Dublin, OH (city) Franklin County	1,919
Parma, OH (city) Cuyahoga County	1,115
Strongsville, OH (city) Cuyahoga County	1,051
Cleveland Heights, OH (city) Cuyahoga County	992
Westlake, OH (city) Cuyahoga County	990

Asian
Top 10 Places Sorted by Percent

Place	Percent
Fairborn, OH (city) Greene County	91.55
Findlay, OH (city) Hancock County	87.35
Sharonville, OH (city) Hamilton County	87.23
Bowling Green, OH (city) Wood County	86.39
Forest Park, OH (city) Hamilton County	84.33
Stow, OH (city) Summit County	82.60
Garfield Heights, OH (city) Cuyahoga County	82.25
Blue Ash, OH (city) Hamilton County	80.96
Maple Heights, OH (city) Cuyahoga County	80.91
Beachwood, OH (city) Cuyahoga County	80.90

Native Hawaiian and Other Pacific Islander
Top 10 Places Sorted by Number

Place	Number
No places met population threshold.	

Native Hawaiian and Other Pacific Islander
Top 10 Places Sorted by Percent

Place	Percent
No places met population threshold.	

Asian Indian
Top 10 Places Sorted by Number

Place	Number
Columbus, OH (city) Franklin County	5,131
Cincinnati, OH (city) Hamilton County	1,392
Cleveland, OH (city) Cuyahoga County	814
Toledo, OH (city) Lucas County	684
Parma, OH (city) Cuyahoga County	566
Strongsville, OH (city) Cuyahoga County	546
Dublin, OH (city) Franklin County	518
Akron, OH (city) Summit County	498
Cleveland Heights, OH (city) Cuyahoga County	430
Westlake, OH (city) Cuyahoga County	407

Asian Indian
Top 10 Places Sorted by Percent

Place	Percent
Sharonville, OH (city) Hamilton County	92.37
Cincinnati, OH (city) Hamilton County	90.33
Parma, OH (city) Cuyahoga County	89.13

Notes: Please refer to the User's Guide for an explanation of data; tables reflect only those areas that meet Summary File 4 population thresholds, therefore there may be less than 10 places listed

PROFILES OF OHIO / Asian Rankings: Foreign Born

Place	
Blue Ash, OH (city) Hamilton County	84.69
Akron, OH (city) Summit County	83.14
Mayfield Heights, OH (city) Cuyahoga County	82.22
Columbus, OH (city) Franklin County	80.01
Toledo, OH (city) Lucas County	79.08
Dublin, OH (city) Franklin County	77.78
Cleveland Heights, OH (city) Cuyahoga County	77.76

Bangladeshi
Top 10 Places Sorted by Number

Place	Number
No places met population threshold.	

Bangladeshi
Top 10 Places Sorted by Percent

Place	Percent
No places met population threshold.	

Cambodian
Top 10 Places Sorted by Number

Place	Number
Columbus, OH (city) Franklin County	783

Cambodian
Top 10 Places Sorted by Percent

Place	Percent
Columbus, OH (city) Franklin County	65.69

Chinese (except Taiwanese)
Top 10 Places Sorted by Number

Place	Number
Columbus, OH (city) Franklin County	4,168
Cleveland, OH (city) Cuyahoga County	1,516
Cincinnati, OH (city) Hamilton County	1,061
Toledo, OH (city) Lucas County	704
Akron, OH (city) Summit County	433
Dublin, OH (city) Franklin County	340
Upper Arlington, OH (city) Franklin County	270
Cleveland Heights, OH (city) Cuyahoga County	266
Solon, OH (city) Cuyahoga County	247
Hudson, OH (city) Summit County	227

Chinese (except Taiwanese)
Top 10 Places Sorted by Percent

Place	Percent
Toledo, OH (city) Lucas County	90.96
Columbus, OH (city) Franklin County	80.98
Akron, OH (city) Summit County	80.93
Cincinnati, OH (city) Hamilton County	80.26
Upper Arlington, OH (city) Franklin County	79.65
Cleveland, OH (city) Cuyahoga County	74.72
Solon, OH (city) Cuyahoga County	71.39
Cleveland Heights, OH (city) Cuyahoga County	67.51
Dublin, OH (city) Franklin County	66.67
Hudson, OH (city) Summit County	63.23

Fijian
Top 10 Places Sorted by Number

Place	Number
No places met population threshold.	

Fijian
Top 10 Places Sorted by Percent

Place	Percent
No places met population threshold.	

Filipino
Top 10 Places Sorted by Number

Place	Number
Columbus, OH (city) Franklin County	787
Cleveland, OH (city) Cuyahoga County	623
Toledo, OH (city) Lucas County	262
Cincinnati, OH (city) Hamilton County	233

Filipino
Top 10 Places Sorted by Percent

Place	Percent
Cleveland, OH (city) Cuyahoga County	74.43
Toledo, OH (city) Lucas County	70.43
Columbus, OH (city) Franklin County	57.07
Cincinnati, OH (city) Hamilton County	48.54

Guamanian or Chamorro
Top 10 Places Sorted by Number

Place	Number
No places met population threshold.	

Guamanian or Chamorro
Top 10 Places Sorted by Percent

Place	Percent
No places met population threshold.	

Hawaiian, Native
Top 10 Places Sorted by Number

Place	Number
No places met population threshold.	

Hawaiian, Native
Top 10 Places Sorted by Percent

Place	Percent
No places met population threshold.	

Hmong
Top 10 Places Sorted by Number

Place	Number
No places met population threshold.	

Hmong
Top 10 Places Sorted by Percent

Place	Percent
No places met population threshold.	

Indonesian
Top 10 Places Sorted by Number

Place	Number
Columbus, OH (city) Franklin County	501

Indonesian
Top 10 Places Sorted by Percent

Place	Percent
Columbus, OH (city) Franklin County	97.47

Japanese
Top 10 Places Sorted by Number

Place	Number
Columbus, OH (city) Franklin County	1,395
Dublin, OH (city) Franklin County	715

Japanese
Top 10 Places Sorted by Percent

Place	Percent
Dublin, OH (city) Franklin County	87.20
Columbus, OH (city) Franklin County	75.61

Korean
Top 10 Places Sorted by Number

Place	Number
Columbus, OH (city) Franklin County	2,019

Korean
Top 10 Places Sorted by Percent

Place	Percent
Columbus, OH (city) Franklin County	79.99

Laotian
Top 10 Places Sorted by Number

Place	Number
Columbus, OH (city) Franklin County	692
Akron, OH (city) Summit County	363

Laotian
Top 10 Places Sorted by Percent

Place	Percent
Columbus, OH (city) Franklin County	70.68
Akron, OH (city) Summit County	63.46

Malaysian
Top 10 Places Sorted by Number

Place	Number
No places met population threshold.	

Malaysian
Top 10 Places Sorted by Percent

Place	Percent
No places met population threshold.	

Pakistani
Top 10 Places Sorted by Number

Place	Number
No places met population threshold.	

Pakistani
Top 10 Places Sorted by Percent

Place	Percent
No places met population threshold.	

Samoan
Top 10 Places Sorted by Number

Place	Number
No places met population threshold.	

Samoan
Top 10 Places Sorted by Percent

Place	Percent
No places met population threshold.	

Sri Lankan
Top 10 Places Sorted by Number

Place	Number
No places met population threshold.	

Sri Lankan
Top 10 Places Sorted by Percent

Place	Percent
No places met population threshold.	

Taiwanese
Top 10 Places Sorted by Number

Place	Number
Columbus, OH (city) Franklin County	406

Taiwanese
Top 10 Places Sorted by Percent

Place	Percent
Columbus, OH (city) Franklin County	87.69

Notes: Please refer to the User's Guide for an explanation of data; tables reflect only those areas that meet Summary File 4 population thresholds, therefore there may be less than 10 places listed

PROFILES OF OHIO / Asian Rankings: Foreign-Born Naturalized Citizens

Thai
Top 10 Places Sorted by Number

Place	Number
Columbus, OH (city) Franklin County	327

Thai
Top 10 Places Sorted by Percent

Place	Percent
Columbus, OH (city) Franklin County	84.06

Tongan
Top 10 Places Sorted by Number

Place	Number
No places met population threshold.	

Tongan
Top 10 Places Sorted by Percent

Place	Percent
No places met population threshold.	

Vietnamese
Top 10 Places Sorted by Number

Place	Number
Columbus, OH (city) Franklin County	1,740
Cleveland, OH (city) Cuyahoga County	758
Akron, OH (city) Summit County	468

Vietnamese
Top 10 Places Sorted by Percent

Place	Percent
Akron, OH (city) Summit County	81.96
Columbus, OH (city) Franklin County	79.78
Cleveland, OH (city) Cuyahoga County	68.47

Foreign-Born Naturalized Citizens

Total Population
Top 10 Places Sorted by Number

Place	Number
Columbus, OH (city) Franklin County	14,197
Cleveland, OH (city) Cuyahoga County	9,755
Parma, OH (city) Cuyahoga County	4,567
Toledo, OH (city) Lucas County	4,487
Cincinnati, OH (city) Hamilton County	4,139
Akron, OH (city) Summit County	3,181
Lakewood, OH (city) Cuyahoga County	2,603
Cleveland Heights, OH (city) Cuyahoga County	1,926
Westlake, OH (city) Cuyahoga County	1,905
Strongsville, OH (city) Cuyahoga County	1,760

Total Population
Top 10 Places Sorted by Percent

Place	Percent
Beachwood, OH (city) Cuyahoga County	10.35
Richmond Heights, OH (city) Cuyahoga County	9.59
Mayfield Heights, OH (city) Cuyahoga County	8.77
Highland Heights, OH (city) Cuyahoga County	7.76
Middleburg Heights, OH (city) Cuyahoga County	6.54
South Euclid, OH (city) Cuyahoga County	6.20
Westlake, OH (city) Cuyahoga County	5.98
Solon, OH (city) Cuyahoga County	5.44
Parma Heights, OH (city) Cuyahoga County	5.38
Parma, OH (city) Cuyahoga County	5.33

Asian
Top 10 Places Sorted by Number

Place	Number
Columbus, OH (city) Franklin County	5,679
Cleveland, OH (city) Cuyahoga County	1,852
Cincinnati, OH (city) Hamilton County	981
Toledo, OH (city) Lucas County	764
Akron, OH (city) Summit County	712
Westlake, OH (city) Cuyahoga County	665
Strongsville, OH (city) Cuyahoga County	645
Beavercreek, OH (city) Greene County	639
Dublin, OH (city) Franklin County	528
Parma, OH (city) Cuyahoga County	471

Asian
Top 10 Places Sorted by Percent

Place	Percent
Garfield Heights, OH (city) Cuyahoga County	52.48
Beavercreek, OH (city) Greene County	52.12
Brunswick, OH (city) Medina County	50.14
Westlake, OH (city) Cuyahoga County	49.11
Huber Heights, OH (city) Montgomery County	45.72
Maple Heights, OH (city) Cuyahoga County	45.34
Riverside, OH (city) Montgomery County	45.29
Strongsville, OH (city) Cuyahoga County	43.88
Beckett Ridge, OH (cdp) Butler County	43.53
Solon, OH (city) Cuyahoga County	43.46

Native Hawaiian and Other Pacific Islander
Top 10 Places Sorted by Number

Place	Number
No places met population threshold.	

Native Hawaiian and Other Pacific Islander
Top 10 Places Sorted by Percent

Place	Percent
No places met population threshold.	

Asian Indian
Top 10 Places Sorted by Number

Place	Number
Columbus, OH (city) Franklin County	1,102
Strongsville, OH (city) Cuyahoga County	322
Cincinnati, OH (city) Hamilton County	264
Westlake, OH (city) Cuyahoga County	258
Beavercreek, OH (city) Greene County	255
Solon, OH (city) Cuyahoga County	229
Parma, OH (city) Cuyahoga County	189
Cleveland, OH (city) Cuyahoga County	188
Cleveland Heights, OH (city) Cuyahoga County	176
North Olmsted, OH (city) Cuyahoga County	159

Asian Indian
Top 10 Places Sorted by Percent

Place	Percent
Beavercreek, OH (city) Greene County	53.80
Solon, OH (city) Cuyahoga County	48.72
Westlake, OH (city) Cuyahoga County	47.69
Strongsville, OH (city) Cuyahoga County	44.29
North Olmsted, OH (city) Cuyahoga County	37.24
Cleveland Heights, OH (city) Cuyahoga County	31.83
Parma, OH (city) Cuyahoga County	29.76
North Royalton, OH (city) Cuyahoga County	27.36
Fairfield, OH (city) Butler County	25.41
Dublin, OH (city) Franklin County	23.12

Bangladeshi
Top 10 Places Sorted by Number

Place	Number
No places met population threshold.	

Bangladeshi
Top 10 Places Sorted by Percent

Place	Percent
No places met population threshold.	

Cambodian
Top 10 Places Sorted by Number

Place	Number
Columbus, OH (city) Franklin County	322

Cambodian
Top 10 Places Sorted by Percent

Place	Percent
Columbus, OH (city) Franklin County	27.01

Chinese (except Taiwanese)
Top 10 Places Sorted by Number

Place	Number
Columbus, OH (city) Franklin County	1,154
Cleveland, OH (city) Cuyahoga County	496
Cincinnati, OH (city) Hamilton County	181
Dublin, OH (city) Franklin County	171
Toledo, OH (city) Lucas County	145
Solon, OH (city) Cuyahoga County	130
Upper Arlington, OH (city) Franklin County	104
Hudson, OH (city) Summit County	102
Cleveland Heights, OH (city) Cuyahoga County	100
Akron, OH (city) Summit County	39

Chinese (except Taiwanese)
Top 10 Places Sorted by Percent

Place	Percent
Solon, OH (city) Cuyahoga County	37.57
Dublin, OH (city) Franklin County	33.53
Upper Arlington, OH (city) Franklin County	30.68
Hudson, OH (city) Summit County	28.41
Cleveland Heights, OH (city) Cuyahoga County	25.38
Cleveland, OH (city) Cuyahoga County	24.45
Columbus, OH (city) Franklin County	22.42
Toledo, OH (city) Lucas County	18.73
Cincinnati, OH (city) Hamilton County	13.69
Akron, OH (city) Summit County	7.29

Fijian
Top 10 Places Sorted by Number

Place	Number
No places met population threshold.	

Fijian
Top 10 Places Sorted by Percent

Place	Percent
No places met population threshold.	

Filipino
Top 10 Places Sorted by Number

Place	Number
Columbus, OH (city) Franklin County	521
Cleveland, OH (city) Cuyahoga County	284
Toledo, OH (city) Lucas County	189
Cincinnati, OH (city) Hamilton County	123

Filipino
Top 10 Places Sorted by Percent

Place	Percent
Toledo, OH (city) Lucas County	50.81
Columbus, OH (city) Franklin County	37.78
Cleveland, OH (city) Cuyahoga County	33.93
Cincinnati, OH (city) Hamilton County	25.62

Guamanian or Chamorro
Top 10 Places Sorted by Number

Place	Number
No places met population threshold.	

Notes: Please refer to the User's Guide for an explanation of data; tables reflect only those areas that meet Summary File 4 population thresholds, therefore there may be less than 10 places listed

PROFILES OF OHIO / Asian Rankings: Educational Attainment: H.S. Graduates

Guamanian or Chamorro
Top 10 Places Sorted by Percent

Place	Percent
No places met population threshold.	

Hawaiian, Native
Top 10 Places Sorted by Number

Place	Number
No places met population threshold.	

Hawaiian, Native
Top 10 Places Sorted by Percent

Place	Percent
No places met population threshold.	

Hmong
Top 10 Places Sorted by Number

Place	Number
No places met population threshold.	

Hmong
Top 10 Places Sorted by Percent

Place	Percent
No places met population threshold.	

Indonesian
Top 10 Places Sorted by Number

Place	Number
Columbus, OH (city) Franklin County	0

Indonesian
Top 10 Places Sorted by Percent

Place	Percent
Columbus, OH (city) Franklin County	0.00

Japanese
Top 10 Places Sorted by Number

Place	Number
Columbus, OH (city) Franklin County	107
Dublin, OH (city) Franklin County	10

Japanese
Top 10 Places Sorted by Percent

Place	Percent
Columbus, OH (city) Franklin County	5.80
Dublin, OH (city) Franklin County	1.22

Korean
Top 10 Places Sorted by Number

Place	Number
Columbus, OH (city) Franklin County	634

Korean
Top 10 Places Sorted by Percent

Place	Percent
Columbus, OH (city) Franklin County	25.12

Laotian
Top 10 Places Sorted by Number

Place	Number
Columbus, OH (city) Franklin County	404
Akron, OH (city) Summit County	151

Laotian
Top 10 Places Sorted by Percent

Place	Percent
Columbus, OH (city) Franklin County	41.27

Akron, OH (city) Summit County — 26.40

Malaysian
Top 10 Places Sorted by Number

Place	Number
No places met population threshold.	

Malaysian
Top 10 Places Sorted by Percent

Place	Percent
No places met population threshold.	

Pakistani
Top 10 Places Sorted by Number

Place	Number
No places met population threshold.	

Pakistani
Top 10 Places Sorted by Percent

Place	Percent
No places met population threshold.	

Samoan
Top 10 Places Sorted by Number

Place	Number
No places met population threshold.	

Samoan
Top 10 Places Sorted by Percent

Place	Percent
No places met population threshold.	

Sri Lankan
Top 10 Places Sorted by Number

Place	Number
No places met population threshold.	

Sri Lankan
Top 10 Places Sorted by Percent

Place	Percent
No places met population threshold.	

Taiwanese
Top 10 Places Sorted by Number

Place	Number
Columbus, OH (city) Franklin County	123

Taiwanese
Top 10 Places Sorted by Percent

Place	Percent
Columbus, OH (city) Franklin County	26.57

Thai
Top 10 Places Sorted by Number

Place	Number
Columbus, OH (city) Franklin County	65

Thai
Top 10 Places Sorted by Percent

Place	Percent
Columbus, OH (city) Franklin County	16.71

Tongan
Top 10 Places Sorted by Number

Place	Number
No places met population threshold.	

Tongan
Top 10 Places Sorted by Percent

Place	Percent
No places met population threshold.	

Vietnamese
Top 10 Places Sorted by Number

Place	Number
Columbus, OH (city) Franklin County	891
Cleveland, OH (city) Cuyahoga County	418
Akron, OH (city) Summit County	183

Vietnamese
Top 10 Places Sorted by Percent

Place	Percent
Columbus, OH (city) Franklin County	40.85
Cleveland, OH (city) Cuyahoga County	37.76
Akron, OH (city) Summit County	32.05

Educational Attainment: H.S. Graduates

Total Populations 25 Years and Over Who are High School Graduates
Top 10 Places Sorted by Number

Place	Number
Columbus, OH (city) Franklin County	369,376
Cleveland, OH (city) Cuyahoga County	204,829
Cincinnati, OH (city) Hamilton County	159,012
Toledo, OH (city) Lucas County	157,014
Akron, OH (city) Summit County	111,556
Dayton, OH (city) Montgomery County	75,651
Parma, OH (city) Cuyahoga County	50,540
Kettering, OH (city) Montgomery County	36,547
Lakewood, OH (city) Cuyahoga County	35,064
Cuyahoga Falls, OH (city) Summit County	31,140

Total Populations 25 Years and Over Who are High School Graduates
Top 10 Places Sorted by Percent

Place	Percent
Upper Arlington, OH (city) Franklin County	97.93
Dublin, OH (city) Franklin County	97.27
Hudson, OH (city) Summit County	97.25
Beckett Ridge, OH (cdp) Butler County	96.63
Worthington, OH (city) Franklin County	96.06
Centerville, OH (city) Montgomery County	95.54
Shaker Heights, OH (city) Cuyahoga County	94.63
Solon, OH (city) Cuyahoga County	94.60
Westerville, OH (city) Franklin County	94.55
Sylvania, OH (city) Lucas County	94.05

Asians 25 Years and Over Who are High School Graduates
Top 10 Places Sorted by Number

Place	Number
Columbus, OH (city) Franklin County	13,017
Cleveland, OH (city) Cuyahoga County	3,289
Cincinnati, OH (city) Hamilton County	3,042
Toledo, OH (city) Lucas County	1,816
Akron, OH (city) Summit County	1,509
Dublin, OH (city) Franklin County	1,464
Parma, OH (city) Cuyahoga County	945
Cleveland Heights, OH (city) Cuyahoga County	926
Strongsville, OH (city) Cuyahoga County	890
Westlake, OH (city) Cuyahoga County	866

Asians 25 Years and Over Who are High School Graduates
Top 10 Places Sorted by Percent

Place	Percent
Kent, OH (city) Portage County	100.00
Athens, OH (city) Athens County	98.17

Notes: Please refer to the User's Guide for an explanation of data; tables reflect only those areas that meet Summary File 4 population thresholds, therefore there may be less than 10 places listed

PROFILES OF OHIO / Asian Rankings: Educational Attainment: H.S. Graduates

Place	Percent
Findlay, OH (city) Hancock County	98.00
Beckett Ridge, OH (cdp) Butler County	97.86
Blue Ash, OH (city) Hamilton County	97.55
Kenwood, OH (cdp) Hamilton County	97.33
Centerville, OH (city) Montgomery County	97.17
South Euclid, OH (city) Cuyahoga County	96.89
Hudson, OH (city) Summit County	96.61
Mason, OH (city) Warren County	95.95

Native Hawaiian and Other Pacific Islanders 25 Years and Over Who are High School Graduates
Top 10 Places Sorted by Number

Place	Number
No places met population threshold.	

Native Hawaiian and Other Pacific Islanders 25 Years and Over Who are High School Graduates
Top 10 Places Sorted by Percent

Place	Percent
No places met population threshold.	

Asian Indians 25 Years and Over Who are High School Graduates
Top 10 Places Sorted by Number

Place	Number
Columbus, OH (city) Franklin County	3,693
Cincinnati, OH (city) Hamilton County	934
Cleveland, OH (city) Cuyahoga County	650
Toledo, OH (city) Lucas County	468
Strongsville, OH (city) Cuyahoga County	453
Dublin, OH (city) Franklin County	422
Parma, OH (city) Cuyahoga County	413
Westlake, OH (city) Cuyahoga County	386
Akron, OH (city) Summit County	340
Cleveland Heights, OH (city) Cuyahoga County	306

Asian Indians 25 Years and Over Who are High School Graduates
Top 10 Places Sorted by Percent

Place	Percent
Blue Ash, OH (city) Hamilton County	100.00
Dublin, OH (city) Franklin County	100.00
North Olmsted, OH (city) Cuyahoga County	98.46
Westlake, OH (city) Cuyahoga County	98.22
Sharonville, OH (city) Hamilton County	96.39
Mayfield Heights, OH (city) Cuyahoga County	94.81
Cleveland Heights, OH (city) Cuyahoga County	94.74
Strongsville, OH (city) Cuyahoga County	93.79
Toledo, OH (city) Lucas County	93.60
Cincinnati, OH (city) Hamilton County	93.49

Bangladeshis 25 Years and Over Who are High School Graduates
Top 10 Places Sorted by Number

Place	Number
No places met population threshold.	

Bangladeshis 25 Years and Over Who are High School Graduates
Top 10 Places Sorted by Percent

Place	Percent
No places met population threshold.	

Cambodians 25 Years and Over Who are High School Graduates
Top 10 Places Sorted by Number

Place	Number
Columbus, OH (city) Franklin County	266

Cambodians 25 Years and Over Who are High School Graduates
Top 10 Places Sorted by Percent

Place	Percent
Columbus, OH (city) Franklin County	46.67

Chinese (except Taiwanese) 25 Years and Over Who are High School Graduates
Top 10 Places Sorted by Number

Place	Number
Columbus, OH (city) Franklin County	3,087
Cincinnati, OH (city) Hamilton County	1,002
Cleveland, OH (city) Cuyahoga County	988
Toledo, OH (city) Lucas County	579
Akron, OH (city) Summit County	342
Cleveland Heights, OH (city) Cuyahoga County	269
Dublin, OH (city) Franklin County	268
Solon, OH (city) Cuyahoga County	220
Upper Arlington, OH (city) Franklin County	205
Hudson, OH (city) Summit County	195

Chinese (except Taiwanese) 25 Years and Over Who are High School Graduates
Top 10 Places Sorted by Percent

Place	Percent
Hudson, OH (city) Summit County	100.00
Solon, OH (city) Cuyahoga County	100.00
Cincinnati, OH (city) Hamilton County	97.85
Cleveland Heights, OH (city) Cuyahoga County	94.06
Dublin, OH (city) Franklin County	89.04
Upper Arlington, OH (city) Franklin County	88.36
Columbus, OH (city) Franklin County	86.45
Toledo, OH (city) Lucas County	85.40
Akron, OH (city) Summit County	81.04
Cleveland, OH (city) Cuyahoga County	68.52

Fijians 25 Years and Over Who are High School Graduates
Top 10 Places Sorted by Number

Place	Number
No places met population threshold.	

Fijians 25 Years and Over Who are High School Graduates
Top 10 Places Sorted by Percent

Place	Percent
No places met population threshold.	

Filipinos 25 Years and Over Who are High School Graduates
Top 10 Places Sorted by Number

Place	Number
Columbus, OH (city) Franklin County	883
Cleveland, OH (city) Cuyahoga County	527
Toledo, OH (city) Lucas County	288
Cincinnati, OH (city) Hamilton County	255

Filipinos 25 Years and Over Who are High School Graduates
Top 10 Places Sorted by Percent

Place	Percent
Toledo, OH (city) Lucas County	93.20
Cincinnati, OH (city) Hamilton County	93.07
Columbus, OH (city) Franklin County	90.47
Cleveland, OH (city) Cuyahoga County	82.99

Guamanians or Chamorros 25 Years and Over Who are High School Graduates
Top 10 Places Sorted by Number

Place	Number
No places met population threshold.	

Guamanians or Chamorros 25 Years and Over Who are High School Graduates
Top 10 Places Sorted by Percent

Place	Percent
No places met population threshold.	

Hawaiian Natives 25 Years and Over Who are High School Graduates
Top 10 Places Sorted by Number

Place	Number
No places met population threshold.	

Hawaiian Natives 25 Years and Over Who are High School Graduates
Top 10 Places Sorted by Percent

Place	Percent
No places met population threshold.	

Hmongs 25 Years and Over Who are High School Graduates
Top 10 Places Sorted by Number

Place	Number
No places met population threshold.	

Hmongs 25 Years and Over Who are High School Graduates
Top 10 Places Sorted by Percent

Place	Percent
No places met population threshold.	

Indonesians 25 Years and Over Who are High School Graduates
Top 10 Places Sorted by Number

Place	Number
Columbus, OH (city) Franklin County	90

Indonesians 25 Years and Over Who are High School Graduates
Top 10 Places Sorted by Percent

Place	Percent
Columbus, OH (city) Franklin County	100.00

Japanese 25 Years and Over Who are High School Graduates
Top 10 Places Sorted by Number

Place	Number
Columbus, OH (city) Franklin County	1,081
Dublin, OH (city) Franklin County	491

Japanese 25 Years and Over Who are High School Graduates
Top 10 Places Sorted by Percent

Place	Percent
Columbus, OH (city) Franklin County	96.95
Dublin, OH (city) Franklin County	96.27

Koreans 25 Years and Over Who are High School Graduates
Top 10 Places Sorted by Number

Place	Number
Columbus, OH (city) Franklin County	1,511

Koreans 25 Years and Over Who are High School Graduates
Top 10 Places Sorted by Percent

Place	Percent
Columbus, OH (city) Franklin County	91.69

Notes: Please refer to the User's Guide for an explanation of data; tables reflect only those areas that meet Summary File 4 population thresholds, therefore there may be less than 10 places listed

PROFILES OF OHIO / Asian Rankings: Educational Attainment: College Graduates

Laotians 25 Years and Over Who are High School Graduates
Top 10 Places Sorted by Number

Place	Number
Columbus, OH (city) Franklin County	320
Akron, OH (city) Summit County	132

Laotians 25 Years and Over Who are High School Graduates
Top 10 Places Sorted by Percent

Place	Percent
Akron, OH (city) Summit County	60.27
Columbus, OH (city) Franklin County	59.37

Malaysians 25 Years and Over Who are High School Graduates
Top 10 Places Sorted by Number

Place	Number
No places met population threshold.	

Malaysians 25 Years and Over Who are High School Graduates
Top 10 Places Sorted by Percent

Place	Percent
No places met population threshold.	

Pakistanis 25 Years and Over Who are High School Graduates
Top 10 Places Sorted by Number

Place	Number
No places met population threshold.	

Pakistanis 25 Years and Over Who are High School Graduates
Top 10 Places Sorted by Percent

Place	Percent
No places met population threshold.	

Samoans 25 Years and Over Who are High School Graduates
Top 10 Places Sorted by Number

Place	Number
No places met population threshold.	

Samoans 25 Years and Over Who are High School Graduates
Top 10 Places Sorted by Percent

Place	Percent
No places met population threshold.	

Sri Lankans 25 Years and Over Who are High School Graduates
Top 10 Places Sorted by Number

Place	Number
No places met population threshold.	

Sri Lankans 25 Years and Over Who are High School Graduates
Top 10 Places Sorted by Percent

Place	Percent
No places met population threshold.	

Taiwanese 25 Years and Over Who are High School Graduates
Top 10 Places Sorted by Number

Place	Number
Columbus, OH (city) Franklin County	295

Taiwanese 25 Years and Over Who are High School Graduates
Top 10 Places Sorted by Percent

Place	Percent
Columbus, OH (city) Franklin County	96.09

Thais 25 Years and Over Who are High School Graduates
Top 10 Places Sorted by Number

Place	Number
Columbus, OH (city) Franklin County	219

Thais 25 Years and Over Who are High School Graduates
Top 10 Places Sorted by Percent

Place	Percent
Columbus, OH (city) Franklin County	86.56

Tongans 25 Years and Over Who are High School Graduates
Top 10 Places Sorted by Number

Place	Number
No places met population threshold.	

Tongans 25 Years and Over Who are High School Graduates
Top 10 Places Sorted by Percent

Place	Percent
No places met population threshold.	

Vietnamese 25 Years and Over Who are High School Graduates
Top 10 Places Sorted by Number

Place	Number
Columbus, OH (city) Franklin County	870
Cleveland, OH (city) Cuyahoga County	381
Akron, OH (city) Summit County	222

Vietnamese 25 Years and Over Who are High School Graduates
Top 10 Places Sorted by Percent

Place	Percent
Akron, OH (city) Summit County	67.27
Columbus, OH (city) Franklin County	63.83
Cleveland, OH (city) Cuyahoga County	54.35

Educational Attainment: College Graduates

Total Populations 25 Years and Over Who are Four-Year College Graduates
Top 10 Places Sorted by Number

Place	Number
Columbus, OH (city) Franklin County	128,058
Cincinnati, OH (city) Hamilton County	55,215
Cleveland, OH (city) Cuyahoga County	33,949
Toledo, OH (city) Lucas County	33,091
Akron, OH (city) Summit County	25,110
Cleveland Heights, OH (city) Cuyahoga County	16,760
Upper Arlington, OH (city) Franklin County	16,063
Dayton, OH (city) Montgomery County	14,477
Lakewood, OH (city) Cuyahoga County	14,193
Dublin, OH (city) Franklin County	12,749

Total Populations 25 Years and Over Who are Four-Year College Graduates
Top 10 Places Sorted by Percent

Place	Percent
Upper Arlington, OH (city) Franklin County	67.46
Hudson, OH (city) Summit County	66.54
Dublin, OH (city) Franklin County	64.66
Athens, OH (city) Athens County	63.81
Shaker Heights, OH (city) Cuyahoga County	61.69
Worthington, OH (city) Franklin County	59.71
Beckett Ridge, OH (cdp) Butler County	54.49
Oxford, OH (city) Butler County	53.56
Beachwood, OH (city) Cuyahoga County	50.86
Kenwood, OH (cdp) Hamilton County	50.58

Asians 25 Years and Over Who are Four-Year College Graduates
Top 10 Places Sorted by Number

Place	Number
Columbus, OH (city) Franklin County	9,085
Cincinnati, OH (city) Hamilton County	2,357
Cleveland, OH (city) Cuyahoga County	1,907
Toledo, OH (city) Lucas County	1,183
Dublin, OH (city) Franklin County	1,027
Akron, OH (city) Summit County	950
Cleveland Heights, OH (city) Cuyahoga County	797
Westlake, OH (city) Cuyahoga County	731
Strongsville, OH (city) Cuyahoga County	703
Parma, OH (city) Cuyahoga County	662

Asians 25 Years and Over Who are Four-Year College Graduates
Top 10 Places Sorted by Percent

Place	Percent
Athens, OH (city) Athens County	86.50
Kent, OH (city) Portage County	84.21
Cleveland Heights, OH (city) Cuyahoga County	82.00
Kenwood, OH (cdp) Hamilton County	81.33
Centerville, OH (city) Montgomery County	81.09
Shaker Heights, OH (city) Cuyahoga County	80.58
Beachwood, OH (city) Cuyahoga County	79.58
Hudson, OH (city) Summit County	79.19
Richmond Heights, OH (city) Cuyahoga County	78.37
Beckett Ridge, OH (cdp) Butler County	77.21

Native Hawaiian and Other Pacific Islanders 25 Years and Over Who are Four-Year College Graduates
Top 10 Places Sorted by Number

Place	Number
No places met population threshold.	

Native Hawaiian and Other Pacific Islanders 25 Years and Over Who are Four-Year College Graduates
Top 10 Places Sorted by Percent

Place	Percent
No places met population threshold.	

Asian Indians 25 Years and Over Who are Four-Year College Graduates
Top 10 Places Sorted by Number

Place	Number
Columbus, OH (city) Franklin County	3,160
Cincinnati, OH (city) Hamilton County	838
Cleveland, OH (city) Cuyahoga County	504
Dublin, OH (city) Franklin County	380
Westlake, OH (city) Cuyahoga County	358
Strongsville, OH (city) Cuyahoga County	341
Toledo, OH (city) Lucas County	305
Parma, OH (city) Cuyahoga County	297
Akron, OH (city) Summit County	285
Solon, OH (city) Cuyahoga County	279

Asian Indians 25 Years and Over Who are Four-Year College Graduates
Top 10 Places Sorted by Percent

Place	Percent
Westlake, OH (city) Cuyahoga County	91.09
Dublin, OH (city) Franklin County	90.05
Sharonville, OH (city) Hamilton County	89.56

Notes: Please refer to the User's Guide for an explanation of data; tables reflect only those areas that meet Summary File 4 population thresholds, therefore there may be less than 10 places listed

Place	
Blue Ash, OH (city) Hamilton County	86.64
Cleveland Heights, OH (city) Cuyahoga County	86.07
Solon, OH (city) Cuyahoga County	85.85
Cincinnati, OH (city) Hamilton County	83.88
Mayfield Heights, OH (city) Cuyahoga County	81.85
North Olmsted, OH (city) Cuyahoga County	79.23
Columbus, OH (city) Franklin County	78.12

Bangladeshis 25 Years and Over Who are Four-Year College Graduates
Top 10 Places Sorted by Number

Place	Number
No places met population threshold.	

Bangladeshis 25 Years and Over Who are Four-Year College Graduates
Top 10 Places Sorted by Percent

Place	Percent
No places met population threshold.	

Cambodians 25 Years and Over Who are Four-Year College Graduates
Top 10 Places Sorted by Number

Place	Number
Columbus, OH (city) Franklin County	54

Cambodians 25 Years and Over Who are Four-Year College Graduates
Top 10 Places Sorted by Percent

Place	Percent
Columbus, OH (city) Franklin County	9.47

Chinese (except Taiwanese) 25 Years and Over Who are Four-Year College Graduates
Top 10 Places Sorted by Number

Place	Number
Columbus, OH (city) Franklin County	2,428
Cincinnati, OH (city) Hamilton County	846
Cleveland, OH (city) Cuyahoga County	558
Toledo, OH (city) Lucas County	474
Akron, OH (city) Summit County	275
Dublin, OH (city) Franklin County	262
Cleveland Heights, OH (city) Cuyahoga County	215
Upper Arlington, OH (city) Franklin County	196
Hudson, OH (city) Summit County	185
Solon, OH (city) Cuyahoga County	165

Chinese (except Taiwanese) 25 Years and Over Who are Four-Year College Graduates
Top 10 Places Sorted by Percent

Place	Percent
Hudson, OH (city) Summit County	94.87
Dublin, OH (city) Franklin County	87.04
Upper Arlington, OH (city) Franklin County	84.48
Cincinnati, OH (city) Hamilton County	82.62
Cleveland Heights, OH (city) Cuyahoga County	75.17
Solon, OH (city) Cuyahoga County	75.00
Toledo, OH (city) Lucas County	69.91
Columbus, OH (city) Franklin County	67.99
Akron, OH (city) Summit County	65.17
Cleveland, OH (city) Cuyahoga County	38.70

Fijians 25 Years and Over Who are Four-Year College Graduates
Top 10 Places Sorted by Number

Place	Number
No places met population threshold.	

Fijians 25 Years and Over Who are Four-Year College Graduates
Top 10 Places Sorted by Percent

Place	Percent
No places met population threshold.	

Filipinos 25 Years and Over Who are Four-Year College Graduates
Top 10 Places Sorted by Number

Place	Number
Columbus, OH (city) Franklin County	518
Cleveland, OH (city) Cuyahoga County	342
Cincinnati, OH (city) Hamilton County	178
Toledo, OH (city) Lucas County	176

Filipinos 25 Years and Over Who are Four-Year College Graduates
Top 10 Places Sorted by Percent

Place	Percent
Cincinnati, OH (city) Hamilton County	64.96
Toledo, OH (city) Lucas County	56.96
Cleveland, OH (city) Cuyahoga County	53.86
Columbus, OH (city) Franklin County	53.07

Guamanians or Chamorros 25 Years and Over Who are Four-Year College Graduates
Top 10 Places Sorted by Number

Place	Number
No places met population threshold.	

Guamanians or Chamorros 25 Years and Over Who are Four-Year College Graduates
Top 10 Places Sorted by Percent

Place	Percent
No places met population threshold.	

Hawaiian Natives 25 Years and Over Who are Four-Year College Graduates
Top 10 Places Sorted by Number

Place	Number
No places met population threshold.	

Hawaiian Natives 25 Years and Over Who are Four-Year College Graduates
Top 10 Places Sorted by Percent

Place	Percent
No places met population threshold.	

Hmongs 25 Years and Over Who are Four-Year College Graduates
Top 10 Places Sorted by Number

Place	Number
No places met population threshold.	

Hmongs 25 Years and Over Who are Four-Year College Graduates
Top 10 Places Sorted by Percent

Place	Percent
No places met population threshold.	

Indonesians 25 Years and Over Who are Four-Year College Graduates
Top 10 Places Sorted by Number

Place	Number
Columbus, OH (city) Franklin County	59

Indonesians 25 Years and Over Who are Four-Year College Graduates
Top 10 Places Sorted by Percent

Place	Percent
Columbus, OH (city) Franklin County	65.56

Japanese 25 Years and Over Who are Four-Year College Graduates
Top 10 Places Sorted by Number

Place	Number
Columbus, OH (city) Franklin County	613
Dublin, OH (city) Franklin County	202

Japanese 25 Years and Over Who are Four-Year College Graduates
Top 10 Places Sorted by Percent

Place	Percent
Columbus, OH (city) Franklin County	54.98
Dublin, OH (city) Franklin County	39.61

Koreans 25 Years and Over Who are Four-Year College Graduates
Top 10 Places Sorted by Number

Place	Number
Columbus, OH (city) Franklin County	1,119

Koreans 25 Years and Over Who are Four-Year College Graduates
Top 10 Places Sorted by Percent

Place	Percent
Columbus, OH (city) Franklin County	67.90

Laotians 25 Years and Over Who are Four-Year College Graduates
Top 10 Places Sorted by Number

Place	Number
Columbus, OH (city) Franklin County	43
Akron, OH (city) Summit County	7

Laotians 25 Years and Over Who are Four-Year College Graduates
Top 10 Places Sorted by Percent

Place	Percent
Columbus, OH (city) Franklin County	7.98
Akron, OH (city) Summit County	3.20

Malaysians 25 Years and Over Who are Four-Year College Graduates
Top 10 Places Sorted by Number

Place	Number
No places met population threshold.	

Malaysians 25 Years and Over Who are Four-Year College Graduates
Top 10 Places Sorted by Percent

Place	Percent
No places met population threshold.	

Pakistanis 25 Years and Over Who are Four-Year College Graduates
Top 10 Places Sorted by Number

Place	Number
No places met population threshold.	

Notes: Please refer to the User's Guide for an explanation of data; tables reflect only those areas that meet Summary File 4 population thresholds, therefore there may be less than 10 places listed

PROFILES OF OHIO / Asian Rankings: Median Household Income

Pakistanis 25 Years and Over Who are Four-Year College Graduates
Top 10 Places Sorted by Percent

Place	Percent
No places met population threshold.	

Samoans 25 Years and Over Who are Four-Year College Graduates
Top 10 Places Sorted by Number

Place	Number
No places met population threshold.	

Samoans 25 Years and Over Who are Four-Year College Graduates
Top 10 Places Sorted by Percent

Place	Percent
No places met population threshold.	

Sri Lankans 25 Years and Over Who are Four-Year College Graduates
Top 10 Places Sorted by Number

Place	Number
No places met population threshold.	

Sri Lankans 25 Years and Over Who are Four-Year College Graduates
Top 10 Places Sorted by Percent

Place	Percent
No places met population threshold.	

Taiwanese 25 Years and Over Who are Four-Year College Graduates
Top 10 Places Sorted by Number

Place	Number
Columbus, OH (city) Franklin County	241

Taiwanese 25 Years and Over Who are Four-Year College Graduates
Top 10 Places Sorted by Percent

Place	Percent
Columbus, OH (city) Franklin County	78.50

Thais 25 Years and Over Who are Four-Year College Graduates
Top 10 Places Sorted by Number

Place	Number
Columbus, OH (city) Franklin County	150

Thais 25 Years and Over Who are Four-Year College Graduates
Top 10 Places Sorted by Percent

Place	Percent
Columbus, OH (city) Franklin County	59.29

Tongans 25 Years and Over Who are Four-Year College Graduates
Top 10 Places Sorted by Number

Place	Number
No places met population threshold.	

Tongans 25 Years and Over Who are Four-Year College Graduates
Top 10 Places Sorted by Percent

Place	Percent
No places met population threshold.	

Vietnamese 25 Years and Over Who are Four-Year College Graduates
Top 10 Places Sorted by Number

Place	Number
Columbus, OH (city) Franklin County	283
Cleveland, OH (city) Cuyahoga County	99
Akron, OH (city) Summit County	75

Vietnamese 25 Years and Over Who are Four-Year College Graduates
Top 10 Places Sorted by Percent

Place	Percent
Akron, OH (city) Summit County	22.73
Columbus, OH (city) Franklin County	20.76
Cleveland, OH (city) Cuyahoga County	14.12

Median Household Income

Total Population
Top 10 Places Sorted by Number

Place	Dollars
Hudson, OH (city) Summit County	99,156
Dublin, OH (city) Franklin County	91,162
Beckett Ridge, OH (cdp) Butler County	80,090
Solon, OH (city) Cuyahoga County	78,903
Upper Arlington, OH (city) Franklin County	72,116
Highland Heights, OH (city) Cuyahoga County	69,750
Westerville, OH (city) Franklin County	69,135
Hilliard, OH (city) Franklin County	69,015
Beavercreek, OH (city) Greene County	68,801
Strongsville, OH (city) Cuyahoga County	68,660

Asian
Top 10 Places Sorted by Number

Place	Dollars
Gahanna, OH (city) Franklin County	110,928
Hudson, OH (city) Summit County	108,230
Westlake, OH (city) Cuyahoga County	105,940
Strongsville, OH (city) Cuyahoga County	102,156
Beckett Ridge, OH (cdp) Butler County	101,799
Solon, OH (city) Cuyahoga County	99,394
Highland Heights, OH (city) Cuyahoga County	90,401
Westerville, OH (city) Franklin County	88,669
Dublin, OH (city) Franklin County	86,889
Mason, OH (city) Warren County	84,308

Native Hawaiian and Other Pacific Islander
Top 10 Places Sorted by Number

Place	Dollars
No places met population threshold.	

Asian Indian
Top 10 Places Sorted by Number

Place	Dollars
Solon, OH (city) Cuyahoga County	134,386
Strongsville, OH (city) Cuyahoga County	107,297
Westlake, OH (city) Cuyahoga County	104,242
Dublin, OH (city) Franklin County	102,288
Beavercreek, OH (city) Greene County	91,015
North Olmsted, OH (city) Cuyahoga County	83,513
Blue Ash, OH (city) Hamilton County	75,506
Mayfield Heights, OH (city) Cuyahoga County	67,250
North Royalton, OH (city) Cuyahoga County	67,188
Fairfield, OH (city) Butler County	62,813

Bangladeshi
Top 10 Places Sorted by Number

Place	Dollars
No places met population threshold.	

Cambodian
Top 10 Places Sorted by Number

Place	Dollars
Columbus, OH (city) Franklin County	31,382

Chinese (except Taiwanese)
Top 10 Places Sorted by Number

Place	Dollars
Dublin, OH (city) Franklin County	118,591
Hudson, OH (city) Summit County	106,977
Solon, OH (city) Cuyahoga County	81,203
Upper Arlington, OH (city) Franklin County	77,418
Columbus, OH (city) Franklin County	34,942
Cleveland Heights, OH (city) Cuyahoga County	34,342
Cincinnati, OH (city) Hamilton County	34,013
Toledo, OH (city) Lucas County	27,031
Akron, OH (city) Summit County	26,528
Cleveland, OH (city) Cuyahoga County	23,313

Fijian
Top 10 Places Sorted by Number

Place	Dollars
No places met population threshold.	

Filipino
Top 10 Places Sorted by Number

Place	Dollars
Cincinnati, OH (city) Hamilton County	50,714
Toledo, OH (city) Lucas County	50,625
Columbus, OH (city) Franklin County	47,750
Cleveland, OH (city) Cuyahoga County	37,917

Guamanian or Chamorro
Top 10 Places Sorted by Number

Place	Dollars
No places met population threshold.	

Hawaiian, Native
Top 10 Places Sorted by Number

Place	Dollars
No places met population threshold.	

Hmong
Top 10 Places Sorted by Number

Place	Dollars
No places met population threshold.	

Indonesian
Top 10 Places Sorted by Number

Place	Dollars
Columbus, OH (city) Franklin County	3,208

Japanese
Top 10 Places Sorted by Number

Place	Dollars
Dublin, OH (city) Franklin County	80,830
Columbus, OH (city) Franklin County	48,243

Korean
Top 10 Places Sorted by Number

Place	Dollars
Columbus, OH (city) Franklin County	16,840

Laotian
Top 10 Places Sorted by Number

Place	Dollars
Akron, OH (city) Summit County	56,400
Columbus, OH (city) Franklin County	39,565

Notes: Please refer to the User's Guide for an explanation of data; tables reflect only those areas that meet Summary File 4 population thresholds, therefore there may be less than 10 places listed

PROFILES OF OHIO / Asian Rankings: Per Capita Income

Malaysian
Top 10 Places Sorted by Number

Place	Dollars
No places met population threshold.	

Pakistani
Top 10 Places Sorted by Number

Place	Dollars
No places met population threshold.	

Samoan
Top 10 Places Sorted by Number

Place	Dollars
No places met population threshold.	

Sri Lankan
Top 10 Places Sorted by Number

Place	Dollars
No places met population threshold.	

Taiwanese
Top 10 Places Sorted by Number

Place	Dollars
Columbus, OH (city) Franklin County	21,146

Thai
Top 10 Places Sorted by Number

Place	Dollars
Columbus, OH (city) Franklin County	16,125

Tongan
Top 10 Places Sorted by Number

Place	Dollars
No places met population threshold.	

Vietnamese
Top 10 Places Sorted by Number

Place	Dollars
Akron, OH (city) Summit County	41,080
Columbus, OH (city) Franklin County	36,611
Cleveland, OH (city) Cuyahoga County	33,295

Per Capita Income

Total Population
Top 10 Places Sorted by Number

Place	Dollars
Upper Arlington, OH (city) Franklin County	42,025
Shaker Heights, OH (city) Cuyahoga County	41,354
Dublin, OH (city) Franklin County	41,122
Hudson, OH (city) Summit County	40,915
Beachwood, OH (city) Cuyahoga County	40,509
Westlake, OH (city) Cuyahoga County	37,142
Solon, OH (city) Cuyahoga County	35,394
Worthington, OH (city) Franklin County	34,495
Beckett Ridge, OH (cdp) Butler County	33,835
Blue Ash, OH (city) Hamilton County	33,801

Asian
Top 10 Places Sorted by Number

Place	Dollars
Westlake, OH (city) Cuyahoga County	46,367
Solon, OH (city) Cuyahoga County	41,367
Gahanna, OH (city) Franklin County	38,218
Hudson, OH (city) Summit County	36,891
Upper Arlington, OH (city) Franklin County	35,630
Wooster, OH (city) Wayne County	34,538
Dublin, OH (city) Franklin County	33,203
Mason, OH (city) Warren County	32,153
Shaker Heights, OH (city) Cuyahoga County	31,910
Strongsville, OH (city) Cuyahoga County	31,692

Native Hawaiian and Other Pacific Islander
Top 10 Places Sorted by Number

Place	Dollars
No places met population threshold.	

Asian Indian
Top 10 Places Sorted by Number

Place	Dollars
Westlake, OH (city) Cuyahoga County	55,467
Solon, OH (city) Cuyahoga County	47,197
Beavercreek, OH (city) Greene County	39,369
Dublin, OH (city) Franklin County	38,436
Strongsville, OH (city) Cuyahoga County	35,842
Mayfield Heights, OH (city) Cuyahoga County	26,494
Fairfield, OH (city) Butler County	25,866
Blue Ash, OH (city) Hamilton County	25,038
Columbus, OH (city) Franklin County	24,873
Cincinnati, OH (city) Hamilton County	24,787

Bangladeshi
Top 10 Places Sorted by Number

Place	Dollars
No places met population threshold.	

Cambodian
Top 10 Places Sorted by Number

Place	Dollars
Columbus, OH (city) Franklin County	17,681

Chinese (except Taiwanese)
Top 10 Places Sorted by Number

Place	Dollars
Solon, OH (city) Cuyahoga County	37,218
Dublin, OH (city) Franklin County	35,393
Hudson, OH (city) Summit County	29,140
Cleveland Heights, OH (city) Cuyahoga County	26,672
Upper Arlington, OH (city) Franklin County	26,190
Columbus, OH (city) Franklin County	19,976
Cincinnati, OH (city) Hamilton County	17,631
Toledo, OH (city) Lucas County	16,701
Akron, OH (city) Summit County	13,508
Cleveland, OH (city) Cuyahoga County	12,750

Fijian
Top 10 Places Sorted by Number

Place	Dollars
No places met population threshold.	

Filipino
Top 10 Places Sorted by Number

Place	Dollars
Columbus, OH (city) Franklin County	29,897
Cincinnati, OH (city) Hamilton County	22,479
Toledo, OH (city) Lucas County	20,428
Cleveland, OH (city) Cuyahoga County	18,238

Guamanian or Chamorro
Top 10 Places Sorted by Number

Place	Dollars
No places met population threshold.	

Hawaiian, Native
Top 10 Places Sorted by Number

Place	Dollars
No places met population threshold.	

Hmong
Top 10 Places Sorted by Number

Place	Dollars
No places met population threshold.	

Indonesian
Top 10 Places Sorted by Number

Place	Dollars
Columbus, OH (city) Franklin County	9,661

Japanese
Top 10 Places Sorted by Number

Place	Dollars
Dublin, OH (city) Franklin County	31,854
Columbus, OH (city) Franklin County	21,840

Korean
Top 10 Places Sorted by Number

Place	Dollars
Columbus, OH (city) Franklin County	16,693

Laotian
Top 10 Places Sorted by Number

Place	Dollars
Columbus, OH (city) Franklin County	12,990
Akron, OH (city) Summit County	11,528

Malaysian
Top 10 Places Sorted by Number

Place	Dollars
No places met population threshold.	

Pakistani
Top 10 Places Sorted by Number

Place	Dollars
No places met population threshold.	

Samoan
Top 10 Places Sorted by Number

Place	Dollars
No places met population threshold.	

Sri Lankan
Top 10 Places Sorted by Number

Place	Dollars
No places met population threshold.	

Taiwanese
Top 10 Places Sorted by Number

Place	Dollars
Columbus, OH (city) Franklin County	26,570

Thai
Top 10 Places Sorted by Number

Place	Dollars
Columbus, OH (city) Franklin County	10,742

Tongan
Top 10 Places Sorted by Number

Place	Dollars
No places met population threshold.	

Vietnamese
Top 10 Places Sorted by Number

Place	Dollars
Akron, OH (city) Summit County	27,728
Cleveland, OH (city) Cuyahoga County	15,747

Notes: Please refer to the User's Guide for an explanation of data; tables reflect only those areas that meet Summary File 4 population thresholds, therefore there may be less than 10 places listed

PROFILES OF OHIO / Asian Rankings: Poverty Status

Columbus, OH (city) Franklin County — 15,203

Poverty Status

Total Populations with Income Below Poverty Level
Top 10 Places Sorted by Number

Place	Number
Cleveland, OH (city) Cuyahoga County	122,479
Columbus, OH (city) Franklin County	102,723
Cincinnati, OH (city) Hamilton County	69,722
Toledo, OH (city) Lucas County	54,903
Akron, OH (city) Summit County	36,975
Dayton, OH (city) Montgomery County	35,756
Athens, OH (city) Athens County	7,247
Oxford, OH (city) Butler County	6,296
Bowling Green, OH (city) Wood County	5,761
Kent, OH (city) Portage County	5,622

Total Populations with Income Below Poverty Level
Top 10 Places Sorted by Percent

Place	Percent
Athens, OH (city) Athens County	51.93
Oxford, OH (city) Butler County	43.66
Cleveland, OH (city) Cuyahoga County	26.27
Bowling Green, OH (city) Wood County	25.27
Kent, OH (city) Portage County	25.23
Dayton, OH (city) Montgomery County	22.99
Cincinnati, OH (city) Hamilton County	21.91
Toledo, OH (city) Lucas County	17.89
Akron, OH (city) Summit County	17.45
Columbus, OH (city) Franklin County	14.81

Asians with Income Below Poverty Level
Top 10 Places Sorted by Number

Place	Number
Columbus, OH (city) Franklin County	4,482
Cleveland, OH (city) Cuyahoga County	1,697
Cincinnati, OH (city) Hamilton County	993
Toledo, OH (city) Lucas County	743
Akron, OH (city) Summit County	631
Athens, OH (city) Athens County	410
Fairborn, OH (city) Greene County	374
Cleveland Heights, OH (city) Cuyahoga County	310
Kent, OH (city) Portage County	235
Oxford, OH (city) Butler County	197

Asians with Income Below Poverty Level
Top 10 Places Sorted by Percent

Place	Percent
Athens, OH (city) Athens County	54.23
Oxford, OH (city) Butler County	52.39
Kent, OH (city) Portage County	44.09
Fairborn, OH (city) Greene County	42.16
Cleveland, OH (city) Cuyahoga County	25.99
Parma Heights, OH (city) Cuyahoga County	25.87
Findlay, OH (city) Hancock County	25.13
Toledo, OH (city) Lucas County	25.09
Cleveland Heights, OH (city) Cuyahoga County	22.83
Beachwood, OH (city) Cuyahoga County	21.11

Native Hawaiian and Other Pacific Islanders with Income Below Poverty Level
Top 10 Places Sorted by Number

Place	Number

No places met population threshold.

Native Hawaiian and Other Pacific Islanders with Income Below Poverty Level
Top 10 Places Sorted by Percent

Place	Percent

No places met population threshold.

Asian Indians with Income Below Poverty Level
Top 10 Places Sorted by Number

Place	Number
Columbus, OH (city) Franklin County	948
Cleveland, OH (city) Cuyahoga County	463
Cincinnati, OH (city) Hamilton County	327
Toledo, OH (city) Lucas County	252
Akron, OH (city) Summit County	160
Cleveland Heights, OH (city) Cuyahoga County	134
Parma, OH (city) Cuyahoga County	45
Beavercreek, OH (city) Greene County	23
North Olmsted, OH (city) Cuyahoga County	23
Sharonville, OH (city) Hamilton County	8

Asian Indians with Income Below Poverty Level
Top 10 Places Sorted by Percent

Place	Percent
Cleveland, OH (city) Cuyahoga County	43.84
Toledo, OH (city) Lucas County	30.00
Akron, OH (city) Summit County	28.02
Cleveland Heights, OH (city) Cuyahoga County	24.23
Cincinnati, OH (city) Hamilton County	21.22
Columbus, OH (city) Franklin County	15.26
Parma, OH (city) Cuyahoga County	7.09
North Olmsted, OH (city) Cuyahoga County	5.46
Beavercreek, OH (city) Greene County	4.85
Sharonville, OH (city) Hamilton County	2.04

Bangladeshis with Income Below Poverty Level
Top 10 Places Sorted by Number

Place	Number

No places met population threshold.

Bangladeshis with Income Below Poverty Level
Top 10 Places Sorted by Percent

Place	Percent

No places met population threshold.

Cambodians with Income Below Poverty Level
Top 10 Places Sorted by Number

Place	Number
Columbus, OH (city) Franklin County	291

Cambodians with Income Below Poverty Level
Top 10 Places Sorted by Percent

Place	Percent
Columbus, OH (city) Franklin County	24.41

Chinese (except Taiwanese) with Income Below Poverty Level
Top 10 Places Sorted by Number

Place	Number
Columbus, OH (city) Franklin County	843
Cleveland, OH (city) Cuyahoga County	448
Cincinnati, OH (city) Hamilton County	236
Toledo, OH (city) Lucas County	218
Cleveland Heights, OH (city) Cuyahoga County	76
Akron, OH (city) Summit County	75
Upper Arlington, OH (city) Franklin County	61
Dublin, OH (city) Franklin County	25
Hudson, OH (city) Summit County	0
Solon, OH (city) Cuyahoga County	0

Chinese (except Taiwanese) with Income Below Poverty Level
Top 10 Places Sorted by Percent

Place	Percent
Toledo, OH (city) Lucas County	28.17
Cleveland, OH (city) Cuyahoga County	23.22
Cleveland Heights, OH (city) Cuyahoga County	19.29
Cincinnati, OH (city) Hamilton County	18.14
Upper Arlington, OH (city) Franklin County	17.99
Columbus, OH (city) Franklin County	16.88
Akron, OH (city) Summit County	14.18
Dublin, OH (city) Franklin County	4.90
Hudson, OH (city) Summit County	0.00
Solon, OH (city) Cuyahoga County	0.00

Fijians with Income Below Poverty Level
Top 10 Places Sorted by Number

Place	Number

No places met population threshold.

Fijians with Income Below Poverty Level
Top 10 Places Sorted by Percent

Place	Percent

No places met population threshold.

Filipinos with Income Below Poverty Level
Top 10 Places Sorted by Number

Place	Number
Columbus, OH (city) Franklin County	71
Cincinnati, OH (city) Hamilton County	54
Cleveland, OH (city) Cuyahoga County	46
Toledo, OH (city) Lucas County	24

Filipinos with Income Below Poverty Level
Top 10 Places Sorted by Percent

Place	Percent
Cincinnati, OH (city) Hamilton County	11.49
Toledo, OH (city) Lucas County	6.45
Cleveland, OH (city) Cuyahoga County	5.50
Columbus, OH (city) Franklin County	5.15

Guamanians or Chamorros with Income Below Poverty Level
Top 10 Places Sorted by Number

Place	Number

No places met population threshold.

Guamanians or Chamorros with Income Below Poverty Level
Top 10 Places Sorted by Percent

Place	Percent

No places met population threshold.

Hawaiian Natives with Income Below Poverty Level
Top 10 Places Sorted by Number

Place	Number

No places met population threshold.

Hawaiian Natives with Income Below Poverty Level
Top 10 Places Sorted by Percent

Place	Percent

No places met population threshold.

Hmongs with Income Below Poverty Level
Top 10 Places Sorted by Number

Place	Number

No places met population threshold.

Hmongs with Income Below Poverty Level
Top 10 Places Sorted by Percent

Place	Percent

No places met population threshold.

Indonesians with Income Below Poverty Level
Top 10 Places Sorted by Number

Place	Number
Columbus, OH (city) Franklin County	321

Notes: Please refer to the User's Guide for an explanation of data; tables reflect only those areas that meet Summary File 4 population thresholds, therefore there may be less than 10 places listed

Indonesians with Income Below Poverty Level
Top 10 Places Sorted by Percent

Place	Percent
Columbus, OH (city) Franklin County	63.31

Japanese with Income Below Poverty Level
Top 10 Places Sorted by Number

Place	Number
Columbus, OH (city) Franklin County	232
Dublin, OH (city) Franklin County	107

Japanese with Income Below Poverty Level
Top 10 Places Sorted by Percent

Place	Percent
Columbus, OH (city) Franklin County	13.35
Dublin, OH (city) Franklin County	13.05

Koreans with Income Below Poverty Level
Top 10 Places Sorted by Number

Place	Number
Columbus, OH (city) Franklin County	688

Koreans with Income Below Poverty Level
Top 10 Places Sorted by Percent

Place	Percent
Columbus, OH (city) Franklin County	28.64

Laotians with Income Below Poverty Level
Top 10 Places Sorted by Number

Place	Number
Columbus, OH (city) Franklin County	187
Akron, OH (city) Summit County	66

Laotians with Income Below Poverty Level
Top 10 Places Sorted by Percent

Place	Percent
Columbus, OH (city) Franklin County	19.10
Akron, OH (city) Summit County	11.81

Malaysians with Income Below Poverty Level
Top 10 Places Sorted by Number

Place	Number
No places met population threshold.	

Malaysians with Income Below Poverty Level
Top 10 Places Sorted by Percent

Place	Percent
No places met population threshold.	

Pakistanis with Income Below Poverty Level
Top 10 Places Sorted by Number

Place	Number
No places met population threshold.	

Pakistanis with Income Below Poverty Level
Top 10 Places Sorted by Percent

Place	Percent
No places met population threshold.	

Samoans with Income Below Poverty Level
Top 10 Places Sorted by Number

Place	Number
No places met population threshold.	

Samoans with Income Below Poverty Level
Top 10 Places Sorted by Percent

Place	Percent
No places met population threshold.	

Sri Lankans with Income Below Poverty Level
Top 10 Places Sorted by Number

Place	Number
No places met population threshold.	

Sri Lankans with Income Below Poverty Level
Top 10 Places Sorted by Percent

Place	Percent
No places met population threshold.	

Taiwanese with Income Below Poverty Level
Top 10 Places Sorted by Number

Place	Number
Columbus, OH (city) Franklin County	123

Taiwanese with Income Below Poverty Level
Top 10 Places Sorted by Percent

Place	Percent
Columbus, OH (city) Franklin County	30.90

Thais with Income Below Poverty Level
Top 10 Places Sorted by Number

Place	Number
Columbus, OH (city) Franklin County	128

Thais with Income Below Poverty Level
Top 10 Places Sorted by Percent

Place	Percent
Columbus, OH (city) Franklin County	33.60

Tongans with Income Below Poverty Level
Top 10 Places Sorted by Number

Place	Number
No places met population threshold.	

Tongans with Income Below Poverty Level
Top 10 Places Sorted by Percent

Place	Percent
No places met population threshold.	

Vietnamese with Income Below Poverty Level
Top 10 Places Sorted by Number

Place	Number
Cleveland, OH (city) Cuyahoga County	314
Columbus, OH (city) Franklin County	301
Akron, OH (city) Summit County	124

Vietnamese with Income Below Poverty Level
Top 10 Places Sorted by Percent

Place	Percent
Cleveland, OH (city) Cuyahoga County	28.36
Akron, OH (city) Summit County	21.72
Columbus, OH (city) Franklin County	14.03

Homeownership

Total Populations Who Own Their Own Homes
Top 10 Places Sorted by Number

Place	Number
Columbus, OH (city) Franklin County	148,315
Cleveland, OH (city) Cuyahoga County	92,498
Toledo, OH (city) Lucas County	77,028
Cincinnati, OH (city) Hamilton County	57,655
Akron, OH (city) Summit County	53,441
Dayton, OH (city) Montgomery County	35,536
Parma, OH (city) Cuyahoga County	27,222
Kettering, OH (city) Montgomery County	17,082
Mentor, OH (city) Lake County	16,436
Cuyahoga Falls, OH (city) Summit County	14,239

Total Populations Who Own Their Own Homes
Top 10 Places Sorted by Percent

Place	Percent
Highland Heights, OH (city) Cuyahoga County	97.30
Hudson, OH (city) Summit County	90.40
Solon, OH (city) Cuyahoga County	87.83
Mentor, OH (city) Lake County	87.44
Beckett Ridge, OH (cdp) Butler County	85.81
Worthington, OH (city) Franklin County	84.68
Beavercreek, OH (city) Greene County	84.21
Mason, OH (city) Warren County	84.13
South Euclid, OH (city) Cuyahoga County	83.94
Maple Heights, OH (city) Cuyahoga County	83.82

Asians Who Own Their Own Homes
Top 10 Places Sorted by Number

Place	Number
Columbus, OH (city) Franklin County	2,688
Cleveland, OH (city) Cuyahoga County	943
Akron, OH (city) Summit County	444
Dublin, OH (city) Franklin County	422
Cincinnati, OH (city) Hamilton County	377
Toledo, OH (city) Lucas County	370
Strongsville, OH (city) Cuyahoga County	319
Westlake, OH (city) Cuyahoga County	313
Beavercreek, OH (city) Greene County	280
Solon, OH (city) Cuyahoga County	250

Asians Who Own Their Own Homes
Top 10 Places Sorted by Percent

Place	Percent
Highland Heights, OH (city) Cuyahoga County	100.00
Mason, OH (city) Warren County	93.63
Beckett Ridge, OH (cdp) Butler County	89.82
Brunswick, OH (city) Medina County	85.19
Solon, OH (city) Cuyahoga County	84.46
Hudson, OH (city) Summit County	83.82
Twinsburg, OH (city) Summit County	78.99
Garfield Heights, OH (city) Cuyahoga County	75.81
Stow, OH (city) Summit County	74.63
Worthington, OH (city) Franklin County	74.02

Native Hawaiian and Other Pacific Islanders Who Own Their Own Homes
Top 10 Places Sorted by Number

Place	Number
No places met population threshold.	

Native Hawaiian and Other Pacific Islanders Who Own Their Own Homes
Top 10 Places Sorted by Percent

Place	Percent
No places met population threshold.	

Asian Indians Who Own Their Own Homes
Top 10 Places Sorted by Number

Place	Number
Columbus, OH (city) Franklin County	513
Strongsville, OH (city) Cuyahoga County	159
Dublin, OH (city) Franklin County	142
Westlake, OH (city) Cuyahoga County	128
Beavercreek, OH (city) Greene County	119
Solon, OH (city) Cuyahoga County	116
Cleveland, OH (city) Cuyahoga County	111
Cincinnati, OH (city) Hamilton County	108

Notes: Please refer to the User's Guide for an explanation of data; tables reflect only those areas that meet Summary File 4 population thresholds, therefore there may be less than 10 places listed

Place	
North Olmsted, OH (city) Cuyahoga County	79
Parma, OH (city) Cuyahoga County	78

Asian Indians Who Own Their Own Homes
Top 10 Places Sorted by Percent

Place	Percent
Solon, OH (city) Cuyahoga County	86.57
Beavercreek, OH (city) Greene County	74.84
Strongsville, OH (city) Cuyahoga County	70.67
North Royalton, OH (city) Cuyahoga County	67.35
North Olmsted, OH (city) Cuyahoga County	62.20
Dublin, OH (city) Franklin County	58.92
Westlake, OH (city) Cuyahoga County	58.72
Cleveland Heights, OH (city) Cuyahoga County	38.59
Blue Ash, OH (city) Hamilton County	36.62
Fairfield, OH (city) Butler County	35.06

Bangladeshis Who Own Their Own Homes
Top 10 Places Sorted by Number

Place	Number
No places met population threshold.	

Bangladeshis Who Own Their Own Homes
Top 10 Places Sorted by Percent

Place	Percent
No places met population threshold.	

Cambodians Who Own Their Own Homes
Top 10 Places Sorted by Number

Place	Number
Columbus, OH (city) Franklin County	125

Cambodians Who Own Their Own Homes
Top 10 Places Sorted by Percent

Place	Percent
Columbus, OH (city) Franklin County	42.96

Chinese (except Taiwanese) Who Own Their Own Homes
Top 10 Places Sorted by Number

Place	Number
Columbus, OH (city) Franklin County	670
Cleveland, OH (city) Cuyahoga County	281
Dublin, OH (city) Franklin County	115
Toledo, OH (city) Lucas County	96
Hudson, OH (city) Summit County	87
Solon, OH (city) Cuyahoga County	76
Akron, OH (city) Summit County	71
Cleveland Heights, OH (city) Cuyahoga County	68
Cincinnati, OH (city) Hamilton County	56
Upper Arlington, OH (city) Franklin County	54

Chinese (except Taiwanese) Who Own Their Own Homes
Top 10 Places Sorted by Percent

Place	Percent
Hudson, OH (city) Summit County	83.65
Solon, OH (city) Cuyahoga County	80.85
Dublin, OH (city) Franklin County	75.66
Upper Arlington, OH (city) Franklin County	47.79
Cleveland, OH (city) Cuyahoga County	37.22
Cleveland Heights, OH (city) Cuyahoga County	35.60
Akron, OH (city) Summit County	33.33
Columbus, OH (city) Franklin County	33.18
Toledo, OH (city) Lucas County	29.72
Cincinnati, OH (city) Hamilton County	9.57

Fijians Who Own Their Own Homes
Top 10 Places Sorted by Number

Place	Number
No places met population threshold.	

Fijians Who Own Their Own Homes
Top 10 Places Sorted by Percent

Place	Percent
No places met population threshold.	

Filipinos Who Own Their Own Homes
Top 10 Places Sorted by Number

Place	Number
Columbus, OH (city) Franklin County	218
Cleveland, OH (city) Cuyahoga County	135
Toledo, OH (city) Lucas County	98
Cincinnati, OH (city) Hamilton County	70

Filipinos Who Own Their Own Homes
Top 10 Places Sorted by Percent

Place	Percent
Toledo, OH (city) Lucas County	73.68
Columbus, OH (city) Franklin County	43.60
Cleveland, OH (city) Cuyahoga County	39.94
Cincinnati, OH (city) Hamilton County	37.43

Guamanians or Chamorros Who Own Their Own Homes
Top 10 Places Sorted by Number

Place	Number
No places met population threshold.	

Guamanians or Chamorros Who Own Their Own Homes
Top 10 Places Sorted by Percent

Place	Percent
No places met population threshold.	

Hawaiian Natives Who Own Their Own Homes
Top 10 Places Sorted by Number

Place	Number
No places met population threshold.	

Hawaiian Natives Who Own Their Own Homes
Top 10 Places Sorted by Percent

Place	Percent
No places met population threshold.	

Hmongs Who Own Their Own Homes
Top 10 Places Sorted by Number

Place	Number
No places met population threshold.	

Hmongs Who Own Their Own Homes
Top 10 Places Sorted by Percent

Place	Percent
No places met population threshold.	

Indonesians Who Own Their Own Homes
Top 10 Places Sorted by Number

Place	Number
Columbus, OH (city) Franklin County	0

Indonesians Who Own Their Own Homes
Top 10 Places Sorted by Percent

Place	Percent
Columbus, OH (city) Franklin County	0.00

Japanese Who Own Their Own Homes
Top 10 Places Sorted by Number

Place	Number
Columbus, OH (city) Franklin County	263
Dublin, OH (city) Franklin County	82

Japanese Who Own Their Own Homes
Top 10 Places Sorted by Percent

Place	Percent
Columbus, OH (city) Franklin County	35.44
Dublin, OH (city) Franklin County	29.93

Koreans Who Own Their Own Homes
Top 10 Places Sorted by Number

Place	Number
Columbus, OH (city) Franklin County	114

Koreans Who Own Their Own Homes
Top 10 Places Sorted by Percent

Place	Percent
Columbus, OH (city) Franklin County	10.09

Laotians Who Own Their Own Homes
Top 10 Places Sorted by Number

Place	Number
Columbus, OH (city) Franklin County	151
Akron, OH (city) Summit County	96

Laotians Who Own Their Own Homes
Top 10 Places Sorted by Percent

Place	Percent
Akron, OH (city) Summit County	86.49
Columbus, OH (city) Franklin County	50.50

Malaysians Who Own Their Own Homes
Top 10 Places Sorted by Number

Place	Number
No places met population threshold.	

Malaysians Who Own Their Own Homes
Top 10 Places Sorted by Percent

Place	Percent
No places met population threshold.	

Pakistanis Who Own Their Own Homes
Top 10 Places Sorted by Number

Place	Number
No places met population threshold.	

Pakistanis Who Own Their Own Homes
Top 10 Places Sorted by Percent

Place	Percent
No places met population threshold.	

Samoans Who Own Their Own Homes
Top 10 Places Sorted by Number

Place	Number
No places met population threshold.	

Samoans Who Own Their Own Homes
Top 10 Places Sorted by Percent

Place	Percent
No places met population threshold.	

Sri Lankans Who Own Their Own Homes
Top 10 Places Sorted by Number

Place	Number
No places met population threshold.	

Sri Lankans Who Own Their Own Homes
Top 10 Places Sorted by Percent

Place	Percent
No places met population threshold.	

Notes: Please refer to the User's Guide for an explanation of data; tables reflect only those areas that meet Summary File 4 population thresholds, therefore there may be less than 10 places listed

Taiwanese Who Own Their Own Homes
Top 10 Places Sorted by Number

Place	Number
Columbus, OH (city) Franklin County	50

Taiwanese Who Own Their Own Homes
Top 10 Places Sorted by Percent

Place	Percent
Columbus, OH (city) Franklin County	31.65

Thais Who Own Their Own Homes
Top 10 Places Sorted by Number

Place	Number
Columbus, OH (city) Franklin County	41

Thais Who Own Their Own Homes
Top 10 Places Sorted by Percent

Place	Percent
Columbus, OH (city) Franklin County	31.78

Tongans Who Own Their Own Homes
Top 10 Places Sorted by Number

Place	Number
No places met population threshold.	

Tongans Who Own Their Own Homes
Top 10 Places Sorted by Percent

Place	Percent
No places met population threshold.	

Vietnamese Who Own Their Own Homes
Top 10 Places Sorted by Number

Place	Number
Columbus, OH (city) Franklin County	359
Cleveland, OH (city) Cuyahoga County	211
Akron, OH (city) Summit County	96

Vietnamese Who Own Their Own Homes
Top 10 Places Sorted by Percent

Place	Percent
Akron, OH (city) Summit County	69.06
Cleveland, OH (city) Cuyahoga County	58.61
Columbus, OH (city) Franklin County	58.56

Median Gross Rent

All Specified Renter-Occupied Housing Units
Top 10 Places Sorted by Number

Place	Dollars/Month
Hudson, OH (city) Summit County	1,303
Beachwood, OH (city) Cuyahoga County	1,145
Beckett Ridge, OH (cdp) Butler County	1,019
Highland Heights, OH (city) Cuyahoga County	1,000
Kenwood, OH (cdp) Hamilton County	953
Dublin, OH (city) Franklin County	929
Westlake, OH (city) Cuyahoga County	866
Beavercreek, OH (city) Greene County	821
Blue Ash, OH (city) Hamilton County	816
Solon, OH (city) Cuyahoga County	814

Specified Housing Units Rented by Asians
Top 10 Places Sorted by Number

Place	Dollars/Month
Hudson, OH (city) Summit County	1,403
Beckett Ridge, OH (cdp) Butler County	1,264
Dublin, OH (city) Franklin County	1,036
Kenwood, OH (cdp) Hamilton County	1,000
Beavercreek, OH (city) Greene County	984
Beachwood, OH (city) Cuyahoga County	961
Westlake, OH (city) Cuyahoga County	943
Hilliard, OH (city) Franklin County	888
Twinsburg, OH (city) Summit County	789
North Royalton, OH (city) Cuyahoga County	783

Specified Housing Units Rented by Native Hawaiian and Other Pacific Islanders
Top 10 Places Sorted by Number

Place	Dollars/Month
No places met population threshold.	

Specified Housing Units Rented by Asian Indians
Top 10 Places Sorted by Number

Place	Dollars/Month
Westlake, OH (city) Cuyahoga County	998
Dublin, OH (city) Franklin County	910
Beavercreek, OH (city) Greene County	867
North Royalton, OH (city) Cuyahoga County	814
Solon, OH (city) Cuyahoga County	771
Blue Ash, OH (city) Hamilton County	757
North Olmsted, OH (city) Cuyahoga County	727
Strongsville, OH (city) Cuyahoga County	704
Fairfield, OH (city) Butler County	677
Cleveland Heights, OH (city) Cuyahoga County	651

Specified Housing Units Rented by Bangladeshis
Top 10 Places Sorted by Number

Place	Dollars/Month
No places met population threshold.	

Specified Housing Units Rented by Cambodians
Top 10 Places Sorted by Number

Place	Dollars/Month
Columbus, OH (city) Franklin County	445

Specified Housing Units Rented by Chinese (except Taiwanese)
Top 10 Places Sorted by Number

Place	Dollars/Month
Hudson, OH (city) Summit County	1,264
Dublin, OH (city) Franklin County	939
Upper Arlington, OH (city) Franklin County	710
Solon, OH (city) Cuyahoga County	675
Cleveland Heights, OH (city) Cuyahoga County	601
Columbus, OH (city) Franklin County	523
Cincinnati, OH (city) Hamilton County	469
Toledo, OH (city) Lucas County	449
Cleveland, OH (city) Cuyahoga County	448
Akron, OH (city) Summit County	428

Specified Housing Units Rented by Fijians
Top 10 Places Sorted by Number

Place	Dollars/Month
No places met population threshold.	

Specified Housing Units Rented by Filipinos
Top 10 Places Sorted by Number

Place	Dollars/Month
Columbus, OH (city) Franklin County	622
Toledo, OH (city) Lucas County	553
Cincinnati, OH (city) Hamilton County	522
Cleveland, OH (city) Cuyahoga County	446

Specified Housing Units Rented by Guamanians or Chamorros
Top 10 Places Sorted by Number

Place	Dollars/Month
No places met population threshold.	

Specified Housing Units Rented by Hawaiian Natives
Top 10 Places Sorted by Number

Place	Dollars/Month
No places met population threshold.	

Specified Housing Units Rented by Hmongs
Top 10 Places Sorted by Number

Place	Dollars/Month
No places met population threshold.	

Specified Housing Units Rented by Indonesians
Top 10 Places Sorted by Number

Place	Dollars/Month
Columbus, OH (city) Franklin County	712

Specified Housing Units Rented by Japanese
Top 10 Places Sorted by Number

Place	Dollars/Month
Dublin, OH (city) Franklin County	1,438
Columbus, OH (city) Franklin County	693

Specified Housing Units Rented by Koreans
Top 10 Places Sorted by Number

Place	Dollars/Month
Columbus, OH (city) Franklin County	613

Specified Housing Units Rented by Laotians
Top 10 Places Sorted by Number

Place	Dollars/Month
Columbus, OH (city) Franklin County	553
Akron, OH (city) Summit County	247

Specified Housing Units Rented by Malaysians
Top 10 Places Sorted by Number

Place	Dollars/Month
No places met population threshold.	

Specified Housing Units Rented by Pakistanis
Top 10 Places Sorted by Number

Place	Dollars/Month
No places met population threshold.	

Specified Housing Units Rented by Samoans
Top 10 Places Sorted by Number

Place	Dollars/Month
No places met population threshold.	

Specified Housing Units Rented by Sri Lankans
Top 10 Places Sorted by Number

Place	Dollars/Month
No places met population threshold.	

Specified Housing Units Rented by Taiwanese
Top 10 Places Sorted by Number

Place	Dollars/Month
Columbus, OH (city) Franklin County	576

Specified Housing Units Rented by Thais
Top 10 Places Sorted by Number

Place	Dollars/Month
Columbus, OH (city) Franklin County	533

Specified Housing Units Rented by Tongans
Top 10 Places Sorted by Number

Place	Dollars/Month
No places met population threshold.	

Notes: Please refer to the User's Guide for an explanation of data; tables reflect only those areas that meet Summary File 4 population thresholds, therefore there may be less than 10 places listed

Specified Housing Units Rented by Vietnamese
Top 10 Places Sorted by Number

Place	Dollars/Month
Columbus, OH (city) Franklin County	534
Akron, OH (city) Summit County	453
Cleveland, OH (city) Cuyahoga County	400

Median Home Value

All Specified Owner-Occupied Housing Units
Top 10 Places Sorted by Number

Place	Dollars
Beachwood, OH (city) Cuyahoga County	244,700
Dublin, OH (city) Franklin County	243,200
Hudson, OH (city) Summit County	236,700
Highland Heights, OH (city) Cuyahoga County	217,500
Solon, OH (city) Cuyahoga County	217,000
Upper Arlington, OH (city) Franklin County	214,700
Shaker Heights, OH (city) Cuyahoga County	201,600
Westlake, OH (city) Cuyahoga County	201,000
Kenwood, OH (cdp) Hamilton County	184,800
Beckett Ridge, OH (cdp) Butler County	184,100

Specified Housing Units Owned and Occupied by Asians
Top 10 Places Sorted by Number

Place	Dollars
Solon, OH (city) Cuyahoga County	250,900
Westlake, OH (city) Cuyahoga County	248,200
Beachwood, OH (city) Cuyahoga County	246,400
Highland Heights, OH (city) Cuyahoga County	242,200
Gahanna, OH (city) Franklin County	232,500
Upper Arlington, OH (city) Franklin County	230,000
Dublin, OH (city) Franklin County	229,500
Hudson, OH (city) Summit County	228,400
Blue Ash, OH (city) Hamilton County	224,200
Strongsville, OH (city) Cuyahoga County	218,500

Specified Housing Units Owned and Occupied by Native Hawaiian and Other Pacific Islanders
Top 10 Places Sorted by Number

Place	Dollars

No places met population threshold.

Specified Housing Units Owned and Occupied by Asian Indians
Top 10 Places Sorted by Number

Place	Dollars
Westlake, OH (city) Cuyahoga County	297,700
Dublin, OH (city) Franklin County	256,400
Solon, OH (city) Cuyahoga County	240,200
Strongsville, OH (city) Cuyahoga County	215,400
North Royalton, OH (city) Cuyahoga County	210,500
Blue Ash, OH (city) Hamilton County	204,200
Beavercreek, OH (city) Greene County	198,300
Cincinnati, OH (city) Hamilton County	187,500
Sharonville, OH (city) Hamilton County	181,000
Fairfield, OH (city) Butler County	172,300

Specified Housing Units Owned and Occupied by Bangladeshis
Top 10 Places Sorted by Number

Place	Dollars

No places met population threshold.

Specified Housing Units Owned and Occupied by Cambodians
Top 10 Places Sorted by Number

Place	Dollars
Columbus, OH (city) Franklin County	88,000

Specified Housing Units Owned and Occupied by Chinese (except Taiwanese)
Top 10 Places Sorted by Number

Place	Dollars
Upper Arlington, OH (city) Franklin County	258,300
Dublin, OH (city) Franklin County	244,600
Solon, OH (city) Cuyahoga County	228,600
Hudson, OH (city) Summit County	215,000
Cincinnati, OH (city) Hamilton County	171,400
Columbus, OH (city) Franklin County	148,700
Cleveland Heights, OH (city) Cuyahoga County	101,800
Toledo, OH (city) Lucas County	98,800
Akron, OH (city) Summit County	85,500
Cleveland, OH (city) Cuyahoga County	82,500

Specified Housing Units Owned and Occupied by Fijians
Top 10 Places Sorted by Number

Place	Dollars

No places met population threshold.

Specified Housing Units Owned and Occupied by Filipinos
Top 10 Places Sorted by Number

Place	Dollars
Columbus, OH (city) Franklin County	141,100
Cincinnati, OH (city) Hamilton County	131,600
Cleveland, OH (city) Cuyahoga County	84,500
Toledo, OH (city) Lucas County	83,200

Specified Housing Units Owned and Occupied by Guamanians or Chamorros
Top 10 Places Sorted by Number

Place	Dollars

No places met population threshold.

Specified Housing Units Owned and Occupied by Hawaiian Natives
Top 10 Places Sorted by Number

Place	Dollars

No places met population threshold.

Specified Housing Units Owned and Occupied by Hmongs
Top 10 Places Sorted by Number

Place	Dollars

No places met population threshold.

Specified Housing Units Owned and Occupied by Indonesians
Top 10 Places Sorted by Number

Place	Dollars
Columbus, OH (city) Franklin County	0

Specified Housing Units Owned and Occupied by Japanese
Top 10 Places Sorted by Number

Place	Dollars
Dublin, OH (city) Franklin County	147,200
Columbus, OH (city) Franklin County	134,700

Specified Housing Units Owned and Occupied by Koreans
Top 10 Places Sorted by Number

Place	Dollars
Columbus, OH (city) Franklin County	122,700

Specified Housing Units Owned and Occupied by Laotians
Top 10 Places Sorted by Number

Place	Dollars
Columbus, OH (city) Franklin County	83,600
Akron, OH (city) Summit County	76,200

Specified Housing Units Owned and Occupied by Malaysians
Top 10 Places Sorted by Number

Place	Dollars

No places met population threshold.

Specified Housing Units Owned and Occupied by Pakistanis
Top 10 Places Sorted by Number

Place	Dollars

No places met population threshold.

Specified Housing Units Owned and Occupied by Samoans
Top 10 Places Sorted by Number

Place	Dollars

No places met population threshold.

Specified Housing Units Owned and Occupied by Sri Lankans
Top 10 Places Sorted by Number

Place	Dollars

No places met population threshold.

Specified Housing Units Owned and Occupied by Taiwanese
Top 10 Places Sorted by Number

Place	Dollars
Columbus, OH (city) Franklin County	245,000

Specified Housing Units Owned and Occupied by Thais
Top 10 Places Sorted by Number

Place	Dollars
Columbus, OH (city) Franklin County	119,100

Specified Housing Units Owned and Occupied by Tongans
Top 10 Places Sorted by Number

Place	Dollars

No places met population threshold.

Specified Housing Units Owned and Occupied by Vietnamese
Top 10 Places Sorted by Number

Place	Dollars
Columbus, OH (city) Franklin County	97,100
Cleveland, OH (city) Cuyahoga County	77,300
Akron, OH (city) Summit County	60,200

Notes: Please refer to the User's Guide for an explanation of data; tables reflect only those areas that meet Summary File 4 population thresholds, therefore there may be less than 10 places listed

OHIO

PHYSICAL FEATURES AND GENERAL CLIMATE. The climate of Ohio is remarkably varied. Less than one-half of its area is occupied by typical plains, while most of eastern and much of southern Ohio is hilly. Topography ranges in elevation from 430 feet above sea level at the junction of the Great Miami and Ohio Rivers up to 1,550 feet on a summit near Bellefontaine. In addition to this high point there are innumerable other hills which rise above 1,400 feet (mean sea level). These are located mainly along the dividing line between the Ohio River and Lake Erie drainage basins. Large areas in the State have elevations above 1,000 feet. An extensive area in northwestern Ohio is occupied by a flat lake plain — once the bottom of glacial Lake Maumee which was much larger than the present Lake Erie. The greater part of eastern Ohio is within the Allegheny Plateau, an unglaciated area consisting of picturesque hills, many of which rise above 1,300 feet and comprise many winding rivers and streams.

The Ohio River, which forms the southern and southeastern boundaries of Ohio, and its tributaries drain the greater portion of the State. A number of streams drain northward into Lake Erie. Although this area comprises nearly a third of the State, the divide between the two drainages is only 20 to 40 miles from the lake shore for a distance of more than 100 miles until it dips south of the arrowhead-shaped Maumee Basin. The largest streams in this region are the Maumee, Sandusky, and Cuyahoga Rivers. Principal tributaries flowing southward into the Ohio River include the Muskingum in the east, the Scioto in the central section, and the Great Miami in the west. A small portion in the west-central region drains westward into the Wabash River basin of Indiana.

Located west of the Appalachian Mountains, Ohio has a climate essentially continental in nature, characterized by moderate extremes of heat and cold, and wetness and dryness. Summers are moderately warm and humid, with occasional days when temperatures exceed 100°F.; winters are reasonably cold, with an average of about two days of subzero weather; and autumns are predominately cool, dry, and invigorating. Spring is the wettest season and vegetation is lush and profuse.

PRECIPITATION. Annual precipitation is slightly in excess of the national average and is well distributed, though with peaks in early spring and summer. In spite of the relatively small range in latitude and the compact shape of Ohio, rainfall varies considerably in amount and seasonal distribution. This is accounted for not only by the presence of Lake Erie on the north, but also by its topography and proximity to rain producing storm paths. Annual precipitation averages about 38 inches, being most generous in spring (about four inches in April) and least in the fall (about 2.5 inches in October). Greatest amounts are measured in the southwest where Wilmington has an average of 44.36 inches; the lake shore is driest, with Gilbralter Island having a normal of only 29.06 inches.

The southern half of the State is visited more frequently by productive rainstorms which, together with the general roughness of terrain, accounts for the larger total precipitation. The lifting of moist air masses over the hills tends to increase the yield of rainfall, especially in winter and spring. There is a marked tendency during the cold season for northeastern counties to receive snowfall amounts substantially in excess of those measured elsewhere. Northerly winds have a long fetch across Lake Huron and the widest part of Lake Erie, thus picking up moisture and heat from the lakes. This moisture is then forced to condense as the air is lifted abruptly over the divide a short distance from the lake. Average snowfall ranges from 60 inches in parts of Lake and adjoining counties down to 16 inches or less along the Ohio River.

TEMPERATURE. The normal annual temperature for the State ranges from 49.6°F. at Hiram in Portage County up to 56.9°F. at Portsmouth on the Ohio River. Variations over the State are due mainly to differences in latitude and topography, but the immediate lake shore area experiences a moderating effect due to its proximity to a large body of water. Widest temperature ranges are found generally among the eastern hills. In an average year, 90°F. heat may be expected about 20 times in summer with 100°F. or more once or twice. Readings of zero or lower are generally to be expected on two to four days each winter, and these are just as likely to occur in the south as the north. However, one winter out of six or eight will pass without experiencing zero readings anywhere in the State.

OTHER CLIMATIC ELEMENTS. The growing season, as defined by the period 32°F. or higher, ranges widely because of latitude and proximity to Lake Erie. The longest is about 200 days on the lake shore and the shortest is in the northeastern valleys within the Ohio River drainage. Dates of the average last freezing temperature in spring range from April 15 to May 18 and the mean first freeze date in fall varies from September 30 to November 6, the latter being on the western lake shore.

Damaging windstorms are mostly associated with heavy thunderstorms or line squalls. Three or four tornadoes may be expected to strike in Ohio each year. Most tornadoes, however, are of limited effect having paths that are short and narrow.

Most floods in Ohio are caused by unusual precipitation. The storms causing floods may bring rainfall of unusual intensity or of unusual duration and extent. Some floods may be caused by a series of ordinary storms which follow one another in rapid succession. Others may result from rain falling at relatively high temperatures on snow-covered areas. At times, though infrequent, flood conditions are caused or aggravated by ice gorges, especially in the tributary streams. Severe thunderstorms frequently cause local flash flooding. General flooding occurs most frequently during January to March and rarely occurs during August to October.

PROFILES OF OHIO / Weather: Weather Stations

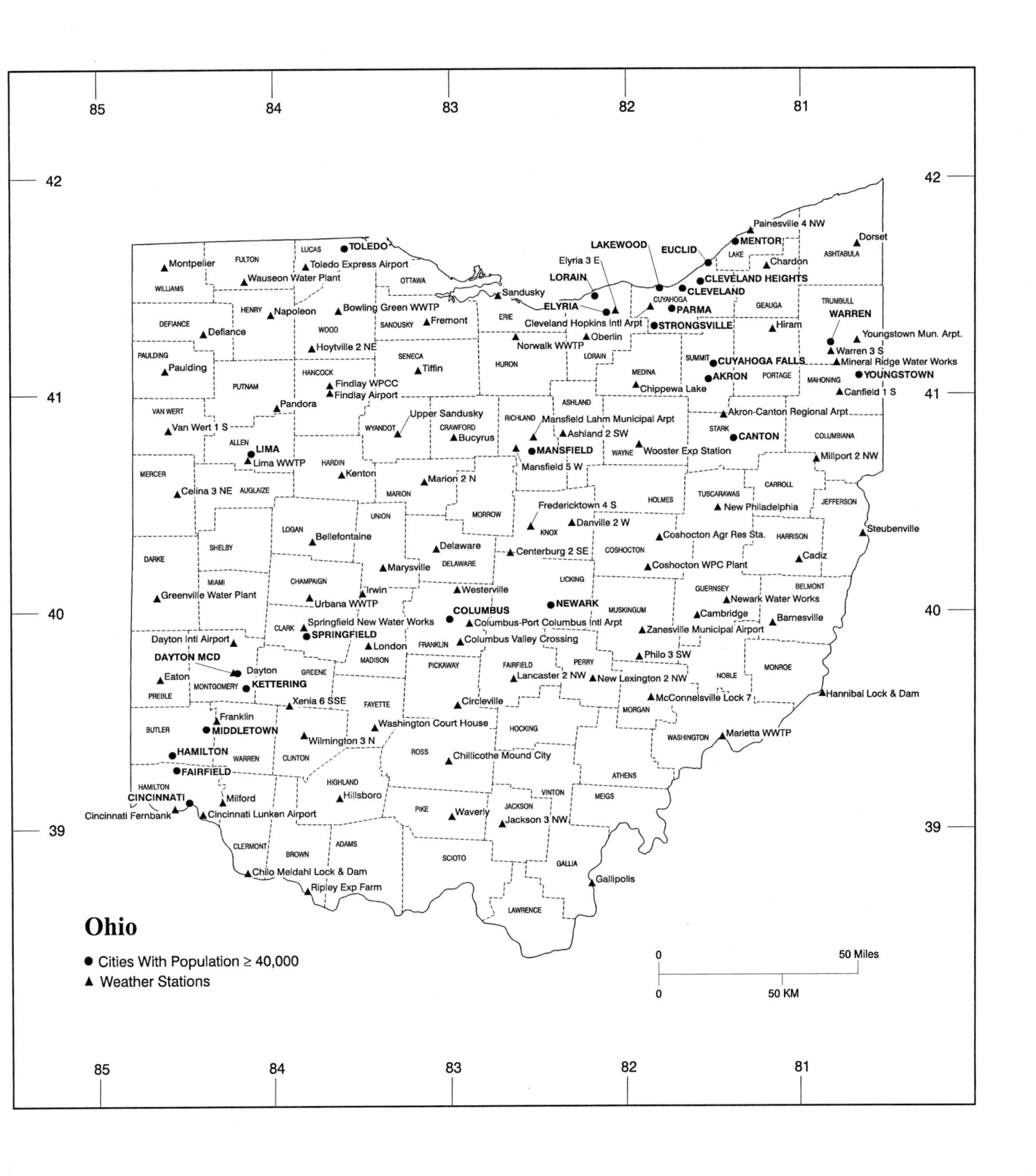

Ohio

- Cities With Population ≥ 40,000
- ▲ Weather Stations

Ohio Weather Stations by County

County	Station Name
Allen	Lima WWTP
Ashland	Ashland 2 SW
Ashtabula	Dorset
Belmont	Barnesville
Boone	Cincinnati Covington Airport
Brown	Ripley Exp. Farm
Champaign	Urbana WWTP
Clark	Springfield New Water Works
Clermont	Chilo Meldahl Lock & Dam Milford
Clinton	Wilmington 3 N
Columbiana	Millport 2 NW
Coshocton	Coshocton Agr. Res. Station Coshocton WPC Plant
Crawford	Bucyrus
Cuyahoga	Cleveland Hopkins Int'l Airport
Darke	Greenville Water Plant
Defiance	Defiance
Delaware	Delaware
Erie	Sandusky
Fairfield	Lancaster 2 NW
Fayette	Washington Court House
Franklin	Columbus Valley Crossing Columbus-Port Columbus Int'l Westerville
Fulton	Wauseon Water Plant
Gallia	Gallipolis
Geauga	Chardon
Greene	Xenia 6 SSE
Guernsey	Cambridge
Hamilton	Cincinnati Fernbank Cincinnati Lunken Airport
Hancock	Findlay Airport Findlay WPCC
Hardin	Kenton

County	Station Name
Harrison	Cadiz
Henry	Napoleon
Highland	Hillsboro
Huron	Norwalk WWTP
Jackson	Jackson 3 NW
Jefferson	Steubenville
Knox	Centerburg 2 SE Danville 2 W Fredericktown 4 S
Lake	Painesville 4 NW
Licking	Newark Water Works
Logan	Bellefontaine
Lorain	Elyria 3 E Oberlin
Lucas	Toledo Express Airport
Madison	London
Mahoning	Canfield 1 S
Marion	Marion 2 N
Medina	Chippewa Lake
Mercer	Celina 3 NE
Monroe	Hannibal Lock & Dam
Montgomery	Dayton Int'l Airport Dayton MCD
Morgan	McConnelsville Lock 7
Muskingum	Philo 3 SW Zanesville Municipal Airport
Ottawa	Put-In-Bay
Paulding	Paulding
Perry	New Lexington 2 NW
Pickaway	Circleville
Pike	Waverly
Portage	Hiram
Preble	Eaton
Putnam	Pandora
Richland	Mansfield 5 W

County	Station Name
Richland (cont.)	Mansfield Lahm Municipal Airport
Ross	Chillicothe Mound City
Sandusky	Fremont
Scioto	Portsmouth Sciotoville
Seneca	Tiffin
Summit	Akron-Canton Regional Airport
Trumbull	Mineral Ridge Water Works Warren 3 S Youngstown Municipal Airport
Tuscarawas	New Philadelphia
Union	Irwin Marysville
Van Wert	Van Wert 1 S
Warren	Franklin
Washington	Marietta WWTP
Wayne	Wooster Exp. Station
Williams	Montpelier
Wood	Bowling Green WWTP Hoytville 2 NE
Wyandot	Upper Sandusky

Ohio Weather Stations by City

City	Station Name	Miles
Akron	Akron-Canton Regional Airport	12
Canton	Akron-Canton Regional Airport	8
Cincinnati	Cincinnati Covington Airport	11
	Cincinnati Fernbank	10
	Cincinnati Lunken Airport	5
	Milford	12
Cleveland	Cleveland Hopkins Int'l Airport	11
Cleveland Heights	Cleveland Hopkins Int'l Airport	17
Columbus	Columbus Valley Crossing	8
	Columbus-Port Columbus Int'l	6
	Westerville	9
Cuyahoga Falls	Akron-Canton Regional Airport	16
Dayton	Dayton MCD	1
	Dayton Int'l Airport	10
	Franklin	16
	Xenia 6 SSE	19
Elyria	Cleveland Hopkins Int'l Airport	13
	Elyria 3 E	3
	Oberlin	10
Euclid	Chardon	17
	Painesville 4 NW	16
Fairfield	Cincinnati Fernbank	17
	Cincinnati Lunken Airport	17
	Franklin	20
	Milford	17
Hamilton	Franklin	17
Kettering	Dayton MCD	5
	Dayton Int'l Airport	15
	Franklin	13
	Xenia 6 SSE	14
Lakewood	Cleveland Hopkins Int'l Airport	6
	Elyria 3 E	15
Lima	Lima WWTP	2
	Pandora	16
Lorain	Cleveland Hopkins Int'l Airport	17
	Elyria 3 E	8
	Oberlin	13
Mansfield	Ashland 2 SW	11
	Mansfield Lahm Municipal Airport	4
	Mansfield 5 W	5
Mentor	Chardon	11
	Painesville 4 NW	5
Middletown	Franklin	4
Parma	Cleveland Hopkins Int'l Airport	6
	Elyria 3 E	17

City	Station Name	Miles
Springfield	London	19
	Springfield New Water Works	3
	Urbana WWTP	12
Strongsville	Chippewa Lake	19
	Cleveland Hopkins Int'l Airport	6
	Elyria 3 E	12
Toledo	Monroe, MI	20
	Bowling Green WWTP	19
	Toledo Express Airport	13
Warren	Canfield 1 S	16
	Hiram	18
	Mineral Ridge Water Works	6
	Warren 3 S	3
	Youngstown Municipal Airport	8
Youngstown	Canfield 1 S	8
	Mineral Ridge Water Works	8
	Warren 3 S	11
	Youngstown Municipal Airport	11
	New Castle 1 N, PA	16

Note: Miles is the distance between the geographic center of the city and the weather station.

Ohio Weather Stations by Elevation

Feet	Station Name
1,348	Mansfield 5 W
1,292	Mansfield Lahm Muni Airport
1,263	Ashland 2 SW
1,259	Cadiz
1,240	Barnesville
1,227	Hiram
1,207	Akron-Canton Regional Airport
1,204	Centerburg 2 SE
1,184	Bellefontaine
1,177	Chippewa Lake
1,177	Youngstown Municipal Airport
1,148	Millport 2 NW
1,138	Canfield 1 S
1,138	Coshocton Agr. Res. Station
1,128	Chardon
1,099	Hillsboro
1,049	Fredericktown 4 S
1,026	Wilmington 3 N
1,023	Greenville Water Plant
1,017	London
1,017	Philo 3 SW
1,017	Wooster Exp. Station
1,007	Irwin
1,000	Eaton
997	Dayton Int'l Airport
997	Marysville
997	Urbana WWTP
994	Kenton
990	Steubenville
977	Dorset
967	Danville 2 W
967	Xenia 6 SSE
964	Marion 2 N
958	Washington Court House
954	Bucyrus
928	Springfield New Water Works
918	Delaware
898	Warren 3 S
892	New Philadelphia
889	Mineral Ridge Water Works
889	New Lexington 2 NW
879	Ripley Exp. Farm
879	Zanesville Municipal Airport
866	Cincinnati Covington Airport
859	Celina 3 NE
859	Lancaster 2 NW
859	Montpelier
853	Upper Sandusky
849	Lima WWTP
833	Newark Water Works
813	Oberlin
807	Columbus-Port Columbus Int'l
807	Westerville
797	Cambridge
797	Findlay Airport
797	Jackson 3 NW
787	Van Wert 1 S
767	Cleveland Hopkins Int'l Airport
767	Findlay WPCC
767	Pandora
757	Coshocton WPC Plant
757	McConnelsville Lock 7
748	Wauseon Water Plant
744	Dayton MCD
738	Tiffin
734	Columbus Valley Crossing
728	Elyria 3 E
725	Paulding
698	Defiance
698	Hoytville 2 NE
679	Napoleon
672	Bowling Green WWTP
672	Circleville
669	Franklin
669	Norwalk WWTP
666	Toledo Express Airport
649	Chillicothe Mound City
620	Hannibal Lock & Dam
597	Fremont
597	Painesville 4 NW
583	Sandusky
577	Marietta WWTP
577	Put-In-Bay
567	Gallipolis
557	Waverly
538	Portsmouth Sciotoville
518	Milford
498	Chilo Meldahl Lock & Dam
498	Cincinnati Fernbank
488	Cincinnati Lunken Airport

Akron-Canton Regional Airport

The station at the Akron-Canton Airport is located about midway between Akron and Canton, a few miles south of the crest separating the Lake Erie and Muskingum River drainage areas. Precipitation at the station and southward drains through the Muskingum River into the Ohio, while northward of the crest the Cuyahoga and other streams flow into Lake Erie. The terrain is rolling with highest elevations near 1,300 feet above sea level and many small lakes provide water for local industry as well as recreational facilities for the densely populated region. The area is mainly industrial, agricultural operations having diminished rapidly in recent years.

Lake Erie has considerable influence on the area weather, tempering cold air masses during the late fall and winter, as well as contributing to the formation of brief, but heavy snow squalls until the lake freezes over.

The arrival of spring is late in this area, allowing growing of normally frost-susceptible fruits. Summers are moderately warm, but quite humid, while the months of September, October, and sometimes November are usually pleasant although with considerable morning fog. The average last occurrence of freezing temperatures in spring is the end of April, and the first occurrence in fall is late October. In past years, growing seasons for most vegetation has varied from 120 to 211 days. Temperatures and occurences of frost vary widely over the area because of the hilly terrain. Due to the influence of Lake Erie, snowfall is usually much heavier north of the station.

Akron-Canton Regional Airport *Summit County*   Elevation: 1,207 ft.   Latitude: 40° 55' N   Longitude: 81° 26' W

	JAN	FEB	MAR	APR	MAY	JUN	JUL	AUG	SEP	OCT	NOV	DEC	YEAR
Mean Maximum Temp. (°F)	33.5	36.8	46.9	59.1	69.7	78.4	82.4	80.7	73.3	61.6	49.2	38.4	59.2
Mean Temp. (°F)	26.0	28.7	37.7	48.5	59.1	68.0	72.2	70.6	63.4	52.1	41.5	31.5	49.9
Mean Minimum Temp. (°F)	18.4	20.5	28.4	37.9	48.6	57.6	61.9	60.5	53.5	42.5	33.8	24.5	40.7
Extreme Maximum Temp. (°F)	65	70	81	88	93	100	101	97	93	81	75	76	101
Extreme Minimum Temp. (°F)	-25	-13	-3	14	27	32	43	41	35	22	2	-16	-25
Days Maximum Temp. ≥ 90°F	0	0	0	0	0	1	4	2	0	0	0	0	7
Days Maximum Temp. ≤ 32°F	14	11	4	0	0	0	0	0	0	0	2	9	40
Days Minimum Temp. ≤ 32°F	28	23	21	9	1	0	0	0	0	3	14	25	124
Days Minimum Temp. ≤ 0°F	3	2	0	0	0	0	0	0	0	0	0	1	6
Heating Degree Days (base 65°F)	1,204	1,020	841	494	216	46	7	14	116	398	697	1,031	6,084
Cooling Degree Days (base 65°F)	0	0	1	7	43	142	249	197	72	5	0	0	716
Mean Precipitation (in.)	2.50	2.30	3.13	3.34	3.94	3.63	3.90	3.52	3.40	2.61	3.08	2.96	38.31
Maximum Precipitation (in.)	8.7	5.2	8.8	6.5	9.6	8.4	11.4	8.2	9.0	8.4	9.4	6.7	65.7
Minimum Precipitation (in.)	0.7	0.3	1.0	0.9	1.0	0.4	0.7	0.5	0.2	0.4	0.6	0.3	23.8
Maximum 24-hr. Precipitation (in.)	2.8	2.0	3.2	2.0	2.6	2.8	3.3	3.7	3.7	2.6	1.9	1.6	3.7
Days With ≥ 0.1" Precipitation	7	6	8	8	8	7	7	7	6	6	7	7	84
Days With ≥ 1.0" Precipitation	0	0	0	1	1	1	1	1	1	0	0	1	7
Mean Snowfall (in.)	12.9	9.5	9.0	2.6	trace	trace	0.0	0.0	trace	0.6	3.2	9.1	46.9
Maximum Snowfall (in.)	38	20	21	21	3	0	0	0	0	7	22	29	72
Maximum 24-hr. Snowfall (in.)	9	10	8	20	3	0	0	0	0	4	7	16	20
Days With ≥ 1.0" Snow Depth	16	12	6	1	0	0	0	0	0	0	1	9	45
Thunderstorm Days	< 1	< 1	2	4	6	7	8	6	3	1	1	< 1	38
Foggy Days	13	12	13	13	14	15	17	19	17	15	13	14	175
Predominant Sky Cover	OVR	OVR	OVR	OVR	OVR	OVR	OVR	OVR	OVR	OVR	OVR	OVR	OVR
Mean Relative Humidity 7am (%)	80	80	79	77	77	80	84	87	88	84	80	81	82
Mean Relative Humidity 4pm (%)	69	65	59	53	52	54	54	55	56	56	64	70	59
Mean Dewpoint (°F)	19	20	27	36	47	56	61	60	53	42	32	24	40
Prevailing Wind Direction	SW	WSW	W	SW	SW	SW	SW	SW	S	S	S	WSW	SW
Prevailing Wind Speed (mph)	13	12	13	12	10	9	8	8	8	9	12	13	10
Maximum Wind Gust (mph)	76	58	64	60	56	63	68	62	52	51	58	61	76

Cincinnati Covington Airport

Greater Cincinnati Airport is located on a gently rolling plateau about 12 miles southwest of downtown Cincinnati and two miles south of the Ohio River at its nearest point. The river valley is rather narrow and steep-sided varying from one to three miles in width and the river bed is 500 feet below the level of the airport.

The climate is continental with a rather wide range of temperatures from winter to summer. A precipitation maximum occurs during winter and spring with a late summer and fall minimum. On the average, the maximum snowfall occurs during January, although the heaviest 24-hour amounts have been recorded during late November and February.

The heaviest precipitation, as well as the precipitation of the longest duration, is normally associated with low pressure disturbances moving in a general southwest to northeast direction through the Ohio valley and south of the Cincinnati area.

Summers are warm and rather humid. The temperature will reach 100 degrees or more in one year out of three. However, the temperature will reach 90 degrees or higher on about 19 days each year. Winters are moderately cold with frequent periods of extensive cloudiness.

The freeze free period lasts on the average 187 days from mid-April to the latter part of October.

Cincinnati Covington Airport *Boone County* Elevation: 866 ft. Latitude: 39° 03' N Longitude: 84° 40' W

	JAN	FEB	MAR	APR	MAY	JUN	JUL	AUG	SEP	OCT	NOV	DEC	YEAR
Mean Maximum Temp. (°F)	37.4	42.0	52.7	64.1	73.8	81.7	85.8	84.2	77.7	65.8	53.1	42.4	63.4
Mean Temp. (°F)	29.1	33.1	42.9	53.2	63.0	71.4	75.8	74.0	67.2	55.2	44.2	34.5	53.6
Mean Minimum Temp. (°F)	20.7	24.2	33.0	42.2	52.2	61.0	65.6	63.8	56.6	44.5	35.3	26.4	43.8
Extreme Maximum Temp. (°F)	70	74	84	89	92	102	103	101	95	87	81	75	103
Extreme Minimum Temp. (°F)	-25	-11	-11	15	30	39	48	43	31	19	1	-20	-25
Days Maximum Temp. ≥ 90°F	0	0	0	0	0	4	8	5	2	0	0	0	19
Days Maximum Temp. ≤ 32°F	11	7	1	0	0	0	0	0	0	0	1	6	26
Days Minimum Temp. ≤ 32°F	26	21	16	5	0	0	0	0	0	3	13	21	105
Days Minimum Temp. ≤ 0°F	3	1	0	0	0	0	0	0	0	0	0	1	5
Heating Degree Days (base 65°F)	1,108	894	681	363	132	17	1	2	64	315	618	941	5,136
Cooling Degree Days (base 65°F)	0	0	3	13	77	225	352	294	132	19	1	1	1,117
Mean Precipitation (in.)	2.81	2.61	3.95	4.06	4.48	4.46	3.75	3.79	2.79	3.00	3.46	3.29	42.45
Maximum Precipitation (in.)	9.4	6.7	12.2	7.2	9.5	7.4	8.4	7.7	8.6	8.6	7.5	7.9	57.6
Minimum Precipitation (in.)	0.6	0.3	1.1	1.0	1.1	0.9	1.2	0.3	0.2	0.3	0.4	0.5	28.0
Maximum 24-hr. Precipitation (in.)	4.0	2.8	5.2	2.1	3.0	3.3	3.9	3.5	3.2	4.3	3.3	2.5	5.2
Days With ≥ 0.1" Precipitation	6	6	9	8	8	7	7	7	5	6	7	7	83
Days With ≥ 1.0" Precipitation	0	1	1	1	1	1	1	1	1	1	1	1	11
Mean Snowfall (in.)	7.7	6.1	4.2	0.6	trace	trace	trace	0.0	0.0	0.4	1.3	3.3	23.6
Maximum Snowfall (in.)	32	20	13	4	trace	0	0	0	0	6	12	13	54
Maximum 24-hr. Snowfall (in.)	8	9	10	3	trace	0	0	0	0	6	9	8	10
Days With ≥ 1.0" Snow Depth	8	7	3	0	0	0	0	0	0	0	0	3	21
Thunderstorm Days	1	1	3	4	6	7	8	6	3	1	1	< 1	41
Foggy Days	13	12	12	9	12	13	16	19	16	14	12	14	162
Predominant Sky Cover	OVR	OVR	OVR	OVR	OVR	OVR	OVR	OVR	OVR	OVR	OVR	OVR	OVR
Mean Relative Humidity 7am (%)	80	79	77	76	80	82	85	88	87	83	79	80	81
Mean Relative Humidity 4pm (%)	65	60	55	50	52	53	54	53	52	51	59	65	56
Mean Dewpoint (°F)	22	24	31	40	51	60	64	63	56	44	34	26	43
Prevailing Wind Direction	SSW	SSW	SSW	SSW	SSW	SW	SSW	SSW	SSW	SSW	SSW	SSW	SSW
Prevailing Wind Speed (mph)	12	12	13	12	9	9	8	7	8	9	12	12	10
Maximum Wind Gust (mph)	71	55	64	71	59	67	83	62	54	59	56	61	83

Cleveland Hopkins Int'l Airport

Cleveland is on the south shore of Lake Erie in northeast Ohio. The metropolitan area has a lake frontage of 31 miles. The surrounding terrain is generally level except for an abrupt ridge on the eastern edge of the city which rises some 500 feet above the shore terrain. The Cuyahoga River, which flows through a rather deep but narrow north-south valley, bisects the city.

Local climate is continental in character but with strong modifying influences by Lake Erie. West to northerly winds blowing off Lake Erie tend to lower daily high temperatures in summer and raise temperatures in winter. Temperatures at Hopkins Airport which is 5 miles south of the lakeshore average from two to four degrees higher than the lakeshore in summer, while overnight low temperatures average from two to four degrees lower than the lakefront during all seasons.

In this area, summers are moderately warm and humid with occasional days when temperatures exceed 90 degrees. Winters are relatively cold and cloudy with an average of five days with sub-zero temperatures. Weather changes occur every few days from the passing of cold fronts.

The daily range in temperature is usually greatest in late summer and least in winter. Annual extremes in temperature normally occur soon after late June and December. Maximum temperatures below freezing occur most often in December, January, and February. Temperatures of 100 degrees or higher are rare. On the average, freezing temperatures in fall are first recorded in October while the last freezing temperature in spring normally occurs in April.

As is characteristic of continental climates, precipitation varies widely from year to year. However, it is normally abundant and well distributed throughout the year with spring being the wettest season. Showers and thunderstorms account for most of the rainfall during the growing season. Thunderstorms are most frequent from April through August. Snowfall may fluctuate widely. Mean annual snowfall increases from west to east in Cuyahoga County ranging from about 45 inches in the west to more than 90 inches in the extreme east.

Damaging winds of 50 mph or greater are usually associated with thunderstorms. Tornadoes, one of the most destructive of all atmospheric storms, occasionally occur in Cuyahoga County.

Cleveland Hopkins Int'l Airport *Cuyahoga Co.* Elevation: 767 ft. Latitude: 41° 24' N Longitude: 81° 51' W

	JAN	FEB	MAR	APR	MAY	JUN	JUL	AUG	SEP	OCT	NOV	DEC	YEAR
Mean Maximum Temp. (°F)	33.1	36.4	46.3	58.0	69.2	78.0	82.4	80.4	73.6	62.0	49.9	38.7	59.0
Mean Temp. (°F)	25.9	28.7	37.6	48.1	58.9	68.0	72.5	70.9	64.1	52.9	42.5	32.0	50.2
Mean Minimum Temp. (°F)	18.7	20.9	28.9	38.2	48.5	57.9	62.5	61.3	54.5	43.7	35.0	25.3	41.3
Extreme Maximum Temp. (°F)	67	71	82	88	91	104	100	99	95	84	77	77	104
Extreme Minimum Temp. (°F)	-20	-10	-5	11	27	31	45	38	34	19	3	-15	-20
Days Maximum Temp. ≥ 90°F	0	0	0	0	0	2	4	2	1	0	0	0	9
Days Maximum Temp. ≤ 32°F	15	12	4	0	0	0	0	0	0	0	1	9	41
Days Minimum Temp. ≤ 32°F	28	23	21	9	1	0	0	0	0	2	13	24	121
Days Minimum Temp. ≤ 0°F	3	2	0	0	0	0	0	0	0	0	0	1	6
Heating Degree Days (base 65°F)	1,205	1,019	844	508	227	51	6	12	106	376	670	1,016	6,040
Cooling Degree Days (base 65°F)	0	0	2	7	45	148	257	203	82	8	1	0	753
Mean Precipitation (in.)	2.43	2.27	2.96	3.34	3.42	3.87	3.57	3.56	3.77	2.75	3.42	3.12	38.48
Maximum Precipitation (in.)	7.0	4.7	6.1	6.6	9.1	9.1	9.1	9.0	7.3	9.5	8.8	8.6	53.8
Minimum Precipitation (in.)	0.4	0.5	0.8	1.2	1.0	0.6	1.2	0.5	0.7	0.6	0.8	0.7	18.8
Maximum 24-hr. Precipitation (in.)	2.5	2.0	2.8	2.1	3.4	3.0	2.7	3.5	2.3	3.4	2.2	2.4	3.5
Days With ≥ 0.1" Precipitation	7	6	8	8	8	7	6	7	7	7	8	8	87
Days With ≥ 1.0" Precipitation	0	0	0	0	1	1	1	1	1	0	1	0	6
Mean Snowfall (in.)	16.4	13.4	10.8	2.5	trace	trace	trace	0.0	trace	0.4	4.9	12.6	61.0
Maximum Snowfall (in.)	43	39	26	13	2	0	0	0	0	8	22	30	97
Maximum 24-hr. Snowfall (in.)	10	14	11	9	2	0	0	0	0	7	13	12	14
Days With ≥ 1.0" Snow Depth	17	14	7	1	0	0	0	0	0	0	3	10	52
Thunderstorm Days	< 1	< 1	2	3	5	6	6	5	3	2	1	< 1	33
Foggy Days	13	12	13	12	13	11	12	14	12	11	12	13	148
Predominant Sky Cover	OVR	OVR	OVR	OVR	OVR	OVR	OVR	OVR	OVR	OVR	OVR	OVR	OVR
Mean Relative Humidity 7am (%)	79	79	79	76	77	79	81	85	84	81	78	78	80
Mean Relative Humidity 4pm (%)	70	67	62	56	54	55	55	58	58	58	65	70	61
Mean Dewpoint (°F)	19	21	27	37	47	57	61	61	54	43	33	24	40
Prevailing Wind Direction	SW	SW	SW	S	N	SSW	SW	SW	S	SSW	SW	SW	SW
Prevailing Wind Speed (mph)	13	13	14	13	9	10	9	8	9	10	13	13	12
Maximum Wind Gust (mph)	82	64	63	78	55	77	67	51	58	54	59	71	82

Columbus-Port Columbus Int'l

Columbus is located in the center of the state and in the drainage area of the Ohio River. The airport is located at the eastern boundary of the city approximately seven miles from the center of the business district.

Four nearly parallel streams run through or adjacent to the city. The Scioto River is the principal stream and flows from the northwest into the center of the city and then flows straight south toward the Ohio River. The Olentangy River runs almost due south and empties into the Scioto just west of the business district. Alum Creek empties into the Big Walnut southeast of the city and the Big Walnut Creek empties into the Scioto a few miles downstream.

The narrow valleys associated with the streams flowing through the city supply the only variation in the micro-climate of the area. The city proper shows the typical metropolitan effect with shrubs and flowers blossoming earlier than in the immediate surroundings and in retarding light frost on clear quiet nights. Many small areas to the southeast and to the north and northeast show marked effects of air drainage as evidenced by the frequent formation of shallow ground fog at daybreak during the summer and fall months and the higher frequency of frost in the spring and fall.

The average occurrence of the last freezing temperature in the spring within the city proper is mid-April, and the first freeze in the fall is very late October, but in the immediate surroundings there is much variation. For example, at Valley Crossing located at the southeastern outskirts of the city, the average occurrence of the last 32 degree temperature in the spring is very early May, while the first 32 degree temperature in the fall is mid-October.

The records show a high frequency of calm or very low wind speeds during the late evening and early morning hours, from June through September. The rolling landscape is conducive to calm winds from the Weather Service location at the airport these are toward the northwest with the wind direction indicated as southeast, at speeds generally 4 mph or less.

Columbus is located in the area of changeable weather. Air masses from central and northwest Canada frequently invade this region. Air from the Gulf of Mexico often reaches central Ohio during the summer and to a much lesser extent in the fall and winter. There are also occasional weather changes brought about by cool outbreaks from the Hudson Bay region of Canada, especially during the spring months. At infrequent intervals the general circulation will bring showers or snow to Columbus from the Atlantic.

Columbus-Port Columbus Int'l *Franklin County*   Elevation: 807 ft.   Latitude: 39° 59' N   Longitude: 82° 53' W

	JAN	FEB	MAR	APR	MAY	JUN	JUL	AUG	SEP	OCT	NOV	DEC	YEAR
Mean Maximum Temp. (°F)	35.2	39.4	50.6	62.4	72.7	81.0	84.7	83.1	76.5	64.5	51.6	40.6	61.9
Mean Temp. (°F)	27.6	31.2	41.0	51.4	61.8	70.4	74.5	72.9	66.0	54.0	43.2	33.4	52.3
Mean Minimum Temp. (°F)	19.9	22.8	31.4	40.3	50.8	59.7	64.2	62.6	55.4	43.5	34.7	26.1	42.6
Extreme Maximum Temp. (°F)	70	74	83	88	93	101	100	101	97	86	80	76	101
Extreme Minimum Temp. (°F)	-22	-13	-6	14	30	35	43	40	33	21	5	-17	-22
Days Maximum Temp. ≥ 90°F	0	0	0	0	1	3	6	4	1	0	0	0	15
Days Maximum Temp. ≤ 32°F	12	9	2	0	0	0	0	0	0	0	1	7	31
Days Minimum Temp. ≤ 32°F	27	22	18	6	0	0	0	0	0	3	13	23	112
Days Minimum Temp. ≤ 0°F	3	1	0	0	0	0	0	0	0	0	0	1	5
Heating Degree Days (base 65°F)	1,154	950	738	412	159	25	3	6	77	345	649	973	5,491
Cooling Degree Days (base 65°F)	0	0	2	9	66	201	319	267	114	12	1	0	991
Mean Precipitation (in.)	2.46	2.16	2.90	3.30	3.88	4.15	4.60	3.72	2.91	2.29	3.21	2.89	38.47
Maximum Precipitation (in.)	8.3	5.1	9.6	6.4	9.1	9.8	12.4	8.6	6.8	5.2	10.7	7.0	53.2
Minimum Precipitation (in.)	0.6	0.3	1.0	0.7	0.9	0.7	1.0	0.6	0.5	0.1	0.6	0.5	24.5
Maximum 24-hr. Precipitation (in.)	4.8	2.1	3.4	2.0	2.1	2.5	5.1	3.2	2.7	1.7	2.4	1.7	5.1
Days With ≥ 0.1" Precipitation	6	6	8	7	8	7	7	7	5	5	7	7	80
Days With ≥ 1.0" Precipitation	0	0	0	1	1	1	1	1	1	0	1	0	7
Mean Snowfall (in.)	10.5	6.1	4.3	1.2	trace	trace	trace	0.0	trace	0.2	1.6	4.5	28.4
Maximum Snowfall (in.)	34	16	14	13	1	0	0	0	trace	5	15	17	48
Maximum 24-hr. Snowfall (in.)	7	9	9	12	1	0	0	0	trace	4	8	8	12
Days With ≥ 1.0" Snow Depth	12	8	3	0	0	0	0	0	0	0	0	4	27
Thunderstorm Days	<1	1	2	4	6	8	8	6	3	1	1	<1	40
Foggy Days	13	11	12	10	13	14	16	19	15	14	12	14	163
Predominant Sky Cover	OVR	OVR	OVR	OVR	OVR	OVR	OVR	SCT	OVR	OVR	OVR	OVR	OVR
Mean Relative Humidity 7am (%)	78	78	76	76	79	81	84	87	87	83	80	80	81
Mean Relative Humidity 4pm (%)	67	62	55	51	52	53	54	53	53	52	61	67	57
Mean Dewpoint (°F)	20	22	29	38	49	59	63	62	55	43	34	25	42
Prevailing Wind Direction	S	S	WNW	S	S	S	S	S	S	S	S	S	S
Prevailing Wind Speed (mph)	9	9	12	9	8	8	7	7	8	8	9	9	9
Maximum Wind Gust (mph)	69	58	62	78	76	68	67	66	62	53	53	61	78

Dayton Int'l Airport

Dayton is located near the center of the Miami River Valley, which is a nearly flat plain, 50 to 200 feet below the general elevation of the adjacent rolling country. Three Miami River tributaries, the Mad River, the Stillwater River, and Wolf Creek converge, fanwise, from the north to join the master stream within the city limits of Dayton. Heavy rains in March 1913 caused the worst flood disaster in the history of the Miami Valley. During the flood more than 400 people lost their lives and property damage amounted to $100 million. After the 1913 flood, dams were built on the streams north of Dayton, forming retarding basins. No floods have occurred at Dayton since the construction of these dams.

The elevation of the city of Dayton is about 750 feet. Terrain north of the city slopes gradually upward to about 1,100 feet at Indian Lake. Ten miles southeast of Indian Lake, near Bellefontaine, is the highest point in the state, with an elevation of about 1,550 feet. South of the city, the terrain slopes gradually downward to about 450 feet where the Miami River empties into the Ohio River.

Precipitation, which is rather evenly distributed throughout the year, and moderate temperatures help to make the Miami Valley a rich agricultural region. High relative humidities during much of the year cause some discomfort to people with allergies. Temperatures of zero or below will be experienced in about four years out of five, while 100 degrees or higher will be recorded in about one year out of five. Extreme temperatures are usually of short duration. The downward slope of about 700 feet in the 163 miles of the Miami River may have some moderating influence on the winter temperatures in the Miami Valley.

Based on the 1951-1980 period, the average last occurrence in the spring of freezing temperatures is mid-April, and the average first occurrence in the autumn is late October.

Cold, polar air, flowing across the Great Lakes, causes much cloudiness during the winter, and is accompanied by frequent snow flurries. These add little to the total snowfall.

Dayton Int'l Airport *Montgomery County*   Elevation: 997 ft.   Latitude: 39° 54' N   Longitude: 84° 13' W

	JAN	FEB	MAR	APR	MAY	JUN	JUL	AUG	SEP	OCT	NOV	DEC	YEAR
Mean Maximum Temp. (°F)	34.3	38.9	49.9	61.9	72.3	81.1	85.1	83.1	76.4	64.2	51.0	39.8	61.5
Mean Temp. (°F)	26.6	30.5	40.5	51.2	61.8	70.7	74.8	72.8	65.7	53.9	42.8	32.4	52.0
Mean Minimum Temp. (°F)	18.9	22.1	31.0	40.5	51.2	60.3	64.5	62.4	54.9	43.6	34.4	24.9	42.4
Extreme Maximum Temp. (°F)	66	73	82	88	92	102	102	102	96	86	79	72	102
Extreme Minimum Temp. (°F)	-25	-12	-7	15	28	40	44	41	32	23	5	-20	-25
Days Maximum Temp. ≥ 90°F	0	0	0	0	0	3	7	4	1	0	0	0	15
Days Maximum Temp. ≤ 32°F	13	9	3	0	0	0	0	0	0	0	1	8	34
Days Minimum Temp. ≤ 32°F	27	22	18	6	0	0	0	0	0	3	14	24	114
Days Minimum Temp. ≤ 0°F	3	2	0	0	0	0	0	0	0	0	0	1	6
Heating Degree Days (base 65°F)	1,184	967	755	417	161	22	2	6	85	349	662	1,006	5,616
Cooling Degree Days (base 65°F)	0	0	2	9	63	201	319	258	109	12	1	0	974
Mean Precipitation (in.)	2.53	2.26	3.29	4.07	4.16	4.21	3.73	3.44	2.59	2.70	3.28	3.06	39.32
Maximum Precipitation (in.)	9.9	5.8	7.6	6.8	9.0	10.9	8.5	8.0	5.7	6.3	8.1	10.0	59.8
Minimum Precipitation (in.)	0.3	0.2	1.1	0.6	1.5	0.3	0.5	0.3	0.3	0.2	0.5	0.4	24.2
Maximum 24-hr. Precipitation (in.)	4.2	2.6	2.9	3.1	3.2	3.8	3.2	3.4	2.6	3.5	2.8	2.8	4.2
Days With ≥ 0.1" Precipitation	6	5	8	8	8	7	7	6	5	6	7	7	80
Days With ≥ 1.0" Precipitation	0	0	0	1	1	1	1	1	1	0	1	1	8
Mean Snowfall (in.)	9.7	6.6	4.7	0.8	trace	0.0	trace	0.0	0.0	0.4	1.5	4.4	28.1
Maximum Snowfall (in.)	40	18	14	5	trace	0	0	0	0	6	13	16	53
Maximum 24-hr. Snowfall (in.)	12	7	11	5	trace	0	0	0	0	5	8	6	12
Days With ≥ 1.0" Snow Depth	12	9	3	0	0	0	0	0	0	0	1	5	30
Thunderstorm Days	< 1	1	2	4	6	7	8	6	3	2	1	< 1	40
Foggy Days	15	12	14	12	13	13	15	18	15	14	14	15	170
Predominant Sky Cover	OVR	OVR	OVR	OVR	OVR	OVR	OVR	OVR	OVR	OVR	OVR	OVR	OVR
Mean Relative Humidity 7am (%)	80	79	79	77	78	80	83	86	87	83	81	81	81
Mean Relative Humidity 4pm (%)	68	64	59	53	52	52	53	53	52	52	63	69	57
Mean Dewpoint (°F)	20	22	30	39	49	58	63	62	54	43	33	25	42
Prevailing Wind Direction	W	WNW	WNW	SSW	SSW	SSW	SW	SW	SSW	SSW	SSW	SSW	SSW
Prevailing Wind Speed (mph)	13	13	13	13	12	10	9	9	9	10	13	13	12
Maximum Wind Gust (mph)	69	52	67	63	60	60	71	61	48	46	54	62	71

Mansfield Lahm Municipal Airport

Mansfield is in the north central highlands at the geographical and climatological junction of central Ohio, northwest Ohio, and northeast Ohio. The station is on a plateau 3 miles north of the city of Mansfield and surrounded by rolling open farmland. The general elevation ranges from around 1,300 to 1,400 feet above sea level with the 1,000-foot contour east to west some 15 miles to the north. The climate is continental, with the modifying effects of Lake Erie most pronounced in winter. Lake Erie is just 38 miles due north.

The lake influence, plus the elevation, produce cloudy skies and considerable snow shower activity from late November into April with any wind flow from northwest through northeast. Because of this, any windshift with a cold frontal passage in winter does not bring the clearing skies, indeed, more snow is often measured from the flurry activity behind the front than from the pre-frontal conditions. A frozen Lake Erie will allow clearing skies, but an open lake dictates overcast and snow flurries. Usually the lake is open enough to set off the flurries and cloudy conditions. The major snow producer will be an intense storm moving out of the southwest with the Gulf of Mexico moisture available. Snow cover is almost constant from December through March due to almost daily snow flurries, but the depth of cover is rarely more than 8 inches. Daytime winter temperatures are not above the freezing mark too often.

Spring is a short period of rapid transition from hard winter to summer conditions. April usually brings abundant shower activity and the crops and vegetation get a quick start.

Summer is a pleasant season with low humidities and no extremely high temperatures. Rarely does the temperature climb above the 90 degree point. Thunderstorms average about once every three days during the season from June through September. Highest winds are associated with the heavier thunderstorms, and while hail does not occur often, it is of major concern to the applegrowers in the area. Flooding problems are confined to the flash-flood type on the small streams in the area.

The growing season is normally about 153 days. Autumn usually produces many clear warm days and cool invigorating nights. Ground fog is at a maximum incidence during the autumn. Little rainfall occurs to interfere with harvest time and county fair time.

Mansfield Lahm Municipal Airport *Richland Co.* Elevation: 1,292 ft. Latitude: 40° 49' N Longitude: 82° 31' W

	JAN	FEB	MAR	APR	MAY	JUN	JUL	AUG	SEP	OCT	NOV	DEC	YEAR
Mean Maximum Temp. (°F)	32.4	35.8	46.4	58.6	69.5	78.0	82.1	80.0	73.4	61.8	48.9	37.6	58.7
Mean Temp. (°F)	25.0	28.0	37.5	48.4	59.1	67.9	72.2	70.4	63.6	52.3	41.3	30.7	49.7
Mean Minimum Temp. (°F)	17.6	20.1	28.4	38.1	48.7	57.7	62.2	60.7	53.7	42.7	33.6	23.8	40.6
Extreme Maximum Temp. (°F)	65	68	82	86	90	101	100	97	92	84	76	73	101
Extreme Minimum Temp. (°F)	-22	-11	-6	8	26	37	43	42	33	20	2	-17	-22
Days Maximum Temp. ≥ 90°F	0	0	0	0	0	1	3	1	1	0	0	0	6
Days Maximum Temp. ≤ 32°F	16	12	4	0	0	0	0	0	0	0	2	10	44
Days Minimum Temp. ≤ 32°F	28	24	21	9	1	0	0	0	0	4	15	25	127
Days Minimum Temp. ≤ 0°F	4	2	0	0	0	0	0	0	0	0	0	1	7
Heating Degree Days (base 65°F)	1,234	1,038	848	499	219	50	7	17	115	396	706	1,056	6,185
Cooling Degree Days (base 65°F)	0	0	2	7	43	143	238	185	73	7	0	0	698
Mean Precipitation (in.)	2.57	2.11	3.33	4.20	4.42	4.42	4.30	4.45	3.51	2.70	3.80	3.24	43.05
Maximum Precipitation (in.)	11.5	5.4	7.0	7.0	8.8	10.0	13.2	8.6	7.8	6.4	12.8	11.2	67.2
Minimum Precipitation (in.)	0.4	0.3	1.2	0.8	1.1	0.6	0.9	0.6	0.7	0.4	0.7	0.7	21.8
Maximum 24-hr. Precipitation (in.)	2.7	2.8	2.4	2.3	2.6	3.7	3.4	3.8	2.3	3.3	3.1	2.6	3.8
Days With ≥ 0.1" Precipitation	6	5	8	9	9	7	7	7	6	6	7	7	84
Days With ≥ 1.0" Precipitation	0	0	1	1	1	1	1	1	1	0	1	1	9
Mean Snowfall (in.)	12.9	9.8	6.9	2.0	trace	trace	0.0	0.0	trace	0.6	2.5	8.6	43.3
Maximum Snowfall (in.)	42	18	17	13	1	0	0	0	0	10	12	23	59
Maximum 24-hr. Snowfall (in.)	10	9	8	12	1	0	0	0	0	8	5	12	12
Days With ≥ 1.0" Snow Depth	17	14	6	1	0	0	0	0	0	0	2	10	50
Thunderstorm Days	<1	<1	2	3	5	6	7	6	3	1	1	<1	34
Foggy Days	13	12	14	13	14	13	14	17	15	13	13	15	166
Predominant Sky Cover	OVR	OVR	OVR	OVR	OVR	OVR	SCT	SCT	OVR	OVR	OVR	OVR	OVR
Mean Relative Humidity 7am (%)	82	81	81	78	78	81	83	87	87	83	82	83	82
Mean Relative Humidity 4pm (%)	72	69	64	56	55	56	56	57	58	56	67	74	62
Mean Dewpoint (°F)	20	21	28	37	47	58	62	61	54	42	33	24	40
Prevailing Wind Direction	WSW	WSW	WSW	WSW	SSW	SSW	SW	SSW	S	S	SW	WSW	WSW
Prevailing Wind Speed (mph)	15	14	15	14	13	12	10	10	9	10	14	14	13
Maximum Wind Gust (mph)	62	59	62	68	60	68	81	69	61	53	69	69	81

Toledo Express Airport

Toledo is located on the western end of Lake Erie at the mouth of the Maumee River. Except for a bank up from the river about 30 feet, the terrain is generally level with only a slight slope toward the river and Lake Erie. The city has quite a diversified industrial section and excellent harbor facilities, making it a large transportation center for rail, water, and motor freight. Generally rich agricultural land is found in the surrounding area, especially up the Maumee Valley toward the Indiana state line.

Rainfall is usually sufficient for general agriculture. The terrain is level and drainage rather poor, therefore, a little less than the normal precipitation during the growing season is better than excessive amounts. Snowfall is generally light in this area, distributed throughout the winter from November to March with frequent thaws.

The nearness of Lake Erie and the other Great Lakes has a moderating effect on the temperature, and extremes are seldom recorded. On average, only fifteen days a year experience temperatures of 90 degrees or higher, and only eight days when it drops to zero or lower. The growing season averages 160 days, but has ranged from over 220 to less than 125 days.

Humidity is rather high throughout the year in this area, and there is an excessive amount of cloudiness. In the winter months the sun shines during only about 30 percent of the daylight hours. December and January, the cloudiest months, sometimes have as little as 16 percent of the possible hours of sunshine.

Severe windstorms, causing more than minor damage, occur infrequently. There are on the average twenty-three days per year having a sustained wind velocity of 32 mph or more.

Flooding in the Toledo area is produced by several factors. Heavy rains of one inch or more will cause a sudden rise in creeks and drainage ditches to the point of overflow. The western shores of Lake Erie are subject to flooding when the lake level is high and prolonged periods of east to northeast winds prevail.

Toledo Express Airport *Lucas County*   Elevation: 666 ft.   Latitude: 41° 35' N   Longitude: 83° 48' W

	JAN	FEB	MAR	APR	MAY	JUN	JUL	AUG	SEP	OCT	NOV	DEC	YEAR
Mean Maximum Temp. (°F)	30.9	34.5	45.8	58.9	70.9	79.9	84.0	81.7	74.6	62.3	48.4	36.4	59.0
Mean Temp. (°F)	23.5	26.5	36.6	48.0	59.3	68.4	72.8	70.6	63.2	51.4	40.2	29.3	49.1
Mean Minimum Temp. (°F)	16.0	18.4	27.3	37.1	47.6	56.9	61.5	59.4	51.8	40.5	31.9	22.2	39.2
Extreme Maximum Temp. (°F)	65	71	81	88	94	104	104	99	98	87	78	69	104
Extreme Minimum Temp. (°F)	-20	-14	-6	8	25	32	40	34	26	15	5	-19	-20
Days Maximum Temp. ≥ 90°F	0	0	0	0	1	3	6	3	1	0	0	0	14
Days Maximum Temp. ≤ 32°F	17	12	4	0	0	0	0	0	0	0	2	10	45
Days Minimum Temp. ≤ 32°F	29	25	22	10	1	0	0	0	0	6	17	26	136
Days Minimum Temp. ≤ 0°F	5	3	0	0	0	0	0	0	0	0	0	1	9
Heating Degree Days (base 65°F)	1,282	1,081	875	510	216	44	6	16	125	421	738	1,099	6,413
Cooling Degree Days (base 65°F)	0	0	1	6	47	161	270	206	77	6	0	0	774
Mean Precipitation (in.)	1.93	1.88	2.65	3.27	3.05	3.77	2.93	3.15	2.87	2.32	2.80	2.61	33.23
Maximum Precipitation (in.)	4.6	5.4	5.7	6.1	5.1	8.5	6.8	8.5	8.1	5.5	6.9	6.8	40.8
Minimum Precipitation (in.)	0.3	0.3	0.6	0.9	1.0	0.3	0.3	0.4	0.6	0.3	0.5	0.5	22.0
Maximum 24-hr. Precipitation (in.)	1.5	2.6	2.6	2.9	1.7	3.1	4.3	2.4	3.3	2.9	2.7	3.5	4.3
Days With ≥ 0.1" Precipitation	5	5	7	8	7	7	6	6	6	6	6	7	76
Days With ≥ 1.0" Precipitation	0	0	0	0	1	1	1	1	1	0	0	0	5
Mean Snowfall (in.)	10.9	8.2	5.7	1.4	trace	trace	trace	trace	trace	0.2	2.7	8.1	37.2
Maximum Snowfall (in.)	31	17	18	12	1	0	0	0	trace	2	18	24	72
Maximum 24-hr. Snowfall (in.)	10	8	9	7	1	0	0	0	trace	2	7	14	14
Days With ≥ 1.0" Snow Depth	17	14	5	1	0	0	0	0	0	0	1	10	48
Thunderstorm Days	< 1	1	2	4	5	7	7	6	4	1	1	< 1	38
Foggy Days	13	11	14	12	12	11	14	18	15	13	14	15	162
Predominant Sky Cover	OVR	OVR	OVR	OVR	OVR	OVR	SCT	SCT	OVR	OVR	OVR	OVR	OVR
Mean Relative Humidity 7am (%)	80	80	81	80	80	82	86	91	91	86	83	83	84
Mean Relative Humidity 4pm (%)	68	65	59	53	51	52	53	56	54	55	65	72	58
Mean Dewpoint (°F)	17	19	27	36	47	57	62	61	54	42	32	23	40
Prevailing Wind Direction	WSW	WSW	ENE	WSW	WSW	SW	SW	SW	SW	SW	WSW	WSW	WSW
Prevailing Wind Speed (mph)	13	13	12	13	12	9	8	8	9	10	13	13	12
Maximum Wind Gust (mph)	62	52	64	63	58	59	66	75	54	49	55	56	75

Youngstown Municipal Airport

The Youngstown Municipal Airport is located in northeastern Ohio approximately eight miles north of the city of Youngstown in Trumbull County. Airport elevation is 1,178 feet, about 200 feet higher than most communities in the Mahoning and Shenango River Valleys. There are numerous natural and man-made lakes in the region, including Lake Erie, 45 miles to the north. Drainage from the area flows southward through the Mahoning and Shenango Rivers which join to form the Beaver River at New Castle, Pennsylvania. The Beaver empties into the Ohio River at Rochester, Pennsylvania.

This entire area experiences frequent outbreaks of cold Canadian air masses which may be modified by passage over Lake Erie. This effect produces widespread cloudiness especially during the cool months of the year. The winter months are characterized by persistent cloudiness and intermittent snow flurries. The daily temperature range during most winter days is quite small. During most winters, the bulk of the snow falls as flurries of 2 inches or less per occurrence, although several snowstorms per year will produce amounts in the four to 10 inch range.

Destructive storms seldom occur, and tornadoes are not common. During recent years flood control projects have all but eliminated the threat of serious river flooding. Flash flooding of small streams and creeks rarely affects residential areas. Certain communities have well known areas of urban flooding during periods of prolonged heavy thunderstorms.

The climate of the Youngstown district has had an important role in the growth and development of this industrial area. Temperatures seldom reach extreme values especially during the summer months. However, high humidity during most days of the year tends to accentuate the temperature. Rainfall, reasonably well distributed throughout the year, provides a more than adequate supply of water for agriculture, industrial, and residential use.

Based on the 1951-1980 period, the average first occurrence of 32 degrees Fahrenheit in the fall is October 14 and the average last occurrence in the spring is May 6.

Youngstown Municipal Airport *Trumbull County* Elevation: 1,177 ft. Latitude: 41° 15' N Longitude: 80° 40' W

	JAN	FEB	MAR	APR	MAY	JUN	JUL	AUG	SEP	OCT	NOV	DEC	YEAR
Mean Maximum Temp. (°F)	31.9	35.5	45.7	58.3	69.4	77.6	81.9	80.1	72.5	60.9	48.3	37.3	58.3
Mean Temp. (°F)	24.7	27.5	36.5	47.7	58.1	66.4	70.7	69.1	62.0	51.1	40.9	30.7	48.8
Mean Minimum Temp. (°F)	17.5	19.5	27.3	37.0	46.7	55.2	59.5	58.1	51.4	41.4	33.5	24.0	39.3
Extreme Maximum Temp. (°F)	67	71	82	88	90	99	100	97	92	83	78	76	100
Extreme Minimum Temp. (°F)	-22	-14	-10	14	24	30	42	32	29	20	1	-12	-22
Days Maximum Temp. ≥ 90°F	0	0	0	0	0	1	3	2	0	0	0	0	6
Days Maximum Temp. ≤ 32°F	16	12	5	0	0	0	0	0	0	0	2	10	45
Days Minimum Temp. ≤ 32°F	28	24	22	11	1	0	0	0	0	5	15	25	131
Days Minimum Temp. ≤ 0°F	3	2	0	0	0	0	0	0	0	0	0	1	6
Heating Degree Days (base 65°F)	1,242	1,052	877	522	244	67	13	25	144	427	716	1,057	6,386
Cooling Degree Days (base 65°F)	0	0	2	7	35	118	208	163	59	6	1	0	599
Mean Precipitation (in.)	2.30	2.03	3.06	3.27	3.42	3.91	4.12	3.38	3.87	2.50	3.17	2.95	37.98
Maximum Precipitation (in.)	7.6	5.3	6.2	6.4	6.2	10.7	9.7	7.9	6.1	8.6	9.1	6.5	48.6
Minimum Precipitation (in.)	0.7	0.5	1.1	1.0	0.8	0.7	1.6	0.5	0.3	0.4	0.9	0.9	23.8
Maximum 24-hr. Precipitation (in.)	2.6	1.9	2.0	1.6	1.9	3.6	3.8	3.5	3.0	4.3	2.7	1.9	4.3
Days With ≥ 0.1" Precipitation	6	6	8	8	8	8	7	6	7	6	7	7	84
Days With ≥ 1.0" Precipitation	0	0	0	1	1	1	1	1	1	0	0	0	6
Mean Snowfall (in.)	14.1	10.5	10.7	2.2	trace	trace	trace	0.0	trace	0.6	4.5	12.1	54.7
Maximum Snowfall (in.)	36	23	31	12	5	0	0	0	trace	8	31	30	91
Maximum 24-hr. Snowfall (in.)	17	9	15	12	5	0	0	0	trace	5	17	12	17
Days With ≥ 1.0" Snow Depth	18	14	7	1	0	0	0	0	0	0	2	11	53
Thunderstorm Days	< 1	< 1	2	3	4	7	7	5	3	1	1	< 1	33
Foggy Days	13	12	14	13	15	16	17	20	17	15	13	14	179
Predominant Sky Cover	OVR	OVR	OVR	OVR	OVR	OVR	OVR	OVR	OVR	OVR	OVR	OVR	OVR
Mean Relative Humidity 7am (%)	81	80	80	77	79	82	85	88	89	85	81	82	82
Mean Relative Humidity 4pm (%)	70	66	60	54	52	54	55	55	57	57	66	72	60
Mean Dewpoint (°F)	18	19	26	36	46	56	60	60	53	42	32	23	39
Prevailing Wind Direction	WSW	WSW	W	SW	SW	SW	SW	SW	SW	SW	SW	WSW	SW
Prevailing Wind Speed (mph)	14	13	13	13	12	9	9	8	9	10	12	14	12
Maximum Wind Gust (mph)	67	54	78	75	70	58	66	58	62	51	53	62	78

526 PROFILES OF OHIO / Weather: Cooperative Stations

Ashland 2 SW *Ashland County* Elevation: 1,263 ft. Latitude: 40° 50' N Longitude: 82° 21' W

	JAN	FEB	MAR	APR	MAY	JUN	JUL	AUG	SEP	OCT	NOV	DEC	YEAR
Mean Maximum Temp. (°F)	32.3	36.1	46.5	59.2	70.2	78.9	83.1	81.0	74.4	62.3	48.8	37.7	59.2
Mean Temp. (°F)	23.9	27.1	36.3	47.5	58.5	67.4	71.5	69.3	62.7	51.2	40.0	29.8	48.8
Mean Minimum Temp. (°F)	15.5	18.0	26.1	35.7	46.6	55.8	59.8	57.6	50.9	40.0	31.2	21.8	38.3
Extreme Maximum Temp. (°F)	65	69	80	87	90	100	99	96	94	85	76	74	100
Extreme Minimum Temp. (°F)	-23	-16	-15	6	25	31	39	37	29	20	0	-18	-23
Days Maximum Temp. ≥ 90°F	0	0	0	0	0	2	5	2	1	0	0	0	10
Days Maximum Temp. ≤ 32°F	16	11	4	0	0	0	0	0	0	0	2	10	43
Days Minimum Temp. ≤ 32°F	29	25	23	12	1	0	0	0	1	7	18	27	143
Days Minimum Temp. ≤ 0°F	5	3	1	0	0	0	0	0	0	0	0	1	10
Heating Degree Days (base 65°F)	1,268	1,064	883	525	235	57	12	23	133	427	744	1,086	6,457
Cooling Degree Days (base 65°F)	0	0	1	5	35	133	221	159	63	5	0	0	622
Mean Precipitation (in.)	2.36	2.10	2.80	3.55	4.05	3.96	4.22	4.09	3.40	2.57	3.17	2.66	38.93
Days With ≥ 0.1" Precipitation	6	5	7	8	9	8	7	6	6	6	7	7	82
Days With ≥ 1.0" Precipitation	0	0	0	1	1	1	1	1	1	0	1	0	7
Mean Snowfall (in.)	10.0	7.9	5.4	1.5	trace	0.0	0.0	0.0	0.0	trace	2.1	7.1	34.0
Days With ≥ 1.0" Snow Depth	16	13	5	1	0	0	0	0	0	0	2	9	46

Barnesville *Belmont County* Elevation: 1,240 ft. Latitude: 39° 59' N Longitude: 81° 09' W

	JAN	FEB	MAR	APR	MAY	JUN	JUL	AUG	SEP	OCT	NOV	DEC	YEAR
Mean Maximum Temp. (°F)	34.5	38.2	48.8	60.4	70.3	78.3	82.1	80.8	74.5	62.8	50.8	40.0	60.1
Mean Temp. (°F)	25.8	28.8	38.3	48.7	58.8	67.2	71.4	69.8	63.2	51.5	41.5	31.8	49.7
Mean Minimum Temp. (°F)	17.0	19.2	27.8	36.9	47.2	56.1	60.6	58.8	51.8	40.0	32.2	23.6	39.3
Extreme Maximum Temp. (°F)	71	72	82	87	90	96	100	96	94	83	77	75	100
Extreme Minimum Temp. (°F)	-23	-20	-5	13	22	31	42	38	28	16	0	-17	-23
Days Maximum Temp. ≥ 90°F	0	0	0	0	0	1	2	2	1	0	0	0	6
Days Maximum Temp. ≤ 32°F	14	10	3	0	0	0	0	0	0	0	1	8	36
Days Minimum Temp. ≤ 32°F	28	24	22	11	2	0	0	0	0	6	16	25	134
Days Minimum Temp. ≤ 0°F	4	2	0	0	0	0	0	0	0	0	0	1	7
Heating Degree Days (base 65°F)	1,208	1,015	821	491	221	51	9	18	118	417	698	1,022	6,089
Cooling Degree Days (base 65°F)	0	0	2	8	37	136	237	185	69	5	0	0	679
Mean Precipitation (in.)	3.01	2.69	3.53	3.85	4.35	4.88	4.73	3.90	3.54	2.97	3.69	3.20	44.34
Days With ≥ 0.1" Precipitation	7	6	8	9	9	8	8	7	6	6	8	8	90
Days With ≥ 1.0" Precipitation	0	0	1	1	1	1	1	1	1	1	1	0	9
Mean Snowfall (in.)	11.6	7.6	5.1	1.2	trace	0.0	0.0	trace	0.0	trace	1.7	5.7	32.9
Days With ≥ 1.0" Snow Depth	14	12	5	0	0	0	0	0	0	0	2	7	40

Bellefontaine *Logan County* Elevation: 1,184 ft. Latitude: 40° 21' N Longitude: 83° 46' W

	JAN	FEB	MAR	APR	MAY	JUN	JUL	AUG	SEP	OCT	NOV	DEC	YEAR
Mean Maximum Temp. (°F)	32.3	37.1	48.1	60.6	71.5	79.6	83.3	81.5	75.9	63.5	49.7	38.2	60.1
Mean Temp. (°F)	24.6	28.6	38.5	49.8	60.8	69.2	73.0	71.3	64.9	53.2	41.3	30.8	50.5
Mean Minimum Temp. (°F)	16.9	20.0	29.0	39.0	50.0	58.7	62.6	61.0	53.9	42.8	33.0	23.2	40.8
Extreme Maximum Temp. (°F)	64	71	82	87	90	101	99	101	95	85	77	71	101
Extreme Minimum Temp. (°F)	-27	-13	-12	9	25	37	45	39	30	17	5	-22	-27
Days Maximum Temp. ≥ 90°F	0	0	0	0	0	2	4	2	1	0	0	0	9
Days Maximum Temp. ≤ 32°F	15	11	3	0	0	0	0	0	0	0	2	9	40
Days Minimum Temp. ≤ 32°F	28	24	21	8	1	0	0	0	0	5	16	25	128
Days Minimum Temp. ≤ 0°F	4	2	0	0	0	0	0	0	0	0	0	1	7
Heating Degree Days (base 65°F)	1,245	1,022	814	457	180	35	4	11	94	370	704	1,054	5,990
Cooling Degree Days (base 65°F)	0	0	1	6	54	169	265	217	94	11	0	0	817
Mean Precipitation (in.)	2.25	1.98	2.75	3.56	3.95	3.97	3.92	3.42	2.67	2.44	3.06	2.95	36.92
Days With ≥ 0.1" Precipitation	6	5	7	8	8	7	7	6	5	6	7	7	79
Days With ≥ 1.0" Precipitation	0	0	0	1	1	1	1	1	1	0	0	1	7
Mean Snowfall (in.)	6.9	4.1	1.7	0.4	trace	0.0	0.0	0.0	0.0	0.2	0.8	3.7	17.8
Days With ≥ 1.0" Snow Depth	11	6	2	0	0	0	0	0	0	0	0	4	23

Bowling Green WWTP *Wood County* Elevation: 672 ft. Latitude: 41° 23' N Longitude: 83° 37' W

	JAN	FEB	MAR	APR	MAY	JUN	JUL	AUG	SEP	OCT	NOV	DEC	YEAR
Mean Maximum Temp. (°F)	31.3	35.4	46.5	59.6	71.7	81.1	84.6	82.2	76.0	63.5	49.2	37.2	59.8
Mean Temp. (°F)	23.8	27.4	37.0	48.4	60.0	69.6	73.3	70.8	64.1	52.4	40.7	29.9	49.8
Mean Minimum Temp. (°F)	16.2	19.3	27.5	37.2	48.3	58.2	61.9	59.4	52.2	41.3	32.2	22.6	39.7
Extreme Maximum Temp. (°F)	64	71	80	88	92	104	101	98	96	88	78	70	104
Extreme Minimum Temp. (°F)	-20	-13	-7	8	25	36	41	38	30	21	6	-19	-20
Days Maximum Temp. ≥ 90°F	0	0	0	0	1	4	6	3	1	0	0	0	15
Days Maximum Temp. ≤ 32°F	16	12	4	0	0	0	0	0	0	0	1	9	42
Days Minimum Temp. ≤ 32°F	29	25	23	10	1	0	0	0	0	5	17	26	136
Days Minimum Temp. ≤ 0°F	4	2	0	0	0	0	0	0	0	0	0	1	7
Heating Degree Days (base 65°F)	1,272	1,056	860	498	200	33	4	14	107	393	722	1,080	6,239
Cooling Degree Days (base 65°F)	0	0	1	7	49	177	269	197	80	9	0	0	789
Mean Precipitation (in.)	1.73	1.59	2.40	3.27	3.53	3.52	3.70	3.28	2.60	2.50	2.69	2.33	33.14
Days With ≥ 0.1" Precipitation	5	4	6	8	7	7	7	6	5	6	6	6	73
Days With ≥ 1.0" Precipitation	0	0	0	1	1	1	1	1	0	0	0	0	5
Mean Snowfall (in.)	7.2	5.4	3.1	0.7	trace	0.0	0.0	0.0	0.0	trace	0.7	4.8	21.9
Days With ≥ 1.0" Snow Depth	14	12	4	0	0	0	0	0	0	0	1	6	37

PROFILES OF OHIO / Weather: Cooperative Stations

Bucyrus *Crawford County* Elevation: 954 ft. Latitude: 40° 49' N Longitude: 82° 58' W

	JAN	FEB	MAR	APR	MAY	JUN	JUL	AUG	SEP	OCT	NOV	DEC	YEAR
Mean Maximum Temp. (°F)	31.5	35.1	45.8	58.7	70.2	79.1	83.1	81.0	74.5	62.0	48.6	37.1	58.9
Mean Temp. (°F)	23.8	26.7	36.3	47.7	58.7	68.0	72.0	69.9	63.0	51.3	40.2	29.8	48.9
Mean Minimum Temp. (°F)	16.0	18.2	26.7	36.6	47.2	56.8	61.0	58.8	51.4	40.4	31.8	22.5	38.9
Extreme Maximum Temp. (°F)	64	69	81	88	91	102	100	99	93	85	76	72	102
Extreme Minimum Temp. (°F)	-26	-18	-11	10	26	37	43	39	27	18	3	-18	-26
Days Maximum Temp. ≥ 90°F	0	0	0	0	0	2	5	2	1	0	0	0	10
Days Maximum Temp. ≤ 32°F	16	12	4	0	0	0	0	0	0	0	2	10	44
Days Minimum Temp. ≤ 32°F	29	25	23	11	1	0	0	0	0	6	17	26	138
Days Minimum Temp. ≤ 0°F	4	3	0	0	0	0	0	0	0	0	0	1	8
Heating Degree Days (base 65°F)	1,271	1,077	885	520	230	49	9	20	128	425	736	1,085	6,435
Cooling Degree Days (base 65°F)	0	0	1	6	41	149	245	185	72	7	0	0	706
Mean Precipitation (in.)	2.24	1.90	2.67	3.52	3.95	4.40	4.48	3.83	3.16	2.37	3.10	2.76	38.38
Days With ≥ 0.1" Precipitation	6	5	7	8	8	7	7	6	6	6	7	7	80
Days With ≥ 1.0" Precipitation	0	0	0	1	1	1	1	1	1	0	1	0	7
Mean Snowfall (in.)	7.9	5.9	3.6	0.8	trace	0.0	0.0	0.0	0.0	trace	1.0	4.0	23.2
Days With ≥ 1.0" Snow Depth	15	10	4	0	0	0	0	0	0	0	1	6	36

Cadiz *Harrison County* Elevation: 1,259 ft. Latitude: 40° 16' N Longitude: 81° 00' W

	JAN	FEB	MAR	APR	MAY	JUN	JUL	AUG	SEP	OCT	NOV	DEC	YEAR
Mean Maximum Temp. (°F)	34.9	39.3	49.9	61.8	71.3	79.0	82.7	81.5	75.6	64.0	51.0	40.4	61.0
Mean Temp. (°F)	27.0	30.4	39.9	50.6	60.6	68.6	72.6	71.3	65.0	53.4	42.4	32.6	51.2
Mean Minimum Temp. (°F)	19.1	21.5	29.7	39.3	49.8	58.1	62.5	61.1	54.5	42.8	33.8	24.8	41.4
Extreme Maximum Temp. (°F)	69	72	81	89	89	97	101	96	94	84	79	75	101
Extreme Minimum Temp. (°F)	-24	-10	-6	14	23	33	42	40	33	21	1	-17	-24
Days Maximum Temp. ≥ 90°F	0	0	0	0	0	1	3	2	1	0	0	0	7
Days Maximum Temp. ≤ 32°F	13	9	3	0	0	0	0	0	0	0	1	8	34
Days Minimum Temp. ≤ 32°F	28	23	20	8	1	0	0	0	0	4	14	25	123
Days Minimum Temp. ≤ 0°F	3	2	0	0	0	0	0	0	0	0	0	1	6
Heating Degree Days (base 65°F)	1,171	970	775	439	180	36	5	9	87	361	670	997	5,700
Cooling Degree Days (base 65°F)	0	0	2	11	47	150	258	211	91	10	1	0	781
Mean Precipitation (in.)	2.79	2.38	3.18	3.39	4.09	4.37	4.43	4.13	3.23	2.59	3.28	3.00	40.86
Days With ≥ 0.1" Precipitation	7	6	8	9	9	8	8	7	6	6	7	7	88
Days With ≥ 1.0" Precipitation	0	0	0	0	1	1	1	1	1	0	0	0	5
Mean Snowfall (in.)	11.5	6.5	5.1	1.2	0.0	0.0	0.0	0.0	0.0	trace	1.7	6.3	32.3
Days With ≥ 1.0" Snow Depth	na	na	na	0	0	0	0	0	0	0	1	na	na

Cambridge *Guernsey County* Elevation: 797 ft. Latitude: 40° 01' N Longitude: 81° 35' W

	JAN	FEB	MAR	APR	MAY	JUN	JUL	AUG	SEP	OCT	NOV	DEC	YEAR
Mean Maximum Temp. (°F)	37.4	41.9	52.9	65.0	74.3	81.7	85.1	83.6	77.4	65.9	53.2	42.4	63.4
Mean Temp. (°F)	28.7	32.2	41.7	52.2	61.6	69.6	73.6	72.2	65.8	53.9	43.6	34.1	52.4
Mean Minimum Temp. (°F)	20.1	22.5	30.5	39.3	48.8	57.5	62.1	60.8	54.0	41.9	33.9	25.7	41.4
Extreme Maximum Temp. (°F)	71	73	83	90	92	99	102	99	96	85	79	77	102
Extreme Minimum Temp. (°F)	-32	-16	-3	14	25	30	42	37	32	19	0	-17	-32
Days Maximum Temp. ≥ 90°F	0	0	0	0	0	3	6	4	1	0	0	0	14
Days Maximum Temp. ≤ 32°F	10	7	1	0	0	0	0	0	0	0	0	6	24
Days Minimum Temp. ≤ 32°F	27	22	19	8	1	0	0	0	0	5	14	23	119
Days Minimum Temp. ≤ 0°F	3	2	0	0	0	0	0	0	0	0	0	1	6
Heating Degree Days (base 65°F)	1,118	920	717	389	154	26	3	7	77	347	638	952	5,348
Cooling Degree Days (base 65°F)	0	0	2	12	56	183	301	247	108	10	0	0	919
Mean Precipitation (in.)	2.67	2.25	2.99	3.39	3.96	4.07	4.32	3.87	2.97	2.61	3.25	2.84	39.19
Days With ≥ 0.1" Precipitation	7	6	8	7	8	8	8	7	6	6	7	7	85
Days With ≥ 1.0" Precipitation	0	0	0	1	1	1	1	1	1	0	1	0	7
Mean Snowfall (in.)	7.4	4.1	2.9	0.6	trace	0.0	0.0	0.0	0.0	trace	0.8	2.6	18.4
Days With ≥ 1.0" Snow Depth	11	7	2	0	0	0	0	0	0	0	0	4	24

Canfield 1 S *Mahoning County* Elevation: 1,138 ft. Latitude: 41° 01' N Longitude: 80° 46' W

	JAN	FEB	MAR	APR	MAY	JUN	JUL	AUG	SEP	OCT	NOV	DEC	YEAR
Mean Maximum Temp. (°F)	34.1	36.9	48.6	60.1	70.9	79.1	82.9	81.7	74.5	62.8	49.7	38.8	60.0
Mean Temp. (°F)	25.2	27.0	37.4	47.3	57.8	66.4	70.4	68.9	61.8	50.6	40.4	30.4	48.6
Mean Minimum Temp. (°F)	16.3	17.1	26.1	34.4	44.7	53.7	57.9	56.0	49.1	38.4	31.0	21.9	37.2
Extreme Maximum Temp. (°F)	65	70	84	94	89	96	101	98	92	84	75	74	101
Extreme Minimum Temp. (°F)	-24	-23	-15	12	20	29	38	27	26	15	-3	-16	-24
Days Maximum Temp. ≥ 90°F	0	0	0	0	0	1	4	2	0	0	0	0	7
Days Maximum Temp. ≤ 32°F	14	11	3	0	0	0	0	0	0	0	1	9	38
Days Minimum Temp. ≤ 32°F	28	25	23	14	4	0	0	0	1	9	18	27	149
Days Minimum Temp. ≤ 0°F	4	3	1	0	0	0	0	0	0	0	0	1	9
Heating Degree Days (base 65°F)	1,227	1,065	851	528	246	63	15	27	147	442	733	1,066	6,410
Cooling Degree Days (base 65°F)	0	0	1	4	28	112	200	153	51	3	0	0	552
Mean Precipitation (in.)	1.97	1.80	2.89	3.03	3.87	4.19	4.37	3.57	3.78	2.77	3.07	2.66	37.97
Days With ≥ 0.1" Precipitation	5	6	7	7	9	8	8	7	7	6	7	6	83
Days With ≥ 1.0" Precipitation	0	0	0	0	1	1	1	1	1	0	0	0	5
Mean Snowfall (in.)	na	na	3.3	0.7	0.0	0.0	0.0	0.0	0.0	0.3	1.1	na	na
Days With ≥ 1.0" Snow Depth	na	na	3	1	0	0	0	0	0	0	1	na	na

PROFILES OF OHIO / Weather: Cooperative Stations

Celina 3 NE *Mercer County*   Elevation: 859 ft.   Latitude: 40° 34' N   Longitude: 84° 32' W

	JAN	FEB	MAR	APR	MAY	JUN	JUL	AUG	SEP	OCT	NOV	DEC	YEAR
Mean Maximum Temp. (°F)	32.5	37.2	48.8	61.9	73.0	81.3	84.6	82.4	76.9	64.6	50.0	38.1	60.9
Mean Temp. (°F)	25.1	29.0	39.4	50.9	61.8	70.7	74.1	71.8	65.8	54.2	42.1	31.2	51.3
Mean Minimum Temp. (°F)	17.7	20.8	29.9	39.8	50.6	59.9	63.6	61.2	54.5	43.7	34.2	24.2	41.7
Extreme Maximum Temp. (°F)	62	69	82	86	94	103	101	101	96	88	76	70	103
Extreme Minimum Temp. (°F)	-23	-16	-9	9	28	40	43	39	30	20	6	-20	-23
Days Maximum Temp. ≥ 90°F	0	0	0	0	0	3	6	3	1	0	0	0	13
Days Maximum Temp. ≤ 32°F	15	10	3	0	0	0	0	0	0	0	1	9	38
Days Minimum Temp. ≤ 32°F	28	24	20	7	1	0	0	0	0	3	14	25	122
Days Minimum Temp. ≤ 0°F	4	2	0	0	0	0	0	0	0	0	0	1	7
Heating Degree Days (base 65°F)	1,230	1,009	788	426	159	25	3	10	83	342	680	1,042	5,797
Cooling Degree Days (base 65°F)	0	0	1	9	67	205	298	232	110	15	0	0	937
Mean Precipitation (in.)	2.13	2.06	2.79	3.52	3.63	3.80	4.51	3.53	2.66	2.33	2.97	2.63	36.56
Days With ≥ 0.1" Precipitation	6	5	7	8	8	7	7	6	6	6	6	7	79
Days With ≥ 1.0" Precipitation	0	0	0	1	1	1	1	1	1	0	0	0	6
Mean Snowfall (in.)	11.4	7.7	4.7	1.1	0.0	0.0	0.0	0.0	0.0	0.3	1.6	6.3	33.1
Days With ≥ 1.0" Snow Depth	14	9	3	0	0	0	0	0	0	0	0	1	6	33

Centerburg 2 SE *Knox County*   Elevation: 1,204 ft.   Latitude: 40° 18' N   Longitude: 82° 39' W

	JAN	FEB	MAR	APR	MAY	JUN	JUL	AUG	SEP	OCT	NOV	DEC	YEAR
Mean Maximum Temp. (°F)	32.2	36.3	47.1	59.6	69.8	78.6	82.3	80.8	74.4	62.2	49.2	37.4	59.2
Mean Temp. (°F)	24.1	27.5	37.5	48.7	59.0	68.0	71.8	70.3	63.4	51.3	40.6	29.8	49.3
Mean Minimum Temp. (°F)	15.6	18.5	27.7	37.5	48.1	57.4	61.3	59.5	52.2	40.4	31.9	22.4	39.4
Extreme Maximum Temp. (°F)	66	72	82	86	89	99	99	97	94	87	78	70	99
Extreme Minimum Temp. (°F)	-29	-16	-6	11	25	32	43	38	31	20	0	-23	-29
Days Maximum Temp. ≥ 90°F	0	0	0	0	0	1	3	2	1	0	0	0	7
Days Maximum Temp. ≤ 32°F	15	11	4	0	0	0	0	0	0	0	2	10	42
Days Minimum Temp. ≤ 32°F	29	25	22	10	1	0	0	0	0	7	17	26	137
Days Minimum Temp. ≤ 0°F	4	3	0	0	0	0	0	0	0	0	0	1	8
Heating Degree Days (base 65°F)	1,262	1,053	848	491	219	44	8	17	118	424	727	1,086	6,297
Cooling Degree Days (base 65°F)	0	0	2	7	42	146	242	195	71	6	0	0	711
Mean Precipitation (in.)	2.45	2.13	2.98	3.66	4.03	4.59	4.56	3.85	3.21	2.80	3.61	3.02	40.89
Days With ≥ 0.1" Precipitation	6	6	7	8	8	8	8	6	5	6	7	7	82
Days With ≥ 1.0" Precipitation	0	0	0	1	1	1	1	1	1	1	1	1	9
Mean Snowfall (in.)	na	3.2	na	0.3	trace	0.0	0.0	0.0	0.0	trace	0.9	na	na
Days With ≥ 1.0" Snow Depth	9	6	3	1	0	0	0	0	0	0	1	5	25

Chardon *Geauga County*   Elevation: 1,128 ft.   Latitude: 41° 35' N   Longitude: 81° 11' W

	JAN	FEB	MAR	APR	MAY	JUN	JUL	AUG	SEP	OCT	NOV	DEC	YEAR
Mean Maximum Temp. (°F)	31.4	34.5	43.9	56.1	67.7	76.3	80.1	78.7	71.9	60.4	48.0	37.0	57.2
Mean Temp. (°F)	22.8	24.8	33.9	44.9	55.9	64.7	69.0	67.5	60.7	49.8	39.8	29.5	46.9
Mean Minimum Temp. (°F)	14.1	15.1	23.8	33.7	44.1	53.1	57.8	56.2	49.3	39.2	31.6	21.9	36.7
Extreme Maximum Temp. (°F)	65	69	82	88	89	100	98	96	91	83	76	73	100
Extreme Minimum Temp. (°F)	-23	-26	-17	5	22	30	38	33	25	15	-2	-21	-26
Days Maximum Temp. ≥ 90°F	0	0	0	0	0	1	2	1	0	0	0	0	4
Days Maximum Temp. ≤ 32°F	17	13	6	1	0	0	0	0	0	0	2	10	49
Days Minimum Temp. ≤ 32°F	29	26	25	15	3	0	0	0	1	7	18	27	151
Days Minimum Temp. ≤ 0°F	5	4	1	0	0	0	0	0	0	0	0	1	11
Heating Degree Days (base 65°F)	1,303	1,130	959	600	296	94	30	40	173	466	748	1,095	6,934
Cooling Degree Days (base 65°F)	0	0	0	4	22	96	169	126	48	3	0	0	468
Mean Precipitation (in.)	3.22	2.70	3.44	3.77	4.08	4.42	4.00	4.58	4.49	3.88	4.29	4.14	47.01
Days With ≥ 0.1" Precipitation	10	8	9	9	9	8	8	7	9	9	10	11	107
Days With ≥ 1.0" Precipitation	0	0	0	1	1	1	1	1	1	1	1	0	8
Mean Snowfall (in.)	26.2	18.9	14.4	2.9	trace	0.0	0.0	0.0	0.0	0.9	10.1	23.6	97.0
Days With ≥ 1.0" Snow Depth	24	20	12	2	0	0	0	0	0	0	6	17	81

Chillicothe Mound City *Ross County*   Elevation: 649 ft.   Latitude: 39° 22' N   Longitude: 83° 00' W

	JAN	FEB	MAR	APR	MAY	JUN	JUL	AUG	SEP	OCT	NOV	DEC	YEAR
Mean Maximum Temp. (°F)	37.6	41.9	52.7	64.0	74.0	82.0	86.2	85.1	78.6	66.5	53.9	42.7	63.8
Mean Temp. (°F)	28.4	31.8	41.5	51.7	61.7	70.2	74.5	72.9	65.8	53.8	43.6	33.7	52.5
Mean Minimum Temp. (°F)	19.1	21.6	30.2	39.3	49.4	58.4	62.8	60.8	52.9	40.7	33.2	24.5	41.1
Extreme Maximum Temp. (°F)	73	76	83	90	93	103	103	105	100	88	82	80	105
Extreme Minimum Temp. (°F)	-29	-14	-10	13	29	35	41	39	31	17	-2	-21	-29
Days Maximum Temp. ≥ 90°F	0	0	0	0	1	4	9	7	2	0	0	0	23
Days Maximum Temp. ≤ 32°F	10	7	2	0	0	0	0	0	0	0	0	6	25
Days Minimum Temp. ≤ 32°F	27	23	20	8	1	0	0	0	0	6	16	24	125
Days Minimum Temp. ≤ 0°F	3	2	0	0	0	0	0	0	0	0	0	1	6
Heating Degree Days (base 65°F)	1,128	932	723	405	159	27	2	7	83	354	637	965	5,422
Cooling Degree Days (base 65°F)	0	0	3	12	62	200	317	265	114	14	1	0	988
Mean Precipitation (in.)	2.49	2.34	3.38	3.52	4.37	3.45	3.91	3.59	2.80	2.55	2.93	2.63	37.96
Days With ≥ 0.1" Precipitation	6	5	7	8	8	7	7	6	5	5	6	6	76
Days With ≥ 1.0" Precipitation	0	1	1	1	1	1	1	1	1	1	0	1	10
Mean Snowfall (in.)	7.1	4.6	3.1	0.4	trace	0.0	0.0	0.0	0.0	0.1	0.4	2.2	17.9
Days With ≥ 1.0" Snow Depth	10	6	2	0	0	0	0	0	0	0	0	3	21

PROFILES OF OHIO / Weather: Cooperative Stations

Chilo Meldahl Lock & Dam *Clermont County* Elevation: 498 ft. Latitude: 38° 48' N Longitude: 84° 10' W

	JAN	FEB	MAR	APR	MAY	JUN	JUL	AUG	SEP	OCT	NOV	DEC	YEAR
Mean Maximum Temp. (°F)	38.5	43.2	53.0	64.9	73.8	82.0	86.2	85.3	79.3	67.6	54.8	43.8	64.4
Mean Temp. (°F)	29.6	33.4	42.1	52.6	62.0	70.8	75.4	74.3	67.7	55.9	45.0	35.1	53.6
Mean Minimum Temp. (°F)	20.4	23.1	31.3	40.3	50.1	59.5	64.3	63.2	56.1	44.1	35.2	26.3	42.8
Extreme Maximum Temp. (°F)	71	73	82	89	91	98	101	107	98	90	82	73	107
Extreme Minimum Temp. (°F)	-22	-8	-4	20	29	39	47	44	33	21	5	-15	-22
Days Maximum Temp. ≥ 90°F	0	0	0	0	0	3	9	7	3	0	0	0	22
Days Maximum Temp. ≤ 32°F	9	6	1	0	0	0	0	0	0	0	0	5	21
Days Minimum Temp. ≤ 32°F	26	23	18	6	0	0	0	0	0	2	12	22	109
Days Minimum Temp. ≤ 0°F	2	1	0	0	0	0	0	0	0	0	0	1	4
Heating Degree Days (base 65°F)	1,091	888	704	373	145	20	1	2	54	289	595	921	5,083
Cooling Degree Days (base 65°F)	0	0	1	9	54	208	344	307	139	17	0	0	1,079
Mean Precipitation (in.)	3.04	2.97	4.17	3.81	4.48	4.29	3.79	3.94	3.11	2.88	3.28	3.29	43.05
Days With ≥ 0.1" Precipitation	7	5	8	8	7	7	6	6	5	5	6	6	76
Days With ≥ 1.0" Precipitation	1	1	1	1	1	1	1	1	1	1	1	1	12
Mean Snowfall (in.)	na	na	1.0	0.0	0.0	0.0	0.0	0.0	0.0	0.0	trace	1.5	na
Days With ≥ 1.0" Snow Depth	4	5	1	0	0	0	0	0	0	0	0	1	11

Chippewa Lake *Medina County* Elevation: 1,177 ft. Latitude: 41° 03' N Longitude: 81° 56' W

	JAN	FEB	MAR	APR	MAY	JUN	JUL	AUG	SEP	OCT	NOV	DEC	YEAR
Mean Maximum Temp. (°F)	32.7	36.7	47.0	59.7	70.7	79.1	83.0	81.3	74.5	62.8	49.6	38.0	59.6
Mean Temp. (°F)	24.6	27.6	36.9	47.9	58.7	67.4	71.5	69.9	63.0	51.9	41.0	30.5	49.2
Mean Minimum Temp. (°F)	16.7	18.3	26.7	36.0	46.5	55.7	59.9	58.3	51.5	40.9	32.3	22.9	38.8
Extreme Maximum Temp. (°F)	64	70	83	88	90	102	102	99	94	84	77	75	102
Extreme Minimum Temp. (°F)	-26	-17	-14	8	23	28	39	34	28	16	-2	-18	-26
Days Maximum Temp. ≥ 90°F	0	0	0	0	0	1	4	2	1	0	0	0	8
Days Maximum Temp. ≤ 32°F	15	11	4	0	0	0	0	0	0	0	2	9	41
Days Minimum Temp. ≤ 32°F	29	25	23	12	2	0	0	0	0	5	17	26	139
Days Minimum Temp. ≤ 0°F	4	3	0	0	0	0	0	0	0	0	0	1	8
Heating Degree Days (base 65°F)	1,244	1,051	864	511	226	52	10	18	123	406	715	1,064	6,284
Cooling Degree Days (base 65°F)	0	0	1	5	36	136	230	183	69	6	0	0	666
Mean Precipitation (in.)	2.28	2.11	2.98	3.37	3.64	3.81	3.88	3.58	3.67	2.51	3.39	3.00	38.22
Days With ≥ 0.1" Precipitation	7	6	8	9	8	8	7	7	6	7	8	8	89
Days With ≥ 1.0" Precipitation	0	0	0	0	1	1	1	1	1	0	1	0	6
Mean Snowfall (in.)	10.7	8.6	6.7	2.1	trace	0.0	0.0	0.0	0.0	0.2	3.3	8.2	39.8
Days With ≥ 1.0" Snow Depth	17	14	6	1	0	0	0	0	0	0	0	2	9	49

Cincinnati Fernbank *Hamilton County* Elevation: 498 ft. Latitude: 39° 07' N Longitude: 84° 42' W

	JAN	FEB	MAR	APR	MAY	JUN	JUL	AUG	SEP	OCT	NOV	DEC	YEAR
Mean Maximum Temp. (°F)	38.1	43.6	53.8	65.1	74.7	82.4	86.6	85.3	78.5	67.2	55.4	43.7	64.6
Mean Temp. (°F)	29.2	33.3	42.6	52.7	62.5	71.0	75.5	74.1	66.7	55.2	45.3	34.8	53.6
Mean Minimum Temp. (°F)	20.2	23.0	31.3	40.1	50.3	59.5	64.4	62.8	54.8	43.1	35.1	25.8	42.5
Extreme Maximum Temp. (°F)	70	77	84	90	93	106	107	105	96	87	88	78	107
Extreme Minimum Temp. (°F)	-25	-10	-10	17	29	41	46	42	33	18	1	-18	-25
Days Maximum Temp. ≥ 90°F	0	0	0	0	1	5	9	7	2	0	0	0	24
Days Maximum Temp. ≤ 32°F	10	6	1	0	0	0	0	0	0	0	0	5	22
Days Minimum Temp. ≤ 32°F	26	22	18	7	0	0	0	0	0	3	13	23	112
Days Minimum Temp. ≤ 0°F	3	1	0	0	0	0	0	0	0	0	0	1	5
Heating Degree Days (base 65°F)	1,104	888	691	377	142	20	1	3	69	315	586	930	5,126
Cooling Degree Days (base 65°F)	0	0	3	12	66	209	342	293	129	21	1	0	1,076
Mean Precipitation (in.)	3.46	2.91	4.35	4.42	5.51	4.62	4.52	4.08	2.88	3.30	3.74	3.64	47.43
Days With ≥ 0.1" Precipitation	7	6	9	10	9	8	7	7	5	6	8	7	89
Days With ≥ 1.0" Precipitation	1	1	1	1	2	1	2	1	1	1	1	1	14
Mean Snowfall (in.)	6.7	na	2.6	0.1	trace	0.0	0.0	0.0	0.0	trace	0.4	2.2	na
Days With ≥ 1.0" Snow Depth	7	6	2	0	0	0	0	0	0	0	0	3	18

Cincinnati Lunken Airport *Hamilton County* Elevation: 488 ft. Latitude: 39° 06' N Longitude: 84° 26' W

	JAN	FEB	MAR	APR	MAY	JUN	JUL	AUG	SEP	OCT	NOV	DEC	YEAR
Mean Maximum Temp. (°F)	38.5	43.5	54.2	65.4	74.7	82.8	86.8	85.2	78.6	67.1	54.6	43.9	64.6
Mean Temp. (°F)	30.4	34.4	44.2	54.3	63.8	72.4	76.8	75.1	68.1	56.0	45.4	35.8	54.7
Mean Minimum Temp. (°F)	22.2	25.4	34.2	43.1	52.9	62.0	66.7	64.9	57.4	44.9	36.1	27.7	44.8
Extreme Maximum Temp. (°F)	70	76	85	90	93	101	105	103	97	87	82	75	105
Extreme Minimum Temp. (°F)	-22	-9	-6	21	32	41	47	43	35	20	7	-14	-22
Days Maximum Temp. ≥ 90°F	0	0	0	0	1	5	11	7	3	0	0	0	27
Days Maximum Temp. ≤ 32°F	10	6	1	0	0	0	0	0	0	0	0	5	22
Days Minimum Temp. ≤ 32°F	25	21	14	3	0	0	0	0	0	2	12	21	98
Days Minimum Temp. ≤ 0°F	1	0	0	0	0	0	0	0	0	0	0	0	1
Heating Degree Days (base 65°F)	1,066	857	639	330	114	11	0	2	52	287	582	899	4,839
Cooling Degree Days (base 65°F)	0	0	2	14	82	243	387	327	142	17	1	0	1,215
Mean Precipitation (in.)	2.70	2.43	3.88	3.74	4.61	4.00	3.83	4.07	3.12	2.95	3.39	3.17	41.89
Days With ≥ 0.1" Precipitation	6	5	9	8	8	8	7	6	5	5	7	7	81
Days With ≥ 1.0" Precipitation	1	0	1	1	1	1	1	1	1	1	1	0	10
Mean Snowfall (in.)	4.6	3.7	2.6	0.2	trace	trace	trace	0.0	0.0	0.1	0.4	1.6	13.2
Days With ≥ 1.0" Snow Depth	7	6	2	0	0	0	0	0	0	0	0	2	17

PROFILES OF OHIO / Weather: Cooperative Stations

Circleville *Pickaway County*   Elevation: 672 ft.   Latitude: 39° 37' N   Longitude: 82° 57' W

	JAN	FEB	MAR	APR	MAY	JUN	JUL	AUG	SEP	OCT	NOV	DEC	YEAR
Mean Maximum Temp. (°F)	37.0	41.2	52.4	64.3	73.9	82.0	85.5	84.2	78.3	66.6	53.3	42.2	63.4
Mean Temp. (°F)	28.9	32.1	41.9	52.3	62.3	70.8	74.6	72.9	66.4	54.8	44.0	34.3	52.9
Mean Minimum Temp. (°F)	20.8	23.0	31.3	40.2	50.5	59.6	63.6	61.5	54.5	42.9	34.6	26.4	42.4
Extreme Maximum Temp. (°F)	70	75	83	90	91	100	100	101	97	87	81	79	101
Extreme Minimum Temp. (°F)	-22	-15	-5	17	30	35	42	40	31	19	5	-19	-22
Days Maximum Temp. ≥ 90°F	0	0	0	0	1	4	7	5	1	0	0	0	18
Days Maximum Temp. ≤ 32°F	11	7	2	0	0	0	0	0	0	0	1	6	27
Days Minimum Temp. ≤ 32°F	26	22	18	7	0	0	0	0	0	4	14	22	113
Days Minimum Temp. ≤ 0°F	2	2	0	0	0	0	0	0	0	0	0	1	5
Heating Degree Days (base 65°F)	1,111	921	713	388	148	21	2	6	71	325	625	944	5,275
Cooling Degree Days (base 65°F)	0	0	2	11	61	200	309	255	110	16	1	0	965
Mean Precipitation (in.)	2.35	2.14	2.77	3.48	4.62	3.88	3.87	3.85	3.11	2.64	3.07	2.67	38.45
Days With ≥ 0.1" Precipitation	6	5	7	8	8	7	7	6	5	6	7	6	78
Days With ≥ 1.0" Precipitation	0	0	0	1	1	1	1	1	1	0	1	0	7
Mean Snowfall (in.)	5.9	4.0	2.0	0.4	0.0	0.0	0.0	0.0	0.0	0.1	0.7	1.8	14.9
Days With ≥ 1.0" Snow Depth	9	6	2	0	0	0	0	0	0	0	0	4	21

Columbus Valley Crossing *Franklin County*   Elevation: 734 ft.   Latitude: 39° 54' N   Longitude: 82° 56' W

	JAN	FEB	MAR	APR	MAY	JUN	JUL	AUG	SEP	OCT	NOV	DEC	YEAR
Mean Maximum Temp. (°F)	36.2	41.0	52.1	64.3	74.0	82.0	85.3	83.5	77.9	66.3	52.9	41.6	63.1
Mean Temp. (°F)	28.1	32.0	41.9	52.4	62.3	71.0	74.6	72.6	66.3	54.7	43.7	33.7	52.8
Mean Minimum Temp. (°F)	20.0	23.1	31.6	40.5	50.7	59.8	63.7	61.6	54.6	43.0	34.4	25.7	42.4
Extreme Maximum Temp. (°F)	70	74	83	90	93	100	100	100	95	87	79	76	100
Extreme Minimum Temp. (°F)	-28	-14	-2	17	30	37	45	38	28	19	2	-21	-28
Days Maximum Temp. ≥ 90°F	0	0	0	0	1	4	7	4	1	0	0	0	17
Days Maximum Temp. ≤ 32°F	11	7	2	0	0	0	0	0	0	0	1	6	27
Days Minimum Temp. ≤ 32°F	27	22	18	7	0	0	0	0	0	4	14	23	115
Days Minimum Temp. ≤ 0°F	3	1	0	0	0	0	0	0	0	0	0	1	5
Heating Degree Days (base 65°F)	1,138	924	712	381	141	18	1	5	72	326	635	965	5,318
Cooling Degree Days (base 65°F)	0	0	1	9	61	203	311	246	110	12	1	0	954
Mean Precipitation (in.)	2.51	2.03	3.00	3.72	4.34	4.08	4.39	4.26	2.88	2.52	3.34	2.89	39.96
Days With ≥ 0.1" Precipitation	6	5	7	7	8	7	7	7	5	6	7	6	78
Days With ≥ 1.0" Precipitation	0	0	0	1	1	1	1	1	1	0	1	0	7
Mean Snowfall (in.)	8.4	5.0	1.9	0.6	trace	0.0	0.0	0.0	0.0	trace	0.6	2.8	19.3
Days With ≥ 1.0" Snow Depth	9	na	1	0	0	0	0	0	0	0	0	3	na

Coshocton Agr. Res. Station *Coshocton County*   Elevation: 1,138 ft.   Latitude: 40° 22' N   Longitude: 81° 48' W

	JAN	FEB	MAR	APR	MAY	JUN	JUL	AUG	SEP	OCT	NOV	DEC	YEAR
Mean Maximum Temp. (°F)	33.3	36.9	47.4	59.2	69.6	78.1	82.0	80.5	74.1	62.4	50.1	38.9	59.4
Mean Temp. (°F)	25.5	28.6	38.2	49.5	60.1	68.6	72.7	71.3	64.7	52.9	41.9	31.6	50.5
Mean Minimum Temp. (°F)	17.7	20.2	29.0	39.7	50.6	59.1	63.3	62.0	55.2	43.3	33.8	24.1	41.5
Extreme Maximum Temp. (°F)	68	71	82	85	91	98	101	97	94	83	78	74	101
Extreme Minimum Temp. (°F)	-26	-15	1	14	28	38	47	39	32	21	1	-17	-26
Days Maximum Temp. ≥ 90°F	0	0	0	0	0	1	3	2	1	0	0	0	7
Days Maximum Temp. ≤ 32°F	15	11	4	0	0	0	0	0	0	0	1	9	40
Days Minimum Temp. ≤ 32°F	28	24	21	7	0	0	0	0	0	3	15	25	123
Days Minimum Temp. ≤ 0°F	3	2	0	0	0	0	0	0	0	0	0	1	6
Heating Degree Days (base 65°F)	1,216	1,022	824	469	196	38	5	11	94	379	687	1,030	5,971
Cooling Degree Days (base 65°F)	0	0	2	9	48	163	270	225	92	10	1	0	820
Mean Precipitation (in.)	2.28	2.04	2.91	3.34	3.79	4.01	4.04	3.53	2.95	2.40	3.10	2.65	37.04
Days With ≥ 0.1" Precipitation	5	5	7	7	7	7	7	6	6	6	6	6	75
Days With ≥ 1.0" Precipitation	0	0	0	1	1	1	1	1	1	0	1	0	7
Mean Snowfall (in.)	na	na	na	trace	0.0	0.0	0.0	0.0	0.0	trace	0.2	na	na
Days With ≥ 1.0" Snow Depth	na	na	na	0	0	0	0	0	0	0	0	na	na

Coshocton WPC Plant *Coshocton County*   Elevation: 757 ft.   Latitude: 40° 14' N   Longitude: 81° 52' W

	JAN	FEB	MAR	APR	MAY	JUN	JUL	AUG	SEP	OCT	NOV	DEC	YEAR
Mean Maximum Temp. (°F)	36.1	40.4	51.2	62.6	72.6	80.4	84.2	82.6	76.1	64.7	52.3	41.2	62.0
Mean Temp. (°F)	27.3	30.6	40.3	50.3	60.4	68.7	72.7	71.2	64.3	52.6	42.3	32.7	51.1
Mean Minimum Temp. (°F)	18.4	20.9	29.4	38.0	48.2	57.0	61.3	59.7	52.4	40.4	32.3	24.1	40.2
Extreme Maximum Temp. (°F)	69	72	84	89	92	101	101	99	96	86	80	77	101
Extreme Minimum Temp. (°F)	-24	-14	-6	12	20	31	41	39	29	19	1	-19	-24
Days Maximum Temp. ≥ 90°F	0	0	0	0	0	2	5	3	1	0	0	0	11
Days Maximum Temp. ≤ 32°F	12	8	2	0	0	0	0	0	0	0	1	6	29
Days Minimum Temp. ≤ 32°F	28	24	21	9	1	0	0	0	0	6	17	25	131
Days Minimum Temp. ≤ 0°F	3	2	0	0	0	0	0	0	0	0	0	1	6
Heating Degree Days (base 65°F)	1,163	964	759	440	182	34	5	11	98	384	673	996	5,709
Cooling Degree Days (base 65°F)	0	0	1	7	47	159	271	219	80	6	1	0	791
Mean Precipitation (in.)	2.54	2.36	3.16	3.79	4.11	4.03	4.45	4.15	3.21	2.69	3.47	3.00	40.96
Days With ≥ 0.1" Precipitation	7	6	8	8	8	8	8	7	6	6	8	7	87
Days With ≥ 1.0" Precipitation	0	0	0	1	1	1	1	1	1	0	1	0	7
Mean Snowfall (in.)	8.8	5.6	3.0	0.8	trace	0.0	0.0	0.0	0.0	trace	0.9	3.6	22.7
Days With ≥ 1.0" Snow Depth	13	8	3	0	0	0	0	0	0	0	1	5	30

PROFILES OF OHIO / Weather: Cooperative Stations

Danville 2 W *Knox County* Elevation: 967 ft. Latitude: 40° 26' N Longitude: 82° 18' W

	JAN	FEB	MAR	APR	MAY	JUN	JUL	AUG	SEP	OCT	NOV	DEC	YEAR
Mean Maximum Temp. (°F)	34.0	38.5	49.6	61.6	72.0	80.3	84.3	82.7	76.2	64.2	51.0	39.6	61.2
Mean Temp. (°F)	25.0	28.4	38.1	48.2	58.4	67.3	71.4	69.7	62.8	50.9	40.7	30.9	49.3
Mean Minimum Temp. (°F)	16.0	18.3	26.7	34.7	44.8	54.2	58.5	56.7	49.3	37.5	30.3	22.1	37.4
Extreme Maximum Temp. (°F)	67	72	83	89	94	102	102	98	96	84	78	74	102
Extreme Minimum Temp. (°F)	-35	-22	-18	9	21	27	35	32	26	15	-2	-22	-35
Days Maximum Temp. ≥ 90°F	0	0	0	0	0	2	5	3	1	0	0	0	11
Days Maximum Temp. ≤ 32°F	14	9	3	0	0	0	0	0	0	0	1	8	35
Days Minimum Temp. ≤ 32°F	28	25	22	14	3	0	0	0	1	11	19	26	149
Days Minimum Temp. ≤ 0°F	5	3	0	0	0	0	0	0	0	0	0	2	10
Heating Degree Days (base 65°F)	1,234	1,026	827	502	230	51	10	21	130	434	724	1,051	6,240
Cooling Degree Days (base 65°F)	0	0	0	3	31	124	220	169	62	4	0	0	613
Mean Precipitation (in.)	2.62	2.38	3.12	3.67	4.22	4.68	4.32	3.75	3.33	2.65	3.37	3.10	41.21
Days With ≥ 0.1" Precipitation	6	6	8	8	9	8	7	6	6	6	7	7	84
Days With ≥ 1.0" Precipitation	0	0	0	1	1	1	1	1	1	0	1	1	8
Mean Snowfall (in.)	12.4	8.4	4.6	1.3	trace	0.0	0.0	0.0	0.0	trace	1.8	7.0	35.5
Days With ≥ 1.0" Snow Depth	16	11	4	1	0	0	0	0	0	0	2	8	42

Dayton MCD *Montgomery County* Elevation: 744 ft. Latitude: 39° 46' N Longitude: 84° 11' W

	JAN	FEB	MAR	APR	MAY	JUN	JUL	AUG	SEP	OCT	NOV	DEC	YEAR
Mean Maximum Temp. (°F)	34.9	39.8	50.5	63.0	74.1	83.1	87.3	85.4	78.8	65.8	52.2	41.0	63.0
Mean Temp. (°F)	27.7	31.5	41.3	52.6	63.7	72.9	77.1	75.0	68.1	55.6	44.2	33.9	53.6
Mean Minimum Temp. (°F)	20.4	23.2	32.0	42.3	53.2	62.6	66.9	64.6	57.3	45.3	36.1	26.7	44.2
Extreme Maximum Temp. (°F)	69	75	84	90	95	103	104	103	97	89	81	75	104
Extreme Minimum Temp. (°F)	-21	-6	2	18	33	42	51	45	35	24	8	-16	-21
Days Maximum Temp. ≥ 90°F	0	0	0	0	2	7	12	8	3	0	0	0	32
Days Maximum Temp. ≤ 32°F	13	8	2	0	0	0	0	0	0	0	1	7	31
Days Minimum Temp. ≤ 32°F	26	22	17	4	0	0	0	0	0	2	11	22	104
Days Minimum Temp. ≤ 0°F	2	1	0	0	0	0	0	0	0	0	0	1	4
Heating Degree Days (base 65°F)	1,152	939	732	382	129	15	1	2	57	306	619	958	5,292
Cooling Degree Days (base 65°F)	0	0	4	16	92	264	397	330	156	23	1	0	1,283
Mean Precipitation (in.)	2.57	2.32	3.07	4.07	4.38	4.11	3.90	3.28	2.57	2.68	3.25	2.93	39.13
Days With ≥ 0.1" Precipitation	6	6	7	8	8	7	7	6	5	5	6	6	77
Days With ≥ 1.0" Precipitation	0	0	0	1	1	1	1	1	1	1	1	1	9
Mean Snowfall (in.)	6.3	3.6	2.4	0.2	0.0	0.0	0.0	0.0	0.0	trace	0.4	2.8	15.7
Days With ≥ 1.0" Snow Depth	11	7	2	0	0	0	0	0	0	0	0	3	23

Defiance *Defiance County* Elevation: 698 ft. Latitude: 41° 17' N Longitude: 84° 23' W

	JAN	FEB	MAR	APR	MAY	JUN	JUL	AUG	SEP	OCT	NOV	DEC	YEAR
Mean Maximum Temp. (°F)	31.1	35.0	45.7	59.1	71.3	80.7	84.6	82.4	75.6	63.1	48.7	36.9	59.5
Mean Temp. (°F)	22.9	26.1	35.9	47.8	59.3	69.0	73.0	70.9	63.8	51.9	40.1	29.3	49.2
Mean Minimum Temp. (°F)	14.7	17.1	26.1	36.4	47.4	57.2	61.5	59.4	51.9	40.6	31.4	21.6	38.8
Extreme Maximum Temp. (°F)	64	71	80	89	92	104	104	99	95	88	77	70	104
Extreme Minimum Temp. (°F)	-22	-19	-6	4	26	38	45	43	29	18	6	-19	-22
Days Maximum Temp. ≥ 90°F	0	0	0	0	1	4	7	4	1	0	0	0	17
Days Maximum Temp. ≤ 32°F	16	12	4	0	0	0	0	0	0	0	1	10	43
Days Minimum Temp. ≤ 32°F	29	25	24	10	1	0	0	0	0	5	18	27	139
Days Minimum Temp. ≤ 0°F	5	4	0	0	0	0	0	0	0	0	0	2	11
Heating Degree Days (base 65°F)	1,298	1,094	895	519	215	41	6	13	114	409	741	1,099	6,444
Cooling Degree Days (base 65°F)	0	0	1	7	48	174	280	216	85	9	0	0	820
Mean Precipitation (in.)	1.90	1.79	2.68	3.45	3.59	3.72	4.03	3.13	3.16	2.62	3.00	2.57	35.64
Days With ≥ 0.1" Precipitation	5	5	7	8	8	7	7	6	6	6	6	6	77
Days With ≥ 1.0" Precipitation	0	0	0	1	1	1	1	1	1	0	1	0	7
Mean Snowfall (in.)	6.8	5.3	2.4	0.6	trace	0.0	0.0	0.0	0.0	trace	1.2	4.5	20.8
Days With ≥ 1.0" Snow Depth	16	12	4	0	0	0	0	0	0	0	0	8	41

Delaware *Delaware County* Elevation: 918 ft. Latitude: 40° 19' N Longitude: 83° 04' W

	JAN	FEB	MAR	APR	MAY	JUN	JUL	AUG	SEP	OCT	NOV	DEC	YEAR
Mean Maximum Temp. (°F)	33.3	37.2	47.9	60.5	71.3	80.0	83.9	82.4	76.2	63.9	49.9	38.9	60.5
Mean Temp. (°F)	24.7	27.8	37.7	48.9	59.5	68.6	72.6	70.7	63.8	51.9	40.6	30.8	49.8
Mean Minimum Temp. (°F)	16.2	18.5	27.5	37.1	47.6	57.1	61.2	59.0	51.4	39.9	31.3	22.6	39.1
Extreme Maximum Temp. (°F)	68	72	82	87	90	101	100	100	96	87	78	74	101
Extreme Minimum Temp. (°F)	-28	-16	-9	14	27	35	41	37	31	16	2	-27	-28
Days Maximum Temp. ≥ 90°F	0	0	0	0	0	3	6	3	1	0	0	0	13
Days Maximum Temp. ≤ 32°F	14	10	3	0	0	0	0	0	0	0	1	8	36
Days Minimum Temp. ≤ 32°F	28	24	22	10	1	0	0	0	0	0	7	18	25	135
Days Minimum Temp. ≤ 0°F	4	3	0	0	0	0	0	0	0	0	0	1	8
Heating Degree Days (base 65°F)	1,243	1,044	839	484	210	41	6	15	111	407	725	1,054	6,179
Cooling Degree Days (base 65°F)	0	0	1	6	46	161	266	206	81	9	0	0	776
Mean Precipitation (in.)	2.29	1.88	2.47	3.44	3.96	4.20	4.12	3.54	2.78	2.45	3.47	2.73	37.33
Days With ≥ 0.1" Precipitation	6	5	7	7	8	8	7	6	5	5	7	7	78
Days With ≥ 1.0" Precipitation	0	0	0	1	1	1	1	1	1	0	1	0	7
Mean Snowfall (in.)	8.1	4.3	2.9	0.9	0.0	0.0	0.0	0.0	0.0	trace	0.8	3.7	20.7
Days With ≥ 1.0" Snow Depth	13	9	3	0	0	0	0	0	0	0	1	5	31

532 PROFILES OF OHIO / Weather: Cooperative Stations

Dorset *Ashtabula County*   Elevation: 977 ft.   Latitude: 41° 41' N   Longitude: 80° 40' W

	JAN	FEB	MAR	APR	MAY	JUN	JUL	AUG	SEP	OCT	NOV	DEC	YEAR
Mean Maximum Temp. (°F)	31.4	34.7	44.3	56.6	68.3	76.9	81.2	79.7	73.1	61.3	48.4	37.0	57.8
Mean Temp. (°F)	23.1	25.3	34.5	45.5	56.3	65.1	69.4	67.9	61.4	50.4	40.3	29.6	47.4
Mean Minimum Temp. (°F)	14.6	15.8	24.7	34.3	44.2	53.2	57.4	56.0	49.6	39.5	32.1	22.2	37.0
Extreme Maximum Temp. (°F)	67	69	83	88	89	99	100	98	95	85	83	74	100
Extreme Minimum Temp. (°F)	-28	-28	-20	-4	22	30	37	30	26	17	2	-22	-28
Days Maximum Temp. ≥ 90°F	0	0	0	0	0	1	2	1	0	0	0	0	4
Days Maximum Temp. ≤ 32°F	17	12	6	1	0	0	0	0	0	0	2	10	48
Days Minimum Temp. ≤ 32°F	29	26	24	14	4	0	0	0	1	6	17	26	147
Days Minimum Temp. ≤ 0°F	5	4	1	0	0	0	0	0	0	0	0	1	11
Heating Degree Days (base 65°F)	1,294	1,116	938	583	290	88	28	36	162	448	736	1,090	6,809
Cooling Degree Days (base 65°F)	0	0	0	5	28	100	180	136	62	3	0	0	514
Mean Precipitation (in.)	2.60	2.26	3.16	3.55	3.69	4.53	4.20	4.06	4.31	3.79	3.88	3.27	43.30
Days With ≥ 0.1" Precipitation	7	7	9	9	9	8	7	7	8	9	10	9	99
Days With ≥ 1.0" Precipitation	0	0	0	0	1	1	1	1	1	1	0	0	6
Mean Snowfall (in.)	17.5	12.9	12.1	2.9	trace	0.0	0.0	0.0	0.0	0.6	8.7	18.4	73.1
Days With ≥ 1.0" Snow Depth	21	18	10	2	0	0	0	0	0	0	5	15	71

Eaton *Preble County*   Elevation: 1,000 ft.   Latitude: 39° 44' N   Longitude: 84° 38' W

	JAN	FEB	MAR	APR	MAY	JUN	JUL	AUG	SEP	OCT	NOV	DEC	YEAR
Mean Maximum Temp. (°F)	33.4	38.4	49.3	61.4	72.3	80.8	84.7	83.3	77.2	64.7	50.9	39.2	61.3
Mean Temp. (°F)	24.4	28.3	38.5	48.9	60.2	68.9	72.8	71.2	64.4	52.1	41.0	30.8	50.1
Mean Minimum Temp. (°F)	15.4	18.2	27.6	36.8	48.0	56.9	60.8	59.0	51.5	39.3	31.1	22.1	38.9
Extreme Maximum Temp. (°F)	65	72	82	87	91	100	102	101	96	90	79	72	102
Extreme Minimum Temp. (°F)	-33	-20	-11	14	25	36	42	38	26	12	-3	-30	-33
Days Maximum Temp. ≥ 90°F	0	0	0	0	0	3	6	4	2	0	0	0	15
Days Maximum Temp. ≤ 32°F	14	10	3	0	0	0	0	0	0	0	1	8	36
Days Minimum Temp. ≤ 32°F	28	25	22	10	1	0	0	0	0	7	18	26	137
Days Minimum Temp. ≤ 0°F	5	3	0	0	0	0	0	0	0	0	0	2	10
Heating Degree Days (base 65°F)	1,251	1,029	816	481	189	36	6	9	103	401	714	1,054	6,089
Cooling Degree Days (base 65°F)	0	0	1	4	47	167	265	220	91	9	0	0	804
Mean Precipitation (in.)	2.46	2.24	3.25	4.11	4.64	3.81	3.65	3.38	2.57	2.72	3.41	3.02	39.26
Days With ≥ 0.1" Precipitation	6	6	7	8	8	7	6	6	5	5	7	6	77
Days With ≥ 1.0" Precipitation	0	0	1	1	1	1	1	1	1	1	1	1	10
Mean Snowfall (in.)	na	na	na	0.5	0.0	0.0	0.0	0.0	0.0	0.0	trace	na	na
Days With ≥ 1.0" Snow Depth	12	9	4	0	0	0	0	0	0	0	1	5	31

Elyria 3 E *Lorain County*   Elevation: 728 ft.   Latitude: 41° 23' N   Longitude: 82° 03' W

	JAN	FEB	MAR	APR	MAY	JUN	JUL	AUG	SEP	OCT	NOV	DEC	YEAR
Mean Maximum Temp. (°F)	34.0	37.6	47.8	60.4	71.7	80.5	84.6	82.5	75.9	64.0	51.0	39.4	60.8
Mean Temp. (°F)	26.5	29.2	38.3	49.4	60.1	69.3	73.6	71.8	65.3	53.9	43.0	32.4	51.1
Mean Minimum Temp. (°F)	18.9	20.7	28.8	38.4	48.5	57.9	62.5	61.0	54.6	43.8	35.0	25.3	41.3
Extreme Maximum Temp. (°F)	66	72	84	89	93	104	102	100	95	86	78	76	104
Extreme Minimum Temp. (°F)	-22	-15	-10	11	27	33	44	40	32	18	7	-14	-22
Days Maximum Temp. ≥ 90°F	0	0	0	0	1	4	8	4	1	0	0	0	18
Days Maximum Temp. ≤ 32°F	14	10	3	0	0	0	0	0	0	0	1	7	35
Days Minimum Temp. ≤ 32°F	28	24	21	9	1	0	0	0	0	2	13	24	122
Days Minimum Temp. ≤ 0°F	3	2	0	0	0	0	0	0	0	0	0	1	6
Heating Degree Days (base 65°F)	1,187	1,005	822	470	196	35	4	9	85	346	653	1,003	5,815
Cooling Degree Days (base 65°F)	0	0	2	9	53	173	289	229	98	11	0	0	864
Mean Precipitation (in.)	2.37	2.17	2.74	3.19	3.42	3.98	3.65	3.76	3.54	2.69	3.18	3.07	37.76
Days With ≥ 0.1" Precipitation	7	6	7	8	8	7	7	7	7	7	8	8	87
Days With ≥ 1.0" Precipitation	0	0	0	0	0	1	1	1	1	0	0	0	4
Mean Snowfall (in.)	12.0	10.2	7.2	1.7	trace	trace	0.0	0.0	0.0	0.1	3.2	9.2	43.6
Days With ≥ 1.0" Snow Depth	16	13	5	0	0	0	0	0	0	0	1	9	44

Findlay Airport *Hancock County*   Elevation: 797 ft.   Latitude: 41° 01' N   Longitude: 83° 40' W

	JAN	FEB	MAR	APR	MAY	JUN	JUL	AUG	SEP	OCT	NOV	DEC	YEAR
Mean Maximum Temp. (°F)	31.1	34.7	46.0	58.5	70.2	78.9	82.8	80.5	74.3	62.0	48.4	36.7	58.7
Mean Temp. (°F)	24.3	27.5	37.6	48.7	60.0	69.0	73.0	70.8	64.0	52.4	41.0	30.3	49.9
Mean Minimum Temp. (°F)	17.5	20.3	29.1	38.8	49.8	59.1	63.1	60.9	53.7	42.7	33.6	23.8	41.0
Extreme Maximum Temp. (°F)	66	72	80	86	94	104	102	99	94	86	79	70	104
Extreme Minimum Temp. (°F)	-20	-14	-12	10	28	39	44	40	30	21	7	-18	-20
Days Maximum Temp. ≥ 90°F	0	0	0	0	1	2	5	2	1	0	0	0	11
Days Maximum Temp. ≤ 32°F	16	12	4	0	0	0	0	0	0	0	2	11	45
Days Minimum Temp. ≤ 32°F	28	23	20	8	0	0	0	0	0	4	15	25	123
Days Minimum Temp. ≤ 0°F	4	2	1	0	0	0	0	0	0	0	0	1	7
Heating Degree Days (base 65°F)	1,252	1,051	844	490	200	36	4	13	108	392	712	1,068	6,170
Cooling Degree Days (base 65°F)	0	0	1	6	51	165	265	200	82	9	0	0	779
Mean Precipitation (in.)	1.80	1.65	2.52	3.24	3.74	4.07	3.88	3.66	2.83	2.17	2.73	2.39	34.68
Days With ≥ 0.1" Precipitation	5	4	7	8	7	7	6	6	6	5	6	6	73
Days With ≥ 1.0" Precipitation	0	0	0	0	1	1	1	1	1	0	0	0	5
Mean Snowfall (in.)	8.2	5.3	3.2	0.7	trace	trace	0.0	0.0	trace	0.1	1.2	5.5	24.2
Days With ≥ 1.0" Snow Depth	15	11	4	0	0	0	0	0	0	0	1	7	38

PROFILES OF OHIO / Weather: Cooperative Stations 533

Findlay WPCC *Hancock County* Elevation: 767 ft. Latitude: 41° 03' N Longitude: 83° 40' W

	JAN	FEB	MAR	APR	MAY	JUN	JUL	AUG	SEP	OCT	NOV	DEC	YEAR
Mean Maximum Temp. (°F)	31.3	35.2	46.5	59.2	71.1	79.8	83.6	81.2	74.6	62.2	48.2	36.5	59.1
Mean Temp. (°F)	24.3	27.7	37.7	49.0	60.6	69.7	73.6	71.4	64.5	52.6	40.7	29.9	50.1
Mean Minimum Temp. (°F)	17.2	20.1	28.8	38.8	50.1	59.5	63.6	61.5	54.2	42.9	33.1	23.4	41.1
Extreme Maximum Temp. (°F)	66	71	81	86	93	104	101	99	96	88	78	70	104
Extreme Minimum Temp. (°F)	-20	-12	-11	8	26	40	47	42	31	19	6	-18	-20
Days Maximum Temp. ≥ 90°F	0	0	0	0	1	3	5	3	1	0	0	0	13
Days Maximum Temp. ≤ 32°F	16	12	4	0	0	0	0	0	0	0	2	11	45
Days Minimum Temp. ≤ 32°F	28	24	21	7	1	0	0	0	0	3	16	25	125
Days Minimum Temp. ≤ 0°F	4	2	0	0	0	0	0	0	0	0	0	1	7
Heating Degree Days (base 65°F)	1,256	1,047	841	480	186	32	3	11	100	387	724	1,080	6,147
Cooling Degree Days (base 65°F)	0	0	2	7	58	187	294	230	97	10	0	0	885
Mean Precipitation (in.)	2.15	1.98	2.72	3.28	3.92	4.13	3.91	4.05	2.95	2.35	2.78	2.73	36.95
Days With ≥ 0.1" Precipitation	6	5	7	8	8	8	6	6	6	6	7	6	79
Days With ≥ 1.0" Precipitation	0	0	0	1	1	1	1	1	1	0	0	0	6
Mean Snowfall (in.)	10.2	6.2	4.3	1.2	trace	0.0	0.0	0.0	0.0	0.2	1.4	6.0	29.5
Days With ≥ 1.0" Snow Depth	16	12	4	0	0	0	0	0	0	0	1	8	41

Franklin *Warren County* Elevation: 669 ft. Latitude: 39° 33' N Longitude: 84° 19' W

	JAN	FEB	MAR	APR	MAY	JUN	JUL	AUG	SEP	OCT	NOV	DEC	YEAR
Mean Maximum Temp. (°F)	36.0	40.5	51.1	62.8	73.2	81.6	85.5	84.2	78.0	65.6	52.8	41.7	62.7
Mean Temp. (°F)	27.2	30.8	40.5	51.1	61.3	70.1	74.1	72.3	65.3	53.0	42.9	33.1	51.8
Mean Minimum Temp. (°F)	18.4	21.0	29.9	39.3	49.3	58.6	62.7	60.4	52.5	40.2	32.9	24.4	40.8
Extreme Maximum Temp. (°F)	68	74	86	88	96	100	101	100	95	90	79	74	101
Extreme Minimum Temp. (°F)	-24	-12	-7	18	29	38	42	39	32	18	5	-21	-24
Days Maximum Temp. ≥ 90°F	0	0	0	0	0	4	7	5	2	0	0	0	18
Days Maximum Temp. ≤ 32°F	11	8	2	0	0	0	0	0	0	0	1	6	28
Days Minimum Temp. ≤ 32°F	27	23	20	8	1	0	0	0	0	7	16	24	126
Days Minimum Temp. ≤ 0°F	3	2	0	0	0	0	0	0	0	0	0	1	6
Heating Degree Days (base 65°F)	1,164	959	753	420	167	26	3	7	90	376	657	982	5,604
Cooling Degree Days (base 65°F)	0	0	2	7	55	188	298	245	99	9	0	0	903
Mean Precipitation (in.)	2.48	2.30	3.20	3.93	4.40	3.67	4.15	3.27	2.65	2.96	3.34	2.99	39.34
Days With ≥ 0.1" Precipitation	6	6	7	8	8	7	7	6	5	6	7	6	79
Days With ≥ 1.0" Precipitation	0	0	0	1	1	1	1	1	1	1	1	0	8
Mean Snowfall (in.)	na	2.4	1.6	trace	0.0	0.0	0.0	0.0	0.0	0.0	0.5	1.4	na
Days With ≥ 1.0" Snow Depth	8	7	2	0	0	0	0	0	0	0	0	2	19

Fredericktown 4 S *Knox County* Elevation: 1,049 ft. Latitude: 40° 25' N Longitude: 82° 32' W

	JAN	FEB	MAR	APR	MAY	JUN	JUL	AUG	SEP	OCT	NOV	DEC	YEAR
Mean Maximum Temp. (°F)	32.2	36.6	47.4	59.6	70.5	79.3	83.1	81.5	75.1	63.1	49.8	38.8	59.7
Mean Temp. (°F)	22.9	26.5	36.6	47.4	58.0	67.0	70.7	68.7	61.9	50.3	39.9	30.3	48.3
Mean Minimum Temp. (°F)	13.5	16.4	25.7	35.2	45.4	54.6	58.2	55.8	48.6	37.5	30.0	21.7	36.9
Extreme Maximum Temp. (°F)	66	70	82	88	91	100	98	98	94	87	78	75	100
Extreme Minimum Temp. (°F)	-30	-26	-21	12	21	34	38	32	26	15	0	-16	-30
Days Maximum Temp. ≥ 90°F	0	0	0	0	0	2	4	2	1	0	0	0	9
Days Maximum Temp. ≤ 32°F	15	11	4	0	0	0	0	0	0	0	1	8	39
Days Minimum Temp. ≤ 32°F	29	26	24	13	2	0	0	0	1	10	19	26	150
Days Minimum Temp. ≤ 0°F	6	4	1	0	0	0	0	0	0	0	0	2	13
Heating Degree Days (base 65°F)	1,300	1,081	876	526	246	56	14	29	147	452	745	1,070	6,542
Cooling Degree Days (base 65°F)	0	0	1	4	32	123	207	147	54	3	0	0	571
Mean Precipitation (in.)	2.58	2.14	2.97	3.56	4.26	4.37	4.15	3.73	3.29	2.61	3.30	2.94	39.90
Days With ≥ 0.1" Precipitation	6	5	7	8	8	8	7	6	6	6	7	7	81
Days With ≥ 1.0" Precipitation	0	0	0	1	1	1	1	1	1	1	1	1	9
Mean Snowfall (in.)	7.8	5.3	3.1	0.7	trace	0.0	0.0	0.0	0.0	0.0	1.0	3.5	21.4
Days With ≥ 1.0" Snow Depth	na	7	2	0	0	0	0	0	0	0	1	3	na

Fremont *Sandusky County* Elevation: 597 ft. Latitude: 41° 20' N Longitude: 83° 07' W

	JAN	FEB	MAR	APR	MAY	JUN	JUL	AUG	SEP	OCT	NOV	DEC	YEAR
Mean Maximum Temp. (°F)	31.3	34.5	44.9	58.1	70.3	79.1	83.5	81.2	74.7	62.2	49.2	36.8	58.8
Mean Temp. (°F)	23.7	26.4	36.2	48.0	59.6	68.8	73.1	70.6	63.7	51.5	41.0	29.6	49.3
Mean Minimum Temp. (°F)	16.0	18.3	27.5	37.9	48.8	58.4	62.5	60.0	52.6	40.7	32.8	22.3	39.8
Extreme Maximum Temp. (°F)	62	72	81	87	92	104	100	99	95	86	77	71	104
Extreme Minimum Temp. (°F)	-20	-11	-5	8	29	38	46	41	31	19	9	-17	-20
Days Maximum Temp. ≥ 90°F	0	0	0	0	1	3	6	2	1	0	0	0	13
Days Maximum Temp. ≤ 32°F	16	12	5	0	0	0	0	0	0	0	1	10	44
Days Minimum Temp. ≤ 32°F	29	25	23	8	0	0	0	0	0	5	15	26	131
Days Minimum Temp. ≤ 0°F	5	3	0	0	0	0	0	0	0	0	0	1	9
Heating Degree Days (base 65°F)	1,275	1,082	887	510	211	43	5	16	116	421	713	1,092	6,371
Cooling Degree Days (base 65°F)	0	0	2	7	53	165	275	201	82	9	0	0	794
Mean Precipitation (in.)	2.09	1.89	2.71	3.31	3.72	4.26	3.44	3.33	3.07	2.56	2.93	2.73	36.04
Days With ≥ 0.1" Precipitation	6	5	7	8	8	7	6	6	6	6	7	7	79
Days With ≥ 1.0" Precipitation	0	0	0	1	1	1	1	1	1	0	0	0	6
Mean Snowfall (in.)	6.7	5.2	3.6	0.3	trace	0.0	0.0	0.0	0.0	trace	0.6	na	na
Days With ≥ 1.0" Snow Depth	8	6	3	0	0	0	0	0	0	0	0	na	na

PROFILES OF OHIO / Weather: Cooperative Stations

Gallipolis *Gallia County*   Elevation: 567 ft.   Latitude: 38° 49' N   Longitude: 82° 11' W

	JAN	FEB	MAR	APR	MAY	JUN	JUL	AUG	SEP	OCT	NOV	DEC	YEAR
Mean Maximum Temp. (°F)	41.9	46.8	57.5	68.2	76.7	83.9	87.4	86.1	80.2	69.3	57.4	46.8	66.8
Mean Temp. (°F)	32.2	35.7	44.9	54.3	63.5	71.6	75.8	74.4	68.1	56.3	46.1	37.0	55.0
Mean Minimum Temp. (°F)	22.4	24.5	32.2	40.4	50.2	59.3	64.1	62.5	55.8	43.2	34.8	27.1	43.0
Extreme Maximum Temp. (°F)	76	77	86	91	96	102	105	105	98	87	82	80	105
Extreme Minimum Temp. (°F)	-28	-14	-8	16	26	34	44	40	31	17	6	-13	-28
Days Maximum Temp. ≥ 90°F	0	0	0	0	1	5	11	8	3	0	0	0	28
Days Maximum Temp. ≤ 32°F	7	4	1	0	0	0	0	0	0	0	0	3	15
Days Minimum Temp. ≤ 32°F	25	21	17	7	1	0	0	0	0	4	14	22	111
Days Minimum Temp. ≤ 0°F	2	1	0	0	0	0	0	0	0	0	0	0	3
Heating Degree Days (base 65°F)	1,012	821	621	329	119	14	1	3	49	281	562	861	4,673
Cooling Degree Days (base 65°F)	0	0	3	16	81	228	359	306	142	19	2	0	1,156
Mean Precipitation (in.)	2.90	2.90	3.60	3.29	3.98	3.88	4.32	3.66	2.98	2.79	3.09	3.27	40.66
Days With ≥ 0.1" Precipitation	7	7	8	8	8	8	7	7	6	6	7	7	86
Days With ≥ 1.0" Precipitation	0	0	0	0	1	1	1	1	1	1	1	1	8
Mean Snowfall (in.)	6.1	4.6	2.2	trace	0.0	0.0	0.0	0.0	0.0	trace	0.3	1.0	14.2
Days With ≥ 1.0" Snow Depth	7	6	1	0	0	0	0	0	0	0	0	1	15

Greenville Water Plant *Darke County*   Elevation: 1,023 ft.   Latitude: 40° 06' N   Longitude: 84° 39' W

	JAN	FEB	MAR	APR	MAY	JUN	JUL	AUG	SEP	OCT	NOV	DEC	YEAR
Mean Maximum Temp. (°F)	32.2	36.7	47.7	60.4	71.5	80.2	84.1	82.4	76.6	64.1	50.0	38.3	60.3
Mean Temp. (°F)	23.6	27.2	37.6	49.0	59.8	68.9	72.7	70.3	63.5	51.6	40.6	29.9	49.6
Mean Minimum Temp. (°F)	15.0	17.7	27.5	37.6	48.1	57.6	61.1	58.2	50.4	39.0	31.1	21.5	38.7
Extreme Maximum Temp. (°F)	63	72	82	89	92	101	104	101	94	87	78	72	104
Extreme Minimum Temp. (°F)	-33	-23	-14	10	26	37	43	36	28	14	1	-21	-33
Days Maximum Temp. ≥ 90°F	0	0	0	0	0	3	5	3	2	0	0	0	13
Days Maximum Temp. ≤ 32°F	15	11	4	0	0	0	0	0	0	0	1	9	40
Days Minimum Temp. ≤ 32°F	29	25	23	9	1	0	0	0	0	8	18	26	139
Days Minimum Temp. ≤ 0°F	5	4	0	0	0	0	0	0	0	0	0	2	11
Heating Degree Days (base 65°F)	1,277	1,060	843	481	202	39	6	17	121	417	727	1,081	6,271
Cooling Degree Days (base 65°F)	0	0	1	6	48	168	260	193	80	8	0	0	764
Mean Precipitation (in.)	2.16	2.05	2.91	3.56	4.04	3.98	4.24	3.18	2.47	2.73	3.11	2.69	37.12
Days With ≥ 0.1" Precipitation	5	5	7	8	8	7	6	6	5	6	7	6	76
Days With ≥ 1.0" Precipitation	0	0	0	1	1	1	1	1	1	1	1	0	8
Mean Snowfall (in.)	8.3	5.6	3.0	0.5	trace	0.0	0.0	0.0	0.0	0.2	0.8	3.3	21.7
Days With ≥ 1.0" Snow Depth	na	na	2	0	0	0	0	0	0	0	na	na	na

Hannibal Lock & Dam *Monroe County*   Elevation: 620 ft.   Latitude: 39° 40' N   Longitude: 80° 52' W

	JAN	FEB	MAR	APR	MAY	JUN	JUL	AUG	SEP	OCT	NOV	DEC	YEAR
Mean Maximum Temp. (°F)	37.1	41.5	51.4	63.0	72.6	80.6	84.1	82.7	76.4	65.0	53.6	42.2	62.5
Mean Temp. (°F)	28.4	31.6	40.3	50.3	60.3	68.6	73.3	72.1	65.4	53.5	43.6	33.6	51.8
Mean Minimum Temp. (°F)	19.6	21.7	29.0	37.6	47.8	56.6	62.4	61.4	54.4	41.9	33.4	25.1	40.9
Extreme Maximum Temp. (°F)	71	73	83	90	91	96	99	100	95	85	80	74	100
Extreme Minimum Temp. (°F)	-24	-11	-8	18	26	38	42	42	34	22	6	-14	-24
Days Maximum Temp. ≥ 90°F	0	0	0	0	0	2	6	4	1	0	0	0	13
Days Maximum Temp. ≤ 32°F	11	6	2	0	0	0	0	0	0	0	0	6	25
Days Minimum Temp. ≤ 32°F	27	23	21	9	1	0	0	0	0	3	15	24	123
Days Minimum Temp. ≤ 0°F	2	1	0	0	0	0	0	0	0	0	0	0	3
Heating Degree Days (base 65°F)	1,129	936	758	439	181	32	3	7	76	357	637	965	5,520
Cooling Degree Days (base 65°F)	0	0	0	5	37	147	272	235	91	8	0	0	795
Mean Precipitation (in.)	3.08	2.57	3.57	3.25	4.12	3.65	4.63	3.41	3.01	2.63	3.33	3.09	40.34
Days With ≥ 0.1" Precipitation	7	7	8	8	9	7	7	6	5	6	7	7	84
Days With ≥ 1.0" Precipitation	1	0	1	0	1	1	1	1	1	1	0	0	8
Mean Snowfall (in.)	na	na	na	trace	0.0	0.0	0.0	0.0	0.0	0.0	trace	na	na
Days With ≥ 1.0" Snow Depth	na	na	1	0	0	0	0	0	0	0	0	na	na

Hillsboro *Highland County*   Elevation: 1,099 ft.   Latitude: 39° 12' N   Longitude: 83° 37' W

	JAN	FEB	MAR	APR	MAY	JUN	JUL	AUG	SEP	OCT	NOV	DEC	YEAR
Mean Maximum Temp. (°F)	35.6	40.5	51.1	62.7	71.7	79.3	83.3	81.9	76.3	64.9	52.3	41.3	61.7
Mean Temp. (°F)	27.8	31.6	41.4	52.0	61.6	69.7	73.9	72.1	65.9	54.6	43.6	33.5	52.3
Mean Minimum Temp. (°F)	19.9	22.8	31.5	41.4	51.4	60.0	64.3	62.3	55.5	44.1	34.9	25.7	42.8
Extreme Maximum Temp. (°F)	72	73	81	87	89	98	100	99	96	87	80	76	100
Extreme Minimum Temp. (°F)	-23	-9	-1	16	32	37	46	40	25	20	4	-21	-23
Days Maximum Temp. ≥ 90°F	0	0	0	0	0	1	4	2	1	0	0	0	8
Days Maximum Temp. ≤ 32°F	12	8	2	0	0	0	0	0	0	0	1	6	29
Days Minimum Temp. ≤ 32°F	27	22	18	5	0	0	0	0	0	3	14	23	112
Days Minimum Temp. ≤ 0°F	2	1	0	0	0	0	0	0	0	0	0	1	4
Heating Degree Days (base 65°F)	1,148	935	729	396	157	25	2	7	76	332	637	970	5,414
Cooling Degree Days (base 65°F)	0	0	2	14	54	176	289	238	105	16	1	0	895
Mean Precipitation (in.)	2.94	2.68	3.79	4.11	4.70	4.21	4.03	4.27	3.36	2.90	3.22	3.12	43.33
Days With ≥ 0.1" Precipitation	7	6	8	8	9	8	7	6	5	6	7	6	83
Days With ≥ 1.0" Precipitation	0	0	1	1	1	1	1	1	1	1	1	1	10
Mean Snowfall (in.)	7.3	5.0	3.8	0.6	trace	0.0	0.0	0.0	0.0	0.2	0.8	2.8	20.5
Days With ≥ 1.0" Snow Depth	9	8	3	0	0	0	0	0	0	0	0	4	24

PROFILES OF OHIO / Weather: Cooperative Stations 535

Hiram *Portage County*   Elevation: 1,227 ft.   Latitude: 41° 18' N   Longitude: 81° 09' W

	JAN	FEB	MAR	APR	MAY	JUN	JUL	AUG	SEP	OCT	NOV	DEC	YEAR
Mean Maximum Temp. (°F)	31.7	35.8	45.8	58.5	69.6	77.3	81.6	79.9	72.8	61.0	48.5	36.9	58.3
Mean Temp. (°F)	24.1	27.4	36.3	47.9	58.8	66.7	71.4	69.8	62.8	51.5	40.7	29.9	48.9
Mean Minimum Temp. (°F)	16.5	18.8	27.1	37.2	47.9	56.1	61.0	59.7	52.9	41.9	33.0	22.8	39.6
Extreme Maximum Temp. (°F)	65	69	81	87	90	100	99	95	91	81	75	73	100
Extreme Minimum Temp. (°F)	-25	-10	-6	12	25	34	44	38	32	21	1	-15	-25
Days Maximum Temp. ≥ 90°F	0	0	0	0	0	1	2	1	0	0	0	0	4
Days Maximum Temp. ≤ 32°F	16	12	4	0	0	0	0	0	0	0	1	10	43
Days Minimum Temp. ≤ 32°F	29	25	23	10	1	0	0	0	0	4	16	27	135
Days Minimum Temp. ≤ 0°F	3	2	0	0	0	0	0	0	0	0	0	1	6
Heating Degree Days (base 65°F)	1,261	1,056	883	514	225	61	9	18	123	418	722	1,082	6,372
Cooling Degree Days (base 65°F)	0	0	1	7	36	121	223	178	63	4	0	0	633
Mean Precipitation (in.)	2.67	2.30	3.38	3.55	3.75	4.08	3.89	3.79	4.15	3.23	3.65	3.47	41.91
Days With ≥ 0.1" Precipitation	8	7	9	9	8	8	7	7	8	8	9	9	97
Days With ≥ 1.0" Precipitation	0	0	0	0	0	1	1	1	1	1	0	0	5
Mean Snowfall (in.)	16.1	12.4	10.2	1.5	trace	0.0	0.0	0.0	0.0	0.2	6.0	15.2	61.6
Days With ≥ 1.0" Snow Depth	20	17	8	1	0	0	0	0	0	0	4	14	64

Hoytville 2 NE *Wood County*   Elevation: 698 ft.   Latitude: 41° 13' N   Longitude: 83° 46' W

	JAN	FEB	MAR	APR	MAY	JUN	JUL	AUG	SEP	OCT	NOV	DEC	YEAR
Mean Maximum Temp. (°F)	31.1	34.8	46.0	59.1	71.2	80.1	83.8	81.4	75.5	63.1	48.8	36.8	59.3
Mean Temp. (°F)	23.1	26.3	36.3	47.7	59.4	68.8	72.5	69.9	63.3	51.5	40.3	29.3	49.0
Mean Minimum Temp. (°F)	15.0	17.7	26.6	36.3	47.5	57.4	61.1	58.3	51.0	39.8	31.7	21.7	38.7
Extreme Maximum Temp. (°F)	65	71	82	88	93	105	101	98	95	87	78	69	105
Extreme Minimum Temp. (°F)	-22	-15	-9	1	25	36	41	37	27	17	8	-19	-22
Days Maximum Temp. ≥ 90°F	0	0	0	0	1	4	5	3	1	0	0	0	14
Days Maximum Temp. ≤ 32°F	16	12	4	0	0	0	0	0	0	0	1	10	43
Days Minimum Temp. ≤ 32°F	29	25	23	11	1	0	0	0	0	7	18	27	141
Days Minimum Temp. ≤ 0°F	5	3	0	0	0	0	0	0	0	0	0	2	10
Heating Degree Days (base 65°F)	1,293	1,087	884	520	218	43	8	22	125	420	735	1,101	6,456
Cooling Degree Days (base 65°F)	0	0	1	7	48	162	255	183	76	8	0	0	740
Mean Precipitation (in.)	1.78	1.70	2.51	3.26	3.41	3.60	3.86	3.54	2.64	2.40	2.79	2.40	33.89
Days With ≥ 0.1" Precipitation	5	4	6	8	7	7	7	6	5	5	7	6	73
Days With ≥ 1.0" Precipitation	0	0	0	1	1	1	1	1	0	0	0	0	5
Mean Snowfall (in.)	7.5	5.5	3.4	1.0	trace	0.0	0.0	0.0	0.0	trace	1.3	5.2	23.9
Days With ≥ 1.0" Snow Depth	15	11	4	1	0	0	0	0	0	0	0	1	8	40

Irwin *Union County*   Elevation: 1,007 ft.   Latitude: 40° 07' N   Longitude: 83° 29' W

	JAN	FEB	MAR	APR	MAY	JUN	JUL	AUG	SEP	OCT	NOV	DEC	YEAR
Mean Maximum Temp. (°F)	34.5	39.6	51.5	64.0	74.3	82.5	85.6	84.2	78.3	66.7	51.8	39.6	62.7
Mean Temp. (°F)	25.8	29.9	40.4	51.1	61.5	70.0	73.3	71.5	65.0	53.8	42.2	31.3	51.3
Mean Minimum Temp. (°F)	17.1	20.2	29.3	38.2	48.6	57.5	61.0	58.8	51.7	40.8	32.5	23.2	39.9
Extreme Maximum Temp. (°F)	66	72	82	88	93	101	101	101	95	88	79	72	101
Extreme Minimum Temp. (°F)	-28	-21	-17	11	27	34	41	35	28	15	2	-19	-28
Days Maximum Temp. ≥ 90°F	0	0	0	0	1	4	7	4	1	0	0	0	17
Days Maximum Temp. ≤ 32°F	13	9	2	0	0	0	0	0	0	0	1	7	32
Days Minimum Temp. ≤ 32°F	28	24	20	10	1	0	0	0	1	7	16	25	132
Days Minimum Temp. ≤ 0°F	5	3	0	0	0	0	0	0	0	0	0	1	9
Heating Degree Days (base 65°F)	1,208	984	759	419	163	24	4	11	90	352	678	1,037	5,729
Cooling Degree Days (base 65°F)	0	0	1	8	58	183	281	230	93	11	0	0	865
Mean Precipitation (in.)	2.25	1.93	2.62	3.52	4.14	4.28	4.67	3.67	2.92	2.57	3.13	2.68	38.38
Days With ≥ 0.1" Precipitation	5	4	6	7	8	7	7	6	5	5	6	6	72
Days With ≥ 1.0" Precipitation	0	0	0	1	1	1	1	1	1	0	1	1	8
Mean Snowfall (in.)	6.8	4.5	2.5	0.8	trace	0.0	0.0	0.0	0.0	trace	1.0	na	na
Days With ≥ 1.0" Snow Depth	10	7	2	0	0	0	0	0	0	0	1	na	na

Jackson 3 NW *Jackson County*   Elevation: 797 ft.   Latitude: 39° 05' N   Longitude: 82° 42' W

	JAN	FEB	MAR	APR	MAY	JUN	JUL	AUG	SEP	OCT	NOV	DEC	YEAR
Mean Maximum Temp. (°F)	38.3	42.9	53.1	64.8	73.9	81.0	84.6	83.3	77.3	65.8	54.0	43.3	63.5
Mean Temp. (°F)	28.6	32.4	41.4	51.5	61.1	69.0	73.3	71.9	65.3	53.2	43.1	33.8	52.1
Mean Minimum Temp. (°F)	19.1	21.9	29.6	38.1	48.2	57.0	61.9	60.5	53.3	40.5	32.2	24.2	40.5
Extreme Maximum Temp. (°F)	74	76	85	91	91	100	101	102	96	86	81	79	102
Extreme Minimum Temp. (°F)	-28	-14	-15	16	26	31	40	36	30	17	-5	-20	-28
Days Maximum Temp. ≥ 90°F	0	0	0	0	0	2	6	4	1	0	0	0	13
Days Maximum Temp. ≤ 32°F	10	6	2	0	0	0	0	0	0	0	0	6	24
Days Minimum Temp. ≤ 32°F	27	23	19	9	2	0	0	0	0	7	16	24	127
Days Minimum Temp. ≤ 0°F	2	2	0	0	0	0	0	0	0	0	0	1	5
Heating Degree Days (base 65°F)	1,120	914	728	407	169	33	4	9	85	370	651	961	5,451
Cooling Degree Days (base 65°F)	0	0	3	10	57	171	288	240	103	12	1	0	885
Mean Precipitation (in.)	2.76	2.76	3.75	3.43	3.96	4.14	4.03	3.92	3.17	2.82	3.12	3.27	41.13
Days With ≥ 0.1" Precipitation	6	7	8	8	8	8	7	7	6	6	6	8	85
Days With ≥ 1.0" Precipitation	0	0	1	0	1	1	1	1	1	0	1	1	8
Mean Snowfall (in.)	na	na	na	0.7	0.0	0.0	0.0	0.0	0.0	0.0	na	na	na
Days With ≥ 1.0" Snow Depth	na	na	na	0	0	0	0	0	0	0	0	na	na

PROFILES OF OHIO / Weather: Cooperative Stations

Kenton *Hardin County*   Elevation: 994 ft.   Latitude: 40° 39' N   Longitude: 83° 36' W

	JAN	FEB	MAR	APR	MAY	JUN	JUL	AUG	SEP	OCT	NOV	DEC	YEAR
Mean Maximum Temp. (°F)	32.4	37.0	47.3	60.2	72.0	80.9	85.1	82.9	76.3	63.9	49.7	37.7	60.5
Mean Temp. (°F)	24.3	28.2	37.7	49.1	60.5	69.5	73.9	71.4	64.5	52.6	40.9	30.0	50.2
Mean Minimum Temp. (°F)	15.9	19.0	28.0	37.9	49.0	58.2	62.4	59.9	52.7	41.1	32.1	22.2	39.8
Extreme Maximum Temp. (°F)	64	71	82	89	93	104	103	103	96	87	78	71	104
Extreme Minimum Temp. (°F)	-22	-17	-5	10	26	36	42	39	27	16	3	-18	-22
Days Maximum Temp. ≥ 90°F	0	0	0	0	1	4	8	4	2	0	0	0	19
Days Maximum Temp. ≤ 32°F	15	10	4	0	0	0	0	0	0	0	2	9	40
Days Minimum Temp. ≤ 32°F	29	25	22	9	1	0	0	0	0	5	16	27	134
Days Minimum Temp. ≤ 0°F	4	3	0	0	0	0	0	0	0	0	0	1	8
Heating Degree Days (base 65°F)	1,256	1,032	841	478	189	37	4	14	103	389	715	1,080	6,138
Cooling Degree Days (base 65°F)	0	0	1	10	60	190	303	237	99	11	0	0	911
Mean Precipitation (in.)	2.23	2.02	2.75	3.48	3.84	3.53	4.01	3.30	2.61	2.14	2.84	2.72	35.47
Days With ≥ 0.1" Precipitation	6	6	7	8	7	7	7	6	5	5	7	7	78
Days With ≥ 1.0" Precipitation	0	0	0	1	1	1	1	1	1	0	0	0	6
Mean Snowfall (in.)	10.0	6.4	4.2	0.6	0.0	0.0	0.0	0.0	0.0	trace	1.2	5.4	27.8
Days With ≥ 1.0" Snow Depth	na	na	4	0	0	0	0	0	0	0	1	6	na

Lancaster 2 NW *Fairfield County*   Elevation: 859 ft.   Latitude: 39° 44' N   Longitude: 82° 38' W

	JAN	FEB	MAR	APR	MAY	JUN	JUL	AUG	SEP	OCT	NOV	DEC	YEAR
Mean Maximum Temp. (°F)	34.5	38.7	49.6	61.6	71.8	80.4	84.2	82.9	76.9	65.1	51.8	40.5	61.5
Mean Temp. (°F)	25.8	29.1	38.9	49.5	59.7	68.9	72.8	71.4	64.6	52.8	42.1	32.0	50.6
Mean Minimum Temp. (°F)	17.0	19.4	28.2	37.4	47.6	57.3	61.6	59.8	52.4	40.4	32.4	23.4	39.7
Extreme Maximum Temp. (°F)	68	71	82	89	92	101	99	101	96	86	80	78	101
Extreme Minimum Temp. (°F)	-24	-15	-7	8	27	34	41	35	30	19	3	-20	-24
Days Maximum Temp. ≥ 90°F	0	0	0	0	0	2	6	4	1	0	0	0	13
Days Maximum Temp. ≤ 32°F	14	9	3	0	0	0	0	0	0	0	1	7	34
Days Minimum Temp. ≤ 32°F	28	23	22	10	1	0	0	0	0	7	16	24	131
Days Minimum Temp. ≤ 0°F	4	2	0	0	0	0	0	0	0	0	0	1	7
Heating Degree Days (base 65°F)	1,209	1,008	803	468	206	37	6	14	104	381	681	1,017	5,934
Cooling Degree Days (base 65°F)	0	0	2	11	48	170	273	233	99	11	1	0	848
Mean Precipitation (in.)	2.28	2.17	2.65	3.22	4.18	3.82	4.37	3.64	2.76	2.46	3.09	2.91	37.55
Days With ≥ 0.1" Precipitation	5	5	6	6	7	6	7	6	5	5	7	6	71
Days With ≥ 1.0" Precipitation	0	0	1	1	1	1	1	1	1	0	1	0	8
Mean Snowfall (in.)	na	na	na	0.7	0.0	0.0	0.0	0.0	0.0	trace	0.3	na	na
Days With ≥ 1.0" Snow Depth	na	na	na	0	0	0	0	0	0	0	na	na	na

Lima WWTP *Allen County*   Elevation: 849 ft.   Latitude: 40° 43' N   Longitude: 84° 08' W

	JAN	FEB	MAR	APR	MAY	JUN	JUL	AUG	SEP	OCT	NOV	DEC	YEAR
Mean Maximum Temp. (°F)	33.1	37.6	48.3	60.9	72.5	80.9	84.7	82.5	76.6	64.3	50.4	38.7	60.9
Mean Temp. (°F)	25.6	29.4	39.1	50.3	61.6	70.5	74.4	72.4	66.0	54.1	42.5	31.7	51.5
Mean Minimum Temp. (°F)	18.0	21.1	29.9	39.7	50.7	60.0	64.1	62.2	55.3	43.9	34.4	24.5	42.0
Extreme Maximum Temp. (°F)	64	71	81	89	93	97	100	99	95	94	77	70	100
Extreme Minimum Temp. (°F)	-21	-15	-3	8	27	40	46	42	30	19	6	-17	-21
Days Maximum Temp. ≥ 90°F	0	0	0	0	1	3	6	3	1	0	0	0	14
Days Maximum Temp. ≤ 32°F	14	10	3	0	0	0	0	0	0	0	2	8	37
Days Minimum Temp. ≤ 32°F	28	23	20	7	1	0	0	0	0	3	14	24	120
Days Minimum Temp. ≤ 0°F	3	1	0	0	0	0	0	0	0	0	0	1	5
Heating Degree Days (base 65°F)	1,217	996	797	443	166	26	2	8	79	344	668	1,027	5,773
Cooling Degree Days (base 65°F)	0	0	2	10	66	201	310	251	113	15	0	0	968
Mean Precipitation (in.)	2.20	1.94	2.70	3.48	3.91	4.04	4.36	3.28	3.08	2.38	3.13	2.65	37.15
Days With ≥ 0.1" Precipitation	6	5	6	8	8	7	7	6	6	6	7	6	78
Days With ≥ 1.0" Precipitation	0	0	0	1	1	1	1	1	1	0	0	0	6
Mean Snowfall (in.)	na	na	na	0.1	0.0	0.0	0.0	0.0	0.0	trace	trace	na	na
Days With ≥ 1.0" Snow Depth	na	na	na	0	0	0	0	0	0	0	0	na	na

London *Madison County*   Elevation: 1,017 ft.   Latitude: 39° 53' N   Longitude: 83° 27' W

	JAN	FEB	MAR	APR	MAY	JUN	JUL	AUG	SEP	OCT	NOV	DEC	YEAR
Mean Maximum Temp. (°F)	34.4	39.1	50.4	62.6	73.2	81.5	85.1	83.0	77.1	65.3	51.3	40.0	61.9
Mean Temp. (°F)	26.3	30.0	39.9	50.4	61.0	69.8	73.5	71.4	64.7	53.2	42.1	32.1	51.2
Mean Minimum Temp. (°F)	18.1	20.8	29.3	38.2	48.7	58.0	61.8	59.7	52.4	41.0	32.8	24.2	40.4
Extreme Maximum Temp. (°F)	67	71	82	88	92	102	100	101	95	88	79	74	102
Extreme Minimum Temp. (°F)	-24	-19	-14	12	26	35	42	38	30	16	0	-18	-24
Days Maximum Temp. ≥ 90°F	0	0	0	0	0	4	7	4	1	0	0	0	16
Days Maximum Temp. ≤ 32°F	13	9	2	0	0	0	0	0	0	0	1	7	32
Days Minimum Temp. ≤ 32°F	27	23	20	9	1	0	0	0	0	6	16	24	126
Days Minimum Temp. ≤ 0°F	4	2	0	0	0	0	0	0	0	0	0	1	7
Heating Degree Days (base 65°F)	1,194	982	774	440	174	30	4	12	99	370	681	1,014	5,774
Cooling Degree Days (base 65°F)	0	0	1	7	55	184	286	222	93	10	0	0	858
Mean Precipitation (in.)	2.38	2.16	2.80	3.59	4.07	4.30	3.99	3.34	2.82	2.58	3.28	2.96	38.27
Days With ≥ 0.1" Precipitation	5	5	7	8	8	7	7	6	5	5	7	7	77
Days With ≥ 1.0" Precipitation	0	0	1	1	1	1	1	1	1	0	1	0	7
Mean Snowfall (in.)	6.9	na	na	0.4	0.0	0.0	0.0	0.0	0.0	0.2	0.5	na	na
Days With ≥ 1.0" Snow Depth	na	na	2	0	0	0	0	0	0	0	0	na	na

PROFILES OF OHIO / Weather: Cooperative Stations 537

Mansfield 5 W *Richland County* Elevation: 1,348 ft. Latitude: 40° 46' N Longitude: 82° 37' W

	JAN	FEB	MAR	APR	MAY	JUN	JUL	AUG	SEP	OCT	NOV	DEC	YEAR
Mean Maximum Temp. (°F)	31.9	35.9	46.6	59.2	69.9	78.2	81.9	80.2	73.5	61.8	48.7	37.5	58.8
Mean Temp. (°F)	23.7	27.1	36.7	47.8	58.5	66.9	70.8	69.2	62.7	51.3	40.2	29.7	48.7
Mean Minimum Temp. (°F)	15.4	18.3	26.7	36.3	47.0	55.5	59.7	58.2	51.7	40.7	31.6	21.9	38.6
Extreme Maximum Temp. (°F)	66	69	81	87	89	100	99	97	94	84	76	69	100
Extreme Minimum Temp. (°F)	-25	-22	-11	5	18	28	38	37	25	15	3	-19	-25
Days Maximum Temp. ≥ 90°F	0	0	0	0	0	1	3	1	0	0	0	0	5
Days Maximum Temp. ≤ 32°F	15	12	5	0	0	0	0	0	0	0	2	10	44
Days Minimum Temp. ≤ 32°F	29	25	23	12	2	0	0	0	1	6	17	26	141
Days Minimum Temp. ≤ 0°F	5	3	1	0	0	0	0	0	0	0	0	1	10
Heating Degree Days (base 65°F)	1,276	1,063	871	518	232	59	14	22	133	426	739	1,087	6,440
Cooling Degree Days (base 65°F)	0	0	1	6	36	127	212	164	66	7	0	0	619
Mean Precipitation (in.)	2.08	1.69	2.65	3.54	4.14	4.16	3.92	3.63	3.27	2.51	2.91	2.55	37.05
Days With ≥ 0.1" Precipitation	5	5	7	8	9	7	7	7	6	6	6	6	79
Days With ≥ 1.0" Precipitation	0	0	0	1	1	1	1	1	1	0	1	0	7
Mean Snowfall (in.)	na	na	na	0.3	trace	0.0	0.0	0.0	0.0	trace	1.0	na	na
Days With ≥ 1.0" Snow Depth	na	na	3	0	0	0	0	0	0	0	1	na	na

Marietta WWTP *Washington County* Elevation: 577 ft. Latitude: 39° 25' N Longitude: 81° 26' W

	JAN	FEB	MAR	APR	MAY	JUN	JUL	AUG	SEP	OCT	NOV	DEC	YEAR
Mean Maximum Temp. (°F)	39.5	43.8	54.2	65.5	74.7	82.2	85.8	84.5	78.2	66.9	54.9	44.7	64.6
Mean Temp. (°F)	30.8	33.9	43.1	53.1	62.6	70.8	74.9	73.5	66.9	55.1	44.8	36.0	53.8
Mean Minimum Temp. (°F)	22.1	24.0	31.9	40.6	50.5	59.4	64.0	62.5	55.5	43.2	34.8	27.2	43.0
Extreme Maximum Temp. (°F)	73	75	85	91	93	99	102	100	96	86	81	78	102
Extreme Minimum Temp. (°F)	-23	-10	0	19	29	37	44	38	33	20	10	-11	-23
Days Maximum Temp. ≥ 90°F	0	0	0	0	1	3	8	6	2	0	0	0	20
Days Maximum Temp. ≤ 32°F	9	5	1	0	0	0	0	0	0	0	0	4	19
Days Minimum Temp. ≤ 32°F	25	22	17	6	1	0	0	0	0	3	14	22	110
Days Minimum Temp. ≤ 0°F	1	1	0	0	0	0	0	0	0	0	0	0	2
Heating Degree Days (base 65°F)	1,053	872	674	362	134	19	1	4	61	313	599	892	4,984
Cooling Degree Days (base 65°F)	0	0	2	11	64	205	332	274	116	13	1	0	1,018
Mean Precipitation (in.)	3.12	2.75	3.69	3.10	4.04	4.40	4.22	4.16	3.31	2.87	3.17	3.37	42.20
Days With ≥ 0.1" Precipitation	8	7	8	8	9	8	7	7	6	6	7	8	89
Days With ≥ 1.0" Precipitation	0	0	1	0	1	1	1	1	1	1	0	0	7
Mean Snowfall (in.)	7.2	na	3.4	0.5	0.0	0.0	0.0	0.0	0.0	trace	0.6	2.6	na
Days With ≥ 1.0" Snow Depth	9	na	1	0	0	0	0	0	0	0	0	2	na

Marion 2 N *Marion County* Elevation: 964 ft. Latitude: 40° 37' N Longitude: 83° 08' W

	JAN	FEB	MAR	APR	MAY	JUN	JUL	AUG	SEP	OCT	NOV	DEC	YEAR
Mean Maximum Temp. (°F)	32.3	36.7	47.3	60.2	71.1	80.3	84.0	82.2	75.7	63.5	49.8	38.0	60.1
Mean Temp. (°F)	24.1	27.7	37.5	48.8	59.7	69.2	73.0	70.8	63.8	52.1	41.0	30.4	49.8
Mean Minimum Temp. (°F)	15.8	18.7	27.6	37.4	48.3	58.0	61.9	59.3	51.9	40.7	32.1	22.8	39.6
Extreme Maximum Temp. (°F)	67	72	81	87	91	103	100	99	97	90	79	73	103
Extreme Minimum Temp. (°F)	-23	-20	-5	8	25	36	43	35	24	17	4	-19	-23
Days Maximum Temp. ≥ 90°F	0	0	0	0	1	4	6	4	2	0	0	0	17
Days Maximum Temp. ≤ 32°F	15	11	4	0	0	0	0	0	0	0	1	9	40
Days Minimum Temp. ≤ 32°F	29	25	22	10	1	0	0	0	0	6	17	26	136
Days Minimum Temp. ≤ 0°F	4	3	0	0	0	0	0	0	0	0	0	1	8
Heating Degree Days (base 65°F)	1,262	1,047	848	488	210	39	6	18	116	401	714	1,064	6,213
Cooling Degree Days (base 65°F)	0	0	2	8	51	172	270	206	83	10	0	0	802
Mean Precipitation (in.)	2.35	1.72	2.31	3.69	4.17	4.24	4.38	3.69	3.03	2.73	3.01	2.84	38.16
Days With ≥ 0.1" Precipitation	5	5	6	9	8	7	7	6	6	6	7	7	79
Days With ≥ 1.0" Precipitation	0	0	0	1	1	1	1	1	1	1	1	0	8
Mean Snowfall (in.)	9.7	5.3	3.2	0.6	0.0	0.0	0.0	0.0	0.0	trace	0.8	4.4	24.0
Days With ≥ 1.0" Snow Depth	14	10	3	0	0	0	0	0	0	0	1	5	33

Marysville *Union County* Elevation: 997 ft. Latitude: 40° 14' N Longitude: 83° 22' W

	JAN	FEB	MAR	APR	MAY	JUN	JUL	AUG	SEP	OCT	NOV	DEC	YEAR
Mean Maximum Temp. (°F)	33.5	37.8	49.0	61.2	72.2	80.4	84.2	82.3	75.7	63.5	50.0	38.7	60.7
Mean Temp. (°F)	25.8	29.2	39.2	50.2	61.1	69.7	73.7	71.7	64.8	53.0	41.7	31.5	51.0
Mean Minimum Temp. (°F)	17.9	20.7	29.4	39.1	50.0	58.8	63.1	61.0	53.8	42.4	33.3	24.1	41.1
Extreme Maximum Temp. (°F)	66	72	82	88	92	101	100	99	96	86	78	72	101
Extreme Minimum Temp. (°F)	-23	-18	-11	12	29	36	44	41	31	18	4	-20	-23
Days Maximum Temp. ≥ 90°F	0	0	0	0	0	3	6	3	1	0	0	0	13
Days Maximum Temp. ≤ 32°F	14	10	3	0	0	0	0	0	0	0	1	8	36
Days Minimum Temp. ≤ 32°F	28	24	21	7	0	0	0	0	0	4	15	25	124
Days Minimum Temp. ≤ 0°F	4	2	0	0	0	0	0	0	0	0	0	1	7
Heating Degree Days (base 65°F)	1,210	1,004	794	445	173	29	3	9	95	374	694	1,033	5,863
Cooling Degree Days (base 65°F)	0	0	2	7	58	180	292	232	95	9	0	0	875
Mean Precipitation (in.)	2.26	1.93	2.59	3.38	3.88	4.32	4.05	3.27	2.64	2.44	2.95	2.66	36.37
Days With ≥ 0.1" Precipitation	6	5	7	7	8	7	7	7	5	6	7	7	78
Days With ≥ 1.0" Precipitation	0	0	0	1	1	1	1	1	1	0	1	0	7
Mean Snowfall (in.)	6.5	4.8	3.3	0.9	0.0	0.0	0.0	0.0	0.0	trace	1.1	3.6	20.2
Days With ≥ 1.0" Snow Depth	13	8	3	0	0	0	0	0	0	0	1	5	30

PROFILES OF OHIO / Weather: Cooperative Stations

McConnelsville Lock 7 *Morgan County* Elevation: 757 ft. Latitude: 39° 39' N Longitude: 81° 51' W

	JAN	FEB	MAR	APR	MAY	JUN	JUL	AUG	SEP	OCT	NOV	DEC	YEAR
Mean Maximum Temp. (°F)	37.9	41.9	52.6	64.5	74.0	81.4	85.0	83.7	77.6	66.2	54.1	43.3	63.5
Mean Temp. (°F)	27.8	30.7	40.2	50.6	60.5	68.8	73.1	71.7	64.9	52.8	42.8	33.4	51.5
Mean Minimum Temp. (°F)	17.6	19.5	27.8	36.7	46.9	56.2	61.2	59.7	52.2	39.4	31.5	23.5	39.3
Extreme Maximum Temp. (°F)	74	75	84	91	94	99	102	99	97	87	81	77	102
Extreme Minimum Temp. (°F)	-32	-15	-11	15	26	32	40	39	31	18	1	-16	-32
Days Maximum Temp. ≥ 90°F	0	0	0	0	1	3	7	5	2	0	0	0	18
Days Maximum Temp. ≤ 32°F	11	6	1	0	0	0	0	0	0	0	0	5	23
Days Minimum Temp. ≤ 32°F	28	24	22	11	2	0	0	0	0	7	18	25	137
Days Minimum Temp. ≤ 0°F	3	3	0	0	0	0	0	0	0	0	0	1	7
Heating Degree Days (base 65°F)	1,145	962	761	433	180	32	4	9	91	377	659	973	5,626
Cooling Degree Days (base 65°F)	0	0	1	7	39	150	265	218	86	7	0	0	773
Mean Precipitation (in.)	3.03	2.49	3.48	3.64	4.37	4.14	4.85	4.35	3.22	2.79	3.38	3.22	42.96
Days With ≥ 0.1" Precipitation	8	7	8	8	9	7	8	7	6	6	7	8	89
Days With ≥ 1.0" Precipitation	0	0	1	1	1	1	1	1	1	1	1	0	9
Mean Snowfall (in.)	7.9	5.7	3.4	0.9	0.0	0.0	0.0	0.0	0.0	0.0	0.7	2.6	21.2
Days With ≥ 1.0" Snow Depth	na	5	2	0	0	0	0	0	0	0	0	2	na

Milford *Clermont County* Elevation: 518 ft. Latitude: 39° 11' N Longitude: 84° 17' W

	JAN	FEB	MAR	APR	MAY	JUN	JUL	AUG	SEP	OCT	NOV	DEC	YEAR
Mean Maximum Temp. (°F)	37.0	41.3	52.4	64.3	74.6	82.4	86.8	85.2	78.5	66.9	53.7	42.5	63.8
Mean Temp. (°F)	27.8	31.1	41.0	51.3	61.7	70.2	74.7	73.1	65.9	53.7	43.0	33.4	52.3
Mean Minimum Temp. (°F)	18.6	20.9	29.6	38.5	48.6	57.9	62.6	61.0	53.2	40.5	32.1	24.3	40.6
Extreme Maximum Temp. (°F)	72	76	84	89	93	97	104	101	98	88	81	75	104
Extreme Minimum Temp. (°F)	-25	-13	-10	18	27	36	40	41	26	12	-3	-22	-25
Days Maximum Temp. ≥ 90°F	0	0	0	0	1	4	10	8	2	0	0	0	25
Days Maximum Temp. ≤ 32°F	11	7	1	0	0	0	0	0	0	0	1	6	26
Days Minimum Temp. ≤ 32°F	27	23	20	9	1	0	0	0	0	6	16	24	126
Days Minimum Temp. ≤ 0°F	3	2	0	0	0	0	0	0	0	0	0	1	6
Heating Degree Days (base 65°F)	1,146	951	739	412	157	23	2	5	80	355	652	973	5,495
Cooling Degree Days (base 65°F)	0	0	2	8	65	202	335	279	112	13	0	0	1,016
Mean Precipitation (in.)	3.14	2.57	3.78	4.18	4.98	4.51	4.03	4.22	3.15	3.14	3.67	3.35	44.72
Days With ≥ 0.1" Precipitation	7	6	8	9	9	8	7	7	6	7	8	7	89
Days With ≥ 1.0" Precipitation	0	0	1	1	1	1	1	1	1	1	1	1	10
Mean Snowfall (in.)	5.8	4.9	2.1	0.4	trace	0.0	0.0	trace	0.0	0.1	0.4	2.2	15.9
Days With ≥ 1.0" Snow Depth	8	7	2	0	0	0	0	0	0	0	0	3	20

Millport 2 NW *Columbiana County* Elevation: 1,148 ft. Latitude: 40° 43' N Longitude: 80° 54' W

	JAN	FEB	MAR	APR	MAY	JUN	JUL	AUG	SEP	OCT	NOV	DEC	YEAR
Mean Maximum Temp. (°F)	34.7	39.1	49.5	61.5	71.3	79.6	83.3	82.0	75.1	63.4	50.7	39.8	60.8
Mean Temp. (°F)	25.6	28.9	38.3	48.5	58.4	66.8	70.8	69.2	62.5	51.1	40.9	31.3	49.4
Mean Minimum Temp. (°F)	16.5	18.7	26.9	35.5	45.4	54.0	58.3	56.5	49.8	38.7	31.1	22.7	37.8
Extreme Maximum Temp. (°F)	67	72	82	90	91	98	103	99	94	82	77	74	103
Extreme Minimum Temp. (°F)	-34	-21	-17	10	20	28	38	27	26	14	-5	-20	-34
Days Maximum Temp. ≥ 90°F	0	0	0	0	0	2	5	3	1	0	0	0	11
Days Maximum Temp. ≤ 32°F	13	8	3	0	0	0	0	0	0	0	1	8	33
Days Minimum Temp. ≤ 32°F	28	24	22	13	3	0	0	0	1	9	18	25	143
Days Minimum Temp. ≤ 0°F	5	3	1	0	0	0	0	0	0	0	0	1	10
Heating Degree Days (base 65°F)	1,214	1,012	823	492	229	54	11	22	131	428	716	1,038	6,170
Cooling Degree Days (base 65°F)	0	0	1	4	29	120	214	164	59	4	0	0	595
Mean Precipitation (in.)	2.47	2.31	3.11	3.24	4.09	3.83	4.15	3.12	3.27	2.53	3.25	3.12	38.49
Days With ≥ 0.1" Precipitation	7	7	8	8	9	8	8	6	7	6	8	8	90
Days With ≥ 1.0" Precipitation	0	0	0	0	1	1	1	1	1	0	0	0	5
Mean Snowfall (in.)	7.8	6.7	6.1	1.3	trace	0.0	0.0	0.0	0.0	trace	2.2	6.1	30.2
Days With ≥ 1.0" Snow Depth	na	na	na	0	0	0	0	0	0	0	1	na	na

Mineral Ridge Water Works *Trumbull County* Elevation: 889 ft. Latitude: 41° 09' N Longitude: 80° 47' W

	JAN	FEB	MAR	APR	MAY	JUN	JUL	AUG	SEP	OCT	NOV	DEC	YEAR
Mean Maximum Temp. (°F)	35.2	39.5	50.1	62.5	73.6	81.5	85.7	83.7	76.9	65.1	51.7	40.9	62.2
Mean Temp. (°F)	26.8	29.9	39.0	49.8	60.3	68.7	73.2	71.5	64.8	53.4	42.7	33.2	51.1
Mean Minimum Temp. (°F)	18.3	20.3	27.8	37.0	47.1	55.9	60.6	59.2	52.7	41.6	33.6	25.4	40.0
Extreme Maximum Temp. (°F)	67	73	82	90	92	98	102	100	94	91	79	74	102
Extreme Minimum Temp. (°F)	-24	-16	-6	13	24	29	41	34	26	14	4	-11	-24
Days Maximum Temp. ≥ 90°F	0	0	0	0	0	4	8	5	1	0	0	0	18
Days Maximum Temp. ≤ 32°F	12	8	2	0	0	0	0	0	0	0	1	7	30
Days Minimum Temp. ≤ 32°F	28	24	22	10	2	0	0	0	0	5	15	25	131
Days Minimum Temp. ≤ 0°F	3	2	0	0	0	0	0	0	0	0	0	0	5
Heating Degree Days (base 65°F)	1,178	984	801	457	188	38	5	12	93	361	664	980	5,761
Cooling Degree Days (base 65°F)	0	0	1	6	50	158	279	223	93	7	0	0	817
Mean Precipitation (in.)	2.16	1.82	2.67	3.11	3.41	4.32	4.19	3.34	3.97	2.55	2.99	2.68	37.21
Days With ≥ 0.1" Precipitation	6	6	7	7	8	8	7	6	7	6	7	7	82
Days With ≥ 1.0" Precipitation	0	0	0	0	0	1	1	1	1	0	0	0	4
Mean Snowfall (in.)	9.8	6.9	7.1	1.1	trace	0.0	0.0	0.0	0.0	trace	1.8	7.8	34.5
Days With ≥ 1.0" Snow Depth	16	13	4	0	0	0	0	0	0	0	1	7	41

PROFILES OF OHIO / Weather: Cooperative Stations

Montpelier Williams County   Elevation: 859 ft.   Latitude: 41° 35' N   Longitude: 84° 36' W

	JAN	FEB	MAR	APR	MAY	JUN	JUL	AUG	SEP	OCT	NOV	DEC	YEAR
Mean Maximum Temp. (°F)	30.3	34.4	45.0	58.3	70.7	80.2	84.1	81.9	74.9	62.1	48.0	36.1	58.8
Mean Temp. (°F)	21.8	25.1	35.1	46.8	58.3	67.8	71.9	69.7	62.2	50.1	39.0	28.3	48.0
Mean Minimum Temp. (°F)	13.3	15.7	25.1	35.2	45.8	55.5	59.7	57.4	49.5	38.1	29.9	20.4	37.1
Extreme Maximum Temp. (°F)	62	71	80	88	92	104	104	102	95	89	76	69	104
Extreme Minimum Temp. (°F)	-25	-22	-7	8	26	36	43	36	28	18	5	-19	-25
Days Maximum Temp. ≥ 90°F	0	0	0	0	1	4	6	3	1	0	0	0	15
Days Maximum Temp. ≤ 32°F	17	12	4	0	0	0	0	0	0	0	2	10	45
Days Minimum Temp. ≤ 32°F	30	27	25	12	2	0	0	0	1	9	20	28	154
Days Minimum Temp. ≤ 0°F	6	4	0	0	0	0	0	0	0	0	0	2	12
Heating Degree Days (base 65°F)	1,332	1,121	922	544	239	50	9	22	140	459	774	1,133	6,745
Cooling Degree Days (base 65°F)	0	0	1	5	39	152	248	187	64	4	0	0	700
Mean Precipitation (in.)	1.92	1.89	2.86	3.60	3.54	3.53	3.47	3.57	3.22	2.55	3.13	2.54	35.82
Days With ≥ 0.1" Precipitation	5	5	7	8	7	7	7	7	6	6	7	7	79
Days With ≥ 1.0" Precipitation	0	0	0	1	1	1	1	1	1	0	0	0	6
Mean Snowfall (in.)	9.9	8.5	4.5	0.8	0.0	0.0	0.0	0.0	0.0	0.2	1.9	8.1	33.9
Days With ≥ 1.0" Snow Depth	17	14	5	0	0	0	0	0	0	0	2	8	46

Napoleon Henry County   Elevation: 679 ft.   Latitude: 41° 22' N   Longitude: 84° 00' W

	JAN	FEB	MAR	APR	MAY	JUN	JUL	AUG	SEP	OCT	NOV	DEC	YEAR
Mean Maximum Temp. (°F)	31.1	35.1	47.3	60.2	72.3	81.5	85.0	83.0	75.9	63.9	49.8	37.1	60.2
Mean Temp. (°F)	23.2	26.5	37.4	48.6	60.1	69.5	73.5	71.3	64.1	52.7	41.2	29.6	49.8
Mean Minimum Temp. (°F)	15.2	17.7	27.4	37.0	47.8	57.4	62.0	59.5	52.3	41.4	32.6	22.0	39.4
Extreme Maximum Temp. (°F)	62	69	80	88	93	105	104	99	95	88	77	70	105
Extreme Minimum Temp. (°F)	-24	-13	-7	5	28	39	40	38	27	22	6	-18	-24
Days Maximum Temp. ≥ 90°F	0	0	0	0	1	4	7	4	1	0	0	0	17
Days Maximum Temp. ≤ 32°F	16	11	3	0	0	0	0	0	0	0	1	9	40
Days Minimum Temp. ≤ 32°F	29	25	22	10	1	0	0	0	1	5	16	26	135
Days Minimum Temp. ≤ 0°F	4	3	0	0	0	0	0	0	0	0	0	2	9
Heating Degree Days (base 65°F)	1,290	1,083	850	493	200	33	4	14	110	383	708	1,091	6,259
Cooling Degree Days (base 65°F)	0	0	1	8	48	160	272	208	79	6	0	0	782
Mean Precipitation (in.)	1.96	1.65	2.68	3.62	3.52	3.40	3.94	3.42	2.72	2.52	2.91	2.47	34.81
Days With ≥ 0.1" Precipitation	5	5	6	8	7	7	7	6	6	6	6	7	76
Days With ≥ 1.0" Precipitation	0	0	0	1	1	1	1	1	0	0	0	0	5
Mean Snowfall (in.)	8.7	5.8	2.8	1.1	0.0	0.0	0.0	0.0	0.0	0.1	0.9	5.2	24.6
Days With ≥ 1.0" Snow Depth	15	12	3	0	0	0	0	0	0	0	0	1	7	38

New Lexington 2 NW Perry County   Elevation: 889 ft.   Latitude: 39° 44' N   Longitude: 82° 13' W

	JAN	FEB	MAR	APR	MAY	JUN	JUL	AUG	SEP	OCT	NOV	DEC	YEAR
Mean Maximum Temp. (°F)	36.7	41.4	52.4	64.2	73.8	81.2	84.7	83.1	77.1	65.7	52.9	42.0	62.9
Mean Temp. (°F)	27.2	30.6	40.3	50.4	60.3	68.6	72.6	71.1	64.6	52.7	42.1	32.8	51.1
Mean Minimum Temp. (°F)	17.6	19.8	28.1	36.6	46.9	56.0	60.5	59.1	52.0	39.6	31.2	23.5	39.2
Extreme Maximum Temp. (°F)	72	74	84	91	92	100	101	100	95	85	80	77	101
Extreme Minimum Temp. (°F)	-35	-20	-11	14	27	32	40	37	30	17	-4	-24	-35
Days Maximum Temp. ≥ 90°F	0	0	0	0	1	3	6	4	1	0	0	0	15
Days Maximum Temp. ≤ 32°F	11	7	2	0	0	0	0	0	0	0	1	6	27
Days Minimum Temp. ≤ 32°F	28	24	21	12	2	0	0	0	0	8	17	25	137
Days Minimum Temp. ≤ 0°F	4	2	0	0	0	0	0	0	0	0	0	1	7
Heating Degree Days (base 65°F)	1,167	964	761	438	183	33	4	11	94	382	683	992	5,712
Cooling Degree Days (base 65°F)	0	0	1	6	39	144	251	203	81	6	0	0	731
Mean Precipitation (in.)	2.87	2.64	3.38	3.76	4.29	4.25	4.68	3.94	2.82	2.65	3.38	3.08	41.74
Days With ≥ 0.1" Precipitation	8	6	8	9	9	8	8	7	6	6	8	7	90
Days With ≥ 1.0" Precipitation	0	0	0	1	1	1	1	1	1	0	1	0	7
Mean Snowfall (in.)	9.2	5.9	3.6	0.5	trace	0.0	0.0	0.0	0.0	trace	0.7	3.0	22.9
Days With ≥ 1.0" Snow Depth	14	9	4	0	0	0	0	0	0	0	1	5	33

New Philadelphia Tuscarawas County   Elevation: 892 ft.   Latitude: 40° 30' N   Longitude: 81° 28' W

	JAN	FEB	MAR	APR	MAY	JUN	JUL	AUG	SEP	OCT	NOV	DEC	YEAR
Mean Maximum Temp. (°F)	34.7	38.7	49.1	61.0	71.9	80.3	84.1	82.9	76.1	64.1	51.2	40.1	61.2
Mean Temp. (°F)	26.2	29.1	38.2	48.7	59.1	68.1	72.2	70.9	63.9	52.0	41.7	32.0	50.2
Mean Minimum Temp. (°F)	17.6	19.4	27.3	36.3	46.3	55.8	60.2	58.8	51.6	39.8	32.2	23.8	39.1
Extreme Maximum Temp. (°F)	69	73	84	90	91	99	102	99	96	87	79	76	102
Extreme Minimum Temp. (°F)	-22	-12	-5	13	25	30	42	36	30	18	4	-16	-22
Days Maximum Temp. ≥ 90°F	0	0	0	0	0	3	6	4	1	0	0	0	14
Days Maximum Temp. ≤ 32°F	13	9	3	0	0	0	0	0	0	0	1	7	33
Days Minimum Temp. ≤ 32°F	28	24	22	12	2	0	0	0	0	7	17	25	137
Days Minimum Temp. ≤ 0°F	3	3	0	0	0	0	0	0	0	0	0	1	7
Heating Degree Days (base 65°F)	1,197	1,008	824	491	218	46	8	16	112	402	692	1,017	6,031
Cooling Degree Days (base 65°F)	0	0	1	7	41	147	253	211	83	7	1	0	751
Mean Precipitation (in.)	2.74	2.40	3.22	3.54	4.08	4.43	4.10	4.21	3.22	2.62	3.28	3.04	40.88
Days With ≥ 0.1" Precipitation	6	6	8	8	8	8	7	7	6	6	7	7	84
Days With ≥ 1.0" Precipitation	0	0	0	1	1	1	1	1	1	0	1	0	7
Mean Snowfall (in.)	9.9	6.6	5.1	1.5	trace	0.0	0.0	0.0	0.0	trace	1.4	5.2	29.7
Days With ≥ 1.0" Snow Depth	15	11	5	0	0	0	0	0	0	0	1	6	38

PROFILES OF OHIO / Weather: Cooperative Stations

Newark Water Works *Licking County* Elevation: 833 ft.   Latitude: 40° 05' N   Longitude: 81° 25' W

	JAN	FEB	MAR	APR	MAY	JUN	JUL	AUG	SEP	OCT	NOV	DEC	YEAR
Mean Maximum Temp. (°F)	35.4	39.9	51.0	63.1	73.3	81.3	84.9	83.0	76.5	64.6	51.8	40.6	62.1
Mean Temp. (°F)	27.3	30.8	40.6	51.1	61.0	69.5	73.4	71.7	64.9	53.0	42.5	32.7	51.5
Mean Minimum Temp. (°F)	19.1	21.6	30.2	39.0	48.7	57.7	61.9	60.3	53.2	41.4	33.1	24.8	40.9
Extreme Maximum Temp. (°F)	69	73	82	89	91	100	100	100	96	87	78	76	100
Extreme Minimum Temp. (°F)	-24	-14	-7	15	29	32	41	38	31	19	3	-17	-24
Days Maximum Temp. ≥ 90°F	0	0	0	0	0	3	6	4	1	0	0	0	14
Days Maximum Temp. ≤ 32°F	12	8	2	0	0	0	0	0	0	0	1	7	30
Days Minimum Temp. ≤ 32°F	27	23	19	9	1	0	0	0	0	5	15	24	123
Days Minimum Temp. ≤ 0°F	3	2	0	0	0	0	0	0	0	0	0	1	6
Heating Degree Days (base 65°F)	1,163	960	751	421	170	29	4	9	93	373	670	994	5,637
Cooling Degree Days (base 65°F)	0	0	1	7	49	170	280	224	90	8	1	0	830
Mean Precipitation (in.)	2.84	2.45	3.16	3.89	4.26	4.40	4.53	4.17	2.96	2.66	3.37	3.17	41.86
Days With ≥ 0.1" Precipitation	7	6	8	8	8	8	8	7	6	6	7	7	86
Days With ≥ 1.0" Precipitation	0	0	0	1	1	1	1	1	1	0	1	0	7
Mean Snowfall (in.)	8.4	5.3	2.8	0.9	trace	0.0	0.0	0.0	0.0	trace	0.5	2.7	20.6
Days With ≥ 1.0" Snow Depth	12	8	3	0	0	0	0	0	0	0	0	4	27

Norwalk WWTP *Huron County* Elevation: 669 ft.   Latitude: 41° 16' N   Longitude: 82° 37' W

	JAN	FEB	MAR	APR	MAY	JUN	JUL	AUG	SEP	OCT	NOV	DEC	YEAR
Mean Maximum Temp. (°F)	32.3	35.4	45.3	57.9	69.5	78.5	82.6	80.7	74.3	62.4	49.3	37.8	58.8
Mean Temp. (°F)	24.4	27.0	36.3	47.4	58.6	67.9	72.1	70.2	63.3	51.9	41.2	30.5	49.2
Mean Minimum Temp. (°F)	16.5	18.6	27.2	37.0	47.7	57.2	61.6	59.6	52.3	41.3	33.1	23.2	39.6
Extreme Maximum Temp. (°F)	65	70	81	87	91	103	98	98	94	85	77	73	103
Extreme Minimum Temp. (°F)	-21	-11	-7	7	26	33	41	41	30	17	6	-17	-21
Days Maximum Temp. ≥ 90°F	0	0	0	0	0	3	5	2	1	0	0	0	11
Days Maximum Temp. ≤ 32°F	16	12	4	0	0	0	0	0	0	0	1	9	42
Days Minimum Temp. ≤ 32°F	29	25	22	10	1	0	0	0	0	5	16	26	134
Days Minimum Temp. ≤ 0°F	4	3	0	0	0	0	0	0	0	0	0	1	8
Heating Degree Days (base 65°F)	1,253	1,065	885	529	237	56	12	20	124	408	708	1,062	6,359
Cooling Degree Days (base 65°F)	0	0	2	8	46	152	250	192	81	9	0	0	740
Mean Precipitation (in.)	2.16	1.79	2.72	3.32	3.50	4.22	3.72	3.81	3.24	2.41	2.98	2.75	36.62
Days With ≥ 0.1" Precipitation	6	5	7	8	8	7	7	6	7	6	7	7	81
Days With ≥ 1.0" Precipitation	0	0	0	0	1	1	1	1	1	0	0	0	5
Mean Snowfall (in.)	8.6	6.2	4.8	0.8	trace	0.0	0.0	trace	0.0	trace	0.9	5.4	26.7
Days With ≥ 1.0" Snow Depth	15	13	5	1	0	0	0	0	0	0	1	8	43

Oberlin *Lorain County* Elevation: 813 ft.   Latitude: 41° 16' N   Longitude: 82° 13' W

	JAN	FEB	MAR	APR	MAY	JUN	JUL	AUG	SEP	OCT	NOV	DEC	YEAR
Mean Maximum Temp. (°F)	33.0	36.8	46.9	59.6	71.2	79.9	83.9	82.0	75.3	63.3	50.0	38.3	60.0
Mean Temp. (°F)	24.6	27.6	36.9	48.0	59.0	67.9	72.2	70.1	63.2	51.8	41.0	30.3	49.4
Mean Minimum Temp. (°F)	16.1	18.4	26.7	36.4	46.8	56.0	60.5	58.2	51.0	40.3	32.1	22.3	38.7
Extreme Maximum Temp. (°F)	65	71	82	87	92	104	100	100	96	85	76	75	104
Extreme Minimum Temp. (°F)	-23	-18	-15	11	24	30	38	32	25	16	4	-18	-23
Days Maximum Temp. ≥ 90°F	0	0	0	0	0	3	6	3	1	0	0	0	13
Days Maximum Temp. ≤ 32°F	15	11	4	0	0	0	0	0	0	0	1	8	39
Days Minimum Temp. ≤ 32°F	29	25	23	11	2	0	0	0	0	5	17	26	138
Days Minimum Temp. ≤ 0°F	4	3	0	0	0	0	0	0	0	0	0	1	8
Heating Degree Days (base 65°F)	1,247	1,049	867	510	222	52	10	17	123	409	712	1,069	6,287
Cooling Degree Days (base 65°F)	0	0	2	6	44	146	246	184	71	6	0	0	705
Mean Precipitation (in.)	2.19	1.96	2.66	3.20	3.55	3.91	3.70	3.41	3.34	2.46	3.18	2.76	36.32
Days With ≥ 0.1" Precipitation	6	6	7	8	8	8	7	6	6	6	8	7	83
Days With ≥ 1.0" Precipitation	0	0	0	0	1	1	1	1	1	0	0	0	5
Mean Snowfall (in.)	11.9	9.7	7.1	1.6	trace	0.0	0.0	0.0	0.0	trace	2.5	8.6	41.4
Days With ≥ 1.0" Snow Depth	na	na	na	1	0	0	0	0	0	0	1	na	na

Painesville 4 NW *Lake County* Elevation: 597 ft.   Latitude: 41° 45' N   Longitude: 81° 18' W

	JAN	FEB	MAR	APR	MAY	JUN	JUL	AUG	SEP	OCT	NOV	DEC	YEAR
Mean Maximum Temp. (°F)	34.3	36.6	45.6	56.3	67.7	76.7	81.4	79.8	74.2	63.2	51.2	40.3	58.9
Mean Temp. (°F)	27.2	29.0	37.1	47.6	58.6	67.8	72.6	71.3	65.4	54.7	44.1	33.7	50.8
Mean Minimum Temp. (°F)	20.1	21.4	28.7	38.8	49.5	58.9	63.8	62.8	56.6	46.1	36.9	27.1	42.6
Extreme Maximum Temp. (°F)	67	74	82	91	92	98	96	93	91	86	78	75	98
Extreme Minimum Temp. (°F)	-19	-8	0	17	29	39	45	39	33	24	5	-11	-19
Days Maximum Temp. ≥ 90°F	0	0	0	0	0	1	2	1	0	0	0	0	4
Days Maximum Temp. ≤ 32°F	13	11	4	0	0	0	0	0	0	0	0	6	34
Days Minimum Temp. ≤ 32°F	27	24	21	7	0	0	0	0	0	1	9	22	111
Days Minimum Temp. ≤ 0°F	2	1	0	0	0	0	0	0	0	0	0	0	3
Heating Degree Days (base 65°F)	1,166	1,009	858	522	229	45	3	7	74	324	624	962	5,823
Cooling Degree Days (base 65°F)	0	0	1	5	38	135	257	213	94	11	0	0	754
Mean Precipitation (in.)	2.28	1.78	2.76	3.15	3.02	3.80	3.13	3.72	4.12	3.28	3.54	2.94	37.52
Days With ≥ 0.1" Precipitation	7	5	7	8	7	7	6	7	7	8	9	8	86
Days With ≥ 1.0" Precipitation	0	0	0	0	0	1	1	1	1	0	1	0	5
Mean Snowfall (in.)	10.2	7.3	5.2	1.2	trace	0.0	0.0	0.0	0.0	trace	2.1	8.8	34.8
Days With ≥ 1.0" Snow Depth	17	11	4	0	0	0	0	0	0	0	1	9	42

Pandora *Putnam County* Elevation: 767 ft. Latitude: 40° 57' N Longitude: 83° 58' W

	JAN	FEB	MAR	APR	MAY	JUN	JUL	AUG	SEP	OCT	NOV	DEC	YEAR
Mean Maximum Temp. (°F)	31.6	35.7	47.1	59.9	71.7	80.5	84.0	81.7	75.4	62.9	48.9	37.1	59.7
Mean Temp. (°F)	24.2	27.6	37.8	49.1	60.6	69.6	73.2	70.8	64.1	52.5	41.0	30.2	50.1
Mean Minimum Temp. (°F)	16.7	19.6	28.5	38.2	49.4	58.7	62.3	59.9	52.8	42.0	33.1	23.2	40.4
Extreme Maximum Temp. (°F)	65	71	82	89	94	103	101	100	96	87	78	71	103
Extreme Minimum Temp. (°F)	-21	-17	-13	6	25	37	44	40	28	19	8	-19	-21
Days Maximum Temp. ≥ 90°F	0	0	0	0	1	3	6	3	1	0	0	0	14
Days Maximum Temp. ≤ 32°F	16	12	4	0	0	0	0	0	0	0	2	10	44
Days Minimum Temp. ≤ 32°F	28	24	21	9	1	0	0	0	0	5	16	26	130
Days Minimum Temp. ≤ 0°F	5	3	0	0	0	0	0	0	0	0	0	1	9
Heating Degree Days (base 65°F)	1,260	1,048	838	481	190	32	4	14	107	390	714	1,073	6,151
Cooling Degree Days (base 65°F)	0	0	2	8	59	179	278	210	87	10	0	0	833
Mean Precipitation (in.)	2.04	1.86	2.74	3.32	3.65	3.97	3.86	3.35	3.01	2.31	2.86	2.66	35.63
Days With ≥ 0.1" Precipitation	6	5	7	8	7	7	7	6	6	5	7	6	77
Days With ≥ 1.0" Precipitation	0	0	0	0	1	1	1	1	1	0	0	0	5
Mean Snowfall (in.)	9.5	7.1	4.2	1.2	trace	0.0	0.0	0.0	trace	0.1	2.0	6.6	30.7
Days With ≥ 1.0" Snow Depth	16	12	5	1	0	0	0	0	0	0	1	8	43

Paulding *Paulding County* Elevation: 725 ft. Latitude: 41° 07' N Longitude: 84° 36' W

	JAN	FEB	MAR	APR	MAY	JUN	JUL	AUG	SEP	OCT	NOV	DEC	YEAR
Mean Maximum Temp. (°F)	30.4	34.5	45.8	58.9	70.9	80.3	84.2	81.9	75.4	62.5	48.7	36.6	59.2
Mean Temp. (°F)	22.0	25.6	36.0	47.6	59.1	68.7	72.4	69.8	62.9	50.7	39.6	28.7	48.6
Mean Minimum Temp. (°F)	13.7	16.6	26.2	36.2	47.2	57.1	60.5	57.7	50.2	38.8	30.4	20.8	37.9
Extreme Maximum Temp. (°F)	62	71	80	87	92	104	100	99	95	85	79	70	104
Extreme Minimum Temp. (°F)	-25	-20	-11	7	25	36	45	39	27	17	5	-20	-25
Days Maximum Temp. ≥ 90°F	0	0	0	0	0	3	6	3	1	0	0	0	13
Days Maximum Temp. ≤ 32°F	17	12	4	0	0	0	0	0	0	0	2	10	45
Days Minimum Temp. ≤ 32°F	30	26	24	10	1	0	0	0	1	7	19	27	145
Days Minimum Temp. ≤ 0°F	6	3	0	0	0	0	0	0	0	0	0	2	11
Heating Degree Days (base 65°F)	1,327	1,106	892	520	221	41	7	20	127	443	755	1,117	6,576
Cooling Degree Days (base 65°F)	0	0	0	4	45	159	251	179	74	5	0	0	717
Mean Precipitation (in.)	1.90	1.73	2.68	3.38	3.78	3.43	3.41	2.95	3.00	2.50	2.95	2.58	34.29
Days With ≥ 0.1" Precipitation	5	4	6	7	7	6	6	5	6	6	6	6	70
Days With ≥ 1.0" Precipitation	0	0	0	1	1	1	1	1	0	0	1	0	6
Mean Snowfall (in.)	5.5	5.3	3.2	0.4	0.0	0.0	0.0	0.0	0.0	trace	1.2	4.1	19.7
Days With ≥ 1.0" Snow Depth	na	na	na	0	0	0	0	0	0	0	1	na	na

Philo 3 SW *Muskingum County* Elevation: 1,017 ft. Latitude: 39° 50' N Longitude: 81° 55' W

	JAN	FEB	MAR	APR	MAY	JUN	JUL	AUG	SEP	OCT	NOV	DEC	YEAR
Mean Maximum Temp. (°F)	34.9	39.6	50.4	62.0	71.0	78.0	81.7	80.6	74.4	63.5	51.0	40.1	60.6
Mean Temp. (°F)	27.3	30.9	40.5	51.0	60.1	67.7	71.5	70.3	63.9	52.9	42.5	32.6	50.9
Mean Minimum Temp. (°F)	19.6	22.2	30.5	39.9	49.3	57.3	61.3	59.8	53.2	42.3	34.0	25.0	41.2
Extreme Maximum Temp. (°F)	67	73	83	89	89	98	102	99	97	85	80	76	102
Extreme Minimum Temp. (°F)	-27	-10	-2	12	25	33	43	39	28	19	2	-18	-27
Days Maximum Temp. ≥ 90°F	0	0	0	0	0	0	3	1	1	0	0	0	5
Days Maximum Temp. ≤ 32°F	13	9	3	0	0	0	0	0	0	0	2	8	35
Days Minimum Temp. ≤ 32°F	27	23	19	7	1	0	0	0	0	5	15	24	121
Days Minimum Temp. ≤ 0°F	2	1	0	0	0	0	0	0	0	0	0	1	4
Heating Degree Days (base 65°F)	1,164	958	759	428	192	42	9	16	109	377	669	998	5,721
Cooling Degree Days (base 65°F)	0	0	3	11	42	126	222	182	75	9	1	0	671
Mean Precipitation (in.)	2.09	2.07	2.70	3.11	4.08	4.18	4.19	3.77	2.83	2.50	2.97	2.54	37.03
Days With ≥ 0.1" Precipitation	6	5	7	7	8	8	7	6	6	6	7	6	79
Days With ≥ 1.0" Precipitation	0	0	0	1	1	1	1	1	1	0	0	0	6
Mean Snowfall (in.)	9.4	5.3	4.3	1.1	trace	0.0	0.0	0.0	0.0	trace	1.1	3.6	24.8
Days With ≥ 1.0" Snow Depth	13	9	3	0	0	0	0	0	0	0	1	5	31

Portsmouth Sciotoville *Scioto County* Elevation: 538 ft. Latitude: 38° 45' N Longitude: 82° 53' W

	JAN	FEB	MAR	APR	MAY	JUN	JUL	AUG	SEP	OCT	NOV	DEC	YEAR
Mean Maximum Temp. (°F)	39.7	44.4	55.1	66.4	75.5	82.8	86.7	85.4	79.3	67.9	55.9	45.2	65.3
Mean Temp. (°F)	30.9	34.6	44.2	54.1	63.5	71.5	75.5	73.8	67.2	55.4	45.4	36.2	54.4
Mean Minimum Temp. (°F)	22.1	24.8	33.4	42.0	51.5	60.0	64.2	62.2	55.0	42.9	34.8	27.1	43.3
Extreme Maximum Temp. (°F)	74	76	84	92	93	101	104	104	100	88	82	76	104
Extreme Minimum Temp. (°F)	-29	-8	0	12	28	38	40	35	31	22	7	-18	-29
Days Maximum Temp. ≥ 90°F	0	0	0	0	1	5	10	7	2	0	0	0	25
Days Maximum Temp. ≤ 32°F	8	5	1	0	0	0	0	0	0	0	0	4	18
Days Minimum Temp. ≤ 32°F	26	22	15	5	0	0	0	0	0	4	13	21	106
Days Minimum Temp. ≤ 0°F	1	1	0	0	0	0	0	0	0	0	0	1	3
Heating Degree Days (base 65°F)	1,049	851	640	337	120	17	1	5	63	306	584	887	4,860
Cooling Degree Days (base 65°F)	0	0	2	13	74	213	330	269	114	14	1	0	1,030
Mean Precipitation (in.)	3.16	2.82	3.65	3.44	4.37	3.86	4.06	4.00	3.05	2.63	3.02	3.33	41.39
Days With ≥ 0.1" Precipitation	7	7	8	8	9	7	8	6	5	6	7	7	85
Days With ≥ 1.0" Precipitation	1	1	1	1	1	1	1	1	1	0	1	1	11
Mean Snowfall (in.)	5.5	3.7	2.3	0.3	trace	0.0	0.0	0.0	0.0	trace	0.3	1.2	13.3
Days With ≥ 1.0" Snow Depth	7	6	2	0	0	0	0	0	0	0	0	1	16

542 PROFILES OF OHIO / Weather: Cooperative Stations

Put-In-Bay *Ottawa County* Elevation: 577 ft. Latitude: 41° 39' N Longitude: 82° 48' W

	JAN	FEB	MAR	APR	MAY	JUN	JUL	AUG	SEP	OCT	NOV	DEC	YEAR
Mean Maximum Temp. (°F)	31.2	33.9	43.1	55.3	67.1	77.3	82.3	80.6	73.7	61.3	48.4	36.9	57.6
Mean Temp. (°F)	24.8	26.7	35.9	47.2	59.2	69.4	74.6	73.5	66.6	54.5	42.6	31.2	50.5
Mean Minimum Temp. (°F)	18.4	19.7	28.6	39.1	51.2	61.5	66.9	66.3	59.4	47.6	36.6	25.5	43.4
Extreme Maximum Temp. (°F)	60	63	78	87	91	99	100	95	97	84	79	68	100
Extreme Minimum Temp. (°F)	-18	-10	-2	13	33	41	51	50	37	30	11	-14	-18
Days Maximum Temp. ≥ 90°F	0	0	0	0	0	1	4	2	1	0	0	0	8
Days Maximum Temp. ≤ 32°F	16	13	4	0	0	0	0	0	0	0	1	8	42
Days Minimum Temp. ≤ 32°F	28	25	21	5	0	0	0	0	0	0	9	23	111
Days Minimum Temp. ≤ 0°F	2	1	0	0	0	0	0	0	0	0	0	1	4
Heating Degree Days (base 65°F)	1,239	1,075	896	532	211	27	1	3	61	329	667	1,040	6,081
Cooling Degree Days (base 65°F)	0	0	0	6	35	162	307	269	105	8	0	0	892
Mean Precipitation (in.)	1.58	1.44	5.21	2.91	3.33	3.41	3.06	3.31	3.16	2.55	2.68	2.15	34.79
Days With ≥ 0.1" Precipitation	5	4	5	7	7	6	6	6	6	6	6	5	69
Days With ≥ 1.0" Precipitation	0	0	0	0	1	1	1	1	1	0	0	0	5
Mean Snowfall (in.)	7.3	5.3	2.8	0.4	trace	0.0	0.0	0.0	0.0	trace	0.2	3.7	19.7
Days With ≥ 1.0" Snow Depth	17	12	5	0	0	0	0	0	0	0	0	7	41

Ripley Exp. Farm *Brown County* Elevation: 879 ft. Latitude: 38° 47' N Longitude: 83° 48' W

	JAN	FEB	MAR	APR	MAY	JUN	JUL	AUG	SEP	OCT	NOV	DEC	YEAR
Mean Maximum Temp. (°F)	38.0	42.8	53.1	64.3	73.4	81.5	85.2	84.0	78.1	66.3	53.6	43.4	63.6
Mean Temp. (°F)	29.1	32.9	42.3	52.7	62.2	70.5	74.4	72.8	66.2	54.3	43.9	34.4	53.0
Mean Minimum Temp. (°F)	20.2	22.9	31.5	41.0	50.9	59.6	63.5	61.6	54.3	42.2	34.1	25.4	42.3
Extreme Maximum Temp. (°F)	73	74	81	88	90	102	103	103	96	87	81	76	103
Extreme Minimum Temp. (°F)	-28	-11	-5	15	30	37	43	39	30	18	2	-22	-28
Days Maximum Temp. ≥ 90°F	0	0	0	0	0	3	7	5	2	0	0	0	17
Days Maximum Temp. ≤ 32°F	10	7	2	0	0	0	0	0	0	0	1	5	25
Days Minimum Temp. ≤ 32°F	27	22	18	6	0	0	0	0	0	5	14	23	115
Days Minimum Temp. ≤ 0°F	3	1	0	0	0	0	0	0	0	0	0	1	5
Heating Degree Days (base 65°F)	1,106	901	699	377	147	22	2	6	76	339	628	942	5,245
Cooling Degree Days (base 65°F)	0	0	2	11	66	200	314	262	111	14	1	0	981
Mean Precipitation (in.)	2.84	2.77	4.14	4.17	4.97	4.49	4.56	4.09	3.25	3.05	3.43	3.57	45.33
Days With ≥ 0.1" Precipitation	6	6	8	9	9	8	7	7	6	6	7	8	87
Days With ≥ 1.0" Precipitation	0	1	1	1	1	1	2	1	1	1	1	1	12
Mean Snowfall (in.)	7.5	5.6	4.1	0.5	trace	0.0	0.0	0.0	0.0	trace	0.9	2.9	21.5
Days With ≥ 1.0" Snow Depth	10	8	3	0	0	0	0	0	0	0	0	4	25

Sandusky *Erie County* Elevation: 583 ft. Latitude: 41° 27' N Longitude: 82° 43' W

	JAN	FEB	MAR	APR	MAY	JUN	JUL	AUG	SEP	OCT	NOV	DEC	YEAR
Mean Maximum Temp. (°F)	32.2	35.0	44.1	56.3	68.0	77.5	82.3	80.3	73.7	62.0	49.3	37.9	58.2
Mean Temp. (°F)	25.1	27.6	36.5	47.8	59.5	69.1	73.7	71.9	64.8	53.3	42.2	31.3	50.2
Mean Minimum Temp. (°F)	18.0	20.2	28.8	39.2	50.9	60.6	65.1	63.4	55.9	44.6	35.0	24.7	42.2
Extreme Maximum Temp. (°F)	65	71	81	88	93	103	99	98	94	86	77	73	103
Extreme Minimum Temp. (°F)	-20	-7	-7	16	32	43	41	45	36	24	9	-16	-20
Days Maximum Temp. ≥ 90°F	0	0	0	0	0	2	4	2	1	0	0	0	9
Days Maximum Temp. ≤ 32°F	16	12	5	0	0	0	0	0	0	0	1	9	43
Days Minimum Temp. ≤ 32°F	28	24	21	5	0	0	0	0	0	2	13	25	118
Days Minimum Temp. ≤ 0°F	3	2	0	0	0	0	0	0	0	0	0	1	6
Heating Degree Days (base 65°F)	1,230	1,049	878	518	212	36	3	7	92	365	678	1,039	6,107
Cooling Degree Days (base 65°F)	0	0	2	7	46	165	285	231	91	10	0	0	837
Mean Precipitation (in.)	1.86	1.71	2.48	3.06	3.29	4.10	3.38	3.58	3.13	2.32	2.75	2.53	34.19
Days With ≥ 0.1" Precipitation	5	4	6	7	7	7	6	6	6	6	6	6	72
Days With ≥ 1.0" Precipitation	0	0	0	0	1	1	1	1	1	0	0	0	5
Mean Snowfall (in.)	8.7	6.0	3.0	0.6	trace	0.0	0.0	0.0	0.0	trace	0.3	4.3	22.9
Days With ≥ 1.0" Snow Depth	14	8	3	0	0	0	0	0	0	0	0	6	31

Springfield New Water Works *Clark County* Elevation: 928 ft. Latitude: 39° 58' N Longitude: 83° 49' W

	JAN	FEB	MAR	APR	MAY	JUN	JUL	AUG	SEP	OCT	NOV	DEC	YEAR
Mean Maximum Temp. (°F)	33.7	37.9	48.6	60.5	71.4	80.0	83.8	82.4	76.3	63.9	50.7	39.6	60.7
Mean Temp. (°F)	25.2	28.5	38.5	49.2	59.9	69.2	72.8	70.9	64.0	52.0	41.5	31.5	50.3
Mean Minimum Temp. (°F)	16.5	19.1	28.4	37.8	48.4	58.2	61.8	59.3	51.7	40.1	32.2	23.3	39.7
Extreme Maximum Temp. (°F)	68	73	81	93	91	98	98	100	95	86	79	72	100
Extreme Minimum Temp. (°F)	-26	-18	-13	14	26	34	43	39	29	15	3	-26	-26
Days Maximum Temp. ≥ 90°F	0	0	0	0	0	2	5	3	1	0	0	0	11
Days Maximum Temp. ≤ 32°F	14	10	3	0	0	0	0	0	0	0	1	8	36
Days Minimum Temp. ≤ 32°F	28	24	21	10	1	0	0	0	0	7	17	25	133
Days Minimum Temp. ≤ 0°F	4	3	0	0	0	0	0	0	0	0	0	1	8
Heating Degree Days (base 65°F)	1,229	1,025	815	476	199	37	6	15	111	405	701	1,032	6,051
Cooling Degree Days (base 65°F)	0	0	2	6	49	176	270	213	86	9	0	0	811
Mean Precipitation (in.)	2.27	1.81	2.51	3.40	4.34	4.45	4.15	3.62	2.90	2.57	2.96	2.71	37.69
Days With ≥ 0.1" Precipitation	5	5	6	7	8	8	7	6	5	5	6	7	75
Days With ≥ 1.0" Precipitation	0	0	0	1	1	1	1	1	1	1	1	0	8
Mean Snowfall (in.)	na	na	na	trace	0.0	0.0	0.0	0.0	0.0	trace	0.1	na	na
Days With ≥ 1.0" Snow Depth	na	na	na	0	0	0	0	0	0	0	0	na	na

PROFILES OF OHIO / Weather: Cooperative Stations 543

Steubenville *Jefferson County* Elevation: 990 ft. Latitude: 40° 23' N Longitude: 80° 38' W

	JAN	FEB	MAR	APR	MAY	JUN	JUL	AUG	SEP	OCT	NOV	DEC	YEAR
Mean Maximum Temp. (°F)	36.5	40.4	50.8	62.4	72.0	79.9	83.3	82.0	75.6	64.1	52.1	41.6	61.7
Mean Temp. (°F)	28.4	31.6	40.6	50.8	60.8	69.2	73.3	72.0	65.5	53.8	43.5	33.8	51.9
Mean Minimum Temp. (°F)	20.3	22.7	30.3	39.2	49.5	58.4	63.2	62.0	55.4	43.5	34.8	26.0	42.1
Extreme Maximum Temp. (°F)	72	74	83	89	90	98	102	96	95	84	80	77	102
Extreme Minimum Temp. (°F)	-22	-8	-1	16	27	34	45	42	34	22	5	-14	-22
Days Maximum Temp. ≥ 90°F	0	0	0	0	0	2	4	2	1	0	0	0	9
Days Maximum Temp. ≤ 32°F	12	8	2	0	0	0	0	0	0	0	1	7	30
Days Minimum Temp. ≤ 32°F	27	22	19	8	1	0	0	0	0	2	13	23	115
Days Minimum Temp. ≤ 0°F	2	1	0	0	0	0	0	0	0	0	0	0	3
Heating Degree Days (base 65°F)	1,128	937	753	427	172	30	3	7	78	348	640	961	5,484
Cooling Degree Days (base 65°F)	0	0	2	8	47	165	280	233	96	9	1	0	841
Mean Precipitation (in.)	2.80	2.43	3.31	3.20	3.98	4.45	4.20	3.72	3.25	2.61	3.42	3.00	40.37
Days With ≥ 0.1" Precipitation	7	6	8	8	9	8	8	7	6	6	8	7	88
Days With ≥ 1.0" Precipitation	0	0	0	0	1	1	1	1	1	0	1	0	6
Mean Snowfall (in.)	na	na	na	trace	0.0	0.0	0.0	0.0	0.0	0.2	0.3	na	na
Days With ≥ 1.0" Snow Depth	na	na	na	0	0	0	0	0	0	0	0	na	na

Tiffin *Seneca County* Elevation: 738 ft. Latitude: 41° 07' N Longitude: 83° 10' W

	JAN	FEB	MAR	APR	MAY	JUN	JUL	AUG	SEP	OCT	NOV	DEC	YEAR
Mean Maximum Temp. (°F)	32.1	36.1	47.6	60.2	71.9	80.3	84.4	82.2	76.0	63.3	49.5	37.8	60.1
Mean Temp. (°F)	24.8	28.2	38.4	49.5	60.7	69.5	73.7	71.4	64.8	52.7	41.6	30.8	50.5
Mean Minimum Temp. (°F)	17.5	20.2	29.2	38.7	49.5	58.6	63.0	60.6	53.6	42.0	33.6	23.8	40.9
Extreme Maximum Temp. (°F)	67	72	82	88	93	105	101	98	95	86	79	72	105
Extreme Minimum Temp. (°F)	-21	-15	-2	8	28	38	44	39	31	19	7	-18	-21
Days Maximum Temp. ≥ 90°F	0	0	0	0	1	3	6	3	1	0	0	0	14
Days Maximum Temp. ≤ 32°F	15	11	3	0	0	0	0	0	0	0	1	9	39
Days Minimum Temp. ≤ 32°F	28	24	20	8	0	0	0	0	0	4	15	25	124
Days Minimum Temp. ≤ 0°F	3	2	0	0	0	0	0	0	0	0	0	1	6
Heating Degree Days (base 65°F)	1,239	1,033	818	469	185	37	4	12	96	384	696	1,054	6,027
Cooling Degree Days (base 65°F)	0	0	2	9	59	178	290	220	93	9	0	0	860
Mean Precipitation (in.)	2.26	1.97	2.69	3.39	3.68	4.19	3.34	3.77	3.14	2.39	3.00	2.93	36.75
Days With ≥ 0.1" Precipitation	6	5	7	8	8	8	7	6	6	6	7	7	81
Days With ≥ 1.0" Precipitation	0	0	0	1	1	1	1	1	1	0	0	0	6
Mean Snowfall (in.)	8.8	6.2	3.7	1.2	trace	0.0	0.0	0.0	0.0	trace	1.2	6.7	27.8
Days With ≥ 1.0" Snow Depth	16	13	4	1	0	0	0	0	0	0	1	8	43

Upper Sandusky *Wyandot County* Elevation: 853 ft. Latitude: 40° 50' N Longitude: 83° 17' W

	JAN	FEB	MAR	APR	MAY	JUN	JUL	AUG	SEP	OCT	NOV	DEC	YEAR
Mean Maximum Temp. (°F)	32.4	36.6	47.6	60.4	71.7	80.6	84.4	82.7	76.4	63.9	49.8	38.1	60.4
Mean Temp. (°F)	24.8	28.2	38.2	49.3	60.3	69.5	73.4	71.5	64.7	52.8	41.4	30.8	50.4
Mean Minimum Temp. (°F)	17.2	19.8	28.7	38.1	48.9	58.3	62.2	60.1	53.0	41.8	32.9	23.5	40.4
Extreme Maximum Temp. (°F)	67	72	82	87	92	104	102	99	95	88	79	72	104
Extreme Minimum Temp. (°F)	-23	-16	-8	9	26	37	43	40	28	18	6	-20	-23
Days Maximum Temp. ≥ 90°F	0	0	0	0	1	3	6	4	1	0	0	0	15
Days Maximum Temp. ≤ 32°F	15	11	3	0	0	0	0	0	0	0	1	9	39
Days Minimum Temp. ≤ 32°F	28	24	20	9	1	0	0	0	0	5	16	25	128
Days Minimum Temp. ≤ 0°F	4	2	0	0	0	0	0	0	0	0	0	1	7
Heating Degree Days (base 65°F)	1,239	1,033	826	474	195	35	5	12	98	383	701	1,052	6,053
Cooling Degree Days (base 65°F)	0	0	2	7	52	174	275	219	90	11	0	0	830
Mean Precipitation (in.)	2.11	1.77	2.63	3.50	3.98	3.72	4.17	3.22	3.03	2.22	3.05	2.63	36.03
Days With ≥ 0.1" Precipitation	6	5	6	8	8	7	7	6	6	6	7	7	79
Days With ≥ 1.0" Precipitation	0	0	0	1	1	1	1	1	1	0	1	0	7
Mean Snowfall (in.)	8.3	5.8	3.6	1.2	trace	0.0	0.0	0.0	0.0	trace	1.4	6.3	26.6
Days With ≥ 1.0" Snow Depth	14	11	4	0	0	0	0	0	0	0	1	6	36

Urbana WWTP *Champaign County* Elevation: 997 ft. Latitude: 40° 06' N Longitude: 83° 47' W

	JAN	FEB	MAR	APR	MAY	JUN	JUL	AUG	SEP	OCT	NOV	DEC	YEAR
Mean Maximum Temp. (°F)	33.4	37.5	48.1	60.5	71.5	80.3	84.4	82.7	76.4	63.7	50.4	39.1	60.7
Mean Temp. (°F)	25.1	28.5	38.3	49.3	60.1	69.2	72.9	70.8	64.0	52.1	41.4	31.1	50.2
Mean Minimum Temp. (°F)	16.8	19.4	28.5	38.1	48.7	58.0	61.5	58.9	51.5	40.5	32.4	23.1	39.8
Extreme Maximum Temp. (°F)	66	68	80	87	93	99	100	101	96	87	76	72	101
Extreme Minimum Temp. (°F)	-26	-18	-8	14	28	36	42	39	28	18	1	-22	-26
Days Maximum Temp. ≥ 90°F	0	0	0	0	0	3	6	3	1	0	0	0	13
Days Maximum Temp. ≤ 32°F	14	10	3	0	0	0	0	0	0	0	1	8	36
Days Minimum Temp. ≤ 32°F	28	24	21	9	1	0	0	0	0	6	16	25	130
Days Minimum Temp. ≤ 0°F	4	3	0	0	0	0	0	0	0	0	0	1	8
Heating Degree Days (base 65°F)	1,230	1,025	820	470	194	35	5	14	108	400	700	1,043	6,044
Cooling Degree Days (base 65°F)	0	0	0	5	46	167	266	205	81	7	0	0	777
Mean Precipitation (in.)	2.33	2.09	2.85	3.52	4.37	4.46	4.97	3.61	2.87	2.78	3.05	2.90	39.80
Days With ≥ 0.1" Precipitation	6	5	7	8	8	8	7	6	5	6	7	6	79
Days With ≥ 1.0" Precipitation	1	0	0	1	1	1	2	1	1	1	1	1	11
Mean Snowfall (in.)	na	na	na	0.5	0.0	0.0	0.0	0.0	0.0	0.1	0.3	na	na
Days With ≥ 1.0" Snow Depth	na	na	na	0	0	0	0	0	0	0	0	na	na

PROFILES OF OHIO / Weather: Cooperative Stations

Van Wert 1 S *Van Wert County*   Elevation: 787 ft.   Latitude: 40° 51' N   Longitude: 84° 35' W

	JAN	FEB	MAR	APR	MAY	JUN	JUL	AUG	SEP	OCT	NOV	DEC	YEAR
Mean Maximum Temp. (°F)	32.2	36.3	47.6	60.7	72.6	81.5	85.2	82.9	76.6	64.1	49.6	37.6	60.6
Mean Temp. (°F)	24.4	27.8	38.0	49.6	61.1	70.4	74.1	71.8	64.9	52.9	41.2	30.3	50.5
Mean Minimum Temp. (°F)	16.6	19.1	28.3	38.4	49.6	59.2	63.0	60.6	53.1	41.6	32.8	23.0	40.5
Extreme Maximum Temp. (°F)	64	72	81	88	94	104	103	99	97	89	77	71	104
Extreme Minimum Temp. (°F)	-22	-14	-9	9	28	39	44	41	30	20	7	-18	-22
Days Maximum Temp. ≥ 90°F	0	0	0	0	1	4	7	4	2	0	0	0	18
Days Maximum Temp. ≤ 32°F	15	10	3	0	0	0	0	0	0	0	1	9	38
Days Minimum Temp. ≤ 32°F	29	25	21	8	1	0	0	0	0	4	16	26	130
Days Minimum Temp. ≤ 0°F	4	3	0	0	0	0	0	0	0	0	0	1	8
Heating Degree Days (base 65°F)	1,253	1,045	831	464	176	28	3	11	97	380	708	1,068	6,064
Cooling Degree Days (base 65°F)	0	0	1	8	62	198	301	232	97	11	0	0	910
Mean Precipitation (in.)	2.00	1.83	2.66	3.57	3.81	4.16	3.93	3.28	2.90	2.63	3.07	2.68	36.52
Days With ≥ 0.1" Precipitation	5	5	7	8	8	7	7	6	6	6	7	6	78
Days With ≥ 1.0" Precipitation	0	0	0	1	1	1	1	1	1	1	1	0	8
Mean Snowfall (in.)	9.3	6.8	2.8	1.2	0.0	0.0	0.0	0.0	0.0	0.2	1.8	7.7	29.8
Days With ≥ 1.0" Snow Depth	12	11	4	0	0	0	0	0	0	0	1	6	34

Warren 3 S *Trumbull County*   Elevation: 898 ft.   Latitude: 41° 12' N   Longitude: 80° 49' W

	JAN	FEB	MAR	APR	MAY	JUN	JUL	AUG	SEP	OCT	NOV	DEC	YEAR
Mean Maximum Temp. (°F)	33.9	37.6	47.9	60.1	71.0	79.1	83.1	81.4	74.2	62.7	50.2	39.3	60.1
Mean Temp. (°F)	25.0	27.6	36.8	47.3	57.8	66.4	70.5	69.0	62.0	50.8	40.7	31.0	48.7
Mean Minimum Temp. (°F)	15.9	17.6	25.5	34.4	44.5	53.5	57.9	56.6	49.7	38.8	31.2	22.6	37.3
Extreme Maximum Temp. (°F)	67	73	82	90	91	99	101	99	93	83	78	76	101
Extreme Minimum Temp. (°F)	-26	-20	-11	10	20	28	38	30	27	16	-7	-17	-26
Days Maximum Temp. ≥ 90°F	0	0	0	0	0	2	4	2	1	0	0	0	9
Days Maximum Temp. ≤ 32°F	14	10	4	0	0	0	0	0	0	0	1	8	37
Days Minimum Temp. ≤ 32°F	29	25	24	14	4	0	0	0	1	9	18	26	150
Days Minimum Temp. ≤ 0°F	4	3	0	0	0	0	0	0	0	0	0	1	8
Heating Degree Days (base 65°F)	1,236	1,049	871	529	246	62	14	24	144	437	722	1,048	6,382
Cooling Degree Days (base 65°F)	0	0	1	5	30	114	208	162	58	3	0	0	581
Mean Precipitation (in.)	2.24	1.67	2.95	3.25	3.59	4.01	4.22	3.32	3.93	2.69	3.10	2.80	37.77
Days With ≥ 0.1" Precipitation	6	5	8	8	8	8	7	7	8	7	7	7	86
Days With ≥ 1.0" Precipitation	0	0	0	1	1	1	1	1	1	0	0	0	6
Mean Snowfall (in.)	11.1	8.2	5.5	0.5	trace	0.0	0.0	0.0	0.0	trace	1.3	7.3	33.9
Days With ≥ 1.0" Snow Depth	16	11	4	0	0	0	0	0	0	0	1	8	40

Washington Court House *Fayette County*   Elevation: 958 ft.   Latitude: 39° 31' N   Longitude: 83° 25' W

	JAN	FEB	MAR	APR	MAY	JUN	JUL	AUG	SEP	OCT	NOV	DEC	YEAR
Mean Maximum Temp. (°F)	35.6	40.4	51.3	63.4	72.4	79.5	82.6	81.8	76.5	65.8	52.4	40.9	61.9
Mean Temp. (°F)	28.0	31.8	41.6	52.2	62.1	70.1	73.6	72.3	66.2	54.9	43.5	33.4	52.5
Mean Minimum Temp. (°F)	20.3	23.2	31.8	40.9	51.7	60.6	64.5	62.8	55.9	44.0	34.6	25.8	43.0
Extreme Maximum Temp. (°F)	69	73	83	89	91	93	97	97	95	86	80	77	97
Extreme Minimum Temp. (°F)	-27	-11	-4	16	30	39	47	42	33	19	1	-20	-27
Days Maximum Temp. ≥ 90°F	0	0	0	0	0	1	3	3	1	0	0	0	8
Days Maximum Temp. ≤ 32°F	12	8	2	0	0	0	0	0	0	0	1	7	30
Days Minimum Temp. ≤ 32°F	27	22	18	6	0	0	0	0	0	3	14	23	113
Days Minimum Temp. ≤ 0°F	2	1	0	0	0	0	0	0	0	0	0	1	4
Heating Degree Days (base 65°F)	1,140	930	722	388	148	22	2	6	71	319	640	974	5,362
Cooling Degree Days (base 65°F)	0	0	2	9	63	186	284	243	113	14	1	0	915
Mean Precipitation (in.)	2.43	2.35	3.32	3.60	4.70	3.79	3.95	3.85	2.64	2.65	3.01	2.81	39.10
Days With ≥ 0.1" Precipitation	6	6	8	8	8	7	7	6	5	6	6	7	80
Days With ≥ 1.0" Precipitation	0	0	1	0	1	1	1	1	1	1	1	0	8
Mean Snowfall (in.)	8.7	6.1	4.1	0.7	trace	0.0	0.0	0.0	0.0	0.2	1.0	3.5	24.3
Days With ≥ 1.0" Snow Depth	11	8	3	0	0	0	0	0	0	0	1	4	27

Wauseon Water Plant *Fulton County*   Elevation: 748 ft.   Latitude: 41° 31' N   Longitude: 84° 09' W

	JAN	FEB	MAR	APR	MAY	JUN	JUL	AUG	SEP	OCT	NOV	DEC	YEAR
Mean Maximum Temp. (°F)	30.8	35.0	46.4	59.8	71.8	80.9	84.3	81.9	75.7	63.2	48.8	36.5	59.6
Mean Temp. (°F)	23.0	26.6	36.9	48.5	59.8	69.1	72.6	70.3	63.6	51.9	40.3	29.2	49.3
Mean Minimum Temp. (°F)	15.3	18.0	27.3	37.2	47.7	57.3	60.8	58.6	51.4	40.6	31.7	22.0	39.0
Extreme Maximum Temp. (°F)	62	69	79	88	93	103	101	98	95	88	76	68	103
Extreme Minimum Temp. (°F)	-24	-16	-7	2	26	37	40	37	28	17	5	-21	-24
Days Maximum Temp. ≥ 90°F	0	0	0	0	0	3	6	3	1	0	0	0	13
Days Maximum Temp. ≤ 32°F	16	11	3	0	0	0	0	0	0	0	2	10	42
Days Minimum Temp. ≤ 32°F	29	26	23	10	1	0	0	0	0	6	18	27	140
Days Minimum Temp. ≤ 0°F	5	3	0	0	0	0	0	0	0	0	0	1	9
Heating Degree Days (base 65°F)	1,295	1,080	867	493	203	34	5	15	112	404	736	1,102	6,346
Cooling Degree Days (base 65°F)	0	0	0	6	51	172	266	197	80	6	0	0	778
Mean Precipitation (in.)	1.85	1.61	2.53	3.37	3.39	3.69	3.44	3.65	3.09	2.60	2.95	2.42	34.59
Days With ≥ 0.1" Precipitation	5	4	6	8	7	7	6	7	6	6	7	6	75
Days With ≥ 1.0" Precipitation	0	0	0	0	1	1	1	1	1	0	0	0	5
Mean Snowfall (in.)	8.7	7.0	4.4	0.9	trace	0.0	0.0	0.0	0.0	trace	2.2	5.8	29.0
Days With ≥ 1.0" Snow Depth	14	12	4	0	0	0	0	0	0	0	2	7	39

PROFILES OF OHIO / Weather: Cooperative Stations

Waverly *Pike County*   Elevation: 557 ft.   Latitude: 39° 07' N   Longitude: 82° 59' W

	JAN	FEB	MAR	APR	MAY	JUN	JUL	AUG	SEP	OCT	NOV	DEC	YEAR
Mean Maximum Temp. (°F)	39.0	44.0	55.0	66.8	75.4	82.9	86.5	85.2	79.2	68.0	55.6	44.7	65.2
Mean Temp. (°F)	29.1	32.8	42.5	52.6	62.1	70.5	74.6	72.8	66.2	54.1	43.9	34.5	53.0
Mean Minimum Temp. (°F)	19.2	21.7	29.9	38.3	48.8	58.1	62.7	60.5	53.1	40.1	32.2	24.3	40.7
Extreme Maximum Temp. (°F)	75	77	88	92	96	101	102	102	99	87	81	79	102
Extreme Minimum Temp. (°F)	-31	-17	-12	15	27	31	41	38	28	17	7	-21	-31
Days Maximum Temp. ≥ 90°F	0	0	0	0	1	5	9	7	2	0	0	0	24
Days Maximum Temp. ≤ 32°F	8	5	1	0	0	0	0	0	0	0	0	4	18
Days Minimum Temp. ≤ 32°F	27	23	20	9	1	0	0	0	0	7	17	23	127
Days Minimum Temp. ≤ 0°F	2	1	0	0	0	0	0	0	0	0	0	1	4
Heating Degree Days (base 65°F)	1,106	902	696	376	146	21	2	6	74	343	627	939	5,238
Cooling Degree Days (base 65°F)	0	0	1	9	59	194	313	251	104	12	0	0	943
Mean Precipitation (in.)	2.69	2.27	3.62	3.56	4.18	3.86	3.99	4.40	2.63	2.56	3.08	3.02	39.86
Days With ≥ 0.1" Precipitation	5	5	8	8	8	7	7	6	5	5	7	7	78
Days With ≥ 1.0" Precipitation	0	0	1	1	1	1	1	1	1	1	0	1	9
Mean Snowfall (in.)	4.7	na	3.0	0.1	0.0	0.0	0.0	0.0	0.0	trace	0.1	1.5	na
Days With ≥ 1.0" Snow Depth	na	na	1	0	0	0	0	0	0	0	0	na	na

Westerville *Franklin County*   Elevation: 807 ft.   Latitude: 40° 08' N   Longitude: 82° 57' W

	JAN	FEB	MAR	APR	MAY	JUN	JUL	AUG	SEP	OCT	NOV	DEC	YEAR
Mean Maximum Temp. (°F)	35.6	40.6	51.8	64.1	74.2	82.1	85.3	84.0	77.9	66.1	52.4	41.0	62.9
Mean Temp. (°F)	27.0	30.8	41.0	51.6	61.8	70.3	73.8	72.3	65.7	54.0	43.1	33.0	52.0
Mean Minimum Temp. (°F)	18.4	21.0	30.1	39.1	49.3	58.3	62.2	60.6	53.5	41.9	33.7	25.0	41.1
Extreme Maximum Temp. (°F)	68	73	82	88	92	100	101	101	97	86	79	76	101
Extreme Minimum Temp. (°F)	-27	-25	-8	14	27	33	41	36	29	17	3	-25	-27
Days Maximum Temp. ≥ 90°F	0	0	0	0	0	3	7	5	2	0	0	0	17
Days Maximum Temp. ≤ 32°F	12	8	2	0	0	0	0	0	0	0	1	7	30
Days Minimum Temp. ≤ 32°F	27	23	19	9	1	0	0	0	0	5	15	24	123
Days Minimum Temp. ≤ 0°F	4	3	0	0	0	0	0	0	0	0	0	1	8
Heating Degree Days (base 65°F)	1,171	959	739	404	155	24	3	8	82	346	652	985	5,528
Cooling Degree Days (base 65°F)	0	0	2	10	65	200	306	257	116	14	1	0	971
Mean Precipitation (in.)	2.52	2.23	2.79	3.61	4.03	4.64	4.04	3.51	2.90	2.62	3.36	2.91	39.16
Days With ≥ 0.1" Precipitation	6	5	7	8	8	8	7	6	5	6	7	7	80
Days With ≥ 1.0" Precipitation	0	0	0	1	1	1	1	1	1	1	0	1	7
Mean Snowfall (in.)	7.7	5.1	2.3	0.7	trace	0.0	0.0	0.0	0.0	trace	0.5	3.3	19.6
Days With ≥ 1.0" Snow Depth	12	7	2	0	0	0	0	0	0	0	0	4	25

Wilmington 3 N *Clinton County*   Elevation: 1,026 ft.   Latitude: 39° 29' N   Longitude: 83° 49' W

	JAN	FEB	MAR	APR	MAY	JUN	JUL	AUG	SEP	OCT	NOV	DEC	YEAR
Mean Maximum Temp. (°F)	35.0	39.1	50.0	61.6	71.8	80.2	83.9	82.6	76.9	64.8	51.6	40.5	61.5
Mean Temp. (°F)	26.7	30.0	39.9	50.3	60.6	69.3	73.0	71.1	64.8	53.1	42.3	32.5	51.1
Mean Minimum Temp. (°F)	18.4	20.9	29.6	38.9	49.3	58.3	62.1	59.5	52.6	41.3	33.0	24.4	40.7
Extreme Maximum Temp. (°F)	69	72	82	87	90	99	99	99	95	86	78	73	99
Extreme Minimum Temp. (°F)	-25	-20	-10	12	27	37	40	37	30	12	2	-24	-25
Days Maximum Temp. ≥ 90°F	0	0	0	0	0	2	5	4	1	0	0	0	12
Days Maximum Temp. ≤ 32°F	13	9	3	0	0	0	0	0	0	0	1	7	33
Days Minimum Temp. ≤ 32°F	27	23	20	8	1	0	0	0	0	6	15	24	124
Days Minimum Temp. ≤ 0°F	3	3	0	0	0	0	0	0	0	0	0	1	7
Heating Degree Days (base 65°F)	1,181	981	774	444	181	32	4	14	98	373	675	1,002	5,759
Cooling Degree Days (base 65°F)	0	0	2	9	48	174	274	215	94	12	1	0	829
Mean Precipitation (in.)	2.57	2.38	3.40	4.06	4.81	4.25	4.35	3.33	2.81	2.89	3.36	2.91	41.12
Days With ≥ 0.1" Precipitation	6	6	8	9	9	8	8	6	5	6	7	6	84
Days With ≥ 1.0" Precipitation	1	0	1	1	1	1	1	1	1	1	1	0	10
Mean Snowfall (in.)	8.2	6.3	3.9	0.7	trace	0.0	0.0	0.0	0.0	0.2	1.4	3.0	23.7
Days With ≥ 1.0" Snow Depth	11	9	3	0	0	0	0	0	0	0	1	4	28

Wooster Exp. Station *Wayne County*   Elevation: 1,017 ft.   Latitude: 40° 47' N   Longitude: 81° 55' W

	JAN	FEB	MAR	APR	MAY	JUN	JUL	AUG	SEP	OCT	NOV	DEC	YEAR
Mean Maximum Temp. (°F)	32.4	36.1	46.9	58.8	69.5	78.0	81.8	80.0	73.0	61.2	48.8	37.7	58.7
Mean Temp. (°F)	25.0	28.0	37.6	48.2	58.6	67.3	71.2	69.4	62.5	51.1	40.9	30.8	49.2
Mean Minimum Temp. (°F)	17.6	19.9	28.4	37.5	47.8	56.6	60.6	58.9	51.8	40.9	32.9	23.8	39.7
Extreme Maximum Temp. (°F)	64	70	80	86	90	100	101	95	92	83	75	74	101
Extreme Minimum Temp. (°F)	-24	-13	-6	14	25	31	41	36	30	17	5	-17	-24
Days Maximum Temp. ≥ 90°F	0	0	0	0	0	1	2	1	0	0	0	0	4
Days Maximum Temp. ≤ 32°F	16	11	4	0	0	0	0	0	0	0	2	10	43
Days Minimum Temp. ≤ 32°F	28	24	21	10	1	0	0	0	0	6	16	25	131
Days Minimum Temp. ≤ 0°F	4	2	0	0	0	0	0	0	0	0	0	1	7
Heating Degree Days (base 65°F)	1,233	1,038	842	503	226	53	10	21	134	429	717	1,055	6,261
Cooling Degree Days (base 65°F)	0	0	1	5	36	133	225	170	60	5	0	0	635
Mean Precipitation (in.)	2.22	1.94	2.76	3.44	3.92	4.02	4.00	3.91	3.43	2.61	3.07	2.65	37.97
Days With ≥ 0.1" Precipitation	6	5	7	8	8	8	7	7	6	6	7	6	81
Days With ≥ 1.0" Precipitation	0	0	0	1	1	1	1	1	1	0	0	0	6
Mean Snowfall (in.)	10.0	7.2	5.1	1.2	trace	0.0	0.0	trace	0.0	trace	1.9	6.3	31.7
Days With ≥ 1.0" Snow Depth	16	13	6	1	0	0	0	0	0	0	1	9	46

Xenia 6 SSE *Greene County* Elevation: 967 ft. Latitude: 39° 37' N Longitude: 83° 54' W

	JAN	FEB	MAR	APR	MAY	JUN	JUL	AUG	SEP	OCT	NOV	DEC	YEAR
Mean Maximum Temp. (°F)	35.8	40.7	52.0	63.4	73.0	80.4	83.7	82.1	76.3	65.1	52.3	41.2	62.2
Mean Temp. (°F)	27.6	31.6	41.9	51.9	61.8	69.8	73.2	71.2	64.9	53.8	43.1	33.1	52.0
Mean Minimum Temp. (°F)	19.3	22.5	31.8	40.4	50.6	59.2	62.7	60.2	53.5	42.4	33.8	24.9	41.8
Extreme Maximum Temp. (°F)	68	74	83	88	91	102	100	98	95	89	80	74	102
Extreme Minimum Temp. (°F)	-28	-20	-5	14	28	37	42	38	25	16	3	-24	-28
Days Maximum Temp. ≥ 90°F	0	0	0	0	0	2	4	2	1	0	0	0	9
Days Maximum Temp. ≤ 32°F	12	8	2	0	0	0	0	0	0	0	1	6	29
Days Minimum Temp. ≤ 32°F	26	22	18	7	1	0	0	0	0	5	15	24	118
Days Minimum Temp. ≤ 0°F	3	2	0	0	0	0	0	0	0	0	0	1	6
Heating Degree Days (base 65°F)	1,154	936	712	395	151	25	3	10	90	353	652	983	5,464
Cooling Degree Days (base 65°F)	0	0	2	10	61	185	279	216	96	12	1	0	862
Mean Precipitation (in.)	2.51	2.23	3.16	3.91	4.42	3.87	4.09	3.66	2.73	2.84	3.23	3.02	39.67
Days With ≥ 0.1" Precipitation	6	6	7	8	8	7	8	7	5	6	7	7	82
Days With ≥ 1.0" Precipitation	0	0	0	1	1	1	1	1	1	1	1	1	9
Mean Snowfall (in.)	8.8	5.6	3.5	0.4	trace	0.0	0.0	0.0	0.0	0.2	0.9	3.3	22.7
Days With ≥ 1.0" Snow Depth	na	na	1	0	0	0	0	0	0	0	0	na	na

Zanesville Municipal Airport *Muskingum County* Elevation: 879 ft. Latitude: 39° 57' N Longitude: 81° 54' W

	JAN	FEB	MAR	APR	MAY	JUN	JUL	AUG	SEP	OCT	NOV	DEC	YEAR
Mean Maximum Temp. (°F)	36.0	40.6	51.3	62.4	72.2	80.1	83.9	82.2	75.6	64.0	52.2	40.9	61.8
Mean Temp. (°F)	28.1	31.7	41.2	51.2	61.1	69.3	73.4	71.8	64.8	53.1	43.2	33.2	51.8
Mean Minimum Temp. (°F)	20.1	22.6	31.1	39.9	49.9	58.5	62.9	61.4	53.9	42.1	34.2	25.5	41.8
Extreme Maximum Temp. (°F)	70	72	83	88	90	101	103	98	96	84	79	76	103
Extreme Minimum Temp. (°F)	-25	-13	-2	16	26	37	42	37	30	18	2	-17	-25
Days Maximum Temp. ≥ 90°F	0	0	0	0	0	2	5	3	1	0	0	0	11
Days Maximum Temp. ≤ 32°F	12	8	2	0	0	0	0	0	0	0	1	7	30
Days Minimum Temp. ≤ 32°F	27	22	18	7	1	0	0	0	0	5	15	23	118
Days Minimum Temp. ≤ 0°F	2	2	0	0	0	0	0	0	0	0	0	1	5
Heating Degree Days (base 65°F)	1,137	934	733	418	170	30	3	9	93	371	648	979	5,525
Cooling Degree Days (base 65°F)	0	0	2	8	52	171	286	230	94	10	1	0	854
Mean Precipitation (in.)	2.53	2.31	3.09	3.54	4.11	4.39	4.19	3.96	2.94	2.56	3.10	2.75	39.47
Days With ≥ 0.1" Precipitation	7	6	8	8	8	7	7	7	6	6	7	7	84
Days With ≥ 1.0" Precipitation	0	0	0	1	1	1	1	1	1	1	0	0	6
Mean Snowfall (in.)	8.6	4.3	3.5	1.4	trace	trace	trace	0.0	trace	trace	1.2	3.5	22.5
Days With ≥ 1.0" Snow Depth	12	8	3	0	0	0	0	0	0	0	1	4	28

Note: See User's Guide for explanation of data.

Annual Extreme Maximum Temperature

Highest

Rank	Station Name	°F
1	Chilo Meldahl Lock & Dam	107
1	Cincinnati Fernbank	107
3	Chillicothe Mound City	105
3	Cincinnati Lunken Airport	105
3	Gallipolis	105
3	Hoytville 2 NE	105
3	Napoleon	105
3	Tiffin	105
9	Bowling Green WWTP	104
9	Cleveland Hopkins Int'l Airport	104
9	Dayton MCD	104
9	Defiance	104
9	Elyria 3 E	104
9	Findlay Airport	104
9	Findlay WPCC	104
9	Fremont	104
9	Greenville Water Plant	104
9	Kenton	104
9	Milford	104
9	Montpelier	104
9	Oberlin	104
9	Paulding	104
9	Portsmouth Sciotoville	104
9	Toledo Express Airport	104
9	Upper Sandusky	104

Lowest

Rank	Station Name	°F
1	Washington Court House	97
2	Painesville 4 NW	98
3	Centerburg 2 SE	99
3	Wilmington 3 N	99
5	Ashland 2 SW	100
5	Barnesville	100
5	Chardon	100
5	Columbus Valley Crossing	100
5	Dorset	100
5	Fredericktown 4 S	100
5	Hannibal Lock & Dam	100
5	Hillsboro	100
5	Hiram	100
5	Lima WWTP	100
5	Mansfield 5 W	100
5	Newark Water Works	100
5	Put-In-Bay	100
5	Springfield New Water Works	100
5	Youngstown Municipal Airport	100
20	Akron-Canton Regional Airport	101
20	Bellefontaine	101
20	Cadiz	101
20	Canfield 1 S	101
20	Circleville	101
20	Columbus-Port Columbus Int'l	101

Annual Mean Maximum Temperature

Highest

Rank	Station Name	°F
1	Gallipolis	66.8
2	Portsmouth Sciotoville	65.3
3	Waverly	65.2
4	Cincinnati Fernbank	64.6
4	Cincinnati Lunken Airport	64.6
4	Marietta WWTP	64.6
7	Chilo Meldahl Lock & Dam	64.4
8	Chillicothe Mound City	63.8
8	Milford	63.8
10	Ripley Exp. Farm	63.6
11	Jackson 3 NW	63.5
11	McConnelsville Lock 7	63.5
13	Cambridge	63.4
13	Circleville	63.4
15	Columbus Valley Crossing	63.1
16	Dayton MCD	63.0
17	New Lexington 2 NW	62.9
17	Westerville	62.9
19	Franklin	62.7
19	Irwin	62.7
21	Hannibal Lock & Dam	62.5
22	Mineral Ridge Water Works	62.2
22	Xenia 6 SSE	62.2
24	Newark Water Works	62.1
25	Coshocton WPC Plant	62.0

Lowest

Rank	Station Name	°F
1	Chardon	57.2
2	Put-In-Bay	57.6
3	Dorset	57.8
4	Sandusky	58.2
5	Hiram	58.3
5	Youngstown Municipal Airport	58.3
7	Findlay Airport	58.7
7	Mansfield Lahm Municipal Airport	58.7
7	Wooster Exp. Station	58.7
10	Fremont	58.8
10	Mansfield 5 W	58.8
10	Montpelier	58.8
10	Norwalk WWTP	58.8
14	Bucyrus	58.9
14	Painesville 4 NW	58.9
16	Cleveland Hopkins Int'l Airport	59.0
16	Toledo Express Airport	59.0
18	Findlay WPCC	59.1
19	Akron-Canton Regional Airport	59.2
19	Ashland 2 SW	59.2
19	Centerburg 2 SE	59.2
19	Paulding	59.2
23	Hoytville 2 NE	59.3
24	Coshocton Agr. Res. Station	59.4
25	Defiance	59.5

Annual Mean Temperature

Highest

Rank	Station Name	°F
1	Gallipolis	55.0
2	Cincinnati Lunken Airport	54.7
3	Portsmouth Sciotoville	54.4
4	Marietta WWTP	53.8
5	Chilo Meldahl Lock & Dam	53.6
5	Cincinnati Fernbank	53.6
5	Dayton MCD	53.6
8	Ripley Exp. Farm	53.0
8	Waverly	53.0
10	Circleville	52.9
11	Columbus Valley Crossing	52.8
12	Chillicothe Mound City	52.5
12	Washington Court House	52.5
14	Cambridge	52.4
15	Columbus-Port Columbus Int'l	52.3
15	Hillsboro	52.3
15	Milford	52.3
18	Jackson 3 NW	52.1
19	Dayton Int'l Airport	52.0
19	Westerville	52.0
19	Xenia 6 SSE	52.0
22	Steubenville	51.9
23	Franklin	51.8
23	Hannibal Lock & Dam	51.8
23	Zanesville Municipal Airport	51.8

Lowest

Rank	Station Name	°F
1	Chardon	46.9
2	Dorset	47.4
3	Montpelier	48.0
4	Fredericktown 4 S	48.3
5	Canfield 1 S	48.6
5	Paulding	48.6
7	Mansfield 5 W	48.7
7	Warren 3 S	48.7
9	Ashland 2 SW	48.8
9	Youngstown Municipal Airport	48.8
11	Bucyrus	48.9
11	Hiram	48.9
13	Hoytville 2 NE	49.0
14	Toledo Express Airport	49.1
15	Chippewa Lake	49.2
15	Defiance	49.2
15	Norwalk WWTP	49.2
15	Wooster Exp. Station	49.2
19	Centerburg 2 SE	49.3
19	Danville 2 W	49.3
19	Fremont	49.3
19	Wauseon Water Plant	49.3
23	Millport 2 NW	49.4
23	Oberlin	49.4
25	Greenville Water Plant	49.6

Annual Mean Minimum Temperature

Highest

Rank	Station Name	°F
1	Cincinnati Lunken Airport	44.8
2	Dayton MCD	44.2
3	Put-In-Bay	43.4
4	Portsmouth Sciotoville	43.3
5	Gallipolis	43.0
5	Marietta WWTP	43.0
5	Washington Court House	43.0
8	Chilo Meldahl Lock & Dam	42.8
8	Hillsboro	42.8
10	Columbus-Port Columbus Int'l	42.6
10	Painesville 4 NW	42.6
12	Cincinnati Fernbank	42.5
13	Circleville	42.4
13	Columbus Valley Crossing	42.4
13	Dayton Int'l Airport	42.4
16	Ripley Exp. Farm	42.3
17	Sandusky	42.2
18	Steubenville	42.1
19	Lima WWTP	42.0
20	Xenia 6 SSE	41.8
20	Zanesville Municipal Airport	41.8
22	Celina 3 NE	41.7
23	Coshocton Agr. Res. Station	41.5
24	Cadiz	41.4
24	Cambridge	41.4

Lowest

Rank	Station Name	°F
1	Chardon	36.7
2	Fredericktown 4 S	36.9
3	Dorset	37.0
4	Montpelier	37.1
5	Canfield 1 S	37.2
6	Warren 3 S	37.3
7	Danville 2 W	37.4
8	Millport 2 NW	37.8
9	Paulding	37.9
10	Ashland 2 SW	38.3
11	Mansfield 5 W	38.6
12	Greenville Water Plant	38.7
12	Hoytville 2 NE	38.7
12	Oberlin	38.7
15	Chippewa Lake	38.8
15	Defiance	38.8
17	Bucyrus	38.9
17	Eaton	38.9
19	Wauseon Water Plant	39.0
20	Delaware	39.1
20	New Philadelphia	39.1
22	New Lexington 2 NW	39.2
22	Toledo Express Airport	39.2
24	Barnesville	39.3
24	McConnelsville Lock 7	39.3

Annual Extreme Minimum Temperature

Highest

Rank	Station Name	°F
1	Put-In-Bay	-18
2	Painesville 4 NW	-19
3	Bowling Green WWTP	-20
3	Cleveland Hopkins Int'l Airport	-20
3	Findlay Airport	-20
3	Findlay WPCC	-20
3	Fremont	-20
3	Sandusky	-20
3	Toledo Express Airport	-20
10	Dayton MCD	-21
10	Lima WWTP	-21
10	Norwalk WWTP	-21
10	Pandora	-21
10	Tiffin	-21
15	Chilo Meldahl Lock & Dam	-22
15	Cincinnati Lunken Airport	-22
15	Circleville	-22
15	Columbus-Port Columbus Int'l	-22
15	Defiance	-22
15	Elyria 3 E	-22
15	Hoytville 2 NE	-22
15	Kenton	-22
15	Mansfield Lahm Municipal Airport	-22
15	New Philadelphia	-22
15	Steubenville	-22

Lowest

Rank	Station Name	°F
1	Danville 2 W	-35
1	New Lexington 2 NW	-35
3	Millport 2 NW	-34
4	Eaton	-33
4	Greenville Water Plant	-33
6	Cambridge	-32
6	McConnelsville Lock 7	-32
8	Waverly	-31
9	Fredericktown 4 S	-30
10	Centerburg 2 SE	-29
10	Chillicothe Mound City	-29
10	Portsmouth Sciotoville	-29
13	Columbus Valley Crossing	-28
13	Delaware	-28
13	Dorset	-28
13	Gallipolis	-28
13	Irwin	-28
13	Jackson 3 NW	-28
13	Ripley Exp. Farm	-28
13	Xenia 6 SSE	-28
21	Bellefontaine	-27
21	Philo 3 SW	-27
21	Washington Court House	-27
21	Westerville	-27
25	Bucyrus	-26

July Mean Maximum Temperature

Highest

Rank	Station Name	°F
1	Gallipolis	87.4
2	Dayton MCD	87.3
3	Cincinnati Lunken Airport	86.8
3	Milford	86.8
5	Portsmouth Sciotoville	86.7
6	Cincinnati Fernbank	86.6
7	Waverly	86.5
8	Chillicothe Mound City	86.2
8	Chilo Meldahl Lock & Dam	86.2
10	Marietta WWTP	85.8
11	Mineral Ridge Water Works	85.7
12	Irwin	85.6
13	Circleville	85.5
13	Franklin	85.5
15	Columbus Valley Crossing	85.3
15	Westerville	85.3
17	Ripley Exp. Farm	85.2
17	Van Wert 1 S	85.2
19	Cambridge	85.1
19	Dayton Int'l Airport	85.1
19	Kenton	85.1
19	London	85.1
23	McConnelsville Lock 7	85.0
23	Napoleon	85.0
25	Newark Water Works	84.9

Lowest

Rank	Station Name	°F
1	Chardon	80.1
2	Dorset	81.2
3	Painesville 4 NW	81.4
4	Hiram	81.6
5	Philo 3 SW	81.7
6	Wooster Exp. Station	81.8
7	Mansfield 5 W	81.9
7	Youngstown Municipal Airport	81.9
9	Coshocton Agr. Res. Station	82.0
10	Barnesville	82.1
10	Mansfield Lahm Municipal Airport	82.1
12	Centerburg 2 SE	82.3
12	Put-In-Bay	82.3
12	Sandusky	82.3
15	Akron-Canton Regional Airport	82.4
15	Cleveland Hopkins Int'l Airport	82.4
17	Norwalk WWTP	82.6
17	Washington Court House	82.6
19	Cadiz	82.7
20	Findlay Airport	82.8
21	Canfield 1 S	82.9
22	Chippewa Lake	83.0
23	Ashland 2 SW	83.1
23	Bucyrus	83.1
23	Fredericktown 4 S	83.1

January Mean Minimum Temperature

Highest

Rank	Station Name	°F
1	Gallipolis	22.4
2	Cincinnati Lunken Airport	22.2
3	Marietta WWTP	22.1
3	Portsmouth Sciotoville	22.1
5	Circleville	20.8
6	Chilo Meldahl Lock & Dam	20.4
6	Dayton MCD	20.4
8	Steubenville	20.3
8	Washington Court House	20.3
10	Cincinnati Fernbank	20.2
10	Ripley Exp. Farm	20.2
12	Cambridge	20.1
12	Painesville 4 NW	20.1
12	Zanesville Municipal Airport	20.1
15	Columbus Valley Crossing	20.0
16	Columbus-Port Columbus Int'l	19.9
16	Hillsboro	19.9
18	Hannibal Lock & Dam	19.6
18	Philo 3 SW	19.6
20	Xenia 6 SSE	19.3
21	Waverly	19.2
22	Cadiz	19.1
22	Chillicothe Mound City	19.1
22	Jackson 3 NW	19.1
22	Newark Water Works	19.1

Lowest

Rank	Station Name	°F
1	Montpelier	13.3
2	Fredericktown 4 S	13.5
3	Paulding	13.7
4	Chardon	14.1
5	Dorset	14.6
6	Defiance	14.7
7	Greenville Water Plant	15.0
7	Hoytville 2 NE	15.0
9	Napoleon	15.2
10	Wauseon Water Plant	15.3
11	Eaton	15.4
11	Mansfield 5 W	15.4
13	Ashland 2 SW	15.5
14	Centerburg 2 SE	15.6
15	Marion 2 N	15.8
16	Kenton	15.9
16	Warren 3 S	15.9
18	Bucyrus	16.0
18	Danville 2 W	16.0
18	Fremont	16.0
18	Toledo Express Airport	16.0
22	Oberlin	16.1
23	Bowling Green WWTP	16.2
23	Delaware	16.2
25	Canfield 1 S	16.3

Number of Annual Heating Degree Days

Highest

Rank	Station Name	Num.
1	Chardon	6,934
2	Dorset	6,809
3	Montpelier	6,745
4	Paulding	6,576
5	Fredericktown 4 S	6,542
6	Ashland 2 SW	6,457
7	Hoytville 2 NE	6,456
8	Defiance	6,444
9	Mansfield 5 W	6,440
10	Bucyrus	6,435
11	Toledo Express Airport	6,413
12	Canfield 1 S	6,410
13	Youngstown Municipal Airport	6,386
14	Warren 3 S	6,382
15	Hiram	6,372
16	Fremont	6,371
17	Norwalk WWTP	6,359
18	Wauseon Water Plant	6,346
19	Centerburg 2 SE	6,297
20	Oberlin	6,287
21	Chippewa Lake	6,284
22	Greenville Water Plant	6,271
23	Wooster Exp. Station	6,261
24	Napoleon	6,259
25	Danville 2 W	6,240

Lowest

Rank	Station Name	Num.
1	Gallipolis	4,673
2	Cincinnati Lunken Airport	4,839
3	Portsmouth Sciotoville	4,860
4	Marietta WWTP	4,984
5	Chilo Meldahl Lock & Dam	5,083
6	Cincinnati Fernbank	5,126
7	Waverly	5,238
8	Ripley Exp. Farm	5,245
9	Circleville	5,275
10	Dayton MCD	5,292
11	Columbus Valley Crossing	5,318
12	Cambridge	5,348
13	Washington Court House	5,362
14	Hillsboro	5,414
15	Chillicothe Mound City	5,422
16	Jackson 3 NW	5,451
17	Xenia 6 SSE	5,464
18	Steubenville	5,484
19	Columbus-Port Columbus Int'l	5,491
20	Milford	5,495
21	Hannibal Lock & Dam	5,520
22	Zanesville Municipal Airport	5,525
23	Westerville	5,528
24	Franklin	5,604
25	Dayton Int'l Airport	5,616

Number of Annual Cooling Degree Days

Highest

Rank	Station Name	Num.
1	Dayton MCD	1,283
2	Cincinnati Lunken Airport	1,215
3	Gallipolis	1,156
4	Chilo Meldahl Lock & Dam	1,079
5	Cincinnati Fernbank	1,076
6	Portsmouth Sciotoville	1,030
7	Marietta WWTP	1,018
8	Milford	1,016
9	Columbus-Port Columbus Int'l	991
10	Chillicothe Mound City	988
11	Ripley Exp. Farm	981
12	Dayton Int'l Airport	974
13	Westerville	971
14	Lima WWTP	968
15	Circleville	965
16	Columbus Valley Crossing	954
17	Waverly	943
18	Celina 3 NE	937
19	Cambridge	919
20	Washington Court House	915
21	Kenton	911
22	Van Wert 1 S	910
23	Franklin	903
24	Hillsboro	895
25	Put-In-Bay	892

Lowest

Rank	Station Name	Num.
1	Chardon	468
2	Dorset	514
3	Canfield 1 S	552
4	Fredericktown 4 S	571
5	Warren 3 S	581
6	Millport 2 NW	595
7	Youngstown Municipal Airport	599
8	Danville 2 W	613
9	Mansfield 5 W	619
10	Ashland 2 SW	622
11	Hiram	633
12	Wooster Exp. Station	635
13	Chippewa Lake	666
14	Philo 3 SW	671
15	Barnesville	679
16	Mansfield Lahm Municipal Airport	698
17	Montpelier	700
18	Oberlin	705
19	Bucyrus	706
20	Centerburg 2 SE	711
21	Akron-Canton Regional Airport	716
22	Paulding	717
23	New Lexington 2 NW	731
24	Hoytville 2 NE	740
24	Norwalk WWTP	740

Annual Precipitation

Highest

Rank	Station Name	Inches
1	Cincinnati Fernbank	47.43
2	Chardon	47.01
3	Ripley Exp. Farm	45.33
4	Milford	44.72
5	Barnesville	44.34
6	Hillsboro	43.33
7	Dorset	43.30
8	Chilo Meldahl Lock & Dam	43.05
8	Mansfield Lahm Municipal Airport	43.05
10	McConnelsville Lock 7	42.96
11	Marietta WWTP	42.20
12	Hiram	41.91
13	Cincinnati Lunken Airport	41.89
14	Newark Water Works	41.86
15	New Lexington 2 NW	41.74
16	Portsmouth Sciotoville	41.39
17	Danville 2 W	41.21
18	Jackson 3 NW	41.13
19	Wilmington 3 N	41.12
20	Coshocton WPC Plant	40.96
21	Centerburg 2 SE	40.89
22	New Philadelphia	40.88
23	Cadiz	40.86
24	Gallipolis	40.66
25	Steubenville	40.37

Lowest

Rank	Station Name	Inches
1	Bowling Green WWTP	33.14
2	Toledo Express Airport	33.23
3	Hoytville 2 NE	33.89
4	Sandusky	34.19
5	Paulding	34.29
6	Wauseon Water Plant	34.59
7	Findlay Airport	34.68
8	Put-In-Bay	34.79
9	Napoleon	34.81
10	Kenton	35.47
11	Pandora	35.63
12	Defiance	35.64
13	Montpelier	35.82
14	Upper Sandusky	36.03
15	Fremont	36.04
16	Oberlin	36.32
17	Marysville	36.37
18	Van Wert 1 S	36.52
19	Celina 3 NE	36.56
20	Norwalk WWTP	36.62
21	Tiffin	36.75
22	Bellefontaine	36.92
23	Findlay WPCC	36.95
24	Philo 3 SW	37.03
25	Coshocton Agr. Res. Station	37.04

Number of Days Annually With ≥ 0.1" Precipitation

Highest

Rank	Station Name	Days
1	Chardon	107
2	Dorset	99
3	Hiram	97
4	Barnesville	90
4	Millport 2 NW	90
4	New Lexington 2 NW	90
7	Chippewa Lake	89
7	Cincinnati Fernbank	89
7	Marietta WWTP	89
7	McConnelsville Lock 7	89
7	Milford	89
12	Cadiz	88
12	Steubenville	88
14	Cleveland Hopkins Int'l Airport	87
14	Coshocton WPC Plant	87
14	Elyria 3 E	87
14	Ripley Exp. Farm	87
18	Gallipolis	86
18	Newark Water Works	86
18	Painesville 4 NW	86
18	Warren 3 S	86
22	Cambridge	85
22	Jackson 3 NW	85
22	Portsmouth Sciotoville	85
25	Akron-Canton Regional Airport	84

Lowest

Rank	Station Name	Days
1	Put-In-Bay	69
2	Paulding	70
3	Lancaster 2 NW	71
4	Irwin	72
4	Sandusky	72
6	Bowling Green WWTP	73
6	Findlay Airport	73
6	Hoytville 2 NE	73
9	Coshocton Agr. Res. Station	75
9	Springfield New Water Works	75
9	Wauseon Water Plant	75
12	Chillicothe Mound City	76
12	Chilo Meldahl Lock & Dam	76
12	Greenville Water Plant	76
12	Napoleon	76
12	Toledo Express Airport	76
17	Dayton MCD	77
17	Defiance	77
17	Eaton	77
17	London	77
17	Pandora	77
22	Circleville	78
22	Columbus Valley Crossing	78
22	Delaware	78
22	Kenton	78

Number of Days Annually With ≥ 1.0" Precipitation

Highest

Rank	Station Name	Days
1	Cincinnati Fernbank	14
2	Chilo Meldahl Lock & Dam	12
2	Ripley Exp. Farm	12
4	Portsmouth Sciotoville	11
4	Urbana WWTP	11
6	Chillicothe Mound City	10
6	Cincinnati Lunken Airport	10
6	Eaton	10
6	Hillsboro	10
6	Milford	10
6	Wilmington 3 N	10
12	Barnesville	9
12	Centerburg 2 SE	9
12	Dayton MCD	9
12	Fredericktown 4 S	9
12	Mansfield Lahm Municipal Airport	9
12	McConnelsville Lock 7	9
12	Waverly	9
12	Xenia 6 SSE	9
20	Chardon	8
20	Danville 2 W	8
20	Dayton Int'l Airport	8
20	Franklin	8
20	Gallipolis	8
20	Greenville Water Plant	8

Lowest

Rank	Station Name	Days
1	Elyria 3 E	4
1	Mineral Ridge Water Works	4
3	Bowling Green WWTP	5
3	Cadiz	5
3	Canfield 1 S	5
3	Findlay Airport	5
3	Hiram	5
3	Hoytville 2 NE	5
3	Millport 2 NW	5
3	Napoleon	5
3	Norwalk WWTP	5
3	Oberlin	5
3	Painesville 4 NW	5
3	Pandora	5
3	Put-In-Bay	5
3	Sandusky	5
3	Toledo Express Airport	5
3	Wauseon Water Plant	5
19	Celina 3 NE	6
19	Chippewa Lake	6
19	Cleveland Hopkins Int'l Airport	6
19	Dorset	6
19	Findlay WPCC	6
19	Fremont	6
19	Kenton	6

Annual Snowfall

Highest

Rank	Station Name	Inches
1	Chardon	97.0
2	Dorset	73.1
3	Hiram	61.6
4	Cleveland Hopkins Int'l Airport	61.0
5	Youngstown Municipal Airport	54.7
6	Akron-Canton Regional Airport	46.9
7	Elyria 3 E	43.6
8	Mansfield Lahm Municipal Airport	43.3
9	Oberlin	41.4
10	Chippewa Lake	39.8
11	Toledo Express Airport	37.2
12	Danville 2 W	35.5
13	Painesville 4 NW	34.8
14	Mineral Ridge Water Works	34.5
15	Ashland 2 SW	34.0
16	Montpelier	33.9
16	Warren 3 S	33.9
18	Celina 3 NE	33.1
19	Barnesville	32.9
20	Cadiz	32.3
21	Wooster Exp. Station	31.7
22	Pandora	30.7
23	Millport 2 NW	30.2
24	Van Wert 1 S	29.8
25	New Philadelphia	29.7

Lowest

Rank	Station Name	Inches
1	Cincinnati Lunken Airport	13.2
2	Portsmouth Sciotoville	13.3
3	Gallipolis	14.2
4	Circleville	14.9
5	Dayton MCD	15.7
6	Milford	15.9
7	Bellefontaine	17.8
8	Chillicothe Mound City	17.9
9	Cambridge	18.4
10	Columbus Valley Crossing	19.3
11	Westerville	19.6
12	Paulding	19.7
12	Put-In-Bay	19.7
14	Marysville	20.2
15	Hillsboro	20.5
16	Newark Water Works	20.6
17	Delaware	20.7
18	Defiance	20.8
19	McConnelsville Lock 7	21.2
20	Fredericktown 4 S	21.4
21	Ripley Exp. Farm	21.5
22	Greenville Water Plant	21.7
23	Bowling Green WWTP	21.9
24	Zanesville Municipal Airport	22.5
25	Coshocton WPC Plant	22.7

Note: See User's Guide for explanation of data.

Deadliest Storm Events in Ohio: April 1981 - April 2006

Rank	Location or County	Date	Storm Event	Fatalities	Injuries	Property Damage ($mil.)	Crop Damage ($mil.)
1	Northern Ohio	8/8/1995	Heat Wave	13	52	0.5	0.0
2	Cincinnati and Dayton Metro Areas	7/20/1999	Excessive Heat	13	0	0.0	0.0
3	Trumbull County	5/31/1985	Tornado (F5)	10	250	250.0	0.0
4	Northern Ohio	8/3/1995	Heat Wave	5	11	0.0	0.0
5	Noble County	6/27/1998	Flash Flood	5	0	10.0	10.0
6	Morrow County	6/13/1981	Tornado (F3)	4	56	25.0	0.0
7	All of Ohio	2/11/1995	Extreme Cold	4	0	0.1	0.0
8	Northern Ohio	1/10/1997	Extreme Cold	4	0	0.2	0.0
9	Blue Ash	4/9/1999	Tornado (F4)	4	65	82.0	0.0
10	Lucas County	6/3/1990	Thunderstorm Wind	3	1	0.0	0.0
11	Cuyahoga County	9/6/1990	Thunderstorm Wind	3	3	0.0	0.0
12	Scioto County	8/9/1995	Flash Flood	3	0	0.1	0.0
13	Northern Ohio	12/9/1995	Extreme Cold	3	0	0.2	0.0
14	Cuyahoga County	7/24/1999	Thunderstorm Wind	3	0	0.0	0.0
15	Hamilton County	7/17/2001	Flash Flood	3	0	3.6	0.0
16	Summit County	7/21/2003	Flash Flood	3	0	100.0	0.0

Most Destructive Storm Events in Ohio: April 1981 - April 2006

Rank	Location or County	Date	Storm Event	Fatalities	Injuries	Property Damage ($mil.)	Crop Damage ($mil.)
1	Portage County	5/31/1985	Tornado (F5)	0	0	250.0	0.0
2	Trumbull County (4:39 pm)	5/31/1985	Tornado (F5)	10	250	250.0	0.0
3	Trumbull County (5:11 pm)	5/31/1985	Tornado (F5)	0	0	250.0	0.0
4	Northern Ohio	1/5/2005	Ice Storm	0	0	124.9	0.0
5	Summit County	7/21/2003	Flash Flood	3	0	100.0	0.0
6	Blue Ash	4/9/1999	Tornado (F4)	4	65	82.0	0.0
7	Westerville	4/20/2003	Hail (1.75 in.)	0	0	80.0	0.0
8	Huber Heights	4/9/2001	Hail (1.75 in.)	0	0	70.0	0.0
9	Powell	4/20/2003	Hail (1.50 in.)	0	0	65.0	0.0
10	Ashland, Crawford, Cuyahoga, Erie, Huron, Lorain, Marion, Medina, Morrow, Richland, Seneca, and Wyandot Counties	12/22/2004	Winter Storm	0	0	54.9	0.0
11	Stark County	7/27/2003	Flash Flood	0	0	52.0	0.0
12	Southern Ohio	2/8/1994	Ice Storm	1	1568	50.0	5.0
13	Crystal Springs	4/28/2002	Tornado (F2)	0	2	45.5	0.0
14	Trumbull County	7/21/2003	Flood	0	0	32.0	0.0
15	Willshire	11/10/2002	Tornado (F4)	2	17	30.0	0.0
16	Athens, Gallia, Lawrence, Meigs, Morgan, Perry, Vinton, and Washington Counties	9/17/2004	Flood	0	0	25.5	0.0
17	Morrow County	6/13/1981	Tornado (F3)	4	56	25.0	0.0
18	Wood County	5/2/1983	Tornado (F3)	1	22	25.0	0.0
19	Cuyahoga County	5/2/1983	Tornado (F3)	1	25	25.0	0.0
20	Licking County	5/31/1985	Tornado (F3)	1	20	25.0	0.0
21	Columbiana County	5/31/1985	Tornado (F2)	0	20	25.0	0.0
22	Coshocton County	5/31/1985	Tornado (F3)	0	0	25.0	0.0
23	Hamilton County	6/2/1990	Tornado (F4)	0	14	25.0	0.0
24	Butler County (9:45 pm)	6/2/1990	Tornado (F4)	0	2	25.0	0.0
25	Butler County (9:50 pm)	6/2/1990	Tornado (F4)	0	0	25.0	0.0
26	Warren County	6/2/1990	Tornado (F4)	0	0	25.0	0.0
27	Williams County	3/27/1991	Tornado (F3)	0	18	25.0	0.0
28	Preble County	11/22/1992	Tornado (F3)	0	0	25.0	0.0
29	Darke County	11/22/1992	Tornado (F3)	0	21	25.0	0.0
30	Trumbull County	7/21/2003	Flash Flood	0	0	25.0	0.0
31	Stark County	5/17/2004	Hail (2.75 in.)	0	0	25.0	0.0

DEMOGRAPHIC MAPS

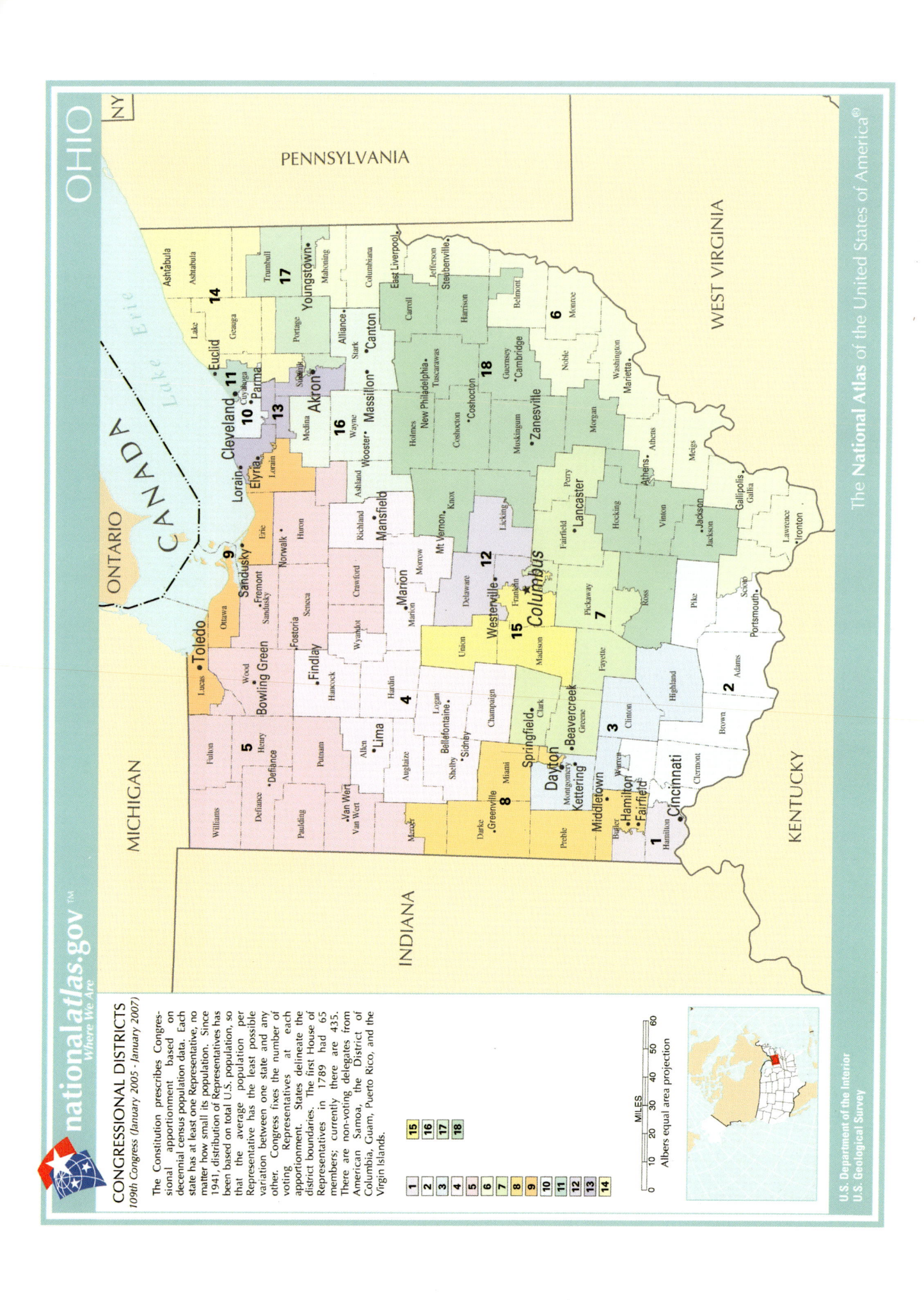

OHIO

CONGRESSIONAL DISTRICTS
109th Congress (January 2005 - January 2007)

The Constitution prescribes Congressional apportionment based on decennial census population data. Each state has at least one Representative, no matter how small its population. Since 1941, distribution of Representatives has been based on total U.S. population, so that the average population per Representative has the least possible variation between one state and any other. Congress fixes the number of voting Representatives at each apportionment. States delineate the district boundaries. The first House of Representatives in 1789 had 65 members; currently there are 435. There are non-voting delegates from American Samoa, the District of Columbia, Guam, Puerto Rico, and the Virgin Islands.

The National Atlas of the United States of America

U.S. Department of the Interior
U.S. Geological Survey

OHIO - Core Based Statistical Areas and Counties

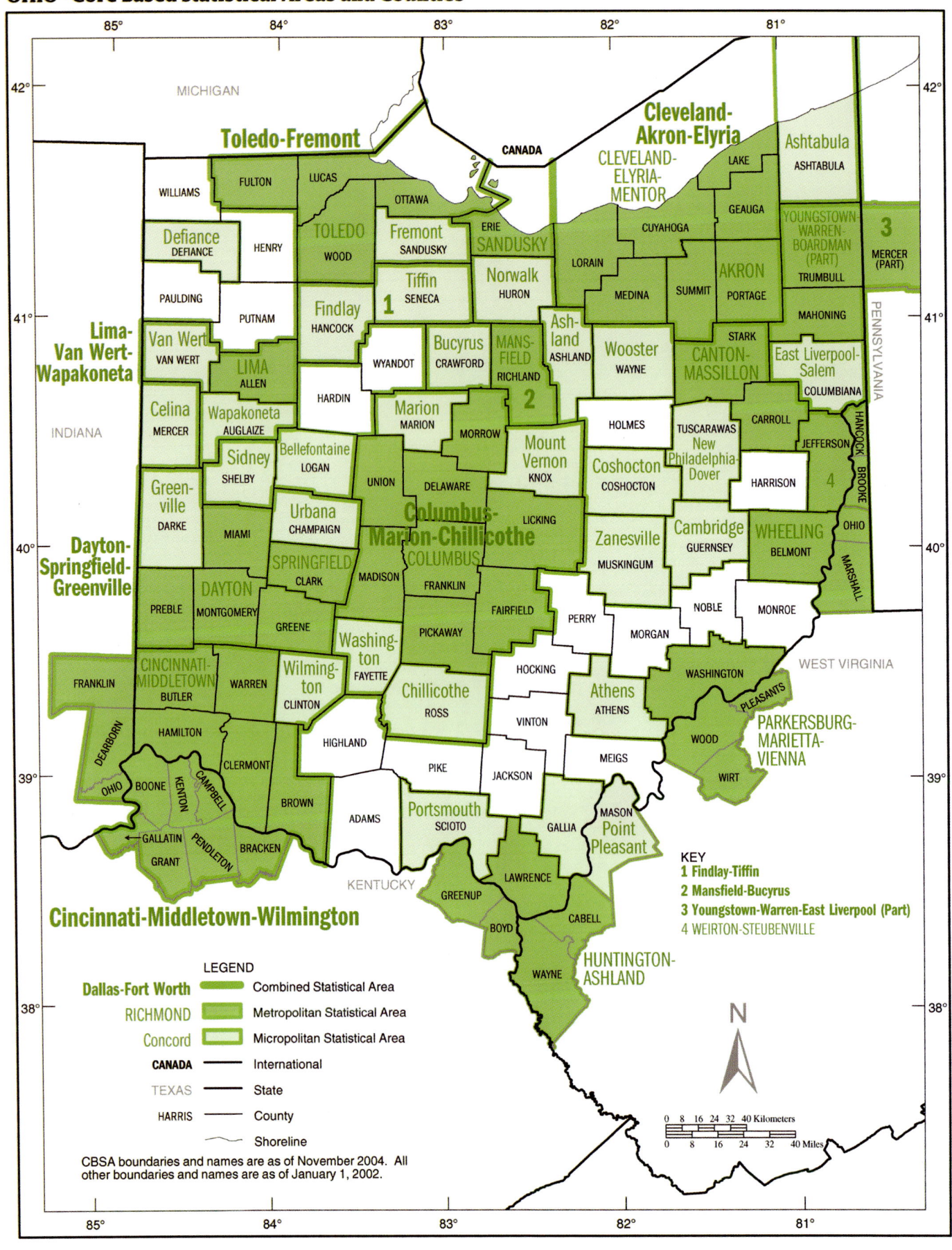

Population (2005)

Legend
- 150,000 and Over
- 75,000 to 149,999
- 50,000 to 74,999
- 25,000 to 49,999
- Under 25,000

Percent White (2005)

Legend
- 95.0 and Over
- 90.0 to 94.9
- 85.0 to 89.9
- Under 85.0

Percent Black (2005)

Legend
- 5.0 and Over
- 2.0 to 4.9
- 1.0 to 1.9
- Under 1.0

Note: Copyright © 1988-2003 Microsoft Corp. and/or its suppliers. All rights reserved. © Copyright 2002 by Geographic Data Technology, Inc. All rights reserved. © 2002 Navigation Technologies. All rights reserved.

Percent Asian (2005)

Legend
- 1.1 and Over
- 0.7 to 1.0
- 0.4 to 0.6
- Under 0.4

Percent Hispanic (2005)

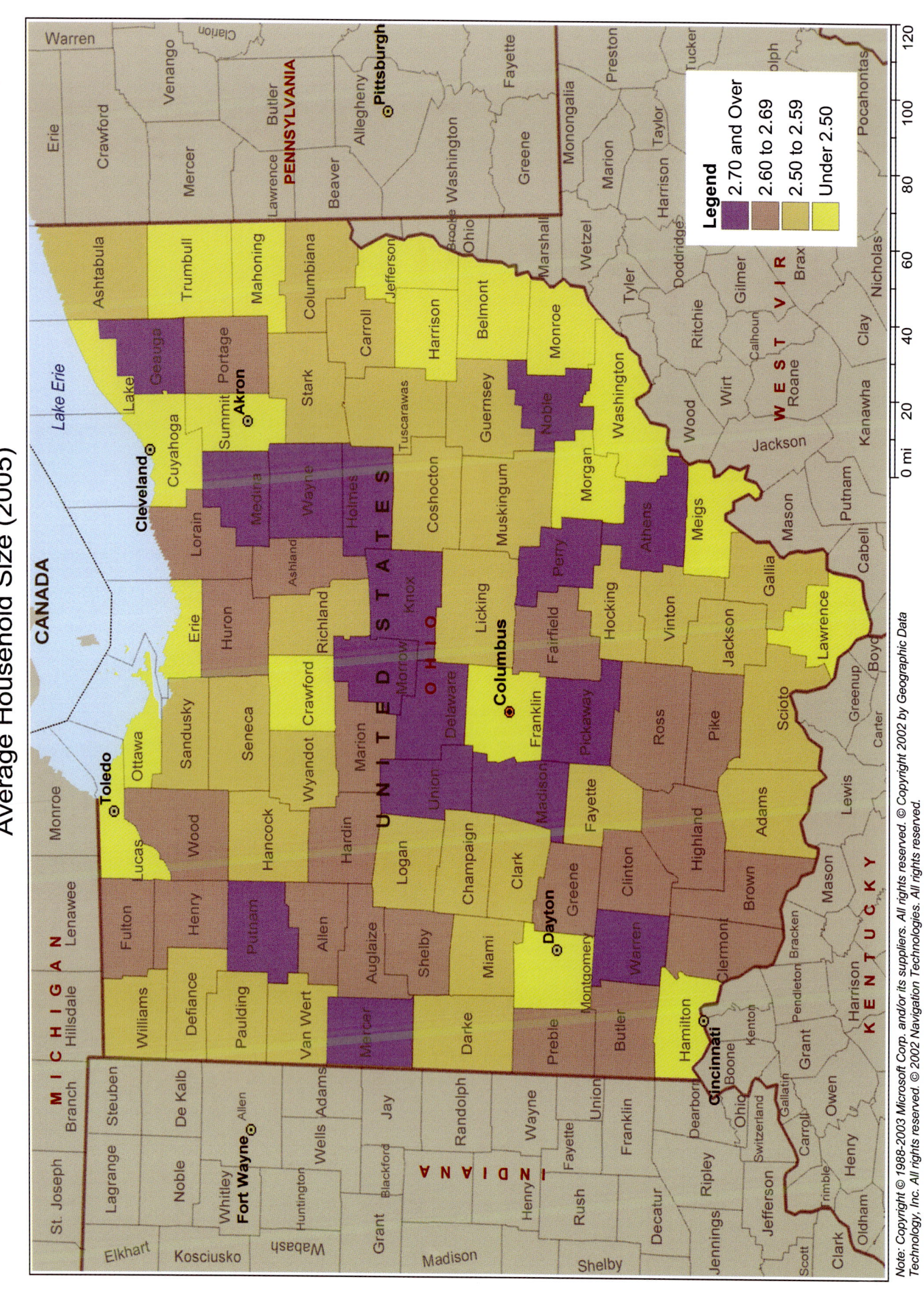

Average Household Size (2005)

Legend
- 2.70 and Over
- 2.60 to 2.69
- 2.50 to 2.59
- Under 2.50

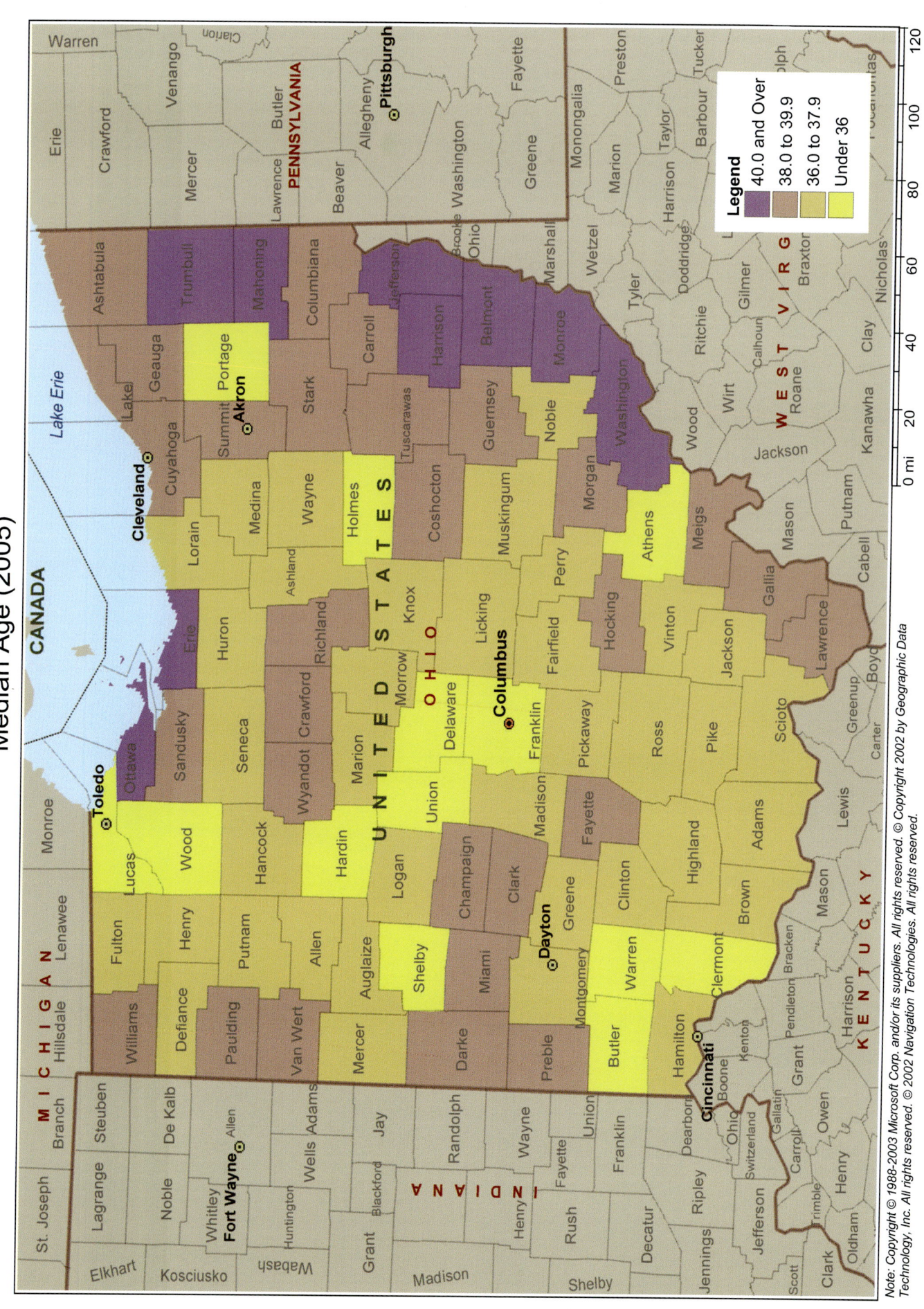

Median Age (2005)

Legend
- 40.0 and Over
- 38.0 to 39.9
- 36.0 to 37.9
- Under 36

Median Household Income (2005)

Legend
- 48,000 and Over
- 44,000 to 47,999
- 40,000 to 43,999
- Under 40,000

Note: Copyright © 1988-2003 Microsoft Corp. and/or its suppliers. All rights reserved. © Copyright 2002 by Geographic Data Technology, Inc. All rights reserved. © 2002 Navigation Technologies. All rights reserved.

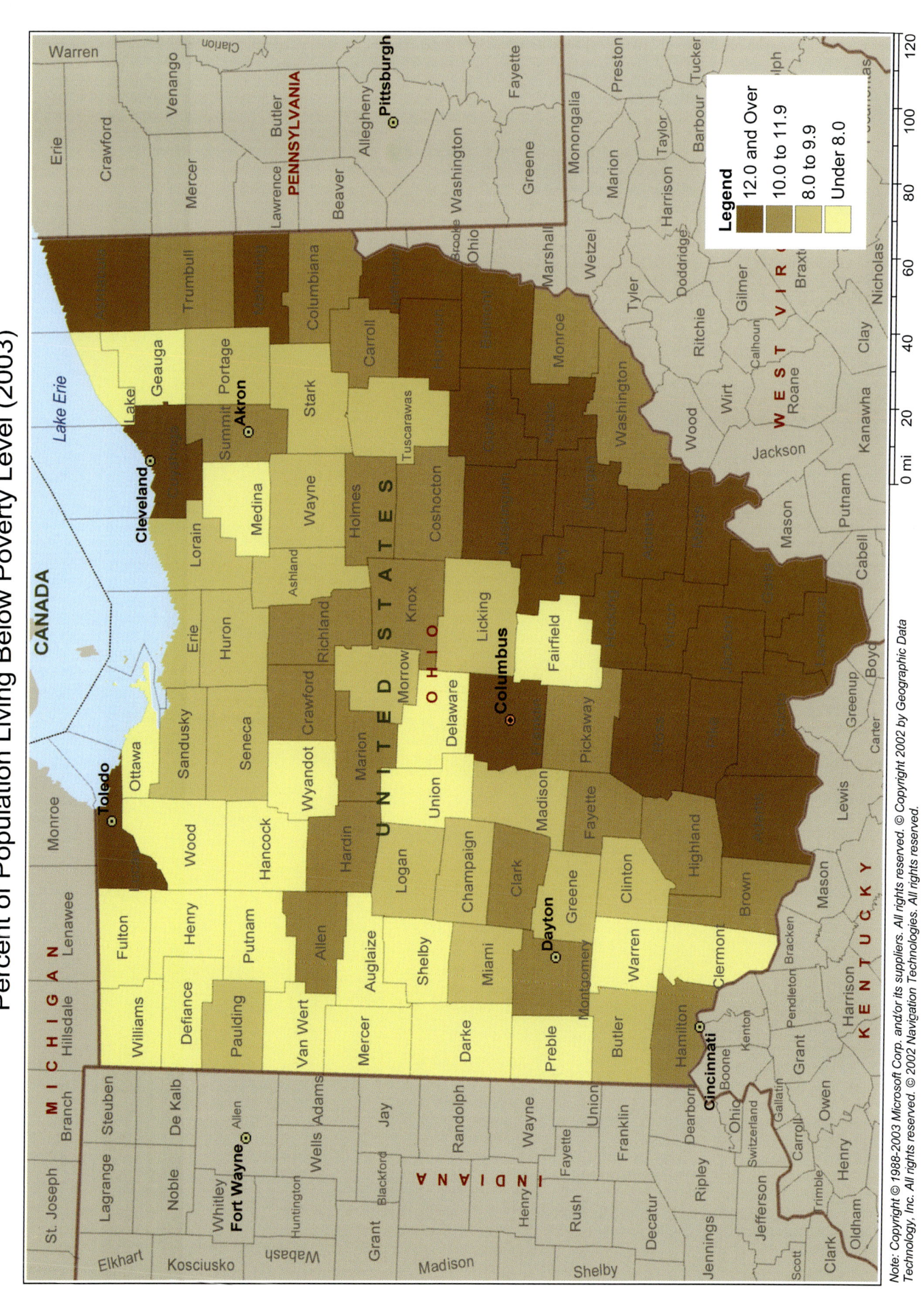

Percent of Population Living Below Poverty Level (2003)

Legend
- 12.0 and Over
- 10.0 to 11.9
- 8.0 to 9.9
- Under 8.0

Note: Copyright © 1988-2003 Microsoft Corp. and/or its suppliers. All rights reserved. © Copyright 2002 by Geographic Data Technology, Inc. All rights reserved. © 2002 Navigation Technologies. All rights reserved.

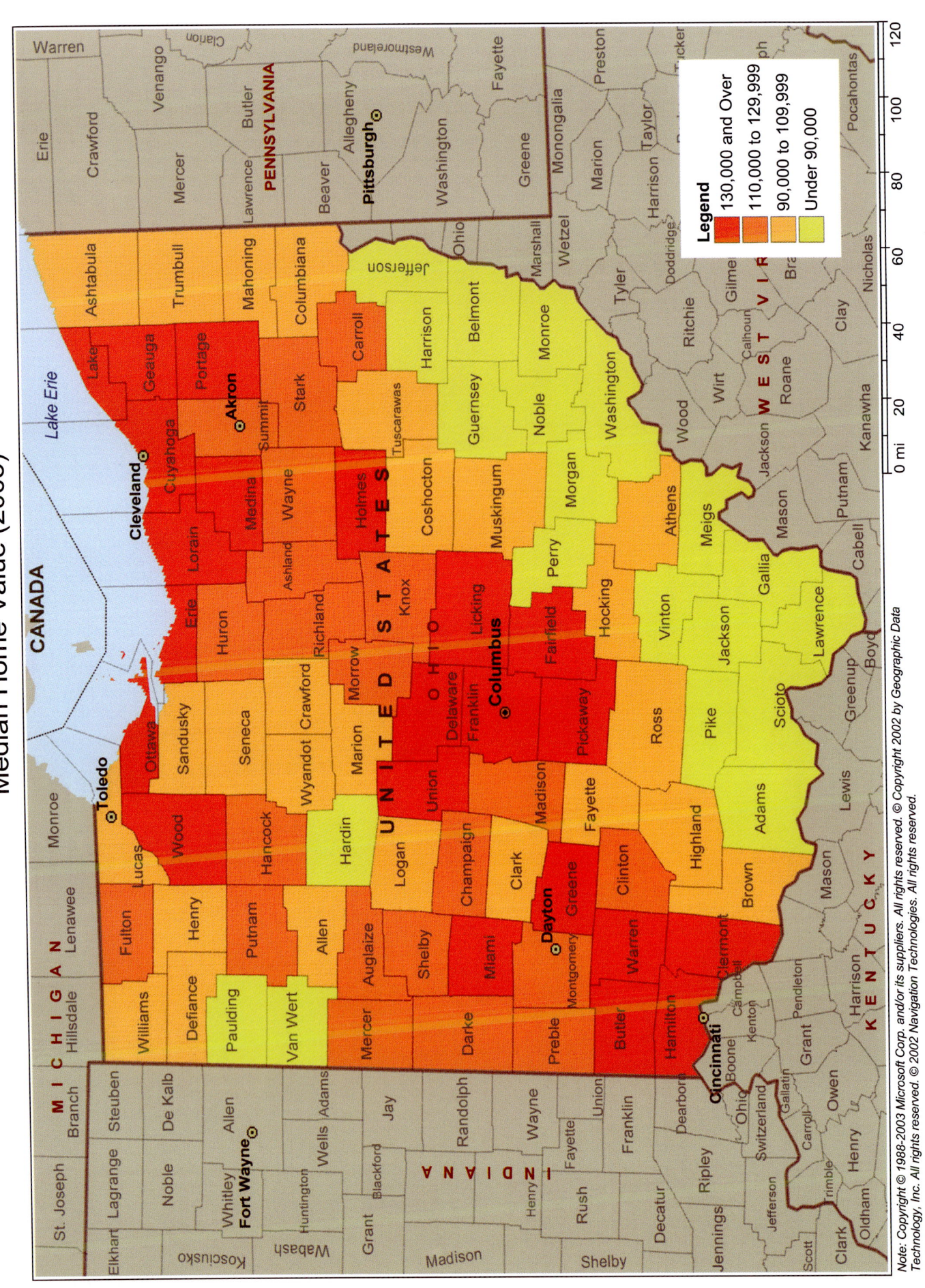

Median Home Value (2005)

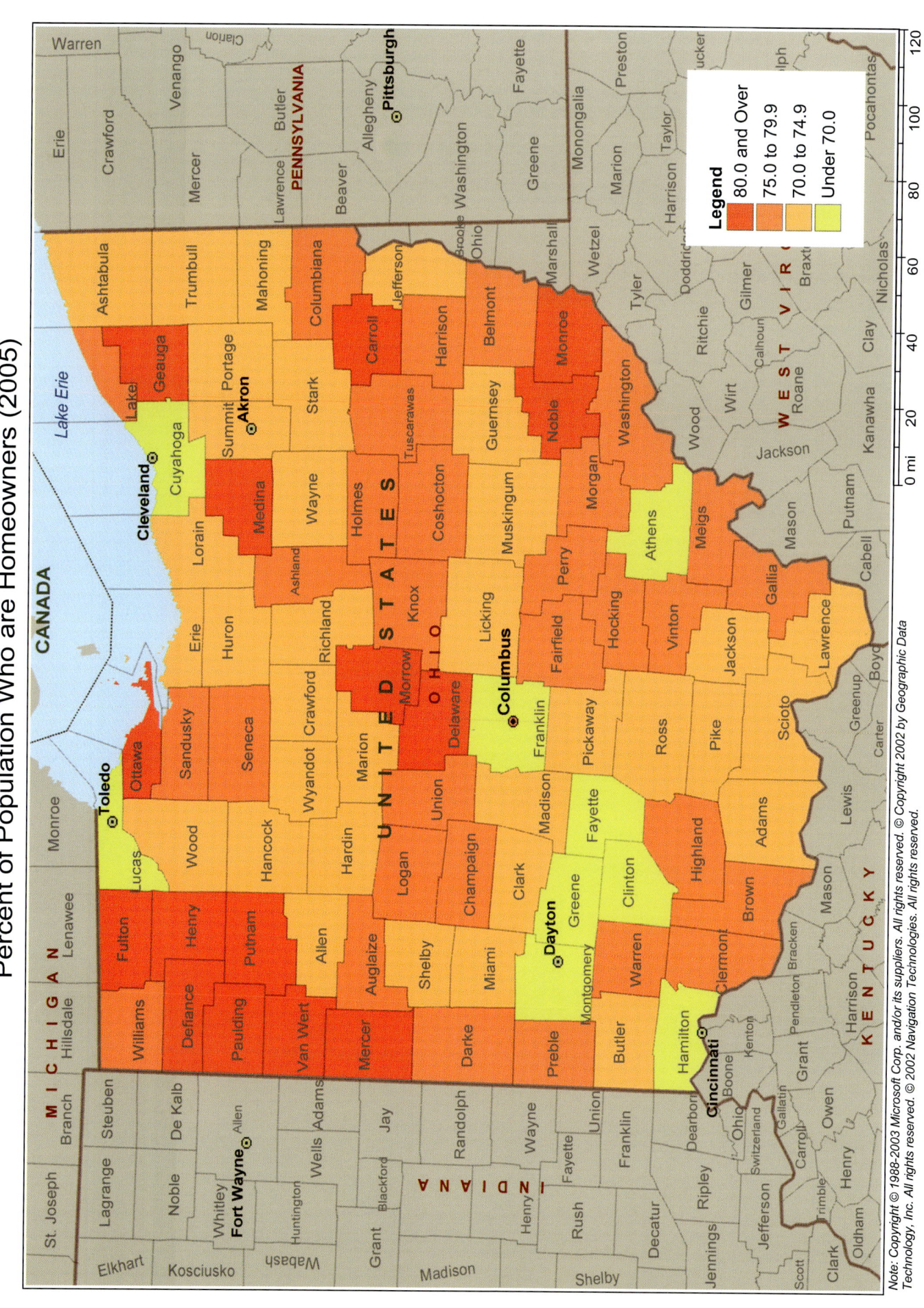

Percent of Population Who are Homeowners (2005)

Legend
- 80.0 and Over
- 75.0 to 79.9
- 70.0 to 74.9
- Under 70.0

Note: Copyright © 1988-2003 Microsoft Corp. and/or its suppliers. All rights reserved. © Copyright 2002 by Geographic Data Technology, Inc. All rights reserved. © 2002 Navigation Technologies. All rights reserved.

Percent High School Graduates* (2005)

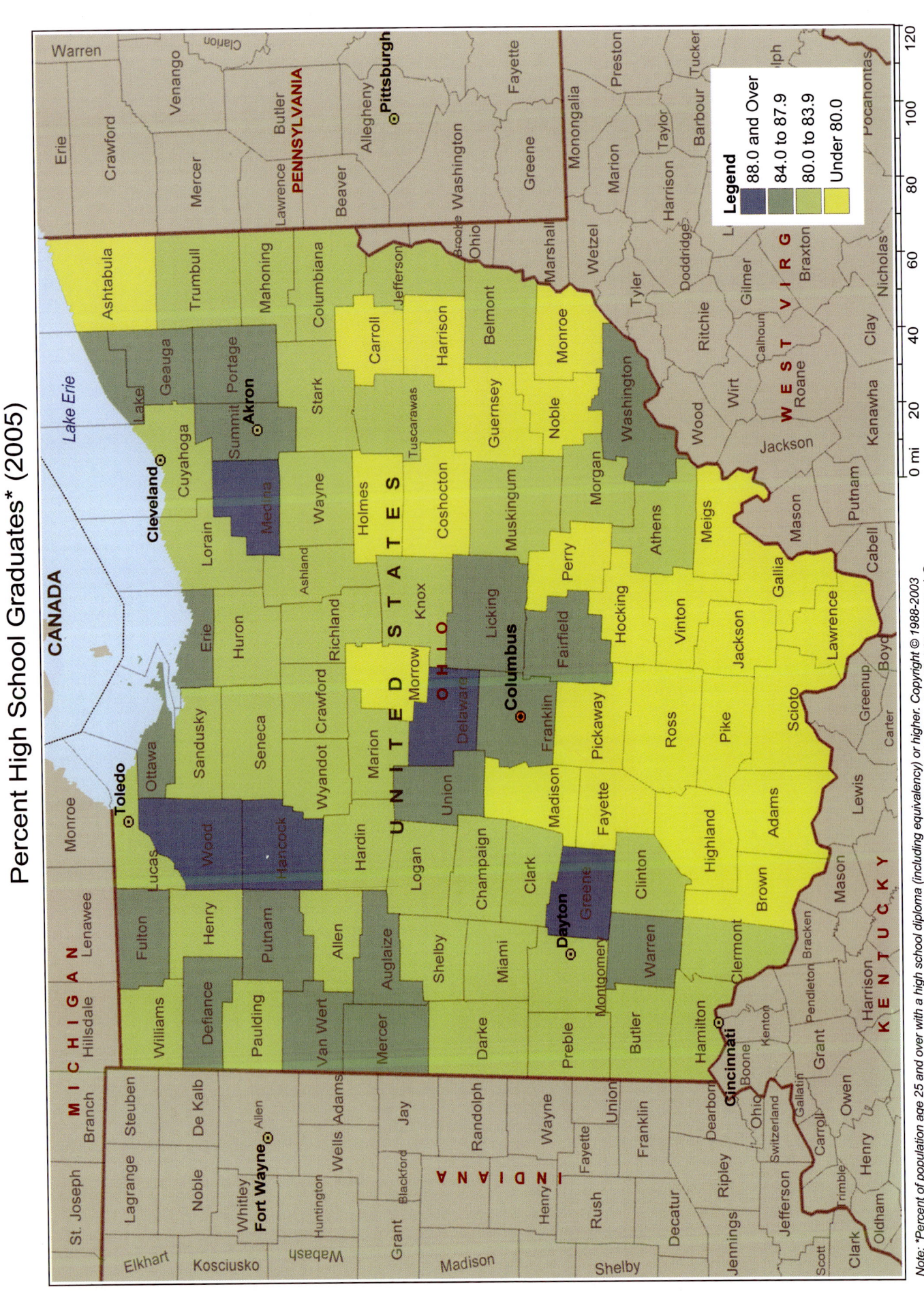

Legend
- 88.0 and Over
- 84.0 to 87.9
- 80.0 to 83.9
- Under 80.0

Note: *Percent of population age 25 and over with a high school diploma (including equivalency) or higher. Copyright © 1988-2003 Microsoft Corp. and/or its suppliers. All rights reserved. © Copyright 2002 by Geographic Data Technology, Inc. All rights reserved. © 2002 Navigation Technologies. All rights reserved.

Percent College Graduates* (2005)

Legend
- 20.0 and Over
- 15.0 to 19.9
- 10.0 to 14.9
- Under 10.0

Note: *Percent of population age 25 and over with a Bachelor's Degree or higher. Copyright © 1988-2003 Microsoft Corp. and/or its suppliers. All rights reserved. © Copyright 2002 by Geographic Data Technology, Inc. All rights reserved. © 2002 Navigation Technologies. All rights reserved.

Percent of Population Who Voted for George Bush in 2004

Legend
- 70.0 and Over
- 60.0 to 69.9
- 50.0 to 59.9
- Under 50.0

Note: Copyright © 1988-2003 Microsoft Corp. and/or its suppliers. All rights reserved. © Copyright 2002 by Geographic Data Technology, Inc. All rights reserved. © 2002 Navigation Technologies. All rights reserved.